NIV

MEN'S
DEVOTIONAL BIBLE

✓ T5-ANT-793

NEW INTERNATIONAL VERSION

ZondervanPublishingHouse

GRAND RAPIDS, MICHIGAN 49530, U.S.A.

You will be pleased to know that a portion of the purchase price of your new NIV Bible has been provided to International Bible Society to help spread the gospel of Jesus Christ around the world!

CONTENTS

INTRODUCTION—NIV MEN'S DEVOTIONAL BIBLE

B ecoming a real man in a fast-paced, demanding world is hard work. It's not easy to build relationships with family and friends, to stand up under job pressures, and still be true to who you are as a man made in God's image. What's a real man supposed to be? What your father was? What your peers want? What your wife and children need? Where can a man find answers to tough questions about being a man? Relax, your search is over! The NIV Men's Devotional Bible is designed just for you—one of today's men tired of trying to measure up to society's standards of manhood and eager to discover the Biblical model of masculinity and maturity.

Written for, by and about today's man, the NIV Men's Devotional Bible will reach you right where you are. But it won't leave you there! With God's Word and the thoughtful reflections of many godly men, the NIV Men's Devotional Bible will transport you step by step on a journey to Christian maturity.

Several features make the NIV Men's Devotional Bible an exceptional devotional guide:

The Bible

The NIV Men's Devotional Bible features the complete text of the Holy Bible, New International Version. The NIV's accuracy and readability make it today's most popular modern translation.

The Devotions

All of the daily and weekend devotions are written by men—men who have struggled with what it means to be a man of integrity and vision; men who want to be good men, good workers, good husbands, good fathers; men who want to share what they've learned with other men. Each devotion is located within the text, in close proximity to the Scripture passage on which it is based.

The Introductions

The introduction to each Bible book succinctly highlights that book's practical themes. Each introduction gives you interesting facts and helpful background information, as well as a practical application to encourage you as you read that particular book and the devotions within it.

Ease of Use

The NIV Men's Devotional Bible is designed to help you see how relevant the Bible is to your particular life situation as a man. The easy-to-use Bible reading/devotional meditation plan will get you into the Word and help you to leave a mark on your friends, your colleagues, your wife and your children.

The devotions in the NIV Men's Devotional Bible take a distinctive pattern following the days of the week: Monday, Tuesday, Wednesday, Thursday, Friday. In recognition of your need for something different on the weekend, we've developed "Weekending"—combining brief, provocative devotional thoughts with short Scripture readings for both Saturday and Sunday.

No matter what day of the week you begin your reading, you simply turn to a devotion for that day. To proceed on to the next reading, look to the bottom of the devotion; you will be directed to the page number on which the next day's devotion can be found. For example, if you start on a Monday, you could turn to the first devotion in the book of Genesis, page 3. Glance at the bottom of Monday's devotion, and you will see the page number where Tuesday's devotion will be found—and so on as you keep reading on through Friday.

Friday's devotion will direct you to a "Weekending," which will provide you with a reflective insight for your weekend and a Scripture reading for both Saturday and Sunday. The bottom of the "Weekending" will send you to the next Monday's devotion. And you are well on your way—through a year of developing a vital relationship with the Lord as you spend time in his Word.

Reading Plan

On page 1417 you will find a plan to help you read through the entire Bible in one year. If you choose to follow this plan, you'll discover great riches as you read the Bible chapter by chapter and book by book.

Author Biographies

You will very likely recognize the names of many of the men who contributed to the NIV Men's Devotional Bible. The author index, found on page 1420, provides information about each man, as well as a list of the pages where his devotions appear.

Subject Index

You feel like a failure as a father; your spiritual discipline is waning; you're weary of the rat race; you're confused about how your sexuality relates to who you are as a man. Whatever your circumstances, the subject index will direct you to just the right words to encourage and motivate you. Look up a wide variety of subjects in this index on page 1427, and turn to the listed page number for a devotion that fits your need.

So come on along. You're invited to open the pages of the NIV Men's Devotional Bible and proceed along the road to authentic masculinity and maturity in Christ. The riches of God's Word await you every step of the way, and the meditations of the men who have shared a bit of themselves will give the encouragement you need to keep moving ahead. As you go, we pray you'll become all that God intends you to be as a man of God in today's world.

PREFACE

THE NEW INTERNATIONAL VERSION is a completely new translation of the Holy Bible made by over a hundred scholars working directly from the best available Hebrew, Aramaic and Greek texts. It had its beginning in 1965 when, after several years of exploratory study by committees from the Christian Reformed Church and the National Association of Evangelicals, a group of scholars met at Palos Heights, Illinois, and concurred in the need for a new translation of the Bible in contemporary English. This group, though not made up of official church representatives, was transdenominational. Its conclusion was endorsed by a large number of leaders from many denominations who met in Chicago in 1966.

Responsibility for the new version was delegated by the Palos Heights group to a self-governing body of fifteen, the Committee on Bible Translation, composed for the most part of biblical scholars from colleges, universities and seminaries. In 1967 the New York Bible Society (now the International Bible Society) generously undertook the financial sponsorship of the project—a sponsorship that made it possible to enlist the help of many distinguished scholars. The fact that participants from the United States, Great Britain, Canada, Australia and New Zealand worked together gave the project its international scope. That they were from many denominations—including Anglican, Assemblies of God, Baptist, Brethren, Christian Reformed, Church of Christ, Evangelical Free, Lutheran, Mennonite, Methodist, Nazarene, Presbyterian, Wesleyan and other churches— helped to safeguard the translation from sectarian bias.

How it was made helps to give the New International Version its distinctiveness. The translation of each book was assigned to a team of scholars. Next, one of the Intermediate Editorial Committees revised the initial translation, with constant reference to the Hebrew, Aramaic or Greek. Their work then went to one of the General Editorial Committees, which checked it in detail and made another thorough revision. This revision in turn was carefully reviewed by the Committee on Bible Translation, which made further changes and then released the final version for publication. In this way the entire Bible underwent three revisions, during each of which the translation was examined for its faithfulness to the original languages and for its English style.

All this involved many thousands of hours of research and discussion regarding the meaning of the texts and the precise way of putting them into English. It may well be that no other translation has been made by a more thorough process of review and revision from committee to committee than this one.

From the beginning of the project, the Committee on Bible Translation held to certain goals for the New International Version: that it would be an accurate translation and one that would have clarity and literary quality and so prove suitable for public and private reading, teaching, preaching, memorizing and liturgical use. The Committee also sought to preserve some measure of continuity with the long tradition of translating the Scriptures into English.

In working toward these goals, the translators were united in their commitment to the authority and infallibility of the Bible as God's Word in written form. They believe that it contains the divine answer to the deepest needs of humanity, that it sheds unique light on our path in a dark world, and that it sets forth the way to our eternal well-being.

The first concern of the translators has been the accuracy of the translation and its fidelity to the thought of the biblical writers. They have weighed the significance of the lexical and grammatical details of the Hebrew, Aramaic and Greek texts. At the same time, they have striven for more than a word-for-word translation. Because thought patterns and syntax differ from language to language, faithful communication of the meaning of the writers of the Bible demands frequent modifications in sentence structure and constant regard for the contextual meanings of words.

A sensitive feeling for style does not always accompany scholarship. Accordingly the Committee on Bible Translation submitted the developing version to a number of stylistic consultants. Two of them read every book of both Old and New Testaments twice—once before and once after the last major revision—and made invaluable suggestions. Samples of the translation were tested for clarity and ease of reading by various kinds of people—young and old, highly educated and less well educated, ministers and laymen.

Concern for clear and natural English—that the New International Version should be idiomatic but not idiosyncratic, contemporary but not dated—motivated the translators and consultants. At the same time, they tried to reflect the differing styles of the biblical writers. In view of the international use of English, the translators sought to avoid obvious Americanisms on the one hand and obvious Anglicisms on the other. A British edition reflects the comparatively few differences of significant idiom and of spelling.

As for the traditional pronouns "thou," "thee" and "thine" in reference to the Deity, the translators judged that to use these archaisms (along with the old verb forms such as "doest," "wouldest" and "hadst") would violate accuracy in translation. Neither Hebrew, Aramaic nor Greek uses special pronouns for the persons of the Godhead. A present-day translation is not enhanced by forms that in the time of the King James Version were used in everyday speech, whether referring to God or man.

For the Old Testament the standard Hebrew text, the Masoretic Text as published in the latest editions of Biblia Hebraica, was used throughout. The Dead Sea Scrolls contain material bearing on an earlier stage of the Hebrew text. They were consulted, as were the Samaritan Pentateuch and the ancient scribal traditions relating to textual changes. Sometimes a variant Hebrew reading in the margin of the Masoretic Text was followed instead of the text itself. Such instances, being variants within the Masoretic tradition, are not specified by footnotes. In rare cases, words in the consonantal text were divided differently from the way they appear in the Masoretic Text. Footnotes indicate this. The translators also consulted the more important early versions—the Septuagint; Aquila, Symmachus and Theodotion; the Vulgate; the Syriac Peshitta; the Targums; and for the Psalms the Juxta Hebraica of Jerome. Readings from these versions were occasionally followed where the Masoretic Text seemed doubtful and where accepted principles of textual criticism showed that one or more of these textual witnesses appeared to provide the correct reading. Such instances are footnoted. Sometimes vowel letters and vowel signs did not, in the judgment of the translators, represent the correct vowels for the original consonantal text. Accordingly some words were read with a different set of vowels. These instances are usually not indicated by footnotes.

The Greek text used in translating the New Testament was an eclectic one. No other piece of ancient literature has such an abundance of manuscript witnesses as does the New Testament. Where existing manuscripts differ, the translators made their choice of readings according to accepted principles of New Testament textual criticism. Footnotes call attention to places where there was uncertainty about what the original text was. The best current printed texts of the Greek New Testament were used.

There is a sense in which the work of translation is never wholly finished. This applies to all great literature and uniquely so to the Bible. In 1973 the New Testament in the New International Version was published. Since then, suggestions for corrections and revisions have been received from various sources. The Committee on Bible Translation carefully considered the suggestions and adopted a number of them. These were incorporated in the first printing of the entire Bible in 1978. Additional revisions were made by the Committee on Bible Translation in 1983 and appear in printings after that date.

As in other ancient documents, the precise meaning of the biblical texts is sometimes uncertain. This is more often the case with the Hebrew and Aramaic texts than with the Greek text. Although archaeological and linguistic discoveries in this century aid in understanding difficult passages, some uncertainties remain. The more significant of these have been called to the reader's attention in the footnotes.

In regard to the divine name YHWH, commonly referred to as the Tetragrammaton, the translators adopted the device used in most English versions of rendering that name as "Lord" in capital letters to distinguish it from Adonai, another Hebrew word rendered "Lord," for which small letters are used. Wherever the two names stand together in the Old Testament as a compound name of God, they are rendered "Sovereign Lord."

Because for most readers today the phrases "the Lord of hosts" and "God of hosts" have little meaning, this version renders them "the Lord Almighty" and "God Almighty." These renderings convey the sense of the Hebrew, namely, "he who is sovereign over all the 'hosts' (powers) in heaven and on earth, especially over the 'hosts' (armies) of Israel." For readers unacquainted with Hebrew this does not make clear the distinction between Sabaoth ("hosts" or "Almighty") and Shaddai (which can also be translated "Almighty"), but the latter occurs infrequently and is always footnoted. When Adonai and YHWH Sabaoth occur together, they are rendered "the Lord, the Lord Almighty."

As for other proper nouns, the familiar spellings of the King James Version are generally retained. Names traditionally spelled with "ch," except where it is final, are usually spelled in this translation with "k" or "c," since the biblical languages do not have the sound that "ch" frequently indicates in English—for example, in chant. For well-known names such as Zechariah, however, the traditional spelling has been retained. Variation in the spelling of names in the original languages has usually not been indicated. Where a person or place has two or more different names in the Hebrew, Aramaic or Greek texts, the more familiar one has generally been used, with footnotes where needed.

To achieve clarity the translators sometimes supplied words not in the original texts but required by the context. If there was uncertainty about such material, it is enclosed in brackets. Also for the sake of clarity or style, nouns, including some proper nouns, are sometimes substituted for pronouns, and vice versa. And though the Hebrew writers often shifted back and forth between first, second and third personal pronouns without change of antecedent, this translation often makes them uniform, in accordance with English style and without the use of footnotes.

Poetical passages are printed as poetry, that is, with indentation of lines with separate stanzas. These are generally designed to reflect the structure of Hebrew poetry. This poetry is normally characterized by parallelism in balanced lines. Most of the poetry in the Bible is in the Old Testament, and scholars differ regarding the scansion of Hebrew lines. The translators determined the stanza divisions for the most part by analysis of the subject matter. The stanzas therefore serve as poetic paragraphs.

As an aid to the reader, italicized sectional headings are inserted in most of the books. They are not to be regarded as part of the NIV text, are not for oral reading, and are not intended to dictate the interpretation of the sections they head.

The footnotes in this version are of several kinds, most of which need no explanation. Those giving alternative translations begin with "Or" and generally introduce the alternative with the last word preceding it in the text, except when it is a single-word alternative; in poetry quoted in a footnote a slant mark indicates a line division. Footnotes introduced by "Or" do not have uniform significance. In some cases two possible translations were considered to have about equal validity. In other cases, though the translators were convinced that the translation in the text was correct, they judged that another interpretation was possible and of sufficient importance to be represented in a footnote.

In the New Testament, footnotes that refer to uncertainty regarding the original text are introduced by "Some manuscripts" or similar expressions. In the Old Testament, evidence for the reading chosen is given first and evidence for the alternative is added after a semicolon (for example: Septuagint; Hebrew father). In such notes the term "Hebrew" refers to the Masoretic Text.

It should be noted that minerals, flora and fauna, architectural details, articles of clothing and jewelry, musical instruments and other articles cannot always be identified with precision. Also measures of capacity in the biblical period are particularly uncertain (see the table of weights and measures following the text).

Like all translations of the Bible, made as they are by imperfect man, this one undoubtedly falls short of its goals. Yet we are grateful to God for the extent to which he has enabled us to realize these goals and for the strength he has given us and our colleagues to complete our task. We offer this version of the Bible to him in whose name and for whose glory it has been made. We pray that it will lead many into a better understanding of the Holy Scriptures and a fuller knowledge of Jesus Christ the incarnate Word, of whom the Scriptures so faithfully testify.

The Committee on Bible Translation

June 1978
(Revised August 1983)

Names of the translators and editors may be secured from the International Bible Society, translation sponsors of the New International Version, 1820 Jet Stream Drive, Colorado Springs, Colorado 80921-3696 U.S.A.

OLD TESTAMENT

MOSES writes Genesis, a book of beginnings, to tell us how God creates the world, how sin comes into the world, and how God loves mankind in spite of his sin. He reports exciting stories about Adam, Noah, Abraham, Isaac, Jacob and Joseph, how God cares for them and stands beside them, no matter what they do. As you read this book, think about how God enters into a personal relationship with you, cares for you, and wants you to make serving him a priority in your life.

GENESIS

The Beginning

1 In the beginning God created the heavens and the earth. ²Now the earth was*a* formless and empty, darkness was over the surface of the deep, and the Spirit of God was hovering over the waters.

³And God said, "Let there be light," and there was light. ⁴God saw that the light was good, and he separated the light from the darkness. ⁵God called the light "day," and the darkness he called "night." And there was evening, and there was morning—the first day.

⁶And God said, "Let there be an expanse between the waters to separate water from water." ⁷So God made the expanse and separated the water under the expanse from the water above it. And it was so. ⁸God called the expanse "sky." And there was evening, and there was morning—the second day.

⁹And God said, "Let the water under the sky be gathered to one place, and let dry ground appear." And it was so.

¹⁰God called the dry ground "land," and the gathered waters he called "seas." And God saw that it was good.

¹¹Then God said, "Let the land produce vegetation: seed-bearing plants and trees on the land that bear fruit with seed in it, according to their various kinds." And it was so. ¹²The land produced vegetation: plants bearing seed according to their kinds and trees bearing fruit with seed in it according to their kinds. And God saw that it was good. ¹³And there was evening, and there was morning—the third day.

¹⁴And God said, "Let there be lights in the expanse of the sky to separate the day from the night, and let them serve as signs to mark seasons and days and years, ¹⁵and let them be lights in the expanse of the sky to give light on the earth." And it was so. ¹⁶God made two great lights—the greater light to govern the day and the lesser light to govern the night. He also made the stars. ¹⁷God set them in the expanse of the sky to give light on the earth, ¹⁸to govern the day and the night, and to separate light from darkness. And God saw that it was good. ¹⁹And there was evening, and there was morning—the fourth day.

²⁰And God said, "Let the water teem with living creatures, and let birds fly above the earth across the expanse of the sky." ²¹So God created the great creatures of the sea and every living and moving thing with which the water teems, according to their kinds, and every winged bird according to its kind. And God saw that it was good. ²²God blessed them and said, "Be fruitful and increase in number and fill the water in the seas, and let the birds increase on the earth." ²³And there was evening, and there was morning—the fifth day.

²⁴And God said, "Let the land produce living creatures according to their kinds: livestock, creatures that move along the ground, and wild animals, each according to its kind." And it was so. ²⁵God made the wild animals according to their kinds, the livestock according to their kinds, and all the creatures that move along the ground

according to their kinds. And God saw that it was good.

²⁶Then God said, "Let us make man in our image, in our likeness, and let them rule over the fish of the sea and the birds of the air, over the livestock, over all the earth,ᵃ and over all the creatures that move along the ground."

²⁷So God created man in his own image, in the image of God he created him; male and female he created them.

²⁸God blessed them and said to them, "Be fruitful and increase in number; fill the earth and subdue it. Rule over the fish of the sea and the birds of the air and over every living creature that moves on the ground."

²⁹Then God said, "I give you every seed-bearing plant on the face of the whole earth and every tree that has fruit with seed in it. They will be yours for food. ³⁰And to all the beasts of the earth and all the birds of the air and all the creatures that move on the ground—everything that has the breath of life in it—I give every green plant for food." And it was so.

³¹God saw all that he had made, and it was very good. And there was evening, and there was morning—the sixth day.

2 Thus the heavens and the earth were completed in all their vast array.

²By the seventh day God had finished the work he had been doing; so on the seventh day he restedᵇ from all his work. ³And God blessed the seventh day and made it holy, because on it he rested from all the work of creating that he had done.

Adam and Eve

⁴This is the account of the heavens and the earth when they were created.

When the Lᴏʀᴅ God made the earth and the heavens— ⁵and no shrub of the field had yet appeared on the earthᶜ and no plant of the field had yet sprung up, for the Lᴏʀᴅ God had not sent rain on the earthᶜ and there was no man to work the ground, ⁶but streamsᵈ came up from the earth and watered the whole surface of the ground— ⁷the Lᴏʀᴅ God formed the

ᵃ26 Hebrew; Syriac *all the wild animals*   ᵇ2 Or *ceased*; also in verse 3   ᶜ5 Or *land*; also in verse 6
ᵈ6 Or *mist*

man[a] from the dust of the ground and breathed into his nostrils the breath of life, and the man became a living being.

⁸Now the Lᴏʀᴅ God had planted a garden in the east, in Eden; and there he put the man he had formed. ⁹And the Lᴏʀᴅ God made all kinds of trees grow out of the ground—trees that were pleasing to the eye and good for food. In the middle of the garden were the tree of life and the tree of the knowledge of good and evil.

¹⁰A river watering the garden flowed from Eden; from there it was separated into four headwaters. ¹¹The name of the first is the Pishon; it winds through the entire land of Havilah, where there is gold. ¹²(The gold of that land is good; aromatic resin[b] and onyx are also there.) ¹³The name of the second river is the Gihon; it winds through the entire land of Cush.[c] ¹⁴The name of the third river is the Tigris; it runs along the east side of

---

[a]7 The Hebrew for *man (adam)* sounds like and may be related to the Hebrew for *ground (adamah)*; it is also the name *Adam* (see Gen. 2:20).   [b]12 Or *good; pearls*   [c]13 Possibly southeast Mesopotamia

---

MONDAY

VERSE FOR THE DAY:	*AUTHOR:*	*PASSAGE FOR THE DAY:*
Genesis 1:26	*Doug Sherman and*	*Genesis 1:26–31*
	William Hendricks	

God and Your Work

GOD is a worker. This alone gives us a clue that work itself must be significant, that it must have *intrinsic* value. For, by definition, God can do nothing that is not inherently good, or else he would violate his own nature and character. The fact that God calls what he does "work" and calls that work "good" means that work has intrinsic worth.

Most of us are already familiar with the profound and often misunderstood truth that man was created in the image of his divine Creator. But since God himself is a worker, we would expect man, who is created in God's image, to be a worker, too . . .

The concept of mankind ruling over the other creatures and subduing the creation and eating from the produce of the earth all points to man as a worker. Not only is God a worker, but man is a worker, too. In fact, Ecclesiastes 3:13 calls this work a gift of God: "That everyone may eat and drink and find satisfaction in all his toil—this is the gift of God."

These and other passages of Scripture lend awesome dignity to your work. As a human created in God's image, you are inherently significant and when you work you are doing something that is very Godlike. It is not only God's work that is significant; human work is significant, too. It is something ordained by God. The fact that you work is, in the words of Genesis 1, "very good." Intrinsically good. Valued by God.

Additional Scripture Readings:
Nehemiah 4:6–23;
2 Thessalonians 3:6–13

Go to page 5 for your next devotional reading.

Asshur. And the fourth river is the Euphrates.

¹⁵The Lord God took the man and put him in the Garden of Eden to work it and take care of it. ¹⁶And the Lord God commanded the man, "You are free to eat from any tree in the garden; ¹⁷but you must not eat from the tree of the knowledge of good and evil, for when you eat of it you will surely die."

¹⁸The Lord God said, "It is not good for the man to be alone. I will make a helper suitable for him."

¹⁹Now the Lord God had formed out of the ground all the beasts of the field and all the birds of the air. He brought them to the man to see what he would name them; and whatever the man called each living creature, that was its name. ²⁰So the man gave names to all the livestock, the birds of the air and all the beasts of the field.

But for Adam*ᵃ* no suitable helper was found. ²¹So the Lord God caused the man to fall into a deep sleep; and while he was sleeping, he took one of the man's ribs*ᵇ* and closed up the place with flesh. ²²Then the Lord God made a woman from the rib*ᶜ* he had taken out of the man, and he brought her to the man.

²³The man said,

"This is now bone of my bones
    and flesh of my flesh;
she shall be called 'woman,*ᵈ*'
    for she was taken out of man."

²⁴For this reason a man will leave his father and mother and be united to his wife, and they will become one flesh.

²⁵The man and his wife were both naked, and they felt no shame.

The Fall of Man

3 Now the serpent was more crafty than any of the wild animals the Lord God had made. He said to the woman, "Did God really say, 'You must not eat from any tree in the garden'?"

²The woman said to the serpent, "We may eat fruit from the trees in the garden, ³but God did say, 'You must not eat fruit from the tree that is in the middle of the garden, and you must not touch it, or you will die.'"

⁴"You will not surely die," the serpent said to the woman. ⁵"For God knows that when you eat of it your eyes will be opened, and you will be like God, knowing good and evil."

⁶When the woman saw that the fruit of the tree was good for food and pleasing to the eye, and also desirable for gaining wisdom, she took some and ate it. She also gave some to her husband, who was with her, and he ate it. ⁷Then the eyes of both of them were opened, and they realized they were naked; so they sewed fig leaves together and made coverings for themselves.

⁸Then the man and his wife heard the sound of the Lord God as he was walking in the garden in the cool of the day, and they hid from the Lord God among the trees of the garden. ⁹But the Lord God called to the man, "Where are you?"

¹⁰He answered, "I heard you in the garden, and I was afraid because I was naked; so I hid."

¹¹And he said, "Who told you that you were naked? Have you eaten from the tree that I commanded you not to eat from?"

¹²The man said, "The woman you put here with me—she gave me some fruit from the tree, and I ate it."

¹³Then the Lord God said to the woman, "What is this you have done?"

The woman said, "The serpent deceived me, and I ate."

¹⁴So the Lord God said to the serpent, "Because you have done this,

"Cursed are you above all the
        livestock
    and all the wild animals!
You will crawl on your belly
    and you will eat dust
    all the days of your life.
¹⁵And I will put enmity
    between you and the woman,
    and between your offspring*ᵉ* and
        hers;
he will crush*ᶠ* your head,
    and you will strike his heel."

¹⁶To the woman he said,

"I will greatly increase your pains in
        childbearing;
    with pain you will give birth to
        children.
Your desire will be for your husband,
    and he will rule over you."

ᵃ20 Or *the man*   *ᵇ21* Or *took part of the man's side*   *ᶜ22* Or *part*   *ᵈ23* The Hebrew for *woman*
sounds like the Hebrew for *man*.   *ᵉ15* Or *seed*   *ᶠ15* Or *strike*

17To Adam he said, "Because you listened to your wife and ate from the tree about which I commanded you, 'You must not eat of it,'

"Cursed is the ground because of
     you;
   through painful toil you will eat of
     it
   all the days of your life.

18It will produce thorns and thistles for
     you,
   and you will eat the plants of the
     field.
19By the sweat of your brow
     you will eat your food
   until you return to the ground,
     since from it you were taken;
   for dust you are
     and to dust you will return."

TUESDAY

VERSE FOR THE DAY:
Genesis 2:17

AUTHOR:
C.S. Lewis

PASSAGE FOR THE DAY:
Genesis 2:15–17

Born to Be Free

GOD created things which had free will. That means creatures that can go either wrong or right. Some people think they can imagine a creature which was free but had no possibility of going wrong; I cannot. If a thing is free to be good it is also free to be bad. And free will is what has made evil possible. Why, then, did God give them free will? Because free will, though it makes evil possible, is also the only thing that makes possible any love or goodness or joy worth having. A world of automata—of creatures that worked like machines—would hardly be worth creating. The happiness which God designs for his higher creatures is the happiness of being freely, voluntarily united to him and to each other in an ecstasy of love and delight compared with which the most rapturous love between a man and a woman on this earth is mere milk and water. And for that they must be free.

Of course God knew what would happen if they used their freedom the wrong way: apparently he thought it worth the risk. Perhaps we feel inclined to disagree with him. But there is a difficulty about disagreeing with God. He is the source from which all your reasoning power comes: you could not be right and he wrong any more than a stream can rise higher than its own source. When you are arguing against him you are arguing against the very power that makes you able to argue at all: it is like cutting off the branch you are sitting on. If God thinks this state of war in the universe a price worth paying for free will—that is, for making a live world in which creatures can do real good or harm and something of real importance can happen, instead of a toy world which only moves when he pulls the strings—then we may take it it is worth paying.

Additional Scripture Readings:
John 8:31–36; Galatians 5:1–15

Go to page 8 for your next devotional reading.

[20]Adam[a] named his wife Eve,[b] because she would become the mother of all the living.

[21]The LORD God made garments of skin for Adam and his wife and clothed them. [22]And the LORD God said, "The man has now become like one of us, knowing good and evil. He must not be allowed to reach out his hand and take also from the tree of life and eat, and live forever." [23]So the LORD God banished him from the Garden of Eden to work the ground from which he had been taken. [24]After he drove the man out, he placed on the east side[c] of the Garden of Eden cherubim and a flaming sword flashing back and forth to guard the way to the tree of life.

Cain and Abel

4 Adam[a] lay with his wife Eve, and she became pregnant and gave birth to Cain.[d] She said, "With the help of the LORD I have brought forth[e] a man." [2]Later she gave birth to his brother Abel.

Now Abel kept flocks, and Cain worked the soil. [3]In the course of time Cain brought some of the fruits of the soil as an offering to the LORD. [4]But Abel brought fat portions from some of the firstborn of his flock. The LORD looked with favor on Abel and his offering, [5]but on Cain and his offering he did not look with favor. So Cain was very angry, and his face was downcast.

[6]Then the LORD said to Cain, "Why are you angry? Why is your face downcast? [7]If you do what is right, will you not be accepted? But if you do not do what is right, sin is crouching at your door; it desires to have you, but you must master it."

[8]Now Cain said to his brother Abel, "Let's go out to the field."[f] And while they were in the field, Cain attacked his brother Abel and killed him.

[9]Then the LORD said to Cain, "Where is your brother Abel?"

"I don't know," he replied. "Am I my brother's keeper?"

[10]The LORD said, "What have you done? Listen! Your brother's blood cries out to me from the ground. [11]Now you are under a curse and driven from the ground, which opened its mouth to receive your brother's blood from your hand. [12]When you work the ground, it will no longer yield its crops for you. You will be a restless wanderer on the earth."

[13]Cain said to the LORD, "My punishment is more than I can bear. [14]Today you are driving me from the land, and I will be hidden from your presence; I will be a restless wanderer on the earth, and whoever finds me will kill me."

[15]But the LORD said to him, "Not so[g]; if anyone kills Cain, he will suffer vengeance seven times over." Then the LORD put a mark on Cain so that no one who found him would kill him. [16]So Cain went out from the LORD's presence and lived in the land of Nod,[h] east of Eden.

[17]Cain lay with his wife, and she became pregnant and gave birth to Enoch. Cain was then building a city, and he named it after his son Enoch. [18]To Enoch was born Irad, and Irad was the father of Mehujael, and Mehujael was the father of Methushael, and Methushael was the father of Lamech.

[19]Lamech married two women, one named Adah and the other Zillah. [20]Adah gave birth to Jabal; he was the father of those who live in tents and raise livestock. [21]His brother's name was Jubal; he was the father of all who play the harp and flute. [22]Zillah also had a son, Tubal-Cain, who forged all kinds of tools out of[i] bronze and iron. Tubal-Cain's sister was Naamah.

[23]Lamech said to his wives,

"Adah and Zillah, listen to me;
    wives of Lamech, hear my words.
I have killed[j] a man for wounding
        me,
    a young man for injuring me.
[24]If Cain is avenged seven times,
    then Lamech seventy-seven times."

[25]Adam lay with his wife again, and she gave birth to a son and named him Seth,[k] saying, "God has granted me another child in place of Abel, since Cain killed him." [26]Seth also had a son, and he named him Enosh.

At that time men began to call on[l] the name of the LORD.

---

a20,1 Or *The man*   *b20 Eve* probably means *living.* the Hebrew for *brought forth* or *acquired.*   *e1* Or *have acquired*   *f8* Samaritan Pentateuch, Septuagint, Vulgate and Syriac; Masoretic Text does not have *"Let's go out to the field."*   *g15* Septuagint, Vulgate and Syriac; Hebrew *Very well*   *h16 Nod* means *wandering* (see verses 12 and 14).   *i22* Or *who instructed all who work in*   *j23* Or *I will kill*   *k25 Seth* probably means *granted.*   *l26* Or *to proclaim*

c24 Or *placed in front*   *d1 Cain* sounds like

From Adam to Noah

5 This is the written account of Adam's line.

When God created man, he made him in the likeness of God. ²He created them male and female and blessed them. And when they were created, he called them "man.ᵃ"

³When Adam had lived 130 years, he had a son in his own likeness, in his own image; and he named him Seth. ⁴After Seth was born, Adam lived 800 years and had other sons and daughters. ⁵Altogether, Adam lived 930 years, and then he died.

⁶When Seth had lived 105 years, he became the fatherᵇ of Enosh. ⁷And after he became the father of Enosh, Seth lived 807 years and had other sons and daughters. ⁸Altogether, Seth lived 912 years, and then he died.

⁹When Enosh had lived 90 years, he became the father of Kenan. ¹⁰And after he became the father of Kenan, Enosh lived 815 years and had other sons and daughters. ¹¹Altogether, Enosh lived 905 years, and then he died.

¹²When Kenan had lived 70 years, he became the father of Mahalalel. ¹³And after he became the father of Mahalalel, Kenan lived 840 years and had other sons and daughters. ¹⁴Altogether, Kenan lived 910 years, and then he died.

¹⁵When Mahalalel had lived 65 years, he became the father of Jared. ¹⁶And after he became the father of Jared, Mahalalel lived 830 years and had other sons and daughters. ¹⁷Altogether, Mahalalel lived 895 years, and then he died.

¹⁸When Jared had lived 162 years, he became the father of Enoch. ¹⁹And after he became the father of Enoch, Jared lived 800 years and had other sons and daughters. ²⁰Altogether, Jared lived 962 years, and then he died.

²¹When Enoch had lived 65 years, he became the father of Methuselah. ²²And after he became the father of Methuselah, Enoch walked with God 300 years and had other sons and daughters. ²³Altogether, Enoch lived 365 years. ²⁴Enoch walked with God; then he was no more, because God took him away.

²⁵When Methuselah had lived 187 years, he became the father of Lamech. ²⁶And after he became the father of Lamech, Methuselah lived 782 years and had other sons and daughters. ²⁷Altogether, Methuselah lived 969 years, and then he died.

²⁸When Lamech had lived 182 years, he had a son. ²⁹He named him Noahᶜ and said, "He will comfort us in the labor and painful toil of our hands caused by the ground the LORD has cursed." ³⁰After Noah was born, Lamech lived 595 years and had other sons and daughters. ³¹Altogether, Lamech lived 777 years, and then he died.

³²After Noah was 500 years old, he became the father of Shem, Ham and Japheth.

The Flood

6 When men began to increase in number on the earth and daughters were born to them, ²the sons of God saw that the daughters of men were beautiful, and they married any of them they chose. ³Then the LORD said, "My Spirit will not contend withᵈ man forever, for he is mortalᵉ; his days will be a hundred and twenty years."

⁴The Nephilim were on the earth in those days — and also afterward — when the sons of God went to the daughters of men and had children by them. They were the heroes of old, men of renown.

⁵The LORD saw how great man's wickedness on the earth had become, and that every inclination of the thoughts of his heart was only evil all the time. ⁶The LORD was grieved that he had made man on the earth, and his heart was filled with pain. ⁷So the LORD said, "I will wipe mankind, whom I have created, from the face of the earth — men and animals, and creatures that move along the ground, and birds of the air — for I am grieved that I have made them." ⁸But Noah found favor in the eyes of the LORD.

⁹This is the account of Noah.

Noah was a righteous man, blameless among the people of his time, and he walked with God. ¹⁰Noah had three sons: Shem, Ham and Japheth.

¹¹Now the earth was corrupt in God's sight and was full of violence. ¹²God saw how corrupt the earth had become, for all the people on earth had corrupted their ways. ¹³So God said to Noah, "I am going to put an end to all people, for the earth is

---

ᵃ2 Hebrew *adam*　　ᵇ6 *Father* may mean *ancestor*; also in verses 7-26.　　ᶜ29 *Noah* sounds like the Hebrew for *comfort*.　　ᵈ3 Or *My spirit will not remain in*　　ᵉ3 Or *corrupt* filled with violence because of them. I am surely going to destroy both them and the earth. **14**So make yourself an ark of cypress[a] wood; make rooms in it and coat it with pitch inside and out. **15**This is how you are to build it: The ark is to be 450 feet long, 75 feet wide and 45 feet high.[b] **16**Make a roof for it and finish[c] the ark to within 18 inches[d] of the top. Put a door in the side of the ark and make lower,

middle and upper decks. **17**I am going to bring floodwaters on the earth to destroy all life under the heavens, every creature that has the breath of life in it. Everything on earth will perish. **18**But I will establish my covenant with you, and you will enter the ark—you and your sons and your wife and your sons' wives with you. **19**You are to bring into the ark two of all living creatures, male and female, to keep them alive

[a]14 The meaning of the Hebrew for this word is uncertain.   [b]15 Hebrew *300 cubits long, 50 cubits wide and 30 cubits high* (about 140 meters long, 23 meters wide and 13.5 meters high)   [c]16 Or *Make an opening for light by finishing*   [d]16 Hebrew *a cubit* (about 0.5 meter)

WEDNESDAY

VERSE FOR THE DAY:
Genesis 5:22

AUTHOR:
Jerry Bridges

PASSAGE FOR THE DAY:
Genesis 5:21–24

Walking With God

THE Bible begins to give us some clues about godliness in its earliest pages. Genesis 5:21–24 tells us about Enoch, the father of Methuselah. In a very short three-verse summary of Enoch's life, Moses twice describes him as one who "walked with God." The author of Hebrews gives Enoch a place in his great "Faith's Hall of Fame" in chapter 11, but he sees Enoch from a slightly different perspective. He describes him as "one who pleased God." Here, then, are two important clues: Enoch walked with God, and Enoch pleased God. It is evident from these two statements that Enoch's life was centered in God; God was the focal point, the polestar of his very existence.

Enoch walked with God; he enjoyed a relationship with God; and he pleased God. We could accurately say he was devoted to God. This is the meaning of godliness. The New Testament word for godliness, in its original meaning, conveys the idea of a personal attitude toward God that results in actions that are pleasing to God. This personal attitude toward God is what we call devotion to God. But it is always *devotion in action*. It is not just a warm, emotional feeling about God, the kind of feeling we may get while singing some grand old hymn of praise or some modern-day chorus of worship. Neither is devotion to God merely a time of private Bible reading and prayer, a practice we sometimes call "devotions." Although this practice is vitally important to a godly person, we must not think of it as defining devotion for us. Devotion is not an activity; it is an attitude toward God.

Additional Scripture Readings:
Micah 6:6–8; 1 John 1:5–10

Go to page 18 for your next devotional reading.

with you. **20**Two of every kind of bird, of every kind of animal and of every kind of creature that moves along the ground will come to you to be kept alive. **21**You are to take every kind of food that is to be eaten and store it away as food for you and for them."

22Noah did everything just as God commanded him.

7 The LORD then said to Noah, "Go into the ark, you and your whole family, because I have found you righteous in this generation. **2**Take with you seven*a* of every kind of clean animal, a male and its mate, and two of every kind of unclean animal, a male and its mate, **3**and also seven of every kind of bird, male and female, to keep their various kinds alive throughout the earth. **4**Seven days from now I will send rain on the earth for forty days and forty nights, and I will wipe from the face of the earth every living creature I have made."

5And Noah did all that the LORD commanded him.

6Noah was six hundred years old when the floodwaters came on the earth. **7**And Noah and his sons and his wife and his sons' wives entered the ark to escape the waters of the flood. **8**Pairs of clean and unclean animals, of birds and of all creatures that move along the ground, **9**male and female, came to Noah and entered the ark, as God had commanded Noah. **10**And after the seven days the floodwaters came on the earth.

11In the six hundredth year of Noah's life, on the seventeenth day of the second month—on that day all the springs of the great deep burst forth, and the floodgates of the heavens were opened. **12**And rain fell on the earth forty days and forty nights.

13On that very day Noah and his sons, Shem, Ham and Japheth, together with his wife and the wives of his three sons, entered the ark. **14**They had with them every wild animal according to its kind, all livestock according to their kinds, every creature that moves along the ground according to its kind and every bird according to its kind, everything with wings. **15**Pairs of all creatures that have the breath of life in them came to Noah and entered the ark. **16**The animals going in were male and female of every living thing, as God had

commanded Noah. Then the LORD shut him in.

17For forty days the flood kept coming on the earth, and as the waters increased they lifted the ark high above the earth. **18**The waters rose and increased greatly on the earth, and the ark floated on the surface of the water. **19**They rose greatly on the earth, and all the high mountains under the entire heavens were covered. **20**The waters rose and covered the mountains to a depth of more than twenty feet.*b,c* **21**Every living thing that moved on the earth perished—birds, livestock, wild animals, all the creatures that swarm over the earth, and all mankind. **22**Everything on dry land that had the breath of life in its nostrils died. **23**Every living thing on the face of the earth was wiped out; men and animals and the creatures that move along the ground and the birds of the air were wiped from the earth. Only Noah was left, and those with him in the ark.

24The waters flooded the earth for a hundred and fifty days.

8 But God remembered Noah and all the wild animals and the livestock that were with him in the ark, and he sent a wind over the earth, and the waters receded. **2**Now the springs of the deep and the floodgates of the heavens had been closed, and the rain had stopped falling from the sky. **3**The water receded steadily from the earth. At the end of the hundred and fifty days the water had gone down, **4**and on the seventeenth day of the seventh month the ark came to rest on the mountains of Ararat. **5**The waters continued to recede until the tenth month, and on the first day of the tenth month the tops of the mountains became visible.

6After forty days Noah opened the window he had made in the ark **7**and sent out a raven, and it kept flying back and forth until the water had dried up from the earth. **8**Then he sent out a dove to see if the water had receded from the surface of the ground. **9**But the dove could find no place to set its feet because there was water over all the surface of the earth; so it returned to Noah in the ark. He reached out his hand and took the dove and brought it back to himself in the ark. **10**He waited seven more days and again sent out the dove from the ark. **11**When the dove returned to him in the evening, there

a2 Or seven pairs; also in verse 3   b20 Hebrew fifteen cubits (about 6.9 meters)   c20 Or rose more than twenty feet, and the mountains were covered in its beak was a freshly plucked olive leaf! Then Noah knew that the water had receded from the earth. [12]He waited seven more days and sent the dove out again, but this time it did not return to him.

[13]By the first day of the first month of Noah's six hundred and first year, the water had dried up from the earth. Noah then removed the covering from the ark and saw that the surface of the ground was dry. [14]By the twenty-seventh day of the second month the earth was completely dry.

[15]Then God said to Noah, [16]"Come out of the ark, you and your wife and your sons and their wives. [17]Bring out every kind of living creature that is with you—the birds, the animals, and all the creatures that move along the ground—so they can multiply on the earth and be fruitful and increase in number upon it."

[18]So Noah came out, together with his sons and his wife and his sons' wives. [19]All the animals and all the creatures that move along the ground and all the birds—everything that moves on the earth—came out of the ark, one kind after another.

[20]Then Noah built an altar to the LORD and, taking some of all the clean animals and clean birds, he sacrificed burnt offerings on it. [21]The LORD smelled the pleasing aroma and said in his heart: "Never again will I curse the ground because of man, even though[a] every inclination of his heart is evil from childhood. And never again will I destroy all living creatures, as I have done.

[22]"As long as the earth endures,
  seedtime and harvest,
  cold and heat,
  summer and winter,
  day and night
  will never cease."

God's Covenant With Noah

9 Then God blessed Noah and his sons, saying to them, "Be fruitful and increase in number and fill the earth. [2]The fear and dread of you will fall upon all the beasts of the earth and all the birds of the air, upon every creature that moves along the ground, and upon all the fish of the sea; they are given into your hands. [3]Everything that lives and moves will be food for you. Just as I gave you the green plants, I now give you everything.

[4]"But you must not eat meat that has its lifeblood still in it. [5]And for your lifeblood I will surely demand an accounting. I will demand an accounting from every animal. And from each man, too, I will demand an accounting for the life of his fellow man.

[6]"Whoever sheds the blood of man,
  by man shall his blood be shed;
  for in the image of God
  has God made man.

[7]As for you, be fruitful and increase in number; multiply on the earth and increase upon it."

[8]Then God said to Noah and to his sons with him: [9]"I now establish my covenant with you and with your descendants after you [10]and with every living creature that was with you—the birds, the livestock and all the wild animals, all those that came out of the ark with you—every living creature on earth. [11]I establish my covenant with you: Never again will all life be cut off by the waters of a flood; never again will there be a flood to destroy the earth."

[12]And God said, "This is the sign of the covenant I am making between me and you and every living creature with you, a covenant for all generations to come: [13]I have set my rainbow in the clouds, and it will be the sign of the covenant between me and the earth. [14]Whenever I bring clouds over the earth and the rainbow appears in the clouds, [15]I will remember my covenant between me and you and all living creatures of every kind. Never again will the waters become a flood to destroy all life. [16]Whenever the rainbow appears in the clouds, I will see it and remember the everlasting covenant between God and all living creatures of every kind on the earth."

[17]So God said to Noah, "This is the sign of the covenant I have established between me and all life on the earth."

The Sons of Noah

[18]The sons of Noah who came out of the ark were Shem, Ham and Japheth. (Ham was the father of Canaan.) [19]These were the three sons of Noah, and from them came the people who were scattered over the earth.

[20]Noah, a man of the soil, proceeded[b] to plant a vineyard. [21]When he drank some of its wine, he became drunk and lay uncovered inside his tent. [22]Ham, the

---

[a]21 Or *man, for*   [b]20 Or *soil, was the first*

father of Canaan, saw his father's nakedness and told his two brothers outside. 23But Shem and Japheth took a garment and laid it across their shoulders; then they walked in backward and covered their father's nakedness. Their faces were turned the other way so that they would not see their father's nakedness.

24When Noah awoke from his wine and found out what his youngest son had done to him, 25he said,

"Cursed be Canaan!
  The lowest of slaves
  will he be to his brothers."

26He also said,

"Blessed be the LORD, the God of
    Shem!
  May Canaan be the slave of Shem.*a*
27May God extend the territory of
    Japheth*b*;
  may Japheth live in the tents of
    Shem,
  and may Canaan be his*c* slave."

28After the flood Noah lived 350 years. 29Altogether, Noah lived 950 years, and then he died.

The Table of Nations

10 This is the account of Shem, Ham and Japheth, Noah's sons, who themselves had sons after the flood.

The Japhethites

2The sons*d* of Japheth:
  Gomer, Magog, Madai, Javan, Tubal, Meshech and Tiras.
3The sons of Gomer:
  Ashkenaz, Riphath and Togarmah.
4The sons of Javan:
  Elishah, Tarshish, the Kittim and the Rodanim.*e* 5(From these the maritime peoples spread out into their territories by their clans within their nations, each with its own language.)

The Hamites

6The sons of Ham:
  Cush, Mizraim,*f* Put and Canaan.

7The sons of Cush:
  Seba, Havilah, Sabtah, Raamah and Sabteca.
  The sons of Raamah:
  Sheba and Dedan.

8Cush was the father*g* of Nimrod, who grew to be a mighty warrior on the earth. 9He was a mighty hunter before the LORD; that is why it is said, "Like Nimrod, a mighty hunter before the LORD." 10The first centers of his kingdom were Babylon, Erech, Akkad and Calneh, in*h* Shinar.*i* 11From that land he went to Assyria, where he built Nineveh, Rehoboth Ir,*j* Calah 12and Resen, which is between Nineveh and Calah; that is the great city.

13Mizraim was the father of
  the Ludites, Anamites, Lehabites, Naphtuhites, 14Pathrusites, Casluhites (from whom the Philistines came) and Caphtorites.
15Canaan was the father of
  Sidon his firstborn,*k* and of the Hittites, 16Jebusites, Amorites, Girgashites, 17Hivites, Arkites, Sinites, 18Arvadites, Zemarites and Hamathites.

Later the Canaanite clans scattered 19and the borders of Canaan reached from Sidon toward Gerar as far as Gaza, and then toward Sodom, Gomorrah, Admah and Zeboiim, as far as Lasha.
20These are the sons of Ham by their clans and languages, in their territories and nations.

The Semites

21Sons were also born to Shem, whose older brother was*l* Japheth; Shem was the ancestor of all the sons of Eber.

22The sons of Shem:
  Elam, Asshur, Arphaxad, Lud and Aram.
23The sons of Aram:
  Uz, Hul, Gether and Meshech.*m*
24Arphaxad was the father of*n* Shelah, and Shelah the father of Eber.
25Two sons were born to Eber:

---

a26 Or *be his slave*   *b27* *Japheth* sounds like the Hebrew for *extend.*   *c27* Or *their*   *d2* *Sons* may mean *descendants* or *successors* or *nations*; also in verses 3, 4, 6, 7, 20-23, 29 and 31.   *e4* Some manuscripts of the Masoretic Text and Samaritan Pentateuch (see also Septuagint and 1 Chron. 1:7); most manuscripts of the Masoretic Text *Dodanim*   *f6* That is, Egypt; also in verse 13   *g8* *Father* may mean *ancestor* or *predecessor* or *founder*; also in verses 13, 15, 24 and 26.   *h10* Or *Erech and Akkad—all of them in*   *i10* That is, Babylonia   *j11* Or *Nineveh with its city squares*   *k15* Or *of the Sidonians, the foremost*   *l21* Or *Shem, the older brother of*   *m23* See Septuagint and 1 Chron. 1:17; Hebrew *Mash*   *n24* Hebrew; Septuagint *father of Cainan, and Cainan was the father of*

One was named Peleg,[a] because in his time the earth was divided; his brother was named Joktan. [26]Joktan was the father of

Almodad, Sheleph, Hazarmaveth, Jerah, [27]Hadoram, Uzal, Diklah, [28]Obal, Abimael, Sheba, [29]Ophir, Havilah and Jobab. All these were sons of Joktan.

[30]The region where they lived stretched from Mesha toward Sephar, in the eastern hill country.

[31]These are the sons of Shem by their clans and languages, in their territories and nations.

[32]These are the clans of Noah's sons, according to their lines of descent, within their nations. From these the nations spread out over the earth after the flood.

The Tower of Babel

11 Now the whole world had one language and a common speech. [2]As men moved eastward,[b] they found a plain in Shinar[c] and settled there. [3]They said to each other, "Come, let's make bricks and bake them thoroughly." They used brick instead of stone, and tar for mortar. [4]Then they said, "Come, let us build ourselves a city, with a tower that reaches to the heavens, so that we may make a name for ourselves and not be scattered over the face of the whole earth."

[5]But the LORD came down to see the city and the tower that the men were building. [6]The LORD said, "If as one people speaking the same language they have begun to do this, then nothing they plan to do will be impossible for them. [7]Come, let us go down and confuse their language so they will not understand each other."

[8]So the LORD scattered them from there over all the earth, and they stopped building the city. [9]That is why it was called Babel[d]—because there the LORD confused the language of the whole world. From there the LORD scattered them over the face of the whole earth.

From Shem to Abram

[10]This is the account of Shem.

Two years after the flood, when Shem was 100 years old, he became the father[e] of Arphaxad. [11]And after he became the father of Arphaxad, Shem lived 500 years and had other sons and daughters.

[12]When Arphaxad had lived 35 years, he became the father of Shelah. [13]And after he became the father of Shelah, Arphaxad lived 403 years and had other sons and daughters.[f]

[14]When Shelah had lived 30 years, he became the father of Eber. [15]And after he became the father of Eber, Shelah lived 403 years and had other sons and daughters.

[16]When Eber had lived 34 years, he became the father of Peleg. [17]And after he became the father of Peleg, Eber lived 430 years and had other sons and daughters.

[18]When Peleg had lived 30 years, he became the father of Reu. [19]And after he became the father of Reu, Peleg lived 209 years and had other sons and daughters.

[20]When Reu had lived 32 years, he became the father of Serug. [21]And after he became the father of Serug, Reu lived 207 years and had other sons and daughters.

[22]When Serug had lived 30 years, he became the father of Nahor. [23]And after he became the father of Nahor, Serug lived 200 years and had other sons and daughters.

[24]When Nahor had lived 29 years, he became the father of Terah. [25]And after he became the father of Terah, Nahor lived 119 years and had other sons and daughters.

[26]After Terah had lived 70 years, he became the father of Abram, Nahor and Haran.

[27]This is the account of Terah.

Terah became the father of Abram, Nahor and Haran. And Haran became the father of Lot. [28]While his father Terah was still alive, Haran died in Ur of the Chaldeans, in the land of his birth. [29]Abram and Nahor both married. The name of Abram's wife was Sarai, and the name of Nahor's wife was Milcah; she was the daughter of Haran, the father of both Milcah and Iscah. [30]Now Sarai was barren; she had no children.

a25 *Peleg* means *division.*   b2 Or *from the east*; or *in the east*   c2 That is, Babylonia   d9 That is, Babylon; *Babel* sounds like the Hebrew for *confused.*   e10 *Father* may mean *ancestor*; also in verses 11-25.   f12,13 Hebrew; Septuagint (see also Luke 3:35, 36 and note at Gen. 10:24) *35 years, he became the father of Cainan.* [13]*And after he became the father of Cainan, Arphaxad lived 430 years and had other sons and daughters, and then he died. When Cainan had lived 130 years, he became the father of Shelah. And after he became the father of Shelah, Cainan lived 330 years and had other sons and daughters*

[31]Terah took his son Abram, his grandson Lot son of Haran, and his daughter-in-law Sarai, the wife of his son Abram, and together they set out from Ur of the Chaldeans to go to Canaan. But when they came to Haran, they settled there.

[32]Terah lived 205 years, and he died in Haran.

The Call of Abram

12 The LORD had said to Abram, "Leave your country, your people and your father's household and go to the land I will show you.

[2]"I will make you into a great nation
　and I will bless you;
I will make your name great,
　and you will be a blessing.
[3]I will bless those who bless you,
　and whoever curses you I will
　　　curse;
and all peoples on earth
　will be blessed through you."

[4]So Abram left, as the LORD had told him; and Lot went with him. Abram was seventy-five years old when he set out from Haran. [5]He took his wife Sarai, his nephew Lot, all the possessions they had accumulated and the people they had acquired in Haran, and they set out for the land of Canaan, and they arrived there.

[6]Abram traveled through the land as far as the site of the great tree of Moreh at Shechem. At that time the Canaanites were in the land. [7]The LORD appeared to Abram and said, "To your offspring[a] I will give this land." So he built an altar there to the LORD, who had appeared to him.

[8]From there he went on toward the hills east of Bethel and pitched his tent, with Bethel on the west and Ai on the east. There he built an altar to the LORD and called on the name of the LORD. [9]Then Abram set out and continued toward the Negev.

Abram in Egypt

[10]Now there was a famine in the land, and Abram went down to Egypt to live there for a while because the famine was severe. [11]As he was about to enter Egypt, he said to his wife Sarai, "I know what a beautiful woman you are. [12]When the Egyptians see you, they will say, 'This is his wife.' Then they will kill me but will let you live. [13]Say you are my sister, so that I will be treated well for your sake and my life will be spared because of you."

[14]When Abram came to Egypt, the Egyptians saw that she was a very beautiful woman. [15]And when Pharaoh's officials saw her, they praised her to Pharaoh, and she was taken into his palace. [16]He treated Abram well for her sake, and Abram acquired sheep and cattle, male and female donkeys, menservants and maidservants, and camels.

[17]But the LORD inflicted serious diseases on Pharaoh and his household because of Abram's wife Sarai. [18]So Pharaoh summoned Abram. "What have you done to me?" he said. "Why didn't you tell me she was your wife? [19]Why did you say, 'She is my sister,' so that I took her to be my wife? Now then, here is your wife. Take her and go!" [20]Then Pharaoh gave orders about Abram to his men, and they sent him on his way, with his wife and everything he had.

Abram and Lot Separate

13 So Abram went up from Egypt to the Negev, with his wife and everything he had, and Lot went with him. [2]Abram had become very wealthy in livestock and in silver and gold.

[3]From the Negev he went from place to place until he came to Bethel, to the place between Bethel and Ai where his tent had been earlier [4]and where he had first built an altar. There Abram called on the name of the LORD.

[5]Now Lot, who was moving about with Abram, also had flocks and herds and tents. [6]But the land could not support them while they stayed together, for their possessions were so great that they were not able to stay together. [7]And quarreling arose between Abram's herdsmen and the herdsmen of Lot. The Canaanites and Perizzites were also living in the land at that time.

[8]So Abram said to Lot, "Let's not have any quarreling between you and me, or between your herdsmen and mine, for we are brothers. [9]Is not the whole land before you? Let's part company. If you go to the left, I'll go to the right; if you go to the right, I'll go to the left."

[10]Lot looked up and saw that the whole plain of the Jordan was well watered, like the garden of the LORD, like the land of Egypt, toward Zoar. (This was before the LORD destroyed Sodom and Gomorrah.)

[a]7 Or seed

¹¹So Lot chose for himself the whole plain of the Jordan and set out toward the east. The two men parted company: ¹²Abram lived in the land of Canaan, while Lot lived among the cities of the plain and pitched his tents near Sodom. ¹³Now the men of Sodom were wicked and were sinning greatly against the LORD.

¹⁴The LORD said to Abram after Lot had parted from him, "Lift up your eyes from where you are and look north and south, east and west. ¹⁵All the land that you see I will give to you and your offspring[a] forever. ¹⁶I will make your offspring like the dust of the earth, so that if anyone could count the dust, then your offspring could be counted. ¹⁷Go, walk through the length and breadth of the land, for I am giving it to you."

¹⁸So Abram moved his tents and went to live near the great trees of Mamre at Hebron, where he built an altar to the LORD.

Abram Rescues Lot

14 At this time Amraphel king of Shinar,[b] Arioch king of Ellasar, Kedorlaomer king of Elam and Tidal king of Goiim ²went to war against Bera king of Sodom, Birsha king of Gomorrah, Shinab king of Admah, Shemeber king of Zeboiim, and the king of Bela (that is, Zoar). ³All these latter kings joined forces in the Valley of Siddim (the Salt Sea[c]). ⁴For twelve years they had been subject to Kedorlaomer, but in the thirteenth year they rebelled.

⁵In the fourteenth year, Kedorlaomer and the kings allied with him went out and defeated the Rephaites in Ashteroth Karnaim, the Zuzites in Ham, the Emites in Shaveh Kiriathaim ⁶and the Horites in the hill country of Seir, as far as El Paran near the desert. ⁷Then they turned back and went to En Mishpat (that is, Kadesh), and they conquered the whole territory of the Amalekites, as well as the Amorites who were living in Hazazon Tamar.

⁸Then the king of Sodom, the king of Gomorrah, the king of Admah, the king of Zeboiim and the king of Bela (that is, Zoar) marched out and drew up their battle lines in the Valley of Siddim ⁹against Kedorlaomer king of Elam, Tidal king of Goiim, Amraphel king of Shinar and Arioch king of Ellasar—four kings against five. ¹⁰Now the Valley of Siddim was full of tar pits, and when the kings of Sodom and Gomorrah fled, some of the men fell into them and the rest fled to the hills. ¹¹The four kings seized all the goods of Sodom and Gomorrah and all their food; then they went away. ¹²They also carried off Abram's nephew Lot and his possessions, since he was living in Sodom.

¹³One who had escaped came and reported this to Abram the Hebrew. Now Abram was living near the great trees of Mamre the Amorite, a brother[d] of Eshcol and Aner, all of whom were allied with Abram. ¹⁴When Abram heard that his relative had been taken captive, he called out the 318 trained men born in his household and went in pursuit as far as Dan. ¹⁵During the night Abram divided his men to attack them and he routed them, pursuing them as far as Hobah, north of Damascus. ¹⁶He recovered all the goods and brought back his relative Lot and his possessions, together with the women and the other people.

¹⁷After Abram returned from defeating Kedorlaomer and the kings allied with him, the king of Sodom came out to meet him in the Valley of Shaveh (that is, the King's Valley).

¹⁸Then Melchizedek king of Salem[e] brought out bread and wine. He was priest of God Most High, ¹⁹and he blessed Abram, saying,

"Blessed be Abram by God Most High,
    Creator[f] of heaven and earth.
²⁰And blessed be[g] God Most High,
    who delivered your enemies into
        your hand."

Then Abram gave him a tenth of everything.

²¹The king of Sodom said to Abram, "Give me the people and keep the goods for yourself."

²²But Abram said to the king of Sodom, "I have raised my hand to the LORD, God Most High, Creator of heaven and earth, and have taken an oath ²³that I will accept nothing belonging to you, not even a thread or the thong of a sandal, so that you will never be able to say, 'I made Abram rich.' ²⁴I will accept nothing but what my men have eaten and the share that belongs to the men who went with me—to Aner, Eshcol and Mamre. Let them have their share."

---

a15 Or seed; also in verse 16   b1 That is, Babylonia; also in verse 9   c3 That is, the Dead Sea
d13 Or a relative; or an ally   e18 That is, Jerusalem   f19 Or Possessor; also in verse 22   g20 Or
And praise be to

God's Covenant With Abram

15 After this, the word of the Lord came to Abram in a vision:

"Do not be afraid, Abram.
  I am your shield,[a]
  your very great reward.[b]"

[2]But Abram said, "O Sovereign Lord, what can you give me since I remain childless and the one who will inherit[c] my estate is Eliezer of Damascus?" [3]And Abram said, "You have given me no children; so a servant in my household will be my heir."

[4]Then the word of the Lord came to him: "This man will not be your heir, but a son coming from your own body will be your heir." [5]He took him outside and said, "Look up at the heavens and count the stars—if indeed you can count them." Then he said to him, "So shall your offspring be."

[6]Abram believed the Lord, and he credited it to him as righteousness.

[7]He also said to him, "I am the Lord, who brought you out of Ur of the Chaldeans to give you this land to take possession of it."

[8]But Abram said, "O Sovereign Lord, how can I know that I will gain possession of it?"

[9]So the Lord said to him, "Bring me a heifer, a goat and a ram, each three years old, along with a dove and a young pigeon."

[10]Abram brought all these to him, cut them in two and arranged the halves opposite each other; the birds, however, he did not cut in half. [11]Then birds of prey came down on the carcasses, but Abram drove them away.

[12]As the sun was setting, Abram fell into a deep sleep, and a thick and dreadful darkness came over him. [13]Then the Lord said to him, "Know for certain that your descendants will be strangers in a country not their own, and they will be enslaved and mistreated four hundred years. [14]But I will punish the nation they serve as slaves, and afterward they will come out with great possessions. [15]You, however, will go to your fathers in peace and be buried at a good old age. [16]In the fourth generation your descendants will come back here, for the sin of the Amorites has not yet reached its full measure."

[17]When the sun had set and darkness had fallen, a smoking firepot with a blazing torch appeared and passed between the pieces. [18]On that day the Lord made a covenant with Abram and said, "To your descendants I give this land, from the river[d] of Egypt to the great river, the Euphrates— [19]the land of the Kenites, Kenizzites, Kadmonites, [20]Hittites, Perizzites, Rephaites, [21]Amorites, Canaanites, Girgashites and Jebusites."

Hagar and Ishmael

16 Now Sarai, Abram's wife, had borne him no children. But she had an Egyptian maidservant named Hagar; [2]so she said to Abram, "The Lord has kept me from having children. Go, sleep with my maidservant; perhaps I can build a family through her."

Abram agreed to what Sarai said. [3]So after Abram had been living in Canaan ten years, Sarai his wife took her Egyptian maidservant Hagar and gave her to her husband to be his wife. [4]He slept with Hagar, and she conceived.

When she knew she was pregnant, she began to despise her mistress. [5]Then Sarai said to Abram, "You are responsible for the wrong I am suffering. I put my servant in your arms, and now that she knows she is pregnant, she despises me. May the Lord judge between you and me."

[6]"Your servant is in your hands," Abram said. "Do with her whatever you think best." Then Sarai mistreated Hagar; so she fled from her.

[7]The angel of the Lord found Hagar near a spring in the desert; it was the spring that is beside the road to Shur. [8]And he said, "Hagar, servant of Sarai, where have you come from, and where are you going?"

"I'm running away from my mistress Sarai," she answered.

[9]Then the angel of the Lord told her, "Go back to your mistress and submit to her." [10]The angel added, "I will so increase your descendants that they will be too numerous to count."

[11]The angel of the Lord also said to her:

"You are now with child
  and you will have a son.
You shall name him Ishmael,[e]
  for the Lord has heard of your
    misery.

---

[a]1 Or *sovereign*   [b]1 Or *shield; / your reward will be very great*   [c]2 The meaning of the Hebrew for this phrase is uncertain.   [d]18 Or *Wadi*   [e]11 *Ishmael* means *God hears.*

[12]He will be a wild donkey of a man;
his hand will be against everyone
and everyone's hand against him,
and he will live in hostility
toward[a] all his brothers."

[13]She gave this name to the LORD who spoke to her: "You are the God who sees me," for she said, "I have now seen[b] the One who sees me." [14]That is why the well was called Beer Lahai Roi[c]; it is still there, between Kadesh and Bered.

[15]So Hagar bore Abram a son, and Abram gave the name Ishmael to the son she had borne. [16]Abram was eighty-six years old when Hagar bore him Ishmael.

The Covenant of Circumcision

17 When Abram was ninety-nine years old, the LORD appeared to him and said, "I am God Almighty[d]; walk before me and be blameless. [2]I will confirm my covenant between me and you and will greatly increase your numbers."

[3]Abram fell facedown, and God said to him, [4]"As for me, this is my covenant with you: You will be the father of many nations. [5]No longer will you be called Abram[e]; your name will be Abraham,[f] for I have made you a father of many nations. [6]I will make you very fruitful; I will make nations of you, and kings will come from you. [7]I will establish my covenant as an everlasting covenant between me and you and your descendants after you for the generations to come, to be your God and the God of your descendants after you. [8]The whole land of Canaan, where you are now an alien, I will give as an everlasting possession to you and your descendants after you; and I will be their God."

[9]Then God said to Abraham, "As for you, you must keep my covenant, you and your descendants after you for the generations to come. [10]This is my covenant with you and your descendants after you, the covenant you are to keep: Every male among you shall be circumcised. [11]You are to undergo circumcision, and it will be the sign of the covenant between me and you. [12]For the generations to come every male among you who is eight days old must be circumcised, including those born in your household or bought with money from a foreigner—those who are

not your offspring. [13]Whether born in your household or bought with your money, they must be circumcised. My covenant in your flesh is to be an everlasting covenant. [14]Any uncircumcised male, who has not been circumcised in the flesh, will be cut off from his people; he has broken my covenant."

[15]God also said to Abraham, "As for Sarai your wife, you are no longer to call her Sarai; her name will be Sarah. [16]I will bless her and will surely give you a son by her. I will bless her so that she will be the mother of nations; kings of peoples will come from her."

[17]Abraham fell facedown; he laughed and said to himself, "Will a son be born to a man a hundred years old? Will Sarah bear a child at the age of ninety?" [18]And Abraham said to God, "If only Ishmael might live under your blessing!"

[19]Then God said, "Yes, but your wife Sarah will bear you a son, and you will call him Isaac.[g] I will establish my covenant with him as an everlasting covenant for his descendants after him. [20]And as for Ishmael, I have heard you: I will surely bless him; I will make him fruitful and will greatly increase his numbers. He will be the father of twelve rulers, and I will make him into a great nation. [21]But my covenant I will establish with Isaac, whom Sarah will bear to you by this time next year." [22]When he had finished speaking with Abraham, God went up from him.

[23]On that very day Abraham took his son Ishmael and all those born in his household or bought with his money, every male in his household, and circumcised them, as God told him. [24]Abraham was ninety-nine years old when he was circumcised, [25]and his son Ishmael was thirteen; [26]Abraham and his son Ishmael were both circumcised on that same day. [27]And every male in Abraham's household, including those born in his household or bought from a foreigner, was circumcised with him.

The Three Visitors

18 The LORD appeared to Abraham near the great trees of Mamre while he was sitting at the entrance to his tent in the heat of the day. [2]Abraham looked up and saw three men standing nearby. When he saw them, he hurried from the

---

[a]12 Or *live to the east / of*   [b]13 Or *seen the back of One who sees me.*   [d]1 Hebrew *El-Shaddai*   [e]5 *Abram* means *exalted father.*   [c]14 *Beer Lahai Roi* means *well of the Living*   [f]5 *Abraham* means *father of many.*   [g]19 *Isaac* means *he laughs.*

entrance of his tent to meet them and bowed low to the ground.

3He said, "If I have found favor in your eyes, my lord,*a* do not pass your servant by. **4**Let a little water be brought, and then you may all wash your feet and rest under this tree. **5**Let me get you something to eat, so you can be refreshed and then go on your way—now that you have come to your servant."

"Very well," they answered, "do as you say."

6So Abraham hurried into the tent to Sarah. "Quick," he said, "get three seahs*b* of fine flour and knead it and bake some bread."

7Then he ran to the herd and selected a choice, tender calf and gave it to a servant, who hurried to prepare it. **8**He then brought some curds and milk and the calf that had been prepared, and set these before them. While they ate, he stood near them under a tree.

9"Where is your wife Sarah?" they asked him.

"There, in the tent," he said.

10Then the Lord*c* said, "I will surely return to you about this time next year, and Sarah your wife will have a son."

Now Sarah was listening at the entrance to the tent, which was behind him. **11**Abraham and Sarah were already old and well advanced in years, and Sarah was past the age of childbearing. **12**So Sarah laughed to herself as she thought, "After I am worn out and my master*d* is old, will I now have this pleasure?"

13Then the Lord said to Abraham, "Why did Sarah laugh and say, 'Will I really have a child, now that I am old?' **14**Is anything too hard for the Lord? I will return to you at the appointed time next year and Sarah will have a son."

15Sarah was afraid, so she lied and said, "I did not laugh."

But he said, "Yes, you did laugh."

Abraham Pleads for Sodom

16When the men got up to leave, they looked down toward Sodom, and Abraham walked along with them to see them on their way. **17**Then the Lord said, "Shall I hide from Abraham what I am about to do? **18**Abraham will surely become a great and powerful nation, and all nations on earth will be blessed through him. **19**For I have chosen him, so that he will direct his children and his household after him to keep the way of the Lord by doing what is right and just, so that the Lord will bring about for Abraham what he has promised him."

20Then the Lord said, "The outcry against Sodom and Gomorrah is so great and their sin so grievous **21**that I will go down and see if what they have done is as bad as the outcry that has reached me. If not, I will know."

22The men turned away and went toward Sodom, but Abraham remained standing before the Lord.*e* **23**Then Abraham approached him and said: "Will you sweep away the righteous with the wicked? **24**What if there are fifty righteous people in the city? Will you really sweep it away and not spare*f* the place for the sake of the fifty righteous people in it? **25**Far be it from you to do such a thing—to kill the righteous with the wicked, treating the righteous and the wicked alike. Far be it from you! Will not the Judge*g* of all the earth do right?"

26The Lord said, "If I find fifty righteous people in the city of Sodom, I will spare the whole place for their sake."

27Then Abraham spoke up again: "Now that I have been so bold as to speak to the Lord, though I am nothing but dust and ashes, **28**what if the number of the righteous is five less than fifty? Will you destroy the whole city because of five people?"

"If I find forty-five there," he said, "I will not destroy it."

29Once again he spoke to him, "What if only forty are found there?"

He said, "For the sake of forty, I will not do it."

30Then he said, "May the Lord not be angry, but let me speak. What if only thirty can be found there?"

He answered, "I will not do it if I find thirty there."

31Abraham said, "Now that I have been so bold as to speak to the Lord, what if only twenty can be found there?"

He said, "For the sake of twenty, I will not destroy it."

32Then he said, "May the Lord not be angry, but let me speak just once more. What if only ten can be found there?"

---

a3 Or *O Lord*   *b6* That is, probably about 20 quarts (about 22 liters)   *c10* Hebrew *Then he*
d12 Or *husband*   *e22* Masoretic Text; an ancient Hebrew scribal tradition *but the Lord remained standing before Abraham*   *f24* Or *forgive*; also in verse 26   *g25* Or *Ruler*

He answered, "For the sake of ten, I will not destroy it."

³³When the LORD had finished speaking with Abraham, he left, and Abraham returned home.

Sodom and Gomorrah Destroyed

19 The two angels arrived at Sodom in the evening, and Lot was sitting in the gateway of the city. When he saw them, he got up to meet them and bowed down with his face to the ground. ²"My lords," he said, "please turn aside to your servant's house. You can wash your feet and spend the night and then go on your way early in the morning."

"No," they answered, "we will spend the night in the square."

³But he insisted so strongly that they did go with him and entered his house. He prepared a meal for them, baking bread without yeast, and they ate. ⁴Before they

---

THURSDAY

VERSE FOR THE DAY:	AUTHOR:	PASSAGE FOR THE DAY:
Genesis 18:12	Max Lucado	Genesis 18:9–15

Paying the Pediatrician

WHEN Abram is pushing a century of years and Sarai ninety . . . God pays them a visit and tells them they had better select a name for their new son [see Genesis 17:17–19].

Abram and Sarai have the same response: laughter. They laugh partly because it is too good to happen and partly because it might. They laugh because they have given up hope, and hope born anew is always funny before it is real.

They laugh at the lunacy of it all . . .

They laugh because that is what you do when someone says he can do the impossible. They laugh a little *at* God, and a lot *with* God—for God is laughing, too. Then, with the smile still on his face, he gets busy doing what he does best—the unbelievable.

He changes a few things—beginning with their names. Abram, the father of one, will now be Abraham, the father of a multitude. Sarai, the barren one, will now be Sarah, the mother.

But their names aren't the only things God changes. He changes their minds. He changes their faith. He changes the number of their tax deductions. He changes the way they define the word *impossible*.

But most of all, he changes Sarah's attitude about trusting God. Were she to hear Jesus' statement about being poor in spirit [see Matthew 5:3], she could give a testimony: "He's right. I do things my way, I get a headache. I let God take over, I get a son. You try to figure that out. All I know is I am the first lady in town to pay her pediatrician with a Social Security check."

Additional Scripture Readings:
Matthew 5:1–12; Luke 1:26–38

Go to page 21 for your next devotional reading.

had gone to bed, all the men from every part of the city of Sodom—both young and old—surrounded the house. ⁵They called to Lot, "Where are the men who came to you tonight? Bring them out to us so that we can have sex with them."

⁶Lot went outside to meet them and shut the door behind him ⁷and said, "No, my friends. Don't do this wicked thing. ⁸Look, I have two daughters who have never slept with a man. Let me bring them out to you, and you can do what you like with them. But don't do anything to these men, for they have come under the protection of my roof."

⁹"Get out of our way," they replied. And they said, "This fellow came here as an alien, and now he wants to play the judge! We'll treat you worse than them." They kept bringing pressure on Lot and moved forward to break down the door.

¹⁰But the men inside reached out and pulled Lot back into the house and shut the door. ¹¹Then they struck the men who were at the door of the house, young and old, with blindness so that they could not find the door.

¹²The two men said to Lot, "Do you have anyone else here—sons-in-law, sons or daughters, or anyone else in the city who belongs to you? Get them out of here, ¹³because we are going to destroy this place. The outcry to the LORD against its people is so great that he has sent us to destroy it."

¹⁴So Lot went out and spoke to his sons-in-law, who were pledged to marry[a] his daughters. He said, "Hurry and get out of this place, because the LORD is about to destroy the city!" But his sons-in-law thought he was joking.

¹⁵With the coming of dawn, the angels urged Lot, saying, "Hurry! Take your wife and your two daughters who are here, or you will be swept away when the city is punished."

¹⁶When he hesitated, the men grasped his hand and the hands of his wife and of his two daughters and led them safely out of the city, for the LORD was merciful to them. ¹⁷As soon as they had brought them out, one of them said, "Flee for your lives! Don't look back, and don't stop anywhere in the plain! Flee to the mountains or you will be swept away!"

¹⁸But Lot said to them, "No, my lords,[b] please! ¹⁹Your[c] servant has found favor in your[c] eyes, and you[c] have shown great kindness to me in sparing my life. But I can't flee to the mountains; this disaster will overtake me, and I'll die. ²⁰Look, here is a town near enough to run to, and it is small. Let me flee to it—it is very small, isn't it? Then my life will be spared."

²¹He said to him, "Very well, I will grant this request too; I will not overthrow the town you speak of. ²²But flee there quickly, because I cannot do anything until you reach it." (That is why the town was called Zoar.[d])

²³By the time Lot reached Zoar, the sun had risen over the land. ²⁴Then the LORD rained down burning sulfur on Sodom and Gomorrah—from the LORD out of the heavens. ²⁵Thus he overthrew those cities and the entire plain, including all those living in the cities—and also the vegetation in the land. ²⁶But Lot's wife looked back, and she became a pillar of salt.

²⁷Early the next morning Abraham got up and returned to the place where he had stood before the LORD. ²⁸He looked down toward Sodom and Gomorrah, toward all the land of the plain, and he saw dense smoke rising from the land, like smoke from a furnace.

²⁹So when God destroyed the cities of the plain, he remembered Abraham, and he brought Lot out of the catastrophe that overthrew the cities where Lot had lived.

Lot and His Daughters

³⁰Lot and his two daughters left Zoar and settled in the mountains, for he was afraid to stay in Zoar. He and his two daughters lived in a cave. ³¹One day the older daughter said to the younger, "Our father is old, and there is no man around here to lie with us, as is the custom all over the earth. ³²Let's get our father to drink wine and then lie with him and preserve our family line through our father."

³³That night they got their father to drink wine, and the older daughter went in and lay with him. He was not aware of it when she lay down or when she got up.

³⁴The next day the older daughter said to the younger, "Last night I lay with my father. Let's get him to drink wine again tonight, and you go in and lie with him so we can preserve our family line through our father." ³⁵So they got their father to drink wine that night also, and the youn-

---

a14 Or *were married to*   b18 Or *No, Lord*; or *No, my lord*   c19 The Hebrew is singular.
d22 *Zoar* means *small*.

ger daughter went and lay with him. Again he was not aware of it when she lay down or when she got up. ³⁶So both of Lot's daughters became pregnant by their father. ³⁷The older daughter had a son, and she named him Moab[a]; he is the father of the Moabites of today. ³⁸The younger daughter also had a son, and she named him Ben-Ammi[b]; he is the father of the Ammonites of today.

Abraham and Abimelech

20 Now Abraham moved on from there into the region of the Negev and lived between Kadesh and Shur. For a while he stayed in Gerar, ²and there Abraham said of his wife Sarah, "She is my sister." Then Abimelech king of Gerar sent for Sarah and took her.

³But God came to Abimelech in a dream one night and said to him, "You are as good as dead because of the woman you have taken; she is a married woman."

⁴Now Abimelech had not gone near her, so he said, "Lord, will you destroy an innocent nation? ⁵Did he not say to me, 'She is my sister,' and didn't she also say, 'He is my brother'? I have done this with a clear conscience and clean hands."

⁶Then God said to him in the dream, "Yes, I know you did this with a clear conscience, and so I have kept you from sinning against me. That is why I did not let you touch her. ⁷Now return the man's wife, for he is a prophet, and he will pray for you and you will live. But if you do not return her, you may be sure that you and all yours will die."

⁸Early the next morning Abimelech summoned all his officials, and when he told them all that had happened, they were very much afraid. ⁹Then Abimelech called Abraham in and said, "What have you done to us? How have I wronged you that you have brought such great guilt upon me and my kingdom? You have done things to me that should not be done." ¹⁰And Abimelech asked Abraham, "What was your reason for doing this?"

¹¹Abraham replied, "I said to myself, 'There is surely no fear of God in this place, and they will kill me because of my wife.' ¹²Besides, she really is my sister, the daughter of my father though not of my mother; and she became my wife. ¹³And when God had me wander from my father's household, I said to her, 'This is how you can show your love to me: Everywhere we go, say of me, "He is my brother." ' "

¹⁴Then Abimelech brought sheep and cattle and male and female slaves and gave them to Abraham, and he returned Sarah his wife to him. ¹⁵And Abimelech said, "My land is before you; live wherever you like."

¹⁶To Sarah he said, "I am giving your brother a thousand shekels[c] of silver. This is to cover the offense against you before all who are with you; you are completely vindicated."

¹⁷Then Abraham prayed to God, and God healed Abimelech, his wife and his slave girls so they could have children again, ¹⁸for the LORD had closed up every womb in Abimelech's household because of Abraham's wife Sarah.

The Birth of Isaac

21 Now the LORD was gracious to Sarah as he had said, and the LORD did for Sarah what he had promised. ²Sarah became pregnant and bore a son to Abraham in his old age, at the very time God had promised him. ³Abraham gave the name Isaac[d] to the son Sarah bore him. ⁴When his son Isaac was eight days old, Abraham circumcised him, as God commanded him. ⁵Abraham was a hundred years old when his son Isaac was born to him.

⁶Sarah said, "God has brought me laughter, and everyone who hears about this will laugh with me." ⁷And she added, "Who would have said to Abraham that Sarah would nurse children? Yet I have borne him a son in his old age."

Hagar and Ishmael Sent Away

⁸The child grew and was weaned, and on the day Isaac was weaned Abraham held a great feast. ⁹But Sarah saw that the son whom Hagar the Egyptian had borne to Abraham was mocking, ¹⁰and she said to Abraham, "Get rid of that slave woman and her son, for that slave woman's son will never share in the inheritance with my son Isaac."

¹¹The matter distressed Abraham greatly because it concerned his son. ¹²But God said to him, "Do not be so distressed about the boy and your maidservant. Listen to whatever Sarah tells you, because it

---

a37 Moab sounds like the Hebrew for *from father.*
c16 That is, about 25 pounds (about 11.5 kilograms)
b38 Ben-Ammi means *son of my people.*
d3 Isaac means *he laughs.*

is through Isaac that your offspring[a] will be reckoned. [13]I will make the son of the maidservant into a nation also, because he is your offspring."

[14]Early the next morning Abraham took some food and a skin of water and gave them to Hagar. He set them on her shoulders and then sent her off with the boy. She went on her way and wandered in the desert of Beersheba.

[15]When the water in the skin was gone, she put the boy under one of the bushes. [16]Then she went off and sat down nearby, about a bowshot away, for she thought, "I cannot watch the boy die." And as she sat there nearby, she[b] began to sob.

[17]God heard the boy crying, and the angel of God called to Hagar from heaven and said to her, "What is the matter, Hagar? Do not be afraid; God has heard the boy crying as he lies there. [18]Lift the boy up and take him by the hand, for I will make him into a great nation."

[19]Then God opened her eyes and she saw a well of water. So she went and filled the skin with water and gave the boy a drink.

[20]God was with the boy as he grew up. He lived in the desert and became an archer. [21]While he was living in the Desert of Paran, his mother got a wife for him from Egypt.

---

[a]12 Or *seed*   [b]16 Hebrew; Septuagint *the child*

FRIDAY

VERSE FOR THE DAY:	AUTHOR:	PASSAGE FOR THE DAY:
Genesis 22:3	*Oswald Chambers*	*Genesis 22:1–14*

Fools for Christ

SACRIFICE in the Bible means that we give to God the best we have; it is the finest form of worship. Sacrifice is not giving up things, but giving to God with joy the best we have. We have dragged down the idea of surrender and of sacrifice; we have taken the life out of the words and made them mean something sad and weary and despicable. In the Bible they mean the very opposite. To go out in surrender to God means the surrendering of the miserable sense of my own unimportance: Am I willing to surrender that mean little sense for the great big idea God has for me? Am I willing to surrender the fact that I am an ignorant, useless, worthless, too-old person? There is more hindrance to God's work because people cling to a sense of unworthiness than because of conceit. "Who am I?" Instantly the trend of the mind is to say—"Oh well, I have not had any education"; "I did not begin soon enough." Am I willing to surrender the whole thing, and go out in surrender to God; to go out of the carnal mind into the spiritual—"fools for Christ's sake" [see 1 Corinthians 4:10]?

Abraham surrendered himself entirely to the supernatural God. Have you got hold of a supernatural God?—not, do you know what God is going to do? You cannot know, but you have faith in him, and therefore he can do what he likes.

Additional Scripture Readings:
1 Corinthians 4:8–13; 1 Peter 2:4–12

Go to page 28 for your next devotional reading.

The Treaty at Beersheba

22At that time Abimelech and Phicol the commander of his forces said to Abraham, "God is with you in everything you do. **23**Now swear to me here before God that you will not deal falsely with me or my children or my descendants. Show to me and the country where you are living as an alien the same kindness I have shown to you."

24Abraham said, "I swear it."

25Then Abraham complained to Abimelech about a well of water that Abimelech's servants had seized. **26**But Abimelech said, "I don't know who has done this. You did not tell me, and I heard about it only today."

27So Abraham brought sheep and cattle and gave them to Abimelech, and the two men made a treaty. **28**Abraham set apart seven ewe lambs from the flock, **29**and Abimelech asked Abraham, "What is the meaning of these seven ewe lambs you have set apart by themselves?"

30He replied, "Accept these seven lambs from my hand as a witness that I dug this well."

31So that place was called Beersheba,*a* because the two men swore an oath there.

32After the treaty had been made at Beersheba, Abimelech and Phicol the commander of his forces returned to the land of the Philistines. **33**Abraham planted a tamarisk tree in Beersheba, and there he called upon the name of the LORD, the Eternal God. **34**And Abraham stayed in the land of the Philistines for a long time.

Abraham Tested

22 Some time later God tested Abraham. He said to him, "Abraham!"

"Here I am," he replied.

2Then God said, "Take your son, your only son, Isaac, whom you love, and go to the region of Moriah. Sacrifice him there as a burnt offering on one of the mountains I will tell you about."

3Early the next morning Abraham got up and saddled his donkey. He took with him two of his servants and his son Isaac. When he had cut enough wood for the burnt offering, he set out for the place God had told him about. **4**On the third day Abraham looked up and saw the place in the distance. **5**He said to his servants,

"Stay here with the donkey while I and the boy go over there. We will worship and then we will come back to you."

6Abraham took the wood for the burnt offering and placed it on his son Isaac, and he himself carried the fire and the knife. As the two of them went on together, **7**Isaac spoke up and said to his father Abraham, "Father?"

"Yes, my son?" Abraham replied.

"The fire and wood are here," Isaac said, "but where is the lamb for the burnt offering?"

8Abraham answered, "God himself will provide the lamb for the burnt offering, my son." And the two of them went on together.

9When they reached the place God had told him about, Abraham built an altar there and arranged the wood on it. He bound his son Isaac and laid him on the altar, on top of the wood. **10**Then he reached out his hand and took the knife to slay his son. **11**But the angel of the LORD called out to him from heaven, "Abraham! Abraham!"

"Here I am," he replied.

12"Do not lay a hand on the boy," he said. "Do not do anything to him. Now I know that you fear God, because you have not withheld from me your son, your only son."

13Abraham looked up and there in a thicket he saw a ram*b* caught by its horns. He went over and took the ram and sacrificed it as a burnt offering instead of his son. **14**So Abraham called that place The LORD Will Provide. And to this day it is said, "On the mountain of the LORD it will be provided."

15The angel of the LORD called to Abraham from heaven a second time **16**and said, "I swear by myself, declares the LORD, that because you have done this and have not withheld your son, your only son, **17**I will surely bless you and make your descendants as numerous as the stars in the sky and as the sand on the seashore. Your descendants will take possession of the cities of their enemies, **18**and through your offspring*c* all nations on earth will be blessed, because you have obeyed me."

19Then Abraham returned to his servants, and they set off together for Beersheba. And Abraham stayed in Beersheba.

---

a31 Beersheba can mean *well of seven* or *well of the oath.*   *b13* Many manuscripts of the Masoretic Text, Samaritan Pentateuch, Septuagint and Syriac; most manuscripts of the Masoretic Text *a ram behind him*   *c18* Or *seed*

Nahor's Sons

20Some time later Abraham was told, "Milcah is also a mother; she has borne sons to your brother Nahor: 21Uz the firstborn, Buz his brother, Kemuel (the father of Aram), 22Kesed, Hazo, Pildash, Jidlaph and Bethuel." 23Bethuel became the father of Rebekah. Milcah bore these eight sons to Abraham's brother Nahor. 24His concubine, whose name was Reumah, also had sons: Tebah, Gaham, Tahash and Maacah.

The Death of Sarah

23 Sarah lived to be a hundred and twenty-seven years old. 2She died at Kiriath Arba (that is, Hebron) in the land of Canaan, and Abraham went to mourn for Sarah and to weep over her.

3Then Abraham rose from beside his dead wife and spoke to the Hittites.a He said, 4"I am an alien and a stranger among you. Sell me some property for a burial site here so I can bury my dead."

5The Hittites replied to Abraham, 6"Sir, listen to us. You are a mighty prince among us. Bury your dead in the choicest of our tombs. None of us will refuse you his tomb for burying your dead."

7Then Abraham rose and bowed down before the people of the land, the Hittites. 8He said to them, "If you are willing to let me bury my dead, then listen to me and intercede with Ephron son of Zohar on my behalf 9so he will sell me the cave of Machpelah, which belongs to him and is at the end of his field. Ask him to sell it to me for the full price as a burial site among you."

10Ephron the Hittite was sitting among his people and he replied to Abraham in the hearing of all the Hittites who had come to the gate of his city. 11"No, my lord," he said. "Listen to me; I giveb you the field, and I giveb you the cave that is in it. I giveb it to you in the presence of my people. Bury your dead."

12Again Abraham bowed down before the people of the land 13and he said to Ephron in their hearing, "Listen to me, if you will. I will pay the price of the field. Accept it from me so I can bury my dead there."

14Ephron answered Abraham, 15"Listen to me, my lord; the land is worth four hundred shekelsc of silver, but what is that between me and you? Bury your dead."

16Abraham agreed to Ephron's terms and weighed out for him the price he had named in the hearing of the Hittites: four hundred shekels of silver, according to the weight current among the merchants.

17So Ephron's field in Machpelah near Mamre — both the field and the cave in it, and all the trees within the borders of the field — was deeded 18to Abraham as his property in the presence of all the Hittites who had come to the gate of the city. 19Afterward Abraham buried his wife Sarah in the cave in the field of Machpelah near Mamre (which is at Hebron) in the land of Canaan. 20So the field and the cave in it were deeded to Abraham by the Hittites as a burial site.

Isaac and Rebekah

24 Abraham was now old and well advanced in years, and the LORD had blessed him in every way. 2He said to the chiefd servant in his household, the one in charge of all that he had, "Put your hand under my thigh. 3I want you to swear by the LORD, the God of heaven and the God of earth, that you will not get a wife for my son from the daughters of the Canaanites, among whom I am living, 4but will go to my country and my own relatives and get a wife for my son Isaac."

5The servant asked him, "What if the woman is unwilling to come back with me to this land? Shall I then take your son back to the country you came from?"

6"Make sure that you do not take my son back there," Abraham said. 7"The LORD, the God of heaven, who brought me out of my father's household and my native land and who spoke to me and promised me on oath, saying, 'To your offspringe I will give this land' — he will send his angel before you so that you can get a wife for my son from there. 8If the woman is unwilling to come back with you, then you will be released from this oath of mine. Only do not take my son back there." 9So the servant put his hand under the thigh of his master Abraham and swore an oath to him concerning this matter.

10Then the servant took ten of his master's camels and left, taking with him all kinds of good things from his master. He set out for Aram Naharaimf and made his way to the town of Nahor. 11He had the camels kneel down near the well out-

---

a3 Or the sons of Heth; also in verses 5, 7, 10, 16, 18 and 20   b11 Or sell   c15 That is, about 10 pounds (about 4.5 kilograms)   d2 Or oldest   e7 Or seed   f10 That is, Northwest Mesopotamia side the town; it was toward evening, the time the women go out to draw water.

[12]Then he prayed, "O LORD, God of my master Abraham, give me success today, and show kindness to my master Abraham. [13]See, I am standing beside this spring, and the daughters of the townspeople are coming out to draw water. [14]May it be that when I say to a girl, 'Please let down your jar that I may have a drink,' and she says, 'Drink, and I'll water your camels too'—let her be the one you have chosen for your servant Isaac. By this I will know that you have shown kindness to my master."

[15]Before he had finished praying, Rebekah came out with her jar on her shoulder. She was the daughter of Bethuel son of Milcah, who was the wife of Abraham's brother Nahor. [16]The girl was very beautiful, a virgin; no man had ever lain with her. She went down to the spring, filled her jar and came up again.

[17]The servant hurried to meet her and said, "Please give me a little water from your jar."

[18]"Drink, my lord," she said, and quickly lowered the jar to her hands and gave him a drink.

[19]After she had given him a drink, she said, "I'll draw water for your camels too, until they have finished drinking." [20]So she quickly emptied her jar into the trough, ran back to the well to draw more water, and drew enough for all his camels. [21]Without saying a word, the man watched her closely to learn whether or not the LORD had made his journey successful.

[22]When the camels had finished drinking, the man took out a gold nose ring weighing a beka[a] and two gold bracelets weighing ten shekels.[b] [23]Then he asked, "Whose daughter are you? Please tell me, is there room in your father's house for us to spend the night?"

[24]She answered him, "I am the daughter of Bethuel, the son that Milcah bore to Nahor." [25]And she added, "We have plenty of straw and fodder, as well as room for you to spend the night."

[26]Then the man bowed down and worshiped the LORD, [27]saying, "Praise be to the LORD, the God of my master Abraham, who has not abandoned his kindness and faithfulness to my master. As for me, the LORD has led me on the journey to the house of my master's relatives."

[28]The girl ran and told her mother's household about these things. [29]Now Rebekah had a brother named Laban, and he hurried out to the man at the spring. [30]As soon as he had seen the nose ring, and the bracelets on his sister's arms, and had heard Rebekah tell what the man said to her, he went out to the man and found him standing by the camels near the spring. [31]"Come, you who are blessed by the LORD," he said. "Why are you standing out here? I have prepared the house and a place for the camels."

[32]So the man went to the house, and the camels were unloaded. Straw and fodder were brought for the camels, and water for him and his men to wash their feet. [33]Then food was set before him, but he said, "I will not eat until I have told you what I have to say."

"Then tell us," Laban said.

[34]So he said, "I am Abraham's servant. [35]The LORD has blessed my master abundantly, and he has become wealthy. He has given him sheep and cattle, silver and gold, menservants and maidservants, and camels and donkeys. [36]My master's wife Sarah has borne him a son in her[c] old age, and he has given him everything he owns. [37]And my master made me swear an oath, and said, 'You must not get a wife for my son from the daughters of the Canaanites, in whose land I live, [38]but go to my father's family and to my own clan, and get a wife for my son.'

[39]"Then I asked my master, 'What if the woman will not come back with me?'

[40]"He replied, 'The LORD, before whom I have walked, will send his angel with you and make your journey a success, so that you can get a wife for my son from my own clan and from my father's family. [41]Then, when you go to my clan, you will be released from my oath even if they refuse to give her to you—you will be released from my oath.'

[42]"When I came to the spring today, I said, 'O LORD, God of my master Abraham, if you will, please grant success to the journey on which I have come. [43]See, I am standing beside this spring; if a maiden comes out to draw water and I say to her, "Please let me drink a little water from your jar," [44]and if she says to me, "Drink, and I'll draw water for your cam-

els too," let her be the one the LORD has chosen for my master's son.'

45"Before I finished praying in my heart, Rebekah came out, with her jar on her shoulder. She went down to the spring and drew water, and I said to her, 'Please give me a drink.'

46"She quickly lowered her jar from her shoulder and said, 'Drink, and I'll water your camels too.' So I drank, and she watered the camels also.

47"I asked her, 'Whose daughter are you?'

"She said, 'The daughter of Bethuel son of Nahor, whom Milcah bore to him.'

"Then I put the ring in her nose and the bracelets on her arms, **48**and I bowed down and worshiped the LORD. I praised the LORD, the God of my master Abraham, who had led me on the right road to get the granddaughter of my master's brother for his son. **49**Now if you will show kindness and faithfulness to my master, tell me; and if not, tell me, so I may know which way to turn."

50Laban and Bethuel answered, "This is from the LORD; we can say nothing to you one way or the other. **51**Here is Rebekah; take her and go, and let her become the wife of your master's son, as the LORD has directed."

52When Abraham's servant heard what they said, he bowed down to the ground before the LORD. **53**Then the servant brought out gold and silver jewelry and articles of clothing and gave them to Rebekah; he also gave costly gifts to her brother and to her mother. **54**Then he and the men who were with him ate and drank and spent the night there.

When they got up the next morning, he said, "Send me on my way to my master."

55But her brother and her mother replied, "Let the girl remain with us ten days or so; then you*a* may go."

56But he said to them, "Do not detain me, now that the LORD has granted success to my journey. Send me on my way so I may go to my master."

57Then they said, "Let's call the girl and ask her about it." **58**So they called Rebekah and asked her, "Will you go with this man?"

"I will go," she said.

59So they sent their sister Rebekah on her way, along with her nurse and Abra-

ham's servant and his men. **60**And they blessed Rebekah and said to her,

"Our sister, may you increase
    to thousands upon thousands;
may your offspring possess
    the gates of their enemies."

61Then Rebekah and her maids got ready and mounted their camels and went back with the man. So the servant took Rebekah and left.

62Now Isaac had come from Beer Lahai Roi, for he was living in the Negev. **63**He went out to the field one evening to meditate,*b* and as he looked up, he saw camels approaching. **64**Rebekah also looked up and saw Isaac. She got down from her camel **65**and asked the servant, "Who is that man in the field coming to meet us?"

"He is my master," the servant answered. So she took her veil and covered herself.

66Then the servant told Isaac all he had done. **67**Isaac brought her into the tent of his mother Sarah, and he married Rebekah. So she became his wife, and he loved her; and Isaac was comforted after his mother's death.

The Death of Abraham

25 Abraham took*c* another wife, whose name was Keturah. **2**She bore him Zimran, Jokshan, Medan, Midian, Ishbak and Shuah. **3**Jokshan was the father of Sheba and Dedan; the descendants of Dedan were the Asshurites, the Letushites and the Leummites. **4**The sons of Midian were Ephah, Epher, Hanoch, Abida and Eldaah. All these were descendants of Keturah.

5Abraham left everything he owned to Isaac. **6**But while he was still living, he gave gifts to the sons of his concubines and sent them away from his son Isaac to the land of the east.

7Altogether, Abraham lived a hundred and seventy-five years. **8**Then Abraham breathed his last and died at a good old age, an old man and full of years; and he was gathered to his people. **9**His sons Isaac and Ishmael buried him in the cave of Machpelah near Mamre, in the field of Ephron son of Zohar the Hittite, **10**the field Abraham had bought from the Hittites.*d* There Abraham was buried with his wife Sarah. **11**After Abraham's death, God

---

*a*55 Or *she*   *b*63 The meaning of the Hebrew for this word is uncertain.   *c*1 Or *had taken*
*d*10 Or *the sons of Heth*

blessed his son Isaac, who then lived near Beer Lahai Roi.

Ishmael's Sons

¹²This is the account of Abraham's son Ishmael, whom Sarah's maidservant, Hagar the Egyptian, bore to Abraham.

¹³These are the names of the sons of Ishmael, listed in the order of their birth: Nebaioth the firstborn of Ishmael, Kedar, Adbeel, Mibsam, ¹⁴Mishma, Dumah, Massa, ¹⁵Hadad, Tema, Jetur, Naphish and Kedemah. ¹⁶These were the sons of Ishmael, and these are the names of the twelve tribal rulers according to their settlements and camps. ¹⁷Altogether, Ishmael lived a hundred and thirty-seven years. He breathed his last and died, and he was gathered to his people. ¹⁸His descendants settled in the area from Havilah to Shur, near the border of Egypt, as you go toward Asshur. And they lived in hostility toward[a] all their brothers.

Jacob and Esau

¹⁹This is the account of Abraham's son Isaac.

Abraham became the father of Isaac, ²⁰and Isaac was forty years old when he married Rebekah daughter of Bethuel the Aramean from Paddan Aram[b] and sister of Laban the Aramean.

²¹Isaac prayed to the LORD on behalf of his wife, because she was barren. The LORD answered his prayer, and his wife Rebekah became pregnant. ²²The babies jostled each other within her, and she said, "Why is this happening to me?" So she went to inquire of the LORD.

²³The LORD said to her,

"Two nations are in your womb,
    and two peoples from within you
        will be separated;
one people will be stronger than the
        other,
    and the older will serve the
        younger."

²⁴When the time came for her to give birth, there were twin boys in her womb. ²⁵The first to come out was red, and his whole body was like a hairy garment; so they named him Esau.[c] ²⁶After this, his brother came out, with his hand grasping Esau's heel; so he was named Jacob.[d]

Isaac was sixty years old when Rebekah gave birth to them.

²⁷The boys grew up, and Esau became a skillful hunter, a man of the open country, while Jacob was a quiet man, staying among the tents. ²⁸Isaac, who had a taste for wild game, loved Esau, but Rebekah loved Jacob.

²⁹Once when Jacob was cooking some stew, Esau came in from the open country, famished. ³⁰He said to Jacob, "Quick, let me have some of that red stew! I'm famished!" (That is why he was also called Edom.[e])

³¹Jacob replied, "First sell me your birthright."

³²"Look, I am about to die," Esau said. "What good is the birthright to me?"

³³But Jacob said, "Swear to me first." So he swore an oath to him, selling his birthright to Jacob.

³⁴Then Jacob gave Esau some bread and some lentil stew. He ate and drank, and then got up and left.

So Esau despised his birthright.

Isaac and Abimelech

26 Now there was a famine in the land—besides the earlier famine of Abraham's time—and Isaac went to Abimelech king of the Philistines in Gerar. ²The LORD appeared to Isaac and said, "Do not go down to Egypt; live in the land where I tell you to live. ³Stay in this land for a while, and I will be with you and will bless you. For to you and your descendants I will give all these lands and will confirm the oath I swore to your father Abraham. ⁴I will make your descendants as numerous as the stars in the sky and will give them all these lands, and through your offspring[f] all nations on earth will be blessed, ⁵because Abraham obeyed me and kept my requirements, my commands, my decrees and my laws." ⁶So Isaac stayed in Gerar.

⁷When the men of that place asked him about his wife, he said, "She is my sister," because he was afraid to say, "She is my wife." He thought, "The men of this place might kill me on account of Rebekah, because she is beautiful."

⁸When Isaac had been there a long time, Abimelech king of the Philistines looked down from a window and saw Isaac caressing his wife Rebekah. ⁹So

Abimelech summoned Isaac and said, "She is really your wife! Why did you say, 'She is my sister'?"

Isaac answered him, "Because I thought I might lose my life on account of her."

[10]Then Abimelech said, "What is this you have done to us? One of the men might well have slept with your wife, and you would have brought guilt upon us."

[11]So Abimelech gave orders to all the people: "Anyone who molests this man or his wife shall surely be put to death."

[12]Isaac planted crops in that land and the same year reaped a hundredfold, because the LORD blessed him. [13]The man became rich, and his wealth continued to grow until he became very wealthy. [14]He had so many flocks and herds and servants that the Philistines envied him. [15]So all the wells that his father's servants had dug in the time of his father Abraham, the Philistines stopped up, filling them with earth.

[16]Then Abimelech said to Isaac, "Move away from us; you have become too powerful for us."

[17]So Isaac moved away from there and encamped in the Valley of Gerar and settled there. [18]Isaac reopened the wells that had been dug in the time of his father Abraham, which the Philistines had stopped up after Abraham died, and he gave them the same names his father had given them.

[19]Isaac's servants dug in the valley and discovered a well of fresh water there. [20]But the herdsmen of Gerar quarreled with Isaac's herdsmen and said, "The water is ours!" So he named the well Esek,[a] because they disputed with him. [21]Then they dug another well, but they quarreled over that one also; so he named it Sitnah.[b] [22]He moved on from there and dug another well, and no one quarreled over it. He named it Rehoboth,[c] saying, "Now the LORD has given us room and we will flourish in the land."

[23]From there he went up to Beersheba. [24]That night the LORD appeared to him and said, "I am the God of your father Abraham. Do not be afraid, for I am with you; I will bless you and will increase the number of your descendants for the sake of my servant Abraham."

[25]Isaac built an altar there and called on the name of the LORD. There he pitched his tent, and there his servants dug a well.

[26]Meanwhile, Abimelech had come to him from Gerar, with Ahuzzath his personal adviser and Phicol the commander of his forces. [27]Isaac asked them, "Why have you come to me, since you were hostile to me and sent me away?"

[28]They answered, "We saw clearly that the LORD was with you; so we said, 'There ought to be a sworn agreement between us'—between us and you. Let us make a treaty with you [29]that you will do us no harm, just as we did not molest you but always treated you well and sent you away in peace. And now you are blessed by the LORD."

[30]Isaac then made a feast for them, and they ate and drank. [31]Early the next morning the men swore an oath to each other. Then Isaac sent them on their way, and they left him in peace.

[32]That day Isaac's servants came and told him about the well they had dug. They said, "We've found water!" [33]He called it Shibah,[d] and to this day the name of the town has been Beersheba.[e]

[34]When Esau was forty years old, he married Judith daughter of Beeri the Hittite, and also Basemath daughter of Elon the Hittite. [35]They were a source of grief to Isaac and Rebekah.

Jacob Gets Isaac's Blessing

27 When Isaac was old and his eyes were so weak that he could no longer see, he called for Esau his older son and said to him, "My son."

"Here I am," he answered.

[2]Isaac said, "I am now an old man and don't know the day of my death. [3]Now then, get your weapons—your quiver and bow—and go out to the open country to hunt some wild game for me. [4]Prepare me the kind of tasty food I like and bring it to me to eat, so that I may give you my blessing before I die."

[5]Now Rebekah was listening as Isaac spoke to his son Esau. When Esau left for the open country to hunt game and bring it back, [6]Rebekah said to her son Jacob, "Look, I overheard your father say to your brother Esau, [7]'Bring me some game and prepare me some tasty food to eat, so that I may give you my blessing in the presence of the LORD before I die.' [8]Now, my son, listen carefully and do what I tell you: [9]Go out to the flock and bring me two choice young goats, so I can prepare some

---

a20 Esek means dispute.   *b21 Sitnah means opposition.*   *c22 Rehoboth means room.*   *d33 Shibah can mean oath or seven.*   *e33 Beersheba can mean well of the oath or well of seven.*

WEEKENDING

REFLECT

To wait on God is to struggle and sometimes to
fail. Sometimes the failures teach us more than
the successes. For the failures teach us that to
wait on God is not only to wait *for* his mercy,
but to wait *by* his mercy . . . The glory hidden
in our failures is the discovery that the very
thing we wait for is what we wait by! The
success of our waiting lies not in who we are,
but in who God is. It is not our strength that
will pull us through to the end, it is God's
amazing grace and mercy.

– *Ben Patterson*

REVIVE
Saturday: Genesis 12:10–20
Sunday: 2 Timothy 1:3–12

Go to page 38 for your next devotional reading.

tasty food for your father, just the way he likes it. **10**Then take it to your father to eat, so that he may give you his blessing before he dies."

11Jacob said to Rebekah his mother, "But my brother Esau is a hairy man, and I'm a man with smooth skin. **12**What if my father touches me? I would appear to be tricking him and would bring down a curse on myself rather than a blessing."

13His mother said to him, "My son, let the curse fall on me. Just do what I say; go and get them for me."

14So he went and got them and brought them to his mother, and she prepared some tasty food, just the way his father liked it. **15**Then Rebekah took the best clothes of Esau her older son, which she had in the house, and put them on her younger son Jacob. **16**She also covered his hands and the smooth part of his neck with the goatskins. **17**Then she handed to her son Jacob the tasty food and the bread she had made.

18He went to his father and said, "My father."

"Yes, my son," he answered. "Who is it?"

19Jacob said to his father, "I am Esau your firstborn. I have done as you told me. Please sit up and eat some of my game so that you may give me your blessing."

20Isaac asked his son, "How did you find it so quickly, my son?"

"The LORD your God gave me success," he replied.

21Then Isaac said to Jacob, "Come near so I can touch you, my son, to know whether you really are my son Esau or not."

22Jacob went close to his father Isaac, who touched him and said, "The voice is the voice of Jacob, but the hands are the hands of Esau." **23**He did not recognize him, for his hands were hairy like those of his brother Esau; so he blessed him. **24**"Are you really my son Esau?" he asked.

"I am," he replied.

25Then he said, "My son, bring me some of your game to eat, so that I may give you my blessing."

Jacob brought it to him and he ate; and he brought some wine and he drank. **26**Then his father Isaac said to him, "Come here, my son, and kiss me."

27So he went to him and kissed him. When Isaac caught the smell of his clothes, he blessed him and said,

"Ah, the smell of my son
    is like the smell of a field
    that the LORD has blessed.
28May God give you of heaven's dew
    and of earth's richness—
    an abundance of grain and new
      wine.
29May nations serve you
    and peoples bow down to you.
Be lord over your brothers,
    and may the sons of your mother
      bow down to you.
May those who curse you be cursed
    and those who bless you be
      blessed."

30After Isaac finished blessing him and Jacob had scarcely left his father's presence, his brother Esau came in from hunting. **31**He too prepared some tasty food and brought it to his father. Then he said to him, "My father, sit up and eat some of my game, so that you may give me your blessing."

32His father Isaac asked him, "Who are you?"

"I am your son," he answered, "your firstborn, Esau."

33Isaac trembled violently and said, "Who was it, then, that hunted game and brought it to me? I ate it just before you came and I blessed him—and indeed he will be blessed!"

34When Esau heard his father's words, he burst out with a loud and bitter cry and said to his father, "Bless me—me too, my father!"

35But he said, "Your brother came deceitfully and took your blessing."

36Esau said, "Isn't he rightly named Jacob[a]? He has deceived me these two times: He took my birthright, and now he's taken my blessing!" Then he asked, "Haven't you reserved any blessing for me?"

37Isaac answered Esau, "I have made him lord over you and have made all his relatives his servants, and I have sustained him with grain and new wine. So what can I possibly do for you, my son?"

38Esau said to his father, "Do you have only one blessing, my father? Bless me too, my father!" Then Esau wept aloud.

39His father Isaac answered him,

"Your dwelling will be
    away from the earth's richness,
    away from the dew of heaven
      above.

---

a36 Jacob means *he grasps the heel* (figuratively, *he deceives*).

40You will live by the sword
and you will serve your brother.
But when you grow restless,
you will throw his yoke
from off your neck."

Jacob Flees to Laban

41Esau held a grudge against Jacob because of the blessing his father had given him. He said to himself, "The days of mourning for my father are near; then I will kill my brother Jacob."

42When Rebekah was told what her older son Esau had said, she sent for her younger son Jacob and said to him, "Your brother Esau is consoling himself with the thought of killing you. **43**Now then, my son, do what I say: Flee at once to my brother Laban in Haran. **44**Stay with him for a while until your brother's fury subsides. **45**When your brother is no longer angry with you and forgets what you did to him, I'll send word for you to come back from there. Why should I lose both of you in one day?"

46Then Rebekah said to Isaac, "I'm disgusted with living because of these Hittite women. If Jacob takes a wife from among the women of this land, from Hittite women like these, my life will not be worth living."

28 So Isaac called for Jacob and blessed[a] him and commanded him: "Do not marry a Canaanite woman. **2**Go at once to Paddan Aram,[b] to the house of your mother's father Bethuel. Take a wife for yourself there, from among the daughters of Laban, your mother's brother. **3**May God Almighty[c] bless you and make you fruitful and increase your numbers until you become a community of peoples. **4**May he give you and your descendants the blessing given to Abraham, so that you may take possession of the land where you now live as an alien, the land God gave to Abraham." **5**Then Isaac sent Jacob on his way, and he went to Paddan Aram, to Laban son of Bethuel the Aramean, the brother of Rebekah, who was the mother of Jacob and Esau.

6Now Esau learned that Isaac had blessed Jacob and had sent him to Paddan Aram to take a wife from there, and that when he blessed him he commanded him, "Do not marry a Canaanite woman," **7**and that Jacob had obeyed his father and mother and had gone to Paddan Aram. **8**Esau then realized how displeasing the Canaanite women were to his father Isaac; **9**so he went to Ishmael and married Mahalath, the sister of Nebaioth and daughter of Ishmael son of Abraham, in addition to the wives he already had.

Jacob's Dream at Bethel

10Jacob left Beersheba and set out for Haran. **11**When he reached a certain place, he stopped for the night because the sun had set. Taking one of the stones there, he put it under his head and lay down to sleep. **12**He had a dream in which he saw a stairway[d] resting on the earth, with its top reaching to heaven, and the angels of God were ascending and descending on it. **13**There above it[e] stood the LORD, and he said: "I am the LORD, the God of your father Abraham and the God of Isaac. I will give you and your descendants the land on which you are lying. **14**Your descendants will be like the dust of the earth, and you will spread out to the west and to the east, to the north and to the south. All peoples on earth will be blessed through you and your offspring. **15**I am with you and will watch over you wherever you go, and I will bring you back to this land. I will not leave you until I have done what I have promised you."

16When Jacob awoke from his sleep, he thought, "Surely the LORD is in this place, and I was not aware of it." **17**He was afraid and said, "How awesome is this place! This is none other than the house of God; this is the gate of heaven."

18Early the next morning Jacob took the stone he had placed under his head and set it up as a pillar and poured oil on top of it. **19**He called that place Bethel,[f] though the city used to be called Luz.

20Then Jacob made a vow, saying, "If God will be with me and will watch over me on this journey I am taking and will give me food to eat and clothes to wear **21**so that I return safely to my father's house, then the LORD[g] will be my God **22**and[h] this stone that I have set up as a pillar will be God's house, and of all that you give me I will give you a tenth."

---

[a]1 Or greeted   [b]2 That is, Northwest Mesopotamia; also in verses 5, 6 and 7   [c]3 Hebrew El-Shaddai
[d]12 Or ladder   [e]13 Or There beside him   [f]19 Bethel means house of God.   [g]20,21 Or Since God
. . . father's house, the LORD   [h]21,22 Or house, and the LORD will be my God, 22then

Jacob Arrives in Paddan Aram

29 Then Jacob continued on his journey and came to the land of the eastern peoples. ²There he saw a well in the field, with three flocks of sheep lying near it because the flocks were watered from that well. The stone over the mouth of the well was large. ³When all the flocks were gathered there, the shepherds would roll the stone away from the well's mouth and water the sheep. Then they would return the stone to its place over the mouth of the well.

⁴Jacob asked the shepherds, "My brothers, where are you from?"

"We're from Haran," they replied.

⁵He said to them, "Do you know Laban, Nahor's grandson?"

"Yes, we know him," they answered.

⁶Then Jacob asked them, "Is he well?"

"Yes, he is," they said, "and here comes his daughter Rachel with the sheep."

⁷"Look," he said, "the sun is still high; it is not time for the flocks to be gathered. Water the sheep and take them back to pasture."

⁸"We can't," they replied, "until all the flocks are gathered and the stone has been rolled away from the mouth of the well. Then we will water the sheep."

⁹While he was still talking with them, Rachel came with her father's sheep, for she was a shepherdess. ¹⁰When Jacob saw Rachel daughter of Laban, his mother's brother, and Laban's sheep, he went over and rolled the stone away from the mouth of the well and watered his uncle's sheep. ¹¹Then Jacob kissed Rachel and began to weep aloud. ¹²He had told Rachel that he was a relative of her father and a son of Rebekah. So she ran and told her father.

¹³As soon as Laban heard the news about Jacob, his sister's son, he hurried to meet him. He embraced him and kissed him and brought him to his home, and there Jacob told him all these things. ¹⁴Then Laban said to him, "You are my own flesh and blood."

Jacob Marries Leah and Rachel

After Jacob had stayed with him for a whole month, ¹⁵Laban said to him, "Just because you are a relative of mine, should you work for me for nothing? Tell me what your wages should be."

¹⁶Now Laban had two daughters; the name of the older was Leah, and the name of the younger was Rachel. ¹⁷Leah had weak*ᵃ* eyes, but Rachel was lovely in form, and beautiful. ¹⁸Jacob was in love with Rachel and said, "I'll work for you seven years in return for your younger daughter Rachel."

¹⁹Laban said, "It's better that I give her to you than to some other man. Stay here with me." ²⁰So Jacob served seven years to get Rachel, but they seemed like only a few days to him because of his love for her.

²¹Then Jacob said to Laban, "Give me my wife. My time is completed, and I want to lie with her."

²²So Laban brought together all the people of the place and gave a feast. ²³But when evening came, he took his daughter Leah and gave her to Jacob, and Jacob lay with her. ²⁴And Laban gave his servant girl Zilpah to his daughter as her maidservant.

²⁵When morning came, there was Leah! So Jacob said to Laban, "What is this you have done to me? I served you for Rachel, didn't I? Why have you deceived me?"

²⁶Laban replied, "It is not our custom here to give the younger daughter in marriage before the older one. ²⁷Finish this daughter's bridal week; then we will give you the younger one also, in return for another seven years of work."

²⁸And Jacob did so. He finished the week with Leah, and then Laban gave him his daughter Rachel to be his wife. ²⁹Laban gave his servant girl Bilhah to his daughter Rachel as her maidservant. ³⁰Jacob lay with Rachel also, and he loved Rachel more than Leah. And he worked for Laban another seven years.

Jacob's Children

³¹When the Lord saw that Leah was not loved, he opened her womb, but Rachel was barren. ³²Leah became pregnant and gave birth to a son. She named him Reuben,*ᵇ* for she said, "It is because the Lord has seen my misery. Surely my husband will love me now."

³³She conceived again, and when she gave birth to a son she said, "Because the Lord heard that I am not loved, he gave me this one too." So she named him Simeon.*ᶜ*

³⁴Again she conceived, and when she gave birth to a son she said, "Now at last

---

ᵃ17 Or *delicate*   *ᵇ32* *Reuben* sounds like the Hebrew for *he has seen my misery*; the name means *see, a son.*   *ᶜ33* *Simeon* probably means *one who hears.*

my husband will become attached to me, because I have borne him three sons." So he was named Levi.[a]

[35]She conceived again, and when she gave birth to a son she said, "This time I will praise the LORD." So she named him Judah.[b] Then she stopped having children.

30 When Rachel saw that she was not bearing Jacob any children, she became jealous of her sister. So she said to Jacob, "Give me children, or I'll die!"

[2]Jacob became angry with her and said, "Am I in the place of God, who has kept you from having children?"

[3]Then she said, "Here is Bilhah, my maidservant. Sleep with her so that she can bear children for me and that through her I too can build a family."

[4]So she gave him her servant Bilhah as a wife. Jacob slept with her, [5]and she became pregnant and bore him a son. [6]Then Rachel said, "God has vindicated me; he has listened to my plea and given me a son." Because of this she named him Dan.[c]

[7]Rachel's servant Bilhah conceived again and bore Jacob a second son. [8]Then Rachel said, "I have had a great struggle with my sister, and I have won." So she named him Naphtali.[d]

[9]When Leah saw that she had stopped having children, she took her maidservant Zilpah and gave her to Jacob as a wife. [10]Leah's servant Zilpah bore Jacob a son. [11]Then Leah said, "What good fortune!"[e] So she named him Gad.[f]

[12]Leah's servant Zilpah bore Jacob a second son. [13]Then Leah said, "How happy I am! The women will call me happy." So she named him Asher.[g]

[14]During wheat harvest, Reuben went out into the fields and found some mandrake plants, which he brought to his mother Leah. Rachel said to Leah, "Please give me some of your son's mandrakes."

[15]But she said to her, "Wasn't it enough that you took away my husband? Will you take my son's mandrakes too?"

"Very well," Rachel said, "he can sleep with you tonight in return for your son's mandrakes."

[16]So when Jacob came in from the fields that evening, Leah went out to meet him.

"You must sleep with me," she said. "I have hired you with my son's mandrakes." So he slept with her that night.

[17]God listened to Leah, and she became pregnant and bore Jacob a fifth son. [18]Then Leah said, "God has rewarded me for giving my maidservant to my husband." So she named him Issachar.[h]

[19]Leah conceived again and bore Jacob a sixth son. [20]Then Leah said, "God has presented me with a precious gift. This time my husband will treat me with honor, because I have borne him six sons." So she named him Zebulun.[i]

[21]Some time later she gave birth to a daughter and named her Dinah.

[22]Then God remembered Rachel; he listened to her and opened her womb. [23]She became pregnant and gave birth to a son and said, "God has taken away my disgrace." [24]She named him Joseph,[j] and said, "May the LORD add to me another son."

Jacob's Flocks Increase

[25]After Rachel gave birth to Joseph, Jacob said to Laban, "Send me on my way so I can go back to my own homeland. [26]Give me my wives and children, for whom I have served you, and I will be on my way. You know how much work I've done for you."

[27]But Laban said to him, "If I have found favor in your eyes, please stay. I have learned by divination that[k] the LORD has blessed me because of you." [28]He added, "Name your wages, and I will pay them."

[29]Jacob said to him, "You know how I have worked for you and how your livestock has fared under my care. [30]The little you had before I came has increased greatly, and the LORD has blessed you wherever I have been. But now, when may I do something for my own household?"

[31]"What shall I give you?" he asked.

"Don't give me anything," Jacob replied. "But if you will do this one thing for me, I will go on tending your flocks and watching over them: [32]Let me go through all your flocks today and remove from them every speckled or spotted sheep, every dark-colored lamb and every spotted

---

a34 Levi sounds like and may be derived from the Hebrew for attached.   b35 Judah sounds like and may be derived from the Hebrew for praise.   c6 Dan here means he has vindicated.   d8 Naphtali means my struggle.   e11 Or "A troop is coming!"   f11 Gad can mean good fortune or a troop.   g13 Asher means happy.   h18 Issachar sounds like the Hebrew for reward.   i20 Zebulun probably means honor.   j24 Joseph means may he add.   k27 Or possibly have become rich and or speckled goat. They will be my wages. ³³And my honesty will testify for me in the future, whenever you check on the wages you have paid me. Any goat in my possession that is not speckled or spotted, or any lamb that is not dark-colored, will be considered stolen."

³⁴"Agreed," said Laban. "Let it be as you have said." ³⁵That same day he removed all the male goats that were streaked or spotted, and all the speckled or spotted female goats (all that had white on them) and all the dark-colored lambs, and he placed them in the care of his sons. ³⁶Then he put a three-day journey between himself and Jacob, while Jacob continued to tend the rest of Laban's flocks.

³⁷Jacob, however, took fresh-cut branches from poplar, almond and plane trees and made white stripes on them by peeling the bark and exposing the white inner wood of the branches. ³⁸Then he placed the peeled branches in all the watering troughs, so that they would be directly in front of the flocks when they came to drink. When the flocks were in heat and came to drink, ³⁹they mated in front of the branches. And they bore young that were streaked or speckled or spotted. ⁴⁰Jacob set apart the young of the flock by themselves, but made the rest face the streaked and dark-colored animals that belonged to Laban. Thus he made separate flocks for himself and did not put them with Laban's animals. ⁴¹Whenever the stronger females were in heat, Jacob would place the branches in the troughs in front of the animals so they would mate near the branches, ⁴²but if the animals were weak, he would not place them there. So the weak animals went to Laban and the strong ones to Jacob. ⁴³In this way the man grew exceedingly prosperous and came to own large flocks, and maidservants and menservants, and camels and donkeys.

Jacob Flees From Laban

31 Jacob heard that Laban's sons were saying, "Jacob has taken everything our father owned and has gained all this wealth from what belonged to our father." ²And Jacob noticed that Laban's attitude toward him was not what it had been.

³Then the LORD said to Jacob, "Go back to the land of your fathers and to your relatives, and I will be with you."

⁴So Jacob sent word to Rachel and Leah to come out to the fields where his flocks were. ⁵He said to them, "I see that your father's attitude toward me is not what it was before, but the God of my father has been with me. ⁶You know that I've worked for your father with all my strength, ⁷yet your father has cheated me by changing my wages ten times. However, God has not allowed him to harm me. ⁸If he said, 'The speckled ones will be your wages,' then all the flocks gave birth to speckled young; and if he said, 'The streaked ones will be your wages,' then all the flocks bore streaked young. ⁹So God has taken away your father's livestock and has given them to me.

¹⁰"In breeding season I once had a dream in which I looked up and saw that the male goats mating with the flock were streaked, speckled or spotted. ¹¹The angel of God said to me in the dream, 'Jacob.' I answered, 'Here I am.' ¹²And he said, 'Look up and see that all the male goats mating with the flock are streaked, speckled or spotted, for I have seen all that Laban has been doing to you. ¹³I am the God of Bethel, where you anointed a pillar and where you made a vow to me. Now leave this land at once and go back to your native land.'"

¹⁴Then Rachel and Leah replied, "Do we still have any share in the inheritance of our father's estate? ¹⁵Does he not regard us as foreigners? Not only has he sold us, but he has used up what was paid for us. ¹⁶Surely all the wealth that God took away from our father belongs to us and our children. So do whatever God has told you."

¹⁷Then Jacob put his children and his wives on camels, ¹⁸and he drove all his livestock ahead of him, along with all the goods he had accumulated in Paddan Aram,^a to go to his father Isaac in the land of Canaan.

¹⁹When Laban had gone to shear his sheep, Rachel stole her father's household gods. ²⁰Moreover, Jacob deceived Laban the Aramean by not telling him he was running away. ²¹So he fled with all he had, and crossing the River,^b he headed for the hill country of Gilead.

Laban Pursues Jacob

²²On the third day Laban was told that Jacob had fled. ²³Taking his relatives with

^a18 That is, Northwest Mesopotamia   ^b21 That is, the Euphrates

him, he pursued Jacob for seven days and caught up with him in the hill country of Gilead. **24**Then God came to Laban the Aramean in a dream at night and said to him, "Be careful not to say anything to Jacob, either good or bad."

25Jacob had pitched his tent in the hill country of Gilead when Laban overtook him, and Laban and his relatives camped there too. **26**Then Laban said to Jacob, "What have you done? You've deceived me, and you've carried off my daughters like captives in war. **27**Why did you run off secretly and deceive me? Why didn't you tell me, so I could send you away with joy and singing to the music of tambourines and harps? **28**You didn't even let me kiss my grandchildren and my daughters good-by. You have done a foolish thing. **29**I have the power to harm you; but last night the God of your father said to me, 'Be careful not to say anything to Jacob, either good or bad.' **30**Now you have gone off because you longed to return to your father's house. But why did you steal my gods?"

31Jacob answered Laban, "I was afraid, because I thought you would take your daughters away from me by force. **32**But if you find anyone who has your gods, he shall not live. In the presence of our relatives, see for yourself whether there is anything of yours here with me; and if so, take it." Now Jacob did not know that Rachel had stolen the gods.

33So Laban went into Jacob's tent and into Leah's tent and into the tent of the two maidservants, but he found nothing. After he came out of Leah's tent, he entered Rachel's tent. **34**Now Rachel had taken the household gods and put them inside her camel's saddle and was sitting on them. Laban searched through everything in the tent but found nothing.

35Rachel said to her father, "Don't be angry, my lord, that I cannot stand up in your presence; I'm having my period." So he searched but could not find the household gods.

36Jacob was angry and took Laban to task. "What is my crime?" he asked Laban. "What sin have I committed that you hunt me down? **37**Now that you have searched through all my goods, what have you found that belongs to your household? Put it here in front of your relatives and

mine, and let them judge between the two of us.

38"I have been with you for twenty years now. Your sheep and goats have not miscarried, nor have I eaten rams from your flocks. **39**I did not bring you animals torn by wild beasts; I bore the loss myself. And you demanded payment from me for whatever was stolen by day or night. **40**This was my situation: The heat consumed me in the daytime and the cold at night, and sleep fled from my eyes. **41**It was like this for the twenty years I was in your household. I worked for you fourteen years for your two daughters and six years for your flocks, and you changed my wages ten times. **42**If the God of my father, the God of Abraham and the Fear of Isaac, had not been with me, you would surely have sent me away empty-handed. But God has seen my hardship and the toil of my hands, and last night he rebuked you."

43Laban answered Jacob, "The women are my daughters, the children are my children, and the flocks are my flocks. All you see is mine. Yet what can I do today about these daughters of mine, or about the children they have borne? **44**Come now, let's make a covenant, you and I, and let it serve as a witness between us."

45So Jacob took a stone and set it up as a pillar. **46**He said to his relatives, "Gather some stones." So they took stones and piled them in a heap, and they ate there by the heap. **47**Laban called it Jegar Sahadutha,*a* and Jacob called it Galeed.*b*

48Laban said, "This heap is a witness between you and me today." That is why it was called Galeed. **49**It was also called Mizpah,*c* because he said, "May the LORD keep watch between you and me when we are away from each other. **50**If you mistreat my daughters or if you take any wives besides my daughters, even though no one is with us, remember that God is a witness between you and me."

51Laban also said to Jacob, "Here is this heap, and here is this pillar I have set up between you and me. **52**This heap is a witness, and this pillar is a witness, that I will not go past this heap to your side to harm you and that you will not go past this heap and pillar to my side to harm me. **53**May the God of Abraham and the God of Nahor, the God of their father, judge between us."

So Jacob took an oath in the name of

---

a47 The Aramaic *Jegar Sahadutha* means *witness heap.*   *b47* The Hebrew *Galeed* means *witness heap.*
c49 Mizpah means *watchtower.*

the Fear of his father Isaac. **54**He offered a sacrifice there in the hill country and invited his relatives to a meal. After they had eaten, they spent the night there.

55Early the next morning Laban kissed his grandchildren and his daughters and blessed them. Then he left and returned home.

Jacob Prepares to Meet Esau

32 Jacob also went on his way, and the angels of God met him. **2**When Jacob saw them, he said, "This is the camp of God!" So he named that place Mahanaim.*a*

3Jacob sent messengers ahead of him to his brother Esau in the land of Seir, the country of Edom. **4**He instructed them: "This is what you are to say to my master Esau: 'Your servant Jacob says, I have been staying with Laban and have remained there till now. **5**I have cattle and donkeys, sheep and goats, menservants and maidservants. Now I am sending this message to my lord, that I may find favor in your eyes.' "

6When the messengers returned to Jacob, they said, "We went to your brother Esau, and now he is coming to meet you, and four hundred men are with him."

7In great fear and distress Jacob divided the people who were with him into two groups,*b* and the flocks and herds and camels as well. **8**He thought, "If Esau comes and attacks one group,*c* the group*c* that is left may escape."

9Then Jacob prayed, "O God of my father Abraham, God of my father Isaac, O LORD, who said to me, 'Go back to your country and your relatives, and I will make you prosper,' **10**I am unworthy of all the kindness and faithfulness you have shown your servant. I had only my staff when I crossed this Jordan, but now I have become two groups. **11**Save me, I pray, from the hand of my brother Esau, for I am afraid he will come and attack me, and also the mothers with their children. **12**But you have said, 'I will surely make you prosper and will make your descendants like the sand of the sea, which cannot be counted.' "

13He spent the night there, and from what he had with him he selected a gift for his brother Esau: **14**two hundred female goats and twenty male goats, two hundred ewes and twenty rams, **15**thirty female

camels with their young, forty cows and ten bulls, and twenty female donkeys and ten male donkeys. **16**He put them in the care of his servants, each herd by itself, and said to his servants, "Go ahead of me, and keep some space between the herds."

17He instructed the one in the lead: "When my brother Esau meets you and asks, 'To whom do you belong, and where are you going, and who owns all these animals in front of you?' **18**then you are to say, 'They belong to your servant Jacob. They are a gift sent to my lord Esau, and he is coming behind us.' "

19He also instructed the second, the third and all the others who followed the herds: "You are to say the same thing to Esau when you meet him. **20**And be sure to say, 'Your servant Jacob is coming behind us.' " For he thought, "I will pacify him with these gifts I am sending on ahead; later, when I see him, perhaps he will receive me." **21**So Jacob's gifts went on ahead of him, but he himself spent the night in the camp.

Jacob Wrestles With God

22That night Jacob got up and took his two wives, his two maidservants and his eleven sons and crossed the ford of the Jabbok. **23**After he had sent them across the stream, he sent over all his possessions. **24**So Jacob was left alone, and a man wrestled with him till daybreak. **25**When the man saw that he could not overpower him, he touched the socket of Jacob's hip so that his hip was wrenched as he wrestled with the man. **26**Then the man said, "Let me go, for it is daybreak."

But Jacob replied, "I will not let you go unless you bless me."

27The man asked him, "What is your name?"

"Jacob," he answered.

28Then the man said, "Your name will no longer be Jacob, but Israel,*d* because you have struggled with God and with men and have overcome."

29Jacob said, "Please tell me your name."

But he replied, "Why do you ask my name?" Then he blessed him there.

30So Jacob called the place Peniel,*e* saying, "It is because I saw God face to face, and yet my life was spared."

31The sun rose above him as he passed Peniel,*f* and he was limping because of

---

a2 Mahanaim means *two camps.*   *b7* Or *camps*; also in verse 10   *c8* Or *camp*   *d28* Israel means *he struggles with God.*   *e30* Peniel means *face of God.*   *f31* Hebrew *Penuel*, a variant of *Peniel* his hip. [32]Therefore to this day the Israelites do not eat the tendon attached to the socket of the hip, because the socket of Jacob's hip was touched near the tendon.

Jacob Meets Esau

33 Jacob looked up and there was Esau, coming with his four hundred men; so he divided the children among Leah, Rachel and the two maidservants. [2]He put the maidservants and their children in front, Leah and her children next, and Rachel and Joseph in the rear. [3]He himself went on ahead and bowed down to the ground seven times as he approached his brother.

[4]But Esau ran to meet Jacob and embraced him; he threw his arms around his neck and kissed him. And they wept. [5]Then Esau looked up and saw the women and children. "Who are these with you?" he asked.

Jacob answered, "They are the children God has graciously given your servant."

[6]Then the maidservants and their children approached and bowed down. [7]Next, Leah and her children came and bowed down. Last of all came Joseph and Rachel, and they too bowed down.

[8]Esau asked, "What do you mean by all these droves I met?"

"To find favor in your eyes, my lord," he said.

[9]But Esau said, "I already have plenty, my brother. Keep what you have for yourself."

[10]"No, please!" said Jacob. "If I have found favor in your eyes, accept this gift from me. For to see your face is like seeing the face of God, now that you have received me favorably. [11]Please accept the present that was brought to you, for God has been gracious to me and I have all I need." And because Jacob insisted, Esau accepted it.

[12]Then Esau said, "Let us be on our way; I'll accompany you."

[13]But Jacob said to him, "My lord knows that the children are tender and that I must care for the ewes and cows that are nursing their young. If they are driven hard just one day, all the animals will die. [14]So let my lord go on ahead of his servant, while I move along slowly at the pace of the droves before me and that

of the children, until I come to my lord in Seir."

[15]Esau said, "Then let me leave some of my men with you."

"But why do that?" Jacob asked. "Just let me find favor in the eyes of my lord."

[16]So that day Esau started on his way back to Seir. [17]Jacob, however, went to Succoth, where he built a place for himself and made shelters for his livestock. That is why the place is called Succoth.[a]

[18]After Jacob came from Paddan Aram,[b] he arrived safely at the[c] city of Shechem in Canaan and camped within sight of the city. [19]For a hundred pieces of silver,[d] he bought from the sons of Hamor, the father of Shechem, the plot of ground where he pitched his tent. [20]There he set up an altar and called it El Elohe Israel.[e]

Dinah and the Shechemites

34 Now Dinah, the daughter Leah had borne to Jacob, went out to visit the women of the land. [2]When Shechem son of Hamor the Hivite, the ruler of that area, saw her, he took her and violated her. [3]His heart was drawn to Dinah daughter of Jacob, and he loved the girl and spoke tenderly to her. [4]And Shechem said to his father Hamor, "Get me this girl as my wife."

[5]When Jacob heard that his daughter Dinah had been defiled, his sons were in the fields with his livestock; so he kept quiet about it until they came home.

[6]Then Shechem's father Hamor went out to talk with Jacob. [7]Now Jacob's sons had come in from the fields as soon as they heard what had happened. They were filled with grief and fury, because Shechem had done a disgraceful thing in[f] Israel by lying with Jacob's daughter—a thing that should not be done.

[8]But Hamor said to them, "My son Shechem has his heart set on your daughter. Please give her to him as his wife. [9]Intermarry with us; give us your daughters and take our daughters for yourselves. [10]You can settle among us; the land is open to you. Live in it, trade[g] in it, and acquire property in it."

[11]Then Shechem said to Dinah's father and brothers, "Let me find favor in your eyes, and I will give you whatever you ask.

---

a17 Succoth means shelters.　　　b18 That is, Northwest Mesopotamia　　　c18 Or arrived at Shalem, a
d19 Hebrew hundred kesitahs; a kesitah was a unit of money of unknown weight and value.　　　e20 El
Elohe Israel can mean God, the God of Israel or mighty is the God of Israel.　　　f7 Or against　　　g10 Or
move about freely; also in verse 21

¹²Make the price for the bride and the gift I am to bring as great as you like, and I'll pay whatever you ask me. Only give me the girl as my wife."

¹³Because their sister Dinah had been defiled, Jacob's sons replied deceitfully as they spoke to Shechem and his father Hamor. ¹⁴They said to them, "We can't do such a thing; we can't give our sister to a man who is not circumcised. That would be a disgrace to us. ¹⁵We will give our consent to you on one condition only: that you become like us by circumcising all your males. ¹⁶Then we will give you our daughters and take your daughters for ourselves. We'll settle among you and become one people with you. ¹⁷But if you will not agree to be circumcised, we'll take our sister*a* and go."

¹⁸Their proposal seemed good to Hamor and his son Shechem. ¹⁹The young man, who was the most honored of all his father's household, lost no time in doing what they said, because he was delighted with Jacob's daughter. ²⁰So Hamor and his son Shechem went to the gate of their city to speak to their fellow townsmen. ²¹"These men are friendly toward us," they said. "Let them live in our land and trade in it; the land has plenty of room for them. We can marry their daughters and they can marry ours. ²²But the men will consent to live with us as one people only on the condition that our males be circumcised, as they themselves are. ²³Won't their livestock, their property and all their other animals become ours? So let us give our consent to them, and they will settle among us."

²⁴All the men who went out of the city gate agreed with Hamor and his son Shechem, and every male in the city was circumcised.

²⁵Three days later, while all of them were still in pain, two of Jacob's sons, Simeon and Levi, Dinah's brothers, took their swords and attacked the unsuspecting city, killing every male. ²⁶They put Hamor and his son Shechem to the sword and took Dinah from Shechem's house and left. ²⁷The sons of Jacob came upon the dead bodies and looted the city where*b* their sister had been defiled. ²⁸They seized their flocks and herds and donkeys and everything else of theirs in the city and out in the fields. ²⁹They carried off all their wealth and all their women and children, taking as plunder everything in the houses.

³⁰Then Jacob said to Simeon and Levi, "You have brought trouble on me by making me a stench to the Canaanites and Perizzites, the people living in this land. We are few in number, and if they join forces against me and attack me, I and my household will be destroyed."

³¹But they replied, "Should he have treated our sister like a prostitute?"

Jacob Returns to Bethel

35 Then God said to Jacob, "Go up to Bethel and settle there, and build an altar there to God, who appeared to you when you were fleeing from your brother Esau."

²So Jacob said to his household and to all who were with him, "Get rid of the foreign gods you have with you, and purify yourselves and change your clothes. ³Then come, let us go up to Bethel, where I will build an altar to God, who answered me in the day of my distress and who has been with me wherever I have gone." ⁴So they gave Jacob all the foreign gods they had and the rings in their ears, and Jacob buried them under the oak at Shechem. ⁵Then they set out, and the terror of God fell upon the towns all around them so that no one pursued them.

⁶Jacob and all the people with him came to Luz (that is, Bethel) in the land of Canaan. ⁷There he built an altar, and he called the place El Bethel,*c* because it was there that God revealed himself to him when he was fleeing from his brother. ⁸Now Deborah, Rebekah's nurse, died and was buried under the oak below Bethel. So it was named Allon Bacuth.*d*

⁹After Jacob returned from Paddan Aram,*e* God appeared to him again and blessed him. ¹⁰God said to him, "Your name is Jacob,*f* but you will no longer be called Jacob; your name will be Israel.*g*" So he named him Israel.

¹¹And God said to him, "I am God Almighty*h*; be fruitful and increase in number. A nation and a community of nations will come from you, and kings will come from your body. ¹²The land I gave to Abraham and Isaac I also give to you, and I will

---

a17 Hebrew *daughter*   *b27* Or *because*   *c7 El Bethel* means *God of Bethel.*   *d8 Allon Bacuth* means *oak of weeping.*   *e9* That is, Northwest Mesopotamia; also in verse 26   *f10 Jacob* means *he grasps the heel* (figuratively, *he deceives*).   *g10 Israel* means *he struggles with God.*   *h11* Hebrew *El-Shaddai* give this land to your descendants after you." [13]Then God went up from him at the place where he had talked with him.

[14]Jacob set up a stone pillar at the place where God had talked with him, and he poured out a drink offering on it; he also poured oil on it. [15]Jacob called the place where God had talked with him Bethel.[a]

The Deaths of Rachel and Isaac

[16]Then they moved on from Bethel. While they were still some distance from Ephrath, Rachel began to give birth and had great difficulty. [17]And as she was having great difficulty in childbirth, the midwife said to her, "Don't be afraid, for you have another son." [18]As she breathed her last — for she was dying — she named her son Ben-Oni.[b] But his father named him Benjamin.[c]

[19]So Rachel died and was buried on the way to Ephrath (that is, Bethlehem). [20]Over her tomb Jacob set up a pillar, and

---

[a]15 *Bethel* means *house of God.*   [b]18 *Ben-Oni* means *son of my trouble.*   [c]18 *Benjamin* means *son of my right hand.*

MONDAY

VERSE FOR THE DAY:
Genesis 35:11

AUTHOR:
D. Bruce Lockerbie

PASSAGE FOR THE DAY:
Genesis 35:9–13

The Grace of Posterity

FOR some men, the responsibilities of fatherhood are simply more than they bargained for. It's not just the intrusion of a newborn child's demands; not just the fearful anticipation of financial burdens, from crib to college. Rather, it's the stark reality that the honeymoon has come to an end. Accompanying that reality may be the fear that, with the onset of family life and the responsibilities of parenthood, the feast of love will grow stale, the wine of love will lose its bouquet. Often, when a man is insecure about himself, afraid of his personal attributes as a husband and lover, he's unable to perceive a marvelous truth about marriage: The love between husband and wife possesses a miraculous ingredient that makes possible the expansion of that love to include others.

However, we all know that today many couples disagree with this position and, of course, it's not for you or me to judge another man and woman's choice. All I can say is that the Bible makes it clear that God our Creator, having made us in his image and likeness, intends for us to "be fruitful and increase in number" (Genesis 1:28). In giving life and love to a child, whether by birth or by adoption, we participate most nearly in what it means to be made in God's image because then we share — if only to a limited degree — the chiefest attributes of God the Father himself. Not to offer love to our own children is to miss one of the foretastes of eternity, the grace of posterity as a sacrament of everlasting life.

Additional Scripture Readings:
Genesis 1:26–31; Psalm 127:3–5

Go to page 42 for your next devotional reading.

to this day that pillar marks Rachel's tomb.

²¹Israel moved on again and pitched his tent beyond Migdal Eder. ²²While Israel was living in that region, Reuben went in and slept with his father's concubine Bilhah, and Israel heard of it.

Jacob had twelve sons:
²³The sons of Leah:
    Reuben the firstborn of Jacob,
    Simeon, Levi, Judah, Issachar and
    Zebulun.
²⁴The sons of Rachel:
    Joseph and Benjamin.
²⁵The sons of Rachel's maidservant
    Bilhah:
    Dan and Naphtali.
²⁶The sons of Leah's maidservant Zilpah:
    Gad and Asher.
These were the sons of Jacob, who were born to him in Paddan Aram.

²⁷Jacob came home to his father Isaac in Mamre, near Kiriath Arba (that is, Hebron), where Abraham and Isaac had stayed. ²⁸Isaac lived a hundred and eighty years. ²⁹Then he breathed his last and died and was gathered to his people, old and full of years. And his sons Esau and Jacob buried him.

Esau's Descendants

36 This is the account of Esau (that is, Edom).

²Esau took his wives from the women of Canaan: Adah daughter of Elon the Hittite, and Oholibamah daughter of Anah and granddaughter of Zibeon the Hivite — ³also Basemath daughter of Ishmael and sister of Nebaioth.

⁴Adah bore Eliphaz to Esau, Basemath bore Reuel, ⁵and Oholibamah bore Jeush, Jalam and Korah. These were the sons of Esau, who were born to him in Canaan.

⁶Esau took his wives and sons and daughters and all the members of his household, as well as his livestock and all his other animals and all the goods he had acquired in Canaan, and moved to a land some distance from his brother Jacob. ⁷Their possessions were too great for them to remain together; the land where they were staying could not support them both because of their livestock. ⁸So Esau (that is, Edom) settled in the hill country of Seir.

⁹This is the account of Esau the father of the Edomites in the hill country of Seir.

¹⁰These are the names of Esau's sons:
    Eliphaz, the son of Esau's wife
    Adah, and Reuel, the son of Esau's
    wife Basemath.
¹¹The sons of Eliphaz:
    Teman, Omar, Zepho, Gatam and
    Kenaz.
¹²Esau's son Eliphaz also had a concubine named Timna, who bore him Amalek. These were grandsons of Esau's wife Adah.
¹³The sons of Reuel:
    Nahath, Zerah, Shammah and
    Mizzah. These were grandsons of
    Esau's wife Basemath.
¹⁴The sons of Esau's wife Oholibamah daughter of Anah and granddaughter of Zibeon, whom she bore to Esau:
    Jeush, Jalam and Korah.

¹⁵These were the chiefs among Esau's descendants:
The sons of Eliphaz the firstborn of
    Esau:
    Chiefs Teman, Omar, Zepho, Kenaz, ¹⁶Korah,ᵃ Gatam and Amalek. These were the chiefs descended from Eliphaz in Edom; they were grandsons of Adah.
¹⁷The sons of Esau's son Reuel:
    Chiefs Nahath, Zerah, Shammah and Mizzah. These were the chiefs descended from Reuel in Edom; they were grandsons of Esau's wife Basemath.
¹⁸The sons of Esau's wife Oholibamah:
    Chiefs Jeush, Jalam and Korah. These were the chiefs descended from Esau's wife Oholibamah daughter of Anah.
¹⁹These were the sons of Esau (that is, Edom), and these were their chiefs.

²⁰These were the sons of Seir the Horite, who were living in the region:
    Lotan, Shobal, Zibeon, Anah, ²¹Dishon, Ezer and Dishan. These sons of Seir in Edom were Horite chiefs.
²²The sons of Lotan:

ᵃ16 Masoretic Text; Samaritan Pentateuch (see also Gen. 36:11 and 1 Chron. 1:36) does not have *Korah.*

Hori and Homam.ᵃ Timna was Lotan's sister.

²³The sons of Shobal:

Alvan, Manahath, Ebal, Shepho and Onam.

²⁴The sons of Zibeon:

Aiah and Anah. This is the Anah who discovered the hot springsᵇ in the desert while he was grazing the donkeys of his father Zibeon.

²⁵The children of Anah:

Dishon and Oholibamah daughter of Anah.

²⁶The sons of Dishonᶜ:

Hemdan, Eshban, Ithran and Keran.

²⁷The sons of Ezer:

Bilhan, Zaavan and Akan.

²⁸The sons of Dishan:

Uz and Aran.

²⁹These were the Horite chiefs:

Lotan, Shobal, Zibeon, Anah, ³⁰Dishon, Ezer and Dishan. These were the Horite chiefs, according to their divisions, in the land of Seir.

The Rulers of Edom

³¹These were the kings who reigned in Edom before any Israelite king reignedᵈ:

³²Bela son of Beor became king of Edom. His city was named Dinhabah.

³³When Bela died, Jobab son of Zerah from Bozrah succeeded him as king.

³⁴When Jobab died, Husham from the land of the Temanites succeeded him as king.

³⁵When Husham died, Hadad son of Bedad, who defeated Midian in the country of Moab, succeeded him as king. His city was named Avith.

³⁶When Hadad died, Samlah from Masrekah succeeded him as king.

³⁷When Samlah died, Shaul from Rehoboth on the riverᵉ succeeded him as king.

³⁸When Shaul died, Baal-Hanan son of Acbor succeeded him as king.

³⁹When Baal-Hanan son of Acbor died, Hadadᶠ succeeded him as king. His city was named Pau, and his wife's name was Mehetabel daughter of Matred, the daughter of Me-Zahab.

⁴⁰These were the chiefs descended from Esau, by name, according to their clans and regions:

Timna, Alvah, Jetheth, ⁴¹Oholibamah, Elah, Pinon, ⁴²Kenaz, Teman, Mibzar, ⁴³Magdiel and Iram. These were the chiefs of Edom, according to their settlements in the land they occupied.

This was Esau the father of the Edomites.

Joseph's Dreams

37 Jacob lived in the land where his father had stayed, the land of Canaan.

²This is the account of Jacob.

Joseph, a young man of seventeen, was tending the flocks with his brothers, the sons of Bilhah and the sons of Zilpah, his father's wives, and he brought their father a bad report about them.

³Now Israel loved Joseph more than any of his other sons, because he had been born to him in his old age; and he made a richly ornamentedᵍ robe for him. ⁴When his brothers saw that their father loved him more than any of them, they hated him and could not speak a kind word to him.

⁵Joseph had a dream, and when he told it to his brothers, they hated him all the more. ⁶He said to them, "Listen to this dream I had: ⁷We were binding sheaves of grain out in the field when suddenly my sheaf rose and stood upright, while your sheaves gathered around mine and bowed down to it."

⁸His brothers said to him, "Do you intend to reign over us? Will you actually rule us?" And they hated him all the more because of his dream and what he had said.

⁹Then he had another dream, and he told it to his brothers. "Listen," he said, "I had another dream, and this time the sun

---

ᵃ22 Hebrew *Hemam,* a variant of *Homam* (see 1 Chron. 1:39)   ᵇ24 Vulgate; Syriac *discovered water;* the meaning of the Hebrew for this word is uncertain.   ᶜ26 Hebrew *Dishan,* a variant of *Dishon*   ᵈ31 Or *before an Israelite king reigned over them*   ᵉ37 Possibly the Euphrates   ᶠ39 Many manuscripts of the Masoretic Text, Samaritan Pentateuch and Syriac (see also 1 Chron. 1:50); most manuscripts of the Masoretic Text *Hadar*   ᵍ3 The meaning of the Hebrew for *richly ornamented* is uncertain; also in verses 23 and 32.

and moon and eleven stars were bowing down to me."

[10]When he told his father as well as his brothers, his father rebuked him and said, "What is this dream you had? Will your mother and I and your brothers actually come and bow down to the ground before you?" [11]His brothers were jealous of him, but his father kept the matter in mind.

Joseph Sold by His Brothers

[12]Now his brothers had gone to graze their father's flocks near Shechem, [13]and Israel said to Joseph, "As you know, your brothers are grazing the flocks near Shechem. Come, I am going to send you to them."

"Very well," he replied.

[14]So he said to him, "Go and see if all is well with your brothers and with the flocks, and bring word back to me." Then he sent him off from the Valley of Hebron.

When Joseph arrived at Shechem, [15]a man found him wandering around in the fields and asked him, "What are you looking for?"

[16]He replied, "I'm looking for my brothers. Can you tell me where they are grazing their flocks?"

[17]"They have moved on from here," the man answered. "I heard them say, 'Let's go to Dothan.'"

So Joseph went after his brothers and found them near Dothan. [18]But they saw him in the distance, and before he reached them, they plotted to kill him.

[19]"Here comes that dreamer!" they said to each other. [20]"Come now, let's kill him and throw him into one of these cisterns and say that a ferocious animal devoured him. Then we'll see what comes of his dreams."

[21]When Reuben heard this, he tried to rescue him from their hands. "Let's not take his life," he said. [22]"Don't shed any blood. Throw him into this cistern here in the desert, but don't lay a hand on him." Reuben said this to rescue him from them and take him back to his father.

[23]So when Joseph came to his brothers, they stripped him of his robe — the richly ornamented robe he was wearing — [24]and they took him and threw him into the cistern. Now the cistern was empty; there was no water in it.

[25]As they sat down to eat their meal, they looked up and saw a caravan of Ish-maelites coming from Gilead. Their camels were loaded with spices, balm and myrrh, and they were on their way to take them down to Egypt.

[26]Judah said to his brothers, "What will we gain if we kill our brother and cover up his blood? [27]Come, let's sell him to the Ishmaelites and not lay our hands on him; after all, he is our brother, our own flesh and blood." His brothers agreed.

[28]So when the Midianite merchants came by, his brothers pulled Joseph up out of the cistern and sold him for twenty shekels[a] of silver to the Ishmaelites, who took him to Egypt.

[29]When Reuben returned to the cistern and saw that Joseph was not there, he tore his clothes. [30]He went back to his brothers and said, "The boy isn't there! Where can I turn now?"

[31]Then they got Joseph's robe, slaughtered a goat and dipped the robe in the blood. [32]They took the ornamented robe back to their father and said, "We found this. Examine it to see whether it is your son's robe."

[33]He recognized it and said, "It is my son's robe! Some ferocious animal has devoured him. Joseph has surely been torn to pieces."

[34]Then Jacob tore his clothes, put on sackcloth and mourned for his son many days. [35]All his sons and daughters came to comfort him, but he refused to be comforted. "No," he said, "in mourning will I go down to the grave[b] to my son." So his father wept for him.

[36]Meanwhile, the Midianites[c] sold Joseph in Egypt to Potiphar, one of Pharaoh's officials, the captain of the guard.

Judah and Tamar

38 At that time, Judah left his brothers and went down to stay with a man of Adullam named Hirah. [2]There Judah met the daughter of a Canaanite man named Shua. He married her and lay with her; [3]she became pregnant and gave birth to a son, who was named Er. [4]She conceived again and gave birth to a son and named him Onan. [5]She gave birth to still another son and named him Shelah. It was at Kezib that she gave birth to him.

[6]Judah got a wife for Er, his firstborn, and her name was Tamar. [7]But Er, Judah's firstborn, was wicked in the LORD's sight; so the LORD put him to death.

---

[a]28 That is, about 8 ounces (about 0.2 kilogram)   [b]35 Hebrew *Sheol*   [c]36 Samaritan Pentateuch, Septuagint, Vulgate and Syriac (see also verse 28); Masoretic Text *Medanites*

⁸Then Judah said to Onan, "Lie with your brother's wife and fulfill your duty to her as a brother-in-law to produce offspring for your brother." ⁹But Onan knew that the offspring would not be his; so whenever he lay with his brother's wife, he spilled his semen on the ground to keep from producing offspring for his brother. ¹⁰What he did was wicked in the LORD's sight; so he put him to death also.

¹¹Judah then said to his daughter-in-law Tamar, "Live as a widow in your father's house until my son Shelah grows up." For he thought, "He may die too, just like his

---

TUESDAY

VERSE FOR THE DAY:	AUTHOR:	PASSAGE FOR THE DAY:
Genesis 37:36	Philip Yancey	Genesis 37:1–36

Redeeming the Hardship

IF YOU read Genesis in one sitting, you cannot help noticing a change in how God related to his people. At first he stayed close by, walking in the garden with them, punishing their individual sins, speaking to them directly, intervening constantly. Even in Abraham's day, he sent extraterrestrial messengers on house calls. By Jacob's time, however, the messages were far more ambiguous: a mysterious dream about a ladder, a late-night wrestling match. And toward the end of Genesis, a man named Joseph received guidance in the most unexpected ways.

Genesis slows down when it gets to Joseph, and it shows God working mostly behind the scenes. God spoke to Joseph not through angels, but through such means as the dreams of a despotic Egyptian pharaoh.

If anyone had a valid reason to be disappointed in God, it was Joseph, whose valiant stabs at goodness brought him nothing but trouble. He interpreted a dream to his brothers, and they threw him in a cistern. He resisted a sexual advance and landed in an Egyptian prison. There, he interpreted another dream to save a cell mate's life, and the cell mate promptly forgot about him. I wonder, as Joseph languished for his virtue in an Egyptian dungeon, did questions like—Is God unfair? Silent? Hidden?—occur to him?

But shift for a moment to the perspective of God the parent. Had he deliberately "pulled back" to allow Joseph's faith to reach a new level of maturity? And could this be why Genesis devotes more space to Joseph than to any other person? Through all his trials, Joseph learned to trust: not that God would prevent hardship, but that he would redeem even the hardship. Choking back tears, Joseph tried to explain his faith to his murderous brothers: "You intended to harm me, but God intended it for good . . ." (Genesis 50:20).

Additional Scripture Readings:
Genesis 50:15–20; Romans 8:28–39

Go to page 59 for your next devotional reading.

brothers." So Tamar went to live in her father's house.

¹²After a long time Judah's wife, the daughter of Shua, died. When Judah had recovered from his grief, he went up to Timnah, to the men who were shearing his sheep, and his friend Hirah the Adullamite went with him.

¹³When Tamar was told, "Your father-in-law is on his way to Timnah to shear his sheep," ¹⁴she took off her widow's clothes, covered herself with a veil to disguise herself, and then sat down at the entrance to Enaim, which is on the road to Timnah. For she saw that, though Shelah had now grown up, she had not been given to him as his wife.

¹⁵When Judah saw her, he thought she was a prostitute, for she had covered her face. ¹⁶Not realizing that she was his daughter-in-law, he went over to her by the roadside and said, "Come now, let me sleep with you."

"And what will you give me to sleep with you?" she asked.

¹⁷"I'll send you a young goat from my flock," he said.

"Will you give me something as a pledge until you send it?" she asked.

¹⁸He said, "What pledge should I give you?"

"Your seal and its cord, and the staff in your hand," she answered. So he gave them to her and slept with her, and she became pregnant by him. ¹⁹After she left, she took off her veil and put on her widow's clothes again.

²⁰Meanwhile Judah sent the young goat by his friend the Adullamite in order to get his pledge back from the woman, but he did not find her. ²¹He asked the men who lived there, "Where is the shrine prostitute who was beside the road at Enaim?"

"There hasn't been any shrine prostitute here," they said.

²²So he went back to Judah and said, "I didn't find her. Besides, the men who lived there said, 'There hasn't been any shrine prostitute here.'"

²³Then Judah said, "Let her keep what she has, or we will become a laughingstock. After all, I did send her this young goat, but you didn't find her."

²⁴About three months later Judah was told, "Your daughter-in-law Tamar is guilty of prostitution, and as a result she is now pregnant."

Judah said, "Bring her out and have her burned to death!"

²⁵As she was being brought out, she sent a message to her father-in-law. "I am pregnant by the man who owns these," she said. And she added, "See if you recognize whose seal and cord and staff these are."

²⁶Judah recognized them and said, "She is more righteous than I, since I wouldn't give her to my son Shelah." And he did not sleep with her again.

²⁷When the time came for her to give birth, there were twin boys in her womb. ²⁸As she was giving birth, one of them put out his hand; so the midwife took a scarlet thread and tied it on his wrist and said, "This one came out first." ²⁹But when he drew back his hand, his brother came out, and she said, "So this is how you have broken out!" And he was named Perez.ᵃ ³⁰Then his brother, who had the scarlet thread on his wrist, came out and he was given the name Zerah.ᵇ

Joseph and Potiphar's Wife

39 Now Joseph had been taken down to Egypt. Potiphar, an Egyptian who was one of Pharaoh's officials, the captain of the guard, bought him from the Ishmaelites who had taken him there.

²The Lord was with Joseph and he prospered, and he lived in the house of his Egyptian master. ³When his master saw that the Lord was with him and that the Lord gave him success in everything he did, ⁴Joseph found favor in his eyes and became his attendant. Potiphar put him in charge of his household, and he entrusted to his care everything he owned. ⁵From the time he put him in charge of his household and of all that he owned, the Lord blessed the household of the Egyptian because of Joseph. The blessing of the Lord was on everything Potiphar had, both in the house and in the field. ⁶So he left in Joseph's care everything he had; with Joseph in charge, he did not concern himself with anything except the food he ate.

Now Joseph was well-built and handsome, ⁷and after a while his master's wife took notice of Joseph and said, "Come to bed with me!"

⁸But he refused. "With me in charge," he told her, "my master does not concern himself with anything in the house; everything he owns he has entrusted to my

ᵃ29 Perez means breaking out.   ᵇ30 Zerah can mean scarlet or brightness.

care. **9**No one is greater in this house than I am. My master has withheld nothing from me except you, because you are his wife. How then could I do such a wicked thing and sin against God?" **10**And though she spoke to Joseph day after day, he refused to go to bed with her or even be with her.

11One day he went into the house to attend to his duties, and none of the household servants was inside. **12**She caught him by his cloak and said, "Come to bed with me!" But he left his cloak in her hand and ran out of the house.

13When she saw that he had left his cloak in her hand and had run out of the house, **14**she called her household servants. "Look," she said to them, "this Hebrew has been brought to us to make sport of us! He came in here to sleep with me, but I screamed. **15**When he heard me scream for help, he left his cloak beside me and ran out of the house."

16She kept his cloak beside her until his master came home. **17**Then she told him this story: "That Hebrew slave you brought us came to me to make sport of me. **18**But as soon as I screamed for help, he left his cloak beside me and ran out of the house."

19When his master heard the story his wife told him, saying, "This is how your slave treated me," he burned with anger. **20**Joseph's master took him and put him in prison, the place where the king's prisoners were confined.

But while Joseph was there in the prison, **21**the Lord was with him; he showed him kindness and granted him favor in the eyes of the prison warden. **22**So the warden put Joseph in charge of all those held in the prison, and he was made responsible for all that was done there. **23**The warden paid no attention to anything under Joseph's care, because the Lord was with Joseph and gave him success in whatever he did.

The Cupbearer and the Baker

40 Some time later, the cupbearer and the baker of the king of Egypt offended their master, the king of Egypt. **2**Pharaoh was angry with his two officials, the chief cupbearer and the chief baker, **3**and put them in custody in the house of the captain of the guard, in the same prison where Joseph was confined. **4**The cap-

tain of the guard assigned them to Joseph, and he attended them.

After they had been in custody for some time, **5**each of the two men — the cupbearer and the baker of the king of Egypt, who were being held in prison — had a dream the same night, and each dream had a meaning of its own.

6When Joseph came to them the next morning, he saw that they were dejected. **7**So he asked Pharaoh's officials who were in custody with him in his master's house, "Why are your faces so sad today?"

8"We both had dreams," they answered, "but there is no one to interpret them."

Then Joseph said to them, "Do not interpretations belong to God? Tell me your dreams."

9So the chief cupbearer told Joseph his dream. He said to him, "In my dream I saw a vine in front of me, **10**and on the vine were three branches. As soon as it budded, it blossomed, and its clusters ripened into grapes. **11**Pharaoh's cup was in my hand, and I took the grapes, squeezed them into Pharaoh's cup and put the cup in his hand."

12"This is what it means," Joseph said to him. "The three branches are three days. **13**Within three days Pharaoh will lift up your head and restore you to your position, and you will put Pharaoh's cup in his hand, just as you used to do when you were his cupbearer. **14**But when all goes well with you, remember me and show me kindness; mention me to Pharaoh and get me out of this prison. **15**For I was forcibly carried off from the land of the Hebrews, and even here I have done nothing to deserve being put in a dungeon."

16When the chief baker saw that Joseph had given a favorable interpretation, he said to Joseph, "I too had a dream: On my head were three baskets of bread.*a* **17**In the top basket were all kinds of baked goods for Pharaoh, but the birds were eating them out of the basket on my head."

18"This is what it means," Joseph said. "The three baskets are three days. **19**Within three days Pharaoh will lift off your head and hang you on a tree.*b* And the birds will eat away your flesh."

20Now the third day was Pharaoh's birthday, and he gave a feast for all his officials. He lifted up the heads of the chief cupbearer and the chief baker in the presence of his officials: **21**He restored the chief cupbearer to his position, so that he

---

a16 Or *three wicker baskets*   *b19* Or *and impale you on a pole* once again put the cup into Pharaoh's hand, [22]but he hanged[a] the chief baker, just as Joseph had said to them in his interpretation.

[23]The chief cupbearer, however, did not remember Joseph; he forgot him.

Pharaoh's Dreams

41 When two full years had passed, Pharaoh had a dream: He was standing by the Nile, [2]when out of the river there came up seven cows, sleek and fat, and they grazed among the reeds. [3]After them, seven other cows, ugly and gaunt, came up out of the Nile and stood beside those on the riverbank. [4]And the cows that were ugly and gaunt ate up the seven sleek, fat cows. Then Pharaoh woke up.

[5]He fell asleep again and had a second dream: Seven heads of grain, healthy and good, were growing on a single stalk. [6]After them, seven other heads of grain sprouted — thin and scorched by the east wind. [7]The thin heads of grain swallowed up the seven healthy, full heads. Then Pharaoh woke up; it had been a dream.

[8]In the morning his mind was troubled, so he sent for all the magicians and wise men of Egypt. Pharaoh told them his dreams, but no one could interpret them for him.

[9]Then the chief cupbearer said to Pharaoh, "Today I am reminded of my shortcomings. [10]Pharaoh was once angry with his servants, and he imprisoned me and the chief baker in the house of the captain of the guard. [11]Each of us had a dream the same night, and each dream had a meaning of its own. [12]Now a young Hebrew was there with us, a servant of the captain of the guard. We told him our dreams, and he interpreted them for us, giving each man the interpretation of his dream. [13]And things turned out exactly as he interpreted them to us: I was restored to my position, and the other man was hanged.[a]"

[14]So Pharaoh sent for Joseph, and he was quickly brought from the dungeon. When he had shaved and changed his clothes, he came before Pharaoh.

[15]Pharaoh said to Joseph, "I had a dream, and no one can interpret it. But I have heard it said of you that when you hear a dream you can interpret it."

[16]"I cannot do it," Joseph replied to Pharaoh, "but God will give Pharaoh the answer he desires."

[17]Then Pharaoh said to Joseph, "In my dream I was standing on the bank of the Nile, [18]when out of the river there came up seven cows, fat and sleek, and they grazed among the reeds. [19]After them, seven other cows came up — scrawny and very ugly and lean. I had never seen such ugly cows in all the land of Egypt. [20]The lean, ugly cows ate up the seven fat cows that came up first. [21]But even after they ate them, no one could tell that they had done so; they looked just as ugly as before. Then I woke up.

[22]"In my dreams I also saw seven heads of grain, full and good, growing on a single stalk. [23]After them, seven other heads sprouted — withered and thin and scorched by the east wind. [24]The thin heads of grain swallowed up the seven good heads. I told this to the magicians, but none could explain it to me."

[25]Then Joseph said to Pharaoh, "The dreams of Pharaoh are one and the same. God has revealed to Pharaoh what he is about to do. [26]The seven good cows are seven years, and the seven good heads of grain are seven years; it is one and the same dream. [27]The seven lean, ugly cows that came up afterward are seven years, and so are the seven worthless heads of grain scorched by the east wind: They are seven years of famine.

[28]"It is just as I said to Pharaoh: God has shown Pharaoh what he is about to do. [29]Seven years of great abundance are coming throughout the land of Egypt, [30]but seven years of famine will follow them. Then all the abundance in Egypt will be forgotten, and the famine will ravage the land. [31]The abundance in the land will not be remembered, because the famine that follows it will be so severe. [32]The reason the dream was given to Pharaoh in two forms is that the matter has been firmly decided by God, and God will do it soon.

[33]"And now let Pharaoh look for a discerning and wise man and put him in charge of the land of Egypt. [34]Let Pharaoh appoint commissioners over the land to take a fifth of the harvest of Egypt during the seven years of abundance. [35]They should collect all the food of these good years that are coming and store up the grain under the authority of Pharaoh, to be kept in the cities for food. [36]This food

---

[a]22,13 Or *impaled*

should be held in reserve for the country, to be used during the seven years of famine that will come upon Egypt, so that the country may not be ruined by the famine."

37The plan seemed good to Pharaoh and to all his officials. **38**So Pharaoh asked them, "Can we find anyone like this man, one in whom is the spirit of God*a*?"

39Then Pharaoh said to Joseph, "Since God has made all this known to you, there is no one so discerning and wise as you. **40**You shall be in charge of my palace, and all my people are to submit to your orders. Only with respect to the throne will I be greater than you."

Joseph in Charge of Egypt

41So Pharaoh said to Joseph, "I hereby put you in charge of the whole land of Egypt." **42**Then Pharaoh took his signet ring from his finger and put it on Joseph's finger. He dressed him in robes of fine linen and put a gold chain around his neck. **43**He had him ride in a chariot as his second-in-command,*b* and men shouted before him, "Make way*c*!" Thus he put him in charge of the whole land of Egypt.

44Then Pharaoh said to Joseph, "I am Pharaoh, but without your word no one will lift hand or foot in all Egypt." **45**Pharaoh gave Joseph the name Zaphenath-Paneah and gave him Asenath daughter of Potiphera, priest of On,*d* to be his wife. And Joseph went throughout the land of Egypt.

46Joseph was thirty years old when he entered the service of Pharaoh king of Egypt. And Joseph went out from Pharaoh's presence and traveled throughout Egypt. **47**During the seven years of abundance the land produced plentifully. **48**Joseph collected all the food produced in those seven years of abundance in Egypt and stored it in the cities. In each city he put the food grown in the fields surrounding it. **49**Joseph stored up huge quantities of grain, like the sand of the sea; it was so much that he stopped keeping records because it was beyond measure.

50Before the years of famine came, two sons were born to Joseph by Asenath daughter of Potiphera, priest of On. **51**Joseph named his firstborn Manasseh*e* and said, "It is because God has made me forget all my trouble and all my father's household." **52**The second son he named Ephraim*f* and said, "It is because God has made me fruitful in the land of my suffering."

53The seven years of abundance in Egypt came to an end, **54**and the seven years of famine began, just as Joseph had said. There was famine in all the other lands, but in the whole land of Egypt there was food. **55**When all Egypt began to feel the famine, the people cried to Pharaoh for food. Then Pharaoh told all the Egyptians, "Go to Joseph and do what he tells you."

56When the famine had spread over the whole country, Joseph opened the storehouses and sold grain to the Egyptians, for the famine was severe throughout Egypt. **57**And all the countries came to Egypt to buy grain from Joseph, because the famine was severe in all the world.

Joseph's Brothers Go to Egypt

42 When Jacob learned that there was grain in Egypt, he said to his sons, "Why do you just keep looking at each other?" **2**He continued, "I have heard that there is grain in Egypt. Go down there and buy some for us, so that we may live and not die."

3Then ten of Joseph's brothers went down to buy grain from Egypt. **4**But Jacob did not send Benjamin, Joseph's brother, with the others, because he was afraid that harm might come to him. **5**So Israel's sons were among those who went to buy grain, for the famine was in the land of Canaan also.

6Now Joseph was the governor of the land, the one who sold grain to all its people. So when Joseph's brothers arrived, they bowed down to him with their faces to the ground. **7**As soon as Joseph saw his brothers, he recognized them, but he pretended to be a stranger and spoke harshly to them. "Where do you come from?" he asked.

"From the land of Canaan," they replied, "to buy food."

8Although Joseph recognized his brothers, they did not recognize him. **9**Then he remembered his dreams about them and said to them, "You are spies! You have come to see where our land is unprotected."

10"No, my lord," they answered. "Your

---

a38 Or *of the gods*   *b43* Or *in the chariot of his second-in-command*; or *in his second chariot*
c43 Or *Bow down*   *d45* That is, Heliopolis; also in verse 50   *e51* *Manasseh* sounds like and may be derived from the Hebrew for *forget.*   *f52* *Ephraim* sounds like the Hebrew for *twice fruitful.*

servants have come to buy food. **11**We are all the sons of one man. Your servants are honest men, not spies."

12"No!" he said to them. "You have come to see where our land is unprotected."

13But they replied, "Your servants were twelve brothers, the sons of one man, who lives in the land of Canaan. The youngest is now with our father, and one is no more."

14Joseph said to them, "It is just as I told you: You are spies! **15**And this is how you will be tested: As surely as Pharaoh lives, you will not leave this place unless your youngest brother comes here. **16**Send one of your number to get your brother; the rest of you will be kept in prison, so that your words may be tested to see if you are telling the truth. If you are not, then as surely as Pharaoh lives, you are spies!" **17**And he put them all in custody for three days.

18On the third day, Joseph said to them, "Do this and you will live, for I fear God: **19**If you are honest men, let one of your brothers stay here in prison, while the rest of you go and take grain back for your starving households. **20**But you must bring your youngest brother to me, so that your words may be verified and that you may not die." This they proceeded to do.

21They said to one another, "Surely we are being punished because of our brother. We saw how distressed he was when he pleaded with us for his life, but we would not listen; that's why this distress has come upon us."

22Reuben replied, "Didn't I tell you not to sin against the boy? But you wouldn't listen! Now we must give an accounting for his blood." **23**They did not realize that Joseph could understand them, since he was using an interpreter.

24He turned away from them and began to weep, but then turned back and spoke to them again. He had Simeon taken from them and bound before their eyes.

25Joseph gave orders to fill their bags with grain, to put each man's silver back in his sack, and to give them provisions for their journey. After this was done for them, **26**they loaded their grain on their donkeys and left.

27At the place where they stopped for the night one of them opened his sack to get feed for his donkey, and he saw his silver in the mouth of his sack. **28**"My silver has been returned," he said to his brothers. "Here it is in my sack."

Their hearts sank and they turned to each other trembling and said, "What is this that God has done to us?"

29When they came to their father Jacob in the land of Canaan, they told him all that had happened to them. They said, **30**"The man who is lord over the land spoke harshly to us and treated us as though we were spying on the land. **31**But we said to him, 'We are honest men; we are not spies. **32**We were twelve brothers, sons of one father. One is no more, and the youngest is now with our father in Canaan.'

33"Then the man who is lord over the land said to us, 'This is how I will know whether you are honest men: Leave one of your brothers here with me, and take food for your starving households and go. **34**But bring your youngest brother to me so I will know that you are not spies but honest men. Then I will give your brother back to you, and you can trade*a* in the land.' "

35As they were emptying their sacks, there in each man's sack was his pouch of silver! When they and their father saw the money pouches, they were frightened. **36**Their father Jacob said to them, "You have deprived me of my children. Joseph is no more and Simeon is no more, and now you want to take Benjamin. Everything is against me!"

37Then Reuben said to his father, "You may put both of my sons to death if I do not bring him back to you. Entrust him to my care, and I will bring him back."

38But Jacob said, "My son will not go down there with you; his brother is dead and he is the only one left. If harm comes to him on the journey you are taking, you will bring my gray head down to the grave*b* in sorrow."

The Second Journey to Egypt

43 Now the famine was still severe in the land. **2**So when they had eaten all the grain they had brought from Egypt, their father said to them, "Go back and buy us a little more food."

3But Judah said to him, "The man warned us solemnly, 'You will not see my face again unless your brother is with you.' **4**If you will send our brother along with us, we will go down and buy food for you. **5**But if you will not send him, we will

---

*a*34 Or *move about freely*   *b*38 Hebrew *Sheol*

not go down, because the man said to us, 'You will not see my face again unless your brother is with you.' "

⁶Israel asked, "Why did you bring this trouble on me by telling the man you had another brother?"

⁷They replied, "The man questioned us closely about ourselves and our family. 'Is your father still living?' he asked us. 'Do you have another brother?' We simply answered his questions. How were we to know he would say, 'Bring your brother down here'?"

⁸Then Judah said to Israel his father, "Send the boy along with me and we will go at once, so that we and you and our children may live and not die. ⁹I myself will guarantee his safety; you can hold me personally responsible for him. If I do not bring him back to you and set him here before you, I will bear the blame before you all my life. ¹⁰As it is, if we had not delayed, we could have gone and returned twice."

¹¹Then their father Israel said to them, "If it must be, then do this: Put some of the best products of the land in your bags and take them down to the man as a gift — a little balm and a little honey, some spices and myrrh, some pistachio nuts and almonds. ¹²Take double the amount of silver with you, for you must return the silver that was put back into the mouths of your sacks. Perhaps it was a mistake. ¹³Take your brother also and go back to the man at once. ¹⁴And may God Almighty[a] grant you mercy before the man so that he will let your other brother and Benjamin come back with you. As for me, if I am bereaved, I am bereaved."

¹⁵So the men took the gifts and double the amount of silver, and Benjamin also. They hurried down to Egypt and presented themselves to Joseph. ¹⁶When Joseph saw Benjamin with them, he said to the steward of his house, "Take these men to my house, slaughter an animal and prepare dinner; they are to eat with me at noon."

¹⁷The man did as Joseph told him and took the men to Joseph's house. ¹⁸Now the men were frightened when they were taken to his house. They thought, "We were brought here because of the silver that was put back into our sacks the first time. He wants to attack us and overpower us and seize us as slaves and take our donkeys."

¹⁹So they went up to Joseph's steward and spoke to him at the entrance to the house. ²⁰"Please, sir," they said, "we came down here the first time to buy food. ²¹But at the place where we stopped for the night we opened our sacks and each of us found his silver — the exact weight — in the mouth of his sack. So we have brought it back with us. ²²We have also brought additional silver with us to buy food. We don't know who put our silver in our sacks."

²³"It's all right," he said. "Don't be afraid. Your God, the God of your father, has given you treasure in your sacks; I received your silver." Then he brought Simeon out to them.

²⁴The steward took the men into Joseph's house, gave them water to wash their feet and provided fodder for their donkeys. ²⁵They prepared their gifts for Joseph's arrival at noon, because they had heard that they were to eat there.

²⁶When Joseph came home, they presented to him the gifts they had brought into the house, and they bowed down before him to the ground. ²⁷He asked them how they were, and then he said, "How is your aged father you told me about? Is he still living?"

²⁸They replied, "Your servant our father is still alive and well." And they bowed low to pay him honor.

²⁹As he looked about and saw his brother Benjamin, his own mother's son, he asked, "Is this your youngest brother, the one you told me about?" And he said, "God be gracious to you, my son." ³⁰Deeply moved at the sight of his brother, Joseph hurried out and looked for a place to weep. He went into his private room and wept there.

³¹After he had washed his face, he came out and, controlling himself, said, "Serve the food."

³²They served him by himself, the brothers by themselves, and the Egyptians who ate with him by themselves, because Egyptians could not eat with Hebrews, for that is detestable to Egyptians. ³³The men had been seated before him in the order of their ages, from the firstborn to the youngest; and they looked at each other in astonishment. ³⁴When portions were served to them from Joseph's table, Benjamin's portion was five times as much as anyone else's. So they feasted and drank freely with him.

---

a 14 Hebrew El-Shaddai

A Silver Cup in a Sack

44 Now Joseph gave these instructions to the steward of his house: "Fill the men's sacks with as much food as they can carry, and put each man's silver in the mouth of his sack. ²Then put my cup, the silver one, in the mouth of the youngest one's sack, along with the silver for his grain." And he did as Joseph said.

³As morning dawned, the men were sent on their way with their donkeys. ⁴They had not gone far from the city when Joseph said to his steward, "Go after those men at once, and when you catch up with them, say to them, 'Why have you repaid good with evil? ⁵Isn't this the cup my master drinks from and also uses for divination? This is a wicked thing you have done.' "

⁶When he caught up with them, he repeated these words to them. ⁷But they said to him, "Why does my lord say such things? Far be it from your servants to do anything like that! ⁸We even brought back to you from the land of Canaan the silver we found inside the mouths of our sacks. So why would we steal silver or gold from your master's house? ⁹If any of your servants is found to have it, he will die; and the rest of us will become my lord's slaves."

¹⁰"Very well, then," he said, "let it be as you say. Whoever is found to have it will become my slave; the rest of you will be free from blame."

¹¹Each of them quickly lowered his sack to the ground and opened it. ¹²Then the steward proceeded to search, beginning with the oldest and ending with the youngest. And the cup was found in Benjamin's sack. ¹³At this, they tore their clothes. Then they all loaded their donkeys and returned to the city.

¹⁴Joseph was still in the house when Judah and his brothers came in, and they threw themselves to the ground before him. ¹⁵Joseph said to them, "What is this you have done? Don't you know that a man like me can find things out by divination?"

¹⁶"What can we say to my lord?" Judah replied. "What can we say? How can we prove our innocence? God has uncovered your servants' guilt. We are now my lord's slaves—we ourselves and the one who was found to have the cup."

¹⁷But Joseph said, "Far be it from me to do such a thing! Only the man who was found to have the cup will become my slave. The rest of you, go back to your father in peace."

¹⁸Then Judah went up to him and said: "Please, my lord, let your servant speak a word to my lord. Do not be angry with your servant, though you are equal to Pharaoh himself. ¹⁹My lord asked his servants, 'Do you have a father or a brother?' ²⁰And we answered, 'We have an aged father, and there is a young son born to him in his old age. His brother is dead, and he is the only one of his mother's sons left, and his father loves him.'

²¹"Then you said to your servants, 'Bring him down to me so I can see him for myself.' ²²And we said to my lord, 'The boy cannot leave his father; if he leaves him, his father will die.' ²³But you told your servants, 'Unless your youngest brother comes down with you, you will not see my face again.' ²⁴When we went back to your servant my father, we told him what my lord had said.

²⁵"Then our father said, 'Go back and buy a little more food.' ²⁶But we said, 'We cannot go down. Only if our youngest brother is with us will we go. We cannot see the man's face unless our youngest brother is with us.'

²⁷"Your servant my father said to us, 'You know that my wife bore me two sons. ²⁸One of them went away from me, and I said, "He has surely been torn to pieces." And I have not seen him since. ²⁹If you take this one from me too and harm comes to him, you will bring my gray head down to the grave[a] in misery.'

³⁰"So now, if the boy is not with us when I go back to your servant my father and if my father, whose life is closely bound up with the boy's life, ³¹sees that the boy isn't there, he will die. Your servants will bring the gray head of our father down to the grave in sorrow. ³²Your servant guaranteed the boy's safety to my father. I said, 'If I do not bring him back to you, I will bear the blame before you, my father, all my life!'

³³"Now then, please let your servant remain here as my lord's slave in place of the boy, and let the boy return with his brothers. ³⁴How can I go back to my father if the boy is not with me? No! Do not let me see the misery that would come upon my father."

<hr>

a29 Hebrew *Sheol*; also in verse 31

Joseph Makes Himself Known

45 Then Joseph could no longer control himself before all his attendants, and he cried out, "Have everyone leave my presence!" So there was no one with Joseph when he made himself known to his brothers. **2**And he wept so loudly that the Egyptians heard him, and Pharaoh's household heard about it.

3Joseph said to his brothers, "I am Joseph! Is my father still living?" But his brothers were not able to answer him, because they were terrified at his presence.

4Then Joseph said to his brothers, "Come close to me." When they had done so, he said, "I am your brother Joseph, the one you sold into Egypt! **5**And now, do not be distressed and do not be angry with yourselves for selling me here, because it was to save lives that God sent me ahead of you. **6**For two years now there has been famine in the land, and for the next five years there will not be plowing and reaping. **7**But God sent me ahead of you to preserve for you a remnant on earth and to save your lives by a great deliverance.*a*

8"So then, it was not you who sent me here, but God. He made me father to Pharaoh, lord of his entire household and ruler of all Egypt. **9**Now hurry back to my father and say to him, 'This is what your son Joseph says: God has made me lord of all Egypt. Come down to me; don't delay. **10**You shall live in the region of Goshen and be near me — you, your children and grandchildren, your flocks and herds, and all you have. **11**I will provide for you there, because five years of famine are still to come. Otherwise you and your household and all who belong to you will become destitute.'

12"You can see for yourselves, and so can my brother Benjamin, that it is really I who am speaking to you. **13**Tell my father about all the honor accorded me in Egypt and about everything you have seen. And bring my father down here quickly."

14Then he threw his arms around his brother Benjamin and wept, and Benjamin embraced him, weeping. **15**And he kissed all his brothers and wept over them. Afterward his brothers talked with him.

16When the news reached Pharaoh's palace that Joseph's brothers had come, Pharaoh and all his officials were pleased.

17Pharaoh said to Joseph, "Tell your brothers, 'Do this: Load your animals and return to the land of Canaan, **18**and bring your father and your families back to me. I will give you the best of the land of Egypt and you can enjoy the fat of the land.'

19"You are also directed to tell them, 'Do this: Take some carts from Egypt for your children and your wives, and get your father and come. **20**Never mind about your belongings, because the best of all Egypt will be yours.'"

21So the sons of Israel did this. Joseph gave them carts, as Pharaoh had commanded, and he also gave them provisions for their journey. **22**To each of them he gave new clothing, but to Benjamin he gave three hundred shekels*b* of silver and five sets of clothes. **23**And this is what he sent to his father: ten donkeys loaded with the best things of Egypt, and ten female donkeys loaded with grain and bread and other provisions for his journey. **24**Then he sent his brothers away, and as they were leaving he said to them, "Don't quarrel on the way!"

25So they went up out of Egypt and came to their father Jacob in the land of Canaan. **26**They told him, "Joseph is still alive! In fact, he is ruler of all Egypt." Jacob was stunned; he did not believe them. **27**But when they told him everything Joseph had said to them, and when he saw the carts Joseph had sent to carry him back, the spirit of their father Jacob revived. **28**And Israel said, "I'm convinced! My son Joseph is still alive. I will go and see him before I die."

Jacob Goes to Egypt

46 So Israel set out with all that was his, and when he reached Beersheba, he offered sacrifices to the God of his father Isaac.

2And God spoke to Israel in a vision at night and said, "Jacob! Jacob!"

"Here I am," he replied.

3"I am God, the God of your father," he said. "Do not be afraid to go down to Egypt, for I will make you into a great nation there. **4**I will go down to Egypt with you, and I will surely bring you back again. And Joseph's own hand will close your eyes."

5Then Jacob left Beersheba, and Israel's sons took their father Jacob and their children and their wives in the carts that Pharaoh had sent to transport him. **6**They also

a7 Or *save you as a great band of survivors*   *b22* That is, about 7 1/2 pounds (about 3.5 kilograms) took with them their livestock and the possessions they had acquired in Canaan, and Jacob and all his offspring went to Egypt. [7]He took with him to Egypt his sons and grandsons and his daughters and granddaughters—all his offspring.

[8]These are the names of the sons of Israel (Jacob and his descendants) who went to Egypt:

Reuben the firstborn of Jacob.
[9]The sons of Reuben:
Hanoch, Pallu, Hezron and Carmi.
[10]The sons of Simeon:
Jemuel, Jamin, Ohad, Jakin, Zohar and Shaul the son of a Canaanite woman.
[11]The sons of Levi:
Gershon, Kohath and Merari.
[12]The sons of Judah:
Er, Onan, Shelah, Perez and Zerah (but Er and Onan had died in the land of Canaan).
The sons of Perez:
Hezron and Hamul.
[13]The sons of Issachar:
Tola, Puah,[a] Jashub[b] and Shimron.
[14]The sons of Zebulun:
Sered, Elon and Jahleel.
[15]These were the sons Leah bore to Jacob in Paddan Aram,[c] besides his daughter Dinah. These sons and daughters of his were thirty-three in all.

[16]The sons of Gad:
Zephon,[d] Haggi, Shuni, Ezbon, Eri, Arodi and Areli.
[17]The sons of Asher:
Imnah, Ishvah, Ishvi and Beriah.
Their sister was Serah.
The sons of Beriah:
Heber and Malkiel.
[18]These were the children born to Jacob by Zilpah, whom Laban had given to his daughter Leah—sixteen in all.

[19]The sons of Jacob's wife Rachel:
Joseph and Benjamin. [20]In Egypt, Manasseh and Ephraim were born to Joseph by Asenath daughter of Potiphera, priest of On.[e]
[21]The sons of Benjamin:
Bela, Beker, Ashbel, Gera, Naa-

man, Ehi, Rosh, Muppim, Huppim and Ard.
[22]These were the sons of Rachel who were born to Jacob—fourteen in all.

[23]The son of Dan:
Hushim.
[24]The sons of Naphtali:
Jahziel, Guni, Jezer and Shillem.
[25]These were the sons born to Jacob by Bilhah, whom Laban had given to his daughter Rachel—seven in all.

[26]All those who went to Egypt with Jacob—those who were his direct descendants, not counting his sons' wives—numbered sixty-six persons. [27]With the two sons[f] who had been born to Joseph in Egypt, the members of Jacob's family, which went to Egypt, were seventy[g] in all.

[28]Now Jacob sent Judah ahead of him to Joseph to get directions to Goshen. When they arrived in the region of Goshen, [29]Joseph had his chariot made ready and went to Goshen to meet his father Israel. As soon as Joseph appeared before him, he threw his arms around his father[h] and wept for a long time.

[30]Israel said to Joseph, "Now I am ready to die, since I have seen for myself that you are still alive."

[31]Then Joseph said to his brothers and to his father's household, "I will go up and speak to Pharaoh and will say to him, 'My brothers and my father's household, who were living in the land of Canaan, have come to me. [32]The men are shepherds; they tend livestock, and they have brought along their flocks and herds and everything they own.' [33]When Pharaoh calls you in and asks, 'What is your occupation?' [34]you should answer, 'Your servants have tended livestock from our boyhood on, just as our fathers did.' Then you will be allowed to settle in the region of Goshen, for all shepherds are detestable to the Egyptians."

47 Joseph went and told Pharaoh, "My father and brothers, with their flocks and herds and everything they own, have come from the land of Canaan and are now in Goshen." [2]He chose five of

---

a13 Samaritan Pentateuch and Syriac (see also 1 Chron. 7:1); Masoretic Text Puvah   b13 Samaritan Pentateuch and some Septuagint manuscripts (see also Num. 26:24 and 1 Chron. 7:1); Masoretic Text Iob   c15 That is, Northwest Mesopotamia   d16 Samaritan Pentateuch and Septuagint (see also Num. 26:15); Masoretic Text Ziphion   e20 That is, Heliopolis   f27 Hebrew; Septuagint the nine children   g27 Hebrew (see also Exodus 1:5 and footnote); Septuagint (see also Acts 7:14) seventy-five   h29 Hebrew around him his brothers and presented them before Pharaoh.

[3]Pharaoh asked the brothers, "What is your occupation?"

"Your servants are shepherds," they replied to Pharaoh, "just as our fathers were." [4]They also said to him, "We have come to live here awhile, because the famine is severe in Canaan and your servants' flocks have no pasture. So now, please let your servants settle in Goshen."

[5]Pharaoh said to Joseph, "Your father and your brothers have come to you, [6]and the land of Egypt is before you; settle your father and your brothers in the best part of the land. Let them live in Goshen. And if you know of any among them with special ability, put them in charge of my own livestock."

[7]Then Joseph brought his father Jacob in and presented him before Pharaoh. After Jacob blessed[a] Pharaoh, [8]Pharaoh asked him, "How old are you?"

[9]And Jacob said to Pharaoh, "The years of my pilgrimage are a hundred and thirty. My years have been few and difficult, and they do not equal the years of the pilgrimage of my fathers." [10]Then Jacob blessed[b] Pharaoh and went out from his presence.

[11]So Joseph settled his father and his brothers in Egypt and gave them property in the best part of the land, the district of Rameses, as Pharaoh directed. [12]Joseph also provided his father and his brothers and all his father's household with food, according to the number of their children.

Joseph and the Famine

[13]There was no food, however, in the whole region because the famine was severe; both Egypt and Canaan wasted away because of the famine. [14]Joseph collected all the money that was to be found in Egypt and Canaan in payment for the grain they were buying, and he brought it to Pharaoh's palace. [15]When the money of the people of Egypt and Canaan was gone, all Egypt came to Joseph and said, "Give us food. Why should we die before your eyes? Our money is used up."

[16]"Then bring your livestock," said Joseph. "I will sell you food in exchange for your livestock, since your money is gone."

[17]So they brought their livestock to Joseph, and he gave them food in exchange for their horses, their sheep and goats, their cattle and donkeys. And he brought them through that year with food in exchange for all their livestock.

[18]When that year was over, they came to him the following year and said, "We cannot hide from our lord the fact that since our money is gone and our livestock belongs to you, there is nothing left for our lord except our bodies and our land. [19]Why should we perish before your eyes—we and our land as well? Buy us and our land in exchange for food, and we with our land will be in bondage to Pharaoh. Give us seed so that we may live and not die, and that the land may not become desolate."

[20]So Joseph bought all the land in Egypt for Pharaoh. The Egyptians, one and all, sold their fields, because the famine was too severe for them. The land became Pharaoh's, [21]and Joseph reduced the people to servitude,[c] from one end of Egypt to the other. [22]However, he did not buy the land of the priests, because they received a regular allotment from Pharaoh and had food enough from the allotment Pharaoh gave them. That is why they did not sell their land.

[23]Joseph said to the people, "Now that I have bought you and your land today for Pharaoh, here is seed for you so you can plant the ground. [24]But when the crop comes in, give a fifth of it to Pharaoh. The other four-fifths you may keep as seed for the fields and as food for yourselves and your households and your children."

[25]"You have saved our lives," they said. "May we find favor in the eyes of our lord; we will be in bondage to Pharaoh."

[26]So Joseph established it as a law concerning land in Egypt—still in force today—that a fifth of the produce belongs to Pharaoh. It was only the land of the priests that did not become Pharaoh's.

[27]Now the Israelites settled in Egypt in the region of Goshen. They acquired property there and were fruitful and increased greatly in number.

[28]Jacob lived in Egypt seventeen years, and the years of his life were a hundred and forty-seven. [29]When the time drew near for Israel to die, he called for his son Joseph and said to him, "If I have found favor in your eyes, put your hand under my thigh and promise that you will show me kindness and faithfulness. Do not bury me in Egypt, [30]but when I rest with my fa-

---

[a]7 Or greeted   [b]10 Or said farewell to   [c]21 Samaritan Pentateuch and Septuagint (see also Vulgate); Masoretic Text and he moved the people into the cities

thers, carry me out of Egypt and bury me where they are buried."

"I will do as you say," he said.

31"Swear to me," he said. Then Joseph swore to him, and Israel worshiped as he leaned on the top of his staff.*a*

Manasseh and Ephraim

48 Some time later Joseph was told, "Your father is ill." So he took his two sons Manasseh and Ephraim along with him. **2**When Jacob was told, "Your son Joseph has come to you," Israel rallied his strength and sat up on the bed.

3Jacob said to Joseph, "God Almighty*b* appeared to me at Luz in the land of Canaan, and there he blessed me **4**and said to me, 'I am going to make you fruitful and will increase your numbers. I will make you a community of peoples, and I will give this land as an everlasting possession to your descendants after you.'

5"Now then, your two sons born to you in Egypt before I came to you here will be reckoned as mine; Ephraim and Manasseh will be mine, just as Reuben and Simeon are mine. **6**Any children born to you after them will be yours; in the territory they inherit they will be reckoned under the names of their brothers. **7**As I was returning from Paddan,*c* to my sorrow Rachel died in the land of Canaan while we were still on the way, a little distance from Ephrath. So I buried her there beside the road to Ephrath" (that is, Bethlehem).

8When Israel saw the sons of Joseph, he asked, "Who are these?"

9"They are the sons God has given me here," Joseph said to his father.

Then Israel said, "Bring them to me so I may bless them."

10Now Israel's eyes were failing because of old age, and he could hardly see. So Joseph brought his sons close to him, and his father kissed them and embraced them.

11Israel said to Joseph, "I never expected to see your face again, and now God has allowed me to see your children too."

12Then Joseph removed them from Israel's knees and bowed down with his face to the ground. **13**And Joseph took both of them, Ephraim on his right toward Israel's left hand and Manasseh on his left toward Israel's right hand, and brought them close to him. **14**But Israel reached out his right hand and put it on Ephraim's head, though he was the younger, and crossing his arms, he put his left hand on Manasseh's head, even though Manasseh was the firstborn.

15Then he blessed Joseph and said,

"May the God before whom my
      fathers
   Abraham and Isaac walked,
the God who has been my shepherd
   all my life to this day,
16the Angel who has delivered me from
      all harm
   —may he bless these boys.
May they be called by my name
   and the names of my fathers
      Abraham and Isaac,
and may they increase greatly
   upon the earth."

17When Joseph saw his father placing his right hand on Ephraim's head he was displeased; so he took hold of his father's hand to move it from Ephraim's head to Manasseh's head. **18**Joseph said to him, "No, my father, this one is the firstborn; put your right hand on his head."

19But his father refused and said, "I know, my son, I know. He too will become a people, and he too will become great. Nevertheless, his younger brother will be greater than he, and his descendants will become a group of nations." **20**He blessed them that day and said,

"In your*d* name will Israel pronounce
      this blessing:
   'May God make you like Ephraim
      and Manasseh.' "

So he put Ephraim ahead of Manasseh.

21Then Israel said to Joseph, "I am about to die, but God will be with you*e* and take you*e* back to the land of your*e* fathers. **22**And to you, as one who is over your brothers, I give the ridge of land*f* I took from the Amorites with my sword and my bow."

Jacob Blesses His Sons

49 Then Jacob called for his sons and said: "Gather around so I can tell you what will happen to you in days to come.

2"Assemble and listen, sons of Jacob;
   listen to your father Israel.

---

a31 Or *Israel bowed down at the head of his bed*   *b3* Hebrew *El-Shaddai*   *c7* That is, Northwest Mesopotamia   *d20* The Hebrew is singular.   *e21* The Hebrew is plural.   *f22* Or *And to you I give one portion more than to your brothers—the portion*

³"Reuben, you are my firstborn,
  my might, the first sign of my
    strength,
  excelling in honor, excelling in
    power.
⁴Turbulent as the waters, you will no
    longer excel,
  for you went up onto your father's
    bed,
  onto my couch and defiled it.

⁵"Simeon and Levi are brothers—
  their swords^a are weapons of
    violence.
⁶Let me not enter their council,
  let me not join their assembly,
  for they have killed men in their anger
  and hamstrung oxen as they
    pleased.
⁷Cursed be their anger, so fierce,
  and their fury, so cruel!
  I will scatter them in Jacob
  and disperse them in Israel.

⁸"Judah,^{b} your brothers will praise
    you;
  your hand will be on the neck of
    your enemies;
  your father's sons will bow down to
    you.
⁹You are a lion's cub, O Judah;
  you return from the prey, my son.
  Like a lion he crouches and lies down,
  like a lioness—who dares to rouse
    him?
¹⁰The scepter will not depart from
    Judah,
  nor the ruler's staff from between
    his feet,
  until he comes to whom it belongs^c
  and the obedience of the nations is
    his.
¹¹He will tether his donkey to a vine,
  his colt to the choicest branch;
  he will wash his garments in wine,
  his robes in the blood of grapes.
¹²His eyes will be darker than wine,
  his teeth whiter than milk.^{d}

¹³"Zebulun will live by the seashore
  and become a haven for ships;
  his border will extend toward Sidon.

¹⁴"Issachar is a rawboned^e donkey
  lying down between two
    saddlebags.^{f}
¹⁵When he sees how good is his resting
    place
  and how pleasant is his land,
  he will bend his shoulder to the
    burden
  and submit to forced labor.

¹⁶"Dan^g will provide justice for his
    people
  as one of the tribes of Israel.
¹⁷Dan will be a serpent by the roadside,
  a viper along the path,
  that bites the horse's heels
  so that its rider tumbles backward.

¹⁸"I look for your deliverance, O LORD.

¹⁹"Gad^h will be attacked by a band of
    raiders,
  but he will attack them at their
    heels.

²⁰"Asher's food will be rich;
  he will provide delicacies fit for a
    king.

²¹"Naphtali is a doe set free
  that bears beautiful fawns.^{i}

²²"Joseph is a fruitful vine,
  a fruitful vine near a spring,
  whose branches climb over a wall.^{j}
²³With bitterness archers attacked him;
  they shot at him with hostility.
²⁴But his bow remained steady,
  his strong arms stayed^k limber,
  because of the hand of the Mighty
    One of Jacob,
  because of the Shepherd, the Rock
    of Israel,
²⁵because of your father's God, who
    helps you,
  because of the Almighty,^{l} who
    blesses you
  with blessings of the heavens above,
  blessings of the deep that lies
    below,
  blessings of the breast and womb.
²⁶Your father's blessings are greater
  than the blessings of the ancient
    mountains,
  than^m the bounty of the age-old
    hills.

Let all these rest on the head of
    Joseph,
  on the brow of the prince among[a]
    his brothers.

27"Benjamin is a ravenous wolf;
  in the morning he devours the prey,
  in the evening he divides the
    plunder."

28All these are the twelve tribes of Israel, and this is what their father said to them when he blessed them, giving each the blessing appropriate to him.

The Death of Jacob

29Then he gave them these instructions: "I am about to be gathered to my people. Bury me with my fathers in the cave in the field of Ephron the Hittite, 30the cave in the field of Machpelah, near Mamre in Canaan, which Abraham bought as a burial place from Ephron the Hittite, along with the field. 31There Abraham and his wife Sarah were buried, there Isaac and his wife Rebekah were buried, and there I buried Leah. 32The field and the cave in it were bought from the Hittites.[b]"

33When Jacob had finished giving instructions to his sons, he drew his feet up into the bed, breathed his last and was gathered to his people.

50 Joseph threw himself upon his father and wept over him and kissed him. 2Then Joseph directed the physicians in his service to embalm his father Israel. So the physicians embalmed him, 3taking a full forty days, for that was the time required for embalming. And the Egyptians mourned for him seventy days.

4When the days of mourning had passed, Joseph said to Pharaoh's court, "If I have found favor in your eyes, speak to Pharaoh for me. Tell him, 5'My father made me swear an oath and said, "I am about to die; bury me in the tomb I dug for myself in the land of Canaan." Now let me go up and bury my father; then I will return.' "

6Pharaoh said, "Go up and bury your father, as he made you swear to do."

7So Joseph went up to bury his father. All Pharaoh's officials accompanied him—the dignitaries of his court and all the dignitaries of Egypt— 8besides all the members of Joseph's household and his brothers and those belonging to his father's household. Only their children and

their flocks and herds were left in Goshen. 9Chariots and horsemen[c] also went up with him. It was a very large company.

10When they reached the threshing floor of Atad, near the Jordan, they lamented loudly and bitterly; and there Joseph observed a seven-day period of mourning for his father. 11When the Canaanites who lived there saw the mourning at the threshing floor of Atad, they said, "The Egyptians are holding a solemn ceremony of mourning." That is why that place near the Jordan is called Abel Mizraim.[d]

12So Jacob's sons did as he had commanded them: 13They carried him to the land of Canaan and buried him in the cave in the field of Machpelah, near Mamre, which Abraham had bought as a burial place from Ephron the Hittite, along with the field. 14After burying his father, Joseph returned to Egypt, together with his brothers and all the others who had gone with him to bury his father.

Joseph Reassures His Brothers

15When Joseph's brothers saw that their father was dead, they said, "What if Joseph holds a grudge against us and pays us back for all the wrongs we did to him?" 16So they sent word to Joseph, saying, "Your father left these instructions before he died: 17'This is what you are to say to Joseph: I ask you to forgive your brothers the sins and the wrongs they committed in treating you so badly.' Now please forgive the sins of the servants of the God of your father." When their message came to him, Joseph wept.

18His brothers then came and threw themselves down before him. "We are your slaves," they said.

19But Joseph said to them, "Don't be afraid. Am I in the place of God? 20You intended to harm me, but God intended it for good to accomplish what is now being done, the saving of many lives. 21So then, don't be afraid. I will provide for you and your children." And he reassured them and spoke kindly to them.

The Death of Joseph

22Joseph stayed in Egypt, along with all his father's family. He lived a hundred and ten years 23and saw the third generation of Ephraim's children. Also the children of

a26 Or the one separated from   b32 Or the sons of Heth   c9 Or charioteers   d11 Abel Mizraim means mourning of the Egyptians.

Makir son of Manasseh were placed at birth on Joseph's knees.[a]

24Then Joseph said to his brothers, "I am about to die. But God will surely come to your aid and take you up out of this land to the land he promised on oath to Abraham, Isaac and Jacob." **25**And Joseph made the sons of Israel swear an oath and said, "God will surely come to your aid, and then you must carry my bones up from this place."

26So Joseph died at the age of a hundred and ten. And after they embalmed him, he was placed in a coffin in Egypt.

IN the first half of this book, Moses recounts the exciting story of God delivering his people from slavery in Egypt. In the second half he tells about their stay at Mount Sinai, where they receive God's law and build the tabernacle. As you read this book, think about how God miraculously delivers you from slavery to Satan and sin through the death of his Son Jesus and how he wants you to obey his will (especially the Ten Commandments) in your daily life.

EXODUS

The Israelites Oppressed

1 These are the names of the sons of Israel who went to Egypt with Jacob, each with his family: **2**Reuben, Simeon, Levi and Judah; **3**Issachar, Zebulun and Benjamin; **4**Dan and Naphtali; Gad and Asher. **5**The descendants of Jacob numbered seventy*a* in all; Joseph was already in Egypt.

6Now Joseph and all his brothers and all that generation died, **7**but the Israelites were fruitful and multiplied greatly and became exceedingly numerous, so that the land was filled with them.

8Then a new king, who did not know about Joseph, came to power in Egypt. **9**"Look," he said to his people, "the Israelites have become much too numerous for us. **10**Come, we must deal shrewdly with them or they will become even more numerous and, if war breaks out, will join our enemies, fight against us and leave the country."

11So they put slave masters over them to oppress them with forced labor, and

---

a 5 Masoretic Text (see also Gen. 46:27); Dead Sea Scrolls and Septuagint (see also Acts 7:14 and note at Gen. 46:27) *seventy-five* they built Pithom and Rameses as store cities for Pharaoh. **12**But the more they were oppressed, the more they multiplied and spread; so the Egyptians came to dread the Israelites **13**and worked them ruthlessly. **14**They made their lives bitter with hard labor in brick and mortar and with all kinds of work in the fields; in all their hard labor the Egyptians used them ruthlessly.

15The king of Egypt said to the Hebrew midwives, whose names were Shiphrah and Puah, **16**"When you help the Hebrew women in childbirth and observe them on the delivery stool, if it is a boy, kill him; but if it is a girl, let her live." **17**The midwives, however, feared God and did not do what the king of Egypt had told them to do; they let the boys live. **18**Then the king of Egypt summoned the midwives and asked them, "Why have you done this? Why have you let the boys live?"

19The midwives answered Pharaoh, "Hebrew women are not like Egyptian women; they are vigorous and give birth before the midwives arrive."

20So God was kind to the midwives and the people increased and became even more numerous. **21**And because the midwives feared God, he gave them families of their own.

22Then Pharaoh gave this order to all his people: "Every boy that is born*a* you must throw into the Nile, but let every girl live."

The Birth of Moses

2 Now a man of the house of Levi married a Levite woman, **2**and she became pregnant and gave birth to a son. When she saw that he was a fine child, she hid him for three months. **3**But when she could hide him no longer, she got a papyrus basket for him and coated it with tar and pitch. Then she placed the child in it and put it among the reeds along the bank of the Nile. **4**His sister stood at a distance to see what would happen to him.

5Then Pharaoh's daughter went down to the Nile to bathe, and her attendants were walking along the river bank. She saw the basket among the reeds and sent her slave girl to get it. **6**She opened it and saw the baby. He was crying, and she felt sorry for him. "This is one of the Hebrew babies," she said.

7Then his sister asked Pharaoh's daughter, "Shall I go and get one of the Hebrew women to nurse the baby for you?"

8"Yes, go," she answered. And the girl went and got the baby's mother. **9**Pharaoh's daughter said to her, "Take this baby and nurse him for me, and I will pay you." So the woman took the baby and nursed him. **10**When the child grew older, she took him to Pharaoh's daughter and he became her son. She named him Moses,*b* saying, "I drew him out of the water."

Moses Flees to Midian

11One day, after Moses had grown up, he went out to where his own people were and watched them at their hard labor. He saw an Egyptian beating a Hebrew, one of his own people. **12**Glancing this way and that and seeing no one, he killed the Egyptian and hid him in the sand. **13**The next day he went out and saw two Hebrews fighting. He asked the one in the wrong, "Why are you hitting your fellow Hebrew?"

14The man said, "Who made you ruler and judge over us? Are you thinking of killing me as you killed the Egyptian?" Then Moses was afraid and thought, "What I did must have become known."

15When Pharaoh heard of this, he tried to kill Moses, but Moses fled from Pharaoh and went to live in Midian, where he sat down by a well. **16**Now a priest of Midian had seven daughters, and they came to draw water and fill the troughs to water their father's flock. **17**Some shepherds came along and drove them away, but Moses got up and came to their rescue and watered their flock.

18When the girls returned to Reuel their father, he asked them, "Why have you returned so early today?"

19They answered, "An Egyptian rescued us from the shepherds. He even drew water for us and watered the flock."

20"And where is he?" he asked his daughters. "Why did you leave him? Invite him to have something to eat."

21Moses agreed to stay with the man, who gave his daughter Zipporah to Moses in marriage. **22**Zipporah gave birth to a son, and Moses named him Gershom,*c* saying, "I have become an alien in a foreign land."

23During that long period, the king of Egypt died. The Israelites groaned in their

---

a22 Masoretic Text; Samaritan Pentateuch, Septuagint and Targums *born to the Hebrews*   *b10 Moses* sounds like the Hebrew for *draw out.*   *c22 Gershom* sounds like the Hebrew for *an alien there.*

slavery and cried out, and their cry for help because of their slavery went up to God. **24**God heard their groaning and he remembered his covenant with Abraham, with Isaac and with Jacob. **25**So God looked on the Israelites and was concerned about them.

Moses and the Burning Bush

3 Now Moses was tending the flock of Jethro his father-in-law, the priest of Midian, and he led the flock to the far side of the desert and came to Horeb, the mountain of God. **2**There the angel of the LORD appeared to him in flames of fire from within a bush. Moses saw that though the bush was on fire it did not burn up. **3**So Moses thought, "I will go over and see this strange sight — why the bush does not burn up."

4When the LORD saw that he had gone over to look, God called to him from within the bush, "Moses! Moses!"

And Moses said, "Here I am."

5"Do not come any closer," God said. "Take off your sandals, for the place where you are standing is holy ground." **6**Then he said, "I am the God of your fa-

WEDNESDAY

VERSE FOR THE DAY:	AUTHOR:	PASSAGE FOR THE DAY:
Exodus 3:6	A.W. Tozer	Exodus 3:1–6

Encountering God

TRUE Christian experience must always include a genuine encounter with God. Without this, religion is but a shadow, a reflection of reality, a cheap copy of the original once enjoyed by someone else of whom we have heard.

It cannot but be a major tragedy in the life of any man to live in a church from childhood to old age and know nothing more real than some synthetic god compounded of theology and logic, but having no eyes to see, nor ears to hear, and no heart to love.

The spiritual giants of old were men who at some time became acutely conscious of the real Presence of God and maintained that consciousness for the rest of their lives.

The first encounter may have been one of terror, as when a "thick and dreadful darkness" came over Abram (Genesis 15:12), or as when Moses at the bush hid his face because he was afraid to look upon God. Usually this fear soon lost its content of terror and changed after a while to delightsome awe, to level off finally into a reverent sense of complete nearness to God. The essential point is this: these were men who experienced God!

How otherwise can the saints and prophets be explained? How otherwise can we account for the amazing power for good they have exercised over countless generations? Is it not that they walked in conscious communion with the real Presence and addressed their prayers to God with the artless conviction that they were addressing Someone actually there?

Additional Scripture Readings:
Exodus 33:12–23; 1 John 3:1–3

Go to page 76 for your next devotional reading.

ther, the God of Abraham, the God of Isaac and the God of Jacob." At this, Moses hid his face, because he was afraid to look at God.

7The Lord said, "I have indeed seen the misery of my people in Egypt. I have heard them crying out because of their slave drivers, and I am concerned about their suffering. **8**So I have come down to rescue them from the hand of the Egyptians and to bring them up out of that land into a good and spacious land, a land flowing with milk and honey—the home of the Canaanites, Hittites, Amorites, Perizzites, Hivites and Jebusites. **9**And now the cry of the Israelites has reached me, and I have seen the way the Egyptians are oppressing them. **10**So now, go. I am sending you to Pharaoh to bring my people the Israelites out of Egypt."

11But Moses said to God, "Who am I, that I should go to Pharaoh and bring the Israelites out of Egypt?"

12And God said, "I will be with you. And this will be the sign to you that it is I who have sent you: When you have brought the people out of Egypt, you*a* will worship God on this mountain."

13Moses said to God, "Suppose I go to the Israelites and say to them, 'The God of your fathers has sent me to you,' and they ask me, 'What is his name?' Then what shall I tell them?"

14God said to Moses, "I AM WHO I AM.*b* This is what you are to say to the Israelites: 'I AM has sent me to you.' "

15God also said to Moses, "Say to the Israelites, 'The Lord,*c* the God of your fathers—the God of Abraham, the God of Isaac and the God of Jacob—has sent me to you.' This is my name forever, the name by which I am to be remembered from generation to generation.

16"Go, assemble the elders of Israel and say to them, 'The Lord, the God of your fathers—the God of Abraham, Isaac and Jacob—appeared to me and said: I have watched over you and have seen what has been done to you in Egypt. **17**And I have promised to bring you up out of your misery in Egypt into the land of the Canaanites, Hittites, Amorites, Perizzites, Hivites and Jebusites—a land flowing with milk and honey.'

18"The elders of Israel will listen to you. Then you and the elders are to go to the king of Egypt and say to him, 'The Lord, the God of the Hebrews, has met with us. Let us take a three-day journey into the desert to offer sacrifices to the Lord our God.' **19**But I know that the king of Egypt will not let you go unless a mighty hand compels him. **20**So I will stretch out my hand and strike the Egyptians with all the wonders that I will perform among them. After that, he will let you go.

21"And I will make the Egyptians favorably disposed toward this people, so that when you leave you will not go empty-handed. **22**Every woman is to ask her neighbor and any woman living in her house for articles of silver and gold and for clothing, which you will put on your sons and daughters. And so you will plunder the Egyptians."

Signs for Moses

4 Moses answered, "What if they do not believe me or listen to me and say, 'The Lord did not appear to you'?"

2Then the Lord said to him, "What is that in your hand?"

"A staff," he replied.

3The Lord said, "Throw it on the ground."

Moses threw it on the ground and it became a snake, and he ran from it. **4**Then the Lord said to him, "Reach out your hand and take it by the tail." So Moses reached out and took hold of the snake and it turned back into a staff in his hand. **5**"This," said the Lord, "is so that they may believe that the Lord, the God of their fathers—the God of Abraham, the God of Isaac and the God of Jacob—has appeared to you."

6Then the Lord said, "Put your hand inside your cloak." So Moses put his hand into his cloak, and when he took it out, it was leprous,*d* like snow.

7"Now put it back into your cloak," he said. So Moses put his hand back into his cloak, and when he took it out, it was restored, like the rest of his flesh.

8Then the Lord said, "If they do not believe you or pay attention to the first miraculous sign, they may believe the second. **9**But if they do not believe these two signs or listen to you, take some water from the Nile and pour it on the dry ground. The water you take from the river will become blood on the ground."

---

*a*12 The Hebrew is plural.   *b*14 Or *I will be what I will be* may be derived from the Hebrew for *I am* in verse 14.   *c*15 The Hebrew for Lord sounds like and   *d*6 The Hebrew word was used for various diseases affecting the skin—not necessarily leprosy.

[10]Moses said to the Lord, "O Lord, I have never been eloquent, neither in the past nor since you have spoken to your servant. I am slow of speech and tongue." [11]The Lord said to him, "Who gave man his mouth? Who makes him deaf or mute? Who gives him sight or makes him blind? Is it not I, the Lord? [12]Now go; I will help you speak and will teach you what to say."

[13]But Moses said, "O Lord, please send someone else to do it."

[14]Then the Lord's anger burned against Moses and he said, "What about your brother, Aaron the Levite? I know he can speak well. He is already on his way to meet you, and his heart will be glad when he sees you. [15]You shall speak to him and put words in his mouth; I will help both of you speak and will teach you what to do. [16]He will speak to the people for you, and it will be as if he were your mouth and as if you were God to him. [17]But take this staff in your hand so you can perform miraculous signs with it."

Moses Returns to Egypt

[18]Then Moses went back to Jethro his father-in-law and said to him, "Let me go back to my own people in Egypt to see if any of them are still alive."

Jethro said, "Go, and I wish you well." [19]Now the Lord had said to Moses in Midian, "Go back to Egypt, for all the men who wanted to kill you are dead." [20]So Moses took his wife and sons, put them on a donkey and started back to Egypt. And he took the staff of God in his hand.

[21]The Lord said to Moses, "When you return to Egypt, see that you perform before Pharaoh all the wonders I have given you the power to do. But I will harden his heart so that he will not let the people go. [22]Then say to Pharaoh, 'This is what the Lord says: Israel is my firstborn son, [23]and I told you, "Let my son go, so he may worship me." But you refused to let him go; so I will kill your firstborn son.' "

[24]At a lodging place on the way, the Lord met ⌊Moses⌋[a] and was about to kill him. [25]But Zipporah took a flint knife, cut off her son's foreskin and touched ⌊Moses'⌋ feet with it.[b] "Surely you are a bridegroom of blood to me," she said. [26]So the Lord let him alone. (At that time she said "bridegroom of blood," referring to circumcision.)

[27]The Lord said to Aaron, "Go into the desert to meet Moses." So he met Moses at the mountain of God and kissed him. [28]Then Moses told Aaron everything the Lord had sent him to say, and also about all the miraculous signs he had commanded him to perform.

[29]Moses and Aaron brought together all the elders of the Israelites, [30]and Aaron told them everything the Lord had said to Moses. He also performed the signs before the people, [31]and they believed. And when they heard that the Lord was concerned about them and had seen their misery, they bowed down and worshiped.

Bricks Without Straw

5 Afterward Moses and Aaron went to Pharaoh and said, "This is what the Lord, the God of Israel, says: 'Let my people go, so that they may hold a festival to me in the desert.' "

[2]Pharaoh said, "Who is the Lord, that I should obey him and let Israel go? I do not know the Lord and I will not let Israel go." [3]Then they said, "The God of the Hebrews has met with us. Now let us take a three-day journey into the desert to offer sacrifices to the Lord our God, or he may strike us with plagues or with the sword."

[4]But the king of Egypt said, "Moses and Aaron, why are you taking the people away from their labor? Get back to your work!" [5]Then Pharaoh said, "Look, the people of the land are now numerous, and you are stopping them from working."

[6]That same day Pharaoh gave this order to the slave drivers and foremen in charge of the people: [7]"You are no longer to supply the people with straw for making bricks; let them go and gather their own straw. [8]But require them to make the same number of bricks as before; don't reduce the quota. They are lazy; that is why they are crying out, 'Let us go and sacrifice to our God.' [9]Make the work harder for the men so that they keep working and pay no attention to lies."

[10]Then the slave drivers and the foremen went out and said to the people, "This is what Pharaoh says: 'I will not give you any more straw. [11]Go and get your own straw wherever you can find it, but your work will not be reduced at all.' " [12]So the people scattered all over Egypt to gather stubble to use for straw. [13]The slave drivers kept pressing them, saying, "Complete the work required of you for each day, just as when you had straw." [14]The Israelite foremen appointed by

---

[a]24 Or ⌊Moses' son⌋; Hebrew him   [b]25 Or and drew near ⌊Moses'⌋ feet

Pharaoh's slave drivers were beaten and were asked, "Why didn't you meet your quota of bricks yesterday or today, as before?"

¹⁵Then the Israelite foremen went and appealed to Pharaoh: "Why have you treated your servants this way? ¹⁶Your servants are given no straw, yet we are told, 'Make bricks!' Your servants are being beaten, but the fault is with your own people."

¹⁷Pharaoh said, "Lazy, that's what you are—lazy! That is why you keep saying, 'Let us go and sacrifice to the LORD.' ¹⁸Now get to work. You will not be given any straw, yet you must produce your full quota of bricks."

¹⁹The Israelite foremen realized they were in trouble when they were told, "You are not to reduce the number of bricks required of you for each day." ²⁰When they left Pharaoh, they found Moses and Aaron waiting to meet them, ²¹and they said, "May the LORD look upon you and judge you! You have made us a stench to Pharaoh and his officials and have put a sword in their hand to kill us."

God Promises Deliverance

²²Moses returned to the LORD and said, "O Lord, why have you brought trouble upon this people? Is this why you sent me? ²³Ever since I went to Pharaoh to speak in your name, he has brought trouble upon this people, and you have not rescued your people at all."

6 Then the LORD said to Moses, "Now you will see what I will do to Pharaoh: Because of my mighty hand he will let them go; because of my mighty hand he will drive them out of his country."

²God also said to Moses, "I am the LORD. ³I appeared to Abraham, to Isaac and to Jacob as God Almighty,ᵃ but by my name the LORDᵇ I did not make myself known to them.ᶜ ⁴I also established my covenant with them to give them the land of Canaan, where they lived as aliens. ⁵Moreover, I have heard the groaning of the Israelites, whom the Egyptians are enslaving, and I have remembered my covenant.

⁶"Therefore, say to the Israelites: 'I am the LORD, and I will bring you out from under the yoke of the Egyptians. I will free you from being slaves to them, and I will redeem you with an outstretched arm and with mighty acts of judgment. ⁷I will take you as my own people, and I will be your God. Then you will know that I am the LORD your God, who brought you out from under the yoke of the Egyptians. ⁸And I will bring you to the land I swore with uplifted hand to give to Abraham, to Isaac and to Jacob. I will give it to you as a possession. I am the LORD.' "

⁹Moses reported this to the Israelites, but they did not listen to him because of their discouragement and cruel bondage.

¹⁰Then the LORD said to Moses, ¹¹"Go, tell Pharaoh king of Egypt to let the Israelites go out of his country."

¹²But Moses said to the LORD, "If the Israelites will not listen to me, why would Pharaoh listen to me, since I speak with faltering lipsᵈ?"

Family Record of Moses and Aaron

¹³Now the LORD spoke to Moses and Aaron about the Israelites and Pharaoh king of Egypt, and he commanded them to bring the Israelites out of Egypt.

¹⁴These were the heads of their familiesᵉ:

The sons of Reuben the firstborn son of Israel were Hanoch and Pallu, Hezron and Carmi. These were the clans of Reuben.

¹⁵The sons of Simeon were Jemuel, Jamin, Ohad, Jakin, Zohar and Shaul the son of a Canaanite woman. These were the clans of Simeon.

¹⁶These were the names of the sons of Levi according to their records: Gershon, Kohath and Merari. Levi lived 137 years.

¹⁷The sons of Gershon, by clans, were Libni and Shimei.

¹⁸The sons of Kohath were Amram, Izhar, Hebron and Uzziel. Kohath lived 133 years.

¹⁹The sons of Merari were Mahli and Mushi.

These were the clans of Levi according to their records.

²⁰Amram married his father's sister Jochebed, who bore him Aaron and Moses. Amram lived 137 years.

²¹The sons of Izhar were Korah, Nepheg and Zicri.

²²The sons of Uzziel were Mishael, Elzaphan and Sithri.

ᵃ3 Hebrew *El-Shaddai*   ᵇ3 See note at Exodus 3:15.   ᶜ3 Or *Almighty, and by my name the LORD did I not let myself be known to them?*   ᵈ12 Hebrew *I am uncircumcised of lips*; also in verse 30   ᵉ14 The Hebrew for *families* here and in verse 25 refers to units larger than clans.

23Aaron married Elisheba, daughter of Amminadab and sister of Nahshon, and she bore him Nadab and Abihu, Eleazar and Ithamar. 24The sons of Korah were Assir, Elkanah and Abiasaph. These were the Korahite clans. 25Eleazar son of Aaron married one of the daughters of Putiel, and she bore him Phinehas.

These were the heads of the Levite families, clan by clan.

26It was this same Aaron and Moses to whom the LORD said, "Bring the Israelites out of Egypt by their divisions." 27They were the ones who spoke to Pharaoh king of Egypt about bringing the Israelites out of Egypt. It was the same Moses and Aaron.

Aaron to Speak for Moses

28Now when the LORD spoke to Moses in Egypt, 29he said to him, "I am the LORD. Tell Pharaoh king of Egypt everything I tell you."

30But Moses said to the LORD, "Since I speak with faltering lips, why would Pharaoh listen to me?"

7 Then the LORD said to Moses, "See, I have made you like God to Pharaoh, and your brother Aaron will be your prophet. 2You are to say everything I command you, and your brother Aaron is to tell Pharaoh to let the Israelites go out of his country. 3But I will harden Pharaoh's heart, and though I multiply my miraculous signs and wonders in Egypt, 4he will not listen to you. Then I will lay my hand on Egypt and with mighty acts of judgment I will bring out my divisions, my people the Israelites. 5And the Egyptians will know that I am the LORD when I stretch out my hand against Egypt and bring the Israelites out of it."

6Moses and Aaron did just as the LORD commanded them. 7Moses was eighty years old and Aaron eighty-three when they spoke to Pharaoh.

Aaron's Staff Becomes a Snake

8The LORD said to Moses and Aaron, 9"When Pharaoh says to you, 'Perform a miracle,' then say to Aaron, 'Take your staff and throw it down before Pharaoh,' and it will become a snake."

10So Moses and Aaron went to Pharaoh and did just as the LORD commanded. Aaron threw his staff down in front of Pharaoh and his officials, and it became a snake. 11Pharaoh then summoned wise men and sorcerers, and the Egyptian magicians also did the same things by their secret arts: 12Each one threw down his staff and it became a snake. But Aaron's staff swallowed up their staffs. 13Yet Pharaoh's heart became hard and he would not listen to them, just as the LORD had said.

The Plague of Blood

14Then the LORD said to Moses, "Pharaoh's heart is unyielding; he refuses to let the people go. 15Go to Pharaoh in the morning as he goes out to the water. Wait on the bank of the Nile to meet him, and take in your hand the staff that was changed into a snake. 16Then say to him, 'The LORD, the God of the Hebrews, has sent me to say to you: Let my people go, so that they may worship me in the desert. But until now you have not listened. 17This is what the LORD says: By this you will know that I am the LORD: With the staff that is in my hand I will strike the water of the Nile, and it will be changed into blood. 18The fish in the Nile will die, and the river will stink; the Egyptians will not be able to drink its water.' "

19The LORD said to Moses, "Tell Aaron, 'Take your staff and stretch out your hand over the waters of Egypt—over the streams and canals, over the ponds and all the reservoirs'—and they will turn to blood. Blood will be everywhere in Egypt, even in the wooden buckets and stone jars."

20Moses and Aaron did just as the LORD had commanded. He raised his staff in the presence of Pharaoh and his officials and struck the water of the Nile, and all the water was changed into blood. 21The fish in the Nile died, and the river smelled so bad that the Egyptians could not drink its water. Blood was everywhere in Egypt.

22But the Egyptian magicians did the same things by their secret arts, and Pharaoh's heart became hard; he would not listen to Moses and Aaron, just as the LORD had said. 23Instead, he turned and went into his palace, and did not take even this to heart. 24And all the Egyptians dug along the Nile to get drinking water, because they could not drink the water of the river.

The Plague of Frogs

25Seven days passed after the LORD struck the Nile. 8 1Then the LORD said to Moses, "Go to Pharaoh and say to him, 'This is what the LORD says: Let my people go, so that they may worship me. ²If you refuse to let them go, I will plague your whole country with frogs. ³The Nile will teem with frogs. They will come up into your palace and your bedroom and onto your bed, into the houses of your officials and on your people, and into your ovens and kneading troughs. ⁴The frogs will go up on you and your people and all your officials.' "

⁵Then the LORD said to Moses, "Tell Aaron, 'Stretch out your hand with your staff over the streams and canals and ponds, and make frogs come up on the land of Egypt.' "

⁶So Aaron stretched out his hand over the waters of Egypt, and the frogs came up and covered the land. ⁷But the magicians did the same things by their secret arts; they also made frogs come up on the land of Egypt.

⁸Pharaoh summoned Moses and Aaron and said, "Pray to the LORD to take the frogs away from me and my people, and I will let your people go to offer sacrifices to the LORD."

⁹Moses said to Pharaoh, "I leave to you the honor of setting the time for me to pray for you and your officials and your people that you and your houses may be rid of the frogs, except for those that remain in the Nile."

¹⁰"Tomorrow," Pharaoh said.

Moses replied, "It will be as you say, so that you may know there is no one like the LORD our God. ¹¹The frogs will leave you and your houses, your officials and your people; they will remain only in the Nile."

¹²After Moses and Aaron left Pharaoh, Moses cried out to the LORD about the frogs he had brought on Pharaoh. ¹³And the LORD did what Moses asked. The frogs died in the houses, in the courtyards and in the fields. ¹⁴They were piled into heaps, and the land reeked of them. ¹⁵But when Pharaoh saw that there was relief, he hardened his heart and would not listen to Moses and Aaron, just as the LORD had said.

The Plague of Gnats

¹⁶Then the LORD said to Moses, "Tell Aaron, 'Stretch out your staff and strike the dust of the ground,' and throughout the land of Egypt the dust will become gnats." ¹⁷They did this, and when Aaron stretched out his hand with the staff and struck the dust of the ground, gnats came

upon men and animals. All the dust throughout the land of Egypt became gnats. ¹⁸But when the magicians tried to produce gnats by their secret arts, they could not. And the gnats were on men and animals.

¹⁹The magicians said to Pharaoh, "This is the finger of God." But Pharaoh's heart was hard and he would not listen, just as the LORD had said.

The Plague of Flies

²⁰Then the LORD said to Moses, "Get up early in the morning and confront Pharaoh as he goes to the water and say to him, 'This is what the LORD says: Let my people go, so that they may worship me. ²¹If you do not let my people go, I will send swarms of flies on you and your officials, on your people and into your houses. The houses of the Egyptians will be full of flies, and even the ground where they are.

²²" 'But on that day I will deal differently with the land of Goshen, where my people live; no swarms of flies will be there, so that you will know that I, the LORD, am in this land. ²³I will make a distinction[a] between my people and your people. This miraculous sign will occur tomorrow.' "

²⁴And the LORD did this. Dense swarms of flies poured into Pharaoh's palace and into the houses of his officials, and throughout Egypt the land was ruined by the flies.

²⁵Then Pharaoh summoned Moses and Aaron and said, "Go, sacrifice to your God here in the land."

²⁶But Moses said, "That would not be right. The sacrifices we offer the LORD our God would be detestable to the Egyptians. And if we offer sacrifices that are detestable in their eyes, will they not stone us? ²⁷We must take a three-day journey into the desert to offer sacrifices to the LORD our God, as he commands us."

²⁸Pharaoh said, "I will let you go to offer sacrifices to the LORD your God in the desert, but you must not go very far. Now pray for me."

²⁹Moses answered, "As soon as I leave you, I will pray to the LORD, and tomorrow the flies will leave Pharaoh and his officials and his people. Only be sure that Pharaoh does not act deceitfully again by not letting the people go to offer sacrifices to the LORD."

³⁰Then Moses left Pharaoh and prayed

---

a23 Septuagint and Vulgate; Hebrew *will put a deliverance*

to the Lord, [31]and the Lord did what Moses asked: The flies left Pharaoh and his officials and his people; not a fly remained. [32]But this time also Pharaoh hardened his heart and would not let the people go.

The Plague on Livestock

9 Then the Lord said to Moses, "Go to Pharaoh and say to him, 'This is what the Lord, the God of the Hebrews, says: "Let my people go, so that they may worship me." [2]If you refuse to let them go and continue to hold them back, [3]the hand of the Lord will bring a terrible plague on your livestock in the field—on your horses and donkeys and camels and on your cattle and sheep and goats. [4]But the Lord will make a distinction between the livestock of Israel and that of Egypt, so that no animal belonging to the Israelites will die.'"

[5]The Lord set a time and said, "Tomorrow the Lord will do this in the land." [6]And the next day the Lord did it: All the livestock of the Egyptians died, but not one animal belonging to the Israelites died. [7]Pharaoh sent men to investigate and found that not even one of the animals of the Israelites had died. Yet his heart was unyielding and he would not let the people go.

The Plague of Boils

[8]Then the Lord said to Moses and Aaron, "Take handfuls of soot from a furnace and have Moses toss it into the air in the presence of Pharaoh. [9]It will become fine dust over the whole land of Egypt, and festering boils will break out on men and animals throughout the land."

[10]So they took soot from a furnace and stood before Pharaoh. Moses tossed it into the air, and festering boils broke out on men and animals. [11]The magicians could not stand before Moses because of the boils that were on them and on all the Egyptians. [12]But the Lord hardened Pharaoh's heart and he would not listen to Moses and Aaron, just as the Lord had said to Moses.

The Plague of Hail

[13]Then the Lord said to Moses, "Get up early in the morning, confront Pharaoh and say to him, 'This is what the Lord, the God of the Hebrews, says: Let my people go, so that they may worship me, [14]or this time I will send the full force of my plagues against you and against your officials and your people, so you may know that there is no one like me in all the earth. [15]For by now I could have stretched out my hand and struck you and your people with a plague that would have wiped you off the earth. [16]But I have raised you up[a] for this very purpose, that I might show you my power and that my name might be proclaimed in all the earth. [17]You still set yourself against my people and will not let them go. [18]Therefore, at this time tomorrow I will send the worst hailstorm that has ever fallen on Egypt, from the day it was founded till now. [19]Give an order now to bring your livestock and everything you have in the field to a place of shelter, because the hail will fall on every man and animal that has not been brought in and is still out in the field, and they will die.'"

[20]Those officials of Pharaoh who feared the word of the Lord hurried to bring their slaves and their livestock inside. [21]But those who ignored the word of the Lord left their slaves and livestock in the field.

[22]Then the Lord said to Moses, "Stretch out your hand toward the sky so that hail will fall all over Egypt—on men and animals and on everything growing in the fields of Egypt." [23]When Moses stretched out his staff toward the sky, the Lord sent thunder and hail, and lightning flashed down to the ground. So the Lord rained hail on the land of Egypt; [24]hail fell and lightning flashed back and forth. It was the worst storm in all the land of Egypt since it had become a nation. [25]Throughout Egypt hail struck everything in the fields—both men and animals; it beat down everything growing in the fields and stripped every tree. [26]The only place it did not hail was the land of Goshen, where the Israelites were.

[27]Then Pharaoh summoned Moses and Aaron. "This time I have sinned," he said to them. "The Lord is in the right, and I and my people are in the wrong. [28]Pray to the Lord, for we have had enough thunder and hail. I will let you go; you don't have to stay any longer."

[29]Moses replied, "When I have gone out of the city, I will spread out my hands in prayer to the Lord. The thunder will stop and there will be no more hail, so you may know that the earth is the Lord's. [30]But I know that you and your officials still do not fear the Lord God."

_a16_ Or _have spared you_

31(The flax and barley were destroyed, since the barley had headed and the flax was in bloom. **32**The wheat and spelt, however, were not destroyed, because they ripen later.)

33Then Moses left Pharaoh and went out of the city. He spread out his hands toward the LORD; the thunder and hail stopped, and the rain no longer poured down on the land. **34**When Pharaoh saw that the rain and hail and thunder had stopped, he sinned again: He and his officials hardened their hearts. **35**So Pharaoh's heart was hard and he would not let the Israelites go, just as the LORD had said through Moses.

The Plague of Locusts

10 Then the LORD said to Moses, "Go to Pharaoh, for I have hardened his heart and the hearts of his officials so that I may perform these miraculous signs of mine among them **2**that you may tell your children and grandchildren how I dealt harshly with the Egyptians and how I performed my signs among them, and that you may know that I am the LORD."

3So Moses and Aaron went to Pharaoh and said to him, "This is what the LORD, the God of the Hebrews, says: 'How long will you refuse to humble yourself before me? Let my people go, so that they may worship me. **4**If you refuse to let them go, I will bring locusts into your country tomorrow. **5**They will cover the face of the ground so that it cannot be seen. They will devour what little you have left after the hail, including every tree that is growing in your fields. **6**They will fill your houses and those of all your officials and all the Egyptians — something neither your fathers nor your forefathers have ever seen from the day they settled in this land till now.' " Then Moses turned and left Pharaoh.

7Pharaoh's officials said to him, "How long will this man be a snare to us? Let the people go, so that they may worship the LORD their God. Do you not yet realize that Egypt is ruined?"

8Then Moses and Aaron were brought back to Pharaoh. "Go, worship the LORD your God," he said. "But just who will be going?"

9Moses answered, "We will go with our young and old, with our sons and daughters, and with our flocks and herds, because we are to celebrate a festival to the LORD."

10Pharaoh said, "The LORD be with you — if I let you go, along with your women and children! Clearly you are bent on evil.*a* **11**No! Have only the men go; and worship the LORD, since that's what you have been asking for." Then Moses and Aaron were driven out of Pharaoh's presence.

12And the LORD said to Moses, "Stretch out your hand over Egypt so that locusts will swarm over the land and devour everything growing in the fields, everything left by the hail."

13So Moses stretched out his staff over Egypt, and the LORD made an east wind blow across the land all that day and all that night. By morning the wind had brought the locusts; **14**they invaded all Egypt and settled down in every area of the country in great numbers. Never before had there been such a plague of locusts, nor will there ever be again. **15**They covered all the ground until it was black. They devoured all that was left after the hail — everything growing in the fields and the fruit on the trees. Nothing green remained on tree or plant in all the land of Egypt.

16Pharaoh quickly summoned Moses and Aaron and said, "I have sinned against the LORD your God and against you. **17**Now forgive my sin once more and pray to the LORD your God to take this deadly plague away from me."

18Moses then left Pharaoh and prayed to the LORD. **19**And the LORD changed the wind to a very strong west wind, which caught up the locusts and carried them into the Red Sea.*b* Not a locust was left anywhere in Egypt. **20**But the LORD hardened Pharaoh's heart, and he would not let the Israelites go.

The Plague of Darkness

21Then the LORD said to Moses, "Stretch out your hand toward the sky so that darkness will spread over Egypt — darkness that can be felt." **22**So Moses stretched out his hand toward the sky, and total darkness covered all Egypt for three days. **23**No one could see anyone else or leave his place for three days. Yet all the Israelites had light in the places where they lived.

24Then Pharaoh summoned Moses and said, "Go, worship the LORD. Even your

---

a 10 Or *Be careful, trouble is in store for you!*   *b 19* Hebrew *Yam Suph*; that is, Sea of Reeds women and children may go with you; only leave your flocks and herds behind."

²⁵But Moses said, "You must allow us to have sacrifices and burnt offerings to present to the LORD our God. ²⁶Our livestock too must go with us; not a hoof is to be left behind. We have to use some of them in worshiping the LORD our God, and until we get there we will not know what we are to use to worship the LORD."

²⁷But the LORD hardened Pharaoh's heart, and he was not willing to let them go. ²⁸Pharaoh said to Moses, "Get out of my sight! Make sure you do not appear before me again! The day you see my face you will die."

²⁹"Just as you say," Moses replied, "I will never appear before you again."

The Plague on the Firstborn

11 Now the LORD had said to Moses, "I will bring one more plague on Pharaoh and on Egypt. After that, he will let you go from here, and when he does, he will drive you out completely. ²Tell the people that men and women alike are to ask their neighbors for articles of silver and gold." ³(The LORD made the Egyptians favorably disposed toward the people, and Moses himself was highly regarded in Egypt by Pharaoh's officials and by the people.)

⁴So Moses said, "This is what the LORD says: 'About midnight I will go throughout Egypt. ⁵Every firstborn son in Egypt will die, from the firstborn son of Pharaoh, who sits on the throne, to the firstborn son of the slave girl, who is at her hand mill, and all the firstborn of the cattle as well. ⁶There will be loud wailing throughout Egypt — worse than there has ever been or ever will be again. ⁷But among the Israelites not a dog will bark at any man or animal.' Then you will know that the LORD makes a distinction between Egypt and Israel. ⁸All these officials of yours will come to me, bowing down before me and saying, 'Go, you and all the people who follow you!' After that I will leave." Then Moses, hot with anger, left Pharaoh.

⁹The LORD had said to Moses, "Pharaoh will refuse to listen to you — so that my wonders may be multiplied in Egypt." ¹⁰Moses and Aaron performed all these wonders before Pharaoh, but the LORD hardened Pharaoh's heart, and he would not let the Israelites go out of his country.

The Passover

12 The LORD said to Moses and Aaron in Egypt, ²"This month is to be for you the first month, the first month of your year. ³Tell the whole community of Israel that on the tenth day of this month each man is to take a lamb*a* for his family, one for each household. ⁴If any household is too small for a whole lamb, they must share one with their nearest neighbor, having taken into account the number of people there are. You are to determine the amount of lamb needed in accordance with what each person will eat. ⁵The animals you choose must be year-old males without defect, and you may take them from the sheep or the goats. ⁶Take care of them until the fourteenth day of the month, when all the people of the community of Israel must slaughter them at twilight. ⁷Then they are to take some of the blood and put it on the sides and tops of the doorframes of the houses where they eat the lambs. ⁸That same night they are to eat the meat roasted over the fire, along with bitter herbs, and bread made without yeast. ⁹Do not eat the meat raw or cooked in water, but roast it over the fire — head, legs and inner parts. ¹⁰Do not leave any of it till morning; if some is left till morning, you must burn it. ¹¹This is how you are to eat it: with your cloak tucked into your belt, your sandals on your feet and your staff in your hand. Eat it in haste; it is the LORD's Passover.

¹²"On that same night I will pass through Egypt and strike down every firstborn — both men and animals — and I will bring judgment on all the gods of Egypt. I am the LORD. ¹³The blood will be a sign for you on the houses where you are; and when I see the blood, I will pass over you. No destructive plague will touch you when I strike Egypt.

¹⁴"This is a day you are to commemorate; for the generations to come you shall celebrate it as a festival to the LORD — a lasting ordinance. ¹⁵For seven days you are to eat bread made without yeast. On the first day remove the yeast from your houses, for whoever eats anything with yeast in it from the first day through the seventh must be cut off from Israel. ¹⁶On the first day hold a sacred assembly, and another one on the seventh day. Do no work at all on these days, except to pre-

a3 The Hebrew word can mean lamb or kid; also in verse 4.

pare food for everyone to eat—that is all you may do.

[17]"Celebrate the Feast of Unleavened Bread, because it was on this very day that I brought your divisions out of Egypt. Celebrate this day as a lasting ordinance for the generations to come. [18]In the first month you are to eat bread made without yeast, from the evening of the fourteenth day until the evening of the twenty-first day. [19]For seven days no yeast is to be found in your houses. And whoever eats anything with yeast in it must be cut off from the community of Israel, whether he is an alien or native-born. [20]Eat nothing made with yeast. Wherever you live, you must eat unleavened bread."

[21]Then Moses summoned all the elders of Israel and said to them, "Go at once and select the animals for your families and slaughter the Passover lamb. [22]Take a bunch of hyssop, dip it into the blood in the basin and put some of the blood on the top and on both sides of the doorframe. Not one of you shall go out the door of his house until morning. [23]When the LORD goes through the land to strike down the Egyptians, he will see the blood on the top and sides of the doorframe and will pass over that doorway, and he will not permit the destroyer to enter your houses and strike you down.

[24]"Obey these instructions as a lasting ordinance for you and your descendants. [25]When you enter the land that the LORD will give you as he promised, observe this ceremony. [26]And when your children ask you, 'What does this ceremony mean to you?' [27]then tell them, 'It is the Passover sacrifice to the LORD, who passed over the houses of the Israelites in Egypt and spared our homes when he struck down the Egyptians.' " Then the people bowed down and worshiped. [28]The Israelites did just what the LORD commanded Moses and Aaron.

[29]At midnight the LORD struck down all the firstborn in Egypt, from the firstborn of Pharaoh, who sat on the throne, to the firstborn of the prisoner, who was in the dungeon, and the firstborn of all the livestock as well. [30]Pharaoh and all his officials and all the Egyptians got up during the night, and there was loud wailing in Egypt, for there was not a house without someone dead.

The Exodus

[31]During the night Pharaoh summoned Moses and Aaron and said, "Up! Leave my people, you and the Israelites! Go, worship the LORD as you have requested. [32]Take your flocks and herds, as you have said, and go. And also bless me."

[33]The Egyptians urged the people to hurry and leave the country. "For otherwise," they said, "we will all die!" [34]So the people took their dough before the yeast was added, and carried it on their shoulders in kneading troughs wrapped in clothing. [35]The Israelites did as Moses instructed and asked the Egyptians for articles of silver and gold and for clothing. [36]The LORD had made the Egyptians favorably disposed toward the people, and they gave them what they asked for; so they plundered the Egyptians.

[37]The Israelites journeyed from Rameses to Succoth. There were about six hundred thousand men on foot, besides women and children. [38]Many other people went up with them, as well as large droves of livestock, both flocks and herds. [39]With the dough they had brought from Egypt, they baked cakes of unleavened bread. The dough was without yeast because they had been driven out of Egypt and did not have time to prepare food for themselves.

[40]Now the length of time the Israelite people lived in Egypt[a] was 430 years. [41]At the end of the 430 years, to the very day, all the LORD's divisions left Egypt. [42]Because the LORD kept vigil that night to bring them out of Egypt, on this night all the Israelites are to keep vigil to honor the LORD for the generations to come.

Passover Restrictions

[43]The LORD said to Moses and Aaron, "These are the regulations for the Passover:

"No foreigner is to eat of it. [44]Any slave you have bought may eat of it after you have circumcised him, [45]but a temporary resident and a hired worker may not eat of it.

[46]"It must be eaten inside one house; take none of the meat outside the house. Do not break any of the bones. [47]The whole community of Israel must celebrate it.

[48]"An alien living among you who wants to celebrate the LORD's Passover

---

[a]40 Masoretic Text; Samaritan Pentateuch and Septuagint *Egypt and Canaan*

must have all the males in his household circumcised; then he may take part like one born in the land. No uncircumcised male may eat of it. **49**The same law applies to the native-born and to the alien living among you."

50All the Israelites did just what the LORD had commanded Moses and Aaron. **51**And on that very day the LORD brought the Israelites out of Egypt by their divisions.

Consecration of the Firstborn

13 The LORD said to Moses, **2**"Consecrate to me every firstborn male. The first offspring of every womb among the Israelites belongs to me, whether man or animal."

3Then Moses said to the people, "Commemorate this day, the day you came out of Egypt, out of the land of slavery, because the LORD brought you out of it with a mighty hand. Eat nothing containing yeast. **4**Today, in the month of Abib, you are leaving. **5**When the LORD brings you into the land of the Canaanites, Hittites, Amorites, Hivites and Jebusites — the land he swore to your forefathers to give you, a land flowing with milk and honey — you are to observe this ceremony in this month: **6**For seven days eat bread made without yeast and on the seventh day hold a festival to the LORD. **7**Eat unleavened bread during those seven days; nothing with yeast in it is to be seen among you, nor shall any yeast be seen anywhere within your borders. **8**On that day tell your son, 'I do this because of what the LORD did for me when I came out of Egypt.' **9**This observance will be for you like a sign on your hand and a reminder on your forehead that the law of the LORD is to be on your lips. For the LORD brought you out of Egypt with his mighty hand. **10**You must keep this ordinance at the appointed time year after year.

11"After the LORD brings you into the land of the Canaanites and gives it to you, as he promised on oath to you and your forefathers, **12**you are to give over to the LORD the first offspring of every womb. All the firstborn males of your livestock belong to the LORD. **13**Redeem with a lamb every firstborn donkey, but if you do not redeem it, break its neck. Redeem every firstborn among your sons.

14"In days to come, when your son asks you, 'What does this mean?' say to him, 'With a mighty hand the LORD brought us out of Egypt, out of the land of slavery. **15**When Pharaoh stubbornly refused to let us go, the LORD killed every firstborn in Egypt, both man and animal. This is why I sacrifice to the LORD the first male offspring of every womb and redeem each of my firstborn sons.' **16**And it will be like a sign on your hand and a symbol on your forehead that the LORD brought us out of Egypt with his mighty hand."

Crossing the Sea

17When Pharaoh let the people go, God did not lead them on the road through the Philistine country, though that was shorter. For God said, "If they face war, they might change their minds and return to Egypt." **18**So God led the people around by the desert road toward the Red Sea.*a* The Israelites went up out of Egypt armed for battle.

19Moses took the bones of Joseph with him because Joseph had made the sons of Israel swear an oath. He had said, "God will surely come to your aid, and then you must carry my bones up with you from this place."*b*

20After leaving Succoth they camped at Etham on the edge of the desert. **21**By day the LORD went ahead of them in a pillar of cloud to guide them on their way and by night in a pillar of fire to give them light, so that they could travel by day or night. **22**Neither the pillar of cloud by day nor the pillar of fire by night left its place in front of the people.

14 Then the LORD said to Moses, **2**"Tell the Israelites to turn back and encamp near Pi Hahiroth, between Migdol and the sea. They are to encamp by the sea, directly opposite Baal Zephon. **3**Pharaoh will think, 'The Israelites are wandering around the land in confusion, hemmed in by the desert.' **4**And I will harden Pharaoh's heart, and he will pursue them. But I will gain glory for myself through Pharaoh and all his army, and the Egyptians will know that I am the LORD." So the Israelites did this.

5When the king of Egypt was told that the people had fled, Pharaoh and his officials changed their minds about them and said, "What have we done? We have let the Israelites go and have lost their services!" **6**So he had his chariot made ready and took his army with him. **7**He took six

---

*a*18 Hebrew *Yam Suph*; that is, Sea of Reeds   *b*19 See Gen. 50:25.

hundred of the best chariots, along with all the other chariots of Egypt, with officers over all of them. [8]The Lord hardened the heart of Pharaoh king of Egypt, so that he pursued the Israelites, who were marching out boldly. [9]The Egyptians—all Pharaoh's horses and chariots, horsemen[a] and troops—pursued the Israelites and overtook them as they camped by the sea near Pi Hahiroth, opposite Baal Zephon.

[10]As Pharaoh approached, the Israelites looked up, and there were the Egyptians, marching after them. They were terrified and cried out to the Lord. [11]They said to Moses, "Was it because there were no graves in Egypt that you brought us to the desert to die? What have you done to us by bringing us out of Egypt? [12]Didn't we say to you in Egypt, 'Leave us alone; let us serve the Egyptians'? It would have been better for us to serve the Egyptians than to die in the desert!"

[13]Moses answered the people, "Do not be afraid. Stand firm and you will see the deliverance the Lord will bring you today. The Egyptians you see today you will never see again. [14]The Lord will fight for you; you need only to be still."

[15]Then the Lord said to Moses, "Why are you crying out to me? Tell the Israelites to move on. [16]Raise your staff and stretch out your hand over the sea to divide the water so that the Israelites can go through the sea on dry ground. [17]I will harden the hearts of the Egyptians so that they will go in after them. And I will gain glory through Pharaoh and all his army, through his chariots and his horsemen. [18]The Egyptians will know that I am the Lord when I gain glory through Pharaoh, his chariots and his horsemen."

[19]Then the angel of God, who had been traveling in front of Israel's army, withdrew and went behind them. The pillar of cloud also moved from in front and stood behind them, [20]coming between the armies of Egypt and Israel. Throughout the night the cloud brought darkness to the one side and light to the other side; so neither went near the other all night long.

[21]Then Moses stretched out his hand over the sea, and all that night the Lord drove the sea back with a strong east wind and turned it into dry land. The waters were divided, [22]and the Israelites went through the sea on dry ground, with a wall of water on their right and on their left.

[23]The Egyptians pursued them, and all Pharaoh's horses and chariots and horsemen followed them into the sea. [24]During the last watch of the night the Lord looked down from the pillar of fire and cloud at the Egyptian army and threw it into confusion. [25]He made the wheels of their chariots come off[b] so that they had difficulty driving. And the Egyptians said, "Let's get away from the Israelites! The Lord is fighting for them against Egypt."

[26]Then the Lord said to Moses, "Stretch out your hand over the sea so that the waters may flow back over the Egyptians and their chariots and horsemen." [27]Moses stretched out his hand over the sea, and at daybreak the sea went back to its place. The Egyptians were fleeing toward[c] it, and the Lord swept them into the sea. [28]The water flowed back and covered the chariots and horsemen—the entire army of Pharaoh that had followed the Israelites into the sea. Not one of them survived.

[29]But the Israelites went through the sea on dry ground, with a wall of water on their right and on their left. [30]That day the Lord saved Israel from the hands of the Egyptians, and Israel saw the Egyptians lying dead on the shore. [31]And when the Israelites saw the great power the Lord displayed against the Egyptians, the people feared the Lord and put their trust in him and in Moses his servant.

The Song of Moses and Miriam

15 Then Moses and the Israelites sang this song to the Lord:

"I will sing to the Lord,
  for he is highly exalted.
The horse and its rider
  he has hurled into the sea.
[2]The Lord is my strength and my song;
  he has become my salvation.
He is my God, and I will praise him,
  my father's God, and I will exalt
    him.
[3]The Lord is a warrior;
  the Lord is his name.
[4]Pharaoh's chariots and his army
  he has hurled into the sea.
The best of Pharaoh's officers
  are drowned in the Red Sea.[d]
[5]The deep waters have covered them;

---

[a]9 Or *charioteers*; also in verses 17, 18, 23, 26 and 28 (see Samaritan Pentateuch, Septuagint and Syriac) of Reeds; also in verse 22
[b]25 Or *He jammed the wheels of their chariots*   [c]27 Or *from*   [d]4 Hebrew *Yam Suph*; that is, Sea

they sank to the depths like a stone.

⁶"Your right hand, O Lᴏʀᴅ,
    was majestic in power.
Your right hand, O Lᴏʀᴅ,
    shattered the enemy.
⁷In the greatness of your majesty
    you threw down those who opposed
      you.
You unleashed your burning anger;
    it consumed them like stubble.
⁸By the blast of your nostrils
    the waters piled up.
The surging waters stood firm like a
      wall;
    the deep waters congealed in the
      heart of the sea.

⁹"The enemy boasted,
    'I will pursue, I will overtake them.
I will divide the spoils;
    I will gorge myself on them.
I will draw my sword
    and my hand will destroy them.'
¹⁰But you blew with your breath,
    and the sea covered them.
They sank like lead
    in the mighty waters.

¹¹"Who among the gods is like you,
    O Lᴏʀᴅ?
Who is like you—
    majestic in holiness,
    awesome in glory,
    working wonders?
¹²You stretched out your right hand
    and the earth swallowed them.

¹³"In your unfailing love you will lead
    the people you have redeemed.
In your strength you will guide them
    to your holy dwelling.
¹⁴The nations will hear and tremble;
    anguish will grip the people of
      Philistia.
¹⁵The chiefs of Edom will be terrified,
    the leaders of Moab will be seized
      with trembling,
the people ᵃ of Canaan will melt
      away;
¹⁶   terror and dread will fall upon
      them.
By the power of your arm
    they will be as still as a stone—
until your people pass by, O Lᴏʀᴅ,
    until the people you bought ᵇ pass
      by.
¹⁷You will bring them in and plant them
    on the mountain of your
      inheritance—

the place, O Lᴏʀᴅ, you made for your
    dwelling,
    the sanctuary, O Lord, your hands
      established.
¹⁸The Lᴏʀᴅ will reign
    for ever and ever."

¹⁹When Pharaoh's horses, chariots and horsemen ᶜ went into the sea, the Lᴏʀᴅ brought the waters of the sea back over them, but the Israelites walked through the sea on dry ground. ²⁰Then Miriam the prophetess, Aaron's sister, took a tambourine in her hand, and all the women followed her, with tambourines and dancing. ²¹Miriam sang to them:

"Sing to the Lᴏʀᴅ,
    for he is highly exalted.
The horse and its rider
    he has hurled into the sea."

The Waters of Marah and Elim

²²Then Moses led Israel from the Red Sea and they went into the Desert of Shur. For three days they traveled in the desert without finding water. ²³When they came to Marah, they could not drink its water because it was bitter. (That is why the place is called Marah.ᵈ) ²⁴So the people grumbled against Moses, saying, "What are we to drink?"

²⁵Then Moses cried out to the Lᴏʀᴅ, and the Lᴏʀᴅ showed him a piece of wood. He threw it into the water, and the water became sweet.

There the Lᴏʀᴅ made a decree and a law for them, and there he tested them. ²⁶He said, "If you listen carefully to the voice of the Lᴏʀᴅ your God and do what is right in his eyes, if you pay attention to his commands and keep all his decrees, I will not bring on you any of the diseases I brought on the Egyptians, for I am the Lᴏʀᴅ, who heals you."

²⁷Then they came to Elim, where there were twelve springs and seventy palm trees, and they camped there near the water.

Manna and Quail

16 The whole Israelite community set out from Elim and came to the Desert of Sin, which is between Elim and Sinai, on the fifteenth day of the second month after they had come out of Egypt. ²In the desert the whole community grumbled against Moses and Aaron. ³The Israelites said to them, "If only we had

---

ᵃ15 Or *rulers*   ᵇ16 Or *created*   ᶜ19 Or *charioteers*   ᵈ23 *Marah* means *bitter.*

died by the Lord's hand in Egypt! There we sat around pots of meat and ate all the food we wanted, but you have brought us out into this desert to starve this entire assembly to death."

[4]Then the Lord said to Moses, "I will rain down bread from heaven for you. The people are to go out each day and gather enough for that day. In this way I will test them and see whether they will follow my instructions. [5]On the sixth day they are to prepare what they bring in, and that is to be twice as much as they gather on the other days."

[6]So Moses and Aaron said to all the Israelites, "In the evening you will know that it was the Lord who brought you out of Egypt, [7]and in the morning you will see the glory of the Lord, because he has heard your grumbling against him. Who are we, that you should grumble against us?" [8]Moses also said, "You will know that it was the Lord when he gives you meat to eat in the evening and all the bread you want in the morning, because he has heard your grumbling against him. Who are we? You are not grumbling against us, but against the Lord."

[9]Then Moses told Aaron, "Say to the entire Israelite community, 'Come before the Lord, for he has heard your grumbling.'"

[10]While Aaron was speaking to the whole Israelite community, they looked toward the desert, and there was the glory of the Lord appearing in the cloud.

[11]The Lord said to Moses, [12]"I have heard the grumbling of the Israelites. Tell them, 'At twilight you will eat meat, and in the morning you will be filled with bread. Then you will know that I am the Lord your God.'"

[13]That evening quail came and covered the camp, and in the morning there was a layer of dew around the camp. [14]When the dew was gone, thin flakes like frost on the ground appeared on the desert floor. [15]When the Israelites saw it, they said to each other, "What is it?" For they did not know what it was.

Moses said to them, "It is the bread the Lord has given you to eat. [16]This is what the Lord has commanded: 'Each one is to gather as much as he needs. Take an omer[a] for each person you have in your tent.'"

[17]The Israelites did as they were told; some gathered much, some little. [18]And when they measured it by the omer, he who gathered much did not have too much, and he who gathered little did not have too little. Each one gathered as much as he needed.

[19]Then Moses said to them, "No one is to keep any of it until morning."

[20]However, some of them paid no attention to Moses; they kept part of it until morning, but it was full of maggots and began to smell. So Moses was angry with them.

[21]Each morning everyone gathered as much as he needed, and when the sun grew hot, it melted away. [22]On the sixth day, they gathered twice as much—two omers[b] for each person—and the leaders of the community came and reported this to Moses. [23]He said to them, "This is what the Lord commanded: 'Tomorrow is to be a day of rest, a holy Sabbath to the Lord. So bake what you want to bake and boil what you want to boil. Save whatever is left and keep it until morning.'"

[24]So they saved it until morning, as Moses commanded, and it did not stink or get maggots in it. [25]"Eat it today," Moses said, "because today is a Sabbath to the Lord. You will not find any of it on the ground today. [26]Six days you are to gather it, but on the seventh day, the Sabbath, there will not be any."

[27]Nevertheless, some of the people went out on the seventh day to gather it, but they found none. [28]Then the Lord said to Moses, "How long will you[c] refuse to keep my commands and my instructions? [29]Bear in mind that the Lord has given you the Sabbath; that is why on the sixth day he gives you bread for two days. Everyone is to stay where he is on the seventh day; no one is to go out." [30]So the people rested on the seventh day.

[31]The people of Israel called the bread manna.[d] It was white like coriander seed and tasted like wafers made with honey. [32]Moses said, "This is what the Lord has commanded: 'Take an omer of manna and keep it for the generations to come, so they can see the bread I gave you to eat in the desert when I brought you out of Egypt.'"

[33]So Moses said to Aaron, "Take a jar and put an omer of manna in it. Then

---

[a]16 That is, probably about 2 quarts (about 2 liters); also in verses 18, 32, 33 and 36   [b]22 That is, probably about 4 quarts (about 4.5 liters)   [c]28 The Hebrew is plural.   [d]31 Manna means What is it? (see verse 15).

place it before the Lord to be kept for the generations to come."

³⁴As the Lord commanded Moses, Aaron put the manna in front of the Testimony, that it might be kept. ³⁵The Israelites ate manna forty years, until they came to a land that was settled; they ate manna until they reached the border of Canaan. ³⁶(An omer is one tenth of an ephah.)

Water From the Rock

17 The whole Israelite community set out from the Desert of Sin, traveling from place to place as the Lord commanded. They camped at Rephidim, but there was no water for the people to drink. ²So they quarreled with Moses and said, "Give us water to drink."

Moses replied, "Why do you quarrel with me? Why do you put the Lord to the test?"

³But the people were thirsty for water there, and they grumbled against Moses. They said, "Why did you bring us up out of Egypt to make us and our children and livestock die of thirst?"

⁴Then Moses cried out to the Lord, "What am I to do with these people? They are almost ready to stone me."

⁵The Lord answered Moses, "Walk on ahead of the people. Take with you some of the elders of Israel and take in your hand the staff with which you struck the Nile, and go. ⁶I will stand there before you by the rock at Horeb. Strike the rock, and water will come out of it for the people to drink." So Moses did this in the sight of the elders of Israel. ⁷And he called the place Massah*ᵃ* and Meribah*ᵇ* because the Israelites quarreled and because they tested the Lord saying, "Is the Lord among us or not?"

The Amalekites Defeated

⁸The Amalekites came and attacked the Israelites at Rephidim. ⁹Moses said to Joshua, "Choose some of our men and go out to fight the Amalekites. Tomorrow I will stand on top of the hill with the staff of God in my hands."

¹⁰So Joshua fought the Amalekites as Moses had ordered, and Moses, Aaron and Hur went to the top of the hill. ¹¹As long as Moses held up his hands, the Israelites were winning, but whenever he lowered his hands, the Amalekites were win-

ning. ¹²When Moses' hands grew tired, they took a stone and put it under him and he sat on it. Aaron and Hur held his hands up — one on one side, one on the other — so that his hands remained steady till sunset. ¹³So Joshua overcame the Amalekite army with the sword.

¹⁴Then the Lord said to Moses, "Write this on a scroll as something to be remembered and make sure that Joshua hears it, because I will completely blot out the memory of Amalek from under heaven."

¹⁵Moses built an altar and called it The Lord is my Banner. ¹⁶He said, "For hands were lifted up to the throne of the Lord. The*ᶜ* Lord will be at war against the Amalekites from generation to generation."

Jethro Visits Moses

18 Now Jethro, the priest of Midian and father-in-law of Moses, heard of everything God had done for Moses and for his people Israel, and how the Lord had brought Israel out of Egypt.

²After Moses had sent away his wife Zipporah, his father-in-law Jethro received her ³and her two sons. One son was named Gershom,*ᵈ* for Moses said, "I have become an alien in a foreign land"; ⁴and the other was named Eliezer,*ᵉ* for he said, "My father's God was my helper; he saved me from the sword of Pharaoh."

⁵Jethro, Moses' father-in-law, together with Moses' sons and wife, came to him in the desert, where he was camped near the mountain of God. ⁶Jethro had sent word to him, "I, your father-in-law Jethro, am coming to you with your wife and her two sons."

⁷So Moses went out to meet his father-in-law and bowed down and kissed him. They greeted each other and then went into the tent. ⁸Moses told his father-in-law about everything the Lord had done to Pharaoh and the Egyptians for Israel's sake and about all the hardships they had met along the way and how the Lord had saved them.

⁹Jethro was delighted to hear about all the good things the Lord had done for Israel in rescuing them from the hand of the Egyptians. ¹⁰He said, "Praise be to the Lord, who rescued you from the hand of the Egyptians and of Pharaoh, and who rescued the people from the hand of the Egyptians. ¹¹Now I know that the Lord is

---

ᵃ7 Massah means *testing.*   *ᵇ7 Meribah* means *quarreling.*   *ᶜ16* Or *"Because a hand was against the throne of the Lord, the*   *ᵈ3 Gershom* sounds like the Hebrew for *an alien there.*   *ᵉ4 Eliezer* means *my God is helper.*

greater than all other gods, for he did this to those who had treated Israel arrogantly." 12Then Jethro, Moses' father-in-law, brought a burnt offering and other sacrifices to God, and Aaron came with all the elders of Israel to eat bread with Moses' father-in-law in the presence of God.

13The next day Moses took his seat to serve as judge for the people, and they stood around him from morning till evening. 14When his father-in-law saw all that Moses was doing for the people, he said, "What is this you are doing for the people? Why do you alone sit as judge, while all these people stand around you from morning till evening?"

15Moses answered him, "Because the people come to me to seek God's will. 16Whenever they have a dispute, it is brought to me, and I decide between the parties and inform them of God's decrees and laws."

17Moses' father-in-law replied, "What you are doing is not good. 18You and these people who come to you will only wear yourselves out. The work is too heavy for you; you cannot handle it alone. 19Listen now to me and I will give you some advice, and may God be with you. You must be the people's representative before God and bring their disputes to him. 20Teach them the decrees and laws, and show them the way to live and the duties they are to perform. 21But select capable men from all the people—men who fear God, trustworthy men who hate dishonest gain—and appoint them as officials over thousands, hundreds, fifties and tens. 22Have them serve as judges for the people at all times, but have them bring every difficult case to you; the simple cases they can decide themselves. That will make your load lighter, because they will share it with you. 23If you do this and God so commands, you will be able to stand the strain, and all these people will go home satisfied."

24Moses listened to his father-in-law and did everything he said. 25He chose capable men from all Israel and made them leaders of the people, officials over thousands, hundreds, fifties and tens. 26They served as judges for the people at all times. The difficult cases they brought to Moses, but the simple ones they decided themselves.

27Then Moses sent his father-in-law on his way, and Jethro returned to his own country.

At Mount Sinai

19 In the third month after the Israelites left Egypt—on the very day—they came to the Desert of Sinai. 2After they set out from Rephidim, they entered the Desert of Sinai, and Israel camped there in the desert in front of the mountain.

3Then Moses went up to God, and the LORD called to him from the mountain and said, "This is what you are to say to the house of Jacob and what you are to tell the people of Israel: 4'You yourselves have seen what I did to Egypt, and how I carried you on eagles' wings and brought you to myself. 5Now if you obey me fully and keep my covenant, then out of all nations you will be my treasured possession. Although the whole earth is mine, 6youa will be for me a kingdom of priests and a holy nation.' These are the words you are to speak to the Israelites."

7So Moses went back and summoned the elders of the people and set before them all the words the LORD had commanded him to speak. 8The people all responded together, "We will do everything the LORD has said." So Moses brought their answer back to the LORD.

9The LORD said to Moses, "I am going to come to you in a dense cloud, so that the people will hear me speaking with you and will always put their trust in you." Then Moses told the LORD what the people had said.

10And the LORD said to Moses, "Go to the people and consecrate them today and tomorrow. Have them wash their clothes 11and be ready by the third day, because on that day the LORD will come down on Mount Sinai in the sight of all the people. 12Put limits for the people around the mountain and tell them, 'Be careful that you do not go up the mountain or touch the foot of it. Whoever touches the mountain shall surely be put to death. 13He shall surely be stoned or shot with arrows; not a hand is to be laid on him. Whether man or animal, he shall not be permitted to live.' Only when the ram's horn sounds a long blast may they go up to the mountain."

14After Moses had gone down the mountain to the people, he consecrated them, and they washed their clothes.

a5,6 Or possession, for the whole earth is mine. 6You

¹⁵Then he said to the people, "Prepare yourselves for the third day. Abstain from sexual relations."

¹⁶On the morning of the third day there was thunder and lightning, with a thick cloud over the mountain, and a very loud trumpet blast. Everyone in the camp trembled. ¹⁷Then Moses led the people out of the camp to meet with God, and they stood at the foot of the mountain. ¹⁸Mount Sinai was covered with smoke, because the LORD descended on it in fire. The smoke billowed up from it like smoke from a furnace, the whole mountain*ᵃ* trembled violently, ¹⁹and the sound of the trumpet grew louder and louder. Then Moses spoke and the voice of God answered him.*ᵇ*

²⁰The LORD descended to the top of Mount Sinai and called Moses to the top of the mountain. So Moses went up ²¹and the LORD said to him, "Go down and warn the people so they do not force their way through to see the LORD and many of them perish. ²²Even the priests, who approach the LORD, must consecrate themselves, or the LORD will break out against them."

²³Moses said to the LORD, "The people cannot come up Mount Sinai, because you yourself warned us, 'Put limits around the mountain and set it apart as holy.'"

²⁴The LORD replied, "Go down and bring Aaron up with you. But the priests and the people must not force their way through to come up to the LORD, or he will break out against them."

²⁵So Moses went down to the people and told them.

The Ten Commandments

20 And God spoke all these words:

²"I am the LORD your God, who brought you out of Egypt, out of the land of slavery.

³"You shall have no other gods before*ᶜ* me.

⁴"You shall not make for yourself an idol in the form of anything in heaven above or on the earth beneath or in the waters below. ⁵You shall not bow down to them or worship them; for I, the LORD your God, am a jealous God, punishing the children for the sin of the fathers to the third and fourth generation of those who hate me, ⁶but showing love to a thousand ˌgenerationsˌ of those who love me and keep my commandments.

⁷"You shall not misuse the name of the LORD your God, for the LORD will not hold anyone guiltless who misuses his name.

⁸"Remember the Sabbath day by keeping it holy. ⁹Six days you shall labor and do all your work, ¹⁰but the seventh day is a Sabbath to the LORD your God. On it you shall not do any work, neither you, nor your son or daughter, nor your manservant or maidservant, nor your animals, nor the alien within your gates. ¹¹For in six days the LORD made the heavens and the earth, the sea, and all that is in them, but he rested on the seventh day. Therefore the LORD blessed the Sabbath day and made it holy.

¹²"Honor your father and your mother, so that you may live long in the land the LORD your God is giving you.

¹³"You shall not murder.

¹⁴"You shall not commit adultery.

¹⁵"You shall not steal.

¹⁶"You shall not give false testimony against your neighbor.

¹⁷"You shall not covet your neighbor's house. You shall not covet your neighbor's wife, or his manservant or maidservant, his ox or donkey, or anything that belongs to your neighbor."

¹⁸When the people saw the thunder and lightning and heard the trumpet and saw the mountain in smoke, they trembled with fear. They stayed at a distance ¹⁹and said to Moses, "Speak to us yourself and we will listen. But do not have God speak to us or we will die."

²⁰Moses said to the people, "Do not be afraid. God has come to test you, so that the fear of God will be with you to keep you from sinning."

²¹The people remained at a distance, while Moses approached the thick darkness where God was.

ᵃ18 Most Hebrew manuscripts; a few Hebrew manuscripts and Septuagint *all the people*   *ᵇ19* Or *and God answered him with thunder*   *ᶜ3* Or *besides*

Idols and Altars

22Then the LORD said to Moses, "Tell the Israelites this: 'You have seen for yourselves that I have spoken to you from heaven: **23**Do not make any gods to be alongside me; do not make for yourselves gods of silver or gods of gold.

24" 'Make an altar of earth for me and sacrifice on it your burnt offerings and fellowship offerings,*a* your sheep and goats and your cattle. Wherever I cause my name to be honored, I will come to you and bless you. **25**If you make an altar of stones for me, do not build it with dressed stones, for you will defile it if you use a tool on it. **26**And do not go up to my altar on steps, lest your nakedness be exposed on it.'

21 "These are the laws you are to set before them:

Hebrew Servants

2"If you buy a Hebrew servant, he is to serve you for six years. But in the seventh year, he shall go free, without paying anything. **3**If he comes alone, he is to go free

a24 Traditionally *peace offerings*

THURSDAY

VERSE FOR THE DAY:	AUTHOR:	PASSAGE FOR THE DAY:
Exodus 20:12	Leonard LeSourd	Exodus 20:12–17

A Special Blessing

LIKE most males, during my youth and early manhood I gave little thought to what I owed my parents—or what it meant to be a son.

When I left the nest I wrote an occasional letter or card to them, called home on Mother's Day, Father's Day and other occasions. Their love for me was accepted and returned casually. Their concern and advice were often shrugged off.

The change in me began when, as the editor of *Guideposts* magazine, I took responsibility for putting together a series of articles on the Ten Commandments. Thus my first real encounter with the fifth commandment: "Honor your father and your mother, so that you may live long in the land the LORD your God is giving you" (Exodus 20:12).

During my previous readings of this verse, I had stopped after the first five words. That seemed to say it. So I would then skip down to the sixth commandment.

But as I lingered over the words that day in my *Guideposts* office, the totality of the promise hit me. God was giving us more than a command; he was telling us *why* it is important to honor our parents . . . "that you may live long in the land the LORD your God is giving you."

A new thought here—that when we war with parents, reject parents or are indifferent to them we may be missing out on a special blessing.

Additional Scripture Readings:
Matthew 15:1–9; Ephesians 6:1–3

Go to page 89 for your next devotional reading.

alone; but if he has a wife when he comes, she is to go with him. **4**If his master gives him a wife and she bears him sons or daughters, the woman and her children shall belong to her master, and only the man shall go free.

5"But if the servant declares, 'I love my master and my wife and children and do not want to go free,' **6**then his master must take him before the judges.*a* He shall take him to the door or the doorpost and pierce his ear with an awl. Then he will be his servant for life.

7"If a man sells his daughter as a servant, she is not to go free as menservants do. **8**If she does not please the master who has selected her for himself,*b* he must let her be redeemed. He has no right to sell her to foreigners, because he has broken faith with her. **9**If he selects her for his son, he must grant her the rights of a daughter. **10**If he marries another woman, he must not deprive the first one of her food, clothing and marital rights. **11**If he does not provide her with these three things, she is to go free, without any payment of money.

Personal Injuries

12"Anyone who strikes a man and kills him shall surely be put to death. **13**However, if he does not do it intentionally, but God lets it happen, he is to flee to a place I will designate. **14**But if a man schemes and kills another man deliberately, take him away from my altar and put him to death.

15"Anyone who attacks*c* his father or his mother must be put to death.

16"Anyone who kidnaps another and either sells him or still has him when he is caught must be put to death.

17"Anyone who curses his father or mother must be put to death.

18"If men quarrel and one hits the other with a stone or with his fist*d* and he does not die but is confined to bed, **19**the one who struck the blow will not be held responsible if the other gets up and walks around outside with his staff; however, he must pay the injured man for the loss of his time and see that he is completely healed.

20"If a man beats his male or female slave with a rod and the slave dies as a direct result, he must be punished, **21**but he is not to be punished if the slave gets up

after a day or two, since the slave is his property.

22"If men who are fighting hit a pregnant woman and she gives birth prematurely*e* but there is no serious injury, the offender must be fined whatever the woman's husband demands and the court allows. **23**But if there is serious injury, you are to take life for life, **24**eye for eye, tooth for tooth, hand for hand, foot for foot, **25**burn for burn, wound for wound, bruise for bruise.

26"If a man hits a manservant or maidservant in the eye and destroys it, he must let the servant go free to compensate for the eye. **27**And if he knocks out the tooth of a manservant or maidservant, he must let the servant go free to compensate for the tooth.

28"If a bull gores a man or a woman to death, the bull must be stoned to death, and its meat must not be eaten. But the owner of the bull will not be held responsible. **29**If, however, the bull has had the habit of goring and the owner has been warned but has not kept it penned up and it kills a man or woman, the bull must be stoned and the owner also must be put to death. **30**However, if payment is demanded of him, he may redeem his life by paying whatever is demanded. **31**This law also applies if the bull gores a son or daughter. **32**If the bull gores a male or female slave, the owner must pay thirty shekels*f* of silver to the master of the slave, and the bull must be stoned.

33"If a man uncovers a pit or digs one and fails to cover it and an ox or a donkey falls into it, **34**the owner of the pit must pay for the loss; he must pay its owner, and the dead animal will be his.

35"If a man's bull injures the bull of another and it dies, they are to sell the live one and divide both the money and the dead animal equally. **36**However, if it was known that the bull had the habit of goring, yet the owner did not keep it penned up, the owner must pay, animal for animal, and the dead animal will be his.

Protection of Property

22 "If a man steals an ox or a sheep and slaughters it or sells it, he must pay back five head of cattle for the ox and four sheep for the sheep.

2"If a thief is caught breaking in and is struck so that he dies, the defender is not

---

a6 Or *before God*   *b8* Or *master so that he does not choose her*   *c15* Or *kills*   *d18* Or *with a tool*
e22 Or *she has a miscarriage*   *f32* That is, about 12 ounces (about 0.3 kilogram)

guilty of bloodshed; **3**but if it happens[a] after sunrise, he is guilty of bloodshed.

"A thief must certainly make restitution, but if he has nothing, he must be sold to pay for his theft.

4"If the stolen animal is found alive in his possession — whether ox or donkey or sheep — he must pay back double.

5"If a man grazes his livestock in a field or vineyard and lets them stray and they graze in another man's field, he must make restitution from the best of his own field or vineyard.

6"If a fire breaks out and spreads into thornbushes so that it burns shocks of grain or standing grain or the whole field, the one who started the fire must make restitution.

7"If a man gives his neighbor silver or goods for safekeeping and they are stolen from the neighbor's house, the thief, if he is caught, must pay back double. **8**But if the thief is not found, the owner of the house must appear before the judges[b] to determine whether he has laid his hands on the other man's property. **9**In all cases of illegal possession of an ox, a donkey, a sheep, a garment, or any other lost property about which somebody says, 'This is mine,' both parties are to bring their cases before the judges. The one whom the judges declare[c] guilty must pay back double to his neighbor.

10"If a man gives a donkey, an ox, a sheep or any other animal to his neighbor for safekeeping and it dies or is injured or is taken away while no one is looking, **11**the issue between them will be settled by the taking of an oath before the Lord that the neighbor did not lay hands on the other person's property. The owner is to accept this, and no restitution is required. **12**But if the animal was stolen from the neighbor, he must make restitution to the owner. **13**If it was torn to pieces by a wild animal, he shall bring in the remains as evidence and he will not be required to pay for the torn animal.

14"If a man borrows an animal from his neighbor and it is injured or dies while the owner is not present, he must make restitution. **15**But if the owner is with the animal, the borrower will not have to pay. If the animal was hired, the money paid for the hire covers the loss.

Social Responsibility

16"If a man seduces a virgin who is not pledged to be married and sleeps with her, he must pay the bride-price, and she shall be his wife. **17**If her father absolutely refuses to give her to him, he must still pay the bride-price for virgins.

18"Do not allow a sorceress to live.

19"Anyone who has sexual relations with an animal must be put to death.

20"Whoever sacrifices to any god other than the Lord must be destroyed.[d]

21"Do not mistreat an alien or oppress him, for you were aliens in Egypt.

22"Do not take advantage of a widow or an orphan. **23**If you do and they cry out to me, I will certainly hear their cry. **24**My anger will be aroused, and I will kill you with the sword; your wives will become widows and your children fatherless.

25"If you lend money to one of my people among you who is needy, do not be like a moneylender; charge him no interest.[e] **26**If you take your neighbor's cloak as a pledge, return it to him by sunset, **27**because his cloak is the only covering he has for his body. What else will he sleep in? When he cries out to me, I will hear, for I am compassionate.

28"Do not blaspheme God[f] or curse the ruler of your people.

29"Do not hold back offerings from your granaries or your vats.[g]

"You must give me the firstborn of your sons. **30**Do the same with your cattle and your sheep. Let them stay with their mothers for seven days, but give them to me on the eighth day.

31"You are to be my holy people. So do not eat the meat of an animal torn by wild beasts; throw it to the dogs.

Laws of Justice and Mercy

23 "Do not spread false reports. Do not help a wicked man by being a malicious witness.

2"Do not follow the crowd in doing wrong. When you give testimony in a lawsuit, do not pervert justice by siding with the crowd, **3**and do not show favoritism to a poor man in his lawsuit.

4"If you come across your enemy's ox or donkey wandering off, be sure to take it back to him. **5**If you see the donkey of someone who hates you fallen down un-

---

[a]3 Or *if he strikes him*   [b]8 Or *before God*; also in verse 9   [c]9 Or *whom God declares*   [d]20 The Hebrew term refers to the irrevocable giving over of things or persons to the Lord, often by totally destroying them.   [e]25 Or *excessive interest*   [f]28 Or *Do not revile the judges*   [g]29 The meaning of the Hebrew for this phrase is uncertain.

der its load, do not leave it there; be sure you help him with it.

⁶"Do not deny justice to your poor people in their lawsuits. ⁷Have nothing to do with a false charge and do not put an innocent or honest person to death, for I will not acquit the guilty.

⁸"Do not accept a bribe, for a bribe blinds those who see and twists the words of the righteous.

⁹"Do not oppress an alien; you yourselves know how it feels to be aliens, because you were aliens in Egypt.

Sabbath Laws

¹⁰"For six years you are to sow your fields and harvest the crops, ¹¹but during the seventh year let the land lie unplowed and unused. Then the poor among your people may get food from it, and the wild animals may eat what they leave. Do the same with your vineyard and your olive grove.

¹²"Six days do your work, but on the seventh day do not work, so that your ox and your donkey may rest and the slave born in your household, and the alien as well, may be refreshed.

¹³"Be careful to do everything I have said to you. Do not invoke the names of other gods; do not let them be heard on your lips.

The Three Annual Festivals

¹⁴"Three times a year you are to celebrate a festival to me.

¹⁵"Celebrate the Feast of Unleavened Bread; for seven days eat bread made without yeast, as I commanded you. Do this at the appointed time in the month of Abib, for in that month you came out of Egypt.

"No one is to appear before me empty-handed.

¹⁶"Celebrate the Feast of Harvest with the firstfruits of the crops you sow in your field.

"Celebrate the Feast of Ingathering at the end of the year, when you gather in your crops from the field.

¹⁷"Three times a year all the men are to appear before the Sovereign LORD.

¹⁸"Do not offer the blood of a sacrifice to me along with anything containing yeast.

"The fat of my festival offerings must not be kept until morning.

¹⁹"Bring the best of the firstfruits of your soil to the house of the LORD your God.

"Do not cook a young goat in its mother's milk.

God's Angel to Prepare the Way

²⁰"See, I am sending an angel ahead of you to guard you along the way and to bring you to the place I have prepared. ²¹Pay attention to him and listen to what he says. Do not rebel against him; he will not forgive your rebellion, since my Name is in him. ²²If you listen carefully to what he says and do all that I say, I will be an enemy to your enemies and will oppose those who oppose you. ²³My angel will go ahead of you and bring you into the land of the Amorites, Hittites, Perizzites, Canaanites, Hivites and Jebusites, and I will wipe them out. ²⁴Do not bow down before their gods or worship them or follow their practices. You must demolish them and break their sacred stones to pieces. ²⁵Worship the LORD your God, and his blessing will be on your food and water. I will take away sickness from among you, ²⁶and none will miscarry or be barren in your land. I will give you a full life span.

²⁷"I will send my terror ahead of you and throw into confusion every nation you encounter. I will make all your enemies turn their backs and run. ²⁸I will send the hornet ahead of you to drive the Hivites, Canaanites and Hittites out of your way. ²⁹But I will not drive them out in a single year, because the land would become desolate and the wild animals too numerous for you. ³⁰Little by little I will drive them out before you, until you have increased enough to take possession of the land.

³¹"I will establish your borders from the Red Sea[a] to the Sea of the Philistines,[b] and from the desert to the River.[c] I will hand over to you the people who live in the land and you will drive them out before you. ³²Do not make a covenant with them or with their gods. ³³Do not let them live in your land, or they will cause you to sin against me, because the worship of their gods will certainly be a snare to you."

The Covenant Confirmed

24 Then he said to Moses, "Come up to the LORD, you and Aaron, Nadab

---

[a]31 Hebrew *Yam Suph*; that is, Sea of Reeds   [b]31 That is, the Mediterranean   [c]31 That is, the Euphrates

and Abihu, and seventy of the elders of Israel. You are to worship at a distance, **2**but Moses alone is to approach the LORD; the others must not come near. And the people may not come up with him."

3When Moses went and told the people all the LORD's words and laws, they responded with one voice, "Everything the LORD has said we will do." **4**Moses then wrote down everything the LORD had said.

He got up early the next morning and built an altar at the foot of the mountain and set up twelve stone pillars representing the twelve tribes of Israel. **5**Then he sent young Israelite men, and they offered burnt offerings and sacrificed young bulls as fellowship offerings*a* to the LORD. **6**Moses took half of the blood and put it in bowls, and the other half he sprinkled on the altar. **7**Then he took the Book of the Covenant and read it to the people. They responded, "We will do everything the LORD has said; we will obey."

8Moses then took the blood, sprinkled it on the people and said, "This is the blood of the covenant that the LORD has made with you in accordance with all these words."

9Moses and Aaron, Nadab and Abihu, and the seventy elders of Israel went up **10**and saw the God of Israel. Under his feet was something like a pavement made of sapphire,*b* clear as the sky itself. **11**But God did not raise his hand against these leaders of the Israelites; they saw God, and they ate and drank.

12The LORD said to Moses, "Come up to me on the mountain and stay here, and I will give you the tablets of stone, with the law and commands I have written for their instruction."

13Then Moses set out with Joshua his aide, and Moses went up on the mountain of God. **14**He said to the elders, "Wait here for us until we come back to you. Aaron and Hur are with you, and anyone involved in a dispute can go to them."

15When Moses went up on the mountain, the cloud covered it, **16**and the glory of the LORD settled on Mount Sinai. For six days the cloud covered the mountain, and on the seventh day the LORD called to Moses from within the cloud. **17**To the Israelites the glory of the LORD looked like a consuming fire on top of the mountain. **18**Then Moses entered the cloud as he went on up the mountain. And he stayed on the mountain forty days and forty nights.

Offerings for the Tabernacle

25 The LORD said to Moses, **2**"Tell the Israelites to bring me an offering. You are to receive the offering for me from each man whose heart prompts him to give. **3**These are the offerings you are to receive from them: gold, silver and bronze; **4**blue, purple and scarlet yarn and fine linen; goat hair; **5**ram skins dyed red and hides of sea cows*c*; acacia wood; **6**olive oil for the light; spices for the anointing oil and for the fragrant incense; **7**and onyx stones and other gems to be mounted on the ephod and breastpiece.

8"Then have them make a sanctuary for me, and I will dwell among them. **9**Make this tabernacle and all its furnishings exactly like the pattern I will show you.

The Ark

10"Have them make a chest of acacia wood—two and a half cubits long, a cubit and a half wide, and a cubit and a half high.*d* **11**Overlay it with pure gold, both inside and out, and make a gold molding around it. **12**Cast four gold rings for it and fasten them to its four feet, with two rings on one side and two rings on the other. **13**Then make poles of acacia wood and overlay them with gold. **14**Insert the poles into the rings on the sides of the chest to carry it. **15**The poles are to remain in the rings of this ark; they are not to be removed. **16**Then put in the ark the Testimony, which I will give you.

17"Make an atonement cover*e* of pure gold—two and a half cubits long and a cubit and a half wide.*f* **18**And make two cherubim out of hammered gold at the ends of the cover. **19**Make one cherub on one end and the second cherub on the other; make the cherubim of one piece with the cover, at the two ends. **20**The cherubim are to have their wings spread upward, overshadowing the cover with them. The cherubim are to face each other, looking toward the cover. **21**Place the cover on top of the ark and put in the ark the Testimony, which I will give you. **22**There, above the cover between the two

---

a5 Traditionally *peace offerings*   *b10* Or *lapis lazuli*   *c5* That is, dugongs   *d10* That is, about 3 3/4 feet (about 1.1 meters) long and 2 1/4 feet (about 0.7 meter) wide and high   *e17* Traditionally *a mercy seat*   *f17* That is, about 3 3/4 feet (about 1.1 meters) long and 2 1/4 feet (about 0.7 meter) wide cherubim that are over the ark of the Testimony, I will meet with you and give you all my commands for the Israelites.

The Table

23"Make a table of acacia wood — two cubits long, a cubit wide and a cubit and a half high.ᵃ 24Overlay it with pure gold and make a gold molding around it. 25Also make around it a rim a handbreadthᵇ wide and put a gold molding on the rim. 26Make four gold rings for the table and fasten them to the four corners, where the four legs are. 27The rings are to be close to the rim to hold the poles used in carrying the table. 28Make the poles of acacia wood, overlay them with gold and carry the table with them. 29And make its plates and dishes of pure gold, as well as its pitchers and bowls for the pouring out of offerings. 30Put the bread of the Presence on this table to be before me at all times.

The Lampstand

31"Make a lampstand of pure gold and hammer it out, base and shaft; its flowerlike cups, buds and blossoms shall be of one piece with it. 32Six branches are to extend from the sides of the lampstand — three on one side and three on the other. 33Three cups shaped like almond flowers with buds and blossoms are to be on one branch, three on the next branch, and the same for all six branches extending from the lampstand. 34And on the lampstand there are to be four cups shaped like almond flowers with buds and blossoms. 35One bud shall be under the first pair of branches extending from the lampstand, a second bud under the second pair, and a third bud under the third pair — six branches in all. 36The buds and branches shall all be of one piece with the lampstand, hammered out of pure gold.

37"Then make its seven lamps and set them up on it so that they light the space in front of it. 38Its wick trimmers and trays are to be of pure gold. 39A talentᶜ of pure gold is to be used for the lampstand and all these accessories. 40See that you make them according to the pattern shown you on the mountain.

The Tabernacle

26 "Make the tabernacle with ten curtains of finely twisted linen and blue, purple and scarlet yarn, with cherubim worked into them by a skilled craftsman. 2All the curtains are to be the same size — twenty-eight cubits long and four cubits wide.ᵈ 3Join five of the curtains together, and do the same with the other five. 4Make loops of blue material along the edge of the end curtain in one set, and do the same with the end curtain in the other set. 5Make fifty loops on one curtain and fifty loops on the end curtain of the other set, with the loops opposite each other. 6Then make fifty gold clasps and use them to fasten the curtains together so that the tabernacle is a unit.

7"Make curtains of goat hair for the tent over the tabernacle — eleven altogether. 8All eleven curtains are to be the same size — thirty cubits long and four cubits wide.ᵉ 9Join five of the curtains together into one set and the other six into another set. Fold the sixth curtain double at the front of the tent. 10Make fifty loops along the edge of the end curtain in one set and also along the edge of the end curtain in the other set. 11Then make fifty bronze clasps and put them in the loops to fasten the tent together as a unit. 12As for the additional length of the tent curtains, the half curtain that is left over is to hang down at the rear of the tabernacle. 13The tent curtains will be a cubitᶠ longer on both sides; what is left will hang over the sides of the tabernacle so as to cover it. 14Make for the tent a covering of ram skins dyed red, and over that a covering of hides of sea cows.ᵍ

15"Make upright frames of acacia wood for the tabernacle. 16Each frame is to be ten cubits long and a cubit and a half wide,ʰ 17with two projections set parallel to each other. Make all the frames of the tabernacle in this way. 18Make twenty frames for the south side of the tabernacle 19and make forty silver bases to go under them — two bases for each frame, one under each projection. 20For the other side, the north side of the tabernacle, make twenty frames 21and forty silver bases — two under each frame. 22Make six frames

---

ᵃ23 That is, about 3 feet (about 0.9 meter) long and 1 1/2 feet (about 0.5 meter) wide and 2 1/4 feet (about 0.7 meter) high   ᵇ25 That is, about 3 inches (about 8 centimeters)   ᶜ39 That is, about 75 pounds (about 34 kilograms)   ᵈ2 That is, about 42 feet (about 12.5 meters) long and 6 feet (about 1.8 meters) wide   ᵉ8 That is, about 45 feet (about 13.5 meters) long and 6 feet (about 1.8 meters) wide ᶠ13 That is, about 1 1/2 feet (about 0.5 meter)   ᵍ14 That is, dugongs   ʰ16 That is, about 15 feet (about 4.5 meters) long and 2 1/4 feet (about 0.7 meter) wide for the far end, that is, the west end of the tabernacle, ²³and make two frames for the corners at the far end. ²⁴At these two corners they must be double from the bottom all the way to the top, and fitted into a single ring; both shall be like that. ²⁵So there will be eight frames and sixteen silver bases — two under each frame.

²⁶"Also make crossbars of acacia wood: five for the frames on one side of the tabernacle, ²⁷five for those on the other side, and five for the frames on the west, at the far end of the tabernacle. ²⁸The center crossbar is to extend from end to end at the middle of the frames. ²⁹Overlay the frames with gold and make gold rings to hold the crossbars. Also overlay the crossbars with gold.

³⁰"Set up the tabernacle according to the plan shown you on the mountain.

³¹"Make a curtain of blue, purple and scarlet yarn and finely twisted linen, with cherubim worked into it by a skilled craftsman. ³²Hang it with gold hooks on four posts of acacia wood overlaid with gold and standing on four silver bases. ³³Hang the curtain from the clasps and place the ark of the Testimony behind the curtain. The curtain will separate the Holy Place from the Most Holy Place. ³⁴Put the atonement cover on the ark of the Testimony in the Most Holy Place. ³⁵Place the table outside the curtain on the north side of the tabernacle and put the lampstand opposite it on the south side.

³⁶"For the entrance to the tent make a curtain of blue, purple and scarlet yarn and finely twisted linen — the work of an embroiderer. ³⁷Make gold hooks for this curtain and five posts of acacia wood overlaid with gold. And cast five bronze bases for them.

The Altar of Burnt Offering

27 "Build an altar of acacia wood, three cubits[a] high; it is to be square, five cubits long and five cubits wide.[b] ²Make a horn at each of the four corners, so that the horns and the altar are of one piece, and overlay the altar with bronze. ³Make all its utensils of bronze — its pots to remove the ashes, and its shovels, sprinkling bowls, meat forks and firepans. ⁴Make a grating for it, a bronze

network, and make a bronze ring at each of the four corners of the network. ⁵Put it under the ledge of the altar so that it is halfway up the altar. ⁶Make poles of acacia wood for the altar and overlay them with bronze. ⁷The poles are to be inserted into the rings so they will be on two sides of the altar when it is carried. ⁸Make the altar hollow, out of boards. It is to be made just as you were shown on the mountain.

The Courtyard

⁹"Make a courtyard for the tabernacle. The south side shall be a hundred cubits[c] long and is to have curtains of finely twisted linen, ¹⁰with twenty posts and twenty bronze bases and with silver hooks and bands on the posts. ¹¹The north side shall also be a hundred cubits long and is to have curtains, with twenty posts and twenty bronze bases and with silver hooks and bands on the posts.

¹²"The west end of the courtyard shall be fifty cubits[d] wide and have curtains, with ten posts and ten bases. ¹³On the east end, toward the sunrise, the courtyard shall also be fifty cubits wide. ¹⁴Curtains fifteen cubits[e] long are to be on one side of the entrance, with three posts and three bases, ¹⁵and curtains fifteen cubits long are to be on the other side, with three posts and three bases.

¹⁶"For the entrance to the courtyard, provide a curtain twenty cubits[f] long, of blue, purple and scarlet yarn and finely twisted linen — the work of an embroiderer — with four posts and four bases. ¹⁷All the posts around the courtyard are to have silver bands and hooks, and bronze bases. ¹⁸The courtyard shall be a hundred cubits long and fifty cubits wide,[g] with curtains of finely twisted linen five cubits[h] high, and with bronze bases. ¹⁹All the other articles used in the service of the tabernacle, whatever their function, including all the tent pegs for it and those for the courtyard, are to be of bronze.

Oil for the Lampstand

²⁰"Command the Israelites to bring you clear oil of pressed olives for the light so that the lamps may be kept burning. ²¹In the Tent of Meeting, outside the curtain

---

a1 That is, about 4 1/2 feet (about 1.3 meters)   b1 That is, about 7 1/2 feet (about 2.3 meters) long and wide   c9 That is, about 150 feet (about 46 meters); also in verse 11   d12 That is, about 75 feet (about 23 meters); also in verse 13   e14 That is, about 22 1/2 feet (about 6.9 meters); also in verse 15   f16 That is, about 30 feet (about 9 meters)   g18 That is, about 150 feet (about 46 meters) long and 75 feet (about 23 meters) wide   h18 That is, about 7 1/2 feet (about 2.3 meters) that is in front of the Testimony, Aaron and his sons are to keep the lamps burning before the LORD from evening till morning. This is to be a lasting ordinance among the Israelites for the generations to come.

The Priestly Garments

28 "Have Aaron your brother brought to you from among the Israelites, along with his sons Nadab and Abihu, Eleazar and Ithamar, so they may serve me as priests. ²Make sacred garments for your brother Aaron, to give him dignity and honor. ³Tell all the skilled men to whom I have given wisdom in such matters that they are to make garments for Aaron, for his consecration, so he may serve me as priest. ⁴These are the garments they are to make: a breastpiece, an ephod, a robe, a woven tunic, a turban and a sash. They are to make these sacred garments for your brother Aaron and his sons, so they may serve me as priests. ⁵Have them use gold, and blue, purple and scarlet yarn, and fine linen.

The Ephod

⁶"Make the ephod of gold, and of blue, purple and scarlet yarn, and of finely twisted linen — the work of a skilled craftsman. ⁷It is to have two shoulder pieces attached to two of its corners, so it can be fastened. ⁸Its skillfully woven waistband is to be like it — of one piece with the ephod and made with gold, and with blue, purple and scarlet yarn, and with finely twisted linen.

⁹"Take two onyx stones and engrave on them the names of the sons of Israel ¹⁰in the order of their birth — six names on one stone and the remaining six on the other. ¹¹Engrave the names of the sons of Israel on the two stones the way a gem cutter engraves a seal. Then mount the stones in gold filigree settings ¹²and fasten them on the shoulder pieces of the ephod as memorial stones for the sons of Israel. Aaron is to bear the names on his shoulders as a memorial before the LORD. ¹³Make gold filigree settings ¹⁴and two braided chains of pure gold, like a rope, and attach the chains to the settings.

The Breastpiece

¹⁵"Fashion a breastpiece for making de-cisions — the work of a skilled craftsman. Make it like the ephod: of gold, and of blue, purple and scarlet yarn, and of finely twisted linen. ¹⁶It is to be square — a span*a* long and a span wide — and folded double. ¹⁷Then mount four rows of precious stones on it. In the first row there shall be a ruby, a topaz and a beryl; ¹⁸in the second row a turquoise, a sapphire*b* and an emerald; ¹⁹in the third row a jacinth, an agate and an amethyst; ²⁰in the fourth row a chrysolite, an onyx and a jasper.*c* Mount them in gold filigree settings. ²¹There are to be twelve stones, one for each of the names of the sons of Israel, each engraved like a seal with the name of one of the twelve tribes.

²²"For the breastpiece make braided chains of pure gold, like a rope. ²³Make two gold rings for it and fasten them to two corners of the breastpiece. ²⁴Fasten the two gold chains to the rings at the corners of the breastpiece, ²⁵and the other ends of the chains to the two settings, attaching them to the shoulder pieces of the ephod at the front. ²⁶Make two gold rings and attach them to the other two corners of the breastpiece on the inside edge next to the ephod. ²⁷Make two more gold rings and attach them to the bottom of the shoulder pieces on the front of the ephod, close to the seam just above the waistband of the ephod. ²⁸The rings of the breastpiece are to be tied to the rings of the ephod with blue cord, connecting it to the waistband, so that the breastpiece will not swing out from the ephod.

²⁹"Whenever Aaron enters the Holy Place, he will bear the names of the sons of Israel over his heart on the breastpiece of decision as a continuing memorial before the LORD. ³⁰Also put the Urim and the Thummim in the breastpiece, so they may be over Aaron's heart whenever he enters the presence of the LORD. Thus Aaron will always bear the means of making decisions for the Israelites over his heart before the LORD.

Other Priestly Garments

³¹"Make the robe of the ephod entirely of blue cloth, ³²with an opening for the head in its center. There shall be a woven edge like a collar*d* around this opening, so that it will not tear. ³³Make pomegranates of blue, purple and scarlet yarn

---

a16 That is, about 9 inches (about 22 centimeters)   *b18* Or *lapis lazuli*   *c20* The precise identification of some of these precious stones is uncertain.   *d32* The meaning of the Hebrew for this word is uncertain.

around the hem of the robe, with gold bells between them. [34]The gold bells and the pomegranates are to alternate around the hem of the robe. [35]Aaron must wear it when he ministers. The sound of the bells will be heard when he enters the Holy Place before the LORD and when he comes out, so that he will not die.

[36]"Make a plate of pure gold and engrave on it as on a seal: HOLY TO THE LORD. [37]Fasten a blue cord to it to attach it to the turban; it is to be on the front of the turban. [38]It will be on Aaron's forehead, and he will bear the guilt involved in the sacred gifts the Israelites consecrate, whatever their gifts may be. It will be on Aaron's forehead continually so that they will be acceptable to the LORD.

[39]"Weave the tunic of fine linen and make the turban of fine linen. The sash is to be the work of an embroiderer. [40]Make tunics, sashes and headbands for Aaron's sons, to give them dignity and honor. [41]After you put these clothes on your brother Aaron and his sons, anoint and ordain them. Consecrate them so they may serve me as priests.

[42]"Make linen undergarments as a covering for the body, reaching from the waist to the thigh. [43]Aaron and his sons must wear them whenever they enter the Tent of Meeting or approach the altar to minister in the Holy Place, so that they will not incur guilt and die.

"This is to be a lasting ordinance for Aaron and his descendants.

Consecration of the Priests

29 "This is what you are to do to consecrate them, so they may serve me as priests: Take a young bull and two rams without defect. [2]And from fine wheat flour, without yeast, make bread, and cakes mixed with oil, and wafers spread with oil. [3]Put them in a basket and present them in it — along with the bull and the two rams. [4]Then bring Aaron and his sons to the entrance to the Tent of Meeting and wash them with water. [5]Take the garments and dress Aaron with the tunic, the robe of the ephod, the ephod itself and the breastpiece. Fasten the ephod on him by its skillfully woven waistband. [6]Put the turban on his head and attach the sacred diadem to the turban. [7]Take the anointing oil and anoint him by pouring it on his head. [8]Bring his sons and dress them in tunics [9]and put headbands on them. Then

tie sashes on Aaron and his sons.[a] The priesthood is theirs by a lasting ordinance. In this way you shall ordain Aaron and his sons.

[10]"Bring the bull to the front of the Tent of Meeting, and Aaron and his sons shall lay their hands on its head. [11]Slaughter it in the LORD's presence at the entrance to the Tent of Meeting. [12]Take some of the bull's blood and put it on the horns of the altar with your finger, and pour out the rest of it at the base of the altar. [13]Then take all the fat around the inner parts, the covering of the liver, and both kidneys with the fat on them, and burn them on the altar. [14]But burn the bull's flesh and its hide and its offal outside the camp. It is a sin offering.

[15]"Take one of the rams, and Aaron and his sons shall lay their hands on its head. [16]Slaughter it and take the blood and sprinkle it against the altar on all sides. [17]Cut the ram into pieces and wash the inner parts and the legs, putting them with the head and the other pieces. [18]Then burn the entire ram on the altar. It is a burnt offering to the LORD, a pleasing aroma, an offering made to the LORD by fire.

[19]"Take the other ram, and Aaron and his sons shall lay their hands on its head. [20]Slaughter it, take some of its blood and put it on the lobes of the right ears of Aaron and his sons, on the thumbs of their right hands, and on the big toes of their right feet. Then sprinkle blood against the altar on all sides. [21]And take some of the blood on the altar and some of the anointing oil and sprinkle it on Aaron and his garments and on his sons and their garments. Then he and his sons and their garments will be consecrated.

[22]"Take from this ram the fat, the fat tail, the fat around the inner parts, the covering of the liver, both kidneys with the fat on them, and the right thigh. (This is the ram for the ordination.) [23]From the basket of bread made without yeast, which is before the LORD, take a loaf, and a cake made with oil, and a wafer. [24]Put all these in the hands of Aaron and his sons and wave them before the LORD as a wave offering. [25]Then take them from their hands and burn them on the altar along with the burnt offering for a pleasing aroma to the LORD, an offering made to the LORD by fire. [26]After you take the breast of the ram for Aaron's ordination, wave it be-

[a]9 Hebrew; Septuagint *on them*

fore the Lord as a wave offering, and it will be your share.

27"Consecrate those parts of the ordination ram that belong to Aaron and his sons: the breast that was waved and the thigh that was presented. 28This is always to be the regular share from the Israelites for Aaron and his sons. It is the contribution the Israelites are to make to the Lord from their fellowship offerings.[a]

29"Aaron's sacred garments will belong to his descendants so that they can be anointed and ordained in them. 30The son who succeeds him as priest and comes to the Tent of Meeting to minister in the Holy Place is to wear them seven days.

31"Take the ram for the ordination and cook the meat in a sacred place. 32At the entrance to the Tent of Meeting, Aaron and his sons are to eat the meat of the ram and the bread that is in the basket. 33They are to eat these offerings by which atonement was made for their ordination and consecration. But no one else may eat them, because they are sacred. 34And if any of the meat of the ordination ram or any bread is left over till morning, burn it up. It must not be eaten, because it is sacred.

35"Do for Aaron and his sons everything I have commanded you, taking seven days to ordain them. 36Sacrifice a bull each day as a sin offering to make atonement. Purify the altar by making atonement for it, and anoint it to consecrate it. 37For seven days make atonement for the altar and consecrate it. Then the altar will be most holy, and whatever touches it will be holy.

38"This is what you are to offer on the altar regularly each day: two lambs a year old. 39Offer one in the morning and the other at twilight. 40With the first lamb offer a tenth of an ephah[b] of fine flour mixed with a quarter of a hin[c] of oil from pressed olives, and a quarter of a hin of wine as a drink offering. 41Sacrifice the other lamb at twilight with the same grain offering and its drink offering as in the morning—a pleasing aroma, an offering made to the Lord by fire.

42"For the generations to come this burnt offering is to be made regularly at the entrance to the Tent of Meeting before the Lord. There I will meet you and speak to you; 43there also I will meet with the Israelites, and the place will be consecrated by my glory.

44"So I will consecrate the Tent of Meeting and the altar and will consecrate Aaron and his sons to serve me as priests. 45Then I will dwell among the Israelites and be their God. 46They will know that I am the Lord their God, who brought them out of Egypt so that I might dwell among them. I am the Lord their God.

The Altar of Incense

30 "Make an altar of acacia wood for burning incense. 2It is to be square, a cubit long and a cubit wide, and two cubits high[d]—its horns of one piece with it. 3Overlay the top and all the sides and the horns with pure gold, and make a gold molding around it. 4Make two gold rings for the altar below the molding—two on opposite sides—to hold the poles used to carry it. 5Make the poles of acacia wood and overlay them with gold. 6Put the altar in front of the curtain that is before the ark of the Testimony—before the atonement cover that is over the Testimony—where I will meet with you.

7"Aaron must burn fragrant incense on the altar every morning when he tends the lamps. 8He must burn incense again when he lights the lamps at twilight so incense will burn regularly before the Lord for the generations to come. 9Do not offer on this altar any other incense or any burnt offering or grain offering, and do not pour a drink offering on it. 10Once a year Aaron shall make atonement on its horns. This annual atonement must be made with the blood of the atoning sin offering for the generations to come. It is most holy to the Lord.".

Atonement Money

11Then the Lord said to Moses, 12"When you take a census of the Israelites to count them, each one must pay the Lord a ransom for his life at the time he is counted. Then no plague will come on them when you number them. 13Each one who crosses over to those already counted is to give a half shekel,[e] according to the sanctuary shekel, which weighs twenty gerahs. This half shekel is an offering to the Lord. 14All who cross over, those twenty years old or more, are to give an offering to the Lord. 15The rich are not to

---

a28 Traditionally peace offerings   b40 That is, probably about 2 quarts (about 2 liters)   c40 That is, probably about 1 quart (about 1 liter)   d2 That is, about 1 1/2 feet (about 0.5 meter) long and wide and about 3 feet (about 0.9 meter) high   e13 That is, about 1/5 ounce (about 6 grams); also in verse 15 give more than a half shekel and the poor are not to give less when you make the offering to the LORD to atone for your lives. ¹⁶Receive the atonement money from the Israelites and use it for the service of the Tent of Meeting. It will be a memorial for the Israelites before the LORD, making atonement for your lives."

Basin for Washing

¹⁷Then the LORD said to Moses, ¹⁸"Make a bronze basin, with its bronze stand, for washing. Place it between the Tent of Meeting and the altar, and put water in it. ¹⁹Aaron and his sons are to wash their hands and feet with water from it. ²⁰Whenever they enter the Tent of Meeting, they shall wash with water so that they will not die. Also, when they approach the altar to minister by presenting an offering made to the LORD by fire, ²¹they shall wash their hands and feet so that they will not die. This is to be a lasting ordinance for Aaron and his descendants for the generations to come."

Anointing Oil

²²Then the LORD said to Moses, ²³"Take the following fine spices: 500 shekels*a* of liquid myrrh, half as much (that is, 250 shekels) of fragrant cinnamon, 250 shekels of fragrant cane, ²⁴500 shekels of cassia—all according to the sanctuary shekel—and a hin*b* of olive oil. ²⁵Make these into a sacred anointing oil, a fragrant blend, the work of a perfumer. It will be the sacred anointing oil. ²⁶Then use it to anoint the Tent of Meeting, the ark of the Testimony, ²⁷the table and all its articles, the lampstand and its accessories, the altar of incense, ²⁸the altar of burnt offering and all its utensils, and the basin with its stand. ²⁹You shall consecrate them so they will be most holy, and whatever touches them will be holy.

³⁰"Anoint Aaron and his sons and consecrate them so they may serve me as priests. ³¹Say to the Israelites, 'This is to be my sacred anointing oil for the generations to come. ³²Do not pour it on men's bodies and do not make any oil with the same formula. It is sacred, and you are to consider it sacred. ³³Whoever makes perfume like it and whoever puts it on anyone other than a priest must be cut off from his people.' "

Incense

³⁴Then the LORD said to Moses, "Take fragrant spices—gum resin, onycha and galbanum—and pure frankincense, all in equal amounts, ³⁵and make a fragrant blend of incense, the work of a perfumer. It is to be salted and pure and sacred. ³⁶Grind some of it to powder and place it in front of the Testimony in the Tent of Meeting, where I will meet with you. It shall be most holy to you. ³⁷Do not make any incense with this formula for yourselves; consider it holy to the LORD. ³⁸Whoever makes any like it to enjoy its fragrance must be cut off from his people."

Bezalel and Oholiab

31 Then the LORD said to Moses, ²"See, I have chosen Bezalel son of Uri, the son of Hur, of the tribe of Judah, ³and I have filled him with the Spirit of God, with skill, ability and knowledge in all kinds of crafts— ⁴to make artistic designs for work in gold, silver and bronze, ⁵to cut and set stones, to work in wood, and to engage in all kinds of craftsmanship. ⁶Moreover, I have appointed Oholiab son of Ahisamach, of the tribe of Dan, to help him. Also I have given skill to all the craftsmen to make everything I have commanded you: ⁷the Tent of Meeting, the ark of the Testimony with the atonement cover on it, and all the other furnishings of the tent— ⁸the table and its articles, the pure gold lampstand and all its accessories, the altar of incense, ⁹the altar of burnt offering and all its utensils, the basin with its stand— ¹⁰and also the woven garments, both the sacred garments for Aaron the priest and the garments for his sons when they serve as priests, ¹¹and the anointing oil and fragrant incense for the Holy Place. They are to make them just as I commanded you."

The Sabbath

¹²Then the LORD said to Moses, ¹³"Say to the Israelites, 'You must observe my Sabbaths. This will be a sign between me and you for the generations to come, so you may know that I am the LORD, who makes you holy.*c*

¹⁴" 'Observe the Sabbath, because it is holy to you. Anyone who desecrates it must be put to death; whoever does any

---

a23 That is, about 12 1/2 pounds (about 6 kilograms)　　*b24* That is, probably about 4 quarts (about 4 liters)　　*c13* Or *who sanctifies you*; or *who sets you apart as holy* work on that day must be cut off from his people. [15]For six days, work is to be done, but the seventh day is a Sabbath of rest, holy to the Lord. Whoever does any work on the Sabbath day must be put to death. [16]The Israelites are to observe the Sabbath, celebrating it for the generations to come as a lasting covenant. [17]It will be a sign between me and the Israelites forever, for in six days the Lord made the heavens and the earth, and on the seventh day he abstained from work and rested.' "

[18]When the Lord finished speaking to Moses on Mount Sinai, he gave him the two tablets of the Testimony, the tablets of stone inscribed by the finger of God.

The Golden Calf

32 When the people saw that Moses was so long in coming down from the mountain, they gathered around Aaron and said, "Come, make us gods[a] who will go before us. As for this fellow Moses who brought us up out of Egypt, we don't know what has happened to him."

[2]Aaron answered them, "Take off the gold earrings that your wives, your sons and your daughters are wearing, and bring them to me." [3]So all the people took off their earrings and brought them to Aaron. [4]He took what they handed him and made it into an idol cast in the shape of a calf, fashioning it with a tool. Then they said, "These are your gods,[b] O Israel, who brought you up out of Egypt."

[5]When Aaron saw this, he built an altar in front of the calf and announced, "Tomorrow there will be a festival to the Lord." [6]So the next day the people rose early and sacrificed burnt offerings and presented fellowship offerings.[c] Afterward they sat down to eat and drink and got up to indulge in revelry.

[7]Then the Lord said to Moses, "Go down, because your people, whom you brought up out of Egypt, have become corrupt. [8]They have been quick to turn away from what I commanded them and have made themselves an idol cast in the shape of a calf. They have bowed down to it and sacrificed to it and have said, 'These are your gods, O Israel, who brought you up out of Egypt.'

[9]"I have seen these people," the Lord said to Moses, "and they are a stiff-necked people. [10]Now leave me alone so that my anger may burn against them and that I

may destroy them. Then I will make you into a great nation."

[11]But Moses sought the favor of the Lord his God. "O Lord," he said, "why should your anger burn against your people, whom you brought out of Egypt with great power and a mighty hand? [12]Why should the Egyptians say, 'It was with evil intent that he brought them out, to kill them in the mountains and to wipe them off the face of the earth'? Turn from your fierce anger; relent and do not bring disaster on your people. [13]Remember your servants Abraham, Isaac and Israel, to whom you swore by your own self: 'I will make your descendants as numerous as the stars in the sky and I will give your descendants all this land I promised them, and it will be their inheritance forever.' " [14]Then the Lord relented and did not bring on his people the disaster he had threatened.

[15]Moses turned and went down the mountain with the two tablets of the Testimony in his hands. They were inscribed on both sides, front and back. [16]The tablets were the work of God; the writing was the writing of God, engraved on the tablets.

[17]When Joshua heard the noise of the people shouting, he said to Moses, "There is the sound of war in the camp."

[18]Moses replied:

"It is not the sound of victory,
  it is not the sound of defeat;
  it is the sound of singing that I
    hear."

[19]When Moses approached the camp and saw the calf and the dancing, his anger burned and he threw the tablets out of his hands, breaking them to pieces at the foot of the mountain. [20]And he took the calf they had made and burned it in the fire; then he ground it to powder, scattered it on the water and made the Israelites drink it.

[21]He said to Aaron, "What did these people do to you, that you led them into such great sin?"

[22]"Do not be angry, my lord," Aaron answered. "You know how prone these people are to evil. [23]They said to me, 'Make us gods who will go before us. As for this fellow Moses who brought us up out of Egypt, we don't know what has happened to him.' [24]So I told them, 'Whoever has

---

[a]1 Or a god; also in verses 23 and 31   [b]4 Or This is your god; also in verse 8   [c]6 Traditionally peace offerings

any gold jewelry, take it off.' Then they gave me the gold, and I threw it into the fire, and out came this calf'

²⁵Moses saw that the people were running wild and that Aaron had let them get out of control and so become a laughingstock to their enemies. ²⁶So he stood at the entrance to the camp and said, "Whoever is for the LORD, come to me." And all the Levites rallied to him.

²⁷Then he said to them, "This is what the LORD, the God of Israel, says: 'Each man strap a sword to his side. Go back and forth through the camp from one end to the other, each killing his brother and friend and neighbor.' " ²⁸The Levites did as Moses commanded, and that day about three thousand of the people died. ²⁹Then Moses said, "You have been set apart to the LORD today, for you were against your own sons and brothers, and he has blessed you this day."

³⁰The next day Moses said to the people, "You have committed a great sin. But now I will go up to the LORD; perhaps I can make atonement for your sin."

³¹So Moses went back to the LORD and said, "Oh, what a great sin these people have committed! They have made themselves gods of gold. ³²But now, please forgive their sin—but if not, then blot me out of the book you have written."

³³The LORD replied to Moses, "Whoever has sinned against me I will blot out of my book. ³⁴Now go, lead the people to the place I spoke of, and my angel will go before you. However, when the time comes for me to punish, I will punish them for their sin."

³⁵And the LORD struck the people with a plague because of what they did with the calf Aaron had made.

33 Then the LORD said to Moses, "Leave this place, you and the people you brought up out of Egypt, and go up to the land I promised on oath to Abraham, Isaac and Jacob, saying, 'I will give it to your descendants.' ²I will send an angel before you and drive out the Canaanites, Amorites, Hittites, Perizzites, Hivites and Jebusites. ³Go up to the land flowing with milk and honey. But I will not go with you, because you are a stiff-necked people and I might destroy you on the way."

⁴When the people heard these distressing words, they began to mourn and no one put on any ornaments. ⁵For the LORD had said to Moses, "Tell the Israelites, 'You are a stiff-necked people. If I were to go with you even for a moment, I might destroy you. Now take off your ornaments and I will decide what to do with you.' " ⁶So the Israelites stripped off their ornaments at Mount Horeb.

The Tent of Meeting

⁷Now Moses used to take a tent and pitch it outside the camp some distance away, calling it the "tent of meeting." Anyone inquiring of the LORD would go to the tent of meeting outside the camp. ⁸And whenever Moses went out to the tent, all the people rose and stood at the entrances to their tents, watching Moses until he entered the tent. ⁹As Moses went into the tent, the pillar of cloud would come down and stay at the entrance, while the LORD spoke with Moses. ¹⁰Whenever the people saw the pillar of cloud standing at the entrance to the tent, they all stood and worshiped, each at the entrance to his tent. ¹¹The LORD would speak to Moses face to face, as a man speaks with his friend. Then Moses would return to the camp, but his young aide Joshua son of Nun did not leave the tent.

Moses and the Glory of the LORD

¹²Moses said to the LORD, "You have been telling me, 'Lead these people,' but you have not let me know whom you will send with me. You have said, 'I know you by name and you have found favor with me.' ¹³If you are pleased with me, teach me your ways so I may know you and continue to find favor with you. Remember that this nation is your people."

¹⁴The LORD replied, "My Presence will go with you, and I will give you rest."

¹⁵Then Moses said to him, "If your Presence does not go with us, do not send us up from here. ¹⁶How will anyone know that you are pleased with me and with your people unless you go with us? What else will distinguish me and your people from all the other people on the face of the earth?"

¹⁷And the LORD said to Moses, "I will do the very thing you have asked, because I am pleased with you and I know you by name."

¹⁸Then Moses said, "Now show me your glory."

¹⁹And the LORD said, "I will cause all my goodness to pass in front of you, and I will proclaim my name, the LORD, in your presence. I will have mercy on whom I will have mercy, and I will have compassion

on whom I will have compassion. **20**But," he said, "you cannot see my face, for no one may see me and live."

21Then the LORD said, "There is a place near me where you may stand on a rock. **22**When my glory passes by, I will put you in a cleft in the rock and cover you with my hand until I have passed by. **23**Then I will remove my hand and you will see my back; but my face must not be seen."

The New Stone Tablets

34 The LORD said to Moses, "Chisel out two stone tablets like the first ones, and I will write on them the words that were on the first tablets, which you broke. **2**Be ready in the morning, and then come up on Mount Sinai. Present yourself to me there on top of the mountain. **3**No one is to come with you or be seen anywhere on the mountain; not even the

---

FRIDAY

VERSE FOR THE DAY:	AUTHOR:	PASSAGE FOR THE DAY:
Exodus 33:14	Archibald Hart	Exodus 33:12–23

Stress-free Living

BECOMING dependent on adrenalin arousal for the good feelings of life can create an association between spirituality and high arousal. In other words, one doesn't feel "spiritual" unless one is also being stimulated by adrenalin arousal.

Many expressions of spirituality have become linked to adrenalin arousal, and this can be very harmful. A great many of the true saints of God have found their peak spiritual experiences in quietness and solitude. But many modern "saints" look for it only in exciting challenges or emotional catharsis . . .

[Many] confuse adrenalin arousal with spiritual growth. If their bodies were stimulated, they felt they were growing spiritually. If they were not stimulated, they felt nothing was happening.

The saddest thing about this kind of confusion is that it actually works *against* spiritual growth. Why? Because when we confuse adrenalin arousal for spirituality we start to worship our own bodies instead of God! We think we are listening for God's voice when we are actually waiting for our adrenalin system to be aroused. Unless the body is "revved up" there is no hunger for God. Unless there is physical stimulation, there is no desire for righteousness.

We need to learn again the truth of 1 Peter 3:3–4, which was meant for wives in the original context but is helpful for all of us to remember as a prescription for stress-free living: "Your beauty . . . should be that of your inner self, the unfading beauty of a gentle and quiet spirit, which is of great worth in God's sight."

Additional Scripture Readings:
Ephesians 3:14–19; 1 Peter 3:3–4

Go to page 91 for your next devotional reading.

flocks and herds may graze in front of the mountain."

4So Moses chiseled out two stone tablets like the first ones and went up Mount Sinai early in the morning, as the LORD had commanded him; and he carried the two stone tablets in his hands. **5**Then the LORD came down in the cloud and stood there with him and proclaimed his name, the LORD. **6**And he passed in front of Moses, proclaiming, "The LORD, the LORD, the compassionate and gracious God, slow to anger, abounding in love and faithfulness, **7**maintaining love to thousands, and forgiving wickedness, rebellion and sin. Yet he does not leave the guilty unpunished; he punishes the children and their children for the sin of the fathers to the third and fourth generation."

8Moses bowed to the ground at once and worshiped. **9**"O Lord, if I have found favor in your eyes," he said, "then let the Lord go with us. Although this is a stiff-necked people, forgive our wickedness and our sin, and take us as your inheritance."

10Then the LORD said: "I am making a covenant with you. Before all your people I will do wonders never before done in any nation in all the world. The people you live among will see how awesome is the work that I, the LORD, will do for you. **11**Obey what I command you today. I will drive out before you the Amorites, Canaanites, Hittites, Perizzites, Hivites and Jebusites. **12**Be careful not to make a treaty with those who live in the land where you are going, or they will be a snare among you. **13**Break down their altars, smash their sacred stones and cut down their Asherah poles.*a* **14**Do not worship any other god, for the LORD, whose name is Jealous, is a jealous God.

15"Be careful not to make a treaty with those who live in the land; for when they prostitute themselves to their gods and sacrifice to them, they will invite you and you will eat their sacrifices. **16**And when you choose some of their daughters as wives for your sons and those daughters prostitute themselves to their gods, they will lead your sons to do the same.

17"Do not make cast idols.

18"Celebrate the Feast of Unleavened Bread. For seven days eat bread made without yeast, as I commanded you. Do this at the appointed time in the month of Abib, for in that month you came out of Egypt.

19"The first offspring of every womb belongs to me, including all the firstborn males of your livestock, whether from herd or flock. **20**Redeem the firstborn donkey with a lamb, but if you do not redeem it, break its neck. Redeem all your firstborn sons.

"No one is to appear before me empty-handed.

21"Six days you shall labor, but on the seventh day you shall rest; even during the plowing season and harvest you must rest.

22"Celebrate the Feast of Weeks with the firstfruits of the wheat harvest, and the Feast of Ingathering at the turn of the year.*b* **23**Three times a year all your men are to appear before the Sovereign LORD, the God of Israel. **24**I will drive out nations before you and enlarge your territory, and no one will covet your land when you go up three times each year to appear before the LORD your God.

25"Do not offer the blood of a sacrifice to me along with anything containing yeast, and do not let any of the sacrifice from the Passover Feast remain until morning.

26"Bring the best of the firstfruits of your soil to the house of the LORD your God.

"Do not cook a young goat in its mother's milk."

27Then the LORD said to Moses, "Write down these words, for in accordance with these words I have made a covenant with you and with Israel." **28**Moses was there with the LORD forty days and forty nights without eating bread or drinking water. And he wrote on the tablets the words of the covenant — the Ten Commandments.

The Radiant Face of Moses

29When Moses came down from Mount Sinai with the two tablets of the Testimony in his hands, he was not aware that his face was radiant because he had spoken with the LORD. **30**When Aaron and all the Israelites saw Moses, his face was radiant, and they were afraid to come near him. **31**But Moses called to them; so Aaron and all the leaders of the community came back to him, and he spoke to them. **32**Afterward all the Israelites came near him, and he gave them all the commands the LORD had given him on Mount Sinai.

---

a13 That is, symbols of the goddess Asherah　　*b22* That is, in the fall

WEEKENDING

REALIZE

The most portentous fact about any person is
not what he at a given time may say or do, but
what he in his deep heart conceives God to be
like . . . A right conception of God is basic to
practical Christian living. There is scarcely an
error in doctrine or a failure in applying
Christian ethics that cannot be traced finally to
imperfect and ignoble thoughts about God.
— *A.W. Tozer*

RECEIVE

It was Jesus himself who reminded us that we
were to call him Father—"Abba Father"—which
is a lot more like calling him Dad. I think Jesus
was telling us that our Father is the one in the
stands who is standing on the seat, waving his
coat in a circle over his head, with tears of
pride and happiness running down his face.
— *Bob Benson*

REVIVE

Saturday: Exodus 15:11–18
Sunday: Isaiah 40:18–31

Go to page 92 for your next devotional reading.

33When Moses finished speaking to them, he put a veil over his face. **34**But whenever he entered the LORD's presence to speak with him, he removed the veil until he came out. And when he came out and told the Israelites what he had been commanded, **35**they saw that his face was radiant. Then Moses would put the veil back over his face until he went in to speak with the LORD.

Sabbath Regulations

35 Moses assembled the whole Israelite community and said to them, "These are the things the LORD has commanded you to do: **2**For six days, work is to be done, but the seventh day shall be your holy day, a Sabbath of rest to the LORD. Whoever does any work on it must be put to death. **3**Do not light a fire in any of your dwellings on the Sabbath day."

Materials for the Tabernacle

4Moses said to the whole Israelite community, "This is what the LORD has commanded: **5**From what you have, take an offering for the LORD. Everyone who is willing is to bring to the LORD an offering of gold, silver and bronze; **6**blue, purple and scarlet yarn and fine linen; goat hair; **7**ram skins dyed red and hides of sea cows*a*; acacia wood; **8**olive oil for the light; spices for the anointing oil and for the fragrant incense; **9**and onyx stones and other gems to be mounted on the ephod and breastpiece.

10"All who are skilled among you are to come and make everything the LORD has

*a*7 That is, dugongs; also in verse 23

MONDAY

VERSE FOR THE DAY:
Exodus 34:29

AUTHOR:
Tim Stafford

PASSAGE FOR THE DAY:
Exodus 34:29–35

Caught Up Again in Love

I KNOW not all marriages are like ours. Tonight, at a [restaurant] table near ours, [my wife] Popie pointed out a quiet battle in progress, tears and all. But our hardness, when it comes, is more often like the hardness of winter, when the sun comes up late and goes down early and you settle into a numbed, close-the-door-it's-freezing-out-there routine. It's not horrible by any means. But compared to our summery times, it's not terribly happy either.

That's why we need, much more often than we take it, a night like tonight. Dinner and a movie. Such a simple thing, yet it reminds us of who we are and why we are married. I think of something Popie says about God: how you can worry that your relationship with him has gone cold, that you've lost your spiritual edge. You can think it will take a lot of time, a month or so of spiritual discipline, to get going again with him.

Then you sit down and discover, in just minutes, that you don't have to do a thing—except take some time. Be alone with him. In what feels like no time you are caught up again in your love.

Additional Scripture Readings:
Psalm 62; Matthew 11:28–30

Go to page 115 for your next devotional reading.

commanded: [11]the tabernacle with its tent and its covering, clasps, frames, crossbars, posts and bases; [12]the ark with its poles and the atonement cover and the curtain that shields it; [13]the table with its poles and all its articles and the bread of the Presence; [14]the lampstand that is for light with its accessories, lamps and oil for the light; [15]the altar of incense with its poles, the anointing oil and the fragrant incense; the curtain for the doorway at the entrance to the tabernacle; [16]the altar of burnt offering with its bronze grating, its poles and all its utensils; the bronze basin with its stand; [17]the curtains of the courtyard with its posts and bases, and the curtain for the entrance to the courtyard; [18]the tent pegs for the tabernacle and for the courtyard, and their ropes; [19]the woven garments worn for ministering in the sanctuary—both the sacred garments for Aaron the priest and the garments for his sons when they serve as priests."

[20]Then the whole Israelite community withdrew from Moses' presence, [21]and everyone who was willing and whose heart moved him came and brought an offering to the LORD for the work on the Tent of Meeting, for all its service, and for the sacred garments. [22]All who were willing, men and women alike, came and brought gold jewelry of all kinds: brooches, earrings, rings and ornaments. They all presented their gold as a wave offering to the LORD. [23]Everyone who had blue, purple or scarlet yarn or fine linen, or goat hair, ram skins dyed red or hides of sea cows brought them. [24]Those presenting an offering of silver or bronze brought it as an offering to the LORD, and everyone who had acacia wood for any part of the work brought it. [25]Every skilled woman spun with her hands and brought what she had spun—blue, purple or scarlet yarn or fine linen. [26]And all the women who were willing and had the skill spun the goat hair. [27]The leaders brought onyx stones and other gems to be mounted on the ephod and breastpiece. [28]They also brought spices and olive oil for the light and for the anointing oil and for the fragrant incense. [29]All the Israelite men and women who were willing brought to the LORD freewill offerings for all the work the LORD through Moses had commanded them to do.

Bezalel and Oholiab

[30]Then Moses said to the Israelites,

"See, the LORD has chosen Bezalel son of Uri, the son of Hur, of the tribe of Judah, [31]and he has filled him with the Spirit of God, with skill, ability and knowledge in all kinds of crafts— [32]to make artistic designs for work in gold, silver and bronze, [33]to cut and set stones, to work in wood and to engage in all kinds of artistic craftsmanship. [34]And he has given both him and Oholiab son of Ahisamach, of the tribe of Dan, the ability to teach others. [35]He has filled them with skill to do all kinds of work as craftsmen, designers, embroiderers in blue, purple and scarlet yarn and fine linen, and weavers—all of them master craftsmen and designers.

36 [1]So Bezalel, Oholiab and every skilled person to whom the LORD has given skill and ability to know how to carry out all the work of constructing the sanctuary are to do the work just as the Lord has commanded."

[2]Then Moses summoned Bezalel and Oholiab and every skilled person to whom the LORD had given ability and who was willing to come and do the work. [3]They received from Moses all the offerings the Israelites had brought to carry out the work of constructing the sanctuary. And the people continued to bring freewill offerings morning after morning. [4]So all the skilled craftsmen who were doing all the work on the sanctuary left their work [5]and said to Moses, "The people are bringing more than enough for doing the work the LORD commanded to be done."

[6]Then Moses gave an order and they sent this word throughout the camp: "No man or woman is to make anything else as an offering for the sanctuary." And so the people were restrained from bringing more, [7]because what they already had was more than enough to do all the work.

The Tabernacle

[8]All the skilled men among the workmen made the tabernacle with ten curtains of finely twisted linen and blue, purple and scarlet yarn, with cherubim worked into them by a skilled craftsman. [9]All the curtains were the same size—twenty-eight cubits long and four cubits wide.[a] [10]They joined five of the curtains together and did the same with the other five. [11]Then they made loops of blue material along the edge of the end curtain in one set, and the same was done with the end curtain in the other set. [12]They also

---

[a]9 That is, about 42 feet (about 12.5 meters) long and 6 feet (about 1.8 meters) wide

made fifty loops on one curtain and fifty loops on the end curtain of the other set, with the loops opposite each other. [13]Then they made fifty gold clasps and used them to fasten the two sets of curtains together so that the tabernacle was a unit.

[14]They made curtains of goat hair for the tent over the tabernacle—eleven altogether. [15]All eleven curtains were the same size—thirty cubits long and four cubits wide.[a] [16]They joined five of the curtains into one set and the other six into another set. [17]Then they made fifty loops along the edge of the end curtain in one set and also along the edge of the end curtain in the other set. [18]They made fifty bronze clasps to fasten the tent together as a unit. [19]Then they made for the tent a covering of ram skins dyed red, and over that a covering of hides of sea cows.[b]

[20]They made upright frames of acacia wood for the tabernacle. [21]Each frame was ten cubits long and a cubit and a half wide,[c] [22]with two projections set parallel to each other. They made all the frames of the tabernacle in this way. [23]They made twenty frames for the south side of the tabernacle [24]and made forty silver bases to go under them—two bases for each frame, one under each projection. [25]For the other side, the north side of the tabernacle, they made twenty frames [26]and forty silver bases—two under each frame. [27]They made six frames for the far end, that is, the west end of the tabernacle, [28]and two frames were made for the corners of the tabernacle at the far end. [29]At these two corners the frames were double from the bottom all the way to the top and fitted into a single ring; both were made alike. [30]So there were eight frames and sixteen silver bases—two under each frame.

[31]They also made crossbars of acacia wood: five for the frames on one side of the tabernacle, [32]five for those on the other side, and five for the frames on the west, at the far end of the tabernacle. [33]They made the center crossbar so that it extended from end to end at the middle of the frames. [34]They overlaid the frames with gold and made gold rings to hold the crossbars. They also overlaid the crossbars with gold.

[35]They made the curtain of blue, purple and scarlet yarn and finely twisted linen, with cherubim worked into it by a skilled craftsman. [36]They made four posts of acacia wood for it and overlaid them with gold. They made gold hooks for them and cast their four silver bases. [37]For the entrance to the tent they made a curtain of blue, purple and scarlet yarn and finely twisted linen—the work of an embroiderer; [38]and they made five posts with hooks for them. They overlaid the tops of the posts and their bands with gold and made their five bases of bronze.

The Ark

37 Bezalel made the ark of acacia wood—two and a half cubits long, a cubit and a half wide, and a cubit and a half high.[d] [2]He overlaid it with pure gold, both inside and out, and made a gold molding around it. [3]He cast four gold rings for it and fastened them to its four feet, with two rings on one side and two rings on the other. [4]Then he made poles of acacia wood and overlaid them with gold. [5]And he inserted the poles into the rings on the sides of the ark to carry it.

[6]He made the atonement cover of pure gold—two and a half cubits long and a cubit and a half wide.[e] [7]Then he made two cherubim out of hammered gold at the ends of the cover. [8]He made one cherub on one end and the second cherub on the other; at the two ends he made them of one piece with the cover. [9]The cherubim had their wings spread upward, overshadowing the cover with them. The cherubim faced each other, looking toward the cover.

The Table

[10]They[f] made the table of acacia wood—two cubits long, a cubit wide, and a cubit and a half high.[g] [11]Then they overlaid it with pure gold and made a gold molding around it. [12]They also made around it a rim a handbreadth[h] wide and put a gold molding on the rim. [13]They cast four gold rings for the table and fastened them to the four corners, where the four

---

[a]15 That is, about 45 feet (about 13.5 meters) long and 6 feet (about 1.8 meters) wide   [b]19 That is, dugongs   [c]21 That is, about 15 feet (about 4.5 meters) long and 2 1/4 feet (about 0.7 meter) wide   [d]1 That is, about 3 3/4 feet (about 1.1 meters) long and 2 1/4 feet (about 0.7 meter) wide and high   [e]6 That is, about 3 3/4 feet (about 1.1 meters) long and 2 1/4 feet (about 0.7 meter) wide   [f]10 Or He; also in verses 11-29   [g]10 That is, about 3 feet (about 0.9 meter) long, 1 1/2 feet (about 0.5 meter) wide, and 2 1/4 feet (about 0.7 meter) high   [h]12 That is, about 3 inches (about 8 centimeters)

legs were. ¹⁴The rings were put close to the rim to hold the poles used in carrying the table. ¹⁵The poles for carrying the table were made of acacia wood and were overlaid with gold. ¹⁶And they made from pure gold the articles for the table—its plates and dishes and bowls and its pitchers for the pouring out of drink offerings.

The Lampstand

¹⁷They made the lampstand of pure gold and hammered it out, base and shaft; its flowerlike cups, buds and blossoms were of one piece with it. ¹⁸Six branches extended from the sides of the lampstand—three on one side and three on the other. ¹⁹Three cups shaped like almond flowers with buds and blossoms were on one branch, three on the next branch and the same for all six branches extending from the lampstand. ²⁰And on the lampstand were four cups shaped like almond flowers with buds and blossoms. ²¹One bud was under the first pair of branches extending from the lampstand, a second bud under the second pair, and a third bud under the third pair—six branches in all. ²²The buds and the branches were all of one piece with the lampstand, hammered out of pure gold.

²³They made its seven lamps, as well as its wick trimmers and trays, of pure gold. ²⁴They made the lampstand and all its accessories from one talent[a] of pure gold.

The Altar of Incense

²⁵They made the altar of incense out of acacia wood. It was square, a cubit long and a cubit wide, and two cubits high[b]—its horns of one piece with it. ²⁶They overlaid the top and all the sides and the horns with pure gold, and made a gold molding around it. ²⁷They made two gold rings below the molding—two on opposite sides—to hold the poles used to carry it. ²⁸They made the poles of acacia wood and overlaid them with gold.

²⁹They also made the sacred anointing oil and the pure, fragrant incense—the work of a perfumer.

The Altar of Burnt Offering

38 They[c] built the altar of burnt offering of acacia wood, three cubits[d] high; it was square, five cubits long and five cubits wide.[e] ²They made a horn at each of the four corners, so that the horns and the altar were of one piece, and they overlaid the altar with bronze. ³They made all its utensils of bronze—its pots, shovels, sprinkling bowls, meat forks and firepans. ⁴They made a grating for the altar, a bronze network, to be under its ledge, halfway up the altar. ⁵They cast bronze rings to hold the poles for the four corners of the bronze grating. ⁶They made the poles of acacia wood and overlaid them with bronze. ⁷They inserted the poles into the rings so they would be on the sides of the altar for carrying it. They made it hollow, out of boards.

Basin for Washing

⁸They made the bronze basin and its bronze stand from the mirrors of the women who served at the entrance to the Tent of Meeting.

The Courtyard

⁹Next they made the courtyard. The south side was a hundred cubits[f] long and had curtains of finely twisted linen, ¹⁰with twenty posts and twenty bronze bases, and with silver hooks and bands on the posts. ¹¹The north side was also a hundred cubits long and had twenty posts and twenty bronze bases, with silver hooks and bands on the posts.

¹²The west end was fifty cubits[g] wide and had curtains, with ten posts and ten bases, with silver hooks and bands on the posts. ¹³The east end, toward the sunrise, was also fifty cubits wide. ¹⁴Curtains fifteen cubits[h] long were on one side of the entrance, with three posts and three bases, ¹⁵and curtains fifteen cubits long were on the other side of the entrance to the courtyard, with three posts and three bases. ¹⁶All the curtains around the courtyard were of finely twisted linen. ¹⁷The bases for the posts were bronze. The hooks and bands on the posts were silver, and their tops were overlaid with silver; so all the posts of the courtyard had silver bands.

¹⁸The curtain for the entrance to the courtyard was of blue, purple and scarlet

a24 That is, about 75 pounds (about 34 kilograms) long and wide, and about 3 feet (about 0.9 meter) high   b25 That is, about 1 1/2 feet (about 0.5 meter)   c1 Or He; also in verses 2-9   d1 That is, about 4 1/2 feet (about 1.3 meters)   e1 That is, about 7 1/2 feet (about 2.3 meters) long and wide   f9 That is, about 150 feet (about 46 meters)   g12 That is, about 75 feet (about 23 meters)   h14 That is, about 22 1/2 feet (about 6.9 meters) yarn and finely twisted linen — the work of an embroiderer. It was twenty cubits[a] long and, like the curtains of the courtyard, five cubits[b] high, **19**with four posts and four bronze bases. Their hooks and bands were silver, and their tops were overlaid with silver. **20**All the tent pegs of the tabernacle and of the surrounding courtyard were bronze.

The Materials Used

21These are the amounts of the materials used for the tabernacle, the tabernacle of the Testimony, which were recorded at Moses' command by the Levites under the direction of Ithamar son of Aaron, the priest. **22**(Bezalel son of Uri, the son of Hur, of the tribe of Judah, made everything the LORD commanded Moses; **23**with him was Oholiab son of Ahisamach, of the tribe of Dan — a craftsman and designer, and an embroiderer in blue, purple and scarlet yarn and fine linen.) **24**The total amount of the gold from the wave offering used for all the work on the sanctuary was 29 talents and 730 shekels,[c] according to the sanctuary shekel.

25The silver obtained from those of the community who were counted in the census was 100 talents and 1,775 shekels,[d] according to the sanctuary shekel — **26**one beka per person, that is, half a shekel,[e] according to the sanctuary shekel, from everyone who had crossed over to those counted, twenty years old or more, a total of 603,550 men. **27**The 100 talents[f] of silver were used to cast the bases for the sanctuary and for the curtain — 100 bases from the 100 talents, one talent for each base. **28**They used the 1,775 shekels[g] to make the hooks for the posts, to overlay the tops of the posts, and to make their bands.

29The bronze from the wave offering was 70 talents and 2,400 shekels.[h] **30**They used it to make the bases for the entrance to the Tent of Meeting, the bronze altar with its bronze grating and all its utensils, **31**the bases for the surrounding courtyard and those for its entrance and all the tent pegs for the tabernacle and those for the surrounding courtyard.

The Priestly Garments

39 From the blue, purple and scarlet yarn they made woven garments for ministering in the sanctuary. They also made sacred garments for Aaron, as the LORD commanded Moses.

The Ephod

2They[i] made the ephod of gold, and of blue, purple and scarlet yarn, and of finely twisted linen. **3**They hammered out thin sheets of gold and cut strands to be worked into the blue, purple and scarlet yarn and fine linen — the work of a skilled craftsman. **4**They made shoulder pieces for the ephod, which were attached to two of its corners, so it could be fastened. **5**Its skillfully woven waistband was like it — of one piece with the ephod and made with gold, and with blue, purple and scarlet yarn, and with finely twisted linen, as the LORD commanded Moses.

6They mounted the onyx stones in gold filigree settings and engraved them like a seal with the names of the sons of Israel. **7**Then they fastened them on the shoulder pieces of the ephod as memorial stones for the sons of Israel, as the LORD commanded Moses.

The Breastpiece

8They fashioned the breastpiece — the work of a skilled craftsman. They made it like the ephod: of gold, and of blue, purple and scarlet yarn, and of finely twisted linen. **9**It was square — a span[j] long and a span wide — and folded double. **10**Then they mounted four rows of precious stones on it. In the first row there was a ruby, a topaz and a beryl; **11**in the second row a turquoise, a sapphire[k] and an emerald; **12**in the third row a jacinth, an agate and an amethyst; **13**in the fourth row a chrysolite, an onyx and a jasper.[l] They were mounted in gold filigree settings. **14**There were twelve stones, one for each of the names of the sons of Israel, each engraved like a seal with the name of one of the twelve tribes.

15For the breastpiece they made braided chains of pure gold, like a rope. **16**They made two gold filigree settings and two

---

a18 That is, about 30 feet (about 9 meters)　　*b18* That is, about 7 1/2 feet (about 2.3 meters)　*c24* The weight of the gold was a little over one ton (about 1 metric ton).　　*d25* The weight of the silver was a little over 3 3/4 tons (about 3.4 metric tons).　　*e26* That is, about 1/5 ounce (about 5.5 grams)　*f27* That is, about 3 3/4 tons (about 3.4 metric tons) (about 20 kilograms)　　*h29* The weight of the bronze was about 2 1/2 tons (about 2.4 metric tons).　*i2* Or *He*; also in verses 7, 8 and 22　*j9* That is, about 9 inches (about 22 centimeters)　　*k11* Or *lapis lazuli*　*l13* The precise identification of some of these precious stones is uncertain.

gold rings, and fastened the rings to two of the corners of the breastpiece. ¹⁷They fastened the two gold chains to the rings at the corners of the breastpiece, ¹⁸and the other ends of the chains to the two settings, attaching them to the shoulder pieces of the ephod at the front. ¹⁹They made two gold rings and attached them to the other two corners of the breastpiece on the inside edge next to the ephod. ²⁰Then they made two more gold rings and attached them to the bottom of the shoulder pieces on the front of the ephod, close to the seam just above the waistband of the ephod. ²¹They tied the rings of the breastpiece to the rings of the ephod with blue cord, connecting it to the waistband so that the breastpiece would not swing out from the ephod—as the LORD commanded Moses.

Other Priestly Garments

²²They made the robe of the ephod entirely of blue cloth—the work of a weaver— ²³with an opening in the center of the robe like the opening of a collar,ᵃ and a band around this opening, so that it would not tear. ²⁴They made pomegranates of blue, purple and scarlet yarn and finely twisted linen around the hem of the robe. ²⁵And they made bells of pure gold and attached them around the hem between the pomegranates. ²⁶The bells and pomegranates alternated around the hem of the robe to be worn for ministering, as the LORD commanded Moses.

²⁷For Aaron and his sons, they made tunics of fine linen—the work of a weaver— ²⁸and the turban of fine linen, the linen headbands and the undergarments of finely twisted linen. ²⁹The sash was of finely twisted linen and blue, purple and scarlet yarn—the work of an embroiderer—as the LORD commanded Moses.

³⁰They made the plate, the sacred diadem, out of pure gold and engraved on it, like an inscription on a seal: HOLY TO THE LORD. ³¹Then they fastened a blue cord to it to attach it to the turban, as the LORD commanded Moses.

Moses Inspects the Tabernacle

³²So all the work on the tabernacle, the Tent of Meeting, was completed. The Israelites did everything just as the LORD commanded Moses. ³³Then they brought the tabernacle to Moses: the tent and all its furnishings, its clasps, frames, crossbars,

posts and bases; ³⁴the covering of ram skins dyed red, the covering of hides of sea cowsᵇ and the shielding curtain; ³⁵the ark of the Testimony with its poles and the atonement cover; ³⁶the table with all its articles and the bread of the Presence; ³⁷the pure gold lampstand with its row of lamps and all its accessories, and the oil for the light; ³⁸the gold altar, the anointing oil, the fragrant incense, and the curtain for the entrance to the tent; ³⁹the bronze altar with its bronze grating, its poles and all its utensils; the basin with its stand; ⁴⁰the curtains of the courtyard with its posts and bases, and the curtain for the entrance to the courtyard; the ropes and tent pegs for the courtyard; all the furnishings for the tabernacle, the Tent of Meeting; ⁴¹and the woven garments worn for ministering in the sanctuary, both the sacred garments for Aaron the priest and the garments for his sons when serving as priests.

⁴²The Israelites had done all the work just as the LORD had commanded Moses. ⁴³Moses inspected the work and saw that they had done it just as the LORD had commanded. So Moses blessed them.

Setting Up the Tabernacle

40 Then the LORD said to Moses: ²"Set up the tabernacle, the Tent of Meeting, on the first day of the first month. ³Place the ark of the Testimony in it and shield the ark with the curtain. ⁴Bring in the table and set out what belongs on it. Then bring in the lampstand and set up its lamps. ⁵Place the gold altar of incense in front of the ark of the Testimony and put the curtain at the entrance to the tabernacle.

⁶"Place the altar of burnt offering in front of the entrance to the tabernacle, the Tent of Meeting; ⁷place the basin between the Tent of Meeting and the altar and put water in it. ⁸Set up the courtyard around it and put the curtain at the entrance to the courtyard.

⁹"Take the anointing oil and anoint the tabernacle and everything in it; consecrate it and all its furnishings, and it will be holy. ¹⁰Then anoint the altar of burnt offering and all its utensils; consecrate the altar, and it will be most holy. ¹¹Anoint the basin and its stand and consecrate them.

¹²"Bring Aaron and his sons to the entrance to the Tent of Meeting and wash

them with water. ¹³Then dress Aaron in the sacred garments, anoint him and consecrate him so he may serve me as priest. ¹⁴Bring his sons and dress them in tunics. ¹⁵Anoint them just as you anointed their father, so they may serve me as priests. Their anointing will be to a priesthood that will continue for all generations to come." ¹⁶Moses did everything just as the LORD commanded him.

¹⁷So the tabernacle was set up on the first day of the first month in the second year. ¹⁸When Moses set up the tabernacle, he put the bases in place, erected the frames, inserted the crossbars and set up the posts. ¹⁹Then he spread the tent over the tabernacle and put the covering over the tent, as the LORD commanded him.

²⁰He took the Testimony and placed it in the ark, attached the poles to the ark and put the atonement cover over it. ²¹Then he brought the ark into the tabernacle and hung the shielding curtain and shielded the ark of the Testimony, as the LORD commanded him.

²²Moses placed the table in the Tent of Meeting on the north side of the tabernacle outside the curtain ²³and set out the bread on it before the LORD, as the LORD commanded him.

²⁴He placed the lampstand in the Tent of Meeting opposite the table on the south side of the tabernacle ²⁵and set up the lamps before the LORD, as the LORD commanded him.

²⁶Moses placed the gold altar in the Tent of Meeting in front of the curtain ²⁷and burned fragrant incense on it, as the LORD commanded him. ²⁸Then he put up the curtain at the entrance to the tabernacle.

²⁹He set the altar of burnt offering near the entrance to the tabernacle, the Tent of Meeting, and offered on it burnt offerings and grain offerings, as the LORD commanded him.

³⁰He placed the basin between the Tent of Meeting and the altar and put water in it for washing, ³¹and Moses and Aaron and his sons used it to wash their hands and feet. ³²They washed whenever they entered the Tent of Meeting or approached the altar, as the LORD commanded Moses.

³³Then Moses set up the courtyard around the tabernacle and altar and put up the curtain at the entrance to the courtyard. And so Moses finished the work.

The Glory of the LORD

³⁴Then the cloud covered the Tent of Meeting, and the glory of the LORD filled the tabernacle. ³⁵Moses could not enter the Tent of Meeting because the cloud had settled upon it, and the glory of the LORD filled the tabernacle.

³⁶In all the travels of the Israelites, whenever the cloud lifted from above the tabernacle, they would set out; ³⁷but if the cloud did not lift, they did not set out — until the day it lifted. ³⁸So the cloud of the LORD was over the tabernacle by day, and fire was in the cloud by night, in the sight of all the house of Israel during all their travels.

*M*OSES writes this book while the Israelites are in the wilderness, before they enter the promised land. In it he reports to them the numerous religious, civil and moral laws that God revealed to him on Mount Sinai. As you read this book, some of it may seem dull and boring. But think about how holy God is, how he wants you to serve him in every part of your life and in all you do.

LEVITICUS

The Burnt Offering

1 The LORD called to Moses and spoke to him from the Tent of Meeting. He said, 2"Speak to the Israelites and say to them: 'When any of you brings an offering to the LORD, bring as your offering an animal from either the herd or the flock.

3 " 'If the offering is a burnt offering from the herd, he is to offer a male without defect. He must present it at the entrance to the Tent of Meeting so that it*a* will be acceptable to the LORD. 4He is to lay his hand on the head of the burnt offering, and it will be accepted on his behalf to make atonement for him. 5He is to slaughter the young bull before the LORD, and then Aaron's sons the priests shall bring the blood and sprinkle it against the altar on all sides at the entrance to the Tent of Meeting. 6He is to skin the burnt offering and cut it into pieces. 7The sons of Aaron the priest are to put fire on the altar and arrange wood on the fire. 8Then Aaron's sons the priests shall arrange the pieces, including the head and the fat, on the burning wood that is on the altar. 9He is to wash the inner parts and the legs with water, and the priest is to burn all of it on the altar. It is a burnt offering, an offering made by fire, an aroma pleasing to the LORD.

10 " 'If the offering is a burnt offering from the flock, from either the sheep or the goats, he is to offer a male without defect. 11He is to slaughter it at the north

*a*3 Or *he*

side of the altar before the LORD, and Aaron's sons the priests shall sprinkle its blood against the altar on all sides. ¹²He is to cut it into pieces, and the priest shall arrange them, including the head and the fat, on the burning wood that is on the altar. ¹³He is to wash the inner parts and the legs with water, and the priest is to bring all of it and burn it on the altar. It is a burnt offering, an offering made by fire, an aroma pleasing to the LORD.

¹⁴" 'If the offering to the LORD is a burnt offering of birds, he is to offer a dove or a young pigeon. ¹⁵The priest shall bring it to the altar, wring off the head and burn it on the altar; its blood shall be drained out on the side of the altar. ¹⁶He is to remove the crop with its contents[a] and throw it to the east side of the altar, where the ashes are. ¹⁷He shall tear it open by the wings, not severing it completely, and then the priest shall burn it on the wood that is on the fire on the altar. It is a burnt offering, an offering made by fire, an aroma pleasing to the LORD.

The Grain Offering

2 " 'When someone brings a grain offering to the LORD, his offering is to be of fine flour. He is to pour oil on it, put incense on it ²and take it to Aaron's sons the priests. The priest shall take a handful of the fine flour and oil, together with all the incense, and burn this as a memorial portion on the altar, an offering made by fire, an aroma pleasing to the LORD. ³The rest of the grain offering belongs to Aaron and his sons; it is a most holy part of the offerings made to the LORD by fire.

⁴" 'If you bring a grain offering baked in an oven, it is to consist of fine flour: cakes made without yeast and mixed with oil, or[b] wafers made without yeast and spread with oil. ⁵If your grain offering is prepared on a griddle, it is to be made of fine flour mixed with oil, and without yeast. ⁶Crumble it and pour oil on it; it is a grain offering. ⁷If your grain offering is cooked in a pan, it is to be made of fine flour and oil. ⁸Bring the grain offering made of these things to the LORD; present it to the priest, who shall take it to the altar. ⁹He shall take out the memorial portion from the grain offering and burn it on the altar as an offering made by fire, an aroma pleasing to the LORD. ¹⁰The rest of the grain offering belongs to Aaron and

his sons; it is a most holy part of the offerings made to the LORD by fire.

¹¹" 'Every grain offering you bring to the LORD must be made without yeast, for you are not to burn any yeast or honey in an offering made to the LORD by fire. ¹²You may bring them to the LORD as an offering of the firstfruits, but they are not to be offered on the altar as a pleasing aroma. ¹³Season all your grain offerings with salt. Do not leave the salt of the covenant of your God out of your grain offerings; add salt to all your offerings.

¹⁴" 'If you bring a grain offering of firstfruits to the LORD, offer crushed heads of new grain roasted in the fire. ¹⁵Put oil and incense on it; it is a grain offering. ¹⁶The priest shall burn the memorial portion of the crushed grain and the oil, together with all the incense, as an offering made to the LORD by fire.

The Fellowship Offering

3 " 'If someone's offering is a fellowship offering,[c] and he offers an animal from the herd, whether male or female, he is to present before the LORD an animal without defect. ²He is to lay his hand on the head of his offering and slaughter it at the entrance to the Tent of Meeting. Then Aaron's sons the priests shall sprinkle the blood against the altar on all sides. ³From the fellowship offering he is to bring a sacrifice made to the LORD by fire: all the fat that covers the inner parts or is connected to them, ⁴both kidneys with the fat on them near the loins, and the covering of the liver, which he will remove with the kidneys. ⁵Then Aaron's sons are to burn it on the altar on top of the burnt offering that is on the burning wood, as an offering made by fire, an aroma pleasing to the LORD.

⁶" 'If he offers an animal from the flock as a fellowship offering to the LORD, he is to offer a male or female without defect. ⁷If he offers a lamb, he is to present it before the LORD. ⁸He is to lay his hand on the head of his offering and slaughter it in front of the Tent of Meeting. Then Aaron's sons shall sprinkle its blood against the altar on all sides. ⁹From the fellowship offering he is to bring a sacrifice made to the LORD by fire: its fat, the entire fat tail cut off close to the backbone, all the fat that covers the inner parts or is connected to them, ¹⁰both kidneys with the fat on them

---

[a]16 Or crop and the feathers; the meaning of the Hebrew for this word is uncertain.   [b]4 Or and
[c]1 Traditionally peace offering; also in verses 3, 6 and 9

near the loins, and the covering of the liver, which he will remove with the kidneys. [11]The priest shall burn them on the altar as food, an offering made to the LORD by fire.

[12]" 'If his offering is a goat, he is to present it before the LORD. [13]He is to lay his hand on its head and slaughter it in front of the Tent of Meeting. Then Aaron's sons shall sprinkle its blood against the altar on all sides. [14]From what he offers he is to make this offering to the LORD by fire: all the fat that covers the inner parts or is connected to them, [15]both kidneys with the fat on them near the loins, and the covering of the liver, which he will remove with the kidneys. [16]The priest shall burn them on the altar as food, an offering made by fire, a pleasing aroma. All the fat is the LORD's.

[17]" 'This is a lasting ordinance for the generations to come, wherever you live: You must not eat any fat or any blood.' "

The Sin Offering

4 The LORD said to Moses, [2]"Say to the Israelites: 'When anyone sins unintentionally and does what is forbidden in any of the LORD's commands—

[3]" 'If the anointed priest sins, bringing guilt on the people, he must bring to the LORD a young bull without defect as a sin offering for the sin he has committed. [4]He is to present the bull at the entrance to the Tent of Meeting before the LORD. He is to lay his hand on its head and slaughter it before the LORD. [5]Then the anointed priest shall take some of the bull's blood and carry it into the Tent of Meeting. [6]He is to dip his finger into the blood and sprinkle some of it seven times before the LORD, in front of the curtain of the sanctuary. [7]The priest shall then put some of the blood on the horns of the altar of fragrant incense that is before the LORD in the Tent of Meeting. The rest of the bull's blood he shall pour out at the base of the altar of burnt offering at the entrance to the Tent of Meeting. [8]He shall remove all the fat from the bull of the sin offering—the fat that covers the inner parts or is connected to them, [9]both kidneys with the fat on them near the loins, and the covering of the liver, which he will remove with the kidneys— [10]just as the fat is removed from the ox[a] sacrificed as a fellowship offer-

ing.[b] Then the priest shall burn them on the altar of burnt offering. [11]But the hide of the bull and all its flesh, as well as the head and legs, the inner parts and offal— [12]that is, all the rest of the bull—he must take outside the camp to a place ceremonially clean, where the ashes are thrown, and burn it in a wood fire on the ash heap.

[13]" 'If the whole Israelite community sins unintentionally and does what is forbidden in any of the LORD's commands, even though the community is unaware of the matter, they are guilty. [14]When they become aware of the sin they committed, the assembly must bring a young bull as a sin offering and present it before the Tent of Meeting. [15]The elders of the community are to lay their hands on the bull's head before the LORD, and the bull shall be slaughtered before the LORD. [16]Then the anointed priest is to take some of the bull's blood into the Tent of Meeting. [17]He shall dip his finger into the blood and sprinkle it before the LORD seven times in front of the curtain. [18]He is to put some of the blood on the horns of the altar that is before the LORD in the Tent of Meeting. The rest of the blood he shall pour out at the base of the altar of burnt offering at the entrance to the Tent of Meeting. [19]He shall remove all the fat from it and burn it on the altar, [20]and do with this bull just as he did with the bull for the sin offering. In this way the priest will make atonement for them, and they will be forgiven. [21]Then he shall take the bull outside the camp and burn it as he burned the first bull. This is the sin offering for the community.

[22]" 'When a leader sins unintentionally and does what is forbidden in any of the commands of the LORD his God, he is guilty. [23]When he is made aware of the sin he committed, he must bring as his offering a male goat without defect. [24]He is to lay his hand on the goat's head and slaughter it at the place where the burnt offering is slaughtered before the LORD. It is a sin offering. [25]Then the priest shall take some of the blood of the sin offering with his finger and put it on the horns of the altar of burnt offering and pour out the rest of the blood at the base of the altar. [26]He shall burn all the fat on the altar as he burned the fat of the fellowship offer-

---

[a]10 The Hebrew word can include both male and female. [b]10 Traditionally *peace offering*; also in verses 26, 31 and 35

ing. In this way the priest will make atonement for the man's sin, and he will be forgiven.

27" 'If a member of the community sins unintentionally and does what is forbidden in any of the LORD's commands, he is guilty. **28**When he is made aware of the sin he committed, he must bring as his offering for the sin he committed a female goat without defect. **29**He is to lay his hand on the head of the sin offering and slaughter it at the place of the burnt offering. **30**Then the priest is to take some of the blood with his finger and put it on the horns of the altar of burnt offering and pour out the rest of the blood at the base of the altar. **31**He shall remove all the fat, just as the fat is removed from the fellowship offering, and the priest shall burn it on the altar as an aroma pleasing to the LORD. In this way the priest will make atonement for him, and he will be forgiven.

32" 'If he brings a lamb as his sin offering, he is to bring a female without defect. **33**He is to lay his hand on its head and slaughter it for a sin offering at the place where the burnt offering is slaughtered. **34**Then the priest shall take some of the blood of the sin offering with his finger and put it on the horns of the altar of burnt offering and pour out the rest of the blood at the base of the altar. **35**He shall remove all the fat, just as the fat is removed from the lamb of the fellowship offering, and the priest shall burn it on the altar on top of the offerings made to the LORD by fire. In this way the priest will make atonement for him for the sin he has committed, and he will be forgiven.

5 " 'If a person sins because he does not speak up when he hears a public charge to testify regarding something he has seen or learned about, he will be held responsible.

2" 'Or if a person touches anything ceremonially unclean—whether the carcasses of unclean wild animals or of unclean livestock or of unclean creatures that move along the ground—even though he is unaware of it, he has become unclean and is guilty.

3" 'Or if he touches human uncleanness—anything that would make him unclean—even though he is unaware of it, when he learns of it he will be guilty.

4" 'Or if a person thoughtlessly takes an oath to do anything, whether good or evil—in any matter one might carelessly swear about—even though he is unaware of it, in any case when he learns of it he will be guilty.

5" 'When anyone is guilty in any of these ways, he must confess in what way he has sinned **6**and, as a penalty for the sin he has committed, he must bring to the LORD a female lamb or goat from the flock as a sin offering; and the priest shall make atonement for him for his sin.

7" 'If he cannot afford a lamb, he is to bring two doves or two young pigeons to the LORD as a penalty for his sin—one for a sin offering and the other for a burnt offering. **8**He is to bring them to the priest, who shall first offer the one for the sin offering. He is to wring its head from its neck, not severing it completely, **9**and is to sprinkle some of the blood of the sin offering against the side of the altar; the rest of the blood must be drained out at the base of the altar. It is a sin offering. **10**The priest shall then offer the other as a burnt offering in the prescribed way and make atonement for him for the sin he has committed, and he will be forgiven.

11" 'If, however, he cannot afford two doves or two young pigeons, he is to bring as an offering for his sin a tenth of an ephah *a* of fine flour for a sin offering. He must not put oil or incense on it, because it is a sin offering. **12**He is to bring it to the priest, who shall take a handful of it as a memorial portion and burn it on the altar on top of the offerings made to the LORD by fire. It is a sin offering. **13**In this way the priest will make atonement for him for any of these sins he has committed, and he will be forgiven. The rest of the offering will belong to the priest, as in the case of the grain offering.' "

The Guilt Offering

14The LORD said to Moses: **15**"When a person commits a violation and sins unintentionally in regard to any of the LORD's holy things, he is to bring to the LORD as a penalty a ram from the flock, one without defect and of the proper value in silver, according to the sanctuary shekel. *b* It is a guilt offering. **16**He must make restitution for what he has failed to do in regard to the holy things, add a fifth of the value to that and give it all to the priest, who will make atonement for him with the ram as a guilt offering, and he will be forgiven. **17**"If a person sins and does what is for-

---

a11 That is, probably about 2 quarts (about 2 liters)   *b15* That is, about 2/5 ounce (about 11.5 grams) bidden in any of the Lord's commands, even though he does not know it, he is guilty and will be held responsible. [18]He is to bring to the priest as a guilt offering a ram from the flock, one without defect and of the proper value. In this way the priest will make atonement for him for the wrong he has committed unintentionally, and he will be forgiven. [19]It is a guilt offering; he has been guilty of[a] wrongdoing against the Lord."

6 The Lord said to Moses: [2]"If anyone sins and is unfaithful to the Lord by deceiving his neighbor about something entrusted to him or left in his care or stolen, or if he cheats him, [3]or if he finds lost property and lies about it, or if he swears falsely, or if he commits any such sin that people may do— [4]when he thus sins and becomes guilty, he must return what he has stolen or taken by extortion, or what was entrusted to him, or the lost property he found, [5]or whatever it was he swore falsely about. He must make restitution in full, add a fifth of the value to it and give it all to the owner on the day he presents his guilt offering. [6]And as a penalty he must bring to the priest, that is, to the Lord, his guilt offering, a ram from the flock, one without defect and of the proper value. [7]In this way the priest will make atonement for him before the Lord, and he will be forgiven for any of these things he did that made him guilty."

The Burnt Offering

[8]The Lord said to Moses: [9]"Give Aaron and his sons this command: 'These are the regulations for the burnt offering: The burnt offering is to remain on the altar hearth throughout the night, till morning, and the fire must be kept burning on the altar. [10]The priest shall then put on his linen clothes, with linen undergarments next to his body, and shall remove the ashes of the burnt offering that the fire has consumed on the altar and place them beside the altar. [11]Then he is to take off these clothes and put on others, and carry the ashes outside the camp to a place that is ceremonially clean. [12]The fire on the altar must be kept burning; it must not go out. Every morning the priest is to add firewood and arrange the burnt offering on the fire and burn the fat of the fellowship offerings[b] on it. [13]The fire must be kept burning on the altar continuously; it must not go out.

The Grain Offering

[14]" 'These are the regulations for the grain offering: Aaron's sons are to bring it before the Lord, in front of the altar. [15]The priest is to take a handful of fine flour and oil, together with all the incense on the grain offering, and burn the memorial portion on the altar as an aroma pleasing to the Lord. [16]Aaron and his sons shall eat the rest of it, but it is to be eaten without yeast in a holy place; they are to eat it in the courtyard of the Tent of Meeting. [17]It must not be baked with yeast; I have given it as their share of the offerings made to me by fire. Like the sin offering and the guilt offering, it is most holy. [18]Any male descendant of Aaron may eat it. It is his regular share of the offerings made to the Lord by fire for the generations to come. Whatever touches them will become holy.[c] ' "

[19]The Lord also said to Moses, [20]"This is the offering Aaron and his sons are to bring to the Lord on the day he[d] is anointed: a tenth of an ephah[e] of fine flour as a regular grain offering, half of it in the morning and half in the evening. [21]Prepare it with oil on a griddle; bring it well-mixed and present the grain offering broken[f] in pieces as an aroma pleasing to the Lord. [22]The son who is to succeed him as anointed priest shall prepare it. It is the Lord's regular share and is to be burned completely. [23]Every grain offering of a priest shall be burned completely; it must not be eaten."

The Sin Offering

[24]The Lord said to Moses, [25]"Say to Aaron and his sons: 'These are the regulations for the sin offering: The sin offering is to be slaughtered before the Lord in the place the burnt offering is slaughtered; it is most holy. [26]The priest who offers it shall eat it; it is to be eaten in a holy place, in the courtyard of the Tent of Meeting. [27]Whatever touches any of the flesh will become holy, and if any of the blood is spattered on a garment, you must wash it in a holy place. [28]The clay pot the meat is cooked in must be broken; but if it is cooked in a bronze pot, the pot is to be scoured and rinsed with water. [29]Any

---

[a]19 Or *has made full expiation for his*   [b]12 Traditionally *peace offerings*   [c]18 Or *Whoever touches them must be holy*; similarly in verse 27   [d]20 Or *each*   [e]20 That is, probably about 2 quarts (about 2 liters)   [f]21 The meaning of the Hebrew for this word is uncertain.

male in a priest's family may eat it; it is most holy. [30]But any sin offering whose blood is brought into the Tent of Meeting to make atonement in the Holy Place must not be eaten; it must be burned.

The Guilt Offering

7 " 'These are the regulations for the guilt offering, which is most holy: [2]The guilt offering is to be slaughtered in the place where the burnt offering is slaughtered, and its blood is to be sprinkled against the altar on all sides. [3]All its fat shall be offered: the fat tail and the fat that covers the inner parts, [4]both kidneys with the fat on them near the loins, and the covering of the liver, which is to be removed with the kidneys. [5]The priest shall burn them on the altar as an offering made to the LORD by fire. It is a guilt offering. [6]Any male in a priest's family may eat it, but it must be eaten in a holy place; it is most holy.

[7]" 'The same law applies to both the sin offering and the guilt offering: They belong to the priest who makes atonement with them. [8]The priest who offers a burnt offering for anyone may keep its hide for himself. [9]Every grain offering baked in an oven or cooked in a pan or on a griddle belongs to the priest who offers it, [10]and every grain offering, whether mixed with oil or dry, belongs equally to all the sons of Aaron.

The Fellowship Offering

[11]" 'These are the regulations for the fellowship offering[a] a person may present to the LORD:

[12]" 'If he offers it as an expression of thankfulness, then along with this thank offering he is to offer cakes of bread made without yeast and mixed with oil, wafers made without yeast and spread with oil, and cakes of fine flour well-kneaded and mixed with oil. [13]Along with his fellowship offering of thanksgiving he is to present an offering with cakes of bread made with yeast. [14]He is to bring one of each kind as an offering, a contribution to the LORD; it belongs to the priest who sprinkles the blood of the fellowship offerings. [15]The meat of his fellowship offering of thanksgiving must be eaten on the day it is offered; he must leave none of it till morning.

[16]" 'If, however, his offering is the result of a vow or is a freewill offering, the sacrifice shall be eaten on the day he offers it, but anything left over may be eaten on the next day. [17]Any meat of the sacrifice left over till the third day must be burned up. [18]If any meat of the fellowship offering is eaten on the third day, it will not be accepted. It will not be credited to the one who offered it, for it is impure; the person who eats any of it will be held responsible.

[19]" 'Meat that touches anything ceremonially unclean must not be eaten; it must be burned up. As for other meat, anyone ceremonially clean may eat it. [20]But if anyone who is unclean eats any meat of the fellowship offering belonging to the LORD, that person must be cut off from his people. [21]If anyone touches something unclean — whether human uncleanness or an unclean animal or any unclean, detestable thing — and then eats any of the meat of the fellowship offering belonging to the LORD, that person must be cut off from his people.' "

Eating Fat and Blood Forbidden

[22]The LORD said to Moses, [23]"Say to the Israelites: 'Do not eat any of the fat of cattle, sheep or goats. [24]The fat of an animal found dead or torn by wild animals may be used for any other purpose, but you must not eat it. [25]Anyone who eats the fat of an animal from which an offering by fire may be[b] made to the LORD must be cut off from his people. [26]And wherever you live, you must not eat the blood of any bird or animal. [27]If anyone eats blood, that person must be cut off from his people.' "

The Priests' Share

[28]The LORD said to Moses, [29]"Say to the Israelites: 'Anyone who brings a fellowship offering to the LORD is to bring part of it as his sacrifice to the LORD. [30]With his own hands he is to bring the offering made to the LORD by fire; he is to bring the fat, together with the breast, and wave the breast before the LORD as a wave offering. [31]The priest shall burn the fat on the altar, but the breast belongs to Aaron and his sons. [32]You are to give the right thigh of your fellowship offerings to the priest as a contribution. [33]The son of Aaron who offers the blood and the fat of the fellowship offering shall have the right thigh as his share. [34]From the fellowship offerings of the Israelites, I have taken the breast that is waved and the thigh that is presented

---

[a]11 Traditionally *peace offering*; also in verses 13-37   [b]25 Or *fire is*

and have given them to Aaron the priest and his sons as their regular share from the Israelites.' "

³⁵This is the portion of the offerings made to the LORD by fire that were allotted to Aaron and his sons on the day they were presented to serve the LORD as priests. ³⁶On the day they were anointed, the LORD commanded that the Israelites give this to them as their regular share for the generations to come.

³⁷These, then, are the regulations for the burnt offering, the grain offering, the sin offering, the guilt offering, the ordination offering and the fellowship offering, ³⁸which the LORD gave Moses on Mount Sinai on the day he commanded the Israelites to bring their offerings to the LORD, in the Desert of Sinai.

The Ordination of Aaron and His Sons

8 The LORD said to Moses, ²"Bring Aaron and his sons, their garments, the anointing oil, the bull for the sin offering, the two rams and the basket containing bread made without yeast, ³and gather the entire assembly at the entrance to the Tent of Meeting." ⁴Moses did as the LORD commanded him, and the assembly gathered at the entrance to the Tent of Meeting.

⁵Moses said to the assembly, "This is what the LORD has commanded to be done." ⁶Then Moses brought Aaron and his sons forward and washed them with water. ⁷He put the tunic on Aaron, tied the sash around him, clothed him with the robe and put the ephod on him. He also tied the ephod to him by its skillfully woven waistband; so it was fastened on him. ⁸He placed the breastpiece on him and put the Urim and Thummim in the breastpiece. ⁹Then he placed the turban on Aaron's head and set the gold plate, the sacred diadem, on the front of it, as the LORD commanded Moses.

¹⁰Then Moses took the anointing oil and anointed the tabernacle and everything in it, and so consecrated them. ¹¹He sprinkled some of the oil on the altar seven times, anointing the altar and all its utensils and the basin with its stand, to consecrate them. ¹²He poured some of the anointing oil on Aaron's head and anointed him to consecrate him. ¹³Then he brought Aaron's sons forward, put tunics on them, tied sashes around them and put headbands on them, as the LORD commanded Moses.

¹⁴He then presented the bull for the sin offering, and Aaron and his sons laid their hands on its head. ¹⁵Moses slaughtered the bull and took some of the blood, and with his finger he put it on all the horns of the altar to purify the altar. He poured out the rest of the blood at the base of the altar. So he consecrated it to make atonement for it. ¹⁶Moses also took all the fat around the inner parts, the covering of the liver, and both kidneys and their fat, and burned it on the altar. ¹⁷But the bull with its hide and its flesh and its offal he burned up outside the camp, as the LORD commanded Moses.

¹⁸He then presented the ram for the burnt offering, and Aaron and his sons laid their hands on its head. ¹⁹Then Moses slaughtered the ram and sprinkled the blood against the altar on all sides. ²⁰He cut the ram into pieces and burned the head, the pieces and the fat. ²¹He washed the inner parts and the legs with water and burned the whole ram on the altar as a burnt offering, a pleasing aroma, an offering made to the LORD by fire, as the LORD commanded Moses.

²²He then presented the other ram, the ram for the ordination, and Aaron and his sons laid their hands on its head. ²³Moses slaughtered the ram and took some of its blood and put it on the lobe of Aaron's right ear, on the thumb of his right hand and on the big toe of his right foot. ²⁴Moses also brought Aaron's sons forward and put some of the blood on the lobes of their right ears, on the thumbs of their right hands and on the big toes of their right feet. Then he sprinkled blood against the altar on all sides. ²⁵He took the fat, the fat tail, all the fat around the inner parts, the covering of the liver, both kidneys and their fat and the right thigh. ²⁶Then from the basket of bread made without yeast, which was before the LORD, he took a cake of bread, and one made with oil, and a wafer; he put these on the fat portions and on the right thigh. ²⁷He put all these in the hands of Aaron and his sons and waved them before the LORD as a wave offering. ²⁸Then Moses took them from their hands and burned them on the altar on top of the burnt offering as an ordination offering, a pleasing aroma, an offering made to the LORD by fire. ²⁹He also took the breast—Moses' share of the ordination ram—and waved it before the LORD as a wave offering, as the LORD commanded Moses.

30Then Moses took some of the anointing oil and some of the blood from the altar and sprinkled them on Aaron and his garments and on his sons and their garments. So he consecrated Aaron and his garments and his sons and their garments.

31Moses then said to Aaron and his sons, "Cook the meat at the entrance to the Tent of Meeting and eat it there with the bread from the basket of ordination offerings, as I commanded, saying,*a* 'Aaron and his sons are to eat it.' **32**Then burn up the rest of the meat and the bread. **33**Do not leave the entrance to the Tent of Meeting for seven days, until the days of your ordination are completed, for your ordination will last seven days. **34**What has been done today was commanded by the Lord to make atonement for you. **35**You must stay at the entrance to the Tent of Meeting day and night for seven days and do what the Lord requires, so you will not die; for that is what I have been commanded." **36**So Aaron and his sons did everything the Lord commanded through Moses.

The Priests Begin Their Ministry

9 On the eighth day Moses summoned Aaron and his sons and the elders of Israel. **2**He said to Aaron, "Take a bull calf for your sin offering and a ram for your burnt offering, both without defect, and present them before the Lord. **3**Then say to the Israelites: 'Take a male goat for a sin offering, a calf and a lamb—both a year old and without defect—for a burnt offering, **4**and an ox*b* and a ram for a fellowship offering*c* to sacrifice before the Lord, together with a grain offering mixed with oil. For today the Lord will appear to you.'"

5They took the things Moses commanded to the front of the Tent of Meeting, and the entire assembly came near and stood before the Lord. **6**Then Moses said, "This is what the Lord has commanded you to do, so that the glory of the Lord may appear to you."

7Moses said to Aaron, "Come to the altar and sacrifice your sin offering and your burnt offering and make atonement for yourself and the people; sacrifice the offering that is for the people and make atonement for them, as the Lord has commanded."

8So Aaron came to the altar and slaughtered the calf as a sin offering for himself. **9**His sons brought the blood to him, and he dipped his finger into the blood and put it on the horns of the altar; the rest of the blood he poured out at the base of the altar. **10**On the altar he burned the fat, the kidneys and the covering of the liver from the sin offering, as the Lord commanded Moses; **11**the flesh and the hide he burned up outside the camp.

12Then he slaughtered the burnt offering. His sons handed him the blood, and he sprinkled it against the altar on all sides. **13**They handed him the burnt offering piece by piece, including the head, and he burned them on the altar. **14**He washed the inner parts and the legs and burned them on top of the burnt offering on the altar.

15Aaron then brought the offering that was for the people. He took the goat for the people's sin offering and slaughtered it and offered it for a sin offering as he did with the first one.

16He brought the burnt offering and offered it in the prescribed way. **17**He also brought the grain offering, took a handful of it and burned it on the altar in addition to the morning's burnt offering.

18He slaughtered the ox and the ram as the fellowship offering for the people. His sons handed him the blood, and he sprinkled it against the altar on all sides. **19**But the fat portions of the ox and the ram—the fat tail, the layer of fat, the kidneys and the covering of the liver—**20**these they laid on the breasts, and then Aaron burned the fat on the altar. **21**Aaron waved the breasts and the right thigh before the Lord as a wave offering, as Moses commanded.

22Then Aaron lifted his hands toward the people and blessed them. And having sacrificed the sin offering, the burnt offering and the fellowship offering, he stepped down.

23Moses and Aaron then went into the Tent of Meeting. When they came out, they blessed the people; and the glory of the Lord appeared to all the people. **24**Fire came out from the presence of the Lord and consumed the burnt offering and the fat portions on the altar. And when all the people saw it, they shouted for joy and fell facedown.

---

a31 Or *I was commanded:*   *b4* The Hebrew word can include both male and female; also in verses 18 and 19.   *c4* Traditionally *peace offering*; also in verses 18 and 22

The Death of Nadab and Abihu

10 Aaron's sons Nadab and Abihu took their censers, put fire in them and added incense; and they offered unauthorized fire before the LORD, contrary to his command. ²So fire came out from the presence of the LORD and consumed them, and they died before the LORD. ³Moses then said to Aaron, "This is what the LORD spoke of when he said:

" 'Among those who approach me
  I will show myself holy;
  in the sight of all the people
  I will be honored.' "

Aaron remained silent.

⁴Moses summoned Mishael and Elzaphan, sons of Aaron's uncle Uzziel, and said to them, "Come here; carry your cousins outside the camp, away from the front of the sanctuary." ⁵So they came and carried them, still in their tunics, outside the camp, as Moses ordered.

⁶Then Moses said to Aaron and his sons Eleazar and Ithamar, "Do not let your hair become unkempt,ᵃ and do not tear your clothes, or you will die and the LORD will be angry with the whole community. But your relatives, all the house of Israel, may mourn for those the LORD has destroyed by fire. ⁷Do not leave the entrance to the Tent of Meeting or you will die, because the LORD's anointing oil is on you." So they did as Moses said.

⁸Then the LORD said to Aaron, ⁹"You and your sons are not to drink wine or other fermented drink whenever you go into the Tent of Meeting, or you will die. This is a lasting ordinance for the generations to come. ¹⁰You must distinguish between the holy and the common, between the unclean and the clean, ¹¹and you must teach the Israelites all the decrees the LORD has given them through Moses."

¹²Moses said to Aaron and his remaining sons, Eleazar and Ithamar, "Take the grain offering left over from the offerings made to the LORD by fire and eat it prepared without yeast beside the altar, for it is most holy. ¹³Eat it in a holy place, because it is your share and your sons' share of the offerings made to the LORD by fire; for so I have been commanded. ¹⁴But you and your sons and your daughters may eat the breast that was waved and the thigh that was presented. Eat them in a ceremonially clean place; they have been given to you and your children as your share of the Israelites' fellowship offerings.ᵇ ¹⁵The thigh that was presented and the breast that was waved must be brought with the fat portions of the offerings made by fire, to be waved before the LORD as a wave offering. This will be the regular share for you and your children, as the LORD has commanded."

¹⁶When Moses inquired about the goat of the sin offering and found that it had been burned up, he was angry with Eleazar and Ithamar, Aaron's remaining sons, and asked, ¹⁷"Why didn't you eat the sin offering in the sanctuary area? It is most holy; it was given to you to take away the guilt of the community by making atonement for them before the LORD. ¹⁸Since its blood was not taken into the Holy Place, you should have eaten the goat in the sanctuary area, as I commanded." ¹⁹Aaron replied to Moses, "Today they sacrificed their sin offering and their burnt offering before the LORD, but such things as this have happened to me. Would the LORD have been pleased if I had eaten the sin offering today?" ²⁰When Moses heard this, he was satisfied.

Clean and Unclean Food

11 The LORD said to Moses and Aaron, ²"Say to the Israelites: 'Of all the animals that live on land, these are the ones you may eat: ³You may eat any animal that has a split hoof completely divided and that chews the cud.

⁴" 'There are some that only chew the cud or only have a split hoof, but you must not eat them. The camel, though it chews the cud, does not have a split hoof; it is ceremonially unclean for you. ⁵The coney,ᶜ though it chews the cud, does not have a split hoof; it is unclean for you. ⁶The rabbit, though it chews the cud, does not have a split hoof; it is unclean for you. ⁷And the pig, though it has a split hoof completely divided, does not chew the cud; it is unclean for you. ⁸You must not eat their meat or touch their carcasses; they are unclean for you.

⁹" 'Of all the creatures living in the water of the seas and the streams, you may eat any that have fins and scales. ¹⁰But all creatures in the seas or streams that do not have fins and scales—whether among all the swarming things or among all the

---

ᵃ6 Or *Do not uncover your heads*   ᵇ14 Traditionally *peace offerings*   ᶜ5 That is, the hyrax or rock badger other living creatures in the water — you are to detest. ¹¹And since you are to detest them, you must not eat their meat and you must detest their carcasses. ¹²Anything living in the water that does not have fins and scales is to be detestable to you.

¹³" 'These are the birds you are to detest and not eat because they are detestable: the eagle, the vulture, the black vulture, ¹⁴the red kite, any kind of black kite, ¹⁵any kind of raven, ¹⁶the horned owl, the screech owl, the gull, any kind of hawk, ¹⁷the little owl, the cormorant, the great owl, ¹⁸the white owl, the desert owl, the osprey, ¹⁹the stork, any kind of heron, the hoopoe and the bat.ᵃ

²⁰" 'All flying insects that walk on all fours are to be detestable to you. ²¹There are, however, some winged creatures that walk on all fours that you may eat: those that have jointed legs for hopping on the ground. ²²Of these you may eat any kind of locust, katydid, cricket or grasshopper. ²³But all other winged creatures that have four legs you are to detest.

²⁴" 'You will make yourselves unclean by these; whoever touches their carcasses will be unclean till evening. ²⁵Whoever picks up one of their carcasses must wash his clothes, and he will be unclean till evening.

²⁶" 'Every animal that has a split hoof not completely divided or that does not chew the cud is unclean for you; whoever touches ⸤the carcass of⸥ any of them will be unclean. ²⁷Of all the animals that walk on all fours, those that walk on their paws are unclean for you; whoever touches their carcasses will be unclean till evening. ²⁸Anyone who picks up their carcasses must wash his clothes, and he will be unclean till evening. They are unclean for you.

²⁹" 'Of the animals that move about on the ground, these are unclean for you: the weasel, the rat, any kind of great lizard, ³⁰the gecko, the monitor lizard, the wall lizard, the skink and the chameleon. ³¹Of all those that move along the ground, these are unclean for you. Whoever touches them when they are dead will be unclean till evening. ³²When one of them dies and falls on something, that article, whatever its use, will be unclean, whether it is made of wood, cloth, hide or sackcloth. Put it in water; it will be unclean till evening, and then it will be clean. ³³If one of them falls into a clay pot, everything in

it will be unclean, and you must break the pot. ³⁴Any food that could be eaten but has water on it from such a pot is unclean, and any liquid that could be drunk from it is unclean. ³⁵Anything that one of their carcasses falls on becomes unclean; an oven or cooking pot must be broken up. They are unclean, and you are to regard them as unclean. ³⁶A spring, however, or a cistern for collecting water remains clean, but anyone who touches one of these carcasses is unclean. ³⁷If a carcass falls on any seeds that are to be planted, they remain clean. ³⁸But if water has been put on the seed and a carcass falls on it, it is unclean for you.

³⁹" 'If an animal that you are allowed to eat dies, anyone who touches the carcass will be unclean till evening. ⁴⁰Anyone who eats some of the carcass must wash his clothes, and he will be unclean till evening. Anyone who picks up the carcass must wash his clothes, and he will be unclean till evening.

⁴¹" 'Every creature that moves about on the ground is detestable; it is not to be eaten. ⁴²You are not to eat any creature that moves about on the ground, whether it moves on its belly or walks on all fours or on many feet; it is detestable. ⁴³Do not defile yourselves by any of these creatures. Do not make yourselves unclean by means of them or be made unclean by them. ⁴⁴I am the Lᴏʀᴅ your God; consecrate yourselves and be holy, because I am holy. Do not make yourselves unclean by any creature that moves about on the ground. ⁴⁵I am the Lᴏʀᴅ who brought you up out of Egypt to be your God; therefore be holy, because I am holy.

⁴⁶" 'These are the regulations concerning animals, birds, every living thing that moves in the water and every creature that moves about on the ground. ⁴⁷You must distinguish between the unclean and the clean, between living creatures that may be eaten and those that may not be eaten.' "

Purification After Childbirth

12 The Lᴏʀᴅ said to Moses, ²"Say to the Israelites: 'A woman who becomes pregnant and gives birth to a son will be ceremonially unclean for seven days, just as she is unclean during her monthly period. ³On the eighth day the boy is to be circumcised. ⁴Then the woman must wait thirty-three days to be puri-

---

ᵃ19 The precise identification of some of the birds, insects and animals in this chapter is uncertain.

fied from her bleeding. She must not touch anything sacred or go to the sanctuary until the days of her purification are over. ⁵If she gives birth to a daughter, for two weeks the woman will be unclean, as during her period. Then she must wait sixty-six days to be purified from her bleeding.

⁶" 'When the days of her purification for a son or daughter are over, she is to bring to the priest at the entrance to the Tent of Meeting a year-old lamb for a burnt offering and a young pigeon or a dove for a sin offering. ⁷He shall offer them before the LORD to make atonement for her, and then she will be ceremonially clean from her flow of blood.

" 'These are the regulations for the woman who gives birth to a boy or a girl. ⁸If she cannot afford a lamb, she is to bring two doves or two young pigeons, one for a burnt offering and the other for a sin offering. In this way the priest will make atonement for her, and she will be clean.' "

Regulations About Infectious Skin Diseases

13 The LORD said to Moses and Aaron, ²"When anyone has a swelling or a rash or a bright spot on his skin that may become an infectious skin disease,ᵃ he must be brought to Aaron the priest or to one of his sonsᵇ who is a priest. ³The priest is to examine the sore on his skin, and if the hair in the sore has turned white and the sore appears to be more than skin deep,ᶜ it is an infectious skin disease. When the priest examines him, he shall pronounce him ceremonially unclean. ⁴If the spot on his skin is white but does not appear to be more than skin deep and the hair in it has not turned white, the priest is to put the infected person in isolation for seven days. ⁵On the seventh day the priest is to examine him, and if he sees that the sore is unchanged and has not spread in the skin, he is to keep him in isolation another seven days. ⁶On the seventh day the priest is to examine him again, and if the sore has faded and has not spread in the skin, the priest shall pronounce him clean; it is only a rash. The man must wash his clothes, and he will be clean. ⁷But if the rash does spread in his skin after he has shown himself to the

priest to be pronounced clean, he must appear before the priest again. ⁸The priest is to examine him, and if the rash has spread in the skin, he shall pronounce him unclean; it is an infectious disease.

⁹"When anyone has an infectious skin disease, he must be brought to the priest. ¹⁰The priest is to examine him, and if there is a white swelling in the skin that has turned the hair white and if there is raw flesh in the swelling, ¹¹it is a chronic skin disease and the priest shall pronounce him unclean. He is not to put him in isolation, because he is already unclean.

¹²"If the disease breaks out all over his skin and, so far as the priest can see, it covers all the skin of the infected person from head to foot, ¹³the priest is to examine him, and if the disease has covered his whole body, he shall pronounce that person clean. Since it has all turned white, he is clean. ¹⁴But whenever raw flesh appears on him, he will be unclean. ¹⁵When the priest sees the raw flesh, he shall pronounce him unclean. The raw flesh is unclean; he has an infectious disease. ¹⁶Should the raw flesh change and turn white, he must go to the priest. ¹⁷The priest is to examine him, and if the sores have turned white, the priest shall pronounce the infected person clean; then he will be clean.

¹⁸"When someone has a boil on his skin and it heals, ¹⁹and in the place where the boil was, a white swelling or reddish-white spot appears, he must present himself to the priest. ²⁰The priest is to examine it, and if it appears to be more than skin deep and the hair in it has turned white, the priest shall pronounce him unclean. It is an infectious skin disease that has broken out where the boil was. ²¹But if, when the priest examines it, there is no white hair in it and it is not more than skin deep and has faded, then the priest is to put him in isolation for seven days. ²²If it is spreading in the skin, the priest shall pronounce him unclean; it is infectious. ²³But if the spot is unchanged and has not spread, it is only a scar from the boil, and the priest shall pronounce him clean.

²⁴"When someone has a burn on his skin and a reddish-white or white spot appears in the raw flesh of the burn, ²⁵the priest is to examine the spot, and if the

---

ᵃ2 Traditionally *leprosy*; the Hebrew word was used for various diseases affecting the skin—not necessarily leprosy; also elsewhere in this chapter.   ᵇ2 Or *descendants*   ᶜ3 Or *be lower than the rest of the skin*; also elsewhere in this chapter hair in it has turned white, and it appears to be more than skin deep, it is an infectious disease that has broken out in the burn. The priest shall pronounce him unclean; it is an infectious skin disease. **26**But if the priest examines it and there is no white hair in the spot and if it is not more than skin deep and has faded, then the priest is to put him in isolation for seven days. **27**On the seventh day the priest is to examine him, and if it is spreading in the skin, the priest shall pronounce him unclean; it is an infectious skin disease. **28**If, however, the spot is unchanged and has not spread in the skin but has faded, it is a swelling from the burn, and the priest shall pronounce him clean; it is only a scar from the burn.

29"If a man or woman has a sore on the head or on the chin, **30**the priest is to examine the sore, and if it appears to be more than skin deep and the hair in it is yellow and thin, the priest shall pronounce that person unclean; it is an itch, an infectious disease of the head or chin. **31**But if, when the priest examines this kind of sore, it does not seem to be more than skin deep and there is no black hair in it, then the priest is to put the infected person in isolation for seven days. **32**On the seventh day the priest is to examine the sore, and if the itch has not spread and there is no yellow hair in it and it does not appear to be more than skin deep, **33**he must be shaved except for the diseased area, and the priest is to keep him in isolation another seven days. **34**On the seventh day the priest is to examine the itch, and if it has not spread in the skin and appears to be no more than skin deep, the priest shall pronounce him clean. He must wash his clothes, and he will be clean. **35**But if the itch does spread in the skin after he is pronounced clean, **36**the priest is to examine him, and if the itch has spread in the skin, the priest does not need to look for yellow hair; the person is unclean. **37**If, however, in his judgment it is unchanged and black hair has grown in it, the itch is healed. He is clean, and the priest shall pronounce him clean.

38"When a man or woman has white spots on the skin, **39**the priest is to examine them, and if the spots are dull white, it is a harmless rash that has broken out on the skin; that person is clean.

40"When a man has lost his hair and is bald, he is clean. **41**If he has lost his hair from the front of his scalp and has a bald forehead, he is clean. **42**But if he has a reddish-white sore on his bald head or forehead, it is an infectious disease breaking out on his head or forehead. **43**The priest is to examine him, and if the swollen sore on his head or forehead is reddish-white like an infectious skin disease, **44**the man is diseased and is unclean. The priest shall pronounce him unclean because of the sore on his head.

45"The person with such an infectious disease must wear torn clothes, let his hair be unkempt,*a* cover the lower part of his face and cry out, 'Unclean! Unclean!' **46**As long as he has the infection he remains unclean. He must live alone; he must live outside the camp.

Regulations About Mildew

47"If any clothing is contaminated with mildew—any woolen or linen clothing, **48**any woven or knitted material of linen or wool, any leather or anything made of leather— **49**and if the contamination in the clothing, or leather, or woven or knitted material, or any leather article, is greenish or reddish, it is a spreading mildew and must be shown to the priest. **50**The priest is to examine the mildew and isolate the affected article for seven days. **51**On the seventh day he is to examine it, and if the mildew has spread in the clothing, or the woven or knitted material, or the leather, whatever its use, it is a destructive mildew; the article is unclean. **52**He must burn up the clothing, or the woven or knitted material of wool or linen, or any leather article that has the contamination in it, because the mildew is destructive; the article must be burned up.

53"But if, when the priest examines it, the mildew has not spread in the clothing, or the woven or knitted material, or the leather article, **54**he shall order that the contaminated article be washed. Then he is to isolate it for another seven days. **55**After the affected article has been washed, the priest is to examine it, and if the mildew has not changed its appearance, even though it has not spread, it is unclean. Burn it with fire, whether the mildew has affected one side or the other. **56**If, when the priest examines it, the mildew has faded after the article has been washed, he is to tear the contaminated part out of the clothing, or the leather, or the woven or knitted material. **57**But if it reappears in

---

a45 Or clothes, uncover his head

the clothing, or in the woven or knitted material, or in the leather article, it is spreading, and whatever has the mildew must be burned with fire. **58**The clothing, or the woven or knitted material, or any leather article that has been washed and is rid of the mildew, must be washed again, and it will be clean."

59These are the regulations concerning contamination by mildew in woolen or linen clothing, woven or knitted material, or any leather article, for pronouncing them clean or unclean.

Cleansing From Infectious Skin Diseases

14 The Lord said to Moses, **2**"These are the regulations for the diseased person at the time of his ceremonial cleansing, when he is brought to the priest: **3**The priest is to go outside the camp and examine him. If the person has been healed of his infectious skin disease,*a* **4**the priest shall order that two live clean birds and some cedar wood, scarlet yarn and hyssop be brought for the one to be cleansed. **5**Then the priest shall order that one of the birds be killed over fresh water in a clay pot. **6**He is then to take the live bird and dip it, together with the cedar wood, the scarlet yarn and the hyssop, into the blood of the bird that was killed over the fresh water. **7**Seven times he shall sprinkle the one to be cleansed of the infectious disease and pronounce him clean. Then he is to release the live bird in the open fields.

8"The person to be cleansed must wash his clothes, shave off all his hair and bathe with water; then he will be ceremonially clean. After this he may come into the camp, but he must stay outside his tent for seven days. **9**On the seventh day he must shave off all his hair; he must shave his head, his beard, his eyebrows and the rest of his hair. He must wash his clothes and bathe himself with water, and he will be clean.

10"On the eighth day he must bring two male lambs and one ewe lamb a year old, each without defect, along with three-tenths of an ephah*b* of fine flour mixed with oil for a grain offering, and one log*c* of oil. **11**The priest who pronounces him clean shall present both the one to be cleansed and his offerings before the Lord at the entrance to the Tent of Meeting.

12"Then the priest is to take one of the male lambs and offer it as a guilt offering, along with the log of oil; he shall wave them before the Lord as a wave offering. **13**He is to slaughter the lamb in the holy place where the sin offering and the burnt offering are slaughtered. Like the sin offering, the guilt offering belongs to the priest; it is most holy. **14**The priest is to take some of the blood of the guilt offering and put it on the lobe of the right ear of the one to be cleansed, on the thumb of his right hand and on the big toe of his right foot. **15**The priest shall then take some of the log of oil, pour it in the palm of his own left hand, **16**dip his right forefinger into the oil in his palm, and with his finger sprinkle some of it before the Lord seven times. **17**The priest is to put some of the oil remaining in his palm on the lobe of the right ear of the one to be cleansed, on the thumb of his right hand and on the big toe of his right foot, on top of the blood of the guilt offering. **18**The rest of the oil in his palm the priest shall put on the head of the one to be cleansed and make atonement for him before the Lord.

19"Then the priest is to sacrifice the sin offering and make atonement for the one to be cleansed from his uncleanness. After that, the priest shall slaughter the burnt offering **20**and offer it on the altar, together with the grain offering, and make atonement for him, and he will be clean.

21"If, however, he is poor and cannot afford these, he must take one male lamb as a guilt offering to be waved to make atonement for him, together with a tenth of an ephah*d* of fine flour mixed with oil for a grain offering, a log of oil, **22**and two doves or two young pigeons, which he can afford, one for a sin offering and the other for a burnt offering.

23"On the eighth day he must bring them for his cleansing to the priest at the entrance to the Tent of Meeting, before the Lord. **24**The priest is to take the lamb for the guilt offering, together with the log of oil, and wave them before the Lord as a wave offering. **25**He shall slaughter the lamb for the guilt offering and take some of its blood and put it on the lobe of the right ear of the one to be cleansed, on the

---

a3 Traditionally *leprosy*; the Hebrew word was used for various diseases affecting the skin—not necessarily leprosy; also elsewhere in this chapter.   *b10* That is, probably about 6 quarts (about 6.5 liters)   *c10* That is, probably about 2/3 pint (about 0.3 liter); also in verses 12, 15, 21 and 24   *d21* That is, probably about 2 quarts (about 2 liters) thumb of his right hand and on the big toe of his right foot. **26**The priest is to pour some of the oil into the palm of his own left hand, **27**and with his right forefinger sprinkle some of the oil from his palm seven times before the LORD. **28**Some of the oil in his palm he is to put on the same places he put the blood of the guilt offering—on the lobe of the right ear of the one to be cleansed, on the thumb of his right hand and on the big toe of his right foot. **29**The rest of the oil in his palm the priest shall put on the head of the one to be cleansed, to make atonement for him before the LORD. **30**Then he shall sacrifice the doves or the young pigeons, which the person can afford, **31**one*a* as a sin offering and the other as a burnt offering, together with the grain offering. In this way the priest will make atonement before the LORD on behalf of the one to be cleansed."

32These are the regulations for anyone who has an infectious skin disease and who cannot afford the regular offerings for his cleansing.

Cleansing From Mildew

33The LORD said to Moses and Aaron, **34**"When you enter the land of Canaan, which I am giving you as your possession, and I put a spreading mildew in a house in that land, **35**the owner of the house must go and tell the priest, 'I have seen something that looks like mildew in my house.' **36**The priest is to order the house to be emptied before he goes in to examine the mildew, so that nothing in the house will be pronounced unclean. After this the priest is to go in and inspect the house. **37**He is to examine the mildew on the walls, and if it has greenish or reddish depressions that appear to be deeper than the surface of the wall, **38**the priest shall go out the doorway of the house and close it up for seven days. **39**On the seventh day the priest shall return to inspect the house. If the mildew has spread on the walls, **40**he is to order that the contaminated stones be torn out and thrown into an unclean place outside the town. **41**He must have all the inside walls of the house scraped and the material that is scraped off dumped into an unclean place outside the town. **42**Then they are to take other stones to replace these and take new clay and plaster the house.

43"If the mildew reappears in the house after the stones have been torn out and the house scraped and plastered, **44**the priest is to go and examine it and, if the mildew has spread in the house, it is a destructive mildew; the house is unclean. **45**It must be torn down—its stones, timbers and all the plaster—and taken out of the town to an unclean place.

46"Anyone who goes into the house while it is closed up will be unclean till evening. **47**Anyone who sleeps or eats in the house must wash his clothes.

48"But if the priest comes to examine it and the mildew has not spread after the house has been plastered, he shall pronounce the house clean, because the mildew is gone. **49**To purify the house he is to take two birds and some cedar wood, scarlet yarn and hyssop. **50**He shall kill one of the birds over fresh water in a clay pot. **51**Then he is to take the cedar wood, the hyssop, the scarlet yarn and the live bird, dip them into the blood of the dead bird and the fresh water, and sprinkle the house seven times. **52**He shall purify the house with the bird's blood, the fresh water, the live bird, the cedar wood, the hyssop and the scarlet yarn. **53**Then he is to release the live bird in the open fields outside the town. In this way he will make atonement for the house, and it will be clean."

54These are the regulations for any infectious skin disease, for an itch, **55**for mildew in clothing or in a house, **56**and for a swelling, a rash or a bright spot, **57**to determine when something is clean or unclean.

These are the regulations for infectious skin diseases and mildew.

Discharges Causing Uncleanness

15 The LORD said to Moses and Aaron, **2**"Speak to the Israelites and say to them: 'When any man has a bodily discharge, the discharge is unclean. **3**Whether it continues flowing from his body or is blocked, it will make him unclean. This is how his discharge will bring about uncleanness:

4" 'Any bed the man with a discharge lies on will be unclean, and anything he sits on will be unclean. **5**Anyone who touches his bed must wash his clothes and bathe with water, and he will be unclean till evening. **6**Whoever sits on anything that the man with a discharge sat on must wash his clothes and bathe with water, and he will be unclean till evening.

7" 'Whoever touches the man who has a

---

a31 Septuagint and Syriac; Hebrew *31such as the person can afford, one* discharge must wash his clothes and bathe with water, and he will be unclean till evening.

8" 'If the man with the discharge spits on someone who is clean, that person must wash his clothes and bathe with water, and he will be unclean till evening.

9" 'Everything the man sits on when riding will be unclean, **10**and whoever touches any of the things that were under him will be unclean till evening; whoever picks up those things must wash his clothes and bathe with water, and he will be unclean till evening.

11" 'Anyone the man with a discharge touches without rinsing his hands with water must wash his clothes and bathe with water, and he will be unclean till evening.

12" 'A clay pot that the man touches must be broken, and any wooden article is to be rinsed with water.

13" 'When a man is cleansed from his discharge, he is to count off seven days for his ceremonial cleansing; he must wash his clothes and bathe himself with fresh water, and he will be clean. **14**On the eighth day he must take two doves or two young pigeons and come before the LORD to the entrance to the Tent of Meeting and give them to the priest. **15**The priest is to sacrifice them, the one for a sin offering and the other for a burnt offering. In this way he will make atonement before the LORD for the man because of his discharge.

16" 'When a man has an emission of semen, he must bathe his whole body with water, and he will be unclean till evening. **17**Any clothing or leather that has semen on it must be washed with water, and it will be unclean till evening. **18**When a man lies with a woman and there is an emission of semen, both must bathe with water, and they will be unclean till evening.

19" 'When a woman has her regular flow of blood, the impurity of her monthly period will last seven days, and anyone who touches her will be unclean till evening.

20" 'Anything she lies on during her period will be unclean, and anything she sits on will be unclean. **21**Whoever touches her bed must wash his clothes and bathe with water, and he will be unclean till evening. **22**Whoever touches anything she sits on must wash his clothes and bathe with water, and he will be unclean till evening.

23Whether it is the bed or anything she was sitting on, when anyone touches it, he will be unclean till evening.

24" 'If a man lies with her and her monthly flow touches him, he will be unclean for seven days; any bed he lies on will be unclean.

25" 'When a woman has a discharge of blood for many days at a time other than her monthly period or has a discharge that continues beyond her period, she will be unclean as long as she has the discharge, just as in the days of her period. **26**Any bed she lies on while her discharge continues will be unclean, as is her bed during her monthly period, and anything she sits on will be unclean, as during her period. **27**Whoever touches them will be unclean; he must wash his clothes and bathe with water, and he will be unclean till evening.

28" 'When she is cleansed from her discharge, she must count off seven days, and after that she will be ceremonially clean. **29**On the eighth day she must take two doves or two young pigeons and bring them to the priest at the entrance to the Tent of Meeting. **30**The priest is to sacrifice one for a sin offering and the other for a burnt offering. In this way he will make atonement for her before the LORD for the uncleanness of her discharge.

31" 'You must keep the Israelites separate from things that make them unclean, so they will not die in their uncleanness for defiling my dwelling place,*a* which is among them.' "

32These are the regulations for a man with a discharge, for anyone made unclean by an emission of semen, **33**for a woman in her monthly period, for a man or a woman with a discharge, and for a man who lies with a woman who is ceremonially unclean.

The Day of Atonement

16 The LORD spoke to Moses after the death of the two sons of Aaron who died when they approached the LORD. **2**The LORD said to Moses: "Tell your brother Aaron not to come whenever he chooses into the Most Holy Place behind the curtain in front of the atonement cover on the ark, or else he will die, because I appear in the cloud over the atonement cover.

3"This is how Aaron is to enter the sanctuary area: with a young bull for a sin offering and a ram for a burnt offering. **4**He

a31 Or *my tabernacle*

is to put on the sacred linen tunic, with linen undergarments next to his body; he is to tie the linen sash around him and put on the linen turban. These are sacred garments; so he must bathe himself with water before he puts them on. **5**From the Israelite community he is to take two male goats for a sin offering and a ram for a burnt offering.

6"Aaron is to offer the bull for his own sin offering to make atonement for himself and his household. **7**Then he is to take the two goats and present them before the Lord at the entrance to the Tent of Meeting. **8**He is to cast lots for the two goats—one lot for the Lord and the other for the scapegoat.*a* **9**Aaron shall bring the goat whose lot falls to the Lord and sacrifice it for a sin offering. **10**But the goat chosen by lot as the scapegoat shall be presented alive before the Lord to be used for making atonement by sending it into the desert as a scapegoat.

11"Aaron shall bring the bull for his own sin offering to make atonement for himself and his household, and he is to slaughter the bull for his own sin offering. **12**He is to take a censer full of burning coals from the altar before the Lord and two handfuls of finely ground fragrant incense and take them behind the curtain. **13**He is to put the incense on the fire before the Lord, and the smoke of the incense will conceal the atonement cover above the Testimony, so that he will not die. **14**He is to take some of the bull's blood and with his finger sprinkle it on the front of the atonement cover; then he shall sprinkle some of it with his finger seven times before the atonement cover.

15"He shall then slaughter the goat for the sin offering for the people and take its blood behind the curtain and do with it as he did with the bull's blood: He shall sprinkle it on the atonement cover and in front of it. **16**In this way he will make atonement for the Most Holy Place because of the uncleanness and rebellion of the Israelites, whatever their sins have been. He is to do the same for the Tent of Meeting, which is among them in the midst of their uncleanness. **17**No one is to be in the Tent of Meeting from the time Aaron goes in to make atonement in the Most Holy Place until he comes out, having made atonement for himself, his

household and the whole community of Israel.

18"Then he shall come out to the altar that is before the Lord and make atonement for it. He shall take some of the bull's blood and some of the goat's blood and put it on all the horns of the altar. **19**He shall sprinkle some of the blood on it with his finger seven times to cleanse it and to consecrate it from the uncleanness of the Israelites.

20"When Aaron has finished making atonement for the Most Holy Place, the Tent of Meeting and the altar, he shall bring forward the live goat. **21**He is to lay both hands on the head of the live goat and confess over it all the wickedness and rebellion of the Israelites—all their sins—and put them on the goat's head. He shall send the goat away into the desert in the care of a man appointed for the task. **22**The goat will carry on itself all their sins to a solitary place; and the man shall release it in the desert.

23"Then Aaron is to go into the Tent of Meeting and take off the linen garments he put on before he entered the Most Holy Place, and he is to leave them there. **24**He shall bathe himself with water in a holy place and put on his regular garments. Then he shall come out and sacrifice the burnt offering for himself and the burnt offering for the people, to make atonement for himself and for the people. **25**He shall also burn the fat of the sin offering on the altar.

26"The man who releases the goat as a scapegoat must wash his clothes and bathe himself with water; afterward he may come into the camp. **27**The bull and the goat for the sin offerings, whose blood was brought into the Most Holy Place to make atonement, must be taken outside the camp; their hides, flesh and offal are to be burned up. **28**The man who burns them must wash his clothes and bathe himself with water; afterward he may come into the camp.

29"This is to be a lasting ordinance for you: On the tenth day of the seventh month you must deny yourselves*b* and not do any work—whether native-born or an alien living among you— **30**because on this day atonement will be made for you, to cleanse you. Then, before the Lord, you will be clean from all your sins. **31**It is a sabbath of rest, and you must deny your-

a8 That is, the goat of removal; Hebrew azazel; also in verses 10 and 26   b29 Or must fast; also in verse 31 selves; it is a lasting ordinance. ³²The priest who is anointed and ordained to succeed his father as high priest is to make atonement. He is to put on the sacred linen garments ³³and make atonement for the Most Holy Place, for the Tent of Meeting and the altar, and for the priests and all the people of the community.

³⁴"This is to be a lasting ordinance for you: Atonement is to be made once a year for all the sins of the Israelites."

And it was done, as the LORD commanded Moses.

TUESDAY

VERSE FOR THE DAY:	AUTHOR:	PASSAGE FOR THE DAY:
Leviticus 16:21	Tim Stafford	Leviticus 16:20–22

Whose Sacrifice Is It?

OUR relationship with God requires sacrifice and forgiveness, but it is not our sacrifice. We could not and would not give up a thing for God. Sin goes far too deep in us. It has twisted us all out of shape, making us hardly recognizable to the one who made us. We push God away, hiding behind excuses of being too busy to find time for him or of not being inspired by our church or of not having an answer to some question about the meaning of suffering or—you name it; the variations are limitless. Behind these excuses we hide our hostility toward God. We hide it even from ourselves. We are constitutionally incapable of sacrificing ourselves for the real God; our nature will not let us forgive him. We can forgive others, conditionally, because they are weak like us. We cannot so easily forgive God for being perfect, for knowing everything, for being above us, for being our maker. We cannot easily accept absolute, eternal dependence. It is the ultimate insult to our pride.

Consequently, our "sacrifices" for God easily become manifestations of our sin, not our love for him. We use them as a bargaining weapon: "If I do this for you, God, will you do this for me?" We try to use these sacrifices to control his behavior and bring him down to our level. But this will never lead us to deeper intimacy with God. If we are to know him, we must know him as he is: our perfect, all-knowing God who sacrificed himself for us when we were helpless. He gave up, not just his glory to become a man, but his own life—the just for the unjust, the deserving for the undeserving. His initiative broke the barrier. Ours not only could not, it would not . . .

God placed on Jesus the sin of the world: our rejection of God . . . He absorbed our full rejection, sacrificing his life to it. When the anger was absorbed, it lost its power. Then we could begin anew, forgiven by him.

Additional Scripture Readings:
Isaiah 53:1–12; 1 Peter 2:21–25

Go to page 119 for your next devotional reading.

Eating Blood Forbidden

17 The LORD said to Moses, [2]"Speak to Aaron and his sons and to all the Israelites and say to them: 'This is what the LORD has commanded: [3]Any Israelite who sacrifices an ox,[a] a lamb or a goat in the camp or outside of it [4]instead of bringing it to the entrance to the Tent of Meeting to present it as an offering to the LORD in front of the tabernacle of the LORD — that man shall be considered guilty of bloodshed; he has shed blood and must be cut off from his people. [5]This is so the Israelites will bring to the LORD the sacrifices they are now making in the open fields. They must bring them to the priest, that is, to the LORD, at the entrance to the Tent of Meeting and sacrifice them as fellowship offerings.[b] [6]The priest is to sprinkle the blood against the altar of the LORD at the entrance to the Tent of Meeting and burn the fat as an aroma pleasing to the LORD. [7]They must no longer offer any of their sacrifices to the goat idols[c] to whom they prostitute themselves. This is to be a lasting ordinance for them and for the generations to come.'

[8]"Say to them: 'Any Israelite or any alien living among them who offers a burnt offering or sacrifice [9]and does not bring it to the entrance to the Tent of Meeting to sacrifice it to the LORD — that man must be cut off from his people.

[10]" 'Any Israelite or any alien living among them who eats any blood — I will set my face against that person who eats blood and will cut him off from his people. [11]For the life of a creature is in the blood, and I have given it to you to make atonement for yourselves on the altar; it is the blood that makes atonement for one's life. [12]Therefore I say to the Israelites, "None of you may eat blood, nor may an alien living among you eat blood."

[13]" 'Any Israelite or any alien living among you who hunts any animal or bird that may be eaten must drain out the blood and cover it with earth, [14]because the life of every creature is its blood. That is why I have said to the Israelites, "You must not eat the blood of any creature, because the life of every creature is its blood; anyone who eats it must be cut off."

[15]" 'Anyone, whether native-born or alien, who eats anything found dead or torn by wild animals must wash his clothes and bathe with water, and he will be ceremonially unclean till evening; then he will be clean. [16]But if he does not wash his clothes and bathe himself, he will be held responsible.' "

Unlawful Sexual Relations

18 The LORD said to Moses, [2]"Speak to the Israelites and say to them: 'I am the LORD your God. [3]You must not do as they do in Egypt, where you used to live, and you must not do as they do in the land of Canaan, where I am bringing you. Do not follow their practices. [4]You must obey my laws and be careful to follow my decrees. I am the LORD your God. [5]Keep my decrees and laws, for the man who obeys them will live by them. I am the LORD.

[6]" 'No one is to approach any close relative to have sexual relations. I am the LORD.

[7]" 'Do not dishonor your father by having sexual relations with your mother. She is your mother; do not have relations with her.

[8]" 'Do not have sexual relations with your father's wife; that would dishonor your father.

[9]" 'Do not have sexual relations with your sister, either your father's daughter or your mother's daughter, whether she was born in the same home or elsewhere.

[10]" 'Do not have sexual relations with your son's daughter or your daughter's daughter; that would dishonor you.

[11]" 'Do not have sexual relations with the daughter of your father's wife, born to your father; she is your sister.

[12]" 'Do not have sexual relations with your father's sister; she is your father's close relative.

[13]" 'Do not have sexual relations with your mother's sister, because she is your mother's close relative.

[14]" 'Do not dishonor your father's brother by approaching his wife to have sexual relations; she is your aunt.

[15]" 'Do not have sexual relations with your daughter-in-law. She is your son's wife; do not have relations with her.

[16]" 'Do not have sexual relations with your brother's wife; that would dishonor your brother.

[17]" 'Do not have sexual relations with both a woman and her daughter. Do not have sexual relations with either her son's daughter or her daughter's daughter; they

---

[a]3 The Hebrew word can include both male and female.   [b]5 Traditionally *peace offerings*   [c]7 Or
demons

are her close relatives. That is wickedness.

18" 'Do not take your wife's sister as a rival wife and have sexual relations with her while your wife is living.

19" 'Do not approach a woman to have sexual relations during the uncleanness of her monthly period.

20" 'Do not have sexual relations with your neighbor's wife and defile yourself with her.

21" 'Do not give any of your children to be sacrificed*a* to Molech, for you must not profane the name of your God. I am the Lord.

22" 'Do not lie with a man as one lies with a woman; that is detestable.

23" 'Do not have sexual relations with an animal and defile yourself with it. A woman must not present herself to an animal to have sexual relations with it; that is a perversion.

24" 'Do not defile yourselves in any of these ways, because this is how the nations that I am going to drive out before you became defiled. **25**Even the land was defiled; so I punished it for its sin, and the land vomited out its inhabitants. **26**But you must keep my decrees and my laws. The native-born and the aliens living among you must not do any of these detestable things, **27**for all these things were done by the people who lived in the land before you, and the land became defiled. **28**And if you defile the land, it will vomit you out as it vomited out the nations that were before you.

29" 'Everyone who does any of these detestable things — such persons must be cut off from their people. **30**Keep my requirements and do not follow any of the detestable customs that were practiced before you came and do not defile yourselves with them. I am the Lord your God.' "

Various Laws

19 The Lord said to Moses, **2**"Speak to the entire assembly of Israel and say to them: 'Be holy because I, the Lord your God, am holy.

3" 'Each of you must respect his mother and father, and you must observe my Sabbaths. I am the Lord your God.

4" 'Do not turn to idols or make gods of cast metal for yourselves. I am the Lord your God.

5" 'When you sacrifice a fellowship offering*b* to the Lord, sacrifice it in such a way that it will be accepted on your behalf. **6**It shall be eaten on the day you sacrifice it or on the next day; anything left over until the third day must be burned up. **7**If any of it is eaten on the third day, it is impure and will not be accepted. **8**Whoever eats it will be held responsible because he has desecrated what is holy to the Lord; that person must be cut off from his people.

9" 'When you reap the harvest of your land, do not reap to the very edges of your field or gather the gleanings of your harvest. **10**Do not go over your vineyard a second time or pick up the grapes that have fallen. Leave them for the poor and the alien. I am the Lord your God.

11" 'Do not steal.

" 'Do not lie.

" 'Do not deceive one another.

12" 'Do not swear falsely by my name and so profane the name of your God. I am the Lord.

13" 'Do not defraud your neighbor or rob him.

" 'Do not hold back the wages of a hired man overnight.

14" 'Do not curse the deaf or put a stumbling block in front of the blind, but fear your God. I am the Lord.

15" 'Do not pervert justice; do not show partiality to the poor or favoritism to the great, but judge your neighbor fairly.

16" 'Do not go about spreading slander among your people.

" 'Do not do anything that endangers your neighbor's life. I am the Lord.

17" 'Do not hate your brother in your heart. Rebuke your neighbor frankly so you will not share in his guilt.

18" 'Do not seek revenge or bear a grudge against one of your people, but love your neighbor as yourself. I am the Lord.

19" 'Keep my decrees.

" 'Do not mate different kinds of animals.

" 'Do not plant your field with two kinds of seed.

" 'Do not wear clothing woven of two kinds of material.

20" 'If a man sleeps with a woman who is a slave girl promised to another man but who has not been ransomed or given her freedom, there must be due punishment. Yet they are not to be put to death, because she had not been freed. **21**The man, however, must bring a ram to the entrance

---

a21 Or *to be passed through ₎the fire₎*   *b5* Traditionally *peace offering* to the Tent of Meeting for a guilt offering to the LORD. ²²With the ram of the guilt offering the priest is to make atonement for him before the LORD for the sin he has committed, and his sin will be forgiven.

²³" 'When you enter the land and plant any kind of fruit tree, regard its fruit as forbidden.ᵃ For three years you are to consider it forbiddenᵃ; it must not be eaten. ²⁴In the fourth year all its fruit will be holy, an offering of praise to the LORD. ²⁵But in the fifth year you may eat its fruit. In this way your harvest will be increased. I am the LORD your God.

²⁶" 'Do not eat any meat with the blood still in it.

" 'Do not practice divination or sorcery.

²⁷" 'Do not cut the hair at the sides of your head or clip off the edges of your beard.

²⁸" 'Do not cut your bodies for the dead or put tattoo marks on yourselves. I am the LORD.

²⁹" 'Do not degrade your daughter by making her a prostitute, or the land will turn to prostitution and be filled with wickedness.

³⁰" 'Observe my Sabbaths and have reverence for my sanctuary. I am the LORD.

³¹" 'Do not turn to mediums or seek out spiritists, for you will be defiled by them. I am the LORD your God.

³²" 'Rise in the presence of the aged, show respect for the elderly and revere your God. I am the LORD.

³³" 'When an alien lives with you in your land, do not mistreat him. ³⁴The alien living with you must be treated as one of your native-born. Love him as yourself, for you were aliens in Egypt. I am the LORD your God.

³⁵" 'Do not use dishonest standards when measuring length, weight or quantity. ³⁶Use honest scales and honest weights, an honest ephahᵇ and an honest hin.ᶜ I am the LORD your God, who brought you out of Egypt.

³⁷" 'Keep all my decrees and all my laws and follow them. I am the LORD.' "

Punishments for Sin

20 The LORD said to Moses, ²"Say to the Israelites: 'Any Israelite or any alien living in Israel who givesᵈ any of his children to Molech must be put to death. The people of the community are to stone him. ³I will set my face against that man

and I will cut him off from his people; for by giving his children to Molech, he has defiled my sanctuary and profaned my holy name. ⁴If the people of the community close their eyes when that man gives one of his children to Molech and they fail to put him to death, ⁵I will set my face against that man and his family and will cut off from their people both him and all who follow him in prostituting themselves to Molech.

⁶" 'I will set my face against the person who turns to mediums and spiritists to prostitute himself by following them, and I will cut him off from his people.

⁷" 'Consecrate yourselves and be holy, because I am the LORD your God. ⁸Keep my decrees and follow them. I am the LORD, who makes you holy.ᵉ

⁹" 'If anyone curses his father or mother, he must be put to death. He has cursed his father or his mother, and his blood will be on his own head.

¹⁰" 'If a man commits adultery with another man's wife—with the wife of his neighbor—both the adulterer and the adulteress must be put to death.

¹¹" 'If a man sleeps with his father's wife, he has dishonored his father. Both the man and the woman must be put to death; their blood will be on their own heads.

¹²" 'If a man sleeps with his daughter-in-law, both of them must be put to death. What they have done is a perversion; their blood will be on their own heads.

¹³" 'If a man lies with a man as one lies with a woman, both of them have done what is detestable. They must be put to death; their blood will be on their own heads.

¹⁴" 'If a man marries both a woman and her mother, it is wicked. Both he and they must be burned in the fire, so that no wickedness will be among you.

¹⁵" 'If a man has sexual relations with an animal, he must be put to death, and you must kill the animal.

¹⁶" 'If a woman approaches an animal to have sexual relations with it, kill both the woman and the animal. They must be put to death; their blood will be on their own heads.

¹⁷" 'If a man marries his sister, the daughter of either his father or his mother, and they have sexual relations, it is a

ᵃ23 Hebrew *uncircumcised*   ᵇ36 An ephah was a dry measure.   ᶜ36 A hin was a liquid measure.
ᵈ2 Or *sacrifices*; also in verses 3 and 4   ᵉ8 Or *who sanctifies you*; or *who sets you apart as holy*

disgrace. They must be cut off before the eyes of their people. He has dishonored his sister and will be held responsible.

18" 'If a man lies with a woman during her monthly period and has sexual relations with her, he has exposed the source of her flow, and she has also uncovered it. Both of them must be cut off from their people.

19" 'Do not have sexual relations with the sister of either your mother or your father, for that would dishonor a close rela-

tive; both of you would be held responsible.

20" 'If a man sleeps with his aunt, he has dishonored his uncle. They will be held responsible; they will die childless.

21" 'If a man marries his brother's wife, it is an act of impurity; he has dishonored his brother. They will be childless.

22" 'Keep all my decrees and laws and follow them, so that the land where I am bringing you to live may not vomit you out. **23**You must not live according to the

---

WEDNESDAY

VERSE FOR THE DAY:
Leviticus 19:18

AUTHOR:
Gary Smalley and John Trent

PASSAGE FOR THE DAY:
Leviticus 19:9–18

Love and Honor

WHEN Jesus was asked to name the great commandments in the Scriptures, he didn't hesitate in the least. He told a young lawyer, "Love the Lord your God with all your heart and with all your soul and with all your mind . . . Love your neighbor as yourself" (Matthew 22:37,39). Loving God, loving others and finding value in ourselves. Without a doubt, these three aspects of love are the most effective weapons against the destructive power of low self-worth.

Genuine love is a gift we give others. It isn't purchased by their actions or contingent upon our emotions at the moment. It may carry with it strong emotional feelings, but it isn't supported by them. Rather, it is a decision we make on a daily basis that someone is special and valuable to us.

Like genuine love, honor is a gift we give to someone. It involves the decision we make *before* we put love into action that a person is of high value. In fact, love for someone often begins to flow once we have made the decision to honor him . . .

We give our children the gift of honor by . . .

· extending it first to our own parents.
· helping them find value in troubled times.
· recognizing our own parenting strengths and style.
· providing a healthy balance in our homes.
· establishing loving boundaries.
· building positive loyalties.
· offering honor to God.

Additional Scripture Readings:
Isaiah 43:1–7; Romans 12:9–13

Go to page 136 for your next devotional reading.

customs of the nations I am going to drive out before you. Because they did all these things, I abhorred them. **24**But I said to you, "You will possess their land; I will give it to you as an inheritance, a land flowing with milk and honey." I am the LORD your God, who has set you apart from the nations.

25" 'You must therefore make a distinction between clean and unclean animals and between unclean and clean birds. Do not defile yourselves by any animal or bird or anything that moves along the ground—those which I have set apart as unclean for you. **26**You are to be holy to me*a* because I, the LORD, am holy, and I have set you apart from the nations to be my own.

27" 'A man or woman who is a medium or spiritist among you must be put to death. You are to stone them; their blood will be on their own heads.' "

Rules for Priests

21 The LORD said to Moses, "Speak to the priests, the sons of Aaron, and say to them: 'A priest must not make himself ceremonially unclean for any of his people who die, **2**except for a close relative, such as his mother or father, his son or daughter, his brother, **3**or an unmarried sister who is dependent on him since she has no husband—for her he may make himself unclean. **4**He must not make himself unclean for people related to him by marriage,*b* and so defile himself.

5" 'Priests must not shave their heads or shave off the edges of their beards or cut their bodies. **6**They must be holy to their God and must not profane the name of their God. Because they present the offerings made to the LORD by fire, the food of their God, they are to be holy. **7**" 'They must not marry women defiled by prostitution or divorced from their husbands, because priests are holy to their God. **8**Regard them as holy, because they offer up the food of your God. Consider them holy, because I the LORD am holy—I who make you holy.*c*

9" 'If a priest's daughter defiles herself by becoming a prostitute, she disgraces her father; she must be burned in the fire.

10" 'The high priest, the one among his brothers who has had the anointing oil poured on his head and who has been ordained to wear the priestly garments, must not let his hair become unkempt*d* or tear his clothes. **11**He must not enter a place where there is a dead body. He must not make himself unclean, even for his father or mother, **12**nor leave the sanctuary of his God or desecrate it, because he has been dedicated by the anointing oil of his God. I am the LORD.

13" 'The woman he marries must be a virgin. **14**He must not marry a widow, a divorced woman, or a woman defiled by prostitution, but only a virgin from his own people, **15**so he will not defile his offspring among his people. I am the LORD, who makes him holy.*e* "

16The LORD said to Moses, **17**"Say to Aaron: 'For the generations to come none of your descendants who has a defect may come near to offer the food of his God. **18**No man who has any defect may come near: no man who is blind or lame, disfigured or deformed; **19**no man with a crippled foot or hand, **20**or who is hunchbacked or dwarfed, or who has any eye defect, or who has festering or running sores or damaged testicles. **21**No descendant of Aaron the priest who has any defect is to come near to present the offerings made to the LORD by fire. He has a defect; he must not come near to offer the food of his God. **22**He may eat the most holy food of his God, as well as the holy food; **23**yet because of his defect, he must not go near the curtain or approach the altar, and so desecrate my sanctuary. I am the LORD, who makes them holy.*f* "

24So Moses told this to Aaron and his sons and to all the Israelites.

22 The LORD said to Moses, **2**"Tell Aaron and his sons to treat with respect the sacred offerings the Israelites consecrate to me, so they will not profane my holy name. I am the LORD.

3"Say to them: 'For the generations to come, if any of your descendants is ceremonially unclean and yet comes near the sacred offerings that the Israelites consecrate to the LORD, that person must be cut off from my presence. I am the LORD.

4" 'If a descendant of Aaron has an infectious skin disease*g* or a bodily discharge, he may not eat the sacred offerings until he is cleansed. He will also be

---

a26 Or *be my holy ones*   *b4* Or *unclean as a leader among his people*   *c8* Or *who sanctify you;* or *who set you apart as holy*   *d10* Or *not uncover his head*   *e15* Or *who sanctifies him;* or *who sets him apart as holy*   *f23* Or *who sanctifies them;* or *who sets them apart as holy*   *g4* Traditionally *leprosy;* the Hebrew word was used for various diseases affecting the skin—not necessarily leprosy.

unclean if he touches something defiled by a corpse or by anyone who has an emission of semen, **5**or if he touches any crawling thing that makes him unclean, or any person who makes him unclean, whatever the uncleanness may be. **6**The one who touches any such thing will be unclean till evening. He must not eat any of the sacred offerings unless he has bathed himself with water. **7**When the sun goes down, he will be clean, and after that he may eat the sacred offerings, for they are his food. **8**He must not eat anything found dead or torn by wild animals, and so become unclean through it. I am the LORD.

9" 'The priests are to keep my requirements so that they do not become guilty and die for treating them with contempt. I am the LORD, who makes them holy.*a*

10" 'No one outside a priest's family may eat the sacred offering, nor may the guest of a priest or his hired worker eat it. **11**But if a priest buys a slave with money, or if a slave is born in his household, that slave may eat his food. **12**If a priest's daughter marries anyone other than a priest, she may not eat any of the sacred contributions. **13**But if a priest's daughter becomes a widow or is divorced, yet has no children, and she returns to live in her father's house as in her youth, she may eat of her father's food. No unauthorized person, however, may eat any of it.

14" 'If anyone eats a sacred offering by mistake, he must make restitution to the priest for the offering and add a fifth of the value to it. **15**The priests must not desecrate the sacred offerings the Israelites present to the LORD **16**by allowing them to eat the sacred offerings and so bring upon them guilt requiring payment. I am the LORD, who makes them holy.' "

Unacceptable Sacrifices

17The LORD said to Moses, **18**"Speak to Aaron and his sons and to all the Israelites and say to them: 'If any of you — either an Israelite or an alien living in Israel — presents a gift for a burnt offering to the LORD, either to fulfill a vow or as a freewill offering, **19**you must present a male without defect from the cattle, sheep or goats in order that it may be accepted on your behalf. **20**Do not bring anything with a de-

fect, because it will not be accepted on your behalf. **21**When anyone brings from the herd or flock a fellowship offering*b* to the LORD to fulfill a special vow or as a freewill offering, it must be without defect or blemish to be acceptable. **22**Do not offer to the LORD the blind, the injured or the maimed, or anything with warts or festering or running sores. Do not place any of these on the altar as an offering made to the LORD by fire. **23**You may, however, present as a freewill offering an ox*c* or a sheep that is deformed or stunted, but it will not be accepted in fulfillment of a vow. **24**You must not offer to the LORD an animal whose testicles are bruised, crushed, torn or cut. You must not do this in your own land, **25**and you must not accept such animals from the hand of a foreigner and offer them as the food of your God. They will not be accepted on your behalf, because they are deformed and have defects.' "

26The LORD said to Moses, **27**"When a calf, a lamb or a goat is born, it is to remain with its mother for seven days. From the eighth day on, it will be acceptable as an offering made to the LORD by fire. **28**Do not slaughter a cow or a sheep and its young on the same day.

29"When you sacrifice a thank offering to the LORD, sacrifice it in such a way that it will be accepted on your behalf. **30**It must be eaten that same day; leave none of it till morning. I am the LORD.

31"Keep my commands and follow them. I am the LORD. **32**Do not profane my holy name. I must be acknowledged as holy by the Israelites. I am the LORD, who makes*d* you holy*e* **33**and who brought you out of Egypt to be your God. I am the LORD."

23 The LORD said to Moses, **2**"Speak to the Israelites and say to them: 'These are my appointed feasts, the appointed feasts of the LORD, which you are to proclaim as sacred assemblies.

The Sabbath

3" 'There are six days when you may work, but the seventh day is a Sabbath of rest, a day of sacred assembly. You are not to do any work; wherever you live, it is a Sabbath to the LORD.

---

a9 Or *who sanctifies them*; or *who sets them apart as holy*; also in verse 16   *b21* Traditionally *peace offering*   *c23* The Hebrew word can include both male and female.   *d32* Or *made*   *e32* Or *who sanctifies you*; or *who sets you apart as holy*

The Passover and Unleavened Bread

4" 'These are the LORD's appointed feasts, the sacred assemblies you are to proclaim at their appointed times: 5The LORD's Passover begins at twilight on the fourteenth day of the first month. 6On the fifteenth day of that month the LORD's Feast of Unleavened Bread begins; for seven days you must eat bread made without yeast. 7On the first day hold a sacred assembly and do no regular work. 8For seven days present an offering made to the LORD by fire. And on the seventh day hold a sacred assembly and do no regular work.' "

Firstfruits

9The LORD said to Moses, 10"Speak to the Israelites and say to them: 'When you enter the land I am going to give you and you reap its harvest, bring to the priest a sheaf of the first grain you harvest. 11He is to wave the sheaf before the LORD so it will be accepted on your behalf; the priest is to wave it on the day after the Sabbath. 12On the day you wave the sheaf, you must sacrifice as a burnt offering to the LORD a lamb a year old without defect, 13together with its grain offering of two-tenths of an ephah[a] of fine flour mixed with oil—an offering made to the LORD by fire, a pleasing aroma—and its drink offering of a quarter of a hin[b] of wine. 14You must not eat any bread, or roasted or new grain, until the very day you bring this offering to your God. This is to be a lasting ordinance for the generations to come, wherever you live.

Feast of Weeks

15" 'From the day after the Sabbath, the day you brought the sheaf of the wave offering, count off seven full weeks. 16Count off fifty days up to the day after the seventh Sabbath, and then present an offering of new grain to the LORD. 17From wherever you live, bring two loaves made of two-tenths of an ephah of fine flour, baked with yeast, as a wave offering of firstfruits to the LORD. 18Present with this bread seven male lambs, each a year old and without defect, one young bull and two rams. They will be a burnt offering to the LORD, together with their grain offerings and drink offerings—an offering made by fire, an aroma pleasing to the LORD. 19Then sacrifice one male goat for a sin offering and two lambs, each a year old, for a fellowship offering.[c] 20The priest is to wave the two lambs before the LORD as a wave offering, together with the bread of the firstfruits. They are a sacred offering to the LORD for the priest. 21On that same day you are to proclaim a sacred assembly and do no regular work. This is to be a lasting ordinance for the generations to come, wherever you live.

22" 'When you reap the harvest of your land, do not reap to the very edges of your field or gather the gleanings of your harvest. Leave them for the poor and the alien. I am the LORD your God.' "

Feast of Trumpets

23The LORD said to Moses, 24"Say to the Israelites: 'On the first day of the seventh month you are to have a day of rest, a sacred assembly commemorated with trumpet blasts. 25Do no regular work, but present an offering made to the LORD by fire.' "

Day of Atonement

26The LORD said to Moses, 27"The tenth day of this seventh month is the Day of Atonement. Hold a sacred assembly and deny yourselves,[d] and present an offering made to the LORD by fire. 28Do no work on that day, because it is the Day of Atonement, when atonement is made for you before the LORD your God. 29Anyone who does not deny himself on that day must be cut off from his people. 30I will destroy from among his people anyone who does any work on that day. 31You shall do no work at all. This is to be a lasting ordinance for the generations to come, wherever you live. 32It is a sabbath of rest for you, and you must deny yourselves. From the evening of the ninth day of the month until the following evening you are to observe your sabbath."

Feast of Tabernacles

33The LORD said to Moses, 34"Say to the Israelites: 'On the fifteenth day of the seventh month the LORD's Feast of Tabernacles begins, and it lasts for seven days. 35The first day is a sacred assembly; do no regular work. 36For seven days present offerings made to the LORD by fire, and on the eighth day hold a sacred assembly and present an offering made to the LORD by

---

a13 That is, probably about 4 quarts (about 4.5 liters); also in verse 17   b13 That is, probably about 1 quart (about 1 liter)   c19 Traditionally *peace offering*   d27 Or *and fast*; also in verses 29 and 32 fire. It is the closing assembly; do no regular work.

³⁷(" 'These are the LORD's appointed feasts, which you are to proclaim as sacred assemblies for bringing offerings made to the LORD by fire — the burnt offerings and grain offerings, sacrifices and drink offerings required for each day. ³⁸These offerings are in addition to those for the LORD's Sabbaths and*a* in addition to your gifts and whatever you have vowed and all the freewill offerings you give to the LORD.)

³⁹" 'So beginning with the fifteenth day of the seventh month, after you have gathered the crops of the land, celebrate the festival to the LORD for seven days; the first day is a day of rest, and the eighth day also is a day of rest. ⁴⁰On the first day you are to take choice fruit from the trees, and palm fronds, leafy branches and poplars, and rejoice before the LORD your God for seven days. ⁴¹Celebrate this as a festival to the LORD for seven days each year. This is to be a lasting ordinance for the generations to come; celebrate it in the seventh month. ⁴²Live in booths for seven days: All native-born Israelites are to live in booths ⁴³so your descendants will know that I had the Israelites live in booths when I brought them out of Egypt. I am the LORD your God.' "

⁴⁴So Moses announced to the Israelites the appointed feasts of the LORD.

Oil and Bread Set Before the LORD

24 The LORD said to Moses, ²"Command the Israelites to bring you clear oil of pressed olives for the light so that the lamps may be kept burning continually. ³Outside the curtain of the Testimony in the Tent of Meeting, Aaron is to tend the lamps before the LORD from evening till morning, continually. This is to be a lasting ordinance for the generations to come. ⁴The lamps on the pure gold lampstand before the LORD must be tended continually.

⁵"Take fine flour and bake twelve loaves of bread, using two-tenths of an ephah*b* for each loaf. ⁶Set them in two rows, six in each row, on the table of pure gold before the LORD. ⁷Along each row put some pure incense as a memorial portion to represent the bread and to be an offering made to the LORD by fire. ⁸This bread is to be set out before the LORD regularly, Sabbath after Sabbath, on behalf of the Israelites, as a lasting covenant. ⁹It belongs to Aaron and his sons, who are to eat it in a holy place, because it is a most holy part of their regular share of the offerings made to the LORD by fire."

A Blasphemer Stoned

¹⁰Now the son of an Israelite mother and an Egyptian father went out among the Israelites, and a fight broke out in the camp between him and an Israelite. ¹¹The son of the Israelite woman blasphemed the Name with a curse; so they brought him to Moses. (His mother's name was Shelomith, the daughter of Dibri the Danite.) ¹²They put him in custody until the will of the LORD should be made clear to them.

¹³Then the LORD said to Moses: ¹⁴"Take the blasphemer outside the camp. All those who heard him are to lay their hands on his head, and the entire assembly is to stone him. ¹⁵Say to the Israelites: 'If anyone curses his God, he will be held responsible; ¹⁶anyone who blasphemes the name of the LORD must be put to death. The entire assembly must stone him. Whether an alien or native-born, when he blasphemes the Name, he must be put to death.

¹⁷" 'If anyone takes the life of a human being, he must be put to death. ¹⁸Anyone who takes the life of someone's animal must make restitution — life for life. ¹⁹If anyone injures his neighbor, whatever he has done must be done to him: ²⁰fracture for fracture, eye for eye, tooth for tooth. As he has injured the other, so he is to be injured. ²¹Whoever kills an animal must make restitution, but whoever kills a man must be put to death. ²²You are to have the same law for the alien and the native-born. I am the LORD your God.' "

²³Then Moses spoke to the Israelites, and they took the blasphemer outside the camp and stoned him. The Israelites did as the LORD commanded Moses.

The Sabbath Year

25 The LORD said to Moses on Mount Sinai, ²"Speak to the Israelites and say to them: 'When you enter the land I am going to give you, the land itself must observe a sabbath to the LORD. ³For six years sow your fields, and for six years prune your vineyards and gather their

---

*a*38 Or *These feasts are in addition to the LORD's Sabbaths, and these offerings are*   *b*5 That is, probably about 4 quarts (about 4.5 liters) crops. **4**But in the seventh year the land is to have a sabbath of rest, a sabbath to the LORD. Do not sow your fields or prune your vineyards. **5**Do not reap what grows of itself or harvest the grapes of your untended vines. The land is to have a year of rest. **6**Whatever the land yields during the sabbath year will be food for you — for yourself, your manservant and maidservant, and the hired worker and temporary resident who live among you, **7**as well as for your livestock and the wild animals in your land. Whatever the land produces may be eaten.

The Year of Jubilee

8" 'Count off seven sabbaths of years — seven times seven years — so that the seven sabbaths of years amount to a period of forty-nine years. **9**Then have the trumpet sounded everywhere on the tenth day of the seventh month; on the Day of Atonement sound the trumpet throughout your land. **10**Consecrate the fiftieth year and proclaim liberty throughout the land to all its inhabitants. It shall be a jubilee for you; each one of you is to return to his family property and each to his own clan. **11**The fiftieth year shall be a jubilee for you; do not sow and do not reap what grows of itself or harvest the untended vines. **12**For it is a jubilee and is to be holy for you; eat only what is taken directly from the fields.

13" 'In this Year of Jubilee everyone is to return to his own property.

14" 'If you sell land to one of your countrymen or buy any from him, do not take advantage of each other. **15**You are to buy from your countryman on the basis of the number of years since the Jubilee. And he is to sell to you on the basis of the number of years left for harvesting crops. **16**When the years are many, you are to increase the price, and when the years are few, you are to decrease the price, because what he is really selling you is the number of crops. **17**Do not take advantage of each other, but fear your God. I am the LORD your God.

18" 'Follow my decrees and be careful to obey my laws, and you will live safely in the land. **19**Then the land will yield its fruit, and you will eat your fill and live there in safety. **20**You may ask, "What will we eat in the seventh year if we do not plant or harvest our crops?" **21**I will send you such a blessing in the sixth year that the land will yield enough for three years.

22While you plant during the eighth year, you will eat from the old crop and will continue to eat from it until the harvest of the ninth year comes in.

23" 'The land must not be sold permanently, because the land is mine and you are but aliens and my tenants. **24**Throughout the country that you hold as a possession, you must provide for the redemption of the land.

25" 'If one of your countrymen becomes poor and sells some of his property, his nearest relative is to come and redeem what his countryman has sold. **26**If, however, a man has no one to redeem it for him but he himself prospers and acquires sufficient means to redeem it, **27**he is to determine the value for the years since he sold it and refund the balance to the man to whom he sold it; he can then go back to his own property. **28**But if he does not acquire the means to repay him, what he sold will remain in the possession of the buyer until the Year of Jubilee. It will be returned in the Jubilee, and he can then go back to his property.

29" 'If a man sells a house in a walled city, he retains the right of redemption a full year after its sale. During that time he may redeem it. **30**If it is not redeemed before a full year has passed, the house in the walled city shall belong permanently to the buyer and his descendants. It is not to be returned in the Jubilee. **31**But houses in villages without walls around them are to be considered as open country. They can be redeemed, and they are to be returned in the Jubilee.

32" 'The Levites always have the right to redeem their houses in the Levitical towns, which they possess. **33**So the property of the Levites is redeemable — that is, a house sold in any town they hold — and is to be returned in the Jubilee, because the houses in the towns of the Levites are their property among the Israelites. **34**But the pastureland belonging to their towns must not be sold; it is their permanent possession.

35" 'If one of your countrymen becomes poor and is unable to support himself among you, help him as you would an alien or a temporary resident, so he can continue to live among you. **36**Do not take interest of any kind[a] from him, but fear your God, so that your countryman may continue to live among you. **37**You must not lend him money at interest or sell him

---

[a] 36 Or *take excessive interest*; similarly in verse 37

food at a profit. **38**I am the LORD your God, who brought you out of Egypt to give you the land of Canaan and to be your God.

39" 'If one of your countrymen becomes poor among you and sells himself to you, do not make him work as a slave. **40**He is to be treated as a hired worker or a temporary resident among you; he is to work for you until the Year of Jubilee. **41**Then he and his children are to be released, and he will go back to his own clan and to the property of his forefathers. **42**Because the Israelites are my servants, whom I brought out of Egypt, they must not be sold as slaves. **43**Do not rule over them ruthlessly, but fear your God.

44" 'Your male and female slaves are to come from the nations around you; from them you may buy slaves. **45**You may also buy some of the temporary residents living among you and members of their clans born in your country, and they will become your property. **46**You can will them to your children as inherited property and can make them slaves for life, but you must not rule over your fellow Israelites ruthlessly.

47" 'If an alien or a temporary resident among you becomes rich and one of your countrymen becomes poor and sells himself to the alien living among you or to a member of the alien's clan, **48**he retains the right of redemption after he has sold himself. One of his relatives may redeem him: **49**An uncle or a cousin or any blood relative in his clan may redeem him. Or if he prospers, he may redeem himself. **50**He and his buyer are to count the time from the year he sold himself up to the Year of Jubilee. The price for his release is to be based on the rate paid to a hired man for that number of years. **51**If many years remain, he must pay for his redemption a larger share of the price paid for him. **52**If only a few years remain until the Year of Jubilee, he is to compute that and pay for his redemption accordingly. **53**He is to be treated as a man hired from year to year; you must see to it that his owner does not rule over him ruthlessly.

54" 'Even if he is not redeemed in any of these ways, he and his children are to be released in the Year of Jubilee, **55**for the Israelites belong to me as servants. They are my servants, whom I brought out of Egypt. I am the LORD your God.

Reward for Obedience

26 " 'Do not make idols or set up an image or a sacred stone for yourselves, and do not place a carved stone in your land to bow down before it. I am the LORD your God.

2" 'Observe my Sabbaths and have reverence for my sanctuary. I am the LORD.

3" 'If you follow my decrees and are careful to obey my commands, **4**I will send you rain in its season, and the ground will yield its crops and the trees of the field their fruit. **5**Your threshing will continue until grape harvest and the grape harvest will continue until planting, and you will eat all the food you want and live in safety in your land.

6" 'I will grant peace in the land, and you will lie down and no one will make you afraid. I will remove savage beasts from the land, and the sword will not pass through your country. **7**You will pursue your enemies, and they will fall by the sword before you. **8**Five of you will chase a hundred, and a hundred of you will chase ten thousand, and your enemies will fall by the sword before you.

9" 'I will look on you with favor and make you fruitful and increase your numbers, and I will keep my covenant with you. **10**You will still be eating last year's harvest when you will have to move it out to make room for the new. **11**I will put my dwelling place*a* among you, and I will not abhor you. **12**I will walk among you and be your God, and you will be my people. **13**I am the LORD your God, who brought you out of Egypt so that you would no longer be slaves to the Egyptians; I broke the bars of your yoke and enabled you to walk with heads held high.

Punishment for Disobedience

14" 'But if you will not listen to me and carry out all these commands, **15**and if you reject my decrees and abhor my laws and fail to carry out all my commands and so violate my covenant, **16**then I will do this to you: I will bring upon you sudden terror, wasting diseases and fever that will destroy your sight and drain away your life. You will plant seed in vain, because your enemies will eat it. **17**I will set my face against you so that you will be defeated by your enemies; those who hate you will rule over you, and you will flee even when no one is pursuing you.

a11 Or my tabernacle

18" 'If after all this you will not listen to me, I will punish you for your sins seven times over. **19**I will break down your stubborn pride and make the sky above you like iron and the ground beneath you like bronze. **20**Your strength will be spent in vain, because your soil will not yield its crops, nor will the trees of the land yield their fruit.

21" 'If you remain hostile toward me and refuse to listen to me, I will multiply your afflictions seven times over, as your sins deserve. **22**I will send wild animals against you, and they will rob you of your children, destroy your cattle and make you so few in number that your roads will be deserted.

23" 'If in spite of these things you do not accept my correction but continue to be hostile toward me, **24**I myself will be hostile toward you and will afflict you for your sins seven times over. **25**And I will bring the sword upon you to avenge the breaking of the covenant. When you withdraw into your cities, I will send a plague among you, and you will be given into enemy hands. **26**When I cut off your supply of bread, ten women will be able to bake your bread in one oven, and they will dole out the bread by weight. You will eat, but you will not be satisfied.

27" 'If in spite of this you still do not listen to me but continue to be hostile toward me, **28**then in my anger I will be hostile toward you, and I myself will punish you for your sins seven times over. **29**You will eat the flesh of your sons and the flesh of your daughters. **30**I will destroy your high places, cut down your incense altars and pile your dead bodies on the lifeless forms of your idols, and I will abhor you. **31**I will turn your cities into ruins and lay waste your sanctuaries, and I will take no delight in the pleasing aroma of your offerings. **32**I will lay waste the land, so that your enemies who live there will be appalled. **33**I will scatter you among the nations and will draw out my sword and pursue you. Your land will be laid waste, and your cities will lie in ruins. **34**Then the land will enjoy its sabbath years all the time that it lies desolate and you are in the country of your enemies; then the land will rest and enjoy its sabbaths. **35**All the time that it lies desolate, the land will have the rest it did not have during the sabbaths you lived in it.

36" 'As for those of you who are left, I will make their hearts so fearful in the lands of their enemies that the sound of a windblown leaf will put them to flight. They will run as though fleeing from the sword, and they will fall, even though no one is pursuing them. **37**They will stumble over one another as though fleeing from the sword, even though no one is pursuing them. So you will not be able to stand before your enemies. **38**You will perish among the nations; the land of your enemies will devour you. **39**Those of you who are left will waste away in the lands of their enemies because of their sins; also because of their fathers' sins they will waste away.

40" 'But if they will confess their sins and the sins of their fathers—their treachery against me and their hostility toward me, **41**which made me hostile toward them so that I sent them into the land of their enemies—then when their uncircumcised hearts are humbled and they pay for their sin, **42**I will remember my covenant with Jacob and my covenant with Isaac and my covenant with Abraham, and I will remember the land. **43**For the land will be deserted by them and will enjoy its sabbaths while it lies desolate without them. They will pay for their sins because they rejected my laws and abhorred my decrees. **44**Yet in spite of this, when they are in the land of their enemies, I will not reject them or abhor them so as to destroy them completely, breaking my covenant with them. I am the Lord their God. **45**But for their sake I will remember the covenant with their ancestors whom I brought out of Egypt in the sight of the nations to be their God. I am the Lord.' "

46These are the decrees, the laws and the regulations that the Lord established on Mount Sinai between himself and the Israelites through Moses.

Redeeming What Is the Lord's

27 The Lord said to Moses, **2**"Speak to the Israelites and say to them: 'If anyone makes a special vow to dedicate persons to the Lord by giving equivalent values, **3**set the value of a male between the ages of twenty and sixty at fifty shekels*a* of silver, according to the sanctuary shekel*b*; **4**and if it is a female, set her value at thirty shekels.*c* **5**If it is a person be-

---

a3 That is, about 1 1/4 pounds (about 0.6 kilogram); also in verse 16   *b3* That is, about 2/5 ounce (about 11.5 grams); also in verse 25   *c4* That is, about 12 ounces (about 0.3 kilogram) tween the ages of five and twenty, set the value of a male at twenty shekels[a] and of a female at ten shekels.[b] [6]If it is a person between one month and five years, set the value of a male at five shekels[c] of silver and that of a female at three shekels[d] of silver. [7]If it is a person sixty years old or more, set the value of a male at fifteen shekels[e] and of a female at ten shekels. [8]If anyone making the vow is too poor to pay the specified amount, he is to present the person to the priest, who will set the value for him according to what the man making the vow can afford.

[9]" 'If what he vowed is an animal that is acceptable as an offering to the LORD, such an animal given to the LORD becomes holy. [10]He must not exchange it or substitute a good one for a bad one, or a bad one for a good one; if he should substitute one animal for another, both it and the substitute become holy. [11]If what he vowed is a ceremonially unclean animal—one that is not acceptable as an offering to the LORD—the animal must be presented to the priest, [12]who will judge its quality as good or bad. Whatever value the priest then sets, that is what it will be. [13]If the owner wishes to redeem the animal, he must add a fifth to its value.

[14]" 'If a man dedicates his house as something holy to the LORD, the priest will judge its quality as good or bad. Whatever value the priest then sets, so it will remain. [15]If the man who dedicates his house redeems it, he must add a fifth to its value, and the house will again become his.

[16]" 'If a man dedicates to the LORD part of his family land, its value is to be set according to the amount of seed required for it—fifty shekels of silver to a homer[f] of barley seed. [17]If he dedicates his field during the Year of Jubilee, the value that has been set remains. [18]But if he dedicates his field after the Jubilee, the priest will determine the value according to the number of years that remain until the next Year of Jubilee, and its set value will be reduced. [19]If the man who dedicates the field wishes to redeem it, he must add a fifth to its value,

and the field will again become his. [20]If, however, he does not redeem the field, or if he has sold it to someone else, it can never be redeemed. [21]When the field is released in the Jubilee, it will become holy, like a field devoted to the LORD; it will become the property of the priests.[g]

[22]" 'If a man dedicates to the LORD a field he has bought, which is not part of his family land, [23]the priest will determine its value up to the Year of Jubilee, and the man must pay its value on that day as something holy to the LORD. [24]In the Year of Jubilee the field will revert to the person from whom he bought it, the one whose land it was. [25]Every value is to be set according to the sanctuary shekel, twenty gerahs to the shekel.

[26]" 'No one, however, may dedicate the firstborn of an animal, since the firstborn already belongs to the LORD; whether an ox[h] or a sheep, it is the LORD's. [27]If it is one of the unclean animals, he may buy it back at its set value, adding a fifth of the value to it. If he does not redeem it, it is to be sold at its set value.

[28]" 'But nothing that a man owns and devotes[i] to the LORD—whether man or animal or family land—may be sold or redeemed; everything so devoted is most holy to the LORD.

[29]" 'No person devoted to destruction[j] may be ransomed; he must be put to death.

[30]" 'A tithe of everything from the land, whether grain from the soil or fruit from the trees, belongs to the LORD; it is holy to the LORD. [31]If a man redeems any of his tithe, he must add a fifth of the value to it. [32]The entire tithe of the herd and flock—every tenth animal that passes under the shepherd's rod—will be holy to the LORD. [33]He must not pick out the good from the bad or make any substitution. If he does make a substitution, both the animal and its substitute become holy and cannot be redeemed.' "

[34]These are the commands the LORD gave Moses on Mount Sinai for the Israelites.

---

[a]5 That is, about 8 ounces (about 0.2 kilogram)   [b]5 That is, about 4 ounces (about 110 grams); also in verse 7   [c]6 That is, about 2 ounces (about 55 grams)   [d]6 That is, about 1 1/4 ounces (about 35 grams)   [e]7 That is, about 6 ounces (about 170 grams)   [f]16 That is, probably about 6 bushels (about 220 liters)   [g]21 Or priest   [h]26 The Hebrew word can include both male and female.   [i]28 The Hebrew term refers to the irrevocable giving over of things or persons to the LORD.   [j]29 The Hebrew term refers to the irrevocable giving over of things or persons to the LORD, often by totally destroying them.

MOSES records in this book the number of the Israelites and how he organizes them around the tabernacle. To this he adds an account of what happens as they wander in the wilderness. Note especially that in spite of their numerous rebellions, God still loves them and watches over them. As you read this book, rejoice in God's love and care in your life in spite of your sins; promise God that you will do your best to trust and obey him.

NUMBERS

The Census

1 The LORD spoke to Moses in the Tent of Meeting in the Desert of Sinai on the first day of the second month of the second year after the Israelites came out of Egypt. He said: ²"Take a census of the whole Israelite community by their clans and families, listing every man by name, one by one. ³You and Aaron are to number by their divisions all the men in Israel twenty years old or more who are able to serve in the army. ⁴One man from each tribe, each the head of his family, is to help you. ⁵These are the names of the men who are to assist you:

from Reuben, Elizur son of Shedeur;

⁶from Simeon, Shelumiel son of Zuri-shaddai;
⁷from Judah, Nahshon son of Amminadab;
⁸from Issachar, Nethanel son of Zuar;
⁹from Zebulun, Eliab son of Helon;
¹⁰from the sons of Joseph:
  from Ephraim, Elishama son of Ammihud;
  from Manasseh, Gamaliel son of Pedahzur;
¹¹from Benjamin, Abidan son of Gideoni;
¹²from Dan, Ahiezer son of Ammishaddai;
¹³from Asher, Pagiel son of Ocran;
¹⁴from Gad, Eliasaph son of Deuel;

15from Naphtali, Ahira son of Enan."

16These were the men appointed from the community, the leaders of their ancestral tribes. They were the heads of the clans of Israel.

17Moses and Aaron took these men whose names had been given, 18and they called the whole community together on the first day of the second month. The people indicated their ancestry by their clans and families, and the men twenty years old or more were listed by name, one by one, 19as the LORD commanded Moses. And so he counted them in the Desert of Sinai:

20From the descendants of Reuben the firstborn son of Israel:

All the men twenty years old or more who were able to serve in the army were listed by name, one by one, according to the records of their clans and families. 21The number from the tribe of Reuben was 46,500.

22From the descendants of Simeon:

All the men twenty years old or more who were able to serve in the army were counted and listed by name, one by one, according to the records of their clans and families. 23The number from the tribe of Simeon was 59,300.

24From the descendants of Gad:

All the men twenty years old or more who were able to serve in the army were listed by name, according to the records of their clans and families. 25The number from the tribe of Gad was 45,650.

26From the descendants of Judah:

All the men twenty years old or more who were able to serve in the army were listed by name, according to the records of their clans and families. 27The number from the tribe of Judah was 74,600.

28From the descendants of Issachar:

All the men twenty years old or more who were able to serve in the army were listed by name, according to the records of their clans and families. 29The number from the tribe of Issachar was 54,400.

30From the descendants of Zebulun:

All the men twenty years old or more who were able to serve in the army were listed by name, according to the records of their clans and families. 31The number from the tribe of Zebulun was 57,400.

32From the sons of Joseph:

From the descendants of Ephraim:

All the men twenty years old or more who were able to serve in the army were listed by name, according to the records of their clans and families. 33The number from the tribe of Ephraim was 40,500.

34From the descendants of Manasseh:

All the men twenty years old or more who were able to serve in the army were listed by name, according to the records of their clans and families. 35The number from the tribe of Manasseh was 32,200.

36From the descendants of Benjamin:

All the men twenty years old or more who were able to serve in the army were listed by name, according to the records of their clans and families. 37The number from the tribe of Benjamin was 35,400.

38From the descendants of Dan:

All the men twenty years old or more who were able to serve in the army were listed by name, according to the records of their clans and families. 39The number from the tribe of Dan was 62,700.

40From the descendants of Asher:

All the men twenty years old or more who were able to serve in the army were listed by name, according to the records of their clans and families. 41The number from the tribe of Asher was 41,500.

42From the descendants of Naphtali:

All the men twenty years old or more who were able to serve in the army were listed by name, according to the records of their clans and families. 43The number from the tribe of Naphtali was 53,400.

44These were the men counted by Moses and Aaron and the twelve leaders of

Israel, each one representing his family. ⁴⁵All the Israelites twenty years old or more who were able to serve in Israel's army were counted according to their families. ⁴⁶The total number was 603,550.

⁴⁷The families of the tribe of Levi, however, were not counted along with the others. ⁴⁸The LORD had said to Moses: ⁴⁹"You must not count the tribe of Levi or include them in the census of the other Israelites. ⁵⁰Instead, appoint the Levites to be in charge of the tabernacle of the Testimony — over all its furnishings and everything belonging to it. They are to carry the tabernacle and all its furnishings; they are to take care of it and encamp around it. ⁵¹Whenever the tabernacle is to move, the Levites are to take it down, and whenever the tabernacle is to be set up, the Levites shall do it. Anyone else who goes near it shall be put to death. ⁵²The Israelites are to set up their tents by divisions, each man in his own camp under his own standard. ⁵³The Levites, however, are to set up their tents around the tabernacle of the Testimony so that wrath will not fall on the Israelite community. The Levites are to be responsible for the care of the tabernacle of the Testimony."

⁵⁴The Israelites did all this just as the LORD commanded Moses.

The Arrangement of the Tribal Camps

2 The LORD said to Moses and Aaron: ²"The Israelites are to camp around the Tent of Meeting some distance from it, each man under his standard with the banners of his family."

³On the east, toward the sunrise, the divisions of the camp of Judah are to encamp under their standard. The leader of the people of Judah is Nahshon son of Amminadab. ⁴His division numbers 74,600.

⁵The tribe of Issachar will camp next to them. The leader of the people of Issachar is Nethanel son of Zuar. ⁶His division numbers 54,400.

⁷The tribe of Zebulun will be next. The leader of the people of Zebulun is Eliab son of Helon. ⁸His division numbers 57,400.

⁹All the men assigned to the camp of Judah, according to their divisions, number 186,400. They will set out first.

¹⁰On the south will be the divisions of the camp of Reuben under their standard. The leader of the people of Reuben is Elizur son of Shedeur. ¹¹His division numbers 46,500.

¹²The tribe of Simeon will camp next to them. The leader of the people of Simeon is Shelumiel son of Zurishaddai. ¹³His division numbers 59,300.

¹⁴The tribe of Gad will be next. The leader of the people of Gad is Eliasaph son of Deuel.^a ¹⁵His division numbers 45,650.

¹⁶All the men assigned to the camp of Reuben, according to their divisions, number 151,450. They will set out second.

¹⁷Then the Tent of Meeting and the camp of the Levites will set out in the middle of the camps. They will set out in the same order as they encamp, each in his own place under his standard.

¹⁸On the west will be the divisions of the camp of Ephraim under their standard. The leader of the people of Ephraim is Elishama son of Ammihud. ¹⁹His division numbers 40,500.

²⁰The tribe of Manasseh will be next to them. The leader of the people of Manasseh is Gamaliel son of Pedahzur. ²¹His division numbers 32,200.

²²The tribe of Benjamin will be next. The leader of the people of Benjamin is Abidan son of Gideoni. ²³His division numbers 35,400.

²⁴All the men assigned to the camp of Ephraim, according to their divisions, number 108,100. They will set out third.

²⁵On the north will be the divisions of the camp of Dan, under their standard. The leader of the people of Dan is Ahiezer son of Ammishaddai. ²⁶His division numbers 62,700.

²⁷The tribe of Asher will camp next to them. The leader of the people of Asher is Pagiel son of Ocran. ²⁸His division numbers 41,500.

²⁹The tribe of Naphtali will be next. The leader of the people of Naphtali

^a14 Many manuscripts of the Masoretic Text, Samaritan Pentateuch and Vulgate (see also Num. 1:14); most manuscripts of the Masoretic Text *Reuel*

is Ahira son of Enan. [30]His division numbers 53,400.

[31]All the men assigned to the camp of Dan number 157,600. They will set out last, under their standards.

[32]These are the Israelites, counted according to their families. All those in the camps, by their divisions, number 603,550. [33]The Levites, however, were not counted along with the other Israelites, as the LORD commanded Moses.

[34]So the Israelites did everything the LORD commanded Moses; that is the way they encamped under their standards, and that is the way they set out, each with his clan and family.

The Levites

3 This is the account of the family of Aaron and Moses at the time the LORD talked with Moses on Mount Sinai.

[2]The names of the sons of Aaron were Nadab the firstborn and Abihu, Eleazar and Ithamar. [3]Those were the names of Aaron's sons, the anointed priests, who were ordained to serve as priests. [4]Nadab and Abihu, however, fell dead before the LORD when they made an offering with unauthorized fire before him in the Desert of Sinai. They had no sons; so only Eleazar and Ithamar served as priests during the lifetime of their father Aaron.

[5]The LORD said to Moses, [6]"Bring the tribe of Levi and present them to Aaron the priest to assist him. [7]They are to perform duties for him and for the whole community at the Tent of Meeting by doing the work of the tabernacle. [8]They are to take care of all the furnishings of the Tent of Meeting, fulfilling the obligations of the Israelites by doing the work of the tabernacle. [9]Give the Levites to Aaron and his sons; they are the Israelites who are to be given wholly to him.[a] [10]Appoint Aaron and his sons to serve as priests; anyone else who approaches the sanctuary must be put to death."

[11]The LORD also said to Moses, [12]"I have taken the Levites from among the Israelites in place of the first male offspring of every Israelite woman. The Levites are mine, [13]for all the firstborn are mine. When I struck down all the firstborn in Egypt, I set apart for myself every first-

born in Israel, whether man or animal. They are to be mine. I am the LORD."

[14]The LORD said to Moses in the Desert of Sinai, [15]"Count the Levites by their families and clans. Count every male a month old or more." [16]So Moses counted them, as he was commanded by the word of the LORD.

[17]These were the names of the sons of Levi:

Gershon, Kohath and Merari.

[18]These were the names of the Gershonite clans:

Libni and Shimei.

[19]The Kohathite clans:

Amram, Izhar, Hebron and Uzziel.

[20]The Merarite clans:

Mahli and Mushi.

These were the Levite clans, according to their families.

[21]To Gershon belonged the clans of the Libnites and Shimeites; these were the Gershonite clans. [22]The number of all the males a month old or more who were counted was 7,500. [23]The Gershonite clans were to camp on the west, behind the tabernacle. [24]The leader of the families of the Gershonites was Eliasaph son of Lael. [25]At the Tent of Meeting the Gershonites were responsible for the care of the tabernacle and tent, its coverings, the curtain at the entrance to the Tent of Meeting, [26]the curtains of the courtyard, the curtain at the entrance to the courtyard surrounding the tabernacle and altar, and the ropes — and everything related to their use.

[27]To Kohath belonged the clans of the Amramites, Izharites, Hebronites and Uzzielites; these were the Kohathite clans. [28]The number of all the males a month old or more was 8,600.[b] The Kohathites were responsible for the care of the sanctuary. [29]The Kohathite clans were to camp on the south side of the tabernacle. [30]The leader of the families of the Kohathite clans was Elizaphan son of Uzziel. [31]They were responsible for the care of the ark, the table, the lampstand, the altars, the articles of the sanctuary used in ministering, the curtain, and everything related to their use. [32]The chief leader of the Levites was Eleazar son of Aaron, the priest. He was appointed over those who were responsible for the care of the sanctuary.

---

[a]9 Most manuscripts of the Masoretic Text; some manuscripts of the Masoretic Text, Samaritan Pentateuch and Septuagint (see also Num. 8:16) *to me*   [b]28 Hebrew; some Septuagint manuscripts *8,300*

[33]To Merari belonged the clans of the Mahlites and the Mushites; these were the Merarite clans. [34]The number of all the males a month old or more who were counted was 6,200. [35]The leader of the families of the Merarite clans was Zuriel son of Abihail; they were to camp on the north side of the tabernacle. [36]The Merarites were appointed to take care of the frames of the tabernacle, its crossbars, posts, bases, all its equipment, and everything related to their use, [37]as well as the posts of the surrounding courtyard with their bases, tent pegs and ropes.

[38]Moses and Aaron and his sons were to camp to the east of the tabernacle, toward the sunrise, in front of the Tent of Meeting. They were responsible for the care of the sanctuary on behalf of the Israelites. Anyone else who approached the sanctuary was to be put to death.

[39]The total number of Levites counted at the LORD's command by Moses and Aaron according to their clans, including every male a month old or more, was 22,000.

[40]The LORD said to Moses, "Count all the firstborn Israelite males who are a month old or more and make a list of their names. [41]Take the Levites for me in place of all the firstborn of the Israelites, and the livestock of the Levites in place of all the firstborn of the livestock of the Israelites. I am the LORD."

[42]So Moses counted all the firstborn of the Israelites, as the LORD commanded him. [43]The total number of firstborn males a month old or more, listed by name, was 22,273.

[44]The LORD also said to Moses, [45]"Take the Levites in place of all the firstborn of Israel, and the livestock of the Levites in place of their livestock. The Levites are to be mine. I am the LORD. [46]To redeem the 273 firstborn Israelites who exceed the number of the Levites, [47]collect five shekels[a] for each one, according to the sanctuary shekel, which weighs twenty gerahs. [48]Give the money for the redemption of the additional Israelites to Aaron and his sons."

[49]So Moses collected the redemption money from those who exceeded the number redeemed by the Levites. [50]From the firstborn of the Israelites he collected silver weighing 1,365 shekels,[b] according to the sanctuary shekel. [51]Moses gave the redemption money to Aaron and his sons, as he was commanded by the word of the LORD.

The Kohathites

4 The LORD said to Moses and Aaron: [2]"Take a census of the Kohathite branch of the Levites by their clans and families. [3]Count all the men from thirty to fifty years of age who come to serve in the work in the Tent of Meeting.

[4]"This is the work of the Kohathites in the Tent of Meeting: the care of the most holy things. [5]When the camp is to move, Aaron and his sons are to go in and take down the shielding curtain and cover the ark of the Testimony with it. [6]Then they are to cover this with hides of sea cows,[c] spread a cloth of solid blue over that and put the poles in place.

[7]"Over the table of the Presence they are to spread a blue cloth and put on it the plates, dishes and bowls, and the jars for drink offerings; the bread that is continually there is to remain on it. [8]Over these they are to spread a scarlet cloth, cover that with hides of sea cows and put its poles in place.

[9]"They are to take a blue cloth and cover the lampstand that is for light, together with its lamps, its wick trimmers and trays, and all its jars for the oil used to supply it. [10]Then they are to wrap it and all its accessories in a covering of hides of sea cows and put it on a carrying frame.

[11]"Over the gold altar they are to spread a blue cloth and cover that with hides of sea cows and put its poles in place.

[12]"They are to take all the articles used for ministering in the sanctuary, wrap them in a blue cloth, cover that with hides of sea cows and put them on a carrying frame.

[13]"They are to remove the ashes from the bronze altar and spread a purple cloth over it. [14]Then they are to place on it all the utensils used for ministering at the altar, including the firepans, meat forks, shovels and sprinkling bowls. Over it they are to spread a covering of hides of sea cows and put its poles in place.

[15]"After Aaron and his sons have finished covering the holy furnishings and

---

[a]47 That is, about 2 ounces (about 55 grams)   [b]50 That is, about 35 pounds (about 15.5 kilograms)
[c]6 That is, dugongs; also in verses 8, 10, 11, 12, 14 and 25

all the holy articles, and when the camp is ready to move, the Kohathites are to come to do the carrying. But they must not touch the holy things or they will die. The Kohathites are to carry those things that are in the Tent of Meeting.

¹⁶"Eleazar son of Aaron, the priest, is to have charge of the oil for the light, the fragrant incense, the regular grain offering and the anointing oil. He is to be in charge of the entire tabernacle and everything in it, including its holy furnishings and articles."

¹⁷The LORD said to Moses and Aaron, ¹⁸"See that the Kohathite tribal clans are not cut off from the Levites. ¹⁹So that they may live and not die when they come near the most holy things, do this for them: Aaron and his sons are to go into the sanctuary and assign to each man his work and what he is to carry. ²⁰But the Kohathites must not go in to look at the holy things, even for a moment, or they will die."

The Gershonites

²¹The LORD said to Moses, ²²"Take a census also of the Gershonites by their families and clans. ²³Count all the men from thirty to fifty years of age who come to serve in the work at the Tent of Meeting.

²⁴"This is the service of the Gershonite clans as they work and carry burdens: ²⁵They are to carry the curtains of the tabernacle, the Tent of Meeting, its covering and the outer covering of hides of sea cows, the curtains for the entrance to the Tent of Meeting, ²⁶the curtains of the courtyard surrounding the tabernacle and altar, the curtain for the entrance, the ropes and all the equipment used in its service. The Gershonites are to do all that needs to be done with these things. ²⁷All their service, whether carrying or doing other work, is to be done under the direction of Aaron and his sons. You shall assign to them as their responsibility all they are to carry. ²⁸This is the service of the Gershonite clans at the Tent of Meeting. Their duties are to be under the direction of Ithamar son of Aaron, the priest.

The Merarites

²⁹"Count the Merarites by their clans and families. ³⁰Count all the men from thirty to fifty years of age who come to serve in the work at the Tent of Meeting. ³¹This is their duty as they perform service at the Tent of Meeting: to carry the frames of the tabernacle, its crossbars, posts and bases, ³²as well as the posts of the surrounding courtyard with their bases, tent pegs, ropes, all their equipment and everything related to their use. Assign to each man the specific things he is to carry. ³³This is the service of the Merarite clans as they work at the Tent of Meeting under the direction of Ithamar son of Aaron, the priest."

The Numbering of the Levite Clans

³⁴Moses, Aaron and the leaders of the community counted the Kohathites by their clans and families. ³⁵All the men from thirty to fifty years of age who came to serve in the work in the Tent of Meeting, ³⁶counted by clans, were 2,750. ³⁷This was the total of all those in the Kohathite clans who served in the Tent of Meeting. Moses and Aaron counted them according to the LORD's command through Moses.

³⁸The Gershonites were counted by their clans and families. ³⁹All the men from thirty to fifty years of age who came to serve in the work at the Tent of Meeting, ⁴⁰counted by their clans and families, were 2,630. ⁴¹This was the total of those in the Gershonite clans who served at the Tent of Meeting. Moses and Aaron counted them according to the LORD's command.

⁴²The Merarites were counted by their clans and families. ⁴³All the men from thirty to fifty years of age who came to serve in the work at the Tent of Meeting, ⁴⁴counted by their clans, were 3,200. ⁴⁵This was the total of those in the Merarite clans. Moses and Aaron counted them according to the LORD's command through Moses.

⁴⁶So Moses, Aaron and the leaders of Israel counted all the Levites by their clans and families. ⁴⁷All the men from thirty to fifty years of age who came to do the work of serving and carrying the Tent of Meeting ⁴⁸numbered 8,580. ⁴⁹At the LORD's command through Moses, each was assigned his work and told what to carry.

Thus they were counted, as the LORD commanded Moses.

The Purity of the Camp

5 The LORD said to Moses, ²"Command the Israelites to send away from the camp anyone who has an infectious skin disease*a* or a discharge of any kind, or who is ceremonially unclean because of a dead body. ³Send away male and female alike; send them outside the camp so they will not defile their camp, where I dwell among them." ⁴The Israelites did this; they sent them outside the camp. They did just as the LORD had instructed Moses.

Restitution for Wrongs

⁵The LORD said to Moses, ⁶"Say to the Israelites: 'When a man or woman wrongs another in any way*b* and so is unfaithful to the LORD, that person is guilty ⁷and must confess the sin he has committed. He must make full restitution for his wrong, add one fifth to it and give it all to the person he has wronged. ⁸But if that person has no close relative to whom restitution can be made for the wrong, the restitution belongs to the LORD and must be given to the priest, along with the ram with which atonement is made for him. ⁹All the sacred contributions the Israelites bring to a priest will belong to him. ¹⁰Each man's sacred gifts are his own, but what he gives to the priest will belong to the priest.' "

The Test for an Unfaithful Wife

¹¹Then the LORD said to Moses, ¹²"Speak to the Israelites and say to them: 'If a man's wife goes astray and is unfaithful to him ¹³by sleeping with another man, and this is hidden from her husband and her impurity is undetected (since there is no witness against her and she has not been caught in the act), ¹⁴and if feelings of jealousy come over her husband and he suspects his wife and she is impure — or if he is jealous and suspects her even though she is not impure — ¹⁵then he is to take his wife to the priest. He must also take an offering of a tenth of an ephah*c* of barley flour on her behalf. He must not pour oil on it or put incense on it, because it is a grain offering for jealousy, a reminder offering to draw attention to guilt.

¹⁶" 'The priest shall bring her and have her stand before the LORD. ¹⁷Then he shall take some holy water in a clay jar and put some dust from the tabernacle floor into the water. ¹⁸After the priest has had the woman stand before the LORD, he shall loosen her hair and place in her hands the reminder offering, the grain offering for jealousy, while he himself holds the bitter water that brings a curse. ¹⁹Then the priest shall put the woman under oath and say to her, "If no other man has slept with you and you have not gone astray and become impure while married to your husband, may this bitter water that brings a curse not harm you. ²⁰But if you have gone astray while married to your husband and you have defiled yourself by sleeping with a man other than your husband" — ²¹here the priest is to put the woman under this curse of the oath — "may the LORD cause your people to curse and denounce you when he causes your thigh to waste away and your abdomen to swell.*d* ²²May this water that brings a curse enter your body so that your abdomen swells and your thigh wastes away.*e*"

" 'Then the woman is to say, "Amen. So be it."

²³" 'The priest is to write these curses on a scroll and then wash them off into the bitter water. ²⁴He shall have the woman drink the bitter water that brings a curse, and this water will enter her and cause bitter suffering. ²⁵The priest is to take from her hands the grain offering for jealousy, wave it before the LORD and bring it to the altar. ²⁶The priest is then to take a handful of the grain offering as a memorial offering and burn it on the altar; after that, he is to have the woman drink the water. ²⁷If she has defiled herself and been unfaithful to her husband, then when she is made to drink the water that brings a curse, it will go into her and cause bitter suffering; her abdomen will swell and her thigh waste away,*f* and she will become accursed among her people. ²⁸If, however, the woman has not defiled herself and is free from impurity, she will be cleared of guilt and will be able to have children.

²⁹" 'This, then, is the law of jealousy when a woman goes astray and defiles herself while married to her husband, ³⁰or when feelings of jealousy come over a man because he suspects his wife. The priest is to have her stand before the LORD and is to apply this entire law to her. ³¹The

---

a2 Traditionally *leprosy*; the Hebrew word was used for various diseases affecting the skin—not necessarily leprosy.   *b6* Or *woman commits any wrong common to mankind*   *c15* That is, probably about 2 quarts (about 2 liters)   *d21* Or *causes you to have a miscarrying womb and barrenness*   *e22* Or *body and cause you to be barren and have a miscarrying womb*   *f27* Or *suffering; she will have barrenness and a miscarrying womb* husband will be innocent of any wrongdoing, but the woman will bear the consequences of her sin.' "

The Nazirite

6 The Lord said to Moses, ²"Speak to the Israelites and say to them: 'If a man or woman wants to make a special vow, a vow of separation to the Lord as a Nazirite, ³he must abstain from wine and other fermented drink and must not drink vinegar made from wine or from other fermented drink. He must not drink grape juice or eat grapes or raisins. ⁴As long as he is a Nazirite, he must not eat anything that comes from the grapevine, not even the seeds or skins.

⁵" 'During the entire period of his vow of separation no razor may be used on his head. He must be holy until the period of his separation to the Lord is over; he must let the hair of his head grow long. ⁶Throughout the period of his separation to the Lord he must not go near a dead body. ⁷Even if his own father or mother or brother or sister dies, he must not make himself ceremonially unclean on account of them, because the symbol of his separation to God is on his head. ⁸Throughout the period of his separation he is consecrated to the Lord.

⁹" 'If someone dies suddenly in his presence, thus defiling the hair he has dedicated, he must shave his head on the day of his cleansing—the seventh day. ¹⁰Then on the eighth day he must bring two doves or two young pigeons to the priest at the entrance to the Tent of Meeting. ¹¹The priest is to offer one as a sin offering and the other as a burnt offering to make atonement for him because he sinned by being in the presence of the dead body. That same day he is to consecrate his head. ¹²He must dedicate himself to the Lord for the period of his separation and must bring a year-old male lamb as a guilt offering. The previous days do not count, because he became defiled during his separation.

¹³" 'Now this is the law for the Nazirite when the period of his separation is over. He is to be brought to the entrance to the Tent of Meeting. ¹⁴There he is to present his offerings to the Lord: a year-old male lamb without defect for a burnt offering, a year-old ewe lamb without defect for a sin offering, a ram without defect for a fellowship offering,ᵃ ¹⁵together with their grain

offerings and drink offerings, and a basket of bread made without yeast—cakes made of fine flour mixed with oil, and wafers spread with oil.

¹⁶" 'The priest is to present them before the Lord and make the sin offering and the burnt offering. ¹⁷He is to present the basket of unleavened bread and is to sacrifice the ram as a fellowship offering to the Lord, together with its grain offering and drink offering.

¹⁸" 'Then at the entrance to the Tent of Meeting, the Nazirite must shave off the hair that he dedicated. He is to take the hair and put it in the fire that is under the sacrifice of the fellowship offering.

¹⁹" 'After the Nazirite has shaved off the hair of his dedication, the priest is to place in his hands a boiled shoulder of the ram, and a cake and a wafer from the basket, both made without yeast. ²⁰The priest shall then wave them before the Lord as a wave offering; they are holy and belong to the priest, together with the breast that was waved and the thigh that was presented. After that, the Nazirite may drink wine.

²¹" 'This is the law of the Nazirite who vows his offering to the Lord in accordance with his separation, in addition to whatever else he can afford. He must fulfill the vow he has made, according to the law of the Nazirite.' "

The Priestly Blessing

²²The Lord said to Moses, ²³"Tell Aaron and his sons, 'This is how you are to bless the Israelites. Say to them:

²⁴" ' "The Lord bless you
  and keep you;
²⁵the Lord make his face shine upon
    you
  and be gracious to you;
²⁶the Lord turn his face toward you
  and give you peace." '

²⁷"So they will put my name on the Israelites, and I will bless them."

Offerings at the Dedication of the Tabernacle

7 When Moses finished setting up the tabernacle, he anointed it and consecrated it and all its furnishings. He also anointed and consecrated the altar and all its utensils. ²Then the leaders of Israel, the heads of families who were the tribal leaders in charge of those who were counted,

ᵃ14 Traditionally *peace offering*; also in verses 17 and 18

THURSDAY

VERSE FOR THE DAY:
Numbers 6:26

AUTHOR:
Dave Dravecky

PASSAGE FOR THE DAY:
Numbers 6:22–27

". . . And Give You Peace"

ON JUNE 18, 1991, Dave Dravecky underwent surgery that would result in the amputation of his cancer-filled left arm. The day after surgery Dravecky looked in the mirror and reflected on the peace the Lord had given him, a peace he would later share with another family.

I was shocked at how radically they had cut the arm back. The incision started at my neck and went in a diagonal to my underarm area. The arm was gone. The shoulder was gone. The shoulder blade was gone. And the left side of my collar bone was gone.

"Okay, God. This is what I've got to live with. Put this behind me; let me go forward."

And when the one-armed man looked back at me, there was peace in his eyes . . .

A couple of days later when I was walking around, pushing my IV, I came to the visitors' room down the hall. An entire family was huddled there, sitting, waiting, paging mindlessly through last month's magazines on the coffee table. I sat down next to the mother. Her husband had cancer throughout his body and the prognosis wasn't good. You could tell they were taking it hard . . .

Her son sat down beside me and asked: "Where do you get your peace?" . . .

I told him that Jesus Christ was the source of my peace. The entire family listened as I shared my faith. When I was finished, the woman said: "But, you know, my husband has never done anything bad. He's worked hard, been a good husband, a good father—yet he's in here with cancer while all sorts of bad people are out on the streets, healthy."

It's hard to understand the suffering in this life, I told her, but this much I did know: You can't blame God for it. Sooner or later our life on this earth is going to pass. Even the best lives someday come to an end. The only thing that will matter then is whether or not we'll get to heaven. I believe in miracles, that God can and does heal people, but more important than that, I believe in the eternal hope of heaven. When I die, that's where I'm going, because heaven is my home.

Additional Scripture Readings:
John 14:1–4,25–27; Philippians 4:2–9

Go to page 146 for your next devotional reading.

made offerings. ³They brought as their gifts before the LORD six covered carts and twelve oxen — an ox from each leader and a cart from every two. These they presented before the tabernacle.

⁴The LORD said to Moses, ⁵"Accept these from them, that they may be used in the work at the Tent of Meeting. Give them to the Levites as each man's work requires."

⁶So Moses took the carts and oxen and gave them to the Levites. ⁷He gave two carts and four oxen to the Gershonites, as their work required, ⁸and he gave four carts and eight oxen to the Merarites, as their work required. They were all under the direction of Ithamar son of Aaron, the priest. ⁹But Moses did not give any to the Kohathites, because they were to carry on their shoulders the holy things, for which they were responsible.

¹⁰When the altar was anointed, the leaders brought their offerings for its dedication and presented them before the altar. ¹¹For the LORD had said to Moses, "Each day one leader is to bring his offering for the dedication of the altar."

¹²The one who brought his offering on the first day was Nahshon son of Amminadab of the tribe of Judah.

¹³His offering was one silver plate weighing a hundred and thirty shekels,ᵃ and one silver sprinkling bowl weighing seventy shekels,ᵇ both according to the sanctuary shekel, each filled with fine flour mixed with oil as a grain offering; ¹⁴one gold dish weighing ten shekels,ᶜ filled with incense; ¹⁵one young bull, one ram and one male lamb a year old, for a burnt offering; ¹⁶one male goat for a sin offering; ¹⁷and two oxen, five rams, five male goats and five male lambs a year old, to be sacrificed as a fellowship offering.ᵈ This was the offering of Nahshon son of Amminadab.

¹⁸On the second day Nethanel son of Zuar, the leader of Issachar, brought his offering.

¹⁹The offering he brought was one silver plate weighing a hundred and thirty shekels, and one silver sprinkling bowl weighing seventy shekels, both according to the sanctuary shekel, each filled with fine flour mixed with oil as a grain offering; ²⁰one gold dish weighing ten shekels, filled with incense; ²¹one young bull, one ram and one male lamb a year old, for a burnt offering; ²²one male goat for a sin offering; ²³and two oxen, five rams, five male goats and five male lambs a year old, to be sacrificed as a fellowship offering. This was the offering of Nethanel son of Zuar.

²⁴On the third day, Eliab son of Helon, the leader of the people of Zebulun, brought his offering.

²⁵His offering was one silver plate weighing a hundred and thirty shekels, and one silver sprinkling bowl weighing seventy shekels, both according to the sanctuary shekel, each filled with fine flour mixed with oil as a grain offering; ²⁶one gold dish weighing ten shekels, filled with incense; ²⁷one young bull, one ram and one male lamb a year old, for a burnt offering; ²⁸one male goat for a sin offering; ²⁹and two oxen, five rams, five male goats and five male lambs a year old, to be sacrificed as a fellowship offering. This was the offering of Eliab son of Helon.

³⁰On the fourth day Elizur son of Shedeur, the leader of the people of Reuben, brought his offering.

³¹His offering was one silver plate weighing a hundred and thirty shekels, and one silver sprinkling bowl weighing seventy shekels, both according to the sanctuary shekel, each filled with fine flour mixed with oil as a grain offering; ³²one gold dish weighing ten shekels, filled with incense; ³³one young bull, one ram and one male lamb a year old, for a burnt offering; ³⁴one male goat for a sin offering; ³⁵and two oxen, five rams, five male goats and five male lambs a year old, to be sacrificed as a fellowship offering. This was the offering of Elizur son of Shedeur.

³⁶On the fifth day Shelumiel son of Zurishaddai, the leader of the people of Simeon, brought his offering.

³⁷His offering was one silver plate weighing a hundred and thirty shekels, and one silver sprinkling bowl

ᵃ13 That is, about 3 1/4 pounds (about 1.5 kilograms); also elsewhere in this chapter   ᵇ13 That is, about 1 3/4 pounds (about 0.8 kilogram); also elsewhere in this chapter   ᶜ14 That is, about 4 ounces (about 110 grams); also elsewhere in this chapter   ᵈ17 Traditionally peace offering; also elsewhere in this chapter weighing seventy shekels, both according to the sanctuary shekel, each filled with fine flour mixed with oil as a grain offering; ³⁸one gold dish weighing ten shekels, filled with incense; ³⁹one young bull, one ram and one male lamb a year old, for a burnt offering; ⁴⁰one male goat for a sin offering; ⁴¹and two oxen, five rams, five male goats and five male lambs a year old, to be sacrificed as a fellowship offering. This was the offering of Shelumiel son of Zurishaddai.

⁴²On the sixth day Eliasaph son of Deuel, the leader of the people of Gad, brought his offering.

⁴³His offering was one silver plate weighing a hundred and thirty shekels, and one silver sprinkling bowl weighing seventy shekels, both according to the sanctuary shekel, each filled with fine flour mixed with oil as a grain offering; ⁴⁴one gold dish weighing ten shekels, filled with incense; ⁴⁵one young bull, one ram and one male lamb a year old, for a burnt offering; ⁴⁶one male goat for a sin offering; ⁴⁷and two oxen, five rams, five male goats and five male lambs a year old, to be sacrificed as a fellowship offering. This was the offering of Eliasaph son of Deuel.

⁴⁸On the seventh day Elishama son of Ammihud, the leader of the people of Ephraim, brought his offering.

⁴⁹His offering was one silver plate weighing a hundred and thirty shekels, and one silver sprinkling bowl weighing seventy shekels, both according to the sanctuary shekel, each filled with fine flour mixed with oil as a grain offering; ⁵⁰one gold dish weighing ten shekels, filled with incense; ⁵¹one young bull, one ram and one male lamb a year old, for a burnt offering; ⁵²one male goat for a sin offering; ⁵³and two oxen, five rams, five male goats and five male lambs a year old, to be sacrificed as a fellowship offering. This was the offering of Elishama son of Ammihud.

⁵⁴On the eighth day Gamaliel son of Pedahzur, the leader of the people of Manasseh, brought his offering.

⁵⁵His offering was one silver plate weighing a hundred and thirty shekels, and one silver sprinkling bowl weighing seventy shekels, both ac-

cording to the sanctuary shekel, each filled with fine flour mixed with oil as a grain offering; ⁵⁶one gold dish weighing ten shekels, filled with incense; ⁵⁷one young bull, one ram and one male lamb a year old, for a burnt offering; ⁵⁸one male goat for a sin offering; ⁵⁹and two oxen, five rams, five male goats and five male lambs a year old, to be sacrificed as a fellowship offering. This was the offering of Gamaliel son of Pedahzur.

⁶⁰On the ninth day Abidan son of Gideoni, the leader of the people of Benjamin, brought his offering.

⁶¹His offering was one silver plate weighing a hundred and thirty shekels, and one silver sprinkling bowl weighing seventy shekels, both according to the sanctuary shekel, each filled with fine flour mixed with oil as a grain offering; ⁶²one gold dish weighing ten shekels, filled with incense; ⁶³one young bull, one ram and one male lamb a year old, for a burnt offering; ⁶⁴one male goat for a sin offering; ⁶⁵and two oxen, five rams, five male goats and five male lambs a year old, to be sacrificed as a fellowship offering. This was the offering of Abidan son of Gideoni.

⁶⁶On the tenth day Ahiezer son of Ammishaddai, the leader of the people of Dan, brought his offering.

⁶⁷His offering was one silver plate weighing a hundred and thirty shekels, and one silver sprinkling bowl weighing seventy shekels, both according to the sanctuary shekel, each filled with fine flour mixed with oil as a grain offering; ⁶⁸one gold dish weighing ten shekels, filled with incense; ⁶⁹one young bull, one ram and one male lamb a year old, for a burnt offering; ⁷⁰one male goat for a sin offering; ⁷¹and two oxen, five rams, five male goats and five male lambs a year old, to be sacrificed as a fellowship offering. This was the offering of Ahiezer son of Ammishaddai.

⁷²On the eleventh day Pagiel son of Ocran, the leader of the people of Asher, brought his offering.

⁷³His offering was one silver plate weighing a hundred and thirty shekels, and one silver sprinkling bowl weighing seventy shekels, both according to the sanctuary shekel, each

filled with fine flour mixed with oil as a grain offering; ⁷⁴one gold dish weighing ten shekels, filled with incense; ⁷⁵one young bull, one ram and one male lamb a year old, for a burnt offering; ⁷⁶one male goat for a sin offering; ⁷⁷and two oxen, five rams, five male goats and five male lambs a year old, to be sacrificed as a fellowship offering. This was the offering of Pagiel son of Ocran.

⁷⁸On the twelfth day Ahira son of Enan, the leader of the people of Naphtali, brought his offering.

⁷⁹His offering was one silver plate weighing a hundred and thirty shekels, and one silver sprinkling bowl weighing seventy shekels, both according to the sanctuary shekel, each filled with fine flour mixed with oil as a grain offering; ⁸⁰one gold dish weighing ten shekels, filled with incense; ⁸¹one young bull, one ram and one male lamb a year old, for a burnt offering; ⁸²one male goat for a sin offering; ⁸³and two oxen, five rams, five male goats and five male lambs a year old, to be sacrificed as a fellowship offering. This was the offering of Ahira son of Enan.

⁸⁴These were the offerings of the Israelite leaders for the dedication of the altar when it was anointed: twelve silver plates, twelve silver sprinkling bowls and twelve gold dishes. ⁸⁵Each silver plate weighed a hundred and thirty shekels, and each sprinkling bowl seventy shekels. Altogether, the silver dishes weighed two thousand four hundred shekels,^a according to the sanctuary shekel. ⁸⁶The twelve gold dishes filled with incense weighed ten shekels each, according to the sanctuary shekel. Altogether, the gold dishes weighed a hundred and twenty shekels.^b ⁸⁷The total number of animals for the burnt offering came to twelve young bulls, twelve rams and twelve male lambs a year old, together with their grain offering. Twelve male goats were used for the sin offering. ⁸⁸The total number of animals for the sacrifice of the fellowship offering came to twenty-four oxen, sixty rams, sixty male goats and sixty male lambs a year old. These were the offerings for the dedication of the altar after it was anointed.

⁸⁹When Moses entered the Tent of Meeting to speak with the LORD, he heard the voice speaking to him from between the two cherubim above the atonement cover on the ark of the Testimony. And he spoke with him.

Setting Up the Lamps

8 The LORD said to Moses, ²"Speak to Aaron and say to him, 'When you set up the seven lamps, they are to light the area in front of the lampstand.'"

³Aaron did so; he set up the lamps so that they faced forward on the lampstand, just as the LORD commanded Moses. ⁴This is how the lampstand was made: It was made of hammered gold—from its base to its blossoms. The lampstand was made exactly like the pattern the LORD had shown Moses.

The Setting Apart of the Levites

⁵The LORD said to Moses: ⁶"Take the Levites from among the other Israelites and make them ceremonially clean. ⁷To purify them, do this: Sprinkle the water of cleansing on them; then have them shave their whole bodies and wash their clothes, and so purify themselves. ⁸Have them take a young bull with its grain offering of fine flour mixed with oil; then you are to take a second young bull for a sin offering. ⁹Bring the Levites to the front of the Tent of Meeting and assemble the whole Israelite community. ¹⁰You are to bring the Levites before the LORD, and the Israelites are to lay their hands on them. ¹¹Aaron is to present the Levites before the LORD as a wave offering from the Israelites, so that they may be ready to do the work of the LORD.

¹²"After the Levites lay their hands on the heads of the bulls, use the one for a sin offering to the LORD and the other for a burnt offering, to make atonement for the Levites. ¹³Have the Levites stand in front of Aaron and his sons and then present them as a wave offering to the LORD. ¹⁴In this way you are to set the Levites apart from the other Israelites, and the Levites will be mine.

¹⁵"After you have purified the Levites and presented them as a wave offering, they are to come to do their work at the Tent of Meeting. ¹⁶They are the Israelites who are to be given wholly to me. I have taken them as my own in place of the firstborn, the first male offspring from every Israelite woman. ¹⁷Every firstborn male in Israel, whether man or animal, is mine.

^a85 That is, about 60 pounds (about 28 kilograms)   ^b86 That is, about 3 pounds (about 1.4 kilograms)

When I struck down all the firstborn in Egypt, I set them apart for myself. ¹⁸And I have taken the Levites in place of all the firstborn sons in Israel. ¹⁹Of all the Israelites, I have given the Levites as gifts to Aaron and his sons to do the work at the Tent of Meeting on behalf of the Israelites and to make atonement for them so that no plague will strike the Israelites when they go near the sanctuary."

²⁰Moses, Aaron and the whole Israelite community did with the Levites just as the LORD commanded Moses. ²¹The Levites purified themselves and washed their clothes. Then Aaron presented them as a wave offering before the LORD and made atonement for them to purify them. ²²After that, the Levites came to do their work at the Tent of Meeting under the supervision of Aaron and his sons. They did with the Levites just as the LORD commanded Moses.

²³The LORD said to Moses, ²⁴"This applies to the Levites: Men twenty-five years old or more shall come to take part in the work at the Tent of Meeting, ²⁵but at the age of fifty, they must retire from their regular service and work no longer. ²⁶They may assist their brothers in performing their duties at the Tent of Meeting, but they themselves must not do the work. This, then, is how you are to assign the responsibilities of the Levites."

The Passover

9 The LORD spoke to Moses in the Desert of Sinai in the first month of the second year after they came out of Egypt. He said, ²"Have the Israelites celebrate the Passover at the appointed time. ³Celebrate it at the appointed time, at twilight on the fourteenth day of this month, in accordance with all its rules and regulations."

⁴So Moses told the Israelites to celebrate the Passover, ⁵and they did so in the Desert of Sinai at twilight on the fourteenth day of the first month. The Israelites did everything just as the LORD commanded Moses.

⁶But some of them could not celebrate the Passover on that day because they were ceremonially unclean on account of a dead body. So they came to Moses and Aaron that same day ⁷and said to Moses, "We have become unclean because of a dead body, but why should we be kept from presenting the LORD's offering with the other Israelites at the appointed time?"

⁸Moses answered them, "Wait until I find out what the LORD commands concerning you."

⁹Then the LORD said to Moses, ¹⁰"Tell the Israelites: 'When any of you or your descendants are unclean because of a dead body or are away on a journey, they may still celebrate the LORD's Passover. ¹¹They are to celebrate it on the fourteenth day of the second month at twilight. They are to eat the lamb, together with unleavened bread and bitter herbs. ¹²They must not leave any of it till morning or break any of its bones. When they celebrate the Passover, they must follow all the regulations. ¹³But if a man who is ceremonially clean and not on a journey fails to celebrate the Passover, that person must be cut off from his people because he did not present the LORD's offering at the appointed time. That man will bear the consequences of his sin.

¹⁴" 'An alien living among you who wants to celebrate the LORD's Passover must do so in accordance with its rules and regulations. You must have the same regulations for the alien and the native-born.' "

The Cloud Above the Tabernacle

¹⁵On the day the tabernacle, the Tent of the Testimony, was set up, the cloud covered it. From evening till morning the cloud above the tabernacle looked like fire. ¹⁶That is how it continued to be; the cloud covered it, and at night it looked like fire. ¹⁷Whenever the cloud lifted from above the Tent, the Israelites set out; wherever the cloud settled, the Israelites encamped. ¹⁸At the LORD's command the Israelites set out, and at his command they encamped. As long as the cloud stayed over the tabernacle, they remained in camp. ¹⁹When the cloud remained over the tabernacle a long time, the Israelites obeyed the LORD's order and did not set out. ²⁰Sometimes the cloud was over the tabernacle only a few days; at the LORD's command they would encamp, and then at his command they would set out. ²¹Sometimes the cloud stayed only from evening till morning, and when it lifted in the morning, they set out. Whether by day or by night, whenever the cloud lifted, they set out. ²²Whether the cloud stayed over the tabernacle for two days or a month or a year, the Israelites would remain in camp and not set out; but when it lifted, they would set out. ²³At the LORD's command they encamped, and at the LORD's command they set out. They

obeyed the Lord's order, in accordance with his command through Moses.

The Silver Trumpets

10 The Lord said to Moses: [2]"Make two trumpets of hammered silver, and use them for calling the community together and for having the camps set out. [3]When both are sounded, the whole community is to assemble before you at the entrance to the Tent of Meeting. [4]If only one is sounded, the leaders—the heads of the clans of Israel—are to assemble before you. [5]When a trumpet blast is sounded, the tribes camping on the east are to set out. [6]At the sounding of a second blast, the camps on the south are to set out. The blast will be the signal for setting out. [7]To gather the assembly, blow the trumpets, but not with the same signal.

[8]"The sons of Aaron, the priests, are to blow the trumpets. This is to be a lasting ordinance for you and the generations to come. [9]When you go into battle in your own land against an enemy who is oppressing you, sound a blast on the trumpets. Then you will be remembered by the Lord your God and rescued from your enemies. [10]Also at your times of rejoicing—your appointed feasts and New Moon festivals—you are to sound the trumpets over your burnt offerings and fellowship offerings,[a] and they will be a memorial for you before your God. I am the Lord your God."

The Israelites Leave Sinai

[11]On the twentieth day of the second month of the second year, the cloud lifted from above the tabernacle of the Testimony. [12]Then the Israelites set out from the Desert of Sinai and traveled from place to place until the cloud came to rest in the Desert of Paran. [13]They set out, this first time, at the Lord's command through Moses.

[14]The divisions of the camp of Judah went first, under their standard. Nahshon son of Amminadab was in command. [15]Nethanel son of Zuar was over the division of the tribe of Issachar, [16]and Eliab son of Helon was over the division of the tribe of Zebulun. [17]Then the tabernacle was taken down, and the Gershonites and Merarites, who carried it, set out.

[18]The divisions of the camp of Reuben went next, under their standard. Elizur son of Shedeur was in command. [19]Shelu-miel son of Zurishaddai was over the division of the tribe of Simeon, [20]and Eliasaph son of Deuel was over the division of the tribe of Gad. [21]Then the Kohathites set out, carrying the holy things. The tabernacle was to be set up before they arrived.

[22]The divisions of the camp of Ephraim went next, under their standard. Elishama son of Ammihud was in command. [23]Gamaliel son of Pedahzur was over the division of the tribe of Manasseh, [24]and Abidan son of Gideoni was over the division of the tribe of Benjamin.

[25]Finally, as the rear guard for all the units, the divisions of the camp of Dan set out, under their standard. Ahiezer son of Ammishaddai was in command. [26]Pagiel son of Ocran was over the division of the tribe of Asher, [27]and Ahira son of Enan was over the division of the tribe of Naphtali. [28]This was the order of march for the Israelite divisions as they set out.

[29]Now Moses said to Hobab son of Reuel the Midianite, Moses' father-in-law, "We are setting out for the place about which the Lord said, 'I will give it to you.' Come with us and we will treat you well, for the Lord has promised good things to Israel."

[30]He answered, "No, I will not go; I am going back to my own land and my own people."

[31]But Moses said, "Please do not leave us. You know where we should camp in the desert, and you can be our eyes. [32]If you come with us, we will share with you whatever good things the Lord gives us."

[33]So they set out from the mountain of the Lord and traveled for three days. The ark of the covenant of the Lord went before them during those three days to find them a place to rest. [34]The cloud of the Lord was over them by day when they set out from the camp.

[35]Whenever the ark set out, Moses said,

"Rise up, O Lord!
    May your enemies be scattered;
    may your foes flee before you."

[36]Whenever it came to rest, he said,

"Return, O Lord,
    to the countless thousands of
        Israel."

Fire From the Lord

11 Now the people complained about their hardships in the hearing of

---

[a]10 Traditionally *peace offerings*

the LORD, and when he heard them his anger was aroused. Then fire from the LORD burned among them and consumed some of the outskirts of the camp. ²When the people cried out to Moses, he prayed to the LORD and the fire died down. ³So that place was called Taberah,ᵃ because fire from the LORD had burned among them.

Quail From the LORD

⁴The rabble with them began to crave other food, and again the Israelites started wailing and said, "If only we had meat to eat! ⁵We remember the fish we ate in Egypt at no cost—also the cucumbers, melons, leeks, onions and garlic. ⁶But now we have lost our appetite; we never see anything but this manna!"

⁷The manna was like coriander seed and looked like resin. ⁸The people went around gathering it, and then ground it in a handmill or crushed it in a mortar. They cooked it in a pot or made it into cakes. And it tasted like something made with olive oil. ⁹When the dew settled on the camp at night, the manna also came down.

¹⁰Moses heard the people of every family wailing, each at the entrance to his tent. The LORD became exceedingly angry, and Moses was troubled. ¹¹He asked the LORD, "Why have you brought this trouble on your servant? What have I done to displease you that you put the burden of all these people on me? ¹²Did I conceive all these people? Did I give them birth? Why do you tell me to carry them in my arms, as a nurse carries an infant, to the land you promised on oath to their forefathers? ¹³Where can I get meat for all these people? They keep wailing to me, 'Give us meat to eat!' ¹⁴I cannot carry all these people by myself; the burden is too heavy for me. ¹⁵If this is how you are going to treat me, put me to death right now—if I have found favor in your eyes—and do not let me face my own ruin."

¹⁶The LORD said to Moses: "Bring me seventy of Israel's elders who are known to you as leaders and officials among the people. Have them come to the Tent of Meeting, that they may stand there with you. ¹⁷I will come down and speak with you there, and I will take of the Spirit that is on you and put the Spirit on them. They will help you carry the burden of the peo-

ple so that you will not have to carry it alone.

¹⁸"Tell the people: 'Consecrate yourselves in preparation for tomorrow, when you will eat meat. The LORD heard you when you wailed, "If only we had meat to eat! We were better off in Egypt!" Now the LORD will give you meat, and you will eat it. ¹⁹You will not eat it for just one day, or two days, or five, ten or twenty days, ²⁰but for a whole month—until it comes out of your nostrils and you loathe it—because you have rejected the LORD, who is among you, and have wailed before him, saying, "Why did we ever leave Egypt?" ' "

²¹But Moses said, "Here I am among six hundred thousand men on foot, and you say, 'I will give them meat to eat for a whole month!' ²²Would they have enough if flocks and herds were slaughtered for them? Would they have enough if all the fish in the sea were caught for them?"

²³The LORD answered Moses, "Is the LORD's arm too short? You will now see whether or not what I say will come true for you."

²⁴So Moses went out and told the people what the LORD had said. He brought together seventy of their elders and had them stand around the Tent. ²⁵Then the LORD came down in the cloud and spoke with him, and he took of the Spirit that was on him and put the Spirit on the seventy elders. When the Spirit rested on them, they prophesied, but they did not do so again.ᵇ

²⁶However, two men, whose names were Eldad and Medad, had remained in the camp. They were listed among the elders, but did not go out to the Tent. Yet the Spirit also rested on them, and they prophesied in the camp. ²⁷A young man ran and told Moses, "Eldad and Medad are prophesying in the camp."

²⁸Joshua son of Nun, who had been Moses' aide since youth, spoke up and said, "Moses, my lord, stop them!"

²⁹But Moses replied, "Are you jealous for my sake? I wish that all the LORD's people were prophets and that the LORD would put his Spirit on them!" ³⁰Then Moses and the elders of Israel returned to the camp.

³¹Now a wind went out from the LORD and drove quail in from the sea. It brought themᶜ down all around the camp to about three feetᵈ above the ground, as far

---

ᵃ3 Taberah means burning.   ᵇ25 Or prophesied and continued to do so   ᶜ31 Or They flew
ᵈ31 Hebrew two cubits (about 1 meter)

as a day's walk in any direction. ³²All that day and night and all the next day the people went out and gathered quail. No one gathered less than ten homers.ᵃ Then they spread them out all around the camp. ³³But while the meat was still between their teeth and before it could be consumed, the anger of the LORD burned against the people, and he struck them with a severe plague. ³⁴Therefore the place was named Kibroth Hattaavah,ᵇ because there they buried the people who had craved other food.

³⁵From Kibroth Hattaavah the people traveled to Hazeroth and stayed there.

Miriam and Aaron Oppose Moses

12 Miriam and Aaron began to talk against Moses because of his Cushite wife, for he had married a Cushite. ²"Has the LORD spoken only through Moses?" they asked. "Hasn't he also spoken through us?" And the LORD heard this.

³(Now Moses was a very humble man, more humble than anyone else on the face of the earth.)

⁴At once the LORD said to Moses, Aaron and Miriam, "Come out to the Tent of Meeting, all three of you." So the three of them came out. ⁵Then the LORD came down in a pillar of cloud; he stood at the entrance to the Tent and summoned Aaron and Miriam. When both of them stepped forward, ⁶he said, "Listen to my words:

"When a prophet of the LORD is
    among you,
  I reveal myself to him in visions,
  I speak to him in dreams.
⁷But this is not true of my servant
    Moses;
  he is faithful in all my house.
⁸With him I speak face to face,
  clearly and not in riddles;
  he sees the form of the LORD.
Why then were you not afraid
  to speak against my servant Moses?"

⁹The anger of the LORD burned against them, and he left them.

¹⁰When the cloud lifted from above the Tent, there stood Miriam—leprous,ᶜ like snow. Aaron turned toward her and saw that she had leprosy; ¹¹and he said to Moses, "Please, my lord, do not hold against us the sin we have so foolishly committed.

¹²Do not let her be like a stillborn infant coming from its mother's womb with its flesh half eaten away."

¹³So Moses cried out to the LORD, "O God, please heal her!"

¹⁴The LORD replied to Moses, "If her father had spit in her face, would she not have been in disgrace for seven days? Confine her outside the camp for seven days; after that she can be brought back." ¹⁵So Miriam was confined outside the camp for seven days, and the people did not move on till she was brought back.

¹⁶After that, the people left Hazeroth and encamped in the Desert of Paran.

Exploring Canaan

13 The LORD said to Moses, ²"Send some men to explore the land of Canaan, which I am giving to the Israelites. From each ancestral tribe send one of its leaders."

³So at the LORD's command Moses sent them out from the Desert of Paran. All of them were leaders of the Israelites. ⁴These are their names:

from the tribe of Reuben, Shammua
    son of Zaccur;
⁵from the tribe of Simeon, Shaphat
    son of Hori;
⁶from the tribe of Judah, Caleb son of
    Jephunneh;
⁷from the tribe of Issachar, Igal son of
    Joseph;
⁸from the tribe of Ephraim, Hoshea
    son of Nun;
⁹from the tribe of Benjamin, Palti son
    of Raphu;
¹⁰from the tribe of Zebulun, Gaddiel
    son of Sodi;
¹¹from the tribe of Manasseh (a tribe
    of Joseph), Gaddi son of Susi;
¹²from the tribe of Dan, Ammiel son of
    Gemalli;
¹³from the tribe of Asher, Sethur son
    of Michael;
¹⁴from the tribe of Naphtali, Nahbi son
    of Vophsi;
¹⁵from the tribe of Gad, Geuel son of
    Maki.

¹⁶These are the names of the men Moses sent to explore the land. (Moses gave Hoshea son of Nun the name Joshua.)

¹⁷When Moses sent them to explore Canaan, he said, "Go up through the Negev

---

ᵃ32 That is, probably about 60 bushels (about 2.2 kiloliters)   ᵇ34 *Kibroth Hattaavah* means *graves of craving.*   ᶜ10 The Hebrew word was used for various diseases affecting the skin—not necessarily leprosy.

and on into the hill country. **18**See what the land is like and whether the people who live there are strong or weak, few or many. **19**What kind of land do they live in? Is it good or bad? What kind of towns do they live in? Are they unwalled or fortified? **20**How is the soil? Is it fertile or poor? Are there trees on it or not? Do your best to bring back some of the fruit of the land." (It was the season for the first ripe grapes.)

21So they went up and explored the land from the Desert of Zin as far as Rehob, toward Lebo*a* Hamath. **22**They went up through the Negev and came to Hebron, where Ahiman, Sheshai and Talmai, the descendants of Anak, lived. (Hebron had been built seven years before Zoan in Egypt.) **23**When they reached the Valley of Eshcol,*b* they cut off a branch bearing a single cluster of grapes. Two of them carried it on a pole between them, along with some pomegranates and figs. **24**That place was called the Valley of Eshcol because of the cluster of grapes the Israelites cut off there. **25**At the end of forty days they returned from exploring the land.

Report on the Exploration

26They came back to Moses and Aaron and the whole Israelite community at Kadesh in the Desert of Paran. There they reported to them and to the whole assembly and showed them the fruit of the land. **27**They gave Moses this account: "We went into the land to which you sent us, and it does flow with milk and honey! Here is its fruit. **28**But the people who live there are powerful, and the cities are fortified and very large. We even saw descendants of Anak there. **29**The Amalekites live in the Negev; the Hittites, Jebusites and Amorites live in the hill country; and the Canaanites live near the sea and along the Jordan."

30Then Caleb silenced the people before Moses and said, "We should go up and take possession of the land, for we can certainly do it."

31But the men who had gone up with him said, "We can't attack those people; they are stronger than we are." **32**And they spread among the Israelites a bad report about the land they had explored. They said, "The land we explored devours those living in it. All the people we saw there are of great size. **33**We saw the Nephilim there (the descendants of Anak come from the Nephilim). We seemed like grasshoppers in our own eyes, and we looked the same to them."

The People Rebel

14 That night all the people of the community raised their voices and wept aloud. **2**All the Israelites grumbled against Moses and Aaron, and the whole assembly said to them, "If only we had died in Egypt! Or in this desert! **3**Why is the LORD bringing us to this land only to let us fall by the sword? Our wives and children will be taken as plunder. Wouldn't it be better for us to go back to Egypt?" **4**And they said to each other, "We should choose a leader and go back to Egypt."

5Then Moses and Aaron fell facedown in front of the whole Israelite assembly gathered there. **6**Joshua son of Nun and Caleb son of Jephunneh, who were among those who had explored the land, tore their clothes **7**and said to the entire Israelite assembly, "The land we passed through and explored is exceedingly good. **8**If the LORD is pleased with us, he will lead us into that land, a land flowing with milk and honey, and will give it to us. **9**Only do not rebel against the LORD. And do not be afraid of the people of the land, because we will swallow them up. Their protection is gone, but the LORD is with us. Do not be afraid of them."

10But the whole assembly talked about stoning them. Then the glory of the LORD appeared at the Tent of Meeting to all the Israelites. **11**The LORD said to Moses, "How long will these people treat me with contempt? How long will they refuse to believe in me, in spite of all the miraculous signs I have performed among them? **12**I will strike them down with a plague and destroy them, but I will make you into a nation greater and stronger than they."

13Moses said to the LORD, "Then the Egyptians will hear about it! By your power you brought these people up from among them. **14**And they will tell the inhabitants of this land about it. They have already heard that you, O LORD, are with these people and that you, O LORD, have been seen face to face, that your cloud stays over them, and that you go before them in a pillar of cloud by day and a pillar of fire by night. **15**If you put these people to death all at one time, the nations who have heard this report about you will

---

*a*21 Or *toward the entrance to*   *b*23 *Eshcol* means *cluster*; also in verse 24.

say, [16]'The LORD was not able to bring these people into the land he promised them on oath; so he slaughtered them in the desert.'

[17]"Now may the Lord's strength be displayed, just as you have declared: [18]'The LORD is slow to anger, abounding in love and forgiving sin and rebellion. Yet he does not leave the guilty unpunished; he punishes the children for the sin of the fathers to the third and fourth generation.' [19]In accordance with your great love, forgive the sin of these people, just as you have pardoned them from the time they left Egypt until now."

[20]The LORD replied, "I have forgiven them, as you asked. [21]Nevertheless, as surely as I live and as surely as the glory of the LORD fills the whole earth, [22]not one of the men who saw my glory and the miraculous signs I performed in Egypt and in the desert but who disobeyed me and tested me ten times— [23]not one of them will ever see the land I promised on oath to their forefathers. No one who has treated me with contempt will ever see it. [24]But because my servant Caleb has a different spirit and follows me wholeheartedly, I will bring him into the land he went to, and his descendants will inherit it. [25]Since the Amalekites and Canaanites are living in the valleys, turn back tomorrow and set out toward the desert along the route to the Red Sea.[a]"

[26]The LORD said to Moses and Aaron: [27]"How long will this wicked community grumble against me? I have heard the complaints of these grumbling Israelites. [28]So tell them, 'As surely as I live, declares the LORD, I will do to you the very things I heard you say: [29]In this desert your bodies will fall—every one of you twenty years old or more who was counted in the census and who has grumbled against me. [30]Not one of you will enter the land I swore with uplifted hand to make your home, except Caleb son of Jephunneh and Joshua son of Nun. [31]As for your children that you said would be taken as plunder, I will bring them in to enjoy the land you have rejected. [32]But you—your bodies will fall in this desert. [33]Your children will be shepherds here for forty years, suffering for your unfaithfulness, until the last of your bodies lies in the desert. [34]For forty years—one year for each of the forty days you explored the land—you will suf-

fer for your sins and know what it is like to have me against you.' [35]I, the LORD, have spoken, and I will surely do these things to this whole wicked community, which has banded together against me. They will meet their end in this desert; here they will die."

[36]So the men Moses had sent to explore the land, who returned and made the whole community grumble against him by spreading a bad report about it— [37]these men responsible for spreading the bad report about the land were struck down and died of a plague before the LORD. [38]Of the men who went to explore the land, only Joshua son of Nun and Caleb son of Jephunneh survived.

[39]When Moses reported this to all the Israelites, they mourned bitterly. [40]Early the next morning they went up toward the high hill country. "We have sinned," they said. "We will go up to the place the LORD promised."

[41]But Moses said, "Why are you disobeying the LORD's command? This will not succeed! [42]Do not go up, because the LORD is not with you. You will be defeated by your enemies, [43]for the Amalekites and Canaanites will face you there. Because you have turned away from the LORD, he will not be with you and you will fall by the sword."

[44]Nevertheless, in their presumption they went up toward the high hill country, though neither Moses nor the ark of the LORD's covenant moved from the camp. [45]Then the Amalekites and Canaanites who lived in that hill country came down and attacked them and beat them down all the way to Hormah.

Supplementary Offerings

15 The LORD said to Moses, [2]"Speak to the Israelites and say to them: 'After you enter the land I am giving you as a home [3]and you present to the LORD offerings made by fire, from the herd or the flock, as an aroma pleasing to the LORD— whether burnt offerings or sacrifices, for special vows or freewill offerings or festival offerings— [4]then the one who brings his offering shall present to the LORD a grain offering of a tenth of an ephah[b] of fine flour mixed with a quarter of a hin[c] of oil. [5]With each lamb for the burnt offering or the sacrifice, prepare a quarter of a hin of wine as a drink offering.

---

[a]25 Hebrew *Yam Suph*; that is, Sea of Reeds   [b]4 That is, probably about 2 quarts (about 2 liters)
[c]4 That is, probably about 1 quart (about 1 liter); also in verse 5

VERSE FOR THE DAY: AUTHOR: PASSAGE FOR THE DAY:
Numbers 14:30   James Schaap   Numbers 13:26 — 14:9

Faith Can Move Mountains

A DOCTOR who is not a Christian once told me that he had seen miracles with his own eyes. The bones of an old woman he treated were rotting with cancer, he said. Yet she walked to his office for appointments. She shouldn't have been able to move, he said. Her pain should have been that bad. But what should have been, wasn't. Why? "Her faith," he told me. As she came closer to her death, she looked forward to life with her Lord. Her faith gave her the ability to take pain that no one "should have been" able to take.

Of course, that doesn't mean that those who feel pain have no faith. What the doctor remembered, he remembered as a miracle. But faith *can* do things we think are impossible . . .

You really can't blame the ten spies for chickening out of going into Canaan . . . They've seen the forts of the Canaanites. Sure, there's milk and honey, and everything's really rosy in this new land. But there are also giants running around. The place is crawling with fighters. No way, they say. No way can we take all those Hittites and Jebusites and Amorites.

Caleb and Joshua pooh-pooh the other ten . . . "The Lord loves us," they claim. "He'll bring us in safely."

But ten-to-two odds don't win elections. The Israelites believe the ten and run scared. And it's easy to understand why. Because it's easier *not* to have faith.

God doesn't like it—not at all. "If you're so scared," he says, "then why don't you just back up and start over?" Then he tells Moses the bad news. Not *one* of those who complained, not one of those who are over twenty years old, will ever make it to the promised land.

That's their punishment for faithlessness. A whole new generation of Israelites will have to be born into the kind of strong faith that their parents lack. Then, God's chosen people will make it.

What the Israelites forgot—and what we so easily forget—is that faith can move mountains.

Additional Scripture Readings: *Go to page 165 for your next*
Matthew 17:14–21;   *devotional reading.*
Philippians 4:10–13

⁶" 'With a ram prepare a grain offering of two-tenths of an ephah*a* of fine flour mixed with a third of a hin*b* of oil, ⁷and a third of a hin of wine as a drink offering. Offer it as an aroma pleasing to the LORD.

⁸" 'When you prepare a young bull as a burnt offering or sacrifice, for a special vow or a fellowship offering*c* to the LORD, ⁹bring with the bull a grain offering of three-tenths of an ephah*d* of fine flour mixed with half a hin*e* of oil. ¹⁰Also bring half a hin of wine as a drink offering. It will be an offering made by fire, an aroma pleasing to the LORD. ¹¹Each bull or ram, each lamb or young goat, is to be prepared in this manner. ¹²Do this for each one, for as many as you prepare.

¹³" 'Everyone who is native-born must do these things in this way when he brings an offering made by fire as an aroma pleasing to the LORD. ¹⁴For the generations to come, whenever an alien or anyone else living among you presents an offering made by fire as an aroma pleasing to the LORD, he must do exactly as you do. ¹⁵The community is to have the same rules for you and for the alien living among you; this is a lasting ordinance for the generations to come. You and the alien shall be the same before the LORD: ¹⁶The same laws and regulations will apply both to you and to the alien living among you.' "

¹⁷The LORD said to Moses, ¹⁸"Speak to the Israelites and say to them: 'When you enter the land to which I am taking you ¹⁹and you eat the food of the land, present a portion as an offering to the LORD. ²⁰Present a cake from the first of your ground meal and present it as an offering from the threshing floor. ²¹Throughout the generations to come you are to give this offering to the LORD from the first of your ground meal.

Offerings for Unintentional Sins

²²" 'Now if you unintentionally fail to keep any of these commands the LORD gave Moses— ²³any of the LORD's commands to you through him, from the day the LORD gave them and continuing through the generations to come— ²⁴and if this is done unintentionally without the community being aware of it, then the whole community is to offer a young bull for a burnt offering as an aroma pleasing

to the LORD, along with its prescribed grain offering and drink offering, and a male goat for a sin offering. ²⁵The priest is to make atonement for the whole Israelite community, and they will be forgiven, for it was not intentional and they have brought to the LORD for their wrong an offering made by fire and a sin offering. ²⁶The whole Israelite community and the aliens living among them will be forgiven, because all the people were involved in the unintentional wrong.

²⁷" 'But if just one person sins unintentionally, he must bring a year-old female goat for a sin offering. ²⁸The priest is to make atonement before the LORD for the one who erred by sinning unintentionally, and when atonement has been made for him, he will be forgiven. ²⁹One and the same law applies to everyone who sins unintentionally, whether he is a native-born Israelite or an alien.

³⁰" 'But anyone who sins defiantly, whether native-born or alien, blasphemes the LORD, and that person must be cut off from his people. ³¹Because he has despised the LORD's word and broken his commands, that person must surely be cut off; his guilt remains on him.' "

The Sabbath-Breaker Put to Death

³²While the Israelites were in the desert, a man was found gathering wood on the Sabbath day. ³³Those who found him gathering wood brought him to Moses and Aaron and the whole assembly, ³⁴and they kept him in custody, because it was not clear what should be done to him. ³⁵Then the LORD said to Moses, "The man must die. The whole assembly must stone him outside the camp." ³⁶So the assembly took him outside the camp and stoned him to death, as the LORD commanded Moses.

Tassels on Garments

³⁷The LORD said to Moses, ³⁸"Speak to the Israelites and say to them: 'Throughout the generations to come you are to make tassels on the corners of your garments, with a blue cord on each tassel. ³⁹You will have these tassels to look at and so you will remember all the commands of the LORD, that you may obey them and not prostitute yourselves by going after the lusts of your own hearts and eyes.

---

a6 That is, probably about 4 quarts (about 4.5 liters) 1.2 liters); also in verse 7 *c8* Traditionally *peace offering* *b6* That is, probably about 1 1/4 quarts (about *d9* That is, probably about 6 quarts (about 6.5 liters) *e9* That is, probably about 2 quarts (about 2 liters); also in verse 10

[40]Then you will remember to obey all my commands and will be consecrated to your God. [41]I am the Lord your God, who brought you out of Egypt to be your God. I am the Lord your God.' "

Korah, Dathan and Abiram

16 Korah son of Izhar, the son of Kohath, the son of Levi, and certain Reubenites—Dathan and Abiram, sons of Eliab, and On son of Peleth—became insolent[a] [2]and rose up against Moses. With them were 250 Israelite men, well-known community leaders who had been appointed members of the council. [3]They came as a group to oppose Moses and Aaron and said to them, "You have gone too far! The whole community is holy, every one of them, and the Lord is with them. Why then do you set yourselves above the Lord's assembly?"

[4]When Moses heard this, he fell facedown. [5]Then he said to Korah and all his followers: "In the morning the Lord will show who belongs to him and who is holy, and he will have that person come near him. The man he chooses he will cause to come near him. [6]You, Korah, and all your followers are to do this: Take censers [7]and tomorrow put fire and incense in them before the Lord. The man the Lord chooses will be the one who is holy. You Levites have gone too far!"

[8]Moses also said to Korah, "Now listen, you Levites! [9]Isn't it enough for you that the God of Israel has separated you from the rest of the Israelite community and brought you near himself to do the work at the Lord's tabernacle and to stand before the community and minister to them? [10]He has brought you and all your fellow Levites near himself, but now you are trying to get the priesthood too. [11]It is against the Lord that you and all your followers have banded together. Who is Aaron that you should grumble against him?"

[12]Then Moses summoned Dathan and Abiram, the sons of Eliab. But they said, "We will not come! [13]Isn't it enough that you have brought us up out of a land flowing with milk and honey to kill us in the desert? And now you also want to lord it over us? [14]Moreover, you haven't brought us into a land flowing with milk and honey or given us an inheritance of fields and vineyards. Will you gouge out the eyes of[b] these men? No, we will not come!"

[15]Then Moses became very angry and said to the Lord, "Do not accept their offering. I have not taken so much as a donkey from them, nor have I wronged any of them."

[16]Moses said to Korah, "You and all your followers are to appear before the Lord tomorrow—you and they and Aaron. [17]Each man is to take his censer and put incense in it—250 censers in all—and present it before the Lord. You and Aaron are to present your censers also." [18]So each man took his censer, put fire and incense in it, and stood with Moses and Aaron at the entrance to the Tent of Meeting. [19]When Korah had gathered all his followers in opposition to them at the entrance to the Tent of Meeting, the glory of the Lord appeared to the entire assembly. [20]The Lord said to Moses and Aaron, [21]"Separate yourselves from this assembly so I can put an end to them at once."

[22]But Moses and Aaron fell facedown and cried out, "O God, God of the spirits of all mankind, will you be angry with the entire assembly when only one man sins?"

[23]Then the Lord said to Moses, [24]"Say to the assembly, 'Move away from the tents of Korah, Dathan and Abiram.' "

[25]Moses got up and went to Dathan and Abiram, and the elders of Israel followed him. [26]He warned the assembly, "Move back from the tents of these wicked men! Do not touch anything belonging to them, or you will be swept away because of all their sins." [27]So they moved away from the tents of Korah, Dathan and Abiram. Dathan and Abiram had come out and were standing with their wives, children and little ones at the entrances to their tents.

[28]Then Moses said, "This is how you will know that the Lord has sent me to do all these things and that it was not my idea: [29]If these men die a natural death and experience only what usually happens to men, then the Lord has not sent me. [30]But if the Lord brings about something totally new, and the earth opens its mouth and swallows them, with everything that belongs to them, and they go down alive into the grave,[c] then you will know that these men have treated the Lord with contempt."

[31]As soon as he finished saying all this, the ground under them split apart [32]and

---

[a]1 Or *Peleth—took ⌊men⌋*   [b]14 Or *you make slaves of*; or *you deceive*   [c]30 Hebrew *Sheol*; also in verse 33

the earth opened its mouth and swallowed them, with their households and all Korah's men and all their possessions. ³³They went down alive into the grave, with everything they owned; the earth closed over them, and they perished and were gone from the community. ³⁴At their cries, all the Israelites around them fled, shouting, "The earth is going to swallow us too!"

³⁵And fire came out from the LORD and consumed the 250 men who were offering the incense.

³⁶The LORD said to Moses, ³⁷"Tell Eleazar son of Aaron, the priest, to take the censers out of the smoldering remains and scatter the coals some distance away, for the censers are holy — ³⁸the censers of the men who sinned at the cost of their lives. Hammer the censers into sheets to overlay the altar, for they were presented before the LORD and have become holy. Let them be a sign to the Israelites."

³⁹So Eleazar the priest collected the bronze censers brought by those who had been burned up, and he had them hammered out to overlay the altar, ⁴⁰as the LORD directed him through Moses. This was to remind the Israelites that no one except a descendant of Aaron should come to burn incense before the LORD, or he would become like Korah and his followers.

⁴¹The next day the whole Israelite community grumbled against Moses and Aaron. "You have killed the LORD's people," they said.

⁴²But when the assembly gathered in opposition to Moses and Aaron and turned toward the Tent of Meeting, suddenly the cloud covered it and the glory of the LORD appeared. ⁴³Then Moses and Aaron went to the front of the Tent of Meeting, ⁴⁴and the LORD said to Moses, ⁴⁵"Get away from this assembly so I can put an end to them at once." And they fell facedown.

⁴⁶Then Moses said to Aaron, "Take your censer and put incense in it, along with fire from the altar, and hurry to the assembly to make atonement for them. Wrath has come out from the LORD; the plague has started." ⁴⁷So Aaron did as Moses said, and ran into the midst of the assembly. The plague had already started among the people, but Aaron offered the incense and made atonement for them. ⁴⁸He stood between the living and the dead, and the plague stopped. ⁴⁹But 14,700 people died from the plague, in ad- dition to those who had died because of Korah. ⁵⁰Then Aaron returned to Moses at the entrance to the Tent of Meeting, for the plague had stopped.

The Budding of Aaron's Staff

17 The LORD said to Moses, ²"Speak to the Israelites and get twelve staffs from them, one from the leader of each of their ancestral tribes. Write the name of each man on his staff. ³On the staff of Levi write Aaron's name, for there must be one staff for the head of each ancestral tribe. ⁴Place them in the Tent of Meeting in front of the Testimony, where I meet with you. ⁵The staff belonging to the man I choose will sprout, and I will rid myself of this constant grumbling against you by the Israelites."

⁶So Moses spoke to the Israelites, and their leaders gave him twelve staffs, one for the leader of each of their ancestral tribes, and Aaron's staff was among them. ⁷Moses placed the staffs before the LORD in the Tent of the Testimony.

⁸The next day Moses entered the Tent of the Testimony and saw that Aaron's staff, which represented the house of Levi, had not only sprouted but had budded, blossomed and produced almonds. ⁹Then Moses brought out all the staffs from the LORD's presence to all the Israelites. They looked at them, and each man took his own staff.

¹⁰The LORD said to Moses, "Put back Aaron's staff in front of the Testimony, to be kept as a sign to the rebellious. This will put an end to their grumbling against me, so that they will not die." ¹¹Moses did just as the LORD commanded him.

¹²The Israelites said to Moses, "We will die! We are lost, we are all lost! ¹³Anyone who even comes near the tabernacle of the LORD will die. Are we all going to die?"

Duties of Priests and Levites

18 The LORD said to Aaron, "You, your sons and your father's family are to bear the responsibility for offenses against the sanctuary, and you and your sons alone are to bear the responsibility for offenses against the priesthood. ²Bring your fellow Levites from your ancestral tribe to join you and assist you when you and your sons minister before the Tent of the Testimony. ³They are to be responsible to you and are to perform all the duties of the Tent, but they must not go near the furnishings of the sanctuary or the altar, or both they and you will die. ⁴They are to

join you and be responsible for the care of the Tent of Meeting—all the work at the Tent—and no one else may come near where you are.

⁵"You are to be responsible for the care of the sanctuary and the altar, so that wrath will not fall on the Israelites again. ⁶I myself have selected your fellow Levites from among the Israelites as a gift to you, dedicated to the LORD to do the work at the Tent of Meeting. ⁷But only you and your sons may serve as priests in connection with everything at the altar and inside the curtain. I am giving you the service of the priesthood as a gift. Anyone else who comes near the sanctuary must be put to death."

Offerings for Priests and Levites

⁸Then the LORD said to Aaron, "I myself have put you in charge of the offerings presented to me; all the holy offerings the Israelites give me I give to you and your sons as your portion and regular share. ⁹You are to have the part of the most holy offerings that is kept from the fire. From all the gifts they bring me as most holy offerings, whether grain or sin or guilt offerings, that part belongs to you and your sons. ¹⁰Eat it as something most holy; every male shall eat it. You must regard it as holy.

¹¹"This also is yours: whatever is set aside from the gifts of all the wave offerings of the Israelites. I give this to you and your sons and daughters as your regular share. Everyone in your household who is ceremonially clean may eat it.

¹²"I give you all the finest olive oil and all the finest new wine and grain they give the LORD as the firstfruits of their harvest. ¹³All the land's firstfruits that they bring to the LORD will be yours. Everyone in your household who is ceremonially clean may eat it.

¹⁴"Everything in Israel that is devoted^a to the LORD is yours. ¹⁵The first offspring of every womb, both man and animal, that is offered to the LORD is yours. But you must redeem every firstborn son and every firstborn male of unclean animals. ¹⁶When they are a month old, you must redeem them at the redemption price set at five shekels^b of silver, according to the sanctuary shekel, which weighs twenty gerahs.

¹⁷"But you must not redeem the first-born of an ox, a sheep or a goat; they are holy. Sprinkle their blood on the altar and burn their fat as an offering made by fire, an aroma pleasing to the LORD. ¹⁸Their meat is to be yours, just as the breast of the wave offering and the right thigh are yours. ¹⁹Whatever is set aside from the holy offerings the Israelites present to the LORD I give to you and your sons and daughters as your regular share. It is an everlasting covenant of salt before the LORD for both you and your offspring."

²⁰The LORD said to Aaron, "You will have no inheritance in their land, nor will you have any share among them; I am your share and your inheritance among the Israelites.

²¹"I give to the Levites all the tithes in Israel as their inheritance in return for the work they do while serving at the Tent of Meeting. ²²From now on the Israelites must not go near the Tent of Meeting, or they will bear the consequences of their sin and will die. ²³It is the Levites who are to do the work at the Tent of Meeting and bear the responsibility for offenses against it. This is a lasting ordinance for the generations to come. They will receive no inheritance among the Israelites. ²⁴Instead, I give to the Levites as their inheritance the tithes that the Israelites present as an offering to the LORD. That is why I said concerning them: 'They will have no inheritance among the Israelites.' "

²⁵The LORD said to Moses, ²⁶"Speak to the Levites and say to them: 'When you receive from the Israelites the tithe I give you as your inheritance, you must present a tenth of that tithe as the LORD's offering. ²⁷Your offering will be reckoned to you as grain from the threshing floor or juice from the winepress. ²⁸In this way you also will present an offering to the LORD from all the tithes you receive from the Israelites. From these tithes you must give the LORD's portion to Aaron the priest. ²⁹You must present as the LORD's portion the best and holiest part of everything given to you.'

³⁰"Say to the Levites: 'When you present the best part, it will be reckoned to you as the product of the threshing floor or the winepress. ³¹You and your households may eat the rest of it anywhere, for it is your wages for your work at the Tent of Meeting. ³²By presenting the best part of it you will not be guilty in this

---

^{a}14 The Hebrew term refers to the irrevocable giving over of things or persons to the LORD. ^{b}16 That is, about 2 ounces (about 55 grams)

matter; then you will not defile the holy offerings of the Israelites, and you will not die.' "

The Water of Cleansing

19 The Lord said to Moses and Aaron: ²"This is a requirement of the law that the Lord has commanded: Tell the Israelites to bring you a red heifer without defect or blemish and that has never been under a yoke. ³Give it to Eleazar the priest; it is to be taken outside the camp and slaughtered in his presence. ⁴Then Eleazar the priest is to take some of its blood on his finger and sprinkle it seven times toward the front of the Tent of Meeting. ⁵While he watches, the heifer is to be burned—its hide, flesh, blood and offal. ⁶The priest is to take some cedar wood, hyssop and scarlet wool and throw them onto the burning heifer. ⁷After that, the priest must wash his clothes and bathe himself with water. He may then come into the camp, but he will be ceremonially unclean till evening. ⁸The man who burns it must also wash his clothes and bathe with water, and he too will be unclean till evening.

⁹"A man who is clean shall gather up the ashes of the heifer and put them in a ceremonially clean place outside the camp. They shall be kept by the Israelite community for use in the water of cleansing; it is for purification from sin. ¹⁰The man who gathers up the ashes of the heifer must also wash his clothes, and he too will be unclean till evening. This will be a lasting ordinance both for the Israelites and for the aliens living among them.

¹¹"Whoever touches the dead body of anyone will be unclean for seven days. ¹²He must purify himself with the water on the third day and on the seventh day; then he will be clean. But if he does not purify himself on the third and seventh days, he will not be clean. ¹³Whoever touches the dead body of anyone and fails to purify himself defiles the Lord's tabernacle. That person must be cut off from Israel. Because the water of cleansing has not been sprinkled on him, he is unclean; his uncleanness remains on him.

¹⁴"This is the law that applies when a person dies in a tent: Anyone who enters the tent and anyone who is in it will be unclean for seven days, ¹⁵and every open container without a lid fastened on it will be unclean.

¹⁶"Anyone out in the open who touches someone who has been killed with a sword or someone who has died a natural death, or anyone who touches a human bone or a grave, will be unclean for seven days.

¹⁷"For the unclean person, put some ashes from the burned purification offering into a jar and pour fresh water over them. ¹⁸Then a man who is ceremonially clean is to take some hyssop, dip it in the water and sprinkle the tent and all the furnishings and the people who were there. He must also sprinkle anyone who has touched a human bone or a grave or someone who has been killed or someone who has died a natural death. ¹⁹The man who is clean is to sprinkle the unclean person on the third and seventh days, and on the seventh day he is to purify him. The person being cleansed must wash his clothes and bathe with water, and that evening he will be clean. ²⁰But if a person who is unclean does not purify himself, he must be cut off from the community, because he has defiled the sanctuary of the Lord. The water of cleansing has not been sprinkled on him, and he is unclean. ²¹This is a lasting ordinance for them.

"The man who sprinkles the water of cleansing must also wash his clothes, and anyone who touches the water of cleansing will be unclean till evening. ²²Anything that an unclean person touches becomes unclean, and anyone who touches it becomes unclean till evening."

Water From the Rock

20 In the first month the whole Israelite community arrived at the Desert of Zin, and they stayed at Kadesh. There Miriam died and was buried.

²Now there was no water for the community, and the people gathered in opposition to Moses and Aaron. ³They quarreled with Moses and said, "If only we had died when our brothers fell dead before the Lord! ⁴Why did you bring the Lord's community into this desert, that we and our livestock should die here? ⁵Why did you bring us up out of Egypt to this terrible place? It has no grain or figs, grapevines or pomegranates. And there is no water to drink!"

⁶Moses and Aaron went from the assembly to the entrance to the Tent of Meeting and fell facedown, and the glory of the Lord appeared to them. ⁷The Lord said to Moses, ⁸"Take the staff, and you and your brother Aaron gather the assembly together. Speak to that rock before their eyes and it will pour out its water.

You will bring water out of the rock for the community so they and their livestock can drink."

⁹So Moses took the staff from the LORD's presence, just as he commanded him. ¹⁰He and Aaron gathered the assembly together in front of the rock and Moses said to them, "Listen, you rebels, must we bring you water out of this rock?" ¹¹Then Moses raised his arm and struck the rock twice with his staff. Water gushed out, and the community and their livestock drank.

¹²But the LORD said to Moses and Aaron, "Because you did not trust in me enough to honor me as holy in the sight of the Israelites, you will not bring this community into the land I give them."

¹³These were the waters of Meribah,ᵃ where the Israelites quarreled with the LORD and where he showed himself holy among them.

Edom Denies Israel Passage

¹⁴Moses sent messengers from Kadesh to the king of Edom, saying:

"This is what your brother Israel says: You know about all the hardships that have come upon us. ¹⁵Our forefathers went down into Egypt, and we lived there many years. The Egyptians mistreated us and our fathers, ¹⁶but when we cried out to the LORD, he heard our cry and sent an angel and brought us out of Egypt.

"Now we are here at Kadesh, a town on the edge of your territory. ¹⁷Please let us pass through your country. We will not go through any field or vineyard, or drink water from any well. We will travel along the king's highway and not turn to the right or to the left until we have passed through your territory."

¹⁸But Edom answered:

"You may not pass through here; if you try, we will march out and attack you with the sword."

¹⁹The Israelites replied:

"We will go along the main road, and if we or our livestock drink any of your water, we will pay for it. We only want to pass through on foot — nothing else."

²⁰Again they answered:

"You may not pass through."

Then Edom came out against them with a large and powerful army. ²¹Since Edom refused to let them go through their territory, Israel turned away from them.

The Death of Aaron

²²The whole Israelite community set out from Kadesh and came to Mount Hor. ²³At Mount Hor, near the border of Edom, the LORD said to Moses and Aaron, ²⁴"Aaron will be gathered to his people. He will not enter the land I give the Israelites, because both of you rebelled against my command at the waters of Meribah. ²⁵Get Aaron and his son Eleazar and take them up Mount Hor. ²⁶Remove Aaron's garments and put them on his son Eleazar, for Aaron will be gathered to his people; he will die there."

²⁷Moses did as the LORD commanded: They went up Mount Hor in the sight of the whole community. ²⁸Moses removed Aaron's garments and put them on his son Eleazar. And Aaron died there on top of the mountain. Then Moses and Eleazar came down from the mountain, ²⁹and when the whole community learned that Aaron had died, the entire house of Israel mourned for him thirty days.

Arad Destroyed

21 When the Canaanite king of Arad, who lived in the Negev, heard that Israel was coming along the road to Atharim, he attacked the Israelites and captured some of them. ²Then Israel made this vow to the LORD: "If you will deliver these people into our hands, we will totally destroyᵇ their cities." ³The LORD listened to Israel's plea and gave the Canaanites over to them. They completely destroyed them and their towns; so the place was named Hormah.ᶜ

The Bronze Snake

⁴They traveled from Mount Hor along the route to the Red Sea,ᵈ to go around Edom. But the people grew impatient on the way; ⁵they spoke against God and against Moses, and said, "Why have you

---

ᵃ13 *Meribah* means *quarreling.*   ᵇ2 The Hebrew term refers to the irrevocable giving over of things or persons to the LORD, often by totally destroying them; also in verse 3.   ᶜ3 *Hormah* means *destruction.*
ᵈ4 Hebrew *Yam Suph*; that is, Sea of Reeds

brought us up out of Egypt to die in the desert? There is no bread! There is no water! And we detest this miserable food!"

6Then the LORD sent venomous snakes among them; they bit the people and many Israelites died. 7The people came to Moses and said, "We sinned when we spoke against the LORD and against you. Pray that the LORD will take the snakes away from us." So Moses prayed for the people.

8The LORD said to Moses, "Make a snake and put it up on a pole; anyone who is bitten can look at it and live." 9So Moses made a bronze snake and put it up on a pole. Then when anyone was bitten by a snake and looked at the bronze snake, he lived.

The Journey to Moab

10The Israelites moved on and camped at Oboth. 11Then they set out from Oboth and camped in Iye Abarim, in the desert that faces Moab toward the sunrise. 12From there they moved on and camped in the Zered Valley. 13They set out from there and camped alongside the Arnon, which is in the desert extending into Amorite territory. The Arnon is the border of Moab, between Moab and the Amorites. 14That is why the Book of the Wars of the LORD says:

". . . Waheb in Suphah*a* and the
    ravines,
   the Arnon 15and*b* the slopes of the
    ravines
  that lead to the site of Ar
   and lie along the border of Moab."

16From there they continued on to Beer, the well where the LORD said to Moses, "Gather the people together and I will give them water."

17Then Israel sang this song:

"Spring up, O well!
  Sing about it,
18about the well that the princes dug,
  that the nobles of the people sank—

  the nobles with scepters and staffs."

Then they went from the desert to Mattanah, 19from Mattanah to Nahaliel, from Nahaliel to Bamoth, 20and from Bamoth to the valley in Moab where the top of Pisgah overlooks the wasteland.

Defeat of Sihon and Og

21Israel sent messengers to say to Sihon king of the Amorites:

22"Let us pass through your country. We will not turn aside into any field or vineyard, or drink water from any well. We will travel along the king's highway until we have passed through your territory."

23But Sihon would not let Israel pass through his territory. He mustered his entire army and marched out into the desert against Israel. When he reached Jahaz, he fought with Israel. 24Israel, however, put him to the sword and took over his land from the Arnon to the Jabbok, but only as far as the Ammonites, because their border was fortified. 25Israel captured all the cities of the Amorites and occupied them, including Heshbon and all its surrounding settlements. 26Heshbon was the city of Sihon king of the Amorites, who had fought against the former king of Moab and had taken from him all his land as far as the Arnon.

27That is why the poets say:

"Come to Heshbon and let it be
    rebuilt;
  let Sihon's city be restored.

28"Fire went out from Heshbon,
  a blaze from the city of Sihon.
 It consumed Ar of Moab,
  the citizens of Arnon's heights.
29Woe to you, O Moab!
  You are destroyed, O people of
    Chemosh!
 He has given up his sons as fugitives
  and his daughters as captives
  to Sihon king of the Amorites.

30"But we have overthrown them;
  Heshbon is destroyed all the way to
    Dibon.
 We have demolished them as far as
    Nophah,
  which extends to Medeba."

31So Israel settled in the land of the Amorites.

32After Moses had sent spies to Jazer, the Israelites captured its surrounding settlements and drove out the Amorites who were there. 33Then they turned and went up along the road toward Bashan, and Og king of Bashan and his whole army

a14 The meaning of the Hebrew for this phrase is uncertain. *b14,15* Or "I have been given from Suphah and the ravines / of the Arnon 15to* marched out to meet them in battle at Edrei.

34The LORD said to Moses, "Do not be afraid of him, for I have handed him over to you, with his whole army and his land. Do to him what you did to Sihon king of the Amorites, who reigned in Heshbon." **35**So they struck him down, together with his sons and his whole army, leaving them no survivors. And they took possession of his land.

Balak Summons Balaam

22 Then the Israelites traveled to the plains of Moab and camped along the Jordan across from Jericho.*a*

2Now Balak son of Zippor saw all that Israel had done to the Amorites, **3**and Moab was terrified because there were so many people. Indeed, Moab was filled with dread because of the Israelites.

4The Moabites said to the elders of Midian, "This horde is going to lick up everything around us, as an ox licks up the grass of the field."

So Balak son of Zippor, who was king of Moab at that time, **5**sent messengers to summon Balaam son of Beor, who was at Pethor, near the River,*b* in his native land. Balak said:

"A people has come out of Egypt; they cover the face of the land and have settled next to me. **6**Now come and put a curse on these people, because they are too powerful for me. Perhaps then I will be able to defeat them and drive them out of the country. For I know that those you bless are blessed, and those you curse are cursed."

7The elders of Moab and Midian left, taking with them the fee for divination. When they came to Balaam, they told him what Balak had said.

8"Spend the night here," Balaam said to them, "and I will bring you back the answer the LORD gives me." So the Moabite princes stayed with him.

9God came to Balaam and asked, "Who are these men with you?"

10Balaam said to God, "Balak son of Zippor, king of Moab, sent me this message: **11**'A people that has come out of Egypt covers the face of the land. Now come and put a curse on them for me. Perhaps then I will be able to fight them and drive them away.'"

12But God said to Balaam, "Do not go with them. You must not put a curse on those people, because they are blessed."

13The next morning Balaam got up and said to Balak's princes, "Go back to your own country, for the LORD has refused to let me go with you."

14So the Moabite princes returned to Balak and said, "Balaam refused to come with us."

15Then Balak sent other princes, more numerous and more distinguished than the first. **16**They came to Balaam and said:

"This is what Balak son of Zippor says: Do not let anything keep you from coming to me, **17**because I will reward you handsomely and do whatever you say. Come and put a curse on these people for me."

18But Balaam answered them, "Even if Balak gave me his palace filled with silver and gold, I could not do anything great or small to go beyond the command of the LORD my God. **19**Now stay here tonight as the others did, and I will find out what else the LORD will tell me."

20That night God came to Balaam and said, "Since these men have come to summon you, go with them, but do only what I tell you."

Balaam's Donkey

21Balaam got up in the morning, saddled his donkey and went with the princes of Moab. **22**But God was very angry when he went, and the angel of the LORD stood in the road to oppose him. Balaam was riding on his donkey, and his two servants were with him. **23**When the donkey saw the angel of the LORD standing in the road with a drawn sword in his hand, she turned off the road into a field. Balaam beat her to get her back on the road.

24Then the angel of the LORD stood in a narrow path between two vineyards, with walls on both sides. **25**When the donkey saw the angel of the LORD, she pressed close to the wall, crushing Balaam's foot against it. So he beat her again.

26Then the angel of the LORD moved on ahead and stood in a narrow place where there was no room to turn, either to the right or to the left. **27**When the donkey saw the angel of the LORD, she lay down under Balaam, and he was angry and beat her with his staff. **28**Then the LORD opened the donkey's mouth, and she said to Ba-

---

*a*1 Hebrew *Jordan of Jericho*; possibly an ancient name for the Jordan River   *b*5 That is, the Euphrates laam, "What have I done to you to make you beat me these three times?"

29Balaam answered the donkey, "You have made a fool of me! If I had a sword in my hand, I would kill you right now."

30The donkey said to Balaam, "Am I not your own donkey, which you have always ridden, to this day? Have I been in the habit of doing this to you?"

"No," he said.

31Then the LORD opened Balaam's eyes, and he saw the angel of the LORD standing in the road with his sword drawn. So he bowed low and fell facedown.

32The angel of the LORD asked him, "Why have you beaten your donkey these three times? I have come here to oppose you because your path is a reckless one before me.*a* **33**The donkey saw me and turned away from me these three times. If she had not turned away, I would certainly have killed you by now, but I would have spared her."

34Balaam said to the angel of the LORD, "I have sinned. I did not realize you were standing in the road to oppose me. Now if you are displeased, I will go back."

35The angel of the LORD said to Balaam, "Go with the men, but speak only what I tell you." So Balaam went with the princes of Balak.

36When Balak heard that Balaam was coming, he went out to meet him at the Moabite town on the Arnon border, at the edge of his territory. **37**Balak said to Balaam, "Did I not send you an urgent summons? Why didn't you come to me? Am I really not able to reward you?"

38"Well, I have come to you now," Balaam replied. "But can I say just anything? I must speak only what God puts in my mouth."

39Then Balaam went with Balak to Kiriath Huzoth. **40**Balak sacrificed cattle and sheep, and gave some to Balaam and the princes who were with him. **41**The next morning Balak took Balaam up to Bamoth Baal, and from there he saw part of the people.

Balaam's First Oracle

23 Balaam said, "Build me seven altars here, and prepare seven bulls and seven rams for me." **2**Balak did as Balaam said, and the two of them offered a bull and a ram on each altar.

3Then Balaam said to Balak, "Stay here beside your offering while I go aside. Per-

haps the LORD will come to meet with me. Whatever he reveals to me I will tell you." Then he went off to a barren height.

4God met with him, and Balaam said, "I have prepared seven altars, and on each altar I have offered a bull and a ram."

5The LORD put a message in Balaam's mouth and said, "Go back to Balak and give him this message."

6So he went back to him and found him standing beside his offering, with all the princes of Moab. **7**Then Balaam uttered his oracle:

"Balak brought me from Aram,
   the king of Moab from the eastern
      mountains.
'Come,' he said, 'curse Jacob for me;
   come, denounce Israel.'
8How can I curse
   those whom God has not cursed?
How can I denounce
   those whom the LORD has not
      denounced?
9From the rocky peaks I see them,
   from the heights I view them.
I see a people who live apart
   and do not consider themselves one
      of the nations.
10Who can count the dust of Jacob
   or number the fourth part of Israel?
Let me die the death of the righteous,
   and may my end be like theirs!"

11Balak said to Balaam, "What have you done to me? I brought you to curse my enemies, but you have done nothing but bless them!"

12He answered, "Must I not speak what the LORD puts in my mouth?"

Balaam's Second Oracle

13Then Balak said to him, "Come with me to another place where you can see them; you will see only a part but not all of them. And from there, curse them for me." **14**So he took him to the field of Zophim on the top of Pisgah, and there he built seven altars and offered a bull and a ram on each altar.

15Balaam said to Balak, "Stay here beside your offering while I meet with him over there."

16The LORD met with Balaam and put a message in his mouth and said, "Go back to Balak and give him this message."

17So he went to him and found him standing beside his offering, with the

---

a32 The meaning of the Hebrew for this clause is uncertain.

princes of Moab. Balak asked him, "What did the LORD say?"

18Then he uttered his oracle:

"Arise, Balak, and listen;
    hear me, son of Zippor.
19God is not a man, that he should lie,
    nor a son of man, that he should
        change his mind.
Does he speak and then not act?
    Does he promise and not fulfill?
20I have received a command to bless;
    he has blessed, and I cannot change
        it.

21"No misfortune is seen in Jacob,
    no misery observed in Israel.*a*
The LORD their God is with them;
    the shout of the King is among
        them.
22God brought them out of Egypt;
    they have the strength of a wild ox.
23There is no sorcery against Jacob,
    no divination against Israel.
It will now be said of Jacob
    and of Israel, 'See what God has
        done!'
24The people rise like a lioness;
    they rouse themselves like a lion
that does not rest till he devours his
        prey
    and drinks the blood of his victims."

25Then Balak said to Balaam, "Neither curse them at all nor bless them at all!" **26**Balaam answered, "Did I not tell you I must do whatever the LORD says?"

Balaam's Third Oracle

27Then Balak said to Balaam, "Come, let me take you to another place. Perhaps it will please God to let you curse them for me from there." **28**And Balak took Balaam to the top of Peor, overlooking the wasteland.

29Balaam said, "Build me seven altars here, and prepare seven bulls and seven rams for me." **30**Balak did as Balaam had said, and offered a bull and a ram on each altar.

24 Now when Balaam saw that it pleased the LORD to bless Israel, he did not resort to sorcery as at other times, but turned his face toward the desert. **2**When Balaam looked out and saw Israel encamped tribe by tribe, the Spirit of God came upon him **3**and he uttered his oracle:

"The oracle of Balaam son of Beor,

the oracle of one whose eye sees
    clearly,
4the oracle of one who hears the words
    of God,
who sees a vision from the
    Almighty,*b*
who falls prostrate, and whose eyes
    are opened:

5"How beautiful are your tents,
    O Jacob,
    your dwelling places, O Israel!

6"Like valleys they spread out,
    like gardens beside a river,
like aloes planted by the LORD,
    like cedars beside the waters.
7Water will flow from their buckets;
    their seed will have abundant water.

"Their king will be greater than Agag;
    their kingdom will be exalted.

8"God brought them out of Egypt;
    they have the strength of a wild ox.
They devour hostile nations
    and break their bones in pieces;
    with their arrows they pierce them.
9Like a lion they crouch and lie down,
    like a lioness—who dares to rouse
        them?

"May those who bless you be blessed
    and those who curse you be
        cursed!"

10Then Balak's anger burned against Balaam. He struck his hands together and said to him, "I summoned you to curse my enemies, but you have blessed them these three times. **11**Now leave at once and go home! I said I would reward you handsomely, but the LORD has kept you from being rewarded."

12Balaam answered Balak, "Did I not tell the messengers you sent me, **13**'Even if Balak gave me his palace filled with silver and gold, I could not do anything of my own accord, good or bad, to go beyond the command of the LORD—and I must say only what the LORD says'? **14**Now I am going back to my people, but come, let me warn you of what this people will do to your people in days to come."

Balaam's Fourth Oracle

15Then he uttered his oracle:

"The oracle of Balaam son of Beor,

the oracle of one whose eye sees
    clearly,
16the oracle of one who hears the words
    of God,
who has knowledge from the Most
    High,
who sees a vision from the Almighty,
who falls prostrate, and whose eyes
    are opened:

17"I see him, but not now;
    I behold him, but not near.
A star will come out of Jacob;
    a scepter will rise out of Israel.
He will crush the foreheads of Moab,
    the skulls*a* of*b* all the sons of
    Sheth.*c*
18Edom will be conquered;
    Seir, his enemy, will be conquered,
    but Israel will grow strong.
19A ruler will come out of Jacob
    and destroy the survivors of the
    city."

Balaam's Final Oracles

20Then Balaam saw Amalek and uttered
his oracle:

"Amalek was first among the nations,
    but he will come to ruin at last."

21Then he saw the Kenites and uttered
his oracle:

"Your dwelling place is secure,
    your nest is set in a rock;
22yet you Kenites will be destroyed
    when Asshur takes you captive."

23Then he uttered his oracle:

"Ah, who can live when God does
    this?*d*
24 Ships will come from the shores of
    Kittim;
they will subdue Asshur and Eber,
    but they too will come to ruin."

25Then Balaam got up and returned
home and Balak went his own way.

Moab Seduces Israel

25 While Israel was staying in Shittim,
the men began to indulge in sexual
immorality with Moabite women, 2who
invited them to the sacrifices to their gods.
The people ate and bowed down before
these gods. 3So Israel joined in worshiping

the Baal of Peor. And the LORD's anger
burned against them.

4The LORD said to Moses, "Take all the
leaders of these people, kill them and expose them in broad daylight before the
LORD, so that the LORD's fierce anger may
turn away from Israel."

5So Moses said to Israel's judges, "Each
of you must put to death those of your
men who have joined in worshiping the
Baal of Peor."

6Then an Israelite man brought to his
family a Midianite woman right before the
eyes of Moses and the whole assembly of
Israel while they were weeping at the entrance to the Tent of Meeting. 7When
Phinehas son of Eleazar, the son of Aaron,
the priest, saw this, he left the assembly,
took a spear in his hand 8and followed the
Israelite into the tent. He drove the spear
through both of them — through the Israelite and into the woman's body. Then the
plague against the Israelites was stopped;
9but those who died in the plague numbered 24,000.

10The LORD said to Moses, 11"Phinehas
son of Eleazar, the son of Aaron, the
priest, has turned my anger away from the
Israelites; for he was as zealous as I am for
my honor among them, so that in my zeal
I did not put an end to them. 12Therefore
tell him I am making my covenant of
peace with him. 13He and his descendants
will have a covenant of a lasting priesthood, because he was zealous for the hon-
or of his God and made atonement for the
Israelites."

14The name of the Israelite who was
killed with the Midianite woman was Zimri son of Salu, the leader of a Simeonite
family. 15And the name of the Midianite
woman who was put to death was Cozbi
daughter of Zur, a tribal chief of a Midianite family.

16The LORD said to Moses, 17"Treat the
Midianites as enemies and kill them, 18be-
cause they treated you as enemies when
they deceived you in the affair of Peor and
their sister Cozbi, the daughter of a Midianite leader, the woman who was killed
when the plague came as a result of Peor."

The Second Census

26 After the plague the LORD said to
Moses and Eleazar son of Aaron,
the priest, 2"Take a census of the whole

---

a 17 Samaritan Pentateuch (see also Jer. 48:45); the meaning of the word in the Masoretic Text is
uncertain.   *b* 17 Or possibly *Moab, / batter*   *c* 17 Or *all the noisy boasters*   *d* 23 Masoretic Text;
with a different word division of the Hebrew *A people will gather from the north.*

Israelite community by families—all those twenty years old or more who are able to serve in the army of Israel." **3**So on the plains of Moab by the Jordan across from Jericho,[a] Moses and Eleazar the priest spoke with them and said, **4**"Take a census of the men twenty years old or more, as the LORD commanded Moses."

These were the Israelites who came out of Egypt:

5The descendants of Reuben, the firstborn son of Israel, were:

through Hanoch, the Hanochite clan;
through Pallu, the Palluite clan;
6through Hezron, the Hezronite clan;
through Carmi, the Carmite clan.

7These were the clans of Reuben; those numbered were 43,730.

8The son of Pallu was Eliab, **9**and the sons of Eliab were Nemuel, Dathan and Abiram. The same Dathan and Abiram were the community officials who rebelled against Moses and Aaron and were among Korah's followers when they rebelled against the LORD. **10**The earth opened its mouth and swallowed them along with Korah, whose followers died when the fire devoured the 250 men. And they served as a warning sign. **11**The line of Korah, however, did not die out.

12The descendants of Simeon by their clans were:

through Nemuel, the Nemuelite clan;
through Jamin, the Jaminite clan;
through Jakin, the Jakinite clan;
13through Zerah, the Zerahite clan;
through Shaul, the Shaulite clan.

14These were the clans of Simeon; there were 22,200 men.

15The descendants of Gad by their clans were:

through Zephon, the Zephonite clan;
through Haggi, the Haggite clan;
through Shuni, the Shunite clan;
16through Ozni, the Oznite clan;
through Eri, the Erite clan;
17through Arodi,[b] the Arodite clan;
through Areli, the Arelite clan.

18These were the clans of Gad; those numbered were 40,500.

19Er and Onan were sons of Judah, but they died in Canaan. **20**The descendants of Judah by their clans were:

through Shelah, the Shelanite clan;
through Perez, the Perezite clan;
through Zerah, the Zerahite clan.

21The descendants of Perez were:

through Hezron, the Hezronite clan;
through Hamul, the Hamulite clan.

22These were the clans of Judah; those numbered were 76,500.

23The descendants of Issachar by their clans were:

through Tola, the Tolaite clan;
through Puah, the Puite[c] clan;
24through Jashub, the Jashubite clan;
through Shimron, the Shimronite clan.

25These were the clans of Issachar; those numbered were 64,300.

26The descendants of Zebulun by their clans were:

through Sered, the Seredite clan;
through Elon, the Elonite clan;
through Jahleel, the Jahleelite clan.

27These were the clans of Zebulun; those numbered were 60,500.

28The descendants of Joseph by their clans through Manasseh and Ephraim were:

29The descendants of Manasseh:

through Makir, the Makirite clan (Makir was the father of Gilead);
through Gilead, the Gileadite clan.
30These were the descendants of Gilead:

through Iezer, the Iezerite clan;
through Helek, the Helekite clan;
31through Asriel, the Asrielite clan;
through Shechem, the Shechemite clan;
32through Shemida, the Shemidaite clan;
through Hepher, the Hepherite clan.

33(Zelophehad son of Hepher had no sons; he had only daughters, whose names were Mahlah, Noah, Hoglah, Milcah and Tirzah.)

---

a3 Hebrew *Jordan of Jericho*; possibly an ancient name for the Jordan River; also in verse 63
b17 Samaritan Pentateuch and Syriac (see also Gen. 46:16); Masoretic Text *Arod*   *c23* Samaritan Pentateuch, Septuagint, Vulgate and Syriac (see also 1 Chron. 7:1); Masoretic Text *through Puvah, the Punite*

34These were the clans of Manasseh; those numbered were 52,700.

35These were the descendants of Ephraim by their clans:

through Shuthelah, the Shuthelahite clan;

through Beker, the Bekerite clan;

through Tahan, the Tahanite clan.

36These were the descendants of Shuthelah:

through Eran, the Eranite clan.

37These were the clans of Ephraim; those numbered were 32,500.

These were the descendants of Joseph by their clans.

38The descendants of Benjamin by their clans were:

through Bela, the Belaite clan;

through Ashbel, the Ashbelite clan;

through Ahiram, the Ahiramite clan;

39through Shupham,[a] the Shuphamite clan;

through Hupham, the Huphamite clan.

40The descendants of Bela through Ard and Naaman were:

through Ard,[b] the Ardite clan;

through Naaman, the Naamite clan.

41These were the clans of Benjamin; those numbered were 45,600.

42These were the descendants of Dan by their clans:

through Shuham, the Shuhamite clan.

These were the clans of Dan: **43**All of them were Shuhamite clans; and those numbered were 64,400.

44The descendants of Asher by their clans were:

through Imnah, the Imnite clan;

through Ishvi, the Ishvite clan;

through Beriah, the Beriite clan;

45and through the descendants of Beriah:

through Heber, the Heberite clan;

through Malkiel, the Malkielite clan.

46(Asher had a daughter named Serah.)

47These were the clans of Asher; those numbered were 53,400.

48The descendants of Naphtali by their clans were:

through Jahzeel, the Jahzeelite clan;

through Guni, the Gunite clan;

49through Jezer, the Jezerite clan;

through Shillem, the Shillemite clan.

50These were the clans of Naphtali; those numbered were 45,400.

51The total number of the men of Israel was 601,730.

52The Lord said to Moses, **53**"The land is to be allotted to them as an inheritance based on the number of names. **54**To a larger group give a larger inheritance, and to a smaller group a smaller one; each is to receive its inheritance according to the number of those listed. **55**Be sure that the land is distributed by lot. What each group inherits will be according to the names for its ancestral tribe. **56**Each inheritance is to be distributed by lot among the larger and smaller groups."

57These were the Levites who were counted by their clans:

through Gershon, the Gershonite clan;

through Kohath, the Kohathite clan;

through Merari, the Merarite clan.

58These also were Levite clans:

the Libnite clan,

the Hebronite clan,

the Mahlite clan,

the Mushite clan,

the Korahite clan.

(Kohath was the forefather of Amram; **59**the name of Amram's wife was Jochebed, a descendant of Levi, who was born to the Levites[c] in Egypt. To Amram she bore Aaron, Moses and their sister Miriam. **60**Aaron was the father of Nadab and Abihu, Eleazar and Ithamar. **61**But Nadab and Abihu died when they made an offering before the Lord with unauthorized fire.)

62All the male Levites a month old or more numbered 23,000. They were not counted along with the other Israelites because they received no inheritance among them.

63These are the ones counted by Moses and Eleazar the priest when they counted the Israelites on the plains of Moab by the

---

a39 A few manuscripts of the Masoretic Text, Samaritan Pentateuch, Vulgate and Syriac (see also Septuagint); most manuscripts of the Masoretic Text *Shephupham*   *b40* Samaritan Pentateuch and Vulgate (see also Septuagint); Masoretic Text does not have *through Ard.*   *c59* Or *Jochebed, a daughter of Levi, who was born to Levi*

Jordan across from Jericho. **64**Not one of them was among those counted by Moses and Aaron the priest when they counted the Israelites in the Desert of Sinai. **65**For the LORD had told those Israelites they would surely die in the desert, and not one of them was left except Caleb son of Jephunneh and Joshua son of Nun.

Zelophehad's Daughters

27 The daughters of Zelophehad son of Hepher, the son of Gilead, the son of Makir, the son of Manasseh, belonged to the clans of Manasseh son of Joseph. The names of the daughters were Mahlah, Noah, Hoglah, Milcah and Tirzah. They approached **2**the entrance to the Tent of Meeting and stood before Moses, Eleazar the priest, the leaders and the whole assembly, and said, **3**"Our father died in the desert. He was not among Korah's followers, who banded together against the LORD, but he died for his own sin and left no sons. **4**Why should our father's name disappear from his clan because he had no son? Give us property among our father's relatives."

5So Moses brought their case before the LORD **6**and the LORD said to him, **7**"What Zelophehad's daughters are saying is right. You must certainly give them property as an inheritance among their father's relatives and turn their father's inheritance over to them.

8"Say to the Israelites, 'If a man dies and leaves no son, turn his inheritance over to his daughter. **9**If he has no daughter, give his inheritance to his brothers. **10**If he has no brothers, give his inheritance to his father's brothers. **11**If his father had no brothers, give his inheritance to the nearest relative in his clan, that he may possess it. This is to be a legal requirement for the Israelites, as the LORD commanded Moses.' "

Joshua to Succeed Moses

12Then the LORD said to Moses, "Go up this mountain in the Abarim range and see the land I have given the Israelites. **13**After you have seen it, you too will be gathered to your people, as your brother Aaron was, **14**for when the community rebelled at the waters in the Desert of Zin, both of you disobeyed my command to honor me as holy before their eyes."

(These were the waters of Meribah Kadesh, in the Desert of Zin.)

15Moses said to the LORD, **16**"May the LORD, the God of the spirits of all mankind, appoint a man over this community **17**to go out and come in before them, one who will lead them out and bring them in, so the LORD's people will not be like sheep without a shepherd."

18So the LORD said to Moses, "Take Joshua son of Nun, a man in whom is the spirit,*a* and lay your hand on him. **19**Have him stand before Eleazar the priest and the entire assembly and commission him in their presence. **20**Give him some of your authority so the whole Israelite community will obey him. **21**He is to stand before Eleazar the priest, who will obtain decisions for him by inquiring of the Urim before the LORD. At his command he and the entire community of the Israelites will go out, and at his command they will come in."

22Moses did as the LORD commanded him. He took Joshua and had him stand before Eleazar the priest and the whole assembly. **23**Then he laid his hands on him and commissioned him, as the LORD instructed through Moses.

Daily Offerings

28 The LORD said to Moses, **2**"Give this command to the Israelites and say to them: 'See that you present to me at the appointed time the food for my offerings made by fire, as an aroma pleasing to me.' **3**Say to them: 'This is the offering made by fire that you are to present to the LORD: two lambs a year old without defect, as a regular burnt offering each day. **4**Prepare one lamb in the morning and the other at twilight, **5**together with a grain offering of a tenth of an ephah*b* of fine flour mixed with a quarter of a hin*c* of oil from pressed olives. **6**This is the regular burnt offering instituted at Mount Sinai as a pleasing aroma, an offering made to the LORD by fire. **7**The accompanying drink offering is to be a quarter of a hin of fermented drink with each lamb. Pour out the drink offering to the LORD at the sanctuary. **8**Prepare the second lamb at twilight, along with the same kind of grain offering and drink offering that you prepare in the morning. This is an offering made by fire, an aroma pleasing to the LORD.

---

*a*18 Or *Spirit*   *b*5 That is, probably about 2 quarts (about 2 liters); also in verses 13, 21 and 29
*c*5 That is, probably about 1 quart (about 1 liter); also in verses 7 and 14

Sabbath Offerings

9 " 'On the Sabbath day, make an offering of two lambs a year old without defect, together with its drink offering and a grain offering of two-tenths of an ephah*a* of fine flour mixed with oil. **10**This is the burnt offering for every Sabbath, in addition to the regular burnt offering and its drink offering.

Monthly Offerings

11 " 'On the first of every month, present to the LORD a burnt offering of two young bulls, one ram and seven male lambs a year old, all without defect. **12**With each bull there is to be a grain offering of three-tenths of an ephah*b* of fine flour mixed with oil; with the ram, a grain offering of two-tenths of an ephah of fine flour mixed with oil; **13**and with each lamb, a grain offering of a tenth of an ephah of fine flour mixed with oil. This is for a burnt offering, a pleasing aroma, an offering made to the LORD by fire. **14**With each bull there is to be a drink offering of half a hin*c* of wine; with the ram, a third of a hin*d*; and with each lamb, a quarter of a hin. This is the monthly burnt offering to be made at each new moon during the year. **15**Besides the regular burnt offering with its drink offering, one male goat is to be presented to the LORD as a sin offering.

The Passover

16 " 'On the fourteenth day of the first month the LORD's Passover is to be held. **17**On the fifteenth day of this month there is to be a festival; for seven days eat bread made without yeast. **18**On the first day hold a sacred assembly and do no regular work. **19**Present to the LORD an offering made by fire, a burnt offering of two young bulls, one ram and seven male lambs a year old, all without defect. **20**With each bull prepare a grain offering of three-tenths of an ephah of fine flour mixed with oil; with the ram, two-tenths; **21**and with each of the seven lambs, one-tenth. **22**Include one male goat as a sin offering to make atonement for you. **23**Prepare these in addition to the regular morning burnt offering. **24**In this way prepare the food for the offering made by fire every day for seven days as an aroma pleasing to the LORD; it is to be prepared in addition to the regular burnt offering and its drink offering. **25**On the seventh day hold a sacred assembly and do no regular work.

Feast of Weeks

26 " 'On the day of firstfruits, when you present to the LORD an offering of new grain during the Feast of Weeks, hold a sacred assembly and do no regular work. **27**Present a burnt offering of two young bulls, one ram and seven male lambs a year old as an aroma pleasing to the LORD. **28**With each bull there is to be a grain offering of three-tenths of an ephah of fine flour mixed with oil; with the ram, two-tenths; **29**and with each of the seven lambs, one-tenth. **30**Include one male goat to make atonement for you. **31**Prepare these together with their drink offerings, in addition to the regular burnt offering and its grain offering. Be sure the animals are without defect.

Feast of Trumpets

29 " 'On the first day of the seventh month hold a sacred assembly and do no regular work. It is a day for you to sound the trumpets. **2**As an aroma pleasing to the LORD, prepare a burnt offering of one young bull, one ram and seven male lambs a year old, all without defect. **3**With the bull prepare a grain offering of three-tenths of an ephah*e* of fine flour mixed with oil; with the ram, two-tenths*f*; **4**and with each of the seven lambs, one-tenth.*g* **5**Include one male goat as a sin offering to make atonement for you. **6**These are in addition to the monthly and daily burnt offerings with their grain offerings and drink offerings as specified. They are offerings made to the LORD by fire—a pleasing aroma.

Day of Atonement

7 " 'On the tenth day of this seventh month hold a sacred assembly. You must deny yourselves*h* and do no work. **8**Present as an aroma pleasing to the LORD a burnt offering of one young bull, one ram and seven male lambs a year old, all

---

a9 That is, probably about 4 quarts (about 4.5 liters); also in verses 12, 20 and 28   *b12* That is, probably about 6 quarts (about 6.5 liters); also in verses 20 and 28   *c14* That is, probably about 2 quarts (about 2 liters)   *d14* That is, probably about 1 1/4 quarts (about 1.2 liters)   *e3* That is, probably about 6 quarts (about 6.5 liters); also in verses 9 and 14   *f3* That is, probably about 4 quarts (about 4.5 liters); also in verses 9 and 14   *g4* That is, probably about 2 quarts (about 2 liters); also in verses 10 and 15   *h7* Or *must fast* without defect. **9**With the bull prepare a grain offering of three-tenths of an ephah of fine flour mixed with oil; with the ram, two-tenths; **10**and with each of the seven lambs, one-tenth. **11**Include one male goat as a sin offering, in addition to the sin offering for atonement and the regular burnt offering with its grain offering, and their drink offerings.

Feast of Tabernacles

12" 'On the fifteenth day of the seventh month, hold a sacred assembly and do no regular work. Celebrate a festival to the Lord for seven days. **13**Present an offering made by fire as an aroma pleasing to the Lord, a burnt offering of thirteen young bulls, two rams and fourteen male lambs a year old, all without defect. **14**With each of the thirteen bulls prepare a grain offering of three-tenths of an ephah of fine flour mixed with oil; with each of the two rams, two-tenths; **15**and with each of the fourteen lambs, one-tenth. **16**Include one male goat as a sin offering, in addition to the regular burnt offering with its grain offering and drink offering.

17" 'On the second day prepare twelve young bulls, two rams and fourteen male lambs a year old, all without defect. **18**With the bulls, rams and lambs, prepare their grain offerings and drink offerings according to the number specified. **19**Include one male goat as a sin offering, in addition to the regular burnt offering with its grain offering, and their drink offerings.

20" 'On the third day prepare eleven bulls, two rams and fourteen male lambs a year old, all without defect. **21**With the bulls, rams and lambs, prepare their grain offerings and drink offerings according to the number specified. **22**Include one male goat as a sin offering, in addition to the regular burnt offering with its grain offering and drink offering.

23" 'On the fourth day prepare ten bulls, two rams and fourteen male lambs a year old, all without defect. **24**With the bulls, rams and lambs, prepare their grain offerings and drink offerings according to the number specified. **25**Include one male goat as a sin offering, in addition to the regular burnt offering with its grain offering and drink offering.

26" 'On the fifth day prepare nine bulls, two rams and fourteen male lambs a year old, all without defect. **27**With the bulls,

rams and lambs, prepare their grain offerings and drink offerings according to the number specified. **28**Include one male goat as a sin offering, in addition to the regular burnt offering with its grain offering and drink offering.

29" 'On the sixth day prepare eight bulls, two rams and fourteen male lambs a year old, all without defect. **30**With the bulls, rams and lambs, prepare their grain offerings and drink offerings according to the number specified. **31**Include one male goat as a sin offering, in addition to the regular burnt offering with its grain offering and drink offering.

32" 'On the seventh day prepare seven bulls, two rams and fourteen male lambs a year old, all without defect. **33**With the bulls, rams and lambs, prepare their grain offerings and drink offerings according to the number specified. **34**Include one male goat as a sin offering, in addition to the regular burnt offering with its grain offering and drink offering.

35" 'On the eighth day hold an assembly and do no regular work. **36**Present an offering made by fire as an aroma pleasing to the Lord, a burnt offering of one bull, one ram and seven male lambs a year old, all without defect. **37**With the bull, the ram and the lambs, prepare their grain offerings and drink offerings according to the number specified. **38**Include one male goat as a sin offering, in addition to the regular burnt offering with its grain offering and drink offering.

39" 'In addition to what you vow and your freewill offerings, prepare these for the Lord at your appointed feasts: your burnt offerings, grain offerings, drink offerings and fellowship offerings.*a*' "

40Moses told the Israelites all that the Lord commanded him.

Vows

30 Moses said to the heads of the tribes of Israel: "This is what the Lord commands: **2**When a man makes a vow to the Lord or takes an oath to obligate himself by a pledge, he must not break his word but must do everything he said.

3"When a young woman still living in her father's house makes a vow to the Lord or obligates herself by a pledge **4**and her father hears about her vow or pledge but says nothing to her, then all her vows and every pledge by which she obligated

_a39_ Traditionally _peace offerings_

herself will stand. [5]But if her father forbids her when he hears about it, none of her vows or the pledges by which she obligated herself will stand; the LORD will release her because her father has forbidden her.

[6]"If she marries after she makes a vow or after her lips utter a rash promise by which she obligates herself [7]and her husband hears about it but says nothing to her, then her vows or the pledges by which she obligated herself will stand. [8]But if her husband forbids her when he hears about it, he nullifies the vow that obligates her or the rash promise by which she obligates herself, and the LORD will release her.

[9]"Any vow or obligation taken by a widow or divorced woman will be binding on her.

[10]"If a woman living with her husband makes a vow or obligates herself by a pledge under oath [11]and her husband hears about it but says nothing to her and does not forbid her, then all her vows or the pledges by which she obligated herself will stand. [12]But if her husband nullifies them when he hears about them, then none of the vows or pledges that came from her lips will stand. Her husband has nullified them, and the LORD will release her. [13]Her husband may confirm or nullify any vow she makes or any sworn pledge to deny herself. [14]But if her husband says nothing to her about it from day to day, then he confirms all her vows or the pledges binding on her. He confirms them by saying nothing to her when he hears about them. [15]If, however, he nullifies them some time after he hears about them, then he is responsible for her guilt."

[16]These are the regulations the LORD gave Moses concerning relationships between a man and his wife, and between a father and his young daughter still living in his house.

Vengeance on the Midianites

31 The LORD said to Moses, [2]"Take vengeance on the Midianites for the Israelites. After that, you will be gathered to your people."

[3]So Moses said to the people, "Arm some of your men to go to war against the Midianites and to carry out the LORD's vengeance on them. [4]Send into battle a thousand men from each of the tribes of Israel." [5]So twelve thousand men armed for battle, a thousand from each tribe, were supplied from the clans of Israel. [6]Moses sent them into battle, a thousand from each tribe, along with Phinehas son of Eleazar, the priest, who took with him articles from the sanctuary and the trumpets for signaling.

[7]They fought against Midian, as the LORD commanded Moses, and killed every man. [8]Among their victims were Evi, Rekem, Zur, Hur and Reba—the five kings of Midian. They also killed Balaam son of Beor with the sword. [9]The Israelites captured the Midianite women and children and took all the Midianite herds, flocks and goods as plunder. [10]They burned all the towns where the Midianites had settled, as well as all their camps. [11]They took all the plunder and spoils, including the people and animals, [12]and brought the captives, spoils and plunder to Moses and Eleazar the priest and the Israelite assembly at their camp on the plains of Moab, by the Jordan across from Jericho.[a]

[13]Moses, Eleazar the priest and all the leaders of the community went to meet them outside the camp. [14]Moses was angry with the officers of the army—the commanders of thousands and commanders of hundreds—who returned from the battle.

[15]"Have you allowed all the women to live?" he asked them. [16]"They were the ones who followed Balaam's advice and were the means of turning the Israelites away from the LORD in what happened at Peor, so that a plague struck the LORD's people. [17]Now kill all the boys. And kill every woman who has slept with a man, [18]but save for yourselves every girl who has never slept with a man.

[19]"All of you who have killed anyone or touched anyone who was killed must stay outside the camp seven days. On the third and seventh days you must purify yourselves and your captives. [20]Purify every garment as well as everything made of leather, goat hair or wood."

[21]Then Eleazar the priest said to the soldiers who had gone into battle, "This is the requirement of the law that the LORD gave Moses: [22]Gold, silver, bronze, iron, tin, lead [23]and anything else that can withstand fire must be put through the fire, and then it will be clean. But it must also be purified with the water of cleansing. And whatever cannot withstand fire must be put through that water. [24]On the sev-

---

[a]12 Hebrew *Jordan of Jericho*; possibly an ancient name for the Jordan River

enth day wash your clothes and you will be clean. Then you may come into the camp."

Dividing the Spoils

25The LORD said to Moses, **26**"You and Eleazar the priest and the family heads of the community are to count all the people and animals that were captured. **27**Divide the spoils between the soldiers who took part in the battle and the rest of the community. **28**From the soldiers who fought in the battle, set apart as tribute for the LORD one out of every five hundred, whether persons, cattle, donkeys, sheep or goats. **29**Take this tribute from their half share and give it to Eleazar the priest as the LORD's part. **30**From the Israelites' half, select one out of every fifty, whether persons, cattle, donkeys, sheep, goats or other animals. Give them to the Levites, who are responsible for the care of the LORD's tabernacle." **31**So Moses and Eleazar the priest did as the LORD commanded Moses.

32The plunder remaining from the spoils that the soldiers took was 675,000 sheep, **33**72,000 cattle, **34**61,000 donkeys **35**and 32,000 women who had never slept with a man.

36The half share of those who fought in the battle was:

337,500 sheep, **37**of which the tribute for the LORD was 675;

3836,000 cattle, of which the tribute for the LORD was 72;

3930,500 donkeys, of which the tribute for the LORD was 61;

4016,000 people, of which the tribute for the LORD was 32.

41Moses gave the tribute to Eleazar the priest as the LORD's part, as the LORD commanded Moses.

42The half belonging to the Israelites, which Moses set apart from that of the fighting men— **43**the community's half— was 337,500 sheep, **44**36,000 cattle, **45**30,500 donkeys **46**and 16,000 people. **47**From the Israelites' half, Moses selected one out of every fifty persons and animals, as the LORD commanded him, and gave them to the Levites, who were responsible for the care of the LORD's tabernacle.

48Then the officers who were over the units of the army—the commanders of thousands and commanders of hundreds—went to Moses **49**and said to him, "Your servants have counted the soldiers under our command, and not one is missing. **50**So we have brought as an offering to the LORD the gold articles each of us acquired—armlets, bracelets, signet rings, earrings and necklaces—to make atonement for ourselves before the LORD."

51Moses and Eleazar the priest accepted from them the gold—all the crafted articles. **52**All the gold from the commanders of thousands and commanders of hundreds that Moses and Eleazar presented as a gift to the LORD weighed 16,750 shekels.*a* **53**Each soldier had taken plunder for himself. **54**Moses and Eleazar the priest accepted the gold from the commanders of thousands and commanders of hundreds and brought it into the Tent of Meeting as a memorial for the Israelites before the LORD.

The Transjordan Tribes

32 The Reubenites and Gadites, who had very large herds and flocks, saw that the lands of Jazer and Gilead were suitable for livestock. **2**So they came to Moses and Eleazar the priest and to the leaders of the community, and said, **3**"Ataroth, Dibon, Jazer, Nimrah, Heshbon, Elealeh, Sebam, Nebo and Beon— **4**the land the LORD subdued before the people of Israel—are suitable for livestock, and your servants have livestock. **5**If we have found favor in your eyes," they said, "let this land be given to your servants as our possession. Do not make us cross the Jordan."

6Moses said to the Gadites and Reubenites, "Shall your countrymen go to war while you sit here? **7**Why do you discourage the Israelites from going over into the land the LORD has given them? **8**This is what your fathers did when I sent them from Kadesh Barnea to look over the land. **9**After they went up to the Valley of Eshcol and viewed the land, they discouraged the Israelites from entering the land the LORD had given them. **10**The LORD's anger was aroused that day and he swore this oath: **11**'Because they have not followed me wholeheartedly, not one of the men twenty years old or more who came up out of Egypt will see the land I promised on oath to Abraham, Isaac and Jacob— **12**not one except Caleb son of Jephunneh the Kenizzite and Joshua son of Nun, for they followed the LORD wholeheartedly.' **13**The LORD's anger burned against Israel and he made them wander in the desert forty

---

a52 That is, about 420 pounds (about 190 kilograms)

WEEKENDING

RENEW

You can read about him in the creeds and in
books of theology, or you can get to know God
by becoming involved with him, by arguing
with him like Job, by wrestling with him like
Jacob, by praying to him like Daniel, and by
living with him in the desert for forty years like
Israel. You can learn about God with your mind
or through your experience. God prefers the
latter. He wants us to know him experientially,
to engage him with our whole lives.

– John Timmer

REVIVE

Saturday: Jeremiah 31:31–34
Sunday: Philippians 3:7–11

Go to page 173 for your next devotional reading.

years, until the whole generation of those who had done evil in his sight was gone.

¹⁴"And here you are, a brood of sinners, standing in the place of your fathers and making the LORD even more angry with Israel. ¹⁵If you turn away from following him, he will again leave all this people in the desert, and you will be the cause of their destruction."

¹⁶Then they came up to him and said, "We would like to build pens here for our livestock and cities for our women and children. ¹⁷But we are ready to arm ourselves and go ahead of the Israelites until we have brought them to their place. Meanwhile our women and children will live in fortified cities, for protection from the inhabitants of the land. ¹⁸We will not return to our homes until every Israelite has received his inheritance. ¹⁹We will not receive any inheritance with them on the other side of the Jordan, because our inheritance has come to us on the east side of the Jordan."

²⁰Then Moses said to them, "If you will do this — if you will arm yourselves before the LORD for battle, ²¹and if all of you will go armed over the Jordan before the LORD until he has driven his enemies out before him — ²²then when the land is subdued before the LORD, you may return and be free from your obligation to the LORD and to Israel. And this land will be your possession before the LORD.

²³"But if you fail to do this, you will be sinning against the LORD; and you may be sure that your sin will find you out. ²⁴Build cities for your women and children, and pens for your flocks, but do what you have promised."

²⁵The Gadites and Reubenites said to Moses, "We your servants will do as our lord commands. ²⁶Our children and wives, our flocks and herds will remain here in the cities of Gilead. ²⁷But your servants, every man armed for battle, will cross over to fight before the LORD, just as our lord says."

²⁸Then Moses gave orders about them to Eleazar the priest and Joshua son of Nun and to the family heads of the Israelite tribes. ²⁹He said to them, "If the Gadites and Reubenites, every man armed for battle, cross over the Jordan with you before the LORD, then when the land is subdued before you, give them the land of Gilead as their possession. ³⁰But if they do not cross over with you armed, they must accept their possession with you in Canaan."

³¹The Gadites and Reubenites answered, "Your servants will do what the LORD has said. ³²We will cross over before the LORD into Canaan armed, but the property we inherit will be on this side of the Jordan."

³³Then Moses gave to the Gadites, the Reubenites and the half-tribe of Manasseh son of Joseph the kingdom of Sihon king of the Amorites and the kingdom of Og king of Bashan — the whole land with its cities and the territory around them.

³⁴The Gadites built up Dibon, Ataroth, Aroer, ³⁵Atroth Shophan, Jazer, Jogbehah, ³⁶Beth Nimrah and Beth Haran as fortified cities, and built pens for their flocks. ³⁷And the Reubenites rebuilt Heshbon, Elealeh and Kiriathaim, ³⁸as well as Nebo and Baal Meon (these names were changed) and Sibmah. They gave names to the cities they rebuilt.

³⁹The descendants of Makir son of Manasseh went to Gilead, captured it and drove out the Amorites who were there. ⁴⁰So Moses gave Gilead to the Makirites, the descendants of Manasseh, and they settled there. ⁴¹Jair, a descendant of Manasseh, captured their settlements and called them Havvoth Jair.ᵃ ⁴²And Nobah captured Kenath and its surrounding settlements and called it Nobah after himself.

Stages in Israel's Journey

33 Here are the stages in the journey of the Israelites when they came out of Egypt by divisions under the leadership of Moses and Aaron. ²At the LORD's command Moses recorded the stages in their journey. This is their journey by stages:

³The Israelites set out from Rameses on the fifteenth day of the first month, the day after the Passover. They marched out boldly in full view of all the Egyptians, ⁴who were burying all their firstborn, whom the LORD had struck down among them; for the LORD had brought judgment on their gods.

⁵The Israelites left Rameses and camped at Succoth.

⁶They left Succoth and camped at Etham, on the edge of the desert.

⁷They left Etham, turned back to Pi

ᵃ41 Or them the settlements of Jair

Hahiroth, to the east of Baal Zephon, and camped near Migdol.

8They left Pi Hahiroth*a* and passed through the sea into the desert, and when they had traveled for three days in the Desert of Etham, they camped at Marah.

9They left Marah and went to Elim, where there were twelve springs and seventy palm trees, and they camped there.

10They left Elim and camped by the Red Sea.*b*

11They left the Red Sea and camped in the Desert of Sin.

12They left the Desert of Sin and camped at Dophkah.

13They left Dophkah and camped at Alush.

14They left Alush and camped at Rephidim, where there was no water for the people to drink.

15They left Rephidim and camped in the Desert of Sinai.

16They left the Desert of Sinai and camped at Kibroth Hattaavah.

17They left Kibroth Hattaavah and camped at Hazeroth.

18They left Hazeroth and camped at Rithmah.

19They left Rithmah and camped at Rimmon Perez.

20They left Rimmon Perez and camped at Libnah.

21They left Libnah and camped at Rissah.

22They left Rissah and camped at Kehelathah.

23They left Kehelathah and camped at Mount Shepher.

24They left Mount Shepher and camped at Haradah.

25They left Haradah and camped at Makheloth.

26They left Makheloth and camped at Tahath.

27They left Tahath and camped at Terah.

28They left Terah and camped at Mithcah.

29They left Mithcah and camped at Hashmonah.

30They left Hashmonah and camped at Moseroth.

31They left Moseroth and camped at Bene Jaakan.

32They left Bene Jaakan and camped at Hor Haggidgad.

33They left Hor Haggidgad and camped at Jotbathah.

34They left Jotbathah and camped at Abronah.

35They left Abronah and camped at Ezion Geber.

36They left Ezion Geber and camped at Kadesh, in the Desert of Zin.

37They left Kadesh and camped at Mount Hor, on the border of Edom. **38**At the LORD's command Aaron the priest went up Mount Hor, where he died on the first day of the fifth month of the fortieth year after the Israelites came out of Egypt. **39**Aaron was a hundred and twenty-three years old when he died on Mount Hor.

40The Canaanite king of Arad, who lived in the Negev of Canaan, heard that the Israelites were coming.

41They left Mount Hor and camped at Zalmonah.

42They left Zalmonah and camped at Punon.

43They left Punon and camped at Oboth.

44They left Oboth and camped at Iye Abarim, on the border of Moab.

45They left Iyim*c* and camped at Dibon Gad.

46They left Dibon Gad and camped at Almon Diblathaim.

47They left Almon Diblathaim and camped in the mountains of Abarim, near Nebo.

48They left the mountains of Abarim and camped on the plains of Moab by the Jordan across from Jericho.*d* **49**There on the plains of Moab they camped along the Jordan from Beth Jeshimoth to Abel Shittim.

50On the plains of Moab by the Jordan across from Jericho the LORD said to Moses, **51**"Speak to the Israelites and say to them: 'When you cross the Jordan into Canaan, **52**drive out all the inhabitants of the land before you. Destroy all their carved images and their cast idols, and demolish all their high places. **53**Take pos-

---

a8 Many manuscripts of the Masoretic Text, Samaritan Pentateuch and Vulgate; most manuscripts of the Masoretic Text *left from before Hahiroth*   *b10* Hebrew *Yam Suph*; that is, Sea of Reeds; also in verse 11   *c45* That is, Iye Abarim   *d48* Hebrew *Jordan of Jericho*; possibly an ancient name for the Jordan River; also in verse 50 session of the land and settle in it, for I have given you the land to possess. [54]Distribute the land by lot, according to your clans. To a larger group give a larger inheritance, and to a smaller group a smaller one. Whatever falls to them by lot will be theirs. Distribute it according to your ancestral tribes.

[55]" 'But if you do not drive out the inhabitants of the land, those you allow to remain will become barbs in your eyes and thorns in your sides. They will give you trouble in the land where you will live. [56]And then I will do to you what I plan to do to them.' "

Boundaries of Canaan

34 The LORD said to Moses, [2]"Command the Israelites and say to them: 'When you enter Canaan, the land that will be allotted to you as an inheritance will have these boundaries:

[3]" 'Your southern side will include some of the Desert of Zin along the border of Edom. On the east, your southern boundary will start from the end of the Salt Sea,[a] [4]cross south of Scorpion[b] Pass, continue on to Zin and go south of Kadesh Barnea. Then it will go to Hazar Addar and over to Azmon, [5]where it will turn, join the Wadi of Egypt and end at the Sea.[c]

[6]" 'Your western boundary will be the coast of the Great Sea. This will be your boundary on the west.

[7]" 'For your northern boundary, run a line from the Great Sea to Mount Hor [8]and from Mount Hor to Lebo[d] Hamath. Then the boundary will go to Zedad, [9]continue to Ziphron and end at Hazar Enan. This will be your boundary on the north.

[10]" 'For your eastern boundary, run a line from Hazar Enan to Shepham. [11]The boundary will go down from Shepham to Riblah on the east side of Ain and continue along the slopes east of the Sea of Kinnereth.[e] [12]Then the boundary will go down along the Jordan and end at the Salt Sea.

" 'This will be your land, with its boundaries on every side.' "

[13]Moses commanded the Israelites: "Assign this land by lot as an inheritance. The LORD has ordered that it be given to the nine and a half tribes, [14]because the families of the tribe of Reuben, the tribe of Gad and the half-tribe of Manasseh have received their inheritance. [15]These two and a half tribes have received their inheritance on the east side of the Jordan of Jericho,[f] toward the sunrise."

[16]The LORD said to Moses, [17]"These are the names of the men who are to assign the land for you as an inheritance: Eleazar the priest and Joshua son of Nun. [18]And appoint one leader from each tribe to help assign the land. [19]These are their names:

Caleb son of Jephunneh,
    from the tribe of Judah;
[20]Shemuel son of Ammihud,
    from the tribe of Simeon;
[21]Elidad son of Kislon,
    from the tribe of Benjamin;
[22]Bukki son of Jogli,
    the leader from the tribe of Dan;
[23]Hanniel son of Ephod,
    the leader from the tribe of Manasseh son of Joseph;
[24]Kemuel son of Shiphtan,
    the leader from the tribe of Ephraim son of Joseph;
[25]Elizaphan son of Parnach,
    the leader from the tribe of Zebulun;
[26]Paltiel son of Azzan,
    the leader from the tribe of Issachar;
[27]Ahihud son of Shelomi,
    the leader from the tribe of Asher;
[28]Pedahel son of Ammihud,
    the leader from the tribe of Naphtali."

[29]These are the men the LORD commanded to assign the inheritance to the Israelites in the land of Canaan.

Towns for the Levites

35 On the plains of Moab by the Jordan across from Jericho,[g] the LORD said to Moses, [2]"Command the Israelites to give the Levites towns to live in from the inheritance the Israelites will possess. And give them pasturelands around the towns. [3]Then they will have towns to live in and pasturelands for their cattle, flocks and all their other livestock.

[4]"The pasturelands around the towns that you give the Levites will extend out fifteen hundred feet[h] from the town wall. [5]Outside the town, measure three thou-

---

[a]3 That is, the Dead Sea; also in verse 12   [b]4 Hebrew *Akrabbim*   [c]5 That is, the Mediterranean; also in verses 6 and 7   [d]8 Or *to the entrance to*   [e]11 That is, Galilee   [f]15 *Jordan of Jericho* was possibly an ancient name for the Jordan River   [g]1 Hebrew *Jordan of Jericho*; possibly an ancient name for the Jordan River   [h]4 Hebrew *a thousand cubits* (about 450 meters)

sand feet[a] on the east side, three thousand on the south side, three thousand on the west and three thousand on the north, with the town in the center. They will have this area as pastureland for the towns.

Cities of Refuge

6"Six of the towns you give the Levites will be cities of refuge, to which a person who has killed someone may flee. In addition, give them forty-two other towns. 7In all you must give the Levites forty-eight towns, together with their pasturelands. 8The towns you give the Levites from the land the Israelites possess are to be given in proportion to the inheritance of each tribe: Take many towns from a tribe that has many, but few from one that has few."

9Then the LORD said to Moses: 10"Speak to the Israelites and say to them: 'When you cross the Jordan into Canaan, 11select some towns to be your cities of refuge, to which a person who has killed someone accidentally may flee. 12They will be places of refuge from the avenger, so that a person accused of murder may not die before he stands trial before the assembly. 13These six towns you give will be your cities of refuge. 14Give three on this side of the Jordan and three in Canaan as cities of refuge. 15These six towns will be a place of refuge for Israelites, aliens and any other people living among them, so that anyone who has killed another accidentally can flee there.

16" 'If a man strikes someone with an iron object so that he dies, he is a murderer; the murderer shall be put to death. 17Or if anyone has a stone in his hand that could kill, and he strikes someone so that he dies, he is a murderer; the murderer shall be put to death. 18Or if anyone has a wooden object in his hand that could kill, and he hits someone so that he dies, he is a murderer; the murderer shall be put to death. 19The avenger of blood shall put the murderer to death; when he meets him, he shall put him to death. 20If anyone with malice aforethought shoves another or throws something at him intentionally so that he dies 21or if in hostility he hits him with his fist so that he dies, that person shall be put to death; he is a murderer. The avenger of blood shall put the murderer to death when he meets him.

22" 'But if without hostility someone suddenly shoves another or throws something at him unintentionally 23or, without seeing him, drops a stone on him that could kill him, and he dies, then since he was not his enemy and he did not intend to harm him, 24the assembly must judge between him and the avenger of blood according to these regulations. 25The assembly must protect the one accused of murder from the avenger of blood and send him back to the city of refuge to which he fled. He must stay there until the death of the high priest, who was anointed with the holy oil.

26" 'But if the accused ever goes outside the limits of the city of refuge to which he has fled 27and the avenger of blood finds him outside the city, the avenger of blood may kill the accused without being guilty of murder. 28The accused must stay in his city of refuge until the death of the high priest; only after the death of the high priest may he return to his own property.

29" 'These are to be legal requirements for you throughout the generations to come, wherever you live.

30" 'Anyone who kills a person is to be put to death as a murderer only on the testimony of witnesses. But no one is to be put to death on the testimony of only one witness.

31" 'Do not accept a ransom for the life of a murderer, who deserves to die. He must surely be put to death.

32" 'Do not accept a ransom for anyone who has fled to a city of refuge and so allow him to go back and live on his own land before the death of the high priest.

33" 'Do not pollute the land where you are. Bloodshed pollutes the land, and atonement cannot be made for the land on which blood has been shed, except by the blood of the one who shed it. 34Do not defile the land where you live and where I dwell, for I, the LORD, dwell among the Israelites.' "

Inheritance of Zelophehad's Daughters

36 The family heads of the clan of Gilead son of Makir, the son of Manasseh, who were from the clans of the descendants of Joseph, came and spoke before Moses and the leaders, the heads of the Israelite families. 2They said, "When the LORD commanded my lord to give the land as an inheritance to the Israelites by lot, he ordered you to give the inheritance of our brother Zelophehad to his daugh-

---

a5 Hebrew *two thousand cubits* (about 900 meters)

ters. ³Now suppose they marry men from other Israelite tribes; then their inheritance will be taken from our ancestral inheritance and added to that of the tribe they marry into. And so part of the inheritance allotted to us will be taken away. ⁴When the Year of Jubilee for the Israelites comes, their inheritance will be added to that of the tribe into which they marry, and their property will be taken from the tribal inheritance of our forefathers."

⁵Then at the LORD's command Moses gave this order to the Israelites: "What the tribe of the descendants of Joseph is saying is right. ⁶This is what the LORD commands for Zelophehad's daughters: They may marry anyone they please as long as they marry within the tribal clan of their father. ⁷No inheritance in Israel is to pass from tribe to tribe, for every Israelite shall keep the tribal land inherited from his forefathers. ⁸Every daughter who inherits land in any Israelite tribe must marry someone in her father's tribal clan, so that every Israelite will possess the inheritance of his fathers. ⁹No inheritance may pass from tribe to tribe, for each Israelite tribe is to keep the land it inherits."

¹⁰So Zelophehad's daughters did as the LORD commanded Moses. ¹¹Zelophehad's daughters — Mahlah, Tirzah, Hoglah, Milcah and Noah — married their cousins on their father's side. ¹²They married within the clans of the descendants of Manasseh son of Joseph, and their inheritance remained in their father's clan and tribe.

¹³These are the commands and regulations the LORD gave through Moses to the Israelites on the plains of Moab by the Jordan across from Jericho.ᵃ

ᵃ13 Hebrew *Jordan of Jericho*; possibly an ancient name for the Jordan River

*I*N this book Moses records his farewell address to the nation of Israel as they wait on the bank of the Jordan River, ready to cross over into the land of Canaan. He reminds them of God's care in the past and of his laws, and he challenges them to rededicate their lives to serving the Lord. As you read this book, think about God's daily care in your life and his desire that you dedicate your life to serving him.

DEUTERONOMY

The Command to Leave Horeb

1 These are the words Moses spoke to all Israel in the desert east of the Jordan—that is, in the Arabah—opposite Suph, between Paran and Tophel, Laban, Hazeroth and Dizahab. ²(It takes eleven days to go from Horeb to Kadesh Barnea by the Mount Seir road.)

³In the fortieth year, on the first day of the eleventh month, Moses proclaimed to the Israelites all that the LORD had commanded him concerning them. ⁴This was after he had defeated Sihon king of the Amorites, who reigned in Heshbon, and at Edrei had defeated Og king of Bashan, who reigned in Ashtaroth.

⁵East of the Jordan in the territory of Moab, Moses began to expound this law, saying:

⁶The LORD our God said to us at Horeb, "You have stayed long enough at this mountain. ⁷Break camp and advance into the hill country of the Amorites; go to all the neighboring peoples in the Arabah, in the mountains, in the western foothills, in the Negev and along the coast, to the land of the Canaanites and to Lebanon, as far as the great river, the Euphrates. ⁸See, I have given you this land. Go in and take possession of the land that the LORD swore he would give to your fathers—to Abraham, Isaac and Jacob—and to their descendants after them."

The Appointment of Leaders

9At that time I said to you, "You are too heavy a burden for me to carry alone. **10**The Lord your God has increased your numbers so that today you are as many as the stars in the sky. **11**May the Lord, the God of your fathers, increase you a thousand times and bless you as he has promised! **12**But how can I bear your problems and your burdens and your disputes all by myself? **13**Choose some wise, understanding and respected men from each of your tribes, and I will set them over you."

14You answered me, "What you propose to do is good."

15So I took the leading men of your tribes, wise and respected men, and appointed them to have authority over you — as commanders of thousands, of hundreds, of fifties and of tens and as tribal officials. **16**And I charged your judges at that time: Hear the disputes between your brothers and judge fairly, whether the case is between brother Israelites or between one of them and an alien. **17**Do not show partiality in judging; hear both small and great alike. Do not be afraid of any man, for judgment belongs to God. Bring me any case too hard for you, and I will hear it. **18**And at that time I told you everything you were to do.

Spies Sent Out

19Then, as the Lord our God commanded us, we set out from Horeb and went toward the hill country of the Amorites through all that vast and dreadful desert that you have seen, and so we reached Kadesh Barnea. **20**Then I said to you, "You have reached the hill country of the Amorites, which the Lord our God is giving us. **21**See, the Lord your God has given you the land. Go up and take possession of it as the Lord, the God of your fathers, told you. Do not be afraid; do not be discouraged."

22Then all of you came to me and said, "Let us send men ahead to spy out the land for us and bring back a report about the route we are to take and the towns we will come to."

23The idea seemed good to me; so I selected twelve of you, one man from each tribe. **24**They left and went up into the hill country, and came to the Valley of Eshcol and explored it. **25**Taking with them some of the fruit of the land, they brought it down to us and reported, "It is a good land that the Lord our God is giving us."

Rebellion Against the Lord

26But you were unwilling to go up; you rebelled against the command of the Lord your God. **27**You grumbled in your tents and said, "The Lord hates us; so he brought us out of Egypt to deliver us into the hands of the Amorites to destroy us. **28**Where can we go? Our brothers have made us lose heart. They say, 'The people are stronger and taller than we are; the cities are large, with walls up to the sky. We even saw the Anakites there.' "

29Then I said to you, "Do not be terrified; do not be afraid of them. **30**The Lord your God, who is going before you, will fight for you, as he did for you in Egypt, before your very eyes, **31**and in the desert. There you saw how the Lord your God carried you, as a father carries his son, all the way you went until you reached this place."

32In spite of this, you did not trust in the Lord your God, **33**who went ahead of you on your journey, in fire by night and in a cloud by day, to search out places for you to camp and to show you the way you should go.

34When the Lord heard what you said, he was angry and solemnly swore: **35**"Not a man of this evil generation shall see the good land I swore to give your forefathers, **36**except Caleb son of Jephunneh. He will see it, and I will give him and his descendants the land he set his feet on, because he followed the Lord wholeheartedly."

37Because of you the Lord became angry with me also and said, "You shall not enter it, either. **38**But your assistant, Joshua son of Nun, will enter it. Encourage him, because he will lead Israel to inherit it. **39**And the little ones that you said would be taken captive, your children who do not yet know good from bad — they will enter the land. I will give it to them and they will take possession of it. **40**But as for you, turn around and set out toward the desert along the route to the Red Sea.*a*"

41Then you replied, "We have sinned against the Lord. We will go up and fight, as the Lord our God commanded us." So every one of you put on his weapons, thinking it easy to go up into the hill country.

---

a40 Hebrew *Yam Suph*; that is, Sea of Reeds

⁴²But the LORD said to me, "Tell them, 'Do not go up and fight, because I will not be with you. You will be defeated by your enemies.' "

⁴³So I told you, but you would not listen. You rebelled against the LORD's command and in your arrogance you marched up into the hill country. ⁴⁴The Amorites who lived in those hills came out against you; they chased you like a swarm of bees and beat you down from Seir all the way to Hormah. ⁴⁵You came back and wept before the LORD, but he paid no attention to your weeping and turned a deaf ear to

---

MONDAY

VERSE FOR THE DAY: Deuteronomy 1:17	*AUTHOR:* Ben Carson	*PASSAGE FOR THE DAY:* Deuteronomy 1:15–18

God Don't Make No Junk

I HAVE watched people react to waiters, secretaries and receptionists, and who, afterward, despite identifying name tags and signs on those workers' desks, could not tell anyone anything about these people whom they considered just invisible, anonymous beings—individuals not worth knowing.

I am glad that I learned differently. Mother worked with [my brother] Curtis and me, teaching us not to prejudge others —not to decide on their value before we knew them. She stressed treating everyone with kindness and giving every person a chance.

As surgeons, if we do not consider all other workers as having value and as worth knowing—we are prejudiced, against which the Bible speaks strongly [see James 2:1–4] . . .

Why can't a janitor know significantly more about certain situations than a neurosurgeon does? A person who performs manual labor can certainly be as intelligent as one who sits at a desk, performing clerical work.

Being nice translates to accepting each person for his or her individual worth. It disturbs me that some still decide that certain people are not worth bothering with simply because of their socio-economic class, job title or national origin. *Everyone has value.* Or, as a popular saying of my growing-up years reminds: "God don't make no junk."

These under-recognized people can teach us, encourage us, and even be important allies for us. Over the years, I have gotten to know a great number of such people whom I still know and talk with often. When I am in the midst of a group of doctors and a clerk comes by to say hello, I want that individual to be treated just as well as the CEO of an important company who comes in as a patient. Medical-assistance patients are as important as wealthy patients are. All of them have medical needs that we can minister to.

Additional Scripture Readings:
Acts 10:34–43; James 2:1–13

Go to page 179 for your next devotional reading.

you. **46**And so you stayed in Kadesh many days — all the time you spent there.

Wanderings in the Desert

2 Then we turned back and set out toward the desert along the route to the Red Sea,[a] as the Lord had directed me. For a long time we made our way around the hill country of Seir.

2Then the Lord said to me, **3**"You have made your way around this hill country long enough; now turn north. **4**Give the people these orders: 'You are about to pass through the territory of your brothers the descendants of Esau, who live in Seir. They will be afraid of you, but be very careful. **5**Do not provoke them to war, for I will not give you any of their land, not even enough to put your foot on. I have given Esau the hill country of Seir as his own. **6**You are to pay them in silver for the food you eat and the water you drink.'"

7The Lord your God has blessed you in all the work of your hands. He has watched over your journey through this vast desert. These forty years the Lord your God has been with you, and you have not lacked anything.

8So we went on past our brothers the descendants of Esau, who live in Seir. We turned from the Arabah road, which comes up from Elath and Ezion Geber, and traveled along the desert road of Moab.

9Then the Lord said to me, "Do not harass the Moabites or provoke them to war, for I will not give you any part of their land. I have given Ar to the descendants of Lot as a possession."

10(The Emites used to live there — a people strong and numerous, and as tall as the Anakites. **11**Like the Anakites, they too were considered Rephaites, but the Moabites called them Emites. **12**Horites used to live in Seir, but the descendants of Esau drove them out. They destroyed the Horites from before them and settled in their place, just as Israel did in the land the Lord gave them as their possession.)

13And the Lord said, "Now get up and cross the Zered Valley." So we crossed the valley.

14Thirty-eight years passed from the time we left Kadesh Barnea until we crossed the Zered Valley. By then, that entire generation of fighting men had perished from the camp, as the Lord had sworn to them. **15**The Lord's hand was against them until he had completely eliminated them from the camp.

16Now when the last of these fighting men among the people had died, **17**the Lord said to me, **18**"Today you are to pass by the region of Moab at Ar. **19**When you come to the Ammonites, do not harass them or provoke them to war, for I will not give you possession of any land belonging to the Ammonites. I have given it as a possession to the descendants of Lot."

20(That too was considered a land of the Rephaites, who used to live there; but the Ammonites called them Zamzummites. **21**They were a people strong and numerous, and as tall as the Anakites. The Lord destroyed them from before the Ammonites, who drove them out and settled in their place. **22**The Lord had done the same for the descendants of Esau, who lived in Seir, when he destroyed the Horites from before them. They drove them out and have lived in their place to this day. **23**And as for the Avvites who lived in villages as far as Gaza, the Caphtorites coming out from Caphtor[b] destroyed them and settled in their place.)

Defeat of Sihon King of Heshbon

24"Set out now and cross the Arnon Gorge. See, I have given into your hand Sihon the Amorite, king of Heshbon, and his country. Begin to take possession of it and engage him in battle. **25**This very day I will begin to put the terror and fear of you on all the nations under heaven. They will hear reports of you and will tremble and be in anguish because of you."

26From the desert of Kedemoth I sent messengers to Sihon king of Heshbon offering peace and saying, **27**"Let us pass through your country. We will stay on the main road; we will not turn aside to the right or to the left. **28**Sell us food to eat and water to drink for their price in silver. Only let us pass through on foot — **29**as the descendants of Esau, who live in Seir, and the Moabites, who live in Ar, did for us — until we cross the Jordan into the land the Lord our God is giving us." **30**But Sihon king of Heshbon refused to let us pass through. For the Lord your God had made his spirit stubborn and his heart obstinate in order to give him into your hands, as he has now done.

31The Lord said to me, "See, I have begun to deliver Sihon and his country over

---

[a]1 Hebrew *Yam Suph*; that is, Sea of Reeds   [b]23 That is, Crete

to you. Now begin to conquer and possess his land."

[32]When Sihon and all his army came out to meet us in battle at Jahaz, [33]the LORD our God delivered him over to us and we struck him down, together with his sons and his whole army. [34]At that time we took all his towns and completely destroyed[a] them—men, women and children. We left no survivors. [35]But the livestock and the plunder from the towns we had captured we carried off for ourselves. [36]From Aroer on the rim of the Arnon Gorge, and from the town in the gorge, even as far as Gilead, not one town was too strong for us. The LORD our God gave us all of them. [37]But in accordance with the command of the LORD our God, you did not encroach on any of the land of the Ammonites, neither the land along the course of the Jabbok nor that around the towns in the hills.

Defeat of Og King of Bashan

3 Next we turned and went up along the road toward Bashan, and Og king of Bashan with his whole army marched out to meet us in battle at Edrei. [2]The LORD said to me, "Do not be afraid of him, for I have handed him over to you with his whole army and his land. Do to him what you did to Sihon king of the Amorites, who reigned in Heshbon."

[3]So the LORD our God also gave into our hands Og king of Bashan and all his army. We struck them down, leaving no survivors. [4]At that time we took all his cities. There was not one of the sixty cities that we did not take from them—the whole region of Argob, Og's kingdom in Bashan. [5]All these cities were fortified with high walls and with gates and bars, and there were also a great many unwalled villages. [6]We completely destroyed[a] them, as we had done with Sihon king of Heshbon, destroying[a] every city—men, women and children. [7]But all the livestock and the plunder from their cities we carried off for ourselves.

[8]So at that time we took from these two kings of the Amorites the territory east of the Jordan, from the Arnon Gorge as far as Mount Hermon. [9](Hermon is called Sirion by the Sidonians; the Amorites call it Senir.) [10]We took all the towns on the plateau, and all Gilead, and all Bashan as far as Salecah and Edrei, towns of Og's kingdom in Bashan. [11](Only Og king of Bashan was left of the remnant of the Rephaites. His bed[b] was made of iron and was more than thirteen feet long and six feet wide.[c] It is still in Rabbah of the Ammonites.)

Division of the Land

[12]Of the land that we took over at that time, I gave the Reubenites and the Gadites the territory north of Aroer by the Arnon Gorge, including half the hill country of Gilead, together with its towns. [13]The rest of Gilead and also all of Bashan, the kingdom of Og, I gave to the half tribe of Manasseh. (The whole region of Argob in Bashan used to be known as a land of the Rephaites. [14]Jair, a descendant of Manasseh, took the whole region of Argob as far as the border of the Geshurites and the Maacathites; it was named after him, so that to this day Bashan is called Havvoth Jair.[d]) [15]And I gave Gilead to Makir. [16]But to the Reubenites and the Gadites I gave the territory extending from Gilead down to the Arnon Gorge (the middle of the gorge being the border) and out to the Jabbok River, which is the border of the Ammonites. [17]Its western border was the Jordan in the Arabah, from Kinnereth to the Sea of the Arabah (the Salt Sea[e]), below the slopes of Pisgah.

[18]I commanded you at that time: "The LORD your God has given you this land to take possession of it. But all your able-bodied men, armed for battle, must cross over ahead of your brother Israelites. [19]However, your wives, your children and your livestock (I know you have much livestock) may stay in the towns I have given you, [20]until the LORD gives rest to your brothers as he has to you, and they too have taken over the land that the LORD your God is giving them, across the Jordan. After that, each of you may go back to the possession I have given you."

Moses Forbidden to Cross the Jordan

[21]At that time I commanded Joshua: "You have seen with your own eyes all that the LORD your God has done to these two kings. The LORD will do the same to all the kingdoms over there where you are going. [22]Do not be afraid of them; the

---

[a]34,6 The Hebrew term refers to the irrevocable giving over of things or persons to the LORD, often by totally destroying them. [b]11 Or *sarcophagus* [c]11 Hebrew *nine cubits long and four cubits wide* (about 4 meters long and 1.8 meters wide) [d]14 Or *called the settlements of Jair* [e]17 That is, the Dead Sea

Lord your God himself will fight for you."

²³At that time I pleaded with the Lord: ²⁴"O Sovereign Lord, you have begun to show to your servant your greatness and your strong hand. For what god is there in heaven or on earth who can do the deeds and mighty works you do? ²⁵Let me go over and see the good land beyond the Jordan—that fine hill country and Lebanon."

²⁶But because of you the Lord was angry with me and would not listen to me. "That is enough," the Lord said. "Do not speak to me anymore about this matter. ²⁷Go up to the top of Pisgah and look west and north and south and east. Look at the land with your own eyes, since you are not going to cross this Jordan. ²⁸But commission Joshua, and encourage and strengthen him, for he will lead this people across and will cause them to inherit the land that you will see." ²⁹So we stayed in the valley near Beth Peor.

Obedience Commanded

4 Hear now, O Israel, the decrees and laws I am about to teach you. Follow them so that you may live and may go in and take possession of the land that the Lord, the God of your fathers, is giving you. ²Do not add to what I command you and do not subtract from it, but keep the commands of the Lord your God that I give you.

³You saw with your own eyes what the Lord did at Baal Peor. The Lord your God destroyed from among you everyone who followed the Baal of Peor, ⁴but all of you who held fast to the Lord your God are still alive today.

⁵See, I have taught you decrees and laws as the Lord my God commanded me, so that you may follow them in the land you are entering to take possession of it. ⁶Observe them carefully, for this will show your wisdom and understanding to the nations, who will hear about all these decrees and say, "Surely this great nation is a wise and understanding people." ⁷What other nation is so great as to have their gods near them the way the Lord our God is near us whenever we pray to him? ⁸And what other nation is so great as to have such righteous decrees and laws as this body of laws I am setting before you today?

⁹Only be careful, and watch yourselves closely so that you do not forget the things your eyes have seen or let them slip from your heart as long as you live. Teach them to your children and to their children after them. ¹⁰Remember the day you stood before the Lord your God at Horeb, when he said to me, "Assemble the people before me to hear my words so that they may learn to revere me as long as they live in the land and may teach them to their children." ¹¹You came near and stood at the foot of the mountain while it blazed with fire to the very heavens, with black clouds and deep darkness. ¹²Then the Lord spoke to you out of the fire. You heard the sound of words but saw no form; there was only a voice. ¹³He declared to you his covenant, the Ten Commandments, which he commanded you to follow and then wrote them on two stone tablets. ¹⁴And the Lord directed me at that time to teach you the decrees and laws you are to follow in the land that you are crossing the Jordan to possess.

Idolatry Forbidden

¹⁵You saw no form of any kind the day the Lord spoke to you at Horeb out of the fire. Therefore watch yourselves very carefully, ¹⁶so that you do not become corrupt and make for yourselves an idol, an image of any shape, whether formed like a man or a woman, ¹⁷or like any animal on earth or any bird that flies in the air, ¹⁸or like any creature that moves along the ground or any fish in the waters below. ¹⁹And when you look up to the sky and see the sun, the moon and the stars— all the heavenly array—do not be enticed into bowing down to them and worshiping things the Lord your God has apportioned to all the nations under heaven. ²⁰But as for you, the Lord took you and brought you out of the iron-smelting furnace, out of Egypt, to be the people of his inheritance, as you now are.

²¹The Lord was angry with me because of you, and he solemnly swore that I would not cross the Jordan and enter the good land the Lord your God is giving you as your inheritance. ²²I will die in this land; I will not cross the Jordan; but you are about to cross over and take possession of that good land. ²³Be careful not to forget the covenant of the Lord your God that he made with you; do not make for yourselves an idol in the form of anything the Lord your God has forbidden. ²⁴For the Lord your God is a consuming fire, a jealous God.

²⁵After you have had children and grandchildren and have lived in the land a long time—if you then become corrupt

and make any kind of idol, doing evil in the eyes of the Lord your God and provoking him to anger, **26**I call heaven and earth as witnesses against you this day that you will quickly perish from the land that you are crossing the Jordan to possess. You will not live there long but will certainly be destroyed. **27**The Lord will scatter you among the peoples, and only a few of you will survive among the nations to which the Lord will drive you. **28**There you will worship man-made gods of wood and stone, which cannot see or hear or eat or smell. **29**But if from there you seek the Lord your God, you will find him if you look for him with all your heart and with all your soul. **30**When you are in distress and all these things have happened to you, then in later days you will return to the Lord your God and obey him. **31**For the Lord your God is a merciful God; he will not abandon or destroy you or forget the covenant with your forefathers, which he confirmed to them by oath.

The Lord Is God

32Ask now about the former days, long before your time, from the day God created man on the earth; ask from one end of the heavens to the other. Has anything so great as this ever happened, or has anything like it ever been heard of? **33**Has any other people heard the voice of God*a* speaking out of fire, as you have, and lived? **34**Has any god ever tried to take for himself one nation out of another nation, by testings, by miraculous signs and wonders, by war, by a mighty hand and an outstretched arm, or by great and awesome deeds, like all the things the Lord your God did for you in Egypt before your very eyes?

35You were shown these things so that you might know that the Lord is God; besides him there is no other. **36**From heaven he made you hear his voice to discipline you. On earth he showed you his great fire, and you heard his words from out of the fire. **37**Because he loved your forefathers and chose their descendants after them, he brought you out of Egypt by his Presence and his great strength, **38**to drive out before you nations greater and stronger than you and to bring you into their land to give it to you for your inheritance, as it is today.

39Acknowledge and take to heart this day that the Lord is God in heaven above

and on the earth below. There is no other. **40**Keep his decrees and commands, which I am giving you today, so that it may go well with you and your children after you and that you may live long in the land the Lord your God gives you for all time.

Cities of Refuge

41Then Moses set aside three cities east of the Jordan, **42**to which anyone who had killed a person could flee if he had unintentionally killed his neighbor without malice aforethought. He could flee into one of these cities and save his life. **43**The cities were these: Bezer in the desert plateau, for the Reubenites; Ramoth in Gilead, for the Gadites; and Golan in Bashan, for the Manassites.

Introduction to the Law

44This is the law Moses set before the Israelites. **45**These are the stipulations, decrees and laws Moses gave them when they came out of Egypt **46**and were in the valley near Beth Peor east of the Jordan, in the land of Sihon king of the Amorites, who reigned in Heshbon and was defeated by Moses and the Israelites as they came out of Egypt. **47**They took possession of his land and the land of Og king of Bashan, the two Amorite kings east of the Jordan. **48**This land extended from Aroer on the rim of the Arnon Gorge to Mount Siyon*b* (that is, Hermon), **49**and included all the Arabah east of the Jordan, as far as the Sea of the Arabah,*c* below the slopes of Pisgah.

The Ten Commandments

5 Moses summoned all Israel and said: Hear, O Israel, the decrees and laws I declare in your hearing today. Learn them and be sure to follow them. **2**The Lord our God made a covenant with us at Horeb. **3**It was not with our fathers that the Lord made this covenant, but with us, with all of us who are alive here today. **4**The Lord spoke to you face to face out of the fire on the mountain. **5**(At that time I stood between the Lord and you to declare to you the word of the Lord, because you were afraid of the fire and did not go up the mountain.) And he said:

> **6**"I am the Lord your God, who brought you out of Egypt, out of the land of slavery.

a33 Or *of a god*   *b48* Hebrew; Syriac (see also Deut. 3:9) *Sirion*   *c49* That is, the Dead Sea

7"You shall have no other gods before[a] me.

8"You shall not make for yourself an idol in the form of anything in heaven above or on the earth beneath or in the waters below. 9You shall not bow down to them or worship them; for I, the Lord your God, am a jealous God, punishing the children for the sin of the fathers to the third and fourth generation of those who hate me, 10but showing love to a thousand ₍generations₎ of those who love me and keep my commandments.

11"You shall not misuse the name of the Lord your God, for the Lord will not hold anyone guiltless who misuses his name.

12"Observe the Sabbath day by keeping it holy, as the Lord your God has commanded you. 13Six days you shall labor and do all your work, 14but the seventh day is a Sabbath to the Lord your God. On it you shall not do any work, neither you, nor your son or daughter, nor your manservant or maidservant, nor your ox, your donkey or any of your animals, nor the alien within your gates, so that your manservant and maidservant may rest, as you do. 15Remember that you were slaves in Egypt and that the Lord your God brought you out of there with a mighty hand and an outstretched arm. Therefore the Lord your God has commanded you to observe the Sabbath day.

16"Honor your father and your mother, as the Lord your God has commanded you, so that you may live long and that it may go well with you in the land the Lord your God is giving you.

17"You shall not murder.

18"You shall not commit adultery.

19"You shall not steal.

20"You shall not give false testimony against your neighbor.

21"You shall not covet your neighbor's wife. You shall not set your desire on your neighbor's house or land, his manservant or maidservant, his ox or donkey, or anything that belongs to your neighbor."

22These are the commandments the Lord proclaimed in a loud voice to your whole assembly there on the mountain from out of the fire, the cloud and the deep darkness; and he added nothing more. Then he wrote them on two stone tablets and gave them to me.

23When you heard the voice out of the darkness, while the mountain was ablaze with fire, all the leading men of your tribes and your elders came to me. 24And you said, "The Lord our God has shown us his glory and his majesty, and we have heard his voice from the fire. Today we have seen that a man can live even if God speaks with him. 25But now, why should we die? This great fire will consume us, and we will die if we hear the voice of the Lord our God any longer. 26For what mortal man has ever heard the voice of the living God speaking out of fire, as we have, and survived? 27Go near and listen to all that the Lord our God says. Then tell us whatever the Lord our God tells you. We will listen and obey."

28The Lord heard you when you spoke to me and the Lord said to me, "I have heard what this people said to you. Everything they said was good. 29Oh, that their hearts would be inclined to fear me and keep all my commands always, so that it might go well with them and their children forever!

30"Go, tell them to return to their tents. 31But you stay here with me so that I may give you all the commands, decrees and laws you are to teach them to follow in the land I am giving them to possess."

32So be careful to do what the Lord your God has commanded you; do not turn aside to the right or to the left. 33Walk in all the way that the Lord your God has commanded you, so that you may live and prosper and prolong your days in the land that you will possess.

Love the Lord Your God

6 These are the commands, decrees and laws the Lord your God directed me to teach you to observe in the land that you are crossing the Jordan to possess, 2so that you, your children and their children after them may fear the Lord your God as long as you live by keeping all his decrees and commands that I give you, and so that

a7 Or besides

you may enjoy long life. ³Hear, O Israel, and be careful to obey so that it may go well with you and that you may increase greatly in a land flowing with milk and honey, just as the Lord, the God of your fathers, promised you.

⁴Hear, O Israel: The Lord our God, the Lord is one.ᵃ ⁵Love the Lord your God with all your heart and with all your soul and with all your strength. ⁶These commandments that I give you today are to be upon your hearts. ⁷Impress them on your children. Talk about them when you sit at home and when you walk along the road, when you lie down and when you get up. ⁸Tie them as symbols on your hands and bind them on your foreheads. ⁹Write them on the doorframes of your houses and on your gates.

¹⁰When the Lord your God brings you into the land he swore to your fathers, to Abraham, Isaac and Jacob, to give you — a

ᵃ4 Or *The Lord our God is one Lord*; or *The Lord is our God, the Lord is one*; or *The Lord is our God, the Lord alone*

TUESDAY

VERSE FOR THE DAY:
Deuteronomy 5:18

AUTHOR:
Steve Farrar

PASSAGE FOR THE DAY:
Deuteronomy 5:16–21

The Only Road to Happiness

IF YOU are on the freeway looking for true happiness, do not take the exit marked "adultery." It may look like a shortcut but it isn't. It's a dead end. Keep driving until you find the exit marked "obedience." That's the only road that will get you to genuine happiness.

What you are looking for cannot be found outside of God's will. It is clearly not his will that you violate your marriage covenant. Paul Kaufman tells the old story about two men from different villages. The first man dreams of great treasure buried in the other village. He travels to this village to find the treasure and there meets the second man who tells him that he too has had a strange dream about a treasure. You can guess where the second man dreamed the treasure was buried.

If you think you have misery now, wait until you commit adultery or get a divorce. You will regret it the rest of your life. When a man leaves his wife for an alliance with another woman, he is not only breaking God's commandment, he is making a decision that will only fuel and magnify his personal disappointment . . .

If you are in miserable circumstances as you read these words, you obviously feel as though you are stuck with small potatoes. But if you will honor God by being obedient, he will honor you by throwing you some kind of banquet. I can't tell you how, I can't tell you when, but I can tell you that he keeps his word. He is the God of surprises, and if you remain faithful in that tough marriage, he will surprise you one day with joy.

Additional Scripture Readings:
Matthew 5:27–30; John 8:3–11

Go to page 180 for your next devotional reading.

land with large, flourishing cities you did not build, [11]houses filled with all kinds of good things you did not provide, wells you did not dig, and vineyards and olive groves you did not plant — then when you eat and are satisfied, [12]be careful that you do not forget the LORD, who brought you out of Egypt, out of the land of slavery.

[13]Fear the LORD your God, serve him only and take your oaths in his name. [14]Do not follow other gods, the gods of the peoples around you; [15]for the LORD your God, who is among you, is a jealous God and his anger will burn against you, and he will destroy you from the face of the land. [16]Do not test the LORD your God as you did at Massah. [17]Be sure to keep the commands of the LORD your God and the

---

WEDNESDAY

VERSE FOR THE DAY:
Deuteronomy 6:7

AUTHOR:
D. Bruce Lockerbie

PASSAGE FOR THE DAY:
Deuteronomy 6:1–9

Character at 4 a.m.

TO ANY father who really cares about his children, nothing is of greater importance than their training for discipline, their instruction in principles. Together these make up their *character*, which Aristotle defined as the decisions a person makes when the choice is not obvious. My father used to say, "Character is the way we act when nobody's looking." For example, it's no test of character to stop your car at a police roadblock. The test comes, rather, when you're driving at four o'clock in the morning along a desolate back road in Iowa. You're heading toward a red light at a deserted intersection and you can see for miles around that there's nobody else on the roads. Do you obey the law, even though there's no cross traffic, or zoom on through at full speed? This is a test of character, a choice made on the basis of respect for law, on the discipline of adhering to the principles of safe driving. You decide to stop on the strength of character instead of responding to convenience or whim. Of course, to the person who is well disciplined in respect for law, as well as other ethical and moral principles, such a simple illustration of choice is automatically invalid. For such a person, the only course of action is already established because *you stop at red lights*; that's all there is to it, whatever the time or traffic conditions. Only for a medical emergency does a driver consider some other option, in response to some higher law. In either case, you do what is right, not what you know to be wrong.

But where does such ingrained knowledge of right and wrong come from? Where does a child learn to make such choices? From a father's training and instruction. This job belongs to every parent, but in a special way God has chosen the father of each family to be his representative in the home.

Additional Scripture Readings:
Proverbs 3:1–11; Hebrews 12:5–11

Go to page 183 for your next devotional reading.

stipulations and decrees he has given you. [18]Do what is right and good in the LORD's sight, so that it may go well with you and you may go in and take over the good land that the LORD promised on oath to your forefathers, [19]thrusting out all your enemies before you, as the LORD said.

[20]In the future, when your son asks you, "What is the meaning of the stipulations, decrees and laws the LORD our God has commanded you?" [21]tell him: "We were slaves of Pharaoh in Egypt, but the LORD brought us out of Egypt with a mighty hand. [22]Before our eyes the LORD sent miraculous signs and wonders — great and terrible — upon Egypt and Pharaoh and his whole household. [23]But he brought us out from there to bring us in and give us the land that he promised on oath to our forefathers. [24]The LORD commanded us to obey all these decrees and to fear the LORD our God, so that we might always prosper and be kept alive, as is the case today. [25]And if we are careful to obey all this law before the LORD our God, as he has commanded us, that will be our righteousness."

Driving Out the Nations

7 When the LORD your God brings you into the land you are entering to possess and drives out before you many nations — the Hittites, Girgashites, Amorites, Canaanites, Perizzites, Hivites and Jebusites, seven nations larger and stronger than you — [2]and when the LORD your God has delivered them over to you and you have defeated them, then you must destroy them totally.[a] Make no treaty with them, and show them no mercy. [3]Do not intermarry with them. Do not give your daughters to their sons or take their daughters for your sons, [4]for they will turn your sons away from following me to serve other gods, and the LORD's anger will burn against you and will quickly destroy you. [5]This is what you are to do to them: Break down their altars, smash their sacred stones, cut down their Asherah poles[b] and burn their idols in the fire. [6]For you are a people holy to the LORD your God. The LORD your God has chosen you out of all the peoples on the face of the earth to be his people, his treasured possession.

[7]The LORD did not set his affection on you and choose you because you were more numerous than other peoples, for you were the fewest of all peoples. [8]But it was because the LORD loved you and kept the oath he swore to your forefathers that he brought you out with a mighty hand and redeemed you from the land of slavery, from the power of Pharaoh king of Egypt. [9]Know therefore that the LORD your God is God; he is the faithful God, keeping his covenant of love to a thousand generations of those who love him and keep his commands. [10]But

those who hate him he will repay to
their face by destruction;
he will not be slow to repay to their
face those who hate him.

[11]Therefore, take care to follow the commands, decrees and laws I give you today. [12]If you pay attention to these laws and are careful to follow them, then the LORD your God will keep his covenant of love with you, as he swore to your forefathers. [13]He will love you and bless you and increase your numbers. He will bless the fruit of your womb, the crops of your land — your grain, new wine and oil — the calves of your herds and the lambs of your flocks in the land that he swore to your forefathers to give you. [14]You will be blessed more than any other people; none of your men or women will be childless, nor any of your livestock without young. [15]The LORD will keep you free from every disease. He will not inflict on you the horrible diseases you knew in Egypt, but he will inflict them on all who hate you. [16]You must destroy all the peoples the LORD your God gives over to you. Do not look on them with pity and do not serve their gods, for that will be a snare to you.

[17]You may say to yourselves, "These nations are stronger than we are. How can we drive them out?" [18]But do not be afraid of them; remember well what the LORD your God did to Pharaoh and to all Egypt. [19]You saw with your own eyes the great trials, the miraculous signs and wonders, the mighty hand and outstretched arm, with which the LORD your God brought you out. The LORD your God will do the same to all the peoples you now fear. [20]Moreover, the LORD your God will send the hornet among them until even the survivors who hide from you have perished.

---

[a]2 The Hebrew term refers to the irrevocable giving over of things or persons to the LORD, often by totally destroying them; also in verse 26.   [b]5 That is, symbols of the goddess Asherah; here and elsewhere in Deuteronomy

[21]Do not be terrified by them, for the LORD your God, who is among you, is a great and awesome God. [22]The LORD your God will drive out those nations before you, little by little. You will not be allowed to eliminate them all at once, or the wild animals will multiply around you. [23]But the LORD your God will deliver them over to you, throwing them into great confusion until they are destroyed. [24]He will give their kings into your hand, and you will wipe out their names from under heaven. No one will be able to stand up against you; you will destroy them. [25]The images of their gods you are to burn in the fire. Do not covet the silver and gold on them, and do not take it for yourselves, or you will be ensnared by it, for it is detestable to the LORD your God. [26]Do not bring a detestable thing into your house or you, like it, will be set apart for destruction. Utterly abhor and detest it, for it is set apart for destruction.

Do Not Forget the LORD

8 Be careful to follow every command I am giving you today, so that you may live and increase and may enter and possess the land that the LORD promised on oath to your forefathers. [2]Remember how the LORD your God led you all the way in the desert these forty years, to humble you and to test you in order to know what was in your heart, whether or not you would keep his commands. [3]He humbled you, causing you to hunger and then feeding you with manna, which neither you nor your fathers had known, to teach you that man does not live on bread alone but on every word that comes from the mouth of the LORD. [4]Your clothes did not wear out and your feet did not swell during these forty years. [5]Know then in your heart that as a man disciplines his son, so the LORD your God disciplines you.

[6]Observe the commands of the LORD your God, walking in his ways and revering him. [7]For the LORD your God is bringing you into a good land—a land with streams and pools of water, with springs flowing in the valleys and hills; [8]a land with wheat and barley, vines and fig trees, pomegranates, olive oil and honey; [9]a land where bread will not be scarce and you will lack nothing; a land where the rocks are iron and you can dig copper out of the hills.

[10]When you have eaten and are satisfied, praise the LORD your God for the good land he has given you. [11]Be careful that you do not forget the LORD your God, failing to observe his commands, his laws and his decrees that I am giving you this day. [12]Otherwise, when you eat and are satisfied, when you build fine houses and settle down, [13]and when your herds and flocks grow large and your silver and gold increase and all you have is multiplied, [14]then your heart will become proud and you will forget the LORD your God, who brought you out of Egypt, out of the land of slavery. [15]He led you through the vast and dreadful desert, that thirsty and waterless land, with its venomous snakes and scorpions. He brought you water out of hard rock. [16]He gave you manna to eat in the desert, something your fathers had never known, to humble and to test you so that in the end it might go well with you. [17]You may say to yourself, "My power and the strength of my hands have produced this wealth for me." [18]But remember the LORD your God, for it is he who gives you the ability to produce wealth, and so confirms his covenant, which he swore to your forefathers, as it is today.

[19]If you ever forget the LORD your God and follow other gods and worship and bow down to them, I testify against you today that you will surely be destroyed. [20]Like the nations the LORD destroyed before you, so you will be destroyed for not obeying the LORD your God.

Not Because of Israel's Righteousness

9 Hear, O Israel. You are now about to cross the Jordan to go in and dispossess nations greater and stronger than you, with large cities that have walls up to the sky. [2]The people are strong and tall—Anakites! You know about them and have heard it said: "Who can stand up against the Anakites?" [3]But be assured today that the LORD your God is the one who goes across ahead of you like a devouring fire. He will destroy them; he will subdue them before you. And you will drive them out and annihilate them quickly, as the LORD has promised you.

[4]After the LORD your God has driven them out before you, do not say to yourself, "The LORD has brought me here to take possession of this land because of my righteousness." No, it is on account of the wickedness of these nations that the LORD is going to drive them out before you. [5]It is not because of your righteousness or your integrity that you are going in to take possession of their land; but on account of the wickedness of these nations, the LORD

your God will drive them out before you, to accomplish what he swore to your fathers, to Abraham, Isaac and Jacob. 6Understand, then, that it is not because of your righteousness that the LORD your God is giving you this good land to possess, for you are a stiff-necked people.

The Golden Calf

7Remember this and never forget how you provoked the LORD your God to anger in the desert. From the day you left Egypt until you arrived here, you have been rebellious against the LORD. 8At Horeb you aroused the LORD's wrath so that he was angry enough to destroy you. 9When I went up on the mountain to receive the tablets of stone, the tablets of the covenant that the LORD had made with you, I stayed on the mountain forty days and forty nights; I ate no bread and drank no water. 10The LORD gave me two stone tablets inscribed by the finger of God. On them were all the commandments the LORD proclaimed to you on the mountain out of the fire, on the day of the assembly.

11At the end of the forty days and forty nights, the LORD gave me the two stone tablets, the tablets of the covenant. 12Then the LORD told me, "Go down from here at once, because your people whom you brought out of Egypt have become cor-

---

THURSDAY

VERSE FOR THE DAY:
Deuteronomy 8:2

AUTHOR:
C.S. Lewis

PASSAGE FOR THE DAY:
Deuteronomy 8:1–5

My Only Real Treasure

I AM not arguing that pain is not painful. Pain hurts. That is what the word means. I am only trying to show that the old Christian doctrine of being made "perfect through suffering" is not incredible. To prove it palatable is beyond my design . . .

My own experience is something like this. I am progressing along the path of life in my ordinary contentedly fallen and godless condition, absorbed in a merry meeting with my friends for the morrow or a bit of work that tickles my vanity today, a holiday or a new book, when suddenly a stab of abdominal pain that threatens serious disease, or a headline in the newspapers that threatens us all with destruction, sends this whole pack of cards tumbling down. At first I am overwhelmed, and all my little happinesses look like broken toys. Then, slowly and reluctantly, bit by bit, I try to bring myself into the frame of mind that I should be in at all times. I remind myself that all these toys were never intended to possess my heart, that my true good is in another world and my only real treasure is Christ. And perhaps, by God's grace, I succeed, and for a day or two become a creature consciously dependent on God and drawing its strength from the right sources. But the moment the threat is withdrawn, my whole nature leaps back to the toys . . . Thus the terrible necessity of tribulation is only too clear. God has had me for but forty-eight hours and then only by dint of taking everything else away from me.

Additional Scripture Readings:
2 Corinthians 12:1–10; James 1:2–18

Go to page 186 for your next devotional reading.

rupt. They have turned away quickly from what I commanded them and have made a cast idol for themselves."

[13]And the LORD said to me, "I have seen this people, and they are a stiff-necked people indeed! [14]Let me alone, so that I may destroy them and blot out their name from under heaven. And I will make you into a nation stronger and more numerous than they."

[15]So I turned and went down from the mountain while it was ablaze with fire. And the two tablets of the covenant were in my hands.[a] [16]When I looked, I saw that you had sinned against the LORD your God; you had made for yourselves an idol cast in the shape of a calf. You had turned aside quickly from the way that the LORD had commanded you. [17]So I took the two tablets and threw them out of my hands, breaking them to pieces before your eyes.

[18]Then once again I fell prostrate before the LORD for forty days and forty nights; I ate no bread and drank no water, because of all the sin you had committed, doing what was evil in the LORD's sight and so provoking him to anger. [19]I feared the anger and wrath of the LORD, for he was angry enough with you to destroy you. But again the LORD listened to me. [20]And the LORD was angry enough with Aaron to destroy him, but at that time I prayed for Aaron too. [21]Also I took that sinful thing of yours, the calf you had made, and burned it in the fire. Then I crushed it and ground it to powder as fine as dust and threw the dust into a stream that flowed down the mountain.

[22]You also made the LORD angry at Taberah, at Massah and at Kibroth Hattaavah. [23]And when the LORD sent you out from Kadesh Barnea, he said, "Go up and take possession of the land I have given you." But you rebelled against the command of the LORD your God. You did not trust him or obey him. [24]You have been rebellious against the LORD ever since I have known you.

[25]I lay prostrate before the LORD those forty days and forty nights because the LORD had said he would destroy you. [26]I prayed to the LORD and said, "O Sovereign LORD, do not destroy your people, your own inheritance that you redeemed by your great power and brought out of Egypt with a mighty hand. [27]Remember your servants Abraham, Isaac and Jacob. Overlook the stubbornness of this people,

their wickedness and their sin. [28]Otherwise, the country from which you brought us will say, 'Because the LORD was not able to take them into the land he had promised them, and because he hated them, he brought them out to put them to death in the desert.' [29]But they are your people, your inheritance that you brought out by your great power and your outstretched arm."

Tablets Like the First Ones

10 At that time the LORD said to me, "Chisel out two stone tablets like the first ones and come up to me on the mountain. Also make a wooden chest.[b] [2]I will write on the tablets the words that were on the first tablets, which you broke. Then you are to put them in the chest."

[3]So I made the ark out of acacia wood and chiseled out two stone tablets like the first ones, and I went up on the mountain with the two tablets in my hands. [4]The LORD wrote on these tablets what he had written before, the Ten Commandments he had proclaimed to you on the mountain, out of the fire, on the day of the assembly. And the LORD gave them to me. [5]Then I came back down the mountain and put the tablets in the ark I had made, as the LORD commanded me, and they are there now.

[6](The Israelites traveled from the wells of the Jaakanites to Moserah. There Aaron died and was buried, and Eleazar his son succeeded him as priest. [7]From there they traveled to Gudgodah and on to Jotbathah, a land with streams of water. [8]At that time the LORD set apart the tribe of Levi to carry the ark of the covenant of the LORD, to stand before the LORD to minister and to pronounce blessings in his name, as they still do today. [9]That is why the Levites have no share or inheritance among their brothers; the LORD is their inheritance, as the LORD your God told them.)

[10]Now I had stayed on the mountain forty days and nights, as I did the first time, and the LORD listened to me at this time also. It was not his will to destroy you. [11]"Go," the LORD said to me, "and lead the people on their way, so that they may enter and possess the land that I swore to their fathers to give them."

Fear the LORD

[12]And now, O Israel, what does the LORD your God ask of you but to fear the

---

[a]15 Or And I had the two tablets of the covenant with me, one in each hand   [b]1 That is, an ark

LORD your God, to walk in all his ways, to love him, to serve the LORD your God with all your heart and with all your soul, [13]and to observe the LORD's commands and decrees that I am giving you today for your own good?

[14]To the LORD your God belong the heavens, even the highest heavens, the earth and everything in it. [15]Yet the LORD set his affection on your forefathers and loved them, and he chose you, their descendants, above all the nations, as it is today. [16]Circumcise your hearts, therefore, and do not be stiff-necked any longer. [17]For the LORD your God is God of gods and Lord of lords, the great God, mighty and awesome, who shows no partiality and accepts no bribes. [18]He defends the cause of the fatherless and the widow, and loves the alien, giving him food and clothing. [19]And you are to love those who are aliens, for you yourselves were aliens in Egypt. [20]Fear the LORD your God and serve him. Hold fast to him and take your oaths in his name. [21]He is your praise; he is your God, who performed for you those great and awesome wonders you saw with your own eyes. [22]Your forefathers who went down into Egypt were seventy in all, and now the LORD your God has made you as numerous as the stars in the sky.

Love and Obey the LORD

11 Love the LORD your God and keep his requirements, his decrees, his laws and his commands always. [2]Remember today that your children were not the ones who saw and experienced the discipline of the LORD your God: his majesty, his mighty hand, his outstretched arm; [3]the signs he performed and the things he did in the heart of Egypt, both to Pharaoh king of Egypt and to his whole country; [4]what he did to the Egyptian army, to its horses and chariots, how he overwhelmed them with the waters of the Red Sea[a] as they were pursuing you, and how the LORD brought lasting ruin on them. [5]It was not your children who saw what he did for you in the desert until you arrived at this place, [6]and what he did to Dathan and Abiram, sons of Eliab the Reubenite, when the earth opened its mouth right in the middle of all Israel and swallowed them up with their households, their tents and every living thing that belonged to them. [7]But it was your own eyes that saw all these great things the LORD has done.

[8]Observe therefore all the commands I am giving you today, so that you may have the strength to go in and take over the land that you are crossing the Jordan to possess, [9]and so that you may live long in the land that the LORD swore to your forefathers to give to them and their descendants, a land flowing with milk and honey. [10]The land you are entering to take over is not like the land of Egypt, from which you have come, where you planted your seed and irrigated it by foot as in a vegetable garden. [11]But the land you are crossing the Jordan to take possession of is a land of mountains and valleys that drinks rain from heaven. [12]It is a land the LORD your God cares for; the eyes of the LORD your God are continually on it from the beginning of the year to its end.

[13]So if you faithfully obey the commands I am giving you today — to love the LORD your God and to serve him with all your heart and with all your soul — [14]then I will send rain on your land in its season, both autumn and spring rains, so that you may gather in your grain, new wine and oil. [15]I will provide grass in the fields for your cattle, and you will eat and be satisfied.

[16]Be careful, or you will be enticed to turn away and worship other gods and bow down to them. [17]Then the LORD's anger will burn against you, and he will shut the heavens so that it will not rain and the ground will yield no produce, and you will soon perish from the good land the LORD is giving you. [18]Fix these words of mine in your hearts and minds; tie them as symbols on your hands and bind them on your foreheads. [19]Teach them to your children, talking about them when you sit at home and when you walk along the road, when you lie down and when you get up. [20]Write them on the doorframes of your houses and on your gates, [21]so that your days and the days of your children may be many in the land that the LORD swore to give your forefathers, as many as the days that the heavens are above the earth.

[22]If you carefully observe all these commands I am giving you to follow — to love the LORD your God, to walk in all his ways and to hold fast to him — [23]then the LORD will drive out all these nations before you, and you will dispossess nations larger and stronger than you. [24]Every place where you set your foot will be yours: Your terri-

---

[a]4 Hebrew *Yam Suph*; that is, Sea of Reeds

tory will extend from the desert to Lebanon, and from the Euphrates River to the western sea.[a] **25**No man will be able to stand against you. The Lord your God, as he promised you, will put the terror and fear of you on the whole land, wherever you go.

26See, I am setting before you today a blessing and a curse— **27**the blessing if you obey the commands of the Lord your God that I am giving you today; **28**the curse if you disobey the commands of the Lord your God and turn from the way that I command you today by following other gods, which you have not known. **29**When the Lord your God has brought you into the land you are entering to possess, you are to proclaim on Mount Gerizim the

[a]24 That is, the Mediterranean

FRIDAY

VERSE FOR THE DAY:
Deuteronomy 10:12

AUTHOR:
Doug Sherman and
William Hendricks

PASSAGE FOR THE DAY:
Deuteronomy 10:12–13

Doing What God Wants Done

IF YOU want to love God through your work, then you need to determine that what you are doing in your job is something God *wants* done, and that you are doing your job *because* God wants it done.

This may take some thought. Suppose you are a piano tuner. Is that something God wants done? It unquestionably is, because the pianist cannot play on a piano that is out of tune. Furthermore, if you have the ear for it, then you have a God-given means of providing for this need and for your income.

Then are you tuning pianos because God wants you to tune pianos? I'm sure you would have many reasons for working at such a job . . . . I would hope that you go to the job with a belief that in doing that job, you are ultimately serving God as well as man. If you are, then by tuning pianos you are loving God; you are doing something he wants done.

I encourage you as a worker to think through your job on this basis. At first it may be hard to see how your work connects with anything that God wants done. But I advise you to think very broadly about the needs that people have and the work that God has given mankind to do . . .

Everything about you is to be involved in loving God. It makes sense that your work must be involved as well. Just think about how much of your heart, soul and might go into your work. Imagine, then, as you spend yourself at that task, being able to say, "I'm here to do something God wants done, and I intend to do it because I love him." The person who can make this statement has turned his work into one of his primary means of obeying the greatest of God's commandments.

Additional Scripture Readings:
Colossians 3:12–17; 1 Peter 4:7–11

*Go to page 189 for your next
devotional reading.*

blessings, and on Mount Ebal the curses. [30]As you know, these mountains are across the Jordan, west of the road,[a] toward the setting sun, near the great trees of Moreh, in the territory of those Canaanites living in the Arabah in the vicinity of Gilgal. [31]You are about to cross the Jordan to enter and take possession of the land the LORD your God is giving you. When you have taken it over and are living there, [32]be sure that you obey all the decrees and laws I am setting before you today.

The One Place of Worship

12 These are the decrees and laws you must be careful to follow in the land that the LORD, the God of your fathers, has given you to possess — as long as you live in the land. [2]Destroy completely all the places on the high mountains and on the hills and under every spreading tree where the nations you are dispossessing worship their gods. [3]Break down their altars, smash their sacred stones and burn their Asherah poles in the fire; cut down the idols of their gods and wipe out their names from those places.

[4]You must not worship the LORD your God in their way. [5]But you are to seek the place the LORD your God will choose from among all your tribes to put his Name there for his dwelling. To that place you must go; [6]there bring your burnt offerings and sacrifices, your tithes and special gifts, what you have vowed to give and your freewill offerings, and the firstborn of your herds and flocks. [7]There, in the presence of the LORD your God, you and your families shall eat and shall rejoice in everything you have put your hand to, because the LORD your God has blessed you.

[8]You are not to do as we do here today, everyone as he sees fit, [9]since you have not yet reached the resting place and the inheritance the LORD your God is giving you. [10]But you will cross the Jordan and settle in the land the LORD your God is giving you as an inheritance, and he will give you rest from all your enemies around you so that you will live in safety. [11]Then to the place the LORD your God will choose as a dwelling for his Name — there you are to bring everything I command you: your burnt offerings and sacrifices, your tithes and special gifts, and all the choice possessions you have vowed to the LORD. [12]And there rejoice before the LORD your God, you, your sons and daughters, your menservants and maidservants, and the Levites from your towns, who have no allotment or inheritance of their own. [13]Be careful not to sacrifice your burnt offerings anywhere you please. [14]Offer them only at the place the LORD will choose in one of your tribes, and there observe everything I command you.

[15]Nevertheless, you may slaughter your animals in any of your towns and eat as much of the meat as you want, as if it were gazelle or deer, according to the blessing the LORD your God gives you. Both the ceremonially unclean and the clean may eat it. [16]But you must not eat the blood; pour it out on the ground like water. [17]You must not eat in your own towns the tithe of your grain and new wine and oil, or the firstborn of your herds and flocks, or whatever you have vowed to give, or your freewill offerings or special gifts. [18]Instead, you are to eat them in the presence of the LORD your God at the place the LORD your God will choose — you, your sons and daughters, your menservants and maidservants, and the Levites from your towns — and you are to rejoice before the LORD your God in everything you put your hand to. [19]Be careful not to neglect the Levites as long as you live in your land.

[20]When the LORD your God has enlarged your territory as he promised you, and you crave meat and say, "I would like some meat," then you may eat as much of it as you want. [21]If the place where the LORD your God chooses to put his Name is too far away from you, you may slaughter animals from the herds and flocks the LORD has given you, as I have commanded you, and in your own towns you may eat as much of them as you want. [22]Eat them as you would gazelle or deer. Both the ceremonially unclean and the clean may eat. [23]But be sure you do not eat the blood, because the blood is the life, and you must not eat the life with the meat. [24]You must not eat the blood; pour it out on the ground like water. [25]Do not eat it, so that it may go well with you and your children after you, because you will be doing what is right in the eyes of the LORD.

[26]But take your consecrated things and whatever you have vowed to give, and go to the place the LORD will choose. [27]Present your burnt offerings on the altar of the LORD your God, both the meat and the blood. The blood of your sacrifices must be poured beside the altar of the

LORD your God, but you may eat the meat. 28Be careful to obey all these regulations I am giving you, so that it may always go well with you and your children after you, because you will be doing what is good and right in the eyes of the LORD your God.

29The LORD your God will cut off before you the nations you are about to invade and dispossess. But when you have driven them out and settled in their land, 30and after they have been destroyed before you, be careful not to be ensnared by inquiring about their gods, saying, "How do these nations serve their gods? We will do the same." 31You must not worship the LORD your God in their way, because in worshiping their gods, they do all kinds of detestable things the LORD hates. They even burn their sons and daughters in the fire as sacrifices to their gods.

32See that you do all I command you; do not add to it or take away from it.

Worshiping Other Gods

13 If a prophet, or one who foretells by dreams, appears among you and announces to you a miraculous sign or wonder, 2and if the sign or wonder of which he has spoken takes place, and he says, "Let us follow other gods" (gods you have not known) "and let us worship them," 3you must not listen to the words of that prophet or dreamer. The LORD your God is testing you to find out whether you love him with all your heart and with all your soul. 4It is the LORD your God you must follow, and him you must revere. Keep his commands and obey him; serve him and hold fast to him. 5That prophet or dreamer must be put to death, because he preached rebellion against the LORD your God, who brought you out of Egypt and redeemed you from the land of slavery; he has tried to turn you from the way the LORD your God commanded you to follow. You must purge the evil from among you.

6If your very own brother, or your son or daughter, or the wife you love, or your closest friend secretly entices you, saying, "Let us go and worship other gods" (gods that neither you nor your fathers have known, 7gods of the peoples around you, whether near or far, from one end of the land to the other), 8do not yield to him or listen to him. Show him no pity. Do not spare him or shield him. 9You must cer-

tainly put him to death. Your hand must be the first in putting him to death, and then the hands of all the people. 10Stone him to death, because he tried to turn you away from the LORD your God, who brought you out of Egypt, out of the land of slavery. 11Then all Israel will hear and be afraid, and no one among you will do such an evil thing again.

12If you hear it said about one of the towns the LORD your God is giving you to live in 13that wicked men have arisen among you and have led the people of their town astray, saying, "Let us go and worship other gods" (gods you have not known), 14then you must inquire, probe and investigate it thoroughly. And if it is true and it has been proved that this detestable thing has been done among you, 15you must certainly put to the sword all who live in that town. Destroy it completely,a both its people and its livestock. 16Gather all the plunder of the town into the middle of the public square and completely burn the town and all its plunder as a whole burnt offering to the LORD your God. It is to remain a ruin forever, never to be rebuilt. 17None of those condemned thingsa shall be found in your hands, so that the LORD will turn from his fierce anger; he will show you mercy, have compassion on you, and increase your numbers, as he promised on oath to your forefathers, 18because you obey the LORD your God, keeping all his commands that I am giving you today and doing what is right in his eyes.

Clean and Unclean Food

14 You are the children of the LORD your God. Do not cut yourselves or shave the front of your heads for the dead, 2for you are a people holy to the LORD your God. Out of all the peoples on the face of the earth, the LORD has chosen you to be his treasured possession.

3Do not eat any detestable thing. 4These are the animals you may eat: the ox, the sheep, the goat, 5the deer, the gazelle, the roe deer, the wild goat, the ibex, the antelope and the mountain sheep.b 6You may eat any animal that has a split hoof divided in two and that chews the cud. 7However, of those that chew the cud or that have a split hoof completely divided you may not eat the camel, the rabbit or the

---

a15,17 The Hebrew term refers to the irrevocable giving over of things or persons to the LORD, often by totally destroying them.   b5 The precise identification of some of the birds and animals in this chapter is uncertain.

WEEKENDING

RECOGNIZE

To believe means to realize not just with the head but also with the heart that God loves *me* in a creative, intimate, unique, reliable and *tender* way. Creative: out of his love I came forth; through his love I am who I am. Intimate: his love reaches out to the deepest in me. Unique: his love embraces me as I am, not as I am considered to be by other people or supposed to be in my own self-image. Reliable: his love will never let me down. Tender . . . Tenderness is what happens to you when you know you are deeply and sincerely *liked* by someone.

– *Brennan Manning*

REVIVE

Saturday: Deuteronomy 7:1–11
Sunday: Isaiah 49:13–18

Go to page 191 for your next devotional reading.

Go to page 191 for your next devotional reading.

coney.ᵃ Although they chew the cud, they do not have a split hoof; they are ceremonially unclean for you. **8**The pig is also unclean; although it has a split hoof, it does not chew the cud. You are not to eat their meat or touch their carcasses.

9Of all the creatures living in the water, you may eat any that has fins and scales. **10**But anything that does not have fins and scales you may not eat; for you it is unclean.

11You may eat any clean bird. **12**But these you may not eat: the eagle, the vulture, the black vulture, **13**the red kite, the black kite, any kind of falcon, **14**any kind of raven, **15**the horned owl, the screech owl, the gull, any kind of hawk, **16**the little owl, the great owl, the white owl, **17**the desert owl, the osprey, the cormorant, **18**the stork, any kind of heron, the hoopoe and the bat.

19All flying insects that swarm are unclean to you; do not eat them. **20**But any winged creature that is clean you may eat.

21Do not eat anything you find already dead. You may give it to an alien living in any of your towns, and he may eat it, or you may sell it to a foreigner. But you are a people holy to the LORD your God.

Do not cook a young goat in its mother's milk.

Tithes

22Be sure to set aside a tenth of all that your fields produce each year. **23**Eat the tithe of your grain, new wine and oil, and the firstborn of your herds and flocks in the presence of the LORD your God at the place he will choose as a dwelling for his Name, so that you may learn to revere the LORD your God always. **24**But if that place is too distant and you have been blessed by the LORD your God and cannot carry your tithe (because the place where the LORD will choose to put his Name is so far away), **25**then exchange your tithe for silver, and take the silver with you and go to the place the LORD your God will choose. **26**Use the silver to buy whatever you like: cattle, sheep, wine or other fermented drink, or anything you wish. Then you and your household shall eat there in the presence of the LORD your God and rejoice. **27**And do not neglect the Levites living in your towns, for they have no allotment or inheritance of their own.

28At the end of every three years, bring all the tithes of that year's produce and store it in your towns, **29**so that the Levites (who have no allotment or inheritance of their own) and the aliens, the fatherless and the widows who live in your towns may come and eat and be satisfied, and so that the LORD your God may bless you in all the work of your hands.

The Year for Canceling Debts

15 At the end of every seven years you must cancel debts. **2**This is how it is to be done: Every creditor shall cancel the loan he has made to his fellow Israelite. He shall not require payment from his fellow Israelite or brother, because the LORD's time for canceling debts has been proclaimed. **3**You may require payment from a foreigner, but you must cancel any debt your brother owes you. **4**However, there should be no poor among you, for in the land the LORD your God is giving you to possess as your inheritance, he will richly bless you, **5**if only you fully obey the LORD your God and are careful to follow all these commands I am giving you today. **6**For the LORD your God will bless you as he has promised, and you will lend to many nations but will borrow from none. You will rule over many nations but none will rule over you.

7If there is a poor man among your brothers in any of the towns of the land that the LORD your God is giving you, do not be hardhearted or tightfisted toward your poor brother. **8**Rather be openhanded and freely lend him whatever he needs. **9**Be careful not to harbor this wicked thought: "The seventh year, the year for canceling debts, is near," so that you do not show ill will toward your needy brother and give him nothing. He may then appeal to the LORD against you, and you will be found guilty of sin. **10**Give generously to him and do so without a grudging heart; then because of this the LORD your God will bless you in all your work and in everything you put your hand to. **11**There will always be poor people in the land. Therefore I command you to be openhanded toward your brothers and toward the poor and needy in your land.

Freeing Servants

12If a fellow Hebrew, a man or a woman, sells himself to you and serves you six years, in the seventh year you must let

ᵃ7 That is, the hyrax or rock badger

him go free. ¹³And when you release him, do not send him away empty-handed. ¹⁴Supply him liberally from your flock, your threshing floor and your winepress. Give to him as the LORD your God has blessed you. ¹⁵Remember that you were slaves in Egypt and the LORD your God redeemed you. That is why I give you this command today.

¹⁶But if your servant says to you, "I do not want to leave you," because he loves you and your family and is well off with you, ¹⁷then take an awl and push it through his ear lobe into the door, and he will become your servant for life. Do the same for your maidservant.

¹⁸Do not consider it a hardship to set your servant free, because his service to you these six years has been worth twice as much as that of a hired hand. And the LORD your God will bless you in everything you do.

MONDAY

VERSE FOR THE DAY:	AUTHOR:	PASSAGE FOR THE DAY:
Deuteronomy 15:4	Charles Colson	Deuteronomy 15:1–11

We Dare Not Fail

OUR technology has brought clinical impersonalization: machines solve all problems; television reduces us all to spectators as life appears in a condensed version from 6:00 to 7:00 each evening, in living color. And the by-product of modern technocracy is the loss of our sense of caring and awareness of one another. But if we Christians get out of our pews, seek justice, do the Word of God and lift up Christ, we will see that sense of community restored.

Think what this can mean for evangelism. The world perceives us as pious and self-centered in our protected sanctuaries and multimillion-dollar church complexes—but that is simply not where most of the sick, hurting and hungry people are, so they never hear our message. But imagine what would happen if the poor and needy could see us where *they* live, as we meet them at their point of need.

And, if we heed that call, we will be reasserting a proud heritage of the evangelical church. In the 19th century, evangelicals were at the forefront of the most significant social reforms in Western society: enacting child labor laws; ending abuses in the coal mines; establishing public education and public hospitals; and abolishing slavery.

The contest for America's moral leadership is still going on; whether the church is willing and able to step up to its Biblical responsibility is still to be decided. It may be the greatest question we face. For if we fail even the simple test of responding to human needs in our own community, what possible claim will we have to assume a role of genuine moral leadership in society? We dare not fail.

Additional Scripture Readings: Isaiah 58:6–14; Matthew 25:31–46

Go to page 198 for your next devotional reading.

The Firstborn Animals

[19]Set apart for the LORD your God every firstborn male of your herds and flocks. Do not put the firstborn of your oxen to work, and do not shear the firstborn of your sheep. [20]Each year you and your family are to eat them in the presence of the LORD your God at the place he will choose. [21]If an animal has a defect, is lame or blind, or has any serious flaw, you must not sacrifice it to the LORD your God. [22]You are to eat it in your own towns. Both the ceremonially unclean and the clean may eat it, as if it were gazelle or deer. [23]But you must not eat the blood; pour it out on the ground like water.

Passover

16 Observe the month of Abib and celebrate the Passover of the LORD your God, because in the month of Abib he brought you out of Egypt by night. [2]Sacrifice as the Passover to the LORD your God an animal from your flock or herd at the place the LORD will choose as a dwelling for his Name. [3]Do not eat it with bread made with yeast, but for seven days eat unleavened bread, the bread of affliction, because you left Egypt in haste — so that all the days of your life you may remember the time of your departure from Egypt. [4]Let no yeast be found in your possession in all your land for seven days. Do not let any of the meat you sacrifice on the evening of the first day remain until morning.

[5]You must not sacrifice the Passover in any town the LORD your God gives you [6]except in the place he will choose as a dwelling for his Name. There you must sacrifice the Passover in the evening, when the sun goes down, on the anniversary[a] of your departure from Egypt. [7]Roast it and eat it at the place the LORD your God will choose. Then in the morning return to your tents. [8]For six days eat unleavened bread and on the seventh day hold an assembly to the LORD your God and do no work.

Feast of Weeks

[9]Count off seven weeks from the time you begin to put the sickle to the standing grain. [10]Then celebrate the Feast of Weeks to the LORD your God by giving a freewill offering in proportion to the blessings the LORD your God has given you. [11]And rejoice before the LORD your God at the place he will choose as a dwelling for his Name — you, your sons and daughters, your menservants and maidservants, the Levites in your towns, and the aliens, the fatherless and the widows living among you. [12]Remember that you were slaves in Egypt, and follow carefully these decrees.

Feast of Tabernacles

[13]Celebrate the Feast of Tabernacles for seven days after you have gathered the produce of your threshing floor and your winepress. [14]Be joyful at your Feast — you, your sons and daughters, your menservants and maidservants, and the Levites, the aliens, the fatherless and the widows who live in your towns. [15]For seven days celebrate the Feast to the LORD your God at the place the LORD will choose. For the LORD your God will bless you in all your harvest and in all the work of your hands, and your joy will be complete.

[16]Three times a year all your men must appear before the LORD your God at the place he will choose: at the Feast of Unleavened Bread, the Feast of Weeks and the Feast of Tabernacles. No man should appear before the LORD empty-handed: [17]Each of you must bring a gift in proportion to the way the LORD your God has blessed you.

Judges

[18]Appoint judges and officials for each of your tribes in every town the LORD your God is giving you, and they shall judge the people fairly. [19]Do not pervert justice or show partiality. Do not accept a bribe, for a bribe blinds the eyes of the wise and twists the words of the righteous. [20]Follow justice and justice alone, so that you may live and possess the land the LORD your God is giving you.

Worshiping Other Gods

[21]Do not set up any wooden Asherah pole[b] beside the altar you build to the LORD your God, [22]and do not erect a sacred stone, for these the LORD your God hates.

17 Do not sacrifice to the LORD your God an ox or a sheep that has any defect or flaw in it, for that would be detestable to him.

[2]If a man or woman living among you in one of the towns the LORD gives you is found doing evil in the eyes of the LORD

---

[a]6 Or down, at the time of day   [b]21 Or Do not plant any tree dedicated to Asherah

your God in violation of his covenant, [3]and contrary to my command has worshiped other gods, bowing down to them or to the sun or the moon or the stars of the sky, [4]and this has been brought to your attention, then you must investigate it thoroughly. If it is true and it has been proved that this detestable thing has been done in Israel, [5]take the man or woman who has done this evil deed to your city gate and stone that person to death. [6]On the testimony of two or three witnesses a man shall be put to death, but no one shall be put to death on the testimony of only one witness. [7]The hands of the witnesses must be the first in putting him to death, and then the hands of all the people. You must purge the evil from among you.

Law Courts

[8]If cases come before your courts that are too difficult for you to judge — whether bloodshed, lawsuits or assaults — take them to the place the LORD your God will choose. [9]Go to the priests, who are Levites, and to the judge who is in office at that time. Inquire of them and they will give you the verdict. [10]You must act according to the decisions they give you at the place the LORD will choose. Be careful to do everything they direct you to do. [11]Act according to the law they teach you and the decisions they give you. Do not turn aside from what they tell you, to the right or to the left. [12]The man who shows contempt for the judge or for the priest who stands ministering there to the LORD your God must be put to death. You must purge the evil from Israel. [13]All the people will hear and be afraid, and will not be contemptuous again.

The King

[14]When you enter the land the LORD your God is giving you and have taken possession of it and settled in it, and you say, "Let us set a king over us like all the nations around us," [15]be sure to appoint over you the king the LORD your God chooses. He must be from among your own brothers. Do not place a foreigner over you, one who is not a brother Israelite. [16]The king, moreover, must not acquire great numbers of horses for himself or make the people return to Egypt to get more of them, for the LORD has told you, "You are not to go back that way again." [17]He must not take many wives, or his

heart will be led astray. He must not accumulate large amounts of silver and gold.

[18]When he takes the throne of his kingdom, he is to write for himself on a scroll a copy of this law, taken from that of the priests, who are Levites. [19]It is to be with him, and he is to read it all the days of his life so that he may learn to revere the LORD his God and follow carefully all the words of this law and these decrees [20]and not consider himself better than his brothers and turn from the law to the right or to the left. Then he and his descendants will reign a long time over his kingdom in Israel.

Offerings for Priests and Levites

18 The priests, who are Levites — indeed the whole tribe of Levi — are to have no allotment or inheritance with Israel. They shall live on the offerings made to the LORD by fire, for that is their inheritance. [2]They shall have no inheritance among their brothers; the LORD is their inheritance, as he promised them.

[3]This is the share due the priests from the people who sacrifice a bull or a sheep: the shoulder, the jowls and the inner parts. [4]You are to give them the firstfruits of your grain, new wine and oil, and the first wool from the shearing of your sheep, [5]for the LORD your God has chosen them and their descendants out of all your tribes to stand and minister in the LORD's name always.

[6]If a Levite moves from one of your towns anywhere in Israel where he is living, and comes in all earnestness to the place the LORD will choose, [7]he may minister in the name of the LORD his God like all his fellow Levites who serve there in the presence of the LORD. [8]He is to share equally in their benefits, even though he has received money from the sale of family possessions.

Detestable Practices

[9]When you enter the land the LORD your God is giving you, do not learn to imitate the detestable ways of the nations there. [10]Let no one be found among you who sacrifices his son or daughter in[a] the fire, who practices divination or sorcery, interprets omens, engages in witchcraft, [11]or casts spells, or who is a medium or spiritist or who consults the dead. [12]Anyone who does these things is detestable to the LORD, and because of these detestable

---

[a]10 Or *who makes his son or daughter pass through*

practices the LORD your God will drive out those nations before you. ¹³You must be blameless before the LORD your God.

The Prophet

¹⁴The nations you will dispossess listen to those who practice sorcery or divination. But as for you, the LORD your God has not permitted you to do so. ¹⁵The LORD your God will raise up for you a prophet like me from among your own brothers. You must listen to him. ¹⁶For this is what you asked of the LORD your God at Horeb on the day of the assembly when you said, "Let us not hear the voice of the LORD our God nor see this great fire anymore, or we will die."

¹⁷The LORD said to me: "What they say is good. ¹⁸I will raise up for them a prophet like you from among their brothers; I will put my words in his mouth, and he will tell them everything I command him. ¹⁹If anyone does not listen to my words that the prophet speaks in my name, I myself will call him to account. ²⁰But a prophet who presumes to speak in my name anything I have not commanded him to say, or a prophet who speaks in the name of other gods, must be put to death."

²¹You may say to yourselves, "How can we know when a message has not been spoken by the LORD?" ²²If what a prophet proclaims in the name of the LORD does not take place or come true, that is a message the LORD has not spoken. That prophet has spoken presumptuously. Do not be afraid of him.

Cities of Refuge

19 When the LORD your God has destroyed the nations whose land he is giving you, and when you have driven them out and settled in their towns and houses, ²then set aside for yourselves three cities centrally located in the land the LORD your God is giving you to possess. ³Build roads to them and divide into three parts the land the LORD your God is giving you as an inheritance, so that anyone who kills a man may flee there.

⁴This is the rule concerning the man who kills another and flees there to save his life — one who kills his neighbor unintentionally, without malice aforethought. ⁵For instance, a man may go into the forest with his neighbor to cut wood, and as he swings his ax to fell a tree, the head may fly off and hit his neighbor and kill him. That man may flee to one of these cities and save his life. ⁶Otherwise, the avenger of blood might pursue him in a rage, overtake him if the distance is too great, and kill him even though he is not deserving of death, since he did it to his neighbor without malice aforethought. ⁷This is why I command you to set aside for yourselves three cities.

⁸If the LORD your God enlarges your territory, as he promised on oath to your forefathers, and gives you the whole land he promised them, ⁹because you carefully follow all these laws I command you today — to love the LORD your God and to walk always in his ways — then you are to set aside three more cities. ¹⁰Do this so that innocent blood will not be shed in your land, which the LORD your God is giving you as your inheritance, and so that you will not be guilty of bloodshed.

¹¹But if a man hates his neighbor and lies in wait for him, assaults and kills him, and then flees to one of these cities, ¹²the elders of his town shall send for him, bring him back from the city, and hand him over to the avenger of blood to die. ¹³Show him no pity. You must purge from Israel the guilt of shedding innocent blood, so that it may go well with you.

¹⁴Do not move your neighbor's boundary stone set up by your predecessors in the inheritance you receive in the land the LORD your God is giving you to possess.

Witnesses

¹⁵One witness is not enough to convict a man accused of any crime or offense he may have committed. A matter must be established by the testimony of two or three witnesses.

¹⁶If a malicious witness takes the stand to accuse a man of a crime, ¹⁷the two men involved in the dispute must stand in the presence of the LORD before the priests and the judges who are in office at the time. ¹⁸The judges must make a thorough investigation, and if the witness proves to be a liar, giving false testimony against his brother, ¹⁹then do to him as he intended to do to his brother. You must purge the evil from among you. ²⁰The rest of the people will hear of this and be afraid, and never again will such an evil thing be done among you. ²¹Show no pity: life for life, eye for eye, tooth for tooth, hand for hand, foot for foot.

Going to War

20 When you go to war against your enemies and see horses and chariots and an army greater than yours, do not be afraid of them, because the LORD your God, who brought you up out of Egypt, will be with you. ²When you are about to go into battle, the priest shall come forward and address the army. ³He shall say: "Hear, O Israel, today you are going into battle against your enemies. Do not be fainthearted or afraid; do not be terrified or give way to panic before them. ⁴For the LORD your God is the one who goes with you to fight for you against your enemies to give you victory."

⁵The officers shall say to the army: "Has anyone built a new house and not dedicated it? Let him go home, or he may die in battle and someone else may dedicate it. ⁶Has anyone planted a vineyard and not begun to enjoy it? Let him go home, or he may die in battle and someone else enjoy it. ⁷Has anyone become pledged to a woman and not married her? Let him go home, or he may die in battle and someone else marry her." ⁸Then the officers shall add, "Is any man afraid or fainthearted? Let him go home so that his brothers will not become disheartened too." ⁹When the officers have finished speaking to the army, they shall appoint commanders over it.

¹⁰When you march up to attack a city, make its people an offer of peace. ¹¹If they accept and open their gates, all the people in it shall be subject to forced labor and shall work for you. ¹²If they refuse to make peace and they engage you in battle, lay siege to that city. ¹³When the LORD your God delivers it into your hand, put to the sword all the men in it. ¹⁴As for the women, the children, the livestock and everything else in the city, you may take these as plunder for yourselves. And you may use the plunder the LORD your God gives you from your enemies. ¹⁵This is how you are to treat all the cities that are at a distance from you and do not belong to the nations nearby.

¹⁶However, in the cities of the nations the LORD your God is giving you as an inheritance, do not leave alive anything that breathes. ¹⁷Completely destroy[a] them — the Hittites, Amorites, Canaanites, Perizzites, Hivites and Jebusites — as the LORD your God has commanded you. ¹⁸Otherwise, they will teach you to follow all the detestable things they do in worshiping their gods, and you will sin against the LORD your God.

¹⁹When you lay siege to a city for a long time, fighting against it to capture it, do not destroy its trees by putting an ax to them, because you can eat their fruit. Do not cut them down. Are the trees of the field people, that you should besiege them?[b] ²⁰However, you may cut down trees that you know are not fruit trees and use them to build siege works until the city at war with you falls.

Atonement for an Unsolved Murder

21 If a man is found slain, lying in a field in the land the LORD your God is giving you to possess, and it is not known who killed him, ²your elders and judges shall go out and measure the distance from the body to the neighboring towns. ³Then the elders of the town nearest the body shall take a heifer that has never been worked and has never worn a yoke ⁴and lead her down to a valley that has not been plowed or planted and where there is a flowing stream. There in the valley they are to break the heifer's neck. ⁵The priests, the sons of Levi, shall step forward, for the LORD your God has chosen them to minister and to pronounce blessings in the name of the LORD and to decide all cases of dispute and assault. ⁶Then all the elders of the town nearest the body shall wash their hands over the heifer whose neck was broken in the valley, ⁷and they shall declare: "Our hands did not shed this blood, nor did our eyes see it done. ⁸Accept this atonement for your people Israel, whom you have redeemed, O LORD, and do not hold your people guilty of the blood of an innocent man." And the bloodshed will be atoned for. ⁹So you will purge from yourselves the guilt of shedding innocent blood, since you have done what is right in the eyes of the LORD.

Marrying a Captive Woman

¹⁰When you go to war against your enemies and the LORD your God delivers them into your hands and you take captives, ¹¹if you notice among the captives a beautiful woman and are attracted to her, you may take her as your wife. ¹²Bring her into your home and have her shave her head, trim her nails ¹³and put aside the clothes she was wearing when captured. After she

---

a17 The Hebrew term refers to the irrevocable giving over of things or persons to the LORD, often by totally destroying them.   *b19* Or *down to use in the siege, for the fruit trees are for the benefit of man.*

has lived in your house and mourned her father and mother for a full month, then you may go to her and be her husband and she shall be your wife. **14**If you are not pleased with her, let her go wherever she wishes. You must not sell her or treat her as a slave, since you have dishonored her.

The Right of the Firstborn

15If a man has two wives, and he loves one but not the other, and both bear him sons but the firstborn is the son of the wife he does not love, **16**when he wills his property to his sons, he must not give the rights of the firstborn to the son of the wife he loves in preference to his actual firstborn, the son of the wife he does not love. **17**He must acknowledge the son of his unloved wife as the firstborn by giving him a double share of all he has. That son is the first sign of his father's strength. The right of the firstborn belongs to him.

A Rebellious Son

18If a man has a stubborn and rebellious son who does not obey his father and mother and will not listen to them when they discipline him, **19**his father and mother shall take hold of him and bring him to the elders at the gate of his town. **20**They shall say to the elders, "This son of ours is stubborn and rebellious. He will not obey us. He is a profligate and a drunkard." **21**Then all the men of his town shall stone him to death. You must purge the evil from among you. All Israel will hear of it and be afraid.

Various Laws

22If a man guilty of a capital offense is put to death and his body is hung on a tree, **23**you must not leave his body on the tree overnight. Be sure to bury him that same day, because anyone who is hung on a tree is under God's curse. You must not desecrate the land the LORD your God is giving you as an inheritance.

22 If you see your brother's ox or sheep straying, do not ignore it but be sure to take it back to him. **2**If the brother does not live near you or if you do not know who he is, take it home with you and keep it until he comes looking for it. Then give it back to him. **3**Do the same if you find your brother's donkey or his cloak or anything he loses. Do not ignore it.

4If you see your brother's donkey or his ox fallen on the road, do not ignore it. Help him get it to its feet.

5A woman must not wear men's clothing, nor a man wear women's clothing, for the LORD your God detests anyone who does this.

6If you come across a bird's nest beside the road, either in a tree or on the ground, and the mother is sitting on the young or on the eggs, do not take the mother with the young. **7**You may take the young, but be sure to let the mother go, so that it may go well with you and you may have a long life.

8When you build a new house, make a parapet around your roof so that you may not bring the guilt of bloodshed on your house if someone falls from the roof.

9Do not plant two kinds of seed in your vineyard; if you do, not only the crops you plant but also the fruit of the vineyard will be defiled.*a*

10Do not plow with an ox and a donkey yoked together.

11Do not wear clothes of wool and linen woven together.

12Make tassels on the four corners of the cloak you wear.

Marriage Violations

13If a man takes a wife and, after lying with her, dislikes her **14**and slanders her and gives her a bad name, saying, "I married this woman, but when I approached her, I did not find proof of her virginity," **15**then the girl's father and mother shall bring proof that she was a virgin to the town elders at the gate. **16**The girl's father will say to the elders, "I gave my daughter in marriage to this man, but he dislikes her. **17**Now he has slandered her and said, 'I did not find your daughter to be a virgin.' But here is the proof of my daughter's virginity." Then her parents shall display the cloth before the elders of the town, **18**and the elders shall take the man and punish him. **19**They shall fine him a hundred shekels of silver*b* and give them to the girl's father, because this man has given an Israelite virgin a bad name. She shall continue to be his wife; he must not divorce her as long as he lives.

20If, however, the charge is true and no proof of the girl's virginity can be found, **21**she shall be brought to the door of her father's house and there the men of her town shall stone her to death. She has done a disgraceful thing in Israel by being

---

*a*9 Or *be forfeited to the sanctuary*   *b*19 That is, about 2 1/2 pounds (about 1 kilogram) promiscuous while still in her father's house. You must purge the evil from among you.

22If a man is found sleeping with another man's wife, both the man who slept with her and the woman must die. You must purge the evil from Israel.

23If a man happens to meet in a town a virgin pledged to be married and he sleeps with her, **24**you shall take both of them to the gate of that town and stone them to death — the girl because she was in a town and did not scream for help, and the man because he violated another man's wife. You must purge the evil from among you.

25But if out in the country a man happens to meet a girl pledged to be married and rapes her, only the man who has done this shall die. **26**Do nothing to the girl; she has committed no sin deserving death. This case is like that of someone who attacks and murders his neighbor, **27**for the man found the girl out in the country, and though the betrothed girl screamed, there was no one to rescue her.

28If a man happens to meet a virgin who is not pledged to be married and rapes her and they are discovered, **29**he shall pay the girl's father fifty shekels of silver.[a] He must marry the girl, for he has violated her. He can never divorce her as long as he lives.

30A man is not to marry his father's wife; he must not dishonor his father's bed.

Exclusion From the Assembly

23 No one who has been emasculated by crushing or cutting may enter the assembly of the Lord.

2No one born of a forbidden marriage[b] nor any of his descendants may enter the assembly of the Lord, even down to the tenth generation.

3No Ammonite or Moabite or any of his descendants may enter the assembly of the Lord, even down to the tenth generation. **4**For they did not come to meet you with bread and water on your way when you came out of Egypt, and they hired Balaam son of Beor from Pethor in Aram Naharaim[c] to pronounce a curse on you. **5**However, the Lord your God would not listen to Balaam but turned the curse into a blessing for you, because the Lord your God loves you. **6**Do not seek a treaty of friendship with them as long as you live.

7Do not abhor an Edomite, for he is your brother. Do not abhor an Egyptian, because you lived as an alien in his country. **8**The third generation of children born to them may enter the assembly of the Lord.

Uncleanness in the Camp

9When you are encamped against your enemies, keep away from everything impure. **10**If one of your men is unclean because of a nocturnal emission, he is to go outside the camp and stay there. **11**But as evening approaches he is to wash himself, and at sunset he may return to the camp.

12Designate a place outside the camp where you can go to relieve yourself. **13**As part of your equipment have something to dig with, and when you relieve yourself, dig a hole and cover up your excrement. **14**For the Lord your God moves about in your camp to protect you and to deliver your enemies to you. Your camp must be holy, so that he will not see among you anything indecent and turn away from you.

Miscellaneous Laws

15If a slave has taken refuge with you, do not hand him over to his master. **16**Let him live among you wherever he likes and in whatever town he chooses. Do not oppress him.

17No Israelite man or woman is to become a shrine prostitute. **18**You must not bring the earnings of a female prostitute or of a male prostitute[d] into the house of the Lord your God to pay any vow, because the Lord your God detests them both.

19Do not charge your brother interest, whether on money or food or anything else that may earn interest. **20**You may charge a foreigner interest, but not a brother Israelite, so that the Lord your God may bless you in everything you put your hand to in the land you are entering to possess.

21If you make a vow to the Lord your God, do not be slow to pay it, for the Lord your God will certainly demand it of you and you will be guilty of sin. **22**But if you refrain from making a vow, you will not be guilty. **23**Whatever your lips utter you must be sure to do, because you made your vow freely to the Lord your God with your own mouth.

---

a29 That is, about 1 1/4 pounds (about 0.6 kilogram)   b2 Or one of illegitimate birth   c4 That is,
Northwest Mesopotamia   d18 Hebrew of a dog

²⁴If you enter your neighbor's vineyard, you may eat all the grapes you want, but do not put any in your basket. ²⁵If you enter your neighbor's grainfield, you may pick kernels with your hands, but you must not put a sickle to his standing grain.

24 If a man marries a woman who becomes displeasing to him because he finds something indecent about her, and he writes her a certificate of divorce, gives it to her and sends her from his house, ²and if after she leaves his house she becomes the wife of another man, ³and her second husband dislikes her and writes her a certificate of divorce, gives it to her and sends her from his house, or if he dies, ⁴then her first husband, who divorced her, is not allowed to marry her again after she has been defiled. That would be detestable in the eyes of the LORD. Do not bring sin upon the land the LORD your God is giving you as an inheritance.

⁵If a man has recently married, he must not be sent to war or have any other duty laid on him. For one year he is to be free to stay at home and bring happiness to the wife he has married.

TUESDAY

VERSE FOR THE DAY:	AUTHOR:	PASSAGE FOR THE DAY:
Deuteronomy 24:1	Donald M. Joy	Deuteronomy 24:1–5

Don't Shoot the Wounded

JESUS is more impatient with Jewish divorce practices than almost anything else. Read one of his sharp exchanges in Matthew 19 again. One group of Jewish leaders followed the school of Hillel, a leading rabbi. Hillel taught that Moses' law in Deuteronomy 24, about discovering "something indecent" about your wife, meant "anything displeasing to you." So Jewish men, who were often polygamous, could dismiss wives for any trivial thing at all, much like firing a domestic employee. But the school of Shammai, another great rabbi, taught that only in case of some tragic past sexual disgrace could a man divorce his wife. So, in Matthew 19, the two groups got Jesus in the "cross fire" and wanted him to take sides. Instead, he took them back to Genesis, to creation, and gave them a kindergarten lesson in the meaning of marriage. He hit the crescendo with the warning: "Therefore what God has joined together, let man not separate"—a line you will hear recited at the end of every Christian wedding today.

But watch Jesus, in John 4, deal with a woman who had been married and divorced five times each, and who, in this shameful condition, was now living with a man to whom she was not married. Jesus clearly believes that divorce is not the end of hope. He puts her back on the track of abundant life. So Jesus is not simply a "purist" who shoots the wounded. He believes that anybody in any tragic condition can be salvaged and brought to wholeness and health today.

Additional Scripture Readings:
Matthew 19:1–12; John 8:3–11

Go to page 212 for your next devotional reading.

⁶Do not take a pair of millstones—not even the upper one—as security for a debt, because that would be taking a man's livelihood as security.

⁷If a man is caught kidnapping one of his brother Israelites and treats him as a slave or sells him, the kidnapper must die. You must purge the evil from among you.

⁸In cases of leprous[a] diseases be very careful to do exactly as the priests, who are Levites, instruct you. You must follow carefully what I have commanded them. ⁹Remember what the Lord your God did to Miriam along the way after you came out of Egypt.

¹⁰When you make a loan of any kind to your neighbor, do not go into his house to get what he is offering as a pledge. ¹¹Stay outside and let the man to whom you are making the loan bring the pledge out to you. ¹²If the man is poor, do not go to sleep with his pledge in your possession. ¹³Return his cloak to him by sunset so that he may sleep in it. Then he will thank you, and it will be regarded as a righteous act in the sight of the Lord your God.

¹⁴Do not take advantage of a hired man who is poor and needy, whether he is a brother Israelite or an alien living in one of your towns. ¹⁵Pay him his wages each day before sunset, because he is poor and is counting on it. Otherwise he may cry to the Lord against you, and you will be guilty of sin.

¹⁶Fathers shall not be put to death for their children, nor children put to death for their fathers; each is to die for his own sin.

¹⁷Do not deprive the alien or the fatherless of justice, or take the cloak of the widow as a pledge. ¹⁸Remember that you were slaves in Egypt and the Lord your God redeemed you from there. That is why I command you to do this.

¹⁹When you are harvesting in your field and you overlook a sheaf, do not go back to get it. Leave it for the alien, the fatherless and the widow, so that the Lord your God may bless you in all the work of your hands. ²⁰When you beat the olives from your trees, do not go over the branches a second time. Leave what remains for the alien, the fatherless and the widow. ²¹When you harvest the grapes in your vineyard, do not go over the vines again. Leave what remains for the alien, the fatherless and the widow. ²²Remember that

you were slaves in Egypt. That is why I command you to do this.

25 When men have a dispute, they are to take it to court and the judges will decide the case, acquitting the innocent and condemning the guilty. ²If the guilty man deserves to be beaten, the judge shall make him lie down and have him flogged in his presence with the number of lashes his crime deserves, ³but he must not give him more than forty lashes. If he is flogged more than that, your brother will be degraded in your eyes.

⁴Do not muzzle an ox while it is treading out the grain.

⁵If brothers are living together and one of them dies without a son, his widow must not marry outside the family. Her husband's brother shall take her and marry her and fulfill the duty of a brother-in-law to her. ⁶The first son she bears shall carry on the name of the dead brother so that his name will not be blotted out from Israel.

⁷However, if a man does not want to marry his brother's wife, she shall go to the elders at the town gate and say, "My husband's brother refuses to carry on his brother's name in Israel. He will not fulfill the duty of a brother-in-law to me." ⁸Then the elders of his town shall summon him and talk to him. If he persists in saying, "I do not want to marry her," ⁹his brother's widow shall go up to him in the presence of the elders, take off one of his sandals, spit in his face and say, "This is what is done to the man who will not build up his brother's family line." ¹⁰That man's line shall be known in Israel as The Family of the Unsandaled.

¹¹If two men are fighting and the wife of one of them comes to rescue her husband from his assailant, and she reaches out and seizes him by his private parts, ¹²you shall cut off her hand. Show her no pity.

¹³Do not have two differing weights in your bag—one heavy, one light. ¹⁴Do not have two differing measures in your house—one large, one small. ¹⁵You must have accurate and honest weights and measures, so that you may live long in the land the Lord your God is giving you. ¹⁶For the Lord your God detests anyone who does these things, anyone who deals dishonestly.

¹⁷Remember what the Amalekites did to you along the way when you came out of Egypt. ¹⁸When you were weary and

---

a8 The Hebrew word was used for various diseases affecting the skin—not necessarily leprosy.

worn out, they met you on your journey and cut off all who were lagging behind; they had no fear of God. [19]When the LORD your God gives you rest from all the enemies around you in the land he is giving you to possess as an inheritance, you shall blot out the memory of Amalek from under heaven. Do not forget!

Firstfruits and Tithes

26 When you have entered the land the LORD your God is giving you as an inheritance and have taken possession of it and settled in it, [2]take some of the firstfruits of all that you produce from the soil of the land the LORD your God is giving you and put them in a basket. Then go to the place the LORD your God will choose as a dwelling for his Name [3]and say to the priest in office at the time, "I declare today to the LORD your God that I have come to the land the LORD swore to our forefathers to give us." [4]The priest shall take the basket from your hands and set it down in front of the altar of the LORD your God. [5]Then you shall declare before the LORD your God: "My father was a wandering Aramean, and he went down into Egypt with a few people and lived there and became a great nation, powerful and numerous. [6]But the Egyptians mistreated us and made us suffer, putting us to hard labor. [7]Then we cried out to the LORD, the God of our fathers, and the LORD heard our voice and saw our misery, toil and oppression. [8]So the LORD brought us out of Egypt with a mighty hand and an outstretched arm, with great terror and with miraculous signs and wonders. [9]He brought us to this place and gave us this land, a land flowing with milk and honey; [10]and now I bring the firstfruits of the soil that you, O LORD, have given me." Place the basket before the LORD your God and bow down before him. [11]And you and the Levites and the aliens among you shall rejoice in all the good things the LORD your God has given to you and your household.

[12]When you have finished setting aside a tenth of all your produce in the third year, the year of the tithe, you shall give it to the Levite, the alien, the fatherless and the widow, so that they may eat in your towns and be satisfied. [13]Then say to the LORD your God: "I have removed from my house the sacred portion and have given it to the Levite, the alien, the fatherless and the widow, according to all you com-

manded. I have not turned aside from your commands nor have I forgotten any of them. [14]I have not eaten any of the sacred portion while I was in mourning, nor have I removed any of it while I was unclean, nor have I offered any of it to the dead. I have obeyed the LORD my God; I have done everything you commanded me. [15]Look down from heaven, your holy dwelling place, and bless your people Israel and the land you have given us as you promised on oath to our forefathers, a land flowing with milk and honey."

Follow the LORD's Commands

[16]The LORD your God commands you this day to follow these decrees and laws; carefully observe them with all your heart and with all your soul. [17]You have declared this day that the LORD is your God and that you will walk in his ways, that you will keep his decrees, commands and laws, and that you will obey him. [18]And the LORD has declared this day that you are his people, his treasured possession as he promised, and that you are to keep all his commands. [19]He has declared that he will set you in praise, fame and honor high above all the nations he has made and that you will be a people holy to the LORD your God, as he promised.

The Altar on Mount Ebal

27 Moses and the elders of Israel commanded the people: "Keep all these commands that I give you today. [2]When you have crossed the Jordan into the land the LORD your God is giving you, set up some large stones and coat them with plaster. [3]Write on them all the words of this law when you have crossed over to enter the land the LORD your God is giving you, a land flowing with milk and honey, just as the LORD, the God of your fathers, promised you. [4]And when you have crossed the Jordan, set up these stones on Mount Ebal, as I command you today, and coat them with plaster. [5]Build there an altar to the LORD your God, an altar of stones. Do not use any iron tool upon them. [6]Build the altar of the LORD your God with fieldstones and offer burnt offerings on it to the LORD your God. [7]Sacrifice fellowship offerings[a] there, eating them and rejoicing in the presence of the LORD your God. [8]And you shall write very clearly all the words of this law on these stones you have set up."

---

[a]7 Traditionally *peace offerings*

Curses From Mount Ebal

9Then Moses and the priests, who are Levites, said to all Israel, "Be silent, O Israel, and listen! You have now become the people of the Lord your God. **10**Obey the Lord your God and follow his commands and decrees that I give you today."

11On the same day Moses commanded the people:

12When you have crossed the Jordan, these tribes shall stand on Mount Gerizim to bless the people: Simeon, Levi, Judah, Issachar, Joseph and Benjamin. **13**And these tribes shall stand on Mount Ebal to pronounce curses: Reuben, Gad, Asher, Zebulun, Dan and Naphtali.

14The Levites shall recite to all the people of Israel in a loud voice:

15"Cursed is the man who carves an image or casts an idol — a thing detestable to the Lord, the work of the craftsman's hands — and sets it up in secret."

Then all the people shall say, "Amen!"

16"Cursed is the man who dishonors his father or his mother."

Then all the people shall say, "Amen!"

17"Cursed is the man who moves his neighbor's boundary stone."

Then all the people shall say, "Amen!"

18"Cursed is the man who leads the blind astray on the road."

Then all the people shall say, "Amen!"

19"Cursed is the man who withholds justice from the alien, the fatherless or the widow."

Then all the people shall say, "Amen!"

20"Cursed is the man who sleeps with his father's wife, for he dishonors his father's bed."

Then all the people shall say, "Amen!"

21"Cursed is the man who has sexual relations with any animal."

Then all the people shall say, "Amen!"

22"Cursed is the man who sleeps with his sister, the daughter of his father or the daughter of his mother."

Then all the people shall say, "Amen!"

23"Cursed is the man who sleeps with his mother-in-law."

Then all the people shall say, "Amen!"

24"Cursed is the man who kills his neighbor secretly."

Then all the people shall say, "Amen!"

25"Cursed is the man who accepts a bribe to kill an innocent person."

Then all the people shall say, "Amen!"

26"Cursed is the man who does not uphold the words of this law by carrying them out."

Then all the people shall say, "Amen!"

Blessings for Obedience

28 If you fully obey the Lord your God and carefully follow all his commands I give you today, the Lord your God will set you high above all the nations on earth. **2**All these blessings will come upon you and accompany you if you obey the Lord your God:

3You will be blessed in the city and blessed in the country.

4The fruit of your womb will be blessed, and the crops of your land and the young of your livestock — the calves of your herds and the lambs of your flocks.

5Your basket and your kneading trough will be blessed.

6You will be blessed when you come in and blessed when you go out.

7The Lord will grant that the enemies who rise up against you will be defeated before you. They will come at you from one direction but flee from you in seven.

8The Lord will send a blessing on your barns and on everything you put your hand to. The Lord your God will bless you in the land he is giving you.

9The Lord will establish you as his holy people, as he promised you on oath, if you keep the commands of the Lord your God and walk in his ways. **10**Then all the peoples on earth will see that you are called by the name of the Lord, and they will fear you. **11**The Lord will grant you abundant prosperity — in the fruit of your womb, the young of your livestock and the crops of your ground — in the land he swore to your forefathers to give you.

12The Lord will open the heavens, the storehouse of his bounty, to send rain on your land in season and to bless all the work of your hands. You will lend to many nations but will borrow from none. ¹³The Lord will make you the head, not the tail. If you pay attention to the commands of the Lord your God that I give you this day and carefully follow them, you will always be at the top, never at the bottom. ¹⁴Do not turn aside from any of the commands I give you today, to the right or to the left, following other gods and serving them.

Curses for Disobedience

¹⁵However, if you do not obey the Lord your God and do not carefully follow all his commands and decrees I am giving you today, all these curses will come upon you and overtake you:

¹⁶You will be cursed in the city and cursed in the country.

¹⁷Your basket and your kneading trough will be cursed.

¹⁸The fruit of your womb will be cursed, and the crops of your land, and the calves of your herds and the lambs of your flocks.

¹⁹You will be cursed when you come in and cursed when you go out.

²⁰The Lord will send on you curses, confusion and rebuke in everything you put your hand to, until you are destroyed and come to sudden ruin because of the evil you have done in forsaking him.ᵃ ²¹The Lord will plague you with diseases until he has destroyed you from the land you are entering to possess. ²²The Lord will strike you with wasting disease, with fever and inflammation, with scorching heat and drought, with blight and mildew, which will plague you until you perish. ²³The sky over your head will be bronze, the ground beneath you iron. ²⁴The Lord will turn the rain of your country into dust and powder; it will come down from the skies until you are destroyed.

²⁵The Lord will cause you to be defeated before your enemies. You will come at them from one direction but flee from them in seven, and you will become a thing of horror to all the kingdoms on earth. ²⁶Your carcasses will be food for all the birds of the air and the beasts of the earth, and there will be no one to frighten them away. ²⁷The Lord will afflict you with the boils of Egypt and with tumors, festering sores and the itch, from which you cannot be cured. ²⁸The Lord will afflict you with madness, blindness and confusion of mind. ²⁹At midday you will grope about like a blind man in the dark. You will be unsuccessful in everything you do; day after day you will be oppressed and robbed, with no one to rescue you.

³⁰You will be pledged to be married to a woman, but another will take her and ravish her. You will build a house, but you will not live in it. You will plant a vineyard, but you will not even begin to enjoy its fruit. ³¹Your ox will be slaughtered before your eyes, but you will eat none of it. Your donkey will be forcibly taken from you and will not be returned. Your sheep will be given to your enemies, and no one will rescue them. ³²Your sons and daughters will be given to another nation, and you will wear out your eyes watching for them day after day, powerless to lift a hand. ³³A people that you do not know will eat what your land and labor produce, and you will have nothing but cruel oppression all your days. ³⁴The sights you see will drive you mad. ³⁵The Lord will afflict your knees and legs with painful boils that cannot be cured, spreading from the soles of your feet to the top of your head.

³⁶The Lord will drive you and the king you set over you to a nation unknown to you or your fathers. There you will worship other gods, gods of wood and stone. ³⁷You will become a thing of horror and an object of scorn and ridicule to all the nations where the Lord will drive you.

³⁸You will sow much seed in the field but you will harvest little, because locusts will devour it. ³⁹You will plant vineyards and cultivate them but you will not drink the wine or gather the grapes, because worms will eat them. ⁴⁰You will have olive trees throughout your country but you will not use the oil, because the olives will drop off. ⁴¹You will have sons and daughters but you will not keep them, because they will go into captivity. ⁴²Swarms of locusts will take over all your trees and the crops of your land.

⁴³The alien who lives among you will rise above you higher and higher, but you will sink lower and lower. ⁴⁴He will lend to you, but you will not lend to him. He will be the head, but you will be the tail.

⁴⁵All these curses will come upon you. They will pursue you and overtake you until you are destroyed, because you did not obey the Lord your God and observe the commands and decrees he gave you.

ᵃ20 Hebrew me

⁴⁶They will be a sign and a wonder to you and your descendants forever. ⁴⁷Because you did not serve the Lord your God joyfully and gladly in the time of prosperity, ⁴⁸therefore in hunger and thirst, in nakedness and dire poverty, you will serve the enemies the Lord sends against you. He will put an iron yoke on your neck until he has destroyed you.

⁴⁹The Lord will bring a nation against you from far away, from the ends of the earth, like an eagle swooping down, a nation whose language you will not understand, ⁵⁰a fierce-looking nation without respect for the old or pity for the young. ⁵¹They will devour the young of your livestock and the crops of your land until you are destroyed. They will leave you no grain, new wine or oil, nor any calves of your herds or lambs of your flocks until you are ruined. ⁵²They will lay siege to all the cities throughout your land until the high fortified walls in which you trust fall down. They will besiege all the cities throughout the land the Lord your God is giving you.

⁵³Because of the suffering that your enemy will inflict on you during the siege, you will eat the fruit of the womb, the flesh of the sons and daughters the Lord your God has given you. ⁵⁴Even the most gentle and sensitive man among you will have no compassion on his own brother or the wife he loves or his surviving children, ⁵⁵and he will not give to one of them any of the flesh of his children that he is eating. It will be all he has left because of the suffering your enemy will inflict on you during the siege of all your cities. ⁵⁶The most gentle and sensitive woman among you—so sensitive and gentle that she would not venture to touch the ground with the sole of her foot—will begrudge the husband she loves and her own son or daughter ⁵⁷the afterbirth from her womb and the children she bears. For she intends to eat them secretly during the siege and in the distress that your enemy will inflict on you in your cities.

⁵⁸If you do not carefully follow all the words of this law, which are written in this book, and do not revere this glorious and awesome name—the Lord your God— ⁵⁹the Lord will send fearful plagues on you and your descendants, harsh and prolonged disasters, and severe and lingering illnesses. ⁶⁰He will bring upon you all the diseases of Egypt that you dreaded, and they will cling to you. ⁶¹The Lord will also bring on you every kind of sickness and disaster not recorded in this Book of the Law, until you are destroyed. ⁶²You who were as numerous as the stars in the sky will be left but few in number, because you did not obey the Lord your God. ⁶³Just as it pleased the Lord to make you prosper and increase in number, so it will please him to ruin and destroy you. You will be uprooted from the land you are entering to possess.

⁶⁴Then the Lord will scatter you among all nations, from one end of the earth to the other. There you will worship other gods—gods of wood and stone, which neither you nor your fathers have known. ⁶⁵Among those nations you will find no repose, no resting place for the sole of your foot. There the Lord will give you an anxious mind, eyes weary with longing, and a despairing heart. ⁶⁶You will live in constant suspense, filled with dread both night and day, never sure of your life. ⁶⁷In the morning you will say, "If only it were evening!" and in the evening, "If only it were morning!"—because of the terror that will fill your hearts and the sights that your eyes will see. ⁶⁸The Lord will send you back in ships to Egypt on a journey I said you should never make again. There you will offer yourselves for sale to your enemies as male and female slaves, but no one will buy you.

Renewal of the Covenant

29 These are the terms of the covenant the Lord commanded Moses to make with the Israelites in Moab, in addition to the covenant he had made with them at Horeb.

²Moses summoned all the Israelites and said to them:

Your eyes have seen all that the Lord did in Egypt to Pharaoh, to all his officials and to all his land. ³With your own eyes you saw those great trials, those miraculous signs and great wonders. ⁴But to this day the Lord has not given you a mind that understands or eyes that see or ears that hear. ⁵During the forty years that I led you through the desert, your clothes did not wear out, nor did the sandals on your feet. ⁶You ate no bread and drank no wine or other fermented drink. I did this so that you might know that I am the Lord your God.

⁷When you reached this place, Sihon king of Heshbon and Og king of Bashan came out to fight against us, but we defeated them. ⁸We took their land and gave

it as an inheritance to the Reubenites, the Gadites and the half-tribe of Manasseh.

⁹Carefully follow the terms of this covenant, so that you may prosper in everything you do. ¹⁰All of you are standing today in the presence of the LORD your God—your leaders and chief men, your elders and officials, and all the other men of Israel, ¹¹together with your children and your wives, and the aliens living in your camps who chop your wood and carry your water. ¹²You are standing here in order to enter into a covenant with the LORD your God, a covenant the LORD is making with you this day and sealing with an oath, ¹³to confirm you this day as his people, that he may be your God as he promised you and as he swore to your fathers, Abraham, Isaac and Jacob. ¹⁴I am making this covenant, with its oath, not only with you ¹⁵who are standing here with us today in the presence of the LORD our God but also with those who are not here today.

¹⁶You yourselves know how we lived in Egypt and how we passed through the countries on the way here. ¹⁷You saw among them their detestable images and idols of wood and stone, of silver and gold. ¹⁸Make sure there is no man or woman, clan or tribe among you today whose heart turns away from the LORD our God to go and worship the gods of those nations; make sure there is no root among you that produces such bitter poison.

¹⁹When such a person hears the words of this oath, he invokes a blessing on himself and therefore thinks, "I will be safe, even though I persist in going my own way." This will bring disaster on the watered land as well as the dry.ᵃ ²⁰The LORD will never be willing to forgive him; his wrath and zeal will burn against that man. All the curses written in this book will fall upon him, and the LORD will blot out his name from under heaven. ²¹The LORD will single him out from all the tribes of Israel for disaster, according to all the curses of the covenant written in this Book of the Law.

²²Your children who follow you in later generations and foreigners who come from distant lands will see the calamities that have fallen on the land and the diseases with which the LORD has afflicted it. ²³The whole land will be a burning waste of salt and sulfur—nothing planted, nothing sprouting, no vegetation growing on

it. It will be like the destruction of Sodom and Gomorrah, Admah and Zeboiim, which the LORD overthrew in fierce anger. ²⁴All the nations will ask: "Why has the LORD done this to this land? Why this fierce, burning anger?"

²⁵And the answer will be: "It is because this people abandoned the covenant of the LORD, the God of their fathers, the covenant he made with them when he brought them out of Egypt. ²⁶They went off and worshiped other gods and bowed down to them, gods they did not know, gods he had not given them. ²⁷Therefore the LORD's anger burned against this land, so that he brought on it all the curses written in this book. ²⁸In furious anger and in great wrath the LORD uprooted them from their land and thrust them into another land, as it is now."

²⁹The secret things belong to the LORD our God, but the things revealed belong to us and to our children forever, that we may follow all the words of this law.

Prosperity After Turning to the LORD

30 When all these blessings and curses I have set before you come upon you and you take them to heart wherever the LORD your God disperses you among the nations, ²and when you and your children return to the LORD your God and obey him with all your heart and with all your soul according to everything I command you today, ³then the LORD your God will restore your fortunesᵇ and have compassion on you and gather you again from all the nations where he scattered you. ⁴Even if you have been banished to the most distant land under the heavens, from there the LORD your God will gather you and bring you back. ⁵He will bring you to the land that belonged to your fathers, and you will take possession of it. He will make you more prosperous and numerous than your fathers. ⁶The LORD your God will circumcise your hearts and the hearts of your descendants, so that you may love him with all your heart and with all your soul, and live. ⁷The LORD your God will put all these curses on your enemies who hate and persecute you. ⁸You will again obey the LORD and follow all his commands I am giving you today. ⁹Then the LORD your God will make you most prosperous in all the work of your hands and in the fruit of your womb, the young of your livestock and the crops of

---

ᵃ19 Or way, in order to add drunkenness to thirst."   ᵇ3 Or will bring you back from captivity your land. The LORD will again delight in you and make you prosperous, just as he delighted in your fathers, [10]if you obey the LORD your God and keep his commands and decrees that are written in this Book of the Law and turn to the LORD your God with all your heart and with all your soul.

The Offer of Life or Death

[11]Now what I am commanding you today is not too difficult for you or beyond your reach. [12]It is not up in heaven, so that you have to ask, "Who will ascend into heaven to get it and proclaim it to us so we may obey it?" [13]Nor is it beyond the sea, so that you have to ask, "Who will cross the sea to get it and proclaim it to us so we may obey it?" [14]No, the word is very near you; it is in your mouth and in your heart so you may obey it.

[15]See, I set before you today life and prosperity, death and destruction. [16]For I command you today to love the LORD your God, to walk in his ways, and to keep his commands, decrees and laws; then you will live and increase, and the LORD your God will bless you in the land you are entering to possess.

[17]But if your heart turns away and you are not obedient, and if you are drawn away to bow down to other gods and worship them, [18]I declare to you this day that you will certainly be destroyed. You will not live long in the land you are crossing the Jordan to enter and possess.

[19]This day I call heaven and earth as witnesses against you that I have set before you life and death, blessings and curses. Now choose life, so that you and your children may live [20]and that you may love the LORD your God, listen to his voice, and hold fast to him. For the LORD is your life, and he will give you many years in the land he swore to give to your fathers, Abraham, Isaac and Jacob.

Joshua to Succeed Moses

31 Then Moses went out and spoke these words to all Israel: [2]"I am now a hundred and twenty years old and I am no longer able to lead you. The LORD has said to me, 'You shall not cross the Jordan.' [3]The LORD your God himself will cross over ahead of you. He will destroy these nations before you, and you will take possession of their land. Joshua also will cross over ahead of you, as the LORD said. [4]And the LORD will do to them what he did to Sihon and Og, the kings of the Amorites, whom he destroyed along with

their land. [5]The LORD will deliver them to you, and you must do to them all that I have commanded you. [6]Be strong and courageous. Do not be afraid or terrified because of them, for the LORD your God goes with you; he will never leave you nor forsake you."

[7]Then Moses summoned Joshua and said to him in the presence of all Israel, "Be strong and courageous, for you must go with this people into the land that the LORD swore to their forefathers to give them, and you must divide it among them as their inheritance. [8]The LORD himself goes before you and will be with you; he will never leave you nor forsake you. Do not be afraid; do not be discouraged."

The Reading of the Law

[9]So Moses wrote down this law and gave it to the priests, the sons of Levi, who carried the ark of the covenant of the LORD, and to all the elders of Israel. [10]Then Moses commanded them: "At the end of every seven years, in the year for canceling debts, during the Feast of Tabernacles, [11]when all Israel comes to appear before the LORD your God at the place he will choose, you shall read this law before them in their hearing. [12]Assemble the people — men, women and children, and the aliens living in your towns — so they can listen and learn to fear the LORD your God and follow carefully all the words of this law. [13]Their children, who do not know this law, must hear it and learn to fear the LORD your God as long as you live in the land you are crossing the Jordan to possess."

Israel's Rebellion Predicted

[14]The LORD said to Moses, "Now the day of your death is near. Call Joshua and present yourselves at the Tent of Meeting, where I will commission him." So Moses and Joshua came and presented themselves at the Tent of Meeting.

[15]Then the LORD appeared at the Tent in a pillar of cloud, and the cloud stood over the entrance to the Tent. [16]And the LORD said to Moses: "You are going to rest with your fathers, and these people will soon prostitute themselves to the foreign gods of the land they are entering. They will forsake me and break the covenant I made with them. [17]On that day I will become angry with them and forsake them; I will hide my face from them, and they will be destroyed. Many disasters and difficulties will come upon them, and on that day

they will ask, 'Have not these disasters come upon us because our God is not with us?' **18**And I will certainly hide my face on that day because of all their wickedness in turning to other gods.

19"Now write down for yourselves this song and teach it to the Israelites and have them sing it, so that it may be a witness for me against them. **20**When I have brought them into the land flowing with milk and honey, the land I promised on oath to their forefathers, and when they eat their fill and thrive, they will turn to other gods and worship them, rejecting me and breaking my covenant. **21**And when many disasters and difficulties come upon them, this song will testify against them, because it will not be forgotten by their descendants. I know what they are disposed to do, even before I bring them into the land I promised them on oath." **22**So Moses wrote down this song that day and taught it to the Israelites.

23The LORD gave this command to Joshua son of Nun: "Be strong and courageous, for you will bring the Israelites into the land I promised them on oath, and I myself will be with you."

24After Moses finished writing in a book the words of this law from beginning to end, **25**he gave this command to the Levites who carried the ark of the covenant of the LORD: **26**"Take this Book of the Law and place it beside the ark of the covenant of the LORD your God. There it will remain as a witness against you. **27**For I know how rebellious and stiff-necked you are. If you have been rebellious against the LORD while I am still alive and with you, how much more will you rebel after I die! **28**Assemble before me all the elders of your tribes and all your officials, so that I can speak these words in their hearing and call heaven and earth to testify against them. **29**For I know that after my death you are sure to become utterly corrupt and to turn from the way I have commanded you. In days to come, disaster will fall upon you because you will do evil in the sight of the LORD and provoke him to anger by what your hands have made."

The Song of Moses

30And Moses recited the words of this song from beginning to end in the hearing of the whole assembly of Israel:

32 Listen, O heavens, and I will speak;
hear, O earth, the words of my mouth.
2Let my teaching fall like rain
and my words descend like dew,
like showers on new grass,
like abundant rain on tender plants.

3I will proclaim the name of the LORD.
Oh, praise the greatness of our God!
4He is the Rock, his works are perfect,
and all his ways are just.
A faithful God who does no wrong,
upright and just is he.

5They have acted corruptly toward him;
to their shame they are no longer his children,
but a warped and crooked generation.*a*
6Is this the way you repay the LORD,
O foolish and unwise people?
Is he not your Father, your Creator,*b*
who made you and formed you?

7Remember the days of old;
consider the generations long past.
Ask your father and he will tell you,
your elders, and they will explain to you.
8When the Most High gave the nations their inheritance,
when he divided all mankind,
he set up boundaries for the peoples
according to the number of the sons of Israel.*c*
9For the LORD's portion is his people,
Jacob his allotted inheritance.

10In a desert land he found him,
in a barren and howling waste.
He shielded him and cared for him;
he guarded him as the apple of his eye,
11like an eagle that stirs up its nest
and hovers over its young,
that spreads its wings to catch them
and carries them on its pinions.
12The LORD alone led him;
no foreign god was with him.

13He made him ride on the heights of the land
and fed him with the fruit of the fields.
He nourished him with honey from the rock,

---

a5 Or *Corrupt are they and not his children, / a generation warped and twisted to their shame*   *b6* Or *Father, who bought you*   *c8* Masoretic Text; Dead Sea Scrolls (see also Septuagint) *sons of God*

and with oil from the flinty crag,
14with curds and milk from herd and
    flock
and with fattened lambs and goats,
with choice rams of Bashan
and the finest kernels of wheat.
You drank the foaming blood of the
    grape.

15Jeshurun*a* grew fat and kicked;
    filled with food, he became heavy
        and sleek.
He abandoned the God who made him
    and rejected the Rock his Savior.
16They made him jealous with their
        foreign gods
    and angered him with their
        detestable idols.
17They sacrificed to demons, which are
        not God—
    gods they had not known,
    gods that recently appeared,
    gods your fathers did not fear.
18You deserted the Rock, who fathered
        you;
    you forgot the God who gave you
        birth.

19The Lord saw this and rejected them
    because he was angered by his sons
        and daughters.
20"I will hide my face from them," he
        said,
    "and see what their end will be;
for they are a perverse generation,
    children who are unfaithful.
21They made me jealous by what is no
        god
    and angered me with their
        worthless idols.
I will make them envious by those
        who are not a people;
I will make them angry by a nation
        that has no understanding.
22For a fire has been kindled by my
        wrath,
    one that burns to the realm of
        death*b* below.
It will devour the earth and its
        harvests
    and set afire the foundations of the
        mountains.

23"I will heap calamities upon them
    and spend my arrows against them.
24I will send wasting famine against
        them,
    consuming pestilence and deadly
        plague;

I will send against them the fangs of
        wild beasts,
    the venom of vipers that glide in
        the dust.
25In the street the sword will make
        them childless;
    in their homes terror will reign.
Young men and young women will
        perish,
    infants and gray-haired men.
26I said I would scatter them
    and blot out their memory from
        mankind,
27but I dreaded the taunt of the enemy,
    lest the adversary misunderstand
and say, 'Our hand has triumphed;
    the Lord has not done all this.' "

28They are a nation without sense,
    there is no discernment in them.
29If only they were wise and would
        understand this
    and discern what their end will be!
30How could one man chase a
        thousand,
    or two put ten thousand to flight,
unless their Rock had sold them,
    unless the Lord had given them up?
31For their rock is not like our Rock,
    as even our enemies concede.
32Their vine comes from the vine of
        Sodom
    and from the fields of Gomorrah.
Their grapes are filled with poison,
    and their clusters with bitterness.
33Their wine is the venom of serpents,
    the deadly poison of cobras.

34"Have I not kept this in reserve
    and sealed it in my vaults?
35It is mine to avenge; I will repay.
    In due time their foot will slip;
their day of disaster is near
    and their doom rushes upon them."

36The Lord will judge his people
    and have compassion on his
        servants
when he sees their strength is gone
    and no one is left, slave or free.
37He will say: "Now where are their
        gods,
    the rock they took refuge in,
38the gods who ate the fat of their
        sacrifices
    and drank the wine of their drink
        offerings?
Let them rise up to help you!
Let them give you shelter!

a15 Jeshurun means the upright one, that is, Israel.   b22 Hebrew to Sheol

³⁹"See now that I myself am He!
  There is no god besides me.
I put to death and I bring to life,
  I have wounded and I will heal,
  and no one can deliver out of my
    hand.
⁴⁰I lift my hand to heaven and declare:
  As surely as I live forever,
⁴¹when I sharpen my flashing sword
  and my hand grasps it in judgment,
I will take vengeance on my
    adversaries
  and repay those who hate me.
⁴²I will make my arrows drunk with
    blood,
  while my sword devours flesh:
the blood of the slain and the
    captives,
  the heads of the enemy leaders."

⁴³Rejoice, O nations, with his
    people,^{a, b}
for he will avenge the blood of his
    servants;
he will take vengeance on his enemies
  and make atonement for his land
    and people.

⁴⁴Moses came with Joshua^c son of
Nun and spoke all the words of this song
in the hearing of the people. ⁴⁵When Moses finished reciting all these words to all
Israel, ⁴⁶he said to them, "Take to heart all
the words I have solemnly declared to you
this day, so that you may command your
children to obey carefully all the words of
this law. ⁴⁷They are not just idle words for
you — they are your life. By them you will
live long in the land you are crossing the
Jordan to possess."

Moses to Die on Mount Nebo

⁴⁸On that same day the LORD told Moses, ⁴⁹"Go up into the Abarim Range to
Mount Nebo in Moab, across from Jericho, and view Canaan, the land I am giving the Israelites as their own possession.
⁵⁰There on the mountain that you have
climbed you will die and be gathered to
your people, just as your brother Aaron
died on Mount Hor and was gathered to
his people. ⁵¹This is because both of you
broke faith with me in the presence of the
Israelites at the waters of Meribah Kadesh
in the Desert of Zin and because you did
not uphold my holiness among the Israelites. ⁵²Therefore, you will see the land
only from a distance; you will not enter
the land I am giving to the people of Israel."

Moses Blesses the Tribes

33 This is the blessing that Moses the
man of God pronounced on the Israelites before his death. ²He said:

"The LORD came from Sinai
  and dawned over them from Seir;
  he shone forth from Mount Paran.
He came with^d myriads of holy ones
  from the south, from his mountain
    slopes.^e
³Surely it is you who love the people;
  all the holy ones are in your hand.
At your feet they all bow down,
  and from you receive instruction,
⁴the law that Moses gave us,
  the possession of the assembly of
    Jacob.
⁵He was king over Jeshurun^f
  when the leaders of the people
    assembled,
  along with the tribes of Israel.

⁶"Let Reuben live and not die,
  nor^g his men be few."

⁷And this he said about Judah:

"Hear, O LORD, the cry of Judah;
  bring him to his people.
With his own hands he defends his
    cause.
  Oh, be his help against his foes!"

⁸About Levi he said:

"Your Thummim and Urim belong
  to the man you favored.
You tested him at Massah;
  you contended with him at the
    waters of Meribah.
⁹He said of his father and mother,
  'I have no regard for them.'
He did not recognize his brothers
  or acknowledge his own children,
but he watched over your word
  and guarded your covenant.
¹⁰He teaches your precepts to Jacob
  and your law to Israel.
He offers incense before you
  and whole burnt offerings on your
    altar.
¹¹Bless all his skills, O LORD,

---

^a43 Or *Make his people rejoice, O nations*   ^b43 Masoretic Text; Dead Sea Scrolls (see also Septuagint)
people, / and let all the angels worship him /   ^c44 Hebrew *Hoshea*, a variant of *Joshua*   ^d2 Or *from*
^e2 The meaning of the Hebrew for this phrase is uncertain.   ^f5 *Jeshurun* means *the upright one,* that is,
Israel; also in verse 26.   ^g6 Or *but let*

and be pleased with the work of his
 hands.
Smite the loins of those who rise up
 against him;
  strike his foes till they rise no
   more."

¹²About Benjamin he said:

"Let the beloved of the Lord rest
 secure in him,
  for he shields him all day long,
  and the one the Lord loves rests
   between his shoulders."

¹³About Joseph he said:

"May the Lord bless his land
 with the precious dew from heaven
  above
 and with the deep waters that lie
  below;
¹⁴with the best the sun brings forth
 and the finest the moon can yield;
¹⁵with the choicest gifts of the ancient
 mountains
 and the fruitfulness of the
  everlasting hills;
¹⁶with the best gifts of the earth and its
 fullness
 and the favor of him who dwelt in
  the burning bush.
Let all these rest on the head of
 Joseph,
 on the brow of the prince among*a*
  his brothers.
¹⁷In majesty he is like a firstborn bull;
 his horns are the horns of a wild
  ox.
With them he will gore the nations,
 even those at the ends of the earth.
Such are the ten thousands of
 Ephraim;
 such are the thousands of
  Manasseh."

¹⁸About Zebulun he said:

"Rejoice, Zebulun, in your going out,
 and you, Issachar, in your tents.
¹⁹They will summon peoples to the
 mountain
 and there offer sacrifices of
  righteousness;
they will feast on the abundance of
 the seas,
 on the treasures hidden in the
  sand."

²⁰About Gad he said:

"Blessed is he who enlarges Gad's
 domain!
 Gad lives there like a lion,
  tearing at arm or head.
²¹He chose the best land for himself;
 the leader's portion was kept for
  him.
When the heads of the people
 assembled,
 he carried out the Lord's righteous
  will,
 and his judgments concerning
  Israel."

²²About Dan he said:

"Dan is a lion's cub,
 springing out of Bashan."

²³About Naphtali he said:

"Naphtali is abounding with the favor
 of the Lord
 and is full of his blessing;
 he will inherit southward to the
  lake."

²⁴About Asher he said:

"Most blessed of sons is Asher;
 let him be favored by his brothers,
 and let him bathe his feet in oil.
²⁵The bolts of your gates will be iron
 and bronze,
 and your strength will equal your
  days.

²⁶"There is no one like the God of
 Jeshurun,
 who rides on the heavens to help
  you
 and on the clouds in his majesty.
²⁷The eternal God is your refuge,
 and underneath are the everlasting
  arms.
He will drive out your enemy before
 you,
 saying, 'Destroy him!'
²⁸So Israel will live in safety alone;
 Jacob's spring is secure
in a land of grain and new wine,
 where the heavens drop dew.
²⁹Blessed are you, O Israel!
 Who is like you,
 a people saved by the Lord?
He is your shield and helper
 and your glorious sword.
Your enemies will cower before you,
 and you will trample down their
  high places."*b*

a16 Or of the one separated from *b29 Or will tread upon their bodies*

The Death of Moses

34 Then Moses climbed Mount Nebo from the plains of Moab to the top of Pisgah, across from Jericho. There the LORD showed him the whole land — from Gilead to Dan, [2] all of Naphtali, the territory of Ephraim and Manasseh, all the land of Judah as far as the western sea, [a] [3] the Negev and the whole region from the Valley of Jericho, the City of Palms, as far as Zoar. [4] Then the LORD said to him, "This is the land I promised on oath to Abraham, Isaac and Jacob when I said, 'I will give it to your descendants.' I have let you see it with your eyes, but you will not cross over into it."

[5] And Moses the servant of the LORD died there in Moab, as the LORD had said. [6] He buried him [b] in Moab, in the valley opposite Beth Peor, but to this day no one knows where his grave is. [7] Moses was a hundred and twenty years old when he died, yet his eyes were not weak nor his strength gone. [8] The Israelites grieved for Moses in the plains of Moab thirty days, until the time of weeping and mourning was over.

[9] Now Joshua son of Nun was filled with the spirit [c] of wisdom because Moses had laid his hands on him. So the Israelites listened to him and did what the LORD had commanded Moses.

[10] Since then, no prophet has risen in Israel like Moses, whom the LORD knew face to face, [11] who did all those miraculous signs and wonders the LORD sent him to do in Egypt — to Pharaoh and to all his officials and to his whole land. [12] For no one has ever shown the mighty power or performed the awesome deeds that Moses did in the sight of all Israel.

---

[a]2 That is, the Mediterranean   [b]6 Or *He was buried*   [c]9 Or *Spirit*

JOSHUA tells the story of how the Israelites conquer their enemies in the promised land and divide it up among the twelve tribes. As long as the people trust God and obey his will, he gives them victory in their battles. By the end of the book, the people choose to serve only the Lord. As you read this book, make your own choice to serve the Lord, to do his will, and to depend on him to give you victory over the evil one.

JOSHUA

The Lord Commands Joshua

1 After the death of Moses the servant of the Lord, the Lord said to Joshua son of Nun, Moses' aide: **2**"Moses my servant is dead. Now then, you and all these people, get ready to cross the Jordan River into the land I am about to give to them — to the Israelites. **3**I will give you every place where you set your foot, as I promised Moses. **4**Your territory will extend from the desert to Lebanon, and from the great river, the Euphrates — all the Hittite country — to the Great Sea*a* on the west. **5**No one will be able to stand up against you all the days of your life. As I was with Moses, so I will be with you; I will never leave you nor forsake you.

6"Be strong and courageous, because you will lead these people to inherit the land I swore to their forefathers to give them. **7**Be strong and very courageous. Be careful to obey all the law my servant Moses gave you; do not turn from it to the right or to the left, that you may be successful wherever you go. **8**Do not let this Book of the Law depart from your mouth; meditate on it day and night, so that you may be careful to do everything written in it. Then you will be prosperous and successful. **9**Have I not commanded you? Be strong and courageous. Do not be terrified; do not be discouraged, for the LORD your God will be with you wherever you go."

¹⁰So Joshua ordered the officers of the people: ¹¹"Go through the camp and tell the people, 'Get your supplies ready. Three days from now you will cross the Jordan here to go in and take possession of the land the LORD your God is giving you for your own.' "

¹²But to the Reubenites, the Gadites and the half-tribe of Manasseh, Joshua said, ¹³"Remember the command that Moses the servant of the LORD gave you: 'The LORD your God is giving you rest and has granted you this land.' ¹⁴Your wives, your children and your livestock may stay in the land that Moses gave you east of the Jordan, but all your fighting men, fully armed, must cross over ahead of your brothers. You are to help your brothers ¹⁵until the LORD gives them rest, as he has done for you, and until they too have taken possession of the land that the LORD your God is giving them. After that, you may go back and occupy your own land, which Moses the servant of the LORD gave you east of the Jordan toward the sunrise."

¹⁶Then they answered Joshua, "Whatever you have commanded us we will do, and wherever you send us we will go. ¹⁷Just as we fully obeyed Moses, so we will obey you. Only may the LORD your God be with you as he was with Moses. ¹⁸Whoever rebels against your word and does not obey your words, whatever you may command them, will be put to death. Only be strong and courageous!"

Rahab and the Spies

2 Then Joshua son of Nun secretly sent two spies from Shittim. "Go, look over the land," he said, "especially Jericho." So

---

WEDNESDAY

VERSE FOR THE DAY:
Joshua 1:9

AUTHOR:
Bruce Larson

PASSAGE FOR THE DAY:
Joshua 1:1–11

A Priesthood of Believers

GOD wants us to be aware always of the people next to us. It's not enough to work honestly and industriously, for Christ calls us to be a priesthood of believers who willingly take responsibility for those who are our neighbors.

God calls the laity to do a job the clergy cannot do in many instances. In a parish I once served, a close friend who was a doctor became quite ill. Though I visited him almost daily, I saw no improvement and no benefit from my visits. One day I went to see this Christian doctor and found him greatly improved and free from fear.

I asked him what had happened, and he told me of a visit a few hours before with a senior surgeon in the area who had prayed with him and given him a prescription. The prescription was to read Joshua 1:9. My friend had been touched by God, and not through a clergyman but through a brother physician.

Additional Scripture Readings:
Luke 10:25–37; 1 Peter 2:4–12

Go to page 234 for your next devotional reading.

they went and entered the house of a prostitute[a] named Rahab and stayed there.

2The king of Jericho was told, "Look! Some of the Israelites have come here tonight to spy out the land." 3So the king of Jericho sent this message to Rahab: "Bring out the men who came to you and entered your house, because they have come to spy out the whole land."

4But the woman had taken the two men and hidden them. She said, "Yes, the men came to me, but I did not know where they had come from. 5At dusk, when it was time to close the city gate, the men left. I don't know which way they went. Go after them quickly. You may catch up with them." 6(But she had taken them up to the roof and hidden them under the stalks of flax she had laid out on the roof.) 7So the men set out in pursuit of the spies on the road that leads to the fords of the Jordan, and as soon as the pursuers had gone out, the gate was shut.

8Before the spies lay down for the night, she went up on the roof 9and said to them, "I know that the LORD has given this land to you and that a great fear of you has fallen on us, so that all who live in this country are melting in fear because of you. 10We have heard how the LORD dried up the water of the Red Sea[b] for you when you came out of Egypt, and what you did to Sihon and Og, the two kings of the Amorites east of the Jordan, whom you completely destroyed.[c] 11When we heard of it, our hearts melted and everyone's courage failed because of you, for the LORD your God is God in heaven above and on the earth below. 12Now then, please swear to me by the LORD that you will show kindness to my family, because I have shown kindness to you. Give me a sure sign 13that you will spare the lives of my father and mother, my brothers and sisters, and all who belong to them, and that you will save us from death."

14"Our lives for your lives!" the men assured her. "If you don't tell what we are doing, we will treat you kindly and faithfully when the LORD gives us the land."

15So she let them down by a rope through the window, for the house she lived in was part of the city wall. 16Now she had said to them, "Go to the hills so the pursuers will not find you. Hide yourselves there three days until they return, and then go on your way."

17The men said to her, "This oath you made us swear will not be binding on us 18unless, when we enter the land, you have tied this scarlet cord in the window through which you let us down, and unless you have brought your father and mother, your brothers and all your family into your house. 19If anyone goes outside your house into the street, his blood will be on his own head; we will not be responsible. As for anyone who is in the house with you, his blood will be on our head if a hand is laid on him. 20But if you tell what we are doing, we will be released from the oath you made us swear."

21"Agreed," she replied. "Let it be as you say." So she sent them away and they departed. And she tied the scarlet cord in the window.

22When they left, they went into the hills and stayed there three days, until the pursuers had searched all along the road and returned without finding them. 23Then the two men started back. They went down out of the hills, forded the river and came to Joshua son of Nun and told him everything that had happened to them. 24They said to Joshua, "The LORD has surely given the whole land into our hands; all the people are melting in fear because of us."

Crossing the Jordan

3 Early in the morning Joshua and all the Israelites set out from Shittim and went to the Jordan, where they camped before crossing over. 2After three days the officers went throughout the camp, 3giving orders to the people: "When you see the ark of the covenant of the LORD your God, and the priests, who are Levites, carrying it, you are to move out from your positions and follow it. 4Then you will know which way to go, since you have never been this way before. But keep a distance of about a thousand yards[d] between you and the ark; do not go near it."

5Joshua told the people, "Consecrate yourselves, for tomorrow the LORD will do amazing things among you."

6Joshua said to the priests, "Take up the ark of the covenant and pass on ahead of the people." So they took it up and went ahead of them.

---

a1 Or possibly *an innkeeper*   b10 Hebrew *Yam Suph*; that is, Sea of Reeds   c10 The Hebrew term refers to the irrevocable giving over of things or persons to the LORD, often by totally destroying them.
d4 Hebrew *about two thousand cubits* (about 900 meters)

⁷And the LORD said to Joshua, "Today I will begin to exalt you in the eyes of all Israel, so they may know that I am with you as I was with Moses. ⁸Tell the priests who carry the ark of the covenant: 'When you reach the edge of the Jordan's waters, go and stand in the river.' "

⁹Joshua said to the Israelites, "Come here and listen to the words of the LORD your God. ¹⁰This is how you will know that the living God is among you and that he will certainly drive out before you the Canaanites, Hittites, Hivites, Perizzites, Girgashites, Amorites and Jebusites. ¹¹See, the ark of the covenant of the Lord of all the earth will go into the Jordan ahead of you. ¹²Now then, choose twelve men from the tribes of Israel, one from each tribe. ¹³And as soon as the priests who carry the ark of the LORD—the Lord of all the earth—set foot in the Jordan, its waters flowing downstream will be cut off and stand up in a heap."

¹⁴So when the people broke camp to cross the Jordan, the priests carrying the ark of the covenant went ahead of them. ¹⁵Now the Jordan is at flood stage all during harvest. Yet as soon as the priests who carried the ark reached the Jordan and their feet touched the water's edge, ¹⁶the water from upstream stopped flowing. It piled up in a heap a great distance away, at a town called Adam in the vicinity of Zarethan, while the water flowing down to the Sea of the Arabah (the Salt Sea ᵃ) was completely cut off. So the people crossed over opposite Jericho. ¹⁷The priests who carried the ark of the covenant of the LORD stood firm on dry ground in the middle of the Jordan, while all Israel passed by until the whole nation had completed the crossing on dry ground.

4 When the whole nation had finished crossing the Jordan, the LORD said to Joshua, ²"Choose twelve men from among the people, one from each tribe, ³and tell them to take up twelve stones from the middle of the Jordan from right where the priests stood and to carry them over with you and put them down at the place where you stay tonight."

⁴So Joshua called together the twelve men he had appointed from the Israelites, one from each tribe, ⁵and said to them, "Go over before the ark of the LORD your God into the middle of the Jordan. Each of you is to take up a stone on his shoulder,

according to the number of the tribes of the Israelites, ⁶to serve as a sign among you. In the future, when your children ask you, 'What do these stones mean?' ⁷tell them that the flow of the Jordan was cut off before the ark of the covenant of the LORD. When it crossed the Jordan, the waters of the Jordan were cut off. These stones are to be a memorial to the people of Israel forever."

⁸So the Israelites did as Joshua commanded them. They took twelve stones from the middle of the Jordan, according to the number of the tribes of the Israelites, as the LORD had told Joshua; and they carried them over with them to their camp, where they put them down. ⁹Joshua set up the twelve stones that had beenᵇ in the middle of the Jordan at the spot where the priests who carried the ark of the covenant had stood. And they are there to this day.

¹⁰Now the priests who carried the ark remained standing in the middle of the Jordan until everything the LORD had commanded Joshua was done by the people, just as Moses had directed Joshua. The people hurried over, ¹¹and as soon as all of them had crossed, the ark of the LORD and the priests came to the other side while the people watched. ¹²The men of Reuben, Gad and the half-tribe of Manasseh crossed over, armed, in front of the Israelites, as Moses had directed them. ¹³About forty thousand armed for battle crossed over before the LORD to the plains of Jericho for war.

¹⁴That day the LORD exalted Joshua in the sight of all Israel; and they revered him all the days of his life, just as they had revered Moses.

¹⁵Then the LORD said to Joshua, ¹⁶"Command the priests carrying the ark of the Testimony to come up out of the Jordan."

¹⁷So Joshua commanded the priests, "Come up out of the Jordan."

¹⁸And the priests came up out of the river carrying the ark of the covenant of the LORD. No sooner had they set their feet on the dry ground than the waters of the Jordan returned to their place and ran at flood stage as before.

¹⁹On the tenth day of the first month the people went up from the Jordan and camped at Gilgal on the eastern border of Jericho. ²⁰And Joshua set up at Gilgal the twelve stones they had taken out of the

ᵃ16 That is, the Dead Sea   ᵇ9 Or Joshua also set up twelve stones

Jordan. **21**He said to the Israelites, "In the future when your descendants ask their fathers, 'What do these stones mean?' **22**tell them, 'Israel crossed the Jordan on dry ground.' **23**For the LORD your God dried up the Jordan before you until you had crossed over. The LORD your God did to the Jordan just what he had done to the Red Sea*a* when he dried it up before us until we had crossed over. **24**He did this so that all the peoples of the earth might know that the hand of the LORD is powerful and so that you might always fear the LORD your God."

Circumcision at Gilgal

5 Now when all the Amorite kings west of the Jordan and all the Canaanite kings along the coast heard how the LORD had dried up the Jordan before the Israelites until we had crossed over, their hearts melted and they no longer had the courage to face the Israelites.

2At that time the LORD said to Joshua, "Make flint knives and circumcise the Israelites again." **3**So Joshua made flint knives and circumcised the Israelites at Gibeath Haaraloth.*b*

4Now this is why he did so: All those who came out of Egypt—all the men of military age—died in the desert on the way after leaving Egypt. **5**All the people that came out had been circumcised, but all the people born in the desert during the journey from Egypt had not. **6**The Israelites had moved about in the desert forty years until all the men who were of military age when they left Egypt had died, since they had not obeyed the LORD. For the LORD had sworn to them that they would not see the land that he had solemnly promised their fathers to give us, a land flowing with milk and honey. **7**So he raised up their sons in their place, and these were the ones Joshua circumcised. They were still uncircumcised because they had not been circumcised on the way. **8**And after the whole nation had been circumcised, they remained where they were in camp until they were healed.

9Then the LORD said to Joshua, "Today I have rolled away the reproach of Egypt from you." So the place has been called Gilgal*c* to this day.

10On the evening of the fourteenth day of the month, while camped at Gilgal on the plains of Jericho, the Israelites cele-

brated the Passover. **11**The day after the Passover, that very day, they ate some of the produce of the land: unleavened bread and roasted grain. **12**The manna stopped the day after*d* they ate this food from the land; there was no longer any manna for the Israelites, but that year they ate of the produce of Canaan.

The Fall of Jericho

13Now when Joshua was near Jericho, he looked up and saw a man standing in front of him with a drawn sword in his hand. Joshua went up to him and asked, "Are you for us or for our enemies?"

14"Neither," he replied, "but as commander of the army of the LORD I have now come." Then Joshua fell facedown to the ground in reverence, and asked him, "What message does my Lord*e* have for his servant?"

15The commander of the LORD's army replied, "Take off your sandals, for the place where you are standing is holy." And Joshua did so.

6 Now Jericho was tightly shut up because of the Israelites. No one went out and no one came in.

2Then the LORD said to Joshua, "See, I have delivered Jericho into your hands, along with its king and its fighting men. **3**March around the city once with all the armed men. Do this for six days. **4**Have seven priests carry trumpets of rams' horns in front of the ark. On the seventh day, march around the city seven times, with the priests blowing the trumpets. **5**When you hear them sound a long blast on the trumpets, have all the people give a loud shout; then the wall of the city will collapse and the people will go up, every man straight in."

6So Joshua son of Nun called the priests and said to them, "Take up the ark of the covenant of the LORD and have seven priests carry trumpets in front of it." **7**And he ordered the people, "Advance! March around the city, with the armed guard going ahead of the ark of the LORD."

8When Joshua had spoken to the people, the seven priests carrying the seven trumpets before the LORD went forward, blowing their trumpets, and the ark of the LORD's covenant followed them. **9**The armed guard marched ahead of the priests who blew the trumpets, and the rear guard followed the ark. All this time the

---

a23 Hebrew *Yam Suph*; that is, Sea of Reeds   *b3* *Gibeath Haaraloth* means *hill of foreskins.*
c9 *Gilgal* sounds like the Hebrew for *roll.*   *d12* Or *the day*   *e14* Or *lord*

trumpets were sounding. **10**But Joshua had commanded the people, "Do not give a war cry, do not raise your voices, do not say a word until the day I tell you to shout. Then shout!" **11**So he had the ark of the LORD carried around the city, circling it once. Then the people returned to camp and spent the night there.

12Joshua got up early the next morning and the priests took up the ark of the LORD. **13**The seven priests carrying the seven trumpets went forward, marching before the ark of the LORD and blowing the trumpets. The armed men went ahead of them and the rear guard followed the ark of the LORD, while the trumpets kept sounding. **14**So on the second day they marched around the city once and returned to the camp. They did this for six days.

15On the seventh day, they got up at daybreak and marched around the city seven times in the same manner, except that on that day they circled the city seven times. **16**The seventh time around, when the priests sounded the trumpet blast, Joshua commanded the people, "Shout! For the LORD has given you the city! **17**The city and all that is in it are to be devoted*a* to the LORD. Only Rahab the prostitute*b* and all who are with her in her house shall be spared, because she hid the spies we sent. **18**But keep away from the devoted things, so that you will not bring about your own destruction by taking any of them. Otherwise you will make the camp of Israel liable to destruction and bring trouble on it. **19**All the silver and gold and the articles of bronze and iron are sacred to the LORD and must go into his treasury."

20When the trumpets sounded, the people shouted, and at the sound of the trumpet, when the people gave a loud shout, the wall collapsed; so every man charged straight in, and they took the city. **21**They devoted the city to the LORD and destroyed with the sword every living thing in it — men and women, young and old, cattle, sheep and donkeys.

22Joshua said to the two men who had spied out the land, "Go into the prostitute's house and bring her out and all who belong to her, in accordance with your oath to her." **23**So the young men who had done the spying went in and brought out Rahab, her father and mother and brothers and all who belonged to her. They brought out her entire family and put them in a place outside the camp of Israel.

24Then they burned the whole city and everything in it, but they put the silver and gold and the articles of bronze and iron into the treasury of the LORD's house. **25**But Joshua spared Rahab the prostitute, with her family and all who belonged to her, because she hid the men Joshua had sent as spies to Jericho — and she lives among the Israelites to this day.

26At that time Joshua pronounced this solemn oath: "Cursed before the LORD is the man who undertakes to rebuild this city, Jericho:

"At the cost of his firstborn son
    will he lay its foundations;
at the cost of his youngest
    will he set up its gates."

27So the LORD was with Joshua, and his fame spread throughout the land.

Achan's Sin

7 But the Israelites acted unfaithfully in regard to the devoted things*c*; Achan son of Carmi, the son of Zimri,*d* the son of Zerah, of the tribe of Judah, took some of them. So the LORD's anger burned against Israel.

2Now Joshua sent men from Jericho to Ai, which is near Beth Aven to the east of Bethel, and told them, "Go up and spy out the region." So the men went up and spied out Ai.

3When they returned to Joshua, they said, "Not all the people will have to go up against Ai. Send two or three thousand men to take it and do not weary all the people, for only a few men are there." **4**So about three thousand men went up; but they were routed by the men of Ai, **5**who killed about thirty-six of them. They chased the Israelites from the city gate as far as the stone quarries*e* and struck them down on the slopes. At this the hearts of the people melted and became like water.

6Then Joshua tore his clothes and fell facedown to the ground before the ark of the LORD, remaining there till evening.

---

a 17 The Hebrew term refers to the irrevocable giving over of things or persons to the LORD, often by totally destroying them; also in verses 18 and 21.　　*b 17* Or possibly *innkeeper*; also in verses 22 and 25
c 1 The Hebrew term refers to the irrevocable giving over of things or persons to the LORD, often by totally destroying them; also in verses 11, 12, 13 and 15.　　*d 1* See Septuagint and 1 Chron. 2:6; Hebrew *Zabdi*; also in verses 17 and 18.　　*e 5* Or *as far as Shebarim*

The elders of Israel did the same, and sprinkled dust on their heads. 7And Joshua said, "Ah, Sovereign Lord, why did you ever bring this people across the Jordan to deliver us into the hands of the Amorites to destroy us? If only we had been content to stay on the other side of the Jordan! 8O Lord, what can I say, now that Israel has been routed by its enemies? 9The Canaanites and the other people of the country will hear about this and they will surround us and wipe out our name from the earth. What then will you do for your own great name?"

10The Lord said to Joshua, "Stand up! What are you doing down on your face? 11Israel has sinned; they have violated my covenant, which I commanded them to keep. They have taken some of the devoted things; they have stolen, they have lied, they have put them with their own possessions. 12That is why the Israelites cannot stand against their enemies; they turn their backs and run because they have been made liable to destruction. I will not be with you anymore unless you destroy whatever among you is devoted to destruction.

13"Go, consecrate the people. Tell them, 'Consecrate yourselves in preparation for tomorrow; for this is what the Lord, the God of Israel, says: That which is devoted is among you, O Israel. You cannot stand against your enemies until you remove it.

14" 'In the morning, present yourselves tribe by tribe. The tribe that the Lord takes shall come forward clan by clan; the clan that the Lord takes shall come forward family by family; and the family that the Lord takes shall come forward man by man. 15He who is caught with the devoted things shall be destroyed by fire, along with all that belongs to him. He has violated the covenant of the Lord and has done a disgraceful thing in Israel!' "

16Early the next morning Joshua had Israel come forward by tribes, and Judah was taken. 17The clans of Judah came forward, and he took the Zerahites. He had the clan of the Zerahites come forward by families, and Zimri was taken. 18Joshua had his family come forward man by man, and Achan son of Carmi, the son of Zimri, the son of Zerah, of the tribe of Judah, was taken.

19Then Joshua said to Achan, "My son, give glory to the Lord,a the God of Israel, and give him the praise.b Tell me what you have done; do not hide it from me."

20Achan replied, "It is true! I have sinned against the Lord, the God of Israel. This is what I have done: 21When I saw in the plunder a beautiful robe from Babylonia,c two hundred shekelsd of silver and a wedge of gold weighing fifty shekels,e I coveted them and took them. They are hidden in the ground inside my tent, with the silver underneath."

22So Joshua sent messengers, and they ran to the tent, and there it was, hidden in his tent, with the silver underneath. 23They took the things from the tent, brought them to Joshua and all the Israelites and spread them out before the Lord.

24Then Joshua, together with all Israel, took Achan son of Zerah, the silver, the robe, the gold wedge, his sons and daughters, his cattle, donkeys and sheep, his tent and all that he had, to the Valley of Achor. 25Joshua said, "Why have you brought this trouble on us? The Lord will bring trouble on you today."

Then all Israel stoned him, and after they had stoned the rest, they burned them. 26Over Achan they heaped up a large pile of rocks, which remains to this day. Then the Lord turned from his fierce anger. Therefore that place has been called the Valley of Achorf ever since.

Ai Destroyed

8 Then the Lord said to Joshua, "Do not be afraid; do not be discouraged. Take the whole army with you, and go up and attack Ai. For I have delivered into your hands the king of Ai, his people, his city and his land. 2You shall do to Ai and its king as you did to Jericho and its king, except that you may carry off their plunder and livestock for yourselves. Set an ambush behind the city."

3So Joshua and the whole army moved out to attack Ai. He chose thirty thousand of his best fighting men and sent them out at night 4with these orders: "Listen carefully. You are to set an ambush behind the city. Don't go very far from it. All of you be on the alert. 5I and all those with me will advance on the city, and when the men come out against us, as they did before, we will flee from them. 6They will pursue us until we have lured them away

a19 A solemn charge to tell the truth is, about 5 pounds (about 2.3 kilograms)　b19 Or *and confess to him*　c21 Hebrew *Shinar*　d21 That e21 That is, about 1 1/4 pounds (about 0.6 kilogram)　f26 *Achor* means *trouble*.

from the city, for they will say, 'They are running away from us as they did before.' So when we flee from them, **7**you are to rise up from ambush and take the city. The LORD your God will give it into your hand. **8**When you have taken the city, set it on fire. Do what the LORD has commanded. See to it; you have my orders."

9Then Joshua sent them off, and they went to the place of ambush and lay in wait between Bethel and Ai, to the west of Ai—but Joshua spent that night with the people. **10**Early the next morning Joshua mustered his men, and he and the leaders of Israel marched before them to Ai. **11**The entire force that was with him marched up and approached the city and arrived in front of it. They set up camp north of Ai, with the valley between them and the city. **12**Joshua had taken about five thousand men and set them in ambush between Bethel and Ai, to the west of the city. **13**They had the soldiers take up their positions—all those in the camp to the north of the city and the ambush to the west of it. That night Joshua went into the valley.

14When the king of Ai saw this, he and all the men of the city hurried out early in the morning to meet Israel in battle at a certain place overlooking the Arabah. But he did not know that an ambush had been set against him behind the city. **15**Joshua and all Israel let themselves be driven back before them, and they fled toward the desert. **16**All the men of Ai were called to pursue them, and they pursued Joshua and were lured away from the city. **17**Not a man remained in Ai or Bethel who did not go after Israel. They left the city open and went in pursuit of Israel.

18Then the LORD said to Joshua, "Hold out toward Ai the javelin that is in your hand, for into your hand I will deliver the city." So Joshua held out his javelin toward Ai. **19**As soon as he did this, the men in the ambush rose quickly from their position and rushed forward. They entered the city and captured it and quickly set it on fire.

20The men of Ai looked back and saw the smoke of the city rising against the sky, but they had no chance to escape in any direction, for the Israelites who had been fleeing toward the desert had turned back against their pursuers. **21**For when Joshua and all Israel saw that the ambush had taken the city and that smoke was going up from the city, they turned around and attacked the men of Ai. **22**The men of the ambush also came out of the city against them, so that they were caught in the middle, with Israelites on both sides. Israel cut them down, leaving them neither survivors nor fugitives. **23**But they took the king of Ai alive and brought him to Joshua.

24When Israel had finished killing all the men of Ai in the fields and in the desert where they had chased them, and when every one of them had been put to the sword, all the Israelites returned to Ai and killed those who were in it. **25**Twelve thousand men and women fell that day—all the people of Ai. **26**For Joshua did not draw back the hand that held out his javelin until he had destroyed*a* all who lived in Ai. **27**But Israel did carry off for themselves the livestock and plunder of this city, as the LORD had instructed Joshua.

28So Joshua burned Ai and made it a permanent heap of ruins, a desolate place to this day. **29**He hung the king of Ai on a tree and left him there until evening. At sunset, Joshua ordered them to take his body from the tree and throw it down at the entrance of the city gate. And they raised a large pile of rocks over it, which remains to this day.

The Covenant Renewed at Mount Ebal

30Then Joshua built on Mount Ebal an altar to the LORD, the God of Israel, **31**as Moses the servant of the LORD had commanded the Israelites. He built it according to what is written in the Book of the Law of Moses—an altar of uncut stones, on which no iron tool had been used. On it they offered to the LORD burnt offerings and sacrificed fellowship offerings.*b* **32**There, in the presence of the Israelites, Joshua copied on stones the law of Moses, which he had written. **33**All Israel, aliens and citizens alike, with their elders, officials and judges, were standing on both sides of the ark of the covenant of the LORD, facing those who carried it—the priests, who were Levites. Half of the people stood in front of Mount Gerizim and half of them in front of Mount Ebal, as Moses the servant of the LORD had formerly commanded when he gave instructions to bless the people of Israel.

a26 The Hebrew term refers to the irrevocable giving over of things or persons to the LORD, often by totally destroying them.   *b31* Traditionally *peace offerings*

34Afterward, Joshua read all the words of the law—the blessings and the curses—just as it is written in the Book of the Law. **35**There was not a word of all that Moses had commanded that Joshua did not read to the whole assembly of Israel, including the women and children, and the aliens who lived among them.

The Gibeonite Deception

9 Now when all the kings west of the Jordan heard about these things—those in the hill country, in the western foothills, and along the entire coast of the Great Sea*a* as far as Lebanon (the kings of the Hittites, Amorites, Canaanites, Perizzites, Hivites and Jebusites)— **2**they came together to make war against Joshua and Israel.

3However, when the people of Gibeon heard what Joshua had done to Jericho and Ai, **4**they resorted to a ruse: They went as a delegation whose donkeys were loaded*b* with worn-out sacks and old wineskins, cracked and mended. **5**The men put worn and patched sandals on their feet and wore old clothes. All the bread of their food supply was dry and moldy. **6**Then they went to Joshua in the camp at Gilgal and said to him and the men of Israel, "We have come from a distant country; make a treaty with us."

7The men of Israel said to the Hivites, "But perhaps you live near us. How then can we make a treaty with you?"

8"We are your servants," they said to Joshua.

But Joshua asked, "Who are you and where do you come from?"

9They answered: "Your servants have come from a very distant country because of the fame of the Lord your God. For we have heard reports of him: all that he did in Egypt, **10**and all that he did to the two kings of the Amorites east of the Jordan—Sihon king of Heshbon, and Og king of Bashan, who reigned in Ashtaroth. **11**And our elders and all those living in our country said to us, 'Take provisions for your journey; go and meet them and say to them, "We are your servants; make a treaty with us."' **12**This bread of ours was warm when we packed it at home on the day we left to come to you. But now see how dry and moldy it is. **13**And these wineskins that we filled were new, but see how cracked they are. And our clothes and sandals are worn out by the very long journey."

14The men of Israel sampled their provisions but did not inquire of the Lord. **15**Then Joshua made a treaty of peace with them to let them live, and the leaders of the assembly ratified it by oath.

16Three days after they made the treaty with the Gibeonites, the Israelites heard that they were neighbors, living near them. **17**So the Israelites set out and on the third day came to their cities: Gibeon, Kephirah, Beeroth and Kiriath Jearim. **18**But the Israelites did not attack them, because the leaders of the assembly had sworn an oath to them by the Lord, the God of Israel.

The whole assembly grumbled against the leaders, **19**but all the leaders answered, "We have given them our oath by the Lord, the God of Israel, and we cannot touch them now. **20**This is what we will do to them: We will let them live, so that wrath will not fall on us for breaking the oath we swore to them." **21**They continued, "Let them live, but let them be woodcutters and water carriers for the entire community." So the leaders' promise to them was kept.

22Then Joshua summoned the Gibeonites and said, "Why did you deceive us by saying, 'We live a long way from you,' while actually you live near us? **23**You are now under a curse: You will never cease to serve as woodcutters and water carriers for the house of my God."

24They answered Joshua, "Your servants were clearly told how the Lord your God had commanded his servant Moses to give you the whole land and to wipe out all its inhabitants from before you. So we feared for our lives because of you, and that is why we did this. **25**We are now in your hands. Do to us whatever seems good and right to you."

26So Joshua saved them from the Israelites, and they did not kill them. **27**That day he made the Gibeonites woodcutters and water carriers for the community and for the altar of the Lord at the place the Lord would choose. And that is what they are to this day.

The Sun Stands Still

10 Now Adoni-Zedek king of Jerusalem heard that Joshua had taken Ai

---

a1 That is, the Mediterranean   *b4* Most Hebrew manuscripts; some Hebrew manuscripts, Vulgate and Syriac (see also Septuagint) *They prepared provisions and loaded their donkeys* and totally destroyed[a] it, doing to Ai and its king as he had done to Jericho and its king, and that the people of Gibeon had made a treaty of peace with Israel and were living near them. [2]He and his people were very much alarmed at this, because Gibeon was an important city, like one of the royal cities; it was larger than Ai, and all its men were good fighters. [3]So Adoni-Zedek king of Jerusalem appealed to Hoham king of Hebron, Piram king of Jarmuth, Japhia king of Lachish and Debir king of Eglon. [4]"Come up and help me attack Gibeon," he said, "because it has made peace with Joshua and the Israelites."

[5]Then the five kings of the Amorites — the kings of Jerusalem, Hebron, Jarmuth, Lachish and Eglon — joined forces. They moved up with all their troops and took up positions against Gibeon and attacked it.

[6]The Gibeonites then sent word to Joshua in the camp at Gilgal: "Do not abandon your servants. Come up to us quickly and save us! Help us, because all the Amorite kings from the hill country have joined forces against us."

[7]So Joshua marched up from Gilgal with his entire army, including all the best fighting men. [8]The LORD said to Joshua, "Do not be afraid of them; I have given them into your hand. Not one of them will be able to withstand you."

[9]After an all-night march from Gilgal, Joshua took them by surprise. [10]The LORD threw them into confusion before Israel, who defeated them in a great victory at Gibeon. Israel pursued them along the road going up to Beth Horon and cut them down all the way to Azekah and Makkedah. [11]As they fled before Israel on the road down from Beth Horon to Azekah, the LORD hurled large hailstones down on them from the sky, and more of them died from the hailstones than were killed by the swords of the Israelites.

[12]On the day the LORD gave the Amorites over to Israel, Joshua said to the LORD in the presence of Israel:

"O sun, stand still over Gibeon,
    O moon, over the Valley of Aijalon."
[13]So the sun stood still,
    and the moon stopped,
till the nation avenged itself on[b] its
    enemies,

as it is written in the Book of Jashar.

The sun stopped in the middle of the sky and delayed going down about a full day. [14]There has never been a day like it before or since, a day when the LORD listened to a man. Surely the LORD was fighting for Israel!

[15]Then Joshua returned with all Israel to the camp at Gilgal.

Five Amorite Kings Killed

[16]Now the five kings had fled and hidden in the cave at Makkedah. [17]When Joshua was told that the five kings had been found hiding in the cave at Makkedah, [18]he said, "Roll large rocks up to the mouth of the cave, and post some men there to guard it. [19]But don't stop! Pursue your enemies, attack them from the rear and don't let them reach their cities, for the LORD your God has given them into your hand."

[20]So Joshua and the Israelites destroyed them completely — almost to a man — but the few who were left reached their fortified cities. [21]The whole army then returned safely to Joshua in the camp at Makkedah, and no one uttered a word against the Israelites.

[22]Joshua said, "Open the mouth of the cave and bring those five kings out to me." [23]So they brought the five kings out of the cave — the kings of Jerusalem, Hebron, Jarmuth, Lachish and Eglon. [24]When they had brought these kings to Joshua, he summoned all the men of Israel and said to the army commanders who had come with him, "Come here and put your feet on the necks of these kings." So they came forward and placed their feet on their necks.

[25]Joshua said to them, "Do not be afraid; do not be discouraged. Be strong and courageous. This is what the LORD will do to all the enemies you are going to fight." [26]Then Joshua struck and killed the kings and hung them on five trees, and they were left hanging on the trees until evening.

[27]At sunset Joshua gave the order and they took them down from the trees and threw them into the cave where they had been hiding. At the mouth of the cave they placed large rocks, which are there to this day.

[28]That day Joshua took Makkedah. He put the city and its king to the sword and

---

[a]1 The Hebrew term refers to the irrevocable giving over of things or persons to the LORD, often by totally destroying them; also in verses 28, 35, 37, 39 and 40.   [b]13 Or nation triumphed over

totally destroyed everyone in it. He left no survivors. And he did to the king of Makkedah as he had done to the king of Jericho.

Southern Cities Conquered

29Then Joshua and all Israel with him moved on from Makkedah to Libnah and attacked it. 30The LORD also gave that city and its king into Israel's hand. The city and everyone in it Joshua put to the sword. He left no survivors there. And he did to its king as he had done to the king of Jericho.

31Then Joshua and all Israel with him moved on from Libnah to Lachish; he took up positions against it and attacked it. 32The LORD handed Lachish over to Israel, and Joshua took it on the second day. The city and everyone in it he put to the sword, just as he had done to Libnah. 33Meanwhile, Horam king of Gezer had come up to help Lachish, but Joshua defeated him and his army — until no survivors were left.

34Then Joshua and all Israel with him moved on from Lachish to Eglon; they took up positions against it and attacked it. 35They captured it that same day and put it to the sword and totally destroyed everyone in it, just as they had done to Lachish.

36Then Joshua and all Israel with him went up from Eglon to Hebron and attacked it. 37They took the city and put it to the sword, together with its king, its villages and everyone in it. They left no survivors. Just as at Eglon, they totally destroyed it and everyone in it.

38Then Joshua and all Israel with him turned around and attacked Debir. 39They took the city, its king and its villages, and put them to the sword. Everyone in it they totally destroyed. They left no survivors. They did to Debir and its king as they had done to Libnah and its king and to Hebron.

40So Joshua subdued the whole region, including the hill country, the Negev, the western foothills and the mountain slopes, together with all their kings. He left no survivors. He totally destroyed all who breathed, just as the LORD, the God of Israel, had commanded. 41Joshua subdued them from Kadesh Barnea to Gaza and from the whole region of Goshen to Gibeon. 42All these kings and their lands Joshua conquered in one campaign, because the LORD, the God of Israel, fought for Israel.

43Then Joshua returned with all Israel to the camp at Gilgal.

Northern Kings Defeated

11 When Jabin king of Hazor heard of this, he sent word to Jobab king of Madon, to the kings of Shimron and Acshaph, 2and to the northern kings who were in the mountains, in the Arabah south of Kinnereth, in the western foothills and in Naphoth Dora on the west; 3to the Canaanites in the east and west; to the Amorites, Hittites, Perizzites and Jebusites in the hill country; and to the Hivites below Hermon in the region of Mizpah. 4They came out with all their troops and a large number of horses and chariots — a huge army, as numerous as the sand on the seashore. 5All these kings joined forces and made camp together at the Waters of Merom, to fight against Israel.

6The LORD said to Joshua, "Do not be afraid of them, because by this time tomorrow I will hand all of them over to Israel, slain. You are to hamstring their horses and burn their chariots."

7So Joshua and his whole army came against them suddenly at the Waters of Merom and attacked them, 8and the LORD gave them into the hand of Israel. They defeated them and pursued them all the way to Greater Sidon, to Misrephoth Maim, and to the Valley of Mizpah on the east, until no survivors were left. 9Joshua did to them as the LORD had directed: He hamstrung their horses and burned their chariots.

10At that time Joshua turned back and captured Hazor and put its king to the sword. (Hazor had been the head of all these kingdoms.) 11Everyone in it they put to the sword. They totally destroyedb them, not sparing anything that breathed, and he burned up Hazor itself.

12Joshua took all these royal cities and their kings and put them to the sword. He totally destroyed them, as Moses the servant of the LORD had commanded. 13Yet Israel did not burn any of the cities built on their mounds — except Hazor, which Joshua burned. 14The Israelites carried off for themselves all the plunder and livestock of these cities, but all the people

---

a2 Or *in the heights of Dor*   b11 The Hebrew term refers to the irrevocable giving over of things or persons to the LORD, often by totally destroying them; also in verses 12, 20 and 21.

they put to the sword until they completely destroyed them, not sparing anyone that breathed. [15]As the LORD commanded his servant Moses, so Moses commanded Joshua, and Joshua did it; he left nothing undone of all that the LORD commanded Moses.

[16]So Joshua took this entire land: the hill country, all the Negev, the whole region of Goshen, the western foothills, the Arabah and the mountains of Israel with their foothills, [17]from Mount Halak, which rises toward Seir, to Baal Gad in the Valley of Lebanon below Mount Hermon. He captured all their kings and struck them down, putting them to death. [18]Joshua waged war against all these kings for a long time. [19]Except for the Hivites living in Gibeon, not one city made a treaty of peace with the Israelites, who took them all in battle. [20]For it was the LORD himself who hardened their hearts to wage war against Israel, so that he might destroy them totally, exterminating them without mercy, as the LORD had commanded Moses.

[21]At that time Joshua went and destroyed the Anakites from the hill country: from Hebron, Debir and Anab, from all the hill country of Judah, and from all the hill country of Israel. Joshua totally destroyed them and their towns. [22]No Anakites were left in Israelite territory; only in Gaza, Gath and Ashdod did any survive. [23]So Joshua took the entire land, just as the LORD had directed Moses, and he gave it as an inheritance to Israel according to their tribal divisions.

Then the land had rest from war.

List of Defeated Kings

12 These are the kings of the land whom the Israelites had defeated and whose territory they took over east of the Jordan, from the Arnon Gorge to Mount Hermon, including all the eastern side of the Arabah:

[2]Sihon king of the Amorites,
who reigned in Heshbon. He ruled from Aroer on the rim of the Arnon Gorge — from the middle of the gorge — to the Jabbok River, which is the border of the Ammonites. This included half of Gilead. [3]He also ruled over the eastern Arabah from the Sea of Kinnereth[a] to the Sea of the Arabah (the Salt Sea[b]), to Beth Jeshi-

moth, and then southward below the slopes of Pisgah.

[4]And the territory of Og king of Bashan, one of the last of the Rephaites, who reigned in Ashtaroth and Edrei. [5]He ruled over Mount Hermon, Salecah, all of Bashan to the border of the people of Geshur and Maacah, and half of Gilead to the border of Sihon king of Heshbon.

[6]Moses, the servant of the LORD, and the Israelites conquered them. And Moses the servant of the LORD gave their land to the Reubenites, the Gadites and the half-tribe of Manasseh to be their possession.

[7]These are the kings of the land that Joshua and the Israelites conquered on the west side of the Jordan, from Baal Gad in the Valley of Lebanon to Mount Halak, which rises toward Seir (their lands Joshua gave as an inheritance to the tribes of Israel according to their tribal divisions — [8]the hill country, the western foothills, the Arabah, the mountain slopes, the desert and the Negev — the lands of the Hittites, Amorites, Canaanites, Perizzites, Hivites and Jebusites):

[9]the king of Jericho	one
the king of Ai (near Bethel)	one
[10]the king of Jerusalem	one
the king of Hebron	one
[11]the king of Jarmuth	one
the king of Lachish	one
[12]the king of Eglon	one
the king of Gezer	one
[13]the king of Debir	one
the king of Geder	one
[14]the king of Hormah	one
the king of Arad	one
[15]the king of Libnah	one
the king of Adullam	one
[16]the king of Makkedah	one
the king of Bethel	one
[17]the king of Tappuah	one
the king of Hepher	one
[18]the king of Aphek	one
the king of Lasharon	one
[19]the king of Madon	one
the king of Hazor	one
[20]the king of Shimron Meron	one
the king of Acshaph	one
[21]the king of Taanach	one
the king of Megiddo	one
[22]the king of Kedesh	one
the king of Jokneam in Carmel	one

---

[a]3 That is, Galilee   [b]3 That is, the Dead Sea

23the king of Dor (in Naphoth Dor*a*) — one
the king of Goyim in Gilgal — one
24the king of Tirzah — one
thirty-one kings in all.

Land Still to Be Taken

13 When Joshua was old and well advanced in years, the LORD said to him, "You are very old, and there are still very large areas of land to be taken over.

2"This is the land that remains: all the regions of the Philistines and Geshurites: **3**from the Shihor River on the east of Egypt to the territory of Ekron on the north, all of it counted as Canaanite (the territory of the five Philistine rulers in Gaza, Ashdod, Ashkelon, Gath and Ekron—that of the Avvites); **4**from the south, all the land of the Canaanites, from Arah of the Sidonians as far as Aphek, the region of the Amorites, **5**the area of the Gebalites*b*; and all Lebanon to the east, from Baal Gad below Mount Hermon to Lebo*c* Hamath.

6"As for all the inhabitants of the mountain regions from Lebanon to Misrephoth Maim, that is, all the Sidonians, I myself will drive them out before the Israelites. Be sure to allocate this land to Israel for an inheritance, as I have instructed you, **7**and divide it as an inheritance among the nine tribes and half of the tribe of Manasseh."

Division of the Land East of the Jordan

8The other half of Manasseh,*d* the Reubenites and the Gadites had received the inheritance that Moses had given them east of the Jordan, as he, the servant of the LORD, had assigned it to them.

9It extended from Aroer on the rim of the Arnon Gorge, and from the town in the middle of the gorge, and included the whole plateau of Medeba as far as Dibon, **10**and all the towns of Sihon king of the Amorites, who ruled in Heshbon, out to the border of the Ammonites. **11**It also included Gilead, the territory of the people of Geshur and Maacah, all of Mount Hermon and all Bashan as far as Salecah— **12**that is, the whole kingdom of Og in Bashan, who had reigned in Ashtaroth and Edrei and had survived as one of the last of the Rephaites. Moses had defeated them and taken over their land. **13**But the Israelites did not drive out the people of Geshur and Maacah, so they continue to live among the Israelites to this day.

14But to the tribe of Levi he gave no inheritance, since the offerings made by fire to the LORD, the God of Israel, are their inheritance, as he promised them.

15This is what Moses had given to the tribe of Reuben, clan by clan:

16The territory from Aroer on the rim of the Arnon Gorge, and from the town in the middle of the gorge, and the whole plateau past Medeba **17**to Heshbon and all its towns on the plateau, including Dibon, Bamoth Baal, Beth Baal Meon, **18**Jahaz, Kedemoth, Mephaath, **19**Kiriathaim, Sibmah, Zereth Shahar on the hill in the valley, **20**Beth Peor, the slopes of Pisgah, and Beth Jeshimoth **21**— all the towns on the plateau and the entire realm of Sihon king of the Amorites, who ruled at Heshbon. Moses had defeated him and the Midianite chiefs, Evi, Rekem, Zur, Hur and Reba—princes allied with Sihon—who lived in that country. **22**In addition to those slain in battle, the Israelites had put to the sword Balaam son of Beor, who practiced divination. **23**The boundary of the Reubenites was the bank of the Jordan. These towns and their villages were the inheritance of the Reubenites, clan by clan.

24This is what Moses had given to the tribe of Gad, clan by clan:

25The territory of Jazer, all the towns of Gilead and half the Ammonite country as far as Aroer, near Rabbah; **26**and from Heshbon to Ramath Mizpah and Betonim, and from Mahanaim to the territory of Debir; **27**and in the valley, Beth Haram, Beth Nimrah, Succoth and Zaphon with the rest of the realm of Sihon king of Heshbon (the east side of the Jordan, the territory up to the end of the Sea of Kinnereth*e*). **28**These towns and their vil-

---

*a*23 Or *in the heights of Dor*   *b*5 That is, the area of Byblos   *c*5 Or *to the entrance to*   *d*8 Hebrew
With it (that is, with the other half of Manasseh)   *e*27 That is, Galilee

lages were the inheritance of the Gadites, clan by clan.

29This is what Moses had given to the half-tribe of Manasseh, that is, to half the family of the descendants of Manasseh, clan by clan:

30The territory extending from Mahanaim and including all of Bashan, the entire realm of Og king of Bashan — all the settlements of Jair in Bashan, sixty towns, 31half of Gilead, and Ashtaroth and Edrei (the royal cities of Og in Bashan). This was for the descendants of Makir son of Manasseh — for half of the sons of Makir, clan by clan.

32This is the inheritance Moses had given when he was in the plains of Moab across the Jordan east of Jericho. 33But to the tribe of Levi, Moses had given no inheritance; the Lord, the God of Israel, is their inheritance, as he promised them.

Division of the Land West of the Jordan

14 Now these are the areas the Israelites received as an inheritance in the land of Canaan, which Eleazar the priest, Joshua son of Nun and the heads of the tribal clans of Israel allotted to them. 2Their inheritances were assigned by lot to the nine-and-a-half tribes, as the Lord had commanded through Moses. 3Moses had granted the two-and-a-half tribes their inheritance east of the Jordan but had not granted the Levites an inheritance among the rest, 4for the sons of Joseph had become two tribes — Manasseh and Ephraim. The Levites received no share of the land but only towns to live in, with pasturelands for their flocks and herds. 5So the Israelites divided the land, just as the Lord had commanded Moses.

Hebron Given to Caleb

6Now the men of Judah approached Joshua at Gilgal, and Caleb son of Jephunneh the Kenizzite said to him, "You know what the Lord said to Moses the man of God at Kadesh Barnea about you and me. 7I was forty years old when Moses the servant of the Lord sent me from Kadesh Barnea to explore the land. And I brought him back a report according to my convictions, 8but my brothers who went up with me made the hearts of the people melt

with fear. I, however, followed the Lord my God wholeheartedly. 9So on that day Moses swore to me, 'The land on which your feet have walked will be your inheritance and that of your children forever, because you have followed the Lord my God wholeheartedly.'*a*

10"Now then, just as the Lord promised, he has kept me alive for forty-five years since the time he said this to Moses, while Israel moved about in the desert. So here I am today, eighty-five years old! 11I am still as strong today as the day Moses sent me out; I'm just as vigorous to go out to battle now as I was then. 12Now give me this hill country that the Lord promised me that day. You yourself heard then that the Anakites were there and their cities were large and fortified, but, the Lord helping me, I will drive them out just as he said."

13Then Joshua blessed Caleb son of Jephunneh and gave him Hebron as his inheritance. 14So Hebron has belonged to Caleb son of Jephunneh the Kenizzite ever since, because he followed the Lord, the God of Israel, wholeheartedly. 15(Hebron used to be called Kiriath Arba after Arba, who was the greatest man among the Anakites.)

Then the land had rest from war.

Allotment for Judah

15 The allotment for the tribe of Judah, clan by clan, extended down to the territory of Edom, to the Desert of Zin in the extreme south.

2Their southern boundary started from the bay at the southern end of the Salt Sea,*b* 3crossed south of Scorpion*c* Pass, continued on to Zin and went over to the south of Kadesh Barnea. Then it ran past Hezron up to Addar and curved around to Karka. 4It then passed along to Azmon and joined the Wadi of Egypt, ending at the sea. This is their*d* southern boundary.

5The eastern boundary is the Salt Sea as far as the mouth of the Jordan.

The northern boundary started from the bay of the sea at the mouth of the Jordan, 6went up to Beth Hoglah and continued north of Beth Arabah to the Stone of Bohan son of Reuben. 7The boundary then went up to Debir from the Valley of Achor and turned north to Gilgal, which faces

---

*a*9 Deut. 1:36   *b*2 That is, the Dead Sea; also in verse 5   *c*3 Hebrew *Akrabbim*   *d*4 Hebrew *your* the Pass of Adummim south of the gorge. It continued along to the waters of En Shemesh and came out at En Rogel. ⁸Then it ran up the Valley of Ben Hinnom along the southern slope of the Jebusite city (that is, Jerusalem). From there it climbed to the top of the hill west of the Hinnom Valley at the northern end of the Valley of Rephaim. ⁹From the hilltop the boundary headed toward the spring of the waters of Nephtoah, came out at the towns of Mount Ephron and went down toward Baalah (that is, Kiriath Jearim). ¹⁰Then it curved westward from Baalah to Mount Seir, ran along the northern slope of Mount Jearim (that is, Kesalon), continued down to Beth Shemesh and crossed to Timnah. ¹¹It went to the northern slope of Ekron, turned toward Shikkeron, passed along to Mount Baalah and reached Jabneel. The boundary ended at the sea.

¹²The western boundary is the coastline of the Great Sea.ᵃ These are the boundaries around the people of Judah by their clans.

¹³In accordance with the Lord's command to him, Joshua gave to Caleb son of Jephunneh a portion in Judah—Kiriath Arba, that is, Hebron. (Arba was the forefather of Anak.) ¹⁴From Hebron Caleb drove out the three Anakites—Sheshai, Ahiman and Talmai—descendants of Anak. ¹⁵From there he marched against the people living in Debir (formerly called Kiriath Sepher). ¹⁶And Caleb said, "I will give my daughter Acsah in marriage to the man who attacks and captures Kiriath Sepher." ¹⁷Othniel son of Kenaz, Caleb's brother, took it; so Caleb gave his daughter Acsah to him in marriage.

¹⁸One day when she came to Othniel, she urged himᵇ to ask her father for a field. When she got off her donkey, Caleb asked her, "What can I do for you?"

¹⁹She replied, "Do me a special favor. Since you have given me land in the Negev, give me also springs of water." So Caleb gave her the upper and lower springs.

²⁰This is the inheritance of the tribe of Judah, clan by clan:

²¹The southernmost towns of the tribe of Judah in the Negev toward the boundary of Edom were:

Kabzeel, Eder, Jagur, ²²Kinah, Dimonah, Adadah, ²³Kedesh, Hazor, Ithnan, ²⁴Ziph, Telem, Bealoth, ²⁵Hazor Hadattah, Kerioth Hezron (that is, Hazor), ²⁶Amam, Shema, Moladah, ²⁷Hazar Gaddah, Heshmon, Beth Pelet, ²⁸Hazar Shual, Beersheba, Biziothiah, ²⁹Baalah, Iim, Ezem, ³⁰Eltolad, Kesil, Hormah, ³¹Ziklag, Madmannah, Sansannah, ³²Lebaoth, Shilhim, Ain and Rimmon—a total of twenty-nine towns and their villages.

³³In the western foothills:

Eshtaol, Zorah, Ashnah, ³⁴Zanoah, En Gannim, Tappuah, Enam, ³⁵Jarmuth, Adullam, Socoh, Azekah, ³⁶Shaaraim, Adithaim and Gederah (or Gederothaim)ᶜ—fourteen towns and their villages.

³⁷Zenan, Hadashah, Migdal Gad, ³⁸Dilean, Mizpah, Joktheel, ³⁹Lachish, Bozkath, Eglon, ⁴⁰Cabbon, Lahmas, Kitlish, ⁴¹Gederoth, Beth Dagon, Naamah and Makkedah—sixteen towns and their villages.

⁴²Libnah, Ether, Ashan, ⁴³Iphtah, Ashnah, Nezib, ⁴⁴Keilah, Aczib and Mareshah—nine towns and their villages.

⁴⁵Ekron, with its surrounding settlements and villages; ⁴⁶west of Ekron, all that were in the vicinity of Ashdod, together with their villages; ⁴⁷Ashdod, its surrounding settlements and villages; and Gaza, its settlements and villages, as far as the Wadi of Egypt and the coastline of the Great Sea.

⁴⁸In the hill country:

Shamir, Jattir, Socoh, ⁴⁹Dannah, Kiriath Sannah (that is, Debir), ⁵⁰Anab, Eshtemoh, Anim, ⁵¹Goshen, Holon and Giloh—eleven towns and their villages.

⁵²Arab, Dumah, Eshan, ⁵³Janim, Beth Tappuah, Aphekah, ⁵⁴Humtah, Kiriath Arba (that is, Hebron) and Zior—nine towns and their villages.

⁵⁵Maon, Carmel, Ziph, Juttah, ⁵⁶Jezreel, Jokdeam, Zanoah, ⁵⁷Kain, Gibeah and Timnah—ten towns and their villages.

⁵⁸Halhul, Beth Zur, Gedor, ⁵⁹Maa-

ᵃ12 That is, the Mediterranean; also in verse 47   ᵇ18 Hebrew and some Septuagint manuscripts; other Septuagint manuscripts (see also note at Judges 1:14) *Othniel, he urged her*   ᶜ36 Or *Gederah and Gederothaim* rath, Beth Anoth and Eltekon—six towns and their villages.

⁶⁰Kiriath Baal (that is, Kiriath Jearim) and Rabbah—two towns and their villages.

⁶¹In the desert:

Beth Arabah, Middin, Secacah, ⁶²Nibshan, the City of Salt and En Gedi—six towns and their villages.

⁶³Judah could not dislodge the Jebusites, who were living in Jerusalem; to this day the Jebusites live there with the people of Judah.

Allotment for Ephraim and Manasseh

16 The allotment for Joseph began at the Jordan of Jericho,ᵃ east of the waters of Jericho, and went up from there through the desert into the hill country of Bethel. ²It went on from Bethel (that is, Luz),ᵇ crossed over to the territory of the Arkites in Ataroth, ³descended westward to the territory of the Japhletites as far as the region of Lower Beth Horon and on to Gezer, ending at the sea.

⁴So Manasseh and Ephraim, the descendants of Joseph, received their inheritance.

⁵This was the territory of Ephraim, clan by clan:

The boundary of their inheritance went from Ataroth Addar in the east to Upper Beth Horon ⁶and continued to the sea. From Micmethath on the north it curved eastward to Taanath Shiloh, passing by it to Janoah on the east. ⁷Then it went down from Janoah to Ataroth and Naarah, touched Jericho and came out at the Jordan. ⁸From Tappuah the border went west to the Kanah Ravine and ended at the sea. This was the inheritance of the tribe of the Ephraimites, clan by clan. ⁹It also included all the towns and their villages that were set aside for the Ephraimites within the inheritance of the Manassites.

¹⁰They did not dislodge the Canaanites living in Gezer; to this day the Canaanites live among the people of Ephraim but are required to do forced labor.

17 This was the allotment for the tribe of Manasseh as Joseph's firstborn,

that is, for Makir, Manasseh's firstborn. Makir was the ancestor of the Gileadites, who had received Gilead and Bashan because the Makirites were great soldiers. ²So this allotment was for the rest of the people of Manasseh—the clans of Abiezer, Helek, Asriel, Shechem, Hepher and Shemida. These are the other male descendants of Manasseh son of Joseph by their clans.

³Now Zelophehad son of Hepher, the son of Gilead, the son of Makir, the son of Manasseh, had no sons but only daughters, whose names were Mahlah, Noah, Hoglah, Milcah and Tirzah. ⁴They went to Eleazar the priest, Joshua son of Nun, and the leaders and said, "The LORD commanded Moses to give us an inheritance among our brothers." So Joshua gave them an inheritance along with the brothers of their father, according to the LORD's command. ⁵Manasseh's share consisted of ten tracts of land besides Gilead and Bashan east of the Jordan, ⁶because the daughters of the tribe of Manasseh received an inheritance among the sons. The land of Gilead belonged to the rest of the descendants of Manasseh.

⁷The territory of Manasseh extended from Asher to Micmethath east of Shechem. The boundary ran southward from there to include the people living at En Tappuah. ⁸(Manasseh had the land of Tappuah, but Tappuah itself, on the boundary of Manasseh, belonged to the Ephraimites.) ⁹Then the boundary continued south to the Kanah Ravine. There were towns belonging to Ephraim lying among the towns of Manasseh, but the boundary of Manasseh was the northern side of the ravine and ended at the sea. ¹⁰On the south the land belonged to Ephraim, on the north to Manasseh. The territory of Manasseh reached the sea and bordered Asher on the north and Issachar on the east. ¹¹Within Issachar and Asher, Manasseh also had Beth Shan, Ibleam and the people of Dor, Endor, Taanach and Megiddo, together with their surrounding settlements (the third in the list is Naphothᶜ). ¹²Yet the Manassites were not able to occupy these towns, for the Canaanites were determined to live in that region. ¹³However, when the Israelites grew stronger,

---

ᵃ1 *Jordan of Jericho* was possibly an ancient name for the Jordan River.   ᵇ2 Septuagint; Hebrew *Bethel to Luz*   ᶜ11 That is, Naphoth Dor they subjected the Canaanites to forced labor but did not drive them out completely.

[14]The people of Joseph said to Joshua, "Why have you given us only one allotment and one portion for an inheritance? We are a numerous people and the LORD has blessed us abundantly."

[15]"If you are so numerous," Joshua answered, "and if the hill country of Ephraim is too small for you, go up into the forest and clear land for yourselves there in the land of the Perizzites and Rephaites."

[16]The people of Joseph replied, "The hill country is not enough for us, and all the Canaanites who live in the plain have iron chariots, both those in Beth Shan and its settlements and those in the Valley of Jezreel."

[17]But Joshua said to the house of Joseph—to Ephraim and Manasseh—"You are numerous and very powerful. You will have not only one allotment [18]but the forested hill country as well. Clear it, and its farthest limits will be yours; though the Canaanites have iron chariots and though they are strong, you can drive them out."

Division of the Rest of the Land

18 The whole assembly of the Israelites gathered at Shiloh and set up the Tent of Meeting there. The country was brought under their control, [2]but there were still seven Israelite tribes who had not yet received their inheritance.

[3]So Joshua said to the Israelites: "How long will you wait before you begin to take possession of the land that the LORD, the God of your fathers, has given you? [4]Appoint three men from each tribe. I will send them out to make a survey of the land and to write a description of it, according to the inheritance of each. Then they will return to me. [5]You are to divide the land into seven parts. Judah is to remain in its territory on the south and the house of Joseph in its territory on the north. [6]After you have written descriptions of the seven parts of the land, bring them here to me and I will cast lots for you in the presence of the LORD our God. [7]The Levites, however, do not get a portion among you, because the priestly service of the LORD is their inheritance. And Gad, Reuben and the half-tribe of Manasseh have already received their inheritance on the east side of the Jordan. Moses the servant of the LORD gave it to them."

[8]As the men started on their way to map out the land, Joshua instructed them, "Go and make a survey of the land and write a description of it. Then return to me, and I will cast lots for you here at Shiloh in the presence of the LORD." [9]So the men left and went through the land. They wrote its description on a scroll, town by town, in seven parts, and returned to Joshua in the camp at Shiloh. [10]Joshua then cast lots for them in Shiloh in the presence of the LORD, and there he distributed the land to the Israelites according to their tribal divisions.

Allotment for Benjamin

[11]The lot came up for the tribe of Benjamin, clan by clan. Their allotted territory lay between the tribes of Judah and Joseph:

[12]On the north side their boundary began at the Jordan, passed the northern slope of Jericho and headed west into the hill country, coming out at the desert of Beth Aven. [13]From there it crossed to the south slope of Luz (that is, Bethel) and went down to Ataroth Addar on the hill south of Lower Beth Horon.

[14]From the hill facing Beth Horon on the south the boundary turned south along the western side and came out at Kiriath Baal (that is, Kiriath Jearim), a town of the people of Judah. This was the western side.

[15]The southern side began at the outskirts of Kiriath Jearim on the west, and the boundary came out at the spring of the waters of Nephtoah. [16]The boundary went down to the foot of the hill facing the Valley of Ben Hinnom, north of the Valley of Rephaim. It continued down the Hinnom Valley along the southern slope of the Jebusite city and so to En Rogel. [17]It then curved north, went to En Shemesh, continued to Geliloth, which faces the Pass of Adummim, and ran down to the Stone of Bohan son of Reuben. [18]It continued to the northern slope of Beth Arabah[a] and on down into the Arabah. [19]It then went to the northern slope of Beth Hoglah and came out at the northern bay of the Salt Sea,[b] at the mouth of the Jordan in the south. This was the southern boundary.

[20]The Jordan formed the boundary on the eastern side.

[a]18 Septuagint; Hebrew *slope facing the Arabah*   [b]19 That is, the Dead Sea

These were the boundaries that marked out the inheritance of the clans of Benjamin on all sides.

21The tribe of Benjamin, clan by clan, had the following cities:

Jericho, Beth Hoglah, Emek Keziz, 22Beth Arabah, Zemaraim, Bethel, 23Avvim, Parah, Ophrah, 24Kephar Ammoni, Ophni and Geba — twelve towns and their villages.

25Gibeon, Ramah, Beeroth, 26Mizpah, Kephirah, Mozah, 27Rekem, Irpeel, Taralah, 28Zelah, Haeleph, the Jebusite city (that is, Jerusalem), Gibeah and Kiriath — fourteen towns and their villages.

This was the inheritance of Benjamin for its clans.

Allotment for Simeon

19 The second lot came out for the tribe of Simeon, clan by clan. Their inheritance lay within the territory of Judah. 2It included:

Beersheba (or Sheba),ᵃ Moladah, 3Hazar Shual, Balah, Ezem, 4Eltolad, Bethul, Hormah, 5Ziklag, Beth Marcaboth, Hazar Susah, 6Beth Lebaoth and Sharuhen — thirteen towns and their villages;

7Ain, Rimmon, Ether and Ashan — four towns and their villages — 8and all the villages around these towns as far as Baalath Beer (Ramah in the Negev).

This was the inheritance of the tribe of the Simeonites, clan by clan. 9The inheritance of the Simeonites was taken from the share of Judah, because Judah's portion was more than they needed. So the Simeonites received their inheritance within the territory of Judah.

Allotment for Zebulun

10The third lot came up for Zebulun, clan by clan:

The boundary of their inheritance went as far as Sarid. 11Going west it ran to Maralah, touched Dabbesheth, and extended to the ravine near Jokneam. 12It turned east from Sarid toward the sunrise to the territory of Kisloth Tabor and went on to Daberath and up to Japhia. 13Then it continued eastward to Gath Hepher and Eth Kazin; it came out at Rimmon and turned toward Neah. 14There the boundary went around on the north to Hannathon and ended at the Valley of Iphtah El. 15Included were Kattath, Nahalal, Shimron, Idalah and Bethlehem. There were twelve towns and their villages.

16These towns and their villages were the inheritance of Zebulun, clan by clan.

Allotment for Issachar

17The fourth lot came out for Issachar, clan by clan. 18Their territory included:

Jezreel, Kesulloth, Shunem, 19Hapharaim, Shion, Anaharath, 20Rabbith, Kishion, Ebez, 21Remeth, En Gannim, En Haddah and Beth Pazzez. 22The boundary touched Tabor, Shahazumah and Beth Shemesh, and ended at the Jordan. There were sixteen towns and their villages.

23These towns and their villages were the inheritance of the tribe of Issachar, clan by clan.

Allotment for Asher

24The fifth lot came out for the tribe of Asher, clan by clan. 25Their territory included:

Helkath, Hali, Beten, Acshaph, 26Allammelech, Amad and Mishal. On the west the boundary touched Carmel and Shihor Libnath. 27It then turned east toward Beth Dagon, touched Zebulun and the Valley of Iphtah El, and went north to Beth Emek and Neiel, passing Cabul on the left. 28It went to Abdon,ᵇ Rehob, Hammon and Kanah, as far as Greater Sidon. 29The boundary then turned back toward Ramah and went to the fortified city of Tyre, turned toward Hosah and came out at the sea in the region of Aczib, 30Ummah, Aphek and Rehob. There were twenty-two towns and their villages.

31These towns and their villages were the inheritance of the tribe of Asher, clan by clan.

Allotment for Naphtali

32The sixth lot came out for Naphtali, clan by clan:

33Their boundary went from Heleph and the large tree in Zaanannim, passing Adami Nekeb and Jabneel to Lakkum and ending at the Jordan.

ᵃ2 Or *Beersheba, Sheba*; 1 Chron. 4:28 does not have *Sheba*.　　ᵇ28 Some Hebrew manuscripts (see also Joshua 21:30); most Hebrew manuscripts *Ebron*

34The boundary ran west through Aznoth Tabor and came out at Hukkok. It touched Zebulun on the south, Asher on the west and the Jordan*a* on the east. **35**The fortified cities were Ziddim, Zer, Hammath, Rakkath, Kinnereth, **36**Adamah, Ramah, Hazor, **37**Kedesh, Edrei, En Hazor, **38**Iron, Migdal El, Horem, Beth Anath and Beth Shemesh. There were nineteen towns and their villages.

39These towns and their villages were the inheritance of the tribe of Naphtali, clan by clan.

Allotment for Dan

40The seventh lot came out for the tribe of Dan, clan by clan. **41**The territory of their inheritance included:

Zorah, Eshtaol, Ir Shemesh, **42**Shaalabbin, Aijalon, Ithlah, **43**Elon, Timnah, Ekron, **44**Eltekeh, Gibbethon, Baalath, **45**Jehud, Bene Berak, Gath Rimmon, **46**Me Jarkon and Rakkon, with the area facing Joppa.

47(But the Danites had difficulty taking possession of their territory, so they went up and attacked Leshem, took it, put it to the sword and occupied it. They settled in Leshem and named it Dan after their forefather.)

48These towns and their villages were the inheritance of the tribe of Dan, clan by clan.

Allotment for Joshua

49When they had finished dividing the land into its allotted portions, the Israelites gave Joshua son of Nun an inheritance among them, **50**as the LORD had commanded. They gave him the town he asked for—Timnath Serah*b* in the hill country of Ephraim. And he built up the town and settled there.

51These are the territories that Eleazar the priest, Joshua son of Nun and the heads of the tribal clans of Israel assigned by lot at Shiloh in the presence of the LORD at the entrance to the Tent of Meeting. And so they finished dividing the land.

Cities of Refuge

20 Then the LORD said to Joshua: **2**"Tell the Israelites to designate the cities of refuge, as I instructed you through Moses, **3**so that anyone who kills a person accidentally and unintentionally may flee there and find protection from the avenger of blood.

4"When he flees to one of these cities, he is to stand in the entrance of the city gate and state his case before the elders of that city. Then they are to admit him into their city and give him a place to live with them. **5**If the avenger of blood pursues him, they must not surrender the one accused, because he killed his neighbor unintentionally and without malice aforethought. **6**He is to stay in that city until he has stood trial before the assembly and until the death of the high priest who is serving at that time. Then he may go back to his own home in the town from which he fled."

7So they set apart Kedesh in Galilee in the hill country of Naphtali, Shechem in the hill country of Ephraim, and Kiriath Arba (that is, Hebron) in the hill country of Judah. **8**On the east side of the Jordan of Jericho*c* they designated Bezer in the desert on the plateau in the tribe of Reuben, Ramoth in Gilead in the tribe of Gad, and Golan in Bashan in the tribe of Manasseh. **9**Any of the Israelites or any alien living among them who killed someone accidentally could flee to these designated cities and not be killed by the avenger of blood prior to standing trial before the assembly.

Towns for the Levites

21 Now the family heads of the Levites approached Eleazar the priest, Joshua son of Nun, and the heads of the other tribal families of Israel **2**at Shiloh in Canaan and said to them, "The LORD commanded through Moses that you give us towns to live in, with pasturelands for our livestock." **3**So, as the LORD had commanded, the Israelites gave the Levites the following towns and pasturelands out of their own inheritance:

4The first lot came out for the Kohathites, clan by clan. The Levites who were descendants of Aaron the priest were allotted thirteen towns from the tribes of Judah, Simeon and Benjamin. **5**The rest of Kohath's descendants were allotted ten towns from the clans of the tribes of Ephraim, Dan and half of Manasseh.

6The descendants of Gershon were allotted thirteen towns from the clans of the tribes of Issachar, Asher, Naphtali and the half-tribe of Manasseh in Bashan.

---

a34 Septuagint; Hebrew *west, and Judah, the Jordan,* 2:9)   *c8 Jordan of Jericho* was possibly an ancient name for the Jordan River.   *b50* Also known as *Timnath Heres* (see Judges

7The descendants of Merari, clan by clan, received twelve towns from the tribes of Reuben, Gad and Zebulun.

8So the Israelites allotted to the Levites these towns and their pasturelands, as the LORD had commanded through Moses.

9From the tribes of Judah and Simeon they allotted the following towns by name **10**(these towns were assigned to the descendants of Aaron who were from the Kohathite clans of the Levites, because the first lot fell to them):

11They gave them Kiriath Arba (that is, Hebron), with its surrounding pastureland, in the hill country of Judah. (Arba was the forefather of Anak.) **12**But the fields and villages around the city they had given to Caleb son of Jephunneh as his possession.

13So to the descendants of Aaron the priest they gave Hebron (a city of refuge for one accused of murder), Libnah, **14**Jattir, Eshtemoa, **15**Holon, Debir, **16**Ain, Juttah and Beth Shemesh, together with their pasturelands — nine towns from these two tribes.

17And from the tribe of Benjamin they gave them Gibeon, Geba, **18**Anathoth and Almon, together with their pasturelands — four towns.

19All the towns for the priests, the descendants of Aaron, were thirteen, together with their pasturelands.

20The rest of the Kohathite clans of the Levites were allotted towns from the tribe of Ephraim:

21In the hill country of Ephraim they were given Shechem (a city of refuge for one accused of murder) and Gezer, **22**Kibzaim and Beth Horon, together with their pasturelands — four towns.

23Also from the tribe of Dan they received Eltekeh, Gibbethon, **24**Aijalon and Gath Rimmon, together with their pasturelands — four towns.

25From half the tribe of Manasseh they received Taanach and Gath Rimmon, together with their pasturelands — two towns.

26All these ten towns and their pasturelands were given to the rest of the Kohathite clans.

27The Levite clans of the Gershonites were given:

from the half-tribe of Manasseh,

Golan in Bashan (a city of refuge for one accused of murder) and Be Eshtarah, together with their pasturelands — two towns;

28from the tribe of Issachar,

Kishion, Daberath, **29**Jarmuth and En Gannim, together with their pasturelands — four towns;

30from the tribe of Asher,

Mishal, Abdon, **31**Helkath and Rehob, together with their pasturelands — four towns;

32from the tribe of Naphtali,

Kedesh in Galilee (a city of refuge for one accused of murder), Hammoth Dor and Kartan, together with their pasturelands — three towns.

33All the towns of the Gershonite clans were thirteen, together with their pasturelands.

34The Merarite clans (the rest of the Levites) were given:

from the tribe of Zebulun,

Jokneam, Kartah, **35**Dimnah and Nahalal, together with their pasturelands — four towns;

36from the tribe of Reuben,

Bezer, Jahaz, **37**Kedemoth and Mephaath, together with their pasturelands — four towns;

38from the tribe of Gad,

Ramoth in Gilead (a city of refuge for one accused of murder), Mahanaim, **39**Heshbon and Jazer, together with their pasturelands — four towns in all.

40All the towns allotted to the Merarite clans, who were the rest of the Levites, were twelve.

41The towns of the Levites in the territory held by the Israelites were forty-eight in all, together with their pasturelands. **42**Each of these towns had pasturelands surrounding it; this was true for all these towns.

43So the LORD gave Israel all the land he had sworn to give their forefathers, and they took possession of it and settled there. **44**The LORD gave them rest on every side, just as he had sworn to their forefathers. Not one of their enemies withstood them; the LORD handed all their enemies over to them. **45**Not one of all the LORD's good promises to the house of Israel failed; every one was fulfilled.

Eastern Tribes Return Home

22 Then Joshua summoned the Reubenites, the Gadites and the half-tribe of Manasseh [2]and said to them, "You have done all that Moses the servant of the LORD commanded, and you have obeyed me in everything I commanded. [3]For a long time now — to this very day — you have not deserted your brothers but have carried out the mission the LORD your God gave you. [4]Now that the LORD your God has given your brothers rest as he promised, return to your homes in the land that Moses the servant of the LORD gave you on the other side of the Jordan. [5]But be very careful to keep the commandment and the law that Moses the servant of the LORD gave you: to love the LORD your God, to walk in all his ways, to obey his commands, to hold fast to him and to serve him with all your heart and all your soul."

[6]Then Joshua blessed them and sent them away, and they went to their homes. [7](To the half-tribe of Manasseh Moses had given land in Bashan, and to the other half of the tribe Joshua gave land on the west side of the Jordan with their brothers.) When Joshua sent them home, he blessed them, [8]saying, "Return to your homes with your great wealth — with large herds of livestock, with silver, gold, bronze and iron, and a great quantity of clothing — and divide with your brothers the plunder from your enemies."

[9]So the Reubenites, the Gadites and the half-tribe of Manasseh left the Israelites at Shiloh in Canaan to return to Gilead, their own land, which they had acquired in accordance with the command of the LORD through Moses.

[10]When they came to Geliloth near the Jordan in the land of Canaan, the Reubenites, the Gadites and the half-tribe of Manasseh built an imposing altar there by the Jordan. [11]And when the Israelites heard that they had built the altar on the border of Canaan at Geliloth near the Jordan on the Israelite side, [12]the whole assembly of Israel gathered at Shiloh to go to war against them.

[13]So the Israelites sent Phinehas son of Eleazar, the priest, to the land of Gilead — to Reuben, Gad and the half-tribe of Manasseh. [14]With him they sent ten of the chief men, one for each of the tribes of Israel, each the head of a family division among the Israelite clans. [15]When they went to Gilead — to Reuben, Gad and the half-tribe of Manasseh —

they said to them: [16]"The whole assembly of the LORD says: 'How could you break faith with the God of Israel like this? How could you turn away from the LORD and build yourselves an altar in rebellion against him now? [17]Was not the sin of Peor enough for us? Up to this very day we have not cleansed ourselves from that sin, even though a plague fell on the community of the LORD! [18]And are you now turning away from the LORD?

" 'If you rebel against the LORD today, tomorrow he will be angry with the whole community of Israel. [19]If the land you possess is defiled, come over to the LORD's land, where the LORD's tabernacle stands, and share the land with us. But do not rebel against the LORD or against us by building an altar for yourselves, other than the altar of the LORD our God. [20]When Achan son of Zerah acted unfaithfully regarding the devoted things,[a] did not wrath come upon the whole community of Israel? He was not the only one who died for his sin.' "

[21]Then Reuben, Gad and the half-tribe of Manasseh replied to the heads of the clans of Israel: [22]"The Mighty One, God, the LORD! The Mighty One, God, the LORD! He knows! And let Israel know! If this has been in rebellion or disobedience to the LORD, do not spare us this day. [23]If we have built our own altar to turn away from the LORD and to offer burnt offerings and grain offerings, or to sacrifice fellowship offerings[b] on it, may the LORD himself call us to account.

[24]"No! We did it for fear that some day your descendants might say to ours, 'What do you have to do with the LORD, the God of Israel? [25]The LORD has made the Jordan a boundary between us and you — you Reubenites and Gadites! You have no share in the LORD.' So your descendants might cause ours to stop fearing the LORD.

[26]"That is why we said, 'Let us get ready and build an altar — but not for burnt offerings or sacrifices.' [27]On the contrary, it is to be a witness between us and you and the generations that follow, that we will worship the LORD at his sanctuary with our burnt offerings, sacrifices and fellowship offerings. Then in the future your descendants will not be able to say to ours, 'You have no share in the LORD.'

[28]"And we said, 'If they ever say this to

---

[a]20 The Hebrew term refers to the irrevocable giving over of things or persons to the LORD, often by totally destroying them.   [b]23 Traditionally *peace offerings*; also in verse 27

us, or to our descendants, we will answer: Look at the replica of the LORD's altar, which our fathers built, not for burnt offerings and sacrifices, but as a witness between us and you.'

²⁹"Far be it from us to rebel against the LORD and turn away from him today by building an altar for burnt offerings, grain offerings and sacrifices, other than the altar of the LORD our God that stands before his tabernacle."

³⁰When Phinehas the priest and the leaders of the community—the heads of the clans of the Israelites—heard what Reuben, Gad and Manasseh had to say, they were pleased. ³¹And Phinehas son of Eleazar, the priest, said to Reuben, Gad and Manasseh, "Today we know that the LORD is with us, because you have not acted unfaithfully toward the LORD in this matter. Now you have rescued the Israelites from the LORD's hand."

³²Then Phinehas son of Eleazar, the priest, and the leaders returned to Canaan from their meeting with the Reubenites and Gadites in Gilead and reported to the Israelites. ³³They were glad to hear the report and praised God. And they talked no more about going to war against them to devastate the country where the Reubenites and the Gadites lived.

³⁴And the Reubenites and the Gadites gave the altar this name: A Witness Between Us that the LORD is God.

Joshua's Farewell to the Leaders

23 After a long time had passed and the LORD had given Israel rest from all their enemies around them, Joshua, by then old and well advanced in years, ²summoned all Israel—their elders, leaders, judges and officials—and said to them: "I am old and well advanced in years. ³You yourselves have seen everything the LORD your God has done to all these nations for your sake; it was the LORD your God who fought for you. ⁴Remember how I have allotted as an inheritance for your tribes all the land of the nations that remain—the nations I conquered—between the Jordan and the Great Sea*a* in the west. ⁵The LORD your God himself will drive them out of your way. He will push them out before you, and you will take possession of their land, as the LORD your God promised you.

⁶"Be very strong; be careful to obey all that is written in the Book of the Law of Moses, without turning aside to the right or to the left. ⁷Do not associate with these nations that remain among you; do not invoke the names of their gods or swear by them. You must not serve them or bow down to them. ⁸But you are to hold fast to the LORD your God, as you have until now.

⁹"The LORD has driven out before you great and powerful nations; to this day no one has been able to withstand you. ¹⁰One of you routs a thousand, because the LORD your God fights for you, just as he promised. ¹¹So be very careful to love the LORD your God.

¹²"But if you turn away and ally yourselves with the survivors of these nations that remain among you and if you intermarry with them and associate with them, ¹³then you may be sure that the LORD your God will no longer drive out these nations before you. Instead, they will become snares and traps for you, whips on your backs and thorns in your eyes, until you perish from this good land, which the LORD your God has given you.

¹⁴"Now I am about to go the way of all the earth. You know with all your heart and soul that not one of all the good promises the LORD your God gave you has failed. Every promise has been fulfilled; not one has failed. ¹⁵But just as every good promise of the LORD your God has come true, so the LORD will bring on you all the evil he has threatened, until he has destroyed you from this good land he has given you. ¹⁶If you violate the covenant of the LORD your God, which he commanded you, and go and serve other gods and bow down to them, the LORD's anger will burn against you, and you will quickly perish from the good land he has given you."

The Covenant Renewed at Shechem

24 Then Joshua assembled all the tribes of Israel at Shechem. He summoned the elders, leaders, judges and officials of Israel, and they presented themselves before God.

²Joshua said to all the people, "This is what the LORD, the God of Israel, says: 'Long ago your forefathers, including Terah the father of Abraham and Nahor, lived beyond the River*b* and worshiped other gods. ³But I took your father Abraham from the land beyond the River and led him throughout Canaan and gave him many descendants. I gave him Isaac, ⁴and to Isaac I gave Jacob and Esau. I assigned

a4 That is, the Mediterranean   *b2* That is, the Euphrates; also in verses 3, 14 and 15 the hill country of Seir to Esau, but Jacob and his sons went down to Egypt.

⁵" 'Then I sent Moses and Aaron, and I afflicted the Egyptians by what I did there, and I brought you out. ⁶When I brought your fathers out of Egypt, you came to the sea, and the Egyptians pursued them with chariots and horsemenᵃ as far as the Red Sea.ᵇ ⁷But they cried to the LORD for help, and he put darkness between you and the Egyptians; he brought the sea over them and covered them. You saw with your own eyes what I did to the Egyptians. Then you lived in the desert for a long time.

⁸" 'I brought you to the land of the Amorites who lived east of the Jordan. They fought against you, but I gave them into your hands. I destroyed them from before you, and you took possession of their land. ⁹When Balak son of Zippor, the king of Moab, prepared to fight against Israel, he sent for Balaam son of Beor to put a curse on you. ¹⁰But I would not listen to Balaam, so he blessed you again and again, and I delivered you out of his hand.

¹¹" 'Then you crossed the Jordan and came to Jericho. The citizens of Jericho fought against you, as did also the Amorites, Perizzites, Canaanites, Hittites, Girgashites, Hivites and Jebusites, but I gave them into your hands. ¹²I sent the hornet ahead of you, which drove them out before you—also the two Amorite kings. You did not do it with your own sword and bow. ¹³So I gave you a land on which you did not toil and cities you did not build; and you live in them and eat from vineyards and olive groves that you did not plant.'

¹⁴"Now fear the LORD and serve him with all faithfulness. Throw away the gods your forefathers worshiped beyond the River and in Egypt, and serve the LORD. ¹⁵But if serving the LORD seems undesirable to you, then choose for yourselves this day whom you will serve, whether the gods your forefathers served beyond the River, or the gods of the Amorites, in whose land you are living. But as for me and my household, we will serve the LORD."

¹⁶Then the people answered, "Far be it from us to forsake the LORD to serve other gods! ¹⁷It was the LORD our God himself who brought us and our fathers up out of Egypt, from that land of slavery, and per-

formed those great signs before our eyes. He protected us on our entire journey and among all the nations through which we traveled. ¹⁸And the LORD drove out before us all the nations, including the Amorites, who lived in the land. We too will serve the LORD, because he is our God."

¹⁹Joshua said to the people, "You are not able to serve the LORD. He is a holy God; he is a jealous God. He will not forgive your rebellion and your sins. ²⁰If you forsake the LORD and serve foreign gods, he will turn and bring disaster on you and make an end of you, after he has been good to you."

²¹But the people said to Joshua, "No! We will serve the LORD."

²²Then Joshua said, "You are witnesses against yourselves that you have chosen to serve the LORD."

"Yes, we are witnesses," they replied.

²³"Now then," said Joshua, "throw away the foreign gods that are among you and yield your hearts to the LORD, the God of Israel."

²⁴And the people said to Joshua, "We will serve the LORD our God and obey him."

²⁵On that day Joshua made a covenant for the people, and there at Shechem he drew up for them decrees and laws. ²⁶And Joshua recorded these things in the Book of the Law of God. Then he took a large stone and set it up there under the oak near the holy place of the LORD.

²⁷"See!" he said to all the people. "This stone will be a witness against us. It has heard all the words the LORD has said to us. It will be a witness against you if you are untrue to your God."

Buried in the Promised Land

²⁸Then Joshua sent the people away, each to his own inheritance.

²⁹After these things, Joshua son of Nun, the servant of the LORD, died at the age of a hundred and ten. ³⁰And they buried him in the land of his inheritance, at Timnath Serahᶜ in the hill country of Ephraim, north of Mount Gaash.

³¹Israel served the LORD throughout the lifetime of Joshua and of the elders who outlived him and who had experienced everything the LORD had done for Israel.

³²And Joseph's bones, which the Israelites had brought up from Egypt, were buried at Shechem in the tract of land that Ja-

ᵃ6 Or charioteers   ᵇ6 Hebrew Yam Suph; that is, Sea of Reeds   ᶜ30 Also known as Timnath Heres
(see Judges 2:9)

THURSDAY

VERSE FOR THE DAY:
Joshua 24:15

AUTHOR:
A. Dudley Dennison

PASSAGE FOR THE DAY:
Joshua 24:14–24

Prescription for Marital Success

REMEDIES for the miseries of marital diseases: First of all, accept your mate for who she is. This is why it's good to know your intended well before taking the final leap. Puppy love with a short leash on courtship can lead to a dog's life. But whether you had a long or a short engagement, the success of your marriage may hinge upon acceptance of your partner's total person. If you truly love your mate, you will continue to be blind to her many faults. Love can be delightfully blind, even after marriage . . .

Reserve time for aloneness and allow neither children, in-laws, neighbors, church activities, pesky salesmen, or work brought home from the office to interfere. Take occasional honeymoons, be they only for a night, just to get away.

Make sex loving and exciting. Do not make love just for the sake of loving, but for the response of your lover. Remember: "The wife's body does not belong to her alone but also to her husband. In the same way, the husband's body does not belong to him alone but also to his wife" (1 Corinthians 7:4).

Develop the art of admitting your faults and proving your repentance by changing your ways. An honest "I'm sorry" is soothing the first time and perhaps even the second and third time, but unless you put your money where your mouth is your confession will be sand in her craw.

You must not throw a lighted match into the spilled gasoline of a tense situation, remembering that "a gentle answer turns away wrath, but a harsh word stirs up anger" (Proverbs 15:1).

Always speak in the plural regarding joint interests. Not "my home" but "our home." Not "my career" but "our career." Not "my baby" but "our baby." Not "my vacation" but "our vacation."

Say with Joshua, "But as for me and my household, we will serve the LORD" (Joshua 24:15). Always worship together and serve together in the same church, and pray together at home.

Additional Scripture Readings:
1 Corinthians 7:1–7;
Ephesians 5:22–33

Go to page 243 for your next
devotional reading.

cob bought for a hundred pieces of silver[a] from the sons of Hamor, the father of Shechem. This became the inheritance of Joseph's descendants.

[33]And Eleazar son of Aaron died and was buried at Gibeah, which had been allotted to his son Phinehas in the hill country of Ephraim.

---

*J*UDGES recounts a regular pattern
that develops for God's people in
their new land: the people serve
idols, God punishes them by an enemy invasion, they cry to the Lord,
and he sends a judge (such as
Deborah, Gideon, Jephthah or
Samson) to save them. As you read
this book, remember that only God
can give you victory over sin and evil
and that you will receive his help
only when you serve him alone.

JUDGES

Israel Fights the Remaining Canaanites

1 After the death of Joshua, the Israelites asked the LORD, "Who will be the
first to go up and fight for us against the
Canaanites?"

²The LORD answered, "Judah is to go; I
have given the land into their hands."

³Then the men of Judah said to the Simeonites their brothers, "Come up with us
into the territory allotted to us, to fight
against the Canaanites. We in turn will go
with you into yours." So the Simeonites
went with them.

⁴When Judah attacked, the LORD gave
the Canaanites and Perizzites into their
hands and they struck down ten thousand
men at Bezek. ⁵It was there that they
found Adoni-Bezek and fought against
him, putting to rout the Canaanites and
Perizzites. ⁶Adoni-Bezek fled, but they
chased him and caught him, and cut off
his thumbs and big toes.

⁷Then Adoni-Bezek said, "Seventy
kings with their thumbs and big toes cut
off have picked up scraps under my table.
Now God has paid me back for what I did
to them." They brought him to Jerusalem,
and he died there.

⁸The men of Judah attacked Jerusalem
also and took it. They put the city to the
sword and set it on fire.

⁹After that, the men of Judah went
down to fight against the Canaanites living in the hill country, the Negev and
the western foothills. ¹⁰They advanced

against the Canaanites living in Hebron (formerly called Kiriath Arba) and defeated Sheshai, Ahiman and Talmai. [11]From there they advanced against the people living in Debir (formerly called Kiriath Sepher). [12]And Caleb said, "I will give my daughter Acsah in marriage to the man who attacks and captures Kiriath Sepher." [13]Othniel son of Kenaz, Caleb's younger brother, took it; so Caleb gave his daughter Acsah to him in marriage.

[14]One day when she came to Othniel, she urged him[a] to ask her father for a field. When she got off her donkey, Caleb asked her, "What can I do for you?"

[15]She replied, "Do me a special favor. Since you have given me land in the Negev, give me also springs of water." Then Caleb gave her the upper and lower springs.

[16]The descendants of Moses' father-in-law, the Kenite, went up from the City of Palms[b] with the men of Judah to live among the people of the Desert of Judah in the Negev near Arad.

[17]Then the men of Judah went with the Simeonites their brothers and attacked the Canaanites living in Zephath, and they totally destroyed[c] the city. Therefore it was called Hormah.[d] [18]The men of Judah also took[e] Gaza, Ashkelon and Ekron—each city with its territory.

[19]The LORD was with the men of Judah. They took possession of the hill country, but they were unable to drive the people from the plains, because they had iron chariots. [20]As Moses had promised, Hebron was given to Caleb, who drove from it the three sons of Anak. [21]The Benjamites, however, failed to dislodge the Jebusites, who were living in Jerusalem; to this day the Jebusites live there with the Benjamites.

[22]Now the house of Joseph attacked Bethel, and the LORD was with them. [23]When they sent men to spy out Bethel (formerly called Luz), [24]the spies saw a man coming out of the city and they said to him, "Show us how to get into the city and we will see that you are treated well." [25]So he showed them, and they put the city to the sword but spared the man and his whole family. [26]He then went to the land of the Hittites, where he built a city and called it Luz, which is its name to this day.

[27]But Manasseh did not drive out the people of Beth Shan or Taanach or Dor or Ibleam or Megiddo and their surrounding settlements, for the Canaanites were determined to live in that land. [28]When Israel became strong, they pressed the Canaanites into forced labor but never drove them out completely. [29]Nor did Ephraim drive out the Canaanites living in Gezer, but the Canaanites continued to live there among them. [30]Neither did Zebulun drive out the Canaanites living in Kitron or Nahalol, who remained among them; but they did subject them to forced labor. [31]Nor did Asher drive out those living in Acco or Sidon or Ahlab or Aczib or Helbah or Aphek or Rehob, [32]and because of this the people of Asher lived among the Canaanite inhabitants of the land. [33]Neither did Naphtali drive out those living in Beth Shemesh or Beth Anath; but the Naphtalites too lived among the Canaanite inhabitants of the land, and those living in Beth Shemesh and Beth Anath became forced laborers for them. [34]The Amorites confined the Danites to the hill country, not allowing them to come down into the plain. [35]And the Amorites were determined also to hold out in Mount Heres, Aijalon and Shaalbim, but when the power of the house of Joseph increased, they too were pressed into forced labor. [36]The boundary of the Amorites was from Scorpion[f] Pass to Sela and beyond.

The Angel of the LORD at Bokim

2 The angel of the LORD went up from Gilgal to Bokim and said, "I brought you up out of Egypt and led you into the land that I swore to give to your forefathers. I said, 'I will never break my covenant with you, [2]and you shall not make a covenant with the people of this land, but you shall break down their altars.' Yet you have disobeyed me. Why have you done this? [3]Now therefore I tell you that I will not drive them out before you; they will be ,thorns, in your sides and their gods will be a snare to you."

[4]When the angel of the LORD had spoken these things to all the Israelites, the people wept aloud, [5]and they called that

---

[a]14 Hebrew; Septuagint and Vulgate *Othniel, he urged her*   [b]16 That is, Jericho   [c]17 The Hebrew term refers to the irrevocable giving over of things or persons to the LORD, often by totally destroying them.   [d]17 *Hormah* means *destruction.*   [e]18 Hebrew; Septuagint *Judah did not take*   [f]36 Hebrew *Akrabbim*

place Bokim.[a] There they offered sacrifices to the Lord.

Disobedience and Defeat

[6]After Joshua had dismissed the Israelites, they went to take possession of the land, each to his own inheritance. [7]The people served the Lord throughout the lifetime of Joshua and of the elders who outlived him and who had seen all the great things the Lord had done for Israel. [8]Joshua son of Nun, the servant of the Lord, died at the age of a hundred and ten. [9]And they buried him in the land of his inheritance, at Timnath Heres[b] in the hill country of Ephraim, north of Mount Gaash.

[10]After that whole generation had been gathered to their fathers, another generation grew up, who knew neither the Lord nor what he had done for Israel. [11]Then the Israelites did evil in the eyes of the Lord and served the Baals. [12]They forsook the Lord, the God of their fathers, who had brought them out of Egypt. They followed and worshiped various gods of the peoples around them. They provoked the Lord to anger [13]because they forsook him and served Baal and the Ashtoreths. [14]In his anger against Israel the Lord handed them over to raiders who plundered them. He sold them to their enemies all around, whom they were no longer able to resist. [15]Whenever Israel went out to fight, the hand of the Lord was against them to defeat them, just as he had sworn to them. They were in great distress.

[16]Then the Lord raised up judges,[c] who saved them out of the hands of these raiders. [17]Yet they would not listen to their judges but prostituted themselves to other gods and worshiped them. Unlike their fathers, they quickly turned from the way in which their fathers had walked, the way of obedience to the Lord's commands. [18]Whenever the Lord raised up a judge for them, he was with the judge and saved them out of the hands of their enemies as long as the judge lived; for the Lord had compassion on them as they groaned under those who oppressed and afflicted them. [19]But when the judge died, the people returned to ways even more corrupt than those of their fathers, following other gods and serving and worshiping them. They refused to give up their evil practices and stubborn ways.

[20]Therefore the Lord was very angry with Israel and said, "Because this nation has violated the covenant that I laid down for their forefathers and has not listened to me, [21]I will no longer drive out before them any of the nations Joshua left when he died. [22]I will use them to test Israel and see whether they will keep the way of the Lord and walk in it as their forefathers did." [23]The Lord had allowed those nations to remain; he did not drive them out at once by giving them into the hands of Joshua.

3 These are the nations the Lord left to test all those Israelites who had not experienced any of the wars in Canaan [2](he did this only to teach warfare to the descendants of the Israelites who had not had previous battle experience): [3]the five rulers of the Philistines, all the Canaanites, the Sidonians, and the Hivites living in the Lebanon mountains from Mount Baal Hermon to Lebo[d] Hamath. [4]They were left to test the Israelites to see whether they would obey the Lord's commands, which he had given their forefathers through Moses.

[5]The Israelites lived among the Canaanites, Hittites, Amorites, Perizzites, Hivites and Jebusites. [6]They took their daughters in marriage and gave their own daughters to their sons, and served their gods.

Othniel

[7]The Israelites did evil in the eyes of the Lord; they forgot the Lord their God and served the Baals and the Asherahs. [8]The anger of the Lord burned against Israel so that he sold them into the hands of Cushan-Rishathaim king of Aram Naharaim,[e] to whom the Israelites were subject for eight years. [9]But when they cried out to the Lord, he raised up for them a deliverer, Othniel son of Kenaz, Caleb's younger brother, who saved them. [10]The Spirit of the Lord came upon him, so that he became Israel's judge[f] and went to war. The Lord gave Cushan-Rishathaim king of Aram into the hands of Othniel, who overpowered him. [11]So the land had peace for forty years, until Othniel son of Kenaz died.

---

[a]5 *Bokim* means *weepers.*   [b]9 Also known as *Timnath Serah* (see Joshua 19:50 and 24:30)   [c]16 Or *leaders*; similarly in verses 17-19   [d]3 Or *to the entrance to*   [e]8 That is, Northwest Mesopotamia   [f]10 Or *leader*

Ehud

12Once again the Israelites did evil in the eyes of the Lord, and because they did this evil the Lord gave Eglon king of Moab power over Israel. **13**Getting the Ammonites and Amalekites to join him, Eglon came and attacked Israel, and they took possession of the City of Palms.*a* **14**The Israelites were subject to Eglon king of Moab for eighteen years.

15Again the Israelites cried out to the Lord, and he gave them a deliverer—Ehud, a left-handed man, the son of Gera the Benjamite. The Israelites sent him with tribute to Eglon king of Moab. **16**Now Ehud had made a double-edged sword about a foot and a half*b* long, which he strapped to his right thigh under his clothing. **17**He presented the tribute to Eglon king of Moab, who was a very fat man. **18**After Ehud had presented the tribute, he sent on their way the men who had carried it. **19**At the idols*c* near Gilgal he himself turned back and said, "I have a secret message for you, O king."

The king said, "Quiet!" And all his attendants left him.

20Ehud then approached him while he was sitting alone in the upper room of his summer palace*d* and said, "I have a message from God for you." As the king rose from his seat, **21**Ehud reached with his left hand, drew the sword from his right thigh and plunged it into the king's belly. **22**Even the handle sank in after the blade, which came out his back. Ehud did not pull the sword out, and the fat closed in over it. **23**Then Ehud went out to the porch*e*; he shut the doors of the upper room behind him and locked them.

24After he had gone, the servants came and found the doors of the upper room locked. They said, "He must be relieving himself in the inner room of the house." **25**They waited to the point of embarrassment, but when he did not open the doors of the room, they took a key and unlocked them. There they saw their lord fallen to the floor, dead.

26While they waited, Ehud got away. He passed by the idols and escaped to Seirah. **27**When he arrived there, he blew a trumpet in the hill country of Ephraim, and the Israelites went down with him from the hills, with him leading them.

28"Follow me," he ordered, "for the Lord has given Moab, your enemy, into your hands." So they followed him down and, taking possession of the fords of the Jordan that led to Moab, they allowed no one to cross over. **29**At that time they struck down about ten thousand Moabites, all vigorous and strong; not a man escaped. **30**That day Moab was made subject to Israel, and the land had peace for eighty years.

Shamgar

31After Ehud came Shamgar son of Anath, who struck down six hundred Philistines with an oxgoad. He too saved Israel.

Deborah

4 After Ehud died, the Israelites once again did evil in the eyes of the Lord. **2**So the Lord sold them into the hands of Jabin, a king of Canaan, who reigned in Hazor. The commander of his army was Sisera, who lived in Harosheth Haggoyim. **3**Because he had nine hundred iron chariots and had cruelly oppressed the Israelites for twenty years, they cried to the Lord for help.

4Deborah, a prophetess, the wife of Lappidoth, was leading*f* Israel at that time. **5**She held court under the Palm of Deborah between Ramah and Bethel in the hill country of Ephraim, and the Israelites came to her to have their disputes decided. **6**She sent for Barak son of Abinoam from Kedesh in Naphtali and said to him, "The Lord, the God of Israel, commands you: 'Go, take with you ten thousand men of Naphtali and Zebulun and lead the way to Mount Tabor. **7**I will lure Sisera, the commander of Jabin's army, with his chariots and his troops to the Kishon River and give him into your hands.'"

8Barak said to her, "If you go with me, I will go; but if you don't go with me, I won't go."

9"Very well," Deborah said, "I will go with you. But because of the way you are going about this,*g* the honor will not be yours, for the Lord will hand Sisera over to a woman." So Deborah went with Barak to Kedesh, **10**where he summoned Zebulun and Naphtali. Ten thousand men fol-

a13 That is, Jericho   *b16* Hebrew *a cubit* (about 0.5 meter)   *c19* Or *the stone quarries*; also in verse 26   *d20* The meaning of the Hebrew for this phrase is uncertain.   *e23* The meaning of the Hebrew for this word is uncertain.   *f4* Traditionally *judging*   *g9* Or *But on the expedition you are undertaking* lowed him, and Deborah also went with him.

11Now Heber the Kenite had left the other Kenites, the descendants of Hobab, Moses' brother-in-law,*ᵃ* and pitched his tent by the great tree in Zaanannim near Kedesh.

12When they told Sisera that Barak son of Abinoam had gone up to Mount Tabor, **13**Sisera gathered together his nine hundred iron chariots and all the men with him, from Harosheth Haggoyim to the Kishon River.

14Then Deborah said to Barak, "Go! This is the day the Lᴏʀᴅ has given Sisera into your hands. Has not the Lᴏʀᴅ gone ahead of you?" So Barak went down Mount Tabor, followed by ten thousand men. **15**At Barak's advance, the Lᴏʀᴅ routed Sisera and all his chariots and army by the sword, and Sisera abandoned his chariot and fled on foot. **16**But Barak pursued the chariots and army as far as Harosheth Haggoyim. All the troops of Sisera fell by the sword; not a man was left.

17Sisera, however, fled on foot to the tent of Jael, the wife of Heber the Kenite, because there were friendly relations between Jabin king of Hazor and the clan of Heber the Kenite.

18Jael went out to meet Sisera and said to him, "Come, my lord, come right in. Don't be afraid." So he entered her tent, and she put a covering over him.

19"I'm thirsty," he said. "Please give me some water." She opened a skin of milk, gave him a drink, and covered him up.

20"Stand in the doorway of the tent," he told her. "If someone comes by and asks you, 'Is anyone here?' say 'No.'"

21But Jael, Heber's wife, picked up a tent peg and a hammer and went quietly to him while he lay fast asleep, exhausted. She drove the peg through his temple into the ground, and he died.

22Barak came by in pursuit of Sisera, and Jael went out to meet him. "Come," she said, "I will show you the man you're looking for." So he went in with her, and there lay Sisera with the tent peg through his temple—dead.

23On that day God subdued Jabin, the Canaanite king, before the Israelites. **24**And the hand of the Israelites grew stronger and stronger against Jabin, the Canaanite king, until they destroyed him.

The Song of Deborah

5 On that day Deborah and Barak son of Abinoam sang this song:

2"When the princes in Israel take the lead,
    when the people willingly offer themselves—
    praise the Lᴏʀᴅ!

3"Hear this, you kings! Listen, you rulers!
    I will sing to*ᵇ* the Lᴏʀᴅ, I will sing;
    I will make music to*ᶜ* the Lᴏʀᴅ, the God of Israel.

4"O Lᴏʀᴅ, when you went out from Seir,
    when you marched from the land of Edom,
    the earth shook, the heavens poured,
    the clouds poured down water.
5The mountains quaked before the Lᴏʀᴅ, the One of Sinai,
    before the Lᴏʀᴅ, the God of Israel.

6"In the days of Shamgar son of Anath,
    in the days of Jael, the roads were abandoned;
    travelers took to winding paths.
7Village life*ᵈ* in Israel ceased,
    ceased until I,*ᵉ* Deborah, arose,
    arose a mother in Israel.
8When they chose new gods,
    war came to the city gates,
and not a shield or spear was seen
    among forty thousand in Israel.
9My heart is with Israel's princes,
    with the willing volunteers among the people.
    Praise the Lᴏʀᴅ!

10"You who ride on white donkeys,
    sitting on your saddle blankets,
    and you who walk along the road,
consider **11**the voice of the singers*ᶠ* at the watering places.
    They recite the righteous acts of the Lᴏʀᴅ,
    the righteous acts of his warriors*ᵍ* in Israel.

"Then the people of the Lᴏʀᴅ
    went down to the city gates.
12'Wake up, wake up, Deborah!
    Wake up, wake up, break out in song!
Arise, O Barak!

*ᵃ*11 Or *father-in-law*   *ᵇ*3 Or *of*   *ᶜ*3 Or */ with song I will praise*   *ᵈ*7 Or *Warriors*   *ᵉ*7 Or *you*
*ᶠ*11 Or *archers*; the meaning of the Hebrew for this word is uncertain.   *ᵍ*11 Or *villagers*

Take captive your captives, O son of
    Abinoam.'

13"Then the men who were left
    came down to the nobles;
the people of the Lord
    came to me with the mighty.
14Some came from Ephraim, whose
    roots were in Amalek;
Benjamin was with the people who
    followed you.
From Makir captains came down,
    from Zebulun those who bear a
    commander's staff.
15The princes of Issachar were with
    Deborah;
yes, Issachar was with Barak,
    rushing after him into the valley.
In the districts of Reuben
    there was much searching of heart.
16Why did you stay among the
    campfires*a*
to hear the whistling for the flocks?
In the districts of Reuben
    there was much searching of heart.
17Gilead stayed beyond the Jordan.
    And Dan, why did he linger by the
    ships?
Asher remained on the coast
    and stayed in his coves.
18The people of Zebulun risked their
    very lives;
so did Naphtali on the heights of
    the field.

19"Kings came, they fought;
    the kings of Canaan fought
at Taanach by the waters of Megiddo,
    but they carried off no silver, no
    plunder.
20From the heavens the stars fought,
    from their courses they fought
    against Sisera.
21The river Kishon swept them away,
    the age-old river, the river Kishon.
March on, my soul; be strong!
22Then thundered the horses' hoofs—
    galloping, galloping go his mighty
    steeds.
23'Curse Meroz,' said the angel of the
    Lord.
    'Curse its people bitterly,
because they did not come to help the
    Lord,
    to help the Lord against the
    mighty.'

24"Most blessed of women be Jael,
    the wife of Heber the Kenite,

most blessed of tent-dwelling
    women.
25He asked for water, and she gave him
    milk;
in a bowl fit for nobles she brought
    him curdled milk.
26Her hand reached for the tent peg,
    her right hand for the workman's
    hammer.
She struck Sisera, she crushed his
    head,
    she shattered and pierced his
    temple.
27At her feet he sank,
    he fell; there he lay.
At her feet he sank, he fell;
    where he sank, there he fell—dead.

28"Through the window peered Sisera's
    mother;
    behind the lattice she cried out,
'Why is his chariot so long in coming?
    Why is the clatter of his chariots
    delayed?'
29The wisest of her ladies answer her;
    indeed, she keeps saying to herself,
30'Are they not finding and dividing the
    spoils:
a girl or two for each man,
    colorful garments as plunder for
    Sisera,
    colorful garments embroidered,
highly embroidered garments for
    my neck—
all this as plunder?'

31"So may all your enemies perish,
      O Lord!
But may they who love you be like
    the sun
when it rises in its strength."

Then the land had peace forty years.

Gideon

6 Again the Israelites did evil in the eyes of the Lord, and for seven years he gave them into the hands of the Midianites. 2Because the power of Midian was so oppressive, the Israelites prepared shelters for themselves in mountain clefts, caves and strongholds. 3Whenever the Israelites planted their crops, the Midianites, Amalekites and other eastern peoples invaded the country. 4They camped on the land and ruined the crops all the way to Gaza and did not spare a living thing for Israel, neither sheep nor cattle nor donkeys. 5They came up with their livestock

---

a16 Or *saddlebags*

and their tents like swarms of locusts. It was impossible to count the men and their camels; they invaded the land to ravage it. ⁶Midian so impoverished the Israelites that they cried out to the Lord for help.

⁷When the Israelites cried to the Lord because of Midian, ⁸he sent them a prophet, who said, "This is what the Lord, the God of Israel, says: I brought you up out of Egypt, out of the land of slavery. ⁹I snatched you from the power of Egypt and from the hand of all your oppressors. I drove them from before you and gave you their land. ¹⁰I said to you, 'I am the Lord your God; do not worship the gods of the Amorites, in whose land you live.' But you have not listened to me."

¹¹The angel of the Lord came and sat down under the oak in Ophrah that belonged to Joash the Abiezrite, where his son Gideon was threshing wheat in a winepress to keep it from the Midianites. ¹²When the angel of the Lord appeared to Gideon, he said, "The Lord is with you, mighty warrior."

¹³"But sir," Gideon replied, "if the Lord is with us, why has all this happened to us? Where are all his wonders that our fathers told us about when they said, 'Did not the Lord bring us up out of Egypt?' But now the Lord has abandoned us and put us into the hand of Midian."

¹⁴The Lord turned to him and said, "Go in the strength you have and save Israel out of Midian's hand. Am I not sending you?"

¹⁵"But Lord,ᵃ" Gideon asked, "how can I save Israel? My clan is the weakest in Manasseh, and I am the least in my family."

¹⁶The Lord answered, "I will be with you, and you will strike down all the Midianites together."

¹⁷Gideon replied, "If now I have found favor in your eyes, give me a sign that it is really you talking to me. ¹⁸Please do not go away until I come back and bring my offering and set it before you."

And the Lord said, "I will wait until you return."

¹⁹Gideon went in, prepared a young goat, and from an ephahᵇ of flour he made bread without yeast. Putting the meat in a basket and its broth in a pot, he brought them out and offered them to him under the oak.

²⁰The angel of God said to him, "Take the meat and the unleavened bread, place them on this rock, and pour out the broth." And Gideon did so. ²¹With the tip of the staff that was in his hand, the angel of the Lord touched the meat and the unleavened bread. Fire flared from the rock, consuming the meat and the bread. And the angel of the Lord disappeared. ²²When Gideon realized that it was the angel of the Lord, he exclaimed, "Ah, Sovereign Lord! I have seen the angel of the Lord face to face!"

²³But the Lord said to him, "Peace! Do not be afraid. You are not going to die."

²⁴So Gideon built an altar to the Lord there and called it The Lord is Peace. To this day it stands in Ophrah of the Abiezrites.

²⁵That same night the Lord said to him, "Take the second bull from your father's herd, the one seven years old.ᶜ Tear down your father's altar to Baal and cut down the Asherah poleᵈ beside it. ²⁶Then build a proper kind ofᵉ altar to the Lord your God on the top of this height. Using the wood of the Asherah pole that you cut down, offer the secondᶠ bull as a burnt offering."

²⁷So Gideon took ten of his servants and did as the Lord told him. But because he was afraid of his family and the men of the town, he did it at night rather than in the daytime.

²⁸In the morning when the men of the town got up, there was Baal's altar, demolished, with the Asherah pole beside it cut down and the second bull sacrificed on the newly built altar!

²⁹They asked each other, "Who did this?"

When they carefully investigated, they were told, "Gideon son of Joash did it."

³⁰The men of the town demanded of Joash, "Bring out your son. He must die, because he has broken down Baal's altar and cut down the Asherah pole beside it."

³¹But Joash replied to the hostile crowd around him, "Are you going to plead Baal's cause? Are you trying to save him? Whoever fights for him shall be put to death by morning! If Baal really is a god, he can defend himself when someone breaks down his altar." ³²So that day they

---

ᵃ15 Or sir   ᵇ19 That is, probably about 3/5 bushel (about 22 liters)   ᶜ25 Or Take a full-grown, mature bull from your father's herd   ᵈ25 That is, a symbol of the goddess Asherah; here and elsewhere in Judges   ᵉ26 Or build with layers of stone an   ᶠ26 Or full-grown; also in verse 28

VERSE FOR THE DAY:
Judges 6:16

AUTHOR:
Bill Hybels

PASSAGE FOR THE DAY:
Judges 6:11–24

Authentic Manhood

TO A generation of men failed by their fathers and lost in a cloud of confusion, God says, "Don't spend a lifetime in aimless drifting. Don't succumb to mindless misinterpretations of masculine identity. Enter into a relationship with me, through Jesus Christ, and allow *me* to lead you into authentic manhood. Become my adopted sons and let me 're-father' you."

To say that God wants to re-father his sons is no empty cliché. Scripture repeatedly presents God's desire to be personally and intimately involved with his children. He wants to provide the warmth, affection, discipline and accountability that characterize a parent's loving relationship.

But divine re-fathering is not a simple, overnight process . . . It requires a commitment to two-way dialogue, through prayer and Bible study. It demands that sons take time to listen to the Father's guidance, and then act on it . . .

God wants to father all of us until we're dead sure of his approval, his guiding power and his promise of heaven. Why?

Because God wants us all to experience a deeper level of security. He wants emasculated men to become secure enough to confront timidity and fear, to take risks and make commitments. He wants macho men to become secure enough to crawl out from under the false pretensions and quit trying to impress people . . .

The freedom of authentic masculinity is an amazing thing to see. It produces a "divine elasticity" in men. Finally they can lead with firmness, then submit with humility. They can challenge with a cutting edge, then encourage with enthusiasm. They can fight aggressively for just causes, then moments later weep over suffering.

These are the masterpieces God had in mind when he created man. God looks at them and says, "Very good. You are magnificent creatures—and authentically male."

Additional Scripture Readings:
1 Corinthians 16:13–14;
2 Timothy 1:3–12

Go to page 249 for your next devotional reading.

called Gideon "Jerub-Baal,*a*" saying, "Let Baal contend with him," because he broke down Baal's altar.

33Now all the Midianites, Amalekites and other eastern peoples joined forces and crossed over the Jordan and camped in the Valley of Jezreel. **34**Then the Spirit of the Lord came upon Gideon, and he blew a trumpet, summoning the Abiezrites to follow him. **35**He sent messengers throughout Manasseh, calling them to arms, and also into Asher, Zebulun and Naphtali, so that they too went up to meet them.

36Gideon said to God, "If you will save Israel by my hand as you have promised — **37**look, I will place a wool fleece on the threshing floor. If there is dew only on the fleece and all the ground is dry, then I will know that you will save Israel by my hand, as you said." **38**And that is what happened. Gideon rose early the next day; he squeezed the fleece and wrung out the dew — a bowlful of water.

39Then Gideon said to God, "Do not be angry with me. Let me make just one more request. Allow me one more test with the fleece. This time make the fleece dry and the ground covered with dew." **40**That night God did so. Only the fleece was dry; all the ground was covered with dew.

Gideon Defeats the Midianites

7 Early in the morning, Jerub-Baal (that is, Gideon) and all his men camped at the spring of Harod. The camp of Midian was north of them in the valley near the hill of Moreh. **2**The Lord said to Gideon, "You have too many men for me to deliver Midian into their hands. In order that Israel may not boast against me that her own strength has saved her, **3**announce now to the people, 'Anyone who trembles with fear may turn back and leave Mount Gilead.'" So twenty-two thousand men left, while ten thousand remained.

4But the Lord said to Gideon, "There are still too many men. Take them down to the water, and I will sift them for you there. If I say, 'This one shall go with you,' he shall go; but if I say, 'This one shall not go with you,' he shall not go."

5So Gideon took the men down to the water. There the Lord told him, "Separate those who lap the water with their tongues like a dog from those who kneel down to drink." **6**Three hundred men lapped with their hands to their mouths. All the rest got down on their knees to drink.

7The Lord said to Gideon, "With the three hundred men that lapped I will save you and give the Midianites into your hands. Let all the other men go, each to his own place." **8**So Gideon sent the rest of the Israelites to their tents but kept the three hundred, who took over the provisions and trumpets of the others.

Now the camp of Midian lay below him in the valley. **9**During that night the Lord said to Gideon, "Get up, go down against the camp, because I am going to give it into your hands. **10**If you are afraid to attack, go down to the camp with your servant Purah **11**and listen to what they are saying. Afterward, you will be encouraged to attack the camp." So he and Purah his servant went down to the outposts of the camp. **12**The Midianites, the Amalekites and all the other eastern peoples had settled in the valley, thick as locusts. Their camels could no more be counted than the sand on the seashore.

13Gideon arrived just as a man was telling a friend his dream. "I had a dream," he was saying. "A round loaf of barley bread came tumbling into the Midianite camp. It struck the tent with such force that the tent overturned and collapsed."

14His friend responded, "This can be nothing other than the sword of Gideon son of Joash, the Israelite. God has given the Midianites and the whole camp into his hands."

15When Gideon heard the dream and its interpretation, he worshiped God. He returned to the camp of Israel and called out, "Get up! The Lord has given the Midianite camp into your hands." **16**Dividing the three hundred men into three companies, he placed trumpets and empty jars in the hands of all of them, with torches inside.

17"Watch me," he told them. "Follow my lead. When I get to the edge of the camp, do exactly as I do. **18**When I and all who are with me blow our trumpets, then from all around the camp blow yours and shout, 'For the Lord and for Gideon.'"

19Gideon and the hundred men with him reached the edge of the camp at the beginning of the middle watch, just after they had changed the guard. They blew their trumpets and broke the jars that were in their hands. **20**The three companies blew the trumpets and smashed the jars. Grasping the torches in their left hands and holding in their right hands the trumpets they were to blow, they shouted, "A sword for the LORD and for Gideon!" 21While each man held his position around the camp, all the Midianites ran, crying out as they fled.

22When the three hundred trumpets sounded, the LORD caused the men throughout the camp to turn on each other with their swords. The army fled to Beth Shittah toward Zererah as far as the border of Abel Meholah near Tabbath. 23Israelites from Naphtali, Asher and all Manasseh were called out, and they pursued the Midianites. 24Gideon sent messengers throughout the hill country of Ephraim, saying, "Come down against the Midianites and seize the waters of the Jordan ahead of them as far as Beth Barah."

So all the men of Ephraim were called out and they took the waters of the Jordan as far as Beth Barah. 25They also captured two of the Midianite leaders, Oreb and Zeeb. They killed Oreb at the rock of Oreb, and Zeeb at the winepress of Zeeb. They pursued the Midianites and brought the heads of Oreb and Zeeb to Gideon, who was by the Jordan.

Zebah and Zalmunna

8 Now the Ephraimites asked Gideon, "Why have you treated us like this? Why didn't you call us when you went to fight Midian?" And they criticized him sharply.

2But he answered them, "What have I accomplished compared to you? Aren't the gleanings of Ephraim's grapes better than the full grape harvest of Abiezer? 3God gave Oreb and Zeeb, the Midianite leaders, into your hands. What was I able to do compared to you?" At this, their resentment against him subsided.

4Gideon and his three hundred men, exhausted yet keeping up the pursuit, came to the Jordan and crossed it. 5He said to the men of Succoth, "Give my troops some bread; they are worn out, and I am still pursuing Zebah and Zalmunna, the kings of Midian."

6But the officials of Succoth said, "Do you already have the hands of Zebah and Zalmunna in your possession? Why should we give bread to your troops?"

7Then Gideon replied, "Just for that, when the LORD has given Zebah and Zal-

munna into my hand, I will tear your flesh with desert thorns and briers."

8From there he went up to Peniel[a] and made the same request of them, but they answered as the men of Succoth had. 9So he said to the men of Peniel, "When I return in triumph, I will tear down this tower."

10Now Zebah and Zalmunna were in Karkor with a force of about fifteen thousand men, all that were left of the armies of the eastern peoples; a hundred and twenty thousand swordsmen had fallen. 11Gideon went up by the route of the nomads east of Nobah and Jogbehah and fell upon the unsuspecting army. 12Zebah and Zalmunna, the two kings of Midian, fled, but he pursued them and captured them, routing their entire army.

13Gideon son of Joash then returned from the battle by the Pass of Heres. 14He caught a young man of Succoth and questioned him, and the young man wrote down for him the names of the seventy-seven officials of Succoth, the elders of the town. 15Then Gideon came and said to the men of Succoth, "Here are Zebah and Zalmunna, about whom you taunted me by saying, 'Do you already have the hands of Zebah and Zalmunna in your possession? Why should we give bread to your exhausted men?'" 16He took the elders of the town and taught the men of Succoth a lesson by punishing them with desert thorns and briers. 17He also pulled down the tower of Peniel and killed the men of the town.

18Then he asked Zebah and Zalmunna, "What kind of men did you kill at Tabor?"

"Men like you," they answered, "each one with the bearing of a prince."

19Gideon replied, "Those were my brothers, the sons of my own mother. As surely as the LORD lives, if you had spared their lives, I would not kill you." 20Turning to Jether, his oldest son, he said, "Kill them!" But Jether did not draw his sword, because he was only a boy and was afraid.

21Zebah and Zalmunna said, "Come, do it yourself. 'As is the man, so is his strength.'" So Gideon stepped forward and killed them, and took the ornaments off their camels' necks.

Gideon's Ephod

22The Israelites said to Gideon, "Rule over us—you, your son and your grandson—because you have saved us out of the hand of Midian."

²³But Gideon told them, "I will not rule over you, nor will my son rule over you. The LORD will rule over you." ²⁴And he said, "I do have one request, that each of you give me an earring from your share of the plunder." (It was the custom of the Ishmaelites to wear gold earrings.)

²⁵They answered, "We'll be glad to give them." So they spread out a garment, and each man threw a ring from his plunder onto it. ²⁶The weight of the gold rings he asked for came to seventeen hundred shekels,ᵃ not counting the ornaments, the pendants and the purple garments worn by the kings of Midian or the chains that were on their camels' necks. ²⁷Gideon made the gold into an ephod, which he placed in Ophrah, his town. All Israel prostituted themselves by worshiping it there, and it became a snare to Gideon and his family.

Gideon's Death

²⁸Thus Midian was subdued before the Israelites and did not raise its head again. During Gideon's lifetime, the land enjoyed peace forty years.

²⁹Jerub-Baal son of Joash went back home to live. ³⁰He had seventy sons of his own, for he had many wives. ³¹His concubine, who lived in Shechem, also bore him a son, whom he named Abimelech. ³²Gideon son of Joash died at a good old age and was buried in the tomb of his father Joash in Ophrah of the Abiezrites.

³³No sooner had Gideon died than the Israelites again prostituted themselves to the Baals. They set up Baal-Berith as their god and ³⁴did not remember the LORD their God, who had rescued them from the hands of all their enemies on every side. ³⁵They also failed to show kindness to the family of Jerub-Baal (that is, Gideon) for all the good things he had done for them.

Abimelech

9 Abimelech son of Jerub-Baal went to his mother's brothers in Shechem and said to them and to all his mother's clan, ²"Ask all the citizens of Shechem, 'Which is better for you: to have all seventy of Jerub-Baal's sons rule over you, or just one man?' Remember, I am your flesh and blood."

³When the brothers repeated all this to the citizens of Shechem, they were inclined to follow Abimelech, for they said, "He is our brother." ⁴They gave him seventy shekelsᵇ of silver from the temple of Baal-Berith, and Abimelech used it to hire reckless adventurers, who became his followers. ⁵He went to his father's home in Ophrah and on one stone murdered his seventy brothers, the sons of Jerub-Baal. But Jotham, the youngest son of Jerub-Baal, escaped by hiding. ⁶Then all the citizens of Shechem and Beth Millo gathered beside the great tree at the pillar in Shechem to crown Abimelech king.

⁷When Jotham was told about this, he climbed up on the top of Mount Gerizim and shouted to them, "Listen to me, citizens of Shechem, so that God may listen to you. ⁸One day the trees went out to anoint a king for themselves. They said to the olive tree, 'Be our king.'

⁹"But the olive tree answered, 'Should I give up my oil, by which both gods and men are honored, to hold sway over the trees?'

¹⁰"Next, the trees said to the fig tree, 'Come and be our king.'

¹¹"But the fig tree replied, 'Should I give up my fruit, so good and sweet, to hold sway over the trees?'

¹²"Then the trees said to the vine, 'Come and be our king.'

¹³"But the vine answered, 'Should I give up my wine, which cheers both gods and men, to hold sway over the trees?'

¹⁴"Finally all the trees said to the thornbush, 'Come and be our king.'

¹⁵"The thornbush said to the trees, 'If you really want to anoint me king over you, come and take refuge in my shade; but if not, then let fire come out of the thornbush and consume the cedars of Lebanon!'

¹⁶"Now if you have acted honorably and in good faith when you made Abimelech king, and if you have been fair to Jerub-Baal and his family, and if you have treated him as he deserves— ¹⁷and to think that my father fought for you, risked his life to rescue you from the hand of Midian ¹⁸(but today you have revolted against my father's family, murdered his seventy sons on a single stone, and made Abimelech, the son of his slave girl, king over the citizens of Shechem because he is your brother)— ¹⁹if then you have acted honorably and in good faith toward

---

ᵃ26 That is, about 43 pounds (about 19.5 kilograms) kilogram)   ᵇ4 That is, about 1 3/4 pounds (about 0.8

Jerub-Baal and his family today, may Abimelech be your joy, and may you be his, too! **20**But if you have not, let fire come out from Abimelech and consume you, citizens of Shechem and Beth Millo, and let fire come out from you, citizens of Shechem and Beth Millo, and consume Abimelech!"

21Then Jotham fled, escaping to Beer, and he lived there because he was afraid of his brother Abimelech.

22After Abimelech had governed Israel three years, **23**God sent an evil spirit between Abimelech and the citizens of Shechem, who acted treacherously against Abimelech. **24**God did this in order that the crime against Jerub-Baal's seventy sons, the shedding of their blood, might be avenged on their brother Abimelech and on the citizens of Shechem, who had helped him murder his brothers. **25**In opposition to him these citizens of Shechem set men on the hilltops to ambush and rob everyone who passed by, and this was reported to Abimelech.

26Now Gaal son of Ebed moved with his brothers into Shechem, and its citizens put their confidence in him. **27**After they had gone out into the fields and gathered the grapes and trodden them, they held a festival in the temple of their god. While they were eating and drinking, they cursed Abimelech. **28**Then Gaal son of Ebed said, "Who is Abimelech, and who is Shechem, that we should be subject to him? Isn't he Jerub-Baal's son, and isn't Zebul his deputy? Serve the men of Hamor, Shechem's father! Why should we serve Abimelech? **29**If only this people were under my command! Then I would get rid of him. I would say to Abimelech, 'Call out your whole army!' "[a]

30When Zebul the governor of the city heard what Gaal son of Ebed said, he was very angry. **31**Under cover he sent messengers to Abimelech, saying, "Gaal son of Ebed and his brothers have come to Shechem and are stirring up the city against you. **32**Now then, during the night you and your men should come and lie in wait in the fields. **33**In the morning at sunrise, advance against the city. When Gaal and his men come out against you, do whatever your hand finds to do."

34So Abimelech and all his troops set out by night and took up concealed positions near Shechem in four companies.

35Now Gaal son of Ebed had gone out and was standing at the entrance to the city gate just as Abimelech and his soldiers came out from their hiding place.

36When Gaal saw them, he said to Zebul, "Look, people are coming down from the tops of the mountains!"

Zebul replied, "You mistake the shadows of the mountains for men."

37But Gaal spoke up again: "Look, people are coming down from the center of the land, and a company is coming from the direction of the soothsayers' tree."

38Then Zebul said to him, "Where is your big talk now, you who said, 'Who is Abimelech that we should be subject to him?' Aren't these the men you ridiculed? Go out and fight them!"

39So Gaal led out[b] the citizens of Shechem and fought Abimelech. **40**Abimelech chased him, and many fell wounded in the flight—all the way to the entrance to the gate. **41**Abimelech stayed in Arumah, and Zebul drove Gaal and his brothers out of Shechem.

42The next day the people of Shechem went out to the fields, and this was reported to Abimelech. **43**So he took his men, divided them into three companies and set an ambush in the fields. When he saw the people coming out of the city, he rose to attack them. **44**Abimelech and the companies with him rushed forward to a position at the entrance to the city gate. Then two companies rushed upon those in the fields and struck them down. **45**All that day Abimelech pressed his attack against the city until he had captured it and killed its people. Then he destroyed the city and scattered salt over it.

46On hearing this, the citizens in the tower of Shechem went into the stronghold of the temple of El-Berith. **47**When Abimelech heard that they had assembled there, **48**he and all his men went up Mount Zalmon. He took an ax and cut off some branches, which he lifted to his shoulders. He ordered the men with him, "Quick! Do what you have seen me do!" **49**So all the men cut branches and followed Abimelech. They piled them against the stronghold and set it on fire over the people inside. So all the people in the tower of Shechem, about a thousand men and women, also died.

50Next Abimelech went to Thebez and besieged it and captured it. **51**Inside the city, however, was a strong tower, to which all the men and women — all the people of the city — fled. They locked themselves in and climbed up on the tower roof. 52Abimelech went to the tower and stormed it. But as he approached the entrance to the tower to set it on fire, 53a woman dropped an upper millstone on his head and cracked his skull.

54Hurriedly he called to his armor-bearer, "Draw your sword and kill me, so that they can't say, 'A woman killed him.' " So his servant ran him through, and he died. 55When the Israelites saw that Abimelech was dead, they went home.

56Thus God repaid the wickedness that Abimelech had done to his father by murdering his seventy brothers. 57God also made the men of Shechem pay for all their wickedness. The curse of Jotham son of Jerub-Baal came on them.

Tola

10 After the time of Abimelech a man of Issachar, Tola son of Puah, the son of Dodo, rose to save Israel. He lived in Shamir, in the hill country of Ephraim. 2He led[a] Israel twenty-three years; then he died, and was buried in Shamir.

Jair

3He was followed by Jair of Gilead, who led Israel twenty-two years. 4He had thirty sons, who rode thirty donkeys. They controlled thirty towns in Gilead, which to this day are called Havvoth Jair.[b] 5When Jair died, he was buried in Kamon.

Jephthah

6Again the Israelites did evil in the eyes of the Lord. They served the Baals and the Ashtoreths, and the gods of Aram, the gods of Sidon, the gods of Moab, the gods of the Ammonites and the gods of the Philistines. And because the Israelites forsook the Lord and no longer served him, 7he became angry with them. He sold them into the hands of the Philistines and the Ammonites, 8who that year shattered and crushed them. For eighteen years they oppressed all the Israelites on the east side of the Jordan in Gilead, the land of the Amorites. 9The Ammonites also crossed the Jordan to fight against Judah, Benjamin and the house of Ephraim; and Israel was in great distress. 10Then the Israelites cried out to the Lord, "We have

sinned against you, forsaking our God and serving the Baals."

11The Lord replied, "When the Egyptians, the Amorites, the Ammonites, the Philistines, 12the Sidonians, the Amalekites and the Maonites[c] oppressed you and you cried to me for help, did I not save you from their hands? 13But you have forsaken me and served other gods, so I will no longer save you. 14Go and cry out to the gods you have chosen. Let them save you when you are in trouble!"

15But the Israelites said to the Lord, "We have sinned. Do with us whatever you think best, but please rescue us now." 16Then they got rid of the foreign gods among them and served the Lord. And he could bear Israel's misery no longer.

17When the Ammonites were called to arms and camped in Gilead, the Israelites assembled and camped at Mizpah. 18The leaders of the people of Gilead said to each other, "Whoever will launch the attack against the Ammonites will be the head of all those living in Gilead."

11 Jephthah the Gileadite was a mighty warrior. His father was Gilead; his mother was a prostitute. 2Gilead's wife also bore him sons, and when they were grown up, they drove Jephthah away. "You are not going to get any inheritance in our family," they said, "because you are the son of another woman." 3So Jephthah fled from his brothers and settled in the land of Tob, where a group of adventurers gathered around him and followed him.

4Some time later, when the Ammonites made war on Israel, 5the elders of Gilead went to get Jephthah from the land of Tob. 6"Come," they said, "be our commander, so we can fight the Ammonites."

7Jephthah said to them, "Didn't you hate me and drive me from my father's house? Why do you come to me now, when you're in trouble?"

8The elders of Gilead said to him, "Nevertheless, we are turning to you now; come with us to fight the Ammonites, and you will be our head over all who live in Gilead."

9Jephthah answered, "Suppose you take me back to fight the Ammonites and the Lord gives them to me — will I really be your head?"

10The elders of Gilead replied, "The Lord is our witness; we will certainly do

---

WEEKENDING

REFLECT

What makes the temptation of power so seemingly irresistible? Maybe it is that power offers an easy substitute for the hard task of love. It seems easier to be God than to love God, easier to control people than to love people, easier to own life than to love life . . .

The long painful history of the church is the history of people ever and again tempted to choose power over love, control over the cross, being a leader over being led. Those who resisted this temptation to the end and thereby give us hope are the true saints.

– *Henri Nouwen*

REVIVE

Saturday: Deuteronomy 8:10–18
Sunday: Matthew 20:20–28

Go to page 255 for your next devotional reading.

as you say." [11]So Jephthah went with the elders of Gilead, and the people made him head and commander over them. And he repeated all his words before the LORD in Mizpah.

[12]Then Jephthah sent messengers to the Ammonite king with the question: "What do you have against us that you have attacked our country?"

[13]The king of the Ammonites answered Jephthah's messengers, "When Israel came up out of Egypt, they took away my land from the Arnon to the Jabbok, all the way to the Jordan. Now give it back peaceably."

[14]Jephthah sent back messengers to the Ammonite king, [15]saying:

"This is what Jephthah says: Israel did not take the land of Moab or the land of the Ammonites. [16]But when they came up out of Egypt, Israel went through the desert to the Red Sea[a] and on to Kadesh. [17]Then Israel sent messengers to the king of Edom, saying, 'Give us permission to go through your country,' but the king of Edom would not listen. They sent also to the king of Moab, and he refused. So Israel stayed at Kadesh.

[18]"Next they traveled through the desert, skirted the lands of Edom and Moab, passed along the eastern side of the country of Moab, and camped on the other side of the Arnon. They did not enter the territory of Moab, for the Arnon was its border.

[19]"Then Israel sent messengers to Sihon king of the Amorites, who ruled in Heshbon, and said to him, 'Let us pass through your country to our own place.' [20]Sihon, however, did not trust Israel[b] to pass through his territory. He mustered all his men and encamped at Jahaz and fought with Israel.

[21]"Then the LORD, the God of Israel, gave Sihon and all his men into Israel's hands, and they defeated them. Israel took over all the land of the Amorites who lived in that country, [22]capturing all of it from the Arnon to the Jabbok and from the desert to the Jordan.

[23]"Now since the LORD, the God of Israel, has driven the Amorites out before his people Israel, what right

have you to take it over? [24]Will you not take what your god Chemosh gives you? Likewise, whatever the LORD our God has given us, we will possess. [25]Are you better than Balak son of Zippor, king of Moab? Did he ever quarrel with Israel or fight with them? [26]For three hundred years Israel occupied Heshbon, Aroer, the surrounding settlements and all the towns along the Arnon. Why didn't you retake them during that time? [27]I have not wronged you, but you are doing me wrong by waging war against me. Let the LORD, the Judge,[c] decide the dispute this day between the Israelites and the Ammonites."

[28]The king of Ammon, however, paid no attention to the message Jephthah sent him.

[29]Then the Spirit of the LORD came upon Jephthah. He crossed Gilead and Manasseh, passed through Mizpah of Gilead, and from there he advanced against the Ammonites. [30]And Jephthah made a vow to the LORD: "If you give the Ammonites into my hands, [31]whatever comes out of the door of my house to meet me when I return in triumph from the Ammonites will be the LORD's, and I will sacrifice it as a burnt offering."

[32]Then Jephthah went over to fight the Ammonites, and the LORD gave them into his hands. [33]He devastated twenty towns from Aroer to the vicinity of Minnith, as far as Abel Keramim. Thus Israel subdued Ammon.

[34]When Jephthah returned to his home in Mizpah, who should come out to meet him but his daughter, dancing to the sound of tambourines! She was an only child. Except for her he had neither son nor daughter. [35]When he saw her, he tore his clothes and cried, "Oh! My daughter! You have made me miserable and wretched, because I have made a vow to the LORD that I cannot break."

[36]"My father," she replied, "you have given your word to the LORD. Do to me just as you promised, now that the LORD has avenged you of your enemies, the Ammonites. [37]But grant me this one request," she said. "Give me two months to roam the hills and weep with my friends, because I will never marry."

[38]"You may go," he said. And he let her

---

[a]16 Hebrew *Yam Suph*; that is, Sea of Reeds   [b]20 Or *however, would not make an agreement for Israel*
[c]27 Or *Ruler*

go for two months. She and the girls went into the hills and wept because she would never marry. **39**After the two months, she returned to her father and he did to her as he had vowed. And she was a virgin.

From this comes the Israelite custom **40**that each year the young women of Israel go out for four days to commemorate the daughter of Jephthah the Gileadite.

Jephthah and Ephraim

12 The men of Ephraim called out their forces, crossed over to Zaphon and said to Jephthah, "Why did you go to fight the Ammonites without calling us to go with you? We're going to burn down your house over your head."

2Jephthah answered, "I and my people were engaged in a great struggle with the Ammonites, and although I called, you didn't save me out of their hands. **3**When I saw that you wouldn't help, I took my life in my hands and crossed over to fight the Ammonites, and the LORD gave me the victory over them. Now why have you come up today to fight me?"

4Jephthah then called together the men of Gilead and fought against Ephraim. The Gileadites struck them down because the Ephraimites had said, "You Gileadites are renegades from Ephraim and Manasseh." **5**The Gileadites captured the fords of the Jordan leading to Ephraim, and whenever a survivor of Ephraim said, "Let me cross over," the men of Gilead asked him, "Are you an Ephraimite?" If he replied, "No," **6**they said, "All right, say 'Shibboleth.' " If he said, "Sibboleth," because he could not pronounce the word correctly, they seized him and killed him at the fords of the Jordan. Forty-two thousand Ephraimites were killed at that time.

7Jephthah led*a* Israel six years. Then Jephthah the Gileadite died, and was buried in a town in Gilead.

Ibzan, Elon and Abdon

8After him, Ibzan of Bethlehem led Israel. **9**He had thirty sons and thirty daughters. He gave his daughters away in marriage to those outside his clan, and for his sons he brought in thirty young women as wives from outside his clan. Ibzan led Israel seven years. **10**Then Ibzan died, and was buried in Bethlehem.

11After him, Elon the Zebulunite led Israel ten years. **12**Then Elon died, and was buried in Aijalon in the land of Zebulun.

13After him, Abdon son of Hillel, from Pirathon, led Israel. **14**He had forty sons and thirty grandsons, who rode on seventy donkeys. He led Israel eight years. **15**Then Abdon son of Hillel died, and was buried at Pirathon in Ephraim, in the hill country of the Amalekites.

The Birth of Samson

13 Again the Israelites did evil in the eyes of the LORD, so the LORD delivered them into the hands of the Philistines for forty years.

2A certain man of Zorah, named Manoah, from the clan of the Danites, had a wife who was sterile and remained childless. **3**The angel of the LORD appeared to her and said, "You are sterile and childless, but you are going to conceive and have a son. **4**Now see to it that you drink no wine or other fermented drink and that you do not eat anything unclean, **5**because you will conceive and give birth to a son. No razor may be used on his head, because the boy is to be a Nazirite, set apart to God from birth, and he will begin the deliverance of Israel from the hands of the Philistines."

6Then the woman went to her husband and told him, "A man of God came to me. He looked like an angel of God, very awesome. I didn't ask him where he came from, and he didn't tell me his name. **7**But he said to me, 'You will conceive and give birth to a son. Now then, drink no wine or other fermented drink and do not eat anything unclean, because the boy will be a Nazirite of God from birth until the day of his death.' "

8Then Manoah prayed to the LORD: "O Lord, I beg you, let the man of God you sent to us come again to teach us how to bring up the boy who is to be born."

9God heard Manoah, and the angel of God came again to the woman while she was out in the field; but her husband Manoah was not with her. **10**The woman hurried to tell her husband, "He's here! The man who appeared to me the other day!"

11Manoah got up and followed his wife. When he came to the man, he said, "Are you the one who talked to my wife?"

"I am," he said.

12So Manoah asked him, "When your words are fulfilled, what is to be the rule for the boy's life and work?"

13The angel of the LORD answered, "Your wife must do all that I have told her.

---

a7 Traditionally *judged*; also in verses 8-14

[14]She must not eat anything that comes from the grapevine, nor drink any wine or other fermented drink nor eat anything unclean. She must do everything I have commanded her."

[15]Manoah said to the angel of the LORD, "We would like you to stay until we prepare a young goat for you."

[16]The angel of the LORD replied, "Even though you detain me, I will not eat any of your food. But if you prepare a burnt offering, offer it to the LORD." (Manoah did not realize that it was the angel of the LORD.)

[17]Then Manoah inquired of the angel of the LORD, "What is your name, so that we may honor you when your word comes true?"

[18]He replied, "Why do you ask my name? It is beyond understanding.[a]"

[19]Then Manoah took a young goat, together with the grain offering, and sacrificed it on a rock to the LORD. And the LORD did an amazing thing while Manoah and his wife watched: [20]As the flame blazed up from the altar toward heaven, the angel of the LORD ascended in the flame. Seeing this, Manoah and his wife fell with their faces to the ground. [21]When the angel of the LORD did not show himself again to Manoah and his wife, Manoah realized that it was the angel of the LORD.

[22]"We are doomed to die!" he said to his wife. "We have seen God!"

[23]But his wife answered, "If the LORD had meant to kill us, he would not have accepted a burnt offering and grain offering from our hands, nor shown us all these things or now told us this."

[24]The woman gave birth to a boy and named him Samson. He grew and the LORD blessed him, [25]and the Spirit of the LORD began to stir him while he was in Mahaneh Dan, between Zorah and Eshtaol.

Samson's Marriage

14 Samson went down to Timnah and saw there a young Philistine woman. [2]When he returned, he said to his father and mother, "I have seen a Philistine woman in Timnah; now get her for me as my wife."

[3]His father and mother replied, "Isn't there an acceptable woman among your relatives or among all our people? Must you go to the uncircumcised Philistines to get a wife?"

But Samson said to his father, "Get her for me. She's the right one for me." [4](His parents did not know that this was from the LORD, who was seeking an occasion to confront the Philistines; for at that time they were ruling over Israel.) [5]Samson went down to Timnah together with his father and mother. As they approached the vineyards of Timnah, suddenly a young lion came roaring toward him. [6]The Spirit of the LORD came upon him in power so that he tore the lion apart with his bare hands as he might have torn a young goat. But he told neither his father nor his mother what he had done. [7]Then he went down and talked with the woman, and he liked her.

[8]Some time later, when he went back to marry her, he turned aside to look at the lion's carcass. In it was a swarm of bees and some honey, [9]which he scooped out with his hands and ate as he went along. When he rejoined his parents, he gave them some, and they too ate it. But he did not tell them that he had taken the honey from the lion's carcass.

[10]Now his father went down to see the woman. And Samson made a feast there, as was customary for bridegrooms. [11]When he appeared, he was given thirty companions.

[12]"Let me tell you a riddle," Samson said to them. "If you can give me the answer within the seven days of the feast, I will give you thirty linen garments and thirty sets of clothes. [13]If you can't tell me the answer, you must give me thirty linen garments and thirty sets of clothes."

"Tell us your riddle," they said. "Let's hear it."

[14]He replied,

"Out of the eater, something to eat;
    out of the strong, something sweet."

For three days they could not give the answer.

[15]On the fourth[b] day, they said to Samson's wife, "Coax your husband into explaining the riddle for us, or we will burn you and your father's household to death. Did you invite us here to rob us?"

[16]Then Samson's wife threw herself on him, sobbing, "You hate me! You don't really love me. You've given my people a riddle, but you haven't told me the answer."

"I haven't even explained it to my father or mother," he replied, "so why should I

[a]18 Or is wonderful   [b]15 Some Septuagint manuscripts and Syriac; Hebrew seventh

explain it to you?" 17She cried the whole seven days of the feast. So on the seventh day he finally told her, because she continued to press him. She in turn explained the riddle to her people.

18Before sunset on the seventh day the men of the town said to him,

"What is sweeter than honey?
  What is stronger than a lion?"

Samson said to them,

"If you had not plowed with my
    heifer,
  you would not have solved my
    riddle."

19Then the Spirit of the LORD came upon him in power. He went down to Ashkelon, struck down thirty of their men, stripped them of their belongings and gave their clothes to those who had explained the riddle. Burning with anger, he went up to his father's house. 20And Samson's wife was given to the friend who had attended him at his wedding.

Samson's Vengeance on the Philistines

15 Later on, at the time of wheat harvest, Samson took a young goat and went to visit his wife. He said, "I'm going to my wife's room." But her father would not let him go in.

2"I was so sure you thoroughly hated her," he said, "that I gave her to your friend. Isn't her younger sister more attractive? Take her instead."

3Samson said to them, "This time I have a right to get even with the Philistines; I will really harm them." 4So he went out and caught three hundred foxes and tied them tail to tail in pairs. He then fastened a torch to every pair of tails, 5lit the torches and let the foxes loose in the standing grain of the Philistines. He burned up the shocks and standing grain, together with the vineyards and olive groves.

6When the Philistines asked, "Who did this?" they were told, "Samson, the Timnite's son-in-law, because his wife was given to his friend."

So the Philistines went up and burned her and her father to death. 7Samson said to them, "Since you've acted like this, I won't stop until I get my revenge on you."

8He attacked them viciously and slaughtered many of them. Then he went down and stayed in a cave in the rock of Etam.

9The Philistines went up and camped in Judah, spreading out near Lehi. 10The men of Judah asked, "Why have you come to fight us?"

"We have come to take Samson prisoner," they answered, "to do to him as he did to us."

11Then three thousand men from Judah went down to the cave in the rock of Etam and said to Samson, "Don't you realize that the Philistines are rulers over us? What have you done to us?"

He answered, "I merely did to them what they did to me."

12They said to him, "We've come to tie you up and hand you over to the Philistines."

Samson said, "Swear to me that you won't kill me yourselves."

13"Agreed," they answered. "We will only tie you up and hand you over to them. We will not kill you." So they bound him with two new ropes and led him up from the rock. 14As he approached Lehi, the Philistines came toward him shouting. The Spirit of the LORD came upon him in power. The ropes on his arms became like charred flax, and the bindings dropped from his hands. 15Finding a fresh jawbone of a donkey, he grabbed it and struck down a thousand men.

16Then Samson said,

"With a donkey's jawbone
  I have made donkeys of them.a
With a donkey's jawbone
  I have killed a thousand men."

17When he finished speaking, he threw away the jawbone; and the place was called Ramath Lehi.b

18Because he was very thirsty, he cried out to the LORD, "You have given your servant this great victory. Must I now die of thirst and fall into the hands of the uncircumcised?" 19Then God opened up the hollow place in Lehi, and water came out of it. When Samson drank, his strength returned and he revived. So the spring was called En Hakkore,c and it is still there in Lehi.

20Samson ledd Israel for twenty years in the days of the Philistines.

---

a16 Or *made a heap or two*; the Hebrew for *donkey* sounds like the Hebrew for *heap*.   b17 *Ramath Lehi* means *jawbone hill*.   c19 *En Hakkore* means *caller's spring*.   d20 Traditionally *judged*

Samson and Delilah

16 One day Samson went to Gaza, where he saw a prostitute. He went in to spend the night with her. ²The people of Gaza were told, "Samson is here!" So they surrounded the place and lay in wait for him all night at the city gate. They made no move during the night, saying, "At dawn we'll kill him."

³But Samson lay there only until the middle of the night. Then he got up and took hold of the doors of the city gate, together with the two posts, and tore them loose, bar and all. He lifted them to his shoulders and carried them to the top of the hill that faces Hebron.

⁴Some time later, he fell in love with a woman in the Valley of Sorek whose name was Delilah. ⁵The rulers of the Philistines went to her and said, "See if you can lure him into showing you the secret of his great strength and how we can overpower him so we may tie him up and subdue him. Each one of us will give you eleven hundred shekels*a* of silver."

⁶So Delilah said to Samson, "Tell me the secret of your great strength and how you can be tied up and subdued."

⁷Samson answered her, "If anyone ties me with seven fresh thongs*b* that have not been dried, I'll become as weak as any other man."

⁸Then the rulers of the Philistines brought her seven fresh thongs that had not been dried, and she tied him with them. ⁹With men hidden in the room, she called to him, "Samson, the Philistines are upon you!" But he snapped the thongs as easily as a piece of string snaps when it comes close to a flame. So the secret of his strength was not discovered.

¹⁰Then Delilah said to Samson, "You have made a fool of me; you lied to me. Come now, tell me how you can be tied."

¹¹He said, "If anyone ties me securely with new ropes that have never been used, I'll become as weak as any other man."

¹²So Delilah took new ropes and tied him with them. Then, with men hidden in the room, she called to him, "Samson, the Philistines are upon you!" But he snapped the ropes off his arms as if they were threads.

¹³Delilah then said to Samson, "Until now, you have been making a fool of me and lying to me. Tell me how you can be tied."

He replied, "If you weave the seven braids of my head into the fabric ⌊on the loom⌋ and tighten it with the pin, I'll become as weak as any other man." So while he was sleeping, Delilah took the seven braids of his head, wove them into the fabric ¹⁴and*c* tightened it with the pin.

Again she called to him, "Samson, the Philistines are upon you!" He awoke from his sleep and pulled up the pin and the loom, with the fabric.

¹⁵Then she said to him, "How can you say, 'I love you,' when you won't confide in me? This is the third time you have made a fool of me and haven't told me the secret of your great strength." ¹⁶With such nagging she prodded him day after day until he was tired to death.

¹⁷So he told her everything. "No razor has ever been used on my head," he said, "because I have been a Nazirite set apart to God since birth. If my head were shaved, my strength would leave me, and I would become as weak as any other man."

¹⁸When Delilah saw that he had told her everything, she sent word to the rulers of the Philistines, "Come back once more; he has told me everything." So the rulers of the Philistines returned with the silver in their hands. ¹⁹Having put him to sleep on her lap, she called a man to shave off the seven braids of his hair, and so began to subdue him.*d* And his strength left him.

²⁰Then she called, "Samson, the Philistines are upon you!"

He awoke from his sleep and thought, "I'll go out as before and shake myself free." But he did not know that the LORD had left him.

²¹Then the Philistines seized him, gouged out his eyes and took him down to Gaza. Binding him with bronze shackles, they set him to grinding in the prison. ²²But the hair on his head began to grow again after it had been shaved.

The Death of Samson

²³Now the rulers of the Philistines assembled to offer a great sacrifice to Dagon their god and to celebrate, saying, "Our god has delivered Samson, our enemy, into our hands."

a5 That is, about 28 pounds (about 13 kilograms)   *b7* Or *bowstrings*; also in verses 8 and 9
c13,14 Some Septuagint manuscripts; Hebrew *"I can, if you weave the seven braids of my head into the fabric ⌊on the loom⌋."* *14So she*   *d19* Hebrew; some Septuagint manuscripts *and he began to weaken*

VERSE FOR THE DAY:
Judges 16:20

AUTHOR:
James C. Schaap

PASSAGE FOR THE DAY:
Judges 16:4–22

Pride Goes Before a Fall

A GREEK philosopher named Aristotle would have loved the story of Samson and Delilah. He would have loved it because the story seemed to fit his definition of the word *tragedy*. Aristotle claimed that tragedy is the account of some strong human being who is destroyed by a single character flaw.

In today's Scripture we read of Samson's downfall. Delilah was in cahoots with her Philistine friends, who offered her big money to try to chain down the man who had become the symbol of strength to the Israelites. "Get him to tell you how he keeps all that strength," they pleaded, "and we'll line your bathtub with silver." (They didn't say exactly that, of course.)

Samson may have had big muscles, but he certainly didn't have Solomon's brains. Four times Delilah tried to subdue him before she finally won. You'd think he would have gotten the hint. The Bible says she nagged him so long he was "tired to death." But he kept joshing along. Why didn't he just throw the woman out on her ear? Why?—because of his pride.

Aristotle had something to say about that too. He claimed that the one character flaw that most often leads the tragic hero to his downfall is nothing other than pride . . .

Samson's tragic fall led to the end of his freedom. He was a prisoner of the Philistines, a sorry figure they used for entertainment. So goes the great hero.

One more thing about this philosopher, Aristotle. He claimed that tragedy should deeply affect those who see it. He said tragedy should lead to a *catharsis* in those who truly understand what has gone on. *Catharsis* is a big word, but its meaning is not so difficult. It means "a cleansing." Having seen a great person fall, people should be cleansed of their own pride, Aristotle wrote. They should see themselves in the great fall of a tragic hero.

That's something for all of us to think about when we're patting ourselves on the back and taking the credit for ourselves instead of giving it to God.

As the old saying puts it, "Pride goeth before a fall."

Additional Scripture Readings:
Proverbs 16:1–5,17–19;
Philippians 2:1–11

Go to page 264 for your next devotional reading.

24When the people saw him, they praised their god, saying,

"Our god has delivered our enemy
into our hands,
the one who laid waste our land
and multiplied our slain."

25While they were in high spirits, they shouted, "Bring out Samson to entertain us." So they called Samson out of the prison, and he performed for them.

When they stood him among the pillars, **26**Samson said to the servant who held his hand, "Put me where I can feel the pillars that support the temple, so that I may lean against them." **27**Now the temple was crowded with men and women; all the rulers of the Philistines were there, and on the roof were about three thousand men and women watching Samson perform. **28**Then Samson prayed to the Lord, "O Sovereign Lord, remember me. O God, please strengthen me just once more, and let me with one blow get revenge on the Philistines for my two eyes." **29**Then Samson reached toward the two central pillars on which the temple stood. Bracing himself against them, his right hand on the one and his left hand on the other, **30**Samson said, "Let me die with the Philistines!" Then he pushed with all his might, and down came the temple on the rulers and all the people in it. Thus he killed many more when he died than while he lived.

31Then his brothers and his father's whole family went down to get him. They brought him back and buried him between Zorah and Eshtaol in the tomb of Manoah his father. He had led*a* Israel twenty years.

Micah's Idols

17 Now a man named Micah from the hill country of Ephraim **2**said to his mother, "The eleven hundred shekels*b* of silver that were taken from you and about which I heard you utter a curse—I have that silver with me; I took it."

Then his mother said, "The Lord bless you, my son!"

3When he returned the eleven hundred shekels of silver to his mother, she said, "I solemnly consecrate my silver to the Lord for my son to make a carved image and a cast idol. I will give it back to you."

4So he returned the silver to his mother, and she took two hundred shekels*c* of silver and gave them to a silversmith, who made them into the image and the idol. And they were put in Micah's house. **5**Now this man Micah had a shrine, and he made an ephod and some idols and installed one of his sons as his priest. **6**In those days Israel had no king; everyone did as he saw fit.

7A young Levite from Bethlehem in Judah, who had been living within the clan of Judah, **8**left that town in search of some other place to stay. On his way*d* he came to Micah's house in the hill country of Ephraim.

9Micah asked him, "Where are you from?"

"I'm a Levite from Bethlehem in Judah," he said, "and I'm looking for a place to stay."

10Then Micah said to him, "Live with me and be my father and priest, and I'll give you ten shekels*e* of silver a year, your clothes and your food." **11**So the Levite agreed to live with him, and the young man was to him like one of his sons. **12**Then Micah installed the Levite, and the young man became his priest and lived in his house. **13**And Micah said, "Now I know that the Lord will be good to me, since this Levite has become my priest."

Danites Settle in Laish

18 In those days Israel had no king.
And in those days the tribe of the Danites was seeking a place of their own where they might settle, because they had not yet come into an inheritance among the tribes of Israel. **2**So the Danites sent five warriors from Zorah and Eshtaol to spy out the land and explore it. These men represented all their clans. They told them, "Go, explore the land."

The men entered the hill country of Ephraim and came to the house of Micah, where they spent the night. **3**When they were near Micah's house, they recognized the voice of the young Levite; so they turned in there and asked him, "Who brought you here? What are you doing in this place? Why are you here?"

4He told them what Micah had done for him, and said, "He has hired me and I am his priest."

[5]Then they said to him, "Please inquire of God to learn whether our journey will be successful."

[6]The priest answered them, "Go in peace. Your journey has the LORD's approval."

[7]So the five men left and came to Laish, where they saw that the people were living in safety, like the Sidonians, unsuspecting and secure. And since their land lacked nothing, they were prosperous.[a] Also, they lived a long way from the Sidonians and had no relationship with anyone else.[b]

[8]When they returned to Zorah and Eshtaol, their brothers asked them, "How did you find things?"

[9]They answered, "Come on, let's attack them! We have seen that the land is very good. Aren't you going to do something? Don't hesitate to go there and take it over. [10]When you get there, you will find an unsuspecting people and a spacious land that God has put into your hands, a land that lacks nothing whatever."

[11]Then six hundred men from the clan of the Danites, armed for battle, set out from Zorah and Eshtaol. [12]On their way they set up camp near Kiriath Jearim in Judah. This is why the place west of Kiriath Jearim is called Mahaneh Dan[c] to this day. [13]From there they went on to the hill country of Ephraim and came to Micah's house.

[14]Then the five men who had spied out the land of Laish said to their brothers, "Do you know that one of these houses has an ephod, other household gods, a carved image and a cast idol? Now you know what to do." [15]So they turned in there and went to the house of the young Levite at Micah's place and greeted him. [16]The six hundred Danites, armed for battle, stood at the entrance to the gate. [17]The five men who had spied out the land went inside and took the carved image, the ephod, the other household gods and the cast idol while the priest and the six hundred armed men stood at the entrance to the gate.

[18]When these men went into Micah's house and took the carved image, the ephod, the other household gods and the cast idol, the priest said to them, "What are you doing?"

[19]They answered him, "Be quiet! Don't say a word. Come with us, and be our father and priest. Isn't it better that you serve a tribe and clan in Israel as priest rather than just one man's household?" [20]Then the priest was glad. He took the ephod, the other household gods and the carved image and went along with the people. [21]Putting their little children, their livestock and their possessions in front of them, they turned away and left.

[22]When they had gone some distance from Micah's house, the men who lived near Micah were called together and overtook the Danites. [23]As they shouted after them, the Danites turned and said to Micah, "What's the matter with you that you called out your men to fight?"

[24]He replied, "You took the gods I made, and my priest, and went away. What else do I have? How can you ask, 'What's the matter with you?'"

[25]The Danites answered, "Don't argue with us, or some hot-tempered men will attack you, and you and your family will lose your lives." [26]So the Danites went their way, and Micah, seeing that they were too strong for him, turned around and went back home.

[27]Then they took what Micah had made, and his priest, and went on to Laish, against a peaceful and unsuspecting people. They attacked them with the sword and burned down their city. [28]There was no one to rescue them because they lived a long way from Sidon and had no relationship with anyone else. The city was in a valley near Beth Rehob.

The Danites rebuilt the city and settled there. [29]They named it Dan after their forefather Dan, who was born to Israel — though the city used to be called Laish. [30]There the Danites set up for themselves the idols, and Jonathan son of Gershom, the son of Moses,[d] and his sons were priests for the tribe of Dan until the time of the captivity of the land. [31]They continued to use the idols Micah had made, all the time the house of God was in Shiloh.

A Levite and His Concubine

19 In those days Israel had no king.
Now a Levite who lived in a remote area in the hill country of Ephraim took a concubine from Bethlehem in Judah. [2]But she was unfaithful to him. She left him and went back to her father's house in

---

[a]7 The meaning of the Hebrew for this clause is uncertain. [b]7 Hebrew; some Septuagint manuscripts with the Arameans [c]12 Mahaneh Dan means Dan's camp. [d]30 An ancient Hebrew scribal tradition, some Septuagint manuscripts and Vulgate; Masoretic Text Manasseh

Bethlehem, Judah. After she had been there four months, ³her husband went to her to persuade her to return. He had with him his servant and two donkeys. She took him into her father's house, and when her father saw him, he gladly welcomed him. ⁴His father-in-law, the girl's father, prevailed upon him to stay; so he remained with him three days, eating and drinking, and sleeping there.

⁵On the fourth day they got up early and he prepared to leave, but the girl's father said to his son-in-law, "Refresh yourself with something to eat; then you can go." ⁶So the two of them sat down to eat and drink together. Afterward the girl's father said, "Please stay tonight and enjoy yourself." ⁷And when the man got up to go, his father-in-law persuaded him, so he stayed there that night. ⁸On the morning of the fifth day, when he rose to go, the girl's father said, "Refresh yourself. Wait till afternoon!" So the two of them ate together.

⁹Then when the man, with his concubine and his servant, got up to leave, his father-in-law, the girl's father, said, "Now look, it's almost evening. Spend the night here; the day is nearly over. Stay and enjoy yourself. Early tomorrow morning you can get up and be on your way home." ¹⁰But, unwilling to stay another night, the man left and went toward Jebus (that is, Jerusalem), with his two saddled donkeys and his concubine.

¹¹When they were near Jebus and the day was almost gone, the servant said to his master, "Come, let's stop at this city of the Jebusites and spend the night."

¹²His master replied, "No. We won't go into an alien city, whose people are not Israelites. We will go on to Gibeah." ¹³He added, "Come, let's try to reach Gibeah or Ramah and spend the night in one of those places." ¹⁴So they went on, and the sun set as they neared Gibeah in Benjamin. ¹⁵There they stopped to spend the night. They went and sat in the city square, but no one took them into his home for the night.

¹⁶That evening an old man from the hill country of Ephraim, who was living in Gibeah (the men of the place were Benjamites), came in from his work in the fields. ¹⁷When he looked and saw the traveler in the city square, the old man asked, "Where are you going? Where did you come from?"

¹⁸He answered, "We are on our way from Bethlehem in Judah to a remote area

in the hill country of Ephraim where I live. I have been to Bethlehem in Judah and now I am going to the house of the LORD. No one has taken me into his house. ¹⁹We have both straw and fodder for our donkeys and bread and wine for ourselves your servants — me, your maidservant, and the young man with us. We don't need anything."

²⁰"You are welcome at my house," the old man said. "Let me supply whatever you need. Only don't spend the night in the square." ²¹So he took him into his house and fed his donkeys. After they had washed their feet, they had something to eat and drink.

²²While they were enjoying themselves, some of the wicked men of the city surrounded the house. Pounding on the door, they shouted to the old man who owned the house, "Bring out the man who came to your house so we can have sex with him."

²³The owner of the house went outside and said to them, "No, my friends, don't be so vile. Since this man is my guest, don't do this disgraceful thing. ²⁴Look, here is my virgin daughter, and his concubine. I will bring them out to you now, and you can use them and do to them whatever you wish. But to this man, don't do such a disgraceful thing."

²⁵But the men would not listen to him. So the man took his concubine and sent her outside to them, and they raped her and abused her throughout the night, and at dawn they let her go. ²⁶At daybreak the woman went back to the house where her master was staying, fell down at the door and lay there until daylight.

²⁷When her master got up in the morning and opened the door of the house and stepped out to continue on his way, there lay his concubine, fallen in the doorway of the house, with her hands on the threshold. ²⁸He said to her, "Get up; let's go." But there was no answer. Then the man put her on his donkey and set out for home.

²⁹When he reached home, he took a knife and cut up his concubine, limb by limb, into twelve parts and sent them into all the areas of Israel. ³⁰Everyone who saw it said, "Such a thing has never been seen or done, not since the day the Israelites came up out of Egypt. Think about it! Consider it! Tell us what to do!"

Israelites Fight the Benjamites

20 Then all the Israelites from Dan to Beersheba and from the land of Gilead came out as one man and assembled before the LORD in Mizpah. ²The leaders of all the people of the tribes of Israel took their places in the assembly of the people of God, four hundred thousand soldiers armed with swords. ³(The Benjamites heard that the Israelites had gone up to Mizpah.) Then the Israelites said, "Tell us how this awful thing happened."

⁴So the Levite, the husband of the murdered woman, said, "I and my concubine came to Gibeah in Benjamin to spend the night. ⁵During the night the men of Gibeah came after me and surrounded the house, intending to kill me. They raped my concubine, and she died. ⁶I took my concubine, cut her into pieces and sent one piece to each region of Israel's inheritance, because they committed this lewd and disgraceful act in Israel. ⁷Now, all you Israelites, speak up and give your verdict."

⁸All the people rose as one man, saying, "None of us will go home. No, not one of us will return to his house. ⁹But now this is what we'll do to Gibeah: We'll go up against it as the lot directs. ¹⁰We'll take ten men out of every hundred from all the tribes of Israel, and a hundred from a thousand, and a thousand from ten thousand, to get provisions for the army. Then, when the army arrives at Gibeahᵃ in Benjamin, it can give them what they deserve for all this vileness done in Israel." ¹¹So all the men of Israel got together and united as one man against the city.

¹²The tribes of Israel sent men throughout the tribe of Benjamin, saying, "What about this awful crime that was committed among you? ¹³Now surrender those wicked men of Gibeah so that we may put them to death and purge the evil from Israel."

But the Benjamites would not listen to their fellow Israelites. ¹⁴From their towns they came together at Gibeah to fight against the Israelites. ¹⁵At once the Benjamites mobilized twenty-six thousand swordsmen from their towns, in addition to seven hundred chosen men from those living in Gibeah. ¹⁶Among all these soldiers there were seven hundred chosen men who were left-handed, each of whom could sling a stone at a hair and not miss.

¹⁷Israel, apart from Benjamin, mustered four hundred thousand swordsmen, all of them fighting men.

¹⁸The Israelites went up to Bethelᵇ and inquired of God. They said, "Who of us shall go first to fight against the Benjamites?"

The LORD replied, "Judah shall go first."

¹⁹The next morning the Israelites got up and pitched camp near Gibeah. ²⁰The men of Israel went out to fight the Benjamites and took up battle positions against them at Gibeah. ²¹The Benjamites came out of Gibeah and cut down twenty-two thousand Israelites on the battlefield that day. ²²But the men of Israel encouraged one another and again took up their positions where they had stationed themselves the first day. ²³The Israelites went up and wept before the LORD until evening, and they inquired of the LORD. They said, "Shall we go up again to battle against the Benjamites, our brothers?"

The LORD answered, "Go up against them."

²⁴Then the Israelites drew near to Benjamin the second day. ²⁵This time, when the Benjamites came out from Gibeah to oppose them, they cut down another eighteen thousand Israelites, all of them armed with swords.

²⁶Then the Israelites, all the people, went up to Bethel, and there they sat weeping before the LORD. They fasted that day until evening and presented burnt offerings and fellowship offeringsᶜ to the LORD. ²⁷And the Israelites inquired of the LORD. (In those days the ark of the covenant of God was there, ²⁸with Phinehas son of Eleazar, the son of Aaron, ministering before it.) They asked, "Shall we go up again to battle with Benjamin our brother, or not?"

The LORD responded, "Go, for tomorrow I will give them into your hands."

²⁹Then Israel set an ambush around Gibeah. ³⁰They went up against the Benjamites on the third day and took up positions against Gibeah as they had done before. ³¹The Benjamites came out to meet them and were drawn away from the city. They began to inflict casualties on the Israelites as before, so that about thirty men fell in the open field and on the roads— the one leading to Bethel and the other to Gibeah. ³²While the Benjamites were saying, "We are defeating them as before," the Israelites were saying, "Let's retreat and draw them away from the city to the roads."

ᵃ10 One Hebrew manuscript; most Hebrew manuscripts Geba, a variant of Gibeah   ᵇ18 Or to the house of God; also in verse 26   ᶜ26 Traditionally peace offerings

33All the men of Israel moved from their places and took up positions at Baal Tamar, and the Israelite ambush charged out of its place on the west^a of Gibeah.^b **34**Then ten thousand of Israel's finest men made a frontal attack on Gibeah. The fighting was so heavy that the Benjamites did not realize how near disaster was. **35**The LORD defeated Benjamin before Israel, and on that day the Israelites struck down 25,100 Benjamites, all armed with swords. **36**Then the Benjamites saw that they were beaten.

Now the men of Israel had given way before Benjamin, because they relied on the ambush they had set near Gibeah. **37**The men who had been in ambush made a sudden dash into Gibeah, spread out and put the whole city to the sword. **38**The men of Israel had arranged with the ambush that they should send up a great cloud of smoke from the city, **39**and then the men of Israel would turn in the battle.

The Benjamites had begun to inflict casualties on the men of Israel (about thirty), and they said, "We are defeating them as in the first battle." **40**But when the column of smoke began to rise from the city, the Benjamites turned and saw the smoke of the whole city going up into the sky. **41**Then the men of Israel turned on them, and the men of Benjamin were terrified, because they realized that disaster had come upon them. **42**So they fled before the Israelites in the direction of the desert, but they could not escape the battle. And the men of Israel who came out of the towns cut them down there. **43**They surrounded the Benjamites, chased them and easily^c overran them in the vicinity of Gibeah on the east. **44**Eighteen thousand Benjamites fell, all of them valiant fighters. **45**As they turned and fled toward the desert to the rock of Rimmon, the Israelites cut down five thousand men along the roads. They kept pressing after the Benjamites as far as Gidom and struck down two thousand more.

46On that day twenty-five thousand Benjamite swordsmen fell, all of them valiant fighters. **47**But six hundred men turned and fled into the desert to the rock of Rimmon, where they stayed four months. **48**The men of Israel went back to Benjamin and put all the towns to the sword, including the animals and every-

thing else they found. All the towns they came across they set on fire.

Wives for the Benjamites

21 The men of Israel had taken an oath at Mizpah: "Not one of us will give his daughter in marriage to a Benjamite."

2The people went to Bethel,^d where they sat before God until evening, raising their voices and weeping bitterly. **3**"O LORD, the God of Israel," they cried, "why has this happened to Israel? Why should one tribe be missing from Israel today?"

4Early the next day the people built an altar and presented burnt offerings and fellowship offerings.^e

5Then the Israelites asked, "Who from all the tribes of Israel has failed to assemble before the LORD?" For they had taken a solemn oath that anyone who failed to assemble before the LORD at Mizpah should certainly be put to death.

6Now the Israelites grieved for their brothers, the Benjamites. "Today one tribe is cut off from Israel," they said. **7**"How can we provide wives for those who are left, since we have taken an oath by the LORD not to give them any of our daughters in marriage?" **8**Then they asked, "Which one of the tribes of Israel failed to assemble before the LORD at Mizpah?" They discovered that no one from Jabesh Gilead had come to the camp for the assembly. **9**For when they counted the people, they found that none of the people of Jabesh Gilead were there.

10So the assembly sent twelve thousand fighting men with instructions to go to Jabesh Gilead and put to the sword those living there, including the women and children. **11**"This is what you are to do," they said. "Kill every male and every woman who is not a virgin." **12**They found among the people living in Jabesh Gilead four hundred young women who had never slept with a man, and they took them to the camp at Shiloh in Canaan.

13Then the whole assembly sent an offer of peace to the Benjamites at the rock of Rimmon. **14**So the Benjamites returned at that time and were given the women of Jabesh Gilead who had been spared. But there were not enough for all of them.

15The people grieved for Benjamin, be-

---

^a33 Some Septuagint manuscripts and Vulgate; the meaning of the Hebrew for this word is uncertain.
^b33 Hebrew *Geba*, a variant of *Gibeah*   ^c43 The meaning of the Hebrew for this word is uncertain.
^d2 Or *to the house of God*   ^e4 Traditionally *peace offerings*

cause the Lord had made a gap in the tribes of Israel. **16**And the elders of the assembly said, "With the women of Benjamin destroyed, how shall we provide wives for the men who are left? **17**The Benjamite survivors must have heirs," they said, "so that a tribe of Israel will not be wiped out. **18**We can't give them our daughters as wives, since we Israelites have taken this oath: 'Cursed be anyone who gives a wife to a Benjamite.' **19**But look, there is the annual festival of the Lord in Shiloh, to the north of Bethel, and east of the road that goes from Bethel to Shechem, and to the south of Lebonah."

20So they instructed the Benjamites, saying, "Go and hide in the vineyards **21**and watch. When the girls of Shiloh come out to join in the dancing, then rush from the vineyards and each of you seize a wife from the girls of Shiloh and go to the land of Benjamin. **22**When their fathers or brothers complain to us, we will say to them, 'Do us a kindness by helping them, because we did not get wives for them during the war, and you are innocent, since you did not give your daughters to them.' "

23So that is what the Benjamites did. While the girls were dancing, each man caught one and carried her off to be his wife. Then they returned to their inheritance and rebuilt the towns and settled in them.

24At that time the Israelites left that place and went home to their tribes and clans, each to his own inheritance.

25In those days Israel had no king; everyone did as he saw fit.

*R*UTH'S story, occurring during the time of the judges, recalls the tragedy of Elimelech's family. They desert God's land during a famine, but God still cares about them. When Naomi returns to Judah, her daughter-in-law Ruth marries Boaz to carry on the family name and becomes an ancestor of David and Jesus. As you read this book, think about how God cares about you even when you sin and how wonderful it is that he sent Jesus, son of David, into the world.

RUTH

Naomi and Ruth

1 In the days when the judges ruled,[a] there was a famine in the land, and a man from Bethlehem in Judah, together with his wife and two sons, went to live for a while in the country of Moab. [2]The man's name was Elimelech, his wife's name Naomi, and the names of his two sons were Mahlon and Kilion. They were Ephrathites from Bethlehem, Judah. And they went to Moab and lived there.

[3]Now Elimelech, Naomi's husband, died, and she was left with her two sons.

[4]They married Moabite women, one named Orpah and the other Ruth. After they had lived there about ten years, [5]both Mahlon and Kilion also died, and Naomi was left without her two sons and her husband.

[6]When she heard in Moab that the LORD had come to the aid of his people by providing food for them, Naomi and her daughters-in-law prepared to return home from there. [7]With her two daughters-in-law she left the place where she had been living and set out on the road that would take them back to the land of Judah.

---

a 1 Traditionally *judged*

[8]Then Naomi said to her two daughters-in-law, "Go back, each of you, to your mother's home. May the LORD show kindness to you, as you have shown to your dead and to me. [9]May the LORD grant that each of you will find rest in the home of another husband."

Then she kissed them and they wept aloud [10]and said to her, "We will go back with you to your people."

[11]But Naomi said, "Return home, my daughters. Why would you come with me? Am I going to have any more sons, who could become your husbands? [12]Return home, my daughters; I am too old to have another husband. Even if I thought there was still hope for me — even if I had a husband tonight and then gave birth to sons — [13]would you wait until they grew up? Would you remain unmarried for them? No, my daughters. It is more bitter for me than for you, because the LORD's hand has gone out against me!"

[14]At this they wept again. Then Orpah kissed her mother-in-law good-by, but Ruth clung to her.

[15]"Look," said Naomi, "your sister-in-law is going back to her people and her gods. Go back with her."

[16]But Ruth replied, "Don't urge me to leave you or to turn back from you. Where you go I will go, and where you stay I will stay. Your people will be my people and your God my God. [17]Where you die I will die, and there I will be buried. May the LORD deal with me, be it ever so severely, if anything but death separates you and me." [18]When Naomi realized that Ruth was determined to go with her, she stopped urging her.

[19]So the two women went on until they came to Bethlehem. When they arrived in Bethlehem, the whole town was stirred because of them, and the women exclaimed, "Can this be Naomi?"

[20]"Don't call me Naomi,[a]" she told them. "Call me Mara,[b] because the Almighty[c] has made my life very bitter. [21]I went away full, but the LORD has brought me back empty. Why call me Naomi? The LORD has afflicted[d] me; the Almighty has brought misfortune upon me."

[22]So Naomi returned from Moab accompanied by Ruth the Moabitess, her daughter-in-law, arriving in Bethlehem as the barley harvest was beginning.

Ruth Meets Boaz

2 Now Naomi had a relative on her husband's side, from the clan of Elimelech, a man of standing, whose name was Boaz.

[2]And Ruth the Moabitess said to Naomi, "Let me go to the fields and pick up the leftover grain behind anyone in whose eyes I find favor."

Naomi said to her, "Go ahead, my daughter." [3]So she went out and began to glean in the fields behind the harvesters. As it turned out, she found herself working in a field belonging to Boaz, who was from the clan of Elimelech.

[4]Just then Boaz arrived from Bethlehem and greeted the harvesters, "The LORD be with you!"

"The LORD bless you!" they called back.

[5]Boaz asked the foreman of his harvesters, "Whose young woman is that?"

[6]The foreman replied, "She is the Moabitess who came back from Moab with Naomi. [7]She said, 'Please let me glean and gather among the sheaves behind the harvesters.' She went into the field and has worked steadily from morning till now, except for a short rest in the shelter."

[8]So Boaz said to Ruth, "My daughter, listen to me. Don't go and glean in another field and don't go away from here. Stay here with my servant girls. [9]Watch the field where the men are harvesting, and follow along after the girls. I have told the men not to touch you. And whenever you are thirsty, go and get a drink from the water jars the men have filled."

[10]At this, she bowed down with her face to the ground. She exclaimed, "Why have I found such favor in your eyes that you notice me — a foreigner?"

[11]Boaz replied, "I've been told all about what you have done for your mother-in-law since the death of your husband — how you left your father and mother and your homeland and came to live with a people you did not know before. [12]May the LORD repay you for what you have done. May you be richly rewarded by the LORD, the God of Israel, under whose wings you have come to take refuge."

[13]"May I continue to find favor in your eyes, my lord," she said. "You have given me comfort and have spoken kindly to your servant — though I do not have the standing of one of your servant girls."

---

[a]20 Naomi means pleasant; also in verse 21.   [b]20 Mara means bitter.   [c]20 Hebrew Shaddai; also in verse 21   [d]21 Or has testified against

¹⁴At mealtime Boaz said to her, "Come over here. Have some bread and dip it in the wine vinegar."

When she sat down with the harvesters, he offered her some roasted grain. She ate all she wanted and had some left over. ¹⁵As she got up to glean, Boaz gave orders to his men, "Even if she gathers among the sheaves, don't embarrass her. ¹⁶Rather, pull out some stalks for her from the bundles and leave them for her to pick up, and don't rebuke her."

¹⁷So Ruth gleaned in the field until evening. Then she threshed the barley she had gathered, and it amounted to about an ephah.ᵃ ¹⁸She carried it back to town,

ᵃ17 That is, probably about 3/5 bushel (about 22 liters)

TUESDAY

VERSE FOR THE DAY: *AUTHOR:*   *PASSAGE FOR THE DAY:*
Ruth 2:4   David Atkinson   *Ruth 2:1–4*

Work and Worship

IT IS not often that the Lord is so openly acknowledged by a manager in conversation with his workforce. "The LORD be with you"—the only time this particular greeting is found in this form, which may indicate that it is more than mere convention—brings an awareness that even the ordinariness of daily work is seen by Boaz and his men in the context of faith in the covenant God whose land it is. There is a warmth, even a thankfulness, about the greeting . . .

There is a similar blessing referred to at the end of Psalm 129: "The blessing of the LORD be upon you; we bless you in the name of the LORD." This is very similar again to the priestly blessing of Numbers 6:24: "The LORD bless you and keep you; the LORD make his face shine upon you and be gracious to you; the LORD turn his face toward you and give you peace." It probably reflects the way the priest dismissed his congregation after worship . . .

The blessing which is appropriate for worship is appropriate also for the work place. Boaz's exchange of blessing with his workforce is very similar to that exchanged at the end of worship. There is no separation in the Old Testament between the "sacred" and the "secular": the whole of life is lived as "before the face of God" . . .

We are moral and rational beings whose lives in all respects reflect the limits of our humanness as creatures dependent on the Creator, and also a limited freedom to respond to him in gratitude and worship, or ignore him in supposed autonomy. It is by gratitude and worship that the richness of true human freedom within God's limits is enjoyed, and become the basis for our own human creativity in love.

Additional Scripture Readings: *Go to page 270 for your next*
Psalm 84:1–12; Ephesians 1:3–10   *devotional reading.*

and her mother-in-law saw how much she had gathered. Ruth also brought out and gave her what she had left over after she had eaten enough.

[19]Her mother-in-law asked her, "Where did you glean today? Where did you work? Blessed be the man who took notice of you!"

Then Ruth told her mother-in-law about the one at whose place she had been working. "The name of the man I worked with today is Boaz," she said.

[20]"The LORD bless him!" Naomi said to her daughter-in-law. "He has not stopped showing his kindness to the living and the dead." She added, "That man is our close relative; he is one of our kinsman-redeemers."

[21]Then Ruth the Moabitess said, "He even said to me, 'Stay with my workers until they finish harvesting all my grain.' "

[22]Naomi said to Ruth her daughter-in-law, "It will be good for you, my daughter, to go with his girls, because in someone else's field you might be harmed."

[23]So Ruth stayed close to the servant girls of Boaz to glean until the barley and wheat harvests were finished. And she lived with her mother-in-law.

Ruth and Boaz at the Threshing Floor

3 One day Naomi her mother-in-law said to her, "My daughter, should I not try to find a home[a] for you, where you will be well provided for? [2]Is not Boaz, with whose servant girls you have been, a kinsman of ours? Tonight he will be winnowing barley on the threshing floor. [3]Wash and perfume yourself, and put on your best clothes. Then go down to the threshing floor, but don't let him know you are there until he has finished eating and drinking. [4]When he lies down, note the place where he is lying. Then go and uncover his feet and lie down. He will tell you what to do."

[5]"I will do whatever you say," Ruth answered. [6]So she went down to the threshing floor and did everything her mother-in-law told her to do.

[7]When Boaz had finished eating and drinking and was in good spirits, he went over to lie down at the far end of the grain pile. Ruth approached quietly, uncovered his feet and lay down. [8]In the middle of the night something startled the man, and

he turned and discovered a woman lying at his feet.

[9]"Who are you?" he asked.

"I am your servant Ruth," she said. "Spread the corner of your garment over me, since you are a kinsman-redeemer."

[10]"The LORD bless you, my daughter," he replied. "This kindness is greater than that which you showed earlier: You have not run after the younger men, whether rich or poor. [11]And now, my daughter, don't be afraid. I will do for you all you ask. All my fellow townsmen know that you are a woman of noble character. [12]Although it is true that I am near of kin, there is a kinsman-redeemer nearer than I. [13]Stay here for the night, and in the morning if he wants to redeem, good; let him redeem. But if he is not willing, as surely as the LORD lives I will do it. Lie here until morning."

[14]So she lay at his feet until morning, but got up before anyone could be recognized; and he said, "Don't let it be known that a woman came to the threshing floor."

[15]He also said, "Bring me the shawl you are wearing and hold it out." When she did so, he poured into it six measures of barley and put it on her. Then he[b] went back to town.

[16]When Ruth came to her mother-in-law, Naomi asked, "How did it go, my daughter?"

Then she told her everything Boaz had done for her [17]and added, "He gave me these six measures of barley, saying, 'Don't go back to your mother-in-law empty-handed.' "

[18]Then Naomi said, "Wait, my daughter, until you find out what happens. For the man will not rest until the matter is settled today."

Boaz Marries Ruth

4 Meanwhile Boaz went up to the town gate and sat there. When the kinsman-redeemer he had mentioned came along, Boaz said, "Come over here, my friend, and sit down." So he went over and sat down.

[2]Boaz took ten of the elders of the town and said, "Sit here," and they did so. [3]Then he said to the kinsman-redeemer, "Naomi, who has come back from Moab, is selling the piece of land that belonged to our brother Elimelech. [4]I thought I

---

*a*1 Hebrew *find rest* (see Ruth 1:9)   *b*15 Most Hebrew manuscripts; many Hebrew manuscripts, Vulgate and Syriac *she* should bring the matter to your attention and suggest that you buy it in the presence of these seated here and in the presence of the elders of my people. If you will redeem it, do so. But if you[a] will not, tell me, so I will know. For no one has the right to do it except you, and I am next in line."

"I will redeem it," he said.

[5]Then Boaz said, "On the day you buy the land from Naomi and from Ruth the Moabitess, you acquire[b] the dead man's widow, in order to maintain the name of the dead with his property."

[6]At this, the kinsman-redeemer said, "Then I cannot redeem it because I might endanger my own estate. You redeem it yourself. I cannot do it."

[7](Now in earlier times in Israel, for the redemption and transfer of property to become final, one party took off his sandal and gave it to the other. This was the method of legalizing transactions in Israel.)

[8]So the kinsman-redeemer said to Boaz, "Buy it yourself." And he removed his sandal.

[9]Then Boaz announced to the elders and all the people, "Today you are witnesses that I have bought from Naomi all the property of Elimelech, Kilion and Mahlon. [10]I have also acquired Ruth the Moabitess, Mahlon's widow, as my wife, in order to maintain the name of the dead with his property, so that his name will not disappear from among his family or from the town records. Today you are witnesses!"

[11]Then the elders and all those at the gate said, "We are witnesses. May the Lord make the woman who is coming into your home like Rachel and Leah, who together built up the house of Israel. May you have standing in Ephrathah and be famous in Bethlehem. [12]Through the offspring the Lord gives you by this young woman, may your family be like that of Perez, whom Tamar bore to Judah."

The Genealogy of David

[13]So Boaz took Ruth and she became his wife. Then he went to her, and the Lord enabled her to conceive, and she gave birth to a son. [14]The women said to Naomi: "Praise be to the Lord, who this day has not left you without a kinsman-redeemer. May he become famous throughout Israel! [15]He will renew your life and sustain you in your old age. For your daughter-in-law, who loves you and who is better to you than seven sons, has given him birth."

[16]Then Naomi took the child, laid him in her lap and cared for him. [17]The women living there said, "Naomi has a son." And they named him Obed. He was the father of Jesse, the father of David.

[18]This, then, is the family line of Perez:

Perez was the father of Hezron,
[19]Hezron the father of Ram,
Ram the father of Amminadab,
[20]Amminadab the father of Nahshon,
Nahshon the father of Salmon,[c]
[21]Salmon the father of Boaz,
Boaz the father of Obed,
[22]Obed the father of Jesse,
and Jesse the father of David.

---

[a]4 Many Hebrew manuscripts, Septuagint, Vulgate and Syriac; most Hebrew manuscripts *he*
[b]5 Hebrew; Vulgate and Syriac *Naomi, you acquire Ruth the Moabitess,*   [c]20 A few Hebrew manuscripts, some Septuagint manuscripts and Vulgate (see also verse 21 and Septuagint of 1 Chron. 2:11); most Hebrew manuscripts *Salma*

THIS book tells the story of Samuel, the last judge, and of Saul, Israel's first king. Saul's sin and disobedience lead God to reject him and anoint David as Israel's second king. In spite of numerous threats to David's life from both the Philistines and from Saul, God keeps him safe. As you read this book, think how God will protect and bless you if you trust in him; be warned that if you disobey God, you may face many difficulties.

1 SAMUEL

The Birth of Samuel

1 There was a certain man from Ramathaim, a Zuphite[a] from the hill country of Ephraim, whose name was Elkanah son of Jeroham, the son of Elihu, the son of Tohu, the son of Zuph, an Ephraimite. ²He had two wives; one was called Hannah and the other Peninnah. Peninnah had children, but Hannah had none.

³Year after year this man went up from his town to worship and sacrifice to the LORD Almighty at Shiloh, where Hophni and Phinehas, the two sons of Eli, were priests of the LORD. ⁴Whenever the day came for Elkanah to sacrifice, he would give portions of the meat to his wife Peninnah and to all her sons and daughters. ⁵But to Hannah he gave a double portion because he loved her, and the LORD had closed her womb. ⁶And because the LORD had closed her womb, her rival kept provoking her in order to irritate her. ⁷This went on year after year. Whenever Hannah went up to the house of the LORD, her rival provoked her till she wept and would not eat. ⁸Elkanah her husband would say to her, "Hannah, why are you weeping? Why don't you eat? Why are you down-

---

a 1 Or from Ramathaim Zuphim

hearted? Don't I mean more to you than ten sons?"

⁹Once when they had finished eating and drinking in Shiloh, Hannah stood up. Now Eli the priest was sitting on a chair by the doorpost of the LORD's temple.ᵃ ¹⁰In bitterness of soul Hannah wept much and prayed to the LORD. ¹¹And she made a vow, saying, "O LORD Almighty, if you will only look upon your servant's misery and remember me, and not forget your servant but give her a son, then I will give him to the LORD for all the days of his life, and no razor will ever be used on his head."

¹²As she kept on praying to the LORD, Eli observed her mouth. ¹³Hannah was praying in her heart, and her lips were moving but her voice was not heard. Eli thought she was drunk ¹⁴and said to her, "How long will you keep on getting drunk? Get rid of your wine."

¹⁵"Not so, my lord," Hannah replied, "I am a woman who is deeply troubled. I have not been drinking wine or beer; I was pouring out my soul to the LORD. ¹⁶Do not take your servant for a wicked woman; I have been praying here out of my great anguish and grief."

¹⁷Eli answered, "Go in peace, and may the God of Israel grant you what you have asked of him."

¹⁸She said, "May your servant find favor in your eyes." Then she went her way and ate something, and her face was no longer downcast.

¹⁹Early the next morning they arose and worshiped before the LORD and then went back to their home at Ramah. Elkanah lay with Hannah his wife, and the LORD remembered her. ²⁰So in the course of time Hannah conceived and gave birth to a son. She named him Samuel,ᵇ saying, "Because I asked the LORD for him."

Hannah Dedicates Samuel

²¹When the man Elkanah went up with all his family to offer the annual sacrifice to the LORD and to fulfill his vow, ²²Hannah did not go. She said to her husband, "After the boy is weaned, I will take him and present him before the LORD, and he will live there always."

²³"Do what seems best to you," Elkanah her husband told her. "Stay here until you have weaned him; only may the LORD

make good hisᶜ word." So the woman stayed at home and nursed her son until she had weaned him.

²⁴After he was weaned, she took the boy with her, young as he was, along with a three-year-old bull,ᵈ an ephahᵉ of flour and a skin of wine, and brought him to the house of the LORD at Shiloh. ²⁵When they had slaughtered the bull, they brought the boy to Eli, ²⁶and she said to him, "As surely as you live, my lord, I am the woman who stood here beside you praying to the LORD. ²⁷I prayed for this child, and the LORD has granted me what I asked of him. ²⁸So now I give him to the LORD. For his whole life he will be given over to the LORD." And he worshiped the LORD there.

Hannah's Prayer

2 Then Hannah prayed and said:

"My heart rejoices in the LORD;
  in the LORD my hornᶠ is lifted high.
My mouth boasts over my enemies,
  for I delight in your deliverance.

²"There is no one holyᵍ like the LORD;
  there is no one besides you;
  there is no Rock like our God.

³"Do not keep talking so proudly
  or let your mouth speak such arrogance,
for the LORD is a God who knows,
  and by him deeds are weighed.

⁴"The bows of the warriors are broken,
  but those who stumbled are armed with strength.
⁵Those who were full hire themselves out for food,
  but those who were hungry hunger no more.
She who was barren has borne seven children,
  but she who has had many sons pines away.

⁶"The LORD brings death and makes alive;
  he brings down to the graveʰ and raises up.
⁷The LORD sends poverty and wealth;
  he humbles and he exalts.
⁸He raises the poor from the dust
  and lifts the needy from the ash heap;

ᵃ9 That is, tabernacle   ᵇ20 *Samuel* sounds like the Hebrew for *heard of God.*   ᶜ23 Masoretic Text; Dead Sea Scrolls, Septuagint and Syriac *your*   ᵈ24 Dead Sea Scrolls, Septuagint and Syriac; Masoretic Text *with three bulls*   ᵉ24 That is, probably about 3/5 bushel (about 22 liters)   ᶠ1 *Horn* here symbolizes strength; also in verse 10.   ᵍ2 Or *no Holy One*   ʰ6 Hebrew *Sheol*

he seats them with princes
and has them inherit a throne of
honor.

"For the foundations of the earth are
the Lord's;
upon them he has set the world.
9He will guard the feet of his saints,
but the wicked will be silenced in
darkness.

"It is not by strength that one prevails;
10 those who oppose the Lord will be
shattered.
He will thunder against them from
heaven;
the Lord will judge the ends of the
earth.

"He will give strength to his king
and exalt the horn of his anointed."

11Then Elkanah went home to Ramah,
but the boy ministered before the Lord
under Eli the priest.

Eli's Wicked Sons

12Eli's sons were wicked men; they had
no regard for the Lord. 13Now it was the
practice of the priests with the people that
whenever anyone offered a sacrifice and
while the meat was being boiled, the servant of the priest would come with a
three-pronged fork in his hand. 14He
would plunge it into the pan or kettle or
caldron or pot, and the priest would take
for himself whatever the fork brought up.
This is how they treated all the Israelites
who came to Shiloh. 15But even before the
fat was burned, the servant of the priest
would come and say to the man who was
sacrificing, "Give the priest some meat to
roast; he won't accept boiled meat from
you, but only raw."

16If the man said to him, "Let the fat be
burned up first, and then take whatever
you want," the servant would then answer, "No, hand it over now; if you don't,
I'll take it by force."

17This sin of the young men was very
great in the Lord's sight, for theya were
treating the Lord's offering with contempt.

18But Samuel was ministering before
the Lord—a boy wearing a linen ephod.
19Each year his mother made him a little
robe and took it to him when she went up
with her husband to offer the annual sacrifice. 20Eli would bless Elkanah and his
wife, saying, "May the Lord give you chil-

dren by this woman to take the place of
the one she prayed for and gave to the
Lord." Then they would go home. 21And
the Lord was gracious to Hannah; she
conceived and gave birth to three sons
and two daughters. Meanwhile, the boy
Samuel grew up in the presence of the
Lord.

22Now Eli, who was very old, heard
about everything his sons were doing to
all Israel and how they slept with the
women who served at the entrance to the
Tent of Meeting. 23So he said to them,
"Why do you do such things? I hear from
all the people about these wicked deeds of
yours. 24No, my sons; it is not a good report that I hear spreading among the
Lord's people. 25If a man sins against another man, Godb may mediate for him;
but if a man sins against the Lord, who
will intercede for him?" His sons, however, did not listen to their father's rebuke,
for it was the Lord's will to put them to
death.

26And the boy Samuel continued to
grow in stature and in favor with the Lord
and with men.

Prophecy Against the House of Eli

27Now a man of God came to Eli and
said to him, "This is what the Lord says:
'Did I not clearly reveal myself to your father's house when they were in Egypt under Pharaoh? 28I chose your father out of
all the tribes of Israel to be my priest, to go
up to my altar, to burn incense, and to
wear an ephod in my presence. I also gave
your father's house all the offerings made
with fire by the Israelites. 29Why do youc
scorn my sacrifice and offering that I prescribed for my dwelling? Why do you hon-
or your sons more than me by fattening
yourselves on the choice parts of every offering made by my people Israel?'

30"Therefore the Lord, the God of Israel,
declares: 'I promised that your house and
your father's house would minister before
me forever.' But now the Lord declares:
'Far be it from me! Those who honor me
I will honor, but those who despise me
will be disdained. 31The time is coming
when I will cut short your strength and
the strength of your father's house, so that
there will not be an old man in your family line 32and you will see distress in my
dwelling. Although good will be done to
Israel, in your family line there will never

---

a17 Or men   b25 Or the judges   c29 The Hebrew is plural.

be an old man. ³³Every one of you that I do not cut off from my altar will be spared only to blind your eyes with tears and to grieve your heart, and all your descendants will die in the prime of life.

³⁴" 'And what happens to your two sons, Hophni and Phinehas, will be a sign to you—they will both die on the same day. ³⁵I will raise up for myself a faithful priest, who will do according to what is in my heart and mind. I will firmly establish his house, and he will minister before my anointed one always. ³⁶Then everyone left in your family line will come and bow down before him for a piece of silver and a crust of bread and plead, "Appoint me to

---

WEDNESDAY

VERSE FOR THE DAY:
1 Samuel 2:8

AUTHOR:
Daniel Taylor

PASSAGE FOR THE DAY:
1 Samuel 2:6–10

Poverty and Wealth

WE ALL are poor in some way or other. The person who thinks money is the measure of success suffers from a kind of poverty of the imagination and intellect as well as of the spirit. Others suffer a kind of poverty of the emotions, unable to intertwine their lives affirmingly with the lives of others. And the Bible tells us we are all poor before God. God offers us all of creation and a relationship with him and we have only our brokenness to offer back. (Thankfully, that is all that he requires.)

All this is not an attempt to dismiss our responsibility to the materially poor . . . It is, rather, an appeal to consider carefully who the poor are and what the Christian response to poverty is.

The Bible makes clear that by far the most serious kind of poverty is spiritual poverty and that this poverty afflicts people of every race, class, nationality, age and sex. It offers as the solution for this poverty a right relationship with God through Jesus Christ.

But the Bible also has much to say about material poverty, and it is clearly on the side of the poor. Poverty in the Bible is rarely attributed, as we usually like to do, to laziness or wickedness on the part of the poor. Much more often it is seen as the product of injustice or greed or mercilessness on the part of those who have much. The Bible repeatedly promises heavy consequences for those who insist on increasing the pile of their own [money] while ignoring the needs of the poor.

Is money the root of all evil? No. The love of money is. But we shouldn't rest too easily because of that distinction. We show what we love by that to which we most happily devote our attention.

Additional Scripture Readings:
2 Corinthians 8:1–9;
1 Timothy 6:6–10

Go to page 286 for your next devotional reading.

some priestly office so I can have food to eat.' ' "

The Lord Calls Samuel

3 The boy Samuel ministered before the Lord under Eli. In those days the word of the Lord was rare; there were not many visions.

²One night Eli, whose eyes were becoming so weak that he could barely see, was lying down in his usual place. ³The lamp of God had not yet gone out, and Samuel was lying down in the temple*a* of the Lord, where the ark of God was. ⁴Then the Lord called Samuel.

Samuel answered, "Here I am." ⁵And he ran to Eli and said, "Here I am; you called me."

But Eli said, "I did not call; go back and lie down." So he went and lay down.

⁶Again the Lord called, "Samuel!" And Samuel got up and went to Eli and said, "Here I am; you called me."

"My son," Eli said, "I did not call; go back and lie down."

⁷Now Samuel did not yet know the Lord: The word of the Lord had not yet been revealed to him.

⁸The Lord called Samuel a third time, and Samuel got up and went to Eli and said, "Here I am; you called me."

Then Eli realized that the Lord was calling the boy. ⁹So Eli told Samuel, "Go and lie down, and if he calls you, say, 'Speak, Lord, for your servant is listening.' " So Samuel went and lay down in his place.

¹⁰The Lord came and stood there, calling as at the other times, "Samuel! Samuel!"

Then Samuel said, "Speak, for your servant is listening."

¹¹And the Lord said to Samuel: "See, I am about to do something in Israel that will make the ears of everyone who hears of it tingle. ¹²At that time I will carry out against Eli everything I spoke against his family—from beginning to end. ¹³For I told him that I would judge his family forever because of the sin he knew about; his sons made themselves contemptible,*b* and he failed to restrain them. ¹⁴Therefore, I swore to the house of Eli, 'The guilt of Eli's house will never be atoned for by sacrifice or offering.' "

¹⁵Samuel lay down until morning and then opened the doors of the house of the Lord. He was afraid to tell Eli the vision, ¹⁶but Eli called him and said, "Samuel, my son."

Samuel answered, "Here I am."

¹⁷"What was it he said to you?" Eli asked. "Do not hide it from me. May God deal with you, be it ever so severely, if you hide from me anything he told you." ¹⁸So Samuel told him everything, hiding nothing from him. Then Eli said, "He is the Lord; let him do what is good in his eyes."

¹⁹The Lord was with Samuel as he grew up, and he let none of his words fall to the ground. ²⁰And all Israel from Dan to Beersheba recognized that Samuel was attested as a prophet of the Lord. ²¹The Lord continued to appear at Shiloh, and there he revealed himself to Samuel through his word.

4 And Samuel's word came to all Israel.

The Philistines Capture the Ark

Now the Israelites went out to fight against the Philistines. The Israelites camped at Ebenezer, and the Philistines at Aphek. ²The Philistines deployed their forces to meet Israel, and as the battle spread, Israel was defeated by the Philistines, who killed about four thousand of them on the battlefield. ³When the soldiers returned to camp, the elders of Israel asked, "Why did the Lord bring defeat upon us today before the Philistines? Let us bring the ark of the Lord's covenant from Shiloh, so that it*c* may go with us and save us from the hand of our enemies."

⁴So the people sent men to Shiloh, and they brought back the ark of the covenant of the Lord Almighty, who is enthroned between the cherubim. And Eli's two sons, Hophni and Phinehas, were there with the ark of the covenant of God.

⁵When the ark of the Lord's covenant came into the camp, all Israel raised such a great shout that the ground shook. ⁶Hearing the uproar, the Philistines asked, "What's all this shouting in the Hebrew camp?"

When they learned that the ark of the Lord had come into the camp, ⁷the Philistines were afraid. "A god has come into the camp," they said. "We're in trouble! Nothing like this has happened before. ⁸Woe to us! Who will deliver us from the hand of these mighty gods? They are the gods who struck the Egyptians with all

a3 That is, tabernacle   *b13* Masoretic Text; an ancient Hebrew scribal tradition and Septuagint *sons blasphemed God*   *c3* Or *he* kinds of plagues in the desert. ⁹Be strong, Philistines! Be men, or you will be subject to the Hebrews, as they have been to you. Be men, and fight!"

¹⁰So the Philistines fought, and the Israelites were defeated and every man fled to his tent. The slaughter was very great; Israel lost thirty thousand foot soldiers. ¹¹The ark of God was captured, and Eli's two sons, Hophni and Phinehas, died.

Death of Eli

¹²That same day a Benjamite ran from the battle line and went to Shiloh, his clothes torn and dust on his head. ¹³When he arrived, there was Eli sitting on his chair by the side of the road, watching, because his heart feared for the ark of God. When the man entered the town and told what had happened, the whole town sent up a cry.

¹⁴Eli heard the outcry and asked, "What is the meaning of this uproar?"

The man hurried over to Eli, ¹⁵who was ninety-eight years old and whose eyes were set so that he could not see. ¹⁶He told Eli, "I have just come from the battle line; I fled from it this very day."

Eli asked, "What happened, my son?"

¹⁷The man who brought the news replied, "Israel fled before the Philistines, and the army has suffered heavy losses. Also your two sons, Hophni and Phinehas, are dead, and the ark of God has been captured."

¹⁸When he mentioned the ark of God, Eli fell backward off his chair by the side of the gate. His neck was broken and he died, for he was an old man and heavy. He had led[a] Israel forty years.

¹⁹His daughter-in-law, the wife of Phinehas, was pregnant and near the time of delivery. When she heard the news that the ark of God had been captured and that her father-in-law and her husband were dead, she went into labor and gave birth, but was overcome by her labor pains. ²⁰As she was dying, the women attending her said, "Don't despair; you have given birth to a son." But she did not respond or pay any attention.

²¹She named the boy Ichabod,[b] saying, "The glory has departed from Israel" — because of the capture of the ark of God and the deaths of her father-in-law and her husband. ²²She said, "The glory has de-

parted from Israel, for the ark of God has been captured."

The Ark in Ashdod and Ekron

5 After the Philistines had captured the ark of God, they took it from Ebenezer to Ashdod. ²Then they carried the ark into Dagon's temple and set it beside Dagon. ³When the people of Ashdod rose early the next day, there was Dagon, fallen on his face on the ground before the ark of the Lord! They took Dagon and put him back in his place. ⁴But the following morning when they rose, there was Dagon, fallen on his face on the ground before the ark of the Lord! His head and hands had been broken off and were lying on the threshold; only his body remained. ⁵That is why to this day neither the priests of Dagon nor any others who enter Dagon's temple at Ashdod step on the threshold.

⁶The Lord's hand was heavy upon the people of Ashdod and its vicinity; he brought devastation upon them and afflicted them with tumors.[c] ⁷When the men of Ashdod saw what was happening, they said, "The ark of the god of Israel must not stay here with us, because his hand is heavy upon us and upon Dagon our god." ⁸So they called together all the rulers of the Philistines and asked them, "What shall we do with the ark of the god of Israel?"

They answered, "Have the ark of the god of Israel moved to Gath." So they moved the ark of the God of Israel.

⁹But after they had moved it, the Lord's hand was against that city, throwing it into a great panic. He afflicted the people of the city, both young and old, with an outbreak of tumors.[d] ¹⁰So they sent the ark of God to Ekron.

As the ark of God was entering Ekron, the people of Ekron cried out, "They have brought the ark of the god of Israel around to us to kill us and our people." ¹¹So they called together all the rulers of the Philistines and said, "Send the ark of the god of Israel away; let it go back to its own place, or it[e] will kill us and our people." For death had filled the city with panic; God's hand was very heavy upon it. ¹²Those who did not die were afflicted with tumors, and the outcry of the city went up to heaven.

---

[a]18 Traditionally *judged*   [b]21 *Ichabod* means *no glory.*   [c]6 Hebrew; Septuagint and Vulgate *tumors.* *And rats appeared in their land, and death and destruction were throughout the city*   [d]9 Or *with tumors in the groin* (see Septuagint)   [e]11 Or *he*

The Ark Returned to Israel

6 When the ark of the LORD had been in Philistine territory seven months, [2]the Philistines called for the priests and the diviners and said, "What shall we do with the ark of the LORD? Tell us how we should send it back to its place."

[3]They answered, "If you return the ark of the god of Israel, do not send it away empty, but by all means send a guilt offering to him. Then you will be healed, and you will know why his hand has not been lifted from you."

[4]The Philistines asked, "What guilt offering should we send to him?"

They replied, "Five gold tumors and five gold rats, according to the number of the Philistine rulers, because the same plague has struck both you and your rulers. [5]Make models of the tumors and of the rats that are destroying the country, and pay honor to Israel's god. Perhaps he will lift his hand from you and your gods and your land. [6]Why do you harden your hearts as the Egyptians and Pharaoh did? When he[a] treated them harshly, did they not send the Israelites out so they could go on their way?

[7]"Now then, get a new cart ready, with two cows that have calved and have never been yoked. Hitch the cows to the cart, but take their calves away and pen them up. [8]Take the ark of the LORD and put it on the cart, and in a chest beside it put the gold objects you are sending back to him as a guilt offering. Send it on its way, [9]but keep watching it. If it goes up to its own territory, toward Beth Shemesh, then the LORD has brought this great disaster on us. But if it does not, then we will know that it was not his hand that struck us and that it happened to us by chance."

[10]So they did this. They took two such cows and hitched them to the cart and penned up their calves. [11]They placed the ark of the LORD on the cart and along with it the chest containing the gold rats and the models of the tumors. [12]Then the cows went straight up toward Beth Shemesh, keeping on the road and lowing all the way; they did not turn to the right or to the left. The rulers of the Philistines followed them as far as the border of Beth Shemesh.

[13]Now the people of Beth Shemesh were harvesting their wheat in the valley, and when they looked up and saw the ark, they rejoiced at the sight. [14]The cart came to the field of Joshua of Beth Shemesh, and there it stopped beside a large rock. The people chopped up the wood of the cart and sacrificed the cows as a burnt offering to the LORD. [15]The Levites took down the ark of the LORD, together with the chest containing the gold objects, and placed them on the large rock. On that day the people of Beth Shemesh offered burnt offerings and made sacrifices to the LORD. [16]The five rulers of the Philistines saw all this and then returned that same day to Ekron.

[17]These are the gold tumors the Philistines sent as a guilt offering to the LORD—one each for Ashdod, Gaza, Ashkelon, Gath and Ekron. [18]And the number of the gold rats was according to the number of Philistine towns belonging to the five rulers—the fortified towns with their country villages. The large rock, on which[b] they set the ark of the LORD, is a witness to this day in the field of Joshua of Beth Shemesh.

[19]But God struck down some of the men of Beth Shemesh, putting seventy[c] of them to death because they had looked into the ark of the LORD. The people mourned because of the heavy blow the LORD had dealt them, [20]and the men of Beth Shemesh asked, "Who can stand in the presence of the LORD, this holy God? To whom will the ark go up from here?"

[21]Then they sent messengers to the people of Kiriath Jearim, saying, "The Philistines have returned the ark of the LORD. Come down and take it up to your place."

7 [1]So the men of Kiriath Jearim came and took up the ark of the LORD. They took it to Abinadab's house on the hill and consecrated Eleazar his son to guard the ark of the LORD.

Samuel Subdues the Philistines at Mizpah

[2]It was a long time, twenty years in all, that the ark remained at Kiriath Jearim, and all the people of Israel mourned and sought after the LORD. [3]And Samuel said to the whole house of Israel, "If you are returning to the LORD with all your hearts, then rid yourselves of the foreign gods and the Ashtoreths and commit your-

---

[a]6 That is, God   [b]18 A few Hebrew manuscripts (see also Septuagint); most Hebrew manuscripts *villages as far as Greater Abel, where*   [c]19 A few Hebrew manuscripts; most Hebrew manuscripts and Septuagint *50,070*

selves to the Lord and serve him only, and he will deliver you out of the hand of the Philistines." **4**So the Israelites put away their Baals and Ashtoreths, and served the Lord only.

5Then Samuel said, "Assemble all Israel at Mizpah and I will intercede with the Lord for you." **6**When they had assembled at Mizpah, they drew water and poured it out before the Lord. On that day they fasted and there they confessed, "We have sinned against the Lord." And Samuel was leader*a* of Israel at Mizpah.

7When the Philistines heard that Israel had assembled at Mizpah, the rulers of the Philistines came up to attack them. And when the Israelites heard of it, they were afraid because of the Philistines. **8**They said to Samuel, "Do not stop crying out to the Lord our God for us, that he may rescue us from the hand of the Philistines." **9**Then Samuel took a suckling lamb and offered it up as a whole burnt offering to the Lord. He cried out to the Lord on Israel's behalf, and the Lord answered him. **10**While Samuel was sacrificing the burnt offering, the Philistines drew near to engage Israel in battle. But that day the Lord thundered with loud thunder against the Philistines and threw them into such a panic that they were routed before the Israelites. **11**The men of Israel rushed out of Mizpah and pursued the Philistines, slaughtering them along the way to a point below Beth Car.

12Then Samuel took a stone and set it up between Mizpah and Shen. He named it Ebenezer,*b* saying, "Thus far has the Lord helped us." **13**So the Philistines were subdued and did not invade Israelite territory again.

Throughout Samuel's lifetime, the hand of the Lord was against the Philistines. **14**The towns from Ekron to Gath that the Philistines had captured from Israel were restored to her, and Israel delivered the neighboring territory from the power of the Philistines. And there was peace between Israel and the Amorites.

15Samuel continued as judge over Israel all the days of his life. **16**From year to year he went on a circuit from Bethel to Gilgal to Mizpah, judging Israel in all those places. **17**But he always went back to Ramah, where his home was, and there he also judged Israel. And he built an altar there to the Lord.

Israel Asks for a King

8 When Samuel grew old, he appointed his sons as judges for Israel. **2**The name of his firstborn was Joel and the name of his second was Abijah, and they served at Beersheba. **3**But his sons did not walk in his ways. They turned aside after dishonest gain and accepted bribes and perverted justice.

4So all the elders of Israel gathered together and came to Samuel at Ramah. **5**They said to him, "You are old, and your sons do not walk in your ways; now appoint a king to lead*c* us, such as all the other nations have."

6But when they said, "Give us a king to lead us," this displeased Samuel; so he prayed to the Lord. **7**And the Lord told him: "Listen to all that the people are saying to you; it is not you they have rejected, but they have rejected me as their king. **8**As they have done from the day I brought them up out of Egypt until this day, forsaking me and serving other gods, so they are doing to you. **9**Now listen to them; but warn them solemnly and let them know what the king who will reign over them will do."

10Samuel told all the words of the Lord to the people who were asking him for a king. **11**He said, "This is what the king who will reign over you will do: He will take your sons and make them serve with his chariots and horses, and they will run in front of his chariots. **12**Some he will assign to be commanders of thousands and commanders of fifties, and others to plow his ground and reap his harvest, and still others to make weapons of war and equipment for his chariots. **13**He will take your daughters to be perfumers and cooks and bakers. **14**He will take the best of your fields and vineyards and olive groves and give them to his attendants. **15**He will take a tenth of your grain and of your vintage and give it to his officials and attendants. **16**Your menservants and maidservants and the best of your cattle*d* and donkeys he will take for his own use. **17**He will take a tenth of your flocks, and you yourselves will become his slaves. **18**When that day comes, you will cry out for relief from the king you have chosen, and the Lord will not answer you in that day."

19But the people refused to listen to Samuel. "No!" they said. "We want a king

---

a6 Traditionally *judge*   *b12* Ebenezer means *stone of help.*   *c5* Traditionally *judge*; also in verses 6 and 20   *d16* Septuagint; Hebrew *young men* over us. **20**Then we will be like all the other nations, with a king to lead us and to go out before us and fight our battles."

21When Samuel heard all that the people said, he repeated it before the LORD. **22**The LORD answered, "Listen to them and give them a king."

Then Samuel said to the men of Israel, "Everyone go back to his town."

Samuel Anoints Saul

9 There was a Benjamite, a man of standing, whose name was Kish son of Abiel, the son of Zeror, the son of Becorath, the son of Aphiah of Benjamin. **2**He had a son named Saul, an impressive young man without equal among the Israelites — a head taller than any of the others.

3Now the donkeys belonging to Saul's father Kish were lost, and Kish said to his son Saul, "Take one of the servants with you and go and look for the donkeys." **4**So he passed through the hill country of Ephraim and through the area around Shalisha, but they did not find them. They went on into the district of Shaalim, but the donkeys were not there. Then he passed through the territory of Benjamin, but they did not find them.

5When they reached the district of Zuph, Saul said to the servant who was with him, "Come, let's go back, or my father will stop thinking about the donkeys and start worrying about us."

6But the servant replied, "Look, in this town there is a man of God; he is highly respected, and everything he says comes true. Let's go there now. Perhaps he will tell us what way to take."

7Saul said to his servant, "If we go, what can we give the man? The food in our sacks is gone. We have no gift to take to the man of God. What do we have?"

8The servant answered him again. "Look," he said, "I have a quarter of a shekel*a* of silver. I will give it to the man of God so that he will tell us what way to take." **9**(Formerly in Israel, if a man went to inquire of God, he would say, "Come, let us go to the seer," because the prophet of today used to be called a seer.)

10"Good," Saul said to his servant. "Come, let's go." So they set out for the town where the man of God was.

11As they were going up the hill to the town, they met some girls coming out to draw water, and they asked them, "Is the seer here?"

12"He is," they answered. "He's ahead of you. Hurry now; he has just come to our town today, for the people have a sacrifice at the high place. **13**As soon as you enter the town, you will find him before he goes up to the high place to eat. The people will not begin eating until he comes, because he must bless the sacrifice; afterward, those who are invited will eat. Go up now; you should find him about this time."

14They went up to the town, and as they were entering it, there was Samuel, coming toward them on his way up to the high place.

15Now the day before Saul came, the LORD had revealed this to Samuel: **16**"About this time tomorrow I will send you a man from the land of Benjamin. Anoint him leader over my people Israel; he will deliver my people from the hand of the Philistines. I have looked upon my people, for their cry has reached me."

17When Samuel caught sight of Saul, the LORD said to him, "This is the man I spoke to you about; he will govern my people."

18Saul approached Samuel in the gateway and asked, "Would you please tell me where the seer's house is?"

19"I am the seer," Samuel replied. "Go up ahead of me to the high place, for today you are to eat with me, and in the morning I will let you go and will tell you all that is in your heart. **20**As for the donkeys you lost three days ago, do not worry about them; they have been found. And to whom is all the desire of Israel turned, if not to you and all your father's family?"

21Saul answered, "But am I not a Benjamite, from the smallest tribe of Israel, and is not my clan the least of all the clans of the tribe of Benjamin? Why do you say such a thing to me?"

22Then Samuel brought Saul and his servant into the hall and seated them at the head of those who were invited — about thirty in number. **23**Samuel said to the cook, "Bring the piece of meat I gave you, the one I told you to lay aside."

24So the cook took up the leg with what was on it and set it in front of Saul. Samuel said, "Here is what has been kept for you. Eat, because it was set aside for you for this occasion, from the time I said, 'I have

---

*a*8 That is, about 1/10 ounce (about 3 grams)

invited guests.'" And Saul dined with Samuel that day.

25After they came down from the high place to the town, Samuel talked with Saul on the roof of his house. 26They rose about daybreak and Samuel called to Saul on the roof, "Get ready, and I will send you on your way." When Saul got ready, he and Samuel went outside together. 27As they were going down to the edge of the town, Samuel said to Saul, "Tell the servant to go on ahead of us"—and the servant did so—"but you stay here awhile, so that I may give you a message from God."

10 Then Samuel took a flask of oil and poured it on Saul's head and kissed him, saying, "Has not the LORD anointed you leader over his inheritance?a 2When you leave me today, you will meet two men near Rachel's tomb, at Zelzah on the border of Benjamin. They will say to you, 'The donkeys you set out to look for have been found. And now your father has stopped thinking about them and is worried about you. He is asking, "What shall I do about my son?"'

3"Then you will go on from there until you reach the great tree of Tabor. Three men going up to God at Bethel will meet you there. One will be carrying three young goats, another three loaves of bread, and another a skin of wine. 4They will greet you and offer you two loaves of bread, which you will accept from them.

5"After that you will go to Gibeah of God, where there is a Philistine outpost. As you approach the town, you will meet a procession of prophets coming down from the high place with lyres, tambourines, flutes and harps being played before them, and they will be prophesying. 6The Spirit of the LORD will come upon you in power, and you will prophesy with them; and you will be changed into a different person. 7Once these signs are fulfilled, do whatever your hand finds to do, for God is with you.

8"Go down ahead of me to Gilgal. I will surely come down to you to sacrifice burnt offerings and fellowship offerings,b but you must wait seven days until I come to you and tell you what you are to do."

Saul Made King

9As Saul turned to leave Samuel, God changed Saul's heart, and all these signs were fulfilled that day. 10When they arrived at Gibeah, a procession of prophets met him; the Spirit of God came upon him in power, and he joined in their prophesying. 11When all those who had formerly known him saw him prophesying with the prophets, they asked each other, "What is this that has happened to the son of Kish? Is Saul also among the prophets?"

12A man who lived there answered, "And who is their father?" So it became a saying: "Is Saul also among the prophets?" 13After Saul stopped prophesying, he went to the high place.

14Now Saul's uncle asked him and his servant, "Where have you been?"

"Looking for the donkeys," he said. "But when we saw they were not to be found, we went to Samuel."

15Saul's uncle said, "Tell me what Samuel said to you."

16Saul replied, "He assured us that the donkeys had been found." But he did not tell his uncle what Samuel had said about the kingship.

17Samuel summoned the people of Israel to the LORD at Mizpah 18and said to them, "This is what the LORD, the God of Israel, says: 'I brought Israel up out of Egypt, and I delivered you from the power of Egypt and all the kingdoms that oppressed you.' 19But you have now rejected your God, who saves you out of all your calamities and distresses. And you have said, 'No, set a king over us.' So now present yourselves before the LORD by your tribes and clans.

20When Samuel brought all the tribes of Israel near, the tribe of Benjamin was chosen. 21Then he brought forward the tribe of Benjamin, clan by clan, and Matri's clan was chosen. Finally Saul son of Kish was chosen. But when they looked for him, he was not to be found. 22So they inquired further of the LORD, "Has the man come here yet?"

And the LORD said, "Yes, he has hidden himself among the baggage."

23They ran and brought him out, and as he stood among the people he was a head taller than any of the others. 24Samuel said to all the people, "Do you see the man the LORD has chosen? There is no one like him among all the people."

a1 Hebrew; Septuagint and Vulgate over his people Israel? You will reign over the LORD's people and save them from the power of their enemies round about. And this will be a sign to you that the LORD has anointed you leader over his inheritance: b8 Traditionally peace offerings

Then the people shouted, "Long live the king!"

²⁵Samuel explained to the people the regulations of the kingship. He wrote them down on a scroll and deposited it before the LORD. Then Samuel dismissed the people, each to his own home.

²⁶Saul also went to his home in Gibeah, accompanied by valiant men whose hearts God had touched. ²⁷But some troublemakers said, "How can this fellow save us?" They despised him and brought him no gifts. But Saul kept silent.

Saul Rescues the City of Jabesh

11 Nahash the Ammonite went up and besieged Jabesh Gilead. And all the men of Jabesh said to him, "Make a treaty with us, and we will be subject to you."

²But Nahash the Ammonite replied, "I will make a treaty with you only on the condition that I gouge out the right eye of every one of you and so bring disgrace on all Israel."

³The elders of Jabesh said to him, "Give us seven days so we can send messengers throughout Israel; if no one comes to rescue us, we will surrender to you."

⁴When the messengers came to Gibeah of Saul and reported these terms to the people, they all wept aloud. ⁵Just then Saul was returning from the fields, behind his oxen, and he asked, "What is wrong with the people? Why are they weeping?" Then they repeated to him what the men of Jabesh had said.

⁶When Saul heard their words, the Spirit of God came upon him in power, and he burned with anger. ⁷He took a pair of oxen, cut them into pieces, and sent the pieces by messengers throughout Israel, proclaiming, "This is what will be done to the oxen of anyone who does not follow Saul and Samuel." Then the terror of the LORD fell on the people, and they turned out as one man. ⁸When Saul mustered them at Bezek, the men of Israel numbered three hundred thousand and the men of Judah thirty thousand.

⁹They told the messengers who had come, "Say to the men of Jabesh Gilead, 'By the time the sun is hot tomorrow, you will be delivered.' " When the messengers went and reported this to the men of Jabesh, they were elated. ¹⁰They said to the Ammonites, "Tomorrow we will surrender to you, and you can do to us whatever seems good to you."

¹¹The next day Saul separated his men into three divisions; during the last watch of the night they broke into the camp of the Ammonites and slaughtered them until the heat of the day. Those who survived were scattered, so that no two of them were left together.

Saul Confirmed as King

¹²The people then said to Samuel, "Who was it that asked, 'Shall Saul reign over us?' Bring these men to us and we will put them to death."

¹³But Saul said, "No one shall be put to death today, for this day the LORD has rescued Israel."

¹⁴Then Samuel said to the people, "Come, let us go to Gilgal and there reaffirm the kingship." ¹⁵So all the people went to Gilgal and confirmed Saul as king in the presence of the LORD. There they sacrificed fellowship offerings[a] before the LORD, and Saul and all the Israelites held a great celebration.

Samuel's Farewell Speech

12 Samuel said to all Israel, "I have listened to everything you said to me and have set a king over you. ²Now you have a king as your leader. As for me, I am old and gray, and my sons are here with you. I have been your leader from my youth until this day. ³Here I stand. Testify against me in the presence of the LORD and his anointed. Whose ox have I taken? Whose donkey have I taken? Whom have I cheated? Whom have I oppressed? From whose hand have I accepted a bribe to make me shut my eyes? If I have done any of these, I will make it right."

⁴"You have not cheated or oppressed us," they replied. "You have not taken anything from anyone's hand."

⁵Samuel said to them, "The LORD is witness against you, and also his anointed is witness this day, that you have not found anything in my hand."

"He is witness," they said.

⁶Then Samuel said to the people, "It is the LORD who appointed Moses and Aaron and brought your forefathers up out of Egypt. ⁷Now then, stand here, because I am going to confront you with evidence before the LORD as to all the righteous acts performed by the LORD for you and your fathers.

---

a 15 Traditionally *peace offerings*

8"After Jacob entered Egypt, they cried to the Lord for help, and the Lord sent Moses and Aaron, who brought your forefathers out of Egypt and settled them in this place.

9"But they forgot the Lord their God; so he sold them into the hand of Sisera, the commander of the army of Hazor, and into the hands of the Philistines and the king of Moab, who fought against them. **10**They cried out to the Lord and said, 'We have sinned; we have forsaken the Lord and served the Baals and the Ashtoreths. But now deliver us from the hands of our enemies, and we will serve you.' **11**Then the Lord sent Jerub-Baal,*a* Barak,*b* Jephthah and Samuel,*c* and he delivered you from the hands of your enemies on every side, so that you lived securely.

12"But when you saw that Nahash king of the Ammonites was moving against you, you said to me, 'No, we want a king to rule over us'—even though the Lord your God was your king. **13**Now here is the king you have chosen, the one you asked for; see, the Lord has set a king over you. **14**If you fear the Lord and serve and obey him and do not rebel against his commands, and if both you and the king who reigns over you follow the Lord your God—good! **15**But if you do not obey the Lord, and if you rebel against his commands, his hand will be against you, as it was against your fathers.

16"Now then, stand still and see this great thing the Lord is about to do before your eyes! **17**Is it not wheat harvest now? I will call upon the Lord to send thunder and rain. And you will realize what an evil thing you did in the eyes of the Lord when you asked for a king."

18Then Samuel called upon the Lord, and that same day the Lord sent thunder and rain. So all the people stood in awe of the Lord and of Samuel.

19The people all said to Samuel, "Pray to the Lord your God for your servants so that we will not die, for we have added to all our other sins the evil of asking for a king."

20"Do not be afraid," Samuel replied. "You have done all this evil; yet do not turn away from the Lord, but serve the Lord with all your heart. **21**Do not turn away after useless idols. They can do you no good, nor can they rescue you, because they are useless. **22**For the sake of his great name the Lord will not reject his people, because the Lord was pleased to make you his own. **23**As for me, far be it from me that I should sin against the Lord by failing to pray for you. And I will teach you the way that is good and right. **24**But be sure to fear the Lord and serve him faithfully with all your heart; consider what great things he has done for you. **25**Yet if you persist in doing evil, both you and your king will be swept away."

Samuel Rebukes Saul

13 Saul was ⌊thirty⌋*d* years old when he became king, and he reigned over Israel ⌊forty-⌋*e* two years.

2Saul*f* chose three thousand men from Israel; two thousand were with him at Micmash and in the hill country of Bethel, and a thousand were with Jonathan at Gibeah in Benjamin. The rest of the men he sent back to their homes.

3Jonathan attacked the Philistine outpost at Geba, and the Philistines heard about it. Then Saul had the trumpet blown throughout the land and said, "Let the Hebrews hear!" **4**So all Israel heard the news: "Saul has attacked the Philistine outpost, and now Israel has become a stench to the Philistines." And the people were summoned to join Saul at Gilgal.

5The Philistines assembled to fight Israel, with three thousand*g* chariots, six thousand charioteers, and soldiers as numerous as the sand on the seashore. They went up and camped at Micmash, east of Beth Aven. **6**When the men of Israel saw that their situation was critical and that their army was hard pressed, they hid in caves and thickets, among the rocks, and in pits and cisterns. **7**Some Hebrews even crossed the Jordan to the land of Gad and Gilead.

Saul remained at Gilgal, and all the troops with him were quaking with fear. **8**He waited seven days, the time set by Samuel; but Samuel did not come to Gilgal, and Saul's men began to scatter. **9**So he said, "Bring me the burnt offering and the fellowship offerings.*h*" And Saul of-

---

a11 Also called *Gideon*   *b11* Some Septuagint manuscripts and Syriac; Hebrew *Bedan*   *c11* Hebrew; some Septuagint manuscripts and Syriac *Samson*   *d1* A few late manuscripts of the Septuagint; Hebrew does not have *thirty*.   *e1* See the round number in Acts 13:21; Hebrew does not have *forty-*.   *f1,2* Or *and when he had reigned over Israel two years,* *2he*   *g5* Some Septuagint manuscripts and Syriac; Hebrew *thirty thousand*   *h9* Traditionally *peace offerings* fered up the burnt offering. [10]Just as he finished making the offering, Samuel arrived, and Saul went out to greet him.

[11]"What have you done?" asked Samuel.

Saul replied, "When I saw that the men were scattering, and that you did not come at the set time, and that the Philistines were assembling at Micmash, [12]I thought, 'Now the Philistines will come down against me at Gilgal, and I have not sought the LORD's favor.' So I felt compelled to offer the burnt offering."

[13]"You acted foolishly," Samuel said. "You have not kept the command the LORD your God gave you; if you had, he would have established your kingdom over Israel for all time. [14]But now your kingdom will not endure; the LORD has sought out a man after his own heart and appointed him leader of his people, because you have not kept the LORD's command."

[15]Then Samuel left Gilgal[a] and went up to Gibeah in Benjamin, and Saul counted the men who were with him. They numbered about six hundred.

Israel Without Weapons

[16]Saul and his son Jonathan and the men with them were staying in Gibeah[b] in Benjamin, while the Philistines camped at Micmash. [17]Raiding parties went out from the Philistine camp in three detachments. One turned toward Ophrah in the vicinity of Shual, [18]another toward Beth Horon, and the third toward the borderland overlooking the Valley of Zeboim facing the desert.

[19]Not a blacksmith could be found in the whole land of Israel, because the Philistines had said, "Otherwise the Hebrews will make swords or spears!" [20]So all Israel went down to the Philistines to have their plowshares, mattocks, axes and sickles[c] sharpened. [21]The price was two thirds of a shekel[d] for sharpening plowshares and mattocks, and a third of a shekel[e] for sharpening forks and axes and for repointing goads.

[22]So on the day of the battle not a soldier with Saul and Jonathan had a sword or spear in his hand; only Saul and his son Jonathan had them.

Jonathan Attacks the Philistines

[23]Now a detachment of Philistines had gone out to the pass at Micmash.

14 [1]One day Jonathan son of Saul said to the young man bearing his armor, "Come, let's go over to the Philistine outpost on the other side." But he did not tell his father.

[2]Saul was staying on the outskirts of Gibeah under a pomegranate tree in Migron. With him were about six hundred men, [3]among whom was Ahijah, who was wearing an ephod. He was a son of Ichabod's brother Ahitub son of Phinehas, the son of Eli, the LORD's priest in Shiloh. No one was aware that Jonathan had left.

[4]On each side of the pass that Jonathan intended to cross to reach the Philistine outpost was a cliff; one was called Bozez, and the other Seneh. [5]One cliff stood to the north toward Micmash, the other to the south toward Geba.

[6]Jonathan said to his young armor-bearer, "Come, let's go over to the outpost of those uncircumcised fellows. Perhaps the LORD will act in our behalf. Nothing can hinder the LORD from saving, whether by many or by few."

[7]"Do all that you have in mind," his armor-bearer said. "Go ahead; I am with you heart and soul."

[8]Jonathan said, "Come, then; we will cross over toward the men and let them see us. [9]If they say to us, 'Wait there until we come to you,' we will stay where we are and not go up to them. [10]But if they say, 'Come up to us,' we will climb up, because that will be our sign that the LORD has given them into our hands."

[11]So both of them showed themselves to the Philistine outpost. "Look!" said the Philistines. "The Hebrews are crawling out of the holes they were hiding in." [12]The men of the outpost shouted to Jonathan and his armor-bearer, "Come up to us and we'll teach you a lesson."

So Jonathan said to his armor-bearer, "Climb up after me; the LORD has given them into the hand of Israel."

[13]Jonathan climbed up, using his hands and feet, with his armor-bearer right behind him. The Philistines fell before Jonathan, and his armor-bearer followed and killed behind him. [14]In that first attack Jonathan and his armor-bearer killed

---

[a]15 Hebrew; Septuagint *Gilgal and went his way; the rest of the people went after Saul to meet the army, and they went out of Gilgal*   [b]16 Two Hebrew manuscripts; most Hebrew manuscripts *Geba,* a variant of *Gibeah*   [c]20 Septuagint; Hebrew *plowshares*   [d]21 Hebrew *pim;* that is, about 1/4 ounce (about 8 grams)   [e]21 That is, about 1/8 ounce (about 4 grams)

some twenty men in an area of about half an acre.*a*

Israel Routs the Philistines

15Then panic struck the whole army — those in the camp and field, and those in the outposts and raiding parties — and the ground shook. It was a panic sent by God.*b* **16**Saul's lookouts at Gibeah in Benjamin saw the army melting away in all directions. **17**Then Saul said to the men who were with him, "Muster the forces and see who has left us." When they did, it was Jonathan and his armor-bearer who were not there. **18**Saul said to Ahijah, "Bring the ark of God." (At that time it was with the Israelites.)*c* **19**While Saul was talking to the priest, the tumult in the Philistine camp increased more and more. So Saul said to the priest, "Withdraw your hand."

20Then Saul and all his men assembled and went to the battle. They found the Philistines in total confusion, striking each other with their swords. **21**Those Hebrews who had previously been with the Philistines and had gone up with them to their camp went over to the Israelites who were with Saul and Jonathan. **22**When all the Israelites who had hidden in the hill country of Ephraim heard that the Philistines were on the run, they joined the battle in hot pursuit. **23**So the LORD rescued Israel that day, and the battle moved on beyond Beth Aven.

Jonathan Eats Honey

24Now the men of Israel were in distress that day, because Saul had bound the people under an oath, saying, "Cursed be any man who eats food before evening comes, before I have avenged myself on my enemies!" So none of the troops tasted food.

25The entire army*d* entered the woods, and there was honey on the ground. **26**When they went into the woods, they saw the honey oozing out, yet no one put his hand to his mouth, because they feared the oath. **27**But Jonathan had not heard that his father had bound the people with the oath, so he reached out the end of the staff that was in his hand and dipped it into the honeycomb. He raised

his hand to his mouth, and his eyes brightened.*e* **28**Then one of the soldiers told him, "Your father bound the army under a strict oath, saying, 'Cursed be any man who eats food today!' That is why the men are faint."

29Jonathan said, "My father has made trouble for the country. See how my eyes brightened*f* when I tasted a little of this honey. **30**How much better it would have been if the men had eaten today some of the plunder they took from their enemies. Would not the slaughter of the Philistines have been even greater?"

31That day, after the Israelites had struck down the Philistines from Micmash to Aijalon, they were exhausted. **32**They pounced on the plunder and, taking sheep, cattle and calves, they butchered them on the ground and ate them, together with the blood. **33**Then someone said to Saul, "Look, the men are sinning against the LORD by eating meat that has blood in it."

"You have broken faith," he said. "Roll a large stone over here at once." **34**Then he said, "Go out among the men and tell them, 'Each of you bring me your cattle and sheep, and slaughter them here and eat them. Do not sin against the LORD by eating meat with blood still in it.'"

So everyone brought his ox that night and slaughtered it there. **35**Then Saul built an altar to the LORD; it was the first time he had done this.

36Saul said, "Let us go down after the Philistines by night and plunder them till dawn, and let us not leave one of them alive."

"Do whatever seems best to you," they replied.

But the priest said, "Let us inquire of God here."

37So Saul asked God, "Shall I go down after the Philistines? Will you give them into Israel's hand?" But God did not answer him that day.

38Saul therefore said, "Come here, all you who are leaders of the army, and let us find out what sin has been committed today. **39**As surely as the LORD who rescues Israel lives, even if it lies with my son Jonathan, he must die." But not one of the men said a word.

40Saul then said to all the Israelites,

---

*a*14 Hebrew *half a yoke*; a "yoke" was the land plowed by a yoke of oxen in one day.   *b*15 Or *a terrible panic*   *c*18 Hebrew; Septuagint *"Bring the ephod." (At that time he wore the ephod before the Israelites.)*   *d*25 Or *Now all the people of the land*   *e*27 Or *his strength was renewed*   *f*29 Or *my strength was renewed*

"You stand over there; I and Jonathan my son will stand over here."

"Do what seems best to you," the men replied.

⁴¹Then Saul prayed to the LORD, the God of Israel, "Give me the right answer."ᵃ And Jonathan and Saul were taken by lot, and the men were cleared. ⁴²Saul said, "Cast the lot between me and Jonathan my son." And Jonathan was taken.

⁴³Then Saul said to Jonathan, "Tell me what you have done."

So Jonathan told him, "I merely tasted a little honey with the end of my staff. And now must I die?"

⁴⁴Saul said, "May God deal with me, be it ever so severely, if you do not die, Jonathan."

⁴⁵But the men said to Saul, "Should Jonathan die — he who has brought about this great deliverance in Israel? Never! As surely as the LORD lives, not a hair of his head will fall to the ground, for he did this today with God's help." So the men rescued Jonathan, and he was not put to death.

⁴⁶Then Saul stopped pursuing the Philistines, and they withdrew to their own land.

⁴⁷After Saul had assumed rule over Israel, he fought against their enemies on every side: Moab, the Ammonites, Edom, the kingsᵇ of Zobah, and the Philistines. Wherever he turned, he inflicted punishment on them.ᶜ ⁴⁸He fought valiantly and defeated the Amalekites, delivering Israel from the hands of those who had plundered them.

Saul's Family

⁴⁹Saul's sons were Jonathan, Ishvi and Malki-Shua. The name of his older daughter was Merab, and that of the younger was Michal. ⁵⁰His wife's name was Ahinoam daughter of Ahimaaz. The name of the commander of Saul's army was Abner son of Ner, and Ner was Saul's uncle. ⁵¹Saul's father Kish and Abner's father Ner were sons of Abiel.

⁵²All the days of Saul there was bitter war with the Philistines, and whenever Saul saw a mighty or brave man, he took him into his service.

The LORD Rejects Saul as King

15 Samuel said to Saul, "I am the one the LORD sent to anoint you king over his people Israel; so listen now to the message from the LORD. ²This is what the LORD Almighty says: 'I will punish the Amalekites for what they did to Israel when they waylaid them as they came up from Egypt. ³Now go, attack the Amalekites and totally destroyᵈ everything that belongs to them. Do not spare them; put to death men and women, children and infants, cattle and sheep, camels and donkeys.' "

⁴So Saul summoned the men and mustered them at Telaim — two hundred thousand foot soldiers and ten thousand men from Judah. ⁵Saul went to the city of Amalek and set an ambush in the ravine. ⁶Then he said to the Kenites, "Go away, leave the Amalekites so that I do not destroy you along with them; for you showed kindness to all the Israelites when they came up out of Egypt." So the Kenites moved away from the Amalekites.

⁷Then Saul attacked the Amalekites all the way from Havilah to Shur, to the east of Egypt. ⁸He took Agag king of the Amalekites alive, and all his people he totally destroyed with the sword. ⁹But Saul and the army spared Agag and the best of the sheep and cattle, the fat calvesᵉ and lambs — everything that was good. These they were unwilling to destroy completely, but everything that was despised and weak they totally destroyed.

¹⁰Then the word of the LORD came to Samuel: ¹¹"I am grieved that I have made Saul king, because he has turned away from me and has not carried out my instructions." Samuel was troubled, and he cried out to the LORD all that night.

¹²Early in the morning Samuel got up and went to meet Saul, but he was told, "Saul has gone to Carmel. There he has set up a monument in his own honor and has turned and gone on down to Gilgal."

¹³When Samuel reached him, Saul said, "The LORD bless you! I have carried out the LORD's instructions."

¹⁴But Samuel said, "What then is this bleating of sheep in my ears? What is this lowing of cattle that I hear?"

ᵃ41 Hebrew; Septuagint *"Why have you not answered your servant today? If the fault is in me or my son Jonathan, respond with Urim, but if the men of Israel are at fault, respond with Thummim."*   ᵇ47 Masoretic Text; Dead Sea Scrolls and Septuagint *king*   ᶜ47 Hebrew; Septuagint *he was victorious*   ᵈ3 The Hebrew term refers to the irrevocable giving over of things or persons to the LORD, often by totally destroying them; also in verses 8, 9, 15, 18, 20 and 21.   ᵉ9 Or *the grown bulls*; the meaning of the Hebrew for this phrase is uncertain.

¹⁵Saul answered, "The soldiers brought them from the Amalekites; they spared the best of the sheep and cattle to sacrifice to the LORD your God, but we totally destroyed the rest."

¹⁶"Stop!" Samuel said to Saul. "Let me tell you what the LORD said to me last night."

"Tell me," Saul replied.

¹⁷Samuel said, "Although you were once small in your own eyes, did you not become the head of the tribes of Israel? The LORD anointed you king over Israel. ¹⁸And he sent you on a mission, saying, 'Go and completely destroy those wicked people, the Amalekites; make war on them until you have wiped them out.' ¹⁹Why did you not obey the LORD? Why did you pounce on the plunder and do evil in the eyes of the LORD?"

²⁰"But I did obey the LORD," Saul said. "I went on the mission the LORD assigned me. I completely destroyed the Amalekites and brought back Agag their king. ²¹The soldiers took sheep and cattle from the plunder, the best of what was devoted to God, in order to sacrifice them to the LORD your God at Gilgal."

²²But Samuel replied:

"Does the LORD delight in burnt
    offerings and sacrifices
  as much as in obeying the voice of
    the LORD?
To obey is better than sacrifice,
  and to heed is better than the fat of
    rams.
²³For rebellion is like the sin of
    divination,
  and arrogance like the evil of
    idolatry.
Because you have rejected the word of
    the LORD,
  he has rejected you as king."

²⁴Then Saul said to Samuel, "I have sinned. I violated the LORD's command and your instructions. I was afraid of the people and so I gave in to them. ²⁵Now I beg you, forgive my sin and come back with me, so that I may worship the LORD."

²⁶But Samuel said to him, "I will not go back with you. You have rejected the word of the LORD, and the LORD has rejected you as king over Israel!"

²⁷As Samuel turned to leave, Saul caught hold of the hem of his robe, and it tore. ²⁸Samuel said to him, "The LORD has torn the kingdom of Israel from you today

and has given it to one of your neighbors—to one better than you. ²⁹He who is the Glory of Israel does not lie or change his mind; for he is not a man, that he should change his mind."

³⁰Saul replied, "I have sinned. But please honor me before the elders of my people and before Israel; come back with me, so that I may worship the LORD your God." ³¹So Samuel went back with Saul, and Saul worshiped the LORD.

³²Then Samuel said, "Bring me Agag king of the Amalekites."

Agag came to him confidently,ᵃ thinking, "Surely the bitterness of death is past."

³³But Samuel said,

"As your sword has made women
    childless,
  so will your mother be childless
    among women."

And Samuel put Agag to death before the LORD at Gilgal.

³⁴Then Samuel left for Ramah, but Saul went up to his home in Gibeah of Saul. ³⁵Until the day Samuel died, he did not go to see Saul again, though Samuel mourned for him. And the LORD was grieved that he had made Saul king over Israel.

Samuel Anoints David

16 The LORD said to Samuel, "How long will you mourn for Saul, since I have rejected him as king over Israel? Fill your horn with oil and be on your way; I am sending you to Jesse of Bethlehem. I have chosen one of his sons to be king."

²But Samuel said, "How can I go? Saul will hear about it and kill me."

The LORD said, "Take a heifer with you and say, 'I have come to sacrifice to the LORD.' ³Invite Jesse to the sacrifice, and I will show you what to do. You are to anoint for me the one I indicate."

⁴Samuel did what the LORD said. When he arrived at Bethlehem, the elders of the town trembled when they met him. They asked, "Do you come in peace?"

⁵Samuel replied, "Yes, in peace; I have come to sacrifice to the LORD. Consecrate yourselves and come to the sacrifice with me." Then he consecrated Jesse and his sons and invited them to the sacrifice.

⁶When they arrived, Samuel saw Eliab and thought, "Surely the LORD's anointed stands here before the LORD."

[7]But the LORD said to Samuel, "Do not consider his appearance or his height, for I have rejected him. The LORD does not look at the things man looks at. Man looks at the outward appearance, but the LORD looks at the heart."

[8]Then Jesse called Abinadab and had him pass in front of Samuel. But Samuel said, "The LORD has not chosen this one either." [9]Jesse then had Shammah pass by, but Samuel said, "Nor has the LORD chosen this one." [10]Jesse had seven of his sons pass before Samuel, but Samuel said to him, "The LORD has not chosen these." [11]So he asked Jesse, "Are these all the sons you have?"

"There is still the youngest," Jesse answered, "but he is tending the sheep."

Samuel said, "Send for him; we will not sit down[a] until he arrives."

[12]So he sent and had him brought in. He was ruddy, with a fine appearance and handsome features.

Then the LORD said, "Rise and anoint him; he is the one."

[13]So Samuel took the horn of oil and anointed him in the presence of his brothers, and from that day on the Spirit of the LORD came upon David in power. Samuel then went to Ramah.

David in Saul's Service

[14]Now the Spirit of the LORD had departed from Saul, and an evil[b] spirit from the LORD tormented him.

[15]Saul's attendants said to him, "See, an evil spirit from God is tormenting you. [16]Let our lord command his servants here to search for someone who can play the harp. He will play when the evil spirit from God comes upon you, and you will feel better."

[17]So Saul said to his attendants, "Find someone who plays well and bring him to me."

[18]One of the servants answered, "I have seen a son of Jesse of Bethlehem who knows how to play the harp. He is a brave man and a warrior. He speaks well and is a fine-looking man. And the LORD is with him."

[19]Then Saul sent messengers to Jesse and said, "Send me your son David, who is with the sheep." [20]So Jesse took a donkey loaded with bread, a skin of wine and a young goat and sent them with his son David to Saul.

[21]David came to Saul and entered his service. Saul liked him very much, and David became one of his armor-bearers. [22]Then Saul sent word to Jesse, saying, "Allow David to remain in my service, for I am pleased with him."

[23]Whenever the spirit from God came upon Saul, David would take his harp and play. Then relief would come to Saul; he would feel better, and the evil spirit would leave him.

David and Goliath

17 Now the Philistines gathered their forces for war and assembled at Socoh in Judah. They pitched camp at Ephes Dammim, between Socoh and Azekah. [2]Saul and the Israelites assembled and camped in the Valley of Elah and drew up their battle line to meet the Philistines. [3]The Philistines occupied one hill and the Israelites another, with the valley between them.

[4]A champion named Goliath, who was from Gath, came out of the Philistine camp. He was over nine feet[c] tall. [5]He had a bronze helmet on his head and wore a coat of scale armor of bronze weighing five thousand shekels[d]; [6]on his legs he wore bronze greaves, and a bronze javelin was slung on his back. [7]His spear shaft was like a weaver's rod, and its iron point weighed six hundred shekels.[e] His shield bearer went ahead of him.

[8]Goliath stood and shouted to the ranks of Israel, "Why do you come out and line up for battle? Am I not a Philistine, and are you not the servants of Saul? Choose a man and have him come down to me. [9]If he is able to fight and kill me, we will become your subjects; but if I overcome him and kill him, you will become our subjects and serve us." [10]Then the Philistine said, "This day I defy the ranks of Israel! Give me a man and let us fight each other." [11]On hearing the Philistine's words, Saul and all the Israelites were dismayed and terrified.

[12]Now David was the son of an Ephrathite named Jesse, who was from Bethlehem in Judah. Jesse had eight sons, and in Saul's time he was old and well advanced in years. [13]Jesse's three oldest sons had followed Saul to the war: The firstborn

---

[a]11 Some Septuagint manuscripts; Hebrew *not gather around*   [b]14 Or *injurious*; also in verses 15, 16 and 23   [c]4 Hebrew *was six cubits and a span* (about 3 meters)   [d]5 That is, about 125 pounds (about 57 kilograms)   [e]7 That is, about 15 pounds (about 7 kilograms)

was Eliab; the second, Abinadab; and the third, Shammah. ¹⁴David was the youngest. The three oldest followed Saul, ¹⁵but David went back and forth from Saul to tend his father's sheep at Bethlehem.

¹⁶For forty days the Philistine came forward every morning and evening and took his stand.

¹⁷Now Jesse said to his son David, "Take this ephah*a* of roasted grain and these ten loaves of bread for your brothers and hurry to their camp. ¹⁸Take along these ten cheeses to the commander of their unit.*b* See how your brothers are and bring back some assurance*c* from them. ¹⁹They are with Saul and all the men of Israel in the Valley of Elah, fighting against the Philistines."

²⁰Early in the morning David left the flock with a shepherd, loaded up and set out, as Jesse had directed. He reached the camp as the army was going out to its battle positions, shouting the war cry. ²¹Israel and the Philistines were drawing up their lines facing each other. ²²David left his things with the keeper of supplies, ran to the battle lines and greeted his brothers. ²³As he was talking with them, Goliath, the Philistine champion from Gath, stepped out from his lines and shouted his usual defiance, and David heard it. ²⁴When the Israelites saw the man, they all ran from him in great fear.

²⁵Now the Israelites had been saying, "Do you see how this man keeps coming out? He comes out to defy Israel. The king will give great wealth to the man who kills him. He will also give him his daughter in marriage and will exempt his father's family from taxes in Israel."

²⁶David asked the men standing near him, "What will be done for the man who kills this Philistine and removes this disgrace from Israel? Who is this uncircumcised Philistine that he should defy the armies of the living God?"

²⁷They repeated to him what they had been saying and told him, "This is what will be done for the man who kills him."

²⁸When Eliab, David's oldest brother, heard him speaking with the men, he burned with anger at him and asked, "Why have you come down here? And with whom did you leave those few sheep in the desert? I know how conceited you are and how wicked your heart is; you came down only to watch the battle."

²⁹"Now what have I done?" said David. "Can't I even speak?" ³⁰He then turned away to someone else and brought up the same matter, and the men answered him as before. ³¹What David said was overheard and reported to Saul, and Saul sent for him.

³²David said to Saul, "Let no one lose heart on account of this Philistine; your servant will go and fight him."

³³Saul replied, "You are not able to go out against this Philistine and fight him; you are only a boy, and he has been a fighting man from his youth."

³⁴But David said to Saul, "Your servant has been keeping his father's sheep. When a lion or a bear came and carried off a sheep from the flock, ³⁵I went after it, struck it and rescued the sheep from its mouth. When it turned on me, I seized it by its hair, struck it and killed it. ³⁶Your servant has killed both the lion and the bear; this uncircumcised Philistine will be like one of them, because he has defied the armies of the living God. ³⁷The LORD who delivered me from the paw of the lion and the paw of the bear will deliver me from the hand of this Philistine."

Saul said to David, "Go, and the LORD be with you."

³⁸Then Saul dressed David in his own tunic. He put a coat of armor on him and a bronze helmet on his head. ³⁹David fastened on his sword over the tunic and tried walking around, because he was not used to them.

"I cannot go in these," he said to Saul, "because I am not used to them." So he took them off. ⁴⁰Then he took his staff in his hand, chose five smooth stones from the stream, put them in the pouch of his shepherd's bag and, with his sling in his hand, approached the Philistine.

⁴¹Meanwhile, the Philistine, with his shield bearer in front of him, kept coming closer to David. ⁴²He looked David over and saw that he was only a boy, ruddy and handsome, and he despised him. ⁴³He said to David, "Am I a dog, that you come at me with sticks?" And the Philistine cursed David by his gods. ⁴⁴"Come here," he said, "and I'll give your flesh to the birds of the air and the beasts of the field!"

⁴⁵David said to the Philistine, "You come against me with sword and spear and javelin, but I come against you in the name of the LORD Almighty, the God of the

a17 That is, probably about 3/5 bushel (about 22 liters) or *some pledge of spoils*   *b18* Hebrew *thousand*   *c18* Or *some token*;

armies of Israel, whom you have defied. [46]This day the LORD will hand you over to me, and I'll strike you down and cut off your head. Today I will give the carcasses of the Philistine army to the birds of the air and the beasts of the earth, and the whole world will know that there is a God in Israel. [47]All those gathered here will know that it is not by sword or spear that the LORD saves; for the battle is the LORD's, and he will give all of you into our hands."

[48]As the Philistine moved closer to attack him, David ran quickly toward the battle line to meet him. [49]Reaching into his bag and taking out a stone, he slung it and struck the Philistine on the forehead. The stone sank into his forehead, and he fell facedown on the ground.

[50]So David triumphed over the Philistine with a sling and a stone; without a sword in his hand he struck down the Philistine and killed him.

[51]David ran and stood over him. He took hold of the Philistine's sword and drew it from the scabbard. After he killed him, he cut off his head with the sword.

When the Philistines saw that their hero was dead, they turned and ran. [52]Then the men of Israel and Judah surged forward with a shout and pursued the Philistines to the entrance of Gath[a] and to the gates of Ekron. Their dead were strewn along the Shaaraim road to Gath and Ekron. [53]When the Israelites returned from chasing the Philistines, they plundered their camp. [54]David took the Philistine's head and brought it to Jerusalem, and he put the Philistine's weapons in his own tent.

[55]As Saul watched David going out to meet the Philistine, he said to Abner, commander of the army, "Abner, whose son is that young man?"

Abner replied, "As surely as you live, O king, I don't know."

[56]The king said, "Find out whose son this young man is."

[57]As soon as David returned from killing the Philistine, Abner took him and brought him before Saul, with David still holding the Philistine's head.

[58]"Whose son are you, young man?" Saul asked him.

David said, "I am the son of your servant Jesse of Bethlehem."

Saul's Jealousy of David

18 After David had finished talking with Saul, Jonathan became one in spirit with David, and he loved him as himself. [2]From that day Saul kept David with him and did not let him return to his father's house. [3]And Jonathan made a covenant with David because he loved him as himself. [4]Jonathan took off the robe he was wearing and gave it to David, along with his tunic, and even his sword, his bow and his belt.

[5]Whatever Saul sent him to do, David did it so successfully[b] that Saul gave him a high rank in the army. This pleased all the people, and Saul's officers as well.

[6]When the men were returning home after David had killed the Philistine, the women came out from all the towns of Israel to meet King Saul with singing and dancing, with joyful songs and with tambourines and lutes. [7]As they danced, they sang:

"Saul has slain his thousands,
   and David his tens of thousands."

[8]Saul was very angry; this refrain galled him. "They have credited David with tens of thousands," he thought, "but me with only thousands. What more can he get but the kingdom?" [9]And from that time on Saul kept a jealous eye on David.

[10]The next day an evil[c] spirit from God came forcefully upon Saul. He was prophesying in his house, while David was playing the harp, as he usually did. Saul had a spear in his hand [11]and he hurled it, saying to himself, "I'll pin David to the wall." But David eluded him twice.

[12]Saul was afraid of David, because the LORD was with David but had left Saul. [13]So he sent David away from him and gave him command over a thousand men, and David led the troops in their campaigns. [14]In everything he did he had great success,[d] because the LORD was with him. [15]When Saul saw how successful[e] he was, he was afraid of him. [16]But all Israel and Judah loved David, because he led them in their campaigns.

[17]Saul said to David, "Here is my older daughter Merab. I will give her to you in marriage; only serve me bravely and fight the battles of the LORD." For Saul said to himself, "I will not raise a hand against him. Let the Philistines do that!"

---

[a]52 Some Septuagint manuscripts; Hebrew *a valley was very wise*   [e]15 Or *wise*   [b]5 Or *wisely*   [c]10 Or *injurious*   [d]14 Or *he*

THURSDAY

VERSE FOR THE DAY:
1 Samuel 18:1

AUTHOR:
David W. Smith

PASSAGE FOR THE DAY:
1 Samuel 18:1–4

A Covenant of Friendship

VIRTUALLY every important relationship or event in our society is acknowledged with ritual and ceremony in the presence of others. Marriage is the best illustration of this . . .

In America the important relationship of friendship is devoid of any type of ceremony and covenant formation. When we decide to commit to a friendship, rarely is there a public testimony or occasion for acknowledgment by family and other friends.

The Bible, however, encourages the establishment of a covenant when men become friends. Jonathan and David, because of their mutual love, decided to make a covenant. A covenant is a promise, a contract, a binding agreement, a formation of unity. "Jonathan become one in spirit with David." *Become one with*, which means "to unite," is the same word used in Genesis to express Jacob's love for his youngest son, Benjamin. [In Genesis 44:30, Judah says that Jacob's "life is closely bound up with the boy's life."]

To show outwardly his inward love, Jonathan took off his robe, tunic, sword, bow and belt and gave them all to his dear friend, David. This symbolic gesture, this outward expression of Jonathan's love, affected greatly their commitment to each other. David, being a peasant and therefore not wealthy, could return only the gift of loyalty and respect to his friend.

The giving and accepting of a tangible token to represent commitment helps solidify friendships like the exchanging of rings during a wedding ceremony . . . I still use the pencil sharpener a friend gave me when I entered college. I still smile when I think of the friend who gave me a sapling for my birthday. He knew I wanted more shade in the backyard of our home.

The gifts are appreciated but it is the giver, the one who thought of me, that I cherish. The commitment of the friend and the covenant between us has been marked by the gift. It is vital that friends know that we care about them personally. The very least we can do is tell them how highly we value them and our relationship with them. In short, we should form covenants with friends.

Additional Scripture Readings:
Ruth 1:15–18; John 15:9–17

Go to page 288 for your next devotional reading.

18But David said to Saul, "Who am I, and what is my family or my father's clan in Israel, that I should become the king's son-in-law?" **19**So*a* when the time came for Merab, Saul's daughter, to be given to David, she was given in marriage to Adriel of Meholah.

20Now Saul's daughter Michal was in love with David, and when they told Saul about it, he was pleased. **21**"I will give her to him," he thought, "so that she may be a snare to him and so that the hand of the Philistines may be against him." So Saul said to David, "Now you have a second opportunity to become my son-in-law."

22Then Saul ordered his attendants: "Speak to David privately and say, 'Look, the king is pleased with you, and his attendants all like you; now become his son-in-law.' "

23They repeated these words to David. But David said, "Do you think it is a small matter to become the king's son-in-law? I'm only a poor man and little known."

24When Saul's servants told him what David had said, **25**Saul replied, "Say to David, 'The king wants no other price for the bride than a hundred Philistine foreskins, to take revenge on his enemies.' " Saul's plan was to have David fall by the hands of the Philistines.

26When the attendants told David these things, he was pleased to become the king's son-in-law. So before the allotted time elapsed, **27**David and his men went out and killed two hundred Philistines. He brought their foreskins and presented the full number to the king so that he might become the king's son-in-law. Then Saul gave him his daughter Michal in marriage.

28When Saul realized that the LORD was with David and that his daughter Michal loved David, **29**Saul became still more afraid of him, and he remained his enemy the rest of his days.

30The Philistine commanders continued to go out to battle, and as often as they did, David met with more success*b* than the rest of Saul's officers, and his name became well known.

Saul Tries to Kill David

19 Saul told his son Jonathan and all the attendants to kill David. But Jonathan was very fond of David **2**and warned him, "My father Saul is looking for a chance to kill you. Be on your guard tomorrow morning; go into hiding and stay there. **3**I will go out and stand with my father in the field where you are. I'll speak to him about you and will tell you what I find out."

4Jonathan spoke well of David to Saul his father and said to him, "Let not the king do wrong to his servant David; he has not wronged you, and what he has done has benefited you greatly. **5**He took his life in his hands when he killed the Philistine. The LORD won a great victory for all Israel, and you saw it and were glad. Why then would you do wrong to an innocent man like David by killing him for no reason?"

6Saul listened to Jonathan and took this oath: "As surely as the LORD lives, David will not be put to death."

7So Jonathan called David and told him the whole conversation. He brought him to Saul, and David was with Saul as before.

8Once more war broke out, and David went out and fought the Philistines. He struck them with such force that they fled before him.

9But an evil*c* spirit from the LORD came upon Saul as he was sitting in his house with his spear in his hand. While David was playing the harp, **10**Saul tried to pin him to the wall with his spear, but David eluded him as Saul drove the spear into the wall. That night David made good his escape.

11Saul sent men to David's house to watch it and to kill him in the morning. But Michal, David's wife, warned him, "If you don't run for your life tonight, tomorrow you'll be killed." **12**So Michal let David down through a window, and he fled and escaped. **13**Then Michal took an idol*d* and laid it on the bed, covering it with a garment and putting some goats' hair at the head.

14When Saul sent the men to capture David, Michal said, "He is ill."

15Then Saul sent the men back to see David and told them, "Bring him up to me in his bed so that I may kill him." **16**But when the men entered, there was the idol in the bed, and at the head was some goats' hair.

17Saul said to Michal, "Why did you deceive me like this and send my enemy away so that he escaped?"

a19 Or *However,*   *b30* Or *David acted more wisely* in verse 16   *c9* Or *injurious*   *d13* Hebrew *teraphim*; also

FRIDAY

VERSE FOR THE DAY:
1 Samuel 19:4

AUTHOR:
David W. Smith

PASSAGE FOR THE DAY:
1 Samuel 19:1–7

Male Friendship

ONE of the finest examples of male friendship is found in the historical record of 1 Samuel in 18:1–3; 23:15–16; and 19:1–7. Here we read about real male friendship, about a relationship that ran deep between Jonathan, the king's son, and David, a shepherd boy and God's future choice for the throne. Their friendship was strong, built solidly on an inward attachment rather than on an outer attraction or social status. [First Samuel 18:1 says they "became one in spirit."] These men demonstrated a mutual acceptance of each other despite their different social backgrounds. Covenant or promise rather than performance permeated their friendship. Jonathan did not have to do favors for David, and David, for example, was not pressured into killing more giants such as Goliath to remain Jonathan's friend. Their promise to be faithful to each other was born of unconditional love (18:3). Consequently, they stood strong together and refused to rely solely on self (23:15–16). Mutuality, not individualism or competition, marked their friendship. Moreover, they were not selfish but loyal to each other (19:1–7). David's interests were more important to Jonathan than his own, and David felt the same way about Jonathan's interests.

If you study the friendship between David and Jonathan, you will walk away with a good understanding of what a healthy friendship between men can and should be like. Concluding from their relationship, I would say that any definition should include the following:

- Unconditional love
- Personal enjoyment
- Mutual acceptance
- Mutual interests
- Mutual commitment
- Mutual loyalty

In short, friendship involves a concern for and involvement with the well-being of another.

Additional Scripture Readings:
Proverbs 17:17; 18:24;
1 John 3:11–24

Go to page 305 for your next devotional reading.

Michal told him, "He said to me, 'Let me get away. Why should I kill you?' "

¹⁸When David had fled and made his escape, he went to Samuel at Ramah and told him all that Saul had done to him. Then he and Samuel went to Naioth and stayed there. ¹⁹Word came to Saul: "David is in Naioth at Ramah"; ²⁰so he sent men to capture him. But when they saw a group of prophets prophesying, with Samuel standing there as their leader, the Spirit of God came upon Saul's men and they also prophesied. ²¹Saul was told about it, and he sent more men, and they prophesied too. Saul sent men a third time, and they also prophesied. ²²Finally, he himself left for Ramah and went to the great cistern at Secu. And he asked, "Where are Samuel and David?"

"Over in Naioth at Ramah," they said.

²³So Saul went to Naioth at Ramah. But the Spirit of God came even upon him, and he walked along prophesying until he came to Naioth. ²⁴He stripped off his robes and also prophesied in Samuel's presence. He lay that way all that day and night. This is why people say, "Is Saul also among the prophets?"

David and Jonathan

20 Then David fled from Naioth at Ramah and went to Jonathan and asked, "What have I done? What is my crime? How have I wronged your father, that he is trying to take my life?"

²"Never!" Jonathan replied. "You are not going to die! Look, my father doesn't do anything, great or small, without confiding in me. Why would he hide this from me? It's not so!"

³But David took an oath and said, "Your father knows very well that I have found favor in your eyes, and he has said to himself, 'Jonathan must not know this or he will be grieved.' Yet as surely as the LORD lives and as you live, there is only a step between me and death."

⁴Jonathan said to David, "Whatever you want me to do, I'll do for you."

⁵So David said, "Look, tomorrow is the New Moon festival, and I am supposed to dine with the king; but let me go and hide in the field until the evening of the day after tomorrow. ⁶If your father misses me at all, tell him, 'David earnestly asked my permission to hurry to Bethlehem, his hometown, because an annual sacrifice is being made there for his whole clan.' ⁷If he says, 'Very well,' then your servant is safe. But if he loses his temper, you can be

sure that he is determined to harm me. ⁸As for you, show kindness to your servant, for you have brought him into a covenant with you before the LORD. If I am guilty, then kill me yourself! Why hand me over to your father?"

⁹"Never!" Jonathan said. "If I had the least inkling that my father was determined to harm you, wouldn't I tell you?"

¹⁰David asked, "Who will tell me if your father answers you harshly?"

¹¹"Come," Jonathan said, "let's go out into the field." So they went there together.

¹²Then Jonathan said to David: "By the LORD, the God of Israel, I will surely sound out my father by this time the day after tomorrow! If he is favorably disposed toward you, will I not send you word and let you know? ¹³But if my father is inclined to harm you, may the LORD deal with me, be it ever so severely, if I do not let you know and send you away safely. May the LORD be with you as he has been with my father. ¹⁴But show me unfailing kindness like that of the LORD as long as I live, so that I may not be killed, ¹⁵and do not ever cut off your kindness from my family—not even when the LORD has cut off every one of David's enemies from the face of the earth."

¹⁶So Jonathan made a covenant with the house of David, saying, "May the LORD call David's enemies to account." ¹⁷And Jonathan had David reaffirm his oath out of love for him, because he loved him as he loved himself.

¹⁸Then Jonathan said to David: "Tomorrow is the New Moon festival. You will be missed, because your seat will be empty. ¹⁹The day after tomorrow, toward evening, go to the place where you hid when this trouble began, and wait by the stone Ezel. ²⁰I will shoot three arrows to the side of it, as though I were shooting at a target. ²¹Then I will send a boy and say, 'Go, find the arrows.' If I say to him, 'Look, the arrows are on this side of you; bring them here,' then come, because, as surely as the LORD lives, you are safe; there is no danger. ²²But if I say to the boy, 'Look, the arrows are beyond you,' then you must go, because the LORD has sent you away. ²³And about the matter you and I discussed—remember, the LORD is witness between you and me forever."

²⁴So David hid in the field, and when the New Moon festival came, the king sat down to eat. ²⁵He sat in his customary

place by the wall, opposite Jonathan,^a and Abner sat next to Saul, but David's place was empty. ²⁶Saul said nothing that day, for he thought, "Something must have happened to David to make him ceremonially unclean—surely he is unclean." ²⁷But the next day, the second day of the month, David's place was empty again. Then Saul said to his son Jonathan, "Why hasn't the son of Jesse come to the meal, either yesterday or today?"

²⁸Jonathan answered, "David earnestly asked me for permission to go to Bethlehem. ²⁹He said, 'Let me go, because our family is observing a sacrifice in the town and my brother has ordered me to be there. If I have found favor in your eyes, let me get away to see my brothers.' That is why he has not come to the king's table."

³⁰Saul's anger flared up at Jonathan and he said to him, "You son of a perverse and rebellious woman! Don't I know that you have sided with the son of Jesse to your own shame and to the shame of the mother who bore you? ³¹As long as the son of Jesse lives on this earth, neither you nor your kingdom will be established. Now send and bring him to me, for he must die!"

³²"Why should he be put to death? What has he done?" Jonathan asked his father. ³³But Saul hurled his spear at him to kill him. Then Jonathan knew that his father intended to kill David.

³⁴Jonathan got up from the table in fierce anger; on that second day of the month he did not eat, because he was grieved at his father's shameful treatment of David.

³⁵In the morning Jonathan went out to the field for his meeting with David. He had a small boy with him, ³⁶and he said to the boy, "Run and find the arrows I shoot." As the boy ran, he shot an arrow beyond him. ³⁷When the boy came to the place where Jonathan's arrow had fallen, Jonathan called out after him, "Isn't the arrow beyond you?" ³⁸Then he shouted, "Hurry! Go quickly! Don't stop!" The boy picked up the arrow and returned to his master. ³⁹(The boy knew nothing of all this; only Jonathan and David knew.) ⁴⁰Then Jonathan gave his weapons to the boy and said, "Go, carry them back to town."

⁴¹After the boy had gone, David got up from the south side [of the stone] and bowed down before Jonathan three times, with his face to the ground. Then they kissed each other and wept together—but David wept the most.

⁴²Jonathan said to David, "Go in peace, for we have sworn friendship with each other in the name of the LORD, saying, 'The LORD is witness between you and me, and between your descendants and my descendants forever.'" Then David left, and Jonathan went back to the town.

David at Nob

21 David went to Nob, to Ahimelech the priest. Ahimelech trembled when he met him, and asked, "Why are you alone? Why is no one with you?"

²David answered Ahimelech the priest, "The king charged me with a certain matter and said to me, 'No one is to know anything about your mission and your instructions.' As for my men, I have told them to meet me at a certain place. ³Now then, what do you have on hand? Give me five loaves of bread, or whatever you can find."

⁴But the priest answered David, "I don't have any ordinary bread on hand; however, there is some consecrated bread here—provided the men have kept themselves from women."

⁵David replied, "Indeed women have been kept from us, as usual whenever^b I set out. The men's things^c are holy even on missions that are not holy. How much more so today!" ⁶So the priest gave him the consecrated bread, since there was no bread there except the bread of the Presence that had been removed from before the LORD and replaced by hot bread on the day it was taken away.

⁷Now one of Saul's servants was there that day, detained before the LORD; he was Doeg the Edomite, Saul's head shepherd.

⁸David asked Ahimelech, "Don't you have a spear or a sword here? I haven't brought my sword or any other weapon, because the king's business was urgent."

⁹The priest replied, "The sword of Goliath the Philistine, whom you killed in the Valley of Elah, is here; it is wrapped in a cloth behind the ephod. If you want it, take it; there is no sword here but that one."

David said, "There is none like it; give it to me."

---

^a25 Septuagint; Hebrew *wall. Jonathan arose* bodies   ^b5 Or *from us in the past few days since*   ^c5 Or

David at Gath

¹⁰That day David fled from Saul and went to Achish king of Gath. ¹¹But the servants of Achish said to him, "Isn't this David, the king of the land? Isn't he the one they sing about in their dances:

" 'Saul has slain his thousands,
and David his tens of thousands'?"

¹²David took these words to heart and was very much afraid of Achish king of Gath. ¹³So he pretended to be insane in their presence; and while he was in their hands he acted like a madman, making marks on the doors of the gate and letting saliva run down his beard.

¹⁴Achish said to his servants, "Look at the man! He is insane! Why bring him to me? ¹⁵Am I so short of madmen that you have to bring this fellow here to carry on like this in front of me? Must this man come into my house?"

David at Adullam and Mizpah

22 David left Gath and escaped to the cave of Adullam. When his brothers and his father's household heard about it, they went down to him there. ²All those who were in distress or in debt or discontented gathered around him, and he became their leader. About four hundred men were with him.

³From there David went to Mizpah in Moab and said to the king of Moab, "Would you let my father and mother come and stay with you until I learn what God will do for me?" ⁴So he left them with the king of Moab, and they stayed with him as long as David was in the stronghold.

⁵But the prophet Gad said to David, "Do not stay in the stronghold. Go into the land of Judah." So David left and went to the forest of Hereth.

Saul Kills the Priests of Nob

⁶Now Saul heard that David and his men had been discovered. And Saul, spear in hand, was seated under the tamarisk tree on the hill at Gibeah, with all his officials standing around him. ⁷Saul said to them, "Listen, men of Benjamin! Will the son of Jesse give all of you fields and vineyards? Will he make all of you commanders of thousands and commanders of hundreds? ⁸Is that why you have all conspired against me? No one tells me when my son makes a covenant with the son of Jesse. None of you is concerned about me or

tells me that my son has incited my servant to lie in wait for me, as he does today."

⁹But Doeg the Edomite, who was standing with Saul's officials, said, "I saw the son of Jesse come to Ahimelech son of Ahitub at Nob. ¹⁰Ahimelech inquired of the Lord for him; he also gave him provisions and the sword of Goliath the Philistine."

¹¹Then the king sent for the priest Ahimelech son of Ahitub and his father's whole family, who were the priests at Nob, and they all came to the king. ¹²Saul said, "Listen now, son of Ahitub."

"Yes, my lord," he answered.

¹³Saul said to him, "Why have you conspired against me, you and the son of Jesse, giving him bread and a sword and inquiring of God for him, so that he has rebelled against me and lies in wait for me, as he does today?"

¹⁴Ahimelech answered the king, "Who of all your servants is as loyal as David, the king's son-in-law, captain of your bodyguard and highly respected in your household? ¹⁵Was that day the first time I inquired of God for him? Of course not! Let not the king accuse your servant or any of his father's family, for your servant knows nothing at all about this whole affair."

¹⁶But the king said, "You will surely die, Ahimelech, you and your father's whole family."

¹⁷Then the king ordered the guards at his side: "Turn and kill the priests of the Lord, because they too have sided with David. They knew he was fleeing, yet they did not tell me."

But the king's officials were not willing to raise a hand to strike the priests of the Lord.

¹⁸The king then ordered Doeg, "You turn and strike down the priests." So Doeg the Edomite turned and struck them down. That day he killed eighty-five men who wore the linen ephod. ¹⁹He also put to the sword Nob, the town of the priests, with its men and women, its children and infants, and its cattle, donkeys and sheep.

²⁰But Abiathar, a son of Ahimelech son of Ahitub, escaped and fled to join David. ²¹He told David that Saul had killed the priests of the Lord. ²²Then David said to Abiathar: "That day, when Doeg the Edomite was there, I knew he would be sure to tell Saul. I am responsible for the death of your father's whole family. ²³Stay with me; don't be afraid; the man who is

seeking your life is seeking mine also. You will be safe with me."

David Saves Keilah

23 When David was told, "Look, the Philistines are fighting against Keilah and are looting the threshing floors," [2] he inquired of the LORD, saying, "Shall I go and attack these Philistines?"

The LORD answered him, "Go, attack the Philistines and save Keilah."

[3] But David's men said to him, "Here in Judah we are afraid. How much more, then, if we go to Keilah against the Philistine forces!"

[4] Once again David inquired of the LORD, and the LORD answered him, "Go down to Keilah, for I am going to give the Philistines into your hand." [5] So David and his men went to Keilah, fought the Philistines and carried off their livestock. He inflicted heavy losses on the Philistines and saved the people of Keilah. [6] (Now Abiathar son of Ahimelech had brought the ephod down with him when he fled to David at Keilah.)

Saul Pursues David

[7] Saul was told that David had gone to Keilah, and he said, "God has handed him over to me, for David has imprisoned himself by entering a town with gates and bars." [8] And Saul called up all his forces for battle, to go down to Keilah to besiege David and his men.

[9] When David learned that Saul was plotting against him, he said to Abiathar the priest, "Bring the ephod." [10] David said, "O LORD, God of Israel, your servant has heard definitely that Saul plans to come to Keilah and destroy the town on account of me. [11] Will the citizens of Keilah surrender me to him? Will Saul come down, as your servant has heard? O LORD, God of Israel, tell your servant."

And the LORD said, "He will."

[12] Again David asked, "Will the citizens of Keilah surrender me and my men to Saul?"

And the LORD said, "They will."

[13] So David and his men, about six hundred in number, left Keilah and kept moving from place to place. When Saul was told that David had escaped from Keilah, he did not go there.

[14] David stayed in the desert strongholds and in the hills of the Desert of Ziph.

Day after day Saul searched for him, but God did not give David into his hands. [15] While David was at Horesh in the Desert of Ziph, he learned that Saul had come out to take his life. [16] And Saul's son Jonathan went to David at Horesh and helped him find strength in God. [17] "Don't be afraid," he said. "My father Saul will not lay a hand on you. You will be king over Israel, and I will be second to you. Even my father Saul knows this." [18] The two of them made a covenant before the LORD. Then Jonathan went home, but David remained at Horesh.

[19] The Ziphites went up to Saul at Gibeah and said, "Is not David hiding among us in the strongholds at Horesh, on the hill of Hakilah, south of Jeshimon? [20] Now, O king, come down whenever it pleases you to do so, and we will be responsible for handing him over to the king."

[21] Saul replied, "The LORD bless you for your concern for me. [22] Go and make further preparation. Find out where David usually goes and who has seen him there. They tell me he is very crafty. [23] Find out about all the hiding places he uses and come back to me with definite information. [a] Then I will go with you; if he is in the area, I will track him down among all the clans of Judah."

[24] So they set out and went to Ziph ahead of Saul. Now David and his men were in the Desert of Maon, in the Arabah south of Jeshimon. [25] Saul and his men began the search, and when David was told about it, he went down to the rock and stayed in the Desert of Maon. When Saul heard this, he went into the Desert of Maon in pursuit of David.

[26] Saul was going along one side of the mountain, and David and his men were on the other side, hurrying to get away from Saul. As Saul and his forces were closing in on David and his men to capture them, [27] a messenger came to Saul, saying, "Come quickly! The Philistines are raiding the land." [28] Then Saul broke off his pursuit of David and went to meet the Philistines. That is why they call this place Sela Hammahlekoth. [b] [29] And David went up from there and lived in the strongholds of En Gedi.

David Spares Saul's Life

24 After Saul returned from pursuing the Philistines, he was told, "David is in the Desert of En Gedi." [2] So Saul took three thousand chosen men from all Israel and set out to look for David and his men near the Crags of the Wild Goats.

³He came to the sheep pens along the way; a cave was there, and Saul went in to relieve himself. David and his men were far back in the cave. ⁴The men said, "This is the day the LORD spoke of when he said*a* to you, 'I will give your enemy into your hands for you to deal with as you wish.' " Then David crept up unnoticed and cut off a corner of Saul's robe.

⁵Afterward, David was conscience-stricken for having cut off a corner of his robe. ⁶He said to his men, "The LORD forbid that I should do such a thing to my master, the LORD's anointed, or lift my hand against him; for he is the anointed of the LORD." ⁷With these words David rebuked his men and did not allow them to attack Saul. And Saul left the cave and went his way.

⁸Then David went out of the cave and called out to Saul, "My lord the king!" When Saul looked behind him, David bowed down and prostrated himself with his face to the ground. ⁹He said to Saul, "Why do you listen when men say, 'David is bent on harming you'? ¹⁰This day you have seen with your own eyes how the LORD delivered you into my hands in the cave. Some urged me to kill you, but I spared you; I said, 'I will not lift my hand against my master, because he is the LORD's anointed.' ¹¹See, my father, look at this piece of your robe in my hand! I cut off the corner of your robe but did not kill you. Now understand and recognize that I am not guilty of wrongdoing or rebellion. I have not wronged you, but you are hunting me down to take my life. ¹²May the LORD judge between you and me. And may the LORD avenge the wrongs you have done to me, but my hand will not touch you. ¹³As the old saying goes, 'From evildoers come evil deeds,' so my hand will not touch you.

¹⁴"Against whom has the king of Israel come out? Whom are you pursuing? A dead dog? A flea? ¹⁵May the LORD be our judge and decide between us. May he consider my cause and uphold it; may he vindicate me by delivering me from your hand."

¹⁶When David finished saying this, Saul asked, "Is that your voice, David my son?" And he wept aloud. ¹⁷"You are more righteous than I," he said. "You have treated me well, but I have treated you badly. ¹⁸You have just now told me of the good you did to me; the LORD delivered me into your hands, but you did not kill me. ¹⁹When a man finds his enemy, does he let him get away unharmed? May the LORD reward you well for the way you treated me today. ²⁰I know that you will surely be king and that the kingdom of Israel will be established in your hands. ²¹Now swear to me by the LORD that you will not cut off my descendants or wipe out my name from my father's family."

²²So David gave his oath to Saul. Then Saul returned home, but David and his men went up to the stronghold.

David, Nabal and Abigail

25 Now Samuel died, and all Israel assembled and mourned for him; and they buried him at his home in Ramah.

Then David moved down into the Desert of Maon.*b* ²A certain man in Maon, who had property there at Carmel, was very wealthy. He had a thousand goats and three thousand sheep, which he was shearing in Carmel. ³His name was Nabal and his wife's name was Abigail. She was an intelligent and beautiful woman, but her husband, a Calebite, was surly and mean in his dealings.

⁴While David was in the desert, he heard that Nabal was shearing sheep. ⁵So he sent ten young men and said to them, "Go up to Nabal at Carmel and greet him in my name. ⁶Say to him: 'Long life to you! Good health to you and your household! And good health to all that is yours!

⁷" 'Now I hear that it is sheep-shearing time. When your shepherds were with us, we did not mistreat them, and the whole time they were at Carmel nothing of theirs was missing. ⁸Ask your own servants and they will tell you. Therefore be favorable toward my young men, since we come at a festive time. Please give your servants and your son David whatever you can find for them.' "

⁹When David's men arrived, they gave Nabal this message in David's name. Then they waited.

¹⁰Nabal answered David's servants, "Who is this David? Who is this son of Jesse? Many servants are breaking away from their masters these days. ¹¹Why should I take my bread and water, and the meat I have slaughtered for my shearers, and

give it to men coming from who knows where?"

¹²David's men turned around and went back. When they arrived, they reported every word. ¹³David said to his men, "Put on your swords!" So they put on their swords, and David put on his. About four hundred men went up with David, while two hundred stayed with the supplies.

¹⁴One of the servants told Nabal's wife Abigail: "David sent messengers from the desert to give our master his greetings, but he hurled insults at them. ¹⁵Yet these men were very good to us. They did not mistreat us, and the whole time we were out in the fields near them nothing was missing. ¹⁶Night and day they were a wall around us all the time we were herding our sheep near them. ¹⁷Now think it over and see what you can do, because disaster is hanging over our master and his whole household. He is such a wicked man that no one can talk to him."

¹⁸Abigail lost no time. She took two hundred loaves of bread, two skins of wine, five dressed sheep, five seahs*a* of roasted grain, a hundred cakes of raisins and two hundred cakes of pressed figs, and loaded them on donkeys. ¹⁹Then she told her servants, "Go on ahead; I'll follow you." But she did not tell her husband Nabal.

²⁰As she came riding her donkey into a mountain ravine, there were David and his men descending toward her, and she met them. ²¹David had just said, "It's been useless—all my watching over this fellow's property in the desert so that nothing of his was missing. He has paid me back evil for good. ²²May God deal with David,*b* be it ever so severely, if by morning I leave alive one male of all who belong to him!"

²³When Abigail saw David, she quickly got off her donkey and bowed down before David with her face to the ground. ²⁴She fell at his feet and said: "My lord, let the blame be on me alone. Please let your servant speak to you; hear what your servant has to say. ²⁵May my lord pay no attention to that wicked man Nabal. He is just like his name—his name is Fool, and folly goes with him. But as for me, your servant, I did not see the men my master sent.

²⁶"Now since the LORD has kept you, my master, from bloodshed and from aveng-

ing yourself with your own hands, as surely as the LORD lives and as you live, may your enemies and all who intend to harm my master be like Nabal. ²⁷And let this gift, which your servant has brought to my master, be given to the men who follow you. ²⁸Please forgive your servant's offense, for the LORD will certainly make a lasting dynasty for my master, because he fights the LORD's battles. Let no wrongdoing be found in you as long as you live. ²⁹Even though someone is pursuing you to take your life, the life of my master will be bound securely in the bundle of the living by the LORD your God. But the lives of your enemies he will hurl away as from the pocket of a sling. ³⁰When the LORD has done for my master every good thing he promised concerning him and has appointed him leader over Israel, ³¹my master will not have on his conscience the staggering burden of needless bloodshed or of having avenged himself. And when the LORD has brought my master success, remember your servant."

³²David said to Abigail, "Praise be to the LORD, the God of Israel, who has sent you today to meet me. ³³May you be blessed for your good judgment and for keeping me from bloodshed this day and from avenging myself with my own hands. ³⁴Otherwise, as surely as the LORD, the God of Israel, lives, who has kept me from harming you, if you had not come quickly to meet me, not one male belonging to Nabal would have been left alive by daybreak."

³⁵Then David accepted from her hand what she had brought him and said, "Go home in peace. I have heard your words and granted your request."

³⁶When Abigail went to Nabal, he was in the house holding a banquet like that of a king. He was in high spirits and very drunk. So she told him nothing until daybreak. ³⁷Then in the morning, when Nabal was sober, his wife told him all these things, and his heart failed him and he became like a stone. ³⁸About ten days later, the LORD struck Nabal and he died.

³⁹When David heard that Nabal was dead, he said, "Praise be to the LORD, who has upheld my cause against Nabal for treating me with contempt. He has kept his servant from doing wrong and has brought Nabal's wrongdoing down on his own head."

a18 That is, probably about a bushel (about 37 liters)   *b22* Some Septuagint manuscripts; Hebrew *with*
David's enemies

Then David sent word to Abigail, asking her to become his wife. ⁴⁰His servants went to Carmel and said to Abigail, "David has sent us to you to take you to become his wife."

⁴¹She bowed down with her face to the ground and said, "Here is your maidservant, ready to serve you and wash the feet of my master's servants." ⁴²Abigail quickly got on a donkey and, attended by her five maids, went with David's messengers and became his wife. ⁴³David had also married Ahinoam of Jezreel, and they both were his wives. ⁴⁴But Saul had given his daughter Michal, David's wife, to Paltiel[a] son of Laish, who was from Gallim.

David Again Spares Saul's Life

26 The Ziphites went to Saul at Gibeah and said, "Is not David hiding on the hill of Hakilah, which faces Jeshimon?"

²So Saul went down to the Desert of Ziph, with his three thousand chosen men of Israel, to search there for David. ³Saul made his camp beside the road on the hill of Hakilah facing Jeshimon, but David stayed in the desert. When he saw that Saul had followed him there, ⁴he sent out scouts and learned that Saul had definitely arrived.[b]

⁵Then David set out and went to the place where Saul had camped. He saw where Saul and Abner son of Ner, the commander of the army, had lain down. Saul was lying inside the camp, with the army encamped around him.

⁶David then asked Ahimelech the Hittite and Abishai son of Zeruiah, Joab's brother, "Who will go down into the camp with me to Saul?"

"I'll go with you," said Abishai.

⁷So David and Abishai went to the army by night, and there was Saul, lying asleep inside the camp with his spear stuck in the ground near his head. Abner and the soldiers were lying around him.

⁸Abishai said to David, "Today God has delivered your enemy into your hands. Now let me pin him to the ground with one thrust of my spear; I won't strike him twice."

⁹But David said to Abishai, "Don't destroy him! Who can lay a hand on the LORD's anointed and be guiltless? ¹⁰As surely as the LORD lives," he said, "the LORD himself will strike him; either his time will come and he will die, or he will

go into battle and perish. ¹¹But the LORD forbid that I should lay a hand on the LORD's anointed. Now get the spear and water jug that are near his head, and let's go."

¹²So David took the spear and water jug near Saul's head, and they left. No one saw or knew about it, nor did anyone wake up. They were all sleeping, because the LORD had put them into a deep sleep.

¹³Then David crossed over to the other side and stood on top of the hill some distance away; there was a wide space between them. ¹⁴He called out to the army and to Abner son of Ner, "Aren't you going to answer me, Abner?"

Abner replied, "Who are you who calls to the king?"

¹⁵David said, "You're a man, aren't you? And who is like you in Israel? Why didn't you guard your lord the king? Someone came to destroy your lord the king. ¹⁶What you have done is not good. As surely as the LORD lives, you and your men deserve to die, because you did not guard your master, the LORD's anointed. Look around you. Where are the king's spear and water jug that were near his head?"

¹⁷Saul recognized David's voice and said, "Is that your voice, David my son?"

David replied, "Yes it is, my lord the king." ¹⁸And he added, "Why is my lord pursuing his servant? What have I done, and what wrong am I guilty of? ¹⁹Now let my lord the king listen to his servant's words. If the LORD has incited you against me, then may he accept an offering. If, however, men have done it, may they be cursed before the LORD! They have now driven me from my share in the LORD's inheritance and have said, 'Go, serve other gods.' ²⁰Now do not let my blood fall to the ground far from the presence of the LORD. The king of Israel has come out to look for a flea—as one hunts a partridge in the mountains."

²¹Then Saul said, "I have sinned. Come back, David my son. Because you considered my life precious today, I will not try to harm you again. Surely I have acted like a fool and have erred greatly."

²²"Here is the king's spear," David answered. "Let one of your young men come over and get it. ²³The LORD rewards every man for his righteousness and faithfulness. The LORD delivered you into my hands today, but I would not lay a hand

on the LORD's anointed. ²⁴As surely as I valued your life today, so may the LORD value my life and deliver me from all trouble."

²⁵Then Saul said to David, "May you be blessed, my son David; you will do great things and surely triumph."

So David went on his way, and Saul returned home.

David Among the Philistines

27 But David thought to himself, "One of these days I will be destroyed by the hand of Saul. The best thing I can do is to escape to the land of the Philistines. Then Saul will give up searching for me anywhere in Israel, and I will slip out of his hand."

²So David and the six hundred men with him left and went over to Achish son of Maoch king of Gath. ³David and his men settled in Gath with Achish. Each man had his family with him, and David had his two wives: Ahinoam of Jezreel and Abigail of Carmel, the widow of Nabal. ⁴When Saul was told that David had fled to Gath, he no longer searched for him.

⁵Then David said to Achish, "If I have found favor in your eyes, let a place be assigned to me in one of the country towns, that I may live there. Why should your servant live in the royal city with you?"

⁶So on that day Achish gave him Ziklag, and it has belonged to the kings of Judah ever since. ⁷David lived in Philistine territory a year and four months.

⁸Now David and his men went up and raided the Geshurites, the Girzites and the Amalekites. (From ancient times these peoples had lived in the land extending to Shur and Egypt.) ⁹Whenever David attacked an area, he did not leave a man or woman alive, but took sheep and cattle, donkeys and camels, and clothes. Then he returned to Achish.

¹⁰When Achish asked, "Where did you go raiding today?" David would say, "Against the Negev of Judah" or "Against the Negev of Jerahmeel" or "Against the Negev of the Kenites." ¹¹He did not leave a man or woman alive to be brought to Gath, for he thought, "They might inform on us and say, 'This is what David did.'" And such was his practice as long as he lived in Philistine territory. ¹²Achish trusted David and said to himself, "He has be-

come so odious to his people, the Israelites, that he will be my servant forever."

Saul and the Witch of Endor

28 In those days the Philistines gathered their forces to fight against Israel. Achish said to David, "You must understand that you and your men will accompany me in the army."

²David said, "Then you will see for yourself what your servant can do."

Achish replied, "Very well, I will make you my bodyguard for life."

³Now Samuel was dead, and all Israel had mourned for him and buried him in his own town of Ramah. Saul had expelled the mediums and spiritists from the land.

⁴The Philistines assembled and came and set up camp at Shunem, while Saul gathered all the Israelites and set up camp at Gilboa. ⁵When Saul saw the Philistine army, he was afraid; terror filled his heart. ⁶He inquired of the LORD, but the LORD did not answer him by dreams or Urim or prophets. ⁷Saul then said to his attendants, "Find me a woman who is a medium, so I may go and inquire of her."

"There is one in Endor," they said.

⁸So Saul disguised himself, putting on other clothes, and at night he and two men went to the woman. "Consult a spirit for me," he said, "and bring up for me the one I name."

⁹But the woman said to him, "Surely you know what Saul has done. He has cut off the mediums and spiritists from the land. Why have you set a trap for my life to bring about my death?"

¹⁰Saul swore to her by the LORD, "As surely as the LORD lives, you will not be punished for this."

¹¹Then the woman asked, "Whom shall I bring up for you?"

"Bring up Samuel," he said.

¹²When the woman saw Samuel, she cried out at the top of her voice and said to Saul, "Why have you deceived me? You are Saul!"

¹³The king said to her, "Don't be afraid. What do you see?"

The woman said, "I see a spirit*a* coming up out of the ground."

¹⁴"What does he look like?" he asked.

"An old man wearing a robe is coming up," she said.

Then Saul knew it was Samuel, and he bowed down and prostrated himself with his face to the ground.

a 13 Or see spirits; or see gods

¹⁵Samuel said to Saul, "Why have you disturbed me by bringing me up?"

"I am in great distress," Saul said. "The Philistines are fighting against me, and God has turned away from me. He no longer answers me, either by prophets or by dreams. So I have called on you to tell me what to do."

¹⁶Samuel said, "Why do you consult me, now that the LORD has turned away from you and become your enemy? ¹⁷The LORD has done what he predicted through me. The LORD has torn the kingdom out of your hands and given it to one of your neighbors—to David. ¹⁸Because you did not obey the LORD or carry out his fierce wrath against the Amalekites, the LORD has done this to you today. ¹⁹The LORD will hand over both Israel and you to the Philistines, and tomorrow you and your sons will be with me. The LORD will also hand over the army of Israel to the Philistines."

²⁰Immediately Saul fell full length on the ground, filled with fear because of Samuel's words. His strength was gone, for he had eaten nothing all that day and night.

²¹When the woman came to Saul and saw that he was greatly shaken, she said, "Look, your maidservant has obeyed you. I took my life in my hands and did what you told me to do. ²²Now please listen to your servant and let me give you some food so you may eat and have the strength to go on your way."

²³He refused and said, "I will not eat."

But his men joined the woman in urging him, and he listened to them. He got up from the ground and sat on the couch.

²⁴The woman had a fattened calf at the house, which she butchered at once. She took some flour, kneaded it and baked bread without yeast. ²⁵Then she set it before Saul and his men, and they ate. That same night they got up and left.

Achish Sends David Back to Ziklag

29 The Philistines gathered all their forces at Aphek, and Israel camped by the spring in Jezreel. ²As the Philistine rulers marched with their units of hundreds and thousands, David and his men were marching at the rear with Achish. ³The commanders of the Philistines asked, "What about these Hebrews?"

Achish replied, "Is this not David, who was an officer of Saul king of Israel? He has already been with me for over a year, and from the day he left Saul until now, I have found no fault in him."

⁴But the Philistine commanders were angry with him and said, "Send the man back, that he may return to the place you assigned him. He must not go with us into battle, or he will turn against us during the fighting. How better could he regain his master's favor than by taking the heads of our own men? ⁵Isn't this the David they sang about in their dances:

" 'Saul has slain his thousands,
    and David his tens of thousands'?"

⁶So Achish called David and said to him, "As surely as the LORD lives, you have been reliable, and I would be pleased to have you serve with me in the army. From the day you came to me until now, I have found no fault in you, but the rulers don't approve of you. ⁷Turn back and go in peace; do nothing to displease the Philistine rulers."

⁸"But what have I done?" asked David. "What have you found against your servant from the day I came to you until now? Why can't I go and fight against the enemies of my lord the king?"

⁹Achish answered, "I know that you have been as pleasing in my eyes as an angel of God; nevertheless, the Philistine commanders have said, 'He must not go up with us into battle.' ¹⁰Now get up early, along with your master's servants who have come with you, and leave in the morning as soon as it is light."

¹¹So David and his men got up early in the morning to go back to the land of the Philistines, and the Philistines went up to Jezreel.

David Destroys the Amalekites

30 David and his men reached Ziklag on the third day. Now the Amalekites had raided the Negev and Ziklag. They had attacked Ziklag and burned it, ²and had taken captive the women and all who were in it, both young and old. They killed none of them, but carried them off as they went on their way.

³When David and his men came to Ziklag, they found it destroyed by fire and their wives and sons and daughters taken captive. ⁴So David and his men wept aloud until they had no strength left to weep. ⁵David's two wives had been captured—Ahinoam of Jezreel and Abigail, the widow of Nabal of Carmel. ⁶David was greatly distressed because the men were talking of stoning him; each one was bitter

in spirit because of his sons and daughters. But David found strength in the LORD his God.

[7]Then David said to Abiathar the priest, the son of Ahimelech, "Bring me the ephod." Abiathar brought it to him, [8]and David inquired of the LORD, "Shall I pursue this raiding party? Will I overtake them?"

"Pursue them," he answered. "You will certainly overtake them and succeed in the rescue."

[9]David and the six hundred men with him came to the Besor Ravine, where some stayed behind, [10]for two hundred men were too exhausted to cross the ravine. But David and four hundred men continued the pursuit.

[11]They found an Egyptian in a field and brought him to David. They gave him water to drink and food to eat— [12]part of a cake of pressed figs and two cakes of raisins. He ate and was revived, for he had not eaten any food or drunk any water for three days and three nights.

[13]David asked him, "To whom do you belong, and where do you come from?"

He said, "I am an Egyptian, the slave of an Amalekite. My master abandoned me when I became ill three days ago. [14]We raided the Negev of the Kerethites and the territory belonging to Judah and the Negev of Caleb. And we burned Ziklag."

[15]David asked him, "Can you lead me down to this raiding party?"

He answered, "Swear to me before God that you will not kill me or hand me over to my master, and I will take you down to them."

[16]He led David down, and there they were, scattered over the countryside, eating, drinking and reveling because of the great amount of plunder they had taken from the land of the Philistines and from Judah. [17]David fought them from dusk until the evening of the next day, and none of them got away, except four hundred young men who rode off on camels and fled. [18]David recovered everything the Amalekites had taken, including his two wives. [19]Nothing was missing: young or old, boy or girl, plunder or anything else they had taken. David brought everything back. [20]He took all the flocks and herds, and his men drove them ahead of the other livestock, saying, "This is David's plunder."

[21]Then David came to the two hundred men who had been too exhausted to follow him and who were left behind at the Besor Ravine. They came out to meet David and the people with him. As David and his men approached, he greeted them. [22]But all the evil men and troublemakers among David's followers said, "Because they did not go out with us, we will not share with them the plunder we recovered. However, each man may take his wife and children and go."

[23]David replied, "No, my brothers, you must not do that with what the LORD has given us. He has protected us and handed over to us the forces that came against us. [24]Who will listen to what you say? The share of the man who stayed with the supplies is to be the same as that of him who went down to the battle. All will share alike." [25]David made this a statute and ordinance for Israel from that day to this.

[26]When David arrived in Ziklag, he sent some of the plunder to the elders of Judah, who were his friends, saying, "Here is a present for you from the plunder of the LORD's enemies."

[27]He sent it to those who were in Bethel, Ramoth Negev and Jattir; [28]to those in Aroer, Siphmoth, Eshtemoa [29]and Racal; to those in the towns of the Jerahmeelites and the Kenites; [30]to those in Hormah, Bor Ashan, Athach [31]and Hebron; and to those in all the other places where David and his men had roamed.

Saul Takes His Life

31 Now the Philistines fought against Israel; the Israelites fled before them, and many fell slain on Mount Gilboa. [2]The Philistines pressed hard after Saul and his sons, and they killed his sons Jonathan, Abinadab and Malki-Shua. [3]The fighting grew fierce around Saul, and when the archers overtook him, they wounded him critically.

[4]Saul said to his armor-bearer, "Draw your sword and run me through, or these uncircumcised fellows will come and run me through and abuse me."

But his armor-bearer was terrified and would not do it; so Saul took his own sword and fell on it. [5]When the armor-bearer saw that Saul was dead, he too fell on his sword and died with him. [6]So Saul and his three sons and his armor-bearer and all his men died together that same day.

[7]When the Israelites along the valley and those across the Jordan saw that the Israelite army had fled and that Saul and his sons had died, they abandoned their

towns and fled. And the Philistines came and occupied them.

⁸The next day, when the Philistines came to strip the dead, they found Saul and his three sons fallen on Mount Gilboa. ⁹They cut off his head and stripped off his armor, and they sent messengers throughout the land of the Philistines to proclaim the news in the temple of their idols and among their people. ¹⁰They put his armor in the temple of the Ashtoreths and fastened his body to the wall of Beth Shan.

¹¹When the people of Jabesh Gilead heard of what the Philistines had done to Saul, ¹²all their valiant men journeyed through the night to Beth Shan. They took down the bodies of Saul and his sons from the wall of Beth Shan and went to Jabesh, where they burned them. ¹³Then they took their bones and buried them under a tamarisk tree at Jabesh, and they fasted seven days.

*T*HIS book tells the story of David's kingship over Israel, noting both his many victories and God's promise that his descendants will be on the throne forever. After David's shameful sin with Bathsheba, severe family problems threaten his kingdom. As you read this book, consider how terrible the consequences of sin can be, but also remember the faithfulness of God, who fulfills his promise by sending his Son to reign forever as David's true son.

2 SAMUEL

David Hears of Saul's Death

1 After the death of Saul, David returned from defeating the Amalekites and stayed in Ziklag two days. **2**On the third day a man arrived from Saul's camp, with his clothes torn and with dust on his head. When he came to David, he fell to the ground to pay him honor.

3"Where have you come from?" David asked him.

He answered, "I have escaped from the Israelite camp."

4"What happened?" David asked. "Tell me."

He said, "The men fled from the battle. Many of them fell and died. And Saul and his son Jonathan are dead."

5Then David said to the young man who brought him the report, "How do you know that Saul and his son Jonathan are dead?"

6"I happened to be on Mount Gilboa," the young man said, "and there was Saul, leaning on his spear, with the chariots and riders almost upon him. **7**When he turned around and saw me, he called out to me, and I said, 'What can I do?'

8"He asked me, 'Who are you?'

" 'An Amalekite,' I answered.

9"Then he said to me, 'Stand over me and kill me! I am in the throes of death, but I'm still alive.'

10"So I stood over him and killed him, because I knew that after he had fallen he could not survive. And I took the crown that was on his head and the band on his arm and have brought them here to my lord."

¹¹Then David and all the men with him took hold of their clothes and tore them. ¹²They mourned and wept and fasted till evening for Saul and his son Jonathan, and for the army of the LORD and the house of Israel, because they had fallen by the sword.

¹³David said to the young man who brought him the report, "Where are you from?"

"I am the son of an alien, an Amalekite," he answered.

¹⁴David asked him, "Why were you not afraid to lift your hand to destroy the LORD's anointed?"

¹⁵Then David called one of his men and said, "Go, strike him down!" So he struck him down, and he died. ¹⁶For David had said to him, "Your blood be on your own head. Your own mouth testified against you when you said, 'I killed the LORD's anointed.'"

David's Lament for Saul and Jonathan

¹⁷David took up this lament concerning Saul and his son Jonathan, ¹⁸and ordered that the men of Judah be taught this lament of the bow (it is written in the Book of Jashar):

¹⁹"Your glory, O Israel, lies slain on
        your heights.
    How the mighty have fallen!

²⁰"Tell it not in Gath,
        proclaim it not in the streets of
            Ashkelon,
    lest the daughters of the Philistines be
        glad,
        lest the daughters of the
            uncircumcised rejoice.

²¹"O mountains of Gilboa,
        may you have neither dew nor
            rain,
        nor fields that yield offerings ̣of
            grain ̣.
    For there the shield of the mighty was
        defiled,
        the shield of Saul—no longer
            rubbed with oil.
²²From the blood of the slain,
        from the flesh of the mighty,
    the bow of Jonathan did not turn
        back,

the sword of Saul did not return
        unsatisfied.

²³"Saul and Jonathan—
    in life they were loved and gracious,
        and in death they were not parted.
They were swifter than eagles,
    they were stronger than lions.

²⁴"O daughters of Israel,
    weep for Saul,
who clothed you in scarlet and finery,
    who adorned your garments with
        ornaments of gold.

²⁵"How the mighty have fallen in battle!
    Jonathan lies slain on your heights.
²⁶I grieve for you, Jonathan my brother;
    you were very dear to me.
Your love for me was wonderful,
    more wonderful than that of
        women.

²⁷"How the mighty have fallen!
    The weapons of war have
        perished!"

David Anointed King Over Judah

2 In the course of time, David inquired of the LORD. "Shall I go up to one of the towns of Judah?" he asked.

The LORD said, "Go up."

David asked, "Where shall I go?"

"To Hebron," the LORD answered.

²So David went up there with his two wives, Ahinoam of Jezreel and Abigail, the widow of Nabal of Carmel. ³David also took the men who were with him, each with his family, and they settled in Hebron and its towns. ⁴Then the men of Judah came to Hebron and there they anointed David king over the house of Judah.

When David was told that it was the men of Jabesh Gilead who had buried Saul, ⁵he sent messengers to the men of Jabesh Gilead to say to them, "The LORD bless you for showing this kindness to Saul your master by burying him. ⁶May the LORD now show you kindness and faithfulness, and I too will show you the same favor because you have done this. ⁷Now then, be strong and brave, for Saul your master is dead, and the house of Judah has anointed me king over them."

War Between the Houses of David and Saul

⁸Meanwhile, Abner son of Ner, the commander of Saul's army, had taken Ish-Bosheth son of Saul and brought him over

to Mahanaim. ⁹He made him king over Gilead, Ashuriᵃ and Jezreel, and also over Ephraim, Benjamin and all Israel.

¹⁰Ish-Bosheth son of Saul was forty years old when he became king over Israel, and he reigned two years. The house of Judah, however, followed David. ¹¹The length of time David was king in Hebron over the house of Judah was seven years and six months.

¹²Abner son of Ner, together with the men of Ish-Bosheth son of Saul, left Mahanaim and went to Gibeon. ¹³Joab son of Zeruiah and David's men went out and met them at the pool of Gibeon. One group sat down on one side of the pool and one group on the other side.

¹⁴Then Abner said to Joab, "Let's have some of the young men get up and fight hand to hand in front of us."

"All right, let them do it," Joab said.

¹⁵So they stood up and were counted off—twelve men for Benjamin and Ish-Bosheth son of Saul, and twelve for David. ¹⁶Then each man grabbed his opponent by the head and thrust his dagger into his opponent's side, and they fell down together. So that place in Gibeon was called Helkath Hazzurim.ᵇ

¹⁷The battle that day was very fierce, and Abner and the men of Israel were defeated by David's men.

¹⁸The three sons of Zeruiah were there: Joab, Abishai and Asahel. Now Asahel was as fleet-footed as a wild gazelle. ¹⁹He chased Abner, turning neither to the right nor to the left as he pursued him. ²⁰Abner looked behind him and asked, "Is that you, Asahel?"

"It is," he answered.

²¹Then Abner said to him, "Turn aside to the right or to the left; take on one of the young men and strip him of his weapons." But Asahel would not stop chasing him.

²²Again Abner warned Asahel, "Stop chasing me! Why should I strike you down? How could I look your brother Joab in the face?"

²³But Asahel refused to give up the pursuit; so Abner thrust the butt of his spear into Asahel's stomach, and the spear came out through his back. He fell there and died on the spot. And every man stopped when he came to the place where Asahel had fallen and died.

²⁴But Joab and Abishai pursued Abner, and as the sun was setting, they came to the hill of Ammah, near Giah on the way to the wasteland of Gibeon. ²⁵Then the men of Benjamin rallied behind Abner. They formed themselves into a group and took their stand on top of a hill.

²⁶Abner called out to Joab, "Must the sword devour forever? Don't you realize that this will end in bitterness? How long before you order your men to stop pursuing their brothers?"

²⁷Joab answered, "As surely as God lives, if you had not spoken, the men would have continued the pursuit of their brothers until morning.ᶜ"

²⁸So Joab blew the trumpet, and all the men came to a halt; they no longer pursued Israel, nor did they fight anymore.

²⁹All that night Abner and his men marched through the Arabah. They crossed the Jordan, continued through the whole Bithronᵈ and came to Mahanaim.

³⁰Then Joab returned from pursuing Abner and assembled all his men. Besides Asahel, nineteen of David's men were found missing. ³¹But David's men had killed three hundred and sixty Benjamites who were with Abner. ³²They took Asahel and buried him in his father's tomb at Bethlehem. Then Joab and his men marched all night and arrived at Hebron by daybreak.

3 The war between the house of Saul and the house of David lasted a long time. David grew stronger and stronger, while the house of Saul grew weaker and weaker.

²Sons were born to David in Hebron:

His firstborn was Amnon the son of Ahinoam of Jezreel;

³his second, Kileab the son of Abigail the widow of Nabal of Carmel;

the third, Absalom the son of Maacah daughter of Talmai king of Geshur;

⁴the fourth, Adonijah the son of Haggith;

the fifth, Shephatiah the son of Abital;

⁵and the sixth, Ithream the son of David's wife Eglah.

ᵃ9 Or *Asher*   ᵇ16 *Helkath Hazzurim* means *field of daggers* or *field of hostilities.*   ᶜ27 Or *spoken this morning, the men would not have taken up the pursuit of their brothers*; or *spoken, the men would have given up the pursuit of their brothers by morning*   ᵈ29 Or *morning*; or *ravine*; the meaning of the Hebrew for this word is uncertain.

These were born to David in Hebron.

Abner Goes Over to David

6During the war between the house of Saul and the house of David, Abner had been strengthening his own position in the house of Saul. **7**Now Saul had had a concubine named Rizpah daughter of Aiah. And Ish-Bosheth said to Abner, "Why did you sleep with my father's concubine?"

8Abner was very angry because of what Ish-Bosheth said and he answered, "Am I a dog's head—on Judah's side? This very day I am loyal to the house of your father Saul and to his family and friends. I haven't handed you over to David. Yet now you accuse me of an offense involving this woman! **9**May God deal with Abner, be it ever so severely, if I do not do for David what the LORD promised him on oath **10**and transfer the kingdom from the house of Saul and establish David's throne over Israel and Judah from Dan to Beersheba." **11**Ish-Bosheth did not dare to say another word to Abner, because he was afraid of him.

12Then Abner sent messengers on his behalf to say to David, "Whose land is it? Make an agreement with me, and I will help you bring all Israel over to you."

13"Good," said David. "I will make an agreement with you. But I demand one thing of you: Do not come into my presence unless you bring Michal daughter of Saul when you come to see me." **14**Then David sent messengers to Ish-Bosheth son of Saul, demanding, "Give me my wife Michal, whom I betrothed to myself for the price of a hundred Philistine foreskins."

15So Ish-Bosheth gave orders and had her taken away from her husband Paltiel son of Laish. **16**Her husband, however, went with her, weeping behind her all the way to Bahurim. Then Abner said to him, "Go back home!" So he went back.

17Abner conferred with the elders of Israel and said, "For some time you have wanted to make David your king. **18**Now do it! For the LORD promised David, 'By my servant David I will rescue my people Israel from the hand of the Philistines and from the hand of all their enemies.' "

19Abner also spoke to the Benjamites in person. Then he went to Hebron to tell David everything that Israel and the whole house of Benjamin wanted to do. **20**When Abner, who had twenty men with him, came to David at Hebron, David prepared a feast for him and his men. **21**Then Abner said to David, "Let me go at once and assemble all Israel for my lord the king, so that they may make a compact with you, and that you may rule over all that your heart desires." So David sent Abner away, and he went in peace.

Joab Murders Abner

22Just then David's men and Joab returned from a raid and brought with them a great deal of plunder. But Abner was no longer with David in Hebron, because David had sent him away, and he had gone in peace. **23**When Joab and all the soldiers with him arrived, he was told that Abner son of Ner had come to the king and that the king had sent him away and that he had gone in peace.

24So Joab went to the king and said, "What have you done? Look, Abner came to you. Why did you let him go? Now he is gone! **25**You know Abner son of Ner; he came to deceive you and observe your movements and find out everything you are doing."

26Joab then left David and sent messengers after Abner, and they brought him back from the well of Sirah. But David did not know it. **27**Now when Abner returned to Hebron, Joab took him aside into the gateway, as though to speak with him privately. And there, to avenge the blood of his brother Asahel, Joab stabbed him in the stomach, and he died.

28Later, when David heard about this, he said, "I and my kingdom are forever innocent before the LORD concerning the blood of Abner son of Ner. **29**May his blood fall upon the head of Joab and upon all his father's house! May Joab's house never be without someone who has a running sore or leprosy*a* or who leans on a crutch or who falls by the sword or who lacks food."

30(Joab and his brother Abishai murdered Abner because he had killed their brother Asahel in the battle at Gibeon.)

31Then David said to Joab and all the people with him, "Tear your clothes and put on sackcloth and walk in mourning in front of Abner." King David himself walked behind the bier. **32**They buried Abner in Hebron, and the king wept aloud at Abner's tomb. All the people wept also.

33The king sang this lament for Abner:

a29 The Hebrew word was used for various diseases affecting the skin—not necessarily leprosy.

"Should Abner have died as the
　　lawless die?
34 Your hands were not bound,
　　your feet were not fettered.
You fell as one falls before wicked
　　men."

And all the people wept over him again.
35Then they all came and urged David
to eat something while it was still day; but
David took an oath, saying, "May God deal
with me, be it ever so severely, if I taste
bread or anything else before the sun
sets!"
36All the people took note and were
pleased; indeed, everything the king did
pleased them. **37**So on that day all the people and all Israel knew that the king had
no part in the murder of Abner son of Ner.
38Then the king said to his men, "Do
you not realize that a prince and a great
man has fallen in Israel this day? **39**And today, though I am the anointed king, I am
weak, and these sons of Zeruiah are too
strong for me. May the LORD repay the
evildoer according to his evil deeds!"

Ish-Bosheth Murdered

4 When Ish-Bosheth son of Saul heard
that Abner had died in Hebron, he lost
courage, and all Israel became alarmed.
2Now Saul's son had two men who were
leaders of raiding bands. One was named
Baanah and the other Recab; they were
sons of Rimmon the Beerothite from the
tribe of Benjamin — Beeroth is considered
part of Benjamin, **3**because the people of
Beeroth fled to Gittaim and have lived
there as aliens to this day.

4(Jonathan son of Saul had a son who
was lame in both feet. He was five years
old when the news about Saul and Jonathan came from Jezreel. His nurse picked
him up and fled, but as she hurried to
leave, he fell and became crippled. His
name was Mephibosheth.)

5Now Recab and Baanah, the sons of
Rimmon the Beerothite, set out for the
house of Ish-Bosheth, and they arrived
there in the heat of the day while he was
taking his noonday rest. **6**They went into
the inner part of the house as if to get
some wheat, and they stabbed him in the
stomach. Then Recab and his brother Baanah slipped away.

7They had gone into the house while he
was lying on the bed in his bedroom. After
they stabbed and killed him, they cut off
his head. Taking it with them, they traveled all night by way of the Arabah. **8**They
brought the head of Ish-Bosheth to David
at Hebron and said to the king, "Here is
the head of Ish-Bosheth son of Saul, your
enemy, who tried to take your life. This
day the LORD has avenged my lord the
king against Saul and his offspring."
9David answered Recab and his brother
Baanah, the sons of Rimmon the Beerothite, "As surely as the LORD lives, who has
delivered me out of all trouble, **10**when a
man told me, 'Saul is dead,' and thought
he was bringing good news, I seized him
and put him to death in Ziklag. That was
the reward I gave him for his news! **11**How
much more — when wicked men have
killed an innocent man in his own house
and on his own bed — should I not now
demand his blood from your hand and rid
the earth of you!"
12So David gave an order to his men,
and they killed them. They cut off their
hands and feet and hung the bodies by the
pool in Hebron. But they took the head of
Ish-Bosheth and buried it in Abner's tomb
at Hebron.

David Becomes King Over Israel

5 All the tribes of Israel came to David
at Hebron and said, "We are your own
flesh and blood. **2**In the past, while Saul
was king over us, you were the one who
led Israel on their military campaigns.
And the LORD said to you, 'You will shepherd my people Israel, and you will become their ruler.' "
3When all the elders of Israel had come
to King David at Hebron, the king made a
compact with them at Hebron before the
LORD, and they anointed David king over
Israel.
4David was thirty years old when he became king, and he reigned forty years. **5**In
Hebron he reigned over Judah seven years
and six months, and in Jerusalem he
reigned over all Israel and Judah thirty-
three years.

David Conquers Jerusalem

6The king and his men marched to Jerusalem to attack the Jebusites, who lived
there. The Jebusites said to David, "You
will not get in here; even the blind and the
lame can ward you off." They thought,
"David cannot get in here." **7**Nevertheless,
David captured the fortress of Zion, the
City of David.
8On that day, David said, "Anyone who
conquers the Jebusites will have to use

WEEKENDING

RESTORE

The most important lesson I've learned in my life is that God is so gracious that he accepts me, my failures, my personality quirks, my shortcomings and all.

It's hard for a perfectionist like me, but I have to admit I can never be good enough. No matter how sound my strategy, how much I study, how hard I work—I'll always be a failure when it comes to being perfect. Yet God loves me anyway. And believing that gives me the greatest sense of peace, calm and security in the world.

It's that belief, that faith, more than anything else, that enabled me to last twenty-nine years on the sidelines of the Dallas Cowboys ... And it's that faith that gives me hope for whatever the future holds for me outside of professional football.

– Tom Landry

REVIVE

Saturday: Psalm 51:1–12
Sunday: Romans 8:28–39

Go to page 312 for your next devotional reading.

the water shaft*a* to reach those 'lame and blind' who are David's enemies.*b*" That is why they say, "The 'blind and lame' will not enter the palace."

⁹David then took up residence in the fortress and called it the City of David. He built up the area around it, from the supporting terraces*c* inward. ¹⁰And he became more and more powerful, because the LORD God Almighty was with him.

¹¹Now Hiram king of Tyre sent messengers to David, along with cedar logs and carpenters and stonemasons, and they built a palace for David. ¹²And David knew that the LORD had established him as king over Israel and had exalted his kingdom for the sake of his people Israel.

¹³After he left Hebron, David took more concubines and wives in Jerusalem, and more sons and daughters were born to him. ¹⁴These are the names of the children born to him there: Shammua, Shobab, Nathan, Solomon, ¹⁵Ibhar, Elishua, Nepheg, Japhia, ¹⁶Elishama, Eliada and Eliphelet.

David Defeats the Philistines

¹⁷When the Philistines heard that David had been anointed king over Israel, they went up in full force to search for him, but David heard about it and went down to the stronghold. ¹⁸Now the Philistines had come and spread out in the Valley of Rephaim; ¹⁹so David inquired of the LORD, "Shall I go and attack the Philistines? Will you hand them over to me?"

The LORD answered him, "Go, for I will surely hand the Philistines over to you."

²⁰So David went to Baal Perazim, and there he defeated them. He said, "As waters break out, the LORD has broken out against my enemies before me." So that place was called Baal Perazim.*d* ²¹The Philistines abandoned their idols there, and David and his men carried them off.

²²Once more the Philistines came up and spread out in the Valley of Rephaim; ²³so David inquired of the LORD, and he answered, "Do not go straight up, but circle around behind them and attack them in front of the balsam trees. ²⁴As soon as you hear the sound of marching in the tops of the balsam trees, move quickly, because that will mean the LORD has gone out in front of you to strike the Philistine army." ²⁵So David did as the LORD commanded him, and he struck down the Philistines all the way from Gibeon*e* to Gezer.

The Ark Brought to Jerusalem

6 David again brought together out of Israel chosen men, thirty thousand in all. ²He and all his men set out from Baalah of Judah*f* to bring up from there the ark of God, which is called by the Name,*g* the name of the LORD Almighty, who is enthroned between the cherubim that are on the ark. ³They set the ark of God on a new cart and brought it from the house of Abinadab, which was on the hill. Uzzah and Ahio, sons of Abinadab, were guiding the new cart ⁴with the ark of God on it,*h* and Ahio was walking in front of it. ⁵David and the whole house of Israel were celebrating with all their might before the LORD, with songs*i* and with harps, lyres, tambourines, sistrums and cymbals.

⁶When they came to the threshing floor of Nacon, Uzzah reached out and took hold of the ark of God, because the oxen stumbled. ⁷The LORD's anger burned against Uzzah because of his irreverent act; therefore God struck him down and he died there beside the ark of God.

⁸Then David was angry because the LORD's wrath had broken out against Uzzah, and to this day that place is called Perez Uzzah.*j*

⁹David was afraid of the LORD that day and said, "How can the ark of the LORD ever come to me?" ¹⁰He was not willing to take the ark of the LORD to be with him in the City of David. Instead, he took it aside to the house of Obed-Edom the Gittite. ¹¹The ark of the LORD remained in the house of Obed-Edom the Gittite for three months, and the LORD blessed him and his entire household.

¹²Now King David was told, "The LORD has blessed the household of Obed-Edom and everything he has, because of the ark of God." So David went down and brought up the ark of God from the house of Obed-

a8 Or *use scaling hooks*   *b8* Or *are hated by David lord who breaks out.*   *c9* Or *the Millo*   *d20* Baal Perazim means *the*   *e25* Septuagint (see also 1 Chron. 14:16); Hebrew *Geba*   *f2* That is, Kiriath Jearim; Hebrew *Baale Judah*, a variant of *Baalah of Judah*   *g2* Hebrew; Septuagint and Vulgate do not have *the Name.*   *h3,4* Dead Sea Scrolls and some Septuagint manuscripts; Masoretic Text *cart* ⁴*and they brought it with the ark of God from the house of Abinadab, which was on the hill*   *i5* See Dead Sea Scrolls, Septuagint and 1 Chronicles 13:8; Masoretic Text *celebrating before the LORD with all kinds of instruments made of pine.*   *j8* Perez Uzzah means *outbreak against Uzzah.*

Edom to the City of David with rejoicing. [13]When those who were carrying the ark of the LORD had taken six steps, he sacrificed a bull and a fattened calf. [14]David, wearing a linen ephod, danced before the LORD with all his might, [15]while he and the entire house of Israel brought up the ark of the LORD with shouts and the sound of trumpets.

[16]As the ark of the LORD was entering the City of David, Michal daughter of Saul watched from a window. And when she saw King David leaping and dancing before the LORD, she despised him in her heart.

[17]They brought the ark of the LORD and set it in its place inside the tent that David had pitched for it, and David sacrificed burnt offerings and fellowship offerings[a] before the LORD. [18]After he had finished sacrificing the burnt offerings and fellowship offerings, he blessed the people in the name of the LORD Almighty. [19]Then he gave a loaf of bread, a cake of dates and a cake of raisins to each person in the whole crowd of Israelites, both men and women. And all the people went to their homes.

[20]When David returned home to bless his household, Michal daughter of Saul came out to meet him and said, "How the king of Israel has distinguished himself today, disrobing in the sight of the slave girls of his servants as any vulgar fellow would!"

[21]David said to Michal, "It was before the LORD, who chose me rather than your father or anyone from his house when he appointed me ruler over the LORD's people Israel—I will celebrate before the LORD. [22]I will become even more undignified than this, and I will be humiliated in my own eyes. But by these slave girls you spoke of, I will be held in honor."

[23]And Michal daughter of Saul had no children to the day of her death.

God's Promise to David

7 After the king was settled in his palace and the LORD had given him rest from all his enemies around him, [2]he said to Nathan the prophet, "Here I am, living in a palace of cedar, while the ark of God remains in a tent."

[3]Nathan replied to the king, "Whatever you have in mind, go ahead and do it, for the LORD is with you."

[4]That night the word of the LORD came to Nathan, saying:

[5]"Go and tell my servant David, 'This is what the LORD says: Are you the one to build me a house to dwell in? [6]I have not dwelt in a house from the day I brought the Israelites up out of Egypt to this day. I have been moving from place to place with a tent as my dwelling. [7]Wherever I have moved with all the Israelites, did I ever say to any of their rulers whom I commanded to shepherd my people Israel, "Why have you not built me a house of cedar?" '

[8]"Now then, tell my servant David, 'This is what the LORD Almighty says: I took you from the pasture and from following the flock to be ruler over my people Israel. [9]I have been with you wherever you have gone, and I have cut off all your enemies from before you. Now I will make your name great, like the names of the greatest men of the earth. [10]And I will provide a place for my people Israel and will plant them so that they can have a home of their own and no longer be disturbed. Wicked people will not oppress them anymore, as they did at the beginning [11]and have done ever since the time I appointed leaders[b] over my people Israel. I will also give you rest from all your enemies.

" 'The LORD declares to you that the LORD himself will establish a house for you: [12]When your days are over and you rest with your fathers, I will raise up your offspring to succeed you, who will come from your own body, and I will establish his kingdom. [13]He is the one who will build a house for my Name, and I will establish the throne of his kingdom forever. [14]I will be his father, and he will be my son. When he does wrong, I will punish him with the rod of men, with floggings inflicted by men. [15]But my love will never be taken away from him, as I took it away from Saul, whom I removed from before you. [16]Your house and your kingdom will endure forever before me[c]; your throne will be established forever.' "

[17]Nathan reported to David all the words of this entire revelation.

[a]17 Traditionally *peace offerings*; also in verse 18   [b]11 Traditionally *judges*   [c]16 Some Hebrew manuscripts and Septuagint; most Hebrew manuscripts *you*

David's Prayer

18Then King David went in and sat before the LORD, and he said:

"Who am I, O Sovereign LORD, and what is my family, that you have brought me this far? **19**And as if this were not enough in your sight, O Sovereign LORD, you have also spoken about the future of the house of your servant. Is this your usual way of dealing with man, O Sovereign LORD? **20**"What more can David say to you? For you know your servant, O Sovereign LORD. **21**For the sake of your word and according to your will, you have done this great thing and made it known to your servant.

22"How great you are, O Sovereign LORD! There is no one like you, and there is no God but you, as we have heard with our own ears. **23**And who is like your people Israel—the one nation on earth that God went out to redeem as a people for himself, and to make a name for himself, and to perform great and awesome wonders by driving out nations and their gods from before your people, whom you redeemed from Egypt?[a] **24**You have established your people Israel as your very own forever, and you, O LORD, have become their God.

25"And now, LORD God, keep forever the promise you have made concerning your servant and his house. Do as you promised, **26**so that your name will be great forever. Then men will say, 'The LORD Almighty is God over Israel!' And the house of your servant David will be established before you.

27"O LORD Almighty, God of Israel, you have revealed this to your servant, saying, 'I will build a house for you.' So your servant has found courage to offer you this prayer. **28**O Sovereign LORD, you are God! Your words are trustworthy, and you have promised these good things to your servant. **29**Now be pleased to bless the house of your servant, that it may continue forever in your sight; for you, O Sovereign LORD, have spoken, and with your blessing the house of your servant will be blessed forever."

David's Victories

8 In the course of time, David defeated the Philistines and subdued them, and he took Metheg Ammah from the control of the Philistines.

2David also defeated the Moabites. He made them lie down on the ground and measured them off with a length of cord. Every two lengths of them were put to death, and the third length was allowed to live. So the Moabites became subject to David and brought tribute.

3Moreover, David fought Hadadezer son of Rehob, king of Zobah, when he went to restore his control along the Euphrates River. **4**David captured a thousand of his chariots, seven thousand charioteers[b] and twenty thousand foot soldiers. He hamstrung all but a hundred of the chariot horses.

5When the Arameans of Damascus came to help Hadadezer king of Zobah, David struck down twenty-two thousand of them. **6**He put garrisons in the Aramean kingdom of Damascus, and the Arameans became subject to him and brought tribute. The LORD gave David victory wherever he went.

7David took the gold shields that belonged to the officers of Hadadezer and brought them to Jerusalem. **8**From Tebah[c] and Berothai, towns that belonged to Hadadezer, King David took a great quantity of bronze.

9When Tou[d] king of Hamath heard that David had defeated the entire army of Hadadezer, **10**he sent his son Joram[e] to King David to greet him and congratulate him on his victory in battle over Hadadezer, who had been at war with Tou. Joram brought with him articles of silver and gold and bronze.

11King David dedicated these articles to the LORD, as he had done with the silver and gold from all the nations he had subdued: **12**Edom[f] and Moab, the Ammonites and the Philistines, and Amalek. He also dedicated the plunder taken from Hadadezer son of Rehob, king of Zobah.

---

a23 See Septuagint and 1 Chron. 17:21; Hebrew *wonders for your land and before your people, whom you redeemed from Egypt, from the nations and their gods.*   *b4* Septuagint (see also Dead Sea Scrolls and 1 Chron. 18:4); Masoretic Text *captured seventeen hundred of his charioteers*   *c8* See some Septuagint manuscripts (see also 1 Chron. 18:8); Hebrew *Betah.*   *d9* Hebrew *Toi,* a variant of *Tou;* also in verse 10   *e10* A variant of *Hadoram*   *f12* Some Hebrew manuscripts, Septuagint and Syriac (see also 1 Chron. 18:11); most Hebrew manuscripts *Aram*

[13]And David became famous after he returned from striking down eighteen thousand Edomites[a] in the Valley of Salt.

[14]He put garrisons throughout Edom, and all the Edomites became subject to David. The LORD gave David victory wherever he went.

David's Officials

[15]David reigned over all Israel, doing what was just and right for all his people. [16]Joab son of Zeruiah was over the army; Jehoshaphat son of Ahilud was recorder; [17]Zadok son of Ahitub and Ahimelech son of Abiathar were priests; Seraiah was secretary; [18]Benaiah son of Jehoiada was over the Kerethites and Pelethites; and David's sons were royal advisers.[b]

David and Mephibosheth

9 David asked, "Is there anyone still left of the house of Saul to whom I can show kindness for Jonathan's sake?"

[2]Now there was a servant of Saul's household named Ziba. They called him to appear before David, and the king said to him, "Are you Ziba?"

"Your servant," he replied.

[3]The king asked, "Is there no one still left of the house of Saul to whom I can show God's kindness?"

Ziba answered the king, "There is still a son of Jonathan; he is crippled in both feet."

[4]"Where is he?" the king asked.

Ziba answered, "He is at the house of Makir son of Ammiel in Lo Debar."

[5]So King David had him brought from Lo Debar, from the house of Makir son of Ammiel.

[6]When Mephibosheth son of Jonathan, the son of Saul, came to David, he bowed down to pay him honor.

David said, "Mephibosheth!"

"Your servant," he replied.

[7]"Don't be afraid," David said to him, "for I will surely show you kindness for the sake of your father Jonathan. I will restore to you all the land that belonged to your grandfather Saul, and you will always eat at my table."

[8]Mephibosheth bowed down and said, "What is your servant, that you should notice a dead dog like me?"

[9]Then the king summoned Ziba, Saul's servant, and said to him, "I have given your master's grandson everything that belonged to Saul and his family. [10]You and your sons and your servants are to farm the land for him and bring in the crops, so that your master's grandson may be provided for. And Mephibosheth, grandson of your master, will always eat at my table." (Now Ziba had fifteen sons and twenty servants.)

[11]Then Ziba said to the king, "Your servant will do whatever my lord the king commands his servant to do." So Mephibosheth ate at David's[c] table like one of the king's sons.

[12]Mephibosheth had a young son named Mica, and all the members of Ziba's household were servants of Mephibosheth. [13]And Mephibosheth lived in Jerusalem, because he always ate at the king's table, and he was crippled in both feet.

David Defeats the Ammonites

10 In the course of time, the king of the Ammonites died, and his son Hanun succeeded him as king. [2]David thought, "I will show kindness to Hanun son of Nahash, just as his father showed kindness to me." So David sent a delegation to express his sympathy to Hanun concerning his father.

When David's men came to the land of the Ammonites, [3]the Ammonite nobles said to Hanun their lord, "Do you think David is honoring your father by sending men to you to express sympathy? Hasn't David sent them to you to explore the city and spy it out and overthrow it?" [4]So Hanun seized David's men, shaved off half of each man's beard, cut off their garments in the middle at the buttocks, and sent them away.

[5]When David was told about this, he sent messengers to meet the men, for they were greatly humiliated. The king said, "Stay at Jericho till your beards have grown, and then come back."

[6]When the Ammonites realized that they had become a stench in David's nostrils, they hired twenty thousand Aramean foot soldiers from Beth Rehob and Zobah, as well as the king of Maacah with a thousand men, and also twelve thousand men from Tob.

[7]On hearing this, David sent Joab out with the entire army of fighting men. [8]The Ammonites came out and drew up in battle formation at the entrance to their city

---

[a]13 A few Hebrew manuscripts, Septuagint and Syriac (see also 1 Chron. 18:12); most Hebrew manuscripts *Aram* (that is, Arameans)   [b]18 Or *were priests*   [c]11 Septuagint; Hebrew *my*

gate, while the Arameans of Zobah and Rehob and the men of Tob and Maacah were by themselves in the open country. ⁹Joab saw that there were battle lines in front of him and behind him; so he selected some of the best troops in Israel and deployed them against the Arameans. ¹⁰He put the rest of the men under the command of Abishai his brother and deployed them against the Ammonites. ¹¹Joab said, "If the Arameans are too strong for me, then you are to come to my rescue; but if the Ammonites are too strong for you, then I will come to rescue you. ¹²Be strong and let us fight bravely for our people and the cities of our God. The LORD will do what is good in his sight."

¹³Then Joab and the troops with him advanced to fight the Arameans, and they fled before him. ¹⁴When the Ammonites saw that the Arameans were fleeing, they fled before Abishai and went inside the city. So Joab returned from fighting the Ammonites and came to Jerusalem.

¹⁵After the Arameans saw that they had been routed by Israel, they regrouped. ¹⁶Hadadezer had Arameans brought from beyond the River*a*; they went to Helam, with Shobach the commander of Hadadezer's army leading them.

¹⁷When David was told of this, he gathered all Israel, crossed the Jordan and went to Helam. The Arameans formed their battle lines to meet David and fought against him. ¹⁸But they fled before Israel, and David killed seven hundred of their charioteers and forty thousand of their foot soldiers.*b* He also struck down Shobach the commander of their army, and he died there. ¹⁹When all the kings who were vassals of Hadadezer saw that they had been defeated by Israel, they made peace with the Israelites and became subject to them.

So the Arameans were afraid to help the Ammonites anymore.

David and Bathsheba

11 In the spring, at the time when kings go off to war, David sent Joab out with the king's men and the whole Israelite army. They destroyed the Ammonites and besieged Rabbah. But David remained in Jerusalem.

²One evening David got up from his bed and walked around on the roof of the pal-

ace. From the roof he saw a woman bathing. The woman was very beautiful, ³and David sent someone to find out about her. The man said, "Isn't this Bathsheba, the daughter of Eliam and the wife of Uriah the Hittite?" ⁴Then David sent messengers to get her. She came to him, and he slept with her. (She had purified herself from her uncleanness.) Then*c* she went back home. ⁵The woman conceived and sent word to David, saying, "I am pregnant."

⁶So David sent this word to Joab: "Send me Uriah the Hittite." And Joab sent him to David. ⁷When Uriah came to him, David asked him how Joab was, how the soldiers were and how the war was going. ⁸Then David said to Uriah, "Go down to your house and wash your feet." So Uriah left the palace, and a gift from the king was sent after him. ⁹But Uriah slept at the entrance to the palace with all his master's servants and did not go down to his house.

¹⁰When David was told, "Uriah did not go home," he asked him, "Haven't you just come from a distance? Why didn't you go home?"

¹¹Uriah said to David, "The ark and Israel and Judah are staying in tents, and my master Joab and my lord's men are camped in the open fields. How could I go to my house to eat and drink and lie with my wife? As surely as you live, I will not do such a thing!"

¹²Then David said to him, "Stay here one more day, and tomorrow I will send you back." So Uriah remained in Jerusalem that day and the next. ¹³At David's invitation, he ate and drank with him, and David made him drunk. But in the evening Uriah went out to sleep on his mat among his master's servants; he did not go home.

¹⁴In the morning David wrote a letter to Joab and sent it with Uriah. ¹⁵In it he wrote, "Put Uriah in the front line where the fighting is fiercest. Then withdraw from him so he will be struck down and die."

¹⁶So while Joab had the city under siege, he put Uriah at a place where he knew the strongest defenders were. ¹⁷When the men of the city came out and fought against Joab, some of the men in David's army fell; moreover, Uriah the Hittite died.

¹⁸Joab sent David a full account of the battle. ¹⁹He instructed the messenger:

---

a16 That is, the Euphrates   *b18* Some Septuagint manuscripts (see also 1 Chron. 19:18); Hebrew *horsemen*   *c4* Or *with her. When she purified herself from her uncleanness.*

"When you have finished giving the king this account of the battle, **20**the king's anger may flare up, and he may ask you, 'Why did you get so close to the city to fight? Didn't you know they would shoot arrows from the wall? **21**Who killed Abimelech son of Jerub-Besheth[a]? Didn't a woman throw an upper millstone on him from the wall, so that he died in Thebez? Why did you get so close to the wall?' If he asks you this, then say to him, 'Also, your servant Uriah the Hittite is dead.' "

22The messenger set out, and when he arrived he told David everything Joab had sent him to say. **23**The messenger said to David, "The men overpowered us and came out against us in the open, but we drove them back to the entrance to the city gate. **24**Then the archers shot arrows at your servants from the wall, and some of the king's men died. Moreover, your servant Uriah the Hittite is dead."

25David told the messenger, "Say this to Joab: 'Don't let this upset you; the sword devours one as well as another. Press the attack against the city and destroy it.' Say this to encourage Joab."

26When Uriah's wife heard that her husband was dead, she mourned for him. **27**After the time of mourning was over, David had her brought to his house, and she became his wife and bore him a son. But the thing David had done displeased the LORD.

Nathan Rebukes David

12 The LORD sent Nathan to David. When he came to him, he said, "There were two men in a certain town, one rich and the other poor. **2**The rich man had a very large number of sheep and cattle, **3**but the poor man had nothing except one little ewe lamb he had bought. He raised it, and it grew up with him and his children. It shared his food, drank from his cup and even slept in his arms. It was like a daughter to him.

4"Now a traveler came to the rich man, but the rich man refrained from taking one of his own sheep or cattle to prepare a meal for the traveler who had come to him. Instead, he took the ewe lamb that belonged to the poor man and prepared it for the one who had come to him."

5David burned with anger against the man and said to Nathan, "As surely as the LORD lives, the man who did this deserves to die! **6**He must pay for that lamb four times over, because he did such a thing and had no pity."

7Then Nathan said to David, "You are the man! This is what the LORD, the God of Israel, says: 'I anointed you king over Israel, and I delivered you from the hand of Saul. **8**I gave your master's house to you, and your master's wives into your arms. I gave you the house of Israel and Judah. And if all this had been too little, I would have given you even more. **9**Why did you despise the word of the LORD by doing what is evil in his eyes? You struck down Uriah the Hittite with the sword and took his wife to be your own. You killed him with the sword of the Ammonites. **10**Now, therefore, the sword will never depart from your house, because you despised me and took the wife of Uriah the Hittite to be your own.'

11"This is what the LORD says: 'Out of your own household I am going to bring calamity upon you. Before your very eyes I will take your wives and give them to one who is close to you, and he will lie with your wives in broad daylight. **12**You did it in secret, but I will do this thing in broad daylight before all Israel.' "

13Then David said to Nathan, "I have sinned against the LORD."

Nathan replied, "The LORD has taken away your sin. You are not going to die. **14**But because by doing this you have made the enemies of the LORD show utter contempt,[b] the son born to you will die."

15After Nathan had gone home, the LORD struck the child that Uriah's wife had borne to David, and he became ill. **16**David pleaded with God for the child. He fasted and went into his house and spent the nights lying on the ground. **17**The elders of his household stood beside him to get him up from the ground, but he refused, and he would not eat any food with them.

18On the seventh day the child died. David's servants were afraid to tell him that the child was dead, for they thought, "While the child was still living, we spoke to David but he would not listen to us. How can we tell him the child is dead? He may do something desperate."

19David noticed that his servants were whispering among themselves and he realized the child was dead. "Is the child dead?" he asked.

---

a21 Also known as *Jerub-Baal* (that is, Gideon)   b14 Masoretic Text; an ancient Hebrew scribal tradition *this you have shown utter contempt for the LORD*

"Yes," they replied, "he is dead."

²⁰Then David got up from the ground. After he had washed, put on lotions and changed his clothes, he went into the house of the LORD and worshiped. Then he went to his own house, and at his request they served him food, and he ate.

²¹His servants asked him, "Why are you acting this way? While the child was alive, you fasted and wept, but now that the child is dead, you get up and eat!"

²²He answered, "While the child was still alive, I fasted and wept. I thought, 'Who knows? The LORD may be gracious to me and let the child live.' ²³But now that he is dead, why should I fast? Can I

MONDAY

VERSE FOR THE DAY:
2 Samuel 12:13

AUTHOR:
Gerald Mann

PASSAGE FOR THE DAY:
2 Samuel 11:1–27

You Can Begin Again

THE Bible says you can begin again after broken relationships. Nothing hurts worse than the loss of intimacy with a significant other. It's as if the world has ended. But you can begin again.

Ever read the twenty-eighth book of the Old Testament? Hosea is its name. The writer was a prophet whose wife left him and became a prostitute. Out of the depths of his hurt, God told him something like this: "Now you know how I feel. The ones I love keep on becoming whores, too. They sell themselves to other gods. But I keep on buying them back."

Hosea goes and pays to redeem his wife. He feels the same way about Gomer as God feels about Israel: "How can I give you up? How can I abandon you? . . . My heart will not let me do it! My love for you is too strong" (Hosea 11:8, [author's translation]) . . .

You can begin again after moral failure . . . after you've done the very thing you said you'd never do . . . after you've compromised the last shred of your integrity.

Ever read in the Bible about David's moral wreck? I call it Bathshebagate. It involved hanky-panky, adultery, and even the murder of Bathsheba's husband. The postman rang twice, and his name was Nathan the prophet. David was exposed. His past righteousness and achievement were nullified.

But now read Psalm 51. David did the only thing you can do when you're caught red-handed. He confessed and asked for a new heart to replace the old one . . . a spiritual and moral transplant.

Bathsheba was pregnant. She lost the baby. But out of the ashes of this moral collapse, another son was born. His name was Solomon . . .

You can begin again after moral failure.

Additional Scripture Readings:
Psalm 51; Hosea 11:1–11

Go to page 326 for your next devotional reading.

bring him back again? I will go to him, but he will not return to me."

24Then David comforted his wife Bathsheba, and he went to her and lay with her. She gave birth to a son, and they named him Solomon. The LORD loved him; **25**and because the LORD loved him, he sent word through Nathan the prophet to name him Jedidiah.*a*

26Meanwhile Joab fought against Rabbah of the Ammonites and captured the royal citadel. **27**Joab then sent messengers to David, saying, "I have fought against Rabbah and taken its water supply. **28**Now muster the rest of the troops and besiege the city and capture it. Otherwise I will take the city, and it will be named after me."

29So David mustered the entire army and went to Rabbah, and attacked and captured it. **30**He took the crown from the head of their king*b*—its weight was a talent*c* of gold, and it was set with precious stones—and it was placed on David's head. He took a great quantity of plunder from the city **31**and brought out the people who were there, consigning them to labor with saws and with iron picks and axes, and he made them work at brickmaking.*d* He did this to all the Ammonite towns. Then David and his entire army returned to Jerusalem.

Amnon and Tamar

13 In the course of time, Amnon son of David fell in love with Tamar, the beautiful sister of Absalom son of David.

2Amnon became frustrated to the point of illness on account of his sister Tamar, for she was a virgin, and it seemed impossible for him to do anything to her.

3Now Amnon had a friend named Jonadab son of Shimeah, David's brother. Jonadab was a very shrewd man. **4**He asked Amnon, "Why do you, the king's son, look so haggard morning after morning? Won't you tell me?"

Amnon said to him, "I'm in love with Tamar, my brother Absalom's sister."

5"Go to bed and pretend to be ill," Jonadab said. "When your father comes to see you, say to him, 'I would like my sister Tamar to come and give me something to

eat. Let her prepare the food in my sight so I may watch her and then eat it from her hand.' "

6So Amnon lay down and pretended to be ill. When the king came to see him, Amnon said to him, "I would like my sister Tamar to come and make some special bread in my sight, so I may eat from her hand."

7David sent word to Tamar at the palace: "Go to the house of your brother Amnon and prepare some food for him." **8**So Tamar went to the house of her brother Amnon, who was lying down. She took some dough, kneaded it, made the bread in his sight and baked it. **9**Then she took the pan and served him the bread, but he refused to eat.

"Send everyone out of here," Amnon said. So everyone left him. **10**Then Amnon said to Tamar, "Bring the food here into my bedroom so I may eat from your hand." And Tamar took the bread she had prepared and brought it to her brother Amnon in his bedroom. **11**But when she took it to him to eat, he grabbed her and said, "Come to bed with me, my sister."

12"Don't, my brother!" she said to him. "Don't force me. Such a thing should not be done in Israel! Don't do this wicked thing. **13**What about me? Where could I get rid of my disgrace? And what about you? You would be like one of the wicked fools in Israel. Please speak to the king; he will not keep me from being married to you." **14**But he refused to listen to her, and since he was stronger than she, he raped her.

15Then Amnon hated her with intense hatred. In fact, he hated her more than he had loved her. Amnon said to her, "Get up and get out!"

16"No!" she said to him. "Sending me away would be a greater wrong than what you have already done to me."

But he refused to listen to her. **17**He called his personal servant and said, "Get this woman out of here and bolt the door after her." **18**So his servant put her out and bolted the door after her. She was wearing a richly ornamented*e* robe, for this was the kind of garment the virgin daughters of the king wore. **19**Tamar put ashes on her head and tore the ornamented*f* robe she was wearing. She put her hand on her

---

a25 Jedidiah means *loved by the* LORD.   *b30* Or *of Milcom* (that is, Molech)   *c30* That is, about 75 pounds (about 34 kilograms)   *d31* The meaning of the Hebrew for this clause is uncertain.   *e18* The meaning of the Hebrew for this phrase is uncertain.   *f19* The meaning of the Hebrew for this word is uncertain.

head and went away, weeping aloud as she went.

20Her brother Absalom said to her, "Has that Amnon, your brother, been with you? Be quiet now, my sister; he is your brother. Don't take this thing to heart." And Tamar lived in her brother Absalom's house, a desolate woman.

21When King David heard all this, he was furious. **22**Absalom never said a word to Amnon, either good or bad; he hated Amnon because he had disgraced his sister Tamar.

Absalom Kills Amnon

23Two years later, when Absalom's sheepshearers were at Baal Hazor near the border of Ephraim, he invited all the king's sons to come there. **24**Absalom went to the king and said, "Your servant has had shearers come. Will the king and his officials please join me?"

25"No, my son," the king replied. "All of us should not go; we would only be a burden to you." Although Absalom urged him, he still refused to go, but gave him his blessing.

26Then Absalom said, "If not, please let my brother Amnon come with us."

The king asked him, "Why should he go with you?" **27**But Absalom urged him, so he sent with him Amnon and the rest of the king's sons.

28Absalom ordered his men, "Listen! When Amnon is in high spirits from drinking wine and I say to you, 'Strike Amnon down,' then kill him. Don't be afraid. Have not I given you this order? Be strong and brave." **29**So Absalom's men did to Amnon what Absalom had ordered. Then all the king's sons got up, mounted their mules and fled.

30While they were on their way, the report came to David: "Absalom has struck down all the king's sons; not one of them is left." **31**The king stood up, tore his clothes and lay down on the ground; and all his servants stood by with their clothes torn.

32But Jonadab son of Shimeah, David's brother, said, "My lord should not think that they killed all the princes; only Amnon is dead. This has been Absalom's expressed intention ever since the day Amnon raped his sister Tamar. **33**My lord the king should not be concerned about the report that all the king's sons are dead. Only Amnon is dead."

34Meanwhile, Absalom had fled.

Now the man standing watch looked up and saw many people on the road west of him, coming down the side of the hill. The watchman went and told the king, "I see men in the direction of Horonaim, on the side of the hill."*a*

35Jonadab said to the king, "See, the king's sons are here; it has happened just as your servant said."

36As he finished speaking, the king's sons came in, wailing loudly. The king, too, and all his servants wept very bitterly.

37Absalom fled and went to Talmai son of Ammihud, the king of Geshur. But King David mourned for his son every day.

38After Absalom fled and went to Geshur, he stayed there three years. **39**And the spirit of the king*b* longed to go to Absalom, for he was consoled concerning Amnon's death.

Absalom Returns to Jerusalem

14 Joab son of Zeruiah knew that the king's heart longed for Absalom. **2**So Joab sent someone to Tekoa and had a wise woman brought from there. He said to her, "Pretend you are in mourning. Dress in mourning clothes, and don't use any cosmetic lotions. Act like a woman who has spent many days grieving for the dead. **3**Then go to the king and speak these words to him." And Joab put the words in her mouth.

4When the woman from Tekoa went*c* to the king, she fell with her face to the ground to pay him honor, and she said, "Help me, O king!"

5The king asked her, "What is troubling you?"

She said, "I am indeed a widow; my husband is dead. **6**I your servant had two sons. They got into a fight with each other in the field, and no one was there to separate them. One struck the other and killed him. **7**Now the whole clan has risen up against your servant; they say, 'Hand over the one who struck his brother down, so that we may put him to death for the life of his brother whom he killed; then we will get rid of the heir as well.' They would put out the only burning coal I have left, leaving my husband neither name nor descendant on the face of the earth."

*a*34 Septuagint; Hebrew does not have this sentence. *b*39 Dead Sea Scrolls and some Septuagint manuscripts; Masoretic Text *But ⸲the spirit of⸳ David the king* *c*4 Many Hebrew manuscripts, Septuagint, Vulgate and Syriac; most Hebrew manuscripts *spoke*

[8]The king said to the woman, "Go home, and I will issue an order in your behalf."

[9]But the woman from Tekoa said to him, "My lord the king, let the blame rest on me and on my father's family, and let the king and his throne be without guilt."

[10]The king replied, "If anyone says anything to you, bring him to me, and he will not bother you again."

[11]She said, "Then let the king invoke the Lord his God to prevent the avenger of blood from adding to the destruction, so that my son will not be destroyed."

"As surely as the Lord lives," he said, "not one hair of your son's head will fall to the ground."

[12]Then the woman said, "Let your servant speak a word to my lord the king."

"Speak," he replied.

[13]The woman said, "Why then have you devised a thing like this against the people of God? When the king says this, does he not convict himself, for the king has not brought back his banished son? [14]Like water spilled on the ground, which cannot be recovered, so we must die. But God does not take away life; instead, he devises ways so that a banished person may not remain estranged from him.

[15]"And now I have come to say this to my lord the king because the people have made me afraid. Your servant thought, 'I will speak to the king; perhaps he will do what his servant asks. [16]Perhaps the king will agree to deliver his servant from the hand of the man who is trying to cut off both me and my son from the inheritance God gave us.'

[17]"And now your servant says, 'May the word of my lord the king bring me rest, for my lord the king is like an angel of God in discerning good and evil. May the Lord your God be with you.' "

[18]Then the king said to the woman, "Do not keep from me the answer to what I am going to ask you."

"Let my lord the king speak," the woman said.

[19]The king asked, "Isn't the hand of Joab with you in all this?"

The woman answered, "As surely as you live, my lord the king, no one can turn to the right or to the left from anything my lord the king says. Yes, it was your servant Joab who instructed me to do this and who put all these words into the mouth of your servant. [20]Your servant Joab did this

to change the present situation. My lord has wisdom like that of an angel of God — he knows everything that happens in the land."

[21]The king said to Joab, "Very well, I will do it. Go, bring back the young man Absalom."

[22]Joab fell with his face to the ground to pay him honor, and he blessed the king. Joab said, "Today your servant knows that he has found favor in your eyes, my lord the king, because the king has granted his servant's request."

[23]Then Joab went to Geshur and brought Absalom back to Jerusalem. [24]But the king said, "He must go to his own house; he must not see my face." So Absalom went to his own house and did not see the face of the king.

[25]In all Israel there was not a man so highly praised for his handsome appearance as Absalom. From the top of his head to the sole of his foot there was no blemish in him. [26]Whenever he cut the hair of his head — he used to cut his hair from time to time when it became too heavy for him — he would weigh it, and its weight was two hundred shekels[a] by the royal standard.

[27]Three sons and a daughter were born to Absalom. The daughter's name was Tamar, and she became a beautiful woman.

[28]Absalom lived two years in Jerusalem without seeing the king's face. [29]Then Absalom sent for Joab in order to send him to the king, but Joab refused to come to him. So he sent a second time, but he refused to come. [30]Then he said to his servants, "Look, Joab's field is next to mine, and he has barley there. Go and set it on fire." So Absalom's servants set the field on fire.

[31]Then Joab did go to Absalom's house and he said to him, "Why have your servants set my field on fire?"

[32]Absalom said to Joab, "Look, I sent word to you and said, 'Come here so I can send you to the king to ask, "Why have I come from Geshur? It would be better for me if I were still there!" ' Now then, I want to see the king's face, and if I am guilty of anything, let him put me to death."

[33]So Joab went to the king and told him this. Then the king summoned Absalom, and he came in and bowed down with his face to the ground before the king. And the king kissed Absalom.

---

[a]26 That is, about 5 pounds (about 2.3 kilograms)

Absalom's Conspiracy

15 In the course of time, Absalom provided himself with a chariot and horses and with fifty men to run ahead of him. [2]He would get up early and stand by the side of the road leading to the city gate. Whenever anyone came with a complaint to be placed before the king for a decision, Absalom would call out to him, "What town are you from?" He would answer, "Your servant is from one of the tribes of Israel." [3]Then Absalom would say to him, "Look, your claims are valid and proper, but there is no representative of the king to hear you." [4]And Absalom would add, "If only I were appointed judge in the land! Then everyone who has a complaint or case could come to me and I would see that he gets justice." [5]Also, whenever anyone approached him to bow down before him, Absalom would reach out his hand, take hold of him and kiss him. [6]Absalom behaved in this way toward all the Israelites who came to the king asking for justice, and so he stole the hearts of the men of Israel.

[7]At the end of four[a] years, Absalom said to the king, "Let me go to Hebron and fulfill a vow I made to the LORD. [8]While your servant was living at Geshur in Aram, I made this vow: 'If the LORD takes me back to Jerusalem, I will worship the LORD in Hebron.[b]'"

[9]The king said to him, "Go in peace." So he went to Hebron.

[10]Then Absalom sent secret messengers throughout the tribes of Israel to say, "As soon as you hear the sound of the trumpets, then say, 'Absalom is king in Hebron.'" [11]Two hundred men from Jerusalem had accompanied Absalom. They had been invited as guests and went quite innocently, knowing nothing about the matter. [12]While Absalom was offering sacrifices, he also sent for Ahithophel the Gilonite, David's counselor, to come from Giloh, his hometown. And so the conspiracy gained strength, and Absalom's following kept on increasing.

David Flees

[13]A messenger came and told David, "The hearts of the men of Israel are with Absalom."

[14]Then David said to all his officials who were with him in Jerusalem, "Come! We must flee, or none of us will escape from Absalom. We must leave immediately, or he will move quickly to overtake us and bring ruin upon us and put the city to the sword."

[15]The king's officials answered him, "Your servants are ready to do whatever our lord the king chooses."

[16]The king set out, with his entire household following him; but he left ten concubines to take care of the palace. [17]So the king set out, with all the people following him, and they halted at a place some distance away. [18]All his men marched past him, along with all the Kerethites and Pelethites; and all the six hundred Gittites who had accompanied him from Gath marched before the king.

[19]The king said to Ittai the Gittite, "Why should you come along with us? Go back and stay with King Absalom. You are a foreigner, an exile from your homeland. [20]You came only yesterday. And today shall I make you wander about with us, when I do not know where I am going? Go back, and take your countrymen. May kindness and faithfulness be with you."

[21]But Ittai replied to the king, "As surely as the LORD lives, and as my lord the king lives, wherever my lord the king may be, whether it means life or death, there will your servant be."

[22]David said to Ittai, "Go ahead, march on." So Ittai the Gittite marched on with all his men and the families that were with him.

[23]The whole countryside wept aloud as all the people passed by. The king also crossed the Kidron Valley, and all the people moved on toward the desert.

[24]Zadok was there, too, and all the Levites who were with him were carrying the ark of the covenant of God. They set down the ark of God, and Abiathar offered sacrifices[c] until all the people had finished leaving the city.

[25]Then the king said to Zadok, "Take the ark of God back into the city. If I find favor in the LORD's eyes, he will bring me back and let me see it and his dwelling place again. [26]But if he says, 'I am not pleased with you,' then I am ready; let him do to me whatever seems good to him."

[27]The king also said to Zadok the priest, "Aren't you a seer? Go back to the city in peace, with your son Ahimaaz and Jona-

---

a7 Some Septuagint manuscripts, Syriac and Josephus; Hebrew forty   *b8 Some Septuagint manuscripts;*
Hebrew does not have in Hebron.   *c24 Or Abiathar went up*

than son of Abiathar. You and Abiathar take your two sons with you. **28**I will wait at the fords in the desert until word comes from you to inform me." **29**So Zadok and Abiathar took the ark of God back to Jerusalem and stayed there.

30But David continued up the Mount of Olives, weeping as he went; his head was covered and he was barefoot. All the people with him covered their heads too and were weeping as they went up. **31**Now David had been told, "Ahithophel is among the conspirators with Absalom." So David prayed, "O LORD, turn Ahithophel's counsel into foolishness."

32When David arrived at the summit, where people used to worship God, Hushai the Arkite was there to meet him, his robe torn and dust on his head. **33**David said to him, "If you go with me, you will be a burden to me. **34**But if you return to the city and say to Absalom, 'I will be your servant, O king; I was your father's servant in the past, but now I will be your servant,' then you can help me by frustrating Ahithophel's advice. **35**Won't the priests Zadok and Abiathar be there with you? Tell them anything you hear in the king's palace. **36**Their two sons, Ahimaaz son of Zadok and Jonathan son of Abiathar, are there with them. Send them to me with anything you hear."

37So David's friend Hushai arrived at Jerusalem as Absalom was entering the city.

David and Ziba

16 When David had gone a short distance beyond the summit, there was Ziba, the steward of Mephibosheth, waiting to meet him. He had a string of donkeys saddled and loaded with two hundred loaves of bread, a hundred cakes of raisins, a hundred cakes of figs and a skin of wine.

2The king asked Ziba, "Why have you brought these?"

Ziba answered, "The donkeys are for the king's household to ride on, the bread and fruit are for the men to eat, and the wine is to refresh those who become exhausted in the desert."

3The king then asked, "Where is your master's grandson?"

Ziba said to him, "He is staying in Jerusalem, because he thinks, 'Today the house of Israel will give me back my grandfather's kingdom.' "

4Then the king said to Ziba, "All that belonged to Mephibosheth is now yours."

"I humbly bow," Ziba said. "May I find favor in your eyes, my lord the king."

Shimei Curses David

5As King David approached Bahurim, a man from the same clan as Saul's family came out from there. His name was Shimei son of Gera, and he cursed as he came out. **6**He pelted David and all the king's officials with stones, though all the troops and the special guard were on David's right and left. **7**As he cursed, Shimei said, "Get out, get out, you man of blood, you scoundrel! **8**The LORD has repaid you for all the blood you shed in the household of Saul, in whose place you have reigned. The LORD has handed the kingdom over to your son Absalom. You have come to ruin because you are a man of blood!"

9Then Abishai son of Zeruiah said to the king, "Why should this dead dog curse my lord the king? Let me go over and cut off his head."

10But the king said, "What do you and I have in common, you sons of Zeruiah? If he is cursing because the LORD said to him, 'Curse David,' who can ask, 'Why do you do this?' "

11David then said to Abishai and all his officials, "My son, who is of my own flesh, is trying to take my life. How much more, then, this Benjamite! Leave him alone; let him curse, for the LORD has told him to. **12**It may be that the LORD will see my distress and repay me with good for the cursing I am receiving today."

13So David and his men continued along the road while Shimei was going along the hillside opposite him, cursing as he went and throwing stones at him and showering him with dirt. **14**The king and all the people with him arrived at their destination exhausted. And there he refreshed himself.

The Advice of Hushai and Ahithophel

15Meanwhile, Absalom and all the men of Israel came to Jerusalem, and Ahithophel was with him. **16**Then Hushai the Arkite, David's friend, went to Absalom and said to him, "Long live the king! Long live the king!"

17Absalom asked Hushai, "Is this the love you show your friend? Why didn't you go with your friend?"

18Hushai said to Absalom, "No, the one chosen by the LORD, by these people, and by all the men of Israel — his I will be, and

I will remain with him. [19]Furthermore, whom should I serve? Should I not serve the son? Just as I served your father, so I will serve you."

[20]Absalom said to Ahithophel, "Give us your advice. What should we do?"

[21]Ahithophel answered, "Lie with your father's concubines whom he left to take care of the palace. Then all Israel will hear that you have made yourself a stench in your father's nostrils, and the hands of everyone with you will be strengthened." [22]So they pitched a tent for Absalom on the roof, and he lay with his father's concubines in the sight of all Israel.

[23]Now in those days the advice Ahithophel gave was like that of one who inquires of God. That was how both David and Absalom regarded all of Ahithophel's advice.

17 Ahithophel said to Absalom, "I would[a] choose twelve thousand men and set out tonight in pursuit of David. [2]I would[b] attack him while he is weary and weak. I would[b] strike him with terror, and then all the people with him will flee. I would[b] strike down only the king [3]and bring all the people back to you. The death of the man you seek will mean the return of all; all the people will be unharmed." [4]This plan seemed good to Absalom and to all the elders of Israel.

[5]But Absalom said, "Summon also Hushai the Arkite, so we can hear what he has to say." [6]When Hushai came to him, Absalom said, "Ahithophel has given this advice. Should we do what he says? If not, give us your opinion."

[7]Hushai replied to Absalom, "The advice Ahithophel has given is not good this time. [8]You know your father and his men; they are fighters, and as fierce as a wild bear robbed of her cubs. Besides, your father is an experienced fighter; he will not spend the night with the troops. [9]Even now, he is hidden in a cave or some other place. If he should attack your troops first,[c] whoever hears about it will say, 'There has been a slaughter among the troops who follow Absalom.' [10]Then even the bravest soldier, whose heart is like the heart of a lion, will melt with fear, for all Israel knows that your father is a fighter and that those with him are brave.

[11]"So I advise you: Let all Israel, from Dan to Beersheba—as numerous as the sand on the seashore—be gathered to you, with you yourself leading them into battle. [12]Then we will attack him wherever he may be found, and we will fall on him as dew settles on the ground. Neither he nor any of his men will be left alive. [13]If he withdraws into a city, then all Israel will bring ropes to that city, and we will drag it down to the valley until not even a piece of it can be found."

[14]Absalom and all the men of Israel said, "The advice of Hushai the Arkite is better than that of Ahithophel." For the LORD had determined to frustrate the good advice of Ahithophel in order to bring disaster on Absalom.

[15]Hushai told Zadok and Abiathar, the priests, "Ahithophel has advised Absalom and the elders of Israel to do such and such, but I have advised them to do so and so. [16]Now send a message immediately and tell David, 'Do not spend the night at the fords in the desert; cross over without fail, or the king and all the people with him will be swallowed up.' "

[17]Jonathan and Ahimaaz were staying at En Rogel. A servant girl was to go and inform them, and they were to go and tell King David, for they could not risk being seen entering the city. [18]But a young man saw them and told Absalom. So the two of them left quickly and went to the house of a man in Bahurim. He had a well in his courtyard, and they climbed down into it. [19]His wife took a covering and spread it out over the opening of the well and scattered grain over it. No one knew anything about it.

[20]When Absalom's men came to the woman at the house, they asked, "Where are Ahimaaz and Jonathan?"

The woman answered them, "They crossed over the brook."[d] The men searched but found no one, so they returned to Jerusalem.

[21]After the men had gone, the two climbed out of the well and went to inform King David. They said to him, "Set out and cross the river at once; Ahithophel has advised such and such against you." [22]So David and all the people with him set out and crossed the Jordan. By daybreak, no one was left who had not crossed the Jordan.

[23]When Ahithophel saw that his advice had not been followed, he saddled his donkey and set out for his house in his hometown. He put his house in order and

---

a1 Or *Let me*   b2 Or *will*   c9 Or *When some of the men fall at the first attack*   d20 Or *"They passed by the sheep pen toward the water."*

then hanged himself. So he died and was buried in his father's tomb.

²⁴David went to Mahanaim, and Absalom crossed the Jordan with all the men of Israel. ²⁵Absalom had appointed Amasa over the army in place of Joab. Amasa was the son of a man named Jether,ᵃ an Israeliteᵇ who had married Abigail,ᶜ the daughter of Nahash and sister of Zeruiah the mother of Joab. ²⁶The Israelites and Absalom camped in the land of Gilead.

²⁷When David came to Mahanaim, Shobi son of Nahash from Rabbah of the Ammonites, and Makir son of Ammiel from Lo Debar, and Barzillai the Gileadite from Rogelim ²⁸brought bedding and bowls and articles of pottery. They also brought wheat and barley, flour and roasted grain, beans and lentils,ᵈ ²⁹honey and curds, sheep, and cheese from cows' milk for David and his people to eat. For they said, "The people have become hungry and tired and thirsty in the desert."

Absalom's Death

18 David mustered the men who were with him and appointed over them commanders of thousands and commanders of hundreds. ²David sent the troops out—a third under the command of Joab, a third under Joab's brother Abishai son of Zeruiah, and a third under Ittai the Gittite. The king told the troops, "I myself will surely march out with you."

³But the men said, "You must not go out; if we are forced to flee, they won't care about us. Even if half of us die, they won't care; but you are worth ten thousand of us.ᵉ It would be better now for you to give us support from the city."

⁴The king answered, "I will do whatever seems best to you."

So the king stood beside the gate while all the men marched out in units of hundreds and of thousands. ⁵The king commanded Joab, Abishai and Ittai, "Be gentle with the young man Absalom for my sake." And all the troops heard the king giving orders concerning Absalom to each of the commanders.

⁶The army marched into the field to fight Israel, and the battle took place in the forest of Ephraim. ⁷There the army of Israel was defeated by David's men, and the casualties that day were great—twenty thousand men. ⁸The battle spread out over the whole countryside, and the forest claimed more lives that day than the sword.

⁹Now Absalom happened to meet David's men. He was riding his mule, and as the mule went under the thick branches of a large oak, Absalom's head got caught in the tree. He was left hanging in midair, while the mule he was riding kept on going.

¹⁰When one of the men saw this, he told Joab, "I just saw Absalom hanging in an oak tree."

¹¹Joab said to the man who had told him this, "What! You saw him? Why didn't you strike him to the ground right there? Then I would have had to give you ten shekelsᶠ of silver and a warrior's belt."

¹²But the man replied, "Even if a thousand shekelsᵍ were weighed out into my hands, I would not lift my hand against the king's son. In our hearing the king commanded you and Abishai and Ittai, 'Protect the young man Absalom for my sake.'ʰ ¹³And if I had put my life in jeopardyⁱ—and nothing is hidden from the king—you would have kept your distance from me."

¹⁴Joab said, "I'm not going to wait like this for you." So he took three javelins in his hand and plunged them into Absalom's heart while Absalom was still alive in the oak tree. ¹⁵And ten of Joab's armorbearers surrounded Absalom, struck him and killed him.

¹⁶Then Joab sounded the trumpet, and the troops stopped pursuing Israel, for Joab halted them. ¹⁷They took Absalom, threw him into a big pit in the forest and piled up a large heap of rocks over him. Meanwhile, all the Israelites fled to their homes.

¹⁸During his lifetime Absalom had taken a pillar and erected it in the King's Valley as a monument to himself, for he thought, "I have no son to carry on the memory of my name." He named the pil-

---

ᵃ25 Hebrew *Ithra*, a variant of *Jether*   ᵇ25 Hebrew and some Septuagint manuscripts; other Septuagint manuscripts (see also 1 Chron. 2:17) *Ishmaelite* or *Jezreelite*   ᶜ25 Hebrew *Abigal*, a variant of *Abigail*   ᵈ28 Most Septuagint manuscripts and Syriac; Hebrew *lentils, and roasted grain*   ᵉ3 Two Hebrew manuscripts, some Septuagint manuscripts and Vulgate; most Hebrew manuscripts *care; for now there are ten thousand like us*   ᶠ11 That is, about 4 ounces (about 115 grams)   ᵍ12 That is, about 25 pounds (about 11 kilograms)   ʰ12 A few Hebrew manuscripts, Septuagint, Vulgate and Syriac; most Hebrew manuscripts may be translated *Absalom, whoever you may be.*   ⁱ13 Or *Otherwise, if I had acted treacherously toward him* lar after himself, and it is called Absalom's Monument to this day.

David Mourns

19Now Ahimaaz son of Zadok said, "Let me run and take the news to the king that the LORD has delivered him from the hand of his enemies."

20"You are not the one to take the news today," Joab told him. "You may take the news another time, but you must not do so today, because the king's son is dead."

21Then Joab said to a Cushite, "Go, tell the king what you have seen." The Cushite bowed down before Joab and ran off.

22Ahimaaz son of Zadok again said to Joab, "Come what may, please let me run behind the Cushite."

But Joab replied, "My son, why do you want to go? You don't have any news that will bring you a reward."

23He said, "Come what may, I want to run."

So Joab said, "Run!" Then Ahimaaz ran by way of the plain*a* and outran the Cushite.

24While David was sitting between the inner and outer gates, the watchman went up to the roof of the gateway by the wall. As he looked out, he saw a man running alone. **25**The watchman called out to the king and reported it.

The king said, "If he is alone, he must have good news." And the man came closer and closer.

26Then the watchman saw another man running, and he called down to the gatekeeper, "Look, another man running alone!"

The king said, "He must be bringing good news, too."

27The watchman said, "It seems to me that the first one runs like Ahimaaz son of Zadok."

"He's a good man," the king said. "He comes with good news."

28Then Ahimaaz called out to the king, "All is well!" He bowed down before the king with his face to the ground and said, "Praise be to the LORD your God! He has delivered up the men who lifted their hands against my lord the king."

29The king asked, "Is the young man Absalom safe?"

Ahimaaz answered, "I saw great confusion just as Joab was about to send the king's servant and me, your servant, but I don't know what it was."

30The king said, "Stand aside and wait here." So he stepped aside and stood there.

31Then the Cushite arrived and said, "My lord the king, hear the good news! The LORD has delivered you today from all who rose up against you."

32The king asked the Cushite, "Is the young man Absalom safe?"

The Cushite replied, "May the enemies of my lord the king and all who rise up to harm you be like that young man."

33The king was shaken. He went up to the room over the gateway and wept. As he went, he said: "O my son Absalom! My son, my son Absalom! If only I had died instead of you—O Absalom, my son, my son!"

19 Joab was told, "The king is weeping and mourning for Absalom." **2**And for the whole army the victory that day was turned into mourning, because on that day the troops heard it said, "The king is grieving for his son." **3**The men stole into the city that day as men steal in who are ashamed when they flee from battle. **4**The king covered his face and cried aloud, "O my son Absalom! O Absalom, my son, my son!"

5Then Joab went into the house to the king and said, "Today you have humiliated all your men, who have just saved your life and the lives of your sons and daughters and the lives of your wives and concubines. **6**You love those who hate you and hate those who love you. You have made it clear today that the commanders and their men mean nothing to you. I see that you would be pleased if Absalom were alive today and all of us were dead. **7**Now go out and encourage your men. I swear by the LORD that if you don't go out, not a man will be left with you by nightfall. This will be worse for you than all the calamities that have come upon you from your youth till now."

8So the king got up and took his seat in the gateway. When the men were told, "The king is sitting in the gateway," they all came before him.

David Returns to Jerusalem

Meanwhile, the Israelites had fled to their homes. **9**Throughout the tribes of Israel, the people were all arguing with each other, saying, "The king delivered us from the hand of our enemies; he is the one who rescued us from the hand of the Phi-

---

a23 That is, the plain of the Jordan

listines. But now he has fled the country because of Absalom; ¹⁰and Absalom, whom we anointed to rule over us, has died in battle. So why do you say nothing about bringing the king back?"

¹¹King David sent this message to Zadok and Abiathar, the priests: "Ask the elders of Judah, 'Why should you be the last to bring the king back to his palace, since what is being said throughout Israel has reached the king at his quarters? ¹²You are my brothers, my own flesh and blood. So why should you be the last to bring back the king?' ¹³And say to Amasa, 'Are you not my own flesh and blood? May God deal with me, be it ever so severely, if from now on you are not the commander of my army in place of Joab.' "

¹⁴He won over the hearts of all the men of Judah as though they were one man. They sent word to the king, "Return, you and all your men." ¹⁵Then the king returned and went as far as the Jordan.

Now the men of Judah had come to Gilgal to go out and meet the king and bring him across the Jordan. ¹⁶Shimei son of Gera, the Benjamite from Bahurim, hurried down with the men of Judah to meet King David. ¹⁷With him were a thousand Benjamites, along with Ziba, the steward of Saul's household, and his fifteen sons and twenty servants. They rushed to the Jordan, where the king was. ¹⁸They crossed at the ford to take the king's household over and to do whatever he wished.

When Shimei son of Gera crossed the Jordan, he fell prostrate before the king ¹⁹and said to him, "May my lord not hold me guilty. Do not remember how your servant did wrong on the day my lord the king left Jerusalem. May the king put it out of his mind. ²⁰For I your servant know that I have sinned, but today I have come here as the first of the whole house of Joseph to come down and meet my lord the king."

²¹Then Abishai son of Zeruiah said, "Shouldn't Shimei be put to death for this? He cursed the LORD's anointed."

²²David replied, "What do you and I have in common, you sons of Zeruiah? This day you have become my adversaries! Should anyone be put to death in Israel today? Do I not know that today I am king over Israel?" ²³So the king said to Shimei, "You shall not die." And the king promised him on oath.

²⁴Mephibosheth, Saul's grandson, also went down to meet the king. He had not taken care of his feet or trimmed his mustache or washed his clothes from the day the king left until the day he returned safely. ²⁵When he came from Jerusalem to meet the king, the king asked him, "Why didn't you go with me, Mephibosheth?"

²⁶He said, "My lord the king, since I your servant am lame, I said, 'I will have my donkey saddled and will ride on it, so I can go with the king.' But Ziba my servant betrayed me. ²⁷And he has slandered your servant to my lord the king. My lord the king is like an angel of God; so do whatever pleases you. ²⁸All my grandfather's descendants deserved nothing but death from my lord the king, but you gave your servant a place among those who eat at your table. So what right do I have to make any more appeals to the king?"

²⁹The king said to him, "Why say more? I order you and Ziba to divide the fields."

³⁰Mephibosheth said to the king, "Let him take everything, now that my lord the king has arrived home safely."

³¹Barzillai the Gileadite also came down from Rogelim to cross the Jordan with the king and to send him on his way from there. ³²Now Barzillai was a very old man, eighty years of age. He had provided for the king during his stay in Mahanaim, for he was a very wealthy man. ³³The king said to Barzillai, "Cross over with me and stay with me in Jerusalem, and I will provide for you."

³⁴But Barzillai answered the king, "How many more years will I live, that I should go up to Jerusalem with the king? ³⁵I am now eighty years old. Can I tell the difference between what is good and what is not? Can your servant taste what he eats and drinks? Can I still hear the voices of men and women singers? Why should your servant be an added burden to my lord the king? ³⁶Your servant will cross over the Jordan with the king for a short distance, but why should the king reward me in this way? ³⁷Let your servant return, that I may die in my own town near the tomb of my father and mother. But here is your servant Kimham. Let him cross over with my lord the king. Do for him whatever pleases you."

³⁸The king said, "Kimham shall cross over with me, and I will do for him whatever pleases you. And anything you desire from me I will do for you."

³⁹So all the people crossed the Jordan, and then the king crossed over. The king kissed Barzillai and gave him his blessing, and Barzillai returned to his home.

⁴⁰When the king crossed over to Gilgal, Kimham crossed with him. All the troops of Judah and half the troops of Israel had taken the king over.

⁴¹Soon all the men of Israel were coming to the king and saying to him, "Why did our brothers, the men of Judah, steal the king away and bring him and his household across the Jordan, together with all his men?"

⁴²All the men of Judah answered the men of Israel, "We did this because the king is closely related to us. Why are you angry about it? Have we eaten any of the king's provisions? Have we taken anything for ourselves?"

⁴³Then the men of Israel answered the men of Judah, "We have ten shares in the king; and besides, we have a greater claim on David than you have. So why do you treat us with contempt? Were we not the first to speak of bringing back our king?"

But the men of Judah responded even more harshly than the men of Israel.

Sheba Rebels Against David

20 Now a troublemaker named Sheba son of Bicri, a Benjamite, happened to be there. He sounded the trumpet and shouted,

"We have no share in David,
    no part in Jesse's son!
Every man to his tent, O Israel!"

²So all the men of Israel deserted David to follow Sheba son of Bicri. But the men of Judah stayed by their king all the way from the Jordan to Jerusalem.

³When David returned to his palace in Jerusalem, he took the ten concubines he had left to take care of the palace and put them in a house under guard. He provided for them, but did not lie with them. They were kept in confinement till the day of their death, living as widows.

⁴Then the king said to Amasa, "Summon the men of Judah to come to me within three days, and be here yourself." ⁵But when Amasa went to summon Judah, he took longer than the time the king had set for him.

⁶David said to Abishai, "Now Sheba son of Bicri will do us more harm than Absalom did. Take your master's men and pursue him, or he will find fortified cities and escape from us." ⁷So Joab's men and the Kerethites and Pelethites and all the mighty warriors went out under the command of Abishai. They marched out from Jerusalem to pursue Sheba son of Bicri.

⁸While they were at the great rock in Gibeon, Amasa came to meet them. Joab was wearing his military tunic, and strapped over it at his waist was a belt with a dagger in its sheath. As he stepped forward, it dropped out of its sheath.

⁹Joab said to Amasa, "How are you, my brother?" Then Joab took Amasa by the beard with his right hand to kiss him. ¹⁰Amasa was not on his guard against the dagger in Joab's hand, and Joab plunged it into his belly, and his intestines spilled out on the ground. Without being stabbed again, Amasa died. Then Joab and his brother Abishai pursued Sheba son of Bicri.

¹¹One of Joab's men stood beside Amasa and said, "Whoever favors Joab, and whoever is for David, let him follow Joab!" ¹²Amasa lay wallowing in his blood in the middle of the road, and the man saw that all the troops came to a halt there. When he realized that everyone who came up to Amasa stopped, he dragged him from the road into a field and threw a garment over him. ¹³After Amasa had been removed from the road, all the men went on with Joab to pursue Sheba son of Bicri.

¹⁴Sheba passed through all the tribes of Israel to Abel Beth Maacah[a] and through the entire region of the Berites, who gathered together and followed him. ¹⁵All the troops with Joab came and besieged Sheba in Abel Beth Maacah. They built a siege ramp up to the city, and it stood against the outer fortifications. While they were battering the wall to bring it down, ¹⁶a wise woman called from the city, "Listen! Listen! Tell Joab to come here so I can speak to him." ¹⁷He went toward her, and she asked, "Are you Joab?"

"I am," he answered.

She said, "Listen to what your servant has to say."

"I'm listening," he said.

¹⁸She continued, "Long ago they used to say, 'Get your answer at Abel,' and that settled it. ¹⁹We are the peaceful and faithful in Israel. You are trying to destroy a city that is a mother in Israel. Why do you want to swallow up the LORD's inheritance?"

²⁰"Far be it from me!" Joab replied, "Far be it from me to swallow up or destroy! ²¹That is not the case. A man named She-

---

a 14 Or *Abel, even Beth Maacah*; also in verse 15

ba son of Bicri, from the hill country of Ephraim, has lifted up his hand against the king, against David. Hand over this one man, and I'll withdraw from the city."

The woman said to Joab, "His head will be thrown to you from the wall."

²²Then the woman went to all the people with her wise advice, and they cut off the head of Sheba son of Bicri and threw it to Joab. So he sounded the trumpet, and his men dispersed from the city, each returning to his home. And Joab went back to the king in Jerusalem.

²³Joab was over Israel's entire army; Benaiah son of Jehoiada was over the Kerethites and Pelethites; ²⁴Adoniram^a was in charge of forced labor; Jehoshaphat son of Ahilud was recorder; ²⁵Sheva was secretary; Zadok and Abiathar were priests; ²⁶and Ira the Jairite was David's priest.

The Gibeonites Avenged

21 During the reign of David, there was a famine for three successive years; so David sought the face of the LORD. The LORD said, "It is on account of Saul and his blood-stained house; it is because he put the Gibeonites to death."

²The king summoned the Gibeonites and spoke to them. (Now the Gibeonites were not a part of Israel but were survivors of the Amorites; the Israelites had sworn to ₍spare₎ them, but Saul in his zeal for Israel and Judah had tried to annihilate them.) ³David asked the Gibeonites, "What shall I do for you? How shall I make amends so that you will bless the LORD's inheritance?"

⁴The Gibeonites answered him, "We have no right to demand silver or gold from Saul or his family, nor do we have the right to put anyone in Israel to death."

"What do you want me to do for you?" David asked.

⁵They answered the king, "As for the man who destroyed us and plotted against us so that we have been decimated and have no place anywhere in Israel, ⁶let seven of his male descendants be given to us to be killed and exposed before the LORD at Gibeah of Saul—the LORD's chosen one."

So the king said, "I will give them to you."

⁷The king spared Mephibosheth son of Jonathan, the son of Saul, because of the oath before the LORD between David and Jonathan son of Saul. ⁸But the king took Armoni and Mephibosheth, the two sons of Aiah's daughter Rizpah, whom she had borne to Saul, together with the five sons of Saul's daughter Merab,^b whom she had borne to Adriel son of Barzillai the Meholathite. ⁹He handed them over to the Gibeonites, who killed and exposed them on a hill before the LORD. All seven of them fell together; they were put to death during the first days of the harvest, just as the barley harvest was beginning.

¹⁰Rizpah daughter of Aiah took sackcloth and spread it out for herself on a rock. From the beginning of the harvest till the rain poured down from the heavens on the bodies, she did not let the birds of the air touch them by day or the wild animals by night. ¹¹When David was told what Aiah's daughter Rizpah, Saul's concubine, had done, ¹²he went and took the bones of Saul and his son Jonathan from the citizens of Jabesh Gilead. (They had taken them secretly from the public square at Beth Shan, where the Philistines had hung them after they struck Saul down on Gilboa.) ¹³David brought the bones of Saul and his son Jonathan from there, and the bones of those who had been killed and exposed were gathered up.

¹⁴They buried the bones of Saul and his son Jonathan in the tomb of Saul's father Kish, at Zela in Benjamin, and did everything the king commanded. After that, God answered prayer in behalf of the land.

Wars Against the Philistines

¹⁵Once again there was a battle between the Philistines and Israel. David went down with his men to fight against the Philistines, and he became exhausted. ¹⁶And Ishbi-Benob, one of the descendants of Rapha, whose bronze spearhead weighed three hundred shekels^c and who was armed with a new ₍sword₎, said he would kill David. ¹⁷But Abishai son of Zeruiah came to David's rescue; he struck the Philistine down and killed him. Then David's men swore to him, saying, "Never again will you go out with us to battle, so that the lamp of Israel will not be extinguished."

¹⁸In the course of time, there was anoth-

---

^a24 Some Septuagint manuscripts (see also 1 Kings 4:6 and 5:14); Hebrew *Adoram*　　　^b8 Two Hebrew manuscripts, some Septuagint manuscripts and Syriac (see also 1 Samuel 18:19); most Hebrew and Septuagint manuscripts *Michal*　　　^c16 That is, about 7 1/2 pounds (about 3.5 kilograms)

er battle with the Philistines, at Gob. At that time Sibbecai the Hushathite killed Saph, one of the descendants of Rapha.

¹⁹In another battle with the Philistines at Gob, Elhanan son of Jaare-Oregim*a* the Bethlehemite killed Goliath*b* the Gittite, who had a spear with a shaft like a weaver's rod.

²⁰In still another battle, which took place at Gath, there was a huge man with six fingers on each hand and six toes on each foot — twenty-four in all. He also was descended from Rapha. ²¹When he taunted Israel, Jonathan son of Shimeah, David's brother, killed him.

²²These four were descendants of Rapha in Gath, and they fell at the hands of David and his men.

David's Song of Praise

22 David sang to the LORD the words of this song when the LORD delivered him from the hand of all his enemies and from the hand of Saul. ²He said:

"The LORD is my rock, my fortress and my deliverer;
3　my God is my rock, in whom I take refuge,
　my shield and the horn*c* of my salvation.
He is my stronghold, my refuge and my savior —
　from violent men you save me.
⁴I call to the LORD, who is worthy of praise,
　and I am saved from my enemies.

⁵"The waves of death swirled about me;
　the torrents of destruction overwhelmed me.
⁶The cords of the grave*d* coiled around me;
　the snares of death confronted me.
⁷In my distress I called to the LORD;
　I called out to my God.
From his temple he heard my voice;
　my cry came to his ears.

⁸"The earth trembled and quaked,
　the foundations of the heavens*e* shook;
　they trembled because he was angry.
⁹Smoke rose from his nostrils;

consuming fire came from his mouth,
　burning coals blazed out of it.
¹⁰He parted the heavens and came down;
　dark clouds were under his feet.
¹¹He mounted the cherubim and flew;
　he soared*f* on the wings of the wind.
¹²He made darkness his canopy around him —
　the dark*g* rain clouds of the sky.
¹³Out of the brightness of his presence
　bolts of lightning blazed forth.
¹⁴The LORD thundered from heaven;
　the voice of the Most High resounded.
¹⁵He shot arrows and scattered the enemies,
　bolts of lightning and routed them.
¹⁶The valleys of the sea were exposed
　and the foundations of the earth laid bare
　at the rebuke of the LORD,
　at the blast of breath from his nostrils.

¹⁷"He reached down from on high and took hold of me;
　he drew me out of deep waters.
¹⁸He rescued me from my powerful enemy,
　from my foes, who were too strong for me.
¹⁹They confronted me in the day of my disaster,
　but the LORD was my support.
²⁰He brought me out into a spacious place;
　he rescued me because he delighted in me.

²¹"The LORD has dealt with me according to my righteousness;
　according to the cleanness of my hands he has rewarded me.
²²For I have kept the ways of the LORD;
　I have not done evil by turning from my God.
²³All his laws are before me;
　I have not turned away from his decrees.
²⁴I have been blameless before him
　and have kept myself from sin.
²⁵The LORD has rewarded me according to my righteousness,

---

a19 Or *son of Jair the weaver*　*b19* Hebrew and Septuagint; 1 Chron. 20:5 *son of Jair killed Lahmi the brother of Goliath*　*c3* *Horn* here symbolizes strength.　*d6* Hebrew *Sheol*　*e8* Hebrew; Vulgate and Syriac (see also Psalm 18:7) *mountains*　*f11* Many Hebrew manuscripts (see also Psalm 18:10); most Hebrew manuscripts *appeared*　*g12* Septuagint and Vulgate (see also Psalm 18:11); Hebrew *massed* according to my cleanness[a] in his sight.

26"To the faithful you show yourself faithful,
  to the blameless you show yourself blameless,
27to the pure you show yourself pure,
  but to the crooked you show yourself shrewd.
28You save the humble,
  but your eyes are on the haughty to bring them low.
29You are my lamp, O LORD;
  the LORD turns my darkness into light.
30With your help I can advance against a troop[b];
  with my God I can scale a wall.

31"As for God, his way is perfect;
  the word of the LORD is flawless.
He is a shield
  for all who take refuge in him.
32For who is God besides the LORD?
  And who is the Rock except our God?
33It is God who arms me with strength[c]
  and makes my way perfect.
34He makes my feet like the feet of a deer;
  he enables me to stand on the heights.
35He trains my hands for battle;
  my arms can bend a bow of bronze.
36You give me your shield of victory;
  you stoop down to make me great.
37You broaden the path beneath me,
  so that my ankles do not turn.

38"I pursued my enemies and crushed them;
  I did not turn back till they were destroyed.
39I crushed them completely, and they could not rise;
  they fell beneath my feet.
40You armed me with strength for battle;
  you made my adversaries bow at my feet.
41You made my enemies turn their backs in flight,
  and I destroyed my foes.
42They cried for help, but there was no one to save them—

to the LORD, but he did not answer.
43I beat them as fine as the dust of the earth;
  I pounded and trampled them like mud in the streets.

44"You have delivered me from the attacks of my people;
  you have preserved me as the head of nations.
People I did not know are subject to me,
45 and foreigners come cringing to me;
  as soon as they hear me, they obey me.
46They all lose heart;
  they come trembling[d] from their strongholds.

47"The LORD lives! Praise be to my Rock!
  Exalted be God, the Rock, my Savior!
48He is the God who avenges me,
  who puts the nations under me,
49 who sets me free from my enemies.
You exalted me above my foes;
  from violent men you rescued me.
50Therefore I will praise you, O LORD, among the nations;
  I will sing praises to your name.
51He gives his king great victories;
  he shows unfailing kindness to his anointed,
  to David and his descendants forever."

The Last Words of David

23 These are the last words of David:

"The oracle of David son of Jesse,
  the oracle of the man exalted by the Most High,
the man anointed by the God of Jacob,
  Israel's singer of songs[e]:

2"The Spirit of the LORD spoke through me;
  his word was on my tongue.
3The God of Israel spoke,
  the Rock of Israel said to me:
'When one rules over men in righteousness,
  when he rules in the fear of God,

---

[a]25 Hebrew; Septuagint and Vulgate (see also Psalm 18:24) *to the cleanness of my hands*   [b]30 Or *can run through a barricade*   [c]33 Dead Sea Scrolls, some Septuagint manuscripts, Vulgate and Syriac (see also Psalm 18:32); Masoretic Text *who is my strong refuge*   [d]46 Some Septuagint manuscripts and Vulgate (see also Psalm 18:45); Masoretic Text *they arm themselves.*   [e]1 Or *Israel's beloved singer*

VERSE FOR THE DAY:
2 Samuel 22:31

AUTHOR:
Walter Trobisch

PASSAGE FOR THE DAY:
2 Samuel 22:31–51

The Sheltered Man

IN CONTRAST to the frustrated man who would like to run away from his responsibilities stands the redeemed man who feels safe and secure. He can be a shelter to others because he himself is sheltered. He is not afraid even if at times he should lose or suffer defeat. He simply gets up again and keeps on keeping on. He is a man who has accepted himself not only with his strengths but also with his weaknesses. His secret: he knows he has been accepted by the heavenly Father. He has a roof over his head. He knows where his home is. He has a place where he can put his feet under the table. He can say with the psalmist, "You prepare a table before me in the presence of my enemies" (Psalm 23:5). He can say, "You have been my refuge, a strong tower against the foe. I long to dwell in your tent forever and take refuge in the shelter of your wings" (Psalm 61:3–4).

This is the longing of all mankind—to have security, to know where one's place is. God created man and then he created a place for him, the Garden of Eden. When man lost God, he lost at the same time his place. Since then, the longing for a place where he belongs, where he feels at home, is in the heart of every human being. Those who have not found a place, the uprooted, the eternal Gypsies will find a place nowhere, not even in marriage. On the other hand, those who have found a place, married or unmarried, will be able to become a place where others feel at home, thus filling one of the deepest needs of our time. In light of this, Jesus' promise "to prepare a place" for us is filled with new meaning (John 14:2). Those who have found him have found their place . . .

The redeemed man . . . is a whole man. He is whole first of all because he *belongs* to a family, the family of God. God, his Father, makes him one of his sons.

He is a whole man because he feels *worthy*. Christ died to give him birth and therefore he can take as his own the worthiness of Christ.

He is a whole man because he feels *competent*. This competence comes from the Holy Spirit. "God did not give us a spirit of timidity, but a spirit of power, of love and of self-discipline" (2 Timothy 1:7).

Additional Scripture Readings:
Psalm 1; Romans 8:1–4

*Go to page 342 for your next
devotional reading.*

⁴he is like the light of morning at
  sunrise
  on a cloudless morning,
  like the brightness after rain
  that brings the grass from the
  earth.'

⁵"Is not my house right with God?
  Has he not made with me an
  everlasting covenant,
  arranged and secured in every part?
  Will he not bring to fruition my
  salvation
  and grant me my every desire?
⁶But evil men are all to be cast aside
  like thorns,
  which are not gathered with the
  hand.
⁷Whoever touches thorns
  uses a tool of iron or the shaft of a
  spear;
  they are burned up where they lie."

David's Mighty Men

⁸These are the names of David's mighty
men:

Josheb-Basshebeth,ᵃ a Tahkemonite,ᵇ
was chief of the Three; he raised his
spear against eight hundred men, whom
he killedᶜ in one encounter.
⁹Next to him was Eleazar son of Dodai
the Ahohite. As one of the three mighty
men, he was with David when they taunted the Philistines gathered ₍at Pas Dammim,₎ᵈ for battle. Then the men of Israel
retreated, ¹⁰but he stood his ground and
struck down the Philistines till his hand
grew tired and froze to the sword. The
LORD brought about a great victory that
day. The troops returned to Eleazar, but
only to strip the dead.
¹¹Next to him was Shammah son of
Agee the Hararite. When the Philistines
banded together at a place where there
was a field full of lentils, Israel's troops
fled from them. ¹²But Shammah took his
stand in the middle of the field. He defended it and struck the Philistines down,
and the LORD brought about a great victory.
¹³During harvest time, three of the thirty chief men came down to David at the
cave of Adullam, while a band of Philistines was encamped in the Valley of Rephaim. ¹⁴At that time David was in the
stronghold, and the Philistine garrison
was at Bethlehem. ¹⁵David longed for water and said, "Oh, that someone would get
me a drink of water from the well near the
gate of Bethlehem!" ¹⁶So the three mighty
men broke through the Philistine lines,
drew water from the well near the gate of
Bethlehem and carried it back to David.
But he refused to drink it; instead, he
poured it out before the LORD. ¹⁷"Far be it
from me, O LORD, to do this!" he said. "Is
it not the blood of men who went at the
risk of their lives?" And David would not
drink it.
  Such were the exploits of the three
mighty men.
¹⁸Abishai the brother of Joab son of Zeruiah was chief of the Three.ᵉ He raised
his spear against three hundred men,
whom he killed, and so he became as famous as the Three. ¹⁹Was he not held in
greater honor than the Three? He became
their commander, even though he was not
included among them.
²⁰Benaiah son of Jehoiada was a valiant
fighter from Kabzeel, who performed
great exploits. He struck down two of
Moab's best men. He also went down into
a pit on a snowy day and killed a lion.
²¹And he struck down a huge Egyptian.
Although the Egyptian had a spear in his
hand, Benaiah went against him with a
club. He snatched the spear from the
Egyptian's hand and killed him with his
own spear. ²²Such were the exploits of Benaiah son of Jehoiada; he too was as famous as the three mighty men. ²³He was
held in greater honor than any of the Thirty, but he was not included among the
Three. And David put him in charge of his
bodyguard.

²⁴Among the Thirty were:
  Asahel the brother of Joab,
  Elhanan son of Dodo from Bethlehem,
²⁵Shammah the Harodite,
  Elika the Harodite,
²⁶Helez the Paltite,
  Ira son of Ikkesh from Tekoa,
²⁷Abiezer from Anathoth,
  Mebunnaiᶠ the Hushathite,
²⁸Zalmon the Ahohite,

ᵃ8 Hebrew; some Septuagint manuscripts suggest Ish-Bosheth, that is, Esh-Baal (see also 1 Chron. 11:11
Jashobeam).   ᵇ8 Probably a variant of Hacmonite (see 1 Chron. 11:11)   ᶜ8 Some Septuagint
manuscripts (see also 1 Chron. 11:11); Hebrew and other Septuagint manuscripts Three; it was Adino the
Eznite who killed eight hundred men   ᵈ9 See 1 Chron. 11:13; Hebrew gathered there.   ᵉ18 Most
Hebrew manuscripts (see also 1 Chron. 11:20); two Hebrew manuscripts and Syriac Thirty   ᶠ27 Hebrew;
some Septuagint manuscripts (see also 1 Chron. 11:29) Sibbecai

Maharai the Netophathite,
[29]Heled[a] son of Baanah the Netophathite,
Ithai son of Ribai from Gibeah in
Benjamin,
[30]Benaiah the Pirathonite,
Hiddai[b] from the ravines of Gaash,
[31]Abi-Albon the Arbathite,
Azmaveth the Barhumite,
[32]Eliahba the Shaalbonite,
the sons of Jashen,
Jonathan [33]son of[c] Shammah the
Hararite,
Ahiam son of Sharar[d] the Hararite,
[34]Eliphelet son of Ahasbai the Maacathite,
Eliam son of Ahithophel the Gilonite,
[35]Hezro the Carmelite,
Paarai the Arbite,
[36]Igal son of Nathan from Zobah,
the son of Hagri,[e]
[37]Zelek the Ammonite,
Naharai the Beerothite, the armor-
bearer of Joab son of Zeruiah,
[38]Ira the Ithrite,
Gareb the Ithrite
[39]and Uriah the Hittite.
There were thirty-seven in all.

David Counts the Fighting Men

24 Again the anger of the Lord burned
against Israel, and he incited David
against them, saying, "Go and take a census of Israel and Judah."

[2]So the king said to Joab and the army
commanders[f] with him, "Go throughout
the tribes of Israel from Dan to Beersheba
and enroll the fighting men, so that I may
know how many there are."

[3]But Joab replied to the king, "May the
Lord your God multiply the troops a hundred times over, and may the eyes of my
lord the king see it. But why does my lord
the king want to do such a thing?"

[4]The king's word, however, overruled
Joab and the army commanders; so they
left the presence of the king to enroll the
fighting men of Israel.

[5]After crossing the Jordan, they camped
near Aroer, south of the town in the gorge,
and then went through Gad and on to Jazer. [6]They went to Gilead and the region
of Tahtim Hodshi, and on to Dan Jaan and
around toward Sidon. [7]Then they went toward the fortress of Tyre and all the towns
of the Hivites and Canaanites. Finally,
they went on to Beersheba in the Negev of
Judah.

[8]After they had gone through the entire
land, they came back to Jerusalem at the
end of nine months and twenty days.

[9]Joab reported the number of the fighting men to the king: In Israel there were
eight hundred thousand able-bodied men
who could handle a sword, and in Judah
five hundred thousand.

[10]David was conscience-stricken after
he had counted the fighting men, and he
said to the Lord, "I have sinned greatly in
what I have done. Now, O Lord, I beg you,
take away the guilt of your servant. I have
done a very foolish thing."

[11]Before David got up the next morning,
the word of the Lord had come to Gad the
prophet, David's seer: [12]"Go and tell David, 'This is what the Lord says: I am giving you three options. Choose one of them
for me to carry out against you.' "

[13]So Gad went to David and said to him,
"Shall there come upon you three[g] years
of famine in your land? Or three months
of fleeing from your enemies while they
pursue you? Or three days of plague in
your land? Now then, think it over and decide how I should answer the one who
sent me."

[14]David said to Gad, "I am in deep distress. Let us fall into the hands of the
Lord, for his mercy is great; but do not let
me fall into the hands of men."

[15]So the Lord sent a plague on Israel
from that morning until the end of the
time designated, and seventy thousand of
the people from Dan to Beersheba died.
[16]When the angel stretched out his hand
to destroy Jerusalem, the Lord was
grieved because of the calamity and said
to the angel who was afflicting the people,
"Enough! Withdraw your hand." The angel of the Lord was then at the threshing
floor of Araunah the Jebusite.

[17]When David saw the angel who was

---

[a]29 Some Hebrew manuscripts and Vulgate (see also 1 Chron. 11:30); most Hebrew manuscripts *Heleb*
[b]30 Hebrew; some Septuagint manuscripts (see also 1 Chron. 11:32) *Hurai*　　[c]33 Some Septuagint
manuscripts (see also 1 Chron. 11:34); Hebrew does not have *son of.*　　[d]33 Hebrew; some Septuagint
manuscripts (see also 1 Chron. 11:35) *Sacar*　　[e]36 Some Septuagint manuscripts (see also 1 Chron.
11:38); Hebrew *Haggadi*　　[f]2 Septuagint (see also verse 4 and 1 Chron. 21:2); Hebrew *Joab the army
commander*　　[g]13 Septuagint (see also 1 Chron. 21:12); Hebrew *seven*

striking down the people, he said to the LORD, "I am the one who has sinned and done wrong. These are but sheep. What have they done? Let your hand fall upon me and my family."

David Builds an Altar

¹⁸On that day Gad went to David and said to him, "Go up and build an altar to the LORD on the threshing floor of Araunah the Jebusite." ¹⁹So David went up, as the LORD had commanded through Gad. ²⁰When Araunah looked and saw the king and his men coming toward him, he went out and bowed down before the king with his face to the ground.

²¹Araunah said, "Why has my lord the king come to his servant?"

"To buy your threshing floor," David answered, "so I can build an altar to the LORD, that the plague on the people may be stopped."

²²Araunah said to David, "Let my lord the king take whatever pleases him and offer it up. Here are oxen for the burnt offering, and here are threshing sledges and ox yokes for the wood. ²³O king, Araunah gives all this to the king." Araunah also said to him, "May the LORD your God accept you."

²⁴But the king replied to Araunah, "No, I insist on paying you for it. I will not sacrifice to the LORD my God burnt offerings that cost me nothing."

So David bought the threshing floor and the oxen and paid fifty shekels^a of silver for them. ²⁵David built an altar to the LORD there and sacrificed burnt offerings and fellowship offerings.^b Then the LORD answered prayer in behalf of the land, and the plague on Israel was stopped.

---

^a24 That is, about 1 1/4 pounds (about 0.6 kilogram)   ^b25 Traditionally *peace offerings*

*T*HIS book begins by covering the excitement of Solomon's building of the temple, but it then goes on to describe the sad events that take place after Solomon begins serving other gods. The kingdom is divided into two nations, Israel and Judah. All of Israel's kings are wicked, half of Judah's are. God sends prophets (like Elijah) to preach God's word and to warn the rulers against idolatry. As you read this book, realize how severe it is to disobey God's word. Like the Israelites on Mount Carmel, confess, "The LORD—he is God" (1 Kings 18:39).

1 KINGS

Adonijah Sets Himself Up as King

1 When King David was old and well advanced in years, he could not keep warm even when they put covers over him. **2**So his servants said to him, "Let us look for a young virgin to attend the king and take care of him. She can lie beside him so that our lord the king may keep warm."

3Then they searched throughout Israel for a beautiful girl and found Abishag, a Shunammite, and brought her to the king. **4**The girl was very beautiful; she took care of the king and waited on him, but the king had no intimate relations with her.

5Now Adonijah, whose mother was Haggith, put himself forward and said, "I will be king." So he got chariots and horses[a] ready, with fifty men to run ahead of him. **6**(His father had never inter-

a5 Or charioteers

fered with him by asking, "Why do you behave as you do?" He was also very handsome and was born next after Absalom.)

⁷Adonijah conferred with Joab son of Zeruiah and with Abiathar the priest, and they gave him their support. ⁸But Zadok the priest, Benaiah son of Jehoiada, Nathan the prophet, Shimei and Rei*ᵃ* and David's special guard did not join Adonijah.

⁹Adonijah then sacrificed sheep, cattle and fattened calves at the Stone of Zoheleth near En Rogel. He invited all his brothers, the king's sons, and all the men of Judah who were royal officials, ¹⁰but he did not invite Nathan the prophet or Benaiah or the special guard or his brother Solomon.

¹¹Then Nathan asked Bathsheba, Solomon's mother, "Have you not heard that Adonijah, the son of Haggith, has become king without our lord David's knowing it? ¹²Now then, let me advise you how you can save your own life and the life of your son Solomon. ¹³Go in to King David and say to him, 'My lord the king, did you not swear to me your servant: "Surely Solomon your son shall be king after me, and he will sit on my throne"? Why then has Adonijah become king?' ¹⁴While you are still there talking to the king, I will come in and confirm what you have said."

¹⁵So Bathsheba went to see the aged king in his room, where Abishag the Shunammite was attending him. ¹⁶Bathsheba bowed low and knelt before the king.

"What is it you want?" the king asked.

¹⁷She said to him, "My lord, you yourself swore to me your servant by the LORD your God: 'Solomon your son shall be king after me, and he will sit on my throne.' ¹⁸But now Adonijah has become king, and you, my lord the king, do not know about it. ¹⁹He has sacrificed great numbers of cattle, fattened calves, and sheep, and has invited all the king's sons, Abiathar the priest and Joab the commander of the army, but he has not invited Solomon your servant. ²⁰My lord the king, the eyes of all Israel are on you, to learn from you who will sit on the throne of my lord the king after him. ²¹Otherwise, as soon as my lord the king is laid to rest with his fathers, I and my son Solomon will be treated as criminals."

²²While she was still speaking with the king, Nathan the prophet arrived. ²³And they told the king, "Nathan the prophet is here." So he went before the king and bowed with his face to the ground.

²⁴Nathan said, "Have you, my lord the king, declared that Adonijah shall be king after you, and that he will sit on your throne? ²⁵Today he has gone down and sacrificed great numbers of cattle, fattened calves, and sheep. He has invited all the king's sons, the commanders of the army and Abiathar the priest. Right now they are eating and drinking with him and saying, 'Long live King Adonijah!' ²⁶But me your servant, and Zadok the priest, and Benaiah son of Jehoiada, and your servant Solomon he did not invite. ²⁷Is this something my lord the king has done without letting his servants know who should sit on the throne of my lord the king after him?"

David Makes Solomon King

²⁸Then King David said, "Call in Bathsheba." So she came into the king's presence and stood before him.

²⁹The king then took an oath: "As surely as the LORD lives, who has delivered me out of every trouble, ³⁰I will surely carry out today what I swore to you by the LORD, the God of Israel: Solomon your son shall be king after me, and he will sit on my throne in my place."

³¹Then Bathsheba bowed low with her face to the ground and, kneeling before the king, said, "May my lord King David live forever!"

³²King David said, "Call in Zadok the priest, Nathan the prophet and Benaiah son of Jehoiada." When they came before the king, ³³he said to them: "Take your lord's servants with you and set Solomon my son on my own mule and take him down to Gihon. ³⁴There have Zadok the priest and Nathan the prophet anoint him king over Israel. Blow the trumpet and shout, 'Long live King Solomon!' ³⁵Then you are to go up with him, and he is to come and sit on my throne and reign in my place. I have appointed him ruler over Israel and Judah."

³⁶Benaiah son of Jehoiada answered the king, "Amen! May the LORD, the God of my lord the king, so declare it. ³⁷As the LORD was with my lord the king, so may he be with Solomon to make his throne even greater than the throne of my lord King David!"

³⁸So Zadok the priest, Nathan the

ᵃ8 Or and his friends

prophet, Benaiah son of Jehoiada, the Kerethites and the Pelethites went down and put Solomon on King David's mule and escorted him to Gihon. **39**Zadok the priest took the horn of oil from the sacred tent and anointed Solomon. Then they sounded the trumpet and all the people shouted, "Long live King Solomon!" **40**And all the people went up after him, playing flutes and rejoicing greatly, so that the ground shook with the sound.

41Adonijah and all the guests who were with him heard it as they were finishing their feast. On hearing the sound of the trumpet, Joab asked, "What's the meaning of all the noise in the city?"

42Even as he was speaking, Jonathan son of Abiathar the priest arrived. Adonijah said, "Come in. A worthy man like you must be bringing good news."

43"Not at all!" Jonathan answered. "Our lord King David has made Solomon king. **44**The king has sent with him Zadok the priest, Nathan the prophet, Benaiah son of Jehoiada, the Kerethites and the Pelethites, and they have put him on the king's mule, **45**and Zadok the priest and Nathan the prophet have anointed him king at Gihon. From there they have gone up cheering, and the city resounds with it. That's the noise you hear. **46**Moreover, Solomon has taken his seat on the royal throne. **47**Also, the royal officials have come to congratulate our lord King David, saying, 'May your God make Solomon's name more famous than yours and his throne greater than yours!' And the king bowed in worship on his bed **48**and said, 'Praise be to the LORD, the God of Israel, who has allowed my eyes to see a successor on my throne today.'"

49At this, all Adonijah's guests rose in alarm and dispersed. **50**But Adonijah, in fear of Solomon, went and took hold of the horns of the altar. **51**Then Solomon was told, "Adonijah is afraid of King Solomon and is clinging to the horns of the altar. He says, 'Let King Solomon swear to me today that he will not put his servant to death with the sword.'"

52Solomon replied, "If he shows himself to be a worthy man, not a hair of his head will fall to the ground; but if evil is found in him, he will die." **53**Then King Solomon sent men, and they brought him down from the altar. And Adonijah came and bowed down to King Solomon, and Solomon said, "Go to your home."

David's Charge to Solomon

2 When the time drew near for David to die, he gave a charge to Solomon his son.

2"I am about to go the way of all the earth," he said. "So be strong, show yourself a man, **3**and observe what the LORD your God requires: Walk in his ways, and keep his decrees and commands, his laws and requirements, as written in the Law of Moses, so that you may prosper in all you do and wherever you go, **4**and that the LORD may keep his promise to me: 'If your descendants watch how they live, and if they walk faithfully before me with all their heart and soul, you will never fail to have a man on the throne of Israel.'

5"Now you yourself know what Joab son of Zeruiah did to me — what he did to the two commanders of Israel's armies, Abner son of Ner and Amasa son of Jether. He killed them, shedding their blood in peacetime as if in battle, and with that blood stained the belt around his waist and the sandals on his feet. **6**Deal with him according to your wisdom, but do not let his gray head go down to the grave*a* in peace.

7"But show kindness to the sons of Barzillai of Gilead and let them be among those who eat at your table. They stood by me when I fled from your brother Absalom.

8"And remember, you have with you Shimei son of Gera, the Benjamite from Bahurim, who called down bitter curses on me the day I went to Mahanaim. When he came down to meet me at the Jordan, I swore to him by the LORD: 'I will not put you to death by the sword.' **9**But now, do not consider him innocent. You are a man of wisdom; you will know what to do to him. Bring his gray head down to the grave in blood."

10Then David rested with his fathers and was buried in the City of David. **11**He had reigned forty years over Israel — seven years in Hebron and thirty-three in Jerusalem. **12**So Solomon sat on the throne of his father David, and his rule was firmly established.

Solomon's Throne Established

13Now Adonijah, the son of Haggith, went to Bathsheba, Solomon's mother. Bathsheba asked him, "Do you come peacefully?"

---

*a*6 Hebrew *Sheol*; also in verse 9

He answered, "Yes, peacefully." **14**Then he added, "I have something to say to you."

"You may say it," she replied.

15"As you know," he said, "the kingdom was mine. All Israel looked to me as their king. But things changed, and the kingdom has gone to my brother; for it has come to him from the Lord. **16**Now I have one request to make of you. Do not refuse me."

"You may make it," she said.

17So he continued, "Please ask King Solomon—he will not refuse you—to give me Abishag the Shunammite as my wife."

18"Very well," Bathsheba replied, "I will speak to the king for you."

19When Bathsheba went to King Solomon to speak to him for Adonijah, the king stood up to meet her, bowed down to her and sat down on his throne. He had a throne brought for the king's mother, and she sat down at his right hand.

20"I have one small request to make of you," she said. "Do not refuse me."

The king replied, "Make it, my mother; I will not refuse you."

21So she said, "Let Abishag the Shunammite be given in marriage to your brother Adonijah."

22King Solomon answered his mother, "Why do you request Abishag the Shunammite for Adonijah? You might as well request the kingdom for him—after all, he is my older brother—yes, for him and for Abiathar the priest and Joab son of Zeruiah!"

23Then King Solomon swore by the Lord: "May God deal with me, be it ever so severely, if Adonijah does not pay with his life for this request! **24**And now, as surely as the Lord lives—he who has established me securely on the throne of my father David and has founded a dynasty for me as he promised—Adonijah shall be put to death today!" **25**So King Solomon gave orders to Benaiah son of Jehoiada, and he struck down Adonijah and he died.

26To Abiathar the priest the king said, "Go back to your fields in Anathoth. You deserve to die, but I will not put you to death now, because you carried the ark of the Sovereign Lord before my father David and shared all my father's hardships." **27**So Solomon removed Abiathar from the priesthood of the Lord, fulfilling the word the Lord had spoken at Shiloh about the house of Eli.

28When the news reached Joab, who had conspired with Adonijah though not with Absalom, he fled to the tent of the Lord and took hold of the horns of the altar. **29**King Solomon was told that Joab had fled to the tent of the Lord and was beside the altar. Then Solomon ordered Benaiah son of Jehoiada, "Go, strike him down!"

30So Benaiah entered the tent of the Lord and said to Joab, "The king says, 'Come out!'"

But he answered, "No, I will die here."

Benaiah reported to the king, "This is how Joab answered me."

31Then the king commanded Benaiah, "Do as he says. Strike him down and bury him, and so clear me and my father's house of the guilt of the innocent blood that Joab shed. **32**The Lord will repay him for the blood he shed, because without the knowledge of my father David he attacked two men and killed them with the sword. Both of them—Abner son of Ner, commander of Israel's army, and Amasa son of Jether, commander of Judah's army—were better men and more upright than he. **33**May the guilt of their blood rest on the head of Joab and his descendants forever. But on David and his descendants, his house and his throne, may there be the Lord's peace forever."

34So Benaiah son of Jehoiada went up and struck down Joab and killed him, and he was buried on his own land*a* in the desert. **35**The king put Benaiah son of Jehoiada over the army in Joab's position and replaced Abiathar with Zadok the priest.

36Then the king sent for Shimei and said to him, "Build yourself a house in Jerusalem and live there, but do not go anywhere else. **37**The day you leave and cross the Kidron Valley, you can be sure you will die; your blood will be on your own head."

38Shimei answered the king, "What you say is good. Your servant will do as my lord the king has said." And Shimei stayed in Jerusalem for a long time.

39But three years later, two of Shimei's slaves ran off to Achish son of Maacah, king of Gath, and Shimei was told, "Your slaves are in Gath." **40**At this, he saddled his donkey and went to Achish at Gath in search of his slaves. So Shimei went away and brought the slaves back from Gath.

41When Solomon was told that Shimei

a34 Or buried in his tomb

had gone from Jerusalem to Gath and had returned, **42**the king summoned Shimei and said to him, "Did I not make you swear by the Lord and warn you, 'On the day you leave to go anywhere else, you can be sure you will die'? At that time you said to me, 'What you say is good. I will obey.' **43**Why then did you not keep your oath to the Lord and obey the command I gave you?"

44The king also said to Shimei, "You know in your heart all the wrong you did to my father David. Now the Lord will repay you for your wrongdoing. **45**But King Solomon will be blessed, and David's throne will remain secure before the Lord forever."

46Then the king gave the order to Benaiah son of Jehoiada, and he went out and struck Shimei down and killed him.

The kingdom was now firmly established in Solomon's hands.

Solomon Asks for Wisdom

3 Solomon made an alliance with Pharaoh king of Egypt and married his daughter. He brought her to the City of David until he finished building his palace and the temple of the Lord, and the wall around Jerusalem. **2**The people, however, were still sacrificing at the high places, because a temple had not yet been built for the Name of the Lord. **3**Solomon showed his love for the Lord by walking according to the statutes of his father David, except that he offered sacrifices and burned incense on the high places.

4The king went to Gibeon to offer sacrifices, for that was the most important high place, and Solomon offered a thousand burnt offerings on that altar. **5**At Gibeon the Lord appeared to Solomon during the night in a dream, and God said, "Ask for whatever you want me to give you."

6Solomon answered, "You have shown great kindness to your servant, my father David, because he was faithful to you and righteous and upright in heart. You have continued this great kindness to him and have given him a son to sit on his throne this very day.

7"Now, O Lord my God, you have made your servant king in place of my father David. But I am only a little child and do not know how to carry out my duties. **8**Your servant is here among the people you have chosen, a great people, too numerous to count or number. **9**So give your

servant a discerning heart to govern your people and to distinguish between right and wrong. For who is able to govern this great people of yours?"

10The Lord was pleased that Solomon had asked for this. **11**So God said to him, "Since you have asked for this and not for long life or wealth for yourself, nor have asked for the death of your enemies but for discernment in administering justice, **12**I will do what you have asked. I will give you a wise and discerning heart, so that there will never have been anyone like you, nor will there ever be. **13**Moreover, I will give you what you have not asked for—both riches and honor—so that in your lifetime you will have no equal among kings. **14**And if you walk in my ways and obey my statutes and commands as David your father did, I will give you a long life." **15**Then Solomon awoke—and he realized it had been a dream.

He returned to Jerusalem, stood before the ark of the Lord's covenant and sacrificed burnt offerings and fellowship offerings.*a* Then he gave a feast for all his court.

A Wise Ruling

16Now two prostitutes came to the king and stood before him. **17**One of them said, "My lord, this woman and I live in the same house. I had a baby while she was there with me. **18**The third day after my child was born, this woman also had a baby. We were alone; there was no one in the house but the two of us.

19"During the night this woman's son died because she lay on him. **20**So she got up in the middle of the night and took my son from my side while I your servant was asleep. She put him by her breast and put her dead son by my breast. **21**The next morning, I got up to nurse my son—and he was dead! But when I looked at him closely in the morning light, I saw that it wasn't the son I had borne."

22The other woman said, "No! The living one is my son; the dead one is yours."

But the first one insisted, "No! The dead one is yours; the living one is mine." And so they argued before the king.

23The king said, "This one says, 'My son is alive and your son is dead,' while that one says, 'No! Your son is dead and mine is alive.'"

24Then the king said, "Bring me a sword." So they brought a sword for the king. **25**He then gave an order: "Cut the living child in two and give half to one and half to the other."

26The woman whose son was alive was filled with compassion for her son and said to the king, "Please, my lord, give her the living baby! Don't kill him!"

But the other said, "Neither I nor you shall have him. Cut him in two!"

27Then the king gave his ruling: "Give the living baby to the first woman. Do not kill him; she is his mother."

28When all Israel heard the verdict the king had given, they held the king in awe, because they saw that he had wisdom from God to administer justice.

Solomon's Officials and Governors

4 So King Solomon ruled over all Israel. **2**And these were his chief officials:

Azariah son of Zadok — the priest;
3Elihoreph and Ahijah, sons of Shisha — secretaries;
Jehoshaphat son of Ahilud — recorder;
4Benaiah son of Jehoiada — commander in chief;
Zadok and Abiathar — priests;
5Azariah son of Nathan — in charge of the district officers;
Zabud son of Nathan — a priest and personal adviser to the king;
6Ahishar — in charge of the palace;
Adoniram son of Abda — in charge of forced labor.

7Solomon also had twelve district governors over all Israel, who supplied provisions for the king and the royal household. Each one had to provide supplies for one month in the year. **8**These are their names:

Ben-Hur — in the hill country of Ephraim;
9Ben-Deker — in Makaz, Shaalbim, Beth Shemesh and Elon Bethhanan;
10Ben-Hesed — in Arubboth (Socoh and all the land of Hepher were his);
11Ben-Abinadab — in Naphoth Dor*a* (he was married to Taphath daughter of Solomon);
12Baana son of Ahilud — in Taanach and Megiddo, and in all of Beth

Shan next to Zarethan below Jezreel, from Beth Shan to Abel Meholah across to Jokmeam;
13Ben-Geber — in Ramoth Gilead (the settlements of Jair son of Manasseh in Gilead were his, as well as the district of Argob in Bashan and its sixty large walled cities with bronze gate bars);
14Ahinadab son of Iddo — in Mahanaim;
15Ahimaaz — in Naphtali (he had married Basemath daughter of Solomon);
16Baana son of Hushai — in Asher and in Aloth;
17Jehoshaphat son of Paruah — in Issachar;
18Shimei son of Ela — in Benjamin;
19Geber son of Uri — in Gilead (the country of Sihon king of the Amorites and the country of Og king of Bashan). He was the only governor over the district.

Solomon's Daily Provisions

20The people of Judah and Israel were as numerous as the sand on the seashore; they ate, they drank and they were happy. **21**And Solomon ruled over all the kingdoms from the River*b* to the land of the Philistines, as far as the border of Egypt. These countries brought tribute and were Solomon's subjects all his life.

22Solomon's daily provisions were thirty cors*c* of fine flour and sixty cors*d* of meal, **23**ten head of stall-fed cattle, twenty of pasture-fed cattle and a hundred sheep and goats, as well as deer, gazelles, roebucks and choice fowl. **24**For he ruled over all the kingdoms west of the River, from Tiphsah to Gaza, and had peace on all sides. **25**During Solomon's lifetime Judah and Israel, from Dan to Beersheba, lived in safety, each man under his own vine and fig tree.

26Solomon had four*e* thousand stalls for chariot horses, and twelve thousand horses.*f*

27The district officers, each in his month, supplied provisions for King Solomon and all who came to the king's table. They saw to it that nothing was lacking. **28**They also brought to the proper place their quotas of barley and straw for the chariot horses and the other horses.

---

*a*11 Or *in the heights of Dor*   *b*21 That is, the Euphrates; also in verse 24   *c*22 That is, probably about 185 bushels (about 6.6 kiloliters)   *d*22 That is, probably about 375 bushels (about 13.2 kiloliters)   *e*26 Some Septuagint manuscripts (see also 2 Chron. 9:25); Hebrew *forty*   *f*26 Or *charioteers*

Solomon's Wisdom

29God gave Solomon wisdom and very great insight, and a breadth of understanding as measureless as the sand on the seashore. **30**Solomon's wisdom was greater than the wisdom of all the men of the East, and greater than all the wisdom of Egypt. **31**He was wiser than any other man, including Ethan the Ezrahite—wiser than Heman, Calcol and Darda, the sons of Mahol. And his fame spread to all the surrounding nations. **32**He spoke three thousand proverbs and his songs numbered a thousand and five. **33**He described plant life, from the cedar of Lebanon to the hyssop that grows out of walls. He also taught about animals and birds, reptiles and fish. **34**Men of all nations came to listen to Solomon's wisdom, sent by all the kings of the world, who had heard of his wisdom.

Preparations for Building the Temple

5 When Hiram king of Tyre heard that Solomon had been anointed king to succeed his father David, he sent his envoys to Solomon, because he had always been on friendly terms with David. **2**Solomon sent back this message to Hiram:

3"You know that because of the wars waged against my father David from all sides, he could not build a temple for the Name of the LORD his God until the LORD put his enemies under his feet. **4**But now the LORD my God has given me rest on every side, and there is no adversary or disaster. **5**I intend, therefore, to build a temple for the Name of the LORD my God, as the LORD told my father David, when he said, 'Your son whom I will put on the throne in your place will build the temple for my Name.'

6"So give orders that cedars of Lebanon be cut for me. My men will work with yours, and I will pay you for your men whatever wages you set. You know that we have no one so skilled in felling timber as the Sidonians."

7When Hiram heard Solomon's message, he was greatly pleased and said, "Praise be to the LORD today, for he has given David a wise son to rule over this great nation."

8So Hiram sent word to Solomon:

"I have received the message you sent me and will do all you want in providing the cedar and pine logs. **9**My men will haul them down from Lebanon to the sea, and I will float them in rafts by sea to the place you specify. There I will separate them and you can take them away. And you are to grant my wish by providing food for my royal household."

10In this way Hiram kept Solomon supplied with all the cedar and pine logs he wanted, **11**and Solomon gave Hiram twenty thousand cors*a* of wheat as food for his household, in addition to twenty thousand baths*b,c* of pressed olive oil. Solomon continued to do this for Hiram year after year. **12**The LORD gave Solomon wisdom, just as he had promised him. There were peaceful relations between Hiram and Solomon, and the two of them made a treaty.

13King Solomon conscripted laborers from all Israel—thirty thousand men. **14**He sent them off to Lebanon in shifts of ten thousand a month, so that they spent one month in Lebanon and two months at home. Adoniram was in charge of the forced labor. **15**Solomon had seventy thousand carriers and eighty thousand stonecutters in the hills, **16**as well as thirty-three hundred*d* foremen who supervised the project and directed the workmen. **17**At the king's command they removed from the quarry large blocks of quality stone to provide a foundation of dressed stone for the temple. **18**The craftsmen of Solomon and Hiram and the men of Gebal*e* cut and prepared the timber and stone for the building of the temple.

Solomon Builds the Temple

6 In the four hundred and eightieth*f* year after the Israelites had come out of Egypt, in the fourth year of Solomon's reign over Israel, in the month of Ziv, the second month, he began to build the temple of the LORD.

2The temple that King Solomon built for the LORD was sixty cubits long, twenty

---

a11 That is, probably about 125,000 bushels (about 4,400 kiloliters)   *b11* Septuagint (see also 2 Chron. 2:10); Hebrew *twenty cors*   *c11* That is, about 115,000 gallons (about 440 kiloliters)   *d16* Hebrew; some Septuagint manuscripts (see also 2 Chron. 2:2, 18) *thirty-six hundred*   *e18* That is, Byblos *f1* Hebrew; Septuagint *four hundred and fortieth* wide and thirty high. *a* **3**The portico at the front of the main hall of the temple extended the width of the temple, that is twenty cubits,*b* and projected ten cubits*c* from the front of the temple. **4**He made narrow clerestory windows in the temple. **5**Against the walls of the main hall and inner sanctuary he built a structure around the building, in which there were side rooms. **6**The lowest floor was five cubits*d* wide, the middle floor six cubits*e* and the third floor seven.*f* He made offset ledges around the outside of the temple so that nothing would be inserted into the temple walls.

7In building the temple, only blocks dressed at the quarry were used, and no hammer, chisel or any other iron tool was heard at the temple site while it was being built.

8The entrance to the lowest*g* floor was on the south side of the temple; a stairway led up to the middle level and from there to the third. **9**So he built the temple and completed it, roofing it with beams and cedar planks. **10**And he built the side rooms all along the temple. The height of each was five cubits, and they were attached to the temple by beams of cedar.

11The word of the LORD came to Solomon: **12**"As for this temple you are building, if you follow my decrees, carry out my regulations and keep all my commands and obey them, I will fulfill through you the promise I gave to David your father. **13**And I will live among the Israelites and will not abandon my people Israel."

14So Solomon built the temple and completed it. **15**He lined its interior walls with cedar boards, paneling them from the floor of the temple to the ceiling, and covered the floor of the temple with planks of pine. **16**He partitioned off twenty cubits*b* at the rear of the temple with cedar boards from floor to ceiling to form within the temple an inner sanctuary, the Most Holy Place. **17**The main hall in front of this room was forty cubits*h* long. **18**The inside of the temple was cedar, carved with gourds and open flowers. Everything was cedar; no stone was to be seen.

19He prepared the inner sanctuary within the temple to set the ark of the covenant of the LORD there. **20**The inner sanctuary was twenty cubits long, twenty wide and twenty high.*i* He overlaid the inside with pure gold, and he also overlaid the altar of cedar. **21**Solomon covered the inside of the temple with pure gold, and he extended gold chains across the front of the inner sanctuary, which was overlaid with gold. **22**So he overlaid the whole interior with gold. He also overlaid with gold the altar that belonged to the inner sanctuary.

23In the inner sanctuary he made a pair of cherubim of olive wood, each ten cubits*c* high. **24**One wing of the first cherub was five cubits long, and the other wing five cubits — ten cubits from wing tip to wing tip. **25**The second cherub also measured ten cubits, for the two cherubim were identical in size and shape. **26**The height of each cherub was ten cubits. **27**He placed the cherubim inside the innermost room of the temple, with their wings spread out. The wing of one cherub touched one wall, while the wing of the other touched the other wall, and their wings touched each other in the middle of the room. **28**He overlaid the cherubim with gold.

29On the walls all around the temple, in both the inner and outer rooms, he carved cherubim, palm trees and open flowers. **30**He also covered the floors of both the inner and outer rooms of the temple with gold.

31For the entrance of the inner sanctuary he made doors of olive wood with five-sided jambs. **32**And on the two olive wood doors he carved cherubim, palm trees and open flowers, and overlaid the cherubim and palm trees with beaten gold. **33**In the same way he made four-sided jambs of olive wood for the entrance to the main hall. **34**He also made two pine doors, each having two leaves that turned in sockets. **35**He carved cherubim, palm trees and open flowers on them and overlaid them with gold hammered evenly over the carvings.

36And he built the inner courtyard of three courses of dressed stone and one course of trimmed cedar beams.

---

*a*2 That is, about 90 feet (about 27 meters) long and 30 feet (about 9 meters) wide and 45 feet (about 13.5 meters) high   *b*3,16 That is, about 30 feet (about 9 meters)   *c*3,23 That is, about 15 feet (about 4.5 meters)   *d*6 That is, about 7 1/2 feet (about 2.3 meters); also in verses 10 and 24   *e*6 That is, about 9 feet (about 2.7 meters)   *f*6 That is, about 10 1/2 feet (about 3.1 meters)   *g*8 Septuagint; Hebrew *middle*   *h*17 That is, about 60 feet (about 18 meters)   *i*20 That is, about 30 feet (about 9 meters) long, wide and high

37The foundation of the temple of the LORD was laid in the fourth year, in the month of Ziv. **38**In the eleventh year in the month of Bul, the eighth month, the temple was finished in all its details according to its specifications. He had spent seven years building it.

Solomon Builds His Palace

7 It took Solomon thirteen years, however, to complete the construction of his palace. **2**He built the Palace of the Forest of Lebanon a hundred cubits long, fifty wide and thirty high,*a* with four rows of cedar columns supporting trimmed cedar beams. **3**It was roofed with cedar above the beams that rested on the columns—forty-five beams, fifteen to a row. **4**Its windows were placed high in sets of three, facing each other. **5**All the doorways had rectangular frames; they were in the front part in sets of three, facing each other.*b*

6He made a colonnade fifty cubits long and thirty wide.*c* In front of it was a portico, and in front of that were pillars and an overhanging roof.

7He built the throne hall, the Hall of Justice, where he was to judge, and he covered it with cedar from floor to ceiling.*d* **8**And the palace in which he was to live, set farther back, was similar in design. Solomon also made a palace like this hall for Pharaoh's daughter, whom he had married.

9All these structures, from the outside to the great courtyard and from foundation to eaves, were made of blocks of high-grade stone cut to size and trimmed with a saw on their inner and outer faces. **10**The foundations were laid with large stones of good quality, some measuring ten cubits*e* and some eight.*f* **11**Above were high-grade stones, cut to size, and cedar beams. **12**The great courtyard was surrounded by a wall of three courses of dressed stone and one course of trimmed cedar beams, as was the inner courtyard of the temple of the LORD with its portico.

The Temple's Furnishings

13King Solomon sent to Tyre and brought Huram,*g* **14**whose mother was a widow from the tribe of Naphtali and whose father was a man of Tyre and a craftsman in bronze. Huram was highly skilled and experienced in all kinds of bronze work. He came to King Solomon and did all the work assigned to him.

15He cast two bronze pillars, each eighteen cubits high and twelve cubits around,*h* by line. **16**He also made two capitals of cast bronze to set on the tops of the pillars; each capital was five cubits*i* high. **17**A network of interwoven chains festooned the capitals on top of the pillars, seven for each capital. **18**He made pomegranates in two rows*j* encircling each network to decorate the capitals on top of the pillars.*k* He did the same for each capital. **19**The capitals on top of the pillars in the portico were in the shape of lilies, four cubits*l* high. **20**On the capitals of both pillars, above the bowl-shaped part next to the network, were the two hundred pomegranates in rows all around. **21**He erected the pillars at the portico of the temple. The pillar to the south he named Jakin*m* and the one to the north Boaz.*n* **22**The capitals on top were in the shape of lilies. And so the work on the pillars was completed.

23He made the Sea of cast metal, circular in shape, measuring ten cubits*e* from rim to rim and five cubits high. It took a line of thirty cubits*o* to measure around it. **24**Below the rim, gourds encircled it—ten to a cubit. The gourds were cast in two rows in one piece with the Sea.

25The Sea stood on twelve bulls, three facing north, three facing west, three facing south and three facing east. The Sea rested on top of them, and their hindquarters were toward the center. **26**It was a handbreadth*p* in thickness, and its rim was like the rim of a cup, like a lily blossom. It held two thousand baths.*q*

27He also made ten movable stands of

---

a2 That is, about 150 feet (about 46 meters) long, 75 feet (about 23 meters) wide and 45 feet (about 13.5 meters) high   *b5* The meaning of the Hebrew for this verse is uncertain.   *c6* That is, about 75 feet (about 23 meters) long and 45 feet (about 13.5 meters) wide   *d7* Vulgate and Syriac; Hebrew *floor* *e10,23* That is, about 15 feet (about 4.5 meters)   *f10* That is, about 12 feet (about 3.6 meters) *g13* Hebrew *Hiram*, a variant of *Huram*; also in verses 40 and 45   *h15* That is, about 27 feet (about 8.1 meters) high and 18 feet (about 5.4 meters) around   *i16* That is, about 7 1/2 feet (about 2.3 meters); also in verse 23   *j18* Two Hebrew manuscripts and Septuagint; most Hebrew manuscripts *made the pillars, and there were two rows*   *k18* Many Hebrew manuscripts and Syriac; most Hebrew manuscripts *pomegranates*   *l19* That is, about 6 feet (about 1.8 meters); also in verse 38   *m21* *Jakin* probably means *he establishes.*   *n21* *Boaz* probably means *in him is strength.*   *o23* That is, about 45 feet (about 13.5 meters)   *p26* That is, about 3 inches (about 8 centimeters)   *q26* That is, probably about 11,500 gallons (about 44 kiloliters); the Septuagint does not have this sentence.

bronze; each was four cubits long, four wide and three high.[a] 28This is how the stands were made: They had side panels attached to uprights. 29On the panels between the uprights were lions, bulls and cherubim — and on the uprights as well. Above and below the lions and bulls were wreaths of hammered work. 30Each stand had four bronze wheels with bronze axles, and each had a basin resting on four supports, cast with wreaths on each side. 31On the inside of the stand there was an opening that had a circular frame one cubit[b] deep. This opening was round, and with its basework it measured a cubit and a half.[c] Around its opening there was engraving. The panels of the stands were square, not round. 32The four wheels were under the panels, and the axles of the wheels were attached to the stand. The diameter of each wheel was a cubit and a half. 33The wheels were made like chariot wheels; the axles, rims, spokes and hubs were all of cast metal.

34Each stand had four handles, one on each corner, projecting from the stand. 35At the top of the stand there was a circular band half a cubit[d] deep. The supports and panels were attached to the top of the stand. 36He engraved cherubim, lions and palm trees on the surfaces of the supports and on the panels, in every available space, with wreaths all around. 37This is the way he made the ten stands. They were all cast in the same molds and were identical in size and shape.

38He then made ten bronze basins, each holding forty baths[e] and measuring four cubits across, one basin to go on each of the ten stands. 39He placed five of the stands on the south side of the temple and five on the north. He placed the Sea on the south side, at the southeast corner of the temple. 40He also made the basins and shovels and sprinkling bowls.

So Huram finished all the work he had undertaken for King Solomon in the temple of the LORD:

41the two pillars;
the two bowl-shaped capitals on top of the pillars;
the two sets of network decorating the two bowl-shaped capitals on top of the pillars;
42the four hundred pomegranates for the two sets of network (two rows of pomegranates for each network, decorating the bowl-shaped capitals on top of the pillars);
43the ten stands with their ten basins;
44the Sea and the twelve bulls under it;
45the pots, shovels and sprinkling bowls.

All these objects that Huram made for King Solomon for the temple of the LORD were of burnished bronze. 46The king had them cast in clay molds in the plain of the Jordan between Succoth and Zarethan. 47Solomon left all these things unweighed, because there were so many; the weight of the bronze was not determined.

48Solomon also made all the furnishings that were in the LORD's temple:

the golden altar;
the golden table on which was the bread of the Presence;
49the lampstands of pure gold (five on the right and five on the left, in front of the inner sanctuary);
the gold floral work and lamps and tongs;
50the pure gold basins, wick trimmers, sprinkling bowls, dishes and censers;
and the gold sockets for the doors of the innermost room, the Most Holy Place, and also for the doors of the main hall of the temple.

51When all the work King Solomon had done for the temple of the LORD was finished, he brought in the things his father David had dedicated — the silver and gold and the furnishings — and he placed them in the treasuries of the LORD's temple.

The Ark Brought to the Temple

8 Then King Solomon summoned into his presence at Jerusalem the elders of Israel, all the heads of the tribes and the chiefs of the Israelite families, to bring up the ark of the LORD's covenant from Zion, the City of David. 2All the men of Israel came together to King Solomon at the time of the festival in the month of Ethanim, the seventh month.

3When all the elders of Israel had arrived, the priests took up the ark, 4and they brought up the ark of the LORD and

a27 That is, about 6 feet (about 1.8 meters) long and wide and about 4 1/2 feet (about 1.3 meters) high   b31 That is, about 1 1/2 feet (about 0.5 meter)   c31 That is, about 2 1/4 feet (about 0.7 meter); also in verse 32   d35 That is, about 3/4 foot (about 0.2 meter)   e38 That is, about 230 gallons (about 880 liters) the Tent of Meeting and all the sacred furnishings in it. The priests and Levites carried them up, [5]and King Solomon and the entire assembly of Israel that had gathered about him were before the ark, sacrificing so many sheep and cattle that they could not be recorded or counted.

[6]The priests then brought the ark of the Lord's covenant to its place in the inner sanctuary of the temple, the Most Holy Place, and put it beneath the wings of the cherubim. [7]The cherubim spread their wings over the place of the ark and overshadowed the ark and its carrying poles. [8]These poles were so long that their ends could be seen from the Holy Place in front of the inner sanctuary, but not from outside the Holy Place; and they are still there today. [9]There was nothing in the ark except the two stone tablets that Moses had placed in it at Horeb, where the Lord made a covenant with the Israelites after they came out of Egypt.

[10]When the priests withdrew from the Holy Place, the cloud filled the temple of the Lord. [11]And the priests could not perform their service because of the cloud, for the glory of the Lord filled his temple.

[12]Then Solomon said, "The Lord has said that he would dwell in a dark cloud; [13]I have indeed built a magnificent temple for you, a place for you to dwell forever."

[14]While the whole assembly of Israel was standing there, the king turned around and blessed them. [15]Then he said:

"Praise be to the Lord, the God of Israel, who with his own hand has fulfilled what he promised with his own mouth to my father David. For he said, [16]'Since the day I brought my people Israel out of Egypt, I have not chosen a city in any tribe of Israel to have a temple built for my Name to be there, but I have chosen David to rule my people Israel.'

[17]"My father David had it in his heart to build a temple for the Name of the Lord, the God of Israel. [18]But the Lord said to my father David, 'Because it was in your heart to build a temple for my Name, you did well to have this in your heart. [19]Nevertheless, you are not the one to build the temple, but your son, who is your own flesh and blood—he is the one who will build the temple for my Name.'

[20]"The Lord has kept the promise he made: I have succeeded David my father and now I sit on the throne of Israel, just as the Lord promised, and I have built the temple for the Name of the Lord, the God of Israel. [21]I have provided a place there for the ark, in which is the covenant of the Lord that he made with our fathers when he brought them out of Egypt."

Solomon's Prayer of Dedication

[22]Then Solomon stood before the altar of the Lord in front of the whole assembly of Israel, spread out his hands toward heaven [23]and said:

"O Lord, God of Israel, there is no God like you in heaven above or on earth below—you who keep your covenant of love with your servants who continue wholeheartedly in your way. [24]You have kept your promise to your servant David my father; with your mouth you have promised and with your hand you have fulfilled it—as it is today.

[25]"Now Lord, God of Israel, keep for your servant David my father the promises you made to him when you said, 'You shall never fail to have a man to sit before me on the throne of Israel, if only your sons are careful in all they do to walk before me as you have done.' [26]And now, O God of Israel, let your word that you promised your servant David my father come true.

[27]"But will God really dwell on earth? The heavens, even the highest heaven, cannot contain you. How much less this temple I have built! [28]Yet give attention to your servant's prayer and his plea for mercy, O Lord my God. Hear the cry and the prayer that your servant is praying in your presence this day. [29]May your eyes be open toward this temple night and day, this place of which you said, 'My Name shall be there,' so that you will hear the prayer your servant prays toward this place. [30]Hear the supplication of your servant and of your people Israel when they pray toward this place. Hear from heaven, your dwelling place, and when you hear, forgive.

[31]"When a man wrongs his neighbor and is required to take an oath and he comes and swears the oath before your altar in this temple, [32]then hear from heaven and act.

Judge between your servants, condemning the guilty and bringing down on his own head what he has done. Declare the innocent not guilty, and so establish his innocence.

³³"When your people Israel have been defeated by an enemy because they have sinned against you, and when they turn back to you and confess your name, praying and making supplication to you in this temple, ³⁴then hear from heaven and forgive the sin of your people Israel and bring them back to the land you gave to their fathers.

³⁵"When the heavens are shut up and there is no rain because your people have sinned against you, and when they pray toward this place and confess your name and turn from their sin because you have afflicted them, ³⁶then hear from heaven and forgive the sin of your servants, your people Israel. Teach them the right way to live, and send rain on the land you gave your people for an inheritance.

³⁷"When famine or plague comes to the land, or blight or mildew, locusts or grasshoppers, or when an enemy besieges them in any of their cities, whatever disaster or disease may come, ³⁸and when a prayer or plea is made by any of your people Israel—each one aware of the afflictions of his own heart, and spreading out his hands toward this temple— ³⁹then hear from heaven, your dwelling place. Forgive and act; deal with each man according to all he does, since you know his heart (for you alone know the hearts of all men), ⁴⁰so that they will fear you all the time they live in the land you gave our fathers.

⁴¹"As for the foreigner who does not belong to your people Israel but has come from a distant land because of your name— ⁴²for men will hear of your great name and your mighty hand and your outstretched arm— when he comes and prays toward this temple, ⁴³then hear from heaven, your dwelling place, and do whatever the foreigner asks of you, so that all the peoples of the earth may know your name and fear you, as do your own people Israel, and may know that this house I have built bears your Name.

⁴⁴"When your people go to war

against their enemies, wherever you send them, and when they pray to the LORD toward the city you have chosen and the temple I have built for your Name, ⁴⁵then hear from heaven their prayer and their plea, and uphold their cause.

⁴⁶"When they sin against you—for there is no one who does not sin— and you become angry with them and give them over to the enemy, who takes them captive to his own land, far away or near; ⁴⁷and if they have a change of heart in the land where they are held captive, and repent and plead with you in the land of their conquerors and say, 'We have sinned, we have done wrong, we have acted wickedly'; ⁴⁸and if they turn back to you with all their heart and soul in the land of their enemies who took them captive, and pray to you toward the land you gave their fathers, toward the city you have chosen and the temple I have built for your Name; ⁴⁹then from heaven, your dwelling place, hear their prayer and their plea, and uphold their cause. ⁵⁰And forgive your people, who have sinned against you; forgive all the offenses they have committed against you, and cause their conquerors to show them mercy; ⁵¹for they are your people and your inheritance, whom you brought out of Egypt, out of that iron-smelting furnace.

⁵²"May your eyes be open to your servant's plea and to the plea of your people Israel, and may you listen to them whenever they cry out to you. ⁵³For you singled them out from all the nations of the world to be your own inheritance, just as you declared through your servant Moses when you, O Sovereign LORD, brought our fathers out of Egypt."

⁵⁴When Solomon had finished all these prayers and supplications to the LORD, he rose from before the altar of the LORD, where he had been kneeling with his hands spread out toward heaven. ⁵⁵He stood and blessed the whole assembly of Israel in a loud voice, saying:

⁵⁶"Praise be to the LORD, who has given rest to his people Israel just as he promised. Not one word has failed of all the good promises he gave

through his servant Moses. **57**May the LORD our God be with us as he was with our fathers; may he never leave us nor forsake us. **58**May he turn our hearts to him, to walk in all his ways and to keep the commands, decrees and regulations he gave our fathers. **59**And may these words of mine, which I have prayed before the LORD, be near to the LORD our God day and night, that he may uphold the cause of his servant and the cause of his people Israel according to each day's need, **60**so that all the peoples of the earth may know that the LORD is God and that there is no other. **61**But your hearts must be fully committed to the LORD our God, to live by his decrees and obey his commands, as at this time."

WEDNESDAY

VERSE FOR THE DAY: *AUTHOR:*   *PASSAGE FOR THE DAY:*
1 Kings 8:23   *Philip Yancey*   *1 Kings 8:22–53*

Solomon's Epitaph

WITH everything imaginable working in his favor, at first it seemed Solomon would gratefully follow God. His prayer of dedication for the temple in 1 Kings 8 is one of the most majestic ever prayed. Yet by the end of his reign Solomon had squandered away nearly every advantage . . .

In one generation, Solomon took Israel from a fledgling kingdom dependent on God for bare survival to a self-sufficient political power. But along the way he lost sight of the original vision to which God had called them. Ironically, by the time of Solomon's death, Israel resembled the Egypt they had escaped: an imperial state held in place by a bloated bureaucracy and slave labor, with an official state religion under the ruler's command. Success in the kingdom of this world had crowded out interest in the kingdom of God. The brief, shining vision of a covenant nation faded away, and God withdrew his sanction. After Solomon's death, Israel split in two and slid toward ruin.

A quotation from Oscar Wilde might provide the best epitaph for Solomon: "In this world there are only two tragedies. One is not getting what one wants, and the other is getting it." Solomon got whatever he wanted, especially when it came to symbols of power and status. Gradually, he depended less on God and more on the props around him: the world's largest harem, a house twice the size of the temple, an army well-stocked with chariots, a strong economy. Success may have eliminated any crisis of disappointment with God, but it also seemed to eliminate Solomon's desire for God at all. The more he enjoyed the world's good gifts, the less he thought about the Giver.

Additional Scripture Readings:
1 Kings 11:1–13; Ecclesiastes 2:1–11

Go to page 354 for your next devotional reading.

The Dedication of the Temple

62Then the king and all Israel with him offered sacrifices before the LORD. **63**Solomon offered a sacrifice of fellowship offerings[a] to the LORD: twenty-two thousand cattle and a hundred and twenty thousand sheep and goats. So the king and all the Israelites dedicated the temple of the LORD.

64On that same day the king consecrated the middle part of the courtyard in front of the temple of the LORD, and there he offered burnt offerings, grain offerings and the fat of the fellowship offerings, because the bronze altar before the LORD was too small to hold the burnt offerings, the grain offerings and the fat of the fellowship offerings.

65So Solomon observed the festival at that time, and all Israel with him—a vast assembly, people from Lebo[b] Hamath to the Wadi of Egypt. They celebrated it before the LORD our God for seven days and seven days more, fourteen days in all. **66**On the following day he sent the people away. They blessed the king and then went home, joyful and glad in heart for all the good things the LORD had done for his servant David and his people Israel.

The LORD Appears to Solomon

9 When Solomon had finished building the temple of the LORD and the royal palace, and had achieved all he had desired to do, **2**the LORD appeared to him a second time, as he had appeared to him at Gibeon. **3**The LORD said to him:

"I have heard the prayer and plea you have made before me; I have consecrated this temple, which you have built, by putting my Name there forever. My eyes and my heart will always be there.

4"As for you, if you walk before me in integrity of heart and uprightness, as David your father did, and do all I command and observe my decrees and laws, **5**I will establish your royal throne over Israel forever, as I promised David your father when I said, 'You shall never fail to have a man on the throne of Israel.'

6"But if you[c] or your sons turn away from me and do not observe the commands and decrees I have given you[c] and go off to serve other gods and worship them, **7**then I will cut off Israel from the land I have given them and will reject this temple I have consecrated for my Name. Israel will then become a byword and an object of ridicule among all peoples. **8**And though this temple is now imposing, all who pass by will be appalled and will scoff and say, 'Why has the LORD done such a thing to this land and to this temple?' **9**People will answer, 'Because they have forsaken the LORD their God, who brought their fathers out of Egypt, and have embraced other gods, worshiping and serving them—that is why the LORD brought all this disaster on them.' "

Solomon's Other Activities

10At the end of twenty years, during which Solomon built these two buildings—the temple of the LORD and the royal palace— **11**King Solomon gave twenty towns in Galilee to Hiram king of Tyre, because Hiram had supplied him with all the cedar and pine and gold he wanted. **12**But when Hiram went from Tyre to see the towns that Solomon had given him, he was not pleased with them. **13**"What kind of towns are these you have given me, my brother?" he asked. And he called them the Land of Cabul,[d] a name they have to this day. **14**Now Hiram had sent to the king 120 talents[e] of gold.

15Here is the account of the forced labor King Solomon conscripted to build the LORD's temple, his own palace, the supporting terraces,[f] the wall of Jerusalem, and Hazor, Megiddo and Gezer. **16**(Pharaoh king of Egypt had attacked and captured Gezer. He had set it on fire. He killed its Canaanite inhabitants and then gave it as a wedding gift to his daughter, Solomon's wife. **17**And Solomon rebuilt Gezer.) He built up Lower Beth Horon, **18**Baalath, and Tadmor[g] in the desert, within his land, **19**as well as all his store cities and the towns for his chariots and for his horses[h]—whatever he desired to build in Jerusalem, in Lebanon and throughout all the territory he ruled.

20All the people left from the Amorites,

Hittites, Perizzites, Hivites and Jebusites (these peoples were not Israelites), 21that is, their descendants remaining in the land, whom the Israelites could not exterminate*a* —these Solomon conscripted for his slave labor force, as it is to this day. 22But Solomon did not make slaves of any of the Israelites; they were his fighting men, his government officials, his officers, his captains, and the commanders of his chariots and charioteers. 23They were also the chief officials in charge of Solomon's projects—550 officials supervising the men who did the work.

24After Pharaoh's daughter had come up from the City of David to the palace Solomon had built for her, he constructed the supporting terraces.

25Three times a year Solomon sacrificed burnt offerings and fellowship offerings*b* on the altar he had built for the LORD, burning incense before the LORD along with them, and so fulfilled the temple obligations.

26King Solomon also built ships at Ezion Geber, which is near Elath in Edom, on the shore of the Red Sea.*c* 27And Hiram sent his men—sailors who knew the sea—to serve in the fleet with Solomon's men. 28They sailed to Ophir and brought back 420 talents*d* of gold, which they delivered to King Solomon.

The Queen of Sheba Visits Solomon

10 When the queen of Sheba heard about the fame of Solomon and his relation to the name of the LORD, she came to test him with hard questions. 2Arriving at Jerusalem with a very great caravan—with camels carrying spices, large quantities of gold, and precious stones—she came to Solomon and talked with him about all that she had on her mind. 3Solomon answered all her questions; nothing was too hard for the king to explain to her. 4When the queen of Sheba saw all the wisdom of Solomon and the palace he had built, 5the food on his table, the seating of his officials, the attending servants in their robes, his cupbearers, and the burnt offerings he made at*e* the temple of the LORD, she was overwhelmed.

6She said to the king, "The report I heard in my own country about your achievements and your wisdom is true. 7But I did not believe these things until I came and saw with my own eyes. Indeed, not even half was told me; in wisdom and wealth you have far exceeded the report I heard. 8How happy your men must be! How happy your officials, who continually stand before you and hear your wisdom! 9Praise be to the LORD your God, who has delighted in you and placed you on the throne of Israel. Because of the LORD's eternal love for Israel, he has made you king, to maintain justice and righteousness."

10And she gave the king 120 talents*f* of gold, large quantities of spices, and precious stones. Never again were so many spices brought in as those the queen of Sheba gave to King Solomon.

11(Hiram's ships brought gold from Ophir; and from there they brought great cargoes of almugwood*g* and precious stones. 12The king used the almugwood to make supports for the temple of the LORD and for the royal palace, and to make harps and lyres for the musicians. So much almugwood has never been imported or seen since that day.)

13King Solomon gave the queen of Sheba all she desired and asked for, besides what he had given her out of his royal bounty. Then she left and returned with her retinue to her own country.

Solomon's Splendor

14The weight of the gold that Solomon received yearly was 666 talents,*h* 15not including the revenues from merchants and traders and from all the Arabian kings and the governors of the land.

16King Solomon made two hundred large shields of hammered gold; six hundred bekas*i* of gold went into each shield. 17He also made three hundred small shields of hammered gold, with three minas*j* of gold in each shield. The king put them in the Palace of the Forest of Lebanon.

18Then the king made a great throne inlaid with ivory and overlaid with fine gold. 19The throne had six steps, and its back had a rounded top. On both sides of the

---

a21 The Hebrew term refers to the irrevocable giving over of things or persons to the LORD, often by totally destroying them.   *b25* Traditionally *peace offerings*   *c26* Hebrew *Yam Suph*; that is, Sea of Reeds   *d28* That is, about 16 tons (about 14.5 metric tons)   *e5* Or *the ascent by which he went up to*   *f10* That is, about 4 1/2 tons (about 4 metric tons)   *g11* Probably a variant of *algumwood*; also in verse 12   *h14* That is, about 25 tons (about 23 metric tons)   *i16* That is, about 7 1/2 pounds (about 3.5 kilograms)   *j17* That is, about 3 3/4 pounds (about 1.7 kilograms) seat were armrests, with a lion standing beside each of them. ²⁰Twelve lions stood on the six steps, one at either end of each step. Nothing like it had ever been made for any other kingdom. ²¹All King Solomon's goblets were gold, and all the household articles in the Palace of the Forest of Lebanon were pure gold. Nothing was made of silver, because silver was considered of little value in Solomon's days. ²²The king had a fleet of trading ships[a] at sea along with the ships of Hiram. Once every three years it returned, carrying gold, silver and ivory, and apes and baboons.

²³King Solomon was greater in riches and wisdom than all the other kings of the earth. ²⁴The whole world sought audience with Solomon to hear the wisdom God had put in his heart. ²⁵Year after year, everyone who came brought a gift — articles of silver and gold, robes, weapons and spices, and horses and mules.

²⁶Solomon accumulated chariots and horses; he had fourteen hundred chariots and twelve thousand horses,[b] which he kept in the chariot cities and also with him in Jerusalem. ²⁷The king made silver as common in Jerusalem as stones, and cedar as plentiful as sycamore-fig trees in the foothills. ²⁸Solomon's horses were imported from Egypt[c] and from Kue[d] — the royal merchants purchased them from Kue. ²⁹They imported a chariot from Egypt for six hundred shekels[e] of silver, and a horse for a hundred and fifty.[f] They also exported them to all the kings of the Hittites and of the Arameans.

Solomon's Wives

11 King Solomon, however, loved many foreign women besides Pharaoh's daughter — Moabites, Ammonites, Edomites, Sidonians and Hittites. ²They were from nations about which the LORD had told the Israelites, "You must not intermarry with them, because they will surely turn your hearts after their gods." Nevertheless, Solomon held fast to them in love. ³He had seven hundred wives of royal birth and three hundred concubines, and his wives led him astray. ⁴As Solomon grew old, his wives turned his heart after other gods, and his heart was not fully devoted to the LORD his God, as the heart of David his father had been. ⁵He followed Ashtoreth the goddess of the Sidonians, and Molech[g] the detestable god of the Ammonites. ⁶So Solomon did evil in the eyes of the LORD; he did not follow the LORD completely, as David his father had done.

⁷On a hill east of Jerusalem, Solomon built a high place for Chemosh the detestable god of Moab, and for Molech the detestable god of the Ammonites. ⁸He did the same for all his foreign wives, who burned incense and offered sacrifices to their gods.

⁹The LORD became angry with Solomon because his heart had turned away from the LORD, the God of Israel, who had appeared to him twice. ¹⁰Although he had forbidden Solomon to follow other gods, Solomon did not keep the LORD's command. ¹¹So the LORD said to Solomon, "Since this is your attitude and you have not kept my covenant and my decrees, which I commanded you, I will most certainly tear the kingdom away from you and give it to one of your subordinates. ¹²Nevertheless, for the sake of David your father, I will not do it during your lifetime. I will tear it out of the hand of your son. ¹³Yet I will not tear the whole kingdom from him, but will give him one tribe for the sake of David my servant and for the sake of Jerusalem, which I have chosen."

Solomon's Adversaries

¹⁴Then the LORD raised up against Solomon an adversary, Hadad the Edomite, from the royal line of Edom. ¹⁵Earlier when David was fighting with Edom, Joab the commander of the army, who had gone up to bury the dead, had struck down all the men in Edom. ¹⁶Joab and all the Israelites stayed there for six months, until they had destroyed all the men in Edom. ¹⁷But Hadad, still only a boy, fled to Egypt with some Edomite officials who had served his father. ¹⁸They set out from Midian and went to Paran. Then taking men from Paran with them, they went to Egypt, to Pharaoh king of Egypt, who gave Hadad a house and land and provided him with food.

¹⁹Pharaoh was so pleased with Hadad that he gave him a sister of his own wife, Queen Tahpenes, in marriage. ²⁰The sister of Tahpenes bore him a son named Genubath, whom Tahpenes brought up in the

---

a22 Hebrew *of ships of Tarshish*   *b26* Or *charioteers*   *c28* Or possibly *Muzur*, a region in Cilicia; also in verse 29   *d28* Probably *Cilicia*   *e29* That is, about 15 pounds (about 7 kilograms)   *f29* That is, about 3 3/4 pounds (about 1.7 kilograms)   *g5* Hebrew *Milcom*; also in verse 33 royal palace. There Genubath lived with Pharaoh's own children.

21While he was in Egypt, Hadad heard that David rested with his fathers and that Joab the commander of the army was also dead. Then Hadad said to Pharaoh, "Let me go, that I may return to my own country."

22"What have you lacked here that you want to go back to your own country?" Pharaoh asked.

"Nothing," Hadad replied, "but do let me go!"

23And God raised up against Solomon another adversary, Rezon son of Eliada, who had fled from his master, Hadadezer king of Zobah. **24**He gathered men around him and became the leader of a band of rebels when David destroyed the forces[a] of Zobah; the rebels went to Damascus, where they settled and took control. **25**Rezon was Israel's adversary as long as Solomon lived, adding to the trouble caused by Hadad. So Rezon ruled in Aram and was hostile toward Israel.

Jeroboam Rebels Against Solomon

26Also, Jeroboam son of Nebat rebelled against the king. He was one of Solomon's officials, an Ephraimite from Zeredah, and his mother was a widow named Zeruah.

27Here is the account of how he rebelled against the king: Solomon had built the supporting terraces[b] and had filled in the gap in the wall of the city of David his father. **28**Now Jeroboam was a man of standing, and when Solomon saw how well the young man did his work, he put him in charge of the whole labor force of the house of Joseph.

29About that time Jeroboam was going out of Jerusalem, and Ahijah the prophet of Shiloh met him on the way, wearing a new cloak. The two of them were alone out in the country, **30**and Ahijah took hold of the new cloak he was wearing and tore it into twelve pieces. **31**Then he said to Jeroboam, "Take ten pieces for yourself, for this is what the Lord, the God of Israel, says: 'See, I am going to tear the kingdom out of Solomon's hand and give you ten tribes. **32**But for the sake of my servant David and the city of Jerusalem, which I have chosen out of all the tribes of Israel, he will have one tribe. **33**I will do this because they have[c] forsaken me and worshiped Ashtoreth the goddess of the Sidonians,

Chemosh the god of the Moabites, and Molech the god of the Ammonites, and have not walked in my ways, nor done what is right in my eyes, nor kept my statutes and laws as David, Solomon's father, did.

34" 'But I will not take the whole kingdom out of Solomon's hand; I have made him ruler all the days of his life for the sake of David my servant, whom I chose and who observed my commands and statutes. **35**I will take the kingdom from his son's hands and give you ten tribes. **36**I will give one tribe to his son so that David my servant may always have a lamp before me in Jerusalem, the city where I chose to put my Name. **37**However, as for you, I will take you, and you will rule over all that your heart desires; you will be king over Israel. **38**If you do whatever I command you and walk in my ways and do what is right in my eyes by keeping my statutes and commands, as David my servant did, I will be with you. I will build you a dynasty as enduring as the one I built for David and will give Israel to you. **39**I will humble David's descendants because of this, but not forever.' "

40Solomon tried to kill Jeroboam, but Jeroboam fled to Egypt, to Shishak the king, and stayed there until Solomon's death.

Solomon's Death

41As for the other events of Solomon's reign—all he did and the wisdom he displayed—are they not written in the book of the annals of Solomon? **42**Solomon reigned in Jerusalem over all Israel forty years. **43**Then he rested with his fathers and was buried in the city of David his father. And Rehoboam his son succeeded him as king.

Israel Rebels Against Rehoboam

12 Rehoboam went to Shechem, for all the Israelites had gone there to make him king. **2**When Jeroboam son of Nebat heard this (he was still in Egypt, where he had fled from King Solomon), he returned from[d] Egypt. **3**So they sent for Jeroboam, and he and the whole assembly of Israel went to Rehoboam and said to him: **4**"Your father put a heavy yoke on us, but now lighten the harsh labor and the heavy yoke he put on us, and we will serve you."

---

a24 Hebrew *destroyed them*   *b27* Or *the Millo*   *c33* Hebrew; Septuagint, Vulgate and Syriac *because he has*   *d2* Or *he remained in*

[5]Rehoboam answered, "Go away for three days and then come back to me." So the people went away.

[6]Then King Rehoboam consulted the elders who had served his father Solomon during his lifetime. "How would you advise me to answer these people?" he asked.

[7]They replied, "If today you will be a servant to these people and serve them and give them a favorable answer, they will always be your servants."

[8]But Rehoboam rejected the advice the elders gave him and consulted the young men who had grown up with him and were serving him. [9]He asked them, "What is your advice? How should we answer these people who say to me, 'Lighten the yoke your father put on us'?"

[10]The young men who had grown up with him replied, "Tell these people who have said to you, 'Your father put a heavy yoke on us, but make our yoke lighter'— tell them, 'My little finger is thicker than my father's waist. [11]My father laid on you a heavy yoke; I will make it even heavier. My father scourged you with whips; I will scourge you with scorpions.'"

[12]Three days later Jeroboam and all the people returned to Rehoboam, as the king had said, "Come back to me in three days." [13]The king answered the people harshly. Rejecting the advice given him by the elders, [14]he followed the advice of the young men and said, "My father made your yoke heavy; I will make it even heavier. My father scourged you with whips; I will scourge you with scorpions." [15]So the king did not listen to the people, for this turn of events was from the LORD, to fulfill the word the LORD had spoken to Jeroboam son of Nebat through Ahijah the Shilonite.

[16]When all Israel saw that the king refused to listen to them, they answered the king:

"What share do we have in David,
   what part in Jesse's son?
To your tents, O Israel!
   Look after your own house,
      O David!"

So the Israelites went home. [17]But as for the Israelites who were living in the towns of Judah, Rehoboam still ruled over them.

[18]King Rehoboam sent out Adoniram,[a] who was in charge of forced labor, but all Israel stoned him to death. King Rehoboam, however, managed to get into his chariot and escape to Jerusalem. [19]So Israel has been in rebellion against the house of David to this day.

[20]When all the Israelites heard that Jeroboam had returned, they sent and called him to the assembly and made him king over all Israel. Only the tribe of Judah remained loyal to the house of David.

[21]When Rehoboam arrived in Jerusalem, he mustered the whole house of Judah and the tribe of Benjamin—a hundred and eighty thousand fighting men—to make war against the house of Israel and to regain the kingdom for Rehoboam son of Solomon.

[22]But this word of God came to Shemaiah the man of God: [23]"Say to Rehoboam son of Solomon king of Judah, to the whole house of Judah and Benjamin, and to the rest of the people, [24]'This is what the LORD says: Do not go up to fight against your brothers, the Israelites. Go home, every one of you, for this is my doing.'" So they obeyed the word of the LORD and went home again, as the LORD had ordered.

Golden Calves at Bethel and Dan

[25]Then Jeroboam fortified Shechem in the hill country of Ephraim and lived there. From there he went out and built up Peniel.[b]

[26]Jeroboam thought to himself, "The kingdom will now likely revert to the house of David. [27]If these people go up to offer sacrifices at the temple of the LORD in Jerusalem, they will again give their allegiance to their lord, Rehoboam king of Judah. They will kill me and return to King Rehoboam."

[28]After seeking advice, the king made two golden calves. He said to the people, "It is too much for you to go up to Jerusalem. Here are your gods, O Israel, who brought you up out of Egypt." [29]One he set up in Bethel, and the other in Dan. [30]And this thing became a sin; the people went even as far as Dan to worship the one there.

[31]Jeroboam built shrines on high places and appointed priests from all sorts of people, even though they were not Levites. [32]He instituted a festival on the fifteenth day of the eighth month, like the festival held in Judah, and offered sacri-

---

[a]18 Some Septuagint manuscripts and Syriac (see also 1 Kings 4:6 and 5:14); Hebrew *Adoram*
[b]25 Hebrew *Penuel*, a variant of *Peniel*

fices on the altar. This he did in Bethel, sacrificing to the calves he had made. And at Bethel he also installed priests at the high places he had made. ³³On the fifteenth day of the eighth month, a month of his own choosing, he offered sacrifices on the altar he had built at Bethel. So he instituted the festival for the Israelites and went up to the altar to make offerings.

The Man of God From Judah

13 By the word of the LORD a man of God came from Judah to Bethel, as Jeroboam was standing by the altar to make an offering. ²He cried out against the altar by the word of the LORD: "O altar, altar! This is what the LORD says: 'A son named Josiah will be born to the house of David. On you he will sacrifice the priests of the high places who now make offerings here, and human bones will be burned on you.' " ³That same day the man of God gave a sign: "This is the sign the LORD has declared: The altar will be split apart and the ashes on it will be poured out."

⁴When King Jeroboam heard what the man of God cried out against the altar at Bethel, he stretched out his hand from the altar and said, "Seize him!" But the hand he stretched out toward the man shriveled up, so that he could not pull it back. ⁵Also, the altar was split apart and its ashes poured out according to the sign given by the man of God by the word of the LORD.

⁶Then the king said to the man of God, "Intercede with the LORD your God and pray for me that my hand may be restored." So the man of God interceded with the LORD, and the king's hand was restored and became as it was before.

⁷The king said to the man of God, "Come home with me and have something to eat, and I will give you a gift."

⁸But the man of God answered the king, "Even if you were to give me half your possessions, I would not go with you, nor would I eat bread or drink water here. ⁹For I was commanded by the word of the LORD: 'You must not eat bread or drink water or return by the way you came.' " ¹⁰So he took another road and did not return by the way he had come to Bethel.

¹¹Now there was a certain old prophet living in Bethel, whose sons came and told him all that the man of God had done there that day. They also told their father what he had said to the king. ¹²Their father asked them, "Which way did he go?" And his sons showed him which road the man of God from Judah had taken. ¹³So he said to his sons, "Saddle the donkey for me." And when they had saddled the donkey for him, he mounted it ¹⁴and rode after the man of God. He found him sitting under an oak tree and asked, "Are you the man of God who came from Judah?"

"I am," he replied.

¹⁵So the prophet said to him, "Come home with me and eat."

¹⁶The man of God said, "I cannot turn back and go with you, nor can I eat bread or drink water with you in this place. ¹⁷I have been told by the word of the LORD: 'You must not eat bread or drink water there or return by the way you came.' "

¹⁸The old prophet answered, "I too am a prophet, as you are. And an angel said to me by the word of the LORD: 'Bring him back with you to your house so that he may eat bread and drink water.' " (But he was lying to him.) ¹⁹So the man of God returned with him and ate and drank in his house.

²⁰While they were sitting at the table, the word of the LORD came to the old prophet who had brought him back. ²¹He cried out to the man of God who had come from Judah, "This is what the LORD says: 'You have defied the word of the LORD and have not kept the command the LORD your God gave you. ²²You came back and ate bread and drank water in the place where he told you not to eat or drink. Therefore your body will not be buried in the tomb of your fathers.' "

²³When the man of God had finished eating and drinking, the prophet who had brought him back saddled his donkey for him. ²⁴As he went on his way, a lion met him on the road and killed him, and his body was thrown down on the road, with both the donkey and the lion standing beside it. ²⁵Some people who passed by saw the body thrown down there, with the lion standing beside the body, and they went and reported it in the city where the old prophet lived.

²⁶When the prophet who had brought him back from his journey heard of it, he said, "It is the man of God who defied the word of the LORD. The LORD has given him over to the lion, which has mauled him and killed him, as the word of the LORD had warned him."

²⁷The prophet said to his sons, "Saddle the donkey for me," and they did so. ²⁸Then he went out and found the body thrown down on the road, with the donkey and the lion standing beside it. The

lion had neither eaten the body nor mauled the donkey. ²⁹So the prophet picked up the body of the man of God, laid it on the donkey, and brought it back to his own city to mourn for him and bury him. ³⁰Then he laid the body in his own tomb, and they mourned over him and said, "Oh, my brother!"

³¹After burying him, he said to his sons, "When I die, bury me in the grave where the man of God is buried; lay my bones beside his bones. ³²For the message he declared by the word of the LORD against the altar in Bethel and against all the shrines on the high places in the towns of Samaria will certainly come true."

³³Even after this, Jeroboam did not change his evil ways, but once more appointed priests for the high places from all sorts of people. Anyone who wanted to become a priest he consecrated for the high places. ³⁴This was the sin of the house of Jeroboam that led to its downfall and to its destruction from the face of the earth.

Ahijah's Prophecy Against Jeroboam

14 At that time Abijah son of Jeroboam became ill, ²and Jeroboam said to his wife, "Go, disguise yourself, so you won't be recognized as the wife of Jeroboam. Then go to Shiloh. Ahijah the prophet is there — the one who told me I would be king over this people. ³Take ten loaves of bread with you, some cakes and a jar of honey, and go to him. He will tell you what will happen to the boy." ⁴So Jeroboam's wife did what he said and went to Ahijah's house in Shiloh.

Now Ahijah could not see; his sight was gone because of his age. ⁵But the LORD had told Ahijah, "Jeroboam's wife is coming to ask you about her son, for he is ill, and you are to give her such and such an answer. When she arrives, she will pretend to be someone else."

⁶So when Ahijah heard the sound of her footsteps at the door, he said, "Come in, wife of Jeroboam. Why this pretense? I have been sent to you with bad news. ⁷Go, tell Jeroboam that this is what the LORD, the God of Israel, says: 'I raised you up from among the people and made you a leader over my people Israel. ⁸I tore the kingdom away from the house of David and gave it to you, but you have not been like my servant David, who kept my commands and followed me with all his heart, doing only what was right in my eyes. ⁹You have done more evil than all who lived before you. You have made for yourself other gods, idols made of metal; you have provoked me to anger and thrust me behind your back.

¹⁰" 'Because of this, I am going to bring disaster on the house of Jeroboam. I will cut off from Jeroboam every last male in Israel — slave or free. I will burn up the house of Jeroboam as one burns dung, until it is all gone. ¹¹Dogs will eat those belonging to Jeroboam who die in the city, and the birds of the air will feed on those who die in the country. The LORD has spoken!'

¹²"As for you, go back home. When you set foot in your city, the boy will die. ¹³All Israel will mourn for him and bury him. He is the only one belonging to Jeroboam who will be buried, because he is the only one in the house of Jeroboam in whom the LORD, the God of Israel, has found anything good.

¹⁴"The LORD will raise up for himself a king over Israel who will cut off the family of Jeroboam. This is the day! What? Yes, even now.ᵃ ¹⁵And the LORD will strike Israel, so that it will be like a reed swaying in the water. He will uproot Israel from this good land that he gave to their forefathers and scatter them beyond the River,ᵇ because they provoked the LORD to anger by making Asherah poles.ᶜ ¹⁶And he will give Israel up because of the sins Jeroboam has committed and has caused Israel to commit."

¹⁷Then Jeroboam's wife got up and left and went to Tirzah. As soon as she stepped over the threshold of the house, the boy died. ¹⁸They buried him, and all Israel mourned for him, as the LORD had said through his servant the prophet Ahijah.

¹⁹The other events of Jeroboam's reign, his wars and how he ruled, are written in the book of the annals of the kings of Israel. ²⁰He reigned for twenty-two years and then rested with his fathers. And Nadab his son succeeded him as king.

Rehoboam King of Judah

²¹Rehoboam son of Solomon was king in Judah. He was forty-one years old when he became king, and he reigned seventeen years in Jerusalem, the city the LORD had

---

ᵃ14 The meaning of the Hebrew for this sentence is uncertain.   ᵇ15 That is, the Euphrates
ᶜ15 That is, symbols of the goddess Asherah; here and elsewhere in 1 Kings

chosen out of all the tribes of Israel in which to put his Name. His mother's name was Naamah; she was an Ammonite.

²²Judah did evil in the eyes of the Lord. By the sins they committed they stirred up his jealous anger more than their fathers had done. ²³They also set up for themselves high places, sacred stones and Asherah poles on every high hill and under every spreading tree. ²⁴There were even male shrine prostitutes in the land; the people engaged in all the detestable practices of the nations the Lord had driven out before the Israelites.

²⁵In the fifth year of King Rehoboam, Shishak king of Egypt attacked Jerusalem. ²⁶He carried off the treasures of the temple of the Lord and the treasures of the royal palace. He took everything, including all the gold shields Solomon had made. ²⁷So King Rehoboam made bronze shields to replace them and assigned these to the commanders of the guard on duty at the entrance to the royal palace. ²⁸Whenever the king went to the Lord's temple, the guards bore the shields, and afterward they returned them to the guardroom.

²⁹As for the other events of Rehoboam's reign, and all he did, are they not written in the book of the annals of the kings of Judah? ³⁰There was continual warfare between Rehoboam and Jeroboam. ³¹And Rehoboam rested with his fathers and was buried with them in the City of David. His mother's name was Naamah; she was an Ammonite. And Abijah[a] his son succeeded him as king.

Abijah King of Judah

15 In the eighteenth year of the reign of Jeroboam son of Nebat, Abijah[b] became king of Judah, ²and he reigned in Jerusalem three years. His mother's name was Maacah daughter of Abishalom.[c]

³He committed all the sins his father had done before him; his heart was not fully devoted to the Lord his God, as the heart of David his forefather had been. ⁴Nevertheless, for David's sake the Lord his God gave him a lamp in Jerusalem by raising up a son to succeed him and by making Jerusalem strong. ⁵For David had done what was right in the eyes of the

Lord and had not failed to keep any of the Lord's commands all the days of his life — except in the case of Uriah the Hittite.

⁶There was war between Rehoboam[d] and Jeroboam throughout ₍Abijah's₎ lifetime. ⁷As for the other events of Abijah's reign, and all he did, are they not written in the book of the annals of the kings of Judah? There was war between Abijah and Jeroboam. ⁸And Abijah rested with his fathers and was buried in the City of David. And Asa his son succeeded him as king.

Asa King of Judah

⁹In the twentieth year of Jeroboam king of Israel, Asa became king of Judah, ¹⁰and he reigned in Jerusalem forty-one years. His grandmother's name was Maacah daughter of Abishalom.

¹¹Asa did what was right in the eyes of the Lord, as his father David had done. ¹²He expelled the male shrine prostitutes from the land and got rid of all the idols his fathers had made. ¹³He even deposed his grandmother Maacah from her position as queen mother, because she had made a repulsive Asherah pole. Asa cut the pole down and burned it in the Kidron Valley. ¹⁴Although he did not remove the high places, Asa's heart was fully committed to the Lord all his life. ¹⁵He brought into the temple of the Lord the silver and gold and the articles that he and his father had dedicated.

¹⁶There was war between Asa and Baasha king of Israel throughout their reigns. ¹⁷Baasha king of Israel went up against Judah and fortified Ramah to prevent anyone from leaving or entering the territory of Asa king of Judah.

¹⁸Asa then took all the silver and gold that was left in the treasuries of the Lord's temple and of his own palace. He entrusted it to his officials and sent them to Ben-Hadad son of Tabrimmon, the son of Hezion, the king of Aram, who was ruling in Damascus. ¹⁹"Let there be a treaty between me and you," he said, "as there was between my father and your father. See, I am sending you a gift of silver and gold. Now break your treaty with Baasha king of Israel so he will withdraw from me."

²⁰Ben-Hadad agreed with King Asa and sent the commanders of his forces against

---

a31 Some Hebrew manuscripts and Septuagint (see also 2 Chron. 12:16); most Hebrew manuscripts *Abijam*
b1 Some Hebrew manuscripts and Septuagint (see also 2 Chron. 12:16); most Hebrew manuscripts *Abijam*; also in verses 7 and 8   *c2* A variant of *Absalom*; also in verse 10   *d6* Most Hebrew manuscripts; some Hebrew manuscripts and Syriac *Abijam* (that is, Abijah)

the towns of Israel. He conquered Ijon, Dan, Abel Beth Maacah and all Kinnereth in addition to Naphtali. 21When Baasha heard this, he stopped building Ramah and withdrew to Tirzah. 22Then King Asa issued an order to all Judah—no one was exempt—and they carried away from Ramah the stones and timber Baasha had been using there. With them King Asa built up Geba in Benjamin, and also Mizpah.

23As for all the other events of Asa's reign, all his achievements, all he did and the cities he built, are they not written in the book of the annals of the kings of Judah? In his old age, however, his feet became diseased. 24Then Asa rested with his fathers and was buried with them in the city of his father David. And Jehoshaphat his son succeeded him as king.

Nadab King of Israel

25Nadab son of Jeroboam became king of Israel in the second year of Asa king of Judah, and he reigned over Israel two years. 26He did evil in the eyes of the Lord, walking in the ways of his father and in his sin, which he had caused Israel to commit.

27Baasha son of Ahijah of the house of Issachar plotted against him, and he struck him down at Gibbethon, a Philistine town, while Nadab and all Israel were besieging it. 28Baasha killed Nadab in the third year of Asa king of Judah and succeeded him as king.

29As soon as he began to reign, he killed Jeroboam's whole family. He did not leave Jeroboam anyone that breathed, but destroyed them all, according to the word of the Lord given through his servant Ahijah the Shilonite— 30because of the sins Jeroboam had committed and had caused Israel to commit, and because he provoked the Lord, the God of Israel, to anger.

31As for the other events of Nadab's reign, and all he did, are they not written in the book of the annals of the kings of Israel? 32There was war between Asa and Baasha king of Israel throughout their reigns.

Baasha King of Israel

33In the third year of Asa king of Judah, Baasha son of Ahijah became king of all Israel in Tirzah, and he reigned twenty-four years. 34He did evil in the eyes of the Lord, walking in the ways of Jeroboam and in his sin, which he had caused Israel to commit.

16 Then the word of the Lord came to Jehu son of Hanani against Baasha: 2"I lifted you up from the dust and made you leader of my people Israel, but you walked in the ways of Jeroboam and caused my people Israel to sin and to provoke me to anger by their sins. 3So I am about to consume Baasha and his house, and I will make your house like that of Jeroboam son of Nebat. 4Dogs will eat those belonging to Baasha who die in the city, and the birds of the air will feed on those who die in the country."

5As for the other events of Baasha's reign, what he did and his achievements, are they not written in the book of the annals of the kings of Israel? 6Baasha rested with his fathers and was buried in Tirzah. And Elah his son succeeded him as king.

7Moreover, the word of the Lord came through the prophet Jehu son of Hanani to Baasha and his house, because of all the evil he had done in the eyes of the Lord, provoking him to anger by the things he did, and becoming like the house of Jeroboam—and also because he destroyed it.

Elah King of Israel

8In the twenty-sixth year of Asa king of Judah, Elah son of Baasha became king of Israel, and he reigned in Tirzah two years.

9Zimri, one of his officials, who had command of half his chariots, plotted against him. Elah was in Tirzah at the time, getting drunk in the home of Arza, the man in charge of the palace at Tirzah. 10Zimri came in, struck him down and killed him in the twenty-seventh year of Asa king of Judah. Then he succeeded him as king.

11As soon as he began to reign and was seated on the throne, he killed off Baasha's whole family. He did not spare a single male, whether relative or friend. 12So Zimri destroyed the whole family of Baasha, in accordance with the word of the Lord spoken against Baasha through the prophet Jehu— 13because of all the sins Baasha and his son Elah had committed and had caused Israel to commit, so that they provoked the Lord, the God of Israel, to anger by their worthless idols.

14As for the other events of Elah's reign, and all he did, are they not written in the book of the annals of the kings of Israel?

Zimri King of Israel

15In the twenty-seventh year of Asa king of Judah, Zimri reigned in Tirzah seven days. The army was encamped near

Gibbethon, a Philistine town. ¹⁶When the Israelites in the camp heard that Zimri had plotted against the king and murdered him, they proclaimed Omri, the commander of the army, king over Israel that very day there in the camp. ¹⁷Then Omri and all the Israelites with him withdrew from Gibbethon and laid siege to Tirzah. ¹⁸When Zimri saw that the city was taken, he went into the citadel of the royal palace and set the palace on fire around him. So he died, ¹⁹because of the sins he had committed, doing evil in the eyes of the LORD and walking in the ways of Jeroboam and in the sin he had committed and had caused Israel to commit.

²⁰As for the other events of Zimri's reign, and the rebellion he carried out, are they not written in the book of the annals of the kings of Israel?

Omri King of Israel

²¹Then the people of Israel were split into two factions; half supported Tibni son of Ginath for king, and the other half supported Omri. ²²But Omri's followers proved stronger than those of Tibni son of Ginath. So Tibni died and Omri became king.

²³In the thirty-first year of Asa king of Judah, Omri became king of Israel, and he reigned twelve years, six of them in Tirzah. ²⁴He bought the hill of Samaria from Shemer for two talents*a* of silver and built a city on the hill, calling it Samaria, after Shemer, the name of the former owner of the hill.

²⁵But Omri did evil in the eyes of the LORD and sinned more than all those before him. ²⁶He walked in all the ways of Jeroboam son of Nebat and in his sin, which he had caused Israel to commit, so that they provoked the LORD, the God of Israel, to anger by their worthless idols.

²⁷As for the other events of Omri's reign, what he did and the things he achieved, are they not written in the book of the annals of the kings of Israel? ²⁸Omri rested with his fathers and was buried in Samaria. And Ahab his son succeeded him as king.

Ahab Becomes King of Israel

²⁹In the thirty-eighth year of Asa king of Judah, Ahab son of Omri became king of Israel, and he reigned in Samaria over Israel twenty-two years. ³⁰Ahab son of Omri did more evil in the eyes of the LORD than

any of those before him. ³¹He not only considered it trivial to commit the sins of Jeroboam son of Nebat, but he also married Jezebel daughter of Ethbaal king of the Sidonians, and began to serve Baal and worship him. ³²He set up an altar for Baal in the temple of Baal that he built in Samaria. ³³Ahab also made an Asherah pole and did more to provoke the LORD, the God of Israel, to anger than did all the kings of Israel before him.

³⁴In Ahab's time, Hiel of Bethel rebuilt Jericho. He laid its foundations at the cost of his firstborn son Abiram, and he set up its gates at the cost of his youngest son Segub, in accordance with the word of the LORD spoken by Joshua son of Nun.

Elijah Fed by Ravens

17 Now Elijah the Tishbite, from Tishbe*b* in Gilead, said to Ahab, "As the LORD, the God of Israel, lives, whom I serve, there will be neither dew nor rain in the next few years except at my word."

²Then the word of the LORD came to Elijah: ³"Leave here, turn eastward and hide in the Kerith Ravine, east of the Jordan. ⁴You will drink from the brook, and I have ordered the ravens to feed you there."

⁵So he did what the LORD had told him. He went to the Kerith Ravine, east of the Jordan, and stayed there. ⁶The ravens brought him bread and meat in the morning and bread and meat in the evening, and he drank from the brook.

The Widow at Zarephath

⁷Some time later the brook dried up because there had been no rain in the land. ⁸Then the word of the LORD came to him: ⁹"Go at once to Zarephath of Sidon and stay there. I have commanded a widow in that place to supply you with food." ¹⁰So he went to Zarephath. When he came to the town gate, a widow was there gathering sticks. He called to her and asked, "Would you bring me a little water in a jar so I may have a drink?" ¹¹As she was going to get it, he called, "And bring me, please, a piece of bread."

¹²"As surely as the LORD your God lives," she replied, "I don't have any bread—only a handful of flour in a jar and a little oil in a jug. I am gathering a few sticks to take home and make a meal for myself and my son, that we may eat it—and die."

¹³Elijah said to her, "Don't be afraid. Go

home and do as you have said. But first make a small cake of bread for me from what you have and bring it to me, and then make something for yourself and your son. ¹⁴For this is what the LORD, the God of Israel, says: 'The jar of flour will not be used up and the jug of oil will not run dry until the day the LORD gives rain on the land.' "

¹⁵She went away and did as Elijah had told her. So there was food every day for Elijah and for the woman and her family. ¹⁶For the jar of flour was not used up and the jug of oil did not run dry, in keeping with the word of the LORD spoken by Elijah.

¹⁷Some time later the son of the woman who owned the house became ill. He grew worse and worse, and finally stopped breathing. ¹⁸She said to Elijah, "What do you have against me, man of God? Did you come to remind me of my sin and kill my son?"

¹⁹"Give me your son," Elijah replied. He took him from her arms, carried him to the upper room where he was staying, and laid him on his bed. ²⁰Then he cried out to the LORD, "O LORD my God, have you brought tragedy also upon this widow I am staying with, by causing her son to die?" ²¹Then he stretched himself out on the boy three times and cried to the LORD, "O LORD my God, let this boy's life return to him!"

²²The LORD heard Elijah's cry, and the boy's life returned to him, and he lived. ²³Elijah picked up the child and carried him down from the room into the house. He gave him to his mother and said, "Look, your son is alive!"

²⁴Then the woman said to Elijah, "Now I know that you are a man of God and that the word of the LORD from your mouth is the truth."

Elijah and Obadiah

18 After a long time, in the third year, the word of the LORD came to Elijah: "Go and present yourself to Ahab, and I will send rain on the land." ²So Elijah went to present himself to Ahab.

Now the famine was severe in Samaria, ³and Ahab had summoned Obadiah, who was in charge of his palace. (Obadiah was a devout believer in the LORD. ⁴While Jezebel was killing off the LORD's prophets, Obadiah had taken a hundred prophets and hidden them in two caves, fifty in each, and had supplied them with food and water.) ⁵Ahab had said to Obadiah,

"Go through the land to all the springs and valleys. Maybe we can find some grass to keep the horses and mules alive so we will not have to kill any of our animals." ⁶So they divided the land they were to cover, Ahab going in one direction and Obadiah in another.

⁷As Obadiah was walking along, Elijah met him. Obadiah recognized him, bowed down to the ground, and said, "Is it really you, my lord Elijah?"

⁸"Yes," he replied. "Go tell your master, 'Elijah is here.' "

⁹"What have I done wrong," asked Obadiah, "that you are handing your servant over to Ahab to be put to death? ¹⁰As surely as the LORD your God lives, there is not a nation or kingdom where my master has not sent someone to look for you. And whenever a nation or kingdom claimed you were not there, he made them swear they could not find you. ¹¹But now you tell me to go to my master and say, 'Elijah is here.' ¹²I don't know where the Spirit of the LORD may carry you when I leave you. If I go and tell Ahab and he doesn't find you, he will kill me. Yet I your servant have worshiped the LORD since my youth. ¹³Haven't you heard, my lord, what I did while Jezebel was killing the prophets of the LORD? I hid a hundred of the LORD's prophets in two caves, fifty in each, and supplied them with food and water. ¹⁴And now you tell me to go to my master and say, 'Elijah is here.' He will kill me!"

¹⁵Elijah said, "As the LORD Almighty lives, whom I serve, I will surely present myself to Ahab today."

Elijah on Mount Carmel

¹⁶So Obadiah went to meet Ahab and told him, and Ahab went to meet Elijah. ¹⁷When he saw Elijah, he said to him, "Is that you, you troubler of Israel?"

¹⁸"I have not made trouble for Israel," Elijah replied. "But you and your father's family have. You have abandoned the LORD's commands and have followed the Baals. ¹⁹Now summon the people from all over Israel to meet me on Mount Carmel. And bring the four hundred and fifty prophets of Baal and the four hundred prophets of Asherah, who eat at Jezebel's table."

²⁰So Ahab sent word throughout all Israel and assembled the prophets on Mount Carmel. ²¹Elijah went before the people and said, "How long will you waver between two opinions? If the LORD is

THURSDAY

VERSE FOR THE DAY:
1 Kings 17:14

AUTHOR:
Ben Carson

PASSAGE FOR THE DAY:
1 Kings 17:7–16

It Will Not Run Dry

WHEN Ben Carson was in the tenth grade, he fell under the influence of peer pressure, continually nagging his mother for an Italian knit shirt, just like "everybody else" had. His mother came up with a plan.

"Benjamin, I'll tell you what. I'm going to turn the budget over to you. You pay for the food and take care of all the other bills. You can have what's left over. I'll bring home every penny in cash and turn it over to you" . . .

"You start Monday morning. Remember, after you pay all the bills, whatever is left, you can have. You can take every penny, every dime, and go downtown and buy all the Italian knit shirts you want."

At last I had won. No more nagging. No more begging for Italian knits and leather jackets. I could buy them myself.

On Monday morning, as she promised, Mother handed me all the money she had made the previous week. Then she handed me a list of expenses for things such as food, gas for the car, and utility bills. Eagerly I worked, allocating the money. Of course, long before I came to clothing I had run out of money.

"There isn't any more money left," I said as I looked up at her. I felt really dejected. All the money was gone and I still hadn't put any money down for lunches or the telephone bill.

"That's right, Bennie. And you know I didn't hold anything back. This is about the same amount I bring in every week."

"I know that," I said. As I looked up at her, for the first time, I felt ashamed for my insistence on Italian knits. "But . . . how do you do it?" I asked.

"Only with the Lord's help," she said.

That was a moment of insight for me. For the first time in my life I truly grasped the meaning of the hardship my mother lived under. No matter how often I looked at the income and compared it with what we had to pay out, it amazed me that my mother had kept [my brother] Curtis and me alive. And she did it with such style that our neighbors were convinced we were financially well off.

"You must be a financial wizard," I said.

"With God advising me," she said and laughed, "I sure am!"

Additional Scripture Readings:
Matthew 6:25–34;
Philippians 4:10–20

Go to page 357 for your next
devotional reading.

God, follow him; but if Baal is God, follow him."

But the people said nothing.

²²Then Elijah said to them, "I am the only one of the LORD's prophets left, but Baal has four hundred and fifty prophets. ²³Get two bulls for us. Let them choose one for themselves, and let them cut it into pieces and put it on the wood but not set fire to it. I will prepare the other bull and put it on the wood but not set fire to it. ²⁴Then you call on the name of your god, and I will call on the name of the LORD. The god who answers by fire — he is God."

Then all the people said, "What you say is good."

²⁵Elijah said to the prophets of Baal, "Choose one of the bulls and prepare it first, since there are so many of you. Call on the name of your god, but do not light the fire." ²⁶So they took the bull given them and prepared it.

Then they called on the name of Baal from morning till noon. "O Baal, answer us!" they shouted. But there was no response; no one answered. And they danced around the altar they had made.

²⁷At noon Elijah began to taunt them. "Shout louder!" he said. "Surely he is a god! Perhaps he is deep in thought, or busy, or traveling. Maybe he is sleeping and must be awakened." ²⁸So they shouted louder and slashed themselves with swords and spears, as was their custom, until their blood flowed. ²⁹Midday passed, and they continued their frantic prophesying until the time for the evening sacrifice. But there was no response, no one answered, no one paid attention.

³⁰Then Elijah said to all the people, "Come here to me." They came to him, and he repaired the altar of the LORD, which was in ruins. ³¹Elijah took twelve stones, one for each of the tribes descended from Jacob, to whom the word of the LORD had come, saying, "Your name shall be Israel." ³²With the stones he built an altar in the name of the LORD, and he dug a trench around it large enough to hold two seahs[a] of seed. ³³He arranged the wood, cut the bull into pieces and laid it on the wood. Then he said to them, "Fill four large jars with water and pour it on the offering and on the wood."

³⁴"Do it again," he said, and they did it again.

"Do it a third time," he ordered, and they did it the third time. ³⁵The water ran down around the altar and even filled the trench.

³⁶At the time of sacrifice, the prophet Elijah stepped forward and prayed: "O LORD, God of Abraham, Isaac and Israel, let it be known today that you are God in Israel and that I am your servant and have done all these things at your command. ³⁷Answer me, O LORD, answer me, so these people will know that you, O LORD, are God, and that you are turning their hearts back again."

³⁸Then the fire of the LORD fell and burned up the sacrifice, the wood, the stones and the soil, and also licked up the water in the trench.

³⁹When all the people saw this, they fell prostrate and cried, "The LORD — he is God! The LORD — he is God!"

⁴⁰Then Elijah commanded them, "Seize the prophets of Baal. Don't let anyone get away!" They seized them, and Elijah had them brought down to the Kishon Valley and slaughtered there.

⁴¹And Elijah said to Ahab, "Go, eat and drink, for there is the sound of a heavy rain." ⁴²So Ahab went off to eat and drink, but Elijah climbed to the top of Carmel, bent down to the ground and put his face between his knees.

⁴³"Go and look toward the sea," he told his servant. And he went up and looked.

"There is nothing there," he said.

Seven times Elijah said, "Go back."

⁴⁴The seventh time the servant reported, "A cloud as small as a man's hand is rising from the sea."

So Elijah said, "Go and tell Ahab, 'Hitch up your chariot and go down before the rain stops you.' "

⁴⁵Meanwhile, the sky grew black with clouds, the wind rose, a heavy rain came on and Ahab rode off to Jezreel. ⁴⁶The power of the LORD came upon Elijah and, tucking his cloak into his belt, he ran ahead of Ahab all the way to Jezreel.

Elijah Flees to Horeb

19 Now Ahab told Jezebel everything Elijah had done and how he had killed all the prophets with the sword. ²So Jezebel sent a messenger to Elijah to say, "May the gods deal with me, be it ever so severely, if by this time tomorrow I do not make your life like that of one of them."

³Elijah was afraid[b] and ran for his life. When he came to Beersheba in Judah, he

---

a32 That is, probably about 13 quarts (about 15 liters)   b3 Or *Elijah saw* left his servant there, ⁴while he himself went a day's journey into the desert. He came to a broom tree, sat down under it and prayed that he might die. "I have had enough, LORD," he said. "Take my life; I am no better than my ancestors." ⁵Then he lay down under the tree and fell asleep.

All at once an angel touched him and said, "Get up and eat." ⁶He looked around, and there by his head was a cake of bread baked over hot coals, and a jar of water. He ate and drank and then lay down again.

⁷The angel of the LORD came back a second time and touched him and said, "Get up and eat, for the journey is too much for you." ⁸So he got up and ate and drank. Strengthened by that food, he traveled forty days and forty nights until he reached Horeb, the mountain of God. ⁹There he went into a cave and spent the night.

The LORD Appears to Elijah

And the word of the LORD came to him: "What are you doing here, Elijah?"

¹⁰He replied, "I have been very zealous for the LORD God Almighty. The Israelites have rejected your covenant, broken down your altars, and put your prophets to death with the sword. I am the only one left, and now they are trying to kill me too."

¹¹The LORD said, "Go out and stand on the mountain in the presence of the LORD, for the LORD is about to pass by."

Then a great and powerful wind tore the mountains apart and shattered the rocks before the LORD, but the LORD was not in the wind. After the wind there was an earthquake, but the LORD was not in the earthquake. ¹²After the earthquake came a fire, but the LORD was not in the fire. And after the fire came a gentle whisper. ¹³When Elijah heard it, he pulled his cloak over his face and went out and stood at the mouth of the cave.

Then a voice said to him, "What are you doing here, Elijah?"

¹⁴He replied, "I have been very zealous for the LORD God Almighty. The Israelites have rejected your covenant, broken down your altars, and put your prophets to death with the sword. I am the only one left, and now they are trying to kill me too."

¹⁵The LORD said to him, "Go back the way you came, and go to the Desert of Damascus. When you get there, anoint Hazael king over Aram. ¹⁶Also, anoint Jehu son of Nimshi king over Israel, and anoint Eli-

sha son of Shaphat from Abel Meholah to succeed you as prophet. ¹⁷Jehu will put to death any who escape the sword of Hazael, and Elisha will put to death any who escape the sword of Jehu. ¹⁸Yet I reserve seven thousand in Israel—all whose knees have not bowed down to Baal and all whose mouths have not kissed him."

The Call of Elisha

¹⁹So Elijah went from there and found Elisha son of Shaphat. He was plowing with twelve yoke of oxen, and he himself was driving the twelfth pair. Elijah went up to him and threw his cloak around him. ²⁰Elisha then left his oxen and ran after Elijah. "Let me kiss my father and mother good-by," he said, "and then I will come with you."

"Go back," Elijah replied. "What have I done to you?"

²¹So Elisha left him and went back. He took his yoke of oxen and slaughtered them. He burned the plowing equipment to cook the meat and gave it to the people, and they ate. Then he set out to follow Elijah and became his attendant.

Ben-Hadad Attacks Samaria

20 Now Ben-Hadad king of Aram mustered his entire army. Accompanied by thirty-two kings with their horses and chariots, he went up and besieged Samaria and attacked it. ²He sent messengers into the city to Ahab king of Israel, saying, "This is what Ben-Hadad says: ³'Your silver and gold are mine, and the best of your wives and children are mine.'"

⁴The king of Israel answered, "Just as you say, my lord the king. I and all I have are yours."

⁵The messengers came again and said, "This is what Ben-Hadad says: 'I sent to demand your silver and gold, your wives and your children. ⁶But about this time tomorrow I am going to send my officials to search your palace and the houses of your officials. They will seize everything you value and carry it away.'"

⁷The king of Israel summoned all the elders of the land and said to them, "See how this man is looking for trouble! When he sent for my wives and my children, my silver and my gold, I did not refuse him."

⁸The elders and the people all answered, "Don't listen to him or agree to his demands."

⁹So he replied to Ben-Hadad's messen-

VERSE FOR THE DAY:
1 Kings 19:8

AUTHOR:
H. Beecher Hicks

PASSAGE FOR THE DAY:
1 Kings 19:1–9

From Wilderness to Mountain

LIFE is always composed of those experiences and encounters which provide both challenge to one's character and the testing of one's spirit . . .

To be sure, life is not only composed of experiences and encounters; it is also composed of question marks. In every life there are always questions which ought to be asked and which demand an answer. The first question of life is always: "Who am I?" and the second question is like unto it, "What am I living for?" However, when life has been lived to a level of maturity, when one's experiences and encounters have led to some ups and down, some joy and some sadness, . . . there is yet another question that every man must ask: "How did I get where I am which is so far from where I am supposed to be?" . . .

[In 1 Kings 19] I see a defeated and desolate Elijah sitting under a broom tree in the solitude of his own sadness . . . I see an Elijah who had come to the point where he had to ask life's most difficult question: "How did I get to where I am which is so far from where I am supposed to be?" . . .

I may as well tell you, there are only three kinds of people in the world: those who are in the wilderness, those who have just come out of the wilderness, and those who are headed into the wilderness . . .

In the midst of that wilderness experience, God . . . sent his angel to feed Elijah. "You don't have enough for your journey?"

"What journey? I'm through. I'm all washed up."

"You're not through yet, Elijah."

"I'm going to send you from where you are to where I want you to be. I'm going to send you from the molehill to the mountain . . . I'm going to send you from the wilderness to the mountain."

In the wilderness there is weakness, but on the mountain there is strength. In the wilderness there is loneliness, but on the mountain there is companionship. In the wilderness there is despair, but on the mountain there is hope.

Additional Scripture Readings:
Deuteronomy 32:10–14;
Psalm 18:30–36

Go to page 360 for your next devotional reading.

gers, "Tell my lord the king, 'Your servant will do all you demanded the first time, but this demand I cannot meet.' " They left and took the answer back to Ben-Hadad.

¹⁰Then Ben-Hadad sent another message to Ahab: "May the gods deal with me, be it ever so severely, if enough dust remains in Samaria to give each of my men a handful."

¹¹The king of Israel answered, "Tell him: 'One who puts on his armor should not boast like one who takes it off.' "

¹²Ben-Hadad heard this message while he and the kings were drinking in their tents,ᵃ and he ordered his men: "Prepare to attack." So they prepared to attack the city.

Ahab Defeats Ben-Hadad

¹³Meanwhile a prophet came to Ahab king of Israel and announced, "This is what the LORD says: 'Do you see this vast army? I will give it into your hand today, and then you will know that I am the LORD.' "

¹⁴"But who will do this?" asked Ahab.

The prophet replied, "This is what the LORD says: 'The young officers of the provincial commanders will do it.' "

"And who will start the battle?" he asked.

The prophet answered, "You will."

¹⁵So Ahab summoned the young officers of the provincial commanders, 232 men. Then he assembled the rest of the Israelites, 7,000 in all. ¹⁶They set out at noon while Ben-Hadad and the 32 kings allied with him were in their tents getting drunk. ¹⁷The young officers of the provincial commanders went out first.

Now Ben-Hadad had dispatched scouts, who reported, "Men are advancing from Samaria."

¹⁸He said, "If they have come out for peace, take them alive; if they have come out for war, take them alive."

¹⁹The young officers of the provincial commanders marched out of the city with the army behind them ²⁰and each one struck down his opponent. At that, the Arameans fled, with the Israelites in pursuit. But Ben-Hadad king of Aram escaped on horseback with some of his horsemen. ²¹The king of Israel advanced and overpowered the horses and chariots and inflicted heavy losses on the Arameans.

²²Afterward, the prophet came to the king of Israel and said, "Strengthen your position and see what must be done, because next spring the king of Aram will attack you again."

²³Meanwhile, the officials of the king of Aram advised him, "Their gods are gods of the hills. That is why they were too strong for us. But if we fight them on the plains, surely we will be stronger than they. ²⁴Do this: Remove all the kings from their commands and replace them with other officers. ²⁵You must also raise an army like the one you lost—horse for horse and chariot for chariot—so we can fight Israel on the plains. Then surely we will be stronger than they." He agreed with them and acted accordingly.

²⁶The next spring Ben-Hadad mustered the Arameans and went up to Aphek to fight against Israel. ²⁷When the Israelites were also mustered and given provisions, they marched out to meet them. The Israelites camped opposite them like two small flocks of goats, while the Arameans covered the countryside.

²⁸The man of God came up and told the king of Israel, "This is what the LORD says: 'Because the Arameans think the LORD is a god of the hills and not a god of the valleys, I will deliver this vast army into your hands, and you will know that I am the LORD.' "

²⁹For seven days they camped opposite each other, and on the seventh day the battle was joined. The Israelites inflicted a hundred thousand casualties on the Aramean foot soldiers in one day. ³⁰The rest of them escaped to the city of Aphek, where the wall collapsed on twenty-seven thousand of them. And Ben-Hadad fled to the city and hid in an inner room.

³¹His officials said to him, "Look, we have heard that the kings of the house of Israel are merciful. Let us go to the king of Israel with sackcloth around our waists and ropes around our heads. Perhaps he will spare your life."

³²Wearing sackcloth around their waists and ropes around their heads, they went to the king of Israel and said, "Your servant Ben-Hadad says: 'Please let me live.' "

The king answered, "Is he still alive? He is my brother."

³³The men took this as a good sign and were quick to pick up his word. "Yes, your brother Ben-Hadad!" they said.

"Go and get him," the king said. When

ᵃ12 Or in Succoth; also in verse 16

Ben-Hadad came out, Ahab had him come up into his chariot.

34"I will return the cities my father took from your father," Ben-Hadad offered. "You may set up your own market areas in Damascus, as my father did in Samaria."

₍Ahab said₎ "On the basis of a treaty I will set you free." So he made a treaty with him, and let him go.

A Prophet Condemns Ahab

35By the word of the LORD one of the sons of the prophets said to his companion, "Strike me with your weapon," but the man refused. **36**So the prophet said, "Because you have not obeyed the LORD, as soon as you leave me a lion will kill you." And after the man went away, a lion found him and killed him.

37The prophet found another man and said, "Strike me, please." So the man struck him and wounded him. **38**Then the prophet went and stood by the road waiting for the king. He disguised himself with his headband down over his eyes. **39**As the king passed by, the prophet called out to him, "Your servant went into the thick of the battle, and someone came to me with a captive and said, 'Guard this man. If he is missing, it will be your life for his life, or you must pay a talent*a* of silver.' **40**While your servant was busy here and there, the man disappeared."

"That is your sentence," the king of Israel said. "You have pronounced it yourself."

41Then the prophet quickly removed the headband from his eyes, and the king of Israel recognized him as one of the prophets. **42**He said to the king, "This is what the LORD says: 'You have set free a man I had determined should die.*b* Therefore it is your life for his life, your people for his people.' " **43**Sullen and angry, the king of Israel went to his palace in Samaria.

Naboth's Vineyard

21 Some time later there was an incident involving a vineyard belonging to Naboth the Jezreelite. The vineyard was in Jezreel, close to the palace of Ahab king of Samaria. **2**Ahab said to Naboth, "Let me have your vineyard to use for a vegetable garden, since it is close to my palace. In exchange I will give you a better

vineyard or, if you prefer, I will pay you whatever it is worth."

3But Naboth replied, "The LORD forbid that I should give you the inheritance of my fathers."

4So Ahab went home, sullen and angry because Naboth the Jezreelite had said, "I will not give you the inheritance of my fathers." He lay on his bed sulking and refused to eat.

5His wife Jezebel came in and asked him, "Why are you so sullen? Why won't you eat?"

6He answered her, "Because I said to Naboth the Jezreelite, 'Sell me your vineyard; or if you prefer, I will give you another vineyard in its place.' But he said, 'I will not give you my vineyard.' "

7Jezebel his wife said, "Is this how you act as king over Israel? Get up and eat! Cheer up. I'll get you the vineyard of Naboth the Jezreelite."

8So she wrote letters in Ahab's name, placed his seal on them, and sent them to the elders and nobles who lived in Naboth's city with him. **9**In those letters she wrote:

> "Proclaim a day of fasting and seat Naboth in a prominent place among the people. **10**But seat two scoundrels opposite him and have them testify that he has cursed both God and the king. Then take him out and stone him to death."

11So the elders and nobles who lived in Naboth's city did as Jezebel directed in the letters she had written to them. **12**They proclaimed a fast and seated Naboth in a prominent place among the people. **13**Then two scoundrels came and sat opposite him and brought charges against Naboth before the people, saying, "Naboth has cursed both God and the king." So they took him outside the city and stoned him to death. **14**Then they sent word to Jezebel: "Naboth has been stoned and is dead."

15As soon as Jezebel heard that Naboth had been stoned to death, she said to Ahab, "Get up and take possession of the vineyard of Naboth the Jezreelite that he refused to sell you. He is no longer alive, but dead." **16**When Ahab heard that Naboth was dead, he got up and went down to take possession of Naboth's vineyard. **17**Then the word of the LORD came to

---

a39 That is, about 75 pounds (about 34 kilograms)   *b42* The Hebrew term refers to the irrevocable giving over of things or persons to the LORD, often by totally destroying them.

WEEKENDING

RESOLVE

If you . . . travel into the future, what would
your legacy look like? Would there be a chain
linking generation to generation with godly men
who in turn produced more godly men? Or is it
going to be generation after generation of
confused leadership from men who have no
clear-cut role model?

The destiny of those future generations is in
your hands. The choices that you make with
your family today will determine the quality of
life in your family tree for generations to come.
That's why one man can make a difference.
And if you save your boys, it will be the
greatest and most fulfilling task of your life.

— *Steve Farrar*

REVIVE

Saturday: Deuteronomy 4:9–14
Sunday: Psalm 78:1–8,65–72

Go to page 369 for your next devotional reading.

Elijah the Tishbite: **18**"Go down to meet Ahab king of Israel, who rules in Samaria. He is now in Naboth's vineyard, where he has gone to take possession of it. **19**Say to him, 'This is what the LORD says: Have you not murdered a man and seized his property?' Then say to him, 'This is what the LORD says: In the place where dogs licked up Naboth's blood, dogs will lick up your blood—yes, yours!' "

20Ahab said to Elijah, "So you have found me, my enemy!"

"I have found you," he answered, "because you have sold yourself to do evil in the eyes of the LORD. **21**'I am going to bring disaster on you. I will consume your descendants and cut off from Ahab every last male in Israel—slave or free. **22**I will make your house like that of Jeroboam son of Nebat and that of Baasha son of Ahijah, because you have provoked me to anger and have caused Israel to sin.'

23"And also concerning Jezebel the LORD says: 'Dogs will devour Jezebel by the wall of*a* Jezreel.'

24"Dogs will eat those belonging to Ahab who die in the city, and the birds of the air will feed on those who die in the country."

25(There was never a man like Ahab, who sold himself to do evil in the eyes of the LORD, urged on by Jezebel his wife. **26**He behaved in the vilest manner by going after idols, like the Amorites the LORD drove out before Israel.)

27When Ahab heard these words, he tore his clothes, put on sackcloth and fasted. He lay in sackcloth and went around meekly.

28Then the word of the LORD came to Elijah the Tishbite: **29**"Have you noticed how Ahab has humbled himself before me? Because he has humbled himself, I will not bring this disaster in his day, but I will bring it on his house in the days of his son."

Micaiah Prophesies Against Ahab

22 For three years there was no war between Aram and Israel. **2**But in the third year Jehoshaphat king of Judah went down to see the king of Israel. **3**The king of Israel had said to his officials, "Don't you know that Ramoth Gilead belongs to us and yet we are doing nothing to retake it from the king of Aram?"

4So he asked Jehoshaphat, "Will you go with me to fight against Ramoth Gilead?"

Jehoshaphat replied to the king of Israel, "I am as you are, my people as your people, my horses as your horses." **5**But Jehoshaphat also said to the king of Israel, "First seek the counsel of the LORD."

6So the king of Israel brought together the prophets—about four hundred men—and asked them, "Shall I go to war against Ramoth Gilead, or shall I refrain?"

"Go," they answered, "for the Lord will give it into the king's hand."

7But Jehoshaphat asked, "Is there not a prophet of the LORD here whom we can inquire of?"

8The king of Israel answered Jehoshaphat, "There is still one man through whom we can inquire of the LORD, but I hate him because he never prophesies anything good about me, but always bad. He is Micaiah son of Imlah."

"The king should not say that," Jehoshaphat replied.

9So the king of Israel called one of his officials and said, "Bring Micaiah son of Imlah at once."

10Dressed in their royal robes, the king of Israel and Jehoshaphat king of Judah were sitting on their thrones at the threshing floor by the entrance of the gate of Samaria, with all the prophets prophesying before them. **11**Now Zedekiah son of Kenaanah had made iron horns and he declared, "This is what the LORD says: 'With these you will gore the Arameans until they are destroyed.' "

12All the other prophets were prophesying the same thing. "Attack Ramoth Gilead and be victorious," they said, "for the LORD will give it into the king's hand."

13The messenger who had gone to summon Micaiah said to him, "Look, as one man the other prophets are predicting success for the king. Let your word agree with theirs, and speak favorably."

14But Micaiah said, "As surely as the LORD lives, I can tell him only what the LORD tells me."

15When he arrived, the king asked him, "Micaiah, shall we go to war against Ramoth Gilead, or shall I refrain?"

"Attack and be victorious," he answered, "for the LORD will give it into the king's hand."

16The king said to him, "How many times must I make you swear to tell me

a23 Most Hebrew manuscripts; a few Hebrew manuscripts, Vulgate and Syriac (see also 2 Kings 9:26) *the plot of ground at* nothing but the truth in the name of the LORD?"

17Then Micaiah answered, "I saw all Israel scattered on the hills like sheep without a shepherd, and the LORD said, 'These people have no master. Let each one go home in peace.' "

18The king of Israel said to Jehoshaphat, "Didn't I tell you that he never prophesies anything good about me, but only bad?"

19Micaiah continued, "Therefore hear the word of the LORD: I saw the LORD sitting on his throne with all the host of heaven standing around him on his right and on his left. **20**And the LORD said, 'Who will entice Ahab into attacking Ramoth Gilead and going to his death there?'

"One suggested this, and another that. **21**Finally, a spirit came forward, stood before the LORD and said, 'I will entice him.'

22" 'By what means?' the LORD asked.

" 'I will go out and be a lying spirit in the mouths of all his prophets,' he said.

" 'You will succeed in enticing him,' said the LORD. 'Go and do it.'

23"So now the LORD has put a lying spirit in the mouths of all these prophets of yours. The LORD has decreed disaster for you."

24Then Zedekiah son of Kenaanah went up and slapped Micaiah in the face. "Which way did the spirit from*a* the LORD go when he went from me to speak to you?" he asked.

25Micaiah replied, "You will find out on the day you go to hide in an inner room."

26The king of Israel then ordered, "Take Micaiah and send him back to Amon the ruler of the city and to Joash the king's son **27**and say, 'This is what the king says: Put this fellow in prison and give him nothing but bread and water until I return safely.' "

28Micaiah declared, "If you ever return safely, the LORD has not spoken through me." Then he added, "Mark my words, all you people!"

Ahab Killed at Ramoth Gilead

29So the king of Israel and Jehoshaphat king of Judah went up to Ramoth Gilead. **30**The king of Israel said to Jehoshaphat, "I will enter the battle in disguise, but you wear your royal robes." So the king of Israel disguised himself and went into battle.

31Now the king of Aram had ordered his thirty-two chariot commanders, "Do not fight with anyone, small or great, except the king of Israel." **32**When the chariot commanders saw Jehoshaphat, they thought, "Surely this is the king of Israel." So they turned to attack him, but when Jehoshaphat cried out, **33**the chariot commanders saw that he was not the king of Israel and stopped pursuing him.

34But someone drew his bow at random and hit the king of Israel between the sections of his armor. The king told his chariot driver, "Wheel around and get me out of the fighting. I've been wounded." **35**All day long the battle raged, and the king was propped up in his chariot facing the Arameans. The blood from his wound ran onto the floor of the chariot, and that evening he died. **36**As the sun was setting, a cry spread through the army: "Every man to his town; everyone to his land!"

37So the king died and was brought to Samaria, and they buried him there. **38**They washed the chariot at a pool in Samaria (where the prostitutes bathed),*b* and the dogs licked up his blood, as the word of the LORD had declared.

39As for the other events of Ahab's reign, including all he did, the palace he built and inlaid with ivory, and the cities he fortified, are they not written in the book of the annals of the kings of Israel? **40**Ahab rested with his fathers. And Ahaziah his son succeeded him as king.

Jehoshaphat King of Judah

41Jehoshaphat son of Asa became king of Judah in the fourth year of Ahab king of Israel. **42**Jehoshaphat was thirty-five years old when he became king, and he reigned in Jerusalem twenty-five years. His mother's name was Azubah daughter of Shilhi. **43**In everything he walked in the ways of his father Asa and did not stray from them; he did what was right in the eyes of the LORD. The high places, however, were not removed, and the people continued to offer sacrifices and burn incense there. **44**Jehoshaphat was also at peace with the king of Israel.

45As for the other events of Jehoshaphat's reign, the things he achieved and his military exploits, are they not written in the book of the annals of the kings of Judah? **46**He rid the land of the rest of the male shrine prostitutes who remained there even after the reign of his father Asa.

*a*24 Or *Spirit of*   *b*38 Or *Samaria and cleaned the weapons*

⁴⁷There was then no king in Edom; a deputy ruled.

⁴⁸Now Jehoshaphat built a fleet of trading ships*ᵃ* to go to Ophir for gold, but they never set sail—they were wrecked at Ezion Geber. ⁴⁹At that time Ahaziah son of Ahab said to Jehoshaphat, "Let my men sail with your men," but Jehoshaphat refused.

⁵⁰Then Jehoshaphat rested with his fathers and was buried with them in the city of David his father. And Jehoram his son succeeded him.

Ahaziah King of Israel

⁵¹Ahaziah son of Ahab became king of Israel in Samaria in the seventeenth year of Jehoshaphat king of Judah, and he reigned over Israel two years. ⁵²He did evil in the eyes of the LORD, because he walked in the ways of his father and mother and in the ways of Jeroboam son of Nebat, who caused Israel to sin. ⁵³He served and worshiped Baal and provoked the LORD, the God of Israel, to anger, just as his father had done.

ᵃ48 Hebrew of ships of Tarshish

THIS book continues the history of Israel and Judah begun in 1 Kings. When good kings reign, the people prosper; but after persistent idolatry, God finally allows the Assyrians to destroy the nation of Israel and the Babylonians to carry the nation of Judah into captivity. Yet God preserves the royal line because of the promise he made David (see 2 Kings 8:19). As you read this book, praise God for his faithful love to you in spite of your sins. But remember that God does eventually punish those who disobey.

2 KINGS

The LORD's Judgment on Ahaziah

1 After Ahab's death, Moab rebelled against Israel. **2**Now Ahaziah had fallen through the lattice of his upper room in Samaria and injured himself. So he sent messengers, saying to them, "Go and consult Baal-Zebub, the god of Ekron, to see if I will recover from this injury."

3But the angel of the LORD said to Elijah the Tishbite, "Go up and meet the messengers of the king of Samaria and ask them, 'Is it because there is no God in Israel that you are going off to consult Baal-Zebub, the god of Ekron?' **4**Therefore this is what the LORD says: 'You will not leave the bed you are lying on. You will certainly die!'" So Elijah went.

5When the messengers returned to the king, he asked them, "Why have you come back?"

6"A man came to meet us," they replied. "And he said to us, 'Go back to the king who sent you and tell him, "This is what the LORD says: Is it because there is no God in Israel that you are sending men to consult Baal-Zebub, the god of Ekron?

Therefore you will not leave the bed you are lying on. You will certainly die!'"'"

[7]The king asked them, "What kind of man was it who came to meet you and told you this?"

[8]They replied, "He was a man with a garment of hair and with a leather belt around his waist."

The king said, "That was Elijah the Tishbite."

[9]Then he sent to Elijah a captain with his company of fifty men. The captain went up to Elijah, who was sitting on the top of a hill, and said to him, "Man of God, the king says, 'Come down!'"

[10]Elijah answered the captain, "If I am a man of God, may fire come down from heaven and consume you and your fifty men!" Then fire fell from heaven and consumed the captain and his men.

[11]At this the king sent to Elijah another captain with his fifty men. The captain said to him, "Man of God, this is what the king says, 'Come down at once!'"

[12]"If I am a man of God," Elijah replied, "may fire come down from heaven and consume you and your fifty men!" Then the fire of God fell from heaven and consumed him and his fifty men.

[13]So the king sent a third captain with his fifty men. This third captain went up and fell on his knees before Elijah. "Man of God," he begged, "please have respect for my life and the lives of these fifty men, your servants! [14]See, fire has fallen from heaven and consumed the first two captains and all their men. But now have respect for my life!"

[15]The angel of the LORD said to Elijah, "Go down with him; do not be afraid of him." So Elijah got up and went down with him to the king.

[16]He told the king, "This is what the LORD says: Is it because there is no God in Israel for you to consult that you have sent messengers to consult Baal-Zebub, the god of Ekron? Because you have done this, you will never leave the bed you are lying on. You will certainly die!" [17]So he died, according to the word of the LORD that Elijah had spoken.

Because Ahaziah had no son, Joram[a] succeeded him as king in the second year of Jehoram son of Jehoshaphat king of Judah. [18]As for all the other events of Ahaziah's reign, and what he did, are they not written in the book of the annals of the kings of Israel?

Elijah Taken Up to Heaven

2 When the LORD was about to take Elijah up to heaven in a whirlwind, Elijah and Elisha were on their way from Gilgal. [2]Elijah said to Elisha, "Stay here; the LORD has sent me to Bethel."

But Elisha said, "As surely as the LORD lives and as you live, I will not leave you." So they went down to Bethel.

[3]The company of the prophets at Bethel came out to Elisha and asked, "Do you know that the LORD is going to take your master from you today?"

"Yes, I know," Elisha replied, "but do not speak of it."

[4]Then Elijah said to him, "Stay here, Elisha; the LORD has sent me to Jericho."

And he replied, "As surely as the LORD lives and as you live, I will not leave you." So they went to Jericho.

[5]The company of the prophets at Jericho went up to Elisha and asked him, "Do you know that the LORD is going to take your master from you today?"

"Yes, I know," he replied, "but do not speak of it."

[6]Then Elijah said to him, "Stay here; the LORD has sent me to the Jordan."

And he replied, "As surely as the LORD lives and as you live, I will not leave you." So the two of them walked on.

[7]Fifty men of the company of the prophets went and stood at a distance, facing the place where Elijah and Elisha had stopped at the Jordan. [8]Elijah took his cloak, rolled it up and struck the water with it. The water divided to the right and to the left, and the two of them crossed over on dry ground.

[9]When they had crossed, Elijah said to Elisha, "Tell me, what can I do for you before I am taken from you?"

"Let me inherit a double portion of your spirit," Elisha replied.

[10]"You have asked a difficult thing," Elijah said, "yet if you see me when I am taken from you, it will be yours—otherwise not."

[11]As they were walking along and talking together, suddenly a chariot of fire and horses of fire appeared and separated the two of them, and Elijah went up to heaven in a whirlwind. [12]Elisha saw this and cried out, "My father! My father! The chariots and horsemen of Israel!" And Elisha saw him no more. Then he took hold of his own clothes and tore them apart.

---

[a]17 Hebrew *Jehoram*, a variant of *Joram*

[13]He picked up the cloak that had fallen from Elijah and went back and stood on the bank of the Jordan. [14]Then he took the cloak that had fallen from him and struck the water with it. "Where now is the LORD, the God of Elijah?" he asked. When he struck the water, it divided to the right and to the left, and he crossed over.

[15]The company of the prophets from Jericho, who were watching, said, "The spirit of Elijah is resting on Elisha." And they went to meet him and bowed to the ground before him. [16]"Look," they said, "we your servants have fifty able men. Let them go and look for your master. Perhaps the Spirit of the LORD has picked him up and set him down on some mountain or in some valley."

"No," Elisha replied, "do not send them."

[17]But they persisted until he was too ashamed to refuse. So he said, "Send them." And they sent fifty men, who searched for three days but did not find him. [18]When they returned to Elisha, who was staying in Jericho, he said to them, "Didn't I tell you not to go?"

Healing of the Water

[19]The men of the city said to Elisha, "Look, our lord, this town is well situated, as you can see, but the water is bad and the land is unproductive."

[20]"Bring me a new bowl," he said, "and put salt in it." So they brought it to him. [21]Then he went out to the spring and threw the salt into it, saying, "This is what the LORD says: 'I have healed this water. Never again will it cause death or make the land unproductive.'" [22]And the water has remained wholesome to this day, according to the word Elisha had spoken.

Elisha Is Jeered

[23]From there Elisha went up to Bethel. As he was walking along the road, some youths came out of the town and jeered at him. "Go on up, you baldhead!" they said. "Go on up, you baldhead!" [24]He turned around, looked at them and called down a curse on them in the name of the LORD. Then two bears came out of the woods and mauled forty-two of the youths. [25]And he went on to Mount Carmel and from there returned to Samaria.

Moab Revolts

3 Joram[a] son of Ahab became king of Israel in Samaria in the eighteenth year of Jehoshaphat king of Judah, and he reigned twelve years. [2]He did evil in the eyes of the LORD, but not as his father and mother had done. He got rid of the sacred stone of Baal that his father had made. [3]Nevertheless he clung to the sins of Jeroboam son of Nebat, which he had caused Israel to commit; he did not turn away from them.

[4]Now Mesha king of Moab raised sheep, and he had to supply the king of Israel with a hundred thousand lambs and with the wool of a hundred thousand rams. [5]But after Ahab died, the king of Moab rebelled against the king of Israel. [6]So at that time King Joram set out from Samaria and mobilized all Israel. [7]He also sent this message to Jehoshaphat king of Judah: "The king of Moab has rebelled against me. Will you go with me to fight against Moab?"

"I will go with you," he replied. "I am as you are, my people as your people, my horses as your horses."

[8]"By what route shall we attack?" he asked.

"Through the Desert of Edom," he answered.

[9]So the king of Israel set out with the king of Judah and the king of Edom. After a roundabout march of seven days, the army had no more water for themselves or for the animals with them.

[10]"What!" exclaimed the king of Israel. "Has the LORD called us three kings together only to hand us over to Moab?"

[11]But Jehoshaphat asked, "Is there no prophet of the LORD here, that we may inquire of the LORD through him?"

An officer of the king of Israel answered, "Elisha son of Shaphat is here. He used to pour water on the hands of Elijah.[b]"

[12]Jehoshaphat said, "The word of the LORD is with him." So the king of Israel and Jehoshaphat and the king of Edom went down to him.

[13]Elisha said to the king of Israel, "What do we have to do with each other? Go to the prophets of your father and the prophets of your mother."

"No," the king of Israel answered, "because it was the LORD who called us three kings together to hand us over to Moab."

---

[a]1 Hebrew *Jehoram*, a variant of *Joram*; also in verse 6   [b]11 That is, he was Elijah's personal servant.

[14]Elisha said, "As surely as the Lord Almighty lives, whom I serve, if I did not have respect for the presence of Jehoshaphat king of Judah, I would not look at you or even notice you. [15]But now bring me a harpist."

While the harpist was playing, the hand of the Lord came upon Elisha [16]and he said, "This is what the Lord says: Make this valley full of ditches. [17]For this is what the Lord says: You will see neither wind nor rain, yet this valley will be filled with water, and you, your cattle and your other animals will drink. [18]This is an easy thing in the eyes of the Lord; he will also hand Moab over to you. [19]You will overthrow every fortified city and every major town. You will cut down every good tree, stop up all the springs, and ruin every good field with stones."

[20]The next morning, about the time for offering the sacrifice, there it was—water flowing from the direction of Edom! And the land was filled with water.

[21]Now all the Moabites had heard that the kings had come to fight against them; so every man, young and old, who could bear arms was called up and stationed on the border. [22]When they got up early in the morning, the sun was shining on the water. To the Moabites across the way, the water looked red—like blood. [23]"That's blood!" they said. "Those kings must have fought and slaughtered each other. Now to the plunder, Moab!"

[24]But when the Moabites came to the camp of Israel, the Israelites rose up and fought them until they fled. And the Israelites invaded the land and slaughtered the Moabites. [25]They destroyed the towns, and each man threw a stone on every good field until it was covered. They stopped up all the springs and cut down every good tree. Only Kir Hareseth was left with its stones in place, but men armed with slings surrounded it and attacked it as well.

[26]When the king of Moab saw that the battle had gone against him, he took with him seven hundred swordsmen to break through to the king of Edom, but they failed. [27]Then he took his firstborn son, who was to succeed him as king, and offered him as a sacrifice on the city wall. The fury against Israel was great; they withdrew and returned to their own land.

The Widow's Oil

4 The wife of a man from the company of the prophets cried out to Elisha, "Your servant my husband is dead, and you know that he revered the Lord. But now his creditor is coming to take my two boys as his slaves."

[2]Elisha replied to her, "How can I help you? Tell me, what do you have in your house?"

"Your servant has nothing there at all," she said, "except a little oil."

[3]Elisha said, "Go around and ask all your neighbors for empty jars. Don't ask for just a few. [4]Then go inside and shut the door behind you and your sons. Pour oil into all the jars, and as each is filled, put it to one side."

[5]She left him and afterward shut the door behind her and her sons. They brought the jars to her and she kept pouring. [6]When all the jars were full, she said to her son, "Bring me another one."

But he replied, "There is not a jar left." Then the oil stopped flowing.

[7]She went and told the man of God, and he said, "Go, sell the oil and pay your debts. You and your sons can live on what is left."

The Shunammite's Son Restored to Life

[8]One day Elisha went to Shunem. And a well-to-do woman was there, who urged him to stay for a meal. So whenever he came by, he stopped there to eat. [9]She said to her husband, "I know that this man who often comes our way is a holy man of God. [10]Let's make a small room on the roof and put in it a bed and a table, a chair and a lamp for him. Then he can stay there whenever he comes to us."

[11]One day when Elisha came, he went up to his room and lay down there. [12]He said to his servant Gehazi, "Call the Shunammite." So he called her, and she stood before him. [13]Elisha said to him, "Tell her, 'You have gone to all this trouble for us. Now what can be done for you? Can we speak on your behalf to the king or the commander of the army?'"

She replied, "I have a home among my own people."

[14]"What can be done for her?" Elisha asked.

Gehazi said, "Well, she has no son and her husband is old."

[15]Then Elisha said, "Call her." So he called her, and she stood in the doorway. [16]"About this time next year," Elisha said, "you will hold a son in your arms."

"No, my lord," she objected. "Don't mislead your servant, O man of God!"

¹⁷But the woman became pregnant, and the next year about that same time she gave birth to a son, just as Elisha had told her.

¹⁸The child grew, and one day he went out to his father, who was with the reapers. ¹⁹"My head! My head!" he said to his father.

His father told a servant, "Carry him to his mother." ²⁰After the servant had lifted him up and carried him to his mother, the boy sat on her lap until noon, and then he died. ²¹She went up and laid him on the bed of the man of God, then shut the door and went out.

²²She called her husband and said, "Please send me one of the servants and a donkey so I can go to the man of God quickly and return."

²³"Why go to him today?" he asked. "It's not the New Moon or the Sabbath."

"It's all right," she said.

²⁴She saddled the donkey and said to her servant, "Lead on; don't slow down for me unless I tell you." ²⁵So she set out and came to the man of God at Mount Carmel.

When he saw her in the distance, the man of God said to his servant Gehazi, "Look! There's the Shunammite! ²⁶Run to meet her and ask her, 'Are you all right? Is your husband all right? Is your child all right?' "

"Everything is all right," she said.

²⁷When she reached the man of God at the mountain, she took hold of his feet. Gehazi came over to push her away, but the man of God said, "Leave her alone! She is in bitter distress, but the LORD has hidden it from me and has not told me why."

²⁸"Did I ask you for a son, my lord?" she said. "Didn't I tell you, 'Don't raise my hopes'?"

²⁹Elisha said to Gehazi, "Tuck your cloak into your belt, take my staff in your hand and run. If you meet anyone, do not greet him, and if anyone greets you, do not answer. Lay my staff on the boy's face."

³⁰But the child's mother said, "As surely as the LORD lives and as you live, I will not leave you." So he got up and followed her.

³¹Gehazi went on ahead and laid the staff on the boy's face, but there was no sound or response. So Gehazi went back to meet Elisha and told him, "The boy has not awakened."

³²When Elisha reached the house, there was the boy lying dead on his couch. ³³He went in, shut the door on the two of them and prayed to the LORD. ³⁴Then he got on the bed and lay upon the boy, mouth to mouth, eyes to eyes, hands to hands. As he stretched himself out upon him, the boy's body grew warm. ³⁵Elisha turned away and walked back and forth in the room and then got on the bed and stretched out upon him once more. The boy sneezed seven times and opened his eyes.

³⁶Elisha summoned Gehazi and said, "Call the Shunammite." And he did. When she came, he said, "Take your son." ³⁷She came in, fell at his feet and bowed to the ground. Then she took her son and went out.

Death in the Pot

³⁸Elisha returned to Gilgal and there was a famine in that region. While the company of the prophets was meeting with him, he said to his servant, "Put on the large pot and cook some stew for these men."

³⁹One of them went out into the fields to gather herbs and found a wild vine. He gathered some of its gourds and filled the fold of his cloak. When he returned, he cut them up into the pot of stew, though no one knew what they were. ⁴⁰The stew was poured out for the men, but as they began to eat it, they cried out, "O man of God, there is death in the pot!" And they could not eat it.

⁴¹Elisha said, "Get some flour." He put it into the pot and said, "Serve it to the people to eat." And there was nothing harmful in the pot.

Feeding of a Hundred

⁴²A man came from Baal Shalishah, bringing the man of God twenty loaves of barley bread baked from the first ripe grain, along with some heads of new grain. "Give it to the people to eat," Elisha said.

⁴³"How can I set this before a hundred men?" his servant asked.

But Elisha answered, "Give it to the people to eat. For this is what the LORD says: 'They will eat and have some left over.' "

⁴⁴Then he set it before them, and they ate and had some left over, according to the word of the LORD.

MONDAY

VERSE FOR THE DAY:
2 Kings 4:35

AUTHOR:
Ben Carson

PASSAGE FOR THE DAY:
2 Kings 4:32–37

It's a Miracle!

*DR. BEN Carson tells of his emotions as he faced the seemingly
inevitable death of a patient, the father of three children.*

Lord, I need a booster here, I remember praying. *You could
do wonders for my faith right now. Somehow bring Rob [not
his real name] out of this situation.* I do not know if I believed
that God would do it or not; I did know that I had to ask . . .

Within two days, Rob was off the respirator. He was soon
talking and walking. His children came to see him, and I experienced a deep, peaceful joy as I watched him playing with
them. For a father, nothing feels better than interacting with
his little ones . . .

A few days after Rob went home there was an interesting development. Since I first entered the field of medicine, I have
met doctors who have difficulty dealing with unanswerable situations. Often they'll finally admit, "Well, there's some explanation, we just don't understand it."

One of the neurosurgeons, an especially brilliant man and
one who doesn't acknowledge a belief in God, pondered this
matter of Rob for several days. He asked question after question, determined to figure out an answer. None of us could offer an explanation for Rob's recovery.

"Absolutely none," I said.

"I know, but I think I've finally figured it out," he said.

"Really?"

"Sure. Simple. It's the mitrochondria at the subcellular level,
and they can go into shock." (That is, some of the energy producing parts of the cells that constitute the central nervous
system had simply started functioning again at a normal level.
Basically it was like turning the lights down low, but not turning them completely off.)

I listened to his explanation before I asked him a question.
"Tell me, did you ever see such a thing before?"

"No, not really, but—"

"This is a miracle," I said. "Why not accept it for what it is?
They don't come any more blatantly than this. Rob was gone
and now he's back. This is the only time I've ever seen an
adult sink to such a low neurological level and then recover."

As my final statement I said, "We don't have to explain miracles; all we have to do is accept them."

Additional Scripture Readings:
Luke 7:18–23; John 11:17–44

*Go to page 372 for your next
devotional reading.*

Naaman Healed of Leprosy

5 Now Naaman was commander of the army of the king of Aram. He was a great man in the sight of his master and highly regarded, because through him the LORD had given victory to Aram. He was a valiant soldier, but he had leprosy.[a]

[2] Now bands from Aram had gone out and had taken captive a young girl from Israel, and she served Naaman's wife. [3] She said to her mistress, "If only my master would see the prophet who is in Samaria! He would cure him of his leprosy."

[4] Naaman went to his master and told him what the girl from Israel had said. [5] "By all means, go," the king of Aram replied. "I will send a letter to the king of Israel." So Naaman left, taking with him ten talents[b] of silver, six thousand shekels[c] of gold and ten sets of clothing. [6] The letter that he took to the king of Israel read: "With this letter I am sending my servant Naaman to you so that you may cure him of his leprosy."

[7] As soon as the king of Israel read the letter, he tore his robes and said, "Am I God? Can I kill and bring back to life? Why does this fellow send someone to me to be cured of his leprosy? See how he is trying to pick a quarrel with me!"

[8] When Elisha the man of God heard that the king of Israel had torn his robes, he sent him this message: "Why have you torn your robes? Have the man come to me and he will know that there is a prophet in Israel." [9] So Naaman went with his horses and chariots and stopped at the door of Elisha's house. [10] Elisha sent a messenger to say to him, "Go, wash yourself seven times in the Jordan, and your flesh will be restored and you will be cleansed."

[11] But Naaman went away angry and said, "I thought that he would surely come out to me and stand and call on the name of the LORD his God, wave his hand over the spot and cure me of my leprosy. [12] Are not Abana and Pharpar, the rivers of Damascus, better than any of the waters of Israel? Couldn't I wash in them and be cleansed?" So he turned and went off in a rage.

[13] Naaman's servants went to him and said, "My father, if the prophet had told you to do some great thing, would you not have done it? How much more, then, when he tells you, 'Wash and be cleansed'!" [14] So he went down and dipped himself in the Jordan seven times, as the man of God had told him, and his flesh was restored and became clean like that of a young boy.

[15] Then Naaman and all his attendants went back to the man of God. He stood before him and said, "Now I know that there is no God in all the world except in Israel. Please accept now a gift from your servant."

[16] The prophet answered, "As surely as the LORD lives, whom I serve, I will not accept a thing." And even though Naaman urged him, he refused.

[17] "If you will not," said Naaman, "please let me, your servant, be given as much earth as a pair of mules can carry, for your servant will never again make burnt offerings and sacrifices to any other god but the LORD. [18] But may the LORD forgive your servant for this one thing: When my master enters the temple of Rimmon to bow down and he is leaning on my arm and I bow there also—when I bow down in the temple of Rimmon, may the LORD forgive your servant for this."

[19] "Go in peace," Elisha said.

After Naaman had traveled some distance, [20] Gehazi, the servant of Elisha the man of God, said to himself, "My master was too easy on Naaman, this Aramean, by not accepting from him what he brought. As surely as the LORD lives, I will run after him and get something from him."

[21] So Gehazi hurried after Naaman. When Naaman saw him running toward him, he got down from the chariot to meet him. "Is everything all right?" he asked.

[22] "Everything is all right," Gehazi answered. "My master sent me to say, 'Two young men from the company of the prophets have just come to me from the hill country of Ephraim. Please give them a talent[d] of silver and two sets of clothing.'"

[23] "By all means, take two talents," said Naaman. He urged Gehazi to accept them, and then tied up the two talents of silver in two bags, with two sets of clothing. He gave them to two of his servants, and they carried them ahead of Gehazi. [24] When Gehazi came to the hill, he took the things

---

a1 The Hebrew word was used for various diseases affecting the skin—not necessarily leprosy; also in verses 3, 6, 7, 11 and 27.   b5 That is, about 750 pounds (about 340 kilograms)   c5 That is, about 150 pounds (about 70 kilograms)   d22 That is, about 75 pounds (about 34 kilograms) from the servants and put them away in the house. He sent the men away and they left. 25Then he went in and stood before his master Elisha.

"Where have you been, Gehazi?" Elisha asked.

"Your servant didn't go anywhere," Gehazi answered.

26But Elisha said to him, "Was not my spirit with you when the man got down from his chariot to meet you? Is this the time to take money, or to accept clothes, olive groves, vineyards, flocks, herds, or menservants and maidservants? 27Naaman's leprosy will cling to you and to your descendants forever." Then Gehazi went from Elisha's presence and he was leprous, as white as snow.

An Axhead Floats

6 The company of the prophets said to Elisha, "Look, the place where we meet with you is too small for us. 2Let us go to the Jordan, where each of us can get a pole; and let us build a place there for us to live."

And he said, "Go."

3Then one of them said, "Won't you please come with your servants?"

"I will," Elisha replied. 4And he went with them.

They went to the Jordan and began to cut down trees. 5As one of them was cutting down a tree, the iron axhead fell into the water. "Oh, my lord," he cried out, "it was borrowed!"

6The man of God asked, "Where did it fall?" When he showed him the place, Elisha cut a stick and threw it there, and made the iron float. 7"Lift it out," he said. Then the man reached out his hand and took it.

Elisha Traps Blinded Arameans

8Now the king of Aram was at war with Israel. After conferring with his officers, he said, "I will set up my camp in such and such a place."

9The man of God sent word to the king of Israel: "Beware of passing that place, because the Arameans are going down there." 10So the king of Israel checked on the place indicated by the man of God. Time and again Elisha warned the king, so that he was on his guard in such places.

11This enraged the king of Aram. He summoned his officers and demanded of them, "Will you not tell me which of us is on the side of the king of Israel?"

12"None of us, my lord the king," said one of his officers, "but Elisha, the prophet who is in Israel, tells the king of Israel the very words you speak in your bedroom."

13"Go, find out where he is," the king ordered, "so I can send men and capture him." The report came back: "He is in Dothan." 14Then he sent horses and chariots and a strong force there. They went by night and surrounded the city.

15When the servant of the man of God got up and went out early the next morning, an army with horses and chariots had surrounded the city. "Oh, my lord, what shall we do?" the servant asked.

16"Don't be afraid," the prophet answered. "Those who are with us are more than those who are with them."

17And Elisha prayed, "O LORD, open his eyes so he may see." Then the LORD opened the servant's eyes, and he looked and saw the hills full of horses and chariots of fire all around Elisha.

18As the enemy came down toward him, Elisha prayed to the LORD, "Strike these people with blindness." So he struck them with blindness, as Elisha had asked.

19Elisha told them, "This is not the road and this is not the city. Follow me, and I will lead you to the man you are looking for." And he led them to Samaria.

20After they entered the city, Elisha said, "LORD, open the eyes of these men so they can see." Then the LORD opened their eyes and they looked, and there they were, inside Samaria.

21When the king of Israel saw them, he asked Elisha, "Shall I kill them, my father? Shall I kill them?"

22"Do not kill them," he answered. "Would you kill men you have captured with your own sword or bow? Set food and water before them so that they may eat and drink and then go back to their master." 23So he prepared a great feast for them, and after they had finished eating and drinking, he sent them away, and they returned to their master. So the bands from Aram stopped raiding Israel's territory.

Famine in Besieged Samaria

24Some time later, Ben-Hadad king of Aram mobilized his entire army and marched up and laid siege to Samaria. 25There was a great famine in the city; the siege lasted so long that a donkey's head sold for eighty shekels[a] of silver, and a quarter of a cab[b] of seed pods[c] for five shekels.[d]

26As the king of Israel was passing by on the wall, a woman cried to him, "Help me, my lord the king!"

27The king replied, "If the LORD does not help you, where can I get help for you? From the threshing floor? From the wine-

press?" 28Then he asked her, "What's the matter?"

She answered, "This woman said to me, 'Give up your son so we may eat him to-day, and tomorrow we'll eat my son.' 29So we cooked my son and ate him. The next day I said to her, 'Give up your son so we may eat him,' but she had hidden him."

30When the king heard the woman's

---

a25 That is, about 2 pounds (about 1 kilogram)   b25 That is, probably about 1/2 pint (about 0.3 liter)
c25 Or of dove's dung   d25 That is, about 2 ounces (about 55 grams)

TUESDAY

VERSE FOR THE DAY: AUTHOR: PASSAGE FOR THE DAY:
2 Kings 6:17   Billy Graham   2 Kings 6:14–17

Hills Full of Horses

GOD'S angels often protect his servants from potential ene-mies. Consider 2 Kings 6:14–17. The king of Aram had dis-patched his army to Dothan, learning that Elisha the prophet was there. Upon dressing in the morning, the prophet's helper exclaimed excitedly to Elisha that the surrounding countryside bristled with armies and implements of war. Elisha assured him, "Don't be afraid . . . Those who are with us are more than those who are with them" (v. 16). Elisha then prayed that God would open the eyes of the young man to see the hosts of protective angels: as he did so, the young man "saw the hills full of horses and chariots of fire all around Elisha." This pas-sage has been one of the great assurances and comforts to me in my ministry.

The angels minister to God's servants in time of hardship and danger. We find another outstanding illustration of this in Acts 27:23–25. Paul on his way to Rome faced shipwreck with more than two hundred others on board. Speaking to the fear-ridden crew he said, "Last night an angel of the God whose I am and whom I serve stood beside me and said, 'Do not be afraid, Paul. You must stand trial before Caesar; and God has graciously given you the lives of all who sail with you'" (vv. 23–24).

Some believe strongly that each Christian may have his own guardian angel assigned to watch over him or her. This guard-ianship possibly begins in infancy, for Jesus said, "See that you do not look down on one of these little ones. For I tell you that their angels in heaven always see the face of my Father in heaven" (Matthew 18:10).

Additional Scripture Readings: Go to page 386 for your next
Psalm 91:9–16; Acts 27:21–26   devotional reading.

words, he tore his robes. As he went along the wall, the people looked, and there, underneath, he had sackcloth on his body. ³¹He said, "May God deal with me, be it ever so severely, if the head of Elisha son of Shaphat remains on his shoulders today!"

³²Now Elisha was sitting in his house, and the elders were sitting with him. The king sent a messenger ahead, but before he arrived, Elisha said to the elders, "Don't you see how this murderer is sending someone to cut off my head? Look, when the messenger comes, shut the door and hold it shut against him. Is not the sound of his master's footsteps behind him?"

³³While he was still talking to them, the messenger came down to him. And ˌthe king˲ said, "This disaster is from the Lord. Why should I wait for the Lord any longer?"

7 Elisha said, "Hear the word of the Lord. This is what the Lord says: About this time tomorrow, a seah*a* of flour will sell for a shekel*b* and two seahs*c* of barley for a shekel at the gate of Samaria."

²The officer on whose arm the king was leaning said to the man of God, "Look, even if the Lord should open the floodgates of the heavens, could this happen?"

"You will see it with your own eyes," answered Elisha, "but you will not eat any of it!"

The Siege Lifted

³Now there were four men with leprosy*d* at the entrance of the city gate. They said to each other, "Why stay here until we die? ⁴If we say, 'We'll go into the city'—the famine is there, and we will die. And if we stay here, we will die. So let's go over to the camp of the Arameans and surrender. If they spare us, we live; if they kill us, then we die."

⁵At dusk they got up and went to the camp of the Arameans. When they reached the edge of the camp, not a man was there, ⁶for the Lord had caused the Arameans to hear the sound of chariots and horses and a great army, so that they said to one another, "Look, the king of Israel has hired the Hittite and Egyptian kings to attack us!" ⁷So they got up and

fled in the dusk and abandoned their tents and their horses and donkeys. They left the camp as it was and ran for their lives.

⁸The men who had leprosy reached the edge of the camp and entered one of the tents. They ate and drank, and carried away silver, gold and clothes, and went off and hid them. They returned and entered another tent and took some things from it and hid them also.

⁹Then they said to each other, "We're not doing right. This is a day of good news and we are keeping it to ourselves. If we wait until daylight, punishment will overtake us. Let's go at once and report this to the royal palace."

¹⁰So they went and called out to the city gatekeepers and told them, "We went into the Aramean camp and not a man was there—not a sound of anyone—only tethered horses and donkeys, and the tents left just as they were." ¹¹The gatekeepers shouted the news, and it was reported within the palace.

¹²The king got up in the night and said to his officers, "I will tell you what the Arameans have done to us. They know we are starving; so they have left the camp to hide in the countryside, thinking, 'They will surely come out, and then we will take them alive and get into the city.'"

¹³One of his officers answered, "Have some men take five of the horses that are left in the city. Their plight will be like that of all the Israelites left here—yes, they will only be like all these Israelites who are doomed. So let us send them to find out what happened."

¹⁴So they selected two chariots with their horses, and the king sent them after the Aramean army. He commanded the drivers, "Go and find out what has happened." ¹⁵They followed them as far as the Jordan, and they found the whole road strewn with the clothing and equipment the Arameans had thrown away in their headlong flight. So the messengers returned and reported to the king. ¹⁶Then the people went out and plundered the camp of the Arameans. So a seah of flour sold for a shekel, and two seahs of barley sold for a shekel, as the Lord had said.

¹⁷Now the king had put the officer on whose arm he leaned in charge of the gate, and the people trampled him in the gate-

---

a1 That is, probably about 7 quarts (about 7.3 liters); also in verses 16 and 18　　*b1* That is, about 2/5 ounce (about 11 grams); also in verses 16 and 18　　*c1* That is, probably about 13 quarts (about 15 liters); also in verses 16 and 18　　*d3* The Hebrew word is used for various diseases affecting the skin—not necessarily leprosy; also in verse 8.

way, and he died, just as the man of God had foretold when the king came down to his house. [18]It happened as the man of God had said to the king: "About this time tomorrow, a seah of flour will sell for a shekel and two seahs of barley for a shekel at the gate of Samaria."

[19]The officer had said to the man of God, "Look, even if the LORD should open the floodgates of the heavens, could this happen?" The man of God had replied, "You will see it with your own eyes, but you will not eat any of it!" [20]And that is exactly what happened to him, for the people trampled him in the gateway, and he died.

The Shunammite's Land Restored

8 Now Elisha had said to the woman whose son he had restored to life, "Go away with your family and stay for a while wherever you can, because the LORD has decreed a famine in the land that will last seven years." [2]The woman proceeded to do as the man of God said. She and her family went away and stayed in the land of the Philistines seven years.

[3]At the end of the seven years she came back from the land of the Philistines and went to the king to beg for her house and land. [4]The king was talking to Gehazi, the servant of the man of God, and had said, "Tell me about all the great things Elisha has done." [5]Just as Gehazi was telling the king how Elisha had restored the dead to life, the woman whose son Elisha had brought back to life came to beg the king for her house and land.

Gehazi said, "This is the woman, my lord the king, and this is her son whom Elisha restored to life." [6]The king asked the woman about it, and she told him.

Then he assigned an official to her case and said to him, "Give back everything that belonged to her, including all the income from her land from the day she left the country until now."

Hazael Murders Ben-Hadad

[7]Elisha went to Damascus, and Ben-Hadad king of Aram was ill. When the king was told, "The man of God has come all the way up here," [8]he said to Hazael, "Take a gift with you and go to meet the man of God. Consult the LORD through him; ask him, 'Will I recover from this illness?' "

[9]Hazael went to meet Elisha, taking with him as a gift forty camel-loads of all the finest wares of Damascus. He went in and stood before him, and said, "Your son Ben-Hadad king of Aram has sent me to ask, 'Will I recover from this illness?' "

[10]Elisha answered, "Go and say to him, 'You will certainly recover'; but[a] the LORD has revealed to me that he will in fact die." [11]He stared at him with a fixed gaze until Hazael felt ashamed. Then the man of God began to weep.

[12]"Why is my lord weeping?" asked Hazael.

"Because I know the harm you will do to the Israelites," he answered. "You will set fire to their fortified places, kill their young men with the sword, dash their little children to the ground, and rip open their pregnant women."

[13]Hazael said, "How could your servant, a mere dog, accomplish such a feat?"

"The LORD has shown me that you will become king of Aram," answered Elisha.

[14]Then Hazael left Elisha and returned to his master. When Ben-Hadad asked, "What did Elisha say to you?" Hazael replied, "He told me that you would certainly recover." [15]But the next day he took a thick cloth, soaked it in water and spread it over the king's face, so that he died. Then Hazael succeeded him as king.

Jehoram King of Judah

[16]In the fifth year of Joram son of Ahab king of Israel, when Jehoshaphat was king of Judah, Jehoram son of Jehoshaphat began his reign as king of Judah. [17]He was thirty-two years old when he became king, and he reigned in Jerusalem eight years. [18]He walked in the ways of the kings of Israel, as the house of Ahab had done, for he married a daughter of Ahab. He did evil in the eyes of the LORD. [19]Nevertheless, for the sake of his servant David, the LORD was not willing to destroy Judah. He had promised to maintain a lamp for David and his descendants forever.

[20]In the time of Jehoram, Edom rebelled against Judah and set up its own king. [21]So Jehoram[b] went to Zair with all his chariots. The Edomites surrounded him and his chariot commanders, but he rose up and broke through by night; his army, however, fled back home. [22]To this day

---

[a]10 The Hebrew may also be read *Go and say, 'You will certainly not recover,' for.*   [b]21 Hebrew *Joram*, a variant of *Jehoram*; also in verses 23 and 24

Edom has been in rebellion against Judah. Libnah revolted at the same time.

23As for the other events of Jehoram's reign, and all he did, are they not written in the book of the annals of the kings of Judah? 24Jehoram rested with his fathers and was buried with them in the City of David. And Ahaziah his son succeeded him as king.

Ahaziah King of Judah

25In the twelfth year of Joram son of Ahab king of Israel, Ahaziah son of Jehoram king of Judah began to reign. 26Ahaziah was twenty-two years old when he became king, and he reigned in Jerusalem one year. His mother's name was Athaliah, a granddaughter of Omri king of Israel. 27He walked in the ways of the house of Ahab and did evil in the eyes of the LORD, as the house of Ahab had done, for he was related by marriage to Ahab's family.

28Ahaziah went with Joram son of Ahab to war against Hazael king of Aram at Ramoth Gilead. The Arameans wounded Joram; 29so King Joram returned to Jezreel to recover from the wounds the Arameans had inflicted on him at Ramoth[a] in his battle with Hazael king of Aram.

Then Ahaziah son of Jehoram king of Judah went down to Jezreel to see Joram son of Ahab, because he had been wounded.

Jehu Anointed King of Israel

9 The prophet Elisha summoned a man from the company of the prophets and said to him, "Tuck your cloak into your belt, take this flask of oil with you and go to Ramoth Gilead. 2When you get there, look for Jehu son of Jehoshaphat, the son of Nimshi. Go to him, get him away from his companions and take him into an inner room. 3Then take the flask and pour the oil on his head and declare, 'This is what the LORD says: I anoint you king over Israel.' Then open the door and run; don't delay!"

4So the young man, the prophet, went to Ramoth Gilead. 5When he arrived, he found the army officers sitting together. "I have a message for you, commander," he said.

"For which of us?" asked Jehu.

"For you, commander," he replied.

6Jehu got up and went into the house. Then the prophet poured the oil on Jehu's head and declared, "This is what the LORD, the God of Israel, says: 'I anoint you king over the LORD's people Israel. 7You are to destroy the house of Ahab your master, and I will avenge the blood of my servants the prophets and the blood of all the LORD's servants shed by Jezebel. 8The whole house of Ahab will perish. I will cut off from Ahab every last male in Israel—slave or free. 9I will make the house of Ahab like the house of Jeroboam son of Nebat and like the house of Baasha son of Ahijah. 10As for Jezebel, dogs will devour her on the plot of ground at Jezreel, and no one will bury her.' " Then he opened the door and ran.

11When Jehu went out to his fellow officers, one of them asked him, "Is everything all right? Why did this madman come to you?"

"You know the man and the sort of things he says," Jehu replied.

12"That's not true!" they said. "Tell us." Jehu said, "Here is what he told me: 'This is what the LORD says: I anoint you king over Israel.' "

13They hurried and took their cloaks and spread them under him on the bare steps. Then they blew the trumpet and shouted, "Jehu is king!"

Jehu Kills Joram and Ahaziah

14So Jehu son of Jehoshaphat, the son of Nimshi, conspired against Joram. (Now Joram and all Israel had been defending Ramoth Gilead against Hazael king of Aram, 15but King Joram[b] had returned to Jezreel to recover from the wounds the Arameans had inflicted on him in the battle with Hazael king of Aram.) Jehu said, "If this is the way you feel, don't let anyone slip out of the city to go and tell the news in Jezreel." 16Then he got into his chariot and rode to Jezreel, because Joram was resting there and Ahaziah king of Judah had gone down to see him.

17When the lookout standing on the tower in Jezreel saw Jehu's troops approaching, he called out, "I see some troops coming."

"Get a horseman," Joram ordered. "Send him to meet them and ask, 'Do you come in peace?' "

18The horseman rode off to meet Jehu and said, "This is what the king says: 'Do you come in peace?' "

---

a29 Hebrew Ramah, a variant of Ramoth and 21-24   b15 Hebrew Jehoram, a variant of Joram; also in verses 17

"What do you have to do with peace?" Jehu replied. "Fall in behind me."

The lookout reported, "The messenger has reached them, but he isn't coming back."

19So the king sent out a second horseman. When he came to them he said, "This is what the king says: 'Do you come in peace?'"

Jehu replied, "What do you have to do with peace? Fall in behind me."

20The lookout reported, "He has reached them, but he isn't coming back either. The driving is like that of Jehu son of Nimshi—he drives like a madman."

21"Hitch up my chariot," Joram ordered. And when it was hitched up, Joram king of Israel and Ahaziah king of Judah rode out, each in his own chariot, to meet Jehu. They met him at the plot of ground that had belonged to Naboth the Jezreelite. **22**When Joram saw Jehu he asked, "Have you come in peace, Jehu?"

"How can there be peace," Jehu replied, "as long as all the idolatry and witchcraft of your mother Jezebel abound?"

23Joram turned about and fled, calling out to Ahaziah, "Treachery, Ahaziah!"

24Then Jehu drew his bow and shot Joram between the shoulders. The arrow pierced his heart and he slumped down in his chariot. **25**Jehu said to Bidkar, his chariot officer, "Pick him up and throw him on the field that belonged to Naboth the Jezreelite. Remember how you and I were riding together in chariots behind Ahab his father when the LORD made this prophecy about him: **26**'Yesterday I saw the blood of Naboth and the blood of his sons, declares the LORD, and I will surely make you pay for it on this plot of ground, declares the LORD.'*a* Now then, pick him up and throw him on that plot, in accordance with the word of the LORD."

27When Ahaziah king of Judah saw what had happened, he fled up the road to Beth Haggan.*b* Jehu chased him, shouting, "Kill him too!" They wounded him in his chariot on the way up to Gur near Ibleam, but he escaped to Megiddo and died there. **28**His servants took him by chariot to Jerusalem and buried him with his fathers in his tomb in the City of David. **29**(In the eleventh year of Joram son of Ahab, Ahaziah had become king of Judah.)

Jezebel Killed

30Then Jehu went to Jezreel. When Jezebel heard about it, she painted her eyes, arranged her hair and looked out of a window. **31**As Jehu entered the gate, she asked, "Have you come in peace, Zimri, you murderer of your master?"*c*

32He looked up at the window and called out, "Who is on my side? Who?" Two or three eunuchs looked down at him. **33**"Throw her down!" Jehu said. So they threw her down, and some of her blood spattered the wall and the horses as they trampled her underfoot.

34Jehu went in and ate and drank. "Take care of that cursed woman," he said, "and bury her, for she was a king's daughter." **35**But when they went out to bury her, they found nothing except her skull, her feet and her hands. **36**They went back and told Jehu, who said, "This is the word of the LORD that he spoke through his servant Elijah the Tishbite: On the plot of ground at Jezreel dogs will devour Jezebel's flesh.*d* **37**Jezebel's body will be like refuse on the ground in the plot at Jezreel, so that no one will be able to say, 'This is Jezebel.'"

Ahab's Family Killed

10 Now there were in Samaria seventy sons of the house of Ahab. So Jehu wrote letters and sent them to Samaria: to the officials of Jezreel,*e* to the elders and to the guardians of Ahab's children. He said, **2**"As soon as this letter reaches you, since your master's sons are with you and you have chariots and horses, a fortified city and weapons, **3**choose the best and most worthy of your master's sons and set him on his father's throne. Then fight for your master's house."

4But they were terrified and said, "If two kings could not resist him, how can we?"

5So the palace administrator, the city governor, the elders and the guardians sent this message to Jehu: "We are your servants and we will do anything you say. We will not appoint anyone as king; you do whatever you think best."

6Then Jehu wrote them a second letter, saying, "If you are on my side and will obey me, take the heads of your master's

---

a26 See 1 Kings 21:19.
murdered his master?"
Vulgate *of the city*
b27 Or *fled by way of the garden house*
d36 See 1 Kings 21:23.
c31 Or *"Did Zimri have peace, who*
e1 Hebrew; some Septuagint manuscripts *and*

sons and come to me in Jezreel by this time tomorrow."

Now the royal princes, seventy of them, were with the leading men of the city, who were rearing them. **7**When the letter arrived, these men took the princes and slaughtered all seventy of them. They put their heads in baskets and sent them to Jehu in Jezreel. **8**When the messenger arrived, he told Jehu, "They have brought the heads of the princes."

Then Jehu ordered, "Put them in two piles at the entrance of the city gate until morning."

9The next morning Jehu went out. He stood before all the people and said, "You are innocent. It was I who conspired against my master and killed him, but who killed all these? **10**Know then, that not a word the LORD has spoken against the house of Ahab will fail. The LORD has done what he promised through his servant Elijah." **11**So Jehu killed everyone in Jezreel who remained of the house of Ahab, as well as all his chief men, his close friends and his priests, leaving him no survivor.

12Jehu then set out and went toward Samaria. At Beth Eked of the Shepherds, **13**he met some relatives of Ahaziah king of Judah and asked, "Who are you?"

They said, "We are relatives of Ahaziah, and we have come down to greet the families of the king and of the queen mother."

14"Take them alive!" he ordered. So they took them alive and slaughtered them by the well of Beth Eked—forty-two men. He left no survivor.

15After he left there, he came upon Jehonadab son of Recab, who was on his way to meet him. Jehu greeted him and said, "Are you in accord with me, as I am with you?"

"I am," Jehonadab answered.

"If so," said Jehu, "give me your hand." So he did, and Jehu helped him up into the chariot. **16**Jehu said, "Come with me and see my zeal for the LORD." Then he had him ride along in his chariot.

17When Jehu came to Samaria, he killed all who were left there of Ahab's family; he destroyed them, according to the word of the LORD spoken to Elijah.

Ministers of Baal Killed

18Then Jehu brought all the people together and said to them, "Ahab served Baal a little; Jehu will serve him much. **19**Now summon all the prophets of Baal, all his ministers and all his priests. See that no one is missing, because I am going to hold a great sacrifice for Baal. Anyone who fails to come will no longer live." But Jehu was acting deceptively in order to destroy the ministers of Baal.

20Jehu said, "Call an assembly in honor of Baal." So they proclaimed it. **21**Then he sent word throughout Israel, and all the ministers of Baal came; not one stayed away. They crowded into the temple of Baal until it was full from one end to the other. **22**And Jehu said to the keeper of the wardrobe, "Bring robes for all the ministers of Baal." So he brought out robes for them.

23Then Jehu and Jehonadab son of Recab went into the temple of Baal. Jehu said to the ministers of Baal, "Look around and see that no servants of the LORD are here with you—only ministers of Baal." **24**So they went in to make sacrifices and burnt offerings. Now Jehu had posted eighty men outside with this warning: "If one of you lets any of the men I am placing in your hands escape, it will be your life for his life."

25As soon as Jehu had finished making the burnt offering, he ordered the guards and officers: "Go in and kill them; let no one escape." So they cut them down with the sword. The guards and officers threw the bodies out and then entered the inner shrine of the temple of Baal. **26**They brought the sacred stone out of the temple of Baal and burned it. **27**They demolished the sacred stone of Baal and tore down the temple of Baal, and people have used it for a latrine to this day.

28So Jehu destroyed Baal worship in Israel. **29**However, he did not turn away from the sins of Jeroboam son of Nebat, which he had caused Israel to commit—the worship of the golden calves at Bethel and Dan.

30The LORD said to Jehu, "Because you have done well in accomplishing what is right in my eyes and have done to the house of Ahab all I had in mind to do, your descendants will sit on the throne of Israel to the fourth generation." **31**Yet Jehu was not careful to keep the law of the LORD, the God of Israel, with all his heart. He did not turn away from the sins of Jeroboam, which he had caused Israel to commit.

32In those days the LORD began to reduce the size of Israel. Hazael overpowered the Israelites throughout their territory [33]east of the Jordan in all the land of Gilead (the region of Gad, Reuben and Manasseh), from Aroer by the Arnon Gorge through Gilead to Bashan.

[34]As for the other events of Jehu's reign, all he did, and all his achievements, are they not written in the book of the annals of the kings of Israel?

[35]Jehu rested with his fathers and was buried in Samaria. And Jehoahaz his son succeeded him as king. [36]The time that Jehu reigned over Israel in Samaria was twenty-eight years.

Athaliah and Joash

11 When Athaliah the mother of Ahaziah saw that her son was dead, she proceeded to destroy the whole royal family. [2]But Jehosheba, the daughter of King Jehoram[a] and sister of Ahaziah, took Joash son of Ahaziah and stole him away from among the royal princes, who were about to be murdered. She put him and his nurse in a bedroom to hide him from Athaliah; so he was not killed. [3]He remained hidden with his nurse at the temple of the LORD for six years while Athaliah ruled the land.

[4]In the seventh year Jehoiada sent for the commanders of units of a hundred, the Carites and the guards and had them brought to him at the temple of the LORD. He made a covenant with them and put them under oath at the temple of the LORD. Then he showed them the king's son. [5]He commanded them, saying, "This is what you are to do: You who are in the three companies that are going on duty on the Sabbath — a third of you guarding the royal palace, [6]a third at the Sur Gate, and a third at the gate behind the guard, who take turns guarding the temple — [7]and you who are in the other two companies that normally go off Sabbath duty are all to guard the temple for the king. [8]Station yourselves around the king, each man with his weapon in his hand. Anyone who approaches your ranks[b] must be put to death. Stay close to the king wherever he goes."

[9]The commanders of units of a hundred did just as Jehoiada the priest ordered. Each one took his men — those who were going on duty on the Sabbath and those who were going off duty — and came to Jehoiada the priest. [10]Then he gave the com-manders the spears and shields that had belonged to King David and that were in the temple of the LORD. [11]The guards, each with his weapon in his hand, stationed themselves around the king — near the altar and the temple, from the south side to the north side of the temple.

[12]Jehoiada brought out the king's son and put the crown on him; he presented him with a copy of the covenant and proclaimed him king. They anointed him, and the people clapped their hands and shouted, "Long live the king!"

[13]When Athaliah heard the noise made by the guards and the people, she went to the people at the temple of the LORD. [14]She looked and there was the king, standing by the pillar, as the custom was. The officers and the trumpeters were beside the king, and all the people of the land were rejoicing and blowing trumpets. Then Athaliah tore her robes and called out, "Treason! Treason!"

[15]Jehoiada the priest ordered the commanders of units of a hundred, who were in charge of the troops: "Bring her out between the ranks[c] and put to the sword anyone who follows her." For the priest had said, "She must not be put to death in the temple of the LORD." [16]So they seized her as she reached the place where the horses enter the palace grounds, and there she was put to death.

[17]Jehoiada then made a covenant between the LORD and the king and people that they would be the LORD's people. He also made a covenant between the king and the people. [18]All the people of the land went to the temple of Baal and tore it down. They smashed the altars and idols to pieces and killed Mattan the priest of Baal in front of the altars.

Then Jehoiada the priest posted guards at the temple of the LORD. [19]He took with him the commanders of hundreds, the Carites, the guards and all the people of the land, and together they brought the king down from the temple of the LORD and went into the palace, entering by way of the gate of the guards. The king then took his place on the royal throne, [20]and all the people of the land rejoiced. And the city was quiet, because Athaliah had been slain with the sword at the palace.

[21]Joash[d] was seven years old when he began to reign.

---

a2 Hebrew *Joram*, a variant of *Jehoram*　　b8 Or *approaches the precincts*　　c15 Or *out from the precincts*　　d21 Hebrew *Jehoash*, a variant of *Joash*

Joash Repairs the Temple

12 In the seventh year of Jehu, Joash[a] became king, and he reigned in Jerusalem forty years. His mother's name was Zibiah; she was from Beersheba. [2]Joash did what was right in the eyes of the LORD all the years Jehoiada the priest instructed him. [3]The high places, however, were not removed; the people continued to offer sacrifices and burn incense there.

[4]Joash said to the priests, "Collect all the money that is brought as sacred offerings to the temple of the LORD—the money collected in the census, the money received from personal vows and the money brought voluntarily to the temple. [5]Let every priest receive the money from one of the treasurers, and let it be used to repair whatever damage is found in the temple."

[6]But by the twenty-third year of King Joash the priests still had not repaired the temple. [7]Therefore King Joash summoned Jehoiada the priest and the other priests and asked them, "Why aren't you repairing the damage done to the temple? Take no more money from your treasurers, but hand it over for repairing the temple." [8]The priests agreed that they would not collect any more money from the people and that they would not repair the temple themselves.

[9]Jehoiada the priest took a chest and bored a hole in its lid. He placed it beside the altar, on the right side as one enters the temple of the LORD. The priests who guarded the entrance put into the chest all the money that was brought to the temple of the LORD. [10]Whenever they saw that there was a large amount of money in the chest, the royal secretary and the high priest came, counted the money that had been brought into the temple of the LORD and put it into bags. [11]When the amount had been determined, they gave the money to the men appointed to supervise the work on the temple. With it they paid those who worked on the temple of the LORD—the carpenters and builders, [12]the masons and stonecutters. They purchased timber and dressed stone for the repair of the temple of the LORD, and met all the other expenses of restoring the temple.

[13]The money brought into the temple was not spent for making silver basins, wick trimmers, sprinkling bowls, trumpets or any other articles of gold or silver for the temple of the LORD; [14]it was paid to the workmen, who used it to repair the temple. [15]They did not require an accounting from those to whom they gave the money to pay the workers, because they acted with complete honesty. [16]The money from the guilt offerings and sin offerings was not brought into the temple of the LORD; it belonged to the priests.

[17]About this time Hazael king of Aram went up and attacked Gath and captured it. Then he turned to attack Jerusalem. [18]But Joash king of Judah took all the sacred objects dedicated by his fathers—Jehoshaphat, Jehoram and Ahaziah, the kings of Judah—and the gifts he himself had dedicated and all the gold found in the treasuries of the temple of the LORD and of the royal palace, and he sent them to Hazael king of Aram, who then withdrew from Jerusalem.

[19]As for the other events of the reign of Joash, and all he did, are they not written in the book of the annals of the kings of Judah? [20]His officials conspired against him and assassinated him at Beth Millo, on the road down to Silla. [21]The officials who murdered him were Jozabad son of Shimeath and Jehozabad son of Shomer. He died and was buried with his fathers in the City of David. And Amaziah his son succeeded him as king.

Jehoahaz King of Israel

13 In the twenty-third year of Joash son of Ahaziah king of Judah, Jehoahaz son of Jehu became king of Israel in Samaria, and he reigned seventeen years. [2]He did evil in the eyes of the LORD by following the sins of Jeroboam son of Nebat, which he had caused Israel to commit, and he did not turn away from them. [3]So the LORD's anger burned against Israel, and for a long time he kept them under the power of Hazael king of Aram and Ben-Hadad his son.

[4]Then Jehoahaz sought the LORD's favor, and the LORD listened to him, for he saw how severely the king of Aram was oppressing Israel. [5]The LORD provided a deliverer for Israel, and they escaped from the power of Aram. So the Israelites lived in their own homes as they had before. [6]But they did not turn away from the sins of the house of Jeroboam, which he had caused Israel to commit; they continued

in them. Also, the Asherah pole[a] remained standing in Samaria.

[7]Nothing had been left of the army of Jehoahaz except fifty horsemen, ten chariots and ten thousand foot soldiers, for the king of Aram had destroyed the rest and made them like the dust at threshing time.

[8]As for the other events of the reign of Jehoahaz, all he did and his achievements, are they not written in the book of the annals of the kings of Israel? [9]Jehoahaz rested with his fathers and was buried in Samaria. And Jehoash[b] his son succeeded him as king.

Jehoash King of Israel

[10]In the thirty-seventh year of Joash king of Judah, Jehoash son of Jehoahaz became king of Israel in Samaria, and he reigned sixteen years. [11]He did evil in the eyes of the LORD and did not turn away from any of the sins of Jeroboam son of Nebat, which he had caused Israel to commit; he continued in them.

[12]As for the other events of the reign of Jehoash, all he did and his achievements, including his war against Amaziah king of Judah, are they not written in the book of the annals of the kings of Israel? [13]Jehoash rested with his fathers, and Jeroboam succeeded him on the throne. Jehoash was buried in Samaria with the kings of Israel.

[14]Now Elisha was suffering from the illness from which he died. Jehoash king of Israel went down to see him and wept over him. "My father! My father!" he cried. "The chariots and horsemen of Israel!"

[15]Elisha said, "Get a bow and some arrows," and he did so. [16]"Take the bow in your hands," he said to the king of Israel. When he had taken it, Elisha put his hands on the king's hands.

[17]"Open the east window," he said, and he opened it. "Shoot!" Elisha said, and he shot. "The LORD's arrow of victory, the arrow of victory over Aram!" Elisha declared. "You will completely destroy the Arameans at Aphek."

[18]Then he said, "Take the arrows," and the king took them. Elisha told him, "Strike the ground." He struck it three times and stopped. [19]The man of God was angry with him and said, "You should have struck the ground five or six times; then you would have defeated Aram and completely destroyed it. But now you will defeat it only three times."

[20]Elisha died and was buried.

Now Moabite raiders used to enter the country every spring. [21]Once while some Israelites were burying a man, suddenly they saw a band of raiders; so they threw the man's body into Elisha's tomb. When the body touched Elisha's bones, the man came to life and stood up on his feet.

[22]Hazael king of Aram oppressed Israel throughout the reign of Jehoahaz. [23]But the LORD was gracious to them and had compassion and showed concern for them because of his covenant with Abraham, Isaac and Jacob. To this day he has been unwilling to destroy them or banish them from his presence.

[24]Hazael king of Aram died, and Ben-Hadad his son succeeded him as king. [25]Then Jehoash son of Jehoahaz recaptured from Ben-Hadad son of Hazael the towns he had taken in battle from his father Jehoahaz. Three times Jehoash defeated him, and so he recovered the Israelite towns.

Amaziah King of Judah

14 In the second year of Jehoash[c] son of Jehoahaz king of Israel, Amaziah son of Joash king of Judah began to reign. [2]He was twenty-five years old when he became king, and he reigned in Jerusalem twenty-nine years. His mother's name was Jehoaddin; she was from Jerusalem. [3]He did what was right in the eyes of the LORD, but not as his father David had done. In everything he followed the example of his father Joash. [4]The high places, however, were not removed; the people continued to offer sacrifices and burn incense there.

[5]After the kingdom was firmly in his grasp, he executed the officials who had murdered his father the king. [6]Yet he did not put the sons of the assassins to death, in accordance with what is written in the Book of the Law of Moses where the LORD commanded: "Fathers shall not be put to death for their children, nor children put to death for their fathers; each is to die for his own sins."[d]

[7]He was the one who defeated ten thousand Edomites in the Valley of Salt and captured Sela in battle, calling it Joktheel, the name it has to this day.

---

[a]6 That is, a symbol of the goddess Asherah; here and elsewhere in 2 Kings   [b]9 Hebrew *Joash*, a variant of *Jehoash*; also in verses 12-14 and 25   [c]1 Hebrew *Joash*, a variant of *Jehoash*; also in verses 13, 23 and 27   [d]6 Deut. 24:16

8Then Amaziah sent messengers to Jehoash son of Jehoahaz, the son of Jehu, king of Israel, with the challenge: "Come, meet me face to face."

9But Jehoash king of Israel replied to Amaziah king of Judah: "A thistle in Lebanon sent a message to a cedar in Lebanon, 'Give your daughter to my son in marriage.' Then a wild beast in Lebanon came along and trampled the thistle underfoot. **10**You have indeed defeated Edom and now you are arrogant. Glory in your victory, but stay at home! Why ask for trouble and cause your own downfall and that of Judah also?"

11Amaziah, however, would not listen, so Jehoash king of Israel attacked. He and Amaziah king of Judah faced each other at Beth Shemesh in Judah. **12**Judah was routed by Israel, and every man fled to his home. **13**Jehoash king of Israel captured Amaziah king of Judah, the son of Joash, the son of Ahaziah, at Beth Shemesh. Then Jehoash went to Jerusalem and broke down the wall of Jerusalem from the Ephraim Gate to the Corner Gate—a section about six hundred feet long.[a] **14**He took all the gold and silver and all the articles found in the temple of the Lord and in the treasuries of the royal palace. He also took hostages and returned to Samaria.

15As for the other events of the reign of Jehoash, what he did and his achievements, including his war against Amaziah king of Judah, are they not written in the book of the annals of the kings of Israel? **16**Jehoash rested with his fathers and was buried in Samaria with the kings of Israel. And Jeroboam his son succeeded him as king.

17Amaziah son of Joash king of Judah lived for fifteen years after the death of Jehoash son of Jehoahaz king of Israel. **18**As for the other events of Amaziah's reign, are they not written in the book of the annals of the kings of Judah?

19They conspired against him in Jerusalem, and he fled to Lachish, but they sent men after him to Lachish and killed him there. **20**He was brought back by horse and was buried in Jerusalem with his fathers, in the City of David.

21Then all the people of Judah took Azariah,[b] who was sixteen years old, and made him king in place of his father Amaziah. **22**He was the one who rebuilt Elath and restored it to Judah after Amaziah rested with his fathers.

Jeroboam II King of Israel

23In the fifteenth year of Amaziah son of Joash king of Judah, Jeroboam son of Jehoash king of Israel became king in Samaria, and he reigned forty-one years. **24**He did evil in the eyes of the Lord and did not turn away from any of the sins of Jeroboam son of Nebat, which he had caused Israel to commit. **25**He was the one who restored the boundaries of Israel from Lebo[c] Hamath to the Sea of the Arabah,[d] in accordance with the word of the Lord, the God of Israel, spoken through his servant Jonah son of Amittai, the prophet from Gath Hepher.

26The Lord had seen how bitterly everyone in Israel, whether slave or free, was suffering; there was no one to help them. **27**And since the Lord had not said he would blot out the name of Israel from under heaven, he saved them by the hand of Jeroboam son of Jehoash.

28As for the other events of Jeroboam's reign, all he did, and his military achievements, including how he recovered for Israel both Damascus and Hamath, which had belonged to Yaudi,[e] are they not written in the book of the annals of the kings of Israel? **29**Jeroboam rested with his fathers, the kings of Israel. And Zechariah his son succeeded him as king.

Azariah King of Judah

15 In the twenty-seventh year of Jeroboam king of Israel, Azariah son of Amaziah king of Judah began to reign. **2**He was sixteen years old when he became king, and he reigned in Jerusalem fifty-two years. His mother's name was Jecoliah; she was from Jerusalem. **3**He did what was right in the eyes of the Lord, just as his father Amaziah had done. **4**The high places, however, were not removed; the people continued to offer sacrifices and burn incense there.

5The Lord afflicted the king with leprosy[f] until the day he died, and he lived in a separate house.[g] Jotham the king's son had charge of the palace and governed the people of the land.

a 13 Hebrew four hundred cubits (about 180 meters)   b 21 Also called Uzzias   c 25 Or from the entrance to   d 25 That is, the Dead Sea   e 28 Or Judah   f 5 The Hebrew word was used for various diseases affecting the skin—not necessarily leprosy.   g 5 Or in a house where he was relieved of responsibility

⁶As for the other events of Azariah's reign, and all he did, are they not written in the book of the annals of the kings of Judah? ⁷Azariah rested with his fathers and was buried near them in the City of David. And Jotham his son succeeded him as king.

Zechariah King of Israel

⁸In the thirty-eighth year of Azariah king of Judah, Zechariah son of Jeroboam became king of Israel in Samaria, and he reigned six months. ⁹He did evil in the eyes of the LORD, as his fathers had done. He did not turn away from the sins of Jeroboam son of Nebat, which he had caused Israel to commit.

¹⁰Shallum son of Jabesh conspired against Zechariah. He attacked him in front of the people,ᵃ assassinated him and succeeded him as king. ¹¹The other events of Zechariah's reign are written in the book of the annals of the kings of Israel. ¹²So the word of the LORD spoken to Jehu was fulfilled: "Your descendants will sit on the throne of Israel to the fourth generation."ᵇ

Shallum King of Israel

¹³Shallum son of Jabesh became king in the thirty-ninth year of Uzziah king of Judah, and he reigned in Samaria one month. ¹⁴Then Menahem son of Gadi went from Tirzah up to Samaria. He attacked Shallum son of Jabesh in Samaria, assassinated him and succeeded him as king. ¹⁵The other events of Shallum's reign, and the conspiracy he led, are written in the book of the annals of the kings of Israel.

¹⁶At that time Menahem, starting out from Tirzah, attacked Tiphsah and everyone in the city and its vicinity, because they refused to open their gates. He sacked Tiphsah and ripped open all the pregnant women.

Menahem King of Israel

¹⁷In the thirty-ninth year of Azariah king of Judah, Menahem son of Gadi became king of Israel, and he reigned in Samaria ten years. ¹⁸He did evil in the eyes of the LORD. During his entire reign he did not turn away from the sins of Jeroboam son of Nebat, which he had caused Israel to commit.

¹⁹Then Pulᶜ king of Assyria invaded the land, and Menahem gave him a thousand talentsᵈ of silver to gain his support and strengthen his own hold on the kingdom. ²⁰Menahem exacted this money from Israel. Every wealthy man had to contribute fifty shekelsᵉ of silver to be given to the king of Assyria. So the king of Assyria withdrew and stayed in the land no longer.

²¹As for the other events of Menahem's reign, and all he did, are they not written in the book of the annals of the kings of Israel? ²²Menahem rested with his fathers. And Pekahiah his son succeeded him as king.

Pekahiah King of Israel

²³In the fiftieth year of Azariah king of Judah, Pekahiah son of Menahem became king of Israel in Samaria, and he reigned two years. ²⁴Pekahiah did evil in the eyes of the LORD. He did not turn away from the sins of Jeroboam son of Nebat, which he had caused Israel to commit. ²⁵One of his chief officers, Pekah son of Remaliah, conspired against him. Taking fifty men of Gilead with him, he assassinated Pekahiah, along with Argob and Arieh, in the citadel of the royal palace at Samaria. So Pekah killed Pekahiah and succeeded him as king.

²⁶The other events of Pekahiah's reign, and all he did, are written in the book of the annals of the kings of Israel.

Pekah King of Israel

²⁷In the fifty-second year of Azariah king of Judah, Pekah son of Remaliah became king of Israel in Samaria, and he reigned twenty years. ²⁸He did evil in the eyes of the LORD. He did not turn away from the sins of Jeroboam son of Nebat, which he had caused Israel to commit.

²⁹In the time of Pekah king of Israel, Tiglath-Pileser king of Assyria came and took Ijon, Abel Beth Maacah, Janoah, Kedesh and Hazor. He took Gilead and Galilee, including all the land of Naphtali, and deported the people to Assyria. ³⁰Then Hoshea son of Elah conspired against Pekah son of Remaliah. He attacked and assassinated him, and then succeeded him

ᵃ10 Hebrew; some Septuagint manuscripts in Ibleam   ᵇ12 2 Kings 10:30   ᶜ19 Also called Tiglath-Pileser   ᵈ19 That is, about 37 tons (about 34 metric tons)   ᵉ20 That is, about 1 1/4 pounds (about 0.6 kilogram) as king in the twentieth year of Jotham son of Uzziah.

³¹As for the other events of Pekah's reign, and all he did, are they not written in the book of the annals of the kings of Israel?

Jotham King of Judah

³²In the second year of Pekah son of Remaliah king of Israel, Jotham son of Uzziah king of Judah began to reign. ³³He was twenty-five years old when he became king, and he reigned in Jerusalem sixteen years. His mother's name was Jerusha daughter of Zadok. ³⁴He did what was right in the eyes of the LORD, just as his father Uzziah had done. ³⁵The high places, however, were not removed; the people continued to offer sacrifices and burn incense there. Jotham rebuilt the Upper Gate of the temple of the LORD.

³⁶As for the other events of Jotham's reign, and what he did, are they not written in the book of the annals of the kings of Judah? ³⁷(In those days the LORD began to send Rezin king of Aram and Pekah son of Remaliah against Judah.) ³⁸Jotham rested with his fathers and was buried with them in the City of David, the city of his father. And Ahaz his son succeeded him as king.

Ahaz King of Judah

16 In the seventeenth year of Pekah son of Remaliah, Ahaz son of Jotham king of Judah began to reign. ²Ahaz was twenty years old when he became king, and he reigned in Jerusalem sixteen years. Unlike David his father, he did not do what was right in the eyes of the LORD his God. ³He walked in the ways of the kings of Israel and even sacrificed his son in[a] the fire, following the detestable ways of the nations the LORD had driven out before the Israelites. ⁴He offered sacrifices and burned incense at the high places, on the hilltops and under every spreading tree.

⁵Then Rezin king of Aram and Pekah son of Remaliah king of Israel marched up to fight against Jerusalem and besieged Ahaz, but they could not overpower him. ⁶At that time, Rezin king of Aram recovered Elath for Aram by driving out the men of Judah. Edomites then moved into Elath and have lived there to this day.

⁷Ahaz sent messengers to say to Tiglath-Pileser king of Assyria, "I am your servant and vassal. Come up and save me out of the hand of the king of Aram and of the king of Israel, who are attacking me." ⁸And Ahaz took the silver and gold found in the temple of the LORD and in the treasuries of the royal palace and sent it as a gift to the king of Assyria. ⁹The king of Assyria complied by attacking Damascus and capturing it. He deported its inhabitants to Kir and put Rezin to death.

¹⁰Then King Ahaz went to Damascus to meet Tiglath-Pileser king of Assyria. He saw an altar in Damascus and sent to Uriah the priest a sketch of the altar, with detailed plans for its construction. ¹¹So Uriah the priest built an altar in accordance with all the plans that King Ahaz had sent from Damascus and finished it before King Ahaz returned. ¹²When the king came back from Damascus and saw the altar, he approached it and presented offerings[b] on it. ¹³He offered up his burnt offering and grain offering, poured out his drink offering, and sprinkled the blood of his fellowship offerings[c] on the altar. ¹⁴The bronze altar that stood before the LORD he brought from the front of the temple—from between the new altar and the temple of the LORD—and put it on the north side of the new altar.

¹⁵King Ahaz then gave these orders to Uriah the priest: "On the large new altar, offer the morning burnt offering and the evening grain offering, the king's burnt offering and his grain offering, and the burnt offering of all the people of the land, and their grain offering and their drink offering. Sprinkle on the altar all the blood of the burnt offerings and sacrifices. But I will use the bronze altar for seeking guidance." ¹⁶And Uriah the priest did just as King Ahaz had ordered.

¹⁷King Ahaz took away the side panels and removed the basins from the movable stands. He removed the Sea from the bronze bulls that supported it and set it on a stone base. ¹⁸He took away the Sabbath canopy[d] that had been built at the temple and removed the royal entryway outside the temple of the LORD, in deference to the king of Assyria.

¹⁹As for the other events of the reign of Ahaz, and what he did, are they not written in the book of the annals of the kings of Judah? ²⁰Ahaz rested with his fathers and was buried with them in the City of

---

[a]3 Or *even made his son pass through*   [b]12 Or *and went up*   [c]13 Traditionally *peace offerings*
[d]18 Or *the dais of his throne* (see Septuagint)

David. And Hezekiah his son succeeded him as king.

Hoshea Last King of Israel

17 In the twelfth year of Ahaz king of Judah, Hoshea son of Elah became king of Israel in Samaria, and he reigned nine years. [2]He did evil in the eyes of the LORD, but not like the kings of Israel who preceded him.

[3]Shalmaneser king of Assyria came up to attack Hoshea, who had been Shalmaneser's vassal and had paid him tribute. [4]But the king of Assyria discovered that Hoshea was a traitor, for he had sent envoys to So[a] king of Egypt, and he no longer paid tribute to the king of Assyria, as he had done year by year. Therefore Shalmaneser seized him and put him in prison. [5]The king of Assyria invaded the entire land, marched against Samaria and laid siege to it for three years. [6]In the ninth year of Hoshea, the king of Assyria captured Samaria and deported the Israelites to Assyria. He settled them in Halah, in Gozan on the Habor River and in the towns of the Medes.

Israel Exiled Because of Sin

[7]All this took place because the Israelites had sinned against the LORD their God, who had brought them up out of Egypt from under the power of Pharaoh king of Egypt. They worshiped other gods [8]and followed the practices of the nations the LORD had driven out before them, as well as the practices that the kings of Israel had introduced. [9]The Israelites secretly did things against the LORD their God that were not right. From watchtower to fortified city they built themselves high places in all their towns. [10]They set up sacred stones and Asherah poles on every high hill and under every spreading tree. [11]At every high place they burned incense, as the nations whom the LORD had driven out before them had done. They did wicked things that provoked the LORD to anger. [12]They worshiped idols, though the LORD had said, "You shall not do this."[b] [13]The LORD warned Israel and Judah through all his prophets and seers: "Turn from your evil ways. Observe my commands and decrees, in accordance with the entire Law that I commanded your fathers to obey and that I delivered to you through my servants the prophets."

[14]But they would not listen and were as stiff-necked as their fathers, who did not trust in the LORD their God. [15]They rejected his decrees and the covenant he had made with their fathers and the warnings he had given them. They followed worthless idols and themselves became worthless. They imitated the nations around them although the LORD had ordered them, "Do not do as they do," and they did the things the LORD had forbidden them to do.

[16]They forsook all the commands of the LORD their God and made for themselves two idols cast in the shape of calves, and an Asherah pole. They bowed down to all the starry hosts, and they worshiped Baal. [17]They sacrificed their sons and daughters in[c] the fire. They practiced divination and sorcery and sold themselves to do evil in the eyes of the LORD, provoking him to anger.

[18]So the LORD was very angry with Israel and removed them from his presence. Only the tribe of Judah was left, [19]and even Judah did not keep the commands of the LORD their God. They followed the practices Israel had introduced. [20]Therefore the LORD rejected all the people of Israel; he afflicted them and gave them into the hands of plunderers, until he thrust them from his presence.

[21]When he tore Israel away from the house of David, they made Jeroboam son of Nebat their king. Jeroboam enticed Israel away from following the LORD and caused them to commit a great sin. [22]The Israelites persisted in all the sins of Jeroboam and did not turn away from them [23]until the LORD removed them from his presence, as he had warned through all his servants the prophets. So the people of Israel were taken from their homeland into exile in Assyria, and they are still there.

Samaria Resettled

[24]The king of Assyria brought people from Babylon, Cuthah, Avva, Hamath and Sepharvaim and settled them in the towns of Samaria to replace the Israelites. They took over Samaria and lived in its towns. [25]When they first lived there, they did not worship the LORD; so he sent lions among them and they killed some of the people. [26]It was reported to the king of Assyria: "The people you deported and resettled in

---

a4 Or *to Sais, to the*; *So* is possibly an abbreviation for *Osorkon*.   b12 Exodus 20:4, 5   c17 Or *They made their sons and daughters pass through* the towns of Samaria do not know what the god of that country requires. He has sent lions among them, which are killing them off, because the people do not know what he requires."

27Then the king of Assyria gave this order: "Have one of the priests you took captive from Samaria go back to live there and teach the people what the god of the land requires." **28**So one of the priests who had been exiled from Samaria came to live in Bethel and taught them how to worship the LORD.

29Nevertheless, each national group made its own gods in the several towns where they settled, and set them up in the shrines the people of Samaria had made at the high places. **30**The men from Babylon made Succoth Benoth, the men from Cuthah made Nergal, and the men from Hamath made Ashima; **31**the Avvites made Nibhaz and Tartak, and the Sepharvites burned their children in the fire as sacrifices to Adrammelech and Anammelech, the gods of Sepharvaim. **32**They worshiped the LORD, but they also appointed all sorts of their own people to officiate for them as priests in the shrines at the high places. **33**They worshiped the LORD, but they also served their own gods in accordance with the customs of the nations from which they had been brought.

34To this day they persist in their former practices. They neither worship the LORD nor adhere to the decrees and ordinances, the laws and commands that the LORD gave the descendants of Jacob, whom he named Israel. **35**When the LORD made a covenant with the Israelites, he commanded them: "Do not worship any other gods or bow down to them, serve them or sacrifice to them. **36**But the LORD, who brought you up out of Egypt with mighty power and outstretched arm, is the one you must worship. To him you shall bow down and to him offer sacrifices. **37**You must always be careful to keep the decrees and ordinances, the laws and commands he wrote for you. Do not worship other gods. **38**Do not forget the covenant I have made with you, and do not worship other gods. **39**Rather, worship the LORD your God; it is he who will deliver you from the hand of all your enemies."

40They would not listen, however, but persisted in their former practices. **41**Even while these people were worshiping the LORD, they were serving their idols. To this day their children and grandchildren continue to do as their fathers did.

Hezekiah King of Judah

18 In the third year of Hoshea son of Elah king of Israel, Hezekiah son of Ahaz king of Judah began to reign. **2**He was twenty-five years old when he became king, and he reigned in Jerusalem twenty-nine years. His mother's name was Abijah[a] daughter of Zechariah. **3**He did what was right in the eyes of the LORD, just as his father David had done. **4**He removed the high places, smashed the sacred stones and cut down the Asherah poles. He broke into pieces the bronze snake Moses had made, for up to that time the Israelites had been burning incense to it. (It was called[b] Nehushtan.[c])

5Hezekiah trusted in the LORD, the God of Israel. There was no one like him among all the kings of Judah, either before him or after him. **6**He held fast to the LORD and did not cease to follow him; he kept the commands the LORD had given Moses. **7**And the LORD was with him; he was successful in whatever he undertook. He rebelled against the king of Assyria and did not serve him. **8**From watchtower to fortified city, he defeated the Philistines, as far as Gaza and its territory.

9In King Hezekiah's fourth year, which was the seventh year of Hoshea son of Elah king of Israel, Shalmaneser king of Assyria marched against Samaria and laid siege to it. **10**At the end of three years the Assyrians took it. So Samaria was captured in Hezekiah's sixth year, which was the ninth year of Hoshea king of Israel. **11**The king of Assyria deported Israel to Assyria and settled them in Halah, in Gozan on the Habor River and in towns of the Medes. **12**This happened because they had not obeyed the LORD their God, but had violated his covenant — all that Moses the servant of the LORD commanded. They neither listened to the commands nor carried them out.

13In the fourteenth year of King Hezekiah's reign, Sennacherib king of Assyria attacked all the fortified cities of Judah and captured them. **14**So Hezekiah king of Judah sent this message to the king of Assyria at Lachish: "I have done wrong. Withdraw from me, and I will pay whatever you demand of me." The king of Assyria

---

a2 Hebrew *Abi*, a variant of *Abijah*   *b4* Or *He called it*   *c4 Nehushtan* sounds like the Hebrew for *bronze* and *snake* and *unclean thing*.

exacted from Hezekiah king of Judah three hundred talents[a] of silver and thirty talents[b] of gold. [15]So Hezekiah gave him all the silver that was found in the temple of the LORD and in the treasuries of the royal palace.

[16]At this time Hezekiah king of Judah stripped off the gold with which he had covered the doors and doorposts of the temple of the LORD, and gave it to the king of Assyria.

Sennacherib Threatens Jerusalem

[17]The king of Assyria sent his supreme commander, his chief officer and his field commander with a large army, from Lachish to King Hezekiah at Jerusalem. They came up to Jerusalem and stopped at the aqueduct of the Upper Pool, on the road to the Washerman's Field. [18]They called for the king; and Eliakim son of Hilkiah the palace administrator, Shebna the

---

[a]14 That is, about 11 tons (about 10 metric tons)   [b]14 That is, about 1 ton (about 1 metric ton)

WEDNESDAY

VERSE FOR THE DAY:	AUTHOR:	PASSAGE FOR THE DAY:
2 Kings 18:3	D. Bruce Lockerbie	2 Kings 18:1–8

A Wholesome Example

EACH of us is human, subject to those frailties that are the consequences of sin. All too soon our admiring sons will discover that we too have feet of clay, that we're also susceptible to error, just as capable as anyone else of committing grievous mistakes. Two things, therefore, every father must learn in determining to set a wholesome example for his children. First, a father must humble himself and admit that he can't be the ultimate and faultless example; he can only serve to reflect the image of a higher Example for his sons and daughters to follow. Second, a father must be quick to acknowledge when he has been wrong, and then seek his children's forgiveness. This may be a father's highest example of Christian virtue; it may also be the hardest for him to attain . . .

It's too bad how often our behavior makes our children weep. "Why is it," a young woman in seminary asks me, "that my father's so unyielding, so incapable of acknowledging a mistake? I'm twenty-two years old and I've never once heard him say, to my mother or any member of the family, 'I'm sorry.' He's a good man, an earnest Christian, an elder in our church, but he just can't face up to the fact that he's human."

"I love him," she goes on, "but I'd love him so much more if he'd just accept himself for who he is and stop pretending to be infallible."

Accepting ourselves for who we are: That's a necessary step in establishing healthy relationships with anyone else—wife or husband, brother or sister, parents or children.

Additional Scripture Readings:
Psalm 51:1–12; 1 Peter 3:8–12

Go to page 416 for your next devotional reading.

secretary, and Joah son of Asaph the recorder went out to them.

[19]The field commander said to them, "Tell Hezekiah:

" 'This is what the great king, the king of Assyria, says: On what are you basing this confidence of yours? [20]You say you have strategy and military strength—but you speak only empty words. On whom are you depending, that you rebel against me? [21]Look now, you are depending on Egypt, that splintered reed of a staff, which pierces a man's hand and wounds him if he leans on it! Such is Pharaoh king of Egypt to all who depend on him. [22]And if you say to me, "We are depending on the LORD our God"—isn't he the one whose high places and altars Hezekiah removed, saying to Judah and Jerusalem, "You must worship before this altar in Jerusalem"?

[23]" 'Come now, make a bargain with my master, the king of Assyria: I will give you two thousand horses—if you can put riders on them! [24]How can you repulse one officer of the least of my master's officials, even though you are depending on Egypt for chariots and horsemen[a]? [25]Furthermore, have I come to attack and destroy this place without word from the LORD? The LORD himself told me to march against this country and destroy it.' "

[26]Then Eliakim son of Hilkiah, and Shebna and Joah said to the field commander, "Please speak to your servants in Aramaic, since we understand it. Don't speak to us in Hebrew in the hearing of the people on the wall."

[27]But the commander replied, "Was it only to your master and you that my master sent me to say these things, and not to the men sitting on the wall—who, like you, will have to eat their own filth and drink their own urine?"

[28]Then the commander stood and called out in Hebrew: "Hear the word of the great king, the king of Assyria! [29]This is what the king says: Do not let Hezekiah deceive you. He cannot deliver you from my hand. [30]Do not let Hezekiah persuade you to trust in the LORD when he says, 'The LORD will surely deliver us; this city

will not be given into the hand of the king of Assyria.'

[31]"Do not listen to Hezekiah. This is what the king of Assyria says: Make peace with me and come out to me. Then every one of you will eat from his own vine and fig tree and drink water from his own cistern, [32]until I come and take you to a land like your own, a land of grain and new wine, a land of bread and vineyards, a land of olive trees and honey. Choose life and not death!

"Do not listen to Hezekiah, for he is misleading you when he says, 'The LORD will deliver us.' [33]Has the god of any nation ever delivered his land from the hand of the king of Assyria? [34]Where are the gods of Hamath and Arpad? Where are the gods of Sepharvaim, Hena and Ivvah? Have they rescued Samaria from my hand? [35]Who of all the gods of these countries has been able to save his land from me? How then can the LORD deliver Jerusalem from my hand?"

[36]But the people remained silent and said nothing in reply, because the king had commanded, "Do not answer him."

[37]Then Eliakim son of Hilkiah the palace administrator, Shebna the secretary and Joah son of Asaph the recorder went to Hezekiah, with their clothes torn, and told him what the field commander had said.

Jerusalem's Deliverance Foretold

19 When King Hezekiah heard this, he tore his clothes and put on sackcloth and went into the temple of the LORD. [2]He sent Eliakim the palace administrator, Shebna the secretary and the leading priests, all wearing sackcloth, to the prophet Isaiah son of Amoz. [3]They told him, "This is what Hezekiah says: This day is a day of distress and rebuke and disgrace, as when children come to the point of birth and there is no strength to deliver them. [4]It may be that the LORD your God will hear all the words of the field commander, whom his master, the king of Assyria, has sent to ridicule the living God, and that he will rebuke him for the words the LORD your God has heard. Therefore pray for the remnant that still survives."

[5]When King Hezekiah's officials came to Isaiah, [6]Isaiah said to them, "Tell your master, 'This is what the LORD says: Do not be afraid of what you have heard—

those words with which the underlings of the king of Assyria have blasphemed me. [7]Listen! I am going to put such a spirit in him that when he hears a certain report, he will return to his own country, and there I will have him cut down with the sword.' "

[8]When the field commander heard that the king of Assyria had left Lachish, he withdrew and found the king fighting against Libnah.

[9]Now Sennacherib received a report that Tirhakah, the Cushite[a] king of Egypt, was marching out to fight against him. So he again sent messengers to Hezekiah with this word: [10]"Say to Hezekiah king of Judah: Do not let the god you depend on deceive you when he says, 'Jerusalem will not be handed over to the king of Assyria.' [11]Surely you have heard what the kings of Assyria have done to all the countries, destroying them completely. And will you be delivered? [12]Did the gods of the nations that were destroyed by my forefathers deliver them: the gods of Gozan, Haran, Rezeph and the people of Eden who were in Tel Assar? [13]Where is the king of Hamath, the king of Arpad, the king of the city of Sepharvaim, or of Hena or Ivvah?"

Hezekiah's Prayer

[14]Hezekiah received the letter from the messengers and read it. Then he went up to the temple of the LORD and spread it out before the LORD. [15]And Hezekiah prayed to the LORD: "O LORD, God of Israel, enthroned between the cherubim, you alone are God over all the kingdoms of the earth. You have made heaven and earth. [16]Give ear, O LORD, and hear; open your eyes, O LORD, and see; listen to the words Sennacherib has sent to insult the living God.

[17]"It is true, O LORD, that the Assyrian kings have laid waste these nations and their lands. [18]They have thrown their gods into the fire and destroyed them, for they were not gods but only wood and stone, fashioned by men's hands. [19]Now, O LORD our God, deliver us from his hand, so that all kingdoms on earth may know that you alone, O LORD, are God."

Isaiah Prophesies Sennacherib's Fall

[20]Then Isaiah son of Amoz sent a message to Hezekiah: "This is what the LORD, the God of Israel, says: I have heard your prayer concerning Sennacherib king of Assyria. [21]This is the word that the LORD has spoken against him:

" 'The Virgin Daughter of Zion
    despises you and mocks you.
The Daughter of Jerusalem
    tosses her head as you flee.
[22]Who is it you have insulted and
        blasphemed?
    Against whom have you raised your
        voice
and lifted your eyes in pride?
    Against the Holy One of Israel!
[23]By your messengers
    you have heaped insults on the
        Lord.
And you have said,
    "With my many chariots
I have ascended the heights of the
        mountains,
    the utmost heights of Lebanon.
I have cut down its tallest cedars,
    the choicest of its pines.
I have reached its remotest parts,
    the finest of its forests.
[24]I have dug wells in foreign lands
    and drunk the water there.
With the soles of my feet
    I have dried up all the streams of
        Egypt."

[25]" 'Have you not heard?
    Long ago I ordained it.
In days of old I planned it;
    now I have brought it to pass,
that you have turned fortified cities
    into piles of stone.
[26]Their people, drained of power,
    are dismayed and put to shame.
They are like plants in the field,
    like tender green shoots,
like grass sprouting on the roof,
    scorched before it grows up.

[27]" 'But I know where you stay
    and when you come and go
    and how you rage against me.
[28]Because you rage against me
    and your insolence has reached my
        ears,
I will put my hook in your nose
    and my bit in your mouth,
and I will make you return
    by the way you came.'

[29]"This will be the sign for you,
O Hezekiah:

"This year you will eat what grows by
    itself,

---

[a]9 That is, from the upper Nile region

and the second year what springs
from that.
But in the third year sow and reap,
plant vineyards and eat their fruit.
³⁰Once more a remnant of the house of
Judah
will take root below and bear fruit
above.
³¹For out of Jerusalem will come a
remnant,
and out of Mount Zion a band of
survivors.

The zeal of the LORD Almighty will accomplish this.

³²"Therefore this is what the LORD says
concerning the king of Assyria:

"He will not enter this city
or shoot an arrow here.
He will not come before it with shield
or build a siege ramp against it.
³³By the way that he came he will
return;
he will not enter this city,
declares the LORD.
³⁴I will defend this city and save it,
for my sake and for the sake of
David my servant."

³⁵That night the angel of the LORD went
out and put to death a hundred and
eighty-five thousand men in the Assyrian
camp. When the people got up the next
morning—there were all the dead bodies!
³⁶So Sennacherib king of Assyria broke
camp and withdrew. He returned to Nineveh and stayed there.
³⁷One day, while he was worshiping in
the temple of his god Nisroch, his sons
Adrammelech and Sharezer cut him down
with the sword, and they escaped to the
land of Ararat. And Esarhaddon his son
succeeded him as king.

Hezekiah's Illness

20 In those days Hezekiah became ill
and was at the point of death. The
prophet Isaiah son of Amoz went to him
and said, "This is what the LORD says: Put
your house in order, because you are going to die; you will not recover."
²Hezekiah turned his face to the wall
and prayed to the LORD, ³"Remember,
O LORD, how I have walked before you
faithfully and with wholehearted devotion
and have done what is good in your eyes."
And Hezekiah wept bitterly.
⁴Before Isaiah had left the middle court,
the word of the LORD came to him: ⁵"Go
back and tell Hezekiah, the leader of my

people, 'This is what the LORD, the God of
your father David, says: I have heard your
prayer and seen your tears; I will heal you.
On the third day from now you will go up
to the temple of the LORD. ⁶I will add fifteen years to your life. And I will deliver
you and this city from the hand of the king
of Assyria. I will defend this city for my
sake and for the sake of my servant David.' "
⁷Then Isaiah said, "Prepare a poultice of
figs." They did so and applied it to the
boil, and he recovered.
⁸Hezekiah had asked Isaiah, "What will
be the sign that the LORD will heal me and
that I will go up to the temple of the LORD
on the third day from now?"
⁹Isaiah answered, "This is the LORD's
sign to you that the LORD will do what he
has promised: Shall the shadow go forward ten steps, or shall it go back ten
steps?"
¹⁰"It is a simple matter for the shadow
to go forward ten steps," said Hezekiah.
"Rather, have it go back ten steps."
¹¹Then the prophet Isaiah called upon
the LORD, and the LORD made the shadow
go back the ten steps it had gone down on
the stairway of Ahaz.

Envoys From Babylon

¹²At that time Merodach-Baladan son of
Baladan king of Babylon sent Hezekiah
letters and a gift, because he had heard of
Hezekiah's illness. ¹³Hezekiah received
the messengers and showed them all that
was in his storehouses—the silver, the
gold, the spices and the fine oil—his armory and everything found among his
treasures. There was nothing in his palace
or in all his kingdom that Hezekiah did
not show them.
¹⁴Then Isaiah the prophet went to King
Hezekiah and asked, "What did those
men say, and where did they come from?"
"From a distant land," Hezekiah replied. "They came from Babylon."
¹⁵The prophet asked, "What did they
see in your palace?"
"They saw everything in my palace,"
Hezekiah said. "There is nothing among
my treasures that I did not show them."
¹⁶Then Isaiah said to Hezekiah, "Hear
the word of the LORD: ¹⁷The time will surely come when everything in your palace,
and all that your fathers have stored up
until this day, will be carried off to Babylon. Nothing will be left, says the LORD.
¹⁸And some of your descendants, your
own flesh and blood, that will be born to

you, will be taken away, and they will become eunuchs in the palace of the king of Babylon."

¹⁹"The word of the LORD you have spoken is good," Hezekiah replied. For he thought, "Will there not be peace and security in my lifetime?"

²⁰As for the other events of Hezekiah's reign, all his achievements and how he made the pool and the tunnel by which he brought water into the city, are they not written in the book of the annals of the kings of Judah? ²¹Hezekiah rested with his fathers. And Manasseh his son succeeded him as king.

Manasseh King of Judah

21 Manasseh was twelve years old when he became king, and he reigned in Jerusalem fifty-five years. His mother's name was Hephzibah. ²He did evil in the eyes of the LORD, following the detestable practices of the nations the LORD had driven out before the Israelites. ³He rebuilt the high places his father Hezekiah had destroyed; he also erected altars to Baal and made an Asherah pole, as Ahab king of Israel had done. He bowed down to all the starry hosts and worshiped them. ⁴He built altars in the temple of the LORD, of which the LORD had said, "In Jerusalem I will put my Name." ⁵In both courts of the temple of the LORD, he built altars to all the starry hosts. ⁶He sacrificed his own son in[a] the fire, practiced sorcery and divination, and consulted mediums and spiritists. He did much evil in the eyes of the LORD, provoking him to anger.

⁷He took the carved Asherah pole he had made and put it in the temple, of which the LORD had said to David and to his son Solomon, "In this temple and in Jerusalem, which I have chosen out of all the tribes of Israel, I will put my Name forever. ⁸I will not again make the feet of the Israelites wander from the land I gave their forefathers, if only they will be careful to do everything I commanded them and will keep the whole Law that my servant Moses gave them." ⁹But the people did not listen. Manasseh led them astray, so that they did more evil than the nations the LORD had destroyed before the Israelites.

¹⁰The LORD said through his servants the prophets: ¹¹"Manasseh king of Judah has committed these detestable sins. He has done more evil than the Amorites who preceded him and has led Judah into sin with his idols. ¹²Therefore this is what the LORD, the God of Israel, says: I am going to bring such disaster on Jerusalem and Judah that the ears of everyone who hears of it will tingle. ¹³I will stretch out over Jerusalem the measuring line used against Samaria and the plumb line used against the house of Ahab. I will wipe out Jerusalem as one wipes a dish, wiping it and turning it upside down. ¹⁴I will forsake the remnant of my inheritance and hand them over to their enemies. They will be looted and plundered by all their foes, ¹⁵because they have done evil in my eyes and have provoked me to anger from the day their forefathers came out of Egypt until this day."

¹⁶Moreover, Manasseh also shed so much innocent blood that he filled Jerusalem from end to end—besides the sin that he had caused Judah to commit, so that they did evil in the eyes of the LORD.

¹⁷As for the other events of Manasseh's reign, and all he did, including the sin he committed, are they not written in the book of the annals of the kings of Judah? ¹⁸Manasseh rested with his fathers and was buried in his palace garden, the garden of Uzza. And Amon his son succeeded him as king.

Amon King of Judah

¹⁹Amon was twenty-two years old when he became king, and he reigned in Jerusalem two years. His mother's name was Meshullemeth daughter of Haruz; she was from Jotbah. ²⁰He did evil in the eyes of the LORD, as his father Manasseh had done. ²¹He walked in all the ways of his father; he worshiped the idols his father had worshiped, and bowed down to them. ²²He forsook the LORD, the God of his fathers, and did not walk in the way of the LORD.

²³Amon's officials conspired against him and assassinated the king in his palace. ²⁴Then the people of the land killed all who had plotted against King Amon, and they made Josiah his son king in his place.

²⁵As for the other events of Amon's reign, and what he did, are they not written in the book of the annals of the kings of Judah? ²⁶He was buried in his grave in the garden of Uzza. And Josiah his son succeeded him as king.

---

[a]6 Or *He made his own son pass through*

The Book of the Law Found

22 Josiah was eight years old when he became king, and he reigned in Jerusalem thirty-one years. His mother's name was Jedidah daughter of Adaiah; she was from Bozkath. **2**He did what was right in the eyes of the LORD and walked in all the ways of his father David, not turning aside to the right or to the left.

3In the eighteenth year of his reign, King Josiah sent the secretary, Shaphan son of Azaliah, the son of Meshullam, to the temple of the LORD. He said: **4**"Go up to Hilkiah the high priest and have him get ready the money that has been brought into the temple of the LORD, which the doorkeepers have collected from the people. **5**Have them entrust it to the men appointed to supervise the work on the temple. And have these men pay the workers who repair the temple of the LORD— **6**the carpenters, the builders and the masons. Also have them purchase timber and dressed stone to repair the temple. **7**But they need not account for the money entrusted to them, because they are acting faithfully."

8Hilkiah the high priest said to Shaphan the secretary, "I have found the Book of the Law in the temple of the LORD." He gave it to Shaphan, who read it. **9**Then Shaphan the secretary went to the king and reported to him: "Your officials have paid out the money that was in the temple of the LORD and have entrusted it to the workers and supervisors at the temple." **10**Then Shaphan the secretary informed the king, "Hilkiah the priest has given me a book." And Shaphan read from it in the presence of the king.

11When the king heard the words of the Book of the Law, he tore his robes. **12**He gave these orders to Hilkiah the priest, Ahikam son of Shaphan, Acbor son of Micaiah, Shaphan the secretary and Asaiah the king's attendant: **13**"Go and inquire of the LORD for me and for the people and for all Judah about what is written in this book that has been found. Great is the LORD's anger that burns against us because our fathers have not obeyed the words of this book; they have not acted in accordance with all that is written there concerning us."

14Hilkiah the priest, Ahikam, Acbor, Shaphan and Asaiah went to speak to the prophetess Huldah, who was the wife of Shallum son of Tikvah, the son of Harhas, keeper of the wardrobe. She lived in Jerusalem, in the Second District.

15She said to them, "This is what the LORD, the God of Israel, says: Tell the man who sent you to me, **16**'This is what the LORD says: I am going to bring disaster on this place and its people, according to everything written in the book the king of Judah has read. **17**Because they have forsaken me and burned incense to other gods and provoked me to anger by all the idols their hands have made,*a* my anger will burn against this place and will not be quenched.' **18**Tell the king of Judah, who sent you to inquire of the LORD, 'This is what the LORD, the God of Israel, says concerning the words you heard: **19**Because your heart was responsive and you humbled yourself before the LORD when you heard what I have spoken against this place and its people, that they would become accursed and laid waste, and because you tore your robes and wept in my presence, I have heard you, declares the LORD. **20**Therefore I will gather you to your fathers, and you will be buried in peace. Your eyes will not see all the disaster I am going to bring on this place.' "

So they took her answer back to the king.

Josiah Renews the Covenant

23 Then the king called together all the elders of Judah and Jerusalem. **2**He went up to the temple of the LORD with the men of Judah, the people of Jerusalem, the priests and the prophets—all the people from the least to the greatest. He read in their hearing all the words of the Book of the Covenant, which had been found in the temple of the LORD. **3**The king stood by the pillar and renewed the covenant in the presence of the LORD—to follow the LORD and keep his commands, regulations and decrees with all his heart and all his soul, thus confirming the words of the covenant written in this book. Then all the people pledged themselves to the covenant.

4The king ordered Hilkiah the high priest, the priests next in rank and the doorkeepers to remove from the temple of the LORD all the articles made for Baal and Asherah and all the starry hosts. He burned them outside Jerusalem in the fields of the Kidron Valley and took the ashes to Bethel. **5**He did away with the pa-

a 17 Or by everything they have done

gan priests appointed by the kings of Judah to burn incense on the high places of the towns of Judah and on those around Jerusalem—those who burned incense to Baal, to the sun and moon, to the constellations and to all the starry hosts. **6**He took the Asherah pole from the temple of the LORD to the Kidron Valley outside Jerusalem and burned it there. He ground it to powder and scattered the dust over the graves of the common people. **7**He also tore down the quarters of the male shrine prostitutes, which were in the temple of the LORD and where women did weaving for Asherah.

8Josiah brought all the priests from the towns of Judah and desecrated the high places, from Geba to Beersheba, where the priests had burned incense. He broke down the shrines*a* at the gates—at the entrance to the Gate of Joshua, the city governor, which is on the left of the city gate. **9**Although the priests of the high places did not serve at the altar of the LORD in Jerusalem, they ate unleavened bread with their fellow priests.

10He desecrated Topheth, which was in the Valley of Ben Hinnom, so no one could use it to sacrifice his son or daughter in*b* the fire to Molech. **11**He removed from the entrance to the temple of the LORD the horses that the kings of Judah had dedicated to the sun. They were in the court near the room of an official named Nathan-Melech. Josiah then burned the chariots dedicated to the sun.

12He pulled down the altars the kings of Judah had erected on the roof near the upper room of Ahaz, and the altars Manasseh had built in the two courts of the temple of the LORD. He removed them from there, smashed them to pieces and threw the rubble into the Kidron Valley. **13**The king also desecrated the high places that were east of Jerusalem on the south of the Hill of Corruption—the ones Solomon king of Israel had built for Ashtoreth the vile goddess of the Sidonians, for Chemosh the vile god of Moab, and for Molech*c* the detestable god of the people of Ammon. **14**Josiah smashed the sacred stones and cut down the Asherah poles and covered the sites with human bones.

15Even the altar at Bethel, the high place made by Jeroboam son of Nebat, who had caused Israel to sin—even that altar and high place he demolished. He burned the high place and ground it to powder, and

burned the Asherah pole also. **16**Then Josiah looked around, and when he saw the tombs that were there on the hillside, he had the bones removed from them and burned on the altar to defile it, in accordance with the word of the LORD proclaimed by the man of God who foretold these things.

17The king asked, "What is that tombstone I see?"

The men of the city said, "It marks the tomb of the man of God who came from Judah and pronounced against the altar of Bethel the very things you have done to it."

18"Leave it alone," he said. "Don't let anyone disturb his bones." So they spared his bones and those of the prophet who had come from Samaria.

19Just as he had done at Bethel, Josiah removed and defiled all the shrines at the high places that the kings of Israel had built in the towns of Samaria that had provoked the LORD to anger. **20**Josiah slaughtered all the priests of those high places on the altars and burned human bones on them. Then he went back to Jerusalem.

21The king gave this order to all the people: "Celebrate the Passover to the LORD your God, as it is written in this Book of the Covenant." **22**Not since the days of the judges who led Israel, nor throughout the days of the kings of Israel and the kings of Judah, had any such Passover been observed. **23**But in the eighteenth year of King Josiah, this Passover was celebrated to the LORD in Jerusalem.

24Furthermore, Josiah got rid of the mediums and spiritists, the household gods, the idols and all the other detestable things seen in Judah and Jerusalem. This he did to fulfill the requirements of the law written in the book that Hilkiah the priest had discovered in the temple of the LORD. **25**Neither before nor after Josiah was there a king like him who turned to the LORD as he did—with all his heart and with all his soul and with all his strength, in accordance with all the Law of Moses.

26Nevertheless, the LORD did not turn away from the heat of his fierce anger, which burned against Judah because of all that Manasseh had done to provoke him to anger. **27**So the LORD said, "I will remove Judah also from my presence as I removed Israel, and I will reject Jerusalem, the city I chose, and this temple,

---

a 8 Or *high places*　　　*b 10* Or *to make his son or daughter pass through*　　　*c 13* Hebrew *Milcom* about which I said, 'There shall my Name be.'*a*"

28As for the other events of Josiah's reign, and all he did, are they not written in the book of the annals of the kings of Judah? **29**While Josiah was king, Pharaoh Neco king of Egypt went up to the Euphrates River to help the king of Assyria. King Josiah marched out to meet him in battle, but Neco faced him and killed him at Megiddo. **30**Josiah's servants brought his body in a chariot from Megiddo to Jerusalem and buried him in his own tomb. And the people of the land took Jehoahaz son of Josiah and anointed him and made him king in place of his father.

Jehoahaz King of Judah

31Jehoahaz was twenty-three years old when he became king, and he reigned in Jerusalem three months. His mother's name was Hamutal daughter of Jeremiah; she was from Libnah. **32**He did evil in the eyes of the LORD, just as his fathers had done. **33**Pharaoh Neco put him in chains at Riblah in the land of Hamath*b* so that he might not reign in Jerusalem, and he imposed on Judah a levy of a hundred talents*c* of silver and a talent*d* of gold. **34**Pharaoh Neco made Eliakim son of Josiah king in place of his father Josiah and changed Eliakim's name to Jehoiakim. But he took Jehoahaz and carried him off to Egypt, and there he died. **35**Jehoiakim paid Pharaoh Neco the silver and gold he demanded. In order to do so, he taxed the land and exacted the silver and gold from the people of the land according to their assessments.

Jehoiakim King of Judah

36Jehoiakim was twenty-five years old when he became king, and he reigned in Jerusalem eleven years. His mother's name was Zebidah daughter of Pedaiah; she was from Rumah. **37**And he did evil in the eyes of the LORD, just as his fathers had done.

24 During Jehoiakim's reign, Nebuchadnezzar king of Babylon invaded the land, and Jehoiakim became his vassal for three years. But then he changed his mind and rebelled against Nebuchadnezzar. **2**The LORD sent Babylonian,*e* Aramean, Moabite and Ammonite raiders against him. He sent them to destroy Judah, in accordance with the word of the LORD proclaimed by his servants the prophets. **3**Surely these things happened to Judah according to the LORD's command, in order to remove them from his presence because of the sins of Manasseh and all he had done, **4**including the shedding of innocent blood. For he had filled Jerusalem with innocent blood, and the LORD was not willing to forgive.

5As for the other events of Jehoiakim's reign, and all he did, are they not written in the book of the annals of the kings of Judah? **6**Jehoiakim rested with his fathers. And Jehoiachin his son succeeded him as king.

7The king of Egypt did not march out from his own country again, because the king of Babylon had taken all his territory, from the Wadi of Egypt to the Euphrates River.

Jehoiachin King of Judah

8Jehoiachin was eighteen years old when he became king, and he reigned in Jerusalem three months. His mother's name was Nehushta daughter of Elnathan; she was from Jerusalem. **9**He did evil in the eyes of the LORD, just as his father had done.

10At that time the officers of Nebuchadnezzar king of Babylon advanced on Jerusalem and laid siege to it, **11**and Nebuchadnezzar himself came up to the city while his officers were besieging it. **12**Jehoiachin king of Judah, his mother, his attendants, his nobles and his officials all surrendered to him.

In the eighth year of the reign of the king of Babylon, he took Jehoiachin prisoner. **13**As the LORD had declared, Nebuchadnezzar removed all the treasures from the temple of the LORD and from the royal palace, and took away all the gold articles that Solomon king of Israel had made for the temple of the LORD. **14**He carried into exile all Jerusalem: all the officers and fighting men, and all the craftsmen and artisans—a total of ten thousand. Only the poorest people of the land were left.

15Nebuchadnezzar took Jehoiachin captive to Babylon. He also took from Jerusalem to Babylon the king's mother, his wives, his officials and the leading men of

---

a27 1 Kings 8:29   *b33* Hebrew; Septuagint (see also 2 Chron. 36:3) *Neco at Riblah in Hamath removed him*   *c33* That is, about 3 3/4 tons (about 3.4 metric tons)   *d33* That is, about 75 pounds (about 34 kilograms)   *e2* Or *Chaldean* the land. ¹⁶The king of Babylon also deported to Babylon the entire force of seven thousand fighting men, strong and fit for war, and a thousand craftsmen and artisans. ¹⁷He made Mattaniah, Jehoiachin's uncle, king in his place and changed his name to Zedekiah.

Zedekiah King of Judah

¹⁸Zedekiah was twenty-one years old when he became king, and he reigned in Jerusalem eleven years. His mother's name was Hamutal daughter of Jeremiah; she was from Libnah. ¹⁹He did evil in the eyes of the LORD, just as Jehoiakim had done. ²⁰It was because of the LORD's anger that all this happened to Jerusalem and Judah, and in the end he thrust them from his presence.

The Fall of Jerusalem

Now Zedekiah rebelled against the king of Babylon.

25 So in the ninth year of Zedekiah's reign, on the tenth day of the tenth month, Nebuchadnezzar king of Babylon marched against Jerusalem with his whole army. He encamped outside the city and built siege works all around it. ²The city was kept under siege until the eleventh year of King Zedekiah. ³By the ninth day of the ₍fourth₎^a month the famine in the city had become so severe that there was no food for the people to eat. ⁴Then the city wall was broken through, and the whole army fled at night through the gate between the two walls near the king's garden, though the Babylonians^b were surrounding the city. They fled toward the Arabah,^c ⁵but the Babylonian^d army pursued the king and overtook him in the plains of Jericho. All his soldiers were separated from him and scattered, ⁶and he was captured. He was taken to the king of Babylon at Riblah, where sentence was pronounced on him. ⁷They killed the sons of Zedekiah before his eyes. Then they put out his eyes, bound him with bronze shackles and took him to Babylon.

⁸On the seventh day of the fifth month, in the nineteenth year of Nebuchadnezzar king of Babylon, Nebuzaradan commander of the imperial guard, an official of the king of Babylon, came to Jerusalem. ⁹He set fire to the temple of the LORD, the royal palace and all the houses of Jerusalem.

Every important building he burned down. ¹⁰The whole Babylonian army, under the commander of the imperial guard, broke down the walls around Jerusalem. ¹¹Nebuzaradan the commander of the guard carried into exile the people who remained in the city, along with the rest of the populace and those who had gone over to the king of Babylon. ¹²But the commander left behind some of the poorest people of the land to work the vineyards and fields.

¹³The Babylonians broke up the bronze pillars, the movable stands and the bronze Sea that were at the temple of the LORD and they carried the bronze to Babylon. ¹⁴They also took away the pots, shovels, wick trimmers, dishes and all the bronze articles used in the temple service. ¹⁵The commander of the imperial guard took away the censers and sprinkling bowls—all that were made of pure gold or silver.

¹⁶The bronze from the two pillars, the Sea and the movable stands, which Solomon had made for the temple of the LORD, was more than could be weighed. ¹⁷Each pillar was twenty-seven feet^e high. The bronze capital on top of one pillar was four and a half feet^f high and was decorated with a network and pomegranates of bronze all around. The other pillar, with its network, was similar.

¹⁸The commander of the guard took as prisoners Seraiah the chief priest, Zephaniah the priest next in rank and the three doorkeepers. ¹⁹Of those still in the city, he took the officer in charge of the fighting men and five royal advisers. He also took the secretary who was chief officer in charge of conscripting the people of the land and sixty of his men who were found in the city. ²⁰Nebuzaradan the commander took them all and brought them to the king of Babylon at Riblah. ²¹There at Riblah, in the land of Hamath, the king had them executed.

So Judah went into captivity, away from her land.

²²Nebuchadnezzar king of Babylon appointed Gedaliah son of Ahikam, the son of Shaphan, to be over the people he had left behind in Judah. ²³When all the army officers and their men heard that the king of Babylon had appointed Gedaliah as governor, they came to Gedaliah at Miz-

---

^a3 See Jer. 52:6.   ^b4 Or *Chaldeans*; also in verses 13, 25 and 26   ^c4 Or *the Jordan Valley*   ^d5 Or *Chaldean*; also in verses 10 and 24   ^e17 Hebrew *eighteen cubits* (about 8.1 meters)   ^f17 Hebrew *three cubits* (about 1.3 meters)

pah—Ishmael son of Nethaniah, Johanan son of Kareah, Seraiah son of Tanhumeth the Netophathite, Jaazaniah the son of the Maacathite, and their men. ²⁴Gedaliah took an oath to reassure them and their men. "Do not be afraid of the Babylonian officials," he said. "Settle down in the land and serve the king of Babylon, and it will go well with you."

²⁵In the seventh month, however, Ishmael son of Nethaniah, the son of Elishama, who was of royal blood, came with ten men and assassinated Gedaliah and also the men of Judah and the Babylonians who were with him at Mizpah. ²⁶At this, all the people from the least to the greatest, together with the army officers, fled to Egypt for fear of the Babylonians.

Jehoiachin Released

²⁷In the thirty-seventh year of the exile of Jehoiachin king of Judah, in the year Evil-Merodach[a] became king of Babylon, he released Jehoiachin from prison on the twenty-seventh day of the twelfth month. ²⁸He spoke kindly to him and gave him a seat of honor higher than those of the other kings who were with him in Babylon. ²⁹So Jehoiachin put aside his prison clothes and for the rest of his life ate regularly at the king's table. ³⁰Day by day the king gave Jehoiachin a regular allowance as long as he lived.

[a]27 Also called Amel-Marduk

THIS book, after listing the genealogies of God's people from Adam to David, describes in great detail how David conducts his administrative, military and religious affairs. Note David's desire for the true worship of God, shown by organizing the priests and Levites and by making extensive plans for building the temple. As you read this book, think about the importance of worshiping the Lord and the priority in your life that such worship deserves.

1 CHRONICLES

Historical Records From Adam to Abraham

To Noah's Sons

1 Adam, Seth, Enosh, **²**Kenan, Mahalalel, Jared, **³**Enoch, Methuselah, Lamech, Noah.

⁴The sons of Noah:*ᵃ*
Shem, Ham and Japheth.

The Japhethites

⁵The sons*ᵇ* of Japheth:
Gomer, Magog, Madai, Javan, Tubal, Meshech and Tiras.
⁶The sons of Gomer:
Ashkenaz, Riphath*ᶜ* and Togarmah.
⁷The sons of Javan:
Elishah, Tarshish, the Kittim and the Rodanim.

The Hamites

⁸The sons of Ham:
Cush, Mizraim,*ᵈ* Put and Canaan.
⁹The sons of Cush:

ᵃ4 Septuagint; Hebrew does not have *The sons of Noah:*   *ᵇ5 Sons* may mean *descendants* or *successors* or *nations*; also in verses 6-10, 17 and 20.   *ᶜ6* Many Hebrew manuscripts and Vulgate (see also Septuagint and Gen. 10:3); most Hebrew manuscripts *Diphath*   *ᵈ8* That is, Egypt; also in verse 11

Seba, Havilah, Sabta, Raamah and Sabteca.

The sons of Raamah:
Sheba and Dedan.
10Cush was the father*a* of
Nimrod, who grew to be a mighty warrior on earth.
11Mizraim was the father of
the Ludites, Anamites, Lehabites, Naphtuhites, 12Pathrusites, Casluhites (from whom the Philistines came) and Caphtorites.
13Canaan was the father of
Sidon his firstborn,*b* and of the Hittites, 14Jebusites, Amorites, Girgashites, 15Hivites, Arkites, Sinites, 16Arvadites, Zemarites and Hamathites.

The Semites

17The sons of Shem:
Elam, Asshur, Arphaxad, Lud and Aram.

The sons of Aram*c*:
Uz, Hul, Gether and Meshech.
18Arphaxad was the father of Shelah, and Shelah the father of Eber.
19Two sons were born to Eber:
One was named Peleg,*d* because in his time the earth was divided; his brother was named Joktan.
20Joktan was the father of
Almodad, Sheleph, Hazarmaveth, Jerah, 21Hadoram, Uzal, Diklah, 22Obal,*e* Abimael, Sheba, 23Ophir, Havilah and Jobab. All these were sons of Joktan.

24Shem, Arphaxad,*f* Shelah,
25Eber, Peleg, Reu,
26Serug, Nahor, Terah
27and Abram (that is, Abraham).

The Family of Abraham

28The sons of Abraham:
Isaac and Ishmael.

Descendants of Hagar

29These were their descendants:
Nebaioth the firstborn of Ishmael, Kedar, Adbeel, Mibsam, 30Mish-

ma, Dumah, Massa, Hadad, Tema, 31Jetur, Naphish and Kedemah. These were the sons of Ishmael.

Descendants of Keturah

32The sons born to Keturah, Abraham's concubine:
Zimran, Jokshan, Medan, Midian, Ishbak and Shuah.

The sons of Jokshan:
Sheba and Dedan.
33The sons of Midian:
Ephah, Epher, Hanoch, Abida and Eldaah.

All these were descendants of Keturah.

Descendants of Sarah

34Abraham was the father of Isaac.
The sons of Isaac:
Esau and Israel.

Esau's Sons

35The sons of Esau:
Eliphaz, Reuel, Jeush, Jalam and Korah.
36The sons of Eliphaz:
Teman, Omar, Zepho,*g* Gatam and Kenaz;
by Timna: Amalek.*h*
37The sons of Reuel:
Nahath, Zerah, Shammah and Mizzah.

The People of Seir in Edom

38The sons of Seir:
Lotan, Shobal, Zibeon, Anah, Dishon, Ezer and Dishan.
39The sons of Lotan:
Hori and Homam. Timna was Lotan's sister.
40The sons of Shobal:
Alvan,*i* Manahath, Ebal, Shepho and Onam.

The sons of Zibeon:
Aiah and Anah.
41The son of Anah:
Dishon.

The sons of Dishon:

---

a10 Father may mean *ancestor* or *predecessor* or *founder*; also in verses 11, 13, 18 and 20.   *b13* Or *of the Sidonians, the foremost*   *c17* One Hebrew manuscript and some Septuagint manuscripts (see also Gen. 10:23); most Hebrew manuscripts do not have this line.   *d19 Peleg* means *division*.   *e22* Some Hebrew manuscripts and Syriac (see also Gen. 10:28); most Hebrew manuscripts *Ebal*   *f24* Hebrew; some Septuagint manuscripts *Arphaxad, Cainan* (see also note at Gen. 11:10)   *g36* Many Hebrew manuscripts, some Septuagint manuscripts and Syriac (see also Gen. 36:11); most Hebrew manuscripts *Zephi*   *h36* Some Septuagint manuscripts (see also Gen. 36:12); Hebrew *Gatam, Kenaz, Timna and Amalek*   *i40* Many Hebrew manuscripts and some Septuagint manuscripts (see also Gen. 36:23); most Hebrew manuscripts *Alian*

Hemdan,[a] Eshban, Ithran and Keran.
42The sons of Ezer:
Bilhan, Zaavan and Akan.[b]
The sons of Dishan[c]:
Uz and Aran.

The Rulers of Edom

43These were the kings who reigned in Edom before any Israelite king reigned[d]:
Bela son of Beor, whose city was named Dinhabah.
44When Bela died, Jobab son of Zerah from Bozrah succeeded him as king.
45When Jobab died, Husham from the land of the Temanites succeeded him as king.
46When Husham died, Hadad son of Bedad, who defeated Midian in the country of Moab, succeeded him as king. His city was named Avith.
47When Hadad died, Samlah from Masrekah succeeded him as king.
48When Samlah died, Shaul from Rehoboth on the river[e] succeeded him as king.
49When Shaul died, Baal-Hanan son of Acbor succeeded him as king.
50When Baal-Hanan died, Hadad succeeded him as king. His city was named Pau,[f] and his wife's name was Mehetabel daughter of Matred, the daughter of Me-Zahab.
51Hadad also died.

The chiefs of Edom were:
Timna, Alvah, Jetheth, **52**Oholibamah, Elah, Pinon, **53**Kenaz, Teman, Mibzar, **54**Magdiel and Iram. These were the chiefs of Edom.

Israel's Sons

2 These were the sons of Israel:
Reuben, Simeon, Levi, Judah, Issachar, Zebulun, **2**Dan, Joseph, Benjamin, Naphtali, Gad and Asher.

Judah

To Hezron's Sons

3The sons of Judah:
Er, Onan and Shelah. These three were born to him by a Canaanite woman, the daughter of Shua. Er, Judah's firstborn, was wicked in the LORD's sight; so the LORD put him to death. **4**Tamar, Judah's daughter-in-law, bore him Perez and Zerah. Judah had five sons in all.

5The sons of Perez:
Hezron and Hamul.
6The sons of Zerah:
Zimri, Ethan, Heman, Calcol and Darda[g]—five in all.
7The son of Carmi:
Achar,[h] who brought trouble on Israel by violating the ban on taking devoted things.[i]
8The son of Ethan:
Azariah.
9The sons born to Hezron were:
Jerahmeel, Ram and Caleb.[j]

From Ram Son of Hezron

10Ram was the father of Amminadab, and Amminadab the father of Nahshon, the leader of the people of Judah. **11**Nahshon was the father of Salmon,[k] Salmon the father of Boaz, **12**Boaz the father of Obed and Obed the father of Jesse.

13Jesse was the father of
Eliab his firstborn; the second son was Abinadab, the third Shimea, **14**the fourth Nethanel, the fifth Raddai, **15**the sixth Ozem and the seventh David. **16**Their sisters were Zeruiah and Abigail. Zeruiah's three sons were Abishai, Joab and Asahel. **17**Abigail was the mother of Amasa, whose father was Jether the Ishmaelite.

---

a41 Many Hebrew manuscripts and some Septuagint manuscripts (see also Gen. 36:26); most Hebrew manuscripts *Hamran*   *b42* Many Hebrew and Septuagint manuscripts (see also Gen. 36:27); most Hebrew manuscripts *Zaavan, Jaakan*   *c42* Hebrew *Dishon*, a variant of *Dishan*   *d43* Or *before an Israelite king reigned over them*   *e48* Possibly the Euphrates   *f50* Many Hebrew manuscripts, some Septuagint manuscripts, Vulgate and Syriac (see also Gen. 36:39); most Hebrew manuscripts *Pai* *g6* Many Hebrew manuscripts, some Septuagint manuscripts and Syriac (see also 1 Kings 4:31); most Hebrew manuscripts *Dara*   *h7* *Achar* means *trouble*; *Achar* is called *Achan* in Joshua.   *i7* The Hebrew term refers to the irrevocable giving over of things or persons to the LORD, often by totally destroying them.   *j9* Hebrew *Kelubai*, a variant of *Caleb*   *k11* Septuagint (see also Ruth 4:21); Hebrew *Salma*

Caleb Son of Hezron

18Caleb son of Hezron had children by his wife Azubah (and by Jerioth). These were her sons: Jesher, Shobab and Ardon. **19**When Azubah died, Caleb married Ephrath, who bore him Hur. **20**Hur was the father of Uri, and Uri the father of Bezalel.

21Later, Hezron lay with the daughter of Makir the father of Gilead (he had married her when he was sixty years old), and she bore him Segub. **22**Segub was the father of Jair, who controlled twenty-three towns in Gilead. **23**(But Geshur and Aram captured Havvoth Jair,*a* as well as Kenath with its surrounding settlements — sixty towns.) All these were descendants of Makir the father of Gilead.

24After Hezron died in Caleb Ephrathah, Abijah the wife of Hezron bore him Ashhur the father*b* of Tekoa.

Jerahmeel Son of Hezron

25The sons of Jerahmeel the firstborn of Hezron:

Ram his firstborn, Bunah, Oren, Ozem and*c* Ahijah. **26**Jerahmeel had another wife, whose name was Atarah; she was the mother of Onam.

27The sons of Ram the firstborn of Jerahmeel:

Maaz, Jamin and Eker.

28The sons of Onam:

Shammai and Jada.

The sons of Shammai:

Nadab and Abishur.

29Abishur's wife was named Abihail, who bore him Ahban and Molid.

30The sons of Nadab:

Seled and Appaim. Seled died without children.

31The son of Appaim:

Ishi, who was the father of Sheshan.

Sheshan was the father of Ahlai.

32The sons of Jada, Shammai's brother:

Jether and Jonathan. Jether died without children.

33The sons of Jonathan:

Peleth and Zaza.

These were the descendants of Jerahmeel.

34Sheshan had no sons — only daughters.

He had an Egyptian servant named Jarha. **35**Sheshan gave his daughter in marriage to his servant Jarha, and she bore him Attai.

36Attai was the father of Nathan,

Nathan the father of Zabad,

37Zabad the father of Ephlal,

Ephlal the father of Obed,

38Obed the father of Jehu,

Jehu the father of Azariah,

39Azariah the father of Helez,

Helez the father of Eleasah,

40Eleasah the father of Sismai,

Sismai the father of Shallum,

41Shallum the father of Jekamiah,

and Jekamiah the father of Elishama.

The Clans of Caleb

42The sons of Caleb the brother of Jerahmeel:

Mesha his firstborn, who was the father of Ziph, and his son Mareshah,*d* who was the father of Hebron.

43The sons of Hebron:

Korah, Tappuah, Rekem and Shema. **44**Shema was the father of Raham, and Raham the father of Jorkeam. Rekem was the father of Shammai. **45**The son of Shammai was Maon, and Maon was the father of Beth Zur.

46Caleb's concubine Ephah was the mother of Haran, Moza and Gazez. Haran was the father of Gazez.

47The sons of Jahdai:

Regem, Jotham, Geshan, Pelet, Ephah and Shaaph.

48Caleb's concubine Maacah was the mother of Sheber and Tirhanah. **49**She also gave birth to Shaaph the father of Madmannah and to Sheva the father of Macbenah and Gibea. Caleb's daughter was Acsah. **50**These were the descendants of Caleb.

---

a23 Or *captured the settlements of Jair*   *b24* *Father* may mean *civic leader* or *military leader*; also in verses 42, 45, 49-52 and possibly elsewhere.   *c25* Or *Oren and Ozem, by*   *d42* The meaning of the Hebrew for this phrase is uncertain.

The sons of Hur the firstborn of Ephrathah:

Shobal the father of Kiriath Jearim, **51**Salma the father of Bethlehem, and Hareph the father of Beth Gader.

52The descendants of Shobal the father of Kiriath Jearim were:

Haroeh, half the Manahathites, **53**and the clans of Kiriath Jearim: the Ithrites, Puthites, Shumathites and Mishraites. From these descended the Zorathites and Eshtaolites.

54The descendants of Salma:

Bethlehem, the Netophathites, Atroth Beth Joab, half the Manahathites, the Zorites, **55**and the clans of scribes*a* who lived at Jabez: the Tirathites, Shimeathites and Sucathites. These are the Kenites who came from Hammath, the father of the house of Recab.*b*

The Sons of David

3 These were the sons of David born to him in Hebron:

The firstborn was Amnon the son of Ahinoam of Jezreel;

the second, Daniel the son of Abigail of Carmel;

2the third, Absalom the son of Maacah daughter of Talmai king of Geshur;

the fourth, Adonijah the son of Haggith;

3the fifth, Shephatiah the son of Abital;

and the sixth, Ithream, by his wife Eglah.

4These six were born to David in Hebron, where he reigned seven years and six months.

David reigned in Jerusalem thirty-three years, **5**and these were the children born to him there:

Shammua,*c* Shobab, Nathan and Solomon. These four were by Bathsheba*d* daughter of Ammiel. **6**There were also Ibhar, Elishua,*e* Eliphelet, **7**Nogah, Nepheg, Japhia, **8**Elishama, Eliada and Eliphelet — nine in all. **9**All these were the sons of David, besides his sons by his concubines. And Tamar was their sister.

The Kings of Judah

10Solomon's son was Rehoboam,

Abijah his son,

Asa his son,

Jehoshaphat his son,

11Jehoram*f* his son,

Ahaziah his son,

Joash his son,

12Amaziah his son,

Azariah his son,

Jotham his son,

13Ahaz his son,

Hezekiah his son,

Manasseh his son,

14Amon his son,

Josiah his son.

15The sons of Josiah:

Johanan the firstborn,

Jehoiakim the second son,

Zedekiah the third,

Shallum the fourth.

16The successors of Jehoiakim:

Jehoiachin*g* his son,

and Zedekiah.

The Royal Line After the Exile

17The descendants of Jehoiachin the captive:

Shealtiel his son, **18**Malkiram, Pedaiah, Shenazzar, Jekamiah, Hoshama and Nedabiah.

19The sons of Pedaiah:

Zerubbabel and Shimei.

The sons of Zerubbabel:

Meshullam and Hananiah. Shelomith was their sister.

20There were also five others:

Hashubah, Ohel, Berekiah, Hasadiah and Jushab-Hesed.

21The descendants of Hananiah:

Pelatiah and Jeshaiah, and the sons of Rephaiah, of Arnan, of Obadiah and of Shecaniah.

22The descendants of Shecaniah:

Shemaiah and his sons:

Hattush, Igal, Bariah, Neariah and Shaphat — six in all.

23The sons of Neariah:

Elioenai, Hizkiah and Azrikam — three in all.

24The sons of Elioenai:

---

*a*55 Or *of the Sopherites*   *b*55 Or *father of Beth Recab*   *c*5 Hebrew *Shimea,* a variant of *Shammua*   *d*5 One Hebrew manuscript and Vulgate (see also Septuagint and 2 Samuel 11:3); most Hebrew manuscripts *Bathshua*   *e*6 Two Hebrew manuscripts (see also 2 Samuel 5:15 and 1 Chron. 14:5); most Hebrew manuscripts *Elishama*   *f*11 Hebrew *Joram,* a variant of *Jehoram*   *g*16 Hebrew *Jeconiah,* a variant of *Jehoiachin;* also in verse 17

Hodaviah, Eliashib, Pelaiah, Akkub, Johanan, Delaiah and Anani—seven in all.

Other Clans of Judah

4 The descendants of Judah:
Perez, Hezron, Carmi, Hur and Shobal.

2Reaiah son of Shobal was the father of Jahath, and Jahath the father of Ahumai and Lahad. These were the clans of the Zorathites.

3These were the sons[a] of Etam:
Jezreel, Ishma and Idbash. Their sister was named Hazzelelponi. 4Penuel was the father of Gedor, and Ezer the father of Hushah.

These were the descendants of Hur, the firstborn of Ephrathah and father[b] of Bethlehem.

5Ashhur the father of Tekoa had two wives, Helah and Naarah.

6Naarah bore him Ahuzzam, Hepher, Temeni and Haahashtari. These were the descendants of Naarah.

7The sons of Helah:
Zereth, Zohar, Ethnan, 8and Koz, who was the father of Anub and Hazzobebah and of the clans of Aharhel son of Harum.

9Jabez was more honorable than his brothers. His mother had named him Jabez,[c] saying, "I gave birth to him in pain." 10Jabez cried out to the God of Israel, "Oh, that you would bless me and enlarge my territory! Let your hand be with me, and keep me from harm so that I will be free from pain." And God granted his request.

11Kelub, Shuhah's brother, was the father of Mehir, who was the father of Eshton. 12Eshton was the father of Beth Rapha, Paseah and Tehinnah the father of Ir Nahash.[d] These were the men of Recah.

13The sons of Kenaz:
Othniel and Seraiah.
The sons of Othniel:
Hathath and Meonothai.[e] 14Meonothai was the father of Ophrah.
Seraiah was the father of Joab,
the father of Ge Harashim.[f] It was called this because its people were craftsmen.

15The sons of Caleb son of Jephunneh:
Iru, Elah and Naam.
The son of Elah:
Kenaz.

16The sons of Jehallelel:
Ziph, Ziphah, Tiria and Asarel.

17The sons of Ezrah:
Jether, Mered, Epher and Jalon. One of Mered's wives gave birth to Miriam, Shammai and Ishbah the father of Eshtemoa. 18(His Judean wife gave birth to Jered the father of Gedor, Heber the father of Soco, and Jekuthiel the father of Zanoah.) These were the children of Pharaoh's daughter Bithiah, whom Mered had married.

19The sons of Hodiah's wife, the sister of Naham:
the father of Keilah the Garmite, and Eshtemoa the Maacathite.

20The sons of Shimon:
Amnon, Rinnah, Ben-Hanan and Tilon.
The descendants of Ishi:
Zoheth and Ben-Zoheth.

21The sons of Shelah son of Judah:
Er the father of Lecah, Laadah the father of Mareshah and the clans of the linen workers at Beth Ashbea, 22Jokim, the men of Cozeba, and Joash and Saraph, who ruled in Moab and Jashubi Lehem. (These records are from ancient times.) 23They were the potters who lived at Netaim and Gederah; they stayed there and worked for the king.

Simeon

24The descendants of Simeon:
Nemuel, Jamin, Jarib, Zerah and Shaul;

25Shallum was Shaul's son, Mibsam his son and Mishma his son.

26The descendants of Mishma:
Hammuel his son, Zaccur his son and Shimei his son.

27Shimei had sixteen sons and six daughters, but his brothers did not have many children; so their entire clan did not become as numerous as the people of Judah. 28They lived in Beersheba, Moladah, Hazar Shual, 29Bilhah, Ezem, Tolad, 30Bethuel, Hormah, Ziklag, 31Beth Marcaboth,

---

a3 Some Septuagint manuscripts (see also Vulgate); Hebrew *father*   b4 *Father* may mean *civic leader* or *military leader*; also in verses 12, 14, 17, 18 and possibly elsewhere.   c9 *Jabez* sounds like the Hebrew for *pain*.   d12 Or *of the city of Nahash*   e13 Some Septuagint manuscripts and Vulgate; Hebrew does not have *and Meonothai*.   f14 *Ge Harashim* means *valley of craftsmen*.

Hazar Susim, Beth Biri and Shaaraim. These were their towns until the reign of David. 32Their surrounding villages were Etam, Ain, Rimmon, Token and Ashan— five towns— 33and all the villages around these towns as far as Baalath.a These were their settlements. And they kept a genealogical record.

34Meshobab, Jamlech, Joshah son of Amaziah, 35Joel, Jehu son of Joshibi- ah, the son of Seraiah, the son of Asi- el, 36also Elioenai, Jaakobah, Jesho- haiah, Asaiah, Adiel, Jesimiel, Bena- iah, 37and Ziza son of Shiphi, the son of Allon, the son of Jedaiah, the son of Shimri, the son of Shemaiah.

38The men listed above by name were leaders of their clans. Their families in- creased greatly, 39and they went to the outskirts of Gedor to the east of the valley in search of pasture for their flocks. 40They found rich, good pasture, and the land was spacious, peaceful and quiet. Some Hamites had lived there formerly. 41The men whose names were listed came in the days of Hezekiah king of Ju- dah. They attacked the Hamites in their dwellings and also the Meunites who were there and completely destroyedb them, as is evident to this day. Then they settled in their place, because there was pasture for their flocks. 42And five hun- dred of these Simeonites, led by Pelatiah, Neariah, Rephaiah and Uzziel, the sons of Ishi, invaded the hill country of Seir. 43They killed the remaining Amalekites who had escaped, and they have lived there to this day.

Reuben

5 The sons of Reuben the firstborn of Is- rael (he was the firstborn, but when he defiled his father's marriage bed, his rights as firstborn were given to the sons of Joseph son of Israel; so he could not be listed in the genealogical record in accor- dance with his birthright, 2and though Ju- dah was the strongest of his brothers and a ruler came from him, the rights of the firstborn belonged to Joseph)— 3the sons of Reuben the firstborn of Israel:

Hanoch, Pallu, Hezron and Carmi.
4The descendants of Joel:
Shemaiah his son, Gog his son, Shimei his son, 5Micah his son,

Reaiah his son, Baal his son, 6and Beerah his son, whom Tig- lath-Pileserc king of Assyria took into exile. Beerah was a leader of the Reubenites.

7Their relatives by clans, listed ac- cording to their genealogical records: Jeiel the chief, Zechariah, 8and Bela son of Azaz, the son of She- ma, the son of Joel. They settled in the area from Aroer to Nebo and Baal Meon. 9To the east they occu- pied the land up to the edge of the desert that extends to the Euphra- tes River, because their livestock had increased in Gilead.

10During Saul's reign they waged war against the Hagrites, who were defeated at their hands; they occu- pied the dwellings of the Hagrites throughout the entire region east of Gilead.

Gad

11The Gadites lived next to them in Ba- shan, as far as Salecah:

12Joel was the chief, Shapham the second, then Janai and Shaphat, in Bashan.

13Their relatives, by families, were: Michael, Meshullam, Sheba, Jorai, Jacan, Zia and Eber—seven in all. 14These were the sons of Abihail son of Huri, the son of Jaroah, the son of Gilead, the son of Michael, the son of Jeshishai, the son of Jahdo, the son of Buz.

15Ahi son of Abdiel, the son of Guni, was head of their family.

16The Gadites lived in Gilead, in Ba- shan and its outlying villages, and on all the pasturelands of Sharon as far as they extended.

17All these were entered in the gene- alogical records during the reigns of Jo- tham king of Judah and Jeroboam king of Israel.

18The Reubenites, the Gadites and the half-tribe of Manasseh had 44,760 men ready for military service—able-bodied men who could handle shield and sword, who could use a bow, and who were trained for battle. 19They waged war against the Hagrites, Jetur, Naphish and

---

a33 Some Septuagint manuscripts (see also Joshua 19:8); Hebrew Baal   b41 The Hebrew term refers to the irrevocable giving over of things or persons to the LORD, often by totally destroying them. c6 Hebrew Tilgath-Pilneser, a variant of Tiglath-Pileser; also in verse 26

Nodab. **20**They were helped in fighting them, and God handed the Hagrites and all their allies over to them, because they cried out to him during the battle. He answered their prayers, because they trusted in him. **21**They seized the livestock of the Hagrites—fifty thousand camels, two hundred fifty thousand sheep and two thousand donkeys. They also took one hundred thousand people captive, **22**and many others fell slain, because the battle was God's. And they occupied the land until the exile.

The Half-Tribe of Manasseh

23The people of the half-tribe of Manasseh were numerous; they settled in the land from Bashan to Baal Hermon, that is, to Senir (Mount Hermon).

24These were the heads of their families: Epher, Ishi, Eliel, Azriel, Jeremiah, Hodaviah and Jahdiel. They were brave warriors, famous men, and heads of their families. **25**But they were unfaithful to the God of their fathers and prostituted themselves to the gods of the peoples of the land, whom God had destroyed before them. **26**So the God of Israel stirred up the spirit of Pul king of Assyria (that is, Tiglath-Pileser king of Assyria), who took the Reubenites, the Gadites and the half-tribe of Manasseh into exile. He took them to Halah, Habor, Hara and the river of Gozan, where they are to this day.

Levi

6   The sons of Levi:
    Gershon, Kohath and Merari.
2The sons of Kohath:
    Amram, Izhar, Hebron and Uzziel.
3The children of Amram:
    Aaron, Moses and Miriam.
    The sons of Aaron:
    Nadab, Abihu, Eleazar and Ithamar.
4Eleazar was the father of Phinehas,
    Phinehas the father of Abishua,
5Abishua the father of Bukki,
    Bukki the father of Uzzi,
6Uzzi the father of Zerahiah,
    Zerahiah the father of Meraioth,
7Meraioth the father of Amariah,
    Amariah the father of Ahitub,
8Ahitub the father of Zadok,
    Zadok the father of Ahimaaz,
9Ahimaaz the father of Azariah,
    Azariah the father of Johanan,
10Johanan the father of Azariah (it was he who served as priest in the temple Solomon built in Jerusalem),
11Azariah the father of Amariah,
    Amariah the father of Ahitub,
12Ahitub the father of Zadok,
    Zadok the father of Shallum,
13Shallum the father of Hilkiah,
    Hilkiah the father of Azariah,
14Azariah the father of Seraiah,
    and Seraiah the father of Jehozadak.
15Jehozadak was deported when the LORD sent Judah and Jerusalem into exile by the hand of Nebuchadnezzar.

16The sons of Levi:
    Gershon,*a* Kohath and Merari.
17These are the names of the sons of Gershon:
    Libni and Shimei.
18The sons of Kohath:
    Amram, Izhar, Hebron and Uzziel.
19The sons of Merari:
    Mahli and Mushi.
    These are the clans of the Levites listed according to their fathers:
20Of Gershon:
    Libni his son, Jehath his son,
    Zimmah his son, **21**Joah his son,
    Iddo his son, Zerah his son
    and Jeatherai his son.
22The descendants of Kohath:
    Amminadab his son, Korah his son,
    Assir his son, **23**Elkanah his son,
    Ebiasaph his son, Assir his son,
24Tahath his son, Uriel his son,
    Uzziah his son and Shaul his son.
25The descendants of Elkanah:
    Amasai, Ahimoth,
    26Elkanah his son,*b* Zophai his son,
    Nahath his son, **27**Eliab his son,
    Jeroham his son, Elkanah his son
    and Samuel his son.*c*
28The sons of Samuel:
    Joel*d* the firstborn
    and Abijah the second son.
29The descendants of Merari:

---

a16 Hebrew *Gershom*, a variant of *Gershon*; also in verses 17, 20, 43, 62 and 71   *b26* Some Hebrew manuscripts, Septuagint and Syriac; most Hebrew manuscripts *Ahimoth 26and Elkanah. The sons of Elkanah:*   *c27* Some Septuagint manuscripts (see also 1 Samuel 1:19,20 and 1 Chron. 6:33,34); Hebrew does not have *and Samuel his son.*   *d28* Some Septuagint manuscripts and Syriac (see also 1 Samuel 8:2 and 1 Chron. 6:33); Hebrew does not have *Joel.*

Mahli, Libni his son,
Shimei his son, Uzzah his son,
30Shimea his son, Haggiah his son
and Asaiah his son.

The Temple Musicians

31These are the men David put in
charge of the music in the house of the
LORD after the ark came to rest there.
32They ministered with music before the
tabernacle, the Tent of Meeting, until Solomon built the temple of the LORD in Jerusalem. They performed their duties according to the regulations laid down for
them.

33Here are the men who served, together with their sons:

From the Kohathites:
Heman, the musician,
the son of Joel, the son of Samuel,
34the son of Elkanah, the son of Jeroham,
the son of Eliel, the son of Toah,
35the son of Zuph, the son of Elkanah,
the son of Mahath, the son of
Amasai,
36the son of Elkanah, the son of Joel,
the son of Azariah, the son of
Zephaniah,
37the son of Tahath, the son of Assir,
the son of Ebiasaph, the son of Korah,
38the son of Izhar, the son of Kohath,
the son of Levi, the son of Israel;
39and Heman's associate Asaph, who
served at his right hand:
Asaph son of Berekiah, the son of
Shimea,
40the son of Michael, the son of Baa-
seiah,*a*
the son of Malkijah, **41**the son of
Ethni,
the son of Zerah, the son of Adaiah,
42the son of Ethan, the son of Zimmah,
the son of Shimei, **43**the son of Jahath,
the son of Gershon, the son of
Levi;
44and from their associates, the Merarites, at his left hand:

Ethan son of Kishi, the son of
Abdi,
the son of Malluch, **45**the son of
Hashabiah,
the son of Amaziah, the son of Hilkiah,
46the son of Amzi, the son of Bani,
the son of Shemer, **47**the son of
Mahli,
the son of Mushi, the son of Merari,
the son of Levi.

48Their fellow Levites were assigned to
all the other duties of the tabernacle, the
house of God. **49**But Aaron and his descendants were the ones who presented offerings on the altar of burnt offering and on
the altar of incense in connection with all
that was done in the Most Holy Place,
making atonement for Israel, in accordance with all that Moses the servant of
God had commanded.

50These were the descendants of
Aaron:
Eleazar his son, Phinehas his son,
Abishua his son, **51**Bukki his son,
Uzzi his son, Zerahiah his son,
52Meraioth his son, Amariah his
son,
Ahitub his son, **53**Zadok his son
and Ahimaaz his son.

54These were the locations of their settlements allotted as their territory (they
were assigned to the descendants of Aaron who were from the Kohathite clan, because the first lot was for them):

55They were given Hebron in Judah with its surrounding pasturelands. **56**But the fields and villages
around the city were given to Caleb
son of Jephunneh.

57So the descendants of Aaron
were given Hebron (a city of refuge),
and Libnah,*b* Jattir, Eshtemoa, **58**Hi-
len, Debir, **59**Ashan, Juttah*c* and
Beth Shemesh, together with their
pasturelands. **60**And from the tribe of
Benjamin they were given Gibeon,*d*
Geba, Alemeth and Anathoth, together with their pasturelands.

These towns, which were distributed among the Kohathite clans, were
thirteen in all.

61The rest of Kohath's descendants

a40 Most Hebrew manuscripts; some Hebrew manuscripts, one Septuagint manuscript and Syriac *Maaseiah*
b57 See Joshua 21:13; Hebrew *given the cities of refuge: Hebron, Libnah.*   *c59* Syriac (see also
Septuagint and Joshua 21:16); Hebrew does not have *Juttah.*   *d60* See Joshua 21:17; Hebrew does not
have *Gibeon.*

were allotted ten towns from the clans of half the tribe of Manasseh.

⁶²The descendants of Gershon, clan by clan, were allotted thirteen towns from the tribes of Issachar, Asher and Naphtali, and from the part of the tribe of Manasseh that is in Bashan.

⁶³The descendants of Merari, clan by clan, were allotted twelve towns from the tribes of Reuben, Gad and Zebulun.

⁶⁴So the Israelites gave the Levites these towns and their pasturelands. ⁶⁵From the tribes of Judah, Simeon and Benjamin they allotted the previously named towns.

⁶⁶Some of the Kohathite clans were given as their territory towns from the tribe of Ephraim.

⁶⁷In the hill country of Ephraim they were given Shechem (a city of refuge), and Gezer,ᵃ ⁶⁸Jokmeam, Beth Horon, ⁶⁹Aijalon and Gath Rimmon, together with their pasturelands.

⁷⁰And from half the tribe of Manasseh the Israelites gave Aner and Bileam, together with their pasturelands, to the rest of the Kohathite clans.

⁷¹The Gershonites received the following:

From the clan of the half-tribe of Manasseh
   they received Golan in Bashan and also Ashtaroth, together with their pasturelands;

⁷²from the tribe of Issachar
   they received Kedesh, Daberath, ⁷³Ramoth and Anem, together with their pasturelands;

⁷⁴from the tribe of Asher
   they received Mashal, Abdon, ⁷⁵Hukok and Rehob, together with their pasturelands;

⁷⁶and from the tribe of Naphtali
   they received Kedesh in Galilee, Hammon and Kiriathaim, together with their pasturelands.

⁷⁷The Merarites (the rest of the Levites) received the following:

From the tribe of Zebulun
   they received Jokneam, Kartah,ᵇ Rimmono and Tabor, together with their pasturelands;

⁷⁸from the tribe of Reuben across the Jordan east of Jericho
   they received Bezer in the desert, Jahzah, ⁷⁹Kedemoth and Mepha-

ath, together with their pasturelands;

⁸⁰and from the tribe of Gad
   they received Ramoth in Gilead, Mahanaim, ⁸¹Heshbon and Jazer, together with their pasturelands.

Issachar

7 The sons of Issachar:
   Tola, Puah, Jashub and Shimron—four in all.
   ²The sons of Tola:
   Uzzi, Rephaiah, Jeriel, Jahmai, Ibsam and Samuel—heads of their families. During the reign of David, the descendants of Tola listed as fighting men in their genealogy numbered 22,600.
   ³The son of Uzzi:
   Izrahiah.
   The sons of Izrahiah:
   Michael, Obadiah, Joel and Isshiah. All five of them were chiefs.
   ⁴According to their family genealogy, they had 36,000 men ready for battle, for they had many wives and children.
   ⁵The relatives who were fighting men belonging to all the clans of Issachar, as listed in their genealogy, were 87,000 in all.

Benjamin

⁶Three sons of Benjamin:
   Bela, Beker and Jediael.
   ⁷The sons of Bela:
   Ezbon, Uzzi, Uzziel, Jerimoth and Iri, heads of families—five in all. Their genealogical record listed 22,034 fighting men.
   ⁸The sons of Beker:
   Zemirah, Joash, Eliezer, Elioenai, Omri, Jeremoth, Abijah, Anathoth and Alemeth. All these were the sons of Beker. ⁹Their genealogical record listed the heads of families and 20,200 fighting men.
   ¹⁰The son of Jediael:
   Bilhan.
   The sons of Bilhan:
   Jeush, Benjamin, Ehud, Kenaanah, Zethan, Tarshish and Ahishahar. ¹¹All these sons of Jediael were heads of families. There were 17,200 fighting men ready to go out to war.
   ¹²The Shuppites and Huppites were

ᵃ67 See Joshua 21:21; Hebrew *given the cities of refuge: Shechem, Gezer.*   ᵇ77 See Septuagint and Joshua 21:34; Hebrew does not have *Jokneam, Kartah.*

the descendants of Ir, and the Hushites the descendants of Aher.

Naphtali

13The sons of Naphtali:

Jahziel, Guni, Jezer and Shillem[a]—the descendants of Bilhah.

Manasseh

14The descendants of Manasseh:

Asriel was his descendant through his Aramean concubine. She gave birth to Makir the father of Gilead. **15**Makir took a wife from among the Huppites and Shuppites. His sister's name was Maacah.

Another descendant was named Zelophehad, who had only daughters.

16Makir's wife Maacah gave birth to a son and named him Peresh. His brother was named Sheresh, and his sons were Ulam and Rakem.

17The son of Ulam:

Bedan.

These were the sons of Gilead son of Makir, the son of Manasseh. **18**His sister Hammoleketh gave birth to Ishhod, Abiezer and Mahlah.

19The sons of Shemida were:

Ahian, Shechem, Likhi and Aniam.

Ephraim

20The descendants of Ephraim:

Shuthelah, Bered his son,
Tahath his son, Eleadah his son,
Tahath his son, **21**Zabad his son
and Shuthelah his son.

Ezer and Elead were killed by the native-born men of Gath, when they went down to seize their livestock. **22**Their father Ephraim mourned for them many days, and his relatives came to comfort him. **23**Then he lay with his wife again, and she became pregnant and gave birth to a son. He named him Beriah,[b] because there had been misfortune in his family. **24**His daughter was Sheerah, who built Lower and Upper Beth Horon as well as Uzzen Sheerah.

25Rephah was his son, Resheph his son,[c]

Telah his son, Tahan his son,
26Ladan his son, Ammihud his son,
Elishama his son, **27**Nun his son
and Joshua his son.

28Their lands and settlements included Bethel and its surrounding villages, Naaran to the east, Gezer and its villages to the west, and Shechem and its villages all the way to Ayyah and its villages. **29**Along the borders of Manasseh were Beth Shan, Taanach, Megiddo and Dor, together with their villages. The descendants of Joseph son of Israel lived in these towns.

Asher

30The sons of Asher:

Imnah, Ishvah, Ishvi and Beriah. Their sister was Serah.

31The sons of Beriah:

Heber and Malkiel, who was the father of Birzaith.

32Heber was the father of Japhlet, Shomer and Hotham and of their sister Shua.

33The sons of Japhlet:

Pasach, Bimhal and Ashvath. These were Japhlet's sons.

34The sons of Shomer:

Ahi, Rohgah,[d] Hubbah and Aram.

35The sons of his brother Helem:

Zophah, Imna, Shelesh and Amal.

36The sons of Zophah:

Suah, Harnepher, Shual, Beri, Imrah, **37**Bezer, Hod, Shamma, Shilshah, Ithran[e] and Beera.

38The sons of Jether:

Jephunneh, Pispah and Ara.

39The sons of Ulla:

Arah, Hanniel and Rizia.

40All these were descendants of Asher—heads of families, choice men, brave warriors and outstanding leaders. The number of men ready for battle, as listed in their genealogy, was 26,000.

The Genealogy of Saul the Benjamite

8 Benjamin was the father of Bela his firstborn,

Ashbel the second son, Aharah the third,
2Nohah the fourth and Rapha the fifth.

3The sons of Bela were:

Addar, Gera, Abihud,[f] **4**Abishua,

---

a13 Some Hebrew and Septuagint manuscripts (see also Gen. 46:24 and Num. 26:49); most Hebrew manuscripts *Shallum*   b23 *Beriah* sounds like the Hebrew for *misfortune.*   c25 Some Septuagint manuscripts; Hebrew does not have *his son.*   d34 Or *of his brother Shomer: Rohgah*   e37 Possibly a variant of *Jether*   f3 Or *Gera the father of Ehud*

Naaman, Ahoah, [5]Gera, Shephuphan and Huram.

[6]These were the descendants of Ehud, who were heads of families of those living in Geba and were deported to Manahath:

[7]Naaman, Ahijah, and Gera, who deported them and who was the father of Uzza and Ahihud.

[8]Sons were born to Shaharaim in Moab after he had divorced his wives Hushim and Baara. [9]By his wife Hodesh he had Jobab, Zibia, Mesha, Malcam, [10]Jeuz, Sakia and Mirmah. These were his sons, heads of families. [11]By Hushim he had Abitub and Elpaal.

[12]The sons of Elpaal:

Eber, Misham, Shemed (who built Ono and Lod with its surrounding villages), [13]and Beriah and Shema, who were heads of families of those living in Aijalon and who drove out the inhabitants of Gath.

[14]Ahio, Shashak, Jeremoth, [15]Zebadiah, Arad, Eder, [16]Michael, Ishpah and Joha were the sons of Beriah.

[17]Zebadiah, Meshullam, Hizki, Heber, [18]Ishmerai, Izliah and Jobab were the sons of Elpaal.

[19]Jakim, Zicri, Zabdi, [20]Elienai, Zillethai, Eliel, [21]Adaiah, Beraiah and Shimrath were the sons of Shimei.

[22]Ishpan, Eber, Eliel, [23]Abdon, Zicri, Hanan, [24]Hananiah, Elam, Anthothijah, [25]Iphdeiah and Penuel were the sons of Shashak.

[26]Shamsherai, Shehariah, Athaliah, [27]Jaareshiah, Elijah and Zicri were the sons of Jeroham.

[28]All these were heads of families, chiefs as listed in their genealogy, and they lived in Jerusalem.

[29]Jeiel[a] the father[b] of Gibeon lived in Gibeon.

His wife's name was Maacah, [30]and his firstborn son was Abdon, followed by Zur, Kish, Baal, Ner,[c] Nadab, [31]Gedor, Ahio, Zeker [32]and Mikloth, who was the father of Shimeah. They too lived near their relatives in Jerusalem.

[33]Ner was the father of Kish, Kish the father of Saul, and Saul the father of Jonathan, Malki-Shua, Abinadab and Esh-Baal.[d]

[34]The son of Jonathan:

Merib-Baal,[e] who was the father of Micah.

[35]The sons of Micah:

Pithon, Melech, Tarea and Ahaz.

[36]Ahaz was the father of Jehoaddah, Jehoaddah was the father of Alemeth, Azmaveth and Zimri, and Zimri was the father of Moza. [37]Moza was the father of Binea; Raphah was his son, Eleasah his son and Azel his son.

[38]Azel had six sons, and these were their names:

Azrikam, Bokeru, Ishmael, Sheariah, Obadiah and Hanan. All these were the sons of Azel.

[39]The sons of his brother Eshek:

Ulam his firstborn, Jeush the second son and Eliphelet the third. [40]The sons of Ulam were brave warriors who could handle the bow. They had many sons and grandsons—150 in all.

All these were the descendants of Benjamin.

9 All Israel was listed in the genealogies recorded in the book of the kings of Israel.

The People in Jerusalem

The people of Judah were taken captive to Babylon because of their unfaithfulness. [2]Now the first to resettle on their own property in their own towns were some Israelites, priests, Levites and temple servants.

[3]Those from Judah, from Benjamin, and from Ephraim and Manasseh who lived in Jerusalem were:

[4]Uthai son of Ammihud, the son of Omri, the son of Imri, the son of Bani, a descendant of Perez son of Judah.

[5]Of the Shilonites:

Asaiah the firstborn and his sons.

[6]Of the Zerahites:

Jeuel.

The people from Judah numbered 690.

[7]Of the Benjamites:

Sallu son of Meshullam, the son of Hodaviah, the son of Hassenuah;

---

[a]29 Some Septuagint manuscripts (see also 1 Chron. 9:35); Hebrew does not have *Jeiel*.　[b]29 *Father* may mean *civic leader* or *military leader*.　[c]30 Some Septuagint manuscripts (see also 1 Chron. 9:36); Hebrew does not have *Ner*.　[d]33 Also known as *Ish-Bosheth*　[e]34 Also known as *Mephibosheth*

[8]Ibneiah son of Jeroham; Elah son of Uzzi, the son of Micri; and Meshullam son of Shephatiah, the son of Reuel, the son of Ibnijah.

[9]The people from Benjamin, as listed in their genealogy, numbered 956. All these men were heads of their families.

[10]Of the priests:

Jedaiah; Jehoiarib; Jakin;

[11]Azariah son of Hilkiah, the son of Meshullam, the son of Zadok, the son of Meraioth, the son of Ahitub, the official in charge of the house of God;

[12]Adaiah son of Jeroham, the son of Pashhur, the son of Malkijah; and Maasai son of Adiel, the son of Jahzerah, the son of Meshullam, the son of Meshillemith, the son of Immer.

[13]The priests, who were heads of families, numbered 1,760. They were able men, responsible for ministering in the house of God.

[14]Of the Levites:

Shemaiah son of Hasshub, the son of Azrikam, the son of Hashabiah, a Merarite; [15]Bakbakkar, Heresh, Galal and Mattaniah son of Mica, the son of Zicri, the son of Asaph; [16]Obadiah son of Shemaiah, the son of Galal, the son of Jeduthun; and Berekiah son of Asa, the son of Elkanah, who lived in the villages of the Netophathites.

[17]The gatekeepers:

Shallum, Akkub, Talmon, Ahiman and their brothers, Shallum their chief [18]being stationed at the King's Gate on the east, up to the present time. These were the gatekeepers belonging to the camp of the Levites. [19]Shallum son of Kore, the son of Ebiasaph, the son of Korah, and his fellow gatekeepers from his family (the Korahites) were responsible for guarding the thresholds of the Tent[a] just as their fathers had been responsible for guarding the entrance to the dwelling of the LORD. [20]In earlier times Phinehas son of Eleazar was in charge of the gatekeepers, and the LORD was with him. [21]Zechariah son of Meshelemiah was the gatekeeper at the entrance to the Tent of Meeting.

[22]Altogether, those chosen to be gatekeepers at the thresholds numbered 212. They were registered by genealogy in their villages. The gatekeepers had been assigned to their positions of trust by David and Samuel the seer. [23]They and their descendants were in charge of guarding the gates of the house of the LORD—the house called the Tent. [24]The gatekeepers were on the four sides: east, west, north and south. [25]Their brothers in their villages had to come from time to time and share their duties for seven-day periods. [26]But the four principal gatekeepers, who were Levites, were entrusted with the responsibility for the rooms and treasuries in the house of God. [27]They would spend the night stationed around the house of God, because they had to guard it; and they had charge of the key for opening it each morning.

[28]Some of them were in charge of the articles used in the temple service; they counted them when they were brought in and when they were taken out. [29]Others were assigned to take care of the furnishings and all the other articles of the sanctuary, as well as the flour and wine, and the oil, incense and spices. [30]But some of the priests took care of mixing the spices. [31]A Levite named Mattithiah, the firstborn son of Shallum the Korahite, was entrusted with the responsibility for baking the offering bread. [32]Some of their Kohathite brothers were in charge of preparing for every Sabbath the bread set out on the table.

[33]Those who were musicians, heads of Levite families, stayed in the rooms of the temple and were exempt from other duties because they were responsible for the work day and night.

[34]All these were heads of Levite families, chiefs as listed in their genealogy, and they lived in Jerusalem.

The Genealogy of Saul

[35]Jeiel the father[b] of Gibeon lived in Gibeon.

His wife's name was Maacah, [36]and his firstborn son was Abdon, followed by Zur, Kish, Baal, Ner, Nadab, [37]Gedor, Ahio, Zechariah and Mikloth. [38]Mikloth was the father of Shimeam. They too lived near their relatives in Jerusalem.

[39]Ner was the father of Kish, Kish the

a19 That is, the temple; also in verses 21 and 23   b35 Father may mean civic leader or military leader.

father of Saul, and Saul the father of Jonathan, Malki-Shua, Abinadab and Esh-Baal.[a]

⁴⁰The son of Jonathan:

Merib-Baal,[b] who was the father of Micah.

⁴¹The sons of Micah:

Pithon, Melech, Tahrea and Ahaz.[c]

⁴²Ahaz was the father of Jadah, Jadah[d] was the father of Alemeth, Azmaveth and Zimri, and Zimri was the father of Moza. ⁴³Moza was the father of Binea; Rephaiah was his son, Eleasah his son and Azel his son.

⁴⁴Azel had six sons, and these were their names:

Azrikam, Bokeru, Ishmael, Sheariah, Obadiah and Hanan. These were the sons of Azel.

Saul Takes His Life

10 Now the Philistines fought against Israel; the Israelites fled before them, and many fell slain on Mount Gilboa. ²The Philistines pressed hard after Saul and his sons, and they killed his sons Jonathan, Abinadab and Malki-Shua. ³The fighting grew fierce around Saul, and when the archers overtook him, they wounded him.

⁴Saul said to his armor-bearer, "Draw your sword and run me through, or these uncircumcised fellows will come and abuse me."

But his armor-bearer was terrified and would not do it; so Saul took his own sword and fell on it. ⁵When the armor-bearer saw that Saul was dead, he too fell on his sword and died. ⁶So Saul and his three sons died, and all his house died together.

⁷When all the Israelites in the valley saw that the army had fled and that Saul and his sons had died, they abandoned their towns and fled. And the Philistines came and occupied them.

⁸The next day, when the Philistines came to strip the dead, they found Saul and his sons fallen on Mount Gilboa. ⁹They stripped him and took his head and his armor, and sent messengers throughout the land of the Philistines to proclaim the news among their idols and their people. ¹⁰They put his armor in the temple of

their gods and hung up his head in the temple of Dagon.

¹¹When all the inhabitants of Jabesh Gilead heard of everything the Philistines had done to Saul, ¹²all their valiant men went and took the bodies of Saul and his sons and brought them to Jabesh. Then they buried their bones under the great tree in Jabesh, and they fasted seven days.

¹³Saul died because he was unfaithful to the LORD; he did not keep the word of the LORD and even consulted a medium for guidance, ¹⁴and did not inquire of the LORD. So the LORD put him to death and turned the kingdom over to David son of Jesse.

David Becomes King Over Israel

11 All Israel came together to David at Hebron and said, "We are your own flesh and blood. ²In the past, even while Saul was king, you were the one who led Israel on their military campaigns. And the LORD your God said to you, 'You will shepherd my people Israel, and you will become their ruler.' "

³When all the elders of Israel had come to King David at Hebron, he made a compact with them at Hebron before the LORD, and they anointed David king over Israel, as the LORD had promised through Samuel.

David Conquers Jerusalem

⁴David and all the Israelites marched to Jerusalem (that is, Jebus). The Jebusites who lived there ⁵said to David, "You will not get in here." Nevertheless, David captured the fortress of Zion, the City of David.

⁶David had said, "Whoever leads the attack on the Jebusites will become commander-in-chief." Joab son of Zeruiah went up first, and so he received the command.

⁷David then took up residence in the fortress, and so it was called the City of David. ⁸He built up the city around it, from the supporting terraces[e] to the surrounding wall, while Joab restored the rest of the city. ⁹And David became more and more powerful, because the LORD Almighty was with him.

David's Mighty Men

¹⁰These were the chiefs of David's

---

[a]39 Also known as *Ish-Bosheth*   [b]40 Also known as *Mephibosheth*   [c]41 Vulgate and Syriac (see also Septuagint and 1 Chron. 8:35); Hebrew does not have *and Ahaz.*   [d]42 Some Hebrew manuscripts and Septuagint (see also 1 Chron. 8:36); most Hebrew manuscripts *Jarah, Jarah*   [e]8 Or *the Millo*

mighty men — they, together with all Israel, gave his kingship strong support to extend it over the whole land, as the LORD had promised — **11**this is the list of David's mighty men:

Jashobeam,[a] a Hacmonite, was chief of the officers[b]; he raised his spear against three hundred men, whom he killed in one encounter.

12Next to him was Eleazar son of Dodai the Ahohite, one of the three mighty men. **13**He was with David at Pas Dammim when the Philistines gathered there for battle. At a place where there was a field full of barley, the troops fled from the Philistines. **14**But they took their stand in the middle of the field. They defended it and struck the Philistines down, and the LORD brought about a great victory.

15Three of the thirty chiefs came down to David to the rock at the cave of Adullam, while a band of Philistines was encamped in the Valley of Rephaim. **16**At that time David was in the stronghold, and the Philistine garrison was at Bethlehem. **17**David longed for water and said, "Oh, that someone would get me a drink of water from the well near the gate of Bethlehem!" **18**So the Three broke through the Philistine lines, drew water from the well near the gate of Bethlehem and carried it back to David. But he refused to drink it; instead, he poured it out before the LORD. **19**"God forbid that I should do this!" he said. "Should I drink the blood of these men who went at the risk of their lives?" Because they risked their lives to bring it back, David would not drink it.

Such were the exploits of the three mighty men.

20Abishai the brother of Joab was chief of the Three. He raised his spear against three hundred men, whom he killed, and so he became as famous as the Three. **21**He was doubly honored above the Three and became their commander, even though he was not included among them.

22Benaiah son of Jehoiada was a valiant fighter from Kabzeel, who performed great exploits. He struck down two of Moab's best men. He also went down into a pit on a snowy day and killed a lion. **23**And he struck down an Egyptian who was seven and a half feet[c] tall. Although the Egyptian had a spear like a weaver's rod in his hand, Benaiah went against him with a club. He snatched the spear from the Egyptian's hand and killed him with his own spear. **24**Such were the exploits of Benaiah son of Jehoiada; he too was as famous as the three mighty men. **25**He was held in greater honor than any of the Thirty, but he was not included among the Three. And David put him in charge of his bodyguard.

26The mighty men were:
Asahel the brother of Joab,
Elhanan son of Dodo from Bethlehem,
27Shammoth the Harorite,
Helez the Pelonite,
28Ira son of Ikkesh from Tekoa,
Abiezer from Anathoth,
29Sibbecai the Hushathite,
Ilai the Ahohite,
30Maharai the Netophathite,
Heled son of Baanah the Netophathite,
31Ithai son of Ribai from Gibeah in Benjamin,
Benaiah the Pirathonite,
32Hurai from the ravines of Gaash,
Abiel the Arbathite,
33Azmaveth the Baharumite,
Eliahba the Shaalbonite,
34the sons of Hashem the Gizonite,
Jonathan son of Shagee the Hararite,
35Ahiam son of Sacar the Hararite,
Eliphal son of Ur,
36Hepher the Mekerathite,
Ahijah the Pelonite,
37Hezro the Carmelite,
Naarai son of Ezbai,
38Joel the brother of Nathan,
Mibhar son of Hagri,
39Zelek the Ammonite,
Naharai the Berothite, the armor-bearer of Joab son of Zeruiah,
40Ira the Ithrite,
Gareb the Ithrite,
41Uriah the Hittite,
Zabad son of Ahlai,
42Adina son of Shiza the Reubenite, who was chief of the Reubenites, and the thirty with him,
43Hanan son of Maacah,
Joshaphat the Mithnite,
44Uzzia the Ashterathite,
Shama and Jeiel the sons of Hotham the Aroerite,
45Jediael son of Shimri,
his brother Joha the Tizite,

46Eliel the Mahavite,
Jeribai and Joshaviah the sons of
Elnaam,
Ithmah the Moabite,
47Eliel, Obed and Jaasiel the Mezo-
baite.

Warriors Join David

12 These were the men who came to David at Ziklag, while he was ban-ished from the presence of Saul son of Kish (they were among the warriors who helped him in battle; **2**they were armed with bows and were able to shoot arrows or to sling stones right-handed or left-handed; they were kinsmen of Saul from the tribe of Benjamin):

3Ahiezer their chief and Joash the sons of Shemaah the Gibeathite; Jezi-el and Pelet the sons of Azmaveth; Beracah, Jehu the Anathothite, **4**and Ishmaiah the Gibeonite, a mighty man among the Thirty, who was a leader of the Thirty; Jeremiah, Jaha-ziel, Johanan, Jozabad the Gedera-thite, **5**Eluzai, Jerimoth, Bealiah, Shemariah and Shephatiah the Haru-phite; **6**Elkanah, Isshiah, Azarel, Joe-zer and Jashobeam the Korahites; **7**and Joelah and Zebadiah the sons of Jeroham from Gedor.

8Some Gadites defected to David at his stronghold in the desert. They were brave warriors, ready for battle and able to han-dle the shield and spear. Their faces were the faces of lions, and they were as swift as gazelles in the mountains.
9Ezer was the chief,
Obadiah the second in command,
Eliab the third,
10Mishmannah the fourth, Jeremiah the fifth,
11Attai the sixth, Eliel the seventh,
12Johanan the eighth, Elzabad the ninth,
13Jeremiah the tenth and Macbannai the eleventh.
14These Gadites were army command-ers; the least was a match for a hundred, and the greatest for a thousand. **15**It was they who crossed the Jordan in the first month when it was overflowing all its banks, and they put to flight everyone liv-ing in the valleys, to the east and to the west.
16Other Benjamites and some men from Judah also came to David in his strong-

hold. **17**David went out to meet them and said to them, "If you have come to me in peace, to help me, I am ready to have you unite with me. But if you have come to be-tray me to my enemies when my hands are free from violence, may the God of our fathers see it and judge you."
18Then the Spirit came upon Amasai, chief of the Thirty, and he said:

"We are yours, O David!
We are with you, O son of Jesse!
Success, success to you,
and success to those who help you,
for your God will help you."

So David received them and made them leaders of his raiding bands.
19Some of the men of Manasseh defect-ed to David when he went with the Philis-tines to fight against Saul. (He and his men did not help the Philistines because, after consultation, their rulers sent him away. They said, "It will cost us our heads if he deserts to his master Saul.") **20**When David went to Ziklag, these were the men of Manasseh who defected to him: Adnah, Jozabad, Jediael, Michael, Jozabad, Elihu and Zillethai, leaders of units of a thou-sand in Manasseh. **21**They helped David against raiding bands, for all of them were brave warriors, and they were command-ers in his army. **22**Day after day men came to help David, until he had a great army, like the army of God.[a]

Others Join David at Hebron

23These are the numbers of the men armed for battle who came to David at He-bron to turn Saul's kingdom over to him, as the LORD had said:
24men of Judah, carrying shield and spear — 6,800 armed for battle;
25men of Simeon, warriors ready for battle — 7,100;
26men of Levi — 4,600, **27**including Je-hoiada, leader of the family of Aar-on, with 3,700 men, **28**and Zadok, a brave young warrior, with 22 of-ficers from his family;
29men of Benjamin, Saul's kinsmen — 3,000, most of whom had re-mained loyal to Saul's house until then;
30men of Ephraim, brave warriors, fa-mous in their own clans — 20,800;
31men of half the tribe of Manasseh, designated by name to come and make David king — 18,000;

a22 Or *a great and mighty army*

[32] men of Issachar, who understood the times and knew what Israel should do — 200 chiefs, with all their relatives under their command;

[33] men of Zebulun, experienced soldiers prepared for battle with every type of weapon, to help David with undivided loyalty — 50,000;

[34] men of Naphtali — 1,000 officers, together with 37,000 men carrying shields and spears;

[35] men of Dan, ready for battle — 28,600;

[36] men of Asher, experienced soldiers prepared for battle — 40,000;

[37] and from east of the Jordan, men of Reuben, Gad and the half-tribe of Manasseh, armed with every type of weapon — 120,000.

[38] All these were fighting men who volunteered to serve in the ranks. They came to Hebron fully determined to make David king over all Israel. All the rest of the Israelites were also of one mind to make David king. [39] The men spent three days there with David, eating and drinking, for their families had supplied provisions for them. [40] Also, their neighbors from as far away as Issachar, Zebulun and Naphtali came bringing food on donkeys, camels, mules and oxen. There were plentiful supplies of flour, fig cakes, raisin cakes, wine, oil, cattle and sheep, for there was joy in Israel.

Bringing Back the Ark

13 David conferred with each of his officers, the commanders of thousands and commanders of hundreds. [2] He then said to the whole assembly of Israel, "If it seems good to you and if it is the will of the Lord our God, let us send word far and wide to the rest of our brothers throughout the territories of Israel, and also to the priests and Levites who are with them in their towns and pasturelands, to come and join us. [3] Let us bring the ark of our God back to us, for we did not inquire of[a] it[b] during the reign of Saul." [4] The whole assembly agreed to do this, because it seemed right to all the people.

[5] So David assembled all the Israelites, from the Shihor River in Egypt to Lebo[c] Hamath, to bring the ark of God from Kiriath Jearim. [6] David and all the Israelites

with him went to Baalah of Judah (Kiriath Jearim) to bring up from there the ark of God the Lord, who is enthroned between the cherubim — the ark that is called by the Name.

[7] They moved the ark of God from Abinadab's house on a new cart, with Uzzah and Ahio guiding it. [8] David and all the Israelites were celebrating with all their might before God, with songs and with harps, lyres, tambourines, cymbals and trumpets.

[9] When they came to the threshing floor of Kidon, Uzzah reached out his hand to steady the ark, because the oxen stumbled. [10] The Lord's anger burned against Uzzah, and he struck him down because he had put his hand on the ark. So he died there before God.

[11] Then David was angry because the Lord's wrath had broken out against Uzzah, and to this day that place is called Perez Uzzah.[d]

[12] David was afraid of God that day and asked, "How can I ever bring the ark of God to me?" [13] He did not take the ark to be with him in the City of David. Instead, he took it aside to the house of Obed-Edom the Gittite. [14] The ark of God remained with the family of Obed-Edom in his house for three months, and the Lord blessed his household and everything he had.

David's House and Family

14 Now Hiram king of Tyre sent messengers to David, along with cedar logs, stonemasons and carpenters to build a palace for him. [2] And David knew that the Lord had established him as king over Israel and that his kingdom had been highly exalted for the sake of his people Israel.

[3] In Jerusalem David took more wives and became the father of more sons and daughters. [4] These are the names of the children born to him there: Shammua, Shobab, Nathan, Solomon, [5] Ibhar, Elishua, Elpelet, [6] Nogah, Nepheg, Japhia, [7] Elishama, Beeliada[e] and Eliphelet.

David Defeats the Philistines

[8] When the Philistines heard that David had been anointed king over all Israel, they went up in full force to search for him, but David heard about it and went out to meet them. [9] Now the Philistines

a3 Or we neglected   b3 Or him   c5 Or to the entrance to   d11 Perez Uzzah means outbreak
against Uzzah.   e7 A variant of Eliada

had come and raided the Valley of Repha-im; [10]so David inquired of God: "Shall I go and attack the Philistines? Will you hand them over to me?"

The LORD answered him, "Go, I will hand them over to you."

[11]So David and his men went up to Baal Perazim, and there he defeated them. He said, "As waters break out, God has broken out against my enemies by my hand." So that place was called Baal Perazim.[a] [12]The Philistines had abandoned their gods there, and David gave orders to burn them in the fire.

[13]Once more the Philistines raided the valley; [14]so David inquired of God again, and God answered him, "Do not go straight up, but circle around them and attack them in front of the balsam trees. [15]As soon as you hear the sound of marching in the tops of the balsam trees, move out to battle, because that will mean God has gone out in front of you to strike the Philistine army." [16]So David did as God commanded him, and they struck down the Philistine army, all the way from Gibeon to Gezer.

[17]So David's fame spread throughout every land, and the LORD made all the nations fear him.

The Ark Brought to Jerusalem

15 After David had constructed buildings for himself in the City of David, he prepared a place for the ark of God and pitched a tent for it. [2]Then David said, "No one but the Levites may carry the ark of God, because the LORD chose them to carry the ark of the LORD and to minister before him forever."

[3]David assembled all Israel in Jerusalem to bring up the ark of the LORD to the place he had prepared for it. [4]He called together the descendants of Aaron and the Levites:

[5]From the descendants of Kohath,
Uriel the leader and 120 relatives;
[6]from the descendants of Merari,
Asaiah the leader and 220 relatives;
[7]from the descendants of Gershon,[b]
Joel the leader and 130 relatives;
[8]from the descendants of Elizaphan,
Shemaiah the leader and 200 relatives;
[9]from the descendants of Hebron,
Eliel the leader and 80 relatives;
[10]from the descendants of Uzziel,
Amminadab the leader and 112 relatives.

[11]Then David summoned Zadok and Abiathar the priests, and Uriel, Asaiah, Joel, Shemaiah, Eliel and Amminadab the Levites. [12]He said to them, "You are the heads of the Levitical families; you and your fellow Levites are to consecrate yourselves and bring up the ark of the LORD, the God of Israel, to the place I have prepared for it. [13]It was because you, the Levites, did not bring it up the first time that the LORD our God broke out in anger against us. We did not inquire of him about how to do it in the prescribed way." [14]So the priests and Levites consecrated themselves in order to bring up the ark of the LORD, the God of Israel. [15]And the Levites carried the ark of God with the poles on their shoulders, as Moses had commanded in accordance with the word of the LORD.

[16]David told the leaders of the Levites to appoint their brothers as singers to sing joyful songs, accompanied by musical instruments: lyres, harps and cymbals.

[17]So the Levites appointed Heman son of Joel; from his brothers, Asaph son of Berekiah; and from their brothers the Merarites, Ethan son of Kushaiah; [18]and with them their brothers next in rank: Zechariah,[c] Jaaziel, Shemiramoth, Jehiel, Unni, Eliab, Benaiah, Maaseiah, Mattithiah, Eliphelehu, Mikneiah, Obed-Edom and Jeiel,[d] the gatekeepers.

[19]The musicians Heman, Asaph and Ethan were to sound the bronze cymbals; [20]Zechariah, Aziel, Shemiramoth, Jehiel, Unni, Eliab, Maaseiah and Benaiah were to play the lyres according to *alamoth*,[e] [21]and Mattithiah, Eliphelehu, Mikneiah, Obed-Edom, Jeiel and Azaziah were to play the harps, directing according to *sheminith*.[e] [22]Kenaniah the head Levite was in charge of the singing; that was his responsibility because he was skillful at it.

[23]Berekiah and Elkanah were to be doorkeepers for the ark. [24]Shebaniah, Joshaphat, Nethanel, Amasai, Zechariah, Benaiah and Eliezer the priests were to blow trumpets before the ark of God.

---

[a]11 Baal Perazim means *the lord who breaks out.*   [b]7 Hebrew *Gershom,* a variant of *Gershon*
[c]18 Three Hebrew manuscripts and most Septuagint manuscripts (see also verse 20 and 1 Chron. 16:5); most Hebrew manuscripts *Zechariah son and* or *Zechariah, Ben and*   [d]18 Hebrew; Septuagint (see also verse 21) *Jeiel and Azaziah*   [e]20,21 Probably a musical term

Obed-Edom and Jehiah were also to be doorkeepers for the ark.

25So David and the elders of Israel and the commanders of units of a thousand went to bring up the ark of the covenant of the Lord from the house of Obed-Edom, with rejoicing. 26Because God had helped the Levites who were carrying the ark of the covenant of the Lord, seven bulls and seven rams were sacrificed. 27Now David was clothed in a robe of fine linen, as were all the Levites who were carrying the ark, and as were the singers, and Kenaniah, who was in charge of the singing of the choirs. David also wore a linen ephod. 28So all Israel brought up the ark of the covenant of the Lord with shouts, with the sounding of rams' horns and trumpets, and of cymbals, and the playing of lyres and harps.

29As the ark of the covenant of the Lord was entering the City of David, Michal daughter of Saul watched from a window. And when she saw King David dancing and celebrating, she despised him in her heart.

16 They brought the ark of God and set it inside the tent that David had pitched for it, and they presented burnt offerings and fellowship offeringsa before God. 2After David had finished sacrificing the burnt offerings and fellowship offerings, he blessed the people in the name of the Lord. 3Then he gave a loaf of bread, a cake of dates and a cake of raisins to each Israelite man and woman.

4He appointed some of the Levites to minister before the ark of the Lord, to make petition, to give thanks, and to praise the Lord, the God of Israel: 5Asaph was the chief, Zechariah second, then Jeiel, Shemiramoth, Jehiel, Mattithiah, Eliab, Benaiah, Obed-Edom and Jeiel. They were to play the lyres and harps, Asaph was to sound the cymbals, 6and Benaiah and Jahaziel the priests were to blow the trumpets regularly before the ark of the covenant of God.

David's Psalm of Thanks

7That day David first committed to Asaph and his associates this psalm of thanks to the Lord:

8Give thanks to the Lord, call on his name;

make known among the nations what he has done.
9Sing to him, sing praise to him; tell of all his wonderful acts.
10Glory in his holy name; let the hearts of those who seek the Lord rejoice.
11Look to the Lord and his strength; seek his face always.
12Remember the wonders he has done, his miracles, and the judgments he pronounced,
13O descendants of Israel his servant, O sons of Jacob, his chosen ones.
14He is the Lord our God; his judgments are in all the earth.
15He remembersb his covenant forever, the word he commanded, for a thousand generations,
16the covenant he made with Abraham, the oath he swore to Isaac.
17He confirmed it to Jacob as a decree, to Israel as an everlasting covenant:
18"To you I will give the land of Canaan as the portion you will inherit."
19When they were but few in number, few indeed, and strangers in it,
20theyc wandered from nation to nation, from one kingdom to another.
21He allowed no man to oppress them; for their sake he rebuked kings:
22"Do not touch my anointed ones; do my prophets no harm."
23Sing to the Lord, all the earth; proclaim his salvation day after day.
24Declare his glory among the nations, his marvelous deeds among all peoples.
25For great is the Lord and most worthy of praise; he is to be feared above all gods.
26For all the gods of the nations are idols, but the Lord made the heavens.
27Splendor and majesty are before him; strength and joy in his dwelling place.
28Ascribe to the Lord, O families of nations, ascribe to the Lord glory and strength,
29 ascribe to the Lord the glory due his name.

a1 Traditionally peace offerings; also in verse 2   b15 Some Septuagint manuscripts (see also Psalm 105:8); Hebrew Remember   c18-20 One Hebrew manuscript, Septuagint and Vulgate (see also Psalm 105:12); most Hebrew manuscripts inherit, / 19though you are but few in number, / few indeed, and strangers in it." / 20They

Bring an offering and come before
　　him;
　　worship the Lord in the splendor of
　　his[a] holiness.
30Tremble before him, all the earth!
　　The world is firmly established; it
　　　cannot be moved.
31Let the heavens rejoice, let the earth
　　be glad;
　　let them say among the nations,
　　　"The Lord reigns!"
32Let the sea resound, and all that is in
　　it;
　　let the fields be jubilant, and
　　　everything in them!
33Then the trees of the forest will sing,
　　they will sing for joy before the
　　　Lord,
　　for he comes to judge the earth.

34Give thanks to the Lord, for he is
　　good;
　　his love endures forever.
35Cry out, "Save us, O God our Savior;
　　gather us and deliver us from the
　　　nations,
　　that we may give thanks to your holy
　　　name,
　　that we may glory in your praise."
36Praise be to the Lord, the God of
　　Israel,
　　from everlasting to everlasting.

Then all the people said "Amen" and
"Praise the Lord."

37David left Asaph and his associates
before the ark of the covenant of the Lord
to minister there regularly, according to
each day's requirements. **38**He also left
Obed-Edom and his sixty-eight associates
to minister with them. Obed-Edom son of
Jeduthun, and also Hosah, were gatekeepers.

39David left Zadok the priest and his fellow priests before the tabernacle of the
Lord at the high place in Gibeon **40**to
present burnt offerings to the Lord on the
altar of burnt offering regularly, morning
and evening, in accordance with everything written in the Law of the Lord,
which he had given Israel. **41**With them
were Heman and Jeduthun and the rest of
those chosen and designated by name to
give thanks to the Lord, "for his love endures forever." **42**Heman and Jeduthun
were responsible for the sounding of the
trumpets and cymbals and for the playing
of the other instruments for sacred song.

The sons of Jeduthun were stationed at
the gate.
43Then all the people left, each for his
own home, and David returned home to
bless his family.

God's Promise to David

17 After David was settled in his palace, he said to Nathan the prophet,
"Here I am, living in a palace of cedar,
while the ark of the covenant of the Lord
is under a tent."

2Nathan replied to David, "Whatever
you have in mind, do it, for God is with
you."

3That night the word of God came to
Nathan, saying:

4"Go and tell my servant David,
'This is what the Lord says: You are
not the one to build me a house to
dwell in. **5**I have not dwelt in a house
from the day I brought Israel up out
of Egypt to this day. I have moved
from one tent site to another, from
one dwelling place to another.
6Wherever I have moved with all the
Israelites, did I ever say to any of their
leaders[b] whom I commanded to
shepherd my people, "Why have you
not built me a house of cedar?" '

7"Now then, tell my servant David,
'This is what the Lord Almighty says:
I took you from the pasture and from
following the flock, to be ruler over
my people Israel. **8**I have been with
you wherever you have gone, and I
have cut off all your enemies from before you. Now I will make your name
like the names of the greatest men of
the earth. **9**And I will provide a place
for my people Israel and will plant
them so that they can have a home of
their own and no longer be disturbed.
Wicked people will not oppress them
anymore, as they did at the beginning
10and have done ever since the time
I appointed leaders over my people
Israel. I will also subdue all your enemies.

" 'I declare to you that the Lord will
build a house for you: **11**When your
days are over and you go to be with
your fathers, I will raise up your offspring to succeed you, one of your
own sons, and I will establish his
kingdom. **12**He is the one who will
build a house for me, and I will estab-

---

[a]29 Or Lord with the splendor of　　[b]6 Traditionally judges; also in verse 10

lish his throne forever. ¹³I will be his father, and he will be my son. I will never take my love away from him, as I took it away from your predecessor. ¹⁴I will set him over my house and my kingdom forever; his throne will be established forever.' "

¹⁵Nathan reported to David all the words of this entire revelation.

David's Prayer

¹⁶Then King David went in and sat before the LORD, and he said:

"Who am I, O LORD God, and what is my family, that you have brought me this far? ¹⁷And as if this were not enough in your sight, O God, you have spoken about the future of the house of your servant. You have

---

THURSDAY

VERSE FOR THE DAY:	AUTHOR:	PASSAGE FOR THE DAY:
1 Chronicles 16:24	Dave Dravecky	1 Chronicles 16:8–36

Declaring God's Glory

AFTER an incredible return to baseball after cancer surgery on his pitching arm, Dave Dravecky's arm broke during the second game he pitched. His arm in a cast, he addressed reporters:

I began with a simple statement, telling the reporters the same thing that I'd been talking about and thinking about constantly for the past twenty-four hours.

I told them that the real miracle in my life had nothing to do with an operation on my arm. It had to do with something Jesus Christ had done for me two thousand years before, when he had died for me and made it possible for me to live in fellowship with him. I just said it as simply as I could, and then I took questions.

With my arm breaking, the focus had shifted. The press had written about my comeback as a miracle, but what could they call this? The opposite of a miracle? If coming back from cancer had lifted people's hopes, should this dash them? That wasn't how I saw it. I saw my life as one continuous adventure in partnership with God. The miracle of my life had begun in Amarillo, and it continued.

I told the writers that I hoped to be able to come back and pitch again. I had no intention of quitting. But that wasn't the basic source of my optimism. My optimism was grounded in Jesus Christ, and that day, particularly, my emotions were flooded with thankfulness for what he'd done for me.

For the press, too, the focus had shifted. Before, they had told the world about my physical recovery. Now they reported on my attitude, as if that were more mysterious and awe-inspiring than my arm.

Additional Scripture Readings:
Romans 8:28–39; 1 Peter 1:3–9

Go to page 428 for your next devotional reading.

looked on me as though I were the most exalted of men, O Lord God.

[18]"What more can David say to you for honoring your servant? For you know your servant, [19]O Lord. For the sake of your servant and according to your will, you have done this great thing and made known all these great promises.

[20]"There is no one like you, O Lord, and there is no God but you, as we have heard with our own ears. [21]And who is like your people Israel—the one nation on earth whose God went out to redeem a people for himself, and to make a name for yourself, and to perform great and awesome wonders by driving out nations from before your people, whom you redeemed from Egypt? [22]You made your people Israel your very own forever, and you, O Lord, have become their God.

[23]"And now, Lord, let the promise you have made concerning your servant and his house be established forever. Do as you promised, [24]so that it will be established and that your name will be great forever. Then men will say, 'The Lord Almighty, the God over Israel, is Israel's God!' And the house of your servant David will be established before you.

[25]"You, my God, have revealed to your servant that you will build a house for him. So your servant has found courage to pray to you. [26]O Lord, you are God! You have promised these good things to your servant. [27]Now you have been pleased to bless the house of your servant, that it may continue forever in your sight; for you, O Lord, have blessed it, and it will be blessed forever."

David's Victories

18 In the course of time, David defeated the Philistines and subdued them, and he took Gath and its surrounding villages from the control of the Philistines.

[2]David also defeated the Moabites, and they became subject to him and brought tribute.

[3]Moreover, David fought Hadadezer king of Zobah, as far as Hamath, when he went to establish his control along the Euphrates River. [4]David captured a thousand of his chariots, seven thousand charioteers and twenty thousand foot soldiers. He hamstrung all but a hundred of the chariot horses.

[5]When the Arameans of Damascus came to help Hadadezer king of Zobah, David struck down twenty-two thousand of them. [6]He put garrisons in the Aramean kingdom of Damascus, and the Arameans became subject to him and brought tribute. The Lord gave David victory everywhere he went.

[7]David took the gold shields carried by the officers of Hadadezer and brought them to Jerusalem. [8]From Tebah[a] and Cun, towns that belonged to Hadadezer, David took a great quantity of bronze, which Solomon used to make the bronze Sea, the pillars and various bronze articles.

[9]When Tou king of Hamath heard that David had defeated the entire army of Hadadezer king of Zobah, [10]he sent his son Hadoram to King David to greet him and congratulate him on his victory in battle over Hadadezer, who had been at war with Tou. Hadoram brought all kinds of articles of gold and silver and bronze.

[11]King David dedicated these articles to the Lord, as he had done with the silver and gold he had taken from all these nations: Edom and Moab, the Ammonites and the Philistines, and Amalek.

[12]Abishai son of Zeruiah struck down eighteen thousand Edomites in the Valley of Salt. [13]He put garrisons in Edom, and all the Edomites became subject to David. The Lord gave David victory everywhere he went.

David's Officials

[14]David reigned over all Israel, doing what was just and right for all his people. [15]Joab son of Zeruiah was over the army; Jehoshaphat son of Ahilud was recorder; [16]Zadok son of Ahitub and Ahimelech[b] son of Abiathar were priests; Shavsha was secretary; [17]Benaiah son of Jehoiada was over the Kerethites and Pelethites; and David's sons were chief officials at the king's side.

The Battle Against the Ammonites

19 In the course of time, Nahash king of the Ammonites died, and his son

---

[a]8 Hebrew *Tibhath*, a variant of *Tebah*   [b]16 Some Hebrew manuscripts, Vulgate and Syriac (see also 2 Samuel 8:17); most Hebrew manuscripts *Abimelech*

succeeded him as king. **2**David thought, "I will show kindness to Hanun son of Nahash, because his father showed kindness to me." So David sent a delegation to express his sympathy to Hanun concerning his father.

When David's men came to Hanun in the land of the Ammonites to express sympathy to him, **3**the Ammonite nobles said to Hanun, "Do you think David is honoring your father by sending men to you to express sympathy? Haven't his men come to you to explore and spy out the country and overthrow it?" **4**So Hanun seized David's men, shaved them, cut off their garments in the middle at the buttocks, and sent them away.

5When someone came and told David about the men, he sent messengers to meet them, for they were greatly humiliated. The king said, "Stay at Jericho till your beards have grown, and then come back."

6When the Ammonites realized that they had become a stench in David's nostrils, Hanun and the Ammonites sent a thousand talents*a* of silver to hire chariots and charioteers from Aram Naharaim,*b* Aram Maacah and Zobah. **7**They hired thirty-two thousand chariots and charioteers, as well as the king of Maacah with his troops, who came and camped near Medeba, while the Ammonites were mustered from their towns and moved out for battle.

8On hearing this, David sent Joab out with the entire army of fighting men. **9**The Ammonites came out and drew up in battle formation at the entrance to their city, while the kings who had come were by themselves in the open country.

10Joab saw that there were battle lines in front of him and behind him; so he selected some of the best troops in Israel and deployed them against the Arameans. **11**He put the rest of the men under the command of Abishai his brother, and they were deployed against the Ammonites. **12**Joab said, "If the Arameans are too strong for me, then you are to rescue me; but if the Ammonites are too strong for you, then I will rescue you. **13**Be strong and let us fight bravely for our people and the cities of our God. The LORD will do what is good in his sight."

14Then Joab and the troops with him advanced to fight the Arameans, and they fled before him. **15**When the Ammonites saw that the Arameans were fleeing, they too fled before his brother Abishai and went inside the city. So Joab went back to Jerusalem.

16After the Arameans saw that they had been routed by Israel, they sent messengers and had Arameans brought from beyond the River,*c* with Shophach the commander of Hadadezer's army leading them.

17When David was told of this, he gathered all Israel and crossed the Jordan; he advanced against them and formed his battle lines opposite them. David formed his lines to meet the Arameans in battle, and they fought against him. **18**But they fled before Israel, and David killed seven thousand of their charioteers and forty thousand of their foot soldiers. He also killed Shophach the commander of their army.

19When the vassals of Hadadezer saw that they had been defeated by Israel, they made peace with David and became subject to him.

So the Arameans were not willing to help the Ammonites anymore.

The Capture of Rabbah

20 In the spring, at the time when kings go off to war, Joab led out the armed forces. He laid waste the land of the Ammonites and went to Rabbah and besieged it, but David remained in Jerusalem. Joab attacked Rabbah and left it in ruins. **2**David took the crown from the head of their king*d*—its weight was found to be a talent*e* of gold, and it was set with precious stones—and it was placed on David's head. He took a great quantity of plunder from the city **3**and brought out the people who were there, consigning them to labor with saws and with iron picks and axes. David did this to all the Ammonite towns. Then David and his entire army returned to Jerusalem.

War With the Philistines

4In the course of time, war broke out with the Philistines, at Gezer. At that time Sibbecai the Hushathite killed Sippai, one of the descendants of the Rephaites, and the Philistines were subjugated.

5In another battle with the Philistines, Elhanan son of Jair killed Lahmi the brother of Goliath the Gittite, who had a spear with a shaft like a weaver's rod.

a6 That is, about 37 tons (about 34 metric tons) the Euphrates   *d2* Or *of Milcom,* that is, Molech   *b6* That is, Northwest Mesopotamia   *c16* That is,   *e2* That is, about 75 pounds (about 34 kilograms)

6In still another battle, which took place at Gath, there was a huge man with six fingers on each hand and six toes on each foot—twenty-four in all. He also was descended from Rapha. **7**When he taunted Israel, Jonathan son of Shimea, David's brother, killed him.

8These were descendants of Rapha in Gath, and they fell at the hands of David and his men.

David Numbers the Fighting Men

21 Satan rose up against Israel and incited David to take a census of Israel. **2**So David said to Joab and the commanders of the troops, "Go and count the Israelites from Beersheba to Dan. Then report back to me so that I may know how many there are."

3But Joab replied, "May the LORD multiply his troops a hundred times over. My lord the king, are they not all my lord's subjects? Why does my lord want to do this? Why should he bring guilt on Israel?"

4The king's word, however, overruled Joab; so Joab left and went throughout Israel and then came back to Jerusalem. **5**Joab reported the number of the fighting men to David: In all Israel there were one million one hundred thousand men who could handle a sword, including four hundred and seventy thousand in Judah.

6But Joab did not include Levi and Benjamin in the numbering, because the king's command was repulsive to him. **7**This command was also evil in the sight of God; so he punished Israel.

8Then David said to God, "I have sinned greatly by doing this. Now, I beg you, take away the guilt of your servant. I have done a very foolish thing."

9The LORD said to Gad, David's seer, **10**"Go and tell David, 'This is what the LORD says: I am giving you three options. Choose one of them for me to carry out against you.' "

11So Gad went to David and said to him, "This is what the LORD says: 'Take your choice: **12**three years of famine, three months of being swept away*a* before your enemies, with their swords overtaking you, or three days of the sword of the LORD—days of plague in the land, with the angel of the LORD ravaging every part of Israel.' Now then, decide how I should answer the one who sent me."

13David said to Gad, "I am in deep distress. Let me fall into the hands of the LORD, for his mercy is very great; but do not let me fall into the hands of men."

14So the LORD sent a plague on Israel, and seventy thousand men of Israel fell dead. **15**And God sent an angel to destroy Jerusalem. But as the angel was doing so, the LORD saw it and was grieved because of the calamity and said to the angel who was destroying the people, "Enough! Withdraw your hand." The angel of the LORD was then standing at the threshing floor of Araunah*b* the Jebusite.

16David looked up and saw the angel of the LORD standing between heaven and earth, with a drawn sword in his hand extended over Jerusalem. Then David and the elders, clothed in sackcloth, fell facedown.

17David said to God, "Was it not I who ordered the fighting men to be counted? I am the one who has sinned and done wrong. These are but sheep. What have they done? O LORD my God, let your hand fall upon me and my family, but do not let this plague remain on your people."

18Then the angel of the LORD ordered Gad to tell David to go up and build an altar to the LORD on the threshing floor of Araunah the Jebusite. **19**So David went up in obedience to the word that Gad had spoken in the name of the LORD.

20While Araunah was threshing wheat, he turned and saw the angel; his four sons who were with him hid themselves. **21**Then David approached, and when Araunah looked and saw him, he left the threshing floor and bowed down before David with his face to the ground.

22David said to him, "Let me have the site of your threshing floor so I can build an altar to the LORD, that the plague on the people may be stopped. Sell it to me at the full price."

23Araunah said to David, "Take it! Let my lord the king do whatever pleases him. Look, I will give the oxen for the burnt offerings, the threshing sledges for the wood, and the wheat for the grain offering. I will give all this."

24But King David replied to Araunah, "No, I insist on paying the full price. I will not take for the LORD what is yours, or sacrifice a burnt offering that costs me nothing."

25So David paid Araunah six hundred shekels*c* of gold for the site. **26**David built

---

a12 Hebrew; Septuagint and Vulgate (see also 2 Samuel 24:13) *of fleeing*   *b15* Hebrew *Ornan*, a variant of *Araunah*; also in verses 18-28   *c25* That is, about 15 pounds (about 7 kilograms) an altar to the LORD there and sacrificed burnt offerings and fellowship offerings.*a* He called on the LORD, and the LORD answered him with fire from heaven on the altar of burnt offering.

²⁷Then the LORD spoke to the angel, and he put his sword back into its sheath. ²⁸At that time, when David saw that the LORD had answered him on the threshing floor of Araunah the Jebusite, he offered sacrifices there. ²⁹The tabernacle of the LORD, which Moses had made in the desert, and the altar of burnt offering were at that time on the high place at Gibeon. ³⁰But David could not go before it to inquire of God, because he was afraid of the sword of the angel of the LORD.

22 Then David said, "The house of the LORD God is to be here, and also the altar of burnt offering for Israel."

Preparations for the Temple

²So David gave orders to assemble the aliens living in Israel, and from among them he appointed stonecutters to prepare dressed stone for building the house of God. ³He provided a large amount of iron to make nails for the doors of the gateways and for the fittings, and more bronze than could be weighed. ⁴He also provided more cedar logs than could be counted, for the Sidonians and Tyrians had brought large numbers of them to David.

⁵David said, "My son Solomon is young and inexperienced, and the house to be built for the LORD should be of great magnificence and fame and splendor in the sight of all the nations. Therefore I will make preparations for it." So David made extensive preparations before his death.

⁶Then he called for his son Solomon and charged him to build a house for the LORD, the God of Israel. ⁷David said to Solomon: "My son, I had it in my heart to build a house for the Name of the LORD my God. ⁸But this word of the LORD came to me: 'You have shed much blood and have fought many wars. You are not to build a house for my Name, because you have shed much blood on the earth in my sight. ⁹But you will have a son who will be a man of peace and rest, and I will give him rest from all his enemies on every side. His name will be Solomon,*b* and I will grant Israel peace and quiet during his reign. ¹⁰He is the one who will build a house for my Name. He will be my son, and I will be his father. And I will establish the throne of his kingdom over Israel forever.'

¹¹"Now, my son, the LORD be with you, and may you have success and build the house of the LORD your God, as he said you would. ¹²May the LORD give you discretion and understanding when he puts you in command over Israel, so that you may keep the law of the LORD your God. ¹³Then you will have success if you are careful to observe the decrees and laws that the LORD gave Moses for Israel. Be strong and courageous. Do not be afraid or discouraged.

¹⁴"I have taken great pains to provide for the temple of the LORD a hundred thousand talents*c* of gold, a million talents*d* of silver, quantities of bronze and iron too great to be weighed, and wood and stone. And you may add to them. ¹⁵You have many workmen: stonecutters, masons and carpenters, as well as men skilled in every kind of work ¹⁶in gold and silver, bronze and iron—craftsmen beyond number. Now begin the work, and the LORD be with you."

¹⁷Then David ordered all the leaders of Israel to help his son Solomon. ¹⁸He said to them, "Is not the LORD your God with you? And has he not granted you rest on every side? For he has handed the inhabitants of the land over to me, and the land is subject to the LORD and to his people. ¹⁹Now devote your heart and soul to seeking the LORD your God. Begin to build the sanctuary of the LORD God, so that you may bring the ark of the covenant of the LORD and the sacred articles belonging to God into the temple that will be built for the Name of the LORD."

The Levites

23 When David was old and full of years, he made his son Solomon king over Israel.

²He also gathered together all the leaders of Israel, as well as the priests and Levites. ³The Levites thirty years old or more were counted, and the total number of men was thirty-eight thousand. ⁴David said, "Of these, twenty-four thousand are to supervise the work of the temple of the LORD and six thousand are to be officials

and judges. **5**Four thousand are to be gatekeepers and four thousand are to praise the LORD with the musical instruments I have provided for that purpose."

6David divided the Levites into groups corresponding to the sons of Levi: Gershon, Kohath and Merari.

Gershonites

7Belonging to the Gershonites:
Ladan and Shimei.

8The sons of Ladan:
Jehiel the first, Zetham and Joel — three in all.

9The sons of Shimei:
Shelomoth, Haziel and Haran — three in all.
These were the heads of the families of Ladan.

10And the sons of Shimei:
Jahath, Ziza,*a* Jeush and Beriah.
These were the sons of Shimei — four in all.

11Jahath was the first and Ziza the second, but Jeush and Beriah did not have many sons; so they were counted as one family with one assignment.

Kohathites

12The sons of Kohath:
Amram, Izhar, Hebron and Uzziel — four in all.

13The sons of Amram:
Aaron and Moses.
Aaron was set apart, he and his descendants forever, to consecrate the most holy things, to offer sacrifices before the LORD, to minister before him and to pronounce blessings in his name forever.

14The sons of Moses the man of God were counted as part of the tribe of Levi.

15The sons of Moses:
Gershom and Eliezer.

16The descendants of Gershom:
Shubael was the first.

17The descendants of Eliezer:
Rehabiah was the first.
Eliezer had no other sons, but the sons of Rehabiah were very numerous.

18The sons of Izhar:
Shelomith was the first.

19The sons of Hebron:
Jeriah the first, Amariah the sec-

ond, Jahaziel the third and Jekameam the fourth.

20The sons of Uzziel:
Micah the first and Isshiah the second.

Merarites

21The sons of Merari:
Mahli and Mushi.
The sons of Mahli:
Eleazar and Kish.

22Eleazar died without having sons: he had only daughters. Their cousins, the sons of Kish, married them.

23The sons of Mushi:
Mahli, Eder and Jerimoth — three in all.

24These were the descendants of Levi by their families — the heads of families as they were registered under their names and counted individually, that is, the workers twenty years old or more who served in the temple of the LORD. **25**For David had said, "Since the LORD, the God of Israel, has granted rest to his people and has come to dwell in Jerusalem forever, **26**the Levites no longer need to carry the tabernacle or any of the articles used in its service." **27**According to the last instructions of David, the Levites were counted from those twenty years old or more.

28The duty of the Levites was to help Aaron's descendants in the service of the temple of the LORD: to be in charge of the courtyards, the side rooms, the purification of all sacred things and the performance of other duties at the house of God. **29**They were in charge of the bread set out on the table, the flour for the grain offerings, the unleavened wafers, the baking and the mixing, and all measurements of quantity and size. **30**They were also to stand every morning to thank and praise the LORD. They were to do the same in the evening **31**and whenever burnt offerings were presented to the LORD on Sabbaths and at New Moon festivals and at appointed feasts. They were to serve before the LORD regularly in the proper number and in the way prescribed for them.

32And so the Levites carried out their responsibilities for the Tent of Meeting, for the Holy Place and, under their brothers the descendants of Aaron, for the service of the temple of the LORD.

a 10 One Hebrew manuscript, Septuagint and Vulgate (see also verse 11); most Hebrew manuscripts *Zina*

The Divisions of Priests

24 These were the divisions of the sons of Aaron:

The sons of Aaron were Nadab, Abihu, Eleazar and Ithamar. [2]But Nadab and Abihu died before their father did, and they had no sons; so Eleazar and Ithamar served as the priests. [3]With the help of Zadok a descendant of Eleazar and Ahimelech a descendant of Ithamar, David separated them into divisions for their appointed order of ministering. [4]A larger number of leaders were found among Eleazar's descendants than among Ithamar's, and they were divided accordingly: sixteen heads of families from Eleazar's descendants and eight heads of families from Ithamar's descendants. [5]They divided them impartially by drawing lots, for there were officials of the sanctuary and officials of God among the descendants of both Eleazar and Ithamar.

[6]The scribe Shemaiah son of Nethanel, a Levite, recorded their names in the presence of the king and of the officials: Zadok the priest, Ahimelech son of Abiathar and the heads of families of the priests and of the Levites — one family being taken from Eleazar and then one from Ithamar.

[7]The first lot fell to Jehoiarib,
  the second to Jedaiah,
[8]the third to Harim,
  the fourth to Seorim,
[9]the fifth to Malkijah,
  the sixth to Mijamin,
[10]the seventh to Hakkoz,
  the eighth to Abijah,
[11]the ninth to Jeshua,
  the tenth to Shecaniah,
[12]the eleventh to Eliashib,
  the twelfth to Jakim,
[13]the thirteenth to Huppah,
  the fourteenth to Jeshebeab,
[14]the fifteenth to Bilgah,
  the sixteenth to Immer,
[15]the seventeenth to Hezir,
  the eighteenth to Happizzez,
[16]the nineteenth to Pethahiah,
  the twentieth to Jehezkel,
[17]the twenty-first to Jakin,
  the twenty-second to Gamul,
[18]the twenty-third to Delaiah
  and the twenty-fourth to Maaziah.

[19]This was their appointed order of ministering when they entered the temple of the LORD, according to the regulations prescribed for them by their forefather Aaron, as the LORD, the God of Israel, had commanded him.

The Rest of the Levites

[20]As for the rest of the descendants of Levi:
  from the sons of Amram: Shubael;
    from the sons of Shubael: Jehdeiah.
  [21]As for Rehabiah, from his sons:
    Isshiah was the first.
[22]From the Izharites: Shelomoth;
  from the sons of Shelomoth: Jahath.
[23]The sons of Hebron: Jeriah the first,[a] Amariah the second, Jahaziel the third and Jekameam the fourth.
[24]The son of Uzziel: Micah;
  from the sons of Micah: Shamir.
  [25]The brother of Micah: Isshiah;
  from the sons of Isshiah: Zechariah.
[26]The sons of Merari: Mahli and Mushi.
  The son of Jaaziah: Beno.
[27]The sons of Merari:
  from Jaaziah: Beno, Shoham, Zaccur and Ibri.
[28]From Mahli: Eleazar, who had no sons.
[29]From Kish: the son of Kish: Jerahmeel.
[30]And the sons of Mushi: Mahli, Eder and Jerimoth.

These were the Levites, according to their families. [31]They also cast lots, just as their brothers the descendants of Aaron did, in the presence of King David and of Zadok, Ahimelech, and the heads of families of the priests and of the Levites. The families of the oldest brother were treated the same as those of the youngest.

The Singers

25 David, together with the commanders of the army, set apart some of the sons of Asaph, Heman and Jeduthun for the ministry of prophesying, accompanied by harps, lyres and cymbals. Here is the list of the men who performed this service:

[2]From the sons of Asaph:
  Zaccur, Joseph, Nethaniah and Asa-

---

*a*23 Two Hebrew manuscripts and some Septuagint manuscripts (see also 1 Chron. 23:19); most Hebrew manuscripts *The sons of Jeriah:*

relah. The sons of Asaph were under the supervision of Asaph, who prophesied under the king's supervision.

³As for Jeduthun, from his sons:
Gedaliah, Zeri, Jeshaiah, Shimei,ᵃ Hashabiah and Mattithiah, six in all, under the supervision of their father Jeduthun, who prophesied, using the harp in thanking and praising the LORD.

⁴As for Heman, from his sons:
Bukkiah, Mattaniah, Uzziel, Shubael and Jerimoth; Hananiah, Hanani, Eliathah, Giddalti and Romamti-Ezer; Joshbekashah, Mallothi, Hothir and Mahazioth. ⁵All these were sons of Heman the king's seer. They were given him through the promises of God to exalt him.ᵇ God gave Heman fourteen sons and three daughters.

⁶All these men were under the supervision of their fathers for the music of the temple of the LORD, with cymbals, lyres and harps, for the ministry at the house of God. Asaph, Jeduthun and Heman were under the supervision of the king. ⁷Along with their relatives—all of them trained and skilled in music for the LORD—they numbered 288. ⁸Young and old alike, teacher as well as student, cast lots for their duties.

⁹The first lot, which was for Asaph, fell to Joseph,
his sons and relatives,ᶜ   12ᵈ
the second to Gedaliah,
he and his relatives and sons,   12
¹⁰the third to Zaccur,
his sons and relatives,   12
¹¹the fourth to Izri,ᵉ
his sons and relatives,   12
¹²the fifth to Nethaniah,
his sons and relatives,   12
¹³the sixth to Bukkiah,
his sons and relatives,   12
¹⁴the seventh to Jesarelah,ᶠ
his sons and relatives,   12
¹⁵the eighth to Jeshaiah,
his sons and relatives,   12
¹⁶the ninth to Mattaniah,
his sons and relatives,   12
¹⁷the tenth to Shimei,
his sons and relatives,   12

¹⁸the eleventh to Azarel,ᵍ
his sons and relatives,   12
¹⁹the twelfth to Hashabiah,
his sons and relatives,   12
²⁰the thirteenth to Shubael,
his sons and relatives,   12
²¹the fourteenth to Mattithiah,
his sons and relatives,   12
²²the fifteenth to Jerimoth,
his sons and relatives,   12
²³the sixteenth to Hananiah,
his sons and relatives,   12
²⁴the seventeenth to Joshbekashah,
his sons and relatives,   12
²⁵the eighteenth to Hanani,
his sons and relatives,   12
²⁶the nineteenth to Mallothi,
his sons and relatives,   12
²⁷the twentieth to Eliathah,
his sons and relatives,   12
²⁸the twenty-first to Hothir,
his sons and relatives,   12
²⁹the twenty-second to Giddalti,
his sons and relatives,   12
³⁰the twenty-third to Mahazioth,
his sons and relatives,   12
³¹the twenty-fourth to Romamti-Ezer,
his sons and relatives,   12

The Gatekeepers

26 The divisions of the gatekeepers:

From the Korahites: Meshelemiah son of Kore, one of the sons of Asaph.

²Meshelemiah had sons:
Zechariah the firstborn,
Jediael the second,
Zebadiah the third,
Jathniel the fourth,
³Elam the fifth,
Jehohanan the sixth
and Eliehoenai the seventh.

⁴Obed-Edom also had sons:
Shemaiah the firstborn,
Jehozabad the second,
Joah the third,
Sacar the fourth,
Nethanel the fifth,
⁵Ammiel the sixth,
Issachar the seventh
and Peullethai the eighth.

ᵃ3 One Hebrew manuscript and some Septuagint manuscripts (see also verse 17); most Hebrew manuscripts do not have *Shimei*.   ᵇ5 Hebrew *exalt the horn*   ᶜ9 See Septuagint; Hebrew does not have *his sons and relatives*.   ᵈ9 See the total in verse 7; Hebrew does not have *twelve*.   ᵉ11 A variant of *Zeri*   ᶠ14 A variant of *Asarelah*   ᵍ18 A variant of *Uzziel*

(For God had blessed Obed-Edom.)

6His son Shemaiah also had sons, who were leaders in their father's family because they were very capable men. **7**The sons of Shemaiah: Othni, Rephael, Obed and Elzabad; his relatives Elihu and Semakiah were also able men. **8**All these were descendants of Obed-Edom; they and their sons and their relatives were capable men with the strength to do the work — descendants of Obed-Edom, 62 in all. **9**Meshelemiah had sons and relatives, who were able men — 18 in all.

10Hosah the Merarite had sons: Shimri the first (although he was not the firstborn, his father had appointed him the first), **11**Hilkiah the second, Tabaliah the third and Zechariah the fourth. The sons and relatives of Hosah were 13 in all.

12These divisions of the gatekeepers, through their chief men, had duties for ministering in the temple of the LORD, just as their relatives had. **13**Lots were cast for each gate, according to their families, young and old alike.

14The lot for the East Gate fell to Shelemiah.*a* Then lots were cast for his son Zechariah, a wise counselor, and the lot for the North Gate fell to him. **15**The lot for the South Gate fell to Obed-Edom, and the lot for the storehouse fell to his sons. **16**The lots for the West Gate and the Shalleketh Gate on the upper road fell to Shuppim and Hosah.

Guard was alongside of guard: **17**There were six Levites a day on the east, four a day on the north, four a day on the south and two at a time at the storehouse. **18**As for the court to the west, there were four at the road and two at the court itself.

19These were the divisions of the gatekeepers who were descendants of Korah and Merari.

The Treasurers and Other Officials

20Their fellow Levites were*b* in charge of the treasuries of the house of God and the treasuries for the dedicated things. **21**The descendants of Ladan, who were Gershonites through Ladan and who were heads of families belonging to Ladan the Gershonite, were Jehieli, **22**the sons of Jehieli, Zetham and his brother Joel. They were in charge of the treasuries of the temple of the LORD.

23From the Amramites, the Izharites, the Hebronites and the Uzzielites:

24Shubael, a descendant of Gershom son of Moses, was the officer in charge of the treasuries. **25**His relatives through Eliezer: Rehabiah his son, Jeshaiah his son, Joram his son, Zicri his son and Shelomith his son. **26**Shelomith and his relatives were in charge of all the treasuries for the things dedicated by King David, by the heads of families who were the commanders of thousands and commanders of hundreds, and by the other army commanders. **27**Some of the plunder taken in battle they dedicated for the repair of the temple of the LORD. **28**And everything dedicated by Samuel the seer and by Saul son of Kish, Abner son of Ner and Joab son of Zeruiah, and all the other dedicated things were in the care of Shelomith and his relatives.

29From the Izharites: Kenaniah and his sons were assigned duties away from the temple, as officials and judges over Israel.

30From the Hebronites: Hashabiah and his relatives — seventeen hundred able men — were responsible in Israel west of the Jordan for all the work of the LORD and for the king's service. **31**As for the Hebronites, Jeriah was their chief according to the genealogical records of their families. In the fortieth year of David's reign a search was made in the records, and capable men among the Hebronites were found at Jazer in Gilead. **32**Jeriah had twenty-seven hundred relatives, who were able men and heads of families, and King David put them in charge of the Reubenites, the Gadites and the half-tribe of Manasseh for every matter pertaining to God and for the affairs of the king.

Army Divisions

27 This is the list of the Israelites — heads of families, commanders of

---

a14 A variant of *Meshelemiah*   *b20* Septuagint; Hebrew *As for the Levites, Ahijah was* thousands and commanders of hundreds, and their officers, who served the king in all that concerned the army divisions that were on duty month by month throughout the year. Each division consisted of 24,000 men.

2In charge of the first division, for the first month, was Jashobeam son of Zabdiel. There were 24,000 men in his division. 3He was a descendant of Perez and chief of all the army officers for the first month.
4In charge of the division for the second month was Dodai the Ahohite; Mikloth was the leader of his division. There were 24,000 men in his division.
5The third army commander, for the third month, was Benaiah son of Jehoiada the priest. He was chief and there were 24,000 men in his division. 6This was the Benaiah who was a mighty man among the Thirty and was over the Thirty. His son Ammizabad was in charge of his division.
7The fourth, for the fourth month, was Asahel the brother of Joab; his son Zebadiah was his successor. There were 24,000 men in his division.
8The fifth, for the fifth month, was the commander Shamhuth the Izrahite. There were 24,000 men in his division.
9The sixth, for the sixth month, was Ira the son of Ikkesh the Tekoite. There were 24,000 men in his division.
10The seventh, for the seventh month, was Helez the Pelonite, an Ephraimite. There were 24,000 men in his division.
11The eighth, for the eighth month, was Sibbecai the Hushathite, a Zerahite. There were 24,000 men in his division.
12The ninth, for the ninth month, was Abiezer the Anathothite, a Benjamite. There were 24,000 men in his division.
13The tenth, for the tenth month, was Maharai the Netophathite, a Zerahite. There were 24,000 men in his division.
14The eleventh, for the eleventh month, was Benaiah the Pirathonite, an Ephraimite. There were 24,000 men in his division.
15The twelfth, for the twelfth month, was

Heldai the Netophathite, from the family of Othniel. There were 24,000 men in his division.

Officers of the Tribes

16The officers over the tribes of Israel:

over the Reubenites: Eliezer son of Zicri;
over the Simeonites: Shephatiah son of Maacah;
17over Levi: Hashabiah son of Kemuel;
over Aaron: Zadok;
18over Judah: Elihu, a brother of David;
over Issachar: Omri son of Michael;
19over Zebulun: Ishmaiah son of Obadiah;
over Naphtali: Jerimoth son of Azriel;
20over the Ephraimites: Hoshea son of Azaziah;
over half the tribe of Manasseh: Joel son of Pedaiah;
21over the half-tribe of Manasseh in Gilead: Iddo son of Zechariah;
over Benjamin: Jaasiel son of Abner;
22over Dan: Azarel son of Jeroham.
These were the officers over the tribes of Israel.

23David did not take the number of the men twenty years old or less, because the LORD had promised to make Israel as numerous as the stars in the sky. 24Joab son of Zeruiah began to count the men but did not finish. Wrath came on Israel on account of this numbering, and the number was not entered in the book[a] of the annals of King David.

The King's Overseers

25Azmaveth son of Adiel was in charge of the royal storehouses.
Jonathan son of Uzziah was in charge of the storehouses in the outlying districts, in the towns, the villages and the watchtowers.
26Ezri son of Kelub was in charge of the field workers who farmed the land.
27Shimei the Ramathite was in charge of the vineyards.
Zabdi the Shiphmite was in charge of the produce of the vineyards for the wine vats.
28Baal-Hanan the Gederite was in charge of the olive and sycamore-fig trees in the western foothills.

a24 Septuagint; Hebrew number

Joash was in charge of the supplies of olive oil.

²⁹Shitrai the Sharonite was in charge of the herds grazing in Sharon.

Shaphat son of Adlai was in charge of the herds in the valleys.

³⁰Obil the Ishmaelite was in charge of the camels.

Jehdeiah the Meronothite was in charge of the donkeys.

³¹Jaziz the Hagrite was in charge of the flocks.

All these were the officials in charge of King David's property.

³²Jonathan, David's uncle, was a counselor, a man of insight and a scribe. Jehiel son of Hacmoni took care of the king's sons.

³³Ahithophel was the king's counselor. Hushai the Arkite was the king's friend. ³⁴Ahithophel was succeeded by Jehoiada son of Benaiah and by Abiathar.

Joab was the commander of the royal army.

David's Plans for the Temple

28 David summoned all the officials of Israel to assemble at Jerusalem: the officers over the tribes, the commanders of the divisions in the service of the king, the commanders of thousands and commanders of hundreds, and the officials in charge of all the property and livestock belonging to the king and his sons, together with the palace officials, the mighty men and all the brave warriors.

²King David rose to his feet and said: "Listen to me, my brothers and my people. I had it in my heart to build a house as a place of rest for the ark of the covenant of the LORD, for the footstool of our God, and I made plans to build it. ³But God said to me, 'You are not to build a house for my Name, because you are a warrior and have shed blood.'

⁴"Yet the LORD, the God of Israel, chose me from my whole family to be king over Israel forever. He chose Judah as leader, and from the house of Judah he chose my family, and from my father's sons he was pleased to make me king over all Israel. ⁵Of all my sons—and the LORD has given me many—he has chosen my son Solomon to sit on the throne of the kingdom of the LORD over Israel. ⁶He said to me: 'Solomon your son is the one who will build my house and my courts, for I have chosen him to be my son, and I will be his father. ⁷I will establish his kingdom forever if he is unswerving in carrying out my commands and laws, as is being done at this time.'

⁸"So now I charge you in the sight of all Israel and of the assembly of the LORD, and in the hearing of our God: Be careful to follow all the commands of the LORD your God, that you may possess this good land and pass it on as an inheritance to your descendants forever.

⁹"And you, my son Solomon, acknowledge the God of your father, and serve him with wholehearted devotion and with a willing mind, for the LORD searches every heart and understands every motive behind the thoughts. If you seek him, he will be found by you; but if you forsake him, he will reject you forever. ¹⁰Consider now, for the LORD has chosen you to build a temple as a sanctuary. Be strong and do the work."

¹¹Then David gave his son Solomon the plans for the portico of the temple, its buildings, its storerooms, its upper parts, its inner rooms and the place of atonement. ¹²He gave him the plans of all that the Spirit had put in his mind for the courts of the temple of the LORD and all the surrounding rooms, for the treasuries of the temple of God and for the treasuries for the dedicated things. ¹³He gave him instructions for the divisions of the priests and Levites, and for all the work of serving in the temple of the LORD, as well as for all the articles to be used in its service. ¹⁴He designated the weight of gold for all the gold articles to be used in various kinds of service, and the weight of silver for all the silver articles to be used in various kinds of service: ¹⁵the weight of gold for the gold lampstands and their lamps, with the weight for each lampstand and its lamps; and the weight of silver for each silver lampstand and its lamps, according to the use of each lampstand; ¹⁶the weight of gold for each table for consecrated bread; the weight of silver for the silver tables; ¹⁷the weight of pure gold for the forks, sprinkling bowls and pitchers; the weight of gold for each gold dish; the weight of silver for each silver dish; ¹⁸and the weight of the refined gold for the altar of incense. He also gave him the plan for the chariot, that is, the cherubim of gold that spread their wings and shelter the ark of the covenant of the LORD.

¹⁹"All this," David said, "I have in writing from the hand of the LORD upon me, and he gave me understanding in all the details of the plan."

20David also said to Solomon his son, "Be strong and courageous, and do the work. Do not be afraid or discouraged, for the LORD God, my God, is with you. He will not fail you or forsake you until all the work for the service of the temple of the LORD is finished. 21The divisions of the priests and Levites are ready for all the work on the temple of God, and every willing man skilled in any craft will help you in all the work. The officials and all the people will obey your every command."

Gifts for Building the Temple

29 Then King David said to the whole assembly: "My son Solomon, the one whom God has chosen, is young and inexperienced. The task is great, because this palatial structure is not for man but for the LORD God. 2With all my resources I have provided for the temple of my God—gold for the gold work, silver for the silver, bronze for the bronze, iron for the iron and wood for the wood, as well as onyx for the settings, turquoise,*a* stones of various colors, and all kinds of fine stone and marble—all of these in large quantities. 3Besides, in my devotion to the temple of my God I now give my personal treasures of gold and silver for the temple of my God, over and above everything I have provided for this holy temple: 4three thousand talents*b* of gold (gold of Ophir) and seven thousand talents*c* of refined silver, for the overlaying of the walls of the buildings, 5for the gold work and the silver work, and for all the work to be done by the craftsmen. Now, who is willing to consecrate himself today to the LORD?"

6Then the leaders of families, the officers of the tribes of Israel, the commanders of thousands and commanders of hundreds, and the officials in charge of the king's work gave willingly. 7They gave toward the work on the temple of God five thousand talents*d* and ten thousand darics*e* of gold, ten thousand talents*f* of silver, eighteen thousand talents*g* of bronze and a hundred thousand talents*h* of iron. 8Any who had precious stones gave them to the treasury of the temple of the LORD in the custody of Jehiel the Gershonite.

9The people rejoiced at the willing response of their leaders, for they had given freely and wholeheartedly to the LORD. David the king also rejoiced greatly.

David's Prayer

10David praised the LORD in the presence of the whole assembly, saying,

"Praise be to you, O LORD,
  God of our father Israel,
  from everlasting to everlasting.
11Yours, O LORD, is the greatness and
    the power
  and the glory and the majesty and
    the splendor,
  for everything in heaven and earth
    is yours.
Yours, O LORD, is the kingdom;
  you are exalted as head over all.
12Wealth and honor come from you;
  you are the ruler of all things.
In your hands are strength and power
  to exalt and give strength to all.
13Now, our God, we give you thanks,
  and praise your glorious name.

14"But who am I, and who are my people, that we should be able to give as generously as this? Everything comes from you, and we have given you only what comes from your hand. 15We are aliens and strangers in your sight, as were all our forefathers. Our days on earth are like a shadow, without hope. 16O LORD our God, as for all this abundance that we have provided for building you a temple for your Holy Name, it comes from your hand, and all of it belongs to you. 17I know, my God, that you test the heart and are pleased with integrity. All these things have I given willingly and with honest intent. And now I have seen with joy how willingly your people who are here have given to you. 18O LORD, God of our fathers Abraham, Isaac and Israel, keep this desire in the hearts of your people forever, and keep their hearts loyal to you. 19And give my son Solomon the wholehearted devotion to keep your commands, requirements and decrees and to do everything to build the palatial structure for which I have provided."

20Then David said to the whole assem-

---

*a*2 The meaning of the Hebrew for this word is uncertain.   *b*4 That is, about 110 tons (about 100 metric tons)   *c*4 That is, about 260 tons (about 240 metric tons)   *d*7 That is, about 190 tons (about 170 metric tons)   *e*7 That is, about 185 pounds (about 84 kilograms)   *f*7 That is, about 375 tons (about 345 metric tons)   *g*7 That is, about 675 tons (about 610 metric tons)   *h*7 That is, about 3,750 tons (about 3,450 metric tons) bly, "Praise the LORD your God." So they all praised the LORD, the God of their fathers; they bowed low and fell prostrate before the LORD and the king.

Solomon Acknowledged as King

²¹The next day they made sacrifices to the LORD and presented burnt offerings to him: a thousand bulls, a thousand rams and a thousand male lambs, together with their drink offerings, and other sacrifices in abundance for all Israel. ²²They ate and drank with great joy in the presence of the LORD that day.

Then they acknowledged Solomon son of David as king a second time, anointing him before the LORD to be ruler and Zadok to be priest. ²³So Solomon sat on the throne of the LORD as king in place of his father David. He prospered and all Israel obeyed him. ²⁴All the officers and mighty men, as well as all of King David's sons, pledged their submission to King Solomon.

²⁵The LORD highly exalted Solomon in the sight of all Israel and bestowed on him royal splendor such as no king over Israel ever had before.

FRIDAY

VERSE FOR THE DAY:	AUTHOR:	PASSAGE FOR THE DAY:
1 Chronicles 29:17	Mike Singletary	1 Chronicles 29:14–19

Be Men of Integrity

A FATHER has to be careful of his promises, because a real man will follow through. There must be a careful balance between centering your whole existence around your kids and nurturing them properly. A well-adjusted child will know that there are times when he or she cannot be with his parents, when Daddy or Mommy have to work. The key is priorities. If you set a date with your child and something comes up at the office, you'd better see if you can postpone the office business. Otherwise, you're telling the child exactly where he fits in your life.

Parents need to be careful not to build their whole lives on their children, because one day those children will be gone. They will find husbands and wives to devote themselves to, and you will be left with each other. Be sure to spend enough alone time with each other now so that you won't have to get reacquainted later.

A real man is a man of integrity. That means going all out in everything he does. When he says something, you can count on it, take it to the bank. If I say I'm going to do something, you can consider it done. The first time I violate that, my credibility is shot. Our reputations are only as good as our last performances.

Unless the real men of this country—and there aren't many left—come together and align themselves under God, we're headed for catastrophe. God is looking for men who will obey and be what he wants them to be.

Additional Scripture Readings:
Ezekiel 22:23–31; 1 John 1:5—2:6

Go to page 433 for your next devotional reading.

The Death of David

²⁶David son of Jesse was king over all Israel. ²⁷He ruled over Israel forty years—seven in Hebron and thirty-three in Jerusalem. ²⁸He died at a good old age, having enjoyed long life, wealth and honor. His son Solomon succeeded him as king.

²⁹As for the events of King David's reign, from beginning to end, they are written in the records of Samuel the seer, the records of Nathan the prophet and the records of Gad the seer, ³⁰together with the details of his reign and power, and the circumstances that surrounded him and Israel and the kingdoms of all the other lands.

*T*HIS book continues the history of God's people begun in 1 Chronicles, concentrating exclusively on the nation of Judah. It stresses God's powerful presence in the lives of those kings who believe the word of the Lord and obey his laws. Even though the people are eventually carried away to Babylon, the book ends with a reminder of God's faithfulness in bringing them back. As you read this book, think about how God keeps his promise to surround you with his love in spite of your sin.

2 CHRONICLES

Solomon Asks for Wisdom

1 Solomon son of David established himself firmly over his kingdom, for the Lord his God was with him and made him exceedingly great.

²Then Solomon spoke to all Israel—to the commanders of thousands and commanders of hundreds, to the judges and to all the leaders in Israel, the heads of families— ³and Solomon and the whole assembly went to the high place at Gibeon, for God's Tent of Meeting was there, which Moses the Lord's servant had made in the desert. ⁴Now David had brought up the ark of God from Kiriath Jearim to the place he had prepared for it, because he had pitched a tent for it in Jerusalem. ⁵But the bronze altar that Bezalel son of Uri, the son of Hur, had made was in Gibeon in front of the tabernacle of the Lord; so Solomon and the assembly inquired of him there. ⁶Solomon went up to the bronze altar before the Lord in the Tent of Meeting and offered a thousand burnt offerings on it.

⁷That night God appeared to Solomon and said to him, "Ask for whatever you want me to give you."

⁸Solomon answered God, "You have shown great kindness to David my father

and have made me king in his place. **9**Now, LORD God, let your promise to my father David be confirmed, for you have made me king over a people who are as numerous as the dust of the earth. **10**Give me wisdom and knowledge, that I may lead this people, for who is able to govern this great people of yours?"

11God said to Solomon, "Since this is your heart's desire and you have not asked for wealth, riches or honor, nor for the death of your enemies, and since you have not asked for a long life but for wisdom and knowledge to govern my people over whom I have made you king, **12**therefore wisdom and knowledge will be given you. And I will also give you wealth, riches and honor, such as no king who was before you ever had and none after you will have."

13Then Solomon went to Jerusalem from the high place at Gibeon, from before the Tent of Meeting. And he reigned over Israel.

14Solomon accumulated chariots and horses; he had fourteen hundred chariots and twelve thousand horses,*a* which he kept in the chariot cities and also with him in Jerusalem. **15**The king made silver and gold as common in Jerusalem as stones, and cedar as plentiful as sycamore-fig trees in the foothills. **16**Solomon's horses were imported from Egypt*b* and from Kue*c*—the royal merchants purchased them from Kue. **17**They imported a chariot from Egypt for six hundred shekels*d* of silver, and a horse for a hundred and fifty.*e* They also exported them to all the kings of the Hittites and of the Arameans.

Preparations for Building the Temple

2 Solomon gave orders to build a temple for the Name of the LORD and a royal palace for himself. **2**He conscripted seventy thousand men as carriers and eighty thousand as stonecutters in the hills and thirty-six hundred as foremen over them.

3Solomon sent this message to Hiram*f* king of Tyre:

"Send me cedar logs as you did for my father David when you sent him cedar to build a palace to live in. **4**Now I am about to build a temple for the Name of the LORD my God and to dedicate it to him for burning fragrant incense before him, for setting out the consecrated bread regularly, and for making burnt offerings every morning and evening and on Sabbaths and New Moons and at the appointed feasts of the LORD our God. This is a lasting ordinance for Israel.

5"The temple I am going to build will be great, because our God is greater than all other gods. **6**But who is able to build a temple for him, since the heavens, even the highest heavens, cannot contain him? Who then am I to build a temple for him, except as a place to burn sacrifices before him?

7"Send me, therefore, a man skilled to work in gold and silver, bronze and iron, and in purple, crimson and blue yarn, and experienced in the art of engraving, to work in Judah and Jerusalem with my skilled craftsmen, whom my father David provided.

8"Send me also cedar, pine and algum*g* logs from Lebanon, for I know that your men are skilled in cutting timber there. My men will work with yours **9**to provide me with plenty of lumber, because the temple I build must be large and magnificent. **10**I will give your servants, the woodsmen who cut the timber, twenty thousand cors*h* of ground wheat, twenty thousand cors of barley, twenty thousand baths*i* of wine and twenty thousand baths of olive oil."

11Hiram king of Tyre replied by letter to Solomon:

"Because the LORD loves his people, he has made you their king."

12And Hiram added:

"Praise be to the LORD, the God of Israel, who made heaven and earth! He has given King David a wise son, endowed with intelligence and discernment, who will build a temple for the LORD and a palace for himself.

13"I am sending you Huram-Abi, a man of great skill, **14**whose mother was from Dan and whose father was

a14 Or *charioteers*   *b16* Or possibly *Muzur*, a region in Cilicia; also in verse 17   *c16* Probably Cilicia
d17 That is, about 15 pounds (about 7 kilograms)   *e17* That is, about 3 3/4 pounds (about 1.7 kilograms)   *f3* Hebrew *Huram*, a variant of *Hiram*; also in verses 11 and 12   *g8* Probably a variant of *almug*; possibly juniper   *h10* That is, probably about 125,000 bushels (about 4,400 kiloliters)
i10 That is, probably about 115,000 gallons (about 440 kiloliters)

from Tyre. He is trained to work in gold and silver, bronze and iron, stone and wood, and with purple and blue and crimson yarn and fine linen. He is experienced in all kinds of engraving and can execute any design given to him. He will work with your craftsmen and with those of my lord, David your father.

15"Now let my lord send his servants the wheat and barley and the olive oil and wine he promised, 16and we will cut all the logs from Lebanon that you need and will float them in rafts by sea down to Joppa. You can then take them up to Jerusalem."

17Solomon took a census of all the aliens who were in Israel, after the census his father David had taken; and they were found to be 153,600. 18He assigned 70,000 of them to be carriers and 80,000 to be stonecutters in the hills, with 3,600 foremen over them to keep the people working.

Solomon Builds the Temple

3 Then Solomon began to build the temple of the LORD in Jerusalem on Mount Moriah, where the LORD had appeared to his father David. It was on the threshing floor of Araunah[a] the Jebusite, the place provided by David. 2He began building on the second day of the second month in the fourth year of his reign.

3The foundation Solomon laid for building the temple of God was sixty cubits long and twenty cubits wide[b] (using the cubit of the old standard). 4The portico at the front of the temple was twenty cubits[c] long across the width of the building and twenty cubits[d] high.

He overlaid the inside with pure gold. 5He paneled the main hall with pine and covered it with fine gold and decorated it with palm tree and chain designs. 6He adorned the temple with precious stones. And the gold he used was gold of Parvaim. 7He overlaid the ceiling beams, doorframes, walls and doors of the temple with

gold, and he carved cherubim on the walls.

8He built the Most Holy Place, its length corresponding to the width of the temple—twenty cubits long and twenty cubits wide. He overlaid the inside with six hundred talents[e] of fine gold. 9The gold nails weighed fifty shekels.[f] He also overlaid the upper parts with gold.

10In the Most Holy Place he made a pair of sculptured cherubim and overlaid them with gold. 11The total wingspan of the cherubim was twenty cubits. One wing of the first cherub was five cubits[g] long and touched the temple wall, while its other wing, also five cubits long, touched the wing of the other cherub. 12Similarly one wing of the second cherub was five cubits long and touched the other temple wall, and its other wing, also five cubits long, touched the wing of the first cherub. 13The wings of these cherubim extended twenty cubits. They stood on their feet, facing the main hall.[h]

14He made the curtain of blue, purple and crimson yarn and fine linen, with cherubim worked into it.

15In the front of the temple he made two pillars, which ⌞together⌟ were thirty-five cubits[i] long, each with a capital on top measuring five cubits. 16He made interwoven chains[j] and put them on top of the pillars. He also made a hundred pomegranates and attached them to the chains. 17He erected the pillars in the front of the temple, one to the south and one to the north. The one to the south he named Jakin[k] and the one to the north Boaz.[l]

The Temple's Furnishings

4 He made a bronze altar twenty cubits long, twenty cubits wide and ten cubits high.[m] 2He made the Sea of cast metal, circular in shape, measuring ten cubits from rim to rim and five cubits[n] high. It took a line of thirty cubits[o] to measure around it. 3Below the rim, figures of bulls encircled it—ten to a cubit.[p] The bulls were cast in two rows in one piece with the Sea.

a1 Hebrew Ornan, a variant of Araunah   b3 That is, about 90 feet (about 27 meters) long and 30 feet (about 9 meters) wide   c4 That is, about 30 feet (about 9 meters); also in verses 8, 11 and 13   d4 Some Septuagint and Syriac manuscripts; Hebrew and a hundred and twenty   e8 That is, about 23 tons (about 21 metric tons)   f9 That is, about 1 1/4 pounds (about 0.6 kilogram)   g11 That is, about 7 1/2 feet (about 2.3 meters); also in verse 15   h13 Or facing inward   i15 That is, about 52 feet (about 16 meters)   j16 Or possibly made chains in the inner sanctuary; the meaning of the Hebrew for this phrase is uncertain.   k17 Jakin probably means he establishes.   l17 Boaz probably means in him is strength.   m1 That is, about 30 feet (about 9 meters) long and wide, and about 15 feet (about 4.5 meters) high   n2 That is, about 7 1/2 feet (about 2.3 meters)   o2 That is, about 45 feet (about 13.5 meters)   p3 That is, about 1 1/2 feet (about 0.5 meter)

WEEKENDING

RETHINK

I find that most professionals, and especially most men, hold a mild skepticism toward the faith. They feel that something abstract like faith can't stand the rigors of the street. They attend church on Sunday, and so forth. But religion is a sort of weekend hobby, like golf or fishing. Come Monday, it's time to put away those toys and get back to the "real world" . . .

This will not do, because Christ is Lord of all of life. If he is not, if he only presides over what we do on Sunday or at home, if he is only an ideal, if Jesus is merely a name in a book we read to our children—then he really isn't our Lord at all. He doesn't really matter in what matters most to most of us: our work.

But Jesus *is* Lord. And as such, he is not interested in merely bridging the gap, but in eliminating it altogether. We must bring the entirety of our lives back together under him.
– *Doug Sherman and William Hendricks*

REVIVE

Saturday: Psalm 24
Sunday: Romans 14:1–12

Go to page 437 for your next devotional reading.

[4]The Sea stood on twelve bulls, three facing north, three facing west, three facing south and three facing east. The Sea rested on top of them, and their hindquarters were toward the center. [5]It was a handbreadth[a] in thickness, and its rim was like the rim of a cup, like a lily blossom. It held three thousand baths.[b]

[6]He then made ten basins for washing and placed five on the south side and five on the north. In them the things to be used for the burnt offerings were rinsed, but the Sea was to be used by the priests for washing.

[7]He made ten gold lampstands according to the specifications for them and placed them in the temple, five on the south side and five on the north.

[8]He made ten tables and placed them in the temple, five on the south side and five on the north. He also made a hundred gold sprinkling bowls.

[9]He made the courtyard of the priests, and the large court and the doors for the court, and overlaid the doors with bronze. [10]He placed the Sea on the south side, at the southeast corner.

[11]He also made the pots and shovels and sprinkling bowls.

So Huram finished the work he had undertaken for King Solomon in the temple of God:

[12]the two pillars;
　the two bowl-shaped capitals on top
　　of the pillars;
　the two sets of network decorating
　　the two bowl-shaped capitals on
　　top of the pillars;
[13]the four hundred pomegranates for
　　the two sets of network (two rows
　　of pomegranates for each net-
　　work, decorating the bowl-shaped
　　capitals on top of the pillars);
[14]the stands with their basins;
[15]the Sea and the twelve bulls un-
　　der it;
[16]the pots, shovels, meat forks and all
　　related articles.

All the objects that Huram-Abi made for King Solomon for the temple of the LORD were of polished bronze. [17]The king had them cast in clay molds in the plain of the Jordan between Succoth and Zarethan.[c] [18]All these things that Solomon made amounted to so much that the weight of the bronze was not determined.

[19]Solomon also made all the furnishings that were in God's temple:

the golden altar;
the tables on which was the bread of
　the Presence;
[20]the lampstands of pure gold with
　their lamps, to burn in front of the
　inner sanctuary as prescribed;
[21]the gold floral work and lamps and
　tongs (they were solid gold);
[22]the pure gold wick trimmers, sprin-
　kling bowls, dishes and censers;
　and the gold doors of the temple:
　the inner doors to the Most Holy
　Place and the doors of the main
　hall.

5 When all the work Solomon had done for the temple of the LORD was finished, he brought in the things his father David had dedicated—the silver and gold and all the furnishings—and he placed them in the treasuries of God's temple.

The Ark Brought to the Temple

[2]Then Solomon summoned to Jerusalem the elders of Israel, all the heads of the tribes and the chiefs of the Israelite families, to bring up the ark of the LORD's covenant from Zion, the City of David. [3]And all the men of Israel came together to the king at the time of the festival in the seventh month.

[4]When all the elders of Israel had arrived, the Levites took up the ark, [5]and they brought up the ark and the Tent of Meeting and all the sacred furnishings in it. The priests, who were Levites, carried them up; [6]and King Solomon and the entire assembly of Israel that had gathered about him were before the ark, sacrificing so many sheep and cattle that they could not be recorded or counted.

[7]The priests then brought the ark of the LORD's covenant to its place in the inner sanctuary of the temple, the Most Holy Place, and put it beneath the wings of the cherubim. [8]The cherubim spread their wings over the place of the ark and covered the ark and its carrying poles. [9]These poles were so long that their ends, extending from the ark, could be seen from in front of the inner sanctuary, but not from outside the Holy Place; and they are still there today. [10]There was nothing in the ark except the two tablets that Moses had placed in it at Horeb, where the LORD

---

[a]5 That is, about 3 inches (about 8 centimeters)　　[b]5 That is, about 17,500 gallons (about 66 kiloliters)
[c]17 Hebrew Zeredatha, a variant of Zarethan

made a covenant with the Israelites after they came out of Egypt.

¹¹The priests then withdrew from the Holy Place. All the priests who were there had consecrated themselves, regardless of their divisions. ¹²All the Levites who were musicians—Asaph, Heman, Jeduthun and their sons and relatives—stood on the east side of the altar, dressed in fine linen and playing cymbals, harps and lyres. They were accompanied by 120 priests sounding trumpets. ¹³The trumpeters and singers joined in unison, as with one voice, to give praise and thanks to the LORD. Accompanied by trumpets, cymbals and other instruments, they raised their voices in praise to the LORD and sang:

"He is good;
  his love endures forever."

Then the temple of the LORD was filled with a cloud, ¹⁴and the priests could not perform their service because of the cloud, for the glory of the LORD filled the temple of God.

6 Then Solomon said, "The LORD has said that he would dwell in a dark cloud; ²I have built a magnificent temple for you, a place for you to dwell forever."

³While the whole assembly of Israel was standing there, the king turned around and blessed them. ⁴Then he said:

"Praise be to the LORD, the God of Israel, who with his hands has fulfilled what he promised with his mouth to my father David. For he said, ⁵'Since the day I brought my people out of Egypt, I have not chosen a city in any tribe of Israel to have a temple built for my Name to be there, nor have I chosen anyone to be the leader over my people Israel. ⁶But now I have chosen Jerusalem for my Name to be there, and I have chosen David to rule my people Israel.'

⁷"My father David had it in his heart to build a temple for the Name of the LORD, the God of Israel. ⁸But the LORD said to my father David, 'Because it was in your heart to build a temple for my Name, you did well to have this in your heart. ⁹Nevertheless, you are not the one to build the temple, but your son, who is your

own flesh and blood—he is the one who will build the temple for my Name.'

¹⁰"The LORD has kept the promise he made. I have succeeded David my father and now I sit on the throne of Israel, just as the LORD promised, and I have built the temple for the Name of the LORD, the God of Israel. ¹¹There I have placed the ark, in which is the covenant of the LORD that he made with the people of Israel."

Solomon's Prayer of Dedication

¹²Then Solomon stood before the altar of the LORD in front of the whole assembly of Israel and spread out his hands. ¹³Now he had made a bronze platform, five cubits*ᵃ* long, five cubits wide and three cubits*ᵇ* high, and had placed it in the center of the outer court. He stood on the platform and then knelt down before the whole assembly of Israel and spread out his hands toward heaven. ¹⁴He said:

"O LORD, God of Israel, there is no God like you in heaven or on earth—you who keep your covenant of love with your servants who continue wholeheartedly in your way. ¹⁵You have kept your promise to your servant David my father; with your mouth you have promised and with your hand you have fulfilled it—as it is today.

¹⁶"Now LORD, God of Israel, keep for your servant David my father the promises you made to him when you said, 'You shall never fail to have a man to sit before me on the throne of Israel, if only your sons are careful in all they do to walk before me according to my law, as you have done.' ¹⁷And now, O LORD, God of Israel, let your word that you promised your servant David come true.

¹⁸"But will God really dwell on earth with men? The heavens, even the highest heavens, cannot contain you. How much less this temple I have built! ¹⁹Yet give attention to your servant's prayer and his plea for mercy, O LORD my God. Hear the cry and the prayer that your servant is praying in your presence. ²⁰May your eyes be open toward this temple day and night, this place of which you

ᵃ13 That is, about 7 1/2 feet (about 2.3 meters)   *ᵇ13* That is, about 4 1/2 feet (about 1.3 meters) said you would put your Name there. May you hear the prayer your servant prays toward this place. ²¹Hear the supplications of your servant and of your people Israel when they pray toward this place. Hear from heaven, your dwelling place; and when you hear, forgive.

²²"When a man wrongs his neighbor and is required to take an oath and he comes and swears the oath before your altar in this temple, ²³then hear from heaven and act. Judge between your servants, repaying the guilty by bringing down on his own head what he has done. Declare the innocent not guilty and so establish his innocence.

²⁴"When your people Israel have been defeated by an enemy because they have sinned against you and when they turn back and confess your name, praying and making supplication before you in this temple, ²⁵then hear from heaven and forgive the sin of your people Israel and bring them back to the land you gave to them and their fathers.

²⁶"When the heavens are shut up and there is no rain because your people have sinned against you, and when they pray toward this place and confess your name and turn from their sin because you have afflicted them, ²⁷then hear from heaven and forgive the sin of your servants, your people Israel. Teach them the right way to live, and send rain on the land you gave your people for an inheritance.

²⁸"When famine or plague comes to the land, or blight or mildew, locusts or grasshoppers, or when enemies besiege them in any of their cities, whatever disaster or disease may come, ²⁹and when a prayer or plea is made by any of your people Israel — each one aware of his afflictions and pains, and spreading out his hands toward this temple — ³⁰then hear from heaven, your dwelling place. Forgive, and deal with each man according to all he does, since you know his heart (for you alone know the hearts of men), ³¹so that they will fear you and walk in your ways all the time they live in the land you gave our fathers.

³²"As for the foreigner who does not belong to your people Israel but has come from a distant land because of your great name and your mighty hand and your outstretched arm — when he comes and prays toward this temple, ³³then hear from heaven, your dwelling place, and do whatever the foreigner asks of you, so that all the peoples of the earth may know your name and fear you, as do your own people Israel, and may know that this house I have built bears your Name.

³⁴"When your people go to war against their enemies, wherever you send them, and when they pray to you toward this city you have chosen and the temple I have built for your Name, ³⁵then hear from heaven their prayer and their plea, and uphold their cause.

³⁶"When they sin against you — for there is no one who does not sin — and you become angry with them and give them over to the enemy, who takes them captive to a land far away or near; ³⁷and if they have a change of heart in the land where they are held captive, and repent and plead with you in the land of their captivity and say, 'We have sinned, we have done wrong and acted wickedly'; ³⁸and if they turn back to you with all their heart and soul in the land of their captivity where they were taken, and pray toward the land you gave their fathers, toward the city you have chosen and toward the temple I have built for your Name; ³⁹then from heaven, your dwelling place, hear their prayer and their pleas, and uphold their cause. And forgive your people, who have sinned against you.

⁴⁰"Now, my God, may your eyes be open and your ears attentive to the prayers offered in this place.

⁴¹"Now arise, O Lord God, and
      come to your resting place,
   you and the ark of your might.
May your priests, O Lord God, be
      clothed with salvation,
   may your saints rejoice in your
      goodness.
⁴²O Lord God, do not reject your
      anointed one.
   Remember the great love
      promised to David your
      servant."

The Dedication of the Temple

7 When Solomon finished praying, fire came down from heaven and consumed the burnt offering and the sacrifices, and the glory of the LORD filled the temple. ²The priests could not enter the temple of the LORD because the glory of the LORD filled it. ³When all the Israelites saw the fire coming down and the glory of the LORD above the temple, they knelt on the pavement with their faces to the ground, and they worshiped and gave thanks to the LORD, saying,

> "He is good;
>   his love endures forever."

⁴Then the king and all the people offered sacrifices before the LORD. ⁵And King Solomon offered a sacrifice of twenty-two thousand head of cattle and a hundred and twenty thousand sheep and goats. So the king and all the people dedicated the temple of God. ⁶The priests took their positions, as did the Levites with the LORD's

---

MONDAY

VERSE FOR THE DAY: AUTHOR: PASSAGE FOR THE DAY:
2 Chronicles 6:30   Oswald Chambers   2 Chronicles 6:28–31

What God Has Done in You

THERE is a sentimental notion that makes us make ourselves out worse than we think we are, because we have a lurking suspicion that if we make ourselves out amazingly bad, someone will say, "Oh no, you are not as bad as that"; but Jesus says we are worse. Our Lord never trusted any man, "for he knew what was in a man" [John 2:24]; but he was not a cynic for he had the profoundest confidence in what he could do for every man, consequently he was never in a moral or intellectual panic, as we are, because we will put our confidence in man and in the things that Jesus put no confidence in. Paul says, "Don't glory in men; don't say, I am of Paul, or I am of Apollos [see 1 Corinthians 1:12; 3:21], and don't think of yourself more highly than you ought to think, but think according to the measure of faith, that is, according to what the grace of God has done in you" [see Romans 12:3]. Never trust (in the fundamental meaning of the word) any other saving Jesus Christ. That will mean you will never be unkind to anybody on the face of the earth, whether it be a degraded criminal or an upright moral man, because you have learned that the only thing to depend on in a man is what God has done in him. When you come to work for Jesus Christ, always ask yourself, "Do I believe Jesus Christ can do anything for that case?" Am I as confident in his power as he is in his own? If you deal with people without any faith in Jesus Christ it will crush the very life out of you. If we believe in Jesus Christ, we can face every problem the world holds.

Additional Scripture Readings:
Jeremiah 9:23–24;
1 Corinthians 3:1–23

*Go to page 460 for your next
devotional reading.*

musical instruments, which King David had made for praising the Lord and which were used when he gave thanks, saying, "His love endures forever." Opposite the Levites, the priests blew their trumpets, and all the Israelites were standing.

[7]Solomon consecrated the middle part of the courtyard in front of the temple of the Lord, and there he offered burnt offerings and the fat of the fellowship offerings,[a] because the bronze altar he had made could not hold the burnt offerings, the grain offerings and the fat portions.

[8]So Solomon observed the festival at that time for seven days, and all Israel with him—a vast assembly, people from Lebo[b] Hamath to the Wadi of Egypt. [9]On the eighth day they held an assembly, for they had celebrated the dedication of the altar for seven days and the festival for seven days more. [10]On the twenty-third day of the seventh month he sent the people to their homes, joyful and glad in heart for the good things the Lord had done for David and Solomon and for his people Israel.

The Lord Appears to Solomon

[11]When Solomon had finished the temple of the Lord and the royal palace, and had succeeded in carrying out all he had in mind to do in the temple of the Lord and in his own palace, [12]the Lord appeared to him at night and said:

"I have heard your prayer and have chosen this place for myself as a temple for sacrifices.

[13]"When I shut up the heavens so that there is no rain, or command locusts to devour the land or send a plague among my people, [14]if my people, who are called by my name, will humble themselves and pray and seek my face and turn from their wicked ways, then will I hear from heaven and will forgive their sin and will heal their land. [15]Now my eyes will be open and my ears attentive to the prayers offered in this place. [16]I have chosen and consecrated this temple so that my Name may be there forever. My eyes and my heart will always be there.

[17]"As for you, if you walk before me as David your father did, and do all I command, and observe my de-

crees and laws, [18]I will establish your royal throne, as I covenanted with David your father when I said, 'You shall never fail to have a man to rule over Israel.'

[19]"But if you[c] turn away and forsake the decrees and commands I have given you[c] and go off to serve other gods and worship them, [20]then I will uproot Israel from my land, which I have given them, and will reject this temple I have consecrated for my Name. I will make it a byword and an object of ridicule among all peoples. [21]And though this temple is now so imposing, all who pass by will be appalled and say, 'Why has the Lord done such a thing to this land and to this temple?' [22]People will answer, 'Because they have forsaken the Lord, the God of their fathers, who brought them out of Egypt, and have embraced other gods, worshiping and serving them—that is why he brought all this disaster on them.' "

Solomon's Other Activities

8 At the end of twenty years, during which Solomon built the temple of the Lord and his own palace, [2]Solomon rebuilt the villages that Hiram[d] had given him, and settled Israelites in them. [3]Solomon then went to Hamath Zobah and captured it. [4]He also built up Tadmor in the desert and all the store cities he had built in Hamath. [5]He rebuilt Upper Beth Horon and Lower Beth Horon as fortified cities, with walls and with gates and bars, [6]as well as Baalath and all his store cities, and all the cities for his chariots and for his horses[e]—whatever he desired to build in Jerusalem, in Lebanon and throughout all the territory he ruled.

[7]All the people left from the Hittites, Amorites, Perizzites, Hivites and Jebusites (these peoples were not Israelites), [8]that is, their descendants remaining in the land, whom the Israelites had not destroyed—these Solomon conscripted for his slave labor force, as it is to this day. [9]But Solomon did not make slaves of the Israelites for his work; they were his fighting men, commanders of his captains, and commanders of his chariots and charioteers. [10]They were also King Solomon's chief officials—two hundred and fifty officials supervising the men.

---

[a]7 Traditionally *peace offerings*   [b]8 Or *from the entrance to*   [c]19 The Hebrew is plural.
[d]2 Hebrew *Huram*, a variant of *Hiram*; also in verse 18   [e]6 Or *charioteers*

11Solomon brought Pharaoh's daughter up from the City of David to the palace he had built for her, for he said, "My wife must not live in the palace of David king of Israel, because the places the ark of the Lord has entered are holy."

12On the altar of the Lord that he had built in front of the portico, Solomon sacrificed burnt offerings to the Lord, 13according to the daily requirement for offerings commanded by Moses for Sabbaths, New Moons and the three annual feasts — the Feast of Unleavened Bread, the Feast of Weeks and the Feast of Tabernacles. 14In keeping with the ordinance of his father David, he appointed the divisions of the priests for their duties, and the Levites to lead the praise and to assist the priests according to each day's requirement. He also appointed the gatekeepers by divisions for the various gates, because this was what David the man of God had ordered. 15They did not deviate from the king's commands to the priests or to the Levites in any matter, including that of the treasuries.

16All Solomon's work was carried out, from the day the foundation of the temple of the Lord was laid until its completion. So the temple of the Lord was finished.

17Then Solomon went to Ezion Geber and Elath on the coast of Edom. 18And Hiram sent him ships commanded by his own officers, men who knew the sea. These, with Solomon's men, sailed to Ophir and brought back four hundred and fifty talents[a] of gold, which they delivered to King Solomon.

The Queen of Sheba Visits Solomon

9 When the queen of Sheba heard of Solomon's fame, she came to Jerusalem to test him with hard questions. Arriving with a very great caravan — with camels carrying spices, large quantities of gold, and precious stones — she came to Solomon and talked with him about all she had on her mind. 2Solomon answered all her questions; nothing was too hard for him to explain to her. 3When the queen of Sheba saw the wisdom of Solomon, as well as the palace he had built, 4the food on his table, the seating of his officials, the attending servants in their robes, the cupbearers in their robes and the burnt offer-

ings he made at[b] the temple of the Lord, she was overwhelmed.

5She said to the king, "The report I heard in my own country about your achievements and your wisdom is true. 6But I did not believe what they said until I came and saw with my own eyes. Indeed, not even half the greatness of your wisdom was told me; you have far exceeded the report I heard. 7How happy your men must be! How happy your officials, who continually stand before you and hear your wisdom! 8Praise be to the Lord your God, who has delighted in you and placed you on his throne as king to rule for the Lord your God. Because of the love of your God for Israel and his desire to uphold them forever, he has made you king over them, to maintain justice and righteousness."

9Then she gave the king 120 talents[c] of gold, large quantities of spices, and precious stones. There had never been such spices as those the queen of Sheba gave to King Solomon.

10(The men of Hiram and the men of Solomon brought gold from Ophir; they also brought algumwood[d] and precious stones. 11The king used the algumwood to make steps for the temple of the Lord and for the royal palace, and to make harps and lyres for the musicians. Nothing like them had ever been seen in Judah.)

12King Solomon gave the queen of Sheba all she desired and asked for; he gave her more than she had brought to him. Then she left and returned with her retinue to her own country.

Solomon's Splendor

13The weight of the gold that Solomon received yearly was 666 talents,[e] 14not including the revenues brought in by merchants and traders. Also all the kings of Arabia and the governors of the land brought gold and silver to Solomon.

15King Solomon made two hundred large shields of hammered gold; six hundred bekas[f] of hammered gold went into each shield. 16He also made three hundred small shields of hammered gold, with three hundred bekas[g] of gold in each shield. The king put them in the Palace of the Forest of Lebanon.

17Then the king made a great throne in-

a18 That is, about 17 tons (about 16 metric tons)   b4 Or the ascent by which he went up to   c9 That is, about 4 1/2 tons (about 4 metric tons)   d10 Probably a variant of almugwood   e13 That is, about 25 tons (about 23 metric tons)   f15 That is, about 7 1/2 pounds (about 3.5 kilograms)   g16 That is, about 3 3/4 pounds (about 1.7 kilograms) laid with ivory and overlaid with pure gold. ¹⁸The throne had six steps, and a footstool of gold was attached to it. On both sides of the seat were armrests, with a lion standing beside each of them. ¹⁹Twelve lions stood on the six steps, one at either end of each step. Nothing like it had ever been made for any other kingdom. ²⁰All King Solomon's goblets were gold, and all the household articles in the Palace of the Forest of Lebanon were pure gold. Nothing was made of silver, because silver was considered of little value in Solomon's day. ²¹The king had a fleet of trading ships*a* manned by Hiram's*b* men. Once every three years it returned, carrying gold, silver and ivory, and apes and baboons.

²²King Solomon was greater in riches and wisdom than all the other kings of the earth. ²³All the kings of the earth sought audience with Solomon to hear the wisdom God had put in his heart. ²⁴Year after year, everyone who came brought a gift—articles of silver and gold, and robes, weapons and spices, and horses and mules.

²⁵Solomon had four thousand stalls for horses and chariots, and twelve thousand horses,*c* which he kept in the chariot cities and also with him in Jerusalem. ²⁶He ruled over all the kings from the River*d* to the land of the Philistines, as far as the border of Egypt. ²⁷The king made silver as common in Jerusalem as stones, and cedar as plentiful as sycamore-fig trees in the foothills. ²⁸Solomon's horses were imported from Egypt*e* and from all other countries.

Solomon's Death

²⁹As for the other events of Solomon's reign, from beginning to end, are they not written in the records of Nathan the prophet, in the prophecy of Ahijah the Shilonite and in the visions of Iddo the seer concerning Jeroboam son of Nebat? ³⁰Solomon reigned in Jerusalem over all Israel forty years. ³¹Then he rested with his fathers and was buried in the city of David his father. And Rehoboam his son succeeded him as king.

Israel Rebels Against Rehoboam

10 Rehoboam went to Shechem, for all the Israelites had gone there to make him king. ²When Jeroboam son of

Nebat heard this (he was in Egypt, where he had fled from King Solomon), he returned from Egypt. ³So they sent for Jeroboam, and he and all Israel went to Rehoboam and said to him: ⁴"Your father put a heavy yoke on us, but now lighten the harsh labor and the heavy yoke he put on us, and we will serve you."

⁵Rehoboam answered, "Come back to me in three days." So the people went away.

⁶Then King Rehoboam consulted the elders who had served his father Solomon during his lifetime. "How would you advise me to answer these people?" he asked.

⁷They replied, "If you will be kind to these people and please them and give them a favorable answer, they will always be your servants."

⁸But Rehoboam rejected the advice the elders gave him and consulted the young men who had grown up with him and were serving him. ⁹He asked them, "What is your advice? How should we answer these people who say to me, 'Lighten the yoke your father put on us'?"

¹⁰The young men who had grown up with him replied, "Tell the people who have said to you, 'Your father put a heavy yoke on us, but make our yoke lighter'—tell them, 'My little finger is thicker than my father's waist. ¹¹My father laid on you a heavy yoke; I will make it even heavier. My father scourged you with whips; I will scourge you with scorpions.' "

¹²Three days later Jeroboam and all the people returned to Rehoboam, as the king had said, "Come back to me in three days." ¹³The king answered them harshly. Rejecting the advice of the elders, ¹⁴he followed the advice of the young men and said, "My father made your yoke heavy; I will make it even heavier. My father scourged you with whips; I will scourge you with scorpions." ¹⁵So the king did not listen to the people, for this turn of events was from God, to fulfill the word the Lord had spoken to Jeroboam son of Nebat through Ahijah the Shilonite.

¹⁶When all Israel saw that the king refused to listen to them, they answered the king:

"What share do we have in David,
    what part in Jesse's son?
To your tents, O Israel!

---

a21 Hebrew *of ships that could go to Tarshish*   *b21* Hebrew *Huram,* a variant of *Hiram*   *c25* Or *charioteers*   *d26* That is, the Euphrates   *e28* Or possibly *Muzur,* a region in Cilicia

Look after your own house,
O David!"

So all the Israelites went home. **17**But as for the Israelites who were living in the towns of Judah, Rehoboam still ruled over them.

18King Rehoboam sent out Adoniram,[a] who was in charge of forced labor, but the Israelites stoned him to death. King Rehoboam, however, managed to get into his chariot and escape to Jerusalem. **19**So Israel has been in rebellion against the house of David to this day.

11 When Rehoboam arrived in Jerusalem, he mustered the house of Judah and Benjamin — a hundred and eighty thousand fighting men — to make war against Israel and to regain the kingdom for Rehoboam.

2But this word of the LORD came to Shemaiah the man of God: **3**"Say to Rehoboam son of Solomon king of Judah and to all the Israelites in Judah and Benjamin, **4**'This is what the LORD says: Do not go up to fight against your brothers. Go home, every one of you, for this is my doing.'" So they obeyed the words of the LORD and turned back from marching against Jeroboam.

Rehoboam Fortifies Judah

5Rehoboam lived in Jerusalem and built up towns for defense in Judah: **6**Bethlehem, Etam, Tekoa, **7**Beth Zur, Soco, Adullam, **8**Gath, Mareshah, Ziph, **9**Adoraim, Lachish, Azekah, **10**Zorah, Aijalon and Hebron. These were fortified cities in Judah and Benjamin. **11**He strengthened their defenses and put commanders in them, with supplies of food, olive oil and wine. **12**He put shields and spears in all the cities, and made them very strong. So Judah and Benjamin were his.

13The priests and Levites from all their districts throughout Israel sided with him. **14**The Levites even abandoned their pasturelands and property, and came to Judah and Jerusalem because Jeroboam and his sons had rejected them as priests of the LORD. **15**And he appointed his own priests for the high places and for the goat and calf idols he had made. **16**Those from every tribe of Israel who set their hearts on seeking the LORD, the God of Israel, followed the Levites to Jerusalem to offer sacrifices to the LORD, the God of their fathers. **17**They strengthened the kingdom of Judah and supported Rehoboam son of Solomon three years, walking in the ways of David and Solomon during this time.

Rehoboam's Family

18Rehoboam married Mahalath, who was the daughter of David's son Jerimoth and of Abihail, the daughter of Jesse's son Eliab. **19**She bore him sons: Jeush, Shemariah and Zaham. **20**Then he married Maacah daughter of Absalom, who bore him Abijah, Attai, Ziza and Shelomith. **21**Rehoboam loved Maacah daughter of Absalom more than any of his other wives and concubines. In all, he had eighteen wives and sixty concubines, twenty-eight sons and sixty daughters.

22Rehoboam appointed Abijah son of Maacah to be the chief prince among his brothers, in order to make him king. **23**He acted wisely, dispersing some of his sons throughout the districts of Judah and Benjamin, and to all the fortified cities. He gave them abundant provisions and took many wives for them.

Shishak Attacks Jerusalem

12 After Rehoboam's position as king was established and he had become strong, he and all Israel[b] with him abandoned the law of the LORD. **2**Because they had been unfaithful to the LORD, Shishak king of Egypt attacked Jerusalem in the fifth year of King Rehoboam. **3**With twelve hundred chariots and sixty thousand horsemen and the innumerable troops of Libyans, Sukkites and Cushites[c] that came with him from Egypt, **4**he captured the fortified cities of Judah and came as far as Jerusalem.

5Then the prophet Shemaiah came to Rehoboam and to the leaders of Judah who had assembled in Jerusalem for fear of Shishak, and he said to them, "This is what the LORD says, 'You have abandoned me; therefore, I now abandon you to Shishak.'"

6The leaders of Israel and the king humbled themselves and said, "The LORD is just."

7When the LORD saw that they humbled themselves, this word of the LORD came to Shemaiah: "Since they have humbled themselves, I will not destroy them but will soon give them deliverance. My wrath will not be poured out on Jerusalem

---

a18 Hebrew *Hadoram*, a variant of *Adoniram*   *b1* That is, Judah, as frequently in 2 Chronicles
c3 That is, people from the upper Nile region

through Shishak. **8**They will, however, become subject to him, so that they may learn the difference between serving me and serving the kings of other lands."

9When Shishak king of Egypt attacked Jerusalem, he carried off the treasures of the temple of the LORD and the treasures of the royal palace. He took everything, including the gold shields Solomon had made. **10**So King Rehoboam made bronze shields to replace them and assigned these to the commanders of the guard on duty at the entrance to the royal palace. **11**Whenever the king went to the LORD's temple, the guards went with him, bearing the shields, and afterward they returned them to the guardroom.

12Because Rehoboam humbled himself, the LORD's anger turned from him, and he was not totally destroyed. Indeed, there was some good in Judah.

13King Rehoboam established himself firmly in Jerusalem and continued as king. He was forty-one years old when he became king, and he reigned seventeen years in Jerusalem, the city the LORD had chosen out of all the tribes of Israel in which to put his Name. His mother's name was Naamah; she was an Ammonite. **14**He did evil because he had not set his heart on seeking the LORD.

15As for the events of Rehoboam's reign, from beginning to end, are they not written in the records of Shemaiah the prophet and of Iddo the seer that deal with genealogies? There was continual warfare between Rehoboam and Jeroboam. **16**Rehoboam rested with his fathers and was buried in the City of David. And Abijah his son succeeded him as king.

Abijah King of Judah

13 In the eighteenth year of the reign of Jeroboam, Abijah became king of Judah, **2**and he reigned in Jerusalem three years. His mother's name was Maacah,*a* a daughter*b* of Uriel of Gibeah.

There was war between Abijah and Jeroboam. **3**Abijah went into battle with a force of four hundred thousand able fighting men, and Jeroboam drew up a battle line against him with eight hundred thousand able troops.

4Abijah stood on Mount Zemaraim, in the hill country of Ephraim, and said, "Jeroboam and all Israel, listen to me! **5**Don't you know that the LORD, the God of Israel,

has given the kingship of Israel to David and his descendants forever by a covenant of salt? **6**Yet Jeroboam son of Nebat, an official of Solomon son of David, rebelled against his master. **7**Some worthless scoundrels gathered around him and opposed Rehoboam son of Solomon when he was young and indecisive and not strong enough to resist them.

8"And now you plan to resist the kingdom of the LORD, which is in the hands of David's descendants. You are indeed a vast army and have with you the golden calves that Jeroboam made to be your gods. **9**But didn't you drive out the priests of the LORD, the sons of Aaron, and the Levites, and make priests of your own as the peoples of other lands do? Whoever comes to consecrate himself with a young bull and seven rams may become a priest of what are not gods.

10"As for us, the LORD is our God, and we have not forsaken him. The priests who serve the LORD are sons of Aaron, and the Levites assist them. **11**Every morning and evening they present burnt offerings and fragrant incense to the LORD. They set out the bread on the ceremonially clean table and light the lamps on the gold lampstand every evening. We are observing the requirements of the LORD our God. But you have forsaken him. **12**God is with us; he is our leader. His priests with their trumpets will sound the battle cry against you. Men of Israel, do not fight against the LORD, the God of your fathers, for you will not succeed."

13Now Jeroboam had sent troops around to the rear, so that while he was in front of Judah the ambush was behind them. **14**Judah turned and saw that they were being attacked at both front and rear. Then they cried out to the LORD. The priests blew their trumpets **15**and the men of Judah raised the battle cry. At the sound of their battle cry, God routed Jeroboam and all Israel before Abijah and Judah. **16**The Israelites fled before Judah, and God delivered them into their hands. **17**Abijah and his men inflicted heavy losses on them, so that there were five hundred thousand casualties among Israel's able men. **18**The men of Israel were subdued on that occasion, and the men of Judah were victorious because they relied on the LORD, the God of their fathers.

19Abijah pursued Jeroboam and took

---

*a*2 Most Septuagint manuscripts and Syriac (see also 2 Chron. 11:20 and 1 Kings 15:2); Hebrew *Micaiah*
*b*2 Or *granddaughter*

from him the towns of Bethel, Jeshanah and Ephron, with their surrounding villages. ²⁰Jeroboam did not regain power during the time of Abijah. And the LORD struck him down and he died.

²¹But Abijah grew in strength. He married fourteen wives and had twenty-two sons and sixteen daughters.

²²The other events of Abijah's reign, what he did and what he said, are written in the annotations of the prophet Iddo.

14 And Abijah rested with his fathers and was buried in the City of David. Asa his son succeeded him as king, and in his days the country was at peace for ten years.

Asa King of Judah

²Asa did what was good and right in the eyes of the LORD his God. ³He removed the foreign altars and the high places, smashed the sacred stones and cut down the Asherah poles.ᵃ ⁴He commanded Judah to seek the LORD, the God of their fathers, and to obey his laws and commands. ⁵He removed the high places and incense altars in every town in Judah, and the kingdom was at peace under him. ⁶He built up the fortified cities of Judah, since the land was at peace. No one was at war with him during those years, for the LORD gave him rest.

⁷"Let us build up these towns," he said to Judah, "and put walls around them, with towers, gates and bars. The land is still ours, because we have sought the LORD our God; we sought him and he has given us rest on every side." So they built and prospered.

⁸Asa had an army of three hundred thousand men from Judah, equipped with large shields and with spears, and two hundred and eighty thousand from Benjamin, armed with small shields and with bows. All these were brave fighting men.

⁹Zerah the Cushite marched out against them with a vast armyᵇ and three hundred chariots, and came as far as Mareshah. ¹⁰Asa went out to meet him, and they took up battle positions in the Valley of Zephathah near Mareshah.

¹¹Then Asa called to the LORD his God and said, "LORD, there is no one like you to help the powerless against the mighty. Help us, O LORD our God, for we rely on you, and in your name we have come against this vast army. O LORD, you are our God; do not let man prevail against you."

¹²The LORD struck down the Cushites before Asa and Judah. The Cushites fled, ¹³and Asa and his army pursued them as far as Gerar. Such a great number of Cushites fell that they could not recover; they were crushed before the LORD and his forces. The men of Judah carried off a large amount of plunder. ¹⁴They destroyed all the villages around Gerar, for the terror of the LORD had fallen upon them. They plundered all these villages, since there was much booty there. ¹⁵They also attacked the camps of the herdsmen and carried off droves of sheep and goats and camels. Then they returned to Jerusalem.

Asa's Reform

15 The Spirit of God came upon Azariah son of Oded. ²He went out to meet Asa and said to him, "Listen to me, Asa and all Judah and Benjamin. The LORD is with you when you are with him. If you seek him, he will be found by you, but if you forsake him, he will forsake you. ³For a long time Israel was without the true God, without a priest to teach and without the law. ⁴But in their distress they turned to the LORD, the God of Israel, and sought him, and he was found by them. ⁵In those days it was not safe to travel about, for all the inhabitants of the lands were in great turmoil. ⁶One nation was being crushed by another and one city by another, because God was troubling them with every kind of distress. ⁷But as for you, be strong and do not give up, for your work will be rewarded."

⁸When Asa heard these words and the prophecy of Azariah son ofᶜ Oded the prophet, he took courage. He removed the detestable idols from the whole land of Judah and Benjamin and from the towns he had captured in the hills of Ephraim. He repaired the altar of the LORD that was in front of the portico of the LORD's temple.

⁹Then he assembled all Judah and Benjamin and the people from Ephraim, Manasseh and Simeon who had settled among them, for large numbers had come over to him from Israel when they saw that the LORD his God was with him.

¹⁰They assembled at Jerusalem in the

ᵃ3 That is, symbols of the goddess Asherah; here and elsewhere in 2 Chronicles   ᵇ9 Hebrew *with an army of a thousand thousands* or *with an army of thousands upon thousands*   ᶜ8 Vulgate and Syriac (see also Septuagint and verse 1); Hebrew does not have *Azariah son of*.

third month of the fifteenth year of Asa's reign. [11]At that time they sacrificed to the LORD seven hundred head of cattle and seven thousand sheep and goats from the plunder they had brought back. [12]They entered into a covenant to seek the LORD, the God of their fathers, with all their heart and soul. [13]All who would not seek the LORD, the God of Israel, were to be put to death, whether small or great, man or woman. [14]They took an oath to the LORD with loud acclamation, with shouting and with trumpets and horns. [15]All Judah rejoiced about the oath because they had sworn it wholeheartedly. They sought God eagerly, and he was found by them. So the LORD gave them rest on every side.

[16]King Asa also deposed his grandmother Maacah from her position as queen mother, because she had made a repulsive Asherah pole. Asa cut the pole down, broke it up and burned it in the Kidron Valley. [17]Although he did not remove the high places from Israel, Asa's heart was fully committed ˌto the LORDˌ all his life. [18]He brought into the temple of God the silver and gold and the articles that he and his father had dedicated.

[19]There was no more war until the thirty-fifth year of Asa's reign.

Asa's Last Years

16 In the thirty-sixth year of Asa's reign Baasha king of Israel went up against Judah and fortified Ramah to prevent anyone from leaving or entering the territory of Asa king of Judah.

[2]Asa then took the silver and gold out of the treasuries of the LORD's temple and of his own palace and sent it to Ben-Hadad king of Aram, who was ruling in Damascus. [3]"Let there be a treaty between me and you," he said, "as there was between my father and your father. See, I am sending you silver and gold. Now break your treaty with Baasha king of Israel so he will withdraw from me."

[4]Ben-Hadad agreed with King Asa and sent the commanders of his forces against the towns of Israel. They conquered Ijon, Dan, Abel Maim[a] and all the store cities of Naphtali. [5]When Baasha heard this, he stopped building Ramah and abandoned his work. [6]Then King Asa brought all the men of Judah, and they carried away from Ramah the stones and timber Baasha had

been using. With them he built up Geba and Mizpah.

[7]At that time Hanani the seer came to Asa king of Judah and said to him: "Because you relied on the king of Aram and not on the LORD your God, the army of the king of Aram has escaped from your hand. [8]Were not the Cushites[b] and Libyans a mighty army with great numbers of chariots and horsemen[c]? Yet when you relied on the LORD, he delivered them into your hand. [9]For the eyes of the LORD range throughout the earth to strengthen those whose hearts are fully committed to him. You have done a foolish thing, and from now on you will be at war."

[10]Asa was angry with the seer because of this; he was so enraged that he put him in prison. At the same time Asa brutally oppressed some of the people.

[11]The events of Asa's reign, from beginning to end, are written in the book of the kings of Judah and Israel. [12]In the thirty-ninth year of his reign Asa was afflicted with a disease in his feet. Though his disease was severe, even in his illness he did not seek help from the LORD, but only from the physicians. [13]Then in the forty-first year of his reign Asa died and rested with his fathers. [14]They buried him in the tomb that he had cut out for himself in the City of David. They laid him on a bier covered with spices and various blended perfumes, and they made a huge fire in his honor.

Jehoshaphat King of Judah

17 Jehoshaphat his son succeeded him as king and strengthened himself against Israel. [2]He stationed troops in all the fortified cities of Judah and put garrisons in Judah and in the towns of Ephraim that his father Asa had captured.

[3]The LORD was with Jehoshaphat because in his early years he walked in the ways his father David had followed. He did not consult the Baals [4]but sought the God of his father and followed his commands rather than the practices of Israel. [5]The LORD established the kingdom under his control; and all Judah brought gifts to Jehoshaphat, so that he had great wealth and honor. [6]His heart was devoted to the ways of the LORD; furthermore, he removed the high places and the Asherah poles from Judah.

[7]In the third year of his reign he sent his

---

[a]4 Also known as *Abel Beth Maacah*　　[b]8 That is, people from the upper Nile region　　[c]8 Or *charioteers*

officials Ben-Hail, Obadiah, Zechariah, Nethanel and Micaiah to teach in the towns of Judah. ⁸With them were certain Levites—Shemaiah, Nethaniah, Zebadiah, Asahel, Shemiramoth, Jehonathan, Adonijah, Tobijah and Tob-Adonijah—and the priests Elishama and Jehoram. ⁹They taught throughout Judah, taking with them the Book of the Law of the LORD; they went around to all the towns of Judah and taught the people.

¹⁰The fear of the LORD fell on all the kingdoms of the lands surrounding Judah, so that they did not make war with Jehoshaphat. ¹¹Some Philistines brought Jehoshaphat gifts and silver as tribute, and the Arabs brought him flocks: seven thousand seven hundred rams and seven thousand seven hundred goats.

¹²Jehoshaphat became more and more powerful; he built forts and store cities in Judah ¹³and had large supplies in the towns of Judah. He also kept experienced fighting men in Jerusalem. ¹⁴Their enrollment by families was as follows:

From Judah, commanders of units of 1,000:
Adnah the commander, with 300,000 fighting men;
¹⁵next, Jehohanan the commander, with 280,000;
¹⁶next, Amasiah son of Zicri, who volunteered himself for the service of the LORD, with 200,000.
¹⁷From Benjamin:
Eliada, a valiant soldier, with 200,000 men armed with bows and shields;
¹⁸next, Jehozabad, with 180,000 men armed for battle.

¹⁹These were the men who served the king, besides those he stationed in the fortified cities throughout Judah.

Micaiah Prophesies Against Ahab

18 Now Jehoshaphat had great wealth and honor, and he allied himself with Ahab by marriage. ²Some years later he went down to visit Ahab in Samaria. Ahab slaughtered many sheep and cattle for him and the people with him and urged him to attack Ramoth Gilead. ³Ahab king of Israel asked Jehoshaphat king of Judah, "Will you go with me against Ramoth Gilead?"

Jehoshaphat replied, "I am as you are, and my people as your people; we will join you in the war." ⁴But Jehoshaphat also said to the king of Israel, "First seek the counsel of the LORD."

⁵So the king of Israel brought together the prophets—four hundred men—and asked them, "Shall we go to war against Ramoth Gilead, or shall I refrain?"

"Go," they answered, "for God will give it into the king's hand."

⁶But Jehoshaphat asked, "Is there not a prophet of the LORD here whom we can inquire of?"

⁷The king of Israel answered Jehoshaphat, "There is still one man through whom we can inquire of the LORD, but I hate him because he never prophesies anything good about me, but always bad. He is Micaiah son of Imlah."

"The king should not say that," Jehoshaphat replied.

⁸So the king of Israel called one of his officials and said, "Bring Micaiah son of Imlah at once."

⁹Dressed in their royal robes, the king of Israel and Jehoshaphat king of Judah were sitting on their thrones at the threshing floor by the entrance to the gate of Samaria, with all the prophets prophesying before them. ¹⁰Now Zedekiah son of Kenaanah had made iron horns, and he declared, "This is what the LORD says: 'With these you will gore the Arameans until they are destroyed.'"

¹¹All the other prophets were prophesying the same thing. "Attack Ramoth Gilead and be victorious," they said, "for the LORD will give it into the king's hand."

¹²The messenger who had gone to summon Micaiah said to him, "Look, as one man the other prophets are predicting success for the king. Let your word agree with theirs, and speak favorably."

¹³But Micaiah said, "As surely as the LORD lives, I can tell him only what my God says."

¹⁴When he arrived, the king asked him, "Micaiah, shall we go to war against Ramoth Gilead, or shall I refrain?"

"Attack and be victorious," he answered, "for they will be given into your hand."

¹⁵The king said to him, "How many times must I make you swear to tell me nothing but the truth in the name of the LORD?"

¹⁶Then Micaiah answered, "I saw all Israel scattered on the hills like sheep without a shepherd, and the LORD said, 'These people have no master. Let each one go home in peace.'"

¹⁷The king of Israel said to Jehoshaphat,

"Didn't I tell you that he never prophesies anything good about me, but only bad?"

[18]Micaiah continued, "Therefore hear the word of the LORD: I saw the LORD sitting on his throne with all the host of heaven standing on his right and on his left. [19]And the LORD said, 'Who will entice Ahab king of Israel into attacking Ramoth Gilead and going to his death there?'

"One suggested this, and another that. [20]Finally, a spirit came forward, stood before the LORD and said, 'I will entice him.'

" 'By what means?' the LORD asked.

[21]" 'I will go and be a lying spirit in the mouths of all his prophets,' he said.

" 'You will succeed in enticing him,' said the LORD. 'Go and do it.'

[22]"So now the LORD has put a lying spirit in the mouths of these prophets of yours. The LORD has decreed disaster for you."

[23]Then Zedekiah son of Kenaanah went up and slapped Micaiah in the face. "Which way did the spirit from[a] the LORD go when he went from me to speak to you?" he asked.

[24]Micaiah replied, "You will find out on the day you go to hide in an inner room."

[25]The king of Israel then ordered, "Take Micaiah and send him back to Amon the ruler of the city and to Joash the king's son, [26]and say, 'This is what the king says: Put this fellow in prison and give him nothing but bread and water until I return safely.' "

[27]Micaiah declared, "If you ever return safely, the LORD has not spoken through me." Then he added, "Mark my words, all you people!"

Ahab Killed at Ramoth Gilead

[28]So the king of Israel and Jehoshaphat king of Judah went up to Ramoth Gilead. [29]The king of Israel said to Jehoshaphat, "I will enter the battle in disguise, but you wear your royal robes." So the king of Israel disguised himself and went into battle.

[30]Now the king of Aram had ordered his chariot commanders, "Do not fight with anyone, small or great, except the king of Israel." [31]When the chariot commanders saw Jehoshaphat, they thought, "This is the king of Israel." So they turned to attack him, but Jehoshaphat cried out, and the LORD helped him. God drew them away from him, [32]for when the chariot commanders saw that he was not the king of Israel, they stopped pursuing him.

[33]But someone drew his bow at random and hit the king of Israel between the sections of his armor. The king told the chariot driver, "Wheel around and get me out of the fighting. I've been wounded." [34]All day long the battle raged, and the king of Israel propped himself up in his chariot facing the Arameans until evening. Then at sunset he died.

19 When Jehoshaphat king of Judah returned safely to his palace in Jerusalem, [2]Jehu the seer, the son of Hanani, went out to meet him and said to the king, "Should you help the wicked and love[b] those who hate the LORD? Because of this, the wrath of the LORD is upon you. [3]There is, however, some good in you, for you have rid the land of the Asherah poles and have set your heart on seeking God."

Jehoshaphat Appoints Judges

[4]Jehoshaphat lived in Jerusalem, and he went out again among the people from Beersheba to the hill country of Ephraim and turned them back to the LORD, the God of their fathers. [5]He appointed judges in the land, in each of the fortified cities of Judah. [6]He told them, "Consider carefully what you do, because you are not judging for man but for the LORD, who is with you whenever you give a verdict. [7]Now let the fear of the LORD be upon you. Judge carefully, for with the LORD our God there is no injustice or partiality or bribery."

[8]In Jerusalem also, Jehoshaphat appointed some of the Levites, priests and heads of Israelite families to administer the law of the LORD and to settle disputes. And they lived in Jerusalem. [9]He gave them these orders: "You must serve faithfully and wholeheartedly in the fear of the LORD. [10]In every case that comes before you from your fellow countrymen who live in the cities—whether bloodshed or other concerns of the law, commands, decrees or ordinances—you are to warn them not to sin against the LORD; otherwise his wrath will come on you and your brothers. Do this, and you will not sin.

[11]"Amariah the chief priest will be over you in any matter concerning the LORD, and Zebadiah son of Ishmael, the leader of the tribe of Judah, will be over you in any matter concerning the king, and the Levites will serve as officials before you. Act with courage, and may the LORD be with those who do well."

---

a23 Or *Spirit of*   *b2* Or *and make alliances with*

Jehoshaphat Defeats Moab and Ammon

20 After this, the Moabites and Ammonites with some of the Meunites[a] came to make war on Jehoshaphat.

²Some men came and told Jehoshaphat, "A vast army is coming against you from Edom,[b] from the other side of the Sea.[c] It is already in Hazazon Tamar" (that is, En Gedi). ³Alarmed, Jehoshaphat resolved to inquire of the LORD, and he proclaimed a fast for all Judah. ⁴The people of Judah came together to seek help from the LORD; indeed, they came from every town in Judah to seek him.

⁵Then Jehoshaphat stood up in the assembly of Judah and Jerusalem at the temple of the LORD in the front of the new courtyard ⁶and said:

"O LORD, God of our fathers, are you not the God who is in heaven? You rule over all the kingdoms of the nations. Power and might are in your hand, and no one can withstand you. ⁷O our God, did you not drive out the inhabitants of this land before your people Israel and give it forever to the descendants of Abraham your friend? ⁸They have lived in it and have built in it a sanctuary for your Name, saying, ⁹'If calamity comes upon us, whether the sword of judgment, or plague or famine, we will stand in your presence before this temple that bears your Name and will cry out to you in our distress, and you will hear us and save us.'

¹⁰"But now here are men from Ammon, Moab and Mount Seir, whose territory you would not allow Israel to invade when they came from Egypt; so they turned away from them and did not destroy them. ¹¹See how they are repaying us by coming to drive us out of the possession you gave us as an inheritance. ¹²O our God, will you not judge them? For we have no power to face this vast army that is attacking us. We do not know what to do, but our eyes are upon you."

¹³All the men of Judah, with their wives and children and little ones, stood there before the LORD.

¹⁴Then the Spirit of the LORD came upon Jahaziel son of Zechariah, the son of Benaiah, the son of Jeiel, the son of Mattaniah, a Levite and descendant of Asaph, as he stood in the assembly.

¹⁵He said: "Listen, King Jehoshaphat and all who live in Judah and Jerusalem! This is what the LORD says to you: 'Do not be afraid or discouraged because of this vast army. For the battle is not yours, but God's. ¹⁶Tomorrow march down against them. They will be climbing up by the Pass of Ziz, and you will find them at the end of the gorge in the Desert of Jeruel. ¹⁷You will not have to fight this battle. Take up your positions; stand firm and see the deliverance the LORD will give you, O Judah and Jerusalem. Do not be afraid; do not be discouraged. Go out to face them tomorrow, and the LORD will be with you.' "

¹⁸Jehoshaphat bowed with his face to the ground, and all the people of Judah and Jerusalem fell down in worship before the LORD. ¹⁹Then some Levites from the Kohathites and Korahites stood up and praised the LORD, the God of Israel, with very loud voice.

²⁰Early in the morning they left for the Desert of Tekoa. As they set out, Jehoshaphat stood and said, "Listen to me, Judah and people of Jerusalem! Have faith in the LORD your God and you will be upheld; have faith in his prophets and you will be successful." ²¹After consulting the people, Jehoshaphat appointed men to sing to the LORD and to praise him for the splendor of his[d] holiness as they went out at the head of the army, saying:

"Give thanks to the LORD,
  for his love endures forever."

²²As they began to sing and praise, the LORD set ambushes against the men of Ammon and Moab and Mount Seir who were invading Judah, and they were defeated. ²³The men of Ammon and Moab rose up against the men from Mount Seir to destroy and annihilate them. After they finished slaughtering the men from Seir, they helped to destroy one another.

²⁴When the men of Judah came to the place that overlooks the desert and looked toward the vast army, they saw only dead

a1 Some Septuagint manuscripts; Hebrew *Ammonites*   b2 One Hebrew manuscript; most Hebrew manuscripts, Septuagint and Vulgate *Aram*   c2 That is, the Dead Sea   d21 Or *him with the splendor of* bodies lying on the ground; no one had escaped. ²⁵So Jehoshaphat and his men went to carry off their plunder, and they found among them a great amount of equipment and clothing*a* and also articles of value — more than they could take away. There was so much plunder that it took three days to collect it. ²⁶On the fourth day they assembled in the Valley of Beracah, where they praised the LORD. This is why it is called the Valley of Beracah*b* to this day.

²⁷Then, led by Jehoshaphat, all the men of Judah and Jerusalem returned joyfully to Jerusalem, for the LORD had given them cause to rejoice over their enemies. ²⁸They entered Jerusalem and went to the temple of the LORD with harps and lutes and trumpets.

²⁹The fear of God came upon all the kingdoms of the countries when they heard how the LORD had fought against the enemies of Israel. ³⁰And the kingdom of Jehoshaphat was at peace, for his God had given him rest on every side.

The End of Jehoshaphat's Reign

³¹So Jehoshaphat reigned over Judah. He was thirty-five years old when he became king of Judah, and he reigned in Jerusalem twenty-five years. His mother's name was Azubah daughter of Shilhi. ³²He walked in the ways of his father Asa and did not stray from them; he did what was right in the eyes of the LORD. ³³The high places, however, were not removed, and the people still had not set their hearts on the God of their fathers.

³⁴The other events of Jehoshaphat's reign, from beginning to end, are written in the annals of Jehu son of Hanani, which are recorded in the book of the kings of Israel.

³⁵Later, Jehoshaphat king of Judah made an alliance with Ahaziah king of Israel, who was guilty of wickedness. ³⁶He agreed with him to construct a fleet of trading ships.*c* After these were built at Ezion Geber, ³⁷Eliezer son of Dodavahu of Mareshah prophesied against Jehoshaphat, saying, "Because you have made an alliance with Ahaziah, the LORD will destroy what you have made." The ships were wrecked and were not able to set sail to trade.*d*

21 Then Jehoshaphat rested with his fathers and was buried with them in the City of David. And Jehoram his son succeeded him as king. ²Jehoram's brothers, the sons of Jehoshaphat, were Azariah, Jehiel, Zechariah, Azariahu, Michael and Shephatiah. All these were sons of Jehoshaphat king of Israel.*e* ³Their father had given them many gifts of silver and gold and articles of value, as well as fortified cities in Judah, but he had given the kingdom to Jehoram because he was his firstborn son.

Jehoram King of Judah

⁴When Jehoram established himself firmly over his father's kingdom, he put all his brothers to the sword along with some of the princes of Israel. ⁵Jehoram was thirty-two years old when he became king, and he reigned in Jerusalem eight years. ⁶He walked in the ways of the kings of Israel, as the house of Ahab had done, for he married a daughter of Ahab. He did evil in the eyes of the LORD. ⁷Nevertheless, because of the covenant the LORD had made with David, the LORD was not willing to destroy the house of David. He had promised to maintain a lamp for him and his descendants forever.

⁸In the time of Jehoram, Edom rebelled against Judah and set up its own king. ⁹So Jehoram went there with his officers and all his chariots. The Edomites surrounded him and his chariot commanders, but he rose up and broke through by night. ¹⁰To this day Edom has been in rebellion against Judah.

Libnah revolted at the same time, because Jehoram had forsaken the LORD, the God of his fathers. ¹¹He had also built high places on the hills of Judah and had caused the people of Jerusalem to prostitute themselves and had led Judah astray.

¹²Jehoram received a letter from Elijah the prophet, which said:

"This is what the LORD, the God of your father David, says: 'You have not walked in the ways of your father Jehoshaphat or of Asa king of Judah. ¹³But you have walked in the ways of the kings of Israel, and you have led Judah and the people of Jerusalem to prostitute themselves, just as the house of Ahab did. You have also

---

*a*25 Some Hebrew manuscripts and Vulgate; most Hebrew manuscripts *corpses*　　*b*26 *Beracah* means *praise.*　　*c*36 Hebrew *of ships that could go to Tarshish*　　*d*37 Hebrew *sail for Tarshish*　　*e*2 That is, Judah, as frequently in 2 Chronicles murdered your own brothers, members of your father's house, men who were better than you. **14**So now the Lord is about to strike your people, your sons, your wives and everything that is yours, with a heavy blow. **15**You yourself will be very ill with a lingering disease of the bowels, until the disease causes your bowels to come out.' "

16The Lord aroused against Jehoram the hostility of the Philistines and of the Arabs who lived near the Cushites. **17**They attacked Judah, invaded it and carried off all the goods found in the king's palace, together with his sons and wives. Not a son was left to him except Ahaziah,*a* the youngest.

18After all this, the Lord afflicted Jehoram with an incurable disease of the bowels. **19**In the course of time, at the end of the second year, his bowels came out because of the disease, and he died in great pain. His people made no fire in his honor, as they had for his fathers.

20Jehoram was thirty-two years old when he became king, and he reigned in Jerusalem eight years. He passed away, to no one's regret, and was buried in the City of David, but not in the tombs of the kings.

Ahaziah King of Judah

22 The people of Jerusalem made Ahaziah, Jehoram's youngest son, king in his place, since the raiders, who came with the Arabs into the camp, had killed all the older sons. So Ahaziah son of Jehoram king of Judah began to reign.

2Ahaziah was twenty-two*b* years old when he became king, and he reigned in Jerusalem one year. His mother's name was Athaliah, a granddaughter of Omri.

3He too walked in the ways of the house of Ahab, for his mother encouraged him in doing wrong. **4**He did evil in the eyes of the Lord, as the house of Ahab had done, for after his father's death they became his advisers, to his undoing. **5**He also followed their counsel when he went with Joram*c* son of Ahab king of Israel to war against Hazael king of Aram at Ramoth Gilead. The Arameans wounded Joram; **6**so he returned to Jezreel to recover from the wounds they had inflicted on him at Ramoth*d* in his battle with Hazael king of Aram.

Then Ahaziah*e* son of Jehoram king of Judah went down to Jezreel to see Joram son of Ahab because he had been wounded.

7Through Ahaziah's visit to Joram, God brought about Ahaziah's downfall. When Ahaziah arrived, he went out with Joram to meet Jehu son of Nimshi, whom the Lord had anointed to destroy the house of Ahab. **8**While Jehu was executing judgment on the house of Ahab, he found the princes of Judah and the sons of Ahaziah's relatives, who had been attending Ahaziah, and he killed them. **9**He then went in search of Ahaziah, and his men captured him while he was hiding in Samaria. He was brought to Jehu and put to death. They buried him, for they said, "He was a son of Jehoshaphat, who sought the Lord with all his heart." So there was no one in the house of Ahaziah powerful enough to retain the kingdom.

Athaliah and Joash

10When Athaliah the mother of Ahaziah saw that her son was dead, she proceeded to destroy the whole royal family of the house of Judah. **11**But Jehosheba,*f* the daughter of King Jehoram, took Joash son of Ahaziah and stole him away from among the royal princes who were about to be murdered and put him and his nurse in a bedroom. Because Jehosheba,*f* the daughter of King Jehoram and wife of the priest Jehoiada, was Ahaziah's sister, she hid the child from Athaliah so she could not kill him. **12**He remained hidden with them at the temple of God for six years while Athaliah ruled the land.

23 In the seventh year Jehoiada showed his strength. He made a covenant with the commanders of units of a hundred: Azariah son of Jeroham, Ishmael son of Jehohanan, Azariah son of Obed, Maaseiah son of Adaiah, and Elishaphat son of Zicri. **2**They went throughout Judah and gathered the Levites and the heads of Israelite families from all the towns. When they came to Jerusalem, **3**the whole assembly made a covenant with the king at the temple of God.

---

a17 Hebrew *Jehoahaz*, a variant of *Ahaziah*   *b2* Some Septuagint manuscripts and Syriac (see also 2 Kings 8:26); Hebrew *forty-two*   *c5* Hebrew *Jehoram*, a variant of *Joram*; also in verses 6 and 7   *d6* Hebrew *Ramah*, a variant of *Ramoth*   *e6* Some Hebrew manuscripts, Septuagint, Vulgate and Syriac (see also 2 Kings 8:29); most Hebrew manuscripts *Azariah*   *f11* Hebrew *Jehoshabeath*, a variant of *Jehosheba*

Jehoiada said to them, "The king's son shall reign, as the Lord promised concerning the descendants of David. ⁴Now this is what you are to do: A third of you priests and Levites who are going on duty on the Sabbath are to keep watch at the doors, ⁵a third of you at the royal palace and a third at the Foundation Gate, and all the other men are to be in the courtyards of the temple of the Lord. ⁶No one is to enter the temple of the Lord except the priests and Levites on duty; they may enter because they are consecrated, but all the other men are to guard what the Lord has assigned to them.ᵃ ⁷The Levites are to station themselves around the king, each man with his weapons in his hand. Anyone who enters the temple must be put to death. Stay close to the king wherever he goes."

⁸The Levites and all the men of Judah did just as Jehoiada the priest ordered. Each one took his men — those who were going on duty on the Sabbath and those who were going off duty — for Jehoiada the priest had not released any of the divisions. ⁹Then he gave the commanders of units of a hundred the spears and the large and small shields that had belonged to King David and that were in the temple of God. ¹⁰He stationed all the men, each with his weapon in his hand, around the king — near the altar and the temple, from the south side to the north side of the temple.

¹¹Jehoiada and his sons brought out the king's son and put the crown on him; they presented him with a copy of the covenant and proclaimed him king. They anointed him and shouted, "Long live the king!"

¹²When Athaliah heard the noise of the people running and cheering the king, she went to them at the temple of the Lord. ¹³She looked, and there was the king, standing by his pillar at the entrance. The officers and the trumpeters were beside the king, and all the people of the land were rejoicing and blowing trumpets, and singers with musical instruments were leading the praises. Then Athaliah tore her robes and shouted, "Treason! Treason!"

¹⁴Jehoiada the priest sent out the commanders of units of a hundred, who were in charge of the troops, and said to them: "Bring her out between the ranksᵇ and put to the sword anyone who follows

her." For the priest had said, "Do not put her to death at the temple of the Lord." ¹⁵So they seized her as she reached the entrance of the Horse Gate on the palace grounds, and there they put her to death.

¹⁶Jehoiada then made a covenant that he and the people and the kingᶜ would be the Lord's people. ¹⁷All the people went to the temple of Baal and tore it down. They smashed the altars and idols and killed Mattan the priest of Baal in front of the altars.

¹⁸Then Jehoiada placed the oversight of the temple of the Lord in the hands of the priests, who were Levites, to whom David had made assignments in the temple, to present the burnt offerings of the Lord as written in the Law of Moses, with rejoicing and singing, as David had ordered. ¹⁹He also stationed doorkeepers at the gates of the Lord's temple so that no one who was in any way unclean might enter.

²⁰He took with him the commanders of hundreds, the nobles, the rulers of the people and all the people of the land and brought the king down from the temple of the Lord. They went into the palace through the Upper Gate and seated the king on the royal throne, ²¹and all the people of the land rejoiced. And the city was quiet, because Athaliah had been slain with the sword.

Joash Repairs the Temple

24 Joash was seven years old when he became king, and he reigned in Jerusalem forty years. His mother's name was Zibiah; she was from Beersheba. ²Joash did what was right in the eyes of the Lord all the years of Jehoiada the priest. ³Jehoiada chose two wives for him, and he had sons and daughters.

⁴Some time later Joash decided to restore the temple of the Lord. ⁵He called together the priests and Levites and said to them, "Go to the towns of Judah and collect the money due annually from all Israel, to repair the temple of your God. Do it now." But the Levites did not act at once.

⁶Therefore the king summoned Jehoiada the chief priest and said to him, "Why haven't you required the Levites to bring in from Judah and Jerusalem the tax imposed by Moses the servant of the Lord and by the assembly of Israel for the Tent of the Testimony?"

ᵃ6 Or *to observe the Lord's command not to enter,* ᵇ14 Or *out from the precincts* ᶜ16 Or *covenant between the Lord and the people and the king that they* (see 2 Kings 11:17)

[7]Now the sons of that wicked woman Athaliah had broken into the temple of God and had used even its sacred objects for the Baals.

[8]At the king's command, a chest was made and placed outside, at the gate of the temple of the LORD. [9]A proclamation was then issued in Judah and Jerusalem that they should bring to the LORD the tax that Moses the servant of God had required of Israel in the desert. [10]All the officials and all the people brought their contributions gladly, dropping them into the chest until it was full. [11]Whenever the chest was brought in by the Levites to the king's officials and they saw that there was a large amount of money, the royal secretary and the officer of the chief priest would come and empty the chest and carry it back to its place. They did this regularly and collected a great amount of money. [12]The king and Jehoiada gave it to the men who carried out the work required for the temple of the LORD. They hired masons and carpenters to restore the LORD's temple, and also workers in iron and bronze to repair the temple.

[13]The men in charge of the work were diligent, and the repairs progressed under them. They rebuilt the temple of God according to its original design and reinforced it. [14]When they had finished, they brought the rest of the money to the king and Jehoiada, and with it were made articles for the LORD's temple: articles for the service and for the burnt offerings, and also dishes and other objects of gold and silver. As long as Jehoiada lived, burnt offerings were presented continually in the temple of the LORD.

[15]Now Jehoiada was old and full of years, and he died at the age of a hundred and thirty. [16]He was buried with the kings in the City of David, because of the good he had done in Israel for God and his temple.

The Wickedness of Joash

[17]After the death of Jehoiada, the officials of Judah came and paid homage to the king, and he listened to them. [18]They abandoned the temple of the LORD, the God of their fathers, and worshiped Asherah poles and idols. Because of their guilt, God's anger came upon Judah and Jerusalem. [19]Although the LORD sent prophets to the people to bring them back to him, and though they testified against them, they would not listen.

[20]Then the Spirit of God came upon Zechariah son of Jehoiada the priest. He stood before the people and said, "This is what God says: 'Why do you disobey the LORD's commands? You will not prosper. Because you have forsaken the LORD, he has forsaken you.'"

[21]But they plotted against him, and by order of the king they stoned him to death in the courtyard of the LORD's temple. [22]King Joash did not remember the kindness Zechariah's father Jehoiada had shown him but killed his son, who said as he lay dying, "May the LORD see this and call you to account."

[23]At the turn of the year,[a] the army of Aram marched against Joash; it invaded Judah and Jerusalem and killed all the leaders of the people. They sent all the plunder to their king in Damascus. [24]Although the Aramean army had come with only a few men, the LORD delivered into their hands a much larger army. Because Judah had forsaken the LORD, the God of their fathers, judgment was executed on Joash. [25]When the Arameans withdrew, they left Joash severely wounded. His officials conspired against him for murdering the son of Jehoiada the priest, and they killed him in his bed. So he died and was buried in the City of David, but not in the tombs of the kings.

[26]Those who conspired against him were Zabad,[b] son of Shimeath an Ammonite woman, and Jehozabad, son of Shimrith[c] a Moabite woman. [27]The account of his sons, the many prophecies about him, and the record of the restoration of the temple of God are written in the annotations on the book of the kings. And Amaziah his son succeeded him as king.

Amaziah King of Judah

25 Amaziah was twenty-five years old when he became king, and he reigned in Jerusalem twenty-nine years. His mother's name was Jehoaddin[d]; she was from Jerusalem. [2]He did what was right in the eyes of the LORD, but not wholeheartedly. [3]After the kingdom was firmly in his control, he executed the officials who had murdered his father the king. [4]Yet he did not put their sons to death, but acted in accordance with what is written in the Law, in the Book of Mo-

---

[a]23 Probably in the spring   [b]26 A variant of *Jozabad*   [c]26 A variant of *Shomer*   [d]1 Hebrew *Jehoaddan*, a variant of *Jehoaddin*

ses, where the LORD commanded: "Fathers shall not be put to death for their children, nor children put to death for their fathers; each is to die for his own sins."[a]

5Amaziah called the people of Judah together and assigned them according to their families to commanders of thousands and commanders of hundreds for all Judah and Benjamin. He then mustered those twenty years old or more and found that there were three hundred thousand men ready for military service, able to handle the spear and shield. 6He also hired a hundred thousand fighting men from Israel for a hundred talents[b] of silver.

7But a man of God came to him and said, "O king, these troops from Israel must not march with you, for the LORD is not with Israel—not with any of the people of Ephraim. 8Even if you go and fight courageously in battle, God will overthrow you before the enemy, for God has the power to help or to overthrow."

9Amaziah asked the man of God, "But what about the hundred talents I paid for these Israelite troops?"

The man of God replied, "The LORD can give you much more than that."

10So Amaziah dismissed the troops who had come to him from Ephraim and sent them home. They were furious with Judah and left for home in a great rage.

11Amaziah then marshaled his strength and led his army to the Valley of Salt, where he killed ten thousand men of Seir. 12The army of Judah also captured ten thousand men alive, took them to the top of a cliff and threw them down so that all were dashed to pieces.

13Meanwhile the troops that Amaziah had sent back and had not allowed to take part in the war raided Judean towns from Samaria to Beth Horon. They killed three thousand people and carried off great quantities of plunder.

14When Amaziah returned from slaughtering the Edomites, he brought back the gods of the people of Seir. He set them up as his own gods, bowed down to them and burned sacrifices to them. 15The anger of the LORD burned against Amaziah, and he sent a prophet to him, who said, "Why do you consult this people's gods, which could not save their own people from your hand?"

16While he was still speaking, the king said to him, "Have we appointed you an adviser to the king? Stop! Why be struck down?"

So the prophet stopped but said, "I know that God has determined to destroy you, because you have done this and have not listened to my counsel."

17After Amaziah king of Judah consulted his advisers, he sent this challenge to Jehoash[c] son of Jehoahaz, the son of Jehu, king of Israel: "Come, meet me face to face."

18But Jehoash king of Israel replied to Amaziah king of Judah: "A thistle in Lebanon sent a message to a cedar in Lebanon, 'Give your daughter to my son in marriage.' Then a wild beast in Lebanon came along and trampled the thistle underfoot. 19You say to yourself that you have defeated Edom, and now you are arrogant and proud. But stay at home! Why ask for trouble and cause your own downfall and that of Judah also?"

20Amaziah, however, would not listen, for God so worked that he might hand them over to ⌊Jehoash⌋, because they sought the gods of Edom. 21So Jehoash king of Israel attacked. He and Amaziah king of Judah faced each other at Beth Shemesh in Judah. 22Judah was routed by Israel, and every man fled to his home. 23Jehoash king of Israel captured Amaziah king of Judah, the son of Joash, the son of Ahaziah,[d] at Beth Shemesh. Then Jehoash brought him to Jerusalem and broke down the wall of Jerusalem from the Ephraim Gate to the Corner Gate—a section about six hundred feet[e] long. 24He took all the gold and silver and all the articles found in the temple of God that had been in the care of Obed-Edom, together with the palace treasures and the hostages, and returned to Samaria.

25Amaziah son of Joash king of Judah lived for fifteen years after the death of Jehoash son of Jehoahaz king of Israel. 26As for the other events of Amaziah's reign, from beginning to end, are they not written in the book of the kings of Judah and Israel? 27From the time that Amaziah turned away from following the LORD, they conspired against him in Jerusalem and he fled to Lachish, but they sent men after him to Lachish and killed him there. 28He was brought back by horse and was

---

a4 Deut. 24:16   b6 That is, about 3 3/4 tons (about 3.4 metric tons); also in verse 9   c17 Hebrew Joash, a variant of Jehoash; also in verses 18, 21, 23 and 25   d23 Hebrew Jehoahaz, a variant of Ahaziah   e23 Hebrew four hundred cubits (about 180 meters) buried with his fathers in the City of Judah.

Uzziah King of Judah

26 Then all the people of Judah took Uzziah,[a] who was sixteen years old, and made him king in place of his father Amaziah. [2]He was the one who rebuilt Elath and restored it to Judah after Amaziah rested with his fathers.

[3]Uzziah was sixteen years old when he became king, and he reigned in Jerusalem fifty-two years. His mother's name was Jecoliah; she was from Jerusalem. [4]He did what was right in the eyes of the LORD, just as his father Amaziah had done. [5]He sought God during the days of Zechariah, who instructed him in the fear[b] of God. As long as he sought the LORD, God gave him success.

[6]He went to war against the Philistines and broke down the walls of Gath, Jabneh and Ashdod. He then rebuilt towns near Ashdod and elsewhere among the Philistines. [7]God helped him against the Philistines and against the Arabs who lived in Gur Baal and against the Meunites. [8]The Ammonites brought tribute to Uzziah, and his fame spread as far as the border of Egypt, because he had become very powerful.

[9]Uzziah built towers in Jerusalem at the Corner Gate, at the Valley Gate and at the angle of the wall, and he fortified them. [10]He also built towers in the desert and dug many cisterns, because he had much livestock in the foothills and in the plain. He had people working his fields and vineyards in the hills and in the fertile lands, for he loved the soil.

[11]Uzziah had a well-trained army, ready to go out by divisions according to their numbers as mustered by Jeiel the secretary and Maaseiah the officer under the direction of Hananiah, one of the royal officials. [12]The total number of family leaders over the fighting men was 2,600. [13]Under their command was an army of 307,500 men trained for war, a powerful force to support the king against his enemies. [14]Uzziah provided shields, spears, helmets, coats of armor, bows and slingstones for the entire army. [15]In Jerusalem he made machines designed by skillful men for use on the towers and on the corner defenses to shoot arrows and hurl large stones. His fame spread far and wide, for he was greatly helped until he became powerful.

[16]But after Uzziah became powerful, his pride led to his downfall. He was unfaithful to the LORD his God, and entered the temple of the LORD to burn incense on the altar of incense. [17]Azariah the priest with eighty other courageous priests of the LORD followed him in. [18]They confronted him and said, "It is not right for you, Uzziah, to burn incense to the LORD. That is for the priests, the descendants of Aaron, who have been consecrated to burn incense. Leave the sanctuary, for you have been unfaithful; and you will not be honored by the LORD God."

[19]Uzziah, who had a censer in his hand ready to burn incense, became angry. While he was raging at the priests in their presence before the incense altar in the LORD's temple, leprosy[c] broke out on his forehead. [20]When Azariah the chief priest and all the other priests looked at him, they saw that he had leprosy on his forehead, so they hurried him out. Indeed, he himself was eager to leave, because the LORD had afflicted him.

[21]King Uzziah had leprosy until the day he died. He lived in a separate house[d]— leprous, and excluded from the temple of the LORD. Jotham his son had charge of the palace and governed the people of the land.

[22]The other events of Uzziah's reign, from beginning to end, are recorded by the prophet Isaiah son of Amoz. [23]Uzziah rested with his fathers and was buried near them in a field for burial that belonged to the kings, for people said, "He had leprosy." And Jotham his son succeeded him as king.

Jotham King of Judah

27 Jotham was twenty-five years old when he became king, and he reigned in Jerusalem sixteen years. His mother's name was Jerusha daughter of Zadok. [2]He did what was right in the eyes of the LORD, just as his father Uzziah had done, but unlike him he did not enter the temple of the LORD. The people, however, continued their corrupt practices. [3]Jotham rebuilt the Upper Gate of the temple

---

a1 Also called *Azariah*   *b5* Many Hebrew manuscripts, Septuagint and Syriac; other Hebrew manuscripts *vision*   *c19* The Hebrew word was used for various diseases affecting the skin—not necessarily leprosy; also in verses 20, 21 and 23.   *d21* Or *in a house where he was relieved of responsibilities* of the LORD and did extensive work on the wall at the hill of Ophel. [4]He built towns in the Judean hills and forts and towers in the wooded areas.

[5]Jotham made war on the king of the Ammonites and conquered them. That year the Ammonites paid him a hundred talents[a] of silver, ten thousand cors[b] of wheat and ten thousand cors of barley. The Ammonites brought him the same amount also in the second and third years.

[6]Jotham grew powerful because he walked steadfastly before the LORD his God.

[7]The other events in Jotham's reign, including all his wars and the other things he did, are written in the book of the kings of Israel and Judah. [8]He was twenty-five years old when he became king, and he reigned in Jerusalem sixteen years. [9]Jotham rested with his fathers and was buried in the City of David. And Ahaz his son succeeded him as king.

Ahaz King of Judah

28 Ahaz was twenty years old when he became king, and he reigned in Jerusalem sixteen years. Unlike David his father, he did not do what was right in the eyes of the LORD. [2]He walked in the ways of the kings of Israel and also made cast idols for worshiping the Baals. [3]He burned sacrifices in the Valley of Ben Hinnom and sacrificed his sons in the fire, following the detestable ways of the nations the LORD had driven out before the Israelites. [4]He offered sacrifices and burned incense at the high places, on the hilltops and under every spreading tree.

[5]Therefore the LORD his God handed him over to the king of Aram. The Arameans defeated him and took many of his people as prisoners and brought them to Damascus.

He was also given into the hands of the king of Israel, who inflicted heavy casualties on him. [6]In one day Pekah son of Remaliah killed a hundred and twenty thousand soldiers in Judah—because Judah had forsaken the LORD, the God of their fathers. [7]Zicri, an Ephraimite warrior, killed Maaseiah the king's son, Azrikam the officer in charge of the palace, and Elkanah, second to the king. [8]The Israelites took captive from their kinsmen two hundred thousand wives, sons and daughters. They also took a great deal of plunder, which they carried back to Samaria.

[9]But a prophet of the LORD named Oded was there, and he went out to meet the army when it returned to Samaria. He said to them, "Because the LORD, the God of your fathers, was angry with Judah, he gave them into your hand. But you have slaughtered them in a rage that reaches to heaven. [10]And now you intend to make the men and women of Judah and Jerusalem your slaves. But aren't you also guilty of sins against the LORD your God? [11]Now listen to me! Send back your fellow countrymen you have taken as prisoners, for the LORD's fierce anger rests on you."

[12]Then some of the leaders in Ephraim—Azariah son of Jehohanan, Berekiah son of Meshillemoth, Jehizkiah son of Shallum, and Amasa son of Hadlai—confronted those who were arriving from the war. [13]"You must not bring those prisoners here," they said, "or we will be guilty before the LORD. Do you intend to add to our sin and guilt? For our guilt is already great, and his fierce anger rests on Israel."

[14]So the soldiers gave up the prisoners and plunder in the presence of the officials and all the assembly. [15]The men designated by name took the prisoners, and from the plunder they clothed all who were naked. They provided them with clothes and sandals, food and drink, and healing balm. All those who were weak they put on donkeys. So they took them back to their fellow countrymen at Jericho, the City of Palms, and returned to Samaria.

[16]At that time King Ahaz sent to the king[c] of Assyria for help. [17]The Edomites had again come and attacked Judah and carried away prisoners, [18]while the Philistines had raided towns in the foothills and in the Negev of Judah. They captured and occupied Beth Shemesh, Aijalon and Gederoth, as well as Soco, Timnah and Gimzo, with their surrounding villages. [19]The LORD had humbled Judah because of Ahaz king of Israel,[d] for he had promoted wickedness in Judah and had been most unfaithful to the LORD. [20]Tiglath-Pileser[e] king of Assyria came to him, but he gave him trouble instead of help. [21]Ahaz took

---

[a]5 That is, about 3 3/4 tons (about 3.4 metric tons)　[b]5 That is, probably about 62,000 bushels (about 2,200 kiloliters)　[c]16 One Hebrew manuscript, Septuagint and Vulgate (see also 2 Kings 16:7); most Hebrew manuscripts *kings*　[d]19 That is, Judah, as frequently in 2 Chronicles　[e]20 Hebrew *Tilgath-Pileser*, a variant of *Tiglath-Pileser*

some of the things from the temple of the Lord and from the royal palace and from the princes and presented them to the king of Assyria, but that did not help him. ²²In his time of trouble King Ahaz became even more unfaithful to the Lord. ²³He offered sacrifices to the gods of Damascus, who had defeated him; for he thought, "Since the gods of the kings of Aram have helped them, I will sacrifice to them so they will help me." But they were his downfall and the downfall of all Israel.

²⁴Ahaz gathered together the furnishings from the temple of God and took them away.ᵃ He shut the doors of the Lord's temple and set up altars at every street corner in Jerusalem. ²⁵In every town in Judah he built high places to burn sacrifices to other gods and provoked the Lord, the God of his fathers, to anger.

²⁶The other events of his reign and all his ways, from beginning to end, are written in the book of the kings of Judah and Israel. ²⁷Ahaz rested with his fathers and was buried in the city of Jerusalem, but he was not placed in the tombs of the kings of Israel. And Hezekiah his son succeeded him as king.

Hezekiah Purifies the Temple

29 Hezekiah was twenty-five years old when he became king, and he reigned in Jerusalem twenty-nine years. His mother's name was Abijah daughter of Zechariah. ²He did what was right in the eyes of the Lord, just as his father David had done.

³In the first month of the first year of his reign, he opened the doors of the temple of the Lord and repaired them. ⁴He brought in the priests and the Levites, assembled them in the square on the east side ⁵and said: "Listen to me, Levites! Consecrate yourselves now and consecrate the temple of the Lord, the God of your fathers. Remove all defilement from the sanctuary. ⁶Our fathers were unfaithful; they did evil in the eyes of the Lord our God and forsook him. They turned their faces away from the Lord's dwelling place and turned their backs on him. ⁷They also shut the doors of the portico and put out the lamps. They did not burn incense or present any burnt offerings at the sanctuary to the God of Israel. ⁸Therefore, the anger of the Lord has fallen on Judah and Jerusalem; he has made them an object of dread and horror and scorn, as you can see with your own eyes. ⁹This is why our fathers have fallen by the sword and why our sons and daughters and our wives are in captivity. ¹⁰Now I intend to make a covenant with the Lord, the God of Israel, so that his fierce anger will turn away from us. ¹¹My sons, do not be negligent now, for the Lord has chosen you to stand before him and serve him, to minister before him and to burn incense."

¹²Then these Levites set to work:
from the Kohathites,
Mahath son of Amasai and Joel son of Azariah;
from the Merarites,
Kish son of Abdi and Azariah son of Jehallelel;
from the Gershonites,
Joah son of Zimmah and Eden son of Joah;
¹³from the descendants of Elizaphan,
Shimri and Jeiel;
from the descendants of Asaph,
Zechariah and Mattaniah;
¹⁴from the descendants of Heman,
Jehiel and Shimei;
from the descendants of Jeduthun,
Shemaiah and Uzziel.

¹⁵When they had assembled their brothers and consecrated themselves, they went in to purify the temple of the Lord, as the king had ordered, following the word of the Lord. ¹⁶The priests went into the sanctuary of the Lord to purify it. They brought out to the courtyard of the Lord's temple everything unclean that they found in the temple of the Lord. The Levites took it and carried it out to the Kidron Valley. ¹⁷They began the consecration on the first day of the first month, and by the eighth day of the month they reached the portico of the Lord. For eight more days they consecrated the temple of the Lord itself, finishing on the sixteenth day of the first month.

¹⁸Then they went in to King Hezekiah and reported: "We have purified the entire temple of the Lord, the altar of burnt offering with all its utensils, and the table for setting out the consecrated bread, with all its articles. ¹⁹We have prepared and consecrated all the articles that King Ahaz removed in his unfaithfulness while he was king. They are now in front of the Lord's altar."

²⁰Early the next morning King Hezekiah gathered the city officials together and went up to the temple of the Lord. ²¹They

ᵃ24 Or *and cut them up*

brought seven bulls, seven rams, seven male lambs and seven male goats as a sin offering for the kingdom, for the sanctuary and for Judah. The king commanded the priests, the descendants of Aaron, to offer these on the altar of the LORD. 22So they slaughtered the bulls, and the priests took the blood and sprinkled it on the altar; next they slaughtered the rams and sprinkled their blood on the altar; then they slaughtered the lambs and sprinkled their blood on the altar. 23The goats for the sin offering were brought before the king and the assembly, and they laid their hands on them. 24The priests then slaughtered the goats and presented their blood on the altar for a sin offering to atone for all Israel, because the king had ordered the burnt offering and the sin offering for all Israel.

25He stationed the Levites in the temple of the LORD with cymbals, harps and lyres in the way prescribed by David and Gad the king's seer and Nathan the prophet; this was commanded by the LORD through his prophets. 26So the Levites stood ready with David's instruments, and the priests with their trumpets.

27Hezekiah gave the order to sacrifice the burnt offering on the altar. As the offering began, singing to the LORD began also, accompanied by trumpets and the instruments of David king of Israel. 28The whole assembly bowed in worship, while the singers sang and the trumpeters played. All this continued until the sacrifice of the burnt offering was completed.

29When the offerings were finished, the king and everyone present with him knelt down and worshiped. 30King Hezekiah and his officials ordered the Levites to praise the LORD with the words of David and of Asaph the seer. So they sang praises with gladness and bowed their heads and worshiped.

31Then Hezekiah said, "You have now dedicated yourselves to the LORD. Come and bring sacrifices and thank offerings to the temple of the LORD." So the assembly brought sacrifices and thank offerings, and all whose hearts were willing brought burnt offerings.

32The number of burnt offerings the assembly brought was seventy bulls, a hundred rams and two hundred male lambs — all of them for burnt offerings to the LORD. 33The animals consecrated as sacrifices amounted to six hundred bulls and three thousand sheep and goats. 34The priests, however, were too few to skin all the burnt offerings; so their kinsmen the Levites helped them until the task was finished and until other priests had been consecrated, for the Levites had been more conscientious in consecrating themselves than the priests had been. 35There were burnt offerings in abundance, together with the fat of the fellowship offerings[a] and the drink offerings that accompanied the burnt offerings.

So the service of the temple of the LORD was reestablished. 36Hezekiah and all the people rejoiced at what God had brought about for his people, because it was done so quickly.

Hezekiah Celebrates the Passover

30 Hezekiah sent word to all Israel and Judah and also wrote letters to Ephraim and Manasseh, inviting them to come to the temple of the LORD in Jerusalem and celebrate the Passover to the LORD, the God of Israel. 2The king and his officials and the whole assembly in Jerusalem decided to celebrate the Passover in the second month. 3They had not been able to celebrate it at the regular time because not enough priests had consecrated themselves and the people had not assembled in Jerusalem. 4The plan seemed right both to the king and to the whole assembly. 5They decided to send a proclamation throughout Israel, from Beersheba to Dan, calling the people to come to Jerusalem and celebrate the Passover to the LORD, the God of Israel. It had not been celebrated in large numbers according to what was written.

6At the king's command, couriers went throughout Israel and Judah with letters from the king and from his officials, which read:

"People of Israel, return to the LORD, the God of Abraham, Isaac and Israel, that he may return to you who are left, who have escaped from the hand of the kings of Assyria. 7Do not be like your fathers and brothers, who were unfaithful to the LORD, the God of their fathers, so that he made them an object of horror, as you see. 8Do not be stiff-necked, as your fathers were; submit to the LORD. Come to the sanctuary, which he has consecrated forever. Serve the LORD your

---

[a]35 Traditionally peace offerings

God, so that his fierce anger will turn away from you. ⁹If you return to the LORD, then your brothers and your children will be shown compassion by their captors and will come back to this land, for the LORD your God is gracious and compassionate. He will not turn his face from you if you return to him."

¹⁰The couriers went from town to town in Ephraim and Manasseh, as far as Zebulun, but the people scorned and ridiculed them. ¹¹Nevertheless, some men of Asher, Manasseh and Zebulun humbled themselves and went to Jerusalem. ¹²Also in Judah the hand of God was on the people to give them unity of mind to carry out what the king and his officials had ordered, following the word of the LORD.

¹³A very large crowd of people assembled in Jerusalem to celebrate the Feast of Unleavened Bread in the second month. ¹⁴They removed the altars in Jerusalem and cleared away the incense altars and threw them into the Kidron Valley.

¹⁵They slaughtered the Passover lamb on the fourteenth day of the second month. The priests and the Levites were ashamed and consecrated themselves and brought burnt offerings to the temple of the LORD. ¹⁶Then they took up their regular positions as prescribed in the Law of Moses the man of God. The priests sprinkled the blood handed to them by the Levites. ¹⁷Since many in the crowd had not consecrated themselves, the Levites had to kill the Passover lambs for all those who were not ceremonially clean and could not consecrate their lambs to the LORD. ¹⁸Although most of the many people who came from Ephraim, Manasseh, Issachar and Zebulun had not purified themselves, yet they ate the Passover, contrary to what was written. But Hezekiah prayed for them, saying, "May the LORD, who is good, pardon everyone ¹⁹who sets his heart on seeking God—the LORD, the God of his fathers—even if he is not clean according to the rules of the sanctuary." ²⁰And the LORD heard Hezekiah and healed the people.

²¹The Israelites who were present in Jerusalem celebrated the Feast of Unleavened Bread for seven days with great rejoicing, while the Levites and priests sang to the LORD every day, accompanied by the LORD's instruments of praise.[a]

²²Hezekiah spoke encouragingly to all the Levites, who showed good understanding of the service of the LORD. For the seven days they ate their assigned portion and offered fellowship offerings[b] and praised the LORD, the God of their fathers.

²³The whole assembly then agreed to celebrate the festival seven more days; so for another seven days they celebrated joyfully. ²⁴Hezekiah king of Judah provided a thousand bulls and seven thousand sheep and goats for the assembly, and the officials provided them with a thousand bulls and ten thousand sheep and goats. A great number of priests consecrated themselves. ²⁵The entire assembly of Judah rejoiced, along with the priests and Levites and all who had assembled from Israel, including the aliens who had come from Israel and those who lived in Judah. ²⁶There was great joy in Jerusalem, for since the days of Solomon son of David king of Israel there had been nothing like this in Jerusalem. ²⁷The priests and the Levites stood to bless the people, and God heard them, for their prayer reached heaven, his holy dwelling place.

31 When all this had ended, the Israelites who were there went out to the towns of Judah, smashed the sacred stones and cut down the Asherah poles. They destroyed the high places and the altars throughout Judah and Benjamin and in Ephraim and Manasseh. After they had destroyed all of them, the Israelites returned to their own towns and to their own property.

Contributions for Worship

²Hezekiah assigned the priests and Levites to divisions—each of them according to their duties as priests or Levites—to offer burnt offerings and fellowship offerings,[b] to minister, to give thanks and to sing praises at the gates of the LORD's dwelling. ³The king contributed from his own possessions for the morning and evening burnt offerings and for the burnt offerings on the Sabbaths, New Moons and appointed feasts as written in the Law of the LORD. ⁴He ordered the people living in Jerusalem to give the portion due the priests and Levites so they could devote themselves to the Law of the LORD. ⁵As soon as the order went out, the Israelites

---

a21 Or *priests praised the* LORD *every day with resounding instruments belonging to the* LORD
b22,2 Traditionally *peace offerings*

generously gave the firstfruits of their grain, new wine, oil and honey and all that the fields produced. They brought a great amount, a tithe of everything. **6**The men of Israel and Judah who lived in the towns of Judah also brought a tithe of their herds and flocks and a tithe of the holy things dedicated to the LORD their God, and they piled them in heaps. **7**They began doing this in the third month and finished in the seventh month. **8**When Hezekiah and his officials came and saw the heaps, they praised the LORD and blessed his people Israel.

9Hezekiah asked the priests and Levites about the heaps; **10**and Azariah the chief priest, from the family of Zadok, answered, "Since the people began to bring their contributions to the temple of the LORD, we have had enough to eat and plenty to spare, because the LORD has blessed his people, and this great amount is left over."

11Hezekiah gave orders to prepare storerooms in the temple of the LORD, and this was done. **12**Then they faithfully brought in the contributions, tithes and dedicated gifts. Conaniah, a Levite, was in charge of these things, and his brother Shimei was next in rank. **13**Jehiel, Azaziah, Nahath, Asahel, Jerimoth, Jozabad, Eliel, Ismakiah, Mahath and Benaiah were supervisors under Conaniah and Shimei his brother, by appointment of King Hezekiah and Azariah the official in charge of the temple of God.

14Kore son of Imnah the Levite, keeper of the East Gate, was in charge of the freewill offerings given to God, distributing the contributions made to the LORD and also the consecrated gifts. **15**Eden, Miniamin, Jeshua, Shemaiah, Amariah and Shecaniah assisted him faithfully in the towns of the priests, distributing to their fellow priests according to their divisions, old and young alike.

16In addition, they distributed to the males three years old or more whose names were in the genealogical records — all who would enter the temple of the LORD to perform the daily duties of their various tasks, according to their responsibilities and their divisions. **17**And they distributed to the priests enrolled by their families in the genealogical records and likewise to the Levites twenty years old or more, according to their responsibilities and their divisions. **18**They included all the little ones, the wives, and the sons and daughters of the whole community listed in these genealogical records. For they were faithful in consecrating themselves.

19As for the priests, the descendants of Aaron, who lived on the farm lands around their towns or in any other towns, men were designated by name to distribute portions to every male among them and to all who were recorded in the genealogies of the Levites.

20This is what Hezekiah did throughout Judah, doing what was good and right and faithful before the LORD his God. **21**In everything that he undertook in the service of God's temple and in obedience to the law and the commands, he sought his God and worked wholeheartedly. And so he prospered.

Sennacherib Threatens Jerusalem

32 After all that Hezekiah had so faithfully done, Sennacherib king of Assyria came and invaded Judah. He laid siege to the fortified cities, thinking to conquer them for himself. **2**When Hezekiah saw that Sennacherib had come and that he intended to make war on Jerusalem, **3**he consulted with his officials and military staff about blocking off the water from the springs outside the city, and they helped him. **4**A large force of men assembled, and they blocked all the springs and the stream that flowed through the land. "Why should the kings*a* of Assyria come and find plenty of water?" they said. **5**Then he worked hard repairing all the broken sections of the wall and building towers on it. He built another wall outside that one and reinforced the supporting terraces*b* of the City of David. He also made large numbers of weapons and shields.

6He appointed military officers over the people and assembled them before him in the square at the city gate and encouraged them with these words: **7**"Be strong and courageous. Do not be afraid or discouraged because of the king of Assyria and the vast army with him, for there is a greater power with us than with him. **8**With him is only the arm of flesh, but with us is the LORD our God to help us and to fight our battles." And the people gained confidence from what Hezekiah the king of Judah said.

---

*a*4 Hebrew; Septuagint and Syriac *king*   *b*5 Or *the Millo*

⁹Later, when Sennacherib king of Assyria and all his forces were laying siege to Lachish, he sent his officers to Jerusalem with this message for Hezekiah king of Judah and for all the people of Judah who were there:

¹⁰"This is what Sennacherib king of Assyria says: On what are you basing your confidence, that you remain in Jerusalem under siege? ¹¹When Hezekiah says, 'The LORD our God will save us from the hand of the king of Assyria,' he is misleading you, to let you die of hunger and thirst. ¹²Did not Hezekiah himself remove this god's high places and altars, saying to Judah and Jerusalem, 'You must worship before one altar and burn sacrifices on it'?

¹³"Do you not know what I and my fathers have done to all the peoples of the other lands? Were the gods of those nations ever able to deliver their land from my hand? ¹⁴Who of all the gods of these nations that my fathers destroyed has been able to save his people from me? How then can your god deliver you from my hand? ¹⁵Now do not let Hezekiah deceive you and mislead you like this. Do not believe him, for no god of any nation or kingdom has been able to deliver his people from my hand or the hand of my fathers. How much less will your god deliver you from my hand!"

¹⁶Sennacherib's officers spoke further against the LORD God and against his servant Hezekiah. ¹⁷The king also wrote letters insulting the LORD, the God of Israel, and saying this against him: "Just as the gods of the peoples of the other lands did not rescue their people from my hand, so the god of Hezekiah will not rescue his people from my hand." ¹⁸Then they called out in Hebrew to the people of Jerusalem who were on the wall, to terrify them and make them afraid in order to capture the city. ¹⁹They spoke about the God of Jerusalem as they did about the gods of the other peoples of the world—the work of men's hands.

²⁰King Hezekiah and the prophet Isaiah son of Amoz cried out in prayer to heaven about this. ²¹And the LORD sent an angel, who annihilated all the fighting men and the leaders and officers in the camp of the Assyrian king. So he withdrew to his own land in disgrace. And when he went into the temple of his god, some of his sons cut him down with the sword.

²²So the LORD saved Hezekiah and the people of Jerusalem from the hand of Sennacherib king of Assyria and from the hand of all others. He took care of them[a] on every side. ²³Many brought offerings to Jerusalem for the LORD and valuable gifts for Hezekiah king of Judah. From then on he was highly regarded by all the nations.

Hezekiah's Pride, Success and Death

²⁴In those days Hezekiah became ill and was at the point of death. He prayed to the LORD, who answered him and gave him a miraculous sign. ²⁵But Hezekiah's heart was proud and he did not respond to the kindness shown him; therefore the LORD's wrath was on him and on Judah and Jerusalem. ²⁶Then Hezekiah repented of the pride of his heart, as did the people of Jerusalem; therefore the LORD's wrath did not come upon them during the days of Hezekiah.

²⁷Hezekiah had very great riches and honor, and he made treasuries for his silver and gold and for his precious stones, spices, shields and all kinds of valuables. ²⁸He also made buildings to store the harvest of grain, new wine and oil; and he made stalls for various kinds of cattle, and pens for the flocks. ²⁹He built villages and acquired great numbers of flocks and herds, for God had given him very great riches.

³⁰It was Hezekiah who blocked the upper outlet of the Gihon spring and channeled the water down to the west side of the City of David. He succeeded in everything he undertook. ³¹But when envoys were sent by the rulers of Babylon to ask him about the miraculous sign that had occurred in the land, God left him to test him and to know everything that was in his heart.

³²The other events of Hezekiah's reign and his acts of devotion are written in the vision of the prophet Isaiah son of Amoz in the book of the kings of Judah and Israel. ³³Hezekiah rested with his fathers and was buried on the hill where the tombs of David's descendants are. All Judah and the people of Jerusalem honored him when he died. And Manasseh his son succeeded him as king.

ᵃ22 Hebrew; Septuagint and Vulgate *He gave them rest*

Manasseh King of Judah

33 Manasseh was twelve years old when he became king, and he reigned in Jerusalem fifty-five years. ²He did evil in the eyes of the LORD, following the detestable practices of the nations the LORD had driven out before the Israelites. ³He rebuilt the high places his father Hez-ekiah had demolished; he also erected altars to the Baals and made Asherah poles. He bowed down to all the starry hosts and worshiped them. ⁴He built altars in the temple of the LORD, of which the LORD had said, "My Name will remain in Jerusalem forever." ⁵In both courts of the temple of the LORD, he built altars to all the starry

---

TUESDAY

VERSE FOR THE DAY:	AUTHOR:	PASSAGE FOR THE DAY:
2 Chronicles 32:19	Frederick Buechner	2 Chronicles 32:10–19

The Gods Are Dying

THE gods are dying. The gods of this world are sick unto death. If someone does not believe this, the next time he happens to wake up in the great silence of the night or of the day, just listen. And after a while, at the heart of the silence, he will hear the sound that gives it away: the soft, crazy thud of the feet of the gods as they stagger across the earth; the huge white hands fluttering like moths; the little moans of bewilderment and anguish. And we all shudder at the sound because to witness the death of gods is a fearsome thing.

Which gods? The gods that we worship. The gods that our enemies worship. Their sacred names? There is Science, for one: he who was to redeem the world from poverty and disease, on whose mighty shoulders mankind was to be borne onward and upward toward the high stars. There is Communism, that holy one so terrible in his predilection for blood sacrifice but so magnificent in his promise of the messianic age: from each according to his ability, to each according to his need . . . And we must not leave out from this role of the dying what often passes for the god of the church: the god who sanctifies our foreign policy and our business methods, our political views and our racial prejudices. The god who, bless him, asks so little and promises so much: peace of mind, the end of our inferiority complexes . . .

These are the gods in whom the world has put its ultimate trust. Some of them are our particular gods, and there are plenty of others, each can name for himself. And where are they now? They are dying, dying, and their twilight thickens into night. Where is the security that they promised? Where is the peace? The terrible truth is that the gods of this world are no more worthy of our ultimate trust than are the men who created them.

Additional Scripture Readings:
Psalm 115:1–11; Isaiah 46:1–9

Go to page 475 for your next devotional reading.

hosts. **6**He sacrificed his sons in*a* the fire in the Valley of Ben Hinnom, practiced sorcery, divination and witchcraft, and consulted mediums and spiritists. He did much evil in the eyes of the LORD, provoking him to anger.

7He took the carved image he had made and put it in God's temple, of which God had said to David and to his son Solomon, "In this temple and in Jerusalem, which I have chosen out of all the tribes of Israel, I will put my Name forever. **8**I will not again make the feet of the Israelites leave the land I assigned to your forefathers, if only they will be careful to do everything I commanded them concerning all the laws, decrees and ordinances given through Moses." **9**But Manasseh led Judah and the people of Jerusalem astray, so that they did more evil than the nations the LORD had destroyed before the Israelites.

10The LORD spoke to Manasseh and his people, but they paid no attention. **11**So the LORD brought against them the army commanders of the king of Assyria, who took Manasseh prisoner, put a hook in his nose, bound him with bronze shackles and took him to Babylon. **12**In his distress he sought the favor of the LORD his God and humbled himself greatly before the God of his fathers. **13**And when he prayed to him, the LORD was moved by his entreaty and listened to his plea; so he brought him back to Jerusalem and to his kingdom. Then Manasseh knew that the LORD is God.

14Afterward he rebuilt the outer wall of the City of David, west of the Gihon spring in the valley, as far as the entrance of the Fish Gate and encircling the hill of Ophel; he also made it much higher. He stationed military commanders in all the fortified cities in Judah.

15He got rid of the foreign gods and removed the image from the temple of the LORD, as well as all the altars he had built on the temple hill and in Jerusalem; and he threw them out of the city. **16**Then he restored the altar of the LORD and sacrificed fellowship offerings*b* and thank offerings on it, and told Judah to serve the LORD, the God of Israel. **17**The people, however, continued to sacrifice at the high places, but only to the LORD their God.

18The other events of Manasseh's reign, including his prayer to his God and the words the seers spoke to him in the name of the LORD, the God of Israel, are written in the annals of the kings of Israel.*c* **19**His prayer and how God was moved by his entreaty, as well as all his sins and unfaithfulness, and the sites where he built high places and set up Asherah poles and idols before he humbled himself — all are written in the records of the seers.*d* **20**Manasseh rested with his fathers and was buried in his palace. And Amon his son succeeded him as king.

Amon King of Judah

21Amon was twenty-two years old when he became king, and he reigned in Jerusalem two years. **22**He did evil in the eyes of the LORD, as his father Manasseh had done. Amon worshiped and offered sacrifices to all the idols Manasseh had made. **23**But unlike his father Manasseh, he did not humble himself before the LORD; Amon increased his guilt.

24Amon's officials conspired against him and assassinated him in his palace. **25**Then the people of the land killed all who had plotted against King Amon, and they made Josiah his son king in his place.

Josiah's Reforms

34 Josiah was eight years old when he became king, and he reigned in Jerusalem thirty-one years. **2**He did what was right in the eyes of the LORD and walked in the ways of his father David, not turning aside to the right or to the left.

3In the eighth year of his reign, while he was still young, he began to seek the God of his father David. In his twelfth year he began to purge Judah and Jerusalem of high places, Asherah poles, carved idols and cast images. **4**Under his direction the altars of the Baals were torn down; he cut to pieces the incense altars that were above them, and smashed the Asherah poles, the idols and the images. These he broke to pieces and scattered over the graves of those who had sacrificed to them. **5**He burned the bones of the priests on their altars, and so he purged Judah and Jerusalem. **6**In the towns of Manasseh, Ephraim and Simeon, as far as Naphtali, and in the ruins around them, **7**he tore down the altars and the Asherah poles and crushed the idols to powder

---

a6 Or *He made his sons pass through*   *b16* Traditionally *peace offerings*   *c18* That is, Judah, as frequently in 2 Chronicles   *d19* One Hebrew manuscript and Septuagint; most Hebrew manuscripts *of Hozai* and cut to pieces all the incense altars throughout Israel. Then he went back to Jerusalem.

⁸In the eighteenth year of Josiah's reign, to purify the land and the temple, he sent Shaphan son of Azaliah and Maaseiah the ruler of the city, with Joah son of Joahaz, the recorder, to repair the temple of the LORD his God.

⁹They went to Hilkiah the high priest and gave him the money that had been brought into the temple of God, which the Levites who were the doorkeepers had collected from the people of Manasseh, Ephraim and the entire remnant of Israel and from all the people of Judah and Benjamin and the inhabitants of Jerusalem. ¹⁰Then they entrusted it to the men appointed to supervise the work on the LORD's temple. These men paid the workers who repaired and restored the temple. ¹¹They also gave money to the carpenters and builders to purchase dressed stone, and timber for joists and beams for the buildings that the kings of Judah had allowed to fall into ruin.

¹²The men did the work faithfully. Over them to direct them were Jahath and Obadiah, Levites descended from Merari, and Zechariah and Meshullam, descended from Kohath. The Levites—all who were skilled in playing musical instruments—¹³had charge of the laborers and supervised all the workers from job to job. Some of the Levites were secretaries, scribes and doorkeepers.

The Book of the Law Found

¹⁴While they were bringing out the money that had been taken into the temple of the LORD, Hilkiah the priest found the Book of the Law of the LORD that had been given through Moses. ¹⁵Hilkiah said to Shaphan the secretary, "I have found the Book of the Law in the temple of the LORD." He gave it to Shaphan.

¹⁶Then Shaphan took the book to the king and reported to him: "Your officials are doing everything that has been committed to them. ¹⁷They have paid out the money that was in the temple of the LORD and have entrusted it to the supervisors and workers." ¹⁸Then Shaphan the secretary informed the king, "Hilkiah the priest has given me a book." And Shaphan read from it in the presence of the king.

¹⁹When the king heard the words of the Law, he tore his robes. ²⁰He gave these orders to Hilkiah, Ahikam son of Shaphan, Abdon son of Micah,ᵃ Shaphan the secretary and Asaiah the king's attendant: ²¹"Go and inquire of the LORD for me and for the remnant in Israel and Judah about what is written in this book that has been found. Great is the LORD's anger that is poured out on us because our fathers have not kept the word of the LORD; they have not acted in accordance with all that is written in this book."

²²Hilkiah and those the king had sent with himᵇ went to speak to the prophetess Huldah, who was the wife of Shallum son of Tokhath,ᶜ the son of Hasrah,ᵈ keeper of the wardrobe. She lived in Jerusalem, in the Second District.

²³She said to them, "This is what the LORD, the God of Israel, says: Tell the man who sent you to me, ²⁴'This is what the LORD says: I am going to bring disaster on this place and its people—all the curses written in the book that has been read in the presence of the king of Judah. ²⁵Because they have forsaken me and burned incense to other gods and provoked me to anger by all that their hands have made,ᵉ my anger will be poured out on this place and will not be quenched.' ²⁶Tell the king of Judah, who sent you to inquire of the LORD, 'This is what the LORD, the God of Israel, says concerning the words you heard: ²⁷Because your heart was responsive and you humbled yourself before God when you heard what he spoke against this place and its people, and because you humbled yourself before me and tore your robes and wept in my presence, I have heard you, declares the LORD. ²⁸Now I will gather you to your fathers, and you will be buried in peace. Your eyes will not see all the disaster I am going to bring on this place and on those who live here.'"

So they took her answer back to the king.

²⁹Then the king called together all the elders of Judah and Jerusalem. ³⁰He went up to the temple of the LORD with the men of Judah, the people of Jerusalem, the priests and the Levites—all the people from the least to the greatest. He read in their hearing all the words of the Book of the Covenant, which had been found in

---

ᵃ20 Also called *Acbor son of Micaiah*   ᵇ22 One Hebrew manuscript, Vulgate and Syriac; most Hebrew manuscripts do not have *had sent with him.*   ᶜ22 Also called *Tikvah*   ᵈ22 Also called *Harhas* ᵉ25 Or *by everything they have done* the temple of the LORD. [31]The king stood by his pillar and renewed the covenant in the presence of the LORD—to follow the LORD and keep his commands, regulations and decrees with all his heart and all his soul, and to obey the words of the covenant written in this book.

[32]Then he had everyone in Jerusalem and Benjamin pledge themselves to it; the people of Jerusalem did this in accordance with the covenant of God, the God of their fathers.

[33]Josiah removed all the detestable idols from all the territory belonging to the Israelites, and he had all who were present in Israel serve the LORD their God. As long as he lived, they did not fail to follow the LORD, the God of their fathers.

Josiah Celebrates the Passover

35 Josiah celebrated the Passover to the LORD in Jerusalem, and the Passover lamb was slaughtered on the fourteenth day of the first month. [2]He appointed the priests to their duties and encouraged them in the service of the LORD's temple. [3]He said to the Levites, who instructed all Israel and who had been consecrated to the LORD: "Put the sacred ark in the temple that Solomon son of David king of Israel built. It is not to be carried about on your shoulders. Now serve the LORD your God and his people Israel. [4]Prepare yourselves by families in your divisions, according to the directions written by David king of Israel and by his son Solomon.

[5]"Stand in the holy place with a group of Levites for each subdivision of the families of your fellow countrymen, the lay people. [6]Slaughter the Passover lambs, consecrate yourselves and prepare the lambs for your fellow countrymen, doing what the LORD commanded through Moses."

[7]Josiah provided for all the lay people who were there a total of thirty thousand sheep and goats for the Passover offerings, and also three thousand cattle—all from the king's own possessions.

[8]His officials also contributed voluntarily to the people and the priests and Levites. Hilkiah, Zechariah and Jehiel, the administrators of God's temple, gave the priests twenty-six hundred Passover offerings and three hundred cattle. [9]Also Conaniah along with Shemaiah and Nethanel, his brothers, and Hashabiah, Jeiel and Jozabad, the leaders of the Levites, provided five thousand Passover offerings and five hundred head of cattle for the Levites.

[10]The service was arranged and the priests stood in their places with the Levites in their divisions as the king had ordered. [11]The Passover lambs were slaughtered, and the priests sprinkled the blood handed to them, while the Levites skinned the animals. [12]They set aside the burnt offerings to give them to the subdivisions of the families of the people to offer to the LORD, as is written in the Book of Moses. They did the same with the cattle. [13]They roasted the Passover animals over the fire as prescribed, and boiled the holy offerings in pots, caldrons and pans and served them quickly to all the people. [14]After this, they made preparations for themselves and for the priests, because the priests, the descendants of Aaron, were sacrificing the burnt offerings and the fat portions until nightfall. So the Levites made preparations for themselves and for the Aaronic priests.

[15]The musicians, the descendants of Asaph, were in the places prescribed by David, Asaph, Heman and Jeduthun the king's seer. The gatekeepers at each gate did not need to leave their posts, because their fellow Levites made the preparations for them.

[16]So at that time the entire service of the LORD was carried out for the celebration of the Passover and the offering of burnt offerings on the altar of the LORD, as King Josiah had ordered. [17]The Israelites who were present celebrated the Passover at that time and observed the Feast of Unleavened Bread for seven days. [18]The Passover had not been observed like this in Israel since the days of the prophet Samuel; and none of the kings of Israel had ever celebrated such a Passover as did Josiah, with the priests, the Levites and all Judah and Israel who were there with the people of Jerusalem. [19]This Passover was celebrated in the eighteenth year of Josiah's reign.

The Death of Josiah

[20]After all this, when Josiah had set the temple in order, Neco king of Egypt went up to fight at Carchemish on the Euphrates, and Josiah marched out to meet him in battle. [21]But Neco sent messengers to him, saying, "What quarrel is there between you and me, O king of Judah? It is not you I am attacking at this time, but the house with which I am at war. God has told me to hurry; so stop opposing God,

who is with me, or he will destroy you."

[22]Josiah, however, would not turn away from him, but disguised himself to engage him in battle. He would not listen to what Neco had said at God's command but went to fight him on the plain of Megiddo.

[23]Archers shot King Josiah, and he told his officers, "Take me away; I am badly wounded." [24]So they took him out of his chariot, put him in the other chariot he had and brought him to Jerusalem, where he died. He was buried in the tombs of his fathers, and all Judah and Jerusalem mourned for him.

[25]Jeremiah composed laments for Josiah, and to this day all the men and women singers commemorate Josiah in the laments. These became a tradition in Israel and are written in the Laments.

[26]The other events of Josiah's reign and his acts of devotion, according to what is written in the Law of the LORD — [27]all the events, from beginning to end, are written in the book of the kings of Israel and Judah. **36** [1]And the people of the land took Jehoahaz son of Josiah and made him king in Jerusalem in place of his father.

Jehoahaz King of Judah

[2]Jehoahaz[a] was twenty-three years old when he became king, and he reigned in Jerusalem three months. [3]The king of Egypt dethroned him in Jerusalem and imposed on Judah a levy of a hundred talents[b] of silver and a talent[c] of gold. [4]The king of Egypt made Eliakim, a brother of Jehoahaz, king over Judah and Jerusalem and changed Eliakim's name to Jehoiakim. But Neco took Eliakim's brother Jehoahaz and carried him off to Egypt.

Jehoiakim King of Judah

[5]Jehoiakim was twenty-five years old when he became king, and he reigned in Jerusalem eleven years. He did evil in the eyes of the LORD his God. [6]Nebuchadnezzar king of Babylon attacked him and bound him with bronze shackles to take him to Babylon. [7]Nebuchadnezzar also took to Babylon articles from the temple of the LORD and put them in his temple[d] there.

[8]The other events of Jehoiakim's reign, the detestable things he did and all that was found against him, are written in the book of the kings of Israel and Judah. And Jehoiachin his son succeeded him as king.

Jehoiachin King of Judah

[9]Jehoiachin was eighteen[e] years old when he became king, and he reigned in Jerusalem three months and ten days. He did evil in the eyes of the LORD. [10]In the spring, King Nebuchadnezzar sent for him and brought him to Babylon, together with articles of value from the temple of the LORD, and he made Jehoiachin's uncle,[f] Zedekiah, king over Judah and Jerusalem.

Zedekiah King of Judah

[11]Zedekiah was twenty-one years old when he became king, and he reigned in Jerusalem eleven years. [12]He did evil in the eyes of the LORD his God and did not humble himself before Jeremiah the prophet, who spoke the word of the LORD. [13]He also rebelled against King Nebuchadnezzar, who had made him take an oath in God's name. He became stiff-necked and hardened his heart and would not turn to the LORD, the God of Israel. [14]Furthermore, all the leaders of the priests and the people became more and more unfaithful, following all the detestable practices of the nations and defiling the temple of the LORD, which he had consecrated in Jerusalem.

The Fall of Jerusalem

[15]The LORD, the God of their fathers, sent word to them through his messengers again and again, because he had pity on his people and on his dwelling place. [16]But they mocked God's messengers, despised his words and scoffed at his prophets until the wrath of the LORD was aroused against his people and there was no remedy. [17]He brought up against them the king of the Babylonians,[g] who killed their young men with the sword in the sanctuary, and spared neither young man nor young woman, old man or aged. God handed all of them over to Nebuchadnezzar. [18]He carried to Babylon all the articles from the temple of God, both large and small, and the treasures of the LORD's temple and the treasures of the king and his officials. [19]They set fire to God's temple

---

[a]2 Hebrew *Joahaz*, a variant of *Jehoahaz*; also in verse 4   [b]3 That is, about 3 3/4 tons (about 3.4 metric tons)   [c]3 That is, about 75 pounds (about 34 kilograms)   [d]7 Or *palace*   [e]9 One Hebrew manuscript, some Septuagint manuscripts and Syriac (see also 2 Kings 24:8); most Hebrew manuscripts *eight*   [f]10 Hebrew *brother*, that is, relative (see 2 Kings 24:17)   [g]17 Or *Chaldeans*

and broke down the wall of Jerusalem; they burned all the palaces and destroyed everything of value there.

20He carried into exile to Babylon the remnant, who escaped from the sword, and they became servants to him and his sons until the kingdom of Persia came to power. **21**The land enjoyed its sabbath rests; all the time of its desolation it rested, until the seventy years were completed in fulfillment of the word of the LORD spoken by Jeremiah.

22In the first year of Cyrus king of Persia, in order to fulfill the word of the LORD spoken by Jeremiah, the LORD moved the heart of Cyrus king of Persia to make a proclamation throughout his realm and to put it in writing:

23"This is what Cyrus king of Persia says:

" 'The LORD, the God of heaven, has given me all the kingdoms of the earth and he has appointed me to build a temple for him at Jerusalem in Judah. Anyone of his people among you — may the LORD his God be with him, and let him go up.' "

*E*ZRA tells how God helps two groups return from Babylon to the promised land, the second group led by Ezra himself. The temple of the Lord is rebuilt despite opposition, the worship of the Lord resumes, and the people realize they must not sin through mixed marriages as their ancestors did. As you read this book, rejoice that God always gives you a second chance to serve him; promise to do your best to remain faithful to his Word.

EZRA

Cyrus Helps the Exiles to Return

1 In the first year of Cyrus king of Persia, in order to fulfill the word of the LORD spoken by Jeremiah, the LORD moved the heart of Cyrus king of Persia to make a proclamation throughout his realm and to put it in writing:

²"This is what Cyrus king of Persia says:

" 'The LORD, the God of heaven, has given me all the kingdoms of the earth and he has appointed me to build a temple for him at Jerusalem in Judah. ³Anyone of his people among you — may his God be with him, and let him go up to Jerusalem in Judah and build the temple of the LORD, the God of Israel, the God who is in Jerusalem. ⁴And the people of any place where survivors may now be living are to provide him with silver and gold, with goods and livestock, and with freewill offerings for the temple of God in Jerusalem.' "

⁵Then the family heads of Judah and Benjamin, and the priests and Levites — everyone whose heart God had moved — prepared to go up and build the house of the LORD in Jerusalem. ⁶All their neighbors assisted them with articles of silver and gold, with goods and livestock, and with valuable gifts, in addition to all the

freewill offerings. [7]Moreover, King Cyrus brought out the articles belonging to the temple of the LORD, which Nebuchadnezzar had carried away from Jerusalem and had placed in the temple of his god.[a] [8]Cyrus king of Persia had them brought by Mithredath the treasurer, who counted them out to Sheshbazzar the prince of Judah.

[9]This was the inventory:

gold dishes	30
silver dishes	1,000
silver pans[b]	29
[10]gold bowls	30
matching silver bowls	410
other articles	1,000

[11]In all, there were 5,400 articles of gold and of silver. Sheshbazzar brought all these along when the exiles came up from Babylon to Jerusalem.

The List of the Exiles Who Returned

2 Now these are the people of the province who came up from the captivity of the exiles, whom Nebuchadnezzar king of Babylon had taken captive to Babylon (they returned to Jerusalem and Judah, each to his own town, [2]in company with Zerubbabel, Jeshua, Nehemiah, Seraiah, Reelaiah, Mordecai, Bilshan, Mispar, Bigvai, Rehum and Baanah):

The list of the men of the people of Israel:

[3]the descendants of Parosh	2,172
[4]of Shephatiah	372
[5]of Arah	775
[6]of Pahath-Moab (through the line of Jeshua and Joab)	2,812
[7]of Elam	1,254
[8]of Zattu	945
[9]of Zaccai	760
[10]of Bani	642
[11]of Bebai	623
[12]of Azgad	1,222
[13]of Adonikam	666
[14]of Bigvai	2,056
[15]of Adin	454
[16]of Ater (through Hezekiah)	98
[17]of Bezai	323
[18]of Jorah	112
[19]of Hashum	223
[20]of Gibbar	95

[21]the men of Bethlehem	123
[22]of Netophah	56
[23]of Anathoth	128
[24]of Azmaveth	42
[25]of Kiriath Jearim,[c] Kephirah and Beeroth	743
[26]of Ramah and Geba	621
[27]of Micmash	122
[28]of Bethel and Ai	223
[29]of Nebo	52
[30]of Magbish	156
[31]of the other Elam	1,254
[32]of Harim	320
[33]of Lod, Hadid and Ono	725
[34]of Jericho	345
[35]of Senaah	3,630

[36]The priests:

the descendants of Jedaiah (through the family of Jeshua)	973
[37]of Immer	1,052
[38]of Pashhur	1,247
[39]of Harim	1,017

[40]The Levites:

the descendants of Jeshua and Kadmiel (through the line of Hodaviah)	74

[41]The singers:

the descendants of Asaph	128

[42]The gatekeepers of the temple:

the descendants of Shallum, Ater, Talmon, Akkub, Hatita and Shobai	139

[43]The temple servants:

the descendants of
Ziha, Hasupha, Tabbaoth,
[44]Keros, Siaha, Padon,
[45]Lebanah, Hagabah, Akkub,
[46]Hagab, Shalmai, Hanan,
[47]Giddel, Gahar, Reaiah,
[48]Rezin, Nekoda, Gazzam,
[49]Uzza, Paseah, Besai,
[50]Asnah, Meunim, Nephussim,
[51]Bakbuk, Hakupha, Harhur,
[52]Bazluth, Mehida, Harsha,
[53]Barkos, Sisera, Temah,
[54]Neziah and Hatipha

[55]The descendants of the servants of Solomon:

the descendants of
Sotai, Hassophereth, Peruda,

⁵⁶Jaala, Darkon, Giddel,
⁵⁷Shephatiah, Hattil,
    Pokereth-Hazzebaim and Ami

⁵⁸The temple servants and the
    descendants of the servants of
    Solomon   392

⁵⁹The following came up from the towns of Tel Melah, Tel Harsha, Kerub, Addon and Immer, but they could not show that their families were descended from Israel:

⁶⁰The descendants of
    Delaiah, Tobiah and
    Nekoda   652

⁶¹And from among the priests:

The descendants of
    Hobaiah, Hakkoz and Barzillai
    (a man who had married a
    daughter of Barzillai the
    Gileadite and was called by that
    name).
⁶²These searched for their family records, but they could not find them and so were excluded from the priesthood as unclean. ⁶³The governor ordered them not to eat any of the most sacred food until there was a priest ministering with the Urim and Thummim.

⁶⁴The whole company numbered 42,360, ⁶⁵besides their 7,337 menservants and maidservants; and they also had 200 men and women singers. ⁶⁶They had 736 horses, 245 mules, ⁶⁷435 camels and 6,720 donkeys.

⁶⁸When they arrived at the house of the Lord in Jerusalem, some of the heads of the families gave freewill offerings toward the rebuilding of the house of God on its site. ⁶⁹According to their ability they gave to the treasury for this work 61,000 drachmas[a] of gold, 5,000 minas[b] of silver and 100 priestly garments.
⁷⁰The priests, the Levites, the singers, the gatekeepers and the temple servants settled in their own towns, along with some of the other people, and the rest of the Israelites settled in their towns.

Rebuilding the Altar

3 When the seventh month came and the Israelites had settled in their towns, the people assembled as one man in Jerusalem. ²Then Jeshua son of Jozadak and his fellow priests and Zerubbabel son of Shealtiel and his associates began to build the altar of the God of Israel to sacrifice burnt offerings on it, in accordance with what is written in the Law of Moses the man of God. ³Despite their fear of the peoples around them, they built the altar on its foundation and sacrificed burnt offerings on it to the Lord, both the morning and evening sacrifices. ⁴Then in accordance with what is written, they celebrated the Feast of Tabernacles with the required number of burnt offerings prescribed for each day. ⁵After that, they presented the regular burnt offerings, the New Moon sacrifices and the sacrifices for all the appointed sacred feasts of the Lord, as well as those brought as freewill offerings to the Lord. ⁶On the first day of the seventh month they began to offer burnt offerings to the Lord, though the foundation of the Lord's temple had not yet been laid.

Rebuilding the Temple

⁷Then they gave money to the masons and carpenters, and gave food and drink and oil to the people of Sidon and Tyre, so that they would bring cedar logs by sea from Lebanon to Joppa, as authorized by Cyrus king of Persia.

⁸In the second month of the second year after their arrival at the house of God in Jerusalem, Zerubbabel son of Shealtiel, Jeshua son of Jozadak and the rest of their brothers (the priests and the Levites and all who had returned from the captivity to Jerusalem) began the work, appointing Levites twenty years of age and older to supervise the building of the house of the Lord. ⁹Jeshua and his sons and brothers and Kadmiel and his sons (descendants of Hodaviah[c]) and the sons of Henadad and their sons and brothers—all Levites—joined together in supervising those working on the house of God.

¹⁰When the builders laid the foundation of the temple of the Lord, the priests in their vestments and with trumpets, and the Levites (the sons of Asaph) with cymbals, took their places to praise the Lord, as prescribed by David king of Israel. ¹¹With praise and thanksgiving they sang to the Lord:

---

a69 That is, about 1,100 pounds (about 500 kilograms)   b69 That is, about 3 tons (about 2.9 metric tons)   c9 Hebrew *Yehudah*, probably a variant of *Hodaviah*

"He is good;
　his love to Israel endures forever."

And all the people gave a great shout of praise to the Lord, because the foundation of the house of the Lord was laid. [12]But many of the older priests and Levites and family heads, who had seen the former temple, wept aloud when they saw the foundation of this temple being laid, while many others shouted for joy. [13]No one could distinguish the sound of the shouts of joy from the sound of weeping, because the people made so much noise. And the sound was heard far away.

Opposition to the Rebuilding

4 When the enemies of Judah and Benjamin heard that the exiles were building a temple for the Lord, the God of Israel, [2]they came to Zerubbabel and to the heads of the families and said, "Let us help you build because, like you, we seek your God and have been sacrificing to him since the time of Esarhaddon king of Assyria, who brought us here."

[3]But Zerubbabel, Jeshua and the rest of the heads of the families of Israel answered, "You have no part with us in building a temple to our God. We alone will build it for the Lord, the God of Israel, as King Cyrus, the king of Persia, commanded us."

[4]Then the peoples around them set out to discourage the people of Judah and make them afraid to go on building.[a] [5]They hired counselors to work against them and frustrate their plans during the entire reign of Cyrus king of Persia and down to the reign of Darius king of Persia.

Later Opposition Under Xerxes and Artaxerxes

[6]At the beginning of the reign of Xerxes,[b] they lodged an accusation against the people of Judah and Jerusalem.

[7]And in the days of Artaxerxes king of Persia, Bishlam, Mithredath, Tabeel and the rest of his associates wrote a letter to Artaxerxes. The letter was written in Aramaic script and in the Aramaic language.[c,d]

[8]Rehum the commanding officer and Shimshai the secretary wrote a letter against Jerusalem to Artaxerxes the king as follows:

[9]Rehum the commanding officer and Shimshai the secretary, together with the rest of their associates—the judges and officials over the men from Tripolis, Persia,[e] Erech and Babylon, the Elamites of Susa, [10]and the other people whom the great and honorable Ashurbanipal[f] deported and settled in the city of Samaria and elsewhere in Trans-Euphrates.

[11](This is a copy of the letter they sent him.)

To King Artaxerxes,

From your servants, the men of Trans-Euphrates:

[12]The king should know that the Jews who came up to us from you have gone to Jerusalem and are rebuilding that rebellious and wicked city. They are restoring the walls and repairing the foundations.

[13]Furthermore, the king should know that if this city is built and its walls are restored, no more taxes, tribute or duty will be paid, and the royal revenues will suffer. [14]Now since we are under obligation to the palace and it is not proper for us to see the king dishonored, we are sending this message to inform the king, [15]so that a search may be made in the archives of your predecessors. In these records you will find that this city is a rebellious city, troublesome to kings and provinces, a place of rebellion from ancient times. That is why this city was destroyed. [16]We inform the king that if this city is built and its walls are restored, you will be left with nothing in Trans-Euphrates.

[17]The king sent this reply:

To Rehum the commanding officer, Shimshai the secretary and the rest of their associates living in Samaria and elsewhere in Trans-Euphrates:

Greetings.

[18]The letter you sent us has been read and translated in my presence.

---

[a]4 Or and troubled them as they built　　[b]6 Hebrew Ahasuerus, a variant of Xerxes' Persian name
[c]7 Or written in Aramaic and translated　　[d]7 The text of Ezra 4:8—6:18 is in Aramaic.　　[e]9 Or officials, magistrates and governors over the men from Ashurbanipal　　[f]10 Aramaic Osnappar, a variant of

19I issued an order and a search was made, and it was found that this city has a long history of revolt against kings and has been a place of rebellion and sedition. 20Jerusalem has had powerful kings ruling over the whole of Trans-Euphrates, and taxes, tribute and duty were paid to them. 21Now issue an order to these men to stop work, so that this city will not be rebuilt until I so order. 22Be careful not to neglect this matter. Why let this threat grow, to the detriment of the royal interests?

23As soon as the copy of the letter of King Artaxerxes was read to Rehum and Shimshai the secretary and their associates, they went immediately to the Jews in Jerusalem and compelled them by force to stop.

24Thus the work on the house of God in Jerusalem came to a standstill until the second year of the reign of Darius king of Persia.

Tattenai's Letter to Darius

5 Now Haggai the prophet and Zechariah the prophet, a descendant of Iddo, prophesied to the Jews in Judah and Jerusalem in the name of the God of Israel, who was over them. 2Then Zerubbabel son of Shealtiel and Jeshua son of Jozadak set to work to rebuild the house of God in Jerusalem. And the prophets of God were with them, helping them.

3At that time Tattenai, governor of Trans-Euphrates, and Shethar-Bozenai and their associates went to them and asked, "Who authorized you to rebuild this temple and restore this structure?" 4They also asked, "What are the names of the men constructing this building?"a 5But the eye of their God was watching over the elders of the Jews, and they were not stopped until a report could go to Darius and his written reply be received.

6This is a copy of the letter that Tattenai, governor of Trans-Euphrates, and Shethar-Bozenai and their associates, the officials of Trans-Euphrates, sent to King Darius. 7The report they sent him read as follows:

To King Darius:

Cordial greetings.

8The king should know that we went to the district of Judah, to the temple of the great God. The people are building it with large stones and placing the timbers in the walls. The work is being carried on with diligence and is making rapid progress under their direction.

9We questioned the elders and asked them, "Who authorized you to rebuild this temple and restore this structure?" 10We also asked them their names, so that we could write down the names of their leaders for your information.

11This is the answer they gave us:

"We are the servants of the God of heaven and earth, and we are rebuilding the temple that was built many years ago, one that a great king of Israel built and finished. 12But because our fathers angered the God of heaven, he handed them over to Nebuchadnezzar the Chaldean, king of Babylon, who destroyed this temple and deported the people to Babylon.

13"However, in the first year of Cyrus king of Babylon, King Cyrus issued a decree to rebuild this house of God. 14He even removed from the templeb of Babylon the gold and silver articles of the house of God, which Nebuchadnezzar had taken from the temple in Jerusalem and brought to the templeb in Babylon.

"Then King Cyrus gave them to a man named Sheshbazzar, whom he had appointed governor, 15and he told him, 'Take these articles and go and deposit them in the temple in Jerusalem. And rebuild the house of God on its site.' 16So this Sheshbazzar came and laid the foundations of the house of God in Jerusalem. From that day to the present it has been under construction but is not yet finished."

17Now if it pleases the king, let a search be made in the royal archives of Babylon to see if King Cyrus did in fact issue a decree to rebuild this house of God in Jerusalem. Then let the king send us his decision in this matter.

---

a4 See Septuagint; Aramaic 4We told them the names of the men constructing this building.   b14 Or palace

The Decree of Darius

6 King Darius then issued an order, and they searched in the archives stored in the treasury at Babylon. [2]A scroll was found in the citadel of Ecbatana in the province of Media, and this was written on it:

Memorandum:

[3]In the first year of King Cyrus, the king issued a decree concerning the temple of God in Jerusalem:

Let the temple be rebuilt as a place to present sacrifices, and let its foundations be laid. It is to be ninety feet[a] high and ninety feet wide, [4]with three courses of large stones and one of timbers. The costs are to be paid by the royal treasury. [5]Also, the gold and silver articles of the house of God, which Nebuchadnezzar took from the temple in Jerusalem and brought to Babylon, are to be returned to their places in the temple in Jerusalem; they are to be deposited in the house of God.

[6]Now then, Tattenai, governor of Trans-Euphrates, and Shethar-Bozenai and you, their fellow officials of that province, stay away from there. [7]Do not interfere with the work on this temple of God. Let the governor of the Jews and the Jewish elders rebuild this house of God on its site.

[8]Moreover, I hereby decree what you are to do for these elders of the Jews in the construction of this house of God:

The expenses of these men are to be fully paid out of the royal treasury, from the revenues of Trans-Euphrates, so that the work will not stop. [9]Whatever is needed — young bulls, rams, male lambs for burnt offerings to the God of heaven, and wheat, salt, wine and oil, as requested by the priests in Jerusalem — must be given them daily without fail, [10]so that they may offer sacrifices pleasing to the God of heaven and pray for the well-being of the king and his sons.

[11]Furthermore, I decree that if anyone changes this edict, a beam is to be pulled from his house and he is to be lifted up and impaled on it. And for this crime his house is to be made a pile of rubble. [12]May God, who has caused his Name to dwell there, overthrow any king or people who lifts a hand to change this decree or to destroy this temple in Jerusalem.

I Darius have decreed it. Let it be carried out with diligence.

Completion and Dedication of the Temple

[13]Then, because of the decree King Darius had sent, Tattenai, governor of Trans-Euphrates, and Shethar-Bozenai and their associates carried it out with diligence. [14]So the elders of the Jews continued to build and prosper under the preaching of Haggai the prophet and Zechariah, a descendant of Iddo. They finished building the temple according to the command of the God of Israel and the decrees of Cyrus, Darius and Artaxerxes, kings of Persia. [15]The temple was completed on the third day of the month Adar, in the sixth year of the reign of King Darius.

[16]Then the people of Israel — the priests, the Levites and the rest of the exiles — celebrated the dedication of the house of God with joy. [17]For the dedication of this house of God they offered a hundred bulls, two hundred rams, four hundred male lambs and, as a sin offering for all Israel, twelve male goats, one for each of the tribes of Israel. [18]And they installed the priests in their divisions and the Levites in their groups for the service of God at Jerusalem, according to what is written in the Book of Moses.

The Passover

[19]On the fourteenth day of the first month, the exiles celebrated the Passover. [20]The priests and Levites had purified themselves and were all ceremonially clean. The Levites slaughtered the Passover lamb for all the exiles, for their brothers the priests and for themselves. [21]So the Israelites who had returned from the exile ate it, together with all who had separated themselves from the unclean practices of their Gentile neighbors in order to seek the LORD, the God of Israel. [22]For seven days they celebrated with joy the Feast of Unleavened Bread, because the LORD had filled them with joy by changing the attitude of the king of Assyria, so that he assisted them in the work on the house of God, the God of Israel.

---

[a]3 Aramaic *sixty cubits* (about 27 meters)

Ezra Comes to Jerusalem

7 After these things, during the reign of Artaxerxes king of Persia, Ezra son of Seraiah, the son of Azariah, the son of Hilkiah, ²the son of Shallum, the son of Zadok, the son of Ahitub, ³the son of Amariah, the son of Azariah, the son of Meraioth, ⁴the son of Zerahiah, the son of Uzzi, the son of Bukki, ⁵the son of Abishua, the son of Phinehas, the son of Eleazar, the son of Aaron the chief priest — ⁶this Ezra came up from Babylon. He was a teacher well versed in the Law of Moses, which the Lord, the God of Israel, had given. The king had granted him everything he asked, for the hand of the Lord his God was on him. ⁷Some of the Israelites, including priests, Levites, singers, gatekeepers and temple servants, also came up to Jerusalem in the seventh year of King Artaxerxes.

⁸Ezra arrived in Jerusalem in the fifth month of the seventh year of the king. ⁹He had begun his journey from Babylon on the first day of the first month, and he arrived in Jerusalem on the first day of the fifth month, for the gracious hand of his God was on him. ¹⁰For Ezra had devoted himself to the study and observance of the Law of the Lord, and to teaching its decrees and laws in Israel.

King Artaxerxes' Letter to Ezra

¹¹This is a copy of the letter King Artaxerxes had given to Ezra the priest and teacher, a man learned in matters concerning the commands and decrees of the Lord for Israel:

¹²ᵃArtaxerxes, king of kings,

To Ezra the priest, a teacher of the Law of the God of heaven:

Greetings.

¹³Now I decree that any of the Israelites in my kingdom, including priests and Levites, who wish to go to Jerusalem with you, may go. ¹⁴You are sent by the king and his seven advisers to inquire about Judah and Jerusalem with regard to the Law of your God, which is in your hand. ¹⁵Moreover, you are to take with you the silver and gold that the king and his advisers have freely given to the God of Israel, whose dwelling is in Jerusalem, ¹⁶together with all the silver and gold you may obtain from the province of Babylon, as well as the freewill offerings of the people and priests for the temple of their God in Jerusalem. ¹⁷With this money be sure to buy bulls, rams and male lambs, together with their grain offerings and drink offerings, and sacrifice them on the altar of the temple of your God in Jerusalem.

¹⁸You and your brother Jews may then do whatever seems best with the rest of the silver and gold, in accordance with the will of your God. ¹⁹Deliver to the God of Jerusalem all the articles entrusted to you for worship in the temple of your God. ²⁰And anything else needed for the temple of your God that you may have occasion to supply, you may provide from the royal treasury.

²¹Now I, King Artaxerxes, order all the treasurers of Trans-Euphrates to provide with diligence whatever Ezra the priest, a teacher of the Law of the God of heaven, may ask of you — ²²up to a hundred talentsᵇ of silver, a hundred corsᶜ of wheat, a hundred bathsᵈ of wine, a hundred bathsᵈ of olive oil, and salt without limit. ²³Whatever the God of heaven has prescribed, let it be done with diligence for the temple of the God of heaven. Why should there be wrath against the realm of the king and of his sons? ²⁴You are also to know that you have no authority to impose taxes, tribute or duty on any of the priests, Levites, singers, gatekeepers, temple servants or other workers at this house of God.

²⁵And you, Ezra, in accordance with the wisdom of your God, which you possess, appoint magistrates and judges to administer justice to all the people of Trans-Euphrates — all who know the laws of your God. And you are to teach any who do not know them. ²⁶Whoever does not obey the law of your God and the law of the king must surely be punished by death, banishment, confiscation of property, or imprisonment.

ᵃ12 The text of Ezra 7:12-26 is in Aramaic.   ᵇ22 That is, about 3 3/4 tons (about 3.4 metric tons)
ᶜ22 That is, probably about 600 bushels (about 22 kiloliters)   ᵈ22 That is, probably about 600 gallons (about 2.2 kiloliters)

27Praise be to the Lord, the God of our fathers, who has put it into the king's heart to bring honor to the house of the Lord in Jerusalem in this way 28and who has extended his good favor to me before the king and his advisers and all the king's powerful officials. Because the hand of the Lord my God was on me, I took courage and gathered leading men from Israel to go up with me.

List of the Family Heads Returning With Ezra

8 These are the family heads and those registered with them who came up with me from Babylon during the reign of King Artaxerxes:

2of the descendants of Phinehas, Gershom;
of the descendants of Ithamar, Daniel;
of the descendants of David, Hattush 3of the descendants of Shecaniah;
of the descendants of Parosh, Zechariah, and with him were registered 150 men;
4of the descendants of Pahath-Moab, Eliehoenai son of Zerahiah, and with him 200 men;
5of the descendants of Zattu,*a* Shecaniah son of Jahaziel, and with him 300 men;
6of the descendants of Adin, Ebed son of Jonathan, and with him 50 men;
7of the descendants of Elam, Jeshaiah son of Athaliah, and with him 70 men;
8of the descendants of Shephatiah, Zebadiah son of Michael, and with him 80 men;
9of the descendants of Joab, Obadiah son of Jehiel, and with him 218 men;
10of the descendants of Bani,*b* Shelomith son of Josiphiah, and with him 160 men;
11of the descendants of Bebai, Zechariah son of Bebai, and with him 28 men;
12of the descendants of Azgad, Johanan son of Hakkatan, and with him 110 men;
13of the descendants of Adonikam, the last ones, whose names were Eliphelet, Jeuel and Shemaiah, and with them 60 men;
14of the descendants of Bigvai, Uthai and Zaccur, and with them 70 men.

The Return to Jerusalem

15I assembled them at the canal that flows toward Ahava, and we camped there three days. When I checked among the people and the priests, I found no Levites there. 16So I summoned Eliezer, Ariel, Shemaiah, Elnathan, Jarib, Elnathan, Nathan, Zechariah and Meshullam, who were leaders, and Joiarib and Elnathan, who were men of learning, 17and I sent them to Iddo, the leader in Casiphia. I told them what to say to Iddo and his kinsmen, the temple servants in Casiphia, so that they might bring attendants to us for the house of our God. 18Because the gracious hand of our God was on us, they brought us Sherebiah, a capable man, from the descendants of Mahli son of Levi, the son of Israel, and Sherebiah's sons and brothers, 18 men; 19and Hashabiah, together with Jeshaiah from the descendants of Merari, and his brothers and nephews, 20 men. 20They also brought 220 of the temple servants — a body that David and the officials had established to assist the Levites. All were registered by name.

21There, by the Ahava Canal, I proclaimed a fast, so that we might humble ourselves before our God and ask him for a safe journey for us and our children, with all our possessions. 22I was ashamed to ask the king for soldiers and horsemen to protect us from enemies on the road, because we had told the king, "The gracious hand of our God is on everyone who looks to him, but his great anger is against all who forsake him." 23So we fasted and petitioned our God about this, and he answered our prayer.

24Then I set apart twelve of the leading priests, together with Sherebiah, Hashabiah and ten of their brothers, 25and I weighed out to them the offering of silver and gold and the articles that the king, his advisers, his officials and all Israel present there had donated for the house of our God. 26I weighed out to them 650 talents*c* of silver, silver articles weighing 100 talents,*d* 100 talents*d* of gold, 2720 bowls of

---

gold valued at 1,000 darics,[a] and two fine articles of polished bronze, as precious as gold.

[28]I said to them, "You as well as these articles are consecrated to the LORD. The silver and gold are a freewill offering to the LORD, the God of your fathers. [29]Guard them carefully until you weigh them out in the chambers of the house of the LORD in Jerusalem before the leading priests and the Levites and the family heads of Israel." [30]Then the priests and Levites received the silver and gold and sacred articles that had been weighed out to be taken to the house of our God in Jerusalem.

[31]On the twelfth day of the first month we set out from the Ahava Canal to go to Jerusalem. The hand of our God was on us, and he protected us from enemies and bandits along the way. [32]So we arrived in Jerusalem, where we rested three days.

[33]On the fourth day, in the house of our God, we weighed out the silver and gold and the sacred articles into the hands of Meremoth son of Uriah, the priest. Eleazar son of Phinehas was with him, and so were the Levites Jozabad son of Jeshua and Noadiah son of Binnui. [34]Everything was accounted for by number and weight, and the entire weight was recorded at that time.

[35]Then the exiles who had returned from captivity sacrificed burnt offerings to the God of Israel: twelve bulls for all Israel, ninety-six rams, seventy-seven male lambs and, as a sin offering, twelve male goats. All this was a burnt offering to the LORD. [36]They also delivered the king's orders to the royal satraps and to the governors of Trans-Euphrates, who then gave assistance to the people and to the house of God.

Ezra's Prayer About Intermarriage

9 After these things had been done, the leaders came to me and said, "The people of Israel, including the priests and the Levites, have not kept themselves separate from the neighboring peoples with their detestable practices, like those of the Canaanites, Hittites, Perizzites, Jebusites, Ammonites, Moabites, Egyptians and Amorites. [2]They have taken some of their daughters as wives for themselves and their sons, and have mingled the holy race with the peoples around them. And the leaders and officials have led the way in this unfaithfulness."

[3]When I heard this, I tore my tunic and cloak, pulled hair from my head and beard and sat down appalled. [4]Then everyone who trembled at the words of the God of Israel gathered around me because of this unfaithfulness of the exiles. And I sat there appalled until the evening sacrifice.

[5]Then, at the evening sacrifice, I rose from my self-abasement, with my tunic and cloak torn, and fell on my knees with my hands spread out to the LORD my God [6]and prayed:

"O my God, I am too ashamed and disgraced to lift up my face to you, my God, because our sins are higher than our heads and our guilt has reached to the heavens. [7]From the days of our forefathers until now, our guilt has been great. Because of our sins, we and our kings and our priests have been subjected to the sword and captivity, to pillage and humiliation at the hand of foreign kings, as it is today.

[8]"But now, for a brief moment, the LORD our God has been gracious in leaving us a remnant and giving us a firm place in his sanctuary, and so our God gives light to our eyes and a little relief in our bondage. [9]Though we are slaves, our God has not deserted us in our bondage. He has shown us kindness in the sight of the kings of Persia: He has granted us new life to rebuild the house of our God and repair its ruins, and he has given us a wall of protection in Judah and Jerusalem.

[10]"But now, O our God, what can we say after this? For we have disregarded the commands [11]you gave through your servants the prophets when you said: 'The land you are entering to possess is a land polluted by the corruption of its peoples. By their detestable practices they have filled it with their impurity from one end to the other. [12]Therefore, do not give your daughters in marriage to their sons or take their daughters for your sons. Do not seek a treaty of friendship with them at any time, that you may be strong and eat the good things of the land and leave it to your children as an everlasting inheritance.'

[13]"What has happened to us is a re-

---

[a]27 That is, about 19 pounds (about 8.5 kilograms)

sult of our evil deeds and our great guilt, and yet, our God, you have punished us less than our sins have deserved and have given us a remnant like this. [14]Shall we again break your commands and intermarry with the peoples who commit such detestable practices? Would you not be angry enough with us to destroy us, leaving us no remnant or survivor? [15]O LORD, God of Israel, you are righteous! We are left this day as a remnant. Here we are before you in our guilt, though because of it not one of us can stand in your presence."

The People's Confession of Sin

10 While Ezra was praying and confessing, weeping and throwing himself down before the house of God, a large crowd of Israelites — men, women and children — gathered around him. They too wept bitterly. [2]Then Shecaniah son of Jehiel, one of the descendants of Elam, said to Ezra, "We have been unfaithful to our God by marrying foreign women from the peoples around us. But in spite of this, there is still hope for Israel. [3]Now let us make a covenant before our God to send away all these women and their children, in accordance with the counsel of my lord and of those who fear the commands of our God. Let it be done according to the Law. [4]Rise up; this matter is in your hands. We will support you, so take courage and do it."

[5]So Ezra rose up and put the leading priests and Levites and all Israel under

---

WEDNESDAY

VERSE FOR THE DAY:	AUTHOR:	PASSAGE FOR THE DAY:
Ezra 9:13	Mike Singletary	Ezra 9:6,13–15

To Know His Grace

IT WOULD be a tragedy if my kids grew up knowing only that their dad was a good football player and husband and father. If they thought I expected them to live every minute of their lives the way they have seen me live as they grew up, they would be frustrated and devastated if they ever failed. I want them to know what they didn't see, when I failed miserably and only came out of it by the grace of God. And you know what? I'm still fighting to stay above water, with his help.

As they get older and able to understand, I'm committed to being open and honest with them. I want them to know of my mistakes so they can avoid them. I also want them to know of my mistakes because they will make their own, and I don't want them to feel they are the first person in the family to fail.

Just like I do with teammates, I want to be able to sit with my kids and tell them some of the things I have done. Not to glorify sin. Not to justify it. Not to say everybody does it so it must be okay. Rather, because I'm not proud of it and because I don't want them to feel unique. Most of all, I want them to know that by the grace of God, he brought me through it and out of it, and he can do the same for them.

Additional Scripture Readings:
2 Corinthians 4:13–18;
Ephesians 2:1–10

Go to page 481 for your next
devotional reading.

oath to do what had been suggested. And they took the oath. ⁶Then Ezra withdrew from before the house of God and went to the room of Jehohanan son of Eliashib. While he was there, he ate no food and drank no water, because he continued to mourn over the unfaithfulness of the exiles.

⁷A proclamation was then issued throughout Judah and Jerusalem for all the exiles to assemble in Jerusalem. ⁸Anyone who failed to appear within three days would forfeit all his property, in accordance with the decision of the officials and elders, and would himself be expelled from the assembly of the exiles.

⁹Within the three days, all the men of Judah and Benjamin had gathered in Jerusalem. And on the twentieth day of the ninth month, all the people were sitting in the square before the house of God, greatly distressed by the occasion and because of the rain. ¹⁰Then Ezra the priest stood up and said to them, "You have been unfaithful; you have married foreign women, adding to Israel's guilt. ¹¹Now make confession to the Lord, the God of your fathers, and do his will. Separate yourselves from the peoples around you and from your foreign wives."

¹²The whole assembly responded with a loud voice: "You are right! We must do as you say. ¹³But there are many people here and it is the rainy season; so we cannot stand outside. Besides, this matter cannot be taken care of in a day or two, because we have sinned greatly in this thing. ¹⁴Let our officials act for the whole assembly. Then let everyone in our towns who has married a foreign woman come at a set time, along with the elders and judges of each town, until the fierce anger of our God in this matter is turned away from us." ¹⁵Only Jonathan son of Asahel and Jahzeiah son of Tikvah, supported by Meshullam and Shabbethai the Levite, opposed this.

¹⁶So the exiles did as was proposed. Ezra the priest selected men who were family heads, one from each family division, and all of them designated by name. On the first day of the tenth month they sat down to investigate the cases, ¹⁷and by the first day of the first month they finished dealing with all the men who had married foreign women.

Those Guilty of Intermarriage

¹⁸Among the descendants of the priests, the following had married foreign women:

From the descendants of Jeshua son of Jozadak, and his brothers: Maaseiah, Eliezer, Jarib and Gedaliah. ¹⁹(They all gave their hands in pledge to put away their wives, and for their guilt they each presented a ram from the flock as a guilt offering.)

²⁰From the descendants of Immer: Hanani and Zebadiah.

²¹From the descendants of Harim: Maaseiah, Elijah, Shemaiah, Jehiel and Uzziah.

²²From the descendants of Pashhur: Elioenai, Maaseiah, Ishmael, Nethanel, Jozabad and Elasah.

²³Among the Levites:

Jozabad, Shimei, Kelaiah (that is, Kelita), Pethahiah, Judah and Eliezer.

²⁴From the singers: Eliashib.

From the gatekeepers: Shallum, Telem and Uri.

²⁵And among the other Israelites:

From the descendants of Parosh: Ramiah, Izziah, Malkijah, Mijamin, Eleazar, Malkijah and Benaiah.

²⁶From the descendants of Elam: Mattaniah, Zechariah, Jehiel, Abdi, Jeremoth and Elijah.

²⁷From the descendants of Zattu: Elioenai, Eliashib, Mattaniah, Jeremoth, Zabad and Aziza.

²⁸From the descendants of Bebai: Jehohanan, Hananiah, Zabbai and Athlai.

²⁹From the descendants of Bani: Meshullam, Malluch, Adaiah, Jashub, Sheal and Jeremoth.

³⁰From the descendants of Pahath-Moab: Adna, Kelal, Benaiah, Maaseiah, Mattaniah, Bezalel, Binnui and Manasseh.

³¹From the descendants of Harim: Eliezer, Ishijah, Malkijah, Shemaiah, Shimeon, ³²Benjamin, Malluch and Shemariah.

³³From the descendants of Hashum: Mattenai, Mattattah, Zabad, Eliphelet, Jeremai, Manasseh and Shimei.

³⁴From the descendants of Bani:

Maadai, Amram, Uel, [35]Benaiah, Bedeiah, Keluhi, [36]Vaniah, Meremoth, Eliashib, [37]Mattaniah, Mattenai and Jaasu.

[38]From the descendants of Binnui:[a] Shimei, [39]Shelemiah, Nathan, Adaiah, [40]Macnadebai, Shashai, Sharai, [41]Azarel, Shelemiah, Shemariah, [42]Shallum, Amariah and Joseph.

[43]From the descendants of Nebo: Jeiel, Mattithiah, Zabad, Zebina, Jaddai, Joel and Benaiah.

[44]All these had married foreign women, and some of them had children by these wives.[b]

---

[a]37,38 See Septuagint (also 1 Esdras 9:34); Hebrew *Jaasu* [38]*and Bani and Binnui,*   [b]44 Or *and they sent them away with their children*

THE book of Nehemiah recounts Nehemiah's time as governor of Canaan when God's people were returning from Babylon. He rebuilds the walls of Jerusalem, along with Ezra he leads God's people in worship, and he administers their affairs. Important to his daily work is prayer, through which he expresses his dependence on God. As you read this book, ask yourself how God wants you to serve his people; be sure that everything you do is accompanied by prayer.

NEHEMIAH

Nehemiah's Prayer

1 The words of Nehemiah son of Hacaliah:

In the month of Kislev in the twentieth year, while I was in the citadel of Susa, ²Hanani, one of my brothers, came from Judah with some other men, and I questioned them about the Jewish remnant that survived the exile, and also about Jerusalem.

³They said to me, "Those who survived the exile and are back in the province are in great trouble and disgrace. The wall of Jerusalem is broken down, and its gates have been burned with fire."

⁴When I heard these things, I sat down and wept. For some days I mourned and fasted and prayed before the God of heaven. ⁵Then I said:

"O LORD, God of heaven, the great and awesome God, who keeps his covenant of love with those who love him and obey his commands, ⁶let your ear be attentive and your eyes open to hear the prayer your servant is praying before you day and night for your servants, the people of Israel. I confess the sins we Israelites, including myself and my father's house, have committed against you.

[7] We have acted very wickedly toward you. We have not obeyed the commands, decrees and laws you gave your servant Moses.

[8] "Remember the instruction you gave your servant Moses, saying, 'If you are unfaithful, I will scatter you among the nations, [9] but if you return to me and obey my commands, then even if your exiled people are at the farthest horizon, I will gather them from there and bring them to the place I have chosen as a dwelling for my Name.'

[10] "They are your servants and your people, whom you redeemed by your great strength and your mighty hand. [11] O Lord, let your ear be attentive to the prayer of this your servant and to the prayer of your servants who delight in revering your name. Give your servant success today by granting him favor in the presence of this man."

I was cupbearer to the king.

Artaxerxes Sends Nehemiah to Jerusalem

2 In the month of Nisan in the twentieth year of King Artaxerxes, when wine was brought for him, I took the wine and gave it to the king. I had not been sad in his presence before; [2] so the king asked me, "Why does your face look so sad when you are not ill? This can be nothing but sadness of heart."

I was very much afraid, [3] but I said to the king, "May the king live forever! Why should my face not look sad when the city where my fathers are buried lies in ruins, and its gates have been destroyed by fire?"

[4] The king said to me, "What is it you want?"

Then I prayed to the God of heaven, [5] and I answered the king, "If it pleases the king and if your servant has found favor in his sight, let him send me to the city in Judah where my fathers are buried so that I can rebuild it."

[6] Then the king, with the queen sitting beside him, asked me, "How long will your journey take, and when will you get back?" It pleased the king to send me; so I set a time.

[7] I also said to him, "If it pleases the king, may I have letters to the governors of Trans-Euphrates, so that they will provide me safe-conduct until I arrive in Judah? [8] And may I have a letter to Asaph, keeper of the king's forest, so he will give me timber to make beams for the gates of the citadel by the temple and for the city wall and for the residence I will occupy?" And because the gracious hand of my God was upon me, the king granted my requests. [9] So I went to the governors of Trans-Euphrates and gave them the king's letters. The king had also sent army officers and cavalry with me.

[10] When Sanballat the Horonite and Tobiah the Ammonite official heard about this, they were very much disturbed that someone had come to promote the welfare of the Israelites.

Nehemiah Inspects Jerusalem's Walls

[11] I went to Jerusalem, and after staying there three days [12] I set out during the night with a few men. I had not told anyone what my God had put in my heart to do for Jerusalem. There were no mounts with me except the one I was riding on. [13] By night I went out through the Valley Gate toward the Jackal[a] Well and the Dung Gate, examining the walls of Jerusalem, which had been broken down, and its gates, which had been destroyed by fire. [14] Then I moved on toward the Fountain Gate and the King's Pool, but there was not enough room for my mount to get through; [15] so I went up the valley by night, examining the wall. Finally, I turned back and reentered through the Valley Gate. [16] The officials did not know where I had gone or what I was doing, because as yet I had said nothing to the Jews or the priests or nobles or officials or any others who would be doing the work.

[17] Then I said to them, "You see the trouble we are in: Jerusalem lies in ruins, and its gates have been burned with fire. Come, let us rebuild the wall of Jerusalem, and we will no longer be in disgrace." [18] I also told them about the gracious hand of my God upon me and what the king had said to me.

They replied, "Let us start rebuilding." So they began this good work.

[19] But when Sanballat the Horonite, Tobiah the Ammonite official and Geshem the Arab heard about it, they mocked and ridiculed us. "What is this you are doing?"

[a] 13 Or Serpent or Fig

they asked. "Are you rebelling against the king?"

[20]I answered them by saying, "The God of heaven will give us success. We his servants will start rebuilding, but as for you, you have no share in Jerusalem or any claim or historic right to it."

Builders of the Wall

3 Eliashib the high priest and his fellow priests went to work and rebuilt the Sheep Gate. They dedicated it and set its doors in place, building as far as the Tower of the Hundred, which they dedicated, and as far as the Tower of Hananel. [2]The men of Jericho built the adjoining section, and Zaccur son of Imri built next to them.

[3]The Fish Gate was rebuilt by the sons of Hassenaah. They laid its beams and put its doors and bolts and bars in place. [4]Meremoth son of Uriah, the son of Hakkoz, repaired the next section. Next to him Meshullam son of Berekiah, the son of Meshezabel, made repairs, and next to him Zadok son of Baana also made repairs. [5]The next section was repaired by the men of Tekoa, but their nobles would not put their shoulders to the work under their supervisors.[a]

[6]The Jeshanah[b] Gate was repaired by Joiada son of Paseah and Meshullam son of Besodeiah. They laid its beams and put its doors and bolts and bars in place. [7]Next to them, repairs were made by men from Gibeon and Mizpah — Melatiah of Gibeon and Jadon of Meronoth — places under the authority of the governor of Trans-Euphrates. [8]Uzziel son of Harhaiah, one of the goldsmiths, repaired the next section; and Hananiah, one of the perfume-makers, made repairs next to that. They restored[c] Jerusalem as far as the Broad Wall. [9]Rephaiah son of Hur, ruler of a half-district of Jerusalem, repaired the next section. [10]Adjoining this, Jedaiah son of Harumaph made repairs opposite his house, and Hattush son of Hashabneiah made repairs next to him. [11]Malkijah son of Harim and Hasshub son of Pahath-Moab repaired another section and the Tower of the Ovens. [12]Shallum son of Hallohesh, ruler of a half-district of Jerusalem, repaired the next section with the help of his daughters.

[13]The Valley Gate was repaired by Hanun and the residents of Zanoah. They rebuilt it and put its doors and bolts and bars in place. They also repaired five hundred yards[d] of the wall as far as the Dung Gate.

[14]The Dung Gate was repaired by Malkijah son of Recab, ruler of the district of Beth Hakkerem. He rebuilt it and put its doors and bolts and bars in place.

[15]The Fountain Gate was repaired by Shallun son of Col-Hozeh, ruler of the district of Mizpah. He rebuilt it, roofing it over and putting its doors and bolts and bars in place. He also repaired the wall of the Pool of Siloam,[e] by the King's Garden, as far as the steps going down from the City of David. [16]Beyond him, Nehemiah son of Azbuk, ruler of a half-district of Beth Zur, made repairs up to a point opposite the tombs[f] of David, as far as the artificial pool and the House of the Heroes.

[17]Next to him, the repairs were made by the Levites under Rehum son of Bani. Beside him, Hashabiah, ruler of half the district of Keilah, carried out repairs for his district. [18]Next to him, the repairs were made by their countrymen under Binnui[g] son of Henadad, ruler of the other half-district of Keilah. [19]Next to him, Ezer son of Jeshua, ruler of Mizpah, repaired another section, from a point facing the ascent to the armory as far as the angle. [20]Next to him, Baruch son of Zabbai zealously repaired another section, from the angle to the entrance of the house of Eliashib the high priest. [21]Next to him, Meremoth son of Uriah, the son of Hakkoz, repaired another section, from the entrance of Eliashib's house to the end of it.

[22]The repairs next to him were made by the priests from the surrounding region. [23]Beyond them, Benjamin and Hasshub made repairs in front of their house; and next to them, Azariah son of Maaseiah, the son of Ananiah, made repairs beside his house. [24]Next to him, Binnui son of Henadad repaired another section, from Azariah's house to the angle and the corner, [25]and Palal son of Uzai worked opposite the angle and the tower projecting from the upper palace near the court of the guard. Next to him, Pedaiah son of Parosh [26]and the temple servants living on

a5 Or their Lord or the governor   b6 Or Old   c8 Or They left out part of   d13 Hebrew a thousand cubits (about 450 meters)   e15 Hebrew Shelah, a variant of Shiloah, that is, Siloam   f16 Hebrew; Septuagint, some Vulgate manuscripts and Syriac tomb   g18 Two Hebrew manuscripts and Syriac (see also Septuagint and verse 24); most Hebrew manuscripts Bavvai

THURSDAY

VERSE FOR THE DAY:
Nehemiah 2:18

AUTHOR:
D. Stuart Briscoe

PASSAGE FOR THE DAY:
Nehemiah 2:11–20

A High Calling

SOME people obviously have the idea that work is a curse, while others look upon it as a calling. Depending upon which view you take, you are spending half of your conscious hours in a generally happy pursuit, or you are largely unfulfilled and unhappy . . .

In medieval Christianity, the predominant idea was that God called certain people and their work was a "calling." The rest just worked. That was how we got this awful division between the clergy and the laity; the clergy were called, the laity just got on with it.

Now this kind of attitude was very common. A few people received a high calling into the priesthood and the rest of the folk just went through the sheer drudgery of their work. Then, along came the Reformation. In the Reformation, one or two ancient Biblical doctrines were rediscovered, including this one: the priesthood of all believers. This is the truth that all believers in Jesus Christ are one in Christ Jesus, and that we are all a kingdom of priests (1 Peter 2:5,9). We all have immediate access to the Father through the Son, and we don't need to go through a priest or any other human agent.

If we accept this as true, we have to accept something else. If everybody is equally a priest before God, everybody is equally called. And if everybody is equally called, then the work you are in—if God wants you in it—is your calling.

We might answer: "Come on. I'm just an electrician" . . . You can rule out "just a" when you talk about your job, if you believe that work is a calling. Paul suggests in 1 Corinthians 7:20 that the work you are involved in is as much a divine calling as that in which a missionary or a pastor is involved. If we have got the idea that we are called to that work, I will guarantee it will change our attitude positively toward work.

When you check in to work tomorrow morning, say to the Lord, "Here I am, Lord, uniquely gifted with skill, time and energy graciously provided by you. I recognize this. And I believe that you have me where you want me, which means that this particular job that I thought last week was a real bummer is, in actual fact, a high calling, and I am going to live and work today as if that is exactly what it is."

Additional Scripture Readings:
1 Corinthians 7:17–24;
1 Peter 2:4–12

Go to page 485 for your next
devotional reading.

the hill of Ophel made repairs up to a point opposite the Water Gate toward the east and the projecting tower. 27Next to them, the men of Tekoa repaired another section, from the great projecting tower to the wall of Ophel.

28Above the Horse Gate, the priests made repairs, each in front of his own house. 29Next to them, Zadok son of Immer made repairs opposite his house. Next to him, Shemaiah son of Shecaniah, the guard at the East Gate, made repairs. 30Next to him, Hananiah son of Shelemiah, and Hanun, the sixth son of Zalaph, repaired another section. Next to them, Meshullam son of Berekiah made repairs opposite his living quarters. 31Next to him, Malkijah, one of the goldsmiths, made repairs as far as the house of the temple servants and the merchants, opposite the Inspection Gate, and as far as the room above the corner; 32and between the room above the corner and the Sheep Gate the goldsmiths and merchants made repairs.

Opposition to the Rebuilding

4 When Sanballat heard that we were rebuilding the wall, he became angry and was greatly incensed. He ridiculed the Jews, 2and in the presence of his associates and the army of Samaria, he said, "What are those feeble Jews doing? Will they restore their wall? Will they offer sacrifices? Will they finish in a day? Can they bring the stones back to life from those heaps of rubble—burned as they are?"

3Tobiah the Ammonite, who was at his side, said, "What they are building—if even a fox climbed up on it, he would break down their wall of stones!"

4Hear us, O our God, for we are despised. Turn their insults back on their own heads. Give them over as plunder in a land of captivity. 5Do not cover up their guilt or blot out their sins from your sight, for they have thrown insults in the face of[a] the builders.

6So we rebuilt the wall till all of it reached half its height, for the people worked with all their heart.

7But when Sanballat, Tobiah, the Arabs, the Ammonites and the men of Ashdod heard that the repairs to Jerusalem's walls had gone ahead and that the gaps were being closed, they were very angry. 8They all plotted together to come and fight against Jerusalem and stir up trouble against it. 9But we prayed to our God and posted a guard day and night to meet this threat.

10Meanwhile, the people in Judah said, "The strength of the laborers is giving out, and there is so much rubble that we cannot rebuild the wall."

11Also our enemies said, "Before they know it or see us, we will be right there among them and will kill them and put an end to the work."

12Then the Jews who lived near them came and told us ten times over, "Wherever you turn, they will attack us."

13Therefore I stationed some of the people behind the lowest points of the wall at the exposed places, posting them by families, with their swords, spears and bows. 14After I looked things over, I stood up and said to the nobles, the officials and the rest of the people, "Don't be afraid of them. Remember the Lord, who is great and awesome, and fight for your brothers, your sons and your daughters, your wives and your homes."

15When our enemies heard that we were aware of their plot and that God had frustrated it, we all returned to the wall, each to his own work.

16From that day on, half of my men did the work, while the other half were equipped with spears, shields, bows and armor. The officers posted themselves behind all the people of Judah 17who were building the wall. Those who carried materials did their work with one hand and held a weapon in the other, 18and each of the builders wore his sword at his side as he worked. But the man who sounded the trumpet stayed with me.

19Then I said to the nobles, the officials and the rest of the people, "The work is extensive and spread out, and we are widely separated from each other along the wall. 20Wherever you hear the sound of the trumpet, join us there. Our God will fight for us!"

21So we continued the work with half the men holding spears, from the first light of dawn till the stars came out. 22At that time I also said to the people, "Have every man and his helper stay inside Jerusalem at night, so they can serve us as guards by night and workmen by day." 23Neither I nor my brothers nor my men nor the guards with me took off our

---

a5 Or *have provoked you to anger before*

clothes; each had his weapon, even when he went for water.[a]

Nehemiah Helps the Poor

5 Now the men and their wives raised a great outcry against their Jewish brothers. [2]Some were saying, "We and our sons and daughters are numerous; in order for us to eat and stay alive, we must get grain."

[3]Others were saying, "We are mortgaging our fields, our vineyards and our homes to get grain during the famine."

[4]Still others were saying, "We have had to borrow money to pay the king's tax on our fields and vineyards. [5]Although we are of the same flesh and blood as our countrymen and though our sons are as good as theirs, yet we have to subject our sons and daughters to slavery. Some of our daughters have already been enslaved, but we are powerless, because our fields and our vineyards belong to others."

[6]When I heard their outcry and these charges, I was very angry. [7]I pondered them in my mind and then accused the nobles and officials. I told them, "You are exacting usury from your own countrymen!" So I called together a large meeting to deal with them [8]and said: "As far as possible, we have bought back our Jewish brothers who were sold to the Gentiles. Now you are selling your brothers, only for them to be sold back to us!" They kept quiet, because they could find nothing to say.

[9]So I continued, "What you are doing is not right. Shouldn't you walk in the fear of our God to avoid the reproach of our Gentile enemies? [10]I and my brothers and my men are also lending the people money and grain. But let the exacting of usury stop! [11]Give back to them immediately their fields, vineyards, olive groves and houses, and also the usury you are charging them—the hundredth part of the money, grain, new wine and oil."

[12]"We will give it back," they said. "And we will not demand anything more from them. We will do as you say."

Then I summoned the priests and made the nobles and officials take an oath to do what they had promised. [13]I also shook out the folds of my robe and said, "In this way may God shake out of his house and possessions every man who does not keep this promise. So may such a man be shaken out and emptied!"

At this the whole assembly said, "Amen," and praised the LORD. And the people did as they had promised.

[14]Moreover, from the twentieth year of King Artaxerxes, when I was appointed to be their governor in the land of Judah, until his thirty-second year—twelve years—neither I nor my brothers ate the food allotted to the governor. [15]But the earlier governors—those preceding me—placed a heavy burden on the people and took forty shekels[b] of silver from them in addition to food and wine. Their assistants also lorded it over the people. But out of reverence for God I did not act like that. [16]Instead, I devoted myself to the work on this wall. All my men were assembled there for the work; we[c] did not acquire any land.

[17]Furthermore, a hundred and fifty Jews and officials ate at my table, as well as those who came to us from the surrounding nations. [18]Each day one ox, six choice sheep and some poultry were prepared for me, and every ten days an abundant supply of wine of all kinds. In spite of all this, I never demanded the food allotted to the governor, because the demands were heavy on these people.

[19]Remember me with favor, O my God, for all I have done for these people.

Further Opposition to the Rebuilding

6 When word came to Sanballat, Tobiah, Geshem the Arab and the rest of our enemies that I had rebuilt the wall and not a gap was left in it—though up to that time I had not set the doors in the gates—[2]Sanballat and Geshem sent me this message: "Come, let us meet together in one of the villages[d] on the plain of Ono."

But they were scheming to harm me; [3]so I sent messengers to them with this reply: "I am carrying on a great project and cannot go down. Why should the work stop while I leave it and go down to you?" [4]Four times they sent me the same message, and each time I gave them the same answer.

[5]Then, the fifth time, Sanballat sent his aide to me with the same message, and in his hand was an unsealed letter [6]in which was written:

---

[a]23 The meaning of the Hebrew for this clause is uncertain.   [b]15 That is, about 1 pound (about 0.5 kilogram)   [c]16 Most Hebrew manuscripts; some Hebrew manuscripts, Septuagint, Vulgate and Syriac I   [d]2 Or in Kephirim

"It is reported among the nations — and Geshem[a] says it is true — that you and the Jews are plotting to revolt, and therefore you are building the wall. Moreover, according to these reports you are about to become their king [7]and have even appointed prophets to make this proclamation about you in Jerusalem: 'There is a king in Judah!' Now this report will get back to the king; so come, let us confer together."

[8]I sent him this reply: "Nothing like what you are saying is happening; you are just making it up out of your head."

[9]They were all trying to frighten us, thinking, "Their hands will get too weak for the work, and it will not be completed."

ᴸBut I prayed˩ "Now strengthen my hands."

[10]One day I went to the house of Shemaiah son of Delaiah, the son of Mehetabel, who was shut in at his home. He said, "Let us meet in the house of God, inside the temple, and let us close the temple doors, because men are coming to kill you — by night they are coming to kill you."

[11]But I said, "Should a man like me run away? Or should one like me go into the temple to save his life? I will not go!" [12]I realized that God had not sent him, but that he had prophesied against me because Tobiah and Sanballat had hired him. [13]He had been hired to intimidate me so that I would commit a sin by doing this, and then they would give me a bad name to discredit me.

[14]Remember Tobiah and Sanballat, O my God, because of what they have done; remember also the prophetess Noadiah and the rest of the prophets who have been trying to intimidate me.

The Completion of the Wall

[15]So the wall was completed on the twenty-fifth of Elul, in fifty-two days. [16]When all our enemies heard about this, all the surrounding nations were afraid and lost their self-confidence, because they realized that this work had been done with the help of our God. [17]Also, in those days the nobles of Judah were sending many letters to Tobiah, and replies from Tobiah kept coming to them. [18]For many in Judah were under oath to him, since he was son-in-law to Shecaniah son of Arah, and his son Jehohanan had married the daughter of Meshullam son of Berekiah. [19]Moreover, they kept reporting to me his good deeds and then telling him what I said. And Tobiah sent letters to intimidate me.

[7] After the wall had been rebuilt and I had set the doors in place, the gatekeepers and the singers and the Levites were appointed. [2]I put in charge of Jerusalem my brother Hanani, along with[b] Hananiah the commander of the citadel, because he was a man of integrity and feared God more than most men do. [3]I said to them, "The gates of Jerusalem are not to be opened until the sun is hot. While the gatekeepers are still on duty, have them shut the doors and bar them. Also appoint residents of Jerusalem as guards, some at their posts and some near their own houses."

The List of the Exiles Who Returned

[4]Now the city was large and spacious, but there were few people in it, and the houses had not yet been rebuilt. [5]So my God put it into my heart to assemble the nobles, the officials and the common people for registration by families. I found the genealogical record of those who had been the first to return. This is what I found written there:

[6]These are the people of the province who came up from the captivity of the exiles whom Nebuchadnezzar king of Babylon had taken captive (they returned to Jerusalem and Judah, each to his own town, [7]in company with Zerubbabel, Jeshua, Nehemiah, Azariah, Raamiah, Nahamani, Mordecai, Bilshan, Mispereth, Bigvai, Nehum and Baanah):

The list of the men of Israel:

[8]the descendants of Parosh	2,172
[9]of Shephatiah	372
[10]of Arah	652
[11]of Pahath-Moab (through the line of Jeshua and Joab)	2,818
[12]of Elam	1,254
[13]of Zattu	845
[14]of Zaccai	760
[15]of Binnui	648
[16]of Bebai	628
[17]of Azgad	2,322
[18]of Adonikam	667

---

[a]6 Hebrew *Gashmu*, a variant of *Geshem*   [b]2 Or *Hanani, that is,*

FRIDAY

VERSE FOR THE DAY:
Nehemiah 6:1

AUTHOR:
H. Beecher Hicks

PASSAGE FOR THE DAY:
Nehemiah 6:1–4

Walls

MY FRIENDS, consider the wall. There are two kinds of walls. There is, first of all, a bearing wall. A bearing wall is a wall you cannot do without. A bearing wall is designed to bear the weight of the structure. The wall with the window in it is a bearing wall because it holds up the weight of the roof. But it cannot be a bearing wall unless it is inextricably, fundamentally connected to the foundation. Now, if the wall that is around your life is not connected to the foundation, it is not a bearing wall. If the walls around your life are not connected to the rock, it will not sustain the weight of your problems, your difficulties, your trials . . . You need to be connected to the rock. "For no one can lay any foundation other than the one already laid, which is Jesus Christ" (1 Corinthians 3:11). There is a bearing wall.

There is also this other wall of which Ephesians [2:14–18] speaks. It is the middle wall. It is the interior wall. You can move that wall, and the building will still stand. Now, the problem with the interior wall is that we create them. We make up our own interior walls. We make up our own middle walls. And what is the middle wall? The middle wall is there because discrimination is there . . . because hatred is there . . .

How are you going to have your walls broken down? The wall is only broken down once you acknowledge your humanity, once you realize that you are no more than anyone else. Your wall comes down when you acknowledge that there is nothing to hide and no defense mechanism to secure you . . .

We need a word just now that will be redemptive for this hour. And the word is that God never leaves us with the middle walls in our lives, because of something that we put in every middle wall. Every middle wall in our lives has one thing in it: it has a door! . . . There *is* a door. It is connected to your heart. But nobody will come bursting in. Nobody will break down your door. The lock is not on the outside. The lock is on the inside. And Jesus says, "Here I am! I stand at the door and knock" [Revelation 3:20].

Additional Scripture Readings:
Ephesians 2:14–22;
Revelation 3:19–22

Go to page 493 for your next
devotional reading.

[19]of Bigvai	2,067
[20]of Adin	655
[21]of Ater (through Hezekiah)	98
[22]of Hashum	328
[23]of Bezai	324
[24]of Hariph	112
[25]of Gibeon	95
[26]the men of Bethlehem and Netophah	188
[27]of Anathoth	128
[28]of Beth Azmaveth	42
[29]of Kiriath Jearim, Kephirah and Beeroth	743
[30]of Ramah and Geba	621
[31]of Micmash	122
[32]of Bethel and Ai	123
[33]of the other Nebo	52
[34]of the other Elam	1,254
[35]of Harim	320
[36]of Jericho	345
[37]of Lod, Hadid and Ono	721
[38]of Senaah	3,930

[39]The priests:

the descendants of Jedaiah (through the family of Jeshua)	973
[40]of Immer	1,052
[41]of Pashhur	1,247
[42]of Harim	1,017

[43]The Levites:

the descendants of Jeshua (through Kadmiel through the line of Hodaviah)	74

[44]The singers:

the descendants of Asaph	148

[45]The gatekeepers:

the descendants of Shallum, Ater, Talmon, Akkub, Hatita and Shobai	138

[46]The temple servants:

the descendants of
Ziha, Hasupha, Tabbaoth,
[47]Keros, Sia, Padon,
[48]Lebana, Hagaba, Shalmai,
[49]Hanan, Giddel, Gahar,
[50]Reaiah, Rezin, Nekoda,
[51]Gazzam, Uzza, Paseah,
[52]Besai, Meunim, Nephussim,
[53]Bakbuk, Hakupha, Harhur,
[54]Bazluth, Mehida, Harsha,
[55]Barkos, Sisera, Temah,
[56]Neziah and Hatipha

[57]The descendants of the servants of Solomon:

the descendants of
Sotai, Sophereth, Perida,
[58]Jaala, Darkon, Giddel,
[59]Shephatiah, Hattil,
Pokereth-Hazzebaim and Amon

[60]The temple servants and the descendants of the servants of Solomon	392

[61]The following came up from the towns of Tel Melah, Tel Harsha, Kerub, Addon and Immer, but they could not show that their families were descended from Israel:

[62]the descendants of Delaiah, Tobiah and Nekoda	642

[63]And from among the priests:

the descendants of
Hobaiah, Hakkoz and Barzillai (a man who had married a daughter of Barzillai the Gileadite and was called by that name).

[64]These searched for their family records, but they could not find them and so were excluded from the priesthood as unclean. [65]The governor, therefore, ordered them not to eat any of the most sacred food until there should be a priest ministering with the Urim and Thummim.

[66]The whole company numbered 42,360, [67]besides their 7,337 menservants and maidservants; and they also had 245 men and women singers. [68]There were 736 horses, 245 mules,[a] [69]435 camels and 6,720 donkeys.

[70]Some of the heads of the families contributed to the work. The governor gave to the treasury 1,000 drachmas[b] of gold, 50 bowls and 530 garments for priests. [71]Some of the heads of the families gave to the treasury for the work 20,000 drachmas[c] of gold and 2,200 minas[d] of silver. [72]The total given by the rest of the

---

[a]68 Some Hebrew manuscripts (see also Ezra 2:66); most Hebrew manuscripts do not have this verse.   [b]70 That is, about 19 pounds (about 8.5 kilograms)   [c]71 That is, about 375 pounds (about 170 kilograms); also in verse 72   [d]71 That is, about 1 1/3 tons (about 1.2 metric tons)

people was 20,000 drachmas of gold, 2,000 minas[a] of silver and 67 garments for priests.

73The priests, the Levites, the gatekeepers, the singers and the temple servants, along with certain of the people and the rest of the Israelites, settled in their own towns.

Ezra Reads the Law

When the seventh month came and the Israelites had settled in their towns, 8 1all the people assembled as one man in the square before the Water Gate. They told Ezra the scribe to bring out the Book of the Law of Moses, which the LORD had commanded for Israel.

2So on the first day of the seventh month Ezra the priest brought the Law before the assembly, which was made up of men and women and all who were able to understand. 3He read it aloud from daybreak till noon as he faced the square before the Water Gate in the presence of the men, women and others who could understand. And all the people listened attentively to the Book of the Law.

4Ezra the scribe stood on a high wooden platform built for the occasion. Beside him on his right stood Mattithiah, Shema, Anaiah, Uriah, Hilkiah and Maaseiah; and on his left were Pedaiah, Mishael, Malkijah, Hashum, Hashbaddanah, Zechariah and Meshullam.

5Ezra opened the book. All the people could see him because he was standing above them; and as he opened it, the people all stood up. 6Ezra praised the LORD, the great God; and all the people lifted their hands and responded, "Amen! Amen!" Then they bowed down and worshiped the LORD with their faces to the ground.

7The Levites—Jeshua, Bani, Sherebiah, Jamin, Akkub, Shabbethai, Hodiah, Maaseiah, Kelita, Azariah, Jozabad, Hanan and Pelaiah—instructed the people in the Law while the people were standing there. 8They read from the Book of the Law of God, making it clear[b] and giving the meaning so that the people could understand what was being read.

9Then Nehemiah the governor, Ezra the priest and scribe, and the Levites who were instructing the people said to them all, "This day is sacred to the LORD your God. Do not mourn or weep." For all the people had been weeping as they listened to the words of the Law.

10Nehemiah said, "Go and enjoy choice food and sweet drinks, and send some to those who have nothing prepared. This day is sacred to our Lord. Do not grieve, for the joy of the LORD is your strength."

11The Levites calmed all the people, saying, "Be still, for this is a sacred day. Do not grieve."

12Then all the people went away to eat and drink, to send portions of food and to celebrate with great joy, because they now understood the words that had been made known to them.

13On the second day of the month, the heads of all the families, along with the priests and the Levites, gathered around Ezra the scribe to give attention to the words of the Law. 14They found written in the Law, which the LORD had commanded through Moses, that the Israelites were to live in booths during the feast of the seventh month 15and that they should proclaim this word and spread it throughout their towns and in Jerusalem: "Go out into the hill country and bring back branches from olive and wild olive trees, and from myrtles, palms and shade trees, to make booths"—as it is written.[c]

16So the people went out and brought back branches and built themselves booths on their own roofs, in their courtyards, in the courts of the house of God and in the square by the Water Gate and the one by the Gate of Ephraim. 17The whole company that had returned from exile built booths and lived in them. From the days of Joshua son of Nun until that day, the Israelites had not celebrated it like this. And their joy was very great.

18Day after day, from the first day to the last, Ezra read from the Book of the Law of God. They celebrated the feast for seven days, and on the eighth day, in accordance with the regulation, there was an assembly.

The Israelites Confess Their Sins

9 On the twenty-fourth day of the same month, the Israelites gathered together, fasting and wearing sackcloth and having dust on their heads. 2Those of Israelite descent had separated themselves from all foreigners. They stood in their places and confessed their sins and the wickedness of their fathers. 3They stood where they

---

a72 That is, about 1 1/4 tons (about 1.1 metric tons) 23:37-40.   b8 Or God, translating it   c15 See Lev.

were and read from the Book of the Law of the LORD their God for a quarter of the day, and spent another quarter in confession and in worshiping the LORD their God. [4]Standing on the stairs were the Levites—Jeshua, Bani, Kadmiel, Shebaniah, Bunni, Sherebiah, Bani and Kenani—who called with loud voices to the LORD their God. [5]And the Levites—Jeshua, Kadmiel, Bani, Hashabneiah, Sherebiah, Hodiah, Shebaniah and Pethahiah—said: "Stand up and praise the LORD your God, who is from everlasting to everlasting.[a]"

"Blessed be your glorious name, and may it be exalted above all blessing and praise. [6]You alone are the LORD. You made the heavens, even the highest heavens, and all their starry host, the earth and all that is on it, the seas and all that is in them. You give life to everything, and the multitudes of heaven worship you.

[7]"You are the LORD God, who chose Abram and brought him out of Ur of the Chaldeans and named him Abraham. [8]You found his heart faithful to you, and you made a covenant with him to give to his descendants the land of the Canaanites, Hittites, Amorites, Perizzites, Jebusites and Girgashites. You have kept your promise because you are righteous.

[9]"You saw the suffering of our forefathers in Egypt; you heard their cry at the Red Sea.[b] [10]You sent miraculous signs and wonders against Pharaoh, against all his officials and all the people of his land, for you knew how arrogantly the Egyptians treated them. You made a name for yourself, which remains to this day. [11]You divided the sea before them, so that they passed through it on dry ground, but you hurled their pursuers into the depths, like a stone into mighty waters. [12]By day you led them with a pillar of cloud, and by night with a pillar of fire to give them light on the way they were to take.

[13]"You came down on Mount Sinai; you spoke to them from heaven. You gave them regulations and laws that are just and right, and decrees and commands that are good. [14]You made known to them your holy Sabbath and gave them commands, decrees and laws through your servant Moses. [15]In their hunger you gave them bread from heaven and in their thirst you brought them water from the rock; you told them to go in and take possession of the land you had sworn with uplifted hand to give them.

[16]"But they, our forefathers, became arrogant and stiff-necked, and did not obey your commands. [17]They refused to listen and failed to remember the miracles you performed among them. They became stiff-necked and in their rebellion appointed a leader in order to return to their slavery. But you are a forgiving God, gracious and compassionate, slow to anger and abounding in love. Therefore you did not desert them, [18]even when they cast for themselves an image of a calf and said, 'This is your god, who brought you up out of Egypt,' or when they committed awful blasphemies.

[19]"Because of your great compassion you did not abandon them in the desert. By day the pillar of cloud did not cease to guide them on their path, nor the pillar of fire by night to shine on the way they were to take. [20]You gave your good Spirit to instruct them. You did not withhold your manna from their mouths, and you gave them water for their thirst. [21]For forty years you sustained them in the desert; they lacked nothing, their clothes did not wear out nor did their feet become swollen.

[22]"You gave them kingdoms and nations, allotting to them even the remotest frontiers. They took over the country of Sihon[c] king of Heshbon and the country of Og king of Bashan. [23]You made their sons as numerous as the stars in the sky, and you brought them into the land that you told their fathers to enter and possess. [24]Their sons went in and took possession of the land. You subdued before them the Canaanites, who lived in the land; you handed the Canaanites over to them, along with their kings and the peoples of the land, to deal with them as they pleased. [25]They captured fortified cities and fertile land; they took posses-

a5 Or *God for ever and ever*   b9 Hebrew *Yam Suph*; that is, Sea of Reeds   c22 One Hebrew manuscript and Septuagint; most Hebrew manuscripts *Sihon, that is, the country of the* sion of houses filled with all kinds of good things, wells already dug, vineyards, olive groves and fruit trees in abundance. They ate to the full and were well-nourished; they reveled in your great goodness.

26"But they were disobedient and rebelled against you; they put your law behind their backs. They killed your prophets, who had admonished them in order to turn them back to you; they committed awful blasphemies. 27So you handed them over to their enemies, who oppressed them. But when they were oppressed they cried out to you. From heaven you heard them, and in your great compassion you gave them deliverers, who rescued them from the hand of their enemies.

28"But as soon as they were at rest, they again did what was evil in your sight. Then you abandoned them to the hand of their enemies so that they ruled over them. And when they cried out to you again, you heard from heaven, and in your compassion you delivered them time after time.

29"You warned them to return to your law, but they became arrogant and disobeyed your commands. They sinned against your ordinances, by which a man will live if he obeys them. Stubbornly they turned their backs on you, became stiff-necked and refused to listen. 30For many years you were patient with them. By your Spirit you admonished them through your prophets. Yet they paid no attention, so you handed them over to the neighboring peoples. 31But in your great mercy you did not put an end to them or abandon them, for you are a gracious and merciful God.

32"Now therefore, O our God, the great, mighty and awesome God, who keeps his covenant of love, do not let all this hardship seem trifling in your eyes—the hardship that has come upon us, upon our kings and leaders, upon our priests and prophets, upon our fathers and all your people, from the days of the kings of Assyria until today. 33In all that has happened to us, you have been just; you have acted faithfully, while we did wrong. 34Our kings, our leaders, our priests and our fathers did not follow your law; they did not pay attention to your commands or the warnings you gave them. 35Even while they were in their kingdom, enjoying your great goodness to them in the spacious and fertile land you gave them, they did not serve you or turn from their evil ways.

36"But see, we are slaves today, slaves in the land you gave our forefathers so they could eat its fruit and the other good things it produces. 37Because of our sins, its abundant harvest goes to the kings you have placed over us. They rule over our bodies and our cattle as they please. We are in great distress.

The Agreement of the People

38"In view of all this, we are making a binding agreement, putting it in writing, and our leaders, our Levites and our priests are affixing their seals to it."

10 Those who sealed it were:

Nehemiah the governor, the son of Hacaliah.

Zedekiah, 2Seraiah, Azariah, Jeremiah, 3Pashhur, Amariah, Malkijah, 4Hattush, Shebaniah, Malluch, 5Harim, Meremoth, Obadiah, 6Daniel, Ginnethon, Baruch, 7Meshullam, Abijah, Mijamin, 8Maaziah, Bilgai and Shemaiah.
These were the priests.

9The Levites:

Jeshua son of Azaniah, Binnui of the sons of Henadad, Kadmiel, 10and their associates: Shebaniah, Hodiah, Kelita, Pelaiah, Hanan, 11Mica, Rehob, Hashabiah, 12Zaccur, Sherebiah, Shebaniah, 13Hodiah, Bani and Beninu.

14The leaders of the people:

Parosh, Pahath-Moab, Elam, Zattu, Bani, 15Bunni, Azgad, Bebai, 16Adonijah, Bigvai, Adin, 17Ater, Hezekiah, Azzur, 18Hodiah, Hashum, Bezai, 19Hariph, Anathoth, Nebai, 20Magpiash, Meshullam, Hezir, 21Meshezabel, Zadok, Jaddua, 22Pelatiah, Hanan, Anaiah, 23Hoshea, Hananiah, Hasshub, 24Hallohesh, Pilha, Shobek,

25Rehum, Hashabnah, Maaseiah,
26Ahiah, Hanan, Anan,
27Malluch, Harim and Baanah.

28"The rest of the people — priests, Levites, gatekeepers, singers, temple servants and all who separated themselves from the neighboring peoples for the sake of the Law of God, together with their wives and all their sons and daughters who are able to understand— 29all these now join their brothers the nobles, and bind themselves with a curse and an oath to follow the Law of God given through Moses the servant of God and to obey carefully all the commands, regulations and decrees of the LORD our Lord.

30"We promise not to give our daughters in marriage to the peoples around us or take their daughters for our sons.

31"When the neighboring peoples bring merchandise or grain to sell on the Sabbath, we will not buy from them on the Sabbath or on any holy day. Every seventh year we will forgo working the land and will cancel all debts.

32"We assume the responsibility for carrying out the commands to give a third of a shekel*a* each year for the service of the house of our God: 33for the bread set out on the table; for the regular grain offerings and burnt offerings; for the offerings on the Sabbaths, New Moon festivals and appointed feasts; for the holy offerings; for sin offerings to make atonement for Israel; and for all the duties of the house of our God.

34"We — the priests, the Levites and the people — have cast lots to determine when each of our families is to bring to the house of our God at set times each year a contribution of wood to burn on the altar of the LORD our God, as it is written in the Law.

35"We also assume responsibility for bringing to the house of the LORD each year the firstfruits of our crops and of every fruit tree.

36"As it is also written in the Law, we will bring the firstborn of our sons and of our cattle, of our herds and of our flocks to the house of our God, to the priests ministering there.

37"Moreover, we will bring to the storerooms of the house of our God, to the priests, the first of our ground meal, of our grain, offerings, of the fruit of all our trees and of our new wine and oil. And we will bring a tithe of our crops to the Levites, for it is the Levites who collect the tithes in all the towns where we work. 38A priest descended from Aaron is to accompany the Levites when they receive the tithes, and the Levites are to bring a tenth of the tithes up to the house of our God, to the storerooms of the treasury. 39The people of Israel, including the Levites, are to bring their contributions of grain, new wine and oil to the storerooms where the articles for the sanctuary are kept and where the ministering priests, the gatekeepers and the singers stay.

"We will not neglect the house of our God."

The New Residents of Jerusalem

11 Now the leaders of the people settled in Jerusalem, and the rest of the people cast lots to bring one out of every ten to live in Jerusalem, the holy city, while the remaining nine were to stay in their own towns. 2The people commended all the men who volunteered to live in Jerusalem.

3These are the provincial leaders who settled in Jerusalem (now some Israelites, priests, Levites, temple servants and descendants of Solomon's servants lived in the towns of Judah, each on his own property in the various towns, 4while other people from both Judah and Benjamin lived in Jerusalem):

From the descendants of Judah:

Athaiah son of Uzziah, the son of Zechariah, the son of Amariah, the son of Shephatiah, the son of Mahalalel, a descendant of Perez; 5and Maaseiah son of Baruch, the son of Col-Hozeh, the son of Hazaiah, the son of Adaiah, the son of Joiarib, the son of Zechariah, a descendant of Shelah. 6The descendants of Perez who lived in Jerusalem totaled 468 able men.

7From the descendants of Benjamin:

Sallu son of Meshullam, the son of Joed, the son of Pedaiah, the son of Kolaiah, the son of Maaseiah, the son

a32 That is, about 1/8 ounce (about 4 grams)

of Ithiel, the son of Jeshaiah, **8**and his followers, Gabbai and Sallai — 928 men. **9**Joel son of Zicri was their chief officer, and Judah son of Hassenuah was over the Second District of the city.

10From the priests:

Jedaiah; the son of Joiarib; Jakin; **11**Seraiah son of Hilkiah, the son of Meshullam, the son of Zadok, the son of Meraioth, the son of Ahitub, supervisor in the house of God, **12**and their associates, who carried on work for the temple — 822 men; Adaiah son of Jeroham, the son of Pelaliah, the son of Amzi, the son of Zechariah, the son of Pashhur, the son of Malkijah, **13**and his associates, who were heads of families — 242 men; Amashsai son of Azarel, the son of Ahzai, the son of Meshillemoth, the son of Immer, **14**and his*a* associates, who were able men — 128. Their chief officer was Zabdiel son of Haggedolim.

15From the Levites:

Shemaiah son of Hasshub, the son of Azrikam, the son of Hashabiah, the son of Bunni; **16**Shabbethai and Jozabad, two of the heads of the Levites, who had charge of the outside work of the house of God; **17**Mattaniah son of Mica, the son of Zabdi, the son of Asaph, the director who led in thanksgiving and prayer; Bakbukiah, second among his associates; and Abda son of Shammua, the son of Galal, the son of Jeduthun. **18**The Levites in the holy city totaled 284.

19The gatekeepers:

Akkub, Talmon and their associates, who kept watch at the gates — 172 men.

20The rest of the Israelites, with the priests and Levites, were in all the towns of Judah, each on his ancestral property. **21**The temple servants lived on the hill of Ophel, and Ziha and Gishpa were in charge of them.

22The chief officer of the Levites in Jerusalem was Uzzi son of Bani, the son of Hashabiah, the son of Mattaniah, the son of Mica. Uzzi was one of Asaph's descendants, who were the singers responsible for the service of the house of God. **23**The singers were under the king's orders, which regulated their daily activity.

24Pethahiah son of Meshezabel, one of the descendants of Zerah son of Judah, was the king's agent in all affairs relating to the people.

25As for the villages with their fields, some of the people of Judah lived in Kiriath Arba and its surrounding settlements, in Dibon and its settlements, in Jekabzeel and its villages, **26**in Jeshua, in Moladah, in Beth Pelet, **27**in Hazar Shual, in Beersheba and its settlements, **28**in Ziklag, in Meconah and its settlements, **29**in En Rimmon, in Zorah, in Jarmuth, **30**Zanoah, Adullam and their villages, in Lachish and its fields, and in Azekah and its settlements. So they were living all the way from Beersheba to the Valley of Hinnom.

31The descendants of the Benjamites from Geba lived in Micmash, Aija, Bethel and its settlements, **32**in Anathoth, Nob and Ananiah, **33**in Hazor, Ramah and Gittaim, **34**in Hadid, Zeboim and Neballat, **35**in Lod and Ono, and in the Valley of the Craftsmen.

36Some of the divisions of the Levites of Judah settled in Benjamin.

Priests and Levites

12 These were the priests and Levites who returned with Zerubbabel son of Shealtiel and with Jeshua:

Seraiah, Jeremiah, Ezra,
2Amariah, Malluch, Hattush,
3Shecaniah, Rehum, Meremoth,
4Iddo, Ginnethon,*b* Abijah,
5Mijamin,*c* Moadiah, Bilgah,
6Shemaiah, Joiarib, Jedaiah,
7Sallu, Amok, Hilkiah and Jedaiah.

These were the leaders of the priests and their associates in the days of Jeshua. **8**The Levites were Jeshua, Binnui, Kadmiel, Sherebiah, Judah, and also Mattaniah, who, together with his associates, was in charge of the songs of thanksgiving. **9**Bakbukiah and Unni, their associates, stood opposite them in the services.

10Jeshua was the father of Joiakim, Joiakim the father of Eliashib, Eliashib the father of Joiada, **11**Joiada the father of Jonathan, and Jonathan the father of Jaddua.

12In the days of Joiakim, these were the heads of the priestly families:

of Seraiah's family, Meraiah;
of Jeremiah's, Hananiah;

---

*a*14 Most Septuagint manuscripts; Hebrew *their* (see also Neh. 12:16); most Hebrew manuscripts *Ginnethoi*   *b*4 Many Hebrew manuscripts and Vulgate (see also   *c*5 A variant of *Miniamin*

¹³of Ezra's, Meshullam;
   of Amariah's, Jehohanan;
¹⁴of Malluch's, Jonathan;
   of Shecaniah's,ᵃ Joseph;
¹⁵of Harim's, Adna;
   of Meremoth's,ᵇ Helkai;
¹⁶of Iddo's, Zechariah;
   of Ginnethon's, Meshullam;
¹⁷of Abijah's, Zicri;
   of Miniamin's and of Moadiah's, Piltai;
¹⁸of Bilgah's, Shammua;
   of Shemaiah's, Jehonathan;
¹⁹of Joiarib's, Mattenai;
   of Jedaiah's, Uzzi;
²⁰of Sallu's, Kallai;
   of Amok's, Eber;
²¹of Hilkiah's, Hashabiah;
   of Jedaiah's, Nethanel.

²²The family heads of the Levites in the days of Eliashib, Joiada, Johanan and Jaddua, as well as those of the priests, were recorded in the reign of Darius the Persian. ²³The family heads among the descendants of Levi up to the time of Johanan son of Eliashib were recorded in the book of the annals. ²⁴And the leaders of the Levites were Hashabiah, Sherebiah, Jeshua son of Kadmiel, and their associates, who stood opposite them to give praise and thanksgiving, one section responding to the other, as prescribed by David the man of God.

²⁵Mattaniah, Bakbukiah, Obadiah, Meshullam, Talmon and Akkub were gatekeepers who guarded the storerooms at the gates. ²⁶They served in the days of Joiakim son of Jeshua, the son of Jozadak, and in the days of Nehemiah the governor and of Ezra the priest and scribe.

Dedication of the Wall of Jerusalem

²⁷At the dedication of the wall of Jerusalem, the Levites were sought out from where they lived and were brought to Jerusalem to celebrate joyfully the dedication with songs of thanksgiving and with the music of cymbals, harps and lyres. ²⁸The singers also were brought together from the region around Jerusalem—from the villages of the Netophathites, ²⁹from Beth Gilgal, and from the area of Geba and Azmaveth, for the singers had built villages for themselves around Jerusalem. ³⁰When the priests and Levites had puri-

fied themselves ceremonially, they purified the people, the gates and the wall.

³¹I had the leaders of Judah go up on topᶜ of the wall. I also assigned two large choirs to give thanks. One was to proceed on topᵈ of the wall to the right, toward the Dung Gate. ³²Hoshaiah and half the leaders of Judah followed them, ³³along with Azariah, Ezra, Meshullam, ³⁴Judah, Benjamin, Shemaiah, Jeremiah, ³⁵as well as some priests with trumpets, and also Zechariah son of Jonathan, the son of Shemaiah, the son of Mattaniah, the son of Micaiah, the son of Zaccur, the son of Asaph, ³⁶and his associates—Shemaiah, Azarel, Milalai, Gilalai, Maai, Nethanel, Judah and Hanani—with musical instruments ⌐prescribed by⌐ David the man of God. Ezra the scribe led the procession. ³⁷At the Fountain Gate they continued directly up the steps of the City of David on the ascent to the wall and passed above the house of David to the Water Gate on the east.

³⁸The second choir proceeded in the opposite direction. I followed them on topᵉ of the wall, together with half the people—past the Tower of the Ovens to the Broad Wall, ³⁹over the Gate of Ephraim, the Jeshanahᶠ Gate, the Fish Gate, the Tower of Hananel and the Tower of the Hundred, as far as the Sheep Gate. At the Gate of the Guard they stopped.

⁴⁰The two choirs that gave thanks then took their places in the house of God; so did I, together with half the officials, ⁴¹as well as the priests—Eliakim, Maaseiah, Miniamin, Micaiah, Elioenai, Zechariah and Hananiah with their trumpets— ⁴²and also Maaseiah, Shemaiah, Eleazar, Uzzi, Jehohanan, Malkijah, Elam and Ezer. The choirs sang under the direction of Jezrahiah. ⁴³And on that day they offered great sacrifices, rejoicing because God had given them great joy. The women and children also rejoiced. The sound of rejoicing in Jerusalem could be heard far away.

⁴⁴At that time men were appointed to be in charge of the storerooms for the contributions, firstfruits and tithes. From the fields around the towns they were to bring into the storerooms the portions required by the Law for the priests and the Levites, for Judah was pleased with the minister-

---

ᵃ14 Very many Hebrew manuscripts, some Septuagint manuscripts and Syriac (see also Neh. 12:3); most Hebrew manuscripts *Shebaniah's*   ᵇ15 Some Septuagint manuscripts (see also Neh. 12:3); Hebrew *Meraioth's*   ᶜ31 Or *go alongside*   ᵈ31 Or *proceed alongside*   ᵉ38 Or *them alongside*   ᶠ39 Or *Old*

WEEKENDING

REGARD

We must dispense with the myth that commitment to Christ means becoming a clergyman, or that work done inside a church building or in a church organization is more holy, somehow, than work done in the marketplace. Christ came to give us a sense of calling in everyday work. This is where the world is changed, and where the kingdom is built.

– Bruce Larson

RENEW

Work done for personal gain dulls my spirit; work that produces something beyond myself excites me.

Inviting God into my work opens the door for new creativity.

Being in the right job, doing the kind of work where I give more than I receive brings a whole new light onto my strength as a man.

– Leonard LeSourd

REVIVE

Saturday: Nehemiah 4:6–20
Sunday: 1 Corinthians 3:5–15

Go to page 500 for your next devotional reading.

ing priests and Levites. **45**They performed the service of their God and the service of purification, as did also the singers and gatekeepers, according to the commands of David and his son Solomon. **46**For long ago, in the days of David and Asaph, there had been directors for the singers and for the songs of praise and thanksgiving to God. **47**So in the days of Zerubbabel and of Nehemiah, all Israel contributed the daily portions for the singers and gatekeepers. They also set aside the portion for the other Levites, and the Levites set aside the portion for the descendants of Aaron.

Nehemiah's Final Reforms

13 On that day the Book of Moses was read aloud in the hearing of the people and there it was found written that no Ammonite or Moabite should ever be admitted into the assembly of God, **2**because they had not met the Israelites with food and water but had hired Balaam to call a curse down on them. (Our God, however, turned the curse into a blessing.) **3**When the people heard this law, they excluded from Israel all who were of foreign descent.

4Before this, Eliashib the priest had been put in charge of the storerooms of the house of our God. He was closely associated with Tobiah, **5**and he had provided him with a large room formerly used to store the grain offerings and incense and temple articles, and also the tithes of grain, new wine and oil prescribed for the Levites, singers and gatekeepers, as well as the contributions for the priests.

6But while all this was going on, I was not in Jerusalem, for in the thirty-second year of Artaxerxes king of Babylon I had returned to the king. Some time later I asked his permission **7**and came back to Jerusalem. Here I learned about the evil thing Eliashib had done in providing Tobiah a room in the courts of the house of God. **8**I was greatly displeased and threw all Tobiah's household goods out of the room. **9**I gave orders to purify the rooms, and then I put back into them the equipment of the house of God, with the grain offerings and the incense.

10I also learned that the portions assigned to the Levites had not been given to them, and that all the Levites and singers responsible for the service had gone back to their own fields. **11**So I rebuked the officials and asked them, "Why is the house of God neglected?" Then I called them together and stationed them at their posts.

12All Judah brought the tithes of grain, new wine and oil into the storerooms. **13**I put Shelemiah the priest, Zadok the scribe, and a Levite named Pedaiah in charge of the storerooms and made Hanan son of Zaccur, the son of Mattaniah, their assistant, because these men were considered trustworthy. They were made responsible for distributing the supplies to their brothers.

14Remember me for this, O my God, and do not blot out what I have so faithfully done for the house of my God and its services.

15In those days I saw men in Judah treading winepresses on the Sabbath and bringing in grain and loading it on donkeys, together with wine, grapes, figs and all other kinds of loads. And they were bringing all this into Jerusalem on the Sabbath. Therefore I warned them against selling food on that day. **16**Men from Tyre who lived in Jerusalem were bringing in fish and all kinds of merchandise and selling them in Jerusalem on the Sabbath to the people of Judah. **17**I rebuked the nobles of Judah and said to them, "What is this wicked thing you are doing—desecrating the Sabbath day? **18**Didn't your forefathers do the same things, so that our God brought all this calamity upon us and upon this city? Now you are stirring up more wrath against Israel by desecrating the Sabbath."

19When evening shadows fell on the gates of Jerusalem before the Sabbath, I ordered the doors to be shut and not opened until the Sabbath was over. I stationed some of my own men at the gates so that no load could be brought in on the Sabbath day. **20**Once or twice the merchants and sellers of all kinds of goods spent the night outside Jerusalem. **21**But I warned them and said, "Why do you spend the night by the wall? If you do this again, I will lay hands on you." From that time on they no longer came on the Sabbath. **22**Then I commanded the Levites to purify themselves and go and guard the gates in order to keep the Sabbath day holy.

Remember me for this also, O my God, and show mercy to me according to your great love.

23Moreover, in those days I saw men of Judah who had married women from Ashdod, Ammon and Moab. [24]Half of their children spoke the language of Ashdod or the language of one of the other peoples, and did not know how to speak the language of Judah. [25]I rebuked them and called curses down on them. I beat some of the men and pulled out their hair. I made them take an oath in God's name and said: "You are not to give your daughters in marriage to their sons, nor are you to take their daughters in marriage for your sons or for yourselves. [26]Was it not because of marriages like these that Solomon king of Israel sinned? Among the many nations there was no king like him. He was loved by his God, and God made him king over all Israel, but even he was led into sin by foreign women. [27]Must we hear now that you too are doing all this terrible wickedness and are being unfaithful to our God by marrying foreign women?"

[28]One of the sons of Joiada son of Eliashib the high priest was son-in-law to Sanballat the Horonite. And I drove him away from me.

[29]Remember them, O my God, because they defiled the priestly office and the covenant of the priesthood and of the Levites.

[30]So I purified the priests and the Levites of everything foreign, and assigned them duties, each to his own task. [31]I also made provision for contributions of wood at designated times, and for the firstfruits.

Remember me with favor, O my God.

ESTHER records God's remarkable, providential care of his exiled people when their enemies threaten to destroy them completely. Though his name is not actually mentioned in the book, God is in control, using Esther's position as queen to reverse the plan of wicked Haman. As you read this book, think how God takes care of you in your everyday life, even making good come out of evil.

ESTHER

Queen Vashti Deposed

1 This is what happened during the time of Xerxes,[a] the Xerxes who ruled over 127 provinces stretching from India to Cush[b]: **2**At that time King Xerxes reigned from his royal throne in the citadel of Susa, **3**and in the third year of his reign he gave a banquet for all his nobles and officials. The military leaders of Persia and Media, the princes, and the nobles of the provinces were present.

4For a full 180 days he displayed the vast wealth of his kingdom and the splendor and glory of his majesty. **5**When these days were over, the king gave a banquet, lasting seven days, in the enclosed garden of the king's palace, for all the people from the least to the greatest, who were in the citadel of Susa. **6**The garden had hangings of white and blue linen, fastened with cords of white linen and purple material to silver rings on marble pillars. There were couches of gold and silver on a mosaic pavement of porphyry, marble, mother-of-pearl and other costly stones. **7**Wine was served in goblets of gold, each one different from the other, and the royal wine was abundant, in keeping with the king's liberality. **8**By the king's command each guest was allowed to drink in his own way, for the king instructed all the wine stewards to serve each man what he wished.

9Queen Vashti also gave a banquet for

the women in the royal palace of King Xerxes.

¹⁰On the seventh day, when King Xerxes was in high spirits from wine, he commanded the seven eunuchs who served him—Mehuman, Biztha, Harbona, Bigtha, Abagtha, Zethar and Carcas— ¹¹to bring before him Queen Vashti, wearing her royal crown, in order to display her beauty to the people and nobles, for she was lovely to look at. ¹²But when the attendants delivered the king's command, Queen Vashti refused to come. Then the king became furious and burned with anger.

¹³Since it was customary for the king to consult experts in matters of law and justice, he spoke with the wise men who understood the times ¹⁴and were closest to the king—Carshena, Shethar, Admatha, Tarshish, Meres, Marsena and Memucan, the seven nobles of Persia and Media who had special access to the king and were highest in the kingdom.

¹⁵"According to law, what must be done to Queen Vashti?" he asked. "She has not obeyed the command of King Xerxes that the eunuchs have taken to her."

¹⁶Then Memucan replied in the presence of the king and the nobles, "Queen Vashti has done wrong, not only against the king but also against all the nobles and the peoples of all the provinces of King Xerxes. ¹⁷For the queen's conduct will become known to all the women, and so they will despise their husbands and say, 'King Xerxes commanded Queen Vashti to be brought before him, but she would not come.' ¹⁸This very day the Persian and Median women of the nobility who have heard about the queen's conduct will respond to all the king's nobles in the same way. There will be no end of disrespect and discord.

¹⁹"Therefore, if it pleases the king, let him issue a royal decree and let it be written in the laws of Persia and Media, which cannot be repealed, that Vashti is never again to enter the presence of King Xerxes. Also let the king give her royal position to someone else who is better than she. ²⁰Then when the king's edict is proclaimed throughout all his vast realm, all the women will respect their husbands, from the least to the greatest."

²¹The king and his nobles were pleased with this advice, so the king did as Memucan proposed. ²²He sent dispatches to all parts of the kingdom, to each province in its own script and to each people in its own language, proclaiming in each people's tongue that every man should be ruler over his own household.

Esther Made Queen

2 Later when the anger of King Xerxes had subsided, he remembered Vashti and what she had done and what he had decreed about her. ²Then the king's personal attendants proposed, "Let a search be made for beautiful young virgins for the king. ³Let the king appoint commissioners in every province of his realm to bring all these beautiful girls into the harem at the citadel of Susa. Let them be placed under the care of Hegai, the king's eunuch, who is in charge of the women; and let beauty treatments be given to them. ⁴Then let the girl who pleases the king be queen instead of Vashti." This advice appealed to the king, and he followed it.

⁵Now there was in the citadel of Susa a Jew of the tribe of Benjamin, named Mordecai son of Jair, the son of Shimei, the son of Kish, ⁶who had been carried into exile from Jerusalem by Nebuchadnezzar king of Babylon, among those taken captive with Jehoiachin[a] king of Judah. ⁷Mordecai had a cousin named Hadassah, whom he had brought up because she had neither father nor mother. This girl, who was also known as Esther, was lovely in form and features, and Mordecai had taken her as his own daughter when her father and mother died.

⁸When the king's order and edict had been proclaimed, many girls were brought to the citadel of Susa and put under the care of Hegai. Esther also was taken to the king's palace and entrusted to Hegai, who had charge of the harem. ⁹The girl pleased him and won his favor. Immediately he provided her with her beauty treatments and special food. He assigned to her seven maids selected from the king's palace and moved her and her maids into the best place in the harem.

¹⁰Esther had not revealed her nationality and family background, because Mordecai had forbidden her to do so. ¹¹Every day he walked back and forth near the courtyard of the harem to find out how Esther was and what was happening to her.

¹²Before a girl's turn came to go in to King Xerxes, she had to complete twelve

ᵃ6 Hebrew Jeconiah, a variant of Jehoiachin

months of beauty treatments prescribed for the women, six months with oil of myrrh and six with perfumes and cosmetics. [13]And this is how she would go to the king: Anything she wanted was given her to take with her from the harem to the king's palace. [14]In the evening she would go there and in the morning return to another part of the harem to the care of Shaashgaz, the king's eunuch who was in charge of the concubines. She would not return to the king unless he was pleased with her and summoned her by name.

[15]When the turn came for Esther (the girl Mordecai had adopted, the daughter of his uncle Abihail) to go to the king, she asked for nothing other than what Hegai, the king's eunuch who was in charge of the harem, suggested. And Esther won the favor of everyone who saw her. [16]She was taken to King Xerxes in the royal residence in the tenth month, the month of Tebeth, in the seventh year of his reign.

[17]Now the king was attracted to Esther more than to any of the other women, and she won his favor and approval more than any of the other virgins. So he set a royal crown on her head and made her queen instead of Vashti. [18]And the king gave a great banquet, Esther's banquet, for all his nobles and officials. He proclaimed a holiday throughout the provinces and distributed gifts with royal liberality.

Mordecai Uncovers a Conspiracy

[19]When the virgins were assembled a second time, Mordecai was sitting at the king's gate. [20]But Esther had kept secret her family background and nationality just as Mordecai had told her to do, for she continued to follow Mordecai's instructions as she had done when he was bringing her up.

[21]During the time Mordecai was sitting at the king's gate, Bigthana[a] and Teresh, two of the king's officers who guarded the doorway, became angry and conspired to assassinate King Xerxes. [22]But Mordecai found out about the plot and told Queen Esther, who in turn reported it to the king, giving credit to Mordecai. [23]And when the report was investigated and found to be true, the two officials were hanged on a gallows.[b] All this was recorded in the book of the annals in the presence of the king.

Haman's Plot to Destroy the Jews

3 After these events, King Xerxes honored Haman son of Hammedatha, the Agagite, elevating him and giving him a seat of honor higher than that of all the other nobles. [2]All the royal officials at the king's gate knelt down and paid honor to Haman, for the king had commanded this concerning him. But Mordecai would not kneel down or pay him honor.

[3]Then the royal officials at the king's gate asked Mordecai, "Why do you disobey the king's command?" [4]Day after day they spoke to him but he refused to comply. Therefore they told Haman about it to see whether Mordecai's behavior would be tolerated, for he had told them he was a Jew.

[5]When Haman saw that Mordecai would not kneel down or pay him honor, he was enraged. [6]Yet having learned who Mordecai's people were, he scorned the idea of killing only Mordecai. Instead Haman looked for a way to destroy all Mordecai's people, the Jews, throughout the whole kingdom of Xerxes.

[7]In the twelfth year of King Xerxes, in the first month, the month of Nisan, they cast the *pur* (that is, the lot) in the presence of Haman to select a day and month. And the lot fell on[c] the twelfth month, the month of Adar.

[8]Then Haman said to King Xerxes, "There is a certain people dispersed and scattered among the peoples in all the provinces of your kingdom whose customs are different from those of all other people and who do not obey the king's laws; it is not in the king's best interest to tolerate them. [9]If it pleases the king, let a decree be issued to destroy them, and I will put ten thousand talents[d] of silver into the royal treasury for the men who carry out this business."

[10]So the king took his signet ring from his finger and gave it to Haman son of Hammedatha, the Agagite, the enemy of the Jews. [11]"Keep the money," the king said to Haman, "and do with the people as you please."

[12]Then on the thirteenth day of the first month the royal secretaries were summoned. They wrote out in the script of each province and in the language of each people all Haman's orders to the king's sa-

---

[a]21 Hebrew *Bigthan*, a variant of *Bigthana*   [b]23 Or *were hung* (or *impaled*) *on poles*; similarly elsewhere in Esther   [c]7 Septuagint; Hebrew does not have *And the lot fell on.*   [d]9 That is, about 375 tons (about 345 metric tons)

traps, the governors of the various provinces and the nobles of the various peoples. These were written in the name of King Xerxes himself and sealed with his own ring. [13]Dispatches were sent by couriers to all the king's provinces with the order to destroy, kill and annihilate all the Jews—young and old, women and little children—on a single day, the thirteenth day of the twelfth month, the month of Adar, and to plunder their goods. [14]A copy of the text of the edict was to be issued as law in every province and made known to the people of every nationality so they would be ready for that day.

[15]Spurred on by the king's command, the couriers went out, and the edict was issued in the citadel of Susa. The king and Haman sat down to drink, but the city of Susa was bewildered.

Mordecai Persuades Esther to Help

4 When Mordecai learned of all that had been done, he tore his clothes, put on sackcloth and ashes, and went out into the city, wailing loudly and bitterly. [2]But he went only as far as the king's gate, because no one clothed in sackcloth was allowed to enter it. [3]In every province to which the edict and order of the king came, there was great mourning among the Jews, with fasting, weeping and wailing. Many lay in sackcloth and ashes.

[4]When Esther's maids and eunuchs came and told her about Mordecai, she was in great distress. She sent clothes for him to put on instead of his sackcloth, but he would not accept them. [5]Then Esther summoned Hathach, one of the king's eunuchs assigned to attend her, and ordered him to find out what was troubling Mordecai and why.

[6]So Hathach went out to Mordecai in the open square of the city in front of the king's gate. [7]Mordecai told him everything that had happened to him, including the exact amount of money Haman had promised to pay into the royal treasury for the destruction of the Jews. [8]He also gave him a copy of the text of the edict for their annihilation, which had been published in Susa, to show to Esther and explain it to her, and he told him to urge her to go into the king's presence to beg for mercy and plead with him for her people.

[9]Hathach went back and reported to Esther what Mordecai had said. [10]Then she instructed him to say to Mordecai, [11]"All the king's officials and the people of the royal provinces know that for any man or woman who approaches the king in the inner court without being summoned the king has but one law: that he be put to death. The only exception to this is for the king to extend the gold scepter to him and spare his life. But thirty days have passed since I was called to go to the king."

[12]When Esther's words were reported to Mordecai, [13]he sent back this answer: "Do not think that because you are in the king's house you alone of all the Jews will escape. [14]For if you remain silent at this time, relief and deliverance for the Jews will arise from another place, but you and your father's family will perish. And who knows but that you have come to royal position for such a time as this?"

[15]Then Esther sent this reply to Mordecai: [16]"Go, gather together all the Jews who are in Susa, and fast for me. Do not eat or drink for three days, night or day. I and my maids will fast as you do. When this is done, I will go to the king, even though it is against the law. And if I perish, I perish."

[17]So Mordecai went away and carried out all of Esther's instructions.

Esther's Request to the King

5 On the third day Esther put on her royal robes and stood in the inner court of the palace, in front of the king's hall. The king was sitting on his royal throne in the hall, facing the entrance. [2]When he saw Queen Esther standing in the court, he was pleased with her and held out to her the gold scepter that was in his hand. So Esther approached and touched the tip of the scepter.

[3]Then the king asked, "What is it, Queen Esther? What is your request? Even up to half the kingdom, it will be given you."

[4]"If it pleases the king," replied Esther, "let the king, together with Haman, come today to a banquet I have prepared for him."

[5]"Bring Haman at once," the king said, "so that we may do what Esther asks."

So the king and Haman went to the banquet Esther had prepared. [6]As they were drinking wine, the king again asked Esther, "Now what is your petition? It will be given you. And what is your request? Even up to half the kingdom, it will be granted."

[7]Esther replied, "My petition and my request is this: [8]If the king regards me with favor and if it pleases the king to grant my petition and fulfill my request, let the king

and Haman come tomorrow to the banquet I will prepare for them. Then I will answer the king's question."

Haman's Rage Against Mordecai

9Haman went out that day happy and in high spirits. But when he saw Mordecai at the king's gate and observed that he neither rose nor showed fear in his presence, he was filled with rage against Mordecai.

10Nevertheless, Haman restrained himself and went home.

Calling together his friends and Zeresh, his wife, **11**Haman boasted to them about his vast wealth, his many sons, and all the ways the king had honored him and how he had elevated him above the other nobles and officials. **12**"And that's not all," Haman added. "I'm the only person Queen Esther invited to accompany the

---

MONDAY

VERSE FOR THE DAY:	AUTHOR:	PASSAGE FOR THE DAY:
Esther 4:14	Charles Swindoll	Esther 4:1–17

Seeing God in the Mundane

THE Book of Esther is often like the dramas played out in our everyday lives. For seldom when enemies are on our heels are our Red Seas parted. Seldom when disaster is at our door are we warned by angelic visitors. Seldom when we are in need of direction are we instructed by God from a burning bush.

It's easy to see God in the miraculous. It's not so easy to see him in the mundane. But that's where most of us live. We live without seeing handwriting on the wall or hearing thunder from Sinai. We live with God not centerstage but directing unobtrusively from the wings.

This is all the more reason why we need to be sensitive to his voice—so we can be aware of and attentive to the subtle ways in which he works. And no book will sharpen our spiritual senses more than Esther . . .

Though God is invisible, he is invincible. That is the message of the Book of Esther. The invisible God who may appear to be absent is the invincible God who is working out his best plan.

That is not only true for a young woman and her people in ancient Persia; that's true for us today in the twentieth century . . .

Esther realized that God had raised her to a position of prominence for a reason. But to understand that reason, she had to ignore her palatial surroundings and listen to the still, small voice of providence. Psalm 46 commands us to do the same . . . "Be still . . . " The Hebrew literally means, "Let go, relax."

What will happen when we do? We'll learn what Esther learned—that God, though invisible, is invincible. But we will only learn that if we listen.

Additional Scripture Readings:
Psalm 46; Matthew 11:28–30

Go to page 508 for your next devotional reading.

king to the banquet she gave. And she has invited me along with the king tomorrow. [13]But all this gives me no satisfaction as long as I see that Jew Mordecai sitting at the king's gate."

[14]His wife Zeresh and all his friends said to him, "Have a gallows built, seventy-five feet[a] high, and ask the king in the morning to have Mordecai hanged on it. Then go with the king to the dinner and be happy." This suggestion delighted Haman, and he had the gallows built.

Mordecai Honored

6 That night the king could not sleep; so he ordered the book of the chronicles, the record of his reign, to be brought in and read to him. [2]It was found recorded there that Mordecai had exposed Bigthana and Teresh, two of the king's officers who guarded the doorway, who had conspired to assassinate King Xerxes.

[3]"What honor and recognition has Mordecai received for this?" the king asked.

"Nothing has been done for him," his attendants answered.

[4]The king said, "Who is in the court?" Now Haman had just entered the outer court of the palace to speak to the king about hanging Mordecai on the gallows he had erected for him.

[5]His attendants answered, "Haman is standing in the court."

"Bring him in," the king ordered.

[6]When Haman entered, the king asked him, "What should be done for the man the king delights to honor?"

Now Haman thought to himself, "Who is there that the king would rather honor than me?" [7]So he answered the king, "For the man the king delights to honor, [8]have them bring a royal robe the king has worn and a horse the king has ridden, one with a royal crest placed on its head. [9]Then let the robe and horse be entrusted to one of the king's most noble princes. Let them robe the man the king delights to honor, and lead him on the horse through the city streets, proclaiming before him, 'This is what is done for the man the king delights to honor!' "

[10]"Go at once," the king commanded Haman. "Get the robe and the horse and do just as you have suggested for Mordecai the Jew, who sits at the king's gate. Do not neglect anything you have recommended."

[11]So Haman got the robe and the horse. He robed Mordecai, and led him on horseback through the city streets, proclaiming before him, "This is what is done for the man the king delights to honor!"

[12]Afterward Mordecai returned to the king's gate. But Haman rushed home, with his head covered in grief, [13]and told Zeresh his wife and all his friends everything that had happened to him.

His advisers and his wife Zeresh said to him, "Since Mordecai, before whom your downfall has started, is of Jewish origin, you cannot stand against him—you will surely come to ruin!" [14]While they were still talking with him, the king's eunuchs arrived and hurried Haman away to the banquet Esther had prepared.

Haman Hanged

7 So the king and Haman went to dine with Queen Esther, [2]and as they were drinking wine on that second day, the king again asked, "Queen Esther, what is your petition? It will be given you. What is your request? Even up to half the kingdom, it will be granted."

[3]Then Queen Esther answered, "If I have found favor with you, O king, and if it pleases your majesty, grant me my life—this is my petition. And spare my people—this is my request. [4]For I and my people have been sold for destruction and slaughter and annihilation. If we had merely been sold as male and female slaves, I would have kept quiet, because no such distress would justify disturbing the king.[b]"

[5]King Xerxes asked Queen Esther, "Who is he? Where is the man who has dared to do such a thing?"

[6]Esther said, "The adversary and enemy is this vile Haman."

Then Haman was terrified before the king and queen. [7]The king got up in a rage, left his wine and went out into the palace garden. But Haman, realizing that the king had already decided his fate, stayed behind to beg Queen Esther for his life.

[8]Just as the king returned from the palace garden to the banquet hall, Haman was falling on the couch where Esther was reclining.

The king exclaimed, "Will he even molest the queen while she is with me in the house?"

---

a14 Hebrew *fifty cubits* (about 23 meters)   *b4* Or *quiet, but the compensation our adversary offers cannot be compared with the loss the king would suffer*

As soon as the word left the king's mouth, they covered Haman's face. [9]Then Harbona, one of the eunuchs attending the king, said, "A gallows seventy-five feet[a] high stands by Haman's house. He had it made for Mordecai, who spoke up to help the king."

The king said, "Hang him on it!" [10]So they hanged Haman on the gallows he had prepared for Mordecai. Then the king's fury subsided.

The King's Edict in Behalf of the Jews

8 That same day King Xerxes gave Queen Esther the estate of Haman, the enemy of the Jews. And Mordecai came into the presence of the king, for Esther had told how he was related to her. [2]The king took off his signet ring, which he had reclaimed from Haman, and presented it to Mordecai. And Esther appointed him over Haman's estate.

[3]Esther again pleaded with the king, falling at his feet and weeping. She begged him to put an end to the evil plan of Haman the Agagite, which he had devised against the Jews. [4]Then the king extended the gold scepter to Esther and she arose and stood before him.

[5]"If it pleases the king," she said, "and if he regards me with favor and thinks it the right thing to do, and if he is pleased with me, let an order be written overruling the dispatches that Haman son of Hammedatha, the Agagite, devised and wrote to destroy the Jews in all the king's provinces. [6]For how can I bear to see disaster fall on my people? How can I bear to see the destruction of my family?"

[7]King Xerxes replied to Queen Esther and to Mordecai the Jew, "Because Haman attacked the Jews, I have given his estate to Esther, and they have hanged him on the gallows. [8]Now write another decree in the king's name in behalf of the Jews as seems best to you, and seal it with the king's signet ring—for no document written in the king's name and sealed with his ring can be revoked."

[9]At once the royal secretaries were summoned—on the twenty-third day of the third month, the month of Sivan. They wrote out all Mordecai's orders to the Jews, and to the satraps, governors and nobles of the 127 provinces stretching from India to Cush.[b] These orders were written in the script of each province and the language of each people and also to the Jews in their own script and language. [10]Mordecai wrote in the name of King Xerxes, sealed the dispatches with the king's signet ring, and sent them by mounted couriers, who rode fast horses especially bred for the king.

[11]The king's edict granted the Jews in every city the right to assemble and protect themselves; to destroy, kill and annihilate any armed force of any nationality or province that might attack them and their women and children; and to plunder the property of their enemies. [12]The day appointed for the Jews to do this in all the provinces of King Xerxes was the thirteenth day of the twelfth month, the month of Adar. [13]A copy of the text of the edict was to be issued as law in every province and made known to the people of every nationality so that the Jews would be ready on that day to avenge themselves on their enemies.

[14]The couriers, riding the royal horses, raced out, spurred on by the king's command. And the edict was also issued in the citadel of Susa.

[15]Mordecai left the king's presence wearing royal garments of blue and white, a large crown of gold and a purple robe of fine linen. And the city of Susa held a joyous celebration. [16]For the Jews it was a time of happiness and joy, gladness and honor. [17]In every province and in every city, wherever the edict of the king went, there was joy and gladness among the Jews, with feasting and celebrating. And many people of other nationalities became Jews because fear of the Jews had seized them.

Triumph of the Jews

9 On the thirteenth day of the twelfth month, the month of Adar, the edict commanded by the king was to be carried out. On this day the enemies of the Jews had hoped to overpower them, but now the tables were turned and the Jews got the upper hand over those who hated them. [2]The Jews assembled in their cities in all the provinces of King Xerxes to attack those seeking their destruction. No one could stand against them, because the people of all the other nationalities were afraid of them. [3]And all the nobles of the provinces, the satraps, the governors and the king's administrators helped the Jews, because fear of Mordecai had seized

---

[a]9 Hebrew fifty cubits (about 23 meters)　　[b]9 That is, the upper Nile region

them. ⁴Mordecai was prominent in the palace; his reputation spread throughout the provinces, and he became more and more powerful.

⁵The Jews struck down all their enemies with the sword, killing and destroying them, and they did what they pleased to those who hated them. ⁶In the citadel of Susa, the Jews killed and destroyed five hundred men. ⁷They also killed Parshandatha, Dalphon, Aspatha, ⁸Poratha, Adalia, Aridatha, ⁹Parmashta, Arisai, Aridai and Vaizatha, ¹⁰the ten sons of Haman son of Hammedatha, the enemy of the Jews. But they did not lay their hands on the plunder.

¹¹The number of those slain in the citadel of Susa was reported to the king that same day. ¹²The king said to Queen Esther, "The Jews have killed and destroyed five hundred men and the ten sons of Haman in the citadel of Susa. What have they done in the rest of the king's provinces? Now what is your petition? It will be given you. What is your request? It will also be granted."

¹³"If it pleases the king," Esther answered, "give the Jews in Susa permission to carry out this day's edict tomorrow also, and let Haman's ten sons be hanged on gallows."

¹⁴So the king commanded that this be done. An edict was issued in Susa, and they hanged the ten sons of Haman. ¹⁵The Jews in Susa came together on the fourteenth day of the month of Adar, and they put to death in Susa three hundred men, but they did not lay their hands on the plunder.

¹⁶Meanwhile, the remainder of the Jews who were in the king's provinces also assembled to protect themselves and get relief from their enemies. They killed seventy-five thousand of them but did not lay their hands on the plunder. ¹⁷This happened on the thirteenth day of the month of Adar, and on the fourteenth they rested and made it a day of feasting and joy.

Purim Celebrated

¹⁸The Jews in Susa, however, had assembled on the thirteenth and fourteenth, and then on the fifteenth they rested and made it a day of feasting and joy. ¹⁹That is why rural Jews—those living in villages—observe the fourteenth of the month of Adar as a day of joy and feasting, a day for giving presents to each other.

²⁰Mordecai recorded these events, and he sent letters to all the Jews throughout the provinces of King Xerxes, near and far, ²¹to have them celebrate annually the fourteenth and fifteenth days of the month of Adar ²²as the time when the Jews got relief from their enemies, and as the month when their sorrow was turned into joy and their mourning into a day of celebration. He wrote them to observe the days as days of feasting and joy and giving presents of food to one another and gifts to the poor.

²³So the Jews agreed to continue the celebration they had begun, doing what Mordecai had written to them. ²⁴For Haman son of Hammedatha, the Agagite, the enemy of all the Jews, had plotted against the Jews to destroy them and had cast the *pur* (that is, the lot) for their ruin and destruction. ²⁵But when the plot came to the king's attention,ᵃ he issued written orders that the evil scheme Haman had devised against the Jews should come back onto his own head, and that he and his sons should be hanged on the gallows. ²⁶(Therefore these days were called Purim, from the word *pur.*) Because of everything written in this letter and because of what they had seen and what had happened to them, ²⁷the Jews took it upon themselves to establish the custom that they and their descendants and all who join them should without fail observe these two days every year, in the way prescribed and at the time appointed. ²⁸These days should be remembered and observed in every generation by every family, and in every province and in every city. And these days of Purim should never cease to be celebrated by the Jews, nor should the memory of them die out among their descendants.

²⁹So Queen Esther, daughter of Abihail, along with Mordecai the Jew, wrote with full authority to confirm this second letter concerning Purim. ³⁰And Mordecai sent letters to all the Jews in the 127 provinces of the kingdom of Xerxes—words of goodwill and assurance— ³¹to establish these days of Purim at their designated times, as Mordecai the Jew and Queen Esther had decreed for them, and as they had established for themselves and their descendants in regard to their times of fasting and lamentation. ³²Esther's decree confirmed these regulations about Purim, and it was written down in the records.

ᵃ25 Or *when Esther came before the king*

The Greatness of Mordecai

10 King Xerxes imposed tribute throughout the empire, to its distant shores. ²And all his acts of power and might, together with a full account of the greatness of Mordecai to which the king had raised him, are they not written in the book of the annals of the kings of Media and Persia? ³Mordecai the Jew was second in rank to King Xerxes, preeminent among the Jews, and held in high esteem by his many fellow Jews, because he worked for the good of his people and spoke up for the welfare of all the Jews.

*J*OB presents a striking example of the news behind the news — of God at work behind the scenes of human suffering. After numerous attempts by Job and his friends to uncover the reasons for his suffering, God himself enters the dialogue with a majestic description of his power and love. As you read this book, realize that God may not answer all your questions about life's suffering; realize too that God does control Satan, who can go no farther than the Lord allows.

JOB

Prologue

1 In the land of Uz there lived a man whose name was Job. This man was blameless and upright; he feared God and shunned evil. ²He had seven sons and three daughters, ³and he owned seven thousand sheep, three thousand camels, five hundred yoke of oxen and five hundred donkeys, and had a large number of servants. He was the greatest man among all the people of the East.

⁴His sons used to take turns holding feasts in their homes, and they would invite their three sisters to eat and drink with them. ⁵When a period of feasting had run its course, Job would send and have them purified. Early in the morning he would sacrifice a burnt offering for each of them, thinking, "Perhaps my children have sinned and cursed God in their hearts." This was Job's regular custom.

Job's First Test

⁶One day the angels*a* came to present themselves before the LORD, and Satan*b* also came with them. ⁷The LORD said to Satan, "Where have you come from?"

Satan answered the LORD, "From roaming through the earth and going back and forth in it."

8Then the LORD said to Satan, "Have you considered my servant Job? There is no one on earth like him; he is blameless and upright, a man who fears God and shuns evil."

9"Does Job fear God for nothing?" Satan replied. 10"Have you not put a hedge around him and his household and everything he has? You have blessed the work of his hands, so that his flocks and herds are spread throughout the land. 11But stretch out your hand and strike everything he has, and he will surely curse you to your face."

12The LORD said to Satan, "Very well, then, everything he has is in your hands, but on the man himself do not lay a finger."

Then Satan went out from the presence of the LORD.

13One day when Job's sons and daughters were feasting and drinking wine at the oldest brother's house, 14a messenger came to Job and said, "The oxen were plowing and the donkeys were grazing nearby, 15and the Sabeans attacked and carried them off. They put the servants to the sword, and I am the only one who has escaped to tell you!"

16While he was still speaking, another messenger came and said, "The fire of God fell from the sky and burned up the sheep and the servants, and I am the only one who has escaped to tell you!"

17While he was still speaking, another messenger came and said, "The Chaldeans formed three raiding parties and swept down on your camels and carried them off. They put the servants to the sword, and I am the only one who has escaped to tell you!"

18While he was still speaking, yet another messenger came and said, "Your sons and daughters were feasting and drinking wine at the oldest brother's house, 19when suddenly a mighty wind swept in from the desert and struck the four corners of the house. It collapsed on them and they are dead, and I am the only one who has escaped to tell you!"

20At this, Job got up and tore his robe and shaved his head. Then he fell to the ground in worship 21and said:

"Naked I came from my mother's
     womb,
   and naked I will depart.a
The LORD gave and the LORD has taken
     away;
   may the name of the LORD be
     praised."

22In all this, Job did not sin by charging God with wrongdoing.

Job's Second Test

2 On another day the angelsb came to present themselves before the LORD, and Satan also came with them to present himself before him. 2And the LORD said to Satan, "Where have you come from?"

Satan answered the LORD, "From roaming through the earth and going back and forth in it."

3Then the LORD said to Satan, "Have you considered my servant Job? There is no one on earth like him; he is blameless and upright, a man who fears God and shuns evil. And he still maintains his integrity, though you incited me against him to ruin him without any reason."

4"Skin for skin!" Satan replied. "A man will give all he has for his own life. 5But stretch out your hand and strike his flesh and bones, and he will surely curse you to your face."

6The LORD said to Satan, "Very well, then, he is in your hands; but you must spare his life."

7So Satan went out from the presence of the LORD and afflicted Job with painful sores from the soles of his feet to the top of his head. 8Then Job took a piece of broken pottery and scraped himself with it as he sat among the ashes.

9His wife said to him, "Are you still holding on to your integrity? Curse God and die!"

10He replied, "You are talking like a foolishc woman. Shall we accept good from God, and not trouble?"

In all this, Job did not sin in what he said.

Job's Three Friends

11When Job's three friends, Eliphaz the Temanite, Bildad the Shuhite and Zophar the Naamathite, heard about all the troubles that had come upon him, they set out from their homes and met together by agreement to go and sympathize with him and comfort him. [12]When they saw him from a distance, they could hardly recognize him; they began to weep aloud, and they tore their robes and sprinkled dust on their heads. [13]Then they sat on the ground with him for seven days and seven nights. No one said a word to him, because they saw how great his suffering was.

Job Speaks

3 After this, Job opened his mouth and cursed the day of his birth. [2]He said:

[3]"May the day of my birth perish,
  and the night it was said, 'A boy is
    born!'
[4]That day—may it turn to darkness;
  may God above not care about it;
  may no light shine upon it.
[5]May darkness and deep shadow[a]
    claim it once more;
  may a cloud settle over it;
  may blackness overwhelm its light.
[6]That night—may thick darkness seize
    it;
  may it not be included among the
    days of the year
  nor be entered in any of the
    months.
[7]May that night be barren;
  may no shout of joy be heard in it.
[8]May those who curse days[b] curse
    that day,
  those who are ready to rouse
    Leviathan.
[9]May its morning stars become dark;
  may it wait for daylight in vain
  and not see the first rays of dawn,
[10]for it did not shut the doors of the
    womb on me
  to hide trouble from my eyes.

[11]"Why did I not perish at birth,
  and die as I came from the womb?
[12]Why were there knees to receive me
  and breasts that I might be nursed?
[13]For now I would be lying down in
    peace;
  I would be asleep and at rest
[14]with kings and counselors of the
    earth,
  who built for themselves places now
    lying in ruins,
[15]with rulers who had gold,
  who filled their houses with silver.
[16]Or why was I not hidden in the
    ground like a stillborn child,
like an infant who never saw the
    light of day?
[17]There the wicked cease from turmoil,
  and there the weary are at rest.
[18]Captives also enjoy their ease;
  they no longer hear the slave
    driver's shout.
[19]The small and the great are there,
  and the slave is freed from his
    master.

[20]"Why is light given to those in misery,
  and life to the bitter of soul,
[21]to those who long for death that does
    not come,
  who search for it more than for
    hidden treasure,
[22]who are filled with gladness
  and rejoice when they reach the
    grave?
[23]Why is life given to a man
  whose way is hidden,
  whom God has hedged in?
[24]For sighing comes to me instead of
    food;
  my groans pour out like water.
[25]What I feared has come upon me;
  what I dreaded has happened to me.
[26]I have no peace, no quietness;
  I have no rest, but only turmoil."

Eliphaz

4 Then Eliphaz the Temanite replied:

[2]"If someone ventures a word with
    you, will you be impatient?
  But who can keep from speaking?
[3]Think how you have instructed many,
  how you have strengthened feeble
    hands.
[4]Your words have supported those who
    stumbled;
  you have strengthened faltering
    knees.
[5]But now trouble comes to you, and
    you are discouraged;
  it strikes you, and you are
    dismayed.
[6]Should not your piety be your
    confidence
  and your blameless ways your hope?

[7]"Consider now: Who, being innocent,
    has ever perished?
  Where were the upright ever
    destroyed?
[8]As I have observed, those who plow
    evil

---

[a]5 Or *and the shadow of death*   [b]8 Or *the sea*

and those who sow trouble reap it.
⁹At the breath of God they are
    destroyed;
at the blast of his anger they perish.
¹⁰The lions may roar and growl,
    yet the teeth of the great lions are
        broken.

¹¹The lion perishes for lack of prey,
    and the cubs of the lioness are
        scattered.

¹²"A word was secretly brought to me,
    my ears caught a whisper of it.
¹³Amid disquieting dreams in the night,

TUESDAY

VERSE FOR THE DAY:
Job 3:26

AUTHOR:
Archibald Hart

PASSAGE FOR THE DAY:
Job 3:11–26

Why Worry?

GOOD stress (also called "eustress," from the Latin *eu*, meaning good) is positive and helpful only because it is *not experienced continuously*. It excites, but then it lets the system go back to normal quickly. If a moment never comes when all the demand for stress is passed—if the body *never* returns to a state of rest and recovery—the result will be bad stress (or "distress," from the Latin *dis*, meaning bad), no matter what originally produced the arousal.

Much of the damaging stress we experience comes from threats that can't be acted on because they exist only in the mind and imagination. This kind of stress—which doesn't go away after the "game is played"—can be as dangerous as any real-life catastrophe.

Take, for example, the effect of those threats created by worry and anxiety. There are people whose thoughts are so active and bothersome that they constantly imagine the worst. This worrying magnifies actual threats and creates imagined ones—both of which trigger the stress response. And because [unlike in the story of Job] they *are* imagined or blown out of proportion, these threats cannot be confronted and resolved. The problem is in the mind, although for the body the threat is real. Further, we don't always recognize our "worry stressors." They hide in the dark hours of the night when we try to sleep or in the unconscious activities of our minds when we are doing our daily chores.

It is these more subtle threats that produce the greatest amount of stress damage. Things that worry us, prod us, scare or frighten us—when there is nothing we can do about them —can be the most destructive of all. Perhaps this is why Jesus (who had many good things to say about controlling stress) told us, "Do not let your hearts be troubled and do not be afraid" (John 14:27).

Additional Scripture Readings:
Matthew 6:25–34; Luke 10:38–42

*Go to page 510 for your next
devotional reading.*

when deep sleep falls on men,
¹⁴fear and trembling seized me
  and made all my bones shake.
¹⁵A spirit glided past my face,
  and the hair on my body stood on
    end.
¹⁶It stopped,
  but I could not tell what it was.
  A form stood before my eyes,
  and I heard a hushed voice:
¹⁷'Can a mortal be more righteous than
    God?
  Can a man be more pure than his
    Maker?
¹⁸If God places no trust in his servants,
  if he charges his angels with error,
¹⁹how much more those who live in
    houses of clay,
  whose foundations are in the dust,
  who are crushed more readily than
    a moth!
²⁰Between dawn and dusk they are
    broken to pieces;
  unnoticed, they perish forever.
²¹Are not the cords of their tent pulled
    up,
  so that they die without wisdom?'ᵃ

5 "Call if you will, but who will
    answer you?
  To which of the holy ones will you
    turn?
²Resentment kills a fool,
  and envy slays the simple.
³I myself have seen a fool taking root,
  but suddenly his house was cursed.
⁴His children are far from safety,
  crushed in court without a defender.
⁵The hungry consume his harvest,
  taking it even from among thorns,
  and the thirsty pant after his wealth.
⁶For hardship does not spring from the
    soil,
  nor does trouble sprout from the
    ground.
⁷Yet man is born to trouble
  as surely as sparks fly upward.

⁸"But if it were I, I would appeal to
    God;
  I would lay my cause before him.
⁹He performs wonders that cannot be
    fathomed,
  miracles that cannot be counted.
¹⁰He bestows rain on the earth;
  he sends water upon the
    countryside.
¹¹The lowly he sets on high,

and those who mourn are lifted to
    safety.
¹²He thwarts the plans of the crafty,
  so that their hands achieve no
    success.
¹³He catches the wise in their craftiness,
  and the schemes of the wily are
    swept away.
¹⁴Darkness comes upon them in the
    daytime;
  at noon they grope as in the night.
¹⁵He saves the needy from the sword in
    their mouth;
  he saves them from the clutches of
    the powerful.
¹⁶So the poor have hope,
  and injustice shuts its mouth.

¹⁷"Blessed is the man whom God
    corrects;
  so do not despise the discipline of
    the Almighty.ᵇ
¹⁸For he wounds, but he also binds up;
  he injures, but his hands also heal.
¹⁹From six calamities he will rescue
    you;
  in seven no harm will befall you.
²⁰In famine he will ransom you from
    death,
  and in battle from the stroke of the
    sword.
²¹You will be protected from the lash of
    the tongue,
  and need not fear when destruction
    comes.
²²You will laugh at destruction and
    famine,
  and need not fear the beasts of the
    earth.
²³For you will have a covenant with the
    stones of the field,
  and the wild animals will be at
    peace with you.
²⁴You will know that your tent is
    secure;
  you will take stock of your property
    and find nothing missing.
²⁵You will know that your children will
    be many,
  and your descendants like the grass
    of the earth.
²⁶You will come to the grave in full
    vigor,
  like sheaves gathered in season.

²⁷"We have examined this, and it is
    true.
  So hear it and apply it to yourself."

ᵃ21 Some interpreters end the quotation after verse 17.   ᵇ17 Hebrew *Shaddai*; here and throughout Job

Job

6 Then Job replied:

²"If only my anguish could be weighed
  and all my misery be placed on the
  scales!
³It would surely outweigh the sand of
  the seas —

no wonder my words have been
  impetuous.
⁴The arrows of the Almighty are in me,
  my spirit drinks in their poison;
  God's terrors are marshaled against
  me.
⁵Does a wild donkey bray when it has
  grass,

WEDNESDAY

VERSE FOR THE DAY:	*AUTHOR:*	*PASSAGE FOR THE DAY:*
Job 4:8	David W. Smith	*Job 4:7–8*

What Not to Do

FOR a Biblical example of what not to do in a friendship, we
can turn to what is probably the oldest book in the Bible
—Job. This great section of Scripture illustrates that, despite
circumstances, man has the capacity for a faith completely
centered on God.

Job lost his health, his children, and much that he owned.
He lost the support of his friends, and his wife was impatient
with his tragic circumstances, advising him to "curse God and
die!" (Job 2:9). Job's multiple sufferings were compounded not
just with a lack of sympathy but with overt emotional harass-
ment and condemnation by his three so-called friends. Zophar,
Eliphaz and Bildad told Job he must have committed some
gross sin for all these calamities to befall him. *Why else would
he be suffering so much?* they reasoned.

Eliphaz summed up their thinking when he asked Job a rhe-
torical question: "Consider now: Who, being innocent, has
ever perished? Where were the upright ever destroyed?" Eliphaz continued without waiting for Job's response. "As I have
observed, those who plow evil and those who sow trouble reap
it" (4:7–8). You can almost hear the judgmental and self-
righteous tone of this man's voice as you read the passage. The
fact is, these pseudo-friends, with their criticism and self-
righteousness, failed to look at Job's pain from a different
point of view. They reached the easy but wrong conclusion
that God must be punishing Job for some unrevealed sin.

If we had to choose a friendship like that between David and
Jonathan [1 Samuel 18:1] or that of Job and his crew, we
would all prefer the kindness and commitment that existed between David and Jonathan. But close friendships don't just
happen. They result from the application of principles recorded throughout the Word of God.

Additional Scripture Readings:
1 Samuel 18:1–3; Romans 12:9–21

*Go to page 517 for your next
devotional reading.*

or an ox bellow when it has fodder?
⁶Is tasteless food eaten without salt,
   or is there flavor in the white of an
      egg*ᵃ*?
⁷I refuse to touch it;
   such food makes me ill.

⁸"Oh, that I might have my request,
   that God would grant what I hope
      for,
⁹that God would be willing to crush
      me,
   to let loose his hand and cut me
      off!
¹⁰Then I would still have this
      consolation—
   my joy in unrelenting pain—
   that I had not denied the words of
      the Holy One.

¹¹"What strength do I have, that I
      should still hope?
   What prospects, that I should be
      patient?
¹²Do I have the strength of stone?
   Is my flesh bronze?
¹³Do I have any power to help myself,
   now that success has been driven
      from me?

¹⁴"A despairing man should have the
      devotion of his friends,
   even though he forsakes the fear of
      the Almighty.
¹⁵But my brothers are as undependable
      as intermittent streams,
   as the streams that overflow
¹⁶when darkened by thawing ice
   and swollen with melting snow,
¹⁷but that cease to flow in the dry
      season,
   and in the heat vanish from their
      channels.
¹⁸Caravans turn aside from their routes;
   they go up into the wasteland and
      perish.
¹⁹The caravans of Tema look for water,
   the traveling merchants of Sheba
      look in hope.
²⁰They are distressed, because they had
      been confident;
   they arrive there, only to be
      disappointed.
²¹Now you too have proved to be of no
      help;
   you see something dreadful and are
      afraid.
²²Have I ever said, 'Give something on
      my behalf,

pay a ransom for me from your
      wealth,
²³deliver me from the hand of the
      enemy,
   ransom me from the clutches of the
      ruthless'?

²⁴"Teach me, and I will be quiet;
   show me where I have been wrong.
²⁵How painful are honest words!
   But what do your arguments prove?
²⁶Do you mean to correct what I say,
   and treat the words of a despairing
      man as wind?
²⁷You would even cast lots for the
      fatherless
   and barter away your friend.

²⁸"But now be so kind as to look at me.
   Would I lie to your face?
²⁹Relent, do not be unjust;
   reconsider, for my integrity is at
      stake.*ᵇ*
³⁰Is there any wickedness on my lips?
   Can my mouth not discern malice?

7 "Does not man have hard service on
      earth?
   Are not his days like those of a
      hired man?
²Like a slave longing for the evening
      shadows,
   or a hired man waiting eagerly for
      his wages,
³so I have been allotted months of
      futility,
   and nights of misery have been
      assigned to me.
⁴When I lie down I think, 'How long
      before I get up?'
   The night drags on, and I toss till
      dawn.
⁵My body is clothed with worms and
      scabs,
   my skin is broken and festering.

⁶"My days are swifter than a weaver's
      shuttle,
   and they come to an end without
      hope.
⁷Remember, O God, that my life is but
      a breath;
   my eyes will never see happiness
      again.
⁸The eye that now sees me will see me
      no longer;
   you will look for me, but I will be
      no more.
⁹As a cloud vanishes and is gone,

so he who goes down to the grave[a]
  does not return.
[10]He will never come to his house
  again;
  his place will know him no more.

[11]"Therefore I will not keep silent;
  I will speak out in the anguish of
    my spirit,
  I will complain in the bitterness of
    my soul.
[12]Am I the sea, or the monster of the
    deep,
  that you put me under guard?
[13]When I think my bed will comfort me
  and my couch will ease my
    complaint,
[14]even then you frighten me with
    dreams
  and terrify me with visions,
[15]so that I prefer strangling and death,
  rather than this body of mine.
[16]I despise my life; I would not live
    forever.
  Let me alone; my days have no
    meaning.

[17]"What is man that you make so much
    of him,
  that you give him so much
    attention,
[18]that you examine him every morning
  and test him every moment?
[19]Will you never look away from me,
  or let me alone even for an instant?
[20]If I have sinned, what have I done to
    you,
  O watcher of men?
  Why have you made me your target?
  Have I become a burden to you?[b]
[21]Why do you not pardon my offenses
  and forgive my sins?
  For I will soon lie down in the dust;
  you will search for me, but I will be
    no more."

Bildad

8 Then Bildad the Shuhite replied:

[2]"How long will you say such things?
  Your words are a blustering wind.
[3]Does God pervert justice?
  Does the Almighty pervert what is
    right?
[4]When your children sinned against
    him,

he gave them over to the penalty of
    their sin.
[5]But if you will look to God
  and plead with the Almighty,
[6]if you are pure and upright,
  even now he will rouse himself on
    your behalf
  and restore you to your rightful
    place.
[7]Your beginnings will seem humble,
  so prosperous will your future be.

[8]"Ask the former generations
  and find out what their fathers
    learned,
[9]for we were born only yesterday and
    know nothing,
  and our days on earth are but a
    shadow.
[10]Will they not instruct you and tell
    you?
  Will they not bring forth words
    from their understanding?
[11]Can papyrus grow tall where there is
    no marsh?
  Can reeds thrive without water?
[12]While still growing and uncut,
  they wither more quickly than
    grass.
[13]Such is the destiny of all who forget
    God;
  so perishes the hope of the godless.
[14]What he trusts in is fragile[c];
  what he relies on is a spider's web.
[15]He leans on his web, but it gives way;
  he clings to it, but it does not hold.
[16]He is like a well-watered plant in the
    sunshine,
  spreading its shoots over the
    garden;
[17]it entwines its roots around a pile of
    rocks
  and looks for a place among the
    stones.
[18]But when it is torn from its spot,
  that place disowns it and says, 'I
    never saw you.'
[19]Surely its life withers away,
  and[d] from the soil other plants
    grow.

[20]"Surely God does not reject a
    blameless man
  or strengthen the hands of
    evildoers.
[21]He will yet fill your mouth with
    laughter

---

[a]9 Hebrew *Sheol*   [b]20 A few manuscripts of the Masoretic Text, an ancient Hebrew scribal tradition
and Septuagint; most manuscripts of the Masoretic Text *I have become a burden to myself.*   [c]14 The
meaning of the Hebrew for this word is uncertain.   [d]19 Or *Surely all the joy it has / is that*

and your lips with shouts of joy.
22Your enemies will be clothed in shame,
and the tents of the wicked will be no more."

Job

9

Then Job replied:

2"Indeed, I know that this is true.
But how can a mortal be righteous before God?
3Though one wished to dispute with him,
he could not answer him one time out of a thousand.
4His wisdom is profound, his power is vast.
Who has resisted him and come out unscathed?
5He moves mountains without their knowing it
and overturns them in his anger.
6He shakes the earth from its place
and makes its pillars tremble.
7He speaks to the sun and it does not shine;
he seals off the light of the stars.
8He alone stretches out the heavens
and treads on the waves of the sea.
9He is the Maker of the Bear and Orion,
the Pleiades and the constellations of the south.
10He performs wonders that cannot be fathomed,
miracles that cannot be counted.
11When he passes me, I cannot see him;
when he goes by, I cannot perceive him.
12If he snatches away, who can stop him?
Who can say to him, 'What are you doing?'
13God does not restrain his anger;
even the cohorts of Rahab cowered at his feet.

14"How then can I dispute with him?
How can I find words to argue with him?
15Though I were innocent, I could not answer him;
I could only plead with my Judge for mercy.
16Even if I summoned him and he responded,

I do not believe he would give me a hearing.
17He would crush me with a storm
and multiply my wounds for no reason.
18He would not let me regain my breath
but would overwhelm me with misery.
19If it is a matter of strength, he is mighty!
And if it is a matter of justice, who will summon him*a*?
20Even if I were innocent, my mouth would condemn me;
if I were blameless, it would pronounce me guilty.

21"Although I am blameless,
I have no concern for myself;
I despise my own life.
22It is all the same; that is why I say,
'He destroys both the blameless and the wicked.'
23When a scourge brings sudden death,
he mocks the despair of the innocent.
24When a land falls into the hands of the wicked,
he blindfolds its judges.
If it is not he, then who is it?

25"My days are swifter than a runner;
they fly away without a glimpse of joy.
26They skim past like boats of papyrus,
like eagles swooping down on their prey.
27If I say, 'I will forget my complaint,
I will change my expression, and smile,'
28I still dread all my sufferings,
for I know you will not hold me innocent.
29Since I am already found guilty,
why should I struggle in vain?
30Even if I washed myself with soap*b*
and my hands with washing soda,
31you would plunge me into a slime pit
so that even my clothes would detest me.

32"He is not a man like me that I might answer him,
that we might confront each other in court.
33If only there were someone to arbitrate between us,
to lay his hand upon us both,

---

a19 See Septuagint; Hebrew *me.*   *b30* Or *snow*

³⁴someone to remove God's rod from
    me,
  so that his terror would frighten me
    no more.
³⁵Then I would speak up without fear of
    him,
  but as it now stands with me, I
    cannot.

10

"I loathe my very life;
    therefore I will give free rein to
    my complaint
  and speak out in the bitterness of
    my soul.
²I will say to God: Do not condemn
    me,
  but tell me what charges you have
    against me.
³Does it please you to oppress me,
    to spurn the work of your hands,
  while you smile on the schemes of
    the wicked?
⁴Do you have eyes of flesh?
  Do you see as a mortal sees?
⁵Are your days like those of a mortal
  or your years like those of a man,
⁶that you must search out my faults
  and probe after my sin —
⁷though you know that I am not guilty
  and that no one can rescue me from
    your hand?

⁸"Your hands shaped me and made me.
  Will you now turn and destroy me?
⁹Remember that you molded me like
    clay.
  Will you now turn me to dust
    again?
¹⁰Did you not pour me out like milk
  and curdle me like cheese,
¹¹clothe me with skin and flesh
  and knit me together with bones
    and sinews?
¹²You gave me life and showed me
    kindness,
  and in your providence watched
    over my spirit.

¹³"But this is what you concealed in
    your heart,
  and I know that this was in your
    mind:
¹⁴If I sinned, you would be watching me
  and would not let my offense go
    unpunished.
¹⁵If I am guilty — woe to me!
  Even if I am innocent, I cannot lift
    my head,
  for I am full of shame

and drowned in^a my affliction.
¹⁶If I hold my head high, you stalk me
    like a lion
  and again display your awesome
    power against me.
¹⁷You bring new witnesses against me
  and increase your anger toward me;
  your forces come against me wave
    upon wave.

¹⁸"Why then did you bring me out of
    the womb?
  I wish I had died before any eye
    saw me.
¹⁹If only I had never come into being,
  or had been carried straight from
    the womb to the grave!
²⁰Are not my few days almost over?
  Turn away from me so I can have a
    moment's joy
²¹before I go to the place of no return,
  to the land of gloom and deep
    shadow,^b
²²to the land of deepest night,
  of deep shadow and disorder,
  where even the light is like
    darkness."

Zophar

11

Then Zophar the Naamathite re-
    plied:

²"Are all these words to go
    unanswered?
  Is this talker to be vindicated?
³Will your idle talk reduce men to
    silence?
  Will no one rebuke you when you
    mock?
⁴You say to God, 'My beliefs are
    flawless
  and I am pure in your sight.'
⁵Oh, how I wish that God would speak,
  that he would open his lips against
    you
⁶and disclose to you the secrets of
    wisdom,
  for true wisdom has two sides.
  Know this: God has even forgotten
    some of your sin.

⁷"Can you fathom the mysteries of
    God?
  Can you probe the limits of the
    Almighty?
⁸They are higher than the heavens —
    what can you do?

^a15 Or and aware of   ^b21 Or and the shadow of death; also in verse 22

They are deeper than the depths of
the grave[a]—what can you
know?
⁹Their measure is longer than the earth
and wider than the sea.

¹⁰"If he comes along and confines you
in prison
and convenes a court, who can
oppose him?
¹¹Surely he recognizes deceitful men;
and when he sees evil, does he not
take note?
¹²But a witless man can no more
become wise
than a wild donkey's colt can be
born a man.[b]

¹³"Yet if you devote your heart to him
and stretch out your hands to him,
¹⁴if you put away the sin that is in your
hand
and allow no evil to dwell in your
tent,
¹⁵then you will lift up your face without
shame;
you will stand firm and without
fear.
¹⁶You will surely forget your trouble,
recalling it only as waters gone by.
¹⁷Life will be brighter than noonday,
and darkness will become like
morning.
¹⁸You will be secure, because there is
hope;
you will look about you and take
your rest in safety.
¹⁹You will lie down, with no one to
make you afraid,
and many will court your favor.
²⁰But the eyes of the wicked will fail,
and escape will elude them;
their hope will become a dying
gasp."

Job

12
Then Job replied:

²"Doubtless you are the people,
and wisdom will die with you!
³But I have a mind as well as you;
I am not inferior to you.
Who does not know all these
things?

⁴"I have become a laughingstock to my
friends,

though I called upon God and he
answered—
a mere laughingstock, though
righteous and blameless!
⁵Men at ease have contempt for
misfortune
as the fate of those whose feet are
slipping.
⁶The tents of marauders are
undisturbed,
and those who provoke God are
secure—
those who carry their god in their
hands.[c]

⁷"But ask the animals, and they will
teach you,
or the birds of the air, and they will
tell you;
⁸or speak to the earth, and it will teach
you,
or let the fish of the sea inform you.
⁹Which of all these does not know
that the hand of the LORD has done
this?
¹⁰In his hand is the life of every
creature
and the breath of all mankind.
¹¹Does not the ear test words
as the tongue tastes food?
¹²Is not wisdom found among the aged?
Does not long life bring
understanding?

¹³"To God belong wisdom and power;
counsel and understanding are his.
¹⁴What he tears down cannot be rebuilt;
the man he imprisons cannot be
released.
¹⁵If he holds back the waters, there is
drought;
if he lets them loose, they devastate
the land.
¹⁶To him belong strength and victory;
both deceived and deceiver are his.
¹⁷He leads counselors away stripped
and makes fools of judges.
¹⁸He takes off the shackles put on by
kings
and ties a loincloth[d] around their
waist.
¹⁹He leads priests away stripped
and overthrows men long
established.
²⁰He silences the lips of trusted advisers
and takes away the discernment of
elders.
²¹He pours contempt on nobles

---

[a]8 Hebrew than Sheol   [b]12 Or wild donkey can be born tame   [c]6 Or secure / in what God's hand
brings them   [d]18 Or shackles of kings / and ties a belt

and disarms the mighty.
²²He reveals the deep things of darkness
and brings deep shadows into the
light.
²³He makes nations great, and destroys
them;
he enlarges nations, and disperses
them.
²⁴He deprives the leaders of the earth of
their reason;
he sends them wandering through a
trackless waste.
²⁵They grope in darkness with no light;
he makes them stagger like
drunkards.

13 "My eyes have seen all this,
my ears have heard and
understood it.
²What you know, I also know;
I am not inferior to you.
³But I desire to speak to the Almighty
and to argue my case with God.
⁴You, however, smear me with lies;
you are worthless physicians, all of
you!
⁵If only you would be altogether silent!
For you, that would be wisdom.
⁶Hear now my argument;
listen to the plea of my lips.
⁷Will you speak wickedly on God's
behalf?
Will you speak deceitfully for him?
⁸Will you show him partiality?
Will you argue the case for God?
⁹Would it turn out well if he examined
you?
Could you deceive him as you
might deceive men?
¹⁰He would surely rebuke you
if you secretly showed partiality.
¹¹Would not his splendor terrify you?
Would not the dread of him fall on
you?
¹²Your maxims are proverbs of ashes;
your defenses are defenses of clay.

¹³"Keep silent and let me speak;
then let come to me what may.
¹⁴Why do I put myself in jeopardy
and take my life in my hands?
¹⁵Though he slay me, yet will I hope in
him;
I will surely[a] defend my ways to
his face.
¹⁶Indeed, this will turn out for my
deliverance,

for no godless man would dare
come before him!
¹⁷Listen carefully to my words;
let your ears take in what I say.
¹⁸Now that I have prepared my case,
I know I will be vindicated.
¹⁹Can anyone bring charges against me?
If so, I will be silent and die.

²⁰"Only grant me these two things,
O God,
and then I will not hide from you:
²¹Withdraw your hand far from me,
and stop frightening me with your
terrors.
²²Then summon me and I will answer,
or let me speak, and you reply.
²³How many wrongs and sins have I
committed?
Show me my offense and my sin.
²⁴Why do you hide your face
and consider me your enemy?
²⁵Will you torment a windblown leaf?
Will you chase after dry chaff?
²⁶For you write down bitter things
against me
and make me inherit the sins of my
youth.
²⁷You fasten my feet in shackles;
you keep close watch on all my
paths
by putting marks on the soles of my
feet.

²⁸"So man wastes away like something
rotten,
like a garment eaten by moths.

14 "Man born of woman
is of few days and full of trouble.
²He springs up like a flower and
withers away;
like a fleeting shadow, he does not
endure.
³Do you fix your eye on such a one?
Will you bring him[b] before you for
judgment?
⁴Who can bring what is pure from the
impure?
No one!
⁵Man's days are determined;
you have decreed the number of his
months
and have set limits he cannot
exceed.
⁶So look away from him and let him
alone,

ª15 Or *He will surely slay me; I have no hope — / yet I will*   ᵇ3 Septuagint, Vulgate and Syriac; Hebrew
me

till he has put in his time like a
hired man.

7"At least there is hope for a tree:
If it is cut down, it will sprout
again,
and its new shoots will not fail.
8Its roots may grow old in the ground
and its stump die in the soil,
9yet at the scent of water it will bud
and put forth shoots like a plant.
10But man dies and is laid low;
he breathes his last and is no more.
11As water disappears from the sea

or a riverbed becomes parched and
dry,
12so man lies down and does not rise;
till the heavens are no more, men
will not awake
or be roused from their sleep.
13"If only you would hide me in the
grave*a*
and conceal me till your anger has
passed!
If only you would set me a time
and then remember me!
14If a man dies, will he live again?

a 13 Hebrew *Sheol*

THURSDAY

VERSE FOR THE DAY:	AUTHOR:	PASSAGE FOR THE DAY:
Job 13:15	Charles Colson	Job 13:13–19

God Is Who He Is

OBEDIENCE is the key to real faith—the unshakable kind of
faith so powerfully illustrated by Job's life. Job lost his home,
his family (except for a nagging wife), his health, even his
hope. The advice of friends was no help. No matter where he
turned, he could find no answers to his plight. Eventually he
stood alone. But though it appeared God had abandoned him,
Job clung to the assurance that *God is who he is*. Job confirmed his obedience with those classic words of faith:
"Though he slay me, yet will I hope in him" (Job 13:15).

This is real faith: believing and acting obediently regardless
of circumstances or contrary evidence. After all, if faith depended on visible evidence, it wouldn't be faith. "We live by
faith, not by sight" (2 Corinthians 5:7), the apostle Paul wrote.

It is absurd for Christians to constantly seek new demonstra-
tions of God's power, to expect a miraculous answer to every
need, from curing ingrown toenails to finding parking spaces;
this only leads to faith in miracles rather than the Maker.

True faith depends not upon mysterious signs, celestial fire-
works, or grandiose dispensations from a God who is seen as a
rich, benevolent uncle; true faith, as Job understood, rests on
the assurance that *God is who he is*. Indeed, on that we must
be willing to stake our very lives.

Additional Scripture Readings:
Habakkuk 3:16–19;
2 Corinthians 5:6–10

*Go to page 524 for your next
devotional reading.*

All the days of my hard service
　　I will wait for my renewal[a] to
　　　come.
15You will call and I will answer you;
　　you will long for the creature your
　　　hands have made.
16Surely then you will count my steps
　　but not keep track of my sin.
17My offenses will be sealed up in a bag;
　　you will cover over my sin.

18"But as a mountain erodes and
　　　crumbles
　　and as a rock is moved from its
　　　place,
19as water wears away stones
　　and torrents wash away the soil,
　　so you destroy man's hope.
20You overpower him once for all, and
　　　he is gone;
　　you change his countenance and
　　　send him away.
21If his sons are honored, he does not
　　　know it;
　　if they are brought low, he does not
　　　see it.
22He feels but the pain of his own body
　　and mourns only for himself."

Eliphaz

15

Then Eliphaz the Temanite replied:

2"Would a wise man answer with
　　　empty notions
　　or fill his belly with the hot east
　　　wind?
3Would he argue with useless words,
　　with speeches that have no value?
4But you even undermine piety
　　and hinder devotion to God.
5Your sin prompts your mouth;
　　you adopt the tongue of the crafty.
6Your own mouth condemns you, not
　　　mine;
　　your own lips testify against you.

7"Are you the first man ever born?
　　Were you brought forth before the
　　　hills?
8Do you listen in on God's council?
　　Do you limit wisdom to yourself?
9What do you know that we do not
　　　know?
　　What insights do you have that we
　　　do not have?
10The gray-haired and the aged are on
　　　our side,
　　men even older than your father.

11Are God's consolations not enough for
　　　you,
　　words spoken gently to you?
12Why has your heart carried you away,
　　and why do your eyes flash,
13so that you vent your rage against
　　　God
　　and pour out such words from your
　　　mouth?

14"What is man, that he could be pure,
　　or one born of woman, that he
　　　could be righteous?
15If God places no trust in his holy
　　　ones,
　　if even the heavens are not pure in
　　　his eyes,
16how much less man, who is vile and
　　　corrupt,
　　who drinks up evil like water!

17"Listen to me and I will explain to
　　　you;
　　let me tell you what I have seen,
18what wise men have declared,
　　hiding nothing received from their
　　　fathers
19(to whom alone the land was given
　　when no alien passed among them):
20All his days the wicked man suffers
　　　torment,
　　the ruthless through all the years
　　　stored up for him.
21Terrifying sounds fill his ears;
　　when all seems well, marauders
　　　attack him.
22He despairs of escaping the darkness;
　　he is marked for the sword.
23He wanders about—food for
　　　vultures[b];
　　he knows the day of darkness is at
　　　hand.
24Distress and anguish fill him with
　　　terror;
　　they overwhelm him, like a king
　　　poised to attack,
25because he shakes his fist at God
　　and vaunts himself against the
　　　Almighty,
26defiantly charging against him
　　with a thick, strong shield.

27"Though his face is covered with fat
　　and his waist bulges with flesh,
28he will inhabit ruined towns
　　and houses where no one lives,
　　houses crumbling to rubble.
29He will no longer be rich and his
　　wealth will not endure,

---

a14 Or *release*　　b23 Or *about, looking for food*

nor will his possessions spread over
the land.
³⁰He will not escape the darkness;
a flame will wither his shoots,
and the breath of God's mouth will
carry him away.
³¹Let him not deceive himself by
trusting what is worthless,
for he will get nothing in return.
³²Before his time he will be paid in full,
and his branches will not flourish.
³³He will be like a vine stripped of its
unripe grapes,
like an olive tree shedding its
blossoms.
³⁴For the company of the godless will
be barren,
and fire will consume the tents of
those who love bribes.
³⁵They conceive trouble and give birth
to evil;
their womb fashions deceit."

Job

16
Then Job replied:

²"I have heard many things like these;
miserable comforters are you all!
³Will your long-winded speeches never
end?
What ails you that you keep on
arguing?
⁴I also could speak like you,
if you were in my place;
I could make fine speeches against
you
and shake my head at you.
⁵But my mouth would encourage you;
comfort from my lips would bring
you relief.

⁶"Yet if I speak, my pain is not
relieved;
and if I refrain, it does not go away.
⁷Surely, O God, you have worn me out;
you have devastated my entire
household.
⁸You have bound me—and it has
become a witness;
my gauntness rises up and testifies
against me.
⁹God assails me and tears me in his
anger
and gnashes his teeth at me;
my opponent fastens on me his
piercing eyes.
¹⁰Men open their mouths to jeer at me;
they strike my cheek in scorn

and unite together against me.
¹¹God has turned me over to evil men
and thrown me into the clutches of
the wicked.
¹²All was well with me, but he shattered
me;
he seized me by the neck and
crushed me.
He has made me his target;
¹³   his archers surround me.
Without pity, he pierces my kidneys
and spills my gall on the ground.
¹⁴Again and again he bursts upon me;
he rushes at me like a warrior.

¹⁵"I have sewed sackcloth over my skin
and buried my brow in the dust.
¹⁶My face is red with weeping,
deep shadows ring my eyes;
¹⁷yet my hands have been free of
violence
and my prayer is pure.

¹⁸"O earth, do not cover my blood;
may my cry never be laid to rest!
¹⁹Even now my witness is in heaven;
my advocate is on high.
²⁰My intercessor is my friend[a]
as my eyes pour out tears to God;
²¹on behalf of a man he pleads with
God
as a man pleads for his friend.

²²"Only a few years will pass
before I go on the journey of no
return.

17
¹My spirit is broken,
my days are cut short,
the grave awaits me.
²Surely mockers surround me;
my eyes must dwell on their
hostility.

³"Give me, O God, the pledge you
demand.
Who else will put up security for
me?
⁴You have closed their minds to
understanding;
therefore you will not let them
triumph.
⁵If a man denounces his friends for
reward,
the eyes of his children will fail.

⁶"God has made me a byword to
everyone,
a man in whose face people spit.
⁷My eyes have grown dim with grief;
my whole frame is but a shadow.

a20 Or *My friends treat me with scorn*

[8]Upright men are appalled at this;
  the innocent are aroused against the
    ungodly.
[9]Nevertheless, the righteous will hold
    to their ways,
  and those with clean hands will
    grow stronger.

[10]"But come on, all of you, try again!
  I will not find a wise man among
    you.
[11]My days have passed, my plans are
    shattered,
  and so are the desires of my heart.
[12]These men turn night into day;
  in the face of darkness they say,
    'Light is near.'
[13]If the only home I hope for is the
    grave,[a]
  if I spread out my bed in darkness,
[14]if I say to corruption, 'You are my
    father,'
  and to the worm, 'My mother' or
    'My sister,'
[15]where then is my hope?
  Who can see any hope for me?
[16]Will it go down to the gates of
    death[a]?
  Will we descend together into the
    dust?"

Bildad

18
Then Bildad the Shuhite replied:

[2]"When will you end these speeches?
  Be sensible, and then we can talk.
[3]Why are we regarded as cattle
  and considered stupid in your sight?
[4]You who tear yourself to pieces in
    your anger,
  is the earth to be abandoned for
    your sake?
  Or must the rocks be moved from
    their place?

[5]"The lamp of the wicked is snuffed
    out;
  the flame of his fire stops burning.
[6]The light in his tent becomes dark;
  the lamp beside him goes out.
[7]The vigor of his step is weakened;
  his own schemes throw him down.
[8]His feet thrust him into a net
  and he wanders into its mesh.
[9]A trap seizes him by the heel;
  a snare holds him fast.
[10]A noose is hidden for him on the
    ground;

a trap lies in his path.
[11]Terrors startle him on every side
  and dog his every step.
[12]Calamity is hungry for him;
  disaster is ready for him when he
    falls.
[13]It eats away parts of his skin;
  death's firstborn devours his limbs.
[14]He is torn from the security of his tent
  and marched off to the king of
    terrors.
[15]Fire resides[b] in his tent;
  burning sulfur is scattered over his
    dwelling.
[16]His roots dry up below
  and his branches wither above.
[17]The memory of him perishes from the
    earth;
  he has no name in the land.
[18]He is driven from light into darkness
  and is banished from the world.
[19]He has no offspring or descendants
    among his people,
  no survivor where once he lived.
[20]Men of the west are appalled at his
    fate;
  men of the east are seized with
    horror.
[21]Surely such is the dwelling of an evil
    man;
  such is the place of one who knows
    not God."

Job

19
Then Job replied:

[2]"How long will you torment me
  and crush me with words?
[3]Ten times now you have reproached
    me;
  shamelessly you attack me.
[4]If it is true that I have gone astray,
  my error remains my concern alone.
[5]If indeed you would exalt yourselves
    above me
  and use my humiliation against me,
[6]then know that God has wronged me
  and drawn his net around me.

[7]"Though I cry, 'I've been wronged!' I
    get no response;
  though I call for help, there is no
    justice.
[8]He has blocked my way so I cannot
    pass;
  he has shrouded my paths in
    darkness.
[9]He has stripped me of my honor

---

a 13,16 Hebrew *Sheol*   b 15 Or *Nothing he had remains*

and removed the crown from my head.

¹⁰He tears me down on every side till I am gone;
he uproots my hope like a tree.

¹¹His anger burns against me;
he counts me among his enemies.

¹²His troops advance in force;
they build a siege ramp against me
and encamp around my tent.

¹³"He has alienated my brothers from me;
my acquaintances are completely estranged from me.

¹⁴My kinsmen have gone away;
my friends have forgotten me.

¹⁵My guests and my maidservants count me a stranger;
they look upon me as an alien.

¹⁶I summon my servant, but he does not answer,
though I beg him with my own mouth.

¹⁷My breath is offensive to my wife;
I am loathsome to my own brothers.

¹⁸Even the little boys scorn me;
when I appear, they ridicule me.

¹⁹All my intimate friends detest me;
those I love have turned against me.

²⁰I am nothing but skin and bones;
I have escaped with only the skin of my teeth.ᵃ

²¹"Have pity on me, my friends, have pity,
for the hand of God has struck me.

²²Why do you pursue me as God does?
Will you never get enough of my flesh?

²³"Oh, that my words were recorded,
that they were written on a scroll,

²⁴that they were inscribed with an iron tool onᵇ lead,
or engraved in rock forever!

²⁵I know that my Redeemerᶜ lives,
and that in the end he will stand upon the earth.ᵈ

²⁶And after my skin has been destroyed,
yetᵉ inᶠ my flesh I will see God;

²⁷I myself will see him
with my own eyes—I, and not another.
How my heart yearns within me!

²⁸"If you say, 'How we will hound him,
since the root of the trouble lies in him,ᵍ'

²⁹you should fear the sword yourselves;
for wrath will bring punishment by the sword,
and then you will know that there is judgment.ʰ"

Zophar

20 Then Zophar the Naamathite replied:

²"My troubled thoughts prompt me to answer
because I am greatly disturbed.

³I hear a rebuke that dishonors me,
and my understanding inspires me to reply.

⁴"Surely you know how it has been from of old,
ever since manⁱ was placed on the earth,

⁵that the mirth of the wicked is brief,
the joy of the godless lasts but a moment.

⁶Though his pride reaches to the heavens
and his head touches the clouds,

⁷he will perish forever, like his own dung;
those who have seen him will say, 'Where is he?'

⁸Like a dream he flies away, no more to be found,
banished like a vision of the night.

⁹The eye that saw him will not see him again;
his place will look on him no more.

¹⁰His children must make amends to the poor;
his own hands must give back his wealth.

¹¹The youthful vigor that fills his bones
will lie with him in the dust.

¹²"Though evil is sweet in his mouth
and he hides it under his tongue,

¹³though he cannot bear to let it go
and keeps it in his mouth,

¹⁴yet his food will turn sour in his stomach;
it will become the venom of serpents within him.

¹⁵He will spit out the riches he swallowed;

ᵃ20 Or only my gums   ᵇ24 Or and   ᶜ25 Or defender   ᵈ25 Or upon my grave   ᵉ26 Or And after I awake, / though this ˌbodyˌ has been destroyed, / then   ᶠ26 Or / apart from   ᵍ28 Many Hebrew manuscripts, Septuagint and Vulgate; most Hebrew manuscripts me   ʰ29 Or / that you may come to know the Almighty   ⁱ4 Or Adam

God will make his stomach vomit
    them up.
¹⁶He will suck the poison of serpents;
    the fangs of an adder will kill him.
¹⁷He will not enjoy the streams,
    the rivers flowing with honey and
      cream.
¹⁸What he toiled for he must give back
    uneaten;
    he will not enjoy the profit from his
      trading.
¹⁹For he has oppressed the poor and left
    them destitute;
    he has seized houses he did not
      build.

²⁰"Surely he will have no respite from
    his craving;
    he cannot save himself by his
      treasure.
²¹Nothing is left for him to devour;
    his prosperity will not endure.
²²In the midst of his plenty, distress will
    overtake him;
    the full force of misery will come
      upon him.
²³When he has filled his belly,
    God will vent his burning anger
      against him
    and rain down his blows upon him.
²⁴Though he flees from an iron weapon,
    a bronze-tipped arrow pierces him.
²⁵He pulls it out of his back,
    the gleaming point out of his liver.
    Terrors will come over him;
²⁶   total darkness lies in wait for his
      treasures.
    A fire unfanned will consume him
    and devour what is left in his tent.
²⁷The heavens will expose his guilt;
    the earth will rise up against him.
²⁸A flood will carry off his house,
    rushing waters*a* on the day of
      God's wrath.
²⁹Such is the fate God allots the wicked,
    the heritage appointed for them by
      God."

Job

21
Then Job replied:

²"Listen carefully to my words;
    let this be the consolation you give
      me.
³Bear with me while I speak,
    and after I have spoken, mock on.

⁴"Is my complaint directed to man?

Why should I not be impatient?
⁵Look at me and be astonished;
    clap your hand over your mouth.
⁶When I think about this, I am
    terrified;
    trembling seizes my body.
⁷Why do the wicked live on,
    growing old and increasing in
      power?
⁸They see their children established
    around them,
    their offspring before their eyes.
⁹Their homes are safe and free from
    fear;
    the rod of God is not upon them.
¹⁰Their bulls never fail to breed;
    their cows calve and do not
      miscarry.
¹¹They send forth their children as a
    flock;
    their little ones dance about.
¹²They sing to the music of tambourine
    and harp;
    they make merry to the sound of
      the flute.
¹³They spend their years in prosperity
    and go down to the grave*b* in
      peace.*c*
¹⁴Yet they say to God, 'Leave us alone!
    We have no desire to know your
      ways.
¹⁵Who is the Almighty, that we should
    serve him?
    What would we gain by praying to
      him?'
¹⁶But their prosperity is not in their
    own hands,
    so I stand aloof from the counsel of
      the wicked.

¹⁷"Yet how often is the lamp of the
    wicked snuffed out?
    How often does calamity come
      upon them,
    the fate God allots in his anger?
¹⁸How often are they like straw before
    the wind,
    like chaff swept away by a gale?
¹⁹It is said, 'God stores up a man's
    punishment for his sons.'
    Let him repay the man himself, so
      that he will know it!
²⁰Let his own eyes see his destruction;
    let him drink of the wrath of the
      Almighty.*d*
²¹For what does he care about the
    family he leaves behind

---

a28 Or *The possessions in his house will be carried off, / washed away*   *b13* Hebrew *Sheol*   *c13* Or
in an instant   *d17-20* Verses 17 and 18 may be taken as exclamations and 19 and 20 as declarations.

when his allotted months come to
an end?

22"Can anyone teach knowledge to God,
since he judges even the highest?
23One man dies in full vigor,
completely secure and at ease,
24his body^a well nourished,
his bones rich with marrow.
25Another man dies in bitterness of
soul,
never having enjoyed anything
good.
26Side by side they lie in the dust,
and worms cover them both.

27"I know full well what you are
thinking,
the schemes by which you would
wrong me.
28You say, 'Where now is the great
man's house,
the tents where wicked men lived?'
29Have you never questioned those who
travel?
Have you paid no regard to their
accounts—
30that the evil man is spared from the
day of calamity,
that he is delivered from^b the day
of wrath?
31Who denounces his conduct to his
face?
Who repays him for what he has
done?
32He is carried to the grave,
and watch is kept over his tomb.
33The soil in the valley is sweet to him;
all men follow after him,
and a countless throng goes^c
before him.

34"So how can you console me with
your nonsense?
Nothing is left of your answers but
falsehood!"

Eliphaz

22 Then Eliphaz the Temanite replied:

2"Can a man be of benefit to God?
Can even a wise man benefit him?
3What pleasure would it give the
Almighty if you were righteous?
What would he gain if your ways
were blameless?

4"Is it for your piety that he rebukes
you
and brings charges against you?
5Is not your wickedness great?
Are not your sins endless?
6You demanded security from your
brothers for no reason;
you stripped men of their clothing,
leaving them naked.
7You gave no water to the weary
and you withheld food from the
hungry,
8though you were a powerful man,
owning land—
an honored man, living on it.
9And you sent widows away
empty-handed
and broke the strength of the
fatherless.
10That is why snares are all around you,
why sudden peril terrifies you,
11why it is so dark you cannot see,
and why a flood of water covers
you.

12"Is not God in the heights of heaven?
And see how lofty are the highest
stars!
13Yet you say, 'What does God know?
Does he judge through such
darkness?
14Thick clouds veil him, so he does not
see us
as he goes about in the vaulted
heavens.'
15Will you keep to the old path
that evil men have trod?
16They were carried off before their
time,
their foundations washed away by a
flood.
17They said to God, 'Leave us alone!
What can the Almighty do to us?'
18Yet it was he who filled their houses
with good things,
so I stand aloof from the counsel of
the wicked.

19"The righteous see their ruin and
rejoice;
the innocent mock them, saying,
20'Surely our foes are destroyed,
and fire devours their wealth.'

21"Submit to God and be at peace with
him;
in this way prosperity will come to
you.

---

^a24 The meaning of the Hebrew for this word is uncertain.   ^b30 Or *man is reserved for the day of
calamity, / that he is brought forth to*   ^c33 Or / *as a countless throng went*

²²Accept instruction from his mouth
and lay up his words in your heart.
²³If you return to the Almighty, you will
be restored:
If you remove wickedness far from
your tent
²⁴and assign your nuggets to the dust,
your gold of Ophir to the rocks in
the ravines,
²⁵then the Almighty will be your gold,
the choicest silver for you.
²⁶Surely then you will find delight in
the Almighty
and will lift up your face to God.
²⁷You will pray to him, and he will hear
you,
and you will fulfill your vows.
²⁸What you decide on will be done,

and light will shine on your ways.
²⁹When men are brought low and you
say, 'Lift them up!'
then he will save the downcast.
³⁰He will deliver even one who is not
innocent,
who will be delivered through the
cleanness of your hands."

Job

23

Then Job replied:

²"Even today my complaint is bitter;
his hand[a] is heavy in spite of[b] my
groaning.
³If only I knew where to find him;
if only I could go to his dwelling!
⁴I would state my case before him
and fill my mouth with arguments.

a2 Septuagint and Syriac; Hebrew / the hand on me

b2 Or heavy on me in

FRIDAY

VERSE FOR THE DAY:	AUTHOR:	PASSAGE FOR THE DAY:
Job 22:21	Bill McCartney	Job 22:21–30

Good Life—Godly Life

I WENT to mass every day, I said my prayers, and I tried to live by the Golden Rule.

[But] what I really had was a tiny taste of success and a tiny taste of religion—but not much Christianity. Sure, I was a good person. I treated others with respect. But someone once described the contrast between a good life and a godly life as the difference between the top of the ocean and the bottom. On top, sometimes it's like glass—serene and calm—and other times it's raging and stormy. But hundreds of fathoms below, it is beautiful and consistent, always calm, always peaceful. Down deep in my heart, I did not have the peace that comes only from knowing Jesus Christ as a personal Savior. Back then in 1970, when I was twenty-nine years old and a head football coach for the first time in my life, I was a church-goer and a professing Christian. But it wasn't until four years later, when I was a rookie assistant coach at the University of Michigan that I discovered a real relationship with Jesus Christ. And when I accepted Christ as Savior and Lord of my life, I began an adventure that has transformed my life.

Additional Scripture Readings:
Ephesians 2:1–10; 2 Peter 1:3–11

*Go to page 527 for your next
devotional reading.*

⁵I would find out what he would
    answer me,
  and consider what he would say.
⁶Would he oppose me with great
    power?
  No, he would not press charges
    against me.
⁷There an upright man could present
    his case before him,
  and I would be delivered forever
    from my judge.

⁸"But if I go to the east, he is not
    there;
  if I go to the west, I do not find
    him.
⁹When he is at work in the north, I do
    not see him;
  when he turns to the south, I catch
    no glimpse of him.
¹⁰But he knows the way that I take;
  when he has tested me, I will come
    forth as gold.
¹¹My feet have closely followed his
    steps;
  I have kept to his way without
    turning aside.
¹²I have not departed from the
    commands of his lips;
  I have treasured the words of his
    mouth more than my daily
    bread.

¹³"But he stands alone, and who can
    oppose him?
  He does whatever he pleases.
¹⁴He carries out his decree against me,
  and many such plans he still has in
    store.
¹⁵That is why I am terrified before him;
  when I think of all this, I fear him.
¹⁶God has made my heart faint;
  the Almighty has terrified me.
¹⁷Yet I am not silenced by the darkness,
  by the thick darkness that covers
    my face.

24 "Why does the Almighty not set
    times for judgment?
  Why must those who know him
    look in vain for such days?
²Men move boundary stones;
  they pasture flocks they have stolen.
³They drive away the orphan's donkey
  and take the widow's ox in pledge.
⁴They thrust the needy from the path
  and force all the poor of the land
    into hiding.

⁵Like wild donkeys in the desert,
  the poor go about their labor of
    foraging food;
  the wasteland provides food for
    their children.
⁶They gather fodder in the fields
  and glean in the vineyards of the
    wicked.
⁷Lacking clothes, they spend the night
    naked;
  they have nothing to cover
    themselves in the cold.
⁸They are drenched by mountain rains
  and hug the rocks for lack of
    shelter.
⁹The fatherless child is snatched from
    the breast;
  the infant of the poor is seized for a
    debt.
¹⁰Lacking clothes, they go about naked;
  they carry the sheaves, but still go
    hungry.
¹¹They crush olives among the
    terracesᵃ;
  they tread the winepresses, yet
    suffer thirst.
¹²The groans of the dying rise from the
    city,
  and the souls of the wounded cry
    out for help.
  But God charges no one with
    wrongdoing.

¹³"There are those who rebel against the
    light,
  who do not know its ways
  or stay in its paths.
¹⁴When daylight is gone, the murderer
    rises up
  and kills the poor and needy;
  in the night he steals forth like a
    thief.
¹⁵The eye of the adulterer watches for
    dusk;
  he thinks, 'No eye will see me,'
  and he keeps his face concealed.
¹⁶In the dark, men break into houses,
  but by day they shut themselves in;
  they want nothing to do with the
    light.
¹⁷For all of them, deep darkness is their
    morningᵇ;
  they make friends with the terrors
    of darkness.ᶜ

¹⁸"Yet they are foam on the surface of
    the water;
  their portion of the land is cursed,

ᵃ11 Or *olives between the millstones*; the meaning of the Hebrew for this word is uncertain.   ᵇ17 Or
them, their morning is like the shadow of death   ᶜ17 Or *of the shadow of death*

so that no one goes to the
vineyards.
19As heat and drought snatch away the
melted snow,
so the grave*a* snatches away those
who have sinned.
20The womb forgets them,
the worm feasts on them;
evil men are no longer remembered
but are broken like a tree.
21They prey on the barren and childless
woman,
and to the widow show no
kindness.
22But God drags away the mighty by his
power;
though they become established,
they have no assurance of life.
23He may let them rest in a feeling of
security,
but his eyes are on their ways.
24For a little while they are exalted, and
then they are gone;
they are brought low and gathered
up like all others;
they are cut off like heads of grain.
25"If this is not so, who can prove me
false
and reduce my words to nothing?"

Bildad

25 Then Bildad the Shuhite replied:

2"Dominion and awe belong to God;
he establishes order in the heights
of heaven.
3Can his forces be numbered?
Upon whom does his light not rise?
4How then can a man be righteous
before God?
How can one born of woman be
pure?
5If even the moon is not bright
and the stars are not pure in his
eyes,
6how much less man, who is but a
maggot—
a son of man, who is only a worm!"

Job

26 Then Job replied:

2"How you have helped the powerless!
How you have saved the arm that is
feeble!
3What advice you have offered to one
without wisdom!

And what great insight you have
displayed!
4Who has helped you utter these
words?
And whose spirit spoke from your
mouth?

5"The dead are in deep anguish,
those beneath the waters and all
that live in them.
6Death*a* is naked before God;
Destruction*b* lies uncovered.
7He spreads out the northern skies
over empty space;
he suspends the earth over nothing.
8He wraps up the waters in his clouds,
yet the clouds do not burst under
their weight.
9He covers the face of the full moon,
spreading his clouds over it.
10He marks out the horizon on the face
of the waters
for a boundary between light and
darkness.
11The pillars of the heavens quake,
aghast at his rebuke.
12By his power he churned up the sea;
by his wisdom he cut Rahab to
pieces.
13By his breath the skies became fair;
his hand pierced the gliding serpent.
14And these are but the outer fringe of
his works;
how faint the whisper we hear of
him!
Who then can understand the
thunder of his power?"

27 And Job continued his discourse:

2"As surely as God lives, who has
denied me justice,
the Almighty, who has made me
taste bitterness of soul,
3as long as I have life within me,
the breath of God in my nostrils,
4my lips will not speak wickedness,
and my tongue will utter no deceit.
5I will never admit you are in the right;
till I die, I will not deny my integrity.
6I will maintain my righteousness and
never let go of it;
my conscience will not reproach me
as long as I live.

7"May my enemies be like the wicked,
my adversaries like the unjust!
8For what hope has the godless when
he is cut off,

---

a19,6 Hebrew *Sheol*   *b6* Hebrew *Abaddon*

WEEKENDING

REJOICE

I think there are two very heartening things
about our day. First, we are all admitting we
need some answers. That in itself is
encouraging.

We are asking. We are seeking. We are
knocking. Because of our training or
background or personality or a combination of
these and other things, we ask in different
ways. But we are asking.

But it also is true that just as surely as we are
looking in different ways, answers are coming
to us in a diversity which reflects the mystery
of God himself. The wonderful thing is that he
is making certain we are receiving and that we
are finding and that doors are being opened
to us.

– *Bob Benson*

REVIVE
Saturday: Job 21:22–34
Sunday: Matthew 7:7–12

Go to page 531 for your next devotional reading.

when God takes away his life?
⁹Does God listen to his cry
  when distress comes upon him?
¹⁰Will he find delight in the Almighty?
  Will he call upon God at all times?

¹¹"I will teach you about the power of
      God;
  the ways of the Almighty I will not
      conceal.
¹²You have all seen this yourselves.
  Why then this meaningless talk?

¹³"Here is the fate God allots to the
      wicked,
  the heritage a ruthless man receives
      from the Almighty:
¹⁴However many his children, their fate
      is the sword;
  his offspring will never have enough
      to eat.
¹⁵The plague will bury those who
      survive him,
  and their widows will not weep for
      them.
¹⁶Though he heaps up silver like dust
  and clothes like piles of clay,
¹⁷what he lays up the righteous will
      wear,
  and the innocent will divide his
      silver.
¹⁸The house he builds is like a moth's
      cocoon,
  like a hut made by a watchman.
¹⁹He lies down wealthy, but will do so
      no more;
  when he opens his eyes, all is gone.
²⁰Terrors overtake him like a flood;
  a tempest snatches him away in the
      night.
²¹The east wind carries him off, and he
      is gone;
  it sweeps him out of his place.
²²It hurls itself against him without
      mercy
  as he flees headlong from its power.
²³It claps its hands in derision
  and hisses him out of his place.

28 "There is a mine for silver
      and a place where gold is refined.
²Iron is taken from the earth,
  and copper is smelted from ore.
³Man puts an end to the darkness;
  he searches the farthest recesses
      for ore in the blackest darkness.
⁴Far from where people dwell he cuts a
      shaft,

in places forgotten by the foot of
      man;
  far from men he dangles and sways.
⁵The earth, from which food comes,
  is transformed below as by fire;
⁶sapphires[a] come from its rocks,
  and its dust contains nuggets of
      gold.
⁷No bird of prey knows that hidden
      path,
  no falcon's eye has seen it.
⁸Proud beasts do not set foot on it,
  and no lion prowls there.
⁹Man's hand assaults the flinty rock
  and lays bare the roots of the
      mountains.
¹⁰He tunnels through the rock;
  his eyes see all its treasures.
¹¹He searches[b] the sources of the rivers
  and brings hidden things to light.

¹²"But where can wisdom be found?
  Where does understanding dwell?
¹³Man does not comprehend its worth;
  it cannot be found in the land of
      the living.
¹⁴The deep says, 'It is not in me';
  the sea says, 'It is not with me.'
¹⁵It cannot be bought with the finest
      gold,
  nor can its price be weighed in
      silver.
¹⁶It cannot be bought with the gold of
      Ophir,
  with precious onyx or sapphires.
¹⁷Neither gold nor crystal can compare
      with it,
  nor can it be had for jewels of gold.
¹⁸Coral and jasper are not worthy of
      mention;
  the price of wisdom is beyond
      rubies.
¹⁹The topaz of Cush cannot compare
      with it;
  it cannot be bought with pure gold.

²⁰"Where then does wisdom come from?
  Where does understanding dwell?
²¹It is hidden from the eyes of every
      living thing,
  concealed even from the birds of
      the air.
²²Destruction[c] and Death say,
  'Only a rumor of it has reached our
      ears.'
²³God understands the way to it
  and he alone knows where it
      dwells,

---

a6 Or *lapis lazuli*; also in verse 16   b11 Septuagint, Aquila and Vulgate; Hebrew *He dams up*
c22 Hebrew *Abaddon*

24for he views the ends of the earth
   and sees everything under the
     heavens.
25When he established the force of the
   wind
   and measured out the waters,
26when he made a decree for the rain
   and a path for the thunderstorm,
27then he looked at wisdom and
     appraised it;
   he confirmed it and tested it.
28And he said to man,
   'The fear of the Lord—that is
     wisdom,
   and to shun evil is understanding.' "

29 Job continued his discourse:

2"How I long for the months gone by,
   for the days when God watched
     over me,
3when his lamp shone upon my head
   and by his light I walked through
     darkness!
4Oh, for the days when I was in my
     prime,
   when God's intimate friendship
     blessed my house,
5when the Almighty was still with me
   and my children were around me,
6when my path was drenched with
     cream
   and the rock poured out for me
     streams of olive oil.

7"When I went to the gate of the city
   and took my seat in the public
     square,
8the young men saw me and stepped
     aside
   and the old men rose to their feet;
9the chief men refrained from speaking
   and covered their mouths with their
     hands;
10the voices of the nobles were hushed,
   and their tongues stuck to the roof
     of their mouths.
11Whoever heard me spoke well of me,
   and those who saw me commended
     me,
12because I rescued the poor who cried
     for help,
   and the fatherless who had none to
     assist him.
13The man who was dying blessed me;
   I made the widow's heart sing.
14I put on righteousness as my clothing;
   justice was my robe and my turban.
15I was eyes to the blind

and feet to the lame.
16I was a father to the needy;
   I took up the case of the stranger.
17I broke the fangs of the wicked
   and snatched the victims from their
     teeth.

18"I thought, 'I will die in my own
     house,
   my days as numerous as the grains
     of sand.
19My roots will reach to the water,
   and the dew will lie all night on my
     branches.
20My glory will remain fresh in me,
   the bow ever new in my hand.'

21"Men listened to me expectantly,
   waiting in silence for my counsel.
22After I had spoken, they spoke no
     more;
   my words fell gently on their ears.
23They waited for me as for showers
   and drank in my words as the
     spring rain.
24When I smiled at them, they scarcely
     believed it;
   the light of my face was precious to
     them.a
25I chose the way for them and sat as
     their chief;
   I dwelt as a king among his troops;
   I was like one who comforts
     mourners.

30 "But now they mock me,
   men younger than I,
   whose fathers I would have disdained
   to put with my sheep dogs.
2Of what use was the strength of their
     hands to me,
   since their vigor had gone from
     them?
3Haggard from want and hunger,
   they roamedb the parched land
   in desolate wastelands at night.
4In the brush they gathered salt herbs,
   and their foodc was the root of the
     broom tree.
5They were banished from their fellow
     men,
   shouted at as if they were thieves.
6They were forced to live in the dry
     stream beds,
   among the rocks and in holes in the
     ground.
7They brayed among the bushes
   and huddled in the undergrowth.
8A base and nameless brood,

a24 The meaning of the Hebrew for this clause is uncertain.   b3 Or gnawed   c4 Or fuel they were driven out of the land.

⁹"And now their sons mock me in
    song;
    I have become a byword among
    them.
¹⁰They detest me and keep their
    distance;
    they do not hesitate to spit in my
    face.
¹¹Now that God has unstrung my bow
    and afflicted me,
    they throw off restraint in my
    presence.
¹²On my right the tribeᵃ attacks;
    they lay snares for my feet,
    they build their siege ramps against
    me.
¹³They break up my road;
    they succeed in destroying me —
    without anyone's helping them.ᵇ
¹⁴They advance as through a gaping
    breach;
    amid the ruins they come rolling in.
¹⁵Terrors overwhelm me;
    my dignity is driven away as by the
    wind,
    my safety vanishes like a cloud.

¹⁶"And now my life ebbs away;
    days of suffering grip me.
¹⁷Night pierces my bones;
    my gnawing pains never rest.
¹⁸In his great power ⌊God⌋ becomes like
    clothing to meᶜ;
    he binds me like the neck of my
    garment.
¹⁹He throws me into the mud,
    and I am reduced to dust and ashes.

²⁰"I cry out to you, O God, but you do
    not answer;
    I stand up, but you merely look at
    me.
²¹You turn on me ruthlessly;
    with the might of your hand you
    attack me.
²²You snatch me up and drive me
    before the wind;
    you toss me about in the storm.
²³I know you will bring me down to
    death,
    to the place appointed for all the
    living.

²⁴"Surely no one lays a hand on a
    broken man
    when he cries for help in his
    distress.

²⁵Have I not wept for those in trouble?
    Has not my soul grieved for the
    poor?
²⁶Yet when I hoped for good, evil came;
    when I looked for light, then came
    darkness.
²⁷The churning inside me never stops;
    days of suffering confront me.
²⁸I go about blackened, but not by the
    sun;
    I stand up in the assembly and cry
    for help.
²⁹I have become a brother of jackals,
    a companion of owls.
³⁰My skin grows black and peels;
    my body burns with fever.
³¹My harp is tuned to mourning,
    and my flute to the sound of
    wailing.

31 "I made a covenant with my eyes
    not to look lustfully at a girl.
²For what is man's lot from God above,
    his heritage from the Almighty on
    high?
³Is it not ruin for the wicked,
    disaster for those who do wrong?
⁴Does he not see my ways
    and count my every step?

⁵"If I have walked in falsehood
    or my foot has hurried after
    deceit —
⁶let God weigh me in honest scales
    and he will know that I am
    blameless —
⁷if my steps have turned from the path,
    if my heart has been led by my
    eyes,
    or if my hands have been defiled,
⁸then may others eat what I have
    sown,
    and may my crops be uprooted.

⁹"If my heart has been enticed by a
    woman,
    or if I have lurked at my neighbor's
    door,
¹⁰then may my wife grind another
    man's grain,
    and may other men sleep with her.
¹¹For that would have been shameful,
    a sin to be judged.
¹²It is a fire that burns to Destructionᵈ;
    it would have uprooted my harvest.

¹³"If I have denied justice to my
    menservants and maidservants

ᵃ12 The meaning of the Hebrew for this word is uncertain.
ᶜ18 Hebrew; Septuagint ⌊God⌋ grasps my clothing
ᵇ13 Or me. / 'No one can help him,' ⌊they
say⌋.   ᵈ12 Hebrew Abaddon

VERSE FOR THE DAY:
Job 31:1

AUTHOR:
Steve Farrar

PASSAGE FOR THE DAY:
Job 31:1–12

A Special Kind of Blindness

A ONE-WOMAN kind of man has purposefully cultivated a special kind of blindness.

In the Old Testament, Job put it this way: "I made a covenant with my eyes not to look lustfully at a girl" (Job 31:1). Job is making a commitment to a special kind of blind love. He's talking *Semper Fidelis*.

Let's carefully observe what Job is saying here. He isn't making a commitment to never *notice* an attractive female. That would not only be ludicrous, but would require total blindness. Good-looking girls and women are everywhere. You can't help but see them.

There is a difference, however, between seeing a beautiful woman and lusting after her. Job's point is simply this: There is a difference between a look and a *lustful* look . . .

A one-woman kind of man is a man who demonstrates his commitment by disciplining his eyes. We are all familiar with the guy who can't walk one block without giving some woman the once-over from head to toe. He will even stop dead in his tracks in the flow of pedestrian traffic to turn and watch her as she goes by. Most of us are a little better socially adjusted than that.

A man who is committed with his eyes will avoid certain kinds of magazines and television programs. I'm writing this in a hotel room in Chicago, hundreds of miles from my wife and kids. A hotel room on the road can be a very dangerous place for a one-woman kind of man who is not prepared for battle.

When I bought a newspaper at the hotel gift shop this morning, it was surrounded by pornographic magazines with alluring covers. "Girls of the Southwest Conference!" blazed the cover. If I don't discipline my eyes and look away, I'm going to start wondering how those girls in the Southwest Conference are getting along. But I'm committed to a special kind of blind love. I must particularly cultivate that blindness away from home. I know I must do this because I know myself. And the self I know has a hard enough time even when I'm *not* away from home.

Additional Scripture Readings:
Proverbs 6:20–29; Matthew 5:27–30

Go to page 539 for your next
devotional reading.

when they had a grievance against
    me,
¹⁴what will I do when God confronts
    me?
    What will I answer when called to
      account?
¹⁵Did not he who made me in the
    womb make them?
    Did not the same one form us both
      within our mothers?

¹⁶"If I have denied the desires of the
    poor
    or let the eyes of the widow grow
      weary,
¹⁷if I have kept my bread to myself,
    not sharing it with the fatherless—
¹⁸but from my youth I reared him as
    would a father,
    and from my birth I guided the
      widow—
¹⁹if I have seen anyone perishing for
    lack of clothing,
    or a needy man without a garment,
²⁰and his heart did not bless me
    for warming him with the fleece
      from my sheep,
²¹if I have raised my hand against the
    fatherless,
    knowing that I had influence in
      court,
²²then let my arm fall from the
    shoulder,
    let it be broken off at the joint.
²³For I dreaded destruction from God,
    and for fear of his splendor I could
      not do such things.

²⁴"If I have put my trust in gold
    or said to pure gold, 'You are my
      security,'
²⁵if I have rejoiced over my great
    wealth,
    the fortune my hands had gained,
²⁶if I have regarded the sun in its
    radiance
    or the moon moving in splendor,
²⁷so that my heart was secretly enticed
    and my hand offered them a kiss of
      homage,
²⁸then these also would be sins to be
    judged,
    for I would have been unfaithful to
      God on high.

²⁹"If I have rejoiced at my enemy's
    misfortune

or gloated over the trouble that
    came to him—
³⁰I have not allowed my mouth to sin
    by invoking a curse against his
      life—
³¹if the men of my household have
    never said,
    'Who has not had his fill of Job's
      meat?'—
³²but no stranger had to spend the night
    in the street,
    for my door was always open to the
      traveler—
³³if I have concealed my sin as men
    do,ᵃ
    by hiding my guilt in my heart
³⁴because I so feared the crowd
    and so dreaded the contempt of the
      clans
    that I kept silent and would not go
      outside

³⁵("Oh, that I had someone to hear me!
    I sign now my defense—let the
      Almighty answer me;
    let my accuser put his indictment in
      writing.
³⁶Surely I would wear it on my
    shoulder,
    I would put it on like a crown.
³⁷I would give him an account of my
    every step;
    like a prince I would approach
      him.)—

³⁸"if my land cries out against me
    and all its furrows are wet with
      tears,
³⁹if I have devoured its yield without
    payment
    or broken the spirit of its tenants,
⁴⁰then let briers come up instead of
    wheat
    and weeds instead of barley."

    The words of Job are ended.

Elihu

32 So these three men stopped answering Job, because he was righteous in his own eyes. ²But Elihu son of Barakel the Buzite, of the family of Ram, became very angry with Job for justifying himself rather than God. ³He was also angry with the three friends, because they had found no way to refute Job, and yet had condemned him.ᵇ ⁴Now Elihu had waited before speaking to Job because

ᵃ33 Or *as Adam did*   ᵇ3 Masoretic Text; an ancient Hebrew scribal tradition *Job, and so had condemned God* they were older than he. **5**But when he saw that the three men had nothing more to say, his anger was aroused.

6So Elihu son of Barakel the Buzite said:

"I am young in years,
and you are old;
that is why I was fearful,
not daring to tell you what I know.
7I thought, 'Age should speak;
advanced years should teach
wisdom.'
8But it is the spirit*a* in a man,
the breath of the Almighty, that
gives him understanding.
9It is not only the old*b* who are wise,
not only the aged who understand
what is right.

10"Therefore I say: Listen to me;
I too will tell you what I know.
11I waited while you spoke,
I listened to your reasoning;
while you were searching for words,
12   I gave you my full attention.
But not one of you has proved Job
wrong;
none of you has answered his
arguments.
13Do not say, 'We have found wisdom;
let God refute him, not man.'
14But Job has not marshaled his words
against me,
and I will not answer him with your
arguments.

15"They are dismayed and have no more
to say;
words have failed them.
16Must I wait, now that they are silent,
now that they stand there with no
reply?
17I too will have my say;
I too will tell what I know.
18For I am full of words,
and the spirit within me compels
me;
19inside I am like bottled-up wine,
like new wineskins ready to burst.
20I must speak and find relief;
I must open my lips and reply.
21I will show partiality to no one,
nor will I flatter any man;
22for if I were skilled in flattery,
my Maker would soon take me
away.

33 "But now, Job, listen to my
words;

pay attention to everything I say.
2I am about to open my mouth;
my words are on the tip of my
tongue.
3My words come from an upright
heart;
my lips sincerely speak what I
know.
4The Spirit of God has made me;
the breath of the Almighty gives me
life.
5Answer me then, if you can;
prepare yourself and confront me.
6I am just like you before God;
I too have been taken from clay.
7No fear of me should alarm you,
nor should my hand be heavy upon
you.

8"But you have said in my hearing—
I heard the very words—
9'I am pure and without sin;
I am clean and free from guilt.
10Yet God has found fault with me;
he considers me his enemy.
11He fastens my feet in shackles;
he keeps close watch on all my
paths.'

12"But I tell you, in this you are not
right,
for God is greater than man.
13Why do you complain to him
that he answers none of man's
words*c*?
14For God does speak—now one way,
now another—
though man may not perceive it.
15In a dream, in a vision of the night,
when deep sleep falls on men
as they slumber in their beds,
16he may speak in their ears
and terrify them with warnings,
17to turn man from wrongdoing
and keep him from pride,
18to preserve his soul from the pit,*d*
his life from perishing by the
sword.*e*
19Or a man may be chastened on a bed
of pain
with constant distress in his bones,
20so that his very being finds food
repulsive
and his soul loathes the choicest
meal.
21His flesh wastes away to nothing,
and his bones, once hidden, now
stick out.

*a*8 Or *Spirit*; also in verse 18   *b*9 Or *many*; or *great*   *c*13 Or *that he does not answer for any of his*
actions   *d*18 Or *preserve him from the grave*   *e*18 Or *from crossing the River*

22His soul draws near to the pit,[a]
  and his life to the messengers of
    death.[b]

23"Yet if there is an angel on his side
    as a mediator, one out of a
      thousand,
  to tell a man what is right for him,
24to be gracious to him and say,
    'Spare him from going down to the
      pit[c];
  I have found a ransom for him'—
25then his flesh is renewed like a
      child's;
  it is restored as in the days of his
    youth.
26He prays to God and finds favor with
    him,
  he sees God's face and shouts for
    joy;
  he is restored by God to his
    righteous state.
27Then he comes to men and says,
    'I sinned, and perverted what was
      right,
  but I did not get what I deserved.
28He redeemed my soul from going
    down to the pit,[d]
  and I will live to enjoy the light.'

29"God does all these things to a man—
    twice, even three times—
30to turn back his soul from the pit,[e]
  that the light of life may shine on
    him.

31"Pay attention, Job, and listen to me;
  be silent, and I will speak.
32If you have anything to say, answer
    me;
  speak up, for I want you to be
    cleared.
33But if not, then listen to me;
  be silent, and I will teach you
    wisdom."

34 Then Elihu said:

2"Hear my words, you wise men;
  listen to me, you men of learning.
3For the ear tests words
  as the tongue tastes food.
4Let us discern for ourselves what is
    right;
  let us learn together what is good.

5"Job says, 'I am innocent,
  but God denies me justice.

6Although I am right,
  I am considered a liar;
  although I am guiltless,
    his arrow inflicts an incurable
      wound.'
7What man is like Job,
  who drinks scorn like water?
8He keeps company with evildoers;
  he associates with wicked men.
9For he says, 'It profits a man nothing
  when he tries to please God.'

10"So listen to me, you men of
    understanding.
  Far be it from God to do evil,
  from the Almighty to do wrong.
11He repays a man for what he has
    done;
  he brings upon him what his
    conduct deserves.
12It is unthinkable that God would do
    wrong,
  that the Almighty would pervert
    justice.
13Who appointed him over the earth?
  Who put him in charge of the
    whole world?
14If it were his intention
  and he withdrew his spirit[f] and
    breath,
15all mankind would perish together
  and man would return to the dust.

16"If you have understanding, hear this;
  listen to what I say.
17Can he who hates justice govern?
  Will you condemn the just and
    mighty One?
18Is he not the One who says to kings,
    'You are worthless,'
  and to nobles, 'You are wicked,'
19who shows no partiality to princes
  and does not favor the rich over the
    poor,
  for they are all the work of his
    hands?
20They die in an instant, in the middle
    of the night;
  the people are shaken and they pass
    away;
  the mighty are removed without
    human hand.

21"His eyes are on the ways of men;
  he sees their every step.

---

[a]22 Or *He draws near to the grave*   [b]22 Or *to the dead*   [c]24 Or *grave*   [d]28 Or *redeemed me from
going down to the grave*   [e]30 Or *turn him back from the grave*   [f]14 Or *Spirit*

22There is no dark place, no deep shadow,
where evildoers can hide.
23God has no need to examine men further,
that they should come before him for judgment.
24Without inquiry he shatters the mighty
and sets up others in their place.
25Because he takes note of their deeds,
he overthrows them in the night and they are crushed.
26He punishes them for their wickedness
where everyone can see them,
27because they turned from following him
and had no regard for any of his ways.
28They caused the cry of the poor to come before him,
so that he heard the cry of the needy.
29But if he remains silent, who can condemn him?
If he hides his face, who can see him?
Yet he is over man and nation alike,
30   to keep a godless man from ruling,
from laying snares for the people.

31"Suppose a man says to God,
'I am guilty but will offend no more.
32Teach me what I cannot see;
if I have done wrong, I will not do so again.'
33Should God then reward you on your terms,
when you refuse to repent?
You must decide, not I;
so tell me what you know.

34"Men of understanding declare,
wise men who hear me say to me,
35'Job speaks without knowledge;
his words lack insight.'
36Oh, that Job might be tested to the utmost
for answering like a wicked man!
37To his sin he adds rebellion;
scornfully he claps his hands among us
and multiplies his words against God."

35 Then Elihu said:

2"Do you think this is just?
You say, 'I will be cleared by God.a'
3Yet you ask him, 'What profit is it to me,b
and what do I gain by not sinning?'
4"I would like to reply to you
and to your friends with you.
5Look up at the heavens and see;
gaze at the clouds so high above you.
6If you sin, how does that affect him?
If your sins are many, what does that do to him?
7If you are righteous, what do you give to him,
or what does he receive from your hand?
8Your wickedness affects only a man like yourself,
and your righteousness only the sons of men.

9"Men cry out under a load of oppression;
they plead for relief from the arm of the powerful.
10But no one says, 'Where is God my Maker,
who gives songs in the night,
11who teaches more to us than toc the beasts of the earth
and makes us wiser thand the birds of the air?'
12He does not answer when men cry out
because of the arrogance of the wicked.
13Indeed, God does not listen to their empty plea;
the Almighty pays no attention to it.
14How much less, then, will he listen
when you say that you do not see him,
that your case is before him
and you must wait for him,
15and further, that his anger never punishes
and he does not take the least notice of wickedness.e
16So Job opens his mouth with empty talk;
without knowledge he multiplies words."

---

a2 Or My righteousness is more than God's   b3 Or you   c11 Or teaches us by   d11 Or us wise by
e15 Symmachus, Theodotion and Vulgate; the meaning of the Hebrew for this word is uncertain.

36

Elihu continued:

2"Bear with me a little longer and I will
     show you
  that there is more to be said in
     God's behalf.
3I get my knowledge from afar;
  I will ascribe justice to my Maker.
4Be assured that my words are not
     false;
  one perfect in knowledge is with
     you.

5"God is mighty, but does not despise
     men;
  he is mighty, and firm in his
     purpose.
6He does not keep the wicked alive
  but gives the afflicted their rights.
7He does not take his eyes off the
     righteous;
  he enthrones them with kings
  and exalts them forever.
8But if men are bound in chains,
  held fast by cords of affliction,
9he tells them what they have done—
  that they have sinned arrogantly.
10He makes them listen to correction
  and commands them to repent of
     their evil.
11If they obey and serve him,
  they will spend the rest of their
     days in prosperity
  and their years in contentment.
12But if they do not listen,
  they will perish by the sword[a]
  and die without knowledge.

13"The godless in heart harbor
     resentment;
  even when he fetters them, they do
     not cry for help.
14They die in their youth,
  among male prostitutes of the
     shrines.
15But those who suffer he delivers in
     their suffering;
  he speaks to them in their affliction.

16"He is wooing you from the jaws of
     distress
  to a spacious place free from
     restriction,
  to the comfort of your table laden
     with choice food.
17But now you are laden with the
     judgment due the wicked;

  judgment and justice have taken
     hold of you.
18Be careful that no one entices you by
     riches;
  do not let a large bribe turn you
     aside.
19Would your wealth
  or even all your mighty efforts
  sustain you so you would not be in
     distress?
20Do not long for the night,
  to drag people away from their
     homes.[b]
21Beware of turning to evil,
  which you seem to prefer to
     affliction.

22"God is exalted in his power.
  Who is a teacher like him?
23Who has prescribed his ways for him,
  or said to him, 'You have done
     wrong'?
24Remember to extol his work,
  which men have praised in song.
25All mankind has seen it;
  men gaze on it from afar.
26How great is God—beyond our
     understanding!
  The number of his years is past
     finding out.

27"He draws up the drops of water,
  which distill as rain to the
     streams[c];
28the clouds pour down their moisture
  and abundant showers fall on
     mankind.
29Who can understand how he spreads
     out the clouds,
  how he thunders from his pavilion?
30See how he scatters his lightning
     about him,
  bathing the depths of the sea.
31This is the way he governs[d] the
     nations
  and provides food in abundance.
32He fills his hands with lightning
  and commands it to strike its mark.
33His thunder announces the coming
     storm;
  even the cattle make known its
     approach.[e]

37

"At this my heart pounds
and leaps from its place.
2Listen! Listen to the roar of his voice,

---

a12 Or will cross the River   b20 The meaning of the Hebrew for verses 18-20 is uncertain.   c27 Or
distill from the mist as rain   d31 Or nourishes   e33 Or announces his coming— / the One zealous
against evil

to the rumbling that comes from his
mouth.
³He unleashes his lightning beneath
the whole heaven
and sends it to the ends of the
earth.
⁴After that comes the sound of his
roar;
he thunders with his majestic voice.
When his voice resounds,
he holds nothing back.
⁵God's voice thunders in marvelous
ways;
he does great things beyond our
understanding.
⁶He says to the snow, 'Fall on the
earth,'
and to the rain shower, 'Be a
mighty downpour.'
⁷So that all men he has made may
know his work,
he stops every man from his
labor.ᵃ
⁸The animals take cover;
they remain in their dens.
⁹The tempest comes out from its
chamber,
the cold from the driving winds.
¹⁰The breath of God produces ice,
and the broad waters become
frozen.
¹¹He loads the clouds with moisture;
he scatters his lightning through
them.
¹²At his direction they swirl around
over the face of the whole earth
to do whatever he commands them.
¹³He brings the clouds to punish men,
or to water his earthᵇ and show his
love.
¹⁴"Listen to this, Job;
stop and consider God's wonders.
¹⁵Do you know how God controls the
clouds
and makes his lightning flash?
¹⁶Do you know how the clouds hang
poised,
those wonders of him who is
perfect in knowledge?
¹⁷You who swelter in your clothes
when the land lies hushed under
the south wind,
¹⁸can you join him in spreading out the
skies,
hard as a mirror of cast bronze?
¹⁹"Tell us what we should say to him;

we cannot draw up our case
because of our darkness.
²⁰Should he be told that I want to
speak?
Would any man ask to be
swallowed up?
²¹Now no one can look at the sun,
bright as it is in the skies
after the wind has swept them
clean.
²²Out of the north he comes in golden
splendor;
God comes in awesome majesty.
²³The Almighty is beyond our reach and
exalted in power;
in his justice and great
righteousness, he does not
oppress.
²⁴Therefore, men revere him,
for does he not have regard for all
the wise in heart?ᶜ"

The LORD Speaks

38 Then the LORD answered Job out of
the storm. He said:

²"Who is this that darkens my counsel
with words without knowledge?
³Brace yourself like a man;
I will question you,
and you shall answer me.

⁴"Where were you when I laid the
earth's foundation?
Tell me, if you understand.
⁵Who marked off its dimensions?
Surely you know!
Who stretched a measuring line
across it?
⁶On what were its footings set,
or who laid its cornerstone—
⁷while the morning stars sang together
and all the angelsᵈ shouted for joy?

⁸"Who shut up the sea behind doors
when it burst forth from the womb,
⁹when I made the clouds its garment
and wrapped it in thick darkness,
¹⁰when I fixed limits for it
and set its doors and bars in place,
¹¹when I said, 'This far you may come
and no farther;
here is where your proud waves
halt'?

¹²"Have you ever given orders to the
morning,
or shown the dawn its place,

ᵃ7 Or / he fills all men with fear by his power   ᵇ13 Or to favor them   ᶜ24 Or for he does not have
regard for any who think they are wise.   ᵈ7 Hebrew the sons of God

¹³that it might take the earth by the
        edges
    and shake the wicked out of it?
¹⁴The earth takes shape like clay under
        a seal;
    its features stand out like those of a
        garment.
¹⁵The wicked are denied their light,
    and their upraised arm is broken.

¹⁶"Have you journeyed to the springs of
        the sea
    or walked in the recesses of the
        deep?
¹⁷Have the gates of death been shown
        to you?
    Have you seen the gates of the
        shadow of death *a* ?
¹⁸Have you comprehended the vast
        expanses of the earth?
    Tell me, if you know all this.

¹⁹"What is the way to the abode of
        light?
    And where does darkness reside?
²⁰Can you take them to their places?
    Do you know the paths to their
        dwellings?
²¹Surely you know, for you were
        already born!
    You have lived so many years!

²²"Have you entered the storehouses of
        the snow
    or seen the storehouses of the hail,
²³which I reserve for times of trouble,
    for days of war and battle?
²⁴What is the way to the place where
        the lightning is dispersed,
    or the place where the east winds
        are scattered over the earth?
²⁵Who cuts a channel for the torrents of
        rain,
    and a path for the thunderstorm,
²⁶to water a land where no man lives,
    a desert with no one in it,
²⁷to satisfy a desolate wasteland
    and make it sprout with grass?
²⁸Does the rain have a father?
    Who fathers the drops of dew?
²⁹From whose womb comes the ice?
    Who gives birth to the frost from
        the heavens
³⁰when the waters become hard as
        stone,
    when the surface of the deep is
        frozen?

³¹"Can you bind the beautiful *b*
        Pleiades?
    Can you loose the cords of Orion?
³²Can you bring forth the constellations
        in their seasons *c*
    or lead out the Bear *d* with its cubs?
³³Do you know the laws of the heavens?
    Can you set up ₍God's *e* ₎ dominion
        over the earth?

³⁴"Can you raise your voice to the
        clouds
    and cover yourself with a flood of
        water?
³⁵Do you send the lightning bolts on
        their way?
    Do they report to you, 'Here we
        are'?
³⁶Who endowed the heart *f* with
        wisdom
    or gave understanding to the
        mind *f* ?
³⁷Who has the wisdom to count the
        clouds?
    Who can tip over the water jars of
        the heavens
³⁸when the dust becomes hard
    and the clods of earth stick
        together?

³⁹"Do you hunt the prey for the lioness
    and satisfy the hunger of the lions
⁴⁰when they crouch in their dens
    or lie in wait in a thicket?
⁴¹Who provides food for the raven
    when its young cry out to God
    and wander about for lack of food?

39 "Do you know when the
        mountain goats give birth?
    Do you watch when the doe bears
        her fawn?
²Do you count the months till they
        bear?
    Do you know the time they give
        birth?
³They crouch down and bring forth
        their young;
    their labor pains are ended.
⁴Their young thrive and grow strong in
        the wilds;
    they leave and do not return.

⁵"Who let the wild donkey go free?
    Who untied his ropes?
⁶I gave him the wasteland as his home,
    the salt flats as his habitat.

---

a17 Or *gates of deep shadows*   *b31* Or *the twinkling;* or *the chains of the*   *c32* Or *the morning star*
in its season   *d32* Or *out Leo*   *e33* Or *his;* or *their*   *f36* The meaning of the Hebrew for this word
is uncertain.

⁷He laughs at the commotion in the
town;
　he does not hear a driver's shout.
⁸He ranges the hills for his pasture
　and searches for any green thing.

⁹"Will the wild ox consent to serve
you?
　Will he stay by your manger at
night?
¹⁰Can you hold him to the furrow with
a harness?
　Will he till the valleys behind you?
¹¹Will you rely on him for his great
strength?

Will you leave your heavy work to
him?
¹²Can you trust him to bring in your
grain
　and gather it to your threshing
floor?

¹³"The wings of the ostrich flap joyfully,
　but they cannot compare with the
pinions and feathers of the
stork.
¹⁴She lays her eggs on the ground
　and lets them warm in the sand,
¹⁵unmindful that a foot may crush
them,

TUESDAY

VERSE FOR THE DAY:　　　*AUTHOR:*　　　*PASSAGE FOR THE DAY:*
Job 38:2　　　　　　　John Fischer　　　　　Job 38:1–33

Questions

WE ARE simply not willing to live with questions.

Questions leave us vulnerable, weak, needy. They open up gaping holes in our personality, our theology or our lifestyle. Questions force an honesty that we are unwilling to confront —an honesty that requires us to live with our lives unresolved. We don't like that, especially when we're trying to sell a theology that Christianity is the answer to every problem we face.

This morning I counted 288 question marks in the book of Job. Many were from the mouth of Job; others were spoken by his counselors who turned out to be much like the side-show con artists of today. "Who is this that darkens my counsel with words without knowledge?" God said of them. But surprisingly, when God finally speaks in the closing chapters, his answer to Job comes in the form of more questions—78 of them, to be exact. Of the 288 question marks in the book of Job, 78 of them belong to God; they are his answer to Job.

Sometimes God answers us with questions—questions that leave us humbled, awed, speechless, weak and believing —believing not because we've found the answer, but because we've seen God. It doesn't matter that we have more questions now than when we started. It matters that we see God, for in the seeing, we discover that the truest answer to all our questions is to worship him.

Additional Scripture Readings:　　　*Go to page 548 for your next*
Job 42:1–6; John 14:5–14　　　　　　　*devotional reading.*

that some wild animal may trample
    them.
¹⁶She treats her young harshly, as if
        they were not hers;
    she cares not that her labor was in
        vain,
¹⁷for God did not endow her with
        wisdom
    or give her a share of good sense.
¹⁸Yet when she spreads her feathers to
        run,
    she laughs at horse and rider.

¹⁹"Do you give the horse his strength
    or clothe his neck with a flowing
        mane?
²⁰Do you make him leap like a locust,
    striking terror with his proud
        snorting?
²¹He paws fiercely, rejoicing in his
        strength,
    and charges into the fray.
²²He laughs at fear, afraid of nothing;
    he does not shy away from the
        sword.
²³The quiver rattles against his side,
    along with the flashing spear and
        lance.
²⁴In frenzied excitement he eats up the
        ground;
    he cannot stand still when the
        trumpet sounds.
²⁵At the blast of the trumpet he snorts,
        'Aha!'
    He catches the scent of battle from
        afar,
    the shout of commanders and the
        battle cry.

²⁶"Does the hawk take flight by your
        wisdom
    and spread his wings toward the
        south?
²⁷Does the eagle soar at your command
    and build his nest on high?
²⁸He dwells on a cliff and stays there at
        night;
    a rocky crag is his stronghold.
²⁹From there he seeks out his food;
    his eyes detect it from afar.
³⁰His young ones feast on blood,
    and where the slain are, there is
        he."

40 The LORD said to Job:

²"Will the one who contends with the
    Almighty correct him?

Let him who accuses God answer
    him!"

³Then Job answered the LORD:

⁴"I am unworthy—how can I reply to
        you?
    I put my hand over my mouth.
⁵I spoke once, but I have no answer—
    twice, but I will say no more."

⁶Then the LORD spoke to Job out of the
storm:

⁷"Brace yourself like a man;
    I will question you,
    and you shall answer me.

⁸"Would you discredit my justice?
    Would you condemn me to justify
        yourself?
⁹Do you have an arm like God's,
    and can your voice thunder like his?
¹⁰Then adorn yourself with glory and
        splendor,
    and clothe yourself in honor and
        majesty.
¹¹Unleash the fury of your wrath,
    look at every proud man and bring
        him low,
¹²look at every proud man and humble
        him,
    crush the wicked where they stand.
¹³Bury them all in the dust together;
    shroud their faces in the grave.
¹⁴Then I myself will admit to you
    that your own right hand can save
        you.

¹⁵"Look at the behemoth,ᵃ
    which I made along with you
    and which feeds on grass like an
        ox.
¹⁶What strength he has in his loins,
    what power in the muscles of his
        belly!
¹⁷His tailᵇ sways like a cedar;
    the sinews of his thighs are
        close-knit.
¹⁸His bones are tubes of bronze,
    his limbs like rods of iron.
¹⁹He ranks first among the works of
        God,
    yet his Maker can approach him
        with his sword.
²⁰The hills bring him their produce,
    and all the wild animals play
        nearby.
²¹Under the lotus plants he lies,
    hidden among the reeds in the
        marsh.

ᵃ15 Possibly the hippopotamus or the elephant   ᵇ17 Possibly trunk

²²The lotuses conceal him in their
    shadow;
  the poplars by the stream surround
    him.
²³When the river rages, he is not
    alarmed;
  he is secure, though the Jordan
    should surge against his mouth.
²⁴Can anyone capture him by the
    eyes,*a*
  or trap him and pierce his nose?

41
"Can you pull in the leviathan*b*
  with a fishhook
or tie down his tongue with a rope?
²Can you put a cord through his nose
  or pierce his jaw with a hook?
³Will he keep begging you for mercy?
  Will he speak to you with gentle
    words?
⁴Will he make an agreement with you
  for you to take him as your slave
    for life?
⁵Can you make a pet of him like a bird
  or put him on a leash for your girls?
⁶Will traders barter for him?
  Will they divide him up among the
    merchants?
⁷Can you fill his hide with harpoons
  or his head with fishing spears?
⁸If you lay a hand on him,
  you will remember the struggle and
    never do it again!
⁹Any hope of subduing him is false;
  the mere sight of him is
    overpowering.
¹⁰No one is fierce enough to rouse him.
  Who then is able to stand against
    me?
¹¹Who has a claim against me that I
    must pay?
  Everything under heaven belongs to
    me.

¹²"I will not fail to speak of his limbs,
  his strength and his graceful form.
¹³Who can strip off his outer coat?
  Who would approach him with a
    bridle?
¹⁴Who dares open the doors of his
    mouth,
  ringed about with his fearsome
    teeth?
¹⁵His back has*c* rows of shields
  tightly sealed together;
¹⁶each is so close to the next
  that no air can pass between.
¹⁷They are joined fast to one another;

they cling together and cannot be
    parted.
¹⁸His snorting throws out flashes of
    light;
  his eyes are like the rays of dawn.
¹⁹Firebrands stream from his mouth;
  sparks of fire shoot out.
²⁰Smoke pours from his nostrils
  as from a boiling pot over a fire of
    reeds.
²¹His breath sets coals ablaze,
  and flames dart from his mouth.
²²Strength resides in his neck;
  dismay goes before him.
²³The folds of his flesh are tightly
    joined;
  they are firm and immovable.
²⁴His chest is hard as rock,
  hard as a lower millstone.
²⁵When he rises up, the mighty are
    terrified;
  they retreat before his thrashing.
²⁶The sword that reaches him has no
    effect,
  nor does the spear or the dart or
    the javelin.
²⁷Iron he treats like straw
  and bronze like rotten wood.
²⁸Arrows do not make him flee;
  slingstones are like chaff to him.
²⁹A club seems to him but a piece of
    straw;
  he laughs at the rattling of the
    lance.
³⁰His undersides are jagged potsherds,
  leaving a trail in the mud like a
    threshing sledge.
³¹He makes the depths churn like a
    boiling caldron
  and stirs up the sea like a pot of
    ointment.
³²Behind him he leaves a glistening
    wake;
  one would think the deep had white
    hair.
³³Nothing on earth is his equal—
  a creature without fear.
³⁴He looks down on all that are
    haughty;
  he is king over all that are proud."

Job

42
Then Job replied to the LORD:

²"I know that you can do all things;
  no plan of yours can be thwarted.

---

a24 Or *by a water hole*   *b1* Possibly *the crocodile*   *c15* Or *His pride is his*

3 You asked, 'Who is this that obscures
　　my counsel without
　　knowledge?'
　Surely I spoke of things I did not
　　understand,
　things too wonderful for me to
　　know.
4 "You said, 'Listen now, and I will
　　speak;
　I will question you,
　　and you shall answer me.'
5 My ears had heard of you
　　but now my eyes have seen you.
6 Therefore I despise myself
　　and repent in dust and ashes."

Epilogue

7 After the LORD had said these things to
Job, he said to Eliphaz the Temanite, "I
am angry with you and your two friends,
because you have not spoken of me what
is right, as my servant Job has. **8** So now
take seven bulls and seven rams and go to
my servant Job and sacrifice a burnt offering for yourselves. My servant Job will
pray for you, and I will accept his prayer
and not deal with you according to your
folly. You have not spoken of me what is
right, as my servant Job has." **9** So Eliphaz
the Temanite, Bildad the Shuhite and Zophar the Naamathite did what the LORD
told them; and the LORD accepted Job's
prayer.

10 After Job had prayed for his friends,
the LORD made him prosperous again and
gave him twice as much as he had before.
11 All his brothers and sisters and everyone
who had known him before came and ate
with him in his house. They comforted
and consoled him over all the trouble the
LORD had brought upon him, and each one
gave him a piece of silver[a] and a gold
ring.

12 The LORD blessed the latter part of
Job's life more than the first. He had fourteen thousand sheep, six thousand camels, a thousand yoke of oxen and a thousand donkeys. **13** And he also had seven
sons and three daughters. **14** The first
daughter he named Jemimah, the second
Keziah and the third Keren-Happuch.
15 Nowhere in all the land were there
found women as beautiful as Job's daughters, and their father granted them an inheritance along with their brothers.

16 After this, Job lived a hundred and
forty years; he saw his children and their
children to the fourth generation. **17** And
so he died, old and full of years.

---

a 11 Hebrew *him a kesitah*; a kesitah was a unit of money of unknown weight and value.

*D*AVID, *the shepherd boy and Israel's greatest king, writes most of the psalms. Together these 150 songs form the greatest collection of prayers ever written. A wide range of human emotion is expressed—joy, excitement, compassion, love, anger, grief, depression. As you read this book, remember that no matter what you are feeling, God wants to hear about it in your prayers to him. He promises to listen to all your concerns and to answer them for Jesus' sake.*

PSALMS

BOOK I
Psalms 1–41

Psalm 1

¹Blessed is the man
   who does not walk in the counsel of
      the wicked
 or stand in the way of sinners
   or sit in the seat of mockers.
²But his delight is in the law of the
      LORD,
   and on his law he meditates day
      and night.
³He is like a tree planted by streams of
      water,

which yields its fruit in season
 and whose leaf does not wither.
   Whatever he does prospers.

⁴Not so the wicked!
   They are like chaff
      that the wind blows away.
⁵Therefore the wicked will not stand in
      the judgment,
   nor sinners in the assembly of the
      righteous.

⁶For the LORD watches over the way of
      the righteous,
   but the way of the wicked will
      perish.

Psalm 2

[1]Why do the nations conspire[a]
and the peoples plot in vain?
[2]The kings of the earth take their stand
and the rulers gather together
against the LORD
and against his Anointed One.[b]
[3]"Let us break their chains," they say,
"and throw off their fetters."

[4]The One enthroned in heaven laughs;
the Lord scoffs at them.
[5]Then he rebukes them in his anger
and terrifies them in his wrath,
saying,
[6]"I have installed my King[c]
on Zion, my holy hill."

[7]I will proclaim the decree of the LORD:

He said to me, "You are my Son[d];
today I have become your Father.[e]
[8]Ask of me,
and I will make the nations your
inheritance,
the ends of the earth your
possession.
[9]You will rule them with an iron
scepter[f];
you will dash them to pieces like
pottery."

[10]Therefore, you kings, be wise;
be warned, you rulers of the earth.
[11]Serve the LORD with fear
and rejoice with trembling.
[12]Kiss the Son, lest he be angry
and you be destroyed in your way,
for his wrath can flare up in a
moment.
Blessed are all who take refuge in
him.

Psalm 3

A psalm of David. When he fled from
his son Absalom.

[1]O LORD, how many are my foes!
How many rise up against me!
[2]Many are saying of me,
"God will not deliver him."   *Selah*[g]

[3]But you are a shield around me,
O LORD;

you bestow glory on me and lift[h]
up my head.
[4]To the LORD I cry aloud,
and he answers me from his holy
hill.   *Selah*

[5]I lie down and sleep;
I wake again, because the LORD
sustains me.
[6]I will not fear the tens of thousands
drawn up against me on every side.

[7]Arise, O LORD!
Deliver me, O my God!
Strike all my enemies on the jaw;
break the teeth of the wicked.

[8]From the LORD comes deliverance.
May your blessing be on your
people.   *Selah*

Psalm 4

For the director of music. With stringed
instruments. A psalm of David.

[1]Answer me when I call to you,
O my righteous God.
Give me relief from my distress;
be merciful to me and hear my
prayer.

[2]How long, O men, will you turn my
glory into shame[i]?
How long will you love delusions
and seek false gods[j] ?   *Selah*
[3]Know that the LORD has set apart the
godly for himself;
the LORD will hear when I call to
him.

[4]In your anger do not sin;
when you are on your beds,
search your hearts and be silent.   *Selah*

[5]Offer right sacrifices
and trust in the LORD.

[6]Many are asking, "Who can show us
any good?"
Let the light of your face shine
upon us, O LORD.
[7]You have filled my heart with greater
joy
than when their grain and new wine
abound.

---

a1 Hebrew; Septuagint *rage*   *b2* Or *anointed one*   *c6* Or *king*   *d7* Or *son*; also in verse 12
e7 Or *have begotten you*   *f9* Or *will break them with a rod of iron*   *g2* A word of uncertain meaning,
occurring frequently in the Psalms; possibly a musical term   *h3* Or LORD, / *my Glorious One, who lifts*
i2 Or *you dishonor my Glorious One*   *j2* Or *seek lies*

8I will lie down and sleep in peace,
    for you alone, O LORD,
    make me dwell in safety.

Psalm 5

For the director of music. For flutes.
A psalm of David.

1Give ear to my words, O LORD,
    consider my sighing.
2Listen to my cry for help,
    my King and my God,
    for to you I pray.
3In the morning, O LORD, you hear my
      voice;
    in the morning I lay my requests
      before you
    and wait in expectation.

4You are not a God who takes pleasure
      in evil;
    with you the wicked cannot dwell.
5The arrogant cannot stand in your
      presence;
    you hate all who do wrong.
6You destroy those who tell lies;
    bloodthirsty and deceitful men
    the LORD abhors.

7But I, by your great mercy,
    will come into your house;
 in reverence will I bow down
    toward your holy temple.
8Lead me, O LORD, in your
      righteousness
    because of my enemies —
    make straight your way before me.

9Not a word from their mouth can be
      trusted;
    their heart is filled with destruction.
Their throat is an open grave;
    with their tongue they speak deceit.
10Declare them guilty, O God!
    Let their intrigues be their downfall.
Banish them for their many sins,
    for they have rebelled against you.

11But let all who take refuge in you be
      glad;
    let them ever sing for joy.
Spread your protection over them,
    that those who love your name may
      rejoice in you.
12For surely, O LORD, you bless the
      righteous;
    you surround them with your favor
      as with a shield.

Psalm 6

For the director of music. With stringed
instruments. According to *sheminith.* [a]
A psalm of David.

1O LORD, do not rebuke me in your
      anger
    or discipline me in your wrath.
2Be merciful to me, LORD, for I am
      faint;
    O LORD, heal me, for my bones are
      in agony.
3My soul is in anguish.
    How long, O LORD, how long?

4Turn, O LORD, and deliver me;
    save me because of your unfailing
      love.
5No one remembers you when he is
      dead.
    Who praises you from the grave [b]?

6I am worn out from groaning;
    all night long I flood my bed with
      weeping
    and drench my couch with tears.
7My eyes grow weak with sorrow;
    they fail because of all my foes.

8Away from me, all you who do evil,
    for the LORD has heard my weeping.
9The LORD has heard my cry for mercy;
    the LORD accepts my prayer.
10All my enemies will be ashamed and
      dismayed;
    they will turn back in sudden
      disgrace.

Psalm 7

A *shiggaion* [c] of David, which he sang
to the LORD concerning Cush,
a Benjamite.

1O LORD my God, I take refuge in you;
    save and deliver me from all who
      pursue me,
2or they will tear me like a lion
    and rip me to pieces with no one to
      rescue me.

3O LORD my God, if I have done this
    and there is guilt on my hands —
4if I have done evil to him who is at
      peace with me
    or without cause have robbed my
      foe —
5then let my enemy pursue and
      overtake me;

---

[a] Title: Probably a musical term   [b] 5 Hebrew *Sheol*   [c] Title: Probably a literary or musical term

let him trample my life to the
  ground
and make me sleep in the dust.
Selah

⁶Arise, O LORD, in your anger;
  rise up against the rage of my
    enemies.
Awake, my God; decree justice.
⁷Let the assembled peoples gather
  around you.
Rule over them from on high;
⁸ let the LORD judge the peoples.
Judge me, O LORD, according to my
  righteousness,
  according to my integrity, O Most
    High.
⁹O righteous God,
  who searches minds and hearts,
bring to an end the violence of the
  wicked
and make the righteous secure.

¹⁰My shield[a] is God Most High,
  who saves the upright in heart.
¹¹God is a righteous judge,
  a God who expresses his wrath
    every day.
¹²If he does not relent,
  he[b] will sharpen his sword;
he will bend and string his bow.
¹³He has prepared his deadly weapons;
  he makes ready his flaming arrows.

¹⁴He who is pregnant with evil
  and conceives trouble gives birth to
    disillusionment.
¹⁵He who digs a hole and scoops it out
  falls into the pit he has made.
¹⁶The trouble he causes recoils on
  himself;
  his violence comes down on his
    own head.

¹⁷I will give thanks to the LORD because
  of his righteousness
and will sing praise to the name of
  the LORD Most High.

Psalm 8

For the director of music. According to
gittith.[c] A psalm of David.

¹O LORD, our Lord,
  how majestic is your name in all
    the earth!

You have set your glory
  above the heavens.
²From the lips of children and infants
  you have ordained praise[d]
because of your enemies,
  to silence the foe and the avenger.

³When I consider your heavens,
  the work of your fingers,
the moon and the stars,
  which you have set in place,
⁴what is man that you are mindful of
  him,
  the son of man that you care for
    him?
⁵You made him a little lower than the
  heavenly beings[e]
and crowned him with glory and
  honor.

⁶You made him ruler over the works of
  your hands;
  you put everything under his feet:
⁷all flocks and herds,
  and the beasts of the field,
⁸the birds of the air,
  and the fish of the sea,
  all that swim the paths of the seas.

⁹O LORD, our Lord,
  how majestic is your name in all
    the earth!

Psalm 9[f]

For the director of music. To ⸤the tune
of⸥ "The Death of the Son." A psalm
of David.

¹I will praise you, O LORD, with all my
  heart;
  I will tell of all your wonders.
²I will be glad and rejoice in you;
  I will sing praise to your name,
    O Most High.

³My enemies turn back;
  they stumble and perish before you.
⁴For you have upheld my right and my
  cause;
  you have sat on your throne,
    judging righteously.
⁵You have rebuked the nations and
  destroyed the wicked;
  you have blotted out their name for
    ever and ever.

---

[a]10 Or *sovereign*   [b]12 Or *If a man does not repent, / God*   [c]Title: Probably a musical term   [d]2 Or
strength   [e]5 Or *than God*   [f]Psalms 9 and 10 may have been originally a single acrostic poem, the
stanzas of which begin with the successive letters of the Hebrew alphabet. In the Septuagint they
constitute one psalm.

⁶Endless ruin has overtaken the enemy,
  you have uprooted their cities;
  even the memory of them has
    perished.

⁷The LORD reigns forever;
  he has established his throne for
    judgment.
⁸He will judge the world in
    righteousness;
  he will govern the peoples with
    justice.
⁹The LORD is a refuge for the
    oppressed,
  a stronghold in times of trouble.
¹⁰Those who know your name will trust
    in you,
  for you, LORD, have never forsaken
    those who seek you.

¹¹Sing praises to the LORD, enthroned in
    Zion;
  proclaim among the nations what
    he has done.
¹²For he who avenges blood remembers;
  he does not ignore the cry of the
    afflicted.

¹³O LORD, see how my enemies
    persecute me!
  Have mercy and lift me up from the
    gates of death,
¹⁴that I may declare your praises
  in the gates of the Daughter of Zion
  and there rejoice in your salvation.
¹⁵The nations have fallen into the pit
    they have dug;
  their feet are caught in the net they
    have hidden.
¹⁶The LORD is known by his justice;
  the wicked are ensnared by the
    work of their hands.
                    Higgaion.ᵃ Selah
¹⁷The wicked return to the grave,ᵇ
  all the nations that forget God.
¹⁸But the needy will not always be
    forgotten,
  nor the hope of the afflicted ever
    perish.

¹⁹Arise, O LORD, let not man triumph;
  let the nations be judged in your
    presence.
²⁰Strike them with terror, O LORD;
  let the nations know they are but
    men.   *Selah*

Psalm 10ᶜ

¹Why, O LORD, do you stand far off?
  Why do you hide yourself in times
    of trouble?

²In his arrogance the wicked man
    hunts down the weak,
  who are caught in the schemes he
    devises.
³He boasts of the cravings of his heart;
  he blesses the greedy and reviles
    the LORD.
⁴In his pride the wicked does not seek
    him;
  in all his thoughts there is no room
    for God.
⁵His ways are always prosperous;
  he is haughty and your laws are far
    from him;
  he sneers at all his enemies.
⁶He says to himself, "Nothing will
    shake me;
  I'll always be happy and never have
    trouble."
⁷His mouth is full of curses and lies
    and threats;
  trouble and evil are under his
    tongue.
⁸He lies in wait near the villages;
  from ambush he murders the
    innocent,
  watching in secret for his victims.
⁹He lies in wait like a lion in cover;
  he lies in wait to catch the helpless;
  he catches the helpless and drags
    them off in his net.
¹⁰His victims are crushed, they collapse;
  they fall under his strength.
¹¹He says to himself, "God has
    forgotten;
  he covers his face and never sees."

¹²Arise, LORD! Lift up your hand, O God.
  Do not forget the helpless.
¹³Why does the wicked man revile God?
  Why does he say to himself,
  "He won't call me to account"?
¹⁴But you, O God, do see trouble and
    grief;
  you consider it to take it in hand.
  The victim commits himself to you;
  you are the helper of the fatherless.
¹⁵Break the arm of the wicked and evil
    man;
  call him to account for his
    wickedness

ᵃ16 Or *Meditation*; possibly a musical notation   ᵇ17 Hebrew *Sheol*   ᶜPsalms 9 and 10 may have
been originally a single acrostic poem, the stanzas of which begin with the successive letters of the
Hebrew alphabet. In the Septuagint they constitute one psalm.

that would not be found out.

¹⁶The LORD is King for ever and ever;
the nations will perish from his
land.

¹⁷You hear, O LORD, the desire of the
afflicted;

you encourage them, and you listen
to their cry,

¹⁸defending the fatherless and the
oppressed,

in order that man, who is of the
earth, may terrify no more.

WEDNESDAY

VERSE FOR THE DAY: AUTHOR: PASSAGE FOR THE DAY:
Psalm 10:14   Thomas Hale   Psalm 10:12–18

Pure Religion

REJECTED *by his Nepali villagers, nine-year-old Krishna asked
surgeon Thomas Hale to allow him to stay at the mission hospital.*

I thought of the precedent it would set. We would be deluged with orphans the minute the word got out. Up until now
we had been very careful not to get involved taking in unwanted children. Wasn't it enough to have come to this place,
to care for the sick until they recovered, to feed them if they
were hungry, and to pay their bills if they had no money? Did
our Christian duty demand adopting them as well?

"Krishna, you must go home. Now."

He burst into tears.

My decision had been right, but I was wrong. Krishna cried
for a long time. Along with his tears, he poured out his heart
to me—his fears, his loneliness, his longing for a home and for
affection. My mind went back to an evening some weeks earlier when I had haltingly tried to explain the meaning of James
1:27 to our Nepali Bible class: "Religion that God our Father
accepts as pure and faultless is this: to look after orphans and
widows in their distress and to keep oneself from being polluted by the world." That passage, I learned, is [one of only
two places] in the New Testament where the word "orphan" is
used. The verse had not impressed me then; in fact, I had been
unable to figure out why James defined "pure and faultless" in
such odd terms. As I sat there listening to Krishna, however,
the verse began to take on a new meaning for me. It meant
that if I were not ready to care for orphans in their distress,
then there was something very wrong with my religion. Not
being content with my exegesis of this verse, God seemed further to be asking me, "If you are not ready to care for *this* orphan in his distress, who are you ever going to care for?"

That day, Krishna did not return to his village.

Additional Scripture Readings:
Psalm 146; James 1:19–27

*Go to page 556 for your next
devotional reading.*

Psalm 11

For the director of music. Of David.

[1]In the Lord I take refuge.
How then can you say to me:
"Flee like a bird to your mountain.
[2]For look, the wicked bend their bows;
they set their arrows against the strings
to shoot from the shadows
at the upright in heart.
[3]When the foundations are being destroyed,
what can the righteous do[a]?"

[4]The Lord is in his holy temple;
the Lord is on his heavenly throne.
He observes the sons of men;
his eyes examine them.
[5]The Lord examines the righteous,
but the wicked[b] and those who love violence
his soul hates.
[6]On the wicked he will rain
fiery coals and burning sulfur;
a scorching wind will be their lot.

[7]For the Lord is righteous,
he loves justice;
upright men will see his face.

Psalm 12

For the director of music. According to
sheminith.[c] A psalm of David.

[1]Help, Lord, for the godly are no more;
the faithful have vanished from among men.
[2]Everyone lies to his neighbor;
their flattering lips speak with deception.

[3]May the Lord cut off all flattering lips
and every boastful tongue
[4]that says, "We will triumph with our tongues;
we own our lips[d]—who is our master?"

[5]"Because of the oppression of the weak
and the groaning of the needy,
I will now arise," says the Lord.
"I will protect them from those who malign them."
[6]And the words of the Lord are flawless,

like silver refined in a furnace of clay,
purified seven times.

[7]O Lord, you will keep us safe
and protect us from such people forever.
[8]The wicked freely strut about
when what is vile is honored among men.

Psalm 13

For the director of music. A psalm
of David.

[1]How long, O Lord? Will you forget me forever?
How long will you hide your face from me?
[2]How long must I wrestle with my thoughts
and every day have sorrow in my heart?
How long will my enemy triumph over me?

[3]Look on me and answer, O Lord my God.
Give light to my eyes, or I will sleep in death;
[4]my enemy will say, "I have overcome him,"
and my foes will rejoice when I fall.

[5]But I trust in your unfailing love;
my heart rejoices in your salvation.
[6]I will sing to the Lord,
for he has been good to me.

Psalm 14

For the director of music. Of David.

[1]The fool[e] says in his heart,
"There is no God."
They are corrupt, their deeds are vile;
there is no one who does good.

[2]The Lord looks down from heaven
on the sons of men
to see if there are any who understand,
any who seek God.
[3]All have turned aside,
they have together become corrupt;
there is no one who does good,
not even one.

---

[a]3 Or what is the Righteous One doing   [b]5 Or The Lord, the Righteous One, examines the wicked, /
[c]Title: Probably a musical term   [d]4 Or / our lips are our plowshares   [e]1 The Hebrew words
rendered fool in Psalms denote one who is morally deficient.

⁴Will evildoers never learn—
  those who devour my people as
    men eat bread
  and who do not call on the Lᴏʀᴅ?
⁵There they are, overwhelmed with
    dread,
  for God is present in the company
    of the righteous.
⁶You evildoers frustrate the plans of
    the poor,
  but the Lᴏʀᴅ is their refuge.

⁷Oh, that salvation for Israel would
    come out of Zion!
  When the Lᴏʀᴅ restores the fortunes
    of his people,
  let Jacob rejoice and Israel be glad!

Psalm 15

A psalm of David.

¹Lᴏʀᴅ, who may dwell in your
    sanctuary?
  Who may live on your holy hill?

²He whose walk is blameless
  and who does what is righteous,
who speaks the truth from his heart
³ and has no slander on his tongue,
who does his neighbor no wrong
  and casts no slur on his fellowman,
⁴who despises a vile man
  but honors those who fear the Lᴏʀᴅ,
who keeps his oath
  even when it hurts,
⁵who lends his money without usury
  and does not accept a bribe against
    the innocent.

He who does these things
  will never be shaken.

Psalm 16

A *miktam*ᵃ of David.

¹Keep me safe, O God,
  for in you I take refuge.

²I said to the Lᴏʀᴅ, "You are my Lord;
  apart from you I have no good
    thing."
³As for the saints who are in the land,
  they are the glorious ones in whom
    is all my delight.ᵇ
⁴The sorrows of those will increase
  who run after other gods.

I will not pour out their libations of
    blood
  or take up their names on my lips.

⁵Lᴏʀᴅ, you have assigned me my
    portion and my cup;
  you have made my lot secure.
⁶The boundary lines have fallen for me
    in pleasant places;
  surely I have a delightful
    inheritance.

⁷I will praise the Lᴏʀᴅ, who counsels
    me;
  even at night my heart instructs me.
⁸I have set the Lᴏʀᴅ always before me.
  Because he is at my right hand,
  I will not be shaken.

⁹Therefore my heart is glad and my
    tongue rejoices;
  my body also will rest secure,
¹⁰because you will not abandon me to
    the grave,ᶜ
  nor will you let your Holy Oneᵈ
    see decay.
¹¹You have madeᵉ known to me the
    path of life;
  you will fill me with joy in your
    presence,
  with eternal pleasures at your right
    hand.

Psalm 17

A prayer of David.

¹Hear, O Lᴏʀᴅ, my righteous plea;
  listen to my cry.
Give ear to my prayer—
  it does not rise from deceitful lips.
²May my vindication come from you;
  may your eyes see what is right.

³Though you probe my heart and
    examine me at night,
  though you test me, you will find
    nothing;
  I have resolved that my mouth will
    not sin.
⁴As for the deeds of men—
  by the word of your lips
I have kept myself
  from the ways of the violent.
⁵My steps have held to your paths;
  my feet have not slipped.

⁶I call on you, O God, for you will
    answer me;

ᵃTitle: Probably a literary or musical term   ᵇ3 Or *As for the pagan priests who are in the land / and the nobles in whom all delight, I said:*   ᶜ10 Hebrew *Sheol*   ᵈ10 Or *your faithful one*   ᵉ11 Or *You will make*

give ear to me and hear my prayer.
⁷Show the wonder of your great love,
  you who save by your right hand
  those who take refuge in you from
    their foes.
⁸Keep me as the apple of your eye;
  hide me in the shadow of your
    wings
⁹from the wicked who assail me,
  from my mortal enemies who
    surround me.

¹⁰They close up their callous hearts,
  and their mouths speak with
    arrogance.
¹¹They have tracked me down, they
    now surround me,
  with eyes alert, to throw me to the
    ground.
¹²They are like a lion hungry for prey,
  like a great lion crouching in cover.

¹³Rise up, O Lord, confront them, bring
    them down;
  rescue me from the wicked by your
    sword.
¹⁴O Lord, by your hand save me from
    such men,
  from men of this world whose
    reward is in this life.

You still the hunger of those you
    cherish;
  their sons have plenty,
  and they store up wealth for their
    children.
¹⁵And I—in righteousness I will see
    your face;
  when I awake, I will be satisfied
    with seeing your likeness.

Psalm 18

For the director of music. Of David the
servant of the Lord. He sang to the
Lord the words of this song when
the Lord delivered him from the hand
of all his enemies and from the
hand of Saul. He said:

¹I love you, O Lord, my strength.

²The Lord is my rock, my fortress and
    my deliverer;
  my God is my rock, in whom I take
    refuge.
  He is my shield and the horn*a* of
    my salvation, my stronghold.
³I call to the Lord, who is worthy of
    praise,

and I am saved from my enemies.

⁴The cords of death entangled me;
  the torrents of destruction
    overwhelmed me.
⁵The cords of the grave*b* coiled around
    me;
  the snares of death confronted me.
⁶In my distress I called to the Lord;
  I cried to my God for help.
  From his temple he heard my voice;
  my cry came before him, into his
    ears.

⁷The earth trembled and quaked,
  and the foundations of the
    mountains shook;
  they trembled because he was
    angry.
⁸Smoke rose from his nostrils;
  consuming fire came from his
    mouth,
  burning coals blazed out of it.
⁹He parted the heavens and came
    down;
  dark clouds were under his feet.
¹⁰He mounted the cherubim and flew;
  he soared on the wings of the wind.
¹¹He made darkness his covering, his
    canopy around him—
  the dark rain clouds of the sky.
¹²Out of the brightness of his presence
    clouds advanced,
  with hailstones and bolts of
    lightning.
¹³The Lord thundered from heaven;
  the voice of the Most High
    resounded.*c*
¹⁴He shot his arrows and scattered ‚the
    enemies„,
  great bolts of lightning and routed
    them.
¹⁵The valleys of the sea were exposed
  and the foundations of the earth
    laid bare
  at your rebuke, O Lord,
  at the blast of breath from your
    nostrils.

¹⁶He reached down from on high and
    took hold of me;
  he drew me out of deep waters.
¹⁷He rescued me from my powerful
    enemy,
  from my foes, who were too strong
    for me.

---

a2 *Horn* here symbolizes strength.   *b5* Hebrew *Sheol*   *c13* Some Hebrew manuscripts and Septuagint
(see also 2 Samuel 22:14); most Hebrew manuscripts *resounded, / amid hailstones and bolts of lightning*

¹⁸They confronted me in the day of my
    disaster,
  but the Lᴏʀᴅ was my support.
¹⁹He brought me out into a spacious
    place;
  he rescued me because he delighted
    in me.
²⁰The Lᴏʀᴅ has dealt with me according
    to my righteousness;
  according to the cleanness of my
    hands he has rewarded me.
²¹For I have kept the ways of the Lᴏʀᴅ;
  I have not done evil by turning
    from my God.
²²All his laws are before me;
  I have not turned away from his
    decrees.
²³I have been blameless before him
  and have kept myself from sin.
²⁴The Lᴏʀᴅ has rewarded me according
    to my righteousness,
  according to the cleanness of my
    hands in his sight.

²⁵To the faithful you show yourself
    faithful,
  to the blameless you show yourself
    blameless,
²⁶to the pure you show yourself pure,
  but to the crooked you show
    yourself shrewd.
²⁷You save the humble
  but bring low those whose eyes are
    haughty.
²⁸You, O Lᴏʀᴅ, keep my lamp burning;
  my God turns my darkness into
    light.
²⁹With your help I can advance against
    a troop*ᵃ*;
  with my God I can scale a wall.

³⁰As for God, his way is perfect;
  the word of the Lᴏʀᴅ is flawless.
  He is a shield
  for all who take refuge in him.
³¹For who is God besides the Lᴏʀᴅ?
  And who is the Rock except our
    God?
³²It is God who arms me with strength
  and makes my way perfect.
³³He makes my feet like the feet of a
    deer;
  he enables me to stand on the
    heights.
³⁴He trains my hands for battle;
  my arms can bend a bow of bronze.

³⁵You give me your shield of victory,
  and your right hand sustains me;
  you stoop down to make me great.
³⁶You broaden the path beneath me,
  so that my ankles do not turn.

³⁷I pursued my enemies and overtook
    them;
  I did not turn back till they were
    destroyed.
³⁸I crushed them so that they could not
    rise;
  they fell beneath my feet.
³⁹You armed me with strength for
    battle;
  you made my adversaries bow at
    my feet.
⁴⁰You made my enemies turn their
    backs in flight,
  and I destroyed my foes.
⁴¹They cried for help, but there was no
    one to save them—
  to the Lᴏʀᴅ, but he did not answer.
⁴²I beat them as fine as dust borne on
    the wind;
  I poured them out like mud in the
    streets.

⁴³You have delivered me from the
    attacks of the people;
  you have made me the head of
    nations;
  people I did not know are subject to
    me.
⁴⁴As soon as they hear me, they obey
    me;
  foreigners cringe before me.
⁴⁵They all lose heart;
  they come trembling from their
    strongholds.

⁴⁶The Lᴏʀᴅ lives! Praise be to my Rock!
  Exalted be God my Savior!
⁴⁷He is the God who avenges me,
  who subdues nations under me,
⁴⁸   who saves me from my enemies.
  You exalted me above my foes;
  from violent men you rescued me.
⁴⁹Therefore I will praise you among the
    nations, O Lᴏʀᴅ;
  I will sing praises to your name.
⁵⁰He gives his king great victories;
  he shows unfailing kindness to his
    anointed,
  to David and his descendants
    forever.

ᵃ29 Or *can run through a barricade*

Psalm 19

For the director of music. A psalm
of David.

¹The heavens declare the glory of God;
    the skies proclaim the work of his
        hands.
²Day after day they pour forth speech;
    night after night they display
        knowledge.
³There is no speech or language
    where their voice is not heard.ᵃ
⁴Their voiceᵇ goes out into all the
        earth,
    their words to the ends of the
        world.

In the heavens he has pitched a tent
        for the sun,
5   which is like a bridegroom coming
        forth from his pavilion,
    like a champion rejoicing to run his
        course.
⁶It rises at one end of the heavens
    and makes its circuit to the other;
    nothing is hidden from its heat.

⁷The law of the LORD is perfect,
    reviving the soul.
The statutes of the LORD are
        trustworthy,
    making wise the simple.
⁸The precepts of the LORD are right,
    giving joy to the heart.
The commands of the LORD are
        radiant,
    giving light to the eyes.
⁹The fear of the LORD is pure,
    enduring forever.
The ordinances of the LORD are sure
    and altogether righteous.
¹⁰They are more precious than gold,
    than much pure gold;
they are sweeter than honey,
    than honey from the comb.
¹¹By them is your servant warned;
    in keeping them there is great
        reward.

¹²Who can discern his errors?
    Forgive my hidden faults.
¹³Keep your servant also from willful
        sins;
    may they not rule over me.
Then will I be blameless,
    innocent of great transgression.

¹⁴May the words of my mouth and the
        meditation of my heart
be pleasing in your sight,
    O LORD, my Rock and my
        Redeemer.

Psalm 20

For the director of music. A psalm
of David.

¹May the LORD answer you when you
        are in distress;
    may the name of the God of Jacob
        protect you.
²May he send you help from the
        sanctuary
    and grant you support from Zion.
³May he remember all your sacrifices
    and accept your burnt offerings.
                                    Selah
⁴May he give you the desire of your
        heart
    and make all your plans succeed.
⁵We will shout for joy when you are
        victorious
    and will lift up our banners in the
        name of our God.
May the LORD grant all your requests.

⁶Now I know that the LORD saves his
        anointed;
    he answers him from his holy
        heaven
    with the saving power of his right
        hand.
⁷Some trust in chariots and some in
        horses,
    but we trust in the name of the
        LORD our God.
⁸They are brought to their knees and
        fall,
    but we rise up and stand firm.

⁹O LORD, save the king!
    Answerᶜ us when we call!

Psalm 21

For the director of music. A psalm
of David.

¹O LORD, the king rejoices in your
        strength.
    How great is his joy in the victories
        you give!
²You have granted him the desire of
        his heart

ᵃ3 Or *They have no speech, there are no words; / no sound is heard from them*   ᵇ4 Septuagint, Jerome
and Syriac; Hebrew *line*   ᶜ9 Or *save! / O King, answer*

and have not withheld the request
of his lips.   *Selah*
³You welcomed him with rich blessings
and placed a crown of pure gold on
his head.
⁴He asked you for life, and you gave it
to him—
length of days, for ever and ever.
⁵Through the victories you gave, his
glory is great;
you have bestowed on him splendor
and majesty.
⁶Surely you have granted him eternal
blessings
and made him glad with the joy of
your presence.
⁷For the king trusts in the Lord;
through the unfailing love of the
Most High
he will not be shaken.

⁸Your hand will lay hold on all your
enemies;
your right hand will seize your foes.
⁹At the time of your appearing
you will make them like a fiery
furnace.
In his wrath the Lord will swallow
them up,
and his fire will consume them.
¹⁰You will destroy their descendants
from the earth,
their posterity from mankind.
¹¹Though they plot evil against you
and devise wicked schemes, they
cannot succeed;
¹²for you will make them turn their
backs
when you aim at them with drawn
bow.

¹³Be exalted, O Lord, in your strength;
we will sing and praise your might.

Psalm 22

For the director of music. To the tune
of, "The Doe of the Morning." A psalm
of David.

¹My God, my God, why have you
forsaken me?
Why are you so far from saving me,
so far from the words of my
groaning?
²O my God, I cry out by day, but you
do not answer,
by night, and am not silent.

³Yet you are enthroned as the Holy
One;
you are the praise of Israel.ᵃ
⁴In you our fathers put their trust;
they trusted and you delivered
them.
⁵They cried to you and were saved;
in you they trusted and were not
disappointed.

⁶But I am a worm and not a man,
scorned by men and despised by
the people.
⁷All who see me mock me;
they hurl insults, shaking their
heads:
⁸"He trusts in the Lord;
let the Lord rescue him.
Let him deliver him,
since he delights in him."

⁹Yet you brought me out of the womb;
you made me trust in you
even at my mother's breast.
¹⁰From birth I was cast upon you;
from my mother's womb you have
been my God.
¹¹Do not be far from me,
for trouble is near
and there is no one to help.

¹²Many bulls surround me;
strong bulls of Bashan encircle me.
¹³Roaring lions tearing their prey
open their mouths wide against me.
¹⁴I am poured out like water,
and all my bones are out of joint.
My heart has turned to wax;
it has melted away within me.
¹⁵My strength is dried up like a
potsherd,
and my tongue sticks to the roof of
my mouth;
you lay meᵇ in the dust of death.
¹⁶Dogs have surrounded me;
a band of evil men has encircled
me,
they have piercedᶜ my hands and
my feet.
¹⁷I can count all my bones;
people stare and gloat over me.
¹⁸They divide my garments among them
and cast lots for my clothing.

¹⁹But you, O Lord, be not far off;
O my Strength, come quickly to
help me.
²⁰Deliver my life from the sword,

ᵃ3 Or *Yet you are holy, / enthroned on the praises of Israel*   ᵇ15 Or *I am laid*   ᶜ16 Some Hebrew
manuscripts, Septuagint and Syriac; most Hebrew manuscripts / *like the lion,*

my precious life from the power of
the dogs.
²¹Rescue me from the mouth of the
lions;
save[a] me from the horns of the
wild oxen.

²²I will declare your name to my
brothers;
in the congregation I will praise
you.
²³You who fear the Lord, praise him!
All you descendants of Jacob, honor
him!
Revere him, all you descendants of
Israel!
²⁴For he has not despised or disdained
the suffering of the afflicted one;
he has not hidden his face from him
but has listened to his cry for help.

²⁵From you comes the theme of my
praise in the great assembly;
before those who fear you[b] will I
fulfill my vows.
²⁶The poor will eat and be satisfied;
they who seek the Lord will praise
him—
may your hearts live forever!
²⁷All the ends of the earth
will remember and turn to the Lord,
and all the families of the nations
will bow down before him,
²⁸for dominion belongs to the Lord
and he rules over the nations.

²⁹All the rich of the earth will feast and
worship;
all who go down to the dust will
kneel before him—
those who cannot keep themselves
alive.
³⁰Posterity will serve him;
future generations will be told about
the Lord.
³¹They will proclaim his righteousness
to a people yet unborn—
for he has done it.

Psalm 23

A psalm of David.

¹The Lord is my shepherd, I shall not
be in want.
² He makes me lie down in green
pastures,
he leads me beside quiet waters,
³ he restores my soul.

He guides me in paths of
righteousness
for his name's sake.
⁴Even though I walk
through the valley of the shadow of
death,[c]
I will fear no evil,
for you are with me;
your rod and your staff,
they comfort me.

⁵You prepare a table before me
in the presence of my enemies.
You anoint my head with oil;
my cup overflows.
⁶Surely goodness and love will follow
me
all the days of my life,
and I will dwell in the house of the
Lord
forever.

Psalm 24

Of David. A psalm.

¹The earth is the Lord's, and
everything in it,
the world, and all who live in it;
²for he founded it upon the seas
and established it upon the waters.

³Who may ascend the hill of the Lord?
Who may stand in his holy place?
⁴He who has clean hands and a pure
heart,
who does not lift up his soul to an
idol
or swear by what is false.[d]
⁵He will receive blessing from the Lord
and vindication from God his
Savior.
⁶Such is the generation of those who
seek him,
who seek your face, O God of
Jacob.[e]   Selah

⁷Lift up your heads, O you gates;
be lifted up, you ancient doors,
that the King of glory may come in.
⁸Who is this King of glory?
The Lord strong and mighty,
the Lord mighty in battle.
⁹Lift up your heads, O you gates;
lift them up, you ancient doors,
that the King of glory may come in.
¹⁰Who is he, this King of glory?
The Lord Almighty—
he is the King of glory.   Selah

---

a21 Or / you have heard   b25 Hebrew him   c4 Or through the darkest valley   d4 Or swear falsely
e6 Two Hebrew manuscripts and Syriac (see also Septuagint); most Hebrew manuscripts face, Jacob

Psalm 25[a]

Of David.

[1]To you, O LORD, I lift up my soul;
[2] in you I trust, O my God.
Do not let me be put to shame,
    nor let my enemies triumph over
    me.
[3]No one whose hope is in you
    will ever be put to shame,
but they will be put to shame
    who are treacherous without
    excuse.

[4]Show me your ways, O LORD,
    teach me your paths;
[5]guide me in your truth and teach me,
    for you are God my Savior,
    and my hope is in you all day long.
[6]Remember, O LORD, your great mercy
    and love,
    for they are from of old.
[7]Remember not the sins of my youth
    and my rebellious ways;
according to your love remember me,
    for you are good, O LORD.

[8]Good and upright is the LORD;

[a]This psalm is an acrostic poem, the verses of which begin with the successive letters of the Hebrew alphabet.

THURSDAY

VERSE FOR THE DAY:	AUTHOR:	PASSAGE FOR THE DAY:
Psalm 24:1	Don Wyrtzen	Psalm 24:1–10

No Loose Ends!

THE creative power of God inspires awe. I'm filled with reverent wonder as I contemplate it. To think that he spoke and worlds came into being! In contrast to God, I work with raw materials that he created. My creativity is derived from his. I put the wrapping paper and ribbon on his packages.

Several years ago, Karen and I traveled to Brazil. Along with lecturing and ministering to missionaries, we scheduled some sightseeing. I will never forget the awesome Iguacu Falls. There in the majestic grandeur of cascading water, I saw the omnipotence of the almighty God. I shouted spontaneously, "How great Thou art!"

Because the Lord made the earth and everything in it, he owns it. He founded the earth (Genesis 1) and established it upon the waters. The heathen nations feared the restless, perilous, foaming seas. But even the violent waters belong to God and reflect the variety and depth of his creative imagination.

The Lord didn't create the earth and then abandon it. He is intimately involved with sustaining it. He watches over what belongs to him. My Lord doesn't like loose ends! He not only sustains his creation; he watches over me too and allows me to reflect his creativity!

I praise you, Lord, for your incredible imagination and creativity. I thank you that I can, in a very small way, imitate it.

Additional Scripture Readings:
Job 36:22–33; Psalm 104:1–30

Go to page 564 for your next devotional reading.

therefore he instructs sinners in his
   ways.
9He guides the humble in what is right
   and teaches them his way.
10All the ways of the LORD are loving
   and faithful
   for those who keep the demands of
      his covenant.
11For the sake of your name, O LORD,
   forgive my iniquity, though it is
      great.
12Who, then, is the man that fears the
      LORD?
   He will instruct him in the way
      chosen for him.
13He will spend his days in prosperity,
   and his descendants will inherit the
      land.
14The LORD confides in those who fear
      him;
   he makes his covenant known to
      them.
15My eyes are ever on the LORD,
   for only he will release my feet
      from the snare.

16Turn to me and be gracious to me,
   for I am lonely and afflicted.
17The troubles of my heart have
      multiplied;
   free me from my anguish.
18Look upon my affliction and my
      distress
   and take away all my sins.
19See how my enemies have increased
   and how fiercely they hate me!
20Guard my life and rescue me;
   let me not be put to shame,
   for I take refuge in you.
21May integrity and uprightness protect
      me,
   because my hope is in you.

22Redeem Israel, O God,
   from all their troubles!

Psalm 26

Of David.

1Vindicate me, O LORD,
   for I have led a blameless life;
   I have trusted in the LORD
      without wavering.
2Test me, O LORD, and try me,
   examine my heart and my mind;
3for your love is ever before me,
   and I walk continually in your truth.
4I do not sit with deceitful men,

nor do I consort with hypocrites;
5I abhor the assembly of evildoers
   and refuse to sit with the wicked.
6I wash my hands in innocence,
   and go about your altar, O LORD,
7proclaiming aloud your praise
   and telling of all your wonderful
      deeds.
8I love the house where you live,
      O LORD,
   the place where your glory dwells.

9Do not take away my soul along with
      sinners,
   my life with bloodthirsty men,
10in whose hands are wicked schemes,
   whose right hands are full of bribes.
11But I lead a blameless life;
   redeem me and be merciful to me.

12My feet stand on level ground;
   in the great assembly I will praise
      the LORD.

Psalm 27

Of David.

1The LORD is my light and my
      salvation—
   whom shall I fear?
The LORD is the stronghold of my
      life—
   of whom shall I be afraid?
2When evil men advance against me
   to devour my flesh,a
when my enemies and my foes attack
      me,
   they will stumble and fall.
3Though an army besiege me,
   my heart will not fear;
though war break out against me,
   even then will I be confident.

4One thing I ask of the LORD,
   this is what I seek:
that I may dwell in the house of the
      LORD
   all the days of my life,
to gaze upon the beauty of the LORD
   and to seek him in his temple.
5For in the day of trouble
   he will keep me safe in his
      dwelling;
he will hide me in the shelter of his
      tabernacle
   and set me high upon a rock.
6Then my head will be exalted

a2 Or to slander me

above the enemies who surround
  me;
at his tabernacle will I sacrifice with
  shouts of joy;
I will sing and make music to the
  LORD.
[7]Hear my voice when I call, O LORD;
  be merciful to me and answer me.
[8]My heart says of you, "Seek his[a]
  face!"
  Your face, LORD, I will seek.
[9]Do not hide your face from me,
  do not turn your servant away in
    anger;
  you have been my helper.
Do not reject me or forsake me,
  O God my Savior.
[10]Though my father and mother forsake
  me,
  the LORD will receive me.
[11]Teach me your way, O LORD;
  lead me in a straight path
  because of my oppressors.
[12]Do not turn me over to the desire of
  my foes,
  for false witnesses rise up against
    me,
  breathing out violence.

[13]I am still confident of this:
  I will see the goodness of the LORD
  in the land of the living.
[14]Wait for the LORD;
  be strong and take heart
  and wait for the LORD.

Psalm 28

Of David.

[1]To you I call, O LORD my Rock;
  do not turn a deaf ear to me.
For if you remain silent,
  I will be like those who have gone
    down to the pit.
[2]Hear my cry for mercy
  as I call to you for help,
  as I lift up my hands
  toward your Most Holy Place.

[3]Do not drag me away with the
  wicked,
  with those who do evil,
who speak cordially with their
    neighbors
  but harbor malice in their hearts.
[4]Repay them for their deeds
  and for their evil work;

repay them for what their hands have
  done
  and bring back upon them what
    they deserve.
[5]Since they show no regard for the
  works of the LORD
  and what his hands have done,
he will tear them down
  and never build them up again.

[6]Praise be to the LORD,
  for he has heard my cry for mercy.
[7]The LORD is my strength and my
  shield;
  my heart trusts in him, and I am
    helped.
My heart leaps for joy
  and I will give thanks to him in
    song.

[8]The LORD is the strength of his people,
  a fortress of salvation for his
    anointed one.
[9]Save your people and bless your
  inheritance;
  be their shepherd and carry them
    forever.

Psalm 29

A psalm of David.

[1]Ascribe to the LORD, O mighty ones,
  ascribe to the LORD glory and
    strength.
[2]Ascribe to the LORD the glory due his
  name;
  worship the LORD in the splendor of
    his[b] holiness.

[3]The voice of the LORD is over the
  waters;
  the God of glory thunders,
  the LORD thunders over the mighty
    waters.
[4]The voice of the LORD is powerful;
  the voice of the LORD is majestic.
[5]The voice of the LORD breaks the
  cedars;
  the LORD breaks in pieces the cedars
    of Lebanon.
[6]He makes Lebanon skip like a calf,
  Sirion[c] like a young wild ox.
[7]The voice of the LORD strikes
  with flashes of lightning.
[8]The voice of the LORD shakes the
  desert;
  the LORD shakes the Desert of
    Kadesh.

[a]8 Or To you, O my heart, he has said, "Seek my   [b]2 Or LORD with the splendor of   [c]6 That is,
Mount Hermon

[9]The voice of the LORD twists the
   oaks[a]
and strips the forests bare.
And in his temple all cry, "Glory!"

[10]The LORD sits[b] enthroned over the
   flood;
   the LORD is enthroned as King
   forever.
[11]The LORD gives strength to his people;
   the LORD blesses his people with
   peace.

Psalm 30

A psalm. A song. For the dedication of
the temple.[c] Of David.

[1]I will exalt you, O LORD,
   for you lifted me out of the depths
   and did not let my enemies gloat
   over me.
[2]O LORD my God, I called to you for
   help
   and you healed me.
[3]O LORD, you brought me up from the
   grave[d];
   you spared me from going down
   into the pit.

[4]Sing to the LORD, you saints of his;
   praise his holy name.
[5]For his anger lasts only a moment,
   but his favor lasts a lifetime;
weeping may remain for a night,
   but rejoicing comes in the morning.

[6]When I felt secure, I said,
   "I will never be shaken."
[7]O LORD, when you favored me,
   you made my mountain[e] stand
   firm;
but when you hid your face,
   I was dismayed.

[8]To you, O LORD, I called;
   to the Lord I cried for mercy:
[9]"What gain is there in my
   destruction,[f]
   in my going down into the pit?
Will the dust praise you?
   Will it proclaim your faithfulness?
[10]Hear, O LORD, and be merciful to me;
   O LORD, be my help."

[11]You turned my wailing into dancing;
   you removed my sackcloth and
   clothed me with joy,
[12]that my heart may sing to you and
   not be silent.

O LORD my God, I will give you
   thanks forever.

Psalm 31

For the director of music. A psalm
of David.

[1]In you, O LORD, I have taken refuge;
   let me never be put to shame;
   deliver me in your righteousness.
[2]Turn your ear to me,
   come quickly to my rescue;
be my rock of refuge,
   a strong fortress to save me.
[3]Since you are my rock and my
   fortress,
   for the sake of your name lead and
   guide me.
[4]Free me from the trap that is set for
   me,
   for you are my refuge.
[5]Into your hands I commit my spirit;
   redeem me, O LORD, the God of
   truth.

[6]I hate those who cling to worthless
   idols;
   I trust in the LORD.
[7]I will be glad and rejoice in your love,
   for you saw my affliction
   and knew the anguish of my soul.
[8]You have not handed me over to the
   enemy
   but have set my feet in a spacious
   place.

[9]Be merciful to me, O LORD, for I am in
   distress;
   my eyes grow weak with sorrow,
   my soul and my body with grief.
[10]My life is consumed by anguish
   and my years by groaning;
my strength fails because of my
   affliction,[g]
   and my bones grow weak.
[11]Because of all my enemies,
   I am the utter contempt of my
   neighbors;
I am a dread to my friends—
   those who see me on the street flee
   from me.
[12]I am forgotten by them as though I
   were dead;
   I have become like broken pottery.
[13]For I hear the slander of many;
   there is terror on every side;
they conspire against me

[a]9 Or LORD makes the deer give birth   [b]10 Or sat   [c]Title: Or palace   [d]3 Hebrew Sheol   [e]7 Or
hill country   [f]9 Or there if I am silenced   [g]10 Or guilt

and plot to take my life.
¹⁴But I trust in you, O Lᴏʀᴅ;
   I say, "You are my God."
¹⁵My times are in your hands;
   deliver me from my enemies
   and from those who pursue me.
¹⁶Let your face shine on your servant;
   save me in your unfailing love.
¹⁷Let me not be put to shame, O Lᴏʀᴅ,
   for I have cried out to you;
but let the wicked be put to shame
   and lie silent in the grave.ᵃ
¹⁸Let their lying lips be silenced,
   for with pride and contempt
   they speak arrogantly against the
      righteous.

¹⁹How great is your goodness,
   which you have stored up for those
      who fear you,
which you bestow in the sight of men
   on those who take refuge in you.
²⁰In the shelter of your presence you
      hide them
   from the intrigues of men;
in your dwelling you keep them safe
   from accusing tongues.

²¹Praise be to the Lᴏʀᴅ,
   for he showed his wonderful love to
      me
   when I was in a besieged city.
²²In my alarm I said,
   "I am cut off from your sight!"
Yet you heard my cry for mercy
   when I called to you for help.

²³Love the Lᴏʀᴅ, all his saints!
   The Lᴏʀᴅ preserves the faithful,
   but the proud he pays back in full.
²⁴Be strong and take heart,
   all you who hope in the Lᴏʀᴅ.

Psalm 32

Of David. A maskil.ᵇ

¹Blessed is he
   whose transgressions are forgiven,
   whose sins are covered.
²Blessed is the man
   whose sin the Lᴏʀᴅ does not count
      against him
   and in whose spirit is no deceit.

³When I kept silent,
   my bones wasted away
   through my groaning all day long.

⁴For day and night
   your hand was heavy upon me;
my strength was sapped
   as in the heat of summer.   Selah
⁵Then I acknowledged my sin to you
   and did not cover up my iniquity.
I said, "I will confess
   my transgressions to the Lᴏʀᴅ" —
and you forgave
   the guilt of my sin.   Selah

⁶Therefore let everyone who is godly
      pray to you
   while you may be found;
surely when the mighty waters rise,
   they will not reach him.
⁷You are my hiding place;
   you will protect me from trouble
   and surround me with songs of
      deliverance.   Selah

⁸I will instruct you and teach you in
      the way you should go;
   I will counsel you and watch over
      you.
⁹Do not be like the horse or the mule,
   which have no understanding
but must be controlled by bit and
      bridle
   or they will not come to you.
¹⁰Many are the woes of the wicked,
   but the Lᴏʀᴅ's unfailing love
   surrounds the man who trusts in
      him.

¹¹Rejoice in the Lᴏʀᴅ and be glad, you
      righteous;
   sing, all you who are upright in
      heart!

Psalm 33

¹Sing joyfully to the Lᴏʀᴅ, you
      righteous;
   it is fitting for the upright to praise
      him.
²Praise the Lᴏʀᴅ with the harp;
   make music to him on the
      ten-stringed lyre.
³Sing to him a new song;
   play skillfully, and shout for joy.

⁴For the word of the Lᴏʀᴅ is right and
      true;
   he is faithful in all he does.

ᵃ17 Hebrew Sheol   ᵇTitle: Probably a literary or musical term

⁵The Lord loves righteousness and
      justice;
  the earth is full of his unfailing
      love.
⁶By the word of the Lord were the
      heavens made,
  their starry host by the breath of his
      mouth.
⁷He gathers the waters of the sea into
      jars*a*;
  he puts the deep into storehouses.
⁸Let all the earth fear the Lord;
  let all the people of the world
      revere him.
⁹For he spoke, and it came to be;
  he commanded, and it stood firm.
¹⁰The Lord foils the plans of the
      nations;
  he thwarts the purposes of the
      peoples.
¹¹But the plans of the Lord stand firm
      forever,
  the purposes of his heart through
      all generations.
¹²Blessed is the nation whose God is the
      Lord,
  the people he chose for his
      inheritance.
¹³From heaven the Lord looks down
  and sees all mankind;
¹⁴from his dwelling place he watches
  all who live on earth—
¹⁵he who forms the hearts of all,
  who considers everything they do.
¹⁶No king is saved by the size of his
      army;
  no warrior escapes by his great
      strength.
¹⁷A horse is a vain hope for deliverance;
  despite all its great strength it
      cannot save.
¹⁸But the eyes of the Lord are on those
      who fear him,
  on those whose hope is in his
      unfailing love,
¹⁹to deliver them from death
  and keep them alive in famine.
²⁰We wait in hope for the Lord;
  he is our help and our shield.
²¹In him our hearts rejoice,
  for we trust in his holy name.
²²May your unfailing love rest upon us,
      O Lord,
  even as we put our hope in you.

Psalm 34*b*

Of David. When he pretended to be
insane before Abimelech, who drove him
away, and he left.

¹I will extol the Lord at all times;
  his praise will always be on my lips.
²My soul will boast in the Lord;
  let the afflicted hear and rejoice.
³Glorify the Lord with me;
  let us exalt his name together.

⁴I sought the Lord, and he answered
      me;
  he delivered me from all my fears.
⁵Those who look to him are radiant;
  their faces are never covered with
      shame.
⁶This poor man called, and the Lord
      heard him;
  he saved him out of all his troubles.
⁷The angel of the Lord encamps
      around those who fear him,
  and he delivers them.

⁸Taste and see that the Lord is good;
  blessed is the man who takes refuge
      in him.
⁹Fear the Lord, you his saints,
  for those who fear him lack
      nothing.
¹⁰The lions may grow weak and hungry,
  but those who seek the Lord lack
      no good thing.

¹¹Come, my children, listen to me;
  I will teach you the fear of the
      Lord.
¹²Whoever of you loves life
  and desires to see many good days,
¹³keep your tongue from evil
  and your lips from speaking lies.
¹⁴Turn from evil and do good;
  seek peace and pursue it.

¹⁵The eyes of the Lord are on the
      righteous
  and his ears are attentive to their
      cry;
¹⁶the face of the Lord is against those
      who do evil,
  to cut off the memory of them from
      the earth.

¹⁷The righteous cry out, and the Lord
      hears them;
  he delivers them from all their
      troubles.

a 7 Or *sea as into a heap*   *b* This psalm is an acrostic poem, the verses of which begin with the
successive letters of the Hebrew alphabet.

[18]The Lord is close to the
    brokenhearted
and saves those who are crushed in
    spirit.

[19]A righteous man may have many
    troubles,
but the Lord delivers him from
    them all;
[20]he protects all his bones,
    not one of them will be broken.

[21]Evil will slay the wicked;
    the foes of the righteous will be
    condemned.
[22]The Lord redeems his servants;
    no one will be condemned who
    takes refuge in him.

Psalm 35

Of David.

[1]Contend, O Lord, with those who
    contend with me;
fight against those who fight against
    me.
[2]Take up shield and buckler;
    arise and come to my aid.
[3]Brandish spear and javelin[a]
    against those who pursue me.
Say to my soul,
    "I am your salvation."

[4]May those who seek my life
    be disgraced and put to shame;
may those who plot my ruin
    be turned back in dismay.
[5]May they be like chaff before the
    wind,
with the angel of the Lord driving
    them away;
[6]may their path be dark and slippery,
    with the angel of the Lord pursuing
    them.
[7]Since they hid their net for me
    without cause
and without cause dug a pit for me,
[8]may ruin overtake them by surprise—
    may the net they hid entangle them,
    may they fall into the pit, to their
    ruin.
[9]Then my soul will rejoice in the Lord
    and delight in his salvation.
[10]My whole being will exclaim,
    "Who is like you, O Lord?
You rescue the poor from those too
    strong for them,

the poor and needy from those who
    rob them."

[11]Ruthless witnesses come forward;
    they question me on things I know
    nothing about.
[12]They repay me evil for good
    and leave my soul forlorn.
[13]Yet when they were ill, I put on
    sackcloth
    and humbled myself with fasting.
When my prayers returned to me
    unanswered,
[14] I went about mourning
    as though for my friend or brother.
I bowed my head in grief
    as though weeping for my mother.
[15]But when I stumbled, they gathered in
    glee;
attackers gathered against me when
    I was unaware.
They slandered me without ceasing.
[16]Like the ungodly they maliciously
    mocked[b];
they gnashed their teeth at me.
[17]O Lord, how long will you look on?
    Rescue my life from their ravages,
    my precious life from these lions.
[18]I will give you thanks in the great
    assembly;
among throngs of people I will
    praise you.

[19]Let not those gloat over me
    who are my enemies without cause;
let not those who hate me without
    reason
    maliciously wink the eye.
[20]They do not speak peaceably,
    but devise false accusations
    against those who live quietly in the
    land.
[21]They gape at me and say, "Aha! Aha!
    With our own eyes we have seen
    it."

[22]O Lord, you have seen this; be not
    silent.
    Do not be far from me, O Lord.
[23]Awake, and rise to my defense!
    Contend for me, my God and Lord.
[24]Vindicate me in your righteousness,
    O Lord my God;
do not let them gloat over me.
[25]Do not let them think, "Aha, just what
    we wanted!"
or say, "We have swallowed him
    up."

[26]May all who gloat over my distress

---

[a]3 Or *and block the way*   [b]16 Septuagint; Hebrew may mean *ungodly circle of mockers.*

be put to shame and confusion;
may all who exalt themselves over me
   be clothed with shame and disgrace.
27May those who delight in my
      vindication
   shout for joy and gladness;
may they always say, "The Lord be
      exalted,
   who delights in the well-being of his
      servant."
28My tongue will speak of your
      righteousness
and of your praises all day long.

Psalm 36

For the director of music. Of David the
servant of the Lord.

1An oracle is within my heart
   concerning the sinfulness of the
      wicked:a
There is no fear of God
   before his eyes.
2For in his own eyes he flatters himself
   too much to detect or hate his sin.
3The words of his mouth are wicked
      and deceitful;
   he has ceased to be wise and to do
      good.
4Even on his bed he plots evil;
   he commits himself to a sinful
      course
   and does not reject what is wrong.

5Your love, O Lord, reaches to the
      heavens,
   your faithfulness to the skies.
6Your righteousness is like the mighty
      mountains,
   your justice like the great deep.
O Lord, you preserve both man and
      beast.
7 How priceless is your unfailing
      love!
Both high and low among men
   findb refuge in the shadow of your
      wings.
8They feast on the abundance of your
      house;
   you give them drink from your river
      of delights.
9For with you is the fountain of life;
   in your light we see light.

10Continue your love to those who
      know you,

your righteousness to the upright in
      heart.
11May the foot of the proud not come
      against me,
   nor the hand of the wicked drive
      me away.
12See how the evildoers lie fallen—
   thrown down, not able to rise!

Psalm 37c

Of David.

1Do not fret because of evil men
   or be envious of those who do
      wrong;
2for like the grass they will soon
      wither,
   like green plants they will soon die
      away.

3Trust in the Lord and do good;
   dwell in the land and enjoy safe
      pasture.
4Delight yourself in the Lord
   and he will give you the desires of
      your heart.

5Commit your way to the Lord;
   trust in him and he will do this:
6He will make your righteousness shine
      like the dawn,
   the justice of your cause like the
      noonday sun.

7Be still before the Lord and wait
      patiently for him;
   do not fret when men succeed in
      their ways,
   when they carry out their wicked
      schemes.

8Refrain from anger and turn from
      wrath;
   do not fret—it leads only to evil.
9For evil men will be cut off,
   but those who hope in the Lord will
      inherit the land.

10A little while, and the wicked will be
      no more;
   though you look for them, they will
      not be found.
11But the meek will inherit the land
   and enjoy great peace.

12The wicked plot against the righteous

a1 Or heart: / Sin proceeds from the wicked.   b7 Or love, O God! / Men find; or love! / Both heavenly
beings and men / find   cThis psalm is an acrostic poem, the stanzas of which begin with the successive
letters of the Hebrew alphabet.

and gnash their teeth at them;
[13]but the Lord laughs at the wicked,
for he knows their day is coming.

[14]The wicked draw the sword
and bend the bow
to bring down the poor and needy,
to slay those whose ways are
upright.

[15]But their swords will pierce their own
hearts,
and their bows will be broken.

[16]Better the little that the righteous have
than the wealth of many wicked;
[17]for the power of the wicked will be
broken,
but the LORD upholds the righteous.

FRIDAY

VERSE FOR THE DAY:
Psalm 37:8

AUTHOR:
Richard P. Walters

PASSAGE FOR THE DAY:
Psalm 37:1–11

An Age of Rage

WE LIVE in an age of rage . . . By studying anger and its power, we can learn self-control so that we do not need to *lose* our temper in rage or *abuse* ourselves with resentment, but can *defuse* anger by resolving circumstances and then *use the energy of anger through Christlike indignation.*

The following summary, written in the form of resolutions, can form a point of departure for us as we continue with life. We should reflect prayerfully about how we can incorporate these ideals in our own lives.

- To keep my life centered on God, as best I can, recognizing that when I do not, my natural self will generate things to become angry about;
- To not condemn myself for feelings of anger;
- To do everything I can to avoid acting on the basis of anger;
- To clean up any problems I create as quickly as possible;
- To recognize God's help in this process;
- To redirect the energy of anger away from hurting people and toward improving conditions for people;
- To be sensitive to injustice and evil, learning to be angry about the misery that sin inflicts on people without becoming controlled by the anger.

It has been my observation, in counseling on problems of anger control, that each person who has sought God's help in the understanding and resolution of his or her anger has, without exception, received that help. These people have described the results as "miraculous." There is, indeed, a miracle involved. It is the miracle of God's love for us, the miracle of his redemptive grace.

Additional Scripture Readings:
Psalm 4; Ephesians 4:25—5:2

Go to page 569 for your next devotional reading.

[18]The days of the blameless are known
   to the LORD,
   and their inheritance will endure
   forever.
[19]In times of disaster they will not
   wither;
   in days of famine they will enjoy
   plenty.
[20]But the wicked will perish:
   The LORD's enemies will be like the
   beauty of the fields,
   they will vanish—vanish like
   smoke.

[21]The wicked borrow and do not repay,
   but the righteous give generously;
[22]those the LORD blesses will inherit the
   land,
   but those he curses will be cut off.

[23]If the LORD delights in a man's way,
   he makes his steps firm;
[24]though he stumble, he will not fall,
   for the LORD upholds him with his
   hand.

[25]I was young and now I am old,
   yet I have never seen the righteous
   forsaken
   or their children begging bread.
[26]They are always generous and lend
   freely;
   their children will be blessed.

[27]Turn from evil and do good;
   then you will dwell in the land
   forever.
[28]For the LORD loves the just
   and will not forsake his faithful
   ones.

They will be protected forever,
   but the offspring of the wicked will
   be cut off;
[29]the righteous will inherit the land
   and dwell in it forever.

[30]The mouth of the righteous man
   utters wisdom,
   and his tongue speaks what is just.
[31]The law of his God is in his heart;
   his feet do not slip.

[32]The wicked lie in wait for the
   righteous,
   seeking their very lives;
[33]but the LORD will not leave them in
   their power
   or let them be condemned when
   brought to trial.

[34]Wait for the LORD
   and keep his way.
He will exalt you to inherit the land;
   when the wicked are cut off, you
   will see it.

[35]I have seen a wicked and ruthless
   man
   flourishing like a green tree in its
   native soil,
[36]but he soon passed away and was no
   more;
   though I looked for him, he could
   not be found.

[37]Consider the blameless, observe the
   upright;
   there is a future[a] for the man of
   peace.
[38]But all sinners will be destroyed;
   the future[b] of the wicked will be
   cut off.

[39]The salvation of the righteous comes
   from the LORD;
   he is their stronghold in time of
   trouble.
[40]The LORD helps them and delivers
   them;
   he delivers them from the wicked
   and saves them,
   because they take refuge in him.

Psalm 38

A psalm of David. A petition.

[1]O LORD, do not rebuke me in your
   anger
   or discipline me in your wrath.
[2]For your arrows have pierced me,
   and your hand has come down
   upon me.
[3]Because of your wrath there is no
   health in my body;
   my bones have no soundness
   because of my sin.
[4]My guilt has overwhelmed me
   like a burden too heavy to bear.

[5]My wounds fester and are loathsome
   because of my sinful folly.
[6]I am bowed down and brought very
   low;
   all day long I go about mourning.
[7]My back is filled with searing pain;
   there is no health in my body.
[8]I am feeble and utterly crushed;
   I groan in anguish of heart.

---

[a]37 Or there will be posterity   [b]38 Or posterity

[9]All my longings lie open before you,
     O Lord;
     my sighing is not hidden from you.
[10]My heart pounds, my strength fails
     me;
     even the light has gone from my
     eyes.
[11]My friends and companions avoid me
     because of my wounds;
     my neighbors stay far away.
[12]Those who seek my life set their
     traps,
     those who would harm me talk of
     my ruin;
     all day long they plot deception.

[13]I am like a deaf man, who cannot
     hear,
     like a mute, who cannot open his
     mouth;
[14]I have become like a man who does
     not hear,
     whose mouth can offer no reply.
[15]I wait for you, O Lord;
     you will answer, O Lord my God.
[16]For I said, "Do not let them gloat
     or exalt themselves over me when
     my foot slips."

[17]For I am about to fall,
     and my pain is ever with me.
[18]I confess my iniquity;
     I am troubled by my sin.
[19]Many are those who are my vigorous
     enemies;
     those who hate me without reason
     are numerous.
[20]Those who repay my good with evil
     slander me when I pursue what is
     good.

[21]O Lord, do not forsake me;
     be not far from me, O my God.
[22]Come quickly to help me,
     O Lord my Savior.

Psalm 39

For the director of music. For Jeduthun.
A psalm of David.

[1]I said, "I will watch my ways
     and keep my tongue from sin;
     I will put a muzzle on my mouth
     as long as the wicked are in my
     presence."
[2]But when I was silent and still,
     not even saying anything good,
     my anguish increased.
[3]My heart grew hot within me,
     and as I meditated, the fire burned;

then I spoke with my tongue:

[4]"Show me, O Lord, my life's end
     and the number of my days;
     let me know how fleeting is my life.
[5]You have made my days a mere
     handbreadth;
     the span of my years is as nothing
     before you.
     Each man's life is but a breath.
                         Selah
[6]Man is a mere phantom as he goes to
     and fro:
     He bustles about, but only in vain;
     he heaps up wealth, not knowing
     who will get it.

[7]"But now, Lord, what do I look for?
     My hope is in you.
[8]Save me from all my transgressions;
     do not make me the scorn of fools.
[9]I was silent; I would not open my
     mouth,
     for you are the one who has done
     this.
[10]Remove your scourge from me;
     I am overcome by the blow of your
     hand.
[11]You rebuke and discipline men for
     their sin;
     you consume their wealth like a
     moth —
     each man is but a breath.   *Selah*

[12]"Hear my prayer, O Lord,
     listen to my cry for help;
     be not deaf to my weeping.
     For I dwell with you as an alien,
     a stranger, as all my fathers were.
[13]Look away from me, that I may
     rejoice again
     before I depart and am no more."

Psalm 40

For the director of music. Of David.
A psalm.

[1]I waited patiently for the Lord;
     he turned to me and heard my cry.
[2]He lifted me out of the slimy pit,
     out of the mud and mire;
     he set my feet on a rock
     and gave me a firm place to stand.
[3]He put a new song in my mouth,
     a hymn of praise to our God.
     Many will see and fear
     and put their trust in the Lord.

[4]Blessed is the man
     who makes the Lord his trust,
     who does not look to the proud,

to those who turn aside to false
gods.*a*
5Many, O LORD my God,
are the wonders you have done.
The things you planned for us
no one can recount to you;
were I to speak and tell of them,
they would be too many to declare.

6Sacrifice and offering you did not
desire,
but my ears you have pierced*b,c*;
burnt offerings and sin offerings
you did not require.
7Then I said, "Here I am, I have
come—
it is written about me in the
scroll.*d*
8I desire to do your will, O my God;
your law is within my heart."

9I proclaim righteousness in the great
assembly;
I do not seal my lips,
as you know, O LORD.
10I do not hide your righteousness in
my heart;
I speak of your faithfulness and
salvation.
I do not conceal your love and your
truth
from the great assembly.

11Do not withhold your mercy from me,
O LORD;
may your love and your truth
always protect me.
12For troubles without number surround
me;
my sins have overtaken me, and I
cannot see.
They are more than the hairs of my
head,
and my heart fails within me.

13Be pleased, O LORD, to save me;
O LORD, come quickly to help me.
14May all who seek to take my life
be put to shame and confusion;
may all who desire my ruin
be turned back in disgrace.
15May those who say to me, "Aha! Aha!"
be appalled at their own shame.
16But may all who seek you
rejoice and be glad in you;
may those who love your salvation
always say,
"The LORD be exalted!"
17Yet I am poor and needy;

may the Lord think of me.
You are my help and my deliverer;
O my God, do not delay.

Psalm 41

*For the director of music. A psalm
of David.*

1Blessed is he who has regard for the
weak;
the LORD delivers him in times of
trouble.
2The LORD will protect him and
preserve his life;
he will bless him in the land
and not surrender him to the desire
of his foes.
3The LORD will sustain him on his
sickbed
and restore him from his bed of
illness.

4I said, "O LORD, have mercy on me;
heal me, for I have sinned against
you."
5My enemies say of me in malice,
"When will he die and his name
perish?"
6Whenever one comes to see me,
he speaks falsely, while his heart
gathers slander;
then he goes out and spreads it
abroad.

7All my enemies whisper together
against me;
they imagine the worst for me,
saying,
8"A vile disease has beset him;
he will never get up from the place
where he lies."
9Even my close friend, whom I trusted,
he who shared my bread,
has lifted up his heel against me.

10But you, O LORD, have mercy on me;
raise me up, that I may repay them.
11I know that you are pleased with me,
for my enemy does not triumph
over me.
12In my integrity you uphold me
and set me in your presence
forever.

13Praise be to the LORD, the God of
Israel,
from everlasting to everlasting.
Amen and Amen.

*a4 Or to falsehood   b6 Hebrew; Septuagint but a body you have prepared for me (see also Symmachus
and Theodotion)   c6 Or opened   d7 Or come / with the scroll written for me*

BOOK II

Psalms 42–72

Psalm 42[a]

For the director of music. A *maskil*[b] of
the Sons of Korah.

[1]As the deer pants for streams of
water,
so my soul pants for you, O God.
[2]My soul thirsts for God, for the living
God.
When can I go and meet with
God?
[3]My tears have been my food
day and night,
while men say to me all day long,
"Where is your God?"
[4]These things I remember
as I pour out my soul:
how I used to go with the multitude,
leading the procession to the house
of God,
with shouts of joy and thanksgiving
among the festive throng.

[5]Why are you downcast, O my
soul?
Why so disturbed within me?
Put your hope in God,
for I will yet praise him,
my Savior and [6]my God.

My[c] soul is downcast within me;
therefore I will remember you
from the land of the Jordan,
the heights of Hermon—from
Mount Mizar.
[7]Deep calls to deep
in the roar of your waterfalls;
all your waves and breakers
have swept over me.

[8]By day the Lord directs his love,
at night his song is with me—
a prayer to the God of my life.

[9]I say to God my Rock,
"Why have you forgotten me?
Why must I go about mourning,
oppressed by the enemy?"
[10]My bones suffer mortal agony
as my foes taunt me,
saying to me all day long,
"Where is your God?"

[11]Why are you downcast, O my soul?
Why so disturbed within me?
Put your hope in God,
for I will yet praise him,
my Savior and my God.

Psalm 43[a]

[1]Vindicate me, O God,
and plead my cause against an
ungodly nation;
rescue me from deceitful and
wicked men.
[2]You are God my stronghold.
Why have you rejected me?
Why must I go about mourning,
oppressed by the enemy?
[3]Send forth your light and your truth,
let them guide me;
let them bring me to your holy
mountain,
to the place where you dwell.
[4]Then will I go to the altar of God,
to God, my joy and my delight.
I will praise you with the harp,
O God, my God.

[5]Why are you downcast, O my soul?
Why so disturbed within me?
Put your hope in God,
for I will yet praise him,
my Savior and my God.

Psalm 44

For the director of music. Of the Sons of
Korah. A *maskil.*[b]

[1]We have heard with our ears, O God;
our fathers have told us
what you did in their days,
in days long ago.
[2]With your hand you drove out the
nations
and planted our fathers;
you crushed the peoples
and made our fathers flourish.
[3]It was not by their sword that they
won the land,
nor did their arm bring them
victory;
it was your right hand, your arm,
and the light of your face, for you
loved them.

[4]You are my King and my God,
who decrees[d] victories for Jacob.

---

[a]In many Hebrew manuscripts Psalms 42 and 43 constitute one psalm.   [b]Title: Probably a literary or
musical term   [c]5,6 A few Hebrew manuscripts, Septuagint and Syriac; most Hebrew manuscripts *praise
him for his saving help. / [6]O my God, my*   [d]4 Septuagint, Aquila and Syriac; Hebrew *King, O God; /
command*

WEEKENDING

RETHINK

Is this society so far gone that it's hopeless?
Have we abandoned our role model
responsibilities for so long that we can't
change? I don't think so. Each of us can change
our own little world. Fathers who are honest
with themselves will admit that we all make
mistakes. We have all made bad decisions.
Some of those decisions have to be reversed. If
you have accepted a promotion and a transfer
that takes you a step up the corporate ladder at
the expense of your kids, maybe you need to
think about taking a step back. More important
than providing a life of ease for your kids is
making sure they know you love them
unconditionally.

– Mike Singletary

REVIVE

Saturday: Psalm 40:4–10
Sunday: 1 Corinthians 13

Go to page 573 for your next devotional reading.

⁵Through you we push back our
    enemies;
  through your name we trample our
    foes.
⁶I do not trust in my bow,
  my sword does not bring me
    victory;
⁷but you give us victory over our
    enemies,
  you put our adversaries to shame.
⁸In God we make our boast all day
    long,
  and we will praise your name
    forever.   *Selah*

⁹But now you have rejected and
    humbled us;
  you no longer go out with our
    armies.
¹⁰You made us retreat before the
    enemy,
  and our adversaries have plundered
    us.
¹¹You gave us up to be devoured like
    sheep
  and have scattered us among the
    nations.
¹²You sold your people for a pittance,
  gaining nothing from their sale.

¹³You have made us a reproach to our
    neighbors,
  the scorn and derision of those
    around us.
¹⁴You have made us a byword among
    the nations;
  the peoples shake their heads at us.
¹⁵My disgrace is before me all day long,
  and my face is covered with shame
¹⁶at the taunts of those who reproach
    and revile me,
  because of the enemy, who is bent
    on revenge.

¹⁷All this happened to us,
  though we had not forgotten you
  or been false to your covenant.
¹⁸Our hearts had not turned back;
  our feet had not strayed from your
    path.
¹⁹But you crushed us and made us a
    haunt for jackals
  and covered us over with deep
    darkness.

²⁰If we had forgotten the name of our
    God
  or spread out our hands to a foreign
    god,
²¹would not God have discovered it,

since he knows the secrets of the
    heart?
²²Yet for your sake we face death all
    day long;
  we are considered as sheep to be
    slaughtered.

²³Awake, O Lord! Why do you sleep?
  Rouse yourself! Do not reject us
    forever.
²⁴Why do you hide your face
  and forget our misery and
    oppression?
²⁵We are brought down to the dust;
  our bodies cling to the ground.
²⁶Rise up and help us;
  redeem us because of your unfailing
    love.

Psalm 45

For the director of music. To the tune
of, "Lilies." Of the Sons of Korah. A
*maskil.*ᵃ A wedding song.

¹My heart is stirred by a noble theme
  as I recite my verses for the king;
  my tongue is the pen of a skillful
    writer.

²You are the most excellent of men
  and your lips have been anointed
    with grace,
  since God has blessed you forever.
³Gird your sword upon your side,
    O mighty one;
  clothe yourself with splendor and
    majesty.
⁴In your majesty ride forth victoriously
  in behalf of truth, humility and
    righteousness;
  let your right hand display awesome
    deeds.
⁵Let your sharp arrows pierce the
    hearts of the king's enemies;
  let the nations fall beneath your
    feet.
⁶Your throne, O God, will last for ever
    and ever;
  a scepter of justice will be the
    scepter of your kingdom.
⁷You love righteousness and hate
    wickedness;
  therefore God, your God, has set
    you above your companions
  by anointing you with the oil of joy.
⁸All your robes are fragrant with myrrh
    and aloes and cassia;
  from palaces adorned with ivory

ᵃTitle: Probably a literary or musical term

the music of the strings makes you
glad.
⁹Daughters of kings are among your
honored women;
at your right hand is the royal bride
in gold of Ophir.

¹⁰Listen, O daughter, consider and give
ear:
Forget your people and your father's
house.
¹¹The king is enthralled by your beauty;
honor him, for he is your lord.
¹²The Daughter of Tyre will come with
a gift,ᵃ
men of wealth will seek your favor.

¹³All glorious is the princess within her
chamber;
her gown is interwoven with gold.
¹⁴In embroidered garments she is led to
the king;
her virgin companions follow her
and are brought to you.
¹⁵They are led in with joy and gladness;
they enter the palace of the king.

¹⁶Your sons will take the place of your
fathers;
you will make them princes
throughout the land.
¹⁷I will perpetuate your memory
through all generations;
therefore the nations will praise you
for ever and ever.

Psalm 46

For the director of music. Of the Sons of
Korah. According to *alamoth*.ᵇ A song.

¹God is our refuge and strength,
an ever-present help in trouble.
²Therefore we will not fear, though the
earth give way
and the mountains fall into the
heart of the sea,
³though its waters roar and foam
and the mountains quake with their
surging.   *Selah*

⁴There is a river whose streams make
glad the city of God,
the holy place where the Most High
dwells.
⁵God is within her, she will not fall;
God will help her at break of day.
⁶Nations are in uproar, kingdoms fall;
he lifts his voice, the earth melts.

⁷The Lord Almighty is with us;
the God of Jacob is our fortress.
        Selah

⁸Come and see the works of the Lord,
the desolations he has brought on
the earth.
⁹He makes wars cease to the ends of
the earth;
he breaks the bow and shatters the
spear,
he burns the shieldsᶜ with fire.
¹⁰"Be still, and know that I am God;
I will be exalted among the nations,
I will be exalted in the earth."

¹¹The Lord Almighty is with us;
the God of Jacob is our fortress.
        Selah

Psalm 47

For the director of music. Of the Sons of
Korah. A psalm.

¹Clap your hands, all you nations;
shout to God with cries of joy.
²How awesome is the Lord Most High,
the great King over all the earth!
³He subdued nations under us,
peoples under our feet.
⁴He chose our inheritance for us,
the pride of Jacob, whom he loved.
        Selah

⁵God has ascended amid shouts of joy,
the Lord amid the sounding of
trumpets.
⁶Sing praises to God, sing praises;
sing praises to our King, sing
praises.

⁷For God is the King of all the earth;
sing to him a psalmᵈ of praise.
⁸God reigns over the nations;
God is seated on his holy throne.
⁹The nobles of the nations assemble
as the people of the God of
Abraham,
for the kingsᵉ of the earth belong to
God;
he is greatly exalted.

Psalm 48

A song. A psalm of the Sons of Korah.

¹Great is the Lord, and most worthy of
praise,

ᵃ12 Or *A Tyrian robe is among the gifts*   ᵇTitle: Probably a musical term   ᶜ9 Or *chariots*   ᵈ7 Or
a maskil (probably a literary or musical term)   ᵉ9 Or *shields*

in the city of our God, his holy
    mountain.
²It is beautiful in its loftiness,
    the joy of the whole earth.
Like the utmost heights of Zaphon^a is
    Mount Zion,
    the^b city of the Great King.
³God is in her citadels;
    he has shown himself to be her
        fortress.

⁴When the kings joined forces,
    when they advanced together,
⁵they saw ˎher ˏ and were astounded;
    they fled in terror.
⁶Trembling seized them there,
    pain like that of a woman in labor.
⁷You destroyed them like ships of
        Tarshish
    shattered by an east wind.

⁸As we have heard,
    so have we seen
in the city of the LORD Almighty,
    in the city of our God:
    God makes her secure forever. *Selah*

⁹Within your temple, O God,
    we meditate on your unfailing love.
¹⁰Like your name, O God,
    your praise reaches to the ends of
        the earth;
    your right hand is filled with
        righteousness.
¹¹Mount Zion rejoices,
    the villages of Judah are glad
    because of your judgments.

¹²Walk about Zion, go around her,
    count her towers,
¹³consider well her ramparts,
    view her citadels,
    that you may tell of them to the
        next generation.
¹⁴For this God is our God for ever and
        ever;
    he will be our guide even to the
        end.

Psalm 49

For the director of music. Of the Sons of
    Korah. A psalm.

¹Hear this, all you peoples;
    listen, all who live in this world,
²both low and high,

rich and poor alike:
³My mouth will speak words of
        wisdom;
    the utterance from my heart will
        give understanding.
⁴I will turn my ear to a proverb;
    with the harp I will expound my
        riddle:

⁵Why should I fear when evil days
        come,
    when wicked deceivers surround
        me—
⁶those who trust in their wealth
    and boast of their great riches?
⁷No man can redeem the life of
        another
    or give to God a ransom for
        him—
⁸the ransom for a life is costly,
    no payment is ever enough—
⁹that he should live on forever
    and not see decay.

¹⁰For all can see that wise men die;
    the foolish and the senseless alike
        perish
    and leave their wealth to others.
¹¹Their tombs will remain their
        houses^c forever,
    their dwellings for endless
        generations,
    though they had^d named lands
        after themselves.

¹²But man, despite his riches, does not
        endure;
    he is^e like the beasts that perish.

¹³This is the fate of those who trust in
        themselves,
    and of their followers, who approve
        their sayings.   *Selah*
¹⁴Like sheep they are destined for the
        grave,^f
    and death will feed on them.
The upright will rule over them in the
        morning;
    their forms will decay in the
        grave,^f
    far from their princely mansions.
¹⁵But God will redeem my life^g from
        the grave;
    he will surely take me to himself.
        Selah

¹⁶Do not be overawed when a man
    grows rich,
  when the splendor of his house
    increases;
¹⁷for he will take nothing with him
    when he dies,
  his splendor will not descend with
    him.
¹⁸Though while he lived he counted
    himself blessed—
  and men praise you when you
    prosper—
¹⁹he will join the generation of his
    fathers,
  who will never see the light ⸤of life⸥.

²⁰A man who has riches without
    understanding
  is like the beasts that perish.

Psalm 50

A psalm of Asaph.

¹The Mighty One, God, the LORD,
  speaks and summons the earth
  from the rising of the sun to the
    place where it sets.
²From Zion, perfect in beauty,
  God shines forth.
³Our God comes and will not be silent;

MONDAY

VERSE FOR THE DAY:
Psalm 49:20

AUTHOR:
Don Wyrtzen

PASSAGE FOR THE DAY:
Psalm 49:16–20

Eternity's Values in View

THE finite nature of wealth . . .
    I must admit that I, along with many others, have been
charmed by "Tinseltown." The accouterments of success seem
so appealing that it's pretty easy to fall for those less-than-
subtle advertising ploys touting fancy foreign engineering or
the architectural wonders of some luxury house. Even in
church we sometimes focus on the trappings—lavish sanctuaries, fine pipe organs, plush carpeting. When materialism and
personal pride fuse together, we're all in grave danger of neglecting or even forgetting God!
    Thoughts of death and the prospect of eternity, however,
can abruptly change one's focus, perspective and priorities.
The psalmist reminds us that, no matter how imposing the
wealthy and powerful may appear, "they can't take it with
them."
    In this life the wealthy often inspire awe, admiration and
praise. But this adulation will be short-lived. The possessions
that are the basis of their pride and self-aggrandizement will
not survive past the grave. Verse 20 describes the final state of
the man who leaves God out of his life. Without understanding, he is like the beasts that perish. His power, influence and
wealth won't carry any weight in eternity.
    Lord, may I learn to live always, not for this life only, but
with "eternity's values in view."

Additional Scripture Readings:
Ecclesiastes 5:8–17;
1 Timothy 6:3–10

*Go to page 576 for your next
devotional reading.*

a fire devours before him,
and around him a tempest rages.
[4]He summons the heavens above,
and the earth, that he may judge his
people:
[5]"Gather to me my consecrated ones,
who made a covenant with me by
sacrifice."
[6]And the heavens proclaim his
righteousness,
for God himself is judge.   *Selah*

[7]"Hear, O my people, and I will speak,
O Israel, and I will testify against
you:
I am God, your God.
[8]I do not rebuke you for your sacrifices
or your burnt offerings, which are
ever before me.
[9]I have no need of a bull from your
stall
or of goats from your pens,
[10]for every animal of the forest is mine,
and the cattle on a thousand hills.
[11]I know every bird in the mountains,
and the creatures of the field are
mine.
[12]If I were hungry I would not tell you,
for the world is mine, and all that is
in it.
[13]Do I eat the flesh of bulls
or drink the blood of goats?
[14]Sacrifice thank offerings to God,
fulfill your vows to the Most High,
[15]and call upon me in the day of
trouble;
I will deliver you, and you will
honor me."

[16]But to the wicked, God says:

"What right have you to recite my
laws
or take my covenant on your lips?
[17]You hate my instruction
and cast my words behind you.
[18]When you see a thief, you join with
him;
you throw in your lot with
adulterers.
[19]You use your mouth for evil
and harness your tongue to deceit.
[20]You speak continually against your
brother
and slander your own mother's son.
[21]These things you have done and I
kept silent;

you thought I was altogether[a] like
you.
But I will rebuke you
and accuse you to your face.

[22]"Consider this, you who forget God,
or I will tear you to pieces, with
none to rescue:
[23]He who sacrifices thank offerings
honors me,
and he prepares the way
so that I may show him[b] the
salvation of God."

Psalm 51

For the director of music. A psalm of
David. When the prophet Nathan came
to him after David had committed
adultery with Bathsheba.

[1]Have mercy on me, O God,
according to your unfailing love;
according to your great compassion
blot out my transgressions.
[2]Wash away all my iniquity
and cleanse me from my sin.

[3]For I know my transgressions,
and my sin is always before me.
[4]Against you, you only, have I sinned
and done what is evil in your sight,
so that you are proved right when you
speak
and justified when you judge.
[5]Surely I was sinful at birth,
sinful from the time my mother
conceived me.
[6]Surely you desire truth in the inner
parts[c];
you teach[d] me wisdom in the
inmost place.

[7]Cleanse me with hyssop, and I will be
clean;
wash me, and I will be whiter than
snow.
[8]Let me hear joy and gladness;
let the bones you have crushed
rejoice.
[9]Hide your face from my sins
and blot out all my iniquity.

[10]Create in me a pure heart, O God,
and renew a steadfast spirit within
me.
[11]Do not cast me from your presence
or take your Holy Spirit from me.

---

a21 Or *thought the 'I* AM' *was*   *b23* Or *and to him who considers his way / I will show*   *c6* The
meaning of the Hebrew for this phrase is uncertain.   *d6* Or *you desired . . . ; / you taught*

¹²Restore to me the joy of your
      salvation
   and grant me a willing spirit, to
      sustain me.

¹³Then I will teach transgressors your
      ways,
   and sinners will turn back to you.
¹⁴Save me from bloodguilt, O God,
   the God who saves me,
   and my tongue will sing of your
      righteousness.
¹⁵O Lord, open my lips,
   and my mouth will declare your
      praise.
¹⁶You do not delight in sacrifice, or I
      would bring it;
   you do not take pleasure in burnt
      offerings.
¹⁷The sacrifices of God are[a] a broken
      spirit;
   a broken and contrite heart,
   O God, you will not despise.

¹⁸In your good pleasure make Zion
      prosper;
   build up the walls of Jerusalem.
¹⁹Then there will be righteous sacrifices,
   whole burnt offerings to delight
      you;
   then bulls will be offered on your
      altar.

Psalm 52

For the director of music. A *maskil*[b]
of David. When Doeg the Edomite had
gone to Saul and told him: "David has
gone to the house of Ahimelech."

¹Why do you boast of evil, you mighty
      man?
   Why do you boast all day long,
   you who are a disgrace in the eyes
      of God?
²Your tongue plots destruction;
   it is like a sharpened razor,
   you who practice deceit.
³You love evil rather than good,
   falsehood rather than speaking the
      truth.   *Selah*
⁴You love every harmful word,
   O you deceitful tongue!

⁵Surely God will bring you down to
      everlasting ruin:

He will snatch you up and tear you
      from your tent;
   he will uproot you from the land of
      the living.   *Selah*
⁶The righteous will see and fear;
   they will laugh at him, saying,
⁷"Here now is the man
   who did not make God his
      stronghold
   but trusted in his great wealth
   and grew strong by destroying
      others!"

⁸But I am like an olive tree
   flourishing in the house of God;
   I trust in God's unfailing love
   for ever and ever.
⁹I will praise you forever for what you
      have done;
   in your name I will hope, for your
      name is good.
   I will praise you in the presence of
      your saints.

Psalm 53

For the director of music. According to
   mahalath.[c] A *maskil*[b] of David.

¹The fool says in his heart,
   "There is no God."
They are corrupt, and their ways are
      vile;
   there is no one who does good.

²God looks down from heaven
   on the sons of men
to see if there are any who
      understand,
   any who seek God.
³Everyone has turned away,
   they have together become corrupt;
there is no one who does good,
   not even one.

⁴Will the evildoers never learn—
   those who devour my people as
      men eat bread
   and who do not call on God?
⁵There they were, overwhelmed with
      dread,
   where there was nothing to dread.
God scattered the bones of those who
      attacked you;

---

[a]17 Or *My sacrifice, O God, is*
term   [b]Title: Probably a literary or musical term   [c]Title: Probably a musical

you put them to shame, for God
    despised them.

⁶Oh, that salvation for Israel would
    come out of Zion!
When God restores the fortunes of
    his people,
    let Jacob rejoice and Israel be glad!

ᵃTitle: Probably a literary or musical term

Psalm 54

For the director of music. With stringed
instruments. A *maskil*ᵃ of David. When
the Ziphites had gone to Saul and said,
"Is not David hiding among us?"

¹Save me, O God, by your name;
    vindicate me by your might.

TUESDAY

VERSE FOR THE DAY: Psalm 51:1	AUTHOR: Larry Crabb	PASSAGE FOR THE DAY: Psalm 51:1–17

A Path Leading Downward

REPENTANT people realize that inexcusable wrong can either
be judged or forgiven, never understood and overlooked, and
so they beg for forgiveness with no thought of deserving it.
Truly repentant people are the ones who begin to grasp God's
amazing grace, the ones who know that they need only confess to experience the forgiveness that is always there in infinite supply.

    Whether we are adulterers or thoughtless spouses, the prob-
lem with all of us is that we stubbornly regard our interper-
sonal failures not as *inexcusably selfish choices*, but as *understandable mistakes*. The things our spouses do to us seem
more like the former; the things we do to them more like the
latter.

    Excuse-making has been a natural tendency in people ever
since Adam blamed Eve and Eve blamed the snake. Without
some means of self-justification, we would be forced to face
ourselves squarely as we really are, corrupt by God's standards
and deserving punishment.

    And seeing ourselves as we are would mean taking our place
as condemned sinners, worthy of judgment, powerless to improve ourselves, humbled that our very best deeds provide no
defense, and utterly at the mercy of a righteously angry Judge.
This doesn't sound like much fun. Surely the path to the top
would never begin with a descent *this* steep! How can joy
emerge from such misery?

    Perhaps the hardest thing to get through our brain-damaged
heads (when Adam fell, he must have fallen on his head) is
that this painful point of nakedness and humility is not only
where life begins, but also where joyful growth continues.

Additional Scripture Readings:
Romans 3:9–26; 1 John 1:5–10

*Go to page 578 for your next
devotional reading.*

²Hear my prayer, O God;
  listen to the words of my mouth.

³Strangers are attacking me;
  ruthless men seek my life—
  men without regard for God.   *Selah*

⁴Surely God is my help;
  the Lord is the one who sustains
    me.

⁵Let evil recoil on those who slander
    me;
  in your faithfulness destroy them.

⁶I will sacrifice a freewill offering to
    you;
  I will praise your name, O LORD,
  for it is good.
⁷For he has delivered me from all my
    troubles,
  and my eyes have looked in
    triumph on my foes.

Psalm 55

For the director of music. With stringed
  instruments. A *maskil*ᵃ of David.

¹Listen to my prayer, O God,
  do not ignore my plea;
² hear me and answer me.
My thoughts trouble me and I am
    distraught
³ at the voice of the enemy,
  at the stares of the wicked;
for they bring down suffering upon
    me
  and revile me in their anger.

⁴My heart is in anguish within me;
  the terrors of death assail me.
⁵Fear and trembling have beset
    me;
  horror has overwhelmed me.
⁶I said, "Oh, that I had the wings of a
    dove!
  I would fly away and be at rest—
⁷I would flee far away
  and stay in the desert;   *Selah*
⁸I would hurry to my place of shelter,
  far from the tempest and storm."

⁹Confuse the wicked, O Lord, confound
    their speech,
  for I see violence and strife in the
    city.

¹⁰Day and night they prowl about on its
    walls;
  malice and abuse are within it.
¹¹Destructive forces are at work in the
    city;
  threats and lies never leave its
    streets.

¹²If an enemy were insulting me,
  I could endure it;
if a foe were raising himself against
    me,
  I could hide from him.
¹³But it is you, a man like myself,
  my companion, my close friend,
¹⁴with whom I once enjoyed sweet
    fellowship
  as we walked with the throng at the
    house of God.

¹⁵Let death take my enemies by
    surprise;
  let them go down alive to the
    grave,ᵇ
  for evil finds lodging among them.

¹⁶But I call to God,
  and the LORD saves me.
¹⁷Evening, morning and noon
  I cry out in distress,
  and he hears my voice.
¹⁸He ransoms me unharmed
  from the battle waged against me,
  even though many oppose me.
¹⁹God, who is enthroned forever,
  will hear them and afflict them—
                                Selah
men who never change their ways
  and have no fear of God.

²⁰My companion attacks his friends;
  he violates his covenant.
²¹His speech is smooth as butter,
  yet war is in his heart;
his words are more soothing than
    oil,
  yet they are drawn swords.

²²Cast your cares on the LORD
  and he will sustain you;
  he will never let the righteous fall.
²³But you, O God, will bring down the
    wicked
  into the pit of corruption;
bloodthirsty and deceitful men
  will not live out half their days.

But as for me, I trust in you.

ᵃTitle: Probably a literary or musical term   ᵇ15 Hebrew *Sheol*

Psalm 56

For the director of music. To the tune of, "A Dove on Distant Oaks." Of David. A *miktam.* [a] When the Philistines had seized him in Gath.

[1] Be merciful to me, O God, for men hotly pursue me;
all day long they press their attack.
[2] My slanderers pursue me all day long;
many are attacking me in their pride.

[a] Title: Probably a literary or musical term

[3] When I am afraid,
I will trust in you.
[4] In God, whose word I praise,
in God I trust; I will not be afraid.
What can mortal man do to me?

[5] All day long they twist my words;
they are always plotting to harm me.
[6] They conspire, they lurk,
they watch my steps,
eager to take my life.
[7] On no account let them escape;

WEDNESDAY

VERSE FOR THE DAY:	AUTHOR:	PASSAGE FOR THE DAY:
Psalm 55:13	David W. Smith	Psalm 55:1–14

Be Men of Faithfulness

BIBLICAL friendship calls for faithfulness. Circumstances should not affect our consistency. In Romans 12:15 Paul tells us to "rejoice with those who rejoice; mourn with those who mourn" . . .

Faithfulness is critical to a close relationship because we depend on those who are close to us. Christ's deepest hurts occurred within his circle of closest companions, and David was wounded emotionally more by the treachery of his close friends than by the efforts of his enemies. He laments in Psalm 55:12–14, "If an enemy were insulting me, I could endure it; if a foe were raising himself against me, I could hide from him. But it is you, a man like myself, my companion, my close friend, with whom I once enjoyed sweet fellowship as we walked with the throng at the house of God." Paul too was left to stand alone when he was deserted by Demas and others (2 Timothy 4:10).

A faithful friend keeps confidences. In Proverbs we read that "a perverse man stirs up dissension, and a gossip separates close friends" (16:28). And in 17:9, "He who covers over an offense promotes love, but whoever repeats the matter separates close friends."

Entering friendship involves revealing yourself in confidence to another, and thus becoming vulnerable. This is as it should be, but it is what makes betrayal so evil and faithfulness so virtuous.

Additional Scripture Readings:
Psalm 41; John 13:18–30

Go to page 582 for your next devotional reading.

in your anger, O God, bring down
  the nations.
⁸Record my lament;
  list my tears on your scroll^a—
  are they not in your record?

⁹Then my enemies will turn back
  when I call for help.
  By this I will know that God is for
    me.
¹⁰In God, whose word I praise,
  in the Lord, whose word I praise—
¹¹in God I trust; I will not be afraid.
  What can man do to me?

¹²I am under vows to you, O God;
  I will present my thank offerings to
    you.
¹³For you have delivered me^b from
    death
and my feet from stumbling,
that I may walk before God
  in the light of life.^c

Psalm 57

For the director of music. ⌐To the tune
of⌐ "Do Not Destroy." Of David. A
miktam.^d When he had fled from Saul
into the cave.

¹Have mercy on me, O God, have
    mercy on me,
  for in you my soul takes refuge.
I will take refuge in the shadow of
    your wings
  until the disaster has passed.

²I cry out to God Most High,
  to God, who fulfills ⌐his purpose⌐ for
    me.
³He sends from heaven and saves me,
  rebuking those who hotly pursue
    me;   *Selah*
  God sends his love and his
    faithfulness.

⁴I am in the midst of lions;
  I lie among ravenous beasts—
men whose teeth are spears and
    arrows,
  whose tongues are sharp swords.

⁵Be exalted, O God, above the heavens;
  let your glory be over all the earth.

⁶They spread a net for my feet—
  I was bowed down in distress.
They dug a pit in my path—

but they have fallen into it
  themselves.   *Selah*

⁷My heart is steadfast, O God,
  my heart is steadfast;
  I will sing and make music.
⁸Awake, my soul!
  Awake, harp and lyre!
  I will awaken the dawn.

⁹I will praise you, O Lord, among the
    nations;
  I will sing of you among the
    peoples.
¹⁰For great is your love, reaching to the
    heavens;
  your faithfulness reaches to the
    skies.

¹¹Be exalted, O God, above the heavens;
  let your glory be over all the earth.

Psalm 58

For the director of music. ⌐To the tune
of⌐ "Do Not Destroy." Of David.
A *miktam.*^d

¹Do you rulers indeed speak justly?
  Do you judge uprightly among men?
²No, in your heart you devise injustice,
  and your hands mete out violence
    on the earth.
³Even from birth the wicked go astray;
  from the womb they are wayward
    and speak lies.
⁴Their venom is like the venom of a
    snake,
  like that of a cobra that has stopped
    its ears,
⁵that will not heed the tune of the
    charmer,
  however skillful the enchanter may
    be.

⁶Break the teeth in their mouths,
    O God;
  tear out, O Lord, the fangs of the
    lions!
⁷Let them vanish like water that flows
    away;
  when they draw the bow, let their
    arrows be blunted.
⁸Like a slug melting away as it moves
    along,
  like a stillborn child, may they not
    see the sun.

⁹Before your pots can feel ⌐the heat of⌐
    the thorns—

---

^a8 Or / put my tears in your wineskin   ^b13 Or my soul   ^c13 Or the land of the living   ^dTitle:
Probably a literary or musical term

whether they be green or dry—the
wicked will be swept away.[a]
[10]The righteous will be glad when they
are avenged,
when they bathe their feet in the
blood of the wicked.
[11]Then men will say,
"Surely the righteous still are
rewarded;
surely there is a God who judges
the earth."

Psalm 59

For the director of music. To the tune
of, "Do Not Destroy." Of David. A
miktam.[b] When Saul had sent men to
watch David's house in order to kill him.

[1]Deliver me from my enemies, O God;
protect me from those who rise up
against me.
[2]Deliver me from evildoers
and save me from bloodthirsty men.

[3]See how they lie in wait for me!
Fierce men conspire against me
for no offense or sin of mine,
O LORD.
[4]I have done no wrong, yet they are
ready to attack me.
Arise to help me; look on my
plight!
[5]O LORD God Almighty, the God of
Israel,
rouse yourself to punish all the
nations;
show no mercy to wicked traitors.
                                    Selah

[6]They return at evening,
snarling like dogs,
and prowl about the city.
[7]See what they spew from their
mouths—
they spew out swords from their
lips,
and they say, "Who can hear us?"
[8]But you, O LORD, laugh at them;
you scoff at all those nations.

[9]O my Strength, I watch for you;
you, O God, are my fortress, [10]my
loving God.

God will go before me
and will let me gloat over those
who slander me.

[11]But do not kill them, O Lord our
shield,[c]
or my people will forget.
In your might make them wander
about,
and bring them down.
[12]For the sins of their mouths,
for the words of their lips,
let them be caught in their pride.
For the curses and lies they utter,
[13]   consume them in wrath,
consume them till they are no more.
Then it will be known to the ends of
the earth
that God rules over Jacob.   Selah

[14]They return at evening,
snarling like dogs,
and prowl about the city.
[15]They wander about for food
and howl if not satisfied.
[16]But I will sing of your strength,
in the morning I will sing of your
love;
for you are my fortress,
my refuge in times of trouble.

[17]O my Strength, I sing praise to you;
you, O God, are my fortress, my
loving God.

Psalm 60

For the director of music. To the tune
of, "The Lily of the Covenant." A
miktam[b] of David. For teaching. When
he fought Aram Naharaim[d] and Aram
Zobah,[e] and when Joab returned and
struck down twelve thousand Edomites
in the Valley of Salt.

[1]You have rejected us, O God, and
burst forth upon us;
you have been angry—now restore
us!
[2]You have shaken the land and torn it
open;
mend its fractures, for it is quaking.
[3]You have shown your people
desperate times;
you have given us wine that makes
us stagger.
[4]But for those who fear you, you have
raised a banner
to be unfurled against the bow.
                                    Selah

---

[a]9 The meaning of the Hebrew for this verse is uncertain.   [b]Title: Probably a literary or musical term
[c]11 Or sovereign   [d]Title: That is, Arameans of Northwest Mesopotamia   [e]Title: That is, Arameans of
central Syria

⁵Save us and help us with your right
    hand,
    that those you love may be
        delivered.
⁶God has spoken from his sanctuary:
    "In triumph I will parcel out
        Shechem
    and measure off the Valley of
        Succoth.
⁷Gilead is mine, and Manasseh is
        mine;
    Ephraim is my helmet,
    Judah my scepter.
⁸Moab is my washbasin,
    upon Edom I toss my sandal;
    over Philistia I shout in triumph."

⁹Who will bring me to the fortified
        city?
    Who will lead me to Edom?
¹⁰Is it not you, O God, you who have
        rejected us
    and no longer go out with our
        armies?
¹¹Give us aid against the enemy,
    for the help of man is worthless.
¹²With God we will gain the victory,
    and he will trample down our
        enemies.

Psalm 61

For the director of music. With stringed
    instruments. Of David.

¹Hear my cry, O God;
    listen to my prayer.

²From the ends of the earth I call to
        you,
    I call as my heart grows faint;
    lead me to the rock that is higher
        than I.
³For you have been my refuge,
    a strong tower against the foe.

⁴I long to dwell in your tent forever
    and take refuge in the shelter of
        your wings.   Selah
⁵For you have heard my vows, O God;
    you have given me the heritage of
        those who fear your name.

⁶Increase the days of the king's life,
    his years for many generations.
⁷May he be enthroned in God's
    presence forever;

appoint your love and faithfulness
    to protect him.
⁸Then will I ever sing praise to your
        name
    and fulfill my vows day after day.

Psalm 62

For the director of music. For Jeduthun.
    A psalm of David.

¹My soul finds rest in God alone;
    my salvation comes from him.
²He alone is my rock and my salvation;
    he is my fortress, I will never be
        shaken.

³How long will you assault a man?
    Would all of you throw him
        down—
    this leaning wall, this tottering
        fence?
⁴They fully intend to topple him
    from his lofty place;
    they take delight in lies.
With their mouths they bless,
    but in their hearts they curse.   Selah

⁵Find rest, O my soul, in God alone;
    my hope comes from him.
⁶He alone is my rock and my salvation;
    he is my fortress, I will not be
        shaken.
⁷My salvation and my honor depend
    on Godᵃ;
    he is my mighty rock, my refuge.
⁸Trust in him at all times, O people;
    pour out your hearts to him,
    for God is our refuge.   Selah

⁹Lowborn men are but a breath,
    the highborn are but a lie;
if weighed on a balance, they are
        nothing;
    together they are only a
        breath.
¹⁰Do not trust in extortion
    or take pride in stolen goods;
though your riches increase,
    do not set your heart on them.

¹¹One thing God has spoken,
    two things have I heard:
that you, O God, are strong,
¹² and that you, O Lord, are loving.
Surely you will reward each person
    according to what he has done.

ᵃ7 Or / God Most High is my salvation and my honor

Psalm 63

A psalm of David. When he was in the
Desert of Judah.

¹O God, you are my God,
  earnestly I seek you;
my soul thirsts for you,
  my body longs for you,
in a dry and weary land
  where there is no water.

²I have seen you in the sanctuary
  and beheld your power and your
  glory.
³Because your love is better than life,
  my lips will glorify you.
⁴I will praise you as long as I live,
  and in your name I will lift up my
  hands.
⁵My soul will be satisfied as with the
  richest of foods;

THURSDAY

VERSE FOR THE DAY:	*AUTHOR:*	*PASSAGE FOR THE DAY:*
Psalm 63:8	*Charles Spurgeon*	*Psalm 63:1–8*

Under the Shadow

LIVE by the day—aye, by the hour. Put not trust in frames
and feelings. Care more for a grain of faith than a ton of excitement. Trust in God alone, and lean not on the reeds of human help. Be not surprised when friends fail you: it is a failing
world. Never count upon immutability in a man: inconstancy
you may reckon upon without fear of disappointment. The
disciples of Jesus forsook him; be not amazed if your adher-
ents wander away to other teachers: as they were not your all
when with you, all is not gone from you with their departure.

Serve God with all your might while the candle is burning,
and then when it goes out for a season, you will have the less
to regret. Be content to be nothing, for that is what you are.
When your own emptiness is painfully forced upon your consciousness, chide yourself that you ever dreamed of being full,
except in the Lord. Set small store by present rewards; be
grateful for earnests by the way, but look for the recompensing
joy hereafter. Continue with double earnestness to serve your
Lord when no visible result is before you. Any simpleton can
follow the narrow path in the light: faith's rare wisdom enables
us to march on in the dark with infallible accuracy, since she
places her hand in that of her great Guide. Between this and
heaven there may be rougher weather yet, but it is all provided
for by our covenant Head.

In nothing let us be turned aside from the path which the divine call has urged us to pursue. Come fair or come foul, the
pulpit is our watchtower, and the ministry our warfare; be it
ours, when we cannot see the face of God, to trust under the
shadow of his wings.

Additional Scripture Readings:
Psalm 17:6–15; John 10:22–30

*Go to page 584 for your next
devotional reading.*

with singing lips my mouth will
  praise you.

6On my bed I remember you;
  I think of you through the watches
    of the night.
7Because you are my help,
  I sing in the shadow of your wings.
8My soul clings to you;
  your right hand upholds me.

9They who seek my life will be
    destroyed;
  they will go down to the depths of
    the earth.
10They will be given over to the sword
  and become food for jackals.

11But the king will rejoice in God;
  all who swear by God's name will
    praise him,
  while the mouths of liars will be
    silenced.

Psalm 64

For the director of music. A psalm
of David.

1Hear me, O God, as I voice my
    complaint;
  protect my life from the threat of
    the enemy.
2Hide me from the conspiracy of the
    wicked,
  from that noisy crowd of evildoers.

3They sharpen their tongues like
    swords
  and aim their words like deadly
    arrows.
4They shoot from ambush at the
    innocent man;
  they shoot at him suddenly, without
    fear.

5They encourage each other in evil
    plans,
  they talk about hiding their snares;
  they say, "Who will see thema?"
6They plot injustice and say,
  "We have devised a perfect plan!"
  Surely the mind and heart of man
    are cunning.

7But God will shoot them with arrows;
  suddenly they will be struck down.
8He will turn their own tongues against
    them
  and bring them to ruin;

all who see them will shake their
  heads in scorn.
9All mankind will fear;
  they will proclaim the works of God
  and ponder what he has done.
10Let the righteous rejoice in the LORD
  and take refuge in him;
  let all the upright in heart praise
    him!

Psalm 65

For the director of music. A psalm
of David. A song.

1Praise awaitsb you, O God, in Zion;
  to you our vows will be fulfilled.
2O you who hear prayer,
  to you all men will come.
3When we were overwhelmed by sins,
  you forgavec our transgressions.
4Blessed are those you choose
  and bring near to live in your
    courts!
We are filled with the good things of
    your house,
  of your holy temple.

5You answer us with awesome deeds of
    righteousness,
  O God our Savior,
the hope of all the ends of the earth
  and of the farthest seas,
6who formed the mountains by your
    power,
  having armed yourself with
    strength,
7who stilled the roaring of the seas,
  the roaring of their waves,
  and the turmoil of the nations.
8Those living far away fear your
    wonders;
  where morning dawns and evening
    fades
  you call forth songs of joy.

9You care for the land and water it;
  you enrich it abundantly.
The streams of God are filled with
    water
  to provide the people with grain,
  for so you have ordained it.d
10You drench its furrows
  and level its ridges;
  you soften it with showers
  and bless its crops.
11You crown the year with your bounty,

a5 Or us   b1 Or befits; the meaning of the Hebrew for this word is uncertain.   c3 Or made
atonement for   d9 Or for that is how you prepare the land

and your carts overflow with
   abundance.
¹²The grasslands of the desert overflow;
   the hills are clothed with gladness.
¹³The meadows are covered with flocks
   and the valleys are mantled with
     grain;
   they shout for joy and sing.

Psalm 66

For the director of music. A song.
A psalm.

¹Shout with joy to God, all the earth!
² Sing the glory of his name;
   make his praise glorious!
³Say to God, "How awesome are your
   deeds!

So great is your power
that your enemies cringe before
   you.
⁴All the earth bows down to you;
   they sing praise to you,
   they sing praise to your name."
                   Selah

⁵Come and see what God has done,
   how awesome his works in man's
     behalf!
⁶He turned the sea into dry land,
   they passed through the waters on
     foot—
come, let us rejoice in him.
⁷He rules forever by his power,
   his eyes watch the nations—
   let not the rebellious rise up against
     him.   *Selah*

FRIDAY

VERSE FOR THE DAY: *AUTHOR:*   *PASSAGE FOR THE DAY:*
Psalm 65:8   W. Phillip Keller   Psalm 65:5–13

Our Father's World

HAVE we, as a people, so immersed in our science and tough
technology, lost touch with the earth our Father formed? It is
remarkable to recall how often Christ himself referred to such
natural objects as sheep, birds, flowers, grass, seed, soil, fish
and trees. He used them in his many parables. He explained
the most profound spiritual truths through natural processes.

Part of our problem is that most of us do not really believe
he created all the majestic and complex diversity of the earth.
In our schools and institutions, through books, films and the
media, we have been seduced to believe the earth in all its
glory has emerged from oblivion by pure chance. We are convinced it is the end product of a blind evolutionary process
that appears headed back to oblivion. No wonder our world is
so deep in despair, so sad and forlorn in its futility.

But for a tiny handful of us this is still "My Father's World."
We know assuredly that it is he who brought it into being. We
are acutely aware that he cares for it deeply. He knows the
most minute detail of every bird, flower or tree upon it. They
are his. He is theirs. And amid all the lovely interaction between Creator and creation he speaks to me. Therein lies part
of his wonder, awe and inspiration.

Additional Scripture Readings:
Psalm 95; Matthew 10:29–31

*Go to page 585 for your next
devotional reading.*

WEEKENDING

REFLECT

The sooner a man becomes satisfied with what he has and stops comparing his financial scorecard and trophies with those of other men, the better he will feel about himself. The apostle Paul states: "I have learned to be content whatever the circumstances. I know what it is to be in need, and I know what it is to have plenty. I have learned the secret of being content in any and every situation, whether well fed or hungry, whether living in plenty or in want" (Philippians 4:11–12). Men who opt to be satisfied with what they possess will have more time and energy for the kinds of nurturing relationships that will meet their basic needs.

– *Stephen Arterburn and David Stoop*

REVIVE

Saturday: 1 Timothy 6:3–10
Sunday: Hebrews 13:5–6

Go to page 587 for your next devotional reading.

8Praise our God, O peoples,
    let the sound of his praise be heard;
9he has preserved our lives
    and kept our feet from slipping.
10For you, O God, tested us;
    you refined us like silver.
11You brought us into prison
    and laid burdens on our backs.
12You let men ride over our heads;
    we went through fire and water,
    but you brought us to a place of
        abundance.

13I will come to your temple with burnt
        offerings
    and fulfill my vows to you—
14vows my lips promised and my mouth
        spoke
    when I was in trouble.
15I will sacrifice fat animals to you
    and an offering of rams;
    I will offer bulls and goats.   *Selah*

16Come and listen, all you who fear
        God;
    let me tell you what he has done
        for me.
17I cried out to him with my mouth;
    his praise was on my tongue.
18If I had cherished sin in my heart,
    the Lord would not have listened;
19but God has surely listened
    and heard my voice in prayer.
20Praise be to God,
    who has not rejected my prayer
    or withheld his love from me!

Psalm 67

For the director of music. With stringed
    instruments. A psalm. A song.

1May God be gracious to us and bless
    us
    and make his face shine upon us,
             Selah
2that your ways may be known on
        earth,
    your salvation among all nations.

3May the peoples praise you, O God;
    may all the peoples praise you.
4May the nations be glad and sing for
        joy,
    for you rule the peoples justly
    and guide the nations of the earth.
             Selah
5May the peoples praise you, O God;
    may all the peoples praise you.

6Then the land will yield its harvest,
    and God, our God, will bless us.
7God will bless us,
    and all the ends of the earth will
        fear him.

Psalm 68

For the director of music. Of David.
    A psalm. A song.

1May God arise, may his enemies be
        scattered;
    may his foes flee before him.
2As smoke is blown away by the wind,
    may you blow them away;
  as wax melts before the fire,
    may the wicked perish before God.
3But may the righteous be glad
    and rejoice before God;
    may they be happy and joyful.

4Sing to God, sing praise to his name,
    extol him who rides on the
        clouds*a*—
  his name is the Lord—
    and rejoice before him.
5A father to the fatherless, a defender
        of widows,
    is God in his holy dwelling.
6God sets the lonely in families,*b*
    he leads forth the prisoners with
        singing;
    but the rebellious live in a
        sun-scorched land.

7When you went out before your
        people, O God,
    when you marched through the
        wasteland,   *Selah*
8the earth shook,
    the heavens poured down rain,
  before God, the One of Sinai,
    before God, the God of Israel.
9You gave abundant showers, O God;
    you refreshed your weary
        inheritance.
10Your people settled in it,
    and from your bounty, O God, you
        provided for the poor.

11The Lord announced the word,
    and great was the company of those
        who proclaimed it:
12"Kings and armies flee in haste;
    in the camps men divide the
        plunder.

---

*a*4 Or / *prepare the way for him who rides through the deserts*   *b*6 Or *the desolate in a homeland*

¹³Even while you sleep among the
  campfires,ᵃ
the wings of ˪my˩ dove are sheathed
  with silver,
its feathers with shining gold."
¹⁴When the Almightyᵇ scattered the
  kings in the land,
it was like snow fallen on Zalmon.

¹⁵The mountains of Bashan are majestic
  mountains;
rugged are the mountains of
  Bashan.
¹⁶Why gaze in envy, O rugged
  mountains,

at the mountain where God chooses
  to reign,
where the LORD himself will dwell
  forever?
¹⁷The chariots of God are tens of
  thousands
and thousands of thousands;
the Lord ˪has come˩ from Sinai into
  his sanctuary.
¹⁸When you ascended on high,
you led captives in your train;
you received gifts from men,
even fromᶜ the rebellious —
that you,ᵈ O LORD God, might
  dwell there.

ᵃ13 Or *saddlebags*   ᵇ14 Hebrew *Shaddai*   ᶜ18 Or *gifts for men, / even*   ᵈ18 Or *they*

MONDAY

VERSE FOR THE DAY: *AUTHOR:*   *PASSAGE FOR THE DAY:*
Psalm 66:10   Joe Gibbs   Psalm 66:8–12

Through Deep Waters

NATIONAL Football League coach Joe Gibbs prayed fervently
as doctors removed a tumor from inside his wife's skull. She
survived the operation and recuperated, yet part of her face remains paralyzed.

"I belong to God," she says. "And I believe he allows things
to come into our lives for a reason. Just because I don't know
the reason doesn't mean there isn't one. Maybe this has just
made me more sensitive to other people with problems."

She's dealing with it. It's been more than ten years now and
is part of our lives. I'm proud to introduce her anywhere. Surgery may have slightly altered her looks, but it did not change
her character. She's still Pat.

I'll tell you, going through something like that with the person you love sure makes losing a football game seem trivial. I
had asked God why he had let me endure that horrible season
in Tampa, and why I had been so blind and faithless when I
had no peace about his leading me to San Diego. In a small
way, I think, he was preparing me for this real trial.

There would be other difficulties in my life but none as difficult or scary as almost losing my wife. I still had a lot to learn
about priorities and my faith and my ego, but I could never
again say that God hadn't led me through some deep waters to
strengthen me for when those new lessons came.

Additional Scripture Readings: *Go to page 595 for your next*
Isaiah 43:1–7; 1 Peter 1:3–9   *devotional reading.*

¹⁹Praise be to the Lord, to God our
Savior,
who daily bears our burdens. *Selah*
²⁰Our God is a God who saves;
from the Sovereign LORD comes
escape from death.

²¹Surely God will crush the heads of his
enemies,
the hairy crowns of those who go
on in their sins.
²²The Lord says, "I will bring them from
Bashan;
I will bring them from the depths of
the sea,
²³that you may plunge your feet in the
blood of your foes,
while the tongues of your dogs have
their share."

²⁴Your procession has come into view,
O God,
the procession of my God and King
into the sanctuary.
²⁵In front are the singers, after them the
musicians;
with them are the maidens playing
tambourines.
²⁶Praise God in the great congregation;
praise the LORD in the assembly of
Israel.
²⁷There is the little tribe of Benjamin,
leading them,
there the great throng of Judah's
princes,
and there the princes of Zebulun
and of Naphtali.

²⁸Summon your power, O God[a];
show us your strength, O God, as
you have done before.
²⁹Because of your temple at Jerusalem
kings will bring you gifts.
³⁰Rebuke the beast among the reeds,
the herd of bulls among the calves
of the nations.
Humbled, may it bring bars of silver.
Scatter the nations who delight in
war.
³¹Envoys will come from Egypt;
Cush[b] will submit herself to God.

³²Sing to God, O kingdoms of the earth,
sing praise to the Lord,   *Selah*
³³to him who rides the ancient skies
above,
who thunders with mighty voice.
³⁴Proclaim the power of God,
whose majesty is over Israel,

whose power is in the skies.
³⁵You are awesome, O God, in your
sanctuary;
the God of Israel gives power and
strength to his people.

Praise be to God!

Psalm 69

For the director of music. To the tune
of, "Lilies." Of David.

¹Save me, O God,
for the waters have come up to my
neck.
²I sink in the miry depths,
where there is no foothold.
I have come into the deep waters;
the floods engulf me.
³I am worn out calling for help;
my throat is parched.
My eyes fail,
looking for my God.
⁴Those who hate me without reason
outnumber the hairs of my head;
many are my enemies without cause,
those who seek to destroy me.
I am forced to restore
what I did not steal.

⁵You know my folly, O God;
my guilt is not hidden from you.

⁶May those who hope in you
not be disgraced because of me,
O Lord, the LORD Almighty;
may those who seek you
not be put to shame because of me,
O God of Israel.
⁷For I endure scorn for your sake,
and shame covers my face.
⁸I am a stranger to my brothers,
an alien to my own mother's sons;
⁹for zeal for your house consumes me,
and the insults of those who insult
you fall on me.
¹⁰When I weep and fast,
I must endure scorn;
¹¹when I put on sackcloth,
people make sport of me.
¹²Those who sit at the gate mock me,
and I am the song of the drunkards.

¹³But I pray to you, O LORD,
in the time of your favor;
in your great love, O God,
answer me with your sure salvation.
¹⁴Rescue me from the mire,

---

[a]28 Many Hebrew manuscripts, Septuagint and Syriac; most Hebrew manuscripts *Your God has summoned
power for you*   [b]31 That is, the upper Nile region

do not let me sink;
    deliver me from those who hate me,
    from the deep waters.
¹⁵Do not let the floodwaters engulf me
    or the depths swallow me up
    or the pit close its mouth over me.
¹⁶Answer me, O Lord, out of the
        goodness of your love;
    in your great mercy turn to me.
¹⁷Do not hide your face from your
        servant;
    answer me quickly, for I am in
        trouble.
¹⁸Come near and rescue me;
    redeem me because of my foes.

¹⁹You know how I am scorned,
        disgraced and shamed;
    all my enemies are before you.
²⁰Scorn has broken my heart
    and has left me helpless;
    I looked for sympathy, but there was
        none,
    for comforters, but I found none.
²¹They put gall in my food
    and gave me vinegar for my thirst.

²²May the table set before them become
        a snare;
    may it become retribution and*a* a
        trap.
²³May their eyes be darkened so they
        cannot see,
    and their backs be bent forever.
²⁴Pour out your wrath on them;
    let your fierce anger overtake them.
²⁵May their place be deserted;
    let there be no one to dwell in their
        tents.
²⁶For they persecute those you wound
    and talk about the pain of those you
        hurt.
²⁷Charge them with crime upon crime;
    do not let them share in your
        salvation.
²⁸May they be blotted out of the book
        of life
    and not be listed with the righteous.

²⁹I am in pain and distress;
    may your salvation, O God, protect
        me.
³⁰I will praise God's name in song
    and glorify him with thanksgiving.
³¹This will please the Lord more than
        an ox,
    more than a bull with its horns and
        hoofs.
³²The poor will see and be glad—

you who seek God, may your hearts
        live!
³³The Lord hears the needy
    and does not despise his captive
        people.

³⁴Let heaven and earth praise him,
    the seas and all that move in them,
³⁵for God will save Zion
    and rebuild the cities of Judah.
    Then people will settle there and
        possess it;
³⁶   the children of his servants will
        inherit it,
    and those who love his name will
        dwell there.

Psalm 70

*For the director of music. Of David.
A petition.*

¹Hasten, O God, to save me;
    O Lord, come quickly to help me.
²May those who seek my life
    be put to shame and confusion;
    may all who desire my ruin
    be turned back in disgrace.
³May those who say to me, "Aha!
        Aha!"
    turn back because of their shame.
⁴But may all who seek you
    rejoice and be glad in you;
    may those who love your salvation
        always say,
    "Let God be exalted!"

⁵Yet I am poor and needy;
    come quickly to me, O God.
You are my help and my deliverer;
    O Lord, do not delay.

Psalm 71

¹In you, O Lord, I have taken refuge;
    let me never be put to shame.
²Rescue me and deliver me in your
        righteousness;
    turn your ear to me and save me.
³Be my rock of refuge,
    to which I can always go;
    give the command to save me,
    for you are my rock and my
        fortress.
⁴Deliver me, O my God, from the hand
        of the wicked,
    from the grasp of evil and cruel
        men.

a22 Or snare / and their fellowship become

⁵For you have been my hope,
  O Sovereign LORD,
  my confidence since my youth.
⁶From birth I have relied on you;
  you brought me forth from my
    mother's womb.
  I will ever praise you.
⁷I have become like a portent to many,
  but you are my strong refuge.
⁸My mouth is filled with your praise,
  declaring your splendor all day
    long.

⁹Do not cast me away when I am old;
  do not forsake me when my
    strength is gone.
¹⁰For my enemies speak against me;
  those who wait to kill me conspire
    together.
¹¹They say, "God has forsaken him;
  pursue him and seize him,
  for no one will rescue him."
¹²Be not far from me, O God;
  come quickly, O my God, to help
    me.
¹³May my accusers perish in shame;
  may those who want to harm me
  be covered with scorn and disgrace.

¹⁴But as for me, I will always have
    hope;
  I will praise you more and more.
¹⁵My mouth will tell of your
    righteousness,
  of your salvation all day long,
  though I know not its measure.
¹⁶I will come and proclaim your mighty
    acts, O Sovereign LORD;
  I will proclaim your righteousness,
  yours alone.
¹⁷Since my youth, O God, you have
    taught me,
  and to this day I declare your
    marvelous deeds.
¹⁸Even when I am old and gray,
  do not forsake me, O God,
  till I declare your power to the next
    generation,
  your might to all who are to come.

¹⁹Your righteousness reaches to the
    skies, O God,
  you who have done great things.
  Who, O God, is like you?
²⁰Though you have made me see
    troubles, many and bitter,
  you will restore my life again;
  from the depths of the earth

you will again bring me up.
²¹You will increase my honor
  and comfort me once again.

²²I will praise you with the harp
  for your faithfulness, O my God;
  I will sing praise to you with the lyre,
  O Holy One of Israel.
²³My lips will shout for joy
  when I sing praise to you—
  I, whom you have redeemed.
²⁴My tongue will tell of your righteous
    acts
  all day long,
  for those who wanted to harm me
  have been put to shame and
    confusion.

Psalm 72

Of Solomon.

¹Endow the king with your justice,
  O God,
  the royal son with your
    righteousness.
²He will*a* judge your people in
    righteousness,
  your afflicted ones with justice.
³The mountains will bring prosperity to
    the people,
  the hills the fruit of righteousness.
⁴He will defend the afflicted among the
    people
  and save the children of the needy;
  he will crush the oppressor.

⁵He will endure*b* as long as the sun,
  as long as the moon, through all
    generations.
⁶He will be like rain falling on a mown
    field,
  like showers watering the earth.
⁷In his days the righteous will flourish;
  prosperity will abound till the moon
    is no more.

⁸He will rule from sea to sea
  and from the River*c* to the ends of
    the earth.*d*
⁹The desert tribes will bow before him
  and his enemies will lick the dust.
¹⁰The kings of Tarshish and of distant
    shores
  will bring tribute to him;
  the kings of Sheba and Seba
  will present him gifts.
¹¹All kings will bow down to him
  and all nations will serve him.

---

*a*2 Or *May he*; similarly in verses 3-11 and 17   *b*5 Septuagint; Hebrew *You will be feared*   *c*8 That is,
the Euphrates   *d*8 Or *the end of the land*

12For he will deliver the needy who cry
out,
the afflicted who have no one to
help.
13He will take pity on the weak and the
needy
and save the needy from death.
14He will rescue them from oppression
and violence,
for precious is their blood in his
sight.

15Long may he live!
May gold from Sheba be given him.
May people ever pray for him
and bless him all day long.
16Let grain abound throughout the land;
on the tops of the hills may it sway.
Let its fruit flourish like Lebanon;
let it thrive like the grass of the
field.
17May his name endure forever;
may it continue as long as the sun.

All nations will be blessed through
him,
and they will call him blessed.

18Praise be to the LORD God, the God of
Israel,
who alone does marvelous deeds.
19Praise be to his glorious name forever;
may the whole earth be filled with
his glory.
Amen and Amen.

20This concludes the prayers of David
son of Jesse.

BOOK III

Psalms 73–89

Psalm 73

A psalm of Asaph.

1Surely God is good to Israel,
to those who are pure in heart.

2But as for me, my feet had almost
slipped;
I had nearly lost my foothold.
3For I envied the arrogant
when I saw the prosperity of the
wicked.

4They have no struggles;

their bodies are healthy and
strong.[a]
5They are free from the burdens
common to man;
they are not plagued by human ills.
6Therefore pride is their necklace;
they clothe themselves with
violence.
7From their callous hearts comes
iniquity[b];
the evil conceits of their minds
know no limits.
8They scoff, and speak with malice;
in their arrogance they threaten
oppression.
9Their mouths lay claim to heaven,
and their tongues take possession of
the earth.
10Therefore their people turn to them
and drink up waters in
abundance.[c]
11They say, "How can God know?
Does the Most High have
knowledge?"

12This is what the wicked are like—
always carefree, they increase in
wealth.

13Surely in vain have I kept my heart
pure;
in vain have I washed my hands in
innocence.
14All day long I have been plagued;
I have been punished every
morning.

15If I had said, "I will speak thus,"
I would have betrayed your
children.
16When I tried to understand all this,
it was oppressive to me
17till I entered the sanctuary of God;
then I understood their final
destiny.

18Surely you place them on slippery
ground;
you cast them down to ruin.
19How suddenly are they destroyed,
completely swept away by terrors!
20As a dream when one awakes,
so when you arise, O Lord,
you will despise them as fantasies.

21When my heart was grieved
and my spirit embittered,
22I was senseless and ignorant;

a4 With a different word division of the Hebrew; Masoretic Text *struggles at their death; / their bodies are healthy* *b7* Syriac (see also Septuagint); Hebrew *Their eyes bulge with fat* *c10* The meaning of the Hebrew for this verse is uncertain.

I was a brute beast before you.

23Yet I am always with you;
    you hold me by my right hand.
24You guide me with your counsel,
    and afterward you will take me into
        glory.
25Whom have I in heaven but you?
    And earth has nothing I desire
        besides you.
26My flesh and my heart may fail,
    but God is the strength of my heart
    and my portion forever.

27Those who are far from you will
        perish;
    you destroy all who are unfaithful
    to you.
28But as for me, it is good to be near
        God.
    I have made the Sovereign Lord my
        refuge;
    I will tell of all your deeds.

Psalm 74

A *maskil*[a] of Asaph.

1Why have you rejected us forever,
    O God?
    Why does your anger smolder
        against the sheep of your
        pasture?
2Remember the people you purchased
    of old,
    the tribe of your inheritance, whom
        you redeemed —
    Mount Zion, where you dwelt.
3Turn your steps toward these
        everlasting ruins,
    all this destruction the enemy has
    brought on the sanctuary.

4Your foes roared in the place where
    you met with us;
    they set up their standards as signs.
5They behaved like men wielding axes
    to cut through a thicket of trees.
6They smashed all the carved paneling
    with their axes and hatchets.
7They burned your sanctuary to the
        ground;
    they defiled the dwelling place of
        your Name.
8They said in their hearts, "We will
    crush them completely!"
    They burned every place where God
        was worshiped in the land.
9We are given no miraculous signs;

no prophets are left,
    and none of us knows how long
        this will be.

10How long will the enemy mock you,
    O God?
    Will the foe revile your name
        forever?
11Why do you hold back your hand,
    your right hand?
    Take it from the folds of your
        garment and destroy them!

12But you, O God, are my king from of
        old;
    you bring salvation upon the earth.
13It was you who split open the sea by
    your power;
    you broke the heads of the monster
    in the waters.
14It was you who crushed the heads of
        Leviathan
    and gave him as food to the
        creatures of the desert.
15It was you who opened up springs
    and streams;
    you dried up the ever flowing
        rivers.
16The day is yours, and yours also the
        night;
    you established the sun and moon.
17It was you who set all the boundaries
    of the earth;
    you made both summer and winter.

18Remember how the enemy has
        mocked you, O Lord,
    how foolish people have reviled
        your name.
19Do not hand over the life of your dove
    to wild beasts;
    do not forget the lives of your
        afflicted people forever.
20Have regard for your covenant,
    because haunts of violence fill the
        dark places of the land.
21Do not let the oppressed retreat in
        disgrace;
    may the poor and needy praise your
        name.

22Rise up, O God, and defend your
        cause;
    remember how fools mock you all
        day long.
23Do not ignore the clamor of your
        adversaries,
    the uproar of your enemies, which
        rises continually.

aTitle: Probably a literary or musical term

Psalm 75

For the director of music. To the tune of, "Do Not Destroy." A psalm of Asaph. A song.

[1] We give thanks to you, O God,
    we give thanks, for your Name is near;
  men tell of your wonderful deeds.

[2] You say, "I choose the appointed time;
    it is I who judge uprightly.
[3] When the earth and all its people quake,
    it is I who hold its pillars firm.
                                        Selah
[4] To the arrogant I say, 'Boast no more,'
    and to the wicked, 'Do not lift up your horns.
[5] Do not lift your horns against heaven;
    do not speak with outstretched neck.' "

[6] No one from the east or the west
    or from the desert can exalt a man.
[7] But it is God who judges:
    He brings one down, he exalts another.
[8] In the hand of the LORD is a cup
    full of foaming wine mixed with spices;
  he pours it out, and all the wicked of the earth
    drink it down to its very dregs.

[9] As for me, I will declare this forever;
    I will sing praise to the God of Jacob.
[10] I will cut off the horns of all the wicked,
    but the horns of the righteous will be lifted up.

Psalm 76

For the director of music. With stringed instruments. A psalm of Asaph. A song.

[1] In Judah God is known;
    his name is great in Israel.
[2] His tent is in Salem,
    his dwelling place in Zion.
[3] There he broke the flashing arrows,
    the shields and the swords, the weapons of war.   Selah

[4] You are resplendent with light,
    more majestic than mountains rich with game.
[5] Valiant men lie plundered,
  they sleep their last sleep;
  not one of the warriors
    can lift his hands.
[6] At your rebuke, O God of Jacob,
    both horse and chariot lie still.
[7] You alone are to be feared.
    Who can stand before you when you are angry?
[8] From heaven you pronounced judgment,
    and the land feared and was quiet—
[9] when you, O God, rose up to judge,
    to save all the afflicted of the land.
                                        Selah
[10] Surely your wrath against men brings you praise,
    and the survivors of your wrath are restrained. [a]
[11] Make vows to the LORD your God and fulfill them;
    let all the neighboring lands
    bring gifts to the One to be feared.
[12] He breaks the spirit of rulers;
    he is feared by the kings of the earth.

Psalm 77

For the director of music. For Jeduthun. Of Asaph. A psalm.

[1] I cried out to God for help;
    I cried out to God to hear me.
[2] When I was in distress, I sought the Lord;
    at night I stretched out untiring hands
  and my soul refused to be comforted.

[3] I remembered you, O God, and I groaned;
    I mused, and my spirit grew faint.
                                        Selah
[4] You kept my eyes from closing;
    I was too troubled to speak.
[5] I thought about the former days,
    the years of long ago;
[6] I remembered my songs in the night.
    My heart mused and my spirit inquired:
[7] "Will the Lord reject forever?
    Will he never show his favor again?
[8] Has his unfailing love vanished forever?
    Has his promise failed for all time?
[9] Has God forgotten to be merciful?

---

[a] 10 Or Surely the wrath of men brings you praise, / and with the remainder of wrath you arm yourself

Has he in anger withheld his
   compassion?"   *Selah*
[10]Then I thought, "To this I will appeal:
   the years of the right hand of the
     Most High."
[11]I will remember the deeds of the
   LORD;
   yes, I will remember your miracles
     of long ago.
[12]I will meditate on all your works
   and consider all your mighty deeds.

[13]Your ways, O God, are holy.
   What god is so great as our God?
[14]You are the God who performs
     miracles;
   you display your power among the
     peoples.
[15]With your mighty arm you redeemed
     your people,
   the descendants of Jacob and
     Joseph.   *Selah*

[16]The waters saw you, O God,
   the waters saw you and writhed;
   the very depths were convulsed.
[17]The clouds poured down water,
   the skies resounded with thunder;
   your arrows flashed back and forth.
[18]Your thunder was heard in the
     whirlwind,
   your lightning lit up the world;
   the earth trembled and quaked.
[19]Your path led through the sea,
   your way through the mighty
     waters,
   though your footprints were not
     seen.

[20]You led your people like a flock
   by the hand of Moses and Aaron.

Psalm 78

A maskil[a] of Asaph.

[1]O my people, hear my teaching;
   listen to the words of my mouth.
[2]I will open my mouth in parables,
   I will utter hidden things, things
     from of old—
[3]what we have heard and known,
   what our fathers have told us.
[4]We will not hide them from their
     children;
   we will tell the next generation
the praiseworthy deeds of the LORD,
   his power, and the wonders he has
     done.

[5]He decreed statutes for Jacob
   and established the law in Israel,
which he commanded our forefathers
   to teach their children,
[6]so the next generation would know
     them,
   even the children yet to be born,
   and they in turn would tell their
     children.
[7]Then they would put their trust in
     God
   and would not forget his deeds
   but would keep his commands.
[8]They would not be like their
     forefathers—
   a stubborn and rebellious
     generation,
   whose hearts were not loyal to God,
   whose spirits were not faithful to
     him.

[9]The men of Ephraim, though armed
     with bows,
   turned back on the day of battle;
[10]they did not keep God's covenant
   and refused to live by his law.
[11]They forgot what he had done,
   the wonders he had shown them.
[12]He did miracles in the sight of their
     fathers
   in the land of Egypt, in the region
     of Zoan.
[13]He divided the sea and led them
     through;
   he made the water stand firm like a
     wall.
[14]He guided them with the cloud by day
   and with light from the fire all
     night.
[15]He split the rocks in the desert
   and gave them water as abundant
     as the seas;
[16]he brought streams out of a rocky
     crag
   and made water flow down like
     rivers.

[17]But they continued to sin against him,
   rebelling in the desert against the
     Most High.
[18]They willfully put God to the test
   by demanding the food they craved.
[19]They spoke against God, saying,
   "Can God spread a table in the
     desert?
[20]When he struck the rock, water
     gushed out,
   and streams flowed abundantly.

---

[a]Title: Probably a literary or musical term

But can he also give us food?
Can he supply meat for his people?"
²¹When the LORD heard them, he was very angry;
his fire broke out against Jacob,
and his wrath rose against Israel,
²²for they did not believe in God
or trust in his deliverance.
²³Yet he gave a command to the skies above
and opened the doors of the heavens;
²⁴he rained down manna for the people to eat,
he gave them the grain of heaven.
²⁵Men ate the bread of angels;
he sent them all the food they could eat.
²⁶He let loose the east wind from the heavens

and led forth the south wind by his power.
²⁷He rained meat down on them like dust,
flying birds like sand on the seashore.
²⁸He made them come down inside their camp,
all around their tents.
²⁹They ate till they had more than enough,
for he had given them what they craved.
³⁰But before they turned from the food they craved,
even while it was still in their mouths,
³¹God's anger rose against them;
he put to death the sturdiest among them,

TUESDAY

VERSE FOR THE DAY:
Psalm 78:4

AUTHOR:
James Dobson

PASSAGE FOR THE DAY:
Psalm 78:1–8

Passing the Baton

[A FATHER'S] most important responsibility, I believe, is to communicate the real meaning of Christianity to his children. This mission can be likened to a three-man relay race. First, your father runs his lap around the track, carrying the baton, which represents the gospel of Jesus Christ. At the appropriate moment, he hands the baton to you, and you begin your journey around the track. Then finally, the time will come when you must get the baton safely in the hands of your children. But as any track coach will testify, *relay races are won or lost in the transfer of the baton*. There is a critical moment when all can be lost by a fumble or miscalculation. The baton is rarely dropped on the back side of the track when the runner has it firmly in his grasp. If failure is to occur, it will probably happen in the exchange between generations.

According to the Christian values that govern my life, my most important reason for living is to get the baton, the gospel, safely in the hands of my children. Of course, I want to place it in as many other hands as possible; *nevertheless, my number one responsibility is to evangelize my own children*. I hope millions of other fathers agree with that ultimate priority.

Additional Scripture Readings:
Deuteronomy 6:4–25; Psalm 145:1–7

Go to page 600 for your next devotional reading.

cutting down the young men of
Israel.

³²In spite of all this, they kept on
sinning;
in spite of his wonders, they did not
believe.
³³So he ended their days in futility
and their years in terror.
³⁴Whenever God slew them, they would
seek him;
they eagerly turned to him again.
³⁵They remembered that God was their
Rock,
that God Most High was their
Redeemer.
³⁶But then they would flatter him with
their mouths,
lying to him with their tongues;
³⁷their hearts were not loyal to him,
they were not faithful to his
covenant.
³⁸Yet he was merciful;
he forgave their iniquities
and did not destroy them.
Time after time he restrained his
anger
and did not stir up his full wrath.
³⁹He remembered that they were but
flesh,
a passing breeze that does not
return.
⁴⁰How often they rebelled against him
in the desert
and grieved him in the wasteland!
⁴¹Again and again they put God to the
test;
they vexed the Holy One of Israel.
⁴²They did not remember his power —
the day he redeemed them from the
oppressor,
⁴³the day he displayed his miraculous
signs in Egypt,
his wonders in the region of Zoan.
⁴⁴He turned their rivers to blood;
they could not drink from their
streams.
⁴⁵He sent swarms of flies that devoured
them,
and frogs that devastated them.
⁴⁶He gave their crops to the
grasshopper,
their produce to the locust.
⁴⁷He destroyed their vines with hail
and their sycamore-figs with sleet.
⁴⁸He gave over their cattle to the hail,
their livestock to bolts of lightning.
⁴⁹He unleashed against them his hot
anger,

his wrath, indignation and
hostility —
a band of destroying angels.
⁵⁰He prepared a path for his anger;
he did not spare them from death
but gave them over to the plague.
⁵¹He struck down all the firstborn of
Egypt,
the firstfruits of manhood in the
tents of Ham.
⁵²But he brought his people out like a
flock;
he led them like sheep through the
desert.
⁵³He guided them safely, so they were
unafraid;
but the sea engulfed their enemies.
⁵⁴Thus he brought them to the border
of his holy land,
to the hill country his right hand
had taken.
⁵⁵He drove out nations before them
and allotted their lands to them as
an inheritance;
he settled the tribes of Israel in
their homes.
⁵⁶But they put God to the test
and rebelled against the Most High;
they did not keep his statutes.
⁵⁷Like their fathers they were disloyal
and faithless,
as unreliable as a faulty bow.
⁵⁸They angered him with their high
places;
they aroused his jealousy with their
idols.
⁵⁹When God heard them, he was very
angry;
he rejected Israel completely.
⁶⁰He abandoned the tabernacle of
Shiloh,
the tent he had set up among men.
⁶¹He sent ͵the ark of͵ his might into
captivity,
his splendor into the hands of the
enemy.
⁶²He gave his people over to the sword;
he was very angry with his
inheritance.
⁶³Fire consumed their young men,
and their maidens had no wedding
songs;
⁶⁴their priests were put to the sword,
and their widows could not weep.
⁶⁵Then the Lord awoke as from sleep,
as a man wakes from the stupor of
wine.
⁶⁶He beat back his enemies;
he put them to everlasting shame.

⁶⁷Then he rejected the tents of Joseph,
  he did not choose the tribe of
    Ephraim;
⁶⁸but he chose the tribe of Judah,
  Mount Zion, which he loved.
⁶⁹He built his sanctuary like the heights,
  like the earth that he established
    forever.
⁷⁰He chose David his servant
  and took him from the sheep pens;
⁷¹from tending the sheep he brought
    him
  to be the shepherd of his people
    Jacob,
  of Israel his inheritance.
⁷²And David shepherded them with
    integrity of heart;
  with skillful hands he led them.

Psalm 79

A psalm of Asaph.

¹O God, the nations have invaded your
    inheritance;
  they have defiled your holy temple,
  they have reduced Jerusalem to
    rubble.
²They have given the dead bodies of
    your servants
  as food to the birds of the air,
  the flesh of your saints to the beasts
    of the earth.
³They have poured out blood like
    water
  all around Jerusalem,
  and there is no one to bury the
    dead.
⁴We are objects of reproach to our
    neighbors,
  of scorn and derision to those
    around us.

⁵How long, O LORD? Will you be angry
    forever?
  How long will your jealousy burn
    like fire?
⁶Pour out your wrath on the nations
  that do not acknowledge you,
  on the kingdoms
  that do not call on your name;
⁷for they have devoured Jacob
  and destroyed his homeland.
⁸Do not hold against us the sins of the
    fathers;
  may your mercy come quickly to
    meet us,
  for we are in desperate need.

⁹Help us, O God our Savior,
  for the glory of your name;

deliver us and forgive our sins
  for your name's sake.
¹⁰Why should the nations say,
  "Where is their God?"
Before our eyes, make known among
    the nations
  that you avenge the outpoured
    blood of your servants.
¹¹May the groans of the prisoners come
    before you;
  by the strength of your arm
  preserve those condemned to die.

¹²Pay back into the laps of our
    neighbors seven times
  the reproach they have hurled at
    you, O Lord.
¹³Then we your people, the sheep of
    your pasture,
  will praise you forever;
from generation to generation
  we will recount your praise.

Psalm 80

*For the director of music. To the tune
of, "The Lilies of the Covenant."
Of Asaph. A psalm.*

¹Hear us, O Shepherd of Israel,
  you who lead Joseph like a flock;
you who sit enthroned between the
    cherubim, shine forth
²   before Ephraim, Benjamin and
      Manasseh.
Awaken your might;
  come and save us.

³Restore us, O God;
  make your face shine upon us,
  that we may be saved.

⁴O LORD God Almighty,
  how long will your anger smolder
  against the prayers of your people?
⁵You have fed them with the bread of
    tears;
  you have made them drink tears by
    the bowlful.
⁶You have made us a source of
    contention to our neighbors,
  and our enemies mock us.

⁷Restore us, O God Almighty;
  make your face shine upon us,
  that we may be saved.

⁸You brought a vine out of Egypt;
  you drove out the nations and
    planted it.
⁹You cleared the ground for it,
  and it took root and filled the land.

[10]The mountains were covered with its
shade,
the mighty cedars with its branches.
[11]It sent out its boughs to the Sea,[a]
its shoots as far as the River.[b]
[12]Why have you broken down its walls
so that all who pass by pick its
grapes?
[13]Boars from the forest ravage it
and the creatures of the field feed
on it.
[14]Return to us, O God Almighty!
Look down from heaven and see!
Watch over this vine,
[15]   the root your right hand has
planted,
the son[c] you have raised up for
yourself.
[16]Your vine is cut down, it is burned
with fire;
at your rebuke your people perish.
[17]Let your hand rest on the man at your
right hand,
the son of man you have raised up
for yourself.
[18]Then we will not turn away from you;
revive us, and we will call on your
name.
[19]Restore us, O LORD God Almighty;
make your face shine upon us,
that we may be saved.

Psalm 81

For the director of music. According to
gittith.[d] Of Asaph.

[1]Sing for joy to God our strength;
shout aloud to the God of Jacob!
[2]Begin the music, strike the
tambourine,
play the melodious harp and lyre.
[3]Sound the ram's horn at the New
Moon,
and when the moon is full, on the
day of our Feast;
[4]this is a decree for Israel,
an ordinance of the God of Jacob.
[5]He established it as a statute for
Joseph
when he went out against Egypt,
where we heard a language we did
not understand.[e]
[6]He says, "I removed the burden from
their shoulders;

their hands were set free from the
basket.
[7]In your distress you called and I
rescued you,
I answered you out of a
thundercloud;
I tested you at the waters of
Meribah.   *Selah*
[8]"Hear, O my people, and I will warn
you —
if you would but listen to me,
O Israel!
[9]You shall have no foreign god among
you;
you shall not bow down to an alien
god.
[10]I am the LORD your God,
who brought you up out of Egypt.
Open wide your mouth and I will
fill it.
[11]"But my people would not listen to
me;
Israel would not submit to me.
[12]So I gave them over to their stubborn
hearts
to follow their own devices.
[13]"If my people would but listen to me,
if Israel would follow my ways,
[14]how quickly would I subdue their
enemies
and turn my hand against their
foes!
[15]Those who hate the LORD would
cringe before him,
and their punishment would last
forever.
[16]But you would be fed with the finest
of wheat;
with honey from the rock I would
satisfy you."

Psalm 82

A psalm of Asaph.

[1]God presides in the great assembly;
he gives judgment among the
"gods":
[2]"How long will you[f] defend the
unjust
and show partiality to the wicked?
                                  Selah
[3]Defend the cause of the weak and
fatherless;

---

*a*11 Probably the Mediterranean   *b*11 That is, the Euphrates   *c*15 Or *branch*   *d*Title: Probably a
musical term   *e*5 Or / *and we heard a voice we had not known*   *f*2 The Hebrew is plural.

maintain the rights of the poor and
oppressed.
4Rescue the weak and needy;
deliver them from the hand of the
wicked.

5"They know nothing, they understand
nothing.
They walk about in darkness;
all the foundations of the earth are
shaken.

6"I said, 'You are "gods";
you are all sons of the Most High.'
7But you will die like mere men;
you will fall like every other ruler."

8Rise up, O God, judge the earth,
for all the nations are your
inheritance.

Psalm 83

A song. A psalm of Asaph.

1O God, do not keep silent;
be not quiet, O God, be not still.
2See how your enemies are astir,
how your foes rear their heads.
3With cunning they conspire against
your people;
they plot against those you cherish.
4"Come," they say, "let us destroy them
as a nation,
that the name of Israel be
remembered no more."

5With one mind they plot together;
they form an alliance against you —
6the tents of Edom and the Ishmaelites,
of Moab and the Hagrites,
7Gebal,[a] Ammon and Amalek,
Philistia, with the people of Tyre.
8Even Assyria has joined them
to lend strength to the descendants
of Lot.   *Selah*

9Do to them as you did to Midian,
as you did to Sisera and Jabin at the
river Kishon,
10who perished at Endor
and became like refuse on the
ground.
11Make their nobles like Oreb and Zeeb,
all their princes like Zebah and
Zalmunna,
12who said, "Let us take possession
of the pasturelands of God."

13Make them like tumbleweed, O my
God,

like chaff before the wind.
14As fire consumes the forest
or a flame sets the mountains
ablaze,
15so pursue them with your tempest
and terrify them with your storm.
16Cover their faces with shame
so that men will seek your name,
O LORD.

17May they ever be ashamed and
dismayed;
may they perish in disgrace.
18Let them know that you, whose name
is the LORD —
that you alone are the Most High
over all the earth.

Psalm 84

*For the director of music. According to
gittith.[b] Of the Sons of Korah. A psalm.*

1How lovely is your dwelling place,
O LORD Almighty!
2My soul yearns, even faints,
for the courts of the LORD;
my heart and my flesh cry out
for the living God.

3Even the sparrow has found a home,
and the swallow a nest for herself,
where she may have her young —
a place near your altar,
O LORD Almighty, my King and my
God.
4Blessed are those who dwell in your
house;
they are ever praising you.   *Selah*

5Blessed are those whose strength is in
you,
who have set their hearts on
pilgrimage.
6As they pass through the Valley of
Baca,
they make it a place of springs;
the autumn rains also cover it with
pools.[c]
7They go from strength to strength,
till each appears before God in Zion.

8Hear my prayer, O LORD God
Almighty;
listen to me, O God of Jacob.   *Selah*
9Look upon our shield,[d] O God;
look with favor on your anointed
one.

a7 That is, Byblos   *b*Title: Probably a musical term   *c6* Or *blessings*   *d9* Or *sovereign*

¹⁰Better is one day in your courts
    than a thousand elsewhere;
I would rather be a doorkeeper in the
        house of my God
than dwell in the tents of the
        wicked.
¹¹For the LORD God is a sun and shield;

the LORD bestows favor and honor;
    no good thing does he withhold
        from those whose walk is blameless.

¹²O LORD Almighty,
    blessed is the man who trusts in
        you.

WEDNESDAY

VERSE FOR THE DAY: *AUTHOR:*   *PASSAGE FOR THE DAY:*
Psalm 84:10   *Don Wyrtzen*   *Psalm 84:8–12*

A Worthy Walk

THESE verses are both a comfort and a challenge. I know I've been "set apart" to Christian service in the ministry of music, but sometimes low-grade motivation obscures my vision. The enchantment of conducting a professional orchestra for the first time, seeing my first published song, listening to my first record have faded, and I'm faced with the daily grind. I must work harder to keep the excitement and creative-energy level high.

The psalmist has no such fears or insecurities. His rock-solid devotion to God supersedes all other concerns. He knows he has been set apart ("anointed") by the Lord, and he is utterly committed to his calling (v. 9). In fact, if necessary, he is willing to serve in some menial position ("a doorkeeper") in the house of the Lord rather than to live in the lavish tents of the wicked (v. 10).

In verse 11 we learn the reason for such devotion. The Lord is pictured as a "sun and shield." He offers warmth, blessing, protection and prosperity. He does not withhold anything good from those whose walk with him is blameless—"a spotless walk, conduct ordered according to God's will, and a truth-loving mode of thought."

Now that the musical honeymoon is over, I need to be more committed, to persist and persevere in practicing my craft. I need to exercise discipline as I'm enjoying inspiration. I also need to follow the example of my ancient colleague—turn to my Source and spend more time in meaningful interaction with his people. Out of the rich texture of meaningful human relationships come songs that touch the heart.

O Lord, today I rededicate my life to your service. Be my sun and shield, and give me the satisfaction of knowing that my walk is worthy of my calling.

Additional Scripture Readings:
Psalm 27; 2 John 4–6

*Go to page 605 for your next
devotional reading.*

Psalm 85

For the director of music. Of the Sons of
Korah. A psalm.

¹You showed favor to your land,
    O Lord;
  you restored the fortunes of Jacob.
²You forgave the iniquity of your
    people
  and covered all their sins.   Selah
³You set aside all your wrath
  and turned from your fierce anger.

⁴Restore us again, O God our Savior,
  and put away your displeasure
    toward us.
⁵Will you be angry with us forever?
  Will you prolong your anger
    through all generations?
⁶Will you not revive us again,
  that your people may rejoice in
    you?
⁷Show us your unfailing love, O Lord,
  and grant us your salvation.

⁸I will listen to what God the Lord will
    say;
  he promises peace to his people, his
    saints—
  but let them not return to folly.
⁹Surely his salvation is near those who
    fear him,
  that his glory may dwell in our
    land.

¹⁰Love and faithfulness meet together;
  righteousness and peace kiss each
    other.
¹¹Faithfulness springs forth from the
    earth,
  and righteousness looks down from
    heaven.
¹²The Lord will indeed give what is
    good,
  and our land will yield its harvest.
¹³Righteousness goes before him
  and prepares the way for his steps.

Psalm 86

A prayer of David.

¹Hear, O Lord, and answer me,
  for I am poor and needy.
²Guard my life, for I am devoted to
    you.
  You are my God; save your servant
    who trusts in you.
³Have mercy on me, O Lord,

  for I call to you all day long.
⁴Bring joy to your servant,
  for to you, O Lord,
  I lift up my soul.

⁵You are forgiving and good, O Lord,
  abounding in love to all who call to
    you.
⁶Hear my prayer, O Lord;
  listen to my cry for mercy.
⁷In the day of my trouble I will call to
    you,
  for you will answer me.

⁸Among the gods there is none like
    you, O Lord;
  no deeds can compare with yours.
⁹All the nations you have made
  will come and worship before you,
    O Lord;
  they will bring glory to your name.
¹⁰For you are great and do marvelous
    deeds;
  you alone are God.

¹¹Teach me your way, O Lord,
  and I will walk in your truth;
give me an undivided heart,
  that I may fear your name.
¹²I will praise you, O Lord my God,
  with all my heart;
  I will glorify your name forever.
¹³For great is your love toward me;
  you have delivered me from the
    depths of the grave.ᵃ

¹⁴The arrogant are attacking me, O God;
  a band of ruthless men seeks my
    life—
  men without regard for you.
¹⁵But you, O Lord, are a compassionate
    and gracious God,
  slow to anger, abounding in love
    and faithfulness.
¹⁶Turn to me and have mercy on me;
  grant your strength to your servant
  and save the son of your
    maidservant.ᵇ
¹⁷Give me a sign of your goodness,
  that my enemies may see it and be
    put to shame,
  for you, O Lord, have helped me
    and comforted me.

Psalm 87

Of the Sons of Korah. A psalm. A song.

¹He has set his foundation on the holy
    mountain;

ᵃ13 Hebrew *Sheol*   ᵇ16 Or *save your faithful son*

² the Lord loves the gates of Zion
    more than all the dwellings of
        Jacob.
³Glorious things are said of you,
    O city of God: *Selah*
⁴"I will record Rahab*ᵃ* and Babylon
    among those who acknowledge
        me —
    Philistia too, and Tyre, along with
        Cush*ᵇ* —
    and will say, 'This*ᶜ* one was born
        in Zion.' "

⁵Indeed, of Zion it will be said,
    "This one and that one were born
        in her,
    and the Most High himself will
        establish her."
⁶The Lord will write in the register of
        the peoples:
    "This one was born in Zion."   *Selah*
⁷As they make music they will sing,
    "All my fountains are in you."

Psalm 88

A song. A psalm of the Sons of Korah.
For the director of music. According to
mahalath leannoth.ᵈ A *maskilᵉ* of
Heman the Ezrahite.

¹O Lord, the God who saves me,
    day and night I cry out before you.
²May my prayer come before you;
    turn your ear to my cry.

³For my soul is full of trouble
    and my life draws near the grave.*ᶠ*
⁴I am counted among those who go
        down to the pit;
    I am like a man without strength.
⁵I am set apart with the dead,
    like the slain who lie in the grave,
    whom you remember no more,
    who are cut off from your care.

⁶You have put me in the lowest pit,
    in the darkest depths.
⁷Your wrath lies heavily upon me;
    you have overwhelmed me with all
        your waves.   *Selah*
⁸You have taken from me my closest
        friends
    and have made me repulsive to
        them.
    I am confined and cannot escape;
⁹ my eyes are dim with grief.

I call to you, O Lord, every day;
    I spread out my hands to you.
¹⁰Do you show your wonders to the
        dead?
    Do those who are dead rise up and
        praise you?   *Selah*
¹¹Is your love declared in the grave,
    your faithfulness in Destruction*ᵍ*?
¹²Are your wonders known in the place
        of darkness,
    or your righteous deeds in the land
        of oblivion?

¹³But I cry to you for help, O Lord;
    in the morning my prayer comes
        before you.
¹⁴Why, O Lord, do you reject me
    and hide your face from me?

¹⁵From my youth I have been afflicted
        and close to death;
    I have suffered your terrors and am
        in despair.
¹⁶Your wrath has swept over me;
    your terrors have destroyed me.
¹⁷All day long they surround me like a
        flood;
    they have completely engulfed me.
¹⁸You have taken my companions and
        loved ones from me;
    the darkness is my closest friend.

Psalm 89

A *maskilᵉ* of Ethan the Ezrahite.

¹I will sing of the Lord's great love
        forever;
    with my mouth I will make your
        faithfulness known through all
        generations.
²I will declare that your love stands
        firm forever,
    that you established your
        faithfulness in heaven itself.

³You said, "I have made a covenant
        with my chosen one,
    I have sworn to David my servant,
⁴'I will establish your line forever
    and make your throne firm through
        all generations.' "   *Selah*

⁵The heavens praise your wonders,
    O Lord,
    your faithfulness too, in the
        assembly of the holy ones.

ᵃ4 A poetic name for Egypt   *ᵇ4* That is, the upper Nile region   *ᶜ4* Or *"O Rahab and Babylon, /*
Philistia, Tyre and Cush, / I will record concerning those who acknowledge me: / 'This   *ᵈ*Title: Possibly a
tune, "The Suffering of Affliction"   *ᵉ*Title: Probably a literary or musical term   *ᶠ3* Hebrew *Sheol*
ᵍ11 Hebrew *Abaddon*

⁶For who in the skies above can
    compare with the Lord?
Who is like the Lord among the
    heavenly beings?
⁷In the council of the holy ones God is
    greatly feared;
he is more awesome than all who
    surround him.
⁸O Lord God Almighty, who is like
    you?
You are mighty, O Lord, and your
    faithfulness surrounds you.

⁹You rule over the surging sea;
when its waves mount up, you still
    them.
¹⁰You crushed Rahab like one of the
    slain;
with your strong arm you scattered
    your enemies.
¹¹The heavens are yours, and yours also
    the earth;
you founded the world and all that
    is in it.
¹²You created the north and the south;
Tabor and Hermon sing for joy at
    your name.
¹³Your arm is endued with power;
your hand is strong, your right hand
    exalted.

¹⁴Righteousness and justice are the
    foundation of your throne;
love and faithfulness go before you.
¹⁵Blessed are those who have learned to
    acclaim you,
who walk in the light of your
    presence, O Lord.
¹⁶They rejoice in your name all day
    long;
they exult in your righteousness.
¹⁷For you are their glory and strength,
and by your favor you exalt our
    horn.ᵃ
¹⁸Indeed, our shieldᵇ belongs to the
    Lord,
our king to the Holy One of Israel.

¹⁹Once you spoke in a vision,
to your faithful people you said:
"I have bestowed strength on a
    warrior;
I have exalted a young man from
    among the people.
²⁰I have found David my servant;
with my sacred oil I have anointed
    him.
²¹My hand will sustain him;
surely my arm will strengthen him.

²²No enemy will subject him to tribute;
no wicked man will oppress him.
²³I will crush his foes before him
and strike down his adversaries.
²⁴My faithful love will be with him,
and through my name his hornᶜ
    will be exalted.
²⁵I will set his hand over the sea,
his right hand over the rivers.
²⁶He will call out to me, 'You are my
    Father,
my God, the Rock my Savior.'
²⁷I will also appoint him my firstborn,
the most exalted of the kings of the
    earth.
²⁸I will maintain my love to him
    forever,
and my covenant with him will
    never fail.
²⁹I will establish his line forever,
his throne as long as the heavens
    endure.

³⁰"If his sons forsake my law
and do not follow my statutes,
³¹if they violate my decrees
and fail to keep my commands,
³²I will punish their sin with the rod,
their iniquity with flogging;
³³but I will not take my love from him,
nor will I ever betray my
    faithfulness.
³⁴I will not violate my covenant
or alter what my lips have uttered.
³⁵Once for all, I have sworn by my
    holiness—
and I will not lie to David—
³⁶that his line will continue forever
and his throne endure before me
    like the sun;
³⁷it will be established forever like the
    moon,
the faithful witness in the sky."
Selah

³⁸But you have rejected, you have
    spurned,
you have been very angry with your
    anointed one.
³⁹You have renounced the covenant
    with your servant
and have defiled his crown in the
    dust.
⁴⁰You have broken through all his walls
and reduced his strongholds to
    ruins.
⁴¹All who pass by have plundered him;
he has become the scorn of his
    neighbors.

ᵃ17 *Horn* here symbolizes strong one.   ᵇ18 Or *sovereign*   ᶜ24 *Horn* here symbolizes strength.

⁴²You have exalted the right hand of his
foes;
    you have made all his enemies
rejoice.
⁴³You have turned back the edge of his
sword
    and have not supported him in
battle.
⁴⁴You have put an end to his splendor
    and cast his throne to the ground.
⁴⁵You have cut short the days of his
youth;
    you have covered him with a
      mantle of shame.   *Selah*

⁴⁶How long, O Lᴏʀᴅ? Will you hide
yourself forever?
    How long will your wrath burn like
fire?
⁴⁷Remember how fleeting is my life.
    For what futility you have created
all men!
⁴⁸What man can live and not see death,
    or save himself from the power of
      the grave*ᵃ* ?   *Selah*
⁴⁹O Lord, where is your former great
love,
    which in your faithfulness you
swore to David?
⁵⁰Remember, Lord, how your servant
has*ᵇ* been mocked,
    how I bear in my heart the taunts
of all the nations,
⁵¹the taunts with which your enemies
have mocked, O Lᴏʀᴅ,
    with which they have mocked every
step of your anointed one.

⁵²Praise be to the Lᴏʀᴅ forever!
    Amen and Amen.

BOOK IV

Psalms 90–106

Psalm 90

A prayer of Moses the man of God.

¹Lord, you have been our dwelling
place
    throughout all generations.
²Before the mountains were born
    or you brought forth the earth and
the world,
    from everlasting to everlasting you
are God.

³You turn men back to dust,

saying, "Return to dust, O sons of
men."
⁴For a thousand years in your sight
    are like a day that has just gone by,
    or like a watch in the night.
⁵You sweep men away in the sleep of
death;
    they are like the new grass of the
morning—
⁶though in the morning it springs up
new,
    by evening it is dry and withered.

⁷We are consumed by your anger
    and terrified by your indignation.
⁸You have set our iniquities before
you,
    our secret sins in the light of your
presence.
⁹All our days pass away under your
wrath;
    we finish our years with a moan.
¹⁰The length of our days is seventy
years—
    or eighty, if we have the strength;
    yet their span*ᶜ* is but trouble and
sorrow,
    for they quickly pass, and we fly
away.

¹¹Who knows the power of your anger?
    For your wrath is as great as the
fear that is due you.
¹²Teach us to number our days aright,
    that we may gain a heart of
wisdom.

¹³Relent, O Lᴏʀᴅ! How long will it be?
    Have compassion on your servants.
¹⁴Satisfy us in the morning with your
unfailing love,
    that we may sing for joy and be
glad all our days.
¹⁵Make us glad for as many days as you
have afflicted us,
    for as many years as we have seen
trouble.
¹⁶May your deeds be shown to your
servants,
    your splendor to their children.

¹⁷May the favor*ᵈ* of the Lord our God
rest upon us;
    establish the work of our hands for
us—
    yes, establish the work of our
hands.

Psalm 91

[1]He who dwells in the shelter of the
Most High
will rest in the shadow of the
Almighty.[a]

[2]I will say[b] of the LORD, "He is my
refuge and my fortress,
my God, in whom I trust."

[3]Surely he will save you from the
fowler's snare

[a]1 Hebrew *Shaddai*   [b]2 Or *He says*

THURSDAY

VERSE FOR THE DAY:
Psalm 90:17

AUTHOR:
Ted Engstrom and David Juroe

PASSAGE FOR THE DAY:
Psalm 90:13–17

Work Benches and Altars

FOR millions, work is a drudgery, a grim necessity. Many hate their work every day of their lives and many find escapes in harmful ways to counterbalance the drudgery. Ask career counselors. Some estimate that as high as 90 percent of the labor market see themselves as *victims*, trapped in an unfulfilled daily round of work.

Certainly if Christianity is going to be relevant, it must have something to say about this problem area. There is a Christian philosophy of the family, education and history. Why not a Christian philosophy or theology of work?

One unfortunate development during the long history of the Christian church was the view during the Medieval period that there was a separation of the laity and the clergy. This difference between the sacred and secular callings still exists. In the architecture of early European cathedrals a screen separated the people from the priests because of the common view which held that working people had not been called of God in their tasks as clergy had. Therefore, they had to worship apart.

Martin Luther saw the fallacy in this and courageously spoke out against it. He tore down this screen, and from him we get the idea of "vocational guidance." He said that man, in his worthier callings, is called just as surely as a man who is called to the priesthood or ministry.

Christianity . . . has always provided a connection between work and worship. Men can dignify labor by doing ordinary things, but as redeemed persons. There lies the difference, and this is where the drudgery dissipates—God is in it. That means that every work bench in a plant is an altar! The psalmist says, "May the favor of the Lord our God rest upon us; establish the work of our hands for us" (Psalm 90:17). So you see, we can please the Lord by our work.

Additional Scripture Readings:
2 Thessalonians 3:6–15;
1 Peter 4:7–11

*Go to page 607 for your next
devotional reading.*

and from the deadly pestilence.
⁴He will cover you with his feathers,
  and under his wings you will find
    refuge;
  his faithfulness will be your shield
    and rampart.
⁵You will not fear the terror of night,
  nor the arrow that flies by day,
⁶nor the pestilence that stalks in the
    darkness,
  nor the plague that destroys at
    midday.
⁷A thousand may fall at your side,
  ten thousand at your right hand,
  but it will not come near you.
⁸You will only observe with your eyes
  and see the punishment of the
    wicked.

⁹If you make the Most High your
    dwelling—
  even the LORD, who is my refuge—
¹⁰then no harm will befall you,
  no disaster will come near your
    tent.
¹¹For he will command his angels
    concerning you
  to guard you in all your ways;
¹²they will lift you up in their hands,
  so that you will not strike your foot
    against a stone.
¹³You will tread upon the lion and the
    cobra;
  you will trample the great lion and
    the serpent.

¹⁴"Because he loves me," says the LORD,
  "I will rescue him;
  I will protect him, for he
    acknowledges my name.
¹⁵He will call upon me, and I will
    answer him;
  I will be with him in trouble,
  I will deliver him and honor him.
¹⁶With long life will I satisfy him
  and show him my salvation."

Psalm 92

A psalm. A song. For the Sabbath day.

¹It is good to praise the LORD
  and make music to your name,
    O Most High,
²to proclaim your love in the morning
  and your faithfulness at night,
³to the music of the ten-stringed lyre
  and the melody of the harp.

⁴For you make me glad by your deeds,
    O LORD;
  I sing for joy at the works of your
    hands.
⁵How great are your works, O LORD,
  how profound your thoughts!
⁶The senseless man does not know,
  fools do not understand,
⁷that though the wicked spring up like
    grass
  and all evildoers flourish,
  they will be forever destroyed.

⁸But you, O LORD, are exalted forever.

⁹For surely your enemies, O LORD,
  surely your enemies will perish;
  all evildoers will be scattered.
¹⁰You have exalted my horn[a] like that
    of a wild ox;
  fine oils have been poured upon
    me.
¹¹My eyes have seen the defeat of my
    adversaries;
  my ears have heard the rout of my
    wicked foes.

¹²The righteous will flourish like a palm
    tree,
  they will grow like a cedar of
    Lebanon;
¹³planted in the house of the LORD,
  they will flourish in the courts of
    our God.
¹⁴They will still bear fruit in old age,
  they will stay fresh and green,
¹⁵proclaiming, "The LORD is upright;
  he is my Rock, and there is no
    wickedness in him."

Psalm 93

¹The LORD reigns, he is robed in
    majesty;
  the LORD is robed in majesty
  and is armed with strength.
  The world is firmly established;
  it cannot be moved.
²Your throne was established long ago;
  you are from all eternity.

³The seas have lifted up, O LORD,
  the seas have lifted up their voice;
  the seas have lifted up their
    pounding waves.
⁴Mightier than the thunder of the great
    waters,
  mightier than the breakers of the
    sea—
  the LORD on high is mighty.

---

a10 Horn here symbolizes strength.

⁵Your statutes stand firm;
  holiness adorns your house
  for endless days, O LORD.

Psalm 94

¹O LORD, the God who avenges,
  O God who avenges, shine forth.
²Rise up, O Judge of the earth;
  pay back to the proud what they
  deserve.
³How long will the wicked, O LORD,
  how long will the wicked be
  jubilant?
⁴They pour out arrogant words;
  all the evildoers are full of boasting.

⁵They crush your people, O LORD;
  they oppress your inheritance.
⁶They slay the widow and the alien;
  they murder the fatherless.
⁷They say, "The LORD does not see;
  the God of Jacob pays no heed."

⁸Take heed, you senseless ones among
  the people;
  you fools, when will you become
  wise?
⁹Does he who implanted the ear not
  hear?
  Does he who formed the eye not
  see?
¹⁰Does he who disciplines nations not
  punish?

FRIDAY

VERSE FOR THE DAY:
Psalm 91:11

AUTHOR:
Billy Graham

PASSAGE FOR THE DAY:
Psalm 91:9–16

Nearer Than You Think

REPORTS continually flow to my attention from many places around the world telling of visitors of the angelic order appearing, ministering, fellowshiping and disappearing. They warn of God's impending judgment; they spell out the tenderness of his love; they meet a desperate need; then they are gone. Of one thing we can be sure: angels never draw attention to themselves but ascribe glory to God and press his message upon the hearers as a delivering and sustaining word of the highest order.

Demonic activity and Satan worship are on the increase in all parts of the world. The devil is alive and more at work than at any other time. The Bible says that since he realizes his time is short, his activity will increase. Through his demonic influences, he does succeed in turning many away from true faith; but we can still say that his evil activities are countered for the people of God by his ministering spirits, the holy ones of the angelic order. They are vigorous in delivering the heirs of salvation from the stratagems of evil men. They cannot fail.

Believers, look up—take courage. The angels are nearer than you think. For after all, "God will command his angels concerning you to guard you in all your ways; they will lift you up in their hands, so that you will not strike your foot against a stone" (Psalm 91:11–12).

Additional Scripture Readings:
Ephesians 6:10–18; Hebrews 1:1–14

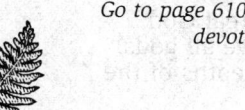

Go to page 610 for your next devotional reading.

Does he who teaches man lack
knowledge?
11The LORD knows the thoughts of man;
he knows that they are futile.

12Blessed is the man you discipline,
O LORD,
the man you teach from your law;
13you grant him relief from days of
trouble,
till a pit is dug for the wicked.
14For the LORD will not reject his people;
he will never forsake his
inheritance.
15Judgment will again be founded on
righteousness,
and all the upright in heart will
follow it.

16Who will rise up for me against the
wicked?
Who will take a stand for me
against evildoers?
17Unless the LORD had given me help,
I would soon have dwelt in the
silence of death.
18When I said, "My foot is slipping,"
your love, O LORD, supported me.
19When anxiety was great within me,
your consolation brought joy to my
soul.

20Can a corrupt throne be allied with
you—
one that brings on misery by its
decrees?
21They band together against the
righteous
and condemn the innocent to death.
22But the LORD has become my fortress,
and my God the rock in whom I
take refuge.
23He will repay them for their sins
and destroy them for their
wickedness;
the LORD our God will destroy them.

Psalm 95

1Come, let us sing for joy to the LORD;
let us shout aloud to the Rock of
our salvation.
2Let us come before him with
thanksgiving
and extol him with music and song.

3For the LORD is the great God,
the great King above all gods.
4In his hand are the depths of the
earth,

and the mountain peaks belong to
him.
5The sea is his, for he made it,
and his hands formed the dry land.

6Come, let us bow down in worship,
let us kneel before the LORD our
Maker;
7for he is our God
and we are the people of his
pasture,
the flock under his care.

Today, if you hear his voice,
8 do not harden your hearts as you
did at Meribah,a
as you did that day at Massahb in
the desert,
9where your fathers tested and tried
me,
though they had seen what I did.
10For forty years I was angry with that
generation;
I said, "They are a people whose
hearts go astray,
and they have not known my
ways."
11So I declared on oath in my anger,
"They shall never enter my rest."

Psalm 96

1Sing to the LORD a new song;
sing to the LORD, all the earth.
2Sing to the LORD, praise his name;
proclaim his salvation day after day.
3Declare his glory among the nations,
his marvelous deeds among all
peoples.

4For great is the LORD and most worthy
of praise;
he is to be feared above all gods.
5For all the gods of the nations are
idols,
but the LORD made the heavens.
6Splendor and majesty are before him;
strength and glory are in his
sanctuary.

7Ascribe to the LORD, O families of
nations,
ascribe to the LORD glory and
strength.
8Ascribe to the LORD the glory due his
name;
bring an offering and come into his
courts.
9Worship the LORD in the splendor of
hisc holiness;

---

a8 Meribah means quarreling.   b8 Massah means testing.   c9 Or LORD with the splendor of tremble before him, all the earth.

¹⁰Say among the nations, "The Lord
     reigns."
   The world is firmly established, it
     cannot be moved;
   he will judge the peoples with
     equity.
¹¹Let the heavens rejoice, let the earth
     be glad;
   let the sea resound, and all that is
     in it;
¹² let the fields be jubilant, and
     everything in them.
   Then all the trees of the forest will
     sing for joy;
¹³ they will sing before the Lord, for
     he comes,
   he comes to judge the earth.
   He will judge the world in
     righteousness
   and the peoples in his truth.

Psalm 97

¹The Lord reigns, let the earth be glad;
   let the distant shores rejoice.

²Clouds and thick darkness surround
     him;
   righteousness and justice are the
     foundation of his throne.
³Fire goes before him
   and consumes his foes on every
     side.
⁴His lightning lights up the world;
   the earth sees and trembles.
⁵The mountains melt like wax before
     the Lord,
   before the Lord of all the earth.
⁶The heavens proclaim his
     righteousness,
   and all the peoples see his glory.

⁷All who worship images are put to
     shame,
   those who boast in idols—
   worship him, all you gods!

⁸Zion hears and rejoices
   and the villages of Judah are glad
   because of your judgments, O Lord.
⁹For you, O Lord, are the Most High
     over all the earth;
   you are exalted far above all gods.

¹⁰Let those who love the Lord hate evil,
   for he guards the lives of his
     faithful ones
   and delivers them from the hand of
     the wicked.
¹¹Light is shed upon the righteous

and joy on the upright in heart.
¹²Rejoice in the Lord, you who are
     righteous,
   and praise his holy name.

Psalm 98

A psalm.

¹Sing to the Lord a new song,
   for he has done marvelous things;
   his right hand and his holy arm
   have worked salvation for him.
²The Lord has made his salvation
     known
   and revealed his righteousness to
     the nations.
³He has remembered his love
   and his faithfulness to the house of
     Israel;
   all the ends of the earth have seen
   the salvation of our God.

⁴Shout for joy to the Lord, all the
     earth,
   burst into jubilant song with music;
⁵make music to the Lord with the
     harp,
   with the harp and the sound of
     singing,
⁶with trumpets and the blast of the
     ram's horn—
   shout for joy before the Lord, the
     King.

⁷Let the sea resound, and everything in
     it,
   the world, and all who live in it.
⁸Let the rivers clap their hands,
   let the mountains sing together for
     joy;
⁹let them sing before the Lord,
   for he comes to judge the earth.
   He will judge the world in
     righteousness
   and the peoples with equity.

Psalm 99

¹The Lord reigns,
   let the nations tremble;
   he sits enthroned between the
     cherubim,
   let the earth shake.
²Great is the Lord in Zion;
   he is exalted over all the nations.
³Let them praise your great and
     awesome name—
   he is holy.

⁴The King is mighty, he loves justice—

WEEKENDING

RECHARGE

It is important for us to grasp the truth that
there is no shame in neediness. For those of us
who were raised to appear strong, neediness is
a horrible condition from which we turn away.
We don't mind giving generously or acting with
compassion toward those who are needy
around us, but we don't let ourselves get to the
place where we must receive help from others.
This fear of unmet needs can drive us to
acquire, achieve and accumulate symbols of
satisfaction . . .

These symbols of satisfaction, while holding
at bay our gnawing sense of insecurity and self-
doubt, also can cloud our view of what is
important. They may also inhibit our pursuing
the very things we need most in life:
relationships in which we are known intimately,
in which we share vulnerably, and in which we
discover love and accountability.

– John F. Westfall

REVIVE

Saturday: 1 Corinthians 1:26–31
Sunday: Philippians 4:10–20

Go to page 614 for your next devotional reading.

you have established equity;
in Jacob you have done
what is just and right.
[5]Exalt the LORD our God
and worship at his footstool;
he is holy.

[6]Moses and Aaron were among his
priests,
Samuel was among those who
called on his name;
they called on the LORD
and he answered them.
[7]He spoke to them from the pillar of
cloud;
they kept his statutes and the
decrees he gave them.

[8]O LORD our God,
you answered them;
you were to Israel[a] a forgiving God,
though you punished their
misdeeds.[b]
[9]Exalt the LORD our God
and worship at his holy mountain,
for the LORD our God is holy.

Psalm 100

A psalm. For giving thanks.

[1]Shout for joy to the LORD, all the
earth.
[2] Worship the LORD with gladness;
come before him with joyful songs.
[3]Know that the LORD is God.
It is he who made us, and we are
his[c];
we are his people, the sheep of his
pasture.

[4]Enter his gates with thanksgiving
and his courts with praise;
give thanks to him and praise his
name.
[5]For the LORD is good and his love
endures forever;
his faithfulness continues through
all generations.

Psalm 101

Of David. A psalm.

[1]I will sing of your love and justice;
to you, O LORD, I will sing praise.
[2]I will be careful to lead a blameless
life—
when will you come to me?

I will walk in my house
with blameless heart.
[3]I will set before my eyes
no vile thing.

The deeds of faithless men I hate;
they will not cling to me.
[4]Men of perverse heart shall be far
from me;
I will have nothing to do with evil.

[5]Whoever slanders his neighbor in
secret,
him will I put to silence;
whoever has haughty eyes and a
proud heart,
him will I not endure.

[6]My eyes will be on the faithful in the
land,
that they may dwell with me;
he whose walk is blameless
will minister to me.

[7]No one who practices deceit
will dwell in my house;
no one who speaks falsely
will stand in my presence.

[8]Every morning I will put to silence
all the wicked in the land;
I will cut off every evildoer
from the city of the LORD.

Psalm 102

A prayer of an afflicted man. When he is
faint and pours out his lament before
the LORD.

[1]Hear my prayer, O LORD;
let my cry for help come to you.
[2]Do not hide your face from me
when I am in distress.
Turn your ear to me;
when I call, answer me quickly.

[3]For my days vanish like smoke;
my bones burn like glowing embers.
[4]My heart is blighted and withered like
grass;
I forget to eat my food.
[5]Because of my loud groaning
I am reduced to skin and bones.
[6]I am like a desert owl,
like an owl among the ruins.
[7]I lie awake; I have become
like a bird alone on a roof.
[8]All day long my enemies taunt me;
those who rail against me use my
name as a curse.

a8 Hebrew them   b8 Or / an avenger of the wrongs done to them   c3 Or and not we ourselves

⁹For I eat ashes as my food
  and mingle my drink with tears
¹⁰because of your great wrath,
    for you have taken me up and
      thrown me aside.
¹¹My days are like the evening shadow;
  I wither away like grass.

¹²But you, O Lord, sit enthroned
    forever;
  your renown endures through all
    generations.
¹³You will arise and have compassion
    on Zion,
  for it is time to show favor to her;
  the appointed time has come.
¹⁴For her stones are dear to your
    servants;
  her very dust moves them to pity.
¹⁵The nations will fear the name of the
    Lord,
  all the kings of the earth will revere
    your glory.
¹⁶For the Lord will rebuild Zion
  and appear in his glory.
¹⁷He will respond to the prayer of the
    destitute;
  he will not despise their plea.

¹⁸Let this be written for a future
    generation,
  that a people not yet created may
    praise the Lord:
¹⁹"The Lord looked down from his
    sanctuary on high,
  from heaven he viewed the earth,
²⁰to hear the groans of the prisoners
  and release those condemned to
    death."
²¹So the name of the Lord will be
    declared in Zion
  and his praise in Jerusalem
²²when the peoples and the kingdoms
  assemble to worship the Lord.

²³In the course of my lifeᵃ he broke
    my strength;
  he cut short my days.
²⁴So I said:
  "Do not take me away, O my God,
    in the midst of my days;
  your years go on through all
    generations.
²⁵In the beginning you laid the
    foundations of the earth,
  and the heavens are the work of
    your hands.
²⁶They will perish, but you remain;

they will all wear out like a
    garment.
Like clothing you will change them
  and they will be discarded.
²⁷But you remain the same,
  and your years will never end.
²⁸The children of your servants will live
    in your presence;
  their descendants will be
    established before you."

Psalm 103

Of David.

¹Praise the Lord, O my soul;
  all my inmost being, praise his holy
    name.
²Praise the Lord, O my soul,
  and forget not all his benefits—
³who forgives all your sins
  and heals all your diseases,
⁴who redeems your life from the pit
  and crowns you with love and
    compassion,
⁵who satisfies your desires with good
    things
  so that your youth is renewed like
    the eagle's.

⁶The Lord works righteousness
  and justice for all the oppressed.

⁷He made known his ways to Moses,
  his deeds to the people of Israel:
⁸The Lord is compassionate and
    gracious,
  slow to anger, abounding in love.
⁹He will not always accuse,
  nor will he harbor his anger forever;
¹⁰he does not treat us as our sins
    deserve
  or repay us according to our
    iniquities.
¹¹For as high as the heavens are above
    the earth,
  so great is his love for those who
    fear him;
¹²as far as the east is from the west,
  so far has he removed our
    transgressions from us.
¹³As a father has compassion on his
    children,
  so the Lord has compassion on
    those who fear him;
¹⁴for he knows how we are formed,
  he remembers that we are dust.
¹⁵As for man, his days are like grass,

ᵃ23 Or By his power

he flourishes like a flower of the
field;
16the wind blows over it and it is gone,
and its place remembers it no more.
17But from everlasting to everlasting
the LORD's love is with those who
fear him,
and his righteousness with their
children's children—
18with those who keep his covenant
and remember to obey his precepts.

19The LORD has established his throne in
heaven,
and his kingdom rules over all.

20Praise the LORD, you his angels,
you mighty ones who do his
bidding,
who obey his word.
21Praise the LORD, all his heavenly hosts,
you his servants who do his will.
22Praise the LORD, all his works
everywhere in his dominion.

Praise the LORD, O my soul.

Psalm 104

1Praise the LORD, O my soul.

O LORD my God, you are very great;
you are clothed with splendor and
majesty.
2He wraps himself in light as with a
garment;
he stretches out the heavens like a
tent
3   and lays the beams of his upper
chambers on their waters.
He makes the clouds his chariot
and rides on the wings of the wind.
4He makes winds his messengers,a
flames of fire his servants.

5He set the earth on its foundations;
it can never be moved.
6You covered it with the deep as with a
garment;
the waters stood above the
mountains.
7But at your rebuke the waters fled,
at the sound of your thunder they
took to flight;
8they flowed over the mountains,
they went down into the valleys,
to the place you assigned for them.
9You set a boundary they cannot cross;
never again will they cover the
earth.

10He makes springs pour water into the
ravines;
it flows between the mountains.
11They give water to all the beasts of
the field;
the wild donkeys quench their
thirst.
12The birds of the air nest by the
waters;
they sing among the branches.
13He waters the mountains from his
upper chambers;
the earth is satisfied by the fruit of
his work.
14He makes grass grow for the cattle,
and plants for man to cultivate—
bringing forth food from the earth:
15wine that gladdens the heart of man,
oil to make his face shine,
and bread that sustains his heart.
16The trees of the LORD are well
watered,
the cedars of Lebanon that he
planted.
17There the birds make their nests;
the stork has its home in the pine
trees.
18The high mountains belong to the
wild goats;
the crags are a refuge for the
coneys.b

19The moon marks off the seasons,
and the sun knows when to go
down.
20You bring darkness, it becomes night,
and all the beasts of the forest
prowl.
21The lions roar for their prey
and seek their food from God.
22The sun rises, and they steal away;
they return and lie down in their
dens.
23Then man goes out to his work,
to his labor until evening.

24How many are your works, O LORD!
In wisdom you made them all;
the earth is full of your creatures.
25There is the sea, vast and spacious,
teeming with creatures beyond
number—
living things both large and small.
26There the ships go to and fro,
and the leviathan, which you
formed to frolic there.

27These all look to you

a4 Or angels   b18 That is, the hyrax or rock badger

to give them their food at the
proper time.
²⁸When you give it to them,
they gather it up;
when you open your hand,
they are satisfied with good things.
²⁹When you hide your face,
they are terrified;
when you take away their breath,

they die and return to the dust.
³⁰When you send your Spirit,
they are created,
and you renew the face of the earth.

³¹May the glory of the LORD endure
forever;
may the LORD rejoice in his works—
³²he who looks at the earth, and it
trembles,

MONDAY

VERSE FOR THE DAY:
Psalm 103:15

AUTHOR:
James Dobson

PASSAGE FOR THE DAY:
Psalm 103:1–22

A Better Way

I HAVE examined America's breathless lifestyle and find it to
be *unacceptable*. At forty-three years of age (I would be forty-
four but I was sick a year), I have been thinking about the
stages of my earthly existence and what they will represent at
its conclusion. There was a time when all of my friends were
graduating from high school. Then I recall so many who entered colleges around the country. And alas, I lived through a
phase when everyone seemed to be getting married. Then a
few years later, we were besieged by baby shower announce-
ments. You see, my generation is slowly but relentlessly moving through the decades, as have 2,400 generations that preceded it. Now, it occurs to me that a time will soon come
when my friends will be dying. ["Wasn't it tragic what happened to Charles Painter yesterday?"]

My aunt, Naomi Dobson, wrote me shortly before her death
in 1978. She said, "It seems like every day another of my close
friends either passes away or is afflicted with a terrible disease." Obviously, she was in that final phase of her generation.
Now she is also gone.

What does this have to do with my life today? How does it
relate to yours? I'm suggesting that we stop and consider the
brevity of our years on earth, perhaps finding new motivation
to preserve the values that will endure. Why should we work
ourselves into an early grave, missing those precious moments
with loved ones who crave our affection and attention? It is a
question that every man and woman should consider.

Let me offer this final word of encouragement for those who
are determined to slow the pace: once you get out from under
constant pressure, you'll wonder why you drove yourself so
hard for all those years. *There is a better way!*

Additional Scripture Readings:
Ecclesiastes 2:17–26; James 4:13–17

*Go to page 621 for your next
devotional reading.*

who touches the mountains, and
   they smoke.

33I will sing to the LORD all my life;
   I will sing praise to my God as long
      as I live.
34May my meditation be pleasing to
      him,
   as I rejoice in the LORD.
35But may sinners vanish from the earth
   and the wicked be no more.

Praise the LORD, O my soul.

Praise the LORD.*a*

Psalm 105

1Give thanks to the LORD, call on his
      name;
   make known among the nations
      what he has done.
2Sing to him, sing praise to him;
   tell of all his wonderful acts.
3Glory in his holy name;
   let the hearts of those who seek the
      LORD rejoice.
4Look to the LORD and his strength;
   seek his face always.

5Remember the wonders he has done,
   his miracles, and the judgments he
      pronounced,
6O descendants of Abraham his
      servant,
   O sons of Jacob, his chosen ones.
7He is the LORD our God;
   his judgments are in all the earth.

8He remembers his covenant forever,
   the word he commanded, for a
      thousand generations,
9the covenant he made with Abraham,
   the oath he swore to Isaac.
10He confirmed it to Jacob as a decree,
   to Israel as an everlasting covenant:
11"To you I will give the land of Canaan
   as the portion you will inherit."

12When they were but few in number,
   few indeed, and strangers in it,
13they wandered from nation to nation,
   from one kingdom to another.
14He allowed no one to oppress them;
   for their sake he rebuked kings:
15"Do not touch my anointed ones;
   do my prophets no harm."

16He called down famine on the land
   and destroyed all their supplies of
      food;

17and he sent a man before them—
   Joseph, sold as a slave.
18They bruised his feet with shackles,
   his neck was put in irons,
19till what he foretold came to pass,
   till the word of the LORD proved him
      true.
20The king sent and released him,
   the ruler of peoples set him free.
21He made him master of his
      household,
   ruler over all he possessed,
22to instruct his princes as he pleased
   and teach his elders wisdom.

23Then Israel entered Egypt;
   Jacob lived as an alien in the land
      of Ham.
24The LORD made his people very
      fruitful;
   he made them too numerous for
      their foes,
25whose hearts he turned to hate his
      people,
   to conspire against his servants.
26He sent Moses his servant,
   and Aaron, whom he had chosen.
27They performed his miraculous signs
      among them,
   his wonders in the land of Ham.
28He sent darkness and made the land
      dark—
   for had they not rebelled against his
      words?
29He turned their waters into blood,
   causing their fish to die.
30Their land teemed with frogs,
   which went up into the bedrooms
      of their rulers.
31He spoke, and there came swarms of
      flies,
   and gnats throughout their country.
32He turned their rain into hail,
   with lightning throughout their
      land;
33he struck down their vines and fig
      trees
   and shattered the trees of their
      country.
34He spoke, and the locusts came,
   grasshoppers without number;
35they ate up every green thing in their
      land,
   ate up the produce of their soil.
36Then he struck down all the firstborn
      in their land,
   the firstfruits of all their manhood.

---

*a*35 Hebrew *Hallelu Yah*; in the Septuagint this line stands at the beginning of Psalm 105.

³⁷He brought out Israel, laden with
    silver and gold,
  and from among their tribes no one
    faltered.
³⁸Egypt was glad when they left,
  because dread of Israel had fallen
    on them.
³⁹He spread out a cloud as a covering,
  and a fire to give light at night.
⁴⁰They asked, and he brought them
    quail
  and satisfied them with the bread of
    heaven.
⁴¹He opened the rock, and water gushed
    out;
  like a river it flowed in the desert.

⁴²For he remembered his holy promise
  given to his servant Abraham.
⁴³He brought out his people with
    rejoicing,
  his chosen ones with shouts of joy;
⁴⁴he gave them the lands of the nations,
  and they fell heir to what others
    had toiled for —
⁴⁵that they might keep his precepts
  and observe his laws.

  Praise the LORD.^a

Psalm 106

¹Praise the LORD.^b

  Give thanks to the LORD, for he is
    good;
  his love endures forever.
²Who can proclaim the mighty acts of
    the LORD
  or fully declare his praise?
³Blessed are they who maintain justice,
  who constantly do what is right.
⁴Remember me, O LORD, when you
    show favor to your people,
  come to my aid when you save
    them,
⁵that I may enjoy the prosperity of
    your chosen ones,
  that I may share in the joy of your
    nation
  and join your inheritance in giving
    praise.

⁶We have sinned, even as our fathers
    did;
  we have done wrong and acted
    wickedly.
⁷When our fathers were in Egypt,

they gave no thought to your
    miracles;
  they did not remember your many
    kindnesses,
  and they rebelled by the sea, the
    Red Sea.^c
⁸Yet he saved them for his name's
    sake,
  to make his mighty power known.
⁹He rebuked the Red Sea, and it dried
    up;
  he led them through the depths as
    through a desert.
¹⁰He saved them from the hand of the
    foe;
  from the hand of the enemy he
    redeemed them.
¹¹The waters covered their adversaries;
  not one of them survived.
¹²Then they believed his promises
  and sang his praise.

¹³But they soon forgot what he had
    done
  and did not wait for his counsel.
¹⁴In the desert they gave in to their
    craving;
  in the wasteland they put God to
    the test.
¹⁵So he gave them what they asked for,
  but sent a wasting disease upon
    them.

¹⁶In the camp they grew envious of
    Moses
  and of Aaron, who was consecrated
    to the LORD.
¹⁷The earth opened up and swallowed
    Dathan;
  it buried the company of Abiram.
¹⁸Fire blazed among their followers;
  a flame consumed the wicked.

¹⁹At Horeb they made a calf
  and worshiped an idol cast from
    metal.
²⁰They exchanged their Glory
  for an image of a bull, which eats
    grass.
²¹They forgot the God who saved them,
  who had done great things in Egypt,
²²miracles in the land of Ham
  and awesome deeds by the Red Sea.
²³So he said he would destroy them —
  had not Moses, his chosen one,
  stood in the breach before him
  to keep his wrath from destroying
    them.

24Then they despised the pleasant land;
   they did not believe his promise.
25They grumbled in their tents
   and did not obey the LORD.
26So he swore to them with uplifted
      hand
   that he would make them fall in the
      desert,
27make their descendants fall among the
      nations
   and scatter them throughout the
      lands.

28They yoked themselves to the Baal of
      Peor
   and ate sacrifices offered to lifeless
      gods;
29they provoked the LORD to anger by
      their wicked deeds,
   and a plague broke out among
      them.
30But Phinehas stood up and intervened,
   and the plague was checked.
31This was credited to him as
      righteousness
   for endless generations to come.

32By the waters of Meribah they
      angered the LORD,
   and trouble came to Moses because
      of them;
33for they rebelled against the Spirit of
      God,
   and rash words came from Moses'
      lips.ᵃ

34They did not destroy the peoples
   as the LORD had commanded them,
35but they mingled with the nations
   and adopted their customs.
36They worshiped their idols,
   which became a snare to them.
37They sacrificed their sons
   and their daughters to demons.
38They shed innocent blood,
   the blood of their sons and
      daughters,
whom they sacrificed to the idols of
      Canaan,
   and the land was desecrated by
      their blood.
39They defiled themselves by what they
      did;
   by their deeds they prostituted
      themselves.

40Therefore the LORD was angry with his
      people
   and abhorred his inheritance.

41He handed them over to the nations,
   and their foes ruled over them.
42Their enemies oppressed them
   and subjected them to their power.
43Many times he delivered them,
   but they were bent on rebellion
   and they wasted away in their sin.

44But he took note of their distress
   when he heard their cry;
45for their sake he remembered his
      covenant
   and out of his great love he
      relented.
46He caused them to be pitied
   by all who held them captive.

47Save us, O LORD our God,
   and gather us from the nations,
that we may give thanks to your holy
      name
   and glory in your praise.

48Praise be to the LORD, the God of
      Israel,
   from everlasting to everlasting.
Let all the people say, "Amen!"

Praise the LORD.

BOOK V
Psalms 107–150

Psalm 107

1Give thanks to the LORD, for he is
      good;
   his love endures forever.
2Let the redeemed of the LORD say
      this —
   those he redeemed from the hand
      of the foe,
3those he gathered from the lands,
   from east and west, from north and
      south.ᵇ

4Some wandered in desert wastelands,
   finding no way to a city where they
      could settle.
5They were hungry and thirsty,
   and their lives ebbed away.
6Then they cried out to the LORD in
      their trouble,
   and he delivered them from their
      distress.
7He led them by a straight way
   to a city where they could settle.

ᵃ33 Or *against his spirit, / and rash words came from his lips*   ᵇ3 Hebrew *north and the sea*

⁸Let them give thanks to the LORD for
    his unfailing love
  and his wonderful deeds for men,
⁹for he satisfies the thirsty
  and fills the hungry with good
    things.

¹⁰Some sat in darkness and the deepest
    gloom,
  prisoners suffering in iron chains,
¹¹for they had rebelled against the
    words of God
  and despised the counsel of the
    Most High.
¹²So he subjected them to bitter labor;
  they stumbled, and there was no
    one to help.
¹³Then they cried to the LORD in their
    trouble,
  and he saved them from their
    distress.
¹⁴He brought them out of darkness and
    the deepest gloom
  and broke away their chains.
¹⁵Let them give thanks to the LORD for
    his unfailing love
  and his wonderful deeds for men,
¹⁶for he breaks down gates of bronze
  and cuts through bars of iron.

¹⁷Some became fools through their
    rebellious ways
  and suffered affliction because of
    their iniquities.
¹⁸They loathed all food
  and drew near the gates of death.
¹⁹Then they cried to the LORD in their
    trouble,
  and he saved them from their
    distress.
²⁰He sent forth his word and healed
    them;
  he rescued them from the grave.
²¹Let them give thanks to the LORD for
    his unfailing love
  and his wonderful deeds for men.
²²Let them sacrifice thank offerings
  and tell of his works with songs of
    joy.

²³Others went out on the sea in ships;
  they were merchants on the mighty
    waters.
²⁴They saw the works of the LORD,
  his wonderful deeds in the deep.
²⁵For he spoke and stirred up a tempest
  that lifted high the waves.
²⁶They mounted up to the heavens and
  went down to the depths;

in their peril their courage melted
    away.
²⁷They reeled and staggered like
    drunken men;
  they were at their wits' end.
²⁸Then they cried out to the LORD in
    their trouble,
  and he brought them out of their
    distress.
²⁹He stilled the storm to a whisper;
  the waves of the sea were hushed.
³⁰They were glad when it grew calm,
  and he guided them to their desired
    haven.
³¹Let them give thanks to the LORD for
    his unfailing love
  and his wonderful deeds for men.
³²Let them exalt him in the assembly of
    the people
  and praise him in the council of the
    elders.

³³He turned rivers into a desert,
  flowing springs into thirsty ground,
³⁴and fruitful land into a salt waste,
  because of the wickedness of those
    who lived there.
³⁵He turned the desert into pools of
    water
  and the parched ground into
    flowing springs;
³⁶there he brought the hungry to live,
  and they founded a city where they
    could settle.
³⁷They sowed fields and planted
    vineyards
  that yielded a fruitful harvest;
³⁸he blessed them, and their numbers
    greatly increased,
  and he did not let their herds
    diminish.

³⁹Then their numbers decreased, and
    they were humbled
  by oppression, calamity and sorrow;
⁴⁰he who pours contempt on nobles
  made them wander in a trackless
    waste.
⁴¹But he lifted the needy out of their
    affliction
  and increased their families like
    flocks.
⁴²The upright see and rejoice,
  but all the wicked shut their
    mouths.

⁴³Whoever is wise, let him heed these
    things
  and consider the great love of the
    LORD.

Psalm 108

A song. A psalm of David.

[1]My heart is steadfast, O God;
  I will sing and make music with all
    my soul.
[2]Awake, harp and lyre!
  I will awaken the dawn.
[3]I will praise you, O LORD, among the
    nations;
  I will sing of you among the
    peoples.
[4]For great is your love, higher than the
    heavens;
  your faithfulness reaches to the
    skies.
[5]Be exalted, O God, above the heavens,
  and let your glory be over all the
    earth.

[6]Save us and help us with your right
    hand,
  that those you love may be
    delivered.
[7]God has spoken from his sanctuary:
  "In triumph I will parcel out
    Shechem
  and measure off the Valley of
    Succoth.
[8]Gilead is mine, Manasseh is mine;
  Ephraim is my helmet,
  Judah my scepter.
[9]Moab is my washbasin,
  upon Edom I toss my sandal;
  over Philistia I shout in triumph."

[10]Who will bring me to the fortified
    city?
  Who will lead me to Edom?
[11]Is it not you, O God, you who have
    rejected us
  and no longer go out with our
    armies?
[12]Give us aid against the enemy,
  for the help of man is worthless.
[13]With God we will gain the victory,
  and he will trample down our
    enemies.

Psalm 109

*For the director of music. Of David.
A psalm.*

[1]O God, whom I praise,
  do not remain silent,
[2]for wicked and deceitful men

have opened their mouths against
    me;
  they have spoken against me with
    lying tongues.
[3]With words of hatred they surround
    me;
  they attack me without cause.
[4]In return for my friendship they
    accuse me,
  but I am a man of prayer.
[5]They repay me evil for good,
  and hatred for my friendship.

[6]Appoint[a] an evil man[b] to oppose
    him;
  let an accuser[c] stand at his right
    hand.
[7]When he is tried, let him be found
    guilty,
  and may his prayers condemn him.
[8]May his days be few;
  may another take his place of
    leadership.
[9]May his children be fatherless
  and his wife a widow.
[10]May his children be wandering
    beggars;
  may they be driven[d] from their
    ruined homes.
[11]May a creditor seize all he has;
  may strangers plunder the fruits of
    his labor.
[12]May no one extend kindness to him
  or take pity on his fatherless
    children.
[13]May his descendants be cut off,
  their names blotted out from the
    next generation.
[14]May the iniquity of his fathers be
    remembered before the LORD;
  may the sin of his mother never be
    blotted out.
[15]May their sins always remain before
    the LORD,
  that he may cut off the memory of
    them from the earth.

[16]For he never thought of doing a
    kindness,
  but hounded to death the poor
  and the needy and the
    brokenhearted.
[17]He loved to pronounce a curse—
  may it[e] come on him;
  he found no pleasure in blessing—
  may it be[f] far from him.
[18]He wore cursing as his garment;
  it entered into his body like water,

a6 Or ,They say, "Appoint (with quotation marks at the end of verse 19)   *b6 Or the Evil One*   *c6 Or
let Satan*   *d10 Septuagint; Hebrew sought*   *e17 Or curse, / and it has*   *f17 Or blessing, / and it is*

into his bones like oil.
19May it be like a cloak wrapped about
     him,
  like a belt tied forever around him.
20May this be the LORD's payment to my
     accusers,
  to those who speak evil of me.

21But you, O Sovereign LORD,
  deal well with me for your name's
     sake;
  out of the goodness of your love,
     deliver me.
22For I am poor and needy,
  and my heart is wounded within
     me.
23I fade away like an evening shadow;
  I am shaken off like a locust.
24My knees give way from fasting;
  my body is thin and gaunt.
25I am an object of scorn to my
     accusers;
  when they see me, they shake their
     heads.

26Help me, O LORD my God;
  save me in accordance with your
     love.
27Let them know that it is your hand,
  that you, O LORD, have done it.
28They may curse, but you will bless;
  when they attack they will be put to
     shame,
  but your servant will rejoice.
29My accusers will be clothed with
     disgrace
  and wrapped in shame as in a
     cloak.

30With my mouth I will greatly extol the
     LORD;
  in the great throng I will praise him.
31For he stands at the right hand of the
     needy one,
  to save his life from those who
     condemn him.

Psalm 110

Of David. A psalm.

1The LORD says to my Lord:
  "Sit at my right hand
  until I make your enemies
  a footstool for your feet."

2The LORD will extend your mighty
     scepter from Zion;
  you will rule in the midst of your
     enemies.
3Your troops will be willing
  on your day of battle.
  Arrayed in holy majesty,
  from the womb of the dawn
  you will receive the dew of your
     youth.a

4The LORD has sworn
  and will not change his mind:
  "You are a priest forever,
  in the order of Melchizedek."

5The Lord is at your right hand;
  he will crush kings on the day of
     his wrath.
6He will judge the nations, heaping up
     the dead
  and crushing the rulers of the whole
     earth.
7He will drink from a brook beside the
     wayb;
  therefore he will lift up his head.

Psalm 111c

1Praise the LORD.d

I will extol the LORD with all my heart
  in the council of the upright and in
     the assembly.

2Great are the works of the LORD;
  they are pondered by all who
     delight in them.
3Glorious and majestic are his deeds,
  and his righteousness endures
     forever.
4He has caused his wonders to be
     remembered;
  the LORD is gracious and
     compassionate.
5He provides food for those who fear
     him;
  he remembers his covenant forever.
6He has shown his people the power of
     his works,
  giving them the lands of other
     nations.
7The works of his hands are faithful
     and just;
  all his precepts are trustworthy.

---

a3 Or / your young men will come to you like the dew   b7 Or / The One who grants succession will set
him in authority   cThis psalm is an acrostic poem, the lines of which begin with the successive letters
of the Hebrew alphabet.   d1 Hebrew Hallelu Yah

8They are steadfast for ever and ever,
     done in faithfulness and
        uprightness.
9He provided redemption for his
     people;
   he ordained his covenant forever —
   holy and awesome is his name.

10The fear of the LORD is the beginning
     of wisdom;
   all who follow his precepts have
     good understanding.
   To him belongs eternal praise.

Psalm 112 *a*

1Praise the LORD. *b*

   Blessed is the man who fears the
      LORD,
    who finds great delight in his
       commands.

2His children will be mighty in the
     land;
   the generation of the upright will be
     blessed.
3Wealth and riches are in his house,

*a*This psalm is an acrostic poem, the lines of which begin with the successive letters of the Hebrew alphabet.   *b*1 Hebrew *Hallelu Yah*

TUESDAY

VERSE FOR THE DAY: AUTHOR: PASSAGE FOR THE DAY:
Psalm 111:10   Don Wyrtzen   Psalm 111:5–10

The Obvious Outcome

THE psalmist develops his theme very specifically here. Our compassionate and gracious Lord has expressed himself by helping his people—by providing a daily supply of food, by remembering his covenant and keeping his promises to make them victorious in conquest, by bequeathing to them the heathen lands around them, by revealing his power. And wonder of wonders, when they continued to grumble and complain against him, he provided a way back to him—a plan of redemption and forgiveness!

My Lord is no less active in my life today. He provides for my basic needs—food, shelter, clothing—by allowing me to serve him through meaningful and fulfilling work. He has blessed me with rich personal relationships with my family and intimate friends. To guide me in facing the hassles of daily living, he has sent his Holy Spirit, and I find myself clinging to him every day.

The conclusion of this psalm reminds me of Proverbs 1:7: "The fear (awesome respect) of the LORD is the beginning of knowledge." It seems that following his precepts in obedience should be the obvious outcome of my gratitude for all he's done for me!

I pray that you will fill me with an awesome respect for you, Lord, so that it will be the most natural thing in the world to obey your rules for right living!

Additional Scripture Readings: *Go to page 623 for your next*
Psalm 19:7–14; John 14:15–21   *devotional reading.*

and his righteousness endures
forever.
[4]Even in darkness light dawns for the
upright,
for the gracious and compassionate
and righteous man.[a]
[5]Good will come to him who is
generous and lends freely,
who conducts his affairs with
justice.
[6]Surely he will never be shaken;
a righteous man will be
remembered forever.
[7]He will have no fear of bad news;
his heart is steadfast, trusting in the
LORD.
[8]His heart is secure, he will have no
fear;
in the end he will look in triumph
on his foes.
[9]He has scattered abroad his gifts to
the poor,
his righteousness endures forever;
his horn[b] will be lifted high in
honor.
[10]The wicked man will see and be
vexed,
he will gnash his teeth and waste
away;
the longings of the wicked will
come to nothing.

Psalm 113

[1]Praise the LORD.[c]

Praise, O servants of the LORD,
praise the name of the LORD.
[2]Let the name of the LORD be praised,
both now and forevermore.
[3]From the rising of the sun to the place
where it sets,
the name of the LORD is to be
praised.

[4]The LORD is exalted over all the
nations,
his glory above the heavens.
[5]Who is like the LORD our God,
the One who sits enthroned on
high,
[6]who stoops down to look
on the heavens and the earth?

[7]He raises the poor from the dust
and lifts the needy from the ash
heap;
[8]he seats them with princes,

with the princes of their people.
[9]He settles the barren woman in her
home
as a happy mother of children.

Praise the LORD.

Psalm 114

[1]When Israel came out of Egypt,
the house of Jacob from a people of
foreign tongue,
[2]Judah became God's sanctuary,
Israel his dominion.

[3]The sea looked and fled,
the Jordan turned back;
[4]the mountains skipped like rams,
the hills like lambs.

[5]Why was it, O sea, that you fled,
O Jordan, that you turned back,
[6]you mountains, that you skipped like
rams,
you hills, like lambs?

[7]Tremble, O earth, at the presence of
the Lord,
at the presence of the God of Jacob,
[8]who turned the rock into a pool,
the hard rock into springs of water.

Psalm 115

[1]Not to us, O LORD, not to us
but to your name be the glory,
because of your love and
faithfulness.

[2]Why do the nations say,
"Where is their God?"
[3]Our God is in heaven;
he does whatever pleases him.
[4]But their idols are silver and gold,
made by the hands of men.
[5]They have mouths, but cannot speak,
eyes, but they cannot see;
[6]they have ears, but cannot hear,
noses, but they cannot smell;
[7]they have hands, but cannot feel,
feet, but they cannot walk;
nor can they utter a sound with
their throats.
[8]Those who make them will be like
them,
and so will all who trust in them.

[9]O house of Israel, trust in the LORD —
he is their help and shield.
[10]O house of Aaron, trust in the LORD —

---

[a]4 Or / for the LORD, is gracious and compassionate and righteous   [b]9 Horn here symbolizes dignity.
[c]1 Hebrew Hallelu Yah; also in verse 9

WEDNESDAY

VERSE FOR THE DAY:
Psalm 115:8

AUTHOR:
Doug Sherman and
William Hendricks

PASSAGE FOR THE DAY:
Psalm 115:2-8

Worshiping Work

MANY workers today are sacrificing themselves on the altar of work. They tolerate immensely harmful symptoms such as anger, chemical dependencies and loneliness in a blind pursuit of self-fulfillment through career success. This may be pathological—but it is also idolatrous! Such a person *worships* his career as though it were a god.

But like all idols, work is impotent in the face of true human need. As Psalm 115:4–7 puts it: "Their idols are silver and gold, made by the hands of men. They have mouths, but cannot speak, eyes, but they cannot see; they have ears, but cannot hear, noses, but they cannot smell; they have hands, but cannot feel, feet, but they cannot walk; nor can they utter a sound with their throats."

In other words, idols are powerless. And work as an idol is just as powerless. Worst of all, those who worship work as an idol are defenseless in the face of true need. In the psalmist's words, "Those who make them will be like them, and so will all who trust in them" (115:8).

I have seen this happen. I have sat with grown men, exceptionally powerful men in business, and watched them weep as they told me their tragic stories, some with personal lives shattered, others with families in shambles, perhaps their character debased or their business in doubt or their circumstances out of control. None of their professional accomplishments, none of the machinery of their companies, none of their wealth is of the slightest help. They are in deep trouble and their god is impotent.

I grieve with such men and women. They have chosen the wrong god. Of course, I also respect the fact that the same thing could happen to me as to anyone. It happens when we take God's gift of work and begin to worship and serve it rather than Christ.

Additional Scripture Readings:
Isaiah 44:6–23; Matthew 6:19–24

Go to page 626 for your next devotional reading.

he is their help and shield.
11You who fear him, trust in the Lord —
he is their help and shield.

12The Lord remembers us and will bless
us:
He will bless the house of Israel,
he will bless the house of Aaron,
13he will bless those who fear the
Lord —
small and great alike.

14May the Lord make you increase,
both you and your children.
15May you be blessed by the Lord,
the Maker of heaven and earth.

16The highest heavens belong to the
Lord,
but the earth he has given to man.
17It is not the dead who praise the Lord,
those who go down to silence;
18it is we who extol the Lord,
both now and forevermore.

Praise the Lord. *a*

Psalm 116

1I love the Lord, for he heard my
voice;
he heard my cry for mercy.
2Because he turned his ear to me,
I will call on him as long as I live.

3The cords of death entangled me,
the anguish of the grave*b* came
upon me;
I was overcome by trouble and
sorrow.
4Then I called on the name of the
Lord:
"O Lord, save me!"

5The Lord is gracious and righteous;
our God is full of compassion.
6The Lord protects the simplehearted;
when I was in great need, he saved
me.

7Be at rest once more, O my soul,
for the Lord has been good to you.

8For you, O Lord, have delivered my
soul from death,
my eyes from tears,
my feet from stumbling,
9that I may walk before the Lord
in the land of the living.
10I believed; therefore*c* I said,
"I am greatly afflicted."

11And in my dismay I said,
"All men are liars."

12How can I repay the Lord
for all his goodness to me?
13I will lift up the cup of salvation
and call on the name of the Lord.
14I will fulfill my vows to the Lord
in the presence of all his people.

15Precious in the sight of the Lord
is the death of his saints.
16O Lord, truly I am your servant;
I am your servant, the son of your
maidservant*d*;
you have freed me from my chains.
17I will sacrifice a thank offering to you
and call on the name of the Lord.
18I will fulfill my vows to the Lord
in the presence of all his people,
19in the courts of the house of the
Lord —
in your midst, O Jerusalem.

Praise the Lord. *a*

Psalm 117

1Praise the Lord, all you nations;
extol him, all you peoples.
2For great is his love toward us,
and the faithfulness of the Lord
endures forever.

Praise the Lord. *a*

Psalm 118

1Give thanks to the Lord, for he is
good;
his love endures forever.

2Let Israel say:
"His love endures forever."
3Let the house of Aaron say:
"His love endures forever."
4Let those who fear the Lord say:
"His love endures forever."

5In my anguish I cried to the Lord,
and he answered by setting me free.
6The Lord is with me; I will not be
afraid.
What can man do to me?
7The Lord is with me; he is my helper.
I will look in triumph on my
enemies.

8It is better to take refuge in the Lord
than to trust in man.

*a*18,19,2 Hebrew *Hallelu Yah*   *b*3 Hebrew *Sheol*   *c*10 Or *believed even when*   *d*16 Or *servant,
your faithful son*

9It is better to take refuge in the LORD
  than to trust in princes.

10All the nations surrounded me,
   but in the name of the LORD I cut
     them off.
11They surrounded me on every side,
   but in the name of the LORD I cut
     them off.
12They swarmed around me like bees,
   but they died out as quickly as
     burning thorns;
   in the name of the LORD I cut them
     off.
13I was pushed back and about to fall,
   but the LORD helped me.
14The LORD is my strength and my song;
   he has become my salvation.

15Shouts of joy and victory
   resound in the tents of the
     righteous:
  "The LORD's right hand has done
     mighty things!
16   The LORD's right hand is lifted high;
   the LORD's right hand has done
     mighty things!"

17I will not die but live,
   and will proclaim what the LORD has
     done.
18The LORD has chastened me severely,
   but he has not given me over to
     death.

19Open for me the gates of
     righteousness;
   I will enter and give thanks to the
     LORD.
20This is the gate of the LORD
   through which the righteous may
     enter.
21I will give you thanks, for you
     answered me;
   you have become my salvation.

22The stone the builders rejected
   has become the capstone;
23the LORD has done this,
   and it is marvelous in our eyes.
24This is the day the LORD has made;
   let us rejoice and be glad in it.

25O LORD, save us;
   O LORD, grant us success.
26Blessed is he who comes in the name
     of the LORD.
   From the house of the LORD we
     bless you.a

27The LORD is God,
   and he has made his light shine
     upon us.
With boughs in hand, join in the
     festal procession
   upb to the horns of the altar.

28You are my God, and I will give you
     thanks;
   you are my God, and I will exalt
     you.

29Give thanks to the LORD, for he is
     good;
   his love endures forever.

Psalm 119c

א Aleph

1Blessed are they whose ways are
     blameless,
   who walk according to the law of
     the LORD.
2Blessed are they who keep his statutes
   and seek him with all their heart.
3They do nothing wrong;
   they walk in his ways.
4You have laid down precepts
   that are to be fully obeyed.
5Oh, that my ways were steadfast
   in obeying your decrees!
6Then I would not be put to shame
   when I consider all your commands.
7I will praise you with an upright heart
   as I learn your righteous laws.
8I will obey your decrees;
   do not utterly forsake me.

ב Beth

9How can a young man keep his way
     pure?
   By living according to your word.
10I seek you with all my heart;
   do not let me stray from your
     commands.
11I have hidden your word in my heart
   that I might not sin against you.
12Praise be to you, O LORD;
   teach me your decrees.
13With my lips I recount
   all the laws that come from your
     mouth.
14I rejoice in following your statutes
   as one rejoices in great riches.
15I meditate on your precepts
   and consider your ways.

a26 The Hebrew is plural.   b27 Or Bind the festal sacrifice with ropes / and take it   cThis psalm is
an acrostic poem; the verses of each stanza begin with the same letter of the Hebrew alphabet.

¹⁶I delight in your decrees;
    I will not neglect your word.

        ג Gimel

¹⁷Do good to your servant, and I will
    live;
    I will obey your word.
¹⁸Open my eyes that I may see

wonderful things in your law.
¹⁹I am a stranger on earth;
    do not hide your commands from
    me.
²⁰My soul is consumed with longing
    for your laws at all times.
²¹You rebuke the arrogant, who are
    cursed

THURSDAY

VERSE FOR THE DAY:	AUTHOR:	PASSAGE FOR THE DAY:
Psalm 119:16	Charles Colson	Psalm 119:9–16

Truth in a Fast-food World

WE TAKE our stand not on the shifting sands of secular relativism but on the holy and inerrant Word of God. Decisions in the world are made on the basis of expedience and changing sociological factors. But the Word is unchanging, immutable, and without it we Christians have nothing.

Taking our stand on Biblical truth can be our only defense against our culture's penchant to reduce all issues to simplistic suppositions and glib answers. We impatiently expect to get solutions to the most profound ambiguities of life the same way we drive up to the fast-food counter: one double burger, chocolate shake, and an order of fries. We are faddists. Just look at the rash of new diets and instant physical-conditioning courses that week after week dominate our bestseller lists.

The problem is, that "easy-answer" mentality is invading the Christian church: we want scorecards by which we can instantly rate our politicians, new catchy acronyms for salvation, time-saving techniques for discipleship. But formulas don't convert people; slick slogans and cute phrases are no substitute for hard spiritual truth.

In our well-intentioned effort to reach unsaved masses, we often make the gospel message itself sound easy, unthreatening, a painless answer to all life's ills. We portray a loving God who forgives all and asks nothing in return. Now, that may tickle the ears of this pleasure-seeking generation, but it is nothing less than heresy.

We must challenge presuppositions—not only of society as a whole but of the evangelical subculture as well. The gospel of Jesus Christ must be the bad news of the conviction of sin before it can be the Good News of redemption. The truth is revealed in God's Holy Word; life can be lived only in absolute and disciplined submission to its authority.

Additional Scripture Readings:
John 8:31–41; 2 Timothy 3:14–17

Go to page 629 for your next devotional reading.

and who stray from your
commands.
²²Remove from me scorn and contempt,
for I keep your statutes.
²³Though rulers sit together and slander
me,
your servant will meditate on your
decrees.
²⁴Your statutes are my delight;
they are my counselors.

ד   Daleth

²⁵I am laid low in the dust;
preserve my life according to your
word.
²⁶I recounted my ways and you
answered me;
teach me your decrees.
²⁷Let me understand the teaching of
your precepts;
then I will meditate on your
wonders.
²⁸My soul is weary with sorrow;
strengthen me according to your
word.
²⁹Keep me from deceitful ways;
be gracious to me through your law.
³⁰I have chosen the way of truth;
I have set my heart on your laws.
³¹I hold fast to your statutes, O LORD;
do not let me be put to shame.
³²I run in the path of your commands,
for you have set my heart free.

ה   He

³³Teach me, O LORD, to follow your
decrees;
then I will keep them to the end.
³⁴Give me understanding, and I will
keep your law
and obey it with all my heart.
³⁵Direct me in the path of your
commands,
for there I find delight.
³⁶Turn my heart toward your statutes
and not toward selfish gain.
³⁷Turn my eyes away from worthless
things;
preserve my life according to your
word.ᵃ
³⁸Fulfill your promise to your servant,
so that you may be feared.
³⁹Take away the disgrace I dread,
for your laws are good.
⁴⁰How I long for your precepts!
Preserve my life in your
righteousness.

ו   Waw

⁴¹May your unfailing love come to me,
O LORD,
your salvation according to your
promise;
⁴²then I will answer the one who taunts
me,
for I trust in your word.
⁴³Do not snatch the word of truth from
my mouth,
for I have put my hope in your
laws.
⁴⁴I will always obey your law,
for ever and ever.
⁴⁵I will walk about in freedom,
for I have sought out your precepts.
⁴⁶I will speak of your statutes before
kings
and will not be put to shame,
⁴⁷for I delight in your commands
because I love them.
⁴⁸I lift up my hands toᵇ your
commands, which I love,
and I meditate on your decrees.

ז   Zayin

⁴⁹Remember your word to your servant,
for you have given me hope.
⁵⁰My comfort in my suffering is this:
Your promise preserves my life.
⁵¹The arrogant mock me without
restraint,
but I do not turn from your law.
⁵²I remember your ancient laws,
O LORD,
and I find comfort in them.
⁵³Indignation grips me because of the
wicked,
who have forsaken your law.
⁵⁴Your decrees are the theme of my
song
wherever I lodge.
⁵⁵In the night I remember your name,
O LORD,
and I will keep your law.
⁵⁶This has been my practice:
I obey your precepts.

ח   Heth

⁵⁷You are my portion, O LORD;
I have promised to obey your
words.
⁵⁸I have sought your face with all my
heart;
be gracious to me according to your
promise.

ᵃ37 Two manuscripts of the Masoretic Text and Dead Sea Scrolls; most manuscripts of the Masoretic Text
life in your way   ᵇ48 Or for

59I have considered my ways
    and have turned my steps to your
       statutes.
60I will hasten and not delay
    to obey your commands.
61Though the wicked bind me with
       ropes,
    I will not forget your law.
62At midnight I rise to give you thanks
    for your righteous laws.
63I am a friend to all who fear you,
    to all who follow your precepts.
64The earth is filled with your love,
       O Lord;
    teach me your decrees.

ט   Teth

65Do good to your servant
    according to your word, O Lord.
66Teach me knowledge and good
       judgment,
    for I believe in your commands.
67Before I was afflicted I went astray,
    but now I obey your word.
68You are good, and what you do is
       good;
    teach me your decrees.
69Though the arrogant have smeared me
       with lies,
    I keep your precepts with all my
       heart.
70Their hearts are callous and unfeeling,
    but I delight in your law.
71It was good for me to be afflicted
    so that I might learn your decrees.
72The law from your mouth is more
       precious to me
    than thousands of pieces of silver
       and gold.

י   Yodh

73Your hands made me and formed me;
    give me understanding to learn your
       commands.
74May those who fear you rejoice when
       they see me,
    for I have put my hope in your
       word.
75I know, O Lord, that your laws are
       righteous,
    and in faithfulness you have
       afflicted me.
76May your unfailing love be my
       comfort,
    according to your promise to your
       servant.
77Let your compassion come to me that
    I may live,
    for your law is my delight.

78May the arrogant be put to shame for
       wronging me without cause;
    but I will meditate on your
       precepts.
79May those who fear you turn to me,
    those who understand your statutes.
80May my heart be blameless toward
       your decrees,
    that I may not be put to shame.

כ   Kaph

81My soul faints with longing for your
       salvation,
    but I have put my hope in your
       word.
82My eyes fail, looking for your
       promise;
    I say, "When will you comfort me?"
83Though I am like a wineskin in the
       smoke,
    I do not forget your decrees.
84How long must your servant wait?
    When will you punish my
       persecutors?
85The arrogant dig pitfalls for me,
    contrary to your law.
86All your commands are trustworthy;
    help me, for men persecute me
       without cause.
87They almost wiped me from the earth,
    but I have not forsaken your
       precepts.
88Preserve my life according to your
       love,
    and I will obey the statutes of your
       mouth.

ל   Lamedh

89Your word, O Lord, is eternal;
    it stands firm in the heavens.
90Your faithfulness continues through
       all generations;
    you established the earth, and it
       endures.
91Your laws endure to this day,
    for all things serve you.
92If your law had not been my delight,
    I would have perished in my
       affliction.
93I will never forget your precepts,
    for by them you have preserved my
       life.
94Save me, for I am yours;
    I have sought out your precepts.
95The wicked are waiting to destroy me,
    but I will ponder your statutes.

⁹⁶To all perfection I see a limit;
but your commands are boundless.

מ Mem

⁹⁷Oh, how I love your law!
I meditate on it all day long.
⁹⁸Your commands make me wiser than
my enemies,
for they are ever with me.
⁹⁹I have more insight than all my
teachers,
for I meditate on your statutes.
¹⁰⁰I have more understanding than the
elders,
for I obey your precepts.
¹⁰¹I have kept my feet from every evil
path
so that I might obey your word.
¹⁰²I have not departed from your laws,
for you yourself have taught me.
¹⁰³How sweet are your words to my
taste,
sweeter than honey to my mouth!

¹⁰⁴I gain understanding from your
precepts;
therefore I hate every wrong path.

נ Nun

¹⁰⁵Your word is a lamp to my feet
and a light for my path.
¹⁰⁶I have taken an oath and
confirmed it,
that I will follow your righteous
laws.
¹⁰⁷I have suffered much;
preserve my life, O LORD, according
to your word.
¹⁰⁸Accept, O LORD, the willing praise of
my mouth,
and teach me your laws.
¹⁰⁹Though I constantly take my life in
my hands,
I will not forget your law.
¹¹⁰The wicked have set a snare for me,
but I have not strayed from your
precepts.

FRIDAY

VERSE FOR THE DAY:	AUTHOR:	PASSAGE FOR THE DAY:
Psalm 119:96	Tom Landry	Psalm 119:89–96

Life Within Limits

MOST successful [football] players not only accept rules and
limitations, I believe they need them. In fact, I believe players
are free to perform at their best only when they know what
the expectations are, where the limits stand.

I see this as a Biblical principle that also applies to life, a
principle our society as a whole has forgotten. You can't enjoy
true freedom without limits.

We often resent rules because they limit what we can do.
Yet without the rules that define a football game, you can't
play the game, let alone enjoy it. The same thing is true in life.
To live and enjoy the freedom we have in America, we have to
live by the rules of society. To live life to its fullest and truly
enjoy it, we need to understand and abide by the rules God
spells out in the Bible. God isn't out to spoil our fun; he knows
that life without limits results in anarchy and misery. It's only
when we have absolute limits that we can be truly free to enjoy the best life has to offer.

Additional Scripture Readings:
Romans 6:15–23; 1 John 2:3–8

*Go to page 633 for your next
devotional reading.*

111Your statutes are my heritage forever;
　　they are the joy of my heart.
112My heart is set on keeping your
　　　decrees
　　to the very end.

ס　Samekh

113I hate double-minded men,
　　but I love your law.
114You are my refuge and my shield;
　　I have put my hope in your word.
115Away from me, you evildoers,
　　that I may keep the commands of
　　　my God!
116Sustain me according to your
　　　promise, and I will live;
　　do not let my hopes be dashed.
117Uphold me, and I will be delivered;
　　I will always have regard for your
　　　decrees.
118You reject all who stray from your
　　　decrees,
　　for their deceitfulness is in vain.
119All the wicked of the earth you
　　　discard like dross;
　　therefore I love your statutes.
120My flesh trembles in fear of you;
　　I stand in awe of your laws.

ע　Ayin

121I have done what is righteous and
　　　just;
　　do not leave me to my oppressors.
122Ensure your servant's well-being;
　　let not the arrogant oppress me.
123My eyes fail, looking for your
　　　salvation,
　　looking for your righteous promise.
124Deal with your servant according to
　　　your love
　　and teach me your decrees.
125I am your servant; give me
　　　discernment
　　that I may understand your statutes.
126It is time for you to act, O Lord;
　　your law is being broken.
127Because I love your commands
　　more than gold, more than pure
　　　gold,
128and because I consider all your
　　　precepts right,
　　I hate every wrong path.

פ　Pe

129Your statutes are wonderful;
　　therefore I obey them.
130The unfolding of your words gives
　　　light;
　　it gives understanding to the simple.

131I open my mouth and pant,
　　longing for your commands.
132Turn to me and have mercy on me,
　　as you always do to those who love
　　　your name.
133Direct my footsteps according to your
　　　word;
　　let no sin rule over me.
134Redeem me from the oppression of
　　　men,
　　that I may obey your precepts.
135Make your face shine upon your
　　　servant
　　and teach me your decrees.
136Streams of tears flow from my eyes,
　　for your law is not obeyed.

צ　Tsadhe

137Righteous are you, O Lord,
　　and your laws are right.
138The statutes you have laid down are
　　　righteous;
　　they are fully trustworthy.
139My zeal wears me out,
　　for my enemies ignore your words.
140Your promises have been thoroughly
　　　tested,
　　and your servant loves them.
141Though I am lowly and despised,
　　I do not forget your precepts.
142Your righteousness is everlasting
　　and your law is true.
143Trouble and distress have come
　　　upon me,
　　but your commands are my delight.
144Your statutes are forever right;
　　give me understanding that I may
　　　live.

ק　Qoph

145I call with all my heart; answer me,
　　　O Lord,
　　and I will obey your decrees.
146I call out to you; save me
　　and I will keep your statutes.
147I rise before dawn and cry for help;
　　I have put my hope in your word.
148My eyes stay open through the
　　　watches of the night,
　　that I may meditate on your
　　　promises.
149Hear my voice in accordance with
　　　your love;
　　preserve my life, O Lord, according
　　　to your laws.
150Those who devise wicked schemes
　　are near,
　　but they are far from your law.
151Yet you are near, O Lord,
　　and all your commands are true.

152Long ago I learned from your statutes
  that you established them to last
    forever.

ㄱ Resh

153Look upon my suffering and
    deliver me,
  for I have not forgotten your law.
154Defend my cause and redeem me;
  preserve my life according to your
    promise.
155Salvation is far from the wicked,
  for they do not seek out your
    decrees.
156Your compassion is great, O Lord;
  preserve my life according to your
    laws.
157Many are the foes who persecute me,
  but I have not turned from your
    statutes.
158I look on the faithless with loathing,
  for they do not obey your word.
159See how I love your precepts;
  preserve my life, O Lord, according
    to your love.
160All your words are true;
  all your righteous laws are eternal.

שׁ Sin and Shin

161Rulers persecute me without cause,
  but my heart trembles at your word.
162I rejoice in your promise
  like one who finds great spoil.
163I hate and abhor falsehood
  but I love your law.
164Seven times a day I praise you
  for your righteous laws.
165Great peace have they who love your
    law,
  and nothing can make them
    stumble.
166I wait for your salvation, O Lord,
  and I follow your commands.
167I obey your statutes,
  for I love them greatly.
168I obey your precepts and your
    statutes,
  for all my ways are known to you.

ת Taw

169May my cry come before you,
    O Lord;
  give me understanding according to
    your word.
170May my supplication come before
    you;
  deliver me according to your
    promise.

171May my lips overflow with praise,
  for you teach me your decrees.
172May my tongue sing of your word,
  for all your commands are
    righteous.
173May your hand be ready to help me,
  for I have chosen your precepts.
174I long for your salvation, O Lord,
  and your law is my delight.
175Let me live that I may praise you,
  and may your laws sustain me.
176I have strayed like a lost sheep.
  Seek your servant,
  for I have not forgotten your
    commands.

Psalm 120

A song of ascents.

1I call on the Lord in my distress,
  and he answers me.
2Save me, O Lord, from lying lips
  and from deceitful tongues.

3What will he do to you,
  and what more besides, O deceitful
    tongue?
4He will punish you with a warrior's
    sharp arrows,
  with burning coals of the broom
    tree.

5Woe to me that I dwell in Meshech,
  that I live among the tents of Kedar!
6Too long have I lived
  among those who hate peace.
7I am a man of peace;
  but when I speak, they are for war.

Psalm 121

A song of ascents.

1I lift up my eyes to the hills —
  where does my help come from?
2My help comes from the Lord,
  the Maker of heaven and earth.

3He will not let your foot slip —
  he who watches over you will not
    slumber;
4indeed, he who watches over Israel
  will neither slumber nor sleep.

5The Lord watches over you —
  the Lord is your shade at your right
    hand;

⁶the sun will not harm you by day,
　nor the moon by night.

⁷The Lord will keep you from all
　　harm—
　he will watch over your life;
⁸the Lord will watch over your coming
　　and going
　both now and forevermore.

Psalm 122

A song of ascents. Of David.

¹I rejoiced with those who said to me,
　"Let us go to the house of the
　　Lord."
²Our feet are standing
　in your gates, O Jerusalem.

³Jerusalem is built like a city
　that is closely compacted together.
⁴That is where the tribes go up,
　the tribes of the Lord,
　to praise the name of the Lord
　according to the statute given to
　　Israel.
⁵There the thrones for judgment stand,
　the thrones of the house of David.

⁶Pray for the peace of Jerusalem:
　"May those who love you be secure.
⁷May there be peace within your walls
　and security within your citadels."
⁸For the sake of my brothers and
　　friends,
　I will say, "Peace be within you."
⁹For the sake of the house of the Lord
　our God,
　I will seek your prosperity.

Psalm 123

A song of ascents.

¹I lift up my eyes to you,
　to you whose throne is in heaven.
²As the eyes of slaves look to the hand
　　of their master,
　as the eyes of a maid look to the
　　hand of her mistress,
　so our eyes look to the Lord our God,
　till he shows us his mercy.

³Have mercy on us, O Lord, have
　　mercy on us,
　for we have endured much
　　contempt.

⁴We have endured much ridicule from
　　the proud,
　much contempt from the arrogant.

Psalm 124

A song of ascents. Of David.

¹If the Lord had not been on our
　　side—
　let Israel say—
²if the Lord had not been on our side
　when men attacked us,
³when their anger flared against us,
　they would have swallowed us
　　alive;
⁴the flood would have engulfed us,
　the torrent would have swept over
　　us,
⁵the raging waters
　would have swept us away.

⁶Praise be to the Lord,
　who has not let us be torn by their
　　teeth.
⁷We have escaped like a bird
　out of the fowler's snare;
　the snare has been broken,
　and we have escaped.
⁸Our help is in the name of the Lord,
　the Maker of heaven and earth.

Psalm 125

A song of ascents.

¹Those who trust in the Lord are like
　　Mount Zion,
　which cannot be shaken but
　　endures forever.
²As the mountains surround Jerusalem,
　so the Lord surrounds his people
　both now and forevermore.

³The scepter of the wicked will not
　　remain
　over the land allotted to the
　　righteous,
　for then the righteous might use
　their hands to do evil.

⁴Do good, O Lord, to those who are
　　good,
　to those who are upright in heart.
⁵But those who turn to crooked ways
　the Lord will banish with the
　　evildoers.

Peace be upon Israel.

WEEKENDING

REALIZE

When you teach your children what God's Word has to say about troubled times, you're providing a lamp to their feet (Psalm 119:105). Biblical principles are like powerful flashlights that can light up even the darkest trial your children may experience.

Because you know this, you can verbally and nonverbally convey this message to your children as they watch your response to their trials. And you can also ask them if they are willing to look for what God has to teach them in the difficulty they've experienced.

– Gary Smalley and John Trent

REVIVE

Saturday: Hebrews 10:32–39
Sunday: 1 Peter 4:12–19

Go to page 635 for your next devotional reading.

Psalm 126

A song of ascents.

¹When the Lord brought back the
    captives to^a Zion,
  we were like men who dreamed.^b
²Our mouths were filled with laughter,
    our tongues with songs of joy.
  Then it was said among the nations,
    "The Lord has done great things for
      them."
³The Lord has done great things for us,
    and we are filled with joy.

⁴Restore our fortunes,^c O Lord,
    like streams in the Negev.
⁵Those who sow in tears
    will reap with songs of joy.
⁶He who goes out weeping,
    carrying seed to sow,
  will return with songs of joy,
    carrying sheaves with him.

Psalm 127

A song of ascents. Of Solomon.

¹Unless the Lord builds the house,
    its builders labor in vain.
  Unless the Lord watches over the city,
    the watchmen stand guard in vain.
²In vain you rise early
    and stay up late,
  toiling for food to eat—
    for he grants sleep to^d those he
      loves.

³Sons are a heritage from the Lord,
    children a reward from him.
⁴Like arrows in the hands of a warrior
    are sons born in one's youth.
⁵Blessed is the man
    whose quiver is full of them.
  They will not be put to shame
    when they contend with their
      enemies in the gate.

Psalm 128

A song of ascents.

¹Blessed are all who fear the Lord,
    who walk in his ways.
²You will eat the fruit of your labor;
    blessings and prosperity will be
      yours.
³Your wife will be like a fruitful vine
    within your house;

  your sons will be like olive shoots
    around your table.
⁴Thus is the man blessed
    who fears the Lord.

⁵May the Lord bless you from Zion
    all the days of your life;
  may you see the prosperity of
    Jerusalem,
⁶ and may you live to see your
    children's children.

  Peace be upon Israel.

Psalm 129

A song of ascents.

¹They have greatly oppressed me from
    my youth—
  let Israel say—
²they have greatly oppressed me from
    my youth,
  but they have not gained the victory
    over me.
³Plowmen have plowed my back
    and made their furrows long.
⁴But the Lord is righteous;
    he has cut me free from the cords
      of the wicked.

⁵May all who hate Zion
    be turned back in shame.
⁶May they be like grass on the roof,
    which withers before it can grow;
⁷with it the reaper cannot fill his
      hands,
  nor the one who gathers fill his
      arms.
⁸May those who pass by not say,
    "The blessing of the Lord be upon
      you;
  we bless you in the name of the
    Lord."

Psalm 130

A song of ascents.

¹Out of the depths I cry to you,
    O Lord;
² O Lord, hear my voice.
  Let your ears be attentive
    to my cry for mercy.

³If you, O Lord, kept a record of sins,
    O Lord, who could stand?
⁴But with you there is forgiveness;
    therefore you are feared.

^a1 Or Lord restored the fortunes of   ^b1 Or men restored to health   ^c4 Or Bring back our captives
^d2 Or eat— / for while they sleep he provides for

⁵I wait for the LORD, my soul waits,
and in his word I put my hope.
⁶My soul waits for the Lord
more than watchmen wait for the
morning,
more than watchmen wait for the
morning.

⁷O Israel, put your hope in the
LORD,
for with the LORD is unfailing
love
and with him is full redemption.
⁸He himself will redeem Israel
from all their sins.

MONDAY

VERSE FOR THE DAY: AUTHOR: PASSAGE FOR THE DAY:
Psalm 127:1   Charles Swindoll   Psalm 127:1–5

A Home Where Love Thrives

THE first two verses of Psalm 127 are the piers and beams of
the home, the foundation from which all else derives its stability and security.

"Unless the Lord builds the house, its builders labor in vain.
Unless the Lord watches over the city, the watchmen stand
guard in vain."

Solomon, the writer of this psalm, compares the home to a
city. When an ancient city was built, it was not uncommon for
its walls to be finished first to keep out the enemy. If the people trusted in the walls to protect them, to give them security,
their trust was misplaced, creating only a false sense of security. Likewise, walls we erect around our families and possessions offer only an illusion of security. Like Jericho's walls,
they can tumble as quickly as a shout. For ultimately, it is not
the watchman or the walls that protect the city; it is the *Lord.*
"The name of the LORD is a strong tower; the righteous run to
it and are safe" (Proverbs 18:10). In the same sense, unless a
husband and wife trust in God, their work and their watchful-
ness are wasted.

In verse 2, Solomon qualifies the phrase *in vain:*

"In vain you rise early and stay up late, toiling for food to
eat—"

Many feel that by working longer hours they can provide
more things to bring happiness to their home or afford a nicer,
newer home in hopes that it will bring happiness . . . It doesn't
satisfy that empty longing in the pit of our soul, that longing
for a home, a *real* home—a home where love thrives, lush and
fragrant. The reason why it's futile burning the candle at both
ends—rising early, staying up late—is that God, not our labors,
is the source of our blessing, as verse 2 indicates: "for he
grants sleep to those he loves" [or, as the alternate translation
reads, "for while they sleep he provides for those he loves"].

Additional Scripture Readings:
Psalm 37:1–9; Matthew 6:25–34

*Go to page 636 for your next
devotional reading.*

Psalm 131

A song of ascents. Of David.

¹My heart is not proud, O LORD,
  my eyes are not haughty;
I do not concern myself with great
    matters
  or things too wonderful for me.
²But I have stilled and quieted my
    soul;
  like a weaned child with its
    mother,
  like a weaned child is my soul
    within me.

³O Israel, put your hope in the LORD
  both now and forevermore.

Psalm 132

A song of ascents.

¹O LORD, remember David
  and all the hardships he endured.
²He swore an oath to the LORD
  and made a vow to the Mighty One
    of Jacob:
³"I will not enter my house
  or go to my bed—
⁴I will allow no sleep to my eyes,

TUESDAY

VERSE FOR THE DAY:	*AUTHOR:*	*PASSAGE FOR THE DAY:*
Psalm 130:1	*Donald Bloesch*	*Psalm 130:1–8*

Empty-handed Praying

THE Biblical Christian can only pray empty-handed, as the
thirteenth-century Dominican preacher William Peraldus expressed it. Or, as Augustine observed, "The best disposition
for praying is that of being desolate, forsaken, stripped of everything." Unlike the ritualist, we know that any sacrifice we
bring before God is stained by sin and therefore unworthy of
acceptance apart from the mediation and intercession of Jesus
Christ. Our hope depends not on the right technique or the
proper phrase or gesture, which borders on magic, but on the
promises of God to look with favor on those who throw themselves on his mercy and who acknowledge the efficacy of the
atoning sacrifice of his Son, Jesus Christ, for their redemption.

As I see it, true prayer is neither mystical rapture nor ritual
observance nor philosophical reflection: it is the outpouring of
the soul before a living God, the crying to God "out of the
depths." Such prayer can only be uttered by one convicted of
sin by the grace of God and moved to confession by the Spirit
of God. True prayer is an encounter with the Holy in which we
realize not only our creatureliness and guilt but also the joy of
knowing that our sins are forgiven through the atoning death
of the divine Savior, Jesus Christ. In such an encounter, we are
impelled not only to bow before God and seek his mercy but
also to offer thanksgiving for grace that goes out to undeserving sinners.

Additional Scripture Readings:
Psalm 142; Philippians 4:4–7

*Go to page 641 for your next
devotional reading.*

no slumber to my eyelids,
⁵till I find a place for the LORD,
  a dwelling for the Mighty One of
    Jacob."

⁶We heard it in Ephrathah,
  we came upon it in the fields of
    Jaar*ᵃ:ᵇ*
⁷"Let us go to his dwelling place;
  let us worship at his footstool—
⁸arise, O LORD, and come to your
    resting place,
  you and the ark of your might.
⁹May your priests be clothed with
    righteousness;
  may your saints sing for joy."

¹⁰For the sake of David your servant,
  do not reject your anointed one.

¹¹The LORD swore an oath to David,
  a sure oath that he will not revoke:
"One of your own descendants
  I will place on your throne—
¹²if your sons keep my covenant
  and the statutes I teach them,
then their sons will sit
  on your throne for ever and ever."

¹³For the LORD has chosen Zion,
  he has desired it for his dwelling:
¹⁴"This is my resting place for ever and
    ever;
  here I will sit enthroned, for I have
    desired it—
¹⁵I will bless her with abundant
    provisions;
  her poor will I satisfy with food.
¹⁶I will clothe her priests with salvation,
  and her saints will ever sing for joy.
¹⁷"Here I will make a hornᶜ grow for
    David
  and set up a lamp for my anointed
    one.
¹⁸I will clothe his enemies with shame,
  but the crown on his head will be
    resplendent."

Psalm 133

A song of ascents. Of David.

¹How good and pleasant it is
  when brothers live together in
    unity!
²It is like precious oil poured on the
    head,
  running down on the beard,

running down on Aaron's beard,
  down upon the collar of his robes.
³It is as if the dew of Hermon
  were falling on Mount Zion.
For there the LORD bestows his
    blessing,
  even life forevermore.

Psalm 134

A song of ascents.

¹Praise the LORD, all you servants of
    the LORD
  who minister by night in the house
    of the LORD.
²Lift up your hands in the sanctuary
  and praise the LORD.

³May the LORD, the Maker of heaven
    and earth,
  bless you from Zion.

Psalm 135

¹Praise the LORD.ᵈ

Praise the name of the LORD;
  praise him, you servants of the
    LORD,
²you who minister in the house of the
    LORD,
  in the courts of the house of our
    God.

³Praise the LORD, for the LORD is good;
  sing praise to his name, for that is
    pleasant.
⁴For the LORD has chosen Jacob to be
    his own,
  Israel to be his treasured
    possession.

⁵I know that the LORD is great,
  that our Lord is greater than all
    gods.
⁶The LORD does whatever pleases him,
  in the heavens and on the earth,
  in the seas and all their depths.
⁷He makes clouds rise from the ends of
    the earth;
  he sends lightning with the rain
  and brings out the wind from his
    storehouses.

⁸He struck down the firstborn of Egypt,
  the firstborn of men and animals.
⁹He sent his signs and wonders into
  your midst, O Egypt,

ᵃ6 That is, Kiriath Jearim   ᵇ6 Or *heard of it in Ephrathah,* / *we found it in the fields of Jaar.* (And no
quotes around verses 7-9)   ᶜ17 *Horn* here symbolizes strong one, that is, king.   ᵈ1 Hebrew *Hallelu
Yah;* also in verses 3 and 21

against Pharaoh and all his servants.
[10]He struck down many nations
　　and killed mighty kings—
[11]Sihon king of the Amorites,
　　Og king of Bashan
　　and all the kings of Canaan—
[12]and he gave their land as an
　　inheritance,
　　an inheritance to his people Israel.

[13]Your name, O Lord, endures forever,
　　your renown, O Lord, through all
　　generations.
[14]For the Lord will vindicate his people
　　and have compassion on his
　　servants.

[15]The idols of the nations are silver and
　　gold,
　　made by the hands of men.
[16]They have mouths, but cannot speak,
　　eyes, but they cannot see;
[17]they have ears, but cannot hear,
　　nor is there breath in their mouths.
[18]Those who make them will be like
　　them,
　　and so will all who trust in them.

[19]O house of Israel, praise the Lord;
　　O house of Aaron, praise the Lord;
[20]O house of Levi, praise the Lord;
　　you who fear him, praise the Lord.
[21]Praise be to the Lord from Zion,
　　to him who dwells in Jerusalem.

Praise the Lord.

Psalm 136

[1]Give thanks to the Lord, for he is
　　good.
　　　His love endures forever.
[2]Give thanks to the God of gods.
　　　His love endures forever.
[3]Give thanks to the Lord of lords:
　　　His love endures forever.

[4]to him who alone does great wonders,
　　　His love endures forever.
[5]who by his understanding made the
　　heavens,
　　　His love endures forever.
[6]who spread out the earth upon the
　　waters,
　　　His love endures forever.
[7]who made the great lights—
　　　His love endures forever.
[8]the sun to govern the day,
　　　His love endures forever.

[9]the moon and stars to govern the
　　night;
　　　His love endures forever.

[10]to him who struck down the firstborn
　　of Egypt
　　　His love endures forever.
[11]and brought Israel out from among
　　them
　　　His love endures forever.
[12]with a mighty hand and outstretched
　　arm;
　　　His love endures forever.
[13]to him who divided the Red Sea[a]
　　asunder
　　　His love endures forever.
[14]and brought Israel through the midst
　　of it,
　　　His love endures forever.
[15]but swept Pharaoh and his army into
　　the Red Sea;
　　　His love endures forever.
[16]to him who led his people through the
　　desert,
　　　His love endures forever.
[17]who struck down great kings,
　　　His love endures forever.
[18]and killed mighty kings—
　　　His love endures forever.
[19]Sihon king of the Amorites
　　　His love endures forever.
[20]and Og king of Bashan—
　　　His love endures forever.
[21]and gave their land as an inheritance,
　　　His love endures forever.
[22]an inheritance to his servant Israel;
　　　His love endures forever.

[23]to the One who remembered us in our
　　low estate
　　　His love endures forever.
[24]and freed us from our enemies,
　　　His love endures forever.
[25]and who gives food to every creature.
　　　His love endures forever.

[26]Give thanks to the God of heaven.
　　　His love endures forever.

Psalm 137

[1]By the rivers of Babylon we sat and
　　wept
　　when we remembered Zion.
[2]There on the poplars
　　we hung our harps,
[3]for there our captors asked us for
　　songs,

---

*a*13 Hebrew *Yam Suph*; that is, Sea of Reeds; also in verse 15

our tormentors demanded songs of
joy;
they said, "Sing us one of the songs
of Zion!"

⁴How can we sing the songs of the
LORD
while in a foreign land?
⁵If I forget you, O Jerusalem,
may my right hand forget ⸤its skill⸥.
⁶May my tongue cling to the roof of
my mouth
if I do not remember you,
if I do not consider Jerusalem
my highest joy.

⁷Remember, O LORD, what the
Edomites did
on the day Jerusalem fell.
"Tear it down," they cried,
"tear it down to its foundations!"

⁸O Daughter of Babylon, doomed to
destruction,
happy is he who repays you
for what you have done to us—
⁹he who seizes your infants
and dashes them against the rocks.

Psalm 138

Of David.

¹I will praise you, O LORD, with all my
heart;
before the "gods" I will sing your
praise.
²I will bow down toward your holy
temple
and will praise your name
for your love and your faithfulness,
for you have exalted above all things
your name and your word.
³When I called, you answered me;
you made me bold and
stouthearted.

⁴May all the kings of the earth praise
you, O LORD,
when they hear the words of your
mouth.
⁵May they sing of the ways of the
LORD,
for the glory of the LORD is great.

⁶Though the LORD is on high, he looks
upon the lowly,
but the proud he knows from afar.
⁷Though I walk in the midst of trouble,
you preserve my life;

you stretch out your hand against the
anger of my foes,
with your right hand you save me.
⁸The LORD will fulfill ⸤his purpose⸥ for
me;
your love, O LORD, endures
forever—
do not abandon the works of your
hands.

Psalm 139

For the director of music. Of David.
A psalm.

¹O LORD, you have searched me
and you know me.
²You know when I sit and when I rise;
you perceive my thoughts from afar.
³You discern my going out and my
lying down;
you are familiar with all my ways.
⁴Before a word is on my tongue
you know it completely, O LORD.

⁵You hem me in—behind and before;
you have laid your hand upon me.
⁶Such knowledge is too wonderful for
me,
too lofty for me to attain.

⁷Where can I go from your Spirit?
Where can I flee from your
presence?
⁸If I go up to the heavens, you are
there;
if I make my bed in the depths,ᵃ
you are there.
⁹If I rise on the wings of the dawn,
if I settle on the far side of the sea,
¹⁰even there your hand will guide me,
your right hand will hold me fast.
¹¹If I say, "Surely the darkness will hide
me
and the light become night around
me,"
¹²even the darkness will not be dark to
you;
the night will shine like the day,
for darkness is as light to you.

¹³For you created my inmost being;
you knit me together in my
mother's womb.
¹⁴I praise you because I am fearfully
and wonderfully made;
your works are wonderful,
I know that full well.
¹⁵My frame was not hidden from you

when I was made in the secret
place.
When I was woven together in the
depths of the earth,
16 your eyes saw my unformed body.
All the days ordained for me
were written in your book
before one of them came to be.

17How precious to*a* me are your
thoughts, O God!
How vast is the sum of them!
18Were I to count them,
they would outnumber the grains of
sand.
When I awake,
I am still with you.

19If only you would slay the wicked,
O God!
Away from me, you bloodthirsty
men!
20They speak of you with evil intent;
your adversaries misuse your name.
21Do I not hate those who hate you,
O LORD,
and abhor those who rise up against
you?
22I have nothing but hatred for them;
I count them my enemies.

23Search me, O God, and know my
heart;
test me and know my anxious
thoughts.
24See if there is any offensive way in
me,
and lead me in the way everlasting.

Psalm 140

For the director of music. A psalm
of David.

1Rescue me, O LORD, from evil men;
protect me from men of violence,
2who devise evil plans in their hearts
and stir up war every day.
3They make their tongues as sharp as a
serpent's;
the poison of vipers is on their lips.
Selah

4Keep me, O LORD, from the hands of
the wicked;
protect me from men of violence
who plan to trip my feet.

5Proud men have hidden a snare for
me;
they have spread out the cords of
their net
and have set traps for me along my
path.   *Selah*
6O LORD, I say to you, "You are my
God."
Hear, O LORD, my cry for mercy.
7O Sovereign LORD, my strong deliverer,
who shields my head in the day of
battle—
8do not grant the wicked their desires,
O LORD;
do not let their plans succeed,
or they will become proud.   *Selah*

9Let the heads of those who surround
me
be covered with the trouble their
lips have caused.
10Let burning coals fall upon them;
may they be thrown into the fire,
into miry pits, never to rise.
11Let slanderers not be established in
the land;
may disaster hunt down men of
violence.

12I know that the LORD secures justice
for the poor
and upholds the cause of the needy.
13Surely the righteous will praise your
name
and the upright will live before you.

Psalm 141

A psalm of David.

1O LORD, I call to you; come quickly to
me.
Hear my voice when I call to you.
2May my prayer be set before you like
incense;
may the lifting up of my hands be
like the evening sacrifice.

3Set a guard over my mouth, O LORD;
keep watch over the door of my
lips.
4Let not my heart be drawn to what is
evil,
to take part in wicked deeds
with men who are evildoers;
let me not eat of their delicacies.

a17 Or concerning

⁵Let a righteous man*ᵃ* strike me — it is a kindness;
let him rebuke me — it is oil on my head.
My head will not refuse it.

Yet my prayer is ever against the deeds of evildoers;
6 their rulers will be thrown down from the cliffs,
and the wicked will learn that my words were well spoken.
⁷They will say, "As one plows and breaks up the earth,

ᵃ5 Or Let the Righteous One   *ᵇ7 Hebrew* Sheol

so our bones have been scattered at the mouth of the grave.*ᵇ*"

⁸But my eyes are fixed on you, O Sovereign LORD;
in you I take refuge — do not give me over to death.
⁹Keep me from the snares they have laid for me,
from the traps set by evildoers.
¹⁰Let the wicked fall into their own nets,
while I pass by in safety.

WEDNESDAY

VERSE FOR THE DAY:
Psalm 139:1

AUTHOR:
W. Phillip Keller

PASSAGE FOR THE DAY:
Psalm 139:1–24

He Knows Me

AS HE [God] begins to share life with us, we really are astonished to discover how well he already knows all about us. He, and only he, is totally familiar with all the intimate intricacies of my genetic makeup. He understands all the unique characteristics which have been inherited from my parents and grandparents. He knows my distinctive and special personality. Because of such incredible insight he understands my behavior far better than any human being. So he deals with me fairly.

Precisely the same principle applies to his comprehension of all the social and unique environmental influences which have shaped my character and molded my mind from birth. I am not an enigma to him. I am one whom he has known since conception. Consequently, he does not reject or despise me. Rather, he begins now to re-create me in his own lovely likeness.

Likewise with my mind, my emotions, my will (heart). He perceives clearly why I think as I do; why I feel as I do in interaction with others; why I make the choices I do from day to day. In all these complex activities, he does not come to condemn me. He comes instead to change and re-direct my energies, my decisions, into noble purposes and lofty service. Bless his Name!

Additional Scripture Readings:
Isaiah 57:14–21; Romans 8:18–27

Go to page 643 for your next devotional reading.

Psalm 142

*A maskil[a] of David. When he was in
the cave. A prayer.*

[1]I cry aloud to the LORD;
    I lift up my voice to the LORD for
        mercy.
[2]I pour out my complaint before him;
    before him I tell my trouble.

[3]When my spirit grows faint within me,
    it is you who know my way.
In the path where I walk
    men have hidden a snare for me.
[4]Look to my right and see;
    no one is concerned for me.
I have no refuge;
    no one cares for my life.

[5]I cry to you, O LORD;
    I say, "You are my refuge,
    my portion in the land of the
        living."
[6]Listen to my cry,
    for I am in desperate need;
rescue me from those who pursue me,
    for they are too strong for me.
[7]Set me free from my prison,
    that I may praise your name.

Then the righteous will gather about
    me
    because of your goodness to me.

Psalm 143

A psalm of David.

[1]O LORD, hear my prayer,
    listen to my cry for mercy;
in your faithfulness and righteousness
    come to my relief.
[2]Do not bring your servant into
        judgment,
    for no one living is righteous before
        you.

[3]The enemy pursues me,
    he crushes me to the ground;
he makes me dwell in darkness
    like those long dead.
[4]So my spirit grows faint within me;
    my heart within me is dismayed.
[5]I remember the days of long ago;
    I meditate on all your works
    and consider what your hands have
        done.
[6]I spread out my hands to you;

my soul thirsts for you like a
        parched land.   *Selah*

[7]Answer me quickly, O LORD;
    my spirit fails.
Do not hide your face from me
    or I will be like those who go down
        to the pit.
[8]Let the morning bring me word of
        your unfailing love,
    for I have put my trust in you.
Show me the way I should go,
    for to you I lift up my soul.
[9]Rescue me from my enemies, O LORD,
    for I hide myself in you.
[10]Teach me to do your will,
    for you are my God;
may your good Spirit
    lead me on level ground.

[11]For your name's sake, O LORD,
    preserve my life;
in your righteousness, bring me out
        of trouble.
[12]In your unfailing love, silence my
        enemies;
    destroy all my foes,
    for I am your servant.

Psalm 144

Of David.

[1]Praise be to the LORD my Rock,
    who trains my hands for war,
    my fingers for battle.
[2]He is my loving God and my fortress,
    my stronghold and my deliverer,
my shield, in whom I take refuge,
    who subdues peoples[b] under me.

[3]O LORD, what is man that you care for
        him,
    the son of man that you think of
        him?
[4]Man is like a breath;
    his days are like a fleeting shadow.

[5]Part your heavens, O LORD, and come
        down;
    touch the mountains, so that they
        smoke.
[6]Send forth lightning and scatter ˌthe
        enemiesˌ;
    shoot your arrows and rout them.
[7]Reach down your hand from on high;
    deliver me and rescue me
from the mighty waters,
    from the hands of foreigners

---

[a]Title: Probably a literary or musical term   [b]2 Many manuscripts of the Masoretic Text, Dead Sea
Scrolls, Aquila, Jerome and Syriac; most manuscripts of the Masoretic Text *subdues my people*

⁸whose mouths are full of lies,
whose right hands are deceitful.

⁹I will sing a new song to you, O God;
on the ten-stringed lyre I will make
music to you,
¹⁰to the One who gives victory to kings,
who delivers his servant David from
the deadly sword.

¹¹Deliver me and rescue me
from the hands of foreigners
whose mouths are full of lies,

whose right hands are deceitful.

¹²Then our sons in their youth
will be like well-nurtured plants,
and our daughters will be like pillars
carved to adorn a palace.
¹³Our barns will be filled
with every kind of provision.
Our sheep will increase by thousands,
by tens of thousands in our fields;
¹⁴   our oxen will draw heavy loads.ᵃ
There will be no breaching of walls,

ᵃ14 Or our chieftains will be firmly established

THURSDAY

VERSE FOR THE DAY:	AUTHOR:	PASSAGE FOR THE DAY:
Psalm 143:8	Don Wyrtzen	Psalm 143:1–12

On Level Ground

AT THE moment of rebirth, when the human spirit is "yielded
and still," the Holy Spirit moves in to make his home and to
provide assistance for our pilgrimage with God.

Even David anticipated something of this divine exchange, I
think. His despairing prayer, filled with strong, virile verbs, is
the night sky against which the dazzling stars of God's grace
through his Spirit are displayed.

Guide—David prays, "Show me the way" (v. 8), sensing that
God's guiding Spirit will not leave him stranded, nor remove
him from the unfailing love that is everlasting.

Enabler—"Rescue me from my enemies" (v. 9), he continues. It is the Spirit of God who enables and empowers. David's
many military coups were a result of divine intervention by the
Enabler.

Teacher—"Teach me to do your will . . . may your good
Spirit lead me on level ground" (v. 10). The Holy Spirit is our
Teacher/Interpreter. It is he who explains spiritual mysteries
and levels the ground of our understanding.

Comforter—"For your name's sake, O LORD, preserve my
life . . . bring me out of trouble" (v. 11). God's Spirit whispers
words of encouragement and calls to our minds his mighty
works in our behalf. He banishes discouragement and puts a
song in our hearts!

O Lord, fill me with your Spirit today. Guide me, enable me,
teach me, comfort me. I need help as I continue my pilgrimage.

Additional Scripture Readings:
Isaiah 57:14–21; John 16:5–16

*Go to page 648 for your next
devotional reading.*

no going into captivity,
no cry of distress in our streets.

15Blessed are the people of whom this is
true;
blessed are the people whose God is
the LORD.

Psalm 145*a*

A psalm of praise. Of David.

1I will exalt you, my God the King;
I will praise your name for ever and
ever.
2Every day I will praise you
and extol your name for ever and
ever.

3Great is the LORD and most worthy of
praise;
his greatness no one can fathom.
4One generation will commend your
works to another;
they will tell of your mighty acts.
5They will speak of the glorious
splendor of your majesty,
and I will meditate on your
wonderful works.*b*
6They will tell of the power of your
awesome works,
and I will proclaim your great
deeds.
7They will celebrate your abundant
goodness
and joyfully sing of your
righteousness.

8The LORD is gracious and
compassionate,
slow to anger and rich in love.
9The LORD is good to all;
he has compassion on all he has
made.
10All you have made will praise you,
O LORD;
your saints will extol you.
11They will tell of the glory of your
kingdom
and speak of your might,
12so that all men may know of your
mighty acts
and the glorious splendor of your
kingdom.
13Your kingdom is an everlasting
kingdom,

and your dominion endures through
all generations.

The LORD is faithful to all his promises
and loving toward all he has
made.*c*
14The LORD upholds all those who fall
and lifts up all who are bowed
down.
15The eyes of all look to you,
and you give them their food at the
proper time.
16You open your hand
and satisfy the desires of every
living thing.

17The LORD is righteous in all his ways
and loving toward all he has made.
18The LORD is near to all who call on
him,
to all who call on him in truth.
19He fulfills the desires of those who
fear him;
he hears their cry and saves them.
20The LORD watches over all who love
him,
but all the wicked he will destroy.

21My mouth will speak in praise of the
LORD.
Let every creature praise his holy
name
for ever and ever.

Psalm 146

1Praise the LORD.*d*

Praise the LORD, O my soul.
2 I will praise the LORD all my life;
I will sing praise to my God as long
as I live.

3Do not put your trust in princes,
in mortal men, who cannot save.
4When their spirit departs, they return
to the ground;
on that very day their plans come to
nothing.

5Blessed is he whose help is the God of
Jacob,
whose hope is in the LORD his God,
6the Maker of heaven and earth,
the sea, and everything in them—
the LORD, who remains faithful
forever.

---

*a*This psalm is an acrostic poem, the verses of which (including verse 13b) begin with the successive
letters of the Hebrew alphabet.   *b*5 Dead Sea Scrolls and Syriac (see also Septuagint); Masoretic Text
On the glorious splendor of your majesty / and on your wonderful works I will meditate   *c*13 One
manuscript of the Masoretic Text, Dead Sea Scrolls and Syriac (see also Septuagint); most manuscripts of
the Masoretic Text do not have the last two lines of verse 13.   *d*1 Hebrew *Hallelu Yah;* also in verse 10

⁷He upholds the cause of the oppressed
and gives food to the hungry.
The LORD sets prisoners free,
⁸ the LORD gives sight to the blind,
the LORD lifts up those who are bowed
down,
the LORD loves the righteous.
⁹The LORD watches over the alien
and sustains the fatherless and the
widow,
but he frustrates the ways of the
wicked.

¹⁰The LORD reigns forever,
your God, O Zion, for all
generations.

Praise the LORD.

Psalm 147

¹Praise the LORD.ᵃ

How good it is to sing praises to our
God,
how pleasant and fitting to praise
him!

²The LORD builds up Jerusalem;
he gathers the exiles of Israel.
³He heals the brokenhearted
and binds up their wounds.
⁴He determines the number of the stars
and calls them each by name.
⁵Great is our Lord and mighty in
power;
his understanding has no limit.
⁶The LORD sustains the humble
but casts the wicked to the ground.

⁷Sing to the LORD with thanksgiving;
make music to our God on the
harp.
⁸He covers the sky with clouds;
he supplies the earth with rain
and makes grass grow on the hills.
⁹He provides food for the cattle
and for the young ravens when they
call.

¹⁰His pleasure is not in the strength of
the horse,
nor his delight in the legs of a man;
¹¹the LORD delights in those who fear
him,
who put their hope in his unfailing
love.

¹²Extol the LORD, O Jerusalem;
praise your God, O Zion,

¹³for he strengthens the bars of your
gates
and blesses your people within you.
¹⁴He grants peace to your borders
and satisfies you with the finest of
wheat.

¹⁵He sends his command to the earth;
his word runs swiftly.
¹⁶He spreads the snow like wool
and scatters the frost like ashes.
¹⁷He hurls down his hail like pebbles.
Who can withstand his icy blast?
¹⁸He sends his word and melts them;
he stirs up his breezes, and the
waters flow.

¹⁹He has revealed his word to Jacob,
his laws and decrees to Israel.
²⁰He has done this for no other nation;
they do not know his laws.

Praise the LORD.

Psalm 148

¹Praise the LORD.ᵇ

Praise the LORD from the heavens,
praise him in the heights above.
²Praise him, all his angels,
praise him, all his heavenly hosts.
³Praise him, sun and moon,
praise him, all you shining stars.
⁴Praise him, you highest heavens
and you waters above the skies.

⁵Let them praise the name of the LORD,
for he commanded and they were
created.
⁶He set them in place for ever and
ever;
he gave a decree that will never
pass away.

⁷Praise the LORD from the earth,
you great sea creatures and all
ocean depths,
⁸lightning and hail, snow and clouds,
stormy winds that do his bidding,
⁹you mountains and all hills,
fruit trees and all cedars,
¹⁰wild animals and all cattle,
small creatures and flying birds,
¹¹kings of the earth and all nations,
you princes and all rulers on earth,
¹²young men and maidens,
old men and children.

¹³Let them praise the name of the LORD,
for his name alone is exalted;

ᵃ1 Hebrew *Hallelu Yah*; also in verse 20   ᵇ1 Hebrew *Hallelu Yah*; also in verse 14

his splendor is above the earth and
the heavens.
[14]He has raised up for his people a
horn,[a]
the praise of all his saints,
of Israel, the people close to his
heart.

Praise the LORD.

Psalm 149

[1]Praise the LORD.[b]

Sing to the LORD a new song,
his praise in the assembly of the
saints.

[2]Let Israel rejoice in their Maker;
let the people of Zion be glad in
their King.
[3]Let them praise his name with
dancing
and make music to him with
tambourine and harp.
[4]For the LORD takes delight in his
people;
he crowns the humble with
salvation.
[5]Let the saints rejoice in this honor
and sing for joy on their beds.

[6]May the praise of God be in their
mouths
and a double-edged sword in their
hands,

[7]to inflict vengeance on the nations
and punishment on the peoples,
[8]to bind their kings with fetters,
their nobles with shackles of iron,
[9]to carry out the sentence written
against them.
This is the glory of all his saints.

Praise the LORD.

Psalm 150

[1]Praise the LORD.[c]

Praise God in his sanctuary;
praise him in his mighty heavens.
[2]Praise him for his acts of power;
praise him for his surpassing
greatness.
[3]Praise him with the sounding of the
trumpet,
praise him with the harp and lyre,
[4]praise him with tambourine and
dancing,
praise him with the strings and
flute,
[5]praise him with the clash of cymbals,
praise him with resounding
cymbals.

[6]Let everything that has breath praise
the LORD.

Praise the LORD.

---

a 14 *Horn* here symbolizes strong one, that is, king.   b 1 Hebrew *Hallelu Yah*; also in verse 9
c 1 Hebrew *Hallelu Yah*; also in verse 6

*S*OLOMON *"spoke three thousand proverbs" (1 Kings 4:32), many of which are collected in this book. These wise sayings describe patterns that operate in everyday life, offering us advice on how to conduct ourselves in various situations. Solomon's fundamental instruction is to fear and trust the Lord. As you read this book, remember that God has something to say about every aspect of your life; seek his wisdom in the decisions you must make each day.*

PROVERBS

Prologue: Purpose and Theme

1 The proverbs of Solomon son of David, king of Israel:

2 for attaining wisdom and discipline;
    for understanding words of insight;
3 for acquiring a disciplined and
        prudent life,
    doing what is right and just and
        fair;
4 for giving prudence to the simple,
    knowledge and discretion to the
        young —
5 let the wise listen and add to their
        learning,
    and let the discerning get
        guidance —
6 for understanding proverbs and
        parables,
    the sayings and riddles of the wise.

7 The fear of the LORD is the beginning
        of knowledge,

but fools*a* despise wisdom and discipline.

Exhortations to Embrace Wisdom

Warning Against Enticement

⁸Listen, my son, to your father's instruction

and do not forsake your mother's teaching.
⁹They will be a garland to grace your head
and a chain to adorn your neck.

¹⁰My son, if sinners entice you, do not give in to them.
¹¹If they say, "Come along with us;

a7 The Hebrew words rendered fool in Proverbs, and often elsewhere in the Old Testament, denote one who is morally deficient.

FRIDAY

VERSE FOR THE DAY: AUTHOR: PASSAGE FOR THE DAY:
Proverbs 1:7   D. Bruce Lockerbie   Proverbs 1:1–7

Discretion to the Young

HOW can we prevent ourselves from creating resentment in our children? Only by obeying the Word of God and staking our lives on its truth. If indeed "the fear of the LORD is the beginning of knowledge" (Proverbs 1:7), then before any father can dispense advice on "doing what is right and just and fair" (Proverbs 1:3), he himself must know the meaning of that reverential awe and the wisdom to which it leads.

The goal of a father's godly instruction must be this spiritual insight called in Proverbs wisdom, knowledge or understanding. But this wisdom isn't a scholastic accomplishment measured by high scores on the College Boards or admission to an Ivy League college. The true test of knowledge, according to Proverbs, goes beyond academic achievement to moral responsibility. It zeroes in on decision-making and shows itself best in the disciplining of the character; this results in "a disciplined and prudent life." To live prudently means to think clearly about one's choices and arrive at decisions controlled not by whim or appetite but by an understanding of the difference between right and wrong. This is what Proverbs also calls "discretion" or "discernment."

What we're talking about, then, is instruction that prepares a child to make wise choices, to be discreet and discerning. Such instruction doesn't presume that the child somehow already knows what's best ... So, from the earliest years, children must be taught and trained to tell the truth rather than lies; to respect the property of others rather than take for themselves; to keep from harming anyone else; to hold the miracle of life, whether animal, vegetable or human life, in highest regard.

Additional Scripture Readings:
Proverbs 3:1–18; James 3:13–18

Go to page 650 for your next devotional reading.

let's lie in wait for someone's blood,
let's waylay some harmless soul;
¹²let's swallow them alive, like the
grave,ᵃ
and whole, like those who go down
to the pit;
¹³we will get all sorts of valuable things
and fill our houses with plunder;
¹⁴throw in your lot with us,
and we will share a common
purse" —
¹⁵my son, do not go along with them,
do not set foot on their paths;
¹⁶for their feet rush into sin,
they are swift to shed blood.
¹⁷How useless to spread a net
in full view of all the birds!
¹⁸These men lie in wait for their own
blood;
they waylay only themselves!
¹⁹Such is the end of all who go after
ill-gotten gain;
it takes away the lives of those who
get it.

Warning Against Rejecting Wisdom

²⁰Wisdom calls aloud in the street,
she raises her voice in the public
squares;
²¹at the head of the noisy streetsᵇ she
cries out,
in the gateways of the city she
makes her speech:

²²"How long will you simple onesᶜ love
your simple ways?
How long will mockers delight in
mockery
and fools hate knowledge?
²³If you had responded to my rebuke,
I would have poured out my heart
to you
and made my thoughts known to
you.
²⁴But since you rejected me when I
called
and no one gave heed when I
stretched out my hand,
²⁵since you ignored all my advice
and would not accept my rebuke,
²⁶I in turn will laugh at your disaster;
I will mock when calamity
overtakes you —
²⁷when calamity overtakes you like a
storm,
when disaster sweeps over you like
a whirlwind,

when distress and trouble
overwhelm you.

²⁸"Then they will call to me but I will
not answer;
they will look for me but will not
find me.
²⁹Since they hated knowledge
and did not choose to fear the LORD,
³⁰since they would not accept my
advice
and spurned my rebuke,
³¹they will eat the fruit of their ways
and be filled with the fruit of their
schemes.
³²For the waywardness of the simple
will kill them,
and the complacency of fools will
destroy them;
³³but whoever listens to me will live in
safety
and be at ease, without fear of
harm."

Moral Benefits of Wisdom

2 My son, if you accept my words
and store up my commands within
you,
²turning your ear to wisdom
and applying your heart to
understanding,
³and if you call out for insight
and cry aloud for understanding,
⁴and if you look for it as for silver
and search for it as for hidden
treasure,
⁵then you will understand the fear of
the LORD
and find the knowledge of God.
⁶For the LORD gives wisdom,
and from his mouth come
knowledge and understanding.
⁷He holds victory in store for the
upright,
he is a shield to those whose walk
is blameless,
⁸for he guards the course of the just
and protects the way of his faithful
ones.
⁹Then you will understand what is
right and just
and fair — every good path.
¹⁰For wisdom will enter your heart,
and knowledge will be pleasant to
your soul.
¹¹Discretion will protect you,
and understanding will guard you.

ᵃ12 Hebrew *Sheol*   ᵇ21 Hebrew; Septuagint / *on the tops of the walls*   ᶜ22 The Hebrew word
rendered *simple* in Proverbs generally denotes one without moral direction and inclined to evil.

WEEKENDING

RETHINK

The home is the greenhouse where godly wisdom is cultivated. The power of consistent Christian living in the context of family relationships is the primary spiritual classroom for authentic Christianity. The home is where the majority of behavioral traits—good and bad—are learned, reinforced and passed along to future generations . . .

A home is . . . filled with fragrant and appealing spiritual riches when each member adopts a servant's spirit. Most family arguments and dissension stem from a failure to yield personal rights. A person filled with the Spirit of Christ strongly desires to serve. He does not seek to establish his own emotional turf but freely edifies and encourages other family members through his servant spirit.

– Charles Stanley

REVIVE

Saturday: Mark 9:33–37
Sunday: Philippians 2:1–11

Go to page 651 for your next devotional reading.

¹²Wisdom will save you from the ways
 of wicked men,
from men whose words are
 perverse,
¹³who leave the straight paths
 to walk in dark ways,
¹⁴who delight in doing wrong
 and rejoice in the perverseness of
 evil,

¹⁵whose paths are crooked
 and who are devious in their
 ways.

¹⁶It will save you also from the
 adulteress,
 from the wayward wife with her
 seductive words,
¹⁷who has left the partner of her youth

MONDAY

VERSE FOR THE DAY:
Proverbs 2:6

AUTHOR:
Steve Farrar

PASSAGE FOR THE DAY:
Proverbs 2:1–11

Save the Boys

WE SAVE our boys by giving them a role model to follow.
When our boys have a clear role model, they intuitively know
how to function when they assume the responsibility of marriage and parenting. But in their generation, there are too
many crippled boys who have no idea what it is to be a man.

It is my God-appointed task to ensure that my sons will be
ready to lead a family. I must equip them to that end. Little
boys are the hope of the next generation. They are the fathers
of tomorrow. They must know who they are and what they are
to do. They must see their role model in action. That's how
they will know what it means to be a male. That puts the ball
in my court . . . and in yours . . .

It's our job to save the boys. So the question is, how are we
going to do that? My boys are eight and five. I've got ten years
left with John before he heads out to college, thirteen with
Josh. That time is simply going to fly by. So I must have a
pretty clear idea of what I need to teach them during those remaining years. I must ask myself: *What do I specifically need
to do in order to train them to become leaders of their families?*

I have five goals for saving my boys. It is my job as their father to model for them the importance of

· knowing and obeying Jesus Christ,
· knowing and displaying godly character,
· knowing and loving my wife,
· knowing and loving my children, and
· knowing my gifts and abilities, so I can work hard and effectively in an area of strength, rather than weakness, and
 contribute effectively to the lives of others—and have a little fun at the same time.

Additional Scripture Readings:
Philippians 3:7–11; 1 Peter 4:7–11

*Go to page 653 for your next
devotional reading.*

and ignored the covenant she made
  before God.ᵃ
¹⁸For her house leads down to death
  and her paths to the spirits of the
    dead.
¹⁹None who go to her return
  or attain the paths of life.

²⁰Thus you will walk in the ways of
    good men
  and keep to the paths of the
    righteous.
²¹For the upright will live in the land,
  and the blameless will remain in it;
²²but the wicked will be cut off from
    the land,
  and the unfaithful will be torn from
    it.

Further Benefits of Wisdom

3 My son, do not forget my teaching,
  but keep my commands in your
    heart,
²for they will prolong your life many
    years
  and bring you prosperity.

³Let love and faithfulness never leave
    you;
  bind them around your neck,
  write them on the tablet of your
    heart.
⁴Then you will win favor and a good
    name
  in the sight of God and man.

⁵Trust in the Lord with all your heart
  and lean not on your own
    understanding;
⁶in all your ways acknowledge him,
  and he will make your paths
    straight.ᵇ

⁷Do not be wise in your own eyes;
  fear the Lord and shun evil.
⁸This will bring health to your body
  and nourishment to your bones.

⁹Honor the Lord with your wealth,
  with the firstfruits of all your crops;
¹⁰then your barns will be filled to
    overflowing,
  and your vats will brim over with
    new wine.

¹¹My son, do not despise the Lord's
    discipline
  and do not resent his rebuke,
¹²because the Lord disciplines those he
    loves,
  as a fatherᶜ the son he delights in.

¹³Blessed is the man who finds wisdom,
  the man who gains understanding,
¹⁴for she is more profitable than silver
  and yields better returns than gold.
¹⁵She is more precious than rubies;
  nothing you desire can compare
    with her.
¹⁶Long life is in her right hand;
  in her left hand are riches and
    honor.
¹⁷Her ways are pleasant ways,
  and all her paths are peace.
¹⁸She is a tree of life to those who
    embrace her;
  those who lay hold of her will be
    blessed.

¹⁹By wisdom the Lord laid the earth's
    foundations,
  by understanding he set the
    heavens in place;
²⁰by his knowledge the deeps were
    divided,
  and the clouds let drop the dew.

²¹My son, preserve sound judgment and
    discernment,
  do not let them out of your sight;
²²they will be life for you,
  an ornament to grace your neck.
²³Then you will go on your way in
    safety,
  and your foot will not stumble;
²⁴when you lie down, you will not be
    afraid;
  when you lie down, your sleep will
    be sweet.
²⁵Have no fear of sudden disaster
  or of the ruin that overtakes the
    wicked,
²⁶for the Lord will be your confidence
  and will keep your foot from being
    snared.

²⁷Do not withhold good from those who
    deserve it,
  when it is in your power to act.
²⁸Do not say to your neighbor,
  "Come back later; I'll give it
    tomorrow"—
  when you now have it with
    you.
²⁹Do not plot harm against your
    neighbor,
  who lives trustfully near you.
³⁰Do not accuse a man for no reason—
  when he has done you no harm.

³¹Do not envy a violent man
  or choose any of his ways,

ᵃ17 Or covenant of her God   ᵇ6 Or will direct your paths   ᶜ12 Hebrew; Septuagint / and he punishes

³²for the LORD detests a perverse man
but takes the upright into his
confidence.

³³The LORD's curse is on the house of
the wicked,
but he blesses the home of the
righteous.
³⁴He mocks proud mockers
but gives grace to the humble.

³⁵The wise inherit honor,
but fools he holds up to shame.

Wisdom Is Supreme

4 Listen, my sons, to a father's
instruction;
pay attention and gain
understanding.
²I give you sound learning,

TUESDAY

VERSE FOR THE DAY:
Proverbs 3:6

AUTHOR:
Bill Hybels

PASSAGE FOR THE DAY:
Proverbs 3:1–6

An Endangered Trait

WE USED to play a game at summer camp in which we would
blindfold one of the kids and have him or her run through a
wooded area, relying on a friend for verbal directions to help
navigate. "Turn to the left; there's a tree coming!" "There's a
log in front of you—*jump!*" Some kids would not trust the verbal directions whatsoever. They would shuffle their feet and
walk very slowly, even though their friends were shouting that
the way was clear. Other kids would trot along, and a few
would go like gangbusters. All the kids, though, had to fight
the urge to tear off the blindfold so that they could see what
was ahead. It takes a great deal of courage to follow another
person's lead.

As Christians, we sometimes feel like those blindfolded children. Paul says in 2 Corinthians 5:7, "We live by faith, not by
sight." We are not alone in the woods, though—God will direct
our paths. But following Jesus Christ demands an enormous
amount of courage. Quite often his leadings sound illogical, irrational, countercultural. Sometimes he is so challenging that I
say, "No, I think I'll just crawl back into my shell and play it
safe." Then a voice inside me says, "Where's your courage, Hybels? Get up and walk. You can trust God."

Cowards do not last long on their spiritual pilgrimages. They
shrivel up and disappear. It takes enormous courage to repent
and become a Christian. It takes enormous courage to follow
God's leadings in the Christian life. Some of his callings demand the best that you can summon. Some of his tests stretch
you to the limit. Some of his adventures evoke great fears and
doubts. Truly, spiritual courage is on the endangered
character-quality list.

Additional Scripture Readings:
Joshua 1:1–9;
1 Corinthians 16:13–14

*Go to page 656 for your next
devotional reading.*

so do not forsake my teaching.
³When I was a boy in my father's house,
  still tender, and an only child of my mother,
⁴he taught me and said,
  "Lay hold of my words with all your heart;
  keep my commands and you will live.
⁵Get wisdom, get understanding;
  do not forget my words or swerve from them.
⁶Do not forsake wisdom, and she will protect you;
  love her, and she will watch over you.
⁷Wisdom is supreme; therefore get wisdom.
  Though it cost all you have,ᵃ get understanding.
⁸Esteem her, and she will exalt you;
  embrace her, and she will honor you.
⁹She will set a garland of grace on your head
  and present you with a crown of splendor."

¹⁰Listen, my son, accept what I say,
  and the years of your life will be many.
¹¹I guide you in the way of wisdom
  and lead you along straight paths.
¹²When you walk, your steps will not be hampered;
  when you run, you will not stumble.
¹³Hold on to instruction, do not let it go;
  guard it well, for it is your life.
¹⁴Do not set foot on the path of the wicked
  or walk in the way of evil men.
¹⁵Avoid it, do not travel on it;
  turn from it and go on your way.
¹⁶For they cannot sleep till they do evil;
  they are robbed of slumber till they make someone fall.
¹⁷They eat the bread of wickedness
  and drink the wine of violence.

¹⁸The path of the righteous is like the first gleam of dawn,
  shining ever brighter till the full light of day.
¹⁹But the way of the wicked is like deep darkness;

they do not know what makes them stumble.

²⁰My son, pay attention to what I say;
  listen closely to my words.
²¹Do not let them out of your sight,
  keep them within your heart;
²²for they are life to those who find them
  and health to a man's whole body.
²³Above all else, guard your heart,
  for it is the wellspring of life.
²⁴Put away perversity from your mouth;
  keep corrupt talk far from your lips.
²⁵Let your eyes look straight ahead,
  fix your gaze directly before you.
²⁶Make levelᵇ paths for your feet
  and take only ways that are firm.
²⁷Do not swerve to the right or the left;
  keep your foot from evil.

Warning Against Adultery

5 My son, pay attention to my wisdom,
  listen well to my words of insight,
²that you may maintain discretion
  and your lips may preserve knowledge.
³For the lips of an adulteress drip honey,
  and her speech is smoother than oil;
⁴but in the end she is bitter as gall,
  sharp as a double-edged sword.
⁵Her feet go down to death;
  her steps lead straight to the grave.ᶜ
⁶She gives no thought to the way of life;
  her paths are crooked, but she knows it not.

⁷Now then, my sons, listen to me;
  do not turn aside from what I say.
⁸Keep to a path far from her,
  do not go near the door of her house,
⁹lest you give your best strength to others
  and your years to one who is cruel,
¹⁰lest strangers feast on your wealth
  and your toil enrich another man's house.
¹¹At the end of your life you will groan,
  when your flesh and body are spent.
¹²You will say, "How I hated discipline!
  How my heart spurned correction!
¹³I would not obey my teachers

or listen to my instructors.
¹⁴I have come to the brink of utter ruin
    in the midst of the whole
    assembly."

¹⁵Drink water from your own cistern,
    running water from your own well.
¹⁶Should your springs overflow in the
    streets,
    your streams of water in the public
    squares?
¹⁷Let them be yours alone,
    never to be shared with strangers.
¹⁸May your fountain be blessed,
    and may you rejoice in the wife of
    your youth.
¹⁹A loving doe, a graceful deer—
    may her breasts satisfy you always,
    may you ever be captivated by her
    love.
²⁰Why be captivated, my son, by an
    adulteress?
    Why embrace the bosom of another
    man's wife?

²¹For a man's ways are in full view of
    the LORD,
    and he examines all his paths.
²²The evil deeds of a wicked man
    ensnare him;
    the cords of his sin hold him fast.
²³He will die for lack of discipline,
    led astray by his own great folly.

Warnings Against Folly

6 My son, if you have put up security
    for your neighbor,
    if you have struck hands in pledge
    for another,
²if you have been trapped by what you
    said,
    ensnared by the words of your
    mouth,
³then do this, my son, to free yourself,
    since you have fallen into your
    neighbor's hands:
 Go and humble yourself;
    press your plea with your neighbor!
⁴Allow no sleep to your eyes,
    no slumber to your eyelids.
⁵Free yourself, like a gazelle from the
    hand of the hunter,
    like a bird from the snare of the
    fowler.

⁶Go to the ant, you sluggard;
    consider its ways and be wise!
⁷It has no commander,
    no overseer or ruler,

⁸yet it stores its provisions in summer
    and gathers its food at harvest.

⁹How long will you lie there, you
    sluggard?
    When will you get up from your
    sleep?
¹⁰A little sleep, a little slumber,
    a little folding of the hands to
    rest—
¹¹and poverty will come on you like a
    bandit
    and scarcity like an armed man.^a

¹²A scoundrel and villain,
    who goes about with a corrupt
    mouth,
¹³   who winks with his eye,
    signals with his feet
    and motions with his fingers,
¹⁴   who plots evil with deceit in his
    heart—
    he always stirs up dissension.
¹⁵Therefore disaster will overtake him in
    an instant;
    he will suddenly be destroyed—
    without remedy.

¹⁶There are six things the LORD hates,
    seven that are detestable to him:
¹⁷   haughty eyes,
    a lying tongue,
    hands that shed innocent blood,
¹⁸   a heart that devises wicked
    schemes,
    feet that are quick to rush into
    evil,
¹⁹   a false witness who pours out lies
    and a man who stirs up
    dissension among brothers.

Warning Against Adultery

²⁰My son, keep your father's commands
    and do not forsake your mother's
    teaching.
²¹Bind them upon your heart forever;
    fasten them around your neck.
²²When you walk, they will guide you;
    when you sleep, they will watch
    over you;
    when you awake, they will speak to
    you.
²³For these commands are a lamp,
    this teaching is a light,
    and the corrections of discipline
    are the way to life,
²⁴keeping you from the immoral
    woman,

^a11 Or *like a vagrant / and scarcity like a beggar*

from the smooth tongue of the
  wayward wife.
²⁵Do not lust in your heart after her
  beauty
or let her captivate you with her
  eyes,
²⁶for the prostitute reduces you to a loaf
  of bread,
and the adulteress preys upon your
  very life.
²⁷Can a man scoop fire into his lap
without his clothes being burned?
²⁸Can a man walk on hot coals
without his feet being scorched?
²⁹So is he who sleeps with another
  man's wife;
no one who touches her will go
  unpunished.

³⁰Men do not despise a thief if he steals
  to satisfy his hunger when he is
  starving.
³¹Yet if he is caught, he must pay
  sevenfold,
though it costs him all the wealth of
  his house.
³²But a man who commits adultery
  lacks judgment;
whoever does so destroys himself.
³³Blows and disgrace are his lot,
and his shame will never be wiped
  away;
³⁴for jealousy arouses a husband's
  fury,
and he will show no mercy when
  he takes revenge.
³⁵He will not accept any compensation;

WEDNESDAY

VERSE FOR THE DAY:	AUTHOR:	PASSAGE FOR THE DAY:
Proverbs 6:20	*Charles Swindoll*	*Proverbs 6:20–29*

He Gives Us Boys

THROUGHOUT history, long before the marines, God has
been looking for a few good men:

"For the eyes of the Lᴏʀᴅ range throughout the earth to
strengthen those whose hearts are fully committed to him"
(2 Chronicles 16:9a).

"I looked for a man among them who would build up the
wall and stand before me in the gap" (Ezekiel 22:30a).

God, give us men. Give us Noahs, to whom you can trust
your mighty plans; give us Abrahams, who are willing to leave
home and homeland to follow your call; give us Josephs, who
would rather endure prison than violate one of your commands; give us Moseses, who are willing to stand as your
mouthpiece against the most powerful leaders in all the world;
give us Daniels, who would rather face a lions' den than compromise their faith; *God, give us men.* However, the reality is
that God *does not* give us men—he gives us *boys.* To us, as
parents, he gives the task of forging these boys into men. To
help equip us for that task, God has provided the book of Proverbs, which is largely the advice of a father to his son . . . . Our
children are our legacy. As a parent, are you taking that
thought seriously?

Additional Scripture Readings:
Deuteronomy 6:1–9,20–25;
Proverbs 1:8–19

*Go to page 663 for your next
devotional reading.*

he will refuse the bribe, however
    great it is.

Warning Against the Adulteress

7 My son, keep my words
    and store up my commands within
      you.
²Keep my commands and you will live;
    guard my teachings as the apple of
      your eye.
³Bind them on your fingers;
    write them on the tablet of your
      heart.
⁴Say to wisdom, "You are my sister,"
    and call understanding your
      kinsman;
⁵they will keep you from the
    adulteress,
    from the wayward wife with her
      seductive words.

⁶At the window of my house
    I looked out through the lattice.
⁷I saw among the simple,
    I noticed among the young men,
    a youth who lacked judgment.
⁸He was going down the street near
      her corner,
    walking along in the direction of
      her house
⁹at twilight, as the day was fading,
    as the dark of night set in.

¹⁰Then out came a woman to meet him,
    dressed like a prostitute and with
      crafty intent.
¹¹(She is loud and defiant,
    her feet never stay at home;
¹²now in the street, now in the squares,
    at every corner she lurks.)
¹³She took hold of him and kissed him
    and with a brazen face she said:

¹⁴"I have fellowship offerings[a] at home;
    today I fulfilled my vows.
¹⁵So I came out to meet you;
    I looked for you and have found
      you!
¹⁶I have covered my bed
    with colored linens from Egypt.
¹⁷I have perfumed my bed
    with myrrh, aloes and cinnamon.
¹⁸Come, let's drink deep of love till
      morning;
    let's enjoy ourselves with love!
¹⁹My husband is not at home;
    he has gone on a long journey.
²⁰He took his purse filled with money

and will not be home till full
    moon."

²¹With persuasive words she led him
    astray;
    she seduced him with her smooth
      talk.
²²All at once he followed her
    like an ox going to the slaughter,
    like a deer[b] stepping into a noose[c]
²³   till an arrow pierces his liver,
    like a bird darting into a snare,
    little knowing it will cost him his
      life.

²⁴Now then, my sons, listen to me;
    pay attention to what I say.
²⁵Do not let your heart turn to her ways
    or stray into her paths.
²⁶Many are the victims she has brought
      down;
    her slain are a mighty throng.
²⁷Her house is a highway to the grave,[d]
    leading down to the chambers of
      death.

Wisdom's Call

8 Does not wisdom call out?
    Does not understanding raise her
      voice?
²On the heights along the way,
    where the paths meet, she takes her
      stand;
³beside the gates leading into the city,
    at the entrances, she cries aloud:
⁴"To you, O men, I call out;
    I raise my voice to all mankind.
⁵You who are simple, gain prudence;
    you who are foolish, gain
      understanding.
⁶Listen, for I have worthy things to say;
    I open my lips to speak what is
      right.
⁷My mouth speaks what is true,
    for my lips detest wickedness.
⁸All the words of my mouth are just;
    none of them is crooked or
      perverse.
⁹To the discerning all of them are
      right;
    they are faultless to those who have
      knowledge.
¹⁰Choose my instruction instead of
      silver,
    knowledge rather than choice gold,
¹¹for wisdom is more precious than
    rubies,

---

a14 Traditionally *peace offerings*   *b22* Syriac (see also Septuagint); Hebrew *fool*   *c22* The meaning of
the Hebrew for this line is uncertain.   *d27* Hebrew *Sheol*

and nothing you desire can compare
with her.

12"I, wisdom, dwell together with
prudence;
I possess knowledge and discretion.
13To fear the LORD is to hate evil;
I hate pride and arrogance,
evil behavior and perverse speech.
14Counsel and sound judgment are
mine;
I have understanding and power.
15By me kings reign
and rulers make laws that are just;
16by me princes govern,
and all nobles who rule on earth.*a*
17I love those who love me,
and those who seek me find me.
18With me are riches and honor,
enduring wealth and prosperity.
19My fruit is better than fine gold;
what I yield surpasses choice silver.
20I walk in the way of righteousness,
along the paths of justice,
21bestowing wealth on those who love
me
and making their treasuries full.

22"The LORD brought me me forth as the
first of his works,*b,c*
before his deeds of old;
23I was appointed*d* from eternity,
from the beginning, before the
world began.
24When there were no oceans, I was
given birth,
when there were no springs
abounding with water;
25before the mountains were settled in
place,
before the hills, I was given birth,
26before he made the earth or its fields
or any of the dust of the world.
27I was there when he set the heavens
in place,
when he marked out the horizon on
the face of the deep,
28when he established the clouds above
and fixed securely the fountains of
the deep,
29when he gave the sea its boundary
so the waters would not overstep
his command,
and when he marked out the
foundations of the earth.
30 Then I was the craftsman at his
side.

I was filled with delight day after day,
rejoicing always in his presence,
31rejoicing in his whole world
and delighting in mankind.

32"Now then, my sons, listen to me;
blessed are those who keep my
ways.
33Listen to my instruction and be wise;
do not ignore it.
34Blessed is the man who listens to me,
watching daily at my doors,
waiting at my doorway.
35For whoever finds me finds life
and receives favor from the LORD.
36But whoever fails to find me harms
himself;
all who hate me love death."

Invitations of Wisdom and of Folly

9 Wisdom has built her house;
she has hewn out its seven pillars.
2She has prepared her meat and mixed
her wine;
she has also set her table.
3She has sent out her maids, and she
calls
from the highest point of the city.
4"Let all who are simple come in here!"
she says to those who lack
judgment.
5"Come, eat my food
and drink the wine I have mixed.
6Leave your simple ways and you will
live;
walk in the way of understanding.

7"Whoever corrects a mocker invites
insult;
whoever rebukes a wicked man
incurs abuse.
8Do not rebuke a mocker or he will
hate you;
rebuke a wise man and he will love
you.
9Instruct a wise man and he will be
wiser still;
teach a righteous man and he will
add to his learning.

10"The fear of the LORD is the beginning
of wisdom,
and knowledge of the Holy One is
understanding.
11For through me your days will be
many,
and years will be added to your life.

---

a16 Many Hebrew manuscripts and Septuagint; most Hebrew manuscripts *and nobles—all righteous rulers*
b22 Or *way;* or *dominion*   *c22* Or *The LORD possessed me at the beginning of his work;* or *The LORD brought me forth at the beginning of his work*   *d23* Or *fashioned*

¹²If you are wise, your wisdom will
      reward you;
   if you are a mocker, you alone will
      suffer."

¹³The woman Folly is loud;
   she is undisciplined and without
      knowledge.
¹⁴She sits at the door of her house,
   on a seat at the highest point of the
      city,
¹⁵calling out to those who pass by,
   who go straight on their way.
¹⁶"Let all who are simple come in here!"
   she says to those who lack
      judgment.
¹⁷"Stolen water is sweet;
   food eaten in secret is delicious!"
¹⁸But little do they know that the dead
      are there,
   that her guests are in the depths of
      the grave.ᵃ

Proverbs of Solomon

10 The proverbs of Solomon:

   A wise son brings joy to his father,
      but a foolish son grief to his
      mother.

²Ill-gotten treasures are of no value,
   but righteousness delivers from
      death.

³The LORD does not let the righteous go
      hungry
   but he thwarts the craving of the
      wicked.

⁴Lazy hands make a man poor,
   but diligent hands bring wealth.

⁵He who gathers crops in summer is a
      wise son,
   but he who sleeps during harvest is
      a disgraceful son.

⁶Blessings crown the head of the
      righteous,
   but violence overwhelms the mouth
      of the wicked.ᵇ

⁷The memory of the righteous will be a
      blessing,
   but the name of the wicked will rot.

⁸The wise in heart accept commands,
   but a chattering fool comes to ruin.

⁹The man of integrity walks securely,
   but he who takes crooked paths will
      be found out.

¹⁰He who winks maliciously causes
      grief,
   and a chattering fool comes to ruin.

¹¹The mouth of the righteous is a
      fountain of life,
   but violence overwhelms the mouth
      of the wicked.

¹²Hatred stirs up dissension,
   but love covers over all wrongs.

¹³Wisdom is found on the lips of the
      discerning,
   but a rod is for the back of him
      who lacks judgment.

¹⁴Wise men store up knowledge,
   but the mouth of a fool invites ruin.

¹⁵The wealth of the rich is their fortified
      city,
   but poverty is the ruin of the poor.

¹⁶The wages of the righteous bring them
      life,
   but the income of the wicked brings
      them punishment.

¹⁷He who heeds discipline shows the
      way to life,
   but whoever ignores correction
      leads others astray.

¹⁸He who conceals his hatred has lying
      lips,
   and whoever spreads slander is a
      fool.

¹⁹When words are many, sin is not
      absent,
   but he who holds his tongue is
      wise.

²⁰The tongue of the righteous is choice
      silver,
   but the heart of the wicked is of
      little value.

²¹The lips of the righteous nourish
      many,
   but fools die for lack of judgment.

²²The blessing of the LORD brings
      wealth,
   and he adds no trouble to it.

²³A fool finds pleasure in evil conduct,
   but a man of understanding delights
      in wisdom.

²⁴What the wicked dreads will overtake
      him;
   what the righteous desire will be
      granted.

ᵃ18 Hebrew *Sheol*   ᵇ6 Or *but the mouth of the wicked conceals violence*; also in verse 11

25When the storm has swept by, the
   wicked are gone,
  but the righteous stand firm forever.

26As vinegar to the teeth and smoke to
   the eyes,
  so is a sluggard to those who send
   him.

27The fear of the LORD adds length to
   life,
  but the years of the wicked are cut
   short.

28The prospect of the righteous is joy,
  but the hopes of the wicked come
   to nothing.

29The way of the LORD is a refuge for
   the righteous,
  but it is the ruin of those who do
   evil.

30The righteous will never be uprooted,
  but the wicked will not remain in
   the land.

31The mouth of the righteous brings
   forth wisdom,
  but a perverse tongue will be cut
   out.

32The lips of the righteous know what is
   fitting,
  but the mouth of the wicked only
   what is perverse.

11 The LORD abhors dishonest
    scales,
  but accurate weights are his delight.

2When pride comes, then comes
   disgrace,
  but with humility comes wisdom.

3The integrity of the upright guides
   them,
  but the unfaithful are destroyed by
   their duplicity.

4Wealth is worthless in the day of
   wrath,
  but righteousness delivers from
   death.

5The righteousness of the blameless
   makes a straight way for them,
  but the wicked are brought down
   by their own wickedness.

6The righteousness of the upright
   delivers them,
  but the unfaithful are trapped by
   evil desires.

7When a wicked man dies, his hope
   perishes;

all he expected from his power
   comes to nothing.

8The righteous man is rescued from
   trouble,
  and it comes on the wicked instead.

9With his mouth the godless destroys
   his neighbor,
  but through knowledge the
   righteous escape.

10When the righteous prosper, the city
   rejoices;
  when the wicked perish, there are
   shouts of joy.

11Through the blessing of the upright a
   city is exalted,
  but by the mouth of the wicked it is
   destroyed.

12A man who lacks judgment derides
   his neighbor,
  but a man of understanding holds
   his tongue.

13A gossip betrays a confidence,
  but a trustworthy man keeps a
   secret.

14For lack of guidance a nation falls,
  but many advisers make victory
   sure.

15He who puts up security for another
   will surely suffer,
  but whoever refuses to strike hands
   in pledge is safe.

16A kindhearted woman gains respect,
  but ruthless men gain only wealth.

17A kind man benefits himself,
  but a cruel man brings trouble on
   himself.

18The wicked man earns deceptive
   wages,
  but he who sows righteousness
   reaps a sure reward.

19The truly righteous man attains life,
  but he who pursues evil goes to his
   death.

20The LORD detests men of perverse
   heart
  but he delights in those whose ways
   are blameless.

21Be sure of this: The wicked will not
   go unpunished,
  but those who are righteous will go
   free.

22Like a gold ring in a pig's snout

is a beautiful woman who shows no discretion.

23The desire of the righteous ends only in good,
but the hope of the wicked only in wrath.

24One man gives freely, yet gains even more;
another withholds unduly, but comes to poverty.

25A generous man will prosper;
he who refreshes others will himself be refreshed.

26People curse the man who hoards grain,
but blessing crowns him who is willing to sell.

27He who seeks good finds goodwill,
but evil comes to him who searches for it.

28Whoever trusts in his riches will fall,
but the righteous will thrive like a green leaf.

29He who brings trouble on his family will inherit only wind,
and the fool will be servant to the wise.

30The fruit of the righteous is a tree of life,
and he who wins souls is wise.

31If the righteous receive their due on earth,
how much more the ungodly and the sinner!

12 Whoever loves discipline loves knowledge,
but he who hates correction is stupid.

2A good man obtains favor from the LORD,
but the LORD condemns a crafty man.

3A man cannot be established through wickedness,
but the righteous cannot be uprooted.

4A wife of noble character is her husband's crown,
but a disgraceful wife is like decay in his bones.

5The plans of the righteous are just,
but the advice of the wicked is deceitful.

6The words of the wicked lie in wait for blood,
but the speech of the upright rescues them.

7Wicked men are overthrown and are no more,
but the house of the righteous stands firm.

8A man is praised according to his wisdom,
but men with warped minds are despised.

9Better to be a nobody and yet have a servant
than pretend to be somebody and have no food.

10A righteous man cares for the needs of his animal,
but the kindest acts of the wicked are cruel.

11He who works his land will have abundant food,
but he who chases fantasies lacks judgment.

12The wicked desire the plunder of evil men,
but the root of the righteous flourishes.

13An evil man is trapped by his sinful talk,
but a righteous man escapes trouble.

14From the fruit of his lips a man is filled with good things
as surely as the work of his hands rewards him.

15The way of a fool seems right to him,
but a wise man listens to advice.

16A fool shows his annoyance at once,
but a prudent man overlooks an insult.

17A truthful witness gives honest testimony,
but a false witness tells lies.

18Reckless words pierce like a sword,
but the tongue of the wise brings healing.

19Truthful lips endure forever,
but a lying tongue lasts only a moment.

20There is deceit in the hearts of those who plot evil,

but joy for those who promote
peace.

21No harm befalls the righteous,
but the wicked have their fill of
trouble.

22The LORD detests lying lips,
but he delights in men who are
truthful.

23A prudent man keeps his knowledge
to himself,
but the heart of fools blurts out
folly.

24Diligent hands will rule,
but laziness ends in slave labor.

25An anxious heart weighs a man down,
but a kind word cheers him up.

26A righteous man is cautious in
friendship,[a]
but the way of the wicked leads
them astray.

27The lazy man does not roast[b] his
game,
but the diligent man prizes his
possessions.

28In the way of righteousness there is
life;
along that path is immortality.

13 A wise son heeds his father's
instruction,
but a mocker does not listen to
rebuke.

2From the fruit of his lips a man enjoys
good things,
but the unfaithful have a craving for
violence.

3He who guards his lips guards his life,
but he who speaks rashly will come
to ruin.

4The sluggard craves and gets nothing,
but the desires of the diligent are
fully satisfied.

5The righteous hate what is false,
but the wicked bring shame and
disgrace.

6Righteousness guards the man of
integrity,
but wickedness overthrows the
sinner.

7One man pretends to be rich, yet has
nothing;
another pretends to be poor, yet has
great wealth.

8A man's riches may ransom his life,
but a poor man hears no threat.

9The light of the righteous shines
brightly,
but the lamp of the wicked is
snuffed out.

10Pride only breeds quarrels,
but wisdom is found in those who
take advice.

11Dishonest money dwindles away,
but he who gathers money little by
little makes it grow.

12Hope deferred makes the heart sick,
but a longing fulfilled is a tree of
life.

13He who scorns instruction will pay for
it,
but he who respects a command is
rewarded.

14The teaching of the wise is a fountain
of life,
turning a man from the snares of
death.

15Good understanding wins favor,
but the way of the unfaithful is
hard.[c]

16Every prudent man acts out of
knowledge,
but a fool exposes his folly.

17A wicked messenger falls into trouble,
but a trustworthy envoy brings
healing.

18He who ignores discipline comes to
poverty and shame,
but whoever heeds correction is
honored.

19A longing fulfilled is sweet to the soul,
but fools detest turning from evil.

20He who walks with the wise grows
wise,
but a companion of fools suffers
harm.

21Misfortune pursues the sinner,
but prosperity is the reward of the
righteous.

²²A good man leaves an inheritance for
    his children's children,
  but a sinner's wealth is stored up
    for the righteous.

²³A poor man's field may produce
    abundant food,
  but injustice sweeps it away.

²⁴He who spares the rod hates his
    son,
  but he who loves him is careful to
    discipline him.

²⁵The righteous eat to their hearts'
    content,
  but the stomach of the wicked goes
    hungry.

14 The wise woman builds her
    house,
  but with her own hands the foolish
    one tears hers down.

²He whose walk is upright fears the
    LORD,
  but he whose ways are devious
    despises him.

THURSDAY

VERSE FOR THE DAY:	AUTHOR:	PASSAGE FOR THE DAY:
Proverbs 13:11	Ron Blue	Proverbs 13:7–11

Lesson on Stewardship

RECENTLY I was walking from the Sunday morning worship
service to my Sunday school class when a teacher stopped me
to ask if I could help him with his lesson on stewardship for
that morning. The class was to start in just a few minutes, but
I agreed to tell him all I could in that brief time. I said a quick
prayer asking for wisdom and the thought came to my mind
that my basic message is threefold.

1. God owns it all.
2. Money is never an end in itself, but is merely a resource
used to accomplish other goals and obligations.
3. Spend less than you earn and do it for a long time, and
you will be financially successful.

There is tremendous freedom of mind in knowing and believing that God owns it all, and that money is nothing more
than a resource provided by God to allow us to accomplish his
purposes on this earth.

Is it wrong then to have a long-term goal of financial independence? I believe not—unless financial independence is defined as having enough to be independent from God. This
whole question is really one of "How much is enough?"

How do you achieve one or more of the long-term goals,
such as financial independence, college education, improving
your lifestyle, getting out of debt, making major contributions
or starting your own business? The answer is simple—spend
less than you earn and do it for a long time—or as the Bible
says, "He who gathers money little by little makes it grow"
(Proverbs 13:11).

Additional Scripture Readings:
Proverbs 10:4; 1 Timothy 6:17–19

Go to page 666 for your next
devotional reading.

³A fool's talk brings a rod to his back,
but the lips of the wise protect
them.

⁴Where there are no oxen, the manger
is empty,
but from the strength of an ox
comes an abundant harvest.

⁵A truthful witness does not deceive,
but a false witness pours out lies.

⁶The mocker seeks wisdom and finds
none,
but knowledge comes easily to the
discerning.

⁷Stay away from a foolish man,
for you will not find knowledge on
his lips.

⁸The wisdom of the prudent is to give
thought to their ways,
but the folly of fools is deception.

⁹Fools mock at making amends for sin,
but goodwill is found among the
upright.

¹⁰Each heart knows its own bitterness,
and no one else can share its joy.

¹¹The house of the wicked will be
destroyed,
but the tent of the upright will
flourish.

¹²There is a way that seems right to a
man,
but in the end it leads to death.

¹³Even in laughter the heart may ache,
and joy may end in grief.

¹⁴The faithless will be fully repaid for
their ways,
and the good man rewarded for his.

¹⁵A simple man believes anything,
but a prudent man gives thought to
his steps.

¹⁶A wise man fears the LORD and shuns
evil,
but a fool is hotheaded and
reckless.

¹⁷A quick-tempered man does foolish
things,
and a crafty man is hated.

¹⁸The simple inherit folly,
but the prudent are crowned with
knowledge.

¹⁹Evil men will bow down in the
presence of the good,
and the wicked at the gates of the
righteous.

²⁰The poor are shunned even by their
neighbors,
but the rich have many friends.

²¹He who despises his neighbor sins,
but blessed is he who is kind to the
needy.

²²Do not those who plot evil go astray?
But those who plan what is good
find^a love and faithfulness.

²³All hard work brings a profit,
but mere talk leads only to poverty.

²⁴The wealth of the wise is their crown,
but the folly of fools yields folly.

²⁵A truthful witness saves lives,
but a false witness is deceitful.

²⁶He who fears the LORD has a secure
fortress,
and for his children it will be a
refuge.

²⁷The fear of the LORD is a fountain of
life,
turning a man from the snares of
death.

²⁸A large population is a king's glory,
but without subjects a prince is
ruined.

²⁹A patient man has great
understanding,
but a quick-tempered man displays
folly.

³⁰A heart at peace gives life to the body,
but envy rots the bones.

³¹He who oppresses the poor shows
contempt for their Maker,
but whoever is kind to the needy
honors God.

³²When calamity comes, the wicked are
brought down,
but even in death the righteous
have a refuge.

³³Wisdom reposes in the heart of the
discerning
and even among fools she lets
herself be known.^b

³⁴Righteousness exalts a nation,
but sin is a disgrace to any people.

^a22 Or *show*   ^b33 Hebrew; Septuagint and Syriac / *but in the heart of fools she is not known*

³⁵A king delights in a wise servant,
but a shameful servant incurs his
wrath.

15

A gentle answer turns away
wrath,
but a harsh word stirs up anger.

²The tongue of the wise commends
knowledge,
but the mouth of the fool gushes
folly.

³The eyes of the LORD are everywhere,
keeping watch on the wicked and
the good.

⁴The tongue that brings healing is a
tree of life,
but a deceitful tongue crushes the
spirit.

⁵A fool spurns his father's discipline,
but whoever heeds correction shows
prudence.

⁶The house of the righteous contains
great treasure,
but the income of the wicked brings
them trouble.

⁷The lips of the wise spread
knowledge;
not so the hearts of fools.

⁸The LORD detests the sacrifice of the
wicked,
but the prayer of the upright pleases
him.

⁹The LORD detests the way of the
wicked
but he loves those who pursue
righteousness.

¹⁰Stern discipline awaits him who leaves
the path;
he who hates correction will die.

¹¹Death and Destruction*ᵃ* lie open
before the LORD —
how much more the hearts of men!

¹²A mocker resents correction;
he will not consult the wise.

¹³A happy heart makes the face
cheerful,
but heartache crushes the spirit.

¹⁴The discerning heart seeks knowledge,
but the mouth of a fool feeds on
folly.

¹⁵All the days of the oppressed are
wretched,
but the cheerful heart has a
continual feast.

¹⁶Better a little with the fear of the LORD
than great wealth with turmoil.

¹⁷Better a meal of vegetables where
there is love
than a fattened calf with hatred.

¹⁸A hot-tempered man stirs up
dissension,
but a patient man calms a quarrel.

¹⁹The way of the sluggard is blocked
with thorns,
but the path of the upright is a
highway.

²⁰A wise son brings joy to his father,
but a foolish man despises his
mother.

²¹Folly delights a man who lacks
judgment,
but a man of understanding keeps a
straight course.

²²Plans fail for lack of counsel,
but with many advisers they
succeed.

²³A man finds joy in giving an apt
reply —
and how good is a timely word!

²⁴The path of life leads upward for the
wise
to keep him from going down to the
grave.*ᵇ*

²⁵The LORD tears down the proud man's
house
but he keeps the widow's
boundaries intact.

²⁶The LORD detests the thoughts of the
wicked,
but those of the pure are pleasing to
him.

²⁷A greedy man brings trouble to his
family,
but he who hates bribes will live.

²⁸The heart of the righteous weighs its
answers,
but the mouth of the wicked gushes
evil.

²⁹The LORD is far from the wicked
but he hears the prayer of the
righteous.

ᵃ11 Hebrew *Sheol and Abaddon*   *ᵇ24* Hebrew *Sheol*

³⁰A cheerful look brings joy to the
heart,
and good news gives health to the
bones.

³¹He who listens to a life-giving rebuke
will be at home among the wise.

³²He who ignores discipline despises
himself,
but whoever heeds correction gains
understanding.

³³The fear of the LORD teaches a man
wisdom,ᵃ
and humility comes before honor.

16 To man belong the plans of the
heart,
but from the LORD comes the reply
of the tongue.

²All a man's ways seem innocent to
him,
but motives are weighed by the
LORD.

ᵃ33 Or *Wisdom teaches the fear of the LORD*

FRIDAY

VERSE FOR THE DAY:
Proverbs 15:10

AUTHOR:
Reggie White

PASSAGE FOR THE DAY:
Proverbs 15:7–10

Accountability

AFTER the Lord, I'm first of all accountable to my wife, Sara. I
know I can depend on her to tell it like it is. God always uses
Sara to affirm or negate whatever may surface in my life. Spiritually, I'm also accountable to some Christian friends who
give me sound spiritual guidance . . .

Any one of them can talk to me for just a few minutes and
discern whether I'm walking close to the Lord or if I might just
need a spiritual kick in the seat of my pants. I can really count
on them to tell me when I'm straying off the path—whether I
ask to do so or not.

Who holds you accountable? You need someone to whom
you can pour out your deepest thoughts and heartaches . . .

We all have blind spots, areas in our lives that hinder our
spiritual growth, but areas we cannot see. For example, we
may express anger to others in a manner that is actually verbally abusive. We feel justified in our correction of them, but
another believer can help us understand that our words should
be the kind to inspire a positive response. In other words,
there is a better way to express our anger, and we may need
help finding that way.

If we are not accountable to someone else, we may never
understand why people reject our advice. We must learn to accept constructive criticism ourselves. We set ourselves up for
the problems in our lives that way. We have to understand the
truth of the proverb: "Stern discipline awaits him who leaves
the path; he who hates correction will die" (Proverbs 15:10).

Additional Scripture Readings:
Proverbs 5:7–23; Hebrews 12:4–13

*Go to page 669 for your next
devotional reading.*

³Commit to the LORD whatever you do,
and your plans will succeed.

⁴The LORD works out everything for his
own ends—
even the wicked for a day of
disaster.

⁵The LORD detests all the proud of
heart.
Be sure of this: They will not go
unpunished.

⁶Through love and faithfulness sin is
atoned for;
through the fear of the LORD a man
avoids evil.

⁷When a man's ways are pleasing to
the LORD,
he makes even his enemies live at
peace with him.

⁸Better a little with righteousness
than much gain with injustice.

⁹In his heart a man plans his course,
but the LORD determines his steps.

¹⁰The lips of a king speak as an oracle,
and his mouth should not betray
justice.

¹¹Honest scales and balances are from
the LORD;
all the weights in the bag are of his
making.

¹²Kings detest wrongdoing,
for a throne is established through
righteousness.

¹³Kings take pleasure in honest lips;
they value a man who speaks the
truth.

¹⁴A king's wrath is a messenger of
death,
but a wise man will appease it.

¹⁵When a king's face brightens, it
means life;
his favor is like a rain cloud in
spring.

¹⁶How much better to get wisdom than
gold,
to choose understanding rather than
silver!

¹⁷The highway of the upright avoids
evil;
he who guards his way guards his
life.

¹⁸Pride goes before destruction,
a haughty spirit before a fall.

¹⁹Better to be lowly in spirit and among
the oppressed
than to share plunder with the
proud.

²⁰Whoever gives heed to instruction
prospers,
and blessed is he who trusts in the
LORD.

²¹The wise in heart are called
discerning,
and pleasant words promote
instruction.ᵃ

²²Understanding is a fountain of life to
those who have it,
but folly brings punishment to
fools.

²³A wise man's heart guides his mouth,
and his lips promote instruction.ᵇ

²⁴Pleasant words are a honeycomb,
sweet to the soul and healing to the
bones.

²⁵There is a way that seems right to a
man,
but in the end it leads to death.

²⁶The laborer's appetite works for him;
his hunger drives him on.

²⁷A scoundrel plots evil,
and his speech is like a scorching
fire.

²⁸A perverse man stirs up dissension,
and a gossip separates close friends.

²⁹A violent man entices his neighbor
and leads him down a path that is
not good.

³⁰He who winks with his eye is plotting
perversity;
he who purses his lips is bent on
evil.

³¹Gray hair is a crown of splendor;
it is attained by a righteous life.

³²Better a patient man than a warrior,
a man who controls his temper than
one who takes a city.

³³The lot is cast into the lap,
but its every decision is from the
LORD.

17 Better a dry crust with peace and
quiet

ᵃ21 Or *words make a man persuasive*   ᵇ23 Or *mouth / and makes his lips persuasive* than a house full of feasting,[a] with strife.

2A wise servant will rule over a disgraceful son,
and will share the inheritance as one of the brothers.

3The crucible for silver and the furnace for gold,
but the LORD tests the heart.

4A wicked man listens to evil lips;
a liar pays attention to a malicious tongue.

5He who mocks the poor shows contempt for their Maker;
whoever gloats over disaster will not go unpunished.

6Children's children are a crown to the aged,
and parents are the pride of their children.

7Arrogant[b] lips are unsuited to a fool—
how much worse lying lips to a ruler!

8A bribe is a charm to the one who gives it;
wherever he turns, he succeeds.

9He who covers over an offense promotes love,
but whoever repeats the matter separates close friends.

10A rebuke impresses a man of discernment
more than a hundred lashes a fool.

11An evil man is bent only on rebellion;
a merciless official will be sent against him.

12Better to meet a bear robbed of her cubs
than a fool in his folly.

13If a man pays back evil for good,
evil will never leave his house.

14Starting a quarrel is like breaching a dam;
so drop the matter before a dispute breaks out.

15Acquitting the guilty and condemning the innocent—
the LORD detests them both.

16Of what use is money in the hand of a fool,
since he has no desire to get wisdom?

17A friend loves at all times,
and a brother is born for adversity.

18A man lacking in judgment strikes hands in pledge
and puts up security for his neighbor.

19He who loves a quarrel loves sin;
he who builds a high gate invites destruction.

20A man of perverse heart does not prosper;
he whose tongue is deceitful falls into trouble.

21To have a fool for a son brings grief;
there is no joy for the father of a fool.

22A cheerful heart is good medicine,
but a crushed spirit dries up the bones.

23A wicked man accepts a bribe in secret
to pervert the course of justice.

24A discerning man keeps wisdom in view,
but a fool's eyes wander to the ends of the earth.

25A foolish son brings grief to his father
and bitterness to the one who bore him.

26It is not good to punish an innocent man,
or to flog officials for their integrity.

27A man of knowledge uses words with restraint,
and a man of understanding is even-tempered.

28Even a fool is thought wise if he keeps silent,
and discerning if he holds his tongue.

18 An unfriendly man pursues selfish ends;
he defies all sound judgment.

2A fool finds no pleasure in understanding
but delights in airing his own opinions.

---

[a]1 Hebrew *sacrifices*   [b]7 Or *Eloquent*

WEEKENDING

RESOLVE

Most of us are poor listeners. Since our mind
moves forward faster than the words to which
we are listening, we are frequently preparing
something to say when we should be
listening . . .

Are we aware of our listening biases? Many
of us tune out children or old people. For years
many women have complained that men do not
listen to them as carefully as they listen to
other men. When we are angry about
something, do we carefully listen to an
explanation?

The world aches for good listeners. Many
doctors report that they daily see patients who
have nothing physically wrong with them. They
merely need someone to listen to them.

– William E. Diehl

REVIVE

Saturday: Proverbs 18:13
Sunday: James 1:19–21

Go to page 672 for your next devotional reading.

[3]When wickedness comes, so does
   contempt,
   and with shame comes disgrace.

[4]The words of a man's mouth are deep
   waters,
   but the fountain of wisdom is a
   bubbling brook.

[5]It is not good to be partial to the
   wicked
   or to deprive the innocent of justice.

[6]A fool's lips bring him strife,
   and his mouth invites a beating.

[7]A fool's mouth is his undoing,
   and his lips are a snare to his soul.

[8]The words of a gossip are like choice
   morsels;
   they go down to a man's inmost
   parts.

[9]One who is slack in his work
   is brother to one who destroys.

[10]The name of the Lord is a strong
   tower;
   the righteous run to it and are safe.

[11]The wealth of the rich is their fortified
   city;
   they imagine it an unscalable wall.

[12]Before his downfall a man's heart is
   proud,
   but humility comes before honor.

[13]He who answers before listening—
   that is his folly and his shame.

[14]A man's spirit sustains him in
   sickness,
   but a crushed spirit who can bear?

[15]The heart of the discerning acquires
   knowledge;
   the ears of the wise seek it out.

[16]A gift opens the way for the giver
   and ushers him into the presence of
   the great.

[17]The first to present his case seems
   right,
   till another comes forward and
   questions him.

[18]Casting the lot settles disputes
   and keeps strong opponents apart.

[19]An offended brother is more
   unyielding than a fortified city,
   and disputes are like the barred
   gates of a citadel.

[20]From the fruit of his mouth a man's
   stomach is filled;
   with the harvest from his lips he is
   satisfied.

[21]The tongue has the power of life and
   death,
   and those who love it will eat its
   fruit.

[22]He who finds a wife finds what is
   good
   and receives favor from the Lord.

[23]A poor man pleads for mercy,
   but a rich man answers harshly.

[24]A man of many companions may
   come to ruin,
   but there is a friend who sticks
   closer than a brother.

19 Better a poor man whose walk is
   blameless
   than a fool whose lips are perverse.

[2]It is not good to have zeal without
   knowledge,
   nor to be hasty and miss the way.

[3]A man's own folly ruins his life,
   yet his heart rages against the Lord.

[4]Wealth brings many friends,
   but a poor man's friend deserts him.

[5]A false witness will not go
   unpunished,
   and he who pours out lies will not
   go free.

[6]Many curry favor with a ruler,
   and everyone is the friend of a man
   who gives gifts.

[7]A poor man is shunned by all his
   relatives—
   how much more do his friends
   avoid him!
Though he pursues them with
   pleading,
   they are nowhere to be found.[a]

[8]He who gets wisdom loves his own
   soul;
   he who cherishes understanding
   prospers.

[9]A false witness will not go
   unpunished,
   and he who pours out lies will
   perish.

[10]It is not fitting for a fool to live in
   luxury—

a7 The meaning of the Hebrew for this sentence is uncertain.

how much worse for a slave to rule
   over princes!

¹¹A man's wisdom gives him patience;
   it is to his glory to overlook an
      offense.

¹²A king's rage is like the roar of a lion,
   but his favor is like dew on the
      grass.

¹³A foolish son is his father's ruin,
   and a quarrelsome wife is like a
      constant dripping.

¹⁴Houses and wealth are inherited from
      parents,
   but a prudent wife is from the Lord.

¹⁵Laziness brings on deep sleep,
   and the shiftless man goes hungry.

¹⁶He who obeys instructions guards his
      life,
   but he who is contemptuous of his
      ways will die.

¹⁷He who is kind to the poor lends to
      the Lord,
   and he will reward him for what he
      has done.

¹⁸Discipline your son, for in that there
      is hope;
   do not be a willing party to his
      death.

¹⁹A hot-tempered man must pay the
      penalty;
   if you rescue him, you will have to
      do it again.

²⁰Listen to advice and accept
      instruction,
   and in the end you will be wise.

²¹Many are the plans in a man's heart,
   but it is the Lord's purpose that
      prevails.

²²What a man desires is unfailing
      love[a];
   better to be poor than a liar.

²³The fear of the Lord leads to life:
   Then one rests content, untouched
      by trouble.

²⁴The sluggard buries his hand in the
      dish;
   he will not even bring it back to his
      mouth!

²⁵Flog a mocker, and the simple will
      learn prudence;

rebuke a discerning man, and he
      will gain knowledge.

²⁶He who robs his father and drives out
      his mother
   is a son who brings shame and
      disgrace.

²⁷Stop listening to instruction, my son,
   and you will stray from the words
      of knowledge.

²⁸A corrupt witness mocks at justice,
   and the mouth of the wicked gulps
      down evil.

²⁹Penalties are prepared for mockers,
   and beatings for the backs of fools.

20 Wine is a mocker and beer a
      brawler;
   whoever is led astray by them is not
      wise.

²A king's wrath is like the roar of a
      lion;
   he who angers him forfeits his life.

³It is to a man's honor to avoid strife,
   but every fool is quick to quarrel.

⁴A sluggard does not plow in season;
   so at harvest time he looks but
      finds nothing.

⁵The purposes of a man's heart are
      deep waters,
   but a man of understanding draws
      them out.

⁶Many a man claims to have unfailing
      love,
   but a faithful man who can find?

⁷The righteous man leads a blameless
      life;
   blessed are his children after him.

⁸When a king sits on his throne to
      judge,
   he winnows out all evil with his eyes.

⁹Who can say, "I have kept my heart
      pure;
   I am clean and without sin"?

¹⁰Differing weights and differing
      measures —
   the Lord detests them both.

¹¹Even a child is known by his actions,
   by whether his conduct is pure and
      right.

a22 Or *A man's greed is his shame*

¹²Ears that hear and eyes that see —
the LORD has made them both.

¹³Do not love sleep or you will grow
poor;
stay awake and you will have food
to spare.

¹⁴"It's no good, it's no good!" says the
buyer;
then off he goes and boasts about
his purchase.

¹⁵Gold there is, and rubies in abundance,
but lips that speak knowledge are a
rare jewel.

¹⁶Take the garment of one who puts up
security for a stranger;
hold it in pledge if he does it for a
wayward woman.

MONDAY

VERSE FOR THE DAY:
Proverbs 20:7

AUTHOR:
Larry Burkett

PASSAGE FOR THE DAY:
Proverbs 20:6–7

Instilling Basic Values

GOD'S instructions are neither complicated nor harsh. In fact, they are designed to free us, not bind us to a set of rigid do's and don'ts. The difficulty is that most American families have been duped into a life of "get rich quick" that includes the way we buy homes, cars, clothes and food. God's principles in the area of finances have been largely ignored for the last forty years, and now we are reaping what has been sown.

I read an article in a business magazine that vividly brought this into focus. It seems that the largest mail order seed company in the country decided to go out of business, despite the fact that sales were higher than ever. Unfortunately, so were nonpayments by their mail order sales force. For nearly fifty years, the company had been supplying seeds to children who would sell them door-to-door, mostly in rural communities, to raise money. In recent years, the nonpayment rate to the company had risen steadily, until in 1981, it reached 70 percent. The average age of these delinquent salesmen was ten years! The final straw came when the company attempted to contact the parents, hoping they would help in collection, only to discover that the parents actually encouraged the kids.

The symptom described is nonpayment of a just debt, but the problem runs much deeper. It involves basic values that parents fail to instill in their children. It's an attitude that my rights come before others. The lack of integrity in the parents is reflected and amplified in the lives of their children.

It's unfortunate that later these parents probably won't understand why irresponsible children become irresponsible adults. *"The righteous man leads a blameless life; blessed are his children after him"* [Proverbs 20:7, italics added].

Additional Scripture Readings:
1 Chronicles 29:14–19; Titus 2:6–8

Go to page 674 for your next devotional reading.

¹⁷Food gained by fraud tastes sweet to a
man,
   but he ends up with a mouth full of
   gravel.

¹⁸Make plans by seeking advice;
   if you wage war, obtain guidance.

¹⁹A gossip betrays a confidence;
   so avoid a man who talks too much.

²⁰If a man curses his father or mother,
   his lamp will be snuffed out in
   pitch darkness.

²¹An inheritance quickly gained at the
beginning
   will not be blessed at the end.

²²Do not say, "I'll pay you back for this
wrong!"
   Wait for the LORD, and he will
   deliver you.

²³The LORD detests differing weights,
   and dishonest scales do not please
   him.

²⁴A man's steps are directed by the
LORD.
   How then can anyone understand
   his own way?

²⁵It is a trap for a man to dedicate
something rashly
   and only later to consider his vows.

²⁶A wise king winnows out the wicked;
   he drives the threshing wheel over
   them.

²⁷The lamp of the LORD searches the
spirit of a man[a];
   it searches out his inmost being.

²⁸Love and faithfulness keep a king
safe;
   through love his throne is made
   secure.

²⁹The glory of young men is their
strength,
   gray hair the splendor of the old.

³⁰Blows and wounds cleanse away evil,
   and beatings purge the inmost
   being.

21 The king's heart is in the hand of
   the LORD;
   he directs it like a watercourse
   wherever he pleases.

²All a man's ways seem right to him,

   but the LORD weighs the heart.

³To do what is right and just
   is more acceptable to the LORD than
   sacrifice.

⁴Haughty eyes and a proud heart,
   the lamp of the wicked, are sin!

⁵The plans of the diligent lead to profit
   as surely as haste leads to poverty.

⁶A fortune made by a lying tongue
   is a fleeting vapor and a deadly
   snare.[b]

⁷The violence of the wicked will drag
   them away,
   for they refuse to do what is right.

⁸The way of the guilty is devious,
   but the conduct of the innocent is
   upright.

⁹Better to live on a corner of the roof
   than share a house with a
   quarrelsome wife.

¹⁰The wicked man craves evil;
   his neighbor gets no mercy from
   him.

¹¹When a mocker is punished, the
   simple gain wisdom;
   when a wise man is instructed, he
   gets knowledge.

¹²The Righteous One[c] takes note of the
   house of the wicked
   and brings the wicked to ruin.

¹³If a man shuts his ears to the cry of
   the poor,
   he too will cry out and not be
   answered.

¹⁴A gift given in secret soothes anger,
   and a bribe concealed in the cloak
   pacifies great wrath.

¹⁵When justice is done, it brings joy to
   the righteous
   but terror to evildoers.

¹⁶A man who strays from the path of
   understanding
   comes to rest in the company of the
   dead.

¹⁷He who loves pleasure will become
   poor;
   whoever loves wine and oil will
   never be rich.

a27 Or *The spirit of man is the* LORD's *lamp*   *b6* Some Hebrew manuscripts, Septuagint and Vulgate;
most Hebrew manuscripts *vapor for those who seek death*   *c12* Or *The righteous man*

18The wicked become a ransom for the righteous,
and the unfaithful for the upright.

19Better to live in a desert
than with a quarrelsome and ill-tempered wife.

20In the house of the wise are stores of choice food and oil,

but a foolish man devours all he has.

21He who pursues righteousness and love
finds life, prosperity*a* and honor.

22A wise man attacks the city of the mighty
and pulls down the stronghold in which they trust.

a21 Or righteousness

TUESDAY

VERSE FOR THE DAY:
Proverbs 21:5

AUTHOR:
Ron Blue

PASSAGE FOR THE DAY:
Proverbs 21:5–6

Trust Her Intuition

NO ONE has ever come to the office or sent a proposal and said, "Let me show you a bad deal." On the front end, every business and investment deal is a good one. It only went bad later! What makes investment and business debts so difficult to evaluate and reject are that they are all presented as good deals, and a person would be foolish to turn them down. Therefore, there never seems to be economic justification alone for turning them down.

This is one of the reasons why I feel it is so important to apply the rule that a husband and wife have perfect unity on their debt decisions. God has granted to women a special sense, which some have called intuition, that cannot be explained, but in many cases, it has kept a husband from making a poor decision . . .

I give two general rules in this area. First of all, if you cannot explain the deal or investment to your wife in such a way that she totally understands it, don't do it. Second, even if you can explain it so that she totally understands it, but she feels uneasy or unsure in any way about it, don't do it. Granted, you may pass up many opportunities. However, one of the surest ways to financial success is to avoid the major mistakes, because not only do you have to make up for the lost investment, but also you lose the earnings that this money could have generated, and the earnings that the earnings could have generated, and the earnings that the earnings that the earnings could have generated, and so on. Again, the Biblical counsel is sound: "He who gathers money little by little makes it grow" (Proverbs 13:11). Or . . . "Get rich slow."

Additional Scripture Readings:
Psalm 37:1–9; Proverbs 13:11

Go to page 676 for your next devotional reading.

23He who guards his mouth and his
  tongue
  keeps himself from calamity.

24The proud and arrogant man—
  "Mocker" is his name;
  he behaves with overweening pride.

25The sluggard's craving will be the
  death of him,
  because his hands refuse to work.
26All day long he craves for more,
  but the righteous give without
  sparing.

27The sacrifice of the wicked is
  detestable—
  how much more so when brought
  with evil intent!

28A false witness will perish,
  and whoever listens to him will be
  destroyed forever.a

29A wicked man puts up a bold front,
  but an upright man gives thought to
  his ways.

30There is no wisdom, no insight, no
  plan
  that can succeed against the LORD.

31The horse is made ready for the day
  of battle,
  but victory rests with the LORD.

22 A good name is more desirable
  than great riches;
  to be esteemed is better than silver
  or gold.

2Rich and poor have this in common:
  The LORD is the Maker of them all.

3A prudent man sees danger and takes
  refuge,
  but the simple keep going and
  suffer for it.

4Humility and the fear of the LORD
  bring wealth and honor and life.

5In the paths of the wicked lie thorns
  and snares,
  but he who guards his soul stays far
  from them.

6Trainb a child in the way he should
  go,
  and when he is old he will not turn
  from it.

7The rich rule over the poor,
  and the borrower is servant to the
  lender.

8He who sows wickedness reaps
  trouble,
  and the rod of his fury will be
  destroyed.

9A generous man will himself be
  blessed,
  for he shares his food with the
  poor.

10Drive out the mocker, and out goes
  strife;
  quarrels and insults are ended.

11He who loves a pure heart and whose
  speech is gracious
  will have the king for his friend.

12The eyes of the LORD keep watch over
  knowledge,
  but he frustrates the words of the
  unfaithful.

13The sluggard says, "There is a lion
  outside!"
  or, "I will be murdered in the
  streets!"

14The mouth of an adulteress is a deep
  pit;
  he who is under the LORD's wrath
  will fall into it.

15Folly is bound up in the heart of a
  child,
  but the rod of discipline will drive it
  far from him.

16He who oppresses the poor to increase
  his wealth
  and he who gives gifts to the rich—
  both come to poverty.

Sayings of the Wise

17Pay attention and listen to the sayings
  of the wise;
  apply your heart to what I teach,
18for it is pleasing when you keep them
  in your heart
  and have all of them ready on your
  lips.
19So that your trust may be in the LORD,
  I teach you today, even you.
20Have I not written thirtyc sayings for
  you,
  sayings of counsel and knowledge,
21teaching you true and reliable words,

---

a28 Or / but the words of an obedient man will live on   b6 Or Start   c20 Or not formerly written; or
not written excellent

so that you can give sound answers
to him who sent you?

²²Do not exploit the poor because they
    are poor
and do not crush the needy in
    court,
²³for the LORD will take up their case
and will plunder those who plunder
    them.

²⁴Do not make friends with a
    hot-tempered man,
do not associate with one easily
    angered,
²⁵or you may learn his ways
and get yourself ensnared.

²⁶Do not be a man who strikes hands in
    pledge
or puts up security for debts;

WEDNESDAY

VERSE FOR THE DAY:
Proverbs 22:6

AUTHOR:
Charles Swindoll

PASSAGE FOR THE DAY:
Proverbs 22:4–6

Understanding the Bents

PROVERBS 22:6 is key in understanding the process of knowing and raising your child:
    "Train a child in the way he should go, and when he is old
he will not turn from it."
    The verse doesn't mean "train up a child as you see him."
Rather, "if you want your training to be meaningful and wise,
be observant and discover your child's way, and adapt your
training accordingly." Strengthening this idea is the word *way.*
This Hebrew term literally means "road" or "path." Metaphori-
cally, it is "a characteristic." Therefore, the thought is, "according to his characteristic, his manner." In Proverbs 22:6, the
word *way* is used in the same sense: "Train up a child in keeping with his characteristics." And his characteristics are distinct and set. There is a bent already established within every
child God places in our care. Each is not, in fact, a pliable
lump of clay but has been bent, prescribed according to a pre-
determined pattern. For example, perhaps you have several
children in your home. If not, perhaps you were from a home
of several children. One may be creative; another, practical.
One may be intelligent; another, just average. One may be out-
going; another, withdrawn. Whatever the case, they're all individuals. They weren't created on the assembly line. They were
handcrafted, individually, by God . . .
    Invariably, parents make two common mistakes. First, they
use the same approach with all their children. Secondly, they
compare them with other children. Both mistakes stem from
not knowing them, from failing to see their individual bents.
Consequently, the crucial concern for us as parents is to understand what the bents are in each of our children.

Additional Scripture Readings:
Psalm 139:1–16;
1 Corinthians 12:14–26

Go to page 679 for your next
devotional reading.

²⁷if you lack the means to pay,
  your very bed will be snatched from
    under you.

²⁸Do not move an ancient boundary
    stone
  set up by your forefathers.

²⁹Do you see a man skilled in his work?
  He will serve before kings;
  he will not serve before obscure
    men.

23 When you sit to dine with a
  ruler,
  note well what ᵃ is before you,
²and put a knife to your throat
  if you are given to gluttony.
³Do not crave his delicacies,
  for that food is deceptive.

⁴Do not wear yourself out to get rich;
  have the wisdom to show restraint.
⁵Cast but a glance at riches, and they
    are gone,
  for they will surely sprout wings
  and fly off to the sky like an eagle.

⁶Do not eat the food of a stingy man,
  do not crave his delicacies;
⁷for he is the kind of man
  who is always thinking about the
    cost.ᵇ
"Eat and drink," he says to you,
  but his heart is not with you.
⁸You will vomit up the little you have
    eaten
  and will have wasted your
    compliments.

⁹Do not speak to a fool,
  for he will scorn the wisdom of
    your words.

¹⁰Do not move an ancient boundary
    stone
  or encroach on the fields of the
    fatherless,
¹¹for their Defender is strong;
  he will take up their case against
    you.

¹²Apply your heart to instruction
  and your ears to words of
    knowledge.

¹³Do not withhold discipline from a
    child;
  if you punish him with the rod, he
    will not die.
¹⁴Punish him with the rod

and save his soul from death.ᶜ

¹⁵My son, if your heart is wise,
  then my heart will be glad;
¹⁶my inmost being will rejoice
  when your lips speak what is right.

¹⁷Do not let your heart envy sinners,
  but always be zealous for the fear
    of the LORD.
¹⁸There is surely a future hope for you,
  and your hope will not be cut off.

¹⁹Listen, my son, and be wise,
  and keep your heart on the right
    path.
²⁰Do not join those who drink too much
    wine
  or gorge themselves on meat,
²¹for drunkards and gluttons become
    poor,
  and drowsiness clothes them in
    rags.

²²Listen to your father, who gave you
    life,
  and do not despise your mother
    when she is old.
²³Buy the truth and do not sell it;
  get wisdom, discipline and
    understanding.
²⁴The father of a righteous man has
    great joy;
  he who has a wise son delights in
    him.
²⁵May your father and mother be glad;
  may she who gave you birth
    rejoice!

²⁶My son, give me your heart
  and let your eyes keep to my ways,
²⁷for a prostitute is a deep pit
  and a wayward wife is a narrow
    well.
²⁸Like a bandit she lies in wait,
  and multiplies the unfaithful among
    men.

²⁹Who has woe? Who has sorrow?
  Who has strife? Who has
    complaints?
  Who has needless bruises? Who has
    bloodshot eyes?
³⁰Those who linger over wine,
  who go to sample bowls of mixed
    wine.
³¹Do not gaze at wine when it is red,
  when it sparkles in the cup,
  when it goes down smoothly!
³²In the end it bites like a snake

ᵃ1 Or who   ᵇ7 Or for as he thinks within himself, / so he is; or for as he puts on a feast, / so he is
ᶜ14 Hebrew Sheol

and poisons like a viper.
33Your eyes will see strange sights
    and your mind imagine confusing
        things.
34You will be like one sleeping on the
        high seas,
    lying on top of the rigging.
35"They hit me," you will say, "but I'm
        not hurt!
    They beat me, but I don't feel it!
    When will I wake up
        so I can find another drink?"

24 Do not envy wicked men,
    do not desire their company;
2for their hearts plot violence,
    and their lips talk about making
        trouble.

3By wisdom a house is built,
    and through understanding it is
        established;
4through knowledge its rooms are filled
    with rare and beautiful treasures.

5A wise man has great power,
    and a man of knowledge increases
        strength;
6for waging war you need guidance,
    and for victory many advisers.

7Wisdom is too high for a fool;
    in the assembly at the gate he has
        nothing to say.

8He who plots evil
    will be known as a schemer.
9The schemes of folly are sin,
    and men detest a mocker.

10If you falter in times of trouble,
    how small is your strength!

11Rescue those being led away to death;
    hold back those staggering toward
        slaughter.
12If you say, "But we knew nothing
        about this,"
    does not he who weighs the heart
        perceive it?
    Does not he who guards your life
        know it?
    Will he not repay each person
        according to what he has done?

13Eat honey, my son, for it is good;
    honey from the comb is sweet to
        your taste.
14Know also that wisdom is sweet to
        your soul;
    if you find it, there is a future hope
        for you,
    and your hope will not be cut off.

15Do not lie in wait like an outlaw
        against a righteous man's
        house,
    do not raid his dwelling place;
16for though a righteous man falls seven
        times, he rises again,
    but the wicked are brought down
        by calamity.

17Do not gloat when your enemy falls;
    when he stumbles, do not let your
        heart rejoice,
18or the Lord will see and disapprove
    and turn his wrath away from him.

19Do not fret because of evil men
    or be envious of the wicked,
20for the evil man has no future hope,
    and the lamp of the wicked will be
        snuffed out.

21Fear the Lord and the king, my son,
    and do not join with the rebellious,
22for those two will send sudden
        destruction upon them,
    and who knows what calamities
        they can bring?

Further Sayings of the Wise

23These also are sayings of the wise:

To show partiality in judging is not
        good:
24Whoever says to the guilty, "You are
        innocent"—
    peoples will curse him and nations
        denounce him.
25But it will go well with those who
        convict the guilty,
    and rich blessing will come upon
        them.

26An honest answer
    is like a kiss on the lips.

27Finish your outdoor work
    and get your fields ready;
    after that, build your house.

28Do not testify against your neighbor
        without cause,
    or use your lips to deceive.
29Do not say, "I'll do to him as he has
        done to me;
    I'll pay that man back for what he
        did."

30I went past the field of the sluggard,
    past the vineyard of the man who
        lacks judgment;
31thorns had come up everywhere,
    the ground was covered with weeds,
    and the stone wall was in ruins.

³²I applied my heart to what I observed
and learned a lesson from what I
saw:
³³A little sleep, a little slumber,
a little folding of the hands to
rest —
³⁴and poverty will come on you like a
bandit
and scarcity like an armed man.ᵃ

More Proverbs of Solomon

25 These are more proverbs of Solomon, copied by the men of Hezekiah king of Judah:

²It is the glory of God to conceal a
matter;
to search out a matter is the glory
of kings.

³As the heavens are high and the earth
is deep,
so the hearts of kings are
unsearchable.

⁴Remove the dross from the silver,
and out comes material forᵇ the
silversmith;
⁵remove the wicked from the king's
presence,

ᵃ34 Or *like a vagrant / and scarcity like a beggar*   ᵇ4 Or *comes a vessel from*

THURSDAY

VERSE FOR THE DAY:
Proverbs 24:33

AUTHOR:
Gary Smalley and John Trent

PASSAGE FOR THE DAY:
Proverbs 24:33–34

The Gift of Honor

WE [SOUND] the call for parents to join the battle against a major destroyer of children—their feeling valueless and insignificant. We can't stress enough how important each day is in waging this war. If we sit back, fold our hands, and neglect building self-worth in our children, one day King Solomon's words may come true in their lives or our own. When this wise king wrote about the sluggard, he made this comment:

"A little sleep, a little slumber, a little folding of the hands to rest—and poverty will come on you like a bandit and scarcity like an armed man."

If we act like tourists or sluggards when it comes to building value into our children, heartache may enter our homes as stealthily as a prowler, or discouragement may burst upon us as forcefully as an armed man.

No matter how old your children are, it's never too late to unfold your hands and start honoring them. When you consistently apply this concept, you save them the heartache of damaged relationships, and you also give them the foundation they will need to truly value God, themselves and others.

Parents, do your children (and yourself) a great favor. Give them a gift that can strengthen them their entire lives—a gift that can continue to build up and bless your children and even your grandchildren—*the gift of honor.*

Additional Scripture Readings:
Proverbs 4:1–27; Mark 10:13–16

*Go to page 686 for your next
devotional reading.*

and his throne will be established
through righteousness.

⁶Do not exalt yourself in the king's
presence,
and do not claim a place among
great men;
⁷it is better for him to say to you,
"Come up here,"
than for him to humiliate you
before a nobleman.

What you have seen with your eyes
⁸   do not bringᵃ hastily to court,
for what will you do in the end
if your neighbor puts you to shame?

⁹If you argue your case with a
neighbor,
do not betray another man's
confidence,
¹⁰or he who hears it may shame you
and you will never lose your bad
reputation.

¹¹A word aptly spoken
is like apples of gold in settings of
silver.

¹²Like an earring of gold or an
ornament of fine gold
is a wise man's rebuke to a listening
ear.

¹³Like the coolness of snow at harvest
time
is a trustworthy messenger to those
who send him;
he refreshes the spirit of his
masters.

¹⁴Like clouds and wind without rain
is a man who boasts of gifts he
does not give.

¹⁵Through patience a ruler can be
persuaded,
and a gentle tongue can break a
bone.

¹⁶If you find honey, eat just enough—
too much of it, and you will vomit.
¹⁷Seldom set foot in your neighbor's
house—
too much of you, and he will hate
you.

¹⁸Like a club or a sword or a sharp
arrow
is the man who gives false
testimony against his neighbor.

¹⁹Like a bad tooth or a lame foot

is reliance on the unfaithful in times
of trouble.

²⁰Like one who takes away a garment
on a cold day,
or like vinegar poured on soda,
is one who sings songs to a heavy
heart.

²¹If your enemy is hungry, give him
food to eat;
if he is thirsty, give him water to
drink.
²²In doing this, you will heap burning
coals on his head,
and the LORD will reward you.

²³As a north wind brings rain,
so a sly tongue brings angry looks.

²⁴Better to live on a corner of the roof
than share a house with a
quarrelsome wife.

²⁵Like cold water to a weary soul
is good news from a distant land.

²⁶Like a muddied spring or a polluted
well
is a righteous man who gives way
to the wicked.

²⁷It is not good to eat too much honey,
nor is it honorable to seek one's
own honor.

²⁸Like a city whose walls are broken
down
is a man who lacks self-control.

26 Like snow in summer or rain in
harvest,
honor is not fitting for a fool.

²Like a fluttering sparrow or a darting
swallow,
an undeserved curse does not come
to rest.

³A whip for the horse, a halter for the
donkey,
and a rod for the backs of fools!

⁴Do not answer a fool according to his
folly,
or you will be like him yourself.

⁵Answer a fool according to his folly,
or he will be wise in his own eyes.

⁶Like cutting off one's feet or drinking
violence
is the sending of a message by the
hand of a fool.

ᵃ7,8 Or *nobleman / on whom you had set your eyes. / ⁸Do not go*

7Like a lame man's legs that hang limp
  is a proverb in the mouth of a fool.

8Like tying a stone in a sling
  is the giving of honor to a fool.

9Like a thornbush in a drunkard's hand
  is a proverb in the mouth of a fool.

10Like an archer who wounds at random
  is he who hires a fool or any
    passer-by.

11As a dog returns to its vomit,
  so a fool repeats his folly.

12Do you see a man wise in his own
    eyes?
  There is more hope for a fool than
    for him.

13The sluggard says, "There is a lion in
    the road,
  a fierce lion roaming the streets!"

14As a door turns on its hinges,
  so a sluggard turns on his bed.

15The sluggard buries his hand in the
    dish;
  he is too lazy to bring it back to his
    mouth.

16The sluggard is wiser in his own eyes
  than seven men who answer
    discreetly.

17Like one who seizes a dog by the ears
  is a passer-by who meddles in a
    quarrel not his own.

18Like a madman shooting
  firebrands or deadly arrows
19is a man who deceives his neighbor
  and says, "I was only joking!"

20Without wood a fire goes out;
  without gossip a quarrel dies down.

21As charcoal to embers and as wood to
    fire,
  so is a quarrelsome man for
    kindling strife.

22The words of a gossip are like choice
    morsels;
  they go down to a man's inmost
    parts.

23Like a coating of glaze*a* over
    earthenware
  are fervent lips with an evil heart.

24A malicious man disguises himself
    with his lips,
  but in his heart he harbors deceit.

25Though his speech is charming, do
    not believe him,
  for seven abominations fill his
    heart.
26His malice may be concealed by
    deception,
  but his wickedness will be exposed
    in the assembly.

27If a man digs a pit, he will fall into it;
  if a man rolls a stone, it will roll
    back on him.

28A lying tongue hates those it hurts,
  and a flattering mouth works ruin.

27 Do not boast about tomorrow,
  for you do not know what a day
    may bring forth.

2Let another praise you, and not your
    own mouth;
  someone else, and not your own
    lips.

3Stone is heavy and sand a burden,
  but provocation by a fool is heavier
    than both.

4Anger is cruel and fury overwhelming,
  but who can stand before jealousy?

5Better is open rebuke
  than hidden love.

6Wounds from a friend can be trusted,
  but an enemy multiplies kisses.

7He who is full loathes honey,
  but to the hungry even what is
    bitter tastes sweet.

8Like a bird that strays from its nest
  is a man who strays from his home.

9Perfume and incense bring joy to the
    heart,
  and the pleasantness of one's friend
    springs from his earnest
    counsel.

10Do not forsake your friend and the
    friend of your father,
  and do not go to your brother's
    house when disaster strikes
    you—
  better a neighbor nearby than a
    brother far away.

11Be wise, my son, and bring joy to my
    heart;
  then I can answer anyone who
    treats me with contempt.

---

a23 With a different word division of the Hebrew; Masoretic Text *of silver dross*

¹²The prudent see danger and take
refuge,
but the simple keep going and
suffer for it.

¹³Take the garment of one who puts up
security for a stranger;
hold it in pledge if he does it for a
wayward woman.

¹⁴If a man loudly blesses his neighbor
early in the morning,
it will be taken as a curse.

¹⁵A quarrelsome wife is like
a constant dripping on a rainy day;
¹⁶restraining her is like restraining the
wind
or grasping oil with the hand.

¹⁷As iron sharpens iron,
so one man sharpens another.

¹⁸He who tends a fig tree will eat its
fruit,
and he who looks after his master
will be honored.

¹⁹As water reflects a face,
so a man's heart reflects the man.

²⁰Death and Destruction[a] are never
satisfied,
and neither are the eyes of man.

²¹The crucible for silver and the furnace
for gold,
but man is tested by the praise he
receives.

²²Though you grind a fool in a mortar,
grinding him like grain with a
pestle,
you will not remove his folly from
him.

²³Be sure you know the condition of
your flocks,
give careful attention to your herds;
²⁴for riches do not endure forever,
and a crown is not secure for all
generations.
²⁵When the hay is removed and new
growth appears
and the grass from the hills is
gathered in,
²⁶the lambs will provide you with
clothing,
and the goats with the price of a
field.
²⁷You will have plenty of goats' milk
to feed you and your family
and to nourish your servant girls.

28 The wicked man flees though no
one pursues,
but the righteous are as bold as a
lion.

²When a country is rebellious, it has
many rulers,
but a man of understanding and
knowledge maintains order.

³A ruler[b] who oppresses the poor
is like a driving rain that leaves no
crops.

⁴Those who forsake the law praise the
wicked,
but those who keep the law resist
them.

⁵Evil men do not understand justice,
but those who seek the LORD
understand it fully.

⁶Better a poor man whose walk is
blameless
than a rich man whose ways are
perverse.

⁷He who keeps the law is a discerning
son,
but a companion of gluttons
disgraces his father.

⁸He who increases his wealth by
exorbitant interest
amasses it for another, who will be
kind to the poor.

⁹If anyone turns a deaf ear to the law,
even his prayers are detestable.

¹⁰He who leads the upright along an
evil path
will fall into his own trap,
but the blameless will receive a
good inheritance.

¹¹A rich man may be wise in his own
eyes,
but a poor man who has
discernment sees through him.

¹²When the righteous triumph, there is
great elation;
but when the wicked rise to power,
men go into hiding.

¹³He who conceals his sins does not
prosper,
but whoever confesses and
renounces them finds mercy.

¹⁴Blessed is the man who always fears
the LORD,

---

a20 Hebrew *Sheol and Abaddon*   *b3* Or *A poor man*

but he who hardens his heart falls
into trouble.

¹⁵Like a roaring lion or a charging bear
is a wicked man ruling over a
helpless people.

¹⁶A tyrannical ruler lacks judgment,
but he who hates ill-gotten gain will
enjoy a long life.

¹⁷A man tormented by the guilt of
murder
will be a fugitive till death;
let no one support him.

¹⁸He whose walk is blameless is kept
safe,
but he whose ways are perverse will
suddenly fall.

¹⁹He who works his land will have
abundant food,
but the one who chases fantasies
will have his fill of poverty.

²⁰A faithful man will be richly blessed,
but one eager to get rich will not go
unpunished.

²¹To show partiality is not good—
yet a man will do wrong for a piece
of bread.

²²A stingy man is eager to get rich
and is unaware that poverty awaits
him.

²³He who rebukes a man will in the end
gain more favor
than he who has a flattering tongue.

²⁴He who robs his father or mother
and says, "It's not wrong"—
he is partner to him who destroys.

²⁵A greedy man stirs up dissension,
but he who trusts in the LORD will
prosper.

²⁶He who trusts in himself is a fool,
but he who walks in wisdom is kept
safe.

²⁷He who gives to the poor will lack
nothing,
but he who closes his eyes to them
receives many curses.

²⁸When the wicked rise to power,
people go into hiding;
but when the wicked perish, the
righteous thrive.

29 A man who remains stiff-necked
after many rebukes

will suddenly be destroyed—
without remedy.

²When the righteous thrive, the people
rejoice;
when the wicked rule, the people
groan.

³A man who loves wisdom brings joy
to his father,
but a companion of prostitutes
squanders his wealth.

⁴By justice a king gives a country
stability,
but one who is greedy for bribes
tears it down.

⁵Whoever flatters his neighbor
is spreading a net for his feet.

⁶An evil man is snared by his own sin,
but a righteous one can sing and be
glad.

⁷The righteous care about justice for
the poor,
but the wicked have no such
concern.

⁸Mockers stir up a city,
but wise men turn away anger.

⁹If a wise man goes to court with a
fool,
the fool rages and scoffs, and there
is no peace.

¹⁰Bloodthirsty men hate a man of
integrity
and seek to kill the upright.

¹¹A fool gives full vent to his anger,
but a wise man keeps himself under
control.

¹²If a ruler listens to lies,
all his officials become wicked.

¹³The poor man and the oppressor have
this in common:
The LORD gives sight to the eyes of
both.

¹⁴If a king judges the poor with fairness,
his throne will always be secure.

¹⁵The rod of correction imparts wisdom,
but a child left to himself disgraces
his mother.

¹⁶When the wicked thrive, so does sin,
but the righteous will see their
downfall.

¹⁷Discipline your son, and he will give
you peace;
he will bring delight to your soul.

¹⁸Where there is no revelation, the
    people cast off restraint;
but blessed is he who keeps the
    law.

¹⁹A servant cannot be corrected by mere
    words;
though he understands, he will not
    respond.

²⁰Do you see a man who speaks in
    haste?
There is more hope for a fool than
    for him.

²¹If a man pampers his servant from
    youth,
he will bring grief*ᵃ* in the end.

²²An angry man stirs up dissension,
    and a hot-tempered one commits
    many sins.

²³A man's pride brings him low,
    but a man of lowly spirit gains
    honor.

²⁴The accomplice of a thief is his own
    enemy;
he is put under oath and dare not
    testify.

²⁵Fear of man will prove to be a snare,
    but whoever trusts in the LORD is
    kept safe.

²⁶Many seek an audience with a ruler,
    but it is from the LORD that man
    gets justice.

²⁷The righteous detest the dishonest;
    the wicked detest the upright.

Sayings of Agur

30 The sayings of Agur son of Jakeh—
    an oracle*ᵇ*:

This man declared to Ithiel,
    to Ithiel and to Ucal:*ᶜ*

²"I am the most ignorant of men;
    I do not have a man's
    understanding.
³I have not learned wisdom,
    nor have I knowledge of the Holy
    One.
⁴Who has gone up to heaven and come
    down?
    Who has gathered up the wind in
    the hollow of his hands?

Who has wrapped up the waters in
    his cloak?
    Who has established all the ends of
    the earth?
What is his name, and the name of
    his son?
    Tell me if you know!

⁵"Every word of God is flawless;
    he is a shield to those who take
    refuge in him.
⁶Do not add to his words,
    or he will rebuke you and prove
    you a liar.

⁷"Two things I ask of you, O LORD;
    do not refuse me before I die:
⁸Keep falsehood and lies far from me;
    give me neither poverty nor riches,
    but give me only my daily bread.
⁹Otherwise, I may have too much and
    disown you
    and say, 'Who is the LORD?'
Or I may become poor and steal,
    and so dishonor the name of my
    God.

¹⁰"Do not slander a servant to his
    master,
    or he will curse you, and you will
    pay for it.

¹¹"There are those who curse their
    fathers
    and do not bless their mothers;
¹²those who are pure in their own eyes
    and yet are not cleansed of their
    filth;
¹³those whose eyes are ever so haughty,
    whose glances are so disdainful;
¹⁴those whose teeth are swords
    and whose jaws are set with knives
to devour the poor from the earth,
    the needy from among mankind.

¹⁵"The leech has two daughters.
    'Give! Give!' they cry.

"There are three things that are never
    satisfied,
    four that never say, 'Enough!':
¹⁶the grave,*ᵈ* the barren womb,
    land, which is never satisfied with
    water,
    and fire, which never says,
    'Enough!'

¹⁷"The eye that mocks a father,
    that scorns obedience to a mother,

will be pecked out by the ravens of
the valley,
will be eaten by the vultures.

18"There are three things that are too
amazing for me,
four that I do not understand:
19the way of an eagle in the sky,
the way of a snake on a rock,
the way of a ship on the high seas,
and the way of a man with a
maiden.

20"This is the way of an adulteress:
She eats and wipes her mouth
and says, 'I've done nothing wrong.'

21"Under three things the earth
trembles,
under four it cannot bear up:
22a servant who becomes king,
a fool who is full of food,
23an unloved woman who is married,
and a maidservant who displaces
her mistress.

24"Four things on earth are small,
yet they are extremely wise:
25Ants are creatures of little strength,
yet they store up their food in the
summer;
26coneys*a* are creatures of little power,
yet they make their home in the
crags;
27locusts have no king,
yet they advance together in ranks;
28a lizard can be caught with the hand,
yet it is found in kings' palaces.

29"There are three things that are stately
in their stride,
four that move with stately bearing:
30a lion, mighty among beasts,
who retreats before nothing;
31a strutting rooster, a he-goat,
and a king with his army around
him.*b*

32"If you have played the fool and
exalted yourself,
or if you have planned evil,
clap your hand over your mouth!
33For as churning the milk produces
butter,
and as twisting the nose produces
blood,
so stirring up anger produces strife."

Sayings of King Lemuel

31 The sayings of King Lemuel—an
oracle*c* his mother taught him:

2"O my son, O son of my womb,
O son of my vows,*d*
3do not spend your strength on
women,
your vigor on those who ruin kings.

4"It is not for kings, O Lemuel—
not for kings to drink wine,
not for rulers to crave beer,
5lest they drink and forget what the
law decrees,
and deprive all the oppressed of
their rights.
6Give beer to those who are perishing,
wine to those who are in anguish;
7let them drink and forget their poverty
and remember their misery no
more.

8"Speak up for those who cannot speak
for themselves,
for the rights of all who are
destitute.
9Speak up and judge fairly;
defend the rights of the poor and
needy."

Epilogue: The Wife of Noble Character

10*e*A wife of noble character who can
find?
She is worth far more than rubies.
11Her husband has full confidence in
her
and lacks nothing of value.
12She brings him good, not harm,
all the days of her life.
13She selects wool and flax
and works with eager hands.
14She is like the merchant ships,
bringing her food from afar.
15She gets up while it is still dark;
she provides food for her family
and portions for her servant girls.
16She considers a field and buys it;
out of her earnings she plants a
vineyard.
17She sets about her work vigorously;
her arms are strong for her tasks.
18She sees that her trading is profitable,
and her lamp does not go out at
night.

---

a26 That is, the hyrax or rock badger   *b31* Or *king secure against revolt*   *c1* Or *of Lemuel king of Massa, which*   *d2* Or / *the answer to my prayers*   *e10* Verses 10-31 are an acrostic, each verse beginning with a successive letter of the Hebrew alphabet.

19In her hand she holds the distaff
and grasps the spindle with her
fingers.
20She opens her arms to the poor
and extends her hands to the needy.
21When it snows, she has no fear for
her household;
for all of them are clothed in
scarlet.
22She makes coverings for her bed;
she is clothed in fine linen and
purple.
23Her husband is respected at the city
gate,
where he takes his seat among the
elders of the land.
24She makes linen garments and sells
them,

and supplies the merchants with
sashes.
25She is clothed with strength and
dignity;
she can laugh at the days to come.
26She speaks with wisdom,
and faithful instruction is on her
tongue.
27She watches over the affairs of her
household
and does not eat the bread of
idleness.
28Her children arise and call her
blessed;
her husband also, and he praises
her:
29"Many women do noble things,
but you surpass them all."

FRIDAY

VERSE FOR THE DAY:
Proverbs 31:10

AUTHOR:
Joe Gibbs

PASSAGE FOR THE DAY:
Proverbs 31:10–31

Praising Your Wife

[MY WIFE] Pat is perfect for me and always has been. During
our long courtship after meeting in high school, we had our
ups and downs and our fights. But we always knew we would
wind up married, best friends, and partners for life. She has a
great sense of humor and gift of gab. We enjoy each other and
we enjoy life. I can't imagine life without her . . .

In the eyes of the world, she's in the background. Her work
is not as visible, and thus, to some people, not as important.
But my work would be nothing without a wife like her. What
most people don't realize is that something is as true in my
family as it is in almost any man's family: What our wives do
and have done is much more valuable in terms of eternity than
anything we could ever do. Ten years from now my name may
appear in the Redskin Hall of Fame because my teams have
won a lot of football games. That will be my legacy. By then I
will be a fan, going to games and cheering along with everyone
else. I have no illusions about that.

But Pat's accomplishments, unknown to most people, will
be honored for eternity. She's been father and mother to our
boys while I spent months leaving the house early and getting
home late, investing my time in a game.

Additional Scripture Readings:
Proverbs 12:4; 1 Peter 3:1–6

*Go to page 690 for your next
devotional reading.*

[30] Charm is deceptive, and beauty is
  fleeting;
but a woman who fears the LORD is
  to be praised.

[31] Give her the reward she has
  earned,
and let her works bring her
  praise at the city gate.

*T*HE Teacher, a king in Jerusalem, searches in this book for a purpose to his life. After various pursuits, frustrated by not finding satisfactory answers, he discovers that happiness is in the Lord and in obeying his word (Ecclesiastes 12:11–14). As you read this book, think about how life without God has no meaning but how life regulated by God and his word is wonderful indeed. Be sure to dedicate your life to the Lord when you are young (Ecclesiastes 12:1).

ECCLESIASTES

Everything Is Meaningless

1 The words of the Teacher,*a* son of David, king in Jerusalem:

2"Meaningless! Meaningless!"
  says the Teacher.
"Utterly meaningless!
  Everything is meaningless."

3What does man gain from all his labor
  at which he toils under the sun?
4Generations come and generations go,
  but the earth remains forever.
5The sun rises and the sun sets,
  and hurries back to where it rises.
6The wind blows to the south
  and turns to the north;
round and round it goes,
  ever returning on its course.
7All streams flow into the sea,
  yet the sea is never full.
To the place the streams come from,
  there they return again.
8All things are wearisome,
  more than one can say.
The eye never has enough of seeing,
  nor the ear its fill of hearing.
9What has been will be again,
  what has been done will be done
  again;

a1 Or leader of the assembly; also in verses 2 and 12

there is nothing new under the sun.
¹⁰Is there anything of which one can
  say,
  "Look! This is something new"?
It was here already, long ago;
  it was here before our time.
¹¹There is no remembrance of men of
  old,
  and even those who are yet to come
will not be remembered
  by those who follow.

Wisdom Is Meaningless

¹²I, the Teacher, was king over Israel in
Jerusalem. ¹³I devoted myself to study
and to explore by wisdom all that is done
under heaven. What a heavy burden God
has laid on men! ¹⁴I have seen all the
things that are done under the sun; all of
them are meaningless, a chasing after the
wind.

¹⁵What is twisted cannot be
  straightened;
  what is lacking cannot be counted.

¹⁶I thought to myself, "Look, I have
grown and increased in wisdom more
than anyone who has ruled over Jerusalem before me; I have experienced much
of wisdom and knowledge." ¹⁷Then I applied myself to the understanding of wisdom, and also of madness and folly, but I
learned that this, too, is a chasing after the
wind.

¹⁸For with much wisdom comes much
  sorrow;
  the more knowledge, the more grief.

Pleasures Are Meaningless

2 I thought in my heart, "Come now, I
will test you with pleasure to find out
what is good." But that also proved to be
meaningless. ²"Laughter," I said, "is foolish. And what does pleasure accomplish?"
³I tried cheering myself with wine, and
embracing folly—my mind still guiding
me with wisdom. I wanted to see what
was worthwhile for men to do under heav-
en during the few days of their lives.

⁴I undertook great projects: I built
houses for myself and planted vineyards.
⁵I made gardens and parks and planted all
kinds of fruit trees in them. ⁶I made reservoirs to water groves of flourishing trees.
⁷I bought male and female slaves and had
other slaves who were born in my house.
I also owned more herds and flocks

than anyone in Jerusalem before me. ⁸I
amassed silver and gold for myself, and
the treasure of kings and provinces. I acquired men and women singers, and a
harem*a* as well—the delights of the heart
of man. ⁹I became greater by far than anyone in Jerusalem before me. In all this my
wisdom stayed with me.

¹⁰I denied myself nothing my eyes
  desired;
  I refused my heart no pleasure.
My heart took delight in all my work,
  and this was the reward for all my
  labor.
¹¹Yet when I surveyed all that my hands
  had done
  and what I had toiled to achieve,
everything was meaningless, a chasing
  after the wind;
  nothing was gained under the sun.

Wisdom and Folly Are Meaningless

¹²Then I turned my thoughts to
  consider wisdom,
  and also madness and folly.
What more can the king's successor
  do
  than what has already been done?
¹³I saw that wisdom is better than folly,
  just as light is better than darkness.
¹⁴The wise man has eyes in his head,
  while the fool walks in the
  darkness;
but I came to realize
  that the same fate overtakes them
  both.

¹⁵Then I thought in my heart,

"The fate of the fool will overtake me
  also.
  What then do I gain by being wise?"
I said in my heart,
  "This too is meaningless."
¹⁶For the wise man, like the fool, will
  not be long remembered;
  in days to come both will be
  forgotten.
Like the fool, the wise man too must
  die!

Toil Is Meaningless

¹⁷So I hated life, because the work that
is done under the sun was grievous to me.
All of it is meaningless, a chasing after the
wind. ¹⁸I hated all the things I had toiled
for under the sun, because I must leave
them to the one who comes after me.

---

*a*8 The meaning of the Hebrew for this phrase is uncertain.

WEEKENDING

RESTORE

When life caves in, you do not need reasons, you need comfort. You do not need some answers; you need some*one*. And Jesus does not come to us with an explanation; he comes to us with his presence.

We are always seeking the reason. We want to know why. Like Job, we finally want God to tell us just what is going on . . . .

But God does not reveal his plan, he reveals himself. He comes to us as warmth when we are cold, fellowship when we are alone, strength when we are weak, peace when we are troubled, courage when we are afraid, songs when we are sad, and bread when we are hungry.

He is with us on our journeys. He is there when we are home. He sits with us at our table. He knows about funerals and weddings and commencements and hospitals and jails and unemployment and labor and laughter and rest and tears. He knows because he is with us. He comes to us again and again.

– *Bob Benson*

REVIVE

Saturday: Isaiah 43:1–7
Sunday: Luke 24:28–35

Go to page 692 for your next devotional reading.

¹⁹And who knows whether he will be a wise man or a fool? Yet he will have control over all the work into which I have poured my effort and skill under the sun. This too is meaningless. ²⁰So my heart began to despair over all my toilsome labor under the sun. ²¹For a man may do his work with wisdom, knowledge and skill, and then he must leave all he owns to someone who has not worked for it. This too is meaningless and a great misfortune. ²²What does a man get for all the toil and anxious striving with which he labors under the sun? ²³All his days his work is pain and grief; even at night his mind does not rest. This too is meaningless.

²⁴A man can do nothing better than to eat and drink and find satisfaction in his work. This too, I see, is from the hand of God, ²⁵for without him, who can eat or find enjoyment? ²⁶To the man who pleases him, God gives wisdom, knowledge and happiness, but to the sinner he gives the task of gathering and storing up wealth to hand it over to the one who pleases God. This too is meaningless, a chasing after the wind.

A Time for Everything

3 There is a time for everything,
  and a season for every activity
      under heaven:

² a time to be born and a time to die,
  a time to plant and a time to
      uproot,
³ a time to kill and a time to heal,
  a time to tear down and a time to
      build,
⁴ a time to weep and a time to laugh,
  a time to mourn and a time to
      dance,
⁵ a time to scatter stones and a time
      to gather them,
  a time to embrace and a time to
      refrain,
⁶ a time to search and a time to give
      up,
  a time to keep and a time to throw
      away,
⁷ a time to tear and a time to mend,
  a time to be silent and a time to
      speak,
⁸ a time to love and a time to hate,
  a time for war and a time for peace.

⁹What does the worker gain from his toil? ¹⁰I have seen the burden God has laid on men. ¹¹He has made everything beautiful in its time. He has also set eternity in the hearts of men; yet they cannot fathom what God has done from beginning to end. ¹²I know that there is nothing better for men than to be happy and do good while they live. ¹³That everyone may eat and drink, and find satisfaction in all his toil — this is the gift of God. ¹⁴I know that everything God does will endure forever; nothing can be added to it and nothing taken from it. God does it so that men will revere him.

¹⁵Whatever is has already been,
  and what will be has been before;
  and God will call the past to
      account.^a

¹⁶And I saw something else under the sun:

In the place of judgment — wickedness
      was there,
  in the place of justice — wickedness
      was there.

¹⁷I thought in my heart,

"God will bring to judgment
  both the righteous and the wicked,
for there will be a time for every
      activity,
  a time for every deed."

¹⁸I also thought, "As for men, God tests them so that they may see that they are like the animals. ¹⁹Man's fate is like that of the animals; the same fate awaits them both: As one dies, so dies the other. All have the same breath^b; man has no advantage over the animal. Everything is meaningless. ²⁰All go to the same place; all come from dust, and to dust all return. ²¹Who knows if the spirit of man rises upward and if the spirit of the animal^c goes down into the earth?"

²²So I saw that there is nothing better for a man than to enjoy his work, because that is his lot. For who can bring him to see what will happen after him?

Oppression, Toil, Friendlessness

4 Again I looked and saw all the oppression that was taking place under the sun:

I saw the tears of the oppressed —
  and they have no comforter;

---

^a15 Or *God calls back the past*   ^b19 Or *spirit*   ^c21 Or *Who knows the spirit of man, which rises upward, or the spirit of the animal, which*

power was on the side of their
    oppressors—
and they have no comforter.
²And I declared that the dead,
    who had already died,
are happier than the living,
    who are still alive.
³But better than both
    is he who has not yet been,

who has not seen the evil
    that is done under the sun.

⁴And I saw that all labor and all achievement spring from man's envy of his neighbor. This too is meaningless, a chasing after the wind.

⁵The fool folds his hands
    and ruins himself.

MONDAY

VERSE FOR THE DAY:
Ecclesiastes 2:23

AUTHOR:
Archibald Hart

PASSAGE FOR THE DAY:
Ecclesiastes 2:17–26

Rest for the Weary

TO AVOID cardiovascular disease and other stress-related disorders, it is not enough to eat the right food and keep cholesterol levels low. It is not enough to exercise regularly and even to take regular vacations. To protect ourselves against dying of or suffering ill effects from stress, we must learn how to switch off our production of adrenalin when it is no longer needed. We've got to become less dependent on the energy hormone for everyday living.

Since anger, frustration, irritation, challenge and excitement are all adrenalin triggers, these psychological triggers must be brought under control. Effective stress management requires that we be healthy in mind and spirit, not just in our bodies. This is what I mean by "adrenalin management." It means controlling the problem at its source.

If you love excitement and enjoy the thrill of challenge, you will have to work a little harder at controlling your adrenalin —because you have a greater tendency to produce too much of it. You may have to work at learning to enjoy life without constant novel stimulation. You will have to train yourself to come down frequently from the "mountaintop" and enjoy the peace of the valley, where recuperation and healing can take place.

The accelerated pace of modern living tends to rob us of natural recovery time, so that must be planned into our lives by deliberate design. Even Jesus was aware of this need for recovery. In Mark 6:31, he told his disciples, "Come with me by yourselves to a quiet place and get some rest."

If Jesus thought it necessary for him and his disciples to rest from time to time, who are we to think we can get by without it?

Additional Scripture Readings:
Matthew 11:28–30; Mark 6:30–34

*Go to page 693 for your next
devotional reading.*

6Better one handful with tranquillity
than two handfuls with toil
and chasing after the wind.

7Again I saw something meaningless under the sun:

8There was a man all alone;
he had neither son nor brother.
There was no end to his toil,
yet his eyes were not content with
his wealth.
"For whom am I toiling," he asked,
"and why am I depriving myself of
enjoyment?"
This too is meaningless—
a miserable business!

9Two are better than one,
because they have a good return for
their work:
10If one falls down,
his friend can help him up.
But pity the man who falls
and has no one to help him up!
11Also, if two lie down together, they
will keep warm.
But how can one keep warm alone?
12Though one may be overpowered,
two can defend themselves.
A cord of three strands is not quickly
broken.

Advancement Is Meaningless

13Better a poor but wise youth than an old but foolish king who no longer knows how to take warning. **14**The youth may

---

TUESDAY

VERSE FOR THE DAY:
Ecclesiastes 3:11

AUTHOR:
Patrick Morley

PASSAGE FOR THE DAY:
Ecclesiastes 3:9–22

A Man's Ultimate Desire

WHAT is the highest hope of a man who does not have Christ? Most men will never see their name in the newspaper. If you were a really great man—someone of national reputation—what would be the most you might expect from history? At the very best, if you were a giant in your time, the most you could expect would be a couple of paragraphs in the World Book Encyclopedia . . .

A man's ultimate desire is for immortality. "He has also set eternity in the hearts of men" (Ecclesiastes 3:11). That's part of what we mean when we say we want to be significant. We want "something" to survive us. In our search for immortality, how do we live on? Is it in our accomplishments, our legacy to our children, or a couple of paragraphs in an encyclopedia? Some wealthy men finance hospital wings and have university buildings named for them to achieve a measure of immortality.

How we decide to answer the questions, *"Who am I?"* and *"Why do I exist?"* is a choice between two time lines: One that's eighty years long and one that lasts forever.

If we do not ultimately find our significance in Christ, then we will not survive the threshold between this world and the next. Our highest hopes will come to a screeching halt. It would be better if we have never been born.

Additional Scripture Readings:
Jeremiah 9:23–24; Philippians 3:7–11

*Go to page 695 for your next
devotional reading.*

have come from prison to the kingship, or he may have been born in poverty within his kingdom. ¹⁵I saw that all who lived and walked under the sun followed the youth, the king's successor. ¹⁶There was no end to all the people who were before them. But those who came later were not pleased with the successor. This too is meaningless, a chasing after the wind.

Stand in Awe of God

5 Guard your steps when you go to the house of God. Go near to listen rather than to offer the sacrifice of fools, who do not know that they do wrong.

²Do not be quick with your mouth,
  do not be hasty in your heart
  to utter anything before God.
 God is in heaven
  and you are on earth,
  so let your words be few.
³As a dream comes when there are
  many cares,
  so the speech of a fool when there
  are many words.

⁴When you make a vow to God, do not delay in fulfilling it. He has no pleasure in fools; fulfill your vow. ⁵It is better not to vow than to make a vow and not fulfill it. ⁶Do not let your mouth lead you into sin. And do not protest to the ₁temple₁ messenger, "My vow was a mistake." Why should God be angry at what you say and destroy the work of your hands? ⁷Much dreaming and many words are meaningless. Therefore stand in awe of God.

Riches Are Meaningless

⁸If you see the poor oppressed in a district, and justice and rights denied, do not be surprised at such things; for one official is eyed by a higher one, and over them both are others higher still. ⁹The increase from the land is taken by all; the king himself profits from the fields.

¹⁰Whoever loves money never has
  money enough;
 whoever loves wealth is never
  satisfied with his income.
 This too is meaningless.

¹¹As goods increase,
  so do those who consume them.
 And what benefit are they to the
  owner
  except to feast his eyes on them?

¹²The sleep of a laborer is sweet,
  whether he eats little or much,

but the abundance of a rich man
  permits him no sleep.

¹³I have seen a grievous evil under the sun:

 wealth hoarded to the harm of its
  owner,
¹⁴ or wealth lost through some
  misfortune,
 so that when he has a son
  there is nothing left for him.
¹⁵Naked a man comes from his mother's
  womb,
  and as he comes, so he departs.
 He takes nothing from his labor
  that he can carry in his hand.

¹⁶This too is a grievous evil:

 As a man comes, so he departs,
  and what does he gain,
  since he toils for the wind?
¹⁷All his days he eats in darkness,
  with great frustration, affliction and
  anger.

¹⁸Then I realized that it is good and proper for a man to eat and drink, and to find satisfaction in his toilsome labor under the sun during the few days of life God has given him—for this is his lot. ¹⁹Moreover, when God gives any man wealth and possessions, and enables him to enjoy them, to accept his lot and be happy in his work—this is a gift of God. ²⁰He seldom reflects on the days of his life, because God keeps him occupied with gladness of heart.

6 I have seen another evil under the sun, and it weighs heavily on men: ²God gives a man wealth, possessions and honor, so that he lacks nothing his heart desires, but God does not enable him to enjoy them, and a stranger enjoys them instead. This is meaningless, a grievous evil.

³A man may have a hundred children and live many years; yet no matter how long he lives, if he cannot enjoy his prosperity and does not receive proper burial, I say that a stillborn child is better off than he. ⁴It comes without meaning, it departs in darkness, and in darkness its name is shrouded. ⁵Though it never saw the sun or knew anything, it has more rest than does that man— ⁶even if he lives a thousand years twice over but fails to enjoy his prosperity. Do not all go to the same place?

⁷All man's efforts are for his mouth,
  yet his appetite is never satisfied.

8What advantage has a wise man
over a fool?
What does a poor man gain
by knowing how to conduct himself
before others?
9Better what the eye sees
than the roving of the appetite.
This too is meaningless,
a chasing after the wind.

10Whatever exists has already been
named,
and what man is has been known;
no man can contend
with one who is stronger than he.

11The more the words,
the less the meaning,
and how does that profit anyone?

12For who knows what is good for a
man in life, during the few and meaningless days he passes through like a shadow? Who can tell him what will happen
under the sun after he is gone?

Wisdom

7 A good name is better than fine
perfume,
and the day of death better than the
day of birth.

WEDNESDAY

VERSE FOR THE DAY:
Ecclesiastes 5:1

AUTHOR:
W. Phillip Keller

PASSAGE FOR THE DAY:
Ecclesiastes 5:1–7

Rendezvous with the Beloved

SO MANY are "empty" within. A strange, painful gnawing vacuum persists in the depths of their person. This inner "aloneness" is ever present. Few know or realize it is a profound
yearning for God himself. In his wondrous design he intended
us for his own companionship. Nor are we ever complete until
we find our fulfillment in him as our constant companion.

Instead, most people recoil in fear from this inner aloneness.
They endeavor to fill this inner vacuum with fun, gaiety,
games, study, work, or other human activities of a thousand
sorts. In desperation they may even resort to sound, music,
drugs, alcohol or sexual adventures. All are an escape from
their selves-in-solitude. Still they are never free of fear.

Yet it is within this inner stillness that our Father can speak
to us most clearly. It is there alone with him that he becomes
real to our inner intuition of spirit. It is there we begin to "see"
him most acutely with the perception of our awakened conscience in response to his Word. There we sense and know his
Presence. He interacts with us in our deepening conviction
through his wondrous Word and by his gracious Spirit.

For the man or woman who comes to know and love God as
Father in such intimacy, the times of solitude are the most exquisite in all of life. They are *"a rendezvous with the Beloved."*
They are anticipated eagerly; awaited with acute expectancy;
relished with enthusiasm. In a word, these times are highlights
of life.

Additional Scripture Readings:
Psalm 42:1–5; Psalm 63:1–11

Go to page 702 for your next
devotional reading.

²It is better to go to a house of
mourning
than to go to a house of feasting,
for death is the destiny of every man;
the living should take this to heart.
³Sorrow is better than laughter,
because a sad face is good for the
heart.
⁴The heart of the wise is in the house
of mourning,
but the heart of fools is in the
house of pleasure.
⁵It is better to heed a wise man's
rebuke
than to listen to the song of fools.
⁶Like the crackling of thorns under the
pot,
so is the laughter of fools.
This too is meaningless.

⁷Extortion turns a wise man into a fool,
and a bribe corrupts the heart.

⁸The end of a matter is better than its
beginning,
and patience is better than pride.
⁹Do not be quickly provoked in your
spirit,
for anger resides in the lap of fools.

¹⁰Do not say, "Why were the old days
better than these?"
For it is not wise to ask such
questions.

¹¹Wisdom, like an inheritance, is a good
thing
and benefits those who see the sun.
¹²Wisdom is a shelter
as money is a shelter,
but the advantage of knowledge is
this:
that wisdom preserves the life of its
possessor.

¹³Consider what God has done:

Who can straighten
what he has made crooked?
¹⁴When times are good, be happy;
but when times are bad, consider:
God has made the one
as well as the other.
Therefore, a man cannot discover
anything about his future.

¹⁵In this meaningless life of mine I have
seen both of these:

a righteous man perishing in his
righteousness,

and a wicked man living long in his
wickedness.
¹⁶Do not be overrighteous,
neither be overwise—
why destroy yourself?
¹⁷Do not be overwicked,
and do not be a fool—
why die before your time?
¹⁸It is good to grasp the one
and not let go of the other.
The man who fears God will avoid
all ₍extremes₎.ᵃ

¹⁹Wisdom makes one wise man more
powerful
than ten rulers in a city.

²⁰There is not a righteous man on earth
who does what is right and never
sins.

²¹Do not pay attention to every word
people say,
or you may hear your servant
cursing you—
²²for you know in your heart
that many times you yourself have
cursed others.

²³All this I tested by wisdom and I said,

"I am determined to be wise"—
but this was beyond me.
²⁴Whatever wisdom may be,
it is far off and most profound—
who can discover it?
²⁵So I turned my mind to understand,
to investigate and to search out
wisdom and the scheme of
things
and to understand the stupidity of
wickedness
and the madness of folly.

²⁶I find more bitter than death
the woman who is a snare,
whose heart is a trap
and whose hands are chains.
The man who pleases God will escape
her,
but the sinner she will ensnare.

²⁷"Look," says the Teacher,ᵇ "this is
what I have discovered:

"Adding one thing to another to
discover the scheme of
things—
²⁸ while I was still searching
but not finding—
I found one ₍upright₎ man among a
thousand,

ᵃ18 Or will follow them both   ᵇ27 Or leader of the assembly

but not one ⌞upright⌟ woman among them all.
²⁹This only have I found:
God made mankind upright,
but men have gone in search of many schemes."

8 Who is like the wise man?
Who knows the explanation of things?
Wisdom brightens a man's face
and changes its hard appearance.

Obey the King

²Obey the king's command, I say, because you took an oath before God. ³Do not be in a hurry to leave the king's presence. Do not stand up for a bad cause, for he will do whatever he pleases. ⁴Since a king's word is supreme, who can say to him, "What are you doing?"

⁵Whoever obeys his command will come to no harm,
and the wise heart will know the proper time and procedure.
⁶For there is a proper time and procedure for every matter,
though a man's misery weighs heavily upon him.

⁷Since no man knows the future,
who can tell him what is to come?
⁸No man has power over the wind to contain it[a];
so no one has power over the day of his death.
As no one is discharged in time of war,
so wickedness will not release those who practice it.

⁹All this I saw, as I applied my mind to everything done under the sun. There is a time when a man lords it over others to his own[b] hurt. ¹⁰Then too, I saw the wicked buried—those who used to come and go from the holy place and receive praise[c] in the city where they did this. This too is meaningless.

¹¹When the sentence for a crime is not quickly carried out, the hearts of the people are filled with schemes to do wrong. ¹²Although a wicked man commits a hundred crimes and still lives a long time, I know that it will go better with God-fearing men, who are reverent before God. ¹³Yet because the wicked do not fear God,

it will not go well with them, and their days will not lengthen like a shadow.

¹⁴There is something else meaningless that occurs on earth: righteous men who get what the wicked deserve, and wicked men who get what the righteous deserve. This too, I say, is meaningless. ¹⁵So I commend the enjoyment of life, because nothing is better for a man under the sun than to eat and drink and be glad. Then joy will accompany him in his work all the days of the life God has given him under the sun.

¹⁶When I applied my mind to know wisdom and to observe man's labor on earth—his eyes not seeing sleep day or night— ¹⁷then I saw all that God has done. No one can comprehend what goes on under the sun. Despite all his efforts to search it out, man cannot discover its meaning. Even if a wise man claims he knows, he cannot really comprehend it.

A Common Destiny for All

9 So I reflected on all this and concluded that the righteous and the wise and what they do are in God's hands, but no man knows whether love or hate awaits him. ²All share a common destiny—the righteous and the wicked, the good and the bad,[d] the clean and the unclean, those who offer sacrifices and those who do not.

As it is with the good man,
so with the sinner;
as it is with those who take oaths,
so with those who are afraid to take them.

³This is the evil in everything that happens under the sun: The same destiny overtakes all. The hearts of men, moreover, are full of evil and there is madness in their hearts while they live, and afterward they join the dead. ⁴Anyone who is among the living has hope[e]—even a live dog is better off than a dead lion!

⁵For the living know that they will die,
but the dead know nothing;
they have no further reward,
and even the memory of them is forgotten.
⁶Their love, their hate
and their jealousy have long since vanished;
never again will they have a part

---

[a]8 Or *over his spirit to retain it*   [b]9 Or *to their* (Aquila); most Hebrew manuscripts *and are forgotten*   [c]10 Some Hebrew manuscripts and Septuagint (Aquila); most Hebrew manuscripts *and are forgotten* Hebrew does not have *and the bad.*   [d]2 Septuagint (Aquila), Vulgate and Syriac; [e]4 Or *What then is to be chosen? With all who live, there is hope*

in anything that happens under the sun.

[7]Go, eat your food with gladness, and drink your wine with a joyful heart, for it is now that God favors what you do. [8]Always be clothed in white, and always anoint your head with oil. [9]Enjoy life with your wife, whom you love, all the days of this meaningless life that God has given you under the sun— all your meaningless days. For this is your lot in life and in your toilsome labor under the sun. [10]Whatever your hand finds to do, do it with all your might, for in the grave,[a] where you are going, there is neither working nor planning nor knowledge nor wisdom.

[11]I have seen something else under the sun:

The race is not to the swift
    or the battle to the strong,
nor does food come to the wise
    or wealth to the brilliant
    or favor to the learned;
but time and chance happen to them
    all.

[12]Moreover, no man knows when his hour will come:

As fish are caught in a cruel net,
    or birds are taken in a snare,
so men are trapped by evil times
    that fall unexpectedly upon them.

Wisdom Better Than Folly

[13]I also saw under the sun this example of wisdom that greatly impressed me: [14]There was once a small city with only a few people in it. And a powerful king came against it, surrounded it and built huge siegeworks against it. [15]Now there lived in that city a man poor but wise, and he saved the city by his wisdom. But nobody remembered that poor man. [16]So I said, "Wisdom is better than strength." But the poor man's wisdom is despised, and his words are no longer heeded.

[17]The quiet words of the wise are more
    to be heeded
    than the shouts of a ruler of fools.
[18]Wisdom is better than weapons of
    war,
    but one sinner destroys much good.

10 As dead flies give perfume a bad
    smell,

so a little folly outweighs wisdom
    and honor.
[2]The heart of the wise inclines to the
    right,
    but the heart of the fool to the left.
[3]Even as he walks along the road,
    the fool lacks sense
    and shows everyone how stupid he
    is.
[4]If a ruler's anger rises against you,
    do not leave your post;
    calmness can lay great errors to
    rest.

[5]There is an evil I have seen under the
    sun,
    the sort of error that arises from a
    ruler:
[6]Fools are put in many high positions,
    while the rich occupy the low ones.
[7]I have seen slaves on horseback,
    while princes go on foot like slaves.

[8]Whoever digs a pit may fall into it;
    whoever breaks through a wall may
    be bitten by a snake.
[9]Whoever quarries stones may be
    injured by them;
    whoever splits logs may be
    endangered by them.

[10]If the ax is dull
    and its edge unsharpened,
more strength is needed
    but skill will bring success.

[11]If a snake bites before it is charmed,
    there is no profit for the charmer.

[12]Words from a wise man's mouth are
    gracious,
    but a fool is consumed by his own
    lips.
[13]At the beginning his words are folly;
    at the end they are wicked
    madness—
[14]   and the fool multiplies words.

No one knows what is coming—
    who can tell him what will happen
    after him?

[15]A fool's work wearies him;
    he does not know the way to town.

[16]Woe to you, O land whose king was a
    servant[b]
and whose princes feast in the
    morning.
[17]Blessed are you, O land whose king is
    of noble birth

---

[a]10 Hebrew *Sheol*   [b]16 Or *king is a child*

and whose princes eat at a proper
  time —
  for strength and not for
  drunkenness.

¹⁸If a man is lazy, the rafters sag;
  if his hands are idle, the house
  leaks.

¹⁹A feast is made for laughter,
  and wine makes life merry,
  but money is the answer for
  everything.

²⁰Do not revile the king even in your
  thoughts,
  or curse the rich in your bedroom,
  because a bird of the air may carry
  your words,
  and a bird on the wing may report
  what you say.

Bread Upon the Waters

11 Cast your bread upon the waters,
  for after many days you will find
  it again.
²Give portions to seven, yes to eight,
  for you do not know what disaster
  may come upon the land.

³If clouds are full of water,
  they pour rain upon the earth.
Whether a tree falls to the south or to
  the north,
  in the place where it falls, there will
  it lie.
⁴Whoever watches the wind will not
  plant;
  whoever looks at the clouds will not
  reap.

⁵As you do not know the path of the
  wind,
  or how the body is formed[a] in a
  mother's womb,
so you cannot understand the work of
  God,
  the Maker of all things.

⁶Sow your seed in the morning,
  and at evening let not your hands
  be idle,
for you do not know which will
  succeed,
  whether this or that,
  or whether both will do equally
  well.

Remember Your Creator While Young

⁷Light is sweet,

and it pleases the eyes to see the
  sun.
⁸However many years a man may live,
  let him enjoy them all.
But let him remember the days of
  darkness,
  for they will be many.
  Everything to come is meaningless.

⁹Be happy, young man, while you are
  young,
  and let your heart give you joy in
  the days of your youth.
Follow the ways of your heart
  and whatever your eyes see,
but know that for all these things
  God will bring you to judgment.
¹⁰So then, banish anxiety from your
  heart
  and cast off the troubles of your
  body,
  for youth and vigor are
  meaningless.

12 Remember your Creator
  in the days of your youth,
before the days of trouble come
  and the years approach when you
  will say,
  "I find no pleasure in them" —
²before the sun and the light
  and the moon and the stars grow
  dark,
  and the clouds return after the rain;
³when the keepers of the house
  tremble,
  and the strong men stoop,
when the grinders cease because they
  are few,
  and those looking through the
  windows grow dim;
⁴when the doors to the street are
  closed
  and the sound of grinding fades;
when men rise up at the sound of
  birds,
  but all their songs grow faint;
⁵when men are afraid of heights
  and of dangers in the streets;
when the almond tree blossoms
  and the grasshopper drags himself
  along
  and desire no longer is stirred.
Then man goes to his eternal home
  and mourners go about the streets.

⁶Remember him — before the silver
  cord is severed,
  or the golden bowl is broken;

ᵃ5 Or *know how life* (or *the spirit*) / *enters the body being formed*

before the pitcher is shattered at the
spring,
or the wheel broken at the well,
[7]and the dust returns to the ground it
came from,
and the spirit returns to God who
gave it.

[8]"Meaningless! Meaningless!" says the
Teacher.[a]
"Everything is meaningless!"

The Conclusion of the Matter

[9]Not only was the Teacher wise, but
also he imparted knowledge to the people. He pondered and searched out
and set in order many proverbs. [10]The
Teacher searched to find just the right
words, and what he wrote was upright
and true.
[11]The words of the wise are like goads,
their collected sayings like firmly embedded nails — given by one Shepherd. [12]Be
warned, my son, of anything in addition
to them.
Of making many books there is no end,
and much study wearies the body.

[13]Now all has been heard;
here is the conclusion of the matter:
Fear God and keep his
commandments,
for this is the whole ˌdutyˌ of man.
[14]For God will bring every deed into
judgment,
including every hidden thing,
whether it is good or evil.

*S*OLOMON'S *"songs numbered a thousand and five" (1 Kings 4:32), of which this is one. It focuses on the spontaneous and exclusive love between a lover and his beloved, demonstrating at the same time the sort of love Christ has for his beloved bride, the church. As you read this book, rejoice not only in the love that can exist between a man and woman, but also bask in the warmth of a personal love relationship with Christ.*

SONG OF SONGS

1 Solomon's Song of Songs.

Beloved[a]

2Let him kiss me with the kisses of his
    mouth—
for your love is more delightful than
    wine.
3Pleasing is the fragrance of your
    perfumes;
your name is like perfume poured
    out.
No wonder the maidens love
    you!

4Take me away with you—let us
    hurry!
Let the king bring me into his
    chambers.

Friends

We rejoice and delight in you[b];
    we will praise your love more than
    wine.

Beloved

How right they are to adore you!
5Dark am I, yet lovely,

---

[a]Primarily on the basis of the gender of the Hebrew pronouns used, male and female speakers are indicated in the margins by the captions *Lover* and *Beloved* respectively. The words of others are marked *Friends.* In some instances the divisions and their captions are debatable.   [b]4 The Hebrew is masculine singular.

O daughters of Jerusalem,
  dark like the tents of Kedar,
  like the tent curtains of Solomon. [a]
6Do not stare at me because I am dark,
  because I am darkened by the sun.
My mother's sons were angry with me
  and made me take care of the
    vineyards;
  my own vineyard I have neglected.
7Tell me, you whom I love, where you
  graze your flock

and where you rest your sheep at
    midday.
  Why should I be like a veiled woman
    beside the flocks of your friends?

Friends

8If you do not know, most beautiful of
    women,
  follow the tracks of the sheep
and graze your young goats
  by the tents of the shepherds.

[a]5 Or *Salma*

THURSDAY

VERSE FOR THE DAY:	AUTHOR:	PASSAGE FOR THE DAY:
Song of Songs 1:2	Richard Foster	Song of Songs 1:1–4

The Vocabulary of Love

FRANKLY, sex in marriage should be a voluptuous experience. It is a gift to celebrate, excellent in every way . . .
  Sexual intercourse is not a given, something that somehow
miraculously takes care of itself once we enter marriage. It
needs nurture, tenderness, training, education and much more.
When two persons enter into sexual intimacy, there must be a
lot of emotional, spiritual and physical give-and-take.
  Men and women respond differently in the sexual experience, and we had better learn the differences. You can find
them cataloged in any number of books. But what you cannot
find is the unique differences that exist between you and your
spouse. The books can only provide hints to point you in the
right general direction. It is up to you to explore the unique
and mysterious ways of your partner.
  Women, the experts tell us, respond to sex more in terms of
relationship, of caring, sharing, than do men. But it is my God-
given responsibility to learn the specific rhythms of my wife.
How often, how intense, how slow, how fast, what gives pleasure, what offends—these and a thousand other things form
the vocabulary of love. I must learn to read the language of her
heart and soul, and she must learn to read mine.
  This is the agony and the ecstasy of sexual intimacy. But we
cannot avoid it even if we want to. Besides, it is the very thing
that provides such infinite variety and lifelong pleasure in our
sexual experience. No wonder the Creator made marriage
permanent—after a lifetime we have only just begun to understand the marvelous inner clockwork of each other.

Additional Scripture Readings:
Proverbs 5:15–20; Matthew 19:1–6

*Go to page 704 for your next
devotional reading.*

Lover

⁹I liken you, my darling, to a mare
  harnessed to one of the chariots of
    Pharaoh.
¹⁰Your cheeks are beautiful with
    earrings,
  your neck with strings of jewels.
¹¹We will make you earrings of gold,
  studded with silver.

Beloved

¹²While the king was at his table,
  my perfume spread its fragrance.
¹³My lover is to me a sachet of myrrh
  resting between my breasts.
¹⁴My lover is to me a cluster of henna
    blossoms
  from the vineyards of En Gedi.

Lover

¹⁵How beautiful you are, my darling!
  Oh, how beautiful!
  Your eyes are doves.

Beloved

¹⁶How handsome you are, my lover!
  Oh, how charming!
  And our bed is verdant.

Lover

¹⁷The beams of our house are cedars;
  our rafters are firs.

Belovedᵃ

2 I am a roseᵇ of Sharon,
  a lily of the valleys.

Lover

²Like a lily among thorns
  is my darling among the maidens.

Beloved

³Like an apple tree among the trees of
    the forest
  is my lover among the young men.
  I delight to sit in his shade,
    and his fruit is sweet to my taste.
⁴He has taken me to the banquet hall,
  and his banner over me is love.
⁵Strengthen me with raisins,
  refresh me with apples,
  for I am faint with love.
⁶His left arm is under my head,
  and his right arm embraces me.
⁷Daughters of Jerusalem, I charge you
  by the gazelles and by the does of
    the field:

Do not arouse or awaken love
  until it so desires.

⁸Listen! My lover!
  Look! Here he comes,
leaping across the mountains,
  bounding over the hills.
⁹My lover is like a gazelle or a young
    stag.
  Look! There he stands behind our
    wall,
gazing through the windows,
  peering through the lattice.
¹⁰My lover spoke and said to me,
  "Arise, my darling,
  my beautiful one, and come with
    me.
¹¹See! The winter is past;
  the rains are over and gone.
¹²Flowers appear on the earth;
  the season of singing has come,
the cooing of doves
  is heard in our land.
¹³The fig tree forms its early fruit;
  the blossoming vines spread their
    fragrance.
Arise, come, my darling;
  my beautiful one, come with me."

Lover

¹⁴My dove in the clefts of the rock,
  in the hiding places on the
    mountainside,
show me your face,
  let me hear your voice;
for your voice is sweet,
  and your face is lovely.
¹⁵Catch for us the foxes,
  the little foxes
that ruin the vineyards,
  our vineyards that are in bloom.

Beloved

¹⁶My lover is mine and I am his;
  he browses among the lilies.
¹⁷Until the day breaks
  and the shadows flee,
turn, my lover,
  and be like a gazelle
or like a young stag
  on the rugged hills.ᶜ

3 All night long on my bed
  I looked for the one my heart loves;
  I looked for him but did not find
    him.
²I will get up now and go about the
    city,
  through its streets and squares;

ᵃ1 Or *Lover*   ᵇ1 Possibly a member of the crocus family   ᶜ17 Or *the hills of Bether*

FRIDAY

VERSE FOR THE DAY:
Song of Songs 2:10

AUTHOR:
Lewis Smedes

PASSAGE FOR THE DAY:
Song of Songs 2:3–13

The Springtime of Fidelity

FIDELITY means a stubborn dedication to growth in personal relationship. A marriage partnership must have room for individual growth; but at the beating heart of any marriage is the delicate, fragile—often painful—but potentially joyful relationship of two persons face to face in personal encounter. The vital core of marriage is the special kind of sexual communion that vibrates on every level—physical, emotional, intellectual and spiritual. All the institutional dimensions are only the framework for the dynamic center. And if partners are faithful in the complex ways mentioned above, their fidelity will mean a steady dedication to the growth of an honest and open relationship in every dimension.

Fidelity is best practiced with an implicit understanding that the relationship happens *within* a permanent, lifelong structure. But within the structure of permanence, relationships are constantly shifting: they are never stagnant, but grow deeper or become shallower. To be faithful means that we can never lazily accept the present as our fated destiny. For relationships never have to be what they are; they can change. The future has possibilities wherever two willing human beings affirm its possibilities for them. No one can make a claim to faithfulness in marriage if he does not keep the door open to the possibilities that his relationship can be better tomorrow than it is today.

Personal relationships are nourished only through communication, and communication between two people enmeshed in daily preoccupations with jobs, budgets, diapers and new math can be very difficult to maintain. For one thing, it takes time . . . And, above all, it takes desire. Personal communication is difficult because it is painful for us to talk about what we are feeling; it is much easier to discuss the unbalanced checking account than to discuss how we feel toward each other. But more, it is difficult because when we talk we are not sure what becomes of our message after it is filtered through the receptive apparatus of the person who receives it . . . Fidelity will give us the job of finding out what the other person is actually hearing from us and of patiently probing what the other person is actually trying to say.

Additional Scripture Readings:
Psalm 85:10–13; Proverbs 3:1–6

*Go to page 706 for your next
devotional reading.*

I will search for the one my heart
   loves.
  So I looked for him but did not find
   him.
[3]The watchmen found me
  as they made their rounds in the
   city.
  "Have you seen the one my heart
   loves?"
[4]Scarcely had I passed them
  when I found the one my heart
   loves.
I held him and would not let him go
  till I had brought him to my
   mother's house,
to the room of the one who
   conceived me.
[5]Daughters of Jerusalem, I charge you
  by the gazelles and by the does of
   the field:
Do not arouse or awaken love
  until it so desires.

[6]Who is this coming up from the
   desert
  like a column of smoke,
perfumed with myrrh and incense
  made from all the spices of the
   merchant?
[7]Look! It is Solomon's carriage,
  escorted by sixty warriors,
  the noblest of Israel,
[8]all of them wearing the sword,
  all experienced in battle,
each with his sword at his side,
  prepared for the terrors of the night.
[9]King Solomon made for himself the
   carriage;
  he made it of wood from Lebanon.
[10]Its posts he made of silver,
  its base of gold.
Its seat was upholstered with purple,
  its interior lovingly inlaid
  by[a] the daughters of Jerusalem.
[11]Come out, you daughters of Zion,
  and look at King Solomon wearing
   the crown,
  the crown with which his mother
   crowned him
on the day of his wedding,
  the day his heart rejoiced.

Lover

4 How beautiful you are, my darling!
  Oh, how beautiful!
  Your eyes behind your veil are
   doves.

Your hair is like a flock of goats
  descending from Mount Gilead.
[2]Your teeth are like a flock of sheep
   just shorn,
  coming up from the washing.
Each has its twin;
  not one of them is alone.
[3]Your lips are like a scarlet ribbon;
  your mouth is lovely.
Your temples behind your veil
  are like the halves of a
   pomegranate.
[4]Your neck is like the tower of David,
  built with elegance[b];
on it hang a thousand shields,
  all of them shields of warriors.
[5]Your two breasts are like two fawns,
  like twin fawns of a gazelle
  that browse among the lilies.
[6]Until the day breaks
  and the shadows flee,
I will go to the mountain of myrrh
  and to the hill of incense.
[7]All beautiful you are, my darling;
  there is no flaw in you.

[8]Come with me from Lebanon, my
   bride,
  come with me from Lebanon.
Descend from the crest of Amana,
  from the top of Senir, the summit of
   Hermon,
from the lions' dens
  and the mountain haunts of the
   leopards.
[9]You have stolen my heart, my sister,
   my bride;
  you have stolen my heart
with one glance of your eyes,
  with one jewel of your necklace.
[10]How delightful is your love, my sister,
   my bride!
  How much more pleasing is your
   love than wine,
and the fragrance of your perfume
   than any spice!
[11]Your lips drop sweetness as the
   honeycomb, my bride;
  milk and honey are under your
   tongue.
The fragrance of your garments is
   like that of Lebanon.
[12]You are a garden locked up, my sister,
   my bride;
  you are a spring enclosed, a sealed
   fountain.

---

[a]10 Or *its inlaid interior a gift of love / from*
uncertain.
[b]4 The meaning of the Hebrew for this word is

WEEKENDING

RETHINK

Our human sexuality, our maleness and femaleness, is not just an accidental arrangement of the human species, not just a convenient way to keep the human race going. No, it is at the center of our true humanity. We exist as male and female in relationship. Our sexualness, our capacity to love and be loved is intimately related to our creation in the image of God. What a high view of human sexuality!

Notice too that the Biblical stress upon relationship helps to enlarge our understanding of human sexuality. The problem with the topless bars and the pornographic literature of our day is not that they emphasize sexuality too much but that they do not emphasize it enough. They totally eliminate relationship and restrain sexuality to the narrow confines of the genitals. They have made sex trivial.

How much richer and fuller is the Biblical perspective! To chat over coffee, to discuss a great book, to view a sunset together—this is sexuality at its best, for male and female are in intimate relationship.

– *Richard Foster*

REVIVE

Saturday: Genesis 1:26–28
Sunday: 1 Corinthians 13

Go to page 707 for your next devotional reading.

13Your plants are an orchard of
   pomegranates
  with choice fruits,
  with henna and nard,
14 nard and saffron,
  calamus and cinnamon,
  with every kind of incense tree,
  with myrrh and aloes
  and all the finest spices.
15You are*a* a garden fountain,
  a well of flowing water
  streaming down from Lebanon.

a15 Or I am (spoken by the Beloved)

Beloved

16Awake, north wind,
  and come, south wind!
Blow on my garden,
  that its fragrance may spread
  abroad.
Let my lover come into his garden
  and taste its choice fruits.

Lover

5 I have come into my garden, my
  sister, my bride;

MONDAY

VERSE FOR THE DAY:	AUTHOR:	PASSAGE FOR THE DAY:
Song of Songs 4:9	Rodney Clapp	Song of Songs 4:8–15

Sweet Surprises

IT'S ODD, when you think about it, that after living together
for eleven years, your wife remains alien enough to surprise
you. You figure you've seen all her tricks and quirks. You
know at which foods she will stick out her tongue. You know
by her walk, when you pick her up after work and watch her
approach the car, if it's been a good or bad day. You know,
before she's read the funny pages, which cartoons she will put
on the refrigerator.

But then one day she surprises you. And you notice anew
the exact spot where the hairline begins on her forehead and
the unique character of her hands. You realize what you had
forgotten for a while—that she's not an extension of yourself,
not a supporting actress in a private drama you are writing and
directing . . .

Sometimes I look at Sandy sleeping, unaware of me, vulnerable as a child, and remember that she lived a good part of her
life before I even entered it. The face of a sleeping woman, of
this sleeping woman, is profound. With its soft lines, with its
hidden eyes, with its closed lips, it says: "Eleven years are
barely enough to get beneath the skin—let alone to the
heart—of the mystery that is a woman."

This woman is my wife. But she is also a sweet stranger, beyond the knowing of a lifetime. She surprises me, and I am
glad for that because it renews our marriage.

Additional Scripture Readings:
Genesis 2:18–25; Proverbs 5:15–20

Go to page 710 for your next
devotional reading.

I have gathered my myrrh with my
spice.
I have eaten my honeycomb and my
honey;
I have drunk my wine and my milk.

Friends

Eat, O friends, and drink;
drink your fill, O lovers.

Beloved

2I slept but my heart was awake.
Listen! My lover is knocking:
"Open to me, my sister, my darling,
my dove, my flawless one.
My head is drenched with dew,
my hair with the dampness of the
night."
3I have taken off my robe—
must I put it on again?
I have washed my feet—
must I soil them again?
4My lover thrust his hand through the
latch-opening;
my heart began to pound for him.
5I arose to open for my lover,
and my hands dripped with myrrh,
my fingers with flowing myrrh,
on the handles of the lock.
6I opened for my lover,
but my lover had left; he was gone.
My heart sank at his departure.*a*
I looked for him but did not find him.
I called him but he did not answer.
7The watchmen found me
as they made their rounds in the
city.
They beat me, they bruised me;
they took away my cloak,
those watchmen of the walls!
8O daughters of Jerusalem, I charge
you—
if you find my lover,
what will you tell him?
Tell him I am faint with love.

Friends

9How is your beloved better than
others,
most beautiful of women?
How is your beloved better than
others,
that you charge us so?

Beloved

10My lover is radiant and ruddy,
outstanding among ten thousand.
11His head is purest gold;

his hair is wavy
and black as a raven.
12His eyes are like doves
by the water streams,
washed in milk,
mounted like jewels.
13His cheeks are like beds of spice
yielding perfume.
His lips are like lilies
dripping with myrrh.
14His arms are rods of gold
set with chrysolite.
His body is like polished ivory
decorated with sapphires.*b*
15His legs are pillars of marble
set on bases of pure gold.
His appearance is like Lebanon,
choice as its cedars.
16His mouth is sweetness itself;
he is altogether lovely.
This is my lover, this my friend,
O daughters of Jerusalem.

Friends

6 Where has your lover gone,
most beautiful of women?
Which way did your lover turn,
that we may look for him with you?

Beloved

2My lover has gone down to his
garden,
to the beds of spices,
to browse in the gardens
and to gather lilies.
3I am my lover's and my lover is mine;
he browses among the lilies.

Lover

4You are beautiful, my darling, as
Tirzah,
lovely as Jerusalem,
majestic as troops with banners.
5Turn your eyes from me;
they overwhelm me.
Your hair is like a flock of goats
descending from Gilead.
6Your teeth are like a flock of sheep
coming up from the washing.
Each has its twin,
not one of them is alone.
7Your temples behind your veil
are like the halves of a
pomegranate.
8Sixty queens there may be,
and eighty concubines,
and virgins beyond number;

---

a6 Or *heart had gone out to him when he spoke*   *b14* Or *lapis lazuli*

9but my dove, my perfect one, is
   unique,
   the only daughter of her mother,
   the favorite of the one who bore
      her.
The maidens saw her and called her
      blessed;
   the queens and concubines praised
      her.

Friends

10Who is this that appears like the
      dawn,
   fair as the moon, bright as the sun,
   majestic as the stars in procession?

Lover

11I went down to the grove of nut trees
   to look at the new growth in the
      valley,
   to see if the vines had budded
   or the pomegranates were in bloom.
12Before I realized it,
   my desire set me among the royal
      chariots of my people.*a*

Friends

13Come back, come back,
   O Shulammite;
   come back, come back, that we may
      gaze on you!

Lover

Why would you gaze on the
      Shulammite
   as on the dance of Mahanaim?

7 How beautiful your sandaled feet,
   O prince's daughter!
Your graceful legs are like jewels,
   the work of a craftsman's hands.
2Your navel is a rounded goblet
   that never lacks blended wine.
Your waist is a mound of wheat
   encircled by lilies.
3Your breasts are like two fawns,
   twins of a gazelle.
4Your neck is like an ivory tower.
Your eyes are the pools of Heshbon
   by the gate of Bath Rabbim.
Your nose is like the tower of
      Lebanon
   looking toward Damascus.
5Your head crowns you like Mount
      Carmel.
   Your hair is like royal tapestry;

the king is held captive by its
      tresses.
6How beautiful you are and how
      pleasing,
   O love, with your delights!
7Your stature is like that of the palm,
   and your breasts like clusters of
      fruit.
8I said, "I will climb the palm tree;
   I will take hold of its fruit."
May your breasts be like the clusters
      of the vine,
   the fragrance of your breath like
      apples,
9   and your mouth like the best wine.

Beloved

May the wine go straight to my lover,
   flowing gently over lips and teeth.*b*
10I belong to my lover,
   and his desire is for me.
11Come, my lover, let us go to the
      countryside,
   let us spend the night in the
      villages.*c*
12Let us go early to the vineyards
   to see if the vines have budded,
   if their blossoms have opened,
   and if the pomegranates are in
      bloom—
   there I will give you my love.
13The mandrakes send out their
      fragrance,
   and at our door is every delicacy,
both new and old,
   that I have stored up for you, my
      lover.

8 If only you were to me like a
   brother,
   who was nursed at my mother's
      breasts!
Then, if I found you outside,
   I would kiss you,
   and no one would despise me.
2I would lead you
   and bring you to my mother's
      house—
   she who has taught me.
I would give you spiced wine to drink,
   the nectar of my pomegranates.
3His left arm is under my head
   and his right arm embraces me.
4Daughters of Jerusalem, I charge you:
   Do not arouse or awaken love
   until it so desires.

a12 Or *among the chariots of Amminadab;* or *among the chariots of the people of the prince*
b9 Septuagint, Aquila, Vulgate and Syriac; Hebrew *lips of sleepers*   *c11* Or *henna bushes*

Friends

⁵Who is this coming up from the
      desert
  leaning on her lover?

Beloved

  Under the apple tree I roused you;
    there your mother conceived you,
there she who was in labor gave
      you birth.
⁶Place me like a seal over your heart,
    like a seal on your arm;
  for love is as strong as death,
    its jealousyᵃ unyielding as the
      grave.ᵇ
  It burns like blazing fire,
    like a mighty flame.ᶜ

ᵃ6 Or *ardor*   ᵇ6 Hebrew *Sheol*   ᶜ6 Or / *like the very flame of the* LORD

TUESDAY

VERSE FOR THE DAY:	AUTHOR:	PASSAGE FOR THE DAY:
Song of Songs 8:6	Paul Plattner	Song of Songs 8:6–7

Peaceful Togetherness

THE different way in which a man and a woman experience
life colors their entire marriage. For the man, sexual union is
an event with a significance of its own, having its own independent experiential value. Through sexual intercourse, he is
able to recover community after having spent some time in a
certain emotional isolation, a certain erotic neutrality, for example, after the day's work. This feeling of belonging, restored
by the sexual event, he now takes with him joyfully and proceeds to discharge in his work the energy he has accumulated
from being with his wife. He is now able to perform with
heightened creativity and new zest because his work now
seems ever so much more meaningful to him. It is for this reason that a man is able to attribute a spiritual meaning to sexual union, indeed a metaphysical significance.

   The woman's story is entirely different. For the feminine
soul, sexual union is both less and more. It is something very
close and palpable. Her spiritual surrender is directed far more
precisely at the person of her husband, perhaps at the hoped-
for child. A woman expects every sexual union to bring her
closer to her husband and to remain closer to him ever after.

   An hour of peaceful togetherness in which the woman
knows that her husband is really beside her, an hour during
which he really participates in everything she tells him and he
tells her, is likely to mean a great deal more to most women
than any stormy sexual encounter during which she loves her
husband, to be sure, but in which her husband actually gives
himself to the experience rather than to his wife.

Additional Scripture Readings:
1 Corinthians 7:1–7;
1 Thessalonians 4:1–8

*Go to page 739 for your next
devotional reading.*

⁷Many waters cannot quench love;
   rivers cannot wash it away.
If one were to give
   all the wealth of his house for love,
   it*a* would be utterly scorned.

Friends

⁸We have a young sister,
   and her breasts are not yet grown.
What shall we do for our sister
   for the day she is spoken for?
⁹If she is a wall,
   we will build towers of silver on
      her.
If she is a door,
   we will enclose her with panels of
      cedar.

Beloved

¹⁰I am a wall,
   and my breasts are like towers.
Thus I have become in his eyes
   like one bringing contentment.

¹¹Solomon had a vineyard in Baal
      Hamon;
   he let out his vineyard to tenants.
Each was to bring for its fruit
   a thousand shekels*b* of silver.
¹²But my own vineyard is mine to
      give;
   the thousand shekels are for you,
      O Solomon,
   and two hundred*c* are for those
      who tend its fruit.

Lover

¹³You who dwell in the gardens
   with friends in attendance,
   let me hear your voice!

Beloved

¹⁴Come away, my lover,
   and be like a gazelle
   or like a young stag
   on the spice-laden mountains.

a7 Or *he*   *b11* That is, about 25 pounds (about 11.5 kilograms); also in verse 12   *c12* That is, about 5 pounds (about 2.3 kilograms)

*I*SAIAH ministers during the events recorded in 2 Chronicles 26–32. He portrays graphically the sins of the kingdom of Judah (idolatry, hypocrisy, materialism, and oppression of the poor) and prophesies that severe judgment is coming. At the same time, he extends to God's people the promise of redemption, offering hope for a glorious future, particularly when the Messiah comes. As you read this book, listen to God's offer to redeem you through Jesus, the Messiah; express your own Christian joy by singing one of Isaiah's songs of thanksgiving.

ISAIAH

1 The vision concerning Judah and Jerusalem that Isaiah son of Amoz saw during the reigns of Uzziah, Jotham, Ahaz and Hezekiah, kings of Judah.

A Rebellious Nation

²Hear, O heavens! Listen, O earth!
   For the LORD has spoken:
"I reared children and brought them
      up,
   but they have rebelled against me.
³The ox knows his master,
   the donkey his owner's manger,
but Israel does not know,
   my people do not understand."

⁴Ah, sinful nation,
   a people loaded with guilt,
a brood of evildoers,
   children given to corruption!
They have forsaken the LORD;
   they have spurned the Holy One of
      Israel
   and turned their backs on him.

⁵Why should you be beaten anymore?
  Why do you persist in rebellion?
Your whole head is injured,
  your whole heart afflicted.
⁶From the sole of your foot to the top
    of your head
  there is no soundness—
only wounds and welts
  and open sores,
not cleansed or bandaged
  or soothed with oil.

⁷Your country is desolate,
  your cities burned with fire;
your fields are being stripped by
    foreigners
  right before you,
  laid waste as when overthrown by
    strangers.
⁸The Daughter of Zion is left
  like a shelter in a vineyard,
like a hut in a field of melons,
  like a city under siege.
⁹Unless the LORD Almighty
  had left us some survivors,
we would have become like Sodom,
  we would have been like Gomorrah.

¹⁰Hear the word of the LORD,
  you rulers of Sodom;
listen to the law of our God,
  you people of Gomorrah!
¹¹"The multitude of your sacrifices—
  what are they to me?" says the
    LORD.
"I have more than enough of burnt
    offerings,
  of rams and the fat of fattened
    animals;
I have no pleasure
  in the blood of bulls and lambs and
    goats.
¹²When you come to appear before me,
  who has asked this of you,
  this trampling of my courts?
¹³Stop bringing meaningless offerings!
  Your incense is detestable to me.
New Moons, Sabbaths and
    convocations—
  I cannot bear your evil assemblies.
¹⁴Your New Moon festivals and your
    appointed feasts
  my soul hates.
They have become a burden to me;
  I am weary of bearing them.
¹⁵When you spread out your hands in
    prayer,
  I will hide my eyes from you;
even if you offer many prayers,

  I will not listen.
Your hands are full of blood;
¹⁶ wash and make yourselves clean.
Take your evil deeds
  out of my sight!
Stop doing wrong,
¹⁷ learn to do right!
Seek justice,
  encourage the oppressed.ᵃ
Defend the cause of the fatherless,
  plead the case of the widow.

¹⁸"Come now, let us reason together,"
  says the LORD.
"Though your sins are like scarlet,
  they shall be as white as snow;
though they are red as crimson,
  they shall be like wool.
¹⁹If you are willing and obedient,
  you will eat the best from the land;
²⁰but if you resist and rebel,
  you will be devoured by the sword."
    For the mouth of the LORD
      has spoken.

²¹See how the faithful city
  has become a harlot!
She once was full of justice;
  righteousness used to dwell in
    her—
  but now murderers!
²²Your silver has become dross,
  your choice wine is diluted with
    water.
²³Your rulers are rebels,
  companions of thieves;
they all love bribes
  and chase after gifts.
They do not defend the cause of the
    fatherless;
  the widow's case does not come
    before them.
²⁴Therefore the Lord, the LORD
    Almighty,
  the Mighty One of Israel, declares:
"Ah, I will get relief from my foes
  and avenge myself on my enemies.
²⁵I will turn my hand against you;
  I will thoroughly purge away your
    dross
  and remove all your impurities.
²⁶I will restore your judges as in days of
    old,
  your counselors as at the beginning.
Afterward you will be called
  the City of Righteousness,
  the Faithful City."
²⁷Zion will be redeemed with justice,

ᵃ17 Or / rebuke the oppressor

her penitent ones with
  righteousness.
28But rebels and sinners will both be
    broken,
  and those who forsake the LORD will
    perish.

29"You will be ashamed because of the
    sacred oaks
  in which you have delighted;
  you will be disgraced because of the
    gardens
  that you have chosen.
30You will be like an oak with fading
    leaves,
  like a garden without water.
31The mighty man will become tinder
  and his work a spark;
  both will burn together,
  with no one to quench the fire."

The Mountain of the LORD

2 This is what Isaiah son of Amoz saw
concerning Judah and Jerusalem:

2In the last days

the mountain of the LORD's temple will
    be established
  as chief among the mountains;
it will be raised above the hills,
  and all nations will stream to it.

3Many peoples will come and say,

"Come, let us go up to the mountain
    of the LORD,
  to the house of the God of Jacob.
He will teach us his ways,
  so that we may walk in his paths."
The law will go out from Zion,
  the word of the LORD from
    Jerusalem.
4He will judge between the nations
  and will settle disputes for many
    peoples.
They will beat their swords into
    plowshares
  and their spears into pruning hooks.
Nation will not take up sword against
    nation,
  nor will they train for war anymore.

5Come, O house of Jacob,
  let us walk in the light of the LORD.

The Day of the LORD

6You have abandoned your people,
  the house of Jacob.
They are full of superstitions from the
    East;

they practice divination like the
    Philistines
  and clasp hands with pagans.
7Their land is full of silver and gold;
  there is no end to their treasures.
Their land is full of horses;
  there is no end to their chariots.
8Their land is full of idols;
  they bow down to the work of their
    hands,
  to what their fingers have made.
9So man will be brought low
  and mankind humbled—
  do not forgive them.a

10Go into the rocks,
  hide in the ground
from dread of the LORD
  and the splendor of his majesty!
11The eyes of the arrogant man will be
    humbled
  and the pride of men brought low;
the LORD alone will be exalted in that
    day.

12The LORD Almighty has a day in store
  for all the proud and lofty,
  for all that is exalted
    (and they will be humbled),
13for all the cedars of Lebanon, tall and
    lofty,
  and all the oaks of Bashan,
14for all the towering mountains
  and all the high hills,
15for every lofty tower
  and every fortified wall,
16for every trading shipb
  and every stately vessel.
17The arrogance of man will be brought
    low
  and the pride of men humbled;
the LORD alone will be exalted in that
    day,
18   and the idols will totally disappear.

19Men will flee to caves in the rocks
  and to holes in the ground
from dread of the LORD
  and the splendor of his majesty,
  when he rises to shake the earth.
20In that day men will throw away
  to the rodents and bats
their idols of silver and idols of gold,
  which they made to worship.
21They will flee to caverns in the rocks
  and to the overhanging crags
from dread of the LORD
  and the splendor of his majesty,
  when he rises to shake the earth.

---

a9 Or not raise them up   b16 Hebrew every ship of Tarshish

22Stop trusting in man,
    who has but a breath in his nostrils.
Of what account is he?

Judgment on Jerusalem and Judah

3 See now, the Lord,
    the LORD Almighty,
is about to take from Jerusalem and
        Judah
    both supply and support:
all supplies of food and all supplies of
        water,
2 the hero and warrior,
    the judge and prophet,
        the soothsayer and elder,
3the captain of fifty and man of rank,
    the counselor, skilled craftsman and
        clever enchanter.

4I will make boys their officials;
    mere children will govern them.
5People will oppress each other—
    man against man, neighbor against
        neighbor.
The young will rise up against the old,
    the base against the honorable.

6A man will seize one of his brothers
    at his father's home, and say,
"You have a cloak, you be our leader;
    take charge of this heap of ruins!"
7But in that day he will cry out,
    "I have no remedy.
I have no food or clothing in my
        house;
    do not make me the leader of the
        people."

8Jerusalem staggers,
    Judah is falling;
their words and deeds are against the
        LORD,
    defying his glorious presence.
9The look on their faces testifies
        against them;
    they parade their sin like Sodom;
    they do not hide it.
Woe to them!
    They have brought disaster upon
        themselves.

10Tell the righteous it will be well with
        them,
    for they will enjoy the fruit of their
        deeds.
11Woe to the wicked! Disaster is upon
        them!
They will be paid back for what their
        hands have done.

12Youths oppress my people,
    women rule over them.

O my people, your guides lead you
        astray;
    they turn you from the path.

13The LORD takes his place in court;
    he rises to judge the people.
14The LORD enters into judgment
    against the elders and leaders of his
        people:
"It is you who have ruined my
        vineyard;
    the plunder from the poor is in your
        houses.
15What do you mean by crushing my
        people
    and grinding the faces of the poor?"
                    declares the Lord,
                        the LORD Almighty.

16The LORD says,
    "The women of Zion are haughty,
walking along with outstretched
        necks,
    flirting with their eyes,
tripping along with mincing steps,
    with ornaments jingling on their
        ankles.
17Therefore the Lord will bring sores on
        the heads of the women of
        Zion;
    the LORD will make their scalps
        bald."

18In that day the Lord will snatch away
their finery: the bangles and headbands
and crescent necklaces, **19**the earrings and
bracelets and veils, **20**the headdresses and
ankle chains and sashes, the perfume bot-
tles and charms, **21**the signet rings and
nose rings, **22**the fine robes and the capes
and cloaks, the purses **23**and mirrors, and
the linen garments and tiaras and shawls.

24Instead of fragrance there will be a
        stench;
    instead of a sash, a rope;
instead of well-dressed hair, baldness;
    instead of fine clothing, sackcloth;
    instead of beauty, branding.
25Your men will fall by the sword,
    your warriors in battle.
26The gates of Zion will lament and
        mourn;
    destitute, she will sit on the ground.

4 In that day seven women
    will take hold of one man
and say, "We will eat our own food
    and provide our own clothes;
only let us be called by your name.
    Take away our disgrace!"

... the LORD

... y the Branch of the LORD will
... and glorious, and the fruit of
... will be the pride and glory of the
... vors in Israel. ³Those who are left in
... on, who remain in Jerusalem, will be
called holy, all who are recorded among
the living in Jerusalem. ⁴The Lord will
wash away the filth of the women of Zion;
he will cleanse the bloodstains from Jerusalem by a spirit*a* of judgment and a spirit*a* of fire. ⁵Then the LORD will create over
all of Mount Zion and over those who assemble there a cloud of smoke by day and
a glow of flaming fire by night; over all the
glory will be a canopy. ⁶It will be a shelter
and shade from the heat of the day, and a
refuge and hiding place from the storm
and rain.

The Song of the Vineyard

5 I will sing for the one I love
  a song about his vineyard:
My loved one had a vineyard
  on a fertile hillside.
²He dug it up and cleared it of stones
  and planted it with the choicest
    vines.
He built a watchtower in it
  and cut out a winepress as well.
Then he looked for a crop of good
    grapes,
  but it yielded only bad fruit.

³"Now you dwellers in Jerusalem and
    men of Judah,
  judge between me and my vineyard.
⁴What more could have been done for
    my vineyard
  than I have done for it?
When I looked for good grapes,
  why did it yield only bad?
⁵Now I will tell you
  what I am going to do to my
    vineyard:
I will take away its hedge,
  and it will be destroyed;
I will break down its wall,
  and it will be trampled.
⁶I will make it a wasteland,
  neither pruned nor cultivated,
  and briers and thorns will grow
    there.
I will command the clouds
  not to rain on it."

⁷The vineyard of the LORD Almighty
  is the house of Israel,
and the men of Judah
  are the garden of his delight.
And he looked for justice, but saw
    bloodshed;
  for righteousness, but heard cries of
    distress.

Woes and Judgments

⁸Woe to you who add house to house
  and join field to field
till no space is left
  and you live alone in the land.

⁹The LORD Almighty has declared in my
hearing:

"Surely the great houses will become
    desolate,
  the fine mansions left without
    occupants.
¹⁰A ten-acre*b* vineyard will produce
  only a bath*c* of wine,
  a homer*d* of seed only an ephah*e*
    of grain."

¹¹Woe to those who rise early in the
    morning
  to run after their drinks,
who stay up late at night
  till they are inflamed with wine.
¹²They have harps and lyres at their
    banquets,
  tambourines and flutes and wine,
but they have no regard for the deeds
    of the LORD,
  no respect for the work of his
    hands.
¹³Therefore my people will go into exile
  for lack of understanding;
their men of rank will die of hunger
  and their masses will be parched
    with thirst.
¹⁴Therefore the grave*f* enlarges its
    appetite
  and opens its mouth without limit;
into it will descend their nobles and
    masses
  with all their brawlers and revelers.
¹⁵So man will be brought low
  and mankind humbled,
  the eyes of the arrogant humbled.
¹⁶But the LORD Almighty will be exalted
  by his justice,
  and the holy God will show himself
    holy by his righteousness.

---

a4 Or *the Spirit*   *b10* Hebrew *ten-yoke*, that is, the land plowed by 10 yoke of oxen in one day
c10 That is, probably about 6 gallons (about 22 liters)   *d10* That is, probably about 6 bushels (about
220 liters)   *e10* That is, probably about 3/5 bushel (about 22 liters)   *f14* Hebrew *Sheol*

[17] Then sheep will graze as in their own
pasture;
lambs will feed[a] among the ruins
of the rich.

[18] Woe to those who draw sin along
with cords of deceit,
and wickedness as with cart ropes,
[19] to those who say, "Let God hurry,
let him hasten his work
so we may see it.
Let it approach,
let the plan of the Holy One of
Israel come,
so we may know it."

[20] Woe to those who call evil good
and good evil,
who put darkness for light
and light for darkness,
who put bitter for sweet
and sweet for bitter.

[21] Woe to those who are wise in their
own eyes
and clever in their own sight.

[22] Woe to those who are heroes at
drinking wine
and champions at mixing drinks,
[23] who acquit the guilty for a bribe,
but deny justice to the innocent.
[24] Therefore, as tongues of fire lick up
straw
and as dry grass sinks down in the
flames,
so their roots will decay
and their flowers blow away like
dust;
for they have rejected the law of the
LORD Almighty
and spurned the word of the Holy
One of Israel.
[25] Therefore the LORD's anger burns
against his people;
his hand is raised and he strikes
them down.
The mountains shake,
and the dead bodies are like refuse
in the streets.

Yet for all this, his anger is not turned
away,
his hand is still upraised.

[26] He lifts up a banner for the distant
nations,
he whistles for those at the ends of
the earth.
Here they come,
swiftly and speedily!

[27] Not one of them grows tired or
stumbles,
not one slumbers or sleeps;
not a belt is loosened at the waist,
not a sandal thong is broken.
[28] Their arrows are sharp,
all their bows are strung;
their horses' hoofs seem like flint,
their chariot wheels like a
whirlwind.
[29] Their roar is like that of the lion,
they roar like young lions;
they growl as they seize their prey
and carry it off with no one to
rescue.
[30] In that day they will roar over it
like the roaring of the sea.
And if one looks at the land,
he will see darkness and distress;
even the light will be darkened by
the clouds.

Isaiah's Commission

6 In the year that King Uzziah died, I saw the Lord seated on a throne, high and exalted, and the train of his robe filled the temple. [2] Above him were seraphs, each with six wings: With two wings they covered their faces, with two they covered their feet, and with two they were flying. [3] And they were calling to one another:

"Holy, holy, holy is the LORD
Almighty;
the whole earth is full of his glory."

[4] At the sound of their voices the doorposts and thresholds shook and the temple was filled with smoke.

[5] "Woe to me!" I cried. "I am ruined! For I am a man of unclean lips, and I live among a people of unclean lips, and my eyes have seen the King, the LORD Almighty."

[6] Then one of the seraphs flew to me with a live coal in his hand, which he had taken with tongs from the altar. [7] With it he touched my mouth and said, "See, this has touched your lips; your guilt is taken away and your sin atoned for."

[8] Then I heard the voice of the Lord saying, "Whom shall I send? And who will go for us?"

And I said, "Here am I. Send me!"
[9] He said, "Go and tell this people:

" 'Be ever hearing, but never
understanding;

---

[a]17 Septuagint; Hebrew / *strangers will eat*

...ing, but never
...ving.'
...heart of this people
...alloused;
...ke their ears dull
...and close their eyes.*a*
Otherwise they might see with their
 eyes,
 hear with their ears,
 understand with their hearts,
and turn and be healed."

11Then I said, "For how long, O Lord?"
And he answered:

"Until the cities lie ruined
 and without inhabitant,
until the houses are left deserted
 and the fields ruined and ravaged,
12until the LORD has sent everyone far
 away
 and the land is utterly forsaken.
13And though a tenth remains in the
 land,
 it will again be laid waste.
But as the terebinth and oak
 leave stumps when they are cut
 down,
 so the holy seed will be the stump
 in the land."

The Sign of Immanuel

7 When Ahaz son of Jotham, the son of
 Uzziah, was king of Judah, King Rezin
of Aram and Pekah son of Remaliah king
of Israel marched up to fight against Jerusalem, but they could not overpower it.
 2Now the house of David was told,
"Aram has allied itself with*b* Ephraim";
so the hearts of Ahaz and his people were
shaken, as the trees of the forest are shak-
en by the wind.
 3Then the LORD said to Isaiah, "Go out,
you and your son Shear-Jashub,*c* to meet
Ahaz at the end of the aqueduct of the Upper Pool, on the road to the Washerman's
Field. **4**Say to him, 'Be careful, keep calm
and don't be afraid. Do not lose heart because of these two smoldering stubs of
firewood—because of the fierce anger of
Rezin and Aram and of the son of Remaliah. **5**Aram, Ephraim and Remaliah's son
have plotted your ruin, saying, **6**"Let us invade Judah; let us tear it apart and divide
it among ourselves, and make the son of

Tabeel king over it." **7**Yet this is what the
Sovereign LORD says:

" 'It will not take place,
 it will not happen,
8for the head of Aram is Damascus,
 and the head of Damascus is only
 Rezin.
Within sixty-five years
 Ephraim will be too shattered to be
 a people.
9The head of Ephraim is Samaria,
 and the head of Samaria is only
 Remaliah's son.
If you do not stand firm in your faith,
 you will not stand at all.' "

 10Again the LORD spoke to Ahaz, **11**"Ask
the LORD your God for a sign, whether in
the deepest depths or in the highest
heights."
 12But Ahaz said, "I will not ask; I will
not put the LORD to the test."
 13Then Isaiah said, "Hear now, you
house of David! Is it not enough to try the
patience of men? Will you try the patience
of my God also? **14**Therefore the Lord himself will give you*d* a sign: The virgin will
be with child and will give birth to a son,
and*e* will call him Immanuel.*f* **15**He will
eat curds and honey when he knows
enough to reject the wrong and choose
the right. **16**But before the boy knows
enough to reject the wrong and choose
the right, the land of the two kings you
dread will be laid waste. **17**The LORD will
bring on you and on your people and on
the house of your father a time unlike any
since Ephraim broke away from Judah—
he will bring the king of Assyria."
 18In that day the LORD will whistle for
flies from the distant streams of Egypt and
for bees from the land of Assyria. **19**They
will all come and settle in the steep ravines and in the crevices in the rocks, on
all the thornbushes and at all the water
holes. **20**In that day the Lord will use a razor hired from beyond the River*g*—the
king of Assyria—to shave your head and
the hair of your legs, and to take off your
beards also. **21**In that day, a man will keep
alive a young cow and two goats. **22**And
because of the abundance of the milk they
give, he will have curds to eat. All who remain in the land will eat curds and honey.

---

*a*9,10 Hebrew; Septuagint *'You will be ever hearing, but never understanding; / you will be ever seeing, but never perceiving.' / 10This people's heart has become calloused; / they hardly hear with their ears, / and they have closed their eyes* *b*2 Or *has set up camp in* *c*3 *Shear-Jashub* means *a remnant will return.* *d*14 The Hebrew is plural. *e*14 Masoretic Text; Dead Sea Scrolls *and he* or *and they* *f*14 *Immanuel* means *God with us.* *g*20 That is, the Euphrates

23In that day, in every place where there were a thousand vines worth a thousand silver shekels,a there will be only briers and thorns. 24Men will go there with bow and arrow, for the land will be covered with briers and thorns. 25As for all the hills once cultivated by the hoe, you will no longer go there for fear of the briers and thorns; they will become places where cattle are turned loose and where sheep run.

Assyria, the LORD's Instrument

8 The LORD said to me, "Take a large scroll and write on it with an ordinary pen: Maher-Shalal-Hash-Baz.b 2And I will call in Uriah the priest and Zechariah son of Jeberekiah as reliable witnesses for me."

3Then I went to the prophetess, and she conceived and gave birth to a son. And the LORD said to me, "Name him Maher-Shal-al-Hash-Baz. 4Before the boy knows how to say 'My father' or 'My mother,' the wealth of Damascus and the plunder of Samaria will be carried off by the king of Assyria."

5The LORD spoke to me again:

6"Because this people has rejected
    the gently flowing waters of Shiloah
and rejoices over Rezin
    and the son of Remaliah,
7therefore the Lord is about to bring
        against them
    the mighty floodwaters of the
        Riverc—
    the king of Assyria with all his
        pomp.
It will overflow all its channels,
    run over all its banks
8and sweep on into Judah, swirling
        over it,
    passing through it and reaching up
        to the neck.
Its outspread wings will cover the
        breadth of your land,
    O Immanueld!"

9Raise the war cry,e you nations, and
        be shattered!
Listen, all you distant lands.
Prepare for battle, and be shattered!
Prepare for battle, and be shattered!
10Devise your strategy, but it will be
        thwarted;

propose your plan, but it will not
        stand,
    for God is with us.f

Fear God

11The LORD spoke to me with his strong hand upon me, warning me not to follow the way of this people. He said:

12"Do not call conspiracy
    everything that these people call
        conspiracyg;
do not fear what they fear,
    and do not dread it.
13The LORD Almighty is the one you are
        to regard as holy,
    he is the one you are to fear,
    he is the one you are to dread,
14and he will be a sanctuary;
    but for both houses of Israel he will
        be
a stone that causes men to stumble
    and a rock that makes them fall.
And for the people of Jerusalem he
        will be
a trap and a snare.
15Many of them will stumble;
    they will fall and be broken,
    they will be snared and captured."

16Bind up the testimony
    and seal up the law among my
        disciples.
17I will wait for the LORD,
    who is hiding his face from the
        house of Jacob.
I will put my trust in him.

18Here am I, and the children the LORD has given me. We are signs and symbols in Israel from the LORD Almighty, who dwells on Mount Zion.

19When men tell you to consult mediums and spiritists, who whisper and mutter, should not a people inquire of their God? Why consult the dead on behalf of the living? 20To the law and to the testimony! If they do not speak according to this word, they have no light of dawn. 21Distressed and hungry, they will roam through the land; when they are famished, they will become enraged and, looking upward, will curse their king and their God. 22Then they will look toward the earth and see only distress and darkness and fearful gloom, and they will be thrust into utter darkness.

---

a23 That is, about 25 pounds (about 11.5 kilograms)   b1 Maher-Shalal-Hash-Baz means quick to the
plunder, swift to the spoil; also in verse 3.   c7 That is, the Euphrates   d8 Immanuel means God with
us.   e9 Or Do your worst   f10 Hebrew Immanuel   g12 Or Do not call for a treaty / every time
these people call for a treaty

719

... *Is Born*

...ess, there will be no more
...or those who were in distress.
...st he humbled the land of Zebu-
...d the land of Naphtali, but in the
...re he will honor Galilee of the Gen-
...les, by the way of the sea, along the Jordan—

²The people walking in darkness
  have seen a great light;
on those living in the land of the
    shadow of death*ᵃ*
  a light has dawned.
³You have enlarged the nation
  and increased their joy;
they rejoice before you
  as people rejoice at the harvest,
as men rejoice
  when dividing the plunder.
⁴For as in the day of Midian's defeat,
  you have shattered
the yoke that burdens them,
  the bar across their shoulders,
  the rod of their oppressor.
⁵Every warrior's boot used in battle
  and every garment rolled in blood
will be destined for burning,
  will be fuel for the fire.
⁶For to us a child is born,
  to us a son is given,
  and the government will be on his
    shoulders.
And he will be called
  Wonderful Counselor,*ᵇ* Mighty
    God,
  Everlasting Father, Prince of Peace.
⁷Of the increase of his government and
    peace
  there will be no end.
He will reign on David's throne
  and over his kingdom,
establishing and upholding it
  with justice and righteousness
  from that time on and forever.
The zeal of the LORD Almighty
  will accomplish this.

The LORD's Anger Against Israel

⁸The Lord has sent a message against
    Jacob;
  it will fall on Israel.
⁹All the people will know it—
  Ephraim and the inhabitants of
    Samaria—
who say with pride
  and arrogance of heart,
¹⁰"The bricks have fallen down,

but we will rebuild with dressed
    stone;
the fig trees have been felled,
  but we will replace them with
    cedars."
¹¹But the LORD has strengthened Rezin's
    foes against them
  and has spurred their enemies on.
¹²Arameans from the east and
    Philistines from the west
  have devoured Israel with open
    mouth.

Yet for all this, his anger is not turned
    away,
  his hand is still upraised.

¹³But the people have not returned to
    him who struck them,
  nor have they sought the LORD
    Almighty.
¹⁴So the LORD will cut off from Israel
    both head and tail,
  both palm branch and reed in a
    single day;
¹⁵the elders and prominent men are the
    head,
  the prophets who teach lies are the
    tail.
¹⁶Those who guide this people mislead
    them,
  and those who are guided are led
    astray.
¹⁷Therefore the Lord will take no
    pleasure in the young men,
  nor will he pity the fatherless and
    widows,
for everyone is ungodly and wicked,
  every mouth speaks vileness.

Yet for all this, his anger is not turned
    away,
  his hand is still upraised.

¹⁸Surely wickedness burns like a fire;
  it consumes briers and thorns,
it sets the forest thickets ablaze,
  so that it rolls upward in a column
    of smoke.
¹⁹By the wrath of the LORD Almighty
  the land will be scorched
and the people will be fuel for the
    fire;
  no one will spare his brother.
²⁰On the right they will devour,
  but still be hungry;
on the left they will eat,
  but not be satisfied.
Each will feed on the flesh of his own
    offspring*ᶜ*:

ᵃ2 Or *land of darkness*   *ᵇ6* Or *Wonderful, Counselor*   *ᶜ20* Or *arm*

21 Manasseh will feed on Ephraim, and
    Ephraim on Manasseh;
  together they will turn against
    Judah.

Yet for all this, his anger is not turned
    away,
  his hand is still upraised.

10 Woe to those who make unjust laws,
  to those who issue oppressive
    decrees,
²to deprive the poor of their rights
  and withhold justice from the
    oppressed of my people,
making widows their prey
  and robbing the fatherless.
³What will you do on the day of
    reckoning,
  when disaster comes from afar?
To whom will you run for help?
  Where will you leave your riches?
⁴Nothing will remain but to cringe
    among the captives
  or fall among the slain.

Yet for all this, his anger is not turned
    away,
  his hand is still upraised.

God's Judgment on Assyria

⁵"Woe to the Assyrian, the rod of my
    anger,
  in whose hand is the club of my
    wrath!
⁶I send him against a godless nation,
  I dispatch him against a people who
    anger me,
to seize loot and snatch plunder,
  and to trample them down like mud
    in the streets.
⁷But this is not what he intends,
  this is not what he has in mind;
his purpose is to destroy,
  to put an end to many nations.
⁸'Are not my commanders all kings?'
  he says.
⁹ 'Has not Calno fared like
    Carchemish?
Is not Hamath like Arpad,
  and Samaria like Damascus?
¹⁰As my hand seized the kingdoms of
    the idols,
  kingdoms whose images excelled
    those of Jerusalem and
    Samaria—
¹¹shall I not deal with Jerusalem and
    her images

as I dealt with Samaria and her
    idols?' "

¹²When the Lord has finished all his
work against Mount Zion and Jerusalem,
he will say, "I will punish the king of Assyria for the willful pride of his heart and
the haughty look in his eyes. ¹³For he
says:

" 'By the strength of my hand I have
    done this,
  and by my wisdom, because I have
    understanding.
I removed the boundaries of nations,
  I plundered their treasures;
  like a mighty one I subdued*ª* their
    kings.
¹⁴As one reaches into a nest,
  so my hand reached for the wealth
    of the nations;
as men gather abandoned eggs,
  so I gathered all the countries;
not one flapped a wing,
  or opened its mouth to chirp.' "

¹⁵Does the ax raise itself above him
    who swings it,
  or the saw boast against him who
    uses it?
As if a rod were to wield him who
    lifts it up,
  or a club brandish him who is not
    wood!
¹⁶Therefore, the Lord, the LORD
    Almighty,
  will send a wasting disease upon his
    sturdy warriors;
under his pomp a fire will be kindled
  like a blazing flame.
¹⁷The Light of Israel will become a fire,
  their Holy One a flame;
in a single day it will burn and
    consume
  his thorns and his briers.
¹⁸The splendor of his forests and fertile
    fields
  it will completely destroy,
  as when a sick man wastes away.
¹⁹And the remaining trees of his forests
    will be so few
  that a child could write them down.

The Remnant of Israel

²⁰In that day the remnant of Israel,
  the survivors of the house of Jacob,
will no longer rely on him
  who struck them down
but will truly rely on the LORD,

ª13 Or / I subdued the mighty,

the Holy One of Israel.
21A remnant will return,*a* a remnant of
      Jacob
   will return to the Mighty God.
22Though your people, O Israel, be like
      the sand by the sea,
   only a remnant will return.
Destruction has been decreed,
   overwhelming and righteous.
23The Lord, the LORD Almighty, will
      carry out
   the destruction decreed upon the
      whole land.

24Therefore, this is what the Lord, the
LORD Almighty, says:

"O my people who live in Zion,
   do not be afraid of the Assyrians,
who beat you with a rod
   and lift up a club against you, as
      Egypt did.
25Very soon my anger against you will
      end
   and my wrath will be directed to
      their destruction."
26The LORD Almighty will lash them
      with a whip,
   as when he struck down Midian at
      the rock of Oreb;
and he will raise his staff over the
      waters,
   as he did in Egypt.
27In that day their burden will be lifted
      from your shoulders,
   their yoke from your neck;
the yoke will be broken
   because you have grown so fat.*b*

28They enter Aiath;
   they pass through Migron;
   they store supplies at Micmash.
29They go over the pass, and say,
   "We will camp overnight at Geba."
Ramah trembles;
   Gibeah of Saul flees.
30Cry out, O Daughter of Gallim!
   Listen, O Laishah!
   Poor Anathoth!
31Madmenah is in flight;
   the people of Gebim take cover.
32This day they will halt at Nob;
   they will shake their fist
at the mount of the Daughter of Zion,
   at the hill of Jerusalem.

33See, the Lord, the LORD Almighty,

will lop off the boughs with great
      power.
The lofty trees will be felled,
   the tall ones will be brought low.
34He will cut down the forest thickets
      with an ax;
   Lebanon will fall before the Mighty
      One.

The Branch From Jesse

11 A shoot will come up from the
      stump of Jesse;
   from his roots a Branch will bear
      fruit.
2The Spirit of the LORD will rest on
      him—
   the Spirit of wisdom and of
      understanding,
   the Spirit of counsel and of power,
   the Spirit of knowledge and of the
      fear of the LORD—
3and he will delight in the fear of the
      LORD.

He will not judge by what he sees
      with his eyes,
   or decide by what he hears with his
      ears;
4but with righteousness he will judge
      the needy,
   with justice he will give decisions
      for the poor of the earth.
He will strike the earth with the rod of
      his mouth;
   with the breath of his lips he will
      slay the wicked.
5Righteousness will be his belt
   and faithfulness the sash around his
      waist.

6The wolf will live with the lamb,
   the leopard will lie down with the
      goat,
the calf and the lion and the
      yearling*c* together;
   and a little child will lead them.
7The cow will feed with the bear,
   their young will lie down together,
   and the lion will eat straw like the
      ox.
8The infant will play near the hole of
      the cobra,
   and the young child put his hand
      into the viper's nest.
9They will neither harm nor destroy
   on all my holy mountain,
for the earth will be full of the
   knowledge of the LORD

---

*a21 Hebrew shear-jashub; also in verse 22   b27 Hebrew; Septuagint broken / from your shoulders
c6 Hebrew; Septuagint lion will feed*

as the waters cover the sea.

¹⁰In that day the Root of Jesse will stand as a banner for the peoples; the nations will rally to him, and his place of rest will be glorious. ¹¹In that day the Lord will reach out his hand a second time to reclaim the remnant that is left of his people from Assyria, from Lower Egypt, from Upper Egypt,ᵃ from Cush,ᵇ from Elam, from Babylonia,ᶜ from Hamath and from the islands of the sea.

¹²He will raise a banner for the nations
  and gather the exiles of Israel;
he will assemble the scattered people
    of Judah
  from the four quarters of the earth.
¹³Ephraim's jealousy will vanish,
  and Judah's enemiesᵈ will be cut
    off;
Ephraim will not be jealous of Judah,
  nor Judah hostile toward Ephraim.
¹⁴They will swoop down on the slopes
    of Philistia to the west;
  together they will plunder the
    people to the east.
They will lay hands on Edom and
    Moab,
  and the Ammonites will be subject
    to them.
¹⁵The Lord will dry up
  the gulf of the Egyptian sea;
with a scorching wind he will sweep
    his hand
  over the Euphrates River.ᵉ
He will break it up into seven streams
  so that men can cross over in
    sandals.
¹⁶There will be a highway for the
    remnant of his people
  that is left from Assyria,
as there was for Israel
  when they came up from Egypt.

Songs of Praise

12 In that day you will say:

"I will praise you, O Lord.
  Although you were angry with me,
your anger has turned away
  and you have comforted me.
²Surely God is my salvation;
  I will trust and not be afraid.
The Lord, the Lord, is my strength
    and my song;
  he has become my salvation."
³With joy you will draw water

from the wells of salvation.

⁴In that day you will say:

"Give thanks to the Lord, call on his
    name;
  make known among the nations
    what he has done,
  and proclaim that his name is
    exalted.
⁵Sing to the Lord, for he has done
    glorious things;
  let this be known to all the world.
⁶Shout aloud and sing for joy, people
    of Zion,
  for great is the Holy One of Israel
    among you."

A Prophecy Against Babylon

13 An oracle concerning Babylon that Isaiah son of Amoz saw:

²Raise a banner on a bare hilltop,
  shout to them;
beckon to them
  to enter the gates of the nobles.
³I have commanded my holy ones;
  I have summoned my warriors to
    carry out my wrath—
  those who rejoice in my triumph.

⁴Listen, a noise on the mountains,
  like that of a great multitude!
Listen, an uproar among the
    kingdoms,
  like nations massing together!
The Lord Almighty is mustering
  an army for war.
⁵They come from faraway lands,
  from the ends of the heavens—
the Lord and the weapons of his
    wrath—
  to destroy the whole country.

⁶Wail, for the day of the Lord is near;
  it will come like destruction from
    the Almighty.ᶠ
⁷Because of this, all hands will go limp,
  every man's heart will melt.
⁸Terror will seize them,
  pain and anguish will grip them;
  they will writhe like a woman in
    labor.
They will look aghast at each other,
  their faces aflame.

⁹See, the day of the Lord is coming
  —a cruel day, with wrath and fierce
    anger—
to make the land desolate

ᵃ11 Hebrew *from Pathros*   ᵇ11 That is, the upper Nile region   ᶜ11 Hebrew *Shinar*   ᵈ13 Or *hostility*   ᵉ15 Hebrew *the River*   ᶠ6 Hebrew *Shaddai*

and destroy the sinners within it.
¹⁰The stars of heaven and their
        constellations
    will not show their light.
The rising sun will be darkened
    and the moon will not give its light.
¹¹I will punish the world for its evil,
    the wicked for their sins.
I will put an end to the arrogance of
        the haughty
    and will humble the pride of the
        ruthless.
¹²I will make man scarcer than pure
        gold, ·
    more rare than the gold of Ophir.
¹³Therefore I will make the heavens
        tremble;
    and the earth will shake from its
        place
at the wrath of the LORD Almighty,
    in the day of his burning anger.

¹⁴Like a hunted gazelle,
    like sheep without a shepherd,
each will return to his own people,
    each will flee to his native land.
¹⁵Whoever is captured will be thrust
        through;
    all who are caught will fall by the
        sword.
¹⁶Their infants will be dashed to pieces
        before their eyes;
    their houses will be looted and their
        wives ravished.

¹⁷See, I will stir up against them the
        Medes,
    who do not care for silver
    and have no delight in gold.
¹⁸Their bows will strike down the young
        men;
    they will have no mercy on infants
    nor will they look with compassion
        on children.
¹⁹Babylon, the jewel of kingdoms,
    the glory of the Babylonians'ᵃ
        pride,
will be overthrown by God
    like Sodom and Gomorrah.
²⁰She will never be inhabited
    or lived in through all generations;
no Arab will pitch his tent there,
    no shepherd will rest his flocks
        there.
²¹But desert creatures will lie there,
    jackals will fill her houses;
there the owls will dwell,

and there the wild goats will leap
        about.
²²Hyenas will howl in her strongholds,
    jackals in her luxurious palaces.
Her time is at hand,
    and her days will not be prolonged.

14 The LORD will have compassion
        on Jacob;
    once again he will choose Israel
    and will settle them in their own
        land.
Aliens will join them
    and unite with the house of Jacob.
²Nations will take them
    and bring them to their own place.
And the house of Israel will possess
        the nations
    as menservants and maidservants in
        the LORD's land.
They will make captives of their
        captors
    and rule over their oppressors.

³On the day the LORD gives you relief
from suffering and turmoil and cruel
bondage, ⁴you will take up this taunt
against the king of Babylon:

How the oppressor has come to an
        end!
    How his furyᵇ has ended!
⁵The LORD has broken the rod of the
        wicked,
    the scepter of the rulers,
⁶which in anger struck down peoples
        with unceasing blows,
    and in fury subdued nations
        with relentless aggression.
⁷All the lands are at rest and at peace;
    they break into singing.
⁸Even the pine trees and the cedars of
        Lebanon
    exult over you and say,
"Now that you have been laid low,
    no woodsman comes to cut us
        down."

⁹The graveᶜ below is all astir
    to meet you at your coming;
it rouses the spirits of the departed to
        greet you—
    all those who were leaders in the
        world;
it makes them rise from their
        thrones—
    all those who were kings over the
        nations.

ᵃ19 Or *Chaldeans'*   ᵇ4 Dead Sea Scrolls, Septuagint and Syriac; the meaning of the word in the
Masoretic Text is uncertain.   ᶜ9 Hebrew *Sheol*; also in verses 11 and 15

¹⁰They will all respond,
    they will say to you,
  "You also have become weak, as we
    are;
    you have become like us."
¹¹All your pomp has been brought
    down to the grave,
  along with the noise of your harps;
maggots are spread out beneath you
  and worms cover you.

¹²How you have fallen from heaven,
    O morning star, son of the dawn!
  You have been cast down to the earth,
    you who once laid low the nations!
¹³You said in your heart,
    "I will ascend to heaven;
  I will raise my throne
    above the stars of God;
  I will sit enthroned on the mount of
    assembly,
    on the utmost heights of the sacred
    mountain.ᵃ
¹⁴I will ascend above the tops of the
    clouds;
  I will make myself like the Most
    High."
¹⁵But you are brought down to the
    grave,
    to the depths of the pit.

¹⁶Those who see you stare at you,
    they ponder your fate:
  "Is this the man who shook the earth
    and made kingdoms tremble,
¹⁷the man who made the world a desert,
    who overthrew its cities
    and would not let his captives go
    home?"

¹⁸All the kings of the nations lie in
    state,
    each in his own tomb.
¹⁹But you are cast out of your tomb
    like a rejected branch;
  you are covered with the slain,
    with those pierced by the sword,
    those who descend to the stones of
    the pit.
  Like a corpse trampled underfoot,
²⁰ you will not join them in burial,
  for you have destroyed your land
    and killed your people.

  The offspring of the wicked
    will never be mentioned again.
²¹Prepare a place to slaughter his sons
    for the sins of their forefathers;
  they are not to rise to inherit the land

and cover the earth with their cities.

²²"I will rise up against them,"
    declares the LORD Almighty.
  "I will cut off from Babylon her name
    and survivors,
    her offspring and descendants,"
                declares the LORD.
²³"I will turn her into a place for owls
    and into swampland;
  I will sweep her with the broom of
    destruction,"
    declares the LORD Almighty.

A Prophecy Against Assyria

²⁴The LORD Almighty has sworn,

  "Surely, as I have planned, so it will
    be,
    and as I have purposed, so it will
    stand.
²⁵I will crush the Assyrian in my land;
    on my mountains I will trample him
    down.
  His yoke will be taken from my
    people,
    and his burden removed from their
    shoulders."

²⁶This is the plan determined for the
    whole world;
  this is the hand stretched out over
    all nations.
²⁷For the LORD Almighty has purposed,
    and who can thwart him?
  His hand is stretched out, and who
    can turn it back?

A Prophecy Against the Philistines

²⁸This oracle came in the year King
Ahaz died:

²⁹Do not rejoice, all you Philistines,
    that the rod that struck you is
    broken;
  from the root of that snake will spring
    up a viper,
    its fruit will be a darting, venomous
    serpent.
³⁰The poorest of the poor will find
    pasture,
    and the needy will lie down in
    safety.
  But your root I will destroy by famine;
    it will slay your survivors.

³¹Wail, O gate! Howl, O city!
    Melt away, all you Philistines!
  A cloud of smoke comes from the
    north,

ᵃ13 Or the north; Hebrew Zaphon

and there is not a straggler in its
ranks.
32What answer shall be given
to the envoys of that nation?
"The LORD has established Zion,
and in her his afflicted people will
find refuge."

A Prophecy Against Moab

15 An oracle concerning Moab:

Ar in Moab is ruined,
destroyed in a night!
Kir in Moab is ruined,
destroyed in a night!
2Dibon goes up to its temple,
to its high places to weep;
Moab wails over Nebo and Medeba.
Every head is shaved
and every beard cut off.
3In the streets they wear sackcloth;
on the roofs and in the public
squares
they all wail,
prostrate with weeping.
4Heshbon and Elealeh cry out,
their voices are heard all the way to
Jahaz.
Therefore the armed men of Moab cry
out,
and their hearts are faint.

5My heart cries out over Moab;
her fugitives flee as far as Zoar,
as far as Eglath Shelishiyah.
They go up the way to Luhith,
weeping as they go;
on the road to Horonaim
they lament their destruction.
6The waters of Nimrim are dried up
and the grass is withered;
the vegetation is gone
and nothing green is left.
7So the wealth they have acquired and
stored up
they carry away over the Ravine of
the Poplars.
8Their outcry echoes along the border
of Moab;
their wailing reaches as far as
Eglaim,
their lamentation as far as Beer
Elim.
9Dimon's*a* waters are full of blood,
but I will bring still more upon
Dimon*a*—
a lion upon the fugitives of Moab

and upon those who remain in the
land.

16 Send lambs as tribute
to the ruler of the land,
from Sela, across the desert,
to the mount of the Daughter of
Zion.
2Like fluttering birds
pushed from the nest,
so are the women of Moab
at the fords of the Arnon.

3"Give us counsel,
render a decision.
Make your shadow like night—
at high noon.
Hide the fugitives,
do not betray the refugees.
4Let the Moabite fugitives stay with
you;
be their shelter from the destroyer."

The oppressor will come to an end,
and destruction will cease;
the aggressor will vanish from the
land.
5In love a throne will be established;
in faithfulness a man will sit on it—
one from the house*b* of David—
one who in judging seeks justice
and speeds the cause of
righteousness.

6We have heard of Moab's pride—
her overweening pride and conceit,
her pride and her insolence—
but her boasts are empty.
7Therefore the Moabites wail,
they wail together for Moab.
Lament and grieve
for the men*c* of Kir Hareseth.
8The fields of Heshbon wither,
the vines of Sibmah also.
The rulers of the nations
have trampled down the choicest
vines,
which once reached Jazer
and spread toward the desert.
Their shoots spread out
and went as far as the sea.
9So I weep, as Jazer weeps,
for the vines of Sibmah.
O Heshbon, O Elealeh,
I drench you with tears!
The shouts of joy over your ripened
fruit

---

a9 Masoretic Text; Dead Sea Scrolls, some Septuagint manuscripts and Vulgate *Dibon*   *b5* Hebrew *tent*
c7 Or *"raisin cakes,"* a wordplay

and over your harvests have been
stilled.
10Joy and gladness are taken away from
the orchards;
no one sings or shouts in the
vineyards;
no one treads out wine at the presses,
for I have put an end to the
shouting.
11My heart laments for Moab like a
harp,
my inmost being for Kir Hareseth.
12When Moab appears at her high place,
she only wears herself out;
when she goes to her shrine to pray,
it is to no avail.

13This is the word the LORD has already
spoken concerning Moab. 14But now the
LORD says: "Within three years, as a servant bound by contract would count
them, Moab's splendor and all her many
people will be despised, and her survivors
will be very few and feeble."

An Oracle Against Damascus

17 An oracle concerning Damascus:

"See, Damascus will no longer be a city
but will become a heap of ruins.
2The cities of Aroer will be deserted
and left to flocks, which will lie
down,
with no one to make them afraid.
3The fortified city will disappear from
Ephraim,
and royal power from Damascus;
the remnant of Aram will be
like the glory of the Israelites,"
declares the LORD Almighty.

4"In that day the glory of Jacob will
fade;
the fat of his body will waste away.
5It will be as when a reaper gathers the
standing grain
and harvests the grain with his
arm—
as when a man gleans heads of grain
in the Valley of Rephaim.
6Yet some gleanings will remain,
as when an olive tree is beaten,
leaving two or three olives on the
topmost branches,
four or five on the fruitful boughs,"
declares the LORD, the God of Israel.

7In that day men will look to their
Maker
and turn their eyes to the Holy One
of Israel.
8They will not look to the altars,
the work of their hands,
and they will have no regard for the
Asherah poles[a]
and the incense altars their fingers
have made.

9In that day their strong cities, which
they left because of the Israelites, will be
like places abandoned to thickets and undergrowth. And all will be desolation.

10You have forgotten God your Savior;
you have not remembered the Rock,
your fortress.
Therefore, though you set out the
finest plants
and plant imported vines,
11though on the day you set them out,
you make them grow,
and on the morning when you plant
them, you bring them to bud,
yet the harvest will be as nothing
in the day of disease and incurable
pain.

12Oh, the raging of many nations—
they rage like the raging sea!
Oh, the uproar of the peoples—
they roar like the roaring of great
waters!
13Although the peoples roar like the
roar of surging waters,
when he rebukes them they flee far
away,
driven before the wind like chaff on
the hills,
like tumbleweed before a gale.
14In the evening, sudden terror!
Before the morning, they are gone!
This is the portion of those who loot
us,
the lot of those who plunder us.

A Prophecy Against Cush

18 Woe to the land of whirring
wings[b]
along the rivers of Cush,[c]
2which sends envoys by sea
in papyrus boats over the water.

Go, swift messengers,
to a people tall and smooth-skinned,
to a people feared far and wide,
an aggressive nation of strange
speech,
whose land is divided by rivers.

---

a8 That is, symbols of the goddess Asherah   b1 Or of locusts   c1 That is, the upper Nile region

[3]All you people of the world,
   you who live on the earth,
when a banner is raised on the
      mountains,
   you will see it,
and when a trumpet sounds,
   you will hear it.
[4]This is what the LORD says to me:
   "I will remain quiet and will look
      on from my dwelling place,
like shimmering heat in the sunshine,
   like a cloud of dew in the heat of
      harvest."
[5]For, before the harvest, when the
      blossom is gone
   and the flower becomes a ripening
      grape,
he will cut off the shoots with pruning
      knives,
   and cut down and take away the
      spreading branches.
[6]They will all be left to the mountain
      birds of prey
   and to the wild animals;
the birds will feed on them all
      summer,
   the wild animals all winter.

[7]At that time gifts will be brought to the
LORD Almighty

from a people tall and
      smooth-skinned,
   from a people feared far and wide,
an aggressive nation of strange
      speech,
   whose land is divided by rivers —

the gifts will be brought to Mount Zion,
the place of the Name of the LORD Almighty.

A Prophecy About Egypt

19

An oracle concerning Egypt:

See, the LORD rides on a swift cloud
   and is coming to Egypt.
The idols of Egypt tremble before him,
   and the hearts of the Egyptians melt
      within them.

[2]"I will stir up Egyptian against
      Egyptian —
   brother will fight against brother,
   neighbor against neighbor,
   city against city,
   kingdom against kingdom.
[3]The Egyptians will lose heart,
   and I will bring their plans to
      nothing;

they will consult the idols and the
      spirits of the dead,
   the mediums and the spiritists.
[4]I will hand the Egyptians over
   to the power of a cruel master,
and a fierce king will rule over them,"
   declares the Lord, the LORD
      Almighty.

[5]The waters of the river will dry up,
   and the riverbed will be parched
      and dry.
[6]The canals will stink;
   the streams of Egypt will dwindle
      and dry up.
The reeds and rushes will wither,
[7]   also the plants along the Nile,
   at the mouth of the river.
Every sown field along the Nile
   will become parched, will blow
      away and be no more.
[8]The fishermen will groan and lament,
   all who cast hooks into the Nile;
those who throw nets on the water
   will pine away.
[9]Those who work with combed flax
   will despair,
   the weavers of fine linen will lose
      hope.
[10]The workers in cloth will be dejected,
   and all the wage earners will be sick
      at heart.

[11]The officials of Zoan are nothing but
      fools;
   the wise counselors of Pharaoh give
      senseless advice.
How can you say to Pharaoh,
   "I am one of the wise men,
   a disciple of the ancient kings"?

[12]Where are your wise men now?
   Let them show you and make
      known
what the LORD Almighty
   has planned against Egypt.
[13]The officials of Zoan have become
      fools,
   the leaders of Memphis[a] are
      deceived;
the cornerstones of her peoples
   have led Egypt astray.
[14]The LORD has poured into them
   a spirit of dizziness;
they make Egypt stagger in all that
      she does,
   as a drunkard staggers around in
      his vomit.
[15]There is nothing Egypt can do —

---

a 13 Hebrew Noph

head or tail, palm branch or reed.

[16]In that day the Egyptians will be like women. They will shudder with fear at the uplifted hand that the LORD Almighty raises against them. [17]And the land of Judah will bring terror to the Egyptians; everyone to whom Judah is mentioned will be terrified, because of what the LORD Almighty is planning against them.

[18]In that day five cities in Egypt will speak the language of Canaan and swear allegiance to the LORD Almighty. One of them will be called the City of Destruction.[a]

[19]In that day there will be an altar to the LORD in the heart of Egypt, and a monument to the LORD at its border. [20]It will be a sign and witness to the LORD Almighty in the land of Egypt. When they cry out to the LORD because of their oppressors, he will send them a savior and defender, and he will rescue them. [21]So the LORD will make himself known to the Egyptians, and in that day they will acknowledge the LORD. They will worship with sacrifices and grain offerings; they will make vows to the LORD and keep them. [22]The LORD will strike Egypt with a plague; he will strike them and heal them. They will turn to the LORD, and he will respond to their pleas and heal them.

[23]In that day there will be a highway from Egypt to Assyria. The Assyrians will go to Egypt and the Egyptians to Assyria. The Egyptians and Assyrians will worship together. [24]In that day Israel will be the third, along with Egypt and Assyria, a blessing on the earth. [25]The LORD Almighty will bless them, saying, "Blessed be Egypt my people, Assyria my handiwork, and Israel my inheritance."

A Prophecy Against Egypt and Cush

20 In the year that the supreme commander, sent by Sargon king of Assyria, came to Ashdod and attacked and captured it — [2]at that time the LORD spoke through Isaiah son of Amoz. He said to him, "Take off the sackcloth from your body and the sandals from your feet." And he did so, going around stripped and barefoot.

[3]Then the LORD said, "Just as my servant Isaiah has gone stripped and barefoot for three years, as a sign and portent against Egypt and Cush,[b] [4]so the king of Assyria will lead away stripped and barefoot the Egyptian captives and Cushite exiles, young and old, with buttocks bared—to Egypt's shame. [5]Those who trusted in Cush and boasted in Egypt will be afraid and put to shame. [6]In that day the people who live on this coast will say, 'See what has happened to those we relied on, those we fled to for help and deliverance from the king of Assyria! How then can we escape?'"

A Prophecy Against Babylon

21 An oracle concerning the Desert by the Sea:

Like whirlwinds sweeping through the
  southland,
  an invader comes from the desert,
  from a land of terror.

[2]A dire vision has been shown to me:
  The traitor betrays, the looter takes
    loot.
  Elam, attack! Media, lay siege!
  I will bring to an end all the
    groaning she caused.

[3]At this my body is racked with pain,
  pangs seize me, like those of a
    woman in labor;
  I am staggered by what I hear,
  I am bewildered by what I see.
[4]My heart falters,
  fear makes me tremble;
  the twilight I longed for
  has become a horror to me.

[5]They set the tables,
  they spread the rugs,
  they eat, they drink!
  Get up, you officers,
  oil the shields!

[6]This is what the Lord says to me:

"Go, post a lookout
  and have him report what he sees.
[7]When he sees chariots
  with teams of horses,
  riders on donkeys
  or riders on camels,
  let him be alert,
  fully alert."

[8]And the lookout[c] shouted,

"Day after day, my lord, I stand on
  the watchtower;

---

[a]18 Most manuscripts of the Masoretic Text; some manuscripts of the Masoretic Text, Dead Sea Scrolls and Vulgate *City of the Sun* (that is, Heliopolis)   [b]3 That is, the upper Nile region; also in verse 5
[c]8 Dead Sea Scrolls and Syriac; Masoretic Text *A lion*

every night I stay at my post.
⁹Look, here comes a man in a chariot
    with a team of horses.
And he gives back the answer:
    'Babylon has fallen, has fallen!
All the images of its gods
    lie shattered on the ground!' "

¹⁰O my people, crushed on the
        threshing floor,
    I tell you what I have heard
from the LORD Almighty,
    from the God of Israel.

A Prophecy Against Edom

¹¹An oracle concerning Dumah ᵃ:

Someone calls to me from Seir,
    "Watchman, what is left of the
        night?
Watchman, what is left of the
        night?"
¹²The watchman replies,
    "Morning is coming, but also the
        night.
If you would ask, then ask;
    and come back yet again."

A Prophecy Against Arabia

¹³An oracle concerning Arabia:

You caravans of Dedanites,
    who camp in the thickets of Arabia,
¹⁴   bring water for the thirsty;
you who live in Tema,
    bring food for the fugitives.
¹⁵They flee from the sword,
    from the drawn sword,
from the bent bow
    and from the heat of battle.

¹⁶This is what the Lord says to me:
"Within one year, as a servant bound by
contract would count it, all the pomp of
Kedar will come to an end. ¹⁷The survivors of the bowmen, the warriors of Kedar, will be few." The LORD, the God of Israel, has spoken.

A Prophecy About Jerusalem

22 An oracle concerning the Valley of
        Vision:

What troubles you now,
    that you have all gone up on the
        roofs,
²O town full of commotion,
    O city of tumult and revelry?
Your slain were not killed by the
        sword,

nor did they die in battle.
³All your leaders have fled together;
    they have been captured without
        using the bow.
All you who were caught were taken
        prisoner together,
    having fled while the enemy was
        still far away.
⁴Therefore I said, "Turn away from me;
    let me weep bitterly.
Do not try to console me
    over the destruction of my people."

⁵The Lord, the LORD Almighty, has a day
    of tumult and trampling and terror
    in the Valley of Vision,
a day of battering down walls
    and of crying out to the mountains.
⁶Elam takes up the quiver,
    with her charioteers and horses;
    Kir uncovers the shield.
⁷Your choicest valleys are full of
        chariots,
    and horsemen are posted at the city
        gates;
⁸   the defenses of Judah are stripped
        away.

And you looked in that day
    to the weapons in the Palace of the
        Forest;
⁹you saw that the City of David
    had many breaches in its defenses;
you stored up water
    in the Lower Pool.
¹⁰You counted the buildings in
        Jerusalem
    and tore down houses to strengthen
        the wall.
¹¹You built a reservoir between the two
        walls
    for the water of the Old Pool,
but you did not look to the One who
        made it,
    or have regard for the One who
        planned it long ago.

¹²The Lord, the LORD Almighty,
    called you on that day
to weep and to wail,
    to tear out your hair and put on
        sackcloth.
¹³But see, there is joy and revelry,
    slaughtering of cattle and killing of
        sheep,
    eating of meat and drinking of
        wine!
"Let us eat and drink," you say,
    "for tomorrow we die!"

ᵃ11 *Dumah* means *silence* or *stillness*, a wordplay on *Edom*.

14The L ORD Almighty has revealed this in my hearing: "Till your dying day this sin will not be atoned for," says the Lord, the L ORD Almighty.

15This is what the Lord, the L ORD Almighty, says:

"Go, say to this steward,
    to Shebna, who is in charge of the palace:
16What are you doing here and who gave you permission
    to cut out a grave for yourself here,
hewing your grave on the height
    and chiseling your resting place in the rock?

17"Beware, the L ORD is about to take firm hold of you
    and hurl you away, O you mighty man.
18He will roll you up tightly like a ball
    and throw you into a large country.
There you will die
    and there your splendid chariots will remain—
    you disgrace to your master's house!
19I will depose you from your office,
    and you will be ousted from your position.

20"In that day I will summon my servant, Eliakim son of Hilkiah. **21**I will clothe him with your robe and fasten your sash around him and hand your authority over to him. He will be a father to those who live in Jerusalem and to the house of Judah. **22**I will place on his shoulder the key to the house of David; what he opens no one can shut, and what he shuts no one can open. **23**I will drive him like a peg into a firm place; he will be a seat[a] of honor for the house of his father. **24**All the glory of his family will hang on him: its offspring and offshoots—all its lesser vessels, from the bowls to all the jars.

25"In that day," declares the L ORD Almighty, "the peg driven into the firm place will give way; it will be sheared off and will fall, and the load hanging on it will be cut down." The L ORD has spoken.

A Prophecy About Tyre

23 An oracle concerning Tyre:

Wail, O ships of Tarshish!
    For Tyre is destroyed
    and left without house or harbor.
From the land of Cyprus[b]
    word has come to them.

2Be silent, you people of the island
    and you merchants of Sidon,
    whom the seafarers have enriched.
3On the great waters
    came the grain of the Shihor;
the harvest of the Nile[c] was the revenue of Tyre,
    and she became the marketplace of the nations.

4Be ashamed, O Sidon, and you,
    O fortress of the sea,
for the sea has spoken:
"I have neither been in labor nor given birth;
    I have neither reared sons nor brought up daughters."
5When word comes to Egypt,
    they will be in anguish at the report from Tyre.

6Cross over to Tarshish;
    wail, you people of the island.
7Is this your city of revelry,
    the old, old city,
whose feet have taken her
    to settle in far-off lands?
8Who planned this against Tyre,
    the bestower of crowns,
whose merchants are princes,
    whose traders are renowned in the earth?
9The L ORD Almighty planned it,
    to bring low the pride of all glory
    and to humble all who are renowned on the earth.

10Till[d] your land as along the Nile,
    O Daughter of Tarshish,
    for you no longer have a harbor.
11The L ORD has stretched out his hand over the sea
    and made its kingdoms tremble.
He has given an order concerning Phoenicia[e]
    that her fortresses be destroyed.
12He said, "No more of your reveling,

---

a23 Or *throne*   *b1* Hebrew *Kittim*   *c2,3* Masoretic Text; one Dead Sea Scroll *Sidon, / who cross over the sea; / your envoys* *3are on the great waters. / The grain of the Shihor, / the harvest of the Nile,* *d10* Dead Sea Scrolls and some Septuagint manuscripts; Masoretic Text *Go through*   *e11* Hebrew *Canaan*

O Virgin Daughter of Sidon, now
   crushed!

"Up, cross over to Cyprus[a];
   even there you will find no rest."
[13]Look at the land of the Babylonians,[b]
   this people that is now of no
      account!
The Assyrians have made it
   a place for desert creatures;
they raised up their siege towers,
   they stripped its fortresses bare
   and turned it into a ruin.

[14]Wail, you ships of Tarshish;
   your fortress is destroyed!

[15]At that time Tyre will be forgotten for
seventy years, the span of a king's life. But
at the end of these seventy years, it will
happen to Tyre as in the song of the prostitute:

[16]"Take up a harp, walk through the
      city,
   O prostitute forgotten;
play the harp well, sing many a song,
   so that you will be remembered."

[17]At the end of seventy years, the LORD
will deal with Tyre. She will return to her
hire as a prostitute and will ply her trade
with all the kingdoms on the face of the
earth. [18]Yet her profit and her earnings
will be set apart for the LORD; they will not
be stored up or hoarded. Her profits will
go to those who live before the LORD, for
abundant food and fine clothes.

The LORD's Devastation of the Earth

24 See, the LORD is going to lay
      waste the earth
   and devastate it;
he will ruin its face
   and scatter its inhabitants—
[2]it will be the same
   for priest as for people,
   for master as for servant,
   for mistress as for maid,
   for seller as for buyer,
   for borrower as for lender,
   for debtor as for creditor.
[3]The earth will be completely laid
      waste
   and totally plundered.
      The LORD has spoken this word.

[4]The earth dries up and withers,
   the world languishes and withers,
   the exalted of the earth languish.
[5]The earth is defiled by its people;

they have disobeyed the laws,
violated the statutes
   and broken the everlasting
      covenant.
[6]Therefore a curse consumes the earth;
   its people must bear their guilt.
Therefore earth's inhabitants are
      burned up,
   and very few are left.
[7]The new wine dries up and the vine
      withers;
   all the merrymakers groan.
[8]The gaiety of the tambourines is
      stilled,
   the noise of the revelers has
      stopped,
   the joyful harp is silent.
[9]No longer do they drink wine with a
      song;
   the beer is bitter to its drinkers.
[10]The ruined city lies desolate;
   the entrance to every house is
      barred.
[11]In the streets they cry out for wine;
   all joy turns to gloom,
   all gaiety is banished from the
      earth.
[12]The city is left in ruins,
   its gate is battered to pieces.
[13]So will it be on the earth
   and among the nations,
as when an olive tree is beaten,
   or as when gleanings are left after
      the grape harvest.

[14]They raise their voices, they shout for
      joy;
   from the west they acclaim the
      LORD's majesty.
[15]Therefore in the east give glory to the
      LORD;
   exalt the name of the LORD, the God
      of Israel,
   in the islands of the sea.
[16]From the ends of the earth we hear
      singing:
   "Glory to the Righteous One."

But I said, "I waste away, I waste
      away!
   Woe to me!
The treacherous betray!
   With treachery the treacherous
      betray!"
[17]Terror and pit and snare await you,
   O people of the earth.
[18]Whoever flees at the sound of terror
   will fall into a pit;
whoever climbs out of the pit

will be caught in a snare.

The floodgates of the heavens are
    opened,
  the foundations of the earth shake.
¹⁹The earth is broken up,
    the earth is split asunder,
    the earth is thoroughly shaken.
²⁰The earth reels like a drunkard,
    it sways like a hut in the wind;
  so heavy upon it is the guilt of its
    rebellion
    that it falls—never to rise again.

²¹In that day the LORD will punish
    the powers in the heavens above
    and the kings on the earth below.
²²They will be herded together
    like prisoners bound in a dungeon;
  they will be shut up in prison
    and be punished*a* after many days.
²³The moon will be abashed, the sun
    ashamed;
  for the LORD Almighty will reign
  on Mount Zion and in Jerusalem,
    and before its elders, gloriously.

Praise to the LORD

25 O LORD, you are my God;
    I will exalt you and praise your
    name,
  for in perfect faithfulness
  you have done marvelous things,
    things planned long ago.
²You have made the city a heap of
    rubble,
    the fortified town a ruin,
  the foreigners' stronghold a city no
    more;
    it will never be rebuilt.
³Therefore strong peoples will honor
    you;
  cities of ruthless nations will revere
    you.
⁴You have been a refuge for the poor,
    a refuge for the needy in his
    distress,
  a shelter from the storm
    and a shade from the heat.
For the breath of the ruthless
    is like a storm driving against a wall
⁵   and like the heat of the desert.
You silence the uproar of foreigners;
    as heat is reduced by the shadow of
    a cloud,
  so the song of the ruthless is stilled.

⁶On this mountain the LORD Almighty
  will prepare

a feast of rich food for all peoples,
  a banquet of aged wine—
    the best of meats and the finest of
    wines.
⁷On this mountain he will destroy
    the shroud that enfolds all peoples,
  the sheet that covers all nations;
⁸   he will swallow up death forever.
The Sovereign LORD will wipe away
    the tears
  from all faces;
  he will remove the disgrace of his
    people
  from all the earth.
          The LORD has spoken.

⁹In that day they will say,

"Surely this is our God;
  we trusted in him, and he saved us.
This is the LORD, we trusted in him;
  let us rejoice and be glad in his
    salvation."

¹⁰The hand of the LORD will rest on this
    mountain;
  but Moab will be trampled under
    him
  as straw is trampled down in the
    manure.
¹¹They will spread out their hands in it,
    as a swimmer spreads out his hands
    to swim.
God will bring down their pride
  despite the cleverness*b* of their
    hands.
¹²He will bring down your high fortified
    walls
    and lay them low;
  he will bring them down to the
    ground,
    to the very dust.

A Song of Praise

26 In that day this song will be sung in
  the land of Judah:

We have a strong city;
  God makes salvation
    its walls and ramparts.
²Open the gates
  that the righteous nation may enter,
    the nation that keeps faith.
³You will keep in perfect peace
  him whose mind is steadfast,
    because he trusts in you.
⁴Trust in the LORD forever,
  for the LORD, the LORD, is the Rock
    eternal.
⁵He humbles those who dwell on high,

---

a22 Or *released*   *b11* The meaning of the Hebrew for this word is uncertain.

he lays the lofty city low;
he levels it to the ground
and casts it down to the dust.
⁶Feet trample it down—
the feet of the oppressed,
the footsteps of the poor.

⁷The path of the righteous is level;
O upright One, you make the way
of the righteous smooth.
⁸Yes, LORD, walking in the way of your
laws,ᵃ
we wait for you;
your name and renown
are the desire of our hearts.
⁹My soul yearns for you in the night;
in the morning my spirit longs for
you.
When your judgments come upon the
earth,
the people of the world learn
righteousness.
¹⁰Though grace is shown to the wicked,
they do not learn righteousness;
even in a land of uprightness they go
on doing evil
and regard not the majesty of the
LORD.
¹¹O LORD, your hand is lifted high,
but they do not see it.
Let them see your zeal for your
people and be put to shame;
let the fire reserved for your
enemies consume them.

¹²LORD, you establish peace for us;
all that we have accomplished you
have done for us.
¹³O LORD, our God, other lords besides
you have ruled over us,
but your name alone do we honor.
¹⁴They are now dead, they live no
more;
those departed spirits do not rise.
You punished them and brought them
to ruin;
you wiped out all memory of them.
¹⁵You have enlarged the nation, O LORD;
you have enlarged the nation.
You have gained glory for yourself;
you have extended all the borders
of the land.

¹⁶LORD, they came to you in their
distress;
when you disciplined them,
they could barely whisper a
prayer.ᵇ

¹⁷As a woman with child and about to
give birth
writhes and cries out in her pain,
so were we in your presence,
O LORD.
¹⁸We were with child, we writhed in
pain,
but we gave birth to wind.
We have not brought salvation to the
earth;
we have not given birth to people of
the world.

¹⁹But your dead will live;
their bodies will rise.
You who dwell in the dust,
wake up and shout for joy.
Your dew is like the dew of the
morning;
the earth will give birth to her dead.

²⁰Go, my people, enter your rooms
and shut the doors behind you;
hide yourselves for a little while
until his wrath has passed by.
²¹See, the LORD is coming out of his
dwelling
to punish the people of the earth for
their sins.
The earth will disclose the blood shed
upon her;
she will conceal her slain no longer.

Deliverance of Israel

27 In that day,

the LORD will punish with his sword,
his fierce, great and powerful sword,
Leviathan the gliding serpent,
Leviathan the coiling serpent;
he will slay the monster of the sea.

²In that day—

"Sing about a fruitful vineyard:
³ I, the LORD, watch over it;
I water it continually.
I guard it day and night
so that no one may harm it.
⁴ I am not angry.
If only there were briers and thorns
confronting me!
I would march against them in
battle;
I would set them all on fire.
⁵Or else let them come to me for
refuge;
let them make peace with me,
yes, let them make peace with me."

ᵃ8 Or *judgments*   ᵇ16 The meaning of the Hebrew for this clause is uncertain.

⁶In days to come Jacob will take root,
    Israel will bud and blossom
    and fill all the world with fruit.

⁷Has ˌthe LORDˌ struck her
    as he struck down those who struck
        her?
  Has she been killed
    as those were killed who killed her?
⁸By warfare*ᵃ* and exile you contend
        with her—
    with his fierce blast he drives her
        out,
    as on a day the east wind blows.
⁹By this, then, will Jacob's guilt be
        atoned for,
    and this will be the full fruitage of
        the removal of his sin:
When he makes all the altar stones
    to be like chalk stones crushed to
        pieces,
    no Asherah poles*ᵇ* or incense altars
    will be left standing.
¹⁰The fortified city stands desolate,
    an abandoned settlement, forsaken
        like the desert;
  there the calves graze,
    there they lie down;
    they strip its branches bare.
¹¹When its twigs are dry, they are
        broken off
    and women come and make fires
        with them.
For this is a people without
        understanding;
    so their Maker has no compassion
        on them,
    and their Creator shows them no
        favor.

¹²In that day the LORD will thresh from
the flowing Euphrates*ᶜ* to the Wadi of
Egypt, and you, O Israelites, will be gathered up one by one. ¹³And in that day a
great trumpet will sound. Those who were
perishing in Assyria and those who were
exiled in Egypt will come and worship the
LORD on the holy mountain in Jerusalem.

Woe to Ephraim

28 Woe to that wreath, the pride of
        Ephraim's drunkards,
    to the fading flower, his glorious
        beauty,
  set on the head of a fertile valley—
    to that city, the pride of those laid
        low by wine!

²See, the Lord has one who is powerful
        and strong.
  Like a hailstorm and a destructive
        wind,
  like a driving rain and a flooding
        downpour,
    he will throw it forcefully to the
        ground.
³That wreath, the pride of Ephraim's
        drunkards,
    will be trampled underfoot.
⁴That fading flower, his glorious
        beauty,
    set on the head of a fertile valley,
  will be like a fig ripe before harvest—
    as soon as someone sees it and
        takes it in his hand,
    he swallows it.

⁵In that day the LORD Almighty
    will be a glorious crown,
  a beautiful wreath
    for the remnant of his people.
⁶He will be a spirit of justice
    to him who sits in judgment,
  a source of strength
    to those who turn back the battle at
        the gate.

⁷And these also stagger from wine
    and reel from beer:
  Priests and prophets stagger from beer
    and are befuddled with wine;
  they reel from beer,
    they stagger when seeing visions,
    they stumble when rendering
        decisions.
⁸All the tables are covered with vomit
    and there is not a spot without filth.

⁹"Who is it he is trying to teach?
    To whom is he explaining his
        message?
  To children weaned from their milk,
    to those just taken from the breast?
¹⁰For it is:
    Do and do, do and do,
    rule on rule, rule on rule*ᵈ*;
    a little here, a little there."

¹¹Very well then, with foreign lips and
        strange tongues
    God will speak to this people,
¹²to whom he said,
    "This is the resting place, let the
        weary rest";
  and, "This is the place of repose"—
    but they would not listen.

ᵃ8 See Septuagint; the meaning of the Hebrew for this word is uncertain.   *ᵇ9* That is, symbols of the
goddess Asherah   *ᶜ12* Hebrew *River*   *ᵈ10* Hebrew / *sav lasav sav lasav / kav lakav kav lakav*
(possibly meaningless sounds; perhaps a mimicking of the prophet's words); also in verse 13

¹³So then, the word of the LORD to them
      will become:
   Do and do, do and do,
   rule on rule, rule on rule;
   a little here, a little there —
so that they will go and fall backward,
   be injured and snared and captured.

¹⁴Therefore hear the word of the LORD,
      you scoffers
   who rule this people in Jerusalem.
¹⁵You boast, "We have entered into a
      covenant with death,
   with the grave[a] we have made an
      agreement.
When an overwhelming scourge
      sweeps by,
   it cannot touch us,
for we have made a lie our refuge
   and falsehood[b] our hiding place."

¹⁶So this is what the Sovereign LORD
says:

   "See, I lay a stone in Zion,
   a tested stone,
a precious cornerstone for a sure
      foundation;
   the one who trusts will never be
      dismayed.
¹⁷I will make justice the measuring line
   and righteousness the plumb line;
hail will sweep away your refuge, the
      lie,
   and water will overflow your hiding
      place.
¹⁸Your covenant with death will be
      annulled;
   your agreement with the grave will
      not stand.
When the overwhelming scourge
      sweeps by,
   you will be beaten down by it.
¹⁹As often as it comes it will carry you
      away;
   morning after morning, by day and
      by night,
   it will sweep through."

The understanding of this message
   will bring sheer terror.
²⁰The bed is too short to stretch out on,
   the blanket too narrow to wrap
      around you.
²¹The LORD will rise up as he did at
      Mount Perazim,
   he will rouse himself as in the
      Valley of Gibeon —
to do his work, his strange work,

and perform his task, his alien task.
²²Now stop your mocking,
   or your chains will become heavier;
the Lord, the LORD Almighty, has told
      me
   of the destruction decreed against
      the whole land.

²³Listen and hear my voice;
   pay attention and hear what I say.
²⁴When a farmer plows for planting,
   does he plow continually?
Does he keep on breaking up and
      harrowing the soil?
²⁵When he has leveled the surface,
   does he not sow caraway and
      scatter cummin?
Does he not plant wheat in its place,[c]
   barley in its plot,[c]
   and spelt in its field?
²⁶His God instructs him
   and teaches him the right way.

²⁷Caraway is not threshed with a sledge,
   nor is a cartwheel rolled over
      cummin;
caraway is beaten out with a rod,
   and cummin with a stick.
²⁸Grain must be ground to make bread;
   so one does not go on threshing it
      forever.
Though he drives the wheels of his
      threshing cart over it,
   his horses do not grind it.
²⁹All this also comes from the LORD
      Almighty,
   wonderful in counsel and
      magnificent in wisdom.

Woe to David's City

29 Woe to you, Ariel, Ariel,
   the city where David settled!
Add year to year
   and let your cycle of festivals go on.
²Yet I will besiege Ariel;
   she will mourn and lament,
   she will be to me like an altar
      hearth.[d]
³I will encamp against you all around;
   I will encircle you with towers
   and set up my siege works against
      you.
⁴Brought low, you will speak from the
      ground;
   your speech will mumble out of the
      dust.
Your voice will come ghostlike from
      the earth;

out of the dust your speech will
  whisper.

⁵But your many enemies will become
    like fine dust,
  the ruthless hordes like blown chaff.
Suddenly, in an instant,
⁶ the LORD Almighty will come
with thunder and earthquake and
    great noise,
  with windstorm and tempest and
    flames of a devouring fire.
⁷Then the hordes of all the nations that
    fight against Ariel,
  that attack her and her fortress and
    besiege her,
will be as it is with a dream,
  with a vision in the night—
⁸as when a hungry man dreams that he
    is eating,
  but he awakens, and his hunger
    remains;
as when a thirsty man dreams that he
    is drinking,
  but he awakens faint, with his thirst
    unquenched.
So will it be with the hordes of all the
    nations
  that fight against Mount Zion.

⁹Be stunned and amazed,
  blind yourselves and be sightless;
be drunk, but not from wine,
  stagger, but not from beer.
¹⁰The LORD has brought over you a deep
    sleep:
  He has sealed your eyes (the
    prophets);
  he has covered your heads (the
    seers).

¹¹For you this whole vision is nothing
but words sealed in a scroll. And if you
give the scroll to someone who can read,
and say to him, "Read this, please," he will
answer, "I can't; it is sealed." ¹²Or if you
give the scroll to someone who cannot
read, and say, "Read this, please," he will
answer, "I don't know how to read."

¹³The Lord says:

"These people come near to me with
    their mouth
  and honor me with their lips,
  but their hearts are far from me.
Their worship of me
  is made up only of rules taught by
    men.ᵃ

¹⁴Therefore once more I will astound
    these people
  with wonder upon wonder;
the wisdom of the wise will perish,
  the intelligence of the intelligent
    will vanish."
¹⁵Woe to those who go to great depths
    to hide their plans from the LORD,
who do their work in darkness and
    think,
  "Who sees us? Who will know?"
¹⁶You turn things upside down,
  as if the potter were thought to be
    like the clay!
Shall what is formed say to him who
    formed it,
  "He did not make me"?
Can the pot say of the potter,
  "He knows nothing"?

¹⁷In a very short time, will not Lebanon
    be turned into a fertile field
  and the fertile field seem like a
    forest?
¹⁸In that day the deaf will hear the
    words of the scroll,
  and out of gloom and darkness
  the eyes of the blind will see.
¹⁹Once more the humble will rejoice in
    the LORD;
  the needy will rejoice in the Holy
    One of Israel.
²⁰The ruthless will vanish,
  the mockers will disappear,
  and all who have an eye for evil
    will be cut down—
²¹those who with a word make a man
    out to be guilty,
  who ensnare the defender in court
  and with false testimony deprive the
    innocent of justice.

²²Therefore this is what the LORD, who
redeemed Abraham, says to the house of
Jacob:

"No longer will Jacob be ashamed;
  no longer will their faces grow pale.
²³When they see among them their
    children,
  the work of my hands,
they will keep my name holy;
  they will acknowledge the holiness
    of the Holy One of Jacob,
  and will stand in awe of the God of
    Israel.
²⁴Those who are wayward in spirit will
    gain understanding;

ᵃ13 Hebrew; Septuagint *They worship me in vain; / their teachings are but rules taught by men*

those who complain will accept
    instruction."

Woe to the Obstinate Nation

30 "Woe to the obstinate children,"
    declares the LORD,
"to those who carry out plans that are
        not mine,
    forming an alliance, but not by my
        Spirit,
    heaping sin upon sin;
²who go down to Egypt
    without consulting me;
who look for help to Pharaoh's
        protection,
    to Egypt's shade for refuge.
³But Pharaoh's protection will be to
        your shame,
    Egypt's shade will bring you
        disgrace.
⁴Though they have officials in Zoan
    and their envoys have arrived in
        Hanes,
⁵everyone will be put to shame
    because of a people useless to them,
who bring neither help nor advantage,
    but only shame and disgrace."

⁶An oracle concerning the animals of
the Negev:

Through a land of hardship and
        distress,
    of lions and lionesses,
    of adders and darting snakes,
the envoys carry their riches on
        donkeys' backs,
    their treasures on the humps of
        camels,
to that unprofitable nation,
⁷   to Egypt, whose help is utterly
        useless.
Therefore I call her
    Rahab the Do-Nothing.

⁸Go now, write it on a tablet for them,
    inscribe it on a scroll,
that for the days to come
    it may be an everlasting witness.
⁹These are rebellious people, deceitful
        children,
    children unwilling to listen to the
        LORD's instruction.
¹⁰They say to the seers,
    "See no more visions!"
and to the prophets,
    "Give us no more visions of what is
        right!
Tell us pleasant things,
    prophesy illusions.
¹¹Leave this way,

get off this path,
    and stop confronting us
    with the Holy One of Israel!"

¹²Therefore, this is what the Holy One
of Israel says:

"Because you have rejected this
        message,
    relied on oppression
    and depended on deceit,
¹³this sin will become for you
    like a high wall, cracked and
        bulging,
    that collapses suddenly, in an
        instant.
¹⁴It will break in pieces like pottery,
    shattered so mercilessly
that among its pieces not a fragment
        will be found
    for taking coals from a hearth
    or scooping water out of a cistern."

¹⁵This is what the Sovereign LORD, the
Holy One of Israel, says:

"In repentance and rest is your
        salvation,
    in quietness and trust is your
        strength,
    but you would have none of it.
¹⁶You said, 'No, we will flee on horses.'
    Therefore you will flee!
You said, 'We will ride off on swift
        horses.'
    Therefore your pursuers will be
        swift!
¹⁷A thousand will flee
    at the threat of one;
at the threat of five
    you will all flee away,
till you are left
    like a flagstaff on a mountaintop,
    like a banner on a hill."

¹⁸Yet the LORD longs to be gracious to
        you;
    he rises to show you compassion.
For the LORD is a God of justice.
    Blessed are all who wait for him!

¹⁹O people of Zion, who live in Jerusalem, you will weep no more. How gracious he will be when you cry for help! As
soon as he hears, he will answer you. ²⁰Al-
though the Lord gives you the bread of adversity and the water of affliction, your
teachers will be hidden no more; with
your own eyes you will see them.
²¹Whether you turn to the right or to the
left, your ears will hear a voice behind
you, saying, "This is the way; walk in it."
²²Then you will defile your idols overlaid

with silver and your images covered with gold; you will throw them away like a menstrual cloth and say to them, "Away with you!"

²³He will also send you rain for the seed you sow in the ground, and the food that comes from the land will be rich and plentiful. In that day your cattle will graze in broad meadows. ²⁴The oxen and donkeys that work the soil will eat fodder and mash, spread out with fork and shovel. ²⁵In the day of great slaughter, when the towers fall, streams of water will flow on every high mountain and every lofty hill. ²⁶The moon will shine like the sun, and the sunlight will be seven times brighter, like the light of seven full days, when the LORD binds up the bruises of his people and heals the wounds he inflicted.

²⁷See, the Name of the LORD comes
    from afar,
with burning anger and dense
    clouds of smoke;
his lips are full of wrath,
    and his tongue is a consuming fire.
²⁸His breath is like a rushing torrent,

WEDNESDAY

VERSE FOR THE DAY:	AUTHOR:	PASSAGE FOR THE DAY:
Isaiah 30:15	Archibald Hart	Isaiah 30:15–18

Traveling by Camel

[ONCE] I was scheduled to speak at a conference in Chicago. I went to my office on a Friday morning, saw three patients, drove to Los Angeles International Airport, flew to Chicago, and got there in time to address an evening meeting. I spoke three times on Saturday and twice on Sunday, then flew back to Los Angeles in time to get to bed. The next morning I went to work as usual.

Such hectic, "rush about" activity takes a heavy stress toll on one's body. And needless to say, four days later I came down with a severe influenza attack—attributable, I believe, to a case of overextension and overstress. My immune system had simply given out.

You see, God designed my body for camel travel and I keep putting it in subsonic jets! Camel travel allows plenty of time for rest. Subsonic flying keeps me tensed and stressed.

Now, I am *not* saying that we should give up flying in jets! I thank God for them every day that I travel. But I am saying we need to recognize that the human frame has its limits, and that we should build in adequate rest and recovery time so as to allow healing and restoration to take place.

This is the problem: People in a hurry never have time for recovery. Their minds have little time to meditate and pray so that problems can be put in perspective. In short, people in our age are showing signs of physiological disintegration because we are living at a pace that is too fast for our bodies. *This is the essence of the stress problem.*

Additional Scripture Readings:
Matthew 11:28–30; Mark 6:30–34

Go to page 749 for your next devotional reading.

rising up to the neck.
He shakes the nations in the sieve of
destruction;
    he places in the jaws of the peoples
    a bit that leads them astray.
29And you will sing
    as on the night you celebrate a holy
    festival;
your hearts will rejoice
    as when people go up with flutes
to the mountain of the LORD,
    to the Rock of Israel.
30The LORD will cause men to hear his
    majestic voice
and will make them see his arm
    coming down
with raging anger and consuming fire,
    with cloudburst, thunderstorm and
    hail.
31The voice of the LORD will shatter
    Assyria;
    with his scepter he will strike them
    down.
32Every stroke the LORD lays on them
    with his punishing rod
will be to the music of tambourines
    and harps,
    as he fights them in battle with the
    blows of his arm.
33Topheth has long been prepared;
    it has been made ready for the king.
Its fire pit has been made deep and
    wide,
    with an abundance of fire and
    wood;
the breath of the LORD,
    like a stream of burning sulfur,
    sets it ablaze.

Woe to Those Who Rely on Egypt

31 Woe to those who go down to
Egypt for help,
who rely on horses,
who trust in the multitude of their
    chariots
    and in the great strength of their
    horsemen,
but do not look to the Holy One of
    Israel,
    or seek help from the LORD.
2Yet he too is wise and can bring
    disaster;
    he does not take back his words.
He will rise up against the house of
    the wicked,
    against those who help evildoers.
3But the Egyptians are men and not
    God;
    their horses are flesh and not spirit.
When the LORD stretches out his hand,

he who helps will stumble,
    he who is helped will fall;
    both will perish together.

4This is what the LORD says to me:

"As a lion growls,
    a great lion over his prey—
and though a whole band of
    shepherds
    is called together against him,
he is not frightened by their shouts
    or disturbed by their clamor—
so the LORD Almighty will come down
    to do battle on Mount Zion and on
    its heights.
5Like birds hovering overhead,
    the LORD Almighty will shield
    Jerusalem;
he will shield it and deliver it,
    he will 'pass over' it and will rescue
    it."

6Return to him you have so greatly revolted against, O Israelites. **7**For in that
day every one of you will reject the idols
of silver and gold your sinful hands have
made.

8"Assyria will fall by a sword that is
    not of man;
    a sword, not of mortals, will devour
    them.
They will flee before the sword
    and their young men will be put to
    forced labor.
9Their stronghold will fall because of
    terror;
    at sight of the battle standard their
    commanders will panic,"
declares the LORD,
    whose fire is in Zion,
    whose furnace is in Jerusalem.

The Kingdom of Righteousness

32 See, a king will reign in
righteousness
and rulers will rule with justice.
2Each man will be like a shelter from
    the wind
    and a refuge from the storm,
like streams of water in the desert
    and the shadow of a great rock in a
    thirsty land.

3Then the eyes of those who see will
    no longer be closed,
    and the ears of those who hear will
    listen.
4The mind of the rash will know and
    understand,

and the stammering tongue will be
    fluent and clear.
⁵No longer will the fool be called noble
    nor the scoundrel be highly
    respected.
⁶For the fool speaks folly,
    his mind is busy with evil:
He practices ungodliness
    and spreads error concerning the
    LORD;
the hungry he leaves empty
    and from the thirsty he withholds
    water.
⁷The scoundrel's methods are wicked,
    he makes up evil schemes
to destroy the poor with lies,
    even when the plea of the needy is
    just.
⁸But the noble man makes noble plans,
    and by noble deeds he stands.

The Women of Jerusalem

⁹You women who are so complacent,
    rise up and listen to me;
you daughters who feel secure,
    hear what I have to say!
¹⁰In little more than a year
    you who feel secure will tremble;
the grape harvest will fail,
    and the harvest of fruit will not
    come.
¹¹Tremble, you complacent women;
    shudder, you daughters who feel
    secure!
Strip off your clothes,
    put sackcloth around your waists.
¹²Beat your breasts for the pleasant
    fields,
    for the fruitful vines
¹³and for the land of my people,
    a land overgrown with thorns and
    briers—
yes, mourn for all houses of
    merriment
    and for this city of revelry.
¹⁴The fortress will be abandoned,
    the noisy city deserted;
citadel and watchtower will become a
    wasteland forever,
    the delight of donkeys, a pasture for
    flocks,
¹⁵till the Spirit is poured upon us from
    on high,
    and the desert becomes a fertile
    field,
    and the fertile field seems like a
    forest.
¹⁶Justice will dwell in the desert

and righteousness live in the fertile
    field.
¹⁷The fruit of righteousness will be
    peace;
    the effect of righteousness will be
    quietness and confidence
    forever.
¹⁸My people will live in peaceful
    dwelling places,
    in secure homes,
    in undisturbed places of rest.
¹⁹Though hail flattens the forest
    and the city is leveled completely,
²⁰how blessed you will be,
    sowing your seed by every stream,
    and letting your cattle and donkeys
    range free.

Distress and Help

33 Woe to you, O destroyer,
    you who have not been
    destroyed!
Woe to you, O traitor,
    you who have not been betrayed!
When you stop destroying,
    you will be destroyed;
when you stop betraying,
    you will be betrayed.

²O LORD, be gracious to us;
    we long for you.
Be our strength every morning,
    our salvation in time of distress.
³At the thunder of your voice, the
    peoples flee;
    when you rise up, the nations
    scatter.
⁴Your plunder, O nations, is harvested
    as by young locusts;
    like a swarm of locusts men pounce
    on it.

⁵The LORD is exalted, for he dwells on
    high;
    he will fill Zion with justice and
    righteousness.
⁶He will be the sure foundation for
    your times,
    a rich store of salvation and wisdom
    and knowledge;
    the fear of the LORD is the key to
    this treasure.ᵃ

⁷Look, their brave men cry aloud in the
    streets;
    the envoys of peace weep bitterly.
⁸The highways are deserted,
    no travelers are on the roads.
The treaty is broken,

ᵃ6 Or *is a treasure from him*

its witnesses[a] are despised,
no one is respected.
⁹The land mourns[b] and wastes away,
Lebanon is ashamed and withers;
Sharon is like the Arabah,
and Bashan and Carmel drop their
leaves.

¹⁰"Now will I arise," says the LORD.
"Now will I be exalted;
now will I be lifted up.
¹¹You conceive chaff,
you give birth to straw;
your breath is a fire that consumes
you.
¹²The peoples will be burned as if to
lime;
like cut thornbushes they will be set
ablaze."

¹³You who are far away, hear what I
have done;
you who are near, acknowledge my
power!
¹⁴The sinners in Zion are terrified;
trembling grips the godless:
"Who of us can dwell with the
consuming fire?
Who of us can dwell with
everlasting burning?"
¹⁵He who walks righteously
and speaks what is right,
who rejects gain from extortion
and keeps his hand from accepting
bribes,
who stops his ears against plots of
murder
and shuts his eyes against
contemplating evil—
¹⁶this is the man who will dwell on the
heights,
whose refuge will be the mountain
fortress.
His bread will be supplied,
and water will not fail him.

¹⁷Your eyes will see the king in his
beauty
and view a land that stretches afar.
¹⁸In your thoughts you will ponder the
former terror:
"Where is that chief officer?
Where is the one who took the
revenue?
Where is the officer in charge of the
towers?"
¹⁹You will see those arrogant people no
more,

those people of an obscure speech,
with their strange, incomprehensible
tongue.

²⁰Look upon Zion, the city of our
festivals;
your eyes will see Jerusalem,
a peaceful abode, a tent that will
not be moved;
its stakes will never be pulled up,
nor any of its ropes broken.
²¹There the LORD will be our Mighty
One.
It will be like a place of broad rivers
and streams.
No galley with oars will ride them,
no mighty ship will sail them.
²²For the LORD is our judge,
the LORD is our lawgiver,
the LORD is our king;
it is he who will save us.

²³Your rigging hangs loose:
The mast is not held secure,
the sail is not spread.
Then an abundance of spoils will be
divided
and even the lame will carry off
plunder.
²⁴No one living in Zion will say, "I am
ill";
and the sins of those who dwell
there will be forgiven.

Judgment Against the Nations

34 Come near, you nations, and
listen;
pay attention, you peoples!
Let the earth hear, and all that is in it,
the world, and all that comes out of
it!
²The LORD is angry with all nations;
his wrath is upon all their armies.
He will totally destroy[c] them,
he will give them over to slaughter.
³Their slain will be thrown out,
their dead bodies will send up a
stench;
the mountains will be soaked with
their blood.
⁴All the stars of the heavens will be
dissolved
and the sky rolled up like a scroll;
all the starry host will fall
like withered leaves from the vine,
like shriveled figs from the fig tree.

---

[a]8 Dead Sea Scrolls; Masoretic Text / the cities   [b]9 Or dries up   [c]2 The Hebrew term refers to the
irrevocable giving over of things or persons to the LORD, often by totally destroying them; also in verse 5.

⁵My sword has drunk its fill in the
    heavens;
  see, it descends in judgment on
    Edom,
  the people I have totally destroyed.
⁶The sword of the Lord is bathed in
    blood,
  it is covered with fat —
the blood of lambs and goats,
  fat from the kidneys of rams.
For the Lord has a sacrifice in Bozrah
  and a great slaughter in Edom.
⁷And the wild oxen will fall with them,
  the bull calves and the great bulls.
Their land will be drenched with
    blood,
  and the dust will be soaked with
    fat.

⁸For the Lord has a day of vengeance,
  a year of retribution, to uphold
    Zion's cause.
⁹Edom's streams will be turned into
    pitch,
  her dust into burning sulfur;
  her land will become blazing pitch!
¹⁰It will not be quenched night and
    day;
  its smoke will rise forever.
From generation to generation it will
    lie desolate;
  no one will ever pass through it
    again.
¹¹The desert owl[a] and screech owl[a]
    will possess it;
  the great owl[a] and the raven will
    nest there.
God will stretch out over Edom
  the measuring line of chaos
  and the plumb line of desolation.
¹²Her nobles will have nothing there to
    be called a kingdom,
  all her princes will vanish away.
¹³Thorns will overrun her citadels,
  nettles and brambles her
    strongholds.
She will become a haunt for jackals,
  a home for owls.
¹⁴Desert creatures will meet with
    hyenas,
  and wild goats will bleat to each
    other;
there the night creatures will also
    repose
  and find for themselves places of
    rest.
¹⁵The owl will nest there and lay eggs,

she will hatch them, and care for
    her young under the shadow of
    her wings;
there also the falcons will gather,
  each with its mate.

¹⁶Look in the scroll of the Lord and
read:

None of these will be missing,
  not one will lack her mate.
For it is his mouth that has given the
    order,
  and his Spirit will gather them
    together.
¹⁷He allots their portions;
  his hand distributes them by
    measure.
They will possess it forever
  and dwell there from generation to
    generation.

Joy of the Redeemed

35 The desert and the parched land
    will be glad;
  the wilderness will rejoice and
    blossom.
Like the crocus, ²it will burst into
    bloom;
  it will rejoice greatly and shout for
    joy.
The glory of Lebanon will be given to
    it,
  the splendor of Carmel and Sharon;
they will see the glory of the Lord,
  the splendor of our God.

³Strengthen the feeble hands,
  steady the knees that give way;
⁴say to those with fearful hearts,
  "Be strong, do not fear;
your God will come,
  he will come with vengeance;
with divine retribution
  he will come to save you."

⁵Then will the eyes of the blind be
    opened
  and the ears of the deaf unstopped.
⁶Then will the lame leap like a deer,
  and the mute tongue shout for joy.
Water will gush forth in the
    wilderness
  and streams in the desert.
⁷The burning sand will become a pool,
  the thirsty ground bubbling springs.
In the haunts where jackals once lay,
  grass and reeds and papyrus will
    grow.

---

a11 The precise identification of these birds is uncertain.

[8]And a highway will be there;
　it will be called the Way of
　　Holiness.
The unclean will not journey on it;
　it will be for those who walk in that
　　Way;
　wicked fools will not go about on
　　it.[a]
[9]No lion will be there,
　nor will any ferocious beast get up
　　on it;
　they will not be found there.
But only the redeemed will walk
　　there,
[10]　and the ransomed of the LORD will
　　return.
They will enter Zion with singing;
　everlasting joy will crown their
　　heads.
Gladness and joy will overtake them,
　and sorrow and sighing will flee
　　away.

Sennacherib Threatens Jerusalem

36 In the fourteenth year of King Hezekiah's reign, Sennacherib king of Assyria attacked all the fortified cities of Judah and captured them. [2]Then the king of Assyria sent his field commander with a large army from Lachish to King Hezekiah at Jerusalem. When the commander stopped at the aqueduct of the Upper Pool, on the road to the Washerman's Field, [3]Eliakim son of Hilkiah the palace administrator, Shebna the secretary, and Joah son of Asaph the recorder went out to him.

[4]The field commander said to them, "Tell Hezekiah,

" 'This is what the great king, the king of Assyria, says: On what are you basing this confidence of yours? [5]You say you have strategy and military strength—but you speak only empty words. On whom are you depending, that you rebel against me? [6]Look now, you are depending on Egypt, that splintered reed of a staff, which pierces a man's hand and wounds him if he leans on it! Such is Pharaoh king of Egypt to all who depend on him. [7]And if you say to me, "We are depending on the LORD our God"—isn't he the one whose high places and altars Hezekiah removed, saying to Judah and Jerusalem, "You must worship before this altar"?

[8]" 'Come now, make a bargain with my master, the king of Assyria: I will give you two thousand horses—if you can put riders on them! [9]How then can you repulse one officer of the least of my master's officials, even though you are depending on Egypt for chariots and horsemen? [10]Furthermore, have I come to attack and destroy this land without the LORD? The LORD himself told me to march against this country and destroy it.' "

[11]Then Eliakim, Shebna and Joah said to the field commander, "Please speak to your servants in Aramaic, since we understand it. Don't speak to us in Hebrew in the hearing of the people on the wall."

[12]But the commander replied, "Was it only to your master and you that my master sent me to say these things, and not to the men sitting on the wall—who, like you, will have to eat their own filth and drink their own urine?"

[13]Then the commander stood and called out in Hebrew, "Hear the words of the great king, the king of Assyria! [14]This is what the king says: Do not let Hezekiah deceive you. He cannot deliver you! [15]Do not let Hezekiah persuade you to trust in the LORD when he says, 'The LORD will surely deliver us; this city will not be given into the hand of the king of Assyria.'

[16]"Do not listen to Hezekiah. This is what the king of Assyria says: Make peace with me and come out to me. Then every one of you will eat from his own vine and fig tree and drink water from his own cistern, [17]until I come and take you to a land like your own—a land of grain and new wine, a land of bread and vineyards.

[18]"Do not let Hezekiah mislead you when he says, 'The LORD will deliver us.' Has the god of any nation ever delivered his land from the hand of the king of Assyria? [19]Where are the gods of Hamath and Arpad? Where are the gods of Sepharvaim? Have they rescued Samaria from my hand? [20]Who of all the gods of these countries has been able to save his land from me? How then can the LORD deliver Jerusalem from my hand?"

[21]But the people remained silent and said nothing in reply, because the king had commanded, "Do not answer him."

[22]Then Eliakim son of Hilkiah the palace administrator, Shebna the secretary,

---

[a]8 Or / the simple will not stray from it

and Joah son of Asaph the recorder went to Hezekiah, with their clothes torn, and told him what the field commander had said.

Jerusalem's Deliverance Foretold

37 When King Hezekiah heard this, he tore his clothes and put on sackcloth and went into the temple of the LORD. [2]He sent Eliakim the palace administrator, Shebna the secretary, and the leading priests, all wearing sackcloth, to the prophet Isaiah son of Amoz. [3]They told him, "This is what Hezekiah says: This day is a day of distress and rebuke and disgrace, as when children come to the point of birth and there is no strength to deliver them. [4]It may be that the LORD your God will hear the words of the field commander, whom his master, the king of Assyria, has sent to ridicule the living God, and that he will rebuke him for the words the LORD your God has heard. Therefore pray for the remnant that still survives."

[5]When King Hezekiah's officials came to Isaiah, [6]Isaiah said to them, "Tell your master, 'This is what the LORD says: Do not be afraid of what you have heard— those words with which the underlings of the king of Assyria have blasphemed me. [7]Listen! I am going to put a spirit in him so that when he hears a certain report, he will return to his own country, and there I will have him cut down with the sword.' "

[8]When the field commander heard that the king of Assyria had left Lachish, he withdrew and found the king fighting against Libnah.

[9]Now Sennacherib received a report that Tirhakah, the Cushite[a] king ˌof Egyptˌ, was marching out to fight against him. When he heard it, he sent messengers to Hezekiah with this word: [10]"Say to Hezekiah king of Judah: Do not let the god you depend on deceive you when he says, 'Jerusalem will not be handed over to the king of Assyria.' [11]Surely you have heard what the kings of Assyria have done to all the countries, destroying them completely. And will you be delivered? [12]Did the gods of the nations that were destroyed by my forefathers deliver them—the gods of Gozan, Haran, Rezeph and the people of Eden who were in Tel Assar? [13]Where is the king of Hamath, the king of Arpad, the king of the city of Sepharvaim, or of Hena or Ivvah?"

Hezekiah's Prayer

[14]Hezekiah received the letter from the messengers and read it. Then he went up to the temple of the LORD and spread it out before the LORD. [15]And Hezekiah prayed to the LORD: [16]"O LORD Almighty, God of Israel, enthroned between the cherubim, you alone are God over all the kingdoms of the earth. You have made heaven and earth. [17]Give ear, O LORD, and hear; open your eyes, O LORD, and see; listen to all the words Sennacherib has sent to insult the living God.

[18]"It is true, O LORD, that the Assyrian kings have laid waste all these peoples and their lands. [19]They have thrown their gods into the fire and destroyed them, for they were not gods but only wood and stone, fashioned by human hands. [20]Now, O LORD our God, deliver us from his hand, so that all kingdoms on earth may know that you alone, O LORD, are God.[b]"

Sennacherib's Fall

[21]Then Isaiah son of Amoz sent a message to Hezekiah: "This is what the LORD, the God of Israel, says: Because you have prayed to me concerning Sennacherib king of Assyria, [22]this is the word the LORD has spoken against him:

"The Virgin Daughter of Zion
    despises and mocks you.
The Daughter of Jerusalem
    tosses her head as you flee.
[23]Who is it you have insulted and
        blasphemed?
    Against whom have you raised your
        voice
and lifted your eyes in pride?
    Against the Holy One of Israel!
[24]By your messengers
    you have heaped insults on the
        Lord.
And you have said,
    'With my many chariots
I have ascended the heights of the
        mountains,
    the utmost heights of Lebanon.
I have cut down its tallest cedars,
    the choicest of its pines.
I have reached its remotest heights,
    the finest of its forests.

---

[a]9 That is, from the upper Nile region   [b]20 Dead Sea Scrolls (see also 2 Kings 19:19); Masoretic Text *alone are the* LORD

²⁵I have dug wells in foreign lands^a
  and drunk the water there.
With the soles of my feet
  I have dried up all the streams of
    Egypt.'

²⁶"Have you not heard?
  Long ago I ordained it.
In days of old I planned it;
  now I have brought it to pass,
that you have turned fortified cities
  into piles of stone.
²⁷Their people, drained of power,
  are dismayed and put to shame.
They are like plants in the field,
  like tender green shoots,
like grass sprouting on the roof,
  scorched^b before it grows up.

²⁸"But I know where you stay
  and when you come and go
  and how you rage against me.
²⁹Because you rage against me
  and because your insolence has
    reached my ears,
I will put my hook in your nose
  and my bit in your mouth,
and I will make you return
  by the way you came.

³⁰"This will be the sign for you,
O Hezekiah:

"This year you will eat what grows by
    itself,
  and the second year what springs
    from that.
But in the third year sow and reap,
  plant vineyards and eat their fruit.
³¹Once more a remnant of the house of
    Judah
  will take root below and bear fruit
    above.
³²For out of Jerusalem will come a
    remnant,
  and out of Mount Zion a band of
    survivors.
The zeal of the LORD Almighty
  will accomplish this.

³³"Therefore this is what the LORD says
concerning the king of Assyria:

"He will not enter this city
  or shoot an arrow here.
He will not come before it with shield
  or build a siege ramp against it.
³⁴By the way that he came he will
    return;

he will not enter this city,"
                    declares the LORD.
³⁵"I will defend this city and save it,
  for my sake and for the sake of
    David my servant!"

³⁶Then the angel of the LORD went out
and put to death a hundred and eighty-
five thousand men in the Assyrian camp.
When the people got up the next morn-
ing—there were all the dead bodies! ³⁷So
Sennacherib king of Assyria broke camp
and withdrew. He returned to Nineveh
and stayed there.

³⁸One day, while he was worshiping in
the temple of his god Nisroch, his sons
Adrammelech and Sharezer cut him down
with the sword, and they escaped to the
land of Ararat. And Esarhaddon his son
succeeded him as king.

Hezekiah's Illness

38 In those days Hezekiah became ill
and was at the point of death. The
prophet Isaiah son of Amoz went to him
and said, "This is what the LORD says: Put
your house in order, because you are going to die; you will not recover."

²Hezekiah turned his face to the wall
and prayed to the LORD, ³"Remember,
O LORD, how I have walked before you
faithfully and with wholehearted devotion
and have done what is good in your eyes."
And Hezekiah wept bitterly.

⁴Then the word of the LORD came to Isa-
iah: ⁵"Go and tell Hezekiah, 'This is what
the LORD, the God of your father David,
says: I have heard your prayer and seen
your tears; I will add fifteen years to your
life. ⁶And I will deliver you and this city
from the hand of the king of Assyria. I will
defend this city.

⁷" 'This is the LORD's sign to you that the
LORD will do what he has promised: ⁸I will
make the shadow cast by the sun go back
the ten steps it has gone down on the
stairway of Ahaz.' " So the sunlight went
back the ten steps it had gone down.

⁹A writing of Hezekiah king of Judah af-
ter his illness and recovery:

¹⁰I said, "In the prime of my life
  must I go through the gates of
    death^c
  and be robbed of the rest of my
    years?"

---

^a25 Dead Sea Scrolls (see also 2 Kings 19:24); Masoretic Text does not have *in foreign lands.*
^b27 Some manuscripts of the Masoretic Text, Dead Sea Scrolls and some Septuagint manuscripts (see also
2 Kings 19:26); most manuscripts of the Masoretic Text *roof / and terraced fields*   ^c10 Hebrew *Sheol*

[11]I said, "I will not again see the LORD,
the LORD, in the land of the living;
no longer will I look on mankind,
or be with those who now dwell in
this world.[a]
[12]Like a shepherd's tent my house
has been pulled down and taken
from me.
Like a weaver I have rolled up my life,
and he has cut me off from the
loom;
day and night you made an end of
me.
[13]I waited patiently till dawn,
but like a lion he broke all my
bones;
day and night you made an end of
me.
[14]I cried like a swift or thrush,
I moaned like a mourning dove.
My eyes grew weak as I looked to the
heavens.
I am troubled; O Lord, come to my
aid!"
[15]But what can I say?
He has spoken to me, and he
himself has done this.
I will walk humbly all my years
because of this anguish of my soul.
[16]Lord, by such things men live;
and my spirit finds life in them too.
You restored me to health
and let me live.
[17]Surely it was for my benefit
that I suffered such anguish.
In your love you kept me
from the pit of destruction;
you have put all my sins
behind your back.
[18]For the grave[b] cannot praise you,
death cannot sing your praise;
those who go down to the pit
cannot hope for your faithfulness.
[19]The living, the living—they praise
you,
as I am doing today;
fathers tell their children
about your faithfulness.

[20]The LORD will save me,
and we will sing with stringed
instruments
all the days of our lives
in the temple of the LORD.

[21]Isaiah had said, "Prepare a poultice of
figs and apply it to the boil, and he will
recover."

[22]Hezekiah had asked, "What will be
the sign that I will go up to the temple of
the LORD?"

Envoys From Babylon

39 At that time Merodach-Baladan
son of Baladan king of Babylon
sent Hezekiah letters and a gift, because
he had heard of his illness and recovery.
[2]Hezekiah received the envoys gladly and
showed them what was in his storehouses—the silver, the gold, the spices,
the fine oil, his entire armory and everything found among his treasures. There
was nothing in his palace or in all his kingdom that Hezekiah did not show them.

[3]Then Isaiah the prophet went to King
Hezekiah and asked, "What did those
men say, and where did they come from?"

"From a distant land," Hezekiah replied. "They came to me from Babylon."

[4]The prophet asked, "What did they see
in your palace?"

"They saw everything in my palace,"
Hezekiah said. "There is nothing among
my treasures that I did not show them."

[5]Then Isaiah said to Hezekiah, "Hear
the word of the LORD Almighty: [6]The time
will surely come when everything in your
palace, and all that your fathers have
stored up until this day, will be carried off
to Babylon. Nothing will be left, says the
LORD. [7]And some of your descendants,
your own flesh and blood who will be
born to you, will be taken away, and they
will become eunuchs in the palace of the
king of Babylon."

[8]"The word of the LORD you have spoken is good," Hezekiah replied. For he
thought, "There will be peace and security
in my lifetime."

Comfort for God's People

40 Comfort, comfort my people,
says your God.
[2]Speak tenderly to Jerusalem,
and proclaim to her
that her hard service has been
completed,
that her sin has been paid for,
that she has received from the LORD's
hand
double for all her sins.

[3]A voice of one calling:
"In the desert prepare

[a]11 A few Hebrew manuscripts; most Hebrew manuscripts *in the place of cessation*   [b]18 Hebrew *Sheol*

the way for the Lord[a];
make straight in the wilderness
a highway for our God.[b]
[4]Every valley shall be raised up,
every mountain and hill made low;
the rough ground shall become level,
the rugged places a plain.
[5]And the glory of the Lord will be
revealed,
and all mankind together will see it.
For the mouth of the Lord
has spoken."

[6]A voice says, "Cry out."
And I said, "What shall I cry?"

"All men are like grass,
and all their glory is like the flowers
of the field.
[7]The grass withers and the flowers fall,
because the breath of the Lord
blows on them.
Surely the people are grass.
[8]The grass withers and the flowers fall,
but the word of our God stands
forever."

[9]You who bring good tidings to Zion,
go up on a high mountain.
You who bring good tidings to
Jerusalem,[c]
lift up your voice with a shout,
lift it up, do not be afraid;
say to the towns of Judah,
"Here is your God!"
[10]See, the Sovereign Lord comes with
power,
and his arm rules for him.
See, his reward is with him,
and his recompense accompanies
him.
[11]He tends his flock like a shepherd:
He gathers the lambs in his arms
and carries them close to his heart;
he gently leads those that have
young.

[12]Who has measured the waters in the
hollow of his hand,
or with the breadth of his hand
marked off the heavens?
Who has held the dust of the earth in
a basket,
or weighed the mountains on the
scales
and the hills in a balance?
[13]Who has understood the mind[d] of
the Lord,

or instructed him as his counselor?
[14]Whom did the Lord consult to
enlighten him,
and who taught him the right way?
Who was it that taught him
knowledge
or showed him the path of
understanding?

[15]Surely the nations are like a drop in a
bucket;
they are regarded as dust on the
scales;
he weighs the islands as though
they were fine dust.
[16]Lebanon is not sufficient for altar
fires,
nor its animals enough for burnt
offerings.
[17]Before him all the nations are as
nothing;
they are regarded by him as
worthless
and less than nothing.

[18]To whom, then, will you compare
God?
What image will you compare him
to?
[19]As for an idol, a craftsman casts it,
and a goldsmith overlays it with
gold
and fashions silver chains for it.
[20]A man too poor to present such an
offering
selects wood that will not rot.
He looks for a skilled craftsman
to set up an idol that will not
topple.

[21]Do you not know?
Have you not heard?
Has it not been told you from the
beginning?
Have you not understood since the
earth was founded?
[22]He sits enthroned above the circle of
the earth,
and its people are like grasshoppers.
He stretches out the heavens like a
canopy,
and spreads them out like a tent to
live in.
[23]He brings princes to naught
and reduces the rulers of this world
to nothing.
[24]No sooner are they planted,

---

[a]3 Or *A voice of one calling in the desert: / "Prepare the way for the Lord*   [b]3 Hebrew; Septuagint *make straight the paths of our God*   [c]9 Or *O Zion, bringer of good tidings, / go up on a high mountain. / O Jerusalem, bringer of good tidings*   [d]13 Or *Spirit*; or *spirit*

no sooner are they sown,
no sooner do they take root in the
ground,
than he blows on them and they
wither,
and a whirlwind sweeps them away
like chaff.

25"To whom will you compare me?
Or who is my equal?" says the Holy
One.
26Lift your eyes and look to the
heavens:
Who created all these?
He who brings out the starry host one
by one,
and calls them each by name.
Because of his great power and
mighty strength,
not one of them is missing.

27Why do you say, O Jacob,
and complain, O Israel,
"My way is hidden from the LORD;
my cause is disregarded by my
God"?
28Do you not know?
Have you not heard?
The LORD is the everlasting God,
the Creator of the ends of the earth.
He will not grow tired or weary,
and his understanding no one can
fathom.
29He gives strength to the weary
and increases the power of the
weak.
30Even youths grow tired and weary,
and young men stumble and fall;
31but those who hope in the LORD
will renew their strength.
They will soar on wings like eagles;

THURSDAY

VERSE FOR THE DAY:
Isaiah 40:29

AUTHOR:
Oswald Chambers

PASSAGE FOR THE DAY:
Isaiah 40:27–31

Soaring on Eagles' Wings

WHENEVER there is the experience of weariness or degradation, you may be certain you have done one of two things—either you have disregarded a law of nature, or you have deliberately got out of touch with God. There is no such thing as weariness in God's work. If you are in tune with the joy of God, the more you spend out in God's service, the more the recuperation goes on, and when once the warning note of weariness is given, it is a sign that something has gone wrong. If only we would heed the warning, we would find it is God's wonderfully gentle way of saying—"Not that way; that must be left alone; this must be given up." Spiritual fatigue comes from the unconscious frittering away of God's time. When you feel weary or are exhausted, don't ask for hot milk, but get back to God. The secret of weariness and nervous disease in the natural world is a lack of a dominating interest, and the same is true in spiritual life. Much of what is called Christian work is veneered spiritual disease; it is Christian activity that counts—dominating life from God, and every moment is filled with an energy that is not our own, a super-abounding life that nothing can stand before.

Additional Scripture Readings:
Exodus 19:1–6; Ephesians 1:15–23

Go to page 754 for your next devotional reading.

they will run and not grow weary,
they will walk and not be faint.

The Helper of Israel

41 "Be silent before me, you islands!
Let the nations renew their
strength!
Let them come forward and speak;
let us meet together at the place of
judgment.

2"Who has stirred up one from the
east,
calling him in righteousness to his
service*a*?
He hands nations over to him
and subdues kings before him.
He turns them to dust with his sword,
to windblown chaff with his bow.
3He pursues them and moves on
unscathed,
by a path his feet have not traveled
before.
4Who has done this and carried it
through,
calling forth the generations from
the beginning?
I, the LORD—with the first of them
and with the last—I am he."

5The islands have seen it and fear;
the ends of the earth tremble.
They approach and come forward;
6   each helps the other
and says to his brother, "Be strong!"
7The craftsman encourages the
goldsmith,
and he who smooths with the
hammer
spurs on him who strikes the anvil.
He says of the welding, "It is good."
He nails down the idol so it will not
topple.

8"But you, O Israel, my servant,
Jacob, whom I have chosen,
you descendants of Abraham my
friend,
9I took you from the ends of the earth,
from its farthest corners I called
you.
I said, 'You are my servant';
I have chosen you and have not
rejected you.
10So do not fear, for I am with you;
do not be dismayed, for I am your
God.
I will strengthen you and help you;

I will uphold you with my righteous
right hand.

11"All who rage against you
will surely be ashamed and
disgraced;
those who oppose you
will be as nothing and perish.
12Though you search for your enemies,
you will not find them.
Those who wage war against you
will be as nothing at all.
13For I am the LORD, your God,
who takes hold of your right hand
and says to you, Do not fear;
I will help you.
14Do not be afraid, O worm Jacob,
O little Israel,
for I myself will help you," declares
the LORD,
your Redeemer, the Holy One of
Israel.
15"See, I will make you into a threshing
sledge,
new and sharp, with many teeth.
You will thresh the mountains and
crush them,
and reduce the hills to chaff.
16You will winnow them, the wind will
pick them up,
and a gale will blow them away.
But you will rejoice in the LORD
and glory in the Holy One of Israel.

17"The poor and needy search for water,
but there is none;
their tongues are parched with
thirst.
But I the LORD will answer them;
I, the God of Israel, will not forsake
them.
18I will make rivers flow on barren
heights,
and springs within the valleys.
I will turn the desert into pools of
water,
and the parched ground into
springs.
19I will put in the desert
the cedar and the acacia, the myrtle
and the olive.
I will set pines in the wasteland,
the fir and the cypress together,
20so that people may see and know,
may consider and understand,
that the hand of the LORD has done
this,
that the Holy One of Israel has
created it.

a2 Or / whom victory meets at every step

21"Present your case," says the LORD.
    "Set forth your arguments," says
        Jacob's King.
22"Bring in ˻your idols˼ to tell us
    what is going to happen.
Tell us what the former things were,
    so that we may consider them
    and know their final outcome.
Or declare to us the things to come,
23   tell us what the future holds,
    so we may know that you are gods.
Do something, whether good or bad,
    so that we will be dismayed and
        filled with fear.
24But you are less than nothing
    and your works are utterly
        worthless;
    he who chooses you is detestable.

25"I have stirred up one from the north,
        and he comes—
    one from the rising sun who calls
        on my name.
He treads on rulers as if they were
        mortar,
    as if he were a potter treading the
        clay.
26Who told of this from the beginning,
        so we could know,
    or beforehand, so we could say, 'He
        was right'?
No one told of this,
    no one foretold it,
    no one heard any words from you.
27I was the first to tell Zion, 'Look, here
        they are!'
    I gave to Jerusalem a messenger of
        good tidings.
28I look but there is no one—
    no one among them to give counsel,
    no one to give answer when I ask
        them.
29See, they are all false!
    Their deeds amount to nothing;
    their images are but wind and
        confusion.

The Servant of the LORD

42 "Here is my servant, whom I
    uphold,
    my chosen one in whom I delight;
I will put my Spirit on him
    and he will bring justice to the
        nations.
2He will not shout or cry out,
    or raise his voice in the streets.
3A bruised reed he will not break,
    and a smoldering wick he will not
        snuff out.

In faithfulness he will bring forth
        justice;
4   he will not falter or be discouraged
till he establishes justice on earth.
    In his law the islands will put their
        hope."

5This is what God the LORD says—
he who created the heavens and
        stretched them out,
    who spread out the earth and all
        that comes out of it,
    who gives breath to its people,
    and life to those who walk on it:
6"I, the LORD, have called you in
        righteousness;
    I will take hold of your hand.
I will keep you and will make you
    to be a covenant for the people
    and a light for the Gentiles,
7to open eyes that are blind,
    to free captives from prison
    and to release from the dungeon
        those who sit in darkness.

8"I am the LORD; that is my name!
    I will not give my glory to another
    or my praise to idols.
9See, the former things have taken
        place,
    and new things I declare;
before they spring into being
    I announce them to you."

Song of Praise to the LORD

10Sing to the LORD a new song,
    his praise from the ends of the
        earth,
    you who go down to the sea, and all
        that is in it,
    you islands, and all who live in
        them.
11Let the desert and its towns raise their
        voices;
    let the settlements where Kedar
        lives rejoice.
Let the people of Sela sing for joy;
    let them shout from the
        mountaintops.
12Let them give glory to the LORD
    and proclaim his praise in the
        islands.
13The LORD will march out like a mighty
        man,
    like a warrior he will stir up his
        zeal;
with a shout he will raise the battle
        cry
    and will triumph over his enemies.

14"For a long time I have kept silent,

I have been quiet and held myself
back.
But now, like a woman in childbirth,
I cry out, I gasp and pant.
15I will lay waste the mountains and
hills
and dry up all their vegetation;
I will turn rivers into islands
and dry up the pools.
16I will lead the blind by ways they
have not known,
along unfamiliar paths I will guide
them;
I will turn the darkness into light
before them
and make the rough places smooth.
These are the things I will do;
I will not forsake them.
17But those who trust in idols,
who say to images, 'You are our
gods,'
will be turned back in utter shame.

Israel Blind and Deaf

18"Hear, you deaf;
look, you blind, and see!
19Who is blind but my servant,
and deaf like the messenger I send?
Who is blind like the one committed
to me,
blind like the servant of the LORD?
20You have seen many things, but have
paid no attention;
your ears are open, but you hear
nothing."
21It pleased the LORD
for the sake of his righteousness
to make his law great and glorious.
22But this is a people plundered and
looted,
all of them trapped in pits
or hidden away in prisons.
They have become plunder,
with no one to rescue them;
they have been made loot,
with no one to say, "Send them
back."

23Which of you will listen to this
or pay close attention in time to
come?
24Who handed Jacob over to become
loot,
and Israel to the plunderers?
Was it not the LORD,
against whom we have sinned?
For they would not follow his ways;
they did not obey his law.

25So he poured out on them his burning
anger,
the violence of war.
It enveloped them in flames, yet they
did not understand;
it consumed them, but they did not
take it to heart.

Israel's Only Savior

43 But now, this is what the LORD
says—
he who created you, O Jacob,
he who formed you, O Israel:
"Fear not, for I have redeemed you;
I have summoned you by name;
you are mine.
2When you pass through the waters,
I will be with you;
and when you pass through the rivers,
they will not sweep over you.
When you walk through the fire,
you will not be burned;
the flames will not set you ablaze.
3For I am the LORD, your God,
the Holy One of Israel, your Savior;
I give Egypt for your ransom,
Cush[a] and Seba in your stead.
4Since you are precious and honored in
my sight,
and because I love you,
I will give men in exchange for you,
and people in exchange for your
life.
5Do not be afraid, for I am with you;
I will bring your children from the
east
and gather you from the west.
6I will say to the north, 'Give them up!'
and to the south, 'Do not hold them
back.'
Bring my sons from afar
and my daughters from the ends of
the earth—
7everyone who is called by my name,
whom I created for my glory,
whom I formed and made."

8Lead out those who have eyes but are
blind,
who have ears but are deaf.
9All the nations gather together
and the peoples assemble.
Which of them foretold this
and proclaimed to us the former
things?
Let them bring in their witnesses to
prove they were right,

a3 That is, the upper Nile region

so that others may hear and say, "It
is true."
10"You are my witnesses," declares the
LORD,
"and my servant whom I have
chosen,
so that you may know and believe me
and understand that I am he.
Before me no god was formed,
nor will there be one after me.
11I, even I, am the LORD,
and apart from me there is no
savior.
12I have revealed and saved and
proclaimed—
I, and not some foreign god among
you.
You are my witnesses," declares the
LORD, "that I am God.
13 Yes, and from ancient days I am he.
No one can deliver out of my hand.
When I act, who can reverse it?"

God's Mercy and Israel's Unfaithfulness

14This is what the LORD says—
your Redeemer, the Holy One of
Israel:
"For your sake I will send to Babylon
and bring down as fugitives all the
Babylonians,*a*
in the ships in which they took
pride.
15I am the LORD, your Holy One,
Israel's Creator, your King."

16This is what the LORD says—
he who made a way through the
sea,
a path through the mighty waters,
17who drew out the chariots and horses,
the army and reinforcements
together,
and they lay there, never to rise again,
extinguished, snuffed out like a
wick:
18"Forget the former things;
do not dwell on the past.
19See, I am doing a new thing!
Now it springs up; do you not
perceive it?
I am making a way in the desert
and streams in the wasteland.
20The wild animals honor me,
the jackals and the owls,
because I provide water in the desert
and streams in the wasteland,

to give drink to my people, my
chosen,
21 the people I formed for myself
that they may proclaim my praise.

22"Yet you have not called upon me,
O Jacob,
you have not wearied yourselves for
me, O Israel.
23You have not brought me sheep for
burnt offerings,
nor honored me with your
sacrifices.
I have not burdened you with grain
offerings
nor wearied you with demands for
incense.
24You have not bought any fragrant
calamus for me,
or lavished on me the fat of your
sacrifices.
But you have burdened me with your
sins
and wearied me with your offenses.

25"I, even I, am he who blots out
your transgressions, for my own
sake,
and remembers your sins no more.
26Review the past for me,
let us argue the matter together;
state the case for your innocence.
27Your first father sinned;
your spokesmen rebelled against
me.
28So I will disgrace the dignitaries of
your temple,
and I will consign Jacob to
destruction*b*
and Israel to scorn.

Israel the Chosen

44 "But now listen, O Jacob, my
servant,
Israel, whom I have chosen.
2This is what the LORD says—
he who made you, who formed you
in the womb,
and who will help you:
Do not be afraid, O Jacob, my servant,
Jeshurun, whom I have chosen.
3For I will pour water on the thirsty
land,
and streams on the dry ground;
I will pour out my Spirit on your
offspring,
and my blessing on your
descendants.

---

*a*14 Or *Chaldeans*   *b*28 The Hebrew term refers to the irrevocable giving over of things or persons to
the LORD, often by totally destroying them.

⁴They will spring up like grass in a
    meadow,
  like poplar trees by flowing streams.
⁵One will say, 'I belong to the LORD';
  another will call himself by the
    name of Jacob;
  still another will write on his hand,
    'The LORD's,'
  and will take the name Israel.

The LORD, Not Idols

⁶"This is what the LORD says—
  Israel's King and Redeemer, the
    LORD Almighty:
  I am the first and I am the last;
    apart from me there is no God.
⁷Who then is like me? Let him
  proclaim it.

Let him declare and lay out before
    me
  what has happened since I established
    my ancient people,
  and what is yet to come—
  yes, let him foretell what will
    come.
⁸Do not tremble, do not be afraid.
  Did I not proclaim this and
    foretell it long ago?
  You are my witnesses. Is there any
    God besides me?
  No, there is no other Rock; I know
    not one."

⁹All who make idols are nothing,
  and the things they treasure are
    worthless.

FRIDAY

VERSE FOR THE DAY:
Isaiah 43:19

AUTHOR:
Patrick Morley

PASSAGE FOR THE DAY:
Isaiah 43:16–21

Rat Race Dropouts

THE number one reason men fail when they are promoted [to a new job] is that they keep doing the old job. In other words, since what they have done in the past is comfortable, they simply continue the old job description instead of taking on the new challenges.

The same is true in the spiritual realm. The number one reason men fail when promoted to "follower of Christ" is that they keep doing the old job. Instead of penetrating the issues of their lives, and responding Biblically, they continue to live an impotent life as if nothing had ever happened. Maybe the language cleans up a little, but essentially—no change.

Perhaps it's time that Christian men in America check out of the rat race. It's an unwinnable race. Isn't it time we started doing the job we were promoted to when we first trusted Christ? "Therefore, if anyone is in Christ, he is a new creation; the old has gone, the new has come!" (2 Corinthians 5:17). We are promised a new spiritual nature, but we must be faithful to do our part—to do the new job.

Is it time for you to start doing the new job? Are you tired of the rat race? Are you concerned that you may be on your way to a life filled with regrets?

Additional Scripture Readings:
Romans 6:1–14;
2 Corinthians 5:16–20

Go to page 755 for your next devotional reading.

WEEKENDING

RESTORE

No matter how difficult life becomes, we belong in families. There may be times when we let down those we love and fail people who care the most, but through it all we discover a group of people who make us feel that we belong, who say, "What happens to you matters to me." Thus we stand together and face all of life with a confidence born of a sure identity in the family . . .

In spite of the pain, frustration and embarrassment, the unavoidable world of life in the family is still God's gift. The caring, nurture and confidence that comes from being seen at our worst and still knowing that we belong is his gift to us. It is the place where we can . . . love one another over the long haul. It is a place where we see his power and grace demonstrated over and over again.

– *John F. Westfall*

REVIVE

Saturday: Isaiah 44:1–5
Sunday: Romans 12:3–8

Go to page 757 for your next devotional reading.

Those who would speak up for them
　　are blind;
　　they are ignorant, to their own
　　　shame.
10Who shapes a god and casts an idol,
　　which can profit him nothing?
11He and his kind will be put to shame;
　　craftsmen are nothing but men.
Let them all come together and take
　　their stand;
　　they will be brought down to terror
　　and infamy.

12The blacksmith takes a tool
　　and works with it in the coals;
he shapes an idol with hammers,
　　he forges it with the might of his
　　　arm.
He gets hungry and loses his strength;
　　he drinks no water and grows faint.
13The carpenter measures with a line
　　and makes an outline with a
　　　marker;
he roughs it out with chisels
　　and marks it with compasses.
He shapes it in the form of man,
　　of man in all his glory,
　　that it may dwell in a shrine.
14He cut down cedars,
　　or perhaps took a cypress or oak.
He let it grow among the trees of the
　　forest,
　　or planted a pine, and the rain
　　made it grow.
15It is man's fuel for burning;
　　some of it he takes and warms
　　　himself,
　　he kindles a fire and bakes bread.
But he also fashions a god and
　　worships it;
　　he makes an idol and bows down to
　　　it.
16Half of the wood he burns in the fire;
　　over it he prepares his meal,
　　he roasts his meat and eats his fill.
He also warms himself and says,
　　"Ah! I am warm; I see the fire."
17From the rest he makes a god, his
　　idol;
　　he bows down to it and worships.
He prays to it and says,
　　"Save me; you are my god."
18They know nothing, they understand
　　nothing;
　　their eyes are plastered over so they
　　cannot see,
　　and their minds closed so they
　　cannot understand.
19No one stops to think,

no one has the knowledge or
　　understanding to say,
"Half of it I used for fuel;
　　I even baked bread over its coals,
　　I roasted meat and I ate.
Shall I make a detestable thing from
　　what is left?
　　Shall I bow down to a block of
　　wood?"
20He feeds on ashes, a deluded heart
　　misleads him;
　　he cannot save himself, or say,
"Is not this thing in my right hand a
　　lie?"

21"Remember these things, O Jacob,
　　for you are my servant, O Israel.
I have made you, you are my servant;
　　O Israel, I will not forget you.
22I have swept away your offenses like a
　　cloud,
　　your sins like the morning mist.
Return to me,
　　for I have redeemed you."

23Sing for joy, O heavens, for the LORD
　　has done this;
　　shout aloud, O earth beneath.
Burst into song, you mountains,
　　you forests and all your trees,
for the LORD has redeemed Jacob,
　　he displays his glory in Israel.

Jerusalem to Be Inhabited

24"This is what the LORD says—
　　your Redeemer, who formed you in
　　the womb:

I am the LORD,
　　who has made all things,
　　who alone stretched out the heavens,
　　who spread out the earth by myself,
25who foils the signs of false prophets
　　and makes fools of diviners,
who overthrows the learning of the
　　wise
　　and turns it into nonsense,
26who carries out the words of his
　　servants
　　and fulfills the predictions of his
　　messengers,
who says of Jerusalem, 'It shall be
　　inhabited,'
　　of the towns of Judah, 'They shall
　　be built,'
　　and of their ruins, 'I will restore
　　them,'
27who says to the watery deep, 'Be dry,
　　and I will dry up your streams,'

28who says of Cyrus, 'He is my shepherd
and will accomplish all that I please;
he will say of Jerusalem, "Let it be rebuilt,"
and of the temple, "Let its foundations be laid." '

45 "This is what the LORD says to his anointed,
to Cyrus, whose right hand I take hold of
to subdue nations before him
and to strip kings of their armor,

to open doors before him
so that gates will not be shut:
2I will go before you
and will level the mountains*a*;
I will break down gates of bronze
and cut through bars of iron.
3I will give you the treasures of darkness,
riches stored in secret places,
so that you may know that I am the LORD,
the God of Israel, who summons you by name.
4For the sake of Jacob my servant,
of Israel my chosen,

a2 Dead Sea Scrolls and Septuagint; the meaning of the word in the Masoretic Text is uncertain.

VERSE FOR THE DAY:
Isaiah 44:11

AUTHOR:
Dan Allender

PASSAGE FOR THE DAY:
Isaiah 44:6–11

False Gods

IDOLATRY is placing our longings for what only God can provide in the hands of a creature instead of the Creator. When I live for my work, or my wife, then I have made them my false god. When I am failed (and I can be absolutely sure that a false god will be impotent at the point of my greatest need), then I will experience the shame of failure and misplaced trust. The writers of Scripture are crystal clear that dependence on a false god will inevitably result in loss, pain and shame (Isaiah 42:17; 44:9–11). A false god will disappoint.

A friend recalled waiting for her father in an airport where she had a two-hour layover. Two days before her scheduled flight, they had planned on this meeting at the airport. As she waited for him, she was aware of a slight fear that he might forget and she cautioned herself against putting too much hope in her father, a bundle of energy who has time for everyone and everything but her. She waited with keen anticipation, rehearsing in her mind the things she wanted to share with him. Time passed; he did not appear. After an hour she quit looking and began to read a book. Every time she would look up to see if he was finally coming, she would feel a wave of self-hatred and shame. Her hope of connection with a man who was her false god—the one who could bestow or retract life—failed her, and she was ashamed.

Additional Scripture Readings:
Psalm 34:1–7; Isaiah 46:1–7

*Go to page 760 for your next
devotional reading.*

I summon you by name
  and bestow on you a title of honor,
  though you do not acknowledge me.
⁵I am the LORD, and there is no other;
  apart from me there is no God.
I will strengthen you,
  though you have not acknowledged
    me,
⁶so that from the rising of the sun
  to the place of its setting
men may know there is none besides
    me.
  I am the LORD, and there is no
    other.
⁷I form the light and create darkness,
  I bring prosperity and create
    disaster;
  I, the LORD, do all these things.

⁸"You heavens above, rain down
    righteousness;
  let the clouds shower it down.
Let the earth open wide,
  let salvation spring up,
let righteousness grow with it;
  I, the LORD, have created it.

⁹"Woe to him who quarrels with his
    Maker,
  to him who is but a potsherd
    among the potsherds on the
    ground.
Does the clay say to the potter,
  'What are you making?'
Does your work say,
  'He has no hands'?
¹⁰Woe to him who says to his father,
  'What have you begotten?'
or to his mother,
  'What have you brought to birth?'

¹¹"This is what the LORD says—
  the Holy One of Israel, and its
    Maker:
Concerning things to come,
  do you question me about my
    children,
  or give me orders about the work of
    my hands?
¹²It is I who made the earth
  and created mankind upon it.
My own hands stretched out the
    heavens;
  I marshaled their starry hosts.
¹³I will raise up Cyrus[a] in my
    righteousness:
  I will make all his ways straight.
He will rebuild my city
  and set my exiles free,

but not for a price or reward,
  says the LORD Almighty."

¹⁴This is what the LORD says:

"The products of Egypt and the
    merchandise of Cush,[b]
  and those tall Sabeans—
they will come over to you
  and will be yours;
they will trudge behind you,
  coming over to you in chains.
They will bow down before you
  and plead with you, saying,
'Surely God is with you, and there is
    no other;
  there is no other god.' "

¹⁵Truly you are a God who hides
    himself,
  O God and Savior of Israel.
¹⁶All the makers of idols will be put to
    shame and disgraced;
  they will go off into disgrace
    together.
¹⁷But Israel will be saved by the LORD
  with an everlasting salvation;
you will never be put to shame or
    disgraced,
  to ages everlasting.

¹⁸For this is what the LORD says—
he who created the heavens,
  he is God;
he who fashioned and made the earth,
  he founded it;
he did not create it to be empty,
  but formed it to be inhabited—
he says:
"I am the LORD,
  and there is no other.
¹⁹I have not spoken in secret,
  from somewhere in a land of
    darkness;
I have not said to Jacob's descendants,
  'Seek me in vain.'
I, the LORD, speak the truth;
  I declare what is right.

²⁰"Gather together and come;
  assemble, you fugitives from the
    nations.
Ignorant are those who carry about
    idols of wood,
  who pray to gods that cannot save.
²¹Declare what is to be, present it—
  let them take counsel together.
Who foretold this long ago,
  who declared it from the distant
    past?

Was it not I, the LORD?
  And there is no God apart from me,
a righteous God and a Savior;
  there is none but me.

22"Turn to me and be saved,
  all you ends of the earth;
for I am God, and there is no other.
23By myself I have sworn,
  my mouth has uttered in all
    integrity
  a word that will not be revoked:
Before me every knee will bow;
  by me every tongue will swear.
24They will say of me, 'In the LORD
    alone
  are righteousness and strength.' "
All who have raged against him
  will come to him and be put to
    shame.
25But in the LORD all the descendants of
    Israel
  will be found righteous and will
    exult.

Gods of Babylon

46 Bel bows down, Nebo stoops
      low;
  their idols are borne by beasts of
    burden.ᵃ
The images that are carried about are
    burdensome,
  a burden for the weary.
2They stoop and bow down together;
  unable to rescue the burden,
  they themselves go off into
    captivity.

3"Listen to me, O house of Jacob,
  all you who remain of the house of
    Israel,
you whom I have upheld since you
    were conceived,
  and have carried since your birth.
4Even to your old age and gray hairs
  I am he, I am he who will sustain
    you.
I have made you and I will carry you;
  I will sustain you and I will rescue
    you.

5"To whom will you compare me or
    count me equal?
  To whom will you liken me that we
    may be compared?
6Some pour out gold from their bags
  and weigh out silver on the scales;
they hire a goldsmith to make it into a
    god,

and they bow down and worship it.
7They lift it to their shoulders and
    carry it;
  they set it up in its place, and there
    it stands.
  From that spot it cannot move.
Though one cries out to it, it does not
    answer;
  it cannot save him from his
    troubles.

8"Remember this, fix it in mind,
  take it to heart, you rebels.
9Remember the former things, those of
    long ago;
  I am God, and there is no other;
  I am God, and there is none like
    me.
10I make known the end from the
    beginning,
  from ancient times, what is still to
    come.
I say: My purpose will stand,
  and I will do all that I please.
11From the east I summon a bird of
    prey;
  from a far-off land, a man to fulfill
    my purpose.
What I have said, that will I bring
    about;
  what I have planned, that will I do.
12Listen to me, you stubborn-hearted,
  you who are far from righteousness.
13I am bringing my righteousness near,
  it is not far away;
  and my salvation will not be
    delayed.
I will grant salvation to Zion,
  my splendor to Israel.

The Fall of Babylon

47 "Go down, sit in the dust,
      Virgin Daughter of Babylon;
sit on the ground without a throne,
  Daughter of the Babylonians.ᵇ
No more will you be called
  tender or delicate.
2Take millstones and grind flour;
  take off your veil.
Lift up your skirts, bare your legs,
  and wade through the streams.
3Your nakedness will be exposed
  and your shame uncovered.
I will take vengeance;
  I will spare no one."

4Our Redeemer—the LORD Almighty is
    his name—
  is the Holy One of Israel.

ᵃ1 Or are but beasts and cattle   ᵇ1 Or Chaldeans; also in verse 5

TUESDAY

VERSE FOR THE DAY:
Isaiah 46:3

AUTHOR:
Walter Trobisch

PASSAGE FOR THE DAY:
Isaiah 46:1–4

The Tender Man

WE MEN tend to hide or deny our feelings because we think they are unmanly. The redeemed man is set free from this in a remarkable way. He is free to be motherly, to portray the tenderness of God.

The Kiga tribe in East Africa gives God the name of Biheko, which means "a God who carries everyone on his back." In this tribe only mothers and older sisters carry children on their backs while fathers never do. To portray Biheko, one of their artists made a wooden carving portraying a man who carries on his back a child with an adult face and in his arms a weaker child. This carving is a symbol of the God who takes care of human beings with the tender care of a mother. We see this God in Isaiah 46:3–4 . . .

We are often not able to be in touch with our feelings because we think we must express everything objectively, without any feeling. But this is a sign that our spiritual lives are poverty-stricken. We cannot mirror, cannot radiate the tenderness of God because we have not experienced it ourselves . . .

God wants to be loved as a father and mother are loved by their children, as a friend by a friend, as a man by his wife and a wife by her husband, as a sick person by a caring nurse and as a guest by his host. God finds great joy when we express our feelings toward him.

But before a man can feel his own feelings and express them, he often has to go back to the past and deal with that hurting child within himself, that frightened child, that hating child. Jesus loves all those wounded children in our hearts. He is the only one who is the same yesterday, today and forever, who can walk into our pasts, the time even before we were born, and place his healing and comforting hand on all those deeply sensitive spots that we try to cover up with the armor of our invulnerability. This wonderful healing of memories is the key to the man who has the courage to be motherly—the courage to express his deepest longings. This is the key to the redeemed man who, because the past hurts have been exposed to the Light and healed, no longer needs to retreat into his fortress, but stands there naked, vulnerable, ready to risk being wounded again. His fear is gone.

Additional Scripture Readings:
Philippians 2:1–11; 1 John 4:13–21

*Go to page 763 for your next
devotional reading.*

⁵"Sit in silence, go into darkness,
  Daughter of the Babylonians;
no more will you be called
  queen of kingdoms.
⁶I was angry with my people
  and desecrated my inheritance;
I gave them into your hand,
  and you showed them no mercy.
Even on the aged
  you laid a very heavy yoke.
⁷You said, 'I will continue forever—
  the eternal queen!'
But you did not consider these things
  or reflect on what might happen.

⁸"Now then, listen, you wanton
    creature,
  lounging in your security
and saying to yourself,
  'I am, and there is none besides me.
I will never be a widow
  or suffer the loss of children.'
⁹Both of these will overtake you
  in a moment, on a single day:
loss of children and widowhood.
They will come upon you in full
    measure,
  in spite of your many sorceries
  and all your potent spells.
¹⁰You have trusted in your wickedness
  and have said, 'No one sees me.'
Your wisdom and knowledge mislead
    you
  when you say to yourself,
  'I am, and there is none besides
    me.'
¹¹Disaster will come upon you,
  and you will not know how to
    conjure it away.
A calamity will fall upon you
  that you cannot ward off with a
    ransom;
a catastrophe you cannot foresee
  will suddenly come upon you.

¹²"Keep on, then, with your magic spells
  and with your many sorceries,
  which you have labored at since
    childhood.
Perhaps you will succeed,
  perhaps you will cause terror.
¹³All the counsel you have received has
  only worn you out!
Let your astrologers come forward,
  those stargazers who make predictions
    month by month,
  let them save you from what is
    coming upon you.
¹⁴Surely they are like stubble;
  the fire will burn them up.
They cannot even save themselves
from the power of the flame.
Here are no coals to warm anyone;
  here is no fire to sit by.
¹⁵That is all they can do for you—
  these you have labored with
  and trafficked with since childhood.
Each of them goes on in his error;
  there is not one that can save you.

Stubborn Israel

48 "Listen to this, O house of Jacob,
  you who are called by the name
    of Israel
and come from the line of Judah,
  you who take oaths in the name of
    the LORD
  and invoke the God of Israel—
  but not in truth or righteousness—
²you who call yourselves citizens of
    the holy city
  and rely on the God of Israel—
  the LORD Almighty is his name:
³I foretold the former things long ago,
  my mouth announced them and I
    made them known;
  then suddenly I acted, and they
    came to pass.
⁴For I knew how stubborn you were;
  the sinews of your neck were iron,
  your forehead was bronze.
⁵Therefore I told you these things long
    ago;
  before they happened I announced
    them to you
so that you could not say,
  'My idols did them;
  my wooden image and metal god
    ordained them.'
⁶You have heard these things; look at
    them all.
  Will you not admit them?

"From now on I will tell you of new
    things,
  of hidden things unknown to you.
⁷They are created now, and not long
    ago;
  you have not heard of them before
    today.
So you cannot say,
  'Yes, I knew of them.'
⁸You have neither heard nor
    understood;
  from of old your ear has not been
    open.
Well do I know how treacherous you
    are;
  you were called a rebel from birth.
⁹For my own name's sake I delay my
    wrath;

for the sake of my praise I hold it
  back from you,
so as not to cut you off.
10See, I have refined you, though not as
  silver;
I have tested you in the furnace of
  affliction.
11For my own sake, for my own sake, I
  do this.
How can I let myself be defamed?
I will not yield my glory to another.

Israel Freed

12"Listen to me, O Jacob,
  Israel, whom I have called:
I am he;
  I am the first and I am the last.
13My own hand laid the foundations of
  the earth,
  and my right hand spread out the
    heavens;
when I summon them,
  they all stand up together.

14"Come together, all of you, and listen:
  Which of the idols has foretold
    these things?
The Lord's chosen ally
  will carry out his purpose against
    Babylon;
  his arm will be against the
    Babylonians.a
15I, even I, have spoken;
  yes, I have called him.
I will bring him,
  and he will succeed in his mission.

16"Come near me and listen to this:

"From the first announcement I have
  not spoken in secret;
  at the time it happens, I am there."

And now the Sovereign Lord has sent
  me,
  with his Spirit.

17This is what the Lord says—
  your Redeemer, the Holy One of
    Israel:
"I am the Lord your God,
  who teaches you what is best for
    you,
  who directs you in the way you
    should go.
18If only you had paid attention to my
  commands,
  your peace would have been like a
    river,

your righteousness like the waves of
  the sea.
19Your descendants would have been
  like the sand,
  your children like its numberless
    grains;
their name would never be cut off
  nor destroyed from before me."

20Leave Babylon,
  flee from the Babylonians!
Announce this with shouts of joy
  and proclaim it.
Send it out to the ends of the earth;
  say, "The Lord has redeemed his
    servant Jacob."
21They did not thirst when he led them
  through the deserts;
  he made water flow for them from
    the rock;
he split the rock
  and water gushed out.

22"There is no peace," says the Lord,
  "for the wicked."

The Servant of the Lord

49 Listen to me, you islands;
     hear this, you distant nations:
Before I was born the Lord called me;
  from my birth he has made mention
    of my name.
2He made my mouth like a sharpened
  sword,
  in the shadow of his hand he hid
    me;
he made me into a polished arrow
  and concealed me in his quiver.
3He said to me, "You are my servant,
  Israel, in whom I will display my
    splendor."
4But I said, "I have labored to no
  purpose;
  I have spent my strength in vain
    and for nothing.
Yet what is due me is in the Lord's
  hand,
  and my reward is with my God."

5And now the Lord says—
  he who formed me in the womb to
    be his servant
to bring Jacob back to him
  and gather Israel to himself,
for I am honored in the eyes of the
  Lord

a14 Or Chaldeans; also in verse 20

and my God has been my
strength —
⁶he says:
"It is too small a thing for you to be
my servant
to restore the tribes of Jacob

and bring back those of Israel I
have kept.
I will also make you a light for the
Gentiles,
that you may bring my salvation to
the ends of the earth."

WEDNESDAY

VERSE FOR THE DAY: *AUTHOR:*   *PASSAGE FOR THE DAY:*
Isaiah 49:6   Michael Card   Isaiah 49:1–7

Embracing the Embracer

IN LUKE 2:22–35 we meet Simeon, a man who has grown old waiting for the Messiah—the consolation of Israel. As he takes the infant Jesus into his arms, Simeon sings his praise to God, proclaiming in the words of Isaiah 49:6 that this baby would not only be a light for Israel, but also for the Gentiles.

We do not know what Simeon was expecting, but we do know what he got. A little baby wrapped in rags, with paupers for parents . . .

There the Holy Baby was, cradled in his mother's arms. What must have gone through Simeon's mind when God pointed out his Promised One. "There he is, the one with the dirty diaper." Simeon was wise enough to expect the unexpected from the Lord. He went straight to Joseph and Mary. Luke gives us the wonderful detail that he took Jesus and held him in his arms [Luke 2:28]. That, for me, is one of the most significant moments of the nativity narratives. In this one simple man two worlds meet.

The Old Testament embraces the New. For what is the Old Testament but a collection of promises? God promised Adam and Eve, I will send someone to crush the head of the serpent [Genesis 3:15]. Now that One had come. As Simeon took him into his arms he responded poetically, perhaps even in a song, as Adam had first responded to Eve, as Mary had responded to the angel. The promise had become flesh. It was "the good news."

It was good news to finally be able to embrace the Promised One. But far and away the best news of all is that he embraces us. That was the reason for his coming. Most of us describe our coming to faith by saying, "I've asked Jesus into my life." We should really say he has invited us into his life!

That was the reason for Simeon's song. Deep inside his tired old heart, he knew that the infant he held in his arms was in truth the One who had been holding him all his life long.

Additional Scripture Readings:
Psalm 73:23–28; Luke 2:25–35

Go to page 766 for your next devotional reading.

⁷This is what the LORD says—
  the Redeemer and Holy One of
    Israel—
to him who was despised and
    abhorred by the nation,
  to the servant of rulers:
"Kings will see you and rise up,
  princes will see and bow down,
because of the LORD, who is faithful,
  the Holy One of Israel, who has
    chosen you."

Restoration of Israel

⁸This is what the LORD says:

"In the time of my favor I will answer
    you,
  and in the day of salvation I will
    help you;
I will keep you and will make you
  to be a covenant for the people,
to restore the land
  and to reassign its desolate
    inheritances,
⁹to say to the captives, 'Come out,'
  and to those in darkness, 'Be free!'

"They will feed beside the roads
  and find pasture on every barren
    hill.
¹⁰They will neither hunger nor thirst,
  nor will the desert heat or the sun
    beat upon them.
He who has compassion on them will
    guide them
  and lead them beside springs of
    water.
¹¹I will turn all my mountains into
    roads,
  and my highways will be raised up.
¹²See, they will come from afar—
  some from the north, some from the
    west,
  some from the region of Aswan.ᵃ"

¹³Shout for joy, O heavens;
  rejoice, O earth;
  burst into song, O mountains!
For the LORD comforts his people
  and will have compassion on his
    afflicted ones.

¹⁴But Zion said, "The LORD has forsaken
    me,
  the Lord has forgotten me."

¹⁵"Can a mother forget the baby at her
    breast

and have no compassion on the
    child she has borne?
Though she may forget,
  I will not forget you!
¹⁶See, I have engraved you on the palms
    of my hands;
  your walls are ever before me.
¹⁷Your sons hasten back,
  and those who laid you waste
    depart from you.
¹⁸Lift up your eyes and look around;
  all your sons gather and come to
    you.
As surely as I live," declares the LORD,
  "you will wear them all as
    ornaments;
  you will put them on, like a bride.

¹⁹"Though you were ruined and made
    desolate
  and your land laid waste,
now you will be too small for your
    people,
  and those who devoured you will
    be far away.
²⁰The children born during your
    bereavement
  will yet say in your hearing,
'This place is too small for us;
  give us more space to live in.'
²¹Then you will say in your heart,
  'Who bore me these?
I was bereaved and barren;
  I was exiled and rejected.
Who brought these up?
I was left all alone,
  but these—where have they come
    from?' "

²²This is what the Sovereign LORD says:

"See, I will beckon to the Gentiles,
  I will lift up my banner to the
    peoples;
they will bring your sons in their arms
  and carry your daughters on their
    shoulders.
²³Kings will be your foster fathers,
  and their queens your nursing
    mothers.
They will bow down before you with
    their faces to the ground;
  they will lick the dust at your feet.
Then you will know that I am the
    LORD;
  those who hope in me will not be
    disappointed."

²⁴Can plunder be taken from warriors,

ᵃ12 Dead Sea Scrolls; Masoretic Text Sinim

or captives rescued from the
   fierce[a]?
25But this is what the LORD says:

"Yes, captives will be taken from
   warriors,
   and plunder retrieved from the
      fierce;
I will contend with those who contend
   with you,
   and your children I will save.
26I will make your oppressors eat their
   own flesh;
   they will be drunk on their own
      blood, as with wine.
Then all mankind will know
   that I, the LORD, am your Savior,
   your Redeemer, the Mighty One of
      Jacob."

Israel's Sin and the Servant's Obedience

50 This is what the LORD says:

"Where is your mother's certificate of
   divorce
   with which I sent her away?
Or to which of my creditors
   did I sell you?
Because of your sins you were sold;
   because of your transgressions your
      mother was sent away.
2When I came, why was there no one?
   When I called, why was there no
      one to answer?
Was my arm too short to ransom you?
   Do I lack the strength to rescue
      you?
By a mere rebuke I dry up the sea,
   I turn rivers into a desert;
their fish rot for lack of water
   and die of thirst.
3I clothe the sky with darkness
   and make sackcloth its covering."

4The Sovereign LORD has given me an
   instructed tongue,
   to know the word that sustains the
      weary.
He wakens me morning by morning,
   wakens my ear to listen like one
      being taught.
5The Sovereign LORD has opened my
   ears,
   and I have not been rebellious;
   I have not drawn back.
6I offered my back to those who beat
   me,

my cheeks to those who pulled out
   my beard;
I did not hide my face
   from mocking and spitting.
7Because the Sovereign LORD helps me,
   I will not be disgraced.
Therefore have I set my face like flint,
   and I know I will not be put to
      shame.
8He who vindicates me is near.
   Who then will bring charges against
      me?
Let us face each other!
Who is my accuser?
   Let him confront me!
9It is the Sovereign LORD who helps
   me.
   Who is he that will condemn me?
They will all wear out like a garment;
   the moths will eat them up.

10Who among you fears the LORD
   and obeys the word of his servant?
Let him who walks in the dark,
   who has no light,
trust in the name of the LORD
   and rely on his God.
11But now, all you who light fires
   and provide yourselves with flaming
      torches,
go, walk in the light of your fires
   and of the torches you have set
      ablaze.
This is what you shall receive from
   my hand:
   You will lie down in torment.

Everlasting Salvation for Zion

51 "Listen to me, you who pursue
   righteousness
   and who seek the LORD:
Look to the rock from which you were
   cut
   and to the quarry from which you
      were hewn;
2look to Abraham, your father,
   and to Sarah, who gave you birth.
When I called him he was but one,
   and I blessed him and made him
      many.
3The LORD will surely comfort Zion
   and will look with compassion on
      all her ruins;
he will make her deserts like Eden,
   her wastelands like the garden of
      the LORD.
Joy and gladness will be found in her,

---

[a]24 Dead Sea Scrolls, Vulgate and Syriac (see also Septuagint and verse 25); Masoretic Text *righteous*

thanksgiving and the sound of
   singing.
4"Listen to me, my people;
   hear me, my nation:
The law will go out from me;
   my justice will become a light to
   the nations.
5My righteousness draws near speedily,

my salvation is on the way,
   and my arm will bring justice to the
   nations.
The islands will look to me
   and wait in hope for my arm.
6Lift up your eyes to the heavens,
   look at the earth beneath;
the heavens will vanish like smoke,

THURSDAY

VERSE FOR THE DAY: *AUTHOR:*   *PASSAGE FOR THE DAY:*
Isaiah 50:9   *Dan Allender*   *Isaiah 50:6–9*

No Condemnation!

IF WE have acknowledged God as the One, and the only One, who has the power to determine our acceptability, then we will feel only grief, not shame over loss and disappointment. The prophet Isaiah, speaking of the Suffering Servant, reflects that hope in a statement that is a foundation for dealing with injustice and wicked misuse: "I offered my back to those who beat me, my cheeks to those who pulled out my beard; I did not hide my face from mocking and spitting. Because the Sovereign Lord helps me, I will not be disgraced. Therefore have I set my face like flint, and I know I will not be put to shame. He who vindicates me is near. Who then will bring charges against me? Let us face each other! Who is my accuser? Let him confront me! It is the Sovereign Lord who helps me. Who is he that will condemn me?" (Isaiah 50:6–9).

The Servant of God understood that faith was not a protective shield against the brutality of those who beat him or the ignominy of those who pulled out his beard. In that culture, nothing could have been more shameful than having one's beard plucked. Nevertheless, no one could stand as his accuser and bring his soul to shame because the Father stood as his advocate and judge.

Legitimate shame (that is, facing our failure to trust God) is the basis of our return to the Father. For most, trusting God means relying on him to keep our body or our world intact. But that is not Biblical trust at its essential core. Trust involves relying on him for what is most essential to our being: the intactness of our soul. A return to the Father ensures that no one can shame or disgrace or possess our soul—that quintessential core of who we are that will live eternally with him—no matter what is done to our body, reputation or temporal security.

Additional Scripture Readings:
1 Corinthians 4:1–5;
Romans 8:1–4,31–39

Go to page 771 for your next devotional reading.

the earth will wear out like a
    garment
and its inhabitants die like flies.
But my salvation will last forever,
    my righteousness will never fail.

[7]"Hear me, you who know what is
    right,
    you people who have my law in
        your hearts:
Do not fear the reproach of men
    or be terrified by their insults.
[8]For the moth will eat them up like a
    garment;
    the worm will devour them like
        wool.
But my righteousness will last forever,
    my salvation through all
        generations."

[9]Awake, awake! Clothe yourself with
    strength,
    O arm of the LORD;
awake, as in days gone by,
    as in generations of old.
Was it not you who cut Rahab to
    pieces,
    who pierced that monster through?
[10]Was it not you who dried up the sea,
    the waters of the great deep,
who made a road in the depths of the
    sea
    so that the redeemed might cross
        over?
[11]The ransomed of the LORD will return.
    They will enter Zion with singing;
    everlasting joy will crown their
        heads.
Gladness and joy will overtake them,
    and sorrow and sighing will flee
        away.

[12]"I, even I, am he who comforts you.
    Who are you that you fear mortal
        men,
    the sons of men, who are but grass,
[13]that you forget the LORD your Maker,
    who stretched out the heavens
    and laid the foundations of the
        earth,
that you live in constant terror every
    day
    because of the wrath of the
        oppressor,
    who is bent on destruction?
For where is the wrath of the
    oppressor?
[14] The cowering prisoners will soon be
    set free;

they will not die in their dungeon,
    nor will they lack bread.
[15]For I am the LORD your God,
    who churns up the sea so that its
        waves roar—
    the LORD Almighty is his name.
[16]I have put my words in your mouth
    and covered you with the shadow of
        my hand—
I who set the heavens in place,
    who laid the foundations of the
        earth,
    and who say to Zion, 'You are my
        people.' "

The Cup of the LORD's Wrath

[17]Awake, awake!
    Rise up, O Jerusalem,
you who have drunk from the hand of
    the LORD
    the cup of his wrath,
you who have drained to its dregs
    the goblet that makes men stagger.
[18]Of all the sons she bore
    there was none to guide her;
of all the sons she reared
    there was none to take her by the
        hand.
[19]These double calamities have come
    upon you—
    who can comfort you?—
ruin and destruction, famine and
    sword—
    who can[a] console you?
[20]Your sons have fainted;
    they lie at the head of every street,
    like antelope caught in a net.
They are filled with the wrath of the
    LORD
    and the rebuke of your God.

[21]Therefore hear this, you afflicted one,
    made drunk, but not with wine.
[22]This is what your Sovereign LORD
    says,
    your God, who defends his people:
"See, I have taken out of your hand
    the cup that made you stagger;
from that cup, the goblet of my wrath,
    you will never drink again.
[23]I will put it into the hands of your
    tormentors,
    who said to you,
    'Fall prostrate that we may walk
        over you.'
And you made your back like the
    ground,
    like a street to be walked over."

---

[a]19 Dead Sea Scrolls, Septuagint, Vulgate and Syriac; Masoretic Text / *how can I*

52
Awake, awake, O Zion,
clothe yourself with strength.
Put on your garments of splendor,
  O Jerusalem, the holy city.
The uncircumcised and defiled
  will not enter you again.
²Shake off your dust;
  rise up, sit enthroned, O Jerusalem.
Free yourself from the chains on your
    neck,
  O captive Daughter of Zion.

³For this is what the LORD says:

"You were sold for nothing,
  and without money you will be
    redeemed."

⁴For this is what the Sovereign LORD
says:

"At first my people went down to
    Egypt to live;
  lately, Assyria has oppressed them.

⁵"And now what do I have here?" declares the LORD.

"For my people have been taken away
    for nothing,
  and those who rule them mock,ᵃ"
              declares the LORD.
"And all day long
  my name is constantly blasphemed.
⁶Therefore my people will know my
    name;
  therefore in that day they will know
that it is I who foretold it.
  Yes, it is I."

⁷How beautiful on the mountains
  are the feet of those who bring good
    news,
who proclaim peace,
  who bring good tidings,
  who proclaim salvation,
who say to Zion,
  "Your God reigns!"
⁸Listen! Your watchmen lift up their
    voices;
  together they shout for joy.
When the LORD returns to Zion,
  they will see it with their own eyes.
⁹Burst into songs of joy together,
  you ruins of Jerusalem,
for the LORD has comforted his people,
  he has redeemed Jerusalem.
¹⁰The LORD will lay bare his holy arm
  in the sight of all the nations,
and all the ends of the earth will see

the salvation of our God.

¹¹Depart, depart, go out from there!
  Touch no unclean thing!
Come out from it and be pure,
  you who carry the vessels of the
    LORD.
¹²But you will not leave in haste
  or go in flight;
for the LORD will go before you,
  the God of Israel will be your rear
    guard.

The Suffering and Glory
of the Servant

¹³See, my servant will act wiselyᵇ;
  he will be raised and lifted up and
    highly exalted.
¹⁴Just as there were many who were
    appalled at himᶜ—
  his appearance was so disfigured
    beyond that of any man
  and his form marred beyond human
    likeness—
¹⁵so will he sprinkle many nations,ᵈ
  and kings will shut their mouths
    because of him.
For what they were not told, they will
    see,
  and what they have not heard, they
    will understand.

53
Who has believed our message
and to whom has the arm of the
    LORD been revealed?
²He grew up before him like a tender
    shoot,
  and like a root out of dry ground.
He had no beauty or majesty to attract
    us to him,
  nothing in his appearance that we
    should desire him.
³He was despised and rejected by men,
  a man of sorrows, and familiar with
    suffering.
Like one from whom men hide their
    faces
  he was despised, and we esteemed
    him not.

⁴Surely he took up our infirmities
  and carried our sorrows,
yet we considered him stricken by
    God,
  smitten by him, and afflicted.
⁵But he was pierced for our
    transgressions,
  he was crushed for our iniquities;

ᵃ5 Dead Sea Scrolls and Vulgate; Masoretic Text *wail*   ᵇ13 Or *will prosper*   ᶜ14 Hebrew *you*
ᵈ15 Hebrew; Septuagint *so will many nations marvel at him*

the punishment that brought us peace
was upon him,
and by his wounds we are healed.
6We all, like sheep, have gone astray,
each of us has turned to his own
way;
and the LORD has laid on him
the iniquity of us all.

7He was oppressed and afflicted,
yet he did not open his mouth;
he was led like a lamb to the
slaughter,
and as a sheep before her shearers
is silent,
so he did not open his mouth.
8By oppression*a* and judgment he was
taken away.
And who can speak of his
descendants?
For he was cut off from the land of
the living;
for the transgression of my people
he was stricken.*b*
9He was assigned a grave with the
wicked,
and with the rich in his death,
though he had done no violence,
nor was any deceit in his mouth.

10Yet it was the LORD's will to crush him
and cause him to suffer,
and though the LORD makes*c* his
life a guilt offering,
he will see his offspring and prolong
his days,
and the will of the LORD will
prosper in his hand.
11After the suffering of his soul,
he will see the light ˌof lifeˌ*d* and be
satisfied*e*;
by his knowledge*f* my righteous
servant will justify many,
and he will bear their iniquities.
12Therefore I will give him a portion
among the great,*g*
and he will divide the spoils with
the strong,*h*
because he poured out his life unto
death,
and was numbered with the
transgressors.
For he bore the sin of many,
and made intercession for the
transgressors.

The Future Glory of Zion

54 "Sing, O barren woman,
you who never bore a child;
burst into song, shout for joy,
you who were never in labor;
because more are the children of the
desolate woman
than of her who has a husband,"
says the LORD.
2"Enlarge the place of your tent,
stretch your tent curtains wide,
do not hold back;
lengthen your cords,
strengthen your stakes.
3For you will spread out to the right
and to the left;
your descendants will dispossess
nations
and settle in their desolate cities.

4"Do not be afraid; you will not suffer
shame.
Do not fear disgrace; you will not
be humiliated.
You will forget the shame of your
youth
and remember no more the
reproach of your widowhood.
5For your Maker is your husband—
the LORD Almighty is his name—
the Holy One of Israel is your
Redeemer;
he is called the God of all the earth.
6The LORD will call you back
as if you were a wife deserted and
distressed in spirit—
a wife who married young,
only to be rejected," says your God.
7"For a brief moment I abandoned you,
but with deep compassion I will
bring you back.
8In a surge of anger
I hid my face from you for a
moment,
but with everlasting kindness
I will have compassion on you,"
says the LORD your Redeemer.

9"To me this is like the days of Noah,
when I swore that the waters of
Noah would never again cover
the earth.
So now I have sworn not to be angry
with you,
never to rebuke you again.

---

a8 Or From arrest   *b8 Or away. / Yet who of his generation considered / that he was cut off from the
land of the living / for the transgression of my people, / to whom the blow was due?*   *c10 Hebrew
though you make*   *d11 Dead Sea Scrolls (see also Septuagint); Masoretic Text does not have the light
ˌof lifeˌ.*   *e11 Or (with Masoretic Text) 11He will see the result of the suffering of his soul / and be
satisfied*   *f11 Or by knowledge of him*   *g12 Or many*   *h12 Or numerous*

¹⁰Though the mountains be shaken
    and the hills be removed,
  yet my unfailing love for you will not
        be shaken
    nor my covenant of peace be
        removed,"
    says the LORD, who has compassion
        on you.

¹¹"O afflicted city, lashed by storms and
        not comforted,
    I will build you with stones of
        turquoise,ᵃ
  your foundations with sapphires.ᵇ
¹²I will make your battlements of
        rubies,
    your gates of sparkling jewels,
    and all your walls of precious
        stones.
¹³All your sons will be taught by the
        LORD,
    and great will be your children's
        peace.
¹⁴In righteousness you will be
        established:
  Tyranny will be far from you;
    you will have nothing to fear.
  Terror will be far removed;
    it will not come near you.
¹⁵If anyone does attack you, it will not
        be my doing;
    whoever attacks you will surrender
        to you.

¹⁶"See, it is I who created the
        blacksmith
    who fans the coals into flame
    and forges a weapon fit for its work.
  And it is I who have created the
        destroyer to work havoc;
¹⁷ no weapon forged against you will
        prevail,
    and you will refute every tongue
        that accuses you.
  This is the heritage of the servants of
        the LORD,
    and this is their vindication from
        me,"
                declares the LORD.

Invitation to the Thirsty

55 "Come, all you who are thirsty,
      come to the waters;
  and you who have no money,
      come, buy and eat!
  Come, buy wine and milk
      without money and without cost.

²Why spend money on what is not
        bread,
    and your labor on what does not
        satisfy?
  Listen, listen to me, and eat what is
        good,
    and your soul will delight in the
        richest of fare.
³Give ear and come to me;
    hear me, that your soul may live.
  I will make an everlasting covenant
        with you,
    my faithful love promised to David.
⁴See, I have made him a witness to the
        peoples,
    a leader and commander of the
        peoples.
⁵Surely you will summon nations you
        know not,
    and nations that do not know you
        will hasten to you,
  because of the LORD your God,
    the Holy One of Israel,
    for he has endowed you with
        splendor."

⁶Seek the LORD while he may be found;
    call on him while he is near.
⁷Let the wicked forsake his way
    and the evil man his thoughts.
  Let him turn to the LORD, and he will
        have mercy on him,
    and to our God, for he will freely
        pardon.

⁸"For my thoughts are not your
        thoughts,
    neither are your ways my ways,"
                declares the LORD.
⁹"As the heavens are higher than the
        earth,
    so are my ways higher than your
        ways
    and my thoughts than your
        thoughts.
¹⁰As the rain and the snow
    come down from heaven,
  and do not return to it
    without watering the earth
  and making it bud and flourish,
    so that it yields seed for the sower
        and bread for the eater,
¹¹so is my word that goes out from my
        mouth:
  It will not return to me empty,
    but will accomplish what I desire
    and achieve the purpose for which I
        sent it.

ᵃ11 The meaning of the Hebrew for this word is uncertain.   ᵇ11 Or *lapis lazuli*

¹²You will go out in joy
and be led forth in peace;
the mountains and hills
will burst into song before you,
and all the trees of the field
will clap their hands.
¹³Instead of the thornbush will grow the
pine tree,
and instead of briers the myrtle will
grow.
This will be for the LORD's renown,
for an everlasting sign,
which will not be destroyed."

Salvation for Others

56 This is what the LORD says:
"Maintain justice
and do what is right,
for my salvation is close at hand
and my righteousness will soon be
revealed.
²Blessed is the man who does this,
the man who holds it fast,
who keeps the Sabbath without
desecrating it,

FRIDAY

VERSE FOR THE DAY: *AUTHOR:*   *PASSAGE FOR THE DAY:*
Isaiah 55:9   Ron Blue   Isaiah 55:8–13

His Ways, and Our Ways

THE spiritual dangers of borrowing money are twofold: First
of all, borrowing *always* presumes upon the future, and, second, borrowing *may* deny God an opportunity to work.

The Bible definitely warns us about presuming upon the future. In James 4:16, presuming upon the future is called
"boasting." In Luke 14:28, Jesus said: "Suppose one of you
wants to build a tower. Will he not first sit down and estimate
the cost to see if he has enough money to complete it?" . . .

The second spiritual danger of debt is that it *may* deny God
an opportunity to work . . . .

I believe that in many cases, when we borrow the money to
fund one item, be it for the purpose of a new car, a television,
a new home, a vacation, or whatever, we are putting the lender
in the place of God. Who needs God to provide for us if someone will lend to us?

We seem to be very unwilling to wait for God's timing and
for God's method to meet our needs and our desires. We prefer to have it done our way, on our timing. Yet, Isaiah 55:8–9
says, "'For my thoughts are not your thoughts, neither are
your ways my ways,' declares the Lord. 'As the heavens are
higher than the earth, so are my ways higher than your ways
and my thoughts than your thoughts.'" Invariably, God's
method of meeting my needs and desires is different from my
method. The question that we need to ask ourselves is, "Does
God provide for what I want by providing borrowed funds, or
is this me meeting my needs and desires in my own way?"

Additional Scripture Readings:
Psalm 145:1–7; James 4:13–16

Go to page 773 for your next
devotional reading.

and keeps his hand from doing any
  evil."

³Let no foreigner who has bound
    himself to the LORD say,
  "The LORD will surely exclude me
    from his people."
And let not any eunuch complain,
  "I am only a dry tree."

⁴For this is what the LORD says:

"To the eunuchs who keep my
    Sabbaths,
  who choose what pleases me
  and hold fast to my covenant —
⁵to them I will give within my temple
    and its walls
  a memorial and a name
  better than sons and daughters;
I will give them an everlasting name
  that will not be cut off.
⁶And foreigners who bind themselves
    to the LORD
  to serve him,
to love the name of the LORD,
  and to worship him,
all who keep the Sabbath without
    desecrating it
  and who hold fast to my
    covenant —
⁷these I will bring to my holy
    mountain
  and give them joy in my house of
    prayer.
Their burnt offerings and sacrifices
  will be accepted on my altar;
for my house will be called
  a house of prayer for all nations."
⁸The Sovereign LORD declares —
  he who gathers the exiles of Israel:
"I will gather still others to them
  besides those already gathered."

God's Accusation Against the Wicked

⁹Come, all you beasts of the field,
  come and devour, all you beasts of
    the forest!
¹⁰Israel's watchmen are blind,
    they all lack knowledge;
  they are all mute dogs,
    they cannot bark;
  they lie around and dream,
    they love to sleep.
¹¹They are dogs with mighty appetites;
    they never have enough.
  They are shepherds who lack
    understanding;
  they all turn to their own way,

each seeks his own gain.
¹²"Come," each one cries, "let me get
    wine!
  Let us drink our fill of beer!
  And tomorrow will be like today,
    or even far better."

57 The righteous perish,
        and no one ponders it in his
          heart;
  devout men are taken away,
    and no one understands
  that the righteous are taken away
    to be spared from evil.
²Those who walk uprightly
    enter into peace;
  they find rest as they lie in death.

³"But you — come here, you sons of a
    sorceress,
  you offspring of adulterers and
    prostitutes!
⁴Whom are you mocking?
  At whom do you sneer
    and stick out your tongue?
  Are you not a brood of rebels,
    the offspring of liars?
⁵You burn with lust among the oaks
    and under every spreading tree;
  you sacrifice your children in the
    ravines
  and under the overhanging crags.
⁶The idols among the smooth stones
    of the ravines are your portion;
  they, they are your lot.
  Yes, to them you have poured out
    drink offerings
  and offered grain offerings.
  In the light of these things, should I
    relent?
⁷You have made your bed on a high
    and lofty hill;
  there you went up to offer your
    sacrifices.
⁸Behind your doors and your doorposts
  you have put your pagan symbols.
  Forsaking me, you uncovered your
    bed,
  you climbed into it and opened it
    wide;
  you made a pact with those whose
    beds you love,
  and you looked on their nakedness.
⁹You went to Molechᵃ with olive oil
  and increased your perfumes.
  You sent your ambassadorsᵇ far
    away;
  you descended to the graveᶜ itself!

ᵃ9 Or *to the king*   ᵇ9 Or *idols*   ᶜ9 Hebrew *Sheol*

WEEKENDING

REALIZE

Lord, make me an
instrument of your peace!
Where there is hatred,
let me sow love;
where there is injury, pardon;
where there is doubt, faith;
where there is despair, hope;
where there is darkness, light;
and where there is sadness, joy.

O Divine Master,
grant that I may not
so much seek to be consoled
as to console;
to be understood
as to understand;
to be loved
as to love;
for it is in giving
that we receive;
it is in pardoning
that we are pardoned;
and it is in dying
that we are born to Eternal Life.

– Francis of Assisi

REVIVE

Saturday: Romans 6:1–14
Sunday: James 3:13–18

Go to page 776 for your next devotional reading.

¹⁰You were wearied by all your ways,
    but you would not say, 'It is
        hopeless.'
You found renewal of your strength,
    and so you did not faint.

¹¹"Whom have you so dreaded and
        feared
    that you have been false to me,
and have neither remembered me
    nor pondered this in your hearts?
Is it not because I have long been
        silent
    that you do not fear me?
¹²I will expose your righteousness and
        your works,
    and they will not benefit you.
¹³When you cry out for help,
    let your collection ₍of idols₎ save
        you!
The wind will carry all of them off,
    a mere breath will blow them away.
But the man who makes me his refuge
    will inherit the land
    and possess my holy mountain."

Comfort for the Contrite

¹⁴And it will be said:

"Build up, build up, prepare the road!
    Remove the obstacles out of the
        way of my people."
¹⁵For this is what the high and lofty
        One says—
    he who lives forever, whose name is
        holy:
"I live in a high and holy place,
    but also with him who is contrite
        and lowly in spirit,
to revive the spirit of the lowly
    and to revive the heart of the
        contrite.
¹⁶I will not accuse forever,
    nor will I always be angry,
for then the spirit of man would grow
        faint before me—
    the breath of man that I have
        created.
¹⁷I was enraged by his sinful greed;
    I punished him, and hid my face in
        anger,
    yet he kept on in his willful ways.
¹⁸I have seen his ways, but I will heal
        him;
    I will guide him and restore comfort
        to him,
¹⁹ creating praise on the lips of the
        mourners in Israel.
Peace, peace, to those far and near,"
    says the Lord. "And I will heal
        them."

²⁰But the wicked are like the tossing
        sea,
    which cannot rest,
    whose waves cast up mire and mud.
²¹"There is no peace," says my God,
    "for the wicked."

True Fasting

58 "Shout it aloud, do not hold
        back.
Raise your voice like a trumpet.
Declare to my people their rebellion
    and to the house of Jacob their sins.
²For day after day they seek me out;
    they seem eager to know my ways,
as if they were a nation that does
        what is right
    and has not forsaken the commands
        of its God.
They ask me for just decisions
    and seem eager for God to come
        near them.
³'Why have we fasted,' they say,
    'and you have not seen it?
Why have we humbled ourselves,
    and you have not noticed?'

"Yet on the day of your fasting, you
        do as you please
    and exploit all your workers.
⁴Your fasting ends in quarreling and
        strife,
    and in striking each other with
        wicked fists.
You cannot fast as you do today
    and expect your voice to be heard
        on high.
⁵Is this the kind of fast I have chosen,
    only a day for a man to humble
        himself?
Is it only for bowing one's head like a
        reed
    and for lying on sackcloth and
        ashes?
Is that what you call a fast,
    a day acceptable to the Lord?

⁶"Is not this the kind of fasting I have
        chosen:
to loose the chains of injustice
    and untie the cords of the yoke,
to set the oppressed free
    and break every yoke?
⁷Is it not to share your food with the
        hungry
    and to provide the poor wanderer
        with shelter—
when you see the naked, to clothe
        him,
    and not to turn away from your
        own flesh and blood?

8Then your light will break forth like
  the dawn,
  and your healing will quickly
    appear;
then your righteousness*a* will go
  before you,
  and the glory of the LORD will be
    your rear guard.
9Then you will call, and the LORD will
  answer;
  you will cry for help, and he will
    say: Here am I.

"If you do away with the yoke of
  oppression,
  with the pointing finger and
    malicious talk,
10and if you spend yourselves in behalf
  of the hungry
  and satisfy the needs of the
    oppressed,
then your light will rise in the
  darkness,
  and your night will become like the
    noonday.
11The LORD will guide you always;
  he will satisfy your needs in a
    sun-scorched land
  and will strengthen your frame.
You will be like a well-watered
  garden,
  like a spring whose waters never
    fail.
12Your people will rebuild the ancient
  ruins
  and will raise up the age-old
    foundations;
you will be called Repairer of Broken
  Walls,
  Restorer of Streets with Dwellings.

13"If you keep your feet from breaking
  the Sabbath
  and from doing as you please on
    my holy day,
if you call the Sabbath a delight
  and the LORD's holy day honorable,
and if you honor it by not going your
  own way
  and not doing as you please or
    speaking idle words,
14then you will find your joy in the
  LORD,
  and I will cause you to ride on the
    heights of the land
  and to feast on the inheritance of
    your father Jacob."
The mouth of the LORD has spoken.

Sin, Confession and Redemption

59 Surely the arm of the LORD is not
  too short to save,
  nor his ear too dull to hear.
2But your iniquities have separated
  you from your God;
  your sins have hidden his face from
    you,
  so that he will not hear.
3For your hands are stained with
  blood,
  your fingers with guilt.
Your lips have spoken lies,
  and your tongue mutters wicked
    things.
4No one calls for justice;
  no one pleads his case with
    integrity.
They rely on empty arguments and
  speak lies;
  they conceive trouble and give birth
    to evil.
5They hatch the eggs of vipers
  and spin a spider's web.
Whoever eats their eggs will die,
  and when one is broken, an adder
    is hatched.
6Their cobwebs are useless for
  clothing;
  they cannot cover themselves with
    what they make.
Their deeds are evil deeds,
  and acts of violence are in their
    hands.
7Their feet rush into sin;
  they are swift to shed innocent
    blood.
Their thoughts are evil thoughts;
  ruin and destruction mark their
    ways.
8The way of peace they do not know;
  there is no justice in their paths.
They have turned them into crooked
  roads;
  no one who walks in them will
    know peace.

9So justice is far from us,
  and righteousness does not reach
    us.
We look for light, but all is darkness;
  for brightness, but we walk in deep
    shadows.
10Like the blind we grope along the
  wall,
  feeling our way like men without
    eyes.

a8 Or *your righteous One*

At midday we stumble as if it were
    twilight;
  among the strong, we are like the
    dead.
[11]We all growl like bears;
  we moan mournfully like doves.
We look for justice, but find none;
  for deliverance, but it is far away.

[12]For our offenses are many in your
    sight,
  and our sins testify against us.
Our offenses are ever with us,
  and we acknowledge our iniquities:
[13]rebellion and treachery against the
    LORD,
  turning our backs on our God,

MONDAY

VERSE FOR THE DAY:
Isaiah 58:6

AUTHOR:
John B. Anderson

PASSAGE FOR THE DAY:
Isaiah 58:6–12

Loving Your Neighbor

I WONDER how many Christians reading these pages have ever held political office, even as a precinct committeeman. If Christians leave opportunities for participation open and unfilled, the void will be filled by those who do not necessarily share a similar ethical concern. We must be careful not to lose by default what could be won with some additional effort on our part . . .

The average American today suffers no twinge of conscience when he passes the sick man on the road. He knows he has paid the "Good Samaritan" to come along after him and take care of this rather unpleasant social obligation. But the import of Christ's teaching is very plain. He expects us to take the role of the Good Samaritan, and not delegate our Christian love and compassion and concern in every instance to a paid professional or functionary. We are enjoined to love our neighbor —not just to pay taxes to employ someone else to love our neighbor . . .

I believe a large part of the problem is the inability of the average member of an affluent suburban church to feel much real empathy for the problems of an inner-city world so remote from his own existence. I am afraid that there are a great many modern Christians who, if our Lord suddenly returned and they found him dining with the publicans and sinners who infest the big city slums, would recoil with the same fastidious horror displayed by the Pharisees and Sadducees two thousand years ago. . .

The church of Jesus Christ ought to play a part in rallying Christians to social action. Indeed, it is only as we play this kind of role that we will get the type of society that we as Christians would like to see. The church can and should encourage social and economic change.

Additional Scripture Readings:
Matthew 25:31–46; Luke 10:25–37

Go to page 781 for your next devotional reading.

fomenting oppression and revolt,
   uttering lies our hearts have
      conceived.
¹⁴So justice is driven back,
   and righteousness stands at a
      distance;
truth has stumbled in the streets,
   honesty cannot enter.
¹⁵Truth is nowhere to be found,
   and whoever shuns evil becomes a
      prey.

The Lord looked and was displeased
   that there was no justice.
¹⁶He saw that there was no one,
   he was appalled that there was no
      one to intervene;
so his own arm worked salvation for
      him,
   and his own righteousness
      sustained him.
¹⁷He put on righteousness as his
      breastplate,
   and the helmet of salvation on his
      head;
he put on the garments of vengeance
   and wrapped himself in zeal as in a
      cloak.
¹⁸According to what they have done,
   so will he repay
wrath to his enemies
   and retribution to his foes;
he will repay the islands their due.
¹⁹From the west, men will fear the
      name of the Lord,
   and from the rising of the sun, they
      will revere his glory.
For he will come like a pent-up flood
   that the breath of the Lord drives
      along.ᵃ

²⁰"The Redeemer will come to Zion,
   to those in Jacob who repent of
      their sins,"
                        declares the Lord.

²¹"As for me, this is my covenant with
them," says the Lord. "My Spirit, who is
on you, and my words that I have put in
your mouth will not depart from your
mouth, or from the mouths of your children, or from the mouths of their descendants from this time on and forever," says
the Lord.

The Glory of Zion

60 "Arise, shine, for your light has
      come,

and the glory of the Lord rises upon
      you.
²See, darkness covers the earth
   and thick darkness is over the
      peoples,
but the Lord rises upon you
   and his glory appears over you.
³Nations will come to your light,
   and kings to the brightness of your
      dawn.

⁴"Lift up your eyes and look about
      you:
   All assemble and come to you;
your sons come from afar,
   and your daughters are carried on
      the arm.
⁵Then you will look and be radiant,
   your heart will throb and swell with
      joy;
the wealth on the seas will be brought
      to you,
   to you the riches of the nations will
      come.
⁶Herds of camels will cover your land,
   young camels of Midian and Ephah.
And all from Sheba will come,
   bearing gold and incense
   and proclaiming the praise of the
      Lord.
⁷All Kedar's flocks will be gathered to
      you,
   the rams of Nebaioth will serve you;
they will be accepted as offerings on
      my altar,
   and I will adorn my glorious
      temple.

⁸"Who are these that fly along like
      clouds,
   like doves to their nests?
⁹Surely the islands look to me;
   in the lead are the ships of
      Tarshish,ᵇ
bringing your sons from afar,
   with their silver and gold,
to the honor of the Lord your God,
   the Holy One of Israel,
for he has endowed you with
      splendor.

¹⁰"Foreigners will rebuild your walls,
   and their kings will serve you.
Though in anger I struck you,
   in favor I will show you
      compassion.
¹¹Your gates will always stand open,

ᵃ19 Or *When the enemy comes in like a flood, / the Spirit of the Lord will put him to flight*   ᵇ9 Or *the trading ships*

they will never be shut, day or
  night,
so that men may bring you the wealth
  of the nations—
  their kings led in triumphal
  procession.
¹²For the nation or kingdom that will
  not serve you will perish;
  it will be utterly ruined.

¹³"The glory of Lebanon will come to
  you,
  the pine, the fir and the cypress
  together,
to adorn the place of my sanctuary;
  and I will glorify the place of my
  feet.
¹⁴The sons of your oppressors will come
  bowing before you;
  all who despise you will bow down
  at your feet
and will call you the City of the Lord,
  Zion of the Holy One of Israel.

¹⁵"Although you have been forsaken
  and hated,
  with no one traveling through,
I will make you the everlasting pride
  and the joy of all generations.
¹⁶You will drink the milk of nations
  and be nursed at royal breasts.
Then you will know that I, the Lord,
  am your Savior,
  your Redeemer, the Mighty One of
  Jacob.
¹⁷Instead of bronze I will bring you
  gold,
  and silver in place of iron.
Instead of wood I will bring you
  bronze,
  and iron in place of stones.
I will make peace your governor
  and righteousness your ruler.
¹⁸No longer will violence be heard in
  your land,
  nor ruin or destruction within your
  borders,
but you will call your walls Salvation
  and your gates Praise.
¹⁹The sun will no more be your light by
  day,
  nor will the brightness of the moon
  shine on you,
for the Lord will be your everlasting
  light,
  and your God will be your glory.
²⁰Your sun will never set again,
  and your moon will wane no more;
  the Lord will be your everlasting light,

and your days of sorrow will end.
²¹Then will all your people be righteous
  and they will possess the land
  forever.
They are the shoot I have planted,
  the work of my hands,
  for the display of my splendor.
²²The least of you will become a
  thousand,
  the smallest a mighty nation.
I am the Lord;
  in its time I will do this swiftly."

The Year of the Lord's Favor

61 The Spirit of the Sovereign Lord
  is on me,
  because the Lord has anointed me
  to preach good news to the poor.
He has sent me to bind up the
  brokenhearted,
  to proclaim freedom for the captives
  and release from darkness for the
  prisoners,ᵃ
²to proclaim the year of the Lord's
  favor
  and the day of vengeance of our
  God,
to comfort all who mourn,
³ and provide for those who grieve in
  Zion—
to bestow on them a crown of beauty
  instead of ashes,
the oil of gladness
  instead of mourning,
and a garment of praise
  instead of a spirit of despair.
They will be called oaks of
  righteousness,
  a planting of the Lord
  for the display of his splendor.

⁴They will rebuild the ancient ruins
  and restore the places long
  devastated;
they will renew the ruined cities
  that have been devastated for
  generations.
⁵Aliens will shepherd your flocks;
  foreigners will work your fields and
  vineyards.
⁶And you will be called priests of the
  Lord,
  you will be named ministers of our
  God.
You will feed on the wealth of
  nations,
  and in their riches you will boast.

⁷Instead of their shame

my people will receive a double
  portion,
and instead of disgrace
  they will rejoice in their inheritance;
and so they will inherit a double
  portion in their land,
  and everlasting joy will be theirs.

8"For I, the LORD, love justice;
  I hate robbery and iniquity.
In my faithfulness I will reward them
  and make an everlasting covenant
    with them.
9Their descendants will be known
    among the nations
  and their offspring among the
    peoples.
All who see them will acknowledge
  that they are a people the LORD has
    blessed."

10I delight greatly in the LORD;
  my soul rejoices in my God.
For he has clothed me with garments
    of salvation
  and arrayed me in a robe of
    righteousness,
as a bridegroom adorns his head like
    a priest,
  and as a bride adorns herself with
    her jewels.
11For as the soil makes the sprout come
    up
  and a garden causes seeds to grow,
so the Sovereign LORD will make
    righteousness and praise
  spring up before all nations.

Zion's New Name

62 For Zion's sake I will not keep
      silent,
  for Jerusalem's sake I will not
    remain quiet,
till her righteousness shines out like
    the dawn,
  her salvation like a blazing torch.
2The nations will see your
    righteousness,
  and all kings your glory;
you will be called by a new name
  that the mouth of the LORD will
    bestow.
3You will be a crown of splendor in the
    LORD's hand,
  a royal diadem in the hand of your
    God.
4No longer will they call you Deserted,
  or name your land Desolate.
But you will be called Hephzibah,a

and your land Beulahb;
for the LORD will take delight in you,
  and your land will be married.
5As a young man marries a maiden,
  so will your sonsc marry you;
as a bridegroom rejoices over his
    bride,
  so will your God rejoice over you.

6I have posted watchmen on your
    walls, O Jerusalem;
  they will never be silent day or
    night.
You who call on the LORD,
  give yourselves no rest,
7and give him no rest till he establishes
    Jerusalem
  and makes her the praise of the
    earth.

8The LORD has sworn by his right hand
    and by his mighty arm:
"Never again will I give your grain
    as food for your enemies,
  and never again will foreigners drink
    the new wine
  for which you have toiled;
9but those who harvest it will eat it
    and praise the LORD,
  and those who gather the grapes will
    drink it
  in the courts of my sanctuary."

10Pass through, pass through the gates!
  Prepare the way for the people.
Build up, build up the highway!
  Remove the stones.
Raise a banner for the nations.

11The LORD has made proclamation
  to the ends of the earth:
"Say to the Daughter of Zion,
  'See, your Savior comes!
See, his reward is with him,
  and his recompense accompanies
    him.'"
12They will be called the Holy People,
  the Redeemed of the LORD;
and you will be called Sought After,
  the City No Longer Deserted.

God's Day of Vengeance and Redemption

63 Who is this coming from Edom,
      from Bozrah, with his garments
        stained crimson?
Who is this, robed in splendor,
  striding forward in the greatness of
    his strength?

a4 Hephzibah means my delight is in her.   b4 Beulah means married.   c5 Or Builder

"It is I, speaking in righteousness,
  mighty to save."

2Why are your garments red,
  like those of one treading the
    winepress?

3"I have trodden the winepress alone;
  from the nations no one was with
    me.
I trampled them in my anger
  and trod them down in my wrath;
their blood spattered my garments,
  and I stained all my clothing.
4For the day of vengeance was in my
    heart,
  and the year of my redemption has
    come.
5I looked, but there was no one to
    help,
  I was appalled that no one gave
    support;
so my own arm worked salvation for
    me,
  and my own wrath sustained me.
6I trampled the nations in my anger;
  in my wrath I made them drunk
  and poured their blood on the
    ground."

Praise and Prayer

7I will tell of the kindnesses of the
    Lord,
  the deeds for which he is to be
    praised,
  according to all the Lord has done
    for us—
yes, the many good things he has
    done
  for the house of Israel,
  according to his compassion and
    many kindnesses.
8He said, "Surely they are my people,
  sons who will not be false to me";
  and so he became their Savior.
9In all their distress he too was
    distressed,
  and the angel of his presence saved
    them.
In his love and mercy he redeemed
    them;
  he lifted them up and carried them
    all the days of old.
10Yet they rebelled
  and grieved his Holy Spirit.
So he turned and became their enemy
  and he himself fought against them.

11Then his people recalled[a] the days of
    old,
  the days of Moses and his people—
where is he who brought them
    through the sea,
  with the shepherd of his flock?
Where is he who set
  his Holy Spirit among them,
12who sent his glorious arm of power
  to be at Moses' right hand,
who divided the waters before them,
  to gain for himself everlasting
    renown,
13who led them through the depths?
Like a horse in open country,
  they did not stumble;
14like cattle that go down to the plain,
  they were given rest by the Spirit of
    the Lord.
This is how you guided your people
  to make for yourself a glorious
    name.

15Look down from heaven and see
  from your lofty throne, holy and
    glorious.
Where are your zeal and your might?
  Your tenderness and compassion
  are withheld from us.
16But you are our Father,
  though Abraham does not know us
  or Israel acknowledge us;
you, O Lord, are our Father,
  our Redeemer from of old is your
    name.
17Why, O Lord, do you make us wander
    from your ways
  and harden our hearts so we do not
    revere you?
Return for the sake of your servants,
  the tribes that are your inheritance.
18For a little while your people
    possessed your holy place,
  but now our enemies have trampled
    down your sanctuary.
19We are yours from of old;
  but you have not ruled over them,
  they have not been called by your
    name.[b]

64 Oh, that you would rend the
  heavens and come down,
that the mountains would tremble
  before you!
2As when fire sets twigs ablaze
  and causes water to boil,

a11 Or *But may he recall*   b19 Or *We are like those you have never ruled, / like those never called by your name*

come down to make your name
  known to your enemies
and cause the nations to quake
  before you!
³For when you did awesome things
  that we did not expect,
you came down, and the mountains
  trembled before you.
⁴Since ancient times no one has heard,
  no ear has perceived,
no eye has seen any God besides you,
  who acts on behalf of those who
  wait for him.
⁵You come to the help of those who
  gladly do right,
  who remember your ways.

But when we continued to sin against
  them,
  you were angry.
How then can we be saved?
⁶All of us have become like one who is
  unclean,
and all our righteous acts are like
  filthy rags;
we all shrivel up like a leaf,
  and like the wind our sins sweep us
  away.
⁷No one calls on your name
  or strives to lay hold of you;
for you have hidden your face from us
  and made us waste away because of
  our sins.

TUESDAY

VERSE FOR THE DAY:	*AUTHOR:*	*PASSAGE FOR THE DAY:*
Isaiah 63:14	Archibald Hart	Isaiah 63:11–14

Avoiding Stress Damage

TOO MUCH stress—especially stress that is not relieved by
times of rest and renewal—can harm us physically, mentally
and spiritually.

So while I cannot say that a Christian should be totally free
of stress, I think I *can* say that Christians should not allow
themselves to become so stressed as to produce damage to
their bodies, minds and spirits.

That is not to say it doesn't happen! To a great extent, Christians are caught up in the same rat race as everyone else. We
have let our values become distorted and don't see life clearly
from God's perspective. We've lost some of our distinctiveness; our lives are almost identical to those of people who are
not committed to Christ. As a result, I believe we are violating
very basic laws that God has set down for our bodies (the
"temple of the Holy Spirit"). And we may be doing all this in
the name of the One who came to save us from our need to
earn salvation!

Christians must wake up to the fact that they are burning
themselves out just as quickly as everyone else is! Change is
occurring so rapidly and hurry sickness is so rampant in our
society that avoiding stress damage takes an extra effort. And
the sad fact is that relatively few people—even Christians—are
making that extra effort.

Additional Scripture Readings:
Isaiah 30:15–18;
1 Corinthians 6:19–20

Go to page 786 for your next
devotional reading.

⁸Yet, O LORD, you are our Father.
   We are the clay, you are the potter;
   we are all the work of your hand.
⁹Do not be angry beyond measure,
   O LORD;
   do not remember our sins forever.
Oh, look upon us, we pray,
   for we are all your people.
¹⁰Your sacred cities have become a
   desert;
   even Zion is a desert, Jerusalem a
   desolation.
¹¹Our holy and glorious temple, where
   our fathers praised you,
   has been burned with fire,
   and all that we treasured lies in
   ruins.
¹²After all this, O LORD, will you hold
   yourself back?
   Will you keep silent and punish us
   beyond measure?

Judgment and Salvation

65 "I revealed myself to those who
   did not ask for me;
I was found by those who did not
   seek me.
To a nation that did not call on my
   name,
   I said, 'Here am I, here am I.'
²All day long I have held out my hands
   to an obstinate people,
who walk in ways not good,
   pursuing their own imaginations —
³a people who continually provoke me
   to my very face,
offering sacrifices in gardens
   and burning incense on altars of
   brick;
⁴who sit among the graves
   and spend their nights keeping
   secret vigil;
who eat the flesh of pigs,
   and whose pots hold broth of
   unclean meat;
⁵who say, 'Keep away; don't come near
   me,
   for I am too sacred for you!'
Such people are smoke in my nostrils,
   a fire that keeps burning all day.

⁶"See, it stands written before me:
   I will not keep silent but will pay
   back in full;
   I will pay it back into their laps —
⁷both your sins and the sins of your
   fathers,"
   says the LORD.
"Because they burned sacrifices on the
   mountains
and defied me on the hills,
I will measure into their laps
   the full payment for their former
   deeds."

⁸This is what the LORD says:

"As when juice is still found in a
   cluster of grapes
and men say, 'Don't destroy it,
   there is yet some good in it,'
so will I do in behalf of my servants;
   I will not destroy them all.
⁹I will bring forth descendants from
   Jacob,
   and from Judah those who will
   possess my mountains;
my chosen people will inherit them,
   and there will my servants live.
¹⁰Sharon will become a pasture for
   flocks,
   and the Valley of Achor a resting
   place for herds,
for my people who seek me.

¹¹"But as for you who forsake the LORD
   and forget my holy mountain,
who spread a table for Fortune
   and fill bowls of mixed wine for
   Destiny,
¹²I will destine you for the sword,
   and you will all bend down for the
   slaughter;
for I called but you did not answer,
   I spoke but you did not listen.
You did evil in my sight
   and chose what displeases me."

¹³Therefore this is what the Sovereign
LORD says:

"My servants will eat,
   but you will go hungry;
my servants will drink,
   but you will go thirsty;
my servants will rejoice,
   but you will be put to shame.
¹⁴My servants will sing
   out of the joy of their hearts,
but you will cry out
   from anguish of heart
   and wail in brokenness of spirit.
¹⁵You will leave your name
   to my chosen ones as a curse;
the Sovereign LORD will put you to
   death,
   but to his servants he will give
   another name.
¹⁶Whoever invokes a blessing in the
   land
will do so by the God of truth;
he who takes an oath in the land

will swear by the God of truth.
For the past troubles will be forgotten
and hidden from my eyes.

New Heavens and a New Earth

[17]"Behold, I will create
new heavens and a new earth.
The former things will not be
remembered,
nor will they come to mind.
[18]But be glad and rejoice forever
in what I will create,
for I will create Jerusalem to be a
delight
and its people a joy.
[19]I will rejoice over Jerusalem
and take delight in my people;
the sound of weeping and of crying
will be heard in it no more.

[20]"Never again will there be in it
an infant who lives but a few days,
or an old man who does not live
out his years;
he who dies at a hundred
will be thought a mere youth;
he who fails to reach[a] a hundred
will be considered accursed.
[21]They will build houses and dwell in
them;
they will plant vineyards and eat
their fruit.
[22]No longer will they build houses and
others live in them,
or plant and others eat.
For as the days of a tree,
so will be the days of my people;
my chosen ones will long enjoy
the works of their hands.
[23]They will not toil in vain
or bear children doomed to
misfortune;
for they will be a people blessed by
the LORD,
they and their descendants with
them.
[24]Before they call I will answer;
while they are still speaking I will
hear.
[25]The wolf and the lamb will feed
together,
and the lion will eat straw like the
ox,
but dust will be the serpent's food.
They will neither harm nor destroy
on all my holy mountain,"
says the LORD.

Judgment and Hope

66 This is what the LORD says:

"Heaven is my throne,
and the earth is my footstool.
Where is the house you will build for
me?
Where will my resting place be?
[2]Has not my hand made all these
things,
and so they came into being?"
declares the LORD.

"This is the one I esteem:
he who is humble and contrite in
spirit,
and trembles at my word.
[3]But whoever sacrifices a bull
is like one who kills a man,
and whoever offers a lamb,
like one who breaks a dog's neck;
whoever makes a grain offering
is like one who presents pig's blood,
and whoever burns memorial incense,
like one who worships an idol.
They have chosen their own ways,
and their souls delight in their
abominations;
[4]so I also will choose harsh treatment
for them
and will bring upon them what they
dread.
For when I called, no one answered,
when I spoke, no one listened.
They did evil in my sight
and chose what displeases me."

[5]Hear the word of the LORD,
you who tremble at his word:
"Your brothers who hate you,
and exclude you because of my
name, have said,
'Let the LORD be glorified,
that we may see your joy!'
Yet they will be put to shame.
[6]Hear that uproar from the city,
hear that noise from the temple!
It is the sound of the LORD
repaying his enemies all they
deserve.

[7]"Before she goes into labor,
she gives birth;
before the pains come upon her,
she delivers a son.
[8]Who has ever heard of such a thing?
Who has ever seen such things?
Can a country be born in a day

or a nation be brought forth in a
    moment?
Yet no sooner is Zion in labor
    than she gives birth to her children.
[9]Do I bring to the moment of birth
    and not give delivery?" says the
    Lord.
"Do I close up the womb
    when I bring to delivery?" says your
    God.
[10]"Rejoice with Jerusalem and be glad
    for her,
    all you who love her;
rejoice greatly with her,
    all you who mourn over her.
[11]For you will nurse and be satisfied
    at her comforting breasts;
you will drink deeply
    and delight in her overflowing
    abundance."

[12]For this is what the Lord says:

"I will extend peace to her like a river,
    and the wealth of nations like a
    flooding stream;
you will nurse and be carried on her
    arm
    and dandled on her knees.
[13]As a mother comforts her child,
    so will I comfort you;
    and you will be comforted over
    Jerusalem."

[14]When you see this, your heart will
    rejoice
    and you will flourish like grass;
the hand of the Lord will be made
    known to his servants,
    but his fury will be shown to his
    foes.
[15]See, the Lord is coming with fire,
    and his chariots are like a
    whirlwind;
he will bring down his anger with
    fury,
    and his rebuke with flames of fire.

[16]For with fire and with his sword
    the Lord will execute judgment
    upon all men,
    and many will be those slain by the
    Lord.

[17]"Those who consecrate and purify themselves to go into the gardens, following the one in the midst of[a] those who eat the flesh of pigs and rats and other abominable things — they will meet their end together," declares the Lord.

[18]"And I, because of their actions and their imaginations, am about to come[b] and gather all nations and tongues, and they will come and see my glory.

[19]"I will set a sign among them, and I will send some of those who survive to the nations — to Tarshish, to the Libyans[c] and Lydians (famous as archers), to Tubal and Greece, and to the distant islands that have not heard of my fame or seen my glory. They will proclaim my glory among the nations. [20]And they will bring all your brothers, from all the nations, to my holy mountain in Jerusalem as an offering to the Lord — on horses, in chariots and wagons, and on mules and camels," says the Lord. "They will bring them, as the Israelites bring their grain offerings, to the temple of the Lord in ceremonially clean vessels. [21]And I will select some of them also to be priests and Levites," says the Lord.

[22]"As the new heavens and the new earth that I make will endure before me," declares the Lord, "so will your name and descendants endure. [23]From one New Moon to another and from one Sabbath to another, all mankind will come and bow down before me," says the Lord. [24]"And they will go out and look upon the dead bodies of those who rebelled against me; their worm will not die, nor will their fire be quenched, and they will be loathsome to all mankind."

---

[a]17 Or *gardens behind one of your temples, and*
uncertain.   [c]19 Some Septuagint manuscripts *Put* (Libyans); Hebrew *Pul*
[b]18 The meaning of the Hebrew for this clause is

JEREMIAH prophesies in the kingdom of Judah as Jerusalem is being destroyed and God's people are being carried away into Babylon because of their sins (see 2 Chronicles 36). It is a time of judgment and of suffering for all the people and for Jeremiah personally. But Jeremiah also cites God's promise of restoration after seventy years, assuring the people of a coming new covenant. As you read this book, remember that sin has its consequences but also that through Jesus, your mediator, God's last word is forgiveness and eternal life.

JEREMIAH

1 The words of Jeremiah son of Hilkiah, one of the priests at Anathoth in the territory of Benjamin. ²The word of the LORD came to him in the thirteenth year of the reign of Josiah son of Amon king of Judah, ³and through the reign of Jehoiakim son of Josiah king of Judah, down to the fifth month of the eleventh year of Zedekiah son of Josiah king of Judah, when the people of Jerusalem went into exile.

The Call of Jeremiah

⁴The word of the LORD came to me, saying,

⁵"Before I formed you in the womb I
knew*ᵃ* you,
before you were born I set you
apart;
I appointed you as a prophet to the
nations."

⁶"Ah, Sovereign LORD," I said, "I do not

ᵃ5 Or *chose*

know how to speak; I am only a child." ⁷But the LORD said to me, "Do not say, 'I am only a child.' You must go to everyone I send you to and say whatever I command you. ⁸Do not be afraid of them, for I am with you and will rescue you," declares the LORD.

⁹Then the LORD reached out his hand and touched my mouth and said to me, "Now, I have put my words in your mouth. ¹⁰See, today I appoint you over nations and kingdoms to uproot and tear down, to destroy and overthrow, to build and to plant."

¹¹The word of the LORD came to me: "What do you see, Jeremiah?"

WEDNESDAY

VERSE FOR THE DAY:	AUTHOR:	PASSAGE FOR THE DAY:
Jeremiah 1:5	Charles Stanley	Jeremiah 1:4–8

Burdens, or Blessings?

SOME parents refer to the child of an unexpected pregnancy as a surprise or an accident. Such talk, however, reveals the parents' limited perspective and often leads to a subconscious grudge against the child. Worse than that, such talk, if overheard by the child, will make him or her feel like a mistake or an unwanted burden and can only contribute to the child's low sense of self-worth. So, please, if one of your children "surprised" you, let it be the best-kept secret in town. There are no surprises from God's point of view. Fortunately for us, God does not have accidents. What may appear to be a surprise to man is always within the sovereign plan of God . . .

The question now arises, What kind of message are you sending to your children? If in fact they are gifts from God, do they know that? How do your children perceive themselves in the context of your life? Do they see themselves as burdens or blessings? How they answer this last question will pretty much determine whether or not you can keep them on your team.

I can remember as a child being the last one chosen when the guys were choosing sides to play basketball. I knew I was a burden to the team and had been chosen simply because I was the only one left. I knew that if I did not show up the next afternoon to play, no one would miss me.

You can imagine how low my enthusiasm level was as I took my place on the court. You can imagine how unmotivated I was to play. I was not an important part of the team; I did not feel like a part of the team at all.

To keep your children on your team, you must let them know that you wanted them to be a part of the team to begin with. The degree to which this is communicated will greatly affect their self-image and thus their ability and desire to function as a part of the family unit.

Additional Scripture Readings:
Psalm 127:3–5; Psalm 139:13–16

Go to page 789 for your next devotional reading.

"I see the branch of an almond tree," I replied.

12The LORD said to me, "You have seen correctly, for I am watching*a* to see that my word is fulfilled."

13The word of the LORD came to me again: "What do you see?"

"I see a boiling pot, tilting away from the north," I answered.

14The LORD said to me, "From the north disaster will be poured out on all who live in the land. **15**I am about to summon all the peoples of the northern kingdoms," declares the LORD.

"Their kings will come and set up
    their thrones
  in the entrance of the gates of
    Jerusalem;
they will come against all her
    surrounding walls
  and against all the towns of Judah.
16I will pronounce my judgments on my
    people
  because of their wickedness in
    forsaking me,
in burning incense to other gods
  and in worshiping what their hands
    have made.

17"Get yourself ready! Stand up and say to them whatever I command you. Do not be terrified by them, or I will terrify you before them. **18**Today I have made you a fortified city, an iron pillar and a bronze wall to stand against the whole land—against the kings of Judah, its officials, its priests and the people of the land. **19**They will fight against you but will not overcome you, for I am with you and will rescue you," declares the LORD.

Israel Forsakes God

2 The word of the LORD came to me: **2**"Go and proclaim in the hearing of Jerusalem:

" 'I remember the devotion of your
    youth,
  how as a bride you loved me
and followed me through the desert,
  through a land not sown.
3Israel was holy to the LORD,
  the firstfruits of his harvest;
all who devoured her were held guilty,
  and disaster overtook them,' "
            declares the LORD.

4Hear the word of the LORD, O house of
    Jacob,
  all you clans of the house of Israel.
5This is what the LORD says:

"What fault did your fathers find in
    me,
  that they strayed so far from me?
They followed worthless idols
  and became worthless themselves.
6They did not ask, 'Where is the LORD,
  who brought us up out of Egypt
and led us through the barren
    wilderness,
  through a land of deserts and rifts,
a land of drought and darkness,*b*
  a land where no one travels and no
    one lives?'
7I brought you into a fertile land
  to eat its fruit and rich produce.
But you came and defiled my land
  and made my inheritance
    detestable.
8The priests did not ask,
  'Where is the LORD?'
Those who deal with the law did not
    know me;
  the leaders rebelled against me.
The prophets prophesied by Baal,
  following worthless idols.

9"Therefore I bring charges against you
    again,"
            declares the LORD.
"And I will bring charges against
    your children's children.
10Cross over to the coasts of Kittim*c*
    and look,
  send to Kedar*d* and observe
    closely;
  see if there has ever been anything
    like this:
11Has a nation ever changed its gods?
  (Yet they are not gods at all.)
But my people have exchanged their*e*
    Glory
  for worthless idols.
12Be appalled at this, O heavens,
  and shudder with great horror,"
            declares the LORD.
13"My people have committed two sins:
They have forsaken me,
  the spring of living water,
and have dug their own cisterns,
  broken cisterns that cannot hold
    water.

---

a12 The Hebrew for *watching* sounds like the Hebrew for *almond tree.*   *b6* Or *and the shadow of death*
c10 That is, Cyprus and western coastlands   *d10* The home of Bedouin tribes in the Syro-Arabian desert   *e11* Masoretic Text; an ancient Hebrew scribal tradition *my*

¹⁴Is Israel a servant, a slave by birth?
  Why then has he become plunder?
¹⁵Lions have roared;
  they have growled at him.
They have laid waste his land;
  his towns are burned and deserted.
¹⁶Also, the men of Memphis*a* and
    Tahpanhes
  have shaved the crown of your
    head.*b*
¹⁷Have you not brought this on
    yourselves
  by forsaking the LORD your God
  when he led you in the way?
¹⁸Now why go to Egypt
  to drink water from the Shihor*c*?
And why go to Assyria
  to drink water from the River*d*?
¹⁹Your wickedness will punish you;
  your backsliding will rebuke you.
Consider then and realize
  how evil and bitter it is for you
when you forsake the LORD your God
  and have no awe of me,"
             declares the Lord,
             the LORD Almighty.

²⁰"Long ago you broke off your yoke
  and tore off your bonds;
  you said, 'I will not serve you!'
Indeed, on every high hill
  and under every spreading tree
  you lay down as a prostitute.
²¹I had planted you like a choice vine
  of sound and reliable stock.
How then did you turn against me
  into a corrupt, wild vine?
²²Although you wash yourself with soda
  and use an abundance of soap,
  the stain of your guilt is still before
    me,"
            declares the Sovereign LORD.
²³"How can you say, 'I am not defiled;
  I have not run after the Baals'?
See how you behaved in the valley;
  consider what you have done.
You are a swift she-camel
  running here and there,
²⁴a wild donkey accustomed to the
    desert,
  sniffing the wind in her craving—
  in her heat who can restrain her?
Any males that pursue her need not
    tire themselves;
  at mating time they will find her.
²⁵Do not run until your feet are bare
  and your throat is dry.

But you said, 'It's no use!
  I love foreign gods,
  and I must go after them.'

²⁶"As a thief is disgraced when he is
    caught,
  so the house of Israel is disgraced—
they, their kings and their officials,
  their priests and their prophets.
²⁷They say to wood, 'You are my
    father,'
  and to stone, 'You gave me birth.'
They have turned their backs to me
  and not their faces;
yet when they are in trouble, they say,
  'Come and save us!'
²⁸Where then are the gods you made for
    yourselves?
  Let them come if they can save you
  when you are in trouble!
For you have as many gods
  as you have towns, O Judah.

²⁹"Why do you bring charges against
    me?
  You have all rebelled against me,"
            declares the LORD.
³⁰"In vain I punished your people;
  they did not respond to correction.
Your sword has devoured your
    prophets
  like a ravening lion.

³¹"You of this generation, consider the
word of the LORD:

"Have I been a desert to Israel
  or a land of great darkness?
Why do my people say, 'We are free
    to roam;
  we will come to you no more'?
³²Does a maiden forget her jewelry,
  a bride her wedding ornaments?
Yet my people have forgotten me,
  days without number.
³³How skilled you are at pursuing love!
  Even the worst of women can learn
    from your ways.
³⁴On your clothes men find
  the lifeblood of the innocent poor,
  though you did not catch them
    breaking in.
Yet in spite of all this
³⁵ you say, 'I am innocent;
  he is not angry with me.'
But I will pass judgment on you
  because you say, 'I have not
    sinned.'
³⁶Why do you go about so much,

---

a16 Hebrew *Noph*   *b16* Or *have cracked your skull*   *c18* That is, a branch of the Nile   *d18* That
is, the Euphrates

VERSE FOR THE DAY:
Jeremiah 2:13

AUTHOR:
William Petersen

PASSAGE FOR THE DAY:
Jeremiah 2:9–19

Five Steps Down

WHAT you are doing doesn't make sense, God says through Jeremiah. You're exchanging the Almighty God of the universe for a bargain-basement Barbie doll. You're exchanging a diamond ring for a daisy chain, the original Gutenberg Bible for a scratch pad. Instead of fresh water from a sparkling fountain, you build cisterns in the sand. No, it doesn't make sense . . .

Perhaps what surprised Jeremiah the most was not that his people had forsaken the Lord, but that they had no awe of him. They took his forgiveness for granted. He was always there to come home to.

Thus, in Jeremiah's mind, there was a downward progression and he saw the steps this way.

- STEP ONE: Forsaking God, the spring of living water;
- STEP TWO: Going after other gods; digging cisterns in the sand;
- STEP THREE: Having lost an awe for God and his justice;
- STEP FOUR: Having lost any shame for sin;
- STEP FIVE: Committing themselves to follow other gods.

Those downward steps are not unique to the Israelites nor to Jeremiah's lifetime. The same steps are taken by many today. You may begin to forsake God by neglecting his Word, by being so busy with other things that you don't spend time with him in prayer and private devotion, by becoming careless in your attendance at services of worship and praise with your brothers and sisters in Christ.

It often starts, however, with your attitude toward the Book. D.L. Moody said about the Bible, "This Book will keep you from sin, or sin will keep you from this Book." Jeremiah knew that too. When people neglected God's Word, when they stopped drinking from the stream of living water, they started digging their own cisterns in the sand.

Additional Scripture Readings:
Psalm 119:97–104; John 4:4–14

Go to page 799 for your next devotional reading.

changing your ways?
You will be disappointed by Egypt
   as you were by Assyria.
37You will also leave that place
   with your hands on your head,
for the LORD has rejected those you
   trust;
   you will not be helped by them.

3 "If a man divorces his wife
   and she leaves him and marries
      another man,
should he return to her again?
   Would not the land be completely
      defiled?
But you have lived as a prostitute with
      many lovers —
   would you now return to me?"
               declares the LORD.
2"Look up to the barren heights and
      see.
   Is there any place where you have
      not been ravished?
By the roadside you sat waiting for
      lovers,
   sat like a nomad[a] in the desert.
You have defiled the land
   with your prostitution and
      wickedness.
3Therefore the showers have been
      withheld,
   and no spring rains have fallen.
Yet you have the brazen look of a
      prostitute;
   you refuse to blush with shame.
4Have you not just called to me:
   'My Father, my friend from my
      youth,
5will you always be angry?
   Will your wrath continue forever?'
This is how you talk,
   but you do all the evil you can."

Unfaithful Israel

6During the reign of King Josiah, the
LORD said to me, "Have you seen what
faithless Israel has done? She has gone up
on every high hill and under every spreading tree and has committed adultery
there. 7I thought that after she had done
all this she would return to me but she did
not, and her unfaithful sister Judah saw it.
8I gave faithless Israel her certificate of divorce and sent her away because of all her
adulteries. Yet I saw that her unfaithful
sister Judah had no fear; she also went out
and committed adultery. 9Because Israel's
immorality mattered so little to her, she

defiled the land and committed adultery
with stone and wood. 10In spite of all this,
her unfaithful sister Judah did not return
to me with all her heart, but only in pretense," declares the LORD.

11The LORD said to me, "Faithless Israel
is more righteous than unfaithful Judah.
12Go, proclaim this message toward the
north:

  " 'Return, faithless Israel,' declares the
      LORD,
  'I will frown on you no longer,
for I am merciful,' declares the LORD,
  'I will not be angry forever.
13Only acknowledge your guilt —
  you have rebelled against the LORD
      your God,
you have scattered your favors to
      foreign gods
  under every spreading tree,
  and have not obeyed me,' "
               declares the LORD.

14"Return, faithless people," declares
the LORD, "for I am your husband. I will
choose you — one from a town and two
from a clan — and bring you to Zion.
15Then I will give you shepherds after my
own heart, who will lead you with knowledge and understanding. 16In those days,
when your numbers have increased greatly in the land," declares the LORD, "men
will no longer say, 'The ark of the covenant of the LORD.' It will never enter their
minds or be remembered; it will not be
missed, nor will another one be made.
17At that time they will call Jerusalem The
Throne of the LORD, and all nations will
gather in Jerusalem to honor the name of
the LORD. No longer will they follow the
stubbornness of their evil hearts. 18In
those days the house of Judah will join the
house of Israel, and together they will
come from a northern land to the land I
gave your forefathers as an inheritance.
19"I myself said,

  " 'How gladly would I treat you like
      sons
  and give you a desirable land,
  the most beautiful inheritance of
      any nation.'
I thought you would call me 'Father'
  and not turn away from following
      me.
20But like a woman unfaithful to her
      husband,

a2 Or an Arab

so you have been unfaithful to me,
   O house of Israel,"
               declares the LORD.

²¹A cry is heard on the barren heights,
   the weeping and pleading of the
      people of Israel,
because they have perverted their
      ways
   and have forgotten the LORD their
      God.

²²"Return, faithless people;
   I will cure you of backsliding."

  "Yes, we will come to you,
   for you are the LORD our God.
²³Surely the ˌidolatrousˌ commotion on
      the hills
   and mountains is a deception;
  surely in the LORD our God
   is the salvation of Israel.
²⁴From our youth shameful gods have
      consumed
   the fruits of our fathers' labor—
  their flocks and herds,
   their sons and daughters.
²⁵Let us lie down in our shame,
   and let our disgrace cover us.
We have sinned against the LORD our
      God,
   both we and our fathers;
from our youth till this day
   we have not obeyed the LORD our
      God."

4 "If you will return, O Israel,
   return to me,"
               declares the LORD.
"If you put your detestable idols out
      of my sight
   and no longer go astray,
²and if in a truthful, just and righteous
      way
   you swear, 'As surely as the LORD
      lives,'
then the nations will be blessed by
      him
   and in him they will glory."

³This is what the LORD says to the men
of Judah and to Jerusalem:

"Break up your unplowed ground
   and do not sow among thorns.
⁴Circumcise yourselves to the LORD,
   circumcise your hearts,
   you men of Judah and people of
      Jerusalem,

or my wrath will break out and burn
   like fire
because of the evil you have done—

burn with no one to quench it.

Disaster From the North

⁵"Announce in Judah and proclaim in
      Jerusalem and say:
  'Sound the trumpet throughout the
      land!'
Cry aloud and say:
  'Gather together!
Let us flee to the fortified cities!'
⁶Raise the signal to go to Zion!
Flee for safety without delay!
For I am bringing disaster from the
   north,
   even terrible destruction."

⁷A lion has come out of his lair;
   a destroyer of nations has set out.
He has left his place
   to lay waste your land.
Your towns will lie in ruins
   without inhabitant.
⁸So put on sackcloth,
   lament and wail,
for the fierce anger of the LORD
   has not turned away from us.

⁹"In that day," declares the LORD,
  "the king and the officials will lose
      heart,
the priests will be horrified,
   and the prophets will be appalled."

¹⁰Then I said, "Ah, Sovereign LORD, how
completely you have deceived this people
and Jerusalem by saying, 'You will have
peace,' when the sword is at our throats."

¹¹At that time this people and Jerusalem will be told, "A scorching wind from
the barren heights in the desert blows toward my people, but not to winnow or
cleanse; ¹²a wind too strong for that
comes from me.ᵃ Now I pronounce my
judgments against them."

¹³Look! He advances like the clouds,
   his chariots come like a whirlwind,
his horses are swifter than eagles.
   Woe to us! We are ruined!
¹⁴O Jerusalem, wash the evil from your
      heart and be saved.
   How long will you harbor wicked
      thoughts?
¹⁵A voice is announcing from Dan,
   proclaiming disaster from the hills
      of Ephraim.

ᵃ12 Or *comes at my command*

16"Tell this to the nations,
  proclaim it to Jerusalem:
'A besieging army is coming from a
    distant land,
  raising a war cry against the cities
    of Judah.
17They surround her like men guarding
    a field,
  because she has rebelled against
    me,'"
                    declares the Lord.
18"Your own conduct and actions
  have brought this upon you.
This is your punishment.
  How bitter it is!
  How it pierces to the heart!"

19Oh, my anguish, my anguish!
  I writhe in pain.
Oh, the agony of my heart!
  My heart pounds within me,
  I cannot keep silent.
For I have heard the sound of the
    trumpet;
  I have heard the battle cry.
20Disaster follows disaster;
  the whole land lies in ruins.
In an instant my tents are destroyed,
  my shelter in a moment.
21How long must I see the battle
    standard
  and hear the sound of the trumpet?

22"My people are fools;
  they do not know me.
They are senseless children;
  they have no understanding.
They are skilled in doing evil;
  they know not how to do good."

23I looked at the earth,
  and it was formless and empty;
and at the heavens,
  and their light was gone.
24I looked at the mountains,
  and they were quaking;
  all the hills were swaying.
25I looked, and there were no people;
  every bird in the sky had flown
    away.
26I looked, and the fruitful land was a
    desert;
  all its towns lay in ruins
  before the Lord, before his fierce
    anger.

27This is what the Lord says:

"The whole land will be ruined,
  though I will not destroy it
    completely.
28Therefore the earth will mourn

and the heavens above grow dark,
  because I have spoken and will not
    relent,
  I have decided and will not turn
    back."

29At the sound of horsemen and archers
  every town takes to flight.
Some go into the thickets;
  some climb up among the rocks.
All the towns are deserted;
  no one lives in them.

30What are you doing, O devastated
    one?
  Why dress yourself in scarlet
  and put on jewels of gold?
Why shade your eyes with paint?
  You adorn yourself in vain.
Your lovers despise you;
  they seek your life.

31I hear a cry as of a woman in labor,
  a groan as of one bearing her first
    child—
the cry of the Daughter of Zion
    gasping for breath,
  stretching out her hands and saying,
"Alas! I am fainting;
  my life is given over to murderers."

Not One Is Upright

5 "Go up and down the streets of
    Jerusalem,
  look around and consider,
  search through her squares.
If you can find but one person
  who deals honestly and seeks the
    truth,
  I will forgive this city.
2Although they say, 'As surely as the
    Lord lives,'
  still they are swearing falsely."

3O Lord, do not your eyes look for
    truth?
  You struck them, but they felt no
    pain;
  you crushed them, but they refused
    correction.
They made their faces harder than
    stone
  and refused to repent.
4I thought, "These are only the poor;
  they are foolish,
for they do not know the way of the
    Lord,
  the requirements of their God.
5So I will go to the leaders
  and speak to them;
surely they know the way of the Lord,
  the requirements of their God."

But with one accord they too had
    broken off the yoke
  and torn off the bonds.
⁶Therefore a lion from the forest will
    attack them,
  a wolf from the desert will ravage
    them,
  a leopard will lie in wait near their
    towns
  to tear to pieces any who venture
    out,
  for their rebellion is great
    and their backslidings many.

⁷"Why should I forgive you?
  Your children have forsaken me
  and sworn by gods that are not
    gods.
  I supplied all their needs,
    yet they committed adultery
    and thronged to the houses of
      prostitutes.
⁸They are well-fed, lusty stallions,
    each neighing for another man's
      wife.
⁹Should I not punish them for this?"
    declares the LORD.
  "Should I not avenge myself
    on such a nation as this?

¹⁰"Go through her vineyards and ravage
    them,
  but do not destroy them completely.
  Strip off her branches,
    for these people do not belong to
      the LORD.
¹¹The house of Israel and the house of
    Judah
  have been utterly unfaithful to me,"
           declares the LORD.

¹²They have lied about the LORD;
  they said, "He will do nothing!
  No harm will come to us;
    we will never see sword or famine.
¹³The prophets are but wind
    and the word is not in them;
  so let what they say be done to
    them."

¹⁴Therefore this is what the LORD God
Almighty says:

"Because the people have spoken
    these words,
  I will make my words in your
    mouth a fire
  and these people the wood it
    consumes.
¹⁵O house of Israel," declares the LORD,
  "I am bringing a distant nation
    against you —

an ancient and enduring nation,
  a people whose language you do
    not know,
  whose speech you do not
    understand.
¹⁶Their quivers are like an open grave;
  all of them are mighty warriors.
¹⁷They will devour your harvests and
    food,
  devour your sons and daughters;
  they will devour your flocks and
    herds,
  devour your vines and fig trees.
  With the sword they will destroy
    the fortified cities in which you
      trust.

¹⁸"Yet even in those days," declares the
LORD, "I will not destroy you completely.
¹⁹And when the people ask, 'Why has the
LORD our God done all this to us?' you will
tell them, 'As you have forsaken me and
served foreign gods in your own land, so
now you will serve foreigners in a land not
your own.'

²⁰"Announce this to the house of Jacob
    and proclaim it in Judah:
²¹Hear this, you foolish and senseless
    people,
  who have eyes but do not see,
  who have ears but do not hear:
²²Should you not fear me?" declares the
    LORD.
  "Should you not tremble in my
    presence?
  I made the sand a boundary for the
    sea,
    an everlasting barrier it cannot
      cross.
  The waves may roll, but they cannot
    prevail;
  they may roar, but they cannot
    cross it.
²³But these people have stubborn and
    rebellious hearts;
  they have turned aside and gone
    away.
²⁴They do not say to themselves,
  'Let us fear the LORD our God,
  who gives autumn and spring rains in
    season,
    who assures us of the regular weeks
      of harvest.'
²⁵Your wrongdoings have kept these
    away;
  your sins have deprived you of
    good.

²⁶"Among my people are wicked men

who lie in wait like men who snare
      birds
and like those who set traps to
      catch men.
27Like cages full of birds,
      their houses are full of deceit;
they have become rich and powerful
28   and have grown fat and sleek.
Their evil deeds have no limit;
      they do not plead the case of the
            fatherless to win it,
      they do not defend the rights of the
            poor.
29Should I not punish them for this?"
      declares the LORD.
"Should I not avenge myself
      on such a nation as this?

30"A horrible and shocking thing
      has happened in the land:
31The prophets prophesy lies,
      the priests rule by their own
            authority,
and my people love it this way.
      But what will you do in the end?

Jerusalem Under Siege

6 "Flee for safety, people of Benjamin!
      Flee from Jerusalem!
Sound the trumpet in Tekoa!
      Raise the signal over Beth
            Hakkerem!
For disaster looms out of the north,
      even terrible destruction.
2I will destroy the Daughter of Zion,
      so beautiful and delicate.
3Shepherds with their flocks will come
            against her;
      they will pitch their tents around
            her,
      each tending his own portion."

4"Prepare for battle against her!
      Arise, let us attack at noon!
But, alas, the daylight is fading,
      and the shadows of evening grow
            long.
5So arise, let us attack at night
      and destroy her fortresses!"

6This is what the LORD Almighty says:

"Cut down the trees
      and build siege ramps against
            Jerusalem.
This city must be punished;
      it is filled with oppression.
7As a well pours out its water,
      so she pours out her wickedness.

Violence and destruction resound in
      her;
      her sickness and wounds are ever
            before me.
8Take warning, O Jerusalem,
      or I will turn away from you
and make your land desolate
      so no one can live in it."

9This is what the LORD Almighty says:

"Let them glean the remnant of Israel
      as thoroughly as a vine;
pass your hand over the branches
      again,
      like one gathering grapes."

10To whom can I speak and give
      warning?
      Who will listen to me?
Their ears are closed a
      so they cannot hear.
The word of the LORD is offensive to
      them;
      they find no pleasure in it.
11But I am full of the wrath of the LORD,
      and I cannot hold it in.

"Pour it out on the children in the
      street
      and on the young men gathered
            together;
both husband and wife will be caught
      in it,
      and the old, those weighed down
            with years.
12Their houses will be turned over to
      others,
      together with their fields and their
            wives,
when I stretch out my hand
      against those who live in the land,"
                        declares the LORD.
13"From the least to the greatest,
      all are greedy for gain;
prophets and priests alike,
      all practice deceit.
14They dress the wound of my people
      as though it were not serious.
'Peace, peace,' they say,
      when there is no peace.
15Are they ashamed of their loathsome
      conduct?
      No, they have no shame at all;
      they do not even know how to
            blush.
So they will fall among the fallen;
      they will be brought down when I
            punish them,"
                        says the LORD.

a10 Hebrew uncircumcised

[16]This is what the LORD says:

"Stand at the crossroads and look;
    ask for the ancient paths,
ask where the good way is, and walk
        in it,
        and you will find rest for your
            souls.
    But you said, 'We will not walk in
        it.'
[17]I appointed watchmen over you and
        said,
    'Listen to the sound of the trumpet!'
    But you said, 'We will not listen.'
[18]Therefore hear, O nations;
    observe, O witnesses,
    what will happen to them.
[19]Hear, O earth:
I am bringing disaster on this people,
    the fruit of their schemes,
because they have not listened to my
        words
    and have rejected my law.
[20]What do I care about incense from
        Sheba
    or sweet calamus from a distant
        land?
Your burnt offerings are not
        acceptable;
    your sacrifices do not please me."

[21]Therefore this is what the LORD says:

"I will put obstacles before this
        people.
    Fathers and sons alike will stumble
        over them;
    neighbors and friends will perish."

[22]This is what the LORD says:

"Look, an army is coming
    from the land of the north;
a great nation is being stirred up
    from the ends of the earth.
[23]They are armed with bow and spear;
    they are cruel and show no mercy.
They sound like the roaring sea
    as they ride on their horses;
they come like men in battle
        formation
    to attack you, O Daughter of Zion."

[24]We have heard reports about them,
    and our hands hang limp.
Anguish has gripped us,
    pain like that of a woman in labor.
[25]Do not go out to the fields
    or walk on the roads,
for the enemy has a sword,
    and there is terror on every side.

[26]O my people, put on sackcloth
    and roll in ashes;
mourn with bitter wailing
    as for an only son,
for suddenly the destroyer
    will come upon us.

[27]"I have made you a tester of metals
    and my people the ore,
that you may observe
    and test their ways.
[28]They are all hardened rebels,
    going about to slander.
They are bronze and iron;
    they all act corruptly.
[29]The bellows blow fiercely
    to burn away the lead with fire,
but the refining goes on in vain;
    the wicked are not purged out.
[30]They are called rejected silver,
    because the LORD has rejected
        them."

False Religion Worthless

7 This is the word that came to Jeremiah from the LORD: [2]"Stand at the gate of the LORD's house and there proclaim this message:

" 'Hear the word of the LORD, all you people of Judah who come through these gates to worship the LORD. [3]This is what the LORD Almighty, the God of Israel, says: Reform your ways and your actions, and I will let you live in this place. [4]Do not trust in deceptive words and say, "This is the temple of the LORD, the temple of the LORD, the temple of the LORD!" [5]If you really change your ways and your actions and deal with each other justly, [6]if you do not oppress the alien, the fatherless or the widow and do not shed innocent blood in this place, and if you do not follow other gods to your own harm, [7]then I will let you live in this place, in the land I gave your forefathers for ever and ever. [8]But look, you are trusting in deceptive words that are worthless.

[9]" 'Will you steal and murder, commit adultery and perjury,[a] burn incense to Baal and follow other gods you have not known, [10]and then come and stand before me in this house, which bears my Name, and say, "We are safe"—safe to do all these detestable things? [11]Has this house, which bears my Name, become a den of robbers to you? But I have been watching! declares the LORD.

[12]" 'Go now to the place in Shiloh where

---
[a]9 Or and swear by false gods

I first made a dwelling for my Name, and see what I did to it because of the wickedness of my people Israel. ¹³While you were doing all these things, declares the LORD, I spoke to you again and again, but you did not listen; I called you, but you did not answer. ¹⁴Therefore, what I did to Shiloh I will now do to the house that bears my Name, the temple you trust in, the place I gave to you and your fathers. ¹⁵I will thrust you from my presence, just as I did all your brothers, the people of Ephraim.'

¹⁶"So do not pray for this people nor offer any plea or petition for them; do not plead with me, for I will not listen to you. ¹⁷Do you not see what they are doing in the towns of Judah and in the streets of Jerusalem? ¹⁸The children gather wood, the fathers light the fire, and the women knead the dough and make cakes of bread for the Queen of Heaven. They pour out drink offerings to other gods to provoke me to anger. ¹⁹But am I the one they are provoking? declares the LORD. Are they not rather harming themselves, to their own shame?

²⁰"'Therefore this is what the Sovereign LORD says: My anger and my wrath will be poured out on this place, on man and beast, on the trees of the field and on the fruit of the ground, and it will burn and not be quenched.

²¹"'This is what the LORD Almighty, the God of Israel, says: Go ahead, add your burnt offerings to your other sacrifices and eat the meat yourselves! ²²For when I brought your forefathers out of Egypt and spoke to them, I did not just give them commands about burnt offerings and sacrifices, ²³but I gave them this command: Obey me, and I will be your God and you will be my people. Walk in all the ways I command you, that it may go well with you. ²⁴But they did not listen or pay attention; instead, they followed the stubborn inclinations of their evil hearts. They went backward and not forward. ²⁵From the time your forefathers left Egypt until now, day after day, again and again I sent you my servants the prophets. ²⁶But they did not listen to me or pay attention. They were stiff-necked and did more evil than their forefathers.'

²⁷"When you tell them all this, they will not listen to you; when you call to them, they will not answer. ²⁸Therefore say to them, 'This is the nation that has not obeyed the LORD its God or responded to correction. Truth has perished; it has vanished from their lips. ²⁹Cut off your hair and throw it away; take up a lament on the barren heights, for the LORD has rejected and abandoned this generation that is under his wrath.

The Valley of Slaughter

³⁰" 'The people of Judah have done evil in my eyes, declares the LORD. They have set up their detestable idols in the house that bears my Name and have defiled it. ³¹They have built the high places of Topheth in the Valley of Ben Hinnom to burn their sons and daughters in the fire—something I did not command, nor did it enter my mind. ³²So beware, the days are coming, declares the LORD, when people will no longer call it Topheth or the Valley of Ben Hinnom, but the Valley of Slaughter, for they will bury the dead in Topheth until there is no more room. ³³Then the carcasses of this people will become food for the birds of the air and the beasts of the earth, and there will be no one to frighten them away. ³⁴I will bring an end to the sounds of joy and gladness and to the voices of bride and bridegroom in the towns of Judah and the streets of Jerusalem, for the land will become desolate.

8 " 'At that time, declares the LORD, the bones of the kings and officials of Judah, the bones of the priests and prophets, and the bones of the people of Jerusalem will be removed from their graves. ²They will be exposed to the sun and the moon and all the stars of the heavens, which they have loved and served and which they have followed and consulted and worshiped. They will not be gathered up or buried, but will be like refuse lying on the ground. ³Wherever I banish them, all the survivors of this evil nation will prefer death to life, declares the LORD Almighty.'

Sin and Punishment

⁴"Say to them, 'This is what the LORD says:

" 'When men fall down, do they not
    get up?
  When a man turns away, does he
    not return?
⁵Why then have these people turned
    away?
  Why does Jerusalem always turn
    away?
They cling to deceit;
  they refuse to return.
⁶I have listened attentively,

but they do not say what is right.
No one repents of his wickedness,
  saying, "What have I done?"
Each pursues his own course
  like a horse charging into battle.
⁷Even the stork in the sky
  knows her appointed seasons,
and the dove, the swift and the thrush
  observe the time of their migration.
But my people do not know
  the requirements of the LORD.

⁸" 'How can you say, "We are wise,
  for we have the law of the LORD,"
when actually the lying pen of the
    scribes
  has handled it falsely?
⁹The wise will be put to shame;
  they will be dismayed and trapped.
Since they have rejected the word of
    the LORD,
  what kind of wisdom do they have?
¹⁰Therefore I will give their wives to
    other men
  and their fields to new owners.
From the least to the greatest,
  all are greedy for gain;
prophets and priests alike,
  all practice deceit.
¹¹They dress the wound of my people
  as though it were not serious.
"Peace, peace," they say,
  when there is no peace.
¹²Are they ashamed of their loathsome
    conduct?
  No, they have no shame at all;
  they do not even know how to
    blush.
So they will fall among the fallen;
  they will be brought down when
    they are punished,
      says the LORD.

¹³" 'I will take away their harvest,
      declares the LORD.
  There will be no grapes on the vine.
There will be no figs on the tree,
  and their leaves will wither.
What I have given them
  will be taken from them.ᵃ' "

¹⁴"Why are we sitting here?
  Gather together!
Let us flee to the fortified cities
  and perish there!
For the LORD our God has doomed us
    to perish

and given us poisoned water to
    drink,
because we have sinned against
    him.
¹⁵We hoped for peace
  but no good has come,
for a time of healing
  but there was only terror.
¹⁶The snorting of the enemy's horses
  is heard from Dan;
at the neighing of their stallions
  the whole land trembles.
They have come to devour
  the land and everything in it,
  the city and all who live there."

¹⁷"See, I will send venomous snakes
    among you,
  vipers that cannot be charmed,
  and they will bite you,"
      declares the LORD.

¹⁸O my Comforterᵇ in sorrow,
  my heart is faint within me.
¹⁹Listen to the cry of my people
  from a land far away:
"Is the LORD not in Zion?
  Is her King no longer there?"

"Why have they provoked me to anger
    with their images,
  with their worthless foreign idols?"

²⁰"The harvest is past,
  the summer has ended,
  and we are not saved."

²¹Since my people are crushed, I am
    crushed;
  I mourn, and horror grips me.
²²Is there no balm in Gilead?
  Is there no physician there?
Why then is there no healing
  for the wound of my people?

9 ¹Oh, that my head were a spring of
    water
  and my eyes a fountain of tears!
I would weep day and night
  for the slain of my people.
²Oh, that I had in the desert
  a lodging place for travelers,
so that I might leave my people
  and go away from them;
for they are all adulterers,
  a crowd of unfaithful people.

³"They make ready their tongue
  like a bow, to shoot lies;
it is not by truth
  that they triumphᶜ in the land.

ᵃ13 The meaning of the Hebrew for this sentence is uncertain.   ᵇ18 The meaning of the Hebrew for
this word is uncertain.   ᶜ3 Or lies; / they are not valiant for truth

They go from one sin to another;
    they do not acknowledge me,"
                  declares the LORD.
4"Beware of your friends;
    do not trust your brothers.
For every brother is a deceiver,*a*
    and every friend a slanderer.
5Friend deceives friend,
    and no one speaks the truth.
They have taught their tongues to lie;
    they weary themselves with sinning.
6You*b* live in the midst of deception;
    in their deceit they refuse to
        acknowledge me,"
                  declares the LORD.

7Therefore this is what the LORD Almighty says:

"See, I will refine and test them,
    for what else can I do
    because of the sin of my people?
8Their tongue is a deadly arrow;
    it speaks with deceit.
.With his mouth each speaks cordially
    to his neighbor,
    but in his heart he sets a trap for
        him.
9Should I not punish them for this?"
    declares the LORD.
"Should I not avenge myself
    on such a nation as this?"

10I will weep and wail for the
        mountains
    and take up a lament concerning
        the desert pastures.
They are desolate and untraveled,
    and the lowing of cattle is not
        heard.
The birds of the air have fled
    and the animals are gone.

11"I will make Jerusalem a heap of
        ruins,
    a haunt of jackals;
and I will lay waste the towns of
        Judah
    so no one can live there."

12What man is wise enough to understand this? Who has been instructed by the LORD and can explain it? Why has the land been ruined and laid waste like a desert that no one can cross?
13The LORD said, "It is because they have forsaken my law, which I set before them; they have not obeyed me or followed my law. 14Instead, they have followed the stubbornness of their hearts; they have followed the Baals, as their fathers taught them." 15Therefore, this is what the LORD Almighty, the God of Israel, says: "See, I will make this people eat bitter food and drink poisoned water. 16I will scatter them among nations that neither they nor their fathers have known, and I will pursue them with the sword until I have destroyed them."

17This is what the LORD Almighty says:

"Consider now! Call for the wailing
        women to come;
    send for the most skillful of them.
18Let them come quickly
    and wail over us
till our eyes overflow with tears
    and water streams from our eyelids.
19The sound of wailing is heard from
        Zion:
    'How ruined we are!
    How great is our shame!
We must leave our land
    because our houses are in ruins.' "

20Now, O women, hear the word of the
        LORD;
    open your ears to the words of his
        mouth.
Teach your daughters how to wail;
    teach one another a lament.
21Death has climbed in through our
        windows
    and has entered our fortresses;
it has cut off the children from the
        streets
    and the young men from the public
        squares.

22Say, "This is what the LORD declares:

" 'The dead bodies of men will lie
    like refuse on the open field,
like cut grain behind the reaper,
    with no one to gather them.' "

23This is what the LORD says:

"Let not the wise man boast of his
        wisdom
    or the strong man boast of his
        strength
    or the rich man boast of his riches,
24but let him who boasts boast about
        this:
    that he understands and knows me,
that I am the LORD, who exercises
        kindness,

---

*a*4 Or *a deceiving Jacob*   *b*6 That is, Jeremiah (the Hebrew is singular)

justice and righteousness on earth,
for in these I delight,"

declares the LORD.

25"The days are coming," declares the LORD, "when I will punish all who are circumcised only in the flesh— 26Egypt, Judah, Edom, Ammon, Moab and all who live in the desert in distant places.ᵃ For all these nations are really uncircumcised, and even the whole house of Israel is uncircumcised in heart."

ᵃ26 Or *desert and who clip the hair by their foreheads*

God and Idols

10 Hear what the LORD says to you, O house of Israel. 2This is what the LORD says:

"Do not learn the ways of the nations
    or be terrified by signs in the sky,
    though the nations are terrified by
        them.
3For the customs of the peoples are
    worthless;
they cut a tree out of the forest,

FRIDAY

VERSE FOR THE DAY:
Jeremiah 9:23

AUTHOR:
Joe Gibbs

PASSAGE FOR THE DAY:
Jeremiah 9:23–24

Like a Little Child

PICTURE almost 53,000 people screaming, players high-fiving each other, me sweating and grinning and eager to get a drink. It was pandemonium. I felt like I had been on that field with my players, fighting my guts out.

I reached down for a cup [of water] and there was [my son] Coy at the back of the table, pretending two empty film canisters were cars. He was playing cars, oblivious to the sweat and the blood and the cheers and the uproar. It was almost as if a magnet made me stand there a second longer. I could hardly turn away.

Here I was in the middle of a big game, one that had just turned our way. It was the most important thing in my life. Yet here was truly my life, this little kid who couldn't have cared less whether I won or lost. I was stunned. His priorities had not been screwed up. He was having fun in his own little world. It hit me that there were millions of people all over the world who didn't know or care that the Redskins were playing the Chiefs. *Really*, I wondered, *where is the true perspective?*

The world says that right then nothing is as important as winning that game. To my son it meant little. And to me, what will mean anything twenty years from now? I may still remember that we won that game, but I may not. I know I'll remember Coy playing cars and showing me what was important.

We all get caught up in the externals of life, whether it's tennis or golf or business deals, and we run the risk of losing the things most important to us: our own kids.

Additional Scripture Readings:
Psalm 127:3–5; Matthew 18:1–6

Go to page 805 for your next devotional reading.

and a craftsman shapes it with his
chisel.
[4]They adorn it with silver and gold;
they fasten it with hammer and
nails
so it will not totter.
[5]Like a scarecrow in a melon patch,
their idols cannot speak;
they must be carried
because they cannot walk.
Do not fear them;
they can do no harm
nor can they do any good."

[6]No one is like you, O Lord;
you are great,
and your name is mighty in power.
[7]Who should not revere you,
O King of the nations?
This is your due.
Among all the wise men of the
nations
and in all their kingdoms,
there is no one like you.
[8]They are all senseless and foolish;
they are taught by worthless
wooden idols.
[9]Hammered silver is brought from
Tarshish
and gold from Uphaz.
What the craftsman and goldsmith
have made
is then dressed in blue and
purple—
all made by skilled workers.
[10]But the Lord is the true God;
he is the living God, the eternal
King.
When he is angry, the earth trembles;
the nations cannot endure his
wrath.

[11]"Tell them this: 'These gods, who did
not make the heavens and the earth, will
perish from the earth and from under the
heavens.' "[a]

[12]But God made the earth by his power;
he founded the world by his
wisdom
and stretched out the heavens by
his understanding.
[13]When he thunders, the waters in the
heavens roar;
he makes clouds rise from the ends
of the earth.
He sends lightning with the rain
and brings out the wind from his
storehouses.

[14]Everyone is senseless and without
knowledge;
every goldsmith is shamed by his
idols.
His images are a fraud;
they have no breath in them.
[15]They are worthless, the objects of
mockery;
when their judgment comes, they
will perish.
[16]He who is the Portion of Jacob is not
like these,
for he is the Maker of all things,
including Israel, the tribe of his
inheritance—
the Lord Almighty is his name.

Coming Destruction

[17]Gather up your belongings to leave
the land,
you who live under siege.
[18]For this is what the Lord says:
"At this time I will hurl out
those who live in this land;
I will bring distress on them
so that they may be captured."

[19]Woe to me because of my injury!
My wound is incurable!
Yet I said to myself,
"This is my sickness, and I must
endure it."
[20]My tent is destroyed;
all its ropes are snapped.
My sons are gone from me and are no
more;
no one is left now to pitch my tent
or to set up my shelter.
[21]The shepherds are senseless
and do not inquire of the Lord;
so they do not prosper
and all their flock is scattered.
[22]Listen! The report is coming—
a great commotion from the land of
the north!
It will make the towns of Judah
desolate,
a haunt of jackals.

Jeremiah's Prayer

[23]I know, O Lord, that a man's life is
not his own;
it is not for man to direct his steps.
[24]Correct me, Lord, but only with
justice—
not in your anger,
lest you reduce me to nothing.
[25]Pour out your wrath on the nations

---

[a]11 The text of this verse is in Aramaic.

that do not acknowledge you,
on the peoples who do not call on
your name.
For they have devoured Jacob;
they have devoured him completely
and destroyed his homeland.

The Covenant Is Broken

11 This is the word that came to Jeremiah from the LORD: **2**"Listen to the terms of this covenant and tell them to the people of Judah and to those who live in Jerusalem. **3**Tell them that this is what the LORD, the God of Israel, says: 'Cursed is the man who does not obey the terms of this covenant— **4**the terms I commanded your forefathers when I brought them out of Egypt, out of the iron-smelting furnace.' I said, 'Obey me and do everything I command you, and you will be my people, and I will be your God. **5**Then I will fulfill the oath I swore to your forefathers, to give them a land flowing with milk and honey'—the land you possess today."

I answered, "Amen, LORD."

6The LORD said to me, "Proclaim all these words in the towns of Judah and in the streets of Jerusalem: 'Listen to the terms of this covenant and follow them. **7**From the time I brought your forefathers up from Egypt until today, I warned them again and again, saying, "Obey me." **8**But they did not listen or pay attention; instead, they followed the stubbornness of their evil hearts. So I brought on them all the curses of the covenant I had commanded them to follow but that they did not keep.' "

9Then the LORD said to me, "There is a conspiracy among the people of Judah and those who live in Jerusalem. **10**They have returned to the sins of their forefathers, who refused to listen to my words. They have followed other gods to serve them. Both the house of Israel and the house of Judah have broken the covenant I made with their forefathers. **11**Therefore this is what the LORD says: 'I will bring on them a disaster they cannot escape. Although they cry out to me, I will not listen to them. **12**The towns of Judah and the people of Jerusalem will go and cry out to the gods to whom they burn incense, but they will not help them at all when disaster strikes. **13**You have as many gods as you have towns, O Judah; and the altars you have set up to burn incense to that

shameful god Baal are as many as the streets of Jerusalem.'

14"Do not pray for this people nor offer any plea or petition for them, because I will not listen when they call to me in the time of their distress.

15"What is my beloved doing in my temple
as she works out her evil schemes with many?
Can consecrated meat avert ∟your punishment⌋?
When you engage in your wickedness, then you rejoice.*a*"

16The LORD called you a thriving olive tree
with fruit beautiful in form.
But with the roar of a mighty storm he will set it on fire,
and its branches will be broken.

17The LORD Almighty, who planted you, has decreed disaster for you, because the house of Israel and the house of Judah have done evil and provoked me to anger by burning incense to Baal.

Plot Against Jeremiah

18Because the LORD revealed their plot to me, I knew it, for at that time he showed me what they were doing. **19**I had been like a gentle lamb led to the slaughter; I did not realize that they had plotted against me, saying,

"Let us destroy the tree and its fruit;
let us cut him off from the land of the living,
that his name be remembered no more."
20But, O LORD Almighty, you who judge righteously
and test the heart and mind,
let me see your vengeance upon them,
for to you I have committed my cause.

21"Therefore this is what the LORD says about the men of Anathoth who are seeking your life and saying, 'Do not prophesy in the name of the LORD or you will die by our hands'— **22**therefore this is what the LORD Almighty says: 'I will punish them. Their young men will die by the sword, their sons and daughters by famine. **23**Not even a remnant will be left to them, because I will bring disaster on the men of

---

a15 Or *Could consecrated meat avert your punishment? / Then you would rejoice*

Anathoth in the year of their punishment.' "

Jeremiah's Complaint

12 You are always righteous,
O Lord,
when I bring a case before you.
Yet I would speak with you about
your justice:
Why does the way of the wicked
prosper?
Why do all the faithless live at ease?
²You have planted them, and they have
taken root;
they grow and bear fruit.
You are always on their lips
but far from their hearts.
³Yet you know me, O Lord;
you see me and test my thoughts
about you.
Drag them off like sheep to be
butchered!
Set them apart for the day of
slaughter!
⁴How long will the land lie parched[a]
and the grass in every field be
withered?
Because those who live in it are
wicked,
the animals and birds have
perished.
Moreover, the people are saying,
"He will not see what happens to
us."

God's Answer

⁵"If you have raced with men on foot
and they have worn you out,
how can you compete with horses?
If you stumble in safe country,[b]
how will you manage in the thickets
by[c] the Jordan?
⁶Your brothers, your own family—
even they have betrayed you;
they have raised a loud cry against
you.
Do not trust them,
though they speak well of you.

⁷"I will forsake my house,
abandon my inheritance;
I will give the one I love
into the hands of her enemies.
⁸My inheritance has become to me
like a lion in the forest.
She roars at me;
therefore I hate her.

⁹Has not my inheritance become to me
like a speckled bird of prey
that other birds of prey surround
and attack?
Go and gather all the wild beasts;
bring them to devour.
¹⁰Many shepherds will ruin my vineyard
and trample down my field;
they will turn my pleasant field
into a desolate wasteland.
¹¹It will be made a wasteland,
parched and desolate before me;
the whole land will be laid waste
because there is no one who cares.
¹²Over all the barren heights in the
desert
destroyers will swarm,
for the sword of the Lord will devour
from one end of the land to the
other;
no one will be safe.
¹³They will sow wheat but reap thorns;
they will wear themselves out but
gain nothing.
So bear the shame of your harvest
because of the Lord's fierce anger."

¹⁴This is what the Lord says: "As for all
my wicked neighbors who seize the inheritance I gave my people Israel, I will uproot them from their lands and I will uproot the house of Judah from among
them. ¹⁵But after I uproot them, I will
again have compassion and will bring
each of them back to his own inheritance
and his own country. ¹⁶And if they learn
well the ways of my people and swear by
my name, saying, 'As surely as the Lord
lives'—even as they once taught my people to swear by Baal—then they will be
established among my people. ¹⁷But if any
nation does not listen, I will completely
uproot and destroy it," declares the Lord.

A Linen Belt

13 This is what the Lord said to me:
"Go and buy a linen belt and put it
around your waist, but do not let it touch
water." ²So I bought a belt, as the Lord directed, and put it around my waist.

³Then the word of the Lord came to me
a second time: ⁴"Take the belt you bought
and are wearing around your waist, and
go now to Perath[d] and hide it there in a
crevice in the rocks." ⁵So I went and hid it
at Perath, as the Lord told me.

⁶Many days later the Lord said to me,

---

a4 Or *land mourn*   *b5* Or *If you put your trust in a land of safety*   *c5* Or *the flooding of*   *d4* Or
possibly *the Euphrates*; also in verses 5-7

"Go now to Perath and get the belt I told you to hide there." ⁷So I went to Perath and dug up the belt and took it from the place where I had hidden it, but now it was ruined and completely useless.

⁸Then the word of the LORD came to me: ⁹"This is what the LORD says: 'In the same way I will ruin the pride of Judah and the great pride of Jerusalem. ¹⁰These wicked people, who refuse to listen to my words, who follow the stubbornness of their hearts and go after other gods to serve and worship them, will be like this belt — completely useless! ¹¹For as a belt is bound around a man's waist, so I bound the whole house of Israel and the whole house of Judah to me,' declares the LORD, 'to be my people for my renown and praise and honor. But they have not listened.'

Wineskins

¹²"Say to them: 'This is what the LORD, the God of Israel, says: Every wineskin should be filled with wine.' And if they say to you, 'Don't we know that every wineskin should be filled with wine?' ¹³then tell them, 'This is what the LORD says: I am going to fill with drunkenness all who live in this land, including the kings who sit on David's throne, the priests, the prophets and all those living in Jerusalem. ¹⁴I will smash them one against the other, fathers and sons alike, declares the LORD. I will allow no pity or mercy or compassion to keep me from destroying them.' "

Threat of Captivity

¹⁵Hear and pay attention,
    do not be arrogant,
    for the LORD has spoken.
¹⁶Give glory to the LORD your God
    before he brings the darkness,
before your feet stumble
    on the darkening hills.
You hope for light,
    but he will turn it to thick darkness
    and change it to deep gloom.
¹⁷But if you do not listen,
    I will weep in secret
    because of your pride;
my eyes will weep bitterly,
    overflowing with tears,
because the LORD's flock will be
    taken captive.

¹⁸Say to the king and to the queen
        mother,
    "Come down from your thrones,
for your glorious crowns
    will fall from your heads."
¹⁹The cities in the Negev will be shut
        up,
    and there will be no one to open
        them.
All Judah will be carried into exile,
    carried completely away.

²⁰Lift up your eyes and see
    those who are coming from the
        north.
Where is the flock that was entrusted
    to you,
    the sheep of which you boasted?
²¹What will you say when ˌthe LORDˌ
        sets over you
    those you cultivated as your special
        allies?
Will not pain grip you
    like that of a woman in labor?
²²And if you ask yourself,
    "Why has this happened to me?" —
it is because of your many sins
    that your skirts have been torn off
    and your body mistreated.
²³Can the Ethiopian[a] change his skin
    or the leopard its spots?
Neither can you do good
    who are accustomed to doing evil.

²⁴"I will scatter you like chaff
    driven by the desert wind.
²⁵This is your lot,
    the portion I have decreed for you,"
                    declares the LORD,
"because you have forgotten me
    and trusted in false gods.
²⁶I will pull up your skirts over your
        face
    that your shame may be seen —
²⁷your adulteries and lustful neighings,
    your shameless prostitution!
I have seen your detestable acts
    on the hills and in the fields.
Woe to you, O Jerusalem!
    How long will you be unclean?"

Drought, Famine, Sword

14 This is the word of the LORD to Jeremiah concerning the drought:

²"Judah mourns,
    her cities languish;
they wail for the land,
    and a cry goes up from Jerusalem.

---

a23 Hebrew *Cushite* (probably a person from the upper Nile region)

³The nobles send their servants for
  water;
  they go to the cisterns
  but find no water.
They return with their jars unfilled;
  dismayed and despairing,
  they cover their heads.
⁴The ground is cracked
  because there is no rain in the land;
  the farmers are dismayed
  and cover their heads.
⁵Even the doe in the field
  deserts her newborn fawn
  because there is no grass.
⁶Wild donkeys stand on the barren
  heights
  and pant like jackals;
  their eyesight fails
  for lack of pasture."

⁷Although our sins testify against us,
  O LORD, do something for the sake
    of your name.
For our backsliding is great;
  we have sinned against you.
⁸O Hope of Israel,
  its Savior in times of distress,
  why are you like a stranger in the
    land,
  like a traveler who stays only a
    night?
⁹Why are you like a man taken by
    surprise,
  like a warrior powerless to save?
You are among us, O LORD,
  and we bear your name;
  do not forsake us!

¹⁰This is what the LORD says about this
people:

"They greatly love to wander;
  they do not restrain their feet.
So the LORD does not accept them;
  he will now remember their
    wickedness
  and punish them for their sins."

¹¹Then the LORD said to me, "Do not
pray for the well-being of this people.
¹²Although they fast, I will not listen to
their cry; though they offer burnt offerings and grain offerings, I will not accept
them. Instead, I will destroy them with the
sword, famine and plague."

¹³But I said, "Ah, Sovereign LORD, the
prophets keep telling them, 'You will not
see the sword or suffer famine. Indeed, I
will give you lasting peace in this place.' "

¹⁴Then the LORD said to me, "The
prophets are prophesying lies in my
name. I have not sent them or appointed
them or spoken to them. They are prophesying to you false visions, divinations,
idolatries*ᵃ* and the delusions of their own
minds. ¹⁵Therefore, this is what the LORD
says about the prophets who are prophesying in my name: I did not send them, yet
they are saying, 'No sword or famine will
touch this land.' Those same prophets will
perish by sword and famine. ¹⁶And the
people they are prophesying to will be
thrown out into the streets of Jerusalem
because of the famine and sword. There
will be no one to bury them or their wives,
their sons or their daughters. I will pour
out on them the calamity they deserve.

¹⁷"Speak this word to them:

" 'Let my eyes overflow with tears
  night and day without ceasing;
for my virgin daughter — my people —
  has suffered a grievous wound,
  a crushing blow.
¹⁸If I go into the country,
  I see those slain by the sword;
if I go into the city,
  I see the ravages of famine.
Both prophet and priest
  have gone to a land they know
    not.' "

¹⁹Have you rejected Judah completely?
  Do you despise Zion?
Why have you afflicted us
  so that we cannot be healed?
We hoped for peace
  but no good has come,
for a time of healing
  but there is only terror.
²⁰O LORD, we acknowledge our
    wickedness
  and the guilt of our fathers;
  we have indeed sinned against you.
²¹For the sake of your name do not
    despise us;
  do not dishonor your glorious
    throne.
Remember your covenant with us
  and do not break it.
²²Do any of the worthless idols of the
    nations bring rain?
  Do the skies themselves send down
    showers?
No, it is you, O LORD our God.
  Therefore our hope is in you,
  for you are the one who does all
    this.

ᵃ14 Or *visions, worthless divinations*

WEEKENDING

REFLECT

If you're a dad, what kind of mark are you leaving on your children, especially your sons? Do you realize that your little boys are watching you like hawks? They're trying to figure out what maleness is all about, and you're their model. I hope they see in you a deep, uncompromising love for God. I hope they see both toughness and tenderness. If they do, then you have served them well; they will be forever grateful. Your little girls, too, will benefit because they'll grow up with a clear vision of the kind of men who make godly husbands.

– Bill Hybels

REVIVE

Saturday: Jeremiah 9:23–24
Sunday: Matthew 5:1–10

Go to page 820 for your next devotional reading.

15

Then the LORD said to me: "Even if Moses and Samuel were to stand before me, my heart would not go out to this people. Send them away from my presence! Let them go! ²And if they ask you, 'Where shall we go?' tell them, 'This is what the LORD says:

" 'Those destined for death, to death;
those for the sword, to the sword;
those for starvation, to starvation;
those for captivity, to captivity.'

³"I will send four kinds of destroyers against them," declares the LORD, "the sword to kill and the dogs to drag away and the birds of the air and the beasts of the earth to devour and destroy. ⁴I will make them abhorrent to all the kingdoms of the earth because of what Manasseh son of Hezekiah king of Judah did in Jerusalem.

⁵"Who will have pity on you,
    O Jerusalem?
Who will mourn for you?
Who will stop to ask how you are?
⁶You have rejected me," declares the
    LORD.
    "You keep on backsliding.
So I will lay hands on you and destroy
    you;
I can no longer show compassion.
⁷I will winnow them with a winnowing
    fork
    at the city gates of the land.
I will bring bereavement and
    destruction on my people,
    for they have not changed their
        ways.
⁸I will make their widows more
        numerous
    than the sand of the sea.
At midday I will bring a destroyer
    against the mothers of their young
        men;
suddenly I will bring down on them
    anguish and terror.
⁹The mother of seven will grow faint
    and breathe her last.
Her sun will set while it is still day;
    she will be disgraced and
        humiliated.
I will put the survivors to the sword
    before their enemies,"
                    declares the LORD.
¹⁰Alas, my mother, that you gave me
        birth,

a man with whom the whole land
    strives and contends!
I have neither lent nor borrowed,
    yet everyone curses me.

¹¹The LORD said,

"Surely I will deliver you for a good
        purpose;
    surely I will make your enemies
        plead with you
    in times of disaster and times of
        distress.

¹²"Can a man break iron—
    iron from the north—or bronze?
¹³Your wealth and your treasures
    I will give as plunder, without
        charge,
because of all your sins
    throughout your country.
¹⁴I will enslave you to your enemies
    in*a* a land you do not know,
for my anger will kindle a fire
    that will burn against you."

¹⁵You understand, O LORD;
    remember me and care for me.
    Avenge me on my persecutors.
You are long-suffering—do not take
        me away;
    think of how I suffer reproach for
        your sake.
¹⁶When your words came, I ate them;
    they were my joy and my heart's
        delight,
for I bear your name,
    O LORD God Almighty.
¹⁷I never sat in the company of revelers,
    never made merry with them;
I sat alone because your hand was on
        me
    and you had filled me with
        indignation.
¹⁸Why is my pain unending
    and my wound grievous and
        incurable?
Will you be to me like a deceptive
        brook,
    like a spring that fails?

¹⁹Therefore this is what the LORD says:

"If you repent, I will restore you
    that you may serve me;
if you utter worthy, not worthless,
        words,
    you will be my spokesman.
Let this people turn to you,
    but you must not turn to them.

---

*a*14 Some Hebrew manuscripts, Septuagint and Syriac (see also Jer. 17:4); most Hebrew manuscripts *I will cause your enemies to bring you / into*

[20]I will make you a wall to this people,
  a fortified wall of bronze;
they will fight against you
  but will not overcome you,
for I am with you
  to rescue and save you,"
                    declares the LORD.
[21]"I will save you from the hands of the
  wicked
  and redeem you from the grasp of
  the cruel."

Day of Disaster

16 Then the word of the LORD came to me: [2]"You must not marry and have sons or daughters in this place." [3]For this is what the LORD says about the sons and daughters born in this land and about the women who are their mothers and the men who are their fathers: [4]"They will die of deadly diseases. They will not be mourned or buried but will be like refuse lying on the ground. They will perish by sword and famine, and their dead bodies will become food for the birds of the air and the beasts of the earth."

[5]For this is what the LORD says: "Do not enter a house where there is a funeral meal; do not go to mourn or show sympathy, because I have withdrawn my blessing, my love and my pity from this people," declares the LORD. [6]"Both high and low will die in this land. They will not be buried or mourned, and no one will cut himself or shave his head for them. [7]No one will offer food to comfort those who mourn for the dead—not even for a father or a mother—nor will anyone give them a drink to console them.

[8]"And do not enter a house where there is feasting and sit down to eat and drink. [9]For this is what the LORD Almighty, the God of Israel, says: Before your eyes and in your days I will bring an end to the sounds of joy and gladness and to the voices of bride and bridegroom in this place.

[10]"When you tell these people all this and they ask you, 'Why has the LORD decreed such a great disaster against us? What wrong have we done? What sin have we committed against the LORD our God?' [11]then say to them, 'It is because your fathers forsook me,' declares the LORD, 'and followed other gods and served and worshiped them. They forsook me and did not keep my law. [12]But you have behaved more wickedly than your fathers. See how each of you is following the stubbornness of his evil heart instead of obeying me. [13]So I will throw you out of this land into a land neither you nor your fathers have known, and there you will serve other gods day and night, for I will show you no favor.'

[14]"However, the days are coming," declares the LORD, "when men will no longer say, 'As surely as the LORD lives, who brought the Israelites up out of Egypt,' [15]but they will say, 'As surely as the LORD lives, who brought the Israelites up out of the land of the north and out of all the countries where he had banished them.' For I will restore them to the land I gave their forefathers.

[16]"But now I will send for many fishermen," declares the LORD, "and they will catch them. After that I will send for many hunters, and they will hunt them down on every mountain and hill and from the crevices of the rocks. [17]My eyes are on all their ways; they are not hidden from me, nor is their sin concealed from my eyes. [18]I will repay them double for their wickedness and their sin, because they have defiled my land with the lifeless forms of their vile images and have filled my inheritance with their detestable idols."

[19]O LORD, my strength and my fortress,
  my refuge in time of distress,
to you the nations will come
  from the ends of the earth and say,
"Our fathers possessed nothing but
    false gods,
  worthless idols that did them no
    good.
[20]Do men make their own gods?
  Yes, but they are not gods!"

[21]"Therefore I will teach them—
  this time I will teach them
  my power and might.
Then they will know
  that my name is the LORD.

17 "Judah's sin is engraved with an
    iron tool,
  inscribed with a flint point,
on the tablets of their hearts
  and on the horns of their altars.
[2]Even their children remember
  their altars and Asherah poles[a]
beside the spreading trees
  and on the high hills.
[3]My mountain in the land

---

a2 That is, symbols of the goddess Asherah

and your[a] wealth and all your
    treasures
I will give away as plunder,
    together with your high places,
    because of sin throughout your
      country.
[4]Through your own fault you will lose
    the inheritance I gave you.
I will enslave you to your enemies
    in a land you do not know,
for you have kindled my anger,
    and it will burn forever."

[5]This is what the LORD says:

"Cursed is the one who trusts in man,
    who depends on flesh for his
      strength
    and whose heart turns away from
      the LORD.
[6]He will be like a bush in the
      wastelands;
    he will not see prosperity when it
      comes.
He will dwell in the parched places of
      the desert,
    in a salt land where no one lives.

[7]"But blessed is the man who trusts in
      the LORD,
    whose confidence is in him.
[8]He will be like a tree planted by the
      water
    that sends out its roots by the
      stream.
It does not fear when heat comes;
    its leaves are always green.
It has no worries in a year of drought
    and never fails to bear fruit."

[9]The heart is deceitful above all things
    and beyond cure.
    Who can understand it?

[10]"I the LORD search the heart
    and examine the mind,
to reward a man according to his
      conduct,
    according to what his deeds
      deserve."

[11]Like a partridge that hatches eggs it
      did not lay
    is the man who gains riches by
      unjust means.
When his life is half gone, they will
      desert him,
    and in the end he will prove to be a
      fool.

[12]A glorious throne, exalted from the
      beginning,
    is the place of our sanctuary.
[13]O LORD, the hope of Israel,
    all who forsake you will be put to
      shame.
Those who turn away from you will
      be written in the dust
because they have forsaken the
      LORD,
    the spring of living water.

[14]Heal me, O LORD, and I will be healed;
    save me and I will be saved,
    for you are the one I praise.
[15]They keep saying to me,
    "Where is the word of the LORD?
    Let it now be fulfilled!"
[16]I have not run away from being your
      shepherd;
    you know I have not desired the
      day of despair.
What passes my lips is open before
      you.
[17]Do not be a terror to me;
    you are my refuge in the day of
      disaster.
[18]Let my persecutors be put to shame,
    but keep me from shame;
let them be terrified,
    but keep me from terror.
Bring on them the day of disaster;
    destroy them with double
      destruction.

Keeping the Sabbath Holy

[19]This is what the LORD said to me: "Go and stand at the gate of the people, through which the kings of Judah go in and out; stand also at all the other gates of Jerusalem. [20]Say to them, 'Hear the word of the LORD, O kings of Judah and all people of Judah and everyone living in Jerusalem who come through these gates. [21]This is what the LORD says: Be careful not to carry a load on the Sabbath day or bring it through the gates of Jerusalem. [22]Do not bring a load out of your houses or do any work on the Sabbath, but keep the Sabbath day holy, as I commanded your forefathers. [23]Yet they did not listen or pay attention; they were stiff-necked and would not listen or respond to discipline. [24]But if you are careful to obey me, declares the LORD, and bring no load through the gates of this city on the Sabbath, but keep the Sabbath day holy by not doing any work on it, [25]then kings

a2,3 Or hills / 3and the mountains of the land. / Your

who sit on David's throne will come through the gates of this city with their officials. They and their officials will come riding in chariots and on horses, accompanied by the men of Judah and those living in Jerusalem, and this city will be inhabited forever. 26People will come from the towns of Judah and the villages around Jerusalem, from the territory of Benjamin and the western foothills, from the hill country and the Negev, bringing burnt offerings and sacrifices, grain offerings, incense and thank offerings to the house of the LORD. 27But if you do not obey me to keep the Sabbath day holy by not carrying any load as you come through the gates of Jerusalem on the Sabbath day, then I will kindle an unquenchable fire in the gates of Jerusalem that will consume her fortresses.' "

At the Potter's House

18 This is the word that came to Jeremiah from the LORD: 2"Go down to the potter's house, and there I will give you my message." 3So I went down to the potter's house, and I saw him working at the wheel. 4But the pot he was shaping from the clay was marred in his hands; so the potter formed it into another pot, shaping it as seemed best to him.

5Then the word of the LORD came to me: 6"O house of Israel, can I not do with you as this potter does?" declares the LORD. "Like clay in the hand of the potter, so are you in my hand, O house of Israel. 7If at any time I announce that a nation or kingdom is to be uprooted, torn down and destroyed, 8and if that nation I warned repents of its evil, then I will relent and not inflict on it the disaster I had planned. 9And if at another time I announce that a nation or kingdom is to be built up and planted, 10and if it does evil in my sight and does not obey me, then I will reconsider the good I had intended to do for it.

11"Now therefore say to the people of Judah and those living in Jerusalem, 'This is what the LORD says: Look! I am preparing a disaster for you and devising a plan against you. So turn from your evil ways, each one of you, and reform your ways and your actions.' 12But they will reply, 'It's no use. We will continue with our own plans; each of us will follow the stubbornness of his evil heart.' "

13Therefore this is what the LORD says:

"Inquire among the nations:
 Who has ever heard anything like
  this?
A most horrible thing has been done
 by Virgin Israel.
14Does the snow of Lebanon
 ever vanish from its rocky slopes?
Do its cool waters from distant
  sources
 ever cease to flow?[a]
15Yet my people have forgotten me;
 they burn incense to worthless
  idols,
which made them stumble in their
  ways
 and in the ancient paths.
They made them walk in bypaths
 and on roads not built up.
16Their land will be laid waste,
 an object of lasting scorn;
all who pass by will be appalled
 and will shake their heads.
17Like a wind from the east,
 I will scatter them before their
  enemies;
I will show them my back and not my
  face
 in the day of their disaster."

18They said, "Come, let's make plans against Jeremiah; for the teaching of the law by the priest will not be lost, nor will counsel from the wise, nor the word from the prophets. So come, let's attack him with our tongues and pay no attention to anything he says."

19Listen to me, O LORD;
 hear what my accusers are saying!
20Should good be repaid with evil?
 Yet they have dug a pit for me.
Remember that I stood before you
 and spoke in their behalf
 to turn your wrath away from them.
21So give their children over to famine;
 hand them over to the power of the
  sword.
Let their wives be made childless and
  widows;
 let their men be put to death,
 their young men slain by the sword
  in battle.
22Let a cry be heard from their houses
 when you suddenly bring invaders
  against them,
for they have dug a pit to capture me
 and have hidden snares for my feet.
23But you know, O LORD,
 all their plots to kill me.

---

a14 The meaning of the Hebrew for this sentence is uncertain.

Do not forgive their crimes
  or blot out their sins from your
    sight.
Let them be overthrown before you;
  deal with them in the time of your
    anger.

19 This is what the LORD says: "Go and buy a clay jar from a potter. Take along some of the elders of the people and of the priests **2**and go out to the Valley of Ben Hinnom, near the entrance of the Potsherd Gate. There proclaim the words I tell you, **3**and say, 'Hear the word of the LORD, O kings of Judah and people of Jerusalem. This is what the LORD Almighty, the God of Israel, says: Listen! I am going to bring a disaster on this place that will make the ears of everyone who hears of it tingle. **4**For they have forsaken me and made this a place of foreign gods; they have burned sacrifices in it to gods that neither they nor their fathers nor the kings of Judah ever knew, and they have filled this place with the blood of the innocent. **5**They have built the high places of Baal to burn their sons in the fire as offerings to Baal—something I did not command or mention, nor did it enter my mind. **6**So beware, the days are coming, declares the LORD, when people will no longer call this place Topheth or the Valley of Ben Hinnom, but the Valley of Slaughter.

7" 'In this place I will ruin*a* the plans of Judah and Jerusalem. I will make them fall by the sword before their enemies, at the hands of those who seek their lives, and I will give their carcasses as food to the birds of the air and the beasts of the earth. **8**I will devastate this city and make it an object of scorn; all who pass by will be appalled and will scoff because of all its wounds. **9**I will make them eat the flesh of their sons and daughters, and they will eat one another's flesh during the stress of the siege imposed on them by the enemies who seek their lives.'

10"Then break the jar while those who go with you are watching, **11**and say to them, 'This is what the LORD Almighty says: I will smash this nation and this city just as this potter's jar is smashed and cannot be repaired. They will bury the dead in Topheth until there is no more room. **12**This is what I will do to this place and to those who live here, declares the

LORD. I will make this city like Topheth. **13**The houses in Jerusalem and those of the kings of Judah will be defiled like this place, Topheth—all the houses where they burned incense on the roofs to all the starry hosts and poured out drink offerings to other gods.' "

14Jeremiah then returned from Topheth, where the LORD had sent him to prophesy, and stood in the court of the LORD's temple and said to all the people, **15**"This is what the LORD Almighty, the God of Israel, says: 'Listen! I am going to bring on this city and the villages around it every disaster I pronounced against them, because they were stiff-necked and would not listen to my words.' "

Jeremiah and Pashhur

20 When the priest Pashhur son of Immer, the chief officer in the temple of the LORD, heard Jeremiah prophesying these things, **2**he had Jeremiah the prophet beaten and put in the stocks at the Upper Gate of Benjamin at the LORD's temple. **3**The next day, when Pashhur released him from the stocks, Jeremiah said to him, "The LORD's name for you is not Pashhur, but Magor-Missabib.*b* **4**For this is what the LORD says: 'I will make you a terror to yourself and to all your friends; with your own eyes you will see them fall by the sword of their enemies. I will hand all Judah over to the king of Babylon, who will carry them away to Babylon or put them to the sword. **5**I will hand over to their enemies all the wealth of this city— all its products, all its valuables and all the treasures of the kings of Judah. They will take it away as plunder and carry it off to Babylon. **6**And you, Pashhur, and all who live in your house will go into exile to Babylon. There you will die and be buried, you and all your friends to whom you have prophesied lies.' "

Jeremiah's Complaint

7O LORD, you deceived*c* me, and I was
    deceived*c*;
  you overpowered me and prevailed.
I am ridiculed all day long;
  everyone mocks me.
8Whenever I speak, I cry out
  proclaiming violence and
    destruction.
So the word of the LORD has brought
  me

---

a7 The Hebrew for *ruin* sounds like the Hebrew for *jar* (see verses 1 and 10).   *b3* *Magor-Missabib* means *terror on every side.*   *c7* Or *persuaded*

insult and reproach all day long.
⁹But if I say, "I will not mention him
   or speak any more in his name,"
his word is in my heart like a fire,
   a fire shut up in my bones.
I am weary of holding it in;
   indeed, I cannot.
¹⁰I hear many whispering,
   "Terror on every side!
   Report him! Let's report him!"
All my friends
   are waiting for me to slip, saying,
"Perhaps he will be deceived;
   then we will prevail over him
   and take our revenge on him."

¹¹But the LORD is with me like a mighty
      warrior;
   so my persecutors will stumble and
      not prevail.
They will fail and be thoroughly
      disgraced;
   their dishonor will never be
      forgotten.
¹²O LORD Almighty, you who examine
      the righteous
   and probe the heart and mind,
let me see your vengeance upon them,
   for to you I have committed my
      cause.

¹³Sing to the LORD!
   Give praise to the LORD!
He rescues the life of the needy
   from the hands of the wicked.

¹⁴Cursed be the day I was born!
   May the day my mother bore me
      not be blessed!
¹⁵Cursed be the man who brought my
      father the news,
   who made him very glad, saying,
   "A child is born to you—a son!"
¹⁶May that man be like the towns
   the LORD overthrew without pity.
May he hear wailing in the morning,
   a battle cry at noon.
¹⁷For he did not kill me in the womb,
   with my mother as my grave,
   her womb enlarged forever.
¹⁸Why did I ever come out of the womb
   to see trouble and sorrow
   and to end my days in shame?

God Rejects Zedekiah's Request

21 The word came to Jeremiah from
   the LORD when King Zedekiah sent
to him Pashhur son of Malkijah and the
priest Zephaniah son of Maaseiah. They
said: ²"Inquire now of the LORD for us because Nebuchadnezzar[a] king of Babylon
is attacking us. Perhaps the LORD will perform wonders for us as in times past so
that he will withdraw from us."

³But Jeremiah answered them, "Tell
Zedekiah, ⁴'This is what the LORD, the God
of Israel, says: I am about to turn against
you the weapons of war that are in your
hands, which you are using to fight the
king of Babylon and the Babylonians[b]
who are outside the wall besieging you.
And I will gather them inside this city. ⁵I
myself will fight against you with an outstretched hand and a mighty arm in anger
and fury and great wrath. ⁶I will strike
down those who live in this city—both
men and animals—and they will die of a
terrible plague. ⁷After that, declares the
LORD, I will hand over Zedekiah king of Judah, his officials and the people in this
city who survive the plague, sword and
famine, to Nebuchadnezzar king of Babylon and to their enemies who seek their
lives. He will put them to the sword; he
will show them no mercy or pity or compassion.'

⁸"Furthermore, tell the people, 'This is
what the LORD says: See, I am setting before you the way of life and the way of
death. ⁹Whoever stays in this city will die
by the sword, famine or plague. But whoever goes out and surrenders to the Babylonians who are besieging you will live;
he will escape with his life. ¹⁰I have determined to do this city harm and not good,
declares the LORD. It will be given into the
hands of the king of Babylon, and he will
destroy it with fire.'

¹¹"Moreover, say to the royal house of
Judah, 'Hear the word of the LORD; ¹²O
house of David, this is what the LORD says:

" 'Administer justice every morning;
   rescue from the hand of his
      oppressor
   the one who has been robbed,
or my wrath will break out and burn
      like fire
   because of the evil you have done—

burn with no one to quench it.
¹³I am against you, ⌊Jerusalem⌋,
   you who live above this valley
   on the rocky plateau,
                     declares the LORD—

---

a2 Hebrew *Nebuchadrezzar*, of which *Nebuchadnezzar* is a variant; here and often in Jeremiah and Ezekiel
b4 Or *Chaldeans*; also in verse 9

you who say, "Who can come against
    us?
    Who can enter our refuge?"
14I will punish you as your deeds
    deserve,
                    declares the LORD.
I will kindle a fire in your forests
    that will consume everything
        around you.' "

Judgment Against Evil Kings

22 This is what the LORD says: "Go
down to the palace of the king of
Judah and proclaim this message there:
2'Hear the word of the LORD, O king of Judah, you who sit on David's throne—you,
your officials and your people who come
through these gates. **3**This is what the
LORD says: Do what is just and right. Rescue from the hand of his oppressor the
one who has been robbed. Do no wrong or
violence to the alien, the fatherless or the
widow, and do not shed innocent blood in
this place. **4**For if you are careful to carry
out these commands, then kings who sit
on David's throne will come through the
gates of this palace, riding in chariots and
on horses, accompanied by their officials
and their people. **5**But if you do not obey
these commands, declares the LORD, I
swear by myself that this palace will become a ruin.' "

6For this is what the LORD says about
the palace of the king of Judah:

"Though you are like Gilead to me,
    like the summit of Lebanon,
I will surely make you like a desert,
    like towns not inhabited.
7I will send destroyers against you,
    each man with his weapons,
and they will cut up your fine cedar
        beams
    and throw them into the fire.

8"People from many nations will pass
by this city and will ask one another,
'Why has the LORD done such a thing to
this great city?' **9**And the answer will be:
'Because they have forsaken the covenant
of the LORD their God and have worshiped
and served other gods.' "

10Do not weep for the dead ⌊king⌋ or
        mourn his loss;
    rather, weep bitterly for him who is
        exiled,
because he will never return
    nor see his native land again.

11For this is what the LORD says about
Shallum[a] son of Josiah, who succeeded
his father as king of Judah but has gone
from this place: "He will never return.
12He will die in the place where they have
led him captive; he will not see this land
again."

13"Woe to him who builds his palace by
        unrighteousness,
    his upper rooms by injustice,
making his countrymen work for
        nothing,
    not paying them for their labor.
14He says, 'I will build myself a great
        palace
    with spacious upper rooms.'
So he makes large windows in it,
    panels it with cedar
    and decorates it in red.

15"Does it make you a king
    to have more and more cedar?
Did not your father have food and
        drink?
    He did what was right and just,
    so all went well with him.
16He defended the cause of the poor
        and needy,
    and so all went well.
Is that not what it means to know
        me?"
    declares the LORD.
17"But your eyes and your heart
    are set only on dishonest gain,
on shedding innocent blood
    and on oppression and extortion."

18Therefore this is what the LORD says
about Jehoiakim son of Josiah king of Judah:

"They will not mourn for him:
    'Alas, my brother! Alas, my sister!'
They will not mourn for him:
    'Alas, my master! Alas, his
        splendor!'
19He will have the burial of a donkey—
    dragged away and thrown
    outside the gates of Jerusalem."

20"Go up to Lebanon and cry out,
    let your voice be heard in Bashan,
cry out from Abarim,
    for all your allies are crushed.
21I warned you when you felt secure,
    but you said, 'I will not listen!'
This has been your way from your
        youth;
    you have not obeyed me.

---

a 11 Also called *Jehoahaz*

22The wind will drive all your shepherds
away,
and your allies will go into exile.
Then you will be ashamed and
disgraced
because of all your wickedness.
23You who live in 'Lebanon,*a*'
who are nestled in cedar buildings,
how you will groan when pangs come
upon you,
pain like that of a woman in labor!

24"As surely as I live," declares the
Lord, "even if you, Jehoiachin*b* son of Jehoiakim king of Judah, were a signet ring
on my right hand, I would still pull you
off. **25**I will hand you over to those who
seek your life, those you fear—to Nebuchadnezzar king of Babylon and to the
Babylonians.*c* **26**I will hurl you and the
mother who gave you birth into another
country, where neither of you was born,
and there you both will die. **27**You will
never come back to the land you long to
return to."

28Is this man Jehoiachin a despised,
broken pot,
an object no one wants?
Why will he and his children be
hurled out,
cast into a land they do not know?
29O land, land, land,
hear the word of the Lord!
30This is what the Lord says:
"Record this man as if childless,
a man who will not prosper in his
lifetime,
for none of his offspring will prosper,
none will sit on the throne of David
or rule anymore in Judah."

The Righteous Branch

23 "Woe to the shepherds who are destroying and scattering the sheep
of my pasture!" declares the Lord. **2**Therefore this is what the Lord, the God of Israel, says to the shepherds who tend my
people: "Because you have scattered my
flock and driven them away and have not
bestowed care on them, I will bestow punishment on you for the evil you have
done," declares the Lord. **3**"I myself will
gather the remnant of my flock out of all
the countries where I have driven them
and will bring them back to their pasture,
where they will be fruitful and increase in

number. **4**I will place shepherds over them
who will tend them, and they will no longer be afraid or terrified, nor will any be
missing," declares the Lord.

5"The days are coming," declares the
Lord,
"when I will raise up to David*d* a
righteous Branch,
a King who will reign wisely
and do what is just and right in the
land.
6In his days Judah will be saved
and Israel will live in safety.
This is the name by which he will be
called:
The Lord Our Righteousness.

7"So then, the days are coming," declares
the Lord, "when people will no longer say,
'As surely as the Lord lives, who brought
the Israelites up out of Egypt,' **8**but they
will say, 'As surely as the Lord lives, who
brought the descendants of Israel up out
of the land of the north and out of all the
countries where he had banished them.'
Then they will live in their own land."

Lying Prophets

9Concerning the prophets:

My heart is broken within me;
all my bones tremble.
I am like a drunken man,
like a man overcome by wine,
because of the Lord
and his holy words.
10The land is full of adulterers;
because of the curse*e* the land lies
parched*f*
and the pastures in the desert are
withered.
The ⌐prophets⌐ follow an evil course
and use their power unjustly.

11"Both prophet and priest are godless;
even in my temple I find their
wickedness,"
declares the Lord.
12"Therefore their path will become
slippery;
they will be banished to darkness
and there they will fall.
I will bring disaster on them
in the year they are punished,"
declares the Lord.

13"Among the prophets of Samaria

a23 That is, the palace in Jerusalem (see 1 Kings 7:2)   *b24* Hebrew *Coniah*, a variant of *Jehoiachin*; also
in verse 28   *c25* Or *Chaldeans*   *d5* Or *up from David's line*   *e10* Or *because of these things*
f10 Or *land mourns*

I saw this repulsive thing:
They prophesied by Baal
and led my people Israel astray.
[14]And among the prophets of Jerusalem
I have seen something horrible:
They commit adultery and live a lie.
They strengthen the hands of
evildoers,
so that no one turns from his
wickedness.
They are all like Sodom to me;
the people of Jerusalem are like
Gomorrah."

[15]Therefore, this is what the LORD Almighty says concerning the prophets:

"I will make them eat bitter food
and drink poisoned water,
because from the prophets of
Jerusalem
ungodliness has spread throughout
the land."

[16]This is what the LORD Almighty says:

"Do not listen to what the prophets
are prophesying to you;
they fill you with false hopes.
They speak visions from their own
minds,
not from the mouth of the LORD.
[17]They keep saying to those who
despise me,
'The LORD says: You will have
peace.'
And to all who follow the
stubbornness of their hearts
they say, 'No harm will come to
you.'
[18]But which of them has stood in the
council of the LORD
to see or to hear his word?
Who has listened and heard his
word?
[19]See, the storm of the LORD
will burst out in wrath,
a whirlwind swirling down
on the heads of the wicked.
[20]The anger of the LORD will not turn
back
until he fully accomplishes
the purposes of his heart.
In days to come
you will understand it clearly.
[21]I did not send these prophets,
yet they have run with their
message;
I did not speak to them,

yet they have prophesied.
[22]But if they had stood in my council,
they would have proclaimed my
words to my people
and would have turned them from
their evil ways
and from their evil deeds.

[23]"Am I only a God nearby,"
declares the LORD,
"and not a God far away?
[24]Can anyone hide in secret places
so that I cannot see him?"
declares the LORD.
"Do not I fill heaven and earth?"
declares the LORD.

[25]"I have heard what the prophets say who prophesy lies in my name. They say, 'I had a dream! I had a dream!' [26]How long will this continue in the hearts of these lying prophets, who prophesy the delusions of their own minds? [27]They think the dreams they tell one another will make my people forget my name, just as their fathers forgot my name through Baal worship. [28]Let the prophet who has a dream tell his dream, but let the one who has my word speak it faithfully. For what has straw to do with grain?" declares the LORD. [29]"Is not my word like fire," declares the LORD, "and like a hammer that breaks a rock in pieces?

[30]"Therefore," declares the LORD, "I am against the prophets who steal from one another words supposedly from me. [31]Yes," declares the LORD, "I am against the prophets who wag their own tongues and yet declare, 'The LORD declares.' [32]Indeed, I am against those who prophesy false dreams," declares the LORD. "They tell them and lead my people astray with their reckless lies, yet I did not send or appoint them. They do not benefit these people in the least," declares the LORD.

False Oracles and False Prophets

[33]"When these people, or a prophet or a priest, ask you, 'What is the oracle[a] of the LORD?' say to them, 'What oracle?[b] I will forsake you, declares the LORD.' [34]If a prophet or a priest or anyone else claims, 'This is the oracle of the LORD,' I will punish that man and his household. [35]This is what each of you keeps on saying to his friend or relative: 'What is the LORD's answer?' or 'What has the LORD spoken?' [36]But you must not mention 'the oracle of

a33 Or burden (see Septuagint and Vulgate)   b33 Hebrew; Septuagint and Vulgate 'You are the burden.
(The Hebrew for oracle and burden is the same.)

the Lord' again, because every man's own word becomes his oracle and so you distort the words of the living God, the Lord Almighty, our God. ³⁷This is what you keep saying to a prophet: 'What is the Lord's answer to you?' or 'What has the Lord spoken?' ³⁸Although you claim, 'This is the oracle of the Lord,' this is what the Lord says: You used the words, 'This is the oracle of the Lord,' even though I told you that you must not claim, 'This is the oracle of the Lord.' ³⁹Therefore, I will surely forget you and cast you out of my presence along with the city I gave to you and your fathers. ⁴⁰I will bring upon you everlasting disgrace — everlasting shame that will not be forgotten."

Two Baskets of Figs

24 After Jehoiachin*ᵃ* son of Jehoiakim king of Judah and the officials, the craftsmen and the artisans of Judah were carried into exile from Jerusalem to Babylon by Nebuchadnezzar king of Babylon, the Lord showed me two baskets of figs placed in front of the temple of the Lord. ²One basket had very good figs, like those that ripen early; the other basket had very poor figs, so bad they could not be eaten.

³Then the Lord asked me, "What do you see, Jeremiah?"

"Figs," I answered. "The good ones are very good, but the poor ones are so bad they cannot be eaten."

⁴Then the word of the Lord came to me: ⁵"This is what the Lord, the God of Israel, says: 'Like these good figs, I regard as good the exiles from Judah, whom I sent away from this place to the land of the Babylonians.*ᵇ* ⁶My eyes will watch over them for their good, and I will bring them back to this land. I will build them up and not tear them down; I will plant them and not uproot them. ⁷I will give them a heart to know me, that I am the Lord. They will be my people, and I will be their God, for they will return to me with all their heart.

⁸" 'But like the poor figs, which are so bad they cannot be eaten,' says the Lord, 'so will I deal with Zedekiah king of Judah, his officials and the survivors from Jerusalem, whether they remain in this land or live in Egypt. ⁹I will make them abhorrent and an offense to all the kingdoms of the earth, a reproach and a byword, an object of ridicule and cursing,

wherever I banish them. ¹⁰I will send the sword, famine and plague against them until they are destroyed from the land I gave to them and their fathers.' "

Seventy Years of Captivity

25 The word came to Jeremiah concerning all the people of Judah in the fourth year of Jehoiakim son of Josiah king of Judah, which was the first year of Nebuchadnezzar king of Babylon. ²So Jeremiah the prophet said to all the people of Judah and to all those living in Jerusalem: ³For twenty-three years — from the thirteenth year of Josiah son of Amon king of Judah until this very day — the word of the Lord has come to me and I have spoken to you again and again, but you have not listened.

⁴And though the Lord has sent all his servants the prophets to you again and again, you have not listened or paid any attention. ⁵They said, "Turn now, each of you, from your evil ways and your evil practices, and you can stay in the land the Lord gave to you and your fathers for ever and ever. ⁶Do not follow other gods to serve and worship them; do not provoke me to anger with what your hands have made. Then I will not harm you."

⁷"But you did not listen to me," declares the Lord, "and you have provoked me with what your hands have made, and you have brought harm to yourselves."

⁸Therefore the Lord Almighty says this: "Because you have not listened to my words, ⁹I will summon all the peoples of the north and my servant Nebuchadnezzar king of Babylon," declares the Lord, "and I will bring them against this land and its inhabitants and against all the surrounding nations. I will completely destroy*ᶜ* them and make them an object of horror and scorn, and an everlasting ruin. ¹⁰I will banish from them the sounds of joy and gladness, the voices of bride and bridegroom, the sound of millstones and the light of the lamp. ¹¹This whole country will become a desolate wasteland, and these nations will serve the king of Babylon seventy years. ¹²But when the seventy years are fulfilled, I will punish the king of Babylon and his nation, the land of the Babylonians,*ᵇ* for their guilt," declares the Lord, "and will make it desolate forever. ¹³I will bring upon that land all the things I have

---

ᵃ1 Hebrew *Jeconiah*, a variant of *Jehoiachin*   *ᵇ5,12* Or *Chaldeans*   *ᶜ9* The Hebrew term refers to the irrevocable giving over of things or persons to the Lord, often by totally destroying them.

spoken against it, all that are written in this book and prophesied by Jeremiah against all the nations. ¹⁴They themselves will be enslaved by many nations and great kings; I will repay them according to their deeds and the work of their hands."

The Cup of God's Wrath

¹⁵This is what the Lord, the God of Israel, said to me: "Take from my hand this cup filled with the wine of my wrath and make all the nations to whom I send you drink it. ¹⁶When they drink it, they will stagger and go mad because of the sword I will send among them."

¹⁷So I took the cup from the Lord's hand and made all the nations to whom he sent me drink it: ¹⁸Jerusalem and the towns of Judah, its kings and officials, to make them a ruin and an object of horror and scorn and cursing, as they are today; ¹⁹Pharaoh king of Egypt, his attendants, his officials and all his people, ²⁰and all the foreign people there; all the kings of Uz; all the kings of the Philistines (those of Ashkelon, Gaza, Ekron, and the people left at Ashdod); ²¹Edom, Moab and Ammon; ²²all the kings of Tyre and Sidon; the kings of the coastlands across the sea; ²³Dedan, Tema, Buz and all who are in distant places*a*; ²⁴all the kings of Arabia and all the kings of the foreign people who live in the desert; ²⁵all the kings of Zimri, Elam and Media; ²⁶and all the kings of the north, near and far, one after the other — all the kingdoms on the face of the earth. And after all of them, the king of Sheshach*b* will drink it too.

²⁷"Then tell them, 'This is what the Lord Almighty, the God of Israel, says: Drink, get drunk and vomit, and fall to rise no more because of the sword I will send among you.' ²⁸But if they refuse to take the cup from your hand and drink, tell them, 'This is what the Lord Almighty says: You must drink it! ²⁹See, I am beginning to bring disaster on the city that bears my Name, and will you indeed go unpunished? You will not go unpunished, for I am calling down a sword upon all who live on the earth, declares the Lord Almighty.'

³⁰"Now prophesy all these words against them and say to them:

" 'The Lord will roar from on high;

he will thunder from his holy dwelling
and roar mightily against his land.
He will shout like those who tread the grapes,
shout against all who live on the earth.
³¹The tumult will resound to the ends of the earth,
for the Lord will bring charges against the nations;
he will bring judgment on all mankind
and put the wicked to the sword,' "
            declares the Lord.

³²This is what the Lord Almighty says:

"Look! Disaster is spreading
from nation to nation;
a mighty storm is rising
from the ends of the earth."

³³At that time those slain by the Lord will be everywhere — from one end of the earth to the other. They will not be mourned or gathered up or buried, but will be like refuse lying on the ground.

³⁴Weep and wail, you shepherds;
roll in the dust, you leaders of the flock.
For your time to be slaughtered has come;
you will fall and be shattered like fine pottery.
³⁵The shepherds will have nowhere to flee,
the leaders of the flock no place to escape.
³⁶Hear the cry of the shepherds,
the wailing of the leaders of the flock,
for the Lord is destroying their pasture.
³⁷The peaceful meadows will be laid waste
because of the fierce anger of the Lord.
³⁸Like a lion he will leave his lair,
and their land will become desolate
because of the sword*c* of the oppressor
and because of the Lord's fierce anger.

Jeremiah Threatened With Death

26 Early in the reign of Jehoiakim son of Josiah king of Judah, this word came from the Lord: ²"This is what the

---

a23 Or *who clip the hair by their foreheads*   *b26 Sheshach* is a cryptogram for Babylon.   *c38* Some Hebrew manuscripts and Septuagint (see also Jer. 46:16 and 50:16); most Hebrew manuscripts *anger*

Lord says: Stand in the courtyard of the Lord's house and speak to all the people of the towns of Judah who come to worship in the house of the Lord. Tell them everything I command you; do not omit a word. ³Perhaps they will listen and each will turn from his evil way. Then I will relent and not bring on them the disaster I was planning because of the evil they have done. ⁴Say to them, 'This is what the Lord says: If you do not listen to me and follow my law, which I have set before you, ⁵and if you do not listen to the words of my servants the prophets, whom I have sent to you again and again (though you have not listened), ⁶then I will make this house like Shiloh and this city an object of cursing among all the nations of the earth.' "

⁷The priests, the prophets and all the people heard Jeremiah speak these words in the house of the Lord. ⁸But as soon as Jeremiah finished telling all the people everything the Lord had commanded him to say, the priests, the prophets and all the people seized him and said, "You must die! ⁹Why do you prophesy in the Lord's name that this house will be like Shiloh and this city will be desolate and deserted?" And all the people crowded around Jeremiah in the house of the Lord.

¹⁰When the officials of Judah heard about these things, they went up from the royal palace to the house of the Lord and took their places at the entrance of the New Gate of the Lord's house. ¹¹Then the priests and the prophets said to the officials and all the people, "This man should be sentenced to death because he has prophesied against this city. You have heard it with your own ears!"

¹²Then Jeremiah said to all the officials and all the people: "The Lord sent me to prophesy against this house and this city all the things you have heard. ¹³Now reform your ways and your actions and obey the Lord your God. Then the Lord will relent and not bring the disaster he has pronounced against you. ¹⁴As for me, I am in your hands; do with me whatever you think is good and right. ¹⁵Be assured, however, that if you put me to death, you will bring the guilt of innocent blood on yourselves and on this city and on those who live in it, for in truth the Lord has sent me to you to speak all these words in your hearing."

¹⁶Then the officials and all the people said to the priests and the prophets, "This man should not be sentenced to death! He has spoken to us in the name of the Lord our God."

¹⁷Some of the elders of the land stepped forward and said to the entire assembly of people, ¹⁸"Micah of Moresheth prophesied in the days of Hezekiah king of Judah. He told all the people of Judah, 'This is what the Lord Almighty says:

" 'Zion will be plowed like a field,
    Jerusalem will become a heap of
        rubble,
    the temple hill a mound overgrown
        with thickets.'ᵃ

¹⁹"Did Hezekiah king of Judah or anyone else in Judah put him to death? Did not Hezekiah fear the Lord and seek his favor? And did not the Lord relent, so that he did not bring the disaster he pronounced against them? We are about to bring a terrible disaster on ourselves!"

²⁰(Now Uriah son of Shemaiah from Kiriath Jearim was another man who prophesied in the name of the Lord; he prophesied the same things against this city and this land as Jeremiah did. ²¹When King Jehoiakim and all his officers and officials heard his words, the king sought to put him to death. But Uriah heard of it and fled in fear to Egypt. ²²King Jehoiakim, however, sent Elnathan son of Acbor to Egypt, along with some other men. ²³They brought Uriah out of Egypt and took him to King Jehoiakim, who had him struck down with a sword and his body thrown into the burial place of the common people.)

²⁴Furthermore, Ahikam son of Shaphan supported Jeremiah, and so he was not handed over to the people to be put to death.

Judah to Serve Nebuchadnezzar

27 Early in the reign of Zedekiahᵇ son of Josiah king of Judah, this word came to Jeremiah from the Lord: ²This is what the Lord said to me: "Make a yoke out of straps and crossbars and put it on your neck. ³Then send word to the kings of Edom, Moab, Ammon, Tyre and Sidon through the envoys who have come to Jerusalem to Zedekiah king of Judah. ⁴Give them a message for their masters and say, 'This is what the Lord Almighty,

---

ᵃ18 Micah 3:12   ᵇ1 A few Hebrew manuscripts and Syriac (see also Jer. 27:3, 12 and 28:1); most Hebrew manuscripts Jehoiakim (Most Septuagint manuscripts do not have this verse.)

the God of Israel, says: "Tell this to your masters: **5**With my great power and outstretched arm I made the earth and its people and the animals that are on it, and I give it to anyone I please. **6**Now I will hand all your countries over to my servant Nebuchadnezzar king of Babylon; I will make even the wild animals subject to him. **7**All nations will serve him and his son and his grandson until the time for his land comes; then many nations and great kings will subjugate him.

8" ' "If, however, any nation or kingdom will not serve Nebuchadnezzar king of Babylon or bow its neck under his yoke, I will punish that nation with the sword, famine and plague, declares the LORD, until I destroy it by his hand. **9**So do not listen to your prophets, your diviners, your interpreters of dreams, your mediums or your sorcerers who tell you, 'You will not serve the king of Babylon.' **10**They prophesy lies to you that will only serve to remove you far from your lands; I will banish you and you will perish. **11**But if any nation will bow its neck under the yoke of the king of Babylon and serve him, I will let that nation remain in its own land to till it and to live there, declares the LORD." ' "

12I gave the same message to Zedekiah king of Judah. I said, "Bow your neck under the yoke of the king of Babylon; serve him and his people, and you will live. **13**Why will you and your people die by the sword, famine and plague with which the LORD has threatened any nation that will not serve the king of Babylon? **14**Do not listen to the words of the prophets who say to you, 'You will not serve the king of Babylon,' for they are prophesying lies to you. **15**'I have not sent them,' declares the LORD. 'They are prophesying lies in my name. Therefore, I will banish you and you will perish, both you and the prophets who prophesy to you.' "

16Then I said to the priests and all these people, "This is what the LORD says: Do not listen to the prophets who say, 'Very soon now the articles from the LORD's house will be brought back from Babylon.' They are prophesying lies to you. **17**Do not listen to them. Serve the king of Babylon, and you will live. Why should this city become a ruin? **18**If they are prophets and have the word of the LORD, let them plead with the LORD Almighty that the furnishings remaining in the house of the LORD and in the palace of the king of Judah and in Jerusalem not be taken to Babylon. **19**For this is what the LORD Almighty says about the pillars, the Sea, the movable stands and the other furnishings that are left in this city, **20**which Nebuchadnezzar king of Babylon did not take away when he carried Jehoiachin*a* son of Jehoiakim king of Judah into exile from Jerusalem to Babylon, along with all the nobles of Judah and Jerusalem— **21**yes, this is what the LORD Almighty, the God of Israel, says about the things that are left in the house of the LORD and in the palace of the king of Judah and in Jerusalem: **22**'They will be taken to Babylon and there they will remain until the day I come for them,' declares the LORD. 'Then I will bring them back and restore them to this place.' "

The False Prophet Hananiah

28 In the fifth month of that same year, the fourth year, early in the reign of Zedekiah king of Judah, the prophet Hananiah son of Azzur, who was from Gibeon, said to me in the house of the LORD in the presence of the priests and all the people: **2**"This is what the LORD Almighty, the God of Israel, says: 'I will break the yoke of the king of Babylon. **3**Within two years I will bring back to this place all the articles of the LORD's house that Nebuchadnezzar king of Babylon removed from here and took to Babylon. **4**I will also bring back to this place Jehoiachin*a* son of Jehoiakim king of Judah and all the other exiles from Judah who went to Babylon,' declares the LORD, 'for I will break the yoke of the king of Babylon.' "

5Then the prophet Jeremiah replied to the prophet Hananiah before the priests and all the people who were standing in the house of the LORD. **6**He said, "Amen! May the LORD do so! May the LORD fulfill the words you have prophesied by bringing the articles of the LORD's house and all the exiles back to this place from Babylon. **7**Nevertheless, listen to what I have to say in your hearing and in the hearing of all the people: **8**From early times the prophets who preceded you and me have prophesied war, disaster and plague against many countries and great kingdoms. **9**But the prophet who prophesies peace will be recognized as one truly sent by the LORD only if his prediction comes true."

10Then the prophet Hananiah took the

---

*a*20,4 Hebrew *Jeconiah*, a variant of *Jehoiachin*

yoke off the neck of the prophet Jeremiah and broke it, [11]and he said before all the people, "This is what the LORD says: 'In the same way will I break the yoke of Nebuchadnezzar king of Babylon off the neck of all the nations within two years.' " At this, the prophet Jeremiah went on his way.

[12]Shortly after the prophet Hananiah had broken the yoke off the neck of the prophet Jeremiah, the word of the LORD came to Jeremiah: [13]"Go and tell Hananiah, 'This is what the LORD says: You have broken a wooden yoke, but in its place you will get a yoke of iron. [14]This is what the LORD Almighty, the God of Israel, says: I will put an iron yoke on the necks of all these nations to make them serve Nebuchadnezzar king of Babylon, and they will serve him. I will even give him control over the wild animals.' "

[15]Then the prophet Jeremiah said to Hananiah the prophet, "Listen, Hananiah! The LORD has not sent you, yet you have persuaded this nation to trust in lies. [16]Therefore, this is what the LORD says: 'I am about to remove you from the face of the earth. This very year you are going to die, because you have preached rebellion against the LORD.' "

[17]In the seventh month of that same year, Hananiah the prophet died.

A Letter to the Exiles

29 This is the text of the letter that the prophet Jeremiah sent from Jerusalem to the surviving elders among the exiles and to the priests, the prophets and all the other people Nebuchadnezzar had carried into exile from Jerusalem to Babylon. [2](This was after King Jehoiachin[a] and the queen mother, the court officials and the leaders of Judah and Jerusalem, the craftsmen and the artisans had gone into exile from Jerusalem.) [3]He entrusted the letter to Elasah son of Shaphan and to Gemariah son of Hilkiah, whom Zedekiah king of Judah sent to King Nebuchadnezzar in Babylon. It said:

[4]This is what the LORD Almighty, the God of Israel, says to all those I carried into exile from Jerusalem to Babylon: [5]"Build houses and settle down; plant gardens and eat what they produce. [6]Marry and have sons and daughters; find wives for your sons and give your daughters in mar-

riage, so that they too may have sons and daughters. Increase in number there; do not decrease. [7]Also, seek the peace and prosperity of the city to which I have carried you into exile. Pray to the LORD for it, because if it prospers, you too will prosper." [8]Yes, this is what the LORD Almighty, the God of Israel, says: "Do not let the prophets and diviners among you deceive you. Do not listen to the dreams you encourage them to have. [9]They are prophesying lies to you in my name. I have not sent them," declares the LORD.

[10]This is what the LORD says: "When seventy years are completed for Babylon, I will come to you and fulfill my gracious promise to bring you back to this place. [11]For I know the plans I have for you," declares the LORD, "plans to prosper you and not to harm you, plans to give you hope and a future. [12]Then you will call upon me and come and pray to me, and I will listen to you. [13]You will seek me and find me when you seek me with all your heart. [14]I will be found by you," declares the LORD, "and will bring you back from captivity.[b] I will gather you from all the nations and places where I have banished you," declares the LORD, "and will bring you back to the place from which I carried you into exile."

[15]You may say, "The LORD has raised up prophets for us in Babylon," [16]but this is what the LORD says about the king who sits on David's throne and all the people who remain in this city, your countrymen who did not go with you into exile— [17]yes, this is what the LORD Almighty says: "I will send the sword, famine and plague against them and I will make them like poor figs that are so bad they cannot be eaten. [18]I will pursue them with the sword, famine and plague and will make them abhorrent to all the kingdoms of the earth and an object of cursing and horror, of scorn and reproach, among all the nations where I drive them. [19]For they have not listened to my words," declares the LORD, "words that I sent to them again and again by my servants the prophets. And you exiles have

---

[a]2 Hebrew *Jeconiah*, a variant of *Jehoiachin*   [b]14 Or *will restore your fortunes*

not listened either," declares the LORD.

²⁰Therefore, hear the word of the LORD, all you exiles whom I have sent away from Jerusalem to Babylon. ²¹This is what the LORD Almighty, the God of Israel, says about Ahab son of Kolaiah and Zedekiah son of Maaseiah, who are prophesying lies to you in my name: "I will hand them over to Nebuchadnezzar king of Babylon, and he will put them to death before your very eyes. ²²Because of them, all the exiles from Judah who are in Bab-

---

MONDAY

VERSE FOR THE DAY:
Jeremiah 29:5

AUTHOR:
Eugene H. Peterson

PASSAGE FOR THE DAY:
Jeremiah 29:4–14

Living at Our Best

EXILE (being where we don't want to be with people we don't want to be with) forces a decision: Will I focus my attention on what is wrong with the world and feel sorry for myself? Or will I focus my energies on how I can live at my best in this place I find myself? It is always easier to complain about problems than to engage in careers of virtue . . .

Daily we face decisions on how we will respond to these exile conditions. We can say: "I don't like it; I want to be where I was ten years ago. How can you expect me to throw myself into what I don't like—that would be sheer hypocrisy. What sense is there in taking risks and tiring myself out among people I don't even like in a place where I have no future."

Or we can say: "I will do my best with what is here. Far more important than the climate of this place, the economics of this place, the neighbors in this place, is the God of this place. God is here with me. What I am experiencing right now is on ground that was created by him and with people whom he loves. It is just as possible to live out the will of God here as any place else. I am full of fear. I don't know my way around. I have much to learn. I'm not sure I can make it. But I had feelings like that back in Jerusalem. Change is hard. Developing intimacy among strangers is always a risk. Building relationships in unfamiliar and hostile surroundings is difficult. But if that is what it means to be alive and human, I will do it" . . .

All of us are given moments, days, months, years of exile. What will we do with them? Wish we were someplace else? Complain? Escape into fantasies? Drug ourselves into oblivion? Or build and plant and marry and seek the shalom of the place we inhabit and the people we are with? Exile reveals what really matters and frees us to pursue what really matters, which is to seek the Lord with all our hearts.

Additional Scripture Readings:
2 Chronicles 6:36–39;
Matthew 6:25–34

Go to page 823 for your next devotional reading.

ylon will use this curse: 'The LORD treat you like Zedekiah and Ahab, whom the king of Babylon burned in the fire.' **23**For they have done outrageous things in Israel; they have committed adultery with their neighbors' wives and in my name have spoken lies, which I did not tell them to do. I know it and am a witness to it," declares the LORD.

Message to Shemaiah

24Tell Shemaiah the Nehelamite, **25**"This is what the LORD Almighty, the God of Israel, says: You sent letters in your own name to all the people in Jerusalem, to Zephaniah son of Maaseiah the priest, and to all the other priests. You said to Zephaniah, **26**'The LORD has appointed you priest in place of Jehoiada to be in charge of the house of the LORD; you should put any madman who acts like a prophet into the stocks and neck-irons. **27**So why have you not reprimanded Jeremiah from Anathoth, who poses as a prophet among you? **28**He has sent this message to us in Babylon: It will be a long time. Therefore build houses and settle down; plant gardens and eat what they produce.' "

29Zephaniah the priest, however, read the letter to Jeremiah the prophet. **30**Then the word of the LORD came to Jeremiah: **31**"Send this message to all the exiles: 'This is what the LORD says about Shemaiah the Nehelamite: Because Shemaiah has prophesied to you, even though I did not send him, and has led you to believe a lie, **32**this is what the LORD says: I will surely punish Shemaiah the Nehelamite and his descendants. He will have no one left among this people, nor will he see the good things I will do for my people, declares the LORD, because he has preached rebellion against me.' "

Restoration of Israel

30 This is the word that came to Jeremiah from the LORD: **2**"This is what the LORD, the God of Israel, says: 'Write in a book all the words I have spoken to you. **3**The days are coming,' declares the LORD, 'when I will bring my people Israel and Judah back from captivity*a* and restore them to the land I gave their forefathers to possess,' says the LORD."

4These are the words the LORD spoke concerning Israel and Judah: **5**"This is what the LORD says:

" 'Cries of fear are heard—
terror, not peace.
6Ask and see:
Can a man bear children?
Then why do I see every strong man
with his hands on his stomach like
a woman in labor,
every face turned deathly pale?
7How awful that day will be!
None will be like it.
It will be a time of trouble for Jacob,
but he will be saved out of it.

8" ' In that day,' declares the LORD
Almighty,
'I will break the yoke off their necks
and will tear off their bonds;
no longer will foreigners enslave
them.
9Instead, they will serve the LORD their
God
and David their king,
whom I will raise up for them.

10" 'So do not fear, O Jacob my servant;
do not be dismayed, O Israel,'
declares the LORD.
'I will surely save you out of a distant
place,
your descendants from the land of
their exile.
Jacob will again have peace and
security,
and no one will make him afraid.
11I am with you and will save you,'
declares the LORD.
'Though I completely destroy all the
nations
among which I scatter you,
I will not completely destroy you.
I will discipline you but only with
justice;
I will not let you go entirely
unpunished.'

12"This is what the LORD says:

" 'Your wound is incurable,
your injury beyond healing.
13There is no one to plead your cause,
no remedy for your sore,
no healing for you.
14All your allies have forgotten you;
they care nothing for you.
I have struck you as an enemy would
and punished you as would the
cruel,

a3 Or *will restore the fortunes of my people Israel and Judah*

because your guilt is so great
and your sins so many.
15Why do you cry out over your wound,
your pain that has no cure?
Because of your great guilt and many
sins
I have done these things to you.
16" 'But all who devour you will be
devoured;
all your enemies will go into exile.
Those who plunder you will be
plundered;
all who make spoil of you I will
despoil.
17But I will restore you to health
and heal your wounds,'
declares the LORD,
'because you are called an outcast,
Zion for whom no one cares.'

18"This is what the LORD says:

" 'I will restore the fortunes of Jacob's
tents
and have compassion on his
dwellings;
the city will be rebuilt on her ruins,
and the palace will stand in its
proper place.
19From them will come songs of
thanksgiving
and the sound of rejoicing.
I will add to their numbers,
and they will not be decreased;
I will bring them honor,
and they will not be disdained.
20Their children will be as in days of
old,
and their community will be
established before me;
I will punish all who oppress them.
21Their leader will be one of their own;
their ruler will arise from among
them.
I will bring him near and he will come
close to me,
for who is he who will devote
himself
to be close to me?'
declares the LORD.
22" 'So you will be my people,
and I will be your God.' "

23See, the storm of the LORD
will burst out in wrath,
a driving wind swirling down
on the heads of the wicked.
24The fierce anger of the LORD will not
turn back

until he fully accomplishes
the purposes of his heart.
In days to come
you will understand this.

31

"At that time," declares the LORD, "I
will be the God of all the clans of
Israel, and they will be my people."
2This is what the LORD says:

"The people who survive the sword
will find favor in the desert;
I will come to give rest to Israel."

3The LORD appeared to us in the past,[a]
saying:

"I have loved you with an everlasting
love;
I have drawn you with
loving-kindness.
4I will build you up again
and you will be rebuilt, O Virgin
Israel.
Again you will take up your
tambourines
and go out to dance with the joyful.
5Again you will plant vineyards
on the hills of Samaria;
the farmers will plant them
and enjoy their fruit.
6There will be a day when watchmen
cry out
on the hills of Ephraim,
'Come, let us go up to Zion,
to the LORD our God.' "

7This is what the LORD says:

"Sing with joy for Jacob;
shout for the foremost of the
nations.
Make your praises heard, and say,
'O LORD, save your people,
the remnant of Israel.'
8See, I will bring them from the land of
the north
and gather them from the ends of
the earth.
Among them will be the blind and the
lame,
expectant mothers and women in
labor;
a great throng will return.
9They will come with weeping;
they will pray as I bring them back.
I will lead them beside streams of
water
on a level path where they will not
stumble,

a3 Or LORD has appeared to us from afar

because I am Israel's father,
and Ephraim is my firstborn son.

¹⁰"Hear the word of the Lord,
O nations;
proclaim it in distant coastlands:

'He who scattered Israel will gather
them
and will watch over his flock like a
shepherd.'

¹¹For the Lord will ransom Jacob

TUESDAY

VERSE FOR THE DAY:
Jeremiah 31:3

AUTHOR:
Ben Carson

PASSAGE FOR THE DAY:
Jeremiah 31:1–6

The Love of the Father

ABOUT my faith in God, I want to express a few heartfelt
thoughts that may sound simplistic or irreverent. As I continue to develop my relationship with him, I have discovered
that God is a nice guy.

I confess that while growing up, I had bought into the concept of God as a stern individual who busily jots down in a
book every mistake we make, so that on Judgment Day he can
call us up and point to each one, saying, "Why did you do
this? I know you did this," and then divulge to everybody
present the unpraiseworthy actions of our lives.

I have slowly matured, and have experienced God's help in
many crises. I have come to realize that God does not want to
punish us but, rather, to *fulfill* our lives. God created us, loves
us, and wants to help us to realize our potential so that we can
be useful to others.

The relationship that God wants with me became particularly clear to me after Candy and I had children of our own. I
realized how much I love my sons and how much I want for
them. Of course I want them to be successful, and want to give
them everything I can to make them happy. And I realize that
God loves me even more than I love my own children.

I cannot give my children everything, but I try to arrange
their environment so that they can learn to stand on their own
feet, to respect others and to become valuable citizens.

If I lavish everything on them, they will never reach those
goals, but as long as my children know that I love them—that I
will stand behind them and do everything within my power to
assure their success in life, I feel that I have done what I can
for them. They will develop confidence in my love for them
and will know that I only want good for them.

As I have considered my relationship with my sons, it makes
it clear to me the relationship that God wants with me and
with all the children he has created in the world.

Additional Scripture Readings:
Hosea 11:1–4,8–11; 1 John 4:7–21

*Go to page 826 for your next
devotional reading.*

and redeem them from the hand of
those stronger than they.
¹²They will come and shout for joy on
the heights of Zion;
they will rejoice in the bounty of
the LORD—
the grain, the new wine and the oil,
the young of the flocks and herds.
They will be like a well-watered
garden,
and they will sorrow no more.
¹³Then maidens will dance and be glad,
young men and old as well.
I will turn their mourning into
gladness;
I will give them comfort and joy
instead of sorrow.
¹⁴I will satisfy the priests with
abundance,
and my people will be filled with
my bounty,"
declares the LORD.

¹⁵This is what the LORD says:

"A voice is heard in Ramah,
mourning and great weeping,
Rachel weeping for her children
and refusing to be comforted,
because her children are no more."

¹⁶This is what the LORD says:

"Restrain your voice from weeping
and your eyes from tears,
for your work will be rewarded,"
declares the LORD.
"They will return from the land of
the enemy.
¹⁷So there is hope for your future,"
declares the LORD.
"Your children will return to their
own land.

¹⁸"I have surely heard Ephraim's
moaning:
'You disciplined me like an unruly
calf,
and I have been disciplined.
Restore me, and I will return,
because you are the LORD my God.
¹⁹After I strayed,
I repented;
after I came to understand,
I beat my breast.
I was ashamed and humiliated
because I bore the disgrace of my
youth.'
²⁰Is not Ephraim my dear son,
the child in whom I delight?

Though I often speak against him,
I still remember him.
Therefore my heart yearns for him;
I have great compassion for him,"
declares the LORD.

²¹"Set up road signs;
put up guideposts.
Take note of the highway,
the road that you take.
Return, O Virgin Israel,
return to your towns.
²²How long will you wander,
O unfaithful daughter?
The LORD will create a new thing on
earth—
a woman will surround[a] a man."

²³This is what the LORD Almighty, the
God of Israel, says: "When I bring them
back from captivity,[b] the people in the
land of Judah and in its towns will once
again use these words: 'The LORD bless
you, O righteous dwelling, O sacred
mountain.' ²⁴People will live together in
Judah and all its towns—farmers and
those who move about with their flocks.
²⁵I will refresh the weary and satisfy the
faint."

²⁶At this I awoke and looked around.
My sleep had been pleasant to me.

²⁷"The days are coming," declares the
LORD, "when I will plant the house of Israel and the house of Judah with the offspring of men and of animals. ²⁸Just as I
watched over them to uproot and tear
down, and to overthrow, destroy and
bring disaster, so I will watch over them to
build and to plant," declares the LORD.
²⁹"In those days people will no longer say,

'The fathers have eaten sour grapes,
and the children's teeth are set on
edge.'

³⁰Instead, everyone will die for his own
sin; whoever eats sour grapes—his own
teeth will be set on edge.

³¹"The time is coming," declares the
LORD,
"when I will make a new covenant
with the house of Israel
and with the house of Judah.
³²It will not be like the covenant
I made with their forefathers
when I took them by the hand
to lead them out of Egypt,
because they broke my covenant,

---

a22 Or *will go about* ₍*seeking*₎; or *will protect*　　b23 Or *I restore their fortunes*

though I was a husband to[a]
them,[b] "

declares the LORD.

33"This is the covenant I will make with
the house of Israel
after that time," declares the LORD.

"I will put my law in their minds
and write it on their hearts.
I will be their God,
and they will be my people.

34No longer will a man teach his
neighbor,
or a man his brother, saying, 'Know
the LORD,'
because they will all know me,
from the least of them to the
greatest,"

declares the LORD.

"For I will forgive their wickedness
and will remember their sins no
more."

35This is what the LORD says,

he who appoints the sun
to shine by day,
who decrees the moon and stars
to shine by night,
who stirs up the sea
so that its waves roar—
the LORD Almighty is his name:

36"Only if these decrees vanish from my
sight,"
declares the LORD,
"will the descendants of Israel ever
cease
to be a nation before me."

37This is what the LORD says:

"Only if the heavens above can be
measured
and the foundations of the earth
below be searched out
will I reject all the descendants of
Israel
because of all they have done,"

declares the LORD.

38"The days are coming," declares the
LORD, "when this city will be rebuilt for me
from the Tower of Hananel to the Corner
Gate. **39**The measuring line will stretch
from there straight to the hill of Gareb and
then turn to Goah. **40**The whole valley
where dead bodies and ashes are thrown,
and all the terraces out to the Kidron Valley on the east as far as the corner of the
Horse Gate, will be holy to the LORD. The

city will never again be uprooted or demolished."

Jeremiah Buys a Field

32 This is the word that came to Jeremiah from the LORD in the tenth
year of Zedekiah king of Judah, which
was the eighteenth year of Nebuchadnezzar. **2**The army of the king of Babylon was
then besieging Jerusalem, and Jeremiah
the prophet was confined in the courtyard
of the guard in the royal palace of Judah.

3Now Zedekiah king of Judah had imprisoned him there, saying, "Why do you
prophesy as you do? You say, 'This is
what the LORD says: I am about to hand
this city over to the king of Babylon, and
he will capture it. **4**Zedekiah king of Judah
will not escape out of the hands of the
Babylonians[c] but will certainly be handed over to the king of Babylon, and will
speak with him face to face and see him
with his own eyes. **5**He will take Zedekiah
to Babylon, where he will remain until I
deal with him, declares the LORD. If you
fight against the Babylonians, you will not
succeed.' "

6Jeremiah said, "The word of the LORD
came to me: **7**Hanamel son of Shallum
your uncle is going to come to you and
say, 'Buy my field at Anathoth, because as
nearest relative it is your right and duty to
buy it.'

8"Then, just as the LORD had said, my
cousin Hanamel came to me in the courtyard of the guard and said, 'Buy my field
at Anathoth in the territory of Benjamin.
Since it is your right to redeem it and possess it, buy it for yourself.'

"I knew that this was the word of the
LORD; **9**so I bought the field at Anathoth
from my cousin Hanamel and weighed
out for him seventeen shekels[d] of silver.
10I signed and sealed the deed, had it witnessed, and weighed out the silver on the
scales. **11**I took the deed of purchase—the
sealed copy containing the terms and conditions, as well as the unsealed copy—
12and I gave this deed to Baruch son of Neriah, the son of Mahseiah, in the presence
of my cousin Hanamel and of the witnesses who had signed the deed and of all
the Jews sitting in the courtyard of the
guard.

13"In their presence I gave Baruch these
instructions: **14**This is what the LORD Almighty, the God of Israel, says: Take these

---

[a]32 Hebrew; Septuagint and Syriac / *and I turned away from*   [b]32 Or *was their master*   [c]4 Or
Chaldeans; also in verses 5, 24, 25, 28, 29 and 43   [d]9 That is, about 7 ounces (about 200 grams)

WEDNESDAY

VERSE FOR THE DAY:
Jeremiah 32:9

AUTHOR:
Eugene H. Peterson

PASSAGE FOR THE DAY:
Jeremiah 32:6–29

Living in Hope

BUYING that field in Anathoth was a deliberate act of hope. All acts of hope expose themselves to ridicule because they seem impractical, failing to conform to visible reality. But in fact they are the reality that is being constructed but is not yet visible. Hope commits us to actions that connect with God's promises.

What we call hoping is often only wishing. We want things we think are impossible, but we have better sense than to spend any money or commit our lives to them. Biblical hope, though, is an act—like buying a field in Anathoth. Hope acts on the conviction that God will complete the work that he has begun even when the appearances, especially when the appearances, oppose it . . .

The great looming fact is this: In the flurry and panic of that day in Jerusalem, not at all unlike any randomly selected day in anyone's week, with the populace divided between a dull acquiescence to the inevitable and wild schemes for escape, the single practical act that stands out from the historical record is that Jeremiah bought a field in Anathoth for seventeen shekels. That act made the word of God visible, made a foothold of it for anyone who wanted to make a way out of chaotic despair into the ordered wholeness of salvation. Many made their way out.

We have to get practical. Really practical. The most practical thing we can do is hear what God says and act in appropriate response to it . . . Hope-determined actions participate in the future that God is bringing into being. These acts are rarely spectacular. Usually they take place outside sacred settings. Almost never are they perceived to be significant by bystanders. It is not easy to act in hope because most of the immediate evidence is against it. As a result, we live in one of the most impractical societies the world has ever seen. If we are to live practically, we must frequently defy the practicalities of our peers. It takes courage to act in hope. But it is the only practical action, for it is the only action that survives the decay of the moment and escapes the scrapheap of yesterday's fashion.

Additional Scripture Readings:
Philippians 1:3–11;
Colossians 1:3–29

*Go to page 846 for your next
devotional reading.*

documents, both the sealed and unsealed copies of the deed of purchase, and put them in a clay jar so they will last a long time. [15]For this is what the LORD Almighty, the God of Israel, says: Houses, fields and vineyards will again be bought in this land.'

[16]"After I had given the deed of purchase to Baruch son of Neriah, I prayed to the LORD:

[17]"Ah, Sovereign LORD, you have made the heavens and the earth by your great power and outstretched arm. Nothing is too hard for you. [18]You show love to thousands but bring the punishment for the fathers' sins into the laps of their children after them. O great and powerful God, whose name is the LORD Almighty, [19]great are your purposes and mighty are your deeds. Your eyes are open to all the ways of men; you reward everyone according to his conduct and as his deeds deserve. [20]You performed miraculous signs and wonders in Egypt and have continued them to this day, both in Israel and among all mankind, and have gained the renown that is still yours. [21]You brought your people Israel out of Egypt with signs and wonders, by a mighty hand and an outstretched arm and with great terror. [22]You gave them this land you had sworn to give their forefathers, a land flowing with milk and honey. [23]They came in and took possession of it, but they did not obey you or follow your law; they did not do what you commanded them to do. So you brought all this disaster upon them.

[24]"See how the siege ramps are built up to take the city. Because of the sword, famine and plague, the city will be handed over to the Babylonians who are attacking it. What you said has happened, as you now see. [25]And though the city will be handed over to the Babylonians, you, O Sovereign LORD, say to me, 'Buy the field with silver and have the transaction witnessed.'"

[26]Then the word of the LORD came to Jeremiah: [27]"I am the LORD, the God of all mankind. Is anything too hard for me? [28]Therefore, this is what the LORD says: I am about to hand this city over to the Babylonians and to Nebuchadnezzar king of Babylon, who will capture it. [29]The Babylonians who are attacking this city will come in and set it on fire; they will burn it down, along with the houses where the people provoked me to anger by burning incense on the roofs to Baal and by pouring out drink offerings to other gods.

[30]"The people of Israel and Judah have done nothing but evil in my sight from their youth; indeed, the people of Israel have done nothing but provoke me with what their hands have made, declares the LORD. [31]From the day it was built until now, this city has so aroused my anger and wrath that I must remove it from my sight. [32]The people of Israel and Judah have provoked me by all the evil they have done—they, their kings and officials, their priests and prophets, the men of Judah and the people of Jerusalem. [33]They turned their backs to me and not their faces; though I taught them again and again, they would not listen or respond to discipline. [34]They set up their abominable idols in the house that bears my Name and defiled it. [35]They built high places for Baal in the Valley of Ben Hinnom to sacrifice their sons and daughters[a] to Molech, though I never commanded, nor did it enter my mind, that they should do such a detestable thing and so make Judah sin.

[36]"You are saying about this city, 'By the sword, famine and plague it will be handed over to the king of Babylon'; but this is what the LORD, the God of Israel, says: [37]I will surely gather them from all the lands where I banish them in my furious anger and great wrath; I will bring them back to this place and let them live in safety. [38]They will be my people, and I will be their God. [39]I will give them singleness of heart and action, so that they will always fear me for their own good and the good of their children after them. [40]I will make an everlasting covenant with them: I will never stop doing good to them, and I will inspire them to fear me, so that they will never turn away from me. [41]I will rejoice in doing them good and will assuredly plant them in this land with all my heart and soul.

[42]"This is what the LORD says: As I have brought all this great calamity on this people, so I will give them all the prosperity I have promised them. [43]Once more fields will be bought in this land of which you say, 'It is a desolate waste, without men or

---

[a]35 Or *to make their sons and daughters pass through the fire*

animals, for it has been handed over to the Babylonians.' **44**Fields will be bought for silver, and deeds will be signed, sealed and witnessed in the territory of Benjamin, in the villages around Jerusalem, in the towns of Judah and in the towns of the hill country, of the western foothills and of the Negev, because I will restore their fortunes,*a* declares the LORD."

Promise of Restoration

33 While Jeremiah was still confined in the courtyard of the guard, the word of the LORD came to him a second time: **2**"This is what the LORD says, he who made the earth, the LORD who formed it and established it — the LORD is his name: **3**'Call to me and I will answer you and tell you great and unsearchable things you do not know.' **4**For this is what the LORD, the God of Israel, says about the houses in this city and the royal palaces of Judah that have been torn down to be used against the siege ramps and the sword **5**in the fight with the Babylonians*b*: 'They will be filled with the dead bodies of the men I will slay in my anger and wrath. I will hide my face from this city because of all its wickedness.

6" 'Nevertheless, I will bring health and healing to it; I will heal my people and will let them enjoy abundant peace and security. **7**I will bring Judah and Israel back from captivity*c* and will rebuild them as they were before. **8**I will cleanse them from all the sin they have committed against me and will forgive all their sins of rebellion against me. **9**Then this city will bring me renown, joy, praise and honor before all nations on earth that hear of all the good things I do for it; and they will be in awe and will tremble at the abundant prosperity and peace I provide for it.'

10"This is what the LORD says: 'You say about this place, "It is a desolate waste, without men or animals." Yet in the towns of Judah and the streets of Jerusalem that are deserted, inhabited by neither men nor animals, there will be heard once more **11**the sounds of joy and gladness, the voices of bride and bridegroom, and the voices of those who bring thank offerings to the house of the LORD, saying,

"Give thanks to the LORD Almighty,
    for the LORD is good;
    his love endures forever."

For I will restore the fortunes of the land as they were before,' says the LORD.

12"This is what the LORD Almighty says: 'In this place, desolate and without men or animals — in all its towns there will again be pastures for shepherds to rest their flocks. **13**In the towns of the hill country, of the western foothills and of the Negev, in the territory of Benjamin, in the villages around Jerusalem and in the towns of Judah, flocks will again pass under the hand of the one who counts them,' says the LORD.

14" 'The days are coming,' declares the LORD, 'when I will fulfill the gracious promise I made to the house of Israel and to the house of Judah.

15" 'In those days and at that time
    I will make a righteous Branch
        sprout from David's line;
    he will do what is just and right in
        the land.
16In those days Judah will be saved
    and Jerusalem will live in safety.
This is the name by which it*d* will be
    called:
    The LORD Our Righteousness.'

17For this is what the LORD says: 'David will never fail to have a man to sit on the throne of the house of Israel, **18**nor will the priests, who are Levites, ever fail to have a man to stand before me continually to offer burnt offerings, to burn grain offerings and to present sacrifices.' "

19The word of the LORD came to Jeremiah: **20**"This is what the LORD says: 'If you can break my covenant with the day and my covenant with the night, so that day and night no longer come at their appointed time, **21**then my covenant with David my servant — and my covenant with the Levites who are priests ministering before me — can be broken and David will no longer have a descendant to reign on his throne. **22**I will make the descendants of David my servant and the Levites who minister before me as countless as the stars of the sky and as measureless as the sand on the seashore.' "

23The word of the LORD came to Jeremiah: **24**"Have you not noticed that these people are saying, 'The LORD has rejected the two kingdoms*e* he chose'? So they despise my people and no longer regard

a44 Or *will bring them back from captivity*   *b5* Or *Chaldeans*   *c7* Or *will restore the fortunes of Judah and Israel*   *d16* Or *he*   *e24* Or *families* them as a nation. **25**This is what the LORD says: 'If I have not established my covenant with day and night and the fixed laws of heaven and earth, **26**then I will reject the descendants of Jacob and David my servant and will not choose one of his sons to rule over the descendants of Abraham, Isaac and Jacob. For I will restore their fortunes[a] and have compassion on them.' "

Warning to Zedekiah

34 While Nebuchadnezzar king of Babylon and all his army and all the kingdoms and peoples in the empire he ruled were fighting against Jerusalem and all its surrounding towns, this word came to Jeremiah from the LORD: **2**"This is what the LORD, the God of Israel, says: Go to Zedekiah king of Judah and tell him, 'This is what the LORD says: I am about to hand this city over to the king of Babylon, and he will burn it down. **3**You will not escape from his grasp but will surely be captured and handed over to him. You will see the king of Babylon with your own eyes, and he will speak with you face to face. And you will go to Babylon.

4" 'Yet hear the promise of the LORD, O Zedekiah king of Judah. This is what the LORD says concerning you: You will not die by the sword; **5**you will die peacefully. As people made a funeral fire in honor of your fathers, the former kings who preceded you, so they will make a fire in your honor and lament, "Alas, O master!" I myself make this promise, declares the LORD.' "

6Then Jeremiah the prophet told all this to Zedekiah king of Judah, in Jerusalem, **7**while the army of the king of Babylon was fighting against Jerusalem and the other cities of Judah that were still holding out—Lachish and Azekah. These were the only fortified cities left in Judah.

Freedom for Slaves

8The word came to Jeremiah from the LORD after King Zedekiah had made a covenant with all the people in Jerusalem to proclaim freedom for the slaves. **9**Everyone was to free his Hebrew slaves, both male and female; no one was to hold a fellow Jew in bondage. **10**So all the officials and people who entered into this covenant agreed that they would free their male and female slaves and no longer hold them in bondage. They agreed, and

set them free. **11**But afterward they changed their minds and took back the slaves they had freed and enslaved them again.

12Then the word of the LORD came to Jeremiah: **13**"This is what the LORD, the God of Israel, says: I made a covenant with your forefathers when I brought them out of Egypt, out of the land of slavery. I said, **14**'Every seventh year each of you must free any fellow Hebrew who has sold himself to you. After he has served you six years, you must let him go free.'[b] Your fathers, however, did not listen to me or pay attention to me. **15**Recently you repented and did what is right in my sight: Each of you proclaimed freedom to his countrymen. You even made a covenant before me in the house that bears my Name. **16**But now you have turned around and profaned my name; each of you has taken back the male and female slaves you had set free to go where they wished. You have forced them to become your slaves again.

17"Therefore, this is what the LORD says: You have not obeyed me; you have not proclaimed freedom for your fellow countrymen. So I now proclaim 'freedom' for you, declares the LORD—'freedom' to fall by the sword, plague and famine. I will make you abhorrent to all the kingdoms of the earth. **18**The men who have violated my covenant and have not fulfilled the terms of the covenant they made before me, I will treat like the calf they cut in two and then walked between its pieces. **19**The leaders of Judah and Jerusalem, the court officials, the priests and all the people of the land who walked between the pieces of the calf, **20**I will hand over to their enemies who seek their lives. Their dead bodies will become food for the birds of the air and the beasts of the earth.

21"I will hand Zedekiah king of Judah and his officials over to their enemies who seek their lives, to the army of the king of Babylon, which has withdrawn from you. **22**I am going to give the order, declares the LORD, and I will bring them back to this city. They will fight against it, take it and burn it down. And I will lay waste the towns of Judah so no one can live there."

The Recabites

35 This is the word that came to Jeremiah from the LORD during the reign of Jehoiakim son of Josiah king of

Judah: [2]"Go to the Recabite family and invite them to come to one of the side rooms of the house of the LORD and give them wine to drink."

[3]So I went to get Jaazaniah son of Jeremiah, the son of Habazziniah, and his brothers and all his sons — the whole family of the Recabites. [4]I brought them into the house of the LORD, into the room of the sons of Hanan son of Igdaliah the man of God. It was next to the room of the officials, which was over that of Maaseiah son of Shallum the doorkeeper. [5]Then I set bowls full of wine and some cups before the men of the Recabite family and said to them, "Drink some wine."

[6]But they replied, "We do not drink wine, because our forefather Jonadab son of Recab gave us this command: 'Neither you nor your descendants must ever drink wine. [7]Also you must never build houses, sow seed or plant vineyards; you must never have any of these things, but must always live in tents. Then you will live a long time in the land where you are nomads.' [8]We have obeyed everything our forefather Jonadab son of Recab commanded us. Neither we nor our wives nor our sons and daughters have ever drunk wine [9]or built houses to live in or had vineyards, fields or crops. [10]We have lived in tents and have fully obeyed everything our forefather Jonadab commanded us. [11]But when Nebuchadnezzar king of Babylon invaded this land, we said, 'Come, we must go to Jerusalem to escape the Babylonian[a] and Aramean armies.' So we have remained in Jerusalem."

[12]Then the word of the LORD came to Jeremiah, saying: [13]"This is what the LORD Almighty, the God of Israel, says: Go and tell the men of Judah and the people of Jerusalem, 'Will you not learn a lesson and obey my words?' declares the LORD. [14]'Jonadab son of Recab ordered his sons not to drink wine and this command has been kept. To this day they do not drink wine, because they obey their forefather's command. But I have spoken to you again and again, yet you have not obeyed me. [15]Again and again I sent all my servants the prophets to you. They said, "Each of you must turn from your wicked ways and reform your actions; do not follow other gods to serve them. Then you will live in the land I have given to you and your fathers." But you have not paid attention or listened to me. [16]The descendants of Jona-

dab son of Recab have carried out the command their forefather gave them, but these people have not obeyed me.'

[17]"Therefore, this is what the LORD God Almighty, the God of Israel, says: 'Listen! I am going to bring on Judah and on everyone living in Jerusalem every disaster I pronounced against them. I spoke to them, but they did not listen; I called to them, but they did not answer.'"

[18]Then Jeremiah said to the family of the Recabites, "This is what the LORD Almighty, the God of Israel, says: 'You have obeyed the command of your forefather Jonadab and have followed all his instructions and have done everything he ordered.' [19]Therefore, this is what the LORD Almighty, the God of Israel, says: 'Jonadab son of Recab will never fail to have a man to serve me.'"

Jehoiakim Burns Jeremiah's Scroll

36 In the fourth year of Jehoiakim son of Josiah king of Judah, this word came to Jeremiah from the LORD: [2]"Take a scroll and write on it all the words I have spoken to you concerning Israel, Judah and all the other nations from the time I began speaking to you in the reign of Josiah till now. [3]Perhaps when the people of Judah hear about every disaster I plan to inflict on them, each of them will turn from his wicked way; then I will forgive their wickedness and their sin."

[4]So Jeremiah called Baruch son of Neriah, and while Jeremiah dictated all the words the LORD had spoken to him, Baruch wrote them on the scroll. [5]Then Jeremiah told Baruch, "I am restricted; I cannot go to the LORD's temple. [6]So you go to the house of the LORD on a day of fasting and read to the people from the scroll the words of the LORD that you wrote as I dictated. Read them to all the people of Judah who come in from their towns. [7]Perhaps they will bring their petition before the LORD, and each will turn from his wicked ways, for the anger and wrath pronounced against this people by the LORD are great."

[8]Baruch son of Neriah did everything Jeremiah the prophet told him to do; at the LORD's temple he read the words of the LORD from the scroll. [9]In the ninth month of the fifth year of Jehoiakim son of Josiah king of Judah, a time of fasting before the LORD was proclaimed for all the people in Jerusalem and those who had come from the towns of Judah. [10]From the room of

---

[a]11 Or *Chaldean*

Gemariah son of Shaphan the secretary, which was in the upper courtyard at the entrance of the New Gate of the temple, Baruch read to all the people at the LORD's temple the words of Jeremiah from the scroll.

¹¹When Micaiah son of Gemariah, the son of Shaphan, heard all the words of the LORD from the scroll, ¹²he went down to the secretary's room in the royal palace, where all the officials were sitting: Elishama the secretary, Delaiah son of Shemaiah, Elnathan son of Acbor, Gemariah son of Shaphan, Zedekiah son of Hananiah, and all the other officials. ¹³After Micaiah told them everything he had heard Baruch read to the people from the scroll, ¹⁴all the officials sent Jehudi son of Nethaniah, the son of Shelemiah, the son of Cushi, to say to Baruch, "Bring the scroll from which you have read to the people and come." So Baruch son of Neriah went to them with the scroll in his hand. ¹⁵They said to him, "Sit down, please, and read it to us."

So Baruch read it to them. ¹⁶When they heard all these words, they looked at each other in fear and said to Baruch, "We must report all these words to the king." ¹⁷Then they asked Baruch, "Tell us, how did you come to write all this? Did Jeremiah dictate it?"

¹⁸"Yes," Baruch replied, "he dictated all these words to me, and I wrote them in ink on the scroll."

¹⁹Then the officials said to Baruch, "You and Jeremiah, go and hide. Don't let anyone know where you are."

²⁰After they put the scroll in the room of Elishama the secretary, they went to the king in the courtyard and reported everything to him. ²¹The king sent Jehudi to get the scroll, and Jehudi brought it from the room of Elishama the secretary and read it to the king and all the officials standing beside him. ²²It was the ninth month and the king was sitting in the winter apartment, with a fire burning in the firepot in front of him. ²³Whenever Jehudi had read three or four columns of the scroll, the king cut them off with a scribe's knife and threw them into the firepot, until the entire scroll was burned in the fire. ²⁴The king and all his attendants who heard all these words showed no fear, nor did they tear their clothes. ²⁵Even though Elnathan, Delaiah and Gemariah urged the king not to burn the scroll, he would not listen to them. ²⁶Instead, the king com-

manded Jerahmeel, a son of the king, Seraiah son of Azriel and Shelemiah son of Abdeel to arrest Baruch the scribe and Jeremiah the prophet. But the LORD had hidden them.

²⁷After the king burned the scroll containing the words that Baruch had written at Jeremiah's dictation, the word of the LORD came to Jeremiah: ²⁸"Take another scroll and write on it all the words that were on the first scroll, which Jehoiakim king of Judah burned up. ²⁹Also tell Jehoiakim king of Judah, 'This is what the LORD says: You burned that scroll and said, "Why did you write on it that the king of Babylon would certainly come and destroy this land and cut off both men and animals from it?" ³⁰Therefore, this is what the LORD says about Jehoiakim king of Judah: He will have no one to sit on the throne of David; his body will be thrown out and exposed to the heat by day and the frost by night. ³¹I will punish him and his children and his attendants for their wickedness; I will bring on them and those living in Jerusalem and the people of Judah every disaster I pronounced against them, because they have not listened.'"

³²So Jeremiah took another scroll and gave it to the scribe Baruch son of Neriah, and as Jeremiah dictated, Baruch wrote on it all the words of the scroll that Jehoiakim king of Judah had burned in the fire. And many similar words were added to them.

Jeremiah in Prison

37 Zedekiah son of Josiah was made king of Judah by Nebuchadnezzar king of Babylon; he reigned in place of Jehoiachin[a] son of Jehoiakim. ²Neither he nor his attendants nor the people of the land paid any attention to the words the LORD had spoken through Jeremiah the prophet.

³King Zedekiah, however, sent Jehucal son of Shelemiah with the priest Zephaniah son of Maaseiah to Jeremiah the prophet with this message: "Please pray to the LORD our God for us."

⁴Now Jeremiah was free to come and go among the people, for he had not yet been put in prison. ⁵Pharaoh's army had marched out of Egypt, and when the Babylonians[b] who were besieging Jerusalem heard the report about them, they withdrew from Jerusalem.

a1 Hebrew *Coniah,* a variant of *Jehoiachin*   *b5* Or *Chaldeans*; also in verses 8, 9, 13 and 14

⁶Then the word of the Lord came to Jeremiah the prophet: ⁷"This is what the Lord, the God of Israel, says: Tell the king of Judah, who sent you to inquire of me, 'Pharaoh's army, which has marched out to support you, will go back to its own land, to Egypt. ⁸Then the Babylonians will return and attack this city; they will capture it and burn it down.'

⁹"This is what the Lord says: Do not deceive yourselves, thinking, 'The Babylonians will surely leave us.' They will not! ¹⁰Even if you were to defeat the entire Babylonian[a] army that is attacking you and only wounded men were left in their tents, they would come out and burn this city down."

¹¹After the Babylonian army had withdrawn from Jerusalem because of Pharaoh's army, ¹²Jeremiah started to leave the city to go to the territory of Benjamin to get his share of the property among the people there. ¹³But when he reached the Benjamin Gate, the captain of the guard, whose name was Irijah son of Shelemiah, the son of Hananiah, arrested him and said, "You are deserting to the Babylonians!"

¹⁴"That's not true!" Jeremiah said. "I am not deserting to the Babylonians." But Irijah would not listen to him; instead, he arrested Jeremiah and brought him to the officials. ¹⁵They were angry with Jeremiah and had him beaten and imprisoned in the house of Jonathan the secretary, which they had made into a prison.

¹⁶Jeremiah was put into a vaulted cell in a dungeon, where he remained a long time. ¹⁷Then King Zedekiah sent for him and had him brought to the palace, where he asked him privately, "Is there any word from the Lord?"

"Yes," Jeremiah replied, "you will be handed over to the king of Babylon."

¹⁸Then Jeremiah said to King Zedekiah, "What crime have I committed against you or your officials or this people, that you have put me in prison? ¹⁹Where are your prophets who prophesied to you, 'The king of Babylon will not attack you or this land'? ²⁰But now, my lord the king, please listen. Let me bring my petition before you: Do not send me back to the house of Jonathan the secretary, or I will die there."

²¹King Zedekiah then gave orders for Jeremiah to be placed in the courtyard of the guard and given bread from the street of the bakers each day until all the bread in the city was gone. So Jeremiah remained in the courtyard of the guard.

Jeremiah Thrown Into a Cistern

38 Shephatiah son of Mattan, Gedaliah son of Pashhur, Jehucal[b] son of Shelemiah, and Pashhur son of Malkijah heard what Jeremiah was telling all the people when he said, ²"This is what the Lord says: 'Whoever stays in this city will die by the sword, famine or plague, but whoever goes over to the Babylonians[c] will live. He will escape with his life; he will live.' ³And this is what the Lord says: 'This city will certainly be handed over to the army of the king of Babylon, who will capture it.' "

⁴Then the officials said to the king, "This man should be put to death. He is discouraging the soldiers who are left in this city, as well as all the people, by the things he is saying to them. This man is not seeking the good of these people but their ruin."

⁵"He is in your hands," King Zedekiah answered. "The king can do nothing to oppose you."

⁶So they took Jeremiah and put him into the cistern of Malkijah, the king's son, which was in the courtyard of the guard. They lowered Jeremiah by ropes into the cistern; it had no water in it, only mud, and Jeremiah sank down into the mud.

⁷But Ebed-Melech, a Cushite,[d] an official[e] in the royal palace, heard that they had put Jeremiah into the cistern. While the king was sitting in the Benjamin Gate, ⁸Ebed-Melech went out of the palace and said to him, ⁹"My lord the king, these men have acted wickedly in all they have done to Jeremiah the prophet. They have thrown him into a cistern, where he will starve to death when there is no longer any bread in the city."

¹⁰Then the king commanded Ebed-Melech the Cushite, "Take thirty men from here with you and lift Jeremiah the prophet out of the cistern before he dies."

¹¹So Ebed-Melech took the men with him and went to a room under the treasury in the palace. He took some old rags and worn-out clothes from there and let them down with ropes to Jeremiah in the cistern. ¹²Ebed-Melech the Cushite said to

---

a10 Or *Chaldean*; also in verse 11   b1 Hebrew *Jucal*, a variant of *Jehucal*   c2 Or *Chaldeans*; also in verses 18, 19 and 23   d7 Probably from the upper Nile region   e7 Or *a eunuch*

Jeremiah, "Put these old rags and worn-out clothes under your arms to pad the ropes." Jeremiah did so, [13]and they pulled him up with the ropes and lifted him out of the cistern. And Jeremiah remained in the courtyard of the guard.

Zedekiah Questions Jeremiah Again

[14]Then King Zedekiah sent for Jeremiah the prophet and had him brought to the third entrance to the temple of the LORD. "I am going to ask you something," the king said to Jeremiah. "Do not hide anything from me."

[15]Jeremiah said to Zedekiah, "If I give you an answer, will you not kill me? Even if I did give you counsel, you would not listen to me."

[16]But King Zedekiah swore this oath secretly to Jeremiah: "As surely as the LORD lives, who has given us breath, I will neither kill you nor hand you over to those who are seeking your life."

[17]Then Jeremiah said to Zedekiah, "This is what the LORD God Almighty, the God of Israel, says: 'If you surrender to the officers of the king of Babylon, your life will be spared and this city will not be burned down; you and your family will live. [18]But if you will not surrender to the officers of the king of Babylon, this city will be handed over to the Babylonians and they will burn it down; you yourself will not escape from their hands.' "

[19]King Zedekiah said to Jeremiah, "I am afraid of the Jews who have gone over to the Babylonians, for the Babylonians may hand me over to them and they will mistreat me."

[20]"They will not hand you over," Jeremiah replied. "Obey the LORD by doing what I tell you. Then it will go well with you, and your life will be spared. [21]But if you refuse to surrender, this is what the LORD has revealed to me: [22]All the women left in the palace of the king of Judah will be brought out to the officials of the king of Babylon. Those women will say to you:

" 'They misled you and overcame
    you —
   those trusted friends of yours.
Your feet are sunk in the mud;
   your friends have deserted you.'

[23]"All your wives and children will be brought out to the Babylonians. You yourself will not escape from their hands but will be captured by the king of Babylon; and this city will[a] be burned down."

[24]Then Zedekiah said to Jeremiah, "Do not let anyone know about this conversation, or you may die. [25]If the officials hear that I talked with you, and they come to you and say, 'Tell us what you said to the king and what the king said to you; do not hide it from us or we will kill you,' [26]then tell them, 'I was pleading with the king not to send me back to Jonathan's house to die there.' "

[27]All the officials did come to Jeremiah and question him, and he told them everything the king had ordered him to say. So they said no more to him, for no one had heard his conversation with the king.

[28]And Jeremiah remained in the courtyard of the guard until the day Jerusalem was captured.

The Fall of Jerusalem

39 This is how Jerusalem was taken: [1]In the ninth year of Zedekiah king of Judah, in the tenth month, Nebuchadnezzar king of Babylon marched against Jerusalem with his whole army and laid siege to it. [2]And on the ninth day of the fourth month of Zedekiah's eleventh year, the city wall was broken through. [3]Then all the officials of the king of Babylon came and took seats in the Middle Gate: Nergal-Sharezer of Samgar, Nebo-Sarsekim[b] a chief officer, Nergal-Sharezer a high official and all the other officials of the king of Babylon. [4]When Zedekiah king of Judah and all the soldiers saw them, they fled; they left the city at night by way of the king's garden, through the gate between the two walls, and headed toward the Arabah.[c]

[5]But the Babylonian[d] army pursued them and overtook Zedekiah in the plains of Jericho. They captured him and took him to Nebuchadnezzar king of Babylon at Riblah in the land of Hamath, where he pronounced sentence on him. [6]There at Riblah the king of Babylon slaughtered the sons of Zedekiah before his eyes and also killed all the nobles of Judah. [7]Then he put out Zedekiah's eyes and bound him with bronze shackles to take him to Babylon.

[8]The Babylonians[e] set fire to the royal palace and the houses of the people and broke down the walls of Jerusalem. [9]Nebuzaradan commander of the imperial

---

[a]23 Or *and you will cause this city to*   [b]3 Or *Nergal-Sharezer, Samgar-Nebo, Sarsekim*   [c]4 Or *the*
Jordan Valley   [d]5 Or *Chaldean*   [e]8 Or *Chaldeans*

guard carried into exile to Babylon the people who remained in the city, along with those who had gone over to him, and the rest of the people. [10]But Nebuzaradan the commander of the guard left behind in the land of Judah some of the poor people, who owned nothing; and at that time he gave them vineyards and fields.

[11]Now Nebuchadnezzar king of Babylon had given these orders about Jeremiah through Nebuzaradan commander of the imperial guard: [12]"Take him and look after him; don't harm him but do for him whatever he asks." [13]So Nebuzaradan the commander of the guard, Nebushazban a chief officer, Nergal-Sharezer a high official and all the other officers of the king of Babylon [14]sent and had Jeremiah taken out of the courtyard of the guard. They turned him over to Gedaliah son of Ahikam, the son of Shaphan, to take him back to his home. So he remained among his own people.

[15]While Jeremiah had been confined in the courtyard of the guard, the word of the LORD came to him: [16]"Go and tell Ebed-Melech the Cushite, 'This is what the LORD Almighty, the God of Israel, says: I am about to fulfill my words against this city through disaster, not prosperity. At that time they will be fulfilled before your eyes. [17]But I will rescue you on that day, declares the LORD; you will not be handed over to those you fear. [18]I will save you; you will not fall by the sword but will escape with your life, because you trust in me, declares the LORD.'"

Jeremiah Freed

40 The word came to Jeremiah from the LORD after Nebuzaradan commander of the imperial guard had released him at Ramah. He had found Jeremiah bound in chains among all the captives from Jerusalem and Judah who were being carried into exile to Babylon. [2]When the commander of the guard found Jeremiah, he said to him, "The LORD your God decreed this disaster for this place. [3]And now the LORD has brought it about; he has done just as he said he would. All this happened because you people sinned against the LORD and did not obey him. [4]But today I am freeing you from the chains on your wrists. Come with me to Babylon, if you like, and I will look after you; but if you do not want to, then don't

come. Look, the whole country lies before you; go wherever you please." [5]However, before Jeremiah turned to go,[a] Nebuzaradan added, "Go back to Gedaliah son of Ahikam, the son of Shaphan, whom the king of Babylon has appointed over the towns of Judah, and live with him among the people, or go anywhere else you please."

Then the commander gave him provisions and a present and let him go. [6]So Jeremiah went to Gedaliah son of Ahikam at Mizpah and stayed with him among the people who were left behind in the land.

Gedaliah Assassinated

[7]When all the army officers and their men who were still in the open country heard that the king of Babylon had appointed Gedaliah son of Ahikam as governor over the land and had put him in charge of the men, women and children who were the poorest in the land and who had not been carried into exile to Babylon, [8]they came to Gedaliah at Mizpah — Ishmael son of Nethaniah, Johanan and Jonathan the sons of Kareah, Seraiah son of Tanhumeth, the sons of Ephai the Netophathite, and Jaazaniah[b] the son of the Maacathite, and their men. [9]Gedaliah son of Ahikam, the son of Shaphan, took an oath to reassure them and their men. "Do not be afraid to serve the Babylonians,[c]" he said. "Settle down in the land and serve the king of Babylon, and it will go well with you. [10]I myself will stay at Mizpah to represent you before the Babylonians who come to us, but you are to harvest the wine, summer fruit and oil, and put them in your storage jars, and live in the towns you have taken over."

[11]When all the Jews in Moab, Ammon, Edom and all the other countries heard that the king of Babylon had left a remnant in Judah and had appointed Gedaliah son of Ahikam, the son of Shaphan, as governor over them, [12]they all came back to the land of Judah, to Gedaliah at Mizpah, from all the countries where they had been scattered. And they harvested an abundance of wine and summer fruit.

[13]Johanan son of Kareah and all the army officers still in the open country came to Gedaliah at Mizpah [14]and said to him, "Don't you know that Baalis king of the Ammonites has sent Ishmael son of

---

a5 Or *Jeremiah answered*   b8 Hebrew *Jezaniah,* a variant of *Jaazaniah*   c9 Or *Chaldeans*; also in verse 10

Nethaniah to take your life?" But Gedaliah son of Ahikam did not believe them.

15Then Johanan son of Kareah said privately to Gedaliah in Mizpah, "Let me go and kill Ishmael son of Nethaniah, and no one will know it. Why should he take your life and cause all the Jews who are gathered around you to be scattered and the remnant of Judah to perish?"

16But Gedaliah son of Ahikam said to Johanan son of Kareah, "Don't do such a thing! What you are saying about Ishmael is not true."

41 In the seventh month Ishmael son of Nethaniah, the son of Elishama, who was of royal blood and had been one of the king's officers, came with ten men to Gedaliah son of Ahikam at Mizpah. While they were eating together there, 2Ishmael son of Nethaniah and the ten men who were with him got up and struck down Gedaliah son of Ahikam, the son of Shaphan, with the sword, killing the one whom the king of Babylon had appointed as governor over the land. 3Ishmael also killed all the Jews who were with Gedaliah at Mizpah, as well as the Babylonian[a] soldiers who were there.

4The day after Gedaliah's assassination, before anyone knew about it, 5eighty men who had shaved off their beards, torn their clothes and cut themselves came from Shechem, Shiloh and Samaria, bringing grain offerings and incense with them to the house of the LORD. 6Ishmael son of Nethaniah went out from Mizpah to meet them, weeping as he went. When he met them, he said, "Come to Gedaliah son of Ahikam." 7When they went into the city, Ishmael son of Nethaniah and the men who were with him slaughtered them and threw them into a cistern. 8But ten of them said to Ishmael, "Don't kill us! We have wheat and barley, oil and honey, hidden in a field." So he let them alone and did not kill them with the others. 9Now the cistern where he threw all the bodies of the men he had killed along with Gedaliah was the one King Asa had made as part of his defense against Baasha king of Israel. Ishmael son of Nethaniah filled it with the dead.

10Ishmael made captives of all the rest of the people who were in Mizpah — the king's daughters along with all the others who were left there, over whom Nebuzaradan commander of the imperial guard had appointed Gedaliah son of Ahikam.

Ishmael son of Nethaniah took them captive and set out to cross over to the Ammonites.

11When Johanan son of Kareah and all the army officers who were with him heard about all the crimes Ishmael son of Nethaniah had committed, 12they took all their men and went to fight Ishmael son of Nethaniah. They caught up with him near the great pool in Gibeon. 13When all the people Ishmael had with him saw Johanan son of Kareah and the army officers who were with him, they were glad. 14All the people Ishmael had taken captive at Mizpah turned and went over to Johanan son of Kareah. 15But Ishmael son of Nethaniah and eight of his men escaped from Johanan and fled to the Ammonites.

Flight to Egypt

16Then Johanan son of Kareah and all the army officers who were with him led away all the survivors from Mizpah whom he had recovered from Ishmael son of Nethaniah after he had assassinated Gedaliah son of Ahikam: the soldiers, women, children and court officials he had brought from Gibeon. 17And they went on, stopping at Geruth Kimham near Bethlehem on their way to Egypt 18to escape the Babylonians.[b] They were afraid of them because Ishmael son of Nethaniah had killed Gedaliah son of Ahikam, whom the king of Babylon had appointed as governor over the land.

42 Then all the army officers, including Johanan son of Kareah and Jezaniah[c] son of Hoshaiah, and all the people from the least to the greatest approached 2Jeremiah the prophet and said to him, "Please hear our petition and pray to the LORD your God for this entire remnant. For as you now see, though we were once many, now only a few are left. 3Pray that the LORD your God will tell us where we should go and what we should do."

4"I have heard you," replied Jeremiah the prophet. "I will certainly pray to the LORD your God as you have requested; I will tell you everything the LORD says and will keep nothing back from you."

5Then they said to Jeremiah, "May the LORD be a true and faithful witness against us if we do not act in accordance with everything the LORD your God sends you to tell us. 6Whether it is favorable or unfavorable, we will obey the LORD our God, to

a3 Or Chaldean   b18 Or Chaldeans   c1 Hebrew; Septuagint (see also 43:2) Azariah whom we are sending you, so that it will go well with us, for we will obey the LORD our God."

⁷Ten days later the word of the LORD came to Jeremiah. ⁸So he called together Johanan son of Kareah and all the army officers who were with him and all the people from the least to the greatest. ⁹He said to them, "This is what the LORD, the God of Israel, to whom you sent me to present your petition, says: ¹⁰'If you stay in this land, I will build you up and not tear you down; I will plant you and not uproot you, for I am grieved over the disaster I have inflicted on you. ¹¹Do not be afraid of the king of Babylon, whom you now fear. Do not be afraid of him, declares the LORD, for I am with you and will save you and deliver you from his hands. ¹²I will show you compassion so that he will have compassion on you and restore you to your land.'

¹³"However, if you say, 'We will not stay in this land,' and so disobey the LORD your God, ¹⁴and if you say, 'No, we will go and live in Egypt, where we will not see war or hear the trumpet or be hungry for bread,' ¹⁵then hear the word of the LORD, O remnant of Judah. This is what the LORD Almighty, the God of Israel, says: 'If you are determined to go to Egypt and you do go to settle there, ¹⁶then the sword you fear will overtake you there, and the famine you dread will follow you into Egypt, and there you will die. ¹⁷Indeed, all who are determined to go to Egypt to settle there will die by the sword, famine and plague; not one of them will survive or escape the disaster I will bring on them.' ¹⁸This is what the LORD Almighty, the God of Israel, says: 'As my anger and wrath have been poured out on those who lived in Jerusalem, so will my wrath be poured out on you when you go to Egypt. You will be an object of cursing and horror, of condemnation and reproach; you will never see this place again.'

¹⁹"O remnant of Judah, the LORD has told you, 'Do not go to Egypt.' Be sure of this: I warn you today ²⁰that you made a fatal mistake[a] when you sent me to the LORD your God and said, 'Pray to the LORD our God for us; tell us everything he says and we will do it.' ²¹I have told you today, but you still have not obeyed the LORD your God in all he sent me to tell you. ²²So

now, be sure of this: You will die by the sword, famine and plague in the place where you want to go to settle."

43 When Jeremiah finished telling the people all the words of the LORD their God — everything the LORD had sent him to tell them — ²Azariah son of Hoshaiah and Johanan son of Kareah and all the arrogant men said to Jeremiah, "You are lying! The LORD our God has not sent you to say, 'You must not go to Egypt to settle there.' ³But Baruch son of Neriah is inciting you against us to hand us over to the Babylonians,[b] so they may kill us or carry us into exile to Babylon."

⁴So Johanan son of Kareah and all the army officers and all the people disobeyed the LORD's command to stay in the land of Judah. ⁵Instead, Johanan son of Kareah and all the army officers led away all the remnant of Judah who had come back to live in the land of Judah from all the nations where they had been scattered. ⁶They also led away all the men, women and children and the king's daughters whom Nebuzaradan commander of the imperial guard had left with Gedaliah son of Ahikam, the son of Shaphan, and Jeremiah the prophet and Baruch son of Neriah. ⁷So they entered Egypt in disobedience to the LORD and went as far as Tahpanhes.

⁸In Tahpanhes the word of the LORD came to Jeremiah: ⁹"While the Jews are watching, take some large stones with you and bury them in clay in the brick pavement at the entrance to Pharaoh's palace in Tahpanhes. ¹⁰Then say to them, 'This is what the LORD Almighty, the God of Israel, says: I will send for my servant Nebuchadnezzar king of Babylon, and I will set his throne over these stones I have buried here; he will spread his royal canopy above them. ¹¹He will come and attack Egypt, bringing death to those destined for death, captivity to those destined for captivity, and the sword to those destined for the sword. ¹²He[c] will set fire to the temples of the gods of Egypt; he will burn their temples and take their gods captive. As a shepherd wraps his garment around him, so will he wrap Egypt around himself and depart from there unscathed. ¹³There in the temple of the sun[d] in Egypt he will demolish the sacred pillars and will burn down the temples of the gods of Egypt.'"

---

a20 Or *you erred in your hearts*   *b3* Or *Chaldeans*   *c12* Or *I*   *d13* Or *in Heliopolis*

Disaster Because of Idolatry

44 This word came to Jeremiah concerning all the Jews living in Lower Egypt—in Migdol, Tahpanhes and Memphis[a]—and in Upper Egypt[b]: ²"This is what the LORD Almighty, the God of Israel, says: You saw the great disaster I brought on Jerusalem and on all the towns of Judah. Today they lie deserted and in ruins ³because of the evil they have done. They provoked me to anger by burning incense and by worshiping other gods that neither they nor you nor your fathers ever knew. ⁴Again and again I sent my servants the prophets, who said, 'Do not do this detestable thing that I hate!' ⁵But they did not listen or pay attention; they did not turn from their wickedness or stop burning incense to other gods. ⁶Therefore, my fierce anger was poured out; it raged against the towns of Judah and the streets of Jerusalem and made them the desolate ruins they are today.

⁷"Now this is what the LORD God Almighty, the God of Israel, says: Why bring such great disaster on yourselves by cutting off from Judah the men and women, the children and infants, and so leave yourselves without a remnant? ⁸Why provoke me to anger with what your hands have made, burning incense to other gods in Egypt, where you have come to live? You will destroy yourselves and make yourselves an object of cursing and reproach among all the nations on earth. ⁹Have you forgotten the wickedness committed by your fathers and by the kings and queens of Judah and the wickedness committed by you and your wives in the land of Judah and the streets of Jerusalem? ¹⁰To this day they have not humbled themselves or shown reverence, nor have they followed my law and the decrees I set before you and your fathers.

¹¹"Therefore, this is what the LORD Almighty, the God of Israel, says: I am determined to bring disaster on you and to destroy all Judah. ¹²I will take away the remnant of Judah who were determined to go to Egypt to settle there. They will all perish in Egypt; they will fall by the sword or die from famine. From the least to the greatest, they will die by sword or famine. They will become an object of cursing and horror, of condemnation and reproach. ¹³I will punish those who live in Egypt with the sword, famine and plague, as I pun-

ished Jerusalem. ¹⁴None of the remnant of Judah who have gone to live in Egypt will escape or survive to return to the land of Judah, to which they long to return and live; none will return except a few fugitives."

¹⁵Then all the men who knew that their wives were burning incense to other gods, along with all the women who were present—a large assembly—and all the people living in Lower and Upper Egypt,[c] said to Jeremiah, ¹⁶"We will not listen to the message you have spoken to us in the name of the LORD! ¹⁷We will certainly do everything we said we would: We will burn incense to the Queen of Heaven and will pour out drink offerings to her just as we and our fathers, our kings and our officials did in the towns of Judah and in the streets of Jerusalem. At that time we had plenty of food and were well off and suffered no harm. ¹⁸But ever since we stopped burning incense to the Queen of Heaven and pouring out drink offerings to her, we have had nothing and have been perishing by sword and famine."

¹⁹The women added, "When we burned incense to the Queen of Heaven and poured out drink offerings to her, did not our husbands know that we were making cakes like her image and pouring out drink offerings to her?"

²⁰Then Jeremiah said to all the people, both men and women, who were answering him, ²¹"Did not the LORD remember and think about the incense burned in the towns of Judah and the streets of Jerusalem by you and your fathers, your kings and your officials and the people of the land? ²²When the LORD could no longer endure your wicked actions and the detestable things you did, your land became an object of cursing and a desolate waste without inhabitants, as it is today. ²³Because you have burned incense and have sinned against the LORD and have not obeyed him or followed his law or his decrees or his stipulations, this disaster has come upon you, as you now see."

²⁴Then Jeremiah said to all the people, including the women, "Hear the word of the LORD, all you people of Judah in Egypt. ²⁵This is what the LORD Almighty, the God of Israel, says: You and your wives have shown by your actions what you promised when you said, 'We will certainly carry out the vows we made to burn incense

a1 Hebrew *Noph*   *b1* Hebrew *in Pathros*   *c15* Hebrew *in Egypt and Pathros* and pour out drink offerings to the Queen of Heaven.'

"Go ahead then, do what you promised! Keep your vows! **26**But hear the word of the LORD, all Jews living in Egypt: 'I swear by my great name,' says the LORD, 'that no one from Judah living anywhere in Egypt will ever again invoke my name or swear, "As surely as the Sovereign LORD lives." **27**For I am watching over them for harm, not for good; the Jews in Egypt will perish by sword and famine until they are all destroyed. **28**Those who escape the sword and return to the land of Judah from Egypt will be very few. Then the whole remnant of Judah who came to live in Egypt will know whose word will stand — mine or theirs.

29" 'This will be the sign to you that I will punish you in this place,' declares the LORD, 'so that you will know that my threats of harm against you will surely stand.' **30**This is what the LORD says: 'I am going to hand Pharaoh Hophra king of Egypt over to his enemies who seek his life, just as I handed Zedekiah king of Judah over to Nebuchadnezzar king of Babylon, the enemy who was seeking his life.' "

A Message to Baruch

45 This is what Jeremiah the prophet told Baruch son of Neriah in the fourth year of Jehoiakim son of Josiah king of Judah, after Baruch had written on a scroll the words Jeremiah was then dictating: **2**"This is what the LORD, the God of Israel, says to you, Baruch: **3**You said, 'Woe to me! The LORD has added sorrow to my pain; I am worn out with groaning and find no rest.' "

4The LORD said, "Say this to him: 'This is what the LORD says: I will overthrow what I have built and uproot what I have planted, throughout the land. **5**Should you then seek great things for yourself? Seek them not. For I will bring disaster on all people, declares the LORD, but wherever you go I will let you escape with your life.' "

A Message About Egypt

46 This is the word of the LORD that came to Jeremiah the prophet concerning the nations:

2Concerning Egypt:

This is the message against the army of Pharaoh Neco king of Egypt, which was defeated at Carchemish on the Euphrates River by Nebuchadnezzar king of Babylon in the fourth year of Jehoiakim son of Josiah king of Judah:

3"Prepare your shields, both large and
    small,
    and march out for battle!
4Harness the horses,
    mount the steeds!
Take your positions
    with helmets on!
Polish your spears,
    put on your armor!
5What do I see?
    They are terrified,
they are retreating,
    their warriors are defeated.
They flee in haste
    without looking back,
    and there is terror on every side,"
        declares the LORD.
6"The swift cannot flee
    nor the strong escape.
In the north by the River Euphrates
    they stumble and fall.

7"Who is this that rises like the Nile,
    like rivers of surging waters?
8Egypt rises like the Nile,
    like rivers of surging waters.
She says, 'I will rise and cover the
    earth;
    I will destroy cities and their
        people.'
9Charge, O horses!
    Drive furiously, O charioteers!
March on, O warriors —
    men of Cush*a* and Put who carry
        shields,
    men of Lydia who draw the bow.
10But that day belongs to the Lord, the
    LORD Almighty —
    a day of vengeance, for vengeance
        on his foes.
The sword will devour till it is
    satisfied,
    till it has quenched its thirst with
        blood.
For the Lord, the LORD Almighty, will
    offer sacrifice
    in the land of the north by the River
        Euphrates.
11"Go up to Gilead and get balm,
    O Virgin Daughter of Egypt.
But you multiply remedies in vain;

---

a9 That is, the upper Nile region

there is no healing for you.
¹²The nations will hear of your shame;
  your cries will fill the earth.
One warrior will stumble over
    another;
  both will fall down together."

¹³This is the message the LORD spoke to Jeremiah the prophet about the coming of Nebuchadnezzar king of Babylon to attack Egypt:

¹⁴"Announce this in Egypt, and proclaim
    it in Migdol;
  proclaim it also in Memphis[a] and
    Tahpanhes:
'Take your positions and get ready,
  for the sword devours those around
    you.'
¹⁵Why will your warriors be laid low?
  They cannot stand, for the LORD will
    push them down.
¹⁶They will stumble repeatedly;
  they will fall over each other.
They will say, 'Get up, let us go back
  to our own people and our native
    lands,
  away from the sword of the
    oppressor.'
¹⁷There they will exclaim,
  'Pharaoh king of Egypt is only a
    loud noise;
  he has missed his opportunity.'

¹⁸"As surely as I live," declares the
    King,
  whose name is the LORD Almighty,
"one will come who is like Tabor
    among the mountains,
  like Carmel by the sea.
¹⁹Pack your belongings for exile,
  you who live in Egypt,
for Memphis will be laid waste
  and lie in ruins without inhabitant.

²⁰"Egypt is a beautiful heifer,
  but a gadfly is coming
  against her from the north.
²¹The mercenaries in her ranks
  are like fattened calves.
They too will turn and flee together,
  they will not stand their ground,
for the day of disaster is coming upon
    them,
  the time for them to be punished.
²²Egypt will hiss like a fleeing serpent
  as the enemy advances in force;
they will come against her with axes,
  like men who cut down trees.

²³They will chop down her forest,"
            declares the LORD,
  "dense though it be.
They are more numerous than locusts,
  they cannot be counted.
²⁴The Daughter of Egypt will be put to
    shame,
  handed over to the people of the
    north."

²⁵The LORD Almighty, the God of Israel, says: "I am about to bring punishment on Amon god of Thebes,[b] on Pharaoh, on Egypt and her gods and her kings, and on those who rely on Pharaoh. ²⁶I will hand them over to those who seek their lives, to Nebuchadnezzar king of Babylon and his officers. Later, however, Egypt will be inhabited as in times past," declares the LORD.

²⁷"Do not fear, O Jacob my servant;
  do not be dismayed, O Israel.
I will surely save you out of a distant
    place,
  your descendants from the land of
    their exile.
Jacob will again have peace and
    security,
  and no one will make him afraid.
²⁸Do not fear, O Jacob my servant,
  for I am with you," declares the LORD.
"Though I completely destroy all the
    nations
  among which I scatter you,
  I will not completely destroy you.
I will discipline you but only with
    justice;
  I will not let you go entirely
    unpunished."

A Message About the Philistines

47 This is the word of the LORD that came to Jeremiah the prophet concerning the Philistines before Pharaoh attacked Gaza:

²This is what the LORD says:

"See how the waters are rising in the
    north;
  they will become an overflowing
    torrent.
They will overflow the land and
    everything in it,
  the towns and those who live in
    them.
The people will cry out;
  all who dwell in the land will wail

a14 Hebrew Noph; also in verse 19   b25 Hebrew No

³at the sound of the hoofs of galloping
steeds,
at the noise of enemy chariots
and the rumble of their wheels.
Fathers will not turn to help their
children;
their hands will hang limp.
⁴For the day has come
to destroy all the Philistines
and to cut off all survivors
who could help Tyre and Sidon.
The LORD is about to destroy the
Philistines,
the remnant from the coasts of
Caphtor. *a*
⁵Gaza will shave her head in mourning;
Ashkelon will be silenced.
O remnant on the plain,
how long will you cut yourselves?

⁶" 'Ah, sword of the LORD,' ⌐you cry,⌐
'how long till you rest?
Return to your scabbard;
cease and be still.'
⁷But how can it rest
when the LORD has commanded it,
when he has ordered it
to attack Ashkelon and the coast?"

A Message About Moab

48 Concerning Moab:

This is what the LORD Almighty, the God
of Israel, says:

"Woe to Nebo, for it will be ruined.
Kiriathaim will be disgraced and
captured;
the stronghold *b* will be disgraced
and shattered.
²Moab will be praised no more;
in Heshbon *c* men will plot her
downfall:
'Come, let us put an end to that
nation.'
You too, O Madmen, *d* will be
silenced;
the sword will pursue you.
³Listen to the cries from Horonaim,
cries of great havoc and destruction.
⁴Moab will be broken;
her little ones will cry out. *e*
⁵They go up the way to Luhith,
weeping bitterly as they go;
on the road down to Horonaim
anguished cries over the destruction
are heard.

⁶Flee! Run for your lives;
become like a bush *f* in the desert.
⁷Since you trust in your deeds and
riches,
you too will be taken captive,
and Chemosh will go into exile,
together with his priests and
officials.
⁸The destroyer will come against every
town,
and not a town will escape.
The valley will be ruined
and the plateau destroyed,
because the LORD has spoken.
⁹Put salt on Moab,
for she will be laid waste *g*;
her towns will become desolate,
with no one to live in them.

¹⁰"A curse on him who is lax in doing
the LORD's work!
A curse on him who keeps his
sword from bloodshed!

¹¹"Moab has been at rest from youth,
like wine left on its dregs,
not poured from one jar to another—
she has not gone into exile.
So she tastes as she did,
and her aroma is unchanged.
¹²But days are coming,"
declares the LORD,
"when I will send men who pour from
jars,
and they will pour her out;
they will empty her jars
and smash her jugs.
¹³Then Moab will be ashamed of
Chemosh,
as the house of Israel was ashamed
when they trusted in Bethel.

¹⁴"How can you say, 'We are warriors,
men valiant in battle'?
¹⁵Moab will be destroyed and her towns
invaded;
her finest young men will go down
in the slaughter,"
declares the King, whose name is
the LORD Almighty.
¹⁶"The fall of Moab is at hand;
her calamity will come quickly.
¹⁷Mourn for her, all who live around
her,
all who know her fame;
say, 'How broken is the mighty
scepter,

---

a4 That is, Crete   *b1* Or / Misgab   *c2* The Hebrew for Heshbon sounds like the Hebrew for plot.
d2 The name of the Moabite town Madmen sounds like the Hebrew for be silenced.   *e4* Hebrew;
Septuagint / proclaim it to Zoar   *f6* Or like Aroer   *g9* Or Give wings to Moab, / for she will fly away

how broken the glorious staff!'

18"Come down from your glory
  and sit on the parched ground,
  O inhabitants of the Daughter of
    Dibon,
for he who destroys Moab
  will come up against you
  and ruin your fortified cities.
19Stand by the road and watch,
  you who live in Aroer.
Ask the man fleeing and the woman
    escaping,
  ask them, 'What has happened?'
20Moab is disgraced, for she is
    shattered.
  Wail and cry out!
Announce by the Arnon
  that Moab is destroyed.
21Judgment has come to the plateau—
  to Holon, Jahzah and Mephaath,
22 to Dibon, Nebo and Beth
      Diblathaim,
23 to Kiriathaim, Beth Gamul and Beth
      Meon,
24 to Kerioth and Bozrah—
  to all the towns of Moab, far and
      near.
25Moab's horn[a] is cut off;
  her arm is broken,"
                    declares the LORD.

26"Make her drunk,
  for she has defied the LORD.
Let Moab wallow in her vomit;
  let her be an object of ridicule.
27Was not Israel the object of your
    ridicule?
Was she caught among thieves,
  that you shake your head in scorn
    whenever you speak of her?
28Abandon your towns and dwell among
    the rocks,
  you who live in Moab.
Be like a dove that makes its nest
  at the mouth of a cave.

29"We have heard of Moab's pride—
  her overweening pride and conceit,
  her pride and arrogance
  and the haughtiness of her heart.
30I know her insolence but it is futile,"
                    declares the LORD,
  "and her boasts accomplish nothing.
31Therefore I wail over Moab,
  for all Moab I cry out,
  I moan for the men of Kir Hareseth.
32I weep for you, as Jazer weeps,
  O vines of Sibmah.

Your branches spread as far as the
    sea;
  they reached as far as the sea of
    Jazer.
The destroyer has fallen
  on your ripened fruit and grapes.
33Joy and gladness are gone
  from the orchards and fields of
    Moab.
I have stopped the flow of wine from
    the presses;
  no one treads them with shouts of
    joy.
Although there are shouts,
  they are not shouts of joy.

34"The sound of their cry rises
  from Heshbon to Elealeh and Jahaz,
  from Zoar as far as Horonaim and
    Eglath Shelishiyah,
  for even the waters of Nimrim are
    dried up.
35In Moab I will put an end
  to those who make offerings on the
    high places
  and burn incense to their gods,"
                    declares the LORD.
36"So my heart laments for Moab like a
    flute;
  it laments like a flute for the men of
    Kir Hareseth.
The wealth they acquired is gone.
37Every head is shaved
  and every beard cut off;
  every hand is slashed
  and every waist is covered with
    sackcloth.
38On all the roofs in Moab
  and in the public squares
there is nothing but mourning,
  for I have broken Moab
  like a jar that no one wants,"
                    declares the LORD.
39"How shattered she is! How they wail!
  How Moab turns her back in
    shame!
Moab has become an object of
    ridicule,
  an object of horror to all those
    around her."

40This is what the LORD says:

"Look! An eagle is swooping down,
  spreading its wings over Moab.
41Kerioth[b] will be captured
  and the strongholds taken.
In that day the hearts of Moab's
    warriors

---

a25 *Horn* here symbolizes strength.   b41 Or *The cities*

will be like the heart of a woman in
    labor.
42Moab will be destroyed as a nation
    because she defied the LORD.
43Terror and pit and snare await you,
    O people of Moab,"
                    declares the LORD.
44"Whoever flees from the terror
    will fall into a pit,
whoever climbs out of the pit
    will be caught in a snare;
for I will bring upon Moab
    the year of her punishment,"
                    declares the LORD.

45"In the shadow of Heshbon
    the fugitives stand helpless,
for a fire has gone out from Heshbon,
    a blaze from the midst of Sihon;
it burns the foreheads of Moab,
    the skulls of the noisy boasters.
46Woe to you, O Moab!
    The people of Chemosh are
        destroyed;
your sons are taken into exile
    and your daughters into captivity.

47"Yet I will restore the fortunes of
    Moab
    in days to come,"
                    declares the LORD.

Here ends the judgment on Moab.

A Message About Ammon

49 Concerning the Ammonites:

This is what the LORD says:

"Has Israel no sons?
    Has she no heirs?
Why then has Molech[a] taken
    possession of Gad?
Why do his people live in its towns?
2But the days are coming,"
    declares the LORD,
"when I will sound the battle cry
    against Rabbah of the Ammonites;
it will become a mound of ruins,
    and its surrounding villages will be
        set on fire.
Then Israel will drive out
    those who drove her out,"
                    says the LORD.
3"Wail, O Heshbon, for Ai is destroyed!
    Cry out, O inhabitants of Rabbah!
Put on sackcloth and mourn;
    rush here and there inside the
        walls,
for Molech will go into exile,

together with his priests and
    officials.
4Why do you boast of your valleys,
    boast of your valleys so fruitful?
O unfaithful daughter,
    you trust in your riches and say,
    'Who will attack me?'
5I will bring terror on you
    from all those around you,"
                    declares the Lord,
                    the LORD Almighty.
"Every one of you will be driven
    away,
    and no one will gather the fugitives.

6"Yet afterward, I will restore the
    fortunes of the Ammonites,"
                    declares the LORD.

A Message About Edom

7Concerning Edom:

This is what the LORD Almighty says:

"Is there no longer wisdom in Teman?
    Has counsel perished from the
        prudent?
    Has their wisdom decayed?
8Turn and flee, hide in deep caves,
    you who live in Dedan,
for I will bring disaster on Esau
    at the time I punish him.
9If grape pickers came to you,
    would they not leave a few grapes?
If thieves came during the night,
    would they not steal only as much
        as they wanted?
10But I will strip Esau bare;
    I will uncover his hiding places,
    so that he cannot conceal himself.
His children, relatives and neighbors
    will perish,
    and he will be no more.
11Leave your orphans; I will protect
    their lives.
    Your widows too can trust in me."

12This is what the LORD says: "If those
who do not deserve to drink the cup must
drink it, why should you go unpunished?
You will not go unpunished, but must
drink it. 13I swear by myself," declares the
LORD, "that Bozrah will become a ruin and
an object of horror, of reproach and of
cursing; and all its towns will be in ruins
forever."

14I have heard a message from the LORD:
    An envoy was sent to the nations to
        say,

"Assemble yourselves to attack it!
Rise up for battle!"

¹⁵"Now I will make you small among
the nations,
despised among men.
¹⁶The terror you inspire
and the pride of your heart have
deceived you,
you who live in the clefts of the rocks,
who occupy the heights of the hill.
Though you build your nest as high
as the eagle's,
from there I will bring you down,"
declares the Lord.
¹⁷"Edom will become an object of
horror;
all who pass by will be appalled
and will scoff
because of all its wounds.
¹⁸As Sodom and Gomorrah were
overthrown,
along with their neighboring
towns,"
says the Lord,
"so no one will live there;
no man will dwell in it.

¹⁹"Like a lion coming up from Jordan's
thickets
to a rich pastureland,
I will chase Edom from its land in an
instant.
Who is the chosen one I will
appoint for this?
Who is like me and who can
challenge me?
And what shepherd can stand
against me?"
²⁰Therefore, hear what the Lord has
planned against Edom,
what he has purposed against those
who live in Teman:
The young of the flock will be
dragged away;
he will completely destroy their
pasture because of them.
²¹At the sound of their fall the earth
will tremble;
their cry will resound to the Red
Sea.^a
²²Look! An eagle will soar and swoop
down,
spreading its wings over Bozrah.
In that day the hearts of Edom's
warriors
will be like the heart of a woman in
labor.

A Message About Damascus

²³Concerning Damascus:

"Hamath and Arpad are dismayed,
for they have heard bad news.
They are disheartened,
troubled like^b the restless sea.
²⁴Damascus has become feeble,
she has turned to flee
and panic has gripped her;
anguish and pain have seized her,
pain like that of a woman in labor.
²⁵Why has the city of renown not been
abandoned,
the town in which I delight?
²⁶Surely, her young men will fall in the
streets;
all her soldiers will be silenced in
that day,"
declares the Lord Almighty.
²⁷"I will set fire to the walls of
Damascus;
it will consume the fortresses of
Ben-Hadad."

A Message About Kedar and Hazor

²⁸Concerning Kedar and the kingdoms
of Hazor, which Nebuchadnezzar king of
Babylon attacked:

This is what the Lord says:

"Arise, and attack Kedar
and destroy the people of the East.
²⁹Their tents and their flocks will be
taken;
their shelters will be carried off
with all their goods and camels.
Men will shout to them,
'Terror on every side!'

³⁰"Flee quickly away!
Stay in deep caves, you who live in
Hazor,"
declares the Lord.
"Nebuchadnezzar king of Babylon has
plotted against you;
he has devised a plan against you.

³¹"Arise and attack a nation at ease,
which lives in confidence,"
declares the Lord,
"a nation that has neither gates nor
bars;
its people live alone.
³²Their camels will become plunder,
and their large herds will be booty.
I will scatter to the winds those who
are in distant places^c

---

a21 Hebrew *Yam Suph*; that is, Sea of Reeds   *b23* Hebrew *on* or *by*   *c32* Or *who clip the hair by*
their foreheads

and will bring disaster on them
　　from every side,"
　　　　　　declares the LORD.
[33]"Hazor will become a haunt of jackals,
　　a desolate place forever.
No one will live there;
　　no man will dwell in it."

A Message About Elam

[34]This is the word of the LORD that came
to Jeremiah the prophet concerning Elam,
early in the reign of Zedekiah king of Judah:

[35]This is what the LORD Almighty says:

"See, I will break the bow of Elam,
　　the mainstay of their might.
[36]I will bring against Elam the four
　　winds
　　from the four quarters of the
　　　heavens;
I will scatter them to the four winds,
　　and there will not be a nation
　　where Elam's exiles do not go.
[37]I will shatter Elam before their foes,
　　before those who seek their lives;
I will bring disaster upon them,
　　even my fierce anger,"
　　　　　　declares the LORD.
"I will pursue them with the sword
　　until I have made an end of them.
[38]I will set my throne in Elam
　　and destroy her king and officials,"
　　　　　　declares the LORD.

[39]"Yet I will restore the fortunes of Elam
　　in days to come,"
　　　　　　declares the LORD.

A Message About Babylon

50 This is the word the LORD spoke
through Jeremiah the prophet concerning Babylon and the land of the Babylonians[a]:

[2]"Announce and proclaim among the
　　nations,
　　lift up a banner and proclaim it;
　　keep nothing back, but say,
'Babylon will be captured;
　　Bel will be put to shame,
　　Marduk filled with terror.
Her images will be put to shame
　　and her idols filled with terror.'
[3]A nation from the north will attack
　　her
　　and lay waste her land.
No one will live in it;

both men and animals will flee
　　away.

[4]"In those days, at that time,"
　　declares the LORD,
"the people of Israel and the people of
　　Judah together
will go in tears to seek the LORD
　　their God.
[5]They will ask the way to Zion
　　and turn their faces toward it.
They will come and bind themselves
　　to the LORD
in an everlasting covenant
　　that will not be forgotten.

[6]"My people have been lost sheep;
　　their shepherds have led them
　　　astray
　　and caused them to roam on the
　　　mountains.
They wandered over mountain and
　　hill
　　and forgot their own resting place.
[7]Whoever found them devoured them;
　　their enemies said, 'We are not
　　　guilty,
for they sinned against the LORD, their
　　true pasture,
　　the LORD, the hope of their fathers.'

[8]"Flee out of Babylon;
　　leave the land of the Babylonians,
　　and be like the goats that lead the
　　　flock.
[9]For I will stir up and bring against
　　Babylon
　　an alliance of great nations from the
　　　land of the north.
They will take up their positions
　　against her,
　　and from the north she will be
　　　captured.
Their arrows will be like skilled
　　warriors
　　who do not return empty-handed.
[10]So Babylonia[b] will be plundered;
　　all who plunder her will have their
　　　fill,"
　　　　　　declares the LORD.

[11]"Because you rejoice and are glad,
　　you who pillage my inheritance,
because you frolic like a heifer
　　threshing grain
　　and neigh like stallions,
[12]your mother will be greatly ashamed;
　　she who gave you birth will be
　　　disgraced.
She will be the least of the nations—

---

[a]1 Or *Chaldeans*; also in verses 8, 25, 35 and 45　　[b]10 Or *Chaldea*

a wilderness, a dry land, a desert.
¹³Because of the LORD's anger she will
not be inhabited
but will be completely desolate.
All who pass Babylon will be horrified
and scoff
because of all her wounds.

¹⁴"Take up your positions around
Babylon,
all you who draw the bow.
Shoot at her! Spare no arrows,
for she has sinned against the LORD.
¹⁵Shout against her on every side!
She surrenders, her towers fall,
her walls are torn down.
Since this is the vengeance of the
LORD,
take vengeance on her;
do to her as she has done to others.
¹⁶Cut off from Babylon the sower,
and the reaper with his sickle at
harvest.
Because of the sword of the oppressor
let everyone return to his own
people,
let everyone flee to his own land.

¹⁷"Israel is a scattered flock
that lions have chased away.
The first to devour him
was the king of Assyria;
the last to crush his bones
was Nebuchadnezzar king of
Babylon."

¹⁸Therefore this is what the LORD Almighty, the God of Israel, says:

"I will punish the king of Babylon and
his land
as I punished the king of Assyria.
¹⁹But I will bring Israel back to his own
pasture
and he will graze on Carmel and
Bashan;
his appetite will be satisfied
on the hills of Ephraim and Gilead.
²⁰In those days, at that time,"
declares the LORD,
"search will be made for Israel's guilt,
but there will be none,
and for the sins of Judah,
but none will be found,
for I will forgive the remnant I
spare.

²¹"Attack the land of Merathaim
and those who live in Pekod.

Pursue, kill and completely destroy[a]
them,"
declares the LORD.
"Do everything I have commanded
you.
²²The noise of battle is in the land,
the noise of great destruction!
²³How broken and shattered
is the hammer of the whole earth!
How desolate is Babylon
among the nations!
²⁴I set a trap for you, O Babylon,
and you were caught before you
knew it;
you were found and captured
because you opposed the LORD.
²⁵The LORD has opened his arsenal
and brought out the weapons of his
wrath,
for the Sovereign LORD Almighty has
work to do
in the land of the Babylonians.
²⁶Come against her from afar.
Break open her granaries;
pile her up like heaps of grain.
Completely destroy her
and leave her no remnant.
²⁷Kill all her young bulls;
let them go down to the slaughter!
Woe to them! For their day has come,
the time for them to be punished.
²⁸Listen to the fugitives and refugees
from Babylon
declaring in Zion
how the LORD our God has taken
vengeance,
vengeance for his temple.

²⁹"Summon archers against Babylon,
all those who draw the bow.
Encamp all around her;
let no one escape.
Repay her for her deeds;
do to her as she has done.
For she has defied the LORD,
the Holy One of Israel.
³⁰Therefore, her young men will fall in
the streets;
all her soldiers will be silenced in
that day,"
declares the LORD.
³¹"See, I am against you, O arrogant
one,"
declares the Lord, the LORD
Almighty,
"for your day has come,
the time for you to be punished.

---

*a21 The Hebrew term refers to the irrevocable giving over of things or persons to the LORD, often by
totally destroying them; also in verse 26.*

³²The arrogant one will stumble and fall
   and no one will help her up;
I will kindle a fire in her towns
   that will consume all who are
     around her."

³³This is what the Lord Almighty says:

"The people of Israel are oppressed,

and the people of Judah as well.
All their captors hold them fast,
   refusing to let them go.
³⁴Yet their Redeemer is strong;
   the Lord Almighty is his name.
He will vigorously defend their cause
   so that he may bring rest to their
     land,

THURSDAY

VERSE FOR THE DAY:	AUTHOR:	PASSAGE FOR THE DAY:
Jeremiah 50:20	Tom Landry	Jeremiah 50:18–20

Reaching Your Potential

THINK for a moment about the factors that most often prevent anyone from reaching his or her greatest potential—in whatever the field. In my experience as a football coach, I've seen two common barriers that most often prevent people from performing to their fullest potential. The first is a pattern of past failures and past mistakes. The second thing holding people back is a fear of failure.

The basic tenets of Christianity address both those problems and remove both barriers. As a Christian I believe my past is forgiven; I can start over with a clean slate. The mistakes of the past need not hold me back. Neither does my fear of failure—because as a Christian I believe God is in ultimate control of my life. While that doesn't mean I'll always win the championship or never get fired, it means I can believe the promises of Romans 8:28, which says God can bring good out of every experience for those who trust in him. So I don't need to worry about failing.

Without the burden of past mistakes or anxiety about failing in the future, I'm free to concentrate on doing my very best in the present. And I believe that's how a real, personal Christian faith can make it easier for anyone to reach his or her highest potential.

Having said that, I realize a lot of people think the idea of a "personal relationship" with God sounds disturbingly exclusive, somehow presumptive, and more than a little pious. I thought the same thing before I read what the Bible said and decided to become a Christian.

According to the Bible, this idea of having a personal relationship with God isn't at all presumptive. It was God's idea. And it's not at all exclusive. It's available to anyone who accepts God's offer.

Additional Scripture Readings:
Isaiah 55:1–7; Romans 10:1–13

*Go to page 856 for your next
devotional reading.*

but unrest to those who live in
Babylon.

[35]"A sword against the Babylonians!"
declares the Lord—
"against those who live in Babylon
and against her officials and wise
men!
[36]A sword against her false prophets!
They will become fools.
A sword against her warriors!
They will be filled with terror.
[37]A sword against her horses and
chariots
and all the foreigners in her ranks!
They will become women.
A sword against her treasures!
They will be plundered.
[38]A drought on[a] her waters!
They will dry up.
For it is a land of idols,
idols that will go mad with terror.

[39]"So desert creatures and hyenas will
live there,
and there the owl will dwell.
It will never again be inhabited
or lived in from generation to
generation.
[40]As God overthrew Sodom and
Gomorrah
along with their neighboring
towns,"
declares the Lord,
"so no one will live there;
no man will dwell in it.

[41]"Look! An army is coming from the
north;
a great nation and many kings
are being stirred up from the ends
of the earth.
[42]They are armed with bows and spears;
they are cruel and without mercy.
They sound like the roaring sea
as they ride on their horses;
they come like men in battle
formation
to attack you, O Daughter of
Babylon.
[43]The king of Babylon has heard reports
about them,
and his hands hang limp.
Anguish has gripped him,
pain like that of a woman in labor.
[44]Like a lion coming up from Jordan's
thickets

to a rich pastureland,
I will chase Babylon from its land in
an instant.
Who is the chosen one I will
appoint for this?
Who is like me and who can
challenge me?
And what shepherd can stand
against me?"
[45]Therefore, hear what the Lord has
planned against Babylon,
what he has purposed against the
land of the Babylonians:
The young of the flock will be
dragged away;
he will completely destroy their
pasture because of them.
[46]At the sound of Babylon's capture the
earth will tremble;
its cry will resound among the
nations.

51

This is what the Lord says:

"See, I will stir up the spirit of a
destroyer
against Babylon and the people of
Leb Kamai.[b]
[2]I will send foreigners to Babylon
to winnow her and to devastate her
land;
they will oppose her on every side
in the day of her disaster.
[3]Let not the archer string his bow,
nor let him put on his armor.
Do not spare her young men;
completely destroy[c] her army.
[4]They will fall down slain in Babylon,[d]
fatally wounded in her streets.
[5]For Israel and Judah have not been
forsaken
by their God, the Lord Almighty,
though their land[e] is full of guilt
before the Holy One of Israel.

[6]"Flee from Babylon!
Run for your lives!
Do not be destroyed because of her
sins.
It is time for the Lord's vengeance;
he will pay her what she deserves.
[7]Babylon was a gold cup in the Lord's
hand;
she made the whole earth drunk.
The nations drank her wine;
therefore they have now gone mad.

---

[a]38 Or A sword against   [b]1 Leb Kamai is a cryptogram for Chaldea, that is, Babylonia.   [c]3 The
Hebrew term refers to the irrevocable giving over of things or persons to the Lord, often by totally
destroying them.   [d]4 Or Chaldea   [e]5 Or / and the land of the Babylonians

⁸Babylon will suddenly fall and be
broken.
Wail over her!
Get balm for her pain;
perhaps she can be healed.

⁹" 'We would have healed Babylon,
but she cannot be healed;
let us leave her and each go to his
own land,
for her judgment reaches to the
skies,
it rises as high as the clouds.'

¹⁰" 'The LORD has vindicated us;
come, let us tell in Zion
what the LORD our God has done.'

¹¹"Sharpen the arrows,
take up the shields!
The LORD has stirred up the kings of
the Medes,
because his purpose is to destroy
Babylon.
The LORD will take vengeance,
vengeance for his temple.
¹²Lift up a banner against the walls of
Babylon!
Reinforce the guard,
station the watchmen,
prepare an ambush!
The LORD will carry out his purpose,
his decree against the people of
Babylon.
¹³You who live by many waters
and are rich in treasures,
your end has come,
the time for you to be cut off.
¹⁴The LORD Almighty has sworn by
himself:
I will surely fill you with men, as
with a swarm of locusts,
and they will shout in triumph over
you.

¹⁵"He made the earth by his power;
he founded the world by his
wisdom
and stretched out the heavens by
his understanding.
¹⁶When he thunders, the waters in the
heavens roar;
he makes clouds rise from the ends
of the earth.
He sends lightning with the rain
and brings out the wind from his
storehouses.

¹⁷"Every man is senseless and without
knowledge;
every goldsmith is shamed by his
idols.
His images are a fraud;
they have no breath in them.
¹⁸They are worthless, the objects of
mockery;
when their judgment comes, they
will perish.
¹⁹He who is the Portion of Jacob is not
like these,
for he is the Maker of all things,
including the tribe of his
inheritance—
the LORD Almighty is his name.

²⁰"You are my war club,
my weapon for battle—
with you I shatter nations,
with you I destroy kingdoms,
²¹with you I shatter horse and rider,
with you I shatter chariot and
driver,
²²with you I shatter man and woman,
with you I shatter old man and
youth,
with you I shatter young man and
maiden,
²³with you I shatter shepherd and flock,
with you I shatter farmer and oxen,
with you I shatter governors and
officials.

²⁴"Before your eyes I will repay Babylon
and all who live in Babyloniaᵃ for all the
wrong they have done in Zion," declares
the LORD.

²⁵"I am against you, O destroying
mountain,
you who destroy the whole earth,"
declares the LORD.
"I will stretch out my hand against
you,
roll you off the cliffs,
and make you a burned-out
mountain.
²⁶No rock will be taken from you for a
cornerstone,
nor any stone for a foundation,
for you will be desolate forever,"
declares the LORD.

²⁷"Lift up a banner in the land!
Blow the trumpet among the
nations!
Prepare the nations for battle against
her;
summon against her these
kingdoms:
Ararat, Minni and Ashkenaz.

ᵃ24 Or *Chaldea*; also in verse 35

Appoint a commander against her;
 send up horses like a swarm of
  locusts.
28Prepare the nations for battle against
  her—
 the kings of the Medes,
 their governors and all their officials,
 and all the countries they rule.
29The land trembles and writhes,
 for the LORD's purposes against
  Babylon stand—
to lay waste the land of Babylon
 so that no one will live there.
30Babylon's warriors have stopped
  fighting;
 they remain in their strongholds.
Their strength is exhausted;
 they have become like women.
Her dwellings are set on fire;
 the bars of her gates are broken.
31One courier follows another
 and messenger follows messenger
to announce to the king of Babylon
 that his entire city is captured,
32the river crossings seized,
 the marshes set on fire,
 and the soldiers terrified."

33This is what the LORD Almighty, the
God of Israel, says:

"The Daughter of Babylon is like a
  threshing floor
 at the time it is trampled;
 the time to harvest her will soon
  come."

34"Nebuchadnezzar king of Babylon has
  devoured us,
 he has thrown us into confusion,
 he has made us an empty jar.
Like a serpent he has swallowed us
 and filled his stomach with our
  delicacies,
 and then has spewed us out.
35May the violence done to our flesh[a]
  be upon Babylon,"
 say the inhabitants of Zion.
"May our blood be on those who live
  in Babylonia,"
 says Jerusalem.

36Therefore, this is what the LORD says:

"See, I will defend your cause
 and avenge you;
I will dry up her sea
 and make her springs dry.
37Babylon will be a heap of ruins,
 a haunt of jackals,

an object of horror and scorn,
 a place where no one lives.
38Her people all roar like young lions,
 they growl like lion cubs.
39But while they are aroused,
 I will set out a feast for them
 and make them drunk,
 so that they shout with laughter—
 then sleep forever and not awake,"
                     declares the LORD.
40"I will bring them down
 like lambs to the slaughter,
 like rams and goats.

41"How Sheshach[b] will be captured,
 the boast of the whole earth seized!
What a horror Babylon will be
 among the nations!
42The sea will rise over Babylon;
 its roaring waves will cover her.
43Her towns will be desolate,
 a dry and desert land,
a land where no one lives,
 through which no man travels.
44I will punish Bel in Babylon
 and make him spew out what he
  has swallowed.
The nations will no longer stream to
  him.
 And the wall of Babylon will fall.

45"Come out of her, my people!
 Run for your lives!
 Run from the fierce anger of the
  LORD.
46Do not lose heart or be afraid
 when rumors are heard in the land;
one rumor comes this year, another
  the next,
 rumors of violence in the land
 and of ruler against ruler.
47For the time will surely come
 when I will punish the idols of
  Babylon;
her whole land will be disgraced
 and her slain will all lie fallen
  within her.
48Then heaven and earth and all that is
  in them
 will shout for joy over Babylon,
for out of the north
 destroyers will attack her,"
                     declares the LORD.

49"Babylon must fall because of Israel's
  slain,
 just as the slain in all the earth
 have fallen because of Babylon.
50You who have escaped the sword,

---

a35 Or done to us and to our children   *b41 Sheshach is a cryptogram for Babylon.*

leave and do not linger!
Remember the LORD in a distant land,
and think on Jerusalem."

51"We are disgraced,
for we have been insulted
and shame covers our faces,
because foreigners have entered
the holy places of the LORD's
house."

52"But days are coming," declares the
LORD,
"when I will punish her idols,
and throughout her land
the wounded will groan.
53Even if Babylon reaches the sky
and fortifies her lofty stronghold,
I will send destroyers against her,"
declares the LORD.

54"The sound of a cry comes from
Babylon,
the sound of great destruction
from the land of the Babylonians.*a*
55The LORD will destroy Babylon;
he will silence her noisy din.
Waves ʼof enemiesʼ will rage like great
waters;
the roar of their voices will resound.
56A destroyer will come against
Babylon;
her warriors will be captured,
and their bows will be broken.
For the LORD is a God of retribution;
he will repay in full.
57I will make her officials and wise men
drunk,
her governors, officers and warriors
as well;
they will sleep forever and not
awake,"
declares the King, whose name is
the LORD Almighty.

58This is what the LORD Almighty says:

"Babylon's thick wall will be leveled
and her high gates set on fire;
the peoples exhaust themselves for
nothing,
the nations' labor is only fuel for
the flames."

59This is the message Jeremiah gave to
the staff officer Seraiah son of Neriah, the
son of Mahseiah, when he went to Babylon with Zedekiah king of Judah in the
fourth year of his reign. 60Jeremiah had
written on a scroll about all the disasters
that would come upon Babylon—all that
had been recorded concerning Babylon.
61He said to Seraiah, "When you get to
Babylon, see that you read all these words
aloud. 62Then say, 'O LORD, you have said
you will destroy this place, so that neither
man nor animal will live in it; it will be
desolate forever.' 63When you finish reading this scroll, tie a stone to it and throw
it into the Euphrates. 64Then say, 'So will
Babylon sink to rise no more because of
the disaster I will bring upon her. And her
people will fall.' "

The words of Jeremiah end here.

The Fall of Jerusalem

52 Zedekiah was twenty-one years old
when he became king, and he
reigned in Jerusalem eleven years. His
mother's name was Hamutal daughter of
Jeremiah; she was from Libnah. 2He did
evil in the eyes of the LORD, just as Jehoiakim had done. 3It was because of the
LORD's anger that all this happened to Jerusalem and Judah, and in the end he
thrust them from his presence.

Now Zedekiah rebelled against the king
of Babylon.

4So in the ninth year of Zedekiah's
reign, on the tenth day of the tenth month,
Nebuchadnezzar king of Babylon
marched against Jerusalem with his
whole army. They camped outside the
city and built siege works all around it.
5The city was kept under siege until the
eleventh year of King Zedekiah.

6By the ninth day of the fourth month
the famine in the city had become so severe that there was no food for the people
to eat. 7Then the city wall was broken
through, and the whole army fled. They
left the city at night through the gate between the two walls near the king's garden, though the Babylonians*b* were surrounding the city. They fled toward the
Arabah,*c* 8but the Babylonian*d* army
pursued King Zedekiah and overtook him
in the plains of Jericho. All his soldiers
were separated from him and scattered,
9and he was captured.

He was taken to the king of Babylon at
Riblah in the land of Hamath, where he
pronounced sentence on him. 10There at
Riblah the king of Babylon slaughtered
the sons of Zedekiah before his eyes; he
also killed all the officials of Judah.

---

*a*54 Or *Chaldeans*   *b*7 Or *Chaldeans*; also in verse 17   *c*7 Or *the Jordan Valley*   *d*8 Or *Chaldean*;
also in verse 14

[11]Then he put out Zedekiah's eyes, bound him with bronze shackles and took him to Babylon, where he put him in prison till the day of his death.

[12]On the tenth day of the fifth month, in the nineteenth year of Nebuchadnezzar king of Babylon, Nebuzaradan commander of the imperial guard, who served the king of Babylon, came to Jerusalem. [13]He set fire to the temple of the LORD, the royal palace and all the houses of Jerusalem. Every important building he burned down. [14]The whole Babylonian army under the commander of the imperial guard broke down all the walls around Jerusalem. [15]Nebuzaradan the commander of the guard carried into exile some of the poorest people and those who remained in the city, along with the rest of the craftsmen[a] and those who had gone over to the king of Babylon. [16]But Nebuzaradan left behind the rest of the poorest people of the land to work the vineyards and fields.

[17]The Babylonians broke up the bronze pillars, the movable stands and the bronze Sea that were at the temple of the LORD and they carried all the bronze to Babylon. [18]They also took away the pots, shovels, wick trimmers, sprinkling bowls, dishes and all the bronze articles used in the temple service. [19]The commander of the imperial guard took away the basins, censers, sprinkling bowls, pots, lampstands, dishes and bowls used for drink offerings — all that were made of pure gold or silver.

[20]The bronze from the two pillars, the Sea and the twelve bronze bulls under it, and the movable stands, which King Solomon had made for the temple of the LORD, was more than could be weighed. [21]Each of the pillars was eighteen cubits high and twelve cubits in circumference[b]; each was four fingers thick, and hollow. [22]The bronze capital on top of the one pillar was five cubits[c] high and was decorated with a network and pomegranates of bronze all around. The other pillar, with its pomegranates, was similar. [23]There were ninety-six pomegranates on the sides; the total number of pomegranates above the surrounding network was a hundred.

[24]The commander of the guard took as prisoners Seraiah the chief priest, Zephaniah the priest next in rank and the three doorkeepers. [25]Of those still in the city, he took the officer in charge of the fighting men, and seven royal advisers. He also took the secretary who was chief officer in charge of conscripting the people of the land and sixty of his men who were found in the city. [26]Nebuzaradan the commander took them all and brought them to the king of Babylon at Riblah. [27]There at Riblah, in the land of Hamath, the king had them executed.

So Judah went into captivity, away from her land. [28]This is the number of the people Nebuchadnezzar carried into exile:

in the seventh year, 3,023 Jews;
[29]in Nebuchadnezzar's eighteenth year, 832 people from Jerusalem;
[30]in his twenty-third year, 745 Jews taken into exile by Nebuzaradan the commander of the imperial guard.
There were 4,600 people in all.

Jehoiachin Released

[31]In the thirty-seventh year of the exile of Jehoiachin king of Judah, in the year Evil-Merodach[d] became king of Babylon, he released Jehoiachin king of Judah and freed him from prison on the twenty-fifth day of the twelfth month. [32]He spoke kindly to him and gave him a seat of honor higher than those of the other kings who were with him in Babylon. [33]So Jehoiachin put aside his prison clothes and for the rest of his life ate regularly at the king's table. [34]Day by day the king of Babylon gave Jehoiachin a regular allowance as long as he lived, till the day of his death.

---

[a]15 Or *populace* [b]21 That is, about 27 feet (about 8.1 meters) high and 18 feet (about 5.4 meters) in circumference [c]22 That is, about 7 1/2 feet (about 2.3 meters) [d]31 Also called *Amel-Marduk*

JEREMIAH writes these laments as he watches the intense suffering of God's people and the utter devastation of Jerusalem and the temple. He does not question God's justice in sending this suffering; instead, in the middle of the suffering, he celebrates God's faithfulness and unfailing love (Lamentations 3:22–32). As you read this book, think about what Jesus suffered to pay the penalty for your sins and rejoice in the incredible love of the God who offers you salvation.

LAMENTATIONS

1ᵃ How deserted lies the city,
   once so full of people!
How like a widow is she,
   who once was great among the
      nations!
She who was queen among the
      provinces
   has now become a slave.

²Bitterly she weeps at night,
   tears are upon her cheeks.
Among all her lovers

there is none to comfort her.
All her friends have betrayed her;
   they have become her enemies.

³After affliction and harsh labor,
   Judah has gone into exile.
She dwells among the nations;
   she finds no resting place.
All who pursue her have overtaken
      her
   in the midst of her distress.

⁴The roads to Zion mourn,

ᵃThis chapter is an acrostic poem, the verses of which begin with the successive letters of the Hebrew alphabet.

for no one comes to her appointed
feasts.
All her gateways are desolate,
her priests groan,
her maidens grieve,
and she is in bitter anguish.

[5]Her foes have become her masters;
her enemies are at ease.
The LORD has brought her grief
because of her many sins.
Her children have gone into exile,
captive before the foe.

[6]All the splendor has departed
from the Daughter of Zion.
Her princes are like deer
that find no pasture;
in weakness they have fled
before the pursuer.

[7]In the days of her affliction and
wandering
Jerusalem remembers all the
treasures
that were hers in days of old.
When her people fell into enemy
hands,
there was no one to help her.
Her enemies looked at her
and laughed at her destruction.

[8]Jerusalem has sinned greatly
and so has become unclean.
All who honored her despise her,
for they have seen her nakedness;
she herself groans
and turns away.

[9]Her filthiness clung to her skirts;
she did not consider her future.
Her fall was astounding;
there was none to comfort her.
"Look, O LORD, on my affliction,
for the enemy has triumphed."

[10]The enemy laid hands
on all her treasures;
she saw pagan nations
enter her sanctuary—
those you had forbidden
to enter your assembly.

[11]All her people groan
as they search for bread;
they barter their treasures for food
to keep themselves alive.
"Look, O LORD, and consider,
for I am despised."

[12]"Is it nothing to you, all you who pass
by?
Look around and see.
Is any suffering like my suffering
that was inflicted on me,
that the LORD brought on me
in the day of his fierce anger?

[13]"From on high he sent fire,
sent it down into my bones.
He spread a net for my feet
and turned me back.
He made me desolate,
faint all the day long.

[14]"My sins have been bound into a
yoke[a];
by his hands they were woven
together.
They have come upon my neck
and the Lord has sapped my
strength.
He has handed me over
to those I cannot withstand.

[15]"The Lord has rejected
all the warriors in my midst;
he has summoned an army against me
to[b] crush my young men.
In his winepress the Lord has
trampled
the Virgin Daughter of Judah.

[16]"This is why I weep
and my eyes overflow with tears.
No one is near to comfort me,
no one to restore my spirit.
My children are destitute
because the enemy has prevailed."

[17]Zion stretches out her hands,
but there is no one to comfort her.
The LORD has decreed for Jacob
that his neighbors become his foes;
Jerusalem has become
an unclean thing among them.

[18]"The LORD is righteous,
yet I rebelled against his command.
Listen, all you peoples;
look upon my suffering.
My young men and maidens
have gone into exile.

[19]"I called to my allies
but they betrayed me.
My priests and my elders
perished in the city
while they searched for food
to keep themselves alive.

---

[a]14 Most Hebrew manuscripts; Septuagint *He kept watch over my sins*   [b]15 Or *has set a time for me /*
when he will

20"See, O Lord, how distressed I am!
    I am in torment within,
and in my heart I am disturbed,
    for I have been most rebellious.
Outside, the sword bereaves;
    inside, there is only death.

21"People have heard my groaning,
    but there is no one to comfort me.
All my enemies have heard of my
        distress;
    they rejoice at what you have done.
May you bring the day you have
        announced
    so they may become like me.

22"Let all their wickedness come before
        you;
    deal with them
as you have dealt with me
    because of all my sins.
My groans are many
    and my heart is faint."

2^a How the Lord has covered the
        Daughter of Zion
    with the cloud of his anger^b!
He has hurled down the splendor of
        Israel
    from heaven to earth;
he has not remembered his footstool
    in the day of his anger.

2Without pity the Lord has swallowed
        up
    all the dwellings of Jacob;
in his wrath he has torn down
    the strongholds of the Daughter of
        Judah.
He has brought her kingdom and its
        princes
    down to the ground in dishonor.

3In fierce anger he has cut off
    every horn^c of Israel.
He has withdrawn his right hand
    at the approach of the enemy.
He has burned in Jacob like a flaming
        fire
    that consumes everything around it.

4Like an enemy he has strung his bow;
    his right hand is ready.
Like a foe he has slain
    all who were pleasing to the eye;
he has poured out his wrath like fire
    on the tent of the Daughter of Zion.

5The Lord is like an enemy;

he has swallowed up Israel.
He has swallowed up all her palaces
    and destroyed her strongholds.
He has multiplied mourning and
        lamentation
    for the Daughter of Judah.

6He has laid waste his dwelling like a
        garden;
    he has destroyed his place of
        meeting.
The Lord has made Zion forget
    her appointed feasts and her
        Sabbaths;
in his fierce anger he has spurned
    both king and priest.

7The Lord has rejected his altar
    and abandoned his sanctuary.
He has handed over to the enemy
    the walls of her palaces;
they have raised a shout in the house
        of the Lord
    as on the day of an appointed feast.

8The Lord determined to tear down
    the wall around the Daughter of
        Zion.
He stretched out a measuring line
    and did not withhold his hand from
        destroying.
He made ramparts and walls lament;
    together they wasted away.

9Her gates have sunk into the ground;
    their bars he has broken and
        destroyed.
Her king and her princes are exiled
    among the nations,
    the law is no more,
and her prophets no longer find
    visions from the Lord.

10The elders of the Daughter of Zion
    sit on the ground in silence;
they have sprinkled dust on their
        heads
    and put on sackcloth.
The young women of Jerusalem
    have bowed their heads to the
        ground.

11My eyes fail from weeping,
    I am in torment within,
my heart is poured out on the ground
    because my people are destroyed,
because children and infants faint
    in the streets of the city.

---

^aThis chapter is an acrostic poem, the verses of which begin with the successive letters of the Hebrew
alphabet.   ^b1 Or *How the Lord in his anger / has treated the Daughter of Zion with contempt*   ^c3 Or
/ *all the strength*; or *every king*; *horn* here symbolizes strength.

¹²They say to their mothers,
  "Where is bread and wine?"
as they faint like wounded men
  in the streets of the city,
as their lives ebb away
  in their mothers' arms.

¹³What can I say for you?
  With what can I compare you,
  O Daughter of Jerusalem?
To what can I liken you,
  that I may comfort you,
  O Virgin Daughter of Zion?
Your wound is as deep as the sea.
  Who can heal you?

¹⁴The visions of your prophets
  were false and worthless;
they did not expose your sin
  to ward off your captivity.
The oracles they gave you
  were false and misleading.

¹⁵All who pass your way
  clap their hands at you;
they scoff and shake their heads
  at the Daughter of Jerusalem:
"Is this the city that was called
  the perfection of beauty,
  the joy of the whole earth?"

¹⁶All your enemies open their mouths
  wide against you;
they scoff and gnash their teeth
  and say, "We have swallowed her
    up.
This is the day we have waited for;
  we have lived to see it."

¹⁷The LORD has done what he planned;
  he has fulfilled his word,
  which he decreed long ago.
He has overthrown you without pity,
  he has let the enemy gloat over
    you,
  he has exalted the horn^a of your
    foes.

¹⁸The hearts of the people
  cry out to the Lord.
O wall of the Daughter of Zion,
  let your tears flow like a river
  day and night;
give yourself no relief,
  your eyes no rest.

¹⁹Arise, cry out in the night,
  as the watches of the night begin;
pour out your heart like water

in the presence of the Lord.
Lift up your hands to him
  for the lives of your children,
who faint from hunger
  at the head of every street.

²⁰"Look, O LORD, and consider:
  Whom have you ever treated like
    this?
Should women eat their offspring,
  the children they have cared for?
Should priest and prophet be killed
  in the sanctuary of the Lord?

²¹"Young and old lie together
  in the dust of the streets;
my young men and maidens
  have fallen by the sword.
You have slain them in the day of
    your anger;
  you have slaughtered them without
    pity.

²²"As you summon to a feast day,
  so you summoned against me
    terrors on every side.
In the day of the LORD's anger
  no one escaped or survived;
those I cared for and reared,
  my enemy has destroyed."

3 ^b I am the man who has seen
    affliction
  by the rod of his wrath.
²He has driven me away and made me
    walk
  in darkness rather than light;
³indeed, he has turned his hand against
    me
  again and again, all day long.

⁴He has made my skin and my flesh
    grow old
  and has broken my bones.
⁵He has besieged me and surrounded
    me
  with bitterness and hardship.
⁶He has made me dwell in darkness
  like those long dead.

⁷He has walled me in so I cannot
    escape;
  he has weighed me down with
    chains.
⁸Even when I call out or cry for help,
  he shuts out my prayer.
⁹He has barred my way with blocks of
    stone;

---

^a 17 *Horn* here symbolizes strength.   ^b This chapter is an acrostic poem; the verses of each stanza begin
with the successive letters of the Hebrew alphabet, and the verses within each stanza begin with the same
letter.

he has made my paths crooked.

¹⁰Like a bear lying in wait,
  like a lion in hiding,
¹¹he dragged me from the path and
      mangled me
  and left me without help.
¹²He drew his bow
  and made me the target for his
      arrows.
¹³He pierced my heart
  with arrows from his quiver.

¹⁴I became the laughingstock of all my
      people;
  they mock me in song all day
      long.
¹⁵He has filled me with bitter herbs
  and sated me with gall.
¹⁶He has broken my teeth with gravel;
  he has trampled me in the dust.
¹⁷I have been deprived of peace;
  I have forgotten what prosperity is.
¹⁸So I say, "My splendor is gone

FRIDAY

VERSE FOR THE DAY:	*AUTHOR:*	*PASSAGE FOR THE DAY:*
Lamentations 3:25	Charles Stanley	Lamentations 3:19–27

Unfailing Compassion

[MANY believers come to God] confident of only one thing —they have blown it, they have done something wrong and forgotten to ask God to forgive them. They know all about the substitutionary death of Christ and all that, but they picture God as an angry old man who just puts up with them. I have talked with folks who even make a differentiation between Christ's attitude toward them and the Father's. They view Christ as the Friend who is working to hold back the wrath of God the Father. They understand Christ's role, as the One who paid for their sins, to mean that he is the only One preventing God from giving them what they really deserve. The assumption is that God wished he could give them what they deserve, in spite of Christ.

You may never have pictured God the Father exactly like that. But how do you picture him when you think about your sin . . . Like most Christians, you would probably acknowledge that God loves you. But do you think he likes you? Or do you think he just puts up with you because, after all, his Son did die for you? . . .

Our heavenly Father desires to have fellowship with each of us. He desired that while we were still sinners, still separated by the debt of sin. Paul writes, "But God demonstrates his own love for us in this: While we were still sinners, Christ died for us" (Romans 5:8). Until all aspects of this verse sink deep into our emotional being, we will never be free of the feelings of condemnation that accompany sin. The strategy that secured our forgiveness was God's idea: he initiated it. He wants us for his very own.

Additional Scripture Readings:
Psalm 103:1–18; Romans 5:6–8

Go to page 858 for your next devotional reading.

and all that I had hoped from the
LORD."

19I remember my affliction and my
wandering,
  the bitterness and the gall.
20I well remember them,
  and my soul is downcast within me.
21Yet this I call to mind
  and therefore I have hope:

22Because of the LORD's great love we
are not consumed,
  for his compassions never fail.
23They are new every morning;
  great is your faithfulness.
24I say to myself, "The LORD is my
portion;
  therefore I will wait for him."

25The LORD is good to those whose hope
is in him,
  to the one who seeks him;
26it is good to wait quietly
  for the salvation of the LORD.
27It is good for a man to bear the yoke
  while he is young.

28Let him sit alone in silence,
  for the LORD has laid it on him.
29Let him bury his face in the dust—
  there may yet be hope.
30Let him offer his cheek to one who
would strike him,
  and let him be filled with disgrace.

31For men are not cast off
  by the Lord forever.
32Though he brings grief, he will show
compassion,
  so great is his unfailing love.
33For he does not willingly bring
affliction
  or grief to the children of men.

34To crush underfoot
  all prisoners in the land,
35to deny a man his rights
  before the Most High,
36to deprive a man of justice—
  would not the Lord see such things?

37Who can speak and have it happen
  if the Lord has not decreed it?
38Is it not from the mouth of the Most
High
  that both calamities and good things
  come?
39Why should any living man complain
  when punished for his sins?

40Let us examine our ways and test
them,
  and let us return to the LORD.

41Let us lift up our hearts and our
hands
  to God in heaven, and say:
42"We have sinned and rebelled
  and you have not forgiven.

43"You have covered yourself with anger
and pursued us;
  you have slain without pity.
44You have covered yourself with a
cloud
  so that no prayer can get through.
45You have made us scum and refuse
  among the nations.

46"All our enemies have opened their
mouths
  wide against us.
47We have suffered terror and pitfalls,
  ruin and destruction."
48Streams of tears flow from my eyes
  because my people are destroyed.

49My eyes will flow unceasingly,
  without relief,
50until the LORD looks down
  from heaven and sees.
51What I see brings grief to my soul
  because of all the women of my
  city.

52Those who were my enemies without
cause
  hunted me like a bird.
53They tried to end my life in a pit
  and threw stones at me;
54the waters closed over my head,
  and I thought I was about to be cut
  off.

55I called on your name, O LORD,
  from the depths of the pit.
56You heard my plea: "Do not close
your ears
  to my cry for relief."
57You came near when I called you,
  and you said, "Do not fear."

58O Lord, you took up my case;
  you redeemed my life.
59You have seen, O LORD, the wrong
done to me.
  Uphold my cause!
60You have seen the depth of their
vengeance,
  all their plots against me.

61O LORD, you have heard their insults,
  all their plots against me—
62what my enemies whisper and mutter
  against me all day long.
63Look at them! Sitting or standing,
  they mock me in their songs.

WEEKENDING

RENEW

Grief is lessened when we have an eternal
center for our lives. The good news of the Bible
is simply this: men and women may have a
relationship with the eternal God through faith
in Jesus Christ. Putting it another way, Jesus
Christ himself may become the hub of our
entire life . . .

A well-loved king of Israel wrote, "Even
though I walk through the valley of the shadow
of death, . . . you are with me" [Psalm 23:4]. In
that relationship with God, experienced by
thousands of men and women like ourselves,
can be found a hub that no experience in life
can destroy.

– Haddon W. Robinson

REVIVE

Saturday: Isaiah 61:1–7
Sunday: John 16:17–33

Go to page 860 for your next devotional reading.

⁶⁴Pay them back what they deserve,
    O Lord,
  for what their hands have done.
⁶⁵Put a veil over their hearts,
    and may your curse be on them!
⁶⁶Pursue them in anger and destroy
    them
  from under the heavens of the Lord.

4 ᵃ How the gold has lost its luster,
    the fine gold become dull!
  The sacred gems are scattered
    at the head of every street.

²How the precious sons of Zion,
    once worth their weight in gold,
  are now considered as pots of clay,
    the work of a potter's hands!

³Even jackals offer their breasts
    to nurse their young,
  but my people have become heartless
    like ostriches in the desert.

⁴Because of thirst the infant's tongue
    sticks to the roof of its mouth;
  the children beg for bread,
    but no one gives it to them.

⁵Those who once ate delicacies
    are destitute in the streets.
  Those nurtured in purple
    now lie on ash heaps.

⁶The punishment of my people
    is greater than that of Sodom,
  which was overthrown in a moment
    without a hand turned to help her.

⁷Their princes were brighter than snow
    and whiter than milk,
  their bodies more ruddy than rubies,
    their appearance like sapphires.ᵇ

⁸But now they are blacker than soot;
    they are not recognized in the
    streets.
  Their skin has shriveled on their
    bones;
  it has become as dry as a stick.

⁹Those killed by the sword are better
    off
  than those who die of famine;
  racked with hunger, they waste away
    for lack of food from the field.

¹⁰With their own hands compassionate
    women
  have cooked their own children,
  who became their food

when my people were destroyed.

¹¹The Lord has given full vent to his
    wrath;
  he has poured out his fierce anger.
  He kindled a fire in Zion
    that consumed her foundations.

¹²The kings of the earth did not believe,
    nor did any of the world's people,
  that enemies and foes could enter
    the gates of Jerusalem.

¹³But it happened because of the sins of
    her prophets
  and the iniquities of her priests,
  who shed within her
    the blood of the righteous.

¹⁴Now they grope through the streets
    like men who are blind.
  They are so defiled with blood
    that no one dares to touch their
    garments.

¹⁵"Go away! You are unclean!" men cry
    to them.
  "Away! Away! Don't touch us!"
  When they flee and wander about,
    people among the nations say,
  "They can stay here no longer."

¹⁶The Lord himself has scattered them;
    he no longer watches over them.
  The priests are shown no honor,
    the elders no favor.

¹⁷Moreover, our eyes failed,
    looking in vain for help;
  from our towers we watched
    for a nation that could not save us.

¹⁸Men stalked us at every step,
    so we could not walk in our streets.
  Our end was near, our days were
    numbered,
  for our end had come.

¹⁹Our pursuers were swifter
    than eagles in the sky;
  they chased us over the mountains
    and lay in wait for us in the desert.

²⁰The Lord's anointed, our very life
    breath,
  was caught in their traps.
  We thought that under his shadow
    we would live among the nations.

²¹Rejoice and be glad, O Daughter of
    Edom,
  you who live in the land of Uz.

ᵃThis chapter is an acrostic poem, the verses of which begin with the successive letters of the Hebrew alphabet.   ᵇ7 Or *lapis lazuli*

But to you also the cup will be
    passed;
  you will be drunk and stripped
    naked.

²²O Daughter of Zion, your punishment
    will end;
  he will not prolong your exile.
  But, O Daughter of Edom, he will
    punish your sin
  and expose your wickedness.

5 Remember, O Lord, what has
    happened to us;

look, and see our disgrace.
²Our inheritance has been turned over
    to aliens,
  our homes to foreigners.
³We have become orphans and
    fatherless,
  our mothers like widows.
⁴We must buy the water we drink;
  our wood can be had only at a
    price.
⁵Those who pursue us are at our heels;
  we are weary and find no rest.
⁶We submitted to Egypt and Assyria
  to get enough bread.

MONDAY

VERSE FOR THE DAY:
Lamentations 3:40

AUTHOR:
Patrick Morley

PASSAGE FOR THE DAY:
Lamentations 3:40–42

Examine Your Ways

THE number one shortcoming of man at the close of the twentieth century (as it has been at the close of every century) is
that *we lead unexamined lives. Most men have not carefully
chiseled their life view by a personal search for truth and obedience to God.*

Instead, we rush from task to busy task, but we don't call
enough time-outs to reflect on life's larger meaning and purpose. Rather, we live myopically from day-to-day-to-day; we
live under the tyranny of today's problems. Our lives . . . are
consumed in action as we react to the seemingly endless menu
of options that vie for our attention, time and money. But as
Ghandi said, "There is more to life than increasing its speed."

Spiritually, too many of us are just "playing church," just going through the motions. We show up on Sunday mornings,
but the message we come away with doesn't do for us what it
does for some of the other members. We don't know exactly
why, and, before we spend much time thinking about it, our
minds wander to the office problems chewing at our gut. We
speed off to the next busy task, and, by Monday afternoon, the
memory of Sunday is as distant as the memory of last year's
vacation.

As a lawyer or accountant is no better than the effort he
puts into keeping up with his profession, so is the Christian no
better than the effort he puts into self-examination of life's big
questions.

Additional Scripture Readings:
Isaiah 30:15–18;
2 Corinthians 13:5–10

*Go to page 871 for your next
devotional reading.*

⁷Our fathers sinned and are no more,
  and we bear their punishment.
⁸Slaves rule over us,
  and there is none to free us from
    their hands.
⁹We get our bread at the risk of our
    lives
  because of the sword in the desert.
¹⁰Our skin is hot as an oven,
  feverish from hunger.
¹¹Women have been ravished in Zion,
  and virgins in the towns of Judah.
¹²Princes have been hung up by their
    hands;
  elders are shown no respect.
¹³Young men toil at the millstones;
  boys stagger under loads of wood.
¹⁴The elders are gone from the city gate;
  the young men have stopped their
    music.
¹⁵Joy is gone from our hearts;

our dancing has turned to
    mourning.
¹⁶The crown has fallen from our head.
  Woe to us, for we have sinned!
¹⁷Because of this our hearts are faint,
  because of these things our eyes
    grow dim
¹⁸for Mount Zion, which lies desolate,
  with jackals prowling over it.

¹⁹You, O LORD, reign forever;
  your throne endures from
    generation to generation.
²⁰Why do you always forget us?
  Why do you forsake us so long?
²¹Restore us to yourself, O LORD, that
    we may return;
  renew our days as of old
²²unless you have utterly rejected us
  and are angry with us beyond
    measure.

EZEKIEL, living among the exiles in Babylon, wants the people to know that God is everywhere. He reminds them that worshiping false gods has brought about this catastrophe, he emphasizes the need for a new personal relationship with God, and he assures them that God wants a new covenant of peace with them. As you read this book, think of the Prince of Peace who has come to give you eternal life in his name. Be sure to make your own personal commitment to Jesus Christ.

EZEKIEL

The Living Creatures and the Glory of the LORD

1 In the[a] thirtieth year, in the fourth month on the fifth day, while I was among the exiles by the Kebar River, the heavens were opened and I saw visions of God.

2On the fifth of the month—it was the fifth year of the exile of King Jehoiachin—**3**the word of the LORD came to Ezekiel the priest, the son of Buzi,[b] by the Kebar River in the land of the Babylonians.[c] There the hand of the LORD was upon him.

4I looked, and I saw a windstorm coming out of the north—an immense cloud with flashing lightning and surrounded by brilliant light. The center of the fire looked like glowing metal, **5**and in the fire was what looked like four living creatures. In appearance their form was that of a man, **6**but each of them had four faces and four wings. **7**Their legs were straight; their feet were like those of a calf and gleamed like burnished bronze. **8**Under their wings on their four sides they had the hands of a man. All four of them had faces and wings, ⁹and their wings touched one another. Each one went straight ahead; they did not turn as they moved.

¹⁰Their faces looked like this: Each of the four had the face of a man, and on the right side each had the face of a lion, and on the left the face of an ox; each also had the face of an eagle. ¹¹Such were their faces. Their wings were spread out upward; each had two wings, one touching the wing of another creature on either side, and two wings covering its body. ¹²Each one went straight ahead. Wherever the spirit would go, they would go, without turning as they went. ¹³The appearance of the living creatures was like burning coals of fire or like torches. Fire moved back and forth among the creatures; it was bright, and lightning flashed out of it. ¹⁴The creatures sped back and forth like flashes of lightning.

¹⁵As I looked at the living creatures, I saw a wheel on the ground beside each creature with its four faces. ¹⁶This was the appearance and structure of the wheels: They sparkled like chrysolite, and all four looked alike. Each appeared to be made like a wheel intersecting a wheel. ¹⁷As they moved, they would go in any one of the four directions the creatures faced; the wheels did not turn about^a as the creatures went. ¹⁸Their rims were high and awesome, and all four rims were full of eyes all around.

¹⁹When the living creatures moved, the wheels beside them moved; and when the living creatures rose from the ground, the wheels also rose. ²⁰Wherever the spirit would go, they would go, and the wheels would rise along with them, because the spirit of the living creatures was in the wheels. ²¹When the creatures moved, they also moved; when the creatures stood still, they also stood still; and when the creatures rose from the ground, the wheels rose along with them, because the spirit of the living creatures was in the wheels.

²²Spread out above the heads of the living creatures was what looked like an expanse, sparkling like ice, and awesome. ²³Under the expanse their wings were stretched out one toward the other, and each had two wings covering its body. ²⁴When the creatures moved, I heard the sound of their wings, like the roar of rushing waters, like the voice of the Almighty,^b like the tumult of an army.

When they stood still, they lowered their wings.

²⁵Then there came a voice from above the expanse over their heads as they stood with lowered wings. ²⁶Above the expanse over their heads was what looked like a throne of sapphire,^c and high above on the throne was a figure like that of a man. ²⁷I saw that from what appeared to be his waist up he looked like glowing metal, as if full of fire, and that from there down he looked like fire; and brilliant light surrounded him. ²⁸Like the appearance of a rainbow in the clouds on a rainy day, so was the radiance around him.

This was the appearance of the likeness of the glory of the LORD. When I saw it, I fell facedown, and I heard the voice of one speaking.

Ezekiel's Call

2 He said to me, "Son of man, stand up on your feet and I will speak to you." ²As he spoke, the Spirit came into me and raised me to my feet, and I heard him speaking to me.

³He said: "Son of man, I am sending you to the Israelites, to a rebellious nation that has rebelled against me; they and their fathers have been in revolt against me to this very day. ⁴The people to whom I am sending you are obstinate and stubborn. Say to them, 'This is what the Sovereign LORD says.' ⁵And whether they listen or fail to listen—for they are a rebellious house—they will know that a prophet has been among them. ⁶And you, son of man, do not be afraid of them or their words. Do not be afraid, though briers and thorns are all around you and you live among scorpions. Do not be afraid of what they say or terrified by them, though they are a rebellious house. ⁷You must speak my words to them, whether they listen or fail to listen, for they are rebellious. ⁸But you, son of man, listen to what I say to you. Do not rebel like that rebellious house; open your mouth and eat what I give you."

⁹Then I looked, and I saw a hand stretched out to me. In it was a scroll, ¹⁰which he unrolled before me. On both sides of it were written words of lament and mourning and woe.

3 And he said to me, "Son of man, eat what is before you, eat this scroll; then go and speak to the house of Israel." ²So I opened my mouth, and he gave me the scroll to eat.

---

^a17 Or *aside*   ^b24 Hebrew *Shaddai*   ^c26 Or *lapis lazuli*

[3]Then he said to me, "Son of man, eat this scroll I am giving you and fill your stomach with it." So I ate it, and it tasted as sweet as honey in my mouth.

[4]He then said to me: "Son of man, go now to the house of Israel and speak my words to them. [5]You are not being sent to a people of obscure speech and difficult language, but to the house of Israel — [6]not to many peoples of obscure speech and difficult language, whose words you cannot understand. Surely if I had sent you to them, they would have listened to you. [7]But the house of Israel is not willing to listen to you because they are not willing to listen to me, for the whole house of Israel is hardened and obstinate. [8]But I will make you as unyielding and hardened as they are. [9]I will make your forehead like the hardest stone, harder than flint. Do not be afraid of them or terrified by them, though they are a rebellious house."

[10]And he said to me, "Son of man, listen carefully and take to heart all the words I speak to you. [11]Go now to your countrymen in exile and speak to them. Say to them, 'This is what the Sovereign Lord says,' whether they listen or fail to listen."

[12]Then the Spirit lifted me up, and I heard behind me a loud rumbling sound — May the glory of the Lord be praised in his dwelling place! — [13]the sound of the wings of the living creatures brushing against each other and the sound of the wheels beside them, a loud rumbling sound. [14]The Spirit then lifted me up and took me away, and I went in bitterness and in the anger of my spirit, with the strong hand of the Lord upon me. [15]I came to the exiles who lived at Tel Abib near the Kebar River. And there, where they were living, I sat among them for seven days — overwhelmed.

Warning to Israel

[16]At the end of seven days the word of the Lord came to me: [17]"Son of man, I have made you a watchman for the house of Israel; so hear the word I speak and give them warning from me. [18]When I say to a wicked man, 'You will surely die,' and you do not warn him or speak out to dissuade him from his evil ways in order to save his life, that wicked man will die for[a] his sin, and I will hold you accountable for his blood. [19]But if you do warn the wicked man and he does not turn from his wick-

edness or from his evil ways, he will die for his sin; but you will have saved yourself.

[20]"Again, when a righteous man turns from his righteousness and does evil, and I put a stumbling block before him, he will die. Since you did not warn him, he will die for his sin. The righteous things he did will not be remembered, and I will hold you accountable for his blood. [21]But if you do warn the righteous man not to sin and he does not sin, he will surely live because he took warning, and you will have saved yourself."

[22]The hand of the Lord was upon me there, and he said to me, "Get up and go out to the plain, and there I will speak to you." [23]So I got up and went out to the plain. And the glory of the Lord was standing there, like the glory I had seen by the Kebar River, and I fell facedown.

[24]Then the Spirit came into me and raised me to my feet. He spoke to me and said: "Go, shut yourself inside your house. [25]And you, son of man, they will tie with ropes; you will be bound so that you cannot go out among the people. [26]I will make your tongue stick to the roof of your mouth so that you will be silent and unable to rebuke them, though they are a rebellious house. [27]But when I speak to you, I will open your mouth and you shall say to them, 'This is what the Sovereign Lord says.' Whoever will listen let him listen, and whoever will refuse let him refuse; for they are a rebellious house.

Siege of Jerusalem Symbolized

4 "Now, son of man, take a clay tablet, put it in front of you and draw the city of Jerusalem on it. [2]Then lay siege to it: Erect siege works against it, build a ramp up to it, set up camps against it and put battering rams around it. [3]Then take an iron pan, place it as an iron wall between you and the city and turn your face toward it. It will be under siege, and you shall besiege it. This will be a sign to the house of Israel.

[4]"Then lie on your left side and put the sin of the house of Israel upon yourself.[b] You are to bear their sin for the number of days you lie on your side. [5]I have assigned you the same number of days as the years of their sin. So for 390 days you will bear the sin of the house of Israel.

[6]"After you have finished this, lie down

again, this time on your right side, and bear the sin of the house of Judah. I have assigned you 40 days, a day for each year. [7]Turn your face toward the siege of Jerusalem and with bared arm prophesy against her. [8]I will tie you up with ropes so that you cannot turn from one side to the other until you have finished the days of your siege.

[9]"Take wheat and barley, beans and lentils, millet and spelt; put them in a storage jar and use them to make bread for yourself. You are to eat it during the 390 days you lie on your side. [10]Weigh out twenty shekels[a] of food to eat each day and eat it at set times. [11]Also measure out a sixth of a hin[b] of water and drink it at set times. [12]Eat the food as you would a barley cake; bake it in the sight of the people, using human excrement for fuel." [13]The LORD said, "In this way the people of Israel will eat defiled food among the nations where I will drive them."

[14]Then I said, "Not so, Sovereign LORD! I have never defiled myself. From my youth until now I have never eaten anything found dead or torn by wild animals. No unclean meat has ever entered my mouth."

[15]"Very well," he said, "I will let you bake your bread over cow manure instead of human excrement."

[16]He then said to me: "Son of man, I will cut off the supply of food in Jerusalem. The people will eat rationed food in anxiety and drink rationed water in despair, [17]for food and water will be scarce. They will be appalled at the sight of each other and will waste away because of[c] their sin.

[5] "Now, son of man, take a sharp sword and use it as a barber's razor to shave your head and your beard. Then take a set of scales and divide up the hair. [2]When the days of your siege come to an end, burn a third of the hair with fire inside the city. Take a third and strike it with the sword all around the city. And scatter a third to the wind. For I will pursue them with drawn sword. [3]But take a few strands of hair and tuck them away in the folds of your garment. [4]Again, take a few of these and throw them into the fire and burn them up. A fire will spread from there to the whole house of Israel.

[5]"This is what the Sovereign LORD says:

This is Jerusalem, which I have set in the center of the nations, with countries all around her. [6]Yet in her wickedness she has rebelled against my laws and decrees more than the nations and countries around her. She has rejected my laws and has not followed my decrees.

[7]"Therefore this is what the Sovereign LORD says: You have been more unruly than the nations around you and have not followed my decrees or kept my laws. You have not even[d] conformed to the standards of the nations around you.

[8]"Therefore this is what the Sovereign LORD says: I myself am against you, Jerusalem, and I will inflict punishment on you in the sight of the nations. [9]Because of all your detestable idols, I will do to you what I have never done before and will never do again. [10]Therefore in your midst fathers will eat their children, and children will eat their fathers. I will inflict punishment on you and will scatter all your survivors to the winds. [11]Therefore as surely as I live, declares the Sovereign LORD, because you have defiled my sanctuary with all your vile images and detestable practices, I myself will withdraw my favor; I will not look on you with pity or spare you. [12]A third of your people will die of the plague or perish by famine inside you; a third will fall by the sword outside your walls; and a third I will scatter to the winds and pursue with drawn sword.

[13]"Then my anger will cease and my wrath against them will subside, and I will be avenged. And when I have spent my wrath upon them, they will know that I the LORD have spoken in my zeal.

[14]"I will make you a ruin and a reproach among the nations around you, in the sight of all who pass by. [15]You will be a reproach and a taunt, a warning and an object of horror to the nations around you when I inflict punishment on you in anger and in wrath and with stinging rebuke. I the LORD have spoken. [16]When I shoot at you with my deadly and destructive arrows of famine, I will shoot to destroy you. I will bring more and more famine upon you and cut off your supply of food. [17]I will send famine and wild beasts against you, and they will leave you childless. Plague and bloodshed will sweep through you, and I will bring the sword against you. I the LORD have spoken."

---

[a]10 That is, about 8 ounces (about 0.2 kilogram)   [b]11 That is, about 2/3 quart (about 0.6 liter)
[c]17 Or *away in*   [d]7 Most Hebrew manuscripts; some Hebrew manuscripts and Syriac *You have*

A Prophecy Against the Mountains of Israel

6 The word of the LORD came to me: ²"Son of man, set your face against the mountains of Israel; prophesy against them ³and say: 'O mountains of Israel, hear the word of the Sovereign LORD. This is what the Sovereign LORD says to the mountains and hills, to the ravines and valleys: I am about to bring a sword against you, and I will destroy your high places. ⁴Your altars will be demolished and your incense altars will be smashed; and I will slay your people in front of your idols. ⁵I will lay the dead bodies of the Israelites in front of their idols, and I will scatter your bones around your altars. ⁶Wherever you live, the towns will be laid waste and the high places demolished, so that your altars will be laid waste and devastated, your idols smashed and ruined, your incense altars broken down, and what you have made wiped out. ⁷Your people will fall slain among you, and you will know that I am the LORD.

⁸" 'But I will spare some, for some of you will escape the sword when you are scattered among the lands and nations. ⁹Then in the nations where they have been carried captive, those who escape will remember me — how I have been grieved by their adulterous hearts, which have turned away from me, and by their eyes, which have lusted after their idols. They will loathe themselves for the evil they have done and for all their detestable practices. ¹⁰And they will know that I am the LORD; I did not threaten in vain to bring this calamity on them.

¹¹" 'This is what the Sovereign LORD says: Strike your hands together and stamp your feet and cry out "Alas!" because of all the wicked and detestable practices of the house of Israel, for they will fall by the sword, famine and plague. ¹²He that is far away will die of the plague, and he that is near will fall by the sword, and he that survives and is spared will die of famine. So will I spend my wrath upon them. ¹³And they will know that I am the LORD, when their people lie slain among their idols around their altars, on every high hill and on all the mountaintops, under every spreading tree and every leafy oak — places where they offered fragrant incense to all their idols. ¹⁴And I will

stretch out my hand against them and make the land a desolate waste from the desert to Diblah[a] — wherever they live. Then they will know that I am the LORD.' "

The End Has Come

7 The word of the LORD came to me: ²"Son of man, this is what the Sovereign LORD says to the land of Israel: The end! The end has come upon the four corners of the land. ³The end is now upon you and I will unleash my anger against you. I will judge you according to your conduct and repay you for all your detestable practices. ⁴I will not look on you with pity or spare you; I will surely repay you for your conduct and the detestable practices among you. Then you will know that I am the LORD.

⁵"This is what the Sovereign LORD says: Disaster! An unheard-of[b] disaster is coming. ⁶The end has come! The end has come! It has roused itself against you. It has come! ⁷Doom has come upon you — you who dwell in the land. The time has come, the day is near; there is panic, not joy, upon the mountains. ⁸I am about to pour out my wrath on you and spend my anger against you; I will judge you according to your conduct and repay you for all your detestable practices. ⁹I will not look on you with pity or spare you; I will repay you in accordance with your conduct and the detestable practices among you. Then you will know that it is I the LORD who strikes the blow.

¹⁰"The day is here! It has come! Doom has burst forth, the rod has budded, arrogance has blossomed! ¹¹Violence has grown into[c] a rod to punish wickedness; none of the people will be left, none of that crowd — no wealth, nothing of value. ¹²The time has come, the day has arrived. Let not the buyer rejoice nor the seller grieve, for wrath is upon the whole crowd. ¹³The seller will not recover the land he has sold as long as both of them live, for the vision concerning the whole crowd will not be reversed. Because of their sins, not one of them will preserve his life. ¹⁴Though they blow the trumpet and get everything ready, no one will go into battle, for my wrath is upon the whole crowd.

¹⁵"Outside is the sword, inside are plague and famine; those in the country will die by the sword, and those in the city will be devoured by famine and plague.

---

a 14 Most Hebrew manuscripts; a few Hebrew manuscripts Riblah   b 5 Most Hebrew manuscripts; some Hebrew manuscripts and Syriac Disaster after   c 11 Or The violent one has become

16All who survive and escape will be in the mountains, moaning like doves of the valleys, each because of his sins. 17Every hand will go limp, and every knee will become as weak as water. 18They will put on sackcloth and be clothed with terror. Their faces will be covered with shame and their heads will be shaved. 19They will throw their silver into the streets, and their gold will be an unclean thing. Their silver and gold will not be able to save them in the day of the Lord's wrath. They will not satisfy their hunger or fill their stomachs with it, for it has made them stumble into sin. 20They were proud of their beautiful jewelry and used it to make their detestable idols and vile images. Therefore I will turn these into an unclean thing for them. 21I will hand it all over as plunder to foreigners and as loot to the wicked of the earth, and they will defile it. 22I will turn my face away from them, and they will desecrate my treasured place; robbers will enter it and desecrate it.

23"Prepare chains, because the land is full of bloodshed and the city is full of violence. 24I will bring the most wicked of the nations to take possession of their houses; I will put an end to the pride of the mighty, and their sanctuaries will be desecrated. 25When terror comes, they will seek peace, but there will be none. 26Calamity upon calamity will come, and rumor upon rumor. They will try to get a vision from the prophet; the teaching of the law by the priest will be lost, as will the counsel of the elders. 27The king will mourn, the prince will be clothed with despair, and the hands of the people of the land will tremble. I will deal with them according to their conduct, and by their own standards I will judge them. Then they will know that I am the Lord."

Idolatry in the Temple

8 In the sixth year, in the sixth month on the fifth day, while I was sitting in my house and the elders of Judah were sitting before me, the hand of the Sovereign Lord came upon me there. 2I looked, and I saw a figure like that of a man.a From what appeared to be his waist down he was like fire, and from there up his appearance was as bright as glowing metal. 3He stretched out what looked like a hand and took me by the hair of my head. The Spirit lifted me up between earth and heaven and in visions of God he took me to Jerusalem, to the entrance to the north gate of the inner court, where the idol that provokes to jealousy stood. 4And there before me was the glory of the God of Israel, as in the vision I had seen in the plain.

5Then he said to me, "Son of man, look toward the north." So I looked, and in the entrance north of the gate of the altar I saw this idol of jealousy.

6And he said to me, "Son of man, do you see what they are doing—the utterly detestable things the house of Israel is doing here, things that will drive me far from my sanctuary? But you will see things that are even more detestable."

7Then he brought me to the entrance to the court. I looked, and I saw a hole in the wall. 8He said to me, "Son of man, now dig into the wall." So I dug into the wall and saw a doorway there.

9And he said to me, "Go in and see the wicked and detestable things they are doing here." 10So I went in and looked, and I saw portrayed all over the walls all kinds of crawling things and detestable animals and all the idols of the house of Israel. 11In front of them stood seventy elders of the house of Israel, and Jaazaniah son of Shaphan was standing among them. Each had a censer in his hand, and a fragrant cloud of incense was rising.

12He said to me, "Son of man, have you seen what the elders of the house of Israel are doing in the darkness, each at the shrine of his own idol? They say, 'The Lord does not see us; the Lord has forsaken the land.'" 13Again, he said, "You will see them doing things that are even more detestable."

14Then he brought me to the entrance to the north gate of the house of the Lord, and I saw women sitting there, mourning for Tammuz. 15He said to me, "Do you see this, son of man? You will see things that are even more detestable than this."

16He then brought me into the inner court of the house of the Lord, and there at the entrance to the temple, between the portico and the altar, were about twenty-five men. With their backs toward the temple of the Lord and their faces toward the east, they were bowing down to the sun in the east.

17He said to me, "Have you seen this, son of man? Is it a trivial matter for the house of Judah to do the detestable things

a2 Or saw a fiery figure

they are doing here? Must they also fill the land with violence and continually provoke me to anger? Look at them putting the branch to their nose! [18]Therefore I will deal with them in anger; I will not look on them with pity or spare them. Although they shout in my ears, I will not listen to them."

Idolaters Killed

9 Then I heard him call out in a loud voice, "Bring the guards of the city here, each with a weapon in his hand." [2]And I saw six men coming from the direction of the upper gate, which faces north, each with a deadly weapon in his hand. With them was a man clothed in linen who had a writing kit at his side. They came in and stood beside the bronze altar.

[3]Now the glory of the God of Israel went up from above the cherubim, where it had been, and moved to the threshold of the temple. Then the LORD called to the man clothed in linen who had the writing kit at his side [4]and said to him, "Go throughout the city of Jerusalem and put a mark on the foreheads of those who grieve and lament over all the detestable things that are done in it."

[5]As I listened, he said to the others, "Follow him through the city and kill, without showing pity or compassion. [6]Slaughter old men, young men and maidens, women and children, but do not touch anyone who has the mark. Begin at my sanctuary." So they began with the elders who were in front of the temple.

[7]Then he said to them, "Defile the temple and fill the courts with the slain. Go!" So they went out and began killing throughout the city. [8]While they were killing and I was left alone, I fell facedown, crying out, "Ah, Sovereign LORD! Are you going to destroy the entire remnant of Israel in this outpouring of your wrath on Jerusalem?"

[9]He answered me, "The sin of the house of Israel and Judah is exceedingly great; the land is full of bloodshed and the city is full of injustice. They say, 'The LORD has forsaken the land; the LORD does not see.' [10]So I will not look on them with pity or spare them, but I will bring down on their own heads what they have done."

[11]Then the man in linen with the writing kit at his side brought back word, saying, "I have done as you commanded."

The Glory Departs From the Temple

10 I looked, and I saw the likeness of a throne of sapphire[a] above the expanse that was over the heads of the cherubim. [2]The LORD said to the man clothed in linen, "Go in among the wheels beneath the cherubim. Fill your hands with burning coals from among the cherubim and scatter them over the city." And as I watched, he went in.

[3]Now the cherubim were standing on the south side of the temple when the man went in, and a cloud filled the inner court. [4]Then the glory of the LORD rose from above the cherubim and moved to the threshold of the temple. The cloud filled the temple, and the court was full of the radiance of the glory of the LORD. [5]The sound of the wings of the cherubim could be heard as far away as the outer court, like the voice of God Almighty[b] when he speaks.

[6]When the LORD commanded the man in linen, "Take fire from among the wheels, from among the cherubim," the man went in and stood beside a wheel. [7]Then one of the cherubim reached out his hand to the fire that was among them. He took up some of it and put it into the hands of the man in linen, who took it and went out. [8](Under the wings of the cherubim could be seen what looked like the hands of a man.)

[9]I looked, and I saw beside the cherubim four wheels, one beside each of the cherubim; the wheels sparkled like chrysolite. [10]As for their appearance, the four of them looked alike; each was like a wheel intersecting a wheel. [11]As they moved, they would go in any one of the four directions the cherubim faced; the wheels did not turn about[c] as the cherubim went. The cherubim went in whatever direction the head faced, without turning as they went. [12]Their entire bodies, including their backs, their hands and their wings, were completely full of eyes, as were their four wheels. [13]I heard the wheels being called "the whirling wheels." [14]Each of the cherubim had four faces: One face was that of a cherub, the second face of a man, the third the face of a lion, and the fourth the face of an eagle.

[15]Then the cherubim rose upward. These were the living creatures I had seen by the Kebar River. [16]When the cherubim moved, the wheels beside them moved;

---

[a]1 Or *lapis lazuli*　　[b]5 Hebrew *El-Shaddai*　　[c]11 Or *aside*

and when the cherubim spread their wings to rise from the ground, the wheels did not leave their side. ¹⁷When the cherubim stood still, they also stood still; and when the cherubim rose, they rose with them, because the spirit of the living creatures was in them.

¹⁸Then the glory of the LORD departed from over the threshold of the temple and stopped above the cherubim. ¹⁹While I watched, the cherubim spread their wings and rose from the ground, and as they went, the wheels went with them. They stopped at the entrance to the east gate of the LORD's house, and the glory of the God of Israel was above them.

²⁰These were the living creatures I had seen beneath the God of Israel by the Kebar River, and I realized that they were cherubim. ²¹Each had four faces and four wings, and under their wings was what looked like the hands of a man. ²²Their faces had the same appearance as those I had seen by the Kebar River. Each one went straight ahead.

Judgment on Israel's Leaders

11 Then the Spirit lifted me up and brought me to the gate of the house of the LORD that faces east. There at the entrance to the gate were twenty-five men, and I saw among them Jaazaniah son of Azzur and Pelatiah son of Benaiah, leaders of the people. ²The LORD said to me, "Son of man, these are the men who are plotting evil and giving wicked advice in this city. ³They say, 'Will it not soon be time to build houses?ᵃ This city is a cooking pot, and we are the meat.' ⁴Therefore prophesy against them; prophesy, son of man."

⁵Then the Spirit of the LORD came upon me, and he told me to say: "This is what the LORD says: That is what you are saying, O house of Israel, but I know what is going through your mind. ⁶You have killed many people in this city and filled its streets with the dead.

⁷"Therefore this is what the Sovereign LORD says: The bodies you have thrown there are the meat and this city is the pot, but I will drive you out of it. ⁸You fear the sword, and the sword is what I will bring against you, declares the Sovereign LORD. ⁹I will drive you out of the city and hand you over to foreigners and inflict punishment on you. ¹⁰You will fall by the sword,

and I will execute judgment on you at the borders of Israel. Then you will know that I am the LORD. ¹¹This city will not be a pot for you, nor will you be the meat in it; I will execute judgment on you at the borders of Israel. ¹²And you will know that I am the LORD, for you have not followed my decrees or kept my laws but have conformed to the standards of the nations around you."

¹³Now as I was prophesying, Pelatiah son of Benaiah died. Then I fell facedown and cried out in a loud voice, "Ah, Sovereign LORD! Will you completely destroy the remnant of Israel?"

¹⁴The word of the LORD came to me: ¹⁵"Son of man, your brothers — your brothers who are your blood relativesᵇ and the whole house of Israel — are those of whom the people of Jerusalem have said, 'They areᶜ far away from the LORD; this land was given to us as our possession.'

Promised Return of Israel

¹⁶"Therefore say: 'This is what the Sovereign LORD says: Although I sent them far away among the nations and scattered them among the countries, yet for a little while I have been a sanctuary for them in the countries where they have gone.'

¹⁷"Therefore say: 'This is what the Sovereign LORD says: I will gather you from the nations and bring you back from the countries where you have been scattered, and I will give you back the land of Israel again.'

¹⁸"They will return to it and remove all its vile images and detestable idols. ¹⁹I will give them an undivided heart and put a new spirit in them; I will remove from them their heart of stone and give them a heart of flesh. ²⁰Then they will follow my decrees and be careful to keep my laws. They will be my people, and I will be their God. ²¹But as for those whose hearts are devoted to their vile images and detestable idols, I will bring down on their own heads what they have done, declares the Sovereign LORD."

²²Then the cherubim, with the wheels beside them, spread their wings, and the glory of the God of Israel was above them. ²³The glory of the LORD went up from within the city and stopped above the mountain east of it. ²⁴The Spirit lifted me up and brought me to the exiles in Babylo-

---

ᵃ3 Or *This is not the time to build houses.*   ᵇ15 Or *are in exile with you* (see Septuagint and Syriac)
ᶜ15 Or *those to whom the people of Jerusalem have said, 'Stay*

nia*a* in the vision given by the Spirit of God.

Then the vision I had seen went up from me, ²⁵and I told the exiles everything the LORD had shown me.

The Exile Symbolized

12 The word of the LORD came to me: ²"Son of man, you are living among a rebellious people. They have eyes to see but do not see and ears to hear but do not hear, for they are a rebellious people.

³"Therefore, son of man, pack your belongings for exile and in the daytime, as they watch, set out and go from where you are to another place. Perhaps they will understand, though they are a rebellious house. ⁴During the daytime, while they watch, bring out your belongings packed for exile. Then in the evening, while they are watching, go out like those who go into exile. ⁵While they watch, dig through the wall and take your belongings out through it. ⁶Put them on your shoulder as they are watching and carry them out at dusk. Cover your face so that you cannot see the land, for I have made you a sign to the house of Israel."

⁷So I did as I was commanded. During the day I brought out my things packed for exile. Then in the evening I dug through the wall with my hands. I took my belongings out at dusk, carrying them on my shoulders while they watched.

⁸In the morning the word of the LORD came to me: ⁹"Son of man, did not that rebellious house of Israel ask you, 'What are you doing?'

¹⁰"Say to them, 'This is what the Sovereign LORD says: This oracle concerns the prince in Jerusalem and the whole house of Israel who are there.' ¹¹Say to them, 'I am a sign to you.'

"As I have done, so it will be done to them. They will go into exile as captives.

¹²"The prince among them will put his things on his shoulder at dusk and leave, and a hole will be dug in the wall for him to go through. He will cover his face so that he cannot see the land. ¹³I will spread my net for him, and he will be caught in my snare; I will bring him to Babylonia, the land of the Chaldeans, but he will not see it, and there he will die. ¹⁴I will scatter to the winds all those around him—his staff and all his troops—and I will pursue them with drawn sword.

¹⁵"They will know that I am the LORD, when I disperse them among the nations and scatter them through the countries. ¹⁶But I will spare a few of them from the sword, famine and plague, so that in the nations where they go they may acknowledge all their detestable practices. Then they will know that I am the LORD."

¹⁷The word of the LORD came to me: ¹⁸"Son of man, tremble as you eat your food, and shudder in fear as you drink your water. ¹⁹Say to the people of the land: 'This is what the Sovereign LORD says about those living in Jerusalem and in the land of Israel: They will eat their food in anxiety and drink their water in despair, for their land will be stripped of everything in it because of the violence of all who live there. ²⁰The inhabited towns will be laid waste and the land will be desolate. Then you will know that I am the LORD.'"

²¹The word of the LORD came to me: ²²"Son of man, what is this proverb you have in the land of Israel: 'The days go by and every vision comes to nothing'? ²³Say to them, 'This is what the Sovereign LORD says: I am going to put an end to this proverb, and they will no longer quote it in Israel.' Say to them, 'The days are near when every vision will be fulfilled. ²⁴For there will be no more false visions or flattering divinations among the people of Israel. ²⁵But I the LORD will speak what I will, and it shall be fulfilled without delay. For in your days, you rebellious house, I will fulfill whatever I say, declares the Sovereign LORD.'"

²⁶The word of the LORD came to me: ²⁷"Son of man, the house of Israel is saying, 'The vision he sees is for many years from now, and he prophesies about the distant future.'

²⁸"Therefore say to them, 'This is what the Sovereign LORD says: None of my words will be delayed any longer; whatever I say will be fulfilled, declares the Sovereign LORD.'"

False Prophets Condemned

13 The word of the LORD came to me: ²"Son of man, prophesy against the prophets of Israel who are now prophesying. Say to those who prophesy out of their own imagination: 'Hear the word of the LORD! ³This is what the Sovereign LORD says: Woe to the foolish*b* prophets who follow their own spirit and have seen nothing! ⁴Your prophets, O Israel, are like

a24 Or Chaldea   b3 Or wicked

jackals among ruins. [5]You have not gone up to the breaks in the wall to repair it for the house of Israel so that it will stand firm in the battle on the day of the LORD. [6]Their visions are false and their divinations a lie. They say, "The LORD declares," when the LORD has not sent them; yet they expect their words to be fulfilled. [7]Have you not seen false visions and uttered lying divinations when you say, "The LORD declares," though I have not spoken?

[8]'Therefore this is what the Sovereign LORD says: Because of your false words and lying visions, I am against you, declares the Sovereign LORD. [9]My hand will be against the prophets who see false visions and utter lying divinations. They will not belong to the council of my people or be listed in the records of the house of Israel, nor will they enter the land of Israel. Then you will know that I am the Sovereign LORD.

[10]"'Because they lead my people astray, saying, "Peace," when there is no peace, and because, when a flimsy wall is built, they cover it with whitewash, [11]therefore tell those who cover it with whitewash that it is going to fall. Rain will come in torrents, and I will send hailstones hurtling down, and violent winds

---

TUESDAY

VERSE FOR THE DAY:
Ezekiel 12:27

AUTHOR:
Tim Stafford

PASSAGE FOR THE DAY:
Ezekiel 12:21–28

The Day of Opportunity

ETERNITY begins now. This is what John's Gospel promises when it says that "whoever believes in the Son has eternal life" (John 3:36). In time, here and now, we set our direction toward infinite time.

We need time to know God, and he has given it to us. Hebrews refers to God's time as Today: "Today, if you hear his voice, do not harden your hearts" (Hebrews 4:7). Today is always a day of opportunity. Hebrews urges us to enter God's rest Today. God's rest I take to be the state in which everything else stops and we have the opportunity we need to know God. It is not sandwiched into small slots of time. It is a river from heaven flowing through our normal events.

God gives us the time we need to know him. But do we take it seriously? We have seen . . . the opportunities we have to know him personally in a multitude of ways: in conversation, in meals together, in visits with his family, in stories, in sacrifice, in praise, in work, to name a few. Time is the medium in which we use these avenues of God's grace. He makes himself available through them, here and now in time. Are we living through our God-given Today in a deadened stupor, stumbling from one activity to the next? Or are we using Today to begin our relationship with God and enjoy it to the utmost? Do we give God our time? Do we use our time to explore his personality? How does our use of time today predict our use of eternity?

Additional Scripture Readings:
Ephesians 5:15–20; Hebrews 4:1–11

Go to page 883 for your next devotional reading.

will burst forth. **12**When the wall collapses, will people not ask you, "Where is the whitewash you covered it with?"

13" 'Therefore this is what the Sovereign Lord says: In my wrath I will unleash a violent wind, and in my anger hailstones and torrents of rain will fall with destructive fury. **14**I will tear down the wall you have covered with whitewash and will level it to the ground so that its foundation will be laid bare. When it*a* falls, you will be destroyed in it; and you will know that I am the Lord. **15**So I will spend my wrath against the wall and against those who covered it with whitewash. I will say to you, "The wall is gone and so are those who whitewashed it, **16**those prophets of Israel who prophesied to Jerusalem and saw visions of peace for her when there was no peace, declares the Sovereign Lord." '

17"Now, son of man, set your face against the daughters of your people who prophesy out of their own imagination. Prophesy against them **18**and say, 'This is what the Sovereign Lord says: Woe to the women who sew magic charms on all their wrists and make veils of various lengths for their heads in order to ensnare people. Will you ensnare the lives of my people but preserve your own? **19**You have profaned me among my people for a few handfuls of barley and scraps of bread. By lying to my people, who listen to lies, you have killed those who should not have died and have spared those who should not live.

20" 'Therefore this is what the Sovereign Lord says: I am against your magic charms with which you ensnare people like birds and I will tear them from your arms; I will set free the people that you ensnare like birds. **21**I will tear off your veils and save my people from your hands, and they will no longer fall prey to your power. Then you will know that I am the Lord. **22**Because you disheartened the righteous with your lies, when I had brought them no grief, and because you encouraged the wicked not to turn from their evil ways and so save their lives, **23**therefore you will no longer see false visions or practice divination. I will save my people from your hands. And then you will know that I am the Lord.' "

Idolaters Condemned

14 Some of the elders of Israel came to me and sat down in front of me. **2**Then the word of the Lord came to me: **3**"Son of man, these men have set up idols in their hearts and put wicked stumbling blocks before their faces. Should I let them inquire of me at all? **4**Therefore speak to them and tell them, 'This is what the Sovereign Lord says: When any Israelite sets up idols in his heart and puts a wicked stumbling block before his face and then goes to a prophet, I the Lord will answer him myself in keeping with his great idolatry. **5**I will do this to recapture the hearts of the people of Israel, who have all deserted me for their idols.'

6"Therefore say to the house of Israel, 'This is what the Sovereign Lord says: Repent! Turn from your idols and renounce all your detestable practices!

7" 'When any Israelite or any alien living in Israel separates himself from me and sets up idols in his heart and puts a wicked stumbling block before his face and then goes to a prophet to inquire of me, I the Lord will answer him myself. **8**I will set my face against that man and make him an example and a byword. I will cut him off from my people. Then you will know that I am the Lord.

9" 'And if the prophet is enticed to utter a prophecy, I the Lord have enticed that prophet, and I will stretch out my hand against him and destroy him from among my people Israel. **10**They will bear their guilt — the prophet will be as guilty as the one who consults him. **11**Then the people of Israel will no longer stray from me, nor will they defile themselves anymore with all their sins. They will be my people, and I will be their God, declares the Sovereign Lord.' "

Judgment Inescapable

12The word of the Lord came to me: **13**"Son of man, if a country sins against me by being unfaithful and I stretch out my hand against it to cut off its food supply and send famine upon it and kill its men and their animals, **14**even if these three men — Noah, Daniel*b* and Job — were in it, they could save only themselves by their righteousness, declares the Sovereign Lord. **15**"Or if I send wild beasts through that

---

a14 Or *the city*   *b14* Or *Danel*; the Hebrew spelling may suggest a person other than the prophet Daniel; also in verse 20.

country and they leave it childless and it becomes desolate so that no one can pass through it because of the beasts, **16**as surely as I live, declares the Sovereign Lord, even if these three men were in it, they could not save their own sons or daughters. They alone would be saved, but the land would be desolate.

17"Or if I bring a sword against that country and say, 'Let the sword pass throughout the land,' and I kill its men and their animals, **18**as surely as I live, declares the Sovereign Lord, even if these three men were in it, they could not save their own sons or daughters. They alone would be saved.

19"Or if I send a plague into that land and pour out my wrath upon it through bloodshed, killing its men and their animals, **20**as surely as I live, declares the Sovereign Lord, even if Noah, Daniel and Job were in it, they could save neither son nor daughter. They would save only themselves by their righteousness.

21"For this is what the Sovereign Lord says: How much worse will it be when I send against Jerusalem my four dreadful judgments—sword and famine and wild beasts and plague—to kill its men and their animals! **22**Yet there will be some survivors—sons and daughters who will be brought out of it. They will come to you, and when you see their conduct and their actions, you will be consoled regarding the disaster I have brought upon Jerusalem—every disaster I have brought upon it. **23**You will be consoled when you see their conduct and their actions, for you will know that I have done nothing in it without cause, declares the Sovereign Lord."

Jerusalem, A Useless Vine

15 The word of the Lord came to me: **2**"Son of man, how is the wood of a vine better than that of a branch on any of the trees in the forest? **3**Is wood ever taken from it to make anything useful? Do they make pegs from it to hang things on? **4**And after it is thrown on the fire as fuel and the fire burns both ends and chars the middle, is it then useful for anything? **5**If it was not useful for anything when it was whole, how much less can it be made into something useful when the fire has burned it and it is charred?

6"Therefore this is what the Sovereign

Lord says: As I have given the wood of the vine among the trees of the forest as fuel for the fire, so will I treat the people living in Jerusalem. **7**I will set my face against them. Although they have come out of the fire, the fire will yet consume them. And when I set my face against them, you will know that I am the Lord. **8**I will make the land desolate because they have been unfaithful, declares the Sovereign Lord."

An Allegory of Unfaithful Jerusalem

16 The word of the Lord came to me: **2**"Son of man, confront Jerusalem with her detestable practices **3**and say, 'This is what the Sovereign Lord says to Jerusalem: Your ancestry and birth were in the land of the Canaanites; your father was an Amorite and your mother a Hittite. **4**On the day you were born your cord was not cut, nor were you washed with water to make you clean, nor were you rubbed with salt or wrapped in cloths. **5**No one looked on you with pity or had compassion enough to do any of these things for you. Rather, you were thrown out into the open field, for on the day you were born you were despised.

6"'Then I passed by and saw you kicking about in your blood, and as you lay there in your blood I said to you, "Live!"[a] **7**I made you grow like a plant of the field. You grew up and developed and became the most beautiful of jewels.[b] Your breasts were formed and your hair grew, you who were naked and bare.

8"'Later I passed by, and when I looked at you and saw that you were old enough for love, I spread the corner of my garment over you and covered your nakedness. I gave you my solemn oath and entered into a covenant with you, declares the Sovereign Lord, and you became mine.

9"'I bathed[c] you with water and washed the blood from you and put ointments on you. **10**I clothed you with an embroidered dress and put leather sandals on you. I dressed you in fine linen and covered you with costly garments. **11**I adorned you with jewelry: I put bracelets on your arms and a necklace around your neck, **12**and I put a ring on your nose, earrings on your ears and a beautiful crown on your head. **13**So you were adorned with gold and silver; your clothes were of fine linen and costly fabric and embroidered

---

a6 A few Hebrew manuscripts, Septuagint and Syriac; most Hebrew manuscripts "Live!" And as you lay there in your blood I said to you, "Live!"   b7 Or became mature   c9 Or I had bathed cloth. Your food was fine flour, honey and olive oil. You became very beautiful and rose to be a queen. ¹⁴And your fame spread among the nations on account of your beauty, because the splendor I had given you made your beauty perfect, declares the Sovereign Lord.

¹⁵" 'But you trusted in your beauty and used your fame to become a prostitute. You lavished your favors on anyone who passed by and your beauty became his.ᵃ ¹⁶You took some of your garments to make gaudy high places, where you carried on your prostitution. Such things should not happen, nor should they ever occur. ¹⁷You also took the fine jewelry I gave you, the jewelry made of my gold and silver, and you made for yourself male idols and engaged in prostitution with them. ¹⁸And you took your embroidered clothes to put on them, and you offered my oil and incense before them. ¹⁹Also the food I provided for you—the fine flour, olive oil and honey I gave you to eat—you offered as fragrant incense before them. That is what happened, declares the Sovereign Lord.

²⁰" 'And you took your sons and daughters whom you bore to me and sacrificed them as food to the idols. Was your prostitution not enough? ²¹You slaughtered my children and sacrificed themᵇ to the idols. ²²In all your detestable practices and your prostitution you did not remember the days of your youth, when you were naked and bare, kicking about in your blood.

²³" 'Woe! Woe to you, declares the Sovereign Lord. In addition to all your other wickedness, ²⁴you built a mound for yourself and made a lofty shrine in every public square. ²⁵At the head of every street you built your lofty shrines and degraded your beauty, offering your body with increasing promiscuity to anyone who passed by. ²⁶You engaged in prostitution with the Egyptians, your lustful neighbors, and provoked me to anger with your increasing promiscuity. ²⁷So I stretched out my hand against you and reduced your territory; I gave you over to the greed of your enemies, the daughters of the Philistines, who were shocked by your lewd conduct. ²⁸You engaged in prostitution with the Assyrians too, because you were insatiable; and even after that, you still

were not satisfied. ²⁹Then you increased your promiscuity to include Babylonia,ᶜ a land of merchants, but even with this you were not satisfied.

³⁰" 'How weak-willed you are, declares the Sovereign Lord, when you do all these things, acting like a brazen prostitute! ³¹When you built your mounds at the head of every street and made your lofty shrines in every public square, you were unlike a prostitute, because you scorned payment.

³²" 'You adulterous wife! You prefer strangers to your own husband! ³³Every prostitute receives a fee, but you give gifts to all your lovers, bribing them to come to you from everywhere for your illicit favors. ³⁴So in your prostitution you are the opposite of others; no one runs after you for your favors. You are the very opposite, for you give payment and none is given to you.

³⁵" 'Therefore, you prostitute, hear the word of the Lord! ³⁶This is what the Sovereign Lord says: Because you poured out your wealthᵈ and exposed your nakedness in your promiscuity with your lovers, and because of all your detestable idols, and because you gave them your children's blood, ³⁷therefore I am going to gather all your lovers, with whom you found pleasure, those you loved as well as those you hated. I will gather them against you from all around and will strip you in front of them, and they will see all your nakedness. ³⁸I will sentence you to the punishment of women who commit adultery and who shed blood; I will bring upon you the blood vengeance of my wrath and jealous anger. ³⁹Then I will hand you over to your lovers, and they will tear down your mounds and destroy your lofty shrines. They will strip you of your clothes and take your fine jewelry and leave you naked and bare. ⁴⁰They will bring a mob against you, who will stone you and hack you to pieces with their swords. ⁴¹They will burn down your houses and inflict punishment on you in the sight of many women. I will put a stop to your prostitution, and you will no longer pay your lovers. ⁴²Then my wrath against you will subside and my jealous anger will turn away from you; I will be calm and no longer angry.

⁴³" 'Because you did not remember the

ᵃ15 Most Hebrew manuscripts; one Hebrew manuscript (see some Septuagint manuscripts) by. Such a thing should not happen   ᵇ21 Or and made them pass through the fire   ᶜ29 Or Chaldea   ᵈ36 Or lust days of your youth but enraged me with all these things, I will surely bring down on your head what you have done, declares the Sovereign LORD. Did you not add lewdness to all your other detestable practices?

44" 'Everyone who quotes proverbs will quote this proverb about you: "Like mother, like daughter." **45**You are a true daughter of your mother, who despised her husband and her children; and you are a true sister of your sisters, who despised their husbands and their children. Your mother was a Hittite and your father an Amorite. **46**Your older sister was Samaria, who lived to the north of you with her daughters; and your younger sister, who lived to the south of you with her daughters, was Sodom. **47**You not only walked in their ways and copied their detestable practices, but in all your ways you soon became more depraved than they. **48**As surely as I live, declares the Sovereign LORD, your sister Sodom and her daughters never did what you and your daughters have done.

49" 'Now this was the sin of your sister Sodom: She and her daughters were arrogant, overfed and unconcerned; they did not help the poor and needy. **50**They were haughty and did detestable things before me. Therefore I did away with them as you have seen. **51**Samaria did not commit half the sins you did. You have done more detestable things than they, and have made your sisters seem righteous by all these things you have done. **52**Bear your disgrace, for you have furnished some justification for your sisters. Because your sins were more vile than theirs, they appear more righteous than you. So then, be ashamed and bear your disgrace, for you have made your sisters appear righteous.

53" 'However, I will restore the fortunes of Sodom and her daughters and of Samaria and her daughters, and your fortunes along with them, **54**so that you may bear your disgrace and be ashamed of all you have done in giving them comfort. **55**And your sisters, Sodom with her daughters and Samaria with her daughters, will return to what they were before; and you and your daughters will return to what you were before. **56**You would not even mention your sister Sodom in the day of your pride, **57**before your wickedness was uncovered. Even so, you are now scorned by the daughters of Edom*a* and all her neighbors and the daughters of the

Philistines — all those around you who despise you. **58**You will bear the consequences of your lewdness and your detestable practices, declares the LORD.

59" 'This is what the Sovereign LORD says: I will deal with you as you deserve, because you have despised my oath by breaking the covenant. **60**Yet I will remember the covenant I made with you in the days of your youth, and I will establish an everlasting covenant with you. **61**Then you will remember your ways and be ashamed when you receive your sisters, both those who are older than you and those who are younger. I will give them to you as daughters, but not on the basis of my covenant with you. **62**So I will establish my covenant with you, and you will know that I am the LORD. **63**Then, when I make atonement for you for all you have done, you will remember and be ashamed and never again open your mouth because of your humiliation, declares the Sovereign LORD.' "

Two Eagles and a Vine

17 The word of the LORD came to me: **2**"Son of man, set forth an allegory and tell the house of Israel a parable. **3**Say to them, 'This is what the Sovereign LORD says: A great eagle with powerful wings, long feathers and full plumage of varied colors came to Lebanon. Taking hold of the top of a cedar, **4**he broke off its topmost shoot and carried it away to a land of merchants, where he planted it in a city of traders.

5" 'He took some of the seed of your land and put it in fertile soil. He planted it like a willow by abundant water, **6**and it sprouted and became a low, spreading vine. Its branches turned toward him, but its roots remained under it. So it became a vine and produced branches and put out leafy boughs.

7" 'But there was another great eagle with powerful wings and full plumage. The vine now sent out its roots toward him from the plot where it was planted and stretched out its branches to him for water. **8**It had been planted in good soil by abundant water so that it would produce branches, bear fruit and become a splendid vine.'

9"Say to them, 'This is what the Sovereign LORD says: Will it thrive? Will it not be uprooted and stripped of its fruit so that it withers? All its new growth will

---

a57 Many Hebrew manuscripts and Syriac; most Hebrew manuscripts, Septuagint and Vulgate *Aram* wither. It will not take a strong arm or many people to pull it up by the roots. ¹⁰Even if it is transplanted, will it thrive? Will it not wither completely when the east wind strikes it — wither away in the plot where it grew?' "

¹¹Then the word of the LORD came to me: ¹²"Say to this rebellious house, 'Do you not know what these things mean?' Say to them: 'The king of Babylon went to Jerusalem and carried off her king and her nobles, bringing them back with him to Babylon. ¹³Then he took a member of the royal family and made a treaty with him, putting him under oath. He also carried away the leading men of the land, ¹⁴so that the kingdom would be brought low, unable to rise again, surviving only by keeping his treaty. ¹⁵But the king rebelled against him by sending his envoys to Egypt to get horses and a large army. Will he succeed? Will he who does such things escape? Will he break the treaty and yet escape?

¹⁶" 'As surely as I live, declares the Sovereign LORD, he shall die in Babylon, in the land of the king who put him on the throne, whose oath he despised and whose treaty he broke. ¹⁷Pharaoh with his mighty army and great horde will be of no help to him in war, when ramps are built and siege works erected to destroy many lives. ¹⁸He despised the oath by breaking the covenant. Because he had given his hand in pledge and yet did all these things, he shall not escape.

¹⁹" 'Therefore this is what the Sovereign LORD says: As surely as I live, I will bring down on his head my oath that he despised and my covenant that he broke. ²⁰I will spread my net for him, and he will be caught in my snare. I will bring him to Babylon and execute judgment upon him there because he was unfaithful to me. ²¹All his fleeing troops will fall by the sword, and the survivors will be scattered to the winds. Then you will know that I the LORD have spoken.

²²" 'This is what the Sovereign LORD says: I myself will take a shoot from the very top of a cedar and plant it; I will break off a tender sprig from its topmost shoots and plant it on a high and lofty mountain. ²³On the mountain heights of Israel I will plant it; it will produce branches and bear fruit and become a splendid cedar. Birds of every kind will nest in it; they will find shelter in the

shade of its branches. ²⁴All the trees of the field will know that I the LORD bring down the tall tree and make the low tree grow tall. I dry up the green tree and make the dry tree flourish.

" 'I the LORD have spoken, and I will do it.' "

The Soul Who Sins Will Die

18 The word of the LORD came to me: ²"What do you people mean by quoting this proverb about the land of Israel:

" 'The fathers eat sour grapes,
    and the children's teeth are set on
    edge'?

³"As surely as I live, declares the Sovereign LORD, you will no longer quote this proverb in Israel. ⁴For every living soul belongs to me, the father as well as the son — both alike belong to me. The soul who sins is the one who will die.

⁵"Suppose there is a righteous man
    who does what is just and right.
⁶He does not eat at the mountain
        shrines
    or look to the idols of the house of
        Israel.
He does not defile his neighbor's wife
    or lie with a woman during her
        period.
⁷He does not oppress anyone,
    but returns what he took in pledge
        for a loan.
He does not commit robbery
    but gives his food to the hungry
    and provides clothing for the naked.
⁸He does not lend at usury
    or take excessive interest.ᵃ
He withholds his hand from doing
        wrong
    and judges fairly between man and
        man.
⁹He follows my decrees
    and faithfully keeps my laws.
That man is righteous;
    he will surely live,
            declares the Sovereign LORD.

¹⁰"Suppose he has a violent son, who sheds blood or does any of these other thingsᵇ ¹¹(though the father has done none of them):

"He eats at the mountain shrines.
He defiles his neighbor's wife.
¹²He oppresses the poor and needy.

ᵃ8 Or *take interest*; similarly in verses 13 and 17   ᵇ10 Or *things to a brother*

He commits robbery.
He does not return what he took in
   pledge.
He looks to the idols.
He does detestable things.
[13]He lends at usury and takes excessive
   interest.

Will such a man live? He will not! Because
he has done all these detestable things, he
will surely be put to death and his blood
will be on his own head.

[14]"But suppose this son has a son who
sees all the sins his father commits, and
though he sees them, he does not do such
things:

[15]"He does not eat at the mountain
   shrines
   or look to the idols of the house of
   Israel.
He does not defile his neighbor's wife.
[16]He does not oppress anyone
   or require a pledge for a loan.
He does not commit robbery
   but gives his food to the hungry
   and provides clothing for the naked.
[17]He withholds his hand from sin[a]
   and takes no usury or excessive
   interest.
He keeps my laws and follows my
   decrees.

He will not die for his father's sin; he will
surely live. [18]But his father will die for his
own sin, because he practiced extortion,
robbed his brother and did what was
wrong among his people.

[19]"Yet you ask, 'Why does the son not
share the guilt of his father?' Since the son
has done what is just and right and has
been careful to keep all my decrees, he
will surely live. [20]The soul who sins is the
one who will die. The son will not share
the guilt of the father, nor will the father
share the guilt of the son. The righteousness of the righteous man will be credited
to him, and the wickedness of the wicked
will be charged against him.

[21]"But if a wicked man turns away from
all the sins he has committed and keeps
all my decrees and does what is just and
right, he will surely live; he will not die.
[22]None of the offenses he has committed
will be remembered against him. Because
of the righteous things he has done, he
will live. [23]Do I take any pleasure in the
death of the wicked? declares the Sover-

eign LORD. Rather, am I not pleased when
they turn from their ways and live?

[24]"But if a righteous man turns from his
righteousness and commits sin and does
the same detestable things the wicked
man does, will he live? None of the righteous things he has done will be remembered. Because of the unfaithfulness he is
guilty of and because of the sins he has
committed, he will die.

[25]"Yet you say, 'The way of the Lord is
not just.' Hear, O house of Israel: Is my
way unjust? Is it not your ways that are
unjust? [26]If a righteous man turns from his
righteousness and commits sin, he will
die for it; because of the sin he has committed he will die. [27]But if a wicked man
turns away from the wickedness he has
committed and does what is just and
right, he will save his life. [28]Because he
considers all the offenses he has committed and turns away from them, he will
surely live; he will not die. [29]Yet the house
of Israel says, 'The way of the Lord is not
just.' Are my ways unjust, O house of Israel? Is it not your ways that are unjust?

[30]"Therefore, O house of Israel, I will
judge you, each one according to his
ways, declares the Sovereign LORD. Repent! Turn away from all your offenses;
then sin will not be your downfall. [31]Rid
yourselves of all the offenses you have
committed, and get a new heart and a new
spirit. Why will you die, O house of Israel?
[32]For I take no pleasure in the death of
anyone, declares the Sovereign LORD. Repent and live!

A Lament for Israel's Princes

19 "Take up a lament concerning the
princes of Israel [2]and say:

" 'What a lioness was your mother
   among the lions!
She lay down among the young lions
   and reared her cubs.
[3]She brought up one of her cubs,
   and he became a strong lion.
He learned to tear the prey
   and he devoured men.
[4]The nations heard about him,
   and he was trapped in their pit.
They led him with hooks
   to the land of Egypt.

[5]" 'When she saw her hope unfulfilled,
   her expectation gone,
she took another of her cubs
   and made him a strong lion.

---

[a]17 Septuagint (see also verse 8); Hebrew *from the poor*

6He prowled among the lions,
   for he was now a strong lion.
He learned to tear the prey
   and he devoured men.
7He broke down[a] their strongholds
   and devastated their towns.
The land and all who were in it
   were terrified by his roaring.
8Then the nations came against him,
   those from regions round about.
They spread their net for him,
   and he was trapped in their pit.
9With hooks they pulled him into a
      cage
   and brought him to the king of
      Babylon.
They put him in prison,
   so his roar was heard no longer
   on the mountains of Israel.

10" 'Your mother was like a vine in your
      vineyard[b]
   planted by the water;
it was fruitful and full of branches
   because of abundant water.
11Its branches were strong,
   fit for a ruler's scepter.
It towered high
   above the thick foliage,
conspicuous for its height
   and for its many branches.
12But it was uprooted in fury
   and thrown to the ground.
The east wind made it shrivel,
   it was stripped of its fruit;
its strong branches withered
   and fire consumed them.
13Now it is planted in the desert,
   in a dry and thirsty land.
14Fire spread from one of its main[c]
      branches
   and consumed its fruit.
No strong branch is left on it
   fit for a ruler's scepter.'

This is a lament and is to be used as a lament."

Rebellious Israel

20 In the seventh year, in the fifth
month on the tenth day, some of
the elders of Israel came to inquire of the
Lord, and they sat down in front of me.

2Then the word of the Lord came to me:
3"Son of man, speak to the elders of Israel
and say to them, 'This is what the Sovereign Lord says: Have you come to inquire
of me? As surely as I live, I will not let you

inquire of me, declares the Sovereign
Lord.'
4"Will you judge them? Will you judge
them, son of man? Then confront them
with the detestable practices of their fathers 5and say to them: 'This is what the
Sovereign Lord says: On the day I chose
Israel, I swore with uplifted hand to the
descendants of the house of Jacob and revealed myself to them in Egypt. With uplifted hand I said to them, "I am the Lord
your God." 6On that day I swore to them
that I would bring them out of Egypt into
a land I had searched out for them, a land
flowing with milk and honey, the most
beautiful of all lands. 7And I said to them,
"Each of you, get rid of the vile images you
have set your eyes on, and do not defile
yourselves with the idols of Egypt. I am
the Lord your God."
8" 'But they rebelled against me and
would not listen to me; they did not get rid
of the vile images they had set their eyes
on, nor did they forsake the idols of Egypt.
So I said I would pour out my wrath on
them and spend my anger against them in
Egypt. 9But for the sake of my name I did
what would keep it from being profaned
in the eyes of the nations they lived
among and in whose sight I had revealed
myself to the Israelites by bringing them
out of Egypt. 10Therefore I led them out of
Egypt and brought them into the desert.
11I gave them my decrees and made
known to them my laws, for the man who
obeys them will live by them. 12Also I gave
them my Sabbaths as a sign between us,
so they would know that I the Lord made
them holy.
13" 'Yet the people of Israel rebelled
against me in the desert. They did not follow my decrees but rejected my laws — although the man who obeys them will live
by them — and they utterly desecrated my
Sabbaths. So I said I would pour out my
wrath on them and destroy them in the
desert. 14But for the sake of my name I did
what would keep it from being profaned
in the eyes of the nations in whose sight
I had brought them out. 15Also with uplifted hand I swore to them in the desert that
I would not bring them into the land I had
given them — a land flowing with milk and
honey, most beautiful of all lands — 16because they rejected my laws and did not
follow my decrees and desecrated my Sabbaths. For their hearts were devoted to

---

[a]7 Targum (see Septuagint); Hebrew He knew   [b]10 Two Hebrew manuscripts; most Hebrew
manuscripts your blood   [c]14 Or from under its

their idols. **17**Yet I looked on them with pity and did not destroy them or put an end to them in the desert. **18**I said to their children in the desert, "Do not follow the statutes of your fathers or keep their laws or defile yourselves with their idols. **19**I am the LORD your God; follow my decrees and be careful to keep my laws. **20**Keep my Sabbaths holy, that they may be a sign between us. Then you will know that I am the LORD your God."

21" 'But the children rebelled against me: They did not follow my decrees, they were not careful to keep my laws—although the man who obeys them will live by them—and they desecrated my Sabbaths. So I said I would pour out my wrath on them and spend my anger against them in the desert. **22**But I withheld my hand, and for the sake of my name I did what would keep it from being profaned in the eyes of the nations in whose sight I had brought them out. **23**Also with uplifted hand I swore to them in the desert that I would disperse them among the nations and scatter them through the countries, **24**because they had not obeyed my laws but had rejected my decrees and desecrated my Sabbaths, and their eyes lusted after their fathers' idols. **25**I also gave them over to statutes that were not good and laws they could not live by; **26**I let them become defiled through their gifts—the sacrifice of every firstborn*a*—that I might fill them with horror so they would know that I am the LORD.'

27"Therefore, son of man, speak to the people of Israel and say to them, 'This is what the Sovereign LORD says: In this also your fathers blasphemed me by forsaking me: **28**When I brought them into the land I had sworn to give them and they saw any high hill or any leafy tree, there they offered their sacrifices, made offerings that provoked me to anger, presented their fragrant incense and poured out their drink offerings. **29**Then I said to them: What is this high place you go to?' " (It is called Bamah*b* to this day.)

Judgment and Restoration

30"Therefore say to the house of Israel: 'This is what the Sovereign LORD says: Will you defile yourselves the way your fathers did and lust after their vile images? **31**When you offer your gifts—the sacrifice of your sons in*c* the fire—you continue

to defile yourselves with all your idols to this day. Am I to let you inquire of me, O house of Israel? As surely as I live, declares the Sovereign LORD, I will not let you inquire of me.

32" 'You say, "We want to be like the nations, like the peoples of the world, who serve wood and stone." But what you have in mind will never happen. **33**As surely as I live, declares the Sovereign LORD, I will rule over you with a mighty hand and an outstretched arm and with outpoured wrath. **34**I will bring you from the nations and gather you from the countries where you have been scattered—with a mighty hand and an outstretched arm and with outpoured wrath. **35**I will bring you into the desert of the nations and there, face to face, I will execute judgment upon you. **36**As I judged your fathers in the desert of the land of Egypt, so I will judge you, declares the Sovereign LORD. **37**I will take note of you as you pass under my rod, and I will bring you into the bond of the covenant. **38**I will purge you of those who revolt and rebel against me. Although I will bring them out of the land where they are living, yet they will not enter the land of Israel. Then you will know that I am the LORD.

39" 'As for you, O house of Israel, this is what the Sovereign LORD says: Go and serve your idols, every one of you! But afterward you will surely listen to me and no longer profane my holy name with your gifts and idols. **40**For on my holy mountain, the high mountain of Israel, declares the Sovereign LORD, there in the land the entire house of Israel will serve me, and there I will accept them. There I will require your offerings and your choice gifts,*d* along with all your holy sacrifices. **41**I will accept you as fragrant incense when I bring you out from the nations and gather you from the countries where you have been scattered, and I will show myself holy among you in the sight of the nations. **42**Then you will know that I am the LORD, when I bring you into the land of Israel, the land I had sworn with uplifted hand to give to your fathers. **43**There you will remember your conduct and all the actions by which you have defiled yourselves, and you will loathe yourselves for all the evil you have done. **44**You will know that I am the LORD, when I deal with you for my name's sake and not ac-

---

a26 Or —*making every firstborn pass through the fire,*   *b29 Bamah means high place.*   *c31* Or
—*making your sons pass through*   *d40* Or *and the gifts of your firstfruits*

cording to your evil ways and your corrupt practices, O house of Israel, declares the Sovereign LORD.' "

Prophecy Against the South

45The word of the LORD came to me: **46**"Son of man, set your face toward the south; preach against the south and prophesy against the forest of the southland. **47**Say to the southern forest: 'Hear the word of the LORD. This is what the Sovereign LORD says: I am about to set fire to you, and it will consume all your trees, both green and dry. The blazing flame will not be quenched, and every face from south to north will be scorched by it. **48**Everyone will see that I the LORD have kindled it; it will not be quenched.' "

49Then I said, "Ah, Sovereign LORD! They are saying of me, 'Isn't he just telling parables?' "

Babylon, God's Sword of Judgment

21 The word of the LORD came to me: **2**"Son of man, set your face against Jerusalem and preach against the sanctuary. Prophesy against the land of Israel **3**and say to her: 'This is what the LORD says: I am against you. I will draw my sword from its scabbard and cut off from you both the righteous and the wicked. **4**Because I am going to cut off the righteous and the wicked, my sword will be unsheathed against everyone from south to north. **5**Then all people will know that I the LORD have drawn my sword from its scabbard; it will not return again.'

6"Therefore groan, son of man! Groan before them with broken heart and bitter grief. **7**And when they ask you, 'Why are you groaning?' you shall say, 'Because of the news that is coming. Every heart will melt and every hand go limp; every spirit will become faint and every knee become as weak as water.' It is coming! It will surely take place, declares the Sovereign LORD."

8The word of the LORD came to me: **9**"Son of man, prophesy and say, 'This is what the Lord says:

" 'A sword, a sword,
　　sharpened and polished—
10sharpened for the slaughter,
　　polished to flash like lightning!

" 'Shall we rejoice in the scepter of my son ˌJudahˌ? The sword despises every such stick.

11" 'The sword is appointed to be
　　polished,
　　to be grasped with the hand;
it is sharpened and polished,
　　made ready for the hand of the
　　　slayer.
12Cry out and wail, son of man,
　　for it is against my people;
　　it is against all the princes of Israel.
They are thrown to the sword
　　along with my people.
Therefore beat your breast.

13" 'Testing will surely come. And what if the scepter ˌof Judahˌ, which the sword despises, does not continue? declares the Sovereign LORD.'

14"So then, son of man, prophesy
　　and strike your hands together.
Let the sword strike twice,
　　even three times.
It is a sword for slaughter—
　　a sword for great slaughter,
　　closing in on them from every side.
15So that hearts may melt
　　and the fallen be many,
I have stationed the sword for
　　slaughter[a]
　　at all their gates.
Oh! It is made to flash like lightning,
　　it is grasped for slaughter.
16O sword, slash to the right,
　　then to the left,
　　wherever your blade is turned.
17I too will strike my hands together,
　　and my wrath will subside.
I the LORD have spoken."

18The word of the LORD came to me: **19**"Son of man, mark out two roads for the sword of the king of Babylon to take, both starting from the same country. Make a signpost where the road branches off to the city. **20**Mark out one road for the sword to come against Rabbah of the Ammonites and another against Judah and fortified Jerusalem. **21**For the king of Babylon will stop at the fork in the road, at the junction of the two roads, to seek an omen: He will cast lots with arrows, he will consult his idols, he will examine the liver. **22**Into his right hand will come the lot for Jerusalem, where he is to set up battering rams, to give the command to slaughter, to sound the battle cry, to set battering rams against the gates, to build a ramp and to erect siege works. **23**It will seem like a false omen to those who have

---

*a*15 Septuagint; the meaning of the Hebrew for this word is uncertain.

sworn allegiance to him, but he will remind them of their guilt and take them captive.

²⁴"Therefore this is what the Sovereign LORD says: 'Because you people have brought to mind your guilt by your open rebellion, revealing your sins in all that you do—because you have done this, you will be taken captive.

²⁵"'O profane and wicked prince of Israel, whose day has come, whose time of punishment has reached its climax, ²⁶this is what the Sovereign LORD says: Take off the turban, remove the crown. It will not be as it was: The lowly will be exalted and the exalted will be brought low. ²⁷A ruin! A ruin! I will make it a ruin! It will not be restored until he comes to whom it rightfully belongs; to him I will give it.'

²⁸"And you, son of man, prophesy and say, 'This is what the Sovereign LORD says about the Ammonites and their insults:

" 'A sword, a sword,
    drawn for the slaughter,
polished to consume
    and to flash like lightning!
²⁹Despite false visions concerning you
    and lying divinations about you,
it will be laid on the necks
    of the wicked who are to be slain,
whose day has come,
    whose time of punishment has
        reached its climax.
³⁰Return the sword to its scabbard.
    In the place where you were
        created,
in the land of your ancestry,
    I will judge you.
³¹I will pour out my wrath upon you
    and breathe out my fiery anger
        against you;
I will hand you over to brutal men,
    men skilled in destruction.
³²You will be fuel for the fire,
    your blood will be shed in your
        land,
you will be remembered no more;
    for I the LORD have spoken.' "

Jerusalem's Sins

22 The word of the LORD came to me: ²"Son of man, will you judge her? Will you judge this city of bloodshed? Then confront her with all her detestable practices ³and say: 'This is what the Sovereign LORD says: O city that brings on herself doom by shedding blood in her midst and defiles herself by making idols, ⁴you have become guilty because of the blood you have shed and have become defiled by the idols you have made. You have brought your days to a close, and the end of your years has come. Therefore I will make you an object of scorn to the nations and a laughingstock to all the countries. ⁵Those who are near and those who are far away will mock you, O infamous city, full of turmoil.

⁶"'See how each of the princes of Israel who are in you uses his power to shed blood. ⁷In you they have treated father and mother with contempt; in you they have oppressed the alien and mistreated the fatherless and the widow. ⁸You have despised my holy things and desecrated my Sabbaths. ⁹In you are slanderous men bent on shedding blood; in you are those who eat at the mountain shrines and commit lewd acts. ¹⁰In you are those who dishonor their fathers' bed; in you are those who violate women during their period, when they are ceremonially unclean. ¹¹In you one man commits a detestable offense with his neighbor's wife, another shamefully defiles his daughter-in-law, and another violates his sister, his own father's daughter. ¹²In you men accept bribes to shed blood; you take usury and excessive interest[a] and make unjust gain from your neighbors by extortion. And you have forgotten me, declares the Sovereign LORD.

¹³"'I will surely strike my hands together at the unjust gain you have made and at the blood you have shed in your midst. ¹⁴Will your courage endure or your hands be strong in the day I deal with you? I the LORD have spoken, and I will do it. ¹⁵I will disperse you among the nations and scatter you through the countries; and I will put an end to your uncleanness. ¹⁶When you have been defiled[b] in the eyes of the nations, you will know that I am the LORD.' "

¹⁷Then the word of the LORD came to me: ¹⁸"Son of man, the house of Israel has become dross to me; all of them are the copper, tin, iron and lead left inside a furnace. They are but the dross of silver. ¹⁹Therefore this is what the Sovereign LORD says: 'Because you have all become dross, I will gather you into Jerusalem. ²⁰As men gather silver, copper, iron, lead and tin into a furnace to melt it with a fiery blast, so will I gather you in my anger and

my wrath and put you inside the city and melt you. **21**I will gather you and I will blow on you with my fiery wrath, and you will be melted inside her. **22**As silver is melted in a furnace, so you will be melted inside her, and you will know that I the Lord have poured out my wrath upon you.' "

23Again the word of the Lord came to me: **24**"Son of man, say to the land, 'You are a land that has had no rain or showers*a* in the day of wrath.' **25**There is a conspiracy of her princes*b* within her like a roaring lion tearing its prey; they devour people, take treasures and precious things and make many widows within her. **26**Her priests do violence to my law and profane my holy things; they do not distinguish between the holy and the common; they teach that there is no difference between the unclean and the clean; and they shut their eyes to the keeping of my Sabbaths, so that I am profaned among them. **27**Her officials within her are like wolves tearing their prey; they shed blood and kill people to make unjust gain. **28**Her prophets whitewash these deeds for them by false visions and lying divinations. They say, 'This is what the Sovereign Lord says' — when the Lord has not spoken. **29**The people of the land practice extortion and commit robbery; they oppress the poor and needy and mistreat the alien, denying them justice.

30"I looked for a man among them who would build up the wall and stand before me in the gap on behalf of the land so I would not have to destroy it, but I found none. **31**So I will pour out my wrath on them and consume them with my fiery anger, bringing down on their own heads all they have done, declares the Sovereign Lord."

Two Adulterous Sisters

23 The word of the Lord came to me: **2**"Son of man, there were two women, daughters of the same mother. **3**They became prostitutes in Egypt, engaging in prostitution from their youth. In that land their breasts were fondled and their virgin bosoms caressed. **4**The older was named Oholah, and her sister was Oholibah. They were mine and gave birth to sons and daughters. Oholah is Samaria, and Oholibah is Jerusalem.

5"Oholah engaged in prostitution while she was still mine; and she lusted after her lovers, the Assyrians — warriors **6**clothed in blue, governors and commanders, all of them handsome young men, and mounted horsemen. **7**She gave herself as a prostitute to all the elite of the Assyrians and defiled herself with all the idols of everyone she lusted after. **8**She did not give up the prostitution she began in Egypt, when during her youth men slept with her, caressed her virgin bosom and poured out their lust upon her.

9"Therefore I handed her over to her lovers, the Assyrians, for whom she lusted. **10**They stripped her naked, took away her sons and daughters and killed her with the sword. She became a byword among women, and punishment was inflicted on her.

11"Her sister Oholibah saw this, yet in her lust and prostitution she was more depraved than her sister. **12**She too lusted after the Assyrians — governors and commanders, warriors in full dress, mounted horsemen, all handsome young men. **13**I saw that she too defiled herself; both of them went the same way.

14"But she carried her prostitution still further. She saw men portrayed on a wall, figures of Chaldeans*c* portrayed in red, **15**with belts around their waists and flowing turbans on their heads; all of them looked like Babylonian chariot officers, natives of Chaldea.*d* **16**As soon as she saw them, she lusted after them and sent messengers to them in Chaldea. **17**Then the Babylonians came to her, to the bed of love, and in their lust they defiled her. After she had been defiled by them, she turned away from them in disgust. **18**When she carried on her prostitution openly and exposed her nakedness, I turned away from her in disgust, just as I had turned away from her sister. **19**Yet she became more and more promiscuous as she recalled the days of her youth, when she was a prostitute in Egypt. **20**There she lusted after her lovers, whose genitals were like those of donkeys and whose emission was like that of horses. **21**So you longed for the lewdness of your youth, when in Egypt your bosom was caressed and your young breasts fondled.*e*

22"Therefore, Oholibah, this is what the Sovereign Lord says: I will stir up your

---

a24 Septuagint; Hebrew *has not been cleansed or rained on*   *b25* Septuagint; Hebrew *prophets*
c14 Or *Babylonians*   *d15* Or *Babylonia*; also in verse 16   *e21* Syriac (see also verse 3); Hebrew
caressed because of your young breasts

lovers against you, those you turned away from in disgust, and I will bring them against you from every side— **23**the Babylonians and all the Chaldeans, the men of Pekod and Shoa and Koa, and all the Assyrians with them, handsome young men, all of them governors and commanders, chariot officers and men of high rank, all mounted on horses. **24**They will come against you with weapons,*a* chariots and wagons and with a throng of people; they will take up positions against you on every side with large and small shields and with helmets. I will turn you over to them for punishment, and they will punish you according to their standards. **25**I will direct my jealous anger against you, and they will deal with you in fury. They will cut off

a24 The meaning of the Hebrew for this word is uncertain.

WEDNESDAY

VERSE FOR THE DAY:	AUTHOR:	PASSAGE FOR THE DAY:
Ezekiel 22:30	Richard Halverson	Ezekiel 22:23–31

Big Men

RARELY do you run into a really bad man in these circles of business—industry—professions and government. They're good men by and large . . .

But you meet so many small men! Not small in stature—but men who think little, talk little, plan little. Like eagles staked to the ground, there's *no soar* to them. *Ceiling is zero*—and their *horizons are pulled in to the hub.*

Not that these men are selfish. (Some of course are.) But it's just that they're *preoccupied most of the time with their own little bailiwick.* They don't allow their minds to stretch and breathe. They don't think—they just rearrange their prejudices . . .

These little men are *indifferent* to problems other than their own. They have *no concern* for those things which do not hold a personal reference. They refuse to be bothered!

Here lies the tragedy of the little man—his unavailability. He is needed but unavailable! Needed by his community—his nation—the world . . . and he doesn't see beyond the four walls of his miserable little existence! . . .

In this desperately crucial, convulsive time, *unavailability is a terrible sin.* The times demand big men. Not men who are big shots (they're useless), but men who are big in heart and mind. Great men! Large-souled men!

Men with a vision—whose feet are on the ground but whose eyes are on the far horizon. Farsighted, selfless men. *Men with a goal!* Men whose hearts God has touched. Men committed —*dedicated to God* and his holy, high purposes! Men of integrity!

Additional Scripture Readings:
Romans 12:1–2;
1 Corinthians 16:13–14

Go to page 919 for your next devotional reading.

your noses and your ears, and those of you who are left will fall by the sword. They will take away your sons and daughters, and those of you who are left will be consumed by fire. ²⁶They will also strip you of your clothes and take your fine jewelry. ²⁷So I will put a stop to the lewdness and prostitution you began in Egypt. You will not look on these things with longing or remember Egypt anymore.

²⁸"For this is what the Sovereign LORD says: I am about to hand you over to those you hate, to those you turned away from in disgust. ²⁹They will deal with you in hatred and take away everything you have worked for. They will leave you naked and bare, and the shame of your prostitution will be exposed. Your lewdness and promiscuity ³⁰have brought this upon you, because you lusted after the nations and defiled yourself with their idols. ³¹You have gone the way of your sister; so I will put her cup into your hand.

³²"This is what the Sovereign LORD says:

"You will drink your sister's cup,
    a cup large and deep;
it will bring scorn and derision,
    for it holds so much.
³³You will be filled with drunkenness
        and sorrow,
    the cup of ruin and desolation,
    the cup of your sister Samaria.
³⁴You will drink it and drain it dry;
    you will dash it to pieces
    and tear your breasts.

I have spoken, declares the Sovereign LORD.

³⁵"Therefore this is what the Sovereign LORD says: Since you have forgotten me and thrust me behind your back, you must bear the consequences of your lewdness and prostitution."

³⁶The LORD said to me: "Son of man, will you judge Oholah and Oholibah? Then confront them with their detestable practices, ³⁷for they have committed adultery and blood is on their hands. They committed adultery with their idols; they even sacrificed their children, whom they bore to me,ᵃ as food for them. ³⁸They have also done this to me: At that same time they defiled my sanctuary and desecrated my Sabbaths. ³⁹On the very day they sacrificed their children to their idols, they entered my sanctuary and des-

ecrated it. That is what they did in my house.

⁴⁰"They even sent messengers for men who came from far away, and when they arrived you bathed yourself for them, painted your eyes and put on your jewelry. ⁴¹You sat on an elegant couch, with a table spread before it on which you had placed the incense and oil that belonged to me.

⁴²"The noise of a carefree crowd was around her; Sabeansᵇ were brought from the desert along with men from the rabble, and they put bracelets on the arms of the woman and her sister and beautiful crowns on their heads. ⁴³Then I said about the one worn out by adultery, 'Now let them use her as a prostitute, for that is all she is.' ⁴⁴And they slept with her. As men sleep with a prostitute, so they slept with those lewd women, Oholah and Oholibah. ⁴⁵But righteous men will sentence them to the punishment of women who commit adultery and shed blood, because they are adulterous and blood is on their hands.

⁴⁶"This is what the Sovereign LORD says: Bring a mob against them and give them over to terror and plunder. ⁴⁷The mob will stone them and cut them down with their swords; they will kill their sons and daughters and burn down their houses.

⁴⁸"So I will put an end to lewdness in the land, that all women may take warning and not imitate you. ⁴⁹You will suffer the penalty for your lewdness and bear the consequences of your sins of idolatry. Then you will know that I am the Sovereign LORD."

The Cooking Pot

24 In the ninth year, in the tenth month on the tenth day, the word of the LORD came to me: ²"Son of man, record this date, this very date, because the king of Babylon has laid siege to Jerusalem this very day. ³Tell this rebellious house a parable and say to them: 'This is what the Sovereign LORD says:

" 'Put on the cooking pot; put it on
    and pour water into it.
⁴Put into it the pieces of meat,
    all the choice pieces—the leg and
        the shoulder.
Fill it with the best of these bones;
⁵   take the pick of the flock.
Pile wood beneath it for the bones;
    bring it to a boil

ᵃ37 Or *even made the children they bore to me pass through the fire*   ᵇ42 Or *drunkards* and cook the bones in it.

⁶" 'For this is what the Sovereign Lord says:

" 'Woe to the city of bloodshed,
  to the pot now encrusted,
  whose deposit will not go away!
Empty it piece by piece
  without casting lots for them.

⁷" 'For the blood she shed is in her
    midst:
She poured it on the bare rock;
she did not pour it on the ground,
  where the dust would cover it.
⁸To stir up wrath and take revenge
I put her blood on the bare rock,
  so that it would not be covered.

⁹" 'Therefore this is what the Sovereign Lord says:

" 'Woe to the city of bloodshed!
  I, too, will pile the wood high.
¹⁰So heap on the wood
  and kindle the fire.
Cook the meat well,
  mixing in the spices;
  and let the bones be charred.
¹¹Then set the empty pot on the coals
  till it becomes hot and its copper
    glows
so its impurities may be melted
  and its deposit burned away.
¹²It has frustrated all efforts;
  its heavy deposit has not been
    removed,
  not even by fire.

¹³" 'Now your impurity is lewdness. Because I tried to cleanse you but you would not be cleansed from your impurity, you will not be clean again until my wrath against you has subsided.

¹⁴" 'I the Lord have spoken. The time has come for me to act. I will not hold back; I will not have pity, nor will I relent. You will be judged according to your conduct and your actions, declares the Sovereign Lord.' "

Ezekiel's Wife Dies

¹⁵The word of the Lord came to me: ¹⁶"Son of man, with one blow I am about to take away from you the delight of your eyes. Yet do not lament or weep or shed any tears. ¹⁷Groan quietly; do not mourn for the dead. Keep your turban fastened and your sandals on your feet; do not cov-

er the lower part of your face or eat the customary food ˌof mournersˌ."

¹⁸So I spoke to the people in the morning, and in the evening my wife died. The next morning I did as I had been commanded.

¹⁹Then the people asked me, "Won't you tell us what these things have to do with us?"

²⁰So I said to them, "The word of the Lord came to me: ²¹Say to the house of Israel, 'This is what the Sovereign Lord says: I am about to desecrate my sanctuary—the stronghold in which you take pride, the delight of your eyes, the object of your affection. The sons and daughters you left behind will fall by the sword. ²²And you will do as I have done. You will not cover the lower part of your face or eat the customary food ˌof mournersˌ. ²³You will keep your turbans on your heads and your sandals on your feet. You will not mourn or weep but will waste away because ofᵃ your sins and groan among yourselves. ²⁴Ezekiel will be a sign to you; you will do just as he has done. When this happens, you will know that I am the Sovereign Lord.'

²⁵"And you, son of man, on the day I take away their stronghold, their joy and glory, the delight of their eyes, their heart's desire, and their sons and daughters as well— ²⁶on that day a fugitive will come to tell you the news. ²⁷At that time your mouth will be opened; you will speak with him and will no longer be silent. So you will be a sign to them, and they will know that I am the Lord."

A Prophecy Against Ammon

25 The word of the Lord came to me: ²"Son of man, set your face against the Ammonites and prophesy against them. ³Say to them, 'Hear the word of the Sovereign Lord. This is what the Sovereign Lord says: Because you said "Aha!" over my sanctuary when it was desecrated and over the land of Israel when it was laid waste and over the people of Judah when they went into exile, ⁴therefore I am going to give you to the people of the East as a possession. They will set up their camps and pitch their tents among you; they will eat your fruit and drink your milk. ⁵I will turn Rabbah into a pasture for camels and Ammon into a resting place for sheep. Then you will know that I am the Lord. ⁶For this is what the Sovereign

ᵃ23 Or *away in*

LORD says: Because you have clapped your hands and stamped your feet, rejoicing with all the malice of your heart against the land of Israel, [7]therefore I will stretch out my hand against you and give you as plunder to the nations. I will cut you off from the nations and exterminate you from the countries. I will destroy you, and you will know that I am the LORD.' "

A Prophecy Against Moab

[8]"This is what the Sovereign LORD says: 'Because Moab and Seir said, "Look, the house of Judah has become like all the other nations," [9]therefore I will expose the flank of Moab, beginning at its frontier towns — Beth Jeshimoth, Baal Meon and Kiriathaim — the glory of that land. [10]I will give Moab along with the Ammonites to the people of the East as a possession, so that the Ammonites will not be remembered among the nations; [11]and I will inflict punishment on Moab. Then they will know that I am the LORD.' "

A Prophecy Against Edom

[12]"This is what the Sovereign LORD says: 'Because Edom took revenge on the house of Judah and became very guilty by doing so, [13]therefore this is what the Sovereign LORD says: I will stretch out my hand against Edom and kill its men and their animals. I will lay it waste, and from Teman to Dedan they will fall by the sword. [14]I will take vengeance on Edom by the hand of my people Israel, and they will deal with Edom in accordance with my anger and my wrath; they will know my vengeance, declares the Sovereign LORD.' "

A Prophecy Against Philistia

[15]"This is what the Sovereign LORD says: 'Because the Philistines acted in vengeance and took revenge with malice in their hearts, and with ancient hostility sought to destroy Judah, [16]therefore this is what the Sovereign LORD says: I am about to stretch out my hand against the Philistines, and I will cut off the Kerethites and destroy those remaining along the coast. [17]I will carry out great vengeance on them and punish them in my wrath. Then they will know that I am the LORD, when I take vengeance on them.' "

A Prophecy Against Tyre

26 In the eleventh year, on the first day of the month, the word of the LORD came to me: [2]"Son of man, because Tyre has said of Jerusalem, 'Aha! The gate to the nations is broken, and its doors have swung open to me; now that she lies in ruins I will prosper,' [3]therefore this is what the Sovereign LORD says: I am against you, O Tyre, and I will bring many nations against you, like the sea casting up its waves. [4]They will destroy the walls of Tyre and pull down her towers; I will scrape away her rubble and make her a bare rock. [5]Out in the sea she will become a place to spread fishnets, for I have spoken, declares the Sovereign LORD. She will become plunder for the nations, [6]and her settlements on the mainland will be ravaged by the sword. Then they will know that I am the LORD.

[7]"For this is what the Sovereign LORD says: From the north I am going to bring against Tyre Nebuchadnezzar[a] king of Babylon, king of kings, with horses and chariots, with horsemen and a great army. [8]He will ravage your settlements on the mainland with the sword; he will set up siege works against you, build a ramp up to your walls and raise his shields against you. [9]He will direct the blows of his battering rams against your walls and demolish your towers with his weapons. [10]His horses will be so many that they will cover you with dust. Your walls will tremble at the noise of the war horses, wagons and chariots when he enters your gates as men enter a city whose walls have been broken through. [11]The hoofs of his horses will trample all your streets; he will kill your people with the sword, and your strong pillars will fall to the ground. [12]They will plunder your wealth and loot your merchandise; they will break down your walls and demolish your fine houses and throw your stones, timber and rubble into the sea. [13]I will put an end to your noisy songs, and the music of your harps will be heard no more. [14]I will make you a bare rock, and you will become a place to spread fishnets. You will never be rebuilt, for I the LORD have spoken, declares the Sovereign LORD.

[15]"This is what the Sovereign LORD says to Tyre: Will not the coastlands tremble at the sound of your fall, when the wounded groan and the slaughter takes place in

---

[a]7 Hebrew *Nebuchadrezzar*, of which *Nebuchadnezzar* is a variant; here and often in Ezekiel and Jeremiah

you? **16**Then all the princes of the coast will step down from their thrones and lay aside their robes and take off their embroidered garments. Clothed with terror, they will sit on the ground, trembling every moment, appalled at you. **17**Then they will take up a lament concerning you and say to you:

" 'How you are destroyed, O city of
   renown,
  peopled by men of the sea!
You were a power on the seas,
  you and your citizens;
you put your terror
  on all who lived there.
18Now the coastlands tremble
  on the day of your fall;
the islands in the sea
  are terrified at your collapse.'

19"This is what the Sovereign Lord says: When I make you a desolate city, like cities no longer inhabited, and when I bring the ocean depths over you and its vast waters cover you, **20**then I will bring you down with those who go down to the pit, to the people of long ago. I will make you dwell in the earth below, as in ancient ruins, with those who go down to the pit, and you will not return or take your place*a* in the land of the living. **21**I will bring you to a horrible end and you will be no more. You will be sought, but you will never again be found, declares the Sovereign Lord."

A Lament for Tyre

27 The word of the Lord came to me: **2**"Son of man, take up a lament concerning Tyre. **3**Say to Tyre, situated at the gateway to the sea, merchant of peoples on many coasts, 'This is what the Sovereign Lord says:

" 'You say, O Tyre,
  "I am perfect in beauty."
4Your domain was on the high seas;
  your builders brought your beauty
    to perfection.
5They made all your timbers
  of pine trees from Senir*b*;
they took a cedar from Lebanon
  to make a mast for you.
6Of oaks from Bashan
  they made your oars;

of cypress wood*c* from the coasts of
  Cyprus*d*
they made your deck, inlaid with
  ivory.
7Fine embroidered linen from Egypt
  was your sail
and served as your banner;
your awnings were of blue and purple
  from the coasts of Elishah.
8Men of Sidon and Arvad were your
  oarsmen;
your skilled men, O Tyre, were
  aboard as your seamen.
9Veteran craftsmen of Gebal*e* were on
  board
  as shipwrights to caulk your seams.
All the ships of the sea and their
  sailors
  came alongside to trade for your
    wares.

10" 'Men of Persia, Lydia and Put
  served as soldiers in your army.
They hung their shields and helmets
  on your walls,
  bringing you splendor.
11Men of Arvad and Helech
  manned your walls on every side;
men of Gammad
  were in your towers.
They hung their shields around your
  walls;
  they brought your beauty to
    perfection.

12" 'Tarshish did business with you because of your great wealth of goods; they exchanged silver, iron, tin and lead for your merchandise.
13" 'Greece, Tubal and Meshech traded with you; they exchanged slaves and articles of bronze for your wares.
14" 'Men of Beth Togarmah exchanged work horses, war horses and mules for your merchandise.
15" 'The men of Rhodes*f* traded with you, and many coastlands were your customers; they paid you with ivory tusks and ebony.
16" 'Aram*g* did business with you because of your many products; they exchanged turquoise, purple fabric, embroidered work, fine linen, coral and rubies for your merchandise.
17" 'Judah and Israel traded with you; they exchanged wheat from Minnith and

---

a20 Septuagint; Hebrew *return, and I will give glory*   *b5* That is, Hermon   *c6* Targum; the Masoretic Text has a different division of the consonants.   *d6* Hebrew *Kittim*   *e9* That is, Byblos
f15 Septuagint; Hebrew *Dedan*   *g16* Most Hebrew manuscripts; some Hebrew manuscripts and Syriac *Edom*

confections,^a honey, oil and balm for your wares.

¹⁸" 'Damascus, because of your many products and great wealth of goods, did business with you in wine from Helbon and wool from Zahar.

¹⁹ 'Danites and Greeks from Uzal bought your merchandise; they exchanged wrought iron, cassia and calamus for your wares.

²⁰ 'Dedan traded in saddle blankets with you.

²¹" 'Arabia and all the princes of Kedar were your customers; they did business with you in lambs, rams and goats.

²²" 'The merchants of Sheba and Raamah traded with you; for your merchandise they exchanged the finest of all kinds of spices and precious stones, and gold.

²³" 'Haran, Canneh and Eden and merchants of Sheba, Asshur and Kilmad traded with you. ²⁴In your marketplace they traded with you beautiful garments, blue fabric, embroidered work and multicolored rugs with cords twisted and tightly knotted.

²⁵" 'The ships of Tarshish serve
    as carriers for your wares.
You are filled with heavy cargo
    in the heart of the sea.
²⁶Your oarsmen take you
    out to the high seas.
But the east wind will break you to
        pieces
    in the heart of the sea.
²⁷Your wealth, merchandise and wares,
    your mariners, seamen and
        shipwrights,
    your merchants and all your soldiers,
    and everyone else on board
will sink into the heart of the sea
    on the day of your shipwreck.
²⁸The shorelands will quake
    when your seamen cry out.
²⁹All who handle the oars
    will abandon their ships;
the mariners and all the seamen
    will stand on the shore.
³⁰They will raise their voice
    and cry bitterly over you;
they will sprinkle dust on their heads
    and roll in ashes.
³¹They will shave their heads because of
        you
    and will put on sackcloth.

They will weep over you with anguish
        of soul
    and with bitter mourning.
³²As they wail and mourn over you,
    they will take up a lament
        concerning you:
"Who was ever silenced like Tyre,
    surrounded by the sea?"
³³When your merchandise went out on
        the seas,
    you satisfied many nations;
with your great wealth and your wares
    you enriched the kings of the earth.
³⁴Now you are shattered by the sea
    in the depths of the waters;
your wares and all your company
    have gone down with you.
³⁵All who live in the coastlands
    are appalled at you;
their kings shudder with horror
    and their faces are distorted with
        fear.
³⁶The merchants among the nations hiss
        at you;
    you have come to a horrible end
    and will be no more.' "

A Prophecy Against the King of Tyre

28 The word of the LORD came to me: ²"Son of man, say to the ruler of Tyre, 'This is what the Sovereign LORD says:

" 'In the pride of your heart
    you say, "I am a god;
I sit on the throne of a god
    in the heart of the seas."
But you are a man and not a god,
    though you think you are as wise as
        a god.
³Are you wiser than Daniel^b?
    Is no secret hidden from you?
⁴By your wisdom and understanding
    you have gained wealth for yourself
and amassed gold and silver
    in your treasuries.
⁵By your great skill in trading
    you have increased your wealth,
and because of your wealth
    your heart has grown proud.

⁶" 'Therefore this is what the Sovereign LORD says:

" 'Because you think you are wise,
    as wise as a god,
⁷I am going to bring foreigners against
        you,

---

^a17 The meaning of the Hebrew for this word is uncertain.   ^b3 Or *Danel*; the Hebrew spelling may suggest a person other than the prophet Daniel.

the most ruthless of nations;
they will draw their swords against
    your beauty and wisdom
    and pierce your shining splendor.
[8]They will bring you down to the pit,
    and you will die a violent death
    in the heart of the seas.
[9]Will you then say, "I am a god,"
    in the presence of those who kill
        you?
    You will be but a man, not a god,
    in the hands of those who slay you.
[10]You will die the death of the
        uncircumcised
    at the hands of foreigners.

I have spoken, declares the Sovereign
Lord.' "

[11]The word of the Lord came to me:
[12]"Son of man, take up a lament concerning the king of Tyre and say to him: 'This
is what the Sovereign Lord says:

" 'You were the model of perfection,
    full of wisdom and perfect in
        beauty.
[13]You were in Eden,
    the garden of God;
every precious stone adorned you:
    ruby, topaz and emerald,
    chrysolite, onyx and jasper,
    sapphire,[a] turquoise and beryl.[b]
Your settings and mountings[c] were
        made of gold;
    on the day you were created they
        were prepared.
[14]You were anointed as a guardian
        cherub,
    for so I ordained you.
You were on the holy mount of God;
    you walked among the fiery stones.
[15]You were blameless in your ways
    from the day you were created
    till wickedness was found in you.
[16]Through your widespread trade
    you were filled with violence,
    and you sinned.
So I drove you in disgrace from the
        mount of God,
    and I expelled you, O guardian
        cherub,
    from among the fiery stones.
[17]Your heart became proud
    on account of your beauty,
and you corrupted your wisdom
    because of your splendor.
So I threw you to the earth;

I made a spectacle of you before
    kings.
[18]By your many sins and dishonest
        trade
    you have desecrated your
        sanctuaries.
So I made a fire come out from you,
    and it consumed you,
and I reduced you to ashes on the
        ground
    in the sight of all who were
        watching.
[19]All the nations who knew you
    are appalled at you;
you have come to a horrible end
    and will be no more.' "

A Prophecy Against Sidon

[20]The word of the Lord came to me:
[21]"Son of man, set your face against Sidon; prophesy against her [22]and say: 'This
is what the Sovereign Lord says:

" 'I am against you, O Sidon,
    and I will gain glory within you.
They will know that I am the Lord,
    when I inflict punishment on her
    and show myself holy within her.
[23]I will send a plague upon her
    and make blood flow in her streets.
The slain will fall within her,
    with the sword against her on every
        side.
Then they will know that I am the
        Lord.

[24]" 'No longer will the people of Israel
have malicious neighbors who are painful
briers and sharp thorns. Then they will
know that I am the Sovereign Lord.
[25]" 'This is what the Sovereign Lord
says: When I gather the people of Israel
from the nations where they have been
scattered, I will show myself holy among
them in the sight of the nations. Then they
will live in their own land, which I gave to
my servant Jacob. [26]They will live there in
safety and will build houses and plant
vineyards; they will live in safety when I
inflict punishment on all their neighbors
who maligned them. Then they will know
that I am the Lord their God.' "

A Prophecy Against Egypt

29 In the tenth year, in the tenth
    month on the twelfth day, the word
of the Lord came to me: [2]"Son of man, set
your face against Pharaoh king of Egypt

---

[a]13 Or *lapis lazuli*   [b]13 The precise identification of some of these precious stones is uncertain.
[c]13 The meaning of the Hebrew for this phrase is uncertain.

and prophesy against him and against all Egypt. ³Speak to him and say: 'This is what the Sovereign LORD says:

" 'I am against you, Pharaoh king of
    Egypt,
  you great monster lying among your
    streams.
You say, "The Nile is mine;
  I made it for myself."
⁴But I will put hooks in your jaws
  and make the fish of your streams
    stick to your scales.
I will pull you out from among your
    streams,
  with all the fish sticking to your
    scales.
⁵I will leave you in the desert,
  you and all the fish of your streams.
You will fall on the open field
  and not be gathered or picked up.
I will give you as food
  to the beasts of the earth and the
    birds of the air.

⁶Then all who live in Egypt will know that I am the LORD.

" 'You have been a staff of reed for the house of Israel. ⁷When they grasped you with their hands, you splintered and you tore open their shoulders; when they leaned on you, you broke and their backs were wrenched.[a]

⁸" 'Therefore this is what the Sovereign LORD says: I will bring a sword against you and kill your men and their animals. ⁹Egypt will become a desolate wasteland. Then they will know that I am the LORD.

" 'Because you said, "The Nile is mine; I made it," ¹⁰therefore I am against you and against your streams, and I will make the land of Egypt a ruin and a desolate waste from Migdol to Aswan, as far as the border of Cush.[b] ¹¹No foot of man or animal will pass through it; no one will live there for forty years. ¹²I will make the land of Egypt desolate among devastated lands, and her cities will lie desolate forty years among ruined cities. And I will disperse the Egyptians among the nations and scatter them through the countries.

¹³" 'Yet this is what the Sovereign LORD says: At the end of forty years I will gather the Egyptians from the nations where they were scattered. ¹⁴I will bring them back from captivity and return them to Upper Egypt,[c] the land of their ancestry. There they will be a lowly kingdom. ¹⁵It will be the lowliest of kingdoms and will never again exalt itself above the other nations. I will make it so weak that it will never again rule over the nations. ¹⁶Egypt will no longer be a source of confidence for the people of Israel but will be a reminder of their sin in turning to her for help. Then they will know that I am the Sovereign LORD.' "

¹⁷In the twenty-seventh year, in the first month on the first day, the word of the LORD came to me: ¹⁸"Son of man, Nebuchadnezzar king of Babylon drove his army in a hard campaign against Tyre; every head was rubbed bare and every shoulder made raw. Yet he and his army got no reward from the campaign he led against Tyre. ¹⁹Therefore this is what the Sovereign LORD says: I am going to give Egypt to Nebuchadnezzar king of Babylon, and he will carry off its wealth. He will loot and plunder the land as pay for his army. ²⁰I have given him Egypt as a reward for his efforts because he and his army did it for me, declares the Sovereign LORD.

²¹"On that day I will make a horn[d] grow for the house of Israel, and I will open your mouth among them. Then they will know that I am the LORD."

A Lament for Egypt

30 The word of the LORD came to me: ²"Son of man, prophesy and say: 'This is what the Sovereign LORD says:

" 'Wail and say,
  "Alas for that day!"
³For the day is near,
  the day of the LORD is near—
a day of clouds,
  a time of doom for the nations.
⁴A sword will come against Egypt,
  and anguish will come upon
    Cush.[e]
When the slain fall in Egypt,
  her wealth will be carried away
  and her foundations torn down.

⁵Cush and Put, Lydia and all Arabia, Libya[f] and the people of the covenant land will fall by the sword along with Egypt.

⁶" 'This is what the LORD says:

" 'The allies of Egypt will fall

and her proud strength will fail.
From Migdol to Aswan
  they will fall by the sword within
    her,
           declares the Sovereign LORD.
7" 'They will be desolate
  among desolate lands,
  and their cities will lie
  among ruined cities.
8Then they will know that I am the
  LORD,
  when I set fire to Egypt
  and all her helpers are crushed.

9" 'On that day messengers will go out
from me in ships to frighten Cush out of
her complacency. Anguish will take hold
of them on the day of Egypt's doom, for it
is sure to come.

10" 'This is what the Sovereign LORD
says:

" 'I will put an end to the hordes of
  Egypt
  by the hand of Nebuchadnezzar
    king of Babylon.
11He and his army—the most ruthless
  of nations—
  will be brought in to destroy the
    land.
They will draw their swords against
  Egypt
  and fill the land with the slain.
12I will dry up the streams of the Nile
  and sell the land to evil men;
by the hand of foreigners
  I will lay waste the land and
    everything in it.
I the LORD have spoken.

13" 'This is what the Sovereign LORD
says:

" 'I will destroy the idols
  and put an end to the images in
    Memphis.*a*
No longer will there be a prince in
  Egypt,
  and I will spread fear throughout
    the land.
14I will lay waste Upper Egypt,*b*
  set fire to Zoan
  and inflict punishment on Thebes.*c*
15I will pour out my wrath on
  Pelusium,*d*
  the stronghold of Egypt,
  and cut off the hordes of Thebes.
16I will set fire to Egypt;

Pelusium will writhe in agony.
Thebes will be taken by storm;
  Memphis will be in constant
    distress.
17The young men of Heliopolis*e* and
  Bubastis*f*
  will fall by the sword,
  and the cities themselves will go
    into captivity.
18Dark will be the day at Tahpanhes
  when I break the yoke of Egypt;
  there her proud strength will come
    to an end.
She will be covered with clouds,
  and her villages will go into
    captivity.
19So I will inflict punishment on Egypt,
  and they will know that I am the
    LORD.' "

20In the eleventh year, in the first
month on the seventh day, the word of the
LORD came to me: **21**"Son of man, I have
broken the arm of Pharaoh king of Egypt.
It has not been bound up for healing or
put in a splint so as to become strong
enough to hold a sword. **22**Therefore this
is what the Sovereign LORD says: I am
against Pharaoh king of Egypt. I will break
both his arms, the good arm as well as the
broken one, and make the sword fall from
his hand. **23**I will disperse the Egyptians
among the nations and scatter them
through the countries. **24**I will strengthen
the arms of the king of Babylon and put
my sword in his hand, but I will break the
arms of Pharaoh, and he will groan before
him like a mortally wounded man. **25**I will
strengthen the arms of the king of Babylon, but the arms of Pharaoh will fall
limp. Then they will know that I am the
LORD, when I put my sword into the hand
of the king of Babylon and he brandishes
it against Egypt. **26**I will disperse the Egyptians among the nations and scatter them
through the countries. Then they will
know that I am the LORD."

A Cedar in Lebanon

31 In the eleventh year, in the third
month on the first day, the word of
the LORD came to me: **2**"Son of man, say to
Pharaoh king of Egypt and to his hordes:

" 'Who can be compared with you in
  majesty?
3Consider Assyria, once a cedar in
  Lebanon,

---

*a*13 Hebrew *Noph*; also in verse 16   *b*14 Hebrew *waste Pathros*   *c*14 Hebrew *No*; also in verses 15
and 16   *d*15 Hebrew *Sin*; also in verse 16   *e*17 Hebrew *Awen* (or *On*)   *f*17 Hebrew *Pi Beseth*

with beautiful branches
　　overshadowing the forest;
it towered on high,
　　its top above the thick foliage.
[4]The waters nourished it,
　　deep springs made it grow tall;
their streams flowed
　　all around its base
and sent their channels
　　to all the trees of the field.
[5]So it towered higher
　　than all the trees of the field;
its boughs increased
　　and its branches grew long,
　　spreading because of abundant
　　　waters.
[6]All the birds of the air
　　nested in its boughs,
all the beasts of the field
　　gave birth under its branches;
all the great nations
　　lived in its shade.
[7]It was majestic in beauty,
　　with its spreading boughs,
for its roots went down
　　to abundant waters.
[8]The cedars in the garden of God
　　could not rival it,
nor could the pine trees
　　equal its boughs,
nor could the plane trees
　　compare with its branches—
no tree in the garden of God
　　could match its beauty.
[9]I made it beautiful
　　with abundant branches,
the envy of all the trees of Eden
　　in the garden of God.

[10]" Therefore this is what the Sovereign
Lord says: Because it towered on high,
lifting its top above the thick foliage, and
because it was proud of its height, [11]I
handed it over to the ruler of the nations,
for him to deal with according to its wickedness. I cast it aside, [12]and the most ruthless of foreign nations cut it down and left
it. Its boughs fell on the mountains and in
all the valleys; its branches lay broken in
all the ravines of the land. All the nations
of the earth came out from under its shade
and left it. [13]All the birds of the air settled
on the fallen tree, and all the beasts of the
field were among its branches. [14]There-
fore no other trees by the waters are ever
to tower proudly on high, lifting their tops
above the thick foliage. No other trees so
well-watered are ever to reach such a

height; they are all destined for death, for
the earth below, among mortal men, with
those who go down to the pit.

[15]"This is what the Sovereign Lord
says: On the day it was brought down to
the grave[a] I covered the deep springs
with mourning for it; I held back its
streams, and its abundant waters were restrained. Because of it I clothed Lebanon
with gloom, and all the trees of the field
withered away. [16]I made the nations tremble at the sound of its fall when I brought
it down to the grave with those who go
down to the pit. Then all the trees of Eden,
the choicest and best of Lebanon, all the
trees that were well-watered, were consoled in the earth below. [17]Those who
lived in its shade, its allies among the nations, had also gone down to the grave
with it, joining those killed by the sword.

[18]" 'Which of the trees of Eden can be
compared with you in splendor and majesty? Yet you, too, will be brought down
with the trees of Eden to the earth below;
you will lie among the uncircumcised,
with those killed by the sword.

" 'This is Pharaoh and all his hordes, declares the Sovereign Lord.' "

A Lament for Pharaoh

32 In the twelfth year, in the twelfth
month on the first day, the word of
the Lord came to me: [2]"Son of man, take
up a lament concerning Pharaoh king of
Egypt and say to him:

" 'You are like a lion among the
　　nations;
you are like a monster in the seas
thrashing about in your streams,
　　churning the water with your feet
　　and muddying the streams.

[3]" 'This is what the Sovereign Lord
says:

" 'With a great throng of people
　　I will cast my net over you,
　　and they will haul you up in my
　　　net.
[4]I will throw you on the land
　　and hurl you on the open field.
I will let all the birds of the air settle
　　on you
　　and all the beasts of the earth gorge
　　themselves on you.
[5]I will spread your flesh on the
　　mountains

---

[a]15 Hebrew *Sheol*; also in verses 16 and 17

and fill the valleys with your
     remains.
⁶I will drench the land with your
     flowing blood
  all the way to the mountains,
  and the ravines will be filled with
     your flesh.
⁷When I snuff you out, I will cover the
     heavens
  and darken their stars;
  I will cover the sun with a cloud,
  and the moon will not give its light.
⁸All the shining lights in the heavens
  I will darken over you;
  I will bring darkness over your land,
       declares the Sovereign LORD.
⁹I will trouble the hearts of many
     peoples
  when I bring about your destruction
     among the nations,
  among*a* lands you have not known.
¹⁰I will cause many peoples to be
     appalled at you,
  and their kings will shudder with
     horror because of you
  when I brandish my sword before
     them.
On the day of your downfall
  each of them will tremble
  every moment for his life.

¹¹" 'For this is what the Sovereign LORD
says:

  " 'The sword of the king of Babylon
     will come against you.
¹²I will cause your hordes to fall
  by the swords of mighty men —
  the most ruthless of all nations.
They will shatter the pride of Egypt,
  and all her hordes will be
     overthrown.
¹³I will destroy all her cattle
  from beside abundant waters
no longer to be stirred by the foot of
     man
  or muddied by the hoofs of cattle.
¹⁴Then I will let her waters settle
  and make her streams flow like oil,
       declares the Sovereign LORD.
¹⁵When I make Egypt desolate
  and strip the land of everything in
     it,
when I strike down all who live there,
  then they will know that I am the
     LORD.'

¹⁶"This is the lament they will chant for
her. The daughters of the nations will
chant it; for Egypt and all her hordes they
will chant it, declares the Sovereign LORD."

¹⁷In the twelfth year, on the fifteenth
day of the month, the word of the LORD
came to me: ¹⁸"Son of man, wail for the
hordes of Egypt and consign to the earth
below both her and the daughters of
mighty nations, with those who go down
to the pit. ¹⁹Say to them, 'Are you more
favored than others? Go down and be laid
among the uncircumcised.' ²⁰They will
fall among those killed by the sword. The
sword is drawn; let her be dragged off
with all her hordes. ²¹From within the
grave*b* the mighty leaders will say of
Egypt and her allies, 'They have come
down and they lie with the uncircumcised, with those killed by the sword.'

²²"Assyria is there with her whole army;
she is surrounded by the graves of all her
slain, all who have fallen by the sword.
²³Their graves are in the depths of the pit
and her army lies around her grave. All
who had spread terror in the land of the
living are slain, fallen by the sword.

²⁴"Elam is there, with all her hordes
around her grave. All of them are slain,
fallen by the sword. All who had spread
terror in the land of the living went down
uncircumcised to the earth below. They
bear their shame with those who go down
to the pit. ²⁵A bed is made for her among
the slain, with all her hordes around her
grave. All of them are uncircumcised,
killed by the sword. Because their terror
had spread in the land of the living, they
bear their shame with those who go down
to the pit; they are laid among the slain.

²⁶"Meshech and Tubal are there, with
all their hordes around their graves. All of
them are uncircumcised, killed by the
sword because they spread their terror in
the land of the living. ²⁷Do they not lie
with the other uncircumcised warriors
who have fallen, who went down to the
grave with their weapons of war, whose
swords were placed under their heads?
The punishment for their sins rested on
their bones, though the terror of these
warriors had stalked through the land of
the living.

²⁸"You too, O Pharaoh, will be broken
and will lie among the uncircumcised,
with those killed by the sword.

²⁹"Edom is there, her kings and all her

a9 Hebrew; Septuagint *bring you into captivity among the nations, / to*   *b21* Hebrew *Sheol*; also in
verse 27

princes; despite their power, they are laid with those killed by the sword. They lie with the uncircumcised, with those who go down to the pit.

30"All the princes of the north and all the Sidonians are there; they went down with the slain in disgrace despite the terror caused by their power. They lie uncircumcised with those killed by the sword and bear their shame with those who go down to the pit.

31"Pharaoh — he and all his army — will see them and he will be consoled for all his hordes that were killed by the sword, declares the Sovereign LORD. 32Although I had him spread terror in the land of the living, Pharaoh and all his hordes will be laid among the uncircumcised, with those killed by the sword, declares the Sovereign LORD."

Ezekiel a Watchman

33 The word of the LORD came to me: 2"Son of man, speak to your countrymen and say to them: 'When I bring the sword against a land, and the people of the land choose one of their men and make him their watchman, 3and he sees the sword coming against the land and blows the trumpet to warn the people, 4then if anyone hears the trumpet but does not take warning and the sword comes and takes his life, his blood will be on his own head. 5Since he heard the sound of the trumpet but did not take warning, his blood will be on his own head. If he had taken warning, he would have saved himself. 6But if the watchman sees the sword coming and does not blow the trumpet to warn the people and the sword comes and takes the life of one of them, that man will be taken away because of his sin, but I will hold the watchman accountable for his blood.'

7"Son of man, I have made you a watchman for the house of Israel; so hear the word I speak and give them warning from me. 8When I say to the wicked, 'O wicked man, you will surely die,' and you do not speak out to dissuade him from his ways, that wicked man will die for[a] his sin, and I will hold you accountable for his blood. 9But if you do warn the wicked man to turn from his ways and he does not do so, he will die for his sin, but you will have saved yourself.

10"Son of man, say to the house of Israel, 'This is what you are saying: "Our offenses and sins weigh us down, and we are wasting away because of[b] them. How then can we live?"' 11Say to them, 'As surely as I live, declares the Sovereign LORD, I take no pleasure in the death of the wicked, but rather that they turn from their ways and live. Turn! Turn from your evil ways! Why will you die, O house of Israel?'

12"Therefore, son of man, say to your countrymen, 'The righteousness of the righteous man will not save him when he disobeys, and the wickedness of the wicked man will not cause him to fall when he turns from it. The righteous man, if he sins, will not be allowed to live because of his former righteousness.' 13If I tell the righteous man that he will surely live, but then he trusts in his righteousness and does evil, none of the righteous things he has done will be remembered; he will die for the evil he has done. 14And if I say to the wicked man, 'You will surely die,' but he then turns away from his sin and does what is just and right — 15if he gives back what he took in pledge for a loan, returns what he has stolen, follows the decrees that give life, and does no evil, he will surely live; he will not die. 16None of the sins he has committed will be remembered against him. He has done what is just and right; he will surely live.

17"Yet your countrymen say, 'The way of the Lord is not just.' But it is their way that is not just. 18If a righteous man turns from his righteousness and does evil, he will die for it. 19And if a wicked man turns away from his wickedness and does what is just and right, he will live by doing so. 20Yet, O house of Israel, you say, 'The way of the Lord is not just.' But I will judge each of you according to his own ways."

Jerusalem's Fall Explained

21In the twelfth year of our exile, in the tenth month on the fifth day, a man who had escaped from Jerusalem came to me and said, "The city has fallen!" 22Now the evening before the man arrived, the hand of the LORD was upon me, and he opened my mouth before the man came to me in the morning. So my mouth was opened and I was no longer silent.

23Then the word of the LORD came to me: 24"Son of man, the people living in those ruins in the land of Israel are saying, 'Abraham was only one man, yet he possessed the land. But we are many; surely

---

a8 Or *in*; also in verse 9   *b10* Or *away in*

the land has been given to us as our possession.' 25Therefore say to them, 'This is what the Sovereign LORD says: Since you eat meat with the blood still in it and look to your idols and shed blood, should you then possess the land? 26You rely on your sword, you do detestable things, and each of you defiles his neighbor's wife. Should you then possess the land?'

27"Say this to them: 'This is what the Sovereign LORD says: As surely as I live, those who are left in the ruins will fall by the sword, those out in the country I will give to the wild animals to be devoured, and those in strongholds and caves will die of a plague. 28I will make the land a desolate waste, and her proud strength will come to an end, and the mountains of Israel will become desolate so that no one will cross them. 29Then they will know that I am the LORD, when I have made the land a desolate waste because of all the detestable things they have done.'

30"As for you, son of man, your countrymen are talking together about you by the walls and at the doors of the houses, saying to each other, 'Come and hear the message that has come from the LORD.' 31My people come to you, as they usually do, and sit before you to listen to your words, but they do not put them into practice. With their mouths they express devotion, but their hearts are greedy for unjust gain. 32Indeed, to them you are nothing more than one who sings love songs with a beautiful voice and plays an instrument well, for they hear your words but do not put them into practice.

33"When all this comes true—and it surely will—then they will know that a prophet has been among them."

Shepherds and Sheep

34 The word of the LORD came to me: 2"Son of man, prophesy against the shepherds of Israel; prophesy and say to them: 'This is what the Sovereign LORD says: Woe to the shepherds of Israel who only take care of themselves! Should not shepherds take care of the flock? 3You eat the curds, clothe yourselves with the wool and slaughter the choice animals, but you do not take care of the flock. 4You have not strengthened the weak or healed the sick or bound up the injured. You have not brought back the strays or searched for the lost. You have ruled them harshly and brutally. 5So they were scattered because there was no shepherd, and when they were scattered they became food for all the wild animals. 6My sheep wandered over all the mountains and on every high hill. They were scattered over the whole earth, and no one searched or looked for them.

7" 'Therefore, you shepherds, hear the word of the LORD: 8As surely as I live, declares the Sovereign LORD, because my flock lacks a shepherd and so has been plundered and has become food for all the wild animals, and because my shepherds did not search for my flock but cared for themselves rather than for my flock, 9therefore, O shepherds, hear the word of the LORD: 10This is what the Sovereign LORD says: I am against the shepherds and will hold them accountable for my flock. I will remove them from tending the flock so that the shepherds can no longer feed themselves. I will rescue my flock from their mouths, and it will no longer be food for them.

11" 'For this is what the Sovereign LORD says: I myself will search for my sheep and look after them. 12As a shepherd looks after his scattered flock when he is with them, so will I look after my sheep. I will rescue them from all the places where they were scattered on a day of clouds and darkness. 13I will bring them out from the nations and gather them from the countries, and I will bring them into their own land. I will pasture them on the mountains of Israel, in the ravines and in all the settlements in the land. 14I will tend them in a good pasture, and the mountain heights of Israel will be their grazing land. There they will lie down in good grazing land, and there they will feed in a rich pasture on the mountains of Israel. 15I myself will tend my sheep and have them lie down, declares the Sovereign LORD. 16I will search for the lost and bring back the strays. I will bind up the injured and strengthen the weak, but the sleek and the strong I will destroy. I will shepherd the flock with justice.

17" 'As for you, my flock, this is what the Sovereign LORD says: I will judge between one sheep and another, and between rams and goats. 18Is it not enough for you to feed on the good pasture? Must you also trample the rest of your pasture with your feet? Is it not enough for you to drink clear water? Must you also muddy the rest with your feet? 19Must my flock feed on what you have trampled and drink what you have muddied with your feet?

20" 'Therefore this is what the Sovereign LORD says to them: See, I myself will judge between the fat sheep and the lean sheep. [21]Because you shove with flank and shoulder, butting all the weak sheep with your horns until you have driven them away, [22]I will save my flock, and they will no longer be plundered. I will judge between one sheep and another. [23]I will place over them one shepherd, my servant David, and he will tend them; he will tend them and be their shepherd. [24]I the LORD will be their God, and my servant David will be prince among them. I the LORD have spoken.

[25]" 'I will make a covenant of peace with them and rid the land of wild beasts so that they may live in the desert and sleep in the forests in safety. [26]I will bless them and the places surrounding my hill.[a] I will send down showers in season; there will be showers of blessing. [27]The trees of the field will yield their fruit and the ground will yield its crops; the people will be secure in their land. They will know that I am the LORD, when I break the bars of their yoke and rescue them from the hands of those who enslaved them. [28]They will no longer be plundered by the nations, nor will wild animals devour them. They will live in safety, and no one will make them afraid. [29]I will provide for them a land renowned for its crops, and they will no longer be victims of famine in the land or bear the scorn of the nations. [30]Then they will know that I, the LORD their God, am with them and that they, the house of Israel, are my people, declares the Sovereign LORD. [31]You my sheep, the sheep of my pasture, are people, and I am your God, declares the Sovereign LORD.' "

A Prophecy Against Edom

35 The word of the LORD came to me: [2]"Son of man, set your face against Mount Seir; prophesy against it [3]and say: 'This is what the Sovereign LORD says: I am against you, Mount Seir, and I will stretch out my hand against you and make you a desolate waste. [4]I will turn your towns into ruins and you will be desolate. Then you will know that I am the LORD.

[5]" 'Because you harbored an ancient hostility and delivered the Israelites over to the sword at the time of their calamity, the time their punishment reached its climax, [6]therefore as surely as I live, declares the Sovereign LORD, I will give you over to bloodshed and it will pursue you. Since you did not hate bloodshed, bloodshed

will pursue you. [7]I will make Mount Seir a desolate waste and cut off from it all who come and go. [8]I will fill your mountains with the slain; those killed by the sword will fall on your hills and in your valleys and in all your ravines. [9]I will make you desolate forever; your towns will not be inhabited. Then you will know that I am the LORD.

[10]" 'Because you have said, "These two nations and countries will be ours and we will take possession of them," even though I the LORD was there, [11]therefore as surely as I live, declares the Sovereign LORD, I will treat you in accordance with the anger and jealousy you showed in your hatred of them and I will make myself known among them when I judge you. [12]Then you will know that I the LORD have heard all the contemptible things you have said against the mountains of Israel. You said, "They have been laid waste and have been given over to us to devour." [13]You boasted against me and spoke against me without restraint, and I heard it. [14]This is what the Sovereign LORD says: While the whole earth rejoices, I will make you desolate. [15]Because you rejoiced when the inheritance of the house of Israel became desolate, that is how I will treat you. You will be desolate, O Mount Seir, you and all of Edom. Then they will know that I am the LORD.' "

A Prophecy to the Mountains of Israel

36 "Son of man, prophesy to the mountains of Israel and say, 'O mountains of Israel, hear the word of the LORD. [2]This is what the Sovereign LORD says: The enemy said of you, "Aha! The ancient heights have become our possession." ' [3]Therefore prophesy and say, 'This is what the Sovereign LORD says: Because they ravaged and hounded you from every side so that you became the possession of the rest of the nations and the object of people's malicious talk and slander, [4]therefore, O mountains of Israel, hear the word of the Sovereign LORD: This is what the Sovereign LORD says to the mountains and hills, to the ravines and valleys, to the desolate ruins and the deserted towns that have been plundered and ridiculed by the rest of the nations around you— [5]this is what the Sovereign LORD says: In my burning zeal I have spoken against the rest of the nations, and

---

[a]26 Or *I will make them and the places surrounding my hill a blessing*

against all Edom, for with glee and with malice in their hearts they made my land their own possession so that they might plunder its pastureland.' ⁶Therefore prophesy concerning the land of Israel and say to the mountains and hills, to the ravines and valleys: 'This is what the Sovereign LORD says: I speak in my jealous wrath because you have suffered the scorn of the nations. ⁷Therefore this is what the Sovereign LORD says: I swear with uplifted hand that the nations around you will also suffer scorn.

⁸" 'But you, O mountains of Israel, will produce branches and fruit for my people Israel, for they will soon come home. ⁹I am concerned for you and will look on you with favor; you will be plowed and sown, ¹⁰and I will multiply the number of people upon you, even the whole house of Israel. The towns will be inhabited and the ruins rebuilt. ¹¹I will increase the number of men and animals upon you, and they will be fruitful and become numerous. I will settle people on you as in the past and will make you prosper more than before. Then you will know that I am the LORD. ¹²I will cause people, my people Israel, to walk upon you. They will possess you, and you will be their inheritance; you will never again deprive them of their children.

¹³" 'This is what the Sovereign LORD says: Because people say to you, "You devour men and deprive your nation of its children," ¹⁴therefore you will no longer devour men or make your nation childless, declares the Sovereign LORD. ¹⁵No longer will I make you hear the taunts of the nations, and no longer will you suffer the scorn of the peoples or cause your nation to fall, declares the Sovereign LORD.' "

¹⁶Again the word of the LORD came to me: ¹⁷"Son of man, when the people of Israel were living in their own land, they defiled it by their conduct and their actions. Their conduct was like a woman's monthly uncleanness in my sight. ¹⁸So I poured out my wrath on them because they had shed blood in the land and because they had defiled it with their idols. ¹⁹I dispersed them among the nations, and they were scattered through the countries; I judged them according to their conduct and their actions. ²⁰And wherever they went among the nations they profaned my holy name, for it was said of them, 'These are the LORD's people, and yet they had to leave his land.' ²¹I had concern for my holy name, which the house of Israel pro-

faned among the nations where they had gone.

²²"Therefore say to the house of Israel, 'This is what the Sovereign LORD says: It is not for your sake, O house of Israel, that I am going to do these things, but for the sake of my holy name, which you have profaned among the nations where you have gone. ²³I will show the holiness of my great name, which has been profaned among the nations, the name you have profaned among them. Then the nations will know that I am the LORD, declares the Sovereign LORD, when I show myself holy through you before their eyes.

²⁴" 'For I will take you out of the nations; I will gather you from all the countries and bring you back into your own land. ²⁵I will sprinkle clean water on you, and you will be clean; I will cleanse you from all your impurities and from all your idols. ²⁶I will give you a new heart and put a new spirit in you; I will remove from you your heart of stone and give you a heart of flesh. ²⁷And I will put my Spirit in you and move you to follow my decrees and be careful to keep my laws. ²⁸You will live in the land I gave your forefathers; you will be my people, and I will be your God. ²⁹I will save you from all your uncleanness. I will call for the grain and make it plentiful and will not bring famine upon you. ³⁰I will increase the fruit of the trees and the crops of the field, so that you will no longer suffer disgrace among the nations because of famine. ³¹Then you will remember your evil ways and wicked deeds, and you will loathe yourselves for your sins and detestable practices. ³²I want you to know that I am not doing this for your sake, declares the Sovereign LORD. Be ashamed and disgraced for your conduct, O house of Israel!

³³" 'This is what the Sovereign LORD says: On the day I cleanse you from all your sins, I will resettle your towns, and the ruins will be rebuilt. ³⁴The desolate land will be cultivated instead of lying desolate in the sight of all who pass through it. ³⁵They will say, "This land that was laid waste has become like the garden of Eden; the cities that were lying in ruins, desolate and destroyed, are now fortified and inhabited." ³⁶Then the nations around you that remain will know that I the LORD have rebuilt what was destroyed and have replanted what was desolate. I the LORD have spoken, and I will do it.'

³⁷"This is what the Sovereign LORD says: Once again I will yield to the plea of the

house of Israel and do this for them: I will make their people as numerous as sheep, **38**as numerous as the flocks for offerings at Jerusalem during her appointed feasts. So will the ruined cities be filled with flocks of people. Then they will know that I am the Lord."

The Valley of Dry Bones

37 The hand of the Lord was upon me, and he brought me out by the Spirit of the Lord and set me in the middle of a valley; it was full of bones. **2**He led me back and forth among them, and I saw a great many bones on the floor of the valley, bones that were very dry. **3**He asked me, "Son of man, can these bones live?"

I said, "O Sovereign Lord, you alone know."

4Then he said to me, "Prophesy to these bones and say to them, 'Dry bones, hear the word of the Lord! **5**This is what the Sovereign Lord says to these bones: I will make breath*a* enter you, and you will come to life. **6**I will attach tendons to you and make flesh come upon you and cover you with skin; I will put breath in you, and you will come to life. Then you will know that I am the Lord.' "

7So I prophesied as I was commanded. And as I was prophesying, there was a noise, a rattling sound, and the bones came together, bone to bone. **8**I looked, and tendons and flesh appeared on them and skin covered them, but there was no breath in them.

9Then he said to me, "Prophesy to the breath; prophesy, son of man, and say to it, 'This is what the Sovereign Lord says: Come from the four winds, O breath, and breathe into these slain, that they may live.' " **10**So I prophesied as he commanded me, and breath entered them; they came to life and stood up on their feet—a vast army.

11Then he said to me: "Son of man, these bones are the whole house of Israel. They say, 'Our bones are dried up and our hope is gone; we are cut off.' **12**Therefore prophesy and say to them: 'This is what the Sovereign Lord says: O my people, I am going to open your graves and bring you up from them; I will bring you back to the land of Israel. **13**Then you, my people, will know that I am the Lord, when I open your graves and bring you up from them. **14**I will put my Spirit in you and you will

live, and I will settle you in your own land. Then you will know that I the Lord have spoken, and I have done it, declares the Lord.' "

One Nation Under One King

15The word of the Lord came to me: **16**"Son of man, take a stick of wood and write on it, 'Belonging to Judah and the Israelites associated with him.' Then take another stick of wood, and write on it, 'Ephraim's stick, belonging to Joseph and all the house of Israel associated with him.' **17**Join them together into one stick so that they will become one in your hand.

18"When your countrymen ask you, 'Won't you tell us what you mean by this?' **19**say to them, 'This is what the Sovereign Lord says: I am going to take the stick of Joseph—which is in Ephraim's hand—and of the Israelite tribes associated with him, and join it to Judah's stick, making them a single stick of wood, and they will become one in my hand.' **20**Hold before their eyes the sticks you have written on **21**and say to them, 'This is what the Sovereign Lord says: I will take the Israelites out of the nations where they have gone. I will gather them from all around and bring them back into their own land. **22**I will make them one nation in the land, on the mountains of Israel. There will be one king over all of them and they will never again be two nations or be divided into two kingdoms. **23**They will no longer defile themselves with their idols and vile images or with any of their offenses, for I will save them from all their sinful backsliding,*b* and I will cleanse them. They will be my people, and I will be their God.

24" 'My servant David will be king over them, and they will all have one shepherd. They will follow my laws and be careful to keep my decrees. **25**They will live in the land I gave to my servant Jacob, the land where your fathers lived. They and their children and their children's children will live there forever, and David my servant will be their prince forever. **26**I will make a covenant of peace with them; it will be an everlasting covenant. I will establish them and increase their numbers, and I will put my sanctuary among them forever. **27**My dwelling place will be with them; I will be their God, and they will be my people. **28**Then the nations will know that

a5 The Hebrew for this word can also mean wind or spirit (see verses 6-14).   b23 Many Hebrew manuscripts (see also Septuagint); most Hebrew manuscripts all their dwelling places where they sinned

I the LORD make Israel holy, when my sanctuary is among them forever.' "

A Prophecy Against Gog

38 The word of the LORD came to me: [2]"Son of man, set your face against Gog, of the land of Magog, the chief prince of[a] Meshech and Tubal; prophesy against him [3]and say: 'This is what the Sovereign LORD says: I am against you, O Gog, chief prince of[b] Meshech and Tubal. [4]I will turn you around, put hooks in your jaws and bring you out with your whole army—your horses, your horsemen fully armed, and a great horde with large and small shields, all of them brandishing their swords. [5]Persia, Cush[c] and Put will be with them, all with shields and helmets, [6]also Gomer with all its troops, and Beth Togarmah from the far north with all its troops—the many nations with you.

[7]" 'Get ready; be prepared, you and all the hordes gathered about you, and take command of them. [8]After many days you will be called to arms. In future years you will invade a land that has recovered from war, whose people were gathered from many nations to the mountains of Israel, which had long been desolate. They had been brought out from the nations, and now all of them live in safety. [9]You and all your troops and the many nations with you will go up, advancing like a storm; you will be like a cloud covering the land.

[10]" 'This is what the Sovereign LORD says: On that day thoughts will come into your mind and you will devise an evil scheme. [11]You will say, "I will invade a land of unwalled villages; I will attack a peaceful and unsuspecting people—all of them living without walls and without gates and bars. [12]I will plunder and loot and turn my hand against the resettled ruins and the people gathered from the nations, rich in livestock and goods, living at the center of the land." [13]Sheba and Dedan and the merchants of Tarshish and all her villages[d] will say to you, "Have you come to plunder? Have you gathered your hordes to loot, to carry off silver and gold, to take away livestock and goods and to seize much plunder?" '

[14]"Therefore, son of man, prophesy and say to Gog: 'This is what the Sovereign LORD says: In that day, when my people Israel are living in safety, will you not take notice of it? [15]You will come from your place in the far north, you and many nations with you, all of them riding on horses, a great horde, a mighty army. [16]You will advance against my people Israel like a cloud that covers the land. In days to come, O Gog, I will bring you against my land, so that the nations may know me when I show myself holy through you before their eyes.

[17]" 'This is what the Sovereign LORD says: Are you not the one I spoke of in former days by my servants the prophets of Israel? At that time they prophesied for years that I would bring you against them. [18]This is what will happen in that day: When Gog attacks the land of Israel, my hot anger will be aroused, declares the Sovereign LORD. [19]In my zeal and fiery wrath I declare that at that time there shall be a great earthquake in the land of Israel. [20]The fish of the sea, the birds of the air, the beasts of the field, every creature that moves along the ground, and all the people on the face of the earth will tremble at my presence. The mountains will be overturned, the cliffs will crumble and every wall will fall to the ground. [21]I will summon a sword against Gog on all my mountains, declares the Sovereign LORD. Every man's sword will be against his brother. [22]I will execute judgment upon him with plague and bloodshed; I will pour down torrents of rain, hailstones and burning sulfur on him and on his troops and on the many nations with him. [23]And so I will show my greatness and my holiness, and I will make myself known in the sight of many nations. Then they will know that I am the LORD.'

39 "Son of man, prophesy against Gog and say: 'This is what the Sovereign LORD says: I am against you, O Gog, chief prince of[b] Meshech and Tubal. [2]I will turn you around and drag you along. I will bring you from the far north and send you against the mountains of Israel. [3]Then I will strike your bow from your left hand and make your arrows drop from your right hand. [4]On the mountains of Israel you will fall, you and all your troops and the nations with you. I will give you as food to all kinds of carrion birds and to the wild animals. [5]You will fall in the open field, for I have spoken, declares the Sovereign LORD. [6]I will send fire on Magog and on those who live in safety in the coastlands, and they will know that I am the LORD.

7 " 'I will make known my holy name among my people Israel. I will no longer let my holy name be profaned, and the nations will know that I the LORD am the Holy One in Israel. 8It is coming! It will surely take place, declares the Sovereign LORD. This is the day I have spoken of.

9 " 'Then those who live in the towns of Israel will go out and use the weapons for fuel and burn them up—the small and large shields, the bows and arrows, the war clubs and spears. For seven years they will use them for fuel. 10They will not need to gather wood from the fields or cut it from the forests, because they will use the weapons for fuel. And they will plunder those who plundered them and loot those who looted them, declares the Sovereign LORD.

11 " 'On that day I will give Gog a burial place in Israel, in the valley of those who travel east toward*a* the Sea.*b* It will block the way of travelers, because Gog and all his hordes will be buried there. So it will be called the Valley of Hamon Gog.*c*

12 " 'For seven months the house of Israel will be burying them in order to cleanse the land. 13All the people of the land will bury them, and the day I am glorified will be a memorable day for them, declares the Sovereign LORD.

14 " 'Men will be regularly employed to cleanse the land. Some will go throughout the land and, in addition to them, others will bury those that remain on the ground. At the end of the seven months they will begin their search. 15As they go through the land and one of them sees a human bone, he will set up a marker beside it until the gravediggers have buried it in the Valley of Hamon Gog. 16(Also a town called Hamonah*d* will be there.) And so they will cleanse the land.'

17"Son of man, this is what the Sovereign LORD says: Call out to every kind of bird and all the wild animals: 'Assemble and come together from all around to the sacrifice I am preparing for you, the great sacrifice on the mountains of Israel. There you will eat flesh and drink blood. 18You will eat the flesh of mighty men and drink the blood of the princes of the earth as if they were rams and lambs, goats and bulls—all of them fattened animals from Bashan. 19At the sacrifice I am preparing

for you, you will eat fat till you are glutted and drink blood till you are drunk. 20At my table you will eat your fill of horses and riders, mighty men and soldiers of every kind,' declares the Sovereign LORD.

21"I will display my glory among the nations, and all the nations will see the punishment I inflict and the hand I lay upon them. 22From that day forward the house of Israel will know that I am the LORD their God. 23And the nations will know that the people of Israel went into exile for their sin, because they were unfaithful to me. So I hid my face from them and handed them over to their enemies, and they all fell by the sword. 24I dealt with them according to their uncleanness and their offenses, and I hid my face from them.

25"Therefore this is what the Sovereign LORD says: I will now bring Jacob back from captivity*e* and will have compassion on all the people of Israel, and I will be zealous for my holy name. 26They will forget their shame and all the unfaithfulness they showed toward me when they lived in safety in their land with no one to make them afraid. 27When I have brought them back from the nations and have gathered them from the countries of their enemies, I will show myself holy through them in the sight of many nations. 28Then they will know that I am the LORD their God, for though I sent them into exile among the nations, I will gather them to their own land, not leaving any behind. 29I will no longer hide my face from them, for I will pour out my Spirit on the house of Israel, declares the Sovereign LORD."

The New Temple Area

40 In the twenty-fifth year of our exile, at the beginning of the year, on the tenth of the month, in the fourteenth year after the fall of the city—on that very day the hand of the LORD was upon me and he took me there. 2In visions of God he took me to the land of Israel and set me on a very high mountain, on whose south side were some buildings that looked like a city. 3He took me there, and I saw a man whose appearance was like bronze; he was standing in the gateway with a linen cord and a measuring rod in his hand. 4The man said to me, "Son of man, look with your eyes and hear with your ears and pay attention to everything I am going to show you, for that is why you have

---

a11 Or *of* 　 *b11* That is, the Dead Sea 　 *c11 Hamon Gog* means *hordes of Gog.* 　 *d16 Hamonah* means *horde.* 　 *e25* Or *now restore the fortunes of Jacob* been brought here. Tell the house of Israel everything you see."

The East Gate to the Outer Court

⁵I saw a wall completely surrounding the temple area. The length of the measuring rod in the man's hand was six long cubits, each of which was a cubit[a] and a handbreadth.[b] He measured the wall; it was one measuring rod thick and one rod high.

⁶Then he went to the gate facing east. He climbed its steps and measured the threshold of the gate; it was one rod deep.[c] ⁷The alcoves for the guards were one rod long and one rod wide, and the projecting walls between the alcoves were five cubits thick. And the threshold of the gate next to the portico facing the temple was one rod deep.

⁸Then he measured the portico of the gateway; ⁹it[d] was eight cubits deep and its jambs were two cubits thick. The portico of the gateway faced the temple.

¹⁰Inside the east gate were three alcoves on each side; the three had the same measurements, and the faces of the projecting walls on each side had the same measurements. ¹¹Then he measured the width of the entrance to the gateway; it was ten cubits and its length was thirteen cubits. ¹²In front of each alcove was a wall one cubit high, and the alcoves were six cubits square. ¹³Then he measured the gateway from the top of the rear wall of one alcove to the top of the opposite one; the distance was twenty-five cubits from one parapet opening to the opposite one. ¹⁴He measured along the faces of the projecting walls all around the inside of the gateway—sixty cubits. The measurement was up to the portico[e] facing the courtyard.[f] ¹⁵The distance from the entrance of the gateway to the far end of its portico was fifty cubits. ¹⁶The alcoves and the projecting walls inside the gateway were surmounted by narrow parapet openings all around, as was the portico; the openings all around faced inward. The faces of the projecting walls were decorated with palm trees.

The Outer Court

¹⁷Then he brought me into the outer court. There I saw some rooms and a pavement that had been constructed all around the court; there were thirty rooms along the pavement. ¹⁸It abutted the sides of the gateways and was as wide as they were long; this was the lower pavement. ¹⁹Then he measured the distance from the inside of the lower gateway to the outside of the inner court; it was a hundred cubits on the east side as well as on the north.

The North Gate

²⁰Then he measured the length and width of the gate facing north, leading into the outer court. ²¹Its alcoves—three on each side—its projecting walls and its portico had the same measurements as those of the first gateway. It was fifty cubits long and twenty-five cubits wide. ²²Its openings, its portico and its palm tree decorations had the same measurements as those of the gate facing east. Seven steps led up to it, with its portico opposite them. ²³There was a gate to the inner court facing the north gate, just as there was on the east. He measured from one gate to the opposite one; it was a hundred cubits.

The South Gate

²⁴Then he led me to the south side and I saw a gate facing south. He measured its jambs and its portico, and they had the same measurements as the others. ²⁵The gateway and its portico had narrow openings all around, like the openings of the others. It was fifty cubits long and twenty-five cubits wide. ²⁶Seven steps led up to it, with its portico opposite them; it had palm tree decorations on the faces of the projecting walls on each side. ²⁷The inner court also had a gate facing south, and he measured from this gate to the outer gate on the south side; it was a hundred cubits.

Gates to the Inner Court

²⁸Then he brought me into the inner court through the south gate, and he measured the south gate; it had the same measurements as the others. ²⁹Its alcoves, its projecting walls and its portico had the same measurements as the others. The gateway and its portico had openings all around. It was fifty cubits long and twenty-five cubits wide. ³⁰(The porticoes of the

---

a5 The common cubit was about 1 1/2 feet (about 0.5 meter).   *b5* That is, about 3 inches (about 8 centimeters)   *c6* Septuagint; Hebrew *deep, the first threshold, one rod deep*   *d8,9* Many Hebrew manuscripts, Septuagint, Vulgate and Syriac; most Hebrew manuscripts *gateway facing the temple; it was one rod deep. 9Then he measured the portico of the gateway; it*   *e14* Septuagint; Hebrew *projecting wall*   *f14* The meaning of the Hebrew for this verse is uncertain.

gateways around the inner court were twenty-five cubits wide and five cubits deep.) [31]Its portico faced the outer court; palm trees decorated its jambs, and eight steps led up to it.

[32]Then he brought me to the inner court on the east side, and he measured the gateway; it had the same measurements as the others. [33]Its alcoves, its projecting walls and its portico had the same measurements as the others. The gateway and its portico had openings all around. It was fifty cubits long and twenty-five cubits wide. [34]Its portico faced the outer court; palm trees decorated the jambs on either side, and eight steps led up to it.

[35]Then he brought me to the north gate and measured it. It had the same measurements as the others, [36]as did its alcoves, its projecting walls and its portico, and it had openings all around. It was fifty cubits long and twenty-five cubits wide. [37]Its portico[a] faced the outer court; palm trees decorated the jambs on either side, and eight steps led up to it.

The Rooms for Preparing Sacrifices

[38]A room with a doorway was by the portico in each of the inner gateways, where the burnt offerings were washed. [39]In the portico of the gateway were two tables on each side, on which the burnt offerings, sin offerings and guilt offerings were slaughtered. [40]By the outside wall of the portico of the gateway, near the steps at the entrance to the north gateway were two tables, and on the other side of the steps were two tables. [41]So there were four tables on one side of the gateway and four on the other — eight tables in all — on which the sacrifices were slaughtered. [42]There were also four tables of dressed stone for the burnt offerings, each a cubit and a half long, a cubit and a half wide and a cubit high. On them were placed the utensils for slaughtering the burnt offerings and the other sacrifices. [43]And double-pronged hooks, each a handbreadth long, were attached to the wall all around. The tables were for the flesh of the offerings.

Rooms for the Priests

[44]Outside the inner gate, within the in-

ner court, were two rooms, one[b] at the side of the north gate and facing south, and another at the side of the south[c] gate and facing north. [45]He said to me, "The room facing south is for the priests who have charge of the temple, [46]and the room facing north is for the priests who have charge of the altar. These are the sons of Zadok, who are the only Levites who may draw near to the LORD to minister before him."

[47]Then he measured the court: It was square — a hundred cubits long and a hundred cubits wide. And the altar was in front of the temple.

The Temple

[48]He brought me to the portico of the temple and measured the jambs of the portico; they were five cubits wide on either side. The width of the entrance was fourteen cubits and its projecting walls were[d] three cubits wide on either side. [49]The portico was twenty cubits wide, and twelve[e] cubits from front to back. It was reached by a flight of stairs,[f] and there were pillars on each side of the jambs.

41 Then the man brought me to the outer sanctuary and measured the jambs; the width of the jambs was six cubits[g] on each side.[h] [2]The entrance was ten cubits wide, and the projecting walls on each side of it were five cubits wide. He also measured the outer sanctuary; it was forty cubits long and twenty cubits wide.

[3]Then he went into the inner sanctuary and measured the jambs of the entrance; each was two cubits wide. The entrance was six cubits wide, and the projecting walls on each side of it were seven cubits wide. [4]And he measured the length of the inner sanctuary; it was twenty cubits, and its width was twenty cubits across the end of the outer sanctuary. He said to me, "This is the Most Holy Place."

[5]Then he measured the wall of the temple; it was six cubits thick, and each side room around the temple was four cubits wide. [6]The side rooms were on three levels, one above another, thirty on each level. There were ledges all around the wall of the temple to serve as supports for the side rooms, so that the supports were not inserted into the wall of the temple. [7]The

---

[a]37 Septuagint (see also verses 31 and 34); Hebrew *jambs*   [b]44 Septuagint; Hebrew *were rooms for singers, which were*   [c]44 Septuagint; Hebrew *east*   [d]48 Septuagint; Hebrew *entrance was*   [e]49 Septuagint; Hebrew *eleven*   [f]49 Hebrew; Septuagint *Ten steps led up to it*   [g]1 The common cubit was about 1 1/2 feet (about 0.5 meter).   [h]1 One Hebrew manuscript and Septuagint; most Hebrew manuscripts *side, the width of the tent*

side rooms all around the temple were wider at each successive level. The structure surrounding the temple was built in ascending stages, so that the rooms widened as one went upward. A stairway went up from the lowest floor to the top floor through the middle floor.

[8]I saw that the temple had a raised base all around it, forming the foundation of the side rooms. It was the length of the rod, six long cubits. [9]The outer wall of the side rooms was five cubits thick. The open area between the side rooms of the temple [10]and the ⌞priests'⌟ rooms was twenty cubits wide all around the temple. [11]There were entrances to the side rooms from the open area, one on the north and another on the south; and the base adjoining the open area was five cubits wide all around.

[12]The building facing the temple courtyard on the west side was seventy cubits wide. The wall of the building was five cubits thick all around, and its length was ninety cubits.

[13]Then he measured the temple; it was a hundred cubits long, and the temple courtyard and the building with its walls were also a hundred cubits long. [14]The width of the temple courtyard on the east, including the front of the temple, was a hundred cubits.

[15]Then he measured the length of the building facing the courtyard at the rear of the temple, including its galleries on each side; it was a hundred cubits.

The outer sanctuary, the inner sanctuary and the portico facing the court, [16]as well as the thresholds and the narrow windows and galleries around the three of them — everything beyond and including the threshold was covered with wood. The floor, the wall up to the windows, and the windows were covered. [17]In the space above the outside of the entrance to the inner sanctuary and on the walls at regular intervals all around the inner and outer sanctuary [18]were carved cherubim and palm trees. Palm trees alternated with cherubim. Each cherub had two faces: [19]the face of a man toward the palm tree on one side and the face of a lion toward the palm tree on the other. They were carved all around the whole temple. [20]From the floor to the area above the entrance, cherubim and palm trees were carved on the wall of the outer sanctuary.

[21]The outer sanctuary had a rectangular doorframe, and the one at the front of the Most Holy Place was similar. [22]There was a wooden altar three cubits high and two cubits square[a]; its corners, its base[b] and its sides were of wood. The man said to me, "This is the table that is before the Lord." [23]Both the outer sanctuary and the Most Holy Place had double doors. [24]Each door had two leaves — two hinged leaves for each door. [25]And on the doors of the outer sanctuary were carved cherubim and palm trees like those carved on the walls, and there was a wooden overhang on the front of the portico. [26]On the sidewalls of the portico were narrow windows with palm trees carved on each side. The side rooms of the temple also had overhangs.

Rooms for the Priests

42 Then the man led me northward into the outer court and brought me to the rooms opposite the temple courtyard and opposite the outer wall on the north side. [2]The building whose door faced north was a hundred cubits[c] long and fifty cubits wide. [3]Both in the section twenty cubits from the inner court and in the section opposite the pavement of the outer court, gallery faced gallery at the three levels. [4]In front of the rooms was an inner passageway ten cubits wide and a hundred cubits[d] long. Their doors were on the north. [5]Now the upper rooms were narrower, for the galleries took more space from them than from the rooms on the lower and middle floors of the building. [6]The rooms on the third floor had no pillars, as the courts had; so they were smaller in floor space than those on the lower and middle floors. [7]There was an outer wall parallel to the rooms and the outer court; it extended in front of the rooms for fifty cubits. [8]While the row of rooms on the side next to the outer court was fifty cubits long, the row on the side nearest the sanctuary was a hundred cubits long. [9]The lower rooms had an entrance on the east side as one enters them from the outer court.

[10]On the south side[e] along the length of the wall of the outer court, adjoining the temple courtyard and opposite the outer wall, were rooms [11]with a passageway in front of them. These were like the

[a]22 Septuagint; Hebrew *long* 1 1/2 feet (about 0.5 meter).   [b]22 Septuagint; Hebrew *length*   [c]2 The common cubit was about [d]4 Septuagint and Syriac; Hebrew *and one cubit*   [e]10 Septuagint; Hebrew *Eastward*

rooms on the north; they had the same length and width, with similar exits and dimensions. Similar to the doorways on the north [12]were the doorways of the rooms on the south. There was a doorway at the beginning of the passageway that was parallel to the corresponding wall extending eastward, by which one enters the rooms.

[13]Then he said to me, "The north and south rooms facing the temple courtyard are the priests' rooms, where the priests who approach the LORD will eat the most holy offerings. There they will put the most holy offerings — the grain offerings, the sin offerings and the guilt offerings — for the place is holy. [14]Once the priests enter the holy precincts, they are not to go into the outer court until they leave behind the garments in which they minister, for these are holy. They are to put on other clothes before they go near the places that are for the people."

[15]When he had finished measuring what was inside the temple area, he led me out by the east gate and measured the area all around: [16]He measured the east side with the measuring rod; it was five hundred cubits.[a] [17]He measured the north side; it was five hundred cubits[b] by the measuring rod. [18]He measured the south side; it was five hundred cubits by the measuring rod. [19]Then he turned to the west side and measured; it was five hundred cubits by the measuring rod. [20]So he measured the area on all four sides. It had a wall around it, five hundred cubits long and five hundred cubits wide, to separate the holy from the common.

The Glory Returns to the Temple

43 Then the man brought me to the gate facing east, [2]and I saw the glory of the God of Israel coming from the east. His voice was like the roar of rushing waters, and the land was radiant with his glory. [3]The vision I saw was like the vision I had seen when he[c] came to destroy the city and like the visions I had seen by the Kebar River, and I fell facedown. [4]The glory of the LORD entered the temple through the gate facing east. [5]Then the Spirit lifted me up and brought me into the inner court, and the glory of the LORD filled the temple.

[6]While the man was standing beside me, I heard someone speaking to me from inside the temple. [7]He said: "Son of man, this is the place of my throne and the place for the soles of my feet. This is where I will live among the Israelites forever. The house of Israel will never again defile my holy name — neither they nor their kings — by their prostitution[d] and the lifeless idols[e] of their kings at their high places. [8]When they placed their threshold next to my threshold and their doorposts beside my doorposts, with only a wall between me and them, they defiled my holy name by their detestable practices. So I destroyed them in my anger. [9]Now let them put away from me their prostitution and the lifeless idols of their kings, and I will live among them forever.

[10]"Son of man, describe the temple to the people of Israel, that they may be ashamed of their sins. Let them consider the plan, [11]and if they are ashamed of all they have done, make known to them the design of the temple — its arrangement, its exits and entrances — its whole design and all its regulations[f] and laws. Write these down before them so that they may be faithful to its design and follow all its regulations.

[12]"This is the law of the temple: All the surrounding area on top of the mountain will be most holy. Such is the law of the temple.

The Altar

[13]"These are the measurements of the altar in long cubits, that cubit being a cubit[g] and a handbreadth[h]: Its gutter is a cubit deep and a cubit wide, with a rim of one span[i] around the edge. And this is the height of the altar: [14]From the gutter on the ground up to the lower ledge it is two cubits high and a cubit wide, and from the smaller ledge up to the larger ledge it is four cubits high and a cubit wide. [15]The altar hearth is four cubits high, and four horns project upward from the hearth. [16]The altar hearth is square, twelve cubits long and twelve cubits wide. [17]The upper ledge also is square, fourteen

a16 See Septuagint of verse 17; Hebrew *rods*; also in verses 18 and 19.   *b17* Septuagint; Hebrew *rods*
c3 Some Hebrew manuscripts and Vulgate; most Hebrew manuscripts *I*   *d7* Or *their spiritual adultery*;
also in verse 9   *e7* Or *the corpses*; also in verse 9   *f11* Some Hebrew manuscripts and Septuagint;
most Hebrew manuscripts *regulations and its whole design*   *g13* The common cubit was about 1 1/2
feet (about 0.5 meter).   *h13* That is, about 3 inches (about 8 centimeters)   *i13* That is, about 9
inches (about 22 centimeters)

cubits long and fourteen cubits wide, with a rim of half a cubit and a gutter of a cubit all around. The steps of the altar face east."

[18]Then he said to me, "Son of man, this is what the Sovereign LORD says: These will be the regulations for sacrificing burnt offerings and sprinkling blood upon the altar when it is built: [19]You are to give a young bull as a sin offering to the priests, who are Levites, of the family of Zadok, who come near to minister before me, declares the Sovereign LORD. [20]You are to take some of its blood and put it on the four horns of the altar and on the four corners of the upper ledge and all around the rim, and so purify the altar and make atonement for it. [21]You are to take the bull for the sin offering and burn it in the designated part of the temple area outside the sanctuary.

[22]"On the second day you are to offer a male goat without defect for a sin offering, and the altar is to be purified as it was purified with the bull. [23]When you have finished purifying it, you are to offer a young bull and a ram from the flock, both without defect. [24]You are to offer them before the LORD, and the priests are to sprinkle salt on them and sacrifice them as a burnt offering to the LORD.

[25]"For seven days you are to provide a male goat daily for a sin offering; you are also to provide a young bull and a ram from the flock, both without defect. [26]For seven days they are to make atonement for the altar and cleanse it; thus they will dedicate it. [27]At the end of these days, from the eighth day on, the priests are to present your burnt offerings and fellowship offerings[a] on the altar. Then I will accept you, declares the Sovereign LORD."

The Prince, the Levites, the Priests

44 Then the man brought me back to the outer gate of the sanctuary, the one facing east, and it was shut. [2]The LORD said to me, "This gate is to remain shut. It must not be opened; no one may enter through it. It is to remain shut because the LORD, the God of Israel, has entered through it. [3]The prince himself is the only one who may sit inside the gateway to eat in the presence of the LORD. He is to enter by way of the portico of the gateway and go out the same way."

[4]Then the man brought me by way of the north gate to the front of the temple.

I looked and saw the glory of the LORD filling the temple of the LORD, and I fell facedown.

[5]The LORD said to me, "Son of man, look carefully, listen closely and give attention to everything I tell you concerning all the regulations regarding the temple of the LORD. Give attention to the entrance of the temple and all the exits of the sanctuary. [6]Say to the rebellious house of Israel, 'This is what the Sovereign LORD says: Enough of your detestable practices, O house of Israel! [7]In addition to all your other detestable practices, you brought foreigners uncircumcised in heart and flesh into my sanctuary, desecrating my temple while you offered me food, fat and blood, and you broke my covenant. [8]Instead of carrying out your duty in regard to my holy things, you put others in charge of my sanctuary. [9]This is what the Sovereign LORD says: No foreigner uncircumcised in heart and flesh is to enter my sanctuary, not even the foreigners who live among the Israelites.

[10]" 'The Levites who went far from me when Israel went astray and who wandered from me after their idols must bear the consequences of their sin. [11]They may serve in my sanctuary, having charge of the gates of the temple and serving in it; they may slaughter the burnt offerings and sacrifices for the people and stand before the people and serve them. [12]But because they served them in the presence of their idols and made the house of Israel fall into sin, therefore I have sworn with uplifted hand that they must bear the consequences of their sin, declares the Sovereign LORD. [13]They are not to come near to serve me as priests or come near any of my holy things or my most holy offerings; they must bear the shame of their detestable practices. [14]Yet I will put them in charge of the duties of the temple and all the work that is to be done in it.

[15]" 'But the priests, who are Levites and descendants of Zadok and who faithfully carried out the duties of my sanctuary when the Israelites went astray from me, are to come near to minister before me; they are to stand before me to offer sacrifices of fat and blood, declares the Sovereign LORD. [16]They alone are to enter my sanctuary; they alone are to come near my table to minister before me and perform my service.

[17]" 'When they enter the gates of the in-

---

[a]27 Traditionally *peace offerings*

ner court, they are to wear linen clothes; they must not wear any woolen garment while ministering at the gates of the inner court or inside the temple. [18]They are to wear linen turbans on their heads and linen undergarments around their waists. They must not wear anything that makes them perspire. [19]When they go out into the outer court where the people are, they are to take off the clothes they have been ministering in and are to leave them in the sacred rooms, and put on other clothes, so that they do not consecrate the people by means of their garments.

[20]" 'They must not shave their heads or let their hair grow long, but they are to keep the hair of their heads trimmed. [21]No priest is to drink wine when he enters the inner court. [22]They must not marry widows or divorced women; they may marry only virgins of Israelite descent or widows of priests. [23]They are to teach my people the difference between the holy and the common and show them how to distinguish between the unclean and the clean.

[24]" 'In any dispute, the priests are to serve as judges and decide it according to my ordinances. They are to keep my laws and my decrees for all my appointed feasts, and they are to keep my Sabbaths holy.

[25]" 'A priest must not defile himself by going near a dead person; however, if the dead person was his father or mother, son or daughter, brother or unmarried sister, then he may defile himself. [26]After he is cleansed, he must wait seven days. [27]On the day he goes into the inner court of the sanctuary to minister in the sanctuary, he is to offer a sin offering for himself, declares the Sovereign LORD.

[28]" 'I am to be the only inheritance the priests have. You are to give them no possession in Israel; I will be their possession. [29]They will eat the grain offerings, the sin offerings and the guilt offerings; and everything in Israel devoted[a] to the LORD will belong to them. [30]The best of all the firstfruits and of all your special gifts will belong to the priests. You are to give them the first portion of your ground meal so that a blessing may rest on your household. [31]The priests must not eat anything,

bird or animal, found dead or torn by wild animals.

Division of the Land

45 " 'When you allot the land as an inheritance, you are to present to the LORD a portion of the land as a sacred district, 25,000 cubits long and 20,000[b] cubits wide; the entire area will be holy. [2]Of this, a section 500 cubits square is to be for the sanctuary, with 50 cubits around it for open land. [3]In the sacred district, measure off a section 25,000 cubits[c] long and 10,000 cubits[d] wide. In it will be the sanctuary, the Most Holy Place. [4]It will be the sacred portion of the land for the priests, who minister in the sanctuary and who draw near to minister before the LORD. It will be a place for their houses as well as a holy place for the sanctuary. [5]An area 25,000 cubits long and 10,000 cubits wide will belong to the Levites, who serve in the temple, as their possession for towns to live in.[e]

[6]" 'You are to give the city as its property an area 5,000 cubits wide and 25,000 cubits long, adjoining the sacred portion; it will belong to the whole house of Israel.

[7]" 'The prince will have the land bordering each side of the area formed by the sacred district and the property of the city. It will extend westward from the west side and eastward from the east side, running lengthwise from the western to the eastern border parallel to one of the tribal portions. [8]This land will be his possession in Israel. And my princes will no longer oppress my people but will allow the house of Israel to possess the land according to their tribes.

[9]" 'This is what the Sovereign LORD says: You have gone far enough, O princes of Israel! Give up your violence and oppression and do what is just and right. Stop dispossessing my people, declares the Sovereign LORD. [10]You are to use accurate scales, an accurate ephah[f] and an accurate bath.[g] [11]The ephah and the bath are to be the same size, the bath containing a tenth of a homer[h] and the ephah a tenth of a homer; the homer is to be the standard measure for both. [12]The shekel[i] is to consist of twenty gerahs. Twenty

---

[a]29 The Hebrew term refers to the irrevocable giving over of things or persons to the LORD.
[b]1 Septuagint (see also verses 3 and 5 and 48:9); Hebrew *10,000*   [c]3 That is, about 7 miles (about 12 kilometers)   [d]3 That is, about 3 miles (about 5 kilometers)   [e]5 Septuagint; Hebrew *temple; they will have as their possession 20 rooms*   [f]10 An ephah was a dry measure.   [g]10 A bath was a liquid measure.   [h]11 A homer was a dry measure.   [i]12 A shekel weighed about 2/5 ounce (about 11.5 grams).

shekels plus twenty-five shekels plus fifteen shekels equal one mina. *a*

Offerings and Holy Days

13" 'This is the special gift you are to offer: a sixth of an ephah from each homer of wheat and a sixth of an ephah from each homer of barley. 14The prescribed portion of oil, measured by the bath, is a tenth of a bath from each cor (which consists of ten baths or one homer, for ten baths are equivalent to a homer). 15Also one sheep is to be taken from every flock of two hundred from the well-watered pastures of Israel. These will be used for the grain offerings, burnt offerings and fellowship offerings *b* to make atonement for the people, declares the Sovereign Lord. 16All the people of the land will participate in this special gift for the use of the prince in Israel. 17It will be the duty of the prince to provide the burnt offerings, grain offerings and drink offerings at the festivals, the New Moons and the Sabbaths — at all the appointed feasts of the house of Israel. He will provide the sin offerings, grain offerings, burnt offerings and fellowship offerings to make atonement for the house of Israel.

18" 'This is what the Sovereign Lord says: In the first month on the first day you are to take a young bull without defect and purify the sanctuary. 19The priest is to take some of the blood of the sin offering and put it on the doorposts of the temple, on the four corners of the upper ledge of the altar and on the gateposts of the inner court. 20You are to do the same on the seventh day of the month for anyone who sins unintentionally or through ignorance; so you are to make atonement for the temple.

21" 'In the first month on the fourteenth day you are to observe the Passover, a feast lasting seven days, during which you shall eat bread made without yeast. 22On that day the prince is to provide a bull as a sin offering for himself and for all the people of the land. 23Every day during the seven days of the Feast he is to provide seven bulls and seven rams without defect as a burnt offering to the Lord, and a male goat for a sin offering. 24He is to provide as a grain offering an ephah for each bull and an ephah for each ram, along with a hin *c* of oil for each ephah.

25" 'During the seven days of the Feast, which begins in the seventh month on the fifteenth day, he is to make the same provision for sin offerings, burnt offerings, grain offerings and oil.

46 " 'This is what the Sovereign Lord says: The gate of the inner court facing east is to be shut on the six working days, but on the Sabbath day and on the day of the New Moon it is to be opened. 2The prince is to enter from the outside through the portico of the gateway and stand by the gatepost. The priests are to sacrifice his burnt offering and his fellowship offerings. *d* He is to worship at the threshold of the gateway and then go out, but the gate will not be shut until evening. 3On the Sabbaths and New Moons the people of the land are to worship in the presence of the Lord at the entrance to that gateway. 4The burnt offering the prince brings to the Lord on the Sabbath day is to be six male lambs and a ram, all without defect. 5The grain offering given with the ram is to be an ephah, *e* and the grain offering with the lambs is to be as much as he pleases, along with a hin *c* of oil for each ephah. 6On the day of the New Moon he is to offer a young bull, six lambs and a ram, all without defect. 7He is to provide as a grain offering one ephah with the bull, one ephah with the ram, and with the lambs as much as he wants to give, along with a hin of oil with each ephah. 8When the prince enters, he is to go in through the portico of the gateway, and he is to come out the same way.

9" 'When the people of the land come before the Lord at the appointed feasts, whoever enters by the north gate to worship is to go out the south gate; and whoever enters by the south gate is to go out the north gate. No one is to return through the gate by which he entered, but each is to go out the opposite gate. 10The prince is to be among them, going in when they go in and going out when they go out.

11" 'At the festivals and the appointed feasts, the grain offering is to be an ephah with a bull, an ephah with a ram, and with the lambs as much as one pleases, along with a hin of oil for each ephah. 12When the prince provides a freewill offering to the Lord — whether a burnt offering or fellowship offerings — the gate facing east is

---

*a*12 That is, 60 shekels; the common mina was 50 shekels.   *b*15 Traditionally *peace offerings*; also in verse 17   *c*24,5 That is, probably about 4 quarts (about 4 liters)   *d*2 Traditionally *peace offerings*; also in verse 12   *e*5 That is, probably about 3/5 bushel (about 22 liters) to be opened for him. He shall offer his burnt offering or his fellowship offerings as he does on the Sabbath day. Then he shall go out, and after he has gone out, the gate will be shut.

¹³" 'Every day you are to provide a year-old lamb without defect for a burnt offering to the LORD; morning by morning you shall provide it. ¹⁴You are also to provide with it morning by morning a grain offering, consisting of a sixth of an ephah with a third of a hin of oil to moisten the flour. The presenting of this grain offering to the LORD is a lasting ordinance. ¹⁵So the lamb and the grain offering and the oil shall be provided morning by morning for a regular burnt offering.

¹⁶" 'This is what the Sovereign LORD says: If the prince makes a gift from his inheritance to one of his sons, it will also belong to his descendants; it is to be their property by inheritance. ¹⁷If, however, he makes a gift from his inheritance to one of his servants, the servant may keep it until the year of freedom; then it will revert to the prince. His inheritance belongs to his sons only; it is theirs. ¹⁸The prince must not take any of the inheritance of the people, driving them off their property. He is to give his sons their inheritance out of his own property, so that none of my people will be separated from his property.' "

¹⁹Then the man brought me through the entrance at the side of the gate to the sacred rooms facing north, which belonged to the priests, and showed me a place at the western end. ²⁰He said to me, "This is the place where the priests will cook the guilt offering and the sin offering and bake the grain offering, to avoid bringing them into the outer court and consecrating the people."

²¹He then brought me to the outer court and led me around to its four corners, and I saw in each corner another court. ²²In the four corners of the outer court were enclosed[a] courts, forty cubits long and thirty cubits wide; each of the courts in the four corners was the same size. ²³Around the inside of each of the four courts was a ledge of stone, with places for fire built all around under the ledge. ²⁴He said to me, "These are the kitchens where those who minister at the temple will cook the sacrifices of the people."

The River From the Temple

47 The man brought me back to the entrance of the temple, and I saw water coming out from under the threshold of the temple toward the east (for the temple faced east). The water was coming down from under the south side of the temple, south of the altar. ²He then brought me out through the north gate and led me around the outside to the outer gate facing east, and the water was flowing from the south side.

³As the man went eastward with a measuring line in his hand, he measured off a thousand cubits[b] and then led me through water that was ankle-deep. ⁴He measured off another thousand cubits and led me through water that was knee-deep. He measured off another thousand and led me through water that was up to the waist. ⁵He measured off another thousand, but now it was a river that I could not cross, because the water had risen and was deep enough to swim in—a river that no one could cross. ⁶He asked me, "Son of man, do you see this?"

Then he led me back to the bank of the river. ⁷When I arrived there, I saw a great number of trees on each side of the river. ⁸He said to me, "This water flows toward the eastern region and goes down into the Arabah,[c] where it enters the Sea.[d] When it empties into the Sea,[d] the water there becomes fresh. ⁹Swarms of living creatures will live wherever the river flows. There will be large numbers of fish, because this water flows there and makes the salt water fresh; so where the river flows everything will live. ¹⁰Fishermen will stand along the shore; from En Gedi to En Eglaim there will be places for spreading nets. The fish will be of many kinds—like the fish of the Great Sea.[e] ¹¹But the swamps and marshes will not become fresh; they will be left for salt. ¹²Fruit trees of all kinds will grow on both banks of the river. Their leaves will not wither, nor will their fruit fail. Every month they will bear, because the water from the sanctuary flows to them. Their fruit will serve for food and their leaves for healing."

The Boundaries of the Land

¹³This is what the Sovereign LORD says:

---

a22 The meaning of the Hebrew for this word is uncertain.   b3 That is, about 1,500 feet (about 450 meters)   c8 Or *the Jordan Valley*   d8 That is, the Dead Sea   e10 That is, the Mediterranean; also in verses 15, 19 and 20

"These are the boundaries by which you are to divide the land for an inheritance among the twelve tribes of Israel, with two portions for Joseph. **14**You are to divide it equally among them. Because I swore with uplifted hand to give it to your forefathers, this land will become your inheritance.

15"This is to be the boundary of the land:

"On the north side it will run from the Great Sea by the Hethlon road past Lebo[a] Hamath to Zedad, **16**Berothah[b] and Sibraim (which lies on the border between Damascus and Hamath), as far as Hazer Hatticon, which is on the border of Hauran. **17**The boundary will extend from the sea to Hazar Enan,[c] along the northern border of Damascus, with the border of Hamath to the north. This will be the north boundary.

18"On the east side the boundary will run between Hauran and Damascus, along the Jordan between Gilead and the land of Israel, to the eastern sea and as far as Tamar.[d] This will be the east boundary.

19"On the south side it will run from Tamar as far as the waters of Meribah Kadesh, then along the Wadi of Egypt to the Great Sea. This will be the south boundary.

20"On the west side, the Great Sea will be the boundary to a point opposite Lebo[e] Hamath. This will be the west boundary.

21"You are to distribute this land among yourselves according to the tribes of Israel. **22**You are to allot it as an inheritance for yourselves and for the aliens who have settled among you and who have children. You are to consider them as native-born Israelites; along with you they are to be allotted an inheritance among the tribes of Israel. **23**In whatever tribe the alien settles, there you are to give him his inheritance," declares the Sovereign LORD.

The Division of the Land

48 "These are the tribes, listed by name: At the northern frontier, Dan will have one portion; it will follow the Hethlon road to Lebo[f] Hamath; Hazar Enan and the northern border of Damascus next to Hamath will be part of its border from the east side to the west side.

2"Asher will have one portion; it will border the territory of Dan from east to west.

3"Naphtali will have one portion; it will border the territory of Asher from east to west.

4"Manasseh will have one portion; it will border the territory of Naphtali from east to west.

5"Ephraim will have one portion; it will border the territory of Manasseh from east to west.

6"Reuben will have one portion; it will border the territory of Ephraim from east to west.

7"Judah will have one portion; it will border the territory of Reuben from east to west.

8"Bordering the territory of Judah from east to west will be the portion you are to present as a special gift. It will be 25,000 cubits[g] wide, and its length from east to west will equal one of the tribal portions; the sanctuary will be in the center of it.

9"The special portion you are to offer to the LORD will be 25,000 cubits long and 10,000 cubits[h] wide. **10**This will be the sacred portion for the priests. It will be 25,000 cubits long on the north side, 10,000 cubits wide on the west side, 10,000 cubits wide on the east side and 25,000 cubits long on the south side. In the center of it will be the sanctuary of the LORD. **11**This will be for the consecrated priests, the Zadokites, who were faithful in serving me and did not go astray as the Levites did when the Israelites went astray. **12**It will be a special gift to them from the sacred portion of the land, a most holy portion, bordering the territory of the Levites.

13"Alongside the territory of the priests, the Levites will have an allotment 25,000 cubits long and 10,000 cubits wide. Its total length will be 25,000 cubits and its width 10,000 cubits. **14**They must not sell or exchange any of it. This is the best of the land and must not pass into other hands, because it is holy to the LORD.

15"The remaining area, 5,000 cubits wide and 25,000 cubits long, will be for the common use of the city, for houses

---

a15 Or *past the entrance to*   b15,16 See Septuagint and Ezekiel 48:1; Hebrew *road to go into Zedad,*
16*Hamath, Berothah*   c17 Hebrew *Enon,* a variant of *Enan*   d18 Septuagint and Syriac; Hebrew
Israel. You will measure to the eastern sea   e20 Or *opposite the entrance to*   f1 Or *to the entrance to*
g8 That is, about 7 miles (about 12 kilometers)   h9 That is, about 3 miles (about 5 kilometers)

and for pastureland. The city will be in the center of it ¹⁶and will have these measurements: the north side 4,500 cubits, the south side 4,500 cubits, the east side 4,500 cubits, and the west side 4,500 cubits. ¹⁷The pastureland for the city will be 250 cubits on the north, 250 cubits on the south, 250 cubits on the east, and 250 cubits on the west. ¹⁸What remains of the area, bordering on the sacred portion and running the length of it, will be 10,000 cubits on the east side and 10,000 cubits on the west side. Its produce will supply food for the workers of the city. ¹⁹The workers from the city who farm it will come from all the tribes of Israel. ²⁰The entire portion will be a square, 25,000 cubits on each side. As a special gift you will set aside the sacred portion, along with the property of the city.

²¹"What remains on both sides of the area formed by the sacred portion and the city property will belong to the prince. It will extend eastward from the 25,000 cubits of the sacred portion to the eastern border, and westward from the 25,000 cubits to the western border. Both these areas running the length of the tribal portions will belong to the prince, and the sacred portion with the temple sanctuary will be in the center of them. ²²So the property of the Levites and the property of the city will lie in the center of the area that belongs to the prince. The area belonging to the prince will lie between the border of Judah and the border of Benjamin.

²³"As for the rest of the tribes: Benjamin will have one portion; it will extend from the east side to the west side.

²⁴"Simeon will have one portion; it will border the territory of Benjamin from east to west.

²⁵"Issachar will have one portion; it will border the territory of Simeon from east to west.

²⁶"Zebulun will have one portion; it will border the territory of Issachar from east to west.

²⁷"Gad will have one portion; it will border the territory of Zebulun from east to west.

²⁸"The southern boundary of Gad will run south from Tamar to the waters of Meribah Kadesh, then along the Wadi ₍of Egypt₎ to the Great Sea.ᵃ

²⁹"This is the land you are to allot as an inheritance to the tribes of Israel, and these will be their portions," declares the Sovereign LORD.

The Gates of the City

³⁰"These will be the exits of the city: Beginning on the north side, which is 4,500 cubits long, ³¹the gates of the city will be named after the tribes of Israel. The three gates on the north side will be the gate of Reuben, the gate of Judah and the gate of Levi.

³²"On the east side, which is 4,500 cubits long, will be three gates: the gate of Joseph, the gate of Benjamin and the gate of Dan.

³³"On the south side, which measures 4,500 cubits, will be three gates: the gate of Simeon, the gate of Issachar and the gate of Zebulun.

³⁴"On the west side, which is 4,500 cubits long, will be three gates: the gate of Gad, the gate of Asher and the gate of Naphtali.

³⁵"The distance all around will be 18,000 cubits.

"And the name of the city from that time on will be:

THE LORD IS THERE."

ᵃ28 That is, the Mediterranean

DANIEL, writing from Babylon during the time of the exile, wants us to know that God controls everything and that the victory always belongs to the Lord and to those who do his will. Even the pagan kings in Babylon must admit this truth. As you read this book, think about how God controls your life and how you will win out over the forces of evil because you obey the Lord.

DANIEL

Daniel's Training in Babylon

1 In the third year of the reign of Jehoiakim king of Judah, Nebuchadnezzar king of Babylon came to Jerusalem and besieged it. ²And the Lord delivered Jehoiakim king of Judah into his hand, along with some of the articles from the temple of God. These he carried off to the temple of his god in Babylonia*a* and put in the treasure house of his god.

³Then the king ordered Ashpenaz, chief of his court officials, to bring in some of the Israelites from the royal family and the nobility— ⁴young men without any physical defect, handsome, showing aptitude for every kind of learning, well informed, quick to understand, and qualified to serve in the king's palace. He was to teach them the language and literature of the Babylonians.*b* ⁵The king assigned them a daily amount of food and wine from the king's table. They were to be trained for three years, and after that they were to enter the king's service.

⁶Among these were some from Judah: Daniel, Hananiah, Mishael and Azariah. ⁷The chief official gave them new names: to Daniel, the name Belteshazzar; to Hananiah, Shadrach; to Mishael, Meshach; and to Azariah, Abednego.

⁸But Daniel resolved not to defile himself with the royal food and wine, and he asked the chief official for permission not to defile himself this way. ⁹Now God had caused the official to show favor and sym-

*a*2 Hebrew *Shinar*   *b*4 Or *Chaldeans*

pathy to Daniel, [10]but the official told Daniel, "I am afraid of my lord the king, who has assigned your[a] food and drink. Why should he see you looking worse than the other young men your age? The king would then have my head because of you."

[11]Daniel then said to the guard whom the chief official had appointed over Daniel, Hananiah, Mishael and Azariah, [12]"Please test your servants for ten days: Give us nothing but vegetables to eat and water to drink. [13]Then compare our appearance with that of the young men who eat the royal food, and treat your servants in accordance with what you see." [14]So he agreed to this and tested them for ten days.

[15]At the end of the ten days they looked healthier and better nourished than any of the young men who ate the royal food. [16]So the guard took away their choice food and the wine they were to drink and gave them vegetables instead.

[17]To these four young men God gave knowledge and understanding of all kinds of literature and learning. And Daniel could understand visions and dreams of all kinds.

[18]At the end of the time set by the king to bring them in, the chief official presented them to Nebuchadnezzar. [19]The king talked with them, and he found none equal to Daniel, Hananiah, Mishael and Azariah; so they entered the king's service. [20]In every matter of wisdom and understanding about which the king questioned them, he found them ten times better than all the magicians and enchanters in his whole kingdom.

[21]And Daniel remained there until the first year of King Cyrus.

Nebuchadnezzar's Dream

2 In the second year of his reign, Nebuchadnezzar had dreams; his mind was troubled and he could not sleep. [2]So the king summoned the magicians, enchanters, sorcerers and astrologers[b] to tell him what he had dreamed. When they came in and stood before the king, [3]he said to them, "I have had a dream that troubles me and I want to know what it means.[c]"

[4]Then the astrologers answered the king in Aramaic,[d] "O king, live forever! Tell your servants the dream, and we will interpret it."

[5]The king replied to the astrologers, "This is what I have firmly decided: If you do not tell me what my dream was and interpret it, I will have you cut into pieces and your houses turned into piles of rubble. [6]But if you tell me the dream and explain it, you will receive from me gifts and rewards and great honor. So tell me the dream and interpret it for me."

[7]Once more they replied, "Let the king tell his servants the dream, and we will interpret it."

[8]Then the king answered, "I am certain that you are trying to gain time, because you realize that this is what I have firmly decided: [9]If you do not tell me the dream, there is just one penalty for you. You have conspired to tell me misleading and wicked things, hoping the situation will change. So then, tell me the dream, and I will know that you can interpret it for me."

[10]The astrologers answered the king, "There is not a man on earth who can do what the king asks! No king, however great and mighty, has ever asked such a thing of any magician or enchanter or astrologer. [11]What the king asks is too difficult. No one can reveal it to the king except the gods, and they do not live among men."

[12]This made the king so angry and furious that he ordered the execution of all the wise men of Babylon. [13]So the decree was issued to put the wise men to death, and men were sent to look for Daniel and his friends to put them to death.

[14]When Arioch, the commander of the king's guard, had gone out to put to death the wise men of Babylon, Daniel spoke to him with wisdom and tact. [15]He asked the king's officer, "Why did the king issue such a harsh decree?" Arioch then explained the matter to Daniel. [16]At this, Daniel went in to the king and asked for time, so that he might interpret the dream for him.

[17]Then Daniel returned to his house and explained the matter to his friends Hananiah, Mishael and Azariah. [18]He urged them to plead for mercy from the God of heaven concerning this mystery, so that he and his friends might not be executed with the rest of the wise men of Babylon. [19]During the night the mystery was revealed to Daniel in a vision. Then

---

[a]10 The Hebrew for *your* and *you* in this verse is plural.   [b]2 Or *Chaldeans*; also in verses 4, 5 and 10
[c]3 Or *was*   [d]4 The text from here through chapter 7 is in Aramaic.

Daniel praised the God of heaven [20]and said:

"Praise be to the name of God for ever and ever;
wisdom and power are his.
[21]He changes times and seasons;
he sets up kings and deposes them.
He gives wisdom to the wise
and knowledge to the discerning.
[22]He reveals deep and hidden things;
he knows what lies in darkness,
and light dwells with him.
[23]I thank and praise you, O God of my fathers:
You have given me wisdom and power,
you have made known to me what we asked of you,
you have made known to us the dream of the king."

Daniel Interprets the Dream

[24]Then Daniel went to Arioch, whom the king had appointed to execute the wise men of Babylon, and said to him, "Do not execute the wise men of Babylon. Take me to the king, and I will interpret his dream for him."

[25]Arioch took Daniel to the king at once and said, "I have found a man among the exiles from Judah who can tell the king what his dream means."

[26]The king asked Daniel (also called Belteshazzar), "Are you able to tell me what I saw in my dream and interpret it?"

[27]Daniel replied, "No wise man, enchanter, magician or diviner can explain to the king the mystery he has asked about, [28]but there is a God in heaven who reveals mysteries. He has shown King Nebuchadnezzar what will happen in days to come. Your dream and the visions that passed through your mind as you lay on your bed are these:

[29]"As you were lying there, O king, your mind turned to things to come, and the revealer of mysteries showed you what is going to happen. [30]As for me, this mystery has been revealed to me, not because I have greater wisdom than other living men, but so that you, O king, may know the interpretation and that you may understand what went through your mind.

[31]"You looked, O king, and there before you stood a large statue—an enormous, dazzling statue, awesome in appearance. [32]The head of the statue was made of pure gold, its chest and arms of silver, its belly and thighs of bronze, [33]its legs of iron, its feet partly of iron and partly of baked clay. [34]While you were watching, a rock was cut out, but not by human hands. It struck the statue on its feet of iron and clay and smashed them. [35]Then the iron, the clay, the bronze, the silver and the gold were broken to pieces at the same time and became like chaff on a threshing floor in the summer. The wind swept them away without leaving a trace. But the rock that struck the statue became a huge mountain and filled the whole earth.

[36]"This was the dream, and now we will interpret it to the king. [37]You, O king, are the king of kings. The God of heaven has given you dominion and power and might and glory; [38]in your hands he has placed mankind and the beasts of the field and the birds of the air. Wherever they live, he has made you ruler over them all. You are that head of gold.

[39]"After you, another kingdom will rise, inferior to yours. Next, a third kingdom, one of bronze, will rule over the whole earth. [40]Finally, there will be a fourth kingdom, strong as iron—for iron breaks and smashes everything—and as iron breaks things to pieces, so it will crush and break all the others. [41]Just as you saw that the feet and toes were partly of baked clay and partly of iron, so this will be a divided kingdom; yet it will have some of the strength of iron in it, even as you saw iron mixed with clay. [42]As the toes were partly iron and partly clay, so this kingdom will be partly strong and partly brittle. [43]And just as you saw the iron mixed with baked clay, so the people will be a mixture and will not remain united, any more than iron mixes with clay.

[44]"In the time of those kings, the God of heaven will set up a kingdom that will never be destroyed, nor will it be left to another people. It will crush all those kingdoms and bring them to an end, but it will itself endure forever. [45]This is the meaning of the vision of the rock cut out of a mountain, but not by human hands—a rock that broke the iron, the bronze, the clay, the silver and the gold to pieces.

"The great God has shown the king what will take place in the future. The dream is true and the interpretation is trustworthy."

[46]Then King Nebuchadnezzar fell prostrate before Daniel and paid him honor and ordered that an offering and incense be presented to him. [47]The king said to Daniel, "Surely your God is the God of gods and the Lord of kings and a revealer

of mysteries, for you were able to reveal this mystery."

[48]Then the king placed Daniel in a high position and lavished many gifts on him. He made him ruler over the entire province of Babylon and placed him in charge of all its wise men. [49]Moreover, at Daniel's request the king appointed Shadrach, Meshach and Abednego administrators over the province of Babylon, while Daniel himself remained at the royal court.

The Image of Gold and the Fiery Furnace

3 King Nebuchadnezzar made an image of gold, ninety feet high and nine feet[a] wide, and set it up on the plain of Dura in the province of Babylon. [2]He then summoned the satraps, prefects, governors, advisers, treasurers, judges, magistrates and all the other provincial officials to come to the dedication of the image he had set up. [3]So the satraps, prefects, governors, advisers, treasurers, judges, magistrates and all the other provincial officials assembled for the dedication of the image that King Nebuchadnezzar had set up, and they stood before it.

[4]Then the herald loudly proclaimed, "This is what you are commanded to do, O peoples, nations and men of every language: [5]As soon as you hear the sound of the horn, flute, zither, lyre, harp, pipes and all kinds of music, you must fall down and worship the image of gold that King Nebuchadnezzar has set up. [6]Whoever does not fall down and worship will immediately be thrown into a blazing furnace."

[7]Therefore, as soon as they heard the sound of the horn, flute, zither, lyre, harp and all kinds of music, all the peoples, nations and men of every language fell down and worshiped the image of gold that King Nebuchadnezzar had set up.

[8]At this time some astrologers[b] came forward and denounced the Jews. [9]They said to King Nebuchadnezzar, "O king, live forever! [10]You have issued a decree, O king, that everyone who hears the sound of the horn, flute, zither, lyre, harp, pipes and all kinds of music must fall down and worship the image of gold, [11]and that whoever does not fall down and worship will be thrown into a blazing furnace. [12]But there are some Jews whom you have set over the affairs of the province of Bab-

ylon—Shadrach, Meshach and Abednego—who pay no attention to you, O king. They neither serve your gods nor worship the image of gold you have set up."

[13]Furious with rage, Nebuchadnezzar summoned Shadrach, Meshach and Abednego. So these men were brought before the king, [14]and Nebuchadnezzar said to them, "Is it true, Shadrach, Meshach and Abednego, that you do not serve my gods or worship the image of gold I have set up? [15]Now when you hear the sound of the horn, flute, zither, lyre, harp, pipes and all kinds of music, if you are ready to fall down and worship the image I made, very good. But if you do not worship it, you will be thrown immediately into a blazing furnace. Then what god will be able to rescue you from my hand?"

[16]Shadrach, Meshach and Abednego replied to the king, "O Nebuchadnezzar, we do not need to defend ourselves before you in this matter. [17]If we are thrown into the blazing furnace, the God we serve is able to save us from it, and he will rescue us from your hand, O king. [18]But even if he does not, we want you to know, O king, that we will not serve your gods or worship the image of gold you have set up."

[19]Then Nebuchadnezzar was furious with Shadrach, Meshach and Abednego, and his attitude toward them changed. He ordered the furnace heated seven times hotter than usual [20]and commanded some of the strongest soldiers in his army to tie up Shadrach, Meshach and Abednego and throw them into the blazing furnace. [21]So these men, wearing their robes, trousers, turbans and other clothes, were bound and thrown into the blazing furnace. [22]The king's command was so urgent and the furnace so hot that the flames of the fire killed the soldiers who took up Shadrach, Meshach and Abednego, [23]and these three men, firmly tied, fell into the blazing furnace.

[24]Then King Nebuchadnezzar leaped to his feet in amazement and asked his advisers, "Weren't there three men that we tied up and threw into the fire?"

They replied, "Certainly, O king."

[25]He said, "Look! I see four men walking around in the fire, unbound and unharmed, and the fourth looks like a son of the gods."

[26]Nebuchadnezzar then approached the opening of the blazing furnace and

---

a1 Aramaic *sixty cubits high and six cubits wide* (about 27 meters high and 2.7 meters wide)   *b8* Or *Chaldeans* shouted, "Shadrach, Meshach and Abednego, servants of the Most High God, come out! Come here!"

So Shadrach, Meshach and Abednego came out of the fire, [27]and the satraps, prefects, governors and royal advisers crowded around them. They saw that the fire had not harmed their bodies, nor was a hair of their heads singed; their robes were not scorched, and there was no smell of fire on them.

[28]Then Nebuchadnezzar said, "Praise be to the God of Shadrach, Meshach and Abednego, who has sent his angel and rescued his servants! They trusted in him and defied the king's command and were willing to give up their lives rather than serve or worship any god except their own God. [29]Therefore I decree that the people of any nation or language who say anything against the God of Shadrach, Meshach and Abednego be cut into pieces and their houses be turned into piles of rubble, for no other god can save in this way."

[30]Then the king promoted Shadrach, Meshach and Abednego in the province of Babylon.

Nebuchadnezzar's Dream of a Tree

4 King Nebuchadnezzar,

To the peoples, nations and men of every language, who live in all the world:

May you prosper greatly!

[2]It is my pleasure to tell you about the miraculous signs and wonders that the Most High God has performed for me.

[3]How great are his signs,
   how mighty his wonders!
His kingdom is an eternal
   kingdom;
  his dominion endures from
    generation to generation.

[4]I, Nebuchadnezzar, was at home in my palace, contented and prosperous. [5]I had a dream that made me afraid. As I was lying in my bed, the images and visions that passed through my mind terrified me. [6]So I commanded that all the wise men of Babylon be brought before me to interpret the dream for me. [7]When the

magicians, enchanters, astrologers[a] and diviners came, I told them the dream, but they could not interpret it for me. [8]Finally, Daniel came into my presence and I told him the dream. (He is called Belteshazzar, after the name of my god, and the spirit of the holy gods is in him.)

[9]I said, "Belteshazzar, chief of the magicians, I know that the spirit of the holy gods is in you, and no mystery is too difficult for you. Here is my dream; interpret it for me. [10]These are the visions I saw while lying in my bed: I looked, and there before me stood a tree in the middle of the land. Its height was enormous. [11]The tree grew large and strong and its top touched the sky; it was visible to the ends of the earth. [12]Its leaves were beautiful, its fruit abundant, and on it was food for all. Under it the beasts of the field found shelter, and the birds of the air lived in its branches; from it every creature was fed.

[13]"In the visions I saw while lying in my bed, I looked, and there before me was a messenger,[b] a holy one, coming down from heaven. [14]He called in a loud voice: 'Cut down the tree and trim off its branches; strip off its leaves and scatter its fruit. Let the animals flee from under it and the birds from its branches. [15]But let the stump and its roots, bound with iron and bronze, remain in the ground, in the grass of the field.

" 'Let him be drenched with the dew of heaven, and let him live with the animals among the plants of the earth. [16]Let his mind be changed from that of a man and let him be given the mind of an animal, till seven times[c] pass by for him.

[17]" 'The decision is announced by messengers, the holy ones declare the verdict, so that the living may know that the Most High is sovereign over the kingdoms of men and gives them to anyone he wishes and sets over them the lowliest of men.'

[18]"This is the dream that I, King Nebuchadnezzar, had. Now, Belteshazzar, tell me what it means, for none of the wise men in my kingdom can interpret it for me. But you can,

---

a7 Or *Chaldeans*   *b13* Or *watchman*; also in verses 17 and 23   *c16* Or *years*; also in verses 23, 25 and 32 because the spirit of the holy gods is in you."

Daniel Interprets the Dream

¹⁹Then Daniel (also called Belteshazzar) was greatly perplexed for a time, and his thoughts terrified him. So the king said, "Belteshazzar, do not let the dream or its meaning alarm you."

Belteshazzar answered, "My lord, if only the dream applied to your enemies and its meaning to your adversaries! ²⁰The tree you saw, which grew large and strong, with its top touching the sky, visible to the whole earth, ²¹with beautiful leaves and abundant fruit, providing food for all, giving shelter to the beasts of the field, and having nesting places in its branches for the birds of the air— ²²you, O king, are that tree! You have become great and strong; your greatness has grown until it reaches the sky, and your dominion extends to distant parts of the earth.

²³"You, O king, saw a messenger, a holy one, coming down from heaven and saying, 'Cut down the tree and destroy it, but leave the stump, bound with iron and bronze, in the grass of the field, while its roots remain in the ground. Let him be drenched with the dew of heaven; let him live like the wild animals, until seven times pass by for him.'

²⁴"This is the interpretation, O king, and this is the decree the Most High has issued against my lord the king: ²⁵You will be driven away from people and will live with the wild animals; you will eat grass like cattle and be drenched with the dew of heaven. Seven times will pass by for you until you acknowledge that the Most High is sovereign over the kingdoms of men and gives them to anyone he wishes. ²⁶The command to leave the stump of the tree with its roots means that your kingdom will be restored to you when you acknowledge that Heaven rules. ²⁷Therefore, O king, be pleased to accept my advice: Renounce your sins by doing what is right, and your wickedness by being kind to the oppressed. It may be that then your prosperity will continue."

The Dream Is Fulfilled

²⁸All this happened to King Nebuchadnezzar. ²⁹Twelve months later, as the king was walking on the roof of the royal palace of Babylon, ³⁰he said, "Is not this the great Babylon I have built as the royal residence, by my mighty power and for the glory of my majesty?"

³¹The words were still on his lips when a voice came from heaven, "This is what is decreed for you, King Nebuchadnezzar: Your royal authority has been taken from you. ³²You will be driven away from people and will live with the wild animals; you will eat grass like cattle. Seven times will pass by for you until you acknowledge that the Most High is sovereign over the kingdoms of men and gives them to anyone he wishes."

³³Immediately what had been said about Nebuchadnezzar was fulfilled. He was driven away from people and ate grass like cattle. His body was drenched with the dew of heaven until his hair grew like the feathers of an eagle and his nails like the claws of a bird.

³⁴At the end of that time, I, Nebuchadnezzar, raised my eyes toward heaven, and my sanity was restored. Then I praised the Most High; I honored and glorified him who lives forever.

His dominion is an eternal dominion;
    his kingdom endures from
        generation to generation.
³⁵All the peoples of the earth
    are regarded as nothing.
He does as he pleases
    with the powers of heaven
    and the peoples of the earth.
No one can hold back his hand
    or say to him: "What have you
        done?"

³⁶At the same time that my sanity was restored, my honor and splendor were returned to me for the glory of my kingdom. My advisers and nobles sought me out, and I was restored to my throne and became even greater than before. ³⁷Now I, Nebuchadnezzar, praise and exalt and glorify the King of heaven, because everything he does is right and all his ways are just. And those who walk in pride he is able to humble.

The Writing on the Wall

5 King Belshazzar gave a great banquet for a thousand of his nobles and drank wine with them. ²While Belshazzar was drinking his wine, he gave orders to bring in the gold and silver goblets that Nebuchadnezzar his father[a] had taken from the temple in Jerusalem, so that the king and his nobles, his wives and his concubines might drink from them. ³So they brought in the gold goblets that had been taken from the temple of God in Jerusalem, and the king and his nobles, his wives and his concubines drank from them. ⁴As they drank the wine, they praised the gods of gold and silver, of bronze, iron, wood and stone.

⁵Suddenly the fingers of a human hand appeared and wrote on the plaster of the wall, near the lampstand in the royal palace. The king watched the hand as it wrote. ⁶His face turned pale and he was so frightened that his knees knocked together and his legs gave way.

⁷The king called out for the enchanters, astrologers[b] and diviners to be brought and said to these wise men of Babylon, "Whoever reads this writing and tells me what it means will be clothed in purple and have a gold chain placed around his neck, and he will be made the third highest ruler in the kingdom."

⁸Then all the king's wise men came in, but they could not read the writing or tell the king what it meant. ⁹So King Belshazzar became even more terrified and his face grew more pale. His nobles were baffled.

¹⁰The queen,[c] hearing the voices of the king and his nobles, came into the banquet hall. "O king, live forever!" she said. "Don't be alarmed! Don't look so pale! ¹¹There is a man in your kingdom who has the spirit of the holy gods in him. In the time of your father he was found to have insight and intelligence and wisdom like that of the gods. King Nebuchadnezzar your father — your father the king, I say — appointed him chief of the magicians, enchanters, astrologers and diviners. ¹²This man Daniel, whom the king called Belteshazzar, was found to have a keen mind and knowledge and understanding, and also the ability to interpret dreams, explain riddles and solve difficult problems. Call for Daniel, and he will tell you what the writing means."

¹³So Daniel was brought before the king, and the king said to him, "Are you Daniel, one of the exiles my father the king brought from Judah? ¹⁴I have heard that the spirit of the gods is in you and that you have insight, intelligence and outstanding wisdom. ¹⁵The wise men and enchanters were brought before me to read this writing and tell me what it means, but they could not explain it. ¹⁶Now I have heard that you are able to give interpretations and to solve difficult problems. If you can read this writing and tell me what it means, you will be clothed in purple and have a gold chain placed around your neck, and you will be made the third highest ruler in the kingdom."

¹⁷Then Daniel answered the king, "You may keep your gifts for yourself and give your rewards to someone else. Nevertheless, I will read the writing for the king and tell him what it means.

¹⁸"O king, the Most High God gave your father Nebuchadnezzar sovereignty and greatness and glory and splendor. ¹⁹Because of the high position he gave him, all the peoples and nations and men of every language dreaded and feared him. Those the king wanted to put to death, he put to death; those he wanted to spare, he spared; those he wanted to promote, he promoted; and those he wanted to humble, he humbled. ²⁰But when his heart became arrogant and hardened with pride, he was deposed from his royal throne and stripped of his glory. ²¹He was driven away from people and given the mind of an animal; he lived with the wild donkeys and ate grass like cattle; and his body was drenched with the dew of heaven, until he acknowledged that the Most High God is sovereign over the kingdoms of men and sets over them anyone he wishes.

²²"But you his son,[d] O Belshazzar, have not humbled yourself, though you knew all this. ²³Instead, you have set yourself up against the Lord of heaven. You had the goblets from his temple brought to you, and you and your nobles, your wives and your concubines drank wine from them. You praised the gods of silver and gold, of bronze, iron, wood and stone, which cannot see or hear or understand. But you did not honor the God who holds in his hand your life and all your

---

[a]2 Or *ancestor*; or *predecessor*; also in verses 11, 13 and 18   [b]7 Or *Chaldeans*; also in verse 11
[c]10 Or *queen mother*   [d]22 Or *descendant*; or *successor*

ways. **24**Therefore he sent the hand that wrote the inscription.

25"This is the inscription that was written:

MENE, MENE, TEKEL, PARSIN*a*

26"This is what these words mean:

Mene[b]: God has numbered the days of your reign and brought it to an end.
27*Tekel*[c]: You have been weighed on the scales and found wanting.
28*Peres*[d]: Your kingdom is divided and given to the Medes and Persians."

29Then at Belshazzar's command, Daniel was clothed in purple, a gold chain was placed around his neck, and he was proclaimed the third highest ruler in the kingdom. **30**That very night Belshazzar, king of the Babylonians,[e] was slain, **31**and Darius the Mede took over the kingdom, at the age of sixty-two.

Daniel in the Den of Lions

6 It pleased Darius to appoint 120 satraps to rule throughout the kingdom, **2**with three administrators over them, one of whom was Daniel. The satraps were made accountable to them so that the king might not suffer loss. **3**Now Daniel so distinguished himself among the administrators and the satraps by his exceptional qualities that the king planned to set him over the whole kingdom. **4**At this, the administrators and the satraps tried to find grounds for charges against Daniel in his conduct of government affairs, but they were unable to do so. They could find no corruption in him, because he was trustworthy and neither corrupt nor negligent. **5**Finally these men said, "We will never find any basis for charges against this man Daniel unless it has something to do with the law of his God."

6So the administrators and the satraps went as a group to the king and said: "O King Darius, live forever! **7**The royal administrators, prefects, satraps, advisers and governors have all agreed that the king should issue an edict and enforce the decree that anyone who prays to any god or man during the next thirty days, except

to you, O king, shall be thrown into the lions' den. **8**Now, O king, issue the decree and put it in writing so that it cannot be altered—in accordance with the laws of the Medes and Persians, which cannot be repealed." **9**So King Darius put the decree in writing.

10Now when Daniel learned that the decree had been published, he went home to his upstairs room where the windows opened toward Jerusalem. Three times a day he got down on his knees and prayed, giving thanks to his God, just as he had done before. **11**Then these men went as a group and found Daniel praying and asking God for help. **12**So they went to the king and spoke to him about his royal decree: "Did you not publish a decree that during the next thirty days anyone who prays to any god or man except to you, O king, would be thrown into the lions' den?"

The king answered, "The decree stands—in accordance with the laws of the Medes and Persians, which cannot be repealed."

13Then they said to the king, "Daniel, who is one of the exiles from Judah, pays no attention to you, O king, or to the decree you put in writing. He still prays three times a day." **14**When the king heard this, he was greatly distressed; he was determined to rescue Daniel and made every effort until sundown to save him.

15Then the men went as a group to the king and said to him, "Remember, O king, that according to the law of the Medes and Persians no decree or edict that the king issues can be changed."

16So the king gave the order, and they brought Daniel and threw him into the lions' den. The king said to Daniel, "May your God, whom you serve continually, rescue you!"

17A stone was brought and placed over the mouth of the den, and the king sealed it with his own signet ring and with the rings of his nobles, so that Daniel's situation might not be changed. **18**Then the king returned to his palace and spent the night without eating and without any entertainment being brought to him. And he could not sleep.

19At the first light of dawn, the king got up and hurried to the lions' den. **20**When he came near the den, he called to Daniel

---

a25 Aramaic *UPARSIN* (that is, *AND PARSIN*)   *b26 Mene* can mean *numbered* or *mina* (a unit of money).   *c27 Tekel* can mean *weighed* or *shekel.*   *d28 Peres* (the singular of *Parsin*) can mean *divided* or *Persia* or *a half mina* or *a half shekel.*   *e30* Or *Chaldeans* in an anguished voice, "Daniel, servant of the living God, has your God, whom you serve continually, been able to rescue you from the lions?"

²¹Daniel answered, "O king, live forever! ²²My God sent his angel, and he shut the mouths of the lions. They have not hurt me, because I was found innocent in his sight. Nor have I ever done any wrong before you O king."

²³The king was overjoyed and gave orders to lift Daniel out of the den. And when Daniel was lifted from the den, no wound was found on him, because he had trusted in his God.

²⁴At the king's command, the men who

THURSDAY

VERSE FOR THE DAY:
Daniel 6:10

AUTHOR:
Donald Bloesch

PASSAGE FOR THE DAY:
Daniel 6:10–14

Guidelines for Prayer

THE Bible does not prescribe the time or length of prayer, but it does offer guidelines. In Psalm 88 prayer is offered in the early morning (v. 13), and in Psalm 55 prayers are said evening, morning and noon (v. 17). The author of Psalm 119 advocates prayer seven times a day (v. 164). Daniel knelt for devotions three times a day (Daniel 6:10). Jesus prayed before sunrise (Mark 1:35) and in the evening when the day's work was over (Mark 6:46). Peter prayed at the third, sixth and ninth hours.

Despite their aversion to prescribed formulas in the life of prayer that function as a new law, the Reformers did make general recommendations. On the basis of Scriptural testimony Luther suggested that prayer should be "the first business of the morning and the last at night." He advised, "Cultivate the habit of falling asleep with the Lord's Prayer on your lips every evening when you go to bed and again every morning when you get up. And if occasion, place and time permit, pray before you do anything else." Calvin urged that we offer prayer "when we arise in the morning, before we begin daily work, when we sit down to a meal, when by God's blessing we have eaten, when we are getting ready to retire."

Just as the Christian is not bound to ritual laws that regulate the preparation for prayer, so he is not absolutely bound to set times for prayer. Yet there are times that are more appropriate for prayer than others: the gathering together for worship, the hours before work and bedtime, the time right before meals, when we need to remind ourselves of the goodness of God. But a Christian should feel free to pray anywhere, anytime, in the midst of daily work and play as well as in the solitude of his room in the early morning or late in the evening.

Additional Scripture Readings:
Luke 18:1–8;
1 Thessalonians 5:16–18

Go to page 923 for your next devotional reading.

had falsely accused Daniel were brought in and thrown into the lions' den, along with their wives and children. And before they reached the floor of the den, the lions overpowered them and crushed all their bones.

25Then King Darius wrote to all the peoples, nations and men of every language throughout the land:

"May you prosper greatly!

26"I issue a decree that in every part of my kingdom people must fear and reverence the God of Daniel.

"For he is the living God
    and he endures forever;
his kingdom will not be destroyed,
    his dominion will never end.
27He rescues and he saves;
    he performs signs and wonders
in the heavens and on the earth.
He has rescued Daniel
    from the power of the lions."

28So Daniel prospered during the reign of Darius and the reign of Cyrus*a* the Persian.

Daniel's Dream of Four Beasts

7 In the first year of Belshazzar king of Babylon, Daniel had a dream, and visions passed through his mind as he was lying on his bed. He wrote down the substance of his dream.

2Daniel said: "In my vision at night I looked, and there before me were the four winds of heaven churning up the great sea. 3Four great beasts, each different from the others, came up out of the sea.

4"The first was like a lion, and it had the wings of an eagle. I watched until its wings were torn off and it was lifted from the ground so that it stood on two feet like a man, and the heart of a man was given to it.

5"And there before me was a second beast, which looked like a bear. It was raised up on one of its sides, and it had three ribs in its mouth between its teeth. It was told, 'Get up and eat your fill of flesh!'

6"After that, I looked, and there before me was another beast, one that looked like a leopard. And on its back it had four wings like those of a bird. This beast had four heads, and it was given authority to rule.

7"After that, in my vision at night I looked, and there before me was a fourth beast—terrifying and frightening and very powerful. It had large iron teeth; it crushed and devoured its victims and trampled underfoot whatever was left. It was different from all the former beasts, and it had ten horns.

8"While I was thinking about the horns, there before me was another horn, a little one, which came up among them; and three of the first horns were uprooted before it. This horn had eyes like the eyes of a man and a mouth that spoke boastfully.

9"As I looked,

"thrones were set in place,
    and the Ancient of Days took his
        seat.
His clothing was as white as snow;
    the hair of his head was white like
        wool.
His throne was flaming with fire,
    and its wheels were all ablaze.
10A river of fire was flowing,
    coming out from before him.
Thousands upon thousands attended
        him;
    ten thousand times ten thousand
        stood before him.
The court was seated,
    and the books were opened.

11"Then I continued to watch because of the boastful words the horn was speaking. I kept looking until the beast was slain and its body destroyed and thrown into the blazing fire. 12(The other beasts had been stripped of their authority, but were allowed to live for a period of time.)

13"In my vision at night I looked, and there before me was one like a son of man, coming with the clouds of heaven. He approached the Ancient of Days and was led into his presence. 14He was given authority, glory and sovereign power; all peoples, nations and men of every language worshiped him. His dominion is an everlasting dominion that will not pass away, and his kingdom is one that will never be destroyed.

The Interpretation of the Dream

15"I, Daniel, was troubled in spirit, and the visions that passed through my mind disturbed me. 16I approached one of those standing there and asked him the true meaning of all this.

"So he told me and gave me the interpretation of these things: 17'The four great

---

a28 Or *Darius, that is, the reign of Cyrus*

beasts are four kingdoms that will rise from the earth. **18**But the saints of the Most High will receive the kingdom and will possess it forever—yes, for ever and ever.'

19"Then I wanted to know the true meaning of the fourth beast, which was different from all the others and most terrifying, with its iron teeth and bronze claws—the beast that crushed and devoured its victims and trampled underfoot whatever was left. **20**I also wanted to know about the ten horns on its head and about the other horn that came up, before which three of them fell—the horn that looked more imposing than the others and that had eyes and a mouth that spoke boastfully. **21**As I watched, this horn was waging war against the saints and defeating them, **22**until the Ancient of Days came and pronounced judgment in favor of the saints of the Most High, and the time came when they possessed the kingdom.

23"He gave me this explanation: 'The fourth beast is a fourth kingdom that will appear on earth. It will be different from all the other kingdoms and will devour the whole earth, trampling it down and crushing it. **24**The ten horns are ten kings who will come from this kingdom. After them another king will arise, different from the earlier ones; he will subdue three kings. **25**He will speak against the Most High and oppress his saints and try to change the set times and the laws. The saints will be handed over to him for a time, times and half a time.*a*

26" 'But the court will sit, and his power will be taken away and completely destroyed forever. **27**Then the sovereignty, power and greatness of the kingdoms under the whole heaven will be handed over to the saints, the people of the Most High. His kingdom will be an everlasting kingdom, and all rulers will worship and obey him.'

28"This is the end of the matter. I, Daniel, was deeply troubled by my thoughts, and my face turned pale, but I kept the matter to myself."

Daniel's Vision of a Ram and a Goat

8 In the third year of King Belshazzar's reign, I, Daniel, had a vision, after the one that had already appeared to me. **2**In my vision I saw myself in the citadel of Susa in the province of Elam; in the vision I was beside the Ulai Canal. **3**I looked up,

and there before me was a ram with two horns, standing beside the canal, and the horns were long. One of the horns was longer than the other but grew up later. **4**I watched the ram as he charged toward the west and the north and the south. No animal could stand against him, and none could rescue from his power. He did as he pleased and became great.

5As I was thinking about this, suddenly a goat with a prominent horn between his eyes came from the west, crossing the whole earth without touching the ground. **6**He came toward the two-horned ram I had seen standing beside the canal and charged at him in great rage. **7**I saw him attack the ram furiously, striking the ram and shattering his two horns. The ram was powerless to stand against him; the goat knocked him to the ground and trampled on him, and none could rescue the ram from his power. **8**The goat became very great, but at the height of his power his large horn was broken off, and in its place four prominent horns grew up toward the four winds of heaven.

9Out of one of them came another horn, which started small but grew in power to the south and to the east and toward the Beautiful Land. **10**It grew until it reached the host of the heavens, and it threw some of the starry host down to the earth and trampled on them. **11**It set itself up to be as great as the Prince of the host; it took away the daily sacrifice from him, and the place of his sanctuary was brought low. **12**Because of rebellion, the host ,of the saints,*b* and the daily sacrifice were given over to it. It prospered in everything it did, and truth was thrown to the ground.

13Then I heard a holy one speaking, and another holy one said to him, "How long will it take for the vision to be fulfilled—the vision concerning the daily sacrifice, the rebellion that causes desolation, and the surrender of the sanctuary and of the host that will be trampled underfoot?"

14He said to me, "It will take 2,300 evenings and mornings; then the sanctuary will be reconsecrated."

The Interpretation of the Vision

15While I, Daniel, was watching the vision and trying to understand it, there before me stood one who looked like a man. **16**And I heard a man's voice from the Ulai calling, "Gabriel, tell this man the meaning of the vision."

---

*a*25 Or *for a year, two years and half a year*   *b*12 Or *rebellion, the armies*

17As he came near the place where I was standing, I was terrified and fell prostrate. "Son of man," he said to me, "understand that the vision concerns the time of the end."

18While he was speaking to me, I was in a deep sleep, with my face to the ground. Then he touched me and raised me to my feet.

19He said: "I am going to tell you what will happen later in the time of wrath, because the vision concerns the appointed time of the end.a 20The two-horned ram that you saw represents the kings of Media and Persia. 21The shaggy goat is the king of Greece, and the large horn between his eyes is the first king. 22The four horns that replaced the one that was broken off represent four kingdoms that will emerge from his nation but will not have the same power.

23"In the latter part of their reign, when rebels have become completely wicked, a stern-faced king, a master of intrigue, will arise. 24He will become very strong, but not by his own power. He will cause astounding devastation and will succeed in whatever he does. He will destroy the mighty men and the holy people. 25He will cause deceit to prosper, and he will consider himself superior. When they feel secure, he will destroy many and take his stand against the Prince of princes. Yet he will be destroyed, but not by human power.

26"The vision of the evenings and mornings that has been given you is true, but seal up the vision, for it concerns the distant future."

27I, Daniel, was exhausted and lay ill for several days. Then I got up and went about the king's business. I was appalled by the vision; it was beyond understanding.

Daniel's Prayer

9 In the first year of Darius son of Xerxesb (a Mede by descent), who was made ruler over the Babylonianc kingdom— 2in the first year of his reign, I, Daniel, understood from the Scriptures, according to the word of the LORD given to Jeremiah the prophet, that the desolation of Jerusalem would last seventy years. 3So I turned to the Lord God and pleaded with him in prayer and petition, in fasting, and in sackcloth and ashes.

4I prayed to the LORD my God and confessed:

"O Lord, the great and awesome God, who keeps his covenant of love with all who love him and obey his commands, 5we have sinned and done wrong. We have been wicked and have rebelled; we have turned away from your commands and laws. 6We have not listened to your servants the prophets, who spoke in your name to our kings, our princes and our fathers, and to all the people of the land.

7"Lord, you are righteous, but this day we are covered with shame — the men of Judah and people of Jerusalem and all Israel, both near and far, in all the countries where you have scattered us because of our unfaithfulness to you. 8O LORD, we and our kings, our princes and our fathers are covered with shame because we have sinned against you. 9The Lord our God is merciful and forgiving, even though we have rebelled against him; 10we have not obeyed the LORD our God or kept the laws he gave us through his servants the prophets. 11All Israel has transgressed your law and turned away, refusing to obey you.

"Therefore the curses and sworn judgments written in the Law of Moses, the servant of God, have been poured out on us, because we have sinned against you. 12You have fulfilled the words spoken against us and against our rulers by bringing upon us great disaster. Under the whole heaven nothing has ever been done like what has been done to Jerusalem. 13Just as it is written in the Law of Moses, all this disaster has come upon us, yet we have not sought the favor of the LORD our God by turning from our sins and giving attention to your truth. 14The LORD did not hesitate to bring the disaster upon us, for the LORD our God is righteous in everything he does; yet we have not obeyed him.

15"Now, O Lord our God, who brought your people out of Egypt with a mighty hand and who made for yourself a name that endures to this day, we have sinned, we have

---

a19 Or because the end will be at the appointed time   b1 Hebrew Ahasuerus   c1 Or Chaldean done wrong. **16**O Lord, in keeping with all your righteous acts, turn away your anger and your wrath from Jerusalem, your city, your holy hill. Our sins and the iniquities of our fathers have made Jerusalem and your people an object of scorn to all those around us.

17"Now, our God, hear the prayers and petitions of your servant. For your sake, O Lord, look with favor on your desolate sanctuary. **18**Give ear, O God, and hear; open your eyes and see the desolation of the city that bears your Name. We do not make requests of you because we are righteous, but because of your great mercy. **19**O Lord, listen! O Lord, forgive! O Lord, hear and act! For your sake, O my God, do not delay, because your city and your people bear your Name."

The Seventy "Sevens"

20While I was speaking and praying, confessing my sin and the sin of my people Israel and making my request to the LORD my God for his holy hill— **21**while I

FRIDAY

VERSE FOR THE DAY:
Daniel 9:5

AUTHOR:
Henri Nouwen

PASSAGE FOR THE DAY:
Daniel 9:4–11

Have Mercy on Me, a Sinner

O LORD Jesus Christ, Son of the living God, have mercy on me, a sinner. I am impressed by my own spiritual insights. I probably know more about prayer, meditation and contemplation than most Christians do. I have read many books about the Christian life, and have even written a few myself. Still, as impressed as I am, I am more impressed by the enormous abyss between my insights and my life.

It seems as if I am standing on one side of a huge canyon and see how I should grow toward you, live in your presence and serve you, but cannot reach the other side of the canyon where you are. I can speak and write, preach and argue about the beauty and goodness of the life I see on the other side, but how, O Lord, can I get there? Sometimes I even have the painful feeling that the clearer the vision, the more aware I am of the depth of the canyon.

Am I doomed to die on the wrong side of the abyss? Am I destined to excite others to reach the promised land while remaining unable to enter there myself? Sometimes I feel imprisoned by my own insights and "spiritual competence." You alone, Lord, can reach out to me and save me. You alone.

I can only keep trying to be faithful, even though I feel faithless most of the time. What else can I do but keep praying to you, even when I feel dark; to keep writing about you, even when I feel numb; to keep speaking in your name, even when I feel alone. Come, Lord Jesus, come. Have mercy on me, a sinner. Amen.

Additional Scripture Readings:
Psalm 51:1–12; Hebrews 4:14–16

Go to page 926 for your next devotional reading.

was still in prayer, Gabriel, the man I had seen in the earlier vision, came to me in swift flight about the time of the evening sacrifice. **22**He instructed me and said to me, "Daniel, I have now come to give you insight and understanding. **23**As soon as you began to pray, an answer was given, which I have come to tell you, for you are highly esteemed. Therefore, consider the message and understand the vision:

24"Seventy 'sevens'[a] are decreed for your people and your holy city to finish[b] transgression, to put an end to sin, to atone for wickedness, to bring in everlasting righteousness, to seal up vision and prophecy and to anoint the most holy.[c]

25"Know and understand this: From the issuing of the decree[d] to restore and rebuild Jerusalem until the Anointed One,[e] the ruler, comes, there will be seven 'sevens,' and sixty-two 'sevens.' It will be rebuilt with streets and a trench, but in times of trouble. **26**After the sixty-two 'sevens,' the Anointed One will be cut off and will have nothing.[f] The people of the ruler who will come will destroy the city and the sanctuary. The end will come like a flood: War will continue until the end, and desolations have been decreed. **27**He will confirm a covenant with many for one 'seven.'[g] In the middle of the 'seven'[g] he will put an end to sacrifice and offering. And on a wing [of the temple] he will set up an abomination that causes desolation, until the end that is decreed is poured out on him.[h]"[i]

Daniel's Vision of a Man

10 In the third year of Cyrus king of Persia, a revelation was given to Daniel (who was called Belteshazzar). Its message was true and it concerned a great war.[j] The understanding of the message came to him in a vision.

2At that time I, Daniel, mourned for three weeks. **3**I ate no choice food; no meat or wine touched my lips; and I used no lotions at all until the three weeks were over.

4On the twenty-fourth day of the first month, as I was standing on the bank of the great river, the Tigris, **5**I looked up and there before me was a man dressed in linen, with a belt of the finest gold around his waist. **6**His body was like chrysolite, his face like lightning, his eyes like flaming torches, his arms and legs like the gleam of burnished bronze, and his voice like the sound of a multitude.

7I, Daniel, was the only one who saw the vision; the men with me did not see it, but such terror overwhelmed them that they fled and hid themselves. **8**So I was left alone, gazing at this great vision; I had no strength left, my face turned deathly pale and I was helpless. **9**Then I heard him speaking, and as I listened to him, I fell into a deep sleep, my face to the ground.

10A hand touched me and set me trembling on my hands and knees. **11**He said, "Daniel, you who are highly esteemed, consider carefully the words I am about to speak to you, and stand up, for I have now been sent to you." And when he said this to me, I stood up trembling.

12Then he continued, "Do not be afraid, Daniel. Since the first day that you set your mind to gain understanding and to humble yourself before your God, your words were heard, and I have come in response to them. **13**But the prince of the Persian kingdom resisted me twenty-one days. Then Michael, one of the chief princes, came to help me, because I was detained there with the king of Persia. **14**Now I have come to explain to you what will happen to your people in the future, for the vision concerns a time yet to come."

15While he was saying this to me, I bowed with my face toward the ground and was speechless. **16**Then one who looked like a man[k] touched my lips, and I opened my mouth and began to speak. I said to the one standing before me, "I am overcome with anguish because of the vision, my lord, and I am helpless. **17**How can I, your servant, talk with you, my lord? My strength is gone and I can hardly breathe."

18Again the one who looked like a man touched me and gave me strength. **19**"Do not be afraid, O man highly esteemed," he said. "Peace! Be strong now; be strong." When he spoke to me, I was strength-

---

[a]24 Or 'weeks'; also in verses 25 and 26　　[b]24 Or restrain　　[c]24 Or Most Holy Place; or most holy One　　[d]25 Or word　　[e]25 Or an anointed one; also in verse 26　　[f]26 Or off and will have no one; or off, but not for himself　　[g]27 Or 'week'　　[h]27 Or it　　[i]27 Or And one who causes desolation will come upon the pinnacle of the abominable [temple], until the end that is decreed is poured out on the desolated [city]　　[j]1 Or true and burdensome　　[k]16 Most manuscripts of the Masoretic Text; one manuscript of the Masoretic Text, Dead Sea Scrolls and Septuagint Then something that looked like a man's hand

ened and said, "Speak, my lord, since you have given me strength."

20So he said, "Do you know why I have come to you? Soon I will return to fight against the prince of Persia, and when I go, the prince of Greece will come; **21**but first I will tell you what is written in the Book of Truth. (No one supports me against them except Michael, your prince.

11 **1**And in the first year of Darius the Mede, I took my stand to support and protect him.)

The Kings of the South and the North

2"Now then, I tell you the truth: Three more kings will appear in Persia, and then a fourth, who will be far richer than all the others. When he has gained power by his wealth, he will stir up everyone against the kingdom of Greece. **3**Then a mighty king will appear, who will rule with great power and do as he pleases. **4**After he has appeared, his empire will be broken up and parceled out toward the four winds of heaven. It will not go to his descendants, nor will it have the power he exercised, because his empire will be uprooted and given to others.

5"The king of the South will become strong, but one of his commanders will become even stronger than he and will rule his own kingdom with great power. **6**After some years, they will become allies. The daughter of the king of the South will go to the king of the North to make an alliance, but she will not retain her power, and he and his power*a* will not last. In those days she will be handed over, together with her royal escort and her father*b* and the one who supported her.

7"One from her family line will arise to take her place. He will attack the forces of the king of the North and enter his fortress; he will fight against them and be victorious. **8**He will also seize their gods, their metal images and their valuable articles of silver and gold and carry them off to Egypt. For some years he will leave the king of the North alone. **9**Then the king of the North will invade the realm of the king of the South but will retreat to his own country. **10**His sons will prepare for war and assemble a great army, which will sweep on like an irresistible flood and carry the battle as far as his fortress.

11"Then the king of the South will march out in a rage and fight against the king of the North, who will raise a large army, but it will be defeated. **12**When the army is carried off, the king of the South will be filled with pride and will slaughter many thousands, yet he will not remain triumphant. **13**For the king of the North will muster another army, larger than the first; and after several years, he will advance with a huge army fully equipped.

14"In those times many will rise against the king of the South. The violent men among your own people will rebel in fulfillment of the vision, but without success. **15**Then the king of the North will come and build up siege ramps and will capture a fortified city. The forces of the South will be powerless to resist; even their best troops will not have the strength to stand. **16**The invader will do as he pleases; no one will be able to stand against him. He will establish himself in the Beautiful Land and will have the power to destroy it. **17**He will determine to come with the might of his entire kingdom and will make an alliance with the king of the South. And he will give him a daughter in marriage in order to overthrow the kingdom, but his plans*c* will not succeed or help him. **18**Then he will turn his attention to the coastlands and will take many of them, but a commander will put an end to his insolence and will turn his insolence back upon him. **19**After this, he will turn back toward the fortresses of his own country but will stumble and fall, to be seen no more.

20"His successor will send out a tax collector to maintain the royal splendor. In a few years, however, he will be destroyed, yet not in anger or in battle.

21"He will be succeeded by a contemptible person who has not been given the honor of royalty. He will invade the kingdom when its people feel secure, and he will seize it through intrigue. **22**Then an overwhelming army will be swept away before him; both it and a prince of the covenant will be destroyed. **23**After coming to an agreement with him, he will act deceitfully, and with only a few people he will rise to power. **24**When the richest provinces feel secure, he will invade them and will achieve what neither his fathers nor his forefathers did. He will distribute plunder, loot and wealth among his followers. He will plot the overthrow of fortresses—but only for a time.

25"With a large army he will stir up his

---

*a*6 Or *offspring*   *b*6 Or *child* (see Vulgate and Syriac)   *c*17 Or *but she*

WEEKENDING

RETHINK

If, indeed, we all have a kind of appetite for eternity, we have allowed ourselves to be caught up in a society that frustrates our longing at every turn. Half our inventions are advertised to save time—the washing machine, the fast car, the jet flight—but for what? Never were people more harried by time: by watches, by buzzers, by time clocks, by precise schedules . . .

If we complain of time and take such joy in the seemingly timeless moment, what does that suggest?

It suggests that we have not always been or will not always be purely temporal creatures. It suggests that we were created for eternity. Not only are we harried by time, we seem unable, despite a thousand generations, even to get used to it. We are always amazed at it—how fast it goes, how slowly it goes, how much of it is gone? We aren't adapted to it, nor at home in it. If that is so, it may appear as a proof, or at least a powerful suggestion, that eternity exists and is our home.

– Sheldon Vanauken

REVIVE

Saturday: Ecclesiastes 3:9–14
Sunday: 2 Corinthians 5:16—6:2

Go to page 931 for your next devotional reading.

strength and courage against the king of the South. The king of the South will wage war with a large and very powerful army, but he will not be able to stand because of the plots devised against him. **26**Those who eat from the king's provisions will try to destroy him; his army will be swept away, and many will fall in battle. **27**The two kings, with their hearts bent on evil, will sit at the same table and lie to each other, but to no avail, because an end will still come at the appointed time. **28**The king of the North will return to his own country with great wealth, but his heart will be set against the holy covenant. He will take action against it and then return to his own country.

29"At the appointed time he will invade the South again, but this time the outcome will be different from what it was before. **30**Ships of the western coastlands*a* will oppose him, and he will lose heart. Then he will turn back and vent his fury against the holy covenant. He will return and show favor to those who forsake the holy covenant.

31"His armed forces will rise up to desecrate the temple fortress and will abolish the daily sacrifice. Then they will set up the abomination that causes desolation. **32**With flattery he will corrupt those who have violated the covenant, but the people who know their God will firmly resist him.

33"Those who are wise will instruct many, though for a time they will fall by the sword or be burned or captured or plundered. **34**When they fall, they will receive a little help, and many who are not sincere will join them. **35**Some of the wise will stumble, so that they may be refined, purified and made spotless until the time of the end, for it will still come at the appointed time.

The King Who Exalts Himself

36"The king will do as he pleases. He will exalt and magnify himself above every god and will say unheard-of things against the God of gods. He will be successful until the time of wrath is completed, for what has been determined must take place. **37**He will show no regard for the gods of his fathers or for the one desired by women, nor will he regard any god, but will exalt himself above them all. **38**Instead of them, he will honor a god of fortresses; a god unknown to his fathers he will honor with gold and silver, with

precious stones and costly gifts. **39**He will attack the mightiest fortresses with the help of a foreign god and will greatly honor those who acknowledge him. He will make them rulers over many people and will distribute the land at a price.*b*

40"At the time of the end the king of the South will engage him in battle, and the king of the North will storm out against him with chariots and cavalry and a great fleet of ships. He will invade many countries and sweep through them like a flood. **41**He will also invade the Beautiful Land. Many countries will fall, but Edom, Moab and the leaders of Ammon will be delivered from his hand. **42**He will extend his power over many countries; Egypt will not escape. **43**He will gain control of the treasures of gold and silver and all the riches of Egypt, with the Libyans and Nubians in submission. **44**But reports from the east and the north will alarm him, and he will set out in a great rage to destroy and annihilate many. **45**He will pitch his royal tents between the seas at*c* the beautiful holy mountain. Yet he will come to his end, and no one will help him.

The End Times

12 "At that time Michael, the great prince who protects your people, will arise. There will be a time of distress such as has not happened from the beginning of nations until then. But at that time your people—everyone whose name is found written in the book—will be delivered. **2**Multitudes who sleep in the dust of the earth will awake: some to everlasting life, others to shame and everlasting contempt. **3**Those who are wise*d* will shine like the brightness of the heavens, and those who lead many to righteousness, like the stars for ever and ever. **4**But you, Daniel, close up and seal the words of the scroll until the time of the end. Many will go here and there to increase knowledge."

5Then I, Daniel, looked, and there before me stood two others, one on this bank of the river and one on the opposite bank. **6**One of them said to the man clothed in linen, who was above the waters of the river, "How long will it be before these astonishing things are fulfilled?"

7The man clothed in linen, who was above the waters of the river, lifted his

---

*a*30 Hebrew *of Kittim*   *b*39 Or *land for a reward*   *c*45 Or *the sea and*   *d*3 Or *who impart wisdom* right hand and his left hand toward heaven, and I heard him swear by him who lives forever, saying, "It will be for a time, times and half a time.*a* When the power of the holy people has been finally broken, all these things will be completed."

8I heard, but I did not understand. So I asked, "My lord, what will the outcome of all this be?"

9He replied, "Go your way, Daniel, because the words are closed up and sealed until the time of the end. **10**Many will be purified, made spotless and refined, but

the wicked will continue to be wicked. None of the wicked will understand, but those who are wise will understand.

11"From the time that the daily sacrifice is abolished and the abomination that causes desolation is set up, there will be 1,290 days. **12**Blessed is the one who waits for and reaches the end of the 1,335 days.

13"As for you, go your way till the end. You will rest, and then at the end of the days you will rise to receive your allotted inheritance."

a7 Or *a year, two years and half a year*

Hosea prophesies during the last days of Israel (see 2 Kings 14:23–17:41), focusing on her sin of spiritual adultery (that is, idolatry). He warns them that God will punish them unless they change their ways. But he also reminds them of God's incredible love, pleading with them to repent. As you read this book, think of God's love in sending his Son Jesus to die for you, in spite of your sins. Repent of your unfaithfulness to the Lord and turn to him.

HOSEA

1 The word of the Lord that came to Hosea son of Beeri during the reigns of Uzziah, Jotham, Ahaz and Hezekiah, kings of Judah, and during the reign of Jeroboam son of Jehoash[a] king of Israel:

Hosea's Wife and Children

²When the Lord began to speak through Hosea, the Lord said to him, "Go, take to yourself an adulterous wife and children of unfaithfulness, because the land is guilty of the vilest adultery in departing from the Lord." ³So he married Gomer daughter of Diblaim, and she conceived and bore him a son.

⁴Then the Lord said to Hosea, "Call him Jezreel, because I will soon punish the house of Jehu for the massacre at Jezreel, and I will put an end to the kingdom of Israel. ⁵In that day I will break Israel's bow in the Valley of Jezreel."

⁶Gomer conceived again and gave birth to a daughter. Then the Lord said to Hosea, "Call her Lo-Ruhamah,[b] for I will no longer show love to the house of Israel, that I should at all forgive them. ⁷Yet I will show love to the house of Judah; and I will save them—not by bow, sword or battle, or by horses and horsemen, but by the Lord their God."

a1 Hebrew *Joash,* a variant of *Jehoash*   *b6* *Lo-Ruhamah* means *not loved.*

⁸After she had weaned Lo-Ruhamah, Gomer had another son. ⁹Then the LORD said, "Call him Lo-Ammi,ᵃ for you are not my people, and I am not your God.

¹⁰"Yet the Israelites will be like the sand on the seashore, which cannot be measured or counted. In the place where it was said to them, 'You are not my people,' they will be called 'sons of the living God.' ¹¹The people of Judah and the people of Israel will be reunited, and they will appoint one leader and will come up out of the land, for great will be the day of Jezreel.

2 "Say of your brothers, 'My people,' and of your sisters, 'My loved one.'

Israel Punished and Restored

²"Rebuke your mother, rebuke her,
　　for she is not my wife,
　　and I am not her husband.
Let her remove the adulterous look
　　from her face
　　and the unfaithfulness from
　　　between her breasts.
³Otherwise I will strip her naked
　　and make her as bare as on the day
　　　she was born;
I will make her like a desert,
　　turn her into a parched land,
　　and slay her with thirst.
⁴I will not show my love to her
　　children,
　　because they are the children of
　　　adultery.
⁵Their mother has been unfaithful
　　and has conceived them in disgrace.
She said, 'I will go after my lovers,
　　who give me my food and my
　　　water,
　　my wool and my linen, my oil and
　　　my drink.'
⁶Therefore I will block her path with
　　thornbushes;
　　I will wall her in so that she cannot
　　　find her way.
⁷She will chase after her lovers but not
　　catch them;
　　she will look for them but not find
　　　them.
Then she will say,
　　'I will go back to my husband as at
　　　first,
　　for then I was better off than now.'
⁸She has not acknowledged that I was
　　the one
　　who gave her the grain, the new
　　　wine and oil,

who lavished on her the silver and
　　gold—
　　which they used for Baal.

⁹"Therefore I will take away my grain
　　when it ripens,
　　and my new wine when it is ready.
I will take back my wool and my
　　linen,
　　intended to cover her nakedness.
¹⁰So now I will expose her lewdness
　　before the eyes of her lovers;
　　no one will take her out of my
　　　hands.
¹¹I will stop all her celebrations:
　　her yearly festivals, her New Moons,
　　her Sabbath days—all her appointed
　　　feasts.
¹²I will ruin her vines and her fig trees,
　　which she said were her pay from
　　　her lovers;
I will make them a thicket,
　　and wild animals will devour them.
¹³I will punish her for the days
　　she burned incense to the Baals;
she decked herself with rings and
　　jewelry,
　　and went after her lovers,
　　but me she forgot,"
　　　　　　　　declares the LORD.

¹⁴"Therefore I am now going to allure
　　her;
　　I will lead her into the desert
　　and speak tenderly to her.
¹⁵There I will give her back her
　　vineyards,
　　and will make the Valley of Achorᵇ
　　　a door of hope.
There she will singᶜ as in the days of
　　her youth,
　　as in the day she came up out of
　　　Egypt.

¹⁶"In that day," declares the LORD,
　　"you will call me 'my husband';
　　you will no longer call me 'my
　　　master.ᵈ'
¹⁷I will remove the names of the Baals
　　from her lips;
　　no longer will their names be
　　　invoked.
¹⁸In that day I will make a covenant for
　　them
　　with the beasts of the field and the
　　　birds of the air
　　and the creatures that move along
　　　the ground.

ᵃ9 *Lo-Ammi* means *not my people.*　　ᵇ15 *Achor* means *trouble.*　　ᶜ15 Or *respond*　　ᵈ16 Hebrew *baal*

Bow and sword and battle
   I will abolish from the land,
   so that all may lie down in safety.
¹⁹I will betroth you to me forever;
   I will betroth you in ᵃ righteousness
      and justice,
   in ᵇ love and compassion.
²⁰I will betroth you in faithfulness,
   and you will acknowledge the LORD.

²¹"In that day I will respond,"
   declares the LORD—
"I will respond to the skies,
   and they will respond to the earth;
²²and the earth will respond to the
      grain,

the new wine and oil,
   and they will respond to Jezreel.ᶜ
²³I will plant her for myself in the land;
   I will show my love to the one I
      called 'Not my loved one.ᵈ'
I will say to those called 'Not my
      people,ᵉ' 'You are my people';
   and they will say, 'You are my
      God.'"

Hosea's Reconciliation With His Wife

3 The LORD said to me, "Go, show your
love to your wife again, though she is
loved by another and is an adulteress.
Love her as the LORD loves the Israelites,

ᵃ19 Or *with*; also in verse 20   ᵇ19 Or *with*   ᶜ22 *Jezreel* means *God plants.*   ᵈ23 Hebrew
Lo-Ruhamah   ᵉ23 Hebrew *Lo-Ammi*

MONDAY

VERSE FOR THE DAY:
Hosea 2:19

AUTHOR:
G.R. Slater

PASSAGE FOR THE DAY:
Hosea 2:16–23

The Divine Glue

THE presence of Christ gives a grace to marriage. By that I
mean a plus, a blessing and a power beyond the ordinary. It is
significant that the marriage of man and woman is the favorite
image which the Bible uses for God's relationship to his people. And Jesus spoke of himself as the bridegroom and believers as his bride. There is something wonderful about a human
relationship which partakes of divine overtones like that.

There is something divine in true marriage. It is like a trian-
gle: it takes three to get married—a man, a woman and God.
Francis de Sales put it this way, "If the glue is good, two pieces
of wood glued together will cleave so fast to each other that
they can be more easily broken in any other place than where
they were joined. God glues the husband to the wife with his
own blood."

This means that every marriage needs the miracle of God's
presence. It needs to invite him in so that he can introduce his
reconciling grace into the material of two lives. That grace is
not a buttress thrown up from the outside to hold up the walls
of marriage when they are unable to stand by themselves. It is
the "glue" which provides the conditions of personal responsibility, patience and understanding by which two persons adhere to each other in willing faithfulness.

Additional Scripture Readings:
Isaiah 54:5–8; 1 Corinthians 6:12–20

*Go to page 933 for your next
devotional reading.*

though they turn to other gods and love the sacred raisin cakes."

[2]So I bought her for fifteen shekels[a] of silver and about a homer and a lethek[b] of barley. [3]Then I told her, "You are to live with[c] me many days; you must not be a prostitute or be intimate with any man, and I will live with[c] you."

[4]For the Israelites will live many days without king or prince, without sacrifice or sacred stones, without ephod or idol. [5]Afterward the Israelites will return and seek the LORD their God and David their king. They will come trembling to the LORD and to his blessings in the last days.

The Charge Against Israel

4 Hear the word of the LORD, you
  Israelites,
  because the LORD has a charge to
    bring
  against you who live in the land:
"There is no faithfulness, no love,
  no acknowledgment of God in the
    land.
[2]There is only cursing,[d] lying and
    murder,
  stealing and adultery;
they break all bounds,
  and bloodshed follows bloodshed.
[3]Because of this the land mourns,[e]
  and all who live in it waste away;
the beasts of the field and the birds of
    the air
  and the fish of the sea are dying.

[4]"But let no man bring a charge,
  let no man accuse another,
for your people are like those
  who bring charges against a priest.
[5]You stumble day and night,
  and the prophets stumble with you.
So I will destroy your mother—
[6] my people are destroyed from lack
    of knowledge.

"Because you have rejected
    knowledge,
  I also reject you as my priests;
because you have ignored the law of
    your God,
  I also will ignore your children.
[7]The more the priests increased,
  the more they sinned against me;

they exchanged[f] their[g] Glory for
  something disgraceful.
[8]They feed on the sins of my people
  and relish their wickedness.
[9]And it will be: Like people, like
    priests.
  I will punish both of them for their
    ways
  and repay them for their deeds.

[10]"They will eat but not have enough;
  they will engage in prostitution but
    not increase,
because they have deserted the LORD
  to give themselves [11]to prostitution,
to old wine and new,
  which take away the understanding
    [12]of my people.
They consult a wooden idol
  and are answered by a stick of
    wood.
A spirit of prostitution leads them
    astray;
  they are unfaithful to their God.
[13]They sacrifice on the mountaintops
  and burn offerings on the hills,
under oak, poplar and terebinth,
  where the shade is pleasant.
Therefore your daughters turn to
    prostitution
  and your daughters-in-law to
    adultery.

[14]"I will not punish your daughters
  when they turn to prostitution,
nor your daughters-in-law
  when they commit adultery,
because the men themselves consort
    with harlots
  and sacrifice with shrine
    prostitutes—
a people without understanding will
    come to ruin!

[15]"Though you commit adultery,
    O Israel,
  let not Judah become guilty.

"Do not go to Gilgal;
  do not go up to Beth Aven.[h]
  And do not swear, 'As surely as the
    LORD lives!'
[16]The Israelites are stubborn,
  like a stubborn heifer.

---

[a]2 That is, about 6 ounces (about 170 grams)   [b]2 That is, probably about 10 bushels (about 330 liters)   [c]3 Or *wait for*   [d]2 That is, to pronounce a curse upon   [e]3 Or *dries up*   [f]7 Syriac and an ancient Hebrew scribal tradition; Masoretic Text *I will exchange*   [g]7 Masoretic Text; an ancient Hebrew scribal tradition *my*   [h]15 *Beth Aven* means *house of wickedness* (a name for Bethel, which means *house of God*).

How then can the LORD pasture them
   like lambs in a meadow?
[17]Ephraim is joined to idols;
   leave him alone!
[18]Even when their drinks are gone,
   they continue their prostitution;
   their rulers dearly love shameful
      ways.
[19]A whirlwind will sweep them away,
   and their sacrifices will bring them
      shame.

Judgment Against Israel

5 "Hear this, you priests!
   Pay attention, you Israelites!
Listen, O royal house!
   This judgment is against you:
You have been a snare at Mizpah,
   a net spread out on Tabor.
[2]The rebels are deep in slaughter.
   I will discipline all of them.
[3]I know all about Ephraim;
   Israel is not hidden from me.

TUESDAY

VERSE FOR THE DAY:
Hosea 4:1

AUTHOR:
Mark Ritchie

PASSAGE FOR THE DAY:
Hosea 4:1–9

The Power of Committed Love

MODERN-DAY thinking was finding that the marriage contract inhibited a good romantic relationship. Hollywood was showing romantic relationships everywhere except within marriage. In fact, it seemed that the marriage contract would be the kiss of death to a good romance . . .

Lucky for us, things aren't always as they seem. Obviously we aren't nearly as well-informed on these matters as all those Hollywood writers and contributors of intellectual articles to *Playboy*. But we found just the opposite to be the case. We found that the marriage commitment was the highest expression of love.

Modern love seems to need the freedom to leave, otherwise it was confining and restricting. The freedom to leave absolutely precluded security of any sort. It means that separation is an option that could be employed on any problem —emotional, financial, sexual, anything. I wondered how I would feel about Nancy if she insisted that she keep open her option to leave me? What if she said, "Mark, I just can't love you unless you give me the freedom to stop loving you and start loving someone else." I compared that to the marriage commitment: "Mark, I love you so much that there is nothing, absolutely nothing that will ever be able to separate us. I seal my love with this vow: I will never, for any reason, leave you." The comparison made me laugh. It's a small wonder that there is so much insecurity in these modern, enlightened relationships. What we had was a statement of real love. It was out of the power of that committed love that we found the deepest emotional security.

Additional Scripture Readings:
Proverbs 14:22; Romans 8:31–39

Go to page 939 for your next
devotional reading.

Ephraim, you have now turned to
    prostitution;
  Israel is corrupt.

⁴"Their deeds do not permit them
    to return to their God.
  A spirit of prostitution is in their
    heart;
  they do not acknowledge the LORD.
⁵Israel's arrogance testifies against
    them;
  the Israelites, even Ephraim,
    stumble in their sin;
  Judah also stumbles with them.
⁶When they go with their flocks and
    herds
  to seek the LORD,
  they will not find him;
  he has withdrawn himself from
    them.
⁷They are unfaithful to the LORD;
  they give birth to illegitimate
    children.
  Now their New Moon festivals
  will devour them and their fields.

⁸"Sound the trumpet in Gibeah,
  the horn in Ramah.
  Raise the battle cry in Beth Aven[a];
  lead on, O Benjamin.
⁹Ephraim will be laid waste
  on the day of reckoning.
  Among the tribes of Israel
  I proclaim what is certain.
¹⁰Judah's leaders are like those
  who move boundary stones.
  I will pour out my wrath on them
  like a flood of water.
¹¹Ephraim is oppressed,
  trampled in judgment,
  intent on pursuing idols.[b]
¹²I am like a moth to Ephraim,
  like rot to the people of Judah.

¹³"When Ephraim saw his sickness,
  and Judah his sores,
  then Ephraim turned to Assyria,
  and sent to the great king for help.
  But he is not able to cure you,
  not able to heal your sores.
¹⁴For I will be like a lion to Ephraim,
  like a great lion to Judah.
  I will tear them to pieces and go
    away;
  I will carry them off, with no one to
    rescue them.
¹⁵Then I will go back to my place
  until they admit their guilt.

And they will seek my face;
  in their misery they will earnestly
    seek me."

Israel Unrepentant

6 "Come, let us return to the LORD.
  He has torn us to pieces
  but he will heal us;
  he has injured us
  but he will bind up our wounds.
²After two days he will revive us;
  on the third day he will restore us,
  that we may live in his presence.
³Let us acknowledge the LORD;
  let us press on to acknowledge him.
  As surely as the sun rises,
  he will appear;
  he will come to us like the winter
    rains,
  like the spring rains that water the
    earth."

⁴"What can I do with you, Ephraim?
  What can I do with you, Judah?
  Your love is like the morning mist,
  like the early dew that disappears.
⁵Therefore I cut you in pieces with my
    prophets,
  I killed you with the words of my
    mouth;
  my judgments flashed like lightning
    upon you.
⁶For I desire mercy, not sacrifice,
  and acknowledgment of God rather
    than burnt offerings.
⁷Like Adam,[c] they have broken the
    covenant—
  they were unfaithful to me there.
⁸Gilead is a city of wicked men,
  stained with footprints of blood.
⁹As marauders lie in ambush for a
    man,
  so do bands of priests;
  they murder on the road to Shechem,
  committing shameful crimes.
¹⁰I have seen a horrible thing
  in the house of Israel.
  There Ephraim is given to prostitution
  and Israel is defiled.

¹¹"Also for you, Judah,
  a harvest is appointed.

"Whenever I would restore the
    fortunes of my people,
7 ¹whenever I would heal Israel,
  the sins of Ephraim are exposed
  and the crimes of Samaria revealed.

a8 Beth Aven means house of wickedness (a name for Bethel, which means house of God).   b11 The
meaning of the Hebrew for this word is uncertain.   c7 Or As at Adam; or Like men

They practice deceit,
    thieves break into houses,
    bandits rob in the streets;
²but they do not realize
    that I remember all their evil deeds.
Their sins engulf them;
    they are always before me.

³"They delight the king with their
        wickedness,
    the princes with their lies.
⁴They are all adulterers,
    burning like an oven
whose fire the baker need not stir
    from the kneading of the dough till
        it rises.
⁵On the day of the festival of our king
    the princes become inflamed with
        wine,
    and he joins hands with the
        mockers.
⁶Their hearts are like an oven;
    they approach him with intrigue.
Their passion smolders all night;
    in the morning it blazes like a
        flaming fire.
⁷All of them are hot as an oven;
    they devour their rulers.
All their kings fall,
    and none of them calls on me.

⁸"Ephraim mixes with the nations;
    Ephraim is a flat cake not turned
        over.
⁹Foreigners sap his strength,
    but he does not realize it.
His hair is sprinkled with gray,
    but he does not notice.
¹⁰Israel's arrogance testifies against him,
    but despite all this
he does not return to the LORD his
        God
    or search for him.

¹¹"Ephraim is like a dove,
    easily deceived and senseless—
now calling to Egypt,
    now turning to Assyria.
¹²When they go, I will throw my net
        over them;
    I will pull them down like birds of
        the air.
When I hear them flocking together,
    I will catch them.
¹³Woe to them,
    because they have strayed from me!
Destruction to them,
    because they have rebelled against
        me!

I long to redeem them
    but they speak lies against me.
¹⁴They do not cry out to me from their
        hearts
    but wail upon their beds.
They gather togetherᵃ for grain and
        new wine
    but turn away from me.
¹⁵I trained them and strengthened them,
    but they plot evil against me.
¹⁶They do not turn to the Most High;
    they are like a faulty bow.
Their leaders will fall by the sword
    because of their insolent words.
For this they will be ridiculed
    in the land of Egypt.

Israel to Reap the Whirlwind

8 "Put the trumpet to your lips!
    An eagle is over the house of the
        LORD
because the people have broken my
        covenant
    and rebelled against my law.
²Israel cries out to me,
    'O our God, we acknowledge you!'
³But Israel has rejected what is good;
    an enemy will pursue him.
⁴They set up kings without my
        consent;
    they choose princes without my
        approval.
With their silver and gold
    they make idols for themselves
    to their own destruction.
⁵Throw out your calf-idol, O Samaria!
    My anger burns against them.
How long will they be incapable of
        purity?
⁶   They are from Israel!
This calf—a craftsman has made it;
    it is not God.
It will be broken in pieces,
    that calf of Samaria.

⁷"They sow the wind
    and reap the whirlwind.
The stalk has no head;
    it will produce no flour.
Were it to yield grain,
    foreigners would swallow it up.
⁸Israel is swallowed up;
    now she is among the nations
    like a worthless thing.
⁹For they have gone up to Assyria
    like a wild donkey wandering alone.
    Ephraim has sold herself to lovers.

ᵃ14 Most Hebrew manuscripts; some Hebrew manuscripts and Septuagint *They slash themselves*

10Although they have sold themselves
　　among the nations,
　I will now gather them together.
They will begin to waste away
　　under the oppression of the mighty
　　　king.

11"Though Ephraim built many altars
　　for sin offerings,
　these have become altars for
　　sinning.
12I wrote for them the many things of
　　my law,
　but they regarded them as
　　something alien.
13They offer sacrifices given to me
　　and they eat the meat,
　but the LORD is not pleased with
　　them.
Now he will remember their
　　wickedness
　and punish their sins:
They will return to Egypt.
14Israel has forgotten his Maker
　　and built palaces;
　Judah has fortified many towns.
But I will send fire upon their cities
　　that will consume their fortresses."

Punishment for Israel

9 Do not rejoice, O Israel;
　do not be jubilant like the other
　　nations.
For you have been unfaithful to your
　　God;
　you love the wages of a prostitute
　　at every threshing floor.
2Threshing floors and winepresses will
　　not feed the people;
　the new wine will fail them.
3They will not remain in the LORD's
　　land;
　Ephraim will return to Egypt
　and eat unclean[a] food in Assyria.
4They will not pour out wine offerings
　　to the LORD,
　nor will their sacrifices please him.
Such sacrifices will be to them like the
　　bread of mourners;
　all who eat them will be unclean.
This food will be for themselves;
　it will not come into the temple of
　　the LORD.

5What will you do on the day of your
　　appointed feasts,
　on the festival days of the LORD?
6Even if they escape from destruction,
Egypt will gather them,
　and Memphis will bury them.
Their treasures of silver will be taken
　　over by briers,
　and thorns will overrun their tents.
7The days of punishment are coming,
　the days of reckoning are at hand.
Let Israel know this.
Because your sins are so many
　　and your hostility so great,
　the prophet is considered a fool,
　the inspired man a maniac.
8The prophet, along with my God,
　is the watchman over Ephraim,[b]
　yet snares await him on all his paths,
　and hostility in the house of his
　　God.
9They have sunk deep into corruption,
　as in the days of Gibeah.
God will remember their wickedness
　and punish them for their sins.

10"When I found Israel,
　it was like finding grapes in the
　　desert;
when I saw your fathers,
　it was like seeing the early fruit on
　　the fig tree.
But when they came to Baal Peor,
　they consecrated themselves to that
　　shameful idol
　and became as vile as the thing
　　they loved.
11Ephraim's glory will fly away like a
　　bird—
　no birth, no pregnancy, no
　　conception.
12Even if they rear children,
　I will bereave them of every one.
Woe to them
　when I turn away from them!
13I have seen Ephraim, like Tyre,
　planted in a pleasant place.
But Ephraim will bring out
　their children to the slayer."

14Give them, O LORD—
　what will you give them?
Give them wombs that miscarry
　and breasts that are dry.

15"Because of all their wickedness in
　　Gilgal,
　I hated them there.
Because of their sinful deeds,
　I will drive them out of my house.
I will no longer love them;
　all their leaders are rebellious.

---

a3 That is, ceremonially unclean　　b8 Or The prophet is the watchman over Ephraim, / the people of my
God

[16]Ephraim is blighted,
   their root is withered,
   they yield no fruit.
Even if they bear children,
   I will slay their cherished offspring."

[17]My God will reject them
   because they have not obeyed him;
   they will be wanderers among the
      nations.

10 Israel was a spreading vine;
   he brought forth fruit for himself.
As his fruit increased,
   he built more altars;
as his land prospered,
   he adorned his sacred stones.
[2]Their heart is deceitful,
   and now they must bear their guilt.
The LORD will demolish their altars
   and destroy their sacred stones.

[3]Then they will say, "We have no king
   because we did not revere the LORD.
But even if we had a king,
   what could he do for us?"
[4]They make many promises,
   take false oaths
   and make agreements;
therefore lawsuits spring up
   like poisonous weeds in a plowed
      field.
[5]The people who live in Samaria fear
   for the calf-idol of Beth Aven.[a]
Its people will mourn over it,
   and so will its idolatrous priests,
those who had rejoiced over its
      splendor,
   because it is taken from them into
      exile.
[6]It will be carried to Assyria
   as tribute for the great king.
Ephraim will be disgraced;
   Israel will be ashamed of its
      wooden idols.[b]
[7]Samaria and its king will float away
   like a twig on the surface of the
      waters.
[8]The high places of wickedness[c] will
      be destroyed—
   it is the sin of Israel.
Thorns and thistles will grow up
   and cover their altars.
Then they will say to the mountains,
      "Cover us!"
   and to the hills, "Fall on us!"

[9]"Since the days of Gibeah, you have
   sinned, O Israel,
   and there you have remained.[d]
Did not war overtake
   the evildoers in Gibeah?
[10]When I please, I will punish them;
   nations will be gathered against
      them
   to put them in bonds for their
      double sin.
[11]Ephraim is a trained heifer
   that loves to thresh;
so I will put a yoke
   on her fair neck.
I will drive Ephraim,
   Judah must plow,
   and Jacob must break up the
      ground.
[12]Sow for yourselves righteousness,
   reap the fruit of unfailing love,
and break up your unplowed ground;
   for it is time to seek the LORD,
until he comes
   and showers righteousness on you.
[13]But you have planted wickedness,
   you have reaped evil,
   you have eaten the fruit of
      deception.
Because you have depended on your
      own strength
   and on your many warriors,
[14]the roar of battle will rise against your
      people,
   so that all your fortresses will be
      devastated—
as Shalman devastated Beth Arbel on
      the day of battle,
   when mothers were dashed to the
      ground with their children.
[15]Thus will it happen to you, O Bethel,
   because your wickedness is great.
When that day dawns,
   the king of Israel will be completely
      destroyed.

God's Love for Israel

11 "When Israel was a child, I loved
      him,
   and out of Egypt I called my son.
[2]But the more I[e] called Israel,
   the further they went from me.[f]
They sacrificed to the Baals
   and they burned incense to images.
[3]It was I who taught Ephraim to walk,
   taking them by the arms;
but they did not realize

---

[a]5 Beth Aven means *house of wickedness* (a name for Bethel, which means *house of God*).   [b]6 Or *its counsel*   [c]8 Hebrew *aven*, a reference to Beth Aven (a derogatory name for Bethel)   [d]9 Or *there a stand was taken*   [e]2 Some Septuagint manuscripts; Hebrew *they*   [f]2 Septuagint; Hebrew *them*

it was I who healed them.
⁴I led them with cords of human
    kindness,
  with ties of love;
  I lifted the yoke from their neck
    and bent down to feed them.

⁵"Will they not return to Egypt
  and will not Assyria rule over them
    because they refuse to repent?
⁶Swords will flash in their cities,
  will destroy the bars of their gates
    and put an end to their plans.
⁷My people are determined to turn
    from me.
  Even if they call to the Most High,
  he will by no means exalt them.

⁸"How can I give you up, Ephraim?
  How can I hand you over, Israel?
  How can I treat you like Admah?
  How can I make you like Zeboiim?
  My heart is changed within me;
    all my compassion is aroused.
⁹I will not carry out my fierce anger,
  nor will I turn and devastate
    Ephraim.
  For I am God, and not man—
    the Holy One among you.
  I will not come in wrath.ᵃ
¹⁰They will follow the LORD;
  he will roar like a lion.
  When he roars,
    his children will come trembling
    from the west.
¹¹They will come trembling
  like birds from Egypt,
    like doves from Assyria.
  I will settle them in their homes,"
    declares the LORD.

Israel's Sin

¹²Ephraim has surrounded me with lies,
  the house of Israel with deceit.
  And Judah is unruly against God,
    even against the faithful Holy One.

12 ¹Ephraim feeds on the wind;
  he pursues the east wind all day
  and multiplies lies and violence.
  He makes a treaty with Assyria
    and sends olive oil to Egypt.
²The LORD has a charge to bring
    against Judah;
  he will punish Jacobᵇ according to
    his ways
  and repay him according to his
    deeds.

³In the womb he grasped his brother's
    heel;
  as a man he struggled with God.
⁴He struggled with the angel and
    overcame him;
  he wept and begged for his favor.
  He found him at Bethel
    and talked with him there—
⁵the LORD God Almighty,
  the LORD is his name of renown!
⁶But you must return to your God;
  maintain love and justice,
  and wait for your God always.

⁷The merchant uses dishonest scales;
  he loves to defraud.
⁸Ephraim boasts,
  "I am very rich; I have become
    wealthy.
  With all my wealth they will not find
    in me
  any iniquity or sin."

⁹"I am the LORD your God,
  ⌊who brought you⌋ out ofᶜ Egypt;
  I will make you live in tents again,
    as in the days of your appointed
    feasts.
¹⁰I spoke to the prophets,
  gave them many visions
  and told parables through them."

¹¹Is Gilead wicked?
  Its people are worthless!
  Do they sacrifice bulls in Gilgal?
    Their altars will be like piles of
    stones
  on a plowed field.
¹²Jacob fled to the country of Aramᵈ;
  Israel served to get a wife,
    and to pay for her he tended sheep.
¹³The LORD used a prophet to bring
    Israel up from Egypt,
  by a prophet he cared for him.
¹⁴But Ephraim has bitterly provoked
    him to anger;
  his Lord will leave upon him the
    guilt of his bloodshed
  and will repay him for his
    contempt.

The LORD's Anger Against Israel

13 When Ephraim spoke, men
    trembled;
  he was exalted in Israel.
  But he became guilty of Baal
    worship and died.
²Now they sin more and more;

ᵃ9 Or come against any city
God / ever since you were in
ᵇ2 Jacob means he grasps the heel (figuratively, he deceives).
ᵈ12 That is, Northwest Mesopotamia
ᶜ9 Or

they make idols for themselves from
their silver,
cleverly fashioned images,
all of them the work of craftsmen.
It is said of these people,
"They offer human sacrifice
and kiss[a] the calf-idols."
[3]Therefore they will be like the
morning mist,
like the early dew that disappears,
like chaff swirling from a threshing
floor,

like smoke escaping through a
window.
[4]"But I am the LORD your God,
ˌwho brought youˌ out of[b] Egypt.
You shall acknowledge no God but
me,
no Savior except me.
[5]I cared for you in the desert,
in the land of burning heat.
[6]When I fed them, they were
satisfied;

[a]2 Or "Men who sacrifice / kiss   [b]4 Or God / ever since you were in

---

WEDNESDAY

VERSE FOR THE DAY:
Hosea 11:4

AUTHOR:
W. Phillip Keller

PASSAGE FOR THE DAY:
Hosea 11:1–11

The Hound of Heaven

ALWAYS, ever, anew, every day his [God's] unlimited kindness and unbounded mercy enfold me. His grace, his generosity, his goodwill, his great good cheer come to me from his own person. Despite my blemishes, my unusual behavior, his intentions toward me are always for my benefit.

Steadily, but surely, I have come to realize that every interaction, every command, every principle he has established is for my ultimate good. His are not repressive rules or regulations to tie me down into drudgery. They are, instead, the parameters ordained to deliver me from self-destruction and launch me into a life of wholesome harmony with him.

In all this my Father has been so exceedingly patient and persevering. Even when I was still a wayward young man, far removed from God, he pursued me in loving concern down the tangled paths of my escapades. He did not give up on me; he did not write me off. He did not despise, reject or abandon me. Instead, he followed me faithfully out into the deep darkness and despair of my lonely wanderings.

Only Christ, my Friend, could possibly care enough to draw me to himself, to bring me back gently to my Father, to patiently lay down his life for me that I might come to know him.

God's ways are not our ways. We are so selfish. He is so self-giving, so self-sharing! We are so short-tempered. He is so patient, so persevering! We are so hard and critical. He is so merciful and kind!

No wonder I have come to love him so deeply!

Additional Scripture Readings:
Psalm 145:8–16; John 12:30–36

*Go to page 945 for your next
devotional reading.*

when they were satisfied, they
    became proud;
then they forgot me.
⁷So I will come upon them like a lion,
    like a leopard I will lurk by the
      path.
⁸Like a bear robbed of her cubs,
    I will attack them and rip them
      open.
Like a lion I will devour them;
    a wild animal will tear them apart.

⁹"You are destroyed, O Israel,
    because you are against me, against
      your helper.
¹⁰Where is your king, that he may save
      you?
    Where are your rulers in all your
      towns,
of whom you said,
    'Give me a king and princes'?
¹¹So in my anger I gave you a king,
    and in my wrath I took him away.
¹²The guilt of Ephraim is stored up,
    his sins are kept on record.
¹³Pains as of a woman in childbirth
    come to him,
but he is a child without wisdom;
when the time arrives,
    he does not come to the opening of
      the womb.

¹⁴"I will ransom them from the power
    of the grave*ᵃ*;
I will redeem them from death.
Where, O death, are your plagues?
Where, O grave,ᵃ is your
    destruction?

"I will have no compassion,
15   even though he thrives among his
      brothers.
An east wind from the LORD will
    come,
    blowing in from the desert;
his spring will fail
    and his well dry up.
His storehouse will be plundered
    of all its treasures.
¹⁶The people of Samaria must bear their
    guilt,
    because they have rebelled against
      their God.

They will fall by the sword;
    their little ones will be dashed to
      the ground,
    their pregnant women ripped open."

Repentance to Bring Blessing

14 Return, O Israel, to the LORD your
      God.
    Your sins have been your downfall!
²Take words with you
    and return to the LORD.
Say to him:
    "Forgive all our sins
and receive us graciously,
    that we may offer the fruit of our
      lips.ᵇ
³Assyria cannot save us;
    we will not mount war-horses.
We will never again say 'Our gods'
    to what our own hands have made,
    for in you the fatherless find
      compassion."

⁴"I will heal their waywardness
    and love them freely,
    for my anger has turned away from
      them.
⁵I will be like the dew to Israel;
    he will blossom like a lily.
Like a cedar of Lebanon
    he will send down his roots;
⁶   his young shoots will grow.
His splendor will be like an olive tree,
    his fragrance like a cedar of
      Lebanon.
⁷Men will dwell again in his shade.
He will flourish like the grain.
He will blossom like a vine,
    and his fame will be like the wine
      from Lebanon.
⁸O Ephraim, what more have Iᶜ to do
    with idols?
    I will answer him and care for him.
I am like a green pine tree;
    your fruitfulness comes from me."

⁹Who is wise? He will realize these
    things.
    Who is discerning? He will
      understand them.
The ways of the LORD are right;
    the righteous walk in them,
    but the rebellious stumble in them.

ᵃ14 Hebrew *Sheol*   ᵇ2 Or *offer our lips as sacrifices of bulls*   ᶜ8 Or *What more has Ephraim*

JOEL uses a famine (due to a devastating plague of locusts) to picture the coming day of the Lord. He calls on God's people to repent and turn to the Lord, promising that everyone who does so will be saved and will receive God's Spirit. As you read this book, listen to God's call to repent of your sins, so that you may be saved and be filled with the Holy Spirit.

JOEL

1 The word of the LORD that came to Joel son of Pethuel.

An Invasion of Locusts

²Hear this, you elders;
 listen, all who live in the land.
Has anything like this ever happened
 in your days
 or in the days of your forefathers?
³Tell it to your children,
 and let your children tell it to their
 children,
 and their children to the next
 generation.
⁴What the locust swarm has left
 the great locusts have eaten;
what the great locusts have left
 the young locusts have eaten;
 what the young locusts have left
 other locusts[a] have eaten.

⁵Wake up, you drunkards, and weep!
 Wail, all you drinkers of wine;
wail because of the new wine,
 for it has been snatched from your
 lips.
⁶A nation has invaded my land,
 powerful and without number;
 it has the teeth of a lion,
 the fangs of a lioness.
⁷It has laid waste my vines
 and ruined my fig trees.
 It has stripped off their bark
 and thrown it away,
 leaving their branches white.

⁸Mourn like a virgin[b] in sackcloth

---

a4 The precise meaning of the four Hebrew words used here for locusts is uncertain.   *b8* Or *young woman*

grieving for the husband*a* of her
youth.

[9]Grain offerings and drink offerings
are cut off from the house of the
LORD.

The priests are in mourning,
those who minister before the LORD.

[10]The fields are ruined,
the ground is dried up*b*;
the grain is destroyed,
the new wine is dried up,
the oil fails.

[11]Despair, you farmers,
wail, you vine growers;
grieve for the wheat and the barley,
because the harvest of the field is
destroyed.

[12]The vine is dried up
and the fig tree is withered;
the pomegranate, the palm and the
apple tree—
all the trees of the field—are dried
up.

Surely the joy of mankind
is withered away.

A Call to Repentance

[13]Put on sackcloth, O priests, and
mourn;
wail, you who minister before the
altar.
Come, spend the night in sackcloth,
you who minister before my God;
for the grain offerings and drink
offerings
are withheld from the house of your
God.

[14]Declare a holy fast;
call a sacred assembly.
Summon the elders
and all who live in the land
to the house of the LORD your God,
and cry out to the LORD.

[15]Alas for that day!
For the day of the LORD is near;
it will come like destruction from
the Almighty.*c*

[16]Has not the food been cut off
before our very eyes—
joy and gladness
from the house of our God?

[17]The seeds are shriveled
beneath the clods.*d*
The storehouses are in ruins,
the granaries have been broken
down,

for the grain has dried up.

[18]How the cattle moan!
The herds mill about
because they have no pasture;
even the flocks of sheep are
suffering.

[19]To you, O LORD, I call,
for fire has devoured the open
pastures
and flames have burned up all the
trees of the field.

[20]Even the wild animals pant for you;
the streams of water have dried up
and fire has devoured the open
pastures.

An Army of Locusts

2 Blow the trumpet in Zion;
sound the alarm on my holy hill.
Let all who live in the land tremble,
for the day of the LORD is coming.
It is close at hand—

[2] a day of darkness and gloom,
a day of clouds and blackness.
Like dawn spreading across the
mountains
a large and mighty army comes,
such as never was of old
nor ever will be in ages to come.

[3]Before them fire devours,
behind them a flame blazes.
Before them the land is like the
garden of Eden,
behind them, a desert waste—
nothing escapes them.

[4]They have the appearance of horses;
they gallop along like cavalry.

[5]With a noise like that of chariots
they leap over the mountaintops,
like a crackling fire consuming
stubble,
like a mighty army drawn up for
battle.

[6]At the sight of them, nations are in
anguish;
every face turns pale.

[7]They charge like warriors;
they scale walls like soldiers.
They all march in line,
not swerving from their course.

[8]They do not jostle each other;
each marches straight ahead.
They plunge through defenses
without breaking ranks.

[9]They rush upon the city;

*a*8 Or *betrothed*   *b*10 Or *ground mourns*   *c*15 Hebrew *Shaddai*   *d*17 The meaning of the Hebrew
for this word is uncertain.

they run along the wall.
They climb into the houses;
  like thieves they enter through the
    windows.

[10]Before them the earth shakes,
  the sky trembles,
the sun and moon are darkened,
  and the stars no longer shine.
[11]The LORD thunders
  at the head of his army;
his forces are beyond number,
  and mighty are those who obey his
    command.
The day of the LORD is great;
  it is dreadful.
  Who can endure it?

Rend Your Heart

[12]"Even now," declares the LORD,
  "return to me with all your heart,
  with fasting and weeping and
    mourning."

[13]Rend your heart
  and not your garments.
Return to the LORD your God,
  for he is gracious and
    compassionate,
  slow to anger and abounding in love,
  and he relents from sending
    calamity.
[14]Who knows? He may turn and have
    pity
  and leave behind a blessing—
grain offerings and drink offerings
  for the LORD your God.

[15]Blow the trumpet in Zion,
  declare a holy fast,
  call a sacred assembly.
[16]Gather the people,
  consecrate the assembly;
bring together the elders,
  gather the children,
  those nursing at the breast.
Let the bridegroom leave his room
  and the bride her chamber.
[17]Let the priests, who minister before
    the LORD,
  weep between the temple porch and
    the altar.
Let them say, "Spare your people,
  O LORD.
Do not make your inheritance an
    object of scorn,
  a byword among the nations.

Why should they say among the
    peoples,
  'Where is their God?' "

The LORD's Answer

[18]Then the LORD will be jealous for his
    land
  and take pity on his people.

[19]The LORD will reply[a] to them:

"I am sending you grain, new wine
    and oil,
  enough to satisfy you fully;
never again will I make you
  an object of scorn to the nations.

[20]"I will drive the northern army far
    from you,
  pushing it into a parched and
    barren land,
with its front columns going into the
    eastern sea[b]
and those in the rear into the
    western sea.[c]
And its stench will go up;
  its smell will rise."

Surely he has done great things.[d]
[21] Be not afraid, O land;
  be glad and rejoice.
Surely the LORD has done great things.
[22] Be not afraid, O wild animals,
  for the open pastures are becoming
    green.
The trees are bearing their fruit;
  the fig tree and the vine yield their
    riches.
[23]Be glad, O people of Zion,
  rejoice in the LORD your God,
for he has given you
  the autumn rains in righteousness.[e]
He sends you abundant showers,
  both autumn and spring rains, as
    before.
[24]The threshing floors will be filled with
    grain;
  the vats will overflow with new
    wine and oil.

[25]"I will repay you for the years the
    locusts have eaten—
  the great locust and the young
    locust,
  the other locusts and the locust
    swarm[f]—
my great army that I sent among you.

---

[a]18,19 Or LORD was jealous . . . / and took pity . . . / [19]The LORD replied   [b]20 That is, the Dead Sea
[c]20 That is, the Mediterranean   [d]20 Or rise. / Surely it has done great things."   [e]23 Or / the teacher
for righteousness: [f]25 The precise meaning of the four Hebrew words used here for locusts is
uncertain.

26You will have plenty to eat, until you
  are full,
  and you will praise the name of the
      LORD your God,
  who has worked wonders for you;
never again will my people be
      shamed.
27Then you will know that I am in
      Israel,
  that I am the LORD your God,
  and that there is no other;
never again will my people be
      shamed.

The Day of the LORD

28"And afterward,
  I will pour out my Spirit on all
      people.
Your sons and daughters will
      prophesy,
  your old men will dream dreams,
  your young men will see visions.
29Even on my servants, both men and
      women,
  I will pour out my Spirit in those
      days.
30I will show wonders in the heavens
  and on the earth,
  blood and fire and billows of
      smoke.
31The sun will be turned to darkness
  and the moon to blood
  before the coming of the great and
      dreadful day of the LORD.
32And everyone who calls
  on the name of the LORD will be
      saved;
  for on Mount Zion and in Jerusalem
      there will be deliverance,
  as the LORD has said,
among the survivors
  whom the LORD calls.

The Nations Judged

3 "In those days and at that time,
      when I restore the fortunes of Judah
      and Jerusalem,
2I will gather all nations
  and bring them down to the Valley
      of Jehoshaphat.[a]
There I will enter into judgment
      against them
  concerning my inheritance, my
      people Israel,
  for they scattered my people among
      the nations
  and divided up my land.
3They cast lots for my people

and traded boys for prostitutes;
they sold girls for wine
  that they might drink.

4"Now what have you against me, O
Tyre and Sidon and all you regions of Philistia? Are you repaying me for something
I have done? If you are paying me back, I
will swiftly and speedily return on your
own heads what you have done. 5For you
took my silver and my gold and carried off
my finest treasures to your temples. 6You
sold the people of Judah and Jerusalem to
the Greeks, that you might send them far
from their homeland.

7"See, I am going to rouse them out of
the places to which you sold them, and I
will return on your own heads what you
have done. 8I will sell your sons and
daughters to the people of Judah, and
they will sell them to the Sabeans, a nation far away." The LORD has spoken.

9Proclaim this among the nations:
  Prepare for war!
Rouse the warriors!
  Let all the fighting men draw near
      and attack.
10Beat your plowshares into swords
  and your pruning hooks into spears.
Let the weakling say,
  "I am strong!"
11Come quickly, all you nations from
      every side,
  and assemble there.

Bring down your warriors, O LORD!

12"Let the nations be roused;
  let them advance into the Valley of
      Jehoshaphat,
  for there I will sit
  to judge all the nations on every
      side.
13Swing the sickle,
  for the harvest is ripe.
Come, trample the grapes,
  for the winepress is full
  and the vats overflow—
so great is their wickedness!"

14Multitudes, multitudes
  in the valley of decision!
For the day of the LORD is near
  in the valley of decision.
15The sun and moon will be darkened,
  and the stars no longer shine.
16The LORD will roar from Zion
  and thunder from Jerusalem;
  the earth and the sky will tremble.

---

a2 *Jehoshaphat* means *the LORD judges*; also in verse 12.

THURSDAY

VERSE FOR THE DAY: AUTHOR: PASSAGE FOR THE DAY:
Joel 2:32   Gerald Oosterveen   Joel 2:28–32

The One Thing That Matters

GERALD *Oosterveen's son Gerard died at the age of 9, nearly 39 months after he was diagnosed with cancer. The night before he died the young boy and his father talked about death and about faith.*

That night it was my turn to stay with him. Sometime during that night, as I read my Bible, the boy asked me what I was reading. I told him and he asked me to read it to him. It was from Joel 2 where the prophet talks about the coming day of the Lord: "And afterward, I will pour out my Spirit on all people. Your sons and daughters will prophesy, your old men will dream dreams, your young men will see visions. Even on my servants, both men and women, I will pour out my Spirit in those days. I will show wonders in the heavens and on the earth, blood and fire and billows of smoke. The sun will be turned to darkness and the moon to blood before the great and dreadful day of the Lord. And everyone who calls on the name of the Lord will be saved."

The boy was pensive for a while. Then he said, "I guess I won't see that, will I, Dad?"

I pondered his question, then gave my explanation. "I don't quite know what to say about this. In a way the Holy Spirit is already given to people today. He surely is at work in you, I can tell. Otherwise you would not love Jesus as much or look forward to being with him in heaven. Only the Holy Spirit can give you that longing. And you will see visions. It will only be a little while and you will see God himself, sitting on his throne in heaven. That is the greatest vision of them all. And you'll see it before any of us in this family. But as for the specific day that the Bible calls, 'the day of the Lord,' no, you won't see that, unless people in heaven are in some way involved in it too. I may not see it either, for that matter. No one knows just when that day comes. It doesn't really matter when it comes, anyway. There is only one thing that matters. That is whether you love Jesus now and believe that he saved you by dying for you on the cross."

"I believe that, Dad."

Additional Scripture Readings:
John 3:10–21; Romans 10:5–13

Go to page 952 for your next devotional reading.

But the Lord will be a refuge for his
people,
a stronghold for the people of Israel.

Blessings for God's People

17"Then you will know that I, the Lord
your God,
dwell in Zion, my holy hill.
Jerusalem will be holy;
never again will foreigners invade
her.

18"In that day the mountains will drip
new wine,
and the hills will flow with milk;
all the ravines of Judah will run
with water.
A fountain will flow out of the Lord's
house
and will water the valley of
acacias.*a*

19But Egypt will be desolate,
Edom a desert waste,
because of violence done to the
people of Judah,
in whose land they shed innocent
blood.
20Judah will be inhabited forever
and Jerusalem through all
generations.
21Their bloodguilt, which I have not
pardoned,
I will pardon."

The Lord dwells in Zion!

AMOS prophesies during the time of Jeroboam II (2 Kings 14:23–29), a time of prosperity for some but extreme poverty for many others. He reprimands those who oppress the poor and make them suffer even more. As you read this book, think about how angry God becomes when you show more interest in your wealth than in obeying him. Remember, though, that God will forgive you, if you confess your sins and seek to do his will.

AMOS

1 The words of Amos, one of the shepherds of Tekoa — what he saw concerning Israel two years before the earthquake, when Uzziah was king of Judah and Jeroboam son of Jehoash[a] was king of Israel.

²He said:

"The LORD roars from Zion
and thunders from Jerusalem;
the pastures of the shepherds dry
up,[b]
and the top of Carmel withers."

Judgment on Israel's Neighbors

³This is what the LORD says:

"For three sins of Damascus,
even for four, I will not turn back
⌐my wrath⌐.
Because she threshed Gilead
with sledges having iron teeth,
⁴I will send fire upon the house of
Hazael
that will consume the fortresses of
Ben-Hadad.
⁵I will break down the gate of Damascus;

---

a1 Hebrew *Joash,* a variant of *Jehoash*   *b2* Or *shepherds mourn*

I will destroy the king who is in[a]
the Valley of Aven[b]
and the one who holds the scepter in
Beth Eden.
The people of Aram will go into
exile to Kir,"
                    says the LORD.

6This is what the LORD says:

"For three sins of Gaza,
even for four, I will not turn back
⌐my wrath⌐.
Because she took captive whole
communities
and sold them to Edom,
7I will send fire upon the walls of Gaza
that will consume her fortresses.
8I will destroy the king[c] of Ashdod
and the one who holds the scepter
in Ashkelon.
I will turn my hand against Ekron,
till the last of the Philistines is
dead,"
            says the Sovereign LORD.

9This is what the LORD says:

"For three sins of Tyre,
even for four, I will not turn back
⌐my wrath⌐.
Because she sold whole communities
of captives to Edom,
disregarding a treaty of
brotherhood,
10I will send fire upon the walls of Tyre
that will consume her fortresses."

11This is what the LORD says:

"For three sins of Edom,
even for four, I will not turn back
⌐my wrath⌐.
Because he pursued his brother with a
sword,
stifling all compassion,[d]
because his anger raged continually
and his fury flamed unchecked,
12I will send fire upon Teman
that will consume the fortresses of
Bozrah."

13This is what the LORD says:

"For three sins of Ammon,
even for four, I will not turn back
⌐my wrath⌐.
Because he ripped open the pregnant
women of Gilead
in order to extend his borders,

14I will set fire to the walls of Rabbah
that will consume her fortresses
amid war cries on the day of battle,
amid violent winds on a stormy
day.
15Her king[e] will go into exile,
he and his officials together,"
                    says the LORD.

2 This is what the LORD says:

"For three sins of Moab,
even for four, I will not turn back
⌐my wrath⌐.
Because he burned, as if to lime,
the bones of Edom's king,
2I will send fire upon Moab
that will consume the fortresses of
Kerioth.[f]
Moab will go down in great tumult
amid war cries and the blast of the
trumpet.
3I will destroy her ruler
and kill all her officials with him,"
                    says the LORD.

4This is what the LORD says:

"For three sins of Judah,
even for four, I will not turn back
⌐my wrath⌐.
Because they have rejected the law of
the LORD
and have not kept his decrees,
because they have been led astray by
false gods,[g]
the gods[h] their ancestors followed,
5I will send fire upon Judah
that will consume the fortresses of
Jerusalem."

Judgment on Israel

6This is what the LORD says:

"For three sins of Israel,
even for four, I will not turn back
⌐my wrath⌐.
They sell the righteous for silver,
and the needy for a pair of sandals.
7They trample on the heads of the poor
as upon the dust of the ground
and deny justice to the oppressed.
Father and son use the same girl
and so profane my holy name.
8They lie down beside every altar
on garments taken in pledge.
In the house of their god
they drink wine taken as fines.

a5 Or the inhabitants of   b5 Aven means wickedness.   c8 Or inhabitants   d11 Or sword / and
destroyed his allies   e15 Or / Molech; Hebrew malcam   f2 Or of her cities   g4 Or by lies
h4 Or lies

⁹"I destroyed the Amorite before them,
  though he was tall as the cedars
  and strong as the oaks.
I destroyed his fruit above
  and his roots below.

¹⁰"I brought you up out of Egypt,
  and I led you forty years in the
    desert
  to give you the land of the
    Amorites.
¹¹I also raised up prophets from among
    your sons
  and Nazirites from among your
    young men.
Is this not true, people of Israel?"
             declares the Lord.
¹²"But you made the Nazirites drink
    wine
  and commanded the prophets not to
    prophesy.

¹³"Now then, I will crush you
  as a cart crushes when loaded with
    grain.
¹⁴The swift will not escape,
  the strong will not muster their
    strength,
  and the warrior will not save his
    life.
¹⁵The archer will not stand his ground,
  the fleet-footed soldier will not get
    away,
  and the horseman will not save his
    life.
¹⁶Even the bravest warriors
  will flee naked on that day,"
             declares the Lord.

Witnesses Summoned Against Israel

3 Hear this word the Lord has spoken
against you, O people of Israel—
against the whole family I brought up out
of Egypt:

²"You only have I chosen
  of all the families of the earth;
therefore I will punish you
  for all your sins."

³Do two walk together
  unless they have agreed to do so?
⁴Does a lion roar in the thicket
  when he has no prey?
Does he growl in his den
  when he has caught nothing?
⁵Does a bird fall into a trap on the
    ground
  where no snare has been set?
Does a trap spring up from the earth

when there is nothing to catch?
⁶When a trumpet sounds in a city,
  do not the people tremble?
When disaster comes to a city,
  has not the Lord caused it?

⁷Surely the Sovereign Lord does
    nothing
  without revealing his plan
  to his servants the prophets.

⁸The lion has roared—
  who will not fear?
The Sovereign Lord has spoken—
  who can but prophesy?

⁹Proclaim to the fortresses of Ashdod
  and to the fortresses of Egypt:
"Assemble yourselves on the
    mountains of Samaria;
  see the great unrest within her
  and the oppression among her
    people."

¹⁰"They do not know how to do right,"
    declares the Lord,
  "who hoard plunder and loot in
    their fortresses."

¹¹Therefore this is what the Sovereign
Lord says:

"An enemy will overrun the land;
  he will pull down your strongholds
  and plunder your fortresses."

¹²This is what the Lord says:

"As a shepherd saves from the lion's
    mouth
  only two leg bones or a piece of an
    ear,
so will the Israelites be saved,
those who sit in Samaria
  on the edge of their beds
  and in Damascus on their
    couches.ᵃ

¹³"Hear this and testify against the
house of Jacob," declares the Lord, the
Lord God Almighty.

¹⁴"On the day I punish Israel for her
    sins,
  I will destroy the altars of Bethel;
the horns of the altar will be cut off
  and fall to the ground.
¹⁵I will tear down the winter house
  along with the summer house;
the houses adorned with ivory will be
    destroyed

ᵃ12 The meaning of the Hebrew for this line is uncertain.

and the mansions will be
demolished,"
declares the Lord.

Israel Has Not Returned to God

4 Hear this word, you cows of Bashan
on Mount Samaria,
you women who oppress the poor
and crush the needy
and say to your husbands, "Bring us
some drinks!"
[2]The Sovereign Lord has sworn by his
holiness:
"The time will surely come
when you will be taken away with
hooks,
the last of you with fishhooks.
[3]You will each go straight out
through breaks in the wall,
and you will be cast out toward
Harmon,[a]"
declares the Lord.

[4]"Go to Bethel and sin;
go to Gilgal and sin yet more.
Bring your sacrifices every morning,
your tithes every three years.[b]
[5]Burn leavened bread as a thank
offering
and brag about your freewill
offerings—
boast about them, you Israelites,
for this is what you love to do,"
declares the Sovereign Lord.

[6]"I gave you empty stomachs[c] in
every city
and lack of bread in every town,
yet you have not returned to me,"
declares the Lord.

[7]"I also withheld rain from you
when the harvest was still three
months away.
I sent rain on one town,
but withheld it from another.
One field had rain;
another had none and dried up.
[8]People staggered from town to town
for water
but did not get enough to drink,
yet you have not returned to me,"
declares the Lord.

[9]"Many times I struck your gardens
and vineyards,
I struck them with blight and
mildew.
Locusts devoured your fig and olive
trees,
yet you have not returned to me,"
declares the Lord.

[10]"I sent plagues among you
as I did to Egypt.
I killed your young men with the
sword,
along with your captured horses.
I filled your nostrils with the stench of
your camps,
yet you have not returned to me,"
declares the Lord.

[11]"I overthrew some of you
as I[d] overthrew Sodom and
Gomorrah.
You were like a burning stick
snatched from the fire,
yet you have not returned to me,"
declares the Lord.

[12]"Therefore this is what I will do to
you, Israel,
and because I will do this to you,
prepare to meet your God, O Israel."

[13]He who forms the mountains,
creates the wind,
and reveals his thoughts to man,
he who turns dawn to darkness,
and treads the high places of the
earth—
the Lord God Almighty is his name.

A Lament and Call to Repentance

5 Hear this word, O house of Israel, this
lament I take up concerning you:

[2]"Fallen is Virgin Israel,
never to rise again,
deserted in her own land,
with no one to lift her up."

[3]This is what the Sovereign Lord says:

"The city that marches out a thousand
strong for Israel
will have only a hundred left;
the town that marches out a hundred
strong
will have only ten left."

[4]This is what the Lord says to the house
of Israel:

"Seek me and live;
[5]   do not seek Bethel,
do not go to Gilgal,
do not journey to Beersheba.

---

[a]3 Masoretic Text; with a different word division of the Hebrew (see Septuagint) *out, O mountain of oppression*   [b]4 Or *tithes on the third day*   [c]6 Hebrew *you cleanness of teeth*   [d]11 Hebrew *God*

For Gilgal will surely go into exile,
    and Bethel will be reduced to
        nothing.*a*"
6Seek the LORD and live,
    or he will sweep through the house
        of Joseph like a fire;
it will devour,
    and Bethel will have no one to
        quench it.

7You who turn justice into bitterness
    and cast righteousness to the
        ground
8(he who made the Pleiades and Orion,
    who turns blackness into dawn
    and darkens day into night,
who calls for the waters of the sea
    and pours them out over the face of
        the land —
    the LORD is his name —
9he flashes destruction on the
        stronghold
    and brings the fortified city to ruin),
10you hate the one who reproves in
        court
    and despise him who tells the truth.

11You trample on the poor
    and force him to give you grain.
Therefore, though you have built
        stone mansions,
    you will not live in them;
though you have planted lush
        vineyards,
    you will not drink their wine.
12For I know how many are your
        offenses
    and how great your sins.

You oppress the righteous and take
        bribes
    and you deprive the poor of justice
        in the courts.
13Therefore the prudent man keeps
        quiet in such times,
    for the times are evil.

14Seek good, not evil,
    that you may live.
Then the LORD God Almighty will be
        with you,
    just as you say he is.
15Hate evil, love good;
    maintain justice in the courts.
Perhaps the LORD God Almighty will
        have mercy
    on the remnant of Joseph.

16Therefore this is what the Lord, the
    LORD God Almighty, says:

"There will be wailing in all the
        streets
    and cries of anguish in every public
        square.
The farmers will be summoned to
        weep
    and the mourners to wail.
17There will be wailing in all the
        vineyards,
    for I will pass through your midst,"
            says the LORD.

The Day of the LORD

18Woe to you who long
    for the day of the LORD!
Why do you long for the day of the
        LORD?
That day will be darkness, not light.
19It will be as though a man fled from a
        lion
    only to meet a bear,
as though he entered his house
    and rested his hand on the wall
    only to have a snake bite him.
20Will not the day of the LORD be
        darkness, not light —
    pitch-dark, without a ray of
        brightness?

21"I hate, I despise your religious feasts;
    I cannot stand your assemblies.
22Even though you bring me burnt
        offerings and grain offerings,
    I will not accept them.
Though you bring choice fellowship
        offerings,*b*
    I will have no regard for them.
23Away with the noise of your songs!
    I will not listen to the music of your
        harps.
24But let justice roll on like a river,
    righteousness like a never-failing
        stream!

25"Did you bring me sacrifices and
        offerings
    forty years in the desert, O house of
        Israel?
26You have lifted up the shrine of your
        king,
    the pedestal of your idols,
    the star of your god*c* —
which you made for yourselves.

---

*a*5 Or *grief*; or *wickedness*; Hebrew *aven*, a reference to Beth Aven (a derogatory name for Bethel)
*b*22 Traditionally *peace offerings*   *c*26 Or *lifted up Sakkuth your king / and Kaiwan your idols, / your star-gods*; Septuagint *lifted up the shrine of Molech / and the star of your god Rephan, / their idols*

27Therefore I will send you into exile
    beyond Damascus,"
says the LORD, whose name is God
    Almighty.

Woe to the Complacent

6 Woe to you who are complacent in
    Zion,

and to you who feel secure on
    Mount Samaria,
you notable men of the foremost
    nation,
to whom the people of Israel
    come!
2Go to Calneh and look at it;
    go from there to great Hamath,

FRIDAY

VERSE FOR THE DAY:
Amos 5:15

AUTHOR:
Charles Colson

PASSAGE FOR THE DAY:
Amos 5:11–17

And Justice for All

WE ARE commanded not only to seek first the kingdom of God—don't stop there—but his righteousness as well.

Righteousness or holy living is often seen by Christians as maintaining chaste sexual standards, tithing, faithful church attendance, being friendly to those around us. Well, those are indeed Christian responsibilities, but only the beginning of holy living.

And many believers categorize their refraining from alcohol, tobacco, cards and dancing as holy living. Though God may call you to that type of witness, it is only skimming the surface at best. That is piety. And we must never, never confuse piety with righteousness.

Righteousness was defined by Yahweh at Mount Sinai and interpreted by the fiery words of his prophets from Isaiah to Amos to Habakkuk and, ultimately, by the life of his Son, Jesus. God's definition of righteousness is based on justice for all people, especially the unfortunate: you shall not sell the poor for a pair of shoes, nor take away the coat of a man who borrows from you; you shall pay your employees a just wage; you shall care for widows and orphans; you shall hate evil and do good. "Remodel your courts into true halls of justice," thundered the prophet Amos (see Amos 5:15). "Let justice roll on like a river, righteousness like a never-failing stream!" (5:24). That's God's standard of righteousness and holy living.

After 10 years in a Soviet gulag, Alexander Solzhenitsyn wrote "Bless you, prison, for having been in my life." For it was there he learned that "the meaning of earthly existence lies, not as we have grown used to thinking, in prospering, but in the development of the soul." I too can say, "Bless you, prison," for it was there that I learned to see justice in the way that Amos and Micah and Jeremiah and Isaiah saw it.

Additional Scripture Readings:
Isaiah 58:6–14; Micah 6:6–8

*Go to page 955 for your next
devotional reading.*

and then go down to Gath in
   Philistia.
Are they better off than your two
   kingdoms?
Is their land larger than yours?
³You put off the evil day
   and bring near a reign of terror.
⁴You lie on beds inlaid with ivory
   and lounge on your couches.
 You dine on choice lambs
   and fattened calves.
⁵You strum away on your harps like
   David
   and improvise on musical
      instruments.
⁶You drink wine by the bowlful
   and use the finest lotions,
   but you do not grieve over the ruin
      of Joseph.
⁷Therefore you will be among the first
   to go into exile;
   your feasting and lounging will end.

The LORD Abhors the Pride of Israel

⁸The Sovereign LORD has sworn by himself—the LORD God Almighty declares:

 "I abhor the pride of Jacob
   and detest his fortresses;
 I will deliver up the city
   and everything in it."

⁹If ten men are left in one house, they
too will die. ¹⁰And if a relative who is to
burn the bodies comes to carry them out
of the house and asks anyone still hiding
there, "Is anyone with you?" and he says,
"No," then he will say, "Hush! We must
not mention the name of the LORD."

¹¹For the LORD has given the command,
   and he will smash the great house
      into pieces
   and the small house into bits.

¹²Do horses run on the rocky crags?
   Does one plow there with oxen?
But you have turned justice into
   poison
   and the fruit of righteousness into
      bitterness—
¹³you who rejoice in the conquest of Lo
   Debar[a]
   and say, "Did we not take
      Karnaim[b] by our own
      strength?"

¹⁴For the LORD God Almighty declares,

"I will stir up a nation against you,
   O house of Israel,
that will oppress you all the way
   from Lebo[c] Hamath to the valley of
      the Arabah."

Locusts, Fire and a Plumb Line

7 This is what the Sovereign LORD
showed me: He was preparing
swarms of locusts after the king's share
had been harvested and just as the second
crop was coming up. ²When they had
stripped the land clean, I cried out, "Sovereign LORD, forgive! How can Jacob survive? He is so small!"

³So the LORD relented.
"This will not happen," the LORD said.

⁴This is what the Sovereign LORD
showed me: The Sovereign LORD was calling for judgment by fire; it dried up the
great deep and devoured the land. ⁵Then
I cried out, "Sovereign LORD, I beg you,
stop! How can Jacob survive? He is so
small!"

⁶So the LORD relented.
"This will not happen either," the Sovereign LORD said.

⁷This is what he showed me: The Lord
was standing by a wall that had been built
true to plumb, with a plumb line in his
hand. ⁸And the LORD asked me, "What do
you see, Amos?"
"A plumb line," I replied.
Then the Lord said, "Look, I am setting
a plumb line among my people Israel; I
will spare them no longer.

⁹"The high places of Isaac will be
   destroyed
   and the sanctuaries of Israel will be
      ruined;
   with my sword I will rise against
      the house of Jeroboam."

Amos and Amaziah

¹⁰Then Amaziah the priest of Bethel
sent a message to Jeroboam king of Israel:
"Amos is raising a conspiracy against you
in the very heart of Israel. The land cannot
bear all his words. ¹¹For this is what Amos
is saying:

" 'Jeroboam will die by the sword,
   and Israel will surely go into exile,
   away from their native land.' "

¹²Then Amaziah said to Amos, "Get out,
you seer! Go back to the land of Judah.

---

a13 Lo Debar means nothing.   b13 Karnaim means horns; horn here symbolizes strength.   c14 Or
from the entrance to

Earn your bread there and do your prophesying there. ¹³Don't prophesy anymore at Bethel, because this is the king's sanctuary and the temple of the kingdom."

¹⁴Amos answered Amaziah, "I was neither a prophet nor a prophet's son, but I was a shepherd, and I also took care of sycamore-fig trees. ¹⁵But the LORD took me from tending the flock and said to me, 'Go, prophesy to my people Israel.' ¹⁶Now then, hear the word of the LORD. You say,

" 'Do not prophesy against Israel,
    and stop preaching against the
        house of Isaac.'

¹⁷"Therefore this is what the LORD says:

" 'Your wife will become a prostitute
        in the city,
    and your sons and daughters will
        fall by the sword.
Your land will be measured and
        divided up,
    and you yourself will die in a
        pagan[a] country.
And Israel will certainly go into exile,
    away from their native land.' "

A Basket of Ripe Fruit

8 This is what the Sovereign LORD showed me: a basket of ripe fruit. ²"What do you see, Amos?" he asked.

"A basket of ripe fruit," I answered.

Then the LORD said to me, "The time is ripe for my people Israel; I will spare them no longer.

³"In that day," declares the Sovereign LORD, "the songs in the temple will turn to wailing.[b] Many, many bodies—flung everywhere! Silence!"

⁴Hear this, you who trample the needy
    and do away with the poor of the
        land,

⁵saying,

"When will the New Moon be over
        that we may sell grain,
    and the Sabbath be ended
        that we may market wheat?"—
skimping the measure,
    boosting the price
    and cheating with dishonest scales,
⁶buying the poor with silver
    and the needy for a pair of sandals,
    selling even the sweepings with the
        wheat.

⁷The LORD has sworn by the Pride of Jacob: "I will never forget anything they have done.

⁸"Will not the land tremble for this,
    and all who live in it mourn?
The whole land will rise like the Nile;
    it will be stirred up and then sink
    like the river of Egypt.

⁹"In that day," declares the Sovereign LORD,

"I will make the sun go down at noon
    and darken the earth in broad
        daylight.
¹⁰I will turn your religious feasts into
        mourning
    and all your singing into weeping.
I will make all of you wear sackcloth
    and shave your heads.
I will make that time like mourning
        for an only son
    and the end of it like a bitter day.

¹¹"The days are coming," declares the
        Sovereign LORD,
    "when I will send a famine through
        the land—
not a famine of food or a thirst for
        water,
    but a famine of hearing the words
        of the LORD.
¹²Men will stagger from sea to sea
    and wander from north to east,
searching for the word of the LORD,
    but they will not find it.

¹³"In that day

"the lovely young women and strong
        young men
    will faint because of thirst.
¹⁴They who swear by the shame[c] of
        Samaria,
    or say, 'As surely as your god lives,
        O Dan,'
    or, 'As surely as the god[d] of
        Beersheba lives'—
they will fall,
    never to rise again."

Israel to Be Destroyed

9 I saw the Lord standing by the altar, and he said:

"Strike the tops of the pillars
    so that the thresholds shake.
Bring them down on the heads of all
        the people;

---

a17 Hebrew *an unclean*   b3 Or *"the temple singers will wail"*   c14 Or *by Ashima; or by the idol*
d14 Or *power*

WEEKENDING

RESPOND

Give me courage Lord
to take risks
not the usual ones
respected
necessary
relatively safe
but those I could avoid
the go for broke ones.
I need courage
not just because
I may fall on my face
or worse
but others seeing me
a sorry spectacle
if it should happen
will say
he didn't know what he was doing
or he's foolhardy . . .
When it comes right down to it Lord
I choose to be your failure
before anyone else's success.
Keep me from reneging
on my choice.

– Joseph Bayly

REVIVE

Saturday: Joshua 1:5–9
Sunday: 1 Corinthians 1:20–31

Go to page 958 for your next devotional reading.

those who are left I will kill with
the sword.
Not one will get away,
none will escape.
2Though they dig down to the depths
of the grave,^{a}
from there my hand will take them.
Though they climb up to the heavens,
from there I will bring them down.
3Though they hide themselves on the
top of Carmel,
there I will hunt them down and
seize them.
Though they hide from me at the
bottom of the sea,
there I will command the serpent to
bite them.
4Though they are driven into exile by
their enemies,
there I will command the sword to
slay them.
I will fix my eyes upon them
for evil and not for good."

5The Lord, the LORD Almighty,
he who touches the earth and it
melts,
and all who live in it mourn—
the whole land rises like the Nile,
then sinks like the river of Egypt—
6he who builds his lofty palace^b in the
heavens
and sets its foundation^c on the
earth,
who calls for the waters of the sea
and pours them out over the face of
the land—
the LORD is his name.

7"Are not you Israelites
the same to me as the Cushites^d?"
declares the LORD.
"Did I not bring Israel up from Egypt,
the Philistines from Caphtor^e
and the Arameans from Kir?

8"Surely the eyes of the Sovereign LORD
are on the sinful kingdom.
I will destroy it
from the face of the earth—
yet I will not totally destroy

the house of Jacob,"
declares the LORD.
9"For I will give the command,
and I will shake the house of Israel
among all the nations
as grain is shaken in a sieve,
and not a pebble will reach the
ground.
10All the sinners among my people
will die by the sword,
all those who say,
'Disaster will not overtake or meet
us.'

Israel's Restoration

11"In that day I will restore
David's fallen tent.
I will repair its broken places,
restore its ruins,
and build it as it used to be,
12so that they may possess the remnant
of Edom
and all the nations that bear my
name,^{f}"
declares the LORD, who will do these
things.

13"The days are coming," declares the
LORD,
"when the reaper will be overtaken by
the plowman
and the planter by the one treading
grapes.
New wine will drip from the
mountains
and flow from all the hills.
14I will bring back my exiled^g people
Israel;
they will rebuild the ruined cities
and live in them.
They will plant vineyards and drink
their wine;
they will make gardens and eat
their fruit.
15I will plant Israel in their own land,
never again to be uprooted
from the land I have given them,"
says the LORD your God.

---

^{a}2 Hebrew *to Sheol* ^{b}6 The meaning of the Hebrew for this phrase is uncertain. ^{c}6 The meaning
of the Hebrew for this word is uncertain. ^{d}7 That is, people from the upper Nile region ^{e}7 That is,
Crete ^{f}12 Hebrew; Septuagint *so that the remnant of men / and all the nations that bear my name
may seek the Lord* ^{g}14 Or *will restore the fortunes of my*

*O*BADIAH prophesies judgment
against Edom for her violence
against Israel, promising that God
will restore his people. As you read
this book, remember that no one can
fight against God's people and hope
to win in the end. The final victory
belongs to Christ and his church.

OBADIAH

¹The vision of Obadiah.

This is what the Sovereign LORD says
about Edom —

We have heard a message from the
   LORD:
   An envoy was sent to the nations to
   say,
"Rise, and let us go against her for
   battle" —

²"See, I will make you small among the
   nations;
   you will be utterly despised.
³The pride of your heart has deceived
   you,
   you who live in the clefts of the
   rocks*a*
and make your home on the
   heights,
you who say to yourself,
   'Who can bring me down to the
   ground?'

⁴Though you soar like the eagle
   and make your nest among the
   stars,
   from there I will bring you down,"
                  declares the LORD.
⁵"If thieves came to you,
   if robbers in the night —
Oh, what a disaster awaits you —
   would they not steal only as much
   as they wanted?
If grape pickers came to you,
   would they not leave a few grapes?
⁶But how Esau will be ransacked,
   his hidden treasures pillaged!
⁷All your allies will force you to the
   border;
   your friends will deceive and
   overpower you;
those who eat your bread will set a
   trap for you,*b*
   but you will not detect it.

⁸"In that day," declares the LORD,

VERSE FOR THE DAY:
Obadiah 3

AUTHOR:
Ben Carson

PASSAGE FOR THE DAY:
Obadiah 2–7

Winning Against Pride

EVEN now, winning against pride is a struggle. Whenever a person does anything extremely well and others recognize it, it will be a struggle. For me, it is worse, because family members of patients frequently say kind things such as, "Oh, you're fantastic! You're great," when we have successful surgeries, and keep repeating, "You're wonderful. You're so gifted." I know that they mean well, but I also know that I do not have a successful surgery without the help of numerous other gifted people backing me up. Moreover, I know that if God had not given me the ability to be a neurosurgeon, I could not accomplish such successes . . .

When some people begin to experience a degree of success, they become overly confident of their own abilities. They behave as if no one else in the world can do what they do. That is to say, they get an exaggerated sense of their own importance and are puffed up with pride, making it difficult for most people to work with them.

These swollen-headed types also usually cease learning. Why shouldn't they? Don't they already know everything in their field (or assume they do)? Despite their talent, they lose their usefulness. They tend to do little but think about themselves. Instead of singing the hymn, "How Great Thou Art," their words sound like "How Great I Am" . . .

I have worked out a simple formula for humility.

IF WE RECOGNIZE THAT:

1. God created this universe, including us, and
2. God shows that he is much more powerful than we are by what he does and has done in our world, and
3. God gives each of us abilities that we cannot supply to ourselves or explain our worthiness of,

THEN WE ARE HUMBLED.

Additional Scripture Readings:
Luke 18:9–14; Romans 12:14–16

Go to page 962 for your next devotional reading.

"will I not destroy the wise men of
Edom,
men of understanding in the
mountains of Esau?
⁹Your warriors, O Teman, will be
terrified,
and everyone in Esau's mountains
will be cut down in the slaughter.
¹⁰Because of the violence against your
brother Jacob,
you will be covered with shame;
you will be destroyed forever.
¹¹On the day you stood aloof
while strangers carried off his
wealth
and foreigners entered his gates
and cast lots for Jerusalem,
you were like one of them.
¹²You should not look down on your
brother
in the day of his misfortune,
nor rejoice over the people of Judah
in the day of their destruction,
nor boast so much
in the day of their trouble.
¹³You should not march through the
gates of my people
in the day of their disaster,
nor look down on them in their
calamity
in the day of their disaster,
nor seize their wealth
in the day of their disaster.
¹⁴You should not wait at the crossroads
to cut down their fugitives,
nor hand over their survivors
in the day of their trouble.

¹⁵"The day of the LORD is near
for all nations.

As you have done, it will be done to
you;
your deeds will return upon your
own head.
¹⁶Just as you drank on my holy hill,
so all the nations will drink
continually;
they will drink and drink
and be as if they had never been.
¹⁷But on Mount Zion will be
deliverance;
it will be holy,
and the house of Jacob
will possess its inheritance.
¹⁸The house of Jacob will be a fire
and the house of Joseph a flame;
the house of Esau will be stubble,
and they will set it on fire and
consume it.
There will be no survivors
from the house of Esau."
The LORD has spoken.

¹⁹People from the Negev will occupy
the mountains of Esau,
and people from the foothills will
possess
the land of the Philistines.
They will occupy the fields of
Ephraim and Samaria,
and Benjamin will possess Gilead.
²⁰This company of Israelite exiles who
are in Canaan
will possess ⸢the land⸣ as far as
Zarephath;
the exiles from Jerusalem who are in
Sepharad
will possess the towns of the Negev.
²¹Deliverers will go up onᵃ Mount Zion
to govern the mountains of Esau.
And the kingdom will be the LORD's.

ᵃ21 Or from

JONAH is sent by God to Nineveh, the city of the enemy of God's people during the time of Jeroboam II (2 Kings 14:23–29). After he tries to run away, God gives him a second chance to prophesy, for the Lord wants the whole world to hear the message of his grace. As you read this book, think about how many times God gives you a second opportunity. Don't forget to tell others about your Lord.

JONAH

Jonah Flees From the LORD

1 The word of the LORD came to Jonah son of Amittai: **2**"Go to the great city of Nineveh and preach against it, because its wickedness has come up before me."

3But Jonah ran away from the LORD and headed for Tarshish. He went down to Joppa, where he found a ship bound for that port. After paying the fare, he went aboard and sailed for Tarshish to flee from the LORD.

4Then the LORD sent a great wind on the sea, and such a violent storm arose that the ship threatened to break up. **5**All the sailors were afraid and each cried out to his own god. And they threw the cargo into the sea to lighten the ship.

But Jonah had gone below deck, where he lay down and fell into a deep sleep. **6**The captain went to him and said, "How can you sleep? Get up and call on your god! Maybe he will take notice of us, and we will not perish."

7Then the sailors said to each other, "Come, let us cast lots to find out who is responsible for this calamity." They cast lots and the lot fell on Jonah. **8**So they asked him, "Tell us, who is responsible for making all this trouble for us? What do you do? Where do you come from? What is your country? From what people are you?"

9He answered, "I am a Hebrew and I worship the LORD, the God of heaven, who made the sea and the land."

10This terrified them and they asked,

"What have you done?" (They knew he was running away from the Lord, because he had already told them so.)

¹¹The sea was getting rougher and rougher. So they asked him, "What should we do to you to make the sea calm down for us?"

¹²"Pick me up and throw me into the sea," he replied, "and it will become calm. I know that it is my fault that this great storm has come upon you."

¹³Instead, the men did their best to row back to land. But they could not, for the sea grew even wilder than before. ¹⁴Then they cried to the Lord, "O Lord, please do not let us die for taking this man's life. Do not hold us accountable for killing an innocent man, for you, O Lord, have done as you pleased." ¹⁵Then they took Jonah and threw him overboard, and the raging sea grew calm. ¹⁶At this the men greatly feared the Lord, and they offered a sacrifice to the Lord and made vows to him.

¹⁷But the Lord provided a great fish to swallow Jonah, and Jonah was inside the fish three days and three nights.

Jonah's Prayer

2 From inside the fish Jonah prayed to the Lord his God. ²He said:

"In my distress I called to the Lord,
  and he answered me.
From the depths of the grave^a I
    called for help,
  and you listened to my cry.
³You hurled me into the deep,
  into the very heart of the seas,
  and the currents swirled about me;
all your waves and breakers
  swept over me.
⁴I said, 'I have been banished
  from your sight;
yet I will look again
  toward your holy temple.'
⁵The engulfing waters threatened me,^b
  the deep surrounded me;
  seaweed was wrapped around my
    head.
⁶To the roots of the mountains I sank
    down;
  the earth beneath barred me in
    forever.
But you brought my life up from the
    pit,
  O Lord my God.
⁷"When my life was ebbing away,
  I remembered you, Lord,

and my prayer rose to you,
  to your holy temple.
⁸"Those who cling to worthless idols
  forfeit the grace that could be theirs.
⁹But I, with a song of thanksgiving,
  will sacrifice to you.
What I have vowed I will make good.
  Salvation comes from the Lord."

¹⁰And the Lord commanded the fish, and it vomited Jonah onto dry land.

Jonah Goes to Nineveh

3 Then the word of the Lord came to Jonah a second time: ²"Go to the great city of Nineveh and proclaim to it the message I give you."

³Jonah obeyed the word of the Lord and went to Nineveh. Now Nineveh was a very important city—a visit required three days. ⁴On the first day, Jonah started into the city. He proclaimed: "Forty more days and Nineveh will be overturned." ⁵The Ninevites believed God. They declared a fast, and all of them, from the greatest to the least, put on sackcloth.

⁶When the news reached the king of Nineveh, he rose from his throne, took off his royal robes, covered himself with sackcloth and sat down in the dust. ⁷Then he issued a proclamation in Nineveh:

"By the decree of the king and his nobles:

Do not let any man or beast, herd or flock, taste anything; do not let them eat or drink. ⁸But let man and beast be covered with sackcloth. Let everyone call urgently on God. Let them give up their evil ways and their violence. ⁹Who knows? God may yet relent and with compassion turn from his fierce anger so that we will not perish."

¹⁰When God saw what they did and how they turned from their evil ways, he had compassion and did not bring upon them the destruction he had threatened.

Jonah's Anger at the Lord's Compassion

4 But Jonah was greatly displeased and became angry. ²He prayed to the Lord, "O Lord, is this not what I said when I was still at home? That is why I was so quick to flee to Tarshish. I knew that you are a gracious and compassionate

^a2 Hebrew *Sheol*   ^b5 Or *waters were at my throat*

God, slow to anger and abounding in love, a God who relents from sending calamity. ³Now, O Lord, take away my life, for it is better for me to die than to live."

⁴But the Lord replied, "Have you any right to be angry?"

⁵Jonah went out and sat down at a place east of the city. There he made himself a shelter, sat in its shade and waited to see what would happen to the city. ⁶Then the Lord God provided a vine and made it grow up over Jonah to give shade for his head to ease his discomfort, and Jonah was very happy about the vine. ⁷But at dawn the next day God provided a worm, which chewed the vine so that it withered. ⁸When the sun rose, God provided a scorching east wind, and the sun blazed

---

TUESDAY

VERSE FOR THE DAY:
Jonah 4:2

AUTHOR:
Philip Yancey

PASSAGE FOR THE DAY:
Jonah 4:1–4

The God Who Relents

THE most amazing feature of the prophets is not their "modern" outlook or their passionate cry of disappointment. The reason these seventeen books merit a close look is that they include God's own reply to the prophets' bracing questions . . .

Despite everything, I am ready to forgive at any moment.

Often, in the midst of a stern reproof, God would stop—literally midsentence—and beg Israel to repent. Ahab, the most wicked king of Israel, got another chance after Mount Carmel, and then another, and another. "I take no pleasure in the death of the wicked," God explained to Ezekiel. "Turn! Turn from your evil ways! Why will you die, O house of Israel?" (Ezekiel 33:11). He told Jeremiah that if he could find just one honest person in Jerusalem, he would spare the whole city [see Jeremiah 5:1].

Nothing expresses God's yearning to forgive better than the Book of Jonah. It contains but one line of prophecy: "Forty more days and Nineveh will be overturned" (3:4). But, to Jonah's disgust, that simple announcement of doom sparked a spiritual revival in hated Nineveh and changed God's plans for punishment. Jonah, sulking under a shriveled vine, admitted he had suspected God's soft heart all along. "I knew that you are a gracious and compassionate God, slow to anger and abounding in love, a God who relents from sending calamity" (4:2). Thus the whole madcap scenario of balky prophet, ocean storm, and whale detour came about because Jonah could not trust God—could not, that is, trust him to be harsh and unrelenting toward Nineveh. As Robert Frost summed up the story, "After Jonah, you could never trust God not to be merciful again."

Additional Scripture Readings:
Psalm 106:40–48; Ephesians 2:1–10

Go to page 969 for your next devotional reading.

on Jonah's head so that he grew faint. He wanted to die, and said, "It would be better for me to die than to live."

9But God said to Jonah, "Do you have a right to be angry about the vine?"

"I do," he said. "I am angry enough to die."

10But the Lord said, "You have been concerned about this vine, though you did not tend it or make it grow. It sprang up overnight and died overnight. **11**But Nineveh has more than a hundred and twenty thousand people who cannot tell their right hand from their left, and many cattle as well. Should I not be concerned about that great city?"

MICAH prophesies during the time of Jotham and Ahaz (2 Chronicles 27–28) against the numerous sins of the kingdom of Judah, insisting that God wants justice in society. He inspires hope by speaking of the coming Messiah and his kingdom of peace. As you read this book, promise the Lord that your lifestyle will be one of justice, mercy and peace in his Son Jesus Christ.

MICAH

1 The word of the LORD that came to Micah of Moresheth during the reigns of Jotham, Ahaz and Hezekiah, kings of Judah—the vision he saw concerning Samaria and Jerusalem.

²Hear, O peoples, all of you,
    listen, O earth and all who are in it,
that the Sovereign LORD may witness
        against you,
    the Lord from his holy temple.

Judgment Against Samaria and Jerusalem

³Look! The LORD is coming from his
        dwelling place;
    he comes down and treads the high
        places of the earth.
⁴The mountains melt beneath him
    and the valleys split apart,
like wax before the fire,
    like water rushing down a slope.
⁵All this is because of Jacob's
        transgression,
    because of the sins of the house of
        Israel.
What is Jacob's transgression?
    Is it not Samaria?
What is Judah's high place?
    Is it not Jerusalem?

⁶"Therefore I will make Samaria a heap
        of rubble,
    a place for planting vineyards.
I will pour her stones into the valley
    and lay bare her foundations.
⁷All her idols will be broken to pieces;
    all her temple gifts will be burned
        with fire;
    I will destroy all her images.

Since she gathered her gifts from the
  wages of prostitutes,
  as the wages of prostitutes they will
    again be used."

Weeping and Mourning

[8]Because of this I will weep and wail;
  I will go about barefoot and naked.
I will howl like a jackal
  and moan like an owl.
[9]For her wound is incurable;
  it has come to Judah.
It[a] has reached the very gate of my
    people,
  even to Jerusalem itself.
[10]Tell it not in Gath[b];
  weep not at all.[c]
In Beth Ophrah[d]
  roll in the dust.
[11]Pass on in nakedness and shame,
  you who live in Shaphir.[e]
Those who live in Zaanan[f]
  will not come out.
Beth Ezel is in mourning;
  its protection is taken from you.
[12]Those who live in Maroth[g] writhe in
    pain,
  waiting for relief,
because disaster has come from the
    LORD,
  even to the gate of Jerusalem.
[13]You who live in Lachish,[h]
  harness the team to the chariot.
You were the beginning of sin
  to the Daughter of Zion,
for the transgressions of Israel
  were found in you.
[14]Therefore you will give parting gifts
  to Moresheth Gath.
The town of Aczib[i] will prove
    deceptive
  to the kings of Israel.
[15]I will bring a conqueror against you
  who live in Mareshah.[j]
He who is the glory of Israel
  will come to Adullam.
[16]Shave your heads in mourning
  for the children in whom you
    delight;
make yourselves as bald as the
    vulture,
  for they will go from you into
    exile.

Man's Plans and God's

2 Woe to those who plan iniquity,
  to those who plot evil on their
    beds!
At morning's light they carry it out
  because it is in their power to do it.
[2]They covet fields and seize them,
  and houses, and take them.
They defraud a man of his home,
  a fellowman of his inheritance.

[3]Therefore, the LORD says:

"I am planning disaster against this
    people,
  from which you cannot save
    yourselves.
You will no longer walk proudly,
  for it will be a time of calamity.
[4]In that day men will ridicule you;
  they will taunt you with this
    mournful song:
'We are utterly ruined;
  my people's possession is divided
    up.
He takes it from me!
  He assigns our fields to traitors.' "

[5]Therefore you will have no one in the
    assembly of the LORD
  to divide the land by lot.

False Prophets

[6]"Do not prophesy," their prophets say.
  "Do not prophesy about these
    things;
  disgrace will not overtake us."
[7]Should it be said, O house of Jacob:
  "Is the Spirit of the LORD angry?
  Does he do such things?"

"Do not my words do good
  to him whose ways are upright?
[8]Lately my people have risen up
  like an enemy.
You strip off the rich robe
  from those who pass by without a
    care,
  like men returning from battle.
[9]You drive the women of my people
  from their pleasant homes.
You take away my blessing
  from their children forever.
[10]Get up, go away!
  For this is not your resting place,
  because it is defiled,

---

[a]9 Or He   [b]10 Gath sounds like the Hebrew for tell.   [c]10 Hebrew; Septuagint may suggest not in
Acco. The Hebrew for in Acco sounds like the Hebrew for weep.   [d]10 Beth Ophrah means house of dust.
[e]11 Shaphir means pleasant.   [f]11 Zaanan sounds like the Hebrew for come out.   [g]12 Maroth
sounds like the Hebrew for bitter.   [h]13 Lachish sounds like the Hebrew for team.   [i]14 Aczib means
deception.   [j]15 Mareshah sounds like the Hebrew for conqueror.

it is ruined, beyond all remedy.
[11]If a liar and deceiver comes and says,
 'I will prophesy for you plenty of
   wine and beer,'
 he would be just the prophet for
   this people!

Deliverance Promised

[12]"I will surely gather all of you,
   O Jacob;
 I will surely bring together the
   remnant of Israel.
 I will bring them together like sheep
   in a pen,
 like a flock in its pasture;
 the place will throng with people.
[13]One who breaks open the way will go
   up before them;
 they will break through the gate and
   go out.
 Their king will pass through before
   them,
 the LORD at their head."

Leaders and Prophets Rebuked

3 Then I said,

"Listen, you leaders of Jacob,
 you rulers of the house of Israel.
Should you not know justice,
[2] you who hate good and love evil;
who tear the skin from my people
 and the flesh from their bones;
[3]who eat my people's flesh,
 strip off their skin
 and break their bones in pieces;
who chop them up like meat for the
   pan,
 like flesh for the pot?"

[4]Then they will cry out to the LORD,
 but he will not answer them.
At that time he will hide his face from
   them
because of the evil they have done.

[5]This is what the LORD says:

"As for the prophets
 who lead my people astray,
if one feeds them,
 they proclaim 'peace';
if he does not,
 they prepare to wage war against
   him.
[6]Therefore night will come over you,
   without visions,
 and darkness, without divination.
The sun will set for the prophets,
 and the day will go dark for them.
[7]The seers will be ashamed

and the diviners disgraced.
They will all cover their faces
 because there is no answer from
   God."

[8]But as for me, I am filled with power,
 with the Spirit of the LORD,
 and with justice and might,
to declare to Jacob his transgression,
 to Israel his sin.
[9]Hear this, you leaders of the house of
   Jacob,
 you rulers of the house of Israel,
who despise justice
 and distort all that is right;
[10]who build Zion with bloodshed,
 and Jerusalem with wickedness.
[11]Her leaders judge for a bribe,
 her priests teach for a price,
 and her prophets tell fortunes for
   money.
Yet they lean upon the LORD and say,
 "Is not the LORD among us?
 No disaster will come upon us."
[12]Therefore because of you,
 Zion will be plowed like a field,
Jerusalem will become a heap of
   rubble,
 the temple hill a mound overgrown
   with thickets.

The Mountain of the LORD

4 In the last days

the mountain of the LORD's temple will
   be established
 as chief among the mountains;
it will be raised above the hills,
 and peoples will stream to it.

[2]Many nations will come and say,

"Come, let us go up to the mountain
   of the LORD,
 to the house of the God of Jacob.
He will teach us his ways,
 so that we may walk in his paths."
The law will go out from Zion,
 the word of the LORD from
   Jerusalem.
[3]He will judge between many peoples
 and will settle disputes for strong
   nations far and wide.
They will beat their swords into
   plowshares
 and their spears into pruning hooks.
Nation will not take up sword against
   nation,
 nor will they train for war anymore.
[4]Every man will sit under his own vine
 and under his own fig tree,

and no one will make them afraid,
for the LORD Almighty has spoken.
⁵All the nations may walk
in the name of their gods;
we will walk in the name of the LORD
our God for ever and ever.

The LORD's Plan

⁶"In that day," declares the LORD,

"I will gather the lame;
I will assemble the exiles
and those I have brought to grief.
⁷I will make the lame a remnant,
those driven away a strong nation.
The LORD will rule over them in
Mount Zion
from that day and forever.
⁸As for you, O watchtower of the flock,
O stronghold*a* of the Daughter of
Zion,
the former dominion will be restored
to you;
kingship will come to the Daughter
of Jerusalem."

⁹Why do you now cry aloud—
have you no king?
Has your counselor perished,
that pain seizes you like that of a
woman in labor?
¹⁰Writhe in agony, O Daughter of Zion,
like a woman in labor,
for now you must leave the city
to camp in the open field.
You will go to Babylon;
there you will be rescued.
There the LORD will redeem you
out of the hand of your enemies.

¹¹But now many nations
are gathered against you.
They say, "Let her be defiled,
let our eyes gloat over Zion!"
¹²But they do not know
the thoughts of the LORD;
they do not understand his plan,
he who gathers them like sheaves to
the threshing floor.

¹³"Rise and thresh, O Daughter of Zion,
for I will give you horns of iron;
I will give you hoofs of bronze
and you will break to pieces many
nations."

You will devote their ill-gotten gains
to the LORD,

their wealth to the Lord of all the
earth.

A Promised Ruler From Bethlehem

5 Marshal your troops, O city of
troops,*b*
for a siege is laid against us.
They will strike Israel's ruler
on the cheek with a rod.

²"But you, Bethlehem Ephrathah,
though you are small among the
clans*c* of Judah,
out of you will come for me
one who will be ruler over Israel,
whose origins*d* are from of old,
from ancient times.*e*"

³Therefore Israel will be abandoned
until the time when she who is in
labor gives birth
and the rest of his brothers return
to join the Israelites.

⁴He will stand and shepherd his flock
in the strength of the LORD,
in the majesty of the name of the
LORD his God.
And they will live securely, for then
his greatness
will reach to the ends of the earth.
⁵ And he will be their peace.

Deliverance and Destruction

When the Assyrian invades our land
and marches through our fortresses,
we will raise against him seven
shepherds,
even eight leaders of men.
⁶They will rule*f* the land of Assyria
with the sword,
the land of Nimrod with drawn
sword.*g*
He will deliver us from the Assyrian
when he invades our land
and marches into our borders.

⁷The remnant of Jacob will be
in the midst of many peoples
like dew from the LORD,
like showers on the grass,
which do not wait for man
or linger for mankind.
⁸The remnant of Jacob will be among
the nations,
in the midst of many peoples,
like a lion among the beasts of the
forest,

---

a8 Or *hill*   *b1* Or *Strengthen your walls, O walled city*   *c2* Or *rulers*   *d2* Hebrew *goings out*
e2 Or *from days of eternity*   *f6* Or *crush*   *g6* Or *Nimrod in its gates*

like a young lion among flocks of
sheep,
which mauls and mangles as it goes,
and no one can rescue.
⁹Your hand will be lifted up in triumph
over your enemies,
and all your foes will be destroyed.

¹⁰"In that day," declares the LORD,

"I will destroy your horses from
among you
and demolish your chariots.
¹¹I will destroy the cities of your land
and tear down all your strongholds.
¹²I will destroy your witchcraft
and you will no longer cast spells.
¹³I will destroy your carved images
and your sacred stones from among
you;
you will no longer bow down
to the work of your hands.
¹⁴I will uproot from among you your
Asherah poles*a*
and demolish your cities.
¹⁵I will take vengeance in anger and
wrath
upon the nations that have not
obeyed me."

The LORD's Case Against Israel

6 Listen to what the LORD says:

"Stand up, plead your case before the
mountains;
let the hills hear what you have to
say.
²Hear, O mountains, the LORD's
accusation;
listen, you everlasting foundations
of the earth.
For the LORD has a case against his
people;
he is lodging a charge against Israel.

³"My people, what have I done to you?
How have I burdened you? Answer
me.
⁴I brought you up out of Egypt
and redeemed you from the land of
slavery.
I sent Moses to lead you,
also Aaron and Miriam.
⁵My people, remember
what Balak king of Moab counseled
and what Balaam son of Beor
answered.

Remember your journey from Shittim
to Gilgal,
that you may know the righteous
acts of the LORD."

⁶With what shall I come before the
LORD
and bow down before the exalted
God?
Shall I come before him with burnt
offerings,
with calves a year old?
⁷Will the LORD be pleased with
thousands of rams,
with ten thousand rivers of oil?
Shall I offer my firstborn for my
transgression,
the fruit of my body for the sin of
my soul?
⁸He has showed you, O man, what is
good.
And what does the LORD require of
you?
To act justly and to love mercy
and to walk humbly with your God.

Israel's Guilt and Punishment

⁹Listen! The LORD is calling to the
city—
and to fear your name is wisdom—
"Heed the rod and the One who
appointed it.*b*
¹⁰Am I still to forget, O wicked house,
your ill-gotten treasures
and the short ephah,*c* which is
accursed?
¹¹Shall I acquit a man with dishonest
scales,
with a bag of false weights?
¹²Her rich men are violent;
her people are liars
and their tongues speak deceitfully.
¹³Therefore, I have begun to destroy
you,
to ruin you because of your sins.
¹⁴You will eat but not be satisfied;
your stomach will still be empty.*d*
You will store up but save nothing,
because what you save I will give to
the sword.
¹⁵You will plant but not harvest;
you will press olives but not use the
oil on yourselves,
you will crush grapes but not drink
the wine.
¹⁶You have observed the statutes of
Omri

---

*a*14 That is, symbols of the goddess Asherah   *b*9 The meaning of the Hebrew for this line is uncertain.
*c*10 An ephah was a dry measure.   *d*14 The meaning of the Hebrew for this word is uncertain.

and all the practices of Ahab's
  house,
and you have followed their
  traditions.
Therefore I will give you over to ruin
and your people to derision;
  you will bear the scorn of the
    nations.*"

*16 Septuagint; Hebrew *scorn due my people*

Israel's Misery

7 What misery is mine!
I am like one who gathers summer
  fruit
at the gleaning of the vineyard;
there is no cluster of grapes to eat,
  none of the early figs that I crave.

WEDNESDAY

VERSE FOR THE DAY: AUTHOR: PASSAGE FOR THE DAY:
Micah 6:8   *John B. Anderson*   *Micah 6:6–8*

Our Brother's Keeper

BECAUSE Christians are not "of the world," they have too often tended to act as if they are not "in the world," and practiced a pietistic separation. Their separation from those things
they believe to be evil has too often been an excuse for separation from those things that are good. They have often abandoned their responsibilities in the world of literature and the
arts, and in the field of government itself.

One can cling to orthodox Christianity without denying the
right of the poor to be clothed and fed, or the right of minori-
ties to their civil rights, or that there is a proper role for government to assume in fighting poverty and promoting human
rights. In fact, I would reverse this statement to say that it is
difficult for me to believe that a Christian cannot be concerned
and compassionate about these problems.

I would without hesitation maintain that man is a sinner,
and that all of his social institutions are affected by sin. Ultimate social change depends upon changing men, and men
cannot be changed simply by redesigning or altering the environment. If they could, Christ's death on the cross would have
been completely unnecessary and the whole rationale of God's
plan for man's redemption would collapse. Believing as I do
that Christ's words to Nicodemus are relevant to the situation
of modern man and that we must be "born again" in no way
relieves me of my responsibility to pursue social justice, to act
in compassion toward my fellowman, and to seek a better
world. For, while man is a sinner, God has implanted within
each of us a conscience, and with it we become responsible for
our own actions and chargeable with the responsibility to do
mercy, seek justice and walk humbly before our God. We cannot escape the fact that we are our brother's keeper.

Additional Scripture Readings:
Amos 5:14–24; Matthew 25:31–40

*Go to page 970 for your next
devotional reading.*

²The godly have been swept from the
land;
not one upright man remains.
All men lie in wait to shed blood;
each hunts his brother with a net.
³Both hands are skilled in doing evil;
the ruler demands gifts,
the judge accepts bribes,
the powerful dictate what they
desire—
they all conspire together.
⁴The best of them is like a brier,
the most upright worse than a thorn
hedge.
The day of your watchmen has come,
the day God visits you.

Now is the time of their confusion.
⁵Do not trust a neighbor;
put no confidence in a friend.
Even with her who lies in your
embrace
be careful of your words.
⁶For a son dishonors his father,
a daughter rises up against her
mother,
a daughter-in-law against her mother-
in-law—
a man's enemies are the members
of his own household.
⁷But as for me, I watch in hope for the
LORD,

THURSDAY

VERSE FOR THE DAY: *AUTHOR:*   *PASSAGE FOR THE DAY:*
Micah 7:18   *Charles Stanley*   *Micah 7:16–20*

Restored Fellowship

THERE is something God wants more than retribution. There
is something he desires more than simply being paid back for
the disrespect shown him. God wants fellowship with us. And
he was willing to put his own system of justice on hold while
he made provision for sinful men and women to be rescued . . .

If God was willing to move quickly to restore fellowship
with Adam and Eve [see Genesis 3:21], does it make sense that
he would move any less quickly to restore fellowship with us?
And if the heavenly Father was willing to move quickly to restore fellowship with sinners, how much more quickly should
we move to restore fellowship with those who have wronged
us?

The big picture is simply this. People turned their backs on
God and God immediately went to work to regain fellowship.
Observations from the Old Testament should be enough to
convince us that God is a God of love and forgiveness. He forgives because he desires to forgive, not because he is under
some constraint. His forgiveness is not handed out on an individual basis depending upon the sin committed. On the contrary, in the Old Testament God set up a system by which *any
man or woman could come to him regardless of the sin committed.* In the New Testament we find that these same principles of forgiveness apply.

Additional Scripture Readings: *Go to page 973 for your next*
Leviticus 16:18–22; Hebrews 10:1–18   *devotional reading.*

I wait for God my Savior;
my God will hear me.

Israel Will Rise

⁸Do not gloat over me, my enemy!
Though I have fallen, I will rise.
Though I sit in darkness,
the LORD will be my light.
⁹Because I have sinned against him,
I will bear the LORD's wrath,
until he pleads my case
and establishes my right.
He will bring me out into the light;
I will see his righteousness.
¹⁰Then my enemy will see it
and will be covered with shame,
she who said to me,
"Where is the LORD your God?"
My eyes will see her downfall;
even now she will be trampled
underfoot
like mire in the streets.

¹¹The day for building your walls will
come,
the day for extending your
boundaries.
¹²In that day people will come to you
from Assyria and the cities of Egypt,
even from Egypt to the Euphrates
and from sea to sea
and from mountain to mountain.
¹³The earth will become desolate
because of its inhabitants,
as the result of their deeds.

Prayer and Praise

¹⁴Shepherd your people with your staff,
the flock of your inheritance,
which lives by itself in a forest,
in fertile pasturelands. ᵃ
Let them feed in Bashan and Gilead
as in days long ago.

¹⁵"As in the days when you came out of
Egypt,
I will show them my wonders."

¹⁶Nations will see and be ashamed,
deprived of all their power.
They will lay their hands on their
mouths
and their ears will become deaf.
¹⁷They will lick dust like a snake,
like creatures that crawl on the
ground.
They will come trembling out of their
dens;
they will turn in fear to the LORD
our God
and will be afraid of you.
¹⁸Who is a God like you,
who pardons sin and forgives the
transgression
of the remnant of his inheritance?
You do not stay angry forever
but delight to show mercy.
¹⁹You will again have compassion on
us;
you will tread our sins underfoot
and hurl all our iniquities into the
depths of the sea.
²⁰You will be true to Jacob,
and show mercy to Abraham,
as you pledged on oath to our fathers
in days long ago.

ᵃ14 Or in the middle of Carmel

NAHUM prophesies against the wicked and cruel nation of Assyria, probably during the time of Josiah (2 Kings 22–23). In so doing he testifies that God, as the judge of the nations, is in control of all that happens. As you read this book, be comforted (Nahum means "comfort") by the thought that God is Lord of history.

NAHUM

1 An oracle concerning Nineveh. The book of the vision of Nahum the Elkoshite.

The Lord's Anger Against Nineveh

2The Lord is a jealous and avenging God;
the Lord takes vengeance and is filled with wrath.
The Lord takes vengeance on his foes
and maintains his wrath against his enemies.
3The Lord is slow to anger and great in power;
the Lord will not leave the guilty unpunished.
His way is in the whirlwind and the storm,
and clouds are the dust of his feet.
4He rebukes the sea and dries it up;
he makes all the rivers run dry.

Bashan and Carmel wither
and the blossoms of Lebanon fade.
5The mountains quake before him
and the hills melt away.
The earth trembles at his presence,
the world and all who live in it.
6Who can withstand his indignation?
Who can endure his fierce anger?
His wrath is poured out like fire;
the rocks are shattered before him.

7The Lord is good,
a refuge in times of trouble.
He cares for those who trust in him,
8 but with an overwhelming flood
he will make an end of ˌNinevehˌ;
he will pursue his foes into darkness.

9Whatever they plot against the Lord
heª will bring to an end;

ª9 Or *What do you foes plot against the* Lord? / *He*

trouble will not come a second
time.
[10]They will be entangled among thorns
and drunk from their wine;
they will be consumed like dry
stubble.[a]
[11]From you, ⌊O Nineveh⌋ has one come
forth
who plots evil against the LORD
and counsels wickedness.

[12]This is what the LORD says:

"Although they have allies and are
numerous,
they will be cut off and pass away.
Although I have afflicted you,
⌊O Judah⌋
I will afflict you no more.
[13]Now I will break their yoke from your
neck
and tear your shackles away."

[14]The LORD has given a command
concerning you, ⌊Nineveh⌋:

[a]10 The meaning of the Hebrew for this verse is uncertain.

FRIDAY

VERSE FOR THE DAY:
Nahum 1:3

AUTHOR:
C.S. Lewis

PASSAGE FOR THE DAY:
Nahum 1:2–6

Retribution's Good Element

WHEN our ancestors referred to pains and sorrows as God's
"vengeance" upon sin they were not necessarily attributing
evil passions to God; they may have been recognizing the
good element in the idea of retribution. Until the evil man
finds evil unmistakably present in his existence, in the form of
pain, he is enclosed in illusion. Once pain has roused him, he
knows that he is in some way or other "up against" the real
universe: he either rebels (with the possibility of a clearer issue and deeper repentance at some later stage) or else makes
some attempt at an adjustment, which, if pursued, will lead
him to religion . . .

No doubt Pain as God's megaphone is a terrible instrument;
it may lead to final and unrepented rebellion. But it gives the
only opportunity the bad man can have for amendment. It removes the veil; it plants the flag of truth within the fortress of
a rebel soul . . .

Everyone has noticed how hard it is to turn our thoughts to
God when everything is going well with us. We "have all we
want" is a terrible saying when "all" does not include God. We
find God an interruption. As Saint Augustine says somewhere,
"God wants to give us something, but cannot, because our
hands are full—there's nowhere for him to put it." Or as a
friend of mine said, "We regard God as an airman regards his
parachute; it's there for emergencies but he hopes he'll never
have to use it."

Additional Scripture Readings:
Psalm 90:11–17;
2 Corinthians 12:1–10

*Go to page 975 for your next
devotional reading.*

"You will have no descendants to
　　bear your name.
I will destroy the carved images and
　　cast idols
　that are in the temple of your gods.
I will prepare your grave,
　　for you are vile."

15Look, there on the mountains,
　　the feet of one who brings good
　　　news,
　who proclaims peace!
Celebrate your festivals, O Judah,
　　and fulfill your vows.
No more will the wicked invade you;
　they will be completely destroyed.

Nineveh to Fall

2 An attacker advances against you,
　　⌐Nineveh⌐.
Guard the fortress,
watch the road,
brace yourselves,
marshal all your strength!

2The Lord will restore the splendor of
　　Jacob
　like the splendor of Israel,
though destroyers have laid them
　　waste
　and have ruined their vines.

3The shields of his soldiers are red;
　the warriors are clad in scarlet.
The metal on the chariots flashes
　on the day they are made ready;
　the spears of pine are brandished.a
4The chariots storm through the
　　streets,
　rushing back and forth through the
　　squares.
They look like flaming torches;
　they dart about like lightning.

5He summons his picked troops,
　yet they stumble on their way.
They dash to the city wall;
　the protective shield is put in place.
6The river gates are thrown open
　and the palace collapses.
7It is decreedb that ⌐the city⌐
　be exiled and carried away.
Its slave girls moan like doves
　and beat upon their breasts.
8Nineveh is like a pool,
　and its water is draining away.
"Stop! Stop!" they cry,
　but no one turns back.
9Plunder the silver!

Plunder the gold!
The supply is endless,
　the wealth from all its treasures!
10She is pillaged, plundered, stripped!
　Hearts melt, knees give way,
　bodies tremble, every face grows
　　pale.

11Where now is the lions' den,
　the place where they fed their
　　young,
where the lion and lioness went,
　and the cubs, with nothing to fear?
12The lion killed enough for his cubs
　and strangled the prey for his mate,
filling his lairs with the kill
　and his dens with the prey.

13"I am against you,"
　declares the Lord Almighty.
"I will burn up your chariots in
　　smoke,
　and the sword will devour your
　　young lions.
I will leave you no prey on the
　　earth.
The voices of your messengers
　will no longer be heard."

Woe to Nineveh

3 Woe to the city of blood,
　full of lies,
full of plunder,
　never without victims!
2The crack of whips,
　the clatter of wheels,
galloping horses
　and jolting chariots!
3Charging cavalry,
　flashing swords
　and glittering spears!
Many casualties,
　piles of dead,
bodies without number,
　people stumbling over the corpses—

4all because of the wanton lust of a
　　harlot,
　alluring, the mistress of sorceries,
who enslaved nations by her
　　prostitution
　and peoples by her witchcraft.

5"I am against you," declares the Lord
　　Almighty.
　"I will lift your skirts over your face.
I will show the nations your
　　nakedness

---

a3 Hebrew; Septuagint and Syriac / the horsemen rush to and fro　　b7 The meaning of the Hebrew for
this word is uncertain.

WEEKENDING

RECEIVE

What we need to know, of course, is not just that God exists, not just that beyond the steely brightness of the stars there is a cosmic intelligence of some kind that keeps the whole show going, but that there is a God right here in the thick of our day-by-day lives who may not be writing messages about himself in the stars but in one way or another is trying to get messages through our blindness as we move around here knee-deep in the fragrant muck and misery and marvel of the world. It is not objective proof of God's existence that we want but the experience of God's presence. That is the miracle we are really after, and that is also, I think, the miracle that we really get.

– Frederick Buechner

REVIVE

Saturday: Ezekiel 37:24–28
Sunday: John 1:1–14

Go to page 980 for your next devotional reading.

and the kingdoms your shame.
⁶I will pelt you with filth,
   I will treat you with contempt
   and make you a spectacle.
⁷All who see you will flee from you
      and say,
   'Nineveh is in ruins — who will
      mourn for her?'
   Where can I find anyone to comfort
      you?"

⁸Are you better than Thebes,ᵃ
   situated on the Nile,
   with water around her?
The river was her defense,
   the waters her wall.
⁹Cushᵇ and Egypt were her boundless
      strength;
   Put and Libya were among her
      allies.
¹⁰Yet she was taken captive
   and went into exile.
Her infants were dashed to pieces
   at the head of every street.
Lots were cast for her nobles,
   and all her great men were put in
      chains.
¹¹You too will become drunk;
   you will go into hiding
   and seek refuge from the enemy.

¹²All your fortresses are like fig trees
   with their first ripe fruit;
when they are shaken,
   the figs fall into the mouth of the
      eater.
¹³Look at your troops —
   they are all women!
The gates of your land
   are wide open to your enemies;

fire has consumed their bars.

¹⁴Draw water for the siege,
   strengthen your defenses!
Work the clay,
   tread the mortar,
   repair the brickwork!
¹⁵There the fire will devour you;
   the sword will cut you down
   and, like grasshoppers, consume
      you.
Multiply like grasshoppers,
   multiply like locusts!
¹⁶You have increased the number of
      your merchants
   till they are more than the stars of
      the sky,
but like locusts they strip the land
   and then fly away.
¹⁷Your guards are like locusts,
   your officials like swarms of locusts
   that settle in the walls on a cold
      day —
but when the sun appears they fly
      away,
   and no one knows where.

¹⁸O king of Assyria, your shepherdsᶜ
      slumber;
   your nobles lie down to rest.
Your people are scattered on the
      mountains
   with no one to gather them.
¹⁹Nothing can heal your wound;
   your injury is fatal.
Everyone who hears the news about
      you
   claps his hands at your fall,
for who has not felt
   your endless cruelty?

ᵃ8 Hebrew *No Amon*   ᵇ9 That is, the upper Nile region   ᶜ18 Or *rulers*

HABAKKUK prophesies in Judah when the power of Babylon is growing (2 Chronicles 35:20–36:8). When he questions God's justice in allowing evil to go unchecked, he receives the answer that God knows what he is doing, leading to a concluding celebration of God's glory and power. As you read this book, remember that the majestic God is in control of your life, no matter what happens to you.

HABAKKUK

1 The oracle that Habakkuk the prophet received.

Habakkuk's Complaint

²How long, O LORD, must I call for
help,
  but you do not listen?
Or cry out to you, "Violence!"
  but you do not save?
³Why do you make me look at
injustice?
  Why do you tolerate wrong?
Destruction and violence are before
me;
  there is strife, and conflict abounds.
⁴Therefore the law is paralyzed,

and justice never prevails.
The wicked hem in the righteous,
  so that justice is perverted.

The LORD's Answer

⁵"Look at the nations and watch —
  and be utterly amazed.
For I am going to do something in
your days
  that you would not believe,
  even if you were told.
⁶I am raising up the Babylonians,ᵃ
  that ruthless and impetuous people,
who sweep across the whole earth
  to seize dwelling places not their
  own.

7They are a feared and dreaded people;
  they are a law to themselves
  and promote their own honor.
8Their horses are swifter than leopards,
  fiercer than wolves at dusk.
Their cavalry gallops headlong;
  their horsemen come from afar.
They fly like a vulture swooping to
  devour;
9 they all come bent on violence.
Their hordes*a* advance like a desert
  wind
  and gather prisoners like sand.
10They deride kings
  and scoff at rulers.
They laugh at all fortified cities;
  they build earthen ramps and
  capture them.
11Then they sweep past like the wind
  and go on —
  guilty men, whose own strength is
  their god."

Habakkuk's Second Complaint

12O LORD, are you not from everlasting?
  My God, my Holy One, we will not
  die.
O LORD, you have appointed them to
  execute judgment;
  O Rock, you have ordained them to
  punish.
13Your eyes are too pure to look on evil;
  you cannot tolerate wrong.
Why then do you tolerate the
  treacherous?
  Why are you silent while the
  wicked
  swallow up those more righteous
  than themselves?
14You have made men like fish in the
  sea,
  like sea creatures that have no ruler.
15The wicked foe pulls all of them up
  with hooks,
  he catches them in his net,
he gathers them up in his dragnet;
  and so he rejoices and is glad.
16Therefore he sacrifices to his net
  and burns incense to his dragnet,
for by his net he lives in luxury
  and enjoys the choicest food.
17Is he to keep on emptying his net,
  destroying nations without mercy?

2 I will stand at my watch
  and station myself on the ramparts;
I will look to see what he will say to
  me,
  and what answer I am to give to
  this complaint.*b*

The LORD's Answer

2Then the LORD replied:

"Write down the revelation
  and make it plain on tablets
  so that a herald*c* may run with it.
3For the revelation awaits an appointed
  time;
  it speaks of the end
  and will not prove false.
Though it linger, wait for it;
  it*d* will certainly come and will not
  delay.

4"See, he is puffed up;
  his desires are not upright —
  but the righteous will live by his
  faith*e* —
5indeed, wine betrays him;
  he is arrogant and never at rest.
Because he is as greedy as the grave*f*
  and like death is never satisfied,
he gathers to himself all the nations
  and takes captive all the peoples.

6"Will not all of them taunt him with
ridicule and scorn, saying,

" 'Woe to him who piles up stolen
  goods
  and makes himself wealthy by
  extortion!
How long must this go on?'
7Will not your debtors*g* suddenly
  arise?
  Will they not wake up and make
  you tremble?
  Then you will become their victim.
8Because you have plundered many
  nations,
  the peoples who are left will
  plunder you.
For you have shed man's blood;
  you have destroyed lands and cities
  and everyone in them.

9"Woe to him who builds his realm by
  unjust gain
  to set his nest on high,
  to escape the clutches of ruin!
10You have plotted the ruin of many
  peoples,

---

*a*9 The meaning of the Hebrew for this word is uncertain.   *b*1 Or *and what to answer when I am*
rebuked   *c*2 Or *so that whoever reads it*   *d*3 Or *Though he linger, wait for him; / he*   *e*4 Or
faithfulness   *f*5 Hebrew *Sheol*   *g*7 Or *creditors*

shaming your own house and
forfeiting your life.
¹¹The stones of the wall will cry out,
and the beams of the woodwork
will echo it.

¹²"Woe to him who builds a city with
bloodshed
and establishes a town by crime!
¹³Has not the LORD Almighty determined
that the people's labor is only fuel
for the fire,
that the nations exhaust themselves
for nothing?
¹⁴For the earth will be filled with the
knowledge of the glory of the
LORD,
as the waters cover the sea.

¹⁵"Woe to him who gives drink to his
neighbors,
pouring it from the wineskin till
they are drunk,
so that he can gaze on their naked
bodies.
¹⁶You will be filled with shame instead
of glory.
Now it is your turn! Drink and be
exposedᵃ!
The cup from the LORD's right hand is
coming around to you,
and disgrace will cover your glory.
¹⁷The violence you have done to
Lebanon will overwhelm you,
and your destruction of animals will
terrify you.
For you have shed man's blood;
you have destroyed lands and cities
and everyone in them.

¹⁸"Of what value is an idol, since a man
has carved it?
Or an image that teaches lies?
For he who makes it trusts in his own
creation;
he makes idols that cannot speak.
¹⁹Woe to him who says to wood, 'Come
to life!'
Or to lifeless stone, 'Wake up!'
Can it give guidance?
It is covered with gold and silver;
there is no breath in it.
²⁰But the LORD is in his holy temple;
let all the earth be silent before
him."

Habakkuk's Prayer

3 A prayer of Habakkuk the prophet. On
shigionoth.ᵇ

²LORD, I have heard of your fame;
I stand in awe of your deeds,
O LORD.
Renew them in our day,
in our time make them known;
in wrath remember mercy.

³God came from Teman,
the Holy One from Mount Paran.
                                    Selahᶜ
His glory covered the heavens
and his praise filled the earth.
⁴His splendor was like the sunrise;
rays flashed from his hand,
where his power was hidden.
⁵Plague went before him;
pestilence followed his steps.
⁶He stood, and shook the earth;
he looked, and made the nations
tremble.
The ancient mountains crumbled
and the age-old hills collapsed.
His ways are eternal.
⁷I saw the tents of Cushan in distress,
the dwellings of Midian in anguish.

⁸Were you angry with the rivers,
O LORD?
Was your wrath against the
streams?
Did you rage against the sea
when you rode with your horses
and your victorious chariots?
⁹You uncovered your bow,
you called for many arrows.   Selah
You split the earth with rivers;
¹⁰ the mountains saw you and
writhed.
Torrents of water swept by;
the deep roared
and lifted its waves on high.

¹¹Sun and moon stood still in the
heavens
at the glint of your flying arrows,
at the lightning of your flashing
spear.
¹²In wrath you strode through the earth
and in anger you threshed the
nations.
¹³You came out to deliver your people,
to save your anointed one.

ᵃ16 Masoretic Text; Dead Sea Scrolls, Aquila, Vulgate and Syriac (see also Septuagint) and stagger
ᵇ1 Probably a literary or musical term   ᶜ3 A word of uncertain meaning; possibly a musical term; also
in verses 9 and 13

You crushed the leader of the land of
   wickedness,
you stripped him from head to foot.
                  Selah
14With his own spear you pierced his
   head
when his warriors stormed out to
   scatter us,
gloating as though about to devour

the wretched who were in hiding.
15You trampled the sea with your
   horses,
churning the great waters.

16I heard and my heart pounded,
   my lips quivered at the sound;
decay crept into my bones,
   and my legs trembled.

MONDAY

VERSE FOR THE DAY:	AUTHOR:	PASSAGE FOR THE DAY:
Habakkuk 3:2	Henri Nouwen	Habakkuk 3:1–19

I Am Man, He Is God

CERTAINLY praying takes some admissions, that is, recognition of your state as a man. But this admission does not lead
to shame, to a feeling of worthlessness or despair, but rather
to the discovery that you are a man and God is God. If you
cling tightly to your own weaknesses, your faults, shortcomings and your twisted past, to all the events, facts and situations which you would prefer to cut out of your own history,
you're only hiding behind a hedge which everyone can see
through. What you've done is narrowed your world to a small
hiding place, where you try to conceal yourself, suspecting
rather pitifully that everyone has been seeing you all along.

    Praying means giving up a false security, no longer looking
for arguments which will protect you if you get pushed into a
corner, no longer setting your hope on a couple of lighter moments which your life might still offer. Praying means to stop
expecting from God that same small-mindedness which you
discover in yourself. To pray is to walk in the full light of God,
and to say simply, without holding back, "I am a man and you
are God." At that moment, conversion occurs, the restoration
of the true relationship. Man is not the one who once in a
while makes a mistake and God is not the one who now and
then forgives. No, man is a sinner and God is love. Conversion
makes this obvious with a stunning simplicity and a disarming
clarity.

    This conversion brings with it the relaxation which lets you
breathe again and puts you at rest in the embrace of a forgiving God. The experience results in a calm and simple joy. For
then you can say: "I don't know the answer and I can't do this
thing, but I don't have to know it, and I don't have to be able
to do it."

Additional Scripture Readings:
Job 42:1–6; Psalm 8

*Go to page 984 for your next
devotional reading.*

Yet I will wait patiently for the day of calamity
  to come on the nation invading us.
17Though the fig tree does not bud
  and there are no grapes on the vines,
though the olive crop fails
  and the fields produce no food,
though there are no sheep in the pen
  and no cattle in the stalls,

18yet I will rejoice in the LORD,
  I will be joyful in God my Savior.

19The Sovereign LORD is my strength;
  he makes my feet like the feet of a deer,
  he enables me to go on the heights.

For the director of music. On my stringed instruments.

*ZEPHANIAH, early in Josiah's
reign and before his reforms
(2 Chronicles 34:1–13), prophesies
about a coming devastating day of
the Lord. But he promises a wonderful future to those who humble themselves, seek the Lord, and live righteously. As you read this book,
remember that a day of judgment is
coming but that you can escape by
turning to the Lord Jesus Christ.*

ZEPHANIAH

1 The word of the LORD that came to
Zephaniah son of Cushi, the son of
Gedaliah, the son of Amariah, the son of
Hezekiah, during the reign of Josiah son
of Amon king of Judah:

Warning of Coming Destruction

2"I will sweep away everything
    from the face of the earth,"
            declares the LORD.
3"I will sweep away both men and
        animals;
    I will sweep away the birds of the
        air
    and the fish of the sea.
The wicked will have only heaps of
    rubble*a*

when I cut off man from the face of
    the earth,"
            declares the LORD.

Against Judah

4"I will stretch out my hand against
        Judah
    and against all who live in
        Jerusalem.
I will cut off from this place every
        remnant of Baal,
    the names of the pagan and the
        idolatrous priests —
5those who bow down on the roofs
    to worship the starry host,
    those who bow down and swear by
        the LORD

---

*a*3 The meaning of the Hebrew for this line is uncertain.

and who also swear by Molech,[a]
⁶those who turn back from following
the LORD
and neither seek the LORD nor
inquire of him.
⁷Be silent before the Sovereign LORD,
for the day of the LORD is near.
The LORD has prepared a sacrifice;
he has consecrated those he has
invited.
⁸On the day of the LORD's sacrifice
I will punish the princes
and the king's sons
and all those clad
in foreign clothes.
⁹On that day I will punish
all who avoid stepping on the
threshold,[b]
who fill the temple of their gods
with violence and deceit.

¹⁰"On that day," declares the LORD,
"a cry will go up from the Fish
Gate,
wailing from the New Quarter,
and a loud crash from the hills.
¹¹Wail, you who live in the market
district[c];
all your merchants will be wiped
out,
all who trade with[d] silver will be
ruined.
¹²At that time I will search Jerusalem
with lamps
and punish those who are
complacent,
who are like wine left on its dregs,
who think, 'The LORD will do nothing,
either good or bad.'
¹³Their wealth will be plundered,
their houses demolished.
They will build houses
but not live in them;
they will plant vineyards
but not drink the wine.

The Great Day of the LORD

¹⁴"The great day of the LORD is near—
near and coming quickly.
Listen! The cry on the day of the LORD
will be bitter,
the shouting of the warrior there.
¹⁵That day will be a day of wrath,
a day of distress and anguish,
a day of trouble and ruin,
a day of darkness and gloom,
a day of clouds and blackness,

¹⁶a day of trumpet and battle cry
against the fortified cities
and against the corner towers.
¹⁷I will bring distress on the people
and they will walk like blind men,
because they have sinned against
the LORD.
Their blood will be poured out like dust
and their entrails like filth.
¹⁸Neither their silver nor their gold
will be able to save them
on the day of the LORD's wrath.
In the fire of his jealousy
the whole world will be consumed,
for he will make a sudden end
of all who live in the earth."

2 Gather together, gather together,
O shameful nation,
²before the appointed time arrives
and that day sweeps on like chaff,
before the fierce anger of the LORD
comes upon you,
before the day of the LORD's wrath
comes upon you.
³Seek the LORD, all you humble of the
land,
you who do what he commands.
Seek righteousness, seek humility;
perhaps you will be sheltered
on the day of the LORD's anger.

Against Philistia

⁴Gaza will be abandoned
and Ashkelon left in ruins.
At midday Ashdod will be emptied
and Ekron uprooted.
⁵Woe to you who live by the sea,
O Kerethite people;
the word of the LORD is against you,
O Canaan, land of the Philistines.

"I will destroy you,
and none will be left."

⁶The land by the sea, where the
Kerethites[e] dwell,
will be a place for shepherds and
sheep pens.
⁷It will belong to the remnant of the
house of Judah;
there they will find pasture.
In the evening they will lie down
in the houses of Ashkelon.
The LORD their God will care for them;
he will restore their fortunes.[f]

---

a5 Hebrew *Malcam*, that is, Milcom   b9 See 1 Samuel 5:5.   c11 Or *the Mortar*   d11 Or *in*
e6 The meaning of the Hebrew for this word is uncertain.   f7 Or *will bring back their captives*

Against Moab and Ammon

8"I have heard the insults of Moab
    and the taunts of the Ammonites,
who insulted my people
    and made threats against their land.
9Therefore, as surely as I live,"
    declares the Lord Almighty, the God
      of Israel,

"surely Moab will become like Sodom,
    the Ammonites like Gomorrah—
a place of weeds and salt pits,
    a wasteland forever.
The remnant of my people will
    plunder them;
    the survivors of my nation will
      inherit their land."

TUESDAY

VERSE FOR THE DAY:	AUTHOR:	PASSAGE FOR THE DAY:
Zephaniah 1:15	Philip Yancey	Zephaniah 1:14–18

A Sign of Mercy

THE most amazing feature of the prophets is not their "modern" outlook or their passionate cry of disappointment. The reason these seventeen books merit a close look is that they include God's own reply to the prophets' bracing questions . . .

My slowness to act is a sign of mercy, not of weakness.

When God did not punish quickly, the people of Israel presumed he had lost his power: "He will do nothing! No harm will come to us; we will never see sword or famine" (Jeremiah 5:12). They were wrong. God's restraint marked an interlude of mercy, a time of probation he was granting Israel. Reluctantly, like a parent out of options, God resorted to punishment.

For Israel, punishment took the form of foreign invasions. But the prophets also speak of a "day of the Lord" at the end of time. Sandwiched between their shining accounts of a new heaven and a new earth are some of the most dreadful apocalyptic visions ever set to words. Before we can hear the last word, said Dietrich Bonhoeffer, we must listen to the next-to-last word. And the more I study the prophets' accounts of the last days, the more content I become with God's apparent "shyness" to intervene in human affairs.

In my own times of disappointment with God, I have called on him to act with power. I have prayed against political tyranny and unfairness and injustice. I have prayed for miracle, for proof of God's existence. But as I read the prophets' descriptions of the day when God finally will take off all the wraps, one prayer overwhelms all others: "God, I hope I'm not around then." God freely admits he is holding back his power, but he restrains himself for our benefit. For all scoffers who call for direct action from the heavens, the prophets have ominous advice: Just wait.

Additional Scripture Readings:
Romans 2:1–11; 2 Peter 3:1–13

Go to page 988 for your next devotional reading.

¹⁰This is what they will get in return for
their pride,
for insulting and mocking the
people of the LORD Almighty.
¹¹The LORD will be awesome to them
when he destroys all the gods of the
land.
The nations on every shore will
worship him,
every one in its own land.

Against Cush

¹²"You too, O Cushites,ᵃ
will be slain by my sword."

Against Assyria

¹³He will stretch out his hand against
the north
and destroy Assyria,
leaving Nineveh utterly desolate
and dry as the desert.
¹⁴Flocks and herds will lie down there,
creatures of every kind.
The desert owl and the screech owl
will roost on her columns.
Their calls will echo through the
windows,
rubble will be in the doorways,
the beams of cedar will be exposed.
¹⁵This is the carefree city
that lived in safety.
She said to herself,
"I am, and there is none besides
me."
What a ruin she has become,
a lair for wild beasts!
All who pass by her scoff
and shake their fists.

The Future of Jerusalem

3 Woe to the city of oppressors,
rebellious and defiled!
²She obeys no one,
she accepts no correction.
She does not trust in the LORD,
she does not draw near to her God.
³Her officials are roaring lions,
her rulers are evening wolves,
who leave nothing for the morning.
⁴Her prophets are arrogant;
they are treacherous men.
Her priests profane the sanctuary
and do violence to the law.
⁵The LORD within her is righteous;
he does no wrong.
Morning by morning he dispenses his
justice,

and every new day he does not fail,
yet the unrighteous know no
shame.

⁶"I have cut off nations;
their strongholds are demolished.
I have left their streets deserted,
with no one passing through.
Their cities are destroyed;
no one will be left—no one at all.
⁷I said to the city,
'Surely you will fear me
and accept correction!'
Then her dwelling would not be cut
off,
nor all my punishments come upon
her.
But they were still eager
to act corruptly in all they did.
⁸Therefore wait for me," declares the
LORD,
"for the day I will stand up to
testify.ᵇ
I have decided to assemble the
nations,
to gather the kingdoms
and to pour out my wrath on them—
all my fierce anger.
The whole world will be consumed
by the fire of my jealous anger.

⁹"Then will I purify the lips of the
peoples,
that all of them may call on the
name of the LORD
and serve him shoulder to shoulder.
¹⁰From beyond the rivers of Cushᶜ
my worshipers, my scattered people,
will bring me offerings.
¹¹On that day you will not be put to
shame
for all the wrongs you have done to
me,
because I will remove from this city
those who rejoice in their pride.
Never again will you be haughty
on my holy hill.
¹²But I will leave within you
the meek and humble,
who trust in the name of the LORD.
¹³The remnant of Israel will do no
wrong;
they will speak no lies,
nor will deceit be found in their
mouths.
They will eat and lie down
and no one will make them afraid."

ᵃ12 That is, people from the upper Nile region   ᵇ8 Septuagint and Syriac; Hebrew *will rise up to*
plunder   ᶜ10 That is, the upper Nile region

¹⁴Sing, O Daughter of Zion;
   shout aloud, O Israel!
Be glad and rejoice with all your
   heart,
   O Daughter of Jerusalem!
¹⁵The LORD has taken away your
   punishment,
   he has turned back your enemy.
The LORD, the King of Israel, is with
   you;
   never again will you fear any harm.
¹⁶On that day they will say to
   Jerusalem,
   "Do not fear, O Zion;
   do not let your hands hang limp.
¹⁷The LORD your God is with you,
   he is mighty to save.
He will take great delight in you,
   he will quiet you with his love,
   he will rejoice over you with
   singing."

¹⁸"The sorrows for the appointed feasts
   I will remove from you;
   they are a burden and a reproach to
   you.ᵃ
¹⁹At that time I will deal
   with all who oppressed you;
I will rescue the lame
   and gather those who have been
   scattered.
I will give them praise and honor
   in every land where they were put
   to shame.
²⁰At that time I will gather you;
   at that time I will bring you
   home.
I will give you honor and praise
   among all the peoples of the
   earth
when I restore your fortunesᵇ
before your very eyes,"
                says the LORD.

ᵃ18 Or "I will gather you who mourn for the appointed feasts; / your reproach is a burden to you
ᵇ20 Or I bring back your captives

HAGGAI encourages the returning exiles (Ezra 4:24–5:2) to set proper priorities by rebuilding the temple of the Lord before they rebuild their own houses. He goes on to envision a time when all nations will come to the temple. As you read this book, decide to seek God's kingdom first, and rejoice in his promise of a new world when people everywhere will worship the Lord together.

HAGGAI

A Call to Build the House of the LORD

1 In the second year of King Darius, on the first day of the sixth month, the word of the LORD came through the prophet Haggai to Zerubbabel son of Shealtiel, governor of Judah, and to Joshua[a] son of Jehozadak, the high priest:

²This is what the LORD Almighty says: "These people say, 'The time has not yet come for the LORD's house to be built.'"

³Then the word of the LORD came through the prophet Haggai: ⁴"Is it a time for you yourselves to be living in your paneled houses, while this house remains a ruin?"

⁵Now this is what the LORD Almighty says: "Give careful thought to your ways.

⁶You have planted much, but have harvested little. You eat, but never have enough. You drink, but never have your fill. You put on clothes, but are not warm. You earn wages, only to put them in a purse with holes in it."

⁷This is what the LORD Almighty says: "Give careful thought to your ways. ⁸Go up into the mountains and bring down timber and build the house, so that I may take pleasure in it and be honored," says the LORD. ⁹"You expected much, but see, it turned out to be little. What you brought home, I blew away. Why?" declares the LORD Almighty. "Because of my house, which remains a ruin, while each of you is busy with his own house. ¹⁰Therefore, because of you the heavens have withheld

[a]1 A variant of *Jeshua*; here and elsewhere in Haggai

their dew and the earth its crops. ¹¹I called for a drought on the fields and the mountains, on the grain, the new wine, the oil and whatever the ground produces, on men and cattle, and on the labor of your hands."

¹²Then Zerubbabel son of Shealtiel, Joshua son of Jehozadak, the high priest, and the whole remnant of the people obeyed the voice of the LORD their God and the message of the prophet Haggai, because the LORD their God had sent him. And the people feared the LORD.

¹³Then Haggai, the LORD's messenger, gave this message of the LORD to the peo-

---

WEDNESDAY

VERSE FOR THE DAY:	AUTHOR:	PASSAGE FOR THE DAY:
Haggai 1:4	David W. Smith	Haggai 1:1–11

Twisted Priorities

MEN often have a distorted order of priorities. Physical things are more important than relationships. Status is obtained by the acquisition of material wealth rather than, say, the number of close friends. An acquaintance of mine years ago used to show disrespect for his wife's comments and attitudes by saying, "That's immaterial." It seems so strange that love, concern and relationships should take second place to the material emphasis of so many men.

This distortion of emphasis on the material is certainly not a recent development. The Old Testament prophet Haggai, for example, warned that we are more concerned about living in paneled houses (*material*) than we are about our relationship with God and our fellowman (*immaterial*).

A man's success is measured by how much wealth and power can be acquired. Divorced men will speak with little shame about their failures at home, but in sharp contrast are quite defensive if they fail in the business world. At a businessmen's lunch a man said, "I have spent the last thirty years reaching the top rung of the world's ladder of success. I now feel in my heart I was for all those years on the wrong ladder." Life had passed him by. Sure he had money, but his wealth was acquired at the expense of intimacy with his family and friends . . .

Men simply fear getting involved with others beyond a superficial level. This lack of intimacy is foreign to the Biblical command to "carry each other's burdens, and in this way you will fulfill the law of Christ" (Galatians 6:2). There is no way to do this while keeping others at arm's length. The Galatian letter (3:27–29) reminds us that we are to enjoy fellowship together, a oneness as believers in Christ. The barriers that separate us should be destroyed.

Additional Scripture Readings:
Galatians 6:1–10; Ephesians 2:11–22

Go to page 992 for your next devotional reading.

ple: "I am with you," declares the LORD. [14]So the LORD stirred up the spirit of Zerubbabel son of Shealtiel, governor of Judah, and the spirit of Joshua son of Jehozadak, the high priest, and the spirit of the whole remnant of the people. They came and began to work on the house of the LORD Almighty, their God, [15]on the twenty-fourth day of the sixth month in the second year of King Darius.

The Promised Glory of the New House

2 On the twenty-first day of the seventh month, the word of the LORD came through the prophet Haggai: [2]"Speak to Zerubbabel son of Shealtiel, governor of Judah, to Joshua son of Jehozadak, the high priest, and to the remnant of the people. Ask them, [3]'Who of you is left who saw this house in its former glory? How does it look to you now? Does it not seem to you like nothing? [4]But now be strong, O Zerubbabel,' declares the LORD. 'Be strong, O Joshua son of Jehozadak, the high priest. Be strong, all you people of the land,' declares the LORD, 'and work. For I am with you,' declares the LORD Almighty. [5]'This is what I covenanted with you when you came out of Egypt. And my Spirit remains among you. Do not fear.'

[6]"This is what the LORD Almighty says: 'In a little while I will once more shake the heavens and the earth, the sea and the dry land. [7]I will shake all nations, and the desired of all nations will come, and I will fill this house with glory,' says the LORD Almighty. [8]'The silver is mine and the gold is mine,' declares the LORD Almighty. [9]'The glory of this present house will be greater than the glory of the former house,' says the LORD Almighty. 'And in this place I will grant peace,' declares the LORD Almighty."

Blessings for a Defiled People

[10]On the twenty-fourth day of the ninth month, in the second year of Darius, the word of the LORD came to the prophet Haggai: [11]"This is what the LORD Almighty says: 'Ask the priests what the law says:

[12]If a person carries consecrated meat in the fold of his garment, and that fold touches some bread or stew, some wine, oil or other food, does it become consecrated?' "

The priests answered, "No."

[13]Then Haggai said, "If a person defiled by contact with a dead body touches one of these things, does it become defiled?"

"Yes," the priests replied, "it becomes defiled."

[14]Then Haggai said, " 'So it is with this people and this nation in my sight,' declares the LORD. 'Whatever they do and whatever they offer there is defiled.

[15]" 'Now give careful thought to this from this day on[a]—consider how things were before one stone was laid on another in the LORD's temple. [16]When anyone came to a heap of twenty measures, there were only ten. When anyone went to a wine vat to draw fifty measures, there were only twenty. [17]I struck all the work of your hands with blight, mildew and hail, yet you did not turn to me,' declares the LORD. [18]'From this day on, from this twenty-fourth day of the ninth month, give careful thought to the day when the foundation of the LORD's temple was laid. Give careful thought: [19]Is there yet any seed left in the barn? Until now, the vine and the fig tree, the pomegranate and the olive tree have not borne fruit.

" 'From this day on I will bless you.' "

Zerubbabel the LORD's Signet Ring

[20]The word of the LORD came to Haggai a second time on the twenty-fourth day of the month: [21]"Tell Zerubbabel governor of Judah that I will shake the heavens and the earth. [22]I will overturn royal thrones and shatter the power of the foreign kingdoms. I will overthrow chariots and their drivers; horses and their riders will fall, each by the sword of his brother.

[23]" 'On that day,' declares the LORD Almighty, 'I will take you, my servant Zerubbabel son of Shealtiel,' declares the LORD, 'and I will make you like my signet ring, for I have chosen you,' declares the LORD Almighty."

---

[a]15 Or to the days past

ZECHARIAH writes to inspire the returning exiles to turn to the Lord and continue rebuilding the temple in Jerusalem (Ezra 4:24–5:2). He encourages them with his visions that show God's control over everything and the coming new kingdom of the Messiah. As you read this book, be sure you have turned to the Lord and let these visions of hope inspire you to continue serving the Lord.

ZECHARIAH

A Call to Return to the LORD

1 In the eighth month of the second year of Darius, the word of the LORD came to the prophet Zechariah son of Berekiah, the son of Iddo:

2"The LORD was very angry with your forefathers. 3Therefore tell the people: This is what the LORD Almighty says: 'Return to me,' declares the LORD Almighty, 'and I will return to you,' says the LORD Almighty. 4Do not be like your forefathers, to whom the earlier prophets proclaimed: This is what the LORD Almighty says: 'Turn from your evil ways and your evil practices.' But they would not listen or pay attention to me, declares the LORD. 5Where are your forefathers now? And the prophets, do they live forever? 6But did not my words and my decrees, which I commanded my servants the prophets, overtake your forefathers?

"Then they repented and said, 'The LORD Almighty has done to us what our ways and practices deserve, just as he determined to do.' "

The Man Among the Myrtle Trees

7On the twenty-fourth day of the eleventh month, the month of Shebat, in the second year of Darius, the word of the LORD came to the prophet Zechariah son of Berekiah, the son of Iddo.

8During the night I had a vision—and there before me was a man riding a red horse! He was standing among the myrtle trees in a ravine. Behind him were red, brown and white horses.

⁹I asked, "What are these, my lord?"

The angel who was talking with me answered, "I will show you what they are."

¹⁰Then the man standing among the myrtle trees explained, "They are the ones the Lord has sent to go throughout the earth."

¹¹And they reported to the angel of the Lord, who was standing among the myrtle trees, "We have gone throughout the earth and found the whole world at rest and in peace."

¹²Then the angel of the Lord said, "Lord Almighty, how long will you withhold mercy from Jerusalem and from the towns of Judah, which you have been angry with these seventy years?" ¹³So the Lord spoke kind and comforting words to the angel who talked with me.

¹⁴Then the angel who was speaking to me said, "Proclaim this word: This is what the Lord Almighty says: 'I am very jealous for Jerusalem and Zion, ¹⁵but I am very angry with the nations that feel secure. I was only a little angry, but they added to the calamity.'

¹⁶"Therefore, this is what the Lord says: 'I will return to Jerusalem with mercy, and there my house will be rebuilt. And the measuring line will be stretched out over Jerusalem,' declares the Lord Almighty.

¹⁷"Proclaim further: This is what the Lord Almighty says: 'My towns will again overflow with prosperity, and the Lord will again comfort Zion and choose Jerusalem.' "

Four Horns and Four Craftsmen

¹⁸Then I looked up—and there before me were four horns! ¹⁹I asked the angel who was speaking to me, "What are these?"

He answered me, "These are the horns that scattered Judah, Israel and Jerusalem."

²⁰Then the Lord showed me four craftsmen. ²¹I asked, "What are these coming to do?"

He answered, "These are the horns that scattered Judah so that no one could raise his head, but the craftsmen have come to terrify them and throw down these horns of the nations who lifted up their horns against the land of Judah to scatter its people."

A Man With a Measuring Line

2 Then I looked up—and there before me was a man with a measuring line in his hand! ²I asked, "Where are you going?"

He answered me, "To measure Jerusalem, to find out how wide and how long it is."

³Then the angel who was speaking to me left, and another angel came to meet him ⁴and said to him: "Run, tell that young man, 'Jerusalem will be a city without walls because of the great number of men and livestock in it. ⁵And I myself will be a wall of fire around it,' declares the Lord, 'and I will be its glory within.'

⁶"Come! Come! Flee from the land of the north," declares the Lord, "for I have scattered you to the four winds of heaven," declares the Lord.

⁷"Come, O Zion! Escape, you who live in the Daughter of Babylon!" ⁸For this is what the Lord Almighty says: "After he has honored me and has sent me against the nations that have plundered you—for whoever touches you touches the apple of his eye—⁹I will surely raise my hand against them so that their slaves will plunder them.ᵃ Then you will know that the Lord Almighty has sent me.

¹⁰"Shout and be glad, O Daughter of Zion. For I am coming, and I will live among you," declares the Lord. ¹¹"Many nations will be joined with the Lord in that day and will become my people. I will live among you and you will know that the Lord Almighty has sent me to you. ¹²The Lord will inherit Judah as his portion in the holy land and will again choose Jerusalem. ¹³Be still before the Lord, all mankind, because he has roused himself from his holy dwelling."

Clean Garments for the High Priest

3 Then he showed me Joshuaᵇ the high priest standing before the angel of the Lord, and Satanᶜ standing at his right side to accuse him. ²The Lord said to Satan, "The Lord rebuke you, Satan! The Lord, who has chosen Jerusalem, rebuke you! Is not this man a burning stick snatched from the fire?"

³Now Joshua was dressed in filthy clothes as he stood before the angel. ⁴The angel said to those who were standing before him, "Take off his filthy clothes."

ᵃ8,9 Or says after . . . eye: ⁹"I . . . plunder them." Zechariah　ᶜ1 Satan means accuser.　ᵇ1 A variant of Jeshua; here and elsewhere in

Then he said to Joshua, "See, I have taken away your sin, and I will put rich garments on you."

⁵Then I said, "Put a clean turban on his head." So they put a clean turban on his head and clothed him, while the angel of the LORD stood by.

⁶The angel of the LORD gave this charge to Joshua: ⁷"This is what the LORD Almighty says: 'If you will walk in my ways and keep my requirements, then you will govern my house and have charge of my courts, and I will give you a place among these standing here.

⁸"'Listen, O high priest Joshua and your associates seated before you, who are men symbolic of things to come: I am going to bring my servant, the Branch. ⁹See, the stone I have set in front of Joshua! There are seven eyes[a] on that one stone, and I will engrave an inscription on it,' says the LORD Almighty, 'and I will

---

ᵃ9 Or *facets*

THURSDAY

VERSE FOR THE DAY:
Zechariah 2:13

AUTHOR:
A.W. Tozer

PASSAGE FOR THE DAY:
Zechariah 2:10–13

Experience Beyond Song

THERE is a notion widely held among Christians that song is the highest possible expression of the joy of the Lord in the soul of a man or woman.

That idea is so near to being true that it may seem spiritually rude to challenge it. However, it does need to be brought to the test of the Scriptures and Christian testimony.

Both the Bible and the testimony of a thousand saints show that there is experience beyond song. There are delights which the heart may enjoy in the awesome presence of God which cannot find expression in language: they belong to the unutterable elements in Christian experience. Not many enjoy them because not many know that they can.

The whole concept of ineffable worship has been lost to this generation of Christians. Our level of life is so low that no one expects to know the deep things of the soul until the Lord returns. So, we cheer ourselves by breaking into song.

Far be it from me to discourage the art of singing. Creation itself took its rise in a burst of song; Christ rose from the dead and sang among his brethren. But still there is something beyond song!

When the Holy Spirit is permitted to exercise his full sway in a redeemed heart there will likely be voluble praise first; then, when the crescendo rises beyond the ability of studied speech to express, comes song. When song breaks down under the weight of glory, then comes silence where the soul, held in deep fascination, feels itself blessed with an unutterable beatitude!

Additional Scripture Readings:
Psalm 46:8–11; Hebrews 12:25–29

Go to page 1001 for your next devotional reading.

remove the sin of this land in a single day.

[10] "'In that day each of you will invite his neighbor to sit under his vine and fig tree,' declares the LORD Almighty."

The Gold Lampstand and the Two Olive Trees

4 Then the angel who talked with me returned and wakened me, as a man is wakened from his sleep. [2] He asked me, "What do you see?"

I answered, "I see a solid gold lampstand with a bowl at the top and seven lights on it, with seven channels to the lights. [3] Also there are two olive trees by it, one on the right of the bowl and the other on its left."

[4] I asked the angel who talked with me, "What are these, my lord?"

[5] He answered, "Do you not know what these are?"

"No, my lord," I replied.

[6] So he said to me, "This is the word of the LORD to Zerubbabel: 'Not by might nor by power, but by my Spirit,' says the LORD Almighty.

[7] "What[a] are you, O mighty mountain? Before Zerubbabel you will become level ground. Then he will bring out the capstone to shouts of 'God bless it! God bless it!'"

[8] Then the word of the LORD came to me: [9] "The hands of Zerubbabel have laid the foundation of this temple; his hands will also complete it. Then you will know that the LORD Almighty has sent me to you.

[10] "Who despises the day of small things? Men will rejoice when they see the plumb line in the hand of Zerubbabel.

"(These seven are the eyes of the LORD, which range throughout the earth.)"

[11] Then I asked the angel, "What are these two olive trees on the right and the left of the lampstand?"

[12] Again I asked him, "What are these two olive branches beside the two gold pipes that pour out golden oil?"

[13] He replied, "Do you not know what these are?"

"No, my lord," I said.

[14] So he said, "These are the two who are anointed to[b] serve the Lord of all the earth."

The Flying Scroll

5 I looked again—and there before me was a flying scroll!

[2] He asked me, "What do you see?"

I answered, "I see a flying scroll, thirty feet long and fifteen feet wide.[c]"

[3] And he said to me, "This is the curse that is going out over the whole land; for according to what it says on one side, every thief will be banished, and according to what it says on the other, everyone who swears falsely will be banished. [4] The LORD Almighty declares, 'I will send it out, and it will enter the house of the thief and the house of him who swears falsely by my name. It will remain in his house and destroy it, both its timbers and its stones.'"

The Woman in a Basket

[5] Then the angel who was speaking to me came forward and said to me, "Look up and see what this is that is appearing."

[6] I asked, "What is it?"

He replied, "It is a measuring basket.[d]" And he added, "This is the iniquity[e] of the people throughout the land."

[7] Then the cover of lead was raised, and there in the basket sat a woman! [8] He said, "This is wickedness," and he pushed her back into the basket and pushed the lead cover down over its mouth.

[9] Then I looked up—and there before me were two women, with the wind in their wings! They had wings like those of a stork, and they lifted up the basket between heaven and earth.

[10] "Where are they taking the basket?" I asked the angel who was speaking to me.

[11] He replied, "To the country of Babylonia[f] to build a house for it. When it is ready, the basket will be set there in its place."

Four Chariots

6 I looked up again—and there before me were four chariots coming out from between two mountains—mountains of bronze! [2] The first chariot had red horses, the second black, [3] the third white, and the fourth dappled—all of them powerful. [4] I asked the angel who was speaking to me, "What are these, my lord?"

[5] The angel answered me, "These are the four spirits[g] of heaven, going out from standing in the presence of the Lord

[a]7 Or Who   [b]14 Or two who bring oil and (about 9 meters long and 4.5 meters wide)   [c]2 Hebrew twenty cubits long and ten cubits wide   [d]6 Hebrew an ephah; also in verses 7-11   [e]6 Or appearance   [f]11 Hebrew Shinar   [g]5 Or winds

of the whole world. ⁶The one with the black horses is going toward the north country, the one with the white horses toward the west,^a and the one with the dappled horses toward the south."

⁷When the powerful horses went out, they were straining to go throughout the earth. And he said, "Go throughout the earth!" So they went throughout the earth.

⁸Then he called to me, "Look, those going toward the north country have given my Spirit^b rest in the land of the north."

A Crown for Joshua

⁹The word of the LORD came to me: ¹⁰"Take silver and gold from the exiles Heldai, Tobijah and Jedaiah, who have arrived from Babylon. Go the same day to the house of Josiah son of Zephaniah. ¹¹Take the silver and gold and make a crown, and set it on the head of the high priest, Joshua son of Jehozadak. ¹²Tell him this is what the LORD Almighty says: 'Here is the man whose name is the Branch, and he will branch out from his place and build the temple of the LORD. ¹³It is he who will build the temple of the LORD, and he will be clothed with majesty and will sit and rule on his throne. And he will be a priest on his throne. And there will be harmony between the two.' ¹⁴The crown will be given to Heldai,^c Tobijah, Jedaiah and Hen^d son of Zephaniah as a memorial in the temple of the LORD. ¹⁵Those who are far away will come and help to build the temple of the LORD, and you will know that the LORD Almighty has sent me to you. This will happen if you diligently obey the LORD your God."

Justice and Mercy, Not Fasting

⁷ In the fourth year of King Darius, the word of the LORD came to Zechariah on the fourth day of the ninth month, the month of Kislev. ²The people of Bethel had sent Sharezer and Regem-Melech, together with their men, to entreat the LORD ³by asking the priests of the house of the LORD Almighty and the prophets, "Should I mourn and fast in the fifth month, as I have done for so many years?"

⁴Then the word of the LORD Almighty came to me: ⁵"Ask all the people of the land and the priests, 'When you fasted and mourned in the fifth and seventh months for the past seventy years, was it really for me that you fasted? ⁶And when you were eating and drinking, were you not just feasting for yourselves? ⁷Are these not the words the LORD proclaimed through the earlier prophets when Jerusalem and its surrounding towns were at rest and prosperous, and the Negev and the western foothills were settled?' "

⁸And the word of the LORD came again to Zechariah: ⁹"This is what the LORD Almighty says: 'Administer true justice; show mercy and compassion to one another. ¹⁰Do not oppress the widow or the fatherless, the alien or the poor. In your hearts do not think evil of each other.'

¹¹"But they refused to pay attention; stubbornly they turned their backs and stopped up their ears. ¹²They made their hearts as hard as flint and would not listen to the law or to the words that the LORD Almighty had sent by his Spirit through the earlier prophets. So the LORD Almighty was very angry.

¹³" 'When I called, they did not listen; so when they called, I would not listen,' says the LORD Almighty. ¹⁴'I scattered them with a whirlwind among all the nations, where they were strangers. The land was left so desolate behind them that no one could come or go. This is how they made the pleasant land desolate.' "

The LORD Promises to Bless Jerusalem

⁸ Again the word of the LORD Almighty came to me. ²This is what the LORD Almighty says: "I am very jealous for Zion; I am burning with jealousy for her."

³This is what the LORD says: "I will return to Zion and dwell in Jerusalem. Then Jerusalem will be called the City of Truth, and the mountain of the LORD Almighty will be called the Holy Mountain."

⁴This is what the LORD Almighty says: "Once again men and women of ripe old age will sit in the streets of Jerusalem, each with cane in hand because of his age. ⁵The city streets will be filled with boys and girls playing there."

⁶This is what the LORD Almighty says: "It may seem marvelous to the remnant of this people at that time, but will it seem marvelous to me?" declares the LORD Almighty.

⁷This is what the LORD Almighty says: "I will save my people from the countries of the east and the west. ⁸I will bring them back to live in Jerusalem; they will be my

---

^a6 Or *horses after them*   ^b8 Or *spirit*   ^c14 Syriac; Hebrew *Helem*   ^d14 Or *and the gracious one, the*

people, and I will be faithful and righteous to them as their God."

⁹This is what the LORD Almighty says: "You who now hear these words spoken by the prophets who were there when the foundation was laid for the house of the LORD Almighty, let your hands be strong so that the temple may be built. ¹⁰Before that time there were no wages for man or beast. No one could go about his business safely because of his enemy, for I had turned every man against his neighbor. ¹¹But now I will not deal with the remnant of this people as I did in the past," declares the LORD Almighty.

¹²"The seed will grow well, the vine will yield its fruit, the ground will produce its crops, and the heavens will drop their dew. I will give all these things as an inheritance to the remnant of this people. ¹³As you have been an object of cursing among the nations, O Judah and Israel, so will I save you, and you will be a blessing. Do not be afraid, but let your hands be strong."

¹⁴This is what the LORD Almighty says: "Just as I had determined to bring disaster upon you and showed no pity when your fathers angered me," says the LORD Almighty, ¹⁵"so now I have determined to do good again to Jerusalem and Judah. Do not be afraid. ¹⁶These are the things you are to do: Speak the truth to each other, and render true and sound judgment in your courts; ¹⁷do not plot evil against your neighbor, and do not love to swear falsely. I hate all this," declares the LORD.

¹⁸Again the word of the LORD Almighty came to me. ¹⁹This is what the LORD Almighty says: "The fasts of the fourth, fifth, seventh and tenth months will become joyful and glad occasions and happy festivals for Judah. Therefore love truth and peace."

²⁰This is what the LORD Almighty says: "Many peoples and the inhabitants of many cities will yet come, ²¹and the inhabitants of one city will go to another and say, 'Let us go at once to entreat the LORD and seek the LORD Almighty. I myself am going.' ²²And many peoples and powerful nations will come to Jerusalem to seek the LORD Almighty and to entreat him."

²³This is what the LORD Almighty says: "In those days ten men from all languages and nations will take firm hold of one Jew by the hem of his robe and say, 'Let us go with you, because we have heard that God is with you.' "

Judgment on Israel's Enemies
An Oracle

9 The word of the LORD is against the land of Hadrach
and will rest upon Damascus—
for the eyes of men and all the tribes of Israel
are on the LORD— *a*
²and upon Hamath too, which borders on it,
and upon Tyre and Sidon, though they are very skillful.
³Tyre has built herself a stronghold;
she has heaped up silver like dust,
and gold like the dirt of the streets.
⁴But the Lord will take away her possessions
and destroy her power on the sea,
and she will be consumed by fire.
⁵Ashkelon will see it and fear;
Gaza will writhe in agony,
and Ekron too, for her hope will wither.
Gaza will lose her king
and Ashkelon will be deserted.
⁶Foreigners will occupy Ashdod,
and I will cut off the pride of the Philistines.
⁷I will take the blood from their mouths,
the forbidden food from between their teeth.
Those who are left will belong to our God
and become leaders in Judah,
and Ekron will be like the Jebusites.
⁸But I will defend my house against marauding forces.
Never again will an oppressor overrun my people,
for now I am keeping watch.

The Coming of Zion's King

⁹Rejoice greatly, O Daughter of Zion!
Shout, Daughter of Jerusalem!
See, your king *b* comes to you,
righteous and having salvation,
gentle and riding on a donkey,
on a colt, the foal of a donkey.
¹⁰I will take away the chariots from Ephraim
and the war-horses from Jerusalem,

---

a 1 Or *Damascus. / For the eye of the LORD is on all mankind, / as well as on the tribes of Israel.*   *b* 9 Or *King*

and the battle bow will be broken.
He will proclaim peace to the nations.
His rule will extend from sea to sea
and from the River[a] to the ends of
the earth.[b]
[11]As for you, because of the blood of
my covenant with you,
I will free your prisoners from the
waterless pit.
[12]Return to your fortress, O prisoners of
hope;
even now I announce that I will
restore twice as much to you.
[13]I will bend Judah as I bend my bow
and fill it with Ephraim.
I will rouse your sons, O Zion,
against your sons, O Greece,
and make you like a warrior's
sword.

The LORD Will Appear

[14]Then the LORD will appear over them;
his arrow will flash like lightning.
The Sovereign LORD will sound the
trumpet;
he will march in the storms of the
south,
[15] and the LORD Almighty will shield
them.
They will destroy
and overcome with slingstones.
They will drink and roar as with wine;
they will be full like a bowl
used for sprinkling[c] the corners of
the altar.
[16]The LORD their God will save them on
that day
as the flock of his people.
They will sparkle in his land
like jewels in a crown.
[17]How attractive and beautiful they will
be!
Grain will make the young men
thrive,
and new wine the young women.

The LORD Will Care for Judah

10 Ask the LORD for rain in the
springtime;
it is the LORD who makes the storm
clouds.
He gives showers of rain to men,
and plants of the field to everyone.
[2]The idols speak deceit,
diviners see visions that lie;
they tell dreams that are false,
they give comfort in vain.

Therefore the people wander like
sheep
oppressed for lack of a shepherd.

[3]"My anger burns against the
shepherds,
and I will punish the leaders;
for the LORD Almighty will care
for his flock, the house of Judah,
and make them like a proud horse
in battle.
[4]From Judah will come the
cornerstone,
from him the tent peg,
from him the battle bow,
from him every ruler.
[5]Together they[d] will be like mighty
men
trampling the muddy streets in
battle.
Because the LORD is with them,
they will fight and overthrow the
horsemen.

[6]"I will strengthen the house of Judah
and save the house of Joseph.
I will restore them
because I have compassion on
them.
They will be as though
I had not rejected them,
for I am the LORD their God
and I will answer them.
[7]The Ephraimites will become like
mighty men,
and their hearts will be glad as with
wine.
Their children will see it and be
joyful;
their hearts will rejoice in the LORD.
[8]I will signal for them
and gather them in.
Surely I will redeem them;
they will be as numerous as before.
[9]Though I scatter them among the
peoples,
yet in distant lands they will
remember me.
They and their children will survive,
and they will return.
[10]I will bring them back from Egypt
and gather them from Assyria.
I will bring them to Gilead and
Lebanon,
and there will not be room enough
for them.
[11]They will pass through the sea of
trouble;

---

a10 That is, the Euphrates   b10 Or the end of the land   c15 Or bowl, / like   d4,5 Or ruler, all of
them together. / 5They

the surging sea will be subdued
and all the depths of the Nile will
dry up.
Assyria's pride will be brought down
and Egypt's scepter will pass away.
¹²I will strengthen them in the LORD
and in his name they will walk,"
declares the LORD.

11
Open your doors, O Lebanon,
so that fire may devour your
cedars!
²Wail, O pine tree, for the cedar has
fallen;
the stately trees are ruined!
Wail, oaks of Bashan;
the dense forest has been cut down!
³Listen to the wail of the shepherds;
their rich pastures are destroyed!
Listen to the roar of the lions;
the lush thicket of the Jordan is
ruined!

Two Shepherds

⁴This is what the LORD my God says:
"Pasture the flock marked for slaughter.
⁵Their buyers slaughter them and go unpunished. Those who sell them say,
'Praise the LORD, I am rich!' Their own
shepherds do not spare them. ⁶For I will
no longer have pity on the people of the
land," declares the LORD. "I will hand everyone over to his neighbor and his king.
They will oppress the land, and I will not
rescue them from their hands."

⁷So I pastured the flock marked for
slaughter, particularly the oppressed of
the flock. Then I took two staffs and called
one Favor and the other Union, and I pastured the flock. ⁸In one month I got rid of
the three shepherds.

The flock detested me, and I grew weary of them ⁹and said, "I will not be your
shepherd. Let the dying die, and the perishing perish. Let those who are left eat
one another's flesh."

¹⁰Then I took my staff called Favor and
broke it, revoking the covenant I had
made with all the nations. ¹¹It was revoked on that day, and so the afflicted of
the flock who were watching me knew it
was the word of the LORD.

¹²I told them, "If you think it best, give
me my pay; but if not, keep it." So they
paid me thirty pieces of silver.

¹³And the LORD said to me, "Throw it to
the potter" — the handsome price at which
they priced me! So I took the thirty pieces
of silver and threw them into the house of
the LORD to the potter.

¹⁴Then I broke my second staff called
Union, breaking the brotherhood between
Judah and Israel.

¹⁵Then the LORD said to me, "Take again
the equipment of a foolish shepherd.
¹⁶For I am going to raise up a shepherd
over the land who will not care for the
lost, or seek the young, or heal the injured, or feed the healthy, but will eat the
meat of the choice sheep, tearing off their
hoofs.

¹⁷"Woe to the worthless shepherd,
who deserts the flock!
May the sword strike his arm and his
right eye!
May his arm be completely
withered,
his right eye totally blinded!"

Jerusalem's Enemies to Be Destroyed

An Oracle

12
This is the word of the LORD concerning Israel. The LORD, who
stretches out the heavens, who lays the
foundation of the earth, and who forms
the spirit of man within him, declares: ²"I
am going to make Jerusalem a cup that
sends all the surrounding peoples reeling.
Judah will be besieged as well as Jerusalem. ³On that day, when all the nations of
the earth are gathered against her, I will
make Jerusalem an immovable rock for all
the nations. All who try to move it will in-
jure themselves. ⁴On that day I will strike
every horse with panic and its rider with
madness," declares the LORD. "I will keep
a watchful eye over the house of Judah,
but I will blind all the horses of the nations. ⁵Then the leaders of Judah will say
in their hearts, 'The people of Jerusalem
are strong, because the LORD Almighty is
their God.'

⁶"On that day I will make the leaders of
Judah like a firepot in a woodpile, like a
flaming torch among sheaves. They will
consume right and left all the surrounding
peoples, but Jerusalem will remain intact
in her place.

⁷"The LORD will save the dwellings of
Judah first, so that the honor of the house
of David and of Jerusalem's inhabitants
may not be greater than that of Judah. ⁸On
that day the LORD will shield those who
live in Jerusalem, so that the feeblest
among them will be like David, and the
house of David will be like God, like the
Angel of the LORD going before them. ⁹On
that day I will set out to destroy all the nations that attack Jerusalem.

Mourning for the One They Pierced

10"And I will pour out on the house of David and the inhabitants of Jerusalem a spirit[a] of grace and supplication. They will look on[b] me, the one they have pierced, and they will mourn for him as one mourns for an only child, and grieve bitterly for him as one grieves for a first-born son. 11On that day the weeping in Jerusalem will be great, like the weeping of Hadad Rimmon in the plain of Megiddo. 12The land will mourn, each clan by itself, with their wives by themselves: the clan of the house of David and their wives, the clan of the house of Nathan and their wives, 13the clan of the house of Levi and their wives, the clan of Shimei and their wives, 14and all the rest of the clans and their wives.

Cleansing From Sin

13 "On that day a fountain will be opened to the house of David and the inhabitants of Jerusalem, to cleanse them from sin and impurity.

2"On that day, I will banish the names of the idols from the land, and they will be remembered no more," declares the LORD Almighty. "I will remove both the prophets and the spirit of impurity from the land. 3And if anyone still prophesies, his father and mother, to whom he was born, will say to him, 'You must die, because you have told lies in the LORD's name.' When he prophesies, his own parents will stab him.

4"On that day every prophet will be ashamed of his prophetic vision. He will not put on a prophet's garment of hair in order to deceive. 5He will say, 'I am not a prophet. I am a farmer; the land has been my livelihood since my youth.[c]' 6If someone asks him, 'What are these wounds on your body[d]?' he will answer, 'The wounds I was given at the house of my friends.'

The Shepherd Struck, the Sheep Scattered

7"Awake, O sword, against my
    shepherd,
    against the man who is close to
    me!"
    declares the LORD Almighty.
"Strike the shepherd,

and the sheep will be scattered,
    and I will turn my hand against the
    little ones.
8In the whole land," declares the LORD,
    "two-thirds will be struck down and
    perish;
    yet one-third will be left in it.
9This third I will bring into the fire;
    I will refine them like silver
    and test them like gold.
They will call on my name
    and I will answer them;
I will say, 'They are my people,'
    and they will say, 'The LORD is our
    God.'"

The LORD Comes and Reigns

14 A day of the LORD is coming when your plunder will be divided among you.

2I will gather all the nations to Jerusalem to fight against it; the city will be captured, the houses ransacked, and the women raped. Half of the city will go into exile, but the rest of the people will not be taken from the city. 3Then the LORD will go out and fight against those nations, as he fights in the day of battle. 4On that day his feet will stand on the Mount of Olives, east of Jerusalem, and the Mount of Olives will be split in two from east to west, forming a great valley, with half of the mountain moving north and half moving south. 5You will flee by my mountain valley, for it will extend to Azel. You will flee as you fled from the earthquake[e] in the days of Uzziah king of Judah. Then the LORD my God will come, and all the holy ones with him.

6On that day there will be no light, no cold or frost. 7It will be a unique day, without daytime or nighttime—a day known to the LORD. When evening comes, there will be light.

8On that day living water will flow out from Jerusalem, half to the eastern sea[f] and half to the western sea,[g] in summer and in winter.

9The LORD will be king over the whole earth. On that day there will be one LORD, and his name the only name.

10The whole land, from Geba to Rimmon, south of Jerusalem, will become like the Arabah. But Jerusalem will be raised up and remain in its place, from the Benja-

---

a10 Or the Spirit   b10 Or to   c5 Or farmer; a man sold me in my youth   d6 Or wounds between your hands   e5 Or 5My mountain valley will be blocked and will extend to Azel. It will be blocked as it was blocked because of the earthquake   f8 That is, the Dead Sea   g8 That is, the Mediterranean min Gate to the site of the First Gate, to the Corner Gate, and from the Tower of Hananel to the royal winepresses. ¹¹It will be inhabited; never again will it be destroyed. Jerusalem will be secure.

¹²This is the plague with which the LORD will strike all the nations that fought against Jerusalem: Their flesh will rot while they are still standing on their feet, their eyes will rot in their sockets, and their tongues will rot in their mouths. ¹³On that day men will be stricken by the LORD with great panic. Each man will seize the hand of another, and they will attack each other. ¹⁴Judah too will fight at Jerusalem. The wealth of all the surrounding nations will be collected—great quantities of gold and silver and clothing. ¹⁵A similar plague will strike the horses and mules, the camels and donkeys, and all the animals in those camps.

¹⁶Then the survivors from all the nations that have attacked Jerusalem will go up year after year to worship the King, the LORD Almighty, and to celebrate the Feast of Tabernacles. ¹⁷If any of the peoples of the earth do not go up to Jerusalem to worship the King, the LORD Almighty, they will have no rain. ¹⁸If the Egyptian people do not go up and take part, they will have no rain. The LORD[a] will bring on them the plague he inflicts on the nations that do not go up to celebrate the Feast of Tabernacles. ¹⁹This will be the punishment of Egypt and the punishment of all the nations that do not go up to celebrate the Feast of Tabernacles.

²⁰On that day HOLY TO THE LORD will be inscribed on the bells of the horses, and the cooking pots in the LORD's house will be like the sacred bowls in front of the altar. ²¹Every pot in Jerusalem and Judah will be holy to the LORD Almighty, and all who come to sacrifice will take some of the pots and cook in them. And on that day there will no longer be a Canaanite[b] in the house of the LORD Almighty.

MALACHI prophesies during the deplorable conditions described in Nehemiah 13. He calls those complacent in their spiritual life to a renewed relationship with God, promising them God's blessing if they do. As you read this book, promise the Lord that you will not be complacent in your faith but will put his will before your own concerns.

MALACHI

1 An oracle: The word of the LORD to Israel through Malachi.*a*

Jacob Loved, Esau Hated

2"I have loved you," says the LORD.

"But you ask, 'How have you loved us?'

"Was not Esau Jacob's brother?" the LORD says. "Yet I have loved Jacob, **3**but Esau I have hated, and I have turned his mountains into a wasteland and left his inheritance to the desert jackals."

4Edom may say, "Though we have been crushed, we will rebuild the ruins."

But this is what the LORD Almighty says: "They may build, but I will demolish. They will be called the Wicked Land, a people always under the wrath of the LORD. **5**You will see it with your own eyes and say, 'Great is the LORD—even beyond the borders of Israel!'

Blemished Sacrifices

6"A son honors his father, and a servant his master. If I am a father, where is the honor due me? If I am a master, where is the respect due me?" says the LORD Almighty. "It is you, O priests, who show contempt for my name.

"But you ask, 'How have we shown contempt for your name?'

7"You place defiled food on my altar.

"But you ask, 'How have we defiled you?'

"By saying that the LORD's table is contemptible. **8**When you bring blind animals for sacrifice, is that not wrong? When you sacrifice crippled or diseased animals, is that not wrong? Try offering them to your governor! Would he be pleased with you? Would he accept you?" says the LORD Almighty.

⁹"Now implore God to be gracious to us. With such offerings from your hands, will he accept you?"—says the LORD Almighty.

¹⁰"Oh, that one of you would shut the temple doors, so that you would not light useless fires on my altar! I am not pleased with you," says the LORD Almighty, "and I will accept no offering from your hands. ¹¹My name will be great among the nations, from the rising to the setting of the sun. In every place incense and pure offerings will be brought to my name, because my name will be great among the nations," says the LORD Almighty. ¹²"But you profane it by saying of the Lord's table, 'It is defiled,' and of its food, 'It is contemptible.' ¹³And you say, 'What a burden!' and you sniff at it contemptuously," says the LORD Almighty.

FRIDAY

VERSE FOR THE DAY:
Malachi 2:15

AUTHOR:
James Dobson

PASSAGE FOR THE DAY:
Malachi 2:13–16

Flat Tires

THERE are times in every good marriage when a husband and wife don't like each other very much. There are occasions when they feel as though they will never love their partners again. Emotions are like that. They flatten out occasionally like an automobile tire with a nail in the tread. Riding on the rim is a pretty bumpy experience for everyone on board.

I attended the fiftieth wedding anniversary for two friends a few years ago and the man made an incredible statement to his guests. He said he and his wife had never had a serious fight or argument in the fifty years since they were married. That was either a lot of baloney or he and his wife had a very boring relationship. Maybe both were true. To the newly married couples . . . I must say: Don't count on having that kind of placid relationship. There *will* be times of conflict and disagreement. There *will* be periods of emotional blandness when you can generate nothing but a yawn for one another. That's life, as they say.

What will you do, then, when unexpected tornadoes blow through your home, or when the doldrums leave your sails sagging and silent? Will you pack it in and go home to Mama? Will you pout and cry and seek ways to strike back? Or will your commitment hold you steady? These questions must be addressed *now*, before Satan has an opportunity to put his noose of discouragement around your neck. Set your jaw and clench your fists. Nothing short of death must ever be permitted to come between the two of you. *Nothing!*

Additional Scripture Readings:
Matthew 19:1–12;
1 Corinthians 7:1–11

Go to page 1002 for your next devotional reading.

WEEKENDING

RESTORE

Accompanying Mother Teresa . . . to the Home
for the Dying, to the lepers and unwanted
children, I found I went through three phases.
The first was horror mixed with pity, the
second compassion pure and simple, and the
third, reaching far beyond compassion,
something I had never experienced before—an
awareness that these dying and derelict men
and women, these lepers with stumps instead of
hands, these unwanted children, were not
pitiable, repulsive or forlorn, but rather dear
and delightful; as it might be, friends of long
standing, brothers and sisters. How is it to be
explained—the very heart and mystery of the
Christian faith? To soothe those battered old
heads, to grasp those poor stumps, to take in
one's arms those children consigned to
dustbins, because it is his head, as they are his
stumps and his children, of whom he said that
whosoever received one such child in his name
received him.

– Malcolm Muggeridge

REVIVE

Saturday: Zechariah 7:8–10
Sunday: Matthew 25:31–40

Go to page 1004 for your next devotional reading.

"When you bring injured, crippled or diseased animals and offer them as sacrifices, should I accept them from your hands?" says the Lord. [14]"Cursed is the cheat who has an acceptable male in his flock and vows to give it, but then sacrifices a blemished animal to the Lord. For I am a great king," says the Lord Almighty, "and my name is to be feared among the nations.

Admonition for the Priests

2 "And now this admonition is for you, O priests. [2]If you do not listen, and if you do not set your heart to honor my name," says the Lord Almighty, "I will send a curse upon you, and I will curse your blessings. Yes, I have already cursed them, because you have not set your heart to honor me.

[3]"Because of you I will rebuke[a] your descendants[b]; I will spread on your faces the offal from your festival sacrifices, and you will be carried off with it. [4]And you will know that I have sent you this admonition so that my covenant with Levi may continue," says the Lord Almighty. [5]"My covenant was with him, a covenant of life and peace, and I gave them to him; this called for reverence and he revered me and stood in awe of my name. [6]True instruction was in his mouth and nothing false was found on his lips. He walked with me in peace and uprightness, and turned many from sin.

[7]"For the lips of a priest ought to preserve knowledge, and from his mouth men should seek instruction—because he is the messenger of the Lord Almighty. [8]But you have turned from the way and by your teaching have caused many to stumble; you have violated the covenant with Levi," says the Lord Almighty. [9]"So I have caused you to be despised and humiliated before all the people, because you have not followed my ways but have shown partiality in matters of the law."

Judah Unfaithful

[10]Have we not all one Father[c]? Did not one God create us? Why do we profane the covenant of our fathers by breaking faith with one another?

[11]Judah has broken faith. A detestable thing has been committed in Israel and in Jerusalem: Judah has desecrated the sanctuary the Lord loves, by marrying the daughter of a foreign god. [12]As for the man who does this, whoever he may be, may the Lord cut him off from the tents of Jacob[d]—even though he brings offerings to the Lord Almighty.

[13]Another thing you do: You flood the Lord's altar with tears. You weep and wail because he no longer pays attention to your offerings or accepts them with pleasure from your hands. [14]You ask, "Why?" It is because the Lord is acting as the witness between you and the wife of your youth, because you have broken faith with her, though she is your partner, the wife of your marriage covenant.

[15]Has not ‚the Lord‚ made them one? In flesh and spirit they are his. And why one? Because he was seeking godly offspring.[e] So guard yourself in your spirit, and do not break faith with the wife of your youth.

[16]"I hate divorce," says the Lord God of Israel, "and I hate a man's covering himself[f] with violence as well as with his garment," says the Lord Almighty.

So guard yourself in your spirit, and do not break faith.

The Day of Judgment

[17]You have wearied the Lord with your words.

"How have we wearied him?" you ask.

By saying, "All who do evil are good in the eyes of the Lord, and he is pleased with them" or "Where is the God of justice?"

3 "See, I will send my messenger, who will prepare the way before me. Then suddenly the Lord you are seeking will come to his temple; the messenger of the covenant, whom you desire, will come," says the Lord Almighty.

[2]But who can endure the day of his coming? Who can stand when he appears? For he will be like a refiner's fire or a launderer's soap. [3]He will sit as a refiner and purifier of silver; he will purify the Levites and refine them like gold and silver. Then the Lord will have men who will bring offerings in righteousness, [4]and the offerings of Judah and Jerusalem will be acceptable to the Lord, as in days gone by, as in former years.

[5]"So I will come near to you for judg-

---

[a]3 Or cut off (see Septuagint)   [b]3 Or will blight your grain   [c]10 Or father   [d]12 Or [12]May the Lord cut off from the tents of Jacob anyone who gives testimony in behalf of the man who does this   [e]15 Or [15]But the one ‚who is our father‚ did not do this, not as long as life remained in him. And what was he seeking? An offspring from God   [f]16 Or his wife

ment. I will be quick to testify against sorcerers, adulterers and perjurers, against those who defraud laborers of their wages, who oppress the widows and the fatherless, and deprive aliens of justice, but do not fear me," says the LORD Almighty.

Robbing God

⁶"I the LORD do not change. So you, O descendants of Jacob, are not destroyed. ⁷Ever since the time of your forefathers you have turned away from my decrees and have not kept them. Return to me, and I will return to you," says the LORD Almighty.

"But you ask, 'How are we to return?'

⁸"Will a man rob God? Yet you rob me.

"But you ask, 'How do we rob you?'

"In tithes and offerings. ⁹You are under

MONDAY

VERSE FOR THE DAY: AUTHOR: PASSAGE FOR THE DAY:
Malachi 4:2   Philip Yancey   Malachi 4:1–6

One Last Message

NO SUMMARY of the prophets would be complete apart from one last message: their loud insistence that the world will not end in "universal final defeat," but in Joy. They spoke in foreboding times to audiences filled with fear, and often their dire predictions of droughts and locust plagues and enemy sieges fueled that fear. But always, in every one of their seventeen books, the prophets of the Old Testament got around to a word of hope. The wounded lover will recover from his pain, Isaiah promises: "For a brief moment I abandoned you, but with deep compassion I will bring you back" (Isaiah 54:7).

Their voices soar like songbirds' when the prophets turn at last to describe the Joy beyond the walls of the world. In that final day, God will roll up the earth like a carpet and weave it anew. Wolves and lambs will feed together in the same field, and a lion graze in peace beside an ox.

One day, says Malachi, we will leap like calves released from the stall. There will be no fear then, and no pain. No infants will die; no tears will fall. Among the nations, peace will flow like a river, and armies will melt their weapons into farm tools. No one will complain about the hiddenness of God in that day. His glory will fill the earth, and the sun will seem dim by contrast.

For the prophets, human history is not an end in itself but a transition time, a parenthesis between Eden and the new heaven and new earth still to be formed by God. Even when everything seems out of control, God is firmly in control, and someday will assert himself.

Additional Scripture Readings: *Go to page 1011 for your next*
Isaiah 11:1–9; Revelation 22:1–6   *devotional reading.*

a curse—the whole nation of you—because you are robbing me. **10**Bring the whole tithe into the storehouse, that there may be food in my house. Test me in this," says the LORD Almighty, "and see if I will not throw open the floodgates of heaven and pour out so much blessing that you will not have room enough for it. **11**I will prevent pests from devouring your crops, and the vines in your fields will not cast their fruit," says the LORD Almighty. **12**"Then all the nations will call you blessed, for yours will be a delightful land," says the LORD Almighty.

13"You have said harsh things against me," says the LORD.

"Yet you ask, 'What have we said against you?'

14"You have said, 'It is futile to serve God. What did we gain by carrying out his requirements and going about like mourners before the LORD Almighty? **15**But now we call the arrogant blessed. Certainly the evildoers prosper, and even those who challenge God escape.' "

16Then those who feared the LORD talked with each other, and the LORD listened and heard. A scroll of remembrance was written in his presence concerning those who feared the LORD and honored his name.

17"They will be mine," says the LORD Almighty, "in the day when I make up my treasured possession.*a* I will spare them, just as in compassion a man spares his son who serves him. **18**And you will again see the distinction between the righteous and the wicked, between those who serve God and those who do not.

The Day of the LORD

4 "Surely the day is coming; it will burn like a furnace. All the arrogant and every evildoer will be stubble, and that day that is coming will set them on fire," says the LORD Almighty. "Not a root or a branch will be left to them. **2**But for you who revere my name, the sun of righteousness will rise with healing in its wings. And you will go out and leap like calves released from the stall. **3**Then you will trample down the wicked; they will be ashes under the soles of your feet on the day when I do these things," says the LORD Almighty.

4"Remember the law of my servant Moses, the decrees and laws I gave him at Horeb for all Israel.

5"See, I will send you the prophet Elijah before that great and dreadful day of the LORD comes. **6**He will turn the hearts of the fathers to their children, and the hearts of the children to their fathers; or else I will come and strike the land with a curse."

a17 Or Almighty, "my treasured possession, in the day when I act

NEW TESTAMENT

MATTHEW writes this Gospel to emphasize how Jesus fulfills God's promises from the Old Testament. He includes numerous sayings of Jesus about living as one of his disciples and as a member of the church, concluding with the command of Jesus to make disciples of all nations. As you read this book, ask yourself whether you are living as a disciple of Jesus, as well as how you can tell others the story of Jesus.

MATTHEW

The Genealogy of Jesus

1 A record of the genealogy of Jesus Christ the son of David, the son of Abraham:

²Abraham was the father of Isaac,
Isaac the father of Jacob,
Jacob the father of Judah and his brothers,
³Judah the father of Perez and Zerah, whose mother was Tamar,
Perez the father of Hezron,
Hezron the father of Ram,
⁴Ram the father of Amminadab,
Amminadab the father of Nahshon,
Nahshon the father of Salmon,
⁵Salmon the father of Boaz, whose mother was Rahab,
Boaz the father of Obed, whose mother was Ruth,
Obed the father of Jesse,
⁶and Jesse the father of King David.

David was the father of Solomon, whose mother had been Uriah's wife,
⁷Solomon the father of Rehoboam,
Rehoboam the father of Abijah,
Abijah the father of Asa,
⁸Asa the father of Jehoshaphat,
Jehoshaphat the father of Jehoram,
Jehoram the father of Uzziah,
⁹Uzziah the father of Jotham,
Jotham the father of Ahaz,
Ahaz the father of Hezekiah,

¹⁰Hezekiah the father of Manasseh,
Manasseh the father of Amon,
Amon the father of Josiah,
¹¹and Josiah the father of Jeconiah[a]
and his brothers at the time of
the exile to Babylon.

¹²After the exile to Babylon:
Jeconiah was the father of Sheal-
tiel,
Shealtiel the father of Zerubbabel,
¹³Zerubbabel the father of Abiud,
Abiud the father of Eliakim,
Eliakim the father of Azor,
¹⁴Azor the father of Zadok,
Zadok the father of Akim,
Akim the father of Eliud,
¹⁵Eliud the father of Eleazar,
Eleazar the father of Matthan,
Matthan the father of Jacob,
¹⁶and Jacob the father of Joseph, the
husband of Mary, of whom was
born Jesus, who is called Christ.

¹⁷Thus there were fourteen generations
in all from Abraham to David, fourteen
from David to the exile to Babylon, and
fourteen from the exile to the Christ.[b]

The Birth of Jesus Christ

¹⁸This is how the birth of Jesus Christ
came about: His mother Mary was
pledged to be married to Joseph, but before they came together, she was found to
be with child through the Holy Spirit.
¹⁹Because Joseph her husband was a righteous man and did not want to expose her
to public disgrace, he had in mind to divorce her quietly.

²⁰But after he had considered this, an
angel of the Lord appeared to him in a
dream and said, "Joseph son of David, do
not be afraid to take Mary home as your
wife, because what is conceived in her is
from the Holy Spirit. ²¹She will give birth
to a son, and you are to give him the name
Jesus,[c] because he will save his people
from their sins."

²²All this took place to fulfill what the
Lord had said through the prophet: ²³"The
virgin will be with child and will give birth
to a son, and they will call him Immanuel"[d]—which means, "God with us."

²⁴When Joseph woke up, he did what
the angel of the Lord had commanded
him and took Mary home as his wife.

²⁵But he had no union with her until she
gave birth to a son. And he gave him the
name Jesus.

The Visit of the Magi

2 After Jesus was born in Bethlehem in
Judea, during the time of King Herod,
Magi[e] from the east came to Jerusalem
²and asked, "Where is the one who has
been born king of the Jews? We saw his
star in the east[f] and have come to worship him."

³When King Herod heard this he was
disturbed, and all Jerusalem with him.
⁴When he had called together all the people's chief priests and teachers of the law,
he asked them where the Christ[g] was to
be born. ⁵"In Bethlehem in Judea," they
replied, "for this is what the prophet has
written:

⁶" 'But you, Bethlehem, in the land of
Judah,
are by no means least among the
rulers of Judah;
for out of you will come a ruler
who will be the shepherd of my
people Israel.'[h]"

⁷Then Herod called the Magi secretly
and found out from them the exact time
the star had appeared. ⁸He sent them to
Bethlehem and said, "Go and make a careful search for the child. As soon as you
find him, report to me, so that I too may
go and worship him."

⁹After they had heard the king, they
went on their way, and the star they had
seen in the east[i] went ahead of them
until it stopped over the place where
the child was. ¹⁰When they saw the star,
they were overjoyed. ¹¹On coming to the
house, they saw the child with his mother
Mary, and they bowed down and worshiped him. Then they opened their treasures and presented him with gifts of gold
and of incense and of myrrh. ¹²And having been warned in a dream not to go back
to Herod, they returned to their country
by another route.

The Escape to Egypt

¹³When they had gone, an angel of the
Lord appeared to Joseph in a dream. "Get
up," he said, "take the child and his mother and escape to Egypt. Stay there until I

---

a11 That is, Jehoiachin; also in verse 12
(Hebrew) both mean "the Anointed One."   c21 Jesus is the Greek form of Joshua, which means the
LORD saves.   d23 Isaiah 7:14   e1 Traditionally Wise Men   f2 Or star when it rose   g4 Or
Messiah   h6 Micah 5:2   i9 Or seen when it rose   b17 Or Messiah. "The Christ" (Greek) and "the Messiah"

tell you, for Herod is going to search for the child to kill him."

[14]So he got up, took the child and his mother during the night and left for Egypt, [15]where he stayed until the death of Herod. And so was fulfilled what the Lord had said through the prophet: "Out of Egypt I called my son."[a]

[16]When Herod realized that he had been outwitted by the Magi, he was furious, and he gave orders to kill all the boys in Bethlehem and its vicinity who were two years old and under, in accordance with the time he had learned from the Magi. [17]Then what was said through the prophet Jeremiah was fulfilled:

[18]"A voice is heard in Ramah,

[a]15 Hosea 11:1

TUESDAY

VERSE FOR THE DAY:
Matthew 1:20

AUTHOR:
Michael Card

PASSAGE FOR THE DAY:
Matthew 1:18–25

How Could It Be?

JOSEPH was the first person to really struggle with the Incarnation. Mary's momentary "How will this be?" [see Luke 1:34] seemed to come and go, like a cool breeze. But Joseph saw no angels. He only dreamed dreams. He had no quickening in his belly to tell him that life had indeed been conceived without his flesh. We know almost nothing about Joseph, apart from his gentleness and willingness to say "No" to himself for Mary's sake and for God's.

Imagine the dilemma of that simple man, finding himself cast in the role of father to the Son of God. Though that beautiful infant was not part of his body, the baby must have quickly taken over Joseph's heart, as most adopted children have a way of doing. As he held that squirming bundle in his arms, Joseph must have asked the question every new father asks himself and God, "How could it be?" . . .

It is an impossible task, being a parent. Not just difficult . . . impossible. To take a life from its first breath on through to maturity—to feed, clothe, educate, and all the rest. How could it be? . . .

How did Joseph do? We regretfully have no scenes of him with Jesus in the carpenter shop. But since Jesus was also known as a carpenter, he must have learned his trade somewhere, and why not from Joseph? We know for certain that Jesus made it to manhood with a wonderfully strong and simple vision of what *father* meant. He must have learned it at least in part from Joseph. Before he shrieked, "Abba!" with a man's tormented voice in the garden of Gethsemane, he must have tenderly called out that same name in an innocent child's voice to that man in the shadows, Joseph.

Additional Scripture Readings:
Mark 14:32–36; Romans 8:12–17

Go to page 1014 for your next devotional reading.

weeping and great mourning,
Rachel weeping for her children
and refusing to be comforted,
because they are no more."[a]

The Return to Nazareth

[19]After Herod died, an angel of the Lord appeared in a dream to Joseph in Egypt [20]and said, "Get up, take the child and his mother and go to the land of Israel, for those who were trying to take the child's life are dead."

[21]So he got up, took the child and his mother and went to the land of Israel. [22]But when he heard that Archelaus was reigning in Judea in place of his father Herod, he was afraid to go there. Having been warned in a dream, he withdrew to the district of Galilee, [23]and he went and lived in a town called Nazareth. So was fulfilled what was said through the prophets: "He will be called a Nazarene."

John the Baptist Prepares the Way

3 In those days John the Baptist came, preaching in the Desert of Judea [2]and saying, "Repent, for the kingdom of heaven is near." [3]This is he who was spoken of through the prophet Isaiah:

"A voice of one calling in the desert,
'Prepare the way for the Lord,
make straight paths for him.' "[b]

[4]John's clothes were made of camel's hair, and he had a leather belt around his waist. His food was locusts and wild honey. [5]People went out to him from Jerusalem and all Judea and the whole region of the Jordan. [6]Confessing their sins, they were baptized by him in the Jordan River.

[7]But when he saw many of the Pharisees and Sadducees coming to where he was baptizing, he said to them: "You brood of vipers! Who warned you to flee from the coming wrath? [8]Produce fruit in keeping with repentance. [9]And do not think you can say to yourselves, 'We have Abraham as our father.' I tell you that out of these stones God can raise up children for Abraham. [10]The ax is already at the root of the trees, and every tree that does not produce good fruit will be cut down and thrown into the fire.

[11]"I baptize you with[c] water for repentance. But after me will come one who is more powerful than I, whose sandals I am not fit to carry. He will baptize you with the Holy Spirit and with fire. [12]His winnowing fork is in his hand, and he will clear his threshing floor, gathering his wheat into the barn and burning up the chaff with unquenchable fire."

The Baptism of Jesus

[13]Then Jesus came from Galilee to the Jordan to be baptized by John. [14]But John tried to deter him, saying, "I need to be baptized by you, and do you come to me?"

[15]Jesus replied, "Let it be so now; it is proper for us to do this to fulfill all righteousness." Then John consented.

[16]As soon as Jesus was baptized, he went up out of the water. At that moment heaven was opened, and he saw the Spirit of God descending like a dove and lighting on him. [17]And a voice from heaven said, "This is my Son, whom I love; with him I am well pleased."

The Temptation of Jesus

4 Then Jesus was led by the Spirit into the desert to be tempted by the devil. [2]After fasting forty days and forty nights, he was hungry. [3]The tempter came to him and said, "If you are the Son of God, tell these stones to become bread."

[4]Jesus answered, "It is written: 'Man does not live on bread alone, but on every word that comes from the mouth of God.'[d]"

[5]Then the devil took him to the holy city and had him stand on the highest point of the temple. [6]"If you are the Son of God," he said, "throw yourself down. For it is written:

" 'He will command his angels
concerning you,
and they will lift you up in their
hands,
so that you will not strike your foot
against a stone.'[e]"

[7]Jesus answered him, "It is also written: 'Do not put the Lord your God to the test.'[f]"

[8]Again, the devil took him to a very high mountain and showed him all the kingdoms of the world and their splendor. [9]"All this I will give you," he said, "if you will bow down and worship me."

[10]Jesus said to him, "Away from me, Satan! For it is written: 'Worship the Lord your God, and serve him only.'[g]"

---

[a]18 Jer. 31:15   [b]3 Isaiah 40:3   [c]11 Or in   [d]4 Deut. 8:3   [e]6 Psalm 91:11,12   [f]7 Deut. 6:16
[g]10 Deut. 6:13

[11]Then the devil left him, and angels came and attended him.

Jesus Begins to Preach

[12]When Jesus heard that John had been put in prison, he returned to Galilee. [13]Leaving Nazareth, he went and lived in Capernaum, which was by the lake in the area of Zebulun and Naphtali — [14]to fulfill what was said through the prophet Isaiah:

[15]"Land of Zebulun and land of
 Naphtali,
 the way to the sea, along the
 Jordan,
 Galilee of the Gentiles —
[16]the people living in darkness
 have seen a great light;
 on those living in the land of the
 shadow of death
 a light has dawned."[a]

[17]From that time on Jesus began to preach, "Repent, for the kingdom of heaven is near."

The Calling of the First Disciples

[18]As Jesus was walking beside the Sea of Galilee, he saw two brothers, Simon called Peter and his brother Andrew. They were casting a net into the lake, for they were fishermen. [19]"Come, follow me," Jesus said, "and I will make you fishers of men." [20]At once they left their nets and followed him.

[21]Going on from there, he saw two other brothers, James son of Zebedee and his brother John. They were in a boat with their father Zebedee, preparing their nets. Jesus called them, [22]and immediately they left the boat and their father and followed him.

Jesus Heals the Sick

[23]Jesus went throughout Galilee, teaching in their synagogues, preaching the good news of the kingdom, and healing every disease and sickness among the people. [24]News about him spread all over Syria, and people brought to him all who were ill with various diseases, those suffering severe pain, the demon-possessed, those having seizures, and the paralyzed, and he healed them. [25]Large crowds from Galilee, the Decapolis,[b] Jerusalem, Judea and the region across the Jordan followed him.

The Beatitudes

5 Now when he saw the crowds, he went up on a mountainside and sat down. His disciples came to him, [2]and he began to teach them, saying:

[3]"Blessed are the poor in spirit,
 for theirs is the kingdom of heaven.
[4]Blessed are those who mourn,
 for they will be comforted.
[5]Blessed are the meek,
 for they will inherit the earth.
[6]Blessed are those who hunger and
 thirst for righteousness,
 for they will be filled.
[7]Blessed are the merciful,
 for they will be shown mercy.
[8]Blessed are the pure in heart,
 for they will see God.
[9]Blessed are the peacemakers,
 for they will be called sons of God.
[10]Blessed are those who are persecuted
 because of righteousness,
 for theirs is the kingdom of heaven.

[11]"Blessed are you when people insult you, persecute you and falsely say all kinds of evil against you because of me. [12]Rejoice and be glad, because great is your reward in heaven, for in the same way they persecuted the prophets who were before you.

Salt and Light

[13]"You are the salt of the earth. But if the salt loses its saltiness, how can it be made salty again? It is no longer good for anything, except to be thrown out and trampled by men.

[14]"You are the light of the world. A city on a hill cannot be hidden. [15]Neither do people light a lamp and put it under a bowl. Instead they put it on its stand, and it gives light to everyone in the house. [16]In the same way, let your light shine before men, that they may see your good deeds and praise your Father in heaven.

The Fulfillment of the Law

[17]"Do not think that I have come to abolish the Law or the Prophets; I have not come to abolish them but to fulfill them. [18]I tell you the truth, until heaven and earth disappear, not the smallest letter, not the least stroke of a pen, will by any means disappear from the Law until everything is accomplished. [19]Anyone who breaks one of the least of these com-

[a]16 Isaiah 9:1,2   [b]25 That is, the Ten Cities

mandments and teaches others to do the same will be called least in the kingdom of heaven, but whoever practices and teaches these commands will be called great in the kingdom of heaven. **20**For I tell you that unless your righteousness surpasses that of the Pharisees and the teachers of the law, you will certainly not enter the kingdom of heaven.

Murder

21"You have heard that it was said to the people long ago, 'Do not murder,*a* and anyone who murders will be subject to judgment.' **22**But I tell you that anyone

who is angry with his brother*b* will be subject to judgment. Again, anyone who says to his brother, 'Raca,*c*' is answerable to the Sanhedrin. But anyone who says, 'You fool!' will be in danger of the fire of hell.

23"Therefore, if you are offering your gift at the altar and there remember that your brother has something against you, **24**leave your gift there in front of the altar. First go and be reconciled to your brother; then come and offer your gift.

25"Settle matters quickly with your adversary who is taking you to court. Do it while you are still with him on the way, or

a21 Exodus 20:13   *b22* Some manuscripts *brother without cause*   *c22* An Aramaic term of contempt

WEDNESDAY

VERSE FOR THE DAY:
Matthew 5:14

AUTHOR:
Thomas Merton

PASSAGE FOR THE DAY:
Matthew 5:14–16

Give Us the Light

ALL of us who have been baptized in Christ and have "put on Christ" as a new identity are bound to be holy as he is holy. We are bound to live worthy lives, and our actions should bear witness to our union with him. He should manifest his presence in us and through us . . .

We are supposed to be the light of the world. We are supposed to be a light to ourselves and to others. That may well be what accounts for the fact that the world is in darkness! What then is meant by the light of Christ in our lives? What is "holiness"? What is divine sonship? Are we really seriously supposed to be saints? Can a man even desire such a thing without making a complete fool of himself in the eyes of everyone else? Is it not presumptuous? Is such a thing even possible at all? To tell the truth, many laypeople and even a good many religious do not believe, in practice, that sanctity is possible for them. Is this just plain common sense? Is it perhaps humility? Or is it defection, defeatism and despair?

If we are called by God to holiness of life and if holiness is beyond our natural power to achieve (which it certainly is) then it follows that God himself must give us the light, the strength and the courage to fulfill the task he requires of us. He will certainly give us the grace we need. If we do not become saints it is because we do not avail ourselves of his gift.

Additional Scripture Readings:
John 1:1–14; 2 Corinthians 4:1–6

Go to page 1016 for your next devotional reading.

he may hand you over to the judge, and the judge may hand you over to the officer, and you may be thrown into prison. [26]I tell you the truth, you will not get out until you have paid the last penny.[a]

Adultery

[27]"You have heard that it was said, 'Do not commit adultery.'[b] [28]But I tell you that anyone who looks at a woman lustfully has already committed adultery with her in his heart. [29]If your right eye causes you to sin, gouge it out and throw it away. It is better for you to lose one part of your body than for your whole body to be thrown into hell. [30]And if your right hand causes you to sin, cut it off and throw it away. It is better for you to lose one part of your body than for your whole body to go into hell.

Divorce

[31]"It has been said, 'Anyone who divorces his wife must give her a certificate of divorce.'[c] [32]But I tell you that anyone who divorces his wife, except for marital unfaithfulness, causes her to become an adulteress, and anyone who marries the divorced woman commits adultery.

Oaths

[33]"Again, you have heard that it was said to the people long ago, 'Do not break your oath, but keep the oaths you have made to the Lord.' [34]But I tell you, Do not swear at all: either by heaven, for it is God's throne; [35]or by the earth, for it is his footstool; or by Jerusalem, for it is the city of the Great King. [36]And do not swear by your head, for you cannot make even one hair white or black. [37]Simply let your 'Yes' be 'Yes,' and your 'No,' 'No'; anything beyond this comes from the evil one.

An Eye for an Eye

[38]"You have heard that it was said, 'Eye for eye, and tooth for tooth.'[d] [39]But I tell you, Do not resist an evil person. If someone strikes you on the right cheek, turn to him the other also. [40]And if someone wants to sue you and take your tunic, let him have your cloak as well. [41]If someone forces you to go one mile, go with him two miles. [42]Give to the one who asks you, and do not turn away from the one who wants to borrow from you.

Love for Enemies

[43]"You have heard that it was said, 'Love your neighbor[e] and hate your enemy.' [44]But I tell you: Love your enemies[f] and pray for those who persecute you, [45]that you may be sons of your Father in heaven. He causes his sun to rise on the evil and the good, and sends rain on the righteous and the unrighteous. [46]If you love those who love you, what reward will you get? Are not even the tax collectors doing that? [47]And if you greet only your brothers, what are you doing more than others? Do not even pagans do that? [48]Be perfect, therefore, as your heavenly Father is perfect.

Giving to the Needy

6 "Be careful not to do your 'acts of righteousness' before men, to be seen by them. If you do, you will have no reward from your Father in heaven.

[2]"So when you give to the needy, do not announce it with trumpets, as the hypocrites do in the synagogues and on the streets, to be honored by men. I tell you the truth, they have received their reward in full. [3]But when you give to the needy, do not let your left hand know what your right hand is doing, [4]so that your giving may be in secret. Then your Father, who sees what is done in secret, will reward you.

Prayer

[5]"And when you pray, do not be like the hypocrites, for they love to pray standing in the synagogues and on the street corners to be seen by men. I tell you the truth, they have received their reward in full. [6]But when you pray, go into your room, close the door and pray to your Father, who is unseen. Then your Father, who sees what is done in secret, will reward you. [7]And when you pray, do not keep on babbling like pagans, for they think they will be heard because of their many words. [8]Do not be like them, for your Father knows what you need before you ask him.

[9]"This, then, is how you should pray:

" 'Our Father in heaven,
  hallowed be your name,
[10]your kingdom come,
  your will be done

---

a26 Greek *kodrantes*   *b27* Exodus 20:14   *c31* Deut. 24:1   *d38* Exodus 21:24; Lev. 24:20; Deut. 19:21   *e43* Lev. 19:18   *f44* Some late manuscripts *enemies, bless those who curse you, do good to those who hate you*

on earth as it is in heaven.
¹¹Give us today our daily bread.
¹²Forgive us our debts,
   as we also have forgiven our
      debtors.
¹³And lead us not into temptation,
   but deliver us from the evil one.ᵃ'

¹⁴For if you forgive men when they sin

against you, your heavenly Father will
also forgive you. ¹⁵But if you do not forgive men their sins, your Father will not
forgive your sins.

Fasting

¹⁶"When you fast, do not look somber
as the hypocrites do, for they disfigure
their faces to show men they are fasting.

ᵃ13 Or *from evil*; some late manuscripts *one*, / *for yours is the kingdom and the power and the glory
forever. Amen.*

THURSDAY

VERSE FOR THE DAY: AUTHOR: PASSAGE FOR THE DAY:
Matthew 6:10   Jack Perry   Matthew 6:5–15

A Most Tragic Search

IN HIS own life, Jesus asked what was the will of God. He received a most searing answer. We can easily say that he was
the Son of God, and came into the world to save sinners, and
thus had to die on the cross. Yes, but he was the Son of Man
as well, and he prayed that the cup might pass from him, and
he asked why God had forsaken him, and his suffering as he
undertook to do the will of God was suffering such as we mortals know. So we cannot take refuge from hard choices in the
divinity of Jesus. Nor can we hide behind some division of the
world into the part Jesus was talking about and the part he
was not. At Calvary, all came together.

Therefore when Jesus told us to say, "Your kingdom come,
your will be done" (Matthew 6:10), he was telling us to em-
bark upon a most tragic search for the will of God in our lives.
Try as I might, I cannot find any place to hide in those crystal,
bleeding sentences. Human words find it hard to express the
depth of Jesus' divine words. But he was saying, in the most
literal way, that God's will should be sought and it should be
obeyed.

To obey God's will for my life—what a shattering thought! If
I took Jesus at his word, would I not be helping the poor, or
giving all I had to the needy, or learning to care for the sick, or
proclaiming the acceptable day of the Lord on the public
streets, or binding the wounds of the war-torn—would I not be
about my Father's business, rather than going on about my
daily routine? If I took Jesus seriously, and truly asked God to
let me do his will in my life, would I be where I am right now?

Additional Scripture Readings: *Go to page 1018 for your next*
Ephesians 5:15–20;   *devotional reading.*
Colossians 1:9–14

I tell you the truth, they have received their reward in full. [17]But when you fast, put oil on your head and wash your face, [18]so that it will not be obvious to men that you are fasting, but only to your Father, who is unseen; and your Father, who sees what is done in secret, will reward you.

Treasures in Heaven

[19]"Do not store up for yourselves treasures on earth, where moth and rust destroy, and where thieves break in and steal. [20]But store up for yourselves treasures in heaven, where moth and rust do not destroy, and where thieves do not break in and steal. [21]For where your treasure is, there your heart will be also.

[22]"The eye is the lamp of the body. If your eyes are good, your whole body will be full of light. [23]But if your eyes are bad, your whole body will be full of darkness. If then the light within you is darkness, how great is that darkness!

[24]"No one can serve two masters. Either he will hate the one and love the other, or he will be devoted to the one and despise the other. You cannot serve both God and Money.

Do Not Worry

[25]"Therefore I tell you, do not worry about your life, what you will eat or drink; or about your body, what you will wear. Is not life more important than food, and the body more important than clothes? [26]Look at the birds of the air; they do not sow or reap or store away in barns, and yet your heavenly Father feeds them. Are you not much more valuable than they? [27]Who of you by worrying can add a single hour to his life[a]? [28]"And why do you worry about clothes? See how the lilies of the field grow. They do not labor or spin. [29]Yet I tell you that not even Solomon in all his splendor was dressed like one of these. [30]If that is how God clothes the grass of the field, which is here today and tomorrow is thrown into the fire, will he not much more clothe you, O you of little faith? [31]So do not worry, saying, 'What shall we eat?' or 'What shall we drink?' or 'What shall we wear?' [32]For the pagans run after all these things, and your heavenly Father knows that you need them. [33]But seek first his kingdom and his righteousness, and all these things will be given to you as well. [34]Therefore do not worry about tomorrow, for tomorrow will worry about itself. Each day has enough trouble of its own.

Judging Others

7 "Do not judge, or you too will be judged. [2]For in the same way you judge others, you will be judged, and with the measure you use, it will be measured to you.

[3]"Why do you look at the speck of sawdust in your brother's eye and pay no attention to the plank in your own eye? [4]How can you say to your brother, 'Let me take the speck out of your eye,' when all the time there is a plank in your own eye? [5]You hypocrite, first take the plank out of your own eye, and then you will see clearly to remove the speck from your brother's eye.

[6]"Do not give dogs what is sacred; do not throw your pearls to pigs. If you do, they may trample them under their feet, and then turn and tear you to pieces.

Ask, Seek, Knock

[7]"Ask and it will be given to you; seek and you will find; knock and the door will be opened to you. [8]For everyone who asks receives; he who seeks finds; and to him who knocks, the door will be opened.

[9]"Which of you, if his son asks for bread, will give him a stone? [10]Or if he asks for a fish, will give him a snake? [11]If you, then, though you are evil, know how to give good gifts to your children, how much more will your Father in heaven give good gifts to those who ask him! [12]So in everything, do to others what you would have them do to you, for this sums up the Law and the Prophets.

The Narrow and Wide Gates

[13]"Enter through the narrow gate. For wide is the gate and broad is the road that leads to destruction, and many enter through it. [14]But small is the gate and narrow the road that leads to life, and only a few find it.

A Tree and Its Fruit

[15]"Watch out for false prophets. They come to you in sheep's clothing, but inwardly they are ferocious wolves. [16]By their fruit you will recognize them. Do people pick grapes from thornbushes, or figs from thistles? [17]Likewise every good tree bears good fruit, but a bad tree bears

a27 Or *single cubit to his height*

FRIDAY

VERSE FOR THE DAY: AUTHOR: PASSAGE FOR THE DAY:
Matthew 7:24   Tom Landry   Matthew 7:24–27

Spiritual Crossroads

I HAD always considered myself a Christian, yet so much of what I now discovered in the Bible went against the grain of the life philosophy I had lived by . . .

All my life I had made my football career the number-one priority and let it dictate the direction of my life. Now here was the Bible saying I needed to make God and his will first and follow his direction for my life.

Gradually I realized the crossroads I faced in my life was really a spiritual crossroads. I had to decide whether or not I believed what the Bible said. All my other questions hung on that one.

The more of the Bible I read and studied, the more it all made sense. The more pieces of life fit together. The more I wanted to believe. And yet that analytical part of my nature kept asking questions, trying to dispel all doubt.

One day I came across a short passage of a poem by Robert Browning that said: "You call for faith, I give you doubt, to prove that faith exists. The greater the doubt, the stronger the faith, I say, if faith overcomes doubt."

When I read that, something clicked in me and I began to understand faith in a new light.

I can't point to a specific moment or a specific time when I had a sudden "born-again" experience. For me, coming to my own personal faith in God took place over a period of months in 1959. But I finally reached a point where faith outweighed the doubts, and I was willing to commit my entire life to God.

I can't say that decision made an immediately visible difference in my life. I can't even say it instantly transformed me into a much better person; I had a lot yet to learn—and I still do—about how God wants me to live my life. But what my new Christian experience did do for me was to place football behind the priorities of my faith and my family and give me a sense of confidence and peace about the future—whatever it would be.

Additional Scripture Readings:
Romans 12:1–2;
1 Thessalonians 4:1–7

Go to page 1020 for your next devotional reading.

bad fruit. [18]A good tree cannot bear bad fruit, and a bad tree cannot bear good fruit. [19]Every tree that does not bear good fruit is cut down and thrown into the fire. [20]Thus, by their fruit you will recognize them.

[21]"Not everyone who says to me, 'Lord, Lord,' will enter the kingdom of heaven, but only he who does the will of my Father who is in heaven. [22]Many will say to me on that day, 'Lord, Lord, did we not prophesy in your name, and in your name drive out demons and perform many miracles?' [23]Then I will tell them plainly, 'I never knew you. Away from me, you evildoers!'

The Wise and Foolish Builders

[24]"Therefore everyone who hears these words of mine and puts them into practice is like a wise man who built his house on the rock. [25]The rain came down, the streams rose, and the winds blew and beat against that house; yet it did not fall, because it had its foundation on the rock. [26]But everyone who hears these words of mine and does not put them into practice is like a foolish man who built his house on sand. [27]The rain came down, the streams rose, and the winds blew and beat against that house, and it fell with a great crash."

[28]When Jesus had finished saying these things, the crowds were amazed at his teaching, [29]because he taught as one who had authority, and not as their teachers of the law.

The Man With Leprosy

8 When he came down from the mountainside, large crowds followed him. [2]A man with leprosy[a] came and knelt before him and said, "Lord, if you are willing, you can make me clean."

[3]Jesus reached out his hand and touched the man. "I am willing," he said. "Be clean!" Immediately he was cured[b] of his leprosy. [4]Then Jesus said to him, "See that you don't tell anyone. But go, show yourself to the priest and offer the gift Moses commanded, as a testimony to them."

The Faith of the Centurion

[5]When Jesus had entered Capernaum, a centurion came to him, asking for help.

[6]"Lord," he said, "my servant lies at home paralyzed and in terrible suffering."

[7]Jesus said to him, "I will go and heal him."

[8]The centurion replied, "Lord, I do not deserve to have you come under my roof. But just say the word, and my servant will be healed. [9]For I myself am a man under authority, with soldiers under me. I tell this one, 'Go,' and he goes; and that one, 'Come,' and he comes. I say to my servant, 'Do this,' and he does it."

[10]When Jesus heard this, he was astonished and said to those following him, "I tell you the truth, I have not found anyone in Israel with such great faith. [11]I say to you that many will come from the east and the west, and will take their places at the feast with Abraham, Isaac and Jacob in the kingdom of heaven. [12]But the subjects of the kingdom will be thrown outside, into the darkness, where there will be weeping and gnashing of teeth."

[13]Then Jesus said to the centurion, "Go! It will be done just as you believed it would." And his servant was healed at that very hour.

Jesus Heals Many

[14]When Jesus came into Peter's house, he saw Peter's mother-in-law lying in bed with a fever. [15]He touched her hand and the fever left her, and she got up and began to wait on him.

[16]When evening came, many who were demon-possessed were brought to him, and he drove out the spirits with a word and healed all the sick. [17]This was to fulfill what was spoken through the prophet Isaiah:

"He took up our infirmities
 and carried our diseases."[c]

The Cost of Following Jesus

[18]When Jesus saw the crowd around him, he gave orders to cross to the other side of the lake. [19]Then a teacher of the law came to him and said, "Teacher, I will follow you wherever you go."

[20]Jesus replied, "Foxes have holes and birds of the air have nests, but the Son of Man has no place to lay his head."

[21]Another disciple said to him, "Lord, first let me go and bury my father."

[22]But Jesus told him, "Follow me, and let the dead bury their own dead."

---

[a]2 The Greek word was used for various diseases affecting the skin—not necessarily leprosy.   [b]3 Greek made clean   [c]17 Isaiah 53:4

WEEKENDING

RENEW

As long as Jesus is one of many options, he is no option. As long as you can carry your burdens alone, you don't need a burden bearer. As long as your situation brings you no grief, you will receive no comfort. And as long as you can take him or leave him, you might as well leave him, because he won't be taken half-heartedly.

But when you mourn, when you get to the point of sorrow for your sins, when you admit that you have no other option but to cast all your cares on him, and when there is truly no other name that you can call, then cast all your cares on him, for he is waiting in the midst of the storm.

— *Max Lucado*

REVIVE

Saturday: Matthew 14:22–33
Sunday: 1 Peter 5:5–7

Go to page 1021 for your next devotional reading.

Jesus Calms the Storm

²³Then he got into the boat and his disciples followed him. ²⁴Without warning, a furious storm came up on the lake, so that the waves swept over the boat. But Jesus was sleeping. ²⁵The disciples went and woke him, saying, "Lord, save us! We're going to drown!"

²⁶He replied, "You of little faith, why are you so afraid?" Then he got up and rebuked the winds and the waves, and it was completely calm.

²⁷The men were amazed and asked, "What kind of man is this? Even the winds and the waves obey him!"

The Healing of Two Demon-possessed Men

²⁸When he arrived at the other side in the region of the Gadarenes,ᵃ two demon-possessed men coming from the tombs met him. They were so violent that no one could pass that way. ²⁹"What do you want with us, Son of God?" they shouted. "Have you come here to torture us before the appointed time?"

³⁰Some distance from them a large herd of pigs was feeding. ³¹The demons begged Jesus, "If you drive us out, send us into the herd of pigs."

³²He said to them, "Go!" So they came

ᵃ28 Some manuscripts *Gergesenes*; others *Gerasenes*

MONDAY

VERSE FOR THE DAY:
Matthew 8:20

AUTHOR:
Charles Colson

PASSAGE FOR THE DAY:
Matthew 8:18–22

Identifying with Jesus

TIME after time I find that men and women in the prisons of America want nothing to do with the church or with Christianity. They cannot relate to our lavish buildings and stained-glass windows because they see the church as a manifestation of the culture that has rejected them and holds them prisoner. But I see those same people come alive when I talk about Jesus the prisoner, the outcast who was followed by a dirty dozen, the One who was laid in a borrowed manger, rode on a borrowed donkey, was arrested, hung on a cross between two thieves, and then buried in a borrowed tomb. They can understand and identify with the Jesus of the Scriptures, not with a Christ who appears to have just stepped out of a Brooks Brothers catalog.

The longer I'm a Christian, the more I realize that the vague deity of American civil religion is a heretical rejection of the Christ of Holy Scripture. So don't confuse your loyalties —never assume the will of the majority and the will of God are synonymous. They may be different—and frequently are.

The Christian is committed to work for justice and righteousness, to bring the gospel of Christ to bear in all areas of life to make a difference in society. But we do it by the integrity of our witness, not by resorting to quick, simplistic clichés.

Additional Scripture Readings:
Luke 4:16–20; Philippians 2:1–11

Go to page 1025 for your next devotional reading.

out and went into the pigs, and the whole herd rushed down the steep bank into the lake and died in the water. 33Those tending the pigs ran off, went into the town and reported all this, including what had happened to the demon-possessed men. 34Then the whole town went out to meet Jesus. And when they saw him, they pleaded with him to leave their region.

Jesus Heals a Paralytic

9 Jesus stepped into a boat, crossed over and came to his own town. 2Some men brought to him a paralytic, lying on a mat. When Jesus saw their faith, he said to the paralytic, "Take heart, son; your sins are forgiven."

3At this, some of the teachers of the law said to themselves, "This fellow is blaspheming!"

4Knowing their thoughts, Jesus said, "Why do you entertain evil thoughts in your hearts? 5Which is easier: to say, 'Your sins are forgiven,' or to say, 'Get up and walk'? 6But so that you may know that the Son of Man has authority on earth to forgive sins...." Then he said to the paralytic, "Get up, take your mat and go home." 7And the man got up and went home. 8When the crowd saw this, they were filled with awe; and they praised God, who had given such authority to men.

The Calling of Matthew

9As Jesus went on from there, he saw a man named Matthew sitting at the tax collector's booth. "Follow me," he told him, and Matthew got up and followed him.

10While Jesus was having dinner at Matthew's house, many tax collectors and "sinners" came and ate with him and his disciples. 11When the Pharisees saw this, they asked his disciples, "Why does your teacher eat with tax collectors and 'sinners'?"

12On hearing this, Jesus said, "It is not the healthy who need a doctor, but the sick. 13But go and learn what this means: 'I desire mercy, not sacrifice.'a For I have not come to call the righteous, but sinners."

Jesus Questioned About Fasting

14Then John's disciples came and asked him, "How is it that we and the Pharisees fast, but your disciples do not fast?"

15Jesus answered, "How can the guests of the bridegroom mourn while he is with them? The time will come when the bridegroom will be taken from them; then they will fast.

16"No one sews a patch of unshrunk cloth on an old garment, for the patch will pull away from the garment, making the tear worse. 17Neither do men pour new wine into old wineskins. If they do, the skins will burst, the wine will run out and the wineskins will be ruined. No, they pour new wine into new wineskins, and both are preserved."

A Dead Girl and a Sick Woman

18While he was saying this, a ruler came and knelt before him and said, "My daughter has just died. But come and put your hand on her, and she will live." 19Jesus got up and went with him, and so did his disciples.

20Just then a woman who had been subject to bleeding for twelve years came up behind him and touched the edge of his cloak. 21She said to herself, "If I only touch his cloak, I will be healed."

22Jesus turned and saw her. "Take heart, daughter," he said, "your faith has healed you." And the woman was healed from that moment.

23When Jesus entered the ruler's house and saw the flute players and the noisy crowd, 24he said, "Go away. The girl is not dead but asleep." But they laughed at him. 25After the crowd had been put outside, he went in and took the girl by the hand, and she got up. 26News of this spread through all that region.

Jesus Heals the Blind and Mute

27As Jesus went on from there, two blind men followed him, calling out, "Have mercy on us, Son of David!"

28When he had gone indoors, the blind men came to him, and he asked them, "Do you believe that I am able to do this?"

"Yes, Lord," they replied.

29Then he touched their eyes and said, "According to your faith will it be done to you"; 30and their sight was restored. Jesus warned them sternly, "See that no one knows about this." 31But they went out and spread the news about him all over that region.

32While they were going out, a man who was demon-possessed and could not talk was brought to Jesus. 33And when the demon was driven out, the man who had

a13 Hosea 6:6

been mute spoke. The crowd was amazed and said, "Nothing like this has ever been seen in Israel."

34But the Pharisees said, "It is by the prince of demons that he drives out demons."

The Workers Are Few

35Jesus went through all the towns and villages, teaching in their synagogues, preaching the good news of the kingdom and healing every disease and sickness. 36When he saw the crowds, he had compassion on them, because they were harassed and helpless, like sheep without a shepherd. 37Then he said to his disciples, "The harvest is plentiful but the workers are few. 38Ask the Lord of the harvest, therefore, to send out workers into his harvest field."

Jesus Sends Out the Twelve

10 He called his twelve disciples to him and gave them authority to drive out evil*a* spirits and to heal every disease and sickness.

2These are the names of the twelve apostles: first, Simon (who is called Peter) and his brother Andrew; James son of Zebedee, and his brother John; 3Philip and Bartholomew; Thomas and Matthew the tax collector; James son of Alphaeus, and Thaddaeus; 4Simon the Zealot and Judas Iscariot, who betrayed him.

5These twelve Jesus sent out with the following instructions: "Do not go among the Gentiles or enter any town of the Samaritans. 6Go rather to the lost sheep of Israel. 7As you go, preach this message: 'The kingdom of heaven is near.' 8Heal the sick, raise the dead, cleanse those who have leprosy,*b* drive out demons. Freely you have received, freely give. 9Do not take along any gold or silver or copper in your belts; 10take no bag for the journey, or extra tunic, or sandals or a staff; for the worker is worth his keep.

11"Whatever town or village you enter, search for some worthy person there and stay at his house until you leave. 12As you enter the home, give it your greeting. 13If the home is deserving, let your peace rest on it; if it is not, let your peace return to you. 14If anyone will not welcome you or listen to your words, shake the dust off your feet when you leave that home or town. 15I tell you the truth, it will be more

bearable for Sodom and Gomorrah on the day of judgment than for that town. 16I am sending you out like sheep among wolves. Therefore be as shrewd as snakes and as innocent as doves.

17"Be on your guard against men; they will hand you over to the local councils and flog you in their synagogues. 18On my account you will be brought before governors and kings as witnesses to them and to the Gentiles. 19But when they arrest you, do not worry about what to say or how to say it. At that time you will be given what to say, 20for it will not be you speaking, but the Spirit of your Father speaking through you.

21"Brother will betray brother to death, and a father his child; children will rebel against their parents and have them put to death. 22All men will hate you because of me, but he who stands firm to the end will be saved. 23When you are persecuted in one place, flee to another. I tell you the truth, you will not finish going through the cities of Israel before the Son of Man comes.

24"A student is not above his teacher, nor a servant above his master. 25It is enough for the student to be like his teacher, and the servant like his master. If the head of the house has been called Beelzebub,*c* how much more the members of his household!

26"So do not be afraid of them. There is nothing concealed that will not be disclosed, or hidden that will not be made known. 27What I tell you in the dark, speak in the daylight; what is whispered in your ear, proclaim from the roofs. 28Do not be afraid of those who kill the body but cannot kill the soul. Rather, be afraid of the One who can destroy both soul and body in hell. 29Are not two sparrows sold for a penny*d*? Yet not one of them will fall to the ground apart from the will of your Father. 30And even the very hairs of your head are all numbered. 31So don't be afraid; you are worth more than many sparrows.

32"Whoever acknowledges me before men, I will also acknowledge him before my Father in heaven. 33But whoever disowns me before men, I will disown him before my Father in heaven.

34"Do not suppose that I have come to bring peace to the earth. I did not come to

---

*a*1 Greek *unclean*   *b*8 The Greek word was used for various diseases affecting the skin—not necessarily leprosy.   *c*25 Greek *Beezeboul* or *Beelzeboul*   *d*29 Greek *an assarion* bring peace, but a sword. ³⁵For I have come to turn

> " 'a man against his father,
>   a daughter against her mother,
>   a daughter-in-law against her mother-in-law—
> ³⁶ a man's enemies will be the
>   members of his own
>   household.'[a]

³⁷"Anyone who loves his father or mother more than me is not worthy of me; anyone who loves his son or daughter more than me is not worthy of me; ³⁸and anyone who does not take his cross and follow me is not worthy of me. ³⁹Whoever finds his life will lose it, and whoever loses his life for my sake will find it.

⁴⁰"He who receives you receives me, and he who receives me receives the one who sent me. ⁴¹Anyone who receives a prophet because he is a prophet will receive a prophet's reward, and anyone who receives a righteous man because he is a righteous man will receive a righteous man's reward. ⁴²And if anyone gives even a cup of cold water to one of these little ones because he is my disciple, I tell you the truth, he will certainly not lose his reward."

Jesus and John the Baptist

11 After Jesus had finished instructing his twelve disciples, he went on from there to teach and preach in the towns of Galilee.[b]

²When John heard in prison what Christ was doing, he sent his disciples ³to ask him, "Are you the one who was to come, or should we expect someone else?"

⁴Jesus replied, "Go back and report to John what you hear and see: ⁵The blind receive sight, the lame walk, those who have leprosy[c] are cured, the deaf hear, the dead are raised, and the good news is preached to the poor. ⁶Blessed is the man who does not fall away on account of me."

⁷As John's disciples were leaving, Jesus began to speak to the crowd about John: "What did you go out into the desert to see? A reed swayed by the wind? ⁸If not, what did you go out to see? A man dressed in fine clothes? No, those who wear fine clothes are in kings' palaces. ⁹Then what

did you go out to see? A prophet? Yes, I tell you, and more than a prophet. ¹⁰This is the one about whom it is written:

> " 'I will send my messenger ahead of
>   you,
>   who will prepare your way before
>   you.'[d]

¹¹I tell you the truth: Among those born of women there has not risen anyone greater than John the Baptist; yet he who is least in the kingdom of heaven is greater than he. ¹²From the days of John the Baptist until now, the kingdom of heaven has been forcefully advancing, and forceful men lay hold of it. ¹³For all the Prophets and the Law prophesied until John. ¹⁴And if you are willing to accept it, he is the Elijah who was to come. ¹⁵He who has ears, let him hear.

¹⁶"To what can I compare this generation? They are like children sitting in the marketplaces and calling out to others:

> ¹⁷" 'We played the flute for you,
>   and you did not dance;
>   we sang a dirge,
>   and you did not mourn.'

¹⁸For John came neither eating nor drinking, and they say, 'He has a demon.' ¹⁹The Son of Man came eating and drinking, and they say, 'Here is a glutton and a drunkard, a friend of tax collectors and "sinners." ' But wisdom is proved right by her actions."

Woe on Unrepentant Cities

²⁰Then Jesus began to denounce the cities in which most of his miracles had been performed, because they did not repent. ²¹"Woe to you, Korazin! Woe to you, Bethsaida! If the miracles that were performed in you had been performed in Tyre and Sidon, they would have repented long ago in sackcloth and ashes. ²²But I tell you, it will be more bearable for Tyre and Sidon on the day of judgment than for you. ²³And you, Capernaum, will you be lifted up to the skies? No, you will go down to the depths.[e] If the miracles that were performed in you had been performed in Sodom, it would have remained to this day. ²⁴But I tell you that it will be more bearable for Sodom on the day of judgment than for you."

---

[a]36 Micah 7:6   [b]1 Greek *in their towns*   [c]5 The Greek word was used for various diseases affecting the skin—not necessarily leprosy.   [d]10 Mal. 3:1   [e]23 Greek *Hades*

Rest for the Weary

25At that time Jesus said, "I praise you, Father, Lord of heaven and earth, because you have hidden these things from the wise and learned, and revealed them to little children. **26**Yes, Father, for this was your good pleasure.

27"All things have been committed to me by my Father. No one knows the Son except the Father, and no one knows the Father except the Son and those to whom the Son chooses to reveal him.

28"Come to me, all you who are weary and burdened, and I will give you rest. **29**Take my yoke upon you and learn from me, for I am gentle and humble in heart, and you will find rest for your souls. **30**For my yoke is easy and my burden is light."

Lord of the Sabbath

12 At that time Jesus went through the grainfields on the Sabbath. His disciples were hungry and began to pick some heads of grain and eat them. **2**When the Pharisees saw this, they said to him, "Look! Your disciples are doing what is unlawful on the Sabbath."

3He answered, "Haven't you read what David did when he and his companions were hungry? **4**He entered the house of God, and he and his companions ate the consecrated bread—which was not lawful for them to do, but only for the priests. **5**Or haven't you read in the Law that on the Sabbath the priests in the temple desecrate the day and yet are innocent? **6**I tell you that one*a* greater than the temple is

a6 Or something; also in verses 41 and 42

TUESDAY

VERSE FOR THE DAY:
Matthew 11:30

AUTHOR:
Dietrich Bonhoeffer

PASSAGE FOR THE DAY:
Matthew 11:28–30

Christ's Kindly Yoke

WHEN the Bible speaks of following Jesus, it is proclaiming a discipleship that will liberate mankind from all man-made dogmas, from every burden and oppression, from every anxiety and torture that afflicts the conscience. If they follow Jesus, men escape from the hard yoke of their own laws, and submit to the kindly yoke of Jesus Christ. But does this mean that we ignore the seriousness of his commands? Far from it. We can only achieve perfect liberty and enjoy fellowship with Jesus when his command, his call to absolute discipleship, is appreciated in its entirety. Only the man who follows the command of Jesus single-mindedly, and unresistingly lets his yoke rest upon him, finds his burden easy, and under its gentle pressure receives the power to persevere in the right way. The command of Jesus is hard, unutterably hard, for those who try to resist it. But for those who willingly submit, the yoke is easy and the burden is light. "His commands are not burdensome" (1 John 5:3). The commandment of Jesus is not a sort of spiritual shock treatment. Jesus asks nothing of us without giving us the strength to perform it. His commandment never seeks to destroy life, but to foster, strengthen and heal it.

Additional Scripture Readings:
Galatians 3:1–14; 1 John 5:1–5

Go to page 1030 for your next devotional reading.

here. [7]If you had known what these words mean, 'I desire mercy, not sacrifice,'[a] you would not have condemned the innocent. [8]For the Son of Man is Lord of the Sabbath."

[9]Going on from that place, he went into their synagogue, [10]and a man with a shriveled hand was there. Looking for a reason to accuse Jesus, they asked him, "Is it lawful to heal on the Sabbath?"

[11]He said to them, "If any of you has a sheep and it falls into a pit on the Sabbath, will you not take hold of it and lift it out? [12]How much more valuable is a man than a sheep! Therefore it is lawful to do good on the Sabbath."

[13]Then he said to the man, "Stretch out your hand." So he stretched it out and it was completely restored, just as sound as the other. [14]But the Pharisees went out and plotted how they might kill Jesus.

God's Chosen Servant

[15]Aware of this, Jesus withdrew from that place. Many followed him, and he healed all their sick, [16]warning them not to tell who he was. [17]This was to fulfill what was spoken through the prophet Isaiah:

[18]"Here is my servant whom I have
        chosen,
    the one I love, in whom I delight;
  I will put my Spirit on him,
    and he will proclaim justice to the
        nations.
[19]He will not quarrel or cry out;
    no one will hear his voice in the
        streets.
[20]A bruised reed he will not break,
    and a smoldering wick he will not
        snuff out,
  till he leads justice to victory.
[21]   In his name the nations will put
        their hope."[b]

Jesus and Beelzebub

[22]Then they brought him a demon-possessed man who was blind and mute, and Jesus healed him, so that he could both talk and see. [23]All the people were astonished and said, "Could this be the Son of David?"

[24]But when the Pharisees heard this, they said, "It is only by Beelzebub,[c] the prince of demons, that this fellow drives out demons."

[25]Jesus knew their thoughts and said to them, "Every kingdom divided against itself will be ruined, and every city or household divided against itself will not stand. [26]If Satan drives out Satan, he is divided against himself. How then can his kingdom stand? [27]And if I drive out demons by Beelzebub, by whom do your people drive them out? So then, they will be your judges. [28]But if I drive out demons by the Spirit of God, then the kingdom of God has come upon you.

[29]"Or again, how can anyone enter a strong man's house and carry off his possessions unless he first ties up the strong man? Then he can rob his house.

[30]"He who is not with me is against me, and he who does not gather with me scatters. [31]And so I tell you, every sin and blasphemy will be forgiven men, but the blasphemy against the Spirit will not be forgiven. [32]Anyone who speaks a word against the Son of Man will be forgiven, but anyone who speaks against the Holy Spirit will not be forgiven, either in this age or in the age to come.

[33]"Make a tree good and its fruit will be good, or make a tree bad and its fruit will be bad, for a tree is recognized by its fruit. [34]You brood of vipers, how can you who are evil say anything good? For out of the overflow of the heart the mouth speaks. [35]The good man brings good things out of the good stored up in him, and the evil man brings evil things out of the evil stored up in him. [36]But I tell you that men will have to give account on the day of judgment for every careless word they have spoken. [37]For by your words you will be acquitted, and by your words you will be condemned."

The Sign of Jonah

[38]Then some of the Pharisees and teachers of the law said to him, "Teacher, we want to see a miraculous sign from you."

[39]He answered, "A wicked and adulterous generation asks for a miraculous sign! But none will be given it except the sign of the prophet Jonah. [40]For as Jonah was three days and three nights in the belly of a huge fish, so the Son of Man will be three days and three nights in the heart of the earth. [41]The men of Nineveh will stand up at the judgment with this generation and condemn it; for they repented at

---

a7 Hosea 6:6   *b21* Isaiah 42:1-4   *c24* Greek *Beezeboul* or *Beelzeboul*; also in verse 27 the preaching of Jonah, and now one[a] greater than Jonah is here. [42]The Queen of the South will rise at the judgment with this generation and condemn it; for she came from the ends of the earth to listen to Solomon's wisdom, and now one greater than Solomon is here.

[43]"When an evil[b] spirit comes out of a man, it goes through arid places seeking rest and does not find it. [44]Then it says, 'I will return to the house I left.' When it arrives, it finds the house unoccupied, swept clean and put in order. [45]Then it goes and takes with it seven other spirits more wicked than itself, and they go in and live there. And the final condition of that man is worse than the first. That is how it will be with this wicked generation."

Jesus' Mother and Brothers

[46]While Jesus was still talking to the crowd, his mother and brothers stood outside, wanting to speak to him. [47]Someone told him, "Your mother and brothers are standing outside, wanting to speak to you."[c]

[48]He replied to him, "Who is my mother, and who are my brothers?" [49]Pointing to his disciples, he said, "Here are my mother and my brothers. [50]For whoever does the will of my Father in heaven is my brother and sister and mother."

The Parable of the Sower

13 That same day Jesus went out of the house and sat by the lake. [2]Such large crowds gathered around him that he got into a boat and sat in it, while all the people stood on the shore. [3]Then he told them many things in parables, saying: "A farmer went out to sow his seed. [4]As he was scattering the seed, some fell along the path, and the birds came and ate it up. [5]Some fell on rocky places, where it did not have much soil. It sprang up quickly, because the soil was shallow. [6]But when the sun came up, the plants were scorched, and they withered because they had no root. [7]Other seed fell among thorns, which grew up and choked the plants. [8]Still other seed fell on good soil, where it produced a crop—a hundred, sixty or thirty times what was sown. [9]He who has ears, let him hear."

[10]The disciples came to him and asked, "Why do you speak to the people in parables?"

[11]He replied, "The knowledge of the secrets of the kingdom of heaven has been given to you, but not to them. [12]Whoever has will be given more, and he will have an abundance. Whoever does not have, even what he has will be taken from him. [13]This is why I speak to them in parables:

"Though seeing, they do not see;
  though hearing, they do not hear or
    understand.

[14]In them is fulfilled the prophecy of Isaiah:

" 'You will be ever hearing but never
    understanding;
  you will be ever seeing but never
    perceiving.
[15]For this people's heart has become
    calloused;
  they hardly hear with their ears,
  and they have closed their eyes.
Otherwise they might see with their
    eyes,
  hear with their ears,
  understand with their hearts
and turn, and I would heal them.'[d]

[16]But blessed are your eyes because they see, and your ears because they hear. [17]For I tell you the truth, many prophets and righteous men longed to see what you see but did not see it, and to hear what you hear but did not hear it.

[18]"Listen then to what the parable of the sower means: [19]When anyone hears the message about the kingdom and does not understand it, the evil one comes and snatches away what was sown in his heart. This is the seed sown along the path. [20]The one who received the seed that fell on rocky places is the man who hears the word and at once receives it with joy. [21]But since he has no root, he lasts only a short time. When trouble or persecution comes because of the word, he quickly falls away. [22]The one who received the seed that fell among the thorns is the man who hears the word, but the worries of this life and the deceitfulness of wealth choke it, making it unfruitful. [23]But the one who received the seed that fell on good soil is the man who hears the word and understands it. He produces a crop, yielding a hundred, sixty or thirty times what was sown."

---

[a]41 Or *something*; also in verse 42   [b]43 Greek *unclean*   [c]47 Some manuscripts do not have verse 47.   [d]15 Isaiah 6:9,10

The Parable of the Weeds

24Jesus told them another parable: "The kingdom of heaven is like a man who sowed good seed in his field. **25**But while everyone was sleeping, his enemy came and sowed weeds among the wheat, and went away. **26**When the wheat sprouted and formed heads, then the weeds also appeared.

27"The owner's servants came to him and said, 'Sir, didn't you sow good seed in your field? Where then did the weeds come from?'

28" 'An enemy did this,' he replied.

"The servants asked him, 'Do you want us to go and pull them up?'

29" 'No,' he answered, 'because while you are pulling the weeds, you may root up the wheat with them. **30**Let both grow together until the harvest. At that time I will tell the harvesters: First collect the weeds and tie them in bundles to be burned; then gather the wheat and bring it into my barn.' "

The Parables of the Mustard Seed and the Yeast

31He told them another parable: "The kingdom of heaven is like a mustard seed, which a man took and planted in his field. **32**Though it is the smallest of all your seeds, yet when it grows, it is the largest of garden plants and becomes a tree, so that the birds of the air come and perch in its branches."

33He told them still another parable: "The kingdom of heaven is like yeast that a woman took and mixed into a large amount*a* of flour until it worked all through the dough."

34Jesus spoke all these things to the crowd in parables; he did not say anything to them without using a parable. **35**So was fulfilled what was spoken through the prophet:

"I will open my mouth in parables,
  I will utter things hidden since the creation of the world."*b*

The Parable of the Weeds Explained

36Then he left the crowd and went into the house. His disciples came to him and said, "Explain to us the parable of the weeds in the field."

37He answered, "The one who sowed the good seed is the Son of Man. **38**The field is the world, and the good seed stands for the sons of the kingdom. The weeds are the sons of the evil one, **39**and the enemy who sows them is the devil. The harvest is the end of the age, and the harvesters are angels.

40"As the weeds are pulled up and burned in the fire, so it will be at the end of the age. **41**The Son of Man will send out his angels, and they will weed out of his kingdom everything that causes sin and all who do evil. **42**They will throw them into the fiery furnace, where there will be weeping and gnashing of teeth. **43**Then the righteous will shine like the sun in the kingdom of their Father. He who has ears, let him hear.

The Parables of the Hidden Treasure and the Pearl

44"The kingdom of heaven is like treasure hidden in a field. When a man found it, he hid it again, and then in his joy went and sold all he had and bought that field.

45"Again, the kingdom of heaven is like a merchant looking for fine pearls. **46**When he found one of great value, he went away and sold everything he had and bought it.

The Parable of the Net

47"Once again, the kingdom of heaven is like a net that was let down into the lake and caught all kinds of fish. **48**When it was full, the fishermen pulled it up on the shore. Then they sat down and collected the good fish in baskets, but threw the bad away. **49**This is how it will be at the end of the age. The angels will come and separate the wicked from the righteous **50**and throw them into the fiery furnace, where there will be weeping and gnashing of teeth.

51"Have you understood all these things?" Jesus asked.

"Yes," they replied.

52He said to them, "Therefore every teacher of the law who has been instructed about the kingdom of heaven is like the owner of a house who brings out of his storeroom new treasures as well as old."

A Prophet Without Honor

53When Jesus had finished these parables, he moved on from there. **54**Coming to his hometown, he began teaching the people in their synagogue, and they were amazed. "Where did this man get this wisdom and these miraculous powers?" they

---

*a*33 Greek *three satas* (probably about 1/2 bushel or 22 liters)   *b*35 Psalm 78:2

asked. **55**"Isn't this the carpenter's son? Isn't his mother's name Mary, and aren't his brothers James, Joseph, Simon and Judas? **56**Aren't all his sisters with us? Where then did this man get all these things?" **57**And they took offense at him.

But Jesus said to them, "Only in his hometown and in his own house is a prophet without honor."

58And he did not do many miracles there because of their lack of faith.

John the Baptist Beheaded

14 At that time Herod the tetrarch heard the reports about Jesus, **2**and he said to his attendants, "This is John the Baptist; he has risen from the dead! That is why miraculous powers are at work in him."

3Now Herod had arrested John and bound him and put him in prison because of Herodias, his brother Philip's wife, **4**for John had been saying to him: "It is not lawful for you to have her." **5**Herod wanted to kill John, but he was afraid of the people, because they considered him a prophet.

6On Herod's birthday the daughter of Herodias danced for them and pleased Herod so much **7**that he promised with an oath to give her whatever she asked. **8**Prompted by her mother, she said, "Give me here on a platter the head of John the Baptist." **9**The king was distressed, but because of his oaths and his dinner guests, he ordered that her request be granted **10**and had John beheaded in the prison. **11**His head was brought in on a platter and given to the girl, who carried it to her mother. **12**John's disciples came and took his body and buried it. Then they went and told Jesus.

Jesus Feeds the Five Thousand

13When Jesus heard what had happened, he withdrew by boat privately to a solitary place. Hearing of this, the crowds followed him on foot from the towns. **14**When Jesus landed and saw a large crowd, he had compassion on them and healed their sick.

15As evening approached, the disciples came to him and said, "This is a remote place, and it's already getting late. Send the crowds away, so they can go to the villages and buy themselves some food."

16Jesus replied, "They do not need to go away. You give them something to eat."

17"We have here only five loaves of bread and two fish," they answered.

18"Bring them here to me," he said. **19**And he directed the people to sit down on the grass. Taking the five loaves and the two fish and looking up to heaven, he gave thanks and broke the loaves. Then he gave them to the disciples, and the disciples gave them to the people. **20**They all ate and were satisfied, and the disciples picked up twelve basketfuls of broken pieces that were left over. **21**The number of those who ate was about five thousand men, besides women and children.

Jesus Walks on the Water

22Immediately Jesus made the disciples get into the boat and go on ahead of him to the other side, while he dismissed the crowd. **23**After he had dismissed them, he went up on a mountainside by himself to pray. When evening came, he was there alone, **24**but the boat was already a considerable distance*a* from land, buffeted by the waves because the wind was against it.

25During the fourth watch of the night Jesus went out to them, walking on the lake. **26**When the disciples saw him walking on the lake, they were terrified. "It's a ghost," they said, and cried out in fear.

27But Jesus immediately said to them: "Take courage! It is I. Don't be afraid."

28"Lord, if it's you," Peter replied, "tell me to come to you on the water."

29"Come," he said.

Then Peter got down out of the boat, walked on the water and came toward Jesus. **30**But when he saw the wind, he was afraid and, beginning to sink, cried out, "Lord, save me!"

31Immediately Jesus reached out his hand and caught him. "You of little faith," he said, "why did you doubt?"

32And when they climbed into the boat, the wind died down. **33**Then those who were in the boat worshiped him, saying, "Truly you are the Son of God."

34When they had crossed over, they landed at Gennesaret. **35**And when the men of that place recognized Jesus, they sent word to all the surrounding country. People brought all their sick to him **36**and begged him to let the sick just touch the edge of his cloak, and all who touched him were healed.

a24 Greek *many stadia*

VERSE FOR THE DAY:	AUTHOR:	PASSAGE FOR THE DAY:
Matthew 14:14	Thomas Hale	Matthew 14:13–21

Giving All We Have

FROM his home in Nepal, missionary surgeon Thomas Hale looks to the future.

The watchword for us all, no matter where God leads us, will be "love." Love is the one quality the world can discern that sets Christians apart and makes Christianity distinct from every other religion. If we fail to act on this truth, we will lose our right to be heard and will enter the post-Christian era for good.

What is our own personal role to be as we face the travail of the coming years? The problems of overpopulation and hunger, already upon us, are too great even for governments to handle, let alone individual Christians. It is one thing to minister to a handful of hungry Nepalis at our door by giving them food, money, seeds or a job, but when individuals become multitudes, what will we do? . . .

It seems that God is telling us simply to share with them whatever we have, and when it runs low, to try to get more, and when there is no more, to leave the issue to him. He is telling us to enter into their suffering without concern for the outcome. He is reminding us that, whatever we have done for the least of our brothers, we have done for him [see Matthew 25:40]. We cannot, as some do, restrict the interpretation of "brothers" to mean fellow-Christians alone. We wince when we hear Christians refer to much of the agony of mankind as the judgment of God; it may be, but it is not for us to say or even to think.

There are moments when we long for Christ to come again and feed the multitudes, not five thousand only, but fifty thousand, even fifty million. He could do it. Those first disciples had only two fish and a few loaves, but they gave him all they had. Is this not his word to us today—to give him all our loaves and fish, to give him everything we have? Then, who can say what he would be able to accomplish in our time through us?

Additional Scripture Readings:
Matthew 25:31–40;
2 Corinthians 9:6–15

Go to page 1034 for your next devotional reading.

Clean and Unclean

15 Then some Pharisees and teachers of the law came to Jesus from Jerusalem and asked, [2]"Why do your disciples break the tradition of the elders? They don't wash their hands before they eat!"

[3]Jesus replied, "And why do you break the command of God for the sake of your tradition? [4]For God said, 'Honor your father and mother'[a] and 'Anyone who curses his father or mother must be put to death.'[b] [5]But you say that if a man says to his father or mother, 'Whatever help you might otherwise have received from me is a gift devoted to God,' [6]he is not to 'honor his father[c]' with it. Thus you nullify the word of God for the sake of your tradition. [7]You hypocrites! Isaiah was right when he prophesied about you:

[8]" 'These people honor me with their
    lips,
  but their hearts are far from me.
[9]They worship me in vain;
  their teachings are but rules taught
    by men.'[d]"

[10]Jesus called the crowd to him and said, "Listen and understand. [11]What goes into a man's mouth does not make him 'unclean,' but what comes out of his mouth, that is what makes him 'unclean.' "

[12]Then the disciples came to him and asked, "Do you know that the Pharisees were offended when they heard this?"

[13]He replied, "Every plant that my heavenly Father has not planted will be pulled up by the roots. [14]Leave them; they are blind guides.[e] If a blind man leads a blind man, both will fall into a pit."

[15]Peter said, "Explain the parable to us."

[16]"Are you still so dull?" Jesus asked them. [17]"Don't you see that whatever enters the mouth goes into the stomach and then out of the body? [18]But the things that come out of the mouth come from the heart, and these make a man 'unclean.' [19]For out of the heart come evil thoughts, murder, adultery, sexual immorality, theft, false testimony, slander. [20]These are what make a man 'unclean'; but eating with unwashed hands does not make him 'unclean.' "

The Faith of the Canaanite Woman

[21]Leaving that place, Jesus withdrew to the region of Tyre and Sidon. [22]A Canaanite woman from that vicinity came to him, crying out, "Lord, Son of David, have mercy on me! My daughter is suffering terribly from demon-possession."

[23]Jesus did not answer a word. So his disciples came to him and urged him, "Send her away, for she keeps crying out after us."

[24]He answered, "I was sent only to the lost sheep of Israel."

[25]The woman came and knelt before him. "Lord, help me!" she said.

[26]He replied, "It is not right to take the children's bread and toss it to their dogs."

[27]"Yes, Lord," she said, "but even the dogs eat the crumbs that fall from their masters' table."

[28]Then Jesus answered, "Woman, you have great faith! Your request is granted." And her daughter was healed from that very hour.

Jesus Feeds the Four Thousand

[29]Jesus left there and went along the Sea of Galilee. Then he went up on a mountainside and sat down. [30]Great crowds came to him, bringing the lame, the blind, the crippled, the mute and many others, and laid them at his feet; and he healed them. [31]The people were amazed when they saw the mute speaking, the crippled made well, the lame walking and the blind seeing. And they praised the God of Israel.

[32]Jesus called his disciples to him and said, "I have compassion for these people; they have already been with me three days and have nothing to eat. I do not want to send them away hungry, or they may collapse on the way."

[33]His disciples answered, "Where could we get enough bread in this remote place to feed such a crowd?"

[34]"How many loaves do you have?" Jesus asked.

"Seven," they replied, "and a few small fish."

[35]He told the crowd to sit down on the ground. [36]Then he took the seven loaves and the fish, and when he had given thanks, he broke them and gave them to the disciples, and they in turn to the people. [37]They all ate and were satisfied. Af-

---

[a]4 Exodus 20:12; Deut. 5:16   [b]4 Exodus 21:17; Lev. 20:9   [c]6 Some manuscripts *father or his mother*
[d]9 Isaiah 29:13   [e]14 Some manuscripts *guides of the blind*

terward the disciples picked up seven basketfuls of broken pieces that were left over. [38]The number of those who ate was four thousand, besides women and children. [39]After Jesus had sent the crowd away, he got into the boat and went to the vicinity of Magadan.

The Demand for a Sign

16 The Pharisees and Sadducees came to Jesus and tested him by asking him to show them a sign from heaven.

[2]He replied,[a] "When evening comes, you say, 'It will be fair weather, for the sky is red,' [3]and in the morning, 'Today it will be stormy, for the sky is red and overcast.' You know how to interpret the appearance of the sky, but you cannot interpret the signs of the times. [4]A wicked and adulterous generation looks for a miraculous sign, but none will be given it except the sign of Jonah." Jesus then left them and went away.

The Yeast of the Pharisees and Sadducees

[5]When they went across the lake, the disciples forgot to take bread. [6]"Be careful," Jesus said to them. "Be on your guard against the yeast of the Pharisees and Sadducees."

[7]They discussed this among themselves and said, "It is because we didn't bring any bread."

[8]Aware of their discussion, Jesus asked, "You of little faith, why are you talking among yourselves about having no bread? [9]Do you still not understand? Don't you remember the five loaves for the five thousand, and how many basketfuls you gathered? [10]Or the seven loaves for the four thousand, and how many basketfuls you gathered? [11]How is it you don't understand that I was not talking to you about bread? But be on your guard against the yeast of the Pharisees and Sadducees." [12]Then they understood that he was not telling them to guard against the yeast used in bread, but against the teaching of the Pharisees and Sadducees.

Peter's Confession of Christ

[13]When Jesus came to the region of Caesarea Philippi, he asked his disciples, "Who do people say the Son of Man is?" [14]They replied, "Some say John the Baptist; others say Elijah; and still others, Jeremiah or one of the prophets."

[15]"But what about you?" he asked. "Who do you say I am?"

[16]Simon Peter answered, "You are the Christ,[b] the Son of the living God."

[17]Jesus replied, "Blessed are you, Simon son of Jonah, for this was not revealed to you by man, but by my Father in heaven. [18]And I tell you that you are Peter,[c] and on this rock I will build my church, and the gates of Hades[d] will not overcome it.[e] [19]I will give you the keys of the kingdom of heaven; whatever you bind on earth will be[f] bound in heaven, and whatever you loose on earth will be[f] loosed in heaven." [20]Then he warned his disciples not to tell anyone that he was the Christ.

Jesus Predicts His Death

[21]From that time on Jesus began to explain to his disciples that he must go to Jerusalem and suffer many things at the hands of the elders, chief priests and teachers of the law, and that he must be killed and on the third day be raised to life.

[22]Peter took him aside and began to rebuke him. "Never, Lord!" he said. "This shall never happen to you!"

[23]Jesus turned and said to Peter, "Get behind me, Satan! You are a stumbling block to me; you do not have in mind the things of God, but the things of men."

[24]Then Jesus said to his disciples, "If anyone would come after me, he must deny himself and take up his cross and follow me. [25]For whoever wants to save his life[g] will lose it, but whoever loses his life for me will find it. [26]What good will it be for a man if he gains the whole world, yet forfeits his soul? Or what can a man give in exchange for his soul? [27]For the Son of Man is going to come in his Father's glory with his angels, and then he will reward each person according to what he has done. [28]I tell you the truth, some who are standing here will not taste death before they see the Son of Man coming in his kingdom."

The Transfiguration

17 After six days Jesus took with him Peter, James and John the brother of James, and led them up a high moun-

---

[a]2 Some early manuscripts do not have the rest of verse 2 and all of verse 3.   [b]16 Or *Messiah*; also in verse 20   [c]18 *Peter* means *rock.*   [d]18 Or *hell*   [e]18 Or *not prove stronger than it*   [f]19 Or *have been*   [g]25 The Greek word means either *life* or *soul*; also in verse 26.

tain by themselves. [2]There he was transfigured before them. His face shone like the sun, and his clothes became as white as the light. [3]Just then there appeared before them Moses and Elijah, talking with Jesus.

[4]Peter said to Jesus, "Lord, it is good for us to be here. If you wish, I will put up three shelters—one for you, one for Moses and one for Elijah."

[5]While he was still speaking, a bright cloud enveloped them, and a voice from the cloud said, "This is my Son, whom I love; with him I am well pleased. Listen to him!"

[6]When the disciples heard this, they fell facedown to the ground, terrified. [7]But Jesus came and touched them. "Get up," he said. "Don't be afraid." [8]When they looked up, they saw no one except Jesus.

[9]As they were coming down the mountain, Jesus instructed them, "Don't tell anyone what you have seen, until the Son of Man has been raised from the dead."

[10]The disciples asked him, "Why then do the teachers of the law say that Elijah must come first?"

[11]Jesus replied, "To be sure, Elijah comes and will restore all things. [12]But I tell you, Elijah has already come, and they did not recognize him, but have done to him everything they wished. In the same way the Son of Man is going to suffer at their hands." [13]Then the disciples understood that he was talking to them about John the Baptist.

The Healing of a Boy With a Demon

[14]When they came to the crowd, a man approached Jesus and knelt before him. [15]"Lord, have mercy on my son," he said. "He has seizures and is suffering greatly. He often falls into the fire or into the water. [16]I brought him to your disciples, but they could not heal him."

[17]"O unbelieving and perverse generation," Jesus replied, "how long shall I stay with you? How long shall I put up with you? Bring the boy here to me." [18]Jesus rebuked the demon, and it came out of the boy, and he was healed from that moment.

[19]Then the disciples came to Jesus in private and asked, "Why couldn't we drive it out?"

[20]He replied, "Because you have so little faith. I tell you the truth, if you have faith as small as a mustard seed, you can say to this mountain, 'Move from here to there' and it will move. Nothing will be impossible for you.[a]"

[22]When they came together in Galilee, he said to them, "The Son of Man is going to be betrayed into the hands of men. [23]They will kill him, and on the third day he will be raised to life." And the disciples were filled with grief.

The Temple Tax

[24]After Jesus and his disciples arrived in Capernaum, the collectors of the two-drachma tax came to Peter and asked, "Doesn't your teacher pay the temple tax[b]?"

[25]"Yes, he does," he replied.

When Peter came into the house, Jesus was the first to speak. "What do you think, Simon?" he asked. "From whom do the kings of the earth collect duty and taxes—from their own sons or from others?"

[26]"From others," Peter answered.

"Then the sons are exempt," Jesus said to him. [27]"But so that we may not offend them, go to the lake and throw out your line. Take the first fish you catch; open its mouth and you will find a four-drachma coin. Take it and give it to them for my tax and yours."

The Greatest in the Kingdom of Heaven

18 At that time the disciples came to Jesus and asked, "Who is the greatest in the kingdom of heaven?"

[2]He called a little child and had him stand among them. [3]And he said: "I tell you the truth, unless you change and become like little children, you will never enter the kingdom of heaven. [4]Therefore, whoever humbles himself like this child is the greatest in the kingdom of heaven.

[5]"And whoever welcomes a little child like this in my name welcomes me. [6]But if anyone causes one of these little ones who believe in me to sin, it would be better for him to have a large millstone hung around his neck and to be drowned in the depths of the sea.

[7]"Woe to the world because of the things that cause people to sin! Such things must come, but woe to the man through whom they come! [8]If your hand or your foot causes you to sin, cut it off

---

[a]20 Some manuscripts you. [21]But this kind does not go out except by prayer and fasting.   [b]24 Greek the two drachmas

and throw it away. It is better for you to enter life maimed or crippled than to have two hands or two feet and be thrown into eternal fire. [9]And if your eye causes you to sin, gouge it out and throw it away. It is better for you to enter life with one eye than to have two eyes and be thrown into the fire of hell.

The Parable of the Lost Sheep

[10]"See that you do not look down on one of these little ones. For I tell you that their angels in heaven always see the face of my Father in heaven.[a]

[12]"What do you think? If a man owns a hundred sheep, and one of them wanders away, will he not leave the ninety-nine on the hills and go to look for the one that wandered off? [13]And if he finds it, I tell you the truth, he is happier about that one sheep than about the ninety-nine that did not wander off. [14]In the same way your Father in heaven is not willing that any of these little ones should be lost.

[a]10 Some manuscripts *heaven.* [11]*The Son of Man came to save what was lost.*

THURSDAY

VERSE FOR THE DAY:	AUTHOR:	PASSAGE FOR THE DAY:
Matthew 17:20	Philip W. Williams	Matthew 17:14–23

"Father" on Our Lips

"IF ONLY I had more faith, I'd be able to handle myself in this situation." How much faith is enough in our mourning? Some of us feel that it is always more than what we have. Jesus said that the amount of faith isn't important: "I tell you the truth, if you have faith as small as a mustard seed, you can say to this mountain, 'Move from here to there' and it will move. Nothing will be impossible for you" [Matthew 17:20].

A grain of mustard seed! Do you recall how small a mustard seed is? Necklaces used to be worn with a mustard seed in the bulb, which magnified it so that it could be seen with normal eyesight. Now if we have faith, though it be that small, nothing will be impossible.

I interpret faith in this instance as basic trust. We don't need a huge quantity of it in order to get on with our bereavement. In fact, if we worry about having a lot of faith, we may miss the mustard seed we do have.

The giver of this grain of faith is God, whose Son, though despondent and despairing in his crisis, maintained his faith. He went through his Gethsemane of grief with the word "Father" still on his lips.

We too can go through the valleys and mountains of our bereavement journey with "Father" on our lips. Our hearts may wonder, doubt and cry out in pain, but these feelings will not obliterate our faith. Even when we think we have lost that mustard seed, we do well to remember that our Father is faithful, for he has loved us first.

Additional Scripture Readings:
Mark 14:32–40; Ephesians 3:14–21

Go to page 1036 for your next devotional reading.

A Brother Who Sins Against You

15"If your brother sins against you,[a] go and show him his fault, just between the two of you. If he listens to you, you have won your brother over. 16But if he will not listen, take one or two others along, so that 'every matter may be established by the testimony of two or three witnesses.'[b] 17If he refuses to listen to them, tell it to the church; and if he refuses to listen even to the church, treat him as you would a pagan or a tax collector.

18"I tell you the truth, whatever you bind on earth will be[c] bound in heaven, and whatever you loose on earth will be[c] loosed in heaven.

19"Again, I tell you that if two of you on earth agree about anything you ask for, it will be done for you by my Father in heaven. 20For where two or three come together in my name, there am I with them."

The Parable of the Unmerciful Servant

21Then Peter came to Jesus and asked, "Lord, how many times shall I forgive my brother when he sins against me? Up to seven times?"

22Jesus answered, "I tell you, not seven times, but seventy-seven times.[d]

23"Therefore, the kingdom of heaven is like a king who wanted to settle accounts with his servants. 24As he began the settlement, a man who owed him ten thousand talents[e] was brought to him. 25Since he was not able to pay, the master ordered that he and his wife and his children and all that he had be sold to repay the debt.

26"The servant fell on his knees before him. 'Be patient with me,' he begged, 'and I will pay back everything.' 27The servant's master took pity on him, canceled the debt and let him go.

28"But when that servant went out, he found one of his fellow servants who owed him a hundred denarii.[f] He grabbed him and began to choke him. 'Pay back what you owe me!' he demanded.

29"His fellow servant fell to his knees and begged him, 'Be patient with me, and I will pay you back.'

30"But he refused. Instead, he went off and had the man thrown into prison until he could pay the debt. 31When the other servants saw what had happened, they were greatly distressed and went and told their master everything that had happened.

32"Then the master called the servant in. 'You wicked servant,' he said, 'I canceled all that debt of yours because you begged me to. 33Shouldn't you have had mercy on your fellow servant just as I had on you?' 34In anger his master turned him over to the jailers to be tortured, until he should pay back all he owed.

35"This is how my heavenly Father will treat each of you unless you forgive your brother from your heart."

Divorce

19 When Jesus had finished saying these things, he left Galilee and went into the region of Judea to the other side of the Jordan. 2Large crowds followed him, and he healed them there.

3Some Pharisees came to him to test him. They asked, "Is it lawful for a man to divorce his wife for any and every reason?"

4"Haven't you read," he replied, "that at the beginning the Creator 'made them male and female,'[g] 5and said, 'For this reason a man will leave his father and mother and be united to his wife, and the two will become one flesh'[h]? 6So they are no longer two, but one. Therefore what God has joined together, let man not separate."

7"Why then," they asked, "did Moses command that a man give his wife a certificate of divorce and send her away?"

8Jesus replied, "Moses permitted you to divorce your wives because your hearts were hard. But it was not this way from the beginning. 9I tell you that anyone who divorces his wife, except for marital unfaithfulness, and marries another woman commits adultery."

10The disciples said to him, "If this is the situation between a husband and wife, it is better not to marry."

11Jesus replied, "Not everyone can accept this word, but only those to whom it has been given. 12For some are eunuchs because they were born that way; others were made that way by men; and others have renounced marriage[i] because of the kingdom of heaven. The one who can accept this should accept it."

---

a15 Some manuscripts do not have against you.   b16 Deut. 19:15   c18 Or have been   d22 Or seventy times seven   e24 That is, millions of dollars   f28 That is, a few dollars   g4 Gen. 1:27   h5 Gen. 2:24   i12 Or have made themselves eunuchs

The Little Children and Jesus

13Then little children were brought to Jesus for him to place his hands on them and pray for them. But the disciples rebuked those who brought them.

14Jesus said, "Let the little children come to me, and do not hinder them, for the kingdom of heaven belongs to such as these." **15**When he had placed his hands on them, he went on from there.

FRIDAY

VERSE FOR THE DAY:
Matthew 19:26

AUTHOR:
Bill Hybels

PASSAGE FOR THE DAY:
Matthew 19:16–30

Cultivating Vision

THE disciples once thought that they had heard Jesus say that respectable, well-to-do, upstanding community leaders could not be saved. If that were true, then their chances of being saved were not very good either. The disciples, who had not yet become visionaries, immediately gave up hope. They saw no solution; salvation was obviously out of reach. Jesus looked at them and said, "Fellas, you're right. With human beings, some problems have no solutions. But with God all things are possible" (Matthew 19:26).

Does your problem seem bigger than life, bigger than God himself? It isn't. God is infinitely bigger than any problem you ever had or will have, and every time you call a problem unsolvable, you mock God. "With God all things are possible." Visionary people face the same problems everyone else faces; but rather than get paralyzed by their problems, visionaries immediately commit themselves to finding a solution. Almost as a reflex reaction to the problem they say, "The situation is bad, all right, but no problem is bigger than God. And right now, before I get bogged down, I need to start down the path of solving it." More often than not, visionaries find a way, with God's help, to deal with their problems and overcome them rather than surrender their lives to them.

Vision is a vitally important quality to cultivate, because life is really just a series of problems, challenges, trials and disappointments. If you allow yourself to be overwhelmed by difficulties, your future is not bright. You will get stuck first on one problem and then on another . . . If, on the other hand, you cultivate vision—if, whenever you are faced with a problem, you immediately explore ways to deal with it—you will not only avert all sorts of discouragement, but you will also discover just how much creativity and wisdom God wants to give his children who look to him for help.

Additional Scripture Readings:
Ephesians 3:14–21;
Philippians 4:10–13

Go to page 1038 for your next devotional reading.

The Rich Young Man

16Now a man came up to Jesus and asked, "Teacher, what good thing must I do to get eternal life?"

17"Why do you ask me about what is good?" Jesus replied. "There is only One who is good. If you want to enter life, obey the commandments."

18"Which ones?" the man inquired.

Jesus replied, " 'Do not murder, do not commit adultery, do not steal, do not give false testimony, **19**honor your father and mother,'*a* and 'love your neighbor as yourself.'*b*"

20"All these I have kept," the young man said. "What do I still lack?"

21Jesus answered, "If you want to be perfect, go, sell your possessions and give to the poor, and you will have treasure in heaven. Then come, follow me."

22When the young man heard this, he went away sad, because he had great wealth.

23Then Jesus said to his disciples, "I tell you the truth, it is hard for a rich man to enter the kingdom of heaven. **24**Again I tell you, it is easier for a camel to go through the eye of a needle than for a rich man to enter the kingdom of God."

25When the disciples heard this, they were greatly astonished and asked, "Who then can be saved?"

26Jesus looked at them and said, "With man this is impossible, but with God all things are possible."

27Peter answered him, "We have left everything to follow you! What then will there be for us?"

28Jesus said to them, "I tell you the truth, at the renewal of all things, when the Son of Man sits on his glorious throne, you who have followed me will also sit on twelve thrones, judging the twelve tribes of Israel. **29**And everyone who has left houses or brothers or sisters or father or mother*c* or children or fields for my sake will receive a hundred times as much and will inherit eternal life. **30**But many who are first will be last, and many who are last will be first.

The Parable of the Workers in the Vineyard

20 "For the kingdom of heaven is like a landowner who went out early in the morning to hire men to work in his vineyard. **2**He agreed to pay them a denar-ius for the day and sent them into his vineyard.

3"About the third hour he went out and saw others standing in the marketplace doing nothing. **4**He told them, 'You also go and work in my vineyard, and I will pay you whatever is right.' **5**So they went.

"He went out again about the sixth hour and the ninth hour and did the same thing. **6**About the eleventh hour he went out and found still others standing around. He asked them, 'Why have you been standing here all day long doing nothing?'

7" 'Because no one has hired us,' they answered.

"He said to them, 'You also go and work in my vineyard.'

8"When evening came, the owner of the vineyard said to his foreman, 'Call the workers and pay them their wages, beginning with the last ones hired and going on to the first.'

9"The workers who were hired about the eleventh hour came and each received a denarius. **10**So when those came who were hired first, they expected to receive more. But each one of them also received a denarius. **11**When they received it, they began to grumble against the landowner. **12**'These men who were hired last worked only one hour,' they said, 'and you have made them equal to us who have borne the burden of the work and the heat of the day.'

13"But he answered one of them, 'Friend, I am not being unfair to you. Didn't you agree to work for a denarius? **14**Take your pay and go. I want to give the man who was hired last the same as I gave you. **15**Don't I have the right to do what I want with my own money? Or are you envious because I am generous?'

16"So the last will be first, and the first will be last."

Jesus Again Predicts His Death

17Now as Jesus was going up to Jerusalem, he took the twelve disciples aside and said to them, **18**"We are going up to Jerusalem, and the Son of Man will be betrayed to the chief priests and the teachers of the law. They will condemn him to death **19**and will turn him over to the Gentiles to be mocked and flogged and crucified. On the third day he will be raised to life!"

---

a19 Exodus 20:12-16; Deut. 5:16-20   *b19* Lev. 19:18   *c29* Some manuscripts *mother or wife*

WEEKENDING

REALIZE

Forgiving is love's revolution against love's unfairness. When we forgive, we ignore the normal laws that strap us to the natural law of getting even and, by the alchemy of love, we release ourselves from our own painful pasts.

We fly over a dues-paying morality in order to create a new future out of the past's unfairness. We free ourselves from the wrong that is locked into our private histories; we unshackle our spirits from malice; and, maybe, if we are lucky, we also restore a relationship that would otherwise be lost forever.

– Lewis B. Smedes

REVIVE

Saturday: Matthew 18:21–35
Sunday: Ephesians 4:29 — 5:2

Go to page 1040 for your next devotional reading.

A Mother's Request

20Then the mother of Zebedee's sons came to Jesus with her sons and, kneeling down, asked a favor of him.

21"What is it you want?" he asked.

She said, "Grant that one of these two sons of mine may sit at your right and the other at your left in your kingdom."

22"You don't know what you are asking," Jesus said to them. "Can you drink the cup I am going to drink?"

"We can," they answered.

23Jesus said to them, "You will indeed drink from my cup, but to sit at my right or left is not for me to grant. These places belong to those for whom they have been prepared by my Father."

24When the ten heard about this, they were indignant with the two brothers. **25**Jesus called them together and said, "You know that the rulers of the Gentiles lord it over them, and their high officials exercise authority over them. **26**Not so with you. Instead, whoever wants to become great among you must be your servant, **27**and whoever wants to be first must be your slave — **28**just as the Son of Man did not come to be served, but to serve, and to give his life as a ransom for many."

Two Blind Men Receive Sight

29As Jesus and his disciples were leaving Jericho, a large crowd followed him. **30**Two blind men were sitting by the roadside, and when they heard that Jesus was going by, they shouted, "Lord, Son of David, have mercy on us!"

31The crowd rebuked them and told them to be quiet, but they shouted all the louder, "Lord, Son of David, have mercy on us!"

32Jesus stopped and called them. "What do you want me to do for you?" he asked.

33"Lord," they answered, "we want our sight."

34Jesus had compassion on them and touched their eyes. Immediately they received their sight and followed him.

The Triumphal Entry

21 As they approached Jerusalem and came to Bethphage on the Mount of Olives, Jesus sent two disciples, **2**saying to them, "Go to the village ahead of you, and at once you will find a donkey tied there, with her colt by her. Untie them and bring them to me. **3**If anyone says anything to you, tell him that the Lord needs them, and he will send them right away."

4This took place to fulfill what was spoken through the prophet:

5"Say to the Daughter of Zion,
'See, your king comes to you,
gentle and riding on a donkey,
  on a colt, the foal of a donkey.' "[a]

6The disciples went and did as Jesus had instructed them. **7**They brought the donkey and the colt, placed their cloaks on them, and Jesus sat on them. **8**A very large crowd spread their cloaks on the road, while others cut branches from the trees and spread them on the road. **9**The crowds that went ahead of him and those that followed shouted,

"Hosanna[b] to the Son of David!"

"Blessed is he who comes in the name
  of the Lord!"[c]

"Hosanna[b] in the highest!"

10When Jesus entered Jerusalem, the whole city was stirred and asked, "Who is this?"

11The crowds answered, "This is Jesus, the prophet from Nazareth in Galilee."

Jesus at the Temple

12Jesus entered the temple area and drove out all who were buying and selling there. He overturned the tables of the money changers and the benches of those selling doves. **13**"It is written," he said to them, " 'My house will be called a house of prayer,'[d] but you are making it a 'den of robbers.'[e]"

14The blind and the lame came to him at the temple, and he healed them. **15**But when the chief priests and the teachers of the law saw the wonderful things he did and the children shouting in the temple area, "Hosanna to the Son of David," they were indignant.

16"Do you hear what these children are saying?" they asked him.

"Yes," replied Jesus, "have you never read,

" 'From the lips of children and
  infants
you have ordained praise'[f]?"

17And he left them and went out of the city to Bethany, where he spent the night.

---

a5 Zech. 9:9   *b9* A Hebrew expression meaning "Save!" which became an exclamation of praise; also in verse 15   *c9* Psalm 118:26   *d13* Isaiah 56:7   *e13* Jer. 7:11   *f16* Psalm 8:2

The Fig Tree Withers

18Early in the morning, as he was on his way back to the city, he was hungry. **19**Seeing a fig tree by the road, he went up to it but found nothing on it except leaves. Then he said to it, "May you never bear fruit again!" Immediately the tree withered.

20When the disciples saw this, they were amazed. "How did the fig tree wither so quickly?" they asked.

21Jesus replied, "I tell you the truth, if you have faith and do not doubt, not only can you do what was done to the fig tree, but also you can say to this mountain, 'Go, throw yourself into the sea,' and it will be done. **22**If you believe, you will receive whatever you ask for in prayer."

MONDAY

VERSE FOR THE DAY:
Matthew 20:26

AUTHOR:
Mike Singletary

PASSAGE FOR THE DAY:
Matthew 20:20–28

Love and the Real Man

TOO many people say love is impossible to understand or define. Love is action. A real man will love a woman the way the Bible says to. The most militant feminist would not condemn a love like that.

I would never say that I am the definition of what a real man is, but I'm not ashamed to say I'm working toward it. I want to be the best man I can be, and before it's over I'm trying to come close. A real man will treat his wife right. He will be a servant rather than a master. He will do the right thing because it's the right thing. He will give a hundred percent no matter what he's called upon to do.

And how will a man know when he's a real man? When he seeks to serve. When he can sit down with his wife and honestly look to fulfill her needs before his own. He should ask, "What can I do for you?"

Society says a man should find a gorgeous wife who will take care of his needs, make him happy and serve him. She becomes part of his orbit, makes him proud, and he gives her everything he thinks she wants. But she's miserable. She's in second place. He can't put her first because that goes against everything he feels and has been taught. Just like everything else God made perfect, the world has flipped this around. There's a counterfeit of the real thing being sold on the market, and it's called lust.

It's exciting. It looks good. It's even satisfying for a while. But it's not true love. It's backwards. It fulfills *our* desires first, even at the expense of the person we're supposed to love. There is a big difference, and we men need to learn and know it. Lust takes, for our benefit. Love gives, for the benefit of the one we love.

Additional Scripture Readings:
Mark 9:33–37; 1 Corinthians 13:1–7

Go to page 1044 for your next devotional reading.

The Authority of Jesus Questioned

23Jesus entered the temple courts, and, while he was teaching, the chief priests and the elders of the people came to him. "By what authority are you doing these things?" they asked. "And who gave you this authority?"

24Jesus replied, "I will also ask you one question. If you answer me, I will tell you by what authority I am doing these things. **25**John's baptism — where did it come from? Was it from heaven, or from men?"

They discussed it among themselves and said, "If we say, 'From heaven,' he will ask, 'Then why didn't you believe him?' **26**But if we say, 'From men' — we are afraid of the people, for they all hold that John was a prophet."

27So they answered Jesus, "We don't know."

Then he said, "Neither will I tell you by what authority I am doing these things.

The Parable of the Two Sons

28"What do you think? There was a man who had two sons. He went to the first and said, 'Son, go and work today in the vineyard.'

29"'I will not,' he answered, but later he changed his mind and went.

30"Then the father went to the other son and said the same thing. He answered, 'I will, sir,' but he did not go.

31"Which of the two did what his father wanted?"

"The first," they answered.

Jesus said to them, "I tell you the truth, the tax collectors and the prostitutes are entering the kingdom of God ahead of you. **32**For John came to you to show you the way of righteousness, and you did not believe him, but the tax collectors and the prostitutes did. And even after you saw this, you did not repent and believe him.

The Parable of the Tenants

33"Listen to another parable: There was a landowner who planted a vineyard. He put a wall around it, dug a winepress in it and built a watchtower. Then he rented the vineyard to some farmers and went away on a journey. **34**When the harvest time approached, he sent his servants to the tenants to collect his fruit.

35"The tenants seized his servants; they beat one, killed another, and stoned a third. **36**Then he sent other servants to them, more than the first time, and the tenants treated them the same way. **37**Last of all, he sent his son to them. 'They will respect my son,' he said.

38"But when the tenants saw the son, they said to each other, 'This is the heir. Come, let's kill him and take his inheritance.' **39**So they took him and threw him out of the vineyard and killed him.

40"Therefore, when the owner of the vineyard comes, what will he do to those tenants?"

41"He will bring those wretches to a wretched end," they replied, "and he will rent the vineyard to other tenants, who will give him his share of the crop at harvest time."

42Jesus said to them, "Have you never read in the Scriptures:

" 'The stone the builders rejected
    has become the capstone[a];
the Lord has done this,
    and it is marvelous in our eyes'[b]?

43"Therefore I tell you that the kingdom of God will be taken away from you and given to a people who will produce its fruit. **44**He who falls on this stone will be broken to pieces, but he on whom it falls will be crushed."[c]

45When the chief priests and the Pharisees heard Jesus' parables, they knew he was talking about them. **46**They looked for a way to arrest him, but they were afraid of the crowd because the people held that he was a prophet.

The Parable of the Wedding Banquet

22 Jesus spoke to them again in parables, saying: **2**"The kingdom of heaven is like a king who prepared a wedding banquet for his son. **3**He sent his servants to those who had been invited to the banquet to tell them to come, but they refused to come.

4"Then he sent some more servants and said, 'Tell those who have been invited that I have prepared my dinner: My oxen and fattened cattle have been butchered, and everything is ready. Come to the wedding banquet.'

5"But they paid no attention and went off — one to his field, another to his business. **6**The rest seized his servants, mistreated them and killed them. **7**The king was enraged. He sent his army and destroyed those murderers and burned their city.

---

a42 Or *cornerstone*   *b42* Psalm 118:22,23   *c44* Some manuscripts do not have verse 44.

[8] "Then he said to his servants, 'The wedding banquet is ready, but those I invited did not deserve to come. [9]Go to the street corners and invite to the banquet anyone you find.' [10]So the servants went out into the streets and gathered all the people they could find, both good and bad, and the wedding hall was filled with guests.

[11] "But when the king came in to see the guests, he noticed a man there who was not wearing wedding clothes. [12]'Friend,' he asked, 'how did you get in here without wedding clothes?' The man was speechless.

[13] "Then the king told the attendants, 'Tie him hand and foot, and throw him outside, into the darkness, where there will be weeping and gnashing of teeth.'

[14] "For many are invited, but few are chosen."

Paying Taxes to Caesar

[15] Then the Pharisees went out and laid plans to trap him in his words. [16]They sent their disciples to him along with the Herodians. "Teacher," they said, "we know you are a man of integrity and that you teach the way of God in accordance with the truth. You aren't swayed by men, because you pay no attention to who they are. [17]Tell us then, what is your opinion? Is it right to pay taxes to Caesar or not?"

[18] But Jesus, knowing their evil intent, said, "You hypocrites, why are you trying to trap me? [19]Show me the coin used for paying the tax." They brought him a denarius, [20]and he asked them, "Whose portrait is this? And whose inscription?"

[21] "Caesar's," they replied.

Then he said to them, "Give to Caesar what is Caesar's, and to God what is God's."

[22] When they heard this, they were amazed. So they left him and went away.

Marriage at the Resurrection

[23] That same day the Sadducees, who say there is no resurrection, came to him with a question. [24]"Teacher," they said, "Moses told us that if a man dies without having children, his brother must marry the widow and have children for him. [25]Now there were seven brothers among us. The first one married and died, and since he had no children, he left his wife to his brother. [26]The same thing happened to the second and third brother, right on

down to the seventh. [27]Finally, the woman died. [28]Now then, at the resurrection, whose wife will she be of the seven, since all of them were married to her?"

[29] Jesus replied, "You are in error because you do not know the Scriptures or the power of God. [30]At the resurrection people will neither marry nor be given in marriage; they will be like the angels in heaven. [31]But about the resurrection of the dead—have you not read what God said to you, [32]'I am the God of Abraham, the God of Isaac, and the God of Jacob'[a]? He is not the God of the dead but of the living."

[33] When the crowds heard this, they were astonished at his teaching.

The Greatest Commandment

[34] Hearing that Jesus had silenced the Sadducees, the Pharisees got together. [35]One of them, an expert in the law, tested him with this question: [36]"Teacher, which is the greatest commandment in the Law?"

[37] Jesus replied: " 'Love the Lord your God with all your heart and with all your soul and with all your mind.'[b] [38]This is the first and greatest commandment. [39]And the second is like it: 'Love your neighbor as yourself.'[c] [40]All the Law and the Prophets hang on these two commandments."

Whose Son Is the Christ?

[41] While the Pharisees were gathered together, Jesus asked them, [42]"What do you think about the Christ[d]? Whose son is he?"

"The son of David," they replied.

[43] He said to them, "How is it then that David, speaking by the Spirit, calls him 'Lord'? For he says,

[44] " 'The Lord said to my Lord:
  "Sit at my right hand
until I put your enemies
  under your feet." '[e]

[45] If then David calls him 'Lord,' how can he be his son?" [46]No one could say a word in reply, and from that day on no one dared to ask him any more questions.

Seven Woes

23 Then Jesus said to the crowds and to his disciples: [2]"The teachers of the law and the Pharisees sit in Moses'

---

[a]32 Exodus 3:6   [b]37 Deut. 6:5   [c]39 Lev. 19:18   [d]42 Or Messiah   [e]44 Psalm 110:1

seat. ³So you must obey them and do everything they tell you. But do not do what they do, for they do not practice what they preach. ⁴They tie up heavy loads and put them on men's shoulders, but they themselves are not willing to lift a finger to move them.

⁵"Everything they do is done for men to see: They make their phylacteries*a* wide and the tassels on their garments long; ⁶they love the place of honor at banquets and the most important seats in the synagogues; ⁷they love to be greeted in the marketplaces and to have men call them 'Rabbi.'

⁸"But you are not to be called 'Rabbi,' for you have only one Master and you are all brothers. ⁹And do not call anyone on earth 'father,' for you have one Father, and he is in heaven. ¹⁰Nor are you to be called 'teacher,' for you have one Teacher, the Christ.*b* ¹¹The greatest among you will be your servant. ¹²For whoever exalts himself will be humbled, and whoever humbles himself will be exalted.

¹³"Woe to you, teachers of the law and Pharisees, you hypocrites! You shut the kingdom of heaven in men's faces. You yourselves do not enter, nor will you let those enter who are trying to.*c*

¹⁵"Woe to you, teachers of the law and Pharisees, you hypocrites! You travel over land and sea to win a single convert, and when he becomes one, you make him twice as much a son of hell as you are.

¹⁶"Woe to you, blind guides! You say, 'If anyone swears by the temple, it means nothing; but if anyone swears by the gold of the temple, he is bound by his oath.' ¹⁷You blind fools! Which is greater: the gold, or the temple that makes the gold sacred? ¹⁸You also say, 'If anyone swears by the altar, it means nothing; but if anyone swears by the gift on it, he is bound by his oath.' ¹⁹You blind men! Which is greater: the gift, or the altar that makes the gift sacred? ²⁰Therefore, he who swears by the altar swears by it and by everything on it. ²¹And he who swears by the temple swears by it and by the one who dwells in it. ²²And he who swears by heaven swears by God's throne and by the one who sits on it.

²³"Woe to you, teachers of the law and Pharisees, you hypocrites! You give a tenth of your spices — mint, dill and cummin. But you have neglected the more important matters of the law — justice, mercy and faithfulness. You should have practiced the latter, without neglecting the former. ²⁴You blind guides! You strain out a gnat but swallow a camel.

²⁵"Woe to you, teachers of the law and Pharisees, you hypocrites! You clean the outside of the cup and dish, but inside they are full of greed and self-indulgence. ²⁶Blind Pharisee! First clean the inside of the cup and dish, and then the outside also will be clean.

²⁷"Woe to you, teachers of the law and Pharisees, you hypocrites! You are like whitewashed tombs, which look beautiful on the outside but on the inside are full of dead men's bones and everything unclean. ²⁸In the same way, on the outside you appear to people as righteous but on the inside you are full of hypocrisy and wickedness.

²⁹"Woe to you, teachers of the law and Pharisees, you hypocrites! You build tombs for the prophets and decorate the graves of the righteous. ³⁰And you say, 'If we had lived in the days of our forefathers, we would not have taken part with them in shedding the blood of the prophets.' ³¹So you testify against yourselves that you are the descendants of those who murdered the prophets. ³²Fill up, then, the measure of the sin of your forefathers!

³³"You snakes! You brood of vipers! How will you escape being condemned to hell? ³⁴Therefore I am sending you prophets and wise men and teachers. Some of them you will kill and crucify; others you will flog in your synagogues and pursue from town to town. ³⁵And so upon you will come all the righteous blood that has been shed on earth, from the blood of righteous Abel to the blood of Zechariah son of Berekiah, whom you murdered between the temple and the altar. ³⁶I tell you the truth, all this will come upon this generation.

³⁷"O Jerusalem, Jerusalem, you who kill the prophets and stone those sent to you, how often I have longed to gather your children together, as a hen gathers her chicks under her wings, but you were

---

a5 That is, boxes containing Scripture verses, worn on forehead and arm   *b10* Or *Messiah*
c13 Some manuscripts *to. ¹⁴Woe to you, teachers of the law and Pharisees, you hypocrites! You devour widows' houses and for a show make lengthy prayers. Therefore you will be punished more severely.*

not willing. [38]Look, your house is left to you desolate. [39]For I tell you, you will not see me again until you say, 'Blessed is he who comes in the name of the Lord.'[a]"

a39 Psalm 118:26

Signs of the End of the Age

24 Jesus left the temple and was walking away when his disciples came up to him to call his attention to its buildings. [2]"Do you see all these things?" he

---

VERSE FOR THE DAY:	*AUTHOR:*	*PASSAGE FOR THE DAY:*
Matthew 23:28	*John Fischer*	*Matthew 23:25–28*

R-rated Hearts

THE way I feel about being around unbelievers will tell me a whole lot about my concept of God and how I stand before him. Jesus put it this way: "Do not judge, or you too will be judged. For in the same way you judge others, you will be judged, and with the measure you use, it will be measured to you" (Matthew 7:1–2).

In other words, you get what you give out. You want a loving God? Then be loving. You want a merciful God? Then be merciful. Want God to forgive you? Then forgive your fellowman. Want God to condemn you? Then be an accusatory person. Want to put yourself above the rest of the world? Then get ready for a God who is going to strain out every judgmental thought you've ever had and measure all the thoughts and intents of your hidden heart by the same standard.

That's enough to send me to my knees, because I know my heart. You and I as Christians need to realize that however acceptable our lives may be for the general audience, we still possess an R-rated heart, and we're as good as dead if we want God to meet us on any other ground than his grace and forgiveness.

The joy of this truth is that once I can believe that forgiveness for myself, then I can believe it for anybody. I have new eyes to see beyond my neighbor's sin and love him or her with the love of Christ.

When we search the Gospels, we never find a place where Jesus was offended by a sinful person. But there are repeated accounts of his being offended by the self-righteousness of so-called holy people who set themselves apart from the rest of humanity in their own eyes. For these people, he didn't even have the time of day, except to warn them of the judgment to come, a judgment brought about by their refusal to see themselves as needy as the next guy.

Additional Scripture Readings:
Luke 6:37–42; Luke 18:9–14

Go to page 1055 for your next devotional reading.

asked. "I tell you the truth, not one stone here will be left on another; every one will be thrown down."

³As Jesus was sitting on the Mount of Olives, the disciples came to him privately. "Tell us," they said, "when will this happen, and what will be the sign of your coming and of the end of the age?"

⁴Jesus answered: "Watch out that no one deceives you. ⁵For many will come in my name, claiming, 'I am the Christ,ᵃ' and will deceive many. ⁶You will hear of wars and rumors of wars, but see to it that you are not alarmed. Such things must happen, but the end is still to come. ⁷Nation will rise against nation, and kingdom against kingdom. There will be famines and earthquakes in various places. ⁸All these are the beginning of birth pains.

⁹"Then you will be handed over to be persecuted and put to death, and you will be hated by all nations because of me. ¹⁰At that time many will turn away from the faith and will betray and hate each other, ¹¹and many false prophets will appear and deceive many people. ¹²Because of the increase of wickedness, the love of most will grow cold, ¹³but he who stands firm to the end will be saved. ¹⁴And this gospel of the kingdom will be preached in the whole world as a testimony to all nations, and then the end will come.

¹⁵"So when you see standing in the holy place 'the abomination that causes desolation,'ᵇ spoken of through the prophet Daniel—let the reader understand—¹⁶then let those who are in Judea flee to the mountains. ¹⁷Let no one on the roof of his house go down to take anything out of the house. ¹⁸Let no one in the field go back to get his cloak. ¹⁹How dreadful it will be in those days for pregnant women and nursing mothers! ²⁰Pray that your flight will not take place in winter or on the Sabbath. ²¹For then there will be great distress, unequaled from the beginning of the world until now—and never to be equaled again. ²²If those days had not been cut short, no one would survive, but for the sake of the elect those days will be shortened. ²³At that time if anyone says to you, 'Look, here is the Christ!' or, 'There he is!' do not believe it. ²⁴For false Christs and false prophets will appear and perform great signs and miracles to deceive even the elect—if that were possible. ²⁵See, I have told you ahead of time.

²⁶"So if anyone tells you, 'There he is, out in the desert,' do not go out; or, 'Here he is, in the inner rooms,' do not believe it. ²⁷For as lightning that comes from the east is visible even in the west, so will be the coming of the Son of Man. ²⁸Wherever there is a carcass, there the vultures will gather.

²⁹"Immediately after the distress of those days

" 'the sun will be darkened,
    and the moon will not give its light;
the stars will fall from the sky,
    and the heavenly bodies will be
        shaken.'ᶜ

³⁰"At that time the sign of the Son of Man will appear in the sky, and all the nations of the earth will mourn. They will see the Son of Man coming on the clouds of the sky, with power and great glory. ³¹And he will send his angels with a loud trumpet call, and they will gather his elect from the four winds, from one end of the heavens to the other.

³²"Now learn this lesson from the fig tree: As soon as its twigs get tender and its leaves come out, you know that summer is near. ³³Even so, when you see all these things, you know that itᵈ is near, right at the door. ³⁴I tell you the truth, this generationᵉ will certainly not pass away until all these things have happened. ³⁵Heaven and earth will pass away, but my words will never pass away.

The Day and Hour Unknown

³⁶"No one knows about that day or hour, not even the angels in heaven, nor the Son,ᶠ but only the Father. ³⁷As it was in the days of Noah, so it will be at the coming of the Son of Man. ³⁸For in the days before the flood, people were eating and drinking, marrying and giving in marriage, up to the day Noah entered the ark; ³⁹and they knew nothing about what would happen until the flood came and took them all away. That is how it will be at the coming of the Son of Man. ⁴⁰Two men will be in the field; one will be taken and the other left. ⁴¹Two women will be grinding with a hand mill; one will be taken and the other left.

⁴²"Therefore keep watch, because you do not know on what day your Lord will come. ⁴³But understand this: If the owner of the house had known at what time of

night the thief was coming, he would have kept watch and would not have let his house be broken into. ⁴⁴So you also must be ready, because the Son of Man will come at an hour when you do not expect him.

⁴⁵"Who then is the faithful and wise servant, whom the master has put in charge of the servants in his household to give them their food at the proper time? ⁴⁶It will be good for that servant whose master finds him doing so when he returns. ⁴⁷I tell you the truth, he will put him in charge of all his possessions. ⁴⁸But suppose that servant is wicked and says to himself, 'My master is staying away a long time,' ⁴⁹and he then begins to beat his fellow servants and to eat and drink with drunkards. ⁵⁰The master of that servant will come on a day when he does not expect him and at an hour he is not aware of. ⁵¹He will cut him to pieces and assign him a place with the hypocrites, where there will be weeping and gnashing of teeth.

The Parable of the Ten Virgins

25 "At that time the kingdom of heaven will be like ten virgins who took their lamps and went out to meet the bridegroom. ²Five of them were foolish and five were wise. ³The foolish ones took their lamps but did not take any oil with them. ⁴The wise, however, took oil in jars along with their lamps. ⁵The bridegroom was a long time in coming, and they all became drowsy and fell asleep.

⁶"At midnight the cry rang out: 'Here's the bridegroom! Come out to meet him!'

⁷"Then all the virgins woke up and trimmed their lamps. ⁸The foolish ones said to the wise, 'Give us some of your oil; our lamps are going out.'

⁹" 'No,' they replied, 'there may not be enough for both us and you. Instead, go to those who sell oil and buy some for yourselves.'

¹⁰"But while they were on their way to buy the oil, the bridegroom arrived. The virgins who were ready went in with him to the wedding banquet. And the door was shut.

¹¹"Later the others also came. 'Sir! Sir!' they said. 'Open the door for us!'

¹²"But he replied, 'I tell you the truth, I don't know you.'

¹³"Therefore keep watch, because you do not know the day or the hour.

The Parable of the Talents

¹⁴"Again, it will be like a man going on a journey, who called his servants and entrusted his property to them. ¹⁵To one he gave five talents[a] of money, to another two talents, and to another one talent, each according to his ability. Then he went on his journey. ¹⁶The man who had received the five talents went at once and put his money to work and gained five more. ¹⁷So also, the one with the two talents gained two more. ¹⁸But the man who had received the one talent went off, dug a hole in the ground and hid his master's money.

¹⁹"After a long time the master of those servants returned and settled accounts with them. ²⁰The man who had received the five talents brought the other five. 'Master,' he said, 'you entrusted me with five talents. See, I have gained five more.'

²¹"His master replied, 'Well done, good and faithful servant! You have been faithful with a few things; I will put you in charge of many things. Come and share your master's happiness!'

²²"The man with the two talents also came. 'Master,' he said, 'you entrusted me with two talents; see, I have gained two more.'

²³"His master replied, 'Well done, good and faithful servant! You have been faithful with a few things; I will put you in charge of many things. Come and share your master's happiness!'

²⁴"Then the man who had received the one talent came. 'Master,' he said, 'I knew that you are a hard man, harvesting where you have not sown and gathering where you have not scattered seed. ²⁵So I was afraid and went out and hid your talent in the ground. See, here is what belongs to you.'

²⁶"His master replied, 'You wicked, lazy servant! So you knew that I harvest where I have not sown and gather where I have not scattered seed? ²⁷Well then, you should have put my money on deposit with the bankers, so that when I returned I would have received it back with interest.

²⁸" 'Take the talent from him and give it to the one who has the ten talents. ²⁹For everyone who has will be given more, and he will have an abundance. Whoever does not have, even what he has will be taken from him. ³⁰And throw that worthless ser-

---

a15 A talent was worth more than a thousand dollars.

vant outside, into the darkness, where there will be weeping and gnashing of teeth.'

The Sheep and the Goats

[31]"When the Son of Man comes in his glory, and all the angels with him, he will sit on his throne in heavenly glory. [32]All the nations will be gathered before him, and he will separate the people one from another as a shepherd separates the sheep from the goats. [33]He will put the sheep on his right and the goats on his left.

[34]"Then the King will say to those on his right, 'Come, you who are blessed by my Father; take your inheritance, the kingdom prepared for you since the creation of the world. [35]For I was hungry and you gave me something to eat, I was thirsty and you gave me something to drink, I was a stranger and you invited me in, [36]I needed clothes and you clothed me, I was sick and you looked after me, I was in prison and you came to visit me.'

[37]"Then the righteous will answer him, 'Lord, when did we see you hungry and feed you, or thirsty and give you something to drink? [38]When did we see you a stranger and invite you in, or needing clothes and clothe you? [39]When did we see you sick or in prison and go to visit you?'

[40]"The King will reply, 'I tell you the truth, whatever you did for one of the least of these brothers of mine, you did for me.'

[41]"Then he will say to those on his left, 'Depart from me, you who are cursed, into the eternal fire prepared for the devil and his angels. [42]For I was hungry and you gave me nothing to eat, I was thirsty and you gave me nothing to drink, [43]I was a stranger and you did not invite me in, I needed clothes and you did not clothe me, I was sick and in prison and you did not look after me.'

[44]"They also will answer, 'Lord, when did we see you hungry or thirsty or a stranger or needing clothes or sick or in prison, and did not help you?'

[45]"He will reply, 'I tell you the truth, whatever you did not do for one of the least of these, you did not do for me.'

[46]"Then they will go away to eternal punishment, but the righteous to eternal life."

The Plot Against Jesus

26 When Jesus had finished saying all these things, he said to his disci-

ples, [2]"As you know, the Passover is two days away—and the Son of Man will be handed over to be crucified."

[3]Then the chief priests and the elders of the people assembled in the palace of the high priest, whose name was Caiaphas, [4]and they plotted to arrest Jesus in some sly way and kill him. [5]"But not during the Feast," they said, "or there may be a riot among the people."

Jesus Anointed at Bethany

[6]While Jesus was in Bethany in the home of a man known as Simon the Leper, [7]a woman came to him with an alabaster jar of very expensive perfume, which she poured on his head as he was reclining at the table.

[8]When the disciples saw this, they were indignant. "Why this waste?" they asked. [9]"This perfume could have been sold at a high price and the money given to the poor."

[10]Aware of this, Jesus said to them, "Why are you bothering this woman? She has done a beautiful thing to me. [11]The poor you will always have with you, but you will not always have me. [12]When she poured this perfume on my body, she did it to prepare me for burial. [13]I tell you the truth, wherever this gospel is preached throughout the world, what she has done will also be told, in memory of her."

Judas Agrees to Betray Jesus

[14]Then one of the Twelve—the one called Judas Iscariot—went to the chief priests [15]and asked, "What are you willing to give me if I hand him over to you?" So they counted out for him thirty silver coins. [16]From then on Judas watched for an opportunity to hand him over.

The Lord's Supper

[17]On the first day of the Feast of Unleavened Bread, the disciples came to Jesus and asked, "Where do you want us to make preparations for you to eat the Passover?"

[18]He replied, "Go into the city to a certain man and tell him, 'The Teacher says: My appointed time is near. I am going to celebrate the Passover with my disciples at your house.' " [19]So the disciples did as Jesus had directed them and prepared the Passover.

[20]When evening came, Jesus was reclining at the table with the Twelve. [21]And while they were eating, he said, "I tell you the truth, one of you will betray me."

²²They were very sad and began to say to him one after the other, "Surely not I, Lord?"

²³Jesus replied, "The one who has dipped his hand into the bowl with me will betray me. ²⁴The Son of Man will go just as it is written about him. But woe to that man who betrays the Son of Man! It would be better for him if he had not been born."

²⁵Then Judas, the one who would betray him, said, "Surely not I, Rabbi?"

Jesus answered, "Yes, it is you."ᵃ

²⁶While they were eating, Jesus took bread, gave thanks and broke it, and gave it to his disciples, saying, "Take and eat; this is my body."

²⁷Then he took the cup, gave thanks and offered it to them, saying, "Drink from it, all of you. ²⁸This is my blood of theᵇ covenant, which is poured out for many for the forgiveness of sins. ²⁹I tell you, I will not drink of this fruit of the vine from now on until that day when I drink it anew with you in my Father's kingdom."

³⁰When they had sung a hymn, they went out to the Mount of Olives.

Jesus Predicts Peter's Denial

³¹Then Jesus told them, "This very night you will all fall away on account of me, for it is written:

" 'I will strike the shepherd,
    and the sheep of the flock will be
    scattered.'ᶜ

³²But after I have risen, I will go ahead of you into Galilee."

³³Peter replied, "Even if all fall away on account of you, I never will."

³⁴"I tell you the truth," Jesus answered, "this very night, before the rooster crows, you will disown me three times."

³⁵But Peter declared, "Even if I have to die with you, I will never disown you." And all the other disciples said the same.

Gethsemane

³⁶Then Jesus went with his disciples to a place called Gethsemane, and he said to them, "Sit here while I go over there and pray." ³⁷He took Peter and the two sons of Zebedee along with him, and he began to be sorrowful and troubled. ³⁸Then he said to them, "My soul is overwhelmed with sorrow to the point of death. Stay here and keep watch with me."

³⁹Going a little farther, he fell with his face to the ground and prayed, "My Father, if it is possible, may this cup be taken from me. Yet not as I will, but as you will."

⁴⁰Then he returned to his disciples and found them sleeping. "Could you men not keep watch with me for one hour?" he asked Peter. ⁴¹"Watch and pray so that you will not fall into temptation. The spirit is willing, but the body is weak."

⁴²He went away a second time and prayed, "My Father, if it is not possible for this cup to be taken away unless I drink it, may your will be done."

⁴³When he came back, he again found them sleeping, because their eyes were heavy. ⁴⁴So he left them and went away once more and prayed the third time, saying the same thing.

⁴⁵Then he returned to the disciples and said to them, "Are you still sleeping and resting? Look, the hour is near, and the Son of Man is betrayed into the hands of sinners. ⁴⁶Rise, let us go! Here comes my betrayer!"

Jesus Arrested

⁴⁷While he was still speaking, Judas, one of the Twelve, arrived. With him was a large crowd armed with swords and clubs, sent from the chief priests and the elders of the people. ⁴⁸Now the betrayer had arranged a signal with them: "The one I kiss is the man; arrest him." ⁴⁹Going at once to Jesus, Judas said, "Greetings, Rabbi!" and kissed him.

⁵⁰Jesus replied, "Friend, do what you came for."ᵈ

Then the men stepped forward, seized Jesus and arrested him. ⁵¹With that, one of Jesus' companions reached for his sword, drew it out and struck the servant of the high priest, cutting off his ear.

⁵²"Put your sword back in its place," Jesus said to him, "for all who draw the sword will die by the sword. ⁵³Do you think I cannot call on my Father, and he will at once put at my disposal more than twelve legions of angels? ⁵⁴But how then would the Scriptures be fulfilled that say it must happen in this way?"

⁵⁵At that time Jesus said to the crowd, "Am I leading a rebellion, that you have come out with swords and clubs to capture me? Every day I sat in the temple

ᵃ25 Or "You yourself have said it"   ᵇ28 Some manuscripts the new   ᶜ31 Zech. 13:7   ᵈ50 Or
"Friend, why have you come?"

courts teaching, and you did not arrest me. ⁵⁶But this has all taken place that the writings of the prophets might be fulfilled." Then all the disciples deserted him and fled.

Before the Sanhedrin

⁵⁷Those who had arrested Jesus took him to Caiaphas, the high priest, where the teachers of the law and the elders had assembled. ⁵⁸But Peter followed him at a distance, right up to the courtyard of the high priest. He entered and sat down with the guards to see the outcome.

⁵⁹The chief priests and the whole Sanhedrin were looking for false evidence against Jesus so that they could put him to death. ⁶⁰But they did not find any, though many false witnesses came forward.

Finally two came forward ⁶¹and declared, "This fellow said, 'I am able to destroy the temple of God and rebuild it in three days.' "

⁶²Then the high priest stood up and said to Jesus, "Are you not going to answer? What is this testimony that these men are bringing against you?" ⁶³But Jesus remained silent.

The high priest said to him, "I charge you under oath by the living God: Tell us if you are the Christ,ᵃ the Son of God."

⁶⁴"Yes, it is as you say," Jesus replied. "But I say to all of you: In the future you will see the Son of Man sitting at the right hand of the Mighty One and coming on the clouds of heaven."

⁶⁵Then the high priest tore his clothes and said, "He has spoken blasphemy! Why do we need any more witnesses? Look, now you have heard the blasphemy. ⁶⁶What do you think?"

"He is worthy of death," they answered.

⁶⁷Then they spit in his face and struck him with their fists. Others slapped him ⁶⁸and said, "Prophesy to us, Christ. Who hit you?"

Peter Disowns Jesus

⁶⁹Now Peter was sitting out in the courtyard, and a servant girl came to him. "You also were with Jesus of Galilee," she said.

⁷⁰But he denied it before them all. "I don't know what you're talking about," he said.

⁷¹Then he went out to the gateway, where another girl saw him and said to the people there, "This fellow was with Jesus of Nazareth."

⁷²He denied it again, with an oath: "I don't know the man!"

⁷³After a little while, those standing there went up to Peter and said, "Surely you are one of them, for your accent gives you away."

⁷⁴Then he began to call down curses on himself and he swore to them, "I don't know the man!"

Immediately a rooster crowed. ⁷⁵Then Peter remembered the word Jesus had spoken: "Before the rooster crows, you will disown me three times." And he went outside and wept bitterly.

Judas Hangs Himself

27 Early in the morning, all the chief priests and the elders of the people came to the decision to put Jesus to death. ²They bound him, led him away and handed him over to Pilate, the governor.

³When Judas, who had betrayed him, saw that Jesus was condemned, he was seized with remorse and returned the thirty silver coins to the chief priests and the elders. ⁴"I have sinned," he said, "for I have betrayed innocent blood."

"What is that to us?" they replied. "That's your responsibility."

⁵So Judas threw the money into the temple and left. Then he went away and hanged himself.

⁶The chief priests picked up the coins and said, "It is against the law to put this into the treasury, since it is blood money." ⁷So they decided to use the money to buy the potter's field as a burial place for foreigners. ⁸That is why it has been called the Field of Blood to this day. ⁹Then what was spoken by Jeremiah the prophet was fulfilled: "They took the thirty silver coins, the price set on him by the people of Israel, ¹⁰and they used them to buy the potter's field, as the Lord commanded me."ᵇ

Jesus Before Pilate

¹¹Meanwhile Jesus stood before the governor, and the governor asked him, "Are you the king of the Jews?"

"Yes, it is as you say," Jesus replied.

¹²When he was accused by the chief priests and the elders, he gave no answer. ¹³Then Pilate asked him, "Don't you hear the testimony they are bringing against you?" ¹⁴But Jesus made no reply, not even to a single charge—to the great amazement of the governor.

¹⁵Now it was the governor's custom at

ᵃ63 Or *Messiah*; also in verse 68   ᵇ10 See Zech. 11:12,13; Jer. 19:1-13; 32:6-9.

the Feast to release a prisoner chosen by the crowd. [16]At that time they had a notorious prisoner, called Barabbas. [17]So when the crowd had gathered, Pilate asked them, "Which one do you want me to release to you: Barabbas, or Jesus who is called Christ?" [18]For he knew it was out of envy that they had handed Jesus over to him.

[19]While Pilate was sitting on the judge's seat, his wife sent him this message: "Don't have anything to do with that innocent man, for I have suffered a great deal today in a dream because of him."

[20]But the chief priests and the elders persuaded the crowd to ask for Barabbas and to have Jesus executed.

[21]"Which of the two do you want me to release to you?" asked the governor.

"Barabbas," they answered.

[22]"What shall I do, then, with Jesus who is called Christ?" Pilate asked.

They all answered, "Crucify him!"

[23]"Why? What crime has he committed?" asked Pilate.

But they shouted all the louder, "Crucify him!"

[24]When Pilate saw that he was getting nowhere, but that instead an uproar was starting, he took water and washed his hands in front of the crowd. "I am innocent of this man's blood," he said. "It is your responsibility!"

[25]All the people answered, "Let his blood be on us and on our children!"

[26]Then he released Barabbas to them. But he had Jesus flogged, and handed him over to be crucified.

The Soldiers Mock Jesus

[27]Then the governor's soldiers took Jesus into the Praetorium and gathered the whole company of soldiers around him. [28]They stripped him and put a scarlet robe on him, [29]and then twisted together a crown of thorns and set it on his head. They put a staff in his right hand and knelt in front of him and mocked him. "Hail, king of the Jews!" they said. [30]They spit on him, and took the staff and struck him on the head again and again. [31]After they had mocked him, they took off the robe and put his own clothes on him. Then they led him away to crucify him.

The Crucifixion

[32]As they were going out, they met a man from Cyrene, named Simon, and they forced him to carry the cross. [33]They came to a place called Golgotha (which means The Place of the Skull). [34]There they offered Jesus wine to drink, mixed with gall; but after tasting it, he refused to drink it. [35]When they had crucified him, they divided up his clothes by casting lots.[a] [36]And sitting down, they kept watch over him there. [37]Above his head they placed the written charge against him: THIS IS JESUS, THE KING OF THE JEWS. [38]Two robbers were crucified with him, one on his right and one on his left. [39]Those who passed by hurled insults at him, shaking their heads [40]and saying, "You who are going to destroy the temple and build it in three days, save yourself! Come down from the cross, if you are the Son of God!"

[41]In the same way the chief priests, the teachers of the law and the elders mocked him. [42]"He saved others," they said, "but he can't save himself! He's the King of Israel! Let him come down now from the cross, and we will believe in him. [43]He trusts in God. Let God rescue him now if he wants him, for he said, 'I am the Son of God.' " [44]In the same way the robbers who were crucified with him also heaped insults on him.

The Death of Jesus

[45]From the sixth hour until the ninth hour darkness came over all the land. [46]About the ninth hour Jesus cried out in a loud voice, *"Eloi, Eloi,[b] lama sabachthani?"* — which means, "My God, my God, why have you forsaken me?"[c] [47]When some of those standing there heard this, they said, "He's calling Elijah." [48]Immediately one of them ran and got a sponge. He filled it with wine vinegar, put it on a stick, and offered it to Jesus to drink. [49]The rest said, "Now leave him alone. Let's see if Elijah comes to save him."

[50]And when Jesus had cried out again in a loud voice, he gave up his spirit. [51]At that moment the curtain of the temple was torn in two from top to bottom. The earth shook and the rocks split. [52]The tombs broke open and the bodies of many holy people who had died were

---

[a]35 A few late manuscripts *lots that the word spoken by the prophet might be fulfilled: "They divided my garments among themselves and cast lots for my clothing"* (Psalm 22:18)   [b]46 Some manuscripts *Eli, Eli*
[c]46 Psalm 22:1

raised to life. [53]They came out of the tombs, and after Jesus' resurrection they went into the holy city and appeared to many people.

[54]When the centurion and those with him who were guarding Jesus saw the earthquake and all that had happened, they were terrified, and exclaimed, "Surely he was the Son[a] of God!"

[55]Many women were there, watching from a distance. They had followed Jesus from Galilee to care for his needs. [56]Among them were Mary Magdalene, Mary the mother of James and Joses, and the mother of Zebedee's sons.

The Burial of Jesus

[57]As evening approached, there came a rich man from Arimathea, named Joseph, who had himself become a disciple of Jesus. [58]Going to Pilate, he asked for Jesus' body, and Pilate ordered that it be given to him. [59]Joseph took the body, wrapped it in a clean linen cloth, [60]and placed it in his own new tomb that he had cut out of the rock. He rolled a big stone in front of the entrance to the tomb and went away. [61]Mary Magdalene and the other Mary were sitting there opposite the tomb.

The Guard at the Tomb

[62]The next day, the one after Preparation Day, the chief priests and the Pharisees went to Pilate. [63]"Sir," they said, "we remember that while he was still alive that deceiver said, 'After three days I will rise again.' [64]So give the order for the tomb to be made secure until the third day. Otherwise, his disciples may come and steal the body and tell the people that he has been raised from the dead. This last deception will be worse than the first."

[65]"Take a guard," Pilate answered. "Go, make the tomb as secure as you know how." [66]So they went and made the tomb secure by putting a seal on the stone and posting the guard.

The Resurrection

28 After the Sabbath, at dawn on the first day of the week, Mary Magdalene and the other Mary went to look at the tomb.

[2]There was a violent earthquake, for an angel of the Lord came down from heaven and, going to the tomb, rolled back the stone and sat on it. [3]His appearance was like lightning, and his clothes were white as snow. [4]The guards were so afraid of him that they shook and became like dead men.

[5]The angel said to the women, "Do not be afraid, for I know that you are looking for Jesus, who was crucified. [6]He is not here; he has risen, just as he said. Come and see the place where he lay. [7]Then go quickly and tell his disciples: 'He has risen from the dead and is going ahead of you into Galilee. There you will see him.' Now I have told you."

[8]So the women hurried away from the tomb, afraid yet filled with joy, and ran to tell his disciples. [9]Suddenly Jesus met them. "Greetings," he said. They came to him, clasped his feet and worshiped him. [10]Then Jesus said to them, "Do not be afraid. Go and tell my brothers to go to Galilee; there they will see me."

The Guards' Report

[11]While the women were on their way, some of the guards went into the city and reported to the chief priests everything that had happened. [12]When the chief priests had met with the elders and devised a plan, they gave the soldiers a large sum of money, [13]telling them, "You are to say, 'His disciples came during the night and stole him away while we were asleep.' [14]If this report gets to the governor, we will satisfy him and keep you out of trouble." [15]So the soldiers took the money and did as they were instructed. And this story has been widely circulated among the Jews to this very day.

The Great Commission

[16]Then the eleven disciples went to Galilee, to the mountain where Jesus had told them to go. [17]When they saw him, they worshiped him; but some doubted. [18]Then Jesus came to them and said, "All authority in heaven and on earth has been given to me. [19]Therefore go and make disciples of all nations, baptizing them in[b] the name of the Father and of the Son and of the Holy Spirit, [20]and teaching them to obey everything I have commanded you. And surely I am with you always, to the very end of the age."

---

[a]54 Or *a son*   [b]19 Or *into*; see Acts 8:16; 19:5; Romans 6:3; 1 Cor. 1:13; 10:2 and Gal. 3:27.

*M*ARK writes this Gospel to tell the basic story about Jesus. He recounts miracles, parables and other sayings of Jesus. Almost half of his book deals with the final week of Jesus' life, ending with his death on the cross and his resurrection from the dead. As you read this book, notice how full of life and emotion Jesus is and how caring he is. Note too why he came into the world—to give his life for you (Mark 10:45). God wants you to accept his Son Jesus as your own personal Savior and Lord.

MARK

John the Baptist Prepares the Way

1 The beginning of the gospel about Jesus Christ, the Son of God.[a]

²It is written in Isaiah the prophet:

"I will send my messenger ahead of
    you,
  who will prepare your way"[b]—
³"a voice of one calling in the desert,
  'Prepare the way for the Lord,
    make straight paths for him.' "[c]

⁴And so John came, baptizing in the desert region and preaching a baptism of repentance for the forgiveness of sins. ⁵The whole Judean countryside and all the people of Jerusalem went out to him. Confessing their sins, they were baptized by him in the Jordan River. ⁶John wore clothing made of camel's hair, with a leather belt around his waist, and he ate locusts and wild honey. ⁷And this was his message: "After me will come one more powerful than I, the thongs of whose sandals I am not worthy to stoop down and untie. ⁸I baptize you with[d] water,

but he will baptize you with the Holy Spirit."

The Baptism and Temptation of Jesus

[9]At that time Jesus came from Nazareth in Galilee and was baptized by John in the Jordan. [10]As Jesus was coming up out of the water, he saw heaven being torn open and the Spirit descending on him like a dove. [11]And a voice came from heaven: "You are my Son, whom I love; with you I am well pleased."

[12]At once the Spirit sent him out into the desert, [13]and he was in the desert forty days, being tempted by Satan. He was with the wild animals, and angels attended him.

The Calling of the First Disciples

[14]After John was put in prison, Jesus went into Galilee, proclaiming the good news of God. [15]"The time has come," he said. "The kingdom of God is near. Repent and believe the good news!"

[16]As Jesus walked beside the Sea of Galilee, he saw Simon and his brother Andrew casting a net into the lake, for they were fishermen. [17]"Come, follow me," Jesus said, "and I will make you fishers of men." [18]At once they left their nets and followed him.

[19]When he had gone a little farther, he saw James son of Zebedee and his brother John in a boat, preparing their nets. [20]Without delay he called them, and they left their father Zebedee in the boat with the hired men and followed him.

Jesus Drives Out an Evil Spirit

[21]They went to Capernaum, and when the Sabbath came, Jesus went into the synagogue and began to teach. [22]The people were amazed at his teaching, because he taught them as one who had authority, not as the teachers of the law. [23]Just then a man in their synagogue who was possessed by an evil[a] spirit cried out, [24]"What do you want with us, Jesus of Nazareth? Have you come to destroy us? I know who you are—the Holy One of God!"

[25]"Be quiet!" said Jesus sternly. "Come out of him!" [26]The evil spirit shook the man violently and came out of him with a shriek.

[27]The people were all so amazed that they asked each other, "What is this? A new teaching—and with authority! He even gives orders to evil spirits and they obey him." [28]News about him spread quickly over the whole region of Galilee.

Jesus Heals Many

[29]As soon as they left the synagogue, they went with James and John to the home of Simon and Andrew. [30]Simon's mother-in-law was in bed with a fever, and they told Jesus about her. [31]So he went to her, took her hand and helped her up. The fever left her and she began to wait on them.

[32]That evening after sunset the people brought to Jesus all the sick and demon-possessed. [33]The whole town gathered at the door, [34]and Jesus healed many who had various diseases. He also drove out many demons, but he would not let the demons speak because they knew who he was.

Jesus Prays in a Solitary Place

[35]Very early in the morning, while it was still dark, Jesus got up, left the house and went off to a solitary place, where he prayed. [36]Simon and his companions went to look for him, [37]and when they found him, they exclaimed: "Everyone is looking for you!"

[38]Jesus replied, "Let us go somewhere else—to the nearby villages—so I can preach there also. That is why I have come." [39]So he traveled throughout Galilee, preaching in their synagogues and driving out demons.

A Man With Leprosy

[40]A man with leprosy[b] came to him and begged him on his knees, "If you are willing, you can make me clean."

[41]Filled with compassion, Jesus reached out his hand and touched the man. "I am willing," he said. "Be clean!" [42]Immediately the leprosy left him and he was cured.

[43]Jesus sent him away at once with a strong warning: [44]"See that you don't tell this to anyone. But go, show yourself to the priest and offer the sacrifices that Moses commanded for your cleansing, as a testimony to them." [45]Instead he went out and began to talk freely, spreading the news. As a result, Jesus could no longer enter a town openly but stayed outside in

---

[a]23 Greek *unclean*; also in verses 26 and 27 affecting the skin—not necessarily leprosy.   [b]40 The Greek word was used for various diseases

lonely places. Yet the people still came to him from everywhere.

Jesus Heals a Paralytic

2 A few days later, when Jesus again entered Capernaum, the people heard that he had come home. [2]So many gathered that there was no room left, not even outside the door, and he preached the word to them. [3]Some men came, bringing to him a paralytic, carried by four of them. [4]Since they could not get him to Jesus because of the crowd, they made an opening in the roof above Jesus and, after digging through it, lowered the mat the paralyzed man was lying on. [5]When Jesus saw their faith, he said to the paralytic, "Son, your sins are forgiven."

[6]Now some teachers of the law were sitting there, thinking to themselves, [7]"Why does this fellow talk like that? He's blaspheming! Who can forgive sins but God alone?"

[8]Immediately Jesus knew in his spirit that this was what they were thinking in their hearts, and he said to them, "Why are you thinking these things? [9]Which is easier: to say to the paralytic, 'Your sins are forgiven,' or to say, 'Get up, take your mat and walk'? [10]But that you may know that the Son of Man has authority on earth to forgive sins . . . ." He said to the paralytic, [11]"I tell you, get up, take your mat and go home." [12]He got up, took his mat and walked out in full view of them all. This amazed everyone and they praised God, saying, "We have never seen anything like this!"

The Calling of Levi

[13]Once again Jesus went out beside the lake. A large crowd came to him, and he began to teach them. [14]As he walked along, he saw Levi son of Alphaeus sitting at the tax collector's booth. "Follow me," Jesus told him, and Levi got up and followed him.

[15]While Jesus was having dinner at Levi's house, many tax collectors and "sinners" were eating with him and his disciples, for there were many who followed him. [16]When the teachers of the law who were Pharisees saw him eating with the "sinners" and tax collectors, they asked his disciples: "Why does he eat with tax collectors and 'sinners'?"

[17]On hearing this, Jesus said to them, "It is not the healthy who need a doctor, but the sick. I have not come to call the righteous, but sinners."

Jesus Questioned About Fasting

[18]Now John's disciples and the Pharisees were fasting. Some people came and asked Jesus, "How is it that John's disciples and the disciples of the Pharisees are fasting, but yours are not?"

[19]Jesus answered, "How can the guests of the bridegroom fast while he is with them? They cannot, so long as they have him with them. [20]But the time will come when the bridegroom will be taken from them, and on that day they will fast.

[21]"No one sews a patch of unshrunk cloth on an old garment. If he does, the new piece will pull away from the old, making the tear worse. [22]And no one pours new wine into old wineskins. If he does, the wine will burst the skins, and both the wine and the wineskins will be ruined. No, he pours new wine into new wineskins."

Lord of the Sabbath

[23]One Sabbath Jesus was going through the grainfields, and as his disciples walked along, they began to pick some heads of grain. [24]The Pharisees said to him, "Look, why are they doing what is unlawful on the Sabbath?"

[25]He answered, "Have you never read what David did when he and his companions were hungry and in need? [26]In the days of Abiathar the high priest, he entered the house of God and ate the consecrated bread, which is lawful only for priests to eat. And he also gave some to his companions."

[27]Then he said to them, "The Sabbath was made for man, not man for the Sabbath. [28]So the Son of Man is Lord even of the Sabbath."

3 Another time he went into the synagogue, and a man with a shriveled hand was there. [2]Some of them were looking for a reason to accuse Jesus, so they watched him closely to see if he would heal him on the Sabbath. [3]Jesus said to the man with the shriveled hand, "Stand up in front of everyone."

[4]Then Jesus asked them, "Which is lawful on the Sabbath: to do good or to do evil, to save life or to kill?" But they remained silent.

[5]He looked around at them in anger and, deeply distressed at their stubborn hearts, said to the man, "Stretch out your hand." He stretched it out, and his hand was completely restored. [6]Then the Phari-

sees went out and began to plot with the Herodians how they might kill Jesus.

Crowds Follow Jesus

7Jesus withdrew with his disciples to the lake, and a large crowd from Galilee followed. **8**When they heard all he was do-ing, many people came to him from Judea, Jerusalem, Idumea, and the regions across the Jordan and around Tyre and Sidon. **9**Because of the crowd he told his disciples to have a small boat ready for him, to keep the people from crowding him. **10**For he had healed many, so that those

---

WEDNESDAY

VERSE FOR THE DAY:	AUTHOR:	PASSAGE FOR THE DAY:
Mark 2:14	Dietrich Bonhoeffer	Mark 2:13–17

No Other Road

THE call goes forth, and is at once followed by the response of obedience. The response of the disciples is an act of obedience, not a confession of faith in Jesus. How could the call immediately evoke obedience? The story is a stumbling block for the natural reason, and it is no wonder that frantic attempts have been made to separate the two events. By hook or by crook a bridge must be found between them. Something must have happened in between, some psychological or historical event. Thus we get the stupid question: Surely the tax collector must have known Jesus before, and that previous acquaintance explains his readiness to hear the Master's call. Unfortunately our text is ruthlessly silent on this point, and in fact it regards the immediate sequence of call and response as a matter of crucial importance. It displays not the slightest interest in the psychological reasons for a man's religious decisions. And why? For the simple reason that the cause behind the immediate following of call by response is Jesus Christ himself. It is Jesus who calls, and because it is Jesus, Levi follows at once.

This encounter is a testimony to the absolute, direct and unaccountable authority of Jesus. There is no need of any preliminaries, and no other consequence but obedience to the call. Because Jesus is the Christ, he has the authority to call and to demand obedience to his word. Jesus summons men to follow him, not as a teacher or a pattern of the good life, but as the Christ, the Son of God. In this short text Jesus Christ and his claim are proclaimed to men. Not a word of praise is given to the disciple for his decision for Christ. We are not expected to contemplate the disciple, but only him who calls, and his absolute authority. According to our text, there is no road to faith or discipleship, no other road—only obedience to the call of Jesus.

Additional Scripture Readings:
Luke 9:18–27; John 12:23–26

Go to page 1057 for your next devotional reading.

with diseases were pushing forward to touch him. [11]Whenever the evil[a] spirits saw him, they fell down before him and cried out, "You are the Son of God." [12]But he gave them strict orders not to tell who he was.

The Appointing of the Twelve Apostles

[13]Jesus went up on a mountainside and called to him those he wanted, and they came to him. [14]He appointed twelve — designating them apostles[b] — that they might be with him and that he might send them out to preach [15]and to have authority to drive out demons. [16]These are the twelve he appointed: Simon (to whom he gave the name Peter); [17]James son of Zebedee and his brother John (to them he gave the name Boanerges, which means Sons of Thunder); [18]Andrew, Philip, Bartholomew, Matthew, Thomas, James son of Alphaeus, Thaddaeus, Simon the Zealot [19]and Judas Iscariot, who betrayed him.

Jesus and Beelzebub

[20]Then Jesus entered a house, and again a crowd gathered, so that he and his disciples were not even able to eat. [21]When his family heard about this, they went to take charge of him, for they said, "He is out of his mind."

[22]And the teachers of the law who came down from Jerusalem said, "He is possessed by Beelzebub[c]! By the prince of demons he is driving out demons."

[23]So Jesus called them and spoke to them in parables: "How can Satan drive out Satan? [24]If a kingdom is divided against itself, that kingdom cannot stand. [25]If a house is divided against itself, that house cannot stand. [26]And if Satan opposes himself and is divided, he cannot stand; his end has come. [27]In fact, no one can enter a strong man's house and carry off his possessions unless he first ties up the strong man. Then he can rob his house. [28]I tell you the truth, all the sins and blasphemies of men will be forgiven them. [29]But whoever blasphemes against the Holy Spirit will never be forgiven; he is guilty of an eternal sin."

[30]He said this because they were saying, "He has an evil spirit."

Jesus' Mother and Brothers

[31]Then Jesus' mother and brothers arrived. Standing outside, they sent someone in to call him. [32]A crowd was sitting around him, and they told him, "Your mother and brothers are outside looking for you."

[33]"Who are my mother and my brothers?" he asked.

[34]Then he looked at those seated in a circle around him and said, "Here are my mother and my brothers! [35]Whoever does God's will is my brother and sister and mother."

The Parable of the Sower

4 Again Jesus began to teach by the lake. The crowd that gathered around him was so large that he got into a boat and sat in it out on the lake, while all the people were along the shore at the water's edge. [2]He taught them many things by parables, and in his teaching said: [3]"Listen! A farmer went out to sow his seed. [4]As he was scattering the seed, some fell along the path, and the birds came and ate it up. [5]Some fell on rocky places, where it did not have much soil. It sprang up quickly, because the soil was shallow. [6]But when the sun came up, the plants were scorched, and they withered because they had no root. [7]Other seed fell among thorns, which grew up and choked the plants, so that they did not bear grain. [8]Still other seed fell on good soil. It came up, grew and produced a crop, multiplying thirty, sixty, or even a hundred times." [9]Then Jesus said, "He who has ears to hear, let him hear."

[10]When he was alone, the Twelve and the others around him asked him about the parables. [11]He told them, "The secret of the kingdom of God has been given to you. But to those on the outside everything is said in parables [12]so that,

" 'they may be ever seeing but never perceiving,
and ever hearing but never understanding;
otherwise they might turn and be forgiven!'[d] "

[13]Then Jesus said to them, "Don't you understand this parable? How then will you understand any parable? [14]The farmer sows the word. [15]Some people are like seed along the path, where the word is sown. As soon as they hear it, Satan comes and takes away the word that was

---

sown in them. ¹⁶Others, like seed sown on rocky places, hear the word and at once receive it with joy. ¹⁷But since they have no root, they last only a short time. When trouble or persecution comes because of the word, they quickly fall away. ¹⁸Still others, like seed sown among thorns, hear the word; ¹⁹but the worries of this life, the deceitfulness of wealth and the desires for other things come in and choke the word, making it unfruitful. ²⁰Others, like seed sown on good soil, hear the word, accept it, and produce a crop—thirty, sixty or even a hundred times what was sown."

A Lamp on a Stand

²¹He said to them, "Do you bring in a lamp to put it under a bowl or a bed? Instead, don't you put it on its stand? ²²For whatever is hidden is meant to be disclosed, and whatever is concealed is meant to be brought out into the open. ²³If anyone has ears to hear, let him hear."

²⁴"Consider carefully what you hear," he continued. "With the measure you use,

---

THURSDAY

VERSE FOR THE DAY:	AUTHOR:	PASSAGE FOR THE DAY:
Mark 3:14	Stephen Arterburn and David Stoop	Mark 3:13–19

Being Christ's Men

A MAN'S identity (as well as a woman's) is based on who he is apart from what he does. Identity is a matter of character, not accomplishment, a matter of being and relating, not doing. This is apparent in the call of Jesus Christ to his disciples, as recorded in the Bible in Mark 3:14–15: "He appointed twelve —designating them apostles—that they might be with him and that he might send them out to preach and to have authority to drive out demons."

Notice that Jesus definitely called the apostles to *do something*: to preach the gospel and drive out demons. But his first call was for them to *be someone*—his men. He wanted a mutually loving, nurturing, caring relationship with these men.

Christ's acceptance and approval of his disciples was always based on the being part of discipleship, not the doing part. The disciples enjoyed some successes in their mission. But they also experienced some failures, particularly during Christ's arrest, trial and crucifixion when "all the disciples deserted him and fled" (Matthew 26:56). Had the disciples based their identity on their performance, they would have reason to consider themselves failures.

But after his resurrection, Jesus didn't reprimand them for what they did or didn't do. Instead he met privately with them several times before his ascension to assure them that they were still his men. Then he gave them the Great Commission (Matthew 28:16–20), and the disciples successfully carried it out because they had a firm grasp on their identity in Christ.

Additional Scripture Readings:
John 20:19–23; Acts 17:24–28

Go to page 1060 for your next devotional reading.

it will be measured to you—and even more. **25**Whoever has will be given more; whoever does not have, even what he has will be taken from him."

The Parable of the Growing Seed

26He also said, "This is what the kingdom of God is like. A man scatters seed on the ground. **27**Night and day, whether he sleeps or gets up, the seed sprouts and grows, though he does not know how. **28**All by itself the soil produces grain— first the stalk, then the head, then the full kernel in the head. **29**As soon as the grain is ripe, he puts the sickle to it, because the harvest has come."

The Parable of the Mustard Seed

30Again he said, "What shall we say the kingdom of God is like, or what parable shall we use to describe it? **31**It is like a mustard seed, which is the smallest seed you plant in the ground. **32**Yet when planted, it grows and becomes the largest of all garden plants, with such big branches that the birds of the air can perch in its shade."

33With many similar parables Jesus spoke the word to them, as much as they could understand. **34**He did not say anything to them without using a parable. But when he was alone with his own disciples, he explained everything.

Jesus Calms the Storm

35That day when evening came, he said to his disciples, "Let us go over to the other side." **36**Leaving the crowd behind, they took him along, just as he was, in the boat. There were also other boats with him. **37**A furious squall came up, and the waves broke over the boat, so that it was nearly swamped. **38**Jesus was in the stern, sleeping on a cushion. The disciples woke him and said to him, "Teacher, don't you care if we drown?"

39He got up, rebuked the wind and said to the waves, "Quiet! Be still!" Then the wind died down and it was completely calm.

40He said to his disciples, "Why are you so afraid? Do you still have no faith?"

41They were terrified and asked each other, "Who is this? Even the wind and the waves obey him!"

The Healing of a Demon-possessed Man

5 They went across the lake to the region of the Gerasenes.*a* **2**When Jesus got out of the boat, a man with an evil*b* spirit came from the tombs to meet him. **3**This man lived in the tombs, and no one could bind him any more, not even with a chain. **4**For he had often been chained hand and foot, but he tore the chains apart and broke the irons on his feet. No one was strong enough to subdue him. **5**Night and day among the tombs and in the hills he would cry out and cut himself with stones.

6When he saw Jesus from a distance, he ran and fell on his knees in front of him. **7**He shouted at the top of his voice, "What do you want with me, Jesus, Son of the Most High God? Swear to God that you won't torture me!" **8**For Jesus had said to him, "Come out of this man, you evil spirit!"

9Then Jesus asked him, "What is your name?"

"My name is Legion," he replied, "for we are many." **10**And he begged Jesus again and again not to send them out of the area.

11A large herd of pigs was feeding on the nearby hillside. **12**The demons begged Jesus, "Send us among the pigs; allow us to go into them." **13**He gave them permission, and the evil spirits came out and went into the pigs. The herd, about two thousand in number, rushed down the steep bank into the lake and were drowned.

14Those tending the pigs ran off and reported this in the town and countryside, and the people went out to see what had happened. **15**When they came to Jesus, they saw the man who had been possessed by the legion of demons, sitting there, dressed and in his right mind; and they were afraid. **16**Those who had seen it told the people what had happened to the demon-possessed man—and told about the pigs as well. **17**Then the people began to plead with Jesus to leave their region.

18As Jesus was getting into the boat, the man who had been demon-possessed begged to go with him. **19**Jesus did not let him, but said, "Go home to your family and tell them how much the Lord has done for you, and how he has had mercy

---

a1 Some manuscripts *Gadarenes*; other manuscripts *Gergesenes*   *b2* Greek *unclean*; also in verses 8 and 13 on you." **20**So the man went away and began to tell in the Decapolis*a* how much Jesus had done for him. And all the people were amazed.

A Dead Girl and a Sick Woman

21When Jesus had again crossed over by boat to the other side of the lake, a large crowd gathered around him while he was by the lake. **22**Then one of the synagogue rulers, named Jairus, came there. Seeing Jesus, he fell at his feet **23**and pleaded earnestly with him, "My little daughter is dying. Please come and put your hands on her so that she will be healed and live." **24**So Jesus went with him.

A large crowd followed and pressed around him. **25**And a woman was there who had been subject to bleeding for twelve years. **26**She had suffered a great deal under the care of many doctors and had spent all she had, yet instead of getting better she grew worse. **27**When she heard about Jesus, she came up behind him in the crowd and touched his cloak, **28**because she thought, "If I just touch his clothes, I will be healed." **29**Immediately her bleeding stopped and she felt in her body that she was freed from her suffering.

30At once Jesus realized that power had gone out from him. He turned around in the crowd and asked, "Who touched my clothes?"

31"You see the people crowding against you," his disciples answered, "and yet you can ask, 'Who touched me?' "

32But Jesus kept looking around to see who had done it. **33**Then the woman, knowing what had happened to her, came and fell at his feet and, trembling with fear, told him the whole truth. **34**He said to her, "Daughter, your faith has healed you. Go in peace and be freed from your suffering."

35While Jesus was still speaking, some men came from the house of Jairus, the synagogue ruler. "Your daughter is dead," they said. "Why bother the teacher any more?"

36Ignoring what they said, Jesus told the synagogue ruler, "Don't be afraid; just believe."

37He did not let anyone follow him except Peter, James and John the brother of James. **38**When they came to the home of the synagogue ruler, Jesus saw a commo-

tion, with people crying and wailing loudly. **39**He went in and said to them, "Why all this commotion and wailing? The child is not dead but asleep." **40**But they laughed at him.

After he put them all out, he took the child's father and mother and the disciples who were with him, and went in where the child was. **41**He took her by the hand and said to her, *"Talitha koum!"* (which means, "Little girl, I say to you, get up!"). **42**Immediately the girl stood up and walked around (she was twelve years old). At this they were completely astonished. **43**He gave strict orders not to let anyone know about this, and told them to give her something to eat.

A Prophet Without Honor

6 Jesus left there and went to his hometown, accompanied by his disciples. **2**When the Sabbath came, he began to teach in the synagogue, and many who heard him were amazed.

"Where did this man get these things?" they asked. "What's this wisdom that has been given him, that he even does miracles! **3**Isn't this the carpenter? Isn't this Mary's son and the brother of James, Joseph,*b* Judas and Simon? Aren't his sisters here with us?" And they took offense at him.

4Jesus said to them, "Only in his hometown, among his relatives and in his own house is a prophet without honor." **5**He could not do any miracles there, except lay his hands on a few sick people and heal them. **6**And he was amazed at their lack of faith.

Jesus Sends Out the Twelve

Then Jesus went around teaching from village to village. **7**Calling the Twelve to him, he sent them out two by two and gave them authority over evil*c* spirits.

8These were his instructions: "Take nothing for the journey except a staff—no bread, no bag, no money in your belts. **9**Wear sandals but not an extra tunic. **10**Whenever you enter a house, stay there until you leave that town. **11**And if any place will not welcome you or listen to you, shake the dust off your feet when you leave, as a testimony against them."

12They went out and preached that people should repent. **13**They drove out many demons and anointed many sick people with oil and healed them.

---

a20 That is, the Ten Cities   *b3* Greek *Joses*, a variant of *Joseph*   *c7* Greek *unclean*

FRIDAY

VERSE FOR THE DAY:
Mark 5:23

AUTHOR:
John E. Crawford

PASSAGE FOR THE DAY:
Mark 5:21–24,35–43

Fathers . . . and Daughters

EVERY thoughtful father knows that girls, as well as boys, can go terribly far wrong without the right guidance at home. The best counseling services in the finest school facilities have rarely been able to make up for a lack of guidance from a good father and mother who love their children and who tackle the job as a team.

Your daughter wants you to be the chief executive of the household on some matters, with her mother the chief on other matters. She wants you both to be intelligent executives so the household runs as smoothly as it can.

She wants to see in her mother a wise, mature woman who loves you, respects you and can talk to you about all important issues in the family. She needs to find a woman's kind of wisdom and courage in her mother . . .

At the same time, that daughter of yours wants to see in you an intelligent man's viewpoint about life, plus the ability to head up the family in fatherly ways. Then she can really love you as her father as well as a fine man . . .

You are the most important man in her young life. She ought to be able to build her life according to what she sees in yours:

- *your kindness* towards others who have not been able to get along in life due to no real fault of their own;
- *your forgiveness* that flows freely and does not allow you to hold tight to grudges or revenge;
- *your wisdom to withhold judgment* until all the facts have come into view;
- *your quiet courage* that wells up out of deep faith in God;
- *your uncommon sense* that probably is a mixture of these traits.

Nobody can show her these facets of a good father nearly as well as you can, if you put your brainpower to it. Her mother can show her the comparable facets of a fine woman, and she can copy them in her own young life. But your example of what a good man is like will be priceless to her. . . even if you sing off tune beside her in the Sunday morning worship.

Additional Scripture Readings:
1 Corinthians 16:13–14;
Colossians 3:12–14

Go to page 1064 for your next devotional reading.

John the Baptist Beheaded

[14]King Herod heard about this, for Jesus' name had become well known. Some were saying,[a] "John the Baptist has been raised from the dead, and that is why miraculous powers are at work in him."

[15]Others said, "He is Elijah."

And still others claimed, "He is a prophet, like one of the prophets of long ago."

[16]But when Herod heard this, he said, "John, the man I beheaded, has been raised from the dead!"

[17]For Herod himself had given orders to have John arrested, and he had him bound and put in prison. He did this because of Herodias, his brother Philip's wife, whom he had married. [18]For John had been saying to Herod, "It is not lawful for you to have your brother's wife." [19]So Herodias nursed a grudge against John and wanted to kill him. But she was not able to, [20]because Herod feared John and protected him, knowing him to be a righteous and holy man. When Herod heard John, he was greatly puzzled[b]; yet he liked to listen to him.

[21]Finally the opportune time came. On his birthday Herod gave a banquet for his high officials and military commanders and the leading men of Galilee. [22]When the daughter of Herodias came in and danced, she pleased Herod and his dinner guests.

The king said to the girl, "Ask me for anything you want, and I'll give it to you." [23]And he promised her with an oath, "Whatever you ask I will give you, up to half my kingdom."

[24]She went out and said to her mother, "What shall I ask for?"

"The head of John the Baptist," she answered.

[25]At once the girl hurried in to the king with the request: "I want you to give me right now the head of John the Baptist on a platter."

[26]The king was greatly distressed, but because of his oaths and his dinner guests, he did not want to refuse her. [27]So he immediately sent an executioner with orders to bring John's head. The man went, beheaded John in the prison, [28]and brought back his head on a platter. He presented it to the girl, and she gave it to her mother. [29]On hearing of this, John's disciples came and took his body and laid it in a tomb.

Jesus Feeds the Five Thousand

[30]The apostles gathered around Jesus and reported to him all they had done and taught. [31]Then, because so many people were coming and going that they did not even have a chance to eat, he said to them, "Come with me by yourselves to a quiet place and get some rest."

[32]So they went away by themselves in a boat to a solitary place. [33]But many who saw them leaving recognized them and ran on foot from all the towns and got there ahead of them. [34]When Jesus landed and saw a large crowd, he had compassion on them, because they were like sheep without a shepherd. So he began teaching them many things.

[35]By this time it was late in the day, so his disciples came to him. "This is a remote place," they said, "and it's already very late. [36]Send the people away so they can go to the surrounding countryside and villages and buy themselves something to eat."

[37]But he answered, "You give them something to eat."

They said to him, "That would take eight months of a man's wages[c]! Are we to go and spend that much on bread and give it to them to eat?"

[38]"How many loaves do you have?" he asked. "Go and see."

When they found out, they said, "Five—and two fish."

[39]Then Jesus directed them to have all the people sit down in groups on the green grass. [40]So they sat down in groups of hundreds and fifties. [41]Taking the five loaves and the two fish and looking up to heaven, he gave thanks and broke the loaves. Then he gave them to his disciples to set before the people. He also divided the two fish among them all. [42]They all ate and were satisfied, [43]and the disciples picked up twelve basketfuls of broken pieces of bread and fish. [44]The number of the men who had eaten was five thousand.

Jesus Walks on the Water

[45]Immediately Jesus made his disciples get into the boat and go on ahead of him to Bethsaida, while he dismissed the

---

[a]14 Some early manuscripts *He was saying*   [b]20 Some early manuscripts *he did many things*   [c]37 Greek *take two hundred denarii*

crowd. **46**After leaving them, he went up on a mountainside to pray.

47When evening came, the boat was in the middle of the lake, and he was alone on land. **48**He saw the disciples straining at the oars, because the wind was against them. About the fourth watch of the night he went out to them, walking on the lake. He was about to pass by them, **49**but when they saw him walking on the lake, they thought he was a ghost. They cried out, **50**because they all saw him and were terrified.

Immediately he spoke to them and said, "Take courage! It is I. Don't be afraid." **51**Then he climbed into the boat with them, and the wind died down. They were completely amazed, **52**for they had not understood about the loaves; their hearts were hardened.

53When they had crossed over, they landed at Gennesaret and anchored there. **54**As soon as they got out of the boat, people recognized Jesus. **55**They ran throughout that whole region and carried the sick on mats to wherever they heard he was. **56**And wherever he went—into villages, towns or countryside—they placed the sick in the marketplaces. They begged him to let them touch even the edge of his cloak, and all who touched him were healed.

Clean and Unclean

7 The Pharisees and some of the teachers of the law who had come from Jerusalem gathered around Jesus and **2**saw some of his disciples eating food with hands that were "unclean," that is, unwashed. **3**(The Pharisees and all the Jews do not eat unless they give their hands a ceremonial washing, holding to the tradition of the elders. **4**When they come from the marketplace they do not eat unless they wash. And they observe many other traditions, such as the washing of cups, pitchers and kettles.[a])

5So the Pharisees and teachers of the law asked Jesus, "Why don't your disciples live according to the tradition of the elders instead of eating their food with 'unclean' hands?"

6He replied, "Isaiah was right when he prophesied about you hypocrites; as it is written:

" 'These people honor me with their lips,
    but their hearts are far from me.
7They worship me in vain;
    their teachings are but rules taught by men.'[b]

8You have let go of the commands of God and are holding on to the traditions of men."

9And he said to them: "You have a fine way of setting aside the commands of God in order to observe[c] your own traditions! **10**For Moses said, 'Honor your father and your mother,'[d] and, 'Anyone who curses his father or mother must be put to death.'[e] **11**But you say that if a man says to his father or mother: 'Whatever help you might otherwise have received from me is Corban' (that is, a gift devoted to God), **12**then you no longer let him do anything for his father or mother. **13**Thus you nullify the word of God by your tradition that you have handed down. And you do many things like that."

14Again Jesus called the crowd to him and said, "Listen to me, everyone, and understand this. **15**Nothing outside a man can make him 'unclean' by going into him. Rather, it is what comes out of a man that makes him 'unclean.'[f]"

17After he had left the crowd and entered the house, his disciples asked him about this parable. **18**"Are you so dull?" he asked. "Don't you see that nothing that enters a man from the outside can make him 'unclean'? **19**For it doesn't go into his heart but into his stomach, and then out of his body." (In saying this, Jesus declared all foods "clean.")

20He went on: "What comes out of a man is what makes him 'unclean.' **21**For from within, out of men's hearts, come evil thoughts, sexual immorality, theft, murder, adultery, **22**greed, malice, deceit, lewdness, envy, slander, arrogance and folly. **23**All these evils come from inside and make a man 'unclean.' "

The Faith of a Syrophoenician Woman

24Jesus left that place and went to the vicinity of Tyre.[g] He entered a house and did not want anyone to know it; yet he could not keep his presence secret. **25**In

---

a4 Some early manuscripts *pitchers, kettles and dining couches*   *b6,7* Isaiah 29:13   *c9* Some manuscripts *set up*   *d10* Exodus 20:12; Deut. 5:16   *e10* Exodus 21:17; Lev. 20:9   *f15* Some early manuscripts *'unclean.' 16If anyone has ears to hear, let him hear.*   *g24* Many early manuscripts *Tyre and Sidon* fact, as soon as she heard about him, a woman whose little daughter was possessed by an evil[a] spirit came and fell at his feet. [26]The woman was a Greek, born in Syrian Phoenicia. She begged Jesus to drive the demon out of her daughter.

[27]"First let the children eat all they want," he told her, "for it is not right to take the children's bread and toss it to their dogs."

[28]"Yes, Lord," she replied, "but even the dogs under the table eat the children's crumbs."

[29]Then he told her, "For such a reply, you may go; the demon has left your daughter."

[30]She went home and found her child lying on the bed, and the demon gone.

The Healing of a Deaf and Mute Man

[31]Then Jesus left the vicinity of Tyre and went through Sidon, down to the Sea of Galilee and into the region of the Decapolis.[b] [32]There some people brought to him a man who was deaf and could hardly talk, and they begged him to place his hand on the man.

[33]After he took him aside, away from the crowd, Jesus put his fingers into the man's ears. Then he spit and touched the man's tongue. [34]He looked up to heaven and with a deep sigh said to him, *"Ephphatha!"* (which means, "Be opened!"). [35]At this, the man's ears were opened, his tongue was loosened and he began to speak plainly.

[36]Jesus commanded them not to tell anyone. But the more he did so, the more they kept talking about it. [37]People were overwhelmed with amazement. "He has done everything well," they said. "He even makes the deaf hear and the mute speak."

Jesus Feeds the Four Thousand

8 During those days another large crowd gathered. Since they had nothing to eat, Jesus called his disciples to him and said, [2]"I have compassion for these people; they have already been with me three days and have nothing to eat. [3]If I send them home hungry, they will collapse on the way, because some of them have come a long distance."

[4]His disciples answered, "But where in this remote place can anyone get enough bread to feed them?"

[5]"How many loaves do you have?" Jesus asked.

"Seven," they replied.

[6]He told the crowd to sit down on the ground. When he had taken the seven loaves and given thanks, he broke them and gave them to his disciples to set before the people, and they did so. [7]They had a few small fish as well; he gave thanks for them also and told the disciples to distribute them. [8]The people ate and were satisfied. Afterward the disciples picked up seven basketfuls of broken pieces that were left over. [9]About four thousand men were present. And having sent them away, [10]he got into the boat with his disciples and went to the region of Dalmanutha.

[11]The Pharisees came and began to question Jesus. To test him, they asked him for a sign from heaven. [12]He sighed deeply and said, "Why does this generation ask for a miraculous sign? I tell you the truth, no sign will be given to it." [13]Then he left them, got back into the boat and crossed to the other side.

The Yeast of the Pharisees and Herod

[14]The disciples had forgotten to bring bread, except for one loaf they had with them in the boat. [15]"Be careful," Jesus warned them. "Watch out for the yeast of the Pharisees and that of Herod."

[16]They discussed this with one another and said, "It is because we have no bread."

[17]Aware of their discussion, Jesus asked them: "Why are you talking about having no bread? Do you still not see or understand? Are your hearts hardened? [18]Do you have eyes but fail to see, and ears but fail to hear? And don't you remember? [19]When I broke the five loaves for the five thousand, how many basketfuls of pieces did you pick up?"

"Twelve," they replied.

[20]"And when I broke the seven loaves for the four thousand, how many basketfuls of pieces did you pick up?"

They answered, "Seven."

[21]He said to them, "Do you still not understand?"

The Healing of a Blind Man at Bethsaida

[22]They came to Bethsaida, and some people brought a blind man and begged Jesus to touch him. [23]He took the blind man by the hand and led him outside the

---

WEEKENDING

RECOGNIZE

What was it that drew men to Jesus? Yes, he
spoke with authority and he did miraculous and
wonderful deeds, but I think the one thing that
men could not ignore was the compassion and
love that came from his heart and on to his face
and into his words and deeds.

If we abide in him as he abides in us, we
begin to see things differently. We begin to look
at things with his eyes.

– Bob Benson

REVIVE

Saturday: Mark 1:40–45
Sunday: Colossians 3:12–17

Go to page 1066 for your next devotional reading.

village. When he had spit on the man's eyes and put his hands on him, Jesus asked, "Do you see anything?"

²⁴He looked up and said, "I see people; they look like trees walking around."

²⁵Once more Jesus put his hands on the man's eyes. Then his eyes were opened, his sight was restored, and he saw everything clearly. ²⁶Jesus sent him home, saying, "Don't go into the village.ᵃ"

Peter's Confession of Christ

²⁷Jesus and his disciples went on to the villages around Caesarea Philippi. On the way he asked them, "Who do people say I am?"

²⁸They replied, "Some say John the Baptist; others say Elijah; and still others, one of the prophets."

²⁹"But what about you?" he asked. "Who do you say I am?"

Peter answered, "You are the Christ.ᵇ"

³⁰Jesus warned them not to tell anyone about him.

Jesus Predicts His Death

³¹He then began to teach them that the Son of Man must suffer many things and be rejected by the elders, chief priests and teachers of the law, and that he must be killed and after three days rise again. ³²He spoke plainly about this, and Peter took him aside and began to rebuke him.

³³But when Jesus turned and looked at his disciples, he rebuked Peter. "Get behind me, Satan!" he said. "You do not have in mind the things of God, but the things of men."

³⁴Then he called the crowd to him along with his disciples and said: "If anyone would come after me, he must deny himself and take up his cross and follow me. ³⁵For whoever wants to save his lifeᶜ will lose it, but whoever loses his life for me and for the gospel will save it. ³⁶What good is it for a man to gain the whole world, yet forfeit his soul? ³⁷Or what can a man give in exchange for his soul? ³⁸If anyone is ashamed of me and my words in this adulterous and sinful generation, the Son of Man will be ashamed of him when he comes in his Father's glory with the holy angels."

9 And he said to them, "I tell you the truth, some who are standing here

will not taste death before they see the kingdom of God come with power."

The Transfiguration

²After six days Jesus took Peter, James and John with him and led them up a high mountain, where they were all alone. There he was transfigured before them. ³His clothes became dazzling white, whiter than anyone in the world could bleach them. ⁴And there appeared before them Elijah and Moses, who were talking with Jesus.

⁵Peter said to Jesus, "Rabbi, it is good for us to be here. Let us put up three shelters—one for you, one for Moses and one for Elijah." ⁶(He did not know what to say, they were so frightened.)

⁷Then a cloud appeared and enveloped them, and a voice came from the cloud: "This is my Son, whom I love. Listen to him!"

⁸Suddenly, when they looked around, they no longer saw anyone with them except Jesus.

⁹As they were coming down the mountain, Jesus gave them orders not to tell anyone what they had seen until the Son of Man had risen from the dead. ¹⁰They kept the matter to themselves, discussing what "rising from the dead" meant.

¹¹And they asked him, "Why do the teachers of the law say that Elijah must come first?"

¹²Jesus replied, "To be sure, Elijah does come first, and restores all things. Why then is it written that the Son of Man must suffer much and be rejected? ¹³But I tell you, Elijah has come, and they have done to him everything they wished, just as it is written about him."

The Healing of a Boy With an Evil Spirit

¹⁴When they came to the other disciples, they saw a large crowd around them and the teachers of the law arguing with them. ¹⁵As soon as all the people saw Jesus, they were overwhelmed with wonder and ran to greet him.

¹⁶"What are you arguing with them about?" he asked.

¹⁷A man in the crowd answered, "Teacher, I brought you my son, who is possessed by a spirit that has robbed him of speech. ¹⁸Whenever it seizes him, it

throws him to the ground. He foams at the
mouth, gnashes his teeth and becomes
rigid. I asked your disciples to drive out
the spirit, but they could not."

¹⁹"O unbelieving generation," Jesus replied, "how long shall I stay with you?
How long shall I put up with you? Bring
the boy to me."

²⁰So they brought him. When the spirit
saw Jesus, it immediately threw the boy
into a convulsion. He fell to the ground
and rolled around, foaming at the mouth.

²¹Jesus asked the boy's father, "How
long has he been like this?"

"From childhood," he answered. ²²"It
has often thrown him into fire or water to
kill him. But if you can do anything, take
pity on us and help us."

²³"'If you can'?" said Jesus. "Everything
is possible for him who believes."

²⁴Immediately the boy's father exclaimed, "I do believe; help me overcome
my unbelief!"

²⁵When Jesus saw that a crowd was
running to the scene, he rebuked the
evil*a* spirit. "You deaf and mute spirit,"
he said, "I command you, come out of him
and never enter him again."

²⁶The spirit shrieked, convulsed him violently and came out. The boy looked so
much like a corpse that many said, "He's
dead." ²⁷But Jesus took him by the hand

a25 Greek *unclean*

MONDAY

VERSE FOR THE DAY:
Mark 9:2

AUTHOR:
Jim Conway

PASSAGE FOR THE DAY:
Mark 9:2–13

Equal Sharing

YOU don't need to be a friend to everyone. Remember the
model of Jesus. He preached to, ministered to, and healed
thousands of people, but he only had twelve disciples. Of
those twelve, only three were invited with him when he was
transfigured on the mountain.

Don't torture yourself by thinking you have to relate equally
to everyone. In fact, don't waste your precious friendship time
on relationships that won't be productive.

It's one thing to reach out to a needy person, but it's another
to have a friendship. In the first situation you're doing social
work or a spiritual ministry of caring. When you are truly a
friend, you and your friend will be giving equally to each
other. Both of you will be nourished by the relationship.

In your life you should always have some people whom you
nourish and who return little or nothing to you. You should
also have people who nourish you, but you may return nothing to them. A third kind of relationship is equal sharing. This
is friendship.

All three categories are important, but don't refer to the first
two as friendships. The first one is your ministry to someone
else, the second type is someone's ministry to you. Only the
third—equal sharing—is true friendship.

Additional Scripture Readings:
Proverbs 18:24; Ecclesiastes 4:8–12

*Go to page 1068 for your next
devotional reading.*

and lifted him to his feet, and he stood up.

28After Jesus had gone indoors, his disciples asked him privately, "Why couldn't we drive it out?"

29He replied, "This kind can come out only by prayer.*a*"

30They left that place and passed through Galilee. Jesus did not want anyone to know where they were, **31**because he was teaching his disciples. He said to them, "The Son of Man is going to be betrayed into the hands of men. They will kill him, and after three days he will rise." **32**But they did not understand what he meant and were afraid to ask him about it.

Who Is the Greatest?

33They came to Capernaum. When he was in the house, he asked them, "What were you arguing about on the road?" **34**But they kept quiet because on the way they had argued about who was the greatest.

35Sitting down, Jesus called the Twelve and said, "If anyone wants to be first, he must be the very last, and the servant of all."

36He took a little child and had him stand among them. Taking him in his arms, he said to them, **37**"Whoever welcomes one of these little children in my name welcomes me; and whoever welcomes me does not welcome me but the one who sent me."

Whoever Is Not Against Us Is for Us

38"Teacher," said John, "we saw a man driving out demons in your name and we told him to stop, because he was not one of us."

39"Do not stop him," Jesus said. "No one who does a miracle in my name can in the next moment say anything bad about me, **40**for whoever is not against us is for us. **41**I tell you the truth, anyone who gives you a cup of water in my name because you belong to Christ will certainly not lose his reward.

Causing to Sin

42"And if anyone causes one of these little ones who believe in me to sin, it would be better for him to be thrown into the sea with a large millstone tied around his neck. **43**If your hand causes you to sin, cut

it off. It is better for you to enter life maimed than with two hands to go into hell, where the fire never goes out.*b* **45**And if your foot causes you to sin, cut it off. It is better for you to enter life crippled than to have two feet and be thrown into hell.*c* **47**And if your eye causes you to sin, pluck it out. It is better for you to enter the kingdom of God with one eye than to have two eyes and be thrown into hell, **48**where

" 'their worm does not die,
and the fire is not quenched.'*d*

49Everyone will be salted with fire. **50**"Salt is good, but if it loses its saltiness, how can you make it salty again? Have salt in yourselves, and be at peace with each other."

Divorce

10 Jesus then left that place and went into the region of Judea and across the Jordan. Again crowds of people came to him, and as was his custom, he taught them.

2Some Pharisees came and tested him by asking, "Is it lawful for a man to divorce his wife?"

3"What did Moses command you?" he replied.

4They said, "Moses permitted a man to write a certificate of divorce and send her away."

5"It was because your hearts were hard that Moses wrote you this law," Jesus replied. **6**"But at the beginning of creation God 'made them male and female.'*e* **7**'For this reason a man will leave his father and mother and be united to his wife,*f* **8**and the two will become one flesh.'*g* So they are no longer two, but one. **9**Therefore what God has joined together, let man not separate."

10When they were in the house again, the disciples asked Jesus about this. **11**He answered, "Anyone who divorces his wife and marries another woman commits adultery against her. **12**And if she divorces her husband and marries another man, she commits adultery."

The Little Children and Jesus

13People were bringing little children to Jesus to have him touch them, but the dis-

*a*29 Some manuscripts *prayer and fasting*   *b*43 Some manuscripts *out,* 44*where* / " 'their worm does not die, / and the fire is not quenched.'   *c*45 Some manuscripts *hell,* 46*where* / " 'their worm does not die, / and the fire is not quenched.'   *d*48 Isaiah 66:24   *e*6 Gen. 1:27   *f*7 Some early manuscripts do not have *and be united to his wife.*   *g*8 Gen. 2:24

ciples rebuked them. **14**When Jesus saw this, he was indignant. He said to them, "Let the little children come to me, and do not hinder them, for the kingdom of God belongs to such as these. **15**I tell you the truth, anyone who will not receive the kingdom of God like a little child will never enter it." **16**And he took the children in his arms, put his hands on them and blessed them.

The Rich Young Man

17As Jesus started on his way, a man ran up to him and fell on his knees before him. "Good teacher," he asked,

"what must I do to inherit eternal life?"

18"Why do you call me good?" Jesus answered. "No one is good—except God alone. **19**You know the commandments: 'Do not murder, do not commit adultery, do not steal, do not give false testimony, do not defraud, honor your father and mother.'*a*"

20"Teacher," he declared, "all these I have kept since I was a boy."

21Jesus looked at him and loved him. "One thing you lack," he said. "Go, sell everything you have and give to the poor, and you will have treasure in heaven. Then come, follow me."

a19 Exodus 20:12-16; Deut. 5:16-20

TUESDAY

VERSE FOR THE DAY:	*AUTHOR:*	*PASSAGE FOR THE DAY:*
Mark 10:9	*Donald M. Joy*	*Mark 10:1–12*

Jesus' View of Sex

IF YOU want to see the highest respect for human sexuality and marriage, read it in the words and actions of Jesus. He says, "What God joins together sexually, be careful not to rip apart." Jesus announces the warning in the face of easy divorce in his teaching recorded in Matthew 19 [and in Mark 10]. He restates the Genesis 2 picture of one man and one woman forming one flesh unity, and suggests that the only alternative to the kind of beautiful sexual intimacy is holy celibacy: being single for the glory of God and the service of God's purposes in the world. It is clear that to be single and sexually unattached is an expression of high human responsibility and high respect for humans everywhere.

Jesus teaches responsible "looking" in the famous "lust" teaching in Matthew 5. We are to sanctify our sexual imagination and to be careful not to fantasize sexual intimacy with inappropriate people. This high target, which keeps all of us focused on our own lifelong intimacy covenant, means looking ahead toward marriage when we are young and looking back to reconstruct a lifelong fidelity for the rest of our lives. This sex-positive focusing of sexual imagination and energy is an invitation to clear and exclusive thinking as the highest respect we can show for everyone. No one has a higher, more positive view of sex than Jesus.

Additional Scripture Readings:
Matthew 5:27–30; Matthew 19:1–12

Go to page 1070 for your next devotional reading.

²²At this the man's face fell. He went away sad, because he had great wealth.

²³Jesus looked around and said to his disciples, "How hard it is for the rich to enter the kingdom of God!"

²⁴The disciples were amazed at his words. But Jesus said again, "Children, how hard it is*a* to enter the kingdom of God! ²⁵It is easier for a camel to go through the eye of a needle than for a rich man to enter the kingdom of God."

²⁶The disciples were even more amazed, and said to each other, "Who then can be saved?"

²⁷Jesus looked at them and said, "With man this is impossible, but not with God; all things are possible with God."

²⁸Peter said to him, "We have left everything to follow you!"

²⁹"I tell you the truth," Jesus replied, "no one who has left home or brothers or sisters or mother or father or children or fields for me and the gospel ³⁰will fail to receive a hundred times as much in this present age (homes, brothers, sisters, mothers, children and fields — and with them, persecutions) and in the age to come, eternal life. ³¹But many who are first will be last, and the last first."

Jesus Again Predicts His Death

³²They were on their way up to Jerusalem, with Jesus leading the way, and the disciples were astonished, while those who followed were afraid. Again he took the Twelve aside and told them what was going to happen to him. ³³"We are going up to Jerusalem," he said, "and the Son of Man will be betrayed to the chief priests and teachers of the law. They will condemn him to death and will hand him over to the Gentiles, ³⁴who will mock him and spit on him, flog him and kill him. Three days later he will rise."

The Request of James and John

³⁵Then James and John, the sons of Zebedee, came to him. "Teacher," they said, "we want you to do for us whatever we ask."

³⁶"What do you want me to do for you?" he asked.

³⁷They replied, "Let one of us sit at your right and the other at your left in your glory."

³⁸"You don't know what you are asking," Jesus said. "Can you drink the cup I drink or be baptized with the baptism I am baptized with?"

³⁹"We can," they answered.

Jesus said to them, "You will drink the cup I drink and be baptized with the baptism I am baptized with, ⁴⁰but to sit at my right or left is not for me to grant. These places belong to those for whom they have been prepared."

⁴¹When the ten heard about this, they became indignant with James and John. ⁴²Jesus called them together and said, "You know that those who are regarded as rulers of the Gentiles lord it over them, and their high officials exercise authority over them. ⁴³Not so with you. Instead, whoever wants to become great among you must be your servant, ⁴⁴and whoever wants to be first must be slave of all. ⁴⁵For even the Son of Man did not come to be served, but to serve, and to give his life as a ransom for many."

Blind Bartimaeus Receives His Sight

⁴⁶Then they came to Jericho. As Jesus and his disciples, together with a large crowd, were leaving the city, a blind man, Bartimaeus (that is, the Son of Timaeus), was sitting by the roadside begging. ⁴⁷When he heard that it was Jesus of Nazareth, he began to shout, "Jesus, Son of David, have mercy on me!"

⁴⁸Many rebuked him and told him to be quiet, but he shouted all the more, "Son of David, have mercy on me!"

⁴⁹Jesus stopped and said, "Call him."

So they called to the blind man, "Cheer up! On your feet! He's calling you." ⁵⁰Throwing his cloak aside, he jumped to his feet and came to Jesus.

⁵¹"What do you want me to do for you?" Jesus asked him.

The blind man said, "Rabbi, I want to see."

⁵²"Go," said Jesus, "your faith has healed you." Immediately he received his sight and followed Jesus along the road.

The Triumphal Entry

11 As they approached Jerusalem and came to Bethphage and Bethany at the Mount of Olives, Jesus sent two of his disciples, ²saying to them, "Go to the village ahead of you, and just as you enter it, you will find a colt tied there, which no one has ever ridden. Untie it and bring it here. ³If anyone asks you, 'Why are you

---

*a*24 Some manuscripts *is for those who trust in riches*

doing this?' tell him, 'The Lord needs it and will send it back here shortly.' "

4They went and found a colt outside in the street, tied at a doorway. As they untied it, **5**some people standing there asked, "What are you doing, untying that colt?" **6**They answered as Jesus had told them to, and the people let them go. **7**When they brought the colt to Jesus and threw their cloaks over it, he sat on it. **8**Many people spread their cloaks on the road, while oth-

ers spread branches they had cut in the fields. **9**Those who went ahead and those who followed shouted,

"Hosanna!*a*"

"Blessed is he who comes in the name of the Lord!"*b*

10"Blessed is the coming kingdom of our father David!"

"Hosanna in the highest!"

a9 A Hebrew expression meaning "Save!" which became an exclamation of praise; also in verse 10
b9 Psalm 118:25,26

WEDNESDAY

VERSE FOR THE DAY:
Mark 10:43

AUTHOR:
Ron Blue

PASSAGE FOR THE DAY:
Mark 10:35–45

A Different Attitude

BOTH the Christian and the non-Christian are concerned with success, but in each case success is always relative to goals. The difference is in perspective. One view sees only the here and now, the other sees the unseen. What one's perspective is (or to put it another way, what one believes) will determine attitudes and actions. That is why the Christian, in managing his or her money, is different.

Individually, God has called us to be: salt and light (see Matthew 5:13–16), servants (see Mark 10:45) and stewards (see Matthew 25:14–30).

The idea of being salt and light says that God wants me to be *not* better than, *but* different from. The Christian, therefore, may or may not have more than his neighbor, but that does not distinguish him. What does distinguish the Christian from the world is the absence of any anxiety, which might have come as a result of the loss of something he has managed or even God's denial of something he wants. Why? Because the Christian's treasure is not on earth. The world and its temporal toys do not possess him. He is prayerful, but not the least bit anxious about the tremendous uncertainty facing our national and world economy.

Obviously that attitude is not "normal" but rather "different," and it comes from having an entirely different perspective. The Christian's perspective is eternal, the attitude is one of holding possessions lightly, and the lifestyle is free from worry and anxiety. Truly that is different!

Additional Scripture Readings:
Matthew 6:19–27; 1 Timothy 6:3–10

Go to page 1073 for your next devotional reading.

[11] Jesus entered Jerusalem and went to the temple. He looked around at everything, but since it was already late, he went out to Bethany with the Twelve.

Jesus Clears the Temple

[12] The next day as they were leaving Bethany, Jesus was hungry. [13] Seeing in the distance a fig tree in leaf, he went to find out if it had any fruit. When he reached it, he found nothing but leaves, because it was not the season for figs. [14] Then he said to the tree, "May no one ever eat fruit from you again." And his disciples heard him say it.

[15] On reaching Jerusalem, Jesus entered the temple area and began driving out those who were buying and selling there. He overturned the tables of the money changers and the benches of those selling doves, [16] and would not allow anyone to carry merchandise through the temple courts. [17] And as he taught them, he said, "Is it not written:

" 'My house will be called
    a house of prayer for all nations'a?

But you have made it 'a den of robbers.'b"

[18] The chief priests and the teachers of the law heard this and began looking for a way to kill him, for they feared him, because the whole crowd was amazed at his teaching.

[19] When evening came, theyc went out of the city.

The Withered Fig Tree

[20] In the morning, as they went along, they saw the fig tree withered from the roots. [21] Peter remembered and said to Jesus, "Rabbi, look! The fig tree you cursed has withered!"

[22] "Haved faith in God," Jesus answered. [23] "I tell you the truth, if anyone says to this mountain, 'Go, throw yourself into the sea,' and does not doubt in his heart but believes that what he says will happen, it will be done for him. [24] Therefore I tell you, whatever you ask for in prayer, believe that you have received it, and it will be yours. [25] And when you stand praying, if you hold anything against anyone, forgive him, so that your Father in heaven may forgive you your sins.e"

The Authority of Jesus Questioned

[27] They arrived again in Jerusalem, and while Jesus was walking in the temple courts, the chief priests, the teachers of the law and the elders came to him. [28] "By what authority are you doing these things?" they asked. "And who gave you authority to do this?"

[29] Jesus replied, "I will ask you one question. Answer me, and I will tell you by what authority I am doing these things. [30] John's baptism — was it from heaven, or from men? Tell me!"

[31] They discussed it among themselves and said, "If we say, 'From heaven,' he will ask, 'Then why didn't you believe him?' [32] But if we say, 'From men' . . . ." (They feared the people, for everyone held that John really was a prophet.)

[33] So they answered Jesus, "We don't know."

Jesus said, "Neither will I tell you by what authority I am doing these things."

The Parable of the Tenants

12 He then began to speak to them in parables: "A man planted a vineyard. He put a wall around it, dug a pit for the winepress and built a watchtower. Then he rented the vineyard to some farmers and went away on a journey. [2] At harvest time he sent a servant to the tenants to collect from them some of the fruit of the vineyard. [3] But they seized him, beat him and sent him away empty-handed. [4] Then he sent another servant to them; they struck this man on the head and treated him shamefully. [5] He sent still another, and that one they killed. He sent many others; some of them they beat, others they killed.

[6] "He had one left to send, a son, whom he loved. He sent him last of all, saying, 'They will respect my son.'

[7] "But the tenants said to one another, 'This is the heir. Come, let's kill him, and the inheritance will be ours.' [8] So they took him and killed him, and threw him out of the vineyard.

[9] "What then will the owner of the vineyard do? He will come and kill those tenants and give the vineyard to others. [10] Haven't you read this scripture:

" 'The stone the builders rejected
    has become the capstonef;

---

a17 Isaiah 56:7   b17 Jer. 7:11   c19 Some early manuscripts he   d22 Some early manuscripts If you have   e25 Some manuscripts sins. 26But if you do not forgive, neither will your Father who is in heaven forgive your sins.   f10 Or cornerstone

[11]the Lord has done this,
and it is marvelous in our eyes'*a*?"

[12]Then they looked for a way to arrest him because they knew he had spoken the parable against them. But they were afraid of the crowd; so they left him and went away.

Paying Taxes to Caesar

[13]Later they sent some of the Pharisees and Herodians to Jesus to catch him in his words. [14]They came to him and said, "Teacher, we know you are a man of integrity. You aren't swayed by men, because you pay no attention to who they are; but you teach the way of God in accordance with the truth. Is it right to pay taxes to Caesar or not? [15]Should we pay or shouldn't we?"

But Jesus knew their hypocrisy. "Why are you trying to trap me?" he asked. "Bring me a denarius and let me look at it." [16]They brought the coin, and he asked them, "Whose portrait is this? And whose inscription?"

"Caesar's," they replied.

[17]Then Jesus said to them, "Give to Caesar what is Caesar's and to God what is God's."

And they were amazed at him.

Marriage at the Resurrection

[18]Then the Sadducees, who say there is no resurrection, came to him with a question. [19]"Teacher," they said, "Moses wrote for us that if a man's brother dies and leaves a wife but no children, the man must marry the widow and have children for his brother. [20]Now there were seven brothers. The first one married and died without leaving any children. [21]The second one married the widow, but he also died, leaving no child. It was the same with the third. [22]In fact, none of the seven left any children. Last of all, the woman died too. [23]At the resurrection*b* whose wife will she be, since the seven were married to her?"

[24]Jesus replied, "Are you not in error because you do not know the Scriptures or the power of God? [25]When the dead rise, they will neither marry nor be given in marriage; they will be like the angels in heaven. [26]Now about the dead rising— have you not read in the book of Moses, in the account of the bush, how God said to him, 'I am the God of Abraham, the God of Isaac, and the God of Jacob'*c*? [27]He is not the God of the dead, but of the living. You are badly mistaken!"

The Greatest Commandment

[28]One of the teachers of the law came and heard them debating. Noticing that Jesus had given them a good answer, he asked him, "Of all the commandments, which is the most important?"

[29]"The most important one," answered Jesus, "is this: 'Hear, O Israel, the Lord our God, the Lord is one.*d* [30]Love the Lord your God with all your heart and with all your soul and with all your mind and with all your strength.'*e* [31]The second is this: 'Love your neighbor as yourself.'*f* There is no commandment greater than these."

[32]"Well said, teacher," the man replied. "You are right in saying that God is one and there is no other but him. [33]To love him with all your heart, with all your understanding and with all your strength, and to love your neighbor as yourself is more important than all burnt offerings and sacrifices."

[34]When Jesus saw that he had answered wisely, he said to him, "You are not far from the kingdom of God." And from then on no one dared ask him any more questions.

Whose Son Is the Christ?

[35]While Jesus was teaching in the temple courts, he asked, "How is it that the teachers of the law say that the Christ*g* is the son of David? [36]David himself, speaking by the Holy Spirit, declared:

" 'The Lord said to my Lord:
"Sit at my right hand
until I put your enemies
under your feet." '*h*

[37]David himself calls him 'Lord.' How then can he be his son?"

The large crowd listened to him with delight.

[38]As he taught, Jesus said, "Watch out for the teachers of the law. They like to walk around in flowing robes and be greeted in the marketplaces, [39]and have the most important seats in the synagogues and the places of honor at banquets. [40]They devour widows' houses and

for a show make lengthy prayers. Such men will be punished most severely."

The Widow's Offering

⁴¹Jesus sat down opposite the place where the offerings were put and watched the crowd putting their money into the temple treasury. Many rich people threw in large amounts. ⁴²But a poor widow came and put in two very small copper

---

THURSDAY

VERSE FOR THE DAY:
Mark 12:33

AUTHOR:
Thomas Hale

PASSAGE FOR THE DAY:
Mark 12:28–34

No Greater Commandment

GOD'S immediate purpose is to communicate his love to people everywhere, and we believe that is why he sent us to Nepal. But though communicating love through medicine may discharge our responsibility as medical workers, it does little for the sick person coming for treatment if all he has to look forward to after recovery is a life of continuing unhappiness and hopelessness. The only way we know to help our Nepali friends in a lasting way is to put them in touch with the God who is the source of love and who sent his Son Jesus into the world to demonstrate it.

We know from personal experience that God's love changes lives; the faith we share with our Nepali friends is not a hand-me-down or merely theoretical faith. His love changed our lives and sent us to Nepal; his love has kept us here. Many are attracted to Nepal by the spectacular mountains, the anticipation of adventure, the dramatic needs—and undoubtedly we were too—but such attractions will never keep people here. Only the love of Christ can do that. There are too many frustrations, too many insurmountable hurdles, for one to be able to carry on for long on one's own. Humanitarian motives are not enough. The humanitarian needs to be able to measure his accomplishments and see the fruit of his labor. But when there is little to show for his efforts, as is so often the case with work in developing countries, the humanitarian becomes discouraged and his idealism starts to fade. With us, however, the primary motive is to serve Christ. Thus, if our service to men is frustrated, rebuffed or wiped away, we need not be disheartened. We are merely instruments to render *his* service. We share *his* love, not our own, and his love never runs dry.

What does Christ's love mean to us? To a Nepali? It means life, abundant life, that begins now and will never end. Jesus came that we "may have life, and have it to the full" [John 10:10]. And after 2,000 years, his offer still stands.

Additional Scripture Readings:
John 10:7–10; 1 John 4:7–12

Go to page 1082 for your next devotional reading.

coins,*a* worth only a fraction of a penny.*b*

43Calling his disciples to him, Jesus said, "I tell you the truth, this poor widow has put more into the treasury than all the others. **44**They all gave out of their wealth; but she, out of her poverty, put in everything—all she had to live on."

Signs of the End of the Age

13 As he was leaving the temple, one of his disciples said to him, "Look, Teacher! What massive stones! What magnificent buildings!"

2"Do you see all these great buildings?" replied Jesus. "Not one stone here will be left on another; every one will be thrown down."

3As Jesus was sitting on the Mount of Olives opposite the temple, Peter, James, John and Andrew asked him privately, **4**"Tell us, when will these things happen? And what will be the sign that they are all about to be fulfilled?"

5Jesus said to them: "Watch out that no one deceives you. **6**Many will come in my name, claiming, 'I am he,' and will deceive many. **7**When you hear of wars and rumors of wars, do not be alarmed. Such things must happen, but the end is still to come. **8**Nation will rise against nation, and kingdom against kingdom. There will be earthquakes in various places, and famines. These are the beginning of birth pains.

9"You must be on your guard. You will be handed over to the local councils and flogged in the synagogues. On account of me you will stand before governors and kings as witnesses to them. **10**And the gospel must first be preached to all nations. **11**Whenever you are arrested and brought to trial, do not worry beforehand about what to say. Just say whatever is given you at the time, for it is not you speaking, but the Holy Spirit.

12"Brother will betray brother to death, and a father his child. Children will rebel against their parents and have them put to death. **13**All men will hate you because of me, but he who stands firm to the end will be saved.

14"When you see 'the abomination that causes desolation'*c* standing where it*d* does not belong—let the reader understand—then let those who are in Judea flee to the mountains. **15**Let no one on the roof of his house go down or enter the house to take anything out. **16**Let no one in the field go back to get his cloak. **17**How dreadful it will be in those days for pregnant women and nursing mothers! **18**Pray that this will not take place in winter, **19**because those will be days of distress unequaled from the beginning, when God created the world, until now—and never to be equaled again. **20**If the Lord had not cut short those days, no one would survive. But for the sake of the elect, whom he has chosen, he has shortened them. **21**At that time if anyone says to you, 'Look, here is the Christ*e*!' or, 'Look, there he is!' do not believe it. **22**For false Christs and false prophets will appear and perform signs and miracles to deceive the elect—if that were possible. **23**So be on your guard; I have told you everything ahead of time.

24"But in those days, following that distress,

" 'the sun will be darkened,
　　and the moon will not give its light;
25the stars will fall from the sky,
　　and the heavenly bodies will be
　　　shaken.'*f*

26"At that time men will see the Son of Man coming in clouds with great power and glory. **27**And he will send his angels and gather his elect from the four winds, from the ends of the earth to the ends of the heavens.

28"Now learn this lesson from the fig tree: As soon as its twigs get tender and its leaves come out, you know that summer is near. **29**Even so, when you see these things happening, you know that it is near, right at the door. **30**I tell you the truth, this generation*g* will certainly not pass away until all these things have happened. **31**Heaven and earth will pass away, but my words will never pass away.

The Day and Hour Unknown

32"No one knows about that day or hour, not even the angels in heaven, nor the Son, but only the Father. **33**Be on guard! Be alert*h*! You do not know when that time will come. **34**It's like a man going away: He leaves his house and puts his servants in charge, each with his assigned

---

*a*42 Greek *two lepta*　　*b*42 Greek *kodrantes*　　*c*14 Daniel 9:27; 11:31; 12:11　　*d*14 Or *he*; also in verse 29　　*e*21 Or *Messiah*　　*f*25 Isaiah 13:10; 34:4　　*g*30 Or *race*　　*h*33 Some manuscripts *alert and pray* task, and tells the one at the door to keep watch.

35"Therefore keep watch because you do not know when the owner of the house will come back—whether in the evening, or at midnight, or when the rooster crows, or at dawn. 36If he comes suddenly, do not let him find you sleeping. 37What I say to you, I say to everyone: 'Watch!' "

Jesus Anointed at Bethany

14 Now the Passover and the Feast of Unleavened Bread were only two days away, and the chief priests and the teachers of the law were looking for some sly way to arrest Jesus and kill him. 2"But not during the Feast," they said, "or the people may riot."

3While he was in Bethany, reclining at the table in the home of a man known as Simon the Leper, a woman came with an alabaster jar of very expensive perfume, made of pure nard. She broke the jar and poured the perfume on his head.

4Some of those present were saying indignantly to one another, "Why this waste of perfume? 5It could have been sold for more than a year's wages[a] and the money given to the poor." And they rebuked her harshly.

6"Leave her alone," said Jesus. "Why are you bothering her? She has done a beautiful thing to me. 7The poor you will always have with you, and you can help them any time you want. But you will not always have me. 8She did what she could. She poured perfume on my body beforehand to prepare for my burial. 9I tell you the truth, wherever the gospel is preached throughout the world, what she has done will also be told, in memory of her."

10Then Judas Iscariot, one of the Twelve, went to the chief priests to betray Jesus to them. 11They were delighted to hear this and promised to give him money. So he watched for an opportunity to hand him over.

The Lord's Supper

12On the first day of the Feast of Unleavened Bread, when it was customary to sacrifice the Passover lamb, Jesus' disciples asked him, "Where do you want us to go and make preparations for you to eat the Passover?"

13So he sent two of his disciples, telling them, "Go into the city, and a man carrying a jar of water will meet you. Follow him. 14Say to the owner of the house he enters, 'The Teacher asks: Where is my guest room, where I may eat the Passover with my disciples?' 15He will show you a large upper room, furnished and ready. Make preparations for us there."

16The disciples left, went into the city and found things just as Jesus had told them. So they prepared the Passover.

17When evening came, Jesus arrived with the Twelve. 18While they were reclining at the table eating, he said, "I tell you the truth, one of you will betray me—one who is eating with me."

19They were saddened, and one by one they said to him, "Surely not I?"

20"It is one of the Twelve," he replied, "one who dips bread into the bowl with me. 21The Son of Man will go just as it is written about him. But woe to that man who betrays the Son of Man! It would be better for him if he had not been born."

22While they were eating, Jesus took bread, gave thanks and broke it, and gave it to his disciples, saying, "Take it; this is my body."

23Then he took the cup, gave thanks and offered it to them, and they all drank from it.

24"This is my blood of the[b] covenant, which is poured out for many," he said to them. 25"I tell you the truth, I will not drink again of the fruit of the vine until that day when I drink it anew in the kingdom of God."

26When they had sung a hymn, they went out to the Mount of Olives.

Jesus Predicts Peter's Denial

27"You will all fall away," Jesus told them, "for it is written:

" 'I will strike the shepherd,
    and the sheep will be scattered.'[c]

28But after I have risen, I will go ahead of you into Galilee."

29Peter declared, "Even if all fall away, I will not."

30"I tell you the truth," Jesus answered, "today—yes, tonight—before the rooster crows twice[d] you yourself will disown me three times."

31But Peter insisted emphatically, "Even if I have to die with you, I will never disown you." And all the others said the same.

---

a5 Greek *than three hundred denarii*   b24 Some manuscripts *the new*   c27 Zech. 13:7   d30 Some early manuscripts do not have *twice*.

Gethsemane

32They went to a place called Gethsemane, and Jesus said to his disciples, "Sit here while I pray." **33**He took Peter, James and John along with him, and he began to be deeply distressed and troubled. **34**"My soul is overwhelmed with sorrow to the point of death," he said to them. "Stay here and keep watch."

35Going a little farther, he fell to the ground and prayed that if possible the hour might pass from him. **36**"*Abba,*[a] Father," he said, "everything is possible for you. Take this cup from me. Yet not what I will, but what you will."

37Then he returned to his disciples and found them sleeping. "Simon," he said to Peter, "are you asleep? Could you not keep watch for one hour? **38**Watch and pray so that you will not fall into temptation. The spirit is willing, but the body is weak."

39Once more he went away and prayed the same thing. **40**When he came back, he again found them sleeping, because their eyes were heavy. They did not know what to say to him.

41Returning the third time, he said to them, "Are you still sleeping and resting? Enough! The hour has come. Look, the Son of Man is betrayed into the hands of sinners. **42**Rise! Let us go! Here comes my betrayer!"

Jesus Arrested

43Just as he was speaking, Judas, one of the Twelve, appeared. With him was a crowd armed with swords and clubs, sent from the chief priests, the teachers of the law, and the elders. **44**Now the betrayer had arranged a signal with them: "The one I kiss is the man; arrest him and lead him away under guard." **45**Going at once to Jesus, Judas said, "Rabbi!" and kissed him. **46**The men seized Jesus and arrested him. **47**Then one of those standing near drew his sword and struck the servant of the high priest, cutting off his ear.

48"Am I leading a rebellion," said Jesus, "that you have come out with swords and clubs to capture me? **49**Every day I was with you, teaching in the temple courts, and you did not arrest me. But the Scriptures must be fulfilled." **50**Then everyone deserted him and fled.

51A young man, wearing nothing but a linen garment, was following Jesus. When they seized him, **52**he fled naked, leaving his garment behind.

Before the Sanhedrin

53They took Jesus to the high priest, and all the chief priests, elders and teachers of the law came together. **54**Peter followed him at a distance, right into the courtyard of the high priest. There he sat with the guards and warmed himself at the fire.

55The chief priests and the whole Sanhedrin were looking for evidence against Jesus so that they could put him to death, but they did not find any. **56**Many testified falsely against him, but their statements did not agree.

57Then some stood up and gave this false testimony against him: **58**"We heard him say, 'I will destroy this man-made temple and in three days will build another, not made by man.' " **59**Yet even then their testimony did not agree.

60Then the high priest stood up before them and asked Jesus, "Are you not going to answer? What is this testimony that these men are bringing against you?" **61**But Jesus remained silent and gave no answer.

Again the high priest asked him, "Are you the Christ,[b] the Son of the Blessed One?"

62"I am," said Jesus. "And you will see the Son of Man sitting at the right hand of the Mighty One and coming on the clouds of heaven."

63The high priest tore his clothes. "Why do we need any more witnesses?" he asked. **64**"You have heard the blasphemy. What do you think?"

They all condemned him as worthy of death. **65**Then some began to spit at him; they blindfolded him, struck him with their fists, and said, "Prophesy!" And the guards took him and beat him.

Peter Disowns Jesus

66While Peter was below in the courtyard, one of the servant girls of the high priest came by. **67**When she saw Peter warming himself, she looked closely at him.

"You also were with that Nazarene, Jesus," she said.

68But he denied it. "I don't know or un-

---

a36 Aramaic for *Father*   *b61* Or *Messiah*

derstand what you're talking about," he said, and went out into the entryway.[a]

69When the servant girl saw him there, she said again to those standing around, "This fellow is one of them." **70**Again he denied it.

After a little while, those standing near said to Peter, "Surely you are one of them, for you are a Galilean."

71He began to call down curses on himself, and he swore to them, "I don't know this man you're talking about."

72Immediately the rooster crowed the second time.[b] Then Peter remembered the word Jesus had spoken to him: "Before the rooster crows twice[c] you will disown me three times." And he broke down and wept.

Jesus Before Pilate

15 Very early in the morning, the chief priests, with the elders, the teachers of the law and the whole Sanhedrin, reached a decision. They bound Jesus, led him away and handed him over to Pilate.

2"Are you the king of the Jews?" asked Pilate.

"Yes, it is as you say," Jesus replied.

3The chief priests accused him of many things. **4**So again Pilate asked him, "Aren't you going to answer? See how many things they are accusing you of."

5But Jesus still made no reply, and Pilate was amazed.

6Now it was the custom at the Feast to release a prisoner whom the people requested. **7**A man called Barabbas was in prison with the insurrectionists who had committed murder in the uprising. **8**The crowd came up and asked Pilate to do for them what he usually did.

9"Do you want me to release to you the king of the Jews?" asked Pilate, **10**knowing it was out of envy that the chief priests had handed Jesus over to him. **11**But the chief priests stirred up the crowd to have Pilate release Barabbas instead.

12"What shall I do, then, with the one you call the king of the Jews?" Pilate asked them.

13"Crucify him!" they shouted.

14"Why? What crime has he committed?" asked Pilate.

But they shouted all the louder, "Crucify him!"

15Wanting to satisfy the crowd, Pilate released Barabbas to them. He had Jesus flogged, and handed him over to be crucified.

The Soldiers Mock Jesus

16The soldiers led Jesus away into the palace (that is, the Praetorium) and called together the whole company of soldiers. **17**They put a purple robe on him, then twisted together a crown of thorns and set it on him. **18**And they began to call out to him, "Hail, king of the Jews!" **19**Again and again they struck him on the head with a staff and spit on him. Falling on their knees, they paid homage to him. **20**And when they had mocked him, they took off the purple robe and put his own clothes on him. Then they led him out to crucify him.

The Crucifixion

21A certain man from Cyrene, Simon, the father of Alexander and Rufus, was passing by on his way in from the country, and they forced him to carry the cross. **22**They brought Jesus to the place called Golgotha (which means The Place of the Skull). **23**Then they offered him wine mixed with myrrh, but he did not take it. **24**And they crucified him. Dividing up his clothes, they cast lots to see what each would get.

25It was the third hour when they crucified him. **26**The written notice of the charge against him read: THE KING OF THE JEWS. **27**They crucified two robbers with him, one on his right and one on his left.[d] **29**Those who passed by hurled insults at him, shaking their heads and saying, "So! You who are going to destroy the temple and build it in three days, **30**come down from the cross and save yourself!"

31In the same way the chief priests and the teachers of the law mocked him among themselves. "He saved others," they said, "but he can't save himself! **32**Let this Christ,[e] this King of Israel, come down now from the cross, that we may see and believe." Those crucified with him also heaped insults on him.

The Death of Jesus

33At the sixth hour darkness came over the whole land until the ninth hour. **34**And

---

[a]68 Some early manuscripts *entryway and the rooster crowed*   [b]72 Some early manuscripts do not have *the second time.*   [c]72 Some early manuscripts do not have *twice.*   [d]27 Some manuscripts *left, 28and the scripture was fulfilled which says, "He was counted with the lawless ones"* (Isaiah 53:12)   [e]32 Or *Messiah*

at the ninth hour Jesus cried out in a loud voice, *"Eloi, Eloi, lama sabachthani?"* — which means, "My God, my God, why have you forsaken me?"*a*

35When some of those standing near heard this, they said, "Listen, he's calling Elijah."

36One man ran, filled a sponge with wine vinegar, put it on a stick, and offered it to Jesus to drink. "Now leave him alone. Let's see if Elijah comes to take him down," he said.

37With a loud cry, Jesus breathed his last.

38The curtain of the temple was torn in two from top to bottom. **39**And when the centurion, who stood there in front of Jesus, heard his cry and*b* saw how he died, he said, "Surely this man was the Son*c* of God!"

40Some women were watching from a distance. Among them were Mary Magdalene, Mary the mother of James the younger and of Joses, and Salome. **41**In Galilee these women had followed him and cared for his needs. Many other women who had come up with him to Jerusalem were also there.

The Burial of Jesus

42It was Preparation Day (that is, the day before the Sabbath). So as evening approached, **43**Joseph of Arimathea, a prominent member of the Council, who was himself waiting for the kingdom of God, went boldly to Pilate and asked for Jesus' body. **44**Pilate was surprised to hear that he was already dead. Summoning the centurion, he asked him if Jesus had already died. **45**When he learned from the centurion that it was so, he gave the body to Joseph. **46**So Joseph bought some linen cloth, took down the body, wrapped it in the linen, and placed it in a tomb cut out of rock. Then he rolled a stone against the entrance of the tomb. **47**Mary Magdalene and Mary the mother of Joses saw where he was laid.

The Resurrection

16 When the Sabbath was over, Mary Magdalene, Mary the mother of James, and Salome bought spices so that they might go to anoint Jesus' body. **2**Very early on the first day of the week, just after sunrise, they were on their way to the tomb **3**and they asked each other, "Who will roll the stone away from the entrance of the tomb?"

4But when they looked up, they saw that the stone, which was very large, had been rolled away. **5**As they entered the tomb, they saw a young man dressed in a white robe sitting on the right side, and they were alarmed.

6"Don't be alarmed," he said. "You are looking for Jesus the Nazarene, who was crucified. He has risen! He is not here. See the place where they laid him. **7**But go, tell his disciples and Peter, 'He is going ahead of you into Galilee. There you will see him, just as he told you.' "

8Trembling and bewildered, the women went out and fled from the tomb. They said nothing to anyone, because they were afraid.

[The earliest manuscripts and some other ancient witnesses do not have Mark 16:9–20.]

9When Jesus rose early on the first day of the week, he appeared first to Mary Magdalene, out of whom he had driven seven demons. **10**She went and told those who had been with him and who were mourning and weeping. **11**When they heard that Jesus was alive and that she had seen him, they did not believe it.

12Afterward Jesus appeared in a different form to two of them while they were walking in the country. **13**These returned and reported it to the rest; but they did not believe them either.

14Later Jesus appeared to the Eleven as they were eating; he rebuked them for their lack of faith and their stubborn refusal to believe those who had seen him after he had risen.

15He said to them, "Go into all the world and preach the good news to all creation. **16**Whoever believes and is baptized will be saved, but whoever does not believe will be condemned. **17**And these signs will accompany those who believe: In my name they will drive out demons; they will speak in new tongues; **18**they will pick up snakes with their hands; and when

---

a 34 Psalm 22:1   *b* 39 Some manuscripts do not have *heard his cry and*   *c* 39 Or *a son* they drink deadly poison, it will not hurt them at all; they will place their hands on sick people, and they will get well."

[19]After the Lord Jesus had spoken to them, he was taken up into heaven and he sat at the right hand of God. [20]Then the disciples went out and preached everywhere, and the Lord worked with them and confirmed his word by the signs that accompanied it.

*L*UKE writes this Gospel to present Jesus as a Savior for the whole human race. The stories emphasize how kind and loving Jesus is to those despised by society (such as tax collectors, Samaritans, the poor, and women). He stresses the importance of prayer in Jesus' life. As you read this book, be sure that you have repented of your sins and have claimed Jesus as your own personal Savior. Ask yourself whether you show the same sort of compassion to others that Jesus showed.

LUKE

Introduction

1 Many have undertaken to draw up an account of the things that have been fulfilled*a* among us, **2**just as they were handed down to us by those who from the first were eyewitnesses and servants of the word. **3**Therefore, since I myself have carefully investigated everything from the beginning, it seemed good also to me to write an orderly account for you, most excellent Theophilus, **4**so that you may know the certainty of the things you have been taught.

The Birth of John the Baptist Foretold

5In the time of Herod king of Judea there was a priest named Zechariah, who belonged to the priestly division of Abijah; his wife Elizabeth was also a descendant of Aaron. **6**Both of them were upright in the sight of God, observing all the Lord's commandments and regulations blamelessly. **7**But they had no children, because Elizabeth was barren; and they were both well along in years.

8Once when Zechariah's division was

a1 Or been surely believed

on duty and he was serving as priest before God, ⁹he was chosen by lot, according to the custom of the priesthood, to go into the temple of the Lord and burn incense. ¹⁰And when the time for the burning of incense came, all the assembled worshipers were praying outside.

¹¹Then an angel of the Lord appeared to him, standing at the right side of the altar of incense. ¹²When Zechariah saw him, he was startled and was gripped with fear. ¹³But the angel said to him: "Do not be afraid, Zechariah; your prayer has been heard. Your wife Elizabeth will bear you a son, and you are to give him the name John. ¹⁴He will be a joy and delight to you, and many will rejoice because of his birth, ¹⁵for he will be great in the sight of the Lord. He is never to take wine or other fermented drink, and he will be filled with the Holy Spirit even from birth.ᵃ ¹⁶Many of the people of Israel will he bring back to the Lord their God. ¹⁷And he will go on before the Lord, in the spirit and power of Elijah, to turn the hearts of the fathers to their children and the disobedient to the wisdom of the righteous—to make ready a people prepared for the Lord."

¹⁸Zechariah asked the angel, "How can I be sure of this? I am an old man and my wife is well along in years."

¹⁹The angel answered, "I am Gabriel. I stand in the presence of God, and I have been sent to speak to you and to tell you this good news. ²⁰And now you will be silent and not able to speak until the day this happens, because you did not believe my words, which will come true at their proper time."

²¹Meanwhile, the people were waiting for Zechariah and wondering why he stayed so long in the temple. ²²When he came out, he could not speak to them. They realized he had seen a vision in the temple, for he kept making signs to them but remained unable to speak.

²³When his time of service was completed, he returned home. ²⁴After this his wife Elizabeth became pregnant and for five months remained in seclusion. ²⁵"The Lord has done this for me," she said. "In these days he has shown his favor and taken away my disgrace among the people."

The Birth of Jesus Foretold

²⁶In the sixth month, God sent the angel Gabriel to Nazareth, a town in Galilee, ²⁷to a virgin pledged to be married to a man named Joseph, a descendant of David. The virgin's name was Mary. ²⁸The angel went to her and said, "Greetings, you who are highly favored! The Lord is with you."

²⁹Mary was greatly troubled at his words and wondered what kind of greeting this might be. ³⁰But the angel said to her, "Do not be afraid, Mary, you have found favor with God. ³¹You will be with child and give birth to a son, and you are to give him the name Jesus. ³²He will be great and will be called the Son of the Most High. The Lord God will give him the throne of his father David, ³³and he will reign over the house of Jacob forever; his kingdom will never end."

³⁴"How will this be," Mary asked the angel, "since I am a virgin?"

³⁵The angel answered, "The Holy Spirit will come upon you, and the power of the Most High will overshadow you. So the holy one to be born will be calledᵇ the Son of God. ³⁶Even Elizabeth your relative is going to have a child in her old age, and she who was said to be barren is in her sixth month. ³⁷For nothing is impossible with God."

³⁸"I am the Lord's servant," Mary answered. "May it be to me as you have said." Then the angel left her.

Mary Visits Elizabeth

³⁹At that time Mary got ready and hurried to a town in the hill country of Judea, ⁴⁰where she entered Zechariah's home and greeted Elizabeth. ⁴¹When Elizabeth heard Mary's greeting, the baby leaped in her womb, and Elizabeth was filled with the Holy Spirit. ⁴²In a loud voice she exclaimed: "Blessed are you among women, and blessed is the child you will bear! ⁴³But why am I so favored, that the mother of my Lord should come to me? ⁴⁴As soon as the sound of your greeting reached my ears, the baby in my womb leaped for joy. ⁴⁵Blessed is she who has believed that what the Lord has said to her will be accomplished!"

Mary's Song

⁴⁶And Mary said:

"My soul glorifies the Lord
⁴⁷   and my spirit rejoices in God my
        Savior,
⁴⁸for he has been mindful
   of the humble state of his servant.

ᵃ15 Or *from his mother's womb*   ᵇ35 Or *So the child to be born will be called holy,*

From now on all generations will call
  me blessed,
49 for the Mighty One has done great
    things for me—
  holy is his name.
50His mercy extends to those who fear
  him,
  from generation to generation.
51He has performed mighty deeds with
  his arm;
  he has scattered those who are
    proud in their inmost thoughts.

52He has brought down rulers from
    their thrones
  but has lifted up the humble.
53He has filled the hungry with good
    things
  but has sent the rich away
    empty.
54He has helped his servant Israel,
  remembering to be merciful
55to Abraham and his descendants
    forever,
  even as he said to our fathers."

FRIDAY

VERSE FOR THE DAY:
Luke 1:17

AUTHOR:
John E. Crawford

PASSAGE FOR THE DAY:
Luke 1:8–17

Do It Now!

THERE is a fine art to being available to a youngster who
might want to talk to you about what has been troubling her.
Of course, she has to know that you love and value her. Otherwise she could not afford to tell you how she really feels
about anything important. We rarely confide in anyone we
think may not truly care about us. Neither do most of us open
up to people who pry. Communication flows most freely when
children and parents feel safe and secure with one another.

Teenagers as well as younger children often need to be able
to spill out deeper anxieties and fears. Without safety valves,
emotional tensions can rise to such levels that something has
to go. Our children are no different from the rest of us in this
need. The right words and conversation not only can ventilate
the mind and heart and diminish neurotic fear and anguish of
spirit, but also can mend and heal.

Pleasant and relaxing excursions with her father can let a
girl see what intelligent, mature men really are like. Every girl
needs a father she can talk to, argue with, race at a picnic, play
ball with in the cool of evening, hug and kiss. These things are
worth doing even if you have to make room in your time
schedule. She is growing up just as swiftly as you are adding
years to yourself. Waiting until next year or the year after that
will find her older and that much less inclined to talk or swim
or go to the concert with you. Out of these experiences come
the kind of deep mutual ties and understanding that have kept
thousands of girls right-minded and trustworthy about sex,
even in a world where morals and ethics sometimes seem ex-
tinct.

Additional Scripture Readings:
Proverbs 15:1–5; Colossians 4:2–6

*Go to page 1084 for your next
devotional reading.*

⁵⁶Mary stayed with Elizabeth for about three months and then returned home.

The Birth of John the Baptist

⁵⁷When it was time for Elizabeth to have her baby, she gave birth to a son. ⁵⁸Her neighbors and relatives heard that the Lord had shown her great mercy, and they shared her joy.

⁵⁹On the eighth day they came to circumcise the child, and they were going to name him after his father Zechariah, ⁶⁰but his mother spoke up and said, "No! He is to be called John."

⁶¹They said to her, "There is no one among your relatives who has that name."

⁶²Then they made signs to his father, to find out what he would like to name the child. ⁶³He asked for a writing tablet, and to everyone's astonishment he wrote, "His name is John." ⁶⁴Immediately his mouth was opened and his tongue was loosed, and he began to speak, praising God. ⁶⁵The neighbors were all filled with awe, and throughout the hill country of Judea people were talking about all these things. ⁶⁶Everyone who heard this wondered about it, asking, "What then is this child going to be?" For the Lord's hand was with him.

Zechariah's Song

⁶⁷His father Zechariah was filled with the Holy Spirit and prophesied:

⁶⁸"Praise be to the Lord, the God of Israel,
 because he has come and has redeemed his people.
⁶⁹He has raised up a horn[a] of salvation for us
 in the house of his servant David
⁷⁰(as he said through his holy prophets of long ago),
⁷¹salvation from our enemies
 and from the hand of all who hate us—
⁷²to show mercy to our fathers
 and to remember his holy covenant,
⁷³ the oath he swore to our father Abraham:
⁷⁴to rescue us from the hand of our enemies,
 and to enable us to serve him without fear
⁷⁵ in holiness and righteousness before him all our days.

⁷⁶And you, my child, will be called a prophet of the Most High;
 for you will go on before the Lord to prepare the way for him,
⁷⁷to give his people the knowledge of salvation
 through the forgiveness of their sins,
⁷⁸because of the tender mercy of our God,
 by which the rising sun will come to us from heaven
⁷⁹to shine on those living in darkness and in the shadow of death,
 to guide our feet into the path of peace."

⁸⁰And the child grew and became strong in spirit; and he lived in the desert until he appeared publicly to Israel.

The Birth of Jesus

2 In those days Caesar Augustus issued a decree that a census should be taken of the entire Roman world. ²(This was the first census that took place while Quirinius was governor of Syria.) ³And everyone went to his own town to register.

⁴So Joseph also went up from the town of Nazareth in Galilee to Judea, to Bethlehem the town of David, because he belonged to the house and line of David. ⁵He went there to register with Mary, who was pledged to be married to him and was expecting a child. ⁶While they were there, the time came for the baby to be born, ⁷and she gave birth to her firstborn, a son. She wrapped him in cloths and placed him in a manger, because there was no room for them in the inn.

The Shepherds and the Angels

⁸And there were shepherds living out in the fields nearby, keeping watch over their flocks at night. ⁹An angel of the Lord appeared to them, and the glory of the Lord shone around them, and they were terrified. ¹⁰But the angel said to them, "Do not be afraid. I bring you good news of great joy that will be for all the people. ¹¹Today in the town of David a Savior has been born to you; he is Christ[b] the Lord. ¹²This will be a sign to you: You will find a baby wrapped in cloths and lying in a manger."

¹³Suddenly a great company of the

---

[a]69 Horn here symbolizes strength. [b]11 Or Messiah. "The Christ" (Greek) and "the Messiah" (Hebrew) both mean "the Anointed One"; also in verse 26.

WEEKENDING

RECALL

When Jesus promised his return, he did not
intend to scare us out of our wits ... He placed
himself firmly ahead of us, as end, just as he
had established himself at the beginning ... If
we cannot join our beginning to our end, we
will live scattered and incoherent lives. The
expectation of Jesus' coming provides a goal
that shapes and unifies life in accordance with
its origins in Christ, in patterns that are
consonant with its completion in Christ. This
urgency is liberating, for it compels us to stay
awake, deeply and earnestly aware of who we
are and what we are doing, keeping us free
from trivia that ... can make prisoners of us as
effectively as any ball and chain.

– *Eugene H. Peterson*

REVIVE

Saturday: Mark 13:32–37
Sunday: Revelation 1:17–18

Go to page 1086 for your next devotional reading.

heavenly host appeared with the angel, praising God and saying,

[14]"Glory to God in the highest,
  and on earth peace to men on
    whom his favor rests."

[15]When the angels had left them and gone into heaven, the shepherds said to one another, "Let's go to Bethlehem and see this thing that has happened, which the Lord has told us about."

[16]So they hurried off and found Mary and Joseph, and the baby, who was lying in the manger. [17]When they had seen him, they spread the word concerning what had been told them about this child, [18]and all who heard it were amazed at what the shepherds said to them. [19]But Mary treasured up all these things and pondered them in her heart. [20]The shepherds returned, glorifying and praising God for all the things they had heard and seen, which were just as they had been told.

Jesus Presented in the Temple

[21]On the eighth day, when it was time to circumcise him, he was named Jesus, the name the angel had given him before he had been conceived.

[22]When the time of their purification according to the Law of Moses had been completed, Joseph and Mary took him to Jerusalem to present him to the Lord [23](as it is written in the Law of the Lord, "Every firstborn male is to be consecrated to the Lord"[a]), [24]and to offer a sacrifice in keeping with what is said in the Law of the Lord: "a pair of doves or two young pigeons."[b]

[25]Now there was a man in Jerusalem called Simeon, who was righteous and devout. He was waiting for the consolation of Israel, and the Holy Spirit was upon him. [26]It had been revealed to him by the Holy Spirit that he would not die before he had seen the Lord's Christ. [27]Moved by the Spirit, he went into the temple courts. When the parents brought in the child Jesus to do for him what the custom of the Law required, [28]Simeon took him in his arms and praised God, saying:

[29]"Sovereign Lord, as you have
      promised,
  you now dismiss[c] your servant in
      peace.
[30]For my eyes have seen your salvation,

[31] which you have prepared in the
      sight of all people,
[32]a light for revelation to the Gentiles
  and for glory to your people Israel."

[33]The child's father and mother marveled at what was said about him. [34]Then Simeon blessed them and said to Mary, his mother: "This child is destined to cause the falling and rising of many in Israel, and to be a sign that will be spoken against, [35]so that the thoughts of many hearts will be revealed. And a sword will pierce your own soul too."

[36]There was also a prophetess, Anna, the daughter of Phanuel, of the tribe of Asher. She was very old; she had lived with her husband seven years after her marriage, [37]and then was a widow until she was eighty-four.[d] She never left the temple but worshiped night and day, fasting and praying. [38]Coming up to them at that very moment, she gave thanks to God and spoke about the child to all who were looking forward to the redemption of Jerusalem.

[39]When Joseph and Mary had done everything required by the Law of the Lord, they returned to Galilee to their own town of Nazareth. [40]And the child grew and became strong; he was filled with wisdom, and the grace of God was upon him.

The Boy Jesus at the Temple

[41]Every year his parents went to Jerusalem for the Feast of the Passover. [42]When he was twelve years old, they went up to the Feast, according to the custom. [43]After the Feast was over, while his parents were returning home, the boy Jesus stayed behind in Jerusalem, but they were unaware of it. [44]Thinking he was in their company, they traveled on for a day. Then they began looking for him among their relatives and friends. [45]When they did not find him, they went back to Jerusalem to look for him. [46]After three days they found him in the temple courts, sitting among the teachers, listening to them and asking them questions. [47]Everyone who heard him was amazed at his understanding and his answers. [48]When his parents saw him, they were astonished. His mother said to him, "Son, why have you treated us like this? Your father and I have been anxiously searching for you."

---

[a]23 Exodus 13:2,12   [b]24 Lev. 12:8   [c]29 Or promised, / now dismiss   [d]37 Or widow for eighty-four years

⁴⁹"Why were you searching for me?" he asked. "Didn't you know I had to be in my Father's house?" ⁵⁰But they did not understand what he was saying to them.

⁵¹Then he went down to Nazareth with them and was obedient to them. But his mother treasured all these things in her heart. ⁵²And Jesus grew in wisdom and stature, and in favor with God and men.

John the Baptist Prepares the Way

3 In the fifteenth year of the reign of Tiberius Caesar—when Pontius Pilate was governor of Judea, Herod tetrarch of Galilee, his brother Philip tetrarch of Iturea and Traconitis, and Lysanias tetrarch of Abilene— ²during the high priesthood of Annas and Caiaphas, the word of God came to John son of Zechariah in the desert. ³He went into all the country

---

MONDAY

VERSE FOR THE DAY:
Luke 2:8

AUTHOR:
Max Lucado

PASSAGE FOR THE DAY:
Luke 2:8–15

You Have to Stoop

THE announcement went first to the shepherds. They didn't ask God if he was sure he knew what he was doing. Had the angel gone to the theologians, they would have first consulted their commentaries. Had he gone to the elite, they would have looked around to see if anyone was watching. Had he gone to the successful, they would have first looked at their calendars.

So he went to the shepherds. Men who didn't have a reputation to protect or an ax to grind or a ladder to climb. Men who didn't know enough to tell God that angels don't sing to sheep and that messiahs aren't found wrapped in rags and sleeping in a feed trough.

A small cathedral outside Bethlehem marks the supposed birthplace of Jesus. Behind a high altar in the church is a cave, a little cavern lit by silver lamps.

You can enter the main edifice and admire the ancient church. You can also enter the quiet cave where a star embedded in the floor recognizes the birth of the King. There is one stipulation, however. You have to stoop. The door is so low you can't go in standing up.

The same is true of the Christ. You can see the world standing tall, but to witness the Savior, you have to get on your knees.

So . . .
while the theologians were sleeping
and the elite were dreaming
and the successful were snoring,
the meek were kneeling.

They were kneeling before the One only the meek will see.
They were kneeling in front of Jesus.

Additional Scripture Readings:
Matthew 5:1–10; Ephesians 4:1–6

*Go to page 1091 for your next
devotional reading.*

around the Jordan, preaching a baptism of repentance for the forgiveness of sins. ⁴As is written in the book of the words of Isaiah the prophet:

"A voice of one calling in the desert,
 'Prepare the way for the Lord,
  make straight paths for him.
⁵Every valley shall be filled in,
  every mountain and hill made low.
The crooked roads shall become
   straight,
  the rough ways smooth.
⁶And all mankind will see God's
   salvation.' "ᵃ

⁷John said to the crowds coming out to be baptized by him, "You brood of vipers! Who warned you to flee from the coming wrath? ⁸Produce fruit in keeping with repentance. And do not begin to say to yourselves, 'We have Abraham as our father.' For I tell you that out of these stones God can raise up children for Abraham. ⁹The ax is already at the root of the trees, and every tree that does not produce good fruit will be cut down and thrown into the fire."

¹⁰"What should we do then?" the crowd asked.

¹¹John answered, "The man with two tunics should share with him who has none, and the one who has food should do the same."

¹²Tax collectors also came to be baptized. "Teacher," they asked, "what should we do?"

¹³"Don't collect any more than you are required to," he told them.

¹⁴Then some soldiers asked him, "And what should we do?"

He replied, "Don't extort money and don't accuse people falsely—be content with your pay."

¹⁵The people were waiting expectantly and were all wondering in their hearts if John might possibly be the Christ.ᵇ ¹⁶John answered them all, "I baptize you withᶜ water. But one more powerful than I will come, the thongs of whose sandals I am not worthy to untie. He will baptize you with the Holy Spirit and with fire. ¹⁷His winnowing fork is in his hand to clear his threshing floor and to gather the wheat into his barn, but he will burn up the chaff with unquenchable fire." ¹⁸And with many other words John exhorted the people and preached the good news to them.

¹⁹But when John rebuked Herod the tetrarch because of Herodias, his brother's wife, and all the other evil things he had done, ²⁰Herod added this to them all: He locked John up in prison.

The Baptism and Genealogy of Jesus

²¹When all the people were being baptized, Jesus was baptized too. And as he was praying, heaven was opened ²²and the Holy Spirit descended on him in bodily form like a dove. And a voice came from heaven: "You are my Son, whom I love; with you I am well pleased."

²³Now Jesus himself was about thirty years old when he began his ministry. He was the son, so it was thought, of Joseph,

the son of Heli, ²⁴the son of Matthat,
the son of Levi, the son of Melki,
the son of Jannai, the son of Joseph,
²⁵the son of Mattathias, the son of
   Amos,
the son of Nahum, the son of Esli,
the son of Naggai, ²⁶the son of Maath,
the son of Mattathias, the son of
   Semein,
the son of Josech, the son of Joda,
²⁷the son of Joanan, the son of Rhesa,
the son of Zerubbabel, the son of
   Shealtiel,
the son of Neri, ²⁸the son of Melki,
the son of Addi, the son of Cosam,
the son of Elmadam, the son of Er,
²⁹the son of Joshua, the son of Eliezer,
the son of Jorim, the son of Matthat,
the son of Levi, ³⁰the son of Simeon,
the son of Judah, the son of Joseph,
the son of Jonam, the son of Eliakim,
³¹the son of Melea, the son of Menna,
the son of Mattatha, the son of Nathan,
the son of David, ³²the son of Jesse,
the son of Obed, the son of Boaz,
the son of Salmon,ᵈ the son of Nahshon,
³³the son of Amminadab, the son of
   Ram,ᵉ
the son of Hezron, the son of Perez,
the son of Judah, ³⁴the son of Jacob,
the son of Isaac, the son of Abraham,
the son of Terah, the son of Nahor,
³⁵the son of Serug, the son of Reu,
the son of Peleg, the son of Eber,

the son of Shelah, ³⁶the son of Cainan,

the son of Arphaxad, the son of Shem,

the son of Noah, the son of Lamech, ³⁷the son of Methuselah, the son of Enoch,

the son of Jared, the son of Mahalalel,

the son of Kenan, ³⁸the son of Enosh,

the son of Seth, the son of Adam,

the son of God.

The Temptation of Jesus

4 Jesus, full of the Holy Spirit, returned from the Jordan and was led by the Spirit in the desert, ²where for forty days he was tempted by the devil. He ate nothing during those days, and at the end of them he was hungry.

³The devil said to him, "If you are the Son of God, tell this stone to become bread."

⁴Jesus answered, "It is written: 'Man does not live on bread alone.'ᵃ"

⁵The devil led him up to a high place and showed him in an instant all the kingdoms of the world. ⁶And he said to him, "I will give you all their authority and splendor, for it has been given to me, and I can give it to anyone I want to. ⁷So if you worship me, it will all be yours."

⁸Jesus answered, "It is written: 'Worship the Lord your God and serve him only.'ᵇ"

⁹The devil led him to Jerusalem and had him stand on the highest point of the temple. "If you are the Son of God," he said, "throw yourself down from here. ¹⁰For it is written:

" 'He will command his angels
    concerning you
to guard you carefully;
¹¹they will lift you up in their hands,
    so that you will not strike your foot
        against a stone.'ᶜ"

¹²Jesus answered, "It says: 'Do not put the Lord your God to the test.'ᵈ"

¹³When the devil had finished all this tempting, he left him until an opportune time.

Jesus Rejected at Nazareth

¹⁴Jesus returned to Galilee in the power of the Spirit, and news about him spread through the whole countryside. ¹⁵He taught in their synagogues, and everyone praised him.

¹⁶He went to Nazareth, where he had been brought up, and on the Sabbath day he went into the synagogue, as was his custom. And he stood up to read. ¹⁷The scroll of the prophet Isaiah was handed to him. Unrolling it, he found the place where it is written:

¹⁸"The Spirit of the Lord is on me,
    because he has anointed me
    to preach good news to the poor.
He has sent me to proclaim freedom
        for the prisoners
    and recovery of sight for the blind,
to release the oppressed,
¹⁹   to proclaim the year of the Lord's
        favor."ᵉ

²⁰Then he rolled up the scroll, gave it back to the attendant and sat down. The eyes of everyone in the synagogue were fastened on him, ²¹and he began by saying to them, "Today this scripture is fulfilled in your hearing."

²²All spoke well of him and were amazed at the gracious words that came from his lips. "Isn't this Joseph's son?" they asked.

²³Jesus said to them, "Surely you will quote this proverb to me: 'Physician, heal yourself! Do here in your hometown what we have heard that you did in Capernaum.' "

²⁴"I tell you the truth," he continued, "no prophet is accepted in his hometown. ²⁵I assure you that there were many widows in Israel in Elijah's time, when the sky was shut for three and a half years and there was a severe famine throughout the land. ²⁶Yet Elijah was not sent to any of them, but to a widow in Zarephath in the region of Sidon. ²⁷And there were many in Israel with leprosyᶠ in the time of Elisha the prophet, yet not one of them was cleansed—only Naaman the Syrian."

²⁸All the people in the synagogue were furious when they heard this. ²⁹They got up, drove him out of the town, and took him to the brow of the hill on which the town was built, in order to throw him down the cliff. ³⁰But he walked right through the crowd and went on his way.

Jesus Drives Out an Evil Spirit

³¹Then he went down to Capernaum, a town in Galilee, and on the Sabbath began

---

a4 Deut. 8:3   *b8* Deut. 6:13   *c11* Psalm 91:11,12   *d12* Deut. 6:16   *e19* Isaiah 61:1,2
f27 The Greek word was used for various diseases affecting the skin—not necessarily leprosy.

to teach the people. **32**They were amazed at his teaching, because his message had authority.

33In the synagogue there was a man possessed by a demon, an evil*a* spirit. He cried out at the top of his voice, **34**"Ha! What do you want with us, Jesus of Nazareth? Have you come to destroy us? I know who you are—the Holy One of God!"

35"Be quiet!" Jesus said sternly. "Come out of him!" Then the demon threw the man down before them all and came out without injuring him.

36All the people were amazed and said to each other, "What is this teaching? With authority and power he gives orders to evil spirits and they come out!" **37**And the news about him spread throughout the surrounding area.

Jesus Heals Many

38Jesus left the synagogue and went to the home of Simon. Now Simon's mother-in-law was suffering from a high fever, and they asked Jesus to help her. **39**So he bent over her and rebuked the fever, and it left her. She got up at once and began to wait on them.

40When the sun was setting, the people brought to Jesus all who had various kinds of sickness, and laying his hands on each one, he healed them. **41**Moreover, demons came out of many people, shouting, "You are the Son of God!" But he rebuked them and would not allow them to speak, because they knew he was the Christ.*b*

42At daybreak Jesus went out to a solitary place. The people were looking for him and when they came to where he was, they tried to keep him from leaving them. **43**But he said, "I must preach the good news of the kingdom of God to the other towns also, because that is why I was sent." **44**And he kept on preaching in the synagogues of Judea.*c*

The Calling of the First Disciples

5 One day as Jesus was standing by the Lake of Gennesaret,*d* with the people crowding around him and listening to the word of God, **2**he saw at the water's edge two boats, left there by the fishermen, who were washing their nets. **3**He got into one of the boats, the one belonging to Simon, and asked him to put out a little from shore. Then he sat down and taught the people from the boat.

4When he had finished speaking, he said to Simon, "Put out into deep water, and let down*e* the nets for a catch."

5Simon answered, "Master, we've worked hard all night and haven't caught anything. But because you say so, I will let down the nets."

6When they had done so, they caught such a large number of fish that their nets began to break. **7**So they signaled their partners in the other boat to come and help them, and they came and filled both boats so full that they began to sink.

8When Simon Peter saw this, he fell at Jesus' knees and said, "Go away from me, Lord; I am a sinful man!" **9**For he and all his companions were astonished at the catch of fish they had taken, **10**and so were James and John, the sons of Zebedee, Simon's partners.

Then Jesus said to Simon, "Don't be afraid; from now on you will catch men." **11**So they pulled their boats up on shore, left everything and followed him.

The Man With Leprosy

12While Jesus was in one of the towns, a man came along who was covered with leprosy.*f* When he saw Jesus, he fell with his face to the ground and begged him, "Lord, if you are willing, you can make me clean."

13Jesus reached out his hand and touched the man. "I am willing," he said. "Be clean!" And immediately the leprosy left him.

14Then Jesus ordered him, "Don't tell anyone, but go, show yourself to the priest and offer the sacrifices that Moses commanded for your cleansing, as a testimony to them."

15Yet the news about him spread all the more, so that crowds of people came to hear him and to be healed of their sicknesses. **16**But Jesus often withdrew to lonely places and prayed.

Jesus Heals a Paralytic

17One day as he was teaching, Pharisees and teachers of the law, who had come from every village of Galilee and from Judea and Jerusalem, were sitting there. And the power of the Lord was present for him to heal the sick. **18**Some men came

---

a33 Greek *unclean*; also in verse 36   *b41* Or *Messiah*   *c44* Or *the land of the Jews*; some manuscripts *Galilee*   *d1* That is, Sea of Galilee   *e4* The Greek verb is plural.   *f12* The Greek word was used for various diseases affecting the skin—not necessarily leprosy.

carrying a paralytic on a mat and tried to take him into the house to lay him before Jesus. **19**When they could not find a way to do this because of the crowd, they went up on the roof and lowered him on his mat through the tiles into the middle of the crowd, right in front of Jesus.

20When Jesus saw their faith, he said, "Friend, your sins are forgiven."

21The Pharisees and the teachers of the law began thinking to themselves, "Who is this fellow who speaks blasphemy? Who can forgive sins but God alone?"

22Jesus knew what they were thinking and asked, "Why are you thinking these things in your hearts? **23**Which is easier: to say, 'Your sins are forgiven,' or to say, 'Get up and walk'? **24**But that you may know that the Son of Man has authority on earth to forgive sins. . . ." He said to the paralyzed man, "I tell you, get up, take your mat and go home." **25**Immediately he stood up in front of them, took what he had been lying on and went home praising God. **26**Everyone was amazed and gave praise to God. They were filled with awe and said, "We have seen remarkable things today."

The Calling of Levi

27After this, Jesus went out and saw a tax collector by the name of Levi sitting at his tax booth. "Follow me," Jesus said to him, **28**and Levi got up, left everything and followed him.

29Then Levi held a great banquet for Jesus at his house, and a large crowd of tax collectors and others were eating with them. **30**But the Pharisees and the teachers of the law who belonged to their sect complained to his disciples, "Why do you eat and drink with tax collectors and 'sinners'?"

31Jesus answered them, "It is not the healthy who need a doctor, but the sick. **32**I have not come to call the righteous, but sinners to repentance."

Jesus Questioned About Fasting

33They said to him, "John's disciples often fast and pray, and so do the disciples of the Pharisees, but yours go on eating and drinking."

34Jesus answered, "Can you make the guests of the bridegroom fast while he is with them? **35**But the time will come when the bridegroom will be taken from them; in those days they will fast."

36He told them this parable: "No one tears a patch from a new garment and sews it on an old one. If he does, he will have torn the new garment, and the patch from the new will not match the old. **37**And no one pours new wine into old wineskins. If he does, the new wine will burst the skins, the wine will run out and the wineskins will be ruined. **38**No, new wine must be poured into new wineskins. **39**And no one after drinking old wine wants the new, for he says, 'The old is better.' "

Lord of the Sabbath

6 One Sabbath Jesus was going through the grainfields, and his disciples began to pick some heads of grain, rub them in their hands and eat the kernels. **2**Some of the Pharisees asked, "Why are you doing what is unlawful on the Sabbath?"

3Jesus answered them, "Have you never read what David did when he and his companions were hungry? **4**He entered the house of God, and taking the consecrated bread, he ate what is lawful only for priests to eat. And he also gave some to his companions." **5**Then Jesus said to them, "The Son of Man is Lord of the Sabbath."

6On another Sabbath he went into the synagogue and was teaching, and a man was there whose right hand was shriveled. **7**The Pharisees and the teachers of the law were looking for a reason to accuse Jesus, so they watched him closely to see if he would heal on the Sabbath. **8**But Jesus knew what they were thinking and said to the man with the shriveled hand, "Get up and stand in front of everyone." So he got up and stood there.

9Then Jesus said to them, "I ask you, which is lawful on the Sabbath: to do good or to do evil, to save life or to destroy it?"

10He looked around at them all, and then said to the man, "Stretch out your hand." He did so, and his hand was completely restored. **11**But they were furious and began to discuss with one another what they might do to Jesus.

The Twelve Apostles

12One of those days Jesus went out to a mountainside to pray, and spent the night praying to God. **13**When morning came, he called his disciples to him and chose twelve of them, whom he also designated apostles: **14**Simon (whom he named Peter), his brother Andrew, James, John, Philip, Bartholomew, **15**Matthew, Thomas, James son of Alphaeus, Simon who was called the Zealot, [16]Judas son of James, and Judas Iscariot, who became a traitor.

Blessings and Woes

[17]He went down with them and stood on a level place. A large crowd of his disciples was there and a great number of people from all over Judea, from Jerusalem, and from the coast of Tyre and Sidon, [18]who had come to hear him and to be healed of their diseases. Those troubled by evil[a] spirits were cured, [19]and the people all tried to touch him, because power was coming from him and healing them all.

[20]Looking at his disciples, he said:

"Blessed are you who are poor,
    for yours is the kingdom of God.
[21]Blessed are you who hunger now,

[a]18 Greek *unclean*

TUESDAY

VERSE FOR THE DAY:
Luke 5:27

AUTHOR:
John Fischer

PASSAGE FOR THE DAY:
Luke 5:27–32

No Messianic Magic Show

TO EACH of his disciples, Jesus simply said, "Follow me." That was an invitation, not a requirement. An invitation respects the freedom of the invitee to accept or decline. Indeed, the "no" answer is perhaps the greatest expression of human dignity possible. That men and women can go to heaven is an expression of God's love; that they can go to hell is an expression of the value he places on their freedom.

God desires—not requires—a relationship with us. It is not a one-sided affair; we are co-participants with him, both in our relationship with him and in our work in the world.

A woman with a hemorrhage struggled through the press of the crowd in order to touch his garment; four men opened a hole in the ceiling of a crowded house and let down their paralyzed friend in front of Jesus; a centurion soldier asked that Jesus only speak a word so his servant would be healed; a blind man went and washed the clay and the darkness from his eyes; a little boy offered his meager lunch to feed a multitude. Even the miracles of Jesus involved human participation. This was not just a Messianic Magic Show; this was God interacting in human experience—giving and taking, relating with us as Son of Man.

God does not pull all the strings. He counts us as too important for that. To find without seeking, to hear without listening, to say yes without the possibility of saying no is to negate the value of my seeking, my hearing and my participating. I am not a puppet.

Nor does he put all the pieces together. He leaves holes; he raises questions. He wants me to ask.

Additional Scripture Readings:
Matthew 22:1–14; Mark 10:17–31

Go to page 1093 for your next devotional reading.

for you will be satisfied.
Blessed are you who weep now,
  for you will laugh.
22Blessed are you when men hate you,
  when they exclude you and insult
    you
  and reject your name as evil,
    because of the Son of Man.

23"Rejoice in that day and leap for joy,
because great is your reward in heaven.
For that is how their fathers treated the
prophets.

24"But woe to you who are rich,
  for you have already received your
    comfort.
25Woe to you who are well fed now,
  for you will go hungry.
Woe to you who laugh now,
  for you will mourn and weep.
26Woe to you when all men speak well
    of you,
  for that is how their fathers treated
    the false prophets.

Love for Enemies

27"But I tell you who hear me: Love
your enemies, do good to those who hate
you, 28bless those who curse you, pray for
those who mistreat you. 29If someone
strikes you on one cheek, turn to him the
other also. If someone takes your cloak,
do not stop him from taking your tunic.
30Give to everyone who asks you, and if
anyone takes what belongs to you, do not
demand it back. 31Do to others as you
would have them do to you.

32"If you love those who love you, what
credit is that to you? Even 'sinners' love
those who love them. 33And if you do
good to those who are good to you, what
credit is that to you? Even 'sinners' do
that. 34And if you lend to those from
whom you expect repayment, what credit
is that to you? Even 'sinners' lend to 'sinners,' expecting to be repaid in full. 35But
love your enemies, do good to them, and
lend to them without expecting to get anything back. Then your reward will be
great, and you will be sons of the Most
High, because he is kind to the ungrateful
and wicked. 36Be merciful, just as your Father is merciful.

Judging Others

37"Do not judge, and you will not be
judged. Do not condemn, and you will not
be condemned. Forgive, and you will be
forgiven. 38Give, and it will be given to
you. A good measure, pressed down,

shaken together and running over, will be
poured into your lap. For with the measure you use, it will be measured to you."

39He also told them this parable: "Can a
blind man lead a blind man? Will they not
both fall into a pit? 40A student is not
above his teacher, but everyone who is
fully trained will be like his teacher.

41"Why do you look at the speck of sawdust in your brother's eye and pay no attention to the plank in your own eye?
42How can you say to your brother,
'Brother, let me take the speck out of your
eye,' when you yourself fail to see the
plank in your own eye? You hypocrite,
first take the plank out of your eye, and
then you will see clearly to remove the
speck from your brother's eye.

A Tree and Its Fruit

43"No good tree bears bad fruit, nor
does a bad tree bear good fruit. 44Each tree
is recognized by its own fruit. People do
not pick figs from thornbushes, or grapes
from briers. 45The good man brings good
things out of the good stored up in his
heart, and the evil man brings evil things
out of the evil stored up in his heart. For
out of the overflow of his heart his mouth
speaks.

The Wise and Foolish Builders

46"Why do you call me, 'Lord, Lord,'
and do not do what I say? 47I will show
you what he is like who comes to me and
hears my words and puts them into practice. 48He is like a man building a house,
who dug down deep and laid the foundation on rock. When a flood came, the torrent struck that house but could not shake
it, because it was well built. 49But the one
who hears my words and does not put
them into practice is like a man who built
a house on the ground without a foundation. The moment the torrent struck that
house, it collapsed and its destruction was
complete."

The Faith of the Centurion

7 When Jesus had finished saying all
  this in the hearing of the people, he
entered Capernaum. 2There a centurion's
servant, whom his master valued highly,
was sick and about to die. 3The centurion
heard of Jesus and sent some elders of the
Jews to him, asking him to come and heal
his servant. 4When they came to Jesus,
they pleaded earnestly with him, "This
man deserves to have you do this, 5be-
cause he loves our nation and has built

our synagogue." ⁶So Jesus went with them.

He was not far from the house when the centurion sent friends to say to him: "Lord, don't trouble yourself, for I do not deserve to have you come under my roof. ⁷That is why I did not even consider myself worthy to come to you. But say the word, and my servant will be healed. ⁸For I myself am a man under authority, with soldiers under me. I tell this one, 'Go,' and he goes; and that one, 'Come,' and he comes. I say to my servant, 'Do this,' and he does it."

⁹When Jesus heard this, he was amazed at him, and turning to the crowd following him, he said, "I tell you, I have not found such great faith even in Israel." ¹⁰Then the men who had been sent returned to the house and found the servant well.

Jesus Raises a Widow's Son

¹¹Soon afterward, Jesus went to a town called Nain, and his disciples and a large crowd went along with him. ¹²As he approached the town gate, a dead person was being carried out — the only son of his mother, and she was a widow. And a large crowd from the town was with her. ¹³When the Lord saw her, his heart went out to her and he said, "Don't cry." ¹⁴Then he went up and touched the cof-

---

WEDNESDAY

VERSE FOR THE DAY:
Luke 6:38

AUTHOR:
Tim LaHaye

PASSAGE FOR THE DAY:
Luke 6:37–42

True Riches

NEVER settle for second-rate or selfish goals. Earl Nightingale, who probably has helped to motivate more people than any other living person, advises that people desiring success should never try to get rich. Above all, set goals for yourself that involve helping other people; the riches will follow. He has certainly captured the Biblical principle, "Give, and it will be given to you" (Luke 6:38). The richest people I know are those who have given themselves unselfishly to other people. Such motivation will affect the way you sell, cook, teach or ply your particular trade. True riches, of course, are totally unrelated to money or material reward. In fact, if a person has earned money without helping people, his money will not buy him happiness.

A perceptive real-estate friend who sold rather expensive homes observed that a big house never brought happiness. But if the people bought a big home with money they earned helping other people, they tended to enjoy that home. He expressed his homespun philosophy in these words, "Instead of being a status symbol, a home should be an expression of how much help a person has been to his fellowman." Of one thing I am sure: happy people have strong goals—and somehow these include helping other people. They can also be assured that they will never run out of people to help.

Additional Scripture Readings:
2 Corinthians 9:6–15;
Galatians 6:7–10

Go to page 1095 for your next
devotional reading.

fin, and those carrying it stood still. He said, "Young man, I say to you, get up!" 15The dead man sat up and began to talk, and Jesus gave him back to his mother.

16They were all filled with awe and praised God. "A great prophet has appeared among us," they said. "God has come to help his people." 17This news about Jesus spread throughout Judea*a* and the surrounding country.

Jesus and John the Baptist

18John's disciples told him about all these things. Calling two of them, 19he sent them to the Lord to ask, "Are you the one who was to come, or should we expect someone else?"

20When the men came to Jesus, they said, "John the Baptist sent us to you to ask, 'Are you the one who was to come, or should we expect someone else?' "

21At that very time Jesus cured many who had diseases, sicknesses and evil spirits, and gave sight to many who were blind. 22So he replied to the messengers, "Go back and report to John what you have seen and heard: The blind receive sight, the lame walk, those who have leprosy*b* are cured, the deaf hear, the dead are raised, and the good news is preached to the poor. 23Blessed is the man who does not fall away on account of me."

24After John's messengers left, Jesus began to speak to the crowd about John: "What did you go out into the desert to see? A reed swayed by the wind? 25If not, what did you go out to see? A man dressed in fine clothes? No, those who wear expensive clothes and indulge in luxury are in palaces. 26But what did you go out to see? A prophet? Yes, I tell you, and more than a prophet. 27This is the one about whom it is written:

" 'I will send my messenger ahead of you,
　who will prepare your way before you.'*c*

28I tell you, among those born of women there is no one greater than John; yet the one who is least in the kingdom of God is greater than he."

29(All the people, even the tax collectors, when they heard Jesus' words, acknowledged that God's way was right, because they had been baptized by John. 30But the Pharisees and experts in the law rejected God's purpose for themselves, because they had not been baptized by John.)

31"To what, then, can I compare the people of this generation? What are they like? 32They are like children sitting in the marketplace and calling out to each other:

" 'We played the flute for you,
　and you did not dance;
we sang a dirge,
　and you did not cry.'

33For John the Baptist came neither eating bread nor drinking wine, and you say, 'He has a demon.' 34The Son of Man came eating and drinking, and you say, 'Here is a glutton and a drunkard, a friend of tax collectors and "sinners." ' 35But wisdom is proved right by all her children."

Jesus Anointed by a Sinful Woman

36Now one of the Pharisees invited Jesus to have dinner with him, so he went to the Pharisee's house and reclined at the table. 37When a woman who had lived a sinful life in that town learned that Jesus was eating at the Pharisee's house, she brought an alabaster jar of perfume, 38and as she stood behind him at his feet weeping, she began to wet his feet with her tears. Then she wiped them with her hair, kissed them and poured perfume on them.

39When the Pharisee who had invited him saw this, he said to himself, "If this man were a prophet, he would know who is touching him and what kind of woman she is—that she is a sinner."

40Jesus answered him, "Simon, I have something to tell you."

"Tell me, teacher," he said.

41"Two men owed money to a certain moneylender. One owed him five hundred denarii,*d* and the other fifty. 42Neither of them had the money to pay him back, so he canceled the debts of both. Now which of them will love him more?"

43Simon replied, "I suppose the one who had the bigger debt canceled."

"You have judged correctly," Jesus said.

44Then he turned toward the woman and said to Simon, "Do you see this woman? I came into your house. You did not give me any water for my feet, but she wet my feet with her tears and wiped them with her hair. 45You did not give me a kiss,

---

a17 Or *the land of the Jews*　　*b22* The Greek word was used for various diseases affecting the skin—not necessarily leprosy.　　*c27* Mal. 3:1　　*d41* A denarius was a coin worth about a day's wages.

but this woman, from the time I entered, has not stopped kissing my feet. ⁴⁶You did not put oil on my head, but she has poured perfume on my feet. ⁴⁷Therefore, I tell you, her many sins have been forgiven—for she loved much. But he who has been forgiven little loves little."

⁴⁸Then Jesus said to her, "Your sins are forgiven."

⁴⁹The other guests began to say among themselves, "Who is this who even forgives sins?"

VERSE FOR THE DAY:
Luke 7:28

AUTHOR:
D. Stuart Briscoe

PASSAGE FOR THE DAY:
Luke 7:24–28

Be Men of Vision

[ONE] characteristic which qualified John as a real man was his vision. In describing him, Jesus had asked, "What did you go out into the desert to see? A reed swayed by the wind? . . . A man dressed in fine clothes? No . . . But what did you go out to see? A prophet? Yes, I tell you, and more than a prophet" [Luke 7:24–26].

What is a prophet? In Jesus' day a prophet was also called a seer—a person who sees. A seer looks past the immediate to the ultimate. He has been given the perspective of God himself and is able to see the meaning behind events. Unfortunately, because we are committed to the cult of immediacy, in the fast pace of our modern day we often do not realize the consequences of what we do. All we are interested in is an immediate solution to a present problem. So we need to develop the ability to see the consequences of our actions—to see past the immediate to the ultimate . . .

A seer has a vision for possibilities. He or she looks through the situation and envisions how it can glorify God, looking past people's exterior to discover what is really making them tick. The seer is a real man, the kind of gifted person we need in our families, homes, work places, and society. We moderns seem to be more concerned about quick fixes and immediacy than we are about the long-term consequences. That is why cosmetic firms are doing so well. As long as we look good we are likely to feel good about ourselves. If we look good and feel good about ourselves, nothing else matters.

Unfortunately, we've bought into a lie. What really matters is not so much whether I look or feel good, but whether I *am* good. The true seer can see *past* the cosmetic (looking good); he can see *through* the feeling good; and he can concentrate on the issues that determine whether we *are good or evil.* This was the vision of John the Baptist, and it has to be the vision of anyone who claims to be a real man.

Additional Scripture Readings:
Psalm 139:23–24; Ephesians 3:14–21

Go to page 1097 for your next devotional reading.

50Jesus said to the woman, "Your faith has saved you; go in peace."

The Parable of the Sower

8 After this, Jesus traveled about from one town and village to another, proclaiming the good news of the kingdom of God. The Twelve were with him, **2**and also some women who had been cured of evil spirits and diseases: Mary (called Magdalene) from whom seven demons had come out; **3**Joanna the wife of Cuza, the manager of Herod's household; Susanna; and many others. These women were helping to support them out of their own means.

4While a large crowd was gathering and people were coming to Jesus from town after town, he told this parable: **5**"A farmer went out to sow his seed. As he was scattering the seed, some fell along the path; it was trampled on, and the birds of the air ate it up. **6**Some fell on rock, and when it came up, the plants withered because they had no moisture. **7**Other seed fell among thorns, which grew up with it and choked the plants. **8**Still other seed fell on good soil. It came up and yielded a crop, a hundred times more than was sown."

When he said this, he called out, "He who has ears to hear, let him hear."

9His disciples asked him what this parable meant. **10**He said, "The knowledge of the secrets of the kingdom of God has been given to you, but to others I speak in parables, so that,

" 'though seeing, they may not see;
   though hearing, they may not
     understand.'*a*

11"This is the meaning of the parable: The seed is the word of God. **12**Those along the path are the ones who hear, and then the devil comes and takes away the word from their hearts, so that they may not believe and be saved. **13**Those on the rock are the ones who receive the word with joy when they hear it, but they have no root. They believe for a while, but in the time of testing they fall away. **14**The seed that fell among thorns stands for those who hear, but as they go on their way they are choked by life's worries, riches and pleasures, and they do not mature. **15**But the seed on good soil stands for those with a noble and good heart, who hear the word, retain it, and by persevering produce a crop.

A Lamp on a Stand

16"No one lights a lamp and hides it in a jar or puts it under a bed. Instead, he puts it on a stand, so that those who come in can see the light. **17**For there is nothing hidden that will not be disclosed, and nothing concealed that will not be known or brought out into the open. **18**Therefore consider carefully how you listen. Whoever has will be given more; whoever does not have, even what he thinks he has will be taken from him."

Jesus' Mother and Brothers

19Now Jesus' mother and brothers came to see him, but they were not able to get near him because of the crowd. **20**Someone told him, "Your mother and brothers are standing outside, wanting to see you."

21He replied, "My mother and brothers are those who hear God's word and put it into practice."

Jesus Calms the Storm

22One day Jesus said to his disciples, "Let's go over to the other side of the lake." So they got into a boat and set out. **23**As they sailed, he fell asleep. A squall came down on the lake, so that the boat was being swamped, and they were in great danger.

24The disciples went and woke him, saying, "Master, Master, we're going to drown!"

He got up and rebuked the wind and the raging waters; the storm subsided, and all was calm. **25**"Where is your faith?" he asked his disciples.

In fear and amazement they asked one another, "Who is this? He commands even the winds and the water, and they obey him."

The Healing of a Demon-possessed Man

26They sailed to the region of the Gerasenes,*b* which is across the lake from Galilee. **27**When Jesus stepped ashore, he was met by a demon-possessed man from the town. For a long time this man had not worn clothes or lived in a house, but had lived in the tombs. **28**When he saw Jesus, he cried out and fell at his feet, shouting at the top of his voice, "What do you want with me, Jesus, Son of the Most High God? I beg you, don't torture me!" **29**For Jesus

---

a10 Isaiah 6:9   *b26* Some manuscripts *Gadarenes*; other manuscripts *Gergesenes*; also in verse 37 had commanded the evil[a] spirit to come out of the man. Many times it had seized him, and though he was chained hand and foot and kept under guard, he had broken his chains and had been driven by the demon into solitary places.

[30]Jesus asked him, "What is your name?"

"Legion," he replied, because many demons had gone into him. [31]And they begged him repeatedly not to order them to go into the Abyss.

[32]A large herd of pigs was feeding there on the hillside. The demons begged Jesus to let them go into them, and he gave them permission. [33]When the demons came out of the man, they went into the pigs, and the herd rushed down the steep bank into the lake and was drowned.

[34]When those tending the pigs saw what had happened, they ran off and reported this in the town and countryside, [35]and the people went out to see what had happened. When they came to Jesus, they found the man from whom the demons had gone out, sitting at Jesus' feet, dressed and in his right mind; and they were afraid. [36]Those who had seen it told the people how the demon-possessed man had been cured. [37]Then all the peo-

a29 Greek unclean

FRIDAY

VERSE FOR THE DAY:
Luke 7:47

AUTHOR:
Philip W. Williams

PASSAGE FOR THE DAY:
Luke 7:36–50

Real Guilt, Real Grace

THERE is always some guilt when any of us loses a loved one. This isn't unusual. None of us can live close to another person and love deeply without hurting that person. We do and say things we later regret. We know they hurt our loved one.

Intimacy, closeness, is built by loving and hurting and reconciling. We can't really learn to love unless we are willing to run the risks of hurting and failing. Losing someone we love reminds us of those hurts and failings, of words we regret saying, incidents we'd like to forget, actions we'd like to take back. We feel guilty.

God has provided some beautiful resources to help us in our guilt. Church worship contains public or private confession and absolution. The Scriptures proclaim an accepting Lord who continually forgives people. This same Lord and Savior died for us in an ultimate act of forgiveness, and he rose to give us new life. He has given us the Lord's Supper to strengthen us and to reconcile us with God.

Guilt is real. The Bible shows us our guilt, but it also reveals a gracious God who forgives us. A college professor once said something that speaks to many life crises, certainly to the guilt of "if only." He said, "The greatest prayer anyone can pray is, 'Create in me a pure heart, O God, and renew a steadfast spirit within me'" [Psalm 51:10].

Additional Scripture Readings:
Psalm 51:1–12; Ephesians 1:3–10

Go to page 1101 for your next devotional reading.

ple of the region of the Gerasenes asked Jesus to leave them, because they were overcome with fear. So he got into the boat and left.

38The man from whom the demons had gone out begged to go with him, but Jesus sent him away, saying, **39**"Return home and tell how much God has done for you." So the man went away and told all over town how much Jesus had done for him.

A Dead Girl and a Sick Woman

40Now when Jesus returned, a crowd welcomed him, for they were all expecting him. **41**Then a man named Jairus, a ruler of the synagogue, came and fell at Jesus' feet, pleading with him to come to his house **42**because his only daughter, a girl of about twelve, was dying.

As Jesus was on his way, the crowds almost crushed him. **43**And a woman was there who had been subject to bleeding for twelve years,*a* but no one could heal her. **44**She came up behind him and touched the edge of his cloak, and immediately her bleeding stopped.

45"Who touched me?" Jesus asked.

When they all denied it, Peter said, "Master, the people are crowding and pressing against you."

46But Jesus said, "Someone touched me; I know that power has gone out from me."

47Then the woman, seeing that she could not go unnoticed, came trembling and fell at his feet. In the presence of all the people, she told why she had touched him and how she had been instantly healed. **48**Then he said to her, "Daughter, your faith has healed you. Go in peace."

49While Jesus was still speaking, someone came from the house of Jairus, the synagogue ruler. "Your daughter is dead," he said. "Don't bother the teacher any more."

50Hearing this, Jesus said to Jairus, "Don't be afraid; just believe, and she will be healed."

51When he arrived at the house of Jairus, he did not let anyone go in with him except Peter, John and James, and the child's father and mother. **52**Meanwhile, all the people were wailing and mourning for her. "Stop wailing," Jesus said. "She is not dead but asleep."

53They laughed at him, knowing that she was dead. **54**But he took her by the hand and said, "My child, get up!" **55**Her

spirit returned, and at once she stood up. Then Jesus told them to give her something to eat. **56**Her parents were astonished, but he ordered them not to tell anyone what had happened.

Jesus Sends Out the Twelve

9 When Jesus had called the Twelve together, he gave them power and authority to drive out all demons and to cure diseases, **2**and he sent them out to preach the kingdom of God and to heal the sick. **3**He told them: "Take nothing for the journey—no staff, no bag, no bread, no money, no extra tunic. **4**Whatever house you enter, stay there until you leave that town. **5**If people do not welcome you, shake the dust off your feet when you leave their town, as a testimony against them." **6**So they set out and went from village to village, preaching the gospel and healing people everywhere.

7Now Herod the tetrarch heard about all that was going on. And he was perplexed, because some were saying that John had been raised from the dead, **8**others that Elijah had appeared, and still others that one of the prophets of long ago had come back to life. **9**But Herod said, "I beheaded John. Who, then, is this I hear such things about?" And he tried to see him.

Jesus Feeds the Five Thousand

10When the apostles returned, they reported to Jesus what they had done. Then he took them with him and they withdrew by themselves to a town called Bethsaida, **11**but the crowds learned about it and followed him. He welcomed them and spoke to them about the kingdom of God, and healed those who needed healing.

12Late in the afternoon the Twelve came to him and said, "Send the crowd away so they can go to the surrounding villages and countryside and find food and lodging, because we are in a remote place here."

13He replied, "You give them something to eat."

They answered, "We have only five loaves of bread and two fish—unless we go and buy food for all this crowd." **14**(About five thousand men were there.)

But he said to his disciples, "Have them sit down in groups of about fifty each." **15**The disciples did so, and everybody sat down. **16**Taking the five loaves and the

---

a43 Many manuscripts years, and she had spent all she had on doctors two fish and looking up to heaven, he gave thanks and broke them. Then he gave them to the disciples to set before the people. **17**They all ate and were satisfied, and the disciples picked up twelve basketfuls of broken pieces that were left over.

Peter's Confession of Christ

18Once when Jesus was praying in private and his disciples were with him, he asked them, "Who do the crowds say I am?"

19They replied, "Some say John the Baptist; others say Elijah; and still others, that one of the prophets of long ago has come back to life."

20"But what about you?" he asked. "Who do you say I am?"

Peter answered, "The Christ*a* of God."

21Jesus strictly warned them not to tell this to anyone. **22**And he said, "The Son of Man must suffer many things and be rejected by the elders, chief priests and teachers of the law, and he must be killed and on the third day be raised to life."

23Then he said to them all: "If anyone would come after me, he must deny himself and take up his cross daily and follow me. **24**For whoever wants to save his life will lose it, but whoever loses his life for me will save it. **25**What good is it for a man to gain the whole world, and yet lose or forfeit his very self? **26**If anyone is ashamed of me and my words, the Son of Man will be ashamed of him when he comes in his glory and in the glory of the Father and of the holy angels. **27**I tell you the truth, some who are standing here will not taste death before they see the kingdom of God."

The Transfiguration

28About eight days after Jesus said this, he took Peter, John and James with him and went up onto a mountain to pray. **29**As he was praying, the appearance of his face changed, and his clothes became as bright as a flash of lightning. **30**Two men, Moses and Elijah, **31**appeared in glorious splendor, talking with Jesus. They spoke about his departure, which he was about to bring to fulfillment at Jerusalem. **32**Peter and his companions were very sleepy, but when they became fully awake, they saw his glory and the two men standing with him. **33**As the men were leaving Jesus, Peter said to him, "Master, it is good for us to be here. Let us put up three shelters—one for you, one for Moses and one for Elijah." (He did not know what he was saying.)

34While he was speaking, a cloud appeared and enveloped them, and they were afraid as they entered the cloud. **35**A voice came from the cloud, saying, "This is my Son, whom I have chosen; listen to him." **36**When the voice had spoken, they found that Jesus was alone. The disciples kept this to themselves, and told no one at that time what they had seen.

The Healing of a Boy With an Evil Spirit

37The next day, when they came down from the mountain, a large crowd met him. **38**A man in the crowd called out, "Teacher, I beg you to look at my son, for he is my only child. **39**A spirit seizes him and he suddenly screams; it throws him into convulsions so that he foams at the mouth. It scarcely ever leaves him and is destroying him. **40**I begged your disciples to drive it out, but they could not."

41"O unbelieving and perverse generation," Jesus replied, "how long shall I stay with you and put up with you? Bring your son here."

42Even while the boy was coming, the demon threw him to the ground in a convulsion. But Jesus rebuked the evil*b* spirit, healed the boy and gave him back to his father. **43**And they were all amazed at the greatness of God.

While everyone was marveling at all that Jesus did, he said to his disciples, **44**"Listen carefully to what I am about to tell you: The Son of Man is going to be betrayed into the hands of men." **45**But they did not understand what this meant. It was hidden from them, so that they did not grasp it, and they were afraid to ask him about it.

Who Will Be the Greatest?

46An argument started among the disciples as to which of them would be the greatest. **47**Jesus, knowing their thoughts, took a little child and had him stand beside him. **48**Then he said to them, "Whoever welcomes this little child in my name welcomes me; and whoever welcomes me welcomes the one who sent me. For he who is least among you all—he is the greatest."

49"Master," said John, "we saw a man driving out demons in your name and we

---

a20 Or Messiah   *b42* Greek unclean

tried to stop him, because he is not one of us."

⁵⁰"Do not stop him," Jesus said, "for whoever is not against you is for you."

Samaritan Opposition

⁵¹As the time approached for him to be taken up to heaven, Jesus resolutely set out for Jerusalem. ⁵²And he sent messengers on ahead, who went into a Samaritan village to get things ready for him; ⁵³but the people there did not welcome him, because he was heading for Jerusalem. ⁵⁴When the disciples James and John saw this, they asked, "Lord, do you want us to call fire down from heaven to destroy them*a*?" ⁵⁵But Jesus turned and rebuked them, ⁵⁶and*b* they went to another village.

The Cost of Following Jesus

⁵⁷As they were walking along the road, a man said to him, "I will follow you wherever you go."

⁵⁸Jesus replied, "Foxes have holes and birds of the air have nests, but the Son of Man has no place to lay his head."

⁵⁹He said to another man, "Follow me." But the man replied, "Lord, first let me go and bury my father."

⁶⁰Jesus said to him, "Let the dead bury their own dead, but you go and proclaim the kingdom of God."

⁶¹Still another said, "I will follow you, Lord; but first let me go back and say good-by to my family."

⁶²Jesus replied, "No one who puts his hand to the plow and looks back is fit for service in the kingdom of God."

Jesus Sends Out the Seventy-two

10 After this the Lord appointed seventy-two*c* others and sent them two by two ahead of him to every town and place where he was about to go. ²He told them, "The harvest is plentiful, but the workers are few. Ask the Lord of the harvest, therefore, to send out workers into his harvest field. ³Go! I am sending you out like lambs among wolves. ⁴Do not take a purse or bag or sandals; and do not greet anyone on the road.

⁵"When you enter a house, first say 'Peace to this house.' ⁶If a man of peace is there, your peace will rest on him; if not, it will return to you. ⁷Stay in that house,

eating and drinking whatever they give you, for the worker deserves his wages. Do not move around from house to house.

⁸"When you enter a town and are welcomed, eat what is set before you. ⁹Heal the sick who are there and tell them, 'The kingdom of God is near you.' ¹⁰But when you enter a town and are not welcomed, go into its streets and say, ¹¹'Even the dust of your town that sticks to our feet we wipe off against you. Yet be sure of this: The kingdom of God is near.' ¹²I tell you, it will be more bearable on that day for Sodom than for that town.

¹³"Woe to you, Korazin! Woe to you, Bethsaida! For if the miracles that were performed in you had been performed in Tyre and Sidon, they would have repented long ago, sitting in sackcloth and ashes. ¹⁴But it will be more bearable for Tyre and Sidon at the judgment than for you. ¹⁵And you, Capernaum, will you be lifted up to the skies? No, you will go down to the depths.*d*

¹⁶"He who listens to you listens to me; he who rejects you rejects me; but he who rejects me rejects him who sent me."

¹⁷The seventy-two returned with joy and said, "Lord, even the demons submit to us in your name."

¹⁸He replied, "I saw Satan fall like lightning from heaven. ¹⁹I have given you authority to trample on snakes and scorpions and to overcome all the power of the enemy; nothing will harm you. ²⁰However, do not rejoice that the spirits submit to you, but rejoice that your names are written in heaven."

²¹At that time Jesus, full of joy through the Holy Spirit, said, "I praise you, Father, Lord of heaven and earth, because you have hidden these things from the wise and learned, and revealed them to little children. Yes, Father, for this was your good pleasure.

²²"All things have been committed to me by my Father. No one knows who the Son is except the Father, and no one knows who the Father is except the Son and those to whom the Son chooses to reveal him."

²³Then he turned to his disciples and said privately, "Blessed are the eyes that see what you see. ²⁴For I tell you that many prophets and kings wanted to see

*a*54 Some manuscripts *them, even as Elijah did*   *b*55,56 Some manuscripts *them. And he said, "You do not know what kind of spirit you are of, for the Son of Man did not come to destroy men's lives, but to save them."* ⁵⁶*And*   *c*1 Some manuscripts *seventy;* also in verse 17   *d*15 Greek *Hades*

WEEKENDING

RENEW

Help me to understand that only a few things
really *are* necessary in life. And when you get
right down to it, only one: to sit at your feet . . .
listening . . . looking into your eyes . . . and
loving you.

Thank you for the privilege of sitting at those
nail-scarred feet. Grant me the grace never to
regard that privilege casually, nor to neglect it,
but to come there humbly, and to come there
often . . . because you are worthy to be adored,
O beautiful Savior . . . because you are worthy
to be adored.

– Ken Gire

REVIVE

Saturday: Psalm 27
Sunday: Luke 10:38–42

Go to page 1105 for your next devotional reading.

what you see but did not see it, and to hear what you hear but did not hear it."

The Parable of the Good Samaritan

25On one occasion an expert in the law stood up to test Jesus. "Teacher," he asked, "what must I do to inherit eternal life?"

26"What is written in the Law?" he replied. "How do you read it?"

27He answered: " 'Love the Lord your God with all your heart and with all your soul and with all your strength and with all your mind'*a*; and, 'Love your neighbor as yourself.'*b*"

28"You have answered correctly," Jesus replied. "Do this and you will live."

29But he wanted to justify himself, so he asked Jesus, "And who is my neighbor?"

30In reply Jesus said: "A man was going down from Jerusalem to Jericho, when he fell into the hands of robbers. They stripped him of his clothes, beat him and went away, leaving him half dead. **31**A priest happened to be going down the same road, and when he saw the man, he passed by on the other side. **32**So too, a Levite, when he came to the place and saw him, passed by on the other side. **33**But a Samaritan, as he traveled, came where the man was; and when he saw him, he took pity on him. **34**He went to him and bandaged his wounds, pouring on oil and wine. Then he put the man on his own donkey, took him to an inn and took care of him. **35**The next day he took out two silver coins*c* and gave them to the innkeeper. 'Look after him,' he said, 'and when I return, I will reimburse you for any extra expense you may have.'

36"Which of these three do you think was a neighbor to the man who fell into the hands of robbers?"

37The expert in the law replied, "The one who had mercy on him."

Jesus told him, "Go and do likewise."

At the Home of Martha and Mary

38As Jesus and his disciples were on their way, he came to a village where a woman named Martha opened her home to him. **39**She had a sister called Mary, who sat at the Lord's feet listening to what he said. **40**But Martha was distracted by all the preparations that had to be made. She came to him and asked, "Lord, don't you care that my sister has left me to do the work by myself? Tell her to help me!"

41"Martha, Martha," the Lord answered, "you are worried and upset about many things, **42**but only one thing is needed.*d* Mary has chosen what is better, and it will not be taken away from her."

Jesus' Teaching on Prayer

11 One day Jesus was praying in a certain place. When he finished, one of his disciples said to him, "Lord, teach us to pray, just as John taught his disciples."

2He said to them, "When you pray, say:

" 'Father,*e*
hallowed be your name,
your kingdom come.*f*
3Give us each day our daily bread.
4Forgive us our sins,
    for we also forgive everyone who
        sins against us.*g*
And lead us not into temptation.*h* ' "

5Then he said to them, "Suppose one of you has a friend, and he goes to him at midnight and says, 'Friend, lend me three loaves of bread, **6**because a friend of mine on a journey has come to me, and I have nothing to set before him.'

7"Then the one inside answers, 'Don't bother me. The door is already locked, and my children are with me in bed. I can't get up and give you anything.' **8**I tell you, though he will not get up and give him the bread because he is his friend, yet because of the man's boldness*i* he will get up and give him as much as he needs.

9"So I say to you: Ask and it will be given to you; seek and you will find; knock and the door will be opened to you. **10**For everyone who asks receives; he who seeks finds; and to him who knocks, the door will be opened.

11"Which of you fathers, if your son asks for*j* a fish, will give him a snake instead? **12**Or if he asks for an egg, will give him a scorpion? **13**If you then, though you are evil, know how to give good gifts to your children, how much more will your Father in heaven give the Holy Spirit to those who ask him!"

---

*a*27 Deut. 6:5   *b*27 Lev. 19:18   *c*35 Greek *two denarii*   *d*42 Some manuscripts *but few things are needed—or only one*   *e*2 Some manuscripts *Our Father in heaven*   *f*2 Some manuscripts *come. May your will be done on earth as it is in heaven.*   *g*4 Greek *everyone who is indebted to us*   *h*4 Some manuscripts *temptation but deliver us from the evil one*   *i*8 Or *persistence*   *j*11 Some manuscripts *for bread, will give him a stone; or if he asks for*

Jesus and Beelzebub

14Jesus was driving out a demon that was mute. When the demon left, the man who had been mute spoke, and the crowd was amazed. **15**But some of them said, "By Beelzebub,*a* the prince of demons, he is driving out demons." **16**Others tested him by asking for a sign from heaven.

17Jesus knew their thoughts and said to them: "Any kingdom divided against itself will be ruined, and a house divided against itself will fall. **18**If Satan is divided against himself, how can his kingdom stand? I say this because you claim that I drive out demons by Beelzebub. **19**Now if I drive out demons by Beelzebub, by whom do your followers drive them out? So then, they will be your judges. **20**But if I drive out demons by the finger of God, then the kingdom of God has come to you.

21"When a strong man, fully armed, guards his own house, his possessions are safe. **22**But when someone stronger attacks and overpowers him, he takes away the armor in which the man trusted and divides up the spoils.

23"He who is not with me is against me, and he who does not gather with me, scatters.

24"When an evil*b* spirit comes out of a man, it goes through arid places seeking rest and does not find it. Then it says, 'I will return to the house I left.' **25**When it arrives, it finds the house swept clean and put in order. **26**Then it goes and takes seven other spirits more wicked than itself, and they go in and live there. And the final condition of that man is worse than the first."

27As Jesus was saying these things, a woman in the crowd called out, "Blessed is the mother who gave you birth and nursed you."

28He replied, "Blessed rather are those who hear the word of God and obey it."

The Sign of Jonah

29As the crowds increased, Jesus said, "This is a wicked generation. It asks for a miraculous sign, but none will be given it except the sign of Jonah. **30**For as Jonah was a sign to the Ninevites, so also will the Son of Man be to this generation. **31**The Queen of the South will rise at the judgment with the men of this generation and condemn them; for she came from the ends of the earth to listen to Solomon's wisdom, and now one*c* greater than Solomon is here. **32**The men of Nineveh will stand up at the judgment with this generation and condemn it; for they repented at the preaching of Jonah, and now one greater than Jonah is here.

The Lamp of the Body

33"No one lights a lamp and puts it in a place where it will be hidden, or under a bowl. Instead he puts it on its stand, so that those who come in may see the light. **34**Your eye is the lamp of your body. When your eyes are good, your whole body also is full of light. But when they are bad, your body also is full of darkness. **35**See to it, then, that the light within you is not darkness. **36**Therefore, if your whole body is full of light, and no part of it dark, it will be completely lighted, as when the light of a lamp shines on you."

Six Woes

37When Jesus had finished speaking, a Pharisee invited him to eat with him; so he went in and reclined at the table. **38**But the Pharisee, noticing that Jesus did not first wash before the meal, was surprised.

39Then the Lord said to him, "Now then, you Pharisees clean the outside of the cup and dish, but inside you are full of greed and wickedness. **40**You foolish people! Did not the one who made the outside make the inside also? **41**But give what is inside ₜthe dish₎*d* to the poor, and everything will be clean for you.

42"Woe to you Pharisees, because you give God a tenth of your mint, rue and all other kinds of garden herbs, but you neglect justice and the love of God. You should have practiced the latter without leaving the former undone.

43"Woe to you Pharisees, because you love the most important seats in the synagogues and greetings in the marketplaces.

44"Woe to you, because you are like unmarked graves, which men walk over without knowing it."

45One of the experts in the law answered him, "Teacher, when you say these things, you insult us also."

46Jesus replied, "And you experts in the law, woe to you, because you load people down with burdens they can hardly carry, and you yourselves will not lift one finger to help them.

---

*a*15 Greek *Beezeboul* or *Beelzeboul*; also in verses 18 and 19 also in verse 32   *b*24 Greek *unclean*   *c*31 Or *something*; *d*41 Or *what you have*

47"Woe to you, because you build tombs for the prophets, and it was your forefathers who killed them. 48So you testify that you approve of what your forefathers did; they killed the prophets, and you build their tombs. 49Because of this, God in his wisdom said, 'I will send them prophets and apostles, some of whom they will kill and others they will persecute.' 50Therefore this generation will be held responsible for the blood of all the prophets that has been shed since the beginning of the world, 51from the blood of Abel to the blood of Zechariah, who was killed between the altar and the sanctuary. Yes, I tell you, this generation will be held responsible for it all.

52"Woe to you experts in the law, because you have taken away the key to knowledge. You yourselves have not entered, and you have hindered those who were entering."

53When Jesus left there, the Pharisees and the teachers of the law began to oppose him fiercely and to besiege him with questions, 54waiting to catch him in something he might say.

Warnings and Encouragements

12 Meanwhile, when a crowd of many thousands had gathered, so that they were trampling on one another, Jesus began to speak first to his disciples, saying: "Be on your guard against the yeast of the Pharisees, which is hypocrisy. 2There is nothing concealed that will not be disclosed, or hidden that will not be made known. 3What you have said in the dark will be heard in the daylight, and what you have whispered in the ear in the inner rooms will be proclaimed from the roofs.

4"I tell you, my friends, do not be afraid of those who kill the body and after that can do no more. 5But I will show you whom you should fear: Fear him who, after the killing of the body, has power to throw you into hell. Yes, I tell you, fear him. 6Are not five sparrows sold for two pennies[a]? Yet not one of them is forgotten by God. 7Indeed, the very hairs of your head are all numbered. Don't be afraid; you are worth more than many sparrows.

8"I tell you, whoever acknowledges me before men, the Son of Man will also acknowledge him before the angels of God. 9But he who disowns me before men will be disowned before the angels of God.

10And everyone who speaks a word against the Son of Man will be forgiven, but anyone who blasphemes against the Holy Spirit will not be forgiven.

11"When you are brought before synagogues, rulers and authorities, do not worry about how you will defend yourselves or what you will say, 12for the Holy Spirit will teach you at that time what you should say."

The Parable of the Rich Fool

13Someone in the crowd said to him, "Teacher, tell my brother to divide the inheritance with me."

14Jesus replied, "Man, who appointed me a judge or an arbiter between you?" 15Then he said to them, "Watch out! Be on your guard against all kinds of greed; a man's life does not consist in the abundance of his possessions."

16And he told them this parable: "The ground of a certain rich man produced a good crop. 17He thought to himself, 'What shall I do? I have no place to store my crops.'

18"Then he said, 'This is what I'll do. I will tear down my barns and build bigger ones, and there I will store all my grain and my goods. 19And I'll say to myself, "You have plenty of good things laid up for many years. Take life easy; eat, drink and be merry."'

20"But God said to him, 'You fool! This very night your life will be demanded from you. Then who will get what you have prepared for yourself?'

21"This is how it will be with anyone who stores up things for himself but is not rich toward God."

Do Not Worry

22Then Jesus said to his disciples: "Therefore I tell you, do not worry about your life, what you will eat; or about your body, what you will wear. 23Life is more than food, and the body more than clothes. 24Consider the ravens: They do not sow or reap, they have no storeroom or barn; yet God feeds them. And how much more valuable you are than birds! 25Who of you by worrying can add a single hour to his life[b]? 26Since you cannot do this very little thing, why do you worry about the rest?

27"Consider how the lilies grow. They do not labor or spin. Yet I tell you, not even Solomon in all his splendor was

---

a6 Greek *two assaria*　　*b25* Or *single cubit to his height* dressed like one of these. 28If that is how God clothes the grass of the field, which is here today, and tomorrow is thrown into the fire, how much more will he clothe you, O you of little faith! 29And do not set your heart on what you will eat or drink; do not worry about it. 30For the pagan world runs after all such things, and your Father knows that you need them. 31But seek his kingdom, and these things will be given to you as well.

32"Do not be afraid, little flock, for your Father has been pleased to give you the kingdom. 33Sell your possessions and give to the poor. Provide purses for yourselves that will not wear out, a treasure in heaven that will not be exhausted, where no thief comes near and no moth destroys. 34For where your treasure is, there your heart will be also.

Watchfulness

35"Be dressed ready for service and keep your lamps burning, 36like men wait-

---

MONDAY

VERSE FOR THE DAY:
Luke 12:15

AUTHOR:
Ron Blue

PASSAGE FOR THE DAY:
Luke 12:13–21

Needs, or Greeds?

PROVERBS 22:7 says, "The rich rule over the poor, and the borrower is servant to the lender." Anyone who has borrowed or been in bondage to debt knows the truth of this verse. The reality is that whenever you have borrowed from anyone, you are a servant to that person. This verse does not prohibit debt, of course, but it certainly cautions against the use of debt. We could say that anyone who uses debt for any purpose, at the very least, is not using Biblical wisdom and, in fact, may be a "fool." Again, a great caution, but not a prohibition, against debt.

1 Timothy 5:8 says, "If anyone does not provide for his relatives, and especially for his immediate family, he has denied the faith and is worse than an unbeliever." The underlying Biblical principle relative to debt in this verse is that by taking on debt you may run the risk of not providing for your own. Because debt mortgages the future and because the negative compound of debt works against you, you may very well end up in the future not providing for your own. Therefore, this verse says that you have denied the faith and are worse than an unbeliever. Obviously, the danger is great and needs to be avoided.

Luke 12:15 says, "Watch out! Be on your guard against all kinds of greed; a man's life does not consist in the abundance of his possessions." The caution in this verse is clear: "Beware, and be on your guard against *every form of greed*." Debt makes it very easy to fund greeds; yet in doing so, we may violate the Biblical principle set forth in this verse. The question to ask is, "Am I funding my *needs* or my *greeds?*"

Additional Scripture Readings:
Matthew 6:28–34; James 4:1–6

Go to page 1111 for your next devotional reading.

ing for their master to return from a wedding banquet, so that when he comes and knocks they can immediately open the door for him. **37**It will be good for those servants whose master finds them watching when he comes. I tell you the truth, he will dress himself to serve, will have them recline at the table and will come and wait on them. **38**It will be good for those servants whose master finds them ready, even if he comes in the second or third watch of the night. **39**But understand this: If the owner of the house had known at what hour the thief was coming, he would not have let his house be broken into. **40**You also must be ready, because the Son of Man will come at an hour when you do not expect him."

41Peter asked, "Lord, are you telling this parable to us, or to everyone?"

42The Lord answered, "Who then is the faithful and wise manager, whom the master puts in charge of his servants to give them their food allowance at the proper time? **43**It will be good for that servant whom the master finds doing so when he returns. **44**I tell you the truth, he will put him in charge of all his possessions. **45**But suppose the servant says to himself, 'My master is taking a long time in coming,' and he then begins to beat the menservants and maidservants and to eat and drink and get drunk. **46**The master of that servant will come on a day when he does not expect him and at an hour he is not aware of. He will cut him to pieces and assign him a place with the unbelievers.

47"That servant who knows his master's will and does not get ready or does not do what his master wants will be beaten with many blows. **48**But the one who does not know and does things deserving punishment will be beaten with few blows. From everyone who has been given much, much will be demanded; and from the one who has been entrusted with much, much more will be asked.

Not Peace but Division

49"I have come to bring fire on the earth, and how I wish it were already kindled! **50**But I have a baptism to undergo, and how distressed I am until it is completed! **51**Do you think I came to bring peace on earth? No, I tell you, but division. **52**From now on there will be five in one family divided against each other, three against two and two against three.

53They will be divided, father against son and son against father, mother against daughter and daughter against mother, mother-in-law against daughter-in-law and daughter-in-law against mother-in-law."

Interpreting the Times

54He said to the crowd: "When you see a cloud rising in the west, immediately you say, 'It's going to rain,' and it does. **55**And when the south wind blows, you say, 'It's going to be hot,' and it is. **56**Hypocrites! You know how to interpret the appearance of the earth and the sky. How is it that you don't know how to interpret this present time?

57"Why don't you judge for yourselves what is right? **58**As you are going with your adversary to the magistrate, try hard to be reconciled to him on the way, or he may drag you off to the judge, and the judge turn you over to the officer, and the officer throw you into prison. **59**I tell you, you will not get out until you have paid the last penny.*a*"

Repent or Perish

13 Now there were some present at that time who told Jesus about the Galileans whose blood Pilate had mixed with their sacrifices. **2**Jesus answered, "Do you think that these Galileans were worse sinners than all the other Galileans because they suffered this way? **3**I tell you, no! But unless you repent, you too will all perish. **4**Or those eighteen who died when the tower in Siloam fell on them—do you think they were more guilty than all the others living in Jerusalem? **5**I tell you, no! But unless you repent, you too will all perish."

6Then he told this parable: "A man had a fig tree, planted in his vineyard, and he went to look for fruit on it, but did not find any. **7**So he said to the man who took care of the vineyard, 'For three years now I've been coming to look for fruit on this fig tree and haven't found any. Cut it down! Why should it use up the soil?'

8" 'Sir,' the man replied, 'leave it alone for one more year, and I'll dig around it and fertilize it. **9**If it bears fruit next year, fine! If not, then cut it down.' "

A Crippled Woman Healed on the Sabbath

10On a Sabbath Jesus was teaching in

a59 Greek lepton

one of the synagogues, **11**and a woman was there who had been crippled by a spirit for eighteen years. She was bent over and could not straighten up at all. **12**When Jesus saw her, he called her forward and said to her, "Woman, you are set free from your infirmity." **13**Then he put his hands on her, and immediately she straightened up and praised God.

14Indignant because Jesus had healed on the Sabbath, the synagogue ruler said to the people, "There are six days for work. So come and be healed on those days, not on the Sabbath."

15The Lord answered him, "You hypocrites! Doesn't each of you on the Sabbath untie his ox or donkey from the stall and lead it out to give it water? **16**Then should not this woman, a daughter of Abraham, whom Satan has kept bound for eighteen long years, be set free on the Sabbath day from what bound her?"

17When he said this, all his opponents were humiliated, but the people were delighted with all the wonderful things he was doing.

The Parables of the Mustard Seed and the Yeast

18Then Jesus asked, "What is the kingdom of God like? What shall I compare it to? **19**It is like a mustard seed, which a man took and planted in his garden. It grew and became a tree, and the birds of the air perched in its branches."

20Again he asked, "What shall I compare the kingdom of God to? **21**It is like yeast that a woman took and mixed into a large amount*a* of flour until it worked all through the dough."

The Narrow Door

22Then Jesus went through the towns and villages, teaching as he made his way to Jerusalem. **23**Someone asked him, "Lord, are only a few people going to be saved?"

He said to them, **24**"Make every effort to enter through the narrow door, because many, I tell you, will try to enter and will not be able to. **25**Once the owner of the house gets up and closes the door, you will stand outside knocking and pleading, 'Sir, open the door for us.'

"But he will answer, 'I don't know you or where you come from.'

26"Then you will say, 'We ate and drank

with you, and you taught in our streets.'

27"But he will reply, 'I don't know you or where you come from. Away from me, all you evildoers!'

28"There will be weeping there, and gnashing of teeth, when you see Abraham, Isaac and Jacob and all the prophets in the kingdom of God, but you yourselves thrown out. **29**People will come from east and west and north and south, and will take their places at the feast in the kingdom of God. **30**Indeed there are those who are last who will be first, and first who will be last."

Jesus' Sorrow for Jerusalem

31At that time some Pharisees came to Jesus and said to him, "Leave this place and go somewhere else. Herod wants to kill you."

32He replied, "Go tell that fox, 'I will drive out demons and heal people today and tomorrow, and on the third day I will reach my goal.' **33**In any case, I must keep going today and tomorrow and the next day—for surely no prophet can die outside Jerusalem!

34"O Jerusalem, Jerusalem, you who kill the prophets and stone those sent to you, how often I have longed to gather your children together, as a hen gathers her chicks under her wings, but you were not willing! **35**Look, your house is left to you desolate. I tell you, you will not see me again until you say, 'Blessed is he who comes in the name of the Lord.'*b*"

Jesus at a Pharisee's House

14 One Sabbath, when Jesus went to eat in the house of a prominent Pharisee, he was being carefully watched. **2**There in front of him was a man suffering from dropsy. **3**Jesus asked the Pharisees and experts in the law, "Is it lawful to heal on the Sabbath or not?" **4**But they remained silent. So taking hold of the man, he healed him and sent him away.

5Then he asked them, "If one of you has a son*c* or an ox that falls into a well on the Sabbath day, will you not immediately pull him out?" **6**And they had nothing to say.

7When he noticed how the guests picked the places of honor at the table, he told them this parable: **8**"When someone invites you to a wedding feast, do not take the place of honor, for a person more dis-

---

*a*21 Greek *three satas* (probably about 1/2 bushel or 22 liters)   *b*35 Psalm 118:26   *c*5 Some manuscripts *donkey* tinguished than you may have been invited. ⁹If so, the host who invited both of you will come and say to you, 'Give this man your seat.' Then, humiliated, you will have to take the least important place. ¹⁰But when you are invited, take the lowest place, so that when your host comes, he will say to you, 'Friend, move up to a better place.' Then you will be honored in the presence of all your fellow guests. ¹¹For everyone who exalts himself will be humbled, and he who humbles himself will be exalted."

¹²Then Jesus said to his host, "When you give a luncheon or dinner, do not invite your friends, your brothers or relatives, or your rich neighbors; if you do, they may invite you back and so you will be repaid. ¹³But when you give a banquet, invite the poor, the crippled, the lame, the blind, ¹⁴and you will be blessed. Although they cannot repay you, you will be repaid at the resurrection of the righteous."

The Parable of the Great Banquet

¹⁵When one of those at the table with him heard this, he said to Jesus, "Blessed is the man who will eat at the feast in the kingdom of God."

¹⁶Jesus replied: "A certain man was preparing a great banquet and invited many guests. ¹⁷At the time of the banquet he sent his servant to tell those who had been invited, 'Come, for everything is now ready.'

¹⁸"But they all alike began to make excuses. The first said, 'I have just bought a field, and I must go and see it. Please excuse me.'

¹⁹"Another said, 'I have just bought five yoke of oxen, and I'm on my way to try them out. Please excuse me.'

²⁰"Still another said, 'I just got married, so I can't come.'

²¹"The servant came back and reported this to his master. Then the owner of the house became angry and ordered his servant, 'Go out quickly into the streets and alleys of the town and bring in the poor, the crippled, the blind and the lame.'

²²"'Sir,' the servant said, 'what you ordered has been done, but there is still room.'

²³"Then the master told his servant, 'Go out to the roads and country lanes and make them come in, so that my house will be full. ²⁴I tell you, not one of those men who were invited will get a taste of my banquet.'"

The Cost of Being a Disciple

²⁵Large crowds were traveling with Jesus, and turning to them he said: ²⁶"If anyone comes to me and does not hate his father and mother, his wife and children, his brothers and sisters—yes, even his own life—he cannot be my disciple. ²⁷And anyone who does not carry his cross and follow me cannot be my disciple.

²⁸"Suppose one of you wants to build a tower. Will he not first sit down and estimate the cost to see if he has enough money to complete it? ²⁹For if he lays the foundation and is not able to finish it, everyone who sees it will ridicule him, ³⁰saying, 'This fellow began to build and was not able to finish.'

³¹"Or suppose a king is about to go to war against another king. Will he not first sit down and consider whether he is able with ten thousand men to oppose the one coming against him with twenty thousand? ³²If he is not able, he will send a delegation while the other is still a long way off and will ask for terms of peace. ³³In the same way, any of you who does not give up everything he has cannot be my disciple.

³⁴"Salt is good, but if it loses its saltiness, how can it be made salty again? ³⁵It is fit neither for the soil nor for the manure pile; it is thrown out.

"He who has ears to hear, let him hear."

The Parable of the Lost Sheep

15 Now the tax collectors and "sinners" were all gathering around to hear him. ²But the Pharisees and the teachers of the law muttered, "This man welcomes sinners and eats with them."

³Then Jesus told them this parable: ⁴"Suppose one of you has a hundred sheep and loses one of them. Does he not leave the ninety-nine in the open country and go after the lost sheep until he finds it? ⁵And when he finds it, he joyfully puts it on his shoulders ⁶and goes home. Then he calls his friends and neighbors together and says, 'Rejoice with me; I have found my lost sheep.' ⁷I tell you that in the same way there will be more rejoicing in heaven over one sinner who repents than over ninety-nine righteous persons who do not need to repent.

The Parable of the Lost Coin

⁸"Or suppose a woman has ten silver

coins[a] and loses one. Does she not light a lamp, sweep the house and search carefully until she finds it? 9And when she finds it, she calls her friends and neighbors together and says, 'Rejoice with me; I have found my lost coin.' 10In the same way, I tell you, there is rejoicing in the presence of the angels of God over one sinner who repents."

The Parable of the Lost Son

11Jesus continued: "There was a man who had two sons. 12The younger one said to his father, 'Father, give me my share of the estate.' So he divided his property between them.

13"Not long after that, the younger son got together all he had, set off for a distant country and there squandered his wealth in wild living. 14After he had spent everything, there was a severe famine in that whole country, and he began to be in need. 15So he went and hired himself out to a citizen of that country, who sent him to his fields to feed pigs. 16He longed to fill his stomach with the pods that the pigs were eating, but no one gave him anything.

17"When he came to his senses, he said, 'How many of my father's hired men have food to spare, and here I am starving to death! 18I will set out and go back to my father and say to him: Father, I have sinned against heaven and against you. 19I am no longer worthy to be called your son; make me like one of your hired men.' 20So he got up and went to his father.

"But while he was still a long way off, his father saw him and was filled with compassion for him; he ran to his son, threw his arms around him and kissed him.

21"The son said to him, 'Father, I have sinned against heaven and against you. I am no longer worthy to be called your son.[b]'

22"But the father said to his servants, 'Quick! Bring the best robe and put it on him. Put a ring on his finger and sandals on his feet. 23Bring the fattened calf and kill it. Let's have a feast and celebrate. 24For this son of mine was dead and is alive again; he was lost and is found.' So they began to celebrate.

25"Meanwhile, the older son was in the field. When he came near the house, he heard music and dancing. 26So he called one of the servants and asked him what was going on. 27'Your brother has come,' he replied, 'and your father has killed the fattened calf because he has him back safe and sound.'

28"The older brother became angry and refused to go in. So his father went out and pleaded with him. 29But he answered his father, 'Look! All these years I've been slaving for you and never disobeyed your orders. Yet you never gave me even a young goat so I could celebrate with my friends. 30But when this son of yours who has squandered your property with prostitutes comes home, you kill the fattened calf for him!'

31" 'My son,' the father said, 'you are always with me, and everything I have is yours. 32But we had to celebrate and be glad, because this brother of yours was dead and is alive again; he was lost and is found.' "

The Parable of the Shrewd Manager

16 Jesus told his disciples: "There was a rich man whose manager was accused of wasting his possessions. 2So he called him in and asked him, 'What is this I hear about you? Give an account of your management, because you cannot be manager any longer.'

3"The manager said to himself, 'What shall I do now? My master is taking away my job. I'm not strong enough to dig, and I'm ashamed to beg— 4I know what I'll do so that, when I lose my job here, people will welcome me into their houses.'

5"So he called in each one of his master's debtors. He asked the first, 'How much do you owe my master?'

6" 'Eight hundred gallons[c] of olive oil,' he replied.

"The manager told him, 'Take your bill, sit down quickly, and make it four hundred.'

7"Then he asked the second, 'And how much do you owe?'

" 'A thousand bushels[d] of wheat,' he replied.

"He told him, 'Take your bill and make it eight hundred.'

8"The master commended the dishonest manager because he had acted shrewdly. For the people of this world are more shrewd in dealing with their own

---

[a]8 Greek *ten drachmas,* each worth about a day's wages like one of your hired men.   [c]6 Greek *one hundred batous* (probably about 3 kiloliters)   [d]7 Greek *one hundred korous* (probably about 35 kiloliters)   [b]21 Some early manuscripts *son. Make me like one of your hired men.*

kind than are the people of the light. **9**I tell you, use worldly wealth to gain friends for yourselves, so that when it is gone, you will be welcomed into eternal dwellings.

10"Whoever can be trusted with very little can also be trusted with much, and whoever is dishonest with very little will also be dishonest with much. **11**So if you have not been trustworthy in handling worldly wealth, who will trust you with true riches? **12**And if you have not been trustworthy with someone else's property, who will give you property of your own?

13"No servant can serve two masters. Either he will hate the one and love the other, or he will be devoted to the one and despise the other. You cannot serve both God and Money."

14The Pharisees, who loved money, heard all this and were sneering at Jesus. **15**He said to them, "You are the ones who justify yourselves in the eyes of men, but God knows your hearts. What is highly valued among men is detestable in God's sight.

Additional Teachings

16"The Law and the Prophets were proclaimed until John. Since that time, the good news of the kingdom of God is being preached, and everyone is forcing his way into it. **17**It is easier for heaven and earth to disappear than for the least stroke of a pen to drop out of the Law.

18"Anyone who divorces his wife and marries another woman commits adultery, and the man who marries a divorced woman commits adultery.

The Rich Man and Lazarus

19"There was a rich man who was dressed in purple and fine linen and lived in luxury every day. **20**At his gate was laid a beggar named Lazarus, covered with sores **21**and longing to eat what fell from the rich man's table. Even the dogs came and licked his sores.

22"The time came when the beggar died and the angels carried him to Abraham's side. The rich man also died and was buried. **23**In hell,*a* where he was in torment, he looked up and saw Abraham far away, with Lazarus by his side. **24**So he called to him, 'Father Abraham, have pity on me and send Lazarus to dip the tip of his finger in water and cool my tongue, because I am in agony in this fire.'

25"But Abraham replied, 'Son, remember that in your lifetime you received your good things, while Lazarus received bad things, but now he is comforted here and you are in agony. **26**And besides all this, between us and you a great chasm has been fixed, so that those who want to go from here to you cannot, nor can anyone cross over from there to us.'

27"He answered, 'Then I beg you, father, send Lazarus to my father's house, **28**for I have five brothers. Let him warn them, so that they will not also come to this place of torment.'

29"Abraham replied, 'They have Moses and the Prophets; let them listen to them.'

30" 'No, father Abraham,' he said, 'but if someone from the dead goes to them, they will repent.'

31"He said to him, 'If they do not listen to Moses and the Prophets, they will not be convinced even if someone rises from the dead.' "

Sin, Faith, Duty

17 Jesus said to his disciples: "Things that cause people to sin are bound to come, but woe to that person through whom they come. **2**It would be better for him to be thrown into the sea with a millstone tied around his neck than for him to cause one of these little ones to sin. **3**So watch yourselves.

"If your brother sins, rebuke him, and if he repents, forgive him. **4**If he sins against you seven times in a day, and seven times comes back to you and says, 'I repent,' forgive him."

5The apostles said to the Lord, "Increase our faith!"

6He replied, "If you have faith as small as a mustard seed, you can say to this mulberry tree, 'Be uprooted and planted in the sea,' and it will obey you.

7"Suppose one of you had a servant plowing or looking after the sheep. Would he say to the servant when he comes in from the field, 'Come along now and sit down to eat'? **8**Would he not rather say, 'Prepare my supper, get yourself ready and wait on me while I eat and drink; after that you may eat and drink'? **9**Would he thank the servant because he did what he was told to do? **10**So you also, when you have done everything you were told to do, should say, 'We are unworthy servants; we have only done our duty.' "

a23 Greek *Hades*

TUESDAY

VERSE FOR THE DAY:
Luke 16:9

AUTHOR:
Bill Hybels

PASSAGE FOR THE DAY:
Luke 16:1–13

A Most Unusual Reaction

IN LUKE 16:1–9 Jesus tells a parable so unusual that many teachers would rather turn the page and go on than try to understand it. It is the parable of a crooked accountant (traditionally, an "unjust steward") who used creative bookkeeping techniques. His boss eventually caught on and decided to give him his termination notice. But while the accountant still had a few days left to work, he said to himself, "I have a problem. I'm going to lose my steady paycheck. I'm too old to dig ditches and too proud to panhandle. I'm going to have to solve this somehow."

So the accountant did an unethical but ingenious thing: he called some of the people who owed his boss money. "How much do you owe us?" he asked.

One man answered, "A hundred measures of wheat."

"I'll tell you what," the accountant said. "Change your copy of the invoice, and I'll change mine. Put down that you owe us only fifty measures."

"Well, thanks," said the man. "That's a very nice thing for you to do. If you ever need a favor, call me up."

"Don't worry," said the accountant, "I will." Then he called another debtor, and another, and repeated his generous offer.

What was the crooked accountant doing? Plainly, the man was using the company's capital to build up a reserve of personal favors so that when he lost his job he would be able to find another one. His boss quickly saw what he was doing, too, and he had a most unusual reaction—he praised his accountant's ingenuity and shrewdness!

Now neither Jesus nor the boss ever praised deceitfulness, dishonesty or creative bookkeeping. But both of them recognized the accountant's vision. When faced with a serious problem, he did not hide, blame somebody, run to the bottle or jump off a cliff. Instead, he faced his problem and came up with a shrewd way to solve it. Jesus commended him because, as soon as he saw his problem, he became solution oriented.

Additional Scripture Readings:
Matthew 10:5–16;
Philippians 4:10–13

Go to page 1114 for your next devotional reading.

Ten Healed of Leprosy

11Now on his way to Jerusalem, Jesus traveled along the border between Samaria and Galilee. **12**As he was going into a village, ten men who had leprosy*a* met him. They stood at a distance **13**and called out in a loud voice, "Jesus, Master, have pity on us!"

14When he saw them, he said, "Go, show yourselves to the priests." And as they went, they were cleansed.

15One of them, when he saw he was healed, came back, praising God in a loud voice. **16**He threw himself at Jesus' feet and thanked him—and he was a Samaritan.

17Jesus asked, "Were not all ten cleansed? Where are the other nine? **18**Was no one found to return and give praise to God except this foreigner?" **19**Then he said to him, "Rise and go; your faith has made you well."

The Coming of the Kingdom of God

20Once, having been asked by the Pharisees when the kingdom of God would come, Jesus replied, "The kingdom of God does not come with your careful observation, **21**nor will people say, 'Here it is,' or 'There it is,' because the kingdom of God is within*b* you."

22Then he said to his disciples, "The time is coming when you will long to see one of the days of the Son of Man, but you will not see it. **23**Men will tell you, 'There he is!' or 'Here he is!' Do not go running off after them. **24**For the Son of Man in his day*c* will be like the lightning, which flashes and lights up the sky from one end to the other. **25**But first he must suffer many things and be rejected by this generation.

26"Just as it was in the days of Noah, so also will it be in the days of the Son of Man. **27**People were eating, drinking, marrying and being given in marriage up to the day Noah entered the ark. Then the flood came and destroyed them all.

28"It was the same in the days of Lot. People were eating and drinking, buying and selling, planting and building. **29**But the day Lot left Sodom, fire and sulfur rained down from heaven and destroyed them all.

30"It will be just like this on the day the Son of Man is revealed. **31**On that day no one who is on the roof of his house, with his goods inside, should go down to get them. Likewise, no one in the field should go back for anything. **32**Remember Lot's wife! **33**Whoever tries to keep his life will lose it, and whoever loses his life will preserve it. **34**I tell you, on that night two people will be in one bed; one will be taken and the other left. **35**Two women will be grinding grain together; one will be taken and the other left.*d*"

37"Where, Lord?" they asked.

He replied, "Where there is a dead body, there the vultures will gather."

The Parable of the Persistent Widow

18 Then Jesus told his disciples a parable to show them that they should always pray and not give up. **2**He said: "In a certain town there was a judge who neither feared God nor cared about men. **3**And there was a widow in that town who kept coming to him with the plea, 'Grant me justice against my adversary.'

4"For some time he refused. But finally he said to himself, 'Even though I don't fear God or care about men, **5**yet because this widow keeps bothering me, I will see that she gets justice, so that she won't eventually wear me out with her coming!' "

6And the Lord said, "Listen to what the unjust judge says. **7**And will not God bring about justice for his chosen ones, who cry out to him day and night? Will he keep putting them off? **8**I tell you, he will see that they get justice, and quickly. However, when the Son of Man comes, will he find faith on the earth?"

The Parable of the Pharisee and the Tax Collector

9To some who were confident of their own righteousness and looked down on everybody else, Jesus told this parable: **10**"Two men went up to the temple to pray, one a Pharisee and the other a tax collector. **11**The Pharisee stood up and prayed about*e* himself: 'God, I thank you that I am not like other men—robbers, evildoers, adulterers—or even like this tax collector. **12**I fast twice a week and give a tenth of all I get.'

13"But the tax collector stood at a distance. He would not even look up to heav-

---

*a*12 The Greek word was used for various diseases affecting the skin—not necessarily leprosy.   *b*21 Or among   *c*24 Some manuscripts do not have *in his day.*   *d*35 Some manuscripts *left. 36Two men will be in the field; one will be taken and the other left.*   *e*11 Or *to*

LUKE 18–19

1113

en, but beat his breast and said, 'God, have mercy on me, a sinner.'

14"I tell you that this man, rather than the other, went home justified before God. For everyone who exalts himself will be humbled, and he who humbles himself will be exalted."

The Little Children and Jesus

15People were also bringing babies to Jesus to have him touch them. When the disciples saw this, they rebuked them. **16**But Jesus called the children to him and said, "Let the little children come to me, and do not hinder them, for the kingdom of God belongs to such as these. **17**I tell you the truth, anyone who will not receive the kingdom of God like a little child will never enter it."

The Rich Ruler

18A certain ruler asked him, "Good teacher, what must I do to inherit eternal life?"

19"Why do you call me good?" Jesus answered. "No one is good—except God alone. **20**You know the commandments: 'Do not commit adultery, do not murder, do not steal, do not give false testimony, honor your father and mother.'*a*"

21"All these I have kept since I was a boy," he said.

22When Jesus heard this, he said to him, "You still lack one thing. Sell everything you have and give to the poor, and you will have treasure in heaven. Then come, follow me."

23When he heard this, he became very sad, because he was a man of great wealth. **24**Jesus looked at him and said, "How hard it is for the rich to enter the kingdom of God! **25**Indeed, it is easier for a camel to go through the eye of a needle than for a rich man to enter the kingdom of God."

26Those who heard this asked, "Who then can be saved?"

27Jesus replied, "What is impossible with men is possible with God."

28Peter said to him, "We have left all we had to follow you!"

29"I tell you the truth," Jesus said to them, "no one who has left home or wife or brothers or parents or children for the sake of the kingdom of God **30**will fail to receive many times as much in this age and, in the age to come, eternal life."

Jesus Again Predicts His Death

31Jesus took the Twelve aside and told them, "We are going up to Jerusalem, and everything that is written by the prophets about the Son of Man will be fulfilled. **32**He will be handed over to the Gentiles. They will mock him, insult him, spit on him, flog him and kill him. **33**On the third day he will rise again."

34The disciples did not understand any of this. Its meaning was hidden from them, and they did not know what he was talking about.

A Blind Beggar Receives His Sight

35As Jesus approached Jericho, a blind man was sitting by the roadside begging. **36**When he heard the crowd going by, he asked what was happening. **37**They told him, "Jesus of Nazareth is passing by."

38He called out, "Jesus, Son of David, have mercy on me!"

39Those who led the way rebuked him and told him to be quiet, but he shouted all the more, "Son of David, have mercy on me!"

40Jesus stopped and ordered the man to be brought to him. When he came near, Jesus asked him, **41**"What do you want me to do for you?"

"Lord, I want to see," he replied.

42Jesus said to him, "Receive your sight; your faith has healed you." **43**Immediately he received his sight and followed Jesus, praising God. When all the people saw it, they also praised God.

Zacchaeus the Tax Collector

19 Jesus entered Jericho and was passing through. **2**A man was there by the name of Zacchaeus; he was a chief tax collector and was wealthy. **3**He wanted to see who Jesus was, but being a short man he could not, because of the crowd. **4**So he ran ahead and climbed a sycamore-fig tree to see him, since Jesus was coming that way.

5When Jesus reached the spot, he looked up and said to him, "Zacchaeus, come down immediately. I must stay at your house today." **6**So he came down at once and welcomed him gladly.

7All the people saw this and began to mutter, "He has gone to be the guest of a 'sinner.'"

8But Zacchaeus stood up and said to the Lord, "Look, Lord! Here and now I give

a20 Exodus 20:12-16; Deut. 5:16-20

half of my possessions to the poor, and if I have cheated anybody out of anything, I will pay back four times the amount."

9Jesus said to him, "Today salvation has come to this house, because this man, too, is a son of Abraham. 10For the Son of Man came to seek and to save what was lost."

The Parable of the Ten Minas

11While they were listening to this, he went on to tell them a parable, because he was near Jerusalem and the people thought that the kingdom of God was going to appear at once. 12He said: "A man of noble birth went to a distant country to

---

WEDNESDAY

VERSE FOR THE DAY:	AUTHOR:	PASSAGE FOR THE DAY:
Luke 18:22	Thomas Hale	Luke 18:18–30

Dim Lights, Glittering Goods

IT IS hard for friends back home to appreciate just how rich even the poorest missionaries are compared with those around them. Our light is dimmed by the glitter of our goods. We are asked every day for a shirt, money, a tin can, a pair of old shoes, food. If we give to them who ask, we have "rice Christians" and a bigger crowd at our door the next day. If we say no, we feel uneasy because we know full well there are seven shirts in the closet we don't really need. The solution for some has been to sell all and live at the level of their neighbors. The rest of us have managed to strike a compromise between that ideal and what we euphemistically call practicality. I am not implying that we are all called to possess nothing, but I am suggesting that if we did, it would help clarify many of Jesus' sayings pertaining not only to poverty but also to discipleship. We can transform everything Jesus said into symbols and metaphors or we can qualify it into thin air; however, in the end the words remain, "Give to the one who asks you, and do not turn away from the one who wants to borrow from you" (Matthew 5:42); "sell everything you have and give to the poor . . . Then come, follow me" (Mark 10:21).

Surely there is a clue here as to how we might remove the barrier between our wealth and their poverty, a barrier that obscures our Christian testimony. Yet in our experience, problems more basic than wealth affect our Christian testimony. Before worrying ourselves over how many shirts to give and how many to keep, we should make sure we are in a place where we can hear what God is saying to us and that we would be willing to "sell everything" if he told us to. If we have really died to self and aren't just kidding ourselves, and if the compassion of Christ is discernible in our lives, then the number of shirts we give and keep is no longer so important, and the barriers created by our wealth largely disappear.

Additional Scripture Readings:
Matthew 5:38–42; Romans 6:1–14

Go to page 1116 for your next devotional reading.

have himself appointed king and then to return. ¹³So he called ten of his servants and gave them ten minas.ᵃ 'Put this money to work,' he said, 'until I come back.'

¹⁴"But his subjects hated him and sent a delegation after him to say, 'We don't want this man to be our king.'

¹⁵"He was made king, however, and returned home. Then he sent for the servants to whom he had given the money, in order to find out what they had gained with it.

¹⁶"The first one came and said, 'Sir, your mina has earned ten more.'

¹⁷"'Well done, my good servant!' his master replied. 'Because you have been trustworthy in a very small matter, take charge of ten cities.'

¹⁸"The second came and said, 'Sir, your mina has earned five more.'

¹⁹"His master answered, 'You take charge of five cities.'

²⁰"Then another servant came and said, 'Sir, here is your mina; I have kept it laid away in a piece of cloth. ²¹I was afraid of you, because you are a hard man. You take out what you did not put in and reap what you did not sow.'

²²"His master replied, 'I will judge you by your own words, you wicked servant! You knew, did you, that I am a hard man, taking out what I did not put in, and reaping what I did not sow? ²³Why then didn't you put my money on deposit, so that when I came back, I could have collected it with interest?'

²⁴"Then he said to those standing by, 'Take his mina away from him and give it to the one who has ten minas.'

²⁵"'Sir,' they said, 'he already has ten!'

²⁶"He replied, 'I tell you that to everyone who has, more will be given, but as for the one who has nothing, even what he has will be taken away. ²⁷But those enemies of mine who did not want me to be king over them — bring them here and kill them in front of me.'"

The Triumphal Entry

²⁸After Jesus had said this, he went on ahead, going up to Jerusalem. ²⁹As he approached Bethphage and Bethany at the hill called the Mount of Olives, he sent two of his disciples, saying to them, ³⁰"Go to the village ahead of you, and as you enter it, you will find a colt tied there, which no one has ever ridden. Untie it and bring it here. ³¹If anyone asks you, 'Why are you

untying it?' tell him, 'The Lord needs it.'"

³²Those who were sent ahead went and found it just as he had told them. ³³As they were untying the colt, its owners asked them, "Why are you untying the colt?"

³⁴They replied, "The Lord needs it."

³⁵They brought it to Jesus, threw their cloaks on the colt and put Jesus on it. ³⁶As he went along, people spread their cloaks on the road.

³⁷When he came near the place where the road goes down the Mount of Olives, the whole crowd of disciples began joyfully to praise God in loud voices for all the miracles they had seen:

³⁸"Blessed is the king who comes in the name of the Lord!"ᵇ

"Peace in heaven and glory in the highest!"

³⁹Some of the Pharisees in the crowd said to Jesus, "Teacher, rebuke your disciples!"

⁴⁰"I tell you," he replied, "if they keep quiet, the stones will cry out."

⁴¹As he approached Jerusalem and saw the city, he wept over it ⁴²and said, "If you, even you, had only known on this day what would bring you peace — but now it is hidden from your eyes. ⁴³The days will come upon you when your enemies will build an embankment against you and encircle you and hem you in on every side. ⁴⁴They will dash you to the ground, you and the children within your walls. They will not leave one stone on another, because you did not recognize the time of God's coming to you."

Jesus at the Temple

⁴⁵Then he entered the temple area and began driving out those who were selling. ⁴⁶"It is written," he said to them, "'My house will be a house of prayer'ᶜ; but you have made it 'a den of robbers.'ᵈ"

⁴⁷Every day he was teaching at the temple. But the chief priests, the teachers of the law and the leaders among the people were trying to kill him. ⁴⁸Yet they could not find any way to do it, because all the people hung on his words.

The Authority of Jesus Questioned

20 One day as he was teaching the people in the temple courts and preaching the gospel, the chief priests

---

ᵃ13 A mina was about three months' wages.   ᵇ38 Psalm 118:26   ᶜ46 Isaiah 56:7   ᵈ46 Jer. 7:11

and the teachers of the law, together with the elders, came up to him. ²"Tell us by what authority you are doing these things," they said. "Who gave you this authority?"

³He replied, "I will also ask you a question. Tell me, ⁴John's baptism—was it from heaven, or from men?"

⁵They discussed it among themselves and said, "If we say, 'From heaven,' he will ask, 'Why didn't you believe him?' ⁶But if we say, 'From men,' all the people will stone us, because they are persuaded that John was a prophet."

⁷So they answered, "We don't know where it was from."

⁸Jesus said, "Neither will I tell you by what authority I am doing these things."

The Parable of the Tenants

⁹He went on to tell the people this parable: "A man planted a vineyard, rented it to some farmers and went away for a long time. ¹⁰At harvest time he sent a servant to the tenants so they would give him some of the fruit of the vineyard. But the tenants beat him and sent him away empty-handed. ¹¹He sent another servant, but that one

---

THURSDAY

VERSE FOR THE DAY:	*AUTHOR:*	*PASSAGE FOR THE DAY:*
Luke 19:8	Jim Conway	Luke 19:1–10

Overwhelming Acceptance

ZACCHAEUS was fascinated with Jesus. Perhaps he was awed by his power with the people, or maybe he saw in Jesus an opportunity for personal wholeness.

As Jesus moved through the town, he saw Zacchaeus up in a tree. But Jesus saw more than that. He saw [as Duncan Buchanan puts it] "a human being, unloved, unloving, bruised and hurt by the circumstances of life, unsuited to his wealth, . . . unacceptable to those around him, unacceptable to himself."

Jesus then did the unexpected, the dramatic. He invited himself to Zacchaeus's house for a meal. Jesus' acceptance of this shriveled little man so overwhelmed Zacchaeus that he repented on the spot and promised a changed lifestyle. "Here and now I give half of my possessions to the poor, and if I have cheated anybody out of anything, I will pay back four times the amount."

Jesus responded with a statement of affirmation and forgiveness that reinstated Zacchaeus not only with God, but with his community: "Today salvation has come to this house." What a great transformation! This man, so rejected by others and himself, found a new acceptance of himself and with God and others.

As you read accounts of Jesus working with a great variety of people, courageously talk to Jesus as you would with any human being. Tell him your needs and ask him to bring about in you the same feelings of love and acceptance that you see taking place in the people of the New Testament.

Additional Scripture Readings:
Luke 8:26–39; John 7:53—8:11

Go to page 1122 for your next devotional reading.

also they beat and treated shamefully and sent away empty-handed. ¹²He sent still a third, and they wounded him and threw him out.

¹³"Then the owner of the vineyard said, 'What shall I do? I will send my son, whom I love; perhaps they will respect him.'

¹⁴"But when the tenants saw him, they talked the matter over. 'This is the heir,' they said. 'Let's kill him, and the inheritance will be ours.' ¹⁵So they threw him out of the vineyard and killed him.

"What then will the owner of the vineyard do to them? ¹⁶He will come and kill those tenants and give the vineyard to others."

When the people heard this, they said, "May this never be!"

¹⁷Jesus looked directly at them and asked, "Then what is the meaning of that which is written:

" 'The stone the builders rejected
   has become the capstone[a]'[b]?

¹⁸Everyone who falls on that stone will be broken to pieces, but he on whom it falls will be crushed."

¹⁹The teachers of the law and the chief priests looked for a way to arrest him immediately, because they knew he had spoken this parable against them. But they were afraid of the people.

Paying Taxes to Caesar

²⁰Keeping a close watch on him, they sent spies, who pretended to be honest. They hoped to catch Jesus in something he said so that they might hand him over to the power and authority of the governor. ²¹So the spies questioned him: "Teacher, we know that you speak and teach what is right, and that you do not show partiality but teach the way of God in accordance with the truth. ²²Is it right for us to pay taxes to Caesar or not?"

²³He saw through their duplicity and said to them, ²⁴"Show me a denarius. Whose portrait and inscription are on it?"

²⁵"Caesar's," they replied.

He said to them, "Then give to Caesar what is Caesar's, and to God what is God's."

²⁶They were unable to trap him in what he had said there in public. And astonished by his answer, they became silent.

The Resurrection and Marriage

²⁷Some of the Sadducees, who say there is no resurrection, came to Jesus with a question. ²⁸"Teacher," they said, "Moses wrote for us that if a man's brother dies and leaves a wife but no children, the man must marry the widow and have children for his brother. ²⁹Now there were seven brothers. The first one married a woman and died childless. ³⁰The second ³¹and then the third married her, and in the same way the seven died, leaving no children. ³²Finally, the woman died too. ³³Now then, at the resurrection whose wife will she be, since the seven were married to her?"

³⁴Jesus replied, "The people of this age marry and are given in marriage. ³⁵But those who are considered worthy of taking part in that age and in the resurrection from the dead will neither marry nor be given in marriage, ³⁶and they can no longer die; for they are like the angels. They are God's children, since they are children of the resurrection. ³⁷But in the account of the bush, even Moses showed that the dead rise, for he calls the Lord 'the God of Abraham, and the God of Isaac, and the God of Jacob.'[c] ³⁸He is not the God of the dead, but of the living, for to him all are alive."

³⁹Some of the teachers of the law responded, "Well said, teacher!" ⁴⁰And no one dared to ask him any more questions.

Whose Son Is the Christ?

⁴¹Then Jesus said to them, "How is it that they say the Christ[d] is the Son of David? ⁴²David himself declares in the Book of Psalms:

" 'The Lord said to my Lord:
   "Sit at my right hand
⁴³until I make your enemies
   a footstool for your feet." '[e]

⁴⁴David calls him 'Lord.' How then can he be his son?"

⁴⁵While all the people were listening, Jesus said to his disciples, ⁴⁶"Beware of the teachers of the law. They like to walk around in flowing robes and love to be greeted in the marketplaces and have the most important seats in the synagogues and the places of honor at banquets. ⁴⁷They devour widows' houses and for a show make lengthy prayers. Such men will be punished most severely."

---

a17 Or *cornerstone*   *b17* Psalm 118:22   *c37* Exodus 3:6   *d41* Or *Messiah*   *e43* Psalm 110:1

The Widow's Offering

21 As he looked up, Jesus saw the rich putting their gifts into the temple treasury. ²He also saw a poor widow put in two very small copper coins.ᵃ ³"I tell you the truth," he said, "this poor widow has put in more than all the others. ⁴All these people gave their gifts out of their wealth; but she out of her poverty put in all she had to live on."

Signs of the End of the Age

⁵Some of his disciples were remarking about how the temple was adorned with beautiful stones and with gifts dedicated to God. But Jesus said, ⁶"As for what you see here, the time will come when not one stone will be left on another; every one of them will be thrown down."

⁷"Teacher," they asked, "when will these things happen? And what will be the sign that they are about to take place?"

⁸He replied: "Watch out that you are not deceived. For many will come in my name, claiming, 'I am he,' and, 'The time is near.' Do not follow them. ⁹When you hear of wars and revolutions, do not be frightened. These things must happen first, but the end will not come right away."

¹⁰Then he said to them: "Nation will rise against nation, and kingdom against kingdom. ¹¹There will be great earthquakes, famines and pestilences in various places, and fearful events and great signs from heaven.

¹²"But before all this, they will lay hands on you and persecute you. They will deliver you to synagogues and prisons, and you will be brought before kings and governors, and all on account of my name. ¹³This will result in your being witnesses to them. ¹⁴But make up your mind not to worry beforehand how you will defend yourselves. ¹⁵For I will give you words and wisdom that none of your adversaries will be able to resist or contradict. ¹⁶You will be betrayed even by parents, brothers, relatives and friends, and they will put some of you to death. ¹⁷All men will hate you because of me. ¹⁸But not a hair of your head will perish. ¹⁹By standing firm you will gain life.

²⁰"When you see Jerusalem being surrounded by armies, you will know that its desolation is near. ²¹Then let those who are in Judea flee to the mountains, let those in the city get out, and let those in the country not enter the city. ²²For this is the time of punishment in fulfillment of all that has been written. ²³How dreadful it will be in those days for pregnant women and nursing mothers! There will be great distress in the land and wrath against this people. ²⁴They will fall by the sword and will be taken as prisoners to all the nations. Jerusalem will be trampled on by the Gentiles until the times of the Gentiles are fulfilled.

²⁵"There will be signs in the sun, moon and stars. On the earth, nations will be in anguish and perplexity at the roaring and tossing of the sea. ²⁶Men will faint from terror, apprehensive of what is coming on the world, for the heavenly bodies will be shaken. ²⁷At that time they will see the Son of Man coming in a cloud with power and great glory. ²⁸When these things begin to take place, stand up and lift up your heads, because your redemption is drawing near."

²⁹He told them this parable: "Look at the fig tree and all the trees. ³⁰When they sprout leaves, you can see for yourselves and know that summer is near. ³¹Even so, when you see these things happening, you know that the kingdom of God is near.

³²"I tell you the truth, this generationᵇ will certainly not pass away until all these things have happened. ³³Heaven and earth will pass away, but my words will never pass away.

³⁴"Be careful, or your hearts will be weighed down with dissipation, drunkenness and the anxieties of life, and that day will close on you unexpectedly like a trap. ³⁵For it will come upon all those who live on the face of the whole earth. ³⁶Be always on the watch, and pray that you may be able to escape all that is about to happen, and that you may be able to stand before the Son of Man."

³⁷Each day Jesus was teaching at the temple, and each evening he went out to spend the night on the hill called the Mount of Olives, ³⁸and all the people came early in the morning to hear him at the temple.

Judas Agrees to Betray Jesus

22 Now the Feast of Unleavened Bread, called the Passover, was approaching, ²and the chief priests and the teachers of the law were looking for some

---

ᵃ2 Greek *two lepta*　ᵇ32 Or *race*

way to get rid of Jesus, for they were afraid of the people. ³Then Satan entered Judas, called Iscariot, one of the Twelve. ⁴And Judas went to the chief priests and the officers of the temple guard and discussed with them how he might betray Jesus. ⁵They were delighted and agreed to give him money. ⁶He consented, and watched for an opportunity to hand Jesus over to them when no crowd was present.

The Last Supper

⁷Then came the day of Unleavened Bread on which the Passover lamb had to be sacrificed. ⁸Jesus sent Peter and John, saying, "Go and make preparations for us to eat the Passover."

⁹"Where do you want us to prepare for it?" they asked.

¹⁰He replied, "As you enter the city, a man carrying a jar of water will meet you. Follow him to the house that he enters, ¹¹and say to the owner of the house, 'The Teacher asks: Where is the guest room, where I may eat the Passover with my disciples?' ¹²He will show you a large upper room, all furnished. Make preparations there."

¹³They left and found things just as Jesus had told them. So they prepared the Passover.

¹⁴When the hour came, Jesus and his apostles reclined at the table. ¹⁵And he said to them, "I have eagerly desired to eat this Passover with you before I suffer. ¹⁶For I tell you, I will not eat it again until it finds fulfillment in the kingdom of God."

¹⁷After taking the cup, he gave thanks and said, "Take this and divide it among you. ¹⁸For I tell you I will not drink again of the fruit of the vine until the kingdom of God comes."

¹⁹And he took bread, gave thanks and broke it, and gave it to them, saying, "This is my body given for you; do this in remembrance of me."

²⁰In the same way, after the supper he took the cup, saying, "This cup is the new covenant in my blood, which is poured out for you. ²¹But the hand of him who is going to betray me is with mine on the table. ²²The Son of Man will go as it has been decreed, but woe to that man who betrays him." ²³They began to question among themselves which of them it might be who would do this.

²⁴Also a dispute arose among them as to which of them was considered to be greatest. ²⁵Jesus said to them, "The kings of the Gentiles lord it over them; and those who exercise authority over them call themselves Benefactors. ²⁶But you are not to be like that. Instead, the greatest among you should be like the youngest, and the one who rules like the one who serves. ²⁷For who is greater, the one who is at the table or the one who serves? Is it not the one who is at the table? But I am among you as one who serves. ²⁸You are those who have stood by me in my trials. ²⁹And I confer on you a kingdom, just as my Father conferred one on me, ³⁰so that you may eat and drink at my table in my kingdom and sit on thrones, judging the twelve tribes of Israel.

³¹"Simon, Simon, Satan has asked to sift you*a* as wheat. ³²But I have prayed for you, Simon, that your faith may not fail. And when you have turned back, strengthen your brothers."

³³But he replied, "Lord, I am ready to go with you to prison and to death."

³⁴Jesus answered, "I tell you, Peter, before the rooster crows today, you will deny three times that you know me."

³⁵Then Jesus asked them, "When I sent you without purse, bag or sandals, did you lack anything?"

"Nothing," they answered.

³⁶He said to them, "But now if you have a purse, take it, and also a bag; and if you don't have a sword, sell your cloak and buy one. ³⁷It is written: 'And he was numbered with the transgressors'*b*; and I tell you that this must be fulfilled in me. Yes, what is written about me is reaching its fulfillment."

³⁸The disciples said, "See, Lord, here are two swords."

"That is enough," he replied.

Jesus Prays on the Mount of Olives

³⁹Jesus went out as usual to the Mount of Olives, and his disciples followed him. ⁴⁰On reaching the place, he said to them, "Pray that you will not fall into temptation." ⁴¹He withdrew about a stone's throw beyond them, knelt down and prayed, ⁴²"Father, if you are willing, take this cup from me; yet not my will, but yours be done." ⁴³An angel from heaven appeared to him and strengthened him. ⁴⁴And being in anguish, he prayed more

---

a31 The Greek is plural.   *b37* Isaiah 53:12

earnestly, and his sweat was like drops of blood falling to the ground.*a*

45When he rose from prayer and went back to the disciples, he found them asleep, exhausted from sorrow. **46**"Why are you sleeping?" he asked them. "Get up and pray so that you will not fall into temptation."

Jesus Arrested

47While he was still speaking a crowd came up, and the man who was called Judas, one of the Twelve, was leading them. He approached Jesus to kiss him, **48**but Jesus asked him, "Judas, are you betraying the Son of Man with a kiss?"

49When Jesus' followers saw what was going to happen, they said, "Lord, should we strike with our swords?" **50**And one of them struck the servant of the high priest, cutting off his right ear.

51But Jesus answered, "No more of this!" And he touched the man's ear and healed him.

52Then Jesus said to the chief priests, the officers of the temple guard, and the elders, who had come for him, "Am I leading a rebellion, that you have come with swords and clubs? **53**Every day I was with you in the temple courts, and you did not lay a hand on me. But this is your hour—when darkness reigns."

Peter Disowns Jesus

54Then seizing him, they led him away and took him into the house of the high priest. Peter followed at a distance. **55**But when they had kindled a fire in the middle of the courtyard and had sat down together, Peter sat down with them. **56**A servant girl saw him seated there in the firelight. She looked closely at him and said, "This man was with him."

57But he denied it. "Woman, I don't know him," he said.

58A little later someone else saw him and said, "You also are one of them."

"Man, I am not!" Peter replied.

59About an hour later another asserted, "Certainly this fellow was with him, for he is a Galilean."

60Peter replied, "Man, I don't know what you're talking about!" Just as he was speaking, the rooster crowed. **61**The Lord turned and looked straight at Peter. Then Peter remembered the word the Lord had spoken to him: "Before the rooster crows today, you will disown me three times." **62**And he went outside and wept bitterly.

The Guards Mock Jesus

63The men who were guarding Jesus began mocking and beating him. **64**They blindfolded him and demanded, "Prophesy! Who hit you?" **65**And they said many other insulting things to him.

Jesus Before Pilate and Herod

66At daybreak the council of the elders of the people, both the chief priests and teachers of the law, met together, and Jesus was led before them. **67**"If you are the Christ,*b*" they said, "tell us."

Jesus answered, "If I tell you, you will not believe me, **68**and if I asked you, you would not answer. **69**But from now on, the Son of Man will be seated at the right hand of the mighty God."

70They all asked, "Are you then the Son of God?"

He replied, "You are right in saying I am."

71Then they said, "Why do we need any more testimony? We have heard it from his own lips."

23 Then the whole assembly rose and led him off to Pilate. **2**And they began to accuse him, saying, "We have found this man subverting our nation. He opposes payment of taxes to Caesar and claims to be Christ,*c* a king."

3So Pilate asked Jesus, "Are you the king of the Jews?"

"Yes, it is as you say," Jesus replied.

4Then Pilate announced to the chief priests and the crowd, "I find no basis for a charge against this man."

5But they insisted, "He stirs up the people all over Judea*d* by his teaching. He started in Galilee and has come all the way here."

6On hearing this, Pilate asked if the man was a Galilean. **7**When he learned that Jesus was under Herod's jurisdiction, he sent him to Herod, who was also in Jerusalem at that time.

8When Herod saw Jesus, he was greatly pleased, because for a long time he had been wanting to see him. From what he had heard about him, he hoped to see him perform some miracle. **9**He plied him with many questions, but Jesus gave him no answer. **10**The chief priests and the teachers of the law were standing there, vehe-

---

*a*44 Some early manuscripts do not have verses 43 and 44. *b*67 Or *Messiah*   *c*2 Or *Messiah*; also in verses 35 and 39   *d*5 Or *over the land of the Jews* mently accusing him. **11**Then Herod and his soldiers ridiculed and mocked him. Dressing him in an elegant robe, they sent him back to Pilate. **12**That day Herod and Pilate became friends—before this they had been enemies.

13Pilate called together the chief priests, the rulers and the people, **14**and said to them, "You brought me this man as one who was inciting the people to rebellion. I have examined him in your presence and have found no basis for your charges against him. **15**Neither has Herod, for he sent him back to us; as you can see, he has done nothing to deserve death. **16**Therefore, I will punish him and then release him.*a*"

18With one voice they cried out, "Away with this man! Release Barabbas to us!" **19**(Barabbas had been thrown into prison for an insurrection in the city, and for murder.)

20Wanting to release Jesus, Pilate appealed to them again. **21**But they kept shouting, "Crucify him! Crucify him!"

22For the third time he spoke to them: "Why? What crime has this man committed? I have found in him no grounds for the death penalty. Therefore I will have him punished and then release him."

23But with loud shouts they insistently demanded that he be crucified, and their shouts prevailed. **24**So Pilate decided to grant their demand. **25**He released the man who had been thrown into prison for insurrection and murder, the one they asked for, and surrendered Jesus to their will.

The Crucifixion

26As they led him away, they seized Simon from Cyrene, who was on his way in from the country, and put the cross on him and made him carry it behind Jesus. **27**A large number of people followed him, including women who mourned and wailed for him. **28**Jesus turned and said to them, "Daughters of Jerusalem, do not weep for me; weep for yourselves and for your children. **29**For the time will come when you will say, 'Blessed are the barren women, the wombs that never bore and the breasts that never nursed!' **30**Then

" 'they will say to the mountains, "Fall on us!"

and to the hills, "Cover us!" '*b*

31For if men do these things when the tree is green, what will happen when it is dry?"

32Two other men, both criminals, were also led out with him to be executed. **33**When they came to the place called the Skull, there they crucified him, along with the criminals—one on his right, the other on his left. **34**Jesus said, "Father, forgive them, for they do not know what they are doing."*c* And they divided up his clothes by casting lots.

35The people stood watching, and the rulers even sneered at him. They said, "He saved others; let him save himself if he is the Christ of God, the Chosen One."

36The soldiers also came up and mocked him. They offered him wine vinegar **37**and said, "If you are the king of the Jews, save yourself."

38There was a written notice above him, which read: THIS IS THE KING OF THE JEWS.

39One of the criminals who hung there hurled insults at him: "Aren't you the Christ? Save yourself and us!"

40But the other criminal rebuked him. "Don't you fear God," he said, "since you are under the same sentence? **41**We are punished justly, for we are getting what our deeds deserve. But this man has done nothing wrong."

42Then he said, "Jesus, remember me when you come into your kingdom.*d*"

43Jesus answered him, "I tell you the truth, today you will be with me in paradise."

Jesus' Death

44It was now about the sixth hour, and darkness came over the whole land until the ninth hour, **45**for the sun stopped shining. And the curtain of the temple was torn in two. **46**Jesus called out with a loud voice, "Father, into your hands I commit my spirit." When he had said this, he breathed his last.

47The centurion, seeing what had happened, praised God and said, "Surely this was a righteous man." **48**When all the people who had gathered to witness this sight saw what took place, they beat their breasts and went away. **49**But all those who knew him, including the women who had followed him from Galilee, stood at a distance, watching these things.

---

*a*16 Some manuscripts *him.*" *17Now he was obliged to release one man to them at the Feast.*   *b*30 Hosea 10:8   *c*34 Some early manuscripts do not have this sentence.   *d*42 Some manuscripts *come with your kingly power*

Jesus' Burial

50Now there was a man named Joseph, a member of the Council, a good and upright man, **51**who had not consented to their decision and action. He came from the Judean town of Arimathea and he was waiting for the kingdom of God. **52**Going to Pilate, he asked for Jesus' body. **53**Then he took it down, wrapped it in linen cloth and placed it in a tomb cut in the rock, one in which no one had yet been laid. **54**It was Preparation Day, and the Sabbath was about to begin.

55The women who had come with Jesus from Galilee followed Joseph and saw the tomb and how his body was laid in it. **56**Then they went home and prepared spices and perfumes. But they rested on the Sabbath in obedience to the commandment.

The Resurrection

24 On the first day of the week, very early in the morning, the women took the spices they had prepared and went to the tomb. **2**They found the stone rolled away from the tomb, **3**but when they entered, they did not find the body of the Lord Jesus. **4**While they were wondering about this, suddenly two men in clothes that gleamed like lightning stood beside them. **5**In their fright the women bowed down with their faces to the ground, but the men said to them, "Why do you look for the living among the dead? **6**He is not here; he has risen! Remember how he told you, while he was

---

FRIDAY

VERSE FOR THE DAY: AUTHOR: PASSAGE FOR THE DAY:
Luke 23:34   Larry Crabb   Luke 23:32–43

The Mind of Christ

IT'S more than interesting to notice how unblemished humanity responds to aloneness and mistreatment. As our Lord hung on the cross, he didn't require others to treat him fairly. Even though he was alone and wrongly treated beyond imagination and even though he mightily wished his pain could be avoided, his commitment to the Father's purpose and to rescuing us from judgment never became secondary to his desire for immediate relief. It would never have occurred to him to use suffering to excuse self-interest.

When *we* hurt, however, we *do* use suffering to excuse our self-interest. Self-centeredness seems understandable. A command to think of another's happiness seems cruel and absurd. When our Lord hurt, other-centeredness came naturally: "Father, forgive them, for they do not know what they are doing" [Luke 23:34]. In us, loneliness and abuse justify whatever effort we make to recover our sense of dignity and worth, to preserve our meager quality of life. In Christ, however, loneliness and abuse provided a backdrop for highlighting the difference between a character that justifies self-interest and one that delights to love: "Today you will be with me in paradise" [Luke 23:43].

Additional Scripture Readings: *Go to page 1124 for your next*
Romans 12:9–16;   *devotional reading.*
Philippians 2:1–11

still with you in Galilee: **7**'The Son of Man must be delivered into the hands of sinful men, be crucified and on the third day be raised again.' " **8**Then they remembered his words.

9When they came back from the tomb, they told all these things to the Eleven and to all the others. **10**It was Mary Magdalene, Joanna, Mary the mother of James, and the others with them who told this to the apostles. **11**But they did not believe the women, because their words seemed to them like nonsense. **12**Peter, however, got up and ran to the tomb. Bending over, he saw the strips of linen lying by themselves, and he went away, wondering to himself what had happened.

On the Road to Emmaus

13Now that same day two of them were going to a village called Emmaus, about seven miles*a* from Jerusalem. **14**They were talking with each other about everything that had happened. **15**As they talked and discussed these things with each other, Jesus himself came up and walked along with them; **16**but they were kept from recognizing him.

17He asked them, "What are you discussing together as you walk along?"

They stood still, their faces downcast. **18**One of them, named Cleopas, asked him, "Are you only a visitor to Jerusalem and do not know the things that have happened there in these days?"

19"What things?" he asked.

"About Jesus of Nazareth," they replied. "He was a prophet, powerful in word and deed before God and all the people. **20**The chief priests and our rulers handed him over to be sentenced to death, and they crucified him; **21**but we had hoped that he was the one who was going to redeem Israel. And what is more, it is the third day since all this took place. **22**In addition, some of our women amazed us. They went to the tomb early this morning **23**but didn't find his body. They came and told us that they had seen a vision of angels, who said he was alive. **24**Then some of our companions went to the tomb and found it just as the women had said, but him they did not see."

25He said to them, "How foolish you are, and how slow of heart to believe all that the prophets have spoken! **26**Did not the Christ*b* have to suffer these things and then enter his glory?" **27**And begin-

ning with Moses and all the Prophets, he explained to them what was said in all the Scriptures concerning himself.

28As they approached the village to which they were going, Jesus acted as if he were going farther. **29**But they urged him strongly, "Stay with us, for it is nearly evening; the day is almost over." So he went in to stay with them.

30When he was at the table with them, he took bread, gave thanks, broke it and began to give it to them. **31**Then their eyes were opened and they recognized him, and he disappeared from their sight. **32**They asked each other, "Were not our hearts burning within us while he talked with us on the road and opened the Scriptures to us?"

33They got up and returned at once to Jerusalem. There they found the Eleven and those with them, assembled together **34**and saying, "It is true! The Lord has risen and has appeared to Simon." **35**Then the two told what had happened on the way, and how Jesus was recognized by them when he broke the bread.

Jesus Appears to the Disciples

36While they were still talking about this, Jesus himself stood among them and said to them, "Peace be with you."

37They were startled and frightened, thinking they saw a ghost. **38**He said to them, "Why are you troubled, and why do doubts rise in your minds? **39**Look at my hands and my feet. It is I myself! Touch me and see; a ghost does not have flesh and bones, as you see I have."

40When he had said this, he showed them his hands and feet. **41**And while they still did not believe it because of joy and amazement, he asked them, "Do you have anything here to eat?" **42**They gave him a piece of broiled fish, **43**and he took it and ate it in their presence.

44He said to them, "This is what I told you while I was still with you: Everything must be fulfilled that is written about me in the Law of Moses, the Prophets and the Psalms."

45Then he opened their minds so they could understand the Scriptures. **46**He told them, "This is what is written: The Christ will suffer and rise from the dead on the third day, **47**and repentance and forgiveness of sins will be preached in his name to all nations, beginning at Jerusalem. **48**You are witnesses of these things. **49**I am

a13 Greek *sixty stadia* (about 11 kilometers)   *b26* Or *Messiah*; also in verse 46

WEEKENDING

REJOICE

You have a present Savior with whom to meet
and wrestle a present death. Surely, in such
company you need not ignore this enemy as the
fearful world does. And the more you recognize
death around you, the sweeter will seem the
love of the Lord. You will know him better; you
will realize the pragmatic and immediate power
of his salvation—for wherever death is, there
can also be the manifestation of his glorious
victory. And you, child—you may stride with
freedom, even *through* the difficulties, grief and
the hard road, mourning and bereavement.

– *Walter Wangerin, Jr.*

REVIVE

Saturday: Psalm 42:5–11
Sunday: 1 Corinthians 15:55–57

Go to page 1128 for your next devotional reading.

going to send you what my Father has promised; but stay in the city until you have been clothed with power from on high."

The Ascension

50When he had led them out to the vicinity of Bethany, he lifted up his hands and blessed them. **51**While he was blessing them, he left them and was taken up into heaven. **52**Then they worshiped him and returned to Jerusalem with great joy. **53**And they stayed continually at the temple, praising God.

JOHN writes this Gospel to present Jesus, the powerful Son of God, who comes in human flesh, gives his life on the cross, and then returns to the Father—all with a view that we may believe in him and receive eternal life. His coming shows us how much the Father and the Son love us, and his parting command is that we should show the same sacrificial love to one another. As you read this book, be sure that you believe that Jesus is the Christ, the Son of God, and promise him that you will love others as he loves you.

JOHN

The Word Became Flesh

1 In the beginning was the Word, and the Word was with God, and the Word was God. **2**He was with God in the beginning.

3Through him all things were made; without him nothing was made that has been made. **4**In him was life, and that life was the light of men. **5**The light shines in the darkness, but the darkness has not understood[a] it.

6There came a man who was sent from God; his name was John. **7**He came as a witness to testify concerning that light, so that through him all men might believe. **8**He himself was not the light; he came only as a witness to the light. **9**The true light that gives light to every man was coming into the world.[b]

[a]5 Or *darkness, and the darkness has not overcome every man who comes into the world*

[b]9 Or *This was the true light that gives light to*

[10]He was in the world, and though the world was made through him, the world did not recognize him. [11]He came to that which was his own, but his own did not receive him. [12]Yet to all who received him, to those who believed in his name, he gave the right to become children of God— [13]children born not of natural descent,[a] nor of human decision or a husband's will, but born of God.

[14]The Word became flesh and made his dwelling among us. We have seen his glory, the glory of the One and Only,[b] who came from the Father, full of grace and truth.

[15]John testifies concerning him. He cries out, saying, "This was he of whom I said, 'He who comes after me has surpassed me because he was before me.'" [16]From the fullness of his grace we have all received one blessing after another. [17]For the law was given through Moses; grace and truth came through Jesus Christ. [18]No one has ever seen God, but God the One and Only,[b,c] who is at the Father's side, has made him known.

John the Baptist Denies Being the Christ

[19]Now this was John's testimony when the Jews of Jerusalem sent priests and Levites to ask him who he was. [20]He did not fail to confess, but confessed freely, "I am not the Christ.[d]"

[21]They asked him, "Then who are you? Are you Elijah?"

He said, "I am not."

"Are you the Prophet?"

He answered, "No."

[22]Finally they said, "Who are you? Give us an answer to take back to those who sent us. What do you say about yourself?"

[23]John replied in the words of Isaiah the prophet, "I am the voice of one calling in the desert, 'Make straight the way for the Lord.'"[e]

[24]Now some Pharisees who had been sent [25]questioned him, "Why then do you baptize if you are not the Christ, nor Elijah, nor the Prophet?"

[26]"I baptize with[f] water," John replied, "but among you stands one you do not know. [27]He is the one who comes after me, the thongs of whose sandals I am not worthy to untie."

[28]This all happened at Bethany on the other side of the Jordan, where John was baptizing.

Jesus the Lamb of God

[29]The next day John saw Jesus coming toward him and said, "Look, the Lamb of God, who takes away the sin of the world! [30]This is the one I meant when I said, 'A man who comes after me has surpassed me because he was before me.' [31]I myself did not know him, but the reason I came baptizing with water was that he might be revealed to Israel."

[32]Then John gave this testimony: "I saw the Spirit come down from heaven as a dove and remain on him. [33]I would not have known him, except that the one who sent me to baptize with water told me, 'The man on whom you see the Spirit come down and remain is he who will baptize with the Holy Spirit.' [34]I have seen and I testify that this is the Son of God."

Jesus' First Disciples

[35]The next day John was there again with two of his disciples. [36]When he saw Jesus passing by, he said, "Look, the Lamb of God!"

[37]When the two disciples heard him say this, they followed Jesus. [38]Turning around, Jesus saw them following and asked, "What do you want?"

They said, "Rabbi" (which means Teacher), "where are you staying?"

[39]"Come," he replied, "and you will see."

So they went and saw where he was staying, and spent that day with him. It was about the tenth hour.

[40]Andrew, Simon Peter's brother, was one of the two who heard what John had said and who had followed Jesus. [41]The first thing Andrew did was to find his brother Simon and tell him, "We have found the Messiah" (that is, the Christ). [42]And he brought him to Jesus.

Jesus looked at him and said, "You are Simon son of John. You will be called Cephas" (which, when translated, is Peter[g]).

Jesus Calls Philip and Nathanael

[43]The next day Jesus decided to leave for Galilee. Finding Philip, he said to him, "Follow me."

---

[a]13 Greek of bloods   [b]14,18 Or the Only Begotten begotten) Son   [d]20 Or Messiah. "The Christ" (Greek) Anointed One"; also in verse 25.   [e]23 Isaiah 40:3 Cephas (Aramaic) and Peter (Greek) mean rock.   [c]18 Some manuscripts but the only (or only) and "the Messiah" (Hebrew) both mean "the   [f]26 Or in; also in verses 31 and 33   [g]42 Both

⁴⁴Philip, like Andrew and Peter, was from the town of Bethsaida. ⁴⁵Philip found Nathanael and told him, "We have found the one Moses wrote about in the Law, and about whom the prophets also wrote—Jesus of Nazareth, the son of Joseph."

⁴⁶"Nazareth! Can anything good come from there?" Nathanael asked.

"Come and see," said Philip.

⁴⁷When Jesus saw Nathanael approaching, he said of him, "Here is a true Israelite, in whom there is nothing false."

⁴⁸"How do you know me?" Nathanael asked.

Jesus answered, "I saw you while you were still under the fig tree before Philip called you."

⁴⁹Then Nathanael declared, "Rabbi, you are the Son of God; you are the King of Israel."

⁵⁰Jesus said, "You believeᵃ because I told you I saw you under the fig tree. You shall see greater things than that." ⁵¹He then added, "I tell youᵇ the truth, youᵇ shall see heaven open, and the angels of God ascending and descending on the Son of Man."

Jesus Changes Water to Wine

2 On the third day a wedding took place at Cana in Galilee. Jesus' mother was there, ²and Jesus and his disciples had

ᵃ50 Or *Do you believe . . . ?*   ᵇ51 The Greek is plural.

MONDAY

VERSE FOR THE DAY:
John 2:16

AUTHOR:
Stephen Arterburn and
David Stoop

PASSAGE FOR THE DAY:
John 2:13–17

Suppressed Anger

A LOT of people, especially Christians, have a problem with Jesus being angry. They may call his outburst in the temple "righteous indignation," but they won't admit that he was angry because "everybody knows that anger is a sin."

This mentality has caused many men to push their anger out of bounds in another direction—denying it, suppressing it, or pretending it isn't there, because to them it's wrong to be angry . . . Suppressed anger is just as harmful to an angry man as explosive hostility and aggression is to those around an angry man.

Jesus didn't suppress his anger any more than he exploded with rage that day in the temple. His anger was up front, out in the open. He responded to the situation quickly, positively and appropriately, then went on with his business.

If a man buries his anger inside, he's only storing up pressure for a later implosion (hurting himself) and/or explosion (hurting others). If he doesn't bring his anger to the surface and deal with it, someday, somewhere, somehow it will express itself in an out-of-bounds manner, and somebody will get hurt.

Additional Scripture Readings:
Ephesians 4:25–32; James 1:19–21

Go to page 1130 for your next devotional reading.

also been invited to the wedding. ³When the wine was gone, Jesus' mother said to him, "They have no more wine."

⁴"Dear woman, why do you involve me?" Jesus replied. "My time has not yet come."

⁵His mother said to the servants, "Do whatever he tells you."

⁶Nearby stood six stone water jars, the kind used by the Jews for ceremonial washing, each holding from twenty to thirty gallons.ᵃ

⁷Jesus said to the servants, "Fill the jars with water"; so they filled them to the brim.

⁸Then he told them, "Now draw some out and take it to the master of the banquet."

They did so, ⁹and the master of the banquet tasted the water that had been turned into wine. He did not realize where it had come from, though the servants who had drawn the water knew. Then he called the bridegroom aside ¹⁰and said, "Everyone brings out the choice wine first and then the cheaper wine after the guests have had too much to drink; but you have saved the best till now."

¹¹This, the first of his miraculous signs, Jesus performed at Cana in Galilee. He thus revealed his glory, and his disciples put their faith in him.

Jesus Clears the Temple

¹²After this he went down to Capernaum with his mother and brothers and his disciples. There they stayed for a few days.

¹³When it was almost time for the Jewish Passover, Jesus went up to Jerusalem. ¹⁴In the temple courts he found men selling cattle, sheep and doves, and others sitting at tables exchanging money. ¹⁵So he made a whip out of cords, and drove all from the temple area, both sheep and cattle; he scattered the coins of the money changers and overturned their tables. ¹⁶To those who sold doves he said, "Get these out of here! How dare you turn my Father's house into a market!"

¹⁷His disciples remembered that it is written: "Zeal for your house will consume me."ᵇ

¹⁸Then the Jews demanded of him, "What miraculous sign can you show us to prove your authority to do all this?"

¹⁹Jesus answered them, "Destroy this temple, and I will raise it again in three days."

²⁰The Jews replied, "It has taken forty-six years to build this temple, and you are going to raise it in three days?" ²¹But the temple he had spoken of was his body. ²²After he was raised from the dead, his disciples recalled what he had said. Then they believed the Scripture and the words that Jesus had spoken.

²³Now while he was in Jerusalem at the Passover Feast, many people saw the miraculous signs he was doing and believed in his name.ᶜ ²⁴But Jesus would not entrust himself to them, for he knew all men. ²⁵He did not need man's testimony about man, for he knew what was in a man.

Jesus Teaches Nicodemus

3 Now there was a man of the Pharisees named Nicodemus, a member of the Jewish ruling council. ²He came to Jesus at night and said, "Rabbi, we know you are a teacher who has come from God. For no one could perform the miraculous signs you are doing if God were not with him."

³In reply Jesus declared, "I tell you the truth, no one can see the kingdom of God unless he is born again.ᵈ"

⁴"How can a man be born when he is old?" Nicodemus asked. "Surely he cannot enter a second time into his mother's womb to be born!"

⁵Jesus answered, "I tell you the truth, no one can enter the kingdom of God unless he is born of water and the Spirit. ⁶Flesh gives birth to flesh, but the Spiritᵉ gives birth to spirit. ⁷You should not be surprised at my saying, 'Youᶠ must be born again.' ⁸The wind blows wherever it pleases. You hear its sound, but you cannot tell where it comes from or where it is going. So it is with everyone born of the Spirit."

⁹"How can this be?" Nicodemus asked.

¹⁰"You are Israel's teacher," said Jesus, "and do you not understand these things? ¹¹I tell you the truth, we speak of what we know, and we testify to what we have seen, but still you people do not accept our testimony. ¹²I have spoken to you of earthly things and you do not believe; how then will you believe if I speak of heavenly things? ¹³No one has ever gone into heaven except the one who came

---

ᵃ6 Greek *two to three metretes* (probably about 75 to 115 liters)   ᵇ17 Psalm 69:9   ᶜ23 Or *and believed in him*   ᵈ3 Or *born from above*; also in verse 7   ᵉ6 Or *but spirit*   ᶠ7 The Greek is plural.

from heaven—the Son of Man.[a] [14]Just as Moses lifted up the snake in the desert, so the Son of Man must be lifted up, [15]that everyone who believes in him may have eternal life.[b]

[16]"For God so loved the world that he gave his one and only Son,[c] that whoever believes in him shall not perish but have eternal life. [17]For God did not send his Son into the world to condemn the world, but to save the world through him. [18]Whoever believes in him is not condemned, but whoever does not believe stands condemned already because he has not believed in the name of God's one and only Son.[d] [19]This is the verdict: Light has come into the world, but men loved darkness instead of light because their deeds were evil. [20]Everyone who does evil hates the light, and will not come into the light for fear that his deeds will be exposed. [21]But whoever lives by the truth comes

[a]13 Some manuscripts *Man, who is in heaven*   [b]15 Or *believes may have eternal life in him*   [c]16 Or *his only begotten Son*   [d]18 Or *God's only begotten Son*

TUESDAY

VERSE FOR THE DAY:	AUTHOR:	PASSAGE FOR THE DAY:
John 3:3	Jim Conway	John 3:3–6

The New Has Come

YOU have been marked, not only by your genetic background but also by the environment in which you were raised. The people who affirmed you gave you a positive view of other human beings. The people who put you down or belittled you have caused you to feel uncertain about yourself and others . . .

Genesis 1 tells us that God created living things to bring forth according to their own kind. Not only are we likely to look like our parents, but it is also inferred that we will respond to life as our parents did. But take heart. The Bible also says, "So God created man in his own image" (Genesis 1:27). You were not only created in your parents' image, but also in God's.

Yes, you have your past, but you also have God. Remember the classic verse: "Therefore, if anyone is in Christ, he is a new creation; the old has gone, the new has come!" (2 Corinthians 5:17).

You are not trapped with your old experiences and genes. You do have the capacity for change! You can be different! But I won't kid you. You must take charge of your life! You must stop saying, "I'll never be different," and begin saying, "I can be different because of God's love working in me."

If you've invited Christ into your life, you have been reborn and the Holy Spirit is working to help you become all that God wants you to be.

Additional Scripture Readings:
2 Corinthians 5:16–21;
Ephesians 4:20–24

Go to page 1132 for your next devotional reading.

into the light, so that it may be seen plainly that what he has done has been done through God."[a]

John the Baptist's Testimony About Jesus

22After this, Jesus and his disciples went out into the Judean countryside, where he spent some time with them, and baptized. 23Now John also was baptizing at Aenon near Salim, because there was plenty of water, and people were constantly coming to be baptized. 24(This was before John was put in prison.) 25An argument developed between some of John's disciples and a certain Jew[b] over the matter of ceremonial washing. 26They came to John and said to him, "Rabbi, that man who was with you on the other side of the Jordan—the one you testified about—well, he is baptizing, and everyone is going to him."

27To this John replied, "A man can receive only what is given him from heaven. 28You yourselves can testify that I said, 'I am not the Christ[c] but am sent ahead of him.' 29The bride belongs to the bridegroom. The friend who attends the bridegroom waits and listens for him, and is full of joy when he hears the bridegroom's voice. That joy is mine, and it is now complete. 30He must become greater; I must become less.

31"The one who comes from above is above all; the one who is from the earth belongs to the earth, and speaks as one from the earth. The one who comes from heaven is above all. 32He testifies to what he has seen and heard, but no one accepts his testimony. 33The man who has accepted it has certified that God is truthful. 34For the one whom God has sent speaks the words of God, for God[d] gives the Spirit without limit. 35The Father loves the Son and has placed everything in his hands. 36Whoever believes in the Son has eternal life, but whoever rejects the Son will not see life, for God's wrath remains on him."[e]

Jesus Talks With a Samaritan Woman

4 The Pharisees heard that Jesus was gaining and baptizing more disciples than John, 2although in fact it was not Jesus who baptized, but his disciples. 3When the Lord learned of this, he left Judea and went back once more to Galilee.

4Now he had to go through Samaria. 5So he came to a town in Samaria called Sychar, near the plot of ground Jacob had given to his son Joseph. 6Jacob's well was there, and Jesus, tired as he was from the journey, sat down by the well. It was about the sixth hour.

7When a Samaritan woman came to draw water, Jesus said to her, "Will you give me a drink?" 8(His disciples had gone into the town to buy food.)

9The Samaritan woman said to him, "You are a Jew and I am a Samaritan woman. How can you ask me for a drink?" (For Jews do not associate with Samaritans.[f])

10Jesus answered her, "If you knew the gift of God and who it is that asks you for a drink, you would have asked him and he would have given you living water."

11"Sir," the woman said, "you have nothing to draw with and the well is deep. Where can you get this living water? 12Are you greater than our father Jacob, who gave us the well and drank from it himself, as did also his sons and his flocks and herds?"

13Jesus answered, "Everyone who drinks this water will be thirsty again, 14but whoever drinks the water I give him will never thirst. Indeed, the water I give him will become in him a spring of water welling up to eternal life."

15The woman said to him, "Sir, give me this water so that I won't get thirsty and have to keep coming here to draw water."

16He told her, "Go, call your husband and come back."

17"I have no husband," she replied.

Jesus said to her, "You are right when you say you have no husband. 18The fact is, you have had five husbands, and the man you now have is not your husband. What you have just said is quite true."

19"Sir," the woman said, "I can see that you are a prophet. 20Our fathers worshiped on this mountain, but you Jews claim that the place where we must worship is in Jerusalem."

21Jesus declared, "Believe me, woman, a time is coming when you will worship the Father neither on this mountain nor in Jerusalem. 22You Samaritans worship what you do not know; we worship what we do know, for salvation is from the Jews. 23Yet a time is coming and has now

---

a21 Some interpreters end the quotation after verse 15.   b25 Some manuscripts and certain Jews
c28 Or Messiah   d34 Greek he   e36 Some interpreters end the quotation after verse 30.   f9 Or do not use dishes Samaritans have used

come when the true worshipers will worship the Father in spirit and truth, for they are the kind of worshipers the Father seeks. 24God is spirit, and his worshipers must worship in spirit and in truth."

25The woman said, "I know that Messiah" (called Christ) "is coming. When he comes, he will explain everything to us."

26Then Jesus declared, "I who speak to you am he."

The Disciples Rejoin Jesus

27Just then his disciples returned and were surprised to find him talking with a woman. But no one asked, "What do you want?" or "Why are you talking with her?"

28Then, leaving her water jar, the woman went back to the town and said to the people, 29"Come, see a man who told me everything I ever did. Could this be the

---

WEDNESDAY

VERSE FOR THE DAY:
John 3:30

AUTHOR:
D. Stuart Briscoe

PASSAGE FOR THE DAY:
John 3:22–36

The Vulnerable Man

SOCIETY'S definition of a real man is erroneous and its requirements of him are so burdensome that he really finds it difficult to *be* a man. He knows inwardly that he isn't able to cope with these heavy demands. For that reason it's time to reevaluate the question, "What is a real man?"

The answer comes loud and clear from Jesus. "Hey! If you want to see a real man, take a look at John the Baptist. Because, of all the men born of women, there's never been a greater one than John" [see Luke 7:28]. John had six characteristics which qualified him as a real man: sincerity, simplicity, conviction, courage, vision and vulnerability . . .

Modern "macho" man in American society is not supposed to be vulnerable. According to research, the five most difficult statements for the modern man to make are (1) I don't know; (2) I was wrong; (3) I need help; (4) I'm afraid; and (5) I'm sorry. In other words, according to the world's definition, real men do not admit any vulnerability. And if they do, their masculinity is in question. But John was not afraid to admit his vulnerability . . .

John the Baptist's vulnerability is shown in two ways—his honesty and his humility. His humility is unbelievable. One of his best-known statements was in reference to Jesus: "He must become greater; I must become less" (John 3:30) . . .

There's nothing phony about John's humility—it's real. He has come to grips with who he really is in relation to Jesus. A humble man is not afraid to admit it. Such a man admits openly, "I must go on decreasing. He must go on increasing."

Additional Scripture Readings:
1 Corinthians 1:26–31;
Colossians 3:12–14

Go to page 1134 for your next devotional reading.

Christ*a*?" **30**They came out of the town and made their way toward him.

31Meanwhile his disciples urged him, "Rabbi, eat something."

32But he said to them, "I have food to eat that you know nothing about."

33Then his disciples said to each other, "Could someone have brought him food?" **34**"My food," said Jesus, "is to do the will of him who sent me and to finish his work. **35**Do you not say, 'Four months more and then the harvest'? I tell you, open your eyes and look at the fields! They are ripe for harvest. **36**Even now the reaper draws his wages, even now he harvests the crop for eternal life, so that the sower and the reaper may be glad together. **37**Thus the saying 'One sows and another reaps' is true. **38**I sent you to reap what you have not worked for. Others have done the hard work, and you have reaped the benefits of their labor."

Many Samaritans Believe

39Many of the Samaritans from that town believed in him because of the woman's testimony, "He told me everything I ever did." **40**So when the Samaritans came to him, they urged him to stay with them, and he stayed two days. **41**And because of his words many more became believers.

42They said to the woman, "We no longer believe just because of what you said; now we have heard for ourselves, and we know that this man really is the Savior of the world."

Jesus Heals the Official's Son

43After the two days he left for Galilee. **44**(Now Jesus himself had pointed out that a prophet has no honor in his own country.) **45**When he arrived in Galilee, the Galileans welcomed him. They had seen all that he had done in Jerusalem at the Passover Feast, for they also had been there.

46Once more he visited Cana in Galilee, where he had turned the water into wine. And there was a certain royal official whose son lay sick at Capernaum. **47**When this man heard that Jesus had arrived in Galilee from Judea, he went to him and begged him to come and heal his son, who was close to death.

48"Unless you people see miraculous

signs and wonders," Jesus told him, "you will never believe."

49The royal official said, "Sir, come down before my child dies."

50Jesus replied, "You may go. Your son will live."

The man took Jesus at his word and departed. **51**While he was still on the way, his servants met him with the news that his boy was living. **52**When he inquired as to the time when his son got better, they said to him, "The fever left him yesterday at the seventh hour."

53Then the father realized that this was the exact time at which Jesus had said to him, "Your son will live." So he and all his household believed.

54This was the second miraculous sign that Jesus performed, having come from Judea to Galilee.

The Healing at the Pool

5 Some time later, Jesus went up to Jerusalem for a feast of the Jews. **2**Now there is in Jerusalem near the Sheep Gate a pool, which in Aramaic is called Bethesda*b* and which is surrounded by five covered colonnades. **3**Here a great number of disabled people used to lie—the blind, the lame, the paralyzed.*c* **5**One who was there had been an invalid for thirty-eight years. **6**When Jesus saw him lying there and learned that he had been in this condition for a long time, he asked him, "Do you want to get well?"

7"Sir," the invalid replied, "I have no one to help me into the pool when the water is stirred. While I am trying to get in, someone else goes down ahead of me."

8Then Jesus said to him, "Get up! Pick up your mat and walk." **9**At once the man was cured; he picked up his mat and walked.

The day on which this took place was a Sabbath, **10**and so the Jews said to the man who had been healed, "It is the Sabbath; the law forbids you to carry your mat."

11But he replied, "The man who made me well said to me, 'Pick up your mat and walk.'"

12So they asked him, "Who is this fellow who told you to pick it up and walk?"

*a*29 Or *Messiah*   *b*2 Some manuscripts *Bethzatha*; other manuscripts *Bethsaida*   *c*3 Some less important manuscripts *paralyzed—and they waited for the moving of the waters.* *4From time to time an angel of the Lord would come down and stir up the waters. The first one into the pool after each such disturbance would be cured of whatever disease he had.*

13The man who was healed had no idea who it was, for Jesus had slipped away into the crowd that was there.

14Later Jesus found him at the temple and said to him, "See, you are well again. Stop sinning or something worse may happen to you." 15The man went away and told the Jews that it was Jesus who had made him well.

Life Through the Son

16So, because Jesus was doing these things on the Sabbath, the Jews persecuted him. 17Jesus said to them, "My Father is always at his work to this very day, and I, too, am working." 18For this reason the Jews tried all the harder to kill him; not only was he breaking the Sabbath, but he was even calling God his own Father, making himself equal with God.

19Jesus gave them this answer: "I tell you the truth, the Son can do nothing by himself; he can do only what he sees his Father doing, because whatever the Father does the Son also does. 20For the Father loves the Son and shows him all he does. Yes, to your amazement he will show him even greater things than these. 21For just as the Father raises the dead and gives them life, even so the Son gives life to whom he is pleased to give it. 22Moreover, the Father judges no one, but has entrusted all judgment to the Son, 23that all may honor the Son just as they honor the Father. He who does not honor the Son does not honor the Father, who sent him.

24"I tell you the truth, whoever hears my word and believes him who sent me has eternal life and will not be condemned; he has crossed over from death to life. 25I tell you the truth, a time is coming and has now come when the dead will hear the voice of the Son of God and those

---

THURSDAY

VERSE FOR THE DAY:	AUTHOR:	PASSAGE FOR THE DAY:
John 4:42	Michael Card	John 4:39–42

Savior of the World

IF CHRISTMAS means anything to you, then it must mean everything. It is a beginning and an end. It is a time of darkness and inexpressible light. It is a time of blessed relief at finally seeing all God's promises come true in one person . . . As our family [each year visits a real barn and] gathers around our faint, flickering candle to read the Christmas story, the loneliness of the stable reminds us of the loneliness of another place on a hill outside Jerusalem. The rough trough seems almost as cruel a place as the cross. The infant cries we hear coming from the stable seem no less desperate than his final cry, and no less forsaken.

Celebrate? you say. Yes, most heartily, amidst the dung of the stable, which is, of course, the refuse of the world. Celebrate at the foot of that ghastly cross because it is the hope of the world. Gather around a cattle trough and celebrate a baby born in poverty and rejected, because he is the Savior of the world!

Additional Scripture Readings:
Matthew 27:45–50; Luke 2:1–14

Go to page 1138 for your next devotional reading.

who hear will live. ²⁶For as the Father has life in himself, so he has granted the Son to have life in himself. ²⁷And he has given him authority to judge because he is the Son of Man.

²⁸"Do not be amazed at this, for a time is coming when all who are in their graves will hear his voice ²⁹and come out—those who have done good will rise to live, and those who have done evil will rise to be condemned. ³⁰By myself I can do nothing; I judge only as I hear, and my judgment is just, for I seek not to please myself but him who sent me.

Testimonies About Jesus

³¹"If I testify about myself, my testimony is not valid. ³²There is another who testifies in my favor, and I know that his testimony about me is valid.

³³"You have sent to John and he has testified to the truth. ³⁴Not that I accept human testimony; but I mention it that you may be saved. ³⁵John was a lamp that burned and gave light, and you chose for a time to enjoy his light.

³⁶"I have testimony weightier than that of John. For the very work that the Father has given me to finish, and which I am doing, testifies that the Father has sent me. ³⁷And the Father who sent me has himself testified concerning me. You have never heard his voice nor seen his form, ³⁸nor does his word dwell in you, for you do not believe the one he sent. ³⁹You diligently study[a] the Scriptures because you think that by them you possess eternal life. These are the Scriptures that testify about me, ⁴⁰yet you refuse to come to me to have life.

⁴¹"I do not accept praise from men, ⁴²but I know you. I know that you do not have the love of God in your hearts. ⁴³I have come in my Father's name, and you do not accept me; but if someone else comes in his own name, you will accept him. ⁴⁴How can you believe if you accept praise from one another, yet make no effort to obtain the praise that comes from the only God[b]?

⁴⁵"But do not think I will accuse you before the Father. Your accuser is Moses, on whom your hopes are set. ⁴⁶If you believed Moses, you would believe me, for he wrote about me. ⁴⁷But since you do not believe what he wrote, how are you going to believe what I say?"

Jesus Feeds the Five Thousand

6 Some time after this, Jesus crossed to the far shore of the Sea of Galilee (that is, the Sea of Tiberias), ²and a great crowd of people followed him because they saw the miraculous signs he had performed on the sick. ³Then Jesus went up on a mountainside and sat down with his disciples. ⁴The Jewish Passover Feast was near.

⁵When Jesus looked up and saw a great crowd coming toward him, he said to Philip, "Where shall we buy bread for these people to eat?" ⁶He asked this only to test him, for he already had in mind what he was going to do.

⁷Philip answered him, "Eight months' wages[c] would not buy enough bread for each one to have a bite!"

⁸Another of his disciples, Andrew, Simon Peter's brother, spoke up, ⁹"Here is a boy with five small barley loaves and two small fish, but how far will they go among so many?"

¹⁰Jesus said, "Have the people sit down." There was plenty of grass in that place, and the men sat down, about five thousand of them. ¹¹Jesus then took the loaves, gave thanks, and distributed to those who were seated as much as they wanted. He did the same with the fish.

¹²When they had all had enough to eat, he said to his disciples, "Gather the pieces that are left over. Let nothing be wasted." ¹³So they gathered them and filled twelve baskets with the pieces of the five barley loaves left over by those who had eaten.

¹⁴After the people saw the miraculous sign that Jesus did, they began to say, "Surely this is the Prophet who is to come into the world." ¹⁵Jesus, knowing that they intended to come and make him king by force, withdrew again to a mountain by himself.

Jesus Walks on the Water

¹⁶When evening came, his disciples went down to the lake, ¹⁷where they got into a boat and set off across the lake for Capernaum. By now it was dark, and Jesus had not yet joined them. ¹⁸A strong wind was blowing and the waters grew rough. ¹⁹When they had rowed three or three and a half miles,[d] they saw Jesus approaching the boat, walking on the water; and they were terrified. ²⁰But he said to them, "It is I; don't be afraid." ²¹Then

---

[a]39 Or *Study diligently* (the imperative)   [b]44 Some early manuscripts *the Only One*   [c]7 Greek *two hundred denarii*   [d]19 Greek *rowed twenty-five or thirty stadia* (about 5 or 6 kilometers)

they were willing to take him into the boat, and immediately the boat reached the shore where they were heading.

²²The next day the crowd that had stayed on the opposite shore of the lake realized that only one boat had been there, and that Jesus had not entered it with his disciples, but that they had gone away alone. ²³Then some boats from Tiberias landed near the place where the people had eaten the bread after the Lord had given thanks. ²⁴Once the crowd realized that neither Jesus nor his disciples were there, they got into the boats and went to Capernaum in search of Jesus.

Jesus the Bread of Life

²⁵When they found him on the other side of the lake, they asked him, "Rabbi, when did you get here?"

²⁶Jesus answered, "I tell you the truth, you are looking for me, not because you saw miraculous signs but because you ate the loaves and had your fill. ²⁷Do not work for food that spoils, but for food that endures to eternal life, which the Son of Man will give you. On him God the Father has placed his seal of approval."

²⁸Then they asked him, "What must we do to do the works God requires?"

²⁹Jesus answered, "The work of God is this: to believe in the one he has sent."

³⁰So they asked him, "What miraculous sign then will you give that we may see it and believe you? What will you do? ³¹Our forefathers ate the manna in the desert; as it is written: 'He gave them bread from heaven to eat.'ᵃ"

³²Jesus said to them, "I tell you the truth, it is not Moses who has given you the bread from heaven, but it is my Father who gives you the true bread from heaven. ³³For the bread of God is he who comes down from heaven and gives life to the world."

³⁴"Sir," they said, "from now on give us this bread."

³⁵Then Jesus declared, "I am the bread of life. He who comes to me will never go hungry, and he who believes in me will never be thirsty. ³⁶But as I told you, you have seen me and still you do not believe. ³⁷All that the Father gives me will come to me, and whoever comes to me I will never drive away. ³⁸For I have come down from heaven not to do my will but to do the will of him who sent me. ³⁹And this is the will of him who sent me, that I shall lose none

of all that he has given me, but raise them up at the last day. ⁴⁰For my Father's will is that everyone who looks to the Son and believes in him shall have eternal life, and I will raise him up at the last day."

⁴¹At this the Jews began to grumble about him because he said, "I am the bread that came down from heaven." ⁴²They said, "Is this not Jesus, the son of Joseph, whose father and mother we know? How can he now say, 'I came down from heaven'?"

⁴³"Stop grumbling among yourselves," Jesus answered. ⁴⁴"No one can come to me unless the Father who sent me draws him, and I will raise him up at the last day. ⁴⁵It is written in the Prophets: 'They will all be taught by God.'ᵇ Everyone who listens to the Father and learns from him comes to me. ⁴⁶No one has seen the Father except the one who is from God; only he has seen the Father. ⁴⁷I tell you the truth, he who believes has everlasting life. ⁴⁸I am the bread of life. ⁴⁹Your forefathers ate the manna in the desert, yet they died. ⁵⁰But here is the bread that comes down from heaven, which a man may eat and not die. ⁵¹I am the living bread that came down from heaven. If anyone eats of this bread, he will live forever. This bread is my flesh, which I will give for the life of the world."

⁵²Then the Jews began to argue sharply among themselves, "How can this man give us his flesh to eat?"

⁵³Jesus said to them, "I tell you the truth, unless you eat the flesh of the Son of Man and drink his blood, you have no life in you. ⁵⁴Whoever eats my flesh and drinks my blood has eternal life, and I will raise him up at the last day. ⁵⁵For my flesh is real food and my blood is real drink. ⁵⁶Whoever eats my flesh and drinks my blood remains in me, and I in him. ⁵⁷Just as the living Father sent me and I live because of the Father, so the one who feeds on me will live because of me. ⁵⁸This is the bread that came down from heaven. Your forefathers ate manna and died, but he who feeds on this bread will live forever." ⁵⁹He said this while teaching in the synagogue in Capernaum.

Many Disciples Desert Jesus

⁶⁰On hearing it, many of his disciples said, "This is a hard teaching. Who can accept it?"

⁶¹Aware that his disciples were grum-

ᵃ31 Exodus 16:4; Neh. 9:15; Psalm 78:24,25   ᵇ45 Isaiah 54:13

bling about this, Jesus said to them, "Does this offend you? **62**What if you see the Son of Man ascend to where he was before! **63**The Spirit gives life; the flesh counts for nothing. The words I have spoken to you are spirit*a* and they are life. **64**Yet there are some of you who do not believe." For Jesus had known from the beginning which of them did not believe and who would betray him. **65**He went on to say, "This is why I told you that no one can come to me unless the Father has enabled him."

66From this time many of his disciples turned back and no longer followed him.

67"You do not want to leave too, do you?" Jesus asked the Twelve.

68Simon Peter answered him, "Lord, to whom shall we go? You have the words of eternal life. **69**We believe and know that you are the Holy One of God."

70Then Jesus replied, "Have I not chosen you, the Twelve? Yet one of you is a devil!" **71**(He meant Judas, the son of Simon Iscariot, who, though one of the Twelve, was later to betray him.)

Jesus Goes to the Feast of Tabernacles

7 After this, Jesus went around in Galilee, purposely staying away from Judea because the Jews there were waiting to take his life. **2**But when the Jewish Feast of Tabernacles was near, **3**Jesus' brothers said to him, "You ought to leave here and go to Judea, so that your disciples may see the miracles you do. **4**No one who wants to become a public figure acts in secret. Since you are doing these things, show yourself to the world." **5**For even his own brothers did not believe in him.

6Therefore Jesus told them, "The right time for me has not yet come; for you any time is right. **7**The world cannot hate you, but it hates me because I testify that what it does is evil. **8**You go to the Feast. I am not yet*b* going up to this Feast, because for me the right time has not yet come." **9**Having said this, he stayed in Galilee.

10However, after his brothers had left for the Feast, he went also, not publicly, but in secret. **11**Now at the Feast the Jews were watching for him and asking, "Where is that man?"

12Among the crowds there was widespread whispering about him. Some said, "He is a good man."

Others replied, "No, he deceives the people." **13**But no one would say anything publicly about him for fear of the Jews.

Jesus Teaches at the Feast

14Not until halfway through the Feast did Jesus go up to the temple courts and begin to teach. **15**The Jews were amazed and asked, "How did this man get such learning without having studied?"

16Jesus answered, "My teaching is not my own. It comes from him who sent me. **17**If anyone chooses to do God's will, he will find out whether my teaching comes from God or whether I speak on my own. **18**He who speaks on his own does so to gain honor for himself, but he who works for the honor of the one who sent him is a man of truth; there is nothing false about him. **19**Has not Moses given you the law? Yet not one of you keeps the law. Why are you trying to kill me?"

20"You are demon-possessed," the crowd answered. "Who is trying to kill you?"

21Jesus said to them, "I did one miracle, and you are all astonished. **22**Yet, because Moses gave you circumcision (though actually it did not come from Moses, but from the patriarchs), you circumcise a child on the Sabbath. **23**Now if a child can be circumcised on the Sabbath so that the law of Moses may not be broken, why are you angry with me for healing the whole man on the Sabbath? **24**Stop judging by mere appearances, and make a right judgment."

Is Jesus the Christ?

25At that point some of the people of Jerusalem began to ask, "Isn't this the man they are trying to kill? **26**Here he is, speaking publicly, and they are not saying a word to him. Have the authorities really concluded that he is the Christ*c*? **27**But we know where this man is from; when the Christ comes, no one will know where he is from."

28Then Jesus, still teaching in the temple courts, cried out, "Yes, you know me, and you know where I am from. I am not here on my own, but he who sent me is true. You do not know him, **29**but I know him because I am from him and he sent me."

30At this they tried to seize him, but no one laid a hand on him, because his time

---

a63 Or *Spirit*   *b8* Some early manuscripts do not have *yet.*   *c26* Or *Messiah*; also in verses 27, 31, 41 and 42 had not yet come. **31**Still, many in the crowd put their faith in him. They said, "When the Christ comes, will he do more miraculous signs than this man?"

32The Pharisees heard the crowd whispering such things about him. Then the chief priests and the Pharisees sent temple guards to arrest him.

33Jesus said, "I am with you for only a short time, and then I go to the one who sent me. **34**You will look for me, but you will not find me; and where I am, you cannot come."

35The Jews said to one another, "Where does this man intend to go that we cannot find him? Will he go where our people live scattered among the Greeks, and teach the Greeks? **36**What did he mean when he said, 'You will look for me, but you will not find me,' and 'Where I am, you cannot come'?"

37On the last and greatest day of the Feast, Jesus stood and said in a loud voice, "If anyone is thirsty, let him come to me and drink. **38**Whoever believes in me, as*a* the Scripture has said, streams of living

a37,38 Or / If anyone is thirsty, let him come to me. / And let him drink, 38who believes in me. / As

---

FRIDAY

VERSE FOR THE DAY:
John 7:37

AUTHOR:
Max Lucado

PASSAGE FOR THE DAY:
John 7:37–44

Thirsty for Righteousness

"IF ANYONE is thirsty," Jesus once said, "let him come to me and drink" (John 7:37).

Admission of thirst doesn't come easy for us. False fountains pacify our cravings with sugary swallows of pleasure. But there comes a time when pleasure doesn't satisfy. There comes a dark hour in every life when the world caves in and we are left trapped in the rubble of reality, parched and dying.

Some would rather die than admit it. Others admit it and escape death.

"God, I need help."

So the thirsty come. A ragged lot we are, bound together by broken dreams and collapsed promises. Fortunes that were never made. Families that were never built. Promises that were never kept . . .

And we are very thirsty.

Not thirsty for fame, possessions, passion or romance. We've drunk from those pools. They are salt water in the desert. They don't quench—they kill.

"Blessed are those who hunger and thirst for righteousness . . ."

Righteousness. That's it. That's what we are thirsty for. We're thirsty for a clean conscience. We crave a clean slate. We yearn for a fresh start. We pray for a hand which will enter the dark cavern of our world and do for us the one thing we can't do for ourselves—make us right again.

Additional Scripture Readings:
Isaiah 55:1–3; Matthew 5:1–10

Go to page 1140 for your next devotional reading.

water will flow from within him." **39**By this he meant the Spirit, whom those who believed in him were later to receive. Up to that time the Spirit had not been given, since Jesus had not yet been glorified.

40On hearing his words, some of the people said, "Surely this man is the Prophet."

41Others said, "He is the Christ."

Still others asked, "How can the Christ come from Galilee? **42**Does not the Scripture say that the Christ will come from David's family*a* and from Bethlehem, the town where David lived?" **43**Thus the people were divided because of Jesus. **44**Some wanted to seize him, but no one laid a hand on him.

Unbelief of the Jewish Leaders

45Finally the temple guards went back to the chief priests and Pharisees, who asked them, "Why didn't you bring him in?"

46"No one ever spoke the way this man does," the guards declared.

47"You mean he has deceived you also?" the Pharisees retorted. **48**"Has any of the rulers or of the Pharisees believed in him? **49**No! But this mob that knows nothing of the law—there is a curse on them."

50Nicodemus, who had gone to Jesus earlier and who was one of their own number, asked, **51**"Does our law condemn anyone without first hearing him to find out what he is doing?"

52They replied, "Are you from Galilee, too? Look into it, and you will find that a prophet*b* does not come out of Galilee."

[The earliest manuscripts
and many other ancient witnesses
do not have John 7:53–8:11.]

53Then each went to his own home.
8 But Jesus went to the Mount of Olives. **2**At dawn he appeared again in the temple courts, where all the people gathered around him, and he sat down to teach them. **3**The teachers of the law and the Pharisees brought in a woman caught in adultery. They made her stand before the group **4**and said to Jesus, "Teacher, this woman was caught in the act of adultery. **5**In the Law Moses commanded us to stone such women. Now what do you

say?" **6**They were using this question as a trap, in order to have a basis for accusing him.

But Jesus bent down and started to write on the ground with his finger. **7**When they kept on questioning him, he straightened up and said to them, "If any one of you is without sin, let him be the first to throw a stone at her." **8**Again he stooped down and wrote on the ground.

9At this, those who heard began to go away one at a time, the older ones first, until only Jesus was left, with the woman still standing there. **10**Jesus straightened up and asked her, "Woman, where are they? Has no one condemned you?"

11"No one, sir," she said.

"Then neither do I condemn you," Jesus declared. "Go now and leave your life of sin."

The Validity of Jesus' Testimony

12When Jesus spoke again to the people, he said, "I am the light of the world. Whoever follows me will never walk in darkness, but will have the light of life."

13The Pharisees challenged him, "Here you are, appearing as your own witness; your testimony is not valid."

14Jesus answered, "Even if I testify on my own behalf, my testimony is valid, for I know where I came from and where I am going. But you have no idea where I come from or where I am going. **15**You judge by human standards; I pass judgment on no one. **16**But if I do judge, my decisions are right, because I am not alone. I stand with the Father, who sent me. **17**In your own Law it is written that the testimony of two men is valid. **18**I am one who testifies for myself; my other witness is the Father, who sent me."

19Then they asked him, "Where is your father?"

"You do not know me or my Father," Jesus replied. "If you knew me, you would know my Father also." **20**He spoke these words while teaching in the temple area near the place where the offerings were put. Yet no one seized him, because his time had not yet come.

21Once more Jesus said to them, "I am going away, and you will look for me, and you will die in your sin. Where I go, you cannot come."

a42 Greek *seed*   *b52* Two early manuscripts *the Prophet*

WEEKENDING

REMIND

Father, we need reminders. I need reminders.
And so we are thankful for the reminders you
give us daily in the form of our children.
Reminders, first, of your generosity, for children
are a gift from you. But reminders, as well, of
our finitude, or our place in this world that you
have created. Reminders that we are stewards
of your creation, not its gods. Reminders that
we tend the seeds that you have sown, but we
do not determine the plant's growth. Reminders
that our final duty is to honor you through our
acts of service to one another, not to serve and
honor ourselves. *May God grant us the wisdom
to be parents whose treasure lies in heaven and
not in the applause of others.*

– S.D. Gaede

REVIVE

Saturday: Psalm 145:1–7
Sunday: John 3:27–36

Go to page 1142 for your next devotional reading.

22This made the Jews ask, "Will he kill himself? Is that why he says, 'Where I go, you cannot come'?"

23But he continued, "You are from below; I am from above. You are of this world; I am not of this world. **24**I told you that you would die in your sins; if you do not believe that I am ˌthe one I claim to be,ˌ*a* you will indeed die in your sins."

25"Who are you?" they asked.

"Just what I have been claiming all along," Jesus replied. **26**"I have much to say in judgment of you. But he who sent me is reliable, and what I have heard from him I tell the world."

27They did not understand that he was telling them about his Father. **28**So Jesus said, "When you have lifted up the Son of Man, then you will know that I am ˌthe one I claim to beˌ and that I do nothing on my own but speak just what the Father has taught me. **29**The one who sent me is with me; he has not left me alone, for I always do what pleases him." **30**Even as he spoke, many put their faith in him.

The Children of Abraham

31To the Jews who had believed him, Jesus said, "If you hold to my teaching, you are really my disciples. **32**Then you will know the truth, and the truth will set you free."

33They answered him, "We are Abraham's descendants*b* and have never been slaves of anyone. How can you say that we shall be set free?"

34Jesus replied, "I tell you the truth, everyone who sins is a slave to sin. **35**Now a slave has no permanent place in the family, but a son belongs to it forever. **36**So if the Son sets you free, you will be free indeed. **37**I know you are Abraham's descendants. Yet you are ready to kill me, because you have no room for my word. **38**I am telling you what I have seen in the Father's presence, and you do what you have heard from your father.*c*"

39"Abraham is our father," they answered.

"If you were Abraham's children," said Jesus, "then you would*d* do the things Abraham did. **40**As it is, you are determined to kill me, a man who has told you the truth that I heard from God. Abraham did not do such things. **41**You are doing the things your own father does."

"We are not illegitimate children," they protested. "The only Father we have is God himself."

The Children of the Devil

42Jesus said to them, "If God were your Father, you would love me, for I came from God and now am here. I have not come on my own; but he sent me. **43**Why is my language not clear to you? Because you are unable to hear what I say. **44**You belong to your father, the devil, and you want to carry out your father's desire. He was a murderer from the beginning, not holding to the truth, for there is no truth in him. When he lies, he speaks his native language, for he is a liar and the father of lies. **45**Yet because I tell the truth, you do not believe me! **46**Can any of you prove me guilty of sin? If I am telling the truth, why don't you believe me? **47**He who belongs to God hears what God says. The reason you do not hear is that you do not belong to God."

The Claims of Jesus About Himself

48The Jews answered him, "Aren't we right in saying that you are a Samaritan and demon-possessed?"

49"I am not possessed by a demon," said Jesus, "but I honor my Father and you dishonor me. **50**I am not seeking glory for myself; but there is one who seeks it, and he is the judge. **51**I tell you the truth, if anyone keeps my word, he will never see death."

52At this the Jews exclaimed, "Now we know that you are demon-possessed! Abraham died and so did the prophets, yet you say that if anyone keeps your word, he will never taste death. **53**Are you greater than our father Abraham? He died, and so did the prophets. Who do you think you are?"

54Jesus replied, "If I glorify myself, my glory means nothing. My Father, whom you claim as your God, is the one who glorifies me. **55**Though you do not know him, I know him. If I said I did not, I would be a liar like you, but I do know him and keep his word. **56**Your father Abraham rejoiced at the thought of seeing my day; he saw it and was glad."

57"You are not yet fifty years old," the Jews said to him, "and you have seen Abraham!"

---

*a*24 Or *I am he;* also in verse 28   *b*33 Greek *seed;* also in verse 37   *c*38 Or *presence. Therefore do what you have heard from the Father.*   *d*39 Some early manuscripts *"If you are Abraham's children,"* said Jesus, *"then"*

⁵⁸"I tell you the truth," Jesus answered, "before Abraham was born, I am!" ⁵⁹At this, they picked up stones to stone him, but Jesus hid himself, slipping away from the temple grounds.

Jesus Heals a Man Born Blind

9 As he went along, he saw a man blind from birth. ²His disciples asked him, "Rabbi, who sinned, this man or his parents, that he was born blind?"

³"Neither this man nor his parents sinned," said Jesus, "but this happened so that the work of God might be displayed in his life. ⁴As long as it is day, we must do the work of him who sent me. Night is coming, when no one can work. ⁵While I am in the world, I am the light of the world."

MONDAY

VERSE FOR THE DAY:
John 8:36

AUTHOR:
Mark Ritchie

PASSAGE FOR THE DAY:
John 8:32–41

Set Free!

MARK Ritchie reflects on God and the death of friends as he visits his hometown cemetery.

I had the overwhelming sense that I knew a God who had his act together, who knew the end from the beginning, who was indeed in the process of putting all the little pieces of this puzzle of human drama together to form a big picture. And the picture was starting to make sense.

Following God had turned out to be nothing but a bargain for me. And the bargain was totally in nonfinancial terms. Of course, I could hardly complain about the financial end of things either. I could still recall the tough times: the old potato I had found and eaten in my college days; the old car with no alternator or reverse; a very pregnant Nancy pushing the car back out of an intersection. They were tough times to be sure, but I wasn't going to say that God hadn't done right by me. I know where I came from, who I am, and where I'm going.

Amazing, I thought to myself . . . The creator of all this majesty of the universe—I know him, he's my friend. I've felt his comfort in my distress. I saw his care that day in Afghanistan when a poor man reached into his pocket to offer me money. I remember well the incredibly comforting feelings he gave me when I had those awful financial setbacks.

And most of all, I had complete freedom from guilt. The carpenter-preacher had said that he could by his death on a cross make people free of their guilt. He had been so credible in other things, I tried him on this one and found he delivered. The same forgiveness he extended to his executioners, he now handed me. My lifelong quest for truth and meaning has truly been met. I have been literally saved by his life.

Additional Scripture Readings:
Romans 8:1–4; 1 Peter 1:3–9

Go to page 1144 for your next devotional reading.

[6]Having said this, he spit on the ground, made some mud with the saliva, and put it on the man's eyes. [7]"Go," he told him, "wash in the Pool of Siloam" (this word means Sent). So the man went and washed, and came home seeing.

[8]His neighbors and those who had formerly seen him begging asked, "Isn't this the same man who used to sit and beg?" [9]Some claimed that he was.

Others said, "No, he only looks like him."

But he himself insisted, "I am the man."

[10]"How then were your eyes opened?" they demanded.

[11]He replied, "The man they call Jesus made some mud and put it on my eyes. He told me to go to Siloam and wash. So I went and washed, and then I could see."

[12]"Where is this man?" they asked him. "I don't know," he said.

The Pharisees Investigate the Healing

[13]They brought to the Pharisees the man who had been blind. [14]Now the day on which Jesus had made the mud and opened the man's eyes was a Sabbath. [15]Therefore the Pharisees also asked him how he had received his sight. "He put mud on my eyes," the man replied, "and I washed, and now I see."

[16]Some of the Pharisees said, "This man is not from God, for he does not keep the Sabbath."

But others asked, "How can a sinner do such miraculous signs?" So they were divided.

[17]Finally they turned again to the blind man, "What have you to say about him? It was your eyes he opened."

The man replied, "He is a prophet."

[18]The Jews still did not believe that he had been blind and had received his sight until they sent for the man's parents. [19]"Is this your son?" they asked. "Is this the one you say was born blind? How is it that now he can see?"

[20]"We know he is our son," the parents answered, "and we know he was born blind. [21]But how he can see now, or who opened his eyes, we don't know. Ask him. He is of age; he will speak for himself." [22]His parents said this because they were afraid of the Jews, for already the Jews had decided that anyone who acknowledged that Jesus was the Christ[a] would be put out of the synagogue. [23]That was

why his parents said, "He is of age; ask him."

[24]A second time they summoned the man who had been blind. "Give glory to God,[b]" they said. "We know this man is a sinner."

[25]He replied, "Whether he is a sinner or not, I don't know. One thing I do know. I was blind but now I see!"

[26]Then they asked him, "What did he do to you? How did he open your eyes?"

[27]He answered, "I have told you already and you did not listen. Why do you want to hear it again? Do you want to become his disciples, too?"

[28]Then they hurled insults at him and said, "You are this fellow's disciple! We are disciples of Moses! [29]We know that God spoke to Moses, but as for this fellow, we don't even know where he comes from."

[30]The man answered, "Now that is remarkable! You don't know where he comes from, yet he opened my eyes. [31]We know that God does not listen to sinners. He listens to the godly man who does his will. [32]Nobody has ever heard of opening the eyes of a man born blind. [33]If this man were not from God, he could do nothing."

[34]To this they replied, "You were steeped in sin at birth; how dare you lecture us!" And they threw him out.

Spiritual Blindness

[35]Jesus heard that they had thrown him out, and when he found him, he said, "Do you believe in the Son of Man?"

[36]"Who is he, sir?" the man asked. "Tell me so that I may believe in him."

[37]Jesus said, "You have now seen him; in fact, he is the one speaking with you."

[38]Then the man said, "Lord, I believe," and he worshiped him.

[39]Jesus said, "For judgment I have come into this world, so that the blind will see and those who see will become blind."

[40]Some Pharisees who were with him heard him say this and asked, "What? Are we blind too?"

[41]Jesus said, "If you were blind, you would not be guilty of sin; but now that you claim you can see, your guilt remains.

The Shepherd and His Flock

10 "I tell you the truth, the man who does not enter the sheep pen by the gate, but climbs in by some other way, is a thief and a robber. [2]The man who enters

---

[a]22 Or *Messiah*   [b]24 A solemn charge to tell the truth (see Joshua 7:19)

by the gate is the shepherd of his sheep. ³The watchman opens the gate for him, and the sheep listen to his voice. He calls his own sheep by name and leads them out. ⁴When he has brought out all his own, he goes on ahead of them, and his sheep follow him because they know his voice. ⁵But they will never follow a stranger; in fact, they will run away from him because they do not recognize a stranger's voice." ⁶Jesus used this figure of speech, but they did not understand what he was telling them.

⁷Therefore Jesus said again, "I tell you the truth, I am the gate for the sheep. ⁸All who ever came before me were thieves and robbers, but the sheep did not listen to them. ⁹I am the gate; whoever enters through me will be saved.ᵃ He will come in and go out, and find pasture. ¹⁰The thief

ᵃ9 Or *kept safe*

TUESDAY

VERSE FOR THE DAY:	AUTHOR:	PASSAGE FOR THE DAY:
John 10:10	Tim LaHaye	John 10:1–10

God's Special Remedy

MOST miserable or depressed people are not conscious of the fact that their misery emanates from the God-vacuum within them. This spiritual deficiency or God-void makes them vulnerable to a variety of mental, emotional and physical maladies or disorders. Whether they are antagonistic to God or just neglect his presence in their lives seems to make no difference. They experience an empty hunger within them for God, but they lack the spiritual resources to help them cope with the problems caused by their ego-dominated decisions. This God-void is universally as old as man. The Bible calls it "death." In the Garden of Eden when Adam and Eve rebelled and disobeyed God, they died spiritually. That spiritual death has been transmitted from generation to generation, conferring a serious void within the life of every human being. Although man can gain momentary happiness on the mental, emotional or physical planes of life, he will never attain lasting happiness as long as the God-void in his spiritual nature is unfulfilled. He will never know abiding joy or have power to control those weaker parts of his nature.

Jesus Christ is God's special remedy to fill the God-void in every human being. That he lived over 1,900 years ago is a matter of historical fact. Why he lived, however, is too often a source of confusion, even though the only authentic record of his life gives us the answer. Jesus Christ himself said, "I have come that they may have life, and have it to the full" (John 10:10). The abundant life he offers not only fills the God-void in a person's spirit, but also provides him with power to eliminate depression and other emotional problems.

Additional Scripture Readings:
Psalm 42:1–8; Philippians 3:7–11

Go to page 1147 for your next devotional reading.

comes only to steal and kill and destroy; I have come that they may have life, and have it to the full.

[11]"I am the good shepherd. The good shepherd lays down his life for the sheep. [12]The hired hand is not the shepherd who owns the sheep. So when he sees the wolf coming, he abandons the sheep and runs away. Then the wolf attacks the flock and scatters it. [13]The man runs away because he is a hired hand and cares nothing for the sheep.

[14]"I am the good shepherd; I know my sheep and my sheep know me— [15]just as the Father knows me and I know the Father—and I lay down my life for the sheep. [16]I have other sheep that are not of this sheep pen. I must bring them also. They too will listen to my voice, and there shall be one flock and one shepherd. [17]The reason my Father loves me is that I lay down my life—only to take it up again. [18]No one takes it from me, but I lay it down of my own accord. I have authority to lay it down and authority to take it up again. This command I received from my Father."

[19]At these words the Jews were again divided. [20]Many of them said, "He is demon-possessed and raving mad. Why listen to him?"

[21]But others said, "These are not the sayings of a man possessed by a demon. Can a demon open the eyes of the blind?"

The Unbelief of the Jews

[22]Then came the Feast of Dedication[a] at Jerusalem. It was winter, [23]and Jesus was in the temple area walking in Solomon's Colonnade. [24]The Jews gathered around him, saying, "How long will you keep us in suspense? If you are the Christ,[b] tell us plainly."

[25]Jesus answered, "I did tell you, but you do not believe. The miracles I do in my Father's name speak for me, [26]but you do not believe because you are not my sheep. [27]My sheep listen to my voice; I know them, and they follow me. [28]I give them eternal life, and they shall never perish; no one can snatch them out of my hand. [29]My Father, who has given them to me, is greater than all[c]; no one can snatch them out of my Father's hand. [30]I and the Father are one."

[31]Again the Jews picked up stones to stone him, [32]but Jesus said to them, "I have shown you many great miracles from the Father. For which of these do you stone me?"

[33]"We are not stoning you for any of these," replied the Jews, "but for blasphemy, because you, a mere man, claim to be God."

[34]Jesus answered them, "Is it not written in your Law, 'I have said you are gods'[d]? [35]If he called them 'gods,' to whom the word of God came—and the Scripture cannot be broken— [36]what about the one whom the Father set apart as his very own and sent into the world? Why then do you accuse me of blasphemy because I said, 'I am God's Son'? [37]Do not believe me unless I do what my Father does. [38]But if I do it, even though you do not believe me, believe the miracles, that you may know and understand that the Father is in me, and I in the Father." [39]Again they tried to seize him, but he escaped their grasp.

[40]Then Jesus went back across the Jordan to the place where John had been baptizing in the early days. Here he stayed [41]and many people came to him. They said, "Though John never performed a miraculous sign, all that John said about this man was true." [42]And in that place many believed in Jesus.

The Death of Lazarus

11 Now a man named Lazarus was sick. He was from Bethany, the village of Mary and her sister Martha. [2]This Mary, whose brother Lazarus now lay sick, was the same one who poured perfume on the Lord and wiped his feet with her hair. [3]So the sisters sent word to Jesus, "Lord, the one you love is sick."

[4]When he heard this, Jesus said, "This sickness will not end in death. No, it is for God's glory so that God's Son may be glorified through it." [5]Jesus loved Martha and her sister and Lazarus. [6]Yet when he heard that Lazarus was sick, he stayed where he was two more days.

[7]Then he said to his disciples, "Let us go back to Judea."

[8]"But Rabbi," they said, "a short while ago the Jews tried to stone you, and yet you are going back there?"

[9]Jesus answered, "Are there not twelve hours of daylight? A man who walks by day will not stumble, for he sees by this world's light. [10]It is when he walks by

---

a22 That is, Hanukkah   *b24* Or *Messiah*   *c29* Many early manuscripts *What my Father has given me is greater than all*   *d34* Psalm 82:6

night that he stumbles, for he has no light."

¹¹After he had said this, he went on to tell them, "Our friend Lazarus has fallen asleep; but I am going there to wake him up."

¹²His disciples replied, "Lord, if he sleeps, he will get better." ¹³Jesus had been speaking of his death, but his disciples thought he meant natural sleep.

¹⁴So then he told them plainly, "Lazarus is dead, ¹⁵and for your sake I am glad I was not there, so that you may believe. But let us go to him."

¹⁶Then Thomas (called Didymus) said to the rest of the disciples, "Let us also go, that we may die with him."

Jesus Comforts the Sisters

¹⁷On his arrival, Jesus found that Lazarus had already been in the tomb for four days. ¹⁸Bethany was less than two miles[a] from Jerusalem, ¹⁹and many Jews had come to Martha and Mary to comfort them in the loss of their brother. ²⁰When Martha heard that Jesus was coming, she went out to meet him, but Mary stayed at home.

²¹"Lord," Martha said to Jesus, "if you had been here, my brother would not have died. ²²But I know that even now God will give you whatever you ask."

²³Jesus said to her, "Your brother will rise again."

²⁴Martha answered, "I know he will rise again in the resurrection at the last day."

²⁵Jesus said to her, "I am the resurrection and the life. He who believes in me will live, even though he dies; ²⁶and whoever lives and believes in me will never die. Do you believe this?"

²⁷"Yes, Lord," she told him, "I believe that you are the Christ,[b] the Son of God, who was to come into the world."

²⁸And after she had said this, she went back and called her sister Mary aside. "The Teacher is here," she said, "and is asking for you." ²⁹When Mary heard this, she got up quickly and went to him. ³⁰Now Jesus had not yet entered the village, but was still at the place where Martha had met him. ³¹When the Jews who had been with Mary in the house, comforting her, noticed how quickly she got up and went out, they followed her, supposing she was going to the tomb to mourn there.

³²When Mary reached the place where Jesus was and saw him, she fell at his feet and said, "Lord, if you had been here, my brother would not have died."

³³When Jesus saw her weeping, and the Jews who had come along with her also weeping, he was deeply moved in spirit and troubled. ³⁴"Where have you laid him?" he asked.

"Come and see, Lord," they replied.

³⁵Jesus wept.

³⁶Then the Jews said, "See how he loved him!"

³⁷But some of them said, "Could not he who opened the eyes of the blind man have kept this man from dying?"

Jesus Raises Lazarus From the Dead

³⁸Jesus, once more deeply moved, came to the tomb. It was a cave with a stone laid across the entrance. ³⁹"Take away the stone," he said.

"But, Lord," said Martha, the sister of the dead man, "by this time there is a bad odor, for he has been there four days."

⁴⁰Then Jesus said, "Did I not tell you that if you believed, you would see the glory of God?"

⁴¹So they took away the stone. Then Jesus looked up and said, "Father, I thank you that you have heard me. ⁴²I knew that you always hear me, but I said this for the benefit of the people standing here, that they may believe that you sent me."

⁴³When he had said this, Jesus called in a loud voice, "Lazarus, come out!" ⁴⁴The dead man came out, his hands and feet wrapped with strips of linen, and a cloth around his face.

Jesus said to them, "Take off the grave clothes and let him go."

The Plot to Kill Jesus

⁴⁵Therefore many of the Jews who had come to visit Mary, and had seen what Jesus did, put their faith in him. ⁴⁶But some of them went to the Pharisees and told them what Jesus had done. ⁴⁷Then the chief priests and the Pharisees called a meeting of the Sanhedrin.

"What are we accomplishing?" they asked. "Here is this man performing many miraculous signs. ⁴⁸If we let him go on like this, everyone will believe in him, and then the Romans will come and take away both our place[c] and our nation."

⁴⁹Then one of them, named Caiaphas, who was high priest that year, spoke up, "You know nothing at all! ⁵⁰You do not re-

---

[a]18 Greek *fifteen stadia* (about 3 kilometers)   [b]27 Or *Messiah*   [c]48 Or *temple*

alize that it is better for you that one man die for the people than that the whole nation perish."

[51]He did not say this on his own, but as high priest that year he prophesied that Jesus would die for the Jewish nation, [52]and not only for that nation but also for the scattered children of God, to bring them together and make them one. [53]So from that day on they plotted to take his life.

[54]Therefore Jesus no longer moved about publicly among the Jews. Instead he withdrew to a region near the desert, to a village called Ephraim, where he stayed with his disciples.

[55]When it was almost time for the Jewish Passover, many went up from the country to Jerusalem for their ceremonial cleansing before the Passover. [56]They kept looking for Jesus, and as they stood in the temple area they asked one another,

---

WEDNESDAY

VERSE FOR THE DAY:
John 11:35

AUTHOR:
Haddon W. Robinson

PASSAGE FOR THE DAY:
John 11:32–37

Big Boys Do *Cry*

MARY, a follower of Jesus, approached her Lord at the sudden death of her brother and with some bitterness and hostility said, "If you had been here, my brother would not have died." Jesus, deeply moved by her tears, asked, "Where have you laid him?" When Mary and her companions took him to the town cemetery, Christ stood before the tomb, and the text states simply and profoundly, "Jesus wept." Seeing his tears, friends of the family remarked, "See how he loved him!" In that incident, once and for all, Jesus refuted by his tears the notion that "big boys don't cry." He who remains history's perfect and complete man stood by a graveside and wept.

A passage from the pen of Paul has been seriously misunderstood. Paul wrote to his friends in Thessalonica, "We do not want you to be ignorant about those who fall asleep, or to grieve like the rest of men, who have no hope" (1 Thessalonians 4:13). Unfortunately, some Christians struggle under "bad grief" because they have left off the last phrase of the sentence and have missed Paul's point completely. Paul does not say we are not to grieve. Grief is an emotion like love, or fear, guilt or anger and probably a mixture of all of these. Religion does not make us immune from or to emotions, and it is as pointless to deny grief as it is to deny laughter. Christians, in company with all men, experience grief, but unlike others, Christians do not grieve as people without hope. The assurance of the resurrection and the trust in God's power to turn bad Fridays into Good Fridays keep grief from being overwhelming; but nonetheless, God gives no crowns to those who refuse to weep.

Additional Scripture Readings:
John 16:19–24;
1 Thessalonians 4:13–18

Go to page 1150 for your next devotional reading.

"What do you think? Isn't he coming to the Feast at all?" [57]But the chief priests and Pharisees had given orders that if anyone found out where Jesus was, he should report it so that they might arrest him.

Jesus Anointed at Bethany

12 Six days before the Passover, Jesus arrived at Bethany, where Lazarus lived, whom Jesus had raised from the dead. [2]Here a dinner was given in Jesus' honor. Martha served, while Lazarus was among those reclining at the table with him. [3]Then Mary took about a pint[a] of pure nard, an expensive perfume; she poured it on Jesus' feet and wiped his feet with her hair. And the house was filled with the fragrance of the perfume.

[4]But one of his disciples, Judas Iscariot, who was later to betray him, objected, [5]"Why wasn't this perfume sold and the money given to the poor? It was worth a year's wages.[b]" [6]He did not say this because he cared about the poor but because he was a thief; as keeper of the money bag, he used to help himself to what was put into it.

[7]"Leave her alone," Jesus replied. "It was intended that she should save this perfume for the day of my burial. [8]You will always have the poor among you, but you will not always have me."

[9]Meanwhile a large crowd of Jews found out that Jesus was there and came, not only because of him but also to see Lazarus, whom he had raised from the dead. [10]So the chief priests made plans to kill Lazarus as well, [11]for on account of him many of the Jews were going over to Jesus and putting their faith in him.

The Triumphal Entry

[12]The next day the great crowd that had come for the Feast heard that Jesus was on his way to Jerusalem. [13]They took palm branches and went out to meet him, shouting,

"Hosanna![c]"

"Blessed is he who comes in the name of the Lord!"[d]

"Blessed is the King of Israel!"

[14]Jesus found a young donkey and sat upon it, as it is written,

[15]"Do not be afraid, O Daughter of Zion;
see, your king is coming,
seated on a donkey's colt."[e]

[16]At first his disciples did not understand all this. Only after Jesus was glorified did they realize that these things had been written about him and that they had done these things to him.

[17]Now the crowd that was with him when he called Lazarus from the tomb and raised him from the dead continued to spread the word. [18]Many people, because they had heard that he had given this miraculous sign, went out to meet him. [19]So the Pharisees said to one another, "See, this is getting us nowhere. Look how the whole world has gone after him!"

Jesus Predicts His Death

[20]Now there were some Greeks among those who went up to worship at the Feast. [21]They came to Philip, who was from Bethsaida in Galilee, with a request. "Sir," they said, "we would like to see Jesus." [22]Philip went to tell Andrew; Andrew and Philip in turn told Jesus.

[23]Jesus replied, "The hour has come for the Son of Man to be glorified. [24]I tell you the truth, unless a kernel of wheat falls to the ground and dies, it remains only a single seed. But if it dies, it produces many seeds. [25]The man who loves his life will lose it, while the man who hates his life in this world will keep it for eternal life. [26]Whoever serves me must follow me; and where I am, my servant also will be. My Father will honor the one who serves me.

[27]"Now my heart is troubled, and what shall I say? 'Father, save me from this hour'? No, it was for this very reason I came to this hour. [28]Father, glorify your name!"

Then a voice came from heaven, "I have glorified it, and will glorify it again." [29]The crowd that was there and heard it said it had thundered; others said an angel had spoken to him.

[30]Jesus said, "This voice was for your benefit, not mine. [31]Now is the time for judgment on this world; now the prince of this world will be driven out. [32]But I, when I am lifted up from the earth, will draw all men to myself." [33]He said this to show the kind of death he was going to die.

---

[a]3 Greek *a litra* (probably about 0.5 liter)   [b]5 Greek *three hundred denarii*   [c]13 A Hebrew expression meaning "Save!" which became an exclamation of praise   [d]13 Psalm 118:25, 26
[e]15 Zech. 9:9

[34]The crowd spoke up, "We have heard from the Law that the Christ[a] will remain forever, so how can you say, 'The Son of Man must be lifted up'? Who is this 'Son of Man'?"

[35]Then Jesus told them, "You are going to have the light just a little while longer. Walk while you have the light, before darkness overtakes you. The man who walks in the dark does not know where he is going. [36]Put your trust in the light while you have it, so that you may become sons of light." When he had finished speaking, Jesus left and hid himself from them.

The Jews Continue in Their Unbelief

[37]Even after Jesus had done all these miraculous signs in their presence, they still would not believe in him. [38]This was to fulfill the word of Isaiah the prophet:

"Lord, who has believed our message
   and to whom has the arm of the
     Lord been revealed?"[b]

[39]For this reason they could not believe, because, as Isaiah says elsewhere:

[40]"He has blinded their eyes
   and deadened their hearts,
so they can neither see with their
     eyes,
   nor understand with their hearts,
   nor turn—and I would heal
     them."[c]

[41]Isaiah said this because he saw Jesus' glory and spoke about him.

[42]Yet at the same time many even among the leaders believed in him. But because of the Pharisees they would not confess their faith for fear they would be put out of the synagogue; [43]for they loved praise from men more than praise from God.

[44]Then Jesus cried out, "When a man believes in me, he does not believe in me only, but in the one who sent me. [45]When he looks at me, he sees the one who sent me. [46]I have come into the world as a light, so that no one who believes in me should stay in darkness.

[47]"As for the person who hears my words but does not keep them, I do not judge him. For I did not come to judge the world, but to save it. [48]There is a judge for the one who rejects me and does not accept my words; that very word which I spoke will condemn him at the last day. [49]For I did not speak of my own accord,

but the Father who sent me commanded me what to say and how to say it. [50]I know that his command leads to eternal life. So whatever I say is just what the Father has told me to say."

Jesus Washes His Disciples' Feet

13 It was just before the Passover Feast. Jesus knew that the time had come for him to leave this world and go to the Father. Having loved his own who were in the world, he now showed them the full extent of his love.[d]

[2]The evening meal was being served, and the devil had already prompted Judas Iscariot, son of Simon, to betray Jesus. [3]Jesus knew that the Father had put all things under his power, and that he had come from God and was returning to God; [4]so he got up from the meal, took off his outer clothing, and wrapped a towel around his waist. [5]After that, he poured water into a basin and began to wash his disciples' feet, drying them with the towel that was wrapped around him.

[6]He came to Simon Peter, who said to him, "Lord, are you going to wash my feet?"

[7]Jesus replied, "You do not realize now what I am doing, but later you will understand."

[8]"No," said Peter, "you shall never wash my feet."

Jesus answered, "Unless I wash you, you have no part with me."

[9]"Then, Lord," Simon Peter replied, "not just my feet but my hands and my head as well!"

[10]Jesus answered, "A person who has had a bath needs only to wash his feet; his whole body is clean. And you are clean, though not every one of you." [11]For he knew who was going to betray him, and that was why he said not every one was clean.

[12]When he had finished washing their feet, he put on his clothes and returned to his place. "Do you understand what I have done for you?" he asked them. [13]"You call me 'Teacher' and 'Lord,' and rightly so, for that is what I am. [14]Now that I, your Lord and Teacher, have washed your feet, you also should wash one another's feet. [15]I have set you an example that you should do as I have done for you. [16]I tell you the truth, no servant is greater than his master, nor is a messenger greater than the one who sent him. [17]Now that

---

[a]34 Or *Messiah*   [b]38 Isaiah 53:1   [c]40 Isaiah 6:10   [d]1 Or *he loved them to the last*

you know these things, you will be blessed if you do them.

Jesus Predicts His Betrayal

18"I am not referring to all of you; I know those I have chosen. But this is to fulfill the scripture: 'He who shares my bread has lifted up his heel against me.'ᵃ 19"I am telling you now before it happens, so that when it does happen you will believe that I am He. 20I tell you the truth, whoever accepts anyone I send accepts me; and whoever accepts me accepts the one who sent me."

21After he had said this, Jesus was troubled in spirit and testified, "I tell you the truth, one of you is going to betray me."

22His disciples stared at one another, at a loss to know which of them he meant. 23One of them, the disciple whom Jesus loved, was reclining next to him. 24Simon Peter motioned to this disciple and said, "Ask him which one he means."

25Leaning back against Jesus, he asked him, "Lord, who is it?"

26Jesus answered, "It is the one to whom I will give this piece of bread when I have dipped it in the dish." Then, dipping the piece of bread, he gave it to Judas Iscariot, son of Simon. 27As soon as Judas took the bread, Satan entered into him.

"What you are about to do, do quickly," Jesus told him, 28but no one at the meal understood why Jesus said this to him. 29Since Judas had charge of the money, some thought Jesus was telling him to buy

ᵃ18 Psalm 41:9

THURSDAY

VERSE FOR THE DAY:
John 13:14

AUTHOR:
Oswald Chambers

PASSAGE FOR THE DAY:
John 13:1–17

Half Mechanical, Half Mysterious

WE HAVE to recognize that we are one-half mechanical and one-half mysterious; to live in either domain and ignore the other is to be a fool or a fanatic. The great supernatural work of God's grace is in the incalculable part of our nature; we have to work out in the mechanical realm what God works in the mysterious realm. People accept creeds, but they will not accept the holy standards of Jesus Christ's teaching. To build on the fundamental work of God's grace and ignore the fact that we have to work it out in a mechanical life produces humbugs, those who make a divorce between the mysterious life and the practical life. In John 13 the mysterious and the mechanical are closely welded together.

You can't wash anybody's feet mysteriously; it is a purely mechanical matter-of-fact job; you can't do it by giving him devotional books or by praying for him; you can only wash anybody's feet by doing something mechanical. Our Lord did not tell the disciples how they were to do it: He simply says—"Do it." He is not questioning whether or not they can do it; he is saying that they must do what the mastery of his ruling shows them they should do.

Additional Scripture Readings:
Philippians 2:12–14; 1 John 3:11–24

Go to page 1153 for your next devotional reading.

what was needed for the Feast, or to give something to the poor. **30**As soon as Judas had taken the bread, he went out. And it was night.

Jesus Predicts Peter's Denial

31When he was gone, Jesus said, "Now is the Son of Man glorified and God is glorified in him. **32**If God is glorified in him,[a] God will glorify the Son in himself, and will glorify him at once.

33"My children, I will be with you only a little longer. You will look for me, and just as I told the Jews, so I tell you now: Where I am going, you cannot come.

34"A new command I give you: Love one another. As I have loved you, so you must love one another. **35**By this all men will know that you are my disciples, if you love one another."

36Simon Peter asked him, "Lord, where are you going?"

Jesus replied, "Where I am going, you cannot follow now, but you will follow later."

37Peter asked, "Lord, why can't I follow you now? I will lay down my life for you."

38Then Jesus answered, "Will you really lay down your life for me? I tell you the truth, before the rooster crows, you will disown me three times!

Jesus Comforts His Disciples

14 "Do not let your hearts be troubled. Trust in God[b]; trust also in me. **2**In my Father's house are many rooms; if it were not so, I would have told you. I am going there to prepare a place for you. **3**And if I go and prepare a place for you, I will come back and take you to be with me that you also may be where I am. **4**You know the way to the place where I am going."

Jesus the Way to the Father

5Thomas said to him, "Lord, we don't know where you are going, so how can we know the way?"

6Jesus answered, "I am the way and the truth and the life. No one comes to the Father except through me. **7**If you really knew me, you would know[c] my Father as well. From now on, you do know him and have seen him."

8Philip said, "Lord, show us the Father and that will be enough for us."

9Jesus answered: "Don't you know me, Philip, even after I have been among you such a long time? Anyone who has seen me has seen the Father. How can you say, 'Show us the Father'? **10**Don't you believe that I am in the Father, and that the Father is in me? The words I say to you are not just my own. Rather, it is the Father, living in me, who is doing his work. **11**Believe me when I say that I am in the Father and the Father is in me; or at least believe on the evidence of the miracles themselves. **12**I tell you the truth, anyone who has faith in me will do what I have been doing. He will do even greater things than these, because I am going to the Father. **13**And I will do whatever you ask in my name, so that the Son may bring glory to the Father. **14**You may ask me for anything in my name, and I will do it.

Jesus Promises the Holy Spirit

15"If you love me, you will obey what I command. **16**And I will ask the Father, and he will give you another Counselor to be with you forever— **17**the Spirit of truth. The world cannot accept him, because it neither sees him nor knows him. But you know him, for he lives with you and will be[d] in you. **18**I will not leave you as orphans; I will come to you. **19**Before long, the world will not see me anymore, but you will see me. Because I live, you also will live. **20**On that day you will realize that I am in my Father, and you are in me, and I am in you. **21**Whoever has my commands and obeys them, he is the one who loves me. He who loves me will be loved by my Father, and I too will love him and show myself to him."

22Then Judas (not Judas Iscariot) said, "But, Lord, why do you intend to show yourself to us and not to the world?"

23Jesus replied, "If anyone loves me, he will obey my teaching. My Father will love him, and we will come to him and make our home with him. **24**He who does not love me will not obey my teaching. These words you hear are not my own; they belong to the Father who sent me.

25"All this I have spoken while still with you. **26**But the Counselor, the Holy Spirit, whom the Father will send in my name, will teach you all things and will remind you of everything I have said to you. **27**Peace I leave with you; my peace I give

---

[a]32 Many early manuscripts do not have *If God is glorified in him.*   [b]1 Or *You trust in God*
[c]7 Some early manuscripts *If you really have known me, you will know and is*   [d]17 Some early manuscripts

you. I do not give to you as the world gives. Do not let your hearts be troubled and do not be afraid.

28"You heard me say, 'I am going away and I am coming back to you.' If you loved me, you would be glad that I am going to the Father, for the Father is greater than I. 29I have told you now before it happens, so that when it does happen you will believe. 30I will not speak with you much longer, for the prince of this world is coming. He has no hold on me, 31but the world must learn that I love the Father and that I do exactly what my Father has commanded me.

"Come now; let us leave.

The Vine and the Branches

15 "I am the true vine, and my Father is the gardener. 2He cuts off every branch in me that bears no fruit, while every branch that does bear fruit he prunes[a] so that it will be even more fruitful. 3You are already clean because of the word I have spoken to you. 4Remain in me, and I will remain in you. No branch can bear fruit by itself; it must remain in the vine. Neither can you bear fruit unless you remain in me.

5"I am the vine; you are the branches. If a man remains in me and I in him, he will bear much fruit; apart from me you can do nothing. 6If anyone does not remain in me, he is like a branch that is thrown away and withers; such branches are picked up, thrown into the fire and burned. 7If you remain in me and my words remain in you, ask whatever you wish, and it will be given you. 8This is to my Father's glory, that you bear much fruit, showing yourselves to be my disciples.

9"As the Father has loved me, so have I loved you. Now remain in my love. 10If you obey my commands, you will remain in my love, just as I have obeyed my Father's commands and remain in his love. 11I have told you this so that my joy may be in you and that your joy may be complete. 12My command is this: Love each other as I have loved you. 13Greater love has no one than this, that he lay down his life for his friends. 14You are my friends if you do what I command. 15I no longer call you servants, because a servant does not know his master's business. Instead, I have called you friends, for everything that I learned from my Father I have made

known to you. 16You did not choose me, but I chose you and appointed you to go and bear fruit—fruit that will last. Then the Father will give you whatever you ask in my name. 17This is my command: Love each other.

The World Hates the Disciples

18"If the world hates you, keep in mind that it hated me first. 19If you belonged to the world, it would love you as its own. As it is, you do not belong to the world, but I have chosen you out of the world. That is why the world hates you. 20Remember the words I spoke to you: 'No servant is greater than his master.'[b] If they persecuted me, they will persecute you also. If they obeyed my teaching, they will obey yours also. 21They will treat you this way because of my name, for they do not know the One who sent me. 22If I had not come and spoken to them, they would not be guilty of sin. Now, however, they have no excuse for their sin. 23He who hates me hates my Father as well. 24If I had not done among them what no one else did, they would not be guilty of sin. But now they have seen these miracles, and yet they have hated both me and my Father. 25But this is to fulfill what is written in their Law: 'They hated me without reason.'[c]

26"When the Counselor comes, whom I will send to you from the Father, the Spirit of truth who goes out from the Father, he will testify about me. 27And you also must testify, for you have been with me from the beginning.

16 "All this I have told you so that you will not go astray. 2They will put you out of the synagogue; in fact, a time is coming when anyone who kills you will think he is offering a service to God. 3They will do such things because they have not known the Father or me. 4I have told you this, so that when the time comes you will remember that I warned you. I did not tell you this at first because I was with you.

The Work of the Holy Spirit

5"Now I am going to him who sent me, yet none of you asks me, 'Where are you going?' 6Because I have said these things, you are filled with grief. 7But I tell you the truth: It is for your good that I am going away. Unless I go away, the Counselor will not come to you; but if I go, I will send him to you. 8When he comes, he will con-

---

a2 The Greek for *prunes* also means *cleans*.   b20 John 13:16   c25 Psalms 35:19; 69:4

vict the world of guilt*a* in regard to sin and righteousness and judgment: [9]in regard to sin, because men do not believe in me; [10]in regard to righteousness, because I am going to the Father, where you can see me no longer; [11]and in regard to judgment, because the prince of this world now stands condemned.

[12]"I have much more to say to you, more than you can now bear. [13]But when he, the Spirit of truth, comes, he will guide you into all truth. He will not speak on his own; he will speak only what he hears, and he will tell you what is yet to come. [14]He will bring glory to me by taking from what is mine and making it known to you. [15]All that belongs to the Father is mine. That is why I said the Spirit will take from what is mine and make it known to you.

[16]"In a little while you will see me no more, and then after a little while you will see me."

The Disciples' Grief Will Turn to Joy

[17]Some of his disciples said to one another, "What does he mean by saying, 'In

a8 Or *will expose the guilt of the world*

FRIDAY

VERSE FOR THE DAY: John 15:5	AUTHOR: Patrick Morley	PASSAGE FOR THE DAY: John 15:1–8

A Man's Most Innate Need

WHAT do you think is man's greatest need? Someone recently mentioned they would like their tombstone to read, "He made a difference." Whether we speak of achieving our full potential, or only of surviving to the next paycheck, men invariably talk about their need to be significant. A man's most innate need is his need to be significant—to find purpose and meaning . . .

The difference in men is in how we go about satisfying our need to be significant. Some men, eager for the spoils of this life, pursue significance by gratifying only their own ambitions. Others, trained by the Scriptures, find it in obeying God.

How we answer the questions, *"Who am I?"* and *"Why do I exist?"* determines how we pursue our significance. Our answers divide us succinctly into two groups: those who pursue significance in appropriate ways and those who pursue significance in inappropriate ways. Our desire to satisfy this need can take us close to or far away from the things of God.

Authentic, lasting significance is hid with Christ. Jesus said, "I am the vine; you are the branches. If a man remains in me and I in him, he will bear much fruit; *apart from me you can do nothing*" (John 15:5, italics added). That is to say, a man cannot find significance in any lasting way apart from Christ. So, if a man is in Christ, and submitted to God's plan and purpose, then he can satisfy his greatest need in a way that endures.

Additional Scripture Readings:
Jeremiah 9:23–24;
Philippians 3:7–11

Go to page 1154 for your next devotional reading.

WEEKENDING

RENEW

There is a striking difference between knowing about God and knowing God. We may know the right God-words yet not experience God. Only in Jesus, the Son of God, can we truly know God the Father . . .

What we think of God makes a tremendous difference in our lives. Where we get our ideas of God makes a tremendous difference too. We can gather up data and develop our own image of God, or we can allow God to reveal himself in a self-portrait—his Son, Jesus Christ . . .

Yes, Jesus, yes. If God is like you, my heart says yes! But it is hard to let go of old ideas, feelings and images. Give me the grace to bring them all to you. Let your Holy Spirit cleanse and replace the false God-images I have carried so long. Let him fill my heart and mind with the vision of yourself. Amen.

— *Reuben R. Welch*

REVIVE

Saturday: Psalm 145:1–7
Sunday: John 3:27–36

Go to page 1156 for your next devotional reading.

a little while you will see me no more, and then after a little while you will see me,' and 'Because I am going to the Father'?" ¹⁸They kept asking, "What does he mean by 'a little while'? We don't understand what he is saying."

¹⁹Jesus saw that they wanted to ask him about this, so he said to them, "Are you asking one another what I meant when I said, 'In a little while you will see me no more, and then after a little while you will see me'? ²⁰I tell you the truth, you will weep and mourn while the world rejoices. You will grieve, but your grief will turn to joy. ²¹A woman giving birth to a child has pain because her time has come; but when her baby is born she forgets the anguish because of her joy that a child is born into the world. ²²So with you: Now is your time of grief, but I will see you again and you will rejoice, and no one will take away your joy. ²³In that day you will no longer ask me anything. I tell you the truth, my Father will give you whatever you ask in my name. ²⁴Until now you have not asked for anything in my name. Ask and you will receive, and your joy will be complete.

²⁵"Though I have been speaking figuratively, a time is coming when I will no longer use this kind of language but will tell you plainly about my Father. ²⁶In that day you will ask in my name. I am not saying that I will ask the Father on your behalf. ²⁷No, the Father himself loves you because you have loved me and have believed that I came from God. ²⁸I came from the Father and entered the world; now I am leaving the world and going back to the Father."

²⁹Then Jesus' disciples said, "Now you are speaking clearly and without figures of speech. ³⁰Now we can see that you know all things and that you do not even need to have anyone ask you questions. This makes us believe that you came from God."

³¹"You believe at last!"ᵃ Jesus answered. ³²"But a time is coming, and has come, when you will be scattered, each to his own home. You will leave me all alone. Yet I am not alone, for my Father is with me.

³³"I have told you these things, so that in me you may have peace. In this world you will have trouble. But take heart! I have overcome the world."

Jesus Prays for Himself

17 After Jesus said this, he looked toward heaven and prayed:

"Father, the time has come. Glorify your Son, that your Son may glorify you. ²For you granted him authority over all people that he might give eternal life to all those you have given him. ³Now this is eternal life: that they may know you, the only true God, and Jesus Christ, whom you have sent. ⁴I have brought you glory on earth by completing the work you gave me to do. ⁵And now, Father, glorify me in your presence with the glory I had with you before the world began.

Jesus Prays for His Disciples

⁶"I have revealed youᵇ to those whom you gave me out of the world. They were yours; you gave them to me and they have obeyed your word. ⁷Now they know that everything you have given me comes from you. ⁸For I gave them the words you gave me and they accepted them. They knew with certainty that I came from you, and they believed that you sent me. ⁹I pray for them. I am not praying for the world, but for those you have given me, for they are yours. ¹⁰All I have is yours, and all you have is mine. And glory has come to me through them. ¹¹I will remain in the world no longer, but they are still in the world, and I am coming to you. Holy Father, protect them by the power of your name—the name you gave me—so that they may be one as we are one. ¹²While I was with them, I protected them and kept them safe by that name you gave me. None has been lost except the one doomed to destruction so that Scripture would be fulfilled.

¹³"I am coming to you now, but I say these things while I am still in the world, so that they may have the full measure of my joy within them. ¹⁴I have given them your word and the world has hated them, for they are not of the world any more than I am of the world. ¹⁵My prayer is not that you take them out of the world but

ᵃ31 Or "Do you now believe?"   ᵇ6 Greek your name; also in verse 26 that you protect them from the evil one. [16]They are not of the world, even as I am not of it. [17]Sanctify[a] them by the truth; your word is truth. [18]As you sent me into the world, I have sent them into the world. [19]For them I sanctify myself, that they too may be truly sanctified.

[a]17 Greek *hagiazo* (*set apart for sacred use* or *make holy*); also in verse 19

MONDAY

VERSE FOR THE DAY:
John 17:11

AUTHOR:
Paul Brand

PASSAGE FOR THE DAY:
John 17:6–12

Unlikely Seekers

I THINK of the churches I have known: Is there another institution in town with such a mosaic assortment of unlikes? Young radicals, uniformed in jeans, share the pews with Republican bankers in three-piece suits. Bored teenagers tune out the sermon even as their eager grandparents turn up their hearing aids. Some members gather as methodically as a school of fish, then quickly break apart to return to their jobs and homes. Others want close communities and migrate together like social amoebae.

I could easily cluck my tongue at the absurdity of the whole enterprise, seemingly doomed to fail. Jesus prayed that we "may be one" as he and God the Father are one (John 17:11). How can any organism composed of such diversity attain even a semblance of unity?

As the doubts rumble inside me, a sober and quieting voice replies, "You have not chosen me, I have chosen you" [see John 15:16]. The chuckle at Christ's Body is caught in my throat like cotton. For if anything is to be believed about the collection of people who follow him, it is that we were called by him. The word church, *ekklēsia*, means "the called-out ones." Our crew of comedians from central casting is the group God wants.

During my life as a missionary surgeon in India and now as a member of the tiny chapel on the grounds of the Carville leprosy hospital, I have seen my share of unlikely seekers after God. And I must admit that most of my worship in the last thirty years has not taken place among people who have shared my taste in music, speech, or even thought. But over those years I have been profoundly—and humbly—impressed that I find God in the faces of my fellow worshipers by sharing with people who are shockingly different from each other and from me.

Additional Scripture Readings:
Romans 12:4–8;
1 Corinthians 12:12–27

Go to page 1161 for your next devotional reading.

Jesus Prays for All Believers

20"My prayer is not for them alone. I pray also for those who will believe in me through their message, 21that all of them may be one, Father, just as you are in me and I am in you. May they also be in us so that the world may believe that you have sent me. 22I have given them the glory that you gave me, that they may be one as we are one: 23I in them and you in me. May they be brought to complete unity to let the world know that you sent me and have loved them even as you have loved me.

24"Father, I want those you have given me to be with me where I am, and to see my glory, the glory you have given me because you loved me before the creation of the world.

25"Righteous Father, though the world does not know you, I know you, and they know that you have sent me. 26I have made you known to them, and will continue to make you known in order that the love you have for me may be in them and that I myself may be in them."

Jesus Arrested

18 When he had finished praying, Jesus left with his disciples and crossed the Kidron Valley. On the other side there was an olive grove, and he and his disciples went into it.

2Now Judas, who betrayed him, knew the place, because Jesus had often met there with his disciples. 3So Judas came to the grove, guiding a detachment of soldiers and some officials from the chief priests and Pharisees. They were carrying torches, lanterns and weapons.

4Jesus, knowing all that was going to happen to him, went out and asked them, "Who is it you want?"

5"Jesus of Nazareth," they replied.

"I am he," Jesus said. (And Judas the traitor was standing there with them.) 6When Jesus said, "I am he," they drew back and fell to the ground.

7Again he asked them, "Who is it you want?"

And they said, "Jesus of Nazareth."

8"I told you that I am he," Jesus answered. "If you are looking for me, then let these men go." 9This happened so that the words he had spoken would be ful-filled: "I have not lost one of those you gave me."a

10Then Simon Peter, who had a sword, drew it and struck the high priest's servant, cutting off his right ear. (The servant's name was Malchus.)

11Jesus commanded Peter, "Put your sword away! Shall I not drink the cup the Father has given me?"

Jesus Taken to Annas

12Then the detachment of soldiers with its commander and the Jewish officials arrested Jesus. They bound him 13and brought him first to Annas, who was the father-in-law of Caiaphas, the high priest that year. 14Caiaphas was the one who had advised the Jews that it would be good if one man died for the people.

Peter's First Denial

15Simon Peter and another disciple were following Jesus. Because this disciple was known to the high priest, he went with Jesus into the high priest's courtyard, 16but Peter had to wait outside at the door. The other disciple, who was known to the high priest, came back, spoke to the girl on duty there and brought Peter in.

17"You are not one of his disciples, are you?" the girl at the door asked Peter.

He replied, "I am not."

18It was cold, and the servants and officials stood around a fire they had made to keep warm. Peter also was standing with them, warming himself.

The High Priest Questions Jesus

19Meanwhile, the high priest questioned Jesus about his disciples and his teaching.

20"I have spoken openly to the world," Jesus replied. "I always taught in synagogues or at the temple, where all the Jews come together. I said nothing in secret. 21Why question me? Ask those who heard me. Surely they know what I said."

22When Jesus said this, one of the officials nearby struck him in the face. "Is this the way you answer the high priest?" he demanded.

23"If I said something wrong," Jesus replied, "testify as to what is wrong. But if I spoke the truth, why did you strike me?" 24Then Annas sent him, still bound, to Caiaphas the high priest.b

a9 John 6:39   b24 Or (Now Annas had sent him, still bound, to Caiaphas the high priest.)

Peter's Second and Third Denials

25As Simon Peter stood warming himself, he was asked, "You are not one of his disciples, are you?"

He denied it, saying, "I am not."

26One of the high priest's servants, a relative of the man whose ear Peter had cut off, challenged him, "Didn't I see you with him in the olive grove?" **27**Again Peter denied it, and at that moment a rooster began to crow.

Jesus Before Pilate

28Then the Jews led Jesus from Caiaphas to the palace of the Roman governor. By now it was early morning, and to avoid ceremonial uncleanness the Jews did not enter the palace; they wanted to be able to eat the Passover. **29**So Pilate came out to them and asked, "What charges are you bringing against this man?"

30"If he were not a criminal," they replied, "we would not have handed him over to you."

31Pilate said, "Take him yourselves and judge him by your own law."

"But we have no right to execute anyone," the Jews objected. **32**This happened so that the words Jesus had spoken indicating the kind of death he was going to die would be fulfilled.

33Pilate then went back inside the palace, summoned Jesus and asked him, "Are you the king of the Jews?"

34"Is that your own idea," Jesus asked, "or did others talk to you about me?"

35"Am I a Jew?" Pilate replied. "It was your people and your chief priests who handed you over to me. What is it you have done?"

36Jesus said, "My kingdom is not of this world. If it were, my servants would fight to prevent my arrest by the Jews. But now my kingdom is from another place."

37"You are a king, then!" said Pilate.

Jesus answered, "You are right in saying I am a king. In fact, for this reason I was born, and for this I came into the world, to testify to the truth. Everyone on the side of truth listens to me."

38"What is truth?" Pilate asked. With this he went out again to the Jews and said, "I find no basis for a charge against him. **39**But it is your custom for me to release to you one prisoner at the time of the Passover. Do you want me to release 'the king of the Jews'?"

40They shouted back, "No, not him! Give us Barabbas!" Now Barabbas had taken part in a rebellion.

Jesus Sentenced to be Crucified

19 Then Pilate took Jesus and had him flogged. **2**The soldiers twisted together a crown of thorns and put it on his head. They clothed him in a purple robe **3**and went up to him again and again, saying, "Hail, king of the Jews!" And they struck him in the face.

4Once more Pilate came out and said to the Jews, "Look, I am bringing him out to you to let you know that I find no basis for a charge against him." **5**When Jesus came out wearing the crown of thorns and the purple robe, Pilate said to them, "Here is the man!"

6As soon as the chief priests and their officials saw him, they shouted, "Crucify! Crucify!"

But Pilate answered, "You take him and crucify him. As for me, I find no basis for a charge against him."

7The Jews insisted, "We have a law, and according to that law he must die, because he claimed to be the Son of God."

8When Pilate heard this, he was even more afraid, **9**and he went back inside the palace. "Where do you come from?" he asked Jesus, but Jesus gave him no answer. **10**"Do you refuse to speak to me?" Pilate said. "Don't you realize I have power either to free you or to crucify you?"

11Jesus answered, "You would have no power over me if it were not given to you from above. Therefore the one who handed me over to you is guilty of a greater sin."

12From then on, Pilate tried to set Jesus free, but the Jews kept shouting, "If you let this man go, you are no friend of Caesar. Anyone who claims to be a king opposes Caesar."

13When Pilate heard this, he brought Jesus out and sat down on the judge's seat at a place known as the Stone Pavement (which in Aramaic is Gabbatha). **14**It was the day of Preparation of Passover Week, about the sixth hour.

"Here is your king," Pilate said to the Jews.

15But they shouted, "Take him away! Take him away! Crucify him!"

"Shall I crucify your king?" Pilate asked.

"We have no king but Caesar," the chief priests answered.

16Finally Pilate handed him over to them to be crucified.

The Crucifixion

So the soldiers took charge of Jesus. [17]Carrying his own cross, he went out to the place of the Skull (which in Aramaic is called Golgotha). [18]Here they crucified him, and with him two others—one on each side and Jesus in the middle.

[19]Pilate had a notice prepared and fastened to the cross. It read: JESUS OF NAZARETH, THE KING OF THE JEWS. [20]Many of the Jews read this sign, for the place where Jesus was crucified was near the city, and the sign was written in Aramaic, Latin and Greek. [21]The chief priests of the Jews protested to Pilate, "Do not write 'The King of the Jews,' but that this man claimed to be king of the Jews."

[22]Pilate answered, "What I have written, I have written."

[23]When the soldiers crucified Jesus, they took his clothes, dividing them into four shares, one for each of them, with the undergarment remaining. This garment was seamless, woven in one piece from top to bottom.

[24]"Let's not tear it," they said to one another. "Let's decide by lot who will get it."

This happened that the scripture might be fulfilled which said,

"They divided my garments among
    them
and cast lots for my clothing."[a]

So this is what the soldiers did.

[25]Near the cross of Jesus stood his mother, his mother's sister, Mary the wife of Clopas, and Mary Magdalene. [26]When Jesus saw his mother there, and the disciple whom he loved standing nearby, he said to his mother, "Dear woman, here is your son," [27]and to the disciple, "Here is your mother." From that time on, this disciple took her into his home.

The Death of Jesus

[28]Later, knowing that all was now completed, and so that the Scripture would be fulfilled, Jesus said, "I am thirsty." [29]A jar of wine vinegar was there, so they soaked a sponge in it, put the sponge on a stalk of the hyssop plant, and lifted it to Jesus' lips. [30]When he had received the drink, Jesus said, "It is finished." With that, he bowed his head and gave up his spirit.

[31]Now it was the day of Preparation, and the next day was to be a special Sabbath. Because the Jews did not want the bodies left on the crosses during the Sabbath, they asked Pilate to have the legs broken and the bodies taken down. [32]The soldiers therefore came and broke the legs of the first man who had been crucified with Jesus, and then those of the other. [33]But when they came to Jesus and found that he was already dead, they did not break his legs. [34]Instead, one of the soldiers pierced Jesus' side with a spear, bringing a sudden flow of blood and water. [35]The man who saw it has given testimony, and his testimony is true. He knows that he tells the truth, and he testifies so that you also may believe. [36]These things happened so that the scripture would be fulfilled: "Not one of his bones will be broken,"[b] [37]and, as another scripture says, "They will look on the one they have pierced."[c]

The Burial of Jesus

[38]Later, Joseph of Arimathea asked Pilate for the body of Jesus. Now Joseph was a disciple of Jesus, but secretly because he feared the Jews. With Pilate's permission, he came and took the body away. [39]He was accompanied by Nicodemus, the man who earlier had visited Jesus at night. Nicodemus brought a mixture of myrrh and aloes, about seventy-five pounds.[d] [40]Taking Jesus' body, the two of them wrapped it, with the spices, in strips of linen. This was in accordance with Jewish burial customs. [41]At the place where Jesus was crucified, there was a garden, and in the garden a new tomb, in which no one had ever been laid. [42]Because it was the Jewish day of Preparation and since the tomb was nearby, they laid Jesus there.

The Empty Tomb

20 Early on the first day of the week, while it was still dark, Mary Magdalene went to the tomb and saw that the stone had been removed from the entrance. [2]So she came running to Simon Peter and the other disciple, the one Jesus loved, and said, "They have taken the Lord out of the tomb, and we don't know where they have put him!"

[3]So Peter and the other disciple started for the tomb. [4]Both were running, but the other disciple outran Peter and reached the tomb first. [5]He bent over and looked

---

[a]24 Psalm 22:18   [b]36 Exodus 12:46; Num. 9:12; Psalm 34:20   [c]37 Zech. 12:10   [d]39 Greek *a hundred litrai* (about 34 kilograms)

in at the strips of linen lying there but did not go in. **6**Then Simon Peter, who was behind him, arrived and went into the tomb. He saw the strips of linen lying there, **7**as well as the burial cloth that had been around Jesus' head. The cloth was folded up by itself, separate from the linen. **8**Finally the other disciple, who had reached the tomb first, also went inside. He saw and believed. **9**(They still did not understand from Scripture that Jesus had to rise from the dead.)

Jesus Appears to Mary Magdalene

10Then the disciples went back to their homes, **11**but Mary stood outside the tomb crying. As she wept, she bent over to look into the tomb **12**and saw two angels in white, seated where Jesus' body had been, one at the head and the other at the foot.

13They asked her, "Woman, why are you crying?"

"They have taken my Lord away," she said, "and I don't know where they have put him." **14**At this, she turned around and saw Jesus standing there, but she did not realize that it was Jesus.

15"Woman," he said, "why are you crying? Who is it you are looking for?"

Thinking he was the gardener, she said, "Sir, if you have carried him away, tell me where you have put him, and I will get him."

16Jesus said to her, "Mary."

She turned toward him and cried out in Aramaic, "Rabboni!" (which means Teacher).

17Jesus said, "Do not hold on to me, for I have not yet returned to the Father. Go instead to my brothers and tell them, 'I am returning to my Father and your Father, to my God and your God.' "

18Mary Magdalene went to the disciples with the news: "I have seen the Lord!" And she told them that he had said these things to her.

Jesus Appears to His Disciples

19On the evening of that first day of the week, when the disciples were together, with the doors locked for fear of the Jews, Jesus came and stood among them and said, "Peace be with you!" **20**After he said this, he showed them his hands and side. The disciples were overjoyed when they saw the Lord.

21Again Jesus said, "Peace be with you! As the Father has sent me, I am sending

you." **22**And with that he breathed on them and said, "Receive the Holy Spirit. **23**If you forgive anyone his sins, they are forgiven; if you do not forgive them, they are not forgiven."

Jesus Appears to Thomas

24Now Thomas (called Didymus), one of the Twelve, was not with the disciples when Jesus came. **25**So the other disciples told him, "We have seen the Lord!"

But he said to them, "Unless I see the nail marks in his hands and put my finger where the nails were, and put my hand into his side, I will not believe it."

26A week later his disciples were in the house again, and Thomas was with them. Though the doors were locked, Jesus came and stood among them and said, "Peace be with you!" **27**Then he said to Thomas, "Put your finger here; see my hands. Reach out your hand and put it into my side. Stop doubting and believe."

28Thomas said to him, "My Lord and my God!"

29Then Jesus told him, "Because you have seen me, you have believed; blessed are those who have not seen and yet have believed."

30Jesus did many other miraculous signs in the presence of his disciples, which are not recorded in this book. **31**But these are written that you may*a* believe that Jesus is the Christ, the Son of God, and that by believing you may have life in his name.

Jesus and the Miraculous Catch of Fish

21 Afterward Jesus appeared again to his disciples, by the Sea of Tiberias.*b* It happened this way: **2**Simon Peter, Thomas (called Didymus), Nathanael from Cana in Galilee, the sons of Zebedee, and two other disciples were together. **3**"I'm going out to fish," Simon Peter told them, and they said, "We'll go with you." So they went out and got into the boat, but that night they caught nothing.

4Early in the morning, Jesus stood on the shore, but the disciples did not realize that it was Jesus.

5He called out to them, "Friends, haven't you any fish?"

"No," they answered.

6He said, "Throw your net on the right side of the boat and you will find some." When they did, they were unable to haul

---

a31 Some manuscripts *may continue to*   *b1* That is, Sea of Galilee the net in because of the large number of fish.

7Then the disciple whom Jesus loved said to Peter, "It is the Lord!" As soon as Simon Peter heard him say, "It is the Lord," he wrapped his outer garment around him (for he had taken it off) and jumped into the water. **8**The other disciples followed in the boat, towing the net full of fish, for they were not far from shore, about a hundred yards.*a* **9**When they landed, they saw a fire of burning coals there with fish on it, and some bread.

10Jesus said to them, "Bring some of the fish you have just caught."

11Simon Peter climbed aboard and dragged the net ashore. It was full of large fish, 153, but even with so many the net was not torn. **12**Jesus said to them, "Come

a8 Greek about two hundred cubits (about 90 meters)

TUESDAY

VERSE FOR THE DAY:
John 20:20

AUTHOR:
Michael Card

PASSAGE FOR THE DAY:
John 20:19–23

Known by the Scars

[AFTER the crucifixion,] Mary recognized his [Jesus'] familiar voice. The disciples at Emmaus recognized him in the breaking of the bread. The weary fishermen knew it was him because of a miraculous catch. We, too, can recognize the resurrected Jesus in all these ways, by his voice, at his Table, by the miracles he still performs.

When Jesus wanted to be recognized the first thing the Bible says he did was show them his scars. He didn't point to his face and say, "Look, it's me." He showed them his hands and feet and side and gently said, "Look, it's me." Jesus is known by his scars . . .

At the far end of history, John, weeping because no one could open the special scroll, was told by an elder standing beside him in the heavenly crowd, "Do not weep! See, the Lion of the tribe of Judah" [Revelation 5:5].

John looked up, expecting to see a lion. But what did he see? A Lamb. And he knew who that Lamb was precisely because it was wounded.

Jesus is known by his scars. When we stand in his presence he won't point to his face but to his scars and say, "Look, it's me!"

Modern-day heretics point to material wealth and say, "Look, it's Jesus!" But the true followers of all ages . . . will tell you, "This is Jesus, for I bear in my own body the marks of his death" [see Galatians 6:17]. As Jesus' resurrected body was recognized by its scars, so his body, the church, should be known by its scars and tears and the unspeakable joy it knows in spite of, and indeed because of, it all.

Additional Scripture Readings:
Galatians 6:11–18; Revelation 5:1–10

Go to page 1164 for your next devotional reading.

and have breakfast." None of the disciples dared ask him, "Who are you?" They knew it was the Lord. [13]Jesus came, took the bread and gave it to them, and did the same with the fish. [14]This was now the third time Jesus appeared to his disciples after he was raised from the dead.

Jesus Reinstates Peter

[15]When they had finished eating, Jesus said to Simon Peter, "Simon son of John, do you truly love me more than these?"

"Yes, Lord," he said, "you know that I love you."

Jesus said, "Feed my lambs."

[16]Again Jesus said, "Simon son of John, do you truly love me?"

He answered, "Yes, Lord, you know that I love you."

Jesus said, "Take care of my sheep."

[17]The third time he said to him, "Simon son of John, do you love me?"

Peter was hurt because Jesus asked him the third time, "Do you love me?" He said, "Lord, you know all things; you know that I love you."

Jesus said, "Feed my sheep. [18]I tell you the truth, when you were younger you dressed yourself and went where you wanted; but when you are old you will stretch out your hands, and someone else will dress you and lead you where you do not want to go." [19]Jesus said this to indicate the kind of death by which Peter would glorify God. Then he said to him, "Follow me!"

[20]Peter turned and saw that the disciple whom Jesus loved was following them. (This was the one who had leaned back against Jesus at the supper and had said, "Lord, who is going to betray you?") [21]When Peter saw him, he asked, "Lord, what about him?"

[22]Jesus answered, "If I want him to remain alive until I return, what is that to you? You must follow me." [23]Because of this, the rumor spread among the brothers that this disciple would not die. But Jesus did not say that he would not die; he only said, "If I want him to remain alive until I return, what is that to you?"

[24]This is the disciple who testifies to these things and who wrote them down. We know that his testimony is true.

[25]Jesus did many other things as well. If every one of them were written down, I suppose that even the whole world would not have room for the books that would be written.

*L*UKE begins the second volume of his history of Christianity (Acts 1:1–3) by telling how Jesus pours out the Holy Spirit on the apostles. The Spirit in turn inspires them to spread the message of salvation from Jerusalem to Rome. In his story Luke stresses how unity and love prevail in the church and how God protects the missionaries from their enemies. As you read this book, think about how powerful the Holy Spirit still is in the church and in your own life and how God protects you against the forces of evil.

ACTS

Jesus Taken Up Into Heaven

1 In my former book, Theophilus, I wrote about all that Jesus began to do and to teach ²until the day he was taken up to heaven, after giving instructions through the Holy Spirit to the apostles he had chosen. ³After his suffering, he showed himself to these men and gave many convincing proofs that he was alive. He appeared to them over a period of forty days and spoke about the kingdom of God. ⁴On one occasion, while he was eating with them, he gave them this command: "Do not leave Jerusalem, but wait for the gift my Father promised, which you have heard me speak about. ⁵For John baptized with*a* water, but in a few days you will be baptized with the Holy Spirit."

⁶So when they met together, they asked him, "Lord, are you at this time going to restore the kingdom to Israel?"

⁷He said to them: "It is not for you to

*a*5 Or *in*

know the times or dates the Father has set by his own authority. **8**But you will receive power when the Holy Spirit comes on you; and you will be my witnesses in Jerusalem, and in all Judea and Samaria, and to the ends of the earth."

9After he said this, he was taken up before their very eyes, and a cloud hid him from their sight.

10They were looking intently up into the sky as he was going, when suddenly two men dressed in white stood beside them. **11**"Men of Galilee," they said, "why do you stand here looking into the sky? This same Jesus, who has been taken from you into heaven, will come back in the same way you have seen him go into heaven."

Matthias Chosen to Replace Judas

12Then they returned to Jerusalem from the hill called the Mount of Olives, a Sab-

---

WEDNESDAY

VERSE FOR THE DAY:	*AUTHOR:*	*PASSAGE FOR THE DAY:*
Acts 1:8	*Reggie White*	*Acts 1:1–8*

Playground Platform

ON A regular basis Philadelphia Eagles' defensive lineman Reggie White visits Philadelphia's inner city to talk to the kids.

I remind them that I grew up in a neighborhood just like theirs. I know what it's like to feel frustrated, to search for peace and a sense of security. I tell them about my upbringing and the most important thing I learned as a kid. I tell them about God and about his love for me.

I tell them that I love them with the love of the Lord Jesus Christ who loved them so much that he gave his life for them. I share that nothing in life satisfies like he does, that they may think power or money or important friends may fill the need they have. I read a few passages of Scripture and then relay to them the plan of salvation. As their heads are bowed on that dirty, old, hot playground, several of the kids pray to receive Christ as their Lord and Savior.

The rest of the crowd is dismissed as I remind them that we will be back the next Friday and that they should tell their friends and bring them back with them. Then I take the kids who have prayed to receive Christ over to the side and explain to them further what has just happened to their lives as a result of asking Jesus to come into their hearts. The next week I talk with them again about the problems they have, about what being a Christian is all about. What a glorious time we have on those Fridays.

Why do I take time out of my hectic schedule to be with these kids in North Philadelphia? Because God has given me a platform, and if I don't use it, I commit sin. Therefore, I choose to obey my Lord. And I enjoy it.

Additional Scripture Readings:
Romans 1:11–17; 2 Timothy 1:3–14

Go to page 1169 for your next devotional reading.

bath day's walk*a* from the city. **13**When they arrived, they went upstairs to the room where they were staying. Those present were Peter, John, James and Andrew; Philip and Thomas, Bartholomew and Matthew; James son of Alphaeus and Simon the Zealot, and Judas son of James. **14**They all joined together constantly in prayer, along with the women and Mary the mother of Jesus, and with his brothers.

15In those days Peter stood up among the believers*b* (a group numbering about a hundred and twenty) **16**and said, "Brothers, the Scripture had to be fulfilled which the Holy Spirit spoke long ago through the mouth of David concerning Judas, who served as guide for those who arrested Jesus— **17**he was one of our number and shared in this ministry."

18(With the reward he got for his wickedness, Judas bought a field; there he fell headlong, his body burst open and all his intestines spilled out. **19**Everyone in Jerusalem heard about this, so they called that field in their language Akeldama, that is, Field of Blood.)

20"For," said Peter, "it is written in the book of Psalms,

" 'May his place be deserted;
let there be no one to dwell in it,'*c*

and,

" 'May another take his place of
leadership.'*d*

21Therefore it is necessary to choose one of the men who have been with us the whole time the Lord Jesus went in and out among us, **22**beginning from John's baptism to the time when Jesus was taken up from us. For one of these must become a witness with us of his resurrection."

23So they proposed two men: Joseph called Barsabbas (also known as Justus) and Matthias. **24**Then they prayed, "Lord, you know everyone's heart. Show us which of these two you have chosen **25**to take over this apostolic ministry, which Judas left to go where he belongs." **26**Then they cast lots, and the lot fell to Matthias; so he was added to the eleven apostles.

The Holy Spirit Comes at Pentecost

2 When the day of Pentecost came, they were all together in one place. **2**Suddenly a sound like the blowing of a violent wind came from heaven and filled the whole house where they were sitting. **3**They saw what seemed to be tongues of fire that separated and came to rest on each of them. **4**All of them were filled with the Holy Spirit and began to speak in other tongues*e* as the Spirit enabled them.

5Now there were staying in Jerusalem God-fearing Jews from every nation under heaven. **6**When they heard this sound, a crowd came together in bewilderment, because each one heard them speaking in his own language. **7**Utterly amazed, they asked: "Are not all these men who are speaking Galileans? **8**Then how is it that each of us hears them in his own native language? **9**Parthians, Medes and Elamites; residents of Mesopotamia, Judea and Cappadocia, Pontus and Asia, **10**Phrygia and Pamphylia, Egypt and the parts of Libya near Cyrene; visitors from Rome **11**(both Jews and converts to Judaism); Cretans and Arabs—we hear them declaring the wonders of God in our own tongues!" **12**Amazed and perplexed, they asked one another, "What does this mean?"

13Some, however, made fun of them and said, "They have had too much wine.*f*"

Peter Addresses the Crowd

14Then Peter stood up with the Eleven, raised his voice and addressed the crowd: "Fellow Jews and all of you who live in Jerusalem, let me explain this to you; listen carefully to what I say. **15**These men are not drunk, as you suppose. It's only nine in the morning! **16**No, this is what was spoken by the prophet Joel:

17" 'In the last days, God says,
I will pour out my Spirit on all
people.
Your sons and daughters will
prophesy,
your young men will see visions,
your old men will dream dreams.
18Even on my servants, both men and
women,
I will pour out my Spirit in those
days,
and they will prophesy.
19I will show wonders in the heaven
above
and signs on the earth below,

---

*a*12 That is, about 3/4 mile (about 1,100 meters)   *b*15 Greek *brothers*   *c*20 Psalm 69:25
*d*20 Psalm 109:8   *e*4 Or *languages*; also in verse 11   *f*13 Or *sweet wine*

blood and fire and billows of
 smoke.
20The sun will be turned to darkness
 and the moon to blood
before the coming of the great and
 glorious day of the Lord.
21And everyone who calls
 on the name of the Lord will be
 saved.'*a*

22"Men of Israel, listen to this: Jesus of Nazareth was a man accredited by God to you by miracles, wonders and signs, which God did among you through him, as you yourselves know. 23This man was handed over to you by God's set purpose and foreknowledge; and you, with the help of wicked men,*b* put him to death by nailing him to the cross. 24But God raised him from the dead, freeing him from the agony of death, because it was impossible for death to keep its hold on him. 25David said about him:

" 'I saw the Lord always before me.
 Because he is at my right hand,
 I will not be shaken.
26Therefore my heart is glad and my
 tongue rejoices;
 my body also will live in hope,
27because you will not abandon me to
 the grave,
 nor will you let your Holy One see
 decay.
28You have made known to me the
 paths of life;
 you will fill me with joy in your
 presence.'*c*

29"Brothers, I can tell you confidently that the patriarch David died and was buried, and his tomb is here to this day. 30But he was a prophet and knew that God had promised him on oath that he would place one of his descendants on his throne. 31Seeing what was ahead, he spoke of the resurrection of the Christ,*d* that he was not abandoned to the grave, nor did his body see decay. 32God has raised this Jesus to life, and we are all witnesses of the fact. 33Exalted to the right hand of God, he has received from the Father the promised Holy Spirit and has poured out what you now see and hear. 34For David did not ascend to heaven, and yet he said,

" 'The Lord said to my Lord:
 "Sit at my right hand

35until I make your enemies
 a footstool for your feet." '*e*

36"Therefore let all Israel be assured of this: God has made this Jesus, whom you crucified, both Lord and Christ."

37When the people heard this, they were cut to the heart and said to Peter and the other apostles, "Brothers, what shall we do?"

38Peter replied, "Repent and be baptized, every one of you, in the name of Jesus Christ for the forgiveness of your sins. And you will receive the gift of the Holy Spirit. 39The promise is for you and your children and for all who are far off — for all whom the Lord our God will call."

40With many other words he warned them; and he pleaded with them, "Save yourselves from this corrupt generation." 41Those who accepted his message were baptized, and about three thousand were added to their number that day.

The Fellowship of the Believers

42They devoted themselves to the apostles' teaching and to the fellowship, to the breaking of bread and to prayer. 43Everyone was filled with awe, and many wonders and miraculous signs were done by the apostles. 44All the believers were together and had everything in common. 45Selling their possessions and goods, they gave to anyone as he had need. 46Every day they continued to meet together in the temple courts. They broke bread in their homes and ate together with glad and sincere hearts, 47praising God and enjoying the favor of all the people. And the Lord added to their number daily those who were being saved.

Peter Heals the Crippled Beggar

3 One day Peter and John were going up to the temple at the time of prayer — at three in the afternoon. 2Now a man crippled from birth was being carried to the temple gate called Beautiful, where he was put every day to beg from those going into the temple courts. 3When he saw Peter and John about to enter, he asked them for money. 4Peter looked straight at him, as did John. Then Peter said, "Look at us!" 5So the man gave them his attention, expecting to get something from them.

---

a21 Joel 2:28-32   *b23* Or *of those not having the law* (that is, Gentiles)   *c28* Psalm 16:8-11
d31 Or *Messiah.* "The Christ" (Greek) and "the Messiah" (Hebrew) both mean "the Anointed One"; also in verse 36.   *e35* Psalm 110:1

⁶Then Peter said, "Silver or gold I do not have, but what I have I give you. In the name of Jesus Christ of Nazareth, walk." ⁷Taking him by the right hand, he helped him up, and instantly the man's feet and ankles became strong. ⁸He jumped to his feet and began to walk. Then he went with them into the temple courts, walking and jumping, and praising God. ⁹When all the people saw him walking and praising God, ¹⁰they recognized him as the same man who used to sit begging at the temple gate called Beautiful, and they were filled with wonder and amazement at what had happened to him.

Peter Speaks to the Onlookers

¹¹While the beggar held on to Peter and John, all the people were astonished and came running to them in the place called Solomon's Colonnade. ¹²When Peter saw this, he said to them: "Men of Israel, why does this surprise you? Why do you stare at us as if by our own power or godliness we had made this man walk? ¹³The God of Abraham, Isaac and Jacob, the God of our fathers, has glorified his servant Jesus. You handed him over to be killed, and you disowned him before Pilate, though he had decided to let him go. ¹⁴You disowned the Holy and Righteous One and asked that a murderer be released to you. ¹⁵You killed the author of life, but God raised him from the dead. We are witnesses of this. ¹⁶By faith in the name of Jesus, this man whom you see and know was made strong. It is Jesus' name and the faith that comes through him that has given this complete healing to him, as you can all see.

¹⁷"Now, brothers, I know that you acted in ignorance, as did your leaders. ¹⁸But this is how God fulfilled what he had foretold through all the prophets, saying that his Christ[a] would suffer. ¹⁹Repent, then, and turn to God, so that your sins may be wiped out, that times of refreshing may come from the Lord, ²⁰and that he may send the Christ, who has been appointed for you—even Jesus. ²¹He must remain in heaven until the time comes for God to restore everything, as he promised long ago through his holy prophets. ²²For Moses said, 'The Lord your God will raise up for you a prophet like me from among your own people; you must listen to everything he tells you. ²³Anyone who does not listen to him will be completely cut off from among his people.'[b]

²⁴"Indeed, all the prophets from Samuel on, as many as have spoken, have foretold these days. ²⁵And you are heirs of the prophets and of the covenant God made with your fathers. He said to Abraham, 'Through your offspring all peoples on earth will be blessed.'[c] ²⁶When God raised up his servant, he sent him first to you to bless you by turning each of you from your wicked ways."

Peter and John Before the Sanhedrin

4 The priests and the captain of the temple guard and the Sadducees came up to Peter and John while they were speaking to the people. ²They were greatly disturbed because the apostles were teaching the people and proclaiming in Jesus the resurrection of the dead. ³They seized Peter and John, and because it was evening, they put them in jail until the next day. ⁴But many who heard the message believed, and the number of men grew to about five thousand.

⁵The next day the rulers, elders and teachers of the law met in Jerusalem. ⁶Annas the high priest was there, and so were Caiaphas, John, Alexander and the other men of the high priest's family. ⁷They had Peter and John brought before them and began to question them: "By what power or what name did you do this?"

⁸Then Peter, filled with the Holy Spirit, said to them: "Rulers and elders of the people! ⁹If we are being called to account today for an act of kindness shown to a cripple and are asked how he was healed, ¹⁰then know this, you and all the people of Israel: It is by the name of Jesus Christ of Nazareth, whom you crucified but whom God raised from the dead, that this man stands before you healed. ¹¹He is

" 'the stone you builders rejected,
    which has become the
        capstone.[d][e]

¹²Salvation is found in no one else, for there is no other name under heaven given to men by which we must be saved."

¹³When they saw the courage of Peter and John and realized that they were unschooled, ordinary men, they were astonished and they took note that these men had been with Jesus. ¹⁴But since they could see the man who had been healed

---

a18 Or *Messiah*; also in verse 20   *b23* Deut. 18:15,18,19   *c25* Gen. 22:18; 26:4   *d11* Or *cornerstone*   *e11* Psalm 118:22

standing there with them, there was nothing they could say. [15]So they ordered them to withdraw from the Sanhedrin and then conferred together. [16]"What are we going to do with these men?" they asked. "Everybody living in Jerusalem knows they have done an outstanding miracle, and we cannot deny it. [17]But to stop this thing from spreading any further among the people, we must warn these men to speak no longer to anyone in this name."

[18]Then they called them in again and commanded them not to speak or teach at all in the name of Jesus. [19]But Peter and John replied, "Judge for yourselves whether it is right in God's sight to obey you rather than God. [20]For we cannot help speaking about what we have seen and heard."

[21]After further threats they let them go. They could not decide how to punish them, because all the people were praising God for what had happened. [22]For the man who was miraculously healed was over forty years old.

The Believers' Prayer

[23]On their release, Peter and John went back to their own people and reported all that the chief priests and elders had said to them. [24]When they heard this, they raised their voices together in prayer to God. "Sovereign Lord," they said, "you made the heaven and the earth and the sea, and everything in them. [25]You spoke by the Holy Spirit through the mouth of your servant, our father David:

" 'Why do the nations rage
    and the peoples plot in vain?
[26]The kings of the earth take their stand
    and the rulers gather together
  against the Lord
    and against his Anointed One.[a][b]

[27]Indeed Herod and Pontius Pilate met together with the Gentiles and the people[c] of Israel in this city to conspire against your holy servant Jesus, whom you anointed. [28]They did what your power and will had decided beforehand should happen. [29]Now, Lord, consider their threats and enable your servants to speak your word with great boldness. [30]Stretch out your hand to heal and perform miraculous signs and wonders through the name of your holy servant Jesus."

[31]After they prayed, the place where they were meeting was shaken. And they were all filled with the Holy Spirit and spoke the word of God boldly.

The Believers Share Their Possessions

[32]All the believers were one in heart and mind. No one claimed that any of his possessions was his own, but they shared everything they had. [33]With great power the apostles continued to testify to the resurrection of the Lord Jesus, and much grace was upon them all. [34]There were no needy persons among them. For from time to time those who owned lands or houses sold them, brought the money from the sales [35]and put it at the apostles' feet, and it was distributed to anyone as he had need.

[36]Joseph, a Levite from Cyprus, whom the apostles called Barnabas (which means Son of Encouragement), [37]sold a field he owned and brought the money and put it at the apostles' feet.

Ananias and Sapphira

5 Now a man named Ananias, together with his wife Sapphira, also sold a piece of property. [2]With his wife's full knowledge he kept back part of the money for himself, but brought the rest and put it at the apostles' feet.

[3]Then Peter said, "Ananias, how is it that Satan has so filled your heart that you have lied to the Holy Spirit and have kept for yourself some of the money you received for the land? [4]Didn't it belong to you before it was sold? And after it was sold, wasn't the money at your disposal? What made you think of doing such a thing? You have not lied to men but to God."

[5]When Ananias heard this, he fell down and died. And great fear seized all who heard what had happened. [6]Then the young men came forward, wrapped up his body, and carried him out and buried him.

[7]About three hours later his wife came in, not knowing what had happened. [8]Peter asked her, "Tell me, is this the price you and Ananias got for the land?"

"Yes," she said, "that is the price."

[9]Peter said to her, "How could you agree to test the Spirit of the Lord? Look! The feet of the men who buried your husband are at the door, and they will carry you out also."

[10]At that moment she fell down at his feet and died. Then the young men came in and, finding her dead, carried her out

---

[a]26 That is, Christ or Messiah   [b]26 Psalm 2:1,2   [c]27 The Greek is plural.

and buried her beside her husband. [11]Great fear seized the whole church and all who heard about these events.

The Apostles Heal Many

[12]The apostles performed many miraculous signs and wonders among the people. And all the believers used to meet together in Solomon's Colonnade. [13]No one else dared join them, even though they were highly regarded by the people. [14]Nevertheless, more and more men and women believed in the Lord and were added to their number. [15]As a result, peo-

---

THURSDAY

VERSE FOR THE DAY:
Acts 4:13

AUTHOR:
Richard Halverson

PASSAGE FOR THE DAY:
Acts 4:8–20

God with a Face

"I WANT a God with a face on," said a little girl to her minister one day—thereby expressing a *childlike*, nevertheless *profound*, desire for reality in religion. She was not satisfied with some nebulous, ethereal abstraction for God.

She wanted something definite, tangible. She wanted a *someone* for a God . . . not a *something*.

Perhaps that is why men do not take God more seriously. They hold a *theory about God*: Their notion of God is foggy, hazy, remote—an idea that is beyond them with *no connection with the everyday*.

A man wants a God with a face on!

"Who is the God you worship?" I have asked men this question on many occasions. "Tell me about him. What is he like? Where does he dwell? Is he real to you?"

Again and again they stop after a few confused mutterings and admit God is quite unreal. When pinned down they have little to say. Why should a man bother about God if that is all he means to him?

But consider Jesus Christ!

Jesus Christ is God in focus! In him we see God clearly, distinctly, sharply, *down to earth*! . . .

If you want to know what God is like, look at his Son. If you want to hear God, listen to his Son! *A man will make no mistake following Christ*!

Let a man begin with Jesus wherever he must to be honest with himself; let him investigate Jesus all the way. Let him go along with Jesus as far as truth dictates—as far as honest inquiry leads.

He will begin to realize that *Jesus is God in focus* . . .

You can't go wrong trusting Christ, following Christ, worshiping Christ! He will lead you to a personal, dynamic experience of God.

Additional Scripture Readings:
Hebrews 1:1–4; 1 John 1:1–4

Go to page 1175 for your next devotional reading.

ple brought the sick into the streets and laid them on beds and mats so that at least Peter's shadow might fall on some of them as he passed by. **16**Crowds gathered also from the towns around Jerusalem, bringing their sick and those tormented by evil*a* spirits, and all of them were healed.

The Apostles Persecuted

17Then the high priest and all his associates, who were members of the party of the Sadducees, were filled with jealousy. **18**They arrested the apostles and put them in the public jail. **19**But during the night an angel of the Lord opened the doors of the jail and brought them out. **20**"Go, stand in the temple courts," he said, "and tell the people the full message of this new life."

21At daybreak they entered the temple courts, as they had been told, and began to teach the people.

When the high priest and his associates arrived, they called together the Sanhedrin — the full assembly of the elders of Israel — and sent to the jail for the apostles. **22**But on arriving at the jail, the officers did not find them there. So they went back and reported, **23**"We found the jail securely locked, with the guards standing at the doors; but when we opened them, we found no one inside." **24**On hearing this report, the captain of the temple guard and the chief priests were puzzled, wondering what would come of this.

25Then someone came and said, "Look! The men you put in jail are standing in the temple courts teaching the people." **26**At that, the captain went with his officers and brought the apostles. They did not use force, because they feared that the people would stone them.

27Having brought the apostles, they made them appear before the Sanhedrin to be questioned by the high priest. **28**"We gave you strict orders not to teach in this name," he said. "Yet you have filled Jerusalem with your teaching and are determined to make us guilty of this man's blood."

29Peter and the other apostles replied: "We must obey God rather than men! **30**The God of our fathers raised Jesus from the dead — whom you had killed by hanging him on a tree. **31**God exalted him to his own right hand as Prince and Savior that he might give repentance and forgiveness of sins to Israel. **32**We are witnesses of these things, and so is the Holy Spirit,

whom God has given to those who obey him."

33When they heard this, they were furious and wanted to put them to death. **34**But a Pharisee named Gamaliel, a teacher of the law, who was honored by all the people, stood up in the Sanhedrin and ordered that the men be put outside for a little while. **35**Then he addressed them: "Men of Israel, consider carefully what you intend to do to these men. **36**Some time ago Theudas appeared, claiming to be somebody, and about four hundred men rallied to him. He was killed, all his followers were dispersed, and it all came to nothing. **37**After him, Judas the Galilean appeared in the days of the census and led a band of people in revolt. He too was killed, and all his followers were scattered. **38**Therefore, in the present case I advise you: Leave these men alone! Let them go! For if their purpose or activity is of human origin, it will fail. **39**But if it is from God, you will not be able to stop these men; you will only find yourselves fighting against God."

40His speech persuaded them. They called the apostles in and had them flogged. Then they ordered them not to speak in the name of Jesus, and let them go.

41The apostles left the Sanhedrin, rejoicing because they had been counted worthy of suffering disgrace for the Name. **42**Day after day, in the temple courts and from house to house, they never stopped teaching and proclaiming the good news that Jesus is the Christ.*b*

The Choosing of the Seven

6 In those days when the number of disciples was increasing, the Grecian Jews among them complained against the Hebraic Jews because their widows were being overlooked in the daily distribution of food. **2**So the Twelve gathered all the disciples together and said, "It would not be right for us to neglect the ministry of the word of God in order to wait on tables. **3**Brothers, choose seven men from among you who are known to be full of the Spirit and wisdom. We will turn this responsibility over to them **4**and will give our attention to prayer and the ministry of the word."

5This proposal pleased the whole group. They chose Stephen, a man full of faith and of the Holy Spirit; also Philip,

*a*16 Greek *unclean*   *b*42 Or *Messiah*

Procorus, Nicanor, Timon, Parmenas, and Nicolas from Antioch, a convert to Judaism. **6**They presented these men to the apostles, who prayed and laid their hands on them.

7So the word of God spread. The number of disciples in Jerusalem increased rapidly, and a large number of priests became obedient to the faith.

Stephen Seized

8Now Stephen, a man full of God's grace and power, did great wonders and miraculous signs among the people. **9**Opposition arose, however, from members of the Synagogue of the Freedmen (as it was called) — Jews of Cyrene and Alexandria as well as the provinces of Cilicia and Asia. These men began to argue with Stephen, **10**but they could not stand up against his wisdom or the Spirit by whom he spoke.

11Then they secretly persuaded some men to say, "We have heard Stephen speak words of blasphemy against Moses and against God."

12So they stirred up the people and the elders and the teachers of the law. They seized Stephen and brought him before the Sanhedrin. **13**They produced false witnesses, who testified, "This fellow never stops speaking against this holy place and against the law. **14**For we have heard him say that this Jesus of Nazareth will destroy this place and change the customs Moses handed down to us."

15All who were sitting in the Sanhedrin looked intently at Stephen, and they saw that his face was like the face of an angel.

Stephen's Speech to the Sanhedrin

7 Then the high priest asked him, "Are these charges true?"

2To this he replied: "Brothers and fathers, listen to me! The God of glory appeared to our father Abraham while he was still in Mesopotamia, before he lived in Haran. **3**'Leave your country and your people,' God said, 'and go to the land I will show you.'*a*

4"So he left the land of the Chaldeans and settled in Haran. After the death of his father, God sent him to this land where you are now living. **5**He gave him no inheritance here, not even a foot of ground. But God promised him that he and his descendants after him would possess the land, even though at that time Abraham

had no child. **6**God spoke to him in this way: 'Your descendants will be strangers in a country not their own, and they will be enslaved and mistreated four hundred years. **7**But I will punish the nation they serve as slaves,' God said, 'and afterward they will come out of that country and worship me in this place.'*b* **8**Then he gave Abraham the covenant of circumcision. And Abraham became the father of Isaac and circumcised him eight days after his birth. Later Isaac became the father of Jacob, and Jacob became the father of the twelve patriarchs.

9"Because the patriarchs were jealous of Joseph, they sold him as a slave into Egypt. But God was with him **10**and rescued him from all his troubles. He gave Joseph wisdom and enabled him to gain the goodwill of Pharaoh king of Egypt; so he made him ruler over Egypt and all his palace.

11"Then a famine struck all Egypt and Canaan, bringing great suffering, and our fathers could not find food. **12**When Jacob heard that there was grain in Egypt, he sent our fathers on their first visit. **13**On their second visit, Joseph told his brothers who he was, and Pharaoh learned about Joseph's family. **14**After this, Joseph sent for his father Jacob and his whole family, seventy-five in all. **15**Then Jacob went down to Egypt, where he and our fathers died. **16**Their bodies were brought back to Shechem and placed in the tomb that Abraham had bought from the sons of Hamor at Shechem for a certain sum of money.

17"As the time drew near for God to fulfill his promise to Abraham, the number of our people in Egypt greatly increased. **18**Then another king, who knew nothing about Joseph, became ruler of Egypt. **19**He dealt treacherously with our people and oppressed our forefathers by forcing them to throw out their newborn babies so that they would die.

20"At that time Moses was born, and he was no ordinary child.*c* For three months he was cared for in his father's house. **21**When he was placed outside, Pharaoh's daughter took him and brought him up as her own son. **22**Moses was educated in all the wisdom of the Egyptians and was powerful in speech and action.

23"When Moses was forty years old, he decided to visit his fellow Israelites. **24**He saw one of them being mistreated by an

a3 Gen. 12:1   *b7* Gen. 15:13,14   *c20* Or *was fair in the sight of God*

Egyptian, so he went to his defense and avenged him by killing the Egyptian. **25**Moses thought that his own people would realize that God was using him to rescue them, but they did not. **26**The next day Moses came upon two Israelites who were fighting. He tried to reconcile them by saying, 'Men, you are brothers; why do you want to hurt each other?'

27"But the man who was mistreating the other pushed Moses aside and said, 'Who made you ruler and judge over us? **28**Do you want to kill me as you killed the Egyptian yesterday?'*a* **29**When Moses heard this, he fled to Midian, where he settled as a foreigner and had two sons.

30"After forty years had passed, an angel appeared to Moses in the flames of a burning bush in the desert near Mount Sinai. **31**When he saw this, he was amazed at the sight. As he went over to look more closely, he heard the Lord's voice: **32**'I am the God of your fathers, the God of Abraham, Isaac and Jacob.'*b* Moses trembled with fear and did not dare to look.

33"Then the Lord said to him, 'Take off your sandals; the place where you are standing is holy ground. **34**I have indeed seen the oppression of my people in Egypt. I have heard their groaning and have come down to set them free. Now come, I will send you back to Egypt.'*c*

35"This is the same Moses whom they had rejected with the words, 'Who made you ruler and judge?' He was sent to be their ruler and deliverer by God himself, through the angel who appeared to him in the bush. **36**He led them out of Egypt and did wonders and miraculous signs in Egypt, at the Red Sea*d* and for forty years in the desert.

37"This is that Moses who told the Israelites, 'God will send you a prophet like me from your own people.'*e* **38**He was in the assembly in the desert, with the angel who spoke to him on Mount Sinai, and with our fathers; and he received living words to pass on to us.

39"But our fathers refused to obey him. Instead, they rejected him and in their hearts turned back to Egypt. **40**They told Aaron, 'Make us gods who will go before us. As for this fellow Moses who led us out of Egypt—we don't know what has happened to him!'*f* **41**That was the time they made an idol in the form of a calf. They

brought sacrifices to it and held a celebration in honor of what their hands had made. **42**But God turned away and gave them over to the worship of the heavenly bodies. This agrees with what is written in the book of the prophets:

" 'Did you bring me sacrifices and
    offerings
forty years in the desert, O house of
    Israel?
43You have lifted up the shrine of
    Molech
and the star of your god Rephan,
    the idols you made to worship.
Therefore I will send you into exile'*g*
    beyond Babylon.

44"Our forefathers had the tabernacle of the Testimony with them in the desert. It had been made as God directed Moses, according to the pattern he had seen. **45**Having received the tabernacle, our fathers under Joshua brought it with them when they took the land from the nations God drove out before them. It remained in the land until the time of David, **46**who enjoyed God's favor and asked that he might provide a dwelling place for the God of Jacob.*h* **47**But it was Solomon who built the house for him.

48"However, the Most High does not live in houses made by men. As the prophet says:

49" 'Heaven is my throne,
    and the earth is my footstool.
What kind of house will you build for
    me?
              says the Lord.
Or where will my resting place be?
50Has not my hand made all these
    things?'*i*

51"You stiff-necked people, with uncircumcised hearts and ears! You are just like your fathers: You always resist the Holy Spirit! **52**Was there ever a prophet your fathers did not persecute? They even killed those who predicted the coming of the Righteous One. And now you have betrayed and murdered him— **53**you who have received the law that was put into effect through angels but have not obeyed it."

The Stoning of Stephen

54When they heard this, they were furi-

a28 Exodus 2:14   *b32* Exodus 3:6   *c34* Exodus 3:5,7,8,10   *d36* That is, Sea of Reeds
e37 Deut. 18:15   *f40* Exodus 32:1   *g43* Amos 5:25-27   *h46* Some early manuscripts *the house of*
Jacob   *i50* Isaiah 66:1,2

ous and gnashed their teeth at him. **55**But Stephen, full of the Holy Spirit, looked up to heaven and saw the glory of God, and Jesus standing at the right hand of God. **56**"Look," he said, "I see heaven open and the Son of Man standing at the right hand of God."

57At this they covered their ears and, yelling at the top of their voices, they all rushed at him, **58**dragged him out of the city and began to stone him. Meanwhile, the witnesses laid their clothes at the feet of a young man named Saul.

59While they were stoning him, Stephen prayed, "Lord Jesus, receive my spirit." **60**Then he fell on his knees and cried out, "Lord, do not hold this sin against them." When he had said this, he fell asleep.

8 And Saul was there, giving approval to his death.

The Church Persecuted and Scattered

On that day a great persecution broke out against the church at Jerusalem, and all except the apostles were scattered throughout Judea and Samaria. **2**Godly men buried Stephen and mourned deeply for him. **3**But Saul began to destroy the church. Going from house to house, he dragged off men and women and put them in prison.

Philip in Samaria

4Those who had been scattered preached the word wherever they went. **5**Philip went down to a city in Samaria and proclaimed the Christ*a* there. **6**When the crowds heard Philip and saw the miraculous signs he did, they all paid close attention to what he said. **7**With shrieks, evil*b* spirits came out of many, and many paralytics and cripples were healed. **8**So there was great joy in that city.

Simon the Sorcerer

9Now for some time a man named Simon had practiced sorcery in the city and amazed all the people of Samaria. He boasted that he was someone great, **10**and all the people, both high and low, gave him their attention and exclaimed, "This man is the divine power known as the Great Power." **11**They followed him because he had amazed them for a long time with his magic. **12**But when they believed Philip as he preached the good news of the kingdom of God and the name of Jesus

Christ, they were baptized, both men and women. **13**Simon himself believed and was baptized. And he followed Philip everywhere, astonished by the great signs and miracles he saw.

14When the apostles in Jerusalem heard that Samaria had accepted the word of God, they sent Peter and John to them. **15**When they arrived, they prayed for them that they might receive the Holy Spirit, **16**because the Holy Spirit had not yet come upon any of them; they had simply been baptized into*c* the name of the Lord Jesus. **17**Then Peter and John placed their hands on them, and they received the Holy Spirit.

18When Simon saw that the Spirit was given at the laying on of the apostles' hands, he offered them money **19**and said, "Give me also this ability so that everyone on whom I lay my hands may receive the Holy Spirit."

20Peter answered: "May your money perish with you, because you thought you could buy the gift of God with money! **21**You have no part or share in this ministry, because your heart is not right before God. **22**Repent of this wickedness and pray to the Lord. Perhaps he will forgive you for having such a thought in your heart. **23**For I see that you are full of bitterness and captive to sin."

24Then Simon answered, "Pray to the Lord for me so that nothing you have said may happen to me."

25When they had testified and proclaimed the word of the Lord, Peter and John returned to Jerusalem, preaching the gospel in many Samaritan villages.

Philip and the Ethiopian

26Now an angel of the Lord said to Philip, "Go south to the road — the desert road — that goes down from Jerusalem to Gaza." **27**So he started out, and on his way he met an Ethiopian*d* eunuch, an important official in charge of all the treasury of Candace, queen of the Ethiopians. This man had gone to Jerusalem to worship, **28**and on his way home was sitting in his chariot reading the book of Isaiah the prophet. **29**The Spirit told Philip, "Go to that chariot and stay near it."

30Then Philip ran up to the chariot and heard the man reading Isaiah the prophet. "Do you understand what you are reading?" Philip asked.

31"How can I," he said, "unless some-

---

*a*5 Or *Messiah*   *b*7 Greek *unclean*   *c*16 Or *in*   *d*27 That is, from the upper Nile region one explains it to me?" So he invited Philip to come up and sit with him.

32The eunuch was reading this passage of Scripture:

> "He was led like a sheep to the
>   slaughter,
> and as a lamb before the shearer is
>   silent,
> so he did not open his mouth.
> **33**In his humiliation he was deprived of
>   justice.
> Who can speak of his descendants?
> For his life was taken from the
>   earth."*a*

34The eunuch asked Philip, "Tell me, please, who is the prophet talking about, himself or someone else?" **35**Then Philip began with that very passage of Scripture and told him the good news about Jesus.

36As they traveled along the road, they came to some water and the eunuch said, "Look, here is water. Why shouldn't I be baptized?"*b* **38**And he gave orders to stop the chariot. Then both Philip and the eunuch went down into the water and Philip baptized him. **39**When they came up out of the water, the Spirit of the Lord suddenly took Philip away, and the eunuch did not see him again, but went on his way rejoicing. **40**Philip, however, appeared at Azotus and traveled about, preaching the gospel in all the towns until he reached Caesarea.

Saul's Conversion

9 Meanwhile, Saul was still breathing out murderous threats against the Lord's disciples. He went to the high priest **2**and asked him for letters to the synagogues in Damascus, so that if he found any there who belonged to the Way, whether men or women, he might take them as prisoners to Jerusalem. **3**As he neared Damascus on his journey, suddenly a light from heaven flashed around him. **4**He fell to the ground and heard a voice say to him, "Saul, Saul, why do you persecute me?"

5"Who are you, Lord?" Saul asked.

"I am Jesus, whom you are persecuting," he replied. **6**"Now get up and go into the city, and you will be told what you must do."

7The men traveling with Saul stood there speechless; they heard the sound but did not see anyone. **8**Saul got up from the ground, but when he opened his eyes he could see nothing. So they led him by the hand into Damascus. **9**For three days he was blind, and did not eat or drink anything.

10In Damascus there was a disciple named Ananias. The Lord called to him in a vision, "Ananias!"

"Yes, Lord," he answered.

11The Lord told him, "Go to the house of Judas on Straight Street and ask for a man from Tarsus named Saul, for he is praying. **12**In a vision he has seen a man named Ananias come and place his hands on him to restore his sight."

13"Lord," Ananias answered, "I have heard many reports about this man and all the harm he has done to your saints in Jerusalem. **14**And he has come here with authority from the chief priests to arrest all who call on your name."

15But the Lord said to Ananias, "Go! This man is my chosen instrument to carry my name before the Gentiles and their kings and before the people of Israel. **16**I will show him how much he must suffer for my name."

17Then Ananias went to the house and entered it. Placing his hands on Saul, he said, "Brother Saul, the Lord — Jesus, who appeared to you on the road as you were coming here — has sent me so that you may see again and be filled with the Holy Spirit." **18**Immediately, something like scales fell from Saul's eyes, and he could see again. He got up and was baptized, **19**and after taking some food, he regained his strength.

Saul in Damascus and Jerusalem

Saul spent several days with the disciples in Damascus. **20**At once he began to preach in the synagogues that Jesus is the Son of God. **21**All those who heard him were astonished and asked, "Isn't he the man who raised havoc in Jerusalem among those who call on this name? And hasn't he come here to take them as prisoners to the chief priests?" **22**Yet Saul grew more and more powerful and baffled the Jews living in Damascus by proving that Jesus is the Christ.*c*

23After many days had gone by, the Jews conspired to kill him, **24**but Saul learned of their plan. Day and night they kept close watch on the city gates in order to kill him. **25**But his followers took him

a33 Isaiah 53:7,8   *b36* Some late manuscripts *baptized?" 37Philip said, "If you believe with all your heart, you may." The eunuch answered, "I believe that Jesus Christ is the Son of God."*   *c22* Or *Messiah*

FRIDAY

VERSE FOR THE DAY:
Acts 9:15

AUTHOR:
Bill McCartney

PASSAGE FOR THE DAY:
Acts 9:1–16

Overpowered by His Presence

I'VE spent a lot of time reading Bible stories about this remarkable man [Paul]. He began as the bitterest enemy the gospel had. He was a murderer, a bigot, he hated Christianity and everything about it and he almost single-handedly drove the church out of Jerusalem. And he was on his way to Damascus to do the same thing there—to find Christians and bind them and bring them back to a kangaroo court and put them to death. Then, at the doorway of Damascus, the Lord Jesus Christ appeared to him in person and struck him down and transformed his life. From then on, Paul was a completely changed man. All his old war buddies, his cronies, were amazed. They couldn't understand what had happened to him. But he stayed true all the rest of his days.

In 2 Corinthians, there's a list as long as a tall man's arm relating all the things Paul endured. He was beaten, stoned, shipwrecked three times, imprisoned, and there were many attempts on his life before he was finally killed, beheaded in Rome because of his love for the gospel. And just before the end of his life, he was able to write to Timothy: "I have fought the good fight, I have finished the race, I have kept the faith. Now there is in store for me the crown of righteousness, which the Lord, the righteous Judge, will award to me on that day —and not only to me, but also to all who have longed for his appearing" (2 Timothy 4:7–8).

Paul said in Colossians that Christ is our life and in Galatians that Christ lives in us and again in Colossians that Christ in us is the hope of glory. I want more than anything in the world for Jesus Christ to live out his life through me. Without him I am nothing; with him I have the promise of everlasting life. Is there any better deal you can cut? Does anything else give you that assurance? It boggles my mind that someone can see life breathed into a baby, watch the grass die and then come to life again, see leaves fall and watch the rebirth of a tree, or gaze on any of the majestic splendor that is this earth and not be overpowered by the presence of an Almighty God!

Additional Scripture Readings:
Philippians 3:7–11;
Colossians 1:24–29

Go to page 1177 for your next devotional reading.

by night and lowered him in a basket through an opening in the wall.

²⁶When he came to Jerusalem, he tried to join the disciples, but they were all afraid of him, not believing that he really was a disciple. ²⁷But Barnabas took him and brought him to the apostles. He told them how Saul on his journey had seen the Lord and that the Lord had spoken to him, and how in Damascus he had preached fearlessly in the name of Jesus. ²⁸So Saul stayed with them and moved about freely in Jerusalem, speaking boldly in the name of the Lord. ²⁹He talked and debated with the Grecian Jews, but they tried to kill him. ³⁰When the brothers learned of this, they took him down to Caesarea and sent him off to Tarsus.

³¹Then the church throughout Judea, Galilee and Samaria enjoyed a time of peace. It was strengthened; and encouraged by the Holy Spirit, it grew in numbers, living in the fear of the Lord.

Aeneas and Dorcas

³²As Peter traveled about the country, he went to visit the saints in Lydda. ³³There he found a man named Aeneas, a paralytic who had been bedridden for eight years. ³⁴"Aeneas," Peter said to him, "Jesus Christ heals you. Get up and take care of your mat." Immediately Aeneas got up. ³⁵All those who lived in Lydda and Sharon saw him and turned to the Lord.

³⁶In Joppa there was a disciple named Tabitha (which, when translated, is Dorcas[a]), who was always doing good and helping the poor. ³⁷About that time she became sick and died, and her body was washed and placed in an upstairs room. ³⁸Lydda was near Joppa; so when the disciples heard that Peter was in Lydda, they sent two men to him and urged him, "Please come at once!"

³⁹Peter went with them, and when he arrived he was taken upstairs to the room. All the widows stood around him, crying and showing him the robes and other clothing that Dorcas had made while she was still with them.

⁴⁰Peter sent them all out of the room; then he got down on his knees and prayed. Turning toward the dead woman, he said, "Tabitha, get up." She opened her eyes, and seeing Peter she sat up. ⁴¹He took her by the hand and helped her to her feet. Then he called the believers and the widows and presented her to them

alive. ⁴²This became known all over Joppa, and many people believed in the Lord. ⁴³Peter stayed in Joppa for some time with a tanner named Simon.

Cornelius Calls for Peter

10 At Caesarea there was a man named Cornelius, a centurion in what was known as the Italian Regiment. ²He and all his family were devout and God-fearing; he gave generously to those in need and prayed to God regularly. ³One day at about three in the afternoon he had a vision. He distinctly saw an angel of God, who came to him and said, "Cornelius!"

⁴Cornelius stared at him in fear. "What is it, Lord?" he asked.

The angel answered, "Your prayers and gifts to the poor have come up as a memorial offering before God. ⁵Now send men to Joppa to bring back a man named Simon who is called Peter. ⁶He is staying with Simon the tanner, whose house is by the sea."

⁷When the angel who spoke to him had gone, Cornelius called two of his servants and a devout soldier who was one of his attendants. ⁸He told them everything that had happened and sent them to Joppa.

Peter's Vision

⁹About noon the following day as they were on their journey and approaching the city, Peter went up on the roof to pray. ¹⁰He became hungry and wanted something to eat, and while the meal was being prepared, he fell into a trance. ¹¹He saw heaven opened and something like a large sheet being let down to earth by its four corners. ¹²It contained all kinds of four-footed animals, as well as reptiles of the earth and birds of the air. ¹³Then a voice told him, "Get up, Peter. Kill and eat."

¹⁴"Surely not, Lord!" Peter replied. "I have never eaten anything impure or unclean."

¹⁵The voice spoke to him a second time, "Do not call anything impure that God has made clean."

¹⁶This happened three times, and immediately the sheet was taken back to heaven.

¹⁷While Peter was wondering about the meaning of the vision, the men sent by Cornelius found out where Simon's house was and stopped at the gate. ¹⁸They called

---

a 36 Both *Tabitha* (Aramaic) and *Dorcas* (Greek) mean *gazelle.*

WEEKENDING

RESOLVE

I'm part of the fellowship of the unashamed. I have the Holy Spirit power. The die has been cast. I have stepped over the line. The decision has been made—I'm a disciple of his. I won't look back, let up, slow down, back away, or be still. My past is redeemed, my present makes sense, my future is secure. I'm finished and done with low living, sight walking, smooth knees, colorless dreams, tamed visions, worldly talking, cheap giving and dwarfed goals.

I no longer need preeminence, prosperity, position, promotions, plaudits or popularity. I don't have to be right, first, tops, recognized, praised, regarded or rewarded. I now live by faith, lean in his presence, walk by patience, am uplifted by prayer, and I labor with power.

*– A young pastor in Zimbabwe, Africa, later
martyred for his faith in Christ*

REVIVE

Saturday: Luke 14:25–35
Sunday: Acts 7:54—8:1a

Go to page 1179 for your next devotional reading.

out, asking if Simon who was known as Peter was staying there.

¹⁹While Peter was still thinking about the vision, the Spirit said to him, "Simon, three*a* men are looking for you. ²⁰So get up and go downstairs. Do not hesitate to go with them, for I have sent them."

²¹Peter went down and said to the men, "I'm the one you're looking for. Why have you come?"

²²The men replied, "We have come from Cornelius the centurion. He is a righteous and God-fearing man, who is respected by all the Jewish people. A holy angel told him to have you come to his house so that he could hear what you have to say." ²³Then Peter invited the men into the house to be his guests.

Peter at Cornelius' House

The next day Peter started out with them, and some of the brothers from Joppa went along. ²⁴The following day he arrived in Caesarea. Cornelius was expecting them and had called together his relatives and close friends. ²⁵As Peter entered the house, Cornelius met him and fell at his feet in reverence. ²⁶But Peter made him get up. "Stand up," he said, "I am only a man myself."

²⁷Talking with him, Peter went inside and found a large gathering of people. ²⁸He said to them: "You are well aware that it is against our law for a Jew to associate with a Gentile or visit him. But God has shown me that I should not call any man impure or unclean. ²⁹So when I was sent for, I came without raising any objection. May I ask why you sent for me?"

³⁰Cornelius answered: "Four days ago I was in my house praying at this hour, at three in the afternoon. Suddenly a man in shining clothes stood before me ³¹and said, 'Cornelius, God has heard your prayer and remembered your gifts to the poor. ³²Send to Joppa for Simon who is called Peter. He is a guest in the home of Simon the tanner, who lives by the sea.' ³³So I sent for you immediately, and it was good of you to come. Now we are all here in the presence of God to listen to everything the Lord has commanded you to tell us."

³⁴Then Peter began to speak: "I now realize how true it is that God does not show favoritism ³⁵but accepts men from every nation who fear him and do what is right. ³⁶You know the message God sent to the people of Israel, telling the good news of peace through Jesus Christ, who is Lord of all. ³⁷You know what has happened throughout Judea, beginning in Galilee after the baptism that John preached — ³⁸how God anointed Jesus of Nazareth with the Holy Spirit and power, and how he went around doing good and healing all who were under the power of the devil, because God was with him.

³⁹"We are witnesses of everything he did in the country of the Jews and in Jerusalem. They killed him by hanging him on a tree, ⁴⁰but God raised him from the dead on the third day and caused him to be seen. ⁴¹He was not seen by all the people, but by witnesses whom God had already chosen — by us who ate and drank with him after he rose from the dead. ⁴²He commanded us to preach to the people and to testify that he is the one whom God appointed as judge of the living and the dead. ⁴³All the prophets testify about him that everyone who believes in him receives forgiveness of sins through his name."

⁴⁴While Peter was still speaking these words, the Holy Spirit came on all who heard the message. ⁴⁵The circumcised believers who had come with Peter were astonished that the gift of the Holy Spirit had been poured out even on the Gentiles. ⁴⁶For they heard them speaking in tongues*b* and praising God.

Then Peter said, ⁴⁷"Can anyone keep these people from being baptized with water? They have received the Holy Spirit just as we have." ⁴⁸So he ordered that they be baptized in the name of Jesus Christ. Then they asked Peter to stay with them for a few days.

Peter Explains His Actions

11 The apostles and the brothers throughout Judea heard that the Gentiles also had received the word of God. ²So when Peter went up to Jerusalem, the circumcised believers criticized him ³and said, "You went into the house of uncircumcised men and ate with them."

⁴Peter began and explained everything to them precisely as it had happened: ⁵"I was in the city of Joppa praying, and in a trance I saw a vision. I saw something like a large sheet being let down from heaven by its four corners, and it came down to where I was. ⁶I looked into it and saw

---

a19 One early manuscript *two*; other manuscripts do not have the number.   *b46* Or *other languages* four-footed animals of the earth, wild beasts, reptiles, and birds of the air. ⁷Then I heard a voice telling me, 'Get up, Peter. Kill and eat.'

⁸"I replied, 'Surely not, Lord! Nothing impure or unclean has ever entered my mouth.'

⁹"The voice spoke from heaven a second time, 'Do not call anything impure that God has made clean.' ¹⁰This happened three times, and then it was all pulled up to heaven again.

¹¹"Right then three men who had been sent to me from Caesarea stopped at the house where I was staying. ¹²The Spirit told me to have no hesitation about going with them. These six brothers also went

with me, and we entered the man's house. ¹³He told us how he had seen an angel appear in his house and say, 'Send to Joppa for Simon who is called Peter. ¹⁴He will bring you a message through which you and all your household will be saved.'

¹⁵"As I began to speak, the Holy Spirit came on them as he had come on us at the beginning. ¹⁶Then I remembered what the Lord had said: 'John baptized with ᵃ water, but you will be baptized with the Holy Spirit.' ¹⁷So if God gave them the same gift as he gave us, who believed in the Lord Jesus Christ, who was I to think that I could oppose God?"

¹⁸When they heard this, they had no further objections and praised God, say-

ᵃ16 Or *in*

MONDAY

VERSE FOR THE DAY: Acts 10:43	*AUTHOR:* Charles Stanley	*PASSAGE FOR THE DAY:* Acts 10:34–43

Whoever Enters

GOD'S gift of forgiveness must be appropriated; that is, it must be accepted on an individual basis. Although it is a universal offer, it has no effect on the sin debt of a man or a woman who has not personally put trust in Christ. It is like a paycheck that is never picked up; it is like a gift certificate that is not redeemed; it is like a lifeline that is ignored by a drowning person.

Christ creatively communicated the concept of appropriation. Through the use of word pictures and parables, he drove home his point to "trust in God; trust also in me" (John 14:1). He told the woman at the well to ask for "living water" (John 4:10). He instructed the Jews to come to him to receive "life" (John 5:40). He told one group they would have to "eat the flesh of the Son of Man and drink his blood" (John 6:53). To the leaders of the Jews, he said, "If anyone keeps my word, he will never see death" (John 8:51). He presented himself to the Pharisees in this way: "I am the gate; whoever enters through me will be saved. He will come in and go out, and find pasture" (John 10:9). He used every conceivable illustration to show his audience that they needed to personally and individually appropriate God's gift of eternal life for themselves.

Additional Scripture Readings:
John 10:1–10; John 15:1–8

Go to page 1183 for your next devotional reading.

ing, "So then, God has granted even the Gentiles repentance unto life."

The Church in Antioch

19Now those who had been scattered by the persecution in connection with Stephen traveled as far as Phoenicia, Cyprus and Antioch, telling the message only to Jews. 20Some of them, however, men from Cyprus and Cyrene, went to Antioch and began to speak to Greeks also, telling them the good news about the Lord Jesus. 21The Lord's hand was with them, and a great number of people believed and turned to the Lord.

22News of this reached the ears of the church at Jerusalem, and they sent Barnabas to Antioch. 23When he arrived and saw the evidence of the grace of God, he was glad and encouraged them all to remain true to the Lord with all their hearts. 24He was a good man, full of the Holy Spirit and faith, and a great number of people were brought to the Lord.

25Then Barnabas went to Tarsus to look for Saul, 26and when he found him, he brought him to Antioch. So for a whole year Barnabas and Saul met with the church and taught great numbers of people. The disciples were called Christians first at Antioch.

27During this time some prophets came down from Jerusalem to Antioch. 28One of them, named Agabus, stood up and through the Spirit predicted that a severe famine would spread over the entire Roman world. (This happened during the reign of Claudius.) 29The disciples, each according to his ability, decided to provide help for the brothers living in Judea. 30This they did, sending their gift to the elders by Barnabas and Saul.

Peter's Miraculous Escape From Prison

12 It was about this time that King Herod arrested some who belonged to the church, intending to persecute them. 2He had James, the brother of John, put to death with the sword. 3When he saw that this pleased the Jews, he proceeded to seize Peter also. This happened during the Feast of Unleavened Bread. 4After arresting him, he put him in prison, handing him over to be guarded by four squads of four soldiers each. Herod intended to bring him out for public trial after the Passover.

5So Peter was kept in prison, but the church was earnestly praying to God for him.

6The night before Herod was to bring him to trial, Peter was sleeping between two soldiers, bound with two chains, and sentries stood guard at the entrance. 7Suddenly an angel of the Lord appeared and a light shone in the cell. He struck Peter on the side and woke him up. "Quick, get up!" he said, and the chains fell off Peter's wrists.

8Then the angel said to him, "Put on your clothes and sandals." And Peter did so. "Wrap your cloak around you and follow me," the angel told him. 9Peter followed him out of the prison, but he had no idea that what the angel was doing was really happening; he thought he was seeing a vision. 10They passed the first and second guards and came to the iron gate leading to the city. It opened for them by itself, and they went through it. When they had walked the length of one street, suddenly the angel left him.

11Then Peter came to himself and said, "Now I know without a doubt that the Lord sent his angel and rescued me from Herod's clutches and from everything the Jewish people were anticipating."

12When this had dawned on him, he went to the house of Mary the mother of John, also called Mark, where many people had gathered and were praying. 13Peter knocked at the outer entrance, and a servant girl named Rhoda came to answer the door. 14When she recognized Peter's voice, she was so overjoyed she ran back without opening it and exclaimed, "Peter is at the door!"

15"You're out of your mind," they told her. When she kept insisting that it was so, they said, "It must be his angel."

16But Peter kept on knocking, and when they opened the door and saw him, they were astonished. 17Peter motioned with his hand for them to be quiet and described how the Lord had brought him out of prison. "Tell James and the brothers about this," he said, and then he left for another place.

18In the morning, there was no small commotion among the soldiers as to what had become of Peter. 19After Herod had a thorough search made for him and did not find him, he cross-examined the guards and ordered that they be executed.

Herod's Death

Then Herod went from Judea to Caesarea and stayed there a while. 20He had been quarreling with the people of Tyre and Sidon; they now joined together and sought an audience with him. Having secured the support of Blastus, a trusted personal servant of the king, they asked for peace, because they depended on the king's country for their food supply.

²¹On the appointed day Herod, wearing his royal robes, sat on his throne and delivered a public address to the people. ²²They shouted, "This is the voice of a god, not of a man." ²³Immediately, because Herod did not give praise to God, an angel of the Lord struck him down, and he was eaten by worms and died.

²⁴But the word of God continued to increase and spread.

²⁵When Barnabas and Saul had finished their mission, they returned from*a* Jerusalem, taking with them John, also called Mark.

Barnabas and Saul Sent Off

13 In the church at Antioch there were prophets and teachers: Barnabas, Simeon called Niger, Lucius of Cyrene, Manaen (who had been brought up with Herod the tetrarch) and Saul. ²While they were worshiping the Lord and fasting, the Holy Spirit said, "Set apart for me Barnabas and Saul for the work to which I have called them." ³So after they had fasted and prayed, they placed their hands on them and sent them off.

On Cyprus

⁴The two of them, sent on their way by the Holy Spirit, went down to Seleucia and sailed from there to Cyprus. ⁵When they arrived at Salamis, they proclaimed the word of God in the Jewish synagogues. John was with them as their helper.

⁶They traveled through the whole island until they came to Paphos. There they met a Jewish sorcerer and false prophet named Bar-Jesus, ⁷who was an attendant of the proconsul, Sergius Paulus. The proconsul, an intelligent man, sent for Barnabas and Saul because he wanted to hear the word of God. ⁸But Elymas the sorcerer (for that is what his name means) opposed them and tried to turn the proconsul from the faith. ⁹Then Saul, who was also called Paul, filled with the Holy Spirit, looked straight at Elymas and said, ¹⁰"You are a child of the devil and an enemy of everything that is right! You are full of all kinds of deceit and trickery. Will you

never stop perverting the right ways of the Lord? ¹¹Now the hand of the Lord is against you. You are going to be blind, and for a time you will be unable to see the light of the sun."

Immediately mist and darkness came over him, and he groped about, seeking someone to lead him by the hand. ¹²When the proconsul saw what had happened, he believed, for he was amazed at the teaching about the Lord.

In Pisidian Antioch

¹³From Paphos, Paul and his companions sailed to Perga in Pamphylia, where John left them to return to Jerusalem. ¹⁴From Perga they went on to Pisidian Antioch. On the Sabbath they entered the synagogue and sat down. ¹⁵After the reading from the Law and the Prophets, the synagogue rulers sent word to them, saying, "Brothers, if you have a message of encouragement for the people, please speak."

¹⁶Standing up, Paul motioned with his hand and said: "Men of Israel and you Gentiles who worship God, listen to me! ¹⁷The God of the people of Israel chose our fathers; he made the people prosper during their stay in Egypt, with mighty power he led them out of that country, ¹⁸he endured their conduct*b* for about forty years in the desert, ¹⁹he overthrew seven nations in Canaan and gave their land to his people as their inheritance. ²⁰All this took about 450 years.

"After this, God gave them judges until the time of Samuel the prophet. ²¹Then the people asked for a king, and he gave them Saul son of Kish, of the tribe of Benjamin, who ruled forty years. ²²After removing Saul, he made David their king. He testified concerning him: 'I have found David son of Jesse a man after my own heart; he will do everything I want him to do.'

²³"From this man's descendants God has brought to Israel the Savior Jesus, as he promised. ²⁴Before the coming of Jesus, John preached repentance and baptism to all the people of Israel. ²⁵As John was completing his work, he said: 'Who do you think I am? I am not that one. No, but he is coming after me, whose sandals I am not worthy to untie.'

²⁶"Brothers, children of Abraham, and you God-fearing Gentiles, it is to us that this message of salvation has been sent.

---

*a*25 Some manuscripts *to*   *b*18 Some manuscripts *and cared for them*

27The people of Jerusalem and their rulers did not recognize Jesus, yet in condemning him they fulfilled the words of the prophets that are read every Sabbath. 28Though they found no proper ground for a death sentence, they asked Pilate to have him executed. 29When they had carried out all that was written about him, they took him down from the tree and laid him in a tomb. 30But God raised him from the dead, 31and for many days he was seen by those who had traveled with him from Galilee to Jerusalem. They are now his witnesses to our people.

32"We tell you the good news: What God promised our fathers 33he has fulfilled for us, their children, by raising up Jesus. As it is written in the second Psalm:

" 'You are my Son;
    today I have become your
        Father.'a,b

34The fact that God raised him from the dead, never to decay, is stated in these words:

" 'I will give you the holy and sure
    blessings promised to David.'c

35So it is stated elsewhere:

" 'You will not let your Holy One see
    decay.'d

36"For when David had served God's purpose in his own generation, he fell asleep; he was buried with his fathers and his body decayed. 37But the one whom God raised from the dead did not see decay.

38"Therefore, my brothers, I want you to know that through Jesus the forgiveness of sins is proclaimed to you. 39Through him everyone who believes is justified from everything you could not be justified from by the law of Moses. 40Take care that what the prophets have said does not happen to you:

41" 'Look, you scoffers,
    wonder and perish,
  for I am going to do something in
        your days
    that you would never believe,
    even if someone told you.'e"

42As Paul and Barnabas were leaving the synagogue, the people invited them to speak further about these things on the next Sabbath. 43When the congregation was dismissed, many of the Jews and devout converts to Judaism followed Paul and Barnabas, who talked with them and urged them to continue in the grace of God.

44On the next Sabbath almost the whole city gathered to hear the word of the Lord. 45When the Jews saw the crowds, they were filled with jealousy and talked abusively against what Paul was saying.

46Then Paul and Barnabas answered them boldly: "We had to speak the word of God to you first. Since you reject it and do not consider yourselves worthy of eternal life, we now turn to the Gentiles. 47For this is what the Lord has commanded us:

" 'I have made youf a light for the
        Gentiles,
  that youf may bring salvation to
        the ends of the earth.'g"

48When the Gentiles heard this, they were glad and honored the word of the Lord; and all who were appointed for eternal life believed.

49The word of the Lord spread through the whole region. 50But the Jews incited the God-fearing women of high standing and the leading men of the city. They stirred up persecution against Paul and Barnabas, and expelled them from their region. 51So they shook the dust from their feet in protest against them and went to Iconium. 52And the disciples were filled with joy and with the Holy Spirit.

In Iconium

14 At Iconium Paul and Barnabas went as usual into the Jewish synagogue. There they spoke so effectively that a great number of Jews and Gentiles believed. 2But the Jews who refused to believe stirred up the Gentiles and poisoned their minds against the brothers. 3So Paul and Barnabas spent considerable time there, speaking boldly for the Lord, who confirmed the message of his grace by enabling them to do miraculous signs and wonders. 4The people of the city were divided; some sided with the Jews, others with the apostles. 5There was a plot afoot among the Gentiles and Jews, together with their leaders, to mistreat them and stone them. 6But they found out about it and fled to the Lycaonian cities of Lystra and Derbe and to the surrounding coun-

a33 Or *have begotten you*   b33 Psalm 2:7   c34 Isaiah 55:3   d35 Psalm 16:10   e41 Hab. 1:5
f47 The Greek is singular.   g47 Isaiah 49:6

try, 7where they continued to preach the good news.

In Lystra and Derbe

8In Lystra there sat a man crippled in his feet, who was lame from birth and had never walked. 9He listened to Paul as he was speaking. Paul looked directly at him, saw that he had faith to be healed 10and called out, "Stand up on your feet!" At that, the man jumped up and began to walk.

11When the crowd saw what Paul had done, they shouted in the Lycaonian language, "The gods have come down to us in human form!" 12Barnabas they called Zeus, and Paul they called Hermes be-cause he was the chief speaker. 13The priest of Zeus, whose temple was just out-side the city, brought bulls and wreaths to the city gates because he and the crowd wanted to offer sacrifices to them.

14But when the apostles Barnabas and Paul heard of this, they tore their clothes and rushed out into the crowd, shouting: 15"Men, why are you doing this? We too are only men, human like you. We are bringing you good news, telling you to turn from these worthless things to the living God, who made heaven and earth and sea and everything in them. 16In the past, he let all nations go their own way. 17Yet he has not left himself without testi-mony: He has shown kindness by giving

---

TUESDAY

VERSE FOR THE DAY:	AUTHOR:	PASSAGE FOR THE DAY:
Acts 13:39	Bill McCartney	Acts 13:38–41

A Personal Relationship

ON A retreat weekend with Christian university students, many of whom he coached, Bill McCartney was confronted with vibrant Christianity.

That day, for the first time in my life, I was confronted with questions about my faith. Did I have a personal relationship with Jesus Christ? Had I surrendered control of my life to Jesus? Had I made him Lord of my life?

In summary, I began to realize that I had been totally with-out a clue about what it's like to be a wholehearted, committed Christian—to have the true spirit of the Lord in my heart.

Right then and there, I made a decision. I decided to commit my life to Jesus Christ.

You see, I've always been a wholehearted guy, and I've al-ways wanted a full measure of whatever was out there. I've never wanted just part of the package, part of the prize. I want it all! Over the previous ten years I'd been a daily communi-cant in the Catholic Church. You don't have that kind of re-solve unless you want something really enthusiastically. I knew I wanted a deeper walk with the Lord. And that day, I re-alized what I had been missing—I hadn't been born again!

I wanted more. I wanted all of it. Right then and there, I prayed hard to receive the full measure of God's love. It was the most exciting moment of my life!

Additional Scripture Readings:
John 3:1–21; Romans 10:5–13

Go to page 1188 for your next devotional reading.

you rain from heaven and crops in their seasons; he provides you with plenty of food and fills your hearts with joy." [18]Even with these words, they had difficulty keeping the crowd from sacrificing to them.

[19]Then some Jews came from Antioch and Iconium and won the crowd over. They stoned Paul and dragged him outside the city, thinking he was dead. [20]But after the disciples had gathered around him, he got up and went back into the city. The next day he and Barnabas left for Derbe.

The Return to Antioch in Syria

[21]They preached the good news in that city and won a large number of disciples. Then they returned to Lystra, Iconium and Antioch, [22]strengthening the disciples and encouraging them to remain true to the faith. "We must go through many hardships to enter the kingdom of God," they said. [23]Paul and Barnabas appointed elders[a] for them in each church and, with prayer and fasting, committed them to the Lord, in whom they had put their trust. [24]After going through Pisidia, they came into Pamphylia, [25]and when they had preached the word in Perga, they went down to Attalia.

[26]From Attalia they sailed back to Antioch, where they had been committed to the grace of God for the work they had now completed. [27]On arriving there, they gathered the church together and reported all that God had done through them and how he had opened the door of faith to the Gentiles. [28]And they stayed there a long time with the disciples.

The Council at Jerusalem

15 Some men came down from Judea to Antioch and were teaching the brothers: "Unless you are circumcised, according to the custom taught by Moses, you cannot be saved." [2]This brought Paul and Barnabas into sharp dispute and debate with them. So Paul and Barnabas were appointed, along with some other believers, to go up to Jerusalem to see the apostles and elders about this question. [3]The church sent them on their way, and as they traveled through Phoenicia and Samaria, they told how the Gentiles had been converted. This news made all the brothers very glad. [4]When they came to Jerusalem, they were welcomed by the church and the apostles and elders, to whom they reported everything God had done through them.

[5]Then some of the believers who belonged to the party of the Pharisees stood up and said, "The Gentiles must be circumcised and required to obey the law of Moses."

[6]The apostles and elders met to consider this question. [7]After much discussion, Peter got up and addressed them: "Brothers, you know that some time ago God made a choice among you that the Gentiles might hear from my lips the message of the gospel and believe. [8]God, who knows the heart, showed that he accepted them by giving the Holy Spirit to them, just as he did to us. [9]He made no distinction between us and them, for he purified their hearts by faith. [10]Now then, why do you try to test God by putting on the necks of the disciples a yoke that neither we nor our fathers have been able to bear? [11]No! We believe it is through the grace of our Lord Jesus that we are saved, just as they are."

[12]The whole assembly became silent as they listened to Barnabas and Paul telling about the miraculous signs and wonders God had done among the Gentiles through them. [13]When they finished, James spoke up: "Brothers, listen to me. [14]Simon[b] has described to us how God at first showed his concern by taking from the Gentiles a people for himself. [15]The words of the prophets are in agreement with this, as it is written:

[16]" 'After this I will return
  and rebuild David's fallen tent.
Its ruins I will rebuild,
  and I will restore it,
[17]that the remnant of men may seek the
  Lord,
  and all the Gentiles who bear my
  name,
says the Lord, who does these
  things'[c]
[18] that have been known for ages.[d]

[19]"It is my judgment, therefore, that we should not make it difficult for the Gentiles who are turning to God. [20]Instead we should write to them, telling them to abstain from food polluted by idols, from

---

[a]23 Or *Barnabas ordained elders*; or *Barnabas had elders elected*   [b]14 Greek *Simeon*, a variant of *Simon*; that is, Peter   [c]17 Amos 9:11,12   [d]17,18 Some manuscripts *things'— / 18known to the Lord for ages is his work*

sexual immorality, from the meat of strangled animals and from blood. [21]For Moses has been preached in every city from the earliest times and is read in the synagogues on every Sabbath."

The Council's Letter to Gentile Believers

[22]Then the apostles and elders, with the whole church, decided to choose some of their own men and send them to Antioch with Paul and Barnabas. They chose Judas (called Barsabbas) and Silas, two men who were leaders among the brothers. [23]With them they sent the following letter:

The apostles and elders, your brothers,

To the Gentile believers in Antioch, Syria and Cilicia:

Greetings.

[24]We have heard that some went out from us without our authorization and disturbed you, troubling your minds by what they said. [25]So we all agreed to choose some men and send them to you with our dear friends Barnabas and Paul— [26]men who have risked their lives for the name of our Lord Jesus Christ. [27]Therefore we are sending Judas and Silas to confirm by word of mouth what we are writing. [28]It seemed good to the Holy Spirit and to us not to burden you with anything beyond the following requirements: [29]You are to abstain from food sacrificed to idols, from blood, from the meat of strangled animals and from sexual immorality. You will do well to avoid these things.

Farewell.

[30]The men were sent off and went down to Antioch, where they gathered the church together and delivered the letter. [31]The people read it and were glad for its encouraging message. [32]Judas and Silas, who themselves were prophets, said much to encourage and strengthen the brothers. [33]After spending some time there, they were sent off by the brothers with the blessing of peace to return to those who had sent them.[a] [35]But Paul and Barnabas remained in Antioch, where

they and many others taught and preached the word of the Lord.

Disagreement Between Paul and Barnabas

[36]Some time later Paul said to Barnabas, "Let us go back and visit the brothers in all the towns where we preached the word of the Lord and see how they are doing." [37]Barnabas wanted to take John, also called Mark, with them, [38]but Paul did not think it wise to take him, because he had deserted them in Pamphylia and had not continued with them in the work. [39]They had such a sharp disagreement that they parted company. Barnabas took Mark and sailed for Cyprus, [40]but Paul chose Silas and left, commended by the brothers to the grace of the Lord. [41]He went through Syria and Cilicia, strengthening the churches.

Timothy Joins Paul and Silas

16 He came to Derbe and then to Lystra, where a disciple named Timothy lived, whose mother was a Jewess and a believer, but whose father was a Greek. [2]The brothers at Lystra and Iconium spoke well of him. [3]Paul wanted to take him along on the journey, so he circumcised him because of the Jews who lived in that area, for they all knew that his father was a Greek. [4]As they traveled from town to town, they delivered the decisions reached by the apostles and elders in Jerusalem for the people to obey. [5]So the churches were strengthened in the faith and grew daily in numbers.

Paul's Vision of the Man of Macedonia

[6]Paul and his companions traveled throughout the region of Phrygia and Galatia, having been kept by the Holy Spirit from preaching the word in the province of Asia. [7]When they came to the border of Mysia, they tried to enter Bithynia, but the Spirit of Jesus would not allow them to. [8]So they passed by Mysia and went down to Troas. [9]During the night Paul had a vision of a man of Macedonia standing and begging him, "Come over to Macedonia and help us." [10]After Paul had seen the vision, we got ready at once to leave for Macedonia, concluding that God had called us to preach the gospel to them.

---

[a]33 Some manuscripts *them,* [34]*but Silas decided to remain there*

Lydia's Conversion in Philippi

[11] From Troas we put out to sea and sailed straight for Samothrace, and the next day on to Neapolis. [12] From there we traveled to Philippi, a Roman colony and the leading city of that district of Macedonia. And we stayed there several days.

[13] On the Sabbath we went outside the city gate to the river, where we expected to find a place of prayer. We sat down and began to speak to the women who had gathered there. [14] One of those listening was a woman named Lydia, a dealer in purple cloth from the city of Thyatira, who was a worshiper of God. The Lord opened her heart to respond to Paul's message. [15] When she and the members of her household were baptized, she invited us to her home. "If you consider me a believer in the Lord," she said, "come and stay at my house." And she persuaded us.

Paul and Silas in Prison

[16] Once when we were going to the place of prayer, we were met by a slave girl who had a spirit by which she predicted the future. She earned a great deal of money for her owners by fortune-telling. [17] This girl followed Paul and the rest of us, shouting, "These men are servants of the Most High God, who are telling you the way to be saved." [18] She kept this up for many days. Finally Paul became so troubled that he turned around and said to the spirit, "In the name of Jesus Christ I command you to come out of her!" At that moment the spirit left her.

[19] When the owners of the slave girl realized that their hope of making money was gone, they seized Paul and Silas and dragged them into the marketplace to face the authorities. [20] They brought them before the magistrates and said, "These men are Jews, and are throwing our city into an uproar [21] by advocating customs unlawful for us Romans to accept or practice."

[22] The crowd joined in the attack against Paul and Silas, and the magistrates ordered them to be stripped and beaten. [23] After they had been severely flogged, they were thrown into prison, and the jailer was commanded to guard them carefully. [24] Upon receiving such orders, he put them in the inner cell and fastened their feet in the stocks.

[25] About midnight Paul and Silas were praying and singing hymns to God, and the other prisoners were listening to them. [26] Suddenly there was such a violent earthquake that the foundations of the prison were shaken. At once all the prison doors flew open, and everybody's chains came loose. [27] The jailer woke up, and when he saw the prison doors open, he drew his sword and was about to kill himself because he thought the prisoners had escaped. [28] But Paul shouted, "Don't harm yourself! We are all here!"

[29] The jailer called for lights, rushed in and fell trembling before Paul and Silas. [30] He then brought them out and asked, "Sirs, what must I do to be saved?"

[31] They replied, "Believe in the Lord Jesus, and you will be saved — you and your household." [32] Then they spoke the word of the Lord to him and to all the others in his house. [33] At that hour of the night the jailer took them and washed their wounds; then immediately he and all his family were baptized. [34] The jailer brought them into his house and set a meal before them; he was filled with joy because he had come to believe in God — he and his whole family.

[35] When it was daylight, the magistrates sent their officers to the jailer with the order: "Release those men." [36] The jailer told Paul, "The magistrates have ordered that you and Silas be released. Now you can leave. Go in peace."

[37] But Paul said to the officers: "They beat us publicly without a trial, even though we are Roman citizens, and threw us into prison. And now do they want to get rid of us quietly? No! Let them come themselves and escort us out."

[38] The officers reported this to the magistrates, and when they heard that Paul and Silas were Roman citizens, they were alarmed. [39] They came to appease them and escorted them from the prison, requesting them to leave the city. [40] After Paul and Silas came out of the prison, they went to Lydia's house, where they met with the brothers and encouraged them. Then they left.

In Thessalonica

17 When they had passed through Amphipolis and Apollonia, they came to Thessalonica, where there was a Jewish synagogue. [2] As his custom was, Paul went into the synagogue, and on three Sabbath days he reasoned with them from the Scriptures, [3] explaining and

proving that the Christ*a* had to suffer and rise from the dead. "This Jesus I am proclaiming to you is the Christ,*a*" he said. 4Some of the Jews were persuaded and joined Paul and Silas, as did a large number of God-fearing Greeks and not a few prominent women.

5But the Jews were jealous; so they rounded up some bad characters from the marketplace, formed a mob and started a riot in the city. They rushed to Jason's house in search of Paul and Silas in order to bring them out to the crowd.*b* 6But when they did not find them, they dragged Jason and some other brothers before the city officials, shouting: "These men who have caused trouble all over the world have now come here, 7and Jason has welcomed them into his house. They are all defying Caesar's decrees, saying that there is another king, one called Jesus." 8When they heard this, the crowd and the city officials were thrown into turmoil. 9Then they made Jason and the others post bond and let them go.

In Berea

10As soon as it was night, the brothers sent Paul and Silas away to Berea. On arriving there, they went to the Jewish synagogue. 11Now the Bereans were of more noble character than the Thessalonians, for they received the message with great eagerness and examined the Scriptures every day to see if what Paul said was true. 12Many of the Jews believed, as did also a number of prominent Greek women and many Greek men.

13When the Jews in Thessalonica learned that Paul was preaching the word of God at Berea, they went there too, agitating the crowds and stirring them up. 14The brothers immediately sent Paul to the coast, but Silas and Timothy stayed at Berea. 15The men who escorted Paul brought him to Athens and then left with instructions for Silas and Timothy to join him as soon as possible.

In Athens

16While Paul was waiting for them in Athens, he was greatly distressed to see that the city was full of idols. 17So he reasoned in the synagogue with the Jews and the God-fearing Greeks, as well as in the marketplace day by day with those who happened to be there. 18A group of Epicurean and Stoic philosophers began to dispute with him. Some of them asked, "What is this babbler trying to say?" Others remarked, "He seems to be advocating foreign gods." They said this because Paul was preaching the good news about Jesus and the resurrection. 19Then they took him and brought him to a meeting of the Areopagus, where they said to him, "May we know what this new teaching is that you are presenting? 20You are bringing some strange ideas to our ears, and we want to know what they mean." 21(All the Athenians and the foreigners who lived there spent their time doing nothing but talking about and listening to the latest ideas.)

22Paul then stood up in the meeting of the Areopagus and said: "Men of Athens! I see that in every way you are very religious. 23For as I walked around and looked carefully at your objects of worship, I even found an altar with this inscription: TO AN UNKNOWN GOD. Now what you worship as something unknown I am going to proclaim to you.

24"The God who made the world and everything in it is the Lord of heaven and earth and does not live in temples built by hands. 25And he is not served by human hands, as if he needed anything, because he himself gives all men life and breath and everything else. 26From one man he made every nation of men, that they should inhabit the whole earth; and he determined the times set for them and the exact places where they should live. 27God did this so that men would seek him and perhaps reach out for him and find him, though he is not far from each one of us. 28'For in him we live and move and have our being.' As some of your own poets have said, 'We are his offspring.'

29"Therefore since we are God's offspring, we should not think that the divine being is like gold or silver or stone—an image made by man's design and skill. 30In the past God overlooked such ignorance, but now he commands all people everywhere to repent. 31For he has set a day when he will judge the world with justice by the man he has appointed. He has given proof of this to all men by raising him from the dead."

32When they heard about the resurrection of the dead, some of them sneered, but others said, "We want to hear you again on this subject." 33At that, Paul left the Council. 34A few men became followers of Paul and believed. Among them was Dionysius, a member of the Areopagus, also a woman named Damaris, and a number of others.

In Corinth

18 After this, Paul left Athens and went to Corinth. ²There he met a Jew named Aquila, a native of Pontus, who had recently come from Italy with his wife Priscilla, because Claudius had ordered all the Jews to leave Rome. Paul went to see them, ³and because he was a tentmaker as they were, he stayed and worked with them. ⁴Every Sabbath he reasoned in the synagogue, trying to persuade Jews and Greeks.

⁵When Silas and Timothy came from Macedonia, Paul devoted himself exclusively to preaching, testifying to the Jews that Jesus was the Christ.ᵃ ⁶But when the Jews opposed Paul and became abusive, he shook out his clothes in protest and said to them, "Your blood be on your own heads! I am clear of my responsibility. From now on I will go to the Gentiles."

⁷Then Paul left the synagogue and went next door to the house of Titius Justus, a worshiper of God. ⁸Crispus, the synagogue ruler, and his entire household believed in the Lord; and many of the Corinthians who heard him believed and were baptized.

⁹One night the Lord spoke to Paul in a vision: "Do not be afraid; keep on speaking, do not be silent. ¹⁰For I am with you,

ᵃ5 Or *Messiah*; also in verse 28

WEDNESDAY

VERSE FOR THE DAY:	AUTHOR:	PASSAGE FOR THE DAY:
Acts 17:11	Tom Landry	Acts 17:10–15

Character Building

HOW do we develop character?

I believe most of a person's character is developed as a child. It's the result of values learned from family and other significant people early in life—which is what makes our role as parents and the role of those who coach kids so important.

We also develop character by going through adversity. Coaches sometimes talk about a losing year being a "character-building season." There's truth to that as I've seen from experience. That strength of character so crucial to the 1970 [Dallas] Cowboys who rallied from almost certain failure to go on to the Super Bowl was forged through those difficult years when we couldn't win the big one.

They were perfect illustrations of what the apostle Paul was saying: "We know that suffering produces perseverance; perseverance, character; and character, hope" [see Romans 5:3–4].

Yet the truth remains, most of our character is established early in life. Adversity can help build it. Coaches can help mold it. But in our adult years, the only thing I've seen that can radically change a person's basic character is a relationship with Jesus Christ.

Additional Scripture Readings:
Proverbs 22:6; 1 Peter 1:3–9

Go to page 1192 for your next devotional reading.

and no one is going to attack and harm you," because I have many people in this city." ¹¹So Paul stayed for a year and a half, teaching them the word of God.

¹²While Gallio was proconsul of Achaia, the Jews made a united attack on Paul and brought him into court. ¹³"This man," they charged, "is persuading the people to worship God in ways contrary to the law."

¹⁴Just as Paul was about to speak, Gallio said to the Jews, "If you Jews were making a complaint about some misdemeanor or serious crime, it would be reasonable for me to listen to you. ¹⁵But since it involves questions about words and names and your own law—settle the matter yourselves. I will not be a judge of such things." ¹⁶So he had them ejected from the court. ¹⁷Then they all turned on Sosthenes the synagogue ruler and beat him in front of the court. But Gallio showed no concern whatever.

Priscilla, Aquila and Apollos

¹⁸Paul stayed on in Corinth for some time. Then he left the brothers and sailed for Syria, accompanied by Priscilla and Aquila. Before he sailed, he had his hair cut off at Cenchrea because of a vow he had taken. ¹⁹They arrived at Ephesus, where Paul left Priscilla and Aquila. He himself went into the synagogue and reasoned with the Jews. ²⁰When they asked him to spend more time with them, he declined. ²¹But as he left, he promised, "I will come back if it is God's will." Then he set sail from Ephesus. ²²When he landed at Caesarea, he went up and greeted the church and then went down to Antioch.

²³After spending some time in Antioch, Paul set out from there and traveled from place to place throughout the region of Galatia and Phrygia, strengthening all the disciples.

²⁴Meanwhile a Jew named Apollos, a native of Alexandria, came to Ephesus. He was a learned man, with a thorough knowledge of the Scriptures. ²⁵He had been instructed in the way of the Lord, and he spoke with great fervor[a] and taught about Jesus accurately, though he knew only the baptism of John. ²⁶He began to speak boldly in the synagogue. When Priscilla and Aquila heard him, they invited him to their home and explained to him the way of God more adequately.

²⁷When Apollos wanted to go to Achaia, the brothers encouraged him and wrote to the disciples there to welcome him. On arriving, he was a great help to those who by grace had believed. ²⁸For he vigorously refuted the Jews in public debate, proving from the Scriptures that Jesus was the Christ.

Paul in Ephesus

19 While Apollos was at Corinth, Paul took the road through the interior and arrived at Ephesus. There he found some disciples ²and asked them, "Did you receive the Holy Spirit when[b] you believed?"

They answered, "No, we have not even heard that there is a Holy Spirit."

³So Paul asked, "Then what baptism did you receive?"

"John's baptism," they replied.

⁴Paul said, "John's baptism was a baptism of repentance. He told the people to believe in the one coming after him, that is, in Jesus." ⁵On hearing this, they were baptized into[c] the name of the Lord Jesus. ⁶When Paul placed his hands on them, the Holy Spirit came on them, and they spoke in tongues[d] and prophesied. ⁷There were about twelve men in all.

⁸Paul entered the synagogue and spoke boldly there for three months, arguing persuasively about the kingdom of God. ⁹But some of them became obstinate; they refused to believe and publicly maligned the Way. So Paul left them. He took the disciples with him and had discussions daily in the lecture hall of Tyrannus. ¹⁰This went on for two years, so that all the Jews and Greeks who lived in the province of Asia heard the word of the Lord.

¹¹God did extraordinary miracles through Paul, ¹²so that even handkerchiefs and aprons that had touched him were taken to the sick, and their illnesses were cured and the evil spirits left them.

¹³Some Jews who went around driving out evil spirits tried to invoke the name of the Lord Jesus over those who were demon-possessed. They would say, "In the name of Jesus, whom Paul preaches, I command you to come out." ¹⁴Seven sons of Sceva, a Jewish chief priest, were doing this. ¹⁵One day, the evil spirit answered them, "Jesus I know, and I know about Paul, but who are you?" ¹⁶Then the man who had the evil spirit jumped on them and overpowered them all. He gave them

---

ᵃ25 Or with fervor in the Spirit   ᵇ2 Or after   ᶜ5 Or in   ᵈ6 Or other languages such a beating that they ran out of the house naked and bleeding.

[17]When this became known to the Jews and Greeks living in Ephesus, they were all seized with fear, and the name of the Lord Jesus was held in high honor. [18]Many of those who believed now came and openly confessed their evil deeds. [19]A number who had practiced sorcery brought their scrolls together and burned them publicly. When they calculated the value of the scrolls, the total came to fifty thousand drachmas.[a] [20]In this way the word of the Lord spread widely and grew in power.

[21]After all this had happened, Paul decided to go to Jerusalem, passing through Macedonia and Achaia. "After I have been there," he said, "I must visit Rome also." [22]He sent two of his helpers, Timothy and Erastus, to Macedonia, while he stayed in the province of Asia a little longer.

The Riot in Ephesus

[23]About that time there arose a great disturbance about the Way. [24]A silversmith named Demetrius, who made silver shrines of Artemis, brought in no little business for the craftsmen. [25]He called them together, along with the workmen in related trades, and said: "Men, you know we receive a good income from this business. [26]And you see and hear how this fellow Paul has convinced and led astray large numbers of people here in Ephesus and in practically the whole province of Asia. He says that man-made gods are no gods at all. [27]There is danger not only that our trade will lose its good name, but also that the temple of the great goddess Artemis will be discredited, and the goddess herself, who is worshiped throughout the province of Asia and the world, will be robbed of her divine majesty."

[28]When they heard this, they were furious and began shouting: "Great is Artemis of the Ephesians!" [29]Soon the whole city was in an uproar. The people seized Gaius and Aristarchus, Paul's traveling companions from Macedonia, and rushed as one man into the theater. [30]Paul wanted to appear before the crowd, but the disciples would not let him. [31]Even some of the officials of the province, friends of Paul, sent him a message begging him not to venture into the theater.

[32]The assembly was in confusion: Some were shouting one thing, some another.

Most of the people did not even know why they were there. [33]The Jews pushed Alexander to the front, and some of the crowd shouted instructions to him. He motioned for silence in order to make a defense before the people. [34]But when they realized he was a Jew, they all shouted in unison for about two hours: "Great is Artemis of the Ephesians!"

[35]The city clerk quieted the crowd and said: "Men of Ephesus, doesn't all the world know that the city of Ephesus is the guardian of the temple of the great Artemis and of her image, which fell from heaven? [36]Therefore, since these facts are undeniable, you ought to be quiet and not do anything rash. [37]You have brought these men here, though they have neither robbed temples nor blasphemed our goddess. [38]If, then, Demetrius and his fellow craftsmen have a grievance against anybody, the courts are open and there are proconsuls. They can press charges. [39]If there is anything further you want to bring up, it must be settled in a legal assembly. [40]As it is, we are in danger of being charged with rioting because of today's events. In that case we would not be able to account for this commotion, since there is no reason for it." [41]After he had said this, he dismissed the assembly.

Through Macedonia and Greece

20 When the uproar had ended, Paul sent for the disciples and, after encouraging them, said good-by and set out for Macedonia. [2]He traveled through that area, speaking many words of encouragement to the people, and finally arrived in Greece, [3]where he stayed three months. Because the Jews made a plot against him just as he was about to sail for Syria, he decided to go back through Macedonia. [4]He was accompanied by Sopater son of Pyrrhus from Berea, Aristarchus and Secundus from Thessalonica, Gaius from Derbe, Timothy also, and Tychicus and Trophimus from the province of Asia. [5]These men went on ahead and waited for us at Troas. [6]But we sailed from Philippi after the Feast of Unleavened Bread, and five days later joined the others at Troas, where we stayed seven days.

Eutychus Raised From the Dead at Troas

[7]On the first day of the week we came together to break bread. Paul spoke to the

people and, because he intended to leave the next day, kept on talking until midnight. **8**There were many lamps in the upstairs room where we were meeting. **9**Seated in a window was a young man named Eutychus, who was sinking into a deep sleep as Paul talked on and on. When he was sound asleep, he fell to the ground from the third story and was picked up dead. **10**Paul went down, threw himself on the young man and put his arms around him. "Don't be alarmed," he said. "He's alive!" **11**Then he went upstairs again and broke bread and ate. After talking until daylight, he left. **12**The people took the young man home alive and were greatly comforted.

Paul's Farewell to the Ephesian Elders

13We went on ahead to the ship and sailed for Assos, where we were going to take Paul aboard. He had made this arrangement because he was going there on foot. **14**When he met us at Assos, we took him aboard and went on to Mitylene. **15**The next day we set sail from there and arrived off Kios. The day after that we crossed over to Samos, and on the following day arrived at Miletus. **16**Paul had decided to sail past Ephesus to avoid spending time in the province of Asia, for he was in a hurry to reach Jerusalem, if possible, by the day of Pentecost.

17From Miletus, Paul sent to Ephesus for the elders of the church. **18**When they arrived, he said to them: "You know how I lived the whole time I was with you, from the first day I came into the province of Asia. **19**I served the Lord with great humility and with tears, although I was severely tested by the plots of the Jews. **20**You know that I have not hesitated to preach anything that would be helpful to you but have taught you publicly and from house to house. **21**I have declared to both Jews and Greeks that they must turn to God in repentance and have faith in our Lord Jesus.

22"And now, compelled by the Spirit, I am going to Jerusalem, not knowing what will happen to me there. **23**I only know that in every city the Holy Spirit warns me that prison and hardships are facing me. **24**However, I consider my life worth nothing to me, if only I may finish the race and complete the task the Lord Jesus has given me — the task of testifying to the gospel of God's grace.

25"Now I know that none of you among whom I have gone about preaching the kingdom will ever see me again. **26**Therefore, I declare to you today that I am innocent of the blood of all men. **27**For I have not hesitated to proclaim to you the whole will of God. **28**Keep watch over yourselves and all the flock of which the Holy Spirit has made you overseers.*a* Be shepherds of the church of God,*b* which he bought with his own blood. **29**I know that after I leave, savage wolves will come in among you and will not spare the flock. **30**Even from your own number men will arise and distort the truth in order to draw away disciples after them. **31**So be on your guard! Remember that for three years I never stopped warning each of you night and day with tears.

32"Now I commit you to God and to the word of his grace, which can build you up and give you an inheritance among all those who are sanctified. **33**I have not coveted anyone's silver or gold or clothing. **34**You yourselves know that these hands of mine have supplied my own needs and the needs of my companions. **35**In everything I did, I showed you that by this kind of hard work we must help the weak, remembering the words the Lord Jesus himself said: 'It is more blessed to give than to receive.' "

36When he had said this, he knelt down with all of them and prayed. **37**They all wept as they embraced him and kissed him. **38**What grieved them most was his statement that they would never see his face again. Then they accompanied him to the ship.

On to Jerusalem

21 After we had torn ourselves away from them, we put out to sea and sailed straight to Cos. The next day we went to Rhodes and from there to Patara. **2**We found a ship crossing over to Phoenicia, went on board and set sail. **3**After sighting Cyprus and passing to the south of it, we sailed on to Syria. We landed at Tyre, where our ship was to unload its cargo. **4**Finding the disciples there, we stayed with them seven days. Through the Spirit they urged Paul not to go on to Jerusalem. **5**But when our time was up, we left and continued on our way. All the disciples

---

a28 Traditionally *bishops*   *b28* Many manuscripts *of the Lord* and their wives and children accompanied us out of the city, and there on the beach we knelt to pray. 6After saying good-by to each other, we went aboard the ship, and they returned home.

7We continued our voyage from Tyre and landed at Ptolemais, where we greeted the brothers and stayed with them for a day. 8Leaving the next day, we reached Caesarea and stayed at the house of Philip the evangelist, one of the Seven. 9He had four unmarried daughters who prophesied.

10After we had been there a number of days, a prophet named Agabus came down from Judea. 11Coming over to us, he took Paul's belt, tied his own hands and feet with it and said, "The Holy Spirit says,

'In this way the Jews of Jerusalem will bind the owner of this belt and will hand him over to the Gentiles.' "

12When we heard this, we and the people there pleaded with Paul not to go up to Jerusalem. 13Then Paul answered, "Why are you weeping and breaking my heart? I am ready not only to be bound, but also to die in Jerusalem for the name of the Lord Jesus." 14When he would not be dissuaded, we gave up and said, "The Lord's will be done."

15After this, we got ready and went up to Jerusalem. 16Some of the disciples from Caesarea accompanied us and brought us to the home of Mnason, where we were to stay. He was a man from Cyprus and one of the early disciples.

THURSDAY

VERSE FOR THE DAY:	AUTHOR:	PASSAGE FOR THE DAY:
Acts 20:24	Patrick Morley	Acts 20:17–24

Running the Race

WE CAN define the rat race as the pursuit of the beautiful, wrinkle-free life. Since there are no winners, the aftermath of running the race and losing takes a heavy toll . . .

If the pursuit of money and possessions stood alone as an issue, we might be able to rationalize some of our money lust. But every balance sheet has two sides, and the other side of this balance sheet is relationships.

When we choose the rat race, fracture lines soon appear in our relationships, and crumbling is not far behind. Unfortunately, all too often, in pursuit of the good life, *most men leave a trail of broken relationships.*

The way in which we measure our standard of living indicates the race we have decided to run. The American Christian faces a true dilemma. We can choose the rat race, or we can choose to not love this world and "throw off everything that hinders and the sin that so easily entangles, and . . . run with perseverance the race marked out for us" (Hebrews 12:1).

We each make our own choice, but the pressure to make the wrong choice is intense and should not be underestimated. As my first Bible study leader was fond of saying, "You can choose your own way, but you can't choose the result." The cause and effect nature of our choice brands us.

Additional Scripture Readings:
2 Timothy 4:6–8; Hebrews 12:1–3

Go to page 1195 for your next devotional reading.

Paul's Arrival at Jerusalem

17When we arrived at Jerusalem, the brothers received us warmly. **18**The next day Paul and the rest of us went to see James, and all the elders were present. **19**Paul greeted them and reported in detail what God had done among the Gentiles through his ministry.

20When they heard this, they praised God. Then they said to Paul: "You see, brother, how many thousands of Jews have believed, and all of them are zealous for the law. **21**They have been informed that you teach all the Jews who live among the Gentiles to turn away from Moses, telling them not to circumcise their children or live according to our customs. **22**What shall we do? They will certainly hear that you have come, **23**so do what we tell you. There are four men with us who have made a vow. **24**Take these men, join in their purification rites and pay their expenses, so that they can have their heads shaved. Then everybody will know there is no truth in these reports about you, but that you yourself are living in obedience to the law. **25**As for the Gentile believers, we have written to them our decision that they should abstain from food sacrificed to idols, from blood, from the meat of strangled animals and from sexual immorality."

26The next day Paul took the men and purified himself along with them. Then he went to the temple to give notice of the date when the days of purification would end and the offering would be made for each of them.

Paul Arrested

27When the seven days were nearly over, some Jews from the province of Asia saw Paul at the temple. They stirred up the whole crowd and seized him, **28**shouting, "Men of Israel, help us! This is the man who teaches all men everywhere against our people and our law and this place. And besides, he has brought Greeks into the temple area and defiled this holy place." **29**(They had previously seen Trophimus the Ephesian in the city with Paul and assumed that Paul had brought him into the temple area.)

30The whole city was aroused, and the people came running from all directions. Seizing Paul, they dragged him from the temple, and immediately the gates were shut. **31**While they were trying to kill him, news reached the commander of the Roman troops that the whole city of Jerusalem was in an uproar. **32**He at once took some officers and soldiers and ran down to the crowd. When the rioters saw the commander and his soldiers, they stopped beating Paul.

33The commander came up and arrested him and ordered him to be bound with two chains. Then he asked who he was and what he had done. **34**Some in the crowd shouted one thing and some another, and since the commander could not get at the truth because of the uproar, he ordered that Paul be taken into the barracks. **35**When Paul reached the steps, the violence of the mob was so great he had to be carried by the soldiers. **36**The crowd that followed kept shouting, "Away with him!"

Paul Speaks to the Crowd

37As the soldiers were about to take Paul into the barracks, he asked the commander, "May I say something to you?"

"Do you speak Greek?" he replied. **38**"Aren't you the Egyptian who started a revolt and led four thousand terrorists out into the desert some time ago?"

39Paul answered, "I am a Jew, from Tarsus in Cilicia, a citizen of no ordinary city. Please let me speak to the people."

40Having received the commander's permission, Paul stood on the steps and motioned to the crowd. When they were all silent, he said to them in Aramaic[a]:

22 **1**"Brothers and fathers, listen now to my defense."

2When they heard him speak to them in Aramaic, they became very quiet.

Then Paul said: **3**"I am a Jew, born in Tarsus of Cilicia, but brought up in this city. Under Gamaliel I was thoroughly trained in the law of our fathers and was just as zealous for God as any of you are today. **4**I persecuted the followers of this Way to their death, arresting both men and women and throwing them into prison, **5**as also the high priest and all the Council can testify. I even obtained letters from them to their brothers in Damascus, and went there to bring these people as prisoners to Jerusalem to be punished.

6"About noon as I came near Damascus, suddenly a bright light from heaven flashed around me. **7**I fell to the ground

---

a40 Or possibly *Hebrew*; also in 22:2

and heard a voice say to me, 'Saul! Saul! Why do you persecute me?'

8" 'Who are you, Lord?' I asked.

" 'I am Jesus of Nazareth, whom you are persecuting,' he replied. 9My companions saw the light, but they did not understand the voice of him who was speaking to me.

10" 'What shall I do, Lord?' I asked.

" 'Get up,' the Lord said, 'and go into Damascus. There you will be told all that you have been assigned to do.' 11My companions led me by the hand into Damascus, because the brilliance of the light had blinded me.

12"A man named Ananias came to see me. He was a devout observer of the law and highly respected by all the Jews living there. 13He stood beside me and said, 'Brother Saul, receive your sight!' And at that very moment I was able to see him.

14"Then he said: 'The God of our fathers has chosen you to know his will and to see the Righteous One and to hear words from his mouth. 15You will be his witness to all men of what you have seen and heard. 16And now what are you waiting for? Get up, be baptized and wash your sins away, calling on his name.'

17"When I returned to Jerusalem and was praying at the temple, I fell into a trance 18and saw the Lord speaking. 'Quick!' he said to me. 'Leave Jerusalem immediately, because they will not accept your testimony about me.'

19" 'Lord,' I replied, 'these men know that I went from one synagogue to another to imprison and beat those who believe in you. 20And when the blood of your martyr[a] Stephen was shed, I stood there giving my approval and guarding the clothes of those who were killing him.'

21"Then the Lord said to me, 'Go; I will send you far away to the Gentiles.' "

Paul the Roman Citizen

22The crowd listened to Paul until he said this. Then they raised their voices and shouted, "Rid the earth of him! He's not fit to live!"

23As they were shouting and throwing off their cloaks and flinging dust into the air, 24the commander ordered Paul to be taken into the barracks. He directed that he be flogged and questioned in order to find out why the people were shouting at him like this. 25As they stretched him out to flog him, Paul said to the centurion

standing there, "Is it legal for you to flog a Roman citizen who hasn't even been found guilty?"

26When the centurion heard this, he went to the commander and reported it. "What are you going to do?" he asked. "This man is a Roman citizen."

27The commander went to Paul and asked, "Tell me, are you a Roman citizen?"

"Yes, I am," he answered.

28Then the commander said, "I had to pay a big price for my citizenship."

"But I was born a citizen," Paul replied.

29Those who were about to question him withdrew immediately. The commander himself was alarmed when he realized that he had put Paul, a Roman citizen, in chains.

Before the Sanhedrin

30The next day, since the commander wanted to find out exactly why Paul was being accused by the Jews, he released him and ordered the chief priests and all the Sanhedrin to assemble. Then he brought Paul and had him stand before them.

23 Paul looked straight at the Sanhedrin and said, "My brothers, I have fulfilled my duty to God in all good conscience to this day." 2At this the high priest Ananias ordered those standing near Paul to strike him on the mouth. 3Then Paul said to him, "God will strike you, you whitewashed wall! You sit there to judge me according to the law, yet you yourself violate the law by commanding that I be struck!"

4Those who were standing near Paul said, "You dare to insult God's high priest?"

5Paul replied, "Brothers, I did not realize that he was the high priest; for it is written: 'Do not speak evil about the ruler of your people.'[b] "

6Then Paul, knowing that some of them were Sadducees and the others Pharisees, called out in the Sanhedrin, "My brothers, I am a Pharisee, the son of a Pharisee. I stand on trial because of my hope in the resurrection of the dead." 7When he said this, a dispute broke out between the Pharisees and the Sadducees, and the assembly was divided. 8(The Sadducees say that there is no resurrection, and that there are neither angels nor spirits, but the Pharisees acknowledge them all.)

[9]There was a great uproar, and some of the teachers of the law who were Pharisees stood up and argued vigorously. "We find nothing wrong with this man," they said. "What if a spirit or an angel has spoken to him?" [10]The dispute became so violent that the commander was afraid Paul would be torn to pieces by them. He ordered the troops to go down and take him away from them by force and bring him into the barracks.

[11]The following night the Lord stood near Paul and said, "Take courage! As you have testified about me in Jerusalem, so you must also testify in Rome."

The Plot to Kill Paul

[12]The next morning the Jews formed a conspiracy and bound themselves with an oath not to eat or drink until they had killed Paul. [13]More than forty men were involved in this plot. [14]They went to the chief priests and elders and said, "We have taken a solemn oath not to eat anything until we have killed Paul. [15]Now then, you and the Sanhedrin petition the

---

FRIDAY

VERSE FOR THE DAY:
Acts 22:16

AUTHOR:
Max Lucado

PASSAGE FOR THE DAY:
Acts 22:12–21

Sin Meets Savior

ANANIAS'S instructions to Paul are worth reading: "What are you waiting for? Get up, be baptized and wash your sins away, calling on his name" (Acts 22:16).

He didn't have to be told twice. The legalist Saul was buried, and the liberator Paul was born. He was never the same afterwards. And neither was the world.

Stirring sermons, dedicated disciples, and six thousand miles of trails. If his sandals weren't slapping, his pen was writing. If he wasn't explaining the mystery of grace, he was articulating the theology that would determine the course of Western civilization.

All of his words could be reduced to one sentence. "We preach Christ crucified" (1 Corinthians 1:23). It wasn't that he lacked other sermon outlines; it was just that he couldn't exhaust the first one . . .

Paul never took a course in missions. He never sat in on a committee meeting. He never read a book on church growth. He was just inspired by the Holy Spirit and punch-drunk on the love that makes the impossible possible: salvation.

The message is gripping: Show a man his failures without Jesus, and the result will be found in the roadside gutter. Give a man religion without reminding him of his filth, and the result will be arrogance in a three-piece suit. But get the two in the same heart—get sin to meet Savior and Savior to meet sin —and the result just might be another Pharisee turned preacher who sets the world on fire.

Additional Scripture Readings:
1 Corinthians 1:18–31;
1 Timothy 1:15–17

Go to page 1200 for your next devotional reading.

commander to bring him before you on the pretext of wanting more accurate information about his case. We are ready to kill him before he gets here."

¹⁶But when the son of Paul's sister heard of this plot, he went into the barracks and told Paul.

¹⁷Then Paul called one of the centurions and said, "Take this young man to the commander; he has something to tell him." ¹⁸So he took him to the commander.

The centurion said, "Paul, the prisoner, sent for me and asked me to bring this young man to you because he has something to tell you."

¹⁹The commander took the young man by the hand, drew him aside and asked, "What is it you want to tell me?"

²⁰He said: "The Jews have agreed to ask you to bring Paul before the Sanhedrin tomorrow on the pretext of wanting more accurate information about him. ²¹Don't give in to them, because more than forty of them are waiting in ambush for him. They have taken an oath not to eat or drink until they have killed him. They are ready now, waiting for your consent to their request."

²²The commander dismissed the young man and cautioned him, "Don't tell anyone that you have reported this to me."

Paul Transferred to Caesarea

²³Then he called two of his centurions and ordered them, "Get ready a detachment of two hundred soldiers, seventy horsemen and two hundred spearmen^a to go to Caesarea at nine tonight. ²⁴Provide mounts for Paul so that he may be taken safely to Governor Felix."

²⁵He wrote a letter as follows:

²⁶Claudius Lysias,

To His Excellency, Governor Felix:

Greetings.

²⁷This man was seized by the Jews and they were about to kill him, but I came with my troops and rescued him, for I had learned that he is a Roman citizen. ²⁸I wanted to know why they were accusing him, so I brought him to their Sanhedrin. ²⁹I found that the accusation had to do with questions about their law, but there was

no charge against him that deserved death or imprisonment. ³⁰When I was informed of a plot to be carried out against the man, I sent him to you at once. I also ordered his accusers to present to you their case against him.

³¹So the soldiers, carrying out their orders, took Paul with them during the night and brought him as far as Antipatris. ³²The next day they let the cavalry go on with him, while they returned to the barracks. ³³When the cavalry arrived in Caesarea, they delivered the letter to the governor and handed Paul over to him. ³⁴The governor read the letter and asked what province he was from. Learning that he was from Cilicia, ³⁵he said, "I will hear your case when your accusers get here." Then he ordered that Paul be kept under guard in Herod's palace.

The Trial Before Felix

24 Five days later the high priest Ananias went down to Caesarea with some of the elders and a lawyer named Tertullus, and they brought their charges against Paul before the governor. ²When Paul was called in, Tertullus presented his case before Felix: "We have enjoyed a long period of peace under you, and your foresight has brought about reforms in this nation. ³Everywhere and in every way, most excellent Felix, we acknowledge this with profound gratitude. ⁴But in order not to weary you further, I would request that you be kind enough to hear us briefly.

⁵"We have found this man to be a troublemaker, stirring up riots among the Jews all over the world. He is a ringleader of the Nazarene sect ⁶and even tried to desecrate the temple; so we seized him. ⁸By^b examining him yourself you will be able to learn the truth about all these charges we are bringing against him."

⁹The Jews joined in the accusation, asserting that these things were true.

¹⁰When the governor motioned for him to speak, Paul replied: "I know that for a number of years you have been a judge over this nation; so I gladly make my defense. ¹¹You can easily verify that no more than twelve days ago I went up to Jerusalem to worship. ¹²My accusers did not find me arguing with anyone at the tem-

ple, or stirring up a crowd in the synagogues or anywhere else in the city. ¹³And they cannot prove to you the charges they are now making against me. ¹⁴However, I admit that I worship the God of our fathers as a follower of the Way, which they call a sect. I believe everything that agrees with the Law and that is written in the Prophets, ¹⁵and I have the same hope in God as these men, that there will be a resurrection of both the righteous and the wicked. ¹⁶So I strive always to keep my conscience clear before God and man.

¹⁷"After an absence of several years, I came to Jerusalem to bring my people gifts for the poor and to present offerings. ¹⁸I was ceremonially clean when they found me in the temple courts doing this. There was no crowd with me, nor was I involved in any disturbance. ¹⁹But there are some Jews from the province of Asia, who ought to be here before you and bring charges if they have anything against me. ²⁰Or these who are here should state what crime they found in me when I stood before the Sanhedrin— ²¹unless it was this one thing I shouted as I stood in their presence: 'It is concerning the resurrection of the dead that I am on trial before you today.'"

²²Then Felix, who was well acquainted with the Way, adjourned the proceedings. "When Lysias the commander comes," he said, "I will decide your case." ²³He ordered the centurion to keep Paul under guard but to give him some freedom and permit his friends to take care of his needs.

²⁴Several days later Felix came with his wife Drusilla, who was a Jewess. He sent for Paul and listened to him as he spoke about faith in Christ Jesus. ²⁵As Paul discoursed on righteousness, self-control and the judgment to come, Felix was afraid and said, "That's enough for now! You may leave. When I find it convenient, I will send for you." ²⁶At the same time he was hoping that Paul would offer him a bribe, so he sent for him frequently and talked with him.

²⁷When two years had passed, Felix was succeeded by Porcius Festus, but because Felix wanted to grant a favor to the Jews, he left Paul in prison.

The Trial Before Festus

25 Three days after arriving in the province, Festus went up from Caesarea to Jerusalem, ²where the chief priests and Jewish leaders appeared before him and presented the charges against Paul. ³They urgently requested Festus, as a favor to them, to have Paul transferred to Jerusalem, for they were preparing an ambush to kill him along the way. ⁴Festus answered, "Paul is being held at Caesarea, and I myself am going there soon. ⁵Let some of your leaders come with me and press charges against the man there, if he has done anything wrong."

⁶After spending eight or ten days with them, he went down to Caesarea, and the next day he convened the court and ordered that Paul be brought before him. ⁷When Paul appeared, the Jews who had come down from Jerusalem stood around him, bringing many serious charges against him, which they could not prove.

⁸Then Paul made his defense: "I have done nothing wrong against the law of the Jews or against the temple or against Caesar."

⁹Festus, wishing to do the Jews a favor, said to Paul, "Are you willing to go up to Jerusalem and stand trial before me there on these charges?"

¹⁰Paul answered: "I am now standing before Caesar's court, where I ought to be tried. I have not done any wrong to the Jews, as you yourself know very well. ¹¹If, however, I am guilty of doing anything deserving death, I do not refuse to die. But if the charges brought against me by these Jews are not true, no one has the right to hand me over to them. I appeal to Caesar!"

¹²After Festus had conferred with his council, he declared: "You have appealed to Caesar. To Caesar you will go!"

Festus Consults King Agrippa

¹³A few days later King Agrippa and Bernice arrived at Caesarea to pay their respects to Festus. ¹⁴Since they were spending many days there, Festus discussed Paul's case with the king. He said: "There is a man here whom Felix left as a prisoner. ¹⁵When I went to Jerusalem, the chief priests and elders of the Jews brought charges against him and asked that he be condemned.

¹⁶"I told them that it is not the Roman custom to hand over any man before he has faced his accusers and has had an opportunity to defend himself against their charges. ¹⁷When they came here with me, I did not delay the case, but convened the court the next day and ordered the man to be brought in. ¹⁸When his accusers got up

to speak, they did not charge him with any of the crimes I had expected. **19**Instead, they had some points of dispute with him about their own religion and about a dead man named Jesus who Paul claimed was alive. **20**I was at a loss how to investigate such matters; so I asked if he would be willing to go to Jerusalem and stand trial there on these charges. **21**When Paul made his appeal to be held over for the Emperor's decision, I ordered him held until I could send him to Caesar."

22Then Agrippa said to Festus, "I would like to hear this man myself."

He replied, "Tomorrow you will hear him."

Paul Before Agrippa

23The next day Agrippa and Bernice came with great pomp and entered the audience room with the high ranking officers and the leading men of the city. At the command of Festus, Paul was brought in. **24**Festus said: "King Agrippa, and all who are present with us, you see this man! The whole Jewish community has petitioned me about him in Jerusalem and here in Caesarea, shouting that he ought not to live any longer. **25**I found he had done nothing deserving of death, but because he made his appeal to the Emperor I decided to send him to Rome. **26**But I have nothing definite to write to His Majesty about him. Therefore I have brought him before all of you, and especially before you, King Agrippa, so that as a result of this investigation I may have something to write. **27**For I think it is unreasonable to send on a prisoner without specifying the charges against him."

26 Then Agrippa said to Paul, "You have permission to speak for yourself."

So Paul motioned with his hand and began his defense: **2**"King Agrippa, I consider myself fortunate to stand before you today as I make my defense against all the accusations of the Jews, **3**and especially so because you are well acquainted with all the Jewish customs and controversies. Therefore, I beg you to listen to me patiently.

4"The Jews all know the way I have lived ever since I was a child, from the beginning of my life in my own country, and also in Jerusalem. **5**They have known me for a long time and can testify, if they are willing, that according to the strictest sect

of our religion, I lived as a Pharisee. **6**And now it is because of my hope in what God has promised our fathers that I am on trial today. **7**This is the promise our twelve tribes are hoping to see fulfilled as they earnestly serve God day and night. O king, it is because of this hope that the Jews are accusing me. **8**Why should any of you consider it incredible that God raises the dead?

9"I too was convinced that I ought to do all that was possible to oppose the name of Jesus of Nazareth. **10**And that is just what I did in Jerusalem. On the authority of the chief priests I put many of the saints in prison, and when they were put to death, I cast my vote against them. **11**Many a time I went from one synagogue to another to have them punished, and I tried to force them to blaspheme. In my obsession against them, I even went to foreign cities to persecute them.

12"On one of these journeys I was going to Damascus with the authority and commission of the chief priests. **13**About noon, O king, as I was on the road, I saw a light from heaven, brighter than the sun, blazing around me and my companions. **14**We all fell to the ground, and I heard a voice saying to me in Aramaic,*a* 'Saul, Saul, why do you persecute me? It is hard for you to kick against the goads.'

15"Then I asked, 'Who are you, Lord?'

" 'I am Jesus, whom you are persecuting,' the Lord replied. **16**'Now get up and stand on your feet. I have appeared to you to appoint you as a servant and as a witness of what you have seen of me and what I will show you. **17**I will rescue you from your own people and from the Gentiles. I am sending you to them **18**to open their eyes and turn them from darkness to light, and from the power of Satan to God, so that they may receive forgiveness of sins and a place among those who are sanctified by faith in me.'

19"So then, King Agrippa, I was not disobedient to the vision from heaven. **20**First to those in Damascus, then to those in Jerusalem and in all Judea, and to the Gentiles also, I preached that they should repent and turn to God and prove their repentance by their deeds. **21**That is why the Jews seized me in the temple courts and tried to kill me. **22**But I have had God's help to this very day, and so I stand here and testify to small and great alike. I am saying nothing beyond what the prophets

a14 Or Hebrew

and Moses said would happen— [23]that the Christ[a] would suffer and, as the first to rise from the dead, would proclaim light to his own people and to the Gentiles."

[24]At this point Festus interrupted Paul's defense. "You are out of your mind, Paul!" he shouted. "Your great learning is driving you insane."

[25]"I am not insane, most excellent Festus," Paul replied. "What I am saying is true and reasonable. [26]The king is familiar with these things, and I can speak freely to him. I am convinced that none of this has escaped his notice, because it was not done in a corner. [27]King Agrippa, do you believe the prophets? I know you do."

[28]Then Agrippa said to Paul, "Do you think that in such a short time you can persuade me to be a Christian?"

[29]Paul replied, "Short time or long—I pray God that not only you but all who are listening to me today may become what I am, except for these chains."

[30]The king rose, and with him the governor and Bernice and those sitting with them. [31]They left the room, and while talking with one another, they said, "This man is not doing anything that deserves death or imprisonment."

[32]Agrippa said to Festus, "This man could have been set free if he had not appealed to Caesar."

Paul Sails for Rome

27 When it was decided that we would sail for Italy, Paul and some other prisoners were handed over to a centurion named Julius, who belonged to the Imperial Regiment. [2]We boarded a ship from Adramyttium about to sail for ports along the coast of the province of Asia, and we put out to sea. Aristarchus, a Macedonian from Thessalonica, was with us.

[3]The next day we landed at Sidon; and Julius, in kindness to Paul, allowed him to go to his friends so they might provide for his needs. [4]From there we put out to sea again and passed to the lee of Cyprus because the winds were against us. [5]When we had sailed across the open sea off the coast of Cilicia and Pamphylia, we landed at Myra in Lycia. [6]There the centurion found an Alexandrian ship sailing for Italy and put us on board. [7]We made slow headway for many days and had difficulty arriving off Cnidus. When the wind did

not allow us to hold our course, we sailed to the lee of Crete, opposite Salmone. [8]We moved along the coast with difficulty and came to a place called Fair Havens, near the town of Lasea.

[9]Much time had been lost, and sailing had already become dangerous because by now it was after the Fast.[b] So Paul warned them, [10]"Men, I can see that our voyage is going to be disastrous and bring great loss to ship and cargo, and to our own lives also." [11]But the centurion, instead of listening to what Paul said, followed the advice of the pilot and of the owner of the ship. [12]Since the harbor was unsuitable to winter in, the majority decided that we should sail on, hoping to reach Phoenix and winter there. This was a harbor in Crete, facing both southwest and northwest.

The Storm

[13]When a gentle south wind began to blow, they thought they had obtained what they wanted; so they weighed anchor and sailed along the shore of Crete. [14]Before very long, a wind of hurricane force, called the "northeaster," swept down from the island. [15]The ship was caught by the storm and could not head into the wind; so we gave way to it and were driven along. [16]As we passed to the lee of a small island called Cauda, we were hardly able to make the lifeboat secure. [17]When the men had hoisted it aboard, they passed ropes under the ship itself to hold it together. Fearing that they would run aground on the sandbars of Syrtis, they lowered the sea anchor and let the ship be driven along. [18]We took such a violent battering from the storm that the next day they began to throw the cargo overboard. [19]On the third day, they threw the ship's tackle overboard with their own hands. [20]When neither sun nor stars appeared for many days and the storm continued raging, we finally gave up all hope of being saved.

[21]After the men had gone a long time without food, Paul stood up before them and said: "Men, you should have taken my advice not to sail from Crete; then you would have spared yourselves this damage and loss. [22]But now I urge you to keep up your courage, because not one of you will be lost; only the ship will be destroyed. [23]Last night an angel of the God whose I am and whom I serve stood be-

[a]23 Or Messiah   [b]9 That is, the Day of Atonement (Yom Kippur)

WEEKENDING

RECOVER

I have some dreams. It is time for us as men to reject this fragile male ego business. We use it to cover up our failures and avoid looking at ourselves. Thus the women and children in our lives, who presumably have better egos than we do, must pick up the slack and take responsibility for our actions and feelings. Come on guys! Let us at least try to struggle honestly. We need to be confronted by our actions, messages and shortcomings if we expect to learn and grow. No more hiding behind excuses. No blaming others. No hiding behind phrases like, "This is just the way I am." Let us have a look at who we are for that is the best indication of who our sons will become.

– E. James Wilder

REVIVE

Saturday: Job 13:1–12
Sunday: 2 Corinthians 13:1–10

Go to page 1205 for your next devotional reading.

side me [24]and said, 'Do not be afraid, Paul. You must stand trial before Caesar; and God has graciously given you the lives of all who sail with you.' [25]So keep up your courage, men, for I have faith in God that it will happen just as he told me. [26]Nevertheless, we must run aground on some island."

The Shipwreck

[27]On the fourteenth night we were still being driven across the Adriatic[a] Sea, when about midnight the sailors sensed they were approaching land. [28]They took soundings and found that the water was a hundred and twenty feet[b] deep. A short time later they took soundings again and found it was ninety feet[c] deep. [29]Fearing that we would be dashed against the rocks, they dropped four anchors from the stern and prayed for daylight. [30]In an attempt to escape from the ship, the sailors let the lifeboat down into the sea, pretending they were going to lower some anchors from the bow. [31]Then Paul said to the centurion and the soldiers, "Unless these men stay with the ship, you cannot be saved." [32]So the soldiers cut the ropes that held the lifeboat and let it fall away.

[33]Just before dawn Paul urged them all to eat. "For the last fourteen days," he said, "you have been in constant suspense and have gone without food — you haven't eaten anything. [34]Now I urge you to take some food. You need it to survive. Not one of you will lose a single hair from his head." [35]After he said this, he took some bread and gave thanks to God in front of them all. Then he broke it and began to eat. [36]They were all encouraged and ate some food themselves. [37]Altogether there were 276 of us on board. [38]When they had eaten as much as they wanted, they lightened the ship by throwing the grain into the sea.

[39]When daylight came, they did not recognize the land, but they saw a bay with a sandy beach, where they decided to run the ship aground if they could. [40]Cutting loose the anchors, they left them in the sea and at the same time untied the ropes that held the rudders. Then they hoisted the foresail to the wind and made for the beach. [41]But the ship struck a sandbar and ran aground. The bow stuck fast and would not move, and the stern was broken to pieces by the pounding of the surf.

[42]The soldiers planned to kill the prisoners to prevent any of them from swimming away and escaping. [43]But the centurion wanted to spare Paul's life and kept them from carrying out their plan. He ordered those who could swim to jump overboard first and get to land. [44]The rest were to get there on planks or on pieces of the ship. In this way everyone reached land in safety.

Ashore on Malta

28 Once safely on shore, we found out that the island was called Malta. [2]The islanders showed us unusual kindness. They built a fire and welcomed us all because it was raining and cold. [3]Paul gathered a pile of brushwood and, as he put it on the fire, a viper, driven out by the heat, fastened itself on his hand. [4]When the islanders saw the snake hanging from his hand, they said to each other, "This man must be a murderer; for though he escaped from the sea, Justice has not allowed him to live." [5]But Paul shook the snake off into the fire and suffered no ill effects. [6]The people expected him to swell up or suddenly fall dead, but after waiting a long time and seeing nothing unusual happen to him, they changed their minds and said he was a god.

[7]There was an estate nearby that belonged to Publius, the chief official of the island. He welcomed us to his home and for three days entertained us hospitably. [8]His father was sick in bed, suffering from fever and dysentery. Paul went in to see him and, after prayer, placed his hands on him and healed him. [9]When this had happened, the rest of the sick on the island came and were cured. [10]They honored us in many ways and when we were ready to sail, they furnished us with the supplies we needed.

Arrival at Rome

[11]After three months we put out to sea in a ship that had wintered in the island. It was an Alexandrian ship with the figurehead of the twin gods Castor and Pollux. [12]We put in at Syracuse and stayed there three days. [13]From there we set sail and arrived at Rhegium. The next day the south wind came up, and on the following day we reached Puteoli. [14]There we found some brothers who invited us to spend a week with them. And so we came to

---

[a]27 In ancient times the name referred to an area extending well south of Italy.   [b]28 Greek twenty orguias (about 37 meters)   [c]28 Greek fifteen orguias (about 27 meters)

Rome. [15]The brothers there had heard that we were coming, and they traveled as far as the Forum of Appius and the Three Taverns to meet us. At the sight of these men Paul thanked God and was encouraged. [16]When we got to Rome, Paul was allowed to live by himself, with a soldier to guard him.

Paul Preaches at Rome Under Guard

[17]Three days later he called together the leaders of the Jews. When they had assembled, Paul said to them: "My brothers, although I have done nothing against our people or against the customs of our ancestors, I was arrested in Jerusalem and handed over to the Romans. [18]They examined me and wanted to release me, because I was not guilty of any crime deserving death. [19]But when the Jews objected, I was compelled to appeal to Caesar — not that I had any charge to bring against my own people. [20]For this reason I have asked to see you and talk with you. It is because of the hope of Israel that I am bound with this chain."

[21]They replied, "We have not received any letters from Judea concerning you, and none of the brothers who have come from there has reported or said anything bad about you. [22]But we want to hear what your views are, for we know that people everywhere are talking against this sect."

[23]They arranged to meet Paul on a certain day, and came in even larger numbers to the place where he was staying. From morning till evening he explained and declared to them the kingdom of God and tried to convince them about Jesus from the Law of Moses and from the Prophets. [24]Some were convinced by what he said, but others would not believe. [25]They disagreed among themselves and began to leave after Paul had made this final statement: "The Holy Spirit spoke the truth to your forefathers when he said through Isaiah the prophet:

[26]" 'Go to this people and say,
"You will be ever hearing but never
    understanding;
    you will be ever seeing but never
        perceiving."
[27]For this people's heart has become
    calloused;
    they hardly hear with their ears,
    and they have closed their eyes.
Otherwise they might see with their
        eyes,
    hear with their ears,
    understand with their hearts
and turn, and I would heal them.'[a]

[28]"Therefore I want you to know that God's salvation has been sent to the Gentiles, and they will listen!"[b]

[30]For two whole years Paul stayed there in his own rented house and welcomed all who came to see him. [31]Boldly and without hindrance he preached the kingdom of God and taught about the Lord Jesus Christ.

---

[a]27 Isaiah 6:9,10   [b]28 Some manuscripts listen!" [29]After he said this, the Jews left, arguing vigorously among themselves.

PAUL, planning a mission trip to Spain (Romans 15:23–29), writes this letter to introduce himself to the church at Rome. In it he summarizes what he has been preaching about sin, Christ, and the way of salvation. Everything you need to know about God's great plan for redemption lies in these sixteen chapters. As you read the book, think about how much God loves you in sending his Son Jesus and how you can say thank you to him by the life you live.

ROMANS

1 Paul, a servant of Christ Jesus, called to be an apostle and set apart for the gospel of God— ²the gospel he promised beforehand through his prophets in the Holy Scriptures ³regarding his Son, who as to his human nature was a descendant of David, ⁴and who through the Spirit*ᵃ* of holiness was declared with power to be the Son of God*ᵇ* by his resurrection from the dead: Jesus Christ our Lord. ⁵Through him and for his name's sake, we received grace and apostleship to call people from among all the Gentiles to the obedience that comes from faith. ⁶And you also are among those who are called to belong to Jesus Christ.

⁷To all in Rome who are loved by God and called to be saints:

Grace and peace to you from God our Father and from the Lord Jesus Christ.

Paul's Longing to Visit Rome

⁸First, I thank my God through Jesus Christ for all of you, because your faith is being reported all over the world. ⁹God, whom I serve with my whole heart in preaching the gospel of his Son, is my wit-

---

ᵃ4 Or *who as to his spirit*   *ᵇ4* Or *was appointed to be the Son of God with power* ness how constantly I remember you ¹⁰in my prayers at all times; and I pray that now at last by God's will the way may be opened for me to come to you.

¹¹I long to see you so that I may impart to you some spiritual gift to make you strong— ¹²that is, that you and I may be mutually encouraged by each other's faith. ¹³I do not want you to be unaware, brothers, that I planned many times to come to you (but have been prevented from doing so until now) in order that I might have a harvest among you, just as I have had among the other Gentiles.

¹⁴I am obligated both to Greeks and non-Greeks, both to the wise and the foolish. ¹⁵That is why I am so eager to preach the gospel also to you who are at Rome.

¹⁶I am not ashamed of the gospel, because it is the power of God for the salvation of everyone who believes: first for the Jew, then for the Gentile. ¹⁷For in the gospel a righteousness from God is revealed, a righteousness that is by faith from first to last,ᵃ just as it is written: "The righteous will live by faith."ᵇ

God's Wrath Against Mankind

¹⁸The wrath of God is being revealed from heaven against all the godlessness and wickedness of men who suppress the truth by their wickedness, ¹⁹since what may be known about God is plain to them, because God has made it plain to them. ²⁰For since the creation of the world God's invisible qualities—his eternal power and divine nature—have been clearly seen, being understood from what has been made, so that men are without excuse.

²¹For although they knew God, they neither glorified him as God nor gave thanks to him, but their thinking became futile and their foolish hearts were darkened. ²²Although they claimed to be wise, they became fools ²³and exchanged the glory of the immortal God for images made to look like mortal man and birds and animals and reptiles.

²⁴Therefore God gave them over in the sinful desires of their hearts to sexual impurity for the degrading of their bodies with one another. ²⁵They exchanged the truth of God for a lie, and worshiped and served created things rather than the Creator—who is forever praised. Amen.

²⁶Because of this, God gave them over to shameful lusts. Even their women exchanged natural relations for unnatural ones. ²⁷In the same way the men also abandoned natural relations with women and were inflamed with lust for one another. Men committed indecent acts with other men, and received in themselves the due penalty for their perversion.

²⁸Furthermore, since they did not think it worthwhile to retain the knowledge of God, he gave them over to a depraved mind, to do what ought not to be done. ²⁹They have become filled with every kind of wickedness, evil, greed and depravity. They are full of envy, murder, strife, deceit and malice. They are gossips, ³⁰slanderers, God-haters, insolent, arrogant and boastful; they invent ways of doing evil; they disobey their parents; ³¹they are senseless, faithless, heartless, ruthless. ³²Although they know God's righteous decree that those who do such things deserve death, they not only continue to do these very things but also approve of those who practice them.

God's Righteous Judgment

2 You, therefore, have no excuse, you who pass judgment on someone else, for at whatever point you judge the other, you are condemning yourself, because you who pass judgment do the same things. ²Now we know that God's judgment against those who do such things is based on truth. ³So when you, a mere man, pass judgment on them and yet do the same things, do you think you will escape God's judgment? ⁴Or do you show contempt for the riches of his kindness, tolerance and patience, not realizing that God's kindness leads you toward repentance?

⁵But because of your stubbornness and your unrepentant heart, you are storing up wrath against yourself for the day of God's wrath, when his righteous judgment will be revealed. ⁶God "will give to each person according to what he has done."ᶜ ⁷To those who by persistence in doing good seek glory, honor and immortality, he will give eternal life. ⁸But for those who are self-seeking and who reject the truth and follow evil, there will be wrath and anger. ⁹There will be trouble and distress for every human being who does evil: first for the Jew, then for the Gentile; ¹⁰but glory, honor and peace for everyone who does good: first for the Jew, then for the Gentile. ¹¹For God does not show favoritism.

ᵃ17 Or *is from faith to faith*   ᵇ17 Hab. 2:4   ᶜ6 Psalm 62:12; Prov. 24:12

VERSE FOR THE DAY:
Romans 1:25

AUTHOR:
John Fischer

PASSAGE FOR THE DAY:
Romans 1:18–25

Ask, Seek, Knock

ASKING is a way of life lived with an open hand. To ask is to depend on someone other than yourself. It is very humbling. Asking indicates:

- I don't know.
- I failed.
- I ran out.
- I can't find it.
- I'm not sure.
- I don't understand.
- I forgot.
- I didn't listen.
- I didn't care.
- I was wrong.
- I'm not prepared.
- I need more information.
- I came up short.

There's an interesting dilemma here for Christians. If Christianity is no more than a system that answers all of life's questions, then to admit any of the above shortcomings is to be something less than a good Christian. But in our own attempts to be good Christians, we undermine our need for God. We want Christianity to work. We want it to exist in a closed system where every question has an answer, every problem has a solution. We want to show the world a neat, clean, open-and-shut case for Christianity. But in the process, we unknowingly shut out God.

Claiming to be wise, we become fools; we exchange the truth of God for a lie and worship the created things (our systems, principles and formulas) rather than the Creator—who is forever blessed. Amen (see Romans 1:22–25).

That's why Jesus says we should ask. Asking puts us back on track with God. It assumes a need relationship with him—a hand-to-mouth spiritual existence. A vulnerable daily dependence. In a society that rushes to fill every felt need, that steals away the soul of a person and offers to sell it back at a price, we need to rekindle what it means to ask God.

Additional Scripture Readings:
Matthew 7:7–12; John 16:19–28

Go to page 1207 for your next devotional reading.

¹²All who sin apart from the law will also perish apart from the law, and all who sin under the law will be judged by the law. ¹³For it is not those who hear the law who are righteous in God's sight, but it is those who obey the law who will be declared righteous. ¹⁴(Indeed, when Gentiles, who do not have the law, do by nature things required by the law, they are a law for themselves, even though they do not have the law, ¹⁵since they show that the requirements of the law are written on their hearts, their consciences also bearing witness, and their thoughts now accusing, now even defending them.) ¹⁶This will take place on the day when God will judge men's secrets through Jesus Christ, as my gospel declares.

The Jews and the Law

¹⁷Now you, if you call yourself a Jew; if you rely on the law and brag about your relationship to God; ¹⁸if you know his will and approve of what is superior because you are instructed by the law; ¹⁹if you are convinced that you are a guide for the blind, a light for those who are in the dark, ²⁰an instructor of the foolish, a teacher of infants, because you have in the law the embodiment of knowledge and truth— ²¹you, then, who teach others, do you not teach yourself? You who preach against stealing, do you steal? ²²You who say that people should not commit adultery, do you commit adultery? You who abhor idols, do you rob temples? ²³You who brag about the law, do you dishonor God by breaking the law? ²⁴As it is written: "God's name is blasphemed among the Gentiles because of you."ᵃ

²⁵Circumcision has value if you observe the law, but if you break the law, you have become as though you had not been circumcised. ²⁶If those who are not circumcised keep the law's requirements, will they not be regarded as though they were circumcised? ²⁷The one who is not circumcised physically and yet obeys the law will condemn you who, even though you have theᵇ written code and circumcision, are a lawbreaker.

²⁸A man is not a Jew if he is only one outwardly, nor is circumcision merely outward and physical. ²⁹No, a man is a Jew if he is one inwardly; and circumcision is circumcision of the heart, by the Spirit, not by the written code. Such a man's praise is not from men, but from God.

God's Faithfulness

3 What advantage, then, is there in being a Jew, or what value is there in circumcision? ²Much in every way! First of all, they have been entrusted with the very words of God.

³What if some did not have faith? Will their lack of faith nullify God's faithfulness? ⁴Not at all! Let God be true, and every man a liar. As it is written:

"So that you may be proved right
        when you speak
    and prevail when you judge."ᶜ

⁵But if our unrighteousness brings out God's righteousness more clearly, what shall we say? That God is unjust in bringing his wrath on us? (I am using a human argument.) ⁶Certainly not! If that were so, how could God judge the world? ⁷Someone might argue, "If my falsehood enhances God's truthfulness and so increases his glory, why am I still condemned as a sinner?" ⁸Why not say— as we are being slanderously reported as saying and as some claim that we say— "Let us do evil that good may result"? Their condemnation is deserved.

No One Is Righteous

⁹What shall we conclude then? Are we any betterᵈ? Not at all! We have already made the charge that Jews and Gentiles alike are all under sin. ¹⁰As it is written:

"There is no one righteous, not even
        one;
¹¹ there is no one who understands,
        no one who seeks God.
¹²All have turned away,
        they have together become
            worthless;
    there is no one who does good,
        not even one."ᵉ
¹³"Their throats are open graves;
        their tongues practice deceit."ᶠ
    "The poison of vipers is on their
        lips."ᵍ
¹⁴ "Their mouths are full of cursing
        and bitterness."ʰ
¹⁵"Their feet are swift to shed blood;
¹⁶ ruin and misery mark their ways,

¹⁷and the way of peace they do not know."[a]

18 "There is no fear of God before their eyes."[b]

¹⁹Now we know that whatever the law says, it says to those who are under the law, so that every mouth may be silenced and the whole world held accountable to

[a]17 Isaiah 59:7,8   [b]18 Psalm 36:1

TUESDAY

VERSE FOR THE DAY:
Romans 2:4

AUTHOR:
Larry Crabb

PASSAGE FOR THE DAY:
Romans 2:1–4

God's Unhurried Ways

IN SPITE of thunderous warnings delivered from well-pounded pulpits, our self-centeredness seems to generate few bad consequences. And every youngster knows that shouting can be easily endured if there are no spankings.

God seems in no hurry to judge. For now, it appears we can live self-centeredly and not pay a price.

But we can interpret God's delay in *two* ways: either our sin doesn't really offend him a great deal or ". . . he is patient with [us], not wanting anyone to perish, but everyone to come to repentance" (2 Peter 3:9).

In our fallen way of thinking, we strongly favor explaining withheld judgment in terms of divine indifference. If God, the ultimate standard of morality who has the power to punish and reward, is not all that bothered by our self-centered ways, then we can carry on with whatever makes us feel good without worrying about punishment for wrongdoing and without giving up our good opinion of ourselves . . .

The truth is we can continue with our everyday failings, at least for a time, without being struck by lightning. And the unpleasant things that happen seem evenly distributed between good people and bad people.

And when we look after ourselves, better things often do come our way. God's unhurried ways can encourage us to think casually about our ongoing struggle with sin . . .

Having dismissed our selfishness as a relatively benign disorder, we are free to keep our focus on what really matters to self-centered people: the immediate quality of our lives. Finding a way to heal our wounds and to restore a sense of personal wholeness continues to be a far more pressing concern than knowing the escape route from judgment and worshiping the One who provided it.

And the disease continues unchecked, ruining relationships and carrying us toward certain judgment.

Additional Scripture Readings:
Ezekiel 12:21–28; 2 Peter 3:3–10

Go to page 1209 for your next devotional reading.

God. [20]Therefore no one will be declared righteous in his sight by observing the law; rather, through the law we become conscious of sin.

Righteousness Through Faith

[21]But now a righteousness from God, apart from law, has been made known, to which the Law and the Prophets testify. [22]This righteousness from God comes through faith in Jesus Christ to all who believe. There is no difference, [23]for all have sinned and fall short of the glory of God, [24]and are justified freely by his grace through the redemption that came by Christ Jesus. [25]God presented him as a sacrifice of atonement,[a] through faith in his blood. He did this to demonstrate his justice, because in his forbearance he had left the sins committed beforehand unpunished— [26]he did it to demonstrate his justice at the present time, so as to be just and the one who justifies those who have faith in Jesus.

[27]Where, then, is boasting? It is excluded. On what principle? On that of observing the law? No, but on that of faith. [28]For we maintain that a man is justified by faith apart from observing the law. [29]Is God the God of Jews only? Is he not the God of Gentiles too? Yes, of Gentiles too, [30]since there is only one God, who will justify the circumcised by faith and the uncircumcised through that same faith. [31]Do we, then, nullify the law by this faith? Not at all! Rather, we uphold the law.

Abraham Justified by Faith

4 What then shall we say that Abraham, our forefather, discovered in this matter? [2]If, in fact, Abraham was justified by works, he had something to boast about—but not before God. [3]What does the Scripture say? "Abraham believed God, and it was credited to him as righteousness."[b]

[4]Now when a man works, his wages are not credited to him as a gift, but as an obligation. [5]However, to the man who does not work but trusts God who justifies the wicked, his faith is credited as righteousness. [6]David says the same thing when he speaks of the blessedness of the man to whom God credits righteousness apart from works:

[7]"Blessed are they
    whose transgressions are forgiven,
    whose sins are covered.
[8]Blessed is the man
    whose sin the Lord will never count
      against him."[c]

[9]Is this blessedness only for the circumcised, or also for the uncircumcised? We have been saying that Abraham's faith was credited to him as righteousness. [10]Under what circumstances was it credited? Was it after he was circumcised, or before? It was not after, but before! [11]And he received the sign of circumcision, a seal of the righteousness that he had by faith while he was still uncircumcised. So then, he is the father of all who believe but have not been circumcised, in order that righteousness might be credited to them. [12]And he is also the father of the circumcised who not only are circumcised but who also walk in the footsteps of the faith that our father Abraham had before he was circumcised.

[13]It was not through law that Abraham and his offspring received the promise that he would be heir of the world, but through the righteousness that comes by faith. [14]For if those who live by law are heirs, faith has no value and the promise is worthless, [15]because law brings wrath. And where there is no law there is no transgression.

[16]Therefore, the promise comes by faith, so that it may be by grace and may be guaranteed to all Abraham's offspring—not only to those who are of the law but also to those who are of the faith of Abraham. He is the father of us all. [17]As it is written: "I have made you a father of many nations."[d] He is our father in the sight of God, in whom he believed—the God who gives life to the dead and calls things that are not as though they were.

[18]Against all hope, Abraham in hope believed and so became the father of many nations, just as it had been said to him, "So shall your offspring be."[e] [19]Without weakening in his faith, he faced the fact that his body was as good as dead—since he was about a hundred years old—and that Sarah's womb was also dead. [20]Yet he did not waver through unbelief regarding the promise of God, but was strengthened in his faith and gave glory to God, [21]being

---

[a]25 Or *as the one who would turn aside his wrath, taking away sin*   [b]3 Gen. 15:6; also in verse 22
[c]8 Psalm 32:1,2   [d]17 Gen. 17:5   [e]18 Gen. 15:5

fully persuaded that God had power to do what he had promised. ²²This is why "it was credited to him as righteousness." ²³The words "it was credited to him" were written not for him alone, ²⁴but also for us, to whom God will credit righteousness — for us who believe in him who raised Jesus our Lord from the dead. ²⁵He

was delivered over to death for our sins and was raised to life for our justification.

Peace and Joy

5 Therefore, since we have been justified through faith, we[a] have peace with God through our Lord Jesus Christ, ²through whom we have gained access by

a1 Or let us

WEDNESDAY

VERSE FOR THE DAY:
Romans 3:25

AUTHOR:
C.S. Lewis

PASSAGE FOR THE DAY:
Romans 3:21–26

Nourishment and the Cross

THE central Christian belief is that Christ's death has somehow put us right with God and given us a fresh start. A good many different theories have been held as to how it works; what all Christians are agreed on is that it does work. I will tell you what I think it is like. All sensible people know that if you are tired and hungry a meal will do you good. But the modern theory of nourishment — all about the vitamins and proteins — is a different thing. People ate their dinners and felt better long before the theory of vitamins was ever heard of: and if the theory of vitamins is some day abandoned they will go on eating their dinners just the same. Theories about Christ's death are not Christianity: they are explanations about how it works. Christians would not all agree as to how important these theories are. But I think they will all agree that the thing itself is infinitely more important than any explanations that theologians have produced . . .

We believe that the death of Christ is just that point in history at which something absolutely unimaginable from outside shows through into our own world. And if we cannot picture even the atoms of which our own world is built, of course we are not going to be able to picture this. Indeed, if we found that we could fully understand it, that very fact would show it was not what it professes to be — the inconceivable, the uncreated, the thing from beyond nature, striking down into nature like lightning. You may ask what good it will be to us if we do not understand it. But that is easily answered. A man can eat his dinner without understanding exactly how food nourishes him. A man can accept what Christ has done without knowing how it works: indeed, he certainly would not know how it works until he has accepted it.

Additional Scripture Readings:
Romans 11:33–36; Ephesians 1:3–14

Go to page 1211 for your next devotional reading.

faith into this grace in which we now stand. And we[a] rejoice in the hope of the glory of God. [3]Not only so, but we[a] also rejoice in our sufferings, because we know that suffering produces perseverance; [4]perseverance, character; and character, hope. [5]And hope does not disappoint us, because God has poured out his love into our hearts by the Holy Spirit, whom he has given us.

[6]You see, at just the right time, when we were still powerless, Christ died for the ungodly. [7]Very rarely will anyone die for a righteous man, though for a good man someone might possibly dare to die. [8]But God demonstrates his own love for us in this: While we were still sinners, Christ died for us.

[9]Since we have now been justified by his blood, how much more shall we be saved from God's wrath through him! [10]For if, when we were God's enemies, we were reconciled to him through the death of his Son, how much more, having been reconciled, shall we be saved through his life! [11]Not only is this so, but we also rejoice in God through our Lord Jesus Christ, through whom we have now received reconciliation.

Death Through Adam, Life Through Christ

[12]Therefore, just as sin entered the world through one man, and death through sin, and in this way death came to all men, because all sinned— [13]for before the law was given, sin was in the world. But sin is not taken into account when there is no law. [14]Nevertheless, death reigned from the time of Adam to the time of Moses, even over those who did not sin by breaking a command, as did Adam, who was a pattern of the one to come.

[15]But the gift is not like the trespass. For if the many died by the trespass of the one man, how much more did God's grace and the gift that came by the grace of the one man, Jesus Christ, overflow to the many! [16]Again, the gift of God is not like the result of the one man's sin: The judgment followed one sin and brought condemnation, but the gift followed many trespasses and brought justification. [17]For if, by the trespass of the one man, death reigned through that one man, how much more will those who receive God's abundant provision of grace and of the gift of righ-

teousness reign in life through the one man, Jesus Christ.

[18]Consequently, just as the result of one trespass was condemnation for all men, so also the result of one act of righteousness was justification that brings life for all men. [19]For just as through the disobedience of the one man the many were made sinners, so also through the obedience of the one man the many will be made righteous.

[20]The law was added so that the trespass might increase. But where sin increased, grace increased all the more, [21]so that, just as sin reigned in death, so also grace might reign through righteousness to bring eternal life through Jesus Christ our Lord.

Dead to Sin, Alive in Christ

6 What shall we say, then? Shall we go on sinning so that grace may increase? [2]By no means! We died to sin; how can we live in it any longer? [3]Or don't you know that all of us who were baptized into Christ Jesus were baptized into his death? [4]We were therefore buried with him through baptism into death in order that, just as Christ was raised from the dead through the glory of the Father, we too may live a new life.

[5]If we have been united with him like this in his death, we will certainly also be united with him in his resurrection. [6]For we know that our old self was crucified with him so that the body of sin might be done away with,[b] that we should no longer be slaves to sin— [7]because anyone who has died has been freed from sin.

[8]Now if we died with Christ, we believe that we will also live with him. [9]For we know that since Christ was raised from the dead, he cannot die again; death no longer has mastery over him. [10]The death he died, he died to sin once for all; but the life he lives, he lives to God.

[11]In the same way, count yourselves dead to sin but alive to God in Christ Jesus. [12]Therefore do not let sin reign in your mortal body so that you obey its evil desires. [13]Do not offer the parts of your body to sin, as instruments of wickedness, but rather offer yourselves to God, as those who have been brought from death to life; and offer the parts of your body to him as instruments of righteousness. [14]For sin shall not be your master, be-

---

[a]2,3 Or let us   [b]6 Or be rendered powerless

cause you are not under law, but under grace.

Slaves to Righteousness

15What then? Shall we sin because we are not under law but under grace? By no means! 16Don't you know that when you offer yourselves to someone to obey him as slaves, you are slaves to the one whom you obey—whether you are slaves to sin, which leads to death, or to obedience, which leads to righteousness? 17But thanks be to God that, though you used to be slaves to sin, you wholeheartedly obeyed the form of teaching to which you were entrusted. 18You have been set free from sin and have become slaves to righteousness.

19I put this in human terms because you are weak in your natural selves. Just as you used to offer the parts of your body in slavery to impurity and to ever-increasing

---

THURSDAY

VERSE FOR THE DAY:
Romans 5:3

AUTHOR:
Gary Smalley and John Trent

PASSAGE FOR THE DAY:
Romans 5:1–11

First Response

OFTEN, the first response by parents can set the tone for how traumatically an event will be taken . . .

When one of my children is hurting, compounding it by reacting with angry words doesn't add to the solution. If anything, such a reaction often freezes things in a problem state.

Responding with initial softness helps the child see that if Dad and Mom aren't panicking, maybe there is a light at the end of the tunnel. If the child sees his parents panicking or moving into anger, he is often barred from responding in any other way . . .

Where does the ability to initiate softness and keep from panicking come from? *From a decision formed in quiet times apart from trials to believe that God works all things unto good* (see Romans 8:28).

In the middle of a fire, there isn't time to think about ways to prevent a fire. Parents who react emotionally in anger or panic to problems instead of having a plan for responding to them can increase the tension in the air. When parents know ahead of time that the very things that have the potential to devalue their children can be used by God to build character into their lives, they are strengthening their grip on their emotions . . .

When a difficulty first happens, don't lecture your children, panic, or become sickeningly pious. Calmly comforting them at the beginning of a trial lays the foundation for them to find value in their experience. Calmness comes from within us when we are confident in God's Word. Painful trials produce maturity, which leads to love!

Additional Scripture Readings:
Hebrews 12:7–11; James 1:2–12

Go to page 1213 for your next devotional reading.

wickedness, so now offer them in slavery to righteousness leading to holiness. [20]When you were slaves to sin, you were free from the control of righteousness. [21]What benefit did you reap at that time from the things you are now ashamed of? Those things result in death! [22]But now that you have been set free from sin and have become slaves to God, the benefit you reap leads to holiness, and the result is eternal life. [23]For the wages of sin is death, but the gift of God is eternal life in[a] Christ Jesus our Lord.

An Illustration From Marriage

7 Do you not know, brothers—for I am speaking to men who know the law— that the law has authority over a man only as long as he lives? [2]For example, by law a married woman is bound to her husband as long as he is alive, but if her husband dies, she is released from the law of marriage. [3]So then, if she marries another man while her husband is still alive, she is called an adulteress. But if her husband dies, she is released from that law and is not an adulteress, even though she marries another man.

[4]So, my brothers, you also died to the law through the body of Christ, that you might belong to another, to him who was raised from the dead, in order that we might bear fruit to God. [5]For when we were controlled by the sinful nature,[b] the sinful passions aroused by the law were at work in our bodies, so that we bore fruit for death. [6]But now, by dying to what once bound us, we have been released from the law so that we serve in the new way of the Spirit, and not in the old way of the written code.

Struggling With Sin

[7]What shall we say, then? Is the law sin? Certainly not! Indeed I would not have known what sin was except through the law. For I would not have known what coveting really was if the law had not said, "Do not covet."[c] [8]But sin, seizing the opportunity afforded by the commandment, produced in me every kind of covetous desire. For apart from law, sin is dead. [9]Once I was alive apart from law; but when the commandment came, sin sprang to life and I died. [10]I found that the very commandment that was intended to bring life actually brought death. [11]For sin, seizing the opportunity afforded by the commandment, deceived me, and through the commandment put me to death. [12]So then, the law is holy, and the commandment is holy, righteous and good.

[13]Did that which is good, then, become death to me? By no means! But in order that sin might be recognized as sin, it produced death in me through what was good, so that through the commandment sin might become utterly sinful.

[14]We know that the law is spiritual; but I am unspiritual, sold as a slave to sin. [15]I do not understand what I do. For what I want to do I do not do, but what I hate I do. [16]And if I do what I do not want to do, I agree that the law is good. [17]As it is, it is no longer I myself who do it, but it is sin living in me. [18]I know that nothing good lives in me, that is, in my sinful nature.[d] For I have the desire to do what is good, but I cannot carry it out. [19]For what I do is not the good I want to do; no, the evil I do not want to do—this I keep on doing. [20]Now if I do what I do not want to do, it is no longer I who do it, but it is sin living in me that does it.

[21]So I find this law at work: When I want to do good, evil is right there with me. [22]For in my inner being I delight in God's law; [23]but I see another law at work in the members of my body, waging war against the law of my mind and making me a prisoner of the law of sin at work within my members. [24]What a wretched man I am! Who will rescue me from this body of death? [25]Thanks be to God— through Jesus Christ our Lord!

So then, I myself in my mind am a slave to God's law, but in the sinful nature a slave to the law of sin.

Life Through the Spirit

8 Therefore, there is now no condemnation for those who are in Christ Jesus,[e] [2]because through Christ Jesus the law of the Spirit of life set me free from the law of sin and death. [3]For what the law was powerless to do in that it was weakened by the sinful nature,[f] God did by sending his own Son in the likeness of sinful man to be a sin offering.[g] And so he condemned sin in sinful man,[h] [4]in order that the righteous requirements of the law

a23 Or through   b5 Or the flesh; also in verse 25   c7 Exodus 20:17; Deut. 5:21   d18 Or my flesh
e1 Some later manuscripts Jesus, who do not live according to the sinful nature but according to the Spirit,
f3 Or the flesh; also in verses 4, 5, 8, 9, 12 and 13   g3 Or man, for sin   h3 Or in the flesh

might be fully met in us, who do not live according to the sinful nature but according to the Spirit.

⁵Those who live according to the sinful nature have their minds set on what that nature desires; but those who live in accordance with the Spirit have their minds set on what the Spirit desires. ⁶The mind of sinful man*a* is death, but the mind con-

trolled by the Spirit is life and peace; ⁷the sinful mind*b* is hostile to God. It does not submit to God's law, nor can it do so. ⁸Those controlled by the sinful nature cannot please God.

⁹You, however, are controlled not by the sinful nature but by the Spirit, if the Spirit of God lives in you. And if anyone does not have the Spirit of Christ, he does

a6 Or mind set on the flesh   *b7 Or the mind set on the flesh*

FRIDAY

VERSE FOR THE DAY:
Romans 8:17

AUTHOR:
Jerry Bridges

PASSAGE FOR THE DAY:
Romans 8:12–17

Saved from Wrath

ONLY the God-fearing Christian can truly appreciate the love of God. He sees the infinite gulf between a holy God and a sinful creature, and the love that bridged that gulf through the death of the Lord Jesus Christ. God's love for us is manyfaceted, but he supremely demonstrated it by sending his Son to die for our sins. All other aspects of his love are secondary, and in fact are made possible for us through the death of Christ . . .

The truly godly person never forgets that he was at one time an object of God's holy and just wrath. He never forgets that Christ Jesus came into the world to save sinners—and he feels along with Paul that he is himself the worst of sinners. But then as he looks to the cross he sees that Jesus was his atoning sacrifice. He sees that Jesus bore his sins in his own body, and that the wrath of God—the wrath which he, a sinner, should have borne—was expended completely and totally upon the holy Son of God. And in this view of Calvary, he sees the love of God.

The love of God has no meaning apart from Calvary. And Calvary has no meaning apart from the holy and just wrath of God. Jesus did not die just to give us peace and a purpose in life; he died to save us from the wrath of God. He died to reconcile us to a holy God who was alienated from us because of our sin. He died to ransom us from the penalty of sin—the punishment of everlasting destruction, shut out from the presence of the Lord. He died that we, the just objects of God's wrath, should become, by his grace, heirs of God and co-heirs with him.

Additional Scripture Readings:
Ephesians 2:1–10;
1 Thessalonians 5:4–11

Go to page 1215 for your next
devotional reading.

not belong to Christ. [10]But if Christ is in you, your body is dead because of sin, yet your spirit is alive because of righteousness. [11]And if the Spirit of him who raised Jesus from the dead is living in you, he who raised Christ from the dead will also give life to your mortal bodies through his Spirit, who lives in you.

[12]Therefore, brothers, we have an obligation—but it is not to the sinful nature, to live according to it. [13]For if you live according to the sinful nature, you will die; but if by the Spirit you put to death the misdeeds of the body, you will live, [14]because those who are led by the Spirit of God are sons of God. [15]For you did not receive a spirit that makes you a slave again to fear, but you received the Spirit of sonship.[a] And by him we cry, "Abba,[b] Father." [16]The Spirit himself testifies with our spirit that we are God's children. [17]Now if we are children, then we are heirs—heirs of God and co-heirs with Christ, if indeed we share in his sufferings in order that we may also share in his glory.

Future Glory

[18]I consider that our present sufferings are not worth comparing with the glory that will be revealed in us. [19]The creation waits in eager expectation for the sons of God to be revealed. [20]For the creation was subjected to frustration, not by its own choice, but by the will of the one who subjected it, in hope [21]that[c] the creation itself will be liberated from its bondage to decay and brought into the glorious freedom of the children of God.

[22]We know that the whole creation has been groaning as in the pains of childbirth right up to the present time. [23]Not only so, but we ourselves, who have the firstfruits of the Spirit, groan inwardly as we wait eagerly for our adoption as sons, the redemption of our bodies. [24]For in this hope we were saved. But hope that is seen is no hope at all. Who hopes for what he already has? [25]But if we hope for what we do not yet have, we wait for it patiently.

[26]In the same way, the Spirit helps us in our weakness. We do not know what we ought to pray for, but the Spirit himself intercedes for us with groans that words cannot express. [27]And he who searches our hearts knows the mind of the Spirit, because the Spirit intercedes for the saints in accordance with God's will.

More Than Conquerors

[28]And we know that in all things God works for the good of those who love him,[d] who[e] have been called according to his purpose. [29]For those God foreknew he also predestined to be conformed to the likeness of his Son, that he might be the firstborn among many brothers. [30]And those he predestined, he also called; those he called, he also justified; those he justified, he also glorified.

[31]What, then, shall we say in response to this? If God is for us, who can be against us? [32]He who did not spare his own Son, but gave him up for us all—how will he not also, along with him, graciously give us all things? [33]Who will bring any charge against those whom God has chosen? It is God who justifies. [34]Who is he that condemns? Christ Jesus, who died—more than that, who was raised to life—is at the right hand of God and is also interceding for us. [35]Who shall separate us from the love of Christ? Shall trouble or hardship or persecution or famine or nakedness or danger or sword? [36]As it is written:

"For your sake we face death all day
    long;
we are considered as sheep to be
    slaughtered."[f]

[37]No, in all these things we are more than conquerors through him who loved us. [38]For I am convinced that neither death nor life, neither angels nor demons,[g] neither the present nor the future, nor any powers, [39]neither height nor depth, nor anything else in all creation, will be able to separate us from the love of God that is in Christ Jesus our Lord.

God's Sovereign Choice

9 I speak the truth in Christ—I am not lying, my conscience confirms it in the Holy Spirit— [2]I have great sorrow and unceasing anguish in my heart. [3]For I could wish that I myself were cursed and cut off from Christ for the sake of my brothers, those of my own race, [4]the people of Israel. Theirs is the adoption as sons; theirs the divine glory, the cov-

---

[a]15 Or adoption   [b]15 Aramaic for Father   [c]20,21 Or subjected it in hope. [21]For   [d]28 Some manuscripts And we know that all things work together for good to those who love God   [e]28 Or works together with those who love him to bring about what is good—with those who   [f]36 Psalm 44:22   [g]38 Or nor heavenly rulers

WEEKENDING

REALIZE

I am personally convinced that this submission, this dying to self, this crucifying of pride [see Philippians 2:1–8] is crucial to our joy. We think of denying self as somber, grim-faced business when it is in truth a prelude to dancing. If you want power, learn to be assertive. If you want joy, learn to be submissive . . .

The reason our death [to self] increases the joy level all around is that it also increases the love level all around. Only when we die to self can we fully love one another. Self is a devilish creature, demanding all of our energy, wanting our constant attention, reaching even into our pocketbooks for favors. How can we be attuned to another's spirit when self is making so much noise? How can we ever hope to love another when self screams for our constant care? When self is alive and well, it offers us an all-or-nothing proposition. We either pacify self, or we crucify it.

— *Judson Edwards*

REVIVE

Saturday: Romans 6:1–14
Sunday: Colossians 3:1–14

Go to page 1216 for your next devotional reading.

enants, the receiving of the law, the temple worship and the promises. **5**Theirs are the patriarchs, and from them is traced the human ancestry of Christ, who is God over all, forever praised!*a* Amen.

6It is not as though God's word had failed. For not all who are descended from Israel are Israel. **7**Nor because they are his descendants are they all Abraham's children. On the contrary, "It is through Isaac that your offspring will be reckoned."*b* **8**In other words, it is not the natural children who are God's children, but it is the children of the promise who are regarded as Abraham's offspring. **9**For this was how the promise was stated: "At the appointed time I will return, and Sarah will have a son."*c*

10Not only that, but Rebekah's children had one and the same father, our father Isaac. **11**Yet, before the twins were born or had done anything good or bad — in order that God's purpose in election might stand: **12**not by works but by him who calls — she was told, "The older will serve the younger."*d* **13**Just as it is written: "Jacob I loved, but Esau I hated."*e*

14What then shall we say? Is God unjust? Not at all! **15**For he says to Moses,

"I will have mercy on whom I have mercy,

a5 Or *Christ, who is over all. God be forever praised!* Or *Christ. God who is over all be forever praised!*
b7 Gen. 21:12   *c9* Gen. 18:10,14   *d12* Gen. 25:23   *e13* Mal. 1:2,3

MONDAY

VERSE FOR THE DAY: AUTHOR: PASSAGE FOR THE DAY:
Romans 8:31   Michael Card   Romans 8:31–39

His Cost, Our Gain

JESUS paid a tremendous price to be with us. Certainly the cross was the most obvious cost. But I believe more is in view.

We focus so much on the fact that Jesus died for us, we sometimes forget that he also lived for us and lives for us still. If Jesus had simply come as himself, and not as one of us, the Bible makes it quite clear that we could not have borne the sight of his presence, any more than Moses could have looked directly at the face of God.

Imagine what it would be like to be at the Father's side one moment and struggling to sleep in a cattle trough the next. Imagine what it would be like to go from hearing the praise of angels to suffering the taunts of stupid men. The cost to Jesus is an indication of the incredible value of what he came to give us. And because no one will ever fully know what that cost Jesus, we can only begin to understand the incredible value of his gift to us.

The apostle Paul realized the indescribable gift of Immanuel in a passage which many consider the height of his inspiration. He concludes, "If God is for us, who can be against us?" God is on our side, right or wrong, because even when we are wrong, he still loves us.

Additional Scripture Readings:
John 1:1–14; Hebrews 7:23–28

Go to page 1218 for your next devotional reading.

and I will have compassion on
　　whom I have compassion."[a]

[16]It does not, therefore, depend on man's desire or effort, but on God's mercy. [17]For the Scripture says to Pharaoh: "I raised you up for this very purpose, that I might display my power in you and that my name might be proclaimed in all the earth."[b] [18]Therefore God has mercy on whom he wants to have mercy, and he hardens whom he wants to harden.

[19]One of you will say to me: "Then why does God still blame us? For who resists his will?" [20]But who are you, O man, to talk back to God? "Shall what is formed say to him who formed it, 'Why did you make me like this?' "[c] [21]Does not the potter have the right to make out of the same lump of clay some pottery for noble purposes and some for common use?

[22]What if God, choosing to show his wrath and make his power known, bore with great patience the objects of his wrath—prepared for destruction? [23]What if he did this to make the riches of his glory known to the objects of his mercy, whom he prepared in advance for glory— [24]even us, whom he also called, not only from the Jews but also from the Gentiles? [25]As he says in Hosea:

"I will call them 'my people' who are
　　not my people;
and I will call her 'my loved one'
　　who is not my loved one,"[d]

[26]and,

"It will happen that in the very place
　　where it was said to them,
'You are not my people,'
they will be called 'sons of the living
　　God.' "[e]

[27]Isaiah cries out concerning Israel:

"Though the number of the Israelites
　　be like the sand by the sea,
only the remnant will be saved.
[28]For the Lord will carry out
　　his sentence on earth with speed
　　and finality."[f]

[29]It is just as Isaiah said previously:

"Unless the Lord Almighty
　　had left us descendants,
we would have become like Sodom,

we would have been like
　　Gomorrah."[g]

Israel's Unbelief

[30]What then shall we say? That the Gentiles, who did not pursue righteousness, have obtained it, a righteousness that is by faith; [31]but Israel, who pursued a law of righteousness, has not attained it. [32]Why not? Because they pursued it not by faith but as if it were by works. They stumbled over the "stumbling stone." [33]As it is written:

"See, I lay in Zion a stone that causes
　　men to stumble
and a rock that makes them fall,
and the one who trusts in him will
　　never be put to shame."[h]

10 Brothers, my heart's desire and prayer to God for the Israelites is that they may be saved. [2]For I can testify about them that they are zealous for God, but their zeal is not based on knowledge. [3]Since they did not know the righteousness that comes from God and sought to establish their own, they did not submit to God's righteousness. [4]Christ is the end of the law so that there may be righteousness for everyone who believes.

[5]Moses describes in this way the righteousness that is by the law: "The man who does these things will live by them."[i] [6]But the righteousness that is by faith says: "Do not say in your heart, 'Who will ascend into heaven?'[j]" (that is, to bring Christ down) [7]"or 'Who will descend into the deep?'[k]" (that is, to bring Christ up from the dead). [8]But what does it say? "The word is near you; it is in your mouth and in your heart,"[l] that is, the word of faith we are proclaiming: [9]That if you confess with your mouth, "Jesus is Lord," and believe in your heart that God raised him from the dead, you will be saved. [10]For it is with your heart that you believe and are justified, and it is with your mouth that you confess and are saved. [11]As the Scripture says, "Anyone who trusts in him will never be put to shame."[m] [12]For there is no difference between Jew and Gentile—the same Lord is Lord of all and richly blesses all who call on him, [13]for, "Everyone who calls on the name of the Lord will be saved."[n] [14]How, then, can they call on the one

[a]15 Exodus 33:19　　[b]17 Exodus 9:16　　[c]20 Isaiah 29:16; 45:9　　[d]25 Hosea 2:23　　[e]26 Hosea 1:10
[f]28 Isaiah 10:22,23　　[g]29 Isaiah 1:9　　[h]33 Isaiah 8:14; 28:16　　[i]5 Lev. 18:5　　[j]6 Deut. 30:12
[k]7 Deut. 30:13　　[l]8 Deut. 30:14　　[m]11 Isaiah 28:16　　[n]13 Joel 2:32

TUESDAY

VERSE FOR THE DAY:
Romans 9:21

AUTHOR:
H. Beecher Hicks

PASSAGE FOR THE DAY:
Romans 9:16–21

In the Potter's Hand

LOOK closely here! Paul said that the potter has power over the clay . . . God molds us and makes us and holds us in his hand. It's no news to you that every potter has the job of molding and making and holding . . .

The reason that God is involved in the pottery process is that God needs instruments and not objects. Any potter can make an object to sit on the shelf. Any potter can make an artifact that is a thing of beauty and a joy forever. Any potter can make an item of retail sale that men can purchase or leave alone. But God does not need objects, God needs instruments. Far too many who are engaged in the Christian enterprise are objects, but they're not instruments.

· An instrument says I'm good for something.
· An instrument says I have purpose.
· An instrument says I have value.
· An instrument says I can be used . . .

Always remember that the potter does have power over the clay. The potter has creative power. He brings into being that which was not . . .

The potter has creative power. He can stoop down in the dust of the earth and pick up lumps of clay and breathe the breath of life into it until it walks and talks like a natural man. The potter has creative power.

But more, the potter has re-creative power. Jeremiah says that sometimes the pot is marred in the potter's hand [see Jeremiah 18:1–4]. Sometimes the pot does not do what it was designed to do. But the potter just takes it and breaks it and molds it and makes it what he would have it to be. I'm glad to know that when I'm marred and broken, the Lord is not through with me yet. I want him to re-create me . . .

We end where we began: God molds us and makes us and holds us in his hand. No matter what happens in this life, I'm in his hand. What a mighty God we serve! Right or wrong, up or down, poverty or wealth, sickness or health, come what may, I am in his hand. Hallelujah, I am in his hand.

Additional Scripture Readings:
Psalm 139:1–10; Isaiah 64:8–12

Go to page 1222 for your next devotional reading.

they have not believed in? And how can they believe in the one of whom they have not heard? And how can they hear without someone preaching to them? [15]And how can they preach unless they are sent? As it is written, "How beautiful are the feet of those who bring good news!"[a]

[16]But not all the Israelites accepted the good news. For Isaiah says, "Lord, who has believed our message?"[b] [17]Consequently, faith comes from hearing the message, and the message is heard through the word of Christ. [18]But I ask: Did they not hear? Of course they did:

"Their voice has gone out into all the earth,
their words to the ends of the world."[c]

[19]Again I ask: Did Israel not understand? First, Moses says,

"I will make you envious by those who are not a nation;
I will make you angry by a nation that has no understanding."[d]

[20]And Isaiah boldly says,

"I was found by those who did not seek me;
I revealed myself to those who did not ask for me."[e]

[21]But concerning Israel he says,

"All day long I have held out my hands
to a disobedient and obstinate people."[f]

The Remnant of Israel

11 I ask then: Did God reject his people? By no means! I am an Israelite myself, a descendant of Abraham, from the tribe of Benjamin. [2]God did not reject his people, whom he foreknew. Don't you know what the Scripture says in the passage about Elijah—how he appealed to God against Israel: [3]"Lord, they have killed your prophets and torn down your altars; I am the only one left, and they are trying to kill me"[g] [4]And what was God's answer to him? "I have reserved for myself seven thousand who have not bowed the knee to Baal."[h] [5]So too, at the present time there is a remnant chosen by grace. [6]And if by grace, then it is no longer by

works; if it were, grace would no longer be grace.[i]

[7]What then? What Israel sought so earnestly it did not obtain, but the elect did. The others were hardened, [8]as it is written:

"God gave them a spirit of stupor,
eyes so that they could not see
and ears so that they could not hear,
to this very day."[j]

[9]And David says:

"May their table become a snare and a trap,
a stumbling block and a retribution for them.
[10]May their eyes be darkened so they cannot see,
and their backs be bent forever."[k]

Ingrafted Branches

[11]Again I ask: Did they stumble so as to fall beyond recovery? Not at all! Rather, because of their transgression, salvation has come to the Gentiles to make Israel envious. [12]But if their transgression means riches for the world, and their loss means riches for the Gentiles, how much greater riches will their fullness bring!

[13]I am talking to you Gentiles. Inasmuch as I am the apostle to the Gentiles, I make much of my ministry [14]in the hope that I may somehow arouse my own people to envy and save some of them. [15]For if their rejection is the reconciliation of the world, what will their acceptance be but life from the dead? [16]If the part of the dough offered as firstfruits is holy, then the whole batch is holy; if the root is holy, so are the branches.

[17]If some of the branches have been broken off, and you, though a wild olive shoot, have been grafted in among the others and now share in the nourishing sap from the olive root, [18]do not boast over those branches. If you do, consider this: You do not support the root, but the root supports you. [19]You will say then, "Branches were broken off so that I could be grafted in." [20]Granted. But they were broken off because of unbelief, and you stand by faith. Do not be arrogant, but be afraid. [21]For if God did not spare the natural branches, he will not spare you either.

---

[a]15 Isaiah 52:7   [b]16 Isaiah 53:1   [c]18 Psalm 19:4   [d]19 Deut. 32:21   [e]20 Isaiah 65:1
[f]21 Isaiah 65:2   [g]3 1 Kings 19:10,14   [h]4 1 Kings 19:18   [i]6 Some manuscripts *by grace. But if by works, then it is no longer grace; if it were, work would no longer be work.*   [j]8 Deut. 29:4; Isaiah 29:10
[k]10 Psalm 69:22,23

[22]Consider therefore the kindness and sternness of God: sternness to those who fell, but kindness to you, provided that you continue in his kindness. Otherwise, you also will be cut off. [23]And if they do not persist in unbelief, they will be grafted in, for God is able to graft them in again. [24]After all, if you were cut out of an olive tree that is wild by nature, and contrary to nature were grafted into a cultivated olive tree, how much more readily will these, the natural branches, be grafted into their own olive tree!

All Israel Will Be Saved

[25]I do not want you to be ignorant of this mystery, brothers, so that you may not be conceited: Israel has experienced a hardening in part until the full number of the Gentiles has come in. [26]And so all Israel will be saved, as it is written:

"The deliverer will come from Zion;
    he will turn godlessness away from
    Jacob.
[27]And this is[a] my covenant with them
    when I take away their sins."[b]

[28]As far as the gospel is concerned, they are enemies on your account; but as far as election is concerned, they are loved on account of the patriarchs, [29]for God's gifts and his call are irrevocable. [30]Just as you who were at one time disobedient to God have now received mercy as a result of their disobedience, [31]so they too have now become disobedient in order that they too may now[c] receive mercy as a result of God's mercy to you. [32]For God has bound all men over to disobedience so that he may have mercy on them all.

Doxology

[33]Oh, the depth of the riches of the
    wisdom and[d] knowledge of
    God!
How unsearchable his judgments,
    and his paths beyond tracing out!
[34]"Who has known the mind of the
    Lord?
Or who has been his counselor?"[e]
[35]"Who has ever given to God,
    that God should repay him?"[f]
[36]For from him and through him and to
    him are all things.
To him be the glory forever! Amen.

Living Sacrifices

12 Therefore, I urge you, brothers, in view of God's mercy, to offer your bodies as living sacrifices, holy and pleasing to God—this is your spiritual[g] act of worship. [2]Do not conform any longer to the pattern of this world, but be transformed by the renewing of your mind. Then you will be able to test and approve what God's will is—his good, pleasing and perfect will.

[3]For by the grace given me I say to every one of you: Do not think of yourself more highly than you ought, but rather think of yourself with sober judgment, in accordance with the measure of faith God has given you. [4]Just as each of us has one body with many members, and these members do not all have the same function, [5]so in Christ we who are many form one body, and each member belongs to all the others. [6]We have different gifts, according to the grace given us. If a man's gift is prophesying, let him use it in proportion to his[h] faith. [7]If it is serving, let him serve; if it is teaching, let him teach; [8]if it is encouraging, let him encourage; if it is contributing to the needs of others, let him give generously; if it is leadership, let him govern diligently; if it is showing mercy, let him do it cheerfully.

Love

[9]Love must be sincere. Hate what is evil; cling to what is good. [10]Be devoted to one another in brotherly love. Honor one another above yourselves. [11]Never be lacking in zeal, but keep your spiritual fervor, serving the Lord. [12]Be joyful in hope, patient in affliction, faithful in prayer. [13]Share with God's people who are in need. Practice hospitality.

[14]Bless those who persecute you; bless and do not curse. [15]Rejoice with those who rejoice; mourn with those who mourn. [16]Live in harmony with one another. Do not be proud, but be willing to associate with people of low position.[i] Do not be conceited.

[17]Do not repay anyone evil for evil. Be careful to do what is right in the eyes of everybody. [18]If it is possible, as far as it depends on you, live at peace with everyone. [19]Do not take revenge, my friends, but leave room for God's wrath, for it is

---

a27 Or will be   b27 Isaiah 59:20,21; 27:9; Jer. 31:33,34   c31 Some manuscripts do not have now.
d33 Or riches and the wisdom and the   e34 Isaiah 40:13   f35 Job 41:11   g1 Or reasonable
h6 Or in agreement with the   i16 Or willing to do menial work

written: "It is mine to avenge; I will re-pay,"*a* says the Lord. **20**On the contrary:

> "If your enemy is hungry, feed him;
> if he is thirsty, give him something
> to drink.
> In doing this, you will heap burning
> coals on his head."*b*

21Do not be overcome by evil, but over-come evil with good.

Submission to the Authorities

13 Everyone must submit himself to the governing authorities, for there is no authority except that which God has established. The authorities that exist have been established by God. **2**Conse-quently, he who rebels against the author-ity is rebelling against what God has insti-tuted, and those who do so will bring judgment on themselves. **3**For rulers hold no terror for those who do right, but for those who do wrong. Do you want to be free from fear of the one in authority? Then do what is right and he will com-mend you. **4**For he is God's servant to do you good. But if you do wrong, be afraid, for he does not bear the sword for noth-ing. He is God's servant, an agent of wrath to bring punishment on the wrongdoer. **5**Therefore, it is necessary to submit to the authorities, not only because of possible punishment but also because of con-science.

6This is also why you pay taxes, for the authorities are God's servants, who give their full time to governing. **7**Give every-one what you owe him: If you owe taxes, pay taxes; if revenue, then revenue; if re-spect, then respect; if honor, then honor.

Love, for the Day Is Near

8Let no debt remain outstanding, ex-cept the continuing debt to love one an-other, for he who loves his fellowman has fulfilled the law. **9**The commandments, "Do not commit adultery," "Do not mur-der," "Do not steal," "Do not covet,"*c* and whatever other commandment there may be, are summed up in this one rule: "Love your neighbor as yourself."*d* **10**Love does no harm to its neighbor. Therefore love is the fulfillment of the law.

11And do this, understanding the present time. The hour has come for you to wake up from your slumber, because our salvation is nearer now than when we first believed. **12**The night is nearly over; the day is almost here. So let us put aside the deeds of darkness and put on the ar-mor of light. **13**Let us behave decently, as in the daytime, not in orgies and drunken-ness, not in sexual immorality and de-bauchery, not in dissension and jealousy. **14**Rather, clothe yourselves with the Lord Jesus Christ, and do not think about how to gratify the desires of the sinful na-ture.*e*

The Weak and the Strong

14 Accept him whose faith is weak, without passing judgment on dis-putable matters. **2**One man's faith allows him to eat everything, but another man, whose faith is weak, eats only vegetables. **3**The man who eats everything must not look down on him who does not, and the man who does not eat everything must not condemn the man who does, for God has accepted him. **4**Who are you to judge someone else's servant? To his own mas-ter he stands or falls. And he will stand, for the Lord is able to make him stand.

5One man considers one day more sa-cred than another; another man considers every day alike. Each one should be fully convinced in his own mind. **6**He who re-gards one day as special, does so to the Lord. He who eats meat, eats to the Lord, for he gives thanks to God; and he who abstains, does so to the Lord and gives thanks to God. **7**For none of us lives to himself alone and none of us dies to him-self alone. **8**If we live, we live to the Lord; and if we die, we die to the Lord. So, whether we live or die, we belong to the Lord.

9For this very reason, Christ died and returned to life so that he might be the Lord of both the dead and the living. **10**You, then, why do you judge your broth-er? Or why do you look down on your brother? For we will all stand before God's judgment seat. **11**It is written:

> " 'As surely as I live,' says the Lord,
> 'every knee will bow before me;
> every tongue will confess to
> God.' "*f*

12So then, each of us will give an account of himself to God.

13Therefore let us stop passing judg-ment on one another. Instead, make up your mind not to put any stumbling block

a19 Deut. 32:35   *b20* Prov. 25:21,22   *c9* Exodus 20:13-15,17; Deut. 5:17-19,21   *d9* Lev. 19:18
e14 Or *the flesh*   *f11* Isaiah 45:23

or obstacle in your brother's way. ¹⁴As one who is in the Lord Jesus, I am fully convinced that no food*a* is unclean in itself. But if anyone regards something as unclean, then for him it is unclean. ¹⁵If your brother is distressed because of what you eat, you are no longer acting in love. Do not by your eating destroy your brother for whom Christ died. ¹⁶Do not allow what you consider good to be spoken of as evil. ¹⁷For the kingdom of God is not a matter of eating and drinking, but of righteousness, peace and joy in the Holy Spir-

it, ¹⁸because anyone who serves Christ in this way is pleasing to God and approved by men.

¹⁹Let us therefore make every effort to do what leads to peace and to mutual edification. ²⁰Do not destroy the work of God for the sake of food. All food is clean, but it is wrong for a man to eat anything that causes someone else to stumble. ²¹It is better not to eat meat or drink wine or to do anything else that will cause your brother to fall.

²²So whatever you believe about these

a14 Or *that nothing*

WEDNESDAY

VERSE FOR THE DAY:
Romans 14:8

AUTHOR:
Philip W. Williams

PASSAGE FOR THE DAY:
Romans 14:5–8

Out of Sorrow

PAIN and despair are threads that run through us as we move through our journey of bereavement.

In pain and despair we can echo the words of the old spiritual, "Nobody knows the trouble I've seen. Nobody knows my sorrow." We may have been moving through our journey slowly, doing well, when suddenly the reality of our loss, this death, hits again! There is no going back, no recapturing or retrieving what was lost. Our loved one is gone. The pain invades and grips, and the fullness we were beginning to feel seeps out. Emptiness takes over. The wound opens wide and we despair. It's as if all life stops again.

One doesn't have to be married 64 years to feel the pain and despair of death. It is not time, but our closeness to our loved one that increases our vulnerability and opens us to deeper pain and despair. Yet when we confront our pain and despair and begin to accept the loss, surrendering ourselves to God in our powerlessness, then pain and despair can give way to hope. The unwanted pain can be accepted and transformed. When we accept our pain as our own, suffering can grow into compassion. It's as if the heart opens, and out of sorrow come warmth and joy.

The life and death of each of us has influence on others: "If we live, we live to the Lord; and if we die, we die to the Lord. So, whether we live or die, we belong to the Lord" (Romans 14:8).

Additional Scripture Readings:
Psalm 23; Philippians 1:19–26

Go to page 1228 for your next devotional reading.

things keep between yourself and God. Blessed is the man who does not condemn himself by what he approves. 23But the man who has doubts is condemned if he eats, because his eating is not from faith; and everything that does not come from faith is sin.

15 We who are strong ought to bear with the failings of the weak and not to please ourselves. 2Each of us should please his neighbor for his good, to build him up. 3For even Christ did not please himself but, as it is written: "The insults of those who insult you have fallen on me."*a* 4For everything that was written in the past was written to teach us, so that through endurance and the encouragement of the Scriptures we might have hope.

5May the God who gives endurance and encouragement give you a spirit of unity among yourselves as you follow Christ Jesus, 6so that with one heart and mouth you may glorify the God and Father of our Lord Jesus Christ.

7Accept one another, then, just as Christ accepted you, in order to bring praise to God. 8For I tell you that Christ has become a servant of the Jews*b* on behalf of God's truth, to confirm the promises made to the patriarchs 9so that the Gentiles may glorify God for his mercy, as it is written:

"Therefore I will praise you among the
      Gentiles;
   I will sing hymns to your name."*c*

10Again, it says,

"Rejoice, O Gentiles, with his
      people."*d*

11And again,

"Praise the Lord, all you Gentiles,
   and sing praises to him, all you
      peoples."*e*

12And again, Isaiah says,

"The Root of Jesse will spring up,
   one who will arise to rule over the
      nations;
   the Gentiles will hope in him."*f*

13May the God of hope fill you with all joy and peace as you trust in him, so that you may overflow with hope by the power of the Holy Spirit.

Paul the Minister to the Gentiles

14I myself am convinced, my brothers, that you yourselves are full of goodness, complete in knowledge and competent to instruct one another. 15I have written you quite boldly on some points, as if to remind you of them again, because of the grace God gave me 16to be a minister of Christ Jesus to the Gentiles with the priestly duty of proclaiming the gospel of God, so that the Gentiles might become an offering acceptable to God, sanctified by the Holy Spirit.

17Therefore I glory in Christ Jesus in my service to God. 18I will not venture to speak of anything except what Christ has accomplished through me in leading the Gentiles to obey God by what I have said and done— 19by the power of signs and miracles, through the power of the Spirit. So from Jerusalem all the way around to Illyricum, I have fully proclaimed the gospel of Christ. 20It has always been my ambition to preach the gospel where Christ was not known, so that I would not be building on someone else's foundation. 21Rather, as it is written:

"Those who were not told about him
      will see,
   and those who have not heard will
      understand."*g*

22This is why I have often been hindered from coming to you.

Paul's Plan to Visit Rome

23But now that there is no more place for me to work in these regions, and since I have been longing for many years to see you, 24I plan to do so when I go to Spain. I hope to visit you while passing through and to have you assist me on my journey there, after I have enjoyed your company for a while. 25Now, however, I am on my way to Jerusalem in the service of the saints there. 26For Macedonia and Achaia were pleased to make a contribution for the poor among the saints in Jerusalem. 27They were pleased to do it, and indeed they owe it to them. For if the Gentiles have shared in the Jews' spiritual blessings, they owe it to the Jews to share with them their material blessings. 28So after I have completed this task and have made sure that they have received this fruit, I will go to Spain and visit you on the way.

a3 Psalm 69:9   *b8* Greek *circumcision*   *c9* 2 Samuel 22:50; Psalm 18:49   *d10* Deut. 32:43
e11 Psalm 117:1   *f12* Isaiah 11:10   *g21* Isaiah 52:15

[29]I know that when I come to you, I will come in the full measure of the blessing of Christ.

[30]I urge you, brothers, by our Lord Jesus Christ and by the love of the Spirit, to join me in my struggle by praying to God for me. [31]Pray that I may be rescued from the unbelievers in Judea and that my service in Jerusalem may be acceptable to the saints there, [32]so that by God's will I may come to you with joy and together with you be refreshed. [33]The God of peace be with you all. Amen.

Personal Greetings

16 I commend to you our sister Phoebe, a servant[a] of the church in Cenchrea. [2]I ask you to receive her in the Lord in a way worthy of the saints and to give her any help she may need from you, for she has been a great help to many people, including me.

[3]Greet Priscilla[b] and Aquila, my fellow workers in Christ Jesus. [4]They risked their lives for me. Not only I but all the churches of the Gentiles are grateful to them.

[5]Greet also the church that meets at their house.

Greet my dear friend Epenetus, who was the first convert to Christ in the province of Asia.

[6]Greet Mary, who worked very hard for you.

[7]Greet Andronicus and Junias, my relatives who have been in prison with me. They are outstanding among the apostles, and they were in Christ before I was.

[8]Greet Ampliatus, whom I love in the Lord.

[9]Greet Urbanus, our fellow worker in Christ, and my dear friend Stachys.

[10]Greet Apelles, tested and approved in Christ.

Greet those who belong to the household of Aristobulus.

[11]Greet Herodion, my relative.

Greet those in the household of Narcissus who are in the Lord.

[12]Greet Tryphena and Tryphosa, those women who work hard in the Lord.

Greet my dear friend Persis, another woman who has worked very hard in the Lord.

[13]Greet Rufus, chosen in the Lord, and his mother, who has been a mother to me, too.

[14]Greet Asyncritus, Phlegon, Hermes, Patrobas, Hermas and the brothers with them.

[15]Greet Philologus, Julia, Nereus and his sister, and Olympas and all the saints with them.

[16]Greet one another with a holy kiss.

All the churches of Christ send greetings.

[17]I urge you, brothers, to watch out for those who cause divisions and put obstacles in your way that are contrary to the teaching you have learned. Keep away from them. [18]For such people are not serving our Lord Christ, but their own appetites. By smooth talk and flattery they deceive the minds of naive people. [19]Everyone has heard about your obedience, so I am full of joy over you; but I want you to be wise about what is good, and innocent about what is evil.

[20]The God of peace will soon crush Satan under your feet.

The grace of our Lord Jesus be with you.

[21]Timothy, my fellow worker, sends his greetings to you, as do Lucius, Jason and Sosipater, my relatives.

[22]I, Tertius, who wrote down this letter, greet you in the Lord.

[23]Gaius, whose hospitality I and the whole church here enjoy, sends you his greetings.

Erastus, who is the city's director of public works, and our brother Quartus send you their greetings.[c]

[25]Now to him who is able to establish you by my gospel and the proclamation of Jesus Christ, according to the revelation of the mystery hidden for long ages past, [26]but now revealed and made known through the prophetic writings by the command of the eternal God, so that all nations might believe and obey him— [27]to the only wise God be glory forever through Jesus Christ! Amen.

---

a1 Or *deaconess*   b3 Greek *Prisca*, a variant of *Priscilla*   c23 Some manuscripts *their greetings.* 24May *the grace of our Lord Jesus Christ be with all of you. Amen.*

PAUL, while staying in Ephesus (Acts 19), writes this letter to the church he started in Corinth (Acts 18:1–17). He addresses various problems he has heard about and answers questions they have asked of him in a letter (see 1 Corinthians 7:1). He places a high priority on being obedient to Christ and on striving for unity, humility and love in the church. As you read this book, make a decision to seek the Lord's will in everything you do and to work hard to be humble, to love others, and to become one in spirit with your fellow believers.

1 CORINTHIANS

1 Paul, called to be an apostle of Christ Jesus by the will of God, and our brother Sosthenes,

²To the church of God in Corinth, to those sanctified in Christ Jesus and called to be holy, together with all those everywhere who call on the name of our Lord Jesus Christ — their Lord and ours:

³Grace and peace to you from God our Father and the Lord Jesus Christ.

Thanksgiving

⁴I always thank God for you because of his grace given you in Christ Jesus. ⁵For in him you have been enriched in every way — in all your speaking and in all your knowledge — ⁶because our testimony about Christ was confirmed in you. ⁷Therefore you do not lack any spiritual gift as you eagerly wait for our Lord Jesus Christ to be revealed. ⁸He will keep you strong to the end, so that you will be blameless on the day of our Lord Jesus

Christ. [9]God, who has called you into fellowship with his Son Jesus Christ our Lord, is faithful.

Divisions in the Church

[10]I appeal to you, brothers, in the name of our Lord Jesus Christ, that all of you agree with one another so that there may be no divisions among you and that you may be perfectly united in mind and thought. [11]My brothers, some from Chloe's household have informed me that there are quarrels among you. [12]What I mean is this: One of you says, "I follow Paul"; another, "I follow Apollos"; another, "I follow Cephas[a]"; still another, "I follow Christ."

[13]Is Christ divided? Was Paul crucified for you? Were you baptized into[b] the name of Paul? [14]I am thankful that I did not baptize any of you except Crispus and Gaius, [15]so no one can say that you were baptized into my name. [16](Yes, I also baptized the household of Stephanas; beyond that, I don't remember if I baptized anyone else.) [17]For Christ did not send me to baptize, but to preach the gospel—not with words of human wisdom, lest the cross of Christ be emptied of its power.

Christ the Wisdom and Power of God

[18]For the message of the cross is foolishness to those who are perishing, but to us who are being saved it is the power of God. [19]For it is written:

"I will destroy the wisdom of the wise;
     the intelligence of the intelligent I
         will frustrate."[c]

[20]Where is the wise man? Where is the scholar? Where is the philosopher of this age? Has not God made foolish the wisdom of the world? [21]For since in the wisdom of God the world through its wisdom did not know him, God was pleased through the foolishness of what was preached to save those who believe. [22]Jews demand miraculous signs and Greeks look for wisdom, [23]but we preach Christ crucified: a stumbling block to Jews and foolishness to Gentiles, [24]but to those whom God has called, both Jews and Greeks, Christ the power of God and the wisdom of God. [25]For the foolishness of God is wiser than man's wisdom, and the weakness of God is stronger than man's strength.

[26]Brothers, think of what you were when you were called. Not many of you were wise by human standards; not many were influential; not many were of noble birth. [27]But God chose the foolish things of the world to shame the wise; God chose the weak things of the world to shame the strong. [28]He chose the lowly things of this world and the despised things—and the things that are not—to nullify the things that are, [29]so that no one may boast before him. [30]It is because of him that you are in Christ Jesus, who has become for us wisdom from God—that is, our righteousness, holiness and redemption. [31]Therefore, as it is written: "Let him who boasts boast in the Lord."[d]

2 When I came to you, brothers, I did not come with eloquence or superior wisdom as I proclaimed to you the testimony about God.[e] [2]For I resolved to know nothing while I was with you except Jesus Christ and him crucified. [3]I came to you in weakness and fear, and with much trembling. [4]My message and my preaching were not with wise and persuasive words, but with a demonstration of the Spirit's power, [5]so that your faith might not rest on men's wisdom, but on God's power.

Wisdom From the Spirit

[6]We do, however, speak a message of wisdom among the mature, but not the wisdom of this age or of the rulers of this age, who are coming to nothing. [7]No, we speak of God's secret wisdom, a wisdom that has been hidden and that God destined for our glory before time began. [8]None of the rulers of this age understood it, for if they had, they would not have crucified the Lord of glory. [9]However, as it is written:

"No eye has seen,
     no ear has heard,
   no mind has conceived
     what God has prepared for those
         who love him"[f]—

[10]but God has revealed it to us by his Spirit.

The Spirit searches all things, even the deep things of God. [11]For who among men knows the thoughts of a man except the man's spirit within him? In the same way no one knows the thoughts of God except the Spirit of God. [12]We have not received

---

the spirit of the world but the Spirit who is from God, that we may understand what God has freely given us. [13]This is what we speak, not in words taught us by human wisdom but in words taught by the Spirit, expressing spiritual truths in spiritual words.[a] [14]The man without the Spirit does not accept the things that come from the Spirit of God, for they are foolishness to him, and he cannot understand them, because they are spiritually discerned. [15]The spiritual man makes judgments about all things, but he himself is not subject to any man's judgment:

[16]"For who has known the mind of the
    Lord
  that he may instruct him?"[b]

But we have the mind of Christ.

On Divisions in the Church

3 Brothers, I could not address you as spiritual but as worldly—mere infants in Christ. [2]I gave you milk, not solid food, for you were not yet ready for it. Indeed, you are still not ready. [3]You are still worldly. For since there is jealousy and quarreling among you, are you not worldly? Are you not acting like mere men? [4]For when one says, "I follow Paul," and another, "I follow Apollos," are you not mere men?

[5]What, after all, is Apollos? And what is Paul? Only servants, through whom you came to believe—as the Lord has assigned to each his task. [6]I planted the seed, Apollos watered it, but God made it grow. [7]So neither he who plants nor he who waters is anything, but only God, who makes things grow. [8]The man who plants and the man who waters have one purpose, and each will be rewarded according to his own labor. [9]For we are God's fellow workers; you are God's field, God's building.

[10]By the grace God has given me, I laid a foundation as an expert builder, and someone else is building on it. But each one should be careful how he builds. [11]For no one can lay any foundation other than the one already laid, which is Jesus Christ. [12]If any man builds on this foundation using gold, silver, costly stones, wood, hay or straw, [13]his work will be shown for what it is, because the Day will bring it to light. It will be revealed with fire, and the fire will test the quality of each man's work. [14]If what he has built survives, he will receive his reward. [15]If it is burned up, he will suffer loss; he himself will be saved, but only as one escaping through the flames.

[16]Don't you know that you yourselves are God's temple and that God's Spirit lives in you? [17]If anyone destroys God's temple, God will destroy him; for God's temple is sacred, and you are that temple.

[18]Do not deceive yourselves. If any one of you thinks he is wise by the standards of this age, he should become a "fool" so that he may become wise. [19]For the wisdom of this world is foolishness in God's sight. As it is written: "He catches the wise in their craftiness"[c]; [20]and again, "The Lord knows that the thoughts of the wise are futile."[d] [21]So then, no more boasting about men! All things are yours, [22]whether Paul or Apollos or Cephas[e] or the world or life or death or the present or the future—all are yours, [23]and you are of Christ, and Christ is of God.

Apostles of Christ

4 So then, men ought to regard us as servants of Christ and as those entrusted with the secret things of God. [2]Now it is required that those who have been given a trust must prove faithful. [3]I care very little if I am judged by you or by any human court; indeed, I do not even judge myself. [4]My conscience is clear, but that does not make me innocent. It is the Lord who judges me. [5]Therefore judge nothing before the appointed time; wait till the Lord comes. He will bring to light what is hidden in darkness and will expose the motives of men's hearts. At that time each will receive his praise from God.

[6]Now, brothers, I have applied these things to myself and Apollos for your benefit, so that you may learn from us the meaning of the saying, "Do not go beyond what is written." Then you will not take pride in one man over against another. [7]For who makes you different from anyone else? What do you have that you did not receive? And if you did receive it, why do you boast as though you did not?

[8]Already you have all you want! Already you have become rich! You have become kings—and that without us! How I wish that you really had become kings so that we might be kings with you! [9]For it seems to me that God has put us apostles

---

[a]13 Or *Spirit, interpreting spiritual truths to spiritual men*   [b]16 Isaiah 40:13   [c]19 Job 5:13
[d]20 Psalm 94:11   [e]22 That is, Peter

on display at the end of the procession, like men condemned to die in the arena. We have been made a spectacle to the whole universe, to angels as well as to men. ¹⁰We are fools for Christ, but you are so wise in Christ! We are weak, but you are strong! You are honored, we are dishonored! ¹¹To this very hour we go hungry and thirsty, we are in rags, we are brutally treated, we are homeless. ¹²We work hard with our own hands. When we are cursed, we bless; when we are persecuted, we endure it; ¹³when we are slandered, we answer kindly. Up to this moment we have become the scum of the earth, the refuse of the world.

¹⁴I am not writing this to shame you, but to warn you, as my dear children. ¹⁵Even though you have ten thousand guardians in Christ, you do not have many fathers, for in Christ Jesus I became your father through the gospel. ¹⁶Therefore I urge you to imitate me. ¹⁷For this reason I am sending to you Timothy, my son whom I love, who is faithful in the Lord. He will remind you of my way of life in

---

THURSDAY

VERSE FOR THE DAY:
1 Corinthians 4:2

AUTHOR:
Steve Farrar

PASSAGE FOR THE DAY:
1 Corinthians 4:1–5

The Spirit of Our Age

WE LIVE in an era where commitment is cheap. It's cheap in marriage, business, politics, and even athletics. Commitment is cheap in professional sports when a running back will sign a six-year, multi-million dollar contract, and then stay out of training camp in his third year because the team won't renegotiate his contract. Why does he want to renegotiate? Because some other backs in the league recently signed new contracts worth more than his. He wants to renegotiate because his contract is no longer personally convenient, and he refuses to keep his commitment until he gets his way. One player recently hinted that if his contract wasn't renegotiated, he wouldn't be able to give 100 percent on the field. Can you blame him? He was only making $685,000 a year.

The spirit of our age, whether expressed in athletics, business, politics or marriage, maintains that commitments should be honored only while convenient. When a commitment becomes inconvenient, bag it. Burton Hillis once said, "There's a mighty big difference between good, sound reasons, and reasons that sound good." Generally speaking, our society believes that only one commitment sounds good: The right to be happy . . .

A boy who has a father who is committed to his mother will have a tremendous advantage when he becomes a husband. He will have an intuitive understanding that his commitment in marriage is not a right to be happy, but to demonstrate a willingness to be responsible. Even when it's inconvenient. Even when it crowds out his personal happiness.

Additional Scripture Readings:
Ruth 1:16–18; 2 Samuel 15:19–22

Go to page 1230 for your next devotional reading.

Christ Jesus, which agrees with what I teach everywhere in every church.

[18]Some of you have become arrogant, as if I were not coming to you. [19]But I will come to you very soon, if the Lord is willing, and then I will find out not only how these arrogant people are talking, but what power they have. [20]For the kingdom of God is not a matter of talk but of power. [21]What do you prefer? Shall I come to you with a whip, or in love and with a gentle spirit?

Expel the Immoral Brother!

5 It is actually reported that there is sexual immorality among you, and of a kind that does not occur even among pagans: A man has his father's wife. [2]And you are proud! Shouldn't you rather have been filled with grief and have put out of your fellowship the man who did this? [3]Even though I am not physically present, I am with you in spirit. And I have already passed judgment on the one who did this, just as if I were present. [4]When you are assembled in the name of our Lord Jesus and I am with you in spirit, and the power of our Lord Jesus is present, [5]hand this man over to Satan, so that the sinful nature[a] may be destroyed and his spirit saved on the day of the Lord.

[6]Your boasting is not good. Don't you know that a little yeast works through the whole batch of dough? [7]Get rid of the old yeast that you may be a new batch without yeast—as you really are. For Christ, our Passover lamb, has been sacrificed. [8]Therefore let us keep the Festival, not with the old yeast, the yeast of malice and wickedness, but with bread without yeast, the bread of sincerity and truth.

[9]I have written you in my letter not to associate with sexually immoral people— [10]not at all meaning the people of this world who are immoral, or the greedy and swindlers, or idolaters. In that case you would have to leave this world. [11]But now I am writing you that you must not associate with anyone who calls himself a brother but is sexually immoral or greedy, an idolater or a slanderer, a drunkard or a swindler. With such a man do not even eat.

[12]What business is it of mine to judge those outside the church? Are you not to judge those inside? [13]God will judge those outside. "Expel the wicked man from among you."[b]

Lawsuits Among Believers

6 If any of you has a dispute with another, dare he take it before the ungodly for judgment instead of before the saints? [2]Do you not know that the saints will judge the world? And if you are to judge the world, are you not competent to judge trivial cases? [3]Do you not know that we will judge angels? How much more the things of this life! [4]Therefore, if you have disputes about such matters, appoint as judges even men of little account in the church![c] [5]I say this to shame you. Is it possible that there is nobody among you wise enough to judge a dispute between believers? [6]But instead, one brother goes to law against another—and this in front of unbelievers!

[7]The very fact that you have lawsuits among you means you have been completely defeated already. Why not rather be wronged? Why not rather be cheated? [8]Instead, you yourselves cheat and do wrong, and you do this to your brothers.

[9]Do you not know that the wicked will not inherit the kingdom of God? Do not be deceived: Neither the sexually immoral nor idolaters nor adulterers nor male prostitutes nor homosexual offenders [10]nor thieves nor the greedy nor drunkards nor slanderers nor swindlers will inherit the kingdom of God. [11]And that is what some of you were. But you were washed, you were sanctified, you were justified in the name of the Lord Jesus Christ and by the Spirit of our God.

Sexual Immorality

[12]"Everything is permissible for me"— but not everything is beneficial. "Everything is permissible for me"—but I will not be mastered by anything. [13]"Food for the stomach and the stomach for food"— but God will destroy them both. The body is not meant for sexual immorality, but for the Lord, and the Lord for the body. [14]By his power God raised the Lord from the dead, and he will raise us also. [15]Do you not know that your bodies are members of Christ himself? Shall I then take the members of Christ and unite them with a prostitute? Never! [16]Do you not know that he who unites himself with a prostitute is one with her in body? For it is said, "The

---

[a]5 Or that his body; or that the flesh　[b]13 Deut. 17:7; 19:19; 21:21; 22:21,24; 24:7　[c]4 Or matters, do you appoint as judges men of little account in the church?

two will become one flesh."*a* **17**But he who unites himself with the Lord is one with him in spirit.

18Flee from sexual immorality. All other sins a man commits are outside his body, but he who sins sexually sins against his own body. **19**Do you not know that your body is a temple of the Holy Spirit, who is in you, whom you have received from God? You are not your own; **20**you were bought at a price. Therefore honor God with your body.

Marriage

7 Now for the matters you wrote about: It is good for a man not to marry.*b* **2**But since there is so much immorality, each man should have his own wife, and each woman her own husband. **3**The husband should fulfill his marital duty to his

---

*a*16 Gen. 2:24   *b*1 Or *"It is good for a man not to have sexual relations with a woman."*

FRIDAY

VERSE FOR THE DAY:	AUTHOR:	PASSAGE FOR THE DAY:
1 Corinthians 6:19	Thomas Merton	1 Corinthians 6:18–20

Sons of God

EVERY baptized Christian is obliged by his baptismal promises to renounce sin and to give himself completely, without compromise, to Christ, in order that he may fulfill his vocation, save his soul, enter into the mystery of God, and there find himself perfectly in the light of Christ.

As Saint Paul reminds us, we are not our own (1 Corinthians 6:19). We belong entirely to Christ. His Spirit has taken possession of us at baptism. We are the temples of the Holy Spirit. Our thoughts, our actions, our desires, are by rights more his than our own. But we have to struggle to ensure that God always receives from us what we owe him by right. If we do not labor to overcome our natural weakness, our disordered and selfish passions, what belongs to God in us will be withdrawn from the sanctifying power of his love and will be corrupted by selfishness, blinded by irrational desire, hardened by pride, and will eventually plunge into the abyss of moral nonentity which is called sin.

Sin is the refusal of spiritual life, the rejection of the inner order and peace that come from our union with the divine will. In a word, sin is the refusal of God's will and of his love. It is not only a refusal to "do" this or that thing willed by God, or a determination to do what he forbids. It is more radically a refusal to be what we are, a rejection of our mysterious, contingent, spiritual reality hidden in the very mystery of God. Sin is our refusal to be what we were created to be—sons of God, images of God. Ultimately sin, while seeming to be an assertion of freedom, is a flight from the freedom and the responsibility of divine sonship.

Additional Scripture Readings:
Romans 8:12–17;
Galatians 3:26—4:7

Go to page 1232 for your next devotional reading.

wife, and likewise the wife to her husband. **4**The wife's body does not belong to her alone but also to her husband. In the same way, the husband's body does not belong to him alone but also to his wife. **5**Do not deprive each other except by mutual consent and for a time, so that you may devote yourselves to prayer. Then come together again so that Satan will not tempt you because of your lack of self-control. **6**I say this as a concession, not as a command. **7**I wish that all men were as I am. But each man has his own gift from God; one has this gift, another has that.

8Now to the unmarried and the widows I say: It is good for them to stay unmarried, as I am. **9**But if they cannot control themselves, they should marry, for it is better to marry than to burn with passion.

10To the married I give this command (not I, but the Lord): A wife must not separate from her husband. **11**But if she does, she must remain unmarried or else be reconciled to her husband. And a husband must not divorce his wife.

12To the rest I say this (I, not the Lord): If any brother has a wife who is not a believer and she is willing to live with him, he must not divorce her. **13**And if a woman has a husband who is not a believer and he is willing to live with her, she must not divorce him. **14**For the unbelieving husband has been sanctified through his wife, and the unbelieving wife has been sanctified through her believing husband. Otherwise your children would be unclean, but as it is, they are holy.

15But if the unbeliever leaves, let him do so. A believing man or woman is not bound in such circumstances; God has called us to live in peace. **16**How do you know, wife, whether you will save your husband? Or, how do you know, husband, whether you will save your wife?

17Nevertheless, each one should retain the place in life that the Lord assigned to him and to which God has called him. This is the rule I lay down in all the churches. **18**Was a man already circumcised when he was called? He should not become uncircumcised. Was a man uncircumcised when he was called? He should not be circumcised. **19**Circumcision is nothing and uncircumcision is nothing. Keeping God's commands is what counts. **20**Each one should remain in the situation which he was in when God called him. **21**Were you a slave when you were called?

Don't let it trouble you—although if you can gain your freedom, do so. **22**For he who was a slave when he was called by the Lord is the Lord's freedman; similarly, he who was a free man when he was called is Christ's slave. **23**You were bought at a price; do not become slaves of men. **24**Brothers, each man, as responsible to God, should remain in the situation God called him to.

25Now about virgins: I have no command from the Lord, but I give a judgment as one who by the Lord's mercy is trustworthy. **26**Because of the present crisis, I think that it is good for you to remain as you are. **27**Are you married? Do not seek a divorce. Are you unmarried? Do not look for a wife. **28**But if you do marry, you have not sinned; and if a virgin marries, she has not sinned. But those who marry will face many troubles in this life, and I want to spare you this.

29What I mean, brothers, is that the time is short. From now on those who have wives should live as if they had none; **30**those who mourn, as if they did not; those who are happy, as if they were not; those who buy something, as if it were not theirs to keep; **31**those who use the things of the world, as if not engrossed in them. For this world in its present form is passing away.

32I would like you to be free from concern. An unmarried man is concerned about the Lord's affairs—how he can please the Lord. **33**But a married man is concerned about the affairs of this world—how he can please his wife— **34**and his interests are divided. An unmarried woman or virgin is concerned about the Lord's affairs: Her aim is to be devoted to the Lord in both body and spirit. But a married woman is concerned about the affairs of this world—how she can please her husband. **35**I am saying this for your own good, not to restrict you, but that you may live in a right way in undivided devotion to the Lord.

36If anyone thinks he is acting improperly toward the virgin he is engaged to, and if she is getting along in years and he feels he ought to marry, he should do as he wants. He is not sinning. They should get married. **37**But the man who has settled the matter in his own mind, who is under no compulsion but has control over his own will, and who has made up his mind not to marry the virgin—this man also does the right thing. **38**So then, he

WEEKENDING

RECOGNIZE

Everyone who comes to know Jesus stumbles
because of him. He fails to meet our wrong
expectations. He calls us to do impossible
things or to become something we think we
could never become. This is his way of teaching
us how much we need him. He breaks us to
pieces so that he can put us back together in
his image.

– Michael Card

RENEW

The rule is this: Christians are people who
remember their own weaknesses and failure.
They are under reconstruction. So they offer
hope and forgiveness to people who fall and
who need Jesus' healing grace and hope.

– Donald M. Joy

REVIVE

Saturday: 1 Corinthians 1:20–31
Sunday: 2 Corinthians 4:1–12

Go to page 1233 for your next devotional reading.

who marries the virgin does right, but he who does not marry her does even better.[a]

39A woman is bound to her husband as long as he lives. But if her husband dies, she is free to marry anyone she wishes, but he must belong to the Lord. **40**In my judgment, she is happier if she stays as she is—and I think that I too have the Spirit of God.

[a] 36-38 Or 36If anyone thinks he is not treating his daughter properly, and if she is getting along in years, and he feels she ought to marry, he should do as he wants. He is not sinning. He should let her get married. 37But the man who has settled the matter in his own mind, who is under no compulsion but has control over his own will, and who has made up his mind to keep the virgin unmarried—this man also does the right thing. 38So then, he who gives his virgin in marriage does right, but he who does not give her in marriage does even better.

MONDAY

VERSE FOR THE DAY:
1 Corinthians 7:32

AUTHOR:
Leonard LeSourd

PASSAGE FOR THE DAY:
1 Corinthians 7:32–38

Dynamic Celibacy

THE key to a dynamic celibacy is to live a selfless life. When a man's life is centered on serving God and helping others, his energies are directed outward and there's no time to dwell on sexual hang-ups.

The apostle Paul discovered this secret. "An unmarried man is concerned about the Lord's affairs—how he can please the Lord . . . The man who . . . has control over his own will, and who has made up his mind not to marry the virgin—this man also does the right thing. So then, he who marries the virgin does right, but he who does not marry her does even better" (1 Corinthians 7:32,37–38).

Is Paul putting down marriage?

Not at all. He is simply holding up another commitment—an even more demanding and absorbing one: one hundred percent, all-out devotion to God. In his ministry to men, Paul is continually exhorting them to find "the best" through self-discipline, whatever their marital status: "Flee the evil desires of youth" (2 Timothy 2:22). "It is God's will that you should be sanctified: that you should avoid sexual immorality . . . For God did not call us to be impure, but to live a holy life" (1 Thessalonians 4:3,7).

Celibacy in no way implies withdrawal from people or a life of seclusion. In fact, because the single person usually has fewer family responsibilities, he is freer to reach out to those around him who need his love. If I were young and single again in today's hurting world, I would opt to learn more about holy living.

Additional Scripture Readings:
1 Thessalonians 4:3–8;
1 Peter 1:13–25

Go to page 1237 for your next devotional reading.

Food Sacrificed to Idols

8 Now about food sacrificed to idols: We know that we all possess knowledge.[a] Knowledge puffs up, but love builds up. [2]The man who thinks he knows something does not yet know as he ought to know. [3]But the man who loves God is known by God.

[4]So then, about eating food sacrificed to idols: We know that an idol is nothing at all in the world and that there is no God but one. [5]For even if there are so-called gods, whether in heaven or on earth (as indeed there are many "gods" and many "lords"), [6]yet for us there is but one God, the Father, from whom all things came and for whom we live; and there is but one Lord, Jesus Christ, through whom all things came and through whom we live.

[7]But not everyone knows this. Some people are still so accustomed to idols that when they eat such food they think of it as having been sacrificed to an idol, and since their conscience is weak, it is defiled. [8]But food does not bring us near to God; we are no worse if we do not eat, and no better if we do.

[9]Be careful, however, that the exercise of your freedom does not become a stumbling block to the weak. [10]For if anyone with a weak conscience sees you who have this knowledge eating in an idol's temple, won't he be emboldened to eat what has been sacrificed to idols? [11]So this weak brother, for whom Christ died, is destroyed by your knowledge. [12]When you sin against your brothers in this way and wound their weak conscience, you sin against Christ. [13]Therefore, if what I eat causes my brother to fall into sin, I will never eat meat again, so that I will not cause him to fall.

The Rights of an Apostle

9 Am I not free? Am I not an apostle? Have I not seen Jesus our Lord? Are you not the result of my work in the Lord? [2]Even though I may not be an apostle to others, surely I am to you! For you are the seal of my apostleship in the Lord.

[3]This is my defense to those who sit in judgment on me. [4]Don't we have the right to food and drink? [5]Don't we have the right to take a believing wife along with us, as do the other apostles and the Lord's brothers and Cephas[b]? [6]Or is it only I and Barnabas who must work for a living?

[7]Who serves as a soldier at his own expense? Who plants a vineyard and does not eat of its grapes? Who tends a flock and does not drink of the milk? [8]Do I say this merely from a human point of view? Doesn't the Law say the same thing? [9]For it is written in the Law of Moses: "Do not muzzle an ox while it is treading out the grain."[c] Is it about oxen that God is concerned? [10]Surely he says this for us, doesn't he? Yes, this was written for us, because when the plowman plows and the thresher threshes, they ought to do so in the hope of sharing in the harvest. [11]If we have sown spiritual seed among you, is it too much if we reap a material harvest from you? [12]If others have this right of support from you, shouldn't we have it all the more?

But we did not use this right. On the contrary, we put up with anything rather than hinder the gospel of Christ. [13]Don't you know that those who work in the temple get their food from the temple, and those who serve at the altar share in what is offered on the altar? [14]In the same way, the Lord has commanded that those who preach the gospel should receive their living from the gospel.

[15]But I have not used any of these rights. And I am not writing this in the hope that you will do such things for me. I would rather die than have anyone deprive me of this boast. [16]Yet when I preach the gospel, I cannot boast, for I am compelled to preach. Woe to me if I do not preach the gospel! [17]If I preach voluntarily, I have a reward; if not voluntarily, I am simply discharging the trust committed to me. [18]What then is my reward? Just this: that in preaching the gospel I may offer it free of charge, and so not make use of my rights in preaching it.

[19]Though I am free and belong to no man, I make myself a slave to everyone, to win as many as possible. [20]To the Jews I became like a Jew, to win the Jews. To those under the law I became like one under the law (though I myself am not under the law), so as to win those under the law. [21]To those not having the law I became like one not having the law (though I am not free from God's law but am under Christ's law), so as to win those not having the law. [22]To the weak I became weak, to win the weak. I have become all things to all men so that by all possible means I might save some. [23]I do all this for the

---

a1 Or *"We all possess knowledge," as you say*   b5 That is, Peter   c9 Deut. 25:4

sake of the gospel, that I may share in its blessings.

²⁴Do you not know that in a race all the runners run, but only one gets the prize? Run in such a way as to get the prize. ²⁵Everyone who competes in the games goes into strict training. They do it to get a crown that will not last; but we do it to get a crown that will last forever. ²⁶Therefore I do not run like a man running aimlessly; I do not fight like a man beating the air. ²⁷No, I beat my body and make it my slave so that after I have preached to others, I myself will not be disqualified for the prize.

Warnings From Israel's History

10 For I do not want you to be ignorant of the fact, brothers, that our forefathers were all under the cloud and that they all passed through the sea. ²They were all baptized into Moses in the cloud and in the sea. ³They all ate the same spiritual food ⁴and drank the same spiritual drink; for they drank from the spiritual rock that accompanied them, and that rock was Christ. ⁵Nevertheless, God was not pleased with most of them; their bodies were scattered over the desert.

⁶Now these things occurred as examples[a] to keep us from setting our hearts on evil things as they did. ⁷Do not be idolaters, as some of them were; as it is written: "The people sat down to eat and drink and got up to indulge in pagan revelry."[b] ⁸We should not commit sexual immorality, as some of them did—and in one day twenty-three thousand of them died. ⁹We should not test the Lord, as some of them did—and were killed by snakes. ¹⁰And do not grumble, as some of them did—and were killed by the destroying angel.

¹¹These things happened to them as examples and were written down as warnings for us, on whom the fulfillment of the ages has come. ¹²So, if you think you are standing firm, be careful that you don't fall! ¹³No temptation has seized you except what is common to man. And God is faithful; he will not let you be tempted beyond what you can bear. But when you are tempted, he will also provide a way out so that you can stand up under it.

Idol Feasts and the Lord's Supper

¹⁴Therefore, my dear friends, flee from idolatry. ¹⁵I speak to sensible people;

judge for yourselves what I say. ¹⁶Is not the cup of thanksgiving for which we give thanks a participation in the blood of Christ? And is not the bread that we break a participation in the body of Christ? ¹⁷Because there is one loaf, we, who are many, are one body, for we all partake of the one loaf.

¹⁸Consider the people of Israel: Do not those who eat the sacrifices participate in the altar? ¹⁹Do I mean then that a sacrifice offered to an idol is anything, or that an idol is anything? ²⁰No, but the sacrifices of pagans are offered to demons, not to God, and I do not want you to be participants with demons. ²¹You cannot drink the cup of the Lord and the cup of demons too; you cannot have a part in both the Lord's table and the table of demons. ²²Are we trying to arouse the Lord's jealousy? Are we stronger than he?

The Believer's Freedom

²³"Everything is permissible"—but not everything is beneficial. "Everything is permissible"—but not everything is constructive. ²⁴Nobody should seek his own good, but the good of others.

²⁵Eat anything sold in the meat market without raising questions of conscience, ²⁶for, "The earth is the Lord's, and everything in it."[c]

²⁷If some unbeliever invites you to a meal and you want to go, eat whatever is put before you without raising questions of conscience. ²⁸But if anyone says to you, "This has been offered in sacrifice," then do not eat it, both for the sake of the man who told you and for conscience' sake[d]— ²⁹the other man's conscience, I mean, not yours. For why should my freedom be judged by another's conscience? ³⁰If I take part in the meal with thankfulness, why am I denounced because of something I thank God for?

³¹So whether you eat or drink or whatever you do, do it all for the glory of God. ³²Do not cause anyone to stumble, whether Jews, Greeks or the church of God— ³³even as I try to please everybody in every way. For I am not seeking my own good but the good of many, so that they

11 may be saved. ¹Follow my example, as I follow the example of Christ.

---

[a]6 Or *types*; also in verse 11   [b]7 Exodus 32:6   [c]26 Psalm 24:1   [d]28 Some manuscripts conscience' sake, for "the earth is the Lord's and everything in it"

Propriety in Worship

[2]I praise you for remembering me in everything and for holding to the teachings,[a] just as I passed them on to you.

[3]Now I want you to realize that the head of every man is Christ, and the head of the woman is man, and the head of Christ is God. [4]Every man who prays or prophesies with his head covered dishonors his head. [5]And every woman who prays or prophesies with her head uncovered dishonors her head—it is just as though her head were shaved. [6]If a woman does not cover her head, she should have her hair cut off; and if it is a disgrace for a woman to have her hair cut or shaved off, she should cover her head. [7]A man ought not to cover his head,[b] since he is the image and glory of God; but the woman is the glory of man. [8]For man did not come from woman, but woman from man; [9]neither was man created for woman, but woman for man. [10]For this reason, and because of the angels, the woman ought to have a sign of authority on her head.

[11]In the Lord, however, woman is not independent of man, nor is man independent of woman. [12]For as woman came from man, so also man is born of woman. But everything comes from God. [13]Judge for yourselves: Is it proper for a woman to pray to God with her head uncovered? [14]Does not the very nature of things teach you that if a man has long hair, it is a disgrace to him, [15]but that if a woman has long hair, it is her glory? For long hair is given to her as a covering. [16]If anyone wants to be contentious about this, we have no other practice—nor do the churches of God.

The Lord's Supper

[17]In the following directives I have no praise for you, for your meetings do more harm than good. [18]In the first place, I hear that when you come together as a church, there are divisions among you, and to some extent I believe it. [19]No doubt there have to be differences among you to show which of you have God's approval. [20]When you come together, it is not the Lord's Supper you eat, [21]for as you eat, each of you goes ahead without waiting for anybody else. One remains hungry, another gets drunk. [22]Don't you have homes to eat and drink in? Or do you despise the church of God and humiliate those who have nothing? What shall I say to you? Shall I praise you for this? Certainly not!

[23]For I received from the Lord what I also passed on to you: The Lord Jesus, on the night he was betrayed, took bread, [24]and when he had given thanks, he broke it and said, "This is my body, which is for you; do this in remembrance of me." [25]In the same way, after supper he took the cup, saying, "This cup is the new covenant in my blood; do this, whenever you drink it, in remembrance of me." [26]For whenever you eat this bread and drink this cup, you proclaim the Lord's death until he comes.

[27]Therefore, whoever eats the bread or drinks the cup of the Lord in an unworthy manner will be guilty of sinning against the body and blood of the Lord. [28]A man ought to examine himself before he eats of the bread and drinks of the cup. [29]For anyone who eats and drinks without recognizing the body of the Lord eats and drinks judgment on himself. [30]That is why many among you are weak and sick, and a number of you have fallen asleep. [31]But if we judged ourselves, we would not come under judgment. [32]When we are judged by the Lord, we are being disciplined so that we will not be condemned with the world.

[33]So then, my brothers, when you come together to eat, wait for each other. [34]If anyone is hungry, he should eat at home, so that when you meet together it may not result in judgment.

And when I come I will give further directions.

Spiritual Gifts

12 Now about spiritual gifts, brothers, I do not want you to be ignorant. [2]You know that when you were pagans, somehow or other you were influenced and led astray to mute idols. [3]Therefore I tell you that no one who is speaking by the Spirit of God says, "Jesus be cursed," and no one can say, "Jesus is Lord," except by the Holy Spirit.

[4]There are different kinds of gifts, but

---

a2 Or traditions   b4-7 Or [4]Every man who prays or prophesies with long hair dishonors his head. [5]And every woman who prays or prophesies with no covering of hair, on her head dishonors her head—she is just like one of the "shorn women." [6]If a woman has no covering, let her be for now with short hair, but since it is a disgrace for a woman to have her hair shorn or shaved, she should grow it again. [7]A man ought not to have long hair the same Spirit. ⁵There are different kinds of service, but the same Lord. ⁶There are different kinds of working, but the same God works all of them in all men.

⁷Now to each one the manifestation of the Spirit is given for the common good. ⁸To one there is given through the Spirit the message of wisdom, to another the message of knowledge by means of the same Spirit, ⁹to another faith by the same Spirit, to another gifts of healing by that one Spirit, ¹⁰to another miraculous powers, to another prophecy, to another distinguishing between spirits, to another speaking in different kinds of tongues,ᵃ and to still another the interpretation of

ᵃ 10 Or *languages*; also in verse 28

TUESDAY

VERSE FOR THE DAY: *AUTHOR:*   *PASSAGE FOR THE DAY:*
1 Corinthians 11:3   David Augsburger   *1 Corinthians 11:2–10*

Headship's New Meaning

DOES the Biblical recognition of man as "head" in marriage endow him with authority and right-to-dominate? Some have thought that Paul's patterning of man's role as "head" after Christ's position as "head-of-the-church" gives great weight to the husband's role.

Does the husband, like Christ, become lord and master? The ultimate word? Since the two, man and Christ, are compared, does that give man all the rights and roles of lord in the home? On the contrary, the purposes of the comparison are specifically stated (in both 1 Corinthians 11:2–10 and Ephesians 5:21–33). Headship means responsibility and initiative: responsibility to act in love; initiative to act in service. As Christ acted in self-giving love and self-humbling service (giving us a whole new meaning to "headship"), so husbands take the initiative in building an atmosphere of loving, self-sacrificing service.

Headmanship is only part of leadership, one facet of one kind of leadership.

Christ cut through our contorted ideas of headship with surgical words: "The kings of the Gentiles lord it over them; and those who exercise authority over them call themselves Benefactors. But you are not to be like that. Instead, the greatest among you should be like the youngest, and the one who rules like the one who serves. For who is greater, the one who is at the table or the one who serves? Is it not the one who is at the table? But I am among you as one who serves" (Luke 22:25–27).

Leadership is accepting responsibilities and performing certain functions in a marriage relationship in a way that advances both together toward their goals.

Additional Scripture Readings: *Go to page 1239 for your next*
Matthew 20:20–28;   *devotional reading.*
Ephesians 5:21–33

tongues.[a] [11]All these are the work of one and the same Spirit, and he gives them to each one, just as he determines.

One Body, Many Parts

[12]The body is a unit, though it is made up of many parts; and though all its parts are many, they form one body. So it is with Christ. [13]For we were all baptized by[b] one Spirit into one body—whether Jews or Greeks, slave or free—and we were all given the one Spirit to drink.

[14]Now the body is not made up of one part but of many. [15]If the foot should say, "Because I am not a hand, I do not belong to the body," it would not for that reason cease to be part of the body. [16]And if the ear should say, "Because I am not an eye, I do not belong to the body," it would not for that reason cease to be part of the body. [17]If the whole body were an eye, where would the sense of hearing be? If the whole body were an ear, where would the sense of smell be? [18]But in fact God has arranged the parts in the body, every one of them, just as he wanted them to be. [19]If they were all one part, where would the body be? [20]As it is, there are many parts, but one body.

[21]The eye cannot say to the hand, "I don't need you!" And the head cannot say to the feet, "I don't need you!" [22]On the contrary, those parts of the body that seem to be weaker are indispensable, [23]and the parts that we think are less honorable we treat with special honor. And the parts that are unpresentable are treated with special modesty, [24]while our presentable parts need no special treatment. But God has combined the members of the body and has given greater honor to the parts that lacked it, [25]so that there should be no division in the body, but that its parts should have equal concern for each other. [26]If one part suffers, every part suffers with it; if one part is honored, every part rejoices with it.

[27]Now you are the body of Christ, and each one of you is a part of it. [28]And in the church God has appointed first of all apostles, second prophets, third teachers, then workers of miracles, also those having gifts of healing, those able to help others, those with gifts of administration, and those speaking in different kinds of tongues. [29]Are all apostles? Are all proph-

ets? Are all teachers? Do all work miracles? [30]Do all have gifts of healing? Do all speak in tongues[c]? Do all interpret? [31]But eagerly desire[d] the greater gifts.

Love

And now I will show you the most excellent way.

13 If I speak in the tongues[e] of men and of angels, but have not love, I am only a resounding gong or a clanging cymbal. [2]If I have the gift of prophecy and can fathom all mysteries and all knowledge, and if I have a faith that can move mountains, but have not love, I am nothing. [3]If I give all I possess to the poor and surrender my body to the flames,[f] but have not love, I gain nothing.

[4]Love is patient, love is kind. It does not envy, it does not boast, it is not proud. [5]It is not rude, it is not self-seeking, it is not easily angered, it keeps no record of wrongs. [6]Love does not delight in evil but rejoices with the truth. [7]It always protects, always trusts, always hopes, always perseveres.

[8]Love never fails. But where there are prophecies, they will cease; where there are tongues, they will be stilled; where there is knowledge, it will pass away. [9]For we know in part and we prophesy in part, [10]but when perfection comes, the imperfect disappears. [11]When I was a child, I talked like a child, I thought like a child, I reasoned like a child. When I became a man, I put childish ways behind me. [12]Now we see but a poor reflection as in a mirror; then we shall see face to face. Now I know in part; then I shall know fully, even as I am fully known.

[13]And now these three remain: faith, hope and love. But the greatest of these is love.

Gifts of Prophecy and Tongues

14 Follow the way of love and eagerly desire spiritual gifts, especially the gift of prophecy. [2]For anyone who speaks in a tongue[g] does not speak to men but to God. Indeed, no one understands him; he utters mysteries with his spirit.[h] [3]But everyone who prophesies speaks to men for their strengthening, encouragement and comfort. [4]He who speaks in a tongue edifies himself, but he who prophesies edifies the church. [5]I would like every one of

---

[a]10 Or *languages*; also in verse 28   [b]13 Or *with*; or *in*   [c]30 Or *other languages*   [d]31 Or *But you are eagerly desiring*   [e]1 Or *languages*   [f]3 Some early manuscripts *body that I may boast*   [g]2 Or *another language*; also in verses 4, 13, 14, 19, 26 and 27   [h]2 Or *by the Spirit*

you to speak in tongues,[a] but I would rather have you prophesy. He who prophesies is greater than one who speaks in tongues,[a] unless he interprets, so that the church may be edified.

⁶Now, brothers, if I come to you and speak in tongues, what good will I be to you, unless I bring you some revelation or knowledge or prophecy or word of instruction? ⁷Even in the case of lifeless things that make sounds, such as the flute or harp, how will anyone know what tune is being played unless there is a distinction in the notes? ⁸Again, if the trumpet does not sound a clear call, who will get ready for battle? ⁹So it is with you. Unless

[a]5 Or *other languages*; also in verses 6, 18, 22, 23 and 39

WEDNESDAY

VERSE FOR THE DAY:	AUTHOR:	PASSAGE FOR THE DAY:
1 Corinthians 12:12	Paul Brand	1 Corinthians 12:12–31

Body Life

I SOMETIMES think of the human body as a community, and then of its individual cells such as the white cell. The cell is the basic unit of an organism; it can live for itself, or it can help form and sustain the larger organism. I recall the apostle Paul's use of analogy in 1 Corinthians 12 where he compares the church of Christ to the human body. That inspired analogy takes on even more meaning to me because of the expanded vistas allowed by the invention of microscopes. Since Paul's analogy renders a basic principle of God's creation, I can augment it like this:

The body is one unit, though it is made up of many cells, and though all of its cells are many, they form one body . . . If the white cell should say, because I am not a brain cell, I do not belong to the body, it would not for that reason cease to be part of the body. And if the muscle cell should say to the optic nerve cell, because I am not an optic nerve, I do not belong to the body, it would not for that reason cease to be part of the body. If the whole body were an optic nerve cell, where would be the ability to walk? If the whole body were an auditory nerve, where would be the sense of sight? But in fact God has arranged the cells in the body, every one of them, just as he wanted them to be. If all cells were the same, where would the body be? As it is, there are many cells, but one body.

That analogy conveys a more precise meaning to me because though a hand or foot or ear cannot have a life separate from the body, a cell does have that potential. It can be part of the body as a loyalist, or it can cling to its own life. Some cells do choose to live in the body, sharing its benefits while maintaining complete independence—they become parasites or cancer cells.

Additional Scripture Readings:
Romans 12:3–8; Ephesians 4:1–16

Go to page 1240 for your next devotional reading.

you speak intelligible words with your tongue, how will anyone know what you are saying? You will just be speaking into the air. [10]Undoubtedly there are all sorts of languages in the world, yet none of them is without meaning. [11]If then I do not grasp the meaning of what someone is saying, I am a foreigner to the speaker, and he is a foreigner to me. [12]So it is with you. Since you are eager to have spiritual gifts, try to excel in gifts that build up the church.

[13]For this reason anyone who speaks in a tongue should pray that he may interpret what he says. [14]For if I pray in a tongue, my spirit prays, but my mind is

---

THURSDAY

VERSE FOR THE DAY:	AUTHOR:	PASSAGE FOR THE DAY:
1 Corinthians 13:4	Larry Crabb	1 Corinthians 13:1–13

Real Love

I WAS sitting on an old worn-velvet loveseat in the preacher's living room. Nestled close beside me was Rachael, my beautiful bride-to-be. It would have been difficult to slide even a thin book between us.

Across from us, in separate chairs perhaps ten feet apart, sat the preacher and his wife, both in their late seventies. She nodded her gray head and smiled and listened and rocked as her hands worked a rapid rhythm with yarn and knitting needles. He was relaxed into an old stuffed recliner, busily jotting notes in a small, well-used black notebook.

As we discussed the details of our wedding ceremony, I found myself watching the old couple, not as preacher and preacher's wife, but as husband and wife. Suddenly something struck me. Those two, sitting in separate chairs with more than three yards between them, conveyed more love with a single meeting of their eyes than my fiancée and I were exchanging with all our snuggling, grinning and whispered endearments.

I still remember thinking, "How do we get from here to there, from where we are in our eager young love to where they are in their loving maturity?"

Marriage is a stage on which real love—the kind the apostle Paul described as the greatest virtue—can be enacted for the world to see: the kind of love that enables us to endure wrong with patience, to resist evil with conviction, to enjoy the good things with gusto, to give richly of ourselves with humility, and to nourish another's soul with long-suffering.

When all these virtues are present, not only is each marriage partner incomparably blessed, but sometimes a couple of young apprentices about to take their place on this same stage can catch a glimpse of what the marriage relationship *could* be—a glimpse that won't let them settle for anything less.

Additional Scripture Readings:
1 Peter 4:7–11; 1 John 4:7–21

Go to page 1242 for your next devotional reading.

unfruitful. **15**So what shall I do? I will pray with my spirit, but I will also pray with my mind; I will sing with my spirit, but I will also sing with my mind. **16**If you are praising God with your spirit, how can one who finds himself among those who do not understand*a* say "Amen" to your thanksgiving, since he does not know what you are saying? **17**You may be giving thanks well enough, but the other man is not edified.

18I thank God that I speak in tongues more than all of you. **19**But in the church I would rather speak five intelligible words to instruct others than ten thousand words in a tongue.

20Brothers, stop thinking like children. In regard to evil be infants, but in your thinking be adults. **21**In the Law it is written:

"Through men of strange tongues
and through the lips of foreigners
I will speak to this people,
    but even then they will not listen to
    me,"*b*

says the Lord.

22Tongues, then, are a sign, not for believers but for unbelievers; prophecy, however, is for believers, not for unbelievers. **23**So if the whole church comes together and everyone speaks in tongues, and some who do not understand*c* or some unbelievers come in, will they not say that you are out of your mind? **24**But if an unbeliever or someone who does not understand*d* comes in while everybody is prophesying, he will be convinced by all that he is a sinner and will be judged by all, **25**and the secrets of his heart will be laid bare. So he will fall down and worship God, exclaiming, "God is really among you!"

Orderly Worship

26What then shall we say, brothers? When you come together, everyone has a hymn, or a word of instruction, a revelation, a tongue or an interpretation. All of these must be done for the strengthening of the church. **27**If anyone speaks in a tongue, two—or at the most three—should speak, one at a time, and someone must interpret. **28**If there is no interpreter, the speaker should keep quiet in the church and speak to himself and God.

29Two or three prophets should speak, and the others should weigh carefully what is said. **30**And if a revelation comes to someone who is sitting down, the first speaker should stop. **31**For you can all prophesy in turn so that everyone may be instructed and encouraged. **32**The spirits of prophets are subject to the control of prophets. **33**For God is not a God of disorder but of peace.

As in all the congregations of the saints, **34**women should remain silent in the churches. They are not allowed to speak, but must be in submission, as the Law says. **35**If they want to inquire about something, they should ask their own husbands at home; for it is disgraceful for a woman to speak in the church.

36Did the word of God originate with you? Or are you the only people it has reached? **37**If anybody thinks he is a prophet or spiritually gifted, let him acknowledge that what I am writing to you is the Lord's command. **38**If he ignores this, he himself will be ignored.*e*

39Therefore, my brothers, be eager to prophesy, and do not forbid speaking in tongues. **40**But everything should be done in a fitting and orderly way.

The Resurrection of Christ

15 Now, brothers, I want to remind you of the gospel I preached to you, which you received and on which you have taken your stand. **2**By this gospel you are saved, if you hold firmly to the word I preached to you. Otherwise, you have believed in vain.

3For what I received I passed on to you as of first importance*f*: that Christ died for our sins according to the Scriptures, **4**that he was buried, that he was raised on the third day according to the Scriptures, **5**and that he appeared to Peter,*g* and then to the Twelve. **6**After that, he appeared to more than five hundred of the brothers at the same time, most of whom are still living, though some have fallen asleep. **7**Then he appeared to James, then to all the apostles, **8**and last of all he appeared to me also, as to one abnormally born.

9For I am the least of the apostles and do not even deserve to be called an apostle, because I persecuted the church of God. **10**But by the grace of God I am what I am, and his grace to me was not without

a16 Or among the inquirers   b21 Isaiah 28:11,12   c23 Or some inquirers   d24 Or or some inquirer
e38 Some manuscripts If he is ignorant of this, let him be ignorant   f3 Or you at the first   g5 Greek Cephas

effect. No, I worked harder than all of them — yet not I, but the grace of God that was with me. **11**Whether, then, it was I or they, this is what we preach, and this is what you believed.

The Resurrection of the Dead

12But if it is preached that Christ has been raised from the dead, how can some of you say that there is no resurrection of the dead? **13**If there is no resurrection of the dead, then not even Christ has been raised. **14**And if Christ has not been raised, our preaching is useless and so is your faith. **15**More than that, we are then found to be false witnesses about God, for we have testified about God that he raised Christ from the dead. But he did not raise him if in fact the dead are not raised. **16**For if the dead are not raised, then Christ has not been raised either. **17**And if Christ has not been raised, your faith is futile; you are still in your sins. **18**Then those also who have fallen asleep in Christ are lost. **19**If only for this life we have hope in Christ, we are to be pitied more than all men.

20But Christ has indeed been raised from the dead, the firstfruits of those who have fallen asleep. **21**For since death came through a man, the resurrection of the dead comes also through a man. **22**For as in Adam all die, so in Christ all will be made alive. **23**But each in his own turn: Christ, the firstfruits; then, when he comes, those who belong to him. **24**Then the end will come, when he hands over the kingdom to God the Father after he

---

FRIDAY

VERSE FOR THE DAY:
1 Corinthians 15:57

AUTHOR:
Philip W. Williams

PASSAGE FOR THE DAY:
1 Corinthians 15:51–58

A Defeated Enemy

IN THE Old Testament it is death that the man of faith sees as a threat to his relationship with God. It was life that was to be felt and experienced in relationship with God. The stranger, death, was the mysterious visitor that could bring this meaningful, covenanted relationship with God to an end.

Jesus did little preaching or teaching about death. He didn't see death as a roadblock to our relationship with God. Jesus emphasized life and its fulfillment. His own death was overcome by his victorious resurrection. Jesus didn't say much about what happened to people after they died, but he promised everlasting life to all who believed in him.

Paul saw death as the enemy, but an enemy defeated by Christ. Death is our foe, but "thanks be to God! He gives us the victory through our Lord Jesus Christ." We take heart and hope in this resurrection victory . . .

Dear Father, my death and the deaths of people I love are a mystery. Although I may not give up searching out the mystery, I do not want to torture myself to know the unknowable. You have penetrated and conquered it. My hope is in you; I need no more. Your saving grace is enough. Thank you, through Christ my Lord. Amen.

Additional Scripture Readings:
Romans 8:31–39; Hebrews 2:14–18

Go to page 1244 for your next devotional reading.

has destroyed all dominion, authority and power. **25**For he must reign until he has put all his enemies under his feet. **26**The last enemy to be destroyed is death. **27**For he "has put everything under his feet."*a* Now when it says that "everything" has been put under him, it is clear that this does not include God himself, who put everything under Christ. **28**When he has done this, then the Son himself will be made subject to him who put everything under him, so that God may be all in all.

29Now if there is no resurrection, what will those do who are baptized for the dead? If the dead are not raised at all, why are people baptized for them? **30**And as for us, why do we endanger ourselves every hour? **31**I die every day—I mean that, brothers—just as surely as I glory over you in Christ Jesus our Lord. **32**If I fought wild beasts in Ephesus for merely human reasons, what have I gained? If the dead are not raised,

"Let us eat and drink,
  for tomorrow we die."*b*

33Do not be misled: "Bad company corrupts good character." **34**Come back to your senses as you ought, and stop sinning; for there are some who are ignorant of God—I say this to your shame.

The Resurrection Body

35But someone may ask, "How are the dead raised? With what kind of body will they come?" **36**How foolish! What you sow does not come to life unless it dies. **37**When you sow, you do not plant the body that will be, but just a seed, perhaps of wheat or of something else. **38**But God gives it a body as he has determined, and to each kind of seed he gives its own body. **39**All flesh is not the same: Men have one kind of flesh, animals have another, birds another and fish another. **40**There are also heavenly bodies and there are earthly bodies; but the splendor of the heavenly bodies is one kind, and the splendor of the earthly bodies is another. **41**The sun has one kind of splendor, the moon another and the stars another; and star differs from star in splendor.

42So will it be with the resurrection of the dead. The body that is sown is perishable, it is raised imperishable; **43**it is sown in dishonor, it is raised in glory; it is sown in weakness, it is raised in power; **44**it is

sown a natural body, it is raised a spiritual body.

If there is a natural body, there is also a spiritual body. **45**So it is written: "The first man Adam became a living being"*c*; the last Adam, a life-giving spirit. **46**The spiritual did not come first, but the natural, and after that the spiritual. **47**The first man was of the dust of the earth, the second man from heaven. **48**As was the earthly man, so are those who are of the earth; and as is the man from heaven, so also are those who are of heaven. **49**And just as we have borne the likeness of the earthly man, so shall we*d* bear the likeness of the man from heaven.

50I declare to you, brothers, that flesh and blood cannot inherit the kingdom of God, nor does the perishable inherit the imperishable. **51**Listen, I tell you a mystery: We will not all sleep, but we will all be changed— **52**in a flash, in the twinkling of an eye, at the last trumpet. For the trumpet will sound, the dead will be raised imperishable, and we will be changed. **53**For the perishable must clothe itself with the imperishable, and the mortal with immortality. **54**When the perishable has been clothed with the imperishable, and the mortal with immortality, then the saying that is written will come true: "Death has been swallowed up in victory."*e*

55"Where, O death, is your victory?
  Where, O death, is your sting?"*f*

56The sting of death is sin, and the power of sin is the law. **57**But thanks be to God! He gives us the victory through our Lord Jesus Christ.

58Therefore, my dear brothers, stand firm. Let nothing move you. Always give yourselves fully to the work of the Lord, because you know that your labor in the Lord is not in vain.

The Collection for God's People

16 Now about the collection for God's people: Do what I told the Galatian churches to do. **2**On the first day of every week, each one of you should set aside a sum of money in keeping with his income, saving it up, so that when I come no collections will have to be made. **3**Then, when I arrive, I will give letters of introduction to the men you approve and send them with your gift to Jerusalem. **4**If it

---

a27 Psalm 8:6   *b32* Isaiah 22:13   *c45* Gen. 2:7   *d49* Some early manuscripts *so let us*
e54 Isaiah 25:8   *f55* Hosea 13:14

WEEKENDING

RESOLVE

More than anything else in heaven or on
earth,
I pray for the power to love my fellow
person,
to break through the damning bigotry,
the crippling prejudice,
the stifling self-centeredness
that smothers God's Spirit within me,
and to channel and communicate divine
love
to lonely, loveless people about me.
And I pray as well for the ability to translate
the message of God's eternal love into
words
that will pierce the benumbed minds of
busy men
and move their hearts to faith and
obedience.

– Leslie Brandt

REVIVE

Saturday: 1 Corinthians 14:1–5
Sunday: 1 Peter 4:7–11

Go to page 1245 for your next devotional reading.

seems advisable for me to go also, they will accompany me.

Personal Requests

5After I go through Macedonia, I will come to you — for I will be going through Macedonia. **6**Perhaps I will stay with you awhile, or even spend the winter, so that you can help me on my journey, wherever I go. **7**I do not want to see you now and make only a passing visit; I hope to spend some time with you, if the Lord permits. **8**But I will stay on at Ephesus until Pentecost, **9**because a great door for effective work has opened to me, and there are many who oppose me.

10If Timothy comes, see to it that he has nothing to fear while he is with you, for he is carrying on the work of the Lord, just as I am. **11**No one, then, should refuse to accept him. Send him on his way in peace so

---

MONDAY

VERSE FOR THE DAY: *1 Corinthians 16:13*	*AUTHOR:* *Bill Hybels*	*PASSAGE FOR THE DAY:* *1 Corinthians 16:13–14*

Be Men of Courage

FOR a marriage relationship to flourish, there must be intimacy. It takes an enormous amount of courage to say to your spouse, "This is me. I'm not proud of it — in fact, I'm a little embarrassed by it — but this is who I am." It also takes courage to look your spouse in the eye and say, "Our marriage is in serious trouble, and we've got to do something about it." What do most people do? They put their problems on the back burner and go their own directions. While they pursue their own careers and their own recreations, the marriage disintegrates from lack of courage. They did not have the courage to put on the gloves and say, "Let's fight for this marriage. Let's go to a marriage retreat. Let's see a marriage counselor. Let's get together with another couple we respect. Let's lay it out on the table and solve these problems instead of running from them." It takes courage to fight off the "greener grass" temptations, to work through layer after layer of masks, cover-ups, and defense mechanisms, to keep working on that marriage year after year. Relational courage does not apply only to the husband-wife relationship . . .

It also takes relational courage to build significant relationships with friends, to look another person in the eye and say, "Isn't it time we stopped talking about the weather and the stock market and started talking about what's going on in your life and mine? Isn't it time we became brothers?" Not many men have the courage to challenge each other, to fight for each other's spiritual and relational growth. But I have learned over the years that I will never be a success in my marriage, with my kids or with my friends, without courage.

Additional Scripture Readings:
Ephesians 6:10–18; Hebrews 3:1–6

Go to page 1248 for your next devotional reading.

that he may return to me. I am expecting him along with the brothers.

12Now about our brother Apollos: I strongly urged him to go to you with the brothers. He was quite unwilling to go now, but he will go when he has the opportunity.

13Be on your guard; stand firm in the faith; be men of courage; be strong. 14Do everything in love.

15You know that the household of Stephanas were the first converts in Achaia, and they have devoted themselves to the service of the saints. I urge you, brothers, 16to submit to such as these and to everyone who joins in the work, and labors at it. 17I was glad when Stephanas, Fortunatus and Achaicus arrived, because they have supplied what was lacking from you. 18For they refreshed my spirit and yours also. Such men deserve recognition.

Final Greetings

19The churches in the province of Asia send you greetings. Aquila and Priscilla*a* greet you warmly in the Lord, and so does the church that meets at their house. 20All the brothers here send you greetings. Greet one another with a holy kiss.

21I, Paul, write this greeting in my own hand.

22If anyone does not love the Lord — a curse be on him. Come, O Lord*b*!

23The grace of the Lord Jesus be with you.

24My love to all of you in Christ Jesus. Amen.*c*

---

a19 Greek *Prisca*, a variant of *Priscilla*   *b22* In Aramaic the expression *Come, O Lord* is *Marana tha*.
c24 Some manuscripts do not have *Amen*.

PAUL writes this second letter to the church in Corinth from Macedonia (Acts 20:1; 2 Corinthians 7:5), while on his way to Corinth (2 Corinthians 13:1). As the most personal of all his letters, he expresses both how exciting and how painful his life as a missionary has been. He also finds it necessary to defend himself against those who are criticizing him. As you read this letter, think about how exciting it can be to serve the Lord, but realize too that being a Christian can sometimes lead to pain and suffering.

2 CORINTHIANS

1 Paul, an apostle of Christ Jesus by the will of God, and Timothy our brother,

To the church of God in Corinth, together with all the saints throughout Achaia:

[2] Grace and peace to you from God our Father and the Lord Jesus Christ.

The God of All Comfort

[3] Praise be to the God and Father of our Lord Jesus Christ, the Father of compassion and the God of all comfort, [4] who comforts us in all our troubles, so that we can comfort those in any trouble with the comfort we ourselves have received from God. [5] For just as the sufferings of Christ flow over into our lives, so also through Christ our comfort overflows. [6] If we are distressed, it is for your comfort and salvation; if we are comforted, it is for your comfort, which produces in you patient endurance of the same sufferings we suffer. [7] And our hope for you is firm, because we know that just as you share in our sufferings, so also you share in our comfort.

[8] We do not want you to be uninformed, brothers, about the hardships we suffered in the province of Asia. We were under great pressure, far beyond our ability to endure, so that we despaired even of life.

9Indeed, in our hearts we felt the sentence of death. But this happened that we might not rely on ourselves but on God, who raises the dead. 10He has delivered us from such a deadly peril, and he will deliver us. On him we have set our hope that he will continue to deliver us, 11as you help us by your prayers. Then many will give thanks on our[a] behalf for the gracious favor granted us in answer to the prayers of many.

Paul's Change of Plans

12Now this is our boast: Our conscience testifies that we have conducted ourselves in the world, and especially in our relations with you, in the holiness and sincerity that are from God. We have done so not according to worldly wisdom but according to God's grace. 13For we do not write you anything you cannot read or understand. And I hope that, 14as you have understood us in part, you will come to

a11 Many manuscripts your

TUESDAY

VERSE FOR THE DAY:	AUTHOR:	PASSAGE FOR THE DAY:
2 Corinthians 1:9	C.S. Lewis	2 Corinthians 1:8–11

He Stoops to Conquer

GOD, who has made us, knows what we are and that our happiness lies in him. Yet we will not seek it in him as long as he leaves us any other resort where it can even plausibly be looked for. While what we call "our own life" remains agreeable we will not surrender it to him ... We are perplexed to see misfortune falling upon decent, inoffensive, worthy people—on capable, hard-working mothers of families or diligent, thrifty little tradespeople, on those who have worked so hard, and so honestly, for their modest stock of happiness and now seem to be entering on the enjoyment of it with the fullest right ...

Let me implore the reader to try to believe, if only for the moment, that God, who made these deserving people, may really be right when he thinks that their modest prosperity and the happiness of their children are not enough to make them blessed: that all this must fall from them in the end, and that if they have not learned to know him they will be wretched. And therefore he troubles them, warning them in advance on an insufficiency that one day they will have to discover ... I call this a Divine humility because it is a poor thing to strike our colors to God when the ship is going down under us; a poor thing to come to him as a last resort, to offer up "our own" when it is no longer worth keeping. If God were proud he would hardly have us on such terms: but he is not proud, he stoops to conquer, he will have us even though we have shown that we prefer everything else to him, and come to him because there is "nothing better" now to be had.

Additional Scripture Readings:
Psalm 146; Jeremiah 17:5–8

Go to page 1252 for your next devotional reading.

understand fully that you can boast of us just as we will boast of you in the day of the Lord Jesus.

[15]Because I was confident of this, I planned to visit you first so that you might benefit twice. [16]I planned to visit you on my way to Macedonia and to come back to you from Macedonia, and then to have you send me on my way to Judea. [17]When I planned this, did I do it lightly? Or do I make my plans in a worldly manner so that in the same breath I say, "Yes, yes" and "No, no"?

[18]But as surely as God is faithful, our message to you is not "Yes" and "No." [19]For the Son of God, Jesus Christ, who was preached among you by me and Silas[a] and Timothy, was not "Yes" and "No," but in him it has always been "Yes." [20]For no matter how many promises God has made, they are "Yes" in Christ. And so through him the "Amen" is spoken by us to the glory of God. [21]Now it is God who makes both us and you stand firm in Christ. He anointed us, [22]set his seal of ownership on us, and put his Spirit in our hearts as a deposit, guaranteeing what is to come.

[23]I call God as my witness that it was in order to spare you that I did not return to Corinth. [24]Not that we lord it over your faith, but we work with you for your joy, because it is by faith you stand firm. [2][1]So I made up my mind that I would not make another painful visit to you. [2]For if I grieve you, who is left to make me glad but you whom I have grieved? [3]I wrote as I did so that when I came I should not be distressed by those who ought to make me rejoice. I had confidence in all of you, that you would all share my joy. [4]For I wrote you out of great distress and anguish of heart and with many tears, not to grieve you but to let you know the depth of my love for you.

Forgiveness for the Sinner

[5]If anyone has caused grief, he has not so much grieved me as he has grieved all of you, to some extent—not to put it too severely. [6]The punishment inflicted on him by the majority is sufficient for him. [7]Now instead, you ought to forgive and comfort him, so that he will not be overwhelmed by excessive sorrow. [8]I urge you, therefore, to reaffirm your love for him. [9]The reason I wrote you was to see

if you would stand the test and be obedient in everything. [10]If you forgive anyone, I also forgive him. And what I have forgiven—if there was anything to forgive—I have forgiven in the sight of Christ for your sake, [11]in order that Satan might not outwit us. For we are not unaware of his schemes.

Ministers of the New Covenant

[12]Now when I went to Troas to preach the gospel of Christ and found that the Lord had opened a door for me, [13]I still had no peace of mind, because I did not find my brother Titus there. So I said good-by to them and went on to Macedonia.

[14]But thanks be to God, who always leads us in triumphal procession in Christ and through us spreads everywhere the fragrance of the knowledge of him. [15]For we are to God the aroma of Christ among those who are being saved and those who are perishing. [16]To the one we are the smell of death; to the other, the fragrance of life. And who is equal to such a task? [17]Unlike so many, we do not peddle the word of God for profit. On the contrary, in Christ we speak before God with sincerity, like men sent from God.

[3] Are we beginning to commend ourselves again? Or do we need, like some people, letters of recommendation to you or from you? [2]You yourselves are our letter, written on our hearts, known and read by everybody. [3]You show that you are a letter from Christ, the result of our ministry, written not with ink but with the Spirit of the living God, not on tablets of stone but on tablets of human hearts.

[4]Such confidence as this is ours through Christ before God. [5]Not that we are competent in ourselves to claim anything for ourselves, but our competence comes from God. [6]He has made us competent as ministers of a new covenant—not of the letter but of the Spirit; for the letter kills, but the Spirit gives life.

The Glory of the New Covenant

[7]Now if the ministry that brought death, which was engraved in letters on stone, came with glory, so that the Israelites could not look steadily at the face of Moses because of its glory, fading though it was, [8]will not the ministry of the Spirit be even more glorious? [9]If the ministry that condemns men is glorious, how much

---

[a]19 Greek *Silvanus*, a variant of *Silas*

more glorious is the ministry that brings righteousness! [10]For what was glorious has no glory now in comparison with the surpassing glory. [11]And if what was fading away came with glory, how much greater is the glory of that which lasts!

[12]Therefore, since we have such a hope, we are very bold. [13]We are not like Moses, who would put a veil over his face to keep the Israelites from gazing at it while the radiance was fading away. [14]But their minds were made dull, for to this day the same veil remains when the old covenant is read. It has not been removed, because only in Christ is it taken away. [15]Even to this day when Moses is read, a veil covers their hearts. [16]But whenever anyone turns to the Lord, the veil is taken away. [17]Now the Lord is the Spirit, and where the Spirit of the Lord is, there is freedom. [18]And we, who with unveiled faces all reflect[a] the Lord's glory, are being transformed into his likeness with ever-increasing glory, which comes from the Lord, who is the Spirit.

Treasures in Jars of Clay

4 Therefore, since through God's mercy we have this ministry, we do not lose heart. [2]Rather, we have renounced secret and shameful ways; we do not use deception, nor do we distort the word of God. On the contrary, by setting forth the truth plainly we commend ourselves to every man's conscience in the sight of God. [3]And even if our gospel is veiled, it is veiled to those who are perishing. [4]The god of this age has blinded the minds of unbelievers, so that they cannot see the light of the gospel of the glory of Christ, who is the image of God. [5]For we do not preach ourselves, but Jesus Christ as Lord, and ourselves as your servants for Jesus' sake. [6]For God, who said, "Let light shine out of darkness,"[b] made his light shine in our hearts to give us the light of the knowledge of the glory of God in the face of Christ.

[7]But we have this treasure in jars of clay to show that this all-surpassing power is from God and not from us. [8]We are hard pressed on every side, but not crushed; perplexed, but not in despair; [9]persecuted, but not abandoned; struck down, but not destroyed. [10]We always carry around in our body the death of Jesus, so that the life of Jesus may also be revealed in our body. [11]For we who are alive are always

being given over to death for Jesus' sake, so that his life may be revealed in our mortal body. [12]So then, death is at work in us, but life is at work in you.

[13]It is written: "I believed; therefore I have spoken."[c] With that same spirit of faith we also believe and therefore speak, [14]because we know that the one who raised the Lord Jesus from the dead will also raise us with Jesus and present us with you in his presence. [15]All this is for your benefit, so that the grace that is reaching more and more people may cause thanksgiving to overflow to the glory of God.

[16]Therefore we do not lose heart. Though outwardly we are wasting away, yet inwardly we are being renewed day by day. [17]For our light and momentary troubles are achieving for us an eternal glory that far outweighs them all. [18]So we fix our eyes not on what is seen, but on what is unseen. For what is seen is temporary, but what is unseen is eternal.

Our Heavenly Dwelling

5 Now we know that if the earthly tent we live in is destroyed, we have a building from God, an eternal house in heaven, not built by human hands. [2]Meanwhile we groan, longing to be clothed with our heavenly dwelling, [3]because when we are clothed, we will not be found naked. [4]For while we are in this tent, we groan and are burdened, because we do not wish to be unclothed but to be clothed with our heavenly dwelling, so that what is mortal may be swallowed up by life. [5]Now it is God who has made us for this very purpose and has given us the Spirit as a deposit, guaranteeing what is to come.

[6]Therefore we are always confident and know that as long as we are at home in the body we are away from the Lord. [7]We live by faith, not by sight. [8]We are confident, I say, and would prefer to be away from the body and at home with the Lord. [9]So we make it our goal to please him, whether we are at home in the body or away from it. [10]For we must all appear before the judgment seat of Christ, that each one may receive what is due him for the things done while in the body, whether good or bad.

The Ministry of Reconciliation

[11]Since, then, we know what it is to fear

---

[a]18 Or *contemplate*   [b]6 Gen. 1:3   [c]13 Psalm 116:10

the Lord, we try to persuade men. What we are is plain to God, and I hope it is also plain to your conscience. [12]We are not trying to commend ourselves to you again, but are giving you an opportunity to take pride in us, so that you can answer those who take pride in what is seen rather than in what is in the heart. [13]If we are out of our mind, it is for the sake of God; if we are in our right mind, it is for you. [14]For Christ's love compels us, because we are convinced that one died for all, and therefore all died. [15]And he died for all, that those who live should no longer live for themselves but for him who died for them and was raised again.

[16]So from now on we regard no one from a worldly point of view. Though we once regarded Christ in this way, we do so no longer. [17]Therefore, if anyone is in Christ, he is a new creation; the old has gone, the new has come! [18]All this is from God, who reconciled us to himself through Christ and gave us the ministry of reconciliation: [19]that God was reconciling the world to himself in Christ, not counting men's sins against them. And he has committed to us the message of reconciliation. [20]We are therefore Christ's ambassadors, as though God were making his appeal through us. We implore you on Christ's behalf: Be reconciled to God. [21]God made him who had no sin to be sin[a] for us, so that in him we might become the righteousness of God.

6 As God's fellow workers we urge you not to receive God's grace in vain. [2]For he says,

"In the time of my favor I heard you,
    and in the day of salvation I helped
    you."[b]

I tell you, now is the time of God's favor, now is the day of salvation.

Paul's Hardships

[3]We put no stumbling block in anyone's path, so that our ministry will not be discredited. [4]Rather, as servants of God we commend ourselves in every way: in great endurance; in troubles, hardships and distresses; [5]in beatings, imprisonments and riots; in hard work, sleepless nights and hunger; [6]in purity, understanding, patience and kindness; in the Holy Spirit and in sincere love; [7]in truthful speech and in the power of God; with

weapons of righteousness in the right hand and in the left; [8]through glory and dishonor, bad report and good report; genuine, yet regarded as impostors; [9]known, yet regarded as unknown; dying, and yet we live on; beaten, and yet not killed; [10]sorrowful, yet always rejoicing; poor, yet making many rich; having nothing, and yet possessing everything.

[11]We have spoken freely to you, Corinthians, and opened wide our hearts to you. [12]We are not withholding our affection from you, but you are withholding yours from us. [13]As a fair exchange—I speak as to my children—open wide your hearts also.

Do Not Be Yoked With Unbelievers

[14]Do not be yoked together with unbelievers. For what do righteousness and wickedness have in common? Or what fellowship can light have with darkness? [15]What harmony is there between Christ and Belial[c]? What does a believer have in common with an unbeliever? [16]What agreement is there between the temple of God and idols? For we are the temple of the living God. As God has said: "I will live with them and walk among them, and I will be their God, and they will be my people."[d]

[17]"Therefore come out from them
    and be separate,
                    says the Lord.
Touch no unclean thing,
    and I will receive you."[e]
[18]"I will be a Father to you,
    and you will be my sons and
    daughters,
            says the Lord Almighty."[f]

7 Since we have these promises, dear friends, let us purify ourselves from everything that contaminates body and spirit, perfecting holiness out of reverence for God.

Paul's Joy

[2]Make room for us in your hearts. We have wronged no one, we have corrupted no one, we have exploited no one. [3]I do not say this to condemn you; I have said before that you have such a place in our hearts that we would live or die with you. [4]I have great confidence in you; I take great pride in you. I am greatly encour-

[a]21 Or *be a sin offering*   [b]2 Isaiah 49:8   [c]15 Greek *Beliar*, a variant of *Belial*   [d]16 Lev. 26:12; Jer. 32:38; Ezek. 37:27   [e]17 Isaiah 52:11; Ezek. 20:34,41   [f]18 2 Samuel 7:14; 7:8

aged; in all our troubles my joy knows no bounds.

5For when we came into Macedonia, this body of ours had no rest, but we were harassed at every turn—conflicts on the outside, fears within. **6**But God, who comforts the downcast, comforted us by the coming of Titus, **7**and not only by his coming but also by the comfort you had given him. He told us about your longing for me, your deep sorrow, your ardent concern for me, so that my joy was greater than ever.

8Even if I caused you sorrow by my letter, I do not regret it. Though I did regret it—I see that my letter hurt you, but only for a little while— **9**yet now I am happy, not because you were made sorry, but because your sorrow led you to repentance. For you became sorrowful as God intended and so were not harmed in any way by us. **10**Godly sorrow brings repentance that leads to salvation and leaves no regret, but worldly sorrow brings death. **11**See what this godly sorrow has produced in you: what earnestness, what eagerness to clear

---

WEDNESDAY

VERSE FOR THE DAY:	*AUTHOR:*	*PASSAGE FOR THE DAY:*
2 Corinthians 5:17	Paul Brand	2 Corinthians 5:16–21

We in Him, He in Us

[THE] unfathomable idea of an actual identity exchange is implicit in conversion. Jesus described the process in terms his hearers could understand. To Nicodemus he called it being "born again" or "born from above," indicating that spiritual life requires an identity change as drastic as a person's first entrance into the world.

As a result of this stuff-exchange, we carry within us not just the image of, or the philosophy of, or faith in, but the actual substance of God. One staggering consequence credits us with the spiritual genes of Christ; as we stand before God, we are judged on the basis of Christ's perfection, not our unworthiness. "If anyone is in Christ, he is a new creation; the old has gone, the new has come! . . . God made him who had no sin to be sin for us, so that in him we might become the righteousness of God" (2 Corinthians 5:17,21). Elsewhere, Paul underscored, "Your life is now hidden with Christ in God" (Colossians 3:3). We are "in him" and he is "in us."

Just as the complete identity code of my body inheres in each individual cell, so also the reality of God permeates every cell in his Body, linking us members with a true, organic bond. I sense that bond when I meet strangers in India or Africa or California who share my loyalty to the Head: instantly we become brothers and sisters, fellow cells in Christ's Body. I share the ecstasy of community in a universal Body that includes every man and woman in whom God resides.

Additional Scripture Readings:
Ephesians 1:15–23;
Colossians 3:1–11

*Go to page 1254 for your next
devotional reading.*

yourselves, what indignation, what alarm, what longing, what concern, what readiness to see justice done. At every point you have proved yourselves to be innocent in this matter. [12]So even though I wrote to you, it was not on account of the one who did the wrong or of the injured party, but rather that before God you could see for yourselves how devoted to us you are. [13]By all this we are encouraged.

In addition to our own encouragement, we were especially delighted to see how happy Titus was, because his spirit has been refreshed by all of you. [14]I had boasted to him about you, and you have not embarrassed me. But just as everything we said to you was true, so our boasting about you to Titus has proved to be true as well. [15]And his affection for you is all the greater when he remembers that you were all obedient, receiving him with fear and trembling. [16]I am glad I can have complete confidence in you.

Generosity Encouraged

8 And now, brothers, we want you to know about the grace that God has given the Macedonian churches. [2]Out of the most severe trial, their overflowing joy and their extreme poverty welled up in rich generosity. [3]For I testify that they gave as much as they were able, and even beyond their ability. Entirely on their own, [4]they urgently pleaded with us for the privilege of sharing in this service to the saints. [5]And they did not do as we expected, but they gave themselves first to the Lord and then to us in keeping with God's will. [6]So we urged Titus, since he had earlier made a beginning, to bring also to completion this act of grace on your part. [7]But just as you excel in everything—in faith, in speech, in knowledge, in complete earnestness and in your love for us[a]—see that you also excel in this grace of giving.

[8]I am not commanding you, but I want to test the sincerity of your love by comparing it with the earnestness of others. [9]For you know the grace of our Lord Jesus Christ, that though he was rich, yet for your sakes he became poor, so that you through his poverty might become rich.

[10]And here is my advice about what is best for you in this matter: Last year you were the first not only to give but also to have the desire to do so. [11]Now finish the work, so that your eager willingness to do it may be matched by your completion of it, according to your means. [12]For if the willingness is there, the gift is acceptable according to what one has, not according to what he does not have.

[13]Our desire is not that others might be relieved while you are hard pressed, but that there might be equality. [14]At the present time your plenty will supply what they need, so that in turn their plenty will supply what you need. Then there will be equality, [15]as it is written: "He who gathered much did not have too much, and he who gathered little did not have too little."[b]

Titus Sent to Corinth

[16]I thank God, who put into the heart of Titus the same concern I have for you. [17]For Titus not only welcomed our appeal, but he is coming to you with much enthusiasm and on his own initiative. [18]And we are sending along with him the brother who is praised by all the churches for his service to the gospel. [19]What is more, he was chosen by the churches to accompany us as we carry the offering, which we administer in order to honor the Lord himself and to show our eagerness to help. [20]We want to avoid any criticism of the way we administer this liberal gift. [21]For we are taking pains to do what is right, not only in the eyes of the Lord but also in the eyes of men.

[22]In addition, we are sending with them our brother who has often proved to us in many ways that he is zealous, and now even more so because of his great confidence in you. [23]As for Titus, he is my partner and fellow worker among you; as for our brothers, they are representatives of the churches and an honor to Christ. [24]Therefore show these men the proof of your love and the reason for our pride in you, so that the churches can see it.

9 There is no need for me to write to you about this service to the saints. [2]For I know your eagerness to help, and I have been boasting about it to the Macedonians, telling them that since last year you in Achaia were ready to give; and your enthusiasm has stirred most of them to action. [3]But I am sending the brothers in order that our boasting about you in this matter should not prove hollow, but that you may be ready, as I said you would be. [4]For if any Macedonians come with

---

[a]7 Some manuscripts *in our love for you*   [b]15 Exodus 16:18

me and find you unprepared, we—not to say anything about you—would be ashamed of having been so confident. **5**So I thought it necessary to urge the brothers to visit you in advance and finish the arrangements for the generous gift you had promised. Then it will be ready as a generous gift, not as one grudgingly given.

Sowing Generously

6Remember this: Whoever sows sparingly will also reap sparingly, and whoev-

---

THURSDAY

VERSE FOR THE DAY:	AUTHOR:	PASSAGE FOR THE DAY:
2 Corinthians 8:7	Daniel Taylor	2 Corinthians 8:1–9

Your Giving Muscles

WE SHOULD give for the same reason that we should exercise our bodies. Our muscles are made so that they are best off when forced to work. If you "save" your muscles by never making them do anything, you actually are hurting them and yourself. You haven't "spent" any energy, but, strangely, the result is you have less strength and energy than if you had. Eventually you become like a jellyfish plopped helplessly on the beach.

Something like this is true of your giving muscles as well. God has made us to be givers. It isn't something we *have* to do in order to please him so much as it's something we need to do to keep ourselves working properly. We are healthy and whole when we are both giving and receiving . . .

Giving is really more an attitude toward life than it is a specific act at one time or another. Giving people offer friendship easily; they are openhanded not only with their money but with emotions. They are quick to encourage and console. They take genuine delight in the good fortune of others. They think of strangers only as people whom they haven't happened yet to meet.

Givers have a certain openness about them. They are not aggressively competitive. They do not speak a lot about their "rights." They generally laugh a lot and have very little self-pity. They do not run constant cost-benefit analyses to see if an opportunity for generosity is to their advantage. They are not attached like lampreys to the things in their lives.

As it happens, giving is to your benefit. It doesn't make you a saint or martyr to give. In giving you are simply reflecting God's image—he who gave everything. Miserliness in all forms —monetary and emotional—diminishes us. The more we keep the less we have. And the less we are.

This is one of life's interesting paradoxes.

Additional Scripture Readings:
2 Corinthians 9:6–15;
Ephesians 4:25—5:2

Go to page 1256 for your next devotional reading.

er sows generously will also reap generously. [7] Each man should give what he has decided in his heart to give, not reluctantly or under compulsion, for God loves a cheerful giver. [8] And God is able to make all grace abound to you, so that in all things at all times, having all that you need, you will abound in every good work. [9] As it is written:

"He has scattered abroad his gifts to
    the poor;
 his righteousness endures
    forever."[a]

[10] Now he who supplies seed to the sower and bread for food will also supply and increase your store of seed and will enlarge the harvest of your righteousness. [11] You will be made rich in every way so that you can be generous on every occasion, and through us your generosity will result in thanksgiving to God.

[12] This service that you perform is not only supplying the needs of God's people but is also overflowing in many expressions of thanks to God. [13] Because of the service by which you have proved yourselves, men will praise God for the obedience that accompanies your confession of the gospel of Christ, and for your generosity in sharing with them and with everyone else. [14] And in their prayers for you their hearts will go out to you, because of the surpassing grace God has given you. [15] Thanks be to God for his indescribable gift!

Paul's Defense of His Ministry

10 By the meekness and gentleness of Christ, I appeal to you—I, Paul, who am "timid" when face to face with you, but "bold" when away! [2] I beg you that when I come I may not have to be as bold as I expect to be toward some people who think that we live by the standards of this world. [3] For though we live in the world, we do not wage war as the world does. [4] The weapons we fight with are not the weapons of the world. On the contrary, they have divine power to demolish strongholds. [5] We demolish arguments and every pretension that sets itself up against the knowledge of God, and we take captive every thought to make it obedient to Christ. [6] And we will be ready to

punish every act of disobedience, once your obedience is complete.

[7] You are looking only on the surface of things.[b] If anyone is confident that he belongs to Christ, he should consider again that we belong to Christ just as much as he. [8] For even if I boast somewhat freely about the authority the Lord gave us for building you up rather than pulling you down, I will not be ashamed of it. [9] I do not want to seem to be trying to frighten you with my letters. [10] For some say, "His letters are weighty and forceful, but in person he is unimpressive and his speaking amounts to nothing." [11] Such people should realize that what we are in our letters when we are absent, we will be in our actions when we are present.

[12] We do not dare to classify or compare ourselves with some who commend themselves. When they measure themselves by themselves and compare themselves with themselves, they are not wise. [13] We, however, will not boast beyond proper limits, but will confine our boasting to the field God has assigned to us, a field that reaches even to you. [14] We are not going too far in our boasting, as would be the case if we had not come to you, for we did get as far as you with the gospel of Christ. [15] Neither do we go beyond our limits by boasting of work done by others.[c] Our hope is that, as your faith continues to grow, our area of activity among you will greatly expand, [16] so that we can preach the gospel in the regions beyond you. For we do not want to boast about work already done in another man's territory. [17] But, "Let him who boasts boast in the Lord."[d] [18] For it is not the one who commends himself who is approved, but the one whom the Lord commends.

Paul and the False Apostles

11 I hope you will put up with a little of my foolishness; but you are already doing that. [2] I am jealous for you with a godly jealousy. I promised you to one husband, to Christ, so that I might present you as a pure virgin to him. [3] But I am afraid that just as Eve was deceived by the serpent's cunning, your minds may somehow be led astray from your sincere and pure devotion to Christ. [4] For if someone comes to you and preaches a Jesus

---

[a]9 Psalm 112:9   [b]7 Or *Look at the obvious facts*   [c]13-15 Or [13]*We, however, will not boast about things that cannot be measured, but we will boast according to the standard of measurement that the God of measure has assigned us—a measurement that relates even to you.* [14] . . . . [15]*Neither do we boast about things that cannot be measured in regard to the work done by others.*   [d]17 Jer. 9:24

other than the Jesus we preached, or if you receive a different spirit from the one you received, or a different gospel from the one you accepted, you put up with it easily enough. ⁵But I do not think I am in the least inferior to those "super-apostles." ⁶I may not be a trained speaker, but I do have knowledge. We have made this perfectly clear to you in every way.

⁷Was it a sin for me to lower myself in order to elevate you by preaching the gospel of God to you free of charge? ⁸I robbed other churches by receiving support from them so as to serve you. ⁹And when I was with you and needed something, I was not a burden to anyone, for the brothers who came from Macedonia supplied what I needed. I have kept myself from being a burden to you in any way, and will continue to do so. ¹⁰As surely as the truth of Christ is in me, nobody in the regions of Achaia will stop this boasting of mine. ¹¹Why? Because I do not love you? God knows I do! ¹²And I will keep on doing what I am doing in order to cut the ground from under those who want an opportunity to be considered equal with us in the things they boast about.

¹³For such men are false apostles, deceitful workmen, masquerading as apostles of Christ. ¹⁴And no wonder, for Satan himself masquerades as an angel of light.

FRIDAY

VERSE FOR THE DAY:
2 Corinthians 10:4

AUTHOR:
Leonard LeSourd

PASSAGE FOR THE DAY:
2 Corinthians 10:1–6

Under Enemy Attack

HUSBANDS, accept the fact that you are under attack by forces you cannot see, that you have a very real enemy in Satan who wants to destroy your marriage.

The fact that a dark force out there wants to break up your marriage should arouse your fighting spirit. "How dare he single me out!" Your home suddenly becomes a place you will go all-out to protect.

As a husband you need to understand exactly what spiritual warfare is. This is not difficult. There are many books on the subject. More and more churches are dealing with it.

Most important for every husband is to accept the authority the Lord gives him when he becomes the spiritual head of his home.

With this authority a husband can pray against the dark forces he may feel pressing in on him and his family. He prays this way against sickness, against temptations, against forces in his community that would corrupt his children. The prayer for his home could go like this: Lord, with the authority you gave me as the head of this household, I come against all perverse spirits, against principalities and the forces of darkness that are trying to upset the peace and order of our home. In the name of Jesus I rebuke these spirits and cast them out. They have no ground in this house. I pray now that you would fill this place with your Spirit, your love, your peace, your joy.

Additional Scripture Readings:
Ephesians 6:10–18;
Hebrews 2:14–18

Go to page 1258 for your next devotional reading.

15It is not surprising, then, if his servants masquerade as servants of righteousness. Their end will be what their actions deserve.

Paul Boasts About His Sufferings

16I repeat: Let no one take me for a fool. But if you do, then receive me just as you would a fool, so that I may do a little boasting. 17In this self-confident boasting I am not talking as the Lord would, but as a fool. 18Since many are boasting in the way the world does, I too will boast. 19You gladly put up with fools since you are so wise! 20In fact, you even put up with anyone who enslaves you or exploits you or takes advantage of you or pushes himself forward or slaps you in the face. 21To my shame I admit that we were too weak for that!

What anyone else dares to boast about—I am speaking as a fool—I also dare to boast about. 22Are they Hebrews? So am I. Are they Israelites? So am I. Are they Abraham's descendants? So am I. 23Are they servants of Christ? (I am out of my mind to talk like this.) I am more. I have worked much harder, been in prison more frequently, been flogged more severely, and been exposed to death again and again. 24Five times I received from the Jews the forty lashes minus one. 25Three times I was beaten with rods, once I was stoned, three times I was shipwrecked, I spent a night and a day in the open sea, 26I have been constantly on the move. I have been in danger from rivers, in danger from bandits, in danger from my own countrymen, in danger from Gentiles; in danger in the city, in danger in the country, in danger at sea; and in danger from false brothers. 27I have labored and toiled and have often gone without sleep; I have known hunger and thirst and have often gone without food; I have been cold and naked. 28Besides everything else, I face daily the pressure of my concern for all the churches. 29Who is weak, and I do not feel weak? Who is led into sin, and I do not inwardly burn?

30If I must boast, I will boast of the things that show my weakness. 31The God and Father of the Lord Jesus, who is to be praised forever, knows that I am not lying. 32In Damascus the governor under King Aretas had the city of the Damascenes guarded in order to arrest me. 33But I was lowered in a basket from a window in the wall and slipped through his hands.

Paul's Vision and His Thorn

12 I must go on boasting. Although there is nothing to be gained, I will go on to visions and revelations from the Lord. 2I know a man in Christ who fourteen years ago was caught up to the third heaven. Whether it was in the body or out of the body I do not know—God knows. 3And I know that this man—whether in the body or apart from the body I do not know, but God knows— 4was caught up to paradise. He heard inexpressible things, things that man is not permitted to tell. 5I will boast about a man like that, but I will not boast about myself, except about my weaknesses. 6Even if I should choose to boast, I would not be a fool, because I would be speaking the truth. But I refrain, so no one will think more of me than is warranted by what I do or say.

7To keep me from becoming conceited because of these surpassingly great revelations, there was given me a thorn in my flesh, a messenger of Satan, to torment me. 8Three times I pleaded with the Lord to take it away from me. 9But he said to me, "My grace is sufficient for you, for my power is made perfect in weakness." Therefore I will boast all the more gladly about my weaknesses, so that Christ's power may rest on me. 10That is why, for Christ's sake, I delight in weaknesses, in insults, in hardships, in persecutions, in difficulties. For when I am weak, then I am strong.

Paul's Concern for the Corinthians

11I have made a fool of myself, but you drove me to it. I ought to have been commended by you, for I am not in the least inferior to the "super-apostles," even though I am nothing. 12The things that mark an apostle—signs, wonders and miracles—were done among you with great perseverance. 13How were you inferior to the other churches, except that I was never a burden to you? Forgive me this wrong!

14Now I am ready to visit you for the third time, and I will not be a burden to you, because what I want is not your possessions but you. After all, children should not have to save up for their parents, but parents for their children. 15So I will very gladly spend for you everything I have and expend myself as well. If I love you more, will you love me less? 16Be that as it may, I have not been a burden to you. Yet, crafty fellow that I am, I caught you

WEEKENDING

REALIZE

Persistent, faithful, plodding belief and hope are necessary if we are to remain free to give. Despair, which descends by dungeon steps to depression, is one of the major afflictions in our society. People seek relief from it sometimes in entertainment, sometimes in violence. Christians make their way out of it step by step, sometimes with great effort, on hardly visible footholds of sharing. The besetting temptation of the life of the Spirit is simply to quit.

– *Eugene H. Peterson*

REJOICE

Giving and gratitude go together like humor and laughter, like having one's back rubbed and the sigh that follows, like a blowing wind and the murmur of wind chimes. Gratitude keeps alive the rhythm of grace given and grace grateful, a lively lilt that lightens a heavy world.

– *Lewis B. Smedes*

REVIVE

Saturday: 2 Corinthians 9:6–15
Sunday: Galatians 6:7–10

Go to page 1259 for your next devotional reading.

by trickery! **17**Did I exploit you through any of the men I sent you? **18**I urged Titus to go to you and I sent our brother with him. Titus did not exploit you, did he? Did we not act in the same spirit and follow the same course?

19Have you been thinking all along that we have been defending ourselves to you? We have been speaking in the sight of God as those in Christ; and everything we do, dear friends, is for your strengthening. **20**For I am afraid that when I come I may not find you as I want you to be, and you may not find me as you want me to be. I fear that there may be quarreling, jealou-sy, outbursts of anger, factions, slander, gossip, arrogance and disorder. **21**I am afraid that when I come again my God will humble me before you, and I will be grieved over many who have sinned earli-er and have not repented of the impurity, sexual sin and debauchery in which they have indulged.

Final Warnings

13 This will be my third visit to you. "Every matter must be established by the testimony of two or three wit-nesses."*a* **2**I already gave you a warning when I was with you the second time. I

a1 Deut. 19:15

MONDAY

VERSE FOR THE DAY:	AUTHOR:	PASSAGE FOR THE DAY:
2 Corinthians 12:14	D. Bruce Lockerbie	2 Corinthians 12:14–18

Here to Stay

THE main reason why a father's task, no less than a mother's, is the toughest job in the world is that it never ends. The chal-lenges are daily, weekly, monthly, year after year. Being a par-ent is a full-time job with no reprieve, no time off even for ill-ness and recuperation. Children, we soon discover, are *here to stay* for at least a score of years. They don't appear like robins in the spring, then fly away at summer's end; or if, as it some-times seems, they do come and go during high school and col-lege years, their absence in no way lessens our burden of re-sponsibility. In fact, as our children get older, instead of relaxing, our task seemingly intensifies.

"It's the only job I know," says Ted Hutchens, a father with two daughters still at home and a son away at college, "that never seems to get any easier, in spite of all those years of ex-perience". . .

The point is clear: Once a parent, always a parent. Fathers and mothers alike, we don't stop caring just because we're no longer the main providers of shelter, food and the comforts of home. It's not merely our bounden duty, as *The Book of Com-mon Prayer* says, as biological parents of these children; it's also our joyful pleasure to care for them, even after they no longer seem to need us.

Additional Scripture Readings:
Philippians 2:14–18;
1 Thessalonians 2:1–12

Go to page 1262 for your next devotional reading.

now repeat it while absent: On my return I will not spare those who sinned earlier or any of the others, ³since you are demanding proof that Christ is speaking through me. He is not weak in dealing with you, but is powerful among you. ⁴For to be sure, he was crucified in weakness, yet he lives by God's power. Likewise, we are weak in him, yet by God's power we will live with him to serve you.

⁵Examine yourselves to see whether you are in the faith; test yourselves. Do you not realize that Christ Jesus is in you — unless, of course, you fail the test? ⁶And I trust that you will discover that we have not failed the test. ⁷Now we pray to God that you will not do anything wrong. Not that people will see that we have stood the test but that you will do what is right even though we may seem to have

failed. ⁸For we cannot do anything against the truth, but only for the truth. ⁹We are glad whenever we are weak but you are strong; and our prayer is for your perfection. ¹⁰This is why I write these things when I am absent, that when I come I may not have to be harsh in my use of authority — the authority the Lord gave me for building you up, not for tearing you down.

Final Greetings

¹¹Finally, brothers, good-by. Aim for perfection, listen to my appeal, be of one mind, live in peace. And the God of love and peace will be with you.

¹²Greet one another with a holy kiss. ¹³All the saints send their greetings.

¹⁴May the grace of the Lord Jesus Christ, and the love of God, and the fellowship of the Holy Spirit be with you all.

PAUL writes this letter to the churches he founded in Galatia (Acts 13:13–14:28), warning them against certain false teachers. He reminds them of the simple message of salvation by faith alone, which he and other church leaders teach, and concludes with advice on how to live a Spirit-filled life. As you read this book, be sure that you are saved by a personal faith in Jesus, and ask God's Spirit to help you walk in Christian love and peace.

GALATIANS

1 Paul, an apostle — sent not from men nor by man, but by Jesus Christ and God the Father, who raised him from the dead — [2]and all the brothers with me,

To the churches in Galatia:

[3]Grace and peace to you from God our Father and the Lord Jesus Christ, [4]who gave himself for our sins to rescue us from the present evil age, according to the will of our God and Father, [5]to whom be glory for ever and ever. Amen.

No Other Gospel

[6]I am astonished that you are so quickly deserting the one who called you by the grace of Christ and are turning to a different gospel — [7]which is really no gospel at all. Evidently some people are throwing you into confusion and are trying to pervert the gospel of Christ. [8]But even if we or an angel from heaven should preach a gospel other than the one we preached to you, let him be eternally condemned! [9]As we have already said, so now I say again: If anybody is preaching to you a gospel other than what you accepted, let him be eternally condemned!

[10]Am I now trying to win the approval of men, or of God? Or am I trying to please men? If I were still trying to please men, I would not be a servant of Christ.

Paul Called by God

11I want you to know, brothers, that the gospel I preached is not something that man made up. **12**I did not receive it from any man, nor was I taught it; rather, I received it by revelation from Jesus Christ.

13For you have heard of my previous way of life in Judaism, how intensely I persecuted the church of God and tried to destroy it. **14**I was advancing in Judaism beyond many Jews of my own age and was extremely zealous for the traditions of my fathers. **15**But when God, who set

---

TUESDAY

VERSE FOR THE DAY:	AUTHOR:	PASSAGE FOR THE DAY:
Galatians 1:4	W. Phillip Keller	Galatians 1:1–5

Friend, Not Foe

SO MANY people are of the opinion that because God is an infinite being he is beyond our human comprehension. They have the notion he is someone distant, far removed from us, who may be appealed to only in great extremity across spans of space.

The truth is just the opposite. He is our Father, our Friend, and can be our Companion on the path of life. Such an association becomes the most cherished relationship in the world. But it can only become such if we begin to understand God's character and the wondrous ways in which he deals with us . . .

Most human beings have despised and rejected God simply because they never grasped *who he was* and *what he was like.* They saw him as a foe, not a friend.

This explains why Christ called out in profound pathos —while the iron spikes tore through his hands and his feet —*"Father, forgive them, for they do not know what they are doing"* [Luke 23:34, italics added]. It was the intense heart-cry of our compassionate, caring God giving us himself, sharing with us his own life, in a superb act of selfless self-sacrifice.

This caliber of divine love eludes us mortals. We are, for the most part, so selfish, so self-centered, so self-preoccupied, we recoil from those spike-torn hands extended to us in mercy, compassion and deep longing. We simply refuse to believe anyone truly can care for us with such pure motives.

Yes, across the terrible, tortured, tragic centuries of our human history mankind has rejected God. They have assumed always that like themselves he was at heart a tyrant—a stern and unjust judge, a formidable potentate to be feared. All because they seldom understood him. They knew nothing of him in intimate, firsthand communion.

Additional Scripture Readings:
John 15:9–17; Romans 5:1–11

Go to page 1264 for your next devotional reading.

me apart from birth[a] and called me by his grace, was pleased [16]to reveal his Son in me so that I might preach him among the Gentiles, I did not consult any man, [17]nor did I go up to Jerusalem to see those who were apostles before I was, but I went immediately into Arabia and later returned to Damascus.

[18]Then after three years, I went up to Jerusalem to get acquainted with Peter[b] and stayed with him fifteen days. [19]I saw none of the other apostles — only James, the Lord's brother. [20]I assure you before God that what I am writing you is no lie. [21]Later I went to Syria and Cilicia. [22]I was personally unknown to the churches of Judea that are in Christ. [23]They only heard the report: "The man who formerly persecuted us is now preaching the faith he once tried to destroy." [24]And they praised God because of me.

Paul Accepted by the Apostles

2 Fourteen years later I went up again to Jerusalem, this time with Barnabas. I took Titus along also. [2]I went in response to a revelation and set before them the gospel that I preach among the Gentiles. But I did this privately to those who seemed to be leaders, for fear that I was running or had run my race in vain. [3]Yet not even Titus, who was with me, was compelled to be circumcised, even though he was a Greek. [4]This matter arose, because some false brothers had infiltrated our ranks to spy on the freedom we have in Christ Jesus and to make us slaves. [5]We did not give in to them for a moment, so that the truth of the gospel might remain with you.

[6]As for those who seemed to be important — whatever they were makes no difference to me; God does not judge by external appearance — those men added nothing to my message. [7]On the contrary, they saw that I had been entrusted with the task of preaching the gospel to the Gentiles,[c] just as Peter had been to the Jews.[d] [8]For God, who was at work in the ministry of Peter as an apostle to the Jews, was also at work in my ministry as an apostle to the Gentiles. [9]James, Peter[e] and John, those reputed to be pillars, gave me and Barnabas the right hand of fellowship when they recognized the grace given to me. They agreed that we should go

to the Gentiles, and they to the Jews. [10]All they asked was that we should continue to remember the poor, the very thing I was eager to do.

Paul Opposes Peter

[11]When Peter came to Antioch, I opposed him to his face, because he was clearly in the wrong. [12]Before certain men came from James, he used to eat with the Gentiles. But when they arrived, he began to draw back and separate himself from the Gentiles because he was afraid of those who belonged to the circumcision group. [13]The other Jews joined him in his hypocrisy, so that by their hypocrisy even Barnabas was led astray.

[14]When I saw that they were not acting in line with the truth of the gospel, I said to Peter in front of them all, "You are a Jew, yet you live like a Gentile and not like a Jew. How is it, then, that you force Gentiles to follow Jewish customs?

[15]"We who are Jews by birth and not 'Gentile sinners' [16]know that a man is not justified by observing the law, but by faith in Jesus Christ. So we, too, have put our faith in Christ Jesus that we may be justified by faith in Christ and not by observing the law, because by observing the law no one will be justified.

[17]"If, while we seek to be justified in Christ, it becomes evident that we ourselves are sinners, does that mean that Christ promotes sin? Absolutely not! [18]If I rebuild what I destroyed, I prove that I am a lawbreaker. [19]For through the law I died to the law so that I might live for God. [20]I have been crucified with Christ and I no longer live, but Christ lives in me. The life I live in the body, I live by faith in the Son of God, who loved me and gave himself for me. [21]I do not set aside the grace of God, for if righteousness could be gained through the law, Christ died for nothing!"[f]

Faith or Observance of the Law

3 You foolish Galatians! Who has bewitched you? Before your very eyes Jesus Christ was clearly portrayed as crucified. [2]I would like to learn just one thing from you: Did you receive the Spirit by observing the law, or by believing what you heard? [3]Are you so foolish? After beginning with the Spirit, are you now trying to

---

a15 Or *from my mother's womb*   b18 Greek *Cephas*   c7 Greek *uncircumcised*   d7 Greek *circumcised*; also in verses 8 and 9   e9 Greek *Cephas*; also in verses 11 and 14   f21 Some interpreters end the quotation after verse 14.

attain your goal by human effort? **⁴**Have you suffered so much for nothing — if it really was for nothing? **⁵**Does God give you his Spirit and work miracles among you because you observe the law, or because you believe what you heard?

⁶Consider Abraham: "He believed God, and it was credited to him as righteousness."*ᵃ* **⁷**Understand, then, that those who believe are children of Abraham. **⁸**The Scripture foresaw that God would justify the Gentiles by faith, and announced the gospel in advance to Abraham: "All nations will be blessed through you."*ᵇ* **⁹**So those who have faith are blessed along with Abraham, the man of faith.

¹⁰All who rely on observing the law are under a curse, for it is written: "Cursed is everyone who does not continue to do everything written in the Book of the Law."*ᶜ* **¹¹**Clearly no one is justified before

ᵃ6 Gen. 15:6   *ᵇ8* Gen. 12:3; 18:18; 22:18   *ᶜ10* Deut. 27:26

WEDNESDAY

VERSE FOR THE DAY:
Galatians 2:10

AUTHOR:
Doug Sherman and
William Hendricks

PASSAGE FOR THE DAY:
Galatians 2:6–10

Remember the Poor

THROUGH our work we can love others and love ourselves. We can love others by serving their needs through the goods we help produce or distribute, or through the services we help provide. And we can love ourselves by gaining an income to provide for our needs and the needs of our families.

But Scripture adds a purely benevolent purpose to work: to earn money in order to give it away to others. In fact, the overwhelming thrust of the Scriptures is that as God sees fit to prosper us, our abundance should begin to spill over and start benefiting others who, for a variety of reasons, are in need. For example, in Psalm 37:25–26, the writer looks back on his life and says: "I was young and now I am old, yet I have never seen the righteous forsaken or their children begging bread. They are always generous and lend freely; their children will be blessed." In other words, as God has prospered the righteous person and his family, it results in generosity toward others . . .

Giving some portion of your income away is a discipline and a privilege taught by Scripture. I believe every Christian, no matter what his level of lifestyle, should use part of his money to meet the financial and material needs of others . . .

God is deeply concerned to see us meet their [the poor's] needs. His concern does not arise because the poor are inherently better but because they are needy. And from the beginning of creation, he has desired to meet human needs. He wants to meet some of them through you and me.

Additional Scripture Readings:
Psalm 72:1–14; 1 Timothy 6:17–19

Go to page 1266 for your next devotional reading.

God by the law, because, "The righteous will live by faith."*a* 12The law is not based on faith; on the contrary, "The man who does these things will live by them."*b* 13Christ redeemed us from the curse of the law by becoming a curse for us, for it is written: "Cursed is everyone who is hung on a tree."*c* 14He redeemed us in order that the blessing given to Abraham might come to the Gentiles through Christ Jesus, so that by faith we might receive the promise of the Spirit.

The Law and the Promise

15Brothers, let me take an example from everyday life. Just as no one can set aside or add to a human covenant that has been duly established, so it is in this case. 16The promises were spoken to Abraham and to his seed. The Scripture does not say "and to seeds," meaning many people, but "and to your seed,"*d* meaning one person, who is Christ. 17What I mean is this: The law, introduced 430 years later, does not set aside the covenant previously established by God and thus do away with the promise. 18For if the inheritance depends on the law, then it no longer depends on a promise; but God in his grace gave it to Abraham through a promise.

19What, then, was the purpose of the law? It was added because of transgressions until the Seed to whom the promise referred had come. The law was put into effect through angels by a mediator. 20A mediator, however, does not represent just one party; but God is one.

21Is the law, therefore, opposed to the promises of God? Absolutely not! For if a law had been given that could impart life, then righteousness would certainly have come by the law. 22But the Scripture declares that the whole world is a prisoner of sin, so that what was promised, being given through faith in Jesus Christ, might be given to those who believe.

23Before this faith came, we were held prisoners by the law, locked up until faith should be revealed. 24So the law was put in charge to lead us to Christ*e* that we might be justified by faith. 25Now that faith has come, we are no longer under the supervision of the law.

Sons of God

26You are all sons of God through faith in Christ Jesus, 27for all of you who were baptized into Christ have clothed yourselves with Christ. 28There is neither Jew nor Greek, slave nor free, male nor female, for you are all one in Christ Jesus. 29If you belong to Christ, then you are Abraham's seed, and heirs according to the promise.

4 What I am saying is that as long as the heir is a child, he is no different from a slave, although he owns the whole estate. 2He is subject to guardians and trustees until the time set by his father. 3So also, when we were children, we were in slavery under the basic principles of the world. 4But when the time had fully come, God sent his Son, born of a woman, born under law, 5to redeem those under law, that we might receive the full rights of sons. 6Because you are sons, God sent the Spirit of his Son into our hearts, the Spirit who calls out, "Abba,*f* Father." 7So you are no longer a slave, but a son; and since you are a son, God has made you also an heir.

Paul's Concern for the Galatians

8Formerly, when you did not know God, you were slaves to those who by nature are not gods. 9But now that you know God — or rather are known by God — how is it that you are turning back to those weak and miserable principles? Do you wish to be enslaved by them all over again? 10You are observing special days and months and seasons and years! 11I fear for you, that somehow I have wasted my efforts on you.

12I plead with you, brothers, become like me, for I became like you. You have done me no wrong. 13As you know, it was because of an illness that I first preached the gospel to you. 14Even though my illness was a trial to you, you did not treat me with contempt or scorn. Instead, you welcomed me as if I were an angel of God, as if I were Christ Jesus himself. 15What has happened to all your joy? I can testify that, if you could have done so, you would have torn out your eyes and given them to me. 16Have I now become your enemy by telling you the truth?

17Those people are zealous to win you over, but for no good. What they want is to alienate you ⸆from us⸆, so that you may be zealous for them. 18It is fine to be zealous, provided the purpose is good, and to

*a*11 Hab. 2:4   *b*12 Lev. 18:5   *c*13 Deut. 21:23   *d*16 Gen. 12:7; 13:15; 24:7   *e*24 Or *charge until*
Christ came   *f*6 Aramaic for *Father*

be so always and not just when I am with you. **¹⁹**My dear children, for whom I am again in the pains of childbirth until Christ is formed in you, **²⁰**how I wish I could be with you now and change my tone, because I am perplexed about you!

Hagar and Sarah

²¹Tell me, you who want to be under the law, are you not aware of what the law says? **²²**For it is written that Abraham had two sons, one by the slave woman and the other by the free woman. **²³**His son by the

---

THURSDAY

VERSE FOR THE DAY:	AUTHOR:	PASSAGE FOR THE DAY:
Galatians 4:19	David Augsburger	Galatians 4:12–20

To Be a Man

MARRIAGE partners tend to become like each other, taking on the other's qualities, or developing the opposite characteristics in negative reaction to the other.

Leadership shared in mutual respect can establish a climate of dignity, freedom and responsibility, creating an atmosphere which is both comforting and stimulating to both—a Christian atmosphere. In it, each is free to grow toward personal maturity and each is eager to see the shape of Christ forming in the other (see Galatians 4:19–20).

But where one seizes power, or both struggle for control, an atmosphere of competition and conflict chokes communication and understanding. Even the unconscious assuming of power by one partner or the other will mold the relationship, perhaps in ways neither desire.

Leadership is a function which should always be shared.

Authority in one area or another is a responsibility which is mutually designated to one or the other through honest negotiation. It can be renegotiated at any time.

Life together is life shared. Shared love, shared work, shared opportunities, shared leadership, even shared initiative. Man, the nominal head, may function officially for both in public matters of leadership. Woman, recognized as his equal in partnership, leads with, and not against, him. Together, they choose to grow.

To be a man—is to possess the strength to love another, not the need to dominate over others.

To be a man—is to experience the courage to accept another, not the compulsion to be an aggressor.

To be a man—is to keep faith with human values in relationships, not to value oneself by position or possessions.

To be a man—is to be free to give love and to be free to accept love in return.

Additional Scripture Readings:
Galatians 5:13–18;
Ephesians 5:21–33

Go to page 1271 for your next devotional reading.

slave woman was born in the ordinary way; but his son by the free woman was born as the result of a promise.

²⁴These things may be taken figuratively, for the women represent two covenants. One covenant is from Mount Sinai and bears children who are to be slaves: This is Hagar. ²⁵Now Hagar stands for Mount Sinai in Arabia and corresponds to the present city of Jerusalem, because she is in slavery with her children. ²⁶But the Jerusalem that is above is free, and she is our mother. ²⁷For it is written:

"Be glad, O barren woman,
    who bears no children;
break forth and cry aloud,
    you who have no labor pains;
because more are the children of the
        desolate woman
    than of her who has a husband."ᵃ

²⁸Now you, brothers, like Isaac, are children of promise. ²⁹At that time the son born in the ordinary way persecuted the son born by the power of the Spirit. It is the same now. ³⁰But what does the Scripture say? "Get rid of the slave woman and her son, for the slave woman's son will never share in the inheritance with the free woman's son."ᵇ ³¹Therefore, brothers, we are not children of the slave woman, but of the free woman.

Freedom in Christ

5 It is for freedom that Christ has set us free. Stand firm, then, and do not let yourselves be burdened again by a yoke of slavery.

²Mark my words! I, Paul, tell you that if you let yourselves be circumcised, Christ will be of no value to you at all. ³Again I declare to every man who lets himself be circumcised that he is obligated to obey the whole law. ⁴You who are trying to be justified by law have been alienated from Christ; you have fallen away from grace. ⁵But by faith we eagerly await through the Spirit the righteousness for which we hope. ⁶For in Christ Jesus neither circumcision nor uncircumcision has any value. The only thing that counts is faith expressing itself through love.

⁷You were running a good race. Who cut in on you and kept you from obeying the truth? ⁸That kind of persuasion does not come from the one who calls you. ⁹"A little yeast works through the whole batch of dough." ¹⁰I am confident in the Lord that you will take no other view. The one who is throwing you into confusion will pay the penalty, whoever he may be. ¹¹Brothers, if I am still preaching circumcision, why am I still being persecuted? In that case the offense of the cross has been abolished. ¹²As for those agitators, I wish they would go the whole way and emasculate themselves!

¹³You, my brothers, were called to be free. But do not use your freedom to indulge the sinful natureᶜ; rather, serve one another in love. ¹⁴The entire law is summed up in a single command: "Love your neighbor as yourself."ᵈ ¹⁵If you keep on biting and devouring each other, watch out or you will be destroyed by each other.

Life by the Spirit

¹⁶So I say, live by the Spirit, and you will not gratify the desires of the sinful nature. ¹⁷For the sinful nature desires what is contrary to the Spirit, and the Spirit what is contrary to the sinful nature. They are in conflict with each other, so that you do not do what you want. ¹⁸But if you are led by the Spirit, you are not under law.

¹⁹The acts of the sinful nature are obvious: sexual immorality, impurity and debauchery; ²⁰idolatry and witchcraft; hatred, discord, jealousy, fits of rage, selfish ambition, dissensions, factions ²¹and envy; drunkenness, orgies, and the like. I warn you, as I did before, that those who live like this will not inherit the kingdom of God.

²²But the fruit of the Spirit is love, joy, peace, patience, kindness, goodness, faithfulness, ²³gentleness and self-control. Against such things there is no law. ²⁴Those who belong to Christ Jesus have crucified the sinful nature with its passions and desires. ²⁵Since we live by the Spirit, let us keep in step with the Spirit. ²⁶Let us not become conceited, provoking and envying each other.

Doing Good to All

6 Brothers, if someone is caught in a sin, you who are spiritual should restore him gently. But watch yourself, or

---

ᵃ27 Isaiah 54:1   ᵇ30 Gen. 21:10   ᶜ13 Or *the flesh*; also in verses 16, 17, 19 and 24   ᵈ14 Lev.
19:18

you also may be tempted. ²Carry each other's burdens, and in this way you will fulfill the law of Christ. ³If anyone thinks he is something when he is nothing, he deceives himself. ⁴Each one should test his own actions. Then he can take pride in himself, without comparing himself to somebody else, ⁵for each one should carry his own load.

⁶Anyone who receives instruction in the word must share all good things with his instructor.

⁷Do not be deceived: God cannot be mocked. A man reaps what he sows. ⁸The one who sows to please his sinful nature, from that nature*ᵃ* will reap destruction; the one who sows to please the Spirit, from the Spirit will reap eternal life. ⁹Let us not become weary in doing good, for at the proper time we will reap a harvest if we do not give up. ¹⁰Therefore, as we have opportunity, let us do good to all people, especially to those who belong to the family of believers.

Not Circumcision but a New Creation

¹¹See what large letters I use as I write to you with my own hand!

¹²Those who want to make a good impression outwardly are trying to compel you to be circumcised. The only reason they do this is to avoid being persecuted for the cross of Christ. ¹³Not even those who are circumcised obey the law, yet they want you to be circumcised that they may boast about your flesh. ¹⁴May I never boast except in the cross of our Lord Jesus Christ, through which*ᵇ* the world has been crucified to me, and I to the world. ¹⁵Neither circumcision nor uncircumcision means anything; what counts is a new creation. ¹⁶Peace and mercy to all who follow this rule, even to the Israel of God.

¹⁷Finally, let no one cause me trouble, for I bear on my body the marks of Jesus.

¹⁸The grace of our Lord Jesus Christ be with your spirit, brothers. Amen.

ᵃ8 Or *his flesh, from the flesh*   *ᵇ14* Or *whom*

PAUL writes this letter from prison (Ephesians 4:1; probably in Rome, see Acts 28:30–31) to the church he started in Ephesus (Acts 19). In the first half he explains God's great plan to redeem the world through Christ, showing what this means for individual Christians and for the whole church. In the second half he gives practical advice on how to live the Christian life. As you read this book, first examine yourself to be sure that you are saved. Then move on to fight against Satan and show your love to your family, your church and your community.

EPHESIANS

1 Paul, an apostle of Christ Jesus by the will of God,

To the saints in Ephesus,*a* the faithful*b* in Christ Jesus:

²Grace and peace to you from God our Father and the Lord Jesus Christ.

Spiritual Blessings in Christ

³Praise be to the God and Father of our Lord Jesus Christ, who has blessed us in the heavenly realms with every spiritual blessing in Christ. ⁴For he chose us in him before the creation of the world to be holy and blameless in his sight. In love ⁵he*c* predestined us to be adopted as his sons through Jesus Christ, in accordance with his pleasure and will— ⁶to the praise of his glorious grace, which he has freely given us in the One he loves. ⁷In him we have

---

a1 Some early manuscripts do not have *in Ephesus.* *b1* Or *believers who are* *c4,5* Or *sight in* *love. ⁵He* redemption through his blood, the forgiveness of sins, in accordance with the riches of God's grace [8]that he lavished on us with all wisdom and understanding. [9]And he[a] made known to us the mystery of his will according to his good pleasure, which he purposed in Christ, [10]to be put into effect when the times will have reached their fulfillment — to bring all things in heaven and on earth together under one head, even Christ.

[11]In him we were also chosen,[b] having been predestined according to the plan of him who works out everything in conformity with the purpose of his will, [12]in order that we, who were the first to hope in Christ, might be for the praise of his glory. [13]And you also were included in Christ when you heard the word of truth, the gospel of your salvation. Having believed, you were marked in him with a seal, the promised Holy Spirit, [14]who is a deposit guaranteeing our inheritance until the redemption of those who are God's possession — to the praise of his glory.

Thanksgiving and Prayer

[15]For this reason, ever since I heard about your faith in the Lord Jesus and your love for all the saints, [16]I have not stopped giving thanks for you, remembering you in my prayers. [17]I keep asking that the God of our Lord Jesus Christ, the glorious Father, may give you the Spirit[c] of wisdom and revelation, so that you may know him better. [18]I pray also that the eyes of your heart may be enlightened in order that you may know the hope to which he has called you, the riches of his glorious inheritance in the saints, [19]and his incomparably great power for us who believe. That power is like the working of his mighty strength, [20]which he exerted in Christ when he raised him from the dead and seated him at his right hand in the heavenly realms, [21]far above all rule and authority, power and dominion, and every title that can be given, not only in the present age but also in the one to come. [22]And God placed all things under his feet and appointed him to be head over everything for the church, [23]which is his body, the fullness of him who fills everything in every way.

Made Alive in Christ

2 As for you, you were dead in your transgressions and sins, [2]in which you used to live when you followed the ways of this world and of the ruler of the kingdom of the air, the spirit who is now at work in those who are disobedient. [3]All of us also lived among them at one time, gratifying the cravings of our sinful nature[d] and following its desires and thoughts. Like the rest, we were by nature objects of wrath. [4]But because of his great love for us, God, who is rich in mercy, [5]made us alive with Christ even when we were dead in transgressions — it is by grace you have been saved. [6]And God raised us up with Christ and seated us with him in the heavenly realms in Christ Jesus, [7]in order that in the coming ages he might show the incomparable riches of his grace, expressed in his kindness to us in Christ Jesus. [8]For it is by grace you have been saved, through faith — and this not from yourselves, it is the gift of God — [9]not by works, so that no one can boast. [10]For we are God's workmanship, created in Christ Jesus to do good works, which God prepared in advance for us to do.

One in Christ

[11]Therefore, remember that formerly you who are Gentiles by birth and called "uncircumcised" by those who call themselves "the circumcision" (that done in the body by the hands of men) — [12]remember that at that time you were separate from Christ, excluded from citizenship in Israel and foreigners to the covenants of the promise, without hope and without God in the world. [13]But now in Christ Jesus you who once were far away have been brought near through the blood of Christ.

[14]For he himself is our peace, who has made the two one and has destroyed the barrier, the dividing wall of hostility, [15]by abolishing in his flesh the law with its commandments and regulations. His purpose was to create in himself one new man out of the two, thus making peace, [16]and in this one body to reconcile both of them to God through the cross, by which he put to death their hostility. [17]He came and preached peace to you who were far away and peace to those who were near.

---

[a]8,9 Or *us. With all wisdom and understanding,* [9]*he* [b]11 Or *were made heirs*   [c]17 Or *a spirit*
[d]3 Or *our flesh*

VERSE FOR THE DAY:
Ephesians 2:8

AUTHOR:
Mark Ritchie

PASSAGE FOR THE DAY:
Ephesians 2:1–10

Saved by Grace

WHILE *working as an engineer in Afghanistan, Mark Ritchie's father had found an opportunity, despite a ban on proselytizing, to teach a new believer from the Bible.*

It was strictly forbidden for any foreigner in Afghanistan to do anything to "Christianize" an Afghan. [The Muslim passenger in our car] told me how, as a student of Western civilization, he had read about the Reformation and the arguments put forward by Erasmus and Luther on the issue of justification by faith in Jesus Christ—not by the Church's system of works.

"When I read it," he said, "I knew that this was the true way. Doing good works is one of the main tenets of Islam; without good works a person could never get to heaven. But anyone who has really tried to be good knows himself well enough to know he could never be good enough. So I became a believer in Jesus Christ. And I asked your father to help me understand more about it."

I had to admit, this was a new one on me. I had never before heard of anyone being converted to Christianity by reading a history textbook. Just wait till the publishers hear about this, I thought, while our Travelall bounced through the narrow side streets of Herat. I could just see the headlines: MUSLIM READS HISTORY BOOK—CONVERTS—DIPLOMATIC SCANDAL BREWS. This could make a textbook writer's head roll.

Once again I found myself surprised. The remote carpenter from Galilee had written his signature so powerfully across history that I found a Muslim in the farthest corner of the globe who came to the same conclusion about him as I had. It had taken me years of study to become convinced that the carpenter was God. Meanwhile, this man, raised in a Muslim home, saw it after one chapter in a Western civilization textbook.

On reflection, I wondered why I should be so surprised. Isn't this what one might expect to find if the itinerant preacher from Nazareth was as he claimed to be, the creator of the universe?

Additional Scripture Readings:
John 1:1–14; Romans 10:8–18

Go to page 1273 for your next devotional reading.

[18]For through him we both have access to the Father by one Spirit.

[19]Consequently, you are no longer foreigners and aliens, but fellow citizens with God's people and members of God's household, [20]built on the foundation of the apostles and prophets, with Christ Jesus himself as the chief cornerstone. [21]In him the whole building is joined together and rises to become a holy temple in the Lord. [22]And in him you too are being built together to become a dwelling in which God lives by his Spirit.

Paul the Preacher to the Gentiles

3 For this reason I, Paul, the prisoner of Christ Jesus for the sake of you Gentiles —

[2]Surely you have heard about the administration of God's grace that was given to me for you, [3]that is, the mystery made known to me by revelation, as I have already written briefly. [4]In reading this, then, you will be able to understand my insight into the mystery of Christ, [5]which was not made known to men in other generations as it has now been revealed by the Spirit to God's holy apostles and prophets. [6]This mystery is that through the gospel the Gentiles are heirs together with Israel, members together of one body, and sharers together in the promise in Christ Jesus.

[7]I became a servant of this gospel by the gift of God's grace given me through the working of his power. [8]Although I am less than the least of all God's people, this grace was given me: to preach to the Gentiles the unsearchable riches of Christ, [9]and to make plain to everyone the administration of this mystery, which for ages past was kept hidden in God, who created all things. [10]His intent was that now, through the church, the manifold wisdom of God should be made known to the rulers and authorities in the heavenly realms, [11]according to his eternal purpose which he accomplished in Christ Jesus our Lord. [12]In him and through faith in him we may approach God with freedom and confidence. [13]I ask you, therefore, not to be discouraged because of my sufferings for you, which are your glory.

A Prayer for the Ephesians

[14]For this reason I kneel before the Father, [15]from whom his whole family[a] in heaven and on earth derives its name. [16]I pray that out of his glorious riches he may strengthen you with power through his Spirit in your inner being, [17]so that Christ may dwell in your hearts through faith. And I pray that you, being rooted and established in love, [18]may have power, together with all the saints, to grasp how wide and long and high and deep is the love of Christ, [19]and to know this love that surpasses knowledge — that you may be filled to the measure of all the fullness of God.

[20]Now to him who is able to do immeasurably more than all we ask or imagine, according to his power that is at work within us, [21]to him be glory in the church and in Christ Jesus throughout all generations, for ever and ever! Amen.

Unity in the Body of Christ

4 As a prisoner for the Lord, then, I urge you to live a life worthy of the calling you have received. [2]Be completely humble and gentle; be patient, bearing with one another in love. [3]Make every effort to keep the unity of the Spirit through the bond of peace. [4]There is one body and one Spirit — just as you were called to one hope when you were called — [5]one Lord, one faith, one baptism; [6]one God and Father of all, who is over all and through all and in all.

[7]But to each one of us grace has been given as Christ apportioned it. [8]This is why it[b] says:

"When he ascended on high,
    he led captives in his train
    and gave gifts to men."[c]

[9](What does "he ascended" mean except that he also descended to the lower, earthly regions[d]? [10]He who descended is the very one who ascended higher than all the heavens, in order to fill the whole universe.) [11]It was he who gave some to be apostles, some to be prophets, some to be evangelists, and some to be pastors and teachers, [12]to prepare God's people for works of service, so that the body of Christ may be built up [13]until we all reach unity in the faith and in the knowledge of the Son of God and become mature, attaining to the whole measure of the fullness of Christ.

[14]Then we will no longer be infants, tossed back and forth by the waves, and blown here and there by every wind of teaching and by the cunning and crafti-

---

[a]15 Or *whom all fatherhood*   [b]8 Or *God*   [c]8 Psalm 68:18   [d]9 Or *the depths of the earth*

WEEKENDING

RETHINK

The right kind of toughness—strength of character—ought to mark the man of today . . . but not only that. Tenderness—gentleness—is equally important.

God considers it so important he places it on the list of nine qualities he feels should mark the life of his children . . .

Our goal is balance . . . always balance. Not either-or, but both-and. Not just *tough*. That alone makes a man cold, distant, intolerant, unbearable. But tough *and* tender . . . gentle, thoughtful, teachable, considerate.

– *Charles Swindoll*

REVIVE

Saturday: Galatians 5:22–23
Sunday: Ephesians 4:1–6

Go to page 1274 for your next devotional reading.

ness of men in their deceitful scheming. ¹⁵Instead, speaking the truth in love, we will in all things grow up into him who is the Head, that is, Christ. ¹⁶From him the whole body, joined and held together by every supporting ligament, grows and builds itself up in love, as each part does its work.

Living as Children of Light

¹⁷So I tell you this, and insist on it in the Lord, that you must no longer live as the Gentiles do, in the futility of their thinking. ¹⁸They are darkened in their understanding and separated from the life of God because of the ignorance that is in them due to the hardening of their hearts. ¹⁹Having lost all sensitivity, they have given themselves over to sensuality so as to indulge in every kind of impurity, with a continual lust for more.

²⁰You, however, did not come to know Christ that way. ²¹Surely you heard of him and were taught in him in accordance with the truth that is in Jesus. ²²You were taught, with regard to your former way of life, to put off your old self, which is being corrupted by its deceitful desires; ²³to be

---

MONDAY

VERSE FOR THE DAY:
Ephesians 4:16

AUTHOR:
Paul Brand

PASSAGE FOR THE DAY:
Ephesians 4:1–16

A Luxuriant Body

WHENEVER I travel overseas, I am struck anew by the world's incredible diversity, and the churches overseas are now beginning to show that cultural self-expression. For too long they were bound up in Western ways (as the early church had been bound in Jewish ways) so that hymns, dress, architecture and church names were the same around the world. Now indigenous churches are bursting out with their own spontaneous expressions of worship to God. I must guard against picturing the Body of Christ as composed only of American or British cells; it is far grander and more luxuriant than that . . .

I have learned that when God looks upon his Body, spread like an archipelago throughout the world, he sees the whole thing. And I think he, understanding the cultural backgrounds and true intent of the worshipers, likes the variety he sees.

Blacks in Murphy, North Carolina, shout their praises to God. Believers in Austria intone them, accompanied by magnificent organs and illuminated by stained glass. Some Africans dance their praise to God, following the beat of a skilled drummer. Sedate Japanese Christians express their gratitude by creating objects of beauty . . .

The Body of Christ, like our own bodies, is composed of individual, unlike cells that are knit together to form one Body. He is the whole thing, and the joy of the Body increases as individual cells realize they can be diverse without becoming isolated outposts.

Additional Scripture Readings:
Romans 12:3–8;
1 Corinthians 12:12–27

Go to page 1276 for your next devotional reading.

made new in the attitude of your minds; [24]and to put on the new self, created to be like God in true righteousness and holiness.

[25]Therefore each of you must put off falsehood and speak truthfully to his neighbor, for we are all members of one body. [26]"In your anger do not sin"[a]: Do not let the sun go down while you are still angry, [27]and do not give the devil a foothold. [28]He who has been stealing must steal no longer, but must work, doing something useful with his own hands, that he may have something to share with those in need.

[29]Do not let any unwholesome talk come out of your mouths, but only what is helpful for building others up according to their needs, that it may benefit those who listen. [30]And do not grieve the Holy Spirit of God, with whom you were sealed for the day of redemption. [31]Get rid of all bitterness, rage and anger, brawling and slander, along with every form of malice. [32]Be kind and compassionate to one another, forgiving each other, just as in Christ God forgave you.

5 Be imitators of God, therefore, as dearly loved children [2]and live a life of love, just as Christ loved us and gave himself up for us as a fragrant offering and sacrifice to God.

[3]But among you there must not be even a hint of sexual immorality, or of any kind of impurity, or of greed, because these are improper for God's holy people. [4]Nor should there be obscenity, foolish talk or coarse joking, which are out of place, but rather thanksgiving. [5]For of this you can be sure: No immoral, impure or greedy person—such a man is an idolater—has any inheritance in the kingdom of Christ and of God.[b] [6]Let no one deceive you with empty words, for because of such things God's wrath comes on those who are disobedient. [7]Therefore do not be partners with them.

[8]For you were once darkness, but now you are light in the Lord. Live as children of light [9](for the fruit of the light consists in all goodness, righteousness and truth) [10]and find out what pleases the Lord. [11]Have nothing to do with the fruitless deeds of darkness, but rather expose them. [12]For it is shameful even to mention what the disobedient do in secret. [13]But everything exposed by the light becomes visible, [14]for it is light that makes everything visible. This is why it is said:

"Wake up, O sleeper,
    rise from the dead,
and Christ will shine on you."

[15]Be very careful, then, how you live—not as unwise but as wise, [16]making the most of every opportunity, because the days are evil. [17]Therefore do not be foolish, but understand what the Lord's will is. [18]Do not get drunk on wine, which leads to debauchery. Instead, be filled with the Spirit. [19]Speak to one another with psalms, hymns and spiritual songs. Sing and make music in your heart to the Lord, [20]always giving thanks to God the Father for everything, in the name of our Lord Jesus Christ.

[21]Submit to one another out of reverence for Christ.

Wives and Husbands

[22]Wives, submit to your husbands as to the Lord. [23]For the husband is the head of the wife as Christ is the head of the church, his body, of which he is the Savior. [24]Now as the church submits to Christ, so also wives should submit to their husbands in everything.

[25]Husbands, love your wives, just as Christ loved the church and gave himself up for her [26]to make her holy, cleansing[c] her by the washing with water through the word, [27]and to present her to himself as a radiant church, without stain or wrinkle or any other blemish, but holy and blameless. [28]In this same way, husbands ought to love their wives as their own bodies. He who loves his wife loves himself. [29]After all, no one ever hated his own body, but he feeds and cares for it, just as Christ does the church— [30]for we are members of his body. [31]"For this reason a man will leave his father and mother and be united to his wife, and the two will become one flesh."[d] [32]This is a profound mystery—but I am talking about Christ and the church. [33]However, each one of you also must love his wife as he loves himself, and the wife must respect her husband.

Children and Parents

6 Children, obey your parents in the Lord, for this is right. [2]"Honor your father and mother"—which is the first commandment with a promise— [3]"that it may

---

[a]26 Psalm 4:4   [b]5 Or *kingdom of the Christ and God*   [c]26 Or *having cleansed*   [d]31 Gen. 2:24

go well with you and that you may enjoy long life on the earth."*a*

4Fathers, do not exasperate your children; instead, bring them up in the training and instruction of the Lord.

Slaves and Masters

5Slaves, obey your earthly masters with respect and fear, and with sincerity of heart, just as you would obey Christ. **6**Obey them not only to win their favor when their eye is on you, but like slaves of Christ, doing the will of God from your heart. **7**Serve wholeheartedly, as if you were serving the Lord, not men, **8**because you know that the Lord will reward everyone for whatever good he does, whether he is slave or free.

9And masters, treat your slaves in the same way. Do not threaten them, since you know that he who is both their Master and yours is in heaven, and there is no favoritism with him.

*a*3 Deut. 5:16

TUESDAY

VERSE FOR THE DAY:	AUTHOR:	PASSAGE FOR THE DAY:
Ephesians 5:22	Mike Singletary	Ephesians 5:21–33

Servant Leadership

MEN took the Scriptures and went too far. They took a man's role of headship and took it as license to rule as a superior. But man's headship was supposed to be patterned after Jesus' style of leadership: servanthood. He said that he who would be the leader should be the servant of all. He never said to keep your wife barefoot, pregnant, and in the kitchen. The Word of God is the same yesterday, today and forever. It teaches that a man is supposed to love his wife as Christ loved the church.

Too many men read the verse about wives submitting to their husbands and misread it to say that a man has the right to subject his wife. It doesn't say that. The whole passage implies that if a man loves his wife in a godly, selfless, servant-like way, she will *want* to submit to his authority. I know that very word *authority* jars the feminist and she asks, "Why should any man be in authority over me?"

If a man exercised his authority in the way it is outlined in the Bible, a woman would not resent it. She would find herself served. She would find her needs met. She would have her say, be able to exercise her gifts, not be pushed back and ignored and treated like a second-class citizen. God's design for marriage is for husbands to love their wives as Christ loved the church and for wives to respect their husbands. Christ loved the church enough to die for it, and that kind of love is worthy of respect.

Additional Scripture Readings:
Mark 10:35–45; John 13:1–17

Go to page 1277 for your next devotional reading.

The Armor of God

[10]Finally, be strong in the Lord and in his mighty power. [11]Put on the full armor of God so that you can take your stand against the devil's schemes. [12]For our struggle is not against flesh and blood, but against the rulers, against the authorities, against the powers of this dark world and against the spiritual forces of evil in the heavenly realms. [13]Therefore put on the full armor of God, so that when the day of evil comes, you may be able to stand your ground, and after you have done everything, to stand. [14]Stand firm then, with the belt of truth buckled around your waist, with the breastplate of righteousness in place, [15]and with your feet fitted with the readiness that comes from the gospel of peace. [16]In addition to all this, take up the shield of faith, with which you can extinguish all the flaming arrows of the evil one. [17]Take the helmet of salvation and the sword of the Spirit, which is the word of God. [18]And pray in the Spirit on all occasions with all kinds of prayers and requests. With this in mind, be alert and always keep on praying for all the saints.

[19]Pray also for me, that whenever I open my mouth, words may be given me so that I will fearlessly make known the mystery of the gospel, [20]for which I am an ambassador in chains. Pray that I may declare it fearlessly, as I should.

Final Greetings

[21]Tychicus, the dear brother and faithful servant in the Lord, will tell you everything, so that you also may know how I

WEDNESDAY

VERSE FOR THE DAY:
Ephesians 6:4

AUTHOR:
Stephen Arterburn and
David Stoop

PASSAGE FOR THE DAY:
Ephesians 6:1–4

Fathers Who Nurture

EXPERIENCE has shown us that the men who are happiest and most content in the masculine role today are those whose fathers invested a great deal of time and energy in their lives. These dads may have worked outside the home, as the vast majority of fathers in our society today do. But they were committed to maintaining a positive, nurturing relationship with their sons. These fathers supported their sons in their chosen careers, attempted to understand their ambitions (even when they differed from their own), and appreciated their achievements. As a result of their investment, their sons are among the most well-adjusted and peaceful husbands and fathers in our society.

However, men with these kinds of fathers are in the minority today. Most men are struggling to recover from relationships with fathers who failed to nurture, affirm and validate them at some level. These fathers have left their sons a legacy of pain, confusion, frustration, anxiety, bitterness, fear and anger. These adult sons are the angry men of our society.

Additional Scripture Readings:
Psalm 103:7–18;
1 Thessalonians 2:7–12

Go to page 1280 for your next devotional reading.

am and what I am doing. **21**I am sending him to you for this very purpose, that you may know how we are, and that he may encourage you.

23Peace to the brothers, and love with faith from God the Father and the Lord Jesus Christ. **24**Grace to all who love our Lord Jesus Christ with an undying love.

PAUL writes this letter to the church he started in Philippi (Acts 16:11–40). Even though he is in prison, he feels happy when he thinks of what Christ means to him and of what the Philippians are doing for him. He gives some very practical advice on how to live the Christian life. As you read this book, remember always to rejoice in the Lord and to be content, whatever the circumstances.

PHILIPPIANS

1 Paul and Timothy, servants of Christ Jesus,

To all the saints in Christ Jesus at Philippi, together with the overseers[a] and deacons:

²Grace and peace to you from God our Father and the Lord Jesus Christ.

Thanksgiving and Prayer

³I thank my God every time I remember you. ⁴In all my prayers for all of you, I always pray with joy ⁵because of your partnership in the gospel from the first day until now, ⁶being confident of this, that he who began a good work in you will carry it on to completion until the day of Christ Jesus.

⁷It is right for me to feel this way about all of you, since I have you in my heart; for whether I am in chains or defending and confirming the gospel, all of you share in God's grace with me. ⁸God can testify how I long for all of you with the affection of Christ Jesus.

⁹And this is my prayer: that your love may abound more and more in knowledge and depth of insight, ¹⁰so that you may be able to discern what is best and may be pure and blameless until the day of Christ, ¹¹filled with the fruit of righteousness that

---

*a*1 Traditionally *bishops*

comes through Jesus Christ — to the glory and praise of God.

Paul's Chains Advance the Gospel

¹²Now I want you to know, brothers, that what has happened to me has really served to advance the gospel. ¹³As a result, it has become clear throughout the whole palace guard*a* and to everyone else that I am in chains for Christ. ¹⁴Because of my chains, most of the brothers in the Lord have been encouraged to speak the word of God more courageously and fearlessly.

¹⁵It is true that some preach Christ out of envy and rivalry, but others out of goodwill. ¹⁶The latter do so in love, knowing that I am put here for the defense of the gospel. ¹⁷The former preach Christ out of selfish ambition, not sincerely, supposing that they can stir up trouble for me while I am in chains.*b* ¹⁸But what does it matter? The important thing is that in every way, whether from false motives or

---

*a*13 Or *whole palace*   *b*16,17 Some late manuscripts have verses 16 and 17 in reverse order.

THURSDAY

VERSE FOR THE DAY:	*AUTHOR:*	*PASSAGE FOR THE DAY:*
Philippians 1:21	*Daniel Taylor*	*Philippians 1:18–26*

Dying to Live

AH, PHYLLIS! . . .

Phyllis had had a tough life, partly of her own doing, and now she was laced with cancer, sleeping in a chair, wearing a wig and waiting to die . . .

Phyllis knew God. She had seen the first and the last, the beginning and the end. She knew who had made her, who had redeemed her, and who (her broken body notwithstanding) was ready to take her back to himself . . .

Phyllis had no money; she was divorced and living alone; she was in constant physical pain; her precious teenage daughter had been killed a few years earlier. It is very odd, by the world's standards, that this woman should be the most contented person I have ever known. Some people would say she had lost touch with reality in order to protect herself against its pain. I think, rather, she had gotten *in touch* with reality in a way that few of us ever do, and had seen its beauty.

So what does this say about dying? I don't know. Maybe it says that dying is one of the things that helps us know what living is. It says that dying hurts, both those who die and those who are left behind, who will die when their turn comes. It also suggests, however, that dying may be the beginning of something rather than the end . . .

We die because we have lived. We live in order to know and love the God who made us. In dying we become more real than we ever can be while part of this sorrowful world.

I will die someday, and so will you. And that is a good thing.

Additional Scripture Readings:
John 12:23–26; Romans 14:8–9

Go to page 1282 for your next devotional reading.

true, Christ is preached. And because of this I rejoice.

Yes, and I will continue to rejoice, [19]for I know that through your prayers and the help given by the Spirit of Jesus Christ, what has happened to me will turn out for my deliverance.[a] [20]I eagerly expect and hope that I will in no way be ashamed, but will have sufficient courage so that now as always Christ will be exalted in my body, whether by life or by death. [21]For to me, to live is Christ and to die is gain. [22]If I am to go on living in the body, this will mean fruitful labor for me. Yet what shall I choose? I do not know! [23]I am torn between the two: I desire to depart and be with Christ, which is better by far; [24]but it is more necessary for you that I remain in the body. [25]Convinced of this, I know that I will remain, and I will continue with all of you for your progress and joy in the faith, [26]so that through my being with you again your joy in Christ Jesus will overflow on account of me.

[27]Whatever happens, conduct yourselves in a manner worthy of the gospel of Christ. Then, whether I come and see you or only hear about you in my absence, I will know that you stand firm in one spirit, contending as one man for the faith of the gospel [28]without being frightened in any way by those who oppose you. This is a sign to them that they will be destroyed, but that you will be saved—and that by God. [29]For it has been granted to you on behalf of Christ not only to believe on him, but also to suffer for him, [30]since you are going through the same struggle you saw I had, and now hear that I still have.

Imitating Christ's Humility

2 If you have any encouragement from being united with Christ, if any comfort from his love, if any fellowship with the Spirit, if any tenderness and compassion, [2]then make my joy complete by being like-minded, having the same love, being one in spirit and purpose. [3]Do nothing out of selfish ambition or vain conceit, but in humility consider others better than yourselves. [4]Each of you should look not only to your own interests, but also to the interests of others.

[5]Your attitude should be the same as that of Christ Jesus:

[6]Who, being in very nature[b] God,

did not consider equality with God
   something to be grasped,
[7]but made himself nothing,
   taking the very nature[c] of a
     servant,
   being made in human likeness.
[8]And being found in appearance as a
   man,
   he humbled himself
   and became obedient to death—
     even death on a cross!
[9]Therefore God exalted him to the
   highest place
   and gave him the name that is
     above every name,
[10]that at the name of Jesus every knee
   should bow,
   in heaven and on earth and under
     the earth,
[11]and every tongue confess that Jesus
   Christ is Lord,
   to the glory of God the Father.

Shining as Stars

[12]Therefore, my dear friends, as you have always obeyed—not only in my presence, but now much more in my absence—continue to work out your salvation with fear and trembling, [13]for it is God who works in you to will and to act according to his good purpose.

[14]Do everything without complaining or arguing, [15]so that you may become blameless and pure, children of God without fault in a crooked and depraved generation, in which you shine like stars in the universe [16]as you hold out[d] the word of life—in order that I may boast on the day of Christ that I did not run or labor for nothing. [17]But even if I am being poured out like a drink offering on the sacrifice and service coming from your faith, I am glad and rejoice with all of you. [18]So you too should be glad and rejoice with me.

Timothy and Epaphroditus

[19]I hope in the Lord Jesus to send Timothy to you soon, that I also may be cheered when I receive news about you. [20]I have no one else like him, who takes a genuine interest in your welfare. [21]For everyone looks out for his own interests, not those of Jesus Christ. [22]But you know that Timothy has proved himself, because as a son with his father he has served with me in the work of the gospel. [23]I hope, therefore, to send him as soon as I see how

---

[a]19 Or salvation   [b]6 Or in the form of   [c]7 Or the form   [d]16 Or hold on to

things go with me. ²⁴And I am confident in the Lord that I myself will come soon.

²⁵But I think it is necessary to send back to you Epaphroditus, my brother, fellow worker and fellow soldier, who is also your messenger, whom you sent to take care of my needs. ²⁶For he longs for all of you and is distressed because you heard he was ill. ²⁷Indeed he was ill, and almost died. But God had mercy on him, and not on him only but also on me, to spare me sorrow upon sorrow. ²⁸Therefore I am all the more eager to send him, so that when you see him again you may be glad and I may have less anxiety. ²⁹Welcome him in the Lord with great joy, and honor men like him, ³⁰because he almost died for the work of Christ, risking his life to make up for the help you could not give me.

No Confidence in the Flesh

3 Finally, my brothers, rejoice in the Lord! It is no trouble for me to write

---

FRIDAY

VERSE FOR THE DAY: AUTHOR: PASSAGE FOR THE DAY:
Philippians 2:3   James Dobson   Philippians 2:1–11

Divine Perspective

TWO people are not compatible simply because they love each other and are both professing Christians. Many young couples assume that the sunshine and flowers that characterized their courtship will continue for the rest of their lives. No way, José. It is naive to expect two unique and strong-willed individuals to mesh together like a couple of machines. Even gears have multiple cogs with rough edges to be honed before they will work in concert.

That honing process usually occurs in the first year or two of marriage. The foundation for all that is to follow is laid in those critical months. What often occurs at this time is a dramatic struggle for power in the relationship. Who will lead? Who will follow? Who will determine how the money is spent? Who will get his or her way in times of disagreement? Everything is up for grabs in the beginning, and the way these early decisions are made will set the stage for the future.

Therein lies the danger. Abraham Lincoln said, "A house divided against itself cannot stand" [see Matthew 12:25]. If both partners come into the relationship prepared to battle in those first two years, the foundation will begin to crumble. The apostle Paul gave us the divine perspective on human relationships —not only in marriage but in every dimension of life. He wrote, "Do nothing out of selfish ambition or vain conceit, but in humility consider others better than yourselves" (Philippians 2:3).

That one verse contains more wisdom than most marriage manuals combined. If heeded, it could virtually eliminate divorce from the catalog of human experience.

Additional Scripture Readings: *Go to page 1283 for your next*
Romans 12:9–13; 1 Peter 5:5–7   *devotional reading.*

WEEKENDING

RECEIVE

God has chosen to be closer to each of us than anyone else can be. He wants us to have an intimate personal relationship to him that allows us to enter into him and he into each of us. Many people who believe in Jesus have never come to know God that way. They have not grasped the wonder and ecstasy of being personally loved by God. They are impressed by his creative power, but they do not know that he lays aside the garments of his station and humbly presents himself in love . . .

For me, the good news is that the great One who is totally other and past finding out has humbled himself and presented himself to us not in power but in love.

– Tony Campolo

REVIVE

Saturday: John 13:1–17
Sunday: Philippians 2:1–11

Go to page 1284 for your next devotional reading.

the same things to you again, and it is a safeguard for you.

²Watch out for those dogs, those men who do evil, those mutilators of the flesh. ³For it is we who are the circumcision, we who worship by the Spirit of God, who glory in Christ Jesus, and who put no confidence in the flesh— ⁴though I myself have reasons for such confidence.

If anyone else thinks he has reasons to put confidence in the flesh, I have more: ⁵circumcised on the eighth day, of the people of Israel, of the tribe of Benjamin, a Hebrew of Hebrews; in regard to the law, a Pharisee; ⁶as for zeal, persecuting the church; as for legalistic righteousness, faultless.

⁷But whatever was to my profit I now consider loss for the sake of Christ. ⁸What is more, I consider everything a loss compared to the surpassing greatness of knowing Christ Jesus my Lord, for whose sake I have lost all things. I consider them rubbish, that I may gain Christ ⁹and be found in him, not having a righteousness of my own that comes from the law, but that which is through faith in Christ—the righteousness that comes from God and is by faith. ¹⁰I want to know Christ and the power of his resurrection and the fellow-

---

MONDAY

VERSE FOR THE DAY:
Philippians 3:14

AUTHOR:
Philip W. Williams

PASSAGE FOR THE DAY:
Philippians 3:12–16

Press On

IN CHRIST, life is intended to have purpose. Perhaps we all too easily become worshipers of life. We may make life itself into an idol. If all our marbles are in a basket called *life*, death may indeed be the unwanted, purposeless intruder. This is not to say we shouldn't "have life, and have it to the full" [John 10:10], as Jesus said. But to make anything, including life, into the "be all and end all," squeezes God out of the picture. It is our relationship with God in life that enables us to make sense out of seeming nonsense. Even when sense and purpose seem to escape us, we trust that one day we will understand. On that day we will come face to face with the author of life.

A courageous statement was made by a person who, in struggling to understand the death of his beloved, said, "I still do not see the purpose. I struggle, but I don't give up. Somehow I feel that in my very struggle with this I am choosing to say that there is meaning and purpose." Giving up may mean the quiet desperation of despair. There is wisdom in the search and struggle.

When Jesus met Martha, she said to him, "If you had been here, my brother would not have died." Jesus answered, "I am the resurrection and the life. He who believes in me will live, even though he dies; and whoever lives and believes in me will never die. Do you believe this?" [John 11:25–26].

Additional Scripture Readings:
2 Corinthians 4:7–18;
Colossians 3:1–4

Go to page 1286 for your next devotional reading.

ship of sharing in his sufferings, becoming like him in his death, [11]and so, somehow, to attain to the resurrection from the dead.

Pressing on Toward the Goal

[12]Not that I have already obtained all this, or have already been made perfect, but I press on to take hold of that for which Christ Jesus took hold of me. [13]Brothers, I do not consider myself yet to have taken hold of it. But one thing I do: Forgetting what is behind and straining toward what is ahead, [14]I press on toward the goal to win the prize for which God has called me heavenward in Christ Jesus.

[15]All of us who are mature should take such a view of things. And if on some point you think differently, that too God will make clear to you. [16]Only let us live up to what we have already attained.

[17]Join with others in following my example, brothers, and take note of those who live according to the pattern we gave you. [18]For, as I have often told you before and now say again even with tears, many live as enemies of the cross of Christ. [19]Their destiny is destruction, their god is their stomach, and their glory is in their shame. Their mind is on earthly things. [20]But our citizenship is in heaven. And we eagerly await a Savior from there, the Lord Jesus Christ, [21]who, by the power that enables him to bring everything under his control, will transform our lowly bodies so that they will be like his glorious body.

4 Therefore, my brothers, you whom I love and long for, my joy and crown, that is how you should stand firm in the Lord, dear friends!

Exhortations

[2]I plead with Euodia and I plead with Syntyche to agree with each other in the Lord. [3]Yes, and I ask you, loyal yokefellow,[a] help these women who have contended at my side in the cause of the gospel, along with Clement and the rest of my fellow workers, whose names are in the book of life.

[4]Rejoice in the Lord always. I will say it again: Rejoice! [5]Let your gentleness be evident to all. The Lord is near. [6]Do not be anxious about anything, but in everything, by prayer and petition, with thanksgiving, present your requests to God. [7]And the peace of God, which transcends all understanding, will guard your hearts and your minds in Christ Jesus.

[8]Finally, brothers, whatever is true, whatever is noble, whatever is right, whatever is pure, whatever is lovely, whatever is admirable—if anything is excellent or praiseworthy—think about such things. [9]Whatever you have learned or received or heard from me, or seen in me—put it into practice. And the God of peace will be with you.

Thanks for Their Gifts

[10]I rejoice greatly in the Lord that at last you have renewed your concern for me. Indeed, you have been concerned, but you had no opportunity to show it. [11]I am not saying this because I am in need, for I have learned to be content whatever the circumstances. [12]I know what it is to be in need, and I know what it is to have plenty. I have learned the secret of being content in any and every situation, whether well fed or hungry, whether living in plenty or in want. [13]I can do everything through him who gives me strength.

[14]Yet it was good of you to share in my troubles. [15]Moreover, as you Philippians know, in the early days of your acquaintance with the gospel, when I set out from Macedonia, not one church shared with me in the matter of giving and receiving, except you only; [16]for even when I was in Thessalonica, you sent me aid again and again when I was in need. [17]Not that I am looking for a gift, but I am looking for what may be credited to your account. [18]I have received full payment and even more; I am amply supplied, now that I have received from Epaphroditus the gifts you sent. They are a fragrant offering, an acceptable sacrifice, pleasing to God. [19]And my God will meet all your needs according to his glorious riches in Christ Jesus. [20]To our God and Father be glory for ever and ever. Amen.

Final Greetings

[21]Greet all the saints in Christ Jesus. The brothers who are with me send greetings. [22]All the saints send you greetings, especially those who belong to Caesar's household. [23]The grace of the Lord Jesus Christ be with your spirit. Amen.[b]

---

[a]3 Or loyal Syzygus   [b]23 Some manuscripts do not have Amen.

VERSE FOR THE DAY:
Philippians 4:6

AUTHOR:
Frederick Buechner

PASSAGE FOR THE DAY:
Philippians 4:2–9

Visions of the Worst

"DO NOT be anxious about anything," Paul writes to the Philippians. In one sense it is like telling a woman with a bad head cold not to sniffle and sneeze so much or a lame man to stop dragging his feet. Or maybe it is more like telling a wino to lay off the booze or a compulsive gambler to stay away from the track.

Is anxiety a disease or an addiction? Perhaps it is something of both. Partly, perhaps, because you can't help it, and partly because for some dark reason you choose not to help it, you torment yourself with detailed visions of the worst that can possibly happen. The nagging headache turns out to be a malignant brain tumor. When your teenage son fails to get off the plane you've gone to meet, you see his picture being tacked up in the post office among the missing and his disappearance never accounted for . . .

Does the terrible fear of disaster conceal an even more terrible hankering for it? Do the accelerated pulse and the knot in the stomach mean that beneath whatever their immediate cause, you are acting out some ancient and unresolved drama of childhood? . . .

But answer or no answer, the worst things will happen at last even so . . . Sorrow, loss, death await us all and everybody we love. Yet "The Lord is near. Do not be anxious about anything," Paul writes, who was evidently in prison at the time and with good reason to be anxious about everything, "but in everything, by prayer and petition, with thanksgiving, present your requests to God."

He does not deny that the worst things will happen finally to all of us, as indeed he must have had a strong suspicion they were soon to happen to him. He does not try to minimize them. He does not try to explain them away as God's will or God's judgment or God's method of testing our spiritual fiber. He simply tells the Philippians that in spite of them—even in the thick of them—they are to keep in constant touch with the One who unimaginably transcends the worst things as he also unimaginably transcends the best.

Additional Scripture Readings:
Matthew 6:25–31; Ephesians 3:14–21

Go to page 1288 for your next devotional reading.

PAUL writes this letter to the church in Colosse at about the same time as he writes Ephesians. False teachers are deceiving some of those to whom he writes (Colossians 2:4). Therefore, Paul stresses the power and glory of Christ and instructs his readers on how to live as Christians. As you read this book, put your faith in this glorious Savior who died for you, and promise him that you will show Christian love and compassion to others.

COLOSSIANS

1 Paul, an apostle of Christ Jesus by the will of God, and Timothy our brother,

2To the holy and faithful*a* brothers in Christ at Colosse:

Grace and peace to you from God our Father.*b*

Thanksgiving and Prayer

3We always thank God, the Father of our Lord Jesus Christ, when we pray for you, **4**because we have heard of your faith in Christ Jesus and of the love you have for all the saints — **5**the faith and love that spring from the hope that is stored up for you in heaven and that you have already heard about in the word of truth, the gospel **6**that has come to you. All over the world this gospel is bearing fruit and growing, just as it has been doing among you since the day you heard it and understood God's grace in all its truth. **7**You learned it from Epaphras, our dear fellow servant, who is a faithful minister of Christ on our*c* behalf, **8**and who also told us of your love in the Spirit.

9For this reason, since the day we heard about you, we have not stopped praying for you and asking God to fill you with the knowledge of his will through all spiritual

a2 Or believing   b2 Some manuscripts Father and the Lord Jesus Christ   c7 Some manuscripts your wisdom and understanding. [10]And we pray this in order that you may live a life worthy of the Lord and may please him in every way: bearing fruit in every good work, growing in the knowledge of God, [11]being strengthened with all power according to his glorious might so that you may have great endurance and patience,

and joyfully [12]giving thanks to the Father, who has qualified you[a] to share in the inheritance of the saints in the kingdom of light. [13]For he has rescued us from the dominion of darkness and brought us into the kingdom of the Son he loves, [14]in whom we have redemption,[b] the forgiveness of sins.

[a]12 Some manuscripts *us*   [b]14 A few late manuscripts *redemption through his blood*

WEDNESDAY

VERSE FOR THE DAY: AUTHOR: PASSAGE FOR THE DAY:
Colossians 2:6   John Fischer   Colossians 2:6–12

The Hourglass of Life

JESUS never closes a mind; he opens it. Jesus is never threatened by a question; he welcomes it. He knows all questions will ultimately end up with him, so fire away!

Jesus is the answer, and when he walks through a question, he always leaves the door open so anyone can get to it from either side. Modern Christians keep wanting to shut the door (once they've passed through, of course).

For many Christians, the experience of truth has been a narrowing experience, and in one sense this is right. All those questions—religions, sins, frustrations, explorations—finally ended up with Jesus. Like following the inside of a cone, all experiences funneled to a point, and at that point was Jesus on the cross for my sin.

The error, however, is when we stop here and move no further. For our experience of truth to grow, we must move through the cross back out into the same reality—the same questions, the same world—with a different perspective.

It's like an hourglass with the cross at the center. All my preconversion experiences narrowed me toward a personal encounter with Christ; but once through, he leads me back out into the world I came from where the lines now, instead of converging, open up into an ever-widening reality. The sands of truth always move this way—in toward the center and out again.

Yes, Jesus is the answer, and it's precisely *because* he is the answer that we can venture out. Because he is Lord of all, we can walk into all and find him Lord. This is not only a privilege, it's a mandate. It's what Christians are called to do in the world.

Additional Scripture Readings:
Romans 12:1–2;
2 Corinthians 3:12—4:6

Go to page 1290 for your next devotional reading.

The Supremacy of Christ

15He is the image of the invisible God, the firstborn over all creation. **16**For by him all things were created: things in heaven and on earth, visible and invisible, whether thrones or powers or rulers or authorities; all things were created by him and for him. **17**He is before all things, and in him all things hold together. **18**And he is the head of the body, the church; he is the beginning and the firstborn from among the dead, so that in everything he might have the supremacy. **19**For God was pleased to have all his fullness dwell in him, **20**and through him to reconcile to himself all things, whether things on earth or things in heaven, by making peace through his blood, shed on the cross.

21Once you were alienated from God and were enemies in your minds because of*a* your evil behavior. **22**But now he has reconciled you by Christ's physical body through death to present you holy in his sight, without blemish and free from accusation— **23**if you continue in your faith, established and firm, not moved from the hope held out in the gospel. This is the gospel that you heard and that has been proclaimed to every creature under heaven, and of which I, Paul, have become a servant.

Paul's Labor for the Church

24Now I rejoice in what was suffered for you, and I fill up in my flesh what is still lacking in regard to Christ's afflictions, for the sake of his body, which is the church. **25**I have become its servant by the commission God gave me to present to you the word of God in its fullness— **26**the mystery that has been kept hidden for ages and generations, but is now disclosed to the saints. **27**To them God has chosen to make known among the Gentiles the glorious riches of this mystery, which is Christ in you, the hope of glory.

28We proclaim him, admonishing and teaching everyone with all wisdom, so that we may present everyone perfect in Christ. **29**To this end I labor, struggling with all his energy, which so powerfully works in me.

2 I want you to know how much I am struggling for you and for those at Laodicea, and for all who have not met me personally. **2**My purpose is that they may be encouraged in heart and united in love, so that they may have the full riches of complete understanding, in order that they may know the mystery of God, namely, Christ, **3**in whom are hidden all the treasures of wisdom and knowledge. **4**I tell you this so that no one may deceive you by fine-sounding arguments. **5**For though I am absent from you in body, I am present with you in spirit and delight to see how orderly you are and how firm your faith in Christ is.

Freedom From Human Regulations Through Life With Christ

6So then, just as you received Christ Jesus as Lord, continue to live in him, **7**rooted and built up in him, strengthened in the faith as you were taught, and overflowing with thankfulness.

8See to it that no one takes you captive through hollow and deceptive philosophy, which depends on human tradition and the basic principles of this world rather than on Christ.

9For in Christ all the fullness of the Deity lives in bodily form, **10**and you have been given fullness in Christ, who is the head over every power and authority. **11**In him you were also circumcised, in the putting off of the sinful nature,*b* not with a circumcision done by the hands of men but with the circumcision done by Christ, **12**having been buried with him in baptism and raised with him through your faith in the power of God, who raised him from the dead.

13When you were dead in your sins and in the uncircumcision of your sinful nature,*c* God made you*d* alive with Christ. He forgave us all our sins, **14**having canceled the written code, with its regulations, that was against us and that stood opposed to us; he took it away, nailing it to the cross. **15**And having disarmed the powers and authorities, he made a public spectacle of them, triumphing over them by the cross.*e*

16Therefore do not let anyone judge you by what you eat or drink, or with regard to a religious festival, a New Moon celebration or a Sabbath day. **17**These are a shadow of the things that were to come; the reality, however, is found in Christ. **18**Do

*a*21 Or *minds, as shown by*   *b*11 Or *the flesh*   *c*13 Or *your flesh*   *d*13 Some manuscripts *us*
*e*15 Or *them in him*

not let anyone who delights in false humility and the worship of angels disqualify you for the prize. Such a person goes into great detail about what he has seen, and his unspiritual mind puffs him up with idle notions. [19]He has lost connection with the Head, from whom the whole body, supported and held together by its ligaments and sinews, grows as God causes it to grow.

[20]Since you died with Christ to the basic principles of this world, why, as though you still belonged to it, do you submit to its rules: [21]"Do not handle! Do not taste! Do not touch!"? [22]These are all destined to perish with use, because they are based

THURSDAY

VERSE FOR THE DAY:
Colossians 3:5

AUTHOR:
Charles Swindoll

PASSAGE FOR THE DAY:
Colossians 3:5–11

Lust Is Lurking

I THINK of the gentleman I met several years ago—a fine itinerant Bible teacher. He said he had been keeping a confidential list of men who were once outstanding expositors of the Scripture, capable and respected men of God . . . who have shipwrecked their faith on the shoals of moral defilement. During the previous week, he said, he had entered the name of *number forty-two* in his book. This sad, sordid statistic, he claims, caused him to be extra cautious and discreet in his own life. Perhaps, by now, he has added a couple dozen more.

A chill ran down my spine when he told that story. No one is immune. You're not. I'm not. Lust is no respecter of persons . . . Its alluring voice can infiltrate the most intelligent mind and cause its victim to believe its lies and respond to its appeal. And beware—it never gives up . . . it never runs out of ideas. Bolt your front door and it'll rattle at the bedroom window, crawl into the living room through the TV screen, or wink at you out of a magazine in the den . . .

Lust is persistent. If it's knocked on your door once, it'll knock again. And again. You are safe just so long as you draw upon your Savior's strength. Try to handle it yourself and you'll lose—every time. This is why we are warned again and again in the New Testament to *flee* sexual temptations. Remember, lust is committed to wage *war* against your soul—in a life-and-death struggle—in hand-to-hand combat. Don't stand before this mortal enemy and argue or fight in your own strength—run for cover . . . If you get yourself into a situation that leaves you defenseless and weak, if your door is left even slightly ajar, you may be sure that this ancient enemy will kick it open with six-guns blazing. So don't leave it open. Don't give lust a foothold—or even a toehold.

Additional Scripture Readings:
1 Corinthians 6:12–20;
1 Thessalonians 4:3–8

Go to page 1291 for your next devotional reading.

on human commands and teachings. ²³Such regulations indeed have an appearance of wisdom, with their self-imposed worship, their false humility and their harsh treatment of the body, but they lack any value in restraining sensual indulgence.

Rules for Holy Living

3 Since, then, you have been raised with Christ, set your hearts on things above, where Christ is seated at the right hand of God. ²Set your minds on things above, not on earthly things. ³For you died, and your life is now hidden

---

FRIDAY

VERSE FOR THE DAY:
Colossians 3:14

AUTHOR:
G.R. Slater

PASSAGE FOR THE DAY:
Colossians 3:12–14

Great Expectations

WE ARE seeking too much from marriage today. Life has become impersonal. Our circle of friends changes often, and there are few long-time friendships. The family has cut itself adrift from formerly close kinship bonds. Now all the closeness and intimacy previously shared in these other ways among many people is being focused on one person, and the whole load is placed on one pair of shoulders—the husband's or the wife's. It is only realistic to recognize the strain that this excessive closeness and extreme demand places upon both husband and wife. One cannot be expected to be mate, brother, father, friend and psychiatrist all rolled up in one . . .

Conflict can be creative, and the love which is "patient and kind" is able to embrace tensions creatively in at least two ways:

First, it makes possible an openness and honesty about one's disappointments. Often a person feels that his faith forbids him to be honest or critical with his mate, but you owe it to your marriage partner to let her know how you feel. Such openness, within the setting of love and acceptance, can be the basis of a new beginning and partnership at a deeper level . . .

Second, this love that is at liberty to be realistic calls us to recognize that marriage is something that must be worked out. It is not like a coat that is put on, but like a flower that grows. As one elderly lady testified, "Love is what you go through together." It is the recognition, therefore, that you have some needs which are not going to be met by the other person, and that there are some things upon which you will never totally agree. Realism demands patience and a willingness to adjust. The art of marriage, it has been said, is in maintaining equilibrium through the various changes and adjustments of life together.

Additional Scripture Readings:
1 Corinthians 13:1–13;
Ephesians 5:21–33

Go to page 1293 for your next devotional reading.

with Christ in God. [4]When Christ, who is your[a] life, appears, then you also will appear with him in glory.

[5]Put to death, therefore, whatever belongs to your earthly nature: sexual immorality, impurity, lust, evil desires and greed, which is idolatry. [6]Because of these, the wrath of God is coming.[b] [7]You used to walk in these ways, in the life you once lived. [8]But now you must rid yourselves of all such things as these: anger, rage, malice, slander, and filthy language from your lips. [9]Do not lie to each other, since you have taken off your old self with its practices [10]and have put on the new self, which is being renewed in knowledge in the image of its Creator. [11]Here there is no Greek or Jew, circumcised or uncircumcised, barbarian, Scythian, slave or free, but Christ is all, and is in all.

[12]Therefore, as God's chosen people, holy and dearly loved, clothe yourselves with compassion, kindness, humility, gentleness and patience. [13]Bear with each other and forgive whatever grievances you may have against one another. Forgive as the Lord forgave you. [14]And over all these virtues put on love, which binds them all together in perfect unity.

[15]Let the peace of Christ rule in your hearts, since as members of one body you were called to peace. And be thankful. [16]Let the word of Christ dwell in you richly as you teach and admonish one another with all wisdom, and as you sing psalms, hymns and spiritual songs with gratitude in your hearts to God. [17]And whatever you do, whether in word or deed, do it all in the name of the Lord Jesus, giving thanks to God the Father through him.

Rules for Christian Households

[18]Wives, submit to your husbands, as is fitting in the Lord.

[19]Husbands, love your wives and do not be harsh with them.

[20]Children, obey your parents in everything, for this pleases the Lord.

[21]Fathers, do not embitter your children, or they will become discouraged.

[22]Slaves, obey your earthly masters in everything; and do it, not only when their eye is on you and to win their favor, but with sincerity of heart and reverence for the Lord. [23]Whatever you do, work at it with all your heart, as working for the Lord, not for men, [24]since you know that you will receive an inheritance from the Lord as a reward. It is the Lord Christ you are serving. [25]Anyone who does wrong will be repaid for his wrong, and there is no favoritism.

4 Masters, provide your slaves with what is right and fair, because you know that you also have a Master in heaven.

Further Instructions

[2]Devote yourselves to prayer, being watchful and thankful. [3]And pray for us, too, that God may open a door for our message, so that we may proclaim the mystery of Christ, for which I am in chains. [4]Pray that I may proclaim it clearly, as I should. [5]Be wise in the way you act toward outsiders; make the most of every opportunity. [6]Let your conversation be always full of grace, seasoned with salt, so that you may know how to answer everyone.

Final Greetings

[7]Tychicus will tell you all the news about me. He is a dear brother, a faithful minister and fellow servant in the Lord. [8]I am sending him to you for the express purpose that you may know about our[c] circumstances and that he may encourage your hearts. [9]He is coming with Onesimus, our faithful and dear brother, who is one of you. They will tell you everything that is happening here.

[10]My fellow prisoner Aristarchus sends you his greetings, as does Mark, the cousin of Barnabas. (You have received instructions about him; if he comes to you, welcome him.) [11]Jesus, who is called Justus, also sends greetings. These are the only Jews among my fellow workers for the kingdom of God, and they have proved a comfort to me. [12]Epaphras, who is one of you and a servant of Christ Jesus, sends greetings. He is always wrestling in prayer for you, that you may stand firm in all the will of God, mature and fully assured. [13]I vouch for him that he is working hard for you and for those at Laodicea and Hierapolis. [14]Our dear friend Luke, the doctor, and Demas send greetings. [15]Give my greetings to the brothers at Laodicea, and to Nympha and the church in her house.

---

a4 Some manuscripts *our*   b6 Some early manuscripts *coming on those who are disobedient*
c8 Some manuscripts *that he may know about your*

WEEKENDING

REFLECT

The magic of a thankful spirit is that it has the power to replace anger with love, resentment with happiness, fear with faith, worry with peace, the desire to dominate with the wish to play on a team, self-preoccupation with concern for the needs of others, guilt with an open door to forgiveness, sexual impurity with honor and respect, jealousy with joy at another's success, lack of creativity with inspired productivity, inferiorities with dignity, a lack of love with an abundance of self-sharing.

– Donald E. Demaray

REVIVE

Saturday: Psalm 100
Sunday: Colossians 3:15–17

Go to page 1294 for your next devotional reading.

¹⁶After this letter has been read to you, see that it is also read in the church of the Laodiceans and that you in turn read the letter from Laodicea.

¹⁷Tell Archippus: "See to it that you complete the work you have received in the Lord."

¹⁸I, Paul, write this greeting in my own hand. Remember my chains. Grace be with you.

MONDAY

VERSE FOR THE DAY:
Colossians 4:3

AUTHOR:
Reggie White

PASSAGE FOR THE DAY:
Colossians 4:2–6

An Open Door

WE ARE walking witnesses for Jesus Christ wherever we go. How can we do less than witness with all our heart. Our styles may be different, but the intensity shouldn't be. I know all Christians can't do it in the same manner as I do, but I have no choice but to do it with all my heart.

A.C. Green is a Christian brother who plays for the Los Angeles Lakers basketball team. He told me that a reporter once asked him how a Christian could play a game like NBA basketball, a game with so much physical contact. A.C.'s response was that his life on the basketball court is the same as his life off the hardwood. He's going to be aggressive and give it all he's got both on and off the court—on, to win the game for his team; off, to win people for Christ.

God has given me an incredible platform as an NFL professional football player. The reason I'm in Philadelphia today is that that's exactly where God wants me to serve him right now. And any time I have a chance to proclaim Jesus Christ as Lord, I'm going to do it. Period!

Additional Scripture Readings:
Matthew 28:16–20; 1 Peter 3:13–16

Go to page 1296 for your next devotional reading.

*P*AUL *writes this letter to the church he began in Thessalonica (Acts 17:1–9), shortly after leaving them and being unable to return (1 Thessalonians 2:17–18). He is excited about their Christian faith, reminds them of his intense love for them, and answers questions about what death means for a Christian. As you read this book, find comfort as a believer that when you die you will still be under God's care and will "be with the Lord forever" (1 Thessalonians 4:17).*

1 THESSALONIANS

1 Paul, Silas*a* and Timothy,

To the church of the Thessalonians in God the Father and the Lord Jesus Christ:

Grace and peace to you.*b*

Thanksgiving for the Thessalonians' Faith

2We always thank God for all of you, mentioning you in our prayers. **3**We continually remember before our God and Father your work produced by faith, your labor prompted by love, and your endurance inspired by hope in our Lord Jesus Christ.

4For we know, brothers loved by God, that he has chosen you, **5**because our gospel came to you not simply with words, but also with power, with the Holy Spirit and with deep conviction. You know how we lived among you for your sake. **6**You became imitators of us and of the Lord; in

---

a1 Greek *Silvanus*, a variant of *Silas Jesus Christ*   *b1* Some early manuscripts *you from God our Father and the Lord* spite of severe suffering, you welcomed the message with the joy given by the Holy Spirit. **7**And so you became a model to all the believers in Macedonia and Achaia. **8**The Lord's message rang out from you not only in Macedonia and Achaia—your faith in God has become known everywhere. Therefore we do not need to say anything about it, **9**for they themselves report what kind of reception you gave us. They tell how you turned to God from idols to serve the living and true God, **10**and to wait for his Son from heaven, whom he raised from the dead—Jesus, who rescues us from the coming wrath.

Paul's Ministry in Thessalonica

2 You know, brothers, that our visit to you was not a failure. **2**We had previously suffered and been insulted in Philippi, as you know, but with the help of our God we dared to tell you his gospel in spite of strong opposition. **3**For the appeal we make does not spring from error or impure motives, nor are we trying to trick you. **4**On the contrary, we speak as men approved by God to be entrusted with the gospel. We are not trying to please men but God, who tests our hearts. **5**You know we never used flattery, nor did we put on a mask to cover up greed—God is our witness. **6**We were not looking for praise

---

TUESDAY

VERSE FOR THE DAY:	AUTHOR:	PASSAGE FOR THE DAY:
1 Thessalonians 1:6	*Mike Singletary*	*1 Thessalonians 1:2–10*

Set Them an Example

I DON'T mind being a role model. I'm flattered when people say they'd like their kids to be like me. To me, being a role model is a heavy responsibility and a gift from God. I accept it openheartedly. But at the same time, I don't feel I should become more important in a kid's life than his father and mother. Very few kids ever actually emulate their heroes. They do what their parents did. Parents are the most important role models in their children's lives, for good or bad.

I may be signing autographs somewhere and a single mom will come up with her son. She'll say, "I'm so glad he got to meet you because you're his hero, and he'll do what you say. If you tell him to listen to his mother and do what I tell him, he'll do it."

That's sad. I often give them both a little encouragement, but I'd rather that kid know that I'm human too. I came from a broken home too. I knew what it was to be disappointed in my father and to be raised by my mother. That mom has the toughest job because she will serve as both the father and the mother role model for that child. He may admire me and look up to me or some other celebrity, but when the chips are down, he'll pattern his life after his parents. If we've got a role model crisis in this country, it's because parents are not good ones.

Additional Scripture Readings:
Philippians 3:17—4:1; Titus 2:6–8

Go to page 1298 for your next devotional reading.

from men, not from you or anyone else. As apostles of Christ we could have been a burden to you, [7]but we were gentle among you, like a mother caring for her little children. [8]We loved you so much that we were delighted to share with you not only the gospel of God but our lives as well, because you had become so dear to us. [9]Surely you remember, brothers, our toil and hardship; we worked night and day in order not to be a burden to anyone while we preached the gospel of God to you.

[10]You are witnesses, and so is God, of how holy, righteous and blameless we were among you who believed. [11]For you know that we dealt with each of you as a father deals with his own children, [12]encouraging, comforting and urging you to live lives worthy of God, who calls you into his kingdom and glory.

[13]And we also thank God continually because, when you received the word of God, which you heard from us, you accepted it not as the word of men, but as it actually is, the word of God, which is at work in you who believe. [14]For you, brothers, became imitators of God's churches in Judea, which are in Christ Jesus: You suffered from your own countrymen the same things those churches suffered from the Jews, [15]who killed the Lord Jesus and the prophets and also drove us out. They displease God and are hostile to all men [16]in their effort to keep us from speaking to the Gentiles so that they may be saved. In this way they always heap up their sins to the limit. The wrath of God has come upon them at last.[a]

Paul's Longing to See the Thessalonians

[17]But, brothers, when we were torn away from you for a short time (in person, not in thought), out of our intense longing we made every effort to see you. [18]For we wanted to come to you—certainly I, Paul, did, again and again—but Satan stopped us. [19]For what is our hope, our joy, or the crown in which we will glory in the presence of our Lord Jesus when he comes? Is it not you? [20]Indeed, you are our glory and joy.

3 So when we could stand it no longer, we thought it best to be left by ourselves in Athens. [2]We sent Timothy, who is our brother and God's fellow worker[b] in spreading the gospel of Christ, to strengthen and encourage you in your faith, [3]so that no one would be unsettled by these trials. You know quite well that we were destined for them. [4]In fact, when we were with you, we kept telling you that we would be persecuted. And it turned out that way, as you well know. [5]For this reason, when I could stand it no longer, I sent to find out about your faith. I was afraid that in some way the tempter might have tempted you and our efforts might have been useless.

Timothy's Encouraging Report

[6]But Timothy has just now come to us from you and has brought good news about your faith and love. He has told us that you always have pleasant memories of us and that you long to see us, just as we also long to see you. [7]Therefore, brothers, in all our distress and persecution we were encouraged about you because of your faith. [8]For now we really live, since you are standing firm in the Lord. [9]How can we thank God enough for you in return for all the joy we have in the presence of our God because of you? [10]Night and day we pray most earnestly that we may see you again and supply what is lacking in your faith.

[11]Now may our God and Father himself and our Lord Jesus clear the way for us to come to you. [12]May the Lord make your love increase and overflow for each other and for everyone else, just as ours does for you. [13]May he strengthen your hearts so that you will be blameless and holy in the presence of our God and Father when our Lord Jesus comes with all his holy ones.

Living to Please God

4 Finally, brothers, we instructed you how to live in order to please God, as in fact you are living. Now we ask you and urge you in the Lord Jesus to do this more and more. [2]For you know what instructions we gave you by the authority of the Lord Jesus. [3]It is God's will that you should be sanctified: that you should avoid sexual immorality; [4]that each of you should learn to control his own body[c] in a way that is holy and honorable, [5]not in passionate lust like the heathen, who do not know

---

[a]16 Or *them fully*　　[b]2 Some manuscripts *brother and fellow worker*; other manuscripts *brother and God's servant*　　[c]4 Or *learn to live with his own wife*; or *learn to acquire a wife*

God; 6and that in this matter no one should wrong his brother or take advantage of him. The Lord will punish men for all such sins, as we have already told you and warned you. 7For God did not call us to be impure, but to live a holy life. 8Therefore, he who rejects this instruction does not reject man but God, who gives you his Holy Spirit.

9Now about brotherly love we do not need to write to you, for you yourselves have been taught by God to love each other. 10And in fact, you do love all the brothers throughout Macedonia. Yet we urge you, brothers, to do so more and more. 11Make it your ambition to lead a quiet life, to mind your own business and to work with your hands, just as we told you, 12so that your daily life may win the respect of outsiders and so that you will not be dependent on anybody.

The Coming of the Lord

13Brothers, we do not want you to be ignorant about those who fall asleep, or to grieve like the rest of men, who have no hope. 14We believe that Jesus died and rose again and so we believe that God will

---

WEDNESDAY

VERSE FOR THE DAY:	AUTHOR:	PASSAGE FOR THE DAY:
1 Thessalonians 4:3	James Dobson	1 Thessalonians 4:3–8

A "New" Recipe

EVEN those outside the Christian faith are now agreeing that the sexual revolution was an unmitigated disaster. As it turns out, abstinence before marriage, and lifelong fidelity were pretty good ideas after all. Some sociologists are all rediscovering the benefits of sexual restraint—as though they had stumbled onto a brand new concept . . .

What I am recommending to my unmarried readers is this: *stay out of bed unless you go there alone!* Not only is virginity the only way to avoid disease, it is also the best foundation for a healthy marriage. That's the way the system was designed by the Creator and no one has yet devised a way to improve on his plan. We are sexual creatures, both physically and psychologically. Our very identity ("Who am I?") begins with gender assignment and the implications of masculinity versus femininity. Virtually every aspect of life is influenced by this biological foundation. Who can deny the hormonal and reproductive forces that shape the way we think and behave? Given this nature and the vast significance it carries, even an atheist should have recognized the dangers of the sexual revolution and the changes it portended. Any upheaval of such proportion was certain to have far-reaching consequences for the stability of the family. How could we have *expected* to preserve symbiotic relationships between men and women when the rules governing our sexual behavior turned upside down? Family disintegration was inevitable.

Additional Scripture Readings:
1 Corinthians 6:12–20;
Colossians 3:5–11

Go to page 1299 for your next devotional reading.

bring with Jesus those who have fallen asleep in him. **15**According to the Lord's own word, we tell you that we who are still alive, who are left till the coming of the Lord, will certainly not precede those who have fallen asleep. **16**For the Lord himself will come down from heaven, with a loud command, with the voice of the archangel and with the trumpet call of God, and the dead in Christ will rise first. **17**After that, we who are still alive and are left will be caught up together with them in the clouds to meet the Lord in the air. And so we will be with the Lord forever. **18**Therefore encourage each other with these words.

5 Now, brothers, about times and dates we do not need to write to you, **2**for you know very well that the day of the Lord will come like a thief in the night. **3**While people are saying, "Peace and safety," destruction will come on them sud-

---

THURSDAY

VERSE FOR THE DAY:
1 Thessalonians 5:17

AUTHOR:
Daniel Taylor

PASSAGE FOR THE DAY:
1 Thessalonians 5:16–18

Prayer Matters to God

DOES prayer "work"? Julie Taylor asked, and her father replied:

How does God decide what to do when we ask him for something? Does it really do any good to ask? Isn't he going to do whatever he wants anyway?

The short answer is, we don't know—or at least I don't. God didn't tell us how these things work. But he has told us one very important thing—we *are* supposed to pray. He says it *does* matter. He says, "Tell me what you want, how you feel. I want to know. I want to hear it from you. It matters to me."

And if God says to do something, it has always been my experience that the best thing is to do it. I have a guess as to why maybe God hasn't told us how this works. (This is only a guess.) I think maybe if we knew how it worked we would stop *talking*. If we thought we had it worked out how prayer got answered, we would keep asking, even demanding, but would stop really talking. We'd put in our orders, you might say, and not really talk with the One who made us. We do that quite a bit even as it is.

So why when we prayed for [our friend] Mr. Cuendet did he get well, but when we prayed for Uncle Clinton, God took him to heaven instead? I don't know. God never promised to tell me why everything happens the way it does. But he did promise me that anytime I wanted to talk, he would be happy to listen. And in a world where so many people feel they are all alone, that's a pretty great thing to know.

One more thing. God not only listens, he talks too. So when you are praying, *keep your ears open!*

Additional Scripture Readings:
Luke 18:1–8; Philippians 4:4–9

Go to page 1302 for your next devotional reading.

denly, as labor pains on a pregnant woman, and they will not escape.

⁴But you, brothers, are not in darkness so that this day should surprise you like a thief. ⁵You are all sons of the light and sons of the day. We do not belong to the night or to the darkness. ⁶So then, let us not be like others, who are asleep, but let us be alert and self-controlled. ⁷For those who sleep, sleep at night, and those who get drunk, get drunk at night. ⁸But since we belong to the day, let us be self-controlled, putting on faith and love as a breastplate, and the hope of salvation as a helmet. ⁹For God did not appoint us to suffer wrath but to receive salvation through our Lord Jesus Christ. ¹⁰He died for us so that, whether we are awake or asleep, we may live together with him. ¹¹Therefore encourage one another and build each other up, just as in fact you are doing.

Final Instructions

¹²Now we ask you, brothers, to respect those who work hard among you, who are over you in the Lord and who admonish you. ¹³Hold them in the highest regard in love because of their work. Live in peace with each other. ¹⁴And we urge you, brothers, warn those who are idle, encourage the timid, help the weak, be patient with everyone. ¹⁵Make sure that nobody pays back wrong for wrong, but always try to be kind to each other and to everyone else.

¹⁶Be joyful always; ¹⁷pray continually; ¹⁸give thanks in all circumstances, for this is God's will for you in Christ Jesus.

¹⁹Do not put out the Spirit's fire; ²⁰do not treat prophecies with contempt. ²¹Test everything. Hold on to the good. ²²Avoid every kind of evil.

²³May God himself, the God of peace, sanctify you through and through. May your whole spirit, soul and body be kept blameless at the coming of our Lord Jesus Christ. ²⁴The one who calls you is faithful and he will do it.

²⁵Brothers, pray for us. ²⁶Greet all the brothers with a holy kiss. ²⁷I charge you before the Lord to have this letter read to all the brothers.

²⁸The grace of our Lord Jesus Christ be with you.

PAUL writes this letter shortly after 1 Thessalonians to clarify some things that the church failed to understand in his first letter. He tells them that the antichrist is coming, but they must continue with their regular schedules until Jesus returns. As you read this book, remember that God wants you to look forward to Christ's return as well as to continue doing your daily work.

2 THESSALONIANS

1 Paul, Silas[a] and Timothy,

To the church of the Thessalonians in God our Father and the Lord Jesus Christ:

²Grace and peace to you from God the Father and the Lord Jesus Christ.

Thanksgiving and Prayer

³We ought always to thank God for you, brothers, and rightly so, because your faith is growing more and more, and the love every one of you has for each other is increasing. ⁴Therefore, among God's churches we boast about your perseverance and faith in all the persecutions and trials you are enduring.

⁵All this is evidence that God's judgment is right, and as a result you will be counted worthy of the kingdom of God, for which you are suffering. ⁶God is just: He will pay back trouble to those who trouble you ⁷and give relief to you who are troubled, and to us as well. This will happen when the Lord Jesus is revealed from heaven in blazing fire with his powerful angels. ⁸He will punish those who do not know God and do not obey the gospel of our Lord Jesus. ⁹They will be punished with everlasting destruction and shut out from the presence of the Lord and from the majesty of his power ¹⁰on the day he comes to be glorified in his holy people and to be marveled at among all those who have believed. This includes you, because you believed our testimony to you.

¹¹With this in mind, we constantly pray

a1 Greek *Silvanus*, a variant of *Silas*

for you, that our God may count you worthy of his calling, and that by his power he may fulfill every good purpose of yours and every act prompted by your faith. [12]We pray this so that the name of our Lord Jesus may be glorified in you, and you in him, according to the grace of our God and the Lord Jesus Christ.[a]

The Man of Lawlessness

2 Concerning the coming of our Lord Jesus Christ and our being gathered to him, we ask you, brothers, [2]not to become easily unsettled or alarmed by some prophecy, report or letter supposed to have come from us, saying that the day of the Lord has already come. [3]Don't let anyone deceive you in any way, for ₊that day will not come₎ until the rebellion occurs and the man of lawlessness[b] is revealed, the man doomed to destruction. [4]He will oppose and will exalt himself over everything that is called God or is worshiped, so that he sets himself up in God's temple, proclaiming himself to be God.

[5]Don't you remember that when I was with you I used to tell you these things? [6]And now you know what is holding him back, so that he may be revealed at the proper time. [7]For the secret power of lawlessness is already at work; but the one who now holds it back will continue to do

---

[a]12 Or *God and Lord, Jesus Christ*   [b]3 Some manuscripts *sin*

FRIDAY

VERSE FOR THE DAY: AUTHOR: PASSAGE FOR THE DAY:
2 Thessalonians 1:11   Frederick Buechner   2 Thessalonians 1:3–12

All Sorts of Voices

IN THE year that King Uzziah died [see Isaiah 6], or in the year that John F. Kennedy died, or in the year that somebody you loved died, you go into the temple if that is your taste, or you hide your face in the little padded temple of your hands, and a voice says, "Whom shall I send into the pain of a world where people die?" and if you are not careful, you may find yourself answering, "Send me." You may hear the voice say, "Go." Just *go*.

Like "duty," "law," "religion," the word "vocation" has a dull ring to it, but in terms of what it means, it is really not dull at all. *Vocare*, to call, of course, and a man's vocation is a man's calling. It is the work that he is called to in this world, the thing that he is summoned to spend his life doing. We can speak of a man's choosing his vocation, but perhaps it is at least as accurate to speak of a vocation's choosing the man, of a call's being given and a man's hearing it, or not hearing it. And maybe that is the place to start: the business of listening and hearing. A man's life is full of all sorts of voices calling him in all sorts of directions. Some of them are voices from inside and some of them are voices from outside. The more alive and alert we are, the more clamorous our lives are. Which do we listen to? What kind of voice do we listen for?

Additional Scripture Readings:
Isaiah 6:1–8; Jeremiah 1:4–10

Go to page 1303 for your next devotional reading.

WEEKENDING

RECALL

To believe in Christ's rising and death's dying is
also to live with the power and the challenge to
rise up now from all our dark graves of
suffering love. If sympathy for the world's
wounds is not enlarged by our anguish, if love
for those around us is not expanded, if
gratitude for what is good does not flame up, if
insight is not deepened, if commitment to what
is important is not strengthened, if aching for a
new day is not intensified, if hope is weakened
and faith diminished, if from the experience of
death comes nothing good, then death has won.
Then death, be proud.

So I shall struggle to live the reality of
Christ's rising and death's dying. In my living,
my son's dying will not be the last word. But as
I rise up, I bear the wounds of his death. My
rising does not remove them. They mark me. If
you want to know who I am, put your hand in.
– Nicholas Wolterstorff

REVIVE

Saturday: John 20:24–31
Sunday: 1 Corinthians 15:54–57

Go to page 1304 for your next devotional reading.

so till he is taken out of the way. [8]And then the lawless one will be revealed, whom the Lord Jesus will overthrow with the breath of his mouth and destroy by the splendor of his coming. [9]The coming of the lawless one will be in accordance with the work of Satan displayed in all kinds of counterfeit miracles, signs and wonders, [10]and in every sort of evil that deceives those who are perishing. They perish because they refused to love the truth and so be saved. [11]For this reason God sends them a powerful delusion so that they will believe the lie [12]and so that all will be condemned who have not believed the truth but have delighted in wickedness.

Stand Firm

[13]But we ought always to thank God for you, brothers loved by the Lord, because from the beginning God chose you[a] to be saved through the sanctifying work of the Spirit and through belief in the truth. [14]He called you to this through our gospel, that you might share in the glory of our Lord

---

[a]13 Some manuscripts *because God chose you as his firstfruits*

MONDAY

VERSE FOR THE DAY:
2 Thessalonians 3:10

AUTHOR:
Thomas Merton

PASSAGE FOR THE DAY:
2 Thessalonians 3:6–15

Work and the Spiritual Life

AN ACTIVITY that is based on the frenzies and impulsions of human ambition is a delusion and an obstacle to grace. It gets in the way of God's will, and it creates more problems than it solves. We must learn to distinguish between the pseudo spirituality of activism and the true vitality and energy of Christian action guided by the Spirit. At the same time we must not create a split in the Christian life by assuming that all activity is somehow dangerous to the spiritual life. The spiritual life is not a life of quiet withdrawal, a hothouse of growth of artificial ascetic practices beyond the reach of people living ordinary lives. It is in the ordinary duties and labors of life that the Christian can and should develop his spiritual union with God.

This is no new principle. But it is perhaps not often easy to apply in practice. A writer or preacher who assumes that it is very easy may seriously mislead those who try to follow his advice. Work in a normal, healthy human context, work with a sane and moderate human measure, integrated in a productive social milieu, is by itself capable of contributing much to the spiritual life. But work that is disordered, irrational, unproductive, dominated by the exhausting frenzies and wastefulness of a worldwide struggle for power and wealth, is not necessarily going to make a valid contribution to the spiritual lives of all those engaged in it.

Additional Scripture Readings:
Ephesians 4:25–32;
1 Thessalonians 4:3–12

Go to page 1307 for your next devotional reading.

Jesus Christ. [15]So then, brothers, stand firm and hold to the teachings[a] we passed on to you, whether by word of mouth or by letter.

[16]May our Lord Jesus Christ himself and God our Father, who loved us and by his grace gave us eternal encouragement and good hope, [17]encourage your hearts and strengthen you in every good deed and word.

Request for Prayer

3 Finally, brothers, pray for us that the message of the Lord may spread rapidly and be honored, just as it was with you. [2]And pray that we may be delivered from wicked and evil men, for not everyone has faith. [3]But the Lord is faithful, and he will strengthen and protect you from the evil one. [4]We have confidence in the Lord that you are doing and will continue to do the things we command. [5]May the Lord direct your hearts into God's love and Christ's perseverance.

Warning Against Idleness

[6]In the name of the Lord Jesus Christ, we command you, brothers, to keep away from every brother who is idle and does not live according to the teaching[b] you received from us. [7]For you yourselves know how you ought to follow our example. We were not idle when we were with

you, [8]nor did we eat anyone's food without paying for it. On the contrary, we worked night and day, laboring and toiling so that we would not be a burden to any of you. [9]We did this, not because we do not have the right to such help, but in order to make ourselves a model for you to follow. [10]For even when we were with you, we gave you this rule: "If a man will not work, he shall not eat."

[11]We hear that some among you are idle. They are not busy; they are busybodies. [12]Such people we command and urge in the Lord Jesus Christ to settle down and earn the bread they eat. [13]And as for you, brothers, never tire of doing what is right.

[14]If anyone does not obey our instruction in this letter, take special note of him. Do not associate with him, in order that he may feel ashamed. [15]Yet do not regard him as an enemy, but warn him as a brother.

Final Greetings

[16]Now may the Lord of peace himself give you peace at all times and in every way. The Lord be with all of you.

[17]I, Paul, write this greeting in my own hand, which is the distinguishing mark in all my letters. This is how I write.

[18]The grace of our Lord Jesus Christ be with you all.

---

[a]15 Or *traditions*   [b]6 Or *tradition*

PAUL writes this letter to young Timothy, who is serving as a pastor in Ephesus. He instructs him how to organize and run the church and how to deal with false teachers and refute what they say. As you read this book, promise God that you will not stray from true faith.

1 TIMOTHY

1 Paul, an apostle of Christ Jesus by the command of God our Savior and of Christ Jesus our hope,

²To Timothy my true son in the faith:

Grace, mercy and peace from God the Father and Christ Jesus our Lord.

Warning Against False Teachers of the Law

³As I urged you when I went into Macedonia, stay there in Ephesus so that you may command certain men not to teach false doctrines any longer ⁴nor to devote themselves to myths and endless genealogies. These promote controversies rather than God's work—which is by faith. ⁵The goal of this command is love, which comes from a pure heart and a good conscience and a sincere faith. ⁶Some have wandered away from these and turned to meaningless talk. ⁷They want to be teach-

ers of the law, but they do not know what they are talking about or what they so confidently affirm.

⁸We know that the law is good if one uses it properly. ⁹We also know that law*a* is made not for the righteous but for lawbreakers and rebels, the ungodly and sinful, the unholy and irreligious; for those who kill their fathers or mothers, for murderers, ¹⁰for adulterers and perverts, for slave traders and liars and perjurers—and for whatever else is contrary to the sound doctrine ¹¹that conforms to the glorious gospel of the blessed God, which he entrusted to me.

The Lord's Grace to Paul

¹²I thank Christ Jesus our Lord, who has given me strength, that he considered me faithful, appointing me to his service. ¹³Even though I was once a blasphemer and a persecutor and a violent man, I was shown mercy because I acted in ignorance

a9 Or that the law

and unbelief. **14**The grace of our Lord was poured out on me abundantly, along with the faith and love that are in Christ Jesus.

15Here is a trustworthy saying that deserves full acceptance: Christ Jesus came into the world to save sinners — of whom I am the worst. **16**But for that very reason I was shown mercy so that in me, the worst of sinners, Christ Jesus might display his unlimited patience as an example for those who would believe on him and receive eternal life. **17**Now to the King eternal, immortal, invisible, the only God, be honor and glory for ever and ever. Amen.

18Timothy, my son, I give you this instruction in keeping with the prophecies once made about you, so that by following them you may fight the good fight, **19**holding on to faith and a good conscience. Some have rejected these and so have shipwrecked their faith. **20**Among them are Hymenaeus and Alexander, whom I have handed over to Satan to be taught not to blaspheme.

TUESDAY

VERSE FOR THE DAY:	AUTHOR:	PASSAGE FOR THE DAY:
1 Timothy 1:15	Jim Conway	1 Timothy 1:12–17

Overcoming Perfectionism

IT MAY sound strange, but frequently a person with a poor self-image tends to be a perfectionist. If you feel inadequate, unsure of other people's love, then you start saying to yourself, "If only I try harder, if I achieve more, if I'm a better person, then I'll feel better about myself and other people will love me."

Perfectionism, however, is never satisfied! If you can't accept any good things that people say of you, then even if you do great things, your accomplishments will not satisfy that insatiable, gulping appetite of perfectionism.

The perfectionist never asks the question, "How much is enough? At what point can I stop? How much perfection will I have to accomplish to receive the love from people that I really want?" There never is an end; only God is perfect.

The perfectionism also fails to realize that God loves unconditionally. God doesn't withhold love until we arrive at perfection. He loves us while we are growing and even while we are his enemies. His love enables us to change and mature.

Tragically, perfectionists think other people will like them better for their perfection. But truthfully, it is just the opposite. People like to be around flexible, tolerant, imperfect people — like themselves. Perfect people frighten them and cause them to withdraw.

Perfectionists are always paying a debt. The irony is that no one is asking that any debt be paid. Perfectionists do all of this because their poor self-images manipulate them into doing it.

Additional Scripture Readings:
Romans 5:1–11; Romans 8:31–39

Go to page 1309 for your next devotional reading.

Instructions on Worship

2 I urge, then, first of all, that requests, prayers, intercession and thanksgiving be made for everyone— ²for kings and all those in authority, that we may live peaceful and quiet lives in all godliness and holiness. ³This is good, and pleases God our Savior, ⁴who wants all men to be saved and to come to a knowledge of the truth. ⁵For there is one God and one mediator between God and men, the man Christ Jesus, ⁶who gave himself as a ransom for all men—the testimony given in its proper time. ⁷And for this purpose I was appointed a herald and an apostle—I am telling the truth, I am not lying—and a teacher of the true faith to the Gentiles.

⁸I want men everywhere to lift up holy hands in prayer, without anger or disputing.

⁹I also want women to dress modestly, with decency and propriety, not with braided hair or gold or pearls or expensive clothes, ¹⁰but with good deeds, appropriate for women who profess to worship God.

¹¹A woman should learn in quietness and full submission. ¹²I do not permit a woman to teach or to have authority over a man; she must be silent. ¹³For Adam was formed first, then Eve. ¹⁴And Adam was not the one deceived; it was the woman who was deceived and became a sinner. ¹⁵But women*a* will be saved*b* through childbearing—if they continue in faith, love and holiness with propriety.

Overseers and Deacons

3 Here is a trustworthy saying: If anyone sets his heart on being an overseer,*c* he desires a noble task. ²Now the overseer must be above reproach, the husband of but one wife, temperate, self-controlled, respectable, hospitable, able to teach, ³not given to drunkenness, not violent but gentle, not quarrelsome, not a lover of money. ⁴He must manage his own family well and see that his children obey him with proper respect. ⁵(If anyone does not know how to manage his own family, how can he take care of God's church?) ⁶He must not be a recent convert, or he may become conceited and fall under the same judgment as the devil. ⁷He must also have a good reputation with outsiders, so

that he will not fall into disgrace and into the devil's trap.

⁸Deacons, likewise, are to be men worthy of respect, sincere, not indulging in much wine, and not pursuing dishonest gain. ⁹They must keep hold of the deep truths of the faith with a clear conscience. ¹⁰They must first be tested; and then if there is nothing against them, let them serve as deacons.

¹¹In the same way, their wives*d* are to be women worthy of respect, not malicious talkers but temperate and trustworthy in everything.

¹²A deacon must be the husband of but one wife and must manage his children and his household well. ¹³Those who have served well gain an excellent standing and great assurance in their faith in Christ Jesus.

¹⁴Although I hope to come to you soon, I am writing you these instructions so that, ¹⁵if I am delayed, you will know how people ought to conduct themselves in God's household, which is the church of the living God, the pillar and foundation of the truth. ¹⁶Beyond all question, the mystery of godliness is great:

He*e* appeared in a body,*f*
    was vindicated by the Spirit,
was seen by angels,
    was preached among the nations,
was believed on in the world,
    was taken up in glory.

Instructions to Timothy

4 The Spirit clearly says that in later times some will abandon the faith and follow deceiving spirits and things taught by demons. ²Such teachings come through hypocritical liars, whose consciences have been seared as with a hot iron. ³They forbid people to marry and order them to abstain from certain foods, which God created to be received with thanksgiving by those who believe and who know the truth. ⁴For everything God created is good, and nothing is to be rejected if it is received with thanksgiving, ⁵because it is consecrated by the word of God and prayer.

⁶If you point these things out to the brothers, you will be a good minister of Christ Jesus, brought up in the truths of the faith and of the good teaching that you have followed. ⁷Have nothing to do with

---

*a*15 Greek *she*   *b*15 Or *restored*   *c*1 Traditionally *bishop*; also in verse 2   *d*11 Or *way*,
deaconesses   *e*16 Some manuscripts *God*   *f*16 Or *in the flesh*

godless myths and old wives' tales; rather, train yourself to be godly. **8**For physical training is of some value, but godliness has value for all things, holding promise for both the present life and the life to come.

9This is a trustworthy saying that deserves full acceptance **10**(and for this we labor and strive), that we have put our hope in the living God, who is the Savior of all men, and especially of those who believe.

11Command and teach these things. **12**Don't let anyone look down on you because you are young, but set an example for the believers in speech, in life, in love, in faith and in purity. **13**Until I come, devote yourself to the public reading of Scripture, to preaching and to teaching. **14**Do not neglect your gift, which was given you through a prophetic message when the body of elders laid their hands on you.

15Be diligent in these matters; give yourself wholly to them, so that everyone may see your progress. **16**Watch your life and doctrine closely. Persevere in them, because if you do, you will save both yourself and your hearers.

WEDNESDAY

VERSE FOR THE DAY:
1 Timothy 3:4

AUTHOR:
J.H. Waterink

PASSAGE FOR THE DAY:
1 Timothy 3:1–7

On Rights and Duties

PERMIT me to make this observation: we must be very careful in speaking of our rights. People who constantly refer to their rights tread on dangerous ground. Is it true that you have the unqualified right to the respect of your children, and that you have every right to exercise authority over your children? No, you certainly do not have an "unqualified right." You can never sever that right from your parental duty before God. [Reformation leader John] Calvin states it beautifully: "Does a person demand his rights? Certainly, I am prepared to grant him his rights, but in so doing I shall say that he has no other rights than the rights to fulfill his duties" . . .

Parents, perform your parental duty toward God and toward your children. Then, and then only, can you speak of your parental rights . . .

Much is being said about the rebellious spirit of children and young people. On the one hand, this spirit of rebellion has come about because children have never learned respect for authority as their parents did not exercise authority; on the other hand, it is also possible that they did not learn respect for authority because the parents misused it. Both are equally dangerous. It is no wonder that there are so many pitfalls in the exercising of authority: he who wields authority wields a God-given weapon, and he must constantly be on guard lest he misuse it for selfish ends. Authority must never be exercised in an arbitrary, unreasonable manner.

Additional Scripture Readings:
Proverbs 22:6; Romans 12:9–16

Go to page 1310 for your next devotional reading.

Advice About Widows, Elders and Slaves

5 Do not rebuke an older man harshly, but exhort him as if he were your father. Treat younger men as brothers, ²older women as mothers, and younger women as sisters, with absolute purity.

³Give proper recognition to those widows who are really in need. ⁴But if a widow has children or grandchildren, these should learn first of all to put their religion into practice by caring for their own family and so repaying their parents and grandparents, for this is pleasing to God. ⁵The widow who is really in need and left all alone puts her hope in God and continues night and day to pray and to ask God for help. ⁶But the widow who lives for pleasure is dead even while she lives. ⁷Give the people these instructions, too, so that no one may be open to blame. ⁸If

---

THURSDAY

VERSE FOR THE DAY:	AUTHOR:	PASSAGE FOR THE DAY:
1 Timothy 5:8	Doug Sherman and William Hendricks	1 Timothy 5:1–8

A God-given Motive

IT IS not always noticed, but the Great Commandments include a legitimate self-interest: "Love your neighbor *as yourself*" [Mark 12:31, italics added]. The idea is that each of us has a responsibility before God to care for himself as God's person. Not just physically, but spiritually, emotionally, relationally, morally, intellectually, and so forth.

Work is an important means toward fulfilling this responsibility. In 2 Thessalonians 3, Paul says that we should pursue gainful employment in order to provide for our needs . . .

So we are actually commanded to work. Furthermore, we are to work in order to provide for our families: "If anyone does not provide for his relatives, and especially for his immediate family, he has denied the faith and is worse than an unbeliever" (1 Timothy 5:8).

This is remarkably strong language! Failing to try to meet even the basic needs of one's family is denying the faith. Why? Because it directly opposes God's command to love those who are our own. In fact, it is to act worse than an unbeliever, because even pagans have the sense and decency to provide a livelihood for their families.

Fortunately, I find that providing for the family is one of the most important reasons why people go to work, as they explain it to me. In fact, because this motive is so common, many people fail to see it as a God-given reason for work. But that won't do. If you work to meet the legitimate needs of your family, then you are fulfilling something important that God wants done in the world.

Additional Scripture Readings:
Ephesians 4:25–28;
2 Thessalonians 3:6–15

Go to page 1312 for your next devotional reading.

anyone does not provide for his relatives, and especially for his immediate family, he has denied the faith and is worse than an unbeliever.

⁹No widow may be put on the list of widows unless she is over sixty, has been faithful to her husband,ᵃ ¹⁰and is well known for her good deeds, such as bringing up children, showing hospitality, washing the feet of the saints, helping those in trouble and devoting herself to all kinds of good deeds.

¹¹As for younger widows, do not put them on such a list. For when their sensual desires overcome their dedication to Christ, they want to marry. ¹²Thus they bring judgment on themselves, because they have broken their first pledge. ¹³Besides, they get into the habit of being idle and going about from house to house. And not only do they become idlers, but also gossips and busybodies, saying things they ought not to. ¹⁴So I counsel younger widows to marry, to have children, to manage their homes and to give the enemy no opportunity for slander. ¹⁵Some have in fact already turned away to follow Satan.

¹⁶If any woman who is a believer has widows in her family, she should help them and not let the church be burdened with them, so that the church can help those widows who are really in need.

¹⁷The elders who direct the affairs of the church well are worthy of double honor, especially those whose work is preaching and teaching. ¹⁸For the Scripture says, "Do not muzzle the ox while it is treading out the grain,"ᵇ and "The worker deserves his wages."ᶜ ¹⁹Do not entertain an accusation against an elder unless it is brought by two or three witnesses. ²⁰Those who sin are to be rebuked publicly, so that the others may take warning.

²¹I charge you, in the sight of God and Christ Jesus and the elect angels, to keep these instructions without partiality, and to do nothing out of favoritism.

²²Do not be hasty in the laying on of hands, and do not share in the sins of others. Keep yourself pure.

²³Stop drinking only water, and use a little wine because of your stomach and your frequent illnesses.

²⁴The sins of some men are obvious, reaching the place of judgment ahead of them; the sins of others trail behind them. ²⁵In the same way, good deeds are obvious, and even those that are not cannot be hidden.

6 All who are under the yoke of slavery should consider their masters worthy of full respect, so that God's name and our teaching may not be slandered. ²Those who have believing masters are not to show less respect for them because they are brothers. Instead, they are to serve them even better, because those who benefit from their service are believers, and dear to them. These are the things you are to teach and urge on them.

Love of Money

³If anyone teaches false doctrines and does not agree to the sound instruction of our Lord Jesus Christ and to godly teaching, ⁴he is conceited and understands nothing. He has an unhealthy interest in controversies and quarrels about words that result in envy, strife, malicious talk, evil suspicions ⁵and constant friction between men of corrupt mind, who have been robbed of the truth and who think that godliness is a means to financial gain.

⁶But godliness with contentment is great gain. ⁷For we brought nothing into the world, and we can take nothing out of it. ⁸But if we have food and clothing, we will be content with that. ⁹People who want to get rich fall into temptation and a trap and into many foolish and harmful desires that plunge men into ruin and destruction. ¹⁰For the love of money is a root of all kinds of evil. Some people, eager for money, have wandered from the faith and pierced themselves with many griefs.

Paul's Charge to Timothy

¹¹But you, man of God, flee from all this, and pursue righteousness, godliness, faith, love, endurance and gentleness. ¹²Fight the good fight of the faith. Take hold of the eternal life to which you were called when you made your good confession in the presence of many witnesses. ¹³In the sight of God, who gives life to everything, and of Christ Jesus, who while testifying before Pontius Pilate made the good confession, I charge you ¹⁴to keep this command without spot or blame until

---

ᵃ9 Or *has had but one husband*   ᵇ18 Deut. 25:4   ᶜ18 Luke 10:7

the appearing of our Lord Jesus Christ, **15**which God will bring about in his own time—God, the blessed and only Ruler, the King of kings and Lord of lords, **16**who alone is immortal and who lives in unapproachable light, whom no one has seen or can see. To him be honor and might forever. Amen.

17Command those who are rich in this present world not to be arrogant nor to put their hope in wealth, which is so uncertain, but to put their hope in God, who richly provides us with everything for our enjoyment. **18**Command them to do good, to be rich in good deeds, and to be generous and willing to share. **19**In this way they will lay up treasure for themselves as a firm foundation for the coming age, so that they may take hold of the life that is truly life.

20Timothy, guard what has been entrusted to your care. Turn away from godless chatter and the opposing ideas of what is falsely called knowledge, **21**which some have professed and in so doing have wandered from the faith.

Grace be with you.

FRIDAY

VERSE FOR THE DAY:
1 Timothy 6:12

AUTHOR:
Orel Hershiser

PASSAGE FOR THE DAY:
1 Timothy 6:11–16

No Excuse for Mediocrity

LOS Angeles Dodgers pitcher and World Series Most Valuable Player award winner Orel Hershiser is competitive. Even so, he has discovered that failure need not be devastating.

I don't like to fail, but I can handle it. That hasn't always been true, but as a Christian of ten years, I know where my strength comes from. I know that even if I give up a home run that makes me a goat, I'll survive. My wife and kids will still love me. God is still in his heaven. The world will not come to an end, regardless of my performance.

It's that same faith, though, that makes me determined to be a good steward of the mind and body I've been blessed with. If my faith merely made me accept defeat and failure, it would be a crutch—a weak, sad alibi. People who criticize Christians for being less competitive—and Christians who *are* less competitive—have missed the point of the faith.

It's my faith that lifts me up when I've failed. It's my faith that reminds me of my true insignificance when the world has been laid at my feet because of my success throwing a ball. To call myself a Christian and then not strive to be the best I can be and do the most I can with what has been given me would be the height of hypocrisy. Being a Christian is no excuse for mediocrity or passive acceptance of defeat. If anything, Christianity demands a higher standard, more devotion to the task.

Additional Scripture Readings:
Psalm 86:1–13;
1 Corinthians 16:13–18

Go to page 1313 for your next devotional reading.

WEEKENDING

REVIEW

Nothing prohibits Christians from obeying God more than the tug of material comforts. Once we have adjusted to a lifestyle that includes many comforts, it is very difficult to surrender them to serve God. Obviously, God doesn't call everyone to leave his vocation and go into what is traditionally called "Christian work." God can and does use Christians everywhere. But in order to be used by God in any capacity, a Christian must be willing to serve God no matter what the costs . . .

Whenever someone asked Christ about what would be expected of him as a follower, he always tested their willingness to surrender everything for God's sake. Without that attitude, we can't even be trusted with material riches because we would spend them on our own indulgences or build bigger barns to store them in.

– Larry Burkett

REVIVE

Saturday: Luke 12:13–21
Sunday: 1 Timothy 6:3–10

Go to page 1315 for your next devotional reading.

THIS second letter to Timothy is written by Paul shortly before Paul dies (2 Timothy 4:6–8). Times are difficult, both morally and spiritually, and Paul wants to encourage Timothy to persevere in his Christian faith and life. As you read this book, be sure to find your daily strength in Jesus Christ and in God's inspired word.

2 TIMOTHY

1 Paul, an apostle of Christ Jesus by the will of God, according to the promise of life that is in Christ Jesus,

²To Timothy, my dear son:

Grace, mercy and peace from God the Father and Christ Jesus our Lord.

Encouragement to Be Faithful

³I thank God, whom I serve, as my forefathers did, with a clear conscience, as night and day I constantly remember you in my prayers. ⁴Recalling your tears, I long to see you, so that I may be filled with joy. ⁵I have been reminded of your sincere faith, which first lived in your grandmother Lois and in your mother Eunice and, I am persuaded, now lives in you also. ⁶For this reason I remind you to fan into flame the gift of God, which is in you through the laying on of my hands. ⁷For God did not give us a spirit of timidity, but a spirit of power, of love and of self-discipline.

⁸So do not be ashamed to testify about our Lord, or ashamed of me his prisoner. But join with me in suffering for the gospel, by the power of God, ⁹who has saved us and called us to a holy life—not because of anything we have done but because of his own purpose and grace. This grace was given us in Christ Jesus before the beginning of time, ¹⁰but it has now been revealed through the appearing of our Savior, Christ Jesus, who has destroyed death and has brought life and immortality to light through the gospel. ¹¹And of this gospel I was appointed a herald and an apostle and a teacher. ¹²That is why I am suffering as I am. Yet I am not ashamed, because I know whom I have

believed, and am convinced that he is able to guard what I have entrusted to him for that day.

¹³What you heard from me, keep as the pattern of sound teaching, with faith and love in Christ Jesus. ¹⁴Guard the good deposit that was entrusted to you—guard it with the help of the Holy Spirit who lives in us.

¹⁵You know that everyone in the province of Asia has deserted me, including Phygelus and Hermogenes.

¹⁶May the Lord show mercy to the household of Onesiphorus, because he often refreshed me and was not ashamed of my chains. ¹⁷On the contrary, when he was in Rome, he searched hard for me until he found me. ¹⁸May the Lord grant that he will find mercy from the Lord on that day! You know very well in how many ways he helped me in Ephesus.

2 You then, my son, be strong in the grace that is in Christ Jesus. ²And the things you have heard me say in the presence of many witnesses entrust to reliable men who will also be qualified to teach others. ³Endure hardship with us like a good soldier of Christ Jesus. ⁴No one serving as a soldier gets involved in civilian affairs—he wants to please his commanding officer. ⁵Similarly, if anyone competes as an athlete, he does not receive the victor's crown unless he competes according to the rules. ⁶The hardworking farmer should be the first to receive a share of the crops. ⁷Reflect on what I am saying, for the Lord will give you insight into all this.

⁸Remember Jesus Christ, raised from

MONDAY

VERSE FOR THE DAY:
2 Timothy 1:8

AUTHOR:
Orel Hershiser

PASSAGE FOR THE DAY:
2 Timothy 1:8–12

Show and Tell

I'M NOT one to wear my faith on my sleeve. Christians can do a disservice to unbelievers by being obnoxious or judgmental. I'm a chapel leader and have been since my second year in the minors. People know where I'm coming from without my having to harp on it all the time. I know that the message of Christ offends because it calls sin sin and says we are all sinners. There's no way to soften that truth. It's jarring and can alienate people until they begin to realize that it's true. My pushing it down everyone's throat will not make it any easier for them to investigate what it's all about.

I just tell people about God naturally, when opportunities arise or when I'm asked. It's amazing how many people notice when you tend to be straight. If you're not a carouser, not a womanizer, not foul-mouthed, not a gossip, it gets around! . . .

We're far from perfect. We fail. There are people who may think we are insincere or who think we're judgmental. I can't defend myself against people who say I'm phony. Only my family, my true friends and I know who I really am inside. I'll have to answer for that someday. I can only do and be what I think God wants me to do and be. I never want to embarrass him or bring him shame.

Additional Scripture Readings:
Romans 1:11–17; 1 Peter 3:13–17

Go to page 1316 for your next devotional reading.

the dead, descended from David. This is my gospel, [9]for which I am suffering even to the point of being chained like a criminal. But God's word is not chained. [10]Therefore I endure everything for the sake of the elect, that they too may obtain the salvation that is in Christ Jesus, with eternal glory.

[11]Here is a trustworthy saying:

If we died with him,
      we will also live with him;
[12]if we endure,
      we will also reign with him.
If we disown him,
      he will also disown us;
[13]if we are faithless,
      he will remain faithful,
      for he cannot disown himself.

A Workman Approved by God

[14]Keep reminding them of these things. Warn them before God against quarreling about words; it is of no value, and only ruins those who listen. [15]Do your best to present yourself to God as one approved, a workman who does not need to be ashamed and who correctly handles the word of truth. [16]Avoid godless chatter, because those who indulge in it will become more and more ungodly. [17]Their teaching will spread like gangrene. Among them are Hymenaeus and Philetus, [18]who have wandered away from the truth. They say that the resurrection has already taken place, and they destroy the faith of some. [19]Nevertheless, God's solid foundation stands firm, sealed with this inscription:

TUESDAY

VERSE FOR THE DAY:	AUTHOR:	PASSAGE FOR THE DAY:
2 Timothy 2:15	Orel Hershiser	2 Timothy 2:14–19

Life's Balancing Agent

MY FAITH has been a balancing agent in my life. Christ thrills me with who I am in him, and reminds me gently who I am not. When I suffer, I know I'm still loved. When I'm on top of the world, I remember that my accomplishments mean nothing in light of eternity. The biggest surprise to me was to discover that Christ is real. He's not some nebulous concept, some idea or system or approach or philosophy. He's a Person, someone I can know.

And he knows me. How do I know? Because while he changed me from sinner to forgiven-sinner, he also realigned my motives. I still had the same character and personality, but my mind was renewed because I now wanted to do what he wanted me to do. The obsession and perfectionism I had used to promote myself was now redirected. I wanted to be the best baseball player I could be, and now that my motives were right, I was free to enjoy my pursuit rather than be frustrated by it. I've seen players worry so much about how they're doing that they are no longer effective.

If anything, I became more dedicated to paying the price, to working out, to listening, to learning. I wanted to soak up all the baseball knowledge I could.

Additional Scripture Readings:
John 10:11–18; Romans 12:1–2

Go to page 1318 for your next devotional reading.

"The Lord knows those who are his,"[a] and, "Everyone who confesses the name of the Lord must turn away from wickedness."

[20]In a large house there are articles not only of gold and silver, but also of wood and clay; some are for noble purposes and some for ignoble. [21]If a man cleanses himself from the latter, he will be an instrument for noble purposes, made holy, useful to the Master and prepared to do any good work.

[22]Flee the evil desires of youth, and pursue righteousness, faith, love and peace, along with those who call on the Lord out of a pure heart. [23]Don't have anything to do with foolish and stupid arguments, because you know they produce quarrels. [24]And the Lord's servant must not quarrel; instead, he must be kind to everyone, able to teach, not resentful. [25]Those who oppose him he must gently instruct, in the hope that God will grant them repentance leading them to a knowledge of the truth, [26]and that they will come to their senses and escape from the trap of the devil, who has taken them captive to do his will.

Godlessness in the Last Days

3 But mark this: There will be terrible times in the last days. [2]People will be lovers of themselves, lovers of money, boastful, proud, abusive, disobedient to their parents, ungrateful, unholy, [3]without love, unforgiving, slanderous, without self-control, brutal, not lovers of the good, [4]treacherous, rash, conceited, lovers of pleasure rather than lovers of God— [5]having a form of godliness but denying its power. Have nothing to do with them.

[6]They are the kind who worm their way into homes and gain control over weak-willed women, who are loaded down with sins and are swayed by all kinds of evil desires, [7]always learning but never able to acknowledge the truth. [8]Just as Jannes and Jambres opposed Moses, so also these men oppose the truth—men of depraved minds, who, as far as the faith is concerned, are rejected. [9]But they will not get very far because, as in the case of those men, their folly will be clear to everyone.

Paul's Charge to Timothy

[10]You, however, know all about my teaching, my way of life, my purpose, faith, patience, love, endurance, [11]perse-cutions, sufferings—what kinds of things happened to me in Antioch, Iconium and Lystra, the persecutions I endured. Yet the Lord rescued me from all of them. [12]In fact, everyone who wants to live a godly life in Christ Jesus will be persecuted, [13]while evil men and impostors will go from bad to worse, deceiving and being deceived. [14]But as for you, continue in what you have learned and have become convinced of, because you know those from whom you learned it, [15]and how from infancy you have known the holy Scriptures, which are able to make you wise for salvation through faith in Christ Jesus. [16]All Scripture is God-breathed and is useful for teaching, rebuking, correcting and training in righteousness, [17]so that the man of God may be thoroughly equipped for every good work.

4 In the presence of God and of Christ Jesus, who will judge the living and the dead, and in view of his appearing and his kingdom, I give you this charge: [2]Preach the Word; be prepared in season and out of season; correct, rebuke and encourage—with great patience and careful instruction. [3]For the time will come when men will not put up with sound doctrine. Instead, to suit their own desires, they will gather around them a great number of teachers to say what their itching ears want to hear. [4]They will turn their ears away from the truth and turn aside to myths. [5]But you, keep your head in all situations, endure hardship, do the work of an evangelist, discharge all the duties of your ministry.

[6]For I am already being poured out like a drink offering, and the time has come for my departure. [7]I have fought the good fight, I have finished the race, I have kept the faith. [8]Now there is in store for me the crown of righteousness, which the Lord, the righteous Judge, will award to me on that day—and not only to me, but also to all who have longed for his appearing.

Personal Remarks

[9]Do your best to come to me quickly, [10]for Demas, because he loved this world, has deserted me and has gone to Thessalonica. Crescens has gone to Galatia, and Titus to Dalmatia. [11]Only Luke is with me. Get Mark and bring him with you, because he is helpful to me in my ministry. [12]I sent Tychicus to Ephesus. [13]When you come, bring the cloak that I left with Car-

[a]19 Num. 16:5 (see Septuagint)

pus at Troas, and my scrolls, especially the parchments.

[14]Alexander the metalworker did me a great deal of harm. The Lord will repay him for what he has done. [15]You too should be on your guard against him, because he strongly opposed our message.

[16]At my first defense, no one came to my support, but everyone deserted me. May it not be held against them. [17]But the Lord stood at my side and gave me strength, so that through me the message might be fully proclaimed and all the Gentiles might hear it. And I was delivered from the lion's mouth. [18]The Lord will rescue me from every evil attack and will bring me safely to his heavenly kingdom. To him be glory for ever and ever. Amen.

Final Greetings

[19]Greet Priscilla[a] and Aquila and the

[a]19 Greek *Prisca*, a variant of *Priscilla*

WEDNESDAY

VERSE FOR THE DAY:	AUTHOR:	PASSAGE FOR THE DAY:
2 Timothy 4:2	Dietrich Bonhoeffer	2 Timothy 3:14—4:5

Preach the Word

WHEN we go to church and listen to the sermon, what we want to hear is his Word—and that not merely for selfish reasons, but for the sake of the many for whom the church and her message are foreign. We have a strange feeling that if Jesus himself—Jesus alone with his Word—could come into our midst at sermon time, we should find quite a different set of men hearing the Word, and quite a different set rejecting it. That is not to deny that the Word of God is to be heard in the preaching that goes on in our church. The real trouble is that the pure Word of Jesus has been overlaid with so much human ballast—burdensome rules and regulations, false hopes and consolations—that it has become extremely difficult to make a genuine decision for Christ.

Of course it is our aim to preach Christ and Christ alone, but, when all is said and done, it is not the fault of our critics that they find our preaching so hard to understand, so overburdened with ideas and expressions that are hopelessly out of touch with the mental climate in which they live . . . Perhaps it would be just as well to ask ourselves whether we do not in fact often act as obstacles to Jesus and his Word . . . Are we not constantly harping on certain ideas at the expense of others that are just as important? Does not our preaching contain too much of our own opinions and convictions, and too little of Jesus Christ? . . . Let us try to get away from the poverty and pettiness of our own little convictions and problems, and seek the wealth and splendor that are vouchsafed to us in Jesus Christ.

Additional Scripture Readings:
Isaiah 55:8–11; Hebrews 4:12–13

Go to page 1321 for your next devotional reading.

household of Onesiphorus. **20**Erastus stayed in Corinth, and I left Trophimus sick in Miletus. **21**Do your best to get here before winter. Eubulus greets you, and so do Pudens, Linus, Claudia and all the brothers.

22The Lord be with your spirit. Grace be with you.

*P*AUL writes to Titus, a pastor serving in Crete, to advise him both on what to teach the churches and on how to organize them, especially with false teachers around. As you read this book, note God's concern for proper order in the church and for true teaching about Christ.

TITUS

1 Paul, a servant of God and an apostle of Jesus Christ for the faith of God's elect and the knowledge of the truth that leads to godliness— ²a faith and knowledge resting on the hope of eternal life, which God, who does not lie, promised before the beginning of time, ³and at his appointed season he brought his word to light through the preaching entrusted to me by the command of God our Savior,

⁴To Titus, my true son in our common faith:

Grace and peace from God the Father and Christ Jesus our Savior.

Titus' Task on Crete

⁵The reason I left you in Crete was that you might straighten out what was left unfinished and appoint*ᵃ* elders in every town, as I directed you. ⁶An elder must be blameless, the husband of but one wife, a man whose children believe and are not open to the charge of being wild and disobedient. ⁷Since an overseer*ᵇ* is entrusted with God's work, he must be blameless—not overbearing, not quick-tempered, not given to drunkenness, not violent, not pursuing dishonest gain. ⁸Rather he must be hospitable, one who loves what is good, who is self-controlled, upright, holy and disciplined. ⁹He must hold firmly to the trustworthy message as it has been taught, so that he can encourage others by sound doctrine and refute those who oppose it.

¹⁰For there are many rebellious people, mere talkers and deceivers, especially those of the circumcision group. ¹¹They

a5 Or *ordain*   *b7* Traditionally *bishop*

must be silenced, because they are ruining whole households by teaching things they ought not to teach — and that for the sake of dishonest gain. [12]Even one of their own prophets has said, "Cretans are always liars, evil brutes, lazy gluttons." [13]This testimony is true. Therefore, rebuke them sharply, so that they will be sound in the faith [14]and will pay no attention to Jewish myths or to the commands of those who reject the truth. [15]To the pure, all things are pure, but to those who are corrupted and do not believe, nothing is pure. In fact, both their minds and consciences are corrupted. [16]They claim to know God, but by their actions they deny him. They are detestable, disobedient and unfit for doing anything good.

THURSDAY

VERSE FOR THE DAY:	AUTHOR:	PASSAGE FOR THE DAY:
Titus 2:11	Orel Hershiser	Titus 2:11–15

From Skepticism to Belief

[A FELLOW minor league baseball player named] Butch said God loved me and wanted a relationship with me. What could *that* mean? I could know God? God could know me? God was perfect and I wasn't. I was just a guy, and he was, well, God. How could I relate to him? Butch said Jesus was the answer. I could relate to him because even though he was perfect, he had also become a man. He was the bridge. He paid for my sin. If I could accept that and believe in Christ, then I could be forgiven and know I was going to heaven.

One September night . . . I pulled out the Gideon Bible and was reading the book of John. My mind was racing. Do I believe in God? Yes. Do I believe the Bible is God's message to man? Yes. Do I believe what the Bible says? Yes. That all have sinned? Yes. That nothing I can do can save me from my sin? Yes. That Jesus already did it for me and that he is the only way to God? Yes. Do I want Christ in my life? Do I want to become a Christian?

I slipped off the bed and knelt beside it. How does one go about praying? I didn't know. I figured if God was God, he would understand if I just told him what was on my mind. I said, "God, I don't know everything about you. I don't think I ever will. But I know I'm a sinner and I know I want to be forgiven. I know I want Christ in my life, and I want to go to heaven. I want to become a Christian. With that, I accept you. Amen."

No tears, no lightning, no wind, no visions. I just got back on the bed and continued to read the Bible. What a relief! I knew I had done the right thing. I had stepped from skepticism to belief.

Additional Scripture Readings:
John 14:1–14; Romans 5:1–11

Go to page 1322 for your next devotional reading.

What Must Be Taught to Various Groups

2 You must teach what is in accord with sound doctrine. ²Teach the older men to be temperate, worthy of respect, self-controlled, and sound in faith, in love and in endurance.

³Likewise, teach the older women to be reverent in the way they live, not to be slanderers or addicted to much wine, but to teach what is good. ⁴Then they can train the younger women to love their husbands and children, ⁵to be self-controlled and pure, to be busy at home, to be kind, and to be subject to their husbands, so that no one will malign the word of God.

⁶Similarly, encourage the young men to be self-controlled. ⁷In everything set them an example by doing what is good. In your teaching show integrity, seriousness ⁸and soundness of speech that cannot be condemned, so that those who oppose you may be ashamed because they have nothing bad to say about us.

⁹Teach slaves to be subject to their masters in everything, to try to please them,

---

FRIDAY

VERSE FOR THE DAY:	AUTHOR:	PASSAGE FOR THE DAY:
Titus 3:7	Dave Dravecky	Titus 3:1–8

A Deep Well of Hope

GOD is personal. That lesson, learned [while on an Amarillo Double-A baseball team], changed our lives forever. It transformed our response to the news [of a tumor in my pitching arm] we heard seven years later at the Cleveland Clinic.

It prevented us from responding to the tumor with bitterness and anger. If I'd still had an image of God as a distant Keeper of the Rules, then it would have seemed very unfair to me that I was getting a tougher deal than a lot of other ballplayers. What was happening wasn't fair, and a Rulekeeper God either didn't exist, or I had good reason for being very angry at him.

But that's not my image of God any longer. He's not the Cosmic Bookkeeper, the one to blame if things don't work out the way you think they should. Life isn't always fair, at least in the short run, but the Bible taught me not to confuse life with God. When you're confronted with trouble you don't ask, "Why me?" You ask God, "What do you want me to do in this situation?"

Because the God who revealed himself in Jesus is full of love. He never deserts his children. Janice and I entered this difficult period, when life was often beyond our control, with a deep conviction that God was for us. Jesus had given his life for us. There was nothing else—no other good thing—he would withhold. We expected to see God's love in whatever came—however strange the twists and turns of the road might be. That fundamental belief gave us a deep well of hope to draw from.

Additional Scripture Readings:
Colossians 1:3–14; 1 Peter 1:3–9

Go to page 1325 for your next devotional reading.

not to talk back to them, [10]and not to steal from them, but to show that they can be fully trusted, so that in every way they will make the teaching about God our Savior attractive.

[11]For the grace of God that brings salvation has appeared to all men. [12]It teaches us to say "No" to ungodliness and worldly passions, and to live self-controlled, upright and godly lives in this present age, [13]while we wait for the blessed hope — the glorious appearing of our great God and Savior, Jesus Christ, [14]who gave himself for us to redeem us from all wickedness and to purify for himself a people that are his very own, eager to do what is good.

[15]These, then, are the things you should teach. Encourage and rebuke with all authority. Do not let anyone despise you.

Doing What Is Good

3 Remind the people to be subject to rulers and authorities, to be obedient, to be ready to do whatever is good, [2]to slander no one, to be peaceable and considerate, and to show true humility toward all men.

[3]At one time we too were foolish, disobedient, deceived and enslaved by all kinds of passions and pleasures. We lived in malice and envy, being hated and hating one another. [4]But when the kindness and love of God our Savior appeared, [5]he saved us, not because of righteous things we had done, but because of his mercy.

He saved us through the washing of rebirth and renewal by the Holy Spirit, [6]whom he poured out on us generously through Jesus Christ our Savior, [7]so that, having been justified by his grace, we might become heirs having the hope of eternal life. [8]This is a trustworthy saying. And I want you to stress these things, so that those who have trusted in God may be careful to devote themselves to doing what is good. These things are excellent and profitable for everyone.

[9]But avoid foolish controversies and genealogies and arguments and quarrels about the law, because these are unprofitable and useless. [10]Warn a divisive person once, and then warn him a second time. After that, have nothing to do with him. [11]You may be sure that such a man is warped and sinful; he is self-condemned.

Final Remarks

[12]As soon as I send Artemas or Tychicus to you, do your best to come to me at Nicopolis, because I have decided to winter there. [13]Do everything you can to help Zenas the lawyer and Apollos on their way and see that they have everything they need. [14]Our people must learn to devote themselves to doing what is good, in order that they may provide for daily necessities and not live unproductive lives.

[15]Everyone with me sends you greetings. Greet those who love us in the faith.

Grace be with you all.

PAUL writes this brief letter to ask Philemon, a Christian brother living (probably) in Colosse, to forgive and take back Onesimus, a runaway slave who has become a Christian and is helping Paul in prison. As you read this book, be willing to forgive others, no matter what they do to you.

PHILEMON

¹Paul, a prisoner of Christ Jesus, and Timothy our brother,

To Philemon our dear friend and fellow worker, ²to Apphia our sister, to Archippus our fellow soldier and to the church that meets in your home:

³Grace to you and peace from God our Father and the Lord Jesus Christ.

Thanksgiving and Prayer

⁴I always thank my God as I remember you in my prayers, ⁵because I hear about your faith in the Lord Jesus and your love for all the saints. ⁶I pray that you may be active in sharing your faith, so that you will have a full understanding of every good thing we have in Christ. ⁷Your love has given me great joy and encouragement, because you, brother, have refreshed the hearts of the saints.

Paul's Plea for Onesimus

⁸Therefore, although in Christ I could be bold and order you to do what you ought to do, ⁹yet I appeal to you on the basis of love. I then, as Paul—an old man and now also a prisoner of Christ Jesus—¹⁰I appeal to you for my son Onesimus,ᵃ who became my son while I was in chains. ¹¹Formerly he was useless to you, but now he has become useful both to you and to me.

¹²I am sending him—who is my very heart—back to you. ¹³I would have liked to keep him with me so that he could take your place in helping me while I am in chains for the gospel. ¹⁴But I did not want to do anything without your consent, so that any favor you do will be spontaneous and not forced. ¹⁵Perhaps the reason he was separated from you for a little while was that you might have him back for

WEEKENDING

RELAX

The little child says
Here I am daddy
as he bursts
on father's sight
from behind the chair
where he's been hiding.
He doesn't say
What can I do for you?
How can I help you?
I want to serve you
seeking somehow
to work and gain
the father's favor
and delight.
He knows they are his
without exhausting effort
to achieve.
They are his always.
Here I am daddy
—Abba Father—
not working
just being
your eternal son.

— Joseph Bayly

REVIVE
Saturday: John 1:10–13
Sunday: Romans 8:12–17

Go to page 1326 for your next devotional reading.

good — ¹⁶no longer as a slave, but better than a slave, as a dear brother. He is very dear to me but even dearer to you, both as a man and as a brother in the Lord.

¹⁷So if you consider me a partner, welcome him as you would welcome me. ¹⁸If he has done you any wrong or owes you anything, charge it to me. ¹⁹I, Paul, am writing this with my own hand. I will pay it back — not to mention that you owe me your very self. ²⁰I do wish, brother, that I may have some benefit from you in the Lord; refresh my heart in Christ. ²¹Confi-

dent of your obedience, I write to you, knowing that you will do even more than I ask.

²²And one thing more: Prepare a guest room for me, because I hope to be restored to you in answer to your prayers.

²³Epaphras, my fellow prisoner in Christ Jesus, sends you greetings. ²⁴And so do Mark, Aristarchus, Demas and Luke, my fellow workers.

²⁵The grace of the Lord Jesus Christ be with your spirit.

MONDAY

VERSE FOR THE DAY:	AUTHOR:	PASSAGE FOR THE DAY:
Philemon 16	Charles Stanley	Philemon 12–18

Grabbing Rattlesnakes

A PERSON who harbors unforgiveness always loses. Regardless of how wrong the other person may have been, refusing to forgive means reaping corruption in life. And that corruption begins in one relationship including the relationship with God, and works its way into all the rest.

Holding on to hurt is like grabbing a rattlesnake by the tail; you are going to be bitten. As the poison of bitterness works its way through the many facets of your personality, death will occur — death that is more far-reaching than your physical death, for it has the potential to destroy those around you as well.

Have you been hurt? Has somebody, somewhere in your past, rejected you in such a way that you still hurt when you think about it? Do you become critical of people in your past the minute their names are mentioned? Did you leave home as a child or a college student with great relief that you were leaving, swearing you would never return? . . .

Whatever your situation, whatever has happened in your past, remember that you are the loser if you do not deal with an unforgiving spirit. And the people around you suffer, too.

Additional Scripture Readings:
Matthew 18:21–35;
Ephesians 4:25–32

Go to page 1329 for your next devotional reading.

THE author of this letter encourages Christians who are being persecuted for their faith by pointing them to the greatness of the Son of God who became man. Christ is the full expression of God's revelation, better than anything in the Old Testament; the author warns his readers to depend on Christ alone. As you read this book, commit yourself firmly to Jesus your Intercessor, and be sure to persevere and grow daily in your Christian faith and life.

HEBREWS

The Son Superior to Angels

1 In the past God spoke to our forefathers through the prophets at many times and in various ways, **2**but in these last days he has spoken to us by his Son, whom he appointed heir of all things, and through whom he made the universe. **3**The Son is the radiance of God's glory and the exact representation of his being, sustaining all things by his powerful word. After he had provided purification for sins, he sat down at the right hand of the Majesty in heaven. **4**So he became as much superior to the angels as the name he has inherited is superior to theirs.

5For to which of the angels did God ever say,

"You are my Son;
  today I have become your
    Father*a*"*b*?

Or again,

"I will be his Father,
  and he will be my Son"*c*?

6And again, when God brings his firstborn into the world, he says,

a5 Or have begotten you   *b5 Psalm 2:7*   *c5 2 Samuel 7:14; 1 Chron. 17:13*

"Let all God's angels worship him."[a]

[7]In speaking of the angels he says,

"He makes his angels winds,
    his servants flames of fire."[b]

[8]But about the Son he says,

"Your throne, O God, will last for ever
    and ever,
  and righteousness will be the
    scepter of your kingdom.
[9]You have loved righteousness and
    hated wickedness;
  therefore God, your God, has set
    you above your companions
  by anointing you with the oil of
    joy."[c]

[10]He also says,

"In the beginning, O Lord, you laid
    the foundations of the earth,
  and the heavens are the work of
    your hands.
[11]They will perish, but you remain;
  they will all wear out like a
    garment.
[12]You will roll them up like a robe;
  like a garment they will be changed.
But you remain the same,
  and your years will never end."[d]

[13]To which of the angels did God ever say,

"Sit at my right hand
until I make your enemies
a footstool for your feet"[e]?

[14]Are not all angels ministering spirits
sent to serve those who will inherit salvation?

Warning to Pay Attention

2 We must pay more careful attention,
therefore, to what we have heard, so
that we do not drift away. [2]For if the message spoken by angels was binding, and
every violation and disobedience received
its just punishment, [3]how shall we escape
if we ignore such a great salvation? This
salvation, which was first announced by
the Lord, was confirmed to us by those
who heard him. [4]God also testified to it by
signs, wonders and various miracles, and
gifts of the Holy Spirit distributed according to his will.

Jesus Made Like His Brothers

[5]It is not to angels that he has subjected
the world to come, about which we are
speaking. [6]But there is a place where
someone has testified:

"What is man that you are mindful of
    him,
  the son of man that you care for
    him?
[7]You made him a little[f] lower than
    the angels;
  you crowned him with glory and
    honor
[8] and put everything under his
    feet."[g]

In putting everything under him, God left
nothing that is not subject to him. Yet at
present we do not see everything subject
to him. [9]But we see Jesus, who was made
a little lower than the angels, now
crowned with glory and honor because he
suffered death, so that by the grace of God
he might taste death for everyone.

[10]In bringing many sons to glory, it was
fitting that God, for whom and through
whom everything exists, should make the
author of their salvation perfect through
suffering. [11]Both the one who makes men
holy and those who are made holy are of
the same family. So Jesus is not ashamed
to call them brothers. [12]He says,

"I will declare your name to my
    brothers;
  in the presence of the congregation
    I will sing your praises."[h]

[13]And again,

"I will put my trust in him."[i]

And again he says,

"Here am I, and the children God has
    given me."[j]

[14]Since the children have flesh and
blood, he too shared in their humanity so
that by his death he might destroy him
who holds the power of death—that is,
the devil— [15]and free those who all their
lives were held in slavery by their fear of
death. [16]For surely it is not angels he
helps, but Abraham's descendants. [17]For
this reason he had to be made like his
brothers in every way, in order that he
might become a merciful and faithful high

---

[a]6 Deut. 32:43 (see Dead Sea Scrolls and Septuagint)   [b]7 Psalm 104:4   [c]9 Psalm 45:6,7
[d]12 Psalm 102:25-27   [e]13 Psalm 110:1   [f]7 Or him for a little while; also in verse 9
[g]8 Psalm 8:4-6   [h]12 Psalm 22:22   [i]13 Isaiah 8:17   [j]13 Isaiah 8:18

TUESDAY

VERSE FOR THE DAY:
Hebrews 2:11

AUTHOR:
Reuben R. Welch

PASSAGE FOR THE DAY:
Hebrews 2:5–18

He Calls Us Brothers

THE warnings at the beginning of chapter 2 [of Hebrews] called the Hebrews to renewed attentiveness, renewed grip and spirit, new heart and enthusiasm, and recovery of the joy of first love.

Perhaps the writer knew that underneath their drift and loss of nerve were secret hurts and failures, hidden burdens and defeats. Very few believers choose to drift; seldom do Christians plan to be lukewarm. But poor performance undermines confidence and failure causes discouragement. Temptation, even when overcome, leaves us battle-scarred and weary. It is sometimes difficult to tell the difference between victory and defeat because issues are never clear-cut and our successes never total. When one has struggled through the testing time and finally endured, it seldom feels like triumph.

At such times . . . we desperately need to know that Jesus is our brother, with us as we struggle on the way, having the compassion that can only come through his shared experience of suffering and temptation. Our approach to the throne of grace (4:16) is not on the basis of our victories. We are not invited because we are worthy. Jesus our brother opens up the way for us to come in our weaknesses, temptations and failures. He is with us in sympathy and help, not at the end of our struggle, but all the way through.

This is the only way, I believe, that we can maintain vitality and energy and joy in the long haul of the Christian life. Someone has to help us *at the time of our struggle*; we need help *while we are trying*; we need a brother *in the hour of trial*, and especially when we fail. Otherwise we fall into the discouragement of trying harder or of never quite measuring up. The subtle shift from trust in Christ to our own self-efforts robs us of hope and joy. We begin to tally hurts, count disappointments and weigh sacrifices. And already the drift has set in. We need the warning, but more than that, we need to know that we are known, understood and loved by someone who has marked out the path, has won the victory and is with us on the way. That someone is Jesus.

Additional Scripture Readings:
Matthew 11:25–30; Hebrews 4:14–16

Go to page 1331 for your next devotional reading.

priest in service to God, and that he might make atonement for[a] the sins of the people. **18**Because he himself suffered when he was tempted, he is able to help those who are being tempted.

Jesus Greater Than Moses

3 Therefore, holy brothers, who share in the heavenly calling, fix your thoughts on Jesus, the apostle and high priest whom we confess. **2**He was faithful to the one who appointed him, just as Moses was faithful in all God's house. **3**Jesus has been found worthy of greater honor than Moses, just as the builder of a house has greater honor than the house itself. **4**For every house is built by someone, but God is the builder of everything. **5**Moses was faithful as a servant in all God's house, testifying to what would be said in the future. **6**But Christ is faithful as a son over God's house. And we are his house, if we hold on to our courage and the hope of which we boast.

Warning Against Unbelief

7So, as the Holy Spirit says:

"Today, if you hear his voice,
8   do not harden your hearts
as you did in the rebellion,
      during the time of testing in the
         desert,
9where your fathers tested and tried
      me
   and for forty years saw what I did.
10That is why I was angry with that
      generation,
   and I said, 'Their hearts are always
      going astray,
   and they have not known my ways.'
11So I declared on oath in my anger,
   'They shall never enter my rest.' "[b]

12See to it, brothers, that none of you has a sinful, unbelieving heart that turns away from the living God. **13**But encourage one another daily, as long as it is called Today, so that none of you may be hardened by sin's deceitfulness. **14**We have come to share in Christ if we hold firmly till the end the confidence we had at first. **15**As has just been said:

"Today, if you hear his voice,
   do not harden your hearts
   as you did in the rebellion."[c]

16Who were they who heard and rebelled? Were they not all those Moses led out of Egypt? **17**And with whom was he angry for forty years? Was it not with those who sinned, whose bodies fell in the desert? **18**And to whom did God swear that they would never enter his rest if not to those who disobeyed[d]? **19**So we see that they were not able to enter, because of their unbelief.

A Sabbath-Rest for the People of God

4 Therefore, since the promise of entering his rest still stands, let us be careful that none of you be found to have fallen short of it. **2**For we also have had the gospel preached to us, just as they did; but the message they heard was of no value to them, because those who heard did not combine it with faith.[e] **3**Now we who have believed enter that rest, just as God has said,

"So I declared on oath in my anger,
   'They shall never enter my rest.' "[f]

And yet his work has been finished since the creation of the world. **4**For somewhere he has spoken about the seventh day in these words: "And on the seventh day God rested from all his work."[g] **5**And again in the passage above he says, "They shall never enter my rest."

6It still remains that some will enter that rest, and those who formerly had the gospel preached to them did not go in, because of their disobedience. **7**Therefore God again set a certain day, calling it Today, when a long time later he spoke through David, as was said before:

"Today, if you hear his voice,
   do not harden your hearts."[c]

8For if Joshua had given them rest, God would not have spoken later about another day. **9**There remains, then, a Sabbath-rest for the people of God; **10**for anyone who enters God's rest also rests from his own work, just as God did from his. **11**Let us, therefore, make every effort to enter that rest, so that no one will fall by following their example of disobedience.

12For the word of God is living and active. Sharper than any double-edged sword, it penetrates even to dividing soul and spirit, joints and marrow; it judges the thoughts and attitudes of the heart.

---

a17 Or *and that he might turn aside God's wrath, taking away*   *b11* Psalm 95:7-11
c15,7 Psalm 95:7,8   *d18* Or *disbelieved*   *e2* Many manuscripts *because they did not share in the faith of those who obeyed*   *f3* Psalm 95:11; also in verse 5   *g4* Gen. 2:2

¹³Nothing in all creation is hidden from God's sight. Everything is uncovered and laid bare before the eyes of him to whom we must give account.

Jesus the Great High Priest

¹⁴Therefore, since we have a great high priest who has gone through the heavens,ᵃ Jesus the Son of God, let us hold firmly to the faith we profess. ¹⁵For we do not have a high priest who is unable to sympathize with our weaknesses, but we have one who has been tempted in every way, just as we are—yet was without sin. ¹⁶Let us then approach the throne of grace with confidence, so that we may receive mercy and find grace to help us in our time of need.

5 Every high priest is selected from among men and is appointed to represent them in matters related to God, to offer gifts and sacrifices for sins. ²He is able to deal gently with those who are ignorant and are going astray, since he himself is

ᵃ14 Or gone into heaven

WEDNESDAY

VERSE FOR THE DAY:
Hebrews 4:16

AUTHOR:
Jim Conway

PASSAGE FOR THE DAY:
Hebrews 4:14–16

Great Physician and Friend

WHY have people been so attracted to Jesus down through the centuries? The Bible answers that question in a simple phrase, "We love because he first loved us" (1 John 4:19).

As you look at the special relationship Jesus had with so many people, you must be convinced that Jesus is on the side of common people. Anybody who was hurt, sick, mistreated, lonely, disenfranchised or condemned—people like you and me—were the ones Jesus came to help.

Matthew wrote, "When the Pharisees saw this, they asked his disciples, 'Why does your teacher eat with tax collectors and "sinners"?' On hearing this, Jesus said, 'It is not the healthy who need a doctor, but the sick'" (Matthew 9:11–12). In essence, Jesus was saying, "My job here on earth is to get sinners back to God, not to worry about the good people."

Jesus does not present himself to us as "holier than thou," but rather as a friend. He said, "I no longer call you servants, because a servant does not know his master's business. Instead, I have called you friends, for everything that I learned from my Father I have made known to you" (John 15:15).

We are not second-class citizens. The Bible says we are part of God's family. Hebrews 4 records that Jesus, who is now in heaven, intercedes for us and that he understands our weaknesses. We are encouraged to "approach the throne of grace with confidence, so that we may receive mercy and find grace to help us in our time of need" (Hebrews 4:16).

Additional Scripture Readings:
Matthew 9:9–13; John 15:9–17

Go to page 1333 for your next devotional reading.

subject to weakness. [3]This is why he has to offer sacrifices for his own sins, as well as for the sins of the people.

[4]No one takes this honor upon himself; he must be called by God, just as Aaron was. [5]So Christ also did not take upon himself the glory of becoming a high priest. But God said to him,

"You are my Son;
today I have become your
Father.[a]"[b]

[6]And he says in another place,

"You are a priest forever,
in the order of Melchizedek."[c]

[7]During the days of Jesus' life on earth, he offered up prayers and petitions with loud cries and tears to the one who could save him from death, and he was heard because of his reverent submission. [8]Although he was a son, he learned obedience from what he suffered [9]and, once made perfect, he became the source of eternal salvation for all who obey him [10]and was designated by God to be high priest in the order of Melchizedek.

Warning Against Falling Away

[11]We have much to say about this, but it is hard to explain because you are slow to learn. [12]In fact, though by this time you ought to be teachers, you need someone to teach you the elementary truths of God's word all over again. You need milk, not solid food! [13]Anyone who lives on milk, being still an infant, is not acquainted with the teaching about righteousness. [14]But solid food is for the mature, who by constant use have trained themselves to distinguish good from evil.

6 Therefore let us leave the elementary teachings about Christ and go on to maturity, not laying again the foundation of repentance from acts that lead to death,[d] and of faith in God, [2]instruction about baptisms, the laying on of hands, the resurrection of the dead, and eternal judgment. [3]And God permitting, we will do so.

[4]It is impossible for those who have once been enlightened, who have tasted the heavenly gift, who have shared in the Holy Spirit, [5]who have tasted the goodness of the word of God and the powers of the coming age, [6]if they fall away, to be brought back to repentance, because[e] to

their loss they are crucifying the Son of God all over again and subjecting him to public disgrace.

[7]Land that drinks in the rain often falling on it and that produces a crop useful to those for whom it is farmed receives the blessing of God. [8]But land that produces thorns and thistles is worthless and is in danger of being cursed. In the end it will be burned.

[9]Even though we speak like this, dear friends, we are confident of better things in your case—things that accompany salvation. [10]God is not unjust; he will not forget your work and the love you have shown him as you have helped his people and continue to help them. [11]We want each of you to show this same diligence to the very end, in order to make your hope sure. [12]We do not want you to become lazy, but to imitate those who through faith and patience inherit what has been promised.

The Certainty of God's Promise

[13]When God made his promise to Abraham, since there was no one greater for him to swear by, he swore by himself, [14]saying, "I will surely bless you and give you many descendants."[f] [15]And so after waiting patiently, Abraham received what was promised.

[16]Men swear by someone greater than themselves, and the oath confirms what is said and puts an end to all argument. [17]Because God wanted to make the unchanging nature of his purpose very clear to the heirs of what was promised, he confirmed it with an oath. [18]God did this so that, by two unchangeable things in which it is impossible for God to lie, we who have fled to take hold of the hope offered to us may be greatly encouraged. [19]We have this hope as an anchor for the soul, firm and secure. It enters the inner sanctuary behind the curtain, [20]where Jesus, who went before us, has entered on our behalf. He has become a high priest forever, in the order of Melchizedek.

Melchizedek the Priest

7 This Melchizedek was king of Salem and priest of God Most High. He met Abraham returning from the defeat of the kings and blessed him, [2]and Abraham gave him a tenth of everything. First, his name means "king of righteousness"; then

---

[a]5 Or *have begotten you*   [b]5 Psalm 2:7   [c]6 Psalm 110:4   [d]1 Or *from useless rituals*   [e]6 Or *repentance while*   [f]14 Gen. 22:17

VERSE FOR THE DAY:
Hebrews 5:14

AUTHOR:
Reggie White

PASSAGE FOR THE DAY:
Hebrews 5:11—6:3

A Good Defense

YOU know, as a Christian, I run into the very same problems on a spiritual level that I do on the football field. I can get blindsided by friends or other people who don't understand me and what I stand for. I probably trust too many persons and when I'm not looking, I have received a crackback block mentally and sometimes physically. I've also been attacked for my beliefs by a double-team and a triple-team.

How do I handle these threats to my faith? The same way I do as a football player.

The first step is training. I must study God's Word on a daily basis. Paul wrote to Timothy: "Do your best to present yourself to God as one approved, a workman who does not need to be ashamed and who correctly handles the word of truth" (2 Timothy 2:15).

There is no way I will ever be able to deal with all that life has to offer without daily and diligently delving into God's Word . . .

The second focus is on my surroundings. I must also be careful not to surround myself too closely with those who don't believe in God's Word. I have many friends who are not Christians and I sure do love them. But we have a different relationship. Unbelievers just don't have as much in common as believers do. They don't have the same goals, morals or social life that believers in Christ have.

It doesn't take too much sense to realize that you become like those with whom you spend the most time. Know your surroundings and control them; don't let your surroundings control you.

Finally, practice what you know is right. Too often we focus on doing what we've always done. We don't progress, keep in shape, work out daily. The warning is clear: "Solid food is for the mature, who by constant use have trained themselves to distinguish good from evil. Therefore let us leave the elementary teachings about Christ and go on to maturity" (Hebrews 5:14—6:1).

Additional Scripture Readings:
2 Corinthians 6:14–18;
1 Timothy 4:6–8

Go to page 1336 for your next devotional reading.

also, "king of Salem" means "king of peace." [3]Without father or mother, without genealogy, without beginning of days or end of life, like the Son of God he remains a priest forever.

[4]Just think how great he was: Even the patriarch Abraham gave him a tenth of the plunder! [5]Now the law requires the descendants of Levi who become priests to collect a tenth from the people — that is, their brothers — even though their brothers are descended from Abraham. [6]This man, however, did not trace his descent from Levi, yet he collected a tenth from Abraham and blessed him who had the promises. [7]And without doubt the lesser person is blessed by the greater. [8]In the one case, the tenth is collected by men who die; but in the other case, by him who is declared to be living. [9]One might even say that Levi, who collects the tenth, paid the tenth through Abraham, [10]because when Melchizedek met Abraham, Levi was still in the body of his ancestor.

Jesus Like Melchizedek

[11]If perfection could have been attained through the Levitical priesthood (for on the basis of it the law was given to the people), why was there still need for another priest to come — one in the order of Melchizedek, not in the order of Aaron? [12]For when there is a change of the priesthood, there must also be a change of the law. [13]He of whom these things are said belonged to a different tribe, and no one from that tribe has ever served at the altar. [14]For it is clear that our Lord descended from Judah, and in regard to that tribe Moses said nothing about priests. [15]And what we have said is even more clear if another priest like Melchizedek appears, [16]one who has become a priest not on the basis of a regulation as to his ancestry but on the basis of the power of an indestructible life. [17]For it is declared:

"You are a priest forever,
    in the order of Melchizedek."[a]

[18]The former regulation is set aside because it was weak and useless [19](for the law made nothing perfect), and a better hope is introduced, by which we draw near to God.

[20]And it was not without an oath! Others became priests without any oath, [21]but he became a priest with an oath when God said to him:

"The Lord has sworn
    and will not change his mind:
'You are a priest forever.' "[a]

[22]Because of this oath, Jesus has become the guarantee of a better covenant.

[23]Now there have been many of those priests, since death prevented them from continuing in office; [24]but because Jesus lives forever, he has a permanent priesthood. [25]Therefore he is able to save completely[b] those who come to God through him, because he always lives to intercede for them.

[26]Such a high priest meets our need — one who is holy, blameless, pure, set apart from sinners, exalted above the heavens. [27]Unlike the other high priests, he does not need to offer sacrifices day after day, first for his own sins, and then for the sins of the people. He sacrificed for their sins once for all when he offered himself. [28]For the law appoints as high priests men who are weak; but the oath, which came after the law, appointed the Son, who has been made perfect forever.

The High Priest of a New Covenant

8 The point of what we are saying is this: We do have such a high priest, who sat down at the right hand of the throne of the Majesty in heaven, [2]and who serves in the sanctuary, the true tabernacle set up by the Lord, not by man.

[3]Every high priest is appointed to offer both gifts and sacrifices, and so it was necessary for this one also to have something to offer. [4]If he were on earth, he would not be a priest, for there are already men who offer the gifts prescribed by the law. [5]They serve at a sanctuary that is a copy and shadow of what is in heaven. This is why Moses was warned when he was about to build the tabernacle: "See to it that you make everything according to the pattern shown you on the mountain."[c] [6]But the ministry Jesus has received is as superior to theirs as the covenant of which he is mediator is superior to the old one, and it is founded on better promises.

[7]For if there had been nothing wrong with that first covenant, no place would have been sought for another. [8]But God found fault with the people and said[d]:

"The time is coming, declares the
　　Lord,
　when I will make a new covenant
　with the house of Israel
　　and with the house of Judah.
⁹It will not be like the covenant
　I made with their forefathers
　when I took them by the hand
　　to lead them out of Egypt,
　because they did not remain faithful
　　to my covenant,
　and I turned away from them,
　　　　　　　declares the Lord.
¹⁰This is the covenant I will make with
　　the house of Israel
　after that time, declares the Lord.
　I will put my laws in their minds
　　and write them on their hearts.
　I will be their God,
　　and they will be my people.
¹¹No longer will a man teach his
　　neighbor,
　or a man his brother, saying, 'Know
　　the Lord,'
　because they will all know me,
　　from the least of them to the
　　greatest.
¹²For I will forgive their wickedness
　　and will remember their sins no
　　more."ᵃ

¹³By calling this covenant "new," he has
made the first one obsolete; and what is
obsolete and aging will soon disappear.

Worship in the Earthly Tabernacle

9 Now the first covenant had regulations for worship and also an earthly
sanctuary. ²A tabernacle was set up. In its
first room were the lampstand, the table
and the consecrated bread; this was called
the Holy Place. ³Behind the second curtain was a room called the Most Holy
Place, ⁴which had the golden altar of incense and the gold-covered ark of the covenant. This ark contained the gold jar of
manna, Aaron's staff that had budded,
and the stone tablets of the covenant.
⁵Above the ark were the cherubim of the
Glory, overshadowing the atonement cov-
er.ᵇ But we cannot discuss these things
in detail now.

⁶When everything had been arranged
like this, the priests entered regularly into
the outer room to carry on their ministry.
⁷But only the high priest entered the inner
room, and that only once a year, and nev-

er without blood, which he offered for
himself and for the sins the people had
committed in ignorance. ⁸The Holy Spirit
was showing by this that the way into the
Most Holy Place had not yet been disclosed as long as the first tabernacle was
still standing. ⁹This is an illustration for
the present time, indicating that the gifts
and sacrifices being offered were not able
to clear the conscience of the worshiper.
¹⁰They are only a matter of food and drink
and various ceremonial washings—external regulations applying until the time of
the new order.

The Blood of Christ

¹¹When Christ came as high priest of
the good things that are already here,ᶜ he
went through the greater and more perfect
tabernacle that is not man-made, that is to
say, not a part of this creation. ¹²He did
not enter by means of the blood of goats
and calves; but he entered the Most Holy
Place once for all by his own blood, having obtained eternal redemption. ¹³The
blood of goats and bulls and the ashes of
a heifer sprinkled on those who are ceremonially unclean sanctify them so that
they are outwardly clean. ¹⁴How much
more, then, will the blood of Christ, who
through the eternal Spirit offered himself
unblemished to God, cleanse our consciences from acts that lead to death,ᵈ so
that we may serve the living God!

¹⁵For this reason Christ is the mediator
of a new covenant, that those who are
called may receive the promised eternal
inheritance—now that he has died as a
ransom to set them free from the sins
committed under the first covenant.

¹⁶In the case of a will,ᵉ it is necessary
to prove the death of the one who made it,
¹⁷because a will is in force only when
somebody has died; it never takes effect
while the one who made it is living. ¹⁸This
is why even the first covenant was not put
into effect without blood. ¹⁹When Moses
had proclaimed every commandment of
the law to all the people, he took the blood
of calves, together with water, scarlet
wool and branches of hyssop, and sprinkled the scroll and all the people. ²⁰He
said, "This is the blood of the covenant,
which God has commanded you to
keep."ᶠ ²¹In the same way, he sprinkled
with the blood both the tabernacle and everything used in its ceremonies. ²²In fact,

ᵃ12 Jer. 31:31-34　　ᵇ5 Traditionally *the mercy seat*　　ᶜ11 Some early manuscripts *are to come*
ᵈ14 Or *from useless rituals*　　ᵉ16 Same Greek word as *covenant*; also in verse 17　　ᶠ20 Exodus 24:8

the law requires that nearly everything be cleansed with blood, and without the shedding of blood there is no forgiveness.

²³It was necessary, then, for the copies of the heavenly things to be purified with these sacrifices, but the heavenly things themselves with better sacrifices than these. ²⁴For Christ did not enter a man-made sanctuary that was only a copy of the true one; he entered heaven itself, now to appear for us in God's presence. ²⁵Nor did he enter heaven to offer himself again and again, the way the high priest enters the Most Holy Place every year with blood that is not his own. ²⁶Then Christ would have had to suffer many times since the creation of the world. But now he has appeared once for all at the end of the ages to do away with sin by the sacrifice of himself. ²⁷Just as man is destined to die once, and after that to face judgment, ²⁸so Christ was sacrificed once to take away the sins of many people; and he will appear a second time, not to bear sin, but to bring salvation to those who are waiting for him.

Christ's Sacrifice Once for All

10 The law is only a shadow of the good things that are coming — not the realities themselves. For this reason it can never, by the same sacrifices repeated

---

FRIDAY

VERSE FOR THE DAY:
Hebrews 9:15

AUTHOR:
Dietrich Bonhoeffer

PASSAGE FOR THE DAY:
Hebrews 9:11–15

Christianity Without Christ

DISCIPLESHIP means adherence to Christ, and, because Christ is the object of that adherence, it must take the form of discipleship. An abstract Christology, a doctrinal system, a general religious knowledge on the subject of grace or on the forgiveness of sins, render discipleship superfluous, and in fact they positively exclude any idea of discipleship whatever, and are essentially inimical to the whole conception of following Christ. With an abstract idea it is possible to enter into a relation of formal knowledge, to become enthusiastic about it, and perhaps even to put it into practice; but it can never be followed in personal obedience.

Christianity without the living Christ is inevitably Christianity without discipleship, and Christianity without discipleship is always Christianity without Christ. It remains an abstract idea, a myth that has a place for the Fatherhood of God, but omits Christ as the living Son. And a Christianity of that kind is nothing more or less than the end of discipleship. In such a religion there is trust in God, but no following of Christ. Because the Son of God became Man, because he is the Mediator, for that reason alone the only true relation we can have with him is to follow him. Discipleship is bound to Christ as the Mediator, and where it is properly understood, it necessarily implies faith in the Son of God as the Mediator. Only the Mediator, the God-Man, can call men to follow him.

Additional Scripture Readings:
John 10:7–18; 1 Timothy 2:1–7

Go to page 1338 for your next devotional reading.

endlessly year after year, make perfect those who draw near to worship. ²If it could, would they not have stopped being offered? For the worshipers would have been cleansed once for all, and would no longer have felt guilty for their sins. ³But those sacrifices are an annual reminder of sins, ⁴because it is impossible for the blood of bulls and goats to take away sins.

⁵Therefore, when Christ came into the world, he said:

> "Sacrifice and offering you did not
>   desire,
>   but a body you prepared for me;
> ⁶with burnt offerings and sin offerings
>   you were not pleased.
> ⁷Then I said, 'Here I am — it is written
>   about me in the scroll —
>   I have come to do your will,
>   O God.' "ᵃ

⁸First he said, "Sacrifices and offerings, burnt offerings and sin offerings you did not desire, nor were you pleased with them" (although the law required them to be made). ⁹Then he said, "Here I am, I have come to do your will." He sets aside the first to establish the second. ¹⁰And by that will, we have been made holy through the sacrifice of the body of Jesus Christ once for all.

¹¹Day after day every priest stands and performs his religious duties; again and again he offers the same sacrifices, which can never take away sins. ¹²But when this priest had offered for all time one sacrifice for sins, he sat down at the right hand of God. ¹³Since that time he waits for his enemies to be made his footstool, ¹⁴because by one sacrifice he has made perfect forever those who are being made holy.

¹⁵The Holy Spirit also testifies to us about this. First he says:

> ¹⁶"This is the covenant I will make with
>   them
>   after that time, says the Lord.
> I will put my laws in their hearts,
>   and I will write them on their
>   minds."ᵇ

¹⁷Then he adds:

> "Their sins and lawless acts
>   I will remember no more."ᶜ

¹⁸And where these have been forgiven, there is no longer any sacrifice for sin.

A Call to Persevere

¹⁹Therefore, brothers, since we have confidence to enter the Most Holy Place by the blood of Jesus, ²⁰by a new and living way opened for us through the curtain, that is, his body, ²¹and since we have a great priest over the house of God, ²²let us draw near to God with a sincere heart in full assurance of faith, having our hearts sprinkled to cleanse us from a guilty conscience and having our bodies washed with pure water. ²³Let us hold unswervingly to the hope we profess, for he who promised is faithful. ²⁴And let us consider how we may spur one another on toward love and good deeds. ²⁵Let us not give up meeting together, as some are in the habit of doing, but let us encourage one another — and all the more as you see the Day approaching.

²⁶If we deliberately keep on sinning after we have received the knowledge of the truth, no sacrifice for sins is left, ²⁷but only a fearful expectation of judgment and of raging fire that will consume the enemies of God. ²⁸Anyone who rejected the law of Moses died without mercy on the testimony of two or three witnesses. ²⁹How much more severely do you think a man deserves to be punished who has trampled the Son of God under foot, who has treated as an unholy thing the blood of the covenant that sanctified him, and who has insulted the Spirit of grace? ³⁰For we know him who said, "It is mine to avenge; I will repay,"ᵈ and again, "The Lord will judge his people."ᵉ ³¹It is a dreadful thing to fall into the hands of the living God.

³²Remember those earlier days after you had received the light, when you stood your ground in a great contest in the face of suffering. ³³Sometimes you were publicly exposed to insult and persecution; at other times you stood side by side with those who were so treated. ³⁴You sympathized with those in prison and joyfully accepted the confiscation of your property, because you knew that you yourselves had better and lasting possessions.

³⁵So do not throw away your confidence; it will be richly rewarded. ³⁶You need to persevere so that when you have done the will of God, you will receive

---

ᵃ7 Psalm 40:6-8 (see Septuagint)   ᵇ16 Jer. 31:33   ᶜ17 Jer. 31:34   ᵈ30 Deut. 32:35   ᵉ30 Deut.
32:36; Psalm 135:14

WEEKENDING

RECEIVE

Prayer is one of the unlimited resources
available to each of us. In this bound-up world,
prayer may be a lost art, but it is always the
starting point when we move toward God. In
prayer we set aside our agendas, letting God's
priorities become our priorities, and we receive
his resources.

– *John F. Westfall*

RESOLVE

You don't have to learn some special prayer
jargon to start a conversation with God.
Honesty and a willingness to establish a
personal relationship with him are the only
initial requirements. God is looking for an
opportunity to reveal himself to you, so if you
put him to the test and then watch for an
answer without too many preconceptions about
how that answer will come, *I can guarantee you
that you'll be in for some exciting surprises.*

– *Pat Boone*

REVIVE

Saturday: Philippians 4:4–9
Sunday: Hebrews 4:14–16

Go to page 1340 for your next devotional reading.

what he has promised. ³⁷For in just a very little while,

"He who is coming will come and will not delay.
³⁸ But my righteous one[a] will live by faith.
And if he shrinks back,
    I will not be pleased with him."[b]

³⁹But we are not of those who shrink back and are destroyed, but of those who believe and are saved.

By Faith

11 Now faith is being sure of what we hope for and certain of what we do not see. ²This is what the ancients were commended for.

³By faith we understand that the universe was formed at God's command, so that what is seen was not made out of what was visible.

⁴By faith Abel offered God a better sacrifice than Cain did. By faith he was commended as a righteous man, when God spoke well of his offerings. And by faith he still speaks, even though he is dead.

⁵By faith Enoch was taken from this life, so that he did not experience death; he could not be found, because God had taken him away. For before he was taken, he was commended as one who pleased God. ⁶And without faith it is impossible to please God, because anyone who comes to him must believe that he exists and that he rewards those who earnestly seek him.

⁷By faith Noah, when warned about things not yet seen, in holy fear built an ark to save his family. By his faith he condemned the world and became heir of the righteousness that comes by faith.

⁸By faith Abraham, when called to go to a place he would later receive as his inheritance, obeyed and went, even though he did not know where he was going. ⁹By faith he made his home in the promised land like a stranger in a foreign country; he lived in tents, as did Isaac and Jacob, who were heirs with him of the same promise. ¹⁰For he was looking forward to the city with foundations, whose architect and builder is God.

¹¹By faith Abraham, even though he was past age—and Sarah herself was barren—was enabled to become a father because he[c] considered him faithful who had made the promise. ¹²And so from this one man, and he as good as dead, came descendants as numerous as the stars in the sky and as countless as the sand on the seashore.

¹³All these people were still living by faith when they died. They did not receive the things promised; they only saw them and welcomed them from a distance. And they admitted that they were aliens and strangers on earth. ¹⁴People who say such things show that they are looking for a country of their own. ¹⁵If they had been thinking of the country they had left, they would have had opportunity to return. ¹⁶Instead, they were longing for a better country—a heavenly one. Therefore God is not ashamed to be called their God, for he has prepared a city for them.

¹⁷By faith Abraham, when God tested him, offered Isaac as a sacrifice. He who had received the promises was about to sacrifice his one and only son, ¹⁸even though God had said to him, "It is through Isaac that your offspring[d] will be reckoned."[e] ¹⁹Abraham reasoned that God could raise the dead, and figuratively speaking, he did receive Isaac back from death.

²⁰By faith Isaac blessed Jacob and Esau in regard to their future.

²¹By faith Jacob, when he was dying, blessed each of Joseph's sons, and worshiped as he leaned on the top of his staff.

²²By faith Joseph, when his end was near, spoke about the exodus of the Israelites from Egypt and gave instructions about his bones.

²³By faith Moses' parents hid him for three months after he was born, because they saw he was no ordinary child, and they were not afraid of the king's edict.

²⁴By faith Moses, when he had grown up, refused to be known as the son of Pharaoh's daughter. ²⁵He chose to be mistreated along with the people of God rather than to enjoy the pleasures of sin for a short time. ²⁶He regarded disgrace for the sake of Christ as of greater value than the treasures of Egypt, because he was looking ahead to his reward. ²⁷By faith he left Egypt, not fearing the king's anger; he persevered because he saw him who is invisible. ²⁸By faith he kept the Passover and the sprinkling of blood, so that the destroyer of the firstborn would not touch the firstborn of Israel.

²⁹By faith the people passed through

---

[a]38 One early manuscript *But the righteous*   [b]38 Hab. 2:3,4   [c]11 Or *By faith even Sarah, who was past age, was enabled to bear children because she*   [d]18 Greek *seed*   [e]18 Gen. 21:12

the Red Sea[a] as on dry land; but when the Egyptians tried to do so, they were drowned.

30By faith the walls of Jericho fell, after the people had marched around them for seven days.

31By faith the prostitute Rahab, because she welcomed the spies, was not killed with those who were disobedient.[b]

32And what more shall I say? I do not have time to tell about Gideon, Barak,

Samson, Jephthah, David, Samuel and the prophets, **33**who through faith conquered kingdoms, administered justice, and gained what was promised; who shut the mouths of lions, **34**quenched the fury of the flames, and escaped the edge of the sword; whose weakness was turned to strength; and who became powerful in battle and routed foreign armies. **35**Women received back their dead, raised to life again. Others were tortured and refused to

a29 That is, Sea of Reeds   *b31* Or *unbelieving*

MONDAY

VERSE FOR THE DAY:	AUTHOR:	PASSAGE FOR THE DAY:
Hebrews 10:22	Reggie White	Hebrews 10:19–25

The Way to Success

YOU cannot be a complete human being without filling the spiritual void that is inside every person. Training camp Christians [those who attempt to barter with God to achieve success] try to fill that void with religion, money, success, sex, drugs, and the list could go on and on. This void can only be filled with a relationship and continued walking with God through his Son, Jesus Christ.

A well-known national television talk-show host once invited a minister of the gospel on his program. To win the sympathy of the TV audience, he tried to embarrass the minister with question after question. To the talk-show host's chagrin, the minister never gave one answer or opinion of his own. He only quoted Scripture.

At one point the talk-show host asked the man of God why Christians were so narrow-minded in thinking that they were the only people in the whole world who knew God and who knew they were going to heaven.

The minister again quoted Scripture, this time from the New Testament: "I am the way and the truth and the life. No one comes to the Father except through me" (John 14:6).

The preacher then stated, "I didn't say that, God did. If you don't agree with it, tell him, not me."

And that's the answer for training camp Christians also. The promises made, but not kept; the functions attended, but not experienced; the hopes dreamed, but not put into action —commitment matters. There is no success for a football player—or a Christian—without it.

Additional Scripture Readings:
John 14:5–14; John 15:1–8

Go to page 1342 for your next devotional reading.

be released, so that they might gain a better resurrection. [36]Some faced jeers and flogging, while still others were chained and put in prison. [37]They were stoned[a]; they were sawed in two; they were put to death by the sword. They went about in sheepskins and goatskins, destitute, persecuted and mistreated — [38]the world was not worthy of them. They wandered in deserts and mountains, and in caves and holes in the ground.

[39]These were all commended for their faith, yet none of them received what had been promised. [40]God had planned something better for us so that only together with us would they be made perfect.

God Disciplines His Sons

12 Therefore, since we are surrounded by such a great cloud of witnesses, let us throw off everything that hinders and the sin that so easily entangles, and let us run with perseverance the race marked out for us. [2]Let us fix our eyes on Jesus, the author and perfecter of our faith, who for the joy set before him endured the cross, scorning its shame, and sat down at the right hand of the throne of God. [3]Consider him who endured such opposition from sinful men, so that you will not grow weary and lose heart.

[4]In your struggle against sin, you have not yet resisted to the point of shedding your blood. [5]And you have forgotten that word of encouragement that addresses you as sons:

"My son, do not make light of the
     Lord's discipline,
  and do not lose heart when he
     rebukes you,
[6]because the Lord disciplines those he
     loves,
  and he punishes everyone he
     accepts as a son."[b]

[7]Endure hardship as discipline; God is treating you as sons. For what son is not disciplined by his father? [8]If you are not disciplined (and everyone undergoes discipline), then you are illegitimate children and not true sons. [9]Moreover, we have all had human fathers who disciplined us and we respected them for it. How much more should we submit to the Father of our spirits and live! [10]Our fathers disciplined us for a little while as they thought

best; but God disciplines us for our good, that we may share in his holiness. [11]No discipline seems pleasant at the time, but painful. Later on, however, it produces a harvest of righteousness and peace for those who have been trained by it.

[12]Therefore, strengthen your feeble arms and weak knees. [13]"Make level paths for your feet,"[c] so that the lame may not be disabled, but rather healed.

Warning Against Refusing God

[14]Make every effort to live in peace with all men and to be holy; without holiness no one will see the Lord. [15]See to it that no one misses the grace of God and that no bitter root grows up to cause trouble and defile many. [16]See that no one is sexually immoral, or is godless like Esau, who for a single meal sold his inheritance rights as the oldest son. [17]Afterward, as you know, when he wanted to inherit this blessing, he was rejected. He could bring about no change of mind, though he sought the blessing with tears.

[18]You have not come to a mountain that can be touched and that is burning with fire; to darkness, gloom and storm; [19]to a trumpet blast or to such a voice speaking words that those who heard it begged that no further word be spoken to them, [20]because they could not bear what was commanded: "If even an animal touches the mountain, it must be stoned."[d] [21]The sight was so terrifying that Moses said, "I am trembling with fear."[e]

[22]But you have come to Mount Zion, to the heavenly Jerusalem, the city of the living God. You have come to thousands upon thousands of angels in joyful assembly, [23]to the church of the firstborn, whose names are written in heaven. You have come to God, the judge of all men, to the spirits of righteous men made perfect, [24]to Jesus the mediator of a new covenant, and to the sprinkled blood that speaks a better word than the blood of Abel.

[25]See to it that you do not refuse him who speaks. If they did not escape when they refused him who warned them on earth, how much less will we, if we turn away from him who warns us from heaven? [26]At that time his voice shook the earth, but now he has promised, "Once more I will shake not only the earth but also the heavens."[f] [27]The words "once

---

[a]37 Some early manuscripts *stoned; they were put to the test;*   [b]6 Prov. 3:11,12   [c]13 Prov. 4:26
[d]20 Exodus 19:12,13   [e]21 Deut. 9:19   [f]26 Haggai 2:6

more" indicate the removing of what can be shaken — that is, created things — so that what cannot be shaken may remain.

28Therefore, since we are receiving a kingdom that cannot be shaken, let us be thankful, and so worship God acceptably with reverence and awe, 29for our "God is a consuming fire."*a*

Concluding Exhortations

13 Keep on loving each other as brothers. 2Do not forget to entertain strangers, for by so doing some people have entertained angels without knowing it. 3Remember those in prison as if you were their fellow prisoners, and those who are mistreated as if you yourselves were suffering.

4Marriage should be honored by all, and the marriage bed kept pure, for God will judge the adulterer and all the sexually immoral. 5Keep your lives free from the love of money and be content with what you have, because God has said,

a29 Deut. 4:24

TUESDAY

VERSE FOR THE DAY:	AUTHOR:	PASSAGE FOR THE DAY:
Hebrews 12:28	Jerry Bridges	Hebrews 12:18–29

With Reverence and Awe

ONE of the more serious sins of Christians today may well be the almost flippant familiarity with which we often address God in prayer. None of the godly men of the Bible ever adopted the casual manner we often do. They always addressed God with reverence. The same writer who tells us that we have confidence to enter the Most Holy Place, the throne room of God, also tells us that we should worship God acceptably with reverence and awe, "for our 'God is a consuming fire'" (Hebrews 10:19 and 12:28–29). The same Paul who tells us that the Holy Spirit dwelling within us causes us to cry, "*Abba*, Father," also tells us that this same God lives in "unapproachable light" (Romans 8:15 and 1 Timothy 6:16).

In our day we must begin to recover a sense of awe and profound reverence for God. We must begin to view him once again in the infinite majesty that alone belongs to him who is the Creator and Supreme Ruler of the entire universe. There is an infinite gap in worth and dignity between God the Creator and man the creature, even though man has been created in the image of God. The fear of God is a heartfelt recognition of this gap — not a put-down of man, but an exaltation of God . . .

We seem to have magnified the love of God almost to the exclusion of the fear of God. Because of this preoccupation we are not honoring God and reverencing him as we should. We should magnify the love of God; but although we revel in his love and mercy, we must never lose sight of his majesty and his holiness.

Additional Scripture Readings:
Psalm 34:8–14; 1 Peter 1:17–21

Go to page 1343 for your next devotional reading.

"Never will I leave you;
    never will I forsake you."ᵃ

⁶So we say with confidence,

"The Lord is my helper; I will not be
    afraid.
   What can man do to me?"ᵇ

ᵃ5 Deut. 31:6   ᵇ6 Psalm 118:6,7

⁷Remember your leaders, who spoke the word of God to you. Consider the outcome of their way of life and imitate their faith. ⁸Jesus Christ is the same yesterday and today and forever.

⁹Do not be carried away by all kinds of strange teachings. It is good for our hearts

WEDNESDAY

VERSE FOR THE DAY:
Hebrews 13:6

AUTHOR:
Dave Dravecky

PASSAGE FOR THE DAY:
Hebrews 13:5–8

Your Only Audience

DAVE Dravecky's first weeks as a major league baseball pitcher were anxious ones because he was pitching poorly. He was frightened.

"Are you forgetting what you've always said?" [my wife] Janice asked. "Remember? You and Byron used to say you should pitch as though Jesus Christ is your only audience."

That took me back to wonderful, hot Texas days, when I'd been just a scrambling Double-A ballplayer. I'd been with some of my closest friends, playing baseball, enjoying the game, and knowing that a loving God had the only opinion of me that really mattered. Those days in Amarillo had been the happiest of my life. The reason had been, above all, that I knew who I was living for. I knew my audience.

To everybody else, you were only as good as your last performance. The pressure was relentless from the crowd, from the manager, even from the expectations of your friends and family back home. Heck, the pressure could be relentless from inside yourself. But God was concerned only that you did your best. And he was bigger than all the rest combined.

Growing up, I had always been at the center of attention. That was exactly how I had wanted it. My performance had been for me, and no one else. I had to be the star.

That kind of motivation can keep you going strong, so long as you succeed. But it's not so good for dealing with failure, or with forces beyond your control. Seeing Jesus Christ as your audience shifted the pressure off yourself. You did your best to bring glory to God, not yourself. If you lost, the loss would hurt, but it wouldn't change anything fundamental. God would still be there.

Additional Scripture Readings:
Jeremiah 9:23–24;
1 Corinthians 10:31—11:1

*Go to page 1346 for your next
devotional reading.*

to be strengthened by grace, not by ceremonial foods, which are of no value to those who eat them. **10**We have an altar from which those who minister at the tabernacle have no right to eat.

11The high priest carries the blood of animals into the Most Holy Place as a sin offering, but the bodies are burned outside the camp. **12**And so Jesus also suffered outside the city gate to make the people holy through his own blood. **13**Let us, then, go to him outside the camp, bearing the disgrace he bore. **14**For here we do not have an enduring city, but we are looking for the city that is to come.

15Through Jesus, therefore, let us continually offer to God a sacrifice of praise — the fruit of lips that confess his name. **16**And do not forget to do good and to share with others, for with such sacrifices God is pleased.

17Obey your leaders and submit to their authority. They keep watch over you as men who must give an account. Obey them so that their work will be a joy, not a burden, for that would be of no advantage to you.

18Pray for us. We are sure that we have a clear conscience and desire to live honorably in every way. **19**I particularly urge you to pray so that I may be restored to you soon.

20May the God of peace, who through the blood of the eternal covenant brought back from the dead our Lord Jesus, that great Shepherd of the sheep, **21**equip you with everything good for doing his will, and may he work in us what is pleasing to him, through Jesus Christ, to whom be glory for ever and ever. Amen.

22Brothers, I urge you to bear with my word of exhortation, for I have written you only a short letter.

23I want you to know that our brother Timothy has been released. If he arrives soon, I will come with him to see you.

24Greet all your leaders and all God's people. Those from Italy send you their greetings.

25Grace be with you all.

JAMES (a brother of Jesus) writes this letter to urge Christians to express their faith in daily living. He reminds them of what Jesus said, especially in the Sermon on the Mount (Matthew 5–7). As you read this book, ask yourself whether others can see by what you do and say that you believe in Jesus.

JAMES

1 James, a servant of God and of the Lord Jesus Christ,

To the twelve tribes scattered among the nations:

Greetings.

Trials and Temptations

²Consider it pure joy, my brothers, whenever you face trials of many kinds, ³because you know that the testing of your faith develops perseverance. ⁴Perseverance must finish its work so that you may be mature and complete, not lacking anything. ⁵If any of you lacks wisdom, he should ask God, who gives generously to all without finding fault, and it will be given to him. ⁶But when he asks, he must believe and not doubt, because he who doubts is like a wave of the sea, blown and tossed by the wind. ⁷That man should not think he will receive anything from the Lord; ⁸he is a double-minded man, unstable in all he does.

⁹The brother in humble circumstances ought to take pride in his high position. ¹⁰But the one who is rich should take pride in his low position, because he will pass away like a wild flower. ¹¹For the sun rises with scorching heat and withers the plant; its blossom falls and its beauty is destroyed. In the same way, the rich man will fade away even while he goes about his business.

¹²Blessed is the man who perseveres under trial, because when he has stood the test, he will receive the crown of life that God has promised to those who love him.

¹³When tempted, no one should say, "God is tempting me." For God cannot be tempted by evil, nor does he tempt anyone; ¹⁴but each one is tempted when, by his own evil desire, he is dragged away and enticed. ¹⁵Then, after desire has con-

ceived, it gives birth to sin; and sin, when it is full-grown, gives birth to death.

16Don't be deceived, my dear brothers. 17Every good and perfect gift is from above, coming down from the Father of the heavenly lights, who does not change like shifting shadows. 18He chose to give us birth through the word of truth, that we might be a kind of firstfruits of all he created.

Listening and Doing

19My dear brothers, take note of this: Everyone should be quick to listen, slow to speak and slow to become angry, 20for man's anger does not bring about the righteous life that God desires. 21Therefore, get rid of all moral filth and the evil that is so prevalent and humbly accept the word planted in you, which can save you.

22Do not merely listen to the word, and so deceive yourselves. Do what it says. 23Anyone who listens to the word but does not do what it says is like a man who looks at his face in a mirror 24and, after looking at himself, goes away and immediately forgets what he looks like. 25But the man who looks intently into the perfect law that gives freedom, and continues

---

THURSDAY

VERSE FOR THE DAY:	AUTHOR:	PASSAGE FOR THE DAY:
James 1:2	Gary Smalley and John Trent	James 1:2–8

Consider It Pure Joy?

AS LOVING parents, one way we can honor our children and build value into their lives is to help them see the positive gain in troubled times. Whether we like it or not, before they leave our homes, our sons or daughters may experience moments or even days of doubt, discouragement, loneliness, disappointment or depression.

They may be betrayed by a friend, fail to get into the college or the profession of their choice, be dumped later in life by a spouse, or perhaps experience the disabling results of experimenting with drugs or alcohol. And with each painful experience their child suffers, Mom and Dad feel the aftershocks in their hearts . . .

It is certainly not wrong to avoid pain when we can. But it is wrong to deny problems, ignore them or try to explain them away. One of the all-time great truths is that life is difficult and often unfair. The better we are at seeing through trials to what they can produce in our lives and our children's lives, the better able we'll be to provide calmness, assurance and genuine love to our children, even in the midst of trying times. In fact, trials have the capacity to bring strength, maturity, courage, genuine love, righteousness and perseverance to those who are willing to be trained by them. The very things we fear might happen to our children can make them stronger people, depending on their response and our response to their difficulties.

Additional Scripture Readings:
Hebrews 12:7–13; 1 Peter 1:3–9

Go to page 1347 for your next devotional reading.

to do this, not forgetting what he has heard, but doing it — he will be blessed in what he does.

²⁶If anyone considers himself religious and yet does not keep a tight rein on his tongue, he deceives himself and his religion is worthless. ²⁷Religion that God our Father accepts as pure and faultless is this: to look after orphans and widows in their distress and to keep oneself from being polluted by the world.

Favoritism Forbidden

2 My brothers, as believers in our glorious Lord Jesus Christ, don't show favoritism. ²Suppose a man comes into your meeting wearing a gold ring and fine clothes, and a poor man in shabby clothes also comes in. ³If you show special attention to the man wearing fine clothes and say, "Here's a good seat for you," but say to the poor man, "You stand there" or "Sit on the floor by my feet," ⁴have you not

---

FRIDAY

VERSE FOR THE DAY:
James 1:22

AUTHOR:
John E. Crawford

PASSAGE FOR THE DAY:
James 1:19–25

Building Lofty Cathedrals

EVERY experienced parent knows that bad behavior in a child rarely happens with no previous signals and no past incidents of disobedience or defiance. There are always signals of trouble ahead. Alert fathers and mothers notice such signals in time to intervene and prevent the youngster from skidding into serious mistakes . . .

Your wisdom in controlling your youngster is one of the best measures of how much you really love and value her. She knows this, whether she has said so in plain words or not. She knows that her mother should have a hand in controlling her too; but you, her father, have an equal share in the job. Your personal examples are very important, too, along with your rules. You won't be able to sell her any double standards on the important issues in life. She will come much closer to following what you do and what you believe than what you say about these issues.

Your daughter does not have to believe that you are the wisest man in all the world to count you as a good father. She does want to be able to come to you with important questions about life. She needs to see that you are learning and growing, too, that you are open to new ideas, new concepts.

Being a real father to your children is one job that no one else can ever do as well as you. Good fathers deserve their full share of top praise, for they are helping to build the loftiest cathedrals in the universe: young hearts and minds that are learning how to make this world a better place in which to live.

Additional Scripture Readings:
Matthew 7:15–20; John 15:1–17

Go to page 1348 for your next devotional reading.

WEEKENDING

RECOGNIZE

The clear duty of real men goes beyond "live and let live." We are mandated to protect widows, orphans, the alien and all those who lack sustaining relationships. As long as men and boys fail to be protective, they will fall prey to the typical male sexual fantasy that sells [pornographic] magazines and films . . .

The only real solution is to teach boys that the source of their power is in the nurturing and protecting image of God created within them. When we express our essential nature, then substitutes, like pornographic fantasies, lose their appeal.

– *E. James Wilder*

REVIVE

Saturday: 1 Thessalonians 4:3–8
Sunday: James 1:22–27

Go to page 1350 for your next devotional reading.

discriminated among yourselves and become judges with evil thoughts?

[5]Listen, my dear brothers: Has not God chosen those who are poor in the eyes of the world to be rich in faith and to inherit the kingdom he promised those who love him? [6]But you have insulted the poor. Is it not the rich who are exploiting you? Are they not the ones who are dragging you into court? [7]Are they not the ones who are slandering the noble name of him to whom you belong?

[8]If you really keep the royal law found in Scripture, "Love your neighbor as yourself,"[a] you are doing right. [9]But if you show favoritism, you sin and are convicted by the law as lawbreakers. [10]For whoever keeps the whole law and yet stumbles at just one point is guilty of breaking all of it. [11]For he who said, "Do not commit adultery,"[b] also said, "Do not murder."[c] If you do not commit adultery but do commit murder, you have become a lawbreaker.

[12]Speak and act as those who are going to be judged by the law that gives freedom, [13]because judgment without mercy will be shown to anyone who has not been merciful. Mercy triumphs over judgment!

Faith and Deeds

[14]What good is it, my brothers, if a man claims to have faith but has no deeds? Can such faith save him? [15]Suppose a brother or sister is without clothes and daily food. [16]If one of you says to him, "Go, I wish you well; keep warm and well fed," but does nothing about his physical needs, what good is it? [17]In the same way, faith by itself, if it is not accompanied by action, is dead.

[18]But someone will say, "You have faith; I have deeds."

Show me your faith without deeds, and I will show you my faith by what I do. [19]You believe that there is one God. Good! Even the demons believe that — and shudder.

[20]You foolish man, do you want evidence that faith without deeds is useless[d]? [21]Was not our ancestor Abraham considered righteous for what he did when he offered his son Isaac on the altar? [22]You see that his faith and his actions were working together, and his faith was made complete by what he did. [23]And the scripture was fulfilled that says, "Abraham believed God, and it was credited to him as righteousness,"[e] and he was called God's friend. [24]You see that a person is justified by what he does and not by faith alone.

[25]In the same way, was not even Rahab the prostitute considered righteous for what she did when she gave lodging to the spies and sent them off in a different direction? [26]As the body without the spirit is dead, so faith without deeds is dead.

Taming the Tongue

3 Not many of you should presume to be teachers, my brothers, because you know that we who teach will be judged more strictly. [2]We all stumble in many ways. If anyone is never at fault in what he says, he is a perfect man, able to keep his whole body in check.

[3]When we put bits into the mouths of horses to make them obey us, we can turn the whole animal. [4]Or take ships as an example. Although they are so large and are driven by strong winds, they are steered by a very small rudder wherever the pilot wants to go. [5]Likewise the tongue is a small part of the body, but it makes great boasts. Consider what a great forest is set on fire by a small spark. [6]The tongue also is a fire, a world of evil among the parts of the body. It corrupts the whole person, sets the whole course of his life on fire, and is itself set on fire by hell.

[7]All kinds of animals, birds, reptiles and creatures of the sea are being tamed and have been tamed by man, [8]but no man can tame the tongue. It is a restless evil, full of deadly poison.

[9]With the tongue we praise our Lord and Father, and with it we curse men, who have been made in God's likeness. [10]Out of the same mouth come praise and cursing. My brothers, this should not be. [11]Can both fresh water and salt[f] water flow from the same spring? [12]My brothers, can a fig tree bear olives, or a grapevine bear figs? Neither can a salt spring produce fresh water.

Two Kinds of Wisdom

[13]Who is wise and understanding among you? Let him show it by his good life, by deeds done in the humility that comes from wisdom. [14]But if you harbor bitter envy and selfish ambition in your

[a]8 Lev. 19:18   [b]11 Exodus 20:14; Deut. 5:18   [c]11 Exodus 20:13; Deut. 5:17   [d]20 Some early manuscripts dead   [e]23 Gen. 15:6   [f]11 Greek bitter (see also verse 14)

hearts, do not boast about it or deny the truth. ¹⁵Such "wisdom" does not come down from heaven but is earthly, unspiritual, of the devil. ¹⁶For where you have envy and selfish ambition, there you find disorder and every evil practice.

¹⁷But the wisdom that comes from heaven is first of all pure; then peace-loving, considerate, submissive, full of mercy and good fruit, impartial and sincere. ¹⁸Peacemakers who sow in peace raise a harvest of righteousness.

MONDAY

VERSE FOR THE DAY:	AUTHOR:	PASSAGE FOR THE DAY:
James 2:9	Paul Brand	James 2:1–11

Loyalty to the Head

THE Bible directs harsh words to those who show favoritism. James spelled out a situation we can all identify with: "Suppose a man comes into your meeting wearing a gold ring and fine clothes, and a poor man in shabby clothes also comes in. If you show special attention to the man wearing fine clothes and say, 'Here's a good seat for you,' but say to the poor man, 'You stand there,' or, 'Sit on the floor by my feet,' have you not discriminated among yourselves and become judges with evil thoughts?" He concludes, "If you show favoritism, you sin and are convicted by the law as lawbreakers. For whoever keeps the whole law and yet stumbles at just one point is guilty of breaking all of it" (James 2:2–4,9–10) . . .

In our rating-conscious society that ranks everything from baseball teams to "the best chili in New York," an attitude of relative worth can easily seep into the church of Christ. But the design of the group of people who follow Jesus should not resemble a military machine or a corporate structure. The church Jesus founded is more like a family in which the son retarded from birth has as much worth as his brother the Rhodes scholar. It is like the body composed of cells most striking in their diversity but most effective in their mutuality.

God requires only one thing of his "cells": that each person be loyal to the Head. If each cell accepts the needs of the whole Body as the purpose of its life, then the Body will live in health. It is a brilliant stroke, the only pure egalitarianism I observe in all of society. He has endowed every person in the Body with the same capacity to respond to him. In Christ's Body, a teacher of three-year-olds has the same value as a bishop, and that teacher's work may be just as significant. A widow's dollar can equal a millionaire's annuity. Shyness, beauty, eloquence, race, sophistication—none of these matter, only loyalty to the Head, and through the Head to each other.

Additional Scripture Readings:
Ephesians 4:7–16;
Colossians 1:15–20

Go to page 1351 for your next devotional reading.

Submit Yourselves to God

4 What causes fights and quarrels among you? Don't they come from your desires that battle within you? **2**You want something but don't get it. You kill and covet, but you cannot have what you want. You quarrel and fight. You do not have, because you do not ask God. **3**When you ask, you do not receive, because you ask with wrong motives, that you may spend what you get on your pleasures.

4You adulterous people, don't you know that friendship with the world is hatred toward God? Anyone who chooses to be a friend of the world becomes an enemy of God. **5**Or do you think Scripture says without reason that the spirit he

---

TUESDAY

VERSE FOR THE DAY:
James 3:17

AUTHOR:
Larry Crabb

PASSAGE FOR THE DAY:
James 3:13–18

The Deadliest Culprit

DESIRING our own good is not sinful in itself, but natural and instinctive. God gave us everything, even our very existence. He wants us to take care of what he gave us. It is the act of putting ourselves at the center of the universe, where God belongs, that is unqualified sin. This is, in fact, the very definition of sin.

When self-interest continues as the dominant commitment of our lives, when we devote our energy to serving ourselves above all others, then we are wrongly self-centered. And this form of self-interest is a far more serious and dangerous problem than the wounds we suffer at the hands of others.

But very few people even notice their commitment to self-interest, and among those who do, even fewer are deeply concerned about it. More often, self-centeredness is encouraged: "Look out for yourself. Who else is going to?" "You shouldn't have to put up with that kind of treatment." "You must learn to take care of yourself before you can properly give to others" . . .

We will not move very far in our efforts to develop good marriages until we understand that repairing a damaged sense of identity and healing the wound in our hearts is *not* the first order of business. It is rather dealing with the subtle, pervasive, stubborn commitment to ourselves.

Self-centeredness is the killer. In every bad relationship, it is the deadliest culprit. Poor communication, temper problems, unhealthy responses to dysfunctional family backgrounds, codependent relationships, and personal incompatibility —everything (unless medically caused) flows out of the cesspool of self-centeredness.

Additional Scripture Readings:
Ezekiel 28:1–10; Philippians 2:1–11

Go to page 1352 for your next devotional reading.

caused to live in us envies intensely?[a] [6]But he gives us more grace. That is why Scripture says:

"God opposes the proud
but gives grace to the humble."[b]

[7]Submit yourselves, then, to God. Resist the devil, and he will flee from you. [8]Come near to God and he will come near to you. Wash your hands, you sinners, and purify your hearts, you double-minded. [9]Grieve, mourn and wail. Change your laughter to mourning and your joy to gloom. [10]Humble yourselves before the Lord, and he will lift you up.

[11]Brothers, do not slander one another. Anyone who speaks against his brother or judges him speaks against the law and judges it. When you judge the law, you are not keeping it, but sitting in judgment on it. [12]There is only one Lawgiver and Judge, the one who is able to save and destroy. But you—who are you to judge your neighbor?

Boasting About Tomorrow

[13]Now listen, you who say, "Today or tomorrow we will go to this or that city, spend a year there, carry on business and make money." [14]Why, you do not even know what will happen tomorrow. What is your life? You are a mist that appears for a little while and then vanishes. [15]Instead, you ought to say, "If it is the Lord's will,

---

[a]5 Or *that God jealously longs for the spirit that he made to live in us*; or *that the Spirit he caused to live in us longs jealously*   [b]6 Prov. 3:34

WEDNESDAY

VERSE FOR THE DAY:	AUTHOR:	PASSAGE FOR THE DAY:
James 5:16	Stephen Arterburn and	James 5:13–20
	David Stoop	

Torn Between Two . . .

IN ORDER to meet the basic psychological needs to know and be known, to love and be loved by others, men need deep caring relationships with other men. It's to this level that James instructed Christians, "Confess your sins to each other and pray for each other so that you may be healed" (James 5:16). A man who doesn't have at least one other man to whom he can be accountable regarding his failures, hurts and temptations is a prime target for masculine anger.

The angry man in our society is caught between mythical masculinity on the one side and true masculinity on the other. He feels the pressure to achieve, to earn, to conquer, to win —and to do all these things on his own. But he also feels the need to love and to nurture those he loves, and to be loved and nurtured by those who love him. He futilely attempts to reconcile the two in his own life. He is torn between being invincible and vulnerable, aloof and involved, self-serving and succoring . . . . The roots of this conflict send up numerous shoots of anger-producing tendencies in his life.

Additional Scripture Readings:
Ecclesiastes 4:7–12;
1 Thessalonians 2:6b-12

Go to page 1355 for your next devotional reading.

we will live and do this or that." [16]As it is, you boast and brag. All such boasting is evil. [17]Anyone, then, who knows the good he ought to do and doesn't do it, sins.

Warning to Rich Oppressors

5 Now listen, you rich people, weep and wail because of the misery that is coming upon you. [2]Your wealth has rotted, and moths have eaten your clothes. [3]Your gold and silver are corroded. Their corrosion will testify against you and eat your flesh like fire. You have hoarded wealth in the last days. [4]Look! The wages you failed to pay the workmen who mowed your fields are crying out against you. The cries of the harvesters have reached the ears of the Lord Almighty. [5]You have lived on earth in luxury and self-indulgence. You have fattened yourselves in the day of slaughter.[a] [6]You have condemned and murdered innocent men, who were not opposing you.

Patience in Suffering

[7]Be patient, then, brothers, until the Lord's coming. See how the farmer waits for the land to yield its valuable crop and how patient he is for the autumn and spring rains. [8]You too, be patient and stand firm, because the Lord's coming is near. [9]Don't grumble against each other, brothers, or you will be judged. The Judge is standing at the door!

[10]Brothers, as an example of patience in the face of suffering, take the prophets who spoke in the name of the Lord. [11]As you know, we consider blessed those who have persevered. You have heard of Job's perseverance and have seen what the Lord finally brought about. The Lord is full of compassion and mercy.

[12]Above all, my brothers, do not swear—not by heaven or by earth or by anything else. Let your "Yes" be yes, and your "No," no, or you will be condemned.

The Prayer of Faith

[13]Is any one of you in trouble? He should pray. Is anyone happy? Let him sing songs of praise. [14]Is any one of you sick? He should call the elders of the church to pray over him and anoint him with oil in the name of the Lord. [15]And the prayer offered in faith will make the sick person well; the Lord will raise him up. If he has sinned, he will be forgiven. [16]Therefore confess your sins to each other and pray for each other so that you may be healed. The prayer of a righteous man is powerful and effective.

[17]Elijah was a man just like us. He prayed earnestly that it would not rain, and it did not rain on the land for three and a half years. [18]Again he prayed, and the heavens gave rain, and the earth produced its crops.

[19]My brothers, if one of you should wander from the truth and someone should bring him back, [20]remember this: Whoever turns a sinner from the error of his way will save him from death and cover over a multitude of sins.

---

[a]5 Or *yourselves as in a day of feasting*

PETER writes this letter to a group of Christians suffering for their faith, reminding them of how much Jesus suffered. He inspires them with hope for the future and shows them how to grow in their faith. As you read this book, decide to do your best to live a holy life as you look forward to the return of Jesus and to the reward he promises to give his followers.

1 PETER

1 Peter, an apostle of Jesus Christ,

To God's elect, strangers in the world, scattered throughout Pontus, Galatia, Cappadocia, Asia and Bithynia, **2**who have been chosen according to the foreknowledge of God the Father, through the sanctifying work of the Spirit, for obedience to Jesus Christ and sprinkling by his blood:

Grace and peace be yours in abundance.

Praise to God for a Living Hope

3Praise be to the God and Father of our Lord Jesus Christ! In his great mercy he has given us new birth into a living hope through the resurrection of Jesus Christ from the dead, **4**and into an inheritance that can never perish, spoil or fade—kept in heaven for you, **5**who through faith are shielded by God's power until the coming of the salvation that is ready to be revealed in the last time. **6**In this you greatly rejoice, though now for a little while you may have had to suffer grief in all kinds of trials. **7**These have come so that your faith—of greater worth than gold, which perishes even though refined by fire—may be proved genuine and may result in praise, glory and honor when Jesus Christ is revealed. **8**Though you have not seen him, you love him; and even though you do not see him now, you believe in him and are filled with an inexpressible and glorious joy, **9**for you are receiving the goal of your faith, the salvation of your souls.

10Concerning this salvation, the prophets, who spoke of the grace that was to come to you, searched intently and with the greatest care, **11**trying to find out the time and circumstances to which the Spirit of Christ in them was pointing when he predicted the sufferings of Christ and the glories that would follow. ¹²It was revealed to them that they were not serving themselves but you, when they spoke of the things that have now been told you by those who have preached the gospel to you by the Holy Spirit sent from heaven. Even angels long to look into these things.

Be Holy

¹³Therefore, prepare your minds for ac-

tion; be self-controlled; set your hope fully on the grace to be given you when Jesus Christ is revealed. ¹⁴As obedient children, do not conform to the evil desires you had when you lived in ignorance. ¹⁵But just as he who called you is holy, so be holy in all you do; ¹⁶for it is written: "Be holy, because I am holy." *a*

¹⁷Since you call on a Father who judges each man's work impartially, live your lives as strangers here in reverent fear. ¹⁸For you know that it was not with per-

a 16 Lev. 11:44,45; 19:2; 20:7

THURSDAY

VERSE FOR THE DAY:	AUTHOR:	PASSAGE FOR THE DAY:
1 Peter 1:15	Thomas Merton	1 Peter 1:13–16

Be Holy in All You Do

THE way of Christian holiness is, in any case, hard and austere. We must fast and pray. We must embrace hardship and sacrifice, for the love of Christ, and in order to improve the condition of man on earth. We may not merely enjoy the good things of life ourselves, occasionally "purifying our intention" to make sure that we are doing it all "for God." Such purely abstract and mental operations are only a pitiful excuse for mediocrity. They do not justify us in the sight of God. It is not enough to make pious gestures. Our love of God and of man cannot be merely symbolic, it has to be completely real. It is not just a mental operation, but the gift and commitment of our inmost self.

Obviously, this means going a little further than the vapid preachments of that popular religion which has led some people to believe that a "religious revival" is taking place among us. Let us not be too sure of that! The mere fact that men are frightened and insecure, that they grasp at optimistic slogans, run more frequently to church, and seek to pacify their troubled souls by cheerful and humanitarian maxims, is surely no indication that our society is becoming "religious." In fact, it may be a symptom of spiritual sickness. It is certainly a good thing to be aware of our symptoms, but that does not justify our palliating them with quack medicines. Let us not therefore delude ourselves with easy and infantile conceptions of holiness . . . Mere external respectability, without deeper or more positive moral values, brings discredit upon the Christian faith.

Additional Scripture Readings:
Matthew 23:25–28; James 2:14–26

Go to page 1357 for your next devotional reading.

ishable things such as silver or gold that you were redeemed from the empty way of life handed down to you from your forefathers, **19**but with the precious blood of Christ, a lamb without blemish or defect. **20**He was chosen before the creation of the world, but was revealed in these last times for your sake. **21**Through him you believe in God, who raised him from the dead and glorified him, and so your faith and hope are in God.

22Now that you have purified yourselves by obeying the truth so that you have sincere love for your brothers, love one another deeply, from the heart.*a* **23**For you have been born again, not of perishable seed, but of imperishable, through the living and enduring word of God. **24**For,

"All men are like grass,
and all their glory is like the flowers of the field;
the grass withers and the flowers fall,
25 but the word of the Lord stands forever."*b*

And this is the word that was preached to you.

2 Therefore, rid yourselves of all malice and all deceit, hypocrisy, envy, and slander of every kind. **2**Like newborn babies, crave pure spiritual milk, so that by it you may grow up in your salvation, **3**now that you have tasted that the Lord is good.

The Living Stone and a Chosen People

4As you come to him, the living Stone—rejected by men but chosen by God and precious to him— **5**you also, like living stones, are being built into a spiritual house to be a holy priesthood, offering spiritual sacrifices acceptable to God through Jesus Christ. **6**For in Scripture it says:

"See, I lay a stone in Zion,
a chosen and precious cornerstone,
and the one who trusts in him
will never be put to shame."*c*

7Now to you who believe, this stone is precious. But to those who do not believe,

"The stone the builders rejected
has become the capstone,*d*"*e*

8and,

"A stone that causes men to stumble
and a rock that makes them fall."*f*

They stumble because they disobey the message—which is also what they were destined for.

9But you are a chosen people, a royal priesthood, a holy nation, a people belonging to God, that you may declare the praises of him who called you out of darkness into his wonderful light. **10**Once you were not a people, but now you are the people of God; once you had not received mercy, but now you have received mercy.

11Dear friends, I urge you, as aliens and strangers in the world, to abstain from sinful desires, which war against your soul. **12**Live such good lives among the pagans that, though they accuse you of doing wrong, they may see your good deeds and glorify God on the day he visits us.

Submission to Rulers and Masters

13Submit yourselves for the Lord's sake to every authority instituted among men: whether to the king, as the supreme authority, **14**or to governors, who are sent by him to punish those who do wrong and to commend those who do right. **15**For it is God's will that by doing good you should silence the ignorant talk of foolish men. **16**Live as free men, but do not use your freedom as a cover-up for evil; live as servants of God. **17**Show proper respect to everyone: Love the brotherhood of believers, fear God, honor the king.

18Slaves, submit yourselves to your masters with all respect, not only to those who are good and considerate, but also to those who are harsh. **19**For it is commendable if a man bears up under the pain of unjust suffering because he is conscious of God. **20**But how is it to your credit if you receive a beating for doing wrong and endure it? But if you suffer for doing good and you endure it, this is commendable before God. **21**To this you were called, because Christ suffered for you, leaving you an example, that you should follow in his steps.

22"He committed no sin,
and no deceit was found in his mouth."*g*

23When they hurled their insults at him, he did not retaliate; when he suffered, he

---

a22 Some early manuscripts *from a pure heart*   *b25* Isaiah 40:6-8   *c6* Isaiah 28:16   *d7* Or
cornerstone   *e7* Psalm 118:22   *f8* Isaiah 8:14   *g22* Isaiah 53:9

made no threats. Instead, he entrusted himself to him who judges justly. ²⁴He himself bore our sins in his body on the tree, so that we might die to sins and live for righteousness; by his wounds you have been healed. ²⁵For you were like sheep going astray, but now you have returned to the Shepherd and Overseer of your souls.

Wives and Husbands

3 Wives, in the same way be submissive to your husbands so that, if any of them do not believe the word, they may be won over without words by the behavior of their wives, ²when they see the purity and reverence of your lives. ³Your beauty should not come from outward adornment, such as braided hair and the

---

FRIDAY

VERSE FOR THE DAY:
1 Peter 2:1

AUTHOR:
Mark Ritchie

PASSAGE FOR THE DAY:
1 Peter 1:22—2:3

Who's the Hypocrite?

[FOR atheist Jean-Paul Sartre,] it was a "misunderstanding" that caused something to come between him and God. It seems that as a young boy he had done something wrong (he was playing with matches and burned a rug) and while attempting to conceal the evidence, his conscience irritated him.

This was the same sort of thing I had gone through as a boy, I thought, that irritating conscience. "I felt his gaze inside my head," he wrote, "and on my hands. I whirled about in the bathroom, horribly visible, a live target." He flew into a rage at such a crude indiscretion by God and cursed him repeatedly. How could God be so crude, Sartre thought, as to invade the private mind of a small child? This "misunderstanding," as he called it, caused God to vegetate and die.

For myself, I could not possibly have been more puzzled. I certainly shared his feeling that the hypocrisy of the so-called godly made Christianity look false and God powerless. But now God was "gazing on *his* hands," irritating *him* for *his* hypocrisy, and it made him angry. He had experienced God for himself as he said, "inside my head," and he liked the idea even less.

Well, which is it, I asked myself? Are we going to disbelieve because of the hypocrisy we see in others or because God won't allow that same hypocrisy in us? It reminded me of the statement of that other famous atheist, Nietzsche, when he wrote, "If you could prove God to me, I would believe in him all the less." It almost seemed as if the closer these great thinkers came to the idea of God, the less clarity of thought they expressed. While I was impressed—in fact, amazed—at their honesty, I began to lose respect for the objectivity with which they searched for truth.

Additional Scripture Readings:
Mark 7:6–13; Romans 3:9–20

Go to page 1358 for your next devotional reading.

WEEKENDING

RENEW

Develop a new kind of trust in God's presence and sovereign lordship in your life. At birth, he gives each of us a unique, authentic self. As we mature, God encourages us to discover that unique self he made each of us to be. He wants us to nurture it and then to let others see it as his handiwork . . .

Let what you do arise out of who you are. Being is more important than doing. As for me, I have decided that whatever I do for the rest of my life, it will not be in order to have an identity. It will be the result of allowing my God-given self to emerge. I'm done with posturing for a public that demands an unattainable and hypocritical perfection.

– Stan Mooneyham

REVIVE

Saturday: Ephesians 4:20–24
Sunday: 1 Peter 2:9–12

Go to page 1359 for your next devotional reading.

wearing of gold jewelry and fine clothes. [4] Instead, it should be that of your inner self, the unfading beauty of a gentle and quiet spirit, which is of great worth in God's sight. [5] For this is the way the holy women of the past who put their hope in God used to make themselves beautiful. They were submissive to their own husbands, [6] like Sarah, who obeyed Abraham and called him her master. You are her daughters if you do what is right and do not give way to fear.

[7] Husbands, in the same way be considerate as you live with your wives, and treat them with respect as the weaker partner and as heirs with you of the gracious gift of life, so that nothing will hinder your prayers.

Suffering for Doing Good

[8] Finally, all of you, live in harmony with one another; be sympathetic, love as brothers, be compassionate and humble. [9] Do not repay evil with evil or insult with insult, but with blessing, because to this you were called so that you may inherit a blessing. [10] For,

"Whoever would love life
and see good days

MONDAY

VERSE FOR THE DAY:
1 Peter 3:7

AUTHOR:
D. Stuart Briscoe

PASSAGE FOR THE DAY:
1 Peter 3:1–7

Real Husbands

THIS revolutionary teaching by Peter—that women were *equally* heirs of the grace of life—amazed the men of that time. For in Peter and Paul's day, men were the legal heirs of life. They strutted around and had everything going their way. The women entertained them, met their sexual needs, managed their homes, and produced sons (and heirs). Women were locked into roles determined by the men.

Husbands, do you look at your wives from Peter's perspective? Are you as concerned about their spiritual fulfillment as you are about your own? Do you treat them with genuine respect?

Many of us men are extremely gifted at being *inconsiderate*. We fail to see the deep hurts and intense fears of our wives. We are notoriously insensitive—and the people we live with have the scars to prove it. It seems to be a characteristic of the male ego. Peter is telling us that because women are co-heirs with men of "the gracious gift of life," they are equally citizens of the kingdom of heaven.

What do *real* husbands do? They adhere to Jesus' teaching known as the Golden Rule: "Do to others as you would have them do to you" [Luke 6:31]. If husbands faithfully followed that precept in relating to their wives, the married women in our world would think they were "on the threshold of heaven, if not halfway through the door!" Men—let's become *real* husbands!

Additional Scripture Readings:
Luke 6:27–36; Ephesians 5:22–33

Go to page 1361 for your next devotional reading.

must keep his tongue from evil
   and his lips from deceitful speech.
[11]He must turn from evil and do good;
   he must seek peace and pursue it.
[12]For the eyes of the Lord are on the
    righteous
   and his ears are attentive to their
    prayer,
but the face of the Lord is against
   those who do evil."[a]

[13]Who is going to harm you if you are eager to do good? [14]But even if you should suffer for what is right, you are blessed. "Do not fear what they fear[b]; do not be frightened."[c] [15]But in your hearts set apart Christ as Lord. Always be prepared to give an answer to everyone who asks you to give the reason for the hope that you have. But do this with gentleness and respect, [16]keeping a clear conscience, so that those who speak maliciously against your good behavior in Christ may be ashamed of their slander. [17]It is better, if it is God's will, to suffer for doing good than for doing evil. [18]For Christ died for sins once for all, the righteous for the unrighteous, to bring you to God. He was put to death in the body but made alive by the Spirit, [19]through whom[d] also he went and preached to the spirits in prison [20]who disobeyed long ago when God waited patiently in the days of Noah while the ark was being built. In it only a few people, eight in all, were saved through water, [21]and this water symbolizes baptism that now saves you also—not the removal of dirt from the body but the pledge[e] of a good conscience toward God. It saves you by the resurrection of Jesus Christ, [22]who has gone into heaven and is at God's right hand—with angels, authorities and powers in submission to him.

Living for God

4 Therefore, since Christ suffered in his body, arm yourselves also with the same attitude, because he who has suffered in his body is done with sin. [2]As a result, he does not live the rest of his earthly life for evil human desires, but rather for the will of God. [3]For you have spent enough time in the past doing what pagans choose to do—living in debauchery, lust, drunkenness, orgies, carousing and detestable idolatry. [4]They think it strange that you do not plunge with them into the same flood of dissipation, and they heap abuse on you. [5]But they will have to give account to him who is ready to judge the living and the dead. [6]For this is the reason the gospel was preached even to those who are now dead, so that they might be judged according to men in regard to the body, but live according to God in regard to the spirit.

[7]The end of all things is near. Therefore be clear minded and self-controlled so that you can pray. [8]Above all, love each other deeply, because love covers over a multitude of sins. [9]Offer hospitality to one another without grumbling. [10]Each one should use whatever gift he has received to serve others, faithfully administering God's grace in its various forms. [11]If anyone speaks, he should do it as one speaking the very words of God. If anyone serves, he should do it with the strength God provides, so that in all things God may be praised through Jesus Christ. To him be the glory and the power for ever and ever. Amen.

Suffering for Being a Christian

[12]Dear friends, do not be surprised at the painful trial you are suffering, as though something strange were happening to you. [13]But rejoice that you participate in the sufferings of Christ, so that you may be overjoyed when his glory is revealed. [14]If you are insulted because of the name of Christ, you are blessed, for the Spirit of glory and of God rests on you. [15]If you suffer, it should not be as a murderer or thief or any other kind of criminal, or even as a meddler. [16]However, if you suffer as a Christian, do not be ashamed, but praise God that you bear that name. [17]For it is time for judgment to begin with the family of God; and if it begins with us, what will the outcome be for those who do not obey the gospel of God? [18]And,

"If it is hard for the righteous to be
    saved,
   what will become of the ungodly
    and the sinner?"[f]

[19]So then, those who suffer according to God's will should commit themselves to their faithful Creator and continue to do good.

---

[a]12 Psalm 34:12-16   [b]14 Or *not fear their threats*   [c]14 Isaiah 8:12   [d]18,19 Or *alive in the spirit,* [19]*through which*   [e]21 Or *response*   [f]18 Prov. 11:31

To Elders and Young Men

5 To the elders among you, I appeal as a fellow elder, a witness of Christ's sufferings and one who also will share in the glory to be revealed: **2**Be shepherds of God's flock that is under your care, serving as overseers—not because you must, but because you are willing, as God wants you to be; not greedy for money, but eager to serve; **3**not lording it over those entrusted to you, but being examples to the flock. **4**And when the Chief Shepherd appears, you will receive the crown of glory that will never fade away.

5Young men, in the same way be submissive to those who are older. All of you, clothe yourselves with humility toward one another, because,

> "God opposes the proud
>   but gives grace to the humble."*a*

6Humble yourselves, therefore, under God's mighty hand, that he may lift you up in due time. **7**Cast all your anxiety on him because he cares for you.

8Be self-controlled and alert. Your ene-

*a*5 Prov. 3:34

TUESDAY

VERSE FOR THE DAY:
1 Peter 5:8

AUTHOR:
Steve Farrar

PASSAGE FOR THE DAY:
1 Peter 5:8–9

Satan's Strategy

THE enemy is no fool. He has a strategically designed game plan, a diabolical method he employs time and time again. When he wants to destroy a family, he focuses on the man. For if he can neutralize the man . . . he has neutralized the family. And the damage that takes place when a man's family leadership is neutralized is beyond calculation.

Satan's approach is the same, whether he's doing combat in the church or in the family. If Satan can neutralize a pastor through financial impropriety or by a sexual escapade, he has neutralized that pastor's church as well. Not only the reputation of the pastor, but the reputation of the church has been tarnished. Satan's strategy has always been to neutralize the leaders. It works in the family, and it works in the church.

What that means is that we should *expect* to be attacked. We should *expect* extreme temptation to come our way. When you get serious about leading your family, you will be opposed.

If a man is passive and indifferent to the things of God and the spiritual leadership of his home, then attack is not necessary. He is already "neutralized" . . .

Gentlemen, I know that you love your families. You love your wife. You love your children. You would be willing to die for them. In most wars, that's what men are asked to do. They go off to war because they're willing to die for their families. That's what he would have you to do.

Additional Scripture Readings:
Job 1:6–12; Ephesians 6:10–18

Go to page 1364 for your next devotional reading.

my the devil prowls around like a roaring lion looking for someone to devour. [9]Resist him, standing firm in the faith, because you know that your brothers throughout the world are undergoing the same kind of sufferings.

[10]And the God of all grace, who called you to his eternal glory in Christ, after you have suffered a little while, will himself restore you and make you strong, firm and steadfast. [11]To him be the power for ever and ever. Amen.

Final Greetings

[12]With the help of Silas,[a] whom I regard as a faithful brother, I have written to you briefly, encouraging you and testifying that this is the true grace of God. Stand fast in it.

[13]She who is in Babylon, chosen together with you, sends you her greetings, and so does my son Mark. [14]Greet one another with a kiss of love.

Peace to all of you who are in Christ.

[a]12 Greek *Silvanus*, a variant of *Silas*

PETER writes a second letter because false teachers are troubling the church and disturbing the faith of some by their heresy, immorality and greed. He wants Christians to grow in the knowledge of the truth of God's Word. As you read this book, remember that God will eventually win the battle against false teaching, and promise the Lord that you will study to increase your knowledge of the Bible.

2 PETER

1 Simon Peter, a servant and apostle of Jesus Christ,

To those who through the righteousness of our God and Savior Jesus Christ have received a faith as precious as ours:

²Grace and peace be yours in abundance through the knowledge of God and of Jesus our Lord.

Making One's Calling and Election Sure

³His divine power has given us everything we need for life and godliness through our knowledge of him who called us by his own glory and goodness. ⁴Through these he has given us his very great and precious promises, so that through them you may participate in the divine nature and escape the corruption in the world caused by evil desires.

⁵For this very reason, make every effort to add to your faith goodness; and to goodness, knowledge; ⁶and to knowledge, self-control; and to self-control, perseverance; and to perseverance, godliness; ⁷and to godliness, brotherly kindness; and to brotherly kindness, love. ⁸For if you possess these qualities in increasing measure, they will keep you from being ineffective and unproductive in your knowledge of our Lord Jesus Christ. ⁹But if anyone does not have them, he is nearsighted and blind, and has forgotten that he has been cleansed from his past sins.

¹⁰Therefore, my brothers, be all the

more eager to make your calling and election sure. For if you do these things, you will never fall, [11]and you will receive a rich welcome into the eternal kingdom of our Lord and Savior Jesus Christ.

Prophecy of Scripture

[12]So I will always remind you of these things, even though you know them and are firmly established in the truth you now have. [13]I think it is right to refresh your memory as long as I live in the tent of this body, [14]because I know that I will soon put it aside, as our Lord Jesus Christ has made clear to me. [15]And I will make every effort to see that after my departure you will always be able to remember these things.

[16]We did not follow cleverly invented stories when we told you about the power and coming of our Lord Jesus Christ, but we were eyewitnesses of his majesty. [17]For he received honor and glory from God the Father when the voice came to

---

WEDNESDAY

VERSE FOR THE DAY:
2 Peter 1:1

AUTHOR:
Thomas Hale

PASSAGE FOR THE DAY:
2 Peter 1:1–2

Faith as Precious as Ours

THOMAS and Cynthia Hale, a surgeon and pediatrician respectively, moved their family to Nepal in 1970 with the understanding that they would not be allowed to "proselytize" the Nepali people.

Some may ask why we have come to Nepal if not to "proselytize" or "Christianize" the country. Our reason for coming, besides the fact that God has called us here, is to communicate the love of God to the Nepali people through our service and through our lives. We have come because God has given us a love for the people, especially for those suffering in body and spirit. This love does not arise from ourselves—it is a gift purely from God. Out of that love has grown a desire to introduce others to the person who has meant more to us than any other: Jesus Christ. To neglect sharing with our Nepali friends the joy of knowing him would make a pretense of our friendship. To withhold from them this greatest gift would be to no longer love them. And so it is not our religion that we desire to introduce to them but Jesus himself. There is no pressure, no enticement, no ulterior motive, no effort to undermine the many wonderful aspects of their own culture, which we not only admire but from which we have learned and profited. Rather we seek to work among the Nepalis as friends and equals, contributing our professional skills where needed and involving ourselves as much as possible in their national aspirations. During the course of all this, it is perfectly natural for us to share with them, as occasions arise, our hearts' deepest feelings. They can take Christ or leave him; we shall serve them regardless.

Additional Scripture Readings:
Colossians 4:2–6; 1 Peter 3:13–17

Go to page 1365 for your next devotional reading.

him from the Majestic Glory, saying, "This is my Son, whom I love; with him I am well pleased."[a] 18We ourselves heard this voice that came from heaven when we were with him on the sacred mountain.

19And we have the word of the prophets made more certain, and you will do well to pay attention to it, as to a light shining in a dark place, until the day dawns and the morning star rises in your hearts. 20Above all, you must understand that no prophecy of Scripture came about by the prophet's own interpretation. 21For prophecy never had its origin in the will of man, but men spoke from God as they were carried along by the Holy Spirit.

False Teachers and Their Destruction

2 But there were also false prophets among the people, just as there will be false teachers among you. They will secretly introduce destructive heresies, even denying the sovereign Lord who bought them—bringing swift destruction on themselves. 2Many will follow their shameful ways and will bring the way of truth into disrepute. 3In their greed these teachers will exploit you with stories they have made up. Their condemnation has

[a]17 Matt. 17:5; Mark 9:7; Luke 9:35

THURSDAY

VERSE FOR THE DAY:	AUTHOR:	PASSAGE FOR THE DAY:
2 Peter 1:19	Frederick Buechner	2 Peter 1:16–21

Our Very Own Story

FOR all its vast diversity and unevenness, it [the Bible] is a book with a plot and a plot that can be readily stated. God makes the world in love. For one reason or another the world chooses to reject God. God will not reject the world but continues his mysterious and relentless pursuit of it to the end of time. That is what he is doing by choosing Israel to be his special people. That is what he is doing through all the passion and poetry and invective of the prophets. That is why history plays such a crucial part in the Old Testament—all those kings and renegades and battles and invasions and apostasies —because it was precisely through people like that and events like those that God was at work, as, later, in the New Testament, he was supremely at work in the person and event of Jesus Christ. Only "*is* at work" would be the more accurate way of putting it because . . . his work goes on still, of course, and at one and the same time the Biblical past not only illumines the present but becomes itself part of that present, part of our own individual pasts. Until you can read the story of Adam and Eve, of Abraham and Sarah, of David and Bathsheba, as your own story . . . you have not really understood it. The Bible . . . is a book finally about ourselves, our own apostasies, our own battles and blessings.

Additional Scripture Readings:
Psalm 119:105–112;
2 Timothy 3:14–17

Go to page 1367 for your next devotional reading.

long been hanging over them, and their destruction has not been sleeping.

[4]For if God did not spare angels when they sinned, but sent them to hell,[a] putting them into gloomy dungeons[b] to be held for judgment; [5]if he did not spare the ancient world when he brought the flood on its ungodly people, but protected Noah, a preacher of righteousness, and seven others; [6]if he condemned the cities of Sodom and Gomorrah by burning them to ashes, and made them an example of what is going to happen to the ungodly; [7]and if he rescued Lot, a righteous man, who was distressed by the filthy lives of lawless men [8](for that righteous man, living among them day after day, was tormented in his righteous soul by the lawless deeds he saw and heard) — [9]if this is so, then the Lord knows how to rescue godly men from trials and to hold the unrighteous for the day of judgment, while continuing their punishment.[c] [10]This is especially true of those who follow the corrupt desire of the sinful nature[d] and despise authority.

Bold and arrogant, these men are not afraid to slander celestial beings; [11]yet even angels, although they are stronger and more powerful, do not bring slanderous accusations against such beings in the presence of the Lord. [12]But these men blaspheme in matters they do not understand. They are like brute beasts, creatures of instinct, born only to be caught and destroyed, and like beasts they too will perish.

[13]They will be paid back with harm for the harm they have done. Their idea of pleasure is to carouse in broad daylight. They are blots and blemishes, reveling in their pleasures while they feast with you.[e] [14]With eyes full of adultery, they never stop sinning; they seduce the unstable; they are experts in greed — an accursed brood! [15]They have left the straight way and wandered off to follow the way of Balaam son of Beor, who loved the wages of wickedness. [16]But he was rebuked for his wrongdoing by a donkey — a beast without speech — who spoke with a man's voice and restrained the prophet's madness.

[17]These men are springs without water and mists driven by a storm. Blackest darkness is reserved for them. [18]For they mouth empty, boastful words and, by appealing to the lustful desires of sinful human nature, they entice people who are just escaping from those who live in error. [19]They promise them freedom, while they themselves are slaves of depravity — for a man is a slave to whatever has mastered him. [20]If they have escaped the corruption of the world by knowing our Lord and Savior Jesus Christ and are again entangled in it and overcome, they are worse off at the end than they were at the beginning. [21]It would have been better for them not to have known the way of righteousness, than to have known it and then to turn their backs on the sacred command that was passed on to them. [22]Of them the proverbs are true: "A dog returns to its vomit,"[f] and, "A sow that is washed goes back to her wallowing in the mud."

The Day of the Lord

3 Dear friends, this is now my second letter to you. I have written both of them as reminders to stimulate you to wholesome thinking. [2]I want you to recall the words spoken in the past by the holy prophets and the command given by our Lord and Savior through your apostles.

[3]First of all, you must understand that in the last days scoffers will come, scoffing and following their own evil desires. [4]They will say, "Where is this 'coming' he promised? Ever since our fathers died, everything goes on as it has since the beginning of creation." [5]But they deliberately forget that long ago by God's word the heavens existed and the earth was formed out of water and by water. [6]By these waters also the world of that time was deluged and destroyed. [7]By the same word the present heavens and earth are reserved for fire, being kept for the day of judgment and destruction of ungodly men.

[8]But do not forget this one thing, dear friends: With the Lord a day is like a thousand years, and a thousand years are like a day. [9]The Lord is not slow in keeping his promise, as some understand slowness. He is patient with you, not wanting anyone to perish, but everyone to come to repentance.

[10]But the day of the Lord will come like a thief. The heavens will disappear with a roar; the elements will be destroyed by

---

[a]4 Greek *Tartarus*　[b]4 Some manuscripts *into chains of darkness*　[c]9 Or *unrighteous for punishment until the day of judgment*　[d]10 Or *the flesh*　[e]13 Some manuscripts *in their love feasts*　[f]22 Prov. 26:11

fire, and the earth and everything in it will be laid bare.ᵃ

¹¹Since everything will be destroyed in this way, what kind of people ought you to be? You ought to live holy and godly lives ¹²as you look forward to the day of God and speed its coming.ᵇ That day will bring about the destruction of the heavens by fire, and the elements will melt in the heat. ¹³But in keeping with his promise we are looking forward to a new heaven and a new earth, the home of righteousness.

¹⁴So then, dear friends, since you are looking forward to this, make every effort to be found spotless, blameless and at peace with him. ¹⁵Bear in mind that our Lord's patience means salvation, just as our dear brother Paul also wrote you with the wisdom that God gave him. ¹⁶He writes the same way in all his letters, speaking in them of these matters. His letters contain some things that are hard to understand, which ignorant and unstable people distort, as they do the other Scriptures, to their own destruction.

ᵃ10 Some manuscripts *be burned up*   ᵇ12 Or *as you wait eagerly for the day of God to come*

FRIDAY

VERSE FOR THE DAY:
2 Peter 3:11

AUTHOR:
Thomas Merton

PASSAGE FOR THE DAY:
2 Peter 3:11–14

Simply a Window

THE true saint is not one who has become convinced that he himself is holy, but one who is overwhelmed by the realization that God, and God alone, is holy. He is so awestruck with the reality of the divine holiness that he begins to see it everywhere. Eventually, he may be able to see it in himself too: but surely he will see it there last of all, because in himself he will continue to experience the nothingness, the pseudo reality of egoism and sin. Yet even in the darkness of our disposition to evil shines the presence and the mercy of the divine Savior. The saint is capable, as [Russian novelist] Dostoevski said, of loving others even in their sin. For what he sees in all things and in all men is the object of the divine compassion.

The saint, then, seeks not his own glory but the glory of God. And in order that God may be glorified in all things, the saint wishes himself to be nothing but a pure instrument of the divine will. He wants himself to be simply a window through which God's mercy shines on the world. And for this he strives to be holy. He strives to practice virtue heroically, not in order to be known as a virtuous and holy man, but in order that the goodness of God may never be obscured by any selfish act of his.

Hence it is that he who loves God, and seeks the glory of God, seeks to become, by God's grace, perfect in love, as the "heavenly Father is perfect" (Matthew 5:48).

Additional Scripture Readings:
2 Corinthians 3:12—4:6;
1 Peter 1:13–16

Go to page 1369 for your next devotional reading.

17Therefore, dear friends, since you already know this, be on your guard so that you may not be carried away by the error of lawless men and fall from your secure position. 18But grow in the grace and knowledge of our Lord and Savior Jesus Christ. To him be glory both now and forever! Amen.

WEEKENDING

REFLECT

Redemption in Jesus Christ initiates a new life, one in which the life of God invades ours, making the passage of time take on the significance of eternity. We can see the design of history's tapestry even though the entire cloth is not yet woven, and we can be sure that the thread of our lives fits into his great design . . .

It is not that we must pump time full of life again with our own activity. That is the way the world is doing it; and rather than find life in time, the world discovers that time becomes scarce, disappears and ends in remorse. We who are alive with God's life will also have God's time. Time itself will become alive again to us. That calls for a dramatically different view of life: a releasing of our inner time with a consequent sense of fulfillment in our tasks and the expectation of a complete "coming together" of all the redeemed time of the saints at the end.

– *William T. McConnell*

REVIVE
Saturday: Ephesians 5:13–16
Sunday: 2 Peter 3:8–16

Go to page 1371 for your next devotional reading.

JOHN writes this first letter to emphasize some of the same themes as his Gospel (such as "walking in the light," "knowing the truth," and "loving one another"). He does so because antichrists are promoting false views of the Son of God. As you read this book, realize how much God wants you to fight sin, to love others and to believe in the true Jesus for eternal life.

1 JOHN

The Word of Life

1 That which was from the beginning, which we have heard, which we have seen with our eyes, which we have looked at and our hands have touched — this we proclaim concerning the Word of life. **2**The life appeared; we have seen it and testify to it, and we proclaim to you the eternal life, which was with the Father and has appeared to us. **3**We proclaim to you what we have seen and heard, so that you also may have fellowship with us. And our fellowship is with the Father and with his Son, Jesus Christ. **4**We write this to make our*ᵃ* joy complete.

Walking in the Light

5This is the message we have heard from him and declare to you: God is light; in him there is no darkness at all. **6**If we claim to have fellowship with him yet walk in the darkness, we lie and do not live by the truth. **7**But if we walk in the light, as he is in the light, we have fellowship with one another, and the blood of Jesus, his Son, purifies us from all*ᵇ* sin.

8If we claim to be without sin, we deceive ourselves and the truth is not in us. **9**If we confess our sins, he is faithful and just and will forgive us our sins and purify us from all unrighteousness. **10**If we claim

ᵃ4 Some manuscripts your   *ᵇ7 Or every*

we have not sinned, we make him out to be a liar and his word has no place in our lives.

2 My dear children, I write this to you so that you will not sin. But if anybody does sin, we have one who speaks to the Father in our defense—Jesus Christ, the Righteous One. **2**He is the atoning sacrifice for our sins, and not only for ours but also for*a* the sins of the whole world.

3We know that we have come to know him if we obey his commands. **4**The man who says, "I know him," but does not do what he commands is a liar, and the truth is not in him. **5**But if anyone obeys his word, God's love*b* is truly made complete in him. This is how we know we are in him: **6**Whoever claims to live in him must walk as Jesus did.

7Dear friends, I am not writing you a new command but an old one, which you have had since the beginning. This old

a2 Or He is the one who turns aside God's wrath, taking away our sins, and not only ours but also
b5 Or word, love for God

MONDAY

VERSE FOR THE DAY:
1 John 1:9

AUTHOR:
Max Lucado

PASSAGE FOR THE DAY:
1 John 1:5–10

Strange Path to Joy

A PRISON of pride is filled with self-made men and women determined to pull themselves up by their own bootstraps even if they land on their rear ends. It doesn't matter what they did or to whom they did it or where they will end up; it only matters that "I did it my way."

You've seen the prisoners. You've seen the alcoholic who won't admit his drinking problem. You've seen the woman who refuses to talk to anyone about her fears. You've seen the businessman who adamantly rejects help, even when his dreams are falling apart.

Perhaps to see such a prisoner all you have to do is look in the mirror.

"*If* we confess our sins, he is faithful and just" (1 John 1:9, [italics added]). The biggest word in Scripture just might be that two-letter one, *if.* For confessing sins—admitting failure—is exactly what prisoners of pride refuse to do . . .

To mourn for your sins is a natural outflow of poverty of spirit. The second beatitude [Blessed are those who mourn] should follow the first [Blessed are the poor in spirit]. But that's not always the case. Many deny their weakness. Many know they are wrong, yet pretend they are right. As a result, they never taste the exquisite sorrow of repentance.

Of all the paths to joy, this one has to be the strangest. True blessedness, Jesus says, begins with deep sadness.

"Blessed are those who know they are in trouble and have enough sense to admit it."

Additional Scripture Readings:
Matthew 5:1–10; Luke 18:9–14

Go to page 1374 for your next devotional reading.

command is the message you have heard. **8**Yet I am writing you a new command; its truth is seen in him and you, because the darkness is passing and the true light is already shining.

9Anyone who claims to be in the light but hates his brother is still in the darkness. **10**Whoever loves his brother lives in the light, and there is nothing in him*a* to make him stumble. **11**But whoever hates his brother is in the darkness and walks around in the darkness; he does not know where he is going, because the darkness has blinded him.

12I write to you, dear children,
   because your sins have been
     forgiven on account of his
     name.
13I write to you, fathers,
   because you have known him who
     is from the beginning.
I write to you, young men,
   because you have overcome the evil
     one.
I write to you, dear children,
   because you have known the
     Father.
14I write to you, fathers,
   because you have known him who
     is from the beginning.
I write to you, young men,
   because you are strong,
   and the word of God lives in you,
   and you have overcome the evil one.

Do Not Love the World

15Do not love the world or anything in the world. If anyone loves the world, the love of the Father is not in him. **16**For everything in the world—the cravings of sinful man, the lust of his eyes and the boasting of what he has and does—comes not from the Father but from the world. **17**The world and its desires pass away, but the man who does the will of God lives forever.

Warning Against Antichrists

18Dear children, this is the last hour; and as you have heard that the antichrist is coming, even now many antichrists have come. This is how we know it is the last hour. **19**They went out from us, but they did not really belong to us. For if they had belonged to us, they would have remained with us; but their going showed that none of them belonged to us.

20But you have an anointing from the Holy One, and all of you know the truth.*b* **21**I do not write to you because you do not know the truth, but because you do know it and because no lie comes from the truth. **22**Who is the liar? It is the man who denies that Jesus is the Christ. Such a man is the antichrist—he denies the Father and the Son. **23**No one who denies the Son has the Father; whoever acknowledges the Son has the Father also.

24See that what you have heard from the beginning remains in you. If it does, you also will remain in the Son and in the Father. **25**And this is what he promised us—even eternal life.

26I am writing these things to you about those who are trying to lead you astray. **27**As for you, the anointing you received from him remains in you, and you do not need anyone to teach you. But as his anointing teaches you about all things and as that anointing is real, not counterfeit—just as it has taught you, remain in him.

Children of God

28And now, dear children, continue in him, so that when he appears we may be confident and unashamed before him at his coming.

29If you know that he is righteous, you know that everyone who does what is right has been born of him.

3 How great is the love the Father has lavished on us, that we should be called children of God! And that is what we are! The reason the world does not know us is that it did not know him. **2**Dear friends, now we are children of God, and what we will be has not yet been made known. But we know that when he appears,*c* we shall be like him, for we shall see him as he is. **3**Everyone who has this hope in him purifies himself, just as he is pure.

4Everyone who sins breaks the law; in fact, sin is lawlessness. **5**But you know that he appeared so that he might take away our sins. And in him is no sin. **6**No one who lives in him keeps on sinning. No one who continues to sin has either seen him or known him.

7Dear children, do not let anyone lead you astray. He who does what is right is righteous, just as he is righteous. **8**He who does what is sinful is of the devil, because the devil has been sinning from the beginning. The reason the Son of God appeared

---

a10 Or *it*   *b20* Some manuscripts *and you know all things*   *c2* Or *when it is made known* was to destroy the devil's work. **9**No one who is born of God will continue to sin, because God's seed remains in him; he cannot go on sinning, because he has been born of God. **10**This is how we know who the children of God are and who the children of the devil are: Anyone who does not do what is right is not a child of God; nor is anyone who does not love his brother.

Love One Another

11This is the message you heard from the beginning: We should love one another. **12**Do not be like Cain, who belonged to the evil one and murdered his brother. And why did he murder him? Because his own actions were evil and his brother's were righteous. **13**Do not be surprised, my brothers, if the world hates you. **14**We know that we have passed from death to life, because we love our brothers. Anyone who does not love remains in death. **15**Anyone who hates his brother is a murderer, and you know that no murderer has eternal life in him.

16This is how we know what love is: Jesus Christ laid down his life for us. And we ought to lay down our lives for our brothers. **17**If anyone has material possessions and sees his brother in need but has no pity on him, how can the love of God be in him? **18**Dear children, let us not love with words or tongue but with actions and in truth. **19**This then is how we know that we belong to the truth, and how we set our hearts at rest in his presence **20**whenever our hearts condemn us. For God is greater than our hearts, and he knows everything.

21Dear friends, if our hearts do not condemn us, we have confidence before God **22**and receive from him anything we ask, because we obey his commands and do what pleases him. **23**And this is his command: to believe in the name of his Son, Jesus Christ, and to love one another as he commanded us. **24**Those who obey his commands live in him, and he in them. And this is how we know that he lives in us: We know it by the Spirit he gave us.

Test the Spirits

4 Dear friends, do not believe every spirit, but test the spirits to see whether they are from God, because many false prophets have gone out into the world.

2This is how you can recognize the Spirit of God: Every spirit that acknowledges that Jesus Christ has come in the flesh is from God, **3**but every spirit that does not acknowledge Jesus is not from God. This is the spirit of the antichrist, which you have heard is coming and even now is already in the world.

4You, dear children, are from God and have overcome them, because the one who is in you is greater than the one who is in the world. **5**They are from the world and therefore speak from the viewpoint of the world, and the world listens to them. **6**We are from God, and whoever knows God listens to us; but whoever is not from God does not listen to us. This is how we recognize the Spirit*a* of truth and the spirit of falsehood.

God's Love and Ours

7Dear friends, let us love one another, for love comes from God. Everyone who loves has been born of God and knows God. **8**Whoever does not love does not know God, because God is love. **9**This is how God showed his love among us: He sent his one and only Son*b* into the world that we might live through him. **10**This is love: not that we loved God, but that he loved us and sent his Son as an atoning sacrifice for*c* our sins. **11**Dear friends, since God so loved us, we also ought to love one another. **12**No one has ever seen God; but if we love one another, God lives in us and his love is made complete in us.

13We know that we live in him and he in us, because he has given us of his Spirit. **14**And we have seen and testify that the Father has sent his Son to be the Savior of the world. **15**If anyone acknowledges that Jesus is the Son of God, God lives in him and he in God. **16**And so we know and rely on the love God has for us.

God is love. Whoever lives in love lives in God, and God in him. **17**In this way, love is made complete among us so that we will have confidence on the day of judgment, because in this world we are like him. **18**There is no fear in love. But perfect love drives out fear, because fear has to do with punishment. The one who fears is not made perfect in love.

19We love because he first loved us. **20**If anyone says, "I love God," yet hates his brother, he is a liar. For anyone who does not love his brother, whom he has seen,

---

*a*6 Or *spirit*   *b*9 Or *his only begotten Son away*   *c*10 Or *as the one who would turn aside his wrath, taking* cannot love God, whom he has not seen. **21**And he has given us this command: Whoever loves God must also love his brother.

Faith in the Son of God

5 Everyone who believes that Jesus is the Christ is born of God, and every-one who loves the father loves his child as well. **2**This is how we know that we love the children of God: by loving God and carrying out his commands. **3**This is love for God: to obey his commands. And his commands are not burdensome, **4**for everyone born of God overcomes the world. This is the victory that has overcome the

---

TUESDAY

VERSE FOR THE DAY:	AUTHOR:	PASSAGE FOR THE DAY:
1 John 4:18	Daniel Taylor	1 John 4:7–21

Significant Living

I AM tempted to say that I am not genuinely afraid about anything—but that isn't true. My main fear now is insignificance. I am afraid, to put it simply, of living a life that doesn't matter. I am afraid of leaving the world exactly as I found it, no different for my having been here. I am afraid, as the writer Henry Thoreau said, of coming to the end of life and finding that I have not lived.

A lot of people say something like that these days, but they think "having lived" means having a lot of adventures or a lot of fun or a lot of money. I don't think that has much to do with it. Significant living comes from filling your life with things which last forever. That's why the usual things people seek to guarantee importance in their lives—money, fame, power—don't work very well. They all come to an end, often during the person's own life, and certainly thereafter.

What are things which last forever? Justice, mercy, forgiveness, compassion and grace are a few. Truth also lasts forever. These are all forms of the greatest value of all—love. And as you know, the source and perfect giver of love is God.

If I want my life to count, to be significant, then I will try to fill it as much as possible with these attitudes and actions . . . If you have made someone else's life better, you have done something eternal. And that means that a significant life will usually have lots of people in it. Because people are the only part of this world which will last forever . . .

This world is filled with threats—some imagined, some real —to our safety, to our sense of being okay. The ultimate security, the only true safety, is to be in right relationship with the God who is the alpha and omega, the beginning and the end. He was there before the beginning. He has no end. He has seen and suffered all. He has known our fears. He sets us free.

Additional Scripture Readings:
Hebrews 2:10–18; Revelation 1:4–8

Go to page 1375 for your next devotional reading.

world, even our faith. **5**Who is it that overcomes the world? Only he who believes that Jesus is the Son of God.

6This is the one who came by water and blood—Jesus Christ. He did not come by water only, but by water and blood. And it is the Spirit who testifies, because the Spirit is the truth. **7**For there are three that testify: **8**the*a* Spirit, the water and the blood; and the three are in agreement. **9**We accept man's testimony, but God's testimony is greater because it is the testimony of God, which he has given about his Son. **10**Anyone who believes in the Son of God has this testimony in his heart.

Anyone who does not believe God has made him out to be a liar, because he has not believed the testimony God has given about his Son. **11**And this is the testimony: God has given us eternal life, and this life is in his Son. **12**He who has the Son has life; he who does not have the Son of God does not have life.

Concluding Remarks

13I write these things to you who believe in the name of the Son of God so that you may know that you have eternal life. **14**This is the confidence we have in approaching God: that if we ask anything ac-

a7,8 Late manuscripts of the Vulgate *testify in heaven: the Father, the Word and the Holy Spirit, and these three are one.* *8And there are three that testify on earth: the* (not found in any Greek manuscript before the sixteenth century)

WEDNESDAY

VERSE FOR THE DAY:	AUTHOR:	PASSAGE FOR THE DAY:
1 John 5:3	Jerry Bridges	1 John 5:1–5

A Solid Foundation

THE *practice of godliness is an exercise or discipline that focuses upon God.* From this Godward attitude arise the character and conduct that we usually think of as godliness. So often we try to develop Christian character and conduct without taking the time to develop God-centered devotion. We try to please God without taking the time to walk with him and develop a relationship with him. This is impossible to do.

Consider the exacting requirements of a godly lifestyle . . . Note the totality of godliness over one's entire life . . . Nothing is excluded. God is at the center of his thoughts. His most ordinary duties are done with an eye to God's glory. In Paul's words to the Corinthians, whether he eats or drinks or whatever he does, he does it all for the glory of God (1 Corinthians 10:31).

Now it is obvious that such a God-centered lifestyle cannot be developed and maintained apart from a solid foundation of devotion to God. Only a strong personal relationship with the living God can keep such a commitment from becoming oppressive and legalistic. John writes that God's commands are not burdensome; a godly life is not wearisome, but this is true only because a godly person is first of all devoted to God.

Additional Scripture Readings:
Psalm 86:1–13; John 15:1–17

Go to page 1378 for your next devotional reading.

cording to his will, he hears us. **15**And if we know that he hears us — whatever we ask — we know that we have what we asked of him.

16If anyone sees his brother commit a sin that does not lead to death, he should pray and God will give him life. I refer to those whose sin does not lead to death. There is a sin that leads to death. I am not saying that he should pray about that. **17**All wrongdoing is sin, and there is sin that does not lead to death.

18We know that anyone born of God does not continue to sin; the one who was born of God keeps him safe, and the evil one cannot harm him. **19**We know that we are children of God, and that the whole world is under the control of the evil one. **20**We know also that the Son of God has come and has given us understanding, so that we may know him who is true. And we are in him who is true — even in his Son Jesus Christ. He is the true God and eternal life.

21Dear children, keep yourselves from idols.

JOHN writes this second letter to warn the church to stand firm against false teachers and to keep loving other Christians. As you read this book, learn how to stand up for your Lord whenever you encounter false teachers.

2 JOHN

¹The elder,

To the chosen lady and her children, whom I love in the truth—and not I only, but also all who know the truth— ²because of the truth, which lives in us and will be with us forever:

³Grace, mercy and peace from God the Father and from Jesus Christ, the Father's Son, will be with us in truth and love.

⁴It has given me great joy to find some of your children walking in the truth, just as the Father commanded us. ⁵And now, dear lady, I am not writing you a new command but one we have had from the beginning. I ask that we love one another. ⁶And this is love: that we walk in obedience to his commands. As you have heard from the beginning, his command is that you walk in love.

⁷Many deceivers, who do not acknowledge Jesus Christ as coming in the flesh, have gone out into the world. Any such person is the deceiver and the antichrist. ⁸Watch out that you do not lose what you have worked for, but that you may be rewarded fully. ⁹Anyone who runs ahead and does not continue in the teaching of Christ does not have God; whoever continues in the teaching has both the Father and the Son. ¹⁰If anyone comes to you and does not bring this teaching, do not take him into your house or welcome him. ¹¹Anyone who welcomes him shares in his wicked work.

¹²I have much to write to you, but I do not want to use paper and ink. Instead, I hope to visit you and talk with you face to face, so that our joy may be complete.

¹³The children of your chosen sister send their greetings.

VERSE FOR THE DAY:
2 John 9

AUTHOR:
David Wiersbe and
Warren Wiersbe

PASSAGE FOR THE DAY:
2 John 8–9

On Gains and Losses

IN THESE two verses, the aged apostle John pointed out two special threats to the church: the danger of losing what we have gained, and the danger of making gains that are really losses. You and I certainly need discernment and wisdom to detect these dangers and overcome the enemy.

As to the first danger, John tells us, "Watch out that you do not lose what you have worked for, but that you may be rewarded fully." Sometimes we are so anxious to move forward in God's work that we fail to conserve and protect the blessings we have already received . . .

The second danger is that of making gains that are really losses. Verse 9 reads, "Anyone who runs ahead and does not continue in the teaching of Christ does not have God." This is a warning against the "progressive theology" that abandons "the faith that was once for all entrusted to the saints" (Jude 3) and ends up denying Jesus Christ. Over the centuries, more than one ministry has gone backwards by trying to move "forward" in developing a so-called up-to-date doctrinal position.

To be sure, there is always more to be learned from the Bible! And the unchanging Word of God must constantly be related to whatever new insight men discover in Scripture. But to go beyond the fundamental truths that the church holds dear is to make "gains" that are really losses. We must know the truth, live the truth, defend the truth and share the truth with others. But we must never go *beyond* that truth . . .

This is why God's work is so important, and why it demands the very best that we can give it. We are on guard duty for God, staying alert to protect our gains and rejecting profits that are really losses. If you ask, "Who is equal to such a task?" (2 Corinthians 2:16), the answer is clear: "Our competence comes from God" (2 Corinthians 3:5).

Additional Scripture Readings:
John 8:31–38; Hebrews 10:35–39

Go to page 1380 for your next devotional reading.

JOHN writes this third letter to commend a church leader for his hospitality and to warn against another one who is unfriendly and even cruel. As you read this book, think how you can act as a friend toward other Christians.

3 JOHN

¹The elder,

To my dear friend Gaius, whom I love in the truth.

²Dear friend, I pray that you may enjoy good health and that all may go well with you, even as your soul is getting along well. ³It gave me great joy to have some brothers come and tell about your faithfulness to the truth and how you continue to walk in the truth. ⁴I have no greater joy than to hear that my children are walking in the truth.

⁵Dear friend, you are faithful in what you are doing for the brothers, even though they are strangers to you. ⁶They have told the church about your love. You will do well to send them on their way in a manner worthy of God. ⁷It was for the sake of the Name that they went out, receiving no help from the pagans. ⁸We ought therefore to show hospitality to such men so that we may work together for the truth.

⁹I wrote to the church, but Diotrephes, who loves to be first, will have nothing to do with us. ¹⁰So if I come, I will call attention to what he is doing, gossiping maliciously about us. Not satisfied with that, he refuses to welcome the brothers. He also stops those who want to do so and puts them out of the church.

¹¹Dear friend, do not imitate what is evil but what is good. Anyone who does what is good is from God. Anyone who does what is evil has not seen God. ¹²Demetrius is well spoken of by everyone — and even by the truth itself. We also speak well of him, and you know that our testimony is true.

¹³I have much to write you, but I do not want to do so with pen and ink. ¹⁴I hope to see you soon, and we will talk face to face.

Peace to you. The friends here send their greetings. Greet the friends there by name.

VERSE FOR THE DAY:
3 John 2

AUTHOR:
D. Stuart Briscoe

PASSAGE FOR THE DAY:
3 John 1–8

Luxuries, or Necessities?

SCRIPTURE makes it very clear that our lives are lived in terms of relationships: with God and with human beings . . .

Third John is a very interesting letter. It is about the shortest book in the Bible, and over and over again in the fourteen verses is the term "dear friend." If you read this letter, you will get a very lovely picture. John, the aged apostle, writing to a group of believers, is pointing out that they are all his friends. He identifies in special ways some intimate friendships with the people there.

John is making a commitment to that fellowship of believers in general, and to individuals in the fellowship in particular, and so should we. There should be a degree in which you and I look in friendly terms toward the fellowship of believers. And when we do that, we should make a commitment to it. On the basis of the friendly commitment to the fellowship of believers, we should then be giving of ourselves in some ways so that we are building up dear-friend relationships.

If we are to know fellowship and friendship, there has to be a commitment to the fellowship as a whole, and there has to be a readiness to identify individually with people for our good and for theirs. For your good and mine, we need friendships. We need fellowships and relationships. And they don't happen by just coming into church and sitting among the people and then going back home. These friendships happen when there is commitment to the group as a whole, and when we get ourselves into situations where we can begin to nurture more personal, more intimate relationships . . .

Do you have friends? What kind of friends? Is Jesus your friend? Does God call you his friend [see James 2:23]? What kind of friends do you have? Are you cautious? Are you careful? Are you committed, and candid? These are qualities we need to have . . . Are real friends luxuries or necessities? What do you think?

Additional Scripture Readings:
John 15:9–17; 1 Peter 1:22—2:3

Go to page 1381 for your next devotional reading.

WEEKENDING

REGARD

Now when the self replaces God at the center of
the universe, some interesting things begin to
happen. The most important . . . is that people
begin to order their world according to their
own wants and aspirations. This, of course, is a
difficult thing to do since the people around
them are doing the same thing, and since a
great many things happen that are not in the
least predictable. Nevertheless, the self is not
easily deterred. It demands fulfillment. And
fulfillment requires control. You cannot
guarantee your own happiness unless you are
able to control events and manage people . . .

But God cannot be controlled. And he would
be within his rights to either ignore our
attempts at control or simply push us and our
petty little pretensions aside. But thanks be to
God, he is not like that. Instead, out of his grace
and mercy he periodically reminds us of the
folly of our ways. And one way he has done
this in my life is through my children.

— S. D. Gaede

REVIVE

Saturday: Job 40:1–14
Sunday: Romans 11:33–36

Go to page 1383 for your next devotional reading.

*J*UDE *(a brother of Jesus and James) writes this short letter to warn Christians against false teachers in the church and to urge them to strengthen their faith and love. As you read this book, begin to grow in faith and love by depending on the Father, Son and Holy Spirit.*

JUDE

¹Jude, a servant of Jesus Christ and a brother of James,

To those who have been called, who are loved by God the Father and kept by[a] Jesus Christ:

²Mercy, peace and love be yours in abundance.

The Sin and Doom of Godless Men

³Dear friends, although I was very eager to write to you about the salvation we share, I felt I had to write and urge you to contend for the faith that was once for all entrusted to the saints. ⁴For certain men whose condemnation was written about[b] long ago have secretly slipped in among you. They are godless men, who change the grace of our God into a license for immorality and deny Jesus Christ our only Sovereign and Lord.

⁵Though you already know all this, I want to remind you that the Lord[c] delivered his people out of Egypt, but later destroyed those who did not believe. ⁶And the angels who did not keep their positions of authority but abandoned their own home—these he has kept in darkness, bound with everlasting chains for judgment on the great Day. ⁷In a similar way, Sodom and Gomorrah and the surrounding towns gave themselves up to sexual immorality and perversion. They serve as an example of those who suffer the punishment of eternal fire.

⁸In the very same way, these dreamers pollute their own bodies, reject authority and slander celestial beings. ⁹But even the archangel Michael, when he was disputing with the devil about the body of Moses, did not dare to bring a slanderous accusation against him, but said, "The Lord rebuke you!" ¹⁰Yet these men speak abusively against whatever they do not under-

stand; and what things they do understand by instinct, like unreasoning
animals—these are the very things that
destroy them.

11Woe to them! They have taken the
way of Cain; they have rushed for profit
into Balaam's error; they have been destroyed in Korah's rebellion.

12These men are blemishes at your love
feasts, eating with you without the slightest qualm—shepherds who feed only
themselves. They are clouds without rain,
blown along by the wind; autumn trees,
without fruit and uprooted—twice dead.
13They are wild waves of the sea, foaming
up their shame; wandering stars, for
whom blackest darkness has been reserved forever.

14Enoch, the seventh from Adam,
prophesied about these men: "See, the
Lord is coming with thousands upon
thousands of his holy ones **15**to judge everyone, and to convict all the ungodly of
all the ungodly acts they have done in the
ungodly way, and of all the harsh words
ungodly sinners have spoken against

MONDAY

VERSE FOR THE DAY:	AUTHOR:	PASSAGE FOR THE DAY:
Jude 21	A.W. Tozer	Jude 20–23

A Raging Torrent

BOTH the Old and New Testaments teach that the essence of
true worship is the love of God.

Our Lord declared this to be the sum of the Law and the
Prophets: "Love the Lord your God with all your heart and
with all your soul and with all your mind and with all your
strength" (Mark 12:30).

Now, love is both a principle and an emotion; it is something both felt and willed. It is capable of almost infinite de-
grees. Love in the human heart may begin so modestly as to
be hardly perceptible and go on to become a raging torrent
that sweeps its possessor before it in total helplessness.

Something like this must have been the experience of the
Apostle Paul, for he felt it necessary to explain to his critics
that his apparent madness was actually the love of God ravish-
ing his willing heart!

In the love that any intelligent creature feels for God there
must always be a measure of mystery. It is even possible that
it is almost wholly mystery, and that our attempt to find reasons is merely a rationalizing of a love already mysteriously
present in the heart as a result of some secret operation of the
Spirit within us.

We can be certain that it is quite impossible to worship God
without loving him. Scripture and reason agree to declare this.
And God is never satisfied with anything less than all. This
may not at first be possible, but the inward operations of the
Holy Spirit will enable us in his time to offer him our poured-
out fullness of love!

Additional Scripture Readings:
Psalm 18:1–6;
2 Corinthians 5:11–15

Go to page 1387 for your next
devotional reading.

him." **16**These men are grumblers and faultfinders; they follow their own evil desires; they boast about themselves and flatter others for their own advantage.

A Call to Persevere

17But, dear friends, remember what the apostles of our Lord Jesus Christ foretold. **18**They said to you, "In the last times there will be scoffers who will follow their own ungodly desires." **19**These are the men who divide you, who follow mere natural instincts and do not have the Spirit.

20But you, dear friends, build yourselves up in your most holy faith and pray in the Holy Spirit. **21**Keep yourselves in God's love as you wait for the mercy of our Lord Jesus Christ to bring you to eternal life.

22Be merciful to those who doubt; **23**snatch others from the fire and save them; to others show mercy, mixed with fear — hating even the clothing stained by corrupted flesh.

Doxology

24To him who is able to keep you from falling and to present you before his glorious presence without fault and with great joy — **25**to the only God our Savior be glory, majesty, power and authority, through Jesus Christ our Lord, before all ages, now and forevermore! Amen.

JOHN, banished to the island of Patmos, writes what Christ reveals to him in order to comfort Christians suffering for their faith. Through visions of God in control of both the present and the future, he offers them hope, assuring them that in the end Christ will achieve victory over Satan, who is doomed to eternal punishment. As you read this book, rejoice in the awesome power of Christ, and remember that regardless of what happens now or in the future, nothing can ever separate you from his love.

REVELATION

Prologue

1 The revelation of Jesus Christ, which God gave him to show his servants what must soon take place. He made it known by sending his angel to his servant John, ²who testifies to everything he saw—that is, the word of God and the testimony of Jesus Christ. ³Blessed is the one who reads the words of this prophecy, and blessed are those who hear it and take to heart what is written in it, because the time is near.

Greetings and Doxology

⁴John,

To the seven churches in the province of Asia:

Grace and peace to you from him who is, and who was, and who is to come, and from the seven spirits*a* before his throne, ⁵and from Jesus Christ, who is the faithful witness, the firstborn from the dead, and the ruler of the kings of the earth.

a4 Or the sevenfold Spirit

To him who loves us and has freed us from our sins by his blood, **6**and has made us to be a kingdom and priests to serve his God and Father — to him be glory and power for ever and ever! Amen.

7Look, he is coming with the clouds,
    and every eye will see him,
even those who pierced him;
    and all the peoples of the earth will
        mourn because of him.
            So shall it be! Amen.

8"I am the Alpha and the Omega," says the Lord God, "who is, and who was, and who is to come, the Almighty."

One Like a Son of Man

9I, John, your brother and companion in the suffering and kingdom and patient endurance that are ours in Jesus, was on the island of Patmos because of the word of God and the testimony of Jesus. **10**On the Lord's Day I was in the Spirit, and I heard behind me a loud voice like a trumpet, **11**which said: "Write on a scroll what you see and send it to the seven churches: to Ephesus, Smyrna, Pergamum, Thyatira, Sardis, Philadelphia and Laodicea."

12I turned around to see the voice that was speaking to me. And when I turned I saw seven golden lampstands, **13**and among the lampstands was someone "like a son of man,"[a] dressed in a robe reaching down to his feet and with a golden sash around his chest. **14**His head and hair were white like wool, as white as snow, and his eyes were like blazing fire. **15**His feet were like bronze glowing in a furnace, and his voice was like the sound of rushing waters. **16**In his right hand he held seven stars, and out of his mouth came a sharp double-edged sword. His face was like the sun shining in all its brilliance.

17When I saw him, I fell at his feet as though dead. Then he placed his right hand on me and said: "Do not be afraid. I am the First and the Last. **18**I am the Living One; I was dead, and behold I am alive for ever and ever! And I hold the keys of death and Hades.

19"Write, therefore, what you have seen, what is now and what will take place later. **20**The mystery of the seven stars that you saw in my right hand and of the seven golden lampstands is this: The seven stars are the angels[b] of the seven churches,

and the seven lampstands are the seven churches.

To the Church in Ephesus

2 "To the angel[c] of the church in Ephesus write:

These are the words of him who holds the seven stars in his right hand and walks among the seven golden lampstands: **2**I know your deeds, your hard work and your perseverance. I know that you cannot tolerate wicked men, that you have tested those who claim to be apostles but are not, and have found them false. **3**You have persevered and have endured hardships for my name, and have not grown weary.

4Yet I hold this against you: You have forsaken your first love. **5**Remember the height from which you have fallen! Repent and do the things you did at first. If you do not repent, I will come to you and remove your lampstand from its place. **6**But you have this in your favor: You hate the practices of the Nicolaitans, which I also hate.

7He who has an ear, let him hear what the Spirit says to the churches. To him who overcomes, I will give the right to eat from the tree of life, which is in the paradise of God.

To the Church in Smyrna

8"To the angel of the church in Smyrna write:

These are the words of him who is the First and the Last, who died and came to life again. **9**I know your afflictions and your poverty — yet you are rich! I know the slander of those who say they are Jews and are not, but are a synagogue of Satan. **10**Do not be afraid of what you are about to suffer. I tell you, the devil will put some of you in prison to test you, and you will suffer persecution for ten days. Be faithful, even to the point of death, and I will give you the crown of life.

11He who has an ear, let him hear what the Spirit says to the churches. He who overcomes will not be hurt at all by the second death.

---

a13 Daniel 7:13   *b20* Or *messengers*   *c1* Or *messenger*; also in verses 8, 12 and 18

To the Church in Pergamum

¹²"To the angel of the church in Pergamum write:

These are the words of him who has the sharp, double-edged sword. ¹³I know where you live — where Satan has his throne. Yet you remain true to my name. You did not renounce your faith in me, even in the days of Antipas, my faithful witness, who was put to death in your city — where Satan lives.

¹⁴Nevertheless, I have a few things against you: You have people there who hold to the teaching of Balaam, who taught Balak to entice the Israelites to sin by eating food sacrificed to idols and by committing sexual immorality. ¹⁵Likewise you also have those who hold to the teaching of the Nicolaitans. ¹⁶Repent therefore! Otherwise, I will soon come to you and will fight against them with the sword of my mouth.

¹⁷He who has an ear, let him hear

TUESDAY

VERSE FOR THE DAY:	AUTHOR:	PASSAGE FOR THE DAY:
Revelation 1:18	Dave Dravecky	Revelation 1:17–20

He Holds the Keys

AS THE baseball season ended, Giants pitcher Dave Dravecky waited for the results of a biopsy on a lump on his pitching arm.

It was an anxious time, waiting, just waiting to hear the news. When the phone rang I always wondered whether it would be the results.

Yet it was a good kind of anxiety, if I can put it that way. Just looking at [my wife] Janice reminded me how much I loved her, of how much she did for me. I stared at her and I stared at my kids, thinking they were the most beautiful sight in the entire universe. Some nights when Tiffany and Jonathan were asleep I would go into their room and listen to them slowly breathing. I thought of how often I didn't have time for them. On so many occasions, when they had asked me to play ball, I'd told them, "I'm busy reading right now; give me ten minutes" — and then the phone would ring and I never would get to play with them. During those days of waiting I did play ball, or whatever else they wanted to play.

I also thought about my eternal destination. I felt a deep sense of security there — that if I were going to die, I knew what would come next. That meant a lot to me.

I don't ordinarily think much about heaven and hell. I'm too busy keeping up with the day-to-day concerns of life. But in those days I found that my perspective shifted. Some things that mattered a lot in the day-to-day routine of living mattered much less. Some things that I seldom considered mattered a great deal more.

Additional Scripture Readings:
Jeremiah 9:23–24; Philippians 3:7–11

Go to page 1389 for your next devotional reading.

what the Spirit says to the churches. To him who overcomes, I will give some of the hidden manna. I will also give him a white stone with a new name written on it, known only to him who receives it.

To the Church in Thyatira

¹⁸"To the angel of the church in Thyatira write:

These are the words of the Son of God, whose eyes are like blazing fire and whose feet are like burnished bronze. ¹⁹I know your deeds, your love and faith, your service and perseverance, and that you are now doing more than you did at first. ²⁰Nevertheless, I have this against you: You tolerate that woman Jezebel, who calls herself a prophetess. By her teaching she misleads my servants into sexual immorality and the eating of food sacrificed to idols. ²¹I have given her time to repent of her immorality, but she is unwilling. ²²So I will cast her on a bed of suffering, and I will make those who commit adultery with her suffer intensely, unless they repent of her ways. ²³I will strike her children dead. Then all the churches will know that I am he who searches hearts and minds, and I will repay each of you according to your deeds. ²⁴Now I say to the rest of you in Thyatira, to you who do not hold to her teaching and have not learned Satan's so-called deep secrets (I will not impose any other burden on you): ²⁵Only hold on to what you have until I come.

²⁶To him who overcomes and does my will to the end, I will give authority over the nations —

²⁷'He will rule them with an iron scepter;
   he will dash them to pieces like pottery' ᵃ —

just as I have received authority from my Father. ²⁸I will also give him the morning star. ²⁹He who has an ear, let him hear what the Spirit says to the churches.

To the Church in Sardis

3 "To the angel ᵇ of the church in Sardis write:

These are the words of him who holds the seven spirits ᶜ of God and the seven stars. I know your deeds; you have a reputation of being alive, but you are dead. ²Wake up! Strengthen what remains and is about to die, for I have not found your deeds complete in the sight of my God. ³Remember, therefore, what you have received and heard; obey it, and repent. But if you do not wake up, I will come like a thief, and you will not know at what time I will come to you.

⁴Yet you have a few people in Sardis who have not soiled their clothes. They will walk with me, dressed in white, for they are worthy. ⁵He who overcomes will, like them, be dressed in white. I will never blot out his name from the book of life, but will acknowledge his name before my Father and his angels. ⁶He who has an ear, let him hear what the Spirit says to the churches.

To the Church in Philadelphia

⁷"To the angel of the church in Philadelphia write:

These are the words of him who is holy and true, who holds the key of David. What he opens no one can shut, and what he shuts no one can open. ⁸I know your deeds. See, I have placed before you an open door that no one can shut. I know that you have little strength, yet you have kept my word and have not denied my name. ⁹I will make those who are of the synagogue of Satan, who claim to be Jews though they are not, but are liars — I will make them come and fall down at your feet and acknowledge that I have loved you. ¹⁰Since you have kept my command to endure patiently, I will also keep you from the hour of trial that is going to come upon the whole world to test those who live on the earth.

¹¹I am coming soon. Hold on to what you have, so that no one will take your crown. ¹²Him who overcomes I will make a pillar in the temple of my God. Never again will he leave it. I will write on him the name of my God and the name of the city of my God, the new Jerusalem, which is

ᵃ27 Psalm 2:9   ᵇ1 Or *messenger*; also in verses 7 and 14   ᶜ1 Or *the sevenfold Spirit* coming down out of heaven from my God; and I will also write on him my new name. [13]He who has an ear, let him hear what the Spirit says to the churches.

To the Church in Laodicea

[14]"To the angel of the church in Laodicea write:

These are the words of the Amen, the faithful and true witness, the ruler of God's creation. [15]I know your deeds, that you are neither cold nor hot. I wish you were either one or the other! [16]So, because you are lukewarm—neither hot nor cold—I am about to spit you out of my mouth. [17]You say, 'I am rich; I have acquired wealth and do not need a thing.' But you do not realize that you are wretched, pitiful, poor, blind and naked. [18]I counsel you to buy from me gold refined in the fire, so you can become rich; and white clothes to wear, so you can cover your shameful nakedness; and salve to put on your eyes, so you can see.

[19]Those whom I love I rebuke and discipline. So be earnest, and repent.

WEDNESDAY

VERSE FOR THE DAY:
Revelation 3:1

AUTHOR:
Dietrich Bonhoeffer

PASSAGE FOR THE DAY:
Revelation 3:1–6

Grace Without Christ

CHEAP grace is the grace we bestow on ourselves. Cheap grace is the preaching of forgiveness without requiring repentance, baptism without church discipline, Communion without confession, absolution without personal confession. Cheap grace is grace without discipleship, grace without the cross, grace without Jesus Christ, living and incarnate.

Costly grace is the treasure hidden in the field; for the sake of it a man will gladly go and sell all that he has. It is the pearl of great price to buy which the merchant will sell all his goods. It is the kingly rule of Christ, for whose sake a man will pluck out the eye that causes him to stumble, it is the call of Jesus Christ at which the disciple leaves his nets and follows him.

Costly grace is the gospel which must be *sought* again and again, the gift which must be *asked* for, the door at which a man must *knock*.

Such grace is *costly* because it calls us to follow, and it is *grace* because it calls us to follow *Jesus Christ*. It is costly because it gives a man the only true life. It is costly because it condemns sin, and grace because it justifies the sinner. Above all, it is *costly* because it cost God the life of his Son: "You were bought at a price" (1 Corinthians 7:23), and what has cost God much cannot be cheap for us. Above all, it is *grace* because God did not reckon his Son too dear a price to pay for our life, but delivered him up for us. Costly grace is the Incarnation of God.

Additional Scripture Readings:
Mark 10:41–45; Romans 5:6–11

Go to page 1391 for your next devotional reading.

20Here I am! I stand at the door and knock. If anyone hears my voice and opens the door, I will come in and eat with him, and he with me.

21To him who overcomes, I will give the right to sit with me on my throne, just as I overcame and sat down with my Father on his throne. 22He who has an ear, let him hear what the Spirit says to the churches."

The Throne in Heaven

4 After this I looked, and there before me was a door standing open in heaven. And the voice I had first heard speaking to me like a trumpet said, "Come up here, and I will show you what must take place after this." 2At once I was in the Spirit, and there before me was a throne in heaven with someone sitting on it. 3And the one who sat there had the appearance of jasper and carnelian. A rainbow, resembling an emerald, encircled the throne. 4Surrounding the throne were twenty-four other thrones, and seated on them were twenty-four elders. They were dressed in white and had crowns of gold on their heads. 5From the throne came flashes of lightning, rumblings and peals of thunder. Before the throne, seven lamps were blazing. These are the seven spirits[a] of God. 6Also before the throne there was what looked like a sea of glass, clear as crystal.

In the center, around the throne, were four living creatures, and they were covered with eyes, in front and in back. 7The first living creature was like a lion, the second was like an ox, the third had a face like a man, the fourth was like a flying eagle. 8Each of the four living creatures had six wings and was covered with eyes all around, even under his wings. Day and night they never stop saying:

"Holy, holy, holy
is the Lord God Almighty,
who was, and is, and is to come."

9Whenever the living creatures give glory, honor and thanks to him who sits on the throne and who lives for ever and ever, 10the twenty-four elders fall down before him who sits on the throne, and worship him who lives for ever and ever. They lay their crowns before the throne and say:

11"You are worthy, our Lord and God,

to receive glory and honor and
power,
for you created all things,
and by your will they were created
and have their being."

The Scroll and the Lamb

5 Then I saw in the right hand of him who sat on the throne a scroll with writing on both sides and sealed with seven seals. 2And I saw a mighty angel proclaiming in a loud voice, "Who is worthy to break the seals and open the scroll?" 3But no one in heaven or on earth or under the earth could open the scroll or even look inside it. 4I wept and wept because no one was found who was worthy to open the scroll or look inside. 5Then one of the elders said to me, "Do not weep! See, the Lion of the tribe of Judah, the Root of David, has triumphed. He is able to open the scroll and its seven seals."

6Then I saw a Lamb, looking as if it had been slain, standing in the center of the throne, encircled by the four living creatures and the elders. He had seven horns and seven eyes, which are the seven spirits[a] of God sent out into all the earth. 7He came and took the scroll from the right hand of him who sat on the throne. 8And when he had taken it, the four living creatures and the twenty-four elders fell down before the Lamb. Each one had a harp and they were holding golden bowls full of incense, which are the prayers of the saints. 9And they sang a new song:

"You are worthy to take the scroll
and to open its seals,
because you were slain,
and with your blood you purchased
men for God
from every tribe and language and
people and nation.
10You have made them to be a kingdom
and priests to serve our God,
and they will reign on the earth."

11Then I looked and heard the voice of many angels, numbering thousands upon thousands, and ten thousand times ten thousand. They encircled the throne and the living creatures and the elders. 12In a loud voice they sang:

"Worthy is the Lamb, who was slain,
to receive power and wealth and
wisdom and strength
and honor and glory and praise!"

a5,6 Or the sevenfold Spirit

¹³Then I heard every creature in heaven and on earth and under the earth and on the sea, and all that is in them, singing:

"To him who sits on the throne and to the Lamb
be praise and honor and glory and power,

for ever and ever!"

¹⁴The four living creatures said, "Amen," and the elders fell down and worshiped.

The Seals

6 I watched as the Lamb opened the first of the seven seals. Then I heard

---

THURSDAY

VERSE FOR THE DAY:	AUTHOR:	PASSAGE FOR THE DAY:
Revelation 3:20	Tim LaHaye	Revelation 3:14–22

Knock-Knock

A VERY emotionally burdened man came to Jesus Christ one night (John 3:1–13), inquiring how he might come into a personal relationship with God. Jesus said, "I tell you the truth, no one can see the kingdom of God unless he is born again." Obviously puzzled by Christ's explanation, Nicodemus asked, "How can a man be born when he is old? . . . Surely he cannot enter a second time into his mother's womb to be born!" Jesus answered, "I tell you the truth, no one can enter the kingdom of God unless he is born of water and the Spirit." The context of this passage clearly indicates that Nicodemus needed a personal spiritual experience. Just as he had been born physically to enter this world, he had to be born spiritually to fulfill his destiny and prepare for the next world. This spiritual birth of power, created by individually receiving Jesus Christ as Lord and Savior, gives a person the external power he needs to cope with his emotional problems. This is particularly true in the case of depression.

Contrary to public opinion, Jesus Christ is not automatically born within a person; otherwise he would not have need for this spiritual birth. Instead, Jesus Christ is external to man's spiritual nature, for man is born void of God. Through his Holy Spirit and the teaching of the Bible, Christ knocks at the door of man's spiritual consciousness, saying, "If anyone hears my voice and opens the door, I will come in and eat with him, and he with me" (Revelation 3:20). This promise of Christ testifies that any individual conscious of his God-void and rebellion against the will of God can invite him into his life. Christ never forces his way into an individual's life, but responds only when invited. At that moment, the individual is spiritually made alive. This gives him a consciousness for God and an increased capacity to cope with all the problems of life, including depression.

Additional Scripture Readings:
John 3:1–21; Romans 8:9–17

Go to page 1402 for your next devotional reading.

one of the four living creatures say in a voice like thunder, "Come!" [2]I looked, and there before me was a white horse! Its rider held a bow, and he was given a crown, and he rode out as a conqueror bent on conquest.

[3]When the Lamb opened the second seal, I heard the second living creature say, "Come!" [4]Then another horse came out, a fiery red one. Its rider was given power to take peace from the earth and to make men slay each other. To him was given a large sword.

[5]When the Lamb opened the third seal, I heard the third living creature say, "Come!" I looked, and there before me was a black horse! Its rider was holding a pair of scales in his hand. [6]Then I heard what sounded like a voice among the four living creatures, saying, "A quart[a] of wheat for a day's wages,[b] and three quarts of barley for a day's wages,[b] and do not damage the oil and the wine!"

[7]When the Lamb opened the fourth seal, I heard the voice of the fourth living creature say, "Come!" [8]I looked, and there before me was a pale horse! Its rider was named Death, and Hades was following close behind him. They were given power over a fourth of the earth to kill by sword, famine and plague, and by the wild beasts of the earth.

[9]When he opened the fifth seal, I saw under the altar the souls of those who had been slain because of the word of God and the testimony they had maintained. [10]They called out in a loud voice, "How long, Sovereign Lord, holy and true, until you judge the inhabitants of the earth and avenge our blood?" [11]Then each of them was given a white robe, and they were told to wait a little longer, until the number of their fellow servants and brothers who were to be killed as they had been was completed.

[12]I watched as he opened the sixth seal. There was a great earthquake. The sun turned black like sackcloth made of goat hair, the whole moon turned blood red, [13]and the stars in the sky fell to earth, as late figs drop from a fig tree when shaken by a strong wind. [14]The sky receded like a scroll, rolling up, and every mountain and island was removed from its place.

[15]Then the kings of the earth, the princes, the generals, the rich, the mighty, and every slave and every free man hid in caves and among the rocks of the moun-

tains. [16]They called to the mountains and the rocks, "Fall on us and hide us from the face of him who sits on the throne and from the wrath of the Lamb! [17]For the great day of their wrath has come, and who can stand?"

144,000 Sealed

7 After this I saw four angels standing at the four corners of the earth, holding back the four winds of the earth to prevent any wind from blowing on the land or on the sea or on any tree. [2]Then I saw another angel coming up from the east, having the seal of the living God. He called out in a loud voice to the four angels who had been given power to harm the land and the sea: [3]"Do not harm the land or the sea or the trees until we put a seal on the foreheads of the servants of our God." [4]Then I heard the number of those who were sealed: 144,000 from all the tribes of Israel.

[5]From the tribe of Judah 12,000 were sealed,
  from the tribe of Reuben 12,000,
  from the tribe of Gad 12,000,
[6]from the tribe of Asher 12,000,
  from the tribe of Naphtali 12,000,
  from the tribe of Manasseh 12,000,
[7]from the tribe of Simeon 12,000,
  from the tribe of Levi 12,000,
  from the tribe of Issachar 12,000,
[8]from the tribe of Zebulun 12,000,
  from the tribe of Joseph 12,000,
  from the tribe of Benjamin 12,000.

The Great Multitude in White Robes

[9]After this I looked and there before me was a great multitude that no one could count, from every nation, tribe, people and language, standing before the throne and in front of the Lamb. They were wearing white robes and were holding palm branches in their hands. [10]And they cried out in a loud voice:

"Salvation belongs to our God,
  who sits on the throne,
  and to the Lamb."

[11]All the angels were standing around the throne and around the elders and the four living creatures. They fell down on their faces before the throne and worshiped God, [12]saying:

"Amen!
Praise and glory

and wisdom and thanks and honor
and power and strength
be to our God for ever and ever.
Amen!"

¹³Then one of the elders asked me, "These in white robes — who are they, and where did they come from?"

¹⁴I answered, "Sir, you know."

And he said, "These are they who have come out of the great tribulation; they have washed their robes and made them white in the blood of the Lamb. ¹⁵Therefore,

"they are before the throne of God
and serve him day and night in his
temple;
and he who sits on the throne will
spread his tent over them.
¹⁶Never again will they hunger;
never again will they thirst.
The sun will not beat upon them,
nor any scorching heat.
¹⁷For the Lamb at the center of the
throne will be their shepherd;
he will lead them to springs of
living water.
And God will wipe away every tear
from their eyes."

The Seventh Seal and the Golden Censer

8 When he opened the seventh seal, there was silence in heaven for about half an hour.

²And I saw the seven angels who stand before God, and to them were given seven trumpets.

³Another angel, who had a golden censer, came and stood at the altar. He was given much incense to offer, with the prayers of all the saints, on the golden altar before the throne. ⁴The smoke of the incense, together with the prayers of the saints, went up before God from the angel's hand. ⁵Then the angel took the censer, filled it with fire from the altar, and hurled it on the earth; and there came peals of thunder, rumblings, flashes of lightning and an earthquake.

The Trumpets

⁶Then the seven angels who had the seven trumpets prepared to sound them.

⁷The first angel sounded his trumpet, and there came hail and fire mixed with blood, and it was hurled down upon the earth. A third of the earth was burned up,

a third of the trees were burned up, and all the green grass was burned up.

⁸The second angel sounded his trumpet, and something like a huge mountain, all ablaze, was thrown into the sea. A third of the sea turned into blood, ⁹a third of the living creatures in the sea died, and a third of the ships were destroyed.

¹⁰The third angel sounded his trumpet, and a great star, blazing like a torch, fell from the sky on a third of the rivers and on the springs of water — ¹¹the name of the star is Wormwood.*a* A third of the waters turned bitter, and many people died from the waters that had become bitter.

¹²The fourth angel sounded his trumpet, and a third of the sun was struck, a third of the moon, and a third of the stars, so that a third of them turned dark. A third of the day was without light, and also a third of the night.

¹³As I watched, I heard an eagle that was flying in midair call out in a loud voice: "Woe! Woe! Woe to the inhabitants of the earth, because of the trumpet blasts about to be sounded by the other three angels!"

9 The fifth angel sounded his trumpet, and I saw a star that had fallen from the sky to the earth. The star was given the key to the shaft of the Abyss. ²When he opened the Abyss, smoke rose from it like the smoke from a gigantic furnace. The sun and sky were darkened by the smoke from the Abyss. ³And out of the smoke locusts came down upon the earth and were given power like that of scorpions of the earth. ⁴They were told not to harm the grass of the earth or any plant or tree, but only those people who did not have the seal of God on their foreheads. ⁵They were not given power to kill them, but only to torture them for five months. And the agony they suffered was like that of the sting of a scorpion when it strikes a man. ⁶During those days men will seek death, but will not find it; they will long to die, but death will elude them.

⁷The locusts looked like horses prepared for battle. On their heads they wore something like crowns of gold, and their faces resembled human faces. ⁸Their hair was like women's hair, and their teeth were like lions' teeth. ⁹They had breastplates like breastplates of iron, and the sound of their wings was like the thundering of many horses and chariots rushing

a11 That is, Bitterness

into battle. ¹⁰They had tails and stings like scorpions, and in their tails they had power to torment people for five months. ¹¹They had as king over them the angel of the Abyss, whose name in Hebrew is Abaddon, and in Greek, Apollyon.*ᵃ*

¹²The first woe is past; two other woes are yet to come.

¹³The sixth angel sounded his trumpet, and I heard a voice coming from the horns*ᵇ* of the golden altar that is before God. ¹⁴It said to the sixth angel who had the trumpet, "Release the four angels who are bound at the great river Euphrates." ¹⁵And the four angels who had been kept ready for this very hour and day and month and year were released to kill a third of mankind. ¹⁶The number of the mounted troops was two hundred million. I heard their number.

¹⁷The horses and riders I saw in my vision looked like this: Their breastplates were fiery red, dark blue, and yellow as sulfur. The heads of the horses resembled the heads of lions, and out of their mouths came fire, smoke and sulfur. ¹⁸A third of mankind was killed by the three plagues of fire, smoke and sulfur that came out of their mouths. ¹⁹The power of the horses was in their mouths and in their tails; for their tails were like snakes, having heads with which they inflict injury.

²⁰The rest of mankind that were not killed by these plagues still did not repent of the work of their hands; they did not stop worshiping demons, and idols of gold, silver, bronze, stone and wood—idols that cannot see or hear or walk. ²¹Nor did they repent of their murders, their magic arts, their sexual immorality or their thefts.

The Angel and the Little Scroll

10 Then I saw another mighty angel coming down from heaven. He was robed in a cloud, with a rainbow above his head; his face was like the sun, and his legs were like fiery pillars. ²He was holding a little scroll, which lay open in his hand. He planted his right foot on the sea and his left foot on the land, ³and he gave a loud shout like the roar of a lion. When he shouted, the voices of the seven thunders spoke. ⁴And when the seven thunders spoke, I was about to write; but I heard a voice from heaven say, "Seal up what the seven thunders have said and do not write it down."

⁵Then the angel I had seen standing on the sea and on the land raised his right hand to heaven. ⁶And he swore by him who lives for ever and ever, who created the heavens and all that is in them, the earth and all that is in it, and the sea and all that is in it, and said, "There will be no more delay! ⁷But in the days when the seventh angel is about to sound his trumpet, the mystery of God will be accomplished, just as he announced to his servants the prophets."

⁸Then the voice that I had heard from heaven spoke to me once more: "Go, take the scroll that lies open in the hand of the angel who is standing on the sea and on the land."

⁹So I went to the angel and asked him to give me the little scroll. He said to me, "Take it and eat it. It will turn your stomach sour, but in your mouth it will be as sweet as honey." ¹⁰I took the little scroll from the angel's hand and ate it. It tasted as sweet as honey in my mouth, but when I had eaten it, my stomach turned sour. ¹¹Then I was told, "You must prophesy again about many peoples, nations, languages and kings."

The Two Witnesses

11 I was given a reed like a measuring rod and was told, "Go and measure the temple of God and the altar, and count the worshipers there. ²But exclude the outer court; do not measure it, because it has been given to the Gentiles. They will trample on the holy city for 42 months. ³And I will give power to my two witnesses, and they will prophesy for 1,260 days, clothed in sackcloth." ⁴These are the two olive trees and the two lampstands that stand before the Lord of the earth. ⁵If anyone tries to harm them, fire comes from their mouths and devours their enemies. This is how anyone who wants to harm them must die. ⁶These men have power to shut up the sky so that it will not rain during the time they are prophesying; and they have power to turn the waters into blood and to strike the earth with every kind of plague as often as they want.

⁷Now when they have finished their testimony, the beast that comes up from the Abyss will attack them, and overpower and kill them. ⁸Their bodies will lie in the street of the great city, which is figuratively called Sodom and Egypt, where also their Lord was crucified. ⁹For three and a

---

ᵃ11 Abaddon *and* Apollyon *mean* Destroyer.   *ᵇ13* That is, projections half days men from every people, tribe, language and nation will gaze on their bodies and refuse them burial. [10]The inhabitants of the earth will gloat over them and will celebrate by sending each other gifts, because these two prophets had tormented those who live on the earth.

[11]But after the three and a half days a breath of life from God entered them, and they stood on their feet, and terror struck those who saw them. [12]Then they heard a loud voice from heaven saying to them, "Come up here." And they went up to heaven in a cloud, while their enemies looked on.

[13]At that very hour there was a severe earthquake and a tenth of the city collapsed. Seven thousand people were killed in the earthquake, and the survivors were terrified and gave glory to the God of heaven.

[14]The second woe has passed; the third woe is coming soon.

The Seventh Trumpet

[15]The seventh angel sounded his trumpet, and there were loud voices in heaven, which said:

"The kingdom of the world has
    become the kingdom of our
    Lord and of his Christ,
and he will reign for ever and ever."

[16]And the twenty-four elders, who were seated on their thrones before God, fell on their faces and worshiped God, [17]saying:

"We give thanks to you, Lord God
    Almighty,
the One who is and who was,
because you have taken your great
    power
and have begun to reign.
[18]The nations were angry;
    and your wrath has come.
The time has come for judging the
    dead,
    and for rewarding your servants the
        prophets
and your saints and those who
    reverence your name,
    both small and great—
and for destroying those who destroy
    the earth."

[19]Then God's temple in heaven was opened, and within his temple was seen the ark of his covenant. And there came flashes of lightning, rumblings, peals of thunder, an earthquake and a great hailstorm.

The Woman and the Dragon

12 A great and wondrous sign appeared in heaven: a woman clothed with the sun, with the moon under her feet and a crown of twelve stars on her head. [2]She was pregnant and cried out in pain as she was about to give birth. [3]Then another sign appeared in heaven: an enormous red dragon with seven heads and ten horns and seven crowns on his heads. [4]His tail swept a third of the stars out of the sky and flung them to the earth. The dragon stood in front of the woman who was about to give birth, so that he might devour her child the moment it was born. [5]She gave birth to a son, a male child, who will rule all the nations with an iron scepter. And her child was snatched up to God and to his throne. [6]The woman fled into the desert to a place prepared for her by God, where she might be taken care of for 1,260 days.

[7]And there was war in heaven. Michael and his angels fought against the dragon, and the dragon and his angels fought back. [8]But he was not strong enough, and they lost their place in heaven. [9]The great dragon was hurled down—that ancient serpent called the devil, or Satan, who leads the whole world astray. He was hurled to the earth, and his angels with him.

[10]Then I heard a loud voice in heaven say:

"Now have come the salvation and the
    power and the kingdom of our
    God,
    and the authority of his Christ.
For the accuser of our brothers,
    who accuses them before our God
        day and night,
    has been hurled down.
[11]They overcame him
    by the blood of the Lamb
    and by the word of their testimony;
they did not love their lives so much
    as to shrink from death.
[12]Therefore rejoice, you heavens
    and you who dwell in them!
But woe to the earth and the sea,
    because the devil has gone down to
        you!
He is filled with fury,
    because he knows that his time is
        short."

[13]When the dragon saw that he had been hurled to the earth, he pursued the woman who had given birth to the male

child. ¹⁴The woman was given the two wings of a great eagle, so that she might fly to the place prepared for her in the desert, where she would be taken care of for a time, times and half a time, out of the serpent's reach. ¹⁵Then from his mouth the serpent spewed water like a river, to overtake the woman and sweep her away with the torrent. ¹⁶But the earth helped the woman by opening its mouth and swallowing the river that the dragon had spewed out of his mouth. ¹⁷Then the dragon was enraged at the woman and went off to make war against the rest of her offspring—those who obey God's commandments and hold to the testimony of Jesus.

13
¹And the dragon*ᵃ* stood on the shore of the sea.

The Beast out of the Sea

And I saw a beast coming out of the sea. He had ten horns and seven heads, with ten crowns on his horns, and on each head a blasphemous name. ²The beast I saw resembled a leopard, but had feet like those of a bear and a mouth like that of a lion. The dragon gave the beast his power and his throne and great authority. ³One of the heads of the beast seemed to have had a fatal wound, but the fatal wound had been healed. The whole world was astonished and followed the beast. ⁴Men worshiped the dragon because he had given authority to the beast, and they also worshiped the beast and asked, "Who is like the beast? Who can make war against him?"

⁵The beast was given a mouth to utter proud words and blasphemies and to exercise his authority for forty-two months. ⁶He opened his mouth to blaspheme God, and to slander his name and his dwelling place and those who live in heaven. ⁷He was given power to make war against the saints and to conquer them. And he was given authority over every tribe, people, language and nation. ⁸All inhabitants of the earth will worship the beast—all whose names have not been written in the book of life belonging to the Lamb that was slain from the creation of the world.*ᵇ*

⁹He who has an ear, let him hear.

¹⁰If anyone is to go into captivity,
   into captivity he will go.
If anyone is to be killed*ᶜ* with the
   sword,

with the sword he will be killed.

This calls for patient endurance and faithfulness on the part of the saints.

The Beast out of the Earth

¹¹Then I saw another beast, coming out of the earth. He had two horns like a lamb, but he spoke like a dragon. ¹²He exercised all the authority of the first beast on his behalf, and made the earth and its inhabitants worship the first beast, whose fatal wound had been healed. ¹³And he performed great and miraculous signs, even causing fire to come down from heaven to earth in full view of men. ¹⁴Because of the signs he was given power to do on behalf of the first beast, he deceived the inhabitants of the earth. He ordered them to set up an image in honor of the beast who was wounded by the sword and yet lived. ¹⁵He was given power to give breath to the image of the first beast, so that it could speak and cause all who refused to worship the image to be killed. ¹⁶He also forced everyone, small and great, rich and poor, free and slave, to receive a mark on his right hand or on his forehead, ¹⁷so that no one could buy or sell unless he had the mark, which is the name of the beast or the number of his name.

¹⁸This calls for wisdom. If anyone has insight, let him calculate the number of the beast, for it is man's number. His number is 666.

The Lamb and the 144,000

14
Then I looked, and there before me was the Lamb, standing on Mount Zion, and with him 144,000 who had his name and his Father's name written on their foreheads. ²And I heard a sound from heaven like the roar of rushing waters and like a loud peal of thunder. The sound I heard was like that of harpists playing their harps. ³And they sang a new song before the throne and before the four living creatures and the elders. No one could learn the song except the 144,000 who had been redeemed from the earth. ⁴These are those who did not defile themselves with women, for they kept themselves pure. They follow the Lamb wherever he goes. They were purchased from among men and offered as firstfruits to God and the Lamb. ⁵No lie was found in their mouths; they are blameless.

---

*ᵃ*1 Some late manuscripts *And I*   *ᵇ*8 Or *written from the creation of the world in the book of life belonging to the Lamb that was slain*   *ᶜ*10 Some manuscripts *anyone kills*

The Three Angels

[6]Then I saw another angel flying in midair, and he had the eternal gospel to proclaim to those who live on the earth — to every nation, tribe, language and people. [7]He said in a loud voice, "Fear God and give him glory, because the hour of his judgment has come. Worship him who made the heavens, the earth, the sea and the springs of water."

[8]A second angel followed and said, "Fallen! Fallen is Babylon the Great, which made all the nations drink the maddening wine of her adulteries."

[9]A third angel followed them and said in a loud voice: "If anyone worships the beast and his image and receives his mark on the forehead or on the hand, [10]he, too, will drink of the wine of God's fury, which has been poured full strength into the cup of his wrath. He will be tormented with burning sulfur in the presence of the holy angels and of the Lamb. [11]And the smoke of their torment rises for ever and ever. There is no rest day or night for those who worship the beast and his image, or for anyone who receives the mark of his name." [12]This calls for patient endurance on the part of the saints who obey God's commandments and remain faithful to Jesus.

[13]Then I heard a voice from heaven say, "Write: Blessed are the dead who die in the Lord from now on."

"Yes," says the Spirit, "they will rest from their labor, for their deeds will follow them."

The Harvest of the Earth

[14]I looked, and there before me was a white cloud, and seated on the cloud was one "like a son of man"[a] with a crown of gold on his head and a sharp sickle in his hand. [15]Then another angel came out of the temple and called in a loud voice to him who was sitting on the cloud, "Take your sickle and reap, because the time to reap has come, for the harvest of the earth is ripe." [16]So he who was seated on the cloud swung his sickle over the earth, and the earth was harvested.

[17]Another angel came out of the temple in heaven, and he too had a sharp sickle. [18]Still another angel, who had charge of the fire, came from the altar and called in a loud voice to him who had the sharp sickle, "Take your sharp sickle and gather the clusters of grapes from the earth's vine, because its grapes are ripe." [19]The angel swung his sickle on the earth, gathered its grapes and threw them into the great winepress of God's wrath. [20]They were trampled in the winepress outside the city, and blood flowed out of the press, rising as high as the horses' bridles for a distance of 1,600 stadia.[b]

Seven Angels With Seven Plagues

15 I saw in heaven another great and marvelous sign: seven angels with the seven last plagues — last, because with them God's wrath is completed. [2]And I saw what looked like a sea of glass mixed with fire and, standing beside the sea, those who had been victorious over the beast and his image and over the number of his name. They held harps given them by God [3]and sang the song of Moses the servant of God and the song of the Lamb:

"Great and marvelous are your deeds,
   Lord God Almighty.
Just and true are your ways,
   King of the ages.
[4]Who will not fear you, O Lord,
   and bring glory to your name?
For you alone are holy.
All nations will come
   and worship before you,
for your righteous acts have been
   revealed."

[5]After this I looked and in heaven the temple, that is, the tabernacle of the Testimony, was opened. [6]Out of the temple came the seven angels with the seven plagues. They were dressed in clean, shining linen and wore golden sashes around their chests. [7]Then one of the four living creatures gave to the seven angels seven golden bowls filled with the wrath of God, who lives for ever and ever. [8]And the temple was filled with smoke from the glory of God and from his power, and no one could enter the temple until the seven plagues of the seven angels were completed.

The Seven Bowls of God's Wrath

16 Then I heard a loud voice from the temple saying to the seven angels, "Go, pour out the seven bowls of God's wrath on the earth."

[2]The first angel went and poured out his bowl on the land, and ugly and painful sores broke out on the people who had the

---

[a]14 Daniel 7:13   [b]20 That is, about 180 miles (about 300 kilometers)

mark of the beast and worshiped his image.

³The second angel poured out his bowl on the sea, and it turned into blood like that of a dead man, and every living thing in the sea died.

⁴The third angel poured out his bowl on the rivers and springs of water, and they became blood. ⁵Then I heard the angel in charge of the waters say:

"You are just in these judgments,
    you who are and who were, the
        Holy One,
    because you have so judged;
⁶for they have shed the blood of your
        saints and prophets,
    and you have given them blood to
        drink as they deserve."

⁷And I heard the altar respond:

"Yes, Lord God Almighty,
    true and just are your judgments."

⁸The fourth angel poured out his bowl on the sun, and the sun was given power to scorch people with fire. ⁹They were seared by the intense heat and they cursed the name of God, who had control over these plagues, but they refused to repent and glorify him.

¹⁰The fifth angel poured out his bowl on the throne of the beast, and his kingdom was plunged into darkness. Men gnawed their tongues in agony ¹¹and cursed the God of heaven because of their pains and their sores, but they refused to repent of what they had done.

¹²The sixth angel poured out his bowl on the great river Euphrates, and its water was dried up to prepare the way for the kings from the East. ¹³Then I saw three evilᵃ spirits that looked like frogs; they came out of the mouth of the dragon, out of the mouth of the beast and out of the mouth of the false prophet. ¹⁴They are spirits of demons performing miraculous signs, and they go out to the kings of the whole world, to gather them for the battle on the great day of God Almighty.

¹⁵"Behold, I come like a thief! Blessed is he who stays awake and keeps his clothes with him, so that he may not go naked and be shamefully exposed."

¹⁶Then they gathered the kings together to the place that in Hebrew is called Armageddon.

¹⁷The seventh angel poured out his bowl into the air, and out of the temple came a loud voice from the throne, saying, "It is done!" ¹⁸Then there came flashes of lightning, rumblings, peals of thunder and a severe earthquake. No earthquake like it has ever occurred since man has been on earth, so tremendous was the quake. ¹⁹The great city split into three parts, and the cities of the nations collapsed. God remembered Babylon the Great and gave her the cup filled with the wine of the fury of his wrath. ²⁰Every island fled away and the mountains could not be found. ²¹From the sky huge hailstones of about a hundred pounds each fell upon men. And they cursed God on account of the plague of hail, because the plague was so terrible.

The Woman on the Beast

17 One of the seven angels who had the seven bowls came and said to me, "Come, I will show you the punishment of the great prostitute, who sits on many waters. ²With her the kings of the earth committed adultery and the inhabitants of the earth were intoxicated with the wine of her adulteries."

³Then the angel carried me away in the Spirit into a desert. There I saw a woman sitting on a scarlet beast that was covered with blasphemous names and had seven heads and ten horns. ⁴The woman was dressed in purple and scarlet, and was glittering with gold, precious stones and pearls. She held a golden cup in her hand, filled with abominable things and the filth of her adulteries. ⁵This title was written on her forehead:

MYSTERY
BABYLON THE GREAT
THE MOTHER OF PROSTITUTES
AND OF THE ABOMINATIONS OF THE EARTH.

⁶I saw that the woman was drunk with the blood of the saints, the blood of those who bore testimony to Jesus.

When I saw her, I was greatly astonished. ⁷Then the angel said to me: "Why are you astonished? I will explain to you the mystery of the woman and of the beast she rides, which has the seven heads and ten horns. ⁸The beast, which you saw, once was, now is not, and will come up out of the Abyss and go to his destruction. The inhabitants of the earth whose names have not been written in the book of life from the creation of the world will be astonished when they see the beast, because

---

ᵃ13 Greek *unclean*

he once was, now is not, and yet will come.

⁹"This calls for a mind with wisdom. The seven heads are seven hills on which the woman sits. ¹⁰They are also seven kings. Five have fallen, one is, the other has not yet come; but when he does come, he must remain for a little while. ¹¹The beast who once was, and now is not, is an eighth king. He belongs to the seven and is going to his destruction.

¹²"The ten horns you saw are ten kings who have not yet received a kingdom, but who for one hour will receive authority as kings along with the beast. ¹³They have one purpose and will give their power and authority to the beast. ¹⁴They will make war against the Lamb, but the Lamb will overcome them because he is Lord of lords and King of kings—and with him will be his called, chosen and faithful followers."

¹⁵Then the angel said to me, "The waters you saw, where the prostitute sits, are peoples, multitudes, nations and languages. ¹⁶The beast and the ten horns you saw will hate the prostitute. They will bring her to ruin and leave her naked; they will eat her flesh and burn her with fire. ¹⁷For God has put it into their hearts to accomplish his purpose by agreeing to give the beast their power to rule, until God's words are fulfilled. ¹⁸The woman you saw is the great city that rules over the kings of the earth."

The Fall of Babylon

18 After this I saw another angel coming down from heaven. He had great authority, and the earth was illuminated by his splendor. ²With a mighty voice he shouted:

"Fallen! Fallen is Babylon the Great!
　She has become a home for demons
and a haunt for every evil[a] spirit,
　a haunt for every unclean and
　　detestable bird.
³For all the nations have drunk
　the maddening wine of her
　　adulteries.
The kings of the earth committed
　　adultery with her,
　and the merchants of the earth grew
　　rich from her excessive
　　luxuries."

⁴Then I heard another voice from heaven say:

"Come out of her, my people,
　so that you will not share in her
　　sins,
　so that you will not receive any of
　　her plagues;
⁵for her sins are piled up to heaven,
　and God has remembered her
　　crimes.
⁶Give back to her as she has given;
　pay her back double for what she
　　has done.
　Mix her a double portion from her
　　own cup.
⁷Give her as much torture and grief
　as the glory and luxury she gave
　　herself.
In her heart she boasts,
　'I sit as queen; I am not a widow,
　and I will never mourn.'
⁸Therefore in one day her plagues will
　　overtake her:
　death, mourning and famine.
She will be consumed by fire,
　for mighty is the Lord God who
　　judges her.

⁹"When the kings of the earth who committed adultery with her and shared her luxury see the smoke of her burning, they will weep and mourn over her. ¹⁰Terrified at her torment, they will stand far off and cry:

" 'Woe! Woe, O great city,
　O Babylon, city of power!
In one hour your doom has come!'

¹¹"The merchants of the earth will weep and mourn over her because no one buys their cargoes any more— ¹²cargoes of gold, silver, precious stones and pearls; fine linen, purple, silk and scarlet cloth; every sort of citron wood, and articles of every kind made of ivory, costly wood, bronze, iron and marble; ¹³cargoes of cinnamon and spice, of incense, myrrh and frankincense, of wine and olive oil, of fine flour and wheat; cattle and sheep; horses and carriages; and bodies and souls of men.

¹⁴"They will say, 'The fruit you longed for is gone from you. All your riches and splendor have vanished, never to be recovered.' ¹⁵The merchants who sold these things and gained their wealth from her will stand far off, terrified at her torment. They will weep and mourn ¹⁶and cry out:

" 'Woe! Woe, O great city,

a2 Greek *unclean*

dressed in fine linen, purple and
  scarlet,
and glittering with gold, precious
  stones and pearls!
17In one hour such great wealth has
  been brought to ruin!'

"Every sea captain, and all who travel
by ship, the sailors, and all who earn their
living from the sea, will stand far off.
18When they see the smoke of her burning, they will exclaim, 'Was there ever a
city like this great city?' 19They will throw
dust on their heads, and with weeping and
mourning cry out:

" 'Woe! Woe, O great city,
  where all who had ships on the sea
  became rich through her wealth!
In one hour she has been brought to
  ruin!
20Rejoice over her, O heaven!
  Rejoice, saints and apostles and
    prophets!
God has judged her for the way she
  treated you.' "

21Then a mighty angel picked up a boul-
der the size of a large millstone and threw
it into the sea, and said:

"With such violence
  the great city of Babylon will be
    thrown down,
  never to be found again.
22The music of harpists and musicians,
  flute players and trumpeters,
will never be heard in you again.
No workman of any trade
  will ever be found in you again.
The sound of a millstone
  will never be heard in you again.
23The light of a lamp
  will never shine in you again.
The voice of bridegroom and bride
  will never be heard in you again.
Your merchants were the world's great
  men.
By your magic spell all the nations
  were led astray.
24In her was found the blood of
  prophets and of the saints,
and of all who have been killed on
  the earth."

Hallelujah!

19 After this I heard what sounded
like the roar of a great multitude in
heaven shouting:

"Hallelujah!

Salvation and glory and power belong
  to our God,
2 for true and just are his judgments.
He has condemned the great prostitute
  who corrupted the earth by her
    adulteries.
He has avenged on her the blood of
  his servants."

3And again they shouted:

"Hallelujah!
The smoke from her goes up for ever
  and ever."

4The twenty-four elders and the four
living creatures fell down and worshiped
God, who was seated on the throne. And
they cried:

"Amen, Hallelujah!"

5Then a voice came from the throne,
saying:

"Praise our God,
  all you his servants,
you who fear him,
  both small and great!"

6Then I heard what sounded like a great
multitude, like the roar of rushing waters
and like loud peals of thunder, shouting:

"Hallelujah!
For our Lord God Almighty reigns.
7Let us rejoice and be glad
  and give him glory!
For the wedding of the Lamb has
  come,
  and his bride has made herself
    ready.
8Fine linen, bright and clean,
  was given her to wear."
(Fine linen stands for the righteous acts of
the saints.)

9Then the angel said to me, "Write:
'Blessed are those who are invited to the
wedding supper of the Lamb!' " And he
added, "These are the true words of God."
10At this I fell at his feet to worship him.
But he said to me, "Do not do it! I am a
fellow servant with you and with your
brothers who hold to the testimony of
Jesus. Worship God! For the testimony of
Jesus is the spirit of prophecy."

The Rider on the White Horse

11I saw heaven standing open and there
before me was a white horse, whose rider
is called Faithful and True. With justice he
judges and makes war. 12His eyes are like
blazing fire, and on his head are many

crowns. He has a name written on him that no one knows but he himself. [13]He is dressed in a robe dipped in blood, and his name is the Word of God. [14]The armies of heaven were following him, riding on white horses and dressed in fine linen, white and clean. [15]Out of his mouth comes a sharp sword with which to strike down the nations. "He will rule them with an iron scepter."[a] He treads the winepress of the fury of the wrath of God Almighty. [16]On his robe and on his thigh he has this name written:

KING OF KINGS AND LORD OF LORDS.

[17]And I saw an angel standing in the sun, who cried in a loud voice to all the birds flying in midair, "Come, gather together for the great supper of God, [18]so that you may eat the flesh of kings, generals, and mighty men, of horses and their riders, and the flesh of all people, free and slave, small and great."

[19]Then I saw the beast and the kings of the earth and their armies gathered together to make war against the rider on the horse and his army. [20]But the beast was captured, and with him the false prophet who had performed the miraculous signs on his behalf. With these signs he had deluded those who had received the mark of the beast and worshiped his image. The two of them were thrown alive into the fiery lake of burning sulfur. [21]The rest of them were killed with the sword that came out of the mouth of the rider on the horse, and all the birds gorged themselves on their flesh.

The Thousand Years

20 And I saw an angel coming down out of heaven, having the key to the Abyss and holding in his hand a great chain. [2]He seized the dragon, that ancient serpent, who is the devil, or Satan, and bound him for a thousand years. [3]He threw him into the Abyss, and locked and sealed it over him, to keep him from deceiving the nations anymore until the thousand years were ended. After that, he must be set free for a short time.

[4]I saw thrones on which were seated those who had been given authority to judge. And I saw the souls of those who had been beheaded because of their testimony for Jesus and because of the word of God. They had not worshiped the beast or his image and had not received his

mark on their foreheads or their hands. They came to life and reigned with Christ a thousand years. [5](The rest of the dead did not come to life until the thousand years were ended.) This is the first resurrection. [6]Blessed and holy are those who have part in the first resurrection. The second death has no power over them, but they will be priests of God and of Christ and will reign with him for a thousand years.

Satan's Doom

[7]When the thousand years are over, Satan will be released from his prison [8]and will go out to deceive the nations in the four corners of the earth — Gog and Magog — to gather them for battle. In number they are like the sand on the seashore. [9]They marched across the breadth of the earth and surrounded the camp of God's people, the city he loves. But fire came down from heaven and devoured them. [10]And the devil, who deceived them, was thrown into the lake of burning sulfur, where the beast and the false prophet had been thrown. They will be tormented day and night for ever and ever.

The Dead Are Judged

[11]Then I saw a great white throne and him who was seated on it. Earth and sky fled from his presence, and there was no place for them. [12]And I saw the dead, great and small, standing before the throne, and books were opened. Another book was opened, which is the book of life. The dead were judged according to what they had done as recorded in the books. [13]The sea gave up the dead that were in it, and death and Hades gave up the dead that were in them, and each person was judged according to what he had done. [14]Then death and Hades were thrown into the lake of fire. The lake of fire is the second death. [15]If anyone's name was not found written in the book of life, he was thrown into the lake of fire.

The New Jerusalem

21 Then I saw a new heaven and a new earth, for the first heaven and the first earth had passed away, and there was no longer any sea. [2]I saw the Holy City, the new Jerusalem, coming down out of heaven from God, prepared as a bride beautifully dressed for her husband. [3]And I heard a loud voice from the throne

FRIDAY

VERSE FOR THE DAY:
Revelation 21:4

AUTHOR:
Gerald Oosterveen

PASSAGE FOR THE DAY:
Revelation 21:1–5

At Home with Jesus

GERALD Oosterveen reflects on the day his 9-year-old son Gerard was buried. Gerard had fought a courageous 39-month
battle with cancer.

Parents are not supposed to bury their children. The old are
not supposed to stand beside the graves of the young. It is unnatural. One is not prepared for it. The death of a child tears
apart a family like the uprooting of one plant out of a cluster
that have been allowed to grow together in one pot. It cannot
be done. All those roots become so intertwined over the years
that nothing short of violence can separate them. And it leaves
all the plants stunted . . .

In the end, God will always be victorious. Satan may ram-
page through the world and through the souls of people, with
God's inscrutable permission, and cause indescribable disaster
and anguish. When he is finished, however, and arrogantly
boasts to God, "Look what I've done," God will silence him
with his majestic, "And now look what I can do." Then Satan
will shamefacedly slink into the corners of his hell while God
goes about his work of redemption and restoration.

Oh, yes, we mourn . . . But we have hope—bright hope for
tomorrow, when all who trust in Jesus Christ as Savior will
move beyond pain and grief forever because we shall be forever with the Lord. And it is not just some pipe dream, some
opium to stupify and mislead hurting people. It is real, because
Christ is real, because in our past there is a blood-stained cross
on which the Prince of Glory died. Because of that bloody,
pain-filled past we have hope when all things are made new
and death shall be no more, nor grief, nor crying.

In a little cemetery in a small, out-of-the-way town there is a
tiny marker. It bears only three lines: 1961–1970 GERARD RI-
CHARD OOSTERVEEN "At Home With Jesus."

Of the three, the last line is the only one that really matters.
The last line sums up a glorious, endless future, an adventure
that for my son has only just begun. Even if he remembers his
life on earth, I am sure his joy has wiped away any recollection
of pain.

Additional Scripture Readings:
Isaiah 65:17–25;
1 Corinthians 15:12–28

*Go to page 1404 for your next
devotional reading.*

saying, "Now the dwelling of God is with men, and he will live with them. They will be his people, and God himself will be with them and be their God. [4]He will wipe every tear from their eyes. There will be no more death or mourning or crying or pain, for the old order of things has passed away."

[5]He who was seated on the throne said, "I am making everything new!" Then he said, "Write this down, for these words are trustworthy and true."

[6]He said to me: "It is done. I am the Alpha and the Omega, the Beginning and the End. To him who is thirsty I will give to drink without cost from the spring of the water of life. [7]He who overcomes will inherit all this, and I will be his God and he will be my son. [8]But the cowardly, the unbelieving, the vile, the murderers, the sexually immoral, those who practice magic arts, the idolaters and all liars — their place will be in the fiery lake of burning sulfur. This is the second death."

[9]One of the seven angels who had the seven bowls full of the seven last plagues came and said to me, "Come, I will show you the bride, the wife of the Lamb." [10]And he carried me away in the Spirit to a mountain great and high, and showed me the Holy City, Jerusalem, coming down out of heaven from God. [11]It shone with the glory of God, and its brilliance was like that of a very precious jewel, like a jasper, clear as crystal. [12]It had a great, high wall with twelve gates, and with twelve angels at the gates. On the gates were written the names of the twelve tribes of Israel. [13]There were three gates on the east, three on the north, three on the south and three on the west. [14]The wall of the city had twelve foundations, and on them were the names of the twelve apostles of the Lamb.

[15]The angel who talked with me had a measuring rod of gold to measure the city, its gates and its walls. [16]The city was laid out like a square, as long as it was wide. He measured the city with the rod and found it to be 12,000 stadia[a] in length, and as wide and high as it is long. [17]He measured its wall and it was 144 cubits[b] thick,[c] by man's measurement, which the angel was using. [18]The wall was made of jasper, and the city of pure gold, as pure as glass. [19]The foundations of the city walls were decorated with every kind of precious stone. The first foundation was jasper, the second sapphire, the third chalcedony, the fourth emerald, [20]the fifth sardonyx, the sixth carnelian, the seventh chrysolite, the eighth beryl, the ninth topaz, the tenth chrysoprase, the eleventh jacinth, and the twelfth amethyst.[d] [21]The twelve gates were twelve pearls, each gate made of a single pearl. The great street of the city was of pure gold, like transparent glass.

[22]I did not see a temple in the city, because the Lord God Almighty and the Lamb are its temple. [23]The city does not need the sun or the moon to shine on it, for the glory of God gives it light, and the Lamb is its lamp. [24]The nations will walk by its light, and the kings of the earth will bring their splendor into it. [25]On no day will its gates ever be shut, for there will be no night there. [26]The glory and honor of the nations will be brought into it. [27]Nothing impure will ever enter it, nor will anyone who does what is shameful or deceitful, but only those whose names are written in the Lamb's book of life.

The River of Life

22 Then the angel showed me the river of the water of life, as clear as crystal, flowing from the throne of God and of the Lamb [2]down the middle of the great street of the city. On each side of the river stood the tree of life, bearing twelve crops of fruit, yielding its fruit every month. And the leaves of the tree are for the healing of the nations. [3]No longer will there be any curse. The throne of God and of the Lamb will be in the city, and his servants will serve him. [4]They will see his face, and his name will be on their foreheads. [5]There will be no more night. They will not need the light of a lamp or the light of the sun, for the Lord God will give them light. And they will reign for ever and ever.

[6]The angel said to me, "These words are trustworthy and true. The Lord, the God of the spirits of the prophets, sent his angel to show his servants the things that must soon take place."

Jesus Is Coming

[7]"Behold, I am coming soon! Blessed is he who keeps the words of the prophecy in this book."

---

[a]16 That is, about 1,400 miles (about 2,200 kilometers)   [b]17 That is, about 200 feet (about 65 meters)
[c]17 Or high   [d]20 The precise identification of some of these precious stones is uncertain.

WEEKENDING

RESPOND

Father of glory, how I thank you for the
assurance of heaven! While I know I could
never deserve such an assurance, I'm so
grateful that you even give it to me as a right
because of my union with your Son, my Savior.

Thank you that while I live in the world I can
seek to serve you fruitfully, and to praise you
by the kind of life I live, as well as by my lips.

I long to give glory, honor and thanks to you
always. May your indwelling Spirit—the Spirit
of glory—ever keep before me the great
privilege of being an heir of your glory, and a
citizen of heaven. May my life in its praise and
worship of you now be the closest possible
approximation to the praise and worship of
heaven.

Father, I worship and adore you, through
Jesus Christ your Son. Amen.

– *Derek Prime*

REVIVE

Saturday: Isaiah 6:1–8
Sunday: Revelation 4:1–11

Go to page 3 for your next devotional reading.

8I, John, am the one who heard and saw these things. And when I had heard and seen them, I fell down to worship at the feet of the angel who had been showing them to me. **9**But he said to me, "Do not do it! I am a fellow servant with you and with your brothers the prophets and of all who keep the words of this book. Worship God!"

10Then he told me, "Do not seal up the words of the prophecy of this book, because the time is near. **11**Let him who does wrong continue to do wrong; let him who is vile continue to be vile; let him who does right continue to do right; and let him who is holy continue to be holy."

12"Behold, I am coming soon! My reward is with me, and I will give to everyone according to what he has done. **13**I am the Alpha and the Omega, the First and the Last, the Beginning and the End.

14"Blessed are those who wash their robes, that they may have the right to the tree of life and may go through the gates into the city. **15**Outside are the dogs, those who practice magic arts, the sexually immoral, the murderers, the idolaters and everyone who loves and practices falsehood.

16"I, Jesus, have sent my angel to give you*a* this testimony for the churches. I am the Root and the Offspring of David, and the bright Morning Star."

17The Spirit and the bride say, "Come!" And let him who hears say, "Come!" Whoever is thirsty, let him come; and whoever wishes, let him take the free gift of the water of life.

18I warn everyone who hears the words of the prophecy of this book: If anyone adds anything to them, God will add to him the plagues described in this book. **19**And if anyone takes words away from this book of prophecy, God will take away from him his share in the tree of life and in the holy city, which are described in this book.

20He who testifies to these things says, "Yes, I am coming soon."

Amen. Come, Lord Jesus.

21The grace of the Lord Jesus be with God's people. Amen.

a16 The Greek is plural.

WEIGHTS AND MEASURES

The figures of the table are calculated on the basis of a shekel equaling 11.5 grams, a cubit equaling 18 inches and an ephah equaling 22 liters. The quart referred to is either a dry quart (slightly larger than a liter) or a liquid quart (slightly smaller than a liter), whichever is applicable. The ton referred to in the footnotes is the American ton of 2,000 pounds.

This table is based upon the best available information, but it is not intended to be mathematically precise; like the measurement equivalents in the footnotes, it merely gives approximate amounts and distances. Weights and measures differed somewhat at various times and places in the ancient world. There is uncertainty particularly about the ephah and the bath; further discoveries may give more light on these units of capacity.

	BIBLICAL UNIT		APPROXIMATE AMERICAN EQUIVALENT	APPROXIMATE METRIC EQUIVALENT
WEIGHTS	talent	(60 minas)	75 pounds	34 kilograms
	mina	(50 shekels)	1 1/4 pounds	0.6 kilogram
	shekel	(2 bekas)	2/5 ounce	11.5 grams
	pim	(2/3 shekel)	1/3 ounce	7.6 grams
	beka	(10 gerahs)	1/5 ounce	5.5 grams
	gerah		1/50 ounce	0.6 gram
LENGTH	cubit		18 inches	0.5 meter
	span		9 inches	23 centimeters
	handbreadth		3 inches	8 centimeters
CAPACITY Dry Measure	cor [homer]	(10 ephahs)	6 bushels	220 liters
	lethek	(5 ephahs)	3 bushels	110 liters
	ephah	(10 omers)	3/5 bushel	22 liters
	seah	(1/3 ephah)	7 quarts	7.3 liters
	omer	(1/10 ephah)	2 quarts	2 liters
	cab	(1/18 ephah)	1 quart	1 liter
Liquid Measure	bath	(1 ephah)	6 gallons	22 liters
	hin	(1/6 bath)	4 quarts	4 liters
	log	(1/72 bath)	1/3 quart	0.3 liter

ACKNOWLEDGMENTS INDEX

Page 3: Taken from YOUR WORK MATTERS TO GOD by Doug Sherman and William Hendricks. Copyright © 1987 by Doug Sherman and William Hendricks. Used by permission of NavPress.

Page 5: Taken from MERE CHRISTIANITY by C.S. Lewis. Copyright © 1942, 1943, 1944 and 1952 by C.S. Lewis Pte. Ltd. Used by permission of Collins Fount, an imprint of HarperCollins Publishers Limited.

Page 8: Taken from THE PRACTICE OF GODLINESS by Jerry Bridges. Copyright © 1983 by Jerry Bridges. Used by permission of NavPress.

Page 18: Taken from THE APPLAUSE OF HEAVEN by Max Lucado. Copyright © 1990 by Max Lucado. Used by permission of Word, Inc., Dallas, Texas.

Page 21: Taken from DAILY THOUGHTS FOR DISCIPLES by Oswald Chambers. Copyright © 1990 by Oswald Chambers Publications Association 1976. Used by permission of Discovery House Publishers.

Page 28: Taken from WAITING by Ben Patterson. Copyright © 1989 by Ben Patterson. Used by permission of Inter-Varsity Press, P.O. Box 1400, Downers Grove, IL 60515.

Page 38: Taken from FATHERLOVE by D. Bruce Lockerbie. Copyright © 1981 by D. Bruce Lockerbie. Used by permission of Doubleday, a division of Bantam Doubleday Dell Publishing Group, Inc.

Page 42: Taken from DISAPPOINTMENT WITH GOD by Philip Yancey. Copyright © 1988 by Philip Yancey. Used by permission of Zondervan Publishing House.

Page 59: Taken from RENEWED DAY BY DAY by A.W. Tozer. Copyright © 1980 by Christian Publications, Inc. Used by permission.

Page 76: Taken from STRONG MEN, WEAK MEN by Leonard LeSourd. Copyright © 1990 by Leonard LeSourd. Published by Chosen Books. Used by permission of Baker Book House.

Page 89: Taken from ADRENALIN AND STRESS by Archibald Hart. Copyright © 1991 by Archibald Hart. Used by permission of Word, Inc., Dallas, Texas.

Page 91: Taken from THE KNOWLEDGE OF THE HOLY by A.W. Tozer. Copyright © 1961 by Aiden Wilson Tozer. Used by permission of HarperCollins Publishers.

Page 91: Taken from "SEE YOU AT THE HOUSE" by Bob Benson. Copyright © 1989 by Generoux Nelson, a division of Thomas Nelson Publishers. Used by permission.

Page 92: Taken from A SCRUFFY HUSBAND IS A HAPPY HUSBAND by Focus on the Family Publishing. Copyright © 1991, edited by Ron R. Lee. Used by permission.

Page 115: Taken from KNOWING THE FACE OF GOD by Tim Stafford. Copyright © 1986 by Tim Stafford. Used by permission of Zondervan Publishing House.

Page 119: Taken from THE GIFT OF HONOR by Gary Smalley and John Trent. Copyright © 1987 by Gary Smalley and John Trent. Used by permission of Thomas Nelson Publishers.

Page 136: Taken from WHEN YOU CAN'T COME BACK by Dave and Jan Dravecky with Ken Gire. Copyright © 1992 by Dave Dravecky. Used by permission of Zondervan Publishing House.

Page 146: Taken from INTERMISSION: BREAKING AWAY WITH GOD by James C. Schaap. Copyright © 1985 by CRC Publications, Grand Rapids, MI 49560. Used by permission.

Page 165: Taken from GOD OF WEAKNESS by John Timmer. Copyright © 1988 by John Timmer. Used by permission of Zondervan Publishing House.

Page 173: Taken from THINK BIG by Ben Carson, M.D. with Cecil Murphey. Copyright © 1992 by Benjamin Carson, M.D. Used by permission of Zondervan Publishing House.

Page 179: Taken from POINT MAN by Steve Farrar. Copyright © 1990 by Steve Farrar. Published by Multnomah Press. Used by permission of Questar Publishers.

Page 180: Taken from FATHERLOVE by D. Bruce Lockerbie. Copyright © 1981 by D. Bruce Lockerbie. Used by permission of Doubleday, a division of Bantam Doubleday Dell Publishing Group, Inc.

Page 183: Taken from THE PROBLEM OF PAIN by C.S. Lewis. Copyright © 1940 by C.S. Lewis Pte. Ltd. Used by permission of Collins Fount, an imprint of HarperCollins Publishers Limited.

Page 186: Taken from YOUR WORK MATTERS TO GOD by Doug Sherman and William Hendricks. Copyright © 1987 by Doug Sherman and William Hendricks. Used by permission of NavPress.

Page 189: Taken from LION AND LAMB by Brennan Manning. Copyright © 1986 by Brennan Manning. Published by Chosen Books. Used by permission of Baker Book House.

Page 191: Taken from DARE TO BE DIFFERENT by Charles Colson. Copyright © 1986 by SP Publications, Inc. Used by permission.

Page 198: Taken from SEX, STRENGTH AND THE SECRETS OF BECOMING A MAN by Donald M. Joy. Copyright © 1990 by Donald M. Joy. Used by permission of Regal Books, Ventura, CA 93003.

Page 212: Taken from DARE TO LIVE NOW by Bruce Larson. Copyright © 1965 by Zondervan Publishing House. Used by permission.

Page 234: Taken from GIVE IT TO ME STRAIGHT, DOCTOR by A. Dudley Dennison, M.D. Copyright © 1972 by The Zondervan Corporation. Used by permission.

Page 243: Taken from HONEST TO GOD? by Bill Hybels. Copyright © 1990 by Bill Hybels. Used by permission of Zondervan Publishing House.

Page 249: Taken from IN THE NAME OF JESUS: REFLECTIONS ON CHRISTIAN LEADERSHIP by Henri J.M. Nouwen. Copyright © 1989 by Henri J.M. Nouwen. Used by permission of The Crossroad Publishing Company.

Page 255: Taken from INTERMISSION: BREAKING AWAY WITH GOD by James C. Schaap. Copyright © 1985 by CRC Publications, Grand Rapids, MI 49560. Used by permission.

Page 264: Taken from THE WINGS OF REFUGE by David Atkinson. Copyright © 1983 by David Atkinson. Used by permission of InterVarsity Press, P.O. Box 1400, Downers Grove, IL 60515.

Page 270: Taken from LETTERS TO MY CHILDREN by Daniel Taylor. Copyright © 1989 by Daniel Taylor. Used by permission of InterVarsity Press, P.O. Box 1400, Downers Grove, IL 60515.

Page 286: Taken from MEN WITHOUT FRIENDS by David W. Smith. Copyright © 1990 by David W. Smith. Used by permission of Thomas Nelson Publishers.

Page 288: Taken from MEN WITHOUT FRIENDS by David W. Smith. Copyright © 1990 by David W. Smith. Used by permission of Thomas Nelson Publishers.

Page 305: Taken from TOM LANDRY: AN AUTOBIOGRAPHY by Tom Landry with Gregg Lewis. Copyright © 1990 by Tom Landry. Used by permission of Zondervan Publishing House.

Page 312: Taken from COMMON SENSE CHRISTIANITY by Gerald Mann. Copyright © 1989 by Gerald Mann Ministries. Used by permission.

Page 326: Taken from THE MISUNDERSTOOD MAN by Walter Trobisch. Copyright © 1983 by InterVarsity Christian Fellowship of the USA. Used by permission.

Page 342: Taken from DISAPPOINTMENT WITH GOD by Philip Yancey. Copyright © 1988 by Philip Yancey. Used by permission of Zondervan Publishing House.

Page 354: Taken from THINK BIG by Ben Carson, M.D. with Cecil Murphey. Copyright © 1992 by Benjamin Carson, M.D. Used by permission of Zondervan Publishing House.

Page 357: Taken from PREACHING THROUGH A STORM by H. Beecher Hicks, Jr. Copyright © 1987 by H. Beecher Hicks, Jr. Used by permission of Zondervan Publishing House.

Page 360: Taken from POINT MAN by Steve Farrar. Copyright © 1990 by Steve Farrar. Published by Multnomah Press. Used by permission of Questar Publishers.

Page 369: Taken from THINK BIG by Ben Carson, M.D. with Cecil Murphey. Copyright © 1992 by Benjamin Carson, M.D. Used by permission of Zondervan Publishing House.

Page 372: Taken from ANGELS by Billy Graham. Copyright © 1975, 1986 by Billy Graham. Used by permission of Word, Inc., Dallas, Texas.

Page 386: Taken from FATHERLOVE by D. Bruce Lockerbie. Copyright © 1981 by D. Bruce Lockerbie. Used by permission of Doubleday, a division of Bantam Doubleday Dell Publishing Group, Inc.

Page 416: Taken from COMEBACK by Dave Dravecky with Tim Stafford. Copyright © 1990 by Dave Dravecky. Used by permission of Zondervan Publishing House

Page 428: Taken from SINGLETARY ON SINGLETARY by Mike Singletary with Jerry B. Jenkins. Copyright © 1991 by Mike Singletary and Jerry B. Jenkins. Used by permission of Thomas Nelson Publishers.

Page 433: Taken from YOUR WORK MATTERS TO GOD by Doug Sherman and William Hendricks. Copyright © 1987 by Doug Sherman and William Hendricks. Used by permission of NavPress.

Page 437: Taken from DAILY THOUGHTS FOR DISCIPLES by Oswald Chambers. Copyright © 1990 by Oswald Chambers Publications Association 1976. Used by permission of Discovery House Publishers.

Page 460: Taken from LISTENING TO YOUR LIFE by Frederick Buechner. Copyright © 1992 by Frederick Buechner. Used by permission of HarperCollins Publishers.

Page 475: Taken from SINGLETARY ON SINGLETARY by Mike Singletary with Jerry Jenkins. Copyright © 1991 by Mike Singletary and Jerry B. Jenkins. Used by permission of Thomas Nelson Publishers.

Page 481: Taken from WHAT IT MEANS TO BE REAL by D. Stuart Briscoe. Copyright © 1988 by D. Stuart Briscoe. Published by Word, Inc. Used by permission.

Page 485: Taken from PREACHING THROUGH A STORM by H. Beecher Hicks, Jr. Copyright © 1987 by H. Beecher Hicks, Jr. Used by permission of Zondervan Publishing House.

Page 493: Taken from DARE TO LIVE NOW by Bruce Larson. Copyright © 1965 by Zondervan Publishing House. Used by permission.

Page 493: Taken from STRONG MEN, WEAK MEN by Leonard LeSourd. Copyright © 1990 by Leonard LeSourd. Published by Chosen Books. Used by permission of Baker Book House.

Page 500: Taken from the Bible study guide ESTHER: A WOMAN FOR SUCH A TIME AS THIS by Charles R. Swindoll. Copyright © 1990; pages 1,2, and 6. Published by Insight for Living, Anaheim, CA 92806. All rights reserved. Used by permission.

Page 508: Taken from ADRENALIN AND STRESS by Archibald Hart. Copyright © 1991 by Archibald Hart. Used by permission of Word, Inc., Dallas, Texas.

Page 510: Taken from MEN WITHOUT FRIENDS by David W. Smith. Copyright © 1990 by David W. Smith. Used by permission of Thomas Nelson Publishers.

Page 517: Taken from LOVING GOD by Charles Colson. Copyright © 1983, 1987 by Charles W. Colson. Used by permission of Zondervan Publishing House.

Page 524: Taken from FROM ASHES TO GLORY by Bill McCartney with Dave Diles. Copyright © 1990 by Bill McCartney. Used by permission of Thomas Nelson Publishers.

Page 527: Taken from "SEE YOU AT THE HOUSE" by Bob Benson. Copyright © 1989 by Generoux Nelson, a division of Thomas Nelson Publishers. Used by permission.

Page 531: Taken from POINT MAN by Steve Farrar. Copyright © 1990 by Steve Farrar. Published by Multnomah Press. Used by permission of Questar Publishers.

Page 539: Taken from TRUE BELIEVERS DON'T ASK WHY by John Fischer. Copyright © 1989 by John Fischer. Used by permission of Bethany House Publishers.

Page 548: Taken from DON'T LET THE GOATS EAT THE LOQUAT TREES by Thomas Hale. Copyright © 1986 by Thomas Hale, Jr. Used by permission of Zondervan Publishing House.

Page 556: Taken from A MUSICIAN LOOKS AT THE PSALMS by Don Wyrtzen. Copyright © 1988 by Donald J. Wyrtzen. Used by permission of Zondervan Publishing House.

Page 564: Taken from ANGER: YOURS AND MINE AND WHAT TO DO ABOUT IT by Richard P. Walters. Copyright © 1981 by The Zondervan Corporation. Used by permission.

Page 569: Taken from SINGLETARY ON SINGLETARY by Mike Singletary with Jerry Jenkins. Copyright © 1991 by Mike Singletary and Jerry B. Jenkins. Used by permission of Thomas Nelson Publishers.

Page 573: Taken from A MUSICIAN LOOKS AT THE PSALMS by Don Wyrtzen. Copyright © 1988 by Donald J. Wyrtzen. Used by permission of Zondervan Publishing House.

Page 576: Taken from MEN AND WOMEN by Lawrence J. Crabb, Jr. Copyright © 1991 by Dr. Lawrence J. Crabb, Jr. Used by permission of Zondervan Publishing House.

Page 578: Taken from MEN WITHOUT FRIENDS by David W. Smith. Copyright © 1990 by David W. Smith. Used by permission of Thomas Nelson Publishers.

Page 582: Taken from LECTURES TO MY STUDENTS by Charles Spurgeon. Used by permission of HarperCollins Publishers Limited.

Page 584: Taken from GOD IS MY DELIGHT by W. Phillip Keller. Copyright © 1991 by W. Phillip Keller and published by Kregel Publications, a division of Kregel, Inc., P.O. Box 2607, Grand Rapids, MI 49501. Used by permission.

Page 585: Taken from THE ANGRY MAN by Stephen Arterburn and David Stoop. Copyright © 1991 by Stephen Arterburn and David Stoop. Used by permission of Word, Inc., Dallas, Texas.

Page 587: Taken from JOE GIBBS: FOURTH AND ONE by Joe Gibbs with Jerry Jenkins. Copyright © 1991 by Joe J. Gibbs and Jerry B. Jenkins. Used by permission of Thomas Nelson Publishers.

Page 595: Taken from STRAIGHT TALK TO MEN AND THEIR WIVES by James C. Dobson. Copyright © 1980. Published by Word, Inc., Dallas Texas. Used by permission.

Page 600: Taken from A MUSICIAN LOOKS AT THE PSALMS by Don Wyrtzen. Copyright © 1988 by Donald J. Wyrtzen. Used by permission of Zondervan Publishing House.

Page 605: Taken from FOR THE WORKAHOLIC I LOVE by Ted W. Engstrom and David J. Juroe. Copyright © 1979 by Ted W. Engstrom and David J. Juroe. Published by Fleming H. Revell Company. Used by permission of Baker Book House.

Page 607: Taken from ANGELS by Billy Graham. Copyright © 1975, 1986 by Billy Graham. Used by permission of Word, Inc., Dallas, Texas.

Page 610: Taken from COLORING OUTSIDE THE LINES by John F. Westfall. Copyright © 1991 by John F. Westfall. Used by permission of HarperCollins Publishers.

Page 614: Taken from STRAIGHT TALK TO MEN AND THEIR WIVES by James C. Dobson. Copyright © 1980. Published by Word, Inc., Dallas Texas. Used by permission.

Page 621: Taken from A MUSICIAN LOOKS AT THE PSALMS by Don Wyrtzen. Copyright © 1988 by Donald J. Wyrtzen. Used by permission of Zondervan Publishing House.

Page 623: Taken from YOUR WORK MATTERS TO GOD by Doug Sherman and William Hendricks. Copyright © 1987 by Doug Sherman and William Hendricks. Used by permission of NavPress.

Page 626: Taken from DARE TO BE DIFFERENT by Charles Colson. Copyright © 1986 by SP Publications, Inc. Used by permission.

Page 629: Taken from TOM LANDRY: AN AUTOBIOGRAPHY by Tom Landry with Gregg Lewis. Copyright © 1990 by Tom Landry. Used by permission of Zondervan Publishing House.

Page 633: Taken from THE GIFT OF HONOR by Gary Smalley and John Trent. Copyright © 1987 by Gary Smalley and John Trent. Used by permission of Thomas Nelson Publishers.

Page 635: Taken from the Bible study guide YOU AND YOUR CHILD by Charles R. Swindoll. Copyright © 1973,1977,1979,1986; pages 1–3,15–16, and 67–68. Published by Insight for Living, Anaheim, CA 92806. All rights reserved. Used by permission.

Page 636: Taken from THE STRUGGLE OF PRAYER by Donald G. Bloesch. Copyright © 1980 by Donald G. Bloesch. Used by permission of HarperCollins Publishers.

Page 641: Taken from GOD IS MY DELIGHT by W. Phillip Keller. Copyright © 1991 by W. Phillip Keller and published by Kregel Publications, a division of Kregel, Inc., P.O. Box 2607, Grand Rapids, MI 49501. Used by permission.

Page 643: Taken from A MUSICIAN LOOKS AT THE PSALMS by Don Wyrtzen. Copyright © 1988 by Donald J. Wyrtzen. Used by permission of Zondervan Publishing House.

Page 648: Taken from FATHERLOVE by D. Bruce Lockerbie. Copyright © 1981 by D. Bruce Lockerbie. Used by permission of Doubleday, a division of Bantam Doubleday Dell Publishing Group, Inc.

Page 650: Taken from A TOUCH OF HIS WISDOM by Charles Stanley. Copyright © 1992 by Charles Stanley. Used by permission of Zondervan Publishing House.

Page 651: Taken from POINT MAN by Steve Farrar. Copyright © 1990 by Steve Farrar. Published by Multnomah Press. Used by permission of Questar Publishers.

Page 653: Taken from WHO YOU ARE WHEN NO ONE'S LOOKING by Bill Hybels. Copyright © 1987 by Bill Hybels. Used by permission of InterVarsity Press, P.O. Box 1400 Downers Grove, IL 60515.

Page 656: Taken from the Bible study guide YOU AND YOUR CHILD by Charles R. Swindoll. Copyright © 1973,1977,1979,1986; pages 1–3,15–16, and 67–68. Published by Insight for Living, Anaheim, CA 92806. All rights reserved. Used by permission.

Page 663: Taken from MASTER YOUR MONEY by Ron Blue. Copyright © 1986 by Ronald W. Blue. Used by permission of Thomas Nelson Publishers.

Page 666: Taken from REGGIE WHITE: MINISTER OF DEFENSE by Reggie White with Terry Hill. Copyright © 1991 by Reggie White with Terry Hill. Used by permission of Word, Inc., Dallas, Texas.

Page 669: Taken from THE MONDAY CONNECTION by William E. Diehl. Copyright © 1991 by William E. Diehl. Used by permission of HarperCollins Publishers.

Page 672: Taken from USING YOUR MONEY WISELY by Larry Burkett. Copyright © 1985 by Christian Financial Concepts. Used by permission.

Page 674: Taken from MASTER YOUR MONEY by Ron Blue. Copyright © 1986 by Ronald W. Blue. Used by permission of Thomas Nelson Publishers.

Page 676: Taken from the Bible study guide YOU AND YOUR CHILD by Charles R. Swindoll. Copyright © 1973,1977,1979,1986; pages 1–3,15–16, and 67–68. Published by Insight for Living, Anaheim, CA 92806. All rights reserved. Used by permission.

Page 679: Taken from THE GIFT OF HONOR by Gary Smalley and John Trent. Copyright © 1987 by Gary Smalley and John Trent. Used by permission of Thomas Nelson Publishers.

Page 686: Taken from JOE GIBBS: FOURTH AND ONE by Joe Gibbs with Jerry Jenkins. Copyright © 1991 by Joe J. Gibbs and Jerry B. Jenkins. Used by permission of Thomas Nelson Publishers.

Page 690: Taken from "SEE YOU AT THE HOUSE" by Bob Benson. Copyright © 1989 by Generoux Nelson, a division of Thomas Nelson Publishers. Used by permission.

Page 692: Taken from ADRENALIN AND STRESS by Archibald Hart. Copyright © 1991 by Archibald Hart. Used by permission of Word, Inc., Dallas, Texas.

Page 693: Taken from THE MAN IN THE MIRROR by Patrick Morley. Copyright © 1989 by Patrick Morley. Published by Wolgemuth and Hyatt, Publishers. Used by permission of Thomas Nelson Publishers.

Page 695: Taken from GOD IS MY DELIGHT by W. Phillip Keller. Copyright © 1991 by W. Phillip Keller and published by Kregel Publications, a division of Kregel, Inc., P.O. Box 2607, Grand Rapids, MI 49501. Used by permission.

Page 702: Taken from MONEY, SEX & POWER by Richard Foster. Copyright © 1985 by Richard J. Foster. Used by permission of HarperCollins Publishers.

Page 704: Taken from SEX FOR CHRISTIANS by Lewis B. Smedes. Copyright © 1976 by Wm. B. Eerdmans Publishing Co. Used by permission.

Page 706: Taken from MONEY, SEX & POWER by Richard Foster. Copyright © 1985 by Richard J. Foster. Used by permission of HarperCollins Publishers.

Page 707: Taken from A SCRUFFY HUSBAND IS A HAPPY HUSBAND by Focus on the Family Publishing. Copyright © 1991, edited by Ron R. Lee. Used by permission.

Page 710: Taken from CONFLICT AND UNDERSTANDING IN MARRIAGE by Paul Plattner. Copyright © 1970 by M. E. Bratcher. Used by permission of Westminster/John Knox Press.

Page 739: Taken from ADRENALIN AND STRESS by Archibald Hart. Copyright © 1991 by Archibald Hart. Used by permission of Word, Inc., Dallas, Texas.

Page 749: Taken from DAILY THOUGHTS FOR DISCIPLES by Oswald Chambers. Copyright © 1990 by Oswald Chambers Publications Association 1976. Used by permission of Discovery House Publishers.

Page 754: Taken from THE MAN IN THE MIRROR by Patrick Morley. Copyright © 1989 by Patrick Morley. Published by Wolgemuth and Hyatt, Publishers. Used by permission of Thomas Nelson Publishers.

Page 755: Taken from COLORING OUTSIDE THE LINES by John F. Westfall. Copyright © 1991 by John F. Westfall. Used by permission of HarperCollins Publishers.

Page 757: Taken from THE WOUNDED HEART by Dan Allender. Copyright © 1990 by Dan B. Allender. Used by permission of NavPress.

Page 760: Taken from THE MISUNDERSTOOD MAN by Walter Trobisch. Copyright © 1983 by InterVarsity Christian Fellowship of the USA. Used by permission.

Page 763: Taken from IMMANUEL: REFLECTIONS ON THE LIFE OF CHRIST by Michael Card. Copyright © 1990 by Michael Card. Used by permission of Thomas Nelson Publishers.

Page 766: Taken from THE WOUNDED HEART by Dan Allender. Copyright © 1990 by Dan B. Allender. Used by permission of NavPress.

Page 771: Taken from MASTER YOUR MONEY by Ron Blue. Copyright © 1986 by Ronald W. Blue. Used by permission of Thomas Nelson Publishers.

Page 773: Public domain

Page 776: Taken from BETWEEN TWO WORLDS by John B. Anderson. Copyright © 1970 by Zondervan Publishing House. Used by permission.

Page 781: Taken from ADRENALIN AND STRESS by Archibald Hart. Copyright © 1991 by Archibald Hart. Used by permission of Word, Inc., Dallas, Texas.

Page 786: Taken from HOW TO KEEP YOUR KIDS ON YOUR TEAM by Charles Stanley. Copyright © 1986 by Charles Stanley. Used by permission of Thomas Nelson Publishers.

Page 789: Taken from JEREMIAH: THE PROPHET WHO WOULDN'T QUIT by William J. Petersen. Copyright © 1984 by SP Publications, Inc. Used by permission.

Page 799: Taken from JOE GIBBS: FOURTH AND ONE by Joe Gibbs with Jerry Jenkins. Copyright © 1991 by Joe J. Gibbs and Jerry B. Jenkins. Used by permission of Thomas Nelson Publishers.

Page 805: Taken from HONEST TO GOD? by Bill Hybels. Copyright © 1990 by Bill Hybels. Used by permission of Zondervan Publishing House.

Page 820: Taken from RUN WITH THE HORSES by Eugene H. Peterson. Copyright © 1983 by InterVarsity Christian Fellowship of the USA. Used by permission of InterVarsity Press, P.O. Box 1400, Downers Grove, IL 60515.

Page 823: Taken from THINK BIG by Ben Carson, M.D. with Cecil Murphey. Copyright © 1992 by Benjamin Carson, M.D. Used by permission of Zondervan Publishing House.

Page 826: Taken from RUN WITH THE HORSES by Eugene H. Peterson. Copyright © 1983 by InterVarsity Christian Fellowship of the USA. Used by permission of InterVarsity Press, P.O. Box 1400, Downers Grove, IL 60515.

Page 846: Taken from TOM LANDRY: AN AUTOBIOGRAPHY by Tom Landry with Gregg Lewis. Copyright © 1990 by Tom Landry. Used by permission of Zondervan Publishing House.

Page 856: Taken from FORGIVENESS by Charles Stanley. Copyright © 1987 by Charles Stanley. Used by permission of Thomas Nelson Publishers.

Page 858: Taken from GRIEF by Haddon W. Robinson. Copyright © 1974 by The Christian Medical Society. Assigned to The Zondervan Corporation, 1976. Used by permission.

Page 860: Taken from THE MAN IN THE MIRROR by Patrick Morley. Copyright © 1989 by Patrick Morley. Published by Wolgemuth and Hyatt, Publishers. Used by permission of Thomas Nelson Publishers.

Page 871: Taken from KNOWING THE FACE OF GOD by Tim Stafford. Copyright © 1986 by Tim Stafford. Used by permission of Zondervan Publishing House.

Page 883: Taken from PERSPECTIVE by Richard C. Halverson. Copyright © 1957,1985 by Cowman Publishing Company. Used by permission of Zondervan Publishing House.

Page 919: Taken from THE STRUGGLE OF PRAYER by Donald G. Bloesch. Copyright © 1980 by Donald G. Bloesch. Used by permission of HarperCollins Publishers.

Page 923: Taken from A CRY FOR MERCY by Henri J.M. Nouwen. Copyright © 1981 by Henri J.M. Nouwen. Used by permission of Doubleday, a division of Bantam Doubleday Dell Publishing Group, Inc.

Page 926: Taken from A SEVERE MERCY by Sheldon Vanauken. Copyright © 1977 by Sheldon Vanauken. Used by permission of HarperCollins Publishers.

Page 931: Taken from MARRIAGE IS FOR LIVING compiled by Bruce Larson. Excerpt from "When the Wine Runs Out" by G.R. Slater. Copyright © 1968 by Zondervan Publishing House. Used by permission.

Page 933: Taken from GOD IN THE PITS by Mark A. Ritchie. Copyright © 1989,1990 by Mark A. Ritchie. Used by permission of Thomas Nelson Publishers.

Page 939: Taken from GOD IS MY DELIGHT by W. Phillip Keller. Copyright © 1991 by W. Phillip Keller and published by Kregel Publications, a division of Kregel, Inc., P.O. Box 2607, Grand Rapids, MI 49501. Used by permission.

Page 945: Taken from TOO EARLY FROST by Gerald Oosterveen. Copyright © 1988 by Gerald Oosterveen. Used by permission of Zondervan Publishing House.

Page 952: Taken from DARE TO BE DIFFERENT by Charles Colson. Copyright © 1986 by SP Publications, Inc. Used by permission.

Page 955: Taken from PSALMS OF MY LIFE by Joseph Bayly, available at your local Christian bookstore. Copyright © 1987 by the estate of Joseph Bayly. Used by permission of David C. Cook Publishing Co.

Page 958: Taken from THINK BIG by Ben Carson, M.D. with Cecil Murphey. Copyright © 1992 by Benjamin Carson, M.D. Used by permission of Zondervan Publishing House.

Page 962: Taken from DISAPPOINTMENT WITH GOD by Philip Yancey. Copyright © 1988 by Philip Yancey. Used by permission of Zondervan Publishing House.

Page 969: Taken from BETWEEN TWO WORLDS by John B. Anderson. Copyright © 1970 by Zondervan Publishing House. Used by permission.

Page 970: Taken from FORGIVENESS by Charles Stanley. Copyright © 1987 by Charles Stanley. Used by permission of Thomas Nelson Publishers.

Page 973: Taken from THE PROBLEM OF PAIN by C.S. Lewis. Copyright © 1940 by C.S. Lewis Pte. Ltd. Used by permission of Collins Fount, an imprint of HarperCollins Publishers Limited.

Page 975: Taken from THE MAGNIFICENT DEFEAT by Frederick Buechner. Copyright © 1966 by The Seabury Press, © 1985 by Harper & Row. Used by permission of HarperCollins Publishers.

Page 980: Taken from WITH OPEN HANDS by Henri J.M. Nouwen. Copyright © 1972 by Ave Maria Press. All rights reserved. Used by permission of the publisher.

Page 984: Taken from DISAPPOINTMENT WITH GOD by Philip Yancey. Copyright © 1988 by Philip Yancey. Used by permission of Zondervan Publishing House.

Page 988: Taken from MEN WITHOUT FRIENDS by David W. Smith. Copyright © 1990 by David W. Smith. Used by permission of Thomas Nelson Publishers.

Page 992: Taken from RENEWED DAY BY DAY by A.W. Tozer. Copyright © 1980 by Christian Publications, Inc. Used by permission.

Page 1001: Taken from LOVE FOR A LIFETIME by James C. Dobson. Copyright © 1987 by James C. Dobson. Published by Multnomah Press. Used by permission of Questar Publishers.

Page 1002: Taken from SOMETHING BEAUTIFUL FOR GOD by Malcolm Muggeridge. Copyright © 1971 by The Mother Teresa Committee. Used by permission of HarperCollins Publishers and HarperCollins Publishers Limited.

Page 1004: Taken from DISAPPOINTMENT WITH GOD by Philip Yancey. Copyright © 1988 by Philip Yancey. Used by permission of Zondervan Publishing House.

Page 1011: Taken from IMMANUEL: REFLECTIONS ON THE LIFE OF CHRIST by Michael Card. Copyright © 1990 by Michael Card. Used by permission of Thomas Nelson Publishers.

Page 1014: Taken from LIFE AND HOLINESS by Thomas Merton. Copyright © 1963 by the Abbey of Gethsemani, Inc. Used by permission.

Page 1016: Taken from LIGHT FROM LIGHT by Jack Perry. Copyright © 1987 by Jack Perry. Used by permission of Zondervan Publishing House.

Page 1018: Taken from TOM LANDRY: AN AUTOBIOGRAPHY by Tom Landry with Gregg Lewis. Copyright © 1990 by Tom Landry. Used by permission of Zondervan Publishing House.

Page 1020: Taken from THE APPLAUSE OF HEAVEN by Max Lucado. Copyright © 1990 by Max Lucado. Used by permission of Word, Inc., Dallas, Texas.

Page 1021: Taken from DARE TO BE DIFFERENT by Charles Colson. Copyright © 1986 by SP Publications, Inc. Used by permission.

Page 1025: Taken from THE COST OF DISCIPLESHIP by Dietrich Bonhoeffer. Copyright © 1959 by SCM Press, Ltd. Used by permission of Macmillan Publishing Company.

Page 1030: Taken from DON'T LET THE GOATS EAT THE LOQUAT TREES by Thomas Hale. Copyright © 1986 by Thomas Hale, Jr. Used by permission of Zondervan Publishing House.

Page 1034: Taken from WHEN A LOVED ONE DIES by Philip W. Williams. Copyright © 1976 by Augsburg Publishing House. Used by permission of Augsburg Fortress.

Page 1036: Taken from WHO YOU ARE WHEN NO ONE'S LOOKING by Bill Hybels. Copyright © 1987 by Bill Hybels. Used by permission of InterVarsity Press, P.O. Box 1400, Downers Grove, IL 60515.

Page 1153: Taken from THE MAN IN THE MIRROR by Patrick Morley. Copyright © 1989 by Patrick Morley. Published by Wolgemuth and Hyatt, Publishers. Used by permission of Thomas Nelson Publishers.

Page 1154: Taken from LET'S LISTEN TO JESUS by Reuben Welch. Revised editions Copyright © 1985, 1988 by The Zondervan Corporation. Used by permission.

Page 1156: Taken from FEARFULLY AND WONDERFULLY MADE by Dr. Paul Brand and Philip Yancey. Copyright © 1980 by Paul Brand and Philip Yancey. Used by permission of Zondervan Publishing House.

Page 1161: Taken from IMMANUEL: REFLECTIONS ON THE LIFE OF CHRIST by Michael Card. Copyright © 1990 by Michael Card. Used by permission of Thomas Nelson Publishers.

Page 1164: Taken from REGGIE WHITE: MINISTER OF DEFENSE by Reggie White with Terry Hill. Copyright © 1991 by Reggie White with Terry Hill. Used by permission of Word, Inc., Dallas, Texas.

Page 1169: Taken from PERSPECTIVE by Richard C. Halverson. Copyright © 1957, 1985 by Cowman Publishing Company. Used by permission of Zondervan Publishing House.

Page 1175: Taken from FROM ASHES TO GLORY by Bill McCartney with Dave Diles. Copyright © 1990 by Bill McCartney. Used by permission of Thomas Nelson Publishers.

Page 1177: Taken from THE SIGNATURE OF JESUS by Brennan Manning. Copyright © 1992 by Brennan Manning. Published by Multnomah Press. Used by permission of Questar Publishers.

Page 1179: Taken from FORGIVENESS by Charles Stanley. Copyright © 1987 by Charles Stanley. Used by permission of Thomas Nelson Publishers.

Page 1183: Taken from FROM ASHES TO GLORY by Bill McCartney with Dave Diles. Copyright © 1990 by Bill McCartney. Used by permission of Thomas Nelson Publishers.

Page 1188: Taken from TOM LANDRY: AN AUTOBIOGRAPHY by Tom Landry with Gregg Lewis. Copyright © 1990 by Tom Landry. Used by permission of Zondervan Publishing House.

Page 1192: Taken from THE MAN IN THE MIRROR by Patrick Morley. Copyright © 1989 by Patrick Morley. Published by Wolgemuth and Hyatt, Publishers. Used by permission of Thomas Nelson Publishers.

Page 1195: Taken from THE APPLAUSE OF HEAVEN by Max Lucado. Copyright © 1990 by Max Lucado. Used by permission of Word, Inc., Dallas, Texas.

Page 1200: Taken from JUST BETWEEN FATHER & SON by E. James Wilder. Copyright © 1990 by E. James Wilder. Used by permission of InterVarsity Press, P.O. Box 1400, Downers Grove, IL 60515.

Page 1205: Taken from TRUE BELIEVERS DON'T ASK WHY by John Fischer. Copyright © 1989 by John Fischer. Used by permission of Bethany House Publishers.

Page 1207: Taken from MEN AND WOMEN by Lawrence J. Crabb, Jr. Copyright © 1991 by Dr. Lawrence J. Crabb, Jr. Used by permission of Zondervan Publishing House.

Page 1209: Taken from MERE CHRISTIANITY by C.S. Lewis. Copyright © 1942, 1943, 1944 and 1952 by C.S. Lewis Pte. Ltd. Used by permission of Collins Fount, an imprint of HarperCollins Publishers Limited.

Page 1211: Taken from THE GIFT OF HONOR by Gary Smalley and John Trent. Copyright © 1987 by Gary Smalley and John Trent. Used by permission of Thomas Nelson Publishers.

Page 1213: Taken from THE PRACTICE OF GODLINESS by Jerry Bridges. Copyright © 1983 by Jerry Bridges. Used by permission of NavPress.

Page 1215: Taken from DANCING INTO ZION by Judson B. Edwards. Copyright © 1986 by Judson Edwards. Used by permission of Zondervan Publishing House.

Page 1216: Taken from IMMANUEL: REFLECTIONS ON THE LIFE OF CHRIST by Michael Card. Copyright © 1990 by Michael Card. Used by permission of Thomas Nelson Publishers.

Page 1218: Taken from CORRESPONDENCE WITH A CRIPPLE FROM TARSUS by H. Beecher Hicks, Jr. Copyright © 1990 by H. Beecher Hicks, Jr. Used by permission of Zondervan Publishing House.

Page 1222: Taken from WHEN A LOVED ONE DIES by Philip W. Williams. Copyright © 1976 by Augsburg Publishing House. Used by permission of Augsburg Fortress.

Page 1228: Taken from POINT MAN by Steve Farrar. Copyright © 1990 by Steve Farrar. Published by Multnomah Press. Used by permission of Questar Publishers.

Page 1230: Taken from LIFE AND HOLINESS by Thomas Merton. Copyright © 1963 by the Abbey of Gethsemani, Inc. Used by permission.

Page 1232: Taken from IMMANUEL: REFLECTIONS ON THE LIFE OF CHRIST by Michael Card. Copyright © 1990 by Michael Card. Used by permission of Thomas Nelson Publishers.

Page 1232: Taken from SEX, STRENGTH AND THE SECRETS OF BECOMING A MAN by Donald M. Joy. Copyright © 1990 by Donald M. Joy. Used by permission of Regal Books, Ventura, CA 93003.

Page 1233: Taken from STRONG MEN, WEAK MEN by Leonard LeSourd. Copyright © 1990 by Leonard LeSourd. Published by Chosen Books. Used by permission of Baker Book House.

Page 1237: Taken from CHERISHABLE: LOVE AND MARRIAGE by David Augsburger. Copyright © 1971 by Herald Press. Used by permission.

Page 1239: Taken from FEARFULLY AND WONDERFULLY MADE by Dr. Paul Brand and Philip Yancey. Copyright © 1980 by Paul Brand and Philip Yancey. Used by permission of Zondervan Publishing House.

Page 1240: Taken from MEN AND WOMEN by Lawrence J. Crabb, Jr. Copyright © 1991 by Dr. Lawrence J. Crabb, Jr. Used by permission of Zondervan Publishing House.

Page 1242: Taken from WHEN A LOVED ONE DIES by Philip W. Williams. Copyright © 1976 by Augsburg Publishing House. Used by permission of Augsburg Fortress.

Page 1244: Taken from EPISTLES/NOW by Leslie Brandt. Copyright © 1974, 1976 by Concordia Publishing House. Used by permission.

Page 1245: Taken from WHO YOU ARE WHEN NO ONE'S LOOKING by Bill Hybels. Copyright © 1987 by Bill Hybels. Used by permission of InterVarsity Press, P.O. Box 1400, Downers Grove, IL 60515.

Page 1248: Taken from THE PROBLEM OF PAIN by C.S. Lewis. Copyright © 1940 by C.S. Lewis Pte. Ltd. Used by permission of Collins Fount, an imprint of HarperCollins Publishers Limited.

Page 1252: Taken from FEARFULLY AND WONDERFULLY MADE by Dr. Paul Brand and Philip Yancey. Copyright © 1980 by Paul Brand and Philip Yancey. Used by permission of Zondervan Publishing House.

Page 1254: Taken from LETTERS TO MY CHILDREN by Daniel Taylor. Copyright © 1989 by Daniel Taylor. Used by permission of InterVarsity Press, P.O. Box 1400, Downers Grove, IL 60515.

Page 1256: Taken from STRONG MEN, WEAK MEN by Leonard LeSourd. Copyright © 1990 by Leonard LeSourd. Published by Chosen Books. Used by permission of Baker Book House.

Page 1258: Taken from TRAVELING LIGHT by Eugene H. Peterson. Copyright © 1988 by Eugene H. Peterson. Used by permission.

Page 1258: Taken from A PRETTY GOOD PERSON by Lewis B. Smedes. Copyright © 1990 by Lewis B. Smedes. Used by permission of HarperCollins Publishers.

Page 1259: Taken from FATHERLOVE by D. Bruce Lockerbie. Copyright © 1981 by D. Bruce Lockerbie. Used by permission of Doubleday, a division of Bantam Doubleday Dell Publishing Group, Inc.

Page 1262: Taken from GOD IS MY DELIGHT by W. Phillip Keller. Copyright © 1991 by W. Phillip Keller and published by Kregel Publications, a division of Kregel, Inc., P.O. Box 2607, Grand Rapids, MI 49501. Used by permission.

Page 1264: Taken from YOUR WORK MATTERS TO GOD by Doug Sherman and William Hendricks. Copyright © 1987 by Doug Sherman and William Hendricks. Used by permission of NavPress.

Page 1266: Taken from CHERISHABLE: LOVE AND MARRIAGE by David Augsburger. Copyright © 1971 by Herald Press. Used by permission.

Page 1271: Taken from GOD IN THE PITS by Mark A. Ritchie. Copyright © 1989,1990 by Mark A. Ritchie. Used by permission of Thomas Nelson Publishers.

Page 1273: Taken from GROWING STRONG IN THE SEASONS OF LIFE by Charles R. Swindoll. Copyright © 1983 by Charles R. Swindoll. Published by Multnomah Press. Used by permission of Questar Publishers.

Page 1274: Taken from FEARFULLY AND WONDERFULLY MADE by Dr. Paul Brand and Philip Yancey. Copyright © 1980 by Paul Brand and Philip Yancey. Used by permission of Zondervan Publishing House.

Page 1276: Taken from SINGLETARY ON SINGLETARY by Mike Singletary with Jerry Jenkins. Copyright © 1991 by Mike Singletary and Jerry B. Jenkins. Used by permission of Thomas Nelson Publishers.

Page 1277: Taken from THE ANGRY MAN by Stephen Arterburn and David Stoop. Copyright © 1991 by Stephen Arterburn and David Stoop. Used by permission of Word, Inc., Dallas, Texas.

Page 1280: Taken from LETTERS TO MY CHILDREN by Daniel Taylor. Copyright © 1989 by Daniel Taylor. Used by permission of InterVarsity Press, P.O. Box 1400, Downers Grove, IL 60515.

Page 1282: Taken from LOVE FOR A LIFETIME by James C. Dobson. Copyright © 1987 by James C. Dobson. Published by Multnomah Press. Used by permission of Questar Publishers.

Page 1283: Taken from THE POWER DELUSION by Tony Campolo. Copyright © 1983 by SP Publications, Inc. Used by permission.

Page 1284: Taken from WHEN A LOVED ONE DIES by Philip W. Williams. Copyright © 1976 by Augsburg Publishing House. Used by permission of Augsburg Fortress.

Page 1286: Taken from LISTENING TO YOUR LIFE by Frederick Buechner. Copyright © 1992 by Frederick Buechner. Used by permission of HarperCollins Publishers.

Page 1288: Taken from TRUE BELIEVERS DON'T ASK WHY by John Fischer. Copyright © 1989 by John Fischer. Used by permission of Bethany House Publishers.

Page 1290: Taken from COME BEFORE WINTER by Charles R. Swindoll. Copyright © 1985 by Charles R. Swindoll, Inc. Published by Multnomah Press. Used by permission of Questar Publishers.

Page 1291: Taken from MARRIAGE IS FOR LIVING compiled by Bruce Larson. Excerpt from "When the Wine Runs Out" by G.R. Slater. Copyright © 1968 by Zondervan Publishing House. Used by permission.

Page 1293: Taken from LAUGHTER, JOY, AND HEALING by Donald E. Demaray. Copyright © 1986 by Baker Book House Company. Used by permission.

Page 1294: Taken from REGGIE WHITE: MINISTER OF DEFENSE by Reggie White with Terry Hill. Copyright © 1991 by Reggie White with Terry Hill. Used by permission of Word, Inc., Dallas, Texas.

Page 1296: Taken from SINGLETARY ON SINGLETARY by Mike Singletary with Jerry Jenkins. Copyright © 1991 by Mike Singletary and Jerry B. Jenkins. Used by permission of Thomas Nelson Publishers.

Page 1298: Taken from LOVE FOR A LIFETIME by James C. Dobson. Copyright © 1987 by James C. Dobson. Published by Multnomah Press. Used by permission of Questar Publishers.

Page 1299: Taken from LETTERS TO MY CHILDREN by Daniel Taylor. Copyright © 1989 by Daniel Taylor. Used by permission of InterVarsity Press, P.O. Box 1400, Downers Grove, IL 60515.

Page 1302: Taken from LISTENING TO YOUR LIFE by Frederick Buechner. Copyright © 1992 by Frederick Buechner. Used by permission of HarperCollins Publishers.

Page 1303: Taken from LAMENT FOR A SON by Nicholas Wolterstorff. Copyright © 1987 by Wm. B. Eerdmans Publishing Co. Used by permission.

Page 1304: Taken from LIFE AND HOLINESS by Thomas Merton. Copyright © 1963 by the Abbey of Gethsemani, Inc. Used by permission.

Page 1307: Taken from FRIENDSHIP by Jim Conway. Copyright © 1989 by Jim Conway. Used by permission of Zondervan Publishing House.

Page 1309: Taken from GUIDING TEEN-AGERS TO MATURITY by J.H. Waterink. Copyright © 1969 by Zondervan Publishing House. Used by permission.

Page 1310: Taken from YOUR WORK MATTERS TO GOD by Doug Sherman and William Hendricks. Copyright © 1987 by Doug Sherman and William Hendricks. Used by permission of NavPress.

Page 1312: Taken from OUT OF THE BLUE by Orel Hershiser. Copyright © 1989 by Orel Leonard Hershiser IV. Published by Wolgemuth and Hyatt, Publishers. Used by permission of Leader Enterprises, Inc.

Page 1313: Taken from USING YOUR MONEY WISELY by Larry Burkett. Copyright © 1985 by Christian Financial Concepts. Used by permission.

Page 1315: Taken from OUT OF THE BLUE by Orel Hershiser. Copyright © 1989 by Orel Leonard Hershiser IV. Published by Wolgemuth and Hyatt, Publishers. Used by permission of Leader Enterprises, Inc.

Page 1316: Taken from OUT OF THE BLUE by Orel Hershiser. Copyright © 1989 by Orel Leonard Hershiser IV. Published by Wolgemuth and Hyatt, Publishers. Used by permission of Leader Enterprises, Inc.

Page 1318: Taken from THE COST OF DISCIPLESHIP by Dietrich Bonhoeffer. Copyright © 1959 by SCM Press, Ltd. Used by permission of Macmillan Publishing Company.

Page 1321: Taken from OUT OF THE BLUE by Orel Hershiser. Copyright © 1989 by Orel Leonard Hershiser IV. Published by Wolgemuth and Hyatt, Publishers. Used by permission of Leader Enterprises, Inc.

Page 1322: Taken from COMEBACK by Dave Dravecky with Tim Stafford. Copyright © 1990 by Dave Dravecky. Used by permission of Zondervan Publishing House

Page 1325: Taken from PSALMS OF MY LIFE by Joseph Bayly, available at your local Christian bookstore. Copyright © 1987 by the estate of Joseph Bayly. Used by permission of David C. Cook Publishing Co.

Page 1326: Taken from FORGIVENESS by Charles Stanley. Copyright © 1987 by Charles Stanley. Used by permission of Thomas Nelson Publishers.

Page 1329: Taken from FAITH FOR THE JOURNEY by Reuben R. Welch. Copyright © 1988 by Reuben R. Welch. Used by permission of Zondervan Publishing House.

Page 1331: Taken from FRIENDSHIP by Jim Conway. Copyright © 1989 by Jim Conway. Used by permission of Zondervan Publishing House.

Page 1333: Taken from REGGIE WHITE: MINISTER OF DEFENSE by Reggie White with Terry Hill. Copyright © 1991 by Reggie White with Terry Hill. Used by permission of Word, Inc., Dallas, Texas.

Page 1336: Taken from THE COST OF DISCIPLESHIP by Dietrich Bonhoeffer. Copyright © 1959 by SCM Press, Ltd. Used by permission of Macmillan Publishing Company.

Page 1338: Taken from COLORING OUTSIDE THE LINES by John F. Westfall. Copyright © 1991 by John F. Westfall. Used by permission of HarperCollins Publishers.

Page 1338: Taken from PRAY TO WIN by Pat Boone. Copyright © 1980 by Pat Boone. Used by permission.

Page 1340: Taken from REGGIE WHITE: MINISTER OF DEFENSE by Reggie White with Terry Hill. Copyright © 1991 by Reggie White with Terry Hill. Used by permission of Word, Inc., Dallas, Texas.

Page 1342: Taken from THE PRACTICE OF GODLINESS by Jerry Bridges. Copyright © 1983 by Jerry Bridges. Used by permission of NavPress.

Page 1343: Taken from COMEBACK by Dave Dravecky with Tim Stafford. Copyright © 1990 by Dave Dravecky. Used by permission of Zondervan Publishing House

Page 1346: Taken from THE GIFT OF HONOR by Gary Smalley and John Trent. Copyright © 1987 by Gary Smalley and John Trent. Used by permission of Thomas Nelson Publishers.

Page 1347: Taken from BEING THE REAL FATHER NOW THAT YOUR TEENAGER WILL NEED by John Crawford. Copyright © 1968 by Fortress Press. Used by permission of Augsburg Fortress.

Page 1348: Taken from JUST BETWEEN FATHER & SON by E. James Wilder. Copyright © 1990 by E. James Wilder. Used by permission of InterVarsity Press, P.O. Box 1400, Downers Grove, IL 60515.

Page 1350: Taken from FEARFULLY AND WONDERFULLY MADE by Dr. Paul Brand and Philip Yancey. Copyright © 1980 by Paul Brand and Philip Yancey. Used by permission of Zondervan Publishing House.

Page 1351: Taken from MEN AND WOMEN by Lawrence J. Crabb, Jr. Copyright © 1991 by Dr. Lawrence J. Crabb, Jr. Used by permission of Zondervan Publishing House.

Page 1352: Taken from THE ANGRY MAN by Stephen Arterburn and David Stoop. Copyright © 1991 by Stephen Arterburn and David Stoop. Used by permission of Word, Inc., Dallas, Texas.

Page 1355: Taken from LIFE AND HOLINESS by Thomas Merton. Copyright © 1963 by the Abbey of Gethsemani, Inc. Used by permission.

Page 1357: Taken from GOD IN THE PITS by Mark A. Ritchie. Copyright © 1989,1990 by Mark A. Ritchie. Used by permission of Thomas Nelson Publishers.

Page 1358: Taken from DANCING ON THE STRAIT AND NARROW by Stan Mooneyham. Copyright © 1989 by W. Stanley Mooneyham. Used by permission.

Page 1359: Taken from WHAT IT MEANS TO BE REAL by D. Stuart Briscoe. Copyright © 1988 by D. Stuart Briscoe. Published by Word, Inc. Used by permission.

Page 1361: Taken from POINT MAN by Steve Farrar. Copyright © 1990 by Steve Farrar. Published by Multnomah Press. Used by permission of Questar Publishers.

Page 1364: Taken from DON'T LET THE GOATS EAT THE LOQUAT TREES by Thomas Hale. Copyright © 1986 by Thomas Hale, Jr. Used by permission of Zondervan Publishing House.

Page 1365: Taken from LISTENING TO YOUR LIFE by Frederick Buechner. Copyright © 1992 by Frederick Buechner. Used by permission of HarperCollins Publishers.

Page 1367: Taken from LIFE AND HOLINESS by Thomas Merton. Copyright © 1963 by the Abbey of Gethsemani, Inc. Used by permission.

Page 1369: Taken from THE GIFT OF TIME by William McConnell. Copyright © 1983 by InterVarsity Christian Fellowship of the USA. Used by permission.

Page 1371: Taken from THE APPLAUSE OF HEAVEN by Max Lucado. Copyright © 1990 by Max Lucado. Used by permission of Word, Inc., Dallas, Texas.

Page 1374: Taken from LETTERS TO MY CHILDREN by Daniel Taylor. Copyright © 1989 by Daniel Taylor. Used by permission of InterVarsity Press, P.O. Box 1400, Downers Grove, IL 60515.

Page 1375: Taken from THE PRACTICE OF GODLINESS by Jerry Bridges. Copyright © 1983 by Jerry Bridges. Used by permission of NavPress.

Page 1378: Taken from DEVOTIONAL TALKS FOR PEOPLE WHO DO GOD'S BUSINESS by David W. Wiersbe and Warren W. Wiersbe. Copyright © 1986 by Baker Book House Company. Used by permission.

Page 1380: Taken from WHAT IT MEANS TO BE REAL by D. Stuart Briscoe. Copyright © 1988 by D. Stuart Briscoe. Published by Word, Inc. Used by permission.

Page 1381: Taken from LIFE IN THE SLOW LANE by S.D. Gaede. Copyright © 1991 by S.D. Gaede. Used by permission of Zondervan Publishing House.

Page 1383: Taken from RENEWED DAY BY DAY by A.W. Tozer. Copyright © 1980 by Christian Publications, Inc. Used by permission.

Page 1387: Taken from COMEBACK by Dave Dravecky with Tim Stafford. Copyright © 1990 by Dave Dravecky. Used by permission of Zondervan Publishing House

Page 1389: Taken from THE COST OF DISCIPLESHIP by Dietrich Bonhoeffer. Copyright © 1959 by SCM Press, Ltd. Used by permission of Macmillan Publishing Company.

Page 1391: Taken from HOW TO WIN OVER DEPRESSION by Tim LaHaye. Copyright © 1974 by The Zondervan Corporation. Used by permission.

Page 1402: Taken from TOO EARLY FROST by Gerald Oosterveen. Copyright © 1988 by Gerald Oosterveen. Used by permission of Zondervan Publishing House.

Page 1404: Taken from CREATED TO PRAISE by Derek Prime. Copyright © 1981 by Derek Prime. Used by permission.

Every effort has been made to give proper credit for each devotion used. If any error or inaccuracy is noted, please inform the publishers.

READING PLAN

This reading plan gives you a structured pattern for reading through the entire Bible in one year.

DATE	PASSAGE
January 1	Genesis 1–4
January 2	Genesis 5–8
January 3	Genesis 9–12
January 4	Genesis 13–17
January 5	Genesis 18–20
January 6	Genesis 21–23
January 7	Genesis 24–25
January 8	Genesis 26–28
January 9	Genesis 29–31
January 10	Genesis 32–35
January 11	Genesis 36–38
January 12	Genesis 39–41
January 13	Genesis 42–43
January 14	Genesis 44–46
January 15	Genesis 47–50
January 16	Exodus 1–4
January 17	Exodus 5–7
January 18	Exodus 8–10
January 19	Exodus 11–13
January 20	Exodus 14–16
January 21	Exodus 17–20
January 22	Exodus 21–23
January 23	Exodus 24–27
January 24	Exodus 28–30
January 25	Exodus 31–34
January 26	Exodus 35–37
January 27	Exodus 38–40
January 28	Leviticus 1–4
January 29	Leviticus 5–7
January 30	Leviticus 8–10
January 31	Leviticus 11–13
February 1	Leviticus 14–15
February 2	Leviticus 16–18
February 3	Leviticus 19–21
February 4	Leviticus 22–23
February 5	Leviticus 24–25
February 6	Leviticus 26–27
February 7	Numbers 1–2
February 8	Numbers 3–4
February 9	Numbers 5–6
February 10	Numbers 7
February 11	Numbers 8–10
February 12	Numbers 11–13
February 13	Numbers 14–15
February 14	Numbers 16–18
February 15	Numbers 19–21
February 16	Numbers 22–24
February 17	Numbers 25–26
February 18	Numbers 27–29
February 19	Numbers 30–32
February 20	Numbers 33–36
February 21	Deuteronomy 1–2
February 22	Deuteronomy 3–4
February 23	Deuteronomy 5–8

DATE	PASSAGE
February 24	Deuteronomy 9–11
February 25	Deuteronomy 12–15
February 26	Deuteronomy 16–19
February 27	Deuteronomy 20–23
February 28	Deuteronomy 24–27
March 1	Deuteronomy 28–29
March 2	Deuteronomy 30–32
March 3	Deuteronomy 33–34
March 4	Joshua 1–4
March 5	Joshua 5–7
March 6	Joshua 8–10
March 7	Joshua 11–13
March 8	Joshua 14–17
March 9	Joshua 18–20
March 10	Joshua 21–22
March 11	Joshua 23–24
March 12	Judges 1–3
March 13	Judges 4–5
March 14	Judges 6–8
March 15	Judges 9–10
March 16	Judges 11–13
March 17	Judges 14–16
March 18	Judges 17–19
March 19	Judges 20–21
March 20	Ruth 1–4
March 21	1 Samuel 1–3
March 22	1 Samuel 4–7
March 23	1 Samuel 8–12
March 24	1 Samuel 13–14
March 25	1 Samuel 15–16
March 26	1 Samuel 17–18
March 27	1 Samuel 19–21
March 28	1 Samuel 22–24
March 29	1 Samuel 25–27
March 30	1 Samuel 28–31
March 31	2 Samuel 1–3
April 1	2 Samuel 4–7
April 2	2 Samuel 8–11
April 3	2 Samuel 12–13
April 4	2 Samuel 14–16
April 5	2 Samuel 17–19
April 6	2 Samuel 20–22
April 7	2 Samuel 23–24
April 8	1 Kings 1–2
April 9	1 Kings 3–5
April 10	1 Kings 6–7
April 11	1 Kings 8–9
April 12	1 Kings 10–12
April 13	1 Kings 13–15
April 14	1 Kings 16–18
April 15	1 Kings 19–20
April 16	1 Kings 21–22
April 17	2 Kings 1–3

DATE	PASSAGE	DATE	PASSAGE
April 18.	2 Kings 4–5	June 23.	Psalms 95–103
April 19.	2 Kings 6–8	June 24.	Psalms 104–106
April 20.	2 Kings 9–10	June 25.	Psalms 107–111
April 21.	2 Kings 11–13	June 26.	Psalms 112–118
April 22.	2 Kings 14–16	June 27.	Psalm 119
April 23.	2 Kings 17–18	June 28.	Psalms 120–133
April 24.	2 Kings 19–21	June 29.	Psalms 134–140
April 25.	2 Kings 22–23	June 30.	Psalms 141–150
April 26.	2 Kings 24–25	July 1.	Proverbs 1–3
April 27.	1 Chronicles 1–2	July 2.	Proverbs 4–7
April 28.	1 Chronicles 3–4	July 3.	Proverbs 8–11
April 29.	1 Chronicles 5–6	July 4.	Proverbs 12–14
April 30.	1 Chronicles 7–9	July 5.	Proverbs 15–17
May 1.	1 Chronicles 10–12	July 6.	Proverbs 18–20
May 2.	1 Chronicles 13–16	July 7.	Proverbs 21–23
May 3.	1 Chronicles 17–19	July 8.	Proverbs 24–26
May 4.	1 Chronicles 20–23	July 9.	Proverbs 27–29
May 5.	1 Chronicles 24–26	July 10.	Proverbs 30–31
May 6.	1 Chronicles 27–29	July 11.	Ecclesiastes 1–4
May 7.	2 Chronicles 1–4	July 12.	Ecclesiastes 5–8
May 8.	2 Chronicles 5–7	July 13.	Ecclesiastes 9–12
May 9.	2 Chronicles 8–11	July 14.	Song of Songs 1–4
May 10.	2 Chronicles 12–16	July 15.	Song of Songs 5–8
May 11.	2 Chronicles 17–20	July 16.	Isaiah 1–3
May 12.	2 Chronicles 21–24	July 17.	Isaiah 4–8
May 13.	2 Chronicles 25–28	July 18.	Isaiah 9–11
May 14.	2 Chronicles 29–31	July 19.	Isaiah 12–14
May 15.	2 Chronicles 32–34	July 20.	Isaiah 15–19
May 16.	2 Chronicles 35–36	July 21.	Isaiah 20–24
May 17.	Ezra 1–4	July 22.	Isaiah 25–28
May 18.	Ezra 5–7	July 23.	Isaiah 29–31
May 19.	Ezra 8–10	July 24.	Isaiah 32–34
May 20.	Nehemiah 1–3	July 25.	Isaiah 35–37
May 21.	Nehemiah 4–7	July 26.	Isaiah 38–40
May 22.	Nehemiah 8–9	July 27.	Isaiah 41–43
May 23.	Nehemiah 10–11	July 28.	Isaiah 44–46
May 24.	Nehemiah 12–13	July 29.	Isaiah 47–49
May 25.	Esther 1–3	July 30.	Isaiah 50–52
May 26.	Esther 4–7	July 31.	Isaiah 53–56
May 27.	Esther 8–10	August 1.	Isaiah 57–59
May 28.	Job 1–4	August 2.	Isaiah 60–63
May 29.	Job 5–8	August 3.	Isaiah 64–66
May 30.	Job 9–12	August 4.	Jeremiah 1–3
May 31.	Job 13–16	August 5.	Jeremiah 4–5
June 1.	Job 17–20	August 6.	Jeremiah 6–8
June 2.	Job 21–24	August 7.	Jeremiah 9–11
June 3.	Job 25–30	August 8.	Jeremiah 12–14
June 4.	Job 31–34	August 9.	Jeremiah 15–17
June 5.	Job 35–38	August 10.	Jeremiah 18–21
June 6.	Job 39–42	August 11.	Jeremiah 22–24
June 7.	Psalms 1–8	August 12.	Jeremiah 25–27
June 8.	Psalms 9–17	August 13.	Jeremiah 28–30
June 9.	Psalms 18–21	August 14.	Jeremiah 31–32
June 10.	Psalms 22–27	August 15.	Jeremiah 33–36
June 11.	Psalms 28–33	August 16.	Jeremiah 37–39
June 12.	Psalms 34–37	August 17.	Jeremiah 40–43
June 13.	Psalms 38–42	August 18.	Jeremiah 44–46
June 14.	Psalms 43–49	August 19.	Jeremiah 47–48
June 15.	Psalms 50–55	August 20.	Jeremiah 49
June 16.	Psalms 56–61	August 21.	Jeremiah 50
June 17.	Psalms 62–68	August 22.	Jeremiah 51–52
June 18.	Psalms 69–72	August 23.	Lamentations 1–2
June 19.	Psalms 73–77	August 24.	Lamentations 3–5
June 20.	Psalms 78–80	August 25.	Ezekiel 1–4
June 21.	Psalms 81–88		
June 22.	Psalms 89–94		

DATE	PASSAGE	DATE	PASSAGE
August 26	Ezekiel 5–8	October 31	Luke 23–24
August 27	Ezekiel 9–12	November 1	John 1–2
August 28	Ezekiel 13–15	November 2	John 3–4
August 29	Ezekiel 16–17	November 3	John 5–6
August 30	Ezekiel 18–20	November 4	John 7–8
August 31	Ezekiel 21–22	November 5	John 9–10
September 1	Ezekiel 23–24	November 6	John 11–12
September 2	Ezekiel 25–27	November 7	John 13–15
September 3	Ezekiel 28–30	November 8	John 16–17
September 4	Ezekiel 31–32	November 9	John 18–19
September 5	Ezekiel 33–35	November 10	John 20–21
September 6	Ezekiel 36–38	November 11	Acts 1–3
September 7	Ezekiel 39–40	November 12	Acts 4–5
September 8	Ezekiel 41–43	November 13	Acts 6–7
September 9	Ezekiel 44–46	November 14	Acts 8–9
September 10	Ezekiel 47–48	November 15	Acts 10–11
September 11	Daniel 1–3	November 16	Acts 12–13
September 12	Daniel 4–5	November 17	Acts 14–15
September 13	Daniel 6–8	November 18	Acts 16–17
September 14	Daniel 9–12	November 19	Acts 18–19
September 15	Hosea 1–4	November 20	Acts 20–21
September 16	Hosea 5–9	November 21	Acts 22–23
September 17	Hosea 10–14	November 22	Acts 24–26
September 18	Joel 1–3	November 23	Acts 27–28
September 19	Amos 1–4	November 24	Romans 1–3
September 20	Amos 5–9	November 25	Romans 4–7
September 21	Obadiah and Jonah	November 26	Romans 8–10
September 22	Micah 1–4	November 27	Romans 11–14
September 23	Micah 5–7	November 28	Romans 15–16
September 24	Nahum 1–3	November 29	1 Corinthians 1–4
September 25	Habakkuk 1–3	November 30	1 Corinthians 5–9
September 26	Zephaniah 1–3	December 1	1 Corinthians 10–13
September 27	Haggai	December 2	1 Corinthians 14–16
September 28	Zechariah 1–5	December 3	2 Corinthians 1–4
September 29	Zechariah 6–10	December 4	2 Corinthians 5–9
September 30	Zechariah 11–14	December 5	2 Corinthians 10–13
October 1	Malachi 1–4	December 6	Galatians 1–3
October 2	Matthew 1–4	December 7	Galatians 4–6
October 3	Matthew 5–6	December 8	Ephesians 1–6
October 4	Matthew 7–9	December 9	Philippians 1–4
October 5	Matthew 10–11	December 10	Colossians 1–4
October 6	Matthew 12–13	December 11	1 Thessalonians 1–5
October 7	Matthew 14–17	December 12	2 Thessalonians 1–3
October 8	Matthew 18–20	December 13	1 Timothy 1–6
October 9	Matthew 21–22	December 14	2 Timothy 1–4
October 10	Matthew 23–24	December 15	Titus and Philemon
October 11	Matthew 25–26	December 16	Hebrews 1–4
October 12	Matthew 27–28	December 17	Hebrews 5–8
October 13	Mark 1–3	December 18	Hebrews 9–10
October 14	Mark 4–5	December 19	Hebrews 11–13
October 15	Mark 6–7	December 20	James 1–5
October 16	Mark 8–9	December 21	1 Peter 1–5
October 17	Mark 10–11	December 22	2 Peter 1–3
October 18	Mark 12–13	December 23	1 John 1–5
October 19	Mark 14	December 24	2, 3 John, Jude
October 20	Mark 15–16	December 25	Revelation 1–3
October 21	Luke 1–2	December 26	Revelation 4–7
October 22	Luke 3–4	December 27	Revelation 8–11
October 23	Luke 5–6	December 28	Revelation 12–14
October 24	Luke 7–8	December 29	Revelation 15–17
October 25	Luke 9–10	December 30	Revelation 18–19
October 26	Luke 11–12	December 31	Revelation 20–22
October 27	Luke 13–15		
October 28	Luke 16–18		
October 29	Luke 19–20		
October 30	Luke 21–22		

AUTHOR BIOGRAPHIES

This index gives you information about each contributor and tells you where his devotions can be found.

Dan B. Allender teaches in the Biblical Counseling department at Colorado Christian University, conducts seminars and teaches counselor training courses. He is the author of *The Wounded Heart* and *Bold Love*, as well as co-author, with Larry Crabb, of *Encouragement: The Key to Caring*. *Devotions are found on pages 757, 766.*

John B. Anderson served 10 terms in Congress as a Representative from Illinois (1961–1980) before launching an unsuccessful bid to become President of the United States in 1980. Since that time he has been visiting professor at a number of universities throughout the U.S. He is the author of *Between Two Worlds*. *Devotions are found on pages 776, 969.*

Stephen Arterburn is founder and chairman of New Life Treatment Centers, Inc. He is the author of *Growing Up Addicted* and *Addicted to "Love."* Among his other books are *The Angry Man*, written with David Stoop. *Devotions are found on pages 585, 1057, 1128, 1277, 1352.*

David Atkinson is Fellow and Chaplain of Corpus Christi College, Oxford, England, and a pastoral counselor. He is the author of numerous books, including *The Message of Job* and *The Wings of Refuge*. *A devotion is found on page 264.*

David Augsburger holds a Ph.D. degree in pastoral psychotherapy and family therapy from the School of Theology at Claremont, California. He has written many books, including *Caring Enough to Confront* and *When Enough Is Enough*. *Devotions are found on pages 1237, 1266.*

Joseph Bayly was the first director of InterVarsity Press and later filled several key positions at David C. Cook Publishing Company, including service as president. The author of several books, including *A View from the Hearse* and *Psalms of My Life*, he died in 1986, joining three sons who preceded him in death. *Devotions are found on pages 955, 1325.*

Bob Benson, the son of a religious music publisher, was one of the Christian world's leading publishing executives, serving for almost 20 years at The John T. Benson Publishing Company in Nashville, Tennessee, before pursuing speaking and writing on a full-time basis. The author of six books, he succumbed to cancer in March, 1986. *Devotions are found on pages 91, 527, 690, 1064.*

Donald Bloesch, a widely respected scholar and a prolific author, is a professor of theology at the University of Dubuque Theological Seminary in Dubuque, Iowa. Among his many books are *The Christian Life and Salvation* and *The Essentials of Evangelical Theology*. *Devotions are found on pages 636, 919.*

Ron Blue, a Certified Public Accountant, is a managing partner of Christian Financial Management, an Atlanta-based firm. He has more than twenty years' experience in helping people plan for their financial future. He has written *Master Your Money* and *Managing Your Money*. *Devotions are found on pages 663, 674, 771, 1070, 1105.*

Dietrich Bonhoeffer was a German Lutheran pastor and theologian who was arrested in 1943 for his involvement in the Confessing Church and in anti-Nazi activities in wartime Germany. On April 9, 1945, he was hanged in a concentration camp. His books include *The Cost of Discipleship* and *Life Together*. *Devotions are found on pages 1025, 1055, 1318, 1336, 1389.*

Pat Boone is a recording artist, author and speaker who has achieved long-lasting success in the entertainment world. Boone, who lives with his wife Shirley in Beverly Hills, is the father of four daughters. He has written a number of books, including *A New Song* and *Pray to Win*. *A devotion is found on page 1338.*

Paul Brand, now retired, served as Chief of the Rehabilitative branch of the U.S. Public Health Service Hospital in Carville, Louisiana. He is known for his brilliant work as a hand surgeon. With Philip Yancey he has written *Fearfully and Wonderfully Made* and *In His Image*. *Devotions are found on pages 1156, 1239, 1252, 1274, 1350.*

Leslie Brandt has had a powerful ministry through his work as an evangelist, retreat leader and author. He is the author of numerous books, including *Psalms/Now*, *Jesus/Now* and *God Is Here—Let's Celebrate*. *A devotion is found on page 1244.*

Jerry Bridges is Vice President of Corporate Affairs of The Navigators, a parachurch organization. He has served on its staff in some capacity since 1955. Among the books he has written are *Transforming Grace*, *The Pursuit of Holiness*, and *The Practice of Godliness*. *Devotions are found on pages 8, 1213, 1342, 1375.*

D. Stuart Briscoe is the author of more than a dozen books and the senior pastor of Elmbrook Church in Waukesha, Wisconsin. Born in England, he was with The Torchbearers missionary fellowship before coming to the U.S. Among his books are *Getting into God* and *What It Means to Be Real*. Devotions are found on pages 481, 1095, 1132, 1359, 1380.

Frederick Buechner, called by USA Today "one of our most original storytellers," is a critically acclaimed author of more than 20 novels and nonfiction works, including *The Book of Bebb*, *Godric*, *Wishful Thinking*, and *The Alphabet of Grace*. A Presbyterian minister, he lives in Vermont. *Devotions are found on pages 460, 975, 1286, 1302, 1365.*

Larry Burkett is founder and president of Financial Concepts, Inc., a ministry dedicated to teaching and counseling on God's principles of finance. He is the author of a number of best-selling, award-winning books, including *The Coming Economic Earthquake*, *Investing for the Future*, and *Debt-Free Living*. *Devotions are found on pages 672, 1313.*

Tony Campolo is professor of sociology at Eastern College in St. Davids, Pennsylvania. A leader in evangelical social action, he has written several books, including *The Kingdom of God Is a Party* and *Wake Up America! A devotion is found on page 1283.*

Michael Card is a singer/songwriter whose song "El Shaddai" was rated the number one song of the decade by Christian radio broadcasters. He has a master's degree in Biblical Studies from Western Kentucky University. In addition to writing songs, Card studies and teaches the Bible. He is the author of *Immanuel* and *The Promise*. *Devotions are found on pages 763, 1011, 1134, 1161, 1216, 1232.*

Benjamin S. Carson gained worldwide recognition in 1987 for his part in the first successful separation of Siamese twins joined at the back of the head. He won a full scholarship to Yale and graduated from the University of Michigan Medical School. The director of pediatric neurosurgery at Johns Hopkins Hospital in Baltimore, Maryland, he has written *Gifted Hands* and *Think Big*. *Devotions are found on pages 173, 354, 369, 823, 958.*

Oswald Chambers was a Bible teacher, conference leader and YMCA chaplain. After his death his widow compiled his writings in *My Utmost for His Highest*, *Daily Thoughts for Disciples* and other popular devotional books. *Devotions are found on pages 21, 437, 749, 1150.*

Rodney Clapp is an editor with InterVarsity Press. A former News Editor with *Christianity Today*, he is the author of scores of magazine articles. He was a contributor to *A Scruffy Husband Is a Happy Husband*. *A devotion is found on page 707.*

Charles W. Colson served as Special Counsel to President Richard M. Nixon from 1969 to 1973. He is founder and chairman of the board of Prison Fellowship Ministries, an international prison outreach. His books include: *Born Again*, *Kingdoms in Conflict*, and *The Body*. *Devotions are found on pages 191, 517, 626, 952, 1021.*

Jim Conway is co-founder and president of Christian Living Resources/Mid-Life Dimensions, a non-profit organization. He is the author of a number of books, including *Men in Mid-Life Crisis* and *Friendship*. With his wife Sally he has written *Your Marriage Can Survive Mid-Life Crisis*. *Devotions are found on pages 1066, 1116, 1130, 1307, 1331.*

Larry Crabb is founder and director of the Institute of Biblical Counseling, a ministry committed to training Christians to resolve life's problems using Biblical principles. He is also professor of Biblical Counseling at Colorado Christian University, and the author of many books, including *Inside Out* and *Men and Women*. *Devotions are found on pages 576, 1122, 1207, 1240, 1351.*

John E. Crawford was a professor of psychology who in his varied career worked as a college director of guidance and a director of research, as well as a consulting psychologist for children. He developed the "Crawford Spatial Relations Test " and wrote ten books, including *Being the Real Father Now That Your Teenager Will Need*. Devotions are found on pages 1060, 1082, 1347.

Donald E. Demaray is professor of preaching at Asbury Theological Seminary. He has written, edited or compiled more than 20 books, including *A Guide to Happiness*, *Alive to God Through Praise*, and *Laughter, Joy and Healing*. *A devotion is found on page 1293.*

A. Dudley Dennison has had an illustrious career as a noted cardiologist, a sought-after speaker and a prolific author of scores of religious and medical articles and numerous books, including *Give It to Me Straight, Doctor* and *Prescription for Life*. *A devotion is found on page 234.*

William E. Diehl is the president of Riverbend Resource Center, Inc., a management consulting firm. He was manager of sales for Bethlehem Steel for 32 years. He is the author of *In Search of Faithfulness*, *Thank God It's Monday*, and *The Monday Connection*. *A devotion is found on page 669.*

James Dobson is founder and president of Focus on the Family, a non-profit organization that produces his nationally syndicated radio program. Among his books are *Hide or Seek*, *Straight Talk to Men and Their Wives*, *Dare to Discipline*, and *Love for a Lifetime*. *Devotions are found on pages 595, 614, 1001, 1282, 1298.*

Dave Dravecky is a former San Francisco Giants baseball pitcher who returned to the game after a cancerous tumor was removed from his pitching arm. He gained national recognition for his comeback and for the dramatic way his arm broke during his second game back. He is the author of *Comeback* and *When You Can't Come Back*, written with his wife Jan. *Devotions are on pages 136, 416, 1322, 1343, 1387.*

Judson Edwards is pastor of the Heritage Baptist Church in Webster, Texas. He is the author of several books, including *Dancing to Zion* and *Regaining Control of Your Life*. *A devotion is found on page 1215.*

Ted Engstrom is President Emeritus of World Vision, a Christian humanitarian organization. He previously served as president of Youth for Christ International and as general manager of Zondervan Publishing House. He is the author of 36 books, including *The Making of a Christian Leader* and *The Pursuit of Excellence*. *A devotion is found on page 605.*

Steve Farrar is president of Strategic Living, based in Dallas, Texas. He has earned a doctorate from Dallas Theological Seminary. He and his wife speak across the United States in the Family Life Marriage Conferences. He is the author of *Point Man*. *Devotions are found on pages 179, 360, 531, 651, 1228, 1361.*

John Fischer is a pioneer in contemporary Christian music. He has been a performing and recording artist for over twenty years. For several years his columns have appeared in the periodical *Contemporary Christian Music*. He is the author of three books, including *Real Christians Don't Dance* and *Making Real What I Already Believe*. *Devotions are found on pages 539, 1044, 1091, 1205, 1288.*

Richard Foster is the Distinguished Professor of Spiritual Formation at Azusa Pacific University and the founder of Renovaré, an infra-church movement committed to the renewal of the church. He is the author of such best-selling books as *Celebration of Discipline* and *The Freedom of Simplicity*. *Devotions are found on pages 702, 706.*

Francis of Assisi founded the Franciscan religious order of the Roman Catholic Church in 1209. He disavowed his stature as the son of a prosperous merchant and lived a life of poverty. His life inspired many and his poetry contributed to the development of Italian literature. *A devotion is found on page 773.*

Stan D. Gaede is Professor of Sociology at Gordon College in Wenham, Massachusetts. The father of three children, he has written several books, including *Belonging, Life in the Slow Lane*, and *Where Gods May Dwell*. *Devotions are found on pages 1140, 1381.*

Joe Gibbs has not only led his football team to the most victories in Washington Redskin history, his record as head coach is one of the most successful ever in the National Football League's history. His autobiography is entitled *Fourth and One*. *Devotions are found on pages 587, 686, 799.*

Ken Gire is a writer living in Fullerton, California, with his wife and four children. He is an award-winning author of such books as *Intimate Moments with the Savior, Incredible Moments with the Savior*, and *A Father's Gift*. *A devotion is found on page 1101.*

Billy Graham has quite possibly reached more people with the gospel than any other person on earth. In addition to being an international evangelist, he is an accomplished author, whose best-selling books include *Answers to Life's Questions, Peace with God*, and *The Secret of Happiness*. *Devotions are found on pages 372, 607.*

Thomas Hale, a surgeon, and his wife Cynthia, a pediatrician, are medical missionaries and have lived in Nepal since 1970. He is the author of two books on their adventures in Nepal: *Don't Let the Goats Eat the Loquat Trees* and *On The Far Side of Liglig Mountain*. *Devotions are found on pages 548, 1030, 1073, 1114, 1364.*

Richard Halverson is chaplain of the United States Senate and former pastor of Fourth Presbyterian Church in Washington, D.C. He has written several books, including *Man to Man* and *Manhood with Meaning*. *Devotions are found on pages 883, 1169.*

Archibald Hart is a clinical psychologist and dean of the Graduate School of Psychology at Fuller Theological Seminary in Pasadena, California. He is the author of several books, including *Unlocking the Mystery of Your Emotions* and *Adrenalin and Stress*. *Devotions are found on pages 89, 508, 692, 739, 781.*

William Hendricks is the president of a communications development group in Dallas, Texas, and the co-author of seven books, including *Living by the Book*, written with Howard Hendricks. He has written several books with Doug Sherman, including *Your Work Matters to God*. *Devotions are found on pages 3, 186, 433, 623, 1264, 1310.*

Orel Hershiser is a major league baseball pitcher for the Los Angeles Dodgers. In 1988 he won the National League Cy Young Award and was named Most Valuable Player in the World Series. At the same time he was named The Sporting News's Major League Player of the year and the Associated Press Professional Athlete of the Year. His autobiography is entitled *Out of the Blue*. Devotions are found on pages 1312, 1315, 1316, 1321.

H. Beecher Hicks, Jr., is Senior Minister of Metropolitan Baptist Church in Washington, D.C. A graduate of Colgate Rochester Divinity School, he is the author of several books, including *Preaching Through a Storm* and *Correspondence with a Cripple from Tarsus*. Devotions are found on pages 357, 485, 1218.

Bill Hybels is pastor of Willow Creek Community Church, which over the past ten years has grown from a fellowship of 125 people to one of over 9,000. He is the author of many books, including *Descending into Greatness* and *Honest to God?* With his wife Lynne he has written *Fit to Be Tied*. Devotions are found on pages 243, 653, 805, 1036, 1111, 1245.

Donald M. Joy is professor of Human Development and Christian Education at Asbury Theological Seminary. He is the author of more than ten books, including *Bonding: Relationships in the Image of God* and *Unfinished Business*. Devotions are found on pages 198, 1068, 1232.

David Juroe is a family counselor with the Yorba Park Medical Group in Orange, California. He has written *Successful Stepparenting* and, with Ted Engstrom, *For the Workaholic I Love*. A devotion is found on page 605.

W. Phillip Keller is a Canadian citizen and the son of missionaries to Kenya. He has lived in various places around the world and now makes his home in British Columbia. He is the author of over 35 books, the most popular of which is *A Shepherd Looks at Psalm 23*. Devotions are found on pages 584, 641, 695, 939, 1262.

Tim LaHaye is founder and president of Family Life Ministries in Washington D.C., and the author of numerous books, including *Spirit-controlled Temperament* and *How to Win Over Depression*. With his wife Beverly he has written *The Act of Marriage*. Devotions are found on pages 1093, 1144, 1391.

Tom Landry is the revolutionary former football coach of the Dallas Cowboys. A Texas native, he coached for the New York Giants football team until becoming the Cowboys' first and only coach until 1989. During his tenure, he led the team to an impressive 271–180–6 record. His autobiography is entitled *Tom Landry*. Devotions are found on pages 305, 629, 846, 1018, 1188.

Bruce Larson is co-pastor of the Crystal Cathedral in Garden Grove, California. Among the books he has written are: *Living Beyond Our Fears* and *The Presence*. With Paul Anderson and Doug Self he has written *Mastering Pastoral Care*. Devotions are found on pages 212, 493.

Leonard E. LeSourd is Chairman of the Board of Directors of Breakthrough, an intercessory prayer ministry. A writer and editor, he has edited hundreds of books and is the author of numerous others, including *Strong Men, Weak Men*. Devotions are found on pages 76, 493, 1233, 1256.

C.S. Lewis was a professor of Medieval and Renaissance Literature at Cambridge University, Cambridge, England. He is the author of numerous books, including *Mere Christianity*, *The Screwtape Letters*, *The Chronicles of Narnia*, and *The Problem of Pain*. Devotions are found on pages 5, 183, 973, 1209, 1248.

D. Bruce Lockerbie was affiliated with Wheaton College before joining the Stony Brook School, where he held the positions of chairman of the Fine Arts department and dean of the faculty, and, more recently, Scholar in Residence. He has written over 30 books, including *Fatherlove*. Devotions are found on pages 38, 180, 386, 648, 1259.

Max Lucado pastors the Oak Hills Church of Christ in San Antonio, Texas, and lectures at conferences. He is the author of numerous books, including: *No Wonder They Call Him the Savior*, *The Applause of Heaven*, and *In the Eye of the Storm*. Devotions are found on pages 18, 1020, 1086, 1138, 1195, 1371.

Gerald Mann is the senior minister of Riverbend Baptist Church in Austin, Texas. The author of *The Seven Deadly Virtues*, *Why Does Jesus Make Me Nervous?*, and *Common Sense Christianity*, he hosts a highly successful radio program. A devotion is found on page 312.

Brennan Manning, who lives with his wife Rosalyn in New Orleans, spends six months each year on the road directing spiritual retreats and proclaiming God's unconditional love. His books include *Lion and Lamb*, *The Ragamuffin Gospel*, and *The Signature of Jesus*. Devotions are found on pages 189, 1177.

Bill McCartney is head football coach at the University of Colorado. Following the 1989 season, he was named United Press International Coach of the Year. He is the founder of Promise Keepers, a national ministry geared to instructing men in their growth in Christlike masculinity. His autobiography is entitled, *From Ashes to Glory*. Devotions are found on pages 524, 1175, 1183.

William McConnell served as a staff worker for InterVarsity campus ministry before living in Brazil, South America, where he worked with the Bible University Alliance. He is now Assistant to the President of InterVarsity Christian Fellowship in Madison, Wisconsin, and is the author of *The Gift of Time*. *A devotion is found on page 1369.*

Thomas Merton was a poet, author and clergyman born in France. He taught at Columbia and St. Bonaventure Universities and worked at a Catholic settlement house in Harlem before joining the Trappist monastery in Gethsemane, Kentucky. Among his books are *Seeds of Contemplation*. *Devotions are found on pages 1014, 1230, 1304, 1355, 1367.*

Stan Mooneyham was the former president of World Vision, a Christian humanitarian organization. He had also served as special assistant to Billy Graham. He wrote several books, including *What Do You Say to a Hungry World?* and *Dancing on the Strait and Narrow*. *A devotion is found on page 1358.*

Patrick M. Morley is founder, chairman and president of Morley Properties, Inc. He teaches a weekly men's Bible study near his home in central Florida, and is the author of *The Man in the Mirror* and *The Rest of Your Life*. *Devotions are found on pages 693, 754, 860, 1153, 1192.*

Malcolm Muggeridge was a journalist, magazine editor, university rector, novelist, and a familiar figure on British television. His book *Jesus Rediscovered* tells of the events leading up to his conversion from atheism to Christianity. Among his other books are *Something Beautiful for God* and his autobiography, *Chronicles of Wasted Time*. *A devotion is found on page 1002.*

Henri J.M. Nouwen, a native of the Netherlands, has taught at the University of Notre Dame, Yale University and Harvard University, and for the last several years has been pastor of the L'Arche Daybreak Community in Richmond Hill, Ontario, Canada, sharing his life with mentally handicapped individuals. He has written over 25 books, including *The Wounded Healer* and *The Genesee Diary*. *Devotions are found on pages 249, 923, 980.*

Gerald Oosterveen is a pastor with experience in parish ministry and chaplaincy ministries. He has most recently served as a hospital chaplain. He is the author of *Serving Mentally Impaired Persons* and *Too Early Frost*. *Devotions are found on pages 945, 1402.*

Ben Patterson is the pastor of New Providence Presbyterian Church in New Providence, New Jersey. He is a contributing editor for *Christianity Today* and *Leadership*, and the author of *The Grand Essentials* and *Waiting*. *A devotion is found on page 28.*

William Petersen is an editor with Baker Book House. The former editor of *Eternity* magazine, he was with Fleming H. Revell Company for many years. He has written more than 20 books, including *Jeremiah: The Prophet Who Wouldn't Quit* and *Meet Me on the Mountain*. *A devotion is found on page 789.*

Eugene Peterson served as a pastor for many years in Bel Air, Maryland, and is now on the faculty at Regent College in Vancouver, B.C., Canada, where he helps students in their devotional and practical approach to God. He has written many books, including *Reversed Thunder* and *Answering God*. *Devotions are found on pages 820, 826, 1084, 1258.*

Jack Perry had a distinguished diplomatic career that included service as a political officer in U.S. embassies in Moscow and Paris and as U.S. ambassador to Bulgaria. He teaches political science and is the director of the Dean Rusk Program in International Studies at Davidson College. He has written *Light from Light*. *A devotion is found on page 1016.*

Paul Plattner was trained as a psychiatrist and psychotherapist. For many years he was a marriage counselor and directed a private clinic near Bern, Switzerland. With Paul Tournier, he organized annual conferences on "the medicine of the person." Among his publications is *Conflict and Understanding in Marriage*. *A devotion is found on page 710.*

Derek Prime serves as minister of Charlotte Chapel, Edinburgh. He is the author of *Created to Praise*. *A devotion is found on page 1404.*

Mark A. Ritchie is a commodities trader on the Chicago Board of Trade and the author of *God in the Pits*. *Devotions are found on pages 933, 1142, 1271, 1357.*

Haddon W. Robinson, former president of Denver Theological Seminary, is distinguished professor of preaching at Gordon-Conwell Seminary in South Hamilton, Massachusetts. He is the author of *Decision Making by the Book* and *Biblical Preaching*. *Devotions are found on pages 858, 1147.*

James C. Schaap is a professor of English at Dordt College in Sioux Center, Iowa. He is the author of several books, including *Intermission* and *Home Free*. *Devotions are found on pages 146, 255.*

Doug Sherman is president and founder of Career Impact Ministries. He is the author of *How to Keep Your Head Up When Your Job's Got You Down*. The books he has written with William Hendricks include *How to Balance Competing Time Demands* and *Your Work Matters to God*. *Devotions are found on pages 3, 186, 433, 623, 1264, 1310.*

Mike Singletary is a powerhouse middle linebacker for the Chicago Bears football team. He earned the National Football League's "Defensive Player of the Year" award in 1984, 1985 and 1988, and was named the "1990 NFL Man of the Year" for his on-field performance and dedicated community service. He is the author of two books: *Calling the Shots* and *Singletary on Singletary*. *Devotions are found on pages 428, 475, 569, 1040, 1276, 1296.*

G.R. Slater served as minister of St. Matthew's United Church in Toronto, Ontario, Canada, and was a contributor to *Marriage Is for Living*. Devotions are found on pages 931, 1291.

Gary Smalley was a family life pastor and is now president of Today's Family, based in Phoenix, Arizona. He is the author of a number of books, including *If Only He Knew* and *Joy That Lasts*. With John Trent he has written *The Gift of Honor* and *The Hidden Value of a Man*. *Devotions are found on pages 119, 633, 679, 1211, 1346.*

Lewis B. Smedes is Professor Emeritus at Fuller Theological Seminary in Pasadena, California, where he served as professor of philosophy and integration. He is the award-winning author of nine books, including *Choices* and *Forgive and Forget*. *Devotions are found on pages 704, 1038, 1258.*

David W. Smith is superintendent of schools at the Delphi School Corporation in Delphi, Indiana. A respected lecturer in the fields of social science and education, he has been a guest on "Focus on the Family" and NBC's "Today" show. He is the author of *Men Without Friends* and *Choosing Your Child's School*. *Devotions are found on pages 286, 288, 510, 578, 988.*

Charles H. Spurgeon was pastor of New Park Street Baptist Church in London, England, for 38 years and the founder of the Pastor's College, where he instructed over 900 men for the ministry. He had over 1,900 different sermons published during his lifetime, and he has written many books, including *Morning and Evening* and *Lectures to My Students*. *A devotion is found on page 582.*

Tim Stafford divides his time between free-lance writing and editorial responsibilities at *Christianity Today*. He is the author of several books, including *Knowing the Face of God* and *As Our Years Increase*. He wrote many of the notes for the best-selling, award-winning *The Student Bible*. *Devotions are found on pages 92, 115, 871.*

Charles Stanley is senior pastor of the 10,000-member First Baptist Church in Atlanta, Georgia, and the broadcast teacher on "In Touch," a national television and radio program. He has written numerous books, including *A Touch of His Wisdom* and *A Touch of His Freedom*. *Devotions are found on pages 650, 786, 856, 970, 1179, 1326.*

David Stoop is a psychologist and co-director of the Minirth-Meier Clinic West. He is the author of *Hope for the Perfectionist* and *Self Talk*. Together with Stephen Arterburn he has written *When Someone You Love Is Someone You Hate* and *The Angry Man*. *Devotions are found on pages 585, 1057, 1128, 1277, 1352.*

Charles R. Swindoll is pastor of First Evangelical Free Church in Fullerton, California. His "Insight for Living" radio broadcasts are heard nationwide, and he is the author of numerous books, including *Improving Your Serve* and *Laugh Again*. *Devotions are found on pages 500, 635, 656, 676, 1273, 1290.*

Daniel Taylor is associate professor of English at Bethel College in St. Paul, Minnesota. Married and the father of four children, he is the author of *The Myth of Certainty* and *Letters to My Children*. *Devotions are found on pages 270, 1254, 1280, 1299, 1374.*

John Timmer served as a missionary in Japan for 14 years before returning to the U.S. to serve as pastor of a church in New Jersey. He currently is pastor of a church in Grand Rapids, Michigan. He is the author of *God of Weakness* and *The Kingdom Equation*. *A devotion is found on page 165.*

A.W. Tozer was born in Pennsylvania in 1897 and was a pastor of the Christian and Missionary Alliance from 1919 until his death in 1963. His books include *The Divine Conquest*, *Christ the Eternal Song*, and *The Knowledge of the Holy*. *Devotions are found on pages 59, 91, 992, 1383.*

John Trent is associate director of Today's Family, based in Phoenix, Arizona. Previously he served as a family life pastor for eight years. He is the author of *Growing Together*. With Gary Smalley, he has written *The Gift of Honor* and *The Hidden Value of a Man*. *Devotions are found on pages 119, 633, 679, 1211, 1346.*

Walter Trobisch had a profound impact on numerous people in his ministry of writing and lecturing, which took him around the world. Until his death in 1979, he lived with his wife Ingrid in Austria, where he carried on a huge counseling service by mail. Among the books he wrote were *I Loved a Girl* and *The Misunderstood Man*. *Devotions are found on pages 326, 370.*

Sheldon Vanauken, a contributing editor to several magazines, is the author of the award-winning book *A Severe Mercy*, which traces his search for faith and his friendship with C.S. Lewis, and tells of the tragedy of his wife's untimely death. He has also written *Gateway to Heaven*. *A devotion is found on page 926.*

Richard Walters has had broad and varied experience in his career as a psychologist, serving in such settings as psychiatric hospitals, general hospitals, local churches and now as a professor of psychology at Bellhaven College in Jackson, Mississippi. He is the author of *Forgive and Be Free* and *The Escape Trap. A devotion is found on page 564.*

Walter Wangerin, Jr., is a prolific writer, the author of such books as *The Book of the Dun Cow, Reliving the Passion*, and *Mourning into Dancing.* A Lutheran pastor, he currently occupies the Jochum Chair at Valparaiso University. *A devotion is found on page 1124.*

J.H. Waterink was an internationally known educator and psychologist, who spent 35 years as Professor of Education and Psychology at the Free University of Amsterdam. He is the author of many books, including *Guiding Teen-agers to Maturity* and *Leading Little Ones to Jesus. A devotion is found on page 1309.*

Reuben Welch joined the faculty at Point Loma Nazarene College in San Diego in 1960 as associate professor of religion. A popular conference speaker, he is the author of several books, including *Faith for the Journey* and *Let's Listen to Jesus. Devotions are found on pages 1154, 1329.*

John Westfall, the co-host and co-producer of the radio show, "Everyday People," is the author of *Coloring Outside the Lines* and *Enough Is Enough.* He and his family live in Walnut Creek, California. *Devotions are found on pages 610, 755, 1338.*

Reggie White is a defensive lineman for the Green Bay Packers football team. He was an All-American lineman for the University of Tennessee and was a member of the Philadelphia Eagles from 1985 –1992. He is a perennial All-Pro and is regularly a league leader in sacks. He has written *Minister of Defense. Devotions are found on pages 666, 1164, 1294, 1333, 1340.*

David Wiersbe is pastor of Hope Evangelical Free Church in Roscoe, Illinois. He is the co-author, with Warren Wiersbe, of *Devotional Talks for People Who Do God's Business* and *Comforting the Bereaved. A devotion is found on page 1378.*

Warren Wiersbe is the general director and Bible teacher of Back to the Bible, speaking regularly on the daily program, which originates in Lincoln, Nebraska. He is the author of more than 80 books, including his BE series of expositional commentaries on the Bible. *A devotion is found on page 1378.*

E. James Wilder is an ordained minister and a licensed clinical psychologist, serving as assistant director of Shepherd's House Counseling Center in Van Nuys, California. He is the author of *Just between Father & Son. Devotions are found on pages 1200, 1348.*

Philip W. Williams is an ordained American Lutheran minister who has worked as an assistant church pastor and as a hospital director of pastoral care and associate director of clinical pastoral education. He is the author of *When a Loved One Dies* and *Water for Our Wilderness. Devotions are found on pages 1034, 1097, 1222, 1242, 1284.*

Nicholas Wolterstorff is a well-known Christian philosopher and author who taught for many years at Calvin College in Grand Rapids, Michigan. He is now professor of philosophical theology at Yale Divinity School. Among the books he has written are *Lament for a Son* and *Reason within the Bounds of Religion. A devotion is found on page 1303.*

Don Wyrtzen received an early start in music, radio and television under the care of his father, Jack Wyrtzen, founder of Word of Life International. He has arranged and composed more than 200 anthems and sacred songs and has written *A Musician Looks at the Psalms. Devotions are found on pages 556, 573, 600, 621, 643.*

Philip Yancey divides his time between free-lance writing and his responsibilities as editor-at-large for *Christianity Today.* He served as General Editor of the best-selling, award-winning *The Student Bible,* and has written numerous books, including *Where is God When It Hurts?* and *Disappointment with God. Devotions are found on pages 42, 342, 962, 984, 1004.*

SUBJECT INDEX

This subject index lists topics and sends you to those places where you can find devotions related to those topics.